THE **HILLIER** MANUAL OF
TREES & SHRUBS

THE **HILLIER** MANUAL OF
TREES & SHRUBS

Consultant Editors
John Hillier & Allen Coombes

David and Charles

A DAVID & CHARLES BOOK

Copyright © David & Charles Limited 2007

David & Charles is an F+W Publications Inc. company
4700 East Galbraith Road
Cincinnati, OH 45236

First published in the UK in 1972
Reprinted 1973, 1974, 1975
New Edition 1977
Fifth Edition 1981
Reprinted 1984, 1988, 1989, 1990, 1991
Sixth Edition 1991
Reprinted 1992
First published in paperback 1993
Reprinted 1994, 1995, 1996
Pocket edition published 1998
New hardback edition 2002
Reprinted 2003, 2004
New paperback edition 2007
Reprinted 2008

Text copyright © Hillier Nurseries 1972, 1977, 1981, 1991, 1993, 1998, 2002, 2007
Layout copyright © David & Charles 1972, 1977, 1981, 1991, 1993, 1998, 2002, 2007

A catalogue record for this book is available from the British Library.

ISBN-13: 978-0-7153-1073-1 hardback
ISBN-10: 0-7153-1073-9 hardback

ISBN-13: 978-0-7153-2664-0 paperback
ISBN-10: 0-7153-2664-3 paperback

Illustrations by Coral Mula

Printed in Singapore by KHL
for David & Charles
Brunel House, Newton Abbot, Devon

Visit our website at www.davidandcharles.co.uk

David & Charles books are available from all good bookshops; alternatively you can contact our Orderline on 0870 9908222 or write to us at FREEPOST EX2 110, D&C Direct, Newton Abbot, TQ12 4ZZ (no stamp required UK only); US customers call 800-289-0963 and Canadian customers call 800-840-5220.

CONTENTS

HOW TO USE THIS MANUAL

DESCRIPTIONS

The descriptions in this manual have, wherever possible, been based on typical plants growing in our nurseries or in the Sir Harold Hillier Gardens and Arboretum. However, as species and varieties are often variable, such characteristics as leaf shape, colour and texture, colour of flower, occurrence of flower and fruit, habit of plant and autumn colour may vary (within the limitations of the species) from those described. Autumn colours are particularly influenced by local and seasonal conditions, but some clones of a species are more reliable than others.

HEIGHTS

The ultimate height of a tree or shrub is largely dependent on such factors as soil, aspect and local weather conditions. With British gardens in mind, we have devised the following scale to give the probable range of each plant growing under average conditions. Allowances must be made for specimens in shade, against walls and under exceptional circumstances.

TREES

Large	Over 18m (over 60ft)
Medium	10 to 18m (35 to 50ft)
Small	Up to 10m (up to 35ft)

SHRUBS

Large	Over 3m (over 10ft)
Medium	1.5 to 3m (6 to 10ft)
Small	1 to 1.5m (3 to 5ft)
Dwarf	0.3 to 1m (1 to 3ft)
Prostrate	Creeping

FLOWERING PERIODS

Flowering periods in this manual should be taken as being approximate, as they will vary according to locality and from year to year depending on the vagaries of the season.

SOIL pH AND THE PLANT

The term pH is used to designate the acid or alkaline reaction of the soil. A pH reading of 7 is neutral while below this the soil becomes increasingly acid and above it progressively alkaline. In this work, the symbol ‡ is used to denote plants unsuitable for chalky soils. It should, however, be realised that there are many trees and shrubs which, though they may be weak and miserable in a *shallow* soil over chalk, will grow well in a *deep* soil over chalk.

HARDINESS

The hardiness of plants is something about which the gardener is forever wondering. It is a subject full of pitfalls, surprises, disappointments and exceptions to the rule. The term hardy is used to indicate that a plant is able to withstand an average winter in any given area. Some plants, particularly those from northerly latitudes, may be perfectly hardy but may be induced into growth during mild periods in spring and then cut back by late frosts, while others may only be hardy if they have had sufficient summer sun to ripen their growth. While the former should not be planted in sheltered positions or frost pockets, the latter should receive as much sun as possible during the year.

Plants that are not generally hardy can often be accommodated by planting in positions that offer a favourable microclimate, such as against a wall or among or under other trees and shrubs. A surprising number of supposedly tender plants can often be grown in this way. It should be remembered that a small garden, particularly if it is in a built-up area, can usually provide much more shelter and warmth than a large garden or park. Tender plants that need protection except in the milder areas are indicated by the symbol †.

BOTANICAL TERMS

Technical and botanical terms have been used in this manual when they are necessary for precision and brevity. There is a complete glossary on pages 482–485.

NOMENCLATURE AND CLASSIFICATION

Plant nomenclature is controlled by two internationally accepted codes.

The botanical names of plants (necessary for both wild and cultivated plants) are covered by the 'International Code of Botanical Nomenclature', while the use of cultivar and group epithets as well as the names of graft hybrids (which are only required for cultivated plants) are covered by the 'International Code of Nomenclature for Cultivated Plants'.

Advances in our knowledge both of plant variation and plant relationships has inevitably resulted in the re-classification of many plants. This, plus the application of the 'Rule of Priority' (ie the use of the earliest legitimate name) has necessitated a number of name changes. For various reasons not all changes are accepted in this manual, but where a plant has been re-named it has been cross-referenced under its old name, which is also included as a synonym after the accepted name.

The following notes on plant nomenclature are provided to assist with understanding the use and arrangement of plant names in this work.

GENERA These are shown in bold capitals, followed by the author:
eg **ACER** L., **PRUNUS** L., **PINUS** L.

FAMILIES These are shown in bold type and follow the generic names:
eg *Malus* Mill.–**Rosaceae**
    (genus) (author) (family)

SPECIES These are shown in bold italics with a lowercase initial and are listed under the genus to which they belong, followed by the author
eg ***Rhododendron***
    ponticum L.
    racemosum Franch.

SUBSPECIES & VARIETIES Botanically recognised subdivisions of a species (distinct forms which occur in the wild) are shown in bold italics with a lowercase initial, followed by the author, and are listed under the species to which they belong. These can be subspecies (subsp.), varietas (var.) or forma (f.)

eg *Sarcococca hookeriana* var. ***digyna*** Franch.
    (genus)   (species)   (variety)

It should be appreciated that when subdivisions of a species are recognised, the name of the species includes these. Thus, in the above example, *Sarcococca hookeriana* refers to var. *digyna* as well as to the typical plant usually known as *S. hookeriana* and often called the typical variety or 'type', which, to be technically accurate, should be referred to as *S. hookeriana* var. *hookeriana*.

CULTIVARS These are distinct forms which are not considered to warrant botanical recognition, selected either from garden or wild plants and maintained in cultivation by propagation. In the manual they are normally listed along with the species to which they belong and are shown in bold type with a capital initial and are enclosed in single quotation marks:

eg *Camellia japonica* **'Jupiter'**
    Fagus sylvatica **'Cristata'**
    (genus) (species) (cultivar)

GROUPS In status these lie between the cultivar and botanical subdivisions of species. Whereas a cultivar should, ideally, show little or no variation, the members of a group can vary considerably but are still not considered to warrant botanical status. A group can include cultivars with similar features, all the products of a cross between two plants, or it can be a previously recognised botanical category which is no longer afforded botanical status. In this work the term **grex**, often used for certain types of plant, particularly rhododendrons, to indicate the products of one cross, is not recognised as distinct from **Group**:

eg *Acer palmatum* **Dissectum Group** includes the forms
    of *Acer palmatum* with foliage similar to 'Dissectum'.
    Rhododendron **Loderi Group** includes all crosses
    between *R. fortunei* and *R. griffithianum.*
    Cedrus atlantica **Glauca Group** includes the blue-
    foliaged forms of *C. atlantica* previously referred to as
    C. atlantica f. *glauca.*

SELLING NAMES In some cases a plant may be better known under a selling name, which may or may or may not be a Trade Mark. The selling name is given without quotation marks followed by the correct cultivar epithet in parentheses:

eg *Sophora microphylla* **Sun King** ('Hilsop')
            (selling name) (cultivar epithet)

PLANT BREEDERS RIGHTS When a plant is subject to Plant Breeders Rights (as of 2001) this is indicated by PBR. following the name:

eg *Jasminum officinale* **Fiona Sunrise** ('Frojas') PBR.

CLONE A group of individuals derived originally from a single individual and maintained in cultivation by vegeta-tive propagation. All such individuals of a clone are exactly alike and are identical with the original. The majority of the cultivars in this manual are clonal in origin and are normally propagated vegetatively.

FORMS Although *forma* is a recognised botanical category below variety, the term form is often used in a more general manner and may refer to a variety, subspecies or cultivar.

HYBRIDS Hybrids between two species are often given a collective name in Latin form. These are shown as for a species but are preceded by a multiplication sign:

eg *Quercus* × *hispanica*

For hybrids given a collective name in English see under **Groups**.

Where no collective name is available for a hybrid, its cultivar name is given and treated in the same way as a cultivar:

eg *Sorbus* 'Winter Cheer'

Where neither collective name nor cultivar name exists for a hybrid, the names of the parents are given, connected by a multiplication sign:

eg *Nothofagus alpina* × *obliqua*

Parents of hybrids, where known, are shown in italics and enclosed in parentheses after the name of the hybrid, or in a few instances are mentioned in the description. Unless it is otherwise indicated, the sequence of the parents is given in alphabetical order:

eg *Viburnum* × *hillieri* (*V. erubescens* × *V. henryi*)
   (hybrid)   (parents)

INTERGENERIC HYBRIDS Natural (sexual) hybrids between species of two different genera are shown in bold type and are preceded by a multiplication sign:

eg × *Mahoberberis* (*Mahonia* × *Berberis*)
    (intergeneric hybrid)   (parents)

GRAFT HYBRIDS (chimaeras) between species of two different genera are shown in bold type and are preceded by a plus sign:

eg + *Laburnocytisus* (*Laburnum* + *Cytisus*)
  (graft hybrid)   (parents)

SUBGENERA, SECTIONS etc. The larger genera are normally subdivided into Subgenera, Sections, Subsections or Series. Where it is felt these may be of use as a reference they have been added in parentheses after the individual species:

eg *Rhododendron forrestii* (Subgenus Hymenanthes, Subsect. Neriiflora)

SYNONYMS Old or invalid names (those by which a plant was previously known), also those names not accepted in this manual, are shown in italics and placed in parentheses after the accepted name:

eg *Poncirus trifoliata* (*Aegle sepiaria*)
    Thuja plicata (*T. lobbii*)
    (accepted name) (synonym)

Where a synonym is accompanied by the abbreviation hort., it indicates that the plant in question is often known incorrectly by this name in gardens:
eg ***Hebe brachysiphon*** (*H. traversii* hort.)

Similarly, the abbreviation auct. following a name, indicates that various authors have used this name incorrectly for this plant. For example, several authors have used the name *Acer orientale* for what is correctly called *Acer semper-virens*. *A. orientale* L. is a synonym of *A. obtusifolium*.

FOREIGN NAMES OF CULTIVARS Translations of the original cultivar epithet are not accepted here and are regarded as synonyms:
eg ***Hamamelis*** × ***intermedia*** **'Feuerzauber'** ('Magic Fire')

COMMON NAMES Common or colloquial names of common usage are included before the description:
eg ***Quercus coccinea*** L. Scarlet oak.
    (botanical name)   (common name)
In addition, the more familiar common names are listed in the text, cross-referenced to the appropriate botanical name.

AUTHORITIES Following names of genera, species, subspecies and varieties, etc, are the names of the authority responsible for publishing that particular combination. Authors names are usually abbreviated, according to Brummit and Powell, *Authors of Plant Names*, Royal Botanic Gardens, Kew, 1992:
eg ***Osmanthus delavayi*** Franch. – name given by the botanist Franchet
    Ilex aquifolium L. – name given by Linnaeus
    Cotoneaster floccosus (Rehder & E.H. Wilson) Flinck & Hylmö – name given by Rehder and Wilson to a variety of *C. salicifolius* which was later recognised as a species by Flinck & Hylmö

ORIGINS

The countries of origin of wild species and varieties, where known, have been included, normally at the end of the description. Distribution of individual plants may vary depending on one's concept of a species. The recommended and now accepted Pinyin system has been adopted for Chinese placenames except for Tibet, which remains as Tibet here, but is correctly Xizang.

DATES OF INTRODUCTION

The dates of introduction into western gardens of species and varieties, where known, have been included at the end of each description: eg I 1869.
    Where no date of introduction is known, the earliest known date of cultivation is included: eg C 1658.

AWARDS

Many plants have been given awards by the Royal Horticultural Society, but the criteria and procedures vary considerably according to the type of award.

Award of Garden Merit ♀ – re-instituted 1992
Recommendations for this award are made by the appropriate committee to the RHS council on the basis of their assessment of the plant's outstanding excellence for garden decoration or use. Plants with this award are subject to periodic review.

First Class Certificate (FCC) – instituted 1859
Award of Merit (AM) – instituted 1888
Recommendations for these awards are made by the appropriate committee to the RHS council, usually after viewing as a cut specimen in a vase, occasionally as a specimen plant. Judgement is therefore 'as seen' on the day, in an 'exhibition' context, FCC indicating outstanding excellence for exhibition, and AM indicating great merit for exhibition.

FCCT and AMT
Recommendations are again made to the RHS council, by the appropriate committee, after trials at one of the RHS gardens or visits to specialist collections. Since 1992 these awards have been superseded by the Award of Garden Merit (see above).

Cory Cup The Reginal Cory Memorial Cup is awarded to the raiser of the best deliberately raised hybrid of that year. Since 1997 it has been awarded to a raiser for hybridisation work in a particular genus.

TREES AND SHRUBS

This section does not include climbers, conifers or bamboos, which are listed under separate headings at the end of this manual. CLIMBERS see p.389, CONIFERS see p.420, BAMBOOS see p.476.

*   Indicates that the plant is evergreen.
†   Indicates that the plant is too tender for exposed positions in all but the mildest localities, although most of them are hardy on walls, or when given evergreen, woodland, or similar protection.
‡   Indicates that the plant requires lime-free or neutral soil, and will not tolerate alkaline or chalky conditions.
×   Indicates that the plant is of hybrid origin.
+   Indicates that the plant is a graft chimaera (graft hybrid).
PBR   Indicates that the plant is subject to plant breeder's rights.
I   Indicates the date of original introduction into western gardens.
C   Indicates the first recorded date of cultivation where the exact date of introduction is not known.
Awards – See p. 8.
Heights – See p. 6.

A

ABELIA R. Br.—**Caprifoliaceae**—A genus of about 30 species of deciduous and evergreen shrubs, natives of E Asia and Mexico, with opposite leaves and profuse funnel-shaped or tubular flowers. In many species the persistent calyx is attractive after the corolla has fallen. Best in full sun.

chinensis R. Br. A small shrub with freely produced, fragrant, white, rose-tinted flowers from July to October. Sepals 5. C and E China. C 1844. AM 1976.

dielsii (Graebn.) Rehder (*A. zanderi* (Graebn.) Rehder) A small to medium-sized shrub with bristly young shoots. Leaves variable in size, to 8cm long, ovate, acuminate, usually entire but lobed on vigorous shoots, bristly when young becoming nearly smooth. Flowers fragrant, white to pale pink, with a cylindrical tube and 5 short, spreading lobes, opening in summer, in pairs at the ends of the shoots. Calyx 4-lobed. China. In cultivation from recent collections.

'Edward Goucher' (*A.* × *grandiflora* × *A. parvifolia*) Small, semi-evergreen shrub with bright, glossy green leaves, bronze when young. Lilac-pink flowers are profusely borne during summer and autumn. Sepals 2. Raised in the USA in 1911. A first-class shrub for a small garden.

engleriana (Graebn.) Rehder (*A. graebneriana* Rehder) A rare species making a vigorous, medium-sized shrub with reddish shoots and glossy green, taper-pointed leaves; flowers apricot with a yellow throat. Plants grown under this name may be *A. parvifolia*. C China. I 1910 by Ernest Wilson. **'Vedrariensis'** (*A. graebneriana* 'Vedrariensis') A form with larger leaves and broader blotches in the throat of the flower.

†*floribunda* Decne. A medium-sized, evergreen or semi-evergreen shrub with abundant tubular flowers, up to 5cm long, of brilliant cherry-red in June. Best against a warm wall. Mexico. I 1841. ♥ 2002.

graebneriana See *A. engleriana*.

× *grandiflora* Rehder. (*A. chinensis* × *A. uniflora*) A vigorous, arching, medium-sized, semi-evergreen shrub with dark glossy green leaves, sometimes borne in 3s or even 4s, on vigorous shoots. Flowers slightly fragrant, white, tinged pale pink, borne over a long period from July to October or later; attractive, pink-tinged sepals. Raised in Italy before 1866 and possibly elsewhere. ♥ 2002. **'Compacta'** Compact, mound-forming habit, to about 1m tall, occasionally producing vigorous shoots which should be removed. Flowers later than the typical form. **Confetti** ('Conti') PBR A small shrub with narrow, white-margined leaves. **'Francis Mason'** Leaves dark green with a golden-yellow margin. Originated as a sport at Mason's Nurseries, New Zealand, in the early 1950s. The variegation is best developed in full sun in a dry soil. **'Goldsport'** ('Goldspot', 'Gold Strike') A sport of 'Francis Mason' with which it is often confused. Foliage golden-yellow to yellow-green, becoming green. **Hopleys** ('Abghop') PBR A sport of 'Francis Mason' raised at Hopleys Nursery in about 1992. Golden-variegated foliage turns pink in autumn. Said to revert less than 'Goldsport'. **'Panache'** Very similar to Confetti, but said to be of independent origin. **'Prostrata'** A low-growing form to about 60cm tall, spreading widely. **'Sunrise'** PBR A form with the leaves narrowly margined with bright gold. Found as a sport in North Carolina.

parvifolia Hemsl. (*A. schumannii* (Graebn.) Rehder) A small shrub giving a continuous display of abundant lilac-pink, slightly fragrant flowers, blotched with orange, over a long period during late summer and autumn. Very hardy, being injured only in very cold winters. W China. I 1910 by Ernest Wilson. ♥ 2002. AM 1926.

schumannii See *A. parvifolia*.

serrata Siebold & Zucc. A dwarf to small shrub of slow growth; white or blush flowers are tinged orange, May to June. Not recommended for shallow chalk soils. Japan. I 1879 by Charles Maries.

spathulata Siebold & Zucc. A small, very hardy shrub with taper-pointed leaves, bronze-margined when young. The showy white flowers, marked with orange, are borne in June. Japan. I 1880 by Charles Maries.

triflora R. Br. ex Wall. A large, erect shrub of graceful habit. White, tinged pink, exquisitely scented flowers are produced in June in 3s in dense clusters. NW Himalaya. I 1847. AM 1959.

umbellata (Graebn. & Buchw.) Rehder. A vigorous, medium-sized to large shrub of spreading habit. The pure white flowers are produced in early June. C and W China. I 1907 by Ernest Wilson.

zanderi See *A. dielsii*.

ABELIOPHYLLUM Nakai—**Oleaceae**—A monotypic genus related to *Forsythia* but with white flowers. Very hardy but needs hot sun to thrive.

distichum Nakai. A small shrub of slow growth. The fragrant, white flowers, sometimes pink-tinged in bud, are produced on the purplish, leafless stems during February. The leaves sometimes turn purple in autumn. Korea. It is very rare in the wild and in danger of extinction. I 1924. FCC 1944. AM 1937. **Roseum Group** This covers forms with pink flowers.

†**ABUTILON** Mill.—**Malvaceae**—A large genus of about 150 species of trees, shrubs and herbs found in tropical and subtropical regions of both hemispheres. The plants described here are suitable for a sunny wall or cool greenhouse; unless otherwise mentioned, they are medium-sized shrubs. Flowers are often large, bell-shaped or open saucer-shaped, produced over a long period. *A. ochsenii* and *A. vitifolium* are sometimes separated in the genus *Corynabutilon*.

'Ashford Red' Large, apple-green leaves and flowers of good texture, size and substance, best described as a deep shade of crushed strawberry. An outstanding plant.

'Canary Bird' Pure yellow flowers. ♀ 2002.

'Cannington Carol' Foliage blotched and spotted yellow; flowers orange-red. ♀ 2002.

'Cannington Peter' Foliage dark green blotched with yellow. Flowers dark red. ♀ 2002.

'John Thompson' Pendent, bell-shaped, golden-yellow flowers. Leaves deeply cordate at the base, 3-lobed, the central lobe long and pointed.

'Kentish Belle' (*A.* × *milleri* × *A.* 'Golden Fleece') A small to medium-sized shrub with purplish stems and dark green, long-pointed, triangular leaves. Bell-like flowers, 4cm long, are pendent on long stalks and produced over a long period during summer and autumn; they have a red calyx and soft apricot petals, the veins faintly stained with red. Raised by A.V. Pike, once Head Gardener at Hever Castle, Kent. ♀ 2002. AM 1968.

'Linda Vista Peach' Bell-shaped, deep orange flowers with red veins particularly at the base, ageing to deep red, calyx dusky red. ♀ 2002.

'Louis Marignac' Dark green foliage; bell-shaped, clear pink flowers.

'Margherita Manns' See *A. ochsenii*.

'Marion' Glowing orange flowers, veined with deep orange-red inside. ♀ 2002.

megapotamicum (Spreng.) St Hil. & Naud. (*A. vexillarium* E. Morris) A small to medium-sized shrub for a warm wall. The conspicuous pendent flowers have a red calyx, yellow petals and purple anthers. Summer and autumn. Brazil. I 1804. ♀ 2002. AM 1949. 'Variegatum' Leaves with mottled yellow variegation. AM 1988.

× *milleri* hort. (*A. megapotamicum* × *A. pictum*) A medium-sized shrub bearing bell-shaped, orange flowers with crimson stamens; leaves dark green. Continuous flowering. ♀ 2002. 'Variegatum' Leaves mottled yellow.

'Nabob' Vigorous with large, dark green leaves and purple-stalked, deep red flowers. ♀ 2002.

ochsenii (Phil.) Phil. (*A.* 'Margherita Manns') A medium to large, slender shrub for a sunny wall, with cup-shaped flowers of a lovely lavender-blue, darker at centre. Chile. I about 1957. AM 1962.

'Orange Glow' Bell-shaped, reddish-orange flowers, 5cm across, orange-yellow inside with pinkish-red veins. Leaves yellow-mottled, less strongly on vigorous shoots. ♀ 2002.

'Patrick Synge' Very vigorous; the bowl-shaped flowers have flame-red petals.

'Red Queen' Deep orange-red, bell-shaped flowers. Leaves maple-like, 3–5-lobed and sharply toothed, truncate to shallowly cordate at the base.

'Saddlers' Widely bell-shaped, glossy, deep red flowers 9cm across.

'Souvenir de Bonn' Large, sharply toothed and lobed leaves, broadly edged with white. Drooping apricot flowers veined with red. ♀ 2002.

× *suntense* C.D. Brickell (*A. ochsenii* × *A. vitifolium*) A large, fast-growing shrub flowering freely between May and July. Raised intentionally by our propagator Peter Dummer in 1967 and, accidentally, from seed obtained from Highdown near Goring, Sussex by Richard Gorer of Sunte House, Hayward's Heath. 'Gorer's White' Flowers white. A selection of the Sunte House seedlings. AM 1977. 'Jermyns' A form selected from the original cross made in our Winchester nursery in 1967, using the form of *A. vitifolium* known as 'Veronica Tennant'. Flowers clear, dark mauve. ♀ 2002. 'Violetta' Flowers deep violet-blue. 'White Charm' Flowers white, slightly cup-shaped, up to 5cm across. Originated as a chance seedling in the Sir Harold Hillier Gardens and Arboretum in 1975.

vexillarium See *A. megapotamicum*.

vitifolium (Cav.) Presl. A large, handsome shrub needing a sunny, sheltered site. Flowers saucer-shaped, pale to deep mauve. May to July. The vine-shaped leaves are downy and grey. Chile. I 1836. FCC 1888. 'Album' Flowers white. AM 1961. 'Tennant's White' A form with freely borne, large, pure white flowers. ♀ 2002. 'Veronica Tennant' A free-flowering selection with large, mauve flowers. ♀ 2002.

†***ACACIA** Mill.—**Leguminosae**—The wattles are a very large genus of some 1200 species of trees and shrubs (very rarely herbs) found throughout tropical and subtropical regions, particularly Africa and Australia (Australia is home to 700 species). The leaves are often bipinnate but in many species, except in young seedlings, they are reduced to phyllodes (a development of the leaf stalk). The acacias are mostly winter- or spring-flowering, cool-greenhouse shrubs but several species attain tree size outdoors in favoured localities. The flowers are usually yellow, in small, rounded

heads or bottlebrushes, the conspicuous feature of which is the stamens. Most become chlorotic on chalk soils.

alpina F. Muell. Alpine wattle. A small, spreading shrub with short, obovate, blue-green phyllodes and pale yellow flowers in spikes to 2cm long. Introduced to our nursery in 1977 by Sir Harold Hillier. Mountains of Victoria and New South Wales.

armata See *A. paradoxa*.

baileyana F. Muell. Cootamundra wattle. Small tree or large shrub with attractive, glaucous, bipinnate leaves and freely produced racemes of bright yellow flowers in winter and spring. New South Wales. I 1888. ♀ 2002. FCC 1936. AM 1927. **'Purpurea'** A spectacular form with deep purple young foliage contrasting with the blue-green older leaves. ♀ 2002.

dealbata Link (*A. decurrens* var. *dealbata* (Link) F. Muell.) Silver wattle. A large shrub or small tree for a sheltered wall. The fern-like leaves are silvery-green. Fragrant flowers in late winter to early spring. The popular golden mimosa of florists. SE Australia, Tasmania. I 1820. ♀ 2002. FCC 1971. AM 1935.

decurrens **var. *dealbata*** See *A. dealbata*.

diffusa See *A. genistifolia*.

'Exeter Hybrid' (*A. longifolia* × *A. riceana*) (*A.* 'Veitchiana') A beautiful, medium to large shrub raised by Veitch in Exeter. The arching branches bear narrow leaves and spikes of rich yellow, fragrant flowers. AM 1961.

genistifolia Link (*A. diffusa* Ker Gawl.) A large, lax, genista-like shrub with narrow, sharp-pointed phyllodes; sulphur-yellow flowers are borne in small heads. I 1818. AM 1934.

longifolia (Andrews) Muhl. ex Willd. Sallow wattle, Sydney golden wattle. Large shrub with long, lance-shaped, dark green phyllodes and bright yellow flowers in 4–8cm spikes. One of the hardiest species, and fairly lime tolerant. SE Australia, Tasmania. I 1792. **var. *sophorae*** See *A. sophorae*.

melanoxylon R. Br. Blackwood. A tree-like species allied to *A. longifolia*, but with pinnate juvenile foliage. S Australia, Tasmania. I 1808.

mucronata Willd. Narrow leaf wattle. A large shrub related to and resembling *A. longifolia*, but with much narrower phyllodes. SE Australia, Tasmania. AM 1933.

paradoxa DC. (*A. armata* R. Br.) Hedge wattle, Kangaroo thorn. A small-leaved, prickly species of dense, bushy habit making a medium-sized to large shrub, with small, narrow, dark green phyllodes; masses of yellow flowers are borne all along the branches in spring. Australia, widely distributed. I 1803. ♀ 2002.

pataczekii D.I. Morris. Wally's wattle. A remarkably hardy species only named in 1974 after its discoverer, Wally Pataczek. A small, shrubby tree with bloomy shoots and blue-green phyllodes to 6cm long, often purple-tinged when young. Flowers lemon-yellow, borne in racemes of small globular heads. Mts of NE Tasmania. C 1975.

pendula A. Cunn. Weeping myall. Small tree with pendent stems, narrow, rigid, silvery-grey phyllodes and cylindrical panicles of yellow flowers. E Australia.

pravissima F. Muell. Ovens wattle. A large shrub or small tree with slender, arching shoots. Triangular phyllodes are 2-veined, glaucous on both sides with a single spine

on the lower side of the broad apex. Flowers yellow in small clusters early spring. SE Australia. ♀ 2002.

retinodes Schltdl. A small tree with narrow, grey-green, willow-like phyllodes. Flowers are freely carried in large, loose panicles during summer. One of the most lime-tolerant species. SE Australia, Tasmania. I 1871. ♀ 2002. AM 1925.

riceana Hensl. Rice's wattle. A large shrub or small tree of graceful habit with slender, weeping shoots and dark green, sharp-pointed phyllodes. Flowers pale yellow, in drooping clusters in spring. Tasmania. AM 1926.

sophorae (Labill.) R. Br. (*A. longifolia* var. *sophorae* (Labill.) F. Muell. Coastal wattle. Close to *A. longifolia* but phyllodes somewhat shorter and broader. Moderately hardy in favoured areas. E Australia.

verticillata (L'Hér.) Willd. Prickly Moses. A large shrub or small tree with whorled, dark green, needle-like phyllodes and cylindrical spikes of bright yellow flowers. SE Australia, Tasmania. I 1780 by Sir Joseph Hooker. AM 1926.

Acacia, false See *Robinia pseudoacacia*.
Acanthopanax See *Eleutherococcus*.
Acanthopanax pentaphyllus See *E. sieboldianus*.
Acanthopanax ricinifolius See *Kalopanax septemlobus*.
Acanthopanax spinosus See *E. sieboldianus*.

†*****ACCA** O. Berg—**Myrtaceae**—A genus of 2 species of evergreen shrubs with opposite leaves and solitary flowers borne in the leaf axils. Natives of South America, they are closely related to the guavas (*Psidium*).

sellowiana (O. Berg) Burrett (*Feijoa sellowiana* O. Berg) Pineapple guava. A large shrub, fairly hardy given a warm, sheltered position. Grey-green leaves, white-felted beneath; flowers have fleshy crimson and white petals and a central bunch of long, crimson stamens. Large, egg-shaped berries are sometimes produced after a long, hot summer. Both petals and fruits are edible, having a rich, aromatic flavour. Brazil, Uruguay. I 1898. AM 1927. **'Variegata'** A slower-growing form with cream- and white-margined leaves. AM 1969.

ACER L.—**Aceraceae**—The maples comprise more than 120 species of mainly deciduous trees and shrubs found throughout N temperate regions with a large number in E Asia. Leaves opposite, palmately lobed in most species, entire or compound. Flowers small but often attractive, usually opening with the young leaves. They are mostly very hardy and of easy culture. Those referred to as Japanese maples will be found under *A. japonicum* and *A. palmatum*.

acuminatum Wall. ex D. Don. A small tree closely related to *A. caudatum*. Leaves on scarlet petioles, usually 3-lobed and sharply toothed, the lobes with slender, tail-like points. W Himalaya.

amplum Rehder. A small tree with polished, green stems. Leaves like those of the Norway maple, 5-lobed, bronze when young. C China. I 1901 by Ernest Wilson.

‡*argutum* Maxim. A small, upright tree with elegant, 5-lobed, pale green leaves, made conspicuous by the reticulate venation. Long-stalked, greenish flowers open with the leaves. Japan. I 1881.

buergerianum Miq. (*A. trifidum* Hook. & Arn. not Thunb.) Small, bushy tree with 3-lobed, long-persistent leaves, often red or orange in autumn. Mature trees have attractive, red-brown, flaking bark. E China, Korea. C 1890. **'Mino-yatsubusa'** A slow-growing, small, dense shrub; the leaves have very slender lobes ending in long, tapering points.

caesium Wall. ex Brandis. Related to *A. pseudoplatanus*, this is a medium-sized tree in gardens, with slightly bloomy shoots. The broad, sycamore-like, 3–5-veined leaves end in short, tapered lobes and are crowded at the ends of the shoots, turning yellow in autumn. NW Himalaya. **subsp. giraldii** (Pax) E. Murray (*A. giraldii* Pax) A form with glaucous-bloomy young stems and long-stalked leaves that are glaucous and reticulate beneath. N and W China. I by George Forrest.

†*calcaratum* Gagnep. (*A. osmastonii* Gamble) Small tree, the young shoots covered by a conspicuous, almost chalky-white bloom, changing to white striations on the pale green older bark. Large leaves, with red petioles, are deeply 5-lobed, green on both surfaces, purplish when unfolding. Sikkim Himalaya.

†*campbellii* Hook. f. & Thoms. ex Hiern. Medium-sized tree with palmately 5–7-lobed leaves, red when young and often colouring well in autumn. Hardy in the British Isles in sheltered woodland. E Himalaya, Burma, W China. I about 1851 by Sir Joseph Hooker. **subsp. flabellatum** (Rehder) E. Murray (*A. flabellatum* Rehder) A small, shrubby tree, resembling *A. campbellii*. Leaves broadly palmate with 7–9 sharply serrated lobes. Not hardy enough for coldest areas. C China, Vietnam. I 1907 by Ernest Wilson. **var. yunnanense** Rehder (*A. flabellatum* var. *yunnanense* (Rehder) Fang) A slender tree with deeply 5-lobed leaves and red petioles. Yunnan, China.

campestre L. Field maple, Hedge maple. A picturesque, medium-sized tree, frequently used in rustic hedges; foliage turns clear yellow, sometimes flushed red, in autumn. Europe (incl. British Isles), W Asia. ♀ 2002. **'Carnival'** A form with the leaves broadly margined with creamy-white. Found as a seedling in Holland before 1989. **'Compactum'** See 'Nanum'. **'Elsrijk'** A Dutch selection of dense, conical habit. A good street tree. C 1953. **'Nanum'** ('Compactum') A shrubby form of dense, bushy habit. C 1839. **'Postelense'** Young leaves golden-yellow, later yellow-green, red-stalked. Shrubby or a mop-headed small tree. C 1896. **'Pulverulentum'** Leaves thickly speckled and blotched with white. C 1859. **Queen Elizabeth** ('Evelyn') An American selection of vigorous, rather upright habit. We have found it to be susceptible to mildew. C 1985. **'Royal Ruby'** Young leaves red-purple becoming dark green. C 1980. **'Schwerinii'** A form with purple young leaves. C 1897. **'Streetwise'** Our own selection, with a neat and compact, upright habit and brilliant yellow autumn colour. The red fruits are striking in late summer and early autumn. Does not suffer from mildew like the American selection, Queen Elizabeth. Selected early 1980s, I in 1998. **'William Caldwell'** A small tree with a compact and narrow, upright habit with good, orange-red autumn colour.

capillipes Maxim. A small tree with striated bark and bright green, 3-lobed leaves, the young growths coral-red. Attractive, autumn tints of orange and red make it among the best of the snake-bark maples. Japan. I 1892 by Charles Sargent. ♀ 2002. AM 1975.

cappadocicum Gled. (*A. laetum* C.A. Mey.) A medium-sized to large tree with broad, 5–7-lobed, glossy leaves turning to rich butter-yellow in autumn. Caucasus and W Asia. I 1838. **'Aureum'** A striking form with red young leaves, turning golden-yellow and remaining so for many weeks. C 1914. ♀ 2002. **'Rubrum'** Young growths blood-red. A most attractive form. I 1838. ♀ 2002. **subsp. sinicum** (Rehder) Hand.-Mazz. A very attractive variety with smaller, usually 5-lobed leaves; young growths coppery-red. Red autumn fruits. Himalayas, C and W China. I 1901 by Ernest Wilson. AM 1958.

carpinifolium Siebold & Zucc. Hornbeam maple. A small to medium-sized tree with leaves remarkably like those of the common hornbeam but opposite, turning gold and brown in autumn. Japan. I 1879 by Charles Maries.

†*catalpifolium* Rehder. A medium-sized to large tree, in the wild resembling *A. cappadocicum*. The large, catalpa-like leaves, to 25cm long, are ovate and taper-pointed, untoothed, and shallowly 3-lobed or unlobed. A recent introduction, rare in cultivation but growing well in mild gardens. SW China.

caudatifolium Hayata (*A. kawakamii* Koidzumi) A small snake-bark maple closely related to *A. rubescens* with which it has been confused, but differing in its dull green leaves which are unlobed or shallowly 3-lobed at the base. They are usually at least twice as long as broad and end in a long, tapering point. Many of the plants distributed recently as *A. caudatifolium* or *A. kawakamii* are *A. rubescens*. Taiwan. I 1971 by J.G.S. Harris.

caudatum Wall. (*A. papilio* King) A medium-sized tree with glabrous shoots and 5-lobed, coarsely toothed leaves, downy beneath. E Himalaya to E Asia. **subsp. multiserratum** (Maxim.) E. Murray (*A. multiserratum* Maxim.) A small tree with downy shoots and 5- to 7-lobed leaves, nearly glabrous beneath. China. I 1907 by Ernest Wilson. **subsp. ukurunduense** (Trautv. & Mey.) E. Murray (*A. ukurunduense* Trautv. & Mey.) A small tree with 5-lobed leaves, deeply veined above and densely pubescent beneath. Flowers tiny, in slender, upright panicles. Colourful autumn tints. Not very tolerant of chalk soils. E Asia.

circinatum Pursh. Vine maple. A large shrub, or occasionally small tree, with almost circular leaves, prettily tinted in summer and turning orange and crimson in autumn. Wine-red and white flowers in April are quite decorative. Grows well even in dry, shady positions. W North America. I 1826 by David Douglas. **'Monroe'** A small shrub, the leaves divided to the base into usually 5 deeply cut lobes. Found in the Willamette National Forest, Oregon in 1960 by Mr Warner Monroe.

cissifolium (Siebold & Zucc.) K. Koch A small tree with trifoliolate, bronze-tinted leaves which turn to red and yellow in autumn. Similar to *A. henryi* but margins of the leaflets coarsely toothed. Not very tolerant of chalk soils. Japan. I before 1870.

× *conspicuum* van Gelderen & Oterdoom (*A. davidii* × *A. pensylvanicum*) Hybrids of this parentage include some of the most striking of the snakebark maples grown for their bark. **'Elephant's Ear'** Very large, unlobed, dark green leaves to 30cm long. Bark purple with white stripes. C 1990. **'Phoenix'** A seedling of 'Silver Vein' with bright red winter shoots, striped white. C 1982. **'Silver Cardinal'** See *A.* 'Silver Cardinal'. **'Silver Vein'** (*A. davidii* 'George Forrest' × *A. pensylvanicum* 'Erythrocladum') A strong-growing, snakebark maple, making a small tree, the arching branches conspicuously streaked green and white. Leaves large, 3-lobed above the middle with a tapering point, rich green above, on long, red stalks, turning butter-yellow in autumn. Raised in our Chandler's Ford nursery by Peter Douwsma from a cross made in 1961.

× *coriaceum* Tausch. (*A. monspessulanum* × *A. opalus*) Small tree of neat, rounded habit with rather leathery, shallowly 3-lobed leaves, often retained well into winter, turning rich yellow before they fall. C 1790.

crataegifolium Siebold & Zucc. Hawthorn maple. A small tree or large shrub with prettily marked bark and small leaves of variable shape; flowers mustard-yellow in slender racemes. C and S Japan. I 1879 by Charles Maries. **'Veitchii'** Leaves heavily mottled with white and pink, brilliant pink and purple in autumn. C 1881.

creticum See *A. sempervirens*.

dasycarpum See *A. saccharinum*.

davidii Franch. A small tree with attractive, green and white striated bark. The shining, dark green, ovate leaves colour richly in autumn. The green fruits are often suffused red and hang all along the branches in autumn. C China. I 1879 by Charles Maries. **'Ernest Wilson'** A more compact tree with branches ascending then arching. Leaves pale green, orange-yellow in autumn, rather cup-shaped at base, petioles pink at first. Rare in cultivation. The original form from W Hubei and W Yunnan, introduced by Charles Maries and later by Ernest Wilson and Frank Kingdon-Ward. **'George Forrest'** ('Horizontale') An open tree of loose habit with vigorous, spreading branches and large, dark green leaves with rhubarb-red stalks. This is the form most commonly met with in cultivation. I by George Forrest from Yunnan in 1921–22. ♀ 2002. AM 1975 (for fruit). **'Karmen'** A small, shrubby tree with conspicuously striped bark. Deep bronze young leaves turn to reddish-green then yellow or orange in autumn. Found in a Dutch garden about 1975. **'Madeline Spitta'** A columnar form with erect branches. Raised at Winkworth Arboretum, Surrey. Leaves glossy, dark green, retained until late autumn, turning orange before they fall. **'Rosalie'** Attractive, purple young shoots in winter, later green, heavily striped with white. Leaves relatively small, yellow in autumn. Raised in Holland in 1985. **'Serpentine'** A small tree with an upright habit, small leaves to 10cm long, turning yellow to orange in autumn, purple shoots and very good, striped bark. Found as a seedling in Holland before 1976. ♀ 2002.

diabolicum K. Koch. Horned maple. A medium-sized, dioecious tree with large, 5-lobed leaves, pendent corymbs of yellow flowers in April and distinctive, bristly, reddish fruits. Japan. I 1880 by Charles Maries. **Purpurascens Group** (f. *purpurascens* (Franch. & Sav.) Rehder) This is the male form. A most ornamental tree with purple-tinged young leaves, red in autumn. In spring its branches are draped with masses of pendent clusters of salmon-coloured flowers. Japan. C 1878.

× *dieckii* (Pax) Pax (*A. lobelii* × *A. platanoides*) A medium-sized to large tree of rapid growth. Leaves large, 5-lobed, turning to dark red-brown or old gold in autumn. Garden origin in the Zoeschen nursery near Berlin before 1886.

distylum Siebold & Zucc. A medium-sized tree with lime-like, undivided, glossy green leaves which are attractively tinted cream and pink when unfolding. Rich yellow autumn colour. Japan. I 1879 by Charles Maries.

divergens Pax (*A. quinquelobum* K. Koch not Gilib.) Large shrub or small tree with small, polished, 5- or occasionally 3-lobed leaves, bronze-edged when young. Related to *A. campestre*. Transcaucasus. I 1923.

erianthum Schwer. A small tree with 5–7-lobed leaves marked beneath by white tufts of hair in the vein axils. Often abundant crops of attractive, pink-winged fruits. Not very tolerant of chalk soils and best in semi-shade. W China. I 1901 by Ernest Wilson.

†*fabri* Hance. A small, semi-evergreen tree with bloomy young stems and oblong-lanceolate, slender-pointed leaves similar to those of *A. laevigatum* but more prominently veined and with axillary tufts of hair beneath. Originally listed as *A. wardii*. China, E Himalaya.

flabellatum See *A. campbellii* subsp. *flabellatum*. **var. yunnanense** See *A. campbellii* subsp. *flabellatum* var. *yunnanense*.

forrestii Diels. A most beautiful, small tree with striated bark; young stems and petioles are attractive coral-red. Not very tolerant of chalk soils. China. I 1906 by George Forrest. **'Alice'** Young foliage pinkish during summer, later dark green. Leaves only shallowly lobed. Raised in Holland from seed collected at Westonbirt Arboretum. C 1981.

franchetii Pax. A small, slow-growing tree with large 3-lobed leaves, showing its close relationship with *A. sterculiaceum*. Relatively large, green, thick-petalled flowers are borne in drooping clusters with the leaves. C and W China. I 1901 by Ernest Wilson.

× *freemanii* E. Murray (*A. rubrum* × *A. saccharinum*) A naturally occurring hybrid found where the two parents grow together and making a large tree. It was, however, first recognised in gardens after being raised by Oliver Freeman in 1933 at the US National Arboretum, Washington, DC. The foliage is intermediate between the parents, turning red and yellow in autumn. **Autumn Blaze** ('Jeffersred') PBR Vigorous, with a dense, oval head and rich green, deeply cut leaves, orange-red in autumn.

fulvescens See *A. longipes*.

ginnala See *A. tataricum* subsp. *ginnala*. **subsp. semenovii** See *A. tataricum* subsp. *semenovii*.

giraldii See *A. caesium* subsp. *giraldii*.

glabrum Torr. Rock maple. A large shrub or small tree of upright habit with variable leaves which may be 3–5-lobed or trifoliolate. W North America. I about 1884. **subsp. douglasii** (Hook.) Wesm. A variety with 3-lobed leaves. I 1902.

grandidentatum See *A. saccharum* subsp. *grandidentatum*.

griseum (Franch.) Pax. Paperbark maple. One of the most beautiful of all small trees. Leaves trifoliolate, often gorgeously coloured red and scarlet in autumn. Old bark on trunk and primary branches flakes and curls back to reveal cinnamon-coloured underbark. C China. I by Ernest Wilson in 1901. ♀ 2002. AM 1922.

grosseri Pax. A small tree, one of the most beautiful of the snakebark maples. The leaves colour magnificently in autumn. C China. I about 1923. **var. *hersii*** (Rehder) Rehder (*A. hersii* Rehder) A small tree with wonderfully marbled bark. Leaves with or without lobes; rich autumn colour. Fruits in conspicuous, long racemes. C China. I 1921. ♀ 2002.

heldreichii Boiss. A very handsome, medium-sized tree with distinctive, deeply cleft, 3-lobed leaves, which almost resemble those of the Boston ivy (*Parthenocissus tricuspidata*). SE Europe. I 1879. **subsp. *visianii*** K. Maly. This differs in its larger leaves and fruits. Some plants grown as the typical form belong here. Former Yugoslavia, Bulgaria.

henryi Pax. A small to medium-sized, spreading tree having stems marked with bluish striations; leaves beautifully tinted when young and turn brilliant red in autumn, resembling those of *A. cissifolium*, but leaflets nearly entire. Yellow flowers, in slender, drooping catkins, appear with the unfolding leaves. C China. I 1903 by Ernest Wilson.

hersii See *A. grosseri* var. *hersii*.

× *hillieri* Lancaster (*A. cappadocicum* × *A. miyabei*) This hybrid, described in 1979, can occur whenever the two parents grow together. It was first recognised in our West Hill nursery, Winchester. **'Summergold'** Leaves golden-yellow, young growths red in summer. Best if slightly shaded. One parent of this form was *A. cappadocicum* 'Aureum'. **'West Hill'** The original form raised in our West Hill nursery in Winchester before 1935 from seed of *A. miyabei* received from Kew. A small to medium-sized, round-headed tree with slightly glossy, 5–7-lobed leaves turning butter-yellow in autumn. This plant was originally listed as *A.* × *hillieri*.

hookeri See *A. sikkimense*.

× *hybridum* Spach. (*A. opalus* × ? *A. pseudoplatanus*) A medium-sized to large tree with 3-lobed leaves and drooping panicles of yellow-green flowers in May. Plants of this parentage occur in the wild with the parents.

hyrcanum Fisch. & C.A. Mey. Small tree of compact habit and slow growth with 3- or 5-lobed leaves, allied to *A. opalus*. SE Europe, SW Asia. C 1865.

insigne See *A. velutinum* var. *glabrescens*.

japonicum Thunb. ex A. Murray. A small tree or large bush with soft green foliage, beautifully coloured in autumn, and softly hairy petioles. Red flowers with yellow anthers, appear in delicate drooping clusters with the young leaves. There are a number of forms; all do best in a moist, well-drained position sheltered from cold winds. Japan. I 1864. **'Aconitifolium'** ('Laciniatum', 'Filicifolium') Leaves deeply lobed and cut, colouring rich ruby-crimson in autumn. C 1888. ♀ 2002. **'Aureum'** See *A. shirasawanum* 'Aureum'. **'Filicifolium'** See 'Aconitifolium'. **'Green Cascade'** Deeply cut leaves on pendent shoots turn yellow, orange and red in autumn. C. 1955. **'Laciniatum'** See 'Aconitifolium'. **'Vitifolium'** Broad, fan-shaped leaves with 10–12 lobes. An extremely beautiful form, colouring brilliantly in autumn. C 1882. ♀ 2002. FCC 1974 (for autumn foliage).

kawakamii See *A. caudatifolium*.

†*laevigatum* Wall. A small, semi-evergreen tree with smooth, green shoots, bloomy when young. Leaves are oblong-lanceolate, acuminate, 15cm or more long, bright green and lustrous, reticulate beneath; adpressed serrate, at least when young. This species has been received from various sources as *A. fargesii*. Himalaya, China. I 1907.

laxiflorum Pax. A rare, small, spreading tree, the bark streaked with green and white. Leaves dark green above, with dark brown hairs on the veins beneath, taper-pointed and shallowly lobed below the middle. Inclined to be calcifuge. W China. I 1908.

leucoderme See *A. saccharum* subsp. *leucoderme*.

lobelii Ten. A fast-growing, medium-sized to large tree, related to *A. cappadocicum*, with bloomy young shoots and wavy-edged, dark green leaves with taper-pointed lobes. Its ascending branches form a compact, conical head, broadening with age. Good for restricted spaces. S Italy. I 1683.

longipes Franch. ex Rehder (*A. fulvescens* Rehder) A small to medium-sized tree, uncommon in gardens, with glabrous shoots, red when young. The leaves are up to 15cm across and densely tomentose beneath, with usually 3, or sometimes 5, entire lobes, which taper to long, fine points, turning clear yellow in autumn. Young fruits have red wings. W Sichuan, China.

macrophyllum Pursh. Oregon maple. A large tree with handsome, very large, shining, dark green leaves, which turn a bright orange in autumn. Large, drooping clusters of fragrant, yellow flowers and later bristly fruits are very ornamental. W North America. I 1812 by Pursh and again in 1826 by David Douglas. **'Kimballiae'** A remarkable form, the leaves deeply cut to the base into 3–5 lobes. The original tree is in the Washington Park Arboretum, Seattle. C 1940. **'Seattle Sentinel'** A dense, columnar form with upright branches. Originated in Seattle, Washington about 1920. It has reached nearly 15m tall in the Sir Harold Hillier Gardens and Arboretum (2000).

mandshuricum Maxim. A large shrub or small tree with trifoliolate leaves and red petioles. Allied to *A. maximowiczianum* but with glabrous leaves. Rich autumn colour. Manchuria, Korea, E Siberia. C 1904.

maximowiczianum Miq. (*A. nikoense* Maxim.) Nikko maple. A very hardy and beautiful tree of small to medium size. The hairy, trifoliolate leaves, glaucous beneath, turn a glorious orange and flame in autumn. Now a rare tree in its native lands. Japan, C China. I 1881. FCC 1971.

maximowiczii Pax. An attractive, small tree with striated stems and 3- or 5-lobed leaves, attractively red-tinted throughout the growing season and becoming more colourful as autumn approaches. C China. I 1910 by Ernest Wilson.

micranthum Siebold & Zucc. A large shrub or small tree. The small, 5-lobed leaves are beautifully tinted throughout the growing season. Autumn foliage usually red. Japan. I 1879.

miyabei Maxim. A small to medium-sized tree of rounded habit. The large, 3–5-lobed leaves recall those of the Norway maple. Japan. I 1892 by Charles Sargent.

mono See *A. pictum.* **var. *ambiguum*** See *A. pictum* f. *ambiguum.* **var. *tricuspis*** See *A. tenellum.*

monspessulanum L. Montpelier maple. Usually a small tree of neat habit; occasionally shrubby. In general appearance it resembles the field maple (*Acer campestre*) but the 3-lobed leaves are perfectly glabrous and glaucous beneath, and the stalks do not possess the milky juice of the common species. S Europe, W Asia. I 1739.

morrisonense See *A. rubescens.*

multiserratum See *A. caudatum* subsp. *multiserratum.*

neglectum See *A.* × *zoeschense.*

negundo L. Box elder. A very popular, fast-growing, bushy-headed, medium to large tree. The young shoots are bright green and the leaves are pinnate with 3–5, sometimes 7–9, leaflets, bright green above, paler beneath. Reverting shoots on variegated forms should be removed. North America, Mexico, Guatemala. C 1688. **'Auratum'** Leaves bright golden-yellow. AM 1901. **subsp.** *californicum* (Torr. & A. Gray) Wesm. A form with softly hairy shoots and leaves. The male tree has flowers in showy pink tassels. California, Arizona. **'Elegans'** ('Elegantissimum') Leaves with bright yellow marginal variegation. Young shoots with white bloom. C 1885. FCC 1898. **'Flamingo'** Young leaves with a broad, soft pink margin, changing to white, often green at first; shoots glaucous bloomed. This form is often grown as a shrub but will reach tree size. The foliage is most effective on plants that are regularly cut back to a short stem. Raised in Holland before 1976. **'Kelly's Gold'** Yellow-green leaves, more vigorous than 'Auratum' and less liable to sunburn, but less intensely coloured. Raised in New Zealand before 1989. **'Variegatum'** ('Argenteo-variegatum') Leaves with a broad, irregular white margin. A most effective tree but tends to revert if not carefully pruned. **var.** *violaceum* (Kirchn.) Jaeger. Young shoots purple or violet, covered with a white bloom, young foliage bronze. Leaves with usually 5–7 leaflets. An attractive tree in spring when draped with its long, pendent, reddish-pink flower tassels. AM 1975.

nigrum See *A. saccharum* subsp. *nigrum.*

nikoense See *A. maximowiczianum.*

nipponicum Hara. A medium-sized tree with stout, green young shoots. Large, long-stalked leaves, to 25cm across, are heart-shaped at the base, with deeply impressed veins and 3–5 shallow, double-toothed lobes, rusty hairy beneath when young. Long, slender, pendent inflorescences from the ends of the short shoots have small, green flowers with conspicuous stamens. A very distinct species that often fruits profusely and seeds itself beneath the tree in the Sir Harold Hillier Gardens and Arboretum, but remains rare in cultivation. Japan. C 1940.

†***oblongum*** Wall. ex DC. A small tree or large shrub suitable only for mild areas. The oblong, semi-persistent leaves are entire though sometimes 3-lobed on young trees and vigorous shoots, glabrous above, glaucous beneath. Himalaya, C and W China. I 1824. **var.** *concolor* Pax. Leaves green on both sides. Our stock is a fairly hardy form introduced by Ernest Wilson from China.

obtusatum See *A. opalus* subsp. *obtusatum.*

*****obtusifolium*** Sibth. & Sm. (*A. orientale* L., *A. syriacum* Boiss. & Gaill.) A large shrub or small bushy tree with ovate, entire or 3-lobed, rigid, dark green leaves. Very hardy. SW Asia, Cyprus. C 1903.

oliverianum Pax. A handsome species forming a large shrub or small tree. Leaves are deeply 5-lobed, some-what resembling *A. palmatum* but cleaner cut. They turn subtle shades of orange, red and purple over a long period in autumn. C China. I 1901 by Ernest Wilson.

opalus Mill. Italian maple. A medium-sized tree of rounded habit with shallowly 5-lobed leaves which are glabrous above, downy, occasionally glabrous beneath. The conspicuous, yellow flowers appear in crowded corymbs on the leafless stems in March. S Europe, N Africa, Caucasus. I 1752. FCC 1977. AM 1967. **subsp.** *obtusatum* (Willd.) Gams. (*A. obtusatum* Willd.) A form with usually larger leaves softly downy beneath, the lobes short and rounded. SE Europe and Italy. I 1805.

orientale See *A. obtusifolium* and *A. sempervirens.*

osmastonii See *A. calcaratum.*

palmatum Thunb. ex A. Murray. Japanese maple. Generally a large shrub or small tree with a low, rounded head. Leaves 5- or 7-lobed of a bright green. Japan, C China, Korea. I 1820.

Cultivars of *Acer palmatum*

Many cultivars have been raised from this species. They exhibit a wide range of forms both in leaf and habit. The majority attain the size of a large bush or occasionally a small tree, and give gorgeous, red, orange or yellow autumnal colours. Though the typical, and certain stronger, forms will tolerate chalk soils, Japanese maples are at their best in a moist but well-drained loam, sheltered from cold winds.

'Albomarginatum' ('Argenteomarginatum') Leaves smaller than normal, green with a white marginal variegation. Liable to revert.

'Asahi-zuru' A fast-growing, large, spreading shrub. Leaves variously blotched with white, sometimes nearly all white or pink when young. One of the best variegated forms. C 1938.

Atropurpureum Group The most popular Japanese maple. A striking colour form; leaves bronzy-crimson throughout the summer, brilliant red in autumn. C 1857. See also 'Bloodgood'.

'Aureum' Leaves suffused soft yellow becoming golden-yellow in summer. C 1881.

'Beni-kagami' A vigorous, large shrub with deeply cut, 7-lobed, wine-red leaves. Attractive, red-winged fruits in autumn. Raised in Japan before 1930.

'Beni-komachi' A medium-sized shrub with leaves very deeply divided into 5 slender, curved lobes, bright red when young, turning red-purple then greenish-red. Autumn colour scarlet.

'Beni-maiko' A small, bushy shrub with brilliant red young foliage, later pinkish then greenish-red.

'Beni-schichihenge' A striking and rare form. Leaves blue-green, deeply 5- to 7-lobed, the lobes margined with pinkish-white or almost entirely bright orange-pink. C 1967.

'Bloodgood' Leaves very deep reddish-purple, holding their colour well; red in autumn. The red fruits are also attractive. ♛ 2002.

'Burgundy Lace' A small, spreading tree with rich wine-red leaves divided to the base into narrow, sharply toothed lobes. C 1958. ♛ 2002.

'Butterfly' A medium-sized shrub of upright habit with rather small, deeply cut, grey-green leaves, margined

Acer palmatum continued:

cream, pink-tinged when young. The margin turns red in autumn. Raised in Japan before 1938.

'Chitoseyama' A superb clone with deeply cut, greenish-bronze leaves which colour richly in autumn. Old plants have a dense, mound-like habit with gracefully drooping branches. ♀ 2002.

'Corallinum' A rarely seen, most distinct cultivar of slow growth, forming a compact, small shrub. Young stems are soft coral-pink; the leaves, usually less than 5cm long, are 5-lobed, bright shrimp-pink when unfolding, changing to pale mottled green by midsummer. C 1900.

var. *coreanum* See 'Korean Gem'.

'Crimson Queen' (Dissectum Group) Leaves very deep reddish-purple, deeply divided into slender, finely cut lobes. The colour is long-lasting. C 1965. ♀ 2002.

'Crippsii' An elegant, slow-growing form with bronzed-red leaves, finely cut into grass-like segments. A plant of weak constitution. AM 1903.

'Deshojo' An upright shrub of medium size. Leaves with slender-pointed lobes are brilliant red when young, turning bright green.

Dissectum Group A group of clones in which the leaves are divided to the base into 5, 7 or 9 pinnatifid lobes. Generally shrubby in habit, mushroom-shaped when young, ultimately a dense, rounded bush, the branches falling from a high crown. Train carefully when young to produce a standard.

'Dissectum' Leaves green. C 1784. ♀ 2002.

'Dissectum Atropurpureum' Leaves deep purple. C 1879. See also 'Crimson Queen' and 'Inaba-shidare'.

'Dissectum Flavescens' Leaves soft yellow-green in spring. C 1928.

'Dissectum Nigrum' ('Ever Red') Dense habit, the deep bronze-red leaves turning red in autumn. C 1938.

'Dissectum Ornatum' See 'Ornatum'.

'Dissectum Palmatifidum' More finely cut foliage than 'Dissectum', but not very constant. FCC 1869.

'Dissectum Variegatum' Leaves bronze-red, some tipped pink and cream. C 1874.

Elegans Group (Heptalobum Group, Septemlobum Group) A group of clones with larger leaves usually 7-lobed, the lobes finely doubly serrate, broadest about the middle.

'Elegans' Leaves up to 13cm long, green, deeply and attractively toothed. C 1874.

'Elegans Purpureum' See 'Hessei'.

'Filigree' (Dissectum Group) A very beautiful and unusual form. Leaves with 7 deeply and finely divided lobes, pale yellow-green with darker veins, turning gold in autumn. C 1955.

'Fireglow' A vigorous, large shrub with deep red-purple foliage. Similar to but considered an improvement on 'Bloodgood'. C 1977.

'Garnet' (Dissectum Group) A strong-growing form, the large, deep garnet-red leaves with finely cut lobes. Raised in Holland. C 1950. ♀ 2002.

'Hagaromo' ('Sessilifolium', 'Decompositum', 'Koshimino') A small tree of erect habit with short-stalked, deeply cut leaves, colouring well in autumn.

Heptalobum Group See Elegans Group.

'Hessei' ('Elegans Purpureum') (Elegans Group) Leaves bronze-crimson. C 1893.

'Higasayama' Large shrub of upright habit. Leaves 7-lobed, edged with white and pink. Tends to revert. Sometimes incorrectly grown as 'Roseomarginatum' for which see 'Kagiri-nishiki'. C 1882.

'Inaba-shidare' (Dissectum Group) Large, red-stalked leaves are deeply divided into finely pointed, deep purplish lobes, crimson in autumn. Strong-growing, retaining its colour well. C 1930. ♀ 2002.

'Kagiri-nishiki' ('Roseomarginatum') Leaves with usually 5 often sickle-shaped lobes, pale green, irregularly edged with white and coral-pink. Charming but not constant and liable to revert. FCC 1865.

'Kamagata' A small shrub with slender, bright green shoots, and deeply 3–5-lobed leaves, red when young, turning brilliant yellow, orange and red in autumn. A seedling raised and selected by J.D. Vertrees.

'Karasugawa' Leaves deeply 5–7-lobed, pink when young becoming streaked and speckled with white and pink. C 1930.

'Katsura' A small shrub with small, 5-lobed leaves which are a bright orange-yellow when young, deeper at the margin and turning yellow and orange in autumn. ♀ 2002.

'Kinshii' A slow-growing, medium-sized shrub, the small leaves deeply cut into 7 slender lobes, turning yellow to orange in autumn. Raised in Japan before 1984.

'Korean Gem' (var. *coreanum* hort. not Nakai, 'Koreanum') Leaves 5-lobed, sometimes with 2 small additional lobes at the base, tinged purple on the margin, becoming rich crimson in autumn, lasting longer than most. Young shoots deep purple.

'Koreanum' See 'Korean Gem'.

'Koshimino' See 'Hagaromo'.

'Linearilobum' Leaves divided to the base into long, narrow, remotely serrate lobes. C 1867. AM 1896.

'Linearilobum Atropurpureum' ('Atrolineare') Similar to 'Linearilobum' but leaves bronze-red. C 1881.

'Little Princess' See 'Mapi-no-machihime'.

'Lutescens' Leaves glossy green turning clear butter-yellow in autumn. C 1928.

'Mapi-no-machihime' ('Little Princess') A dwarf, densely branched shrub with small, pale green leaves, to 4cm across, edged with red. C 1990.

'Nigrum' A form with leaves of deep purple. C 1928. ♀ 2002.

'Orange Dream' Large, upright shrub with green shoots. The 5–7-lobed leaves are bright orange-yellow turning yellow in autumn. C 1990.

'Ornatum' (Dissectum Group) Leaves bronze-tinted. C 1867.

'Ôsakazuki' (Elegans Group) Leaves green, turning in autumn to fiery scarlet, probably the most brilliant of all Japanese maples. C 1882. ♀ 2002.

'Ôshio-beni' Leaves deep orange-red, later bronze-green, brilliant scarlet in autumn. C 1898.

'Red Filigree Lace' (Dissectum Group) Deep red-purple, 7-lobed leaves, finely cut into thread-like segments. A seedling of 'Dissectum' found in Oregon.

'Red Pygmy' A slow-growing, shrubby form resembling 'Linearilobum Atropurpureum' but less than 2m tall and

Acer palmatum continued:

across, and retaining its colour longer. Leaves reddish-purple, often divided to the base into long, very slender lobes with some leaves bearing broader lobes. Selected in Holland before 1969. ♀ 2002.

'Reticulatum' See 'Shigitatsu-sawa'.

'Ribesifolium' See 'Shishigashira'.

'Roseomarginatum' See 'Kagiri-nishiki'.

'Rubrum' Large leaves are blood-red in spring, paling towards late summer. C 1864.

'Rufescens' A distinct, wide-spreading shrub with broad, deeply cleft leaves, green in summer and attractively tinted in autumn. C 1888.

'Sango-kaku' ('Senkaki') Coral bark maple. An invaluable shrub or small tree for winter effect, all the younger branches being a conspicuous coral-red. Leaves turning soft canary-yellow in autumn. C 1882. ♀ 2002. AM 1950.

'Seiryû' (Dissectum Group) An unusual form of upright habit. Leaves bright green, red-tinged when young, the lobes finely cut, orange-yellow splashed crimson in autumn. Makes a large shrub. C 1882. ♀ 2002.

'Senkaki' See 'Sango-kaku'.

Septemlobum Group See Elegans Group.

'Sessilifolium' See 'Hagaromo'.

'Sherwood Flame' A large, spreading shrub with dark purple leaves, deeply cut into 7 sharply toothed lobes. Raised in Oregon before 1970.

'Shigitatsu-sawa' ('Reticulatum') Leaves soft yellow-green with green margins and dark veins. C 1882.

'Shishigashira' ('Ribesifolium') This slow-growing form of distinctive, upright growth is almost fastigiate but has a broad crown. Leaves are deeply cut and dark green, changing to old gold in autumn. C 1882.

'Shishio Improved' A dense, bushy, medium-sized to large shrub with small leaves, brilliant red when young, later green. C 1965.

'Shojo-nomura' Leaves deeply divided into 7 sharply toothed and taper-pointed lobes, purple-red when young turning to green flushed orange-red in summer.

'Trompenburg' A large shrub with deep purplish-red young leaves, later green, red in autumn. They are divided nearly to the base, the lobes narrow with the margins rolled under. An outstanding plant raised in Holland. C 1965. ♀ 2002.

'Tsuma–beni' A slow-growing, small to medium-sized shrub, the pale green, 5-lobed leaves conspicuously marked with red-purple at the tips of the lobes when young becoming dark green in summer and red in autumn.

'Ukigumo' A striking, variegated form, the deeply 5-lobed leaves heavily mottled and edged white and pink. A small to medium-sized shrub. The name means passing cloud.

'Versicolor' Leaves green with white, pink-tinged blotches and spots. Liable to revert. C 1861.

'Villa Taranto' Similar to 'Linearilobum' but making a dome-shaped bush, the leaves with 5 slender leaflets. Reddish young leaves contrast well with the green older foliage, yellow in autumn. Propagated from a plant at Villa Taranto, Italy. C 1967.

'Yezo-nishiki' A fast-growing, small tree of upright habit, later arching. Young foliage bright red-purple,

deeper in summer, the 7-lobed leaves brilliant red in autumn.

papilio See A. caudatum.

†paxii Franch. A striking, small, semi-evergreen tree with shallowly 3-lobed or entire, leathery leaves, glaucous beneath. Yunnan, China.

pensylvanicum L. (A. striatum Du Roi) Moosewood. A small tree, young stems green, beautifully striped with white and pale jade-green. Leaves, up to 18cm across, are 3-lobed, turning bright yellow in the autumn. Not very tolerant of chalk soils. E North America. I 1755. ♀ 2002. **'Erythrocladum'** A lovely form with brilliant candy-pink, white-striated young shoots in winter. Bark on the main trunk yellow. A plant of weak constitution when grown as a tree, it is much more effective as a multi-stemmed specimen, branched low down. FCC 1977. AM 1976.

†pentaphyllum Diels. A rare, handsome, but unfortunately tender species making a small tree. The leaves, on long, slender, scarlet petioles, are divided to the base into 5 linear-lanceolate segments, green above, glaucous and reticulate below. Sichuan, China. I from seed collected by T.T. Yü in 1937, more recently reintroduced by Mikinori Ogisu.

pictum Thunb. ex Murray (A. mono Maxim.) A medium-sized tree with palmately 5–7-lobed leaves, which usually turn bright yellow in autumn. Japan, China, Korea. I 1881 by Charles Maries. **f. ambiguum** (Pax) H. Ohashi (A. mono var. ambiguum (Pax) Rehder) A rare variety with leaves minutely downy beneath. Autumn colour usually yellow. Origin unknown. C 1892.

platanoides L. Norway maple. A handsome, fast-growing tree of large size. The conspicuous clusters of yellow flowers are produced on the bare stems in April, usually following those of A. opalus. In autumn the foliage turns clear bright yellow, occasionally red. Europe, Caucasus. Long cultivated. ♀ 2002. AM 1967. **'Cleveland'** A selection of strong, upright habit making an oval head of branches with large, deep green leaves. Popular as a street tree in North America. C 1948. **'Columnare'** A large, erect, columnar form. Raised in France in 1855. **'Crimson King'** A handsome, large tree with leaves of deep crimson-purple and deep yellow flowers tinged red. A seedling of 'Schwedleri' raised in Belgium in 1937. ♀ 2002. **'Crimson Sentry'** A narrowly columnar form with reddish-purple leaves, not as dark as 'Crimson King' of which it was a sport. C 1974. **'Cucullatum'** A large, erect tree. Leaves long-stalked, fan-shaped at the base, prominently 7–9-veined and shallowly 7- to 9-lobed, each lobe divided into 3 or more, slender-pointed teeth. Similar in effect to 'Laciniatum' but lobes not as pointed. C 1866. **'Deborah'** Leaves with wavy margins, brilliant red when young, turning to dark green, orange in autumn. A seedling of 'Schwedleri' raised in Canada before 1975. **'Dissectum'** Almost identical to 'Palmatifidum', but leaves darker and glossier green, the lobes with crinkled margins and straight or down-pointing lobes. C 1869. **'Drummondii'** A very striking cultivar, the leaves with a broad, creamy-white marginal band. Any reverting shoots should be removed. C 1903. AM 1956. **'Emerald Queen'** A vigorous form with glossy dark green leaves, yellow in autumn. Upright when young, broadening with age. Selected in Oregon, USA in 1959. **'Erectum'** An erect, usually slow-growing cultivar of medium size with short ascending branches. Found in Rochester, New York before 1931. **'Globosum'** A striking, small tree with short branches forming a dense, mop-shaped head. C 1873. **'Laciniatum'** Eagle's claw maple. An erect, large tree, the leaves fan-shaped at the base, 5-veined and deeply 5-lobed, the lobes ending in long, slender, claw-like points. C 1683. **'Lorbergii'** See 'Palmatifidum'. **'Meyering'** A Dutch selection of upright habit. Young leaves bronze-tinged, soon green, brilliant orange-red in autumn. C 1958. **'Palmatifidum'** ('Lorbergii') Medium-sized tree; leaves pale green, the 5 deep lobes with entire margins and long-pointed tips ascending from the leaf plane. C 1866. **Princeton Gold** ('Prigo') PBR. Leaves bright yellow when young on red petioles. **'Reitenbachii'** A medium-sized tree. Leaves red on emerging, gradually turning to green and finally assuming red autumn tints. C 1874. **'Schwedleri'** Leaves and young growths rich crimson-purple. Most effective when pruned hard every other autumn. C 1864. ♀ 2002. **subsp.** *turkestanicum* (Pax) de Jong (*A. turkestanicum* Pax) A small, bushy tree with 3- to 5- or 7-lobed leaves. W Asia. **'Walderseei'** An unusual form with leaves that are densely speckled with white flecks, appearing greyish from a distance. A tree of rather weak constitution and difficult to propagate. C 1904.

platanoides L. × *truncatum* Bunge. This hybrid is intermediate in leaf shape between the parents and makes a medium-sized tree, smaller than *A. platanoides*. It is a handsome tree, effective in flower and autumn colour. Some named cultivars such as 'Norwegian Sunset' and 'Pacific Sunset' are grown in the USA. A tree in the Sir Harold Hillier Gardens and Arboretum was raised from seed received as *A. truncatum*.

pseudoplatanus L. Sycamore. A picturesque, large tree, and one of the best for exposed situations in any soil. Long planted and naturalised in many parts of the British Isles. Native of Europe and W Asia. **'Atropurpureum'** ('Purpureum Spaethii') A selected form with leaves purple beneath. C 1862. **'Brilliantissimum'** A distinct, small, slow-growing tree. The young leaves are glorious shrimp-pink, changing to pale yellow-green and finally green. C 1905. ♀ 2002. FCC 1977. AM 1925. **'Corstorphinense'** Corstorphine plane. Leaves golden-yellow when young. It was under this tree at Corstorphine near Edinburgh, in 1679, that Lord Forrester was murdered with his own sword by his first wife's sister who was later executed for the deed. The original tree was said to be haunted by their ghosts. **'Erectum'** A large tree with erect branches. C 1949. '**Erythrocarpum'** A form with conspicuous and attractive, red seed wings. C 1864. **'Esk Sunset'** Leaves pink when young, becoming green, conspicuously blotched and mottled with pale pink, grey-green and white, purple-red beneath. A striking, slow-growing selection from New Zealand. **'Leopoldii'** Leaves yellowish-pink at first, later green, speckled and splashed yellow and pink. C 1864. FCC 1865. **'Negenia'** Vigorous and conical with large, dark green, red-stalked leaves. Selected in 1948 in Holland where it is planted as a street tree. **'Nizetii'** Leaves heavily blotched and streaked pale green and

white, purple-tinged beneath. C 1887. **'Prinz Handjéry'** A small, slow-growing tree, similar to 'Brilliantissimum' but slightly larger, with leaves purple-tinged beneath. C 1883. FCC 1890. **Purpureum Group** (f. *purpureum* Loud.) A large, picturesque tree, the undersurfaces of the leaves being conspicuously coloured purple; effective in a breeze. **'Purpureum Spaethii'** See 'Atropurpureum'. **'Simon-Louis Frères'** Leaves pink when young becoming blotched and streaked green and white, green beneath. C 1881. **'Worley'** ('Worleei') Golden sycamore. Medium-sized tree. Leaves soft yellow-green at first, then golden, finally green. Raised in Germany before 1893.

pseudosieboldianum (Pax) Komar. A very graceful, large shrub or small tree of spreading habit, uncommon in gardens, with glabrous, bloomy young shoots. Leaves up to 15cm across, but often less, with usually 11 sharply toothed lobes which reach about half way to the base, glossy green beneath and with hairs on the veins and in the vein axils. Flowers in upright or spreading corymbs; petals white, calyx red. NE China, Korea.

‡*pycnanthum* K. Koch. A rare, medium-sized to large tree, closely related to *A. rubrum* from which it differs in its smaller, shallowly lobed leaves which are bronze when young, turning deep red-purple in autumn. Male trees in particular are striking in early spring when the red flowers open. Some of the largest specimens in Britain are at the Sir Harold Hillier Gardens and Arboretum, one was 14m tall in 2000. We first received seed of this species from Japan in 1960.

quinquelobum See *A. divergens*.

rubescens Hayata (*A. morrisonense* Li) A small, spreading snakebark maple, the bark green striped with white. Leaves to about 9cm long and nearly as wide, on a red petiole, very glossy on both sides, usually with 5 sharply toothed lobes, the terminal lobe tapered to a fine point. A plant raised from seed of a cultivated specimen in a British garden appears to have produced a hybrid with *A. capillipes*. Taiwan. See also *A. caudatifolium*. **'Millicent'** Leaves heavily blotched and speckled with white and grey-green. A seedling selected at Mallet Court Nursery.

‡*rubrum* L. Red maple, Canadian maple. A free-growing, ultimately large tree. The palmate leaves are dark green above, glaucous beneath and turn rich red and scarlet in autumn. Although fairly lime-tolerant, it rarely colours as well on chalky soils. E North America. C 1656. AM 1969. **'Armstrong'** A vigorous, upright form with deeply cut leaves, orange-yellow in autumn. Selected in 1947. **'Columnare'** Eventually a tall tree of narrowly columnar habit, a fiery pillar in autumn. It has reached 18.9m tall at the Sir Harold Hillier Gardens and Arboretum (2000). C 1889. **'October Glory'** An American selection with long-lasting, brilliant red autumn colour. C 1964. ♀ 2002. AM 1988. **Red Sunset** ('Franksred') PBR A form of upright habit with particularly good red autumn colour. C 1968. **'Scanlon'** A medium-sized tree of American origin eventually forming a broadly columnar head of branches. Rich autumn colour. C 1948. **'Schlesingeri'** A clone notable for its outstanding, very early autumn colour – a rich deep scarlet. C 1888. AM 1976.

rufinerve Siebold & Zucc. A medium-sized tree; young stems glaucous, older stems and trunk green with conspicuous, white striations. Leaves 3-lobed, recalling those of *A. pensylvanicum*. Bright red and yellow autumn colours. Japan. I 1879. ♀ 2002. AM 1986 (for autumn colour). **'Albolimbatum'** See 'Hatsuyuki'. **'Erythrocladum'** A slow-growing form with pale yellow summer shoots turning red in winter. C 1953. **'Hatsuyuki'** ('Albolimbatum') Leaves mottled and margined white. Autumn colour brilliant red and purple. C 1869.

saccharinum L. (*A. dasycarpum* Ehrh., *A. eriocarpum* Michx.) Silver maple. A large, fast-growing tree with deeply 5-lobed leaves, silvery-white beneath, creating a delightful effect when ruffled by the wind. Attractive autumn tints. E North America. I 1725. **'Fastigiatum'** See 'Pyramidale'. **Laciniatum Group** (f. *laciniatum* (Carrière) Rehder) This name covers forms with deeply cut leaves. See also 'Wieri'. **'Lutescens'** Leaves orange-yellow when young, soft yellow-green during summer. C 1881. **'Pendulum'** A form with somewhat pendent branches. C 1875. **'Pyramidale'** ('Fastigiatum') An upright form. C 1885. **'Wieri'** (Laciniatum Group) A selection with pendent lower branches and leaves deeply divided into sharply cut lobes. Found in 1873.

saccharum Marshall. Sugar maple. An ultimately large ornamental tree resembling the Norway maple (*A. platanoides*). One of America's finest autumn-colouring trees but usually not as good in the British Isles. The colour varies, orange, gold, scarlet and crimson being exhibited by different individuals. C and E North America, where the sap is used to make maple syrup. Forms of this species are also found in Mexico and Guatemala. I 1735. **subsp. grandidentatum** (Torr. & A. Gray) Desmarais (*A. grandidentatum* Torr. & A. Gray) Usually a small, rather slow-growing tree with 3-lobed leaves. Attractive autumn tints of red and orange. W North America, New Mexico. I 1882. **subsp. leucoderme** (Small) Desmarais (*A. leucoderme* Small) Chalk maple. A small tree with 3- to 5-lobed leaves. Lovely autumn tints. SE USA. C 1900. **'Newton Sentry'** ('Columnare') A striking but slow-growing form of subsp. *nigrum*. Columnar habit with upright branches and no central leader; in early autumn turns into a pillar of orange. See also 'Temple's Upright'. C 1871. **subsp. nigrum** (Michx. f.) Desmarais (*A. nigrum* Michx. f.) Black maple. A medium to large tree with deeply furrowed bark and large, 3- sometimes 5-lobed leaves of a dull, dark green, turning yellow in autumn. The petioles have stipules near the base. E North America. I 1812. **'Temple's Upright'** ('Monumentale') A conical tree with a strong central leader and ascending branches. Has been confused with 'Newton Sentry'. C 1887.

sempervirens L. (*A. creticum* auct. not L., *A. orientale* auct. not L.) Cretan maple. A slow-growing, often semi-evergreen, large shrub or small tree. The small leaves, up to 4cm long, are various shapes – ovate and entire to 3-lobed – glabrous and bright green and often retained until Christmas. Related to *A. monspessulanum*. E Mediterranean region. I 1752.

shirasawanum Koidz. A small, bushy tree or large shrub of elegant habit, related to *A. japonicum*, with bloomy shoots. The rounded, bright green leaves, with petioles

glabrous or nearly so, have usually 11 sharply toothed lobes and turn orange and red in autumn. Flowers with a pink calyx and cream petals, in spreading or almost upright clusters. Japan. C 1888. **'Aureum'** (*A. japonicum* 'Aureum') A beautiful, slow-growing form with soft yellow leaves. Can scorch in full sun. ♀ 2002. FCC 1884.

sieboldianum Miq. A small tree or large shrub similar to *A. japonicum* but with flowers yellow, not red, and leaves finely toothed. Japan. C 1880. AM 1966.

†*sikkimense* Miq. (*A. hookeri* Miq.) A medium-sized, semi-evergreen tree with red young shoots and large, usually entire leaves. Only suitable for the mildest areas. E Himalaya, N Burma, Yunnan. I 1892.

'Silver Cardinal' (*A.* × *conspicuum* 'Silver Cardinal') A small tree with red young shoots and white-striped bark. Leaves glossy dark green, the blade to 13cm long, on a 10cm red petiole. They are shallowly 5-lobed, the terminal lobe long and tapering, variously blotched, mottled and streaked with white and pink when young. It is said to be a seedling of *A. pensylvanicum* but appears close to *A. rubescens*. AM 1985.

'Silver Vein' See *A.* × *conspicuum* 'Silver Vein'.

spicatum Lam. Mountain maple. A small tree or large shrub. Leaves 3- or sometimes 5-lobed, colouring red and yellow in autumn. Flowers in slender, erect panicles, later replaced by attractive, red fruits. Not very tolerant of chalk soils. C and E North America. I 1750.

stachyophyllum Hiern (*A. tetramerum* Pax) A rare, small tree of upright habit, the young shoots and petioles flushed scarlet. Leaves ovate, sharply 3-lobed and dentate, ending in a long point. E Himalaya, W China. I 1901.

sterculiaceum Wall. (*A. villosum* Wall.) A remarkable tree with very large, palmately lobed leaves, and drooping clusters of large fruits. Striking when bearing its racemes of large flowers in spring. Often gives good autumn colour. Himalaya. I before 1850.

striatum See *A. pensylvanicum*.

syriacum See *A. obtusifolium*.

tataricum L. Tatarian maple. A large shrub or small tree of spreading habit. The leaves are dull, pale green and doubly toothed, tapering to a slender point. On young plants and vigorous shoots they may be lobed and resemble those of *A. ginnala* to which it is closely related. Flowers greenish-white, produced in erect panicles in May and June. SE Europe, SW Asia. I 1759. **subsp. ginnala** (Maxim.) Wesm. (*A. ginnala* Maxim.) Amur maple. A large shrub or small tree of vigorous, spreading habit. The bright green, 3-lobed leaves turn to orange and vivid crimson in autumn. Manchuria, China and Japan. I 1860. **subsp. ginnala 'Flame'** is compact and shrubby with brilliant red autumn colour. It has been grown from seed. **subsp. semenovii** (Reg. & Herd.) E. Murray (*A. ginnala* subsp. *semenovii* (Reg. & Herd.) Pax) Shrubby variety with smaller, occasionally 5-lobed leaves. Afghanistan, C Asia. C 1880.

tegmentosum Maxim. A small, spreading tree with bloomy young shoots, the green bark conspicuously streaked with white. Leaves bright green, to 20cm across, with 3–5 taper-pointed lobes, turning yellow in autumn. One of the most striking of snake-bark maples. NE Asia.

tenellum Pax (*A. mono* var. *tricuspis* (Rehder) Rehder) A small tree, often shrubby, related to *A. pictum*. The small, glossy green leaves, to 10cm across, are shallowly 3-lobed or almost entire, turning yellow in autumn. C China. I 1901 by Ernest Wilson.

tetramerum See *A. stachyophyllum*.

trautvetteri Medwed. A medium-sized tree with large, deeply 5-lobed leaves, deep golden-yellow in autumn; flowers are in upright panicles. Fruits with showy, broad, red wings in summer. A handsome foliage tree, conspicuous when the bright red buds open in spring. Caucasus, E Turkey. I 1866. AM 1975.

trifidum See *A. buergerianum*.

triflorum Komar. A very rare, slow-growing, small tree related and similar to *A. maximowiczianum*, but with characteristic pale grey-brown, flaking bark. Leaves trifoliolate, glaucous beneath. One of the most consistent small trees for the brilliance of its autumn colour. Manchuria, Korea. I 1923. ♀ 2002.

truncatum Bunge. A small, round-headed tree bearing 5–7-lobed, bright green leaves which are truncate or occasionally heart-shaped at the base. Corymbs of showy, yellow-green flowers emerge with the leaves. China. I 1881. **'Akikaze-nishiki'** Leaf lobes irregularly margined with creamy-white.

tschonoskii Maxim. A very rare, small tree or large shrub with 5-lobed leaves turning a lovely colour in autumn. Not very tolerant of chalk soils. Japan. I 1902. **subsp. koreanum** A.E. Murray (var. *rubripes* Kom.) Leaves larger, more deeply lobed, young shoots and petioles bright red. NE China, North and South Korea. **var. rubripes** See subsp. *koreanum*.

turkestanicum See *A. platanoides* subsp. *turkestanicum*.

ukurunduense Trautv. & C.A. Mey. See *A. caudatum* subsp. *ukurunduense*.

velutinum Boiss. A large tree with broad, 3- to 5-lobed sycamore-like leaves, softly downy beneath. Bright yellow flowers in dense, upright panicles appear after the leaves emerge. Caucasus, N Iran. **var. glabrescens** (Boiss. & Buhse) Murray (*A. insigne* Boiss.) Leaves smooth and glaucous beneath. **var. vanvolxemii** (Mast.) Rehder. Very large leaves, blue-green beneath and hairy only on the veins. I 1873.

villosum See *A. sterculiaceum*.

†*wardii* W.W. Sm. The true species of this name is a small tree with purple shoots and 3-lobed leaves from Upper Burma, Yunnan and Tibet. I by George Forrest but possibly no longer in cultivation. The plant previously listed under this name is *A. fabri* q.v.

'White Tigress' A small, bushy-headed, often multi-stemmed tree with the bark on the trunk and branches conspicuously streaked with blue-green and white. Leaves to about 15cm long and across, with 5 shallow, taper-pointed lobes, matt-green above, yellow in autumn. Fruits in red-stalked racemes to 15cm long. Of American origin, it is thought to be a hybrid of *A. tegmentosum*.

wilsonii Rehder. A large shrub or sometimes small tree with glabrous, generally 3-lobed leaves, occasionally with 2 small basal lobes. Young foliage is bright shrimp- to coral-pink, passing to soft pale green with age. SW China. I 1907 by Ernest Wilson.

× *zoeschense* Pax (*A. neglectum* Lange not Walpers.) A medium-sized tree with 5-lobed, somewhat purple-tinged, dark green leaves. Clearly a hybrid of *A. campestre* possibly with *A. cappadocicum* but leaves larger and more angular. Garden origin. **'Annae'** A form with deep purple-red young foliage. C 1908.

*†**ACRADENIA** Kippist—**Rutaceae**—A genus of 2 species. *A. euodiiformis* occurs in E Australia.

frankliniae Kippist. A small to medium-sized, evergreen shrub of upright habit succeeding well in mild areas. It has dark green, trifoliolate, aromatic leaves and flat clusters of white flowers in May, and occasionally, like the related *Choisya ternata*, in autumn. It has grown undamaged by frost at the Sir Harold Hillier Gardens and Arboretum since 1988. W Tasmania. I 1845.

Adam's needle See *Yucca gloriosa*.

*†**ADENOCARPUS** DC.—**Leguminosae**—About 15 species of very leafy, evergreen shrubs, related to *Laburnum*, with trifoliolate leaves and broom-like, golden-yellow flowers. Natives of the Mediterranean region, Canary Islands and mountains of tropical Africa.

†*anagyrifolius* Coss. & Balansa. Small to medium-sized shrub with glandular stems and slightly glaucous, trifoliolate leaves. Golden-yellow pea-flowers in summer. Pods warty. Morocco. **var. leiocarpus** Maire. A form with smooth pods.

decorticans Boiss. Vigorous shrub, densely clothed with silvery, hairy, trifoliolate leaves. Flowers in May and June. Essentially for a sunny wall. Spain. AM 1947.

†*foliolosus* (Aiton) DC. A small shrub with small, hairy leaves, densely crowded along the stems, and numerous short, dense, terminal racemes of yellow pea-flowers in spring.

AESCULUS L.—**Hippocastanaceae**—The horse chestnuts and buckeyes are among the most ornamental of late spring- and early summer-flowering trees. All have deciduous, compound, palmate leaves and flowers in panicles, and all are easily cultivated, thriving in any soil. About 13 species in North America, SE Europe and E Asia. Harmful if eaten.

arguta See *A. glabra* var. *arguta*.

× *bushii* Schneid. (*A. glabra* × *A. pavia*) (*A.* × *mississippiensis* Sarg.) A small to medium-sized tree with individual flowers of red, pink and yellow in May or June. Mississippi, Arkansas (USA).

californica (Spach) Nutt. A low, widespreading tree or shrub. Leaves relatively small, with 5–7 rather blue-green leaflets. The fragrant, white or pink-tinted flowers are borne in dense, erect panicles up to 20cm long during summer. California. I about 1850 by William Lobb.

× *carnea* Hayne (*A. hippocastanum* × *A. pavia*) (*A. rubicunda* Loisel.) Red horse chestnut. A large tree, much used for avenues and parks. Flowers rose-pink in panicles up to 20cm long. Similar to *A. hippocastanum* but generally smaller and more compact with smaller, darker green leaflets. C 1820. **'Briotii'** A compact form with deeper pink flowers. Raised in 1858. ♀ 2002. AM 1965. **'Plantierensis'** (*A.* × *carnea* × *A. hippocastanum*) Perhaps the best form. A large tree resembling *A. hippo-*

castanum but with pale pink flowers. A back-cross that does not set seed. Raised in France in about 1894.

chinensis Bunge. The Chinese horse chestnut is a very distinct, small, slow-growing and rare tree with small, white flowers carried in long, slender, cylindrical racemes. The leaves have 5 or 7 narrow, bright green leaflets. Some plants received under this name are *A. indica*. N China. I 1912 by William Purdom.

'Dallimorei' (*A. flava* + *A. hippocastanum*) A vigorous tree, probably eventually of large size with stout shoots and brown winter buds, the scales edged with green, not sticky. Flowers in large panicles in late spring to early summer, creamy-yellow at first with a deeper yellow blotch becoming white blotched with brick-red. Bristly fruits occasionally start to ripen but fall in summer before maturing. Originated from a grafted tree of *A. flava* in Kent before 1956. An unusual alternative to the common and the red horse chestnut which deserves wider planting.

flava Sol. (*A. octandra* Marshall) Sweet buckeye. A medium-sized or large tree; flowers nearest to yellow in a horse chestnut, borne in May and June; leaves with 5–7 leaflets, usually giving good autumn tints. SE USA. I 1764. ♀ 2002.

georgiana See *A. sylvatica*.

glabra Willd. (*A. glabra* f. *pallida* (Willd.) Schelle) Ohio buckeye. A small to medium-sized tree with rough bark. Leaves, usually with 5 leaflets, are orange-yellow in autumn. Yellow-green flowers with exserted stamens appear in May, followed by prickly fruits. SE and C USA. I 1809. **var. arguta** (Buckley) B.L. Rob. (*A. arguta* Buckley) Texas buckeye, White buckeye. Small, shrubby tree with leaves of 7–9 deeply double-toothed leaflets. Soft cream flowers in May. Oklahoma, Texas (USA). I 1909. **f. pallida** See *A. glabra*.

glaucescens See *A.* × *neglecta*.

hippocastanum L. Common horse chestnut. Possibly the most beautiful of large, flowering trees hardy in the British Isles. Exceptionally attractive in May when covered with its stout candles of white flowers with a yellow then red blotch. Provides the familiar conkers of children's games in autumn. Native of the wild border region between Greece and Albania. I into W Europe in 1576 and to the British Isles early in the 17th century. ♀ 2002. 'Baumannii' ('Flore Pleno') Flowers double, white; does not set seed. Arose as a sport in about 1820. ♀ 2002. 'Digitata' ('Pumila') A curious, dwarf form with smaller, deeply incised leaves. 'Flore Pleno' See 'Baumannii'. 'Hampton Court Gold' Leaves soft yellow when young becoming greenish-yellow. Slow-growing and can burn in full sun. Derives from a tree, which is about 12m tall, in the 'Wilderness' garden at Hampton Court. **Laciniata Group** (f. *laciniata* (Jacques) Schelle) A slow-growing form with narrowly, deeply and irregularly incised leaves. Old plants have slender, drooping branches. 'Pumila' See 'Digitata'. 'Pyramidalis' An unusual form of broadly pyramidal habit. C 1895.

× *hybrida* DC. (*A. flava* × *A. pavia*) (*A. lyonii* hort., *A. versicolor* Wender.) Small to medium-sized tree with glossy, dark green leaves producing red and yellow flowers, in panicles 10–18cm long, in June. Occurs wild in the Alleghany Mountains and has arisen in cultivation.

indica (Wall. ex Cambess.) Hook. Indian horse chestnut. A magnificent, large tree with panicles of pink-flushed flowers, occasionally as much as 40cm long and 13cm wide, in June and July. Leaves, with 7 leaflets, are bronze when young, becoming glossy dark green, then turning orange or yellow in autumn. A splendid specimen grows on chalk soil on the site of our West Hill nursery, Winchester (15m tall in 1990). NW Himalaya. I 1851. FCC 1933. AM 1922. 'Sydney Pearce' A free-flowering, upright form with dark olive-green leaves. Flowers in large panicles have individual blossoms up to 2.5cm across, the petals white, marked yellow and prettily suffused pink. Raised at Kew in 1928. ♀ 2002. AM 1967.

× *mississippiensis* See *A.* × *bushii*.

× *mutabilis* (Spach) Schelle (*A. pavia* × *A. sylvatica*) A large shrub or small tree with red and yellow flowers in May and June. C 1834. 'Harbisonii' A form with bright red flowers raised at the Arnold Arboretum, Boston, USA. C 1905. 'Induta' ('Rosea Nana') Flowers apricot with yellow markings during summer. C 1905. AM 1959.

× *neglecta* Lindl. (*A. glaucescens* Sarg.) (*A. flava* × *A. sylvatica*) A medium-sized tree bearing panicles of pale yellow flowers in May and June. Rich autumn colour. SE USA. C 1826. 'Erythroblastos' A spectacular, rather slow-growing form with young leaves of brilliant shrimp-pink changing to pale yellow-green later in the season. C 1935. ♀ 2002. AM 1962. **var. georgiana** See *A. sylvatica*.

octandra See *A. flava*.

parviflora Walter. Bottlebrush buckeye. A spreading shrub, 2.5m or more high, flowering freely in July and August. Flowers are white with long-exserted red anthers, in slender panicles 20–30cm long. Leaves bronze when young and attractively coloured yellow in autumn. SE USA. I 1785. ♀ 2002. AM 1955.

pavia L. (*A. splendens* Sarg.) Red buckeye. A beautiful, medium-sized to large shrub or small tree, leaves with 5 glossy green leaflets; crimson flowers, in panicles 15cm long, open in June to July. S USA. I 1711. ♀ 2002. 'Atrosanguinea' Flowers a little deeper red. 'Humilis' Low, spreading growth; red flowers. C 1826.

splendens. See *A. pavia*.

sylvatica Bartr. (*A. georgiana* Sarg., *A. neglecta* var. *georgiana* (Sarg.) Sarg.) A large shrub or small tree with dense panicles of orange-red flowers. SE USA. I 1905.

turbinata Blume. Japanese horse chestnut. A large tree with outsize foliage attractively veined and tinted in autumn. Long panicles of yellowish-white flowers, each with a red spot, appear in May or June, a little later than *A. hippocastanum*. Japan. Fruits large, pear-shaped, not spiny. I before 1880.

wilsonii Rehder. A very rare tree with larger leaves than those of *A. chinensis*. Small, white flowers with a yellow, later red, centre appear in June. I 1908 by Ernest Wilson from China.

‡†***AGAPETES** D. Don ex G. Don (*Pentapterygium* Klotzsch)—**Ericaceae**—A genus of about 95 evergreen species of usually bristly, often epiphytic shrubs, natives of the Himalaya and E Asia to NE Australia. Suitable for cool conservatory cultivation or for a sheltered shaded wall in the mildest areas.

incurvata (Griff.) Sleum. (*Pentapterygium rugosum* Hook. f.) A handsome, small shrub with rather stiff and upright stems; leaves, larger and broader than those of *A. serpens*, are 7.5–10cm long, rugose and toothed. Nodding flowers are 2.5cm long and white, marbled purple or red; fruits purple. Khasia Hills, Assam and Bhutan. C 1860. AM 1934.

'Ludgvan Cross' (*A. incurvata* × *A. serpens*) (*Pentapterygium* 'Ludgvan Cross') A striking hybrid, intermediate in size and character between its parents. Flowers are large, pale pink, conspicuously veined with deeper pink, and have a crimson calyx. Garden origin. ♀ 2002.

serpens (Wight) Sleum. (*Pentapterygium serpens* (Wight) Klotzsch) A beautiful, long-flowering shrub to 2m high with long, sinuous, arching branches. Leaves lanceolate, 12mm long; flowers bright red with darker markings, pendent, borne all along the slender branches like curious Japanese lanterns. E Himalaya. C 1884. ♀ 2002. AM 1900. **'Nepal Cream'** A form with creamy-green flowers introduced from the Milke Danda in Nepal by Harry van de Laar.

‡*AGARISTA D. Don ex G. Don—Ericaceae—About 30 species of evergreen shrubs and trees related to *Lyonia* and *Pieris*, natives of South and Central America, the SE USA and Africa.

populifolia (Lam.) Judd (*Leucothoe populifolia* (Lam.) Dipp.) A vigorous, medium-sized shrub of considerable quality. Leaves, to 10cm long, are lanceolate to ovate-lanceolate. Flowers white, in short racemes. Subject to injury in the coldest areas. SE USA. I 1765.

†*AGATHOSMA Willd.—Rutaceae—A genus of about 135 species of heath-like evergreens, natives of South Africa.

pulchella (L.) Link (*Barosma pulchella* (L.) Bartl. & Wendl., *Diosma pulchella* L.) An attractive, aromatic, heath-like shrub with terminal clusters of lilac-pink flowers. A pleasing plant but only suitable for the mildest areas or cool greenhouses. I 1787.

AGERATINA Spach—Compositae—A large genus of some 250 species of shrubs and herbs with opposite leaves and flowerheads in corymbs. Natives mainly of Mexico, Central America and N South America, with a few species in the USA.

†*ligustrina* (DC.) R. King & H. Robinson (*Eupatorium ligustrinum* DC. *E. micranthum* Lessing, *E. weinmannianum* Reg. & Koern.) An evergreen shrub producing large, flat heads of small, white flowers in late summer and autumn. In favoured districts grows to 2.5m. Mexico to Costa Rica. I 1867. ♀ 2002.

AILANTHUS Desf.—Simaroubaceae—A genus of about 5 handsome, fast-growing, deciduous trees with large, pinnate leaves from E Asia to Australia. Extremely tolerant of atmospheric pollution.

altissima (Mill.) Swingle (*A. giraldii* Dode, *A. glandulosa* Desf.) Tree of heaven. A large, imposing tree with distinctive, ash-like leaves, up to 1m long on young specimens. Female trees produce large, conspicuous bunches of reddish, key-like fruits. N China. Widely naturalised in regions with hot summers. I 1751 by Peter Collinson. AM 1953. **'Pendulifolia'** A graceful tree with very large, drooping leaves. C 1899.

flavescens See *Toona sinensis*.
giraldii See *A. altissima*.
glandulosa See *A. altissima*.
vilmoriniana Dode. Very close to *A. altissima* from which it differs in the occasional bristly shoots and sometimes rich red rachis. W China. I 1897 by Père Farges.

Alabama snow wreath See *Neviusia alabamensis*.

ALANGIUM Lindl.—Alangiaceae—A genus of about 20 species of trees, shrubs and climbers found mainly in warm regions of the Old World. *A. platanifolium* makes an attractive foliage plant with unusual flowers shaped like a miniature lily.

chinense (Lour.) Harms. A handsome shrub with large, maple-like leaves. The fragrant flowers have 6 recurved petals and open in June and July. Widely distributed in E Asia and Africa.

platanifolium Harms. Large shrub with 3–5-, occasionally 7-lobed leaves and cymes of white, yellow-anthered flowers in June and July. Japan, China, Korea, Manchuria, Taiwan. I 1879 by Charles Maries.

ALBIZIA Durazz.—Leguminosae—Deciduous, mimosa-like shrubs, small trees and climbers valuable for their handsome foliage and attractive, fluffy heads of flowers. Full sun. About 150 species mainly in the Old World tropics and South America.

distachya See *Paraserianthes lophantha*.
julibrissin (Willd.) Durazz. Silk tree. The hardiest species; a small, spreading, graceful tree with pink flowerheads in late summer to early autumn. Iran to China, Taiwan. I 1745. **'Rosea'** A very hardy form with dense heads of bright pink flowers. I 1918 by Ernest Wilson from Korea. ♀ 2002.
lophantha See *Paraserianthes lophantha*.

Alder See *Alnus*. **Alder, white** See *Clethra acuminata*.

†*ALLOCASUARINA L. Johnson—Casuarinaceae—The Sheokes are a genus of evergreen trees and shrubs with about 65 species distributed from the Malay archipelago to the Pacific islands and Australia. An interesting genus with no clear relatives, they show reduction in many features. Once thought to be very primitive, they are now considered to be highly evolved. All are very tender.

nana (Sieber ex Spreng.) L.A.S. Johnson (*Casuarina nana* Sieber ex Spreng.) Dwarf sheoke. Small, densely branched Australian shrub with slender, rush-like stems. Only for the mildest areas.

Allspice See *Calycanthus*.
Almond See *Prunus dulcis*.

ALNUS Ehrh.—Betulaceae—The alders will grow in almost any soil, except very shallow chalk soils, and are particularly useful for damp situations. The most lime-tolerant species are *A. cordata*, *A. glutinosa* and *A. viridis*. *A. orientalis* and *A. nitida* require deep soils. Deciduous trees and shrubs with about 35 species mainly in N temperate regions but extending through Mexico to the Andes of N Argentina. Male and female flowers are borne on the same plant, the male catkins long and drooping, often very ornamental in late winter or early spring, the females short, becoming a woody cone.

cordata Desf. Italian alder. A splendid, medium to large, conical tree for all types of soil, growing rapidly even on chalk soils; notable for its bright green, glistening foliage, and large, ochre-yellow male catkins. Corsica and S Italy. Corsican trees have rounder leaves. I 1820. ♀ 2002. FCC 1987. AM 1976.

crispa See *A. viridis* subsp. *crispa*.

fauriei Lev. A large, dense shrub or small tree with glabrous young shoots. Broadly wedge-shaped leaves, to 10cm long and 13cm across, are rounded to cuneate and entire at the base with a broad, truncate and emarginate apex. They are glabrous above with conspicuous tufts of brown hairs in the vein axils and along the midrib at the base beneath. N and C Japan.

firma Siebold & Zucc. Japanese green alder. A densely branched, small tree or large shrub with occasionally downy branches and ovate, acuminate, sharply toothed, many-veined leaves often remaining green until late autumn. Kyushu, Japan. The following variety is the plant most often cultivated. **var. *hirtella*** Franch. & Sav. A graceful variety making a large shrub or small tree with handsome, hornbeam-like foliage. Japan. I 1894.

glutinosa (L.) Gaertn. Common alder. A small to medium-sized, bushy tree with sticky young growths and yellow catkins in March. Once used extensively in the manufacture of clogs in the north of England. In recent years thousands of alders in Britain have been killed by the fungus *Phytophthora*. Europe (incl. British Isles), W Asia, N Africa. Corsican trees are more spreading with thinner twigs and smaller leaves. **'Aurea'** Leaves pale yellow, particularly noticeable in spring and early summer. Raised about 1860. FCC 1867. **subsp. *betuloides*** Ansin. A form with smooth, white or grey-white bark found in a small area of E Turkey. Only described in 1993, it was introduced to the Sir Harold Hillier Gardens and Arboretum in the same year. **'Fastigiata'** See 'Pyramidalis'. **'Imperialis'** An attractive and very graceful form with deeply and finely cut leaves. C 1859. ♀ 2002. AM 1973. **Incisa Group** (f. *incisa* (Willd.) Koehne) Leaves small, deeply cut or pinnate with broad, rounded, dentate lobes. There are shrubby and arboreal forms. **'Laciniata'** Like 'Imperialis' but stronger growing with a stiffer habit and the leaves not so finely divided. Arose in France before 1819. **'Pyramidalis'** ('Fastigiata') A form with branches at an acute angle making a narrowly conical tree.

hirsuta (Spach) Rupr. (*A. tinctoria* Sarg.) A medium-sized tree, similar in many respects to *A. incana* but with leaves generally larger, and more deeply lobed, glaucous beneath. NE Asia and Japan. I 1879 by Charles Maries.

incana (L.) Moench. Grey alder. An exceptionally hardy tree or large shrub with leaves grey beneath. Ideal for cold or wet situations. The North American plant once referred to as this species is now known as *A. rugosa* q.v. Europe, Caucasus. I 1780. **'Aurea'** Young shoots and foliage are yellow and the catkins conspicuously red-tinted. AM 1995. **'Laciniata'** ('Acuminata') Leaves dissected. C 1861. FCC 1873. **'Pendula'** A handsome, small, weeping tree forming a large mound of pendent

branches and grey-green leaves. Originated in Holland before 1900. **'Ramulis Coccineis'** This attractive tree does not appear to differ in any way from 'Aurea' (see above).

japonica (Thunb.) Steud. A striking species, in time making a medium-sized to large tree. Deep-rooted and often suckering freely. Leaves are elliptic, relatively narrow and pointed. Flowers open early, often in January, but male catkins short and not showy. Korea, Manchuria, Japan, Taiwan. I before 1880.

maritima (Marshall) Nutt. A large shrub or small tree with downy young shoots. Broadly elliptic to obovate leaves, to 8cm long, are broadly cuneate at the base, shallowly toothed at the margin and glossy green above, downy beneath. The short catkins form in summer and expand from September to October. Delaware and Maryland (USA). I 1878.

maximowiczii Callier. A large shrub with rather thick twigs, broad leaves and clusters of short, fat, yellow or maroon catkins in late spring. Japan, Kamchatka, Korea. I 1914. AM 1996 (for flower, to a form from Ullung-Do).

nitida (Spach) Endl. Himalayan alder. Medium-sized tree with smooth, glossy, ovate, normally entire leaves. Distinct because its long male catkins are produced in autumn. NW Himalaya. I 1882 by R.E. Ellis.

oregona See *A. rubra*.

orientalis Decne. Oriental alder. Medium-sized tree with sticky buds, glossy green, ovate, undulate, coarsely toothed leaves and clusters of yellow catkins in March. Syria, Turkey, Cyprus. Shoots and leaves of Cypriot trees are very glutinous and darker green than Turkish trees. I 1924.

rhombifolia Nutt. White alder. Medium-sized to large tree of spreading habit with often diamond-shaped, downy but shiny leaves. Foliage spicily scented. Often weak-growing because of difficulty in 'nodulating'. W North America. I 1895.

rubra Bong. (*A. oregona* Nutt.) Red alder. Medium-sized, fast-growing tree of graceful habit, in spring festooned with 10–15cm-long male catkins. Leaves large, regularly and handsomely lobed, glaucous beneath. W North America. I before 1880. **'Pinnatisecta'** Leaves with more deeply cut lobes. C 1939.

rugosa (Du Roi) Spreng. Speckled alder. A small tree or shrub related to *A. incana* and sometimes regarded as a subspecies of it. Leaves ovate-elliptic; branches with pale lenticels. E North America.

serrulata (Aiton) Willd. Smooth alder. A large shrub or small tree with short catkins in spring before the leaves appear, related to *A. incana* but differing in its obovate, nearly entire leaves, green beneath. E USA. I 1769.

sinuata (Reg.) Rydb. (*A. sitchensis* Sarg.) Sitka alder. A small tree or large shrub related to *A. viridis* with thin, broad, double-toothed leaves. The conspicuous male catkins are up to 13cm long and hang in great profusion. Bark of older plants a striking metallic-grey. W North America, NE Asia. I 1903.

sitchensis Sarg. See *A. sinuata*.

× *spaethii* Callier (*A. japonica* × *A. subcordata*) A fast-growing tree of medium size with large leaves that are purplish when young. Outstanding when in catkin. Garden origin. C 1908.

subcordata C.A. Mey. Caucasian alder. A fast-growing, medium-sized to large tree with broad, sometimes slightly heart-shaped leaves up to 15cm long. Male catkins are borne very early. Caucasus, N Iran. I 1838.

tenuifolia Nutt. An upright, small tree or large shrub with thin, shiny, oval leaves, cordate or rounded at the base. W North America. I 1891.

viridis (Chaix) DC. Green alder. A medium-sized to large shrub forming a clump of long, erect, hazel-like stems. The common alder of the C European Alps. Europe (Alps, Tatra and Carpathians), where it grows on mountain slopes. I 1820. **subsp.** *crispa* (Aiton) Turrill (*A. crispa* (Aiton) Pursh) American green alder. This differs from the European form in its larger size and its larger, more finely toothed leaves. E North America. **var.** *mollis* (Fern.) Fern. (*A. crispa* var. *mollis* Fern.) is a form of this with softly downy shoots and leaf undersides. **subsp.** *suaveolens* (Req.) P.W. Ball. Leaves rounder, more finely toothed. Corsica.

†**ALOYSIA** Juss.—**Verbenaceae**—About 35 species of aromatic shrubs, natives of the SW USA, Central and South America. Only *A. triphylla* is commonly grown.

*chamaedryfolia Cham. An aromatic, medium-sized to large shrub of open, spreading habit. Leaves opposite, broadly ovate, sharply toothed and scabrid. Tiny, scented, lavender, becoming white, flowers are borne in slender spikes in late summer and autumn. Brazil, Argentina.

triphylla (L'Hér.) Britt. (*Lippia citriodora* (Ort.) Kunth) Lemon verbena. A medium-sized to large shrub with lanceolate, lemon-scented leaves, normally in whorls of 3. The tiny, pale purple flowers are profusely borne in terminal panicles in August. Best against a warm wall. Argentina, Chile. I 1784.

AMELANCHIER Medik.—**Rosaceae**—Commonly known as Juneberry, serviceberry or snowy mespilus, this is a genus of about 10 species of beautiful and very hardy, small trees or shrubs, mainly natives of North America, but also found in Europe and Asia. (Several of the European species are presumed to have originated from plants introduced from North America.) They thrive in moist, well-drained, lime-free soils, the most lime-tolerant species being *A. alnifolia*, *A. asiatica* and *A. rotundifolia* (*A. ovalis*). The abundant racemes of white flowers are produced in spring before the leaves are fully developed. The foliage is often richly coloured in autumn.

alnifolia (Nutt.) Nutt. A medium-sized shrub with rounded leaves. In spring, after the leaves appear, bears short, dense, terminal racemes of flowers, followed by black fruits. W North America. I 1918. **var.** *cusickii* (Fern.) C.L.Hitchc. (*A. cusickii* Fern.) Flowers relatively large, in few-flowered racemes after the smooth leaves emerge. Fruits scarlet at first, gradually turning black. NW USA. C 1934. **var.** *semiintegrifolia* (Hook.) C.L.Hitchc. (*A. florida* Lindl.) An erect-branched, large shrub or small tree with rounded or oval leaves and purplish fruits. Flowers borne in upright racemes in May. Autumn tints include a rich clear yellow. W North America. I 1826 by David Douglas.

asiatica (Siebold & Zucc.) Walp. An elegant, large shrub with slender, arching shoots, flowering in May, after the leaves emerge, and intermittently over a long period. Leaves pale green and smooth above when young, silky white-hairy beneath, becoming dark green, then orange-red in autumn. Fruits like blackcurrants. E Asia. I 1865.

'Ballerina' A vigorous, large shrub or small tree with finely toothed leaves, bronze when young turning red and purple in autumn. Large, white flowers are very profusely borne. Selected in Holland from plants sent from our nursery in 1970. Probably a hybrid of *A. laevis*. ♀ 2002.

bartramiana (Tausch) Roem. Mountain Juneberry. A clump-forming, medium-sized shrub with upright branches. Distinct in its leaves not folded as they expand, nearly glabrous, bronze-tinged when young. Flowers white in small clusters of usually no more than 3, followed by purple-black fruits. NE North America.

canadensis (L.) Medik. (*A. oblongifolia* Roem.) Medium to large, suckering shrub with tall, erect stems, oblong leaves and erect racemes. Grows well in moist situations. See also *A. lamarckii* and *A. laevis* with which this species has been confused. North America. AM 1938.

cusickii See *A. alnifolia* var. *cusickii*.

florida Lindl. See *A. alnifolia* var. *semiintegrifolia*.

× *grandiflora* Rehder (*A. arborea* × *A. laevis*) A large, spreading shrub with bronze young leaves and profuse clusters of large, white flowers. This hybrid has originated in the wild as well as in cultivation. Best known here in the following forms. See also *A. lamarckii*. **'Robin Hill'** A large shrub or small tree of dense, upright habit. Flowers pink in bud, opening pale pink, becoming white. **'Rubescens'** An attractive form with pale pink flowers, deep pink in bud. Raised in New York before 1920.

humilis Wiegand. Erect, suckering shrub of medium size. Shoots deep red; leaves elliptic-oblong and densely white-tomentose beneath. Flowers are borne in dense, upright racemes in May as the leaves emerge. Fruits almost black, bloomy. E USA. I 1904.

laevis Wiegand. A small tree or occasionally large shrub usually grown, wrongly, as *A. canadensis*. A picture of striking beauty in early May when the profuse, white, fragrant flowers are interspersed with delicate pink young foliage. The leaves assume rich autumnal tints. North America. C 1870. **'Snowflakes'** Slender, large shrub or small tree, the leaves yellow flushed red in autumn. The large white flowers are borne in nodding racemes.

lamarckii Schröd. A large shrub or small tree of bushy, spreading habit. Leaves oval to oblong, coppery-red and silky when young, colouring richly in autumn. Flowers in lax, ample racemes are scattered along the branches as the young leaves unfold. Fruits black. The best species for general planting, a tree in full flower being a beautiful spectacle. Naturalised in Belgium, Holland, NW Germany and several parts of England where it has been variously, but wrongly, referred to the following species: *A. canadensis*, *A. laevis* and *A. confusa*. ♀ 2002. AM 1976. **'Rubescens'** See *A.* × *grandiflora* 'Rubescens'.

oblongifolia See *A. canadensis*.

ovalis See *A. rotundifolia*.

rotundifolia (Lam.) Dum.-Cours. (*A. ovalis* Medik., *A. vulgaris* Moench) A medium-sized to large shrub of upright habit. Flowers large in short, erect racemes. Leaves ovate, dark green above, white-woolly beneath when young. Fruit red becoming black. C and S Europe,

N Africa, W Asia. I 1596. **'Edelweiss'** A Dutch selection with large, white flowers, profusely borne. C 1988. **'Helvetia'** A compact and very hardy form, making a small, rounded shrub. Originally found in the wild in Switzerland. C 1988.

sanguinea (Pursh) DC. Medium-sized shrub with oval-oblong or rounded leaves and loose, lax flower racemes in May after the leaves have emerged. Fruits black, bloomy. SE Canada, NE USA. I 1824.

spicata (Lam.) K. Koch. A medium-sized to large, erect-branched, suckering shrub of bushy habit with the leaves white-hairy beneath when young. Flowers in dense, erect racemes in April and May before or with the leaves. Fruits blue-black. North America.

stolonifera Wiegand. A small to medium-sized, suckering shrub forming a dense thicket of erect stems. Flowers in short, erect racemes in May as the white-hairy young leaves emerge. North America. I 1883.

vulgaris See *A. rotundifolia*.

× **AMELASORBUS** Rehder—**Rosaceae**—An interesting natural intergeneric hybrid between *Amelanchier* and *Sorbus*. Occurs with the parents in Idaho and Oregon, USA.

jackii Rehder (*Amelanchier alnifolia* × *Sorbus scopulina*) This unusual shrub has oval to elliptic leaves sometimes with distinct leaflets at the base. In spring, produces 5cm-long clusters of white flowers followed by dark red fruits covered with a blue bloom.

†**AMICIA** Kunth—**Leguminosae**—A small genus of about 8 species of Central and South American subshrubs. The following is the only one in general cultivation and requires a well-drained soil and a warm, sunny, sheltered site.

zygomeris DC. A medium-sized shrub of extremely vigorous habit with erect, greenish, downy stems which are hollow and generally herbaceous in nature. Leaves pinnate, with 4 obovate, notched leaflets, arising from a pair of inflated, purple-tinged leafy stipules. The yellow, purple-splashed, pea-like flowers are produced in short axillary racemes during autumn, often too late to avoid early frosts. Mexico. I 1826.

†*****AMOMYRTUS** (Burrett) Legrand & Kausel—**Myrtaceae**—Two species of aromatic evergreen trees from Chile and Argentina, the following previously listed under *Myrtus*.

luma (Molina) Legrand & Kausel (*Myrtus lechleriana* (Miq.) Sealy) A large shrub or small tree of dense habit, well furnished to the ground. Leaves, recalling those of *Vaccinium ovatum*, are strikingly copper-coloured when young, ovate, dark polished green with reddish stalks. Clusters of fragrant blossoms in May; berries red then black, edible. Chile. I 1927 by Harold Comber. AM 1945.

AMORPHA L.—**Leguminosae**—A genus of about 15 species of deciduous, sun-loving shrubs or subshrubs with pinnate leaves and dense, spike-like racemes of small, usually violet or blue pea-like flowers in summer. The flowers are unusual in having only one petal. Natives of North America and Mexico.

canescens Nutt. Lead plant. A small subshrub with grey-hairy pinnate leaves; violet flowers with orange anthers are produced in dense cylindrical racemes, 10–15cm long, in late summer and early autumn. E North America. I 1812.

fruticosa L. False indigo. A variable, medium to large shrub with pinnate leaves and slender racemes of purplish-blue flowers in July. S USA. I 1724. **'Pendula'** A form with pendent branches.

Amphiraphis albescens See *Aster albescens*.
Amur cork tree See *Phellodendron amurense*.

†**ANAGYRIS** L.—**Leguminosae**—A genus of 2 tender, sun-loving shrubs or small trees related to *Piptanthus*. *A. latifolia* Brouss. is a rare native of the Canary Islands.

foetida L. A large shrub or small tree with sage-green, trifoliolate leaves, which are foetid when crushed, and short racemes of yellow pea-like flowers in late spring. Mediterranean region. C 1750.

ANDRACHNE L.—**Euphorbiaceae**— A small genus of about 20 species of herbs and small shrubs, native mainly of N temperate regions. They need a well-drained soil in full sun and are largely of botanical interest.

colchica Fischer & C.A. Mey. A dense, dwarf shrub bearing clusters of small, yellowish-green flowers in summer and autumn. Caucasus. C 1900.

‡*****ANDROMEDA** L.—**Ericaceae**—A genus of 2 species of low-growing, slender-stemmed shrubs for a peat garden or damp, acid soils.

glaucophylla Link. A dwarf shrub with slender, erect stems, narrow leaves and terminal clusters of pale pink, pitcher-shaped flowers in late spring and early summer. Differs from *A. polifolia* in the leaves being minutely white-tomentulose beneath. NE North America. C 1879. **f.** *latifolia* (Aiton) Rehder. A form of looser, more straggly growth with broader leaves.

polifolia L. Bog rosemary. A charming dwarf shrub, a rare native of the British Isles. The slender stems bear narrow, glaucous-green leaves, glabrous and white beneath, and terminal clusters of soft pink flowers in May or early June. Europe, N Asia, North America. C 1768. **'Alba'** A rather straggly form with light blue foliage and white flowers. **'Compacta'** A gem for a cool peat bed; bears clusters of bright pink flowers from May onwards. Compact habit. ♥ 2002. AM 1964. **'Compacta Alba'** A compact, dwarf form with white flowers. ♥ 2002. **'Kirigamine'** Introduced to cultivation from Mt Kirigamine in Japan, this form bears profuse pink flowers. **'Macrophylla'** A form with relatively broad leaves and deep pink flowers. ♥ 2002. FCC 1981. **'Major'** A taller form with broader leaves. **'Minima'** A decumbent or nearly prostrate form with linear, dark green leaves and pink flowers. AM 1985. **'Nana'** A compact form making a low mound only 30cm or so tall, twice as much across. Flowers pink. **'Nikko'** A neat-growing form of compact habit. An improvement on 'Compacta'.

Angel's trumpet See *Brugmansia*.
Angelica tree, Japanese See *Aralia elata*.
Anise, Florida See *Illicium floridanum*.
Anise, Japanese See *Illicium anisatum*.

†***ANOPTERUS** Labill.—**Escalloniaceae**—A genus of 2 species related to *Escallonia*.

glandulosus Labill. Tasmanian laurel. A rare Tasmanian evergreen shrub or small tree, with coarsely toothed, obovate, leathery leaves. A beautiful plant, producing terminal racemes of lily-of-the-valley-like flowers in April and May. Hardy only in favoured localities. I about 1840. AM 1926.

ANTHYLLIS L.—**Leguminosae**—A genus of some 20 species of annual and perennial herbs and shrubs with usually pinnate leaves and clustered pea-like flowers. Natives of Europe, W Asia and N Africa. The following require full sun and well-drained soil.

†*barba-jovis* L. Jupiter's beard. A medium-sized shrub with pinnate, silvery leaves and cream-coloured flowers borne in terminal clusters in early summer. SW Europe, Mediterranean region. C 1640.

hermanniae L. An attractive, dwarf shrub, suitable for a rock garden, with small, narrow, simple, sometimes trifoliolate leaves; masses of small, pea-shaped, yellow flowers with orange markings on the standards are borne in June and July. Mediterranean region. I early 18th century.

montana L. A prostrate subshrub with silky-hairy, pinnate leaves bearing 17–31 leaflets. Pink flowers are borne in dense, clover-like heads in June. S Europe. **'Rubra'** A selection with crimson flowers. ♀ 2002. AM 1956.

APHANANTHE Planch.—**Ulmaceae**—About 5 species of deciduous and evergreen trees, natives of E Asia, Australia and Madagascar.

aspera (Blume) Planch. A small tree in the British Isles but reaching a large size in its native habitat. Shoots and leaves have adpressed hairs making them rough to the touch. Ovate leaves, to 10cm long, are long-acuminate, prominently serrate, usually truncate and somewhat oblique at the base. Japan, Korea, China. I 1895.

Apricot See *Prunus armeniaca*.
Apricot, black or purple See *Prunus × dasycarpa*.

ARALIA L.—**Araliaceae**—About 55 species of perennial herbs and deciduous shrubs, rarely climbers, native mainly of North America and E Asia but also found in Central and South America and SE Asia. The following are mainly grown for their beautiful, large, compound leaves.

chinensis L. Chinese angelica tree. A tall, suckering shrub or small tree, with stout, spiny stems. Leaves are doubly pinnate, 1–1.25m long and 0.6m or more wide; small, white flowers in huge panicles, the panicles with a central axis, appear in August and September. Most plants grown under this name are probably *A. elata*. NE Asia. I about 1830.

elata (Miq.) Seem. Japanese angelica tree. Usually seen as a large, suckering shrub but occasionally making a small, sparsely branched tree. The huge, doubly pinnate leaves are gathered mainly in a ruff-like arrangement towards the tips of the stems and often colour well in autumn. White flowers, in large panicles branched from the base, appear in early autumn. Japan. I about 1830. ♀ 2002. AM 1959. **'Aureovariegata'** Leaflets irregu-

larly margined and splashed with yellow. In spring the two variegated forms are distinct but later in summer the leaves of both become variegated silver-white. **'Variegata'** A handsome form with leaflets irregularly margined and blotched creamy-white. A form distributed under the name of 'Silver Umbrella' is very similar. See note under 'Aureovariegata'. I 1865. ♀ 2002. AM 1902.

sieboldii See *Fatsia japonica*.

spinosa L. Hercules' club, Devil's walking-stick. A North American species with viciously spiny stems. Greenish-white flowers, in panicles with a central axis, appear in July, much earlier than *A. elata*, but they are less showy. In fruit when the other species is in flower. SE USA. I 1688. AM 1974 (for fruit).

*****ARBUTUS** L.—**Ericaceae**—The strawberry trees are among the most ornamental and highly prized of small, evergreen trees, belonging to the Old and New Worlds and attaining, with few exceptions, 3–6m. The glossy, dark green leaves, panicles of white, pitcher-shaped flowers and strawberry-like fruits are all very attractive. There are about 15 species, which, apart from the following, occur in the Canary Islands, SW USA, Mexico and Central America.

†*andrachne* L. The beautiful Grecian strawberry tree. White, pitcher-shaped flowers in spring. Stems cinnamon-brown with flaking bark. Tender when young; hardy when mature, if rightly sited. SE Europe. I 1724.

× *andrachnoides* Link (*A. andrachne* × *A. unedo*) (*A. × hybrida* Ker-Gawl.) Intermediate between the Killarney strawberry tree (*A. unedo*) and the Grecian species (*A. andrachne*). Remarkably beautiful, cinnamon-red branches, lime-tolerant and quite hardy. Flowers during late autumn and winter. Found in the wild in Greece. C 1800. ♀ 2002. AM 1953.

'Marina' A small to medium-sized tree with cinnamon-brown peeling bark and glossy dark green leaves to 12cm long, bronze when young. The drooping, urn-shaped flowers are white, flushed with deep pink, and open in large, upright, open panicles during late summer and autumn, followed by yellow then red fruits. Grown in California since at least 1933, it is thought to have been introduced from Europe in 1917 and is possibly a seedling of *A. × andrachnoides* or a hybrid with *A. canariensis*. It was introduced to cultivation in 1984.

‡*menziesii* Pursh. The noble Madroña of California, occasionally seen as a tree up to 18m, this has beautiful, smooth, reddish-brown bark, peeling in late summer to reveal green young bark. Flowers are in conspicuous panicles in late spring, followed by small, orange-yellow fruits. Hardy in the home counties when rightly sited. One of the many fine introductions of David Douglas. W North America. I 1827 by David Douglas. ♀ 2002. AM 1926.

unedo L. Killarney strawberry tree. A small tree often of gnarled appearance when old, with deep brown, shredding bark. Flowers and fruits produced simultaneously in late autumn. Withstands gales in coastal districts. Unusual among ericaceous plants for its lime tolerance. Mediterranean region, SW Ireland. ♀ 2002. FCC 1933. **'Atlantic'** A form selected for its profuse flowers and fruits, even on young plants. **'Compacta'** A small, dense shrub, often shy-flowering and fruiting. **'Elfin King'** A bushy form making a medium-sized shrub, free-flowering and fruiting when small. **'Integerrima'** A slow-growing shrubby form with entire leaves. White flowers occasionally produced. **'Quercifolia'** A distinct form with coarsely toothed leaves tapering to an entire base. **'Rubra'** A choice form with pink-flushed flowers and abundant fruits. C 1835. ♀ 2002. AM 1925.

Arcterica nana See *Pieris nana.*

‡***ARCTOSTAPHYLOS** Adans.—**Ericaceae**—Distinctive evergreens, varying from prostrate shrubs to small trees, the larger species usually with attractive bark. White to pink flowers are small and nodding, borne in clusters, followed by berry-like fruits. About 50 species mainly in W North America and Mexico. Allied to *Rhododendron* they succeed under similar soil conditions but love the sun.

alpina (L.) Spreng. (*Arctous alpinus* (L.) Nied.) Mountain bearberry. A rare, native shrublet forming a dense mat of prostrate, reddish stems. In late spring bears terminal clusters of urn-shaped, white, pink-flushed flowers. Fruits are black. Northern latitudes of Europe (incl. Scotland), Asia, North America. C 1789. **'Vancouver Jade'** A vigorous form to 40cm tall with red young shoots, bright green leaves and pink flowers. Selected in Victoria, British Columbia before 1974.

†*diversifolia Parry (*Comarostaphylis diversifolia* (Parry) Greene) Summer holly. A medium to large shrub or small tree recalling *Arbutus unedo*. Elliptic-obovate leaves, to 4.5cm long, are coarsely toothed at the margin, blunt to shallowly emarginate at the apex, and glossy green above, thinly downy beneath. White flowers in more or less erect or spreading terminal racemes in spring are followed by small, deep red fruits. S California, Baja California. C 1896.

manzanita Parry. Common manzanita. A beautiful, tall-growing shrub with attractive, dark red-brown peeling bark, sea-green leaves and spikes of pink or white, pitcher-shaped flowers. California. I 1897. FCC 1923.

myrtifolia Parry. Ione manzanita. A rare, tiny, Californian shrublet with white, bell-shaped flowers, tipped pink.

nevadensis A. Gray. Pinemat manzanita. A prostrate, Californian species bearing white, urn-shaped flowers in racemes or panicles. Fruits red.

pumila Nutt. Dune manzanita. A very attractive, prostrate species with small, downy, grey-green leaves. Flowers white or pinkish, followed by brown fruits. California. C 1933.

†*tomentosa* (Pursh) Lindl. Shaggy-barked manzanita. A small shrub with attractive, shredding bark and densely grey-tomentose branches. Leaves sage-green, heavily hairy beneath; flowers white in spring. W North America. C 1835.

uva-ursi (L.) Spreng. Red bearberry. An interesting native, creeping alpine shrub; small, white flowers tinged pink; fruits red. A good plant for sandy banks. Cool-temperate regions of N hemisphere. **'Clyde Robin'** A low-growing, widespreading form with bright green leaves. **'Massachusetts'** Small, dark green leaves and profuse white flowers. **'Point Reyes'** Prostrate with arching branches, peeling bark and grey leaves. Flowers blush-pink.

Arctous alpinus See *Arctostaphylos alpina.*

‡†***ARDISIA** Sw.—**Myrsinaceae**—A large genus of some 250 species of mainly tropical, evergreen trees and shrubs found largely in E Asia and Central and South America.

japonica (Thunb.) Blume. An attractive, dwarf evergreen for pot culture or a lime-free soil in very mild areas. Reaching 30cm in height, it produces whorls of glossy leaves and bright red berries. China, Japan. C 1834.

ARISTOTELIA L'Hér.—**Elaeocarpaceae**—A small genus of about 5 species of mainly evergreen, Australasian and South American shrubs needing some protection in cold districts. Male and female flowers often occur on separate plants.

†*chilensis (Molina) Stutz (*A. macqui* L'Hér.) An interesting evergreen attaining 5m in mild districts. Leaves 13cm long, lustrous green; female plants bear small, black berries. Suitable for maritime exposure. Chile. I 1773. **'Variegata'** Leaves conspicuously margined with yellow. A form is also in cultivated in which the leaves have a central yellow-green blotch.

*fruticosa Hook. f. Mountain wineberry. An intricately branched and remarkably hardy, medium-sized shrub recalling *Corokia cotoneaster;* leaves leathery, varying from linear to oblong-obovate. The tiny flowers are followed by small berries which are variable in colour. New Zealand.

†*serrata* (J.R. Forst. & G. Forst.) W.R.B. Oliv. (*A. racemosa* (A.Cunn.) Hook. f.) Wineberry. A graceful, small tree from New Zealand, with heart-shaped, long-pointed leaves, 5–10cm long, which are jaggedly toothed and downy when young. The flowers are small and rose-pink, the berries dark red. Well-developed specimens may be seen in mild areas. I 1873.

ARONIA Medik.—**Rosaceae**—The chokeberries are attractive shrubs, related to *Pyrus* and *Sorbus*, with white flowers in spring, followed by conspicuous clusters of red or black fruits, and brilliant autumn colours. Not recommended for shallow chalk soils. 2 species in North America.

arbutifolia (L.) Pers. Red chokeberry. A medium-sized shrub with narrow, dark green leaves, grey-felted beneath. Notable for its bright red fruits and exceptionally brilliant autumn colours. E North America. C 1700. **'Brilliant'** ('Brilliantissima') A form selected in North America for its fruit and originally listed as *A. melanocarpa* 'Brilliant'. It has apparently been raised from seed and several forms may be grown under this name. **'Erecta'** A compact, erect-branched shrub, arching with age, and with rich autumn colour. AM 1974.

floribunda See *A.* × *prunifolia.*

melanocarpa (Michx.) Elliott. Black chokeberry. Small shrub with obovate, dark glossy green leaves and white, hawthorn-like flowers in spring, followed by lustrous black fruits. Plants grown under this name with good autumn colour may belong to *A.* × *prunifolia*. E North America. I about 1700. FCC 1980. AM 1972. **'Autumn Magic'** See *A.* × *prunifolia* 'Autumn Magic'. **'Brilliant'** See *A. arbutifolia* 'Brilliant'.

× *prunifolia* (Marshall) Rehder (*A. arbutifolia* × *A. melanocarpa*) (*A. floribunda* Spach) Purple chokeberry. Intermediate in character between the two preceding species. Fruits purple-black. E USA. I 1800. **'Autumn Magic'** (*A. melanocarpa* 'Autumn Magic') Compact, with red-purple autumn colour. Fruits purple-black. **'Viking'** Vigorous, to 2m, with large clusters of small, white flowers profusely borne.

Arrow wood See *Viburnum recognitum*.
Arrow wood, downy See *Viburnum rafinesquianum*.
Arrow wood, southern See *Viburnum dentatum*.

ARTEMISIA L.—**Compositae**—A large genus of some 300 species of often aromatic, perennial herbs, shrubs and sub-shrubs with attractive, green or grey foliage. Natives mainly of the temperate N hemisphere but also found in South Africa and South America. They prefer dry, well-drained soil in full sun.
abrotanum L. Southernwood, Lad's love. A small, erect, grey-downy shrub with sweetly aromatic, finely divided leaves. S Europe. C in England since 16th century. ♀ 2002.
†*arborescens* L. A small shrub of rounded habit. The billowy filigree of its silvery leaves makes it a charming subject for a grey or blue border. S Europe. I 1640. AM 1966. **'Faith Raven'** A particularly hardy form collected near the summit of Mt. Filerimo, Rhodes by Faith Raven in 1968. There has been confusion between this form and *A.* 'Powis Castle'.
'Powis Castle' (*A. absinthium* × *A. arborescens*) A beautiful, small shrub, with deeply cut, silvery-grey leaves. Its origin is unknown but it was taken from a Yorkshire garden to the National Trust garden at Powis Castle from where it was distributed. It is hardier than *A. arborescens* and retains its compact habit. The best of its type for general garden use and excellent groundcover in full sun. C 1968. ♀ 2002. AM 1983.
tridentata Nutt. Sage brush. A medium-sized shrub of spreading habit. The grey, aromatic leaves are wedge-shaped, 3-toothed at the apex and occur in clusters along the stems. Large clusters of small, yellow flowerheads are borne in late summer and autumn. Recent work suggests that the genus *Seriphidium*, in which this species is sometimes included, should be included in *Artemisia*. W USA. I 1895.

Ash See *Fraxinus*.

ASIMINA Adans.—**Annonaceae**—A small genus of about 8 species of evergreen and deciduous shrubs and small trees. The following is the only hardy member of the family, which includes the custard apple (*Annona cherimola* Mill.). Not to be confused with the true pawpaw or papaya (*Carica papaya* L.) a tender tree from tropical South America, widely grown in the tropics for its fruit.
triloba (L.) Dunal. In the British Isles the pawpaw forms a large, deciduous shrub with obovate leaves up to 20cm long. The unusual, purplish flowers are borne in May to June as the leaves emerge. The curious fruits, which frequently form on a plant in the Sir Harold Hillier Gardens and Arboretum, are edible when ripe. SE USA. One of the first American plants to be introduced by Peter Collinson in 1736.

Aspen See *Populus tremula*.

†***ASTELIA** Banks & Sol.—**Asteliaceae**—A small genus of 25 species of evergreen, dioecious, clump-forming perennials, native to the Pacific Islands, Australia and New Zealand.
nervosa Banks & Sol. Dense tufts of sedge-like, green, conspicuously veined leaves and small, fragrant flowers in dense panicles; female plants bear orange berries. New Zealand.

ASTER L.—**Compositae**—A large genus of some 250 species of mainly perennial herbs; widely distributed. The following is suitable for any well-drained soil in a sunny position.
albescens (DC.) Hand.-Mazz. (*Microglossa albescens* (DC.) C.B. Clarke, *Amphiraphis albescens* DC.) A small shrub, up to 1m tall, producing pale lilac-blue, daisy-like flowers in terminal corymbs in July. Himalaya, China. I about 1840.

Asteranthera See under CLIMBERS.

ASTRAGALUS L.—**Leguminosae**—The goat's thorns belong to a large genus of about 2000 species of annual and perennial herbs and shrubs widely distributed mainly in N temperate regions but also in South America and South Africa.
angustifolius Lam. Very dwarf and slow-growing with branches densely set with spines and grey, spine-tipped, pinnate leaves. Pea-shaped, blue-tinged, white flowers are borne in clusters in May and June. A rock-garden shrub. SE Europe, SW Asia.

‡†***ATHEROSPERMA** Labill.—**Monimiaceae**—A monotypic genus from Australia.
moschatum Labill. An interesting evergreen, small tree with lanceolate leaves, white-downy beneath. The whole plant is very fragrant and yields an essential oil. Cream-coloured, solitary flowers. Tasmania, SE Australia. I 1824. AM 1989.

ATRAPHAXIS L.—**Polygonaceae**—The shrubby buckwheats are a small group of interesting, but not spectacular, usually low, spreading plants for dry, sunny positions. About 20 species from N Africa to Greece and SW and C Asia.
frutescens (L.) K. Koch. A small shrub with slender, upright, wiry stems, narrow, sea-green leaves and clusters of tiny, pink and white flowers in late summer. SE Europe and Caucasus to Siberia and Turkestan. I 1770.

ATRIPLEX L.—**Chenopodiaceae**—More than 100 species of annual and perennial herbs and shrubs, widely distributed, the following grown for their silvery-grey foliage. They thrive in coastal districts on saline soil as well as inland. The flowers are inconspicuous.
canescens (Pursh) Nutt. Grey sage brush. A lax, semi-evergreen bush of medium size; leaves narrow, greyish-white. W North America. Long cultivated.
halimus L. Tree purslane. A medium-sized, semi-evergreen shrub with silvery-grey leaves. S Europe. C since early 17th century.

*****AUCUBA** Thunb.—**Aucubaceae**—Evergreen, shade-loving, dioecious shrubs, forming dense, rounded bushes

2–3m high, thriving in almost any soil or situation, however sunless. Very handsome when well grown, especially the variegated forms (which retain their colour best in an open position), and the berrying (female) clones. 3 species found in the Himalaya and E Asia.

albopunctifolia F.T. Wang. This unusual Chinese species has blue-green shoots and slender, taper-pointed leaves that are up to 15cm long and 2.5cm across, edged with small, pointed teeth above the middle and spotted with pale yellow. Sichuan, China. I by Mikinori Ogisu. A plant grown by Roy Lancaster is male with purple flowers.

japonica Thunb. Spotted laurel. A medium-sized shrub with green leaves often referred to as *concolor* or *viridis*. Flowers produced in April; the males are small, reddish-purple with conspicuous creamy-white anthers. The male plant is commonest in cultivation. Japan. I 1783. FCC 1864. **var. borealis** Miyabe & Kudo. An extremely hardy, dwarf, slow-growing variety from the forests of N Japan. **'Crassifolia'** A small to medium-sized shrub with thick, broad, deep green leaves, toothed in the upper half. Male. **'Crotonifolia'** ('Crotonoides') Leaves large, boldly spotted and blotched with gold. The best golden-variegated aucuba. Female. There also appears to be a male form. ♀ 2002. **'Dentata'** Leaves undulate, coarsely toothed in the upper half. **'Fructu-albo'** ('Fructuluteo') Leaves sparingly spotted and blotched pale green and gold. Fruits yellowish-white. FCC 1883. **'Gold Dust'** Leaves conspicuously speckled and blotched gold. Female. **'Golden King'** Similar to 'Crotonifolia' but with a more striking variegation. Male. Best in semi-shade. ♀ 2002. **'Grandis'** A form with very large, elliptic, deep green leaves. Male. FCC 1867. **'Hillieri'** A noble form with large, lustrous, dark green leaves and pointed fruits. Female. **'Lance Leaf'** A striking form with polished, deep green, lance-shaped leaves. A male counterpart of 'Longifolia'. **'Longifolia'** Leaves long, lanceolate and bright green. Female. ♀ 2002. FCC 1864. **'Maculata'** See 'Variegata'. **'Nana Rotundifolia'** A small, free-berrying form. Leaves small, rich green, with an occasional spot, and sharply toothed in the upper half. Stems an unusual shade of sea-green. Female. **'Picturata'** Leaves with a conspicuous, central yellow blotch, the broad margin spotted with yellow. Frequently reverts. Male and female forms occur. **'Rozannie'** Broad, dark green leaves, toothed above the middle. A compact female form, with large, red fruits freely borne. It is not monoecious as often stated. C 1984. ♀ 2002. **'Salicifolia'** A free-berrying form differing from 'Longifolia' in its narrower leaves, and sea-green stems. Female. **'Speckles'** A male counterpart to 'Variegata'. **'Sulphurea'** See 'Sulphurea Marginata'. **'Sulphurea Marginata'** A distinct form with sea-green stems. Leaves green with a pale yellow margin. Inclined to revert in shade. Usually grown as 'Sulphurea'. Female. FCC 1865. **'Variegata'** ('Maculata') Leaves speckled yellow. Female. It is this form that was first introduced from Japan in 1783. FCC 1865.

†*AUSTROMYRTUS (Nied.) Burret—Myrtaceae—A genus of about 37 species of evergreen natives of Australia and New Guinea, previously included in *Myrtus*.

bidwillii (Benth.) Burret (*Myrtus bidwillii* Benth.) A small, erect shrub with dainty leaves rather like those of *Lonicera nitida* in shape and size. Australia (New South Wales, Queensland).

Azalea See under *Rhododendron*.
Azalea mollis See *Rhododendron molle*.
Azalea pontica See *Rhododendron luteum*.
Azalea procumbens See *Loiseleuria procumbens*.
Azalea, mountain See *Loiseleuria procumbens*.

†*AZARA Ruiz & Pav.—Flacourtiaceae—A genus of 10 species of evergreen shrubs or small trees, natives of South America. All the following make attractive foliage plants but, except in mild areas, need to be grown in a sheltered position or against a wall. The leaves often appear paired owing to the prominent stipules. Flowers fragrant, mustard-yellow, without petals but with numerous, conspicuous stamens.

alpina Poepp. & Endl. A small shrub of upright habit with glabrous, glossy dark green, oblong-elliptic leaves to 4.5cm long, edged with small teeth. Distinct in having the stipules the same shape and nearly the same size as their associated leaves. An additional, much smaller stipule is occasionally borne. Yellow flowers are borne in small clusters in the leaf axils in late spring. Chile, Argentina.

dentata Ruiz & Pav. Medium-sized shrub much confused in cultivation with *A. serrata*, differing in its smaller, rigid leaves, green above, densely grey-felted beneath. It is also less hardy. Flowers in midsummer on the new shoots. Chile. I about 1830. **'Variegata'** See *A. integrifolia* 'Variegata'.

gilliesii See *A. petiolaris*.

integrifolia Ruiz & Pav. (*A. integrifolia* var. *browneae* (Phil.) Reiche) A tall wall shrub with oval leaves; the chrome-yellow flower clusters are conspicuous in late winter and early spring. Chile, Argentina. I 1832. AM 1934. **var. browneae** See *A. integrifolia*. **'Variegata'** Leaves with pretty pink and cream variegation. Raised at Kew about 1870. It has recently been distributed as *A. dentata* 'Variegata'.

lanceolata Hook. f. A medium-sized or large shrub, closely related to *A. serrata*, with attractive, narrow, bright green leaves; bears multitudes of small, fragrant, mustard-yellow flowers in April or May. Chile, Argentina. I 1926 by Harold Comber. AM 1931.

microphylla Hook. f. An elegant, small tree with large sprays of dainty foliage; yellow, vanilla-scented flowers appear on the undersides of the twigs in early spring. The hardiest species. Chile, Argentina. I 1861 by Richard Pearce. ♀ 2002. FCC 1872. **'Variegata'** Leaves prettily margined with cream; slow-growing. C 1916.

paraguayensus See *A. serrata* 'Maurice Mason'.

petiolaris (D. Don) Johnst. (*A. gilliesii* Hook. & Arn.) A tall shrub that is notable for the fragrance of its small, yellow flowers, which appear early in the year in February and March. Leaves ovate to oblong, comparatively large, leathery, toothed, teeth with sharp points. Has withstood 15°C of frost without injury but the flower buds can be damaged in cold weather. Chile. I 1859. AM 1933.

serrata Ruiz & Pav. A large shrub for wall or sheltered site, with distinctive, oval, serrate leaves and conspicuous clusters of yellow flowers in May-June from buds on the old wood formed the previous year. Small, white berries are produced in a hot summer. Hardier than most. Chile. ♀ 2002. **'Andes Gold'** The most commonly grown form, often as *A. dentata*. It is vigorous and of upright habit with broad, glossy green leaves, glabrous when mature. AM 1957 (as *A. dentata*). **'Maurice Mason'** (*A. paraguayensis* hort.) Spreading habit with semi-pendent shoots and large, dark green, roughly hairy leaves. This selection has also been distributed as *A. uruguayensis*. I by Maurice Mason from Bariloche, Argentina in 1976 as *A. paraguayensis*.

uruguayensis (Spegazzini) Sleumer. A medium-sized to large, very distinct shrub, sometimes a small tree, young shoots glabrous. Leaves oblong, entire, to 10cm long, bronze when young later bloomy, becoming glossy green above, paler and dull green beneath, with a pair of conspicuous, rounded stipules. The small, yellow flowers are borne in drooping spikes from the leaf axils in early spring. See also *A. serrata* 'Maurice Mason'. Uruguay, Brazil.

B

BACCHARIS L.—**Compositae**—A large genus of some 350 species of dioecious, small trees, shrubs and herbs found in North and South America. They bear flowers in small heads. The following are rapid growers and useful seaside shrubs.

halimifolia L. Bush groundsel. A useful and vigorous shrub up to 4m. Has variable, stalked, sage-green leaves, to 7cm long, and large, terminal panicles of white, groundsel-like flowers in September-October. E North America. I 1683.

magellanica (Lam.) Pers. A prostrate, dioecious, evergreen shrub carpeting the ground and creeping over rocks in the manner of *Cotoneaster congestus*, to about 25cm tall. The tiny, leathery leaves, to 8mm long, are wedge-shaped, entire or with 1–2 teeth at each margin, and dotted with glands on both sides. Flowers creamy-white, in small heads to 7mm long at the ends of the shoots in summer. Chile, Argentina.

patagonica Hook. & Arn. Medium-sized shrub with red shoots and short, stalkless, evergreen, polished, dark green leaves. Yellowish-white flowerheads appear singly in the upper leaf axils in May. Patagonia.

BALLOTA L.—**Labiatae**—About 35 species of herbs and subshrubs occurring in Europe, mainly in the Mediterranean region and W Asia, with a few species in N Africa. The following require a sunny, well-drained position.

acetabulosa L. Very similar to *B. pseudodictamnus* but with less densely hairy stems and a broader calyx. SE Europe. ♀ 2002. AM 1996 (for flower).

pseudodictamnus Benth. A dwarf subshrub entirely covered with greyish-white wool. Leaves orbicular-cordate. A most effective foliage plant particularly if pruned back each spring and an excellent addition to a grey garden. Lilac-pink flowers are produced in whorls in July. Mediterranean region. ♀ 2002.

Bamboos See p. 476.

†***BANKSIA** L. f.—**Proteaceae**—An interesting genus of some 70 species of Australian trees and shrubs with handsome foliage and cone-shaped flowerheads recalling the bottle-brushes. Only suitable for the mildest localities, or worthy of a conservatory.

integrifolia L. f. Medium-sized shrub of dense habit. Leathery leaves, olive-green above and white beneath; flowers yellow. E Australia. I 1788.

marginata Cav. Medium-sized shrub with somewhat spiny leaves, 5cm long, deep green above, snowy-white beneath; lemon-green flowers. SE Australia, Tasmania.

serrata L. f. A tall shrub with long, narrow leaves, curiously squared at the apex, and silvery-grey flowers. Not very lime-tolerant. E Australia.

Barberry See *Berberis*.
Barosma pulchella See *Agathosma pulchella*.
Basswood See *Tilia americana*.

†***BAUERA** Banks ex Andrews—**Baueraceae**—A small genus of 3 species of tender, small, slender-stemmed,

evergreen shrubs found in E Australia. Leaves opposite, sessile, trifoliolate.

rubioides Andrews. An attractive, small, late spring-flowering shrub suitable for mild gardens, also making an excellent pot plant for a conservatory; the 8-petalled flowers are white with a slight pink flush. Tasmania, SE Australia. AM 1941.

Bay See *Laurus nobilis*.
Bay, loblolly See *Gordonia lasianthus*.
Bay, red See *Persea borbonia*.
Bay, swamp See *Magnolia virginiana*.
Bay, sweet See *Magnolia virginiana*.
Bayberry See *Myrica pensylvanica*.
Bayberry, California See *Myrica californica*.
Bearberry, mountain See *Arctostaphylos alpina*.
Bearberry, red See *Arctostaphylos uva-ursi*.
Beauty bush See *Kolkwitzia amabilis*.
Beech See *Fagus*.
Beech, blue See *Carpinus caroliniana*.
Beech, southern See *Nothofagus*.

BERBERIS L.—**Berberidaceae**—The barberries are a large genus of more than 400 evergreen or deciduous species widely distributed in N temperate regions, Africa and South America. They are generally of easy cultivation, thriving in sun or shade and in almost any soil that is not waterlogged. They vary in habit from dwarf to large shrubs; those described here are of medium size unless otherwise stated. The flowers vary from pale yellow to orange and appear during spring. The fruits are often very showy and many species give brilliant autumn colour.

*actinacantha Martelli (*B. crispa* Gay) A remarkable, small shrub with fragrant, chrome-yellow flowers. Hard and rigid leaves, with an occasional spine, vary from long-stalked and orbicular to ovate, 2.5cm across, to tiny elliptic and sessile. Chile. I about 1830. **Hakeoides Group** (*B. hakeoides* (Hook. f.) C.K. Schneid.) A very distinct and quite remarkable form of loose habit with shoots, often unbranched, up to 3m high. Leaves usually in pairs, are rounded and spiny. Flowers golden-yellow, produced in clusters all along the shoots, in April and May. Chile. I 1861. AM 1901.

aggregata C.K. Schneid. A dense bush, usually less than 1.5m high. Numerous, paniculate clusters of pale yellow flowers are followed in autumn by masses of red berries, backed by the rich coloration of the dying leaves. A parent of many hybrids. W China. I 1908 by Ernest Wilson. AM 1913.

amoena Dunn (*B. leptoclada* Diels) A small shrub similar to *B. wilsoniae* var. *stapfiana*. Leaves sea-green, semi-persistent; most striking when displaying its coral-red fruits. China.

angulosa Hook. f. & Thoms. Small shrub with solitary, large, yellow flowers and dark purplish berries. Leaves dark green, whitish beneath, spiny towards the apex. Himalaya. I about 1850.

*× *antoniana* Ahrendt (*B. buxifolia* × *B. darwinii*) A small, rounded bush with almost spineless, dark green leaves;

very pretty when bearing its single, long-stalked, deep yellow flowers, or blue-black berries. Garden origin at the Daisy Hill Nursery, N Ireland before 1912.

aristata See *B. chitria* and *B. floribunda*.

†*asiatica* Roxb. A striking, unmistakable and vigorous species with leathery, obovate leaves, up to 8cm long, sea-green above, white beneath, conspicuously veined. Berries red, finally blue-black. Nepal, Bhutan, Assam. I 1820.

atrocarpa C.K. Schneid. (*B. levis* hort.) A small shrub with stout shoots and narrow, dark green leaves, differing from *B. sargentiana* in that they are smaller and less prominently veined. Flowers freely borne on elegant, arching branches. W Sichuan, China. I 1909.

'Barbarossa' See *B.* × *carminea* 'Barbarossa'.

bergmanniae C.K. Schneid. A compact, pyramidal shrub, up to 3m high, with clusters of large, spiny, leathery leaves. Dense clusters of flowers in May-June are followed by blue-black berries. W China. I 1908 by Ernest Wilson.

'Blenheim' (*B. darwinii* × *B. actinacantha* Hakeoides Group) A large shrub of upright habit with densely clustered, sharply toothed leaves and deep golden-yellow flowers. Originated in our West Hill nursery, Winchester, and was sent to Blenheim Palace as *B. darwinii*.

'Bountiful' See *B.* × *carminea* 'Bountiful'.

brachypoda Maxim. A rare species with narrow, elongated racemes of yellow flowers in May, followed by bright red, oblong berries. The leaves, young shoots and spines are characteristically downy. C and NW China. I 1907.

× bristolensis Ahrendt (*B. calliantha* × *B. verruculosa*) A small shrub of dense, rounded habit with small, prickly leaves, glossy dark green above, white pruinose beneath. An excellent dwarf hedge if clipped. Garden origin.

'Buccaneer' See *B.* × *carminea* 'Buccaneer'.

buxifolia See *B. microphylla*.

cabrerae See *B. montana*.

calliantha Mulligan. A small shrub with small, holly-like leaves conspicuously glaucous beneath. Young stems crimson. Flowers pale yellow, solitary or in pairs in May, relatively large; fruits blue-black. SE Tibet. I 1924 by Kingdon-Ward. AM 1942.

candidula C.K. Schneid. (*B. hypoleuca* hort.) A dense, dome-shaped bush, up to 1m high, with small, shining, dark green leaves, silvery-white beneath, and single, bright yellow flowers. W China. I 1895 by Père Farges.

× *carminea* Ahrendt (*B. aggregata* × *B. wilsoniae*) A colourful group of hybrids from an original cross made at the RHS Gardens, Wisley. Vigorous, small to medium-sized shrubs of semi-erect or spreading habit, sometimes forming large mounds, glorious in the autumn when fuming with their red, scarlet or pink berries. **'Barbarossa'** A vigorous shrub, 1.5–2m tall, with arching branches weighed down by profuse red berries. C 1942. **'Bountiful'** A spreading bush about 1m tall. Very decorative in the autumn when laden with clusters of coral-red berries on arching branches. **'Buccaneer'** An erect-branched, medium-sized shrub with large, deep red berries, carried in large clusters and lasting until December. **'Pirate King'** A small, dense shrub of vigorous growth; berries fiery orange-red.

× *chenaultii* Ahrendt (*B. gagnepainii* × *B. verruculosa*) A small, dense shrub with arching, verrucose stems and ovate-lanceolate leaves, undulate and spiny at the margin, dull green above, pruinose-grey at first beneath. Raised about 1926.

chillanensis See *B. montana*.

chinensis Poir. Large shrub with red-brown stems, oblance-olate leaves, few flowered racemes and dark red berries. SW Russia. C 1808.

chitria Ker Gawl. (*B. aristata* hort. in part) Large-sized, large-leaved species with long, drooping bunches of conspicuous dark red, bloomy berries each about 1.5cm long. Himalaya. I 1818.

chrysosphaera Mulligan. A small to medium-sized shrub with clusters of narrow leaves, glossy green above, white beneath. Flowers canary-yellow, strikingly large for a *Berberis*. A Kingdon-Ward introduction from SE Tibet in 1933–34.

†*comberi* Sprague. A very distinct, small, spineless shrub that is difficult to establish, with thick, holly-like leaves; flowers solitary, orange-yellow. Discovered in the Argentine Andes by Harold Comber in 1925 and introduced by him.

concinna Hook. f. Small, compact shrub with shining, dark green leaves, white beneath. The solitary, yellow flowers are followed by large, oblong, red berries up to 2cm long. Himalaya. I about 1850 by Sir Joseph Hooker. AM 1918.

congestiflora Gay. A large shrub producing flowers in dense clusters at intervals along the stems. Closely related to *B. actinacantha*, but differing in its thinner-textured leaves, glaucous beneath and shorter pedicels. Chile. I 1925 by Harold Comber.

coxii C.K. Schneid. A handsome species with leathery leaves, 2.5–5cm long, dark green and lustrous above, glaucous beneath. Relatively large, pale yellow flowers, in small clusters, in May, are followed by blue-black berries. Upper Burma. I 1919 by Reginald Farrer and named after E.H.M. Cox, his companion in Burma.

crispa See *B. actinacantha*.

darwinii Hook. This early-flowering species is one of the finest of all flowering shrubs. Leaves 3-pointed, dark shining green above. Flowers bright orange tinged red, in drooping clusters, borne over a long period in spring. Chile, Chiloe, Argentina. First discovered in 1835 by Charles Darwin on the voyage of the *Beagle*. I 1849 by William Lobb. ♥ 2002. FCC 1967. **'Nana'** See *B.* × *stenophylla* 'Nana'. **'Prostrata'** See *B.* × *stenophylla* 'Prostrata'.

diaphana Maxim. A shrub, 1–2m high, with grey-green leaves giving good autumn colour. Flowers are in small clusters of up to 5; berries are bright red. NW China. I 1872.

dictyophylla Franch. (*B. dictyophylla* 'Albicaulis') A shrub, to 2m, colouring well in autumn. Young stems red and covered with white bloom; leaves chalk-white beneath. The large, solitary, red berries are also covered with white bloom. W China. I 1916. ♥ 2002. **var. *approximata*** (Sprague) Rehder (*B. approximata* Sprague) A tall, spreading shrub, colouring well in autumn. E Sichuan. **var. *epruinosa*** C.K. Schneid. Less bloomy in all its parts. Yunnan. C 1930.

dielsiana Fedde. A large, vigorous shrub with slightly angled, red-brown stems, narrowly elliptic leaves and racemes of yellow flowers, followed by red berries. E China. I 1910.

dumicola C.K. Schneid. An uncommon species allied to *B. sargentiana*. Its orange-tinged flowers are followed by bloomy, black berries. NW Yunnan. I 1914.

empetrifolia Lam. Dwarf shrub with slender, arching stems, narrow leaves and small, golden-yellow flowers borne singly in May. Intolerant of shallow chalk soils. Argentina, Chile. I 1827.

floribunda G. Don (*B. aristata* hort. in part) A semi-evergreen species, ultimately 3m high. Flowers are bright yellow, often tinged red, borne in racemes 5–10cm long, and are followed by red berries covered with bloom. Nepal. I 1818.

formosana See *B. kawakamii*.

forrestii Ahrendt. Large shrub with loosely arching stems, obovate leaves and long racemes of yellow flowers followed by red berries. W China. I about 1910.

franchetiana C.K. Schneid. This species is mainly represented in cultivation by the following form. var. *macrobotrys* Ahrendt. A large shrub with arching stems, yellow flowers and red berries. W China. I 1937.

francisci-ferdinandii C.K. Schneid. Vigorous, large shrub, producing large, drooping bunches of sealing-wax-red berries. W China. I 1900 by Ernest Wilson.

×frikartii C.K. Schneid. ex Van de Laar (*B. candidula × B. verruculosa*) Shrubs of dense habit with angled shoots and dark glossy green, spiny leaves, glaucous beneath. Pale yellow, relatively large flowers, borne singly or in pairs, are followed by blue-black berries. The original form of this hybrid was raised in Switzerland in 1928 and has been named 'Stäfa'. **'Amstelveen'** A dense, small shrub with attractive, drooping shoots and glossy green leaves, white beneath. Raised in Holland about 1960. ♥ 2002. **'Telstar'** Similar to 'Amstelveen' but taller, to 1.2m, and more compact. Raised in Holland about 1960.

gagnepainii C.K. Schneid. A small, dense shrub producing erect stems closely set with narrow, undulate leaves. Berries black, covered by a blue bloom. Forms an impenetrable hedge. The commonly cultivated form is var. *lanceifolia* Ahrendt. W China. I about 1904 by Ernest Wilson. **'Fernspray'** A compact selection of var. *lanceifolia* with long, slender, wavy-edged leaves. C 1953.

'Georgei' A rare and attractive shrub with arching branches bearing yellow flowers in pendent, red-stalked racemes in May. The elliptic-obovate, toothed leaves colour well in autumn when the profuse, crimson berries in large, pendent clusters are most conspicuous. Origin unknown. ♥ 2002. FCC 1985. AM 1979.

gilgiana Fedde. A small shrub with red-brown shoots and leaves 2.5–4cm long, grey beneath; berries deep blood-red. China. I 1910 by William Purdom.

glaucocarpa Stapf. A large, semi-evergreen shrub, notable for its profuse conspicuous clusters of blue-black berries heavily covered with a white bloom. W Himalaya. I 1832. AM 1983 (for flower). AM 1943 (for fruit).

'Goldilocks' (*B. darwinii × B. valdiviana*) A vigorous, large shrub with upright and arching branches and dark glossy green, spiny leaves. Deep golden-yellow flowers are profusely borne in hanging, red-stalked clusters over a long period during spring. Raised by our propagator

Peter Dummer from a cross made in 1978. The same hybrid also occurs in the wild. FCC and Cory Cup 1991.

gyalaica Ahrendt. A shrub related to *B. sherriffii*. Berries oblong-elliptic, blackish-purple with blue bloom. The leaves turn red in autumn. SE Tibet. I about 1925 by Kingdon-Ward.

hakeoides See *B. actinacantha* Hakeoides Group.

henryana C.K. Schneid. A distinct species with long, pear-shaped leaves and elliptic-oblong, red berries. C China.

heteropoda Schrenk. This species is most frequently grown in the following form. The typical variety differs in its oblong berries. var. *sphaerocarpa* (Kar. & Kir.) Ahrendt. Shrub with few flowered racemes of orange-yellow blooms followed by globose, slightly blue-bloomy, black berries. NW China.

hispanica Boiss. & Reut. An open shrub, about 2m high, with rather small, elliptic and light green leaves, orange-yellow flowers and oval, blue-black berries. S Spain, N Africa.

hookeri Lem. (*B. wallichiana* Hook. not DC.) A Himalayan species forming a compact, dense shrub not more than 1–1.5m high. Leaves glaucous beneath. Berries green at first then black. Nepal, Sikkim, Bhutan. I 1848. var. *viridis* C.K. Schneid. Leaves green beneath. This is the commonest form in cultivation. There are intermediates between it and the typical variety and it is no longer regarded as distinct.

×hybridogagnepainii Suringar (*B. candidula × B. gagnepainii*) A small shrub of dense growth. Leaves ovate, with revolute, spiny margins, dull green above, green beneath. Ideal as a small hedge or as undercover.

hypokerina Airy Shaw. An outstanding, small shrub forming a thicket of purple stems. Leaves, as much as 10cm long, are holly-like, silvery-white beneath. Berries dark blue with white bloom. Called silver holly by its discoverer, Kingdon-Ward, who also introduced it. Does not thrive in thin chalky soil. Upper Burma. I 1926.

ilicifolia L. f. Holly-leaved barberry. A very rare species of small to medium size. Leaves spiny and dark shining green. Flowers orange-yellow in short, dense racemes in May. Argentina, Chile. I 1843 by Sir Joseph Hooker. AM 1962. (For a plant sometimes grown under this name see × *Mahoberberis neubertii*.)

incrassata See *B. insignis* subsp. *incrassata*.

insignis Hook. f. & Thoms. (*B. insignis* var. *tongloensis* C.K. Schneid.) A noble shrub forming a dense clump of erect, yellowish stems, remarkable for their lack of spines. Leaves, usually in clusters of three, are lanceolate, large, up to 18cm long, with bold teeth, dark polished green above, yellowish-green and glossy beneath. Dense clusters of large flowers are followed by black, ovoid berries. Often regarded as tender but has proved quite hardy at our nurseries. N India, Nepal, Bhutan. Introduced from Sikkim by Sir Joseph Hooker in 1850. subsp. *incrassata* (Ahrendt) D.F. Chamb. & Hu (*B. incrassata* Ahrendt) Differs in its rounded berries. NE Upper Burma, SE Tibet. I 1931.

×interposita Ahrendt (*B. hookeri × B. verruculosa*) A vigorous, small shrub, developing into a dense, rounded mound of arching stems. Leaves 1.5–2cm long, sharply spiny, glossy dark green above, pruinose below, often green by autumn. **'Wallich's Purple'** A dense, small bush with arching shoots, the leaves bronze-red when young, later glossy green.

× *irwinii* and cultivars. See under *B.* × *stenophylla*.

jamesiana Forrest & W.W. Sm. A large, erect-branched species giving rich autumn tints. Flowers in racemes, followed by pendent clusters of translucent, coral-red berries. Yunnan. I 1913 by George Forrest. AM 1925.

*julianae C.K. Schneid. An excellent, dense shrub, to 3m, with strongly spiny stems and clusters of stiff, narrow, spine-toothed leaves, copper-tinted when young. Slightly scented, yellow flowers are in dense, axillary clusters. A good screening or hedging plant. China. I 1900 by Ernest Wilson. ♀ 2002.

*kawakamii Hayata. (*B. kawakamii* var. *formosana* Ahrendt, *B. formosana* (Ahrendt) Ahrendt) A small, spiny species, densely furnished with short, rather broad leaves, copper-tinted when young. Dense clusters of rich yellow flowers in March and April. Taiwan. I about 1919 by Ernest Wilson.

koreana Palib. An attractive species with large leaves colouring well in autumn, flowers in drooping racemes and conspicuous red, waxen, ovoid berries. Korea. AM 1996 (for fruit).

*lempergiana Ahrendt. A distinct species, akin to *B. julianae*, but with broader, paler leaves. Berries oval and bloomy, produced in clusters. Zhejiang, China. I 1935 and originally named from a plant raised in our nurseries.

leptoclada See *B. amoena*.

levis See *B. atrocarpa*.

liechtensteinii C.K. Schneid. A semi-evergreen shrub with ovoid, red berries in short racemes. W China. I 1908.

linearifolia See *B. trigona*.

*× lologensis Sandwith (*B. darwinii* × *B. trigona*) A very beautiful shrub, offspring of two superb species. Leaves variable in shape, entire and spiny on the same bush; flowers apricot-yellow. A natural hybrid found with the parents in Argentina by Comber in 1927. AM 1931. **'Apricot Queen'** Broadly upright with large, bright orange flowers. ♀ 2002. **'Mystery Fire'** Upright habit, with profuse clusters of orange-yellow flowers, deeper coloured in bud. Similar to 'Apricot Queen' but much easier to propagate from cuttings. **'Stapehill'** A form with freely borne, rich orange flowers.

*lycium Royle. A semi-evergreen species of medium height. Leaves up to 5cm long, light sea-green; flowers bright yellow in elongated racemes, followed by purple, bloomy berries. Himalaya. I about 1850 by Sir Joseph Hooker.

× *macracantha* Schrad. (*B. aristata* × *B. vulgaris*) A tall shrub up to 4m high. The yellow flowers are produced in racemes of 10–20 blooms and are followed by purple berries. Garden origin.

*manipurana Ahrendt (*B. knightii* hort., *B. xanthoxylon* hort., *B. hookeri* var. *latifolia* hort.) A vigorous, evergreen species, reaching about 3m, with large, lustrous leaves, yellow flowers and oblong, blue-black berries. An excellent hedging plant. Manipur. I 1882. AM 1980.

*× media Groot. (*B.* × *chenaultii* × *B. thunbergii*) This hybrid is represented in gardens by the following forms. **'Parkjuweel'** A small shrub of dense, prickly habit. Leaves obovate, almost spineless, colouring richly in autumn, occasionally remaining until the following spring. Flowers borne singly or in small clusters of up to 4, followed by dull, red-purple fruits. Garden origin in Holland about 1956. **'Red Jewel'** A dense, small, - semi-evergreen shrub similar to 'Parkjuweel' but with somewhat broader leaves becoming deep metallic purple. A sport of 'Parkjuweel'. ♀ 2002.

'Mentorensis' (*B. julianae* × *B. thunbergii*) A vigorous and very dense, deciduous or semi-evergreen shrub, up to 2m tall, with small, obovate leaves, entire or toothed towards the apex. Pale yellow flowers, tinged red, are followed by dark brown-red berries. Garden origin in the USA in 1924.

micrantha Ahrendt. Dense shrub with dark red berries in dense racemes. Bhutan. I 1838.

microphylla G. Forst. (*B. buxifolia* Lam., *B. dulcis* Sweet) A semi-evergreen species of medium size with small, obovate, dark green leaves, glaucous grey beneath and spiny at the tip; solitary deep orange-yellow flowers in April-May are followed by purple-blue, grape-like berries. Argentina, Chile. I about 1826. AM 1961. **'Nana'** See 'Pygmaea'. **'Pygmaea'** A slow-growing, dense, evergreen mound about 50cm high with rounded leaves. Virtually thornless and rarely flowers. Originally grown as 'Nana'. C 1867.

mitifolia Stapf. A distinct species. A small to medium-sized shrub with spike-like racemes of yellow flowers, pubescent leaves, turning red in autumn, and elongated, crimson berries. W China. I 1901 by Ernest Wilson.

montana Gay (*B. cabrerae* Job, *B. chillanensis* (C.K. Schneid.) Sprague *B. chillanensis* var. *hirsutipes* Sprague) A stiffly branched, medium to large, upright shrub with obovate, usually untoothed leaves to 18mm long. Flowers solitary or in clusters of up to 3, followed by black fruits. Argentina, Chile. I 1925–1927 by Harold Comber. AM 1935 FCC 1982 AM 1932 (the last two as *B. chillanensis* var. *hirsutipes*).

morrisonensis Hayata. Mount Morrison barberry. A low, compact, free-flowering shrub with large, bright red berries and brilliant autumn tints of scarlet and gold. Taiwan. I 1912.

mucrifolia Ahrendt. A dwarf shrub of dense, compact habit, with erect, slender, spiny stems and small, mucronate leaves. Flowers usually solitary; berries bright red. Nepal. I about 1954.

oblonga (Regel) C.K. Schneid. Medium to large shrub. Flowers in densely packed racemes; berries purple-black with white bloom. Turkestan. I 1876.

orthobotrys Aitch. A shrub of vigorous, upright habit bearing large, bright red, oval berries. Bright autumn tints. Kashmir, Afghanistan, Nepal. AM 1919. **var. canescens** Ahrendt (*B.* 'Unique') A form with narrower leaves, pruinose beneath. Kashmir, Nepal.

× *ottawensis* C.K. Schneid. (*B. thunbergii* × *B. vulgaris*) A shrub with green, rounded or oval leaves and red berries in drooping clusters. C 1893. **Purpurea Group** (f. *purpurea* (C.K. Schneid.) Rehder) This name covers all forms with purple leaves. See also under 'Superba'. **'Silver Miles'** Leaves red-purple flushed with silvery grey. **'Superba'** A vigorous hybrid of medium to large size. A first-class shrub with rich, vinous-purple foliage, yellow flowers and red berries. Usually grown as 'Purpurea'. Garden origin. ♀ 2002. AM 1979.

pallens Franch. A large shrub. Berries ovoid, bright red; leaves richly tinted in autumn. W China. I 1929.

panlanensis See *B. sanguinea*.

parisepala Ahrendt. Slow-growing, small shrub related to *B. angulosa*. Leaves often red-tinted in autumn; berries large, red. SE Tibet, Bhutan, Nepal. I about 1928.

'Parkjuweel' See *B.* × *media* 'Parkjuweel'.

'Pirate King' See *B.* × *carminea* 'Pirate King'.

poiretii C.K. Schneid. Attractive shrub, up to 1.5m high, with elegant, drooping branches and abundant, pale yellow flowers followed by slender, bright red berries. N China, Amurland. I about 1860.

polyantha Hemsl. Erect shrub with large and abundant, drooping flower panicles followed by grape-like clusters of red berries. One of the most constant in the vivid red of its autumn colour. W China. I 1904. AM 1917.

prattii C.K. Schneid. Medium-sized to large shrub with flowers in erect panicles followed by ovoid, bright coral berries. A lovely shrub of great ornamental beauty when heavy with fruits in autumn. W China. The plant most commonly grown is var. *laxipendula* Ahrendt with drooping panicles. AM 1953.

*pruinosa Franch. A vigorous shrub with distinct, spine-toothed, sea-green foliage, white beneath. The soft yellow flowers are followed by abundant crops of blue-black berries covered with white bloom. Yunnan. I to France in 1894 by Delavay. AM 1924. **var.** *longifolia* Ahrendt. A form with longer, narrower leaves. Possibly a hybrid.

'Red Jewel' See *B.* × *media* 'Red Jewel'.

*replicata W.W. Sm. A graceful, slow-growing shrub, attaining about 1.5m; leaves narrow, recurved at the edges and glaucous beneath; berries ellipsoid, black-purple. Yunnan. I 1917 by George Forrest. AM 1923.

'Rubrostilla' A beautiful, small shrub of garden origin; very showy in autumn with large, oblong, coral-red berries, among the largest in the genus. Garden origin, a hybrid of *B. wilsoniae*. FCC 1916.

*sanguinea C.K. Schneid. (*B. panlanensis* Ahrendt) A charming, compact shrub of very neat growth. Leaves linear, sea-green and spine-toothed. An ideal hedging plant. W China. I 1908. **'Panlanensis'** The commonly grown form described above.

*sargentiana C.K. Schneid. A hardy species up to 2m tall. The evergreen leaves are leathery, elliptic-oblong, net-veined and up to 13cm long; berries blue-black. W China. I 1907 by Ernest Wilson. FCC 1916. AM 1915.

sherriffii Ahrendt. An elegant shrub with elliptic, entire leaves, conspicuous when bearing its large, drooping panicles of bloomy, blue-black berries. SE Tibet. I 1938 by Ludlow, Sherriff and Taylor.

sieboldii Miq. A small, suckering shrub of compact habit, with oval leaves which colour richly in the autumn. Racemes of pale yellow flowers followed by globose, shining, orange berries. Japan. I 1892. AM 1999.

sikkimensis (C.K. Schneid.) Ahrendt. A small shrub with angled shoots and short racemes of ovoid, dark red berries. Sikkim. I about 1924.

silva-taroucana C.K. Schneid. A large, elegant shrub with young growths attractively tinged reddish-purple. The long racemes of yellow flowers are followed by egg-shaped, scarlet berries. China. I 1912.

*soulieana C.K. Schneid. A sparsely branched shrub of stiff habit. Narrow leaves have pronounced spinose teeth, and yellow flowers are borne in clusters in the leaf axils in May. Berries black, covered with a glaucous bloom. C China. I 1897.

*× stenophylla Lindl. (*B. darwinii* × *B. empetrifolia*) An indispensable shrub, ultimately medium-sized and graceful, its long, arching branches wreathed with yellow flowers in April. C 1860. ♀ 2002. FCC 1864. **'Autumnalis'** Small shrub of graceful habit producing a second crop of flowers in autumn. C 1929. **'Claret Cascade'** Flowers rich orange, flushed red outside, young foliage purple-tinged. **'Coccinea'** (*B.* × *irwinii* 'Coccinea') A small shrub with crimson buds opening orange. C 1920. AM 1925. **'Corallina'** (*B.* × *irwinii* 'Corallina') A small shrub of lax habit. Buds coral-red opening yellow. C 1912. **'Corallina Compacta'** (*B.* × *irwinii* 'Corallina Compacta') A dwarf shrub rarely exceeding 30cm. Buds coral-red opening yellow. C 1930. ♀ 2002. AM 1981. **'Crawley Gem'** A small shrub forming a dense mound of arching stems flooded in spring with orange flowers, red-tipped in bud. C 1930. **'Cream Showers'** See 'Lemon Queen'. **'Etna'** A seedling raised in our nurseries before 1935. A small shrub with shining, dark green leaves. In April the whole bush erupts into flower from red buds and the leaves are hidden by clusters of fiery orange blossoms. **'Gracilis'** (*B.* × *irwinii* 'Gracilis') A small shrub of lax habit. Leaves bright green. Flowers golden-yellow. C 1907. **'Gracilis Nana'** (*B.* × *irwinii* 'Gracilis Nana') A dwarf, slow-growing shrub of dense habit, with golden-yellow flowers. C 1909. **'Irwinii'** (*B.* × *irwinii* Bijh.) A small, compact shrub; flowers deep yellow. C 1900. **'Lemon Queen'** ('Cream Showers') An unusual form with creamy-white flowers. A sport of 'Pink Pearl'. **'Nana'** (*B. darwinii* 'Nana') Small, compact shrub with rich yellow flowers. **'Picturata'** (*B.* × *irwinii* 'Picturata') A small, floriferous shrub; flowers deep yellow. **'Pink Pearl'** A curious form of chameleon nature. Leaves dark green or mottled and striped pink and cream. Flowers may be creamy-yellow, orange, pink or bicoloured on different shoots of the same bush. Unfortunately, this unusual form reverts badly. **'Prostrata'** (*B. darwinii* 'Prostrata') Attractive, low shrub; the orange buds open golden-yellow. **'Semperflorens'** Small shrub with red buds opening orange, still flowering when the typical form has finished. C 1930.

†**sublevis* W.W. Sm. Shrub with ribbed, strongly spiny stems and narrow, spine-edged leaves. Primrose-yellow, fragrant flowers. W China. C 1935.

*taliensis C.K. Schneid. A rigid, slow-growing hummock, scarcely exceeding 1m in height. Its lanceolate leaves are dark glossy green. Flowers lemon-yellow; berries blue-black. Yunnan. I 1922 by George Forrest.

taylorii Ahrendt. Shrub with dense panicles of greenish-yellow flowers followed by ovoid, black berries with a blue bloom. SE Tibet. I 1938 by Ludlow, Sherriff and Taylor.

temolaica Ahrendt. One of the most striking barberries. A vigorous shrub, up to 3m high, with stout, erect-spreading branches. Young shoots and leaves are conspicuously glaucous, the shoots becoming a dark, bloomy, purple-brown with age. Berries are egg-shaped, red and covered with bloom. Introduced from SE Tibet by Kingdon-Ward in 1924. ♥ 2002.

thunbergii DC. An invaluable, small shrub, compact in growth and unsurpassed in the brilliance of its autumn foliage and bright red berries. Japan. I about 1864. ♥ 2002. FCC 1890. **Atropurpurea Group** (f. *atropurpurea* (Chenault) Rehder) Foliage rich reddish-purple, throughout spring and summer, and increasing in intensity as winter approaches. C 1913. AM 1926. **'Atropurpurea Nana'** ('Crimson Pygmy', 'Little Favourite') A charming, dwarf form of this popular purple-foliaged shrub, suitable for a rock garden or as a dwarf hedge. Raised in Holland in 1942. ♥ 2002. **'Aurea'** Leaves bright yellow becoming pale green by late summer. C 1950. **'Bagatelle'** Similar to 'Atropurpurea Nana' but much more compact. Raised in Holland in 1971 by crossing 'Atropurpurea Nana' with 'Kobold'. ♥ 2002. **Bonanza Gold** ('Bogozam') PBR A dwarf shrub with orange-red shoots and yellow-green later green foliage which does not burn in sun. **'Cheal's Scarlet'** Leaves bronze-tinged during summer turning brilliant scarlet in early autumn. **'Dart's Red Lady'** Very deep purple leaves turn brilliant red in autumn. **'Erecta'** A small, compact, fastigiate shrub forming a dense clump; excellent for low hedges. Superb autumn colours. **'Golden Ring'** Leaves reddish-purple with a narrow gold margin. Similar forms can be found when Atropurpurea is raised from seed. C 1950. ♥ 2002. **'Green Carpet'** A low shrub, to about 1m high, with widespreading, arching shoots. The rounded leaves turn red in autumn. Selected in Holland about 1956. **'Harlequin'** Similar to 'Rose Glow' but leaves smaller and more heavily mottled pink. C 1969. AM 1978. **'Helmond Pillar'** A form of narrow, upright habit with rich purple foliage. **'Kelleriis'** A compact, spreading bush, the leaves mottled creamy-white. In autumn the white portion of the leaf turns through pink to deep crimson. Raised in Denmark. The more recent 'Silver Beauty' is similar. **'Kobold'** A dwarf form of very dense, rounded habit. Free-fruiting. Raised in Holland about 1960. **'Minor'** An interesting, dense, dwarf shrub scarcely exceeding 50cm. **'Pink Queen'** The best pink-variegated form with reddish leaves heavily flecked grey and white. Raised in Holland before 1958. **'Red Chief'** A small shrub of upright habit, later with arching branches. Stems are bright red; leaves narrow, deep red-purple. Selected in Holland in 1942. ♥ 2002. **'Red Pillar'** A most attractive form of 'Erecta' with reddish-purple leaves that turn brilliant scarlet in autumn. **'Rose Glow'** A very striking, small, colourful shrub. The leaves of the young shoots are purple, mottled silver-pink and bright rose, later becoming purple. Selected in Holland about 1957 but now superseded by other forms. ♥ 2002. **'Silver Beauty'** See under 'Kelleriis'.

*trigona Kunze ex Poeppig & Endl. (*B. linearifolia* Phil.) An erect shrub of medium size and rather ungainly habit, with narrow, dark glossy green, spine-tipped leaves. The orange-red flowers, produced early in spring and sometimes again in the autumn, are the richest coloured of the genus. I 1927 from Argentina by Harold Comber. Native also of Chile. FCC 1931. **'Jewel'** A splendid form and possibly the best in the genus for flower. Flowers scarlet in bud opening to bright orange, relatively large. C 1937.

AM 1978. **'Orange King'** A selected form with larger flowers of a rich orange.

tsangpoensis Ahrendt. A most interesting species, forming a dwarf, widespreading mound, the slender, yellow stems often extending a considerable distance along the ground. Attractive autumn tints and red berries. SE Tibet. I 1925.

umbellata G.Don. Semi-evergreen except in severe winters, this shrub has shoots that are bright red at first, and yellow flowers in long-stalked corymbs followed by egg-shaped, red berries. Nepal. I 1848.

'Unique' See *B. orthobotrys* var. *canescens*.

*valdiviana Phil. A large, stately species with distinctive, large, leathery, polished, almost spineless leaves, like a smooth-leaved holly. Flowers saffron-yellow in long, drooping racemes. A first-class hardy plant deserving wider planting. Chile. I 1902 and again by Clarence Elliott in 1930. AM 1939.

validisepala Ahrendt. A species allied to *B. yunnanensis* and differing in its shorter spines and smaller flowers and berries. Yunnan. I about 1930.

*veitchii C.K. Schneid. (*B. acuminata* Veitch) A shrub, to about 2m high, with long, lanceolate, spine-toothed leaves and red young shoots; long-stalked, bronze-yellow flowers in axillary clusters are followed by black berries. C China. I 1900 by Ernest Wilson.

vernae C.K. Schneid. (*B. caroli* var. *hoanghensis* C.K. Schneid.) A very graceful shrub with flowers in dense, slender racemes all along the stems; berries globose, salmon-red. China. I 1910. AM 1926.

*verruculosa Hemsl. & E.H. Wilson. A very pleasing, compact, slow-growing shrub, 1.5–2m high, with rough, minutely warty, drooping stems densely covered with small, glossy, dark green leaves, white beneath. Usually solitary flowers are golden-yellow. W China. I 1904 by Ernest Wilson. ♥ 2002. AM 1911.

virescens Hook. f. & Thoms. A tall, erect-branched shrub with red shoots and brilliant red autumn colour. Berries reddish, bloomy. Sikkim. I 1849.

virgetorum C.K. Schneid. A shrub, up to 2m high, with comparatively large, obovate, spineless leaves and oblong-elliptic, reddish berries. China. I about 1909.

vulgaris L. The common barberry produces pendent clusters of egg-shaped, translucent, bright red berries. The bark and wood were once used in the treatment of jaundice. Now rarely grown as it is a host to wheat rust. Europe (incl. British Isles), N Africa, temperate Asia. Naturalised in North America. **'Atropurpurea'** Purple-leaf barberry. A striking shrub, its deep vinous-purple foliage contrasting with nodding racemes of yellow flowers. AM 1905.

wilsoniae Hemsl. A splendid, small shrub forming dense mounds of thorny stems. Small, sea-green leaves turn attractive shades in autumn blending with the coral of the fruit clusters. W China. I about 1904 by Ernest Wilson and named after his wife. Reintroduced by Roy Lancaster as seed collected in the mountains above Kunming, Yunnan. FCC 1907. **'Globosa'** A dwarf, compact, globular form. **var. guhtzunica** (Ahrendt) Ahrendt. This variety resembles var. *subcaulialata*, and has attractive, sea-green leaves and reddish-purple young shoots; clusters of berries are translucent white changing to coral-red. W China. I 1938 by Dr Yü. **var. *stapfiana*** (C.K. Schneid.) C.K. Schneid. This semi-evergreen shrub with its soft yellow flowers is a little taller and has more glaucous, sea-green, spathulate leaves and elliptic, coral-red berries. W China. I 1896. **var. *subcaulialata*** (C.K. Schneid.) C.K. Schneid. A taller variety with larger leaves. W China. I 1908.

× ***wintonensis*** Ahrendt. This dense shrub is a hybrid of *B. bergmanniae*, resembling it but having very narrow leaves. The flowers appearing in February are exceptionally freely borne and are followed by blue-black, bloomy berries. Raised in our nurseries in about 1935.

yunnanensis Franch. An attractive shrub of rounded habit with relatively large, golden-yellow flowers, brilliant autumn colours and bright red berries. W China. I 1885 by Delavay.

zabeliana C.K. Schneid. A neat, compact bush with plum-red berries and good autumn colour. Kashmir, Afghanistan.

†*****BESCHORNERIA*** Kunth—Agavaceae—A small genus related to *Agave*. About 10 species, natives of Mexico.

yuccoides K. Koch. A striking, yucca-like plant with pink flower stems to about 2m carrying drooping racemes of bright green flowers shading to bronzy-red at the base, with red bracts. This remarkable plant flourished for more than twenty years on chalk at the foot of a south-facing wall at our Winchester nursery. Requires full sun and a well-drained position. I before 1859. ♀ 2002. AM 1933.

BETULA L.—**Betulaceae**—The birches comprise about 60 species of deciduous trees and shrubs found in N temperate regions. They include some of the most elegant trees, many of which are noteworthy for their stem colour and attractive, yellow leaves in autumn. Male and female catkins are borne on the same tree, the males pendent and elongating in spring, the females shorter and erect. They succeed on most soils, both damp and dry, but do not reach maximum size on shallow chalk soils.

alba See *B. pendula* and *B. pubescens*.

albosinensis Burkill. Beautiful, medium-sized species with glossy green leaves on slightly rough shoots. The attractive, peeling bark is pinkish to coppery-red, cream when first exposed. W China. I 1901 by Ernest Wilson. ♀ 2002. **'Bowling Green'** This form, with honey-coloured, peeling bark, was named from one of the trees at Werrington, grown from seed collected by Ernest Wilson in W Sichuan, China in October 1910 (Wilson 4106). The original tree has since died. **'China Ruby'** Leaves matt blue-green on densely warty shoots. Freshly exposed bark is creamy-white flushed grey and pink, maturing to coppery-red. This is the form we have grown for many years as *B. albosinensis*. **'Chinese Garden'** Propagated from the other tree of Wilson 4106 at Werrington (see under 'Bowling Green'), this differs in its darker, pinkish bark. **'Hergest'** Matt green, sharply toothed leaves on warty and downy shoots. Bark glossy brown with white lenticels on the branches shading to pinkish-white and white at the base. A fast-growing form, a spontaneous seedling at Hergest Croft, Herefordshire. **var. *septentrionalis*** C.K. Schneid. This splendid variety has striking, grey-pink bark, coppery-pink on the main branches. It also differs in its matt green leaves. I 1908 by Ernest Wilson. ♀ 2002.

alleghaniensis Britton. (*B. lutea* Michx.) A medium-sized tree with smooth, shining, amber or golden-brown bark which peels prettily. Ovate-oblong, downy leaves turn rich yellow in autumn. Shoots scented of wintergreen. E North America. I about 1767.

apoiensis Nakai. A variable shrub, closely related to *B. ermanii*, either upright in habit or low and spreading, with persistently and densely warty shoots red when young. Glossy dark green, ovate leaves are borne on short, warty petioles and have about 8 pairs of veins, ending in triangular teeth. Japan, only on Mt Apoi, Hokkaido.

× ***aurata*** Borkh. (*B. pendula* × *B. pubescens*) A small to medium-sized tree, variable in leaf shape and texture but generally intermediate between the parents. Frequent with the parents in the wild.

× ***caerulea*** Blanch. (*B. caerulea-grandis* Blanch.) (*B. cordifolia* × *B. populifolia*) A small tree with orange-tinted, creamy-white bark and ovate, sharply pointed leaves. Occurring with the parents in the wild. I 1905.

caerulea-grandis See *B.* × *caerulea*.

calcicola (W.W. Sm.) P.C. Li. A medium-sized, upright shrub with stout shoots densely clothed with long, yellow hairs when young, grey and downy the second year. Leaves broadly ovate, short-stalked, silky-hairy when young becoming dark green with 16 or more pairs of closely spaced impressed veins. I 1986 by Roy Lancaster who found it growing in limestone crevices on Yulongshan (Jade Dragon Mountains), NW Yunnan (Lancaster 1690 and 1691).

chichibuensis Hara. A very graceful, large shrub of spreading habit with arching shoots, silky-hairy when young becoming glossy red-brown with white lenticels the second year. Ovate, taper-pointed leaves have about 18 pairs of impressed veins ending in fine teeth. A species that grows on limestone rocks in the wild, and found only in two small areas of C and NE Japan.

chinensis Maxim. Large shrub, occasionally a small tree, without conspicuous bark. An uncommon species of neat habit with small, oval, sharply toothed leaves on slender, downy shoots. China. I 1906.

'Conyngham' (*B. albosinensis* var. *septentrionalis* × *B. pendula*) A vigorous tree with arching and slightly pendent branches. Leaves variable, some resembling *B. albosinensis*, others showing the shape and lobing of *B. pendula*. The peeling bark is grey-brown, creamy-white flushed with grey-pink when freshly exposed. Under different conditions the bark can have a red flush. This was a chance seedling of *B. albosinensis* var. *septentrionalis* raised by Kenneth Ashburner.

costata Trautv. The true species of this name is a native of NE Asia and is rare in cultivation. Plants grown as *B. costata* are usually a form of *B. ermanii* (see below).

cylindrostachya Lindl. A rare, small tree which is proving fairly hardy in our nurseries. Stout, downy, drooping shoots bear large, ovate to ovate-oblong, glossy, short-stalked leaves, downy on both sides and occasionally to 15cm long. An interesting species requiring a sheltered position and happiest in milder areas of the British Isles. Himalaya.

davurica Pall. A medium-sized tree with peculiarly rugged, silvery-grey bark, dark brown on the main branches. Dark green leaves with triangular teeth are borne on very rough shoots. Tends to be early leafing and perhaps more suited for northerly and colder areas. Manchuria, N China, Korea. I 1882.

delavayi Franch. A large shrub or small tree with arching shoots, red and silky when young becoming yellow-brown, later red-brown and lenticellate. Leaves ovate, glossy dark green with 10–12 pairs of impressed veins, edged with small, pointed teeth. SW China.

ermanii Cham. (*B. ermanii* var. *subcordata* (Reg.) Koidz.) A graceful, vigorous tree with very rough shoots and bright green, often heart-shaped, conspicuously veined leaves. Creamy-white and pinkish bark, is fawn when first exposed with numerous pale brown lenticels; brown to red-brown on the branches. NE Asia. **'Grayswood Hill'** A form selected for its excellent white bark. Many plants grown as *B. costata* belong here. ♥ 2002. **'Hakkoda Orange'** A form selected by Kenneth Ashburner for its orange, flaking and peeling bark. It was raised from seed collected on Mt Hakkoda, N Honshu, Japan by Sekei Takahashi, in 1981. **'Mt Apoi'** A slow-growing selection, suitable for small gardens, with good, creamy-white bark. Raised from seed collected on Mt Apoi, Hokkaido, Japan.

'Fetisowii' A hybrid originally from C Asia, forming a graceful, narrow-headed tree notable for its peeling, chalk-white bark extending up the trunk to the branches. Plants grown under this name are probably seedlings of the original.

fontinalis See *B. occidentalis*.

glandulifera (Reg.) B.T. Butler (*B. pumila* var. *glandulifera* Reg.) Medium-sized shrub with small, obovate, sometimes orbicular leaves, gland dotted. Male catkins pink, passing to yellow. North Amcrica.

grossa Siebold & Zucc. Japanese cherry birch. Medium-sized tree with smooth, dark grey bark and hornbeam-like leaves. The twigs have a distinctive smell when bruised. Japan. I 1896.

humilis Schrank. A small to medium-sized shrub with hairy and warty twigs and small leaves. Europe and N Asia.

jacquemontii See *B. utilis* var. *jacquemontii*.

'Jermyns' See *B. utilis* var. *jacquemontii* 'Jermyns'.

kenaica W.H. Evans (*B. papyrifera* var. *kenaica* (W.H. Evans) A. Henry) A small tree closely related to *B. papyrifera* differing in its smaller size and smaller leaves with fewer veins. Bark reddish-brown to pinkish-white. Alaska and part of Yukon. I 1891.

× *koehnei* C.K. Schneid. (*B. papyrifera* × *B. pendula*) Medium-sized tree of graceful habit with drooping lower branches and blue-green leaves with jagged teeth. Outstanding for its pure white bark on the trunk and larger branches.

lenta L. Cherry birch. Rarely a tall tree in the British Isles, though attaining 25m in its native land, this has a smooth, dark, reddish-brown or purple trunk. The young bark is sweet and aromatic. Leaves turn rich yellow in autumn. E North America. I 1759. **var. *uber*** See *B. uber*.

luminifera H.J.P. Winkl. A remarkable, large tree. The large, deep green, lustrous leaves persist until a sharp frost in late autumn. W China. I 1901 by Ernest Wilson.

lutea See *B. alleghaniensis*.

lyalliana See *B. papyrifera* var. *commutata*.

mandshurica See *B. platyphylla*. **var. *szechuanica*** See *B. szechuanica*.

maximowicziana Reg. Monarch birch. This, the largest-leaved birch, reaches 30m in its native habitat. As seen in the British Isles it is a fast-growing, wide-headed tree of medium height with an orange-brown trunk, finally grey and pinkish, peeling in narrow strips, coppery on the branches. Heart-shaped leaves, up to 15cm long, turn a lovely clear butter-yellow in autumn. Japan. I 1893.

medwediewii Reg. A large shrub or small, shrubby tree with stout, erect branches. Distinct in its large, terminal buds and large, corrugated leaves which turn yellow in autumn. Transcaucasus. I 1897. AM 1975 (for autumn colour).

middendorffii Trautv. & C.A. Mey. Medium to large shrub with usually resinous-glandular stems and small, rounded leaves. Closely related to *B. humilis*. NE Asia. C 1904.

minor (Tuck.) Fernald (*B. papyrifera* var. *minor* (Tuck.) S. Watson) Dwarf white birch. A shrubby species or occasionally a small, bushy tree, with reddish-brown bark. It is possibly of hybrid origin. Mountains of NE USA and E Canada. I 1904.

nana L. Dwarf birch. A small, native shrub with tiny, neat, rounded leaves. N temperate regions. Similar species occur in North America and NE Asia.

neoalaskana Sarg. (*B. papyrifera* var. *humilis* (Reg.) Fernald & Raup, *B. papyrifera* var. *neoalaskana* (Sarg.) Raup) Yukon white birch. A handsome, large tree with the young shoots densely glandular-resinous. Bark peeling, white to pinkish or red-brown. W Canada, Alaska. I 1905.

nigra L. River birch, Red birch. A beautiful, fast-growing tree, remarkable for its pinkish-orange, shaggy bark, which becomes brown and ridged on old trees. As its common name suggests, it is one of the finest trees for planting in damp ground. Soft green, diamond-shaped leaves are glaucous beneath. C and E USA. I 1736 by Peter Collinson. **'Heritage'** An outstanding form found as a seedling in the USA in 1968. A vigorous tree with peeling, light brown to creamy bark and dark, glossy green leaves. ♥ 2002.

occidentalis Hook. (*B. fontinalis* Sarg., *B. papyrifera* var. *occidentalis* (Hook.) Sarg.) A large shrub or small to medium-sized tree with bronze-red to reddish-brown bark, often not peeling strongly. Leaves sharply double-toothed on shoots that are covered in glandular warts. W North America.

papyrifera Marshall. (*B. papyrifera* var. *commutata* (Regel) Fernald) Paper birch, Canoe birch. A striking, large tree with white, papery bark and yellow autumn foliage. Forms with brown bark occur in the wild. These have been called var. *commutata* and have been confused with *B. occidentalis*. North America. I 1750. **var. *commutata*** See *B. papyrifera*. **var. *humilis*** See *B. neoalaskana*. **var. *kenaica*** See *B. kenaica*. **var. *minor*** See *B. minor*. **var. *neoalaskana*** See *B. neoalaskana*. **'St. George'** A form with white and pale tan bark contrasting with the dark brown of the branches. Leaves smooth and relatively small, on warty shoots. Selected by Kevin Croucher from plants raised from seed collected by Kenneth

Ashburner in St. John's, New Foundland. **'Vancouver'** A very vigorous form with large, downy leaves, the bark an attractive combination of brown, pink and white. Autumn colour rich orange, late. Selected by Kevin Croucher from a batch of seedlings raised by Kenneth Ashburner from seed he collected near Abbotsford, Vancouver in 1981.

pendula Roth (*B. verrucosa* Ehrh., *B. alba* L. in part) The common silver birch, aptly described as 'Lady of the Woods'. A medium-sized, white-stemmed tree, thriving in drier soils than *B. pubescens*, from which it is distinguished by its rough, warty shoots and sharply cut, diamond-shaped leaves. Unlike *B. pubescens* old trees develop rough, black bark at the base. Europe (incl. British Isles), N Asia. ♀ 2002. **'Dalecarlica'** The plant commonly grown under this name is correctly 'Laciniata'; the true 'Dalecarlica' differs in being not as weeping and with more deeply cut leaves. It was originally found in Sweden in 1767 and is rare in cultivation. Forms similar to both occur wild in Sweden. **'Dentata Viscosa'** A small, bushy tree with coarsely toothed leaves and sticky young growths. Of no special horticultural merit. C 1912. **'Fastigiata'** An erect form of medium size and rather stiff habit. 'Obelisk' is similar but perhaps not becoming as wide. C 1870. **'Golden Cloud'** A selection with yellow leaves. Tends to scorch badly. **'Gracilis'** A small tree with arching branches and slender, weeping shoots. Leaves finely and deeply cut. **'Laciniata'** Swedish birch. A tall, slender, graceful tree with drooping branchlets and prettily cut leaves. Often incorrectly grown as 'Dalecarlica' q.v. ♀ 2002. **'Obelisk'** See under 'Fastigiata'. **'Purpurea'** Purple leaf birch. A slow-growing tree with purple leaves. Rather weak constitution. C 1872. FCC 1874. **'Tristis'** A graceful, tall tree with slender, pendent branches, forming a narrow, symmetrical head. A tree of outstanding merit. C 1867. ♀ 2002. **'Youngii'** Young's weeping birch. Ultimately a beautiful, dome-shaped or mushroom-headed, small, weeping tree.

platyphylla Suk. (*B. mandshurica* (Reg.) Nakai) A large tree with white bark. Allied to *B. pendula* but differing in its larger leaves. NE Asia. Rare in cultivation. **var. *japonica*** (Miq.) Hara (*B. mandshurica* var. *japonica* (Miq.) Rehder, *B. tauschii* (Reg.) Koidz.) Japanese white birch. A medium-sized tree with pure white bark and white, resinous shoots, related to *B. pendula* but with larger leaves. Japan. C 1887. **var. *rockii*** See *B. rockii*. **var. *szechuanica*** See *B. szechuanica*.

populifolia Marshall. The grey birch is the American counterpart of the European silver birch. A small tree with ashen-white bark, purplish-brown on the branches, thriving equally well in dry or boggy ground. Leaves on rough shoots are bright green and sharply toothed. E North America. I 1750.

pubescens Ehrh. (*B. alba* L. in part) Common white birch. This species thrives on a variety of soils and especially in damp localities; it is distinguished from *B. pendula* by the less weeping habit, smooth-downy shoots, more rounded leaves and the bark being white to the base. Europe (incl. British Isles), N Asia. **subsp. *carpatica*** See subsp. *tortuosa*. **subsp. *tortuosa*** (Ledeb.) Nyman (subsp. *carpatica* (Willd.) Asch. & Graebn., *B. coriacea*

Gunnarsson) A small tree, with a wide distribution from Iceland to the Carpathians, forming a densely branched head. An extremely tough, hardy tree, ideal for exposed, windy situations.

pumila L. A small to large shrub of upright habit with downy young shoots and pointed, coarsely toothed leaves. E North America. I 1762. **var. *glandulifera*** See *B. glandulifera*.

rockii (Rehder) Jansson (*B. platyphylla* var. *rockii* (Rehder) Rehder) A small, white-barked tree, allied to *B. platyphylla* and *B. szechuanica*, introduced by the American collector Joseph Rock from Lake Koko Nor, China. W China.

szechuanica (C.K. Schneid.) Jansson (*B. platyphylla* var. *szechuanica* (C.K. Schneid.) Rehder, *B. mandschurica* var. *szechuanica* (C.K. Schneid.) Rehder) A vigorous, medium-sized tree with glossy, blue-green leaves and chalk-white bark. W China, SE Tibet. I 1908 by Ernest Wilson.

tatewakiana M. Okhi & Watan. A small to medium-sized shrub with densely glandular branches, downy when young. Leaves, 1.5–2.5cm long, are leathery, ovate to obovate, serrate in the upper half and downy beneath. A rare species, native of bogs in N Japan.

'Trost Dwarf' A weak-growing, small shrub with slender, arching branches and small, finely cut leaves. Susceptible to rust.

uber (Ashe) Fernald (*B. lenta* var. *uber* Ashe) Virginia roundleaf birch. Although described in 1918 this species was not refound until as recently as 1974, as a small population of only 17 trees. It is closely related to *B. lenta* from which it differs in its smaller stature, to 10m tall, and its smaller, rounded to broadly oval leaves, to 5cm long. Seed collected from this population produces a range of hybrids with *B. lenta* with which it grows. Virginia, USA.

utilis D. Don (*B. bhojpattra* Lindl.) Himalayan birch. A widely distributed species occurring throughout the Himalaya from Afghanistan to SW China and very variable in bark colour. The typical form is an attractive, medium-sized tree, with orange- or dark coppery-brown, peeling bark, often bloomed grey-pink, and occurs in the eastern half of the range from SW China to Nepal. I 1849 by Sir Joseph Hooker. **var. *jacquemontii*** (Spach) H.J.P. Winkl. (*B. jacquemontii* Spach) Differs from the typical form in its white bark. For grafted plants originally distributed by us under this name see 'Silver Shadow'. N India, C and W Nepal. C 1880. **'Doorenbos'** ('Snow Queen') A medium-sized tree with striking, white, peeling bark, pale orange when freshly exposed. The Dutch clone is readily available as *B. jacquemontii*. ♀ 2002. **'Grayswood Ghost'** A striking form with bright white bark and glossy green leaves. Propagated from a tree which once grew at Grayswood Hill, Surrey. ♀ 2002. **'Jermyns'** A very vigorous, medium-sized, broadly conical tree; the very fine, white bark is retained into maturity. Catkins long and showy, up to 17cm. Selected in our nurseries from plants received from Belgium. A specimen has reached more than 20m in the Sir Harold Hillier Gardens and Arboretum (2000). ♀ 2002. **'Kashmir White'** A form of var. *occidentalis* with good, white bark selected from an introduction by Roy

Lancaster from Kashmir in 1978. **'Kyelang'** A form of var. *occidentalis* selected by Kenneth Ashburner with white, peeling bark and white, resinous buds. It was the best seedling in a batch raised from seed collected by the Indian Forestry Service in Kyelang, in the NW Himalaya, in about 1975. **var. *occidentalis*** (Kitam.) Ashburner & A.D. Schill. A form with pure white, peeling bark and densely warty shoots. Buds covered with white resin. Veins 7–10. W Himalaya. **'Ramdana River'** A form with very white bark and glossy leaves. Raised from seed collected in Garwhal, Uttar Pradesh, India, by Kenneth Ashburner in 1991. There may be more than one clone grown under this name. **'Silver Shadow'** One of the loveliest birches with dazzling white stems, this is a very distinct form of var. *jacquemontii*, making a small to medium-sized tree with striking, white bark and large, drooping, dark green leaves. The original tree grew for many years in our West Hill Nursery, Winchester. Previously distributed by us as *B. jacquemontii*. ♀ 2002. **'Snow Queen'** See 'Doorenboos'.
verrucosa See *B. pendula*.

Bilberry See *Vaccinium myrtillus*.
Bilberry, Cascade See *Vaccinium deliciosum*.
Bilberry, dwarf See *Vaccinium caespitosum*.
Bilberry, red See *Vaccinium parvifolium*.
Birch See *Betula*.
Bird of paradise See *Clianthus puniceus*.
Bitternut See *Carya cordiformis*.
Black haw See *Viburnum prunifolium*.
Black haw, southern See *Viburnum rufidulum*.
Blackthorn See *Prunus spinosa*.
Blackwood See *Acacia melanoxylon*.
Bladder nut See *Staphylea*.
Bladder senna See *Colutea*.
Blaeberry See *Vaccinium myrtillus*.
Blue haw See *Viburnum cassinoides*.
Blueberry, black highbush See *Vaccinium atrococcum*.
Blueberry, box See *Vaccinium ovatum*.
Blueberry, creeping See *Vaccinium crassifolium*.
Blueberry, evergreen See *Vaccinium myrsinites*.
Blueberry, high-bush See *Vaccinium corymbosum*.
Blueberry, low-bush See *Vaccimium angustifolium*.
Blueberry, rabbiteye See *Vaccimium virgatum*.
Blueberry, swamp See *Vaccinium corymbosum*.

BOENNINGHAUSENIA Rchb. ex Meisn.—**Rutaceae**—A monotypic genus allied to *Ruta*.
albiflora (Hook.) Rchb. A late summer-flowering subshrub, somewhat like a white *Thalictrum* in both flower and foliage. Good on chalk soils. E Asia.

Bog rosemary See *Andromeda polifolia*.
Boldo See *Peumus boldus*.
Bottlebrush See *Callistemon*.

†**BOUVARDIA** Salisb.—**Rubiaceae**—A genus of about 20 species of evergreen herbs and shrubs, natives of Mexico and tropical South America.
ternifolia (Cav.) Schltdl. (*B. triphylla* Salisb) A small, showy plant with glossy green leaves, usually in threes, and orange-scarlet, tubular flowers, 5cm long, in late summer and autumn. Suitable for a conservatory. Mexico. I 1794.
triphylla See *B. ternifolia*.

†***BOWKERIA** Harv.—**Scrophulariaceae**—A small genus of some 5 species of tender, evergreen, South African shrubs and small trees.
gerrardiana See *B. verticillata*.
verticillata (Eckl. & Zeyh.) Druce (*B. gerrardiana* Harv. ex Hiern) A medium-sized shrub, producing white calceolaria-like flowers during summer. Requires conservatory cultivation except in the mildest areas. Natal. I about 1890.

Box See *Buxus*.
Box elder See *Acer negundo*.

***BRACHYGLOTTIS** J.R. Forst. & G. Forst.—**Compositae**—A genus of some 30 species of evergreen shrubs, trees and herbaceous perennials from New Zealand and Tasmania, closely related to *Senecio*. The shrubby members are evergreen and bear heads or panicles of white or yellow daisy flowers, some species lacking ray florets, during summer. All are sun-lovers and make excellent seaside shrubs. Most will not withstand low Continental temperatures but are excellent wind resisters. Unless otherwise stated, the following are natives of New Zealand.
bidwillii (Hook. f.) B. Nord. (*Senecio bidwillii* Hook. f.) A striking, dwarf, alpine shrub of compact, rigid habit, occasionally very slowly reaching 75cm. Leaves elliptic to obovate, up to 2.5cm long, remarkably thick, shining above and covered beneath, like the stems, in a soft, white or buff tomentum. Flowers not conspicuous.
buchananii (Armstr.) B. Nord. (*Senecio buchananii* (Armstr.) Kirk) A densely branched, small shrub with leathery leaves to 5cm long, silvery-tomentose beneath. Flowers yellow to cream, without ray florets, opening in small clusters.
†*compacta* (Kirk) B. Nord. (*Senecio compactus* Kirk) A small, compact shrub, attaining 0.9–1m, like B. 'Sunshine' but less spreading. Leaves oval, 2.5–5cm long, wavy-edged, white-felted beneath, as are the young shoots and flower stalks. Flowerheads bright yellow in few-flowered racemes. Subject to injury in severe winters. See also B. Dunedin Group. North Island where it is restricted to one locality.
'Drysdale' (Dunedin Group) A small shrub like 'Sunshine' but with slightly larger flowers and scalloped leaves.
Dunedin Group (*Senecio* Dunedin Hybrids) This name covers the various hybrids and backcrosses that have occurred between B. *compacta*, B. *greyi* and B. *laxifolius* and are now more commonly grown than any of the parents. For the most frequently seen form, originally grown as *Senecio greyi* and *S. laxifolius*, see B. 'Sunshine'.
elaeagnifolia (Hook. f.) B. Nord. (*Senecio elaeagnifolius* Hook. f.) A rigid, densely branched shrub of medium size with oval, leathery leaves, 7.5–15cm long, glossy above, thickly buff-felted beneath, as are the young shoots and flower stalks. Flowerheads in terminal panicles, of little ornament. An excellent coastal shrub. North Island.
†*greyi* (Hook. f.) B. Nord. (*Senecio greyi* Hook. f.) A small, spreading shrub with grey-hairy shoots. Leaves white-

tomentose on both sides when young, becoming glossy green above. Flowerheads bright yellow. Very rare in cultivation, the plant usually grown under this name is *B*. 'Sunshine', see also under Dunedin Group. North Island.

†*hectoris* (Buchanan) B. Nord. (*Senecio hectoris* Buchanan) A medium-sized to large, semi-evergreen shrub of erect, rather open habit. Leaves oblanceolate, 13–25cm long, often pinnately lobed at base and conspicuously toothed, white-tomentose beneath. Flowerheads white, 4–6cm across, in large terminal corymbs. H.G. Hillier was first introduced to this unusual species by the late Sir Herbert Maxwell, who was growing it in sheltering woodland. Unlike its allies, this handsome, large-leaved species cannot be expected to grow in an exposed, windy position. South Island. I 1910.

†*huntii* (F. v. Muell.) B. Nord. (*Senecio huntii* F. v. Muell.) Rautini. A medium-sized shrub of compact, rounded habit, with glandular-downy young shoots and narrowly obovate leaves up to 11cm long. Flowerheads yellow, in terminal panicles. Chatham Islands. I 1909.

†*kirkii* (Hook. f. ex Kirk) C.J. Webb (*Senecio kirkii* Hook. f. ex Kirk, *S. glastifolius* Hook. f.) Kohurang. A glabrous shrub of medium size, with brittle stems. Leaves fleshy, varying in shape from narrow-obovate to elliptic-oblong, few-toothed or dentate. Flowerheads white, in large, flat terminal corymbs. Only for the mildest areas or conservatory. North Island.

laxifolia (Buchanan) B. Nord. (*Senecio laxifolius* Buchanan) A small shrub related to *B. greyi*, but with smaller, thinner, broader pointed leaves. Flowerheads white, in loose terminal panicles. The true species is rare in cultivation. See also *B*. Dunedin Group. South Island.

†'**Leonard Cockayne**' (*Senecio* 'Leonard Cockayne') (*B. greyi* × *B. rotundifolia*) A wide-spreading, medium-sized shrub with white-backed, wavy-margined, grey-green leaves up to 15cm long. Yellow flowerheads are borne in large panicles. Excellent in coastal areas.

'**Moira Read**' (Dunedin Group) (*Senecio* 'Moira Read') A small shrub similar to 'Sunshine' but with creamy-yellow-blotched leaves.

monroi (Hook. f.) B. Nord. (*Senecio monroi* Hook. f.) A small shrub of dense habit often forming a broad dome, easily recognised by its oblong or oval, conspicuously undulate leaves, covered beneath with a dense, white felt, as are the young shoots and flower stalks. Flowerheads yellow, in dense terminal corymbs. As attractive and useful in gardens as *B*. 'Sunshine'. South Island. ♥ 2002.

†*perdicioides* (Hook. f.) B. Nord. (*Senecio perdicioides* Hook. f.) Raukumara. A small to medium-sized shrub, with dull green, glabrous leaves, finely toothed and 2.5–5cm long. Flowerheads yellow in terminal corymbs. Only for the mildest areas. North Island.

repanda J.R. Forst. & G. Forst. A large shrub with very large, soft green leaves, white beneath, and mignonette-scented flowers in large panicles. Creates a tropical effect. The leaves were used as primitive postcards by Maori tribes in remote areas of New Zealand. Only for the mildest areas or a conservatory. '**Purpurea**' Leaves purple above, white beneath. It was found in the Wanganui district of New Zealand. AM 1977.

rotundifolia J.R. Forst. & G. Forst. (*Senecio reinoldii* Endl., *S. rotundifolius* (J.R. Forst. & G. Forst.) Hook. f.)

Muttonbird scrub. A medium-sized shrub of dense, rounded habit with thick, leathery, rounded leaves, 5–13cm long, glabrous and shining green above, felted beneath. Flowerheads yellowish in terminal panicles, not conspicuous. One of the best shrubs for windswept seaside gardens. It will take the full blast of the Atlantic Ocean. South Island, Stewart Island, etc.

'**Sunshine**' (Dunedin Group) (*Senecio greyi* hort. not Hook. f.) A popular and attractive, grey shrub forming a dense, broad mound up to 1m high and twice as much across. Leaves silvery-grey when young becoming green above. Flowerheads yellow, in large open corymbs. A hybrid between the true *B. greyi* and another species, possibly *B. compacta*. ♥ 2002.

Bramble See *Rubus*.
Bridal wreath See *Spiraea* 'Arguta'.
Broadleaf See *Griselinia littoralis*.
Broom See *Cytisus* and *Genista*.
Broom, blue See *Erinacea anthyllis*.
Broom, butchers' See *Ruscus aculeatus*.
Broom, common See *Cytisus scoparius*.
Broom, hedgehog See *Erinacea anthyllis*.
Broom, Mount Etna See *Genista aetnensis*.
Broom, purple See *Chamaecytisus purpureus*.
Broom, Spanish See *Spartium junceum*.
Broom, Warminster See *Cytisus* × *praecox* 'Warminster'.
Broom, weeping See *Chordospartium stevensonii*.

BROUSSONETIA L'Hér. ex Vent.—**Moraceae**—A small genus of dioecious, deciduous shrubs and trees with about 7 species found in E and SE Asia and Polynesia. The male flowers are produced in catkin-like spikes, the females in globose heads.

kazinoki Siebold & Zucc. A rare, large, spreading shrub with ovate, toothed leaves which are variously lobed. Mainly differs from *B. papyrifera* in its glabrous young shoots and leaves. China, Japan.

papyrifera (L.) Vent. Paper mulberry. A large shrub or small tree with simple to variously lobed, roughly hairy leaves. Male plants have stout, drooping catkins. The female is decorative: its has spherical flower clusters with long exserted stigmas, followed by peculiar, globular heads of orange-red fruits. The flowers open here in late spring to early summer, but are much earlier in warmer climes. In Japan paper is made from its bark. E Asia, naturalised in the USA. I early in the 18th century. '**Laciniata**' ('Dissecta') A dwarf form with curious, finely and deeply divided leaves. Raised in France about 1830.

Bruckenthalia spiculifolia See *Erica spiculifolia*.

†**BRUGMANSIA** Pers. (*Datura* L. in part)—**Solanaceae**—Angel's trumpets. A genus of 5 species of poisonous shrubs and trees, native to South America, particularly the Andes. Grown outside only in the south-west and the Isles of Scilly but suitable for a conservatory. They are conspicuous in their large, hanging, trumpet-shaped flowers. Previously included in *Datura*, which is now restricted to annual species with upright flowers.

× *candida* Pers. (*B. aurea* × *B. versicolor*) This splendid hybrid occurs in the wild in Ecuador where the flowers can be white, yellow or pink. The following form is grown. **'Grand Marnier'** A large shrub with large, hanging, trumpet-shaped flowers of a beautiful, peach colour, the lobes ending in long, tail-like points. ♀ 2002. **'Knightii'** A large shrub with large, hanging, double, white flowers. AM 1957. ♀ 2002.

sanguinea (Ruiz & Pav.) D. Don (*Datura sanguinea* Ruiz & Pav.) Tree-like shrub, up to 3m, taller in the Isles of Scilly. It has large, softly hairy leaves, toothed on young plants, and large, orange-red trumpets hanging from the branches in May and June. Colombia to N Chile.

suaveolens (Humb. & Bonpl. ex Willd.) Bercht. & J. Presl. (*Datura suaveolens* Humb. & Bonpl. ex Willd.) A large, tree-like shrub with flannel-like, untoothed leaves and large, pendent, trumpet-shaped, fragrant, white flowers from June to August. An excellent conservatory subject. Brazil. ♀ 2002.

‡***BRYANTHUS** S.G. Gmelin—**Ericaceae**—A monotypic genus related to *Phyllodoce*.

gmelinii D. Don (*B. musciformis* Nakai) A rare shrublet with prostrate branches, closely set with small, linear leaves. Rose-pink flowers are borne, three or more together, on slender, erect stalks. N Japan, Kamchatka. C 1834.

Buckeye See *Aesculus*.
Buckthorn See *Rhamnus*.
Buckthorn, Sea See *Hippophae rhamnoides*.

BUDDLEJA L.—**Buddlejaceae**—(*Buddleia* L.) About 100 species of evergreen or deciduous, mainly shrubs and small trees found in Africa, Asia and in the Americas, from the S USA to South America. A genus including several species of the greatest garden value, thriving in almost any soil and revelling in full sun. The flowering period is July to September unless otherwise stated. All have opposite leaves except *B. alternifolia*. Many species almost double their height when grown against a sunny wall.

agathosma See *B. crispa*.

albiflora Hemsl. A large, deciduous shrub similar in general appearance to *B. davidii* but with stems rounded, not 4-angled as in the common species. Flowers are pale lilac in long, slender, terminal panicles. Horticulturally inferior to *B. davidii*. China. I 1900.

alternifolia Maxim. A large, deciduous shrub or occasionally a small tree with graceful, arching branches bearing long, narrow, dark green, alternate leaves and wreathed in June with delicately fragrant, lilac flowers. China. I 1915. ♀ 2002. AM 1922. **'Argentea'** A form having leaves covered with closely adpressed, silky hairs giving them a silvery sheen.

†*asiatica* Lour. A large, evergreen shrub or small tree with long, lax stems, narrowly lanceolate leaves, white beneath, and terminal and axillary, drooping, cylindrical panicles of sweetly scented, white flowers during winter. Widely distributed in E Asia from Nepal and China to the Philippines. I 1876. ♀ 2002. FCC 1906.

†*auriculata* Benth. A medium-sized, evergreen shrub of open habit. Leaves white-felted beneath. Winter flowers, in long, cylindrical panicles, are strongly fragrant and creamy-white with a yellow throat. Suitable for a warm wall. S Africa, from Zimbabwe to Cape Province. AM 1923.

†*candida* Dunn. A medium-sized shrub distinguished by soft, flannel-like, fawn-grey leaves and small racemes of violet flowers. E Himalaya. I 1928.

caryopteridifolia Hook. f. & Thoms. A vigorous, deciduous or semi-evergreen, large shrub or small tree with dark green leaves. The large, tubular, deep rose flowers are produced in terminal, drooping panicles in June. While tender as a young plant, mature specimens withstood zero temperatures at our Winchester nursery and survived all winters since 1925. E Himalaya. I 1849. FCC 1896. **'Kewensis'** A form with rich red flowers. AM 1947.

crispa Benth. (*B. agathosma* Diels, *B. caryopteridifolia* W.W. Sm., *B. farreri* Balf. f. & W.W. Sm., *B. sterniana* Cotton, *B. paniculata* hort., *B. tibetica* W.W. Sm.) A medium-sized to large, deciduous shrub, the deeply toothed leaves and stems covered with a dense, white felt. Fragrant, lilac flowers, with an orange throat, are produced in terminal, cylindrical panicles in late summer. N India. I 1850. AM 1961.

davidii Franch. (*B. variabilis* Hemsl.) Butterfly bush. This universally grown, medium-sized, deciduous shrub gives the best results when hard pruned in March. The fragrant flowers, in long racemes, are very attractive to butterflies. Does well near the sea. Naturalised in many towns and cities in the British Isles. C and W China. Japan. C 1890. AM 1898. **var. *alba*** Rehder & E.H. Wilson. White flowers. **'Amplissima'** Huge panicles, deep mauve. C 1911. **'Black Knight'** Long trusses of very deep violet. C 1959. ♀ 2002. **'Blue Horizon'** Large panicles of rich blue flowers, each with a small, orange eye, open from purple buds; panicles occasionally branched at the base. **'Border Beauty'** Deep crimson-purple; compact habit. C 1962. **'Charming'** Lavender-pink. **'Dartmoor'** An unusual form with magenta flowers in large, branched panicles. Found by Mr Hayles near Yelverton on Dartmoor in 1971. ♀ 2002. FCC 1990. AM 1973. **'Dubonnet'** Strong-growing with massive panicles of deep purple. C 1940. **'Empire Blue'** Rich violet-blue with an orange eye. C 1941. ♀ 2002. **'Fascinating'** ('Fascination') Wide, full panicles of vivid lilac-pink. C 1940. **'Fortune'** Long, cylindrical racemes of soft lilac with an orange eye. C 1936. **'Fromow's Purple'** Deep purple-violet, in large, handsome panicles. C 1949. **'Harlequin'** Leaves conspicuously variegated creamy-white; flowers reddish-purple. Lower-growing than most cultivars. Tends to revert. 'Variegata' is similar, but inferior. A sport of 'Royal Red'. C 1964. **'Ile de France'** Long, elegant racemes of rich violet. C 1930. **var. *magnifica*** (E.H. Wilson) Rehder & E.H. Wilson. Bluish-purple with reflexed petal lobes. I 1900 by Ernest Wilson. FCC 1905. AM 1905. **Masquerade** ('Notbud') PBR Deep purple-red flowers, leaves edged with creamy-white. A sport of 'Harlequin'. **var. *nanhoensis*** (Chitt.) Rehder. An elegant, slender-branched variety with narrow leaves and long, narrowly cylindrical panicles of mauve flowers. I 1914 by Reginald Farrer from Gansu. 'Alba' is a lovely form with white flowers. **Nanho Blue** ('Mongo') Flowers pale blue. ♀ 2002. **'Nanho Purple'** ('Monum') Violet-purple with an orange centre. Spreading habit. C 1980. ♀ 2002. **'Peace'** Large panicles of white flowers with an orange eye. C 1945. AM 1952. **'Pink Delight'** See B. 'Pink Delight'. **'Pink Pearl'** Lilac-pink with a soft yellow eye, in dense panicles. **'Pixie Blue'** A compact, small shrub reaching about 1.5 to 2m tall, with pale blue flowers. **'Pixie Red'** Similar to 'Pixie Blue' but with purple-red flowers. **'Pixie White'** Similar to 'Pixie Blue' but with pure white flowers. **'Royal Red'** Massive panicles of red-purple. C 1941. ♀ 2002. AM 1950. **'Salicifolia'** A low-growing form with linear leaves and slender, narrow racemes. **Santana** ('Thia') A sport of 'Royal Red' found in 1988. Leaves margined bright creamy-yellow. **'Summer Beauty'** Compact with silvery-grey foliage and large panicles of rose-pink flowers. **'Variegata'** See under 'Harlequin'. **var. veitchiana** (Veitch) Rehder. Lavender, in large panicles. C 1893. FCC 1902. **'White Ball'** A compact, small shrub with rather small, grey-white leaves and bearing short panicles of white flowers. Raised in Holland in 1993. **'White Bouquet'** Fragrant, white, yellow-eyed flowers in large panicles. C 1942. **'White Cloud'** Pure white flowers in dense panicles. **'White Harlequin'** Similar to 'Harlequin' but with white flowers. **'White Profusion'** Large panicles of pure white, yellow-eyed flowers. C 1945. ♀ 2002.

fallowiana Balf. f. & W.W. Sm. Medium-sized to large, deciduous shrub with white-woolly stems and leaves and very fragrant, pale lavender-blue flowers in large panicles. Requires a sheltered position. N Burma, SW China. C 1921. **var. alba** Sabourin. Creamy-white flowers with an orange eye. ♀ 2002. AM 1978.

farreri See B. crispa.

†*forrestii* Diels. A large, deciduous shrub with young leaves pubescent beneath. Flowers fragrant, usually pale lilac, produced in cylindrical racemes in late summer to early autumn. Requires a sheltered position. E Himalaya, SW China. I 1903.

globosa Hope. The Chilean orange ball tree. A striking, erect, medium-sized shrub with handsome, deciduous foliage. In June laden with orange-yellow, ball-like inflorescences. Andes of Chile, Peru and Argentina. I 1774. ♀ 2002. **'Lemon Ball'** A form with lemon-yellow flowers.

japonica Hemsl. (B. curviflora hort. not André) A medium-sized shrub of arching habit with 4-winged shoots producing drooping, dense, terminal panicles of lavender, woolly flowers during summer. S Japan. I about 1896.

†× *lewisiana* Everett (B. asiatica × B. madagascariensis) (B. × madagasiatica Pike) Hybrids of garden origin between two floriferous species. **'Margaret Pike'** A large, strong-growing shrub with wand-like, white-woolly stems. Flowers of soft yellow are carried in long, dense, terminal racemes during winter. FCC 1954. AM 1953.

lindleyana Fortune. Medium-sized, deciduous shrub with long, slender, curved racemes of purple-violet flowers, which are individually strikingly beautiful. China, Japan. I 1843 by Robert Fortune.

'Lochinch' (B. davidii × B. fallowiana) A medium-sized, deciduous shrub of bushy, compact habit with grey-pubescent young stems and leaves. Later the leaves become green and glabrous above, remaining white-tomentose beneath. Flowers scented, violet-blue with a deep orange eye, in dense, conical panicles. ♀ 2002.

†*loricata* Leeuwenb. Mountain sage. A large shrub or small tree in the wild with narrow, elliptic leaves to 9cm long, puckered above, densely covered with rusty hairs beneath. Flowers cream, sometimes with an orange eye, in dense, terminal panicles in summer. South Africa.

× *madagasiatica* See B. × lewisiana.

†*madagascariensis* Lam. A beautiful, tall evergreen with yellow flowers in long panicles during winter. Suitable for a conservatory. Mountains of Madagascar, widely naturalised in warm regions. I 1827. ♀ 2002.

myriantha Diels. A medium-sized shrub with lanceolate leaves, white- or yellow-tomentose beneath. Purple, downy flowers are borne in slender panicles in late summer. W China, Burma. C 1933.

nivea Duthie. A vigorous, medium-sized shrub with large leaves. The whole plant is woolly-white with a thick, white, felted down. Flowers small, lilac-purple in August. China. I 1901.

†*officinalis* Maxim. Semi-evergreen with leaves clothed beneath with grey wool. Delicate mauve, fragrant flowers in panicles are borne throughout winter if given cool greenhouse treatment. W and C China. I 1908 by Ernest Wilson. ♀ 2002. AM 1911.

× *pikei* H.R. Fletcher (B. alternifolia × B. caryopteridifolia) This cross was made in June 1950 by Mr A.V. Pike, then Head Gardener at Hever Castle, Kent. **'Hever'** A medium-sized, hardy shrub with opposite, sometimes alternate leaves. Lilac-mauve, strongly scented flowers, with a bright orange throat, are borne in terminal panicles, 15–30cm long. AM 1953.

'Pink Delight' (B. davidii 'Pink Delight') A recent hybrid involving B. davidii 'Fascinating', B. davidii var. nanhoensis 'Alba' and B. 'West Hill'. Deciduous with long panicles of bright pink flowers. ♀ 2002. AM 1988.

†*pterocaulis* A.B. Jacks. A rare species from Yunnan and Burma having long, pointed leaves and stout, spiky, lilac inflorescences.

†*salviifolia* (L.) Lam. South African sage wood. A medium-sized shrub, hardy in the south-west of England. Leaves are sage-like; flowers are fragrant, white or pale lilac, with an orange eye. South Africa. C 1783.

sterniana See B. crispa.

tibetica See B. crispa.

'West Hill' (B. davidii × B. fallowiana) A medium-sized, deciduous shrub of spreading habit. The long, arching stems are thinly covered with a loose tomentum. The leaves are grey-pubescent above, later almost glabrous and green, and white-tomentose beneath. Flowers fragrant, pale lavender with an orange eye, produced in large, terminal, curved panicles in late summer. This attractive shrub was for many years distributed as B. fallowiana.

× *weyeriana* Weyer ex Rehder (B. davidii var. magnifica × B. globosa) An unusual, deciduous hybrid with ball-shaped heads of orange-yellow, often mauve-tinged, flowers in long slender panicles on the young wood in summer. Garden origin. **'Golden Glow'** Orange-yellow flushed lilac, vigorous. AM 1923. **'Moonlight'** Creamy-yellow flushed lilac-pink. AM 1923. **'Sungold'** A sport of 'Golden Glow' with deep orange flowers. C 1966. ♀ 2002.

Bullbay See *Magnolia grandiflora*.
Bunchberry See *Cornus canadensis*.

BUPLEURUM L.—Umbelliferae—A genus of about 75 species, mostly herbs and subshrubs, found in Europe, Asia, North and South Africa and North America, of which the following is the only woody species normally cultivated in the open in Britain.

fruticosum L. One of the best evergreen shrubs of medium size for exposed places near the sea and for all types of soil. Sea-green foliage and umbels of yellow flowers from July to September. S Europe, NW Africa. Long cultivated. AM 1979.

†*BURSARIA Cav.—Pittosporaceae—A small genus of 3 or 4 evergreen species related to *Pittosporum* and found in Australia and Tasmania.

spinosa Cav. An evergreen shrub, to about 2.5m, with dainty foliage and panicles of small, fragrant, white flowers in summer. AM 1928.

Bush clover See *Lespedeza*.
Bush poppy See *Dendromecon rigida*.
Butcher's broom See *Ruscus aculeatus*.

†*BUTIA (Becc.) Becc.—Palmae—A genus of about 8 species of single-stemmed, monoecious palms, natives of South America. The following is suitable for growing outside only in the mildest parts of the country but elsewhere is suitable for a large container if moved into a frost-free conservatory during winter.

capitata (Mart.) Becc. Jelly palm. A slow-growing, small tree, to about 6m tall, the stout trunk densely covered in the remains of old leaf bases. Very large leaves, to 2.5m long, are strongly arching with numerous, slender, grey-blue leaflets, to 75cm long, sometimes divided at the tip, and ascending from the spiny leaf stalk to form a V-shape. Mature plants bear inflorescences, to 1m long, with numerous small, creamy-yellow to reddish flowers followed by egg-shaped yellow to orange fruits about 2.5cm long, Brazil, Uruguay.

Butterfly bush See *Buddleja davidii*.
Butternut See *Juglans cinerea*.
Button bush See *Cephalanthus occidentalis*.

*BUXUS L.—Buxaceae—The boxes comprise about 30 species of evergreen shrubs and small trees with opposite, leathery leaves. The small, petalless flowers are produced in clusters in the leaf axils in spring, male and female flowers occurring on the same plant. Widely distributed in the Old World, the West Indies and Central America. The following thrive on most soils, in sun or shade. Many are useful for hedging purposes

balearica Lam. Balearic Islands box. A large shrub or small, erect-growing tree with large, firm, bright green, leathery leaves, 4cm long by 2cm broad. Balearic Isles and SW Spain. I before 1780 by J. Fothergill. ♀ 2002.

harlandii hort. not Hance. A hardy, dwarf shrub of distinct habit, forming a dense, compact dome of bright green, oblanceolate leaves. Probably a form of *B. microphylla* var. *sinica*. The true *B. harlandii* Hance, from C and S China, is more tender and has only recently been introduced to cultivation.

microphylla Siebold & Zucc. A dwarf or small shrub of dense, rounded habit. Leaves are narrowly oblong, thin in texture and up to 1.5cm long. Of Japanese origin but unknown in the wild. I 1860. **'Compacta'** A dwarf form with tiny leaves, slowly forming a dense, compact bun. Suitable for a rock garden or trough. C 1928. **'Faulkner'** Compact, low-spreading habit, with bright green, nearly rounded leaves. Good for ground cover or low hedges. **'Green Pillow'** A slow-growing form of American origin, a dwarf shrub forming a compact hummock. Leaves larger than those of 'Compacta' and a brighter green. var. *japonica* (Müll.-Arg.) Rehder & E.H. Wilson (*B. japonica* Müll.-Arg.) A distinct, small to medium-sized shrub of open, spreading habit with broadly obovate, thick, leathery leaves and 4-angled twigs. Japan. I 1800. var. *koreana* Nakai. A dwarf variety differing in its loose, spreading habit and dark green, often bronze-tinted leaves. Korea. I 1919. **'Richard'** A dwarf cultivar with obovate, thick and firm, bright green leaves with a deep apical notch. USA. var. *sinica* Rehder & E.H. Wilson. Taller and more spreading, also looser in habit, with slightly larger leaves and pubescent branches. China. I 1900.

sempervirens L. Common box. A large shrub or small tree producing luxuriant masses of small, dark green leaves. Distributed through S Europe, N Africa and W Asia. Naturalised and possibly wild in S England.

Cultivars of *Buxus sempervirens*

The common box has given rise to innumerable forms and variations, many of which are suitable for hedging and topiary. ♀ 2002.

'Agram' A columnar form selection from the USA. Leaves elliptic, emarginate, medium to large, deep shining green.

'Arborescens' A large shrub or occasionally a small tree with medium to large, dark green leaves. Excellent for screening.

'Argentea' A widespreading shrub. Leaves dark green, shaded grey and margined creamy-white. Tends to revert. C 1783.

'Aurea Maculata' See 'Aureovariegata'.
'Aurea Maculata Pendula' See 'Aurea Pendula'.
'Aurea Marginata' See 'Marginata'.
'Aurea Pendula' ('Aurea Maculata Pendula') An attractive cultivar, forming a large bush or a small tree, with weeping branchlets and leaves mottled and blotched creamy-yellow.

'Aureovariegata' ('Aurea Maculata') A medium to large shrub of dense, bushy habit. Leaves green, variously striped, splashed and mottled creamy-yellow. C 1770.

'Blauer Heinz' A slow-growing, very compact form, the branches upright from the base, bearing deep blue-green foliage. C 1987.

'Elata' See 'Longifolia'.

Buxus sempervirens **continued:**

'Elegantissima' A small to medium-sized, slow-growing shrub of dense, compact, dome-shaped habit. Leaves small, often misshapen, green with irregular creamy-white margin. Makes an attractive specimen shrub. The best silver box. C 1872. ♀ 2002.

'Gold Tip' See 'Notata'.

'Graham Blandy' ('Greenpeace') A fairly fast-growing form of narrow habit with upright branches. Excellent as a dot plant. C 1985.

'Greenpeace' See 'Graham Blandy'.

'Handsworthensis' ('Handsworthii') A large shrub, initially of erect habit but spreading in maturity. Rounded or oblong leaves are thick, leathery and dark green. Excellent as a tall hedge or screen. C 1872.

'Hardwickensis' A large, strong-growing shrub of stiff habit. The stout shoots are well clothed with leathery leaves, more rounded and bullate than those of the related 'Handsworthensis'.

'Horizontalis' See 'Prostrata'.

'Japonica Aurea' See 'Latifolia Maculata'.

'Latifolia' A large shrub of dense but spreading habit. Comparatively large leaves are deep shining green.

'Latifolia Bullata' Similar in habit to 'Latifolia Macrophylla' but with blistered and puckered leaves.

'Latifolia Macrophylla' A medium to large shrub of loose, spreading habit. Leaves large, broadly ovate to rounded, dark shining green.

'Latifolia Maculata' ('Japonica Aurea') A small to medium-sized shrub of dense, compact habit when young, forming a large mound. The large leaves are irregularly blotched dull yellow. When grown in the open the bright yellow young growths are attractive in spring. Makes an excellent, dense hedge. ♀ 2002.

'Longifolia' ('Elata') A large shrub or small tree producing dense sprays of large, narrowly oblong leaves. An attractive cultivar of elegant habit, particularly when grown on a single stem. C 1864. 'Salicifolia' has been confused with this but is more vigorous with narrower leaves and weeping branches.

'Marginata' ('Aurea Marginata') A large cultivar of erect habit. The medium-sized leaves, often puckered and misshapen, are green, irregularly splashed and mar-gined yellow. Tends to revert when allowed to grow too freely. A branch sport of 'Hardwickensis'. C 1838.

'Myosotidifolia' An erect, slow-growing, small to medium-sized shrub of compact, twiggy habit, with small, dark green leaves. C 1896.

'Myrtifolia' Usually seen as a small or medium-sized shrub, but in time reaching a large size. Leaves small, narrow, occurring in characteristic dense, flattened sprays, sometimes becoming bronzed in winter. C 1782.

'Notata' ('Gold Tip') This is one of the most common forms of box in commercial horticulture. The upper leaves of the terminal shoots are often tipped with yellow.

'Pendula' A large shrub of loose, open growth. The branchlets are pendent and bear masses of dark green leaves. Makes an unusual small tree when trained to a single stem. C 1869.

'Prostrata' ('Horizontalis') A strong-growing, medium-sized shrub with horizontally spreading branches. C 1908.

'Rosmarinifolia' ('Thymifolia') A dwarf shrub of neat habit. The small, distinct, dark sage-green leaves are linear to linear-lanceolate and rough. C 1859.

'Rotundifolia' A small, slow-growing form with rounded leaves. C 1859.

'Salicifolia' See under 'Longifolia'.

'Suffruticosa' Edging box. A dwarf or small shrub commonly used as a formal edging to paths and flower beds. Leaves are medium size, ovate and bright shining green. C 1753. ♀ 2002.

'Thymifolia' See 'Rosmarinifolia'.

'Vardar Valley' A dwarf, spreading form making a low, compact mound. Raised from seed collected in the Vardar river valley by Dr Edgar Anderson in 1934. A specimen in the Sir Harold Hillier Gardens and Arboretum is 1.5m tall and `5m across after 25 years (1990).

'Waterfall' A large shrub with long, pendent shoots and glossy dark green foliage, blue-green when young. A selection from plants grown as 'Pendula' at the Sir Harold Hillier Gardens and Arboretum.

wallichiana Baill. Himalayan box. A rare species in cultivation, usually of open, lax habit and of medium size. Leaves narrowly oblong-lanceolate, to 5cm or more long. Very hardy but subject to injury in severe winters. NW Himalaya. I 1850.

C

Cabbage tree See *Cordyline australis.*

†**CAESALPINIA** L.—**Leguminosae**—A genus of about 100 species of trees, shrubs and climbers, with showy flowers and bipinnate leaves, found throughout tropical and subtropical regions. Spectacular shrubs for sunny, sheltered sites.

decapetala (Roth) Alston (*C. japonica* Siebold & Zucc., *C. sepiaria* Roxb.) Handsome, large shrub, armed with prominent spines. Flowers, 20–30 in a raceme, are bright yellow, with scarlet stamens and open in June. Acacia-like leaves are a refreshing shade of soft green. E and SE Asia. I 1881. FCC 1888.

gilliesii (Hook.) Benth. (*Poinciana gilliesii* Hook.) A large shrub, popularly known as bird of paradise, with dainty leaflets, arranged bipinnately. Long, erect racemes bear 30–40 flowers with rich yellow petals and a cluster of scarlet stamens, 5–8cm long, in July and August. Requires a hot, sunny wall. Argentina, Uruguay. I 1829. AM 1927.

japonica See *C. decapetala.*

sepiaria See *C. decapetala.*

spinosa (Molina) Kuntze (*C. tinctoria* (Dombey ex Kunth) Benth. ex Taub.) A strong-growing, scandent shrub with attractively divided leaves and elegant flowers in summer. N South America.

tinctoria See *C. spinosa.*

Calamondin See × *Citrofortunella microcarpa.*

†**CALCEOLARIA** L.—**Scrophulariaceae**—A large genus with some 300–400 species of shrubs and herbs distributed from Mexico to South America and including many popular greenhouse plants. The shrubby members are sun-loving evergreens with pouch-shaped flowers in terminal panicles. All require a well-drained position at the foot of a sunny wall.

*integrifolia Murr. Handsome, small shrub bearing corymbs of large, yellow flowers in late summer. Chiloe. I 1822. ♀ 2002. **var. *angustifolia*** Lindl. A variety with narrow leaves. AM 1960.

violacea See *Jovellana violacea.*

†****CALDCLUVIA** D. Don—**Cunoniaceae**—A genus of 11 species from tropical SE Asia to Australia and New Zealand with one species in Chile. The following is only suitable for the mildest areas.

paniculata (Cav.) D. Don. A large, erect-branched shrub or small tree with somewhat angled and flattened shoots. Leaves are opposite, oblong-elliptic, to 13cm long and 4cm wide, and glossy green above, with serrate margins and conspicuously elevated veins, resembling those of the sweet chestnut. Small, white flowers are borne in axillary corymbs in midsummer. Chile. I 1832 and again by Harold Comber in 1925.

Calico bush See *Kalmia latifolia.*
California fuchsia See *Zauschneria californica.*
California lilac See *Ceanothus.*

CALLICARPA L.—**Verbenaceae**—About 140 species of shrubs and small trees found mainly in tropical and subtropical regions. The following are particularly notable for their soft rose-madder autumn colour and conspicuous, violet or lilac-purple, small, rounded fruits, which are freely produced where several plants are grown together. Small, pink flowers are borne in cymes.

bodinieri H. Lév. Medium-sized shrub with long leaves and deep lilac fruits. Foliage deep rose-purple in autumn. C and W China. I about 1845. **var. *giraldii*** (Rehder) Rehder (*C. giraldiana* C.K. Schneid.) A medium-sized to large shrub with long, scurfy-pubescent stems and elliptic to lanceolate, long-pointed leaves. Lilac flowers during late summer are followed by masses of small, dark lilac or pale violet fruits. E to W China. C 1900. FCC 1924. **var. *giraldii* 'Profusion'** A free-fruiting selection with bronze-purple young foliage and dense clusters of violet fruits. ♀ 2002. FCC 1992.

dichotoma (Lour.) K. Koch (*C. purpurea* Juss., *C. koreana* hort.) A compact shrub to about 1.5m. Ovate to obovate leaves are coarsely serrated; pink flowers in July, followed by deep lilac fruits. China, Korea, N Taiwan. I 1857. AM 1962.

giraldiana See *C. bodinieri* var. *giraldii.*

japonica Thunb. An attractive, small, compact shrub with oval leaves, pale pink flowers and violet fruits. Japan. I 1845. **var. *angustata*** Rehder (*C. longifolia* Hemsl.) A form with narrow leaves as much as 23cm long. China, Taiwan. I 1907. **'Leucocarpa'** An attractive and unusual form with white fruits. **var. *luxurians*** Rehder. A form with larger leaves and flower clusters. Japan.

koreana See *C. dichotoma.*

†****CALLISTEMON** R. Br.—**Myrtaceae**—With about 30 species of shrubs and small trees found only in Australia and Tasmania, the bottlebrushes are magnificent sun-loving evergreens, but are only suited to the mildest districts. Flowers with long colourful stamens are produced in cylindrical spikes during summer; the spike axes grow on to produce more foliage. Not successful on shallow chalky soils.

citrinus (Curtis) Skeels (*C. lanceolatus* (Sm.) DC.) A vigorous, spreading shrub of medium size with narrow, rigid leaves, lemon-scented when crushed. Bears red flowers in dense spikes during summer. E Australia. I 1788. **'Firebrand'** A form of low, spreading habit, only about 60cm tall, with mauve-pink bottlebrushes. **'Mauve Mist'** A compact shrub with attractive, silky-hairy, pink young foliage and dense, mauve-pink bottlebrushes. Raised in Australia before 1967. **'Splendens'** A graceful shrub, 1.5–2m high, producing brilliant scarlet flowers throughout summer, and thriving in the open in the milder southern countries. ♀ 2002. AM 1926.

linearis DC. Small, narrow leaves and long, cylindrical spikes of scarlet flowers. Hardy in sheltered positions along the South Coast. New South Wales. I 1788. ♀ 2002. See also *C. subulatus.*

pallidus DC. A medium-sized shrub related to *C. salignus*, with narrowly elliptic leaves and cream-coloured flowers. Tasmania, Victoria. AM 1984.

pityoides F. Muell. (*C. sieberi* auct. not DC., *C. pithyoides* Miq.) Alpine bottlebrush. This is the hardiest species, having survived many hard winters outside in the Sir Harold Hillier Gardens and Arboretum. A medium-sized shrub with densely arranged, small, narrow leaves and pale yellow flowers in short spikes. SE Australia. (The name *C. sieberi* DC. is the correct name for the species previously known as *C. paludosus* F. Muell.).

rigidus R. Br. A medium-sized shrub with narrow, rigid leaves, up to 13cm long, and densely crowded, dark red flowers in spikes 8–10cm long. E Australia.

salignus DC. One of the hardiest of the bottlebrushes, in favourable localities attaining a height and width of about 2.5m. Leaves narrow, willow-like; flowers pale yellow. SE Australia. I 1788. ♀ 2002. AM 1948.

sieberi See *C. pityoides*.

speciosus DC. A medium-sized shrub with narrow, sharp-pointed leaves and deep scarlet flowers. I 1823.

subulatus Cheel. A small shrub with sharp-pointed, bright green leaves, silky-hairy when young, and crimson flowers in late summer. The hardiest red-flowered species, it has been confused with *C. linearis*. SE Australia.

viminalis (Gaertn.) Cheel. Weeping bottlebrush. Small shrub to small tree with arching or weeping branches, light green, lanceolate leaves and bright red flower spikes. **'Captain Cook'** A low-growing, spreading form with large clusters of deep crimson flowers in summer. **'Little John'** A compact dwarf form, less than 1m tall, with grey-green foliage and profuse spikes of bright red flowers.

viridiflorus (Sims) Sweet. A dense and very hardy, medium-sized shrub, the young foliage flushed pink and downy. Leaves with long white hairs at first, later glabrous, 2–3cm long by 5mm, sharply pointed. Flowers are borne in dense clusters, to 7cm long, in midsummer; filaments pale yellow-green. The flower clusters are sometimes borne on the young shoots and extend in length as they grow. Tasmania.

‡***CALLUNA** Salisb.—**Ericaceae**—A genus of a single species, differing from *Erica* in its 4-parted corolla and the large 4-parted calyx.

vulgaris (L.) Hull (*Erica vulgaris* L.) Heather, Ling. One of our most familiar native shrublets, covering large tracts of mountain and moorland in northern and western parts of the British Isles, and equally well known on the heaths and commons of the south. Native of Europe and Asia Minor.

Cultivars of *Calluna vulgaris*

A great number of forms of this species are cultivated in gardens, varying in colour of flower and foliage, time of flowering and habit. All are easily grown plants for lime-free soils even tolerating moist positions. Though tolerant of shade, they are freer-flowering and happier in full sun. One of the most beautiful shrubs, especially the double-flowered forms, for cutting for indoor decoration; the dried flowers retain their colour indefinitely. Forms in which the flowers do not open but remain attractive in bud over a long period have been called bud-flowering heathers.

Pruning, consisting of the removal of the old inflorescences, may be carried out after flowering. In the case of cultivars with coloured foliage and those with attractive dried inflorescences, it is best left until late March.

Flowering times:
Early—July to August
Mid—August to September
Late—October to November

Alba Group (f. *alba* (Weston) Braun-Blanq.) White heather. A white-flowered form. Mid. 50cm. Popularly connected with Scotland but liable to appear wherever the species grows.

'Alba Aurea' Bright green foliage with yellow tips; flowers white. Mid. 10cm.

'Alba Elata' Dense habit. Flowers white. Mid to late. 60cm.

'Alba Plena' ('Alba Flore Pleno') A popular, free-flowering cultivar with white, double flowers. Mid. 50cm. A sport of 'Alba Elegans'. AMT 1960. AM 1938.

'Alba Pumila' Dwarf form of compact habit. Flowers white. Mid. 10cm.

'Alba Rigida' An attractive plant with distinctive, horizontal branching habit. Flowers white. Mid. 15cm. AMT 1964.

'Alexandra' PBR (bud-flowering) Compact and upright with dark green foliage. Buds profuse, red and white turning to deep crimson. Mid to late. 30cm. C 1993. ♀ 2002.

'Alicia' PBR (bud-flowering) Compact and upright with bright green foliage and profuse, large, white buds over a long period. A cross between 'Marleen' and 'Long White'. Mid to late. 45cm. C 1996. ♀ 2002.

'Allegro' Deep red. Mid to late. 50cm. ♀ 2002.

'Alportii' Tall, erect growth. Flowers crimson. Mid. 60cm.

'Alportii Praecox' Similar to 'Alportii' but a little dwarfer and flowering 2–3 weeks earlier. Early. 50cm.

'Anette' PBR A sport of 'Melanie' with clear pink buds over a long period. Excellent for dried decorations. Mid to late. 35cm. C 1993. ♀ 2002.

'Annemarie' This excellent cultivar is an improvement on 'H.E. Beale'. Double flowers open light purple, deepening to carmine-rose. It has a compact habit and dark green foliage. 50cm. Mid to late. ♀ 2002.

'Anthony Davis' Profuse white flowers. Silvery-grey foliage. Mid. 45cm. ♀ 2002.

'Arabella' PBR Upright with dark green foliage and profuse brilliant blood-red flowers. Mid. 30cm.

'Argentea' Young shoots of a bright pale green in spring. Flowers mauve. Mid. 30cm.

'August Beauty' Free-flowering, white. Mid. 50cm. AMT 1960.

'Aurea' An attractive form. Foliage gold-tinted, turning bronze-red in winter. Flowers purple. Mid. 30cm. AMT 1961.

'Barnett Anley' Compact and erect, dark green foliage. Flowers petunia-purple in densely packed racemes. Mid. 50cm. FCCT 1962. AMT 1960.

'Battle of Arnhem' Interesting over a long period with light purple-red flowers and dark green foliage, turning bronze in winter. Late. 60cm.

'Beoley Crimson' Deep crimson, upright habit. Mid to late. 60cm.

Calluna vulgaris continued:

'Beoley Gold' A strong-growing form with bright yellow foliage and short sprays of white flowers. Mid. 50cm. ♀ 2002. AMT 1968.

'Blazeaway' A startling foliage plant. The green foliage changes to rich red in winter. Flowers lilac-mauve. Mid. 50cm.

'Boskoop' Foliage rich gold turning orange-red in winter. Flowers lilac-pink. Mid. 30cm.

'Camla' See 'County Wicklow'.

'Coccinea' Grey-green foliage. Dark crimson flowers contrast with the pale grey young shoots. Mid. 25cm.

'County Wicklow' ('Camla') Dwarf and spreading. Flowers shell-pink, double. Mid. 25cm. ♀ 2002. FCCT 1961. AMT 1960.

'Cramond' Vigorous with dark green foliage. Rich pink flowers in long spikes. Mid. 50cm. Raised at Cramond near Edinburgh before 1963. AMT 1970.

'Cuprea' An old cultivar with young shoots golden in summer, ruddy-bronze in autumn and winter. Flowers pale mauve. Mid. 30cm. FCC 1873.

'C.W. Nix' A choice plant with dark green foliage and long, tapered racemes of glowing, dark crimson flowers. Mid. 60cm. AMT 1961.

'Dark Beauty' PBR A sport of 'Darkness', found in Holland in 1990. Compact habit with semi-double, deep pink flowers, darker with age. Foliage dark green. Mid to late. 25cm. ♀ 2002.

'Dark Star' A shrub of neat, dense habit and dark green foliage with semi-double, crimson flowers. Mid to late. 20cm. ♀ 2002.

'Darkness' A dense bush with bright green foliage and deep purplish-pink flowers in short, dense racemes. Mid. 30cm. ♀ 2002.

'Drum-ra' A pretty cultivar with white flowers. Mid. 50cm. AMT 1961.

'Elsie Purnell' Flowers lively silvery-pink, double, deeper coloured in bud. Mid to late. 60–80cm. ♀ 2002. AMT 1963.

'Fairy' Clear yellow foliage, orange to bronze-red in winter. Flowers pale purplish-pink, profuse. Mid. 30cm. C 1966.

'Finale' A spreading plant with fresh green foliage and amethyst flowers. Mid to late. 30cm.

'Firefly' Reddish-brown foliage turning deep orange-red in winter. Flowers deep lilac. Mid. 45cm. ♀ 2002.

'Flamingo' Dark green foliage, pinkish-red in spring. Flowers lavender. Mid. 30cm.

'Flore Pleno' An old cultivar with lilac-pink, double flowers. Mid. 50cm. AM 1929.

'Foxii Nana' Dwarf, forming a dense cushion of green. Flowers, when produced, light purple. Mid. 10cm.

'Fred J. Chapple' Compact and vigorous, flowers mallow-purple. Mid. 25cm. AMT 1961.

'Glencoe' Dark green foliage and double, silvery-pink flowers. Mid to late. 45cm.

'Gold Haze' Foliage bright golden hue. Flowers white. Mid. 50–60cm. ♀ 2002. FCCT 1963. AMT 1961.

'Golden Carpet' Low-growing with orange-yellow foliage and short racemes of purplish-pink flowers. Mid. 10cm. AMT 1971.

'Golden Feather' A most attractive clone with feathery, golden foliage changing to a gentle orange in winter. Sparse, mauve flowers. Mid. 50cm. FCCT 1967. AMT 1965.

'Goldsworth Crimson' A strong-growing plant. Flowers deep crimson. Mid to late. 50–80cm.

'Guinea Gold' Vigorous with white flowers and yellow foliage. Mid to late. 45cm.

'Hammondii' A strong-growing cultivar with dark green foliage. Flowers white. Useful as a low hedge. Mid. 80cm.

'Hammondii Aureifolia' Tips of young shoots coloured golden-yellow in spring. Flowers white. Mid. 50–60cm.

'Hammondii Rubrifolia' Similar in habit to 'Hammondii Aureifolia' but tips of young shoots red-tinged in spring. Flowers purple. Mid. 50–60cm.

'H.E. Beale' A splendid cultivar producing very long racemes of double, bright rose-pink flowers, excellent for cutting. Mid to late. 60cm. FCC 1943.

'Hibernica' A dwarf clone, extremely free-flowering, the mauve flowers often outnumbering and smothering the leaves. Late. 15cm.

'Hiemalis' Erect-growing; flowers soft mauve. Mid to late. 50cm.

var. *hirsuta* (Waitz) Gray. This variety includes plants with grey, hairy leaves and stems. Found occasionally in the wild. Mid. 40cm.

'Hirsuta Compacta' See 'Sister Anne'.

'Hookstone' Erect; salmon-pink flowers in long racemes. Mid. 50–60cm.

'Humpty Dumpty' An amusing form of compact but uneven habit. Flowers white, not freely produced. Mid. 15cm.

'Ineke' Golden foliage, rose-violet flowers. Mid. 30cm.

'Jan Dekker' Spreading habit with excellent downy grey foliage. Flowers mauve. Mid. 15cm.

'J.H. Hamilton' Perhaps the finest double heather. A dwarf with large, pink, double flowers. Early. 25cm. ♀ 2002. FCCT 1961. AMT 1960. AM 1935.

'Jimmy Dyce' A somewhat prostrate form with dark green foliage. Double, lilac-pink flowers. Mid to late. 20cm.

'Joan Sparkes' Flowers mauve, double, occasionally producing single flowers. A sport of 'Alba Plena'. Mid. 25cm. AM 1957.

'Joy Vanstone' Golden foliage, deepening to rich orange in winter. Flowers orchid-pink. Mid. 50cm. ♀ 2002. AMT 1971.

'Kerstin' Upright growth with deep lilac-grey, downy foliage, tipped with pale yellow and red in spring. Flowers mauve. Found in a garden in Sweden. Mid. 30cm. ♀ 2002.

'Kinlochruel' Flowers double, white; foliage bright green, bronze in winter. A sport of 'County Wicklow'. Mid. 25cm. ♀ 2002. FCC 1982. AM 1980.

'Kirby White' Dark green foliage tipped gold when young. White flowers. Mid. 30cm.

'Loch Turret' Flowers white, foliage emerald-green. Early. 30cm.

'Mair's Variety' Tall; flowers white, especially suitable for cutting. Mid. 80cm. ♀ 2002. FCCT 1963. AMT 1961.

'Marleen' (bud-flowering) White buds tipped purple, borne over a long period. Dark green foliage. A seedling found in Holland. Mid to late. 60cm. C 1972.

Calluna vulgaris continued:

'Melanie' (bud-flowering) ('Hammondii' × 'Marleen') Upright habit with dark green foliage. Pure white buds in long racemes. Mid to late. 45cm. C 1991.

'Minima' Dwarf, compact form. Flowers, when produced, purple. Mid. 80cm.

'Mousehole' Dwarf, compact habit. Dark green foliage and pale purple flowers. Mid. Found in Cornwall. 10cm.

'Mrs Ronald Gray' A charming, prostrate mat. Flowers reddish-purple. Mid. 5–8cm.

'Mullion' Semi-prostrate with numerous branches and densely packed racemes of deep pink flowers. Mid. 15–25cm. ♀ 2002. AMT 1963.

'Multicolor' Bright green foliage, tipped red in winter, gold and coral in summer. Flowers phlox-purple. Early to mid. 10cm. AMT 1962 (for winter foliage). AMT 1961 (for flower).

'My Dream' A sport of 'H.E. Beale' with dark green foliage and double white flowers. It can revert and produce pink flowers. Mid to late. 60cm. ♀ 2002.

'Nana Compacta' Low, compact habit and profuse, purplish-pink flowers. Mid. 20cm.

'Orange Queen' Gold young spring foliage turns to deep orange. Flowers pink. Mid. 60cm.

'Peter Sparkes' Flowers deep pink, double, in long racemes. Useful for cutting. Mid to late. 50cm. ♀ 2002. FCCT 1962. AM 1958.

'Pygmaea' Very dwarf, spreading branchlets and dark green foliage. Flowers purple, rarely produced. Mid. 8cm. AMT 1962.

'Radnor' Very compact with bright green foliage. Flowers double, pale lilac-pink with white inner petals. Mid. 25cm. ♀ 2002.

'Red Carpet' Low and spreading with a semi-prostrate habit. Foliage gold in summer, orange-red in winter. Flowers mauve. Mid. 20cm.

'Red Star' Open habit; bears the reddest flowers of all the double-flowered red cultivars. 40cm. Mid to late.

'Robert Chapman' The spring foliage is gold and changes first to orange then finally red. Flowers are soft purple. Mid. 30–60cm. ♀ 2002. AMT 1962.

'Roland Haagen' A bushy plant with pale purple flowers and bronze-yellow foliage, turning orange- to bronze-red in winter. Mid. 30cm. ♀ 2002.

'Romina' (bud-flowering) Upright with dark green foliage and profuse, densely clustered, deep purple-red buds. Mid to late. 45cm. C 1990.

'Rosalind' Golden foliage and pink flowers. Mid. 30–60cm. AMT 1961.

'Ruth Sparkes' Foliage bright yellow-green but inclined to revert. Flowers white, double. Sport of 'Alba Plena'. Mid. 25cm.

'Schurig's Sensation' A sport of 'H.E. Beale' found in Germany, this has dark green foliage and double deep pink flowers. Mid to late. 30cm.

'Serlei' Erect with dark green foliage. Flowers white, in long racemes. Mid to late. 60cm. FCCT 1962. AMT 1961.

'Serlei Aurea' Similar to 'Serlei' but possesses foliage of a bright golden hue. Mid to late. 60cm. ♀ 2002. AMT 1961.

'Serlei Rubra' ('Serlei Grandiflora') Similar to 'Serlei' but the flowers are dark reddish-purple. Mid to late. 60cm.

'Silver Knight' Upright habit with grey foliage. Flowers mauve-pink. Mid. 30cm.

'Silver Queen' A very beautiful plant. Foliage silvery-grey; flowers pale mauve. Mid. 60cm. ♀ 2002.

'Silver Rose' Bright rose-pink flowers and silvery foliage on upright shoots. The combination of flower and foliage is delightful. Mid. 40cm. ♀ 2002.

'Sir John Charrington' Vigorous, spreading habit. Yellow leaves tinged red in winter, reddish in winter; flowers lilac-pink. Early. 40cm. ♀ 2002. AMT 1970.

'Sirsson' A seedling of 'Sir John Charrington' with gold summer foliage turning bright orange-red in winter. Flowers pink. Mid. 30cm.

'Sister Anne' ('Hirsuta Compacta') Compact mounds of pretty, grey foliage and pink flowers. Mid. 8–10cm. ♀ 2002.

'Spitfire' Golden foliage turning bronze-red in winter. Flowers pink. Mid. 25–30cm.

'Spring Cream' Very vigorous with dark green foliage tipped with cream in the spring. Long spikes of white flowers. Mid. 50cm. ♀ 2002.

'Spring Glow' Young foliage attractively tipped with pink and red. Flowers lilac. Mid. 50cm.

'Spring Torch' Young foliage orange-red. Flowers purplish-pink. Upright habit. Mid. 25cm.

'Sunrise' Golden-yellow foliage turns orange-red in winter. Flowers purple. Mid. 30cm. C 1970.

'Sunset' Foliage variegated yellow, gold and orange. Flowers pink. Mid. 25–30cm. ♀ 2002. FCCT 1968. AMT 1967.

'Tenuis' Loose-growing; flowers red-purple in long racemes. Early to mid. 25cm.

'Tib' A lovely, floriferous cultivar. Flowers rosy-red, double. Early. 30–60cm. ♀ 2002. FCCT 1962. AMT 1960.

'Tricolorifolia' Young growths turning from bronze to red, finally deep green. Flowers pink. Mid. 60cm.

'Underwoodii' (bud-flowering) Pale mauve buds remain closed and gradually change to an effective silvery-white, lasting well into winter. Mid to late. 30cm. C 1939. AMT 1960.

'Velvet Fascination' A sport from 'Silver Knight' of upright habit with silver-grey foliage, darker in winter. Flowers white. Mid. 60cm. ♀ 2002.

'White Coral' A sport of 'Kinlochruel' with bright green foliage and double white flowers. Mid. 20cm.

'White Gown' Long racemes of white flowers. Mid to late. 60–80cm.

'White Lawn' A prostrate plant with deep green foliage and white flowers. Mid. 10cm. ♀ 2002.

'Wickwar Flame' Bright orange and yellow summer foliage turns copper and gold in winter. Flowers mauve-pink. Mid. 30cm. Raised by George Osmond. ♀ 2002.

'Winter Chocolate' Foliage greenish-yellow and orange, becoming dark chocolate, tipped red in winter. Flowers lilac-pink. Mid. 30cm.

CALOPHACA Fisch. ex DC.—**Leguminosae**—A small genus of low shrubs and herbs for a sunny, well-drained site. About 5 species found from SW to E Asia.

grandiflora Reg. Dwarf, often procumbent shrub with pinnate leaves and axillary racemes of bright yellow pea-flowers in June or July. Turkestan. I 1880.

wolgarica (L. f.) Fisch. A very hardy, prostrate shrub with pinnate leaves, bearing yellow pea-flowers in June and July. Needs full sun and good drainage. SE Russia. I 1786.

CALYCANTHUS L.—Calycanthaceae—The allspices belong to a small genus of 3 species, all medium-sized, deciduous shrubs with opposite leaves and aromatic bark, confined in the wild to North America. They are easy to cultivate, with conspicuous, red-brown flowers, composed of numerous sepals and petals, during summer and early autumn.

fertilis See *C. floridus* var. *laevigatus*. **'Purpureus'** See *C. floridus* 'Purpureus'.

floridus L. Carolina allspice. A dense, bushy shrub with dark glossy green, aromatic leaves, downy beneath. Brownish-red flowers, with numerous petals, are borne over a long period in summer. SE USA. I 1726. **'Athens'** A form with very fragrant, pale yellow flowers. **var. laevigatus** (Willd.) Torr. & A. Gray (*C. fertilis* Walter, *C. glaucus* Willd.) Leaves smooth or only slightly downy beneath. I 1806. **'Purpureus'** (*C. fertilis* 'Purpureus') Leaves tinged purple beneath. A form of var. *laevigatus*.

occidentalis Hook. & Arn. (*C. macrophyllus* hort.) A Californian species with flowers and leaves that are larger than *C. floridus*, differing also in the exposed leaf buds. I 1831 by David Douglas.

praecox See *Chimonanthus praecox*.

sinensis See *Sinocalycanthus sinensis*.

‡***CAMELLIA** L.—Theaceae—More than 200 species of mainly tender, evergreen shrubs and trees found in E and SE Asia, concentrated in S China; the majority in cultivation are as hardy as laurel. Camellias are magnificent, flowering evergreens, a little more lime-tolerant than *Rhododendrons*, and thrive in a good, acid or neutral, peaty soil. A woodland site with light overhead shade is ideal but they can be grown successfully and often flower more freely when planted in full sun as, for example, when against a south- or west-facing wall. In such positions careful attention to watering and mulching is vital to avoid bud-dropping. Early morning spring sunshine after a frost will damage open flowers so in some areas of the British Isles a north- or west-facing site is better unless light overhead shade of trees is available. It is recommended that all the very large-flowered forms are grown under protection as their flowers are more susceptible to wind and frost damage. Camellias are ideal plants for tubs or a cool greenhouse or conservatory.

FLOWER FORM:

Single	One row of not over eight regular, irregular or loose petals and conspicuous stamens.
Semi-double	Two or more rows of regular, irregular or loose petals and conspicuous stamens.
Anemone form	One or more rows of large, outer petals lying flat or wavy; the centre a convex mass of intermingled petaloids and stamens.
Peony form	A deep, rounded flower consisting of a convex mass of petals, petaloids and sometimes stamens.
Double	Imbricated petals showing stamens in a concave centre when open.
Formal double	Fully imbricated, many rows of petals with no stamens.

FLOWER SIZE:

Very large	Over 12.5cm (5in) across
Large	10–12.5cm (4–5in) across
Medium	7.5–10cm (3–4in) across
Small	5–7.5cm (2–3in) across

Flower size, form and colour are subject to some variation in certain cultivars, type of soil, aspect and general cultivation all playing a part.

'Barbara Clark' (*C. saluenensis* × *C. reticulata* 'Captain Rawes') Rose-pink, medium, semi-double with notched petals. Vigorous, compact, upright habit. C 1958.

'Barbara Hillier' A beautiful, large shrub with handsome, large, polished leaves and large, single, satin-pink flowers. A first-class shrub, a hybrid between *C. japonica* and *C. reticulata* which originated at Embley Park.

'Black Lace' (*C. reticulata* 'Crimson Robe' × *C.* × *williamsii* 'Donation') Rose-form to semi-double, 11cm across, with no stamens. Dark red with a silvery sheen, the numerous incurved petals have black edges. Compact, upright habit with glossy dark green leaves. ♔ 2002.

'Candle Glow' (*C. cuspidata* × *C. japonica*) White with light pink centre, medium, single; compact habit. C 1980.

chrysantha See *C. nitidissima*.

'Cornish Snow' (*C. cuspidata* × *C. saluenensis*) This delightful free-growing, medium-sized to large hybrid bears multitudes of small, single, white flowers along the branchlets. Garden origin about 1930. ♔ 2002. AM 1948.

'Cornish Snow Michael' See *C.* 'Michael'.

'Cornish Snow Winton' See *C.* 'Winton'.

'Cornish Spring' (*C. cuspidata* × *C. japonica* 'Rosea Simplex') Pink, small, single; vigorous, upright habit. C 1972. ♔ 2002.

cuspidata (Kochs) hort. ex Bean. A large shrub with small leaves, copper-tinted when young, and small, creamy-white flowers. Widely distributed in China. I 1900 by Ernest Wilson. AM 1912.

†**'Dr Clifford Parks'** (*C. reticulata* 'Crimson Robe' × *C. japonica* 'Kramer's Supreme') Red with orange cast, very large, semi-double to peony or anemone form. Vigorous, upright habit. C 1971. ♔ 2002.

'Felice Harris' (*C. sasanqua* 'Narumigata' × *C.* 'Buddha') Very pale pink with deeper veins, medium, semi-double. Dark, slightly glaucous green leaves. Vigorous, upright, compact habit. C 1960. AMT 1979.

†**'Forty-niner'** (*C. japonica* 'Indian Summer' × *C. reticulata* 'Houye Diechi') A bushy, vigorous, upright plant with glossy foliage occasionally flecked with white. Its large flowers are peony form and rich red. AM 1996.

'Francie L.' (*C. reticulata* 'Buddha' × *C. saluenensis* 'Apple Blossom') Rose-pink, very large, semi-double with wavy petals. A vigorous shrub, good on a wall. AM 1972. ♔ 2002.

'Freedom Bell' Deep pink, medium, semi-double, to 7cm across, bell-shaped, with a centre of numerous stamens;

free-flowering; dense, bushy, upright habit. ♈ 2002.

†*granthamiana* Sealy. A large shrub with large, parchment-white flowers. The leaves are distinct with their conspicuously impressed venation, bronze when unfolding. A remarkable species from Hong Kong and Guangdong, SE China, discovered in 1955. AM 1974.

heterophylla Hu. The original plant to which this name was given was found in a temple garden in Yunnan. Previously regarded as a hybrid between *C. japonica* and *C. reticulata* it is now considered to be a garden form of the latter. For hybrids previously listed here see individual entries.

hiemalis Nakai. A large shrub bearing pink or white flowers with 7 or more petals, up to 7cm across, in early spring. It was named from a Japanese garden plant and may be a hybrid of *C. sasanqua* introduced from China. **'Dazzler'** Spreading habit with brilliant deep shocking pink, semi-double flowers. **'Sparkling Burgundy'** ('Hinodegumo' × 'Shôwa-no-sakae') Anemone-centred, deep pink, to 10cm across, about 40 petals mixed with stamens and petaloid stamens. Free-flowering and reliable. C 1950. ♈ 2002.

'Inspiration' (*C. reticulata* × *C. saluenensis*) A medium-sized shrub with large, semi-double flowers of deep pink. ♈ 2002. FCCT 1979. AM 1954.

japonica L. Common camellia. A large, evergreen shrub with characteristically polished leaves. The wild species, a native of Japan and China, was originally introduced in 1739 and was later followed by various cultivars from China and Japan. **subsp. rusticana** See *C. rusticana*.

Cultivars of *Camellia japonica*

As the rose has become the plaything of the commercial hybridist, so the camellia has become the toy of both the commercial and the amateur gardener. Far too many scarcely separable sports (mutations) have been made separate entities. In fact, a single bush may embrace three cultivars. At the present time, named cultivars of this species are numbered in thousands and are constantly being added to. The majority are medium-sized, the more vigorous clones reaching a large size after many years. In most areas flowers are normally produced from February to early or mid-May, but their size and colour may vary depending on the age of the plant, the growing conditions and season.

'Abundance' White; medium, peony form. Slow, upright growth.

'Adelina Patti' Single bright pink, cup-shaped flowers, 8cm across, with carmine veins and basal flush, margined white; anthers yellow. Upright habit with pendent shoots and very glossy foliage. I from Japan in 1888. AM 1996. ♈ 2002.

'Admiral Nimitz' ('Kishu-tsukasa') Deep rose-pink, large, formal double. Vigorous, compact and erect growth.

'Adolphe Audusson' Blood-red with conspicuous stamens, large, semi-double. Vigorous, compact growth. A first-class, well proved plant. ♈ 2002. FCC 1956. AM 1934.

'Akashigata' ('Lady Clare') Deep clear peach-pink, large, semi-double. Vigorous, spreading growth. Still one of the best of all camellias. ♈ 2002. AM 1927.

'Alba Plena' ('Alba Grandiflora') White, large, formal double. Erect, bushy growth. Probably the best double white for general planting. AM 1948. ♈ 2002.

'Alba Simplex' White with conspicuous stamens, large, single. The most proven single white.

'Alexander Hunter' Large, bright crimson, single to semi-double with golden stamens. ♈ 2002.

'Althaeiflora' Dark red, large, peony form. Large specimens are to be found in old gardens. AM 1950.

'Anemoniflora' Dark crimson, medium, anemone form. Vigorous, erect growth.

'Annie Wylam' Medium, peony to rose form, double, bright pink, shading to a white centre, with numerous slender, petaloid stamens, borne over a long period. C 1960. ♈ 2002. AM 1981.

'Apollo' Rose-red, occasionally blotched white, medium, semi-double. Growth vigorous and open. One of the most satisfactory camellias for British gardens. It is often confused with 'Jupiter' from which it differs in its more numerous, deeper coloured petals, also in its longer, pointed leaves which possess a characteristic twisted tip. AM 1956.

'Apple Blossom' ('Joy Sander') Pale blush-pink, deepening at margin, medium, semi-double. ♈ 2002. AM 1933.

'Arajishi' See *C. rusticana* 'Arajishi'.

'Augusto Leal de Gouveia Pinto' ('Augusto Pinto') Light lavender-pink to carmine, each petal bordered white, large, semi-double to double. AM 1958.

'Australis' Rose-red, medium, peony form. Vigorous, compact, upright habit. C 1951. ♈ 2002.

'Ave Maria' Medium, formal double to peony form, very pale creamy pink. Good, dark green foliage. C 1943. ♈ 2002.

'Ballet Dancer' Cream shading to coral-pink at the margins, medium, full peony form. Compact, upright habit. C 1960. ♈ 2002. AM 1976.

'Benten' Rose-red, small, single. Leaves with a broad, creamy-white margin. Rather tender and weak-growing. C 1930.

'Berenice Boddy' Light pink, deeper beneath, medium, semi-double. Vigorous and erect growth. ♈ 2002.

'Betty Foy Sanders' Semi-double, 11cm across, with 24 petals and occasional petaloid stamens, white with red stripes and yellow anthers, borne over a long period. Upright habit with dark green, twisted and wavy-edged leaves. C 1947.

'Betty Sheffield' White, striped and blotched red and pink, medium to large, semi-double to loose peony form. Leaves tend to burn in exposed situations. It and its forms often produce sports and reversions. C 1949.

'Betty Sheffield Blush' Light pink with several darker markings, large, semi-double to loose peony form. A sport of 'Betty Sheffield'.

'Betty Sheffield Pink' Deep pink. A sport of 'Betty Sheffield'.

'Betty Sheffield Supreme' White, each petal bordered deep pink to red, large, semi-double to loose peony form. A sport of 'Betty Sheffield'.

'Blood of China' Deep salmon-red, large, semi-double to loose peony form. Vigorous and compact growth.

'Bob Hope' Very dark red, large, semi-double. Compact. C 1972. AM 1992. ♈ 2002.

Camellia japonica continued:

'Bob's Tinsie' Brilliant red, small, anemone form. Compact, upright habit. C 1962. ♀ 2002.

'Bokuhan' Small, to 6cm across, anemone form, red with a white centre. Vigorous upright growth. Known in Japan since 1719. ♀ 2002.

'Brushfield's Yellow' Creamy-white with pale primrose centre, medium, anemone form. Compact, upright habit. C 1968. ♀ 2002.

'C.M. Hovey' Carmine, medium, formal double. Vigorous, compact growth. ♀ 2002. FCC 1879.

'C.M. Wilson' Light pink, very large, anemone form. Slow, spreading growth. A sport of 'Elegans'. AM 1956.

'Carter's Sunburst' Pale pink, striped or marked deeper pink, large or very large, semi-double to peony form or formal double. Compact habit. C 1958. ♀ 2002. AM 1977.

'Cecile Brunazzi' Light pink, medium, semi-double to loose peony form with large outer petals and twisted, upright centre petals. Open, upright habit. C 1951.

'Chandleri Elegans' See 'Elegans'.

'Clarise Carleton' Red, large to very large, semi-double. Vigorous, upright habit. C 1955.

'Commander Mulroy' Medium, formal double, 8cm across, blush-pink to white with a pink centre and edge. Dense, upright habit. C 1950. ♀ 2002.

'Compte de Gomer' Pale pink, striped and speckled rose-pink, medium, double. Medium, compact growth.

'Contessa Lavinia Maggi' See 'Lavinia Maggi'.

'Coquettii' Delft-rose, medium, double. Slow, compact and erect growth. ♀ 2002. AM 1956.

'Daikagura' Bright rose-pink blotched white, large, peony form. Slow, compact growth.

'Daitarin' See 'Dewatairin'.

'Debutante' Light pink, medium, peony form. Vigorous, erect growth.

'Desire' ('Debutante' × 'Doctor Tinsley') Medium to large, formal double, 10cm across, pale pink with a deeper edge. Vigorous, upright habit with dark green foliage. C 1973. ♀ 2002.

'Devonia' ('Devoniensis') White, medium, single, rather cup-shaped. Vigorous, erect growth. AM 1900.

'Dewatairin' ('Daitarin', 'Hatsusakura') Light rose-pink, large, single, mass of petaloids in centre. Vigorous, erect growth. AM 1953.

'Dobreei' Geranium-lake with darker veins, medium, semi-double. Vigorous, erect growth.

'Doctor Tinsley' Pale pink shading to deep pink at margins, medium, semi-double. Compact, upright growth. ♀ 2002.

'Donckelaeri' See 'Masayoshi'.

'Drama Girl' Deep salmon-rose-pink, very large, semi-double. Vigorous, open, slightly pendent growth. ♀ 2002. FCC 1969 (for a cool greenhouse). AM 1966 (for a cool greenhouse).

'Elegans' ('Chandleri Elegans') Deep peach-pink, very large, anemone form. Growth spreading. A well proved cultivar for general cultivation. C 1822. ♀ 2002. FCC 1958. AM 1953.

'Elegans Champagne' Similar to 'Elegans' but white, the creamy central petaloids sometimes flushed pink. A sport of 'Elegans Splendor'. Good for exhibition but with poor foliage and constitution. C 1975.

'Extravaganza' White, vividly marked and striped light red, large to very large, anemone form. Compact, upright habit. A seedling of 'Gauntlettii'. C 1957.

'Fimbriata Superba' See 'Fred Sander'.

'Fire Falls' Loosely double, hemispherical flowers of vivid red. Opening early and flowering over a long period. A seedling of 'Professor Sargent'. C 1953. ♀ 2002.

'Fleur Dipater' ('Peachblossom') Light pink, medium, semi-double. Growth medium and compact. A shade deeper than 'Hagoromo'.

'Flora' White, large, single, with waxy petals.

'Frau Minna Seidel' See 'Otome'.

'Fred Sander' ('Fimbriata Superba') Crimson flowers with curled, fimbriated petals, medium, semi-double. Vigorous, compact, erect growth. A sport of 'Tricolor'. C 1913. AM 1921.

'Furo-an' Soft pink, medium, single. AM 1956.

'Gauntlettii' ('Lotus', 'Sode-gashuki') White, very large, semi-double, waterlily form. A vigorous cultivar with spreading branches but a weak constitution.

'Geisha Girl' Light pink with darker stripes and blotches, large, semi-double. Open, upright growth.

'Général Lamorcière' ('Marguérite Gouillon') Delicate pink, slightly striped and flecked deeper pink, medium, full peony form. Vigorous and bushy.

'Gigantea' ('Kelvingtoniana') Red with conspicuous, white variegations, large, 11cm across, semi-double to loose peony form. A widespreading, sparsely branched, well proved cultivar. Although originally described as red, the variegated form has long been the more commonly grown form. The red form has been called 'Gigantea Red'. C 1830. FCC 1869.

'Gloire de Nantes' Rose-pink, large, semi-double. Medium, compact and erect habit. A splendid, early-flowering cultivar. ♀ 2002. AM 1956.

'Grand Prix' Brilliant red, very large, semi-double with irregular petals. Vigorous, upright habit. C 1968. ♀ 2002.

'Grand Slam' Brilliant dark red, large to very large, semi-double to anemone form. Vigorous, open, upright habit. C 1962. ♀ 2002. AM 1975.

'Guest of Honor' Salmon-pink, very large, semi-double to loose peony form. Vigorous, compact, erect growth. Shy-flowering in the open and best under glass. AM 1967.

'Guilio Nuccio' Coral rose-pink, very large, semi-double. Vigorous, erect growth. ♀ 2002. AM 1962.

'Hagoromo' ('Magnoliiflora') Blush-pink with forward-pointing petals, rather like the expanding buds of *Magnolia stellata*, medium, semi-double. Medium, compact growth. ♀ 2002. AM 1953.

'Hakurakuten' White, large, semi-double to loose peony form with curved and fluted petals. Vigorous and erect growth. ♀ 2002. AM 1977.

'Hanafuki' Soft pink, sometimes splashed white, large, semi-double, cup-shaped. Medium and compact growth. AM 1956.

'Hatsusakura' See 'Dewatairin'.

'Hawaii' Pale pink, medium to large, peony form with fringed petals. A sport of 'C.M. Wilson'. C 1961.

'High Hat' Light pink, large, peony form. Slow, compact growth. A sport of 'Daikagura'.

Camellia japonica continued:

'Imbricata Rubra' Light red, medium, formal double. Distinct leaves, inclined to curl.

'James Allan' Fiery red, large, variable in form, single, semi-double, peony or anemone form. Medium and open growth.

'Jingle Bells' Red, small, anemone form. Vigorous, upright habit. A sport of 'Tinker Bell'. C 1959.

'Joseph Pfingstl' Dark red, medium to large, semi-double to loose peony form. Vigorous. C 1948. ♀ 2002.

'Joshua E. Youtz' White, large, peony form. Slow, compact growth.

'Joy Sander' See 'Apple Blossom'.

'Jupiter' Bright scarlet, sometimes blotched white, medium, single to semi-double with a conspicuous bunch of stamens. Vigorous, erect growth. This is one of the best camellias for general planting. ♀ 2002. AM 1953.

'Kelvingtoniana' See 'Gigantea'.

'Kimberley' Carmine with red stamens, medium, single, cup-shaped. Vigorous, compact, erect growth. AM 1934.

'Konronkoku' ('Kouron-jura') Very dark self-red, medium, formal double. One of the darkest of all camellias. Medium, semi-erect growth. ♀ 2002. AM 1960.

'Kramer's Supreme' Red, large to very large, peony form, slight fragrance. Compact, upright habit. C 1957.

'Lady Clare' See 'Akashigata'.

'Lady de Saumerez' Bright red with white spots, medium, semi-double. Vigorous, compact growth. A well proven cultivar for English gardens. A sport of 'Tricolor'.

'Lady McCulloch' White with crimson blotches, medium, semi-double.

'Lady Vansittart' White with rose-pink stripes, medium, semi-double, with wavy-edged petals. Slow, bushy growth and undulate leaves. Sometimes produces sports, see 'Yours Truly'. I from Japan in 1887.

'Lalla Rookh' ('Laurel Leaf') Pink with white marbling, large, formal double. Slow, compact growth and laurel-like foliage.

'Lanarth' Cardinal-red, medium, nearly single. Vigorous, erect growth. AM 1960.

'Latifolia' Soft rose-red, medium, semi-double. Vigorous, bushy growth. A broad-leaved, hardy cultivar succeeding well in the open.

'Laurel Leaf' See 'Lalla Rookh'.

'Lavinia Maggi' ('Contessa Lavinia Maggi') White or pale pink with broad, rose-cerise stripes, large, formal double. ♀ 2002. FCC 1862.

'Le Lys' ('Madame de Bisschop', 'Victor de Bisschop') White, medium, semi-double. Open, vigorous growth.

'Lily Pons' Large, single to semi-double, pure white, to 15cm across, with long, narrow petals. C 1955. ♀ 2002.

'Lotus' See 'Gauntlettii'.

'Lovelight' Large, semi-double, white, 13cm across, with golden stamens. Vigorous upright habit. A seedling of 'Gauntlettii'. C 1951. ♀ 2002.

'Madame de Bisschop' See 'Le Lys'.

'Magnoliiflora' See 'Hagoromo'.

'Margaret Davis' White with rose-red streaks and vermilion edges, medium, peony form. A sport of 'Aspasia MacArthur'. C 1961. AM 1984.

'Margaret Davis Picotee' Medium, peony form, creamy-white, edged vermilion. A sport of 'Margaret Davis'. C 1982. ♀ 2002.

'Margherita Coleoni' Dark red, medium, double to formal double. Vigorous, erect growth.

'Marguérite Gouillon' See 'Général Lamorcière'.

'Mars' Turkey-red, large, semi-double with a conspicuous bunch of stamens. Open, loose growth. Often confused in cultivation with both 'Apollo' and 'Mercury'. ♀ 2002.

'Mary Charlotte' Light pink, medium, anemone form. Compact, upright growth.

'Masayoshi' ('Donckelaeri') Red, often marbled white, large, semi-double. Growth slow and bushy. A first-class plant for the open garden. I by P.F. von Siebold before 1834. ♀ 2002. AM 1960.

'Mathotiana' ('Mathotiana Rubra') Crimson, large, double to formal double. Compact and upright growth.

'Mathotiana Alba' White, rarely with a pink spot, large, formal double. Not suitable for an exposed site. ♀ 2002.

'Mathotiana Rosea' Clear pink, large, formal double. Vigorous, compact and erect. A sport of 'Mathotiana Alba'. AM 1954. ♀ 2002.

'Mathotiana Rubra' See 'Mathotiana'.

'Mattie Cole' Rose-carmine, large, single. C 1955.

'Mercury' Deep soft crimson with slightly darker veins, large, semi-double. Medium, compact growth. ♀ 2002. AM 1948.

'Mikenjaku' ('Lady Buller', 'Nagasaki') Rose-pink with white marbling, large, semi-double. Leaves often mottled yellow. Growth spreading. A well proven cultivar for English gardens. AM 1953.

'Miss Charleston' Deep red with golden stamens, very large, high-centred, semi-double to peony form. Medium, neat, upright habit.

'Momiji-gari' Scarlet, large, single, with flared, white stamens. One of the Japanese Higo Camellias.

'Morning Glow' White, large, formal double. Vigorous, compact and erect growth.

'Mrs D.W. Davis' Blush-pink, very large, semi-double. Vigorous, compact growth. Requires shelter but makes an excellent conservatory shrub. FCC 1968. AM 1960.

'Nagasaki' See 'Mikenjaku'.

'Nobilissima' White with yellow shading, medium, peony form. Growth fairly erect. One of the earliest to flower.

'Nuccio's Gem' White, medium to large, formal double. Compact, upright habit. C 1970. ♀ 2002.

'Nuccio's Jewel' White flushed with orchid-pink, medium, peony form. Bushy habit. C 1977. ♀ 2002.

'Nuccio's Pearl' White flushed with orchid-pink, medium, formal double. Compact, upright habit. C 1977.

'Otome' ('Frau Minna Seidel', 'Pink Perfection') Shell-pink, small, formal double. Vigorous and erect growth.

'Peachblossom' See 'Fleur Dipater'.

'Pink Champagne' Soft pink, large, semi-double to peony form with irregular petals. Vigorous, open habit. AM 1960.

'Pink Perfection' See 'Otome'.

'Premier' Clear rose-red, large, full peony form. Vigorous, upright habit. Best under glass. C 1965.

'Preston Rose' ('Duchesse de Rohan') Salmon-pink, medium, peony form. Vigorous.

Camellia japonica continued:

'Pride of Descanso' See 'Yukibotan'.

'Purity' See 'Shiragiku'.

'Quercifolia' Crimson, medium, single; fishtail foliage.

'R.L. Wheeler' Rose-pink, large to very large, semi-double to anemone form. Vigorous growth. ♀ 2002. FCC 1975. AM 1959.

'Rôgetsu' White with cream-coloured stamens, medium, single, with rounded petals frilled at the margins.

'Rubescens Major' Crimson flowers with darker veining, large, double. Compact and bushy habit. ♀ 2002. AM 1959.

'San Dimas' Semi-double, dark red flowers, 10cm across, with yellow anthers, profusely borne. Compact and upright with very dark green foliage. C 1965. ♀ 2002.

'Scentsation' Pink, sweetly scented, medium to large, peony form. Compact, vigorous, upright bush. ♀ 2002. AM 1995.

'Shiragiku' ('Purity') White, medium, double to formal double. Vigorous and upright growth.

'Shiro-daikagura' See *C. rusticana* 'Shiro-daikagura'.

'Sieboldii' See 'Tricolor'.

'Silver Anniversary' White with golden stamens, large, semi-double, irregular petals. Vigorous, upright habit. C 1960.

'Sode-gashuki' See 'Gauntlettii'.

'Souvenir de Bahuaud-Litou' Light pink, large, formal double. Vigorous and erect growth. A sport of 'Mathotiana Alba'. ♀ 2002.

'Splendens' Red, large, semi-double.

'Suibijin' ('Yoibijin') Pale pink, small, single. Medium, open growth.

'Sylva' Flowers brilliant scarlet, single, chalice-shaped with a boss of bright yellow anthers. Upright habit. ♀ 2002.

'Tammia' White with a pink centre and edge, miniature to small, formal double with incurved petals. Compact, upright habit. C 1971.

'Tiffany' Light orchid-pink, deeper at margin, large to very large, loose peony to anemone form. Upright habit. Best under glass. C 1962.

'Tinker Bell' White with red and rose-pink stripes, small, anemone form. Vigorous, upright habit. C 1958.

'Tinsie' Red outer petals, white peony centre, miniature, anemone form. Vigorous, upright habit. C 1930.

'Tom Thumb' Small to medium, formal double. Pink, each petal edged white. C 1957. ♀ 2002.

'Tomorrow' Rose, very large, semi-double to peony form. Vigorous, open, slightly pendent growth. Best under glass. C 1953. AM 1960.

'Tomorrow's Dawn' Deep soft pink to light pink shading to white at margin with occasional red streaks and white petaloids; very large, semi-double, with irregular petals and large petaloids, to full peony form. Vigorous, open growth. A sport of 'Tomorrow'. Best under glass. C 1960.

'Tricolor' ('Sieboldii') White with carmine streaks, medium, semi-double. Compact. A well proven cultivar for English gardens. ♀ 2002.

'Ville de Nantes' Dark red usually blotched white, large, semi-double with erect, fimbriated petals. Slow and bushy growth. A sport of 'Donckelaeri'.

'Waiwhetu Beauty' Light pink, medium, semi-double. Vigorous growth.

'Wilamina' Medium, formal double, clear soft pink with deeper edge and white centre. Compact, narrow upright habit. C 1951. ♀ 2002.

'Wildfire' Semi-double, red, 10cm across, with yellow stamens. Vigorous upright habit. C 1943.

'Yoibijin' See 'Suibijin'.

'Yours Truly' Pink with deep pink streaks and white borders, medium, semi-double. Slow, bushy growth; undulate leaves. A sport of 'Lady Vansittart'. AM 1960.

'Yukibotan' ('Pride of Descanso') White, large, semi-double to loose peony form with irregular petals. Vigorous.

†'Lasca Beauty' A vigorous and beautiful shrub bearing very large, semi-double, soft pink flowers with yellow anthers. Introduced at Los Angeles State and County Arboretum (LASCA) by Dr Clifford Parks.

'Leonard Messel' (*C. reticulata* × *C.* × *williamsii* 'Mary Christian') A very beautiful, large shrub that originated at Nymans in Sussex, where it proves to be hardy. Large, rich clear pink, semi-double flowers. The dark green leaves incline, like the flower, towards *C. reticulata*. ♀ 2002. FCC and Cory Cup 1970. AM 1958.

†'Mandalay Queen' A *C. reticulata* seedling, probably a hybrid, bearing very large, rich rose-pink, semi-double flowers with yellow anthers and variegated petaloids. It is vigorous and upright.

'Mary Phoebe Taylor' See *C.* × *williamsii* 'Mary Phoebe Taylor'.

'Michael' (*C. cuspidata* × *C. saluenensis*) A beautiful, medium-sized to large shrub, similar to 'Cornish Snow' but with larger, single, white flowers. The best form of this hybrid.

†*nitidissima* C.W. Chi (*C. chrysantha* (Hu) Tuyama) One of a number of Chinese species with yellow flowers, this remarkable plant is unfortunately very tender. It makes a large shrub with deep yellow flowers composed of 8–10 petals and purple young foliage similar to *C. granthamiana*. In North America, Australia, Japan and China attempts are currently being made to cross it with hardier species. Native to Guangxi (S China) and Vietnam.

oleifera Abel. A medium-sized to large shrub with elliptic, toothed leaves, to 6cm long, and small, fragrant, white flowers in autumn. This species has grown undamaged in the Sir Harold Hillier Gardens and Arboretum for many years. It has been used by the U.S. National Arboretum, Washington to develop hardy hybrids for the E USA. EC and S China. SE Asia. I 1818.

†*reticulata* Lindl. One of the most beautiful of all flowering shrubs. The semi-double form 'Captain Rawes', introduced by Robert Fortune in 1820, was regarded in western gardens as the type plant to which Lindley gave the name *C. reticulata*, until 1924 when that great plant collector George Forrest sent home the single-flowered wild form from W China, which is generally grown as Wild Type or Wild Form. It makes a large, compact shrub of much better constitution than the more popular named cultivars. It is hardy in all but the coldest and most exposed gardens and has been uninjured here since it was planted in 1954. There has been extremely little variation between the hundreds of plants raised from the seed. The handsome, rigid, leathery, net-veined leaves are an excel-

lent foil for the large, single, rose-pink flowers, which are inclined to be trumpet-shaped before finally expanding, and are usually freely produced during late winter and early spring. Yunnan, China. AM 1944.

The tender forms of this species introduced in 1948 ('Butterfly Wings', 'Crimson Robe', 'Lion Head', 'Noble Pearl', 'Professor Tsai', 'Purple Gown' and 'Shot Silk') suffer badly from virus and are now little grown.

The following cultivars with single or semi-double flowers are large shrubs or small trees and are only suitable for the conservatory, except in mild areas. **'Arch of Triumph'** Deep pink to wine-red, very large, loose peony form. Vigorous, upright habit. A seedling of *C. reticulata* (Wild Type). C 1970. **'Captain Rawes'** ('Semi-plena') Carmine rose-pink, very large, semi-double. The original form, introduced in 1820 by Robert Fortune from Guangzhou (Canton), is a magnificent shrub. FCC 1963. **'Flore Pleno'** See 'Songzilin'. **'Mary Williams'** Crimson to rose, large, single. A vigorous and hardy shrub raised as a seedling of the Wild Type at Caerhays Castle, Cornwall by that great gardener J.C. Williams. FCC 1964. AM 1942. **'Miss Tulare'** Bright red to rose-red, large to very large, double to full peony form. Vigorous, upright habit. A seedling of 'Crimson Robe'. C 1975. AM 1995. **'Pagoda'** See 'Songzilin'. **'Robert Fortune'** See 'Songzilin'. **'Semi-plena'** See 'Captain Rawes'. **'Songzilin'** ('Flore Pleno', 'Pagoda', 'Robert Fortune') Deep crimson, large, double. Growth compact. I by Robert Fortune about 1850. FCC 1865. **'Trewithen Pink'** Deep rose, large, semi-double. A vigorous, hardy clone selected by G.H. Johnstone who made Trewithen one of the great Cornish gardens, and wrote a standard work on magnolias. AM 1950. **'William Hertrich'** Deep cherry-red, very large, semi-double with slightly reflexed outer petals and upright, loosely arranged inner petals. A seedling of *C. reticulata* 'Cornelian'. C 1962. AM 1981.

'Royalty' (*C. japonica* 'Clarise Carlton' × *C. reticulata* 'Cornelian') Bright pink, deeper in centre, very large, semi-double with crinkled petals. C 1968. AM 1986. ♀ 2002.

rusticana Honda (*C. japonica* subsp. *rusticana* (Honda) Kitam.) Snow camellia. A tough, hardy species from the mountains of N Japan (Hondo), differing from *C. japonica* in its widespreading petals, which open out flat, and its shorter stamens, which are almost free to the base. Flowers red, comparatively small. I 1954. **'Arajishi'** Similar to 'Beni-arajishi' but the petals are marked with white. **'Beni-arajishi'** Rose-red, medium, peony form. Growth vigorous and open. Distinct in its thick, coarsely toothed, tapering leaves. **'Shiro-daikagura'** ('Daikagura White') White, medium, loose peony form. Medium, compact and erect growth.

†*saluenensis* Stapf ex Bean. A beautiful, medium to large shrub, somewhat similar to *C. reticulata* but with smaller leaves and medium-sized flowers, the latter being a lovely, soft pink, single, carried in great profusion. Yunnan, W China. I 1924.

'Salutation' (*C. reticulata* × *C. saluenensis*) A splendid hybrid of medium to large size with matt green leaves and semi-double, soft silvery-pink flowers, 13cm across, during late winter and early spring. A deliberate cross

raised at Borde Hill, Sussex, by Col Stephenson Clarke, possibly the greatest all-round amateur gardener of the 20th century, who left to posterity one of the most complete arboretums. AM 1936.

sasanqua Thunb. An attractive, winter- and early spring-flowering plant producing small but fragrant, usually white flowers. This delightful species with its numerous progeny is worthy of wall protection; all flower best under glass. As they mature they withstand British winters with only a little occasional damage, but they are not generally so reliable as forms of *C. japonica* and require the Californian sun to do them justice. Of the following only 'Crimson King' and 'Narumigata' are free-flowering outside in the British Isles though others can perform well following very hot summers. Japan. I 1896. **'Blanchette'** White, single. **'Briar Rose'** Soft, clear pink, single. **'Crimson King'** Bright red, single. Proving one of the most reliable and prolific flowering. ♀ 2002. **'Duff Allan'** White, flushed with pink, large, single. **'Fukuzutsumi'** Large, cup-shaped, white flowers. C 1891. **'Hiryu'** Crimson, single to semi-double. **'Hugh Evans'** Single, deep rose-pink flowers, 7cm across, profusely borne. Vigorous, upright habit. C 1943. ♀ 2002. **'Jean May'** Small to medium, peony form to double, 8cm across, blush to shell-pink, deeper in the centre, nearly white at the margin. Vigorous upright habit. C 1951. ♀ 2002. **'Mine-no-yuki'** White, large, peony form. AM 1964. **'Momozono-nishiki'** Rose, shaded white, semi-double with curled petals. **'Narumigata'** Large, creamy-white with pink shading towards the margin, fragrant. One of the most reliable flowering forms of this species. AM 1953 (as *C. oleifera*). **'Rainbow'** White, edged with pink. Vigorous growth. C 1956. **'Rosea Plena'** Pink, double. **'Rubra'** Rich red, single. **'Tanya'** Small, 4cm across, deep rose-pink with deeper margin, single, profusely borne. Compact and low growing with small leaves. Raised in the USA from Japanese seed in 1927. **'Tricolor'** White with pink and red stripes, single. **'Usubeni'** Soft pink, occasionally marbled white, semi-double. **'Variegata'** Blush-white. Leaves grey-green, margined white. **'Versicolor'** White centre, edged lavender with pink in between, single.

'Satan's Robe' (*C.* 'Satan's Satin' × *C. reticulata* 'Crimson Robe') Oriental red, large, semi-double. Vigorous, upright habit. C 1965. AM 1984.

'Show Girl' (*C. reticulata* 'Damanoa' × *C. sasanqua* 'Narumigata') Large to very large, semi-double to peony form, pink. C 1978.

sinensis (L.) Kuntze (*C. thea* Link, *Thea sinensis* L.) The tea plant of commerce, geographically a variable species in size and leaf shape. The form we have been growing in the Sir Harold Hillier Gardens and Arboretum for well over forty years has proved a slow-growing, compact, rather small shrub with small, nodding, white flowers in November and December. China, widely cultivated for tea production. I 1740.

'Spring Festival' A large shrub of narrow, upright habit, a seedling of *C. cuspidata* raised in California. Flowers pink, fading to light pink, miniature, double. C 1975. ♀ 2002.

†*taliensis* (W.W. Sm.) Melch. An interesting species related to *C. sinensis*. A large shrub or small tree with bright

green, laurel-like leaves and small, axillary, cream flowers with conspicuous yellow stamens. Yunnan, W China. I 1914 by George Forrest.

thea See *C. sinensis*.

'Tom Knudsen' (*C. japonica* × *C. reticulata*) Very deep, velvety red, rose form to formal double or sometimes peony form, 11cm across. Bushy, upright habit. C 1946. ♀ 2002.

'Tristrem Carlyon' (*C. japonica* 'Rosea Simplex' × *C.* 'Salutation') Rose-pink, medium, peony form, with numerous petaloid stamens. Vigorous, upright habit. C 1972. ♀ 2002. AM 1977.

†tsai Hu. A tender, very graceful, large shrub, resembling *C. cuspidata*. Flowers white, small but numerous; foliage copper-coloured when young. W China, Burma, N Vietnam. I 1924 by George Forrest. FCC 1985. AM 1960.

× vernalis (Mak.) Mak. (*C. japonica* × *C. sasanqua*) Intermediate between its parents, this hybrid has pure white, slightly fragrant flowers with petals arranged in 3 rows. Flowering from February to May. **'Yuletide'** Brilliant red, small, single, 7.5cm across, with yellow stamens. Bushy and upright with dark green foliage. C 1954.

× williamsii W.W. Sm. (*C. japonica* × *C. saluenensis*) One of the most valuable hybrid shrubs ever produced and perhaps the best camellia for general planting in the British Isles.

Cultivars of *Camellia* × *williamsii*

The cultivars originating from this cross are exquisitely beautiful and exceedingly free-flowering over a long period from November to May. In foliage they tend towards the *C. japonica* parent and in flowers towards *C. saluenensis*. First raised by J.C. Williams at Caerhays Castle, Cornwall about 1925.

'Anticipation' Deep rose, large, peony form. Upright habit. The *C. japonica* parent was 'Leviathan'. C 1962. ♀ 2002. FCCT 1975.

'Bartley Pink' Bright cherry-pink, small, single. C 1955. AMT 1985.

'Bow Bells' Bright rose, single, continuously over a long period.

'Bowen Bryant' Deep pink, large, semi-double on shrubs with a vigorous, upright habit. C 1960. ♀ 2002. AMT 1981.

'Brigadoon' Rose-pink, medium, semi-double. Compact, upright habit. The *C. japonica* parent was 'Princess Baciocchi'. C 1960. ♀ 2002. FCCT 1975. AMT 1974.

'Caerhays' Lilac-rose, medium, anemone form. Spreading, somewhat pendent habit gained from its parent *C. japonica* 'Lady Clare'. C 1948. AM 1969.

'C.F. Coates' Deep rose, medium, single. Leaves peculiarly 3-lobed at the apex, derived from the *C. japonica* parent 'Quercifolia', hence sometimes known as the fishtail camellia. C 1935.

'Charles Michael' Pale pink, large, semi-double with long petals. C 1951.

'China Clay' White, medium, semi-double. Open habit. The *C. japonica* parent was 'Marjorie Magnificent'. C 1972. ♀ 2002. AM 1976.

'Citation' Silver blush-pink, large, semi-double with irregular petals. Vigorous, open and erect growth. C 1950. AM 1960.

'Clarrie Fawcett' Semi-double, amaranth-pink flowers profusely borne. A seedling of *C. saluenensis* raised in Australia. C 1948.

'Coppelia' Carmine-rose, single. C 1950. AMT 1987.

'Crinkles' Rose-pink, large, semi-double with crinkled petals. Bushy and erect. C 1955.

'Daintiness' Salmon-pink, large, semi-double. Open habit. The *C. japonica* parent was 'Magnoliiflora'. C 1975. ♀ 2002. AM 1986.

'Debbie' Clear pink, large, peony form. The *C. japonica* parent was 'Debutante'. C 1965. ♀ 2002. AM 1971.

'Donation' Orchid-pink, large, semi-double. Perhaps the most beautiful camellia raised in the 20th century. Vigorous, erect. Raised at Borde Hill, Sussex, before 1941. The *C. japonica* parent was 'Donckelaeri'. ♀ 2002. FCCT 1974. FCC 1952. AM 1941.

'E.G. Waterhouse' Light pink, medium, formal double. Upright habit. C 1954. AMT 1989.

'E.T.R. Carlyon' (*C.* × *williamsii* 'J.C. Williams' × *C. japonica* 'Adolphe Audusson') White, medium, semi-double to rose form, double. Vigorous, upright habit. C 1972. ♀ 2002.

'Elegant Beauty' Deep rose-pink, large, anemone form. Open, straggly habit and best with some pruning. C 1962. ♀ 2002. AMT 1976.

'Elizabeth Rothschild' Soft rose-pink, medium, semi-double. C 1950.

'Elsie Jury' Clear pink, shaded orchid-pink, large, full peony form. Open, spreading habit. Requires a sheltered position. The *C. japonica* parent was 'Pukekura White'. C 1964. ♀ 2002. FCCT 1975.

'First Flush' Appleblossom-pink, medium, semi-double. Free and early flowering.

'Francis Hanger' White, single. Growth erect, inclined towards *C. japonica*. Leaves strongly undulate. AM 1953.

'Galaxie' White with pink stripes, medium to large, semi-double to rose form, double, cupped with twisted petals. The first striped *williamsii* hybrid. Slow-growing and free-flowering. ♀ 2002.

'George Blandford' Pinkish-mauve, medium, semi-double to peony form, very early. Stiffly spreading habit. AM 1965. AMT 1974. ♀ 2002.

'Glenn's Orbit' Deep orchid-pink, large, semi-double to loose peony form. Vigorous, upright habit. A seedling of 'Donation'. ♀ 2002. AMT 1976. AM 1962.

'Golden Spangles' Phlox-pink, small, single. Leaves with yellow-green central blotch. Found at Wisley in 1957. AMT 1987.

'Hiraethlyn' Palest pink, perfect single form. The *C. japonica* parent is said to be 'Flora'. C 1950. AMT 1989.

'J.C. Williams' Phlox-pink, medium, single. The first clone of *C.* × *williamsii* to be named, and one of the most beautiful of all camellias. Raised by J.C. Williams at Caerhays. ♀ 2002. AMT 1977. FCC 1942.

'Jenefer Carlyon' Silvery-pink, large, semi-double. Spreading habit. Cory Cup 1984.

'Jermyns' Clear, self peach-pink, broad petals. A first-class selection raised in our nurseries.

Camellia × williamsii continued:

'Joan Trehane' Clear rose-pink, very large, rose form, double to formal double, 35 petals, a few petaloids among the cream stamens. Dense, spreading habit. ♀ 2002.

'Julia Hamiter' Blush-pink to white, medium, semi-double to double. Compact habit. A seedling of C. × williamsii 'Donation'. C 1964. ♀ 2002.

'Jury's Yellow' White, medium, anemone form with wavy petals and central mass of creamy-yellow petaloids. Compact, upright habit. C 1976. ♀ 2002.

'Lady Gowrie' Pink, large, semi-double. Vigorous and compact growth. C 1954.

'Les Jury' Strong pillar-box red, double, with bronze young foliage. Compact upright habit. ♀ 2002.

'Mary Christian' Clear pink, small, single. ♀ 2002. FCCT 1977. AM 1942.

'Mary Phoebe Taylor' Light rose-pink, very large, peony-form flowers. A seedling of C. saluenensis raised in New Zealand. C 1975. ♀ 2002.

'Mildred Veitch' Orchid-pink, large, semi-double to anemone form with a loose centre. Compact, upright habit. The C. japonica parent was 'Elegans'. C 1962. AMT 1977. AM 1967.

'Muskoka' Deep pink with darker stripes, medium, semi-double. ♀ 2002.

'Night Rider' (C. japonica 'Kuro-tsubaki' × C. × williamsii 'Ruby Bells') Very dark red, semi-double flowers with narrow, waxy petals. Upright habit with purple-red young foliage.

'November Pink' Phlox-pink, medium, single. Usually the earliest of the group to flower. AM 1950.

'Rose Parade' Deep rose-pink, medium, formal double. Vigorous, compact, upright habit. A cross between 'Donation' and C. japonica. C 1969.

'Rosemary Williams' Rose-pink, medium, single. Compact, upright. C 1961.

'Ruby Wedding' Currant-red, anemone to peony form. Dense, upright habit. Flowering profusely in mid-season. A Jury hybrid from New Zealand.

'Saint Ewe' Rose-pink, medium, single, cupped. ♀ 2002. FCCT 1974. AM 1947.

'Saint Michael' Pink, medium, single, free-flowering. Vigorous, erect with a slightly spreading habit.

'Senorita' (C. japonica 'Hikarugenji' × C. saluenensis) Rose-pink with deeper margins, medium-sized, loose peony form with wavy petals, opening late. Vigorous and compact, upright habit with glossy dark green foliage. Raised in New Zealand before 1957. ♀ 2002.

'Tiptoe' (C. japonica × C. × williamsii 'Farfalla') Silvery-pink with cherry-pink edges, medium, semi-double. Compact, upright, bushy habit. C 1965. AMT 1985.

'Tregrehan' Apricot-pink, medium, semi-double to double. Vigorous, upright habit. C. japonica parent was 'Marjorie Magnificent'. Raised by Gillian Carlyon. C 1972.

'Water Lily' Lavender flushed bright pink, medium, formal double. Vigorous, upright habit. C 1967. ♀ 2002.

'Wilber Foss' (C. japonica 'Beau Harp' × C. saluenensis) Large, full peony form, 12cm across, brilliant red-pink. Vigorous and compact, upright habit with dark green foliage. Raised in New Zealand before 1972. ♀ 2002.

'Winton' (C. cuspidata × C. saluenensis) Similar to 'Cornish Snow' but flowers a soft almond-pink.

Camphor tree See Cinnamomum camphora.

†***CAMPHOROSMA** L.—Chenopodiaceae—A small genus of about 10 species of aromatic, heath-like shrubs, natives of the E Mediterranean region to C Asia.

monspeliaca L. A small shrub with inconspicuous flowers and sage-green leaves. Suitable for sunny, dry positions in coastal areas. N Africa, S Europe to C Asia.

Candleberry See Myrica cerifera.

†***CANTUA** Lam.—Polemoniaceae—A small genus of about 6 species of shrubs and trees found in the N Andes of South America. It is one of the few woody representatives of the family.

buxifolia Juss. (C. dependens Pers.) Magic tree. A very beautiful, small shrub with graceful, drooping corymbs of bright cherry-red, tubular flowers in April. Semi-evergreen in mild localities. Requires a warm, sheltered wall. Andes of Bolivia, Peru and Chile. I 1849. AM 1905.

Cape figwort See Phygelius capensis.
Cape honeysuckle See Tecoma capensis.

CARAGANA Lam.—Leguminosae—About 80 species of usually spiny shrubs or small trees distributed between E Europe and Japan, mainly occurring in C Asia. Leaves are even pinnate, with the terminal leaflet reduced to a spine, but sometimes appear odd pinnate owing to the reduction of one of the leaflets at the base of the spine. The spines are formed from either the leaf rachis, the persistent stipules or both. The pea-like flowers are normally yellow and are borne in early summer. Good in dry soils.

arborescens Lam. Pea tree. A small, shrubby tree. One of the toughest and most accommodating of all plants, succeeding in the most exposed areas, on all types of soil. Flowers yellow. Siberia and Manchuria. I 1752. **'Lorbergii'** An extremely graceful, medium-sized shrub with narrow, almost grass-like leaflets and much smaller flowers. C about 1906. **'Nana'** A remarkable dwarf shrub making an outstanding dot plant for a rock garden. **'Pendula'** A very attractive, weeping form. C 1856. **'Walker'** Foliage similar to 'Lorbergii' but growth prostrate. Usually top-grafted to produce a weeping standard with hanging branches. Raised in Canada by crossing 'Lorbergii' with 'Pendula'.

boisii C.K. Schneid. A yellow-flowered species attaining about 2m. Differs from C. arborescens in its downy seedpods. Tibet, China. C 1904.

brevispina Royle. A medium-sized, spreading shrub of open habit with arching branches and pink-tinged, downy young shoots. Leaves pinnate with usually 8–10 leaflets, softly downy when young, the persistent rachis developing into a spine up to 6cm long. Flowers are yellow flushed with green, reddish with age, and borne in pairs or threes on slender peduncles in June. NW Himalaya. I 1849.

chamlagu See C. sinica.

decorticans Hemsl. A shrubby or tree-like species, ultimately 5–5.5m. Leaves with 10–12 leaflets and tiny stipules. Flowers light yellow, about 2.5cm long. Afghanistan. I 1879.

franchetiana Komar. A tall shrub of open, spreading habit. The bright yellow flowers are 2.5cm long; the pinnate leaves have 12–18 leaflets and are bright apple-green. China. I 1913 by George Forrest.

frutex (L.) K. Koch (*C. frutescens* DC.) A spineless, glabrous shrub, up to 3m, producing bright yellow flowers in May. Leaves with 4 leaflets. Widely distributed from E Europe to C Asia. I 1752.

jubata (Pall.) Poir. A curious, small, slow-growing shrub of irregular form, thickly covered with coarse, brownish-grey hairs and slender spines. Leaves have 12–14 leaflets; the rachis, margin and midrib beneath are covered in long, white hairs. Large, white flowers are produced singly in late spring. Siberia. Mongolia. I 1796.

maximowicziana Komar. A small, semi-pendent species, 1.2–2m high, with spiny branchlets, bearing solitary, yellow flowers, 2.5cm long. China, Tibet. I 1910 by Ernest Wilson.

microphylla Lam. A spreading, medium shrub with bright yellow flowers, usually in pairs. Siberia, N China. I 1789.

pygmaea (L.) DC. A small shrub, sometimes prostrate, with long, slender, somewhat pendent branches. The 2.5cm long, yellow flowers hang on drooping stalks beneath the branches in May or June. Leaves have 4 narrow leaflets and a small, terminal spine. China to Siberia. I 1751.

sinica (Buc'hoz) Rehder (*C. chamlagu* Lam.) A rounded, bushy shrub of medium size, displaying buff-yellow, pea-shaped flowers in May and June. Leaves have 2 pairs of glossy green leaflets on a persistent, spine-tipped rachis. China. I 1773.

× *sophorifolia* Tausch (*C. arborescens* × *C. microphylla*) Intermediate between its parents and of equal garden value. Leaves with 8–10 leaflets.

tragacanthoides (Pall.) Poir. A low, spreading, very spiny shrub. Bright yellow flowers in June are followed by grey, silky seedpods. Leaves with 4 obovate, dark blue-green leaflets. Tibet, China and Siberia. I 1816.

turkestanica Kom. An uncommon, spiny species of loose habit with yellow flowers.

†**CARMICHAELIA** R. Br.—**Leguminosae**—About 40 species of erect or prostrate, broom-like shrubs. Many have distinctive, flattened stems that do the work normally done by the leaves. All require a sunny, well-drained position. Mainly in New Zealand, one on Lord Howe Island.

australis R. Br. A small to medium-sized shrub with flattened, young stems and tiny, pale purple, pea flowers during June and July. C 1823. AM 1927.

enysii Kirk. Occasionally forms a hummock, up to 20cm, with a dense mat of branchlets; flowers small, lilac-pink. I 1892.

flagelliformis Colenso. An erect shrub, 1m or more high, with compressed branchlets. Flowers small, blue-purple with darker veining.

petriei Kirk. Distinguished by its stout branchlets and erect growth; fragrant, thickly clustered racemes of violet-purple flowers.

williamsii Kirk. Distinguished from other cultivated species by its branchlets, which are 6–12mm wide, and by its larger flowers, which are creamy-yellow; attains about 1.5m. Only for the mildest localities. I 1925.

× **CARMISPARTIUM** G. Hutchins ex M.D. Griffiths (*Carmichaelia* × *Notospartium*)—**Leguminosae**—An intergeneric hybrid first raised from seed imported from New Zealand.

hutchinsii M.D. Griffiths (*C. astonii* × *N. glabrescens*) A small, semi-pendent shrub with flattened shoots. Racemes of small pea flowers are borne in summer. **'County Park'** Flowers white, blotched in the centre and veined with deep rose-pink. Raised by Graham Hutchins from seed of *Carmichaelia astonii* received in 1981.

Carob tree See *Ceratonia siliqua*.

***CARPENTERIA** Torr.—**Hydrangeaceae**—A monotypic genus for a warm, sunny position.

californica Torr. Tree anemone. A beautiful, medium-sized evergreen, producing large, white flowers with golden anthers in July. Needs a sunny site, preferably backed by a wall. California. I about 1880. ♥ 2002. FCC 1888. **'Bodnant'** A large-flowered form similar to 'Ladham's Variety' but hardier. Selected at Bodnant in the 1960s by Charles Puddle. **'Elizabeth'** A Californian selection with larger flowers and more flowers in each cluster. Named after Elizabeth McClintock. **'Ladham's Variety'** A vigorous, free-flowering clone with larger flowers often measuring 8cm across. FCC 1980. AM 1924.

CARPINUS L.—**Corylaceae**—The hornbeams are picturesque and easily grown trees. They are suitable for clay or chalky soils, and very attractive when laden with their hop-like fruit clusters. More than 30 species mainly in China but widely distributed in N temperate regions south to Central America.

betulus L. Common hornbeam. Recommended both for single specimens and for hedging, resembling beech in the latter respect. A medium-sized to large tree with a characteristic grey fluted trunk and ovate, serrate, ribbed leaves. Europe (incl. British Isles), Asia Minor. ♥ 2002. **'Columnaris'** A small, columnar tree of dense, compact growth, conical when young. Slower growing and smaller than 'Fastigiata'. C 1891. **'Fastigiata'** ('Pyramidalis') A medium-sized tree of erect, pyramidal habit. Quite narrow as a young tree but broadening as it matures. C 1883. ♥ 2002. **'Frans Fontaine'** A fastigiate form that retains its habit with age. Selected from a street in Eindhoven, Holland. **'Incisa'** A form with small, narrow, deeply and usually singly toothed leaves; inclined to revert. 'Quercifolia' is similar. C 1789. **'Pendula'** A dwarf, mushroom-headed tree with steeply pendent branches. **'Purpurea'** The young leaves have a purple tinge, but soon become green. A collector's plant. C 1873. **'Pyramidalis'** See 'Fastigiata'. **'Quercifolia'** See under 'Incisa'. **'Streetwise'** Our own selection, with an upright habit similar to 'Frans Fontaine'. Distinct, deeply pleated leaves with a wavy edge, yellow-green flushed bronze when young, turning orange and yellow in autumn. Selected in the early 1980s, introduced in

1998. **'Variegata'** A form in which some leaves are splashed creamy-white. Often reverts with age. C 1770.

caroliniana Walter (*C. americana* Michx.) The American hornbeam or blue beech forms a beautiful, small tree with grey fluted bark. It is not so tall as our native species. The spreading branches arch at their tips. Leaves polished apple-green, tinted as autumn approaches. E North America with a variety in Mexico and Central America. I 1812.

cordata Blume. A slow-growing, small tree with comparatively broad, deeply veined leaves, heart-shaped at the base. Fruits green, in large clusters. Japan, NE Asia, N and W China. I 1879.

coreana Nakai. A large, bushy shrub or small tree, the young shoots covered in white hairs. Leaves broadly to narrowly ovate, to 6cm long, sharply double-toothed at the margin; glossy green above, hairy on the veins beneath. Fruit clusters small, about 4cm long, with sharply toothed bracts. First introduced to our nursery by Sir Harold Hillier when he collected in Korea in 1976. Korea.

fangiana Hu. One of the most exciting of recent introductions, this medium-sized tree is remarkable in its finely toothed leaves which are bronze when young and up to nearly 20cm long, with as many as 30 prominent veins. Even more remarkable are the slender, pendent fruiting catkins up to nearly 30cm long. SW China. I to the University of British Columbia Botanic Gardens in 1986 where it flowered and fruited in 1995, and to Britain in 1992 by Mikinori Ogisu who collected seed in SW Sichuan in 1991.

henryana (H. Winkl.) H. Winkl. Medium-sized tree. Leaves ovate lanceolate, up to 9cm long. C and W China. I 1907 by Ernest Wilson.

japonica Blume. A very beautiful, widespreading, small tree or large shrub with prominently corrugated leaves and conspicuous fruiting catkins. In general appearance recalls *Alnus firma*. Japan. I 1895. ♀ 2002.

laxiflora (Siebold & Zucc.) Blume. Medium-sized tree with rather drooping branches, ovate-oblong, slenderly pointed leaves and conspicuous, loose clusters of green fruiting keys. Japan, Korea. I 1914. **var.** *macrostachya* Oliv. Differs in its larger leaves and fruit clusters. Throughout the summer the young growths are bright red. W and C China. I 1900 by Augustine Henry.

orientalis Mill. Small, bushy tree or shrub with small, sharply toothed leaves. SE Europe, SW Asia, Caucasus. I 1735.

× *schuschaensis* H. Winkl. (*C. betulus* × *C. orientalis*) A vigorous, medium-sized tree of upright habit with glossy red, sparsely downy young shoots. Leaves ovate, sharply toothed, to 11cm long, on vigorous shoots, glossy green above, paler and glossy with sparse hairs beneath, petiole, red, 1cm long. Fruit clusters, to 8cm long, have sharply toothed bracts each with 2 small lobes at the base. A naturally occurring hybrid. I by Roy Lancaster and Mrs Ala in 1972 (Ala and Lancaster 5).

tschonoskii Maxim. Small ornamental tree with leaves 4–8cm long. Japan, Korea. I 1901.

turczaninowii Hance. An attractive, small, shrubby tree recalling *Nothofagus dombeyi*, with slender stems and small leaves. The young, emerging leaves are bright red.

N China. Korea, Japan. I 1914 by Reginald Farrer. ♀ 2002. **var.** *ovalifolia* H. Winkl. The form most often cultivated with slightly larger, serrated leaves. W China. I 1889 by Augustine Henry.

†**CARPODETUS** J.R. Forst. & G. Forst.—**Escalloniaceae**— A small genus of 10 species of evergreen trees found in New Zealand and New Guinea.

serratus J.R. Forst. & G. Forst. A graceful, tall evergreen with small, dark green leaves and small, white flowers, in cymose panicles in summer. Needs a sheltered site. New Zealand.

CARRIEREA Franch.—**Flacourtiaceae**—A small genus of 3 species. Small trees from SE Asia.

calycina Franch. A very rare, large shrub or small tree, forming a broad head with glabrous, shining dark green leaves and cup-shaped flowers of creamy-white in terminal candelabra-like racemes in June. Fruit an oblong or spindle-shaped, woody capsule. W China. I 1908 by Ernest Wilson.

CARYA Nutt.—**Juglandaceae**—The hickories belong to a genus of about 17 species of fast-growing, stately, large trees, allied to the walnuts (*Juglans*) and mainly confined to E North America but also occurring in Mexico and SE Asia. They are distinguished from *Juglans* and *Pterocarya* by lacking the chambered pith found in those genera. The large, compound leaves, often over 30cm long, turn clear yellow in the autumn, and the picturesque, grey trunks are attractive in winter. Difficult subjects to transplant, they are best planted when small.

amara See *C. cordiformis*.

cordiformis (Wangenh.) K. Koch (*C. amara* (Michx.) Nutt.) Bitternut. Eventually a large tree with thin, brown, scaly bark. Characteristic yellow winter buds. Leaves with usually 7, occasionally 5 or 9, lanceolate leaflets. Perhaps the best hickory for general planting. E North America. I 1766. AM 1989.

glabra (Mill.) Sweet (*C. porcina* (Michx. f.) Nutt.) Pignut. A medium-sized to large tree with smooth, regularly folded bark. Leaves composed of 5–7 taper-pointed leaflets, the terminal one large and obovate, 13–18cm long. E North America. I 1799. AM 1967.

illinoinensis (Wangenh.) K. Koch (*C. pecan* (Marshall) Engl. & Graebn., *C. oliviformis* (Michx.) Nutt.) Pecan. A large and valuable nut-bearing tree in North America, but not so successful in the British Isles. Distinguished by its numerous leaflets, usually 11–17 on each leaf. SE and SC USA. I about 1760.

laciniosa (Michx. f.) Loud. (*C. sulcata* Nutt.) Big shellbark hickory, Kingnut. A medium-sized tree in the British Isles, with large, handsome leaves, with usually 7, occasionally 9, ovate leaflets, the terminal one larger and obovate. Mature trees with shaggy bark. E USA. I 1804.

oliviformis See *C. illinoinensis*.

ovata (Mill.) K. Koch (*C. alba* Nutt. not K. Koch) Shagbark hickory, Shellbark hickory. The most valuable nut-producing species in the USA. A handsome tree of medium to large size. Leaves composed of 5 long-pointed leaflets, the 3 upper ones large and obovate. Rich yellow autumn foliage. Can fruit in the British Isles after hot summers. E North America. C 1629.

pecan See *C. illinoinensis*.

tomentosa (Poir.) Nutt. (*C. alba* K. Koch not Nutt.) Mockernut, Big-bud hickory. A medium-sized, stately tree, occasionally over 18m, with downy young shoots. Leaves, over 30cm long, are composed of 7, sometimes 5 or 9, ovate leaflets, the terminal leaflet larger and obovate. All are downy and glandular beneath and turn rich butter-yellow in autumn. It is easily recognised by its fragrant, ornamental foliage and large winter buds. SE Canada, E USA. I 1766.

CARYOPTERIS Bunge—**Verbenaceae**—Small, showy, late summer-flowering shrubs and herbaceous perennials with opposite aromatic leaves, best grown in well-drained soil, in full sun. Excellent for chalky soils. About 6 species in E Asia from the Himalaya to Japan.

× *clandonensis* A. Simmonds (*C. incana* × *C. mongholica*) A variable hybrid first raised by Mr Arthur Simmonds when he sowed seed from *C. mongholica* next to which grew *C. incana*. **'Arthur Simmonds'** This attractive hybrid, often sold as 'Heavenly Blue' (see below) thrives almost anywhere, producing its bright blue flowers in August and September. An ideal subject for mass effect, it can be kept to a height of about 60cm. Deservedly one of the most popular, small hybrid shrubs raised in the 20th century, this is a fitting plant to commemorate A. Simmonds who raised it before 1933 and was perhaps the greatest secretary ever to have served the Royal Horticultural Society. ♀ 2002. FCC 1941. AM 1933. **'Blue Mist'** ('Pershore') Compact with powder-blue flowers. **'Dark Knight'** Deep purple-blue flowers and silvery green foliage. **'Ferndown'** A seeding selection with slightly darker flowers of blue-violet. AM 1953. **'First Choice'** Flowers larger and darker than most, deep inky-blue in bud, opening rich cobalt-blue over a long period. A compact selection raised by Peter Catt. ♀ 2002. **Grand Bleu** ('Inoveris') PBR A form raised in France with flowers of an intense deep blue. **'Heavenly Blue'** A clone of American origin. The habit is a little more compact than that of 'Arthur Simmonds' and the blue colour a shade deeper. **'Kew Blue'** A seedling of 'Arthur Simmonds' with slightly darker flowers. Raised at Kew in 1945. **'Pershore'** See 'Blue Mist'. **'Worcester Gold'** Although becoming reasonably well known, this small shrub with golden-yellow-flushed leaves has a tendency, on occasion, to look somewhat chlorotic, even when quite healthy. ♀ 2002.

incana (Houtt.) Miq. (*C. tangutica* Maxim., *C. mastacanthus* Schauer) A small shrub covered by a greyish, felt-like pubescence. Flowers violet-blue. The dominant parent of *C.* × *clandonensis*. Japan. Korea, China, Taiwan. I 1844. AM 1899. **'Blue Cascade'** A form with weeping branches which is proving to be very hardy. It has also been distributed as *C. incana* weeping form.

mastacanthus See *C. incana*.

mongholica Bunge. Distinct in its dwarf habit, narrow leaves and comparatively large, rich blue flowers. A plant of weak constitution. Mongolia, China. C 1844. AM 1928.

tangutica See *C. incana*.

Cassia corymbosa See *Senna corymbosa*, *S.* × *floribunda* and *S. septemtrionalis*.

Cassia obtusa See under *Senna* × *floribunda* and *S. septemtrionalis*.

Cassinia fulvida See *Ozothamnus leptophyllus* Fulvidus Group.

Cassinia leptophylla See *Ozothamnus leptophyllus*.

Cassinia vauvilliersii See *Ozothamnus leptophyllus*.

Cassinia vauvilliersii var. *albida* See *Ozothamnus leptophyllus* Albidus Group.

‡***CASSIOPE** D. Don—**Ericaceae**—About 12 species of attractive, dwarf shrublets, related to *Calluna* and *Erica*, with densely overlapping leaves and solitary, bell-shaped flowers. Natives of N Arctic and mountain regions, they require moist, peaty soil and conditions simulating open moorlands.

'Badenoch' A slender-branched hybrid (probably *C. fastigiata* × *C. lycopodiodes*) forming a loose clump of narrow stems up to 10cm bearing white bells on thread-like pedicels.

'Bearsden' (*C. fastigiata* × *C. lycopodioides*) Similar to 'Badenoch' with 4-angled shoots bearing tightly adpressed, pointed leaves and white, bell-shaped flowers in April and May. Originated as a chance seedling about 1955. AM 1971.

'Edinburgh' (*C. fastigiata* × *C. tetragona*) Slender, dark green stems up to 18cm high and, in spring, white flowers with the green calyx edged red. A chance seedling raised at the Royal Botanic Garden, Edinburgh. Perhaps the most accommodating of a pernickety genus. ♀ 2002. AM 1957.

fastigiata (Wall.) D. Don. A dwarf shrublet, up to 30cm high, with white-margined, adpressed leaves, giving a 4-angled effect to the stems. The white, bell-shaped flowers are carried on hair-like stalks in April and May. Himalaya. I about 1849. FCC 1863.

lycopodioides (Pall.) D. Don. A prostrate mat of thread-like branchlets above which little, white bells dangle from the slenderest of stalks. NE Asia, NW North America. ♀ 2002. FCC 1962. AM 1937. **'Rigida'** (*C. rigida* hort.) Similar but with comparatively large, white, semi-pendent flowers. AM 1938.

mertensiana (Bong.) D. Don. Dwarf shrub, 15–30cm high with erect or spreading, 4-angled stems and pure white flowers in April. Mountains of W North America, where it is referred to as white heather. I about 1885. AM 1927. **subsp. gracilis** Piper. A low-growing form with darker shoots and larger flowers.

'Muirhead' (*C. lycopodioides* × *C. wardii*) A tiny shrublet with curved, repeatedly forked shoots and small, nodding, white flowers in spring. ♀ 2002. FCC 1962. AM 1953.

'Randle Cooke' (*C. fastigiata* × *C. lycopodioides*) A mat-forming shrublet with stems up to 15cm high. White bell flowers appear along the stems in late April. Garden origin 1957. ♀ 2002. AM 1964.

rigida hort. See *C. lycopodioides* 'Rigida'.

tetragona (L.) D. Don (*Andromeda tetragona* L.) Forms tufts of erect shoots covered with closely imbricated, deep green leaves, from which the nodding, white, bell-shaped flowers appear in April and May. North America, Asia, Europe. I 1810.

wardii Marquand. A dwarf, erect-branched shrublet with leaves distinctly arranged in 4 rows and edged with fine white hairs. Flowers are bell-shaped and white tinged red. E Himalaya. I 1938. FCC 1982. AM 1949.

CASTANEA Mill.—**Fagaceae**—The chestnuts are a genus of some 12 species of deciduous trees and shrubs found in the temperate N hemisphere. Sharply serrate leaves are common to all species, and the twigs lack a terminal bud. The tiny, yellowish, unisexual flowers are borne in long, slender catkins, some male, some male and female, and although individually not conspicuous can be very ornamental *en masse*. They are long-lived, drought-resistant trees thriving on well-drained, preferably rather light soils. They are moderately lime-tolerant and may be grown with fair success given deep soils over chalk, but become chlorotic on shallow chalky soils.

alnifolia Nutt. Trailing chinquapin. A small, suckering shrub to 1m tall. Leaves elliptic, to 12cm long, edged with shallow, bristle-tipped teeth, glossy green above, and a tawny pubescence beneath when young becoming glabrous or nearly so. SE USA.

ashei See *C. pumila* var. *ashei*.

crenata Siebold & Zucc. (*C. japonica* Blume) Japanese chestnut. A small tree or large shrub with long, bristle-toothed leaves. Japan. I 1895.

dentata (Marshall) Borkh. (*C. americana* (Michx.) Raf.) The American sweet chestnut, rare in cultivation and becoming so in its native haunts owing to the devastating effects of chestnut blight, which was introduced to the USA in 1904. Differs from the European species mainly in its narrower, always glabrous leaves. E North America. C 1800.

henryi (Skan) Rehder & E.H. Wilson. In nature a tree upwards of 20m high; in cultivation in our part of Hampshire a rare and very distinct shrub, making late, unripened growth which is cut back by winter frost. C and W China. I 1900 by Ernest Wilson.

mollissima Blume. Chinese chestnut. Medium to large tree with ovate or oblong, coarsely serrate leaves. China, Korea. I 1908 by Ernest Wilson.

× *neglecta* Dode (*C. dentata* × *C. pumila*) Similar to *C. pumila*, but leaves less white-pubescent beneath; fruits a little larger.

ozarkensis Ashe (*C. arkansana* Ashe) Ozark chestnut. Generally a medium-sized tree with long, coarsely serrate leaves. Closely related to *C. pumila* but with glabrous shoots and leaves nearly so. C USA. I 1891.

pumila (L.) Mill. Chinquapin. A large, suckering shrub or small tree with downy young shoots. Leaves are white-tomentose beneath at least when young. Distinguished from the closely related *C. alnifolia* by its acute not obtuse leaves, which are tomentose beneath. E and S USA. I 1699. **var.** *ashei* Sudw. (*C. ashei* (Sudw.) Sudw. ex Ashe) Coastal chinquapin. This differs from the typical variety in the less densely spiny involucres. Specimens in the Sir Harold Hillier Gardens and Arboretum have been known to fruit prolifically (autumn 1989), the fruits opening to release the nuts before falling. Coastal SE USA.

sativa Mill. Sweet chestnut, Spanish chestnut. A fast-growing tree, a large specimen being extremely ornamental

particularly in July when laden with its yellowish-green male and female catkins. Hotter than average summers are required to produce good crops of nuts. A valuable timber tree, and especially useful for coppicing. Native of S Europe, N Africa and Asia Minor. Long cultivated and naturalised in the British Isles, where it is believed to have been introduced by the Romans. ♀ 2002. **'Albomarginata'** Leaves with a creamy-white margin. Fruits with white spines. ♀ 2002. AM 1964. **'Aureomarginata'** See 'Variegata'. **'Heterophylla'** Leaves variously shaped, sometimes linear with irregularly lobed margins. Inclined to revert. **'Marron de Lyon'** ('Macrocarpa') The best fruiting clone, bearing at a very early age. **'Variegata'** ('Aureomarginata') Leaves bordered yellow.

seguinii Dode. Large shrub or small tree with long, coarsely serrate leaves. E and C China. I 1853.

†***CASTANOPSIS** (D. Don) Spach—**Fagaceae**—A genus of about 134 species of evergreen trees related to *Quercus* and *Castanea*, differing from the former in their erect male spikes, and from the latter in having terminal buds and the female flowers on separate spikes. Natives mainly of tropical and subtropical SE Asia, particularly Malaysia.

chrysophylla See *Chrysolepis chrysophylla*.

cuspidata (Thunb. ex Murray) Schottky (*Quercus cuspidata* Thunb. ex Murray) A large shrub or small, bushy tree with glabrous twigs. The leathery, shining, dark green leaves are oval with a slenderly drawn-out apex. Requires a sheltered position. Japan, Korea. I 1830.

Casuarina nana See *Allocasuarina nana*.

Catalina ironwood See *Lyonothamnus floribundus*.

CATALPA Scop.—**Bignoniaceae**—A small genus of about 11 species of beautiful, late summer-flowering trees, with large, opposite or whorled leaves, mostly of low, widespreading habit, natives of North America and China. The foxglove-like flowers, which do not occur in young plants, are borne in conspicuous panicles. When planting avoid exposed areas, where the large leaves would become tattered. Suitable for growing in all types of well-drained soils.

bignonioides Walter. Indian bean tree. A medium-sized tree with large, heart-shaped leaves which are usually entire and end in a tapered point. Flowers white with yellow and purple markings, borne in large open panicles in July and August, followed by slender, pendulous pods up to 30cm long. E USA. I 1726. ♀ 2002. AM 1933. **'Aurea'** Golden Indian bean tree. An outstanding form with large, velvety, soft yellow leaves that are almost green by the time the flowers open. C 1877. ♀ 2002. AM 1974. **'Koehnei'** ('Aureomarginata') Leaves with a broad yellow margin, green in late summer. C 1903. **'Nana'** A compact, rounded bush or a small, round-headed tree if grafted as a standard. Originated in France about 1850. **'Variegata'** Leaves variegated white or creamy-yellow.

bungei C.A. Mey. A small tree. Flowers white with purple spots, in clusters, 8–30cm long, in July but not freely produced. The broadly palmate leaves have slender, acuminate lobes. A tree that requires hot summers to thrive; any unripened growth can be damaged in winter. N China. I 1905.

× *erubescens* Carrière (*C. bignonioides* × *C. ovata*) (*C.* × *hybrida* Späth) This hybrid first arose before 1869. The following forms are cultivated. **'J.C. Teas'** A medium-sized tree, intermediate between the parents. Leaves broad ovate; 3-lobed and entire on the same tree, purple when unfolding; flowers in late July, like those of *C. bignonioides*, but smaller and more numerous. Raised in the USA about 1874. Originally listed as *C.* × *erubescens*. **'Purpurea'** Young leaves and shoots dark purple, almost black, gradually becoming dark green. C 1886. ♀ 2002. AM 1970.

fargesii Bureau. One of the best of the midsummer-flowering trees. It is allied to its Chinese neighbour, *C. bungei*, and in cultivation it forms a tree of medium size with leaves smaller than those of the Indian bean tree. The conspicuous flowers are of typical form, lilac-pink with red-brown spots and stained with yellow. They are carried in corymbs of 7–15. China. I 1901 by Ernest Wilson. AM 1973. **f. *duclouxii*** (Dode) Gilmour (*C. duclouxii* Dode) A tree equal in merit to the typical form and with similar flowers, but differing in the leaves being less pubescent and having more conspicuous acuminate lobes. China. I 1907 by Ernest Wilson. AM 1934.

× *hybrida* See *C.* × *erubescens*.

ovata G. Don (*C. kaempferi* Siebold) A tree, 11m or more in height. Leaves usually 3-lobed. Small, white flowers with yellow and red markings, produced in many-flowered, narrowly pyramidal panicles in July and August. China. I 1849 by P.F. von Siebold. AM 1933.

speciosa (Warder ex Barney) Engelm. Western catalpa. A tall tree with large, heart-shaped leaves. The purple-spotted, white flowers, appearing in July, are slightly larger than those of *C. bignonioides*, but there are fewer in the panicle. C USA. I 1880. AM 1956.

CEANOTHUS L.—Rhamnaceae—The Californian lilacs include some 55 species of evergreen and deciduous shrubs and trees widely distributed over the USA, S Canada and Mexico south to Guatemala but occurring mainly in California, where the following species are native unless otherwise stated. They vary from prostrate plants to very vigorous, tall shrubs, but are mostly medium-sized. They provide us with the best blue-flowered shrubs that can be grown out-of-doors in the British Isles. *Ceanothus* require full sun and good drainage; all are lime-tolerant up to a point, but only a few give a good account of themselves in a really poor, shallow chalky soil and some can become chlorotic. Most are excellent for seaside gardens, and in colder areas are ideal for growing against a wall. The deciduous kinds may have the laterals cut back to within 8 or 10cm of the previous year's growth in March. The evergreen kinds need little, if any, pruning, but when desirable, light pruning should be carried out immediately after flowering.

†****'A.T. Johnson'** A vigorous and floriferous hybrid with rich blue flowers in spring and again in autumn. Leaves ovate, glossy green, grey-downy beneath. AM 1934.

americanus L. New Jersey tea. A small, very hardy shrub bearing dense panicles of dull white flowers in June and July. The leaves are said to have been used as a substitute for tea, especially during the American Civil War. E and C USA. I 1713.

†**arboreus Greene. Feltleaf ceanothus. A vigorous, large, spreading shrub or small tree with large, ovate leaves. Flowers deep vivid blue, fragrant, borne abundantly in large panicles in spring. **'Trewithen Blue'** An improved selection with large panicles of deep blue, slightly scented flowers. Originated at Trewithen Gardens, near Truro, home of one of the finest collections of trees and shrubs in Cornwall. ♀ 2002. AM 1967.

*'Autumnal Blue'** Possibly the hardiest evergreen hybrid ceanothus; bears abundant panicles of rich sky-blue flowers in late summer, autumn and often spring as well. Leaves broadly ovate, 3-veined, bright glossy green. ♀ 2002. AM 1930.

*'Blue Cushion'** Compact, with a low-spreading habit, good for groundcover. Bright blue flowers late spring to early summer.

*'Blue Jeans'** A vigorous small, spreading shrub of dense habit, with rigid shoots and dark green foliage. Clusters of amethyst-blue flowers are borne in mid-spring.

*'Blue Mound'** A dense, bushy, small to medium-sized shrub with glossy green, wavy-edged leaves and dense clusters of bright blue flowers produced in May and June and usually again in late summer and autumn. A seedling of *C. griseus* raised in our nurseries, it is a hybrid, possibly with *C. impressus*. ♀ 2002.

'Brilliant' See *C.* × *veitchianus*.

†***'Burkwoodii'** (*C.* 'Indigo' × *C. floribundus*) A medium-sized, rounded shrub of dense habit with oval, glossy green leaves. Flowers rich dark blue throughout summer and autumn. ♀ 2002. AM 1930.

†***'Cascade'** A lovely hybrid of the evergreen, spring-flowered group, bearing bright blue flowers in elongated, long-stalked clusters. ♀ 2002. AM 1946.

'Ceres' See *C.* × *pallidus* 'Ceres'.

'Charles Detriche' See *C.* × *delileanus* 'Charles Detriche'.

†*coeruleus* Lag. Azure ceanothus. A medium-sized shrub with semi-evergreen, ovate, dark green leaves and long panicles of sky-blue flowers in summer and autumn. Mexico to Guatemala. I 1818.

*'Concha'** (*C. impressus* × *C. papillosus* subsp. *roweanus*) A dense, medium-sized shrub with arching branches and narrow, dark green leaves. Clusters of deep blue flowers are profusely borne from red buds. ♀ 2002. FCC 1992. AM 1986.

†**crassifolius Torr. Hoaryleaf ceanothus. Medium-sized shrub with tomentose branches and opposite, thick, leathery, sharply toothed leaves. White flowers in spring.

†**cyaneus Eastw. San Diego ceanothus. A dense, bushy, medium-sized shrub. Bright green, shiny, ovate leaves and intense blue flowers, borne in long-stalked panicles, in early summer. I 1925. AM 1934.

*'Cynthia Postan'** (*C. griseus* var. *horizontalis* × *C. papillosus* var. *roweanus*) A medium-sized, spreading shrub with arching shoots; the glossy dark green leaves, to 4cm long, have impressed veins and crisped margins. Dense clusters of rich blue flowers open in late spring to early summer. Raised at Cambridge Botanic Garden from seed of *C. papillosus* var. *roweanus* collected by Lady Cynthia Postan from Tilden Regional Parks Botanic Garden, Berkeley, California in 1965.

*‘**Dark Star**’ (*C. impressus* × *C. papillosus* subsp. *roweanus*) An arching, medium-sized shrub bearing small, ovate leaves up to 8mm long with deeply impressed veins. Deep purplish-blue, honey-scented flowers are borne in clusters in early spring. ♀ 2002. AM 1992.

*‘**Delight**’ (*C. papillosus* × *C. rigidus*) A splendid hybrid, and one of the hardiest. Flowers rich blue, in long panicles in spring. AM 1933.

× *delileanus* Spach (*C. americanus* × *C. coeruleus*) (*C. arnouldii* Carrière) A small to medium-sized shrub producing its panicles of soft blue flowers throughout summer. Many of the popular deciduous hybrids are selected clones of this cross. ‘**Charles Détriché**’ A medium-sized shrub with flowers of rich dark blue during summer. ‘**Gloire de Plantières**’ A small shrub with panicles of deep blue flowers in summer. ‘**Gloire de Versailles**’ The most popular deciduous ceanothus. Large panicles of powder-blue flowers in summer and autumn. ♀ 2002. FCC 1872. ‘**Henri Desfossé**’ A hybrid resembling ‘Gloire de Versailles’, but with flowers a deeper almost violet-blue, summer. AM 1926. †‘**Indigo**’ True indigo-blue flowers in summer. AM 1902. ‘**Topaze**’ Light indigo-blue flowers in summer. ♀ 2002. AM 1961.

†**dentatus* Torr. & A. Gray. Cropleaf ceanothus. The true species is a low, spreading shrub with tiny, oblong, glandular leaves and clusters of bright blue flowers in May. I 1848. See also *C.* × *lobbianus* and *C.* × *veitchianus* which have been confused with this species.

†**‘**Dignity**’ A beautiful hybrid, somewhat similar to ‘Delight’, frequently flowering again in autumn.

†**divergens* Parry. Calistoga ceanothus. An attractive, semi-prostrate species with opposite, spine-toothed, bright green leaves, grey beneath. The rigid branches are smothered with racemose inflorescences of deep blue flowers in spring.

†**‘**Edinburgh**’ (‘Edinensis’) (*C. foliosus* × *C. griseus*) Rich blue flowers and olive-green foliage. An attractive plant. Originated at the Royal Botanic Garden, Edinburgh about 1934. ♀ 2002.

*fendleri A. Gray. A low, spring-flowering, spiny shrub with downy shoots; white or mauve-tinted flowers in terminal clusters. SW USA, Mexico. I 1893.

†**foliosus* Parry. Wavyleaf ceanothus. Forms a spreading shrub with small, glossy leaves and heads of rich blue flowers in spring.

‘**Gloire de Plantières**’ See *C.* × *delileanus* ‘Gloire de Plantières’.

‘**Gloire de Versailles**’ See *C.* × *delileanus* ‘Gloire de Versailles’.

†**gloriosus* J.T. Howell (*C. rigidus* var. *grandifolius* Torr.) Glory mat, Point Reyes ceanothus. A remarkable prostrate shrub bearing opposite, dark glossy green, toothed leaves and clusters of lavender-blue flowers in April and May. In the Sir Harold Hillier Gardens and Arboretum it has formed a flat carpet 4m across. ‘**Anchor Bay**’ A form of dense habit with glossy foliage and slightly deeper blue flowers. C 1976. ‘**Emily Brown**’ A spreading mound, to 90cm tall, with dark green foliage and deep lavender-blue flowers. var. *exaltatus* J.T. Howell. Glory bush, Navarro ceanothus. A more upright variety.

*griseus (Trel.) McMinn (*C. thyrsiflorus* var. *griseus* Trel.) Known in California as the Carmel ceanothus. A medium-sized to large shrub resembling *C. thyrsiflorus*, with broadly ovate, dark green leaves, grey beneath. The form cultivated in the British Isles has pale lilac-blue flowers in May. var. *horizontalis* McMinn. A low-growing form of spreading habit reaching about 1m tall. ‘**Silver Surprise**’ Leaves with an irregular creamy-white margin. A sport of ‘Yankee Point’. ‘**Yankee Point**’ A compact selection with particularly dark green leaves and deeper blue flowers.

‘**Henri Desfossé**’ See *C.* × *delileanus* ‘Henri Desfossé’.

*impressus Trel. Santa Barbara ceanothus. A small to medium-sized shrub with very distinct small leaves with deeply impressed veins. Flowers deep blue in spring. Among the hardiest of the evergreen sorts. FCC 1957. AM 1944. ‘**Puget Blue**’ See *C.* ‘Puget Blue’.

*incanus Torr. & A. Gray. Coast whitethorn. A spreading, medium-sized shrub with 3-veined, ovate, grey-green leaves and thorny, whitish branches. Slightly fragrant, creamy-white flowers in April and May.

‘**Indigo**’ See *C.* × *delileanus* ‘Indigo’.

†*integerrimus* Hook. & Arn. Deer bush. Large, semi-evergreen shrub. The 3-nerved leaves are dull sea-green. Flowers pale blue in large panicles in June. I 1853.

†**‘**Italian Skies**’ A vigorous, medium-sized, spreading shrub with small, dark green leaves and deep blue flowers in May. A seedling of *C. foliosus* raised in 1956 by E.B. Anderson. ♀ 2002.

†**jepsonii* Greene. Musk brush. A small, spreading shrub with opposite, dark green, holly-like, leathery leaves and rich blue flowers in spring.

†**× lobbianus* Hook. (*C. dentatus* × *C. griseus*) (*C. dentatus* hort.) A large shrub, excellent for covering a wall. Leaves small, oblong, 3-veined and edged with small teeth. Bright blue flowers are profusely borne in May and June. Discovered by William Lobb near Monterey in California about 1853 and introduced by him. ‘**Russellianus**’ This form is distinguished by its very glossy, small leaves and its long-stalked, bright blue flowerheads.

‘**Marie Simon**’ See *C.* × *pallidus* ‘Marie Simon’.

†**megacarpus* Nutt. Bigpod ceanothus. Medium-sized shrub with small, crowded, wedge-shaped leaves and panicles of white flowers in spring.

× mendocinensis McMinn (*C. thyrsiflorus* × *C. velutinus* var. *laevigatus*) Mendocino ceanothus. A small to medium-sized shrub with long, arching shoots and broad, ovate, dark glossy green, rather sticky leaves. Racemes of pale blue flowers are borne in spring. A naturally occurring hybrid.

× *pallidus* Lindl. (? *C.* × *delileanus* × *C. ovatus*) This very hardy, small to medium-sized garden hybrid of European origin has light blue flowers in summer. There are several cultivars. ‘**Ceres**’ Panicles of lilac-pink flowers during summer. ‘**Marie Simon**’ Pink flowers in panicles on the young growths in summer. ‘**Perle Rose**’ Bright rose-carmine; summer. ‘**Plenus**’ (*C.* ‘Albus Plenus’) An equally hardy, summer-flowering hybrid with double, white flowers, pink in bud.

†**papillosus* Torr. & A. Gray. A distinct species, a large shrub with comparatively long, narrow, viscid leaves. Gives a brilliant display of rich blue flowers in late spring. I 1850 by William Lobb. AM 1980. **subsp.**

roweanus (McMinn) Munz. A form with narrower leaves. It has been confused with the typical form.

'Perle Rose' See *C.* × *pallidus* 'Perle Rose'.

*'**Pin Cushion'** A low, spreading, compact shrub, to 90cm tall and 2m across, with arching shoots and oval, glossy green leaves, to 2.5cm long. Clusters of bright blue flowers open in late spring to early summer.

'Pinquet-Guindon' Lavender, suffused pink, a curious colour combination; summer. Raised by Lemoine.

*prostratus Benth. Known in California as squaw carpet, this creeping evergreen ceanothus makes a dense mat up to 1.5m wide with opposite, leathery, dark green, toothed leaves. Quantities of bright blue flowers in spring. AM 1935.

*'**Puget Blue'** (*C. impressus* 'Puget Blue') A dense, medium-sized shrub producing deep blue flowers over a long period during late spring and early summer. Raised at the University of Washington Arboretum, Seattle before 1945. Originally said to be a form of *C. impressus* but the longer, narrower leaves with glandular papillae above and on the margin indicate that it could be a hybrid with *C. papillosus*. ♀ 2002. AM 1971.

*pumilus Greene. Siskiyou mat. A creeping, alpine species. Leaves opposite, narrowly oblong, usually 3-toothed at the apex. Flowers pale blue in spring. Leaves narrower than those of *C. prostratus*.

†*purpureus Jeps. Hollyleaf ceanothus. A dwarf, spreading shrub with leathery, holly-like, opposite leaves and lavender-purple flower clusters in late spring.

†*rigidus Nutt. (*C. rigidus* var. *pallens* Sprague) Monterey ceanothus. A low, spreading, densely branched, compact shrub with distinctive, dark glossy green, leathery and toothed, wedge-shaped leaves; purple-blue flowers in spring. I 1847. **'Snowball'** A form with white flowers.

†*sorediatus Hook. & Arn. Jim brush. A small to medium-sized shrub with rigid branches and glandular-toothed, 3-veined leaves, glossy dark green above. Flowers varying from pale to dark blue in spring.

*'**Snow Flurries'** A medium-sized to large shrub with glossy green foliage and pure white flowers.

*'**Southmead'** A dense shrub of medium size with small, oblong leaves, glossy dark green above. Flowers rich blue in May and June. ♀ 2002. AM 1964.

†*spinosus Nutt. Greenbark ceanothus. A large shrub, only rarely spiny in cultivation. Leaves leathery, glossy green on both surfaces. Flowers rich blue in spring.

*thyrsiflorus Eschsch. Blue blossom. A large shrub, one of the hardiest evergreen species. Leaves broadly elliptic, dark green and 3-veined. Flowers bright blue in early summer. I 1837. AM 1935. **El Dorado** ('Perado') PBR A sport of Zanzibar found in 1996, differing in the broader green blotch on the leaves. **'Millerton Point'** A vigorous, medium-sized shrub with fresh green leaves; bears large clusters of white flowers in late spring and early summer. AM 1993. **var. repens** McMinn. Creeping blue blossom. A vigorous, mound-forming, hardy form, producing early in its life generous quantities of Cambridge blue flowers. It is variable in habit. ♀ 2002. **'Skylark'** A medium-sized shrub with glossy green leaves to 5cm long. Clusters of deep blue flowers are profusely borne over a long period during late spring and early summer. ♀ 2002. **Zanzibar** ('Pershore Zanzibar') PBR Leaves mainly pale yellow or yellow-green with a small central blotch of deep green. A sport found at Pershore College in 1982 making a medium-sized shrub with arching branches.

'Topaz' See *C.* × *delileanus* 'Topaz'.

*× **veitchianus** Hook. (*C. rigidus* × *C. thyrsiflorus*) (*C.* 'Brilliant', *C. dentatus floribundus* hort.) A large shrub with small, glossy green, wedge-shaped leaves and deep blue flowers in May and June. For hardiness, freedom of flowering and richness of colour, this shrub well merits its popularity. A natural hybrid discovered and introduced by William Lobb about 1853.

*velutinus **var. hookeri** Torr. & A. Gray (var. *laevigatus* (Hook.) Torr. & A. Gray) A widespreading shrub with large, glossy, somewhat viscid leaves. Flowers grey-white in dense panicles in autumn. Has been uninjured with us, even in the most severe winters. The typical variety is a small shrub with the leaves velvety beneath.

†*verrucosus Nutt. Wartystem ceanothus. This is a vigorous, medium-sized shrub with rigid, verrucose stems and crowded, leathery leaves which have a single vein and are sometimes notched at the apex. The flowers are white with darker centres and appear in spring. AM 1977.

'Yankee Point' See *C. griseus* 'Yankee Point'.

Cedrela sinensis See *Toona sinensis*.

CELTIS L.—Ulmaceae—The nettle trees or hackberries are elegant, fast-growing, medium-sized, deciduous trees allied to the elms. There are about 60 species in N temperate regions and the tropics.

australis L. Small to medium-sized tree with characteristic broad, lanceolate leaves, rough to the touch above. S Europe, N Africa, Asia Minor. C in England since the 16th century.

caucasica Willd. Caucasian nettle tree. Medium-sized tree with ovate, coarsely toothed leaves. E Bulgaria, W Asia, Himalaya. I 1885.

glabrata Planch. Small tree or large shrub that forms a rounded head. Distinct in its glabrous leaves which are markedly unequal at the base. W Asia. C 1870.

jessoensis Koidz. A small to medium-sized tree with narrowly, occasionally broadly, ovate leaves, obliquely rounded at the base, acuminate at the apex, and pale green or glaucous beneath. Japan, Korea. I 1892.

labilis C.K. Schneid. Small tree with long-acuminate leaves. China. I 1907 by Ernest Wilson.

laevigata Willd. (*C. mississippiensis* Bosc) Mississippi hackberry. A handsome, large tree with lanceolate, entire or few-toothed leaves. SE USA. C 1811.

occidentalis L. Hackberry. Medium-sized tree; mature specimens have rough, warted, corky bark and produce black fruits in profusion. North America. I 1656. **var. cordata** (Pers.) Willd. (*C. occidentalis* var. *crassifolia* (Lam.) A. Gray) A vigorous tree with arching stems bearing heart-shaped leaves, larger than those of the typical form.

pumila (Muhl.) Pursh. A large shrub of dense habit or a small tree with ovate leaves, downy when young. W USA. I 1876.

reticulata Torr. Small to medium-sized tree with ovate, conspicuously reticulate leaves, which may be entire or coarsely toothed in the upper half. Fruits orange-red. SW USA. I 1890.

sinensis Pers. A small tree with very striking polished foliage. E China. Korea, Japan. I 1910.

tournefortii Lam. A small hackberry with polished green leaves and red and yellow fruits. SE Europe. SW Asia. I 1738.

CEPHALANTHUS L.—**Rubiaceae**—A small genus of evergreen and deciduous trees and shrubs. About 6 species in North and Central America, E Asia and Africa.

occidentalis L. The button bush is an easily cultivated but rarely grown, medium-sized shrub with ovate leaves, 5–15cm long, and creamy-white flowers, produced during August in small, globular heads. E and S USA, Mexico, Cuba. I 1735. **'Angustifolius'** A form with lanceolate or narrow-elliptic leaves, often in whorls of 3.

†***CERATONIA** L.—**Leguminosae**—A genus of 2 species of evergreen trees native to SW Asia. The following requires a sheltered, sunny position.

siliqua L. Carob tree, St. John's bread. Supposedly the source of 'locusts and wild honey', this is a large shrub with dark green, pinnate leaves. Extensively planted in the Mediterranean region where it forms a picturesque round-headed tree. Mediterranean region (naturalised), SW Asia.

CERATOSTIGMA Bunge—**Plumbaginaceae**—A small genus of about 8 species found in E Asia and tropical E Africa. The cultivated species are small, ornamental shrubs often referred to as hardy plumbago, useful on account of their blue flowers produced over a long period in early autumn. Suitable for dry, well-drained soil, preferably in full sun.

griffithii C.B. Clarke. A beautiful species that produces deep blue flowers. The leaves often turn conspicuously red late in autumn and often persist well into the New Year. Himalaya, W China. In our nurseries it survived the hard winter of 1963.

†*minus* Prain (*C. polhillii* Bulley) A slender species resembling *C. willmottianum* but smaller in all its parts. Flowers slate-blue. W China.

willmottianum Stapf. Forms a subshrub of about 1m high, suitable either for a shrub or herbaceous border. The rich blue flowers appear in July and continue until autumn. The foliage is tinted red in the autumn. W China. I 1908 by Ernest Wilson. ♀ 2002. AM 1917. **Desert Skies** ('Palmgold') PBR A selection with bright yellow foliage contrasting effectively with blue flowers. It is unfortunately a plant of weak constitution.

Forest Blue ('Lice') PBR Selected by Peter Catt for its branching habit, making a compact, bushy plant which flowers more freely.

CERCIDIPHYLLUM Siebold & Zucc.—**Cercidiphyllaceae**—A genus of 2 species, deciduous trees, native to E Asia and grown for their autumn colour. The tiny red flowers emerge with the young leaves, males and females on separate plants. The affinities of this genus, which is the only one in the family, have been disputed. It has been thought to be related to either *Euptelea* or *Liriodendron*.

japonicum Siebold & Zucc. Katsura tree. An attractive tree with leaves similar to those of the Judas Tree (*Cercis siliquastrum*) but opposite and smaller. In the British Isles forms a small to medium-sized tree. In favourable seasons it assumes pale yellow or smoky-pink autumnal colouring, at the same time producing a sweetly pungent scent, like burnt sugar. May be grown in any deep, fertile soil. Japan, China. I 1881. ♀ 2002. **var. magnificum** See *C. magnificum*. **'Pendulum'** A rare and unusual form with long, pendent branches. Long cultivated in Japan where similar forms occur in the wild and may belong to *C. magnificum* or be hybrids between the two varieties. There may be more than one form in cultivation. ♀ 2002. **'Rotfuchs'** A form of erect habit with deep red-purple foliage. Raised by Karl Fuchs from seed collected in the Exotenwald, Weinheim, Germany in 1977. **var. sinense** Rehder & E.H. Wilson. Stated to be more tree-like in habit but differing very little from the typical form. China. I 1907 by Ernest Wilson.

magnificum (Nakai) Nakai (*C. japonicum* var. *magnificum* Nakai) A rare tree of medium size. Differs in its smoother bark and its larger, more cordate leaves with coarser serrations. Lovely yellow autumn tints. Japan. Recent introductions were made by Mikinori Ogisu from Honshu in 1995 and by Roy Lancaster from Mt Hakoda in 1998.

CERCIS L.—**Leguminosae**—A distinct genus of small trees with broad, rounded, heart-shaped leaves and beautiful pea flowers in spring. There are 6 or 7 species widely distributed in N temperate regions. The apparently simple leaves are derived from the fusion of 2 leaflets of an evenly pinnate leaf. They require full sun and good drainage.

canadensis L. North American redbud. A small tree with a broad, round head, unfortunately not very free-flowering in the British Isles. Flowers pale rose in May and June. It may be distinguished from *C. siliquastrum* by its thinner, brighter green leaves. SE Canada. E USA, NE Mexico. I 1730. **'Forest Pansy'** A splendid selection with deep reddish-purple foliage. Flowers pink but not conspicuous. ♀ 2002. **var. texensis** (S. Watson) Hopkins (*C. reniformis* S. Watson) Texas redbud. Differs from the typical form in being more shrubby and in having rich, glossy green leaves, blunt at the tip, and glabrous shoots. Oklahoma, Texas.

chinensis Bunge (*C. japonica* Planch.) A species with glossy green, heart-shaped leaves, up to 12.5cm across, and bright pink flowers in May. Not suitable for cold areas. China. **'Avondale'** A New Zealand selection, the deep purple buds densely crowding the shoots in spring and opening to deep pink flowers.

occidentalis A. Gray. Western redbud. A shrub, or occasionally a small tree up to 5m. Leaves rounded or notched at apex, rather leathery; rose-coloured flowers are produced in clusters on short stalks. SW USA.

racemosa Oliv. A small tree of upright habit. Flowers pink in drooping racemes, freely produced in May, but not on young trees. Flowered and fruited profusely in the Sir Harold Hillier Gardens and Arboretum in 1990, where it has reached 13.2m tall (2000). China. I 1907 by Ernest Wilson. AM 1927.

reniformis See *C. canadensis* var. *texensis*.

siliquastrum L. Judas tree. Clustered, rosy-lilac flowers wreathe the branches in May. The purple-tinted seed pods are often conspicuous from July onwards. E Mediterranean region. I 16th century. Legend has it that this is the tree on which Judas hanged himself. ♀ 2002. **'Alba'** Flowers white; foliage pale green. AM 1972. **'Bodnant'** A form with deep purple flowers. FCC 1944.

*CERCOCARPUS Kunth—**Rosaceae**—About 6 species of evergreen or semi-evergreen, small trees or large shrubs from W North America and Mexico, known for their hard, heavy wood which has given rise to the common name mountain mahogany. They have little ornamental value in Britain but are sometimes planted in their native lands.

betuloides Torr. & A. Gray (*C. betulifolius* Hook.) A large, graceful, lax shrub with small, obovate leaves. W USA, Mexico.

ledifolius Nutt. A small tree or large shrub with furrowed bark. Leaves are narrow, lanceolate, thick and leathery. W North America. I 1879.

montanus Raf. A medium-sized shrub of open habit, with obovate, prominently veined leaves, coarsely toothed at the apex. In common with other species its flowers are not beautiful but the fruits possess a slender, twisted, silky white tail, 5–10cm long. W North America. C 1913.

†*CESTRUM L.—**Solanaceae**—A large genus of some 200 species of shrubs and small trees, natives of Central and South America and the West Indies. The cultivated species are showy, medium-sized shrubs suitable for a warm wall or conservatory.

aurantiacum Lindl. Long, tubular flowers, deep orange-yellow in large, terminal panicles. Guatemala. I 1840. AM 1961.

elegans (Brogn.) Schltdl. (*C. purpureum* (Lindl.) Standl.) Clusters of bright red flowers over a long period. Mexico. I 1840. AM 1975.

'Newellii' A seedling resembling *C. elegans* in habit with large, orange-red flowers. Garden origin. ♀ 2002. FCC 1876. AM 1951.

parqui L'Hér. Willow-leaved jessamine. Yellowish-green flowers, fragrant at night, are borne in June and July. Hardy in sunny, sheltered places in the south and west of Britain. It grows well at Hyde Hall, Essex, where it is occasionally cut to the ground in cold winters but quickly recovers. Chile. I 1787. ♀ 2002. AM 1990.

purpureum See *C. elegans*.

CHAENOMELES L.—**Rosaceae**—Familiarly known as japonica and once listed under *Cydonia*, the ornamental quinces are among the most beautiful and easily cultivated of the early spring-flowering shrubs. The saucer-shaped flowers, in varying shades of red, orange and white, are followed by large, yellow quinces. They thrive in an open border or against a wall, even if shaded. When treated as wall shrubs, they may be cut back immediately after flowering. 3 species in E Asia.

× *californica* W.B. Clarke ex Weber (*C. cathayensis* × *C.* × *superba*) A group of small shrubs with stiff, erect, spiny branches, narrow leaves and pink or rosy-red flowers. Raised by Messrs. Clarke and Co of California.

'Enchantress' Flowers deep rose-pink, freely produced. One of the original cultivars. C 1938. AM 1943.

cathayensis (Hemsl.) C.K. Schneid. (*C. lagenaria* var. *wilsonii* Rehder) A large, sparsely branched shrub with formidable spines and long, narrow, finely toothed leaves. White flowers, flushed salmon-pink, appear in spring; very large fruits are occasionally 15cm or more long. C China. I about 1800.

japonica (Thunb.) Spach (*Cydonia japonica* (Thunb.) Pers., *Cydonia maulei* T. Moore) A small, spreading shrub with bright orange-flame flowers followed by rounded, yellow, fragrant fruits. Japan. I about 1869. FCC 1890. **var. *alpina*** Maxim. A dwarf form with ascending branchlets and procumbent stems. Flowers bright orange; fruits smaller.

lagenaria See *C. speciosa*. **var. *wilsonii*** See *C. cathayensis*.

sinensis See *Pseudocydonia sinensis*.

speciosa (Sweet) Nakai (*C. lagenaria* (Loisel.) Koidz., *Cydonia speciosa* Sweet) This is the well-known, early-flowering japonica, a much-branched, spreading shrub of medium size. Seedling-raised plants bear flowers of mixed colours, but predominantly red. China. I 1796 by Sir Joseph Banks. **'Apple Blossom'** See 'Moerloosei'. **'Atrococcinea'** Deep crimson. C 1909. **'Brilliant'** Clear scarlet, large. C 1939. **'Cardinalis'** Crimson-scarlet. C 1835. AM 1893. **'Contorta'** White, tinged pink, twisted branches. I from Japan about 1929. **'Eximia'** Deep brick-red. C 1880. **'Falconnet Charlet'** Attractive, salmon-pink, double. C 1915. **'Geisha Girl'** Deep apricot-peach, double. ♀ 2002. **'Kermesina Semiplena'** Scarlet, semi-double. C 1887. **'Knap Hill Radiance'** Bright red, large. AM 1948. **'Moerloosei'** ('Apple Blossom') Delicate pink and white, in thick clusters. C 1856. ♀ 2002. AM 1957. **'Nivalis'** Pure white, large. C 1881. **'Phylis Moore'** Almond-pink, semi-double; large clusters. C 1930. AM 1931. **'Red Ruffles'** Clear red, large, semi-double. C 1950. **'Rosea Plena'** Rose-pink, double. C 1878. **'Rubra Grandiflora'** Crimson, extra large. Low, spreading habit. C 1867. **'Sanguinea Plena'** Red, double. C 1880. **'Simonii'** Blood-red, flat, semi-double. Dwarf, spreading habit. An exceptionally beautiful cultivar. C 1882. AM 1907. **'Snow'** Pure white, large. C 1945. **'Spitfire'** Deep crimson-red, large. Erect habit. C 1949. **'Umbilicata'** Deep salmon-pink. I from Japan by P.F. von Siebold before 1847. AM 1983. **'Versicolor Lutescens'** Pale creamy-yellow, flushed pink, large. Low-growing. C 1865. **'Yukigotan'** Greenish-white, double.

× *superba* (Frahm) Rehder (*C. japonica* × *C. speciosa*) These hybrids are small to medium-sized shrubs of vigorous habit. **'Boule de Feu'** Orange-red. C 1913. **'Cameo'** Peach-pink, double. **'Crimson and Gold'** Deep crimson petals, golden anthers. C 1939. ♀ 2002. AM 1979. **'Elly Mossel'** Orange-red, large. Somewhat spreading habit. **'Ernst Finken'** Fiery red, abundant. Vigorous growth. C 1952. **'Etna'** (*C. speciosa* 'Simonii' × *C.* × *superba*) Rich vermilion. Small shrub. **'Fire Dance'** (*C. speciosa* 'Simonii' × *C.* × *superba*) Glowing signal-red. Spreading habit. C 1953. **'Hever Castle'** Shrimp-pink. Originated at Hever Castle, Kent before 1940. **'Incendie'** Orange-red of a distinct shade, semi-double. C 1912. **'Jet Trail'** Pure white, profuse. **'Knap Hill Scarlet'** Bright orange-scarlet, profusely borne throughout spring and early summer. C 1891. ♀ 2002. AM 1961. **'Lemon & Lime'** A small, spreading shrub with lemon and lime-coloured flowers opening from ivory-white buds followed by golden-yellow fruits. A sport found in the Surrey garden of Dr G.F. Crickmay before 1989. **'Nicoline'** ('Incendie' × 'Rowallane') Scarlet-red. Spreading habit. C 1954. ♀ 2002. **'Pink Lady'** Clear rose-pink, darker in bud, profuse and early. Spreading habit. C 1946. ♀ 2002. **'Red Chief'** Bright red, large, double. C 1953. **'Rowallane'** Blood-crimson, large. C 1920. ♀ 2002. **'Vermilion'** Brilliant vermilion. C 1913.

CHAMAEBATIARIA (Porter) Maxim.—**Rosaceae**—A monotypic genus related to *Sorbaria*.
millefolium (Torr.) Maxim. Desert sweet, Fern bush. A small shrub with erect, downy, aromatic stems, sticky when young, and elegant, finely divided leaves. White flowers in terminal panicles in summer. Requires a sunny position. W North America. I 1891.

CHAMAECYTISUS Link—**Leguminosae**—About 30 species of deciduous shrubs, natives of Europe and W Asia. They are closely related to *Cytisus*.
albus (Hacq.) Rothm. (*Cytisus albus* Hacq., *C. leucanthus* Waldst. & Kit.) A dwarf shrub with spreading, downy stems. White or cream flowers are borne in terminal heads in June and July. C and SE Europe. I 1806.
austriacus (L.) Link (*Cytisus autsriacus* L.) A valuable, late-flowering, dwarf shrub producing a succession of heads of bright yellow flowers from July to September. The foliage is covered with silky, adpressed hairs. C and SE Europe to C Russia. I 1741.
hirsutus (L.) Link (*Cytisus hirsutus* L.) An extremely variable, dwarf or small, hairy shrub of loose habit, producing long, leafy racemes of yellow or buff-stained flowers in May and June. S and C Europe. I during 18th century.
polytrichus (Bieb.) Rothm. (*Cytisus demissus* Boiss.) A prostrate shrub no more than 10cm high. A gem for a rock garden bearing exceptionally large, yellow flowers, with brown keels, in May. SE Europe. Found on Mount Olympus, Greece at about 2,300m.
purpureus (Scop.) Link (*Cytisus purpureus* Scop.) Purple broom. A pretty shrub about 45cm high. Lilac-purple flowers are produced in May. C and SE Europe. I 1792. AM 1980. **Albus Group** (*Cytisus purpureus* f. *albus* (Sweet) Zabel) A slightly dwarfer form with white flowers. C 1838. **'Atropurpureus'** ('Incarnatus') A superb, dwarf shrub with deep purple flowers. ♀ 2002.
ratisbonensis (Schaeff.) Rothm. (*Cytisus ratisbonensis* Schaeff., *C. biflorus* L'Hér.) An attractive, small shrub of loose habit somewhat resembling *C. hirsutus*. Yellow flowers, sometimes with a reddish stain, are arranged in long, arching, leafy racemes in May and June. C Europe to Caucasus, W Siberia. I about 1800.
supinus (L.) Link (*Cytisus supinus* L., *C. capitatus* Scop.) A compact shrub, about 0.6–1m, very variable in the wild. Large, yellow flowers are borne in terminal clusters from July onwards. C and S Europe. I 1755.

× *versicolor* (Dippel) T. Karlsson (*C. hirsutus* × *C. purpureus*) (*Cytisus* × *versicolor* Dippel) Dwarf habit. Flowers pale buff, shaded lilac-pink; May to June. Garden origin about 1850. **'Hillieri'** A low shrub with arching branches. The large flowers are yellow, flushed pale bronze, changing to buff-pink, and are borne in May and June. Raised in our nurseries in about 1933.

‡***CHAMAEDAPHNE** Moench (*Cassandra* D. Don)—**Ericaceae**—A monotypic genus related to *Leucothoe*.
calyculata (L.) Moench. Leatherleaf. A small, wiry shrub for a lime-free soil. Heath-like, white flowers are borne all along the arching branches in March and April. E North America, N & C Europe, N Asia. I 1748. **'Nana'** A very attractive, dwarf, compact form.

Chamaepericlymenum canadense See *Cornus canadensis*.

†***CHAMAEROPS** L.—**Palmae**—A monotypic genus, interesting in being a native European palm though many others are commonly planted. The only other palm found wild in Europe is *Phoenix theophrasti* W. Greuter, which is restricted to the coast of Crete.
excelsa See *Trachycarpus fortunei*.
humilis L. Dwarf fan palm. A miniature palm from SW Europe and N Africa where it covers mountain sides in coastal areas. Rarely exceeds 1.5m high but occasionally forms a short trunk. Large leaves are deeply palmately divided into very stiff segments. Hardy in mild localities. I 1731 by Philip Miller. ♀ 2002. **var. argentea** André (var. *cerifera* Becc.) A striking form with silvery blue foliage. Morocco. **'Vulcano'** A selection of compact habit with the leaves silvery beneath. Originates from the small island of Vulcano, north of Sicily.

Chaste tree See *Vitex agnus-castus*.
Checkerberry See *Gaultheria procumbens*.
Cherry See *Prunus*.
Cherry, Cornelian See *Cornus mas*.
Chestnut, golden See *Chrysolepis chrysophylla*.
Chestnut, horse See *Aesculus hippocastanum*.
Chestnut, Spanish See *Castanea sativa*.
Chestnut, sweet See *Castanea sativa*.
Chilean fire bush See *Embothrium coccineum*.

***CHILIOTRICHUM** Cass.—**Compositae**—2 species of evergreen shrubs related to *Olearia* and native to South America.
diffusum (J.R. Forst.) Kuntze (*C. amelloides* DC., *C. rosmarinifolium* Less.) A small shrub with linear leaves 2–5cm long, white-tomentose beneath, becoming brown. Conspicuous white daisy flowers in summer. A variable species found over a wide area in S South America. Some forms are hardier than others. I about 1926 by Harold Comber.

CHIMONANTHUS Lindl.—**Calycanthaceae**—The wintersweets consist of 6 species of deciduous and evergreen shrubs found in China, but only the following species is in general cultivation. It is a medium-sized, easily grown deciduous shrub, best planted against a sunny wall to ripen growth. Succeeds in any well-drained soil, and excellent on chalk. When treated as a wall shrub, long growths may be cut back immediately after flowering.

fragrans See *C. praecox*.

praecox (L.) Link (*C. fragrans* (Loisel.) Lindl., *Calycanthus praecox* L.) Sweetly scented, pale, waxy-yellow flowers, stained purple at the centre, appear on the leafless branches during winter but are not produced on young plants. China. I 1766. **'Grandiflorus'** A form with deeper yellow flowers conspicuously stained with red. ♀ 2002. FCC 1991. AM 1928. **'Luteus'** Distinguished by its rather large, unstained flowers, which are a uniform, clear waxy-yellow and open later than those of the typical form. ♀ 2002. FCC 1970. AM 1948.

China tree See *Koelreuteria paniculata*.
Chinquapin See *Castanea pumila*.
Chinquapin, coastal See *Castanea pumila* var. *ashei*.
Chinquapin, trailing See *Castanea alnifolia*.

CHIONANTHUS L.—**Oleaceae**—The fringe trees belong to a genus of about 100 species of wide distribution in the tropics with 2 hardy species, one from the New and one from the Old World. Both are easy to cultivate, producing an abundance of white flowers during June and July. These are conspicuous by their 4 or 5 narrow, strap-shaped petals. Flowers are not carried by young plants. Best in full sun.

retusus Lindl. Chinese fringe tree. Given a continental climate, this is one of the most handsome of large shrubs, bearing a profusion of snow-white flowers, followed by damson-like fruits. China, Korea. I 1845 by Robert Fortune. FCC 1885.

virginicus L. The North American fringe tree is ultimately a large shrub with larger and more noteworthy leaves than its Chinese counterpart; flowers white, slightly fragrant. E North America. I 1736. AM 1931.

× **CHITALPA** T.S. Elias & Wisura (*Catalpa* × *Chilopsis*)—**Bignoniaceae**—The following forms of this hybrid are known. They have proved most successful in cultivation in the SW USA; although they have been introduced to Britain, their performance here is uncertain, and they are likely to require a warm, sunny position in well-drained soil.

taschkentensis T.S. Elias & Wisura (*Catalpa bignonioides* × *Chilopsis linearis*) These hybrids were first raised at the Uzbek Academy of Sciences Botanical Garden in Tashkent, Uzbekistan in the 1960s and were introduced to the USA in 1977. They make small, deciduous trees with alternate, lance-shaped leaves to 20cm long, sometimes opposite or in whorls of 3. Flowers in terminal racemes of up to 40, pink to white, marked inside with purple and yellow. **'Morning Cloud'** A vigorous and upright form with very pale pink to white flowers. **'Pink Dawn'** A lower growing, spreading selection with pale pink flowers.

Chittamwood See *Cotinus obovatus*.
Chloranthus brachystachys See *Sarcandra glabra*.

*****CHOISYA** Kunth—**Rutaceae**—A small genus of 5 species of evergreen, aromatic shrubs, natives of Mexico and the SW USA.

arizonica See *C. dumosa* var. *arizonica*.

'Aztec Pearl' (*C. dumosa* var. *arizonica* × *C. ternata*) This remarkable hybrid, the first in the genus, was raised by our propagator Peter Moore in 1982. An elegant, small shrub with aromatic leaves attractively divided into 3–5 slender, bright green leaflets. Fragrant flowers, profusely borne in May and again in late summer, are like those of *C. ternata* but larger, pink-flushed in bud, and opening white, flushed pink on the petal backs. They are in clusters of 3–5 in the leaf axils. ♀ 2002. AM 1990.

dumosa (Torr.) A. Gray. A small, intricately branched, aromatic shrub with slender warty shoots and leaves clustered at the ends of the shoots; the leaves have up to 13 slender, glandular-warty leaflets. Flowers small, white, singly or in small clusters in the leaf axils. SW USA, N Mexico. **var.** *arizonica* (Standley) Benson (*C. arizonica* Standley) Flowers larger, to 2.5cm across, white flushed pink outside and slightly fragrant. Leaves with usually 5 leaflets. Mountains of S Arizona. **var.** *mollis* (Standley) Benson (*C. mollis* Standley) Similar to the typical form but with densely hairy shoots and leaves with 3–5 leaflets.

Goldfingers ('Limo') PBR (*C. dumosa* var. *arizonica* × *C. ternata* Sundance) This exciting new introduction was raised by our ex-propagator Peter Moore, now Assistant Manager and Propagator at Longstock Park Nursery, in 1996. It differs from *C. ternata* Sundance in its softer yellow foliage, and leaves with 3–5, narrower and shallowly toothed leaflets. Fragrant white flowers, slightly flushed with pink, open in late spring and often again in early autumn.

mollis See *C. dumosa* var. *mollis*.

ternata Kunth. Mexican orange blossom. A medium-sized shrub of rounded habit. The trifoliolate leaves are shining dark green, aromatic when crushed. White, sweetly scented flowers are borne in clusters of up to 6 from the leaf axils throughout late spring and early summer, usually flowering again in autumn. A useful shrub for sun or shade. SW Mexico. I 1825. ♀ 2002. FCC 1880. **Moonshine** ('Walcho') PBR A sport of *C. ternata* found in 1992 with broader leaflets and larger flowers. **Sundance** ('Lich') PBR A striking form with bright yellow young foliage. ♀ 2002. AM 1995 (for foliage).

Chokeberry See *Aronia*.

CHORDOSPARTIUM Cheeseman—**Leguminosae**—A monotypic genus related to *Carmichaelia*.

stevensonii Cheeseman. Weeping broom. A rare, medium-sized, broom-like, leafless shrub, bearing racemes of lavender-pink flowers in summer. In habit resembles a miniature weeping willow. New Zealand (South Island) where it is rare in the wild. The stems of young plants appear brown and lifeless for the first 3–4 years. I 1923. AM 1943.

Chosenia arbutifolia See *Salix arbutifolia*.
Christ's thorn See *Paliurus spina-christi*.
Christmas berry See *Heteromeles salicifolia*.

*****CHRYSOLEPIS** Hjelmq.—**Fagaceae**—A genus of 2 species of evergreens, closely related to *Castanea* and *Castanopsis*. Both are native to W North America.

chrysophylla (Hook.) Hjelmq. (*Castanopsis chrysophylla* (Hook.) DC.) Golden chestnut. A small to medium-sized tree or large shrub. Leaves leathery and pointed, dark green above, yellow beneath. Fruits produced in dense green, prickly clusters. Succeeds best in a well-drained, acid or neutral soil. W USA. I 1844. AM 1935. **'Obovata'** ('Obtusata') A distinct form with obtuse leaves 5cm or more long. Free-fruiting. A small tree in our Chandler's Ford nursery survived the severest winters without any ill effect, as have its descendants in the Sir Harold Hillier Gardens and Arboretum where one has reached 4m tall (1990).

vacciniifolia See *Quercus vacciniifolia*.

†***CINNAMOMUM** Schaeff.—**Lauraceae**—A genus of trees and shrubs mainly of economic importance. About 250 species natives of E and SE Asia to Australia. The following are suitable for the mildest areas only and have aromatic, 3-veined leaves. The cinnamon of commerce is obtained from the bark of *C. zeylanicum* Blume.

camphora (L.) Siebold. Camphor tree. A handsome foliage shrub, but too tender for any but the mildest localities. The wood yields the camphor of commerce. Tropical Asia and Malaya to China and Japan. I 1727.

daphnoides Siebold & Zucc. A distinct species, making a large shrub or small tree in mild areas, with leathery, obovate, 3-veined leaves, rounded at the tip, to 3cm long, and closely silvery-hairy beneath. S Japan.

glanduliferum (Wall.) Meissn. A rare, Chinese species with broadly ovate, leathery leaves, light green above, white beneath; aromatic when crushed.

japonicum Siebold ex Nees. An attractive, large, bushy shrub or small tree with reddish shoots and petioles. Leaves ovate-lanceolate, acuminate, glossy green above, glabrous and glaucous beneath. Hardy in a sheltered position here. Japan, Korea, China.

†**CIONURA** Griseb.—**Asclepiadaceae**—A monotypic genus related to *Periploca* and once included in *Marsdenia*, which now contains only tropical species. Easily grown in full sun in any well-drained soil.

erecta (L.) Griseb. (*Marsdenia erecta* (L.) R. Br.) An interesting, lax shrub, up to 2m, with attractively marbled, silvery-green, cordate-ovate leaves and cymes of fragrant, white flowers from May to July. Sap milky-white. Requires a warm border or wall. E Mediterranean region. C since the 16th century.

***CISTUS** L.—**Cistaceae**—The sun roses consist of about 20 species of usually small shrubs found in the wild from the Canary Islands throughout the Mediterranean region to the Caucasus. Numerous hybrids have originated both in the wild and in cultivation. They revel in full sun and are excellent for dry banks, rock gardens and similar positions. The flowers, though individually short-lived, are very freely produced mainly in June and July, and, unless otherwise stated, are white. Where no height is given, it may be assumed to be about 1m. Natives of S Europe and N Africa. Most *Cistus* will tolerate moderate frost, provided that they are given good drainage and are not fed, but they are susceptible to wind-rock if raised in peat compost. They will withstand maritime exposure and do well on chalk. Pinch back the young growth after flowering to encourage a compact habit. We are grateful for the assistance of Robert G. Page for assistance with the revision of this section.

†× *aguilarii* Pau (*C. ladanifer* × *C. populifolius*) A vigorous plant with bright green, wavy-edged leaves and very large flowers 8cm across. Will tolerate moderate pruning. Spain. **'Maculatus'** A most handsome plant, the flowers having a central ring of crimson blotches; leaves narrower. Will not tolerate pruning. ♀ 2002. AM 1936.

albanicus See *C. sintenisii*.

albidus L. A small, compact shrub with whitish-hoary leaves. Flowers pale rose-lilac with a yellow eye. SW Europe, N Africa. C 1640.

'Ann Baker' A seedling of *C.* × *dansereaui* 'Decumbens', the pollen parent is unknown. It makes a vigorous shrub of arching habit with broadly lanceolate, sessile leaves to 6cm or more. The neat, shallowly saucer-shaped white flowers, 7cm across, are blotched with deep red and stained yellow at the base of the petals. Raised by Eric Sammons in 1960, it is a useful late-flowering hybrid, continuing into August and even September.

'Anne Palmer' (*C. crispus* × *C. ladanifer* var. *sulcatus*) A small shrub with sticky shoots bearing long, white hairs and wavy-edged leaves. Flowers, to 7cm across, are soft pink. Raised by Captain Collingwood Ingram before 1960 and named after Lady Anne Palmer, now Lady Anne Berry, who gave her garden Rosemoor in N Devon to the Royal Horticultural Society in 1987. AM 1964. Cory Cup 1960.

× *argenteus* Dans. (*C.* × *canescens* × *C. laurifolius*) Triple hybrids of cultivated origin, represented by the following selections. **'Blushing Peggy Sammons'** A sport of 'Peggy Sammons' with deep magenta-pink flowers. **'Peggy Sammons'** A vigorous, small to medium-sized, lax shrub of erect habit, with grey-green, downy stems and leaves. Flowers are purple-pink with paler centres. Raised in 1955 by J.E. Sammons. ♀ 2002. **'Golden Treasure'** ('Nepond') A sport of 'Peggy Sammons' found in 1993 making an upright, small shrub with deep rose flowers. Sage-green leaves, irregularly margined golden-yellow in spring and summer, deepening late summer into autumn. ♀ 2002. **'Silver Pink'** An exceptionally hardy plant. Bears long clusters of flowers that are a lovely shade of peach-pink. Originated as a chance hybrid in our nurseries about 1910. AM 1919. The name is often misapplied to 'Grayswood Pink'. **'Stripey'** A sport from 'Peggy Sammons' with white petals irregularly striped with pink, found at Ventnor Botanic Garden.

atchleyi See *C. sintenisii*.

'Blanche' See *C. ladanifer* 'Blanche'.

× *bornetianus* Demoly (*C. albidus* × *C. laurifolius*) A vigorous hybrid, not known in the wild, named from the cultivar described below. It was raised by Eric Sammons in 1991 and found in his garden following his death in 1994. **'Jester'** A small shrub somewhat resembling 'Peggy Sammons' but more compact, with narrow, grey-green, slightly wavy-edged leaves and soft, rich pink flowers, the petals white at the base.

'Candy Stripe' A sport of 'Grayswood Pink' found in 1991. It resembles the parent but has the leaves broadly margined with creamy-yellow.

× **canescens** Sweet (*C. albidus* × *C. creticus*) A commonly cultivated fertile hybrid, making a small shrub with grey-green leaves and usually pink flowers. It is most often sold under the name of one of its parents. **'Albus'** A form with white flowers 5cm across.

'Chelsea Bonnet' (*C. libanotis* × *C. monspeliensis*) A small, upright shrub with narrow, glossy green leaves. Profuse pure white flowers with 5 notched petals and a yellow centre.

clusii Dunal. A dwarf, very hardy shrub with slender, aromatic, rosemary-like leaves to 2.5cm long, white beneath with recurved margins. Flowers white with a yellow centre, about 2.5cm across. SW Europe, North Africa. C 1826.

× **corbariensis** See *C.* × *hybridus*.

creticus L. (*C. villosus* L.) An extremely variable, small shrub with often shaggily hairy stems; flowers vary from purple to rose, with a yellow centre. Widely distributed in the E Mediterranean region. C 1650. **'Albus'** Flowers white.

× **crispatus** Dans. (*C. creticus* × *C. crispus*) A low-growing hybrid of cultivated origin, mainly grown in the following form. **'Warley Rose'** A compact dwarf shrub of spreading habit with grey-green foliage and profuse, bright deep pink flowers.

crispus L. A small, spreading shrub of dense habit with wavy-edged, 3-veined, grey-green leaves and rosy-pink flowers with crumpled petals. W Mediterranean region. I about 1656. See also *C.* × *pulverulentus*.

× **cyprius** Lam. (*C. ladanifer* × *C. laurifolius*) A hardy, vigorous hybrid about 2m high with glossy green, sticky leaves. Clusters of white flowers, 8cm wide, with crimson basal blotches. France, Spain, Morocco. ♥ 2002. AMT 1925. **'Albiflorus'** Flowers without blotches. **nothovar. ellipticus** Demoly. Includes hybrids between *C. ladanifer* var. *sulcatus* and *C. laurifolius*, of which 'Elma' is a selection. **'Elma'** (*C. ladanifer* var. *sulcatus* × *C. laurifolius*) Beautifully formed, extra large, pure white flowers contrast with deep green, polished, lanceolate leaves, glaucous beneath. Sturdy, bushy habit to 2m. ♥ 2002. AM 1949.

× **dansereaui** P. Silva (*C. inflatus* × *C. ladanifer*) (*C.* × *lusitanicus* Maund not Mill.) A vigorous, small, upright shrub with lance-shaped, dark green, sticky, wavy-edged leaves. Large, white flowers with or without crimson basal blotches. See also 'Jenkyn Place'. Portugal. **'Decumbens'** A low, spreading form, 1.2m or more across and 0.6m high. C 1835. ♥ 2002. **'Jenkyn Place'** A very floriferous form continuing to flower throughout summer. The original form described by Maund as *C.* × *lusitanicus*, redistributed in the 1980s as *C.* × *florentinus* from a plant at Jenkyn Place. C 1830. **'Portmeirion'** A floriferous cultivar, slightly lower growing than 'Jenkyn Place' with neat, unblotched, white flowers 6cm across. A form of unknown origin which has been grown as *C.* 'Elma'.

'Elma' See *C.* × *cyprius* 'Elma'.

× **florentinus** Lam. (*C. monspeliensis* × *C. salviifolius*) A floriferous, white-flowered, natural hybrid, seldom above 0.6m high. Common in the wild wherever the parents grow together, but very rare in cultivation. Most plants offered under this name are either × *Halimiocistus*

'Ingwersenii', or a widely grown complex hybrid cistus of uncertain parentage. S Europe, Algiers. AMT 1925. **'Fontfroide'** A recently introduced form of the true plant with greyish leaves. Very floriferous.

formosus See *Halimium lasianthum*.

× **glaucus** See *C.* × *ledon*.

Golden Treasure See *C.* × *argenteus* Golden Treasure.

'Gordon Cooper' (*C.* 'Ruby Cluster' × *C. salviifolius*) A very attractive hybrid raised by Bob Page in 1993. A vigorous, and floriferous shrub, the windmill-like flowers have white petals prominently blotched with deep red at the base. It was named after the curator of The Hollies in Leeds, who died in 1998.

'Grayswood Pink' A very hardy, low, spreading shrub with soft grey-green leaves complemented by profuse clear pink flowers to 5cm across. It is of uncertain status but is somewhat akin to *C. parviflorus*, under which name it is sometimes grown. ♥ 2002.

hirsutus See *C. inflatus*.

× **hybridus** Pourr. (*C.* × *corbariensis* Pourr.) (*C. populifolius* × *C. salviifolius*) One of the hardiest. Very neat, white flowers. There are several clones in cultivation. Some have shrimp-pink buds, but less neat flowers. France, Spain.

inflatus Pourr. ex Demoly (*C. hirsutus* Lam., *C. psilosepalus* auct. not Sweet) A dwarf, floriferous species with white flowers stained yellow at the base, conspicuous yellow stamens and recurved, apparently inflated sepals. Portugal, W Spain, W France. C 1634.

Jessamy Group A series of hybrids raised by Eric Sammons in the early 1980s, by crossing *C.* 'Little Gem' with *C. laurifolius*. He raised the fertile 'Little Gem' by backcrossing a seedling of *C.* × *dansereaui* 'Decumbens', possibly pollinated by *C. laurifolius*, several times with *C. inflatus*. They were referred to by Eric Sammons as the Triple Series and were named by Bob Page using Eric's initials, JES. The members of this group are vigorous, small, arching shrubs with profuse, blotched or unblotched flowers in midsummer. **'Jessamy Beauty'** Flowers white, the largest in this group, to 7cm across, with dark red blotches. **'Jessamy Bride'** Flowers cupped, white and unblotched, about 5cm across. **'Jessamy Charm'** Flowers white, about 6.5cm across, with neat, even red blotches.

†**ladanifer** L. Gum cistus. A tall, erect species with sticky, lance-shaped, dark green leaves. The solitary flowers, up to 10cm across, are white with a dark red basal stain; petals crumpled. Many plants sold under this name are the hybrid *C.* × *cyprius*. SW Europe and N Africa. C 1629. ♥ 2002. **'Albiflorus'** Flowers pure white. **'Blanche'** (*C.* 'Blanche') A selection from the plants originally called 'Paladin' which it resembles, but with unblotched flowers. FCC and Cory Cup 1976. AM 1967. **'Minstrel'** Very large white flowers, 10cm across, with deep maroon-red, half-moon-shaped, feathered blotches at the base. A seedling raised by Bob Page. **'Paladin'** (*C.* 'Paladin') A most attractive intermediate form between var. *ladanifer* and var. *sulcatus* raised by Capt. Collingwood Ingram. The name was applied by him to a batch of similar seedlings. Leaves glossy green, white beneath and large, white flowers blotched with maroon. AM 1946. **'Pat'** (*C.* 'Pat', *C.* 'Paladin Pat') A beautiful

selection of 'Paladin', more compact but with very large (13cm wide), white, maroon-blotched flowers. AM 1955. **var. *petiolatus*** Maire. A form with broader, paler green, very sticky and healthier foliage. Flowers white, with or without blotches. S Spain, North Africa. **var. *petiolatus* 'Bennett's White'** Pure white flowers to 9cm across, the petals with distinctive ruffled edges. **var. *sulcatus*** Demoly (*C. palhinhae* Ingram, *C. ladanifer* f. *latifolius* Daveau) This strikingly handsome and distinct form is proving remarkably hardy. Low-growing and compact, with glossy, sticky leaves, it has pure white flowers nearly 10cm across. Introduced from SW Portugal in 1939 by Capt. Collingwood Ingram and Senhor Palhinha. AM 1944. **var. *sulcatus* f. *bicolor*** Demoly. Petals boldly blotched with red-purple.

laurifolius L. The hardiest species, sometimes exceeding 2m in height. Leaves leathery, dark glaucous green; flowers white with yellow centre. SW Europe to Turkey and North Africa. I 1731. ♀ 2002.

× *laxus* Aiton (*C. psilosepalus* Sweet) (*C. inflatus* × *C. populifolius*) Intermediate in character between its parents with short-stalked, wavy-edged leaves. Flowers white with yellow centre. Spain, Portugal. C 1656. **'Snow White'** (*C. inflatus* × *C. populifolius* subsp. *major*) Profusely borne pure white flowers. Vigorous and very hardy. Can be pruned. Raised by J.E. Sammons in 1956.

× *ledon* Lam. (*C.* × *glaucus* Pourr.) (*C. laurifolius* × *C. monspeliensis*) An attractive, very hardy shrub, to 1.2m high, with narrow leaves and white flowers, 4–5cm across. France, Spain.

libanotis L. (*C. bourgaeanus* Coss.) A dwarf, lax shrub. Leaves linear, dark green, up to 5cm long; flowers small, white. SW Portugal, SW Spain. **'Major'** A vigorous form with larger flowers and leaves.

× *loretii* See *C.* × *stenophyllus*. This name is also frequently misapplied to both *C.* × *dansereaui* 'Decumbens' and *C.* × *dansereaui* 'Jenkyn Place'.

× *lusitanicus* See *C.* × *dansereaui*.

†*monspeliensis* L. Montpelier rock rose. A tall, frequently sprawling shrub distinguished by its linear-oblong, sticky and deeply veined leaves and pure white flowers, 2.5cm across with a yellow blotch inside. SW Europe, Canary Islands. C 1634.

†× *obtusifolius* Sweet (*C. inflatus* × *C. salviifolius*) A dwarf shrub of rounded habit with mid-green leaves. Flowers, 2.5–4cm across, are white with a yellow basal stain. France, Spain, Portugal. The name is often misapplied to a complex hybrid of uncertain parentage. C 1827. **'Thrive'** The most commonly grown form of this hybrid. Very free-flowering, profuse white flowers with a conspicuous centre of yellow stamens over a long period. Thrive is also a national charity that gives disabled and disadvantaged people the opportunity to improve their health, skills and quality of life through gardening.

'Paladin' See *C. ladanifer* 'Paladin'.

palhinhae See *C. ladanifer* var. *sulcatus*.

†*parviflorus* Lam. Shrub with small, grey-green leaves gritty to the touch, and small, clear pink flowers. Only suitable for the mildest localities. The name is misapplied to *C.* 'Grayswood Pink'. SE Italy to Cyprus and SW Turkey. C 1825.

'Pat' See *C. ladanifer* 'Pat'.

'Peggy Sammons' See *C.* × *argenteus* 'Peggy Sammons'.

× *platysepalus* Sweet (*C. monspeliensis* × *C. inflatus*) A vigorous hybrid with an attractive, arching habit, intermediate between its parents; covering itself with white flowers stained yellow at the base. Spain, Portugal.

populifolius L. An erect shrub with poplar-like leaves and white flowers stained yellow at the base. One of the hardiest. SW Europe. C 1634. AM 1930. **var. *lasiocalyx*** See subsp. *major*. **subsp. *major*** (Dunal) Heywood (var. *lasiocalyx* (Willk.) Warburg) This has larger, wavy-edged leaves, red buds and white flowers with silky-haired sepals and has proved one of the hardiest. S Spain, S Portugal, Morocco. ♀ 2002.

psilosepalus See *C. inflatus* and *C.* × *laxus*.

†× *pulverulentus* Pourr. (*C. albidus* × *C. crispus*) (*C. crispus* hort.) A dwarf shrub of spreading habit with sage-green, wavy leaves. The flowers are a vivid cerise. France, Spain. C 1929. **'Sunset'** Deep magenta-pink flowers. ♀ 2002. **'Warley Rose'** See *C.* × *crispatus* 'Warley Rose'.

†× *purpureus* Lam. (*C. creticus* × *C. ladanifer*) A small shrub with reddish stems and narrow, rather wavy-edged, dark green leaves. Large, rosy-crimson flowers with conspicuous, maroon basal blotches and a contrasting central cluster of yellow stamens. I 1790. ♀ 2002. AMT 1925. **'Alan Fradd'** A sport with large, white, maroon-blotched flowers over a long period. It often produces a proportion of partially reverted flowers with one or more petals having a wedge of the original rosy-crimson background colour. **'Betty Taudevin'** The commonly grown form described above. **f. *holorhodos*** Demoly. Flowers with unblotched petals, paler in the centre. Foliage grey. **f. *stictus*** Demoly. Flowers pale pink with prominent blotches. Foliage grey.

× *ralletii* Demoly (*C. creticus* × *C. symphytifolius*) A vigorous and strikingly beautiful hybrid of cultivated origin, reaching 2m tall. Large flowers of a rich, warm pink are borne in huge inflorescences of up to 30 or more flowers. Of uncertain hardiness.

× *rodiaei* Verg. (*C. albidus* × *C. ladanifer*) This hybrid was first found near Esterel in France in May 1932 by M.J. Rodie. The following forms were raised by Eric Sammons from a cross made in 1979. **'Jessabel'** Large, nearly red flowers, to 9cm across, blotched in the centre with deep maroon. Leaves dark green, slightly sticky, to 6cm long. **'Jessica'** Reddish-pink flowers to 8cm across, the blotches paler than those of 'Jessabel'. Leaves grey-felted. Flowers over a longer period than 'Jessabel'.

†× *salviifolius* L. A shrub of very variable habit with sage-like leaves; the white flowers have a yellow basal stain. S Europe. C 1548. **'Avalanche'** A form of low, spreading habit with arching branches, good for groundcover. **'Prostratus'** A prostrate, spreading form.

'Silver Pink' See *C.* × *argenteus* 'Silver Pink'.

sintenisii de Litardière (*C. albanicus* Heywood, *C. atchleyi* Warburg) A dwarf shrub of compact, dome-shaped habit with pale green leaves and small racemes of white flowers. Introduced by Sir Oscar Warburg from material collected by W. Ingwersen and S. Atchley in N Greece in 1929.

†× *skanbergii* Lojac. (*C. monspeliensis* × *C. parviflorus*) One of the most beautiful with clear pink flowers. Cyprus, Crete, Lampedusa. ♀ 2002.

'Snow Fire' (*C. populifolius* subsp. *major* × blotched *C. inflatus* hybrid) A vigorous hybrid raised by Eric Sammons in about 1979. Similar to *C.* × *laxus* 'Snow White' but each petal with a conspicuous large, maroon blotch at the base. ♀ 2002.

× *stenophyllus* Link (*C.* × *loretii* Rouy & Foucaud) (*C. ladanifer* × *C. monspeliensis*) A vigorous, upright shrub, to 2m or more, with narrow leaves and bearing large, white flowers with scarlet basal blotches. Occurs in the wild in France and Spain.

'Sunset' See *C.* × *pulverulentus* 'Sunset'.

†*symphytifolius* Lam. (*C. vaginatus* Aiton) A very distinct, tall plant, for mild localities, the large leaves with long, sticky hairs. Flowers vivid magenta with golden anthers. Canary Isles. I 1799.

× *verguinii* Coste & Soulié (*C. ladanifer* × *C. salviifolius*) A compact, small shrub bearing large, white flowers with maroon blotches. S France. **f. albiflorus** Demoly. Larger flowers without blotches. Has a stronger constitution than the blotched form. Attractive, arching habit.

villosus See *C. creticus*.

CITHAREXYLUM L.—**Verbenaceae**—A genus of about 70 species of trees and shrubs related to *Lantana* and natives of the S USA, the West Indies, Mexico and South America.

†*spicatum* Rusby. Evergreen shrub with purplish stems and opposite, leathery, dark glossy green, lanceolate leaves. Tiny, fragrant, lilac, verbena-like flowers are produced in drooping spikes during summer. Only suitable for the mildest gardens. Bolivia.

Citrange See × *Citroncirus webberi*.

†*× **CITROFORTUNELLA** J. Ingram & H.E. Moore—**Rutaceae**—(*Citrus* × *Fortunella*) The following is commonly grown in warm regions for its edible fruits and also in colder regions as an ornamental house or conservatory plant.

microcarpa (Bunge) Wijnands (× *C. mitis* (Blanco) J. Ingram & H. Moore) (*Citrus reticulata* × *Fortunella margarita*) Calamondin. Large shrub or small tree of upright habit with slightly spiny shoots and glossy dark green, aromatic leaves. Flowers pure white, sweetly fragrant, followed by long-persistent, rounded, orange-red fruits, about 4.5cm across, with a juicy acid flesh. ♀ 2002.

mitis See × *C. microcarpa*.

× **CITRONCIRUS** J. Ingram & H.E. Moore—**Rutaceae**—(*Citrus* × *Poncirus*) An intergeneric hybrid of which only the following is known. Another intergeneric hybrid, × *Citrofortunella*, contains citrus fruits such as the limequats and the calamondin.

webberi J. Ingram & H.E Moore (*Citrus sinensis* × *Poncirus trifoliata*) Citrange. A large, semi-evergreen, vigorous shrub with long spines. Leaves large, trifoliolate, with narrowly winged petioles; flowers, when produced, are large, up to 6cm across, white and fragrant. Fruits, the size of a golf ball or larger, are orange or yellow. Hardy in southern England. Garden origin 1897.

†*****CITRONELLA** D. Don—**Icacinaceae**—(*Villaresia* Ruiz & Pav.) About 20 species of evergreen trees and shrubs mainly natives of the tropics.

mucronata (Ruiz & Pav.) D. Don (*Villaresia mucronata* Ruiz & Pav.) A large, evergreen shrub attaining tree size in favoured areas of south-west England. Ovate, leathery, glossy green leaves are spine-toothed, rather holly-like, on young trees, becoming smooth and entire on older specimens. The small, fragrant, creamy-white flowers are borne in dense panicles in June. Black, egg-shaped fruits, 5–7.5cm long, are regularly produced, even on young plants. C Chile. I 1840.

†**CITRUS** L.—**Rutaceae**—A genus of about 15 species of partially armed, semi-evergreen trees or shrubs of great economic importance for their fruits. Originally native to SE Asia, they are now extensively cultivated in warm-temperate and subtropical regions of the world. A few may be grown against sunny walls in very warm, sheltered gardens, but most are best given conservatory treatment.

ichangensis Swingle. Ichang lemon. Small to medium-sized shrub with ovate-elliptic, tapered leaves and conspicuously winged petioles, the wings as broad as the leaf blades. Flowers, when produced, are white. Fruits lemon-shaped. This remarkably hardy shrub grew outside at the Sir Harold Hillier Gardens and Arboretum for nearly 30 years. It can fruit freely on a warm wall. C and SW China. I about 1907.

japonica See *Fortunella japonica*.

limon (L.) Burm. f. Lemon. A small tree with sharply spiny shoots and dark green, aromatic leaves, bronze when young. Flowers fragrant, white, red-purple on the outside of the lobes, opening from red buds and followed by the familiar fruits, to 12cm long. Origin uncertain, possibly NW India, long cultivated in warm regions of the world.

× *meyeri* Tan. Thought to be a hybrid between the lemon, *C. limon*, and the sweet orange, *C. sinensis*, the following is among the most popular in the genus as a conservatory or patio plant. **'Meyer'** (*C.* 'Meyer's Lemon') A medium-sized to large shrub with short-stalked, large, dark green leaves. Clusters of fragrant, white flowers, flushed purple-pink on the backs of the petals, open from deep purple-pink buds and are followed by freely produced, large, yellow fruits. ♀ 2002. AM 1982.

trifoliata See *Poncirus trifoliata*.

Cladothamnus pyroliflorus See *Elliottia pyroliflora*.

CLADRASTIS Raf.—**Leguminosae**—A small genus of some 5 species of trees with pinnate leaves, natives of E Asia with one species in the SE USA. The following are very ornamental but the flowers, similar to those of the false acacia (*Robinia pseudoacacia*), do not appear on young trees.

kentukea (Dum.-Cours.) Rudd (*C. lutea* (Michx. f.) K. Koch, *C. tinctoria* Raf.) Yellowwood, Virgilia. A very handsome, medium-sized tree producing, in June, long, drooping, wisteria-like panicles of fragrant, white flowers. The leaves turn clear yellow before falling. SE USA. I 1812. AM 1924. **'Perkins Pink'** (*C. lutea* 'Rosea') A form with pale pink flowers. Seedlings of this plant have also been distributed. Originally found in a garden near Boston.

lutea See *C. kentukea*. **'Rosea'** See *C. kentukea* 'Perkins Pink'.

sinensis Hemsl. The Chinese yellowwood is a remarkably beautiful and distinct, July-flowering tree of medium size. The compound leaves, which open very late in summer, are soft green above, glaucous beneath; the pink-tinged, white, slightly fragrant flowers are borne in large panicles. China. I 1901 by Ernest Wilson. AM 1923.

CLERODENDRUM L.—Verbenaceae—A large genus of some 400 species of trees, shrubs and climbers with opposite leaves and showy flowers found mainly in tropical regions. Apart from the hardy species, many are grown for greenhouse decoration.

bungei Steud. (*C. foetidum* Bunge) A remarkable semi-woody, suckering shrub of medium height. Dark coloured, erect stems bear large, heart-shaped leaves and large, terminal corymbs of rosy-red, fragrant flowers in August and September. China. I 1844 by Robert Fortune. AM 1926.

trichotomum Thunb. A strong-growing, large shrub valuable for autumn effects. White, very fragrant flowers, enclosed in maroon calyces, appear in August and September, and are followed by bright blue berries still with their colourful calyces. China, Japan. C 1880. FCC 1893. **var. *fargesii*** (Dode) Rehder. Differs in having smooth leaves and stems, and usually more free-fruiting. W China. I by the Abbé Farges in 1898. ♀ 2002. AM 1911. **var. *fargesii*** **'Carnival'** Leaves green and blue-green with a broad, irregular yellow margin when young, becoming blue-green and grey-green margined creamy-white.

‡**CLETHRA** L.—Clethraceae—About 60 species of deciduous and evergreen shrubs or small trees, natives of the S USA, Central and South America, SE Asia and Madeira. Closely related to the Ericaceae, they require lime-free soil and produce small, white, fragrant flowers in long racemes or panicles in July or August. Several have peeling bark.

acuminata Michx. White alder. A large shrub with racemes of fragrant, cream-coloured flowers; leaves yellow in autumn. E USA. I 1806.

alnifolia L. The sweet pepper bush usually does not much exceed 2m in height. Bears erect, terminal racemes of white or nearly white, sweetly scented flowers in August. E North America. I 1731. **'Hummingbird'** A compact, small shrub with glossy dark green leaves, yellow in autumn. Profuse flowers open early in short racemes. **'Paniculata'** A superior form with flowers in terminal panicles. I 1770. ♀ 2002. AM 1956. **'Pink Spires'** A vigorous, pink-flowered selection, similar to 'Rosea' but flowers not fading. Leaves glossy dark green. **'Rosea'** A lovely clone with pink-tinged buds and flowers, fading to white. Also distinct in its leaves, which carry a very healthy gloss. I 1906. **'Ruby Spice'** A sport of 'Pink Spires', found in a Connecticut nursery in 1992, with flowers a rich unfading pink in short racemes.

†**arborea* Aiton. A magnificent, large shrub or small tree with lily-of-the-valley-like flowers produced in large, terminal panicles. Only suitable for the mildest areas. Madeira. I 1784. AM 1912.

barbinervis Siebold & Zucc. (*C. canescens* hort.) A medium-sized, handsome species with long racemes of fragrant flowers. Leaves red and yellow in autumn. Japan, South Korea (Cheju do). I 1870. ♀ 2002. AM 1985.

delavayi Franch. A magnificent, large shrub requiring a sheltered site. The long, broad, many-flowered racemes of white, lily-of-the-valley-like flowers are horizontally disposed over the whole plant. Injured only by exceptionally severe frost. W China (Yunnan). I 1913. FCC 1927.

fargesii Franch. (*C. wilsonii* hort.) A very beautiful species, about 2.5m, producing pure white, fragrant flowers in panicles up to 25cm long in July. Rich yellow autumn colour. C China. I 1900 by Ernest Wilson. AM 1924.

†*monostachya* Rehder & E.H. Wilson. A large shrub with long, terminal racemes of pure white flowers. One of the most beautiful of late summer-flowering shrubs. C China. I 1903 by Ernest Wilson.

tomentosa Lam. A lovely medium-sized, summer-flowering shrub resembling *C. alnifolia*, but with greyer foliage and later flowers. SE USA. I 1731.

‡***CLEYERA** Thunb.—Theaceae—A small genus of about 18 species of evergreen trees and shrubs mostly from Mexico and Central America but with one species in E Asia. They are related to *Eurya*, but differ in their bisexual flowers and normally entire leaves.

fortunei See *C. japonica* 'Fortunei'.

japonica Thunb. (*C. ochnacea* DC., *Eurya ochnacea* (DC.) Szyszyl., *Ternstroemia japonica*) A slow-growing shrub, up to 3m, with a distinctive habit; the branches are rigidly spreading and densely leafy. Leaves entire, leathery, dark, shining green above often turning red in winter. Flowers small, white, very numerous in summer but not conspicuous. Japan, China, Korea, Taiwan. C 1870. **'Fortunei'** (*C. fortunei* Hook. f., *C. japonica* 'Tricolor', *Eurya fortunei*, *E. latifolia* 'Variegata') Dark, shining green leaves are marbled grey and have a cream margin that is flushed deep rose when young. A most attractive evergreen for favoured localities, where it forms a large shrub. I 1861 from Japan. AM 1963. **'Tricolor'** See 'Fortunei'.

ochnacea See *C. japonica*.

†**CLIANTHUS** Soland. ex Lindl.—Leguminosae—A genus of 2 species of shrubs. The following requires a hot, sunny position in well-drained soil and makes an excellent conservatory shrub. *C. formosus* G. Don is the spectacular Sturt's desert pea of Australia.

puniceus (G. Don) Lindl. (*C. puniceus* 'Red Cardinal') Parrot's bill, Lobster's claw. A vigorous, semi-evergreen, scandent shrub of medium size with pinnate leaves, 8–15cm long, composed of 11–25 oblong leaflets. The curious, claw-like flowers are brilliant red and carried in pendent racemes during early summer. When grown outside it succeeds best against a warm south- or west-facing wall. New Zealand (North Island) where it is now extremely rare. I 1831. ♀ 2002. AM 1938. **'Albus'** ('White Heron') Flowers white. ♀ 2002. AM 1938. **'Roseus'** ('Flamingo') Flowers deep rose-pink. **'White Heron'** See 'Albus'.

Cliffbush See *Jamesia americana*.

*CNEORUM L.—**Cneoraceae**—A genus of 3 species of evergreen shrubs found in the Mediterranean region, the Canary Islands and Cuba.

†*tricoccon* L. A dwarf shrub with small, yellow flowers and 3-sided, brownish-red fruits. Sunny, well-drained position. W Mediterranean region. C 1793.

Coffeeberry See *Rhamnus californica*.
Coffeeberry, hoary See *Rhamnus tomentella*.

†***COLEONEMA** Bartl. & H.L. Wendl.—**Rutaceae**—A small genus of 8 species of small, tender, evergreen shrubs, natives of South Africa.

album (Thunb.) Bartl. & H.L. Wendl. A dainty, small, white-flowered shrub for the mildest areas, with aromatic, heath-like foliage. An excellent pot plant.

COLLETIA Comm. ex Juss.—**Rhamnaceae**—A genus of 5 species of spiny shrubs native to S South America. The following are very distinct among cultivated plants being quite or almost leafless and bearing opposite, very prominent spines. The attractive, small, scented flowers are usually produced in summer and autumn.

armata See *C. hystrix*.
cruciata See *C. paradoxa*.
hystrix Clos (*C. armata* Miers) This robust shrub, attaining about 2.5m, has strong, stout, rounded spines. In late summer and autumn the branches are crowded with small, fragrant, pitcher-shaped, white flowers. Chile, N Argentina. I about 1882. AM 1973. **'Rosea'** (*C. armata* 'Rosea') Flowers pink in bud; a delightful shrub. AM 1972. FCC 1994.
infausta See *C. spinosissima*.
paradoxa (Spreng.) Escal. (*C. cruciata* Gillies & Hook., *C. bictoniensis* Lindl.) A remarkable, rather slow-growing shrub with branchlets transformed into formidable, flat, triangular spines. It is crowded with small, pitcher-shaped white flowers in late summer and autumn. E Argentina, Uruguay, S Brazil. I 1824. AM 1959.
†*spinosissima* J.F. Gmel. (*C. infausta* N.E. Br.) A spiny shrub of medium size, related to and resembling *C. hystrix*, but completely glabrous. Flowers white or greenish-white, from March to June. Ecuador to Argentina. I 1823.

†***COLQUHOUNIA** Wall.—**Labiatae**—A genus of about 3 species of evergreen subshrubs, native to the Himalaya and SE Asia.

coccinea Wall. A showy shrub with large, downy leaves and scarlet, tubular flowers in autumn. Requires a sunny site, preferably against a wall, where it will attain 2.5–3m. Occasionally cut back by sharp frost, but usually shoots again in early summer. Himalaya. I before 1850. AM 1981 to 'Jumbesi' introduced from Nepal by Tony Schilling (Schilling 2098). AM 1978. **var.** *vestita* (Prain) Wall. (*C. coccinea* var. *mollis* (Schltdl.) Prain) A form with slightly woollier leaves, and orange and yellow flowers. Nepal.

COLUTEA L.—**Leguminosae**—Some 25 species of deciduous shrubs with a distribution ranging from S Europe to N Africa and the W Himalaya. They are easily grown, with pinnate leaves and conspicuous, pea flowers throughout the summer, followed by distinctive, large, inflated seedpods giving the common name bladder sennas. If encroaching on other plants or getting out of hand they may be hard pruned in March.

aborescens L. A vigorous bush up to 4m high; flowers yellow. S Europe, Mediterranean region. Often naturalised on railway embankments. I in the 16th century. **'Bullata'** A slow-growing, dense form.
buhsei (Boiss.) Shap. A vigorous, large shrub of upright habit to 5m with blue-green, pinnate leaves with 7–9 leaflets. Large, golden-yellow pea flowers in racemes of 2–7 are borne over a long period from June to autumn followed by conspicuous bladders. N Iran and neighbouring former USSR. I by Roy Lancaster and Mrs Ala (A. and L. 7) from N Iran in 1972. AM 1987.
× *media* Willd. (*C. arborescens* × *C. orientalis*) A strong-growing, medium-sized shrub with greyish leaves and rich, bronze-yellow flowers. Garden origin. C 1809. **'Copper Beauty'** A selected form with blue-green leaves and freely borne, bright orange flowers, followed by profuse reddish pods.
multiflora Shap. ex Ali. An arching, medium-sized shrub with purplish-red shoots and deep blue-green leaves with 11–15 leaflets. Racemes of up to 14 crimson buds open to small, brick-red flowers, becoming orange, in July. I by Tony Schilling from Nepal (Schl. 2165).
orientalis Mill. Rounded shrub of medium size with attractive, glaucous leaves and copper-coloured flowers. Caucasian region. I 1710.

Comarostaphylis diversifolia See *Arctostaphylos diversifolia*.

‡**COMPTONIA** Aiton—**Myricaceae**—A genus of a single species related to, and once included under, *Myrica*.

peregrina (L.) Coult. Sweet fern. A small, suckering, aromatic shrub with downy stems and narrow, downy leaves, shaped somewhat like the fronds of a small spleenwort fern. Small, glistening, brown catkins appear in spring. Thrives in lime-free soil and, if given sufficient moisture, is best in full sun. E North America. I 1714.

CONVOLVULUS L.—**Convolvulaceae**—A large genus of more than 200 species of mainly trailing perennials but including several shrubby species. Widely distributed, mostly in temperate regions, with many species in the Mediterranean area.

†*cneorum L. A shrub with silvery, silky leaves and large, pale pink and white, funnel-shaped flowers in May. Full sun and well-drained position. Good for a rock garden. SE Europe. C 1640. ♛ 2002. AM 1977.

*COPROSMA J.R. Forst. & G. Forst.—**Rubiaceae**—About 90 species of usually dioecious, evergreen shrubs or small trees with opposite leaves, mainly found in New Zealand but also occurring in Tasmania, the East Indies, New Guinea and Chile. Flowers are small but many species have attractive fruits, only produced, however, if male and female plants are grown together. In addition to the following, there are 3 other species that are proving very hardy: *C. nitida* Hook. f., from SE Australia, introduced by Harold Comber, and *C. pseudocuneata* W.R.B. Oliv. and *C.*

tenuifolia Cheesm., both introduced from New Zealand to our nurseries by Sir Harold Hillier.

acerosa A. Cunn. One of the hardiest of the genus. A low, wiry shrub, with small, linear leaves; suitable for a rock garden. Female plants have translucent blue berries. New Zealand. *C. brunnea* (Kirk) Cockayne ex Cheesem. is similar, differing in having dark brown leaves and stems.

brunnea See under *C. acerosa*.

†× *cunninghamii* Hook. f. (*C. propinqua* × *C. robusta*) Medium-sized shrub, a natural hybrid, with linear-lanceolate, leathery leaves about 5cm long. Pale, translucent berries. New Zealand.

†× *kirkii* Cheesem. (*C. acerosa* × *C. repens*) This hybrid occurs in the wild where the parents meet. Hardier than *C. repens*. **'Prostrata'** A dense, low, widespreading shrub forming an intricately branched mound. Leaves oblong-lanceolate, to 2 × 0.5cm, glossy green. Excellent groundcover in mild areas. **'Variegata'** A form with white-margined leaves. AM 1982 (as a cool greenhouse plant).

†*lucida* J.R. Forst. & G. Forst. A medium-sized shrub with large, glossy, obovate leaves; fruits, when produced, are reddish-orange. New Zealand.

petriei Cheesem. Creeping shrub forming dense mats. Female plants bear conspicuous blue berries. Quite hardy in a rock garden. New Zealand. AM 1992 (for fruit).

propinqua A. Cunn. A wiry-stemmed shrub of medium size, related to *C. acerosa*. Has small, linear leaves and blue fruits. New Zealand.

Coral berry See *Symphoricarpos orbiculatus*.
Coral tree See *Erythrina crista-galli*.

†***CORDYLINE** Comm. ex R. Br. (*Dracaena* L. in part)—**Agavaceae**—A small genus of about 15 species of evergreen trees and shrubs native to New Zealand, Australia, SE Asia and the Pacific Islands.

australis (G. Forst.) Hook. f. (*Dracaena australis* Hook. f.) The cabbage tree of New Zealand, this plant is a conspicuous feature of many gardens in south-west England. A small tree, usually forming a single trunk and bearing several stout, ascending branches. Each branch is crowned by a large, dense mass of long, sword-like leaves. Small, creamy-white and fragrant flowers are produced in large, terminal panicles in early summer. I 1823. ♀ 2002. AM 1953. **'Albertii'** A form with matt-green leaves that have red midribs, cream stripes and pink margins. ♀ 2002. **'Coffee Cream'** Coffee-coloured foliage. **'Pink Stripe'** Leaves striped with pink and green. **'Purple Tower'** Foliage deep plum-purple. **'Purpurea'** ('Atropurpurea') A form with purple leaves. **'Red Star'** Bronzy-red foliage. **'Sundance'** A small tree bearing yellow leaves with midribs and bases attractively flushed deep pink. ♀ 2002. **'Torbay Dazzler'** A small form with creamy-white-margined leaves. ♀ 2002. **'Torbay Red'** A striking form with deep burgundy-red foliage. ♀ 2002.

indivisa (G. Forst.) Steud. (*Dracaena indivisa* G. Forst.) A tender species differing from *C. australis* in its normally unbranched stem and dense head of much broader leaves. New Zealand. I about 1850. FCC 1860.

CORIARIA L.—**Coriariaceae**—An interesting, small genus of some 8 species of shrubs and herbs with angled branchlets characterised by the frond-like arrangement of their leaves, and the persistence of their attractive flower petals which become thick and fleshy, enclosing the seeds. At least some parts may be poisonous. Widely distributed.

japonica A. Gray. A pleasing small, low-growing shrub, the arching stems making good groundcover. The red fruits are most conspicuous and the autumn foliage is attractively tinted. Japan. I before 1893. AM 1908.

microphylla Poir. (*C. thymifolia* Humb.) A dwarf, suckering, groundcovering shrub throwing out graceful, frond-like stems with pinnate leaves, the whole creating dense, fern-like clumps. The insignificant flowers are followed in late summer by racemes of tiny, blackcurrant-like fruits. Mexico to Peru.

myrtifolia L. A graceful shrub, to 1.5m, with glistening, black fruits. Both leaves and fruits are poisonous. Mediterranean region. I 1629.

†*nepalensis* Wall. A small to medium-sized, spreading shrub with black-purple fruits. Foliage attractively tinted in autumn. Himalaya. Upper Burma. *C. sinica* Maxim., a hardier relative of this species, was introduced from China in 1907 by Ernest Wilson.

sarmentosa G. Forst. Described as a subshrub in the wild, but proving herbaceous in cultivation, this species forms thickets of stout, quadrangular, arching shoots, spreading by underground stems. Glossy green, 3-veined leaves, to 6.5cm long, are borne on very short red stalks, the leaf veins often red towards the base as well. Flowers in long axillary racemes in spring. Continues to flower on young shoots as the glossy black fruits ripen in summer. I to the Sir Harold Hillier Gardens and Arboretum from a collection by Roy Lancaster. New Zealand.

sinica See under *C. napalensis*.

terminalis Hemsl. A small, attractive subshrub. The frond-like leaves give rich autumn tints. Conspicuous black fruits. Sikkim, Tibet, China. I 1897. AM 1931. **var. fructurubro** Hemsl. A form with very effective, translucent, currant-red fruits. There seems no record of the origin of this attractive form, which links the black-fruited Chinese type with the yellow-fruited Sikkim form. **var. xanthocarpa** Rehder. Translucent, yellow fruits. Sikkim, E Nepal. FCC 1970. AM 1904.

thymifolia See *C. microphylla*.

Corkwood See *Leitneria floribunda*.
Cornel See *Cornus*.

CORNUS L.—**Cornaceae**—The dogwoods or cornels range from creeping shrubs to trees, the majority being 2–3m high, and comprise some 50 species widely distributed, mainly in temperate regions. They are ornamental in diverse ways, and mostly of easy cultivation. All have opposite leaves, except *C. alternifolia* and *C. controversa*. Those grown for their attractive coloured stems should be hard pruned every other year in March.

   The genus is sometimes split into several genera (here regarded as synonyms of *Cornus*) in which case *Cornus* L. *sensu stricto* is regarded as containing (of the species listed here) only *C. mas*, *C. officinalis*, and *C. chinensis*. The other genera involved are: *Swida* Opiz (*Thelycrania*

(Dumort.) Fourr.), *Chamaepericlymenum* Hill and *Benthamidia* Spach (*Benthamia* Lindl., *Cynoxylon* Raf., *Dendrobenthamidia* Hutch.).

alba L. (*Swida alba* (L.) Opiz) Red-barked dogwood. This well-known species, succeeding in wet or dry soils, forms a thicket of stems up to 3m high; the young branches are rich red in winter. Leaves colour well in autumn. Fruits white or tinged blue. Siberia to Manchuria, North Korea. I 1741. **'Atrosanguinea'** See 'Sibirica'. **'Aurea'** A charming form with leaves suffused soft yellow. ♀ 2002. **'Bud's Yellow'** See *C. stolonifera* 'Bud's Yellow'. **'Elegantissima'** Leaves broadly margined and mottled white. C 1900. ♀ 2002. **'Gouchaultii'** Similar to 'Spaethii' with which it is often confused but the leaves duller and with a pinkish tinge. C 1888. **'Hessei'** (*C. hessei* Koehne) A remarkable and rare, dwarf shrub of dense, spreading habit, with crowded, narrow, purple-tinged leaves which turn deep purple in autumn as the white fruits ripen. Flowers are profusely borne in dense heads up to 4cm across; purple-tinged in bud, opening creamy-white. Raised in Germany by Hesse. See also *C. sanguinea* 'Compressa'. **Ivory Halo** ('Bailhalo') PBR A compact selection from Bailey Nurseries, Minnesota. Leaves margined with creamy-white, young shoots red in winter. C 1995. **'Kesselringii'** Stems almost black-purple. Very striking. C 1907. **'Siberian Pearls'** A form with profuse white berries becoming tinged with blue. **'Sibirica'** ('Atrosanguinea', 'Westonbirt') A less robust form with brilliant crimson winter shoots. There is very little of this plant now at Westonbirt Arboretum, Gloucestershire. C 1838. ♀ 2002. AM 1961. **'Sibirica Variegata'** A medium-sized shrub with leaves with a broad, creamy-white margin turning interesting shades in autumn. The winter shoots are deep red. It is similar to 'Elegantissima' but not as vigorous and therefore useful in a smaller garden. **'Spaethii'** A superb form with conspicuously golden-variegated leaves. C 1884. ♀ 2002. FCC 1889. **'Variegata'** Leaves greyish-green with an irregular, creamy-white margin. **'Westonbirt'** See 'Sibirica'.

alternifolia L. f. (*Swida alternifolia* (L. f.) Small) Pagoda dogwood. A large shrub, occasionally a small tree, with horizontally spreading branches. Leaves alternate, sometimes giving rich autumn tints. E North America. I 1760. **'Argentea'** ('Variegata') One of the very best silver-variegated shrubs, forming a dense bush of 2.5–3m. Leaves small with a regular, creamy-white margin. C 1900. ♀ 2002. FCC 1974.

amomum Mill. (*Swida amomum* (Mill.) Small) Medium-sized shrub, notable for its rich blue fruits and for its purple winter shoots. E North America. I 1683. AM 1968. **'Blue Cloud'** A striking form with metallic-blue fruits, profusely borne and turning whitish as they age. Good foliage colour in autumn and stem colour in winter. The name was suggested by Sir Harold Hillier when, in the early 1980s, accompanied by P.C. de Jong and H.J. Ilsink, they encountered this plant in fruit in the Sir Harold Hillier Gardens and Arboretum. **'Cinderella'** Leaves with a broad, irregular creamy margin. **subsp. obliqua** (Raf.) J.S. Wilson Raf. (*C. amomum* Raf., *C. purpusii* Koehne) Very similar to *C. amomum* but

usually more loosely branched; the berries are blue or occasionally white. North America. I 1888.

'Ascona' (*C. florida* × *C. nuttallii*) A widespreading, large shrub with purple shoots. Flowerheads freely borne when young, 7.5cm across with 4 pointed, white bracts. The leaves colour well in autumn. C 1959.

asperifolia Michx. In its typical form this large shrub is found in the SE USA, mainly in the coastal plain. It reaches 5m tall and has pale blue fruits. Mainly represented in gardens by the following form. **var. drummondii** (C.A. Mey.) Coult. & W.H. Evans (*C. asperifolia* hort., *C. drummondii* C.A. Mey.) A large shrub or small tree with red-brown twigs. Leaves ovate, slender-pointed, downy on both sides and rough to the touch; fruits white. E and C USA. C 1836.

baileyi See *C. stolonifera*.

bretschneideri L. Henry. A medium-sized shrub which usually has reddish shoots and ovate leaves. Flowers creamy-white in cymes, followed by bluish-black fruits. N China. I about 1800.

‡**canadensis** L. (*Chamaepericlymenum canadense* (L.) Aschers. & Graebn.) Creeping dogwood or bunchberry is not strictly a shrub, the 15cm shoots being renewed from ground level annually. It forms attractive carpets in summer starred with white flowers, followed by tight heads of vivid red fruits. Does best in sandy peat or leaf-mould. North America. I 1774. ♀ 2002. AM 1937.

candidissima See *C. racemosa*.

†*capitata Wall. (Benthamidia capitata (Wall.) Hara, Benthamia fragifera Lindl.) In the mildest districts this beautiful species makes a small tree. Flowerheads, surrounded by attractive, sulphur-yellow bracts in June and July, are followed in October by large, strawberry-like fruits. Himalaya, W and C China. I 1825. AM 1974 (for fruit), AM 1922 (for flower).

†*chinensis Wangerin (KW 19300) A large shrub or small tree, not to be confused with *C. kousa* var. *chinensis*, with green young stems and large, conspicuously veined leaves. Yellow flowers are produced in large, sessile clusters on the naked branches in late winter. Collected by Kingdon-Ward in N Assam in 1950. The species also occurs in W China.

controversa Hemsl. (*Swida controversa* (Hemsl.) Soják) A magnificent tree-like species with alternate leaves. The sweeping, tabulated branches are clothed during May with broad clusters of cream-coloured flowers. In autumn, small, black fruits are produced and, at the same time, the foliage often turns rich purple-red. Japan, China, Taiwan. I before 1880. AM 1984. **'Frans Type'** ('Variegata Frans Type') Leaves grey-green with a very narrow, sometimes barely noticeable, white margin. Occasionally produces sports very similar to 'Variegata'. Said to have originated in N France and probably a sport of 'Variegata'. **'Pagoda'** A bushy form of spreading habit, branching from the base. The particularly large fruits ripen early on red stalks. **'Variegata'** A very ornamental, small tree, retaining the horizontal branching, but slower-growing and with striking silver-margined leaves. C 1890. ♀ 2002.

drummondii See *C. asperifolia* var. *drummondii*.

'Eddie's White Wonder' (*C. florida* × *C. nuttallii*) A superb, hardy, large shrub or small tree of compact, upright habit producing large, white flowerheads in spring. Leaves colouring brilliantly in autumn. Highly praised by its American raisers, this splendid plant has proved itself to be a first-rate ornamental in Britain. Its hybrid nature is clearly shown by the bracts, which only partially enclose the flower buds in winter. ♀ 2002. FCC 1977. AM and Cory Cup 1972.

florida L. (*Benthamidia florida* Spach) The beautiful, North American flowering dogwood. A large shrub or small, bushy tree. Flower buds enclosed by bracts during winter. When they open in May, each flowerhead has 4 conspicuous, white, petal-like bracts. Foliage richly coloured in autumn. Not successful on poor, shallow, chalk soils. Recently many plants have been killed in the eastern USA by anthracnose, caused by the fungus *Discula destructiva*. A non-virulent form of this has also been found on plants in Britain. E USA. C 1730. AM 1951. **'Apple Blossom'** A cultivar of American origin. Flower bracts apple-blossom-pink. **'Cherokee Brave'** Vigorous with deep pink bracts, white at the base. Large, rich green leaves, burgundy-red when young. Considered an improvement on 'Cherokee Chief'. **'Cherokee Chief'** An American selection with bracts of beautiful, deep rose-red. C 1958. ♀ 2002. **'Cherokee Daybreak'** Leaves grey-green with an irregular margin which is yellow-green at first, becoming white flushed with pink, turning pink to red in autumn. Bracts white. **'Cherokee Princess'** Large, white bracts, profusely borne. **'Cherokee Sunset'** Leaves pink when young, developing a broad, irregular yellow margin and turning pink to red and purple in autumn. Bracts red. **'Cloud Nine'** Large, showy white bracts; free-flowering even when young. C 1962. **'First Lady'** Considered by many to be an improvement on 'Rainbow', this plant has leaves that are variegated with yellow. C 1969. **'Hohmann's Golden'** Similar to 'Rainbow' but of more spreading habit. **'Pendula'** An unusual form with pendent branches making a small shrub. C 1880. **'Rainbow'** A form of dense, upright habit. Deep yellow-margined leaves turn to deep red-purple, margined scarlet, in autumn. Bracts large, white. C 1967. **'Red Giant'** Large, deep pink bracts tipped with white. Young foliage flushed bronze. C 1981. **Rubra Group** (f. *rubra* (Weston) Schelle) This name covers all forms in which the bracts are pink to red. Hillier's plant is a beautiful form with rosy-pink bracts; young leaves reddish. C 1889. FCC 1927. **'Spring Song'** An American cultivar with bright, deep rose-red bracts. C 1962. **'Stoke's Pink'** A vigorous form with clear pale pink bracts. Selected in Louisiana, USA. **'Tricolor'** See 'Welchii'. **subsp. urbiniana** (Rose) Rickett. Bracts white, remaining joined at the tip. NE Mexico. **'Welchii'** ('Tricolor') Leaves green with an irregular, creamy-white margin, flushed rose, turning bronze-purple, edged rosy-red, in autumn. A superb but slow-growing, variegated shrub. **'White Cloud'** An American selection with bronzed foliage, noted for its freedom of flowering and the whiteness of its large floral bracts. C 1946.

foemina Mill. (*C. stricta* Lam.) Swamp dogwood. A large shrub, sometimes tree-like, closely related to *C. racemosa* but with rounded flower clusters. Leaves ovate to lanceolate, taper-pointed and short stalked, dark green above, paler beneath. Fruits pale blue. E USA.

glabrata Benth. (*Swida glabrata* (Benth.) A. Heller) Brown dogwood. A large shrub of dense habit. Leaves lanceolate, glossy green on both sides. Fruits white or tinged blue. W North America. I 1894.

hemsleyi C.K. Schneid & Wangerin (*Swida hemsleyi* (C.K. Schneid & Wangerin) Soják) A large, vigorous shrub with reddish shoots and leaves greyish-downy beneath; fruits blue-black. Distinct in the dark brown hairs on the young shoots and leaves. China. I 1908.

hessei See *C. alba* 'Hessei'.

kousa Hance (*Benthamia japonica* Siebold & Zucc., *Benthamidia japonica* (Siebold & Zucc.) Hara) A large, elegant shrub. Numerous flowers with conspicuous, white bracts are poised on slender, erect stalks, covering the spreading branches in June. Fruits strawberry-like. There are conspicuous tufts of dark-coloured down in the axils of the leaf veins beneath. Rich bronze and crimson autumn colour. Not recommended for poor, shallow, chalk soils. Japan, Korea. I 1875. FCC 1892. AM 1958. **'China Girl'** Vigorous with large-bracted flowerheads profusely borne even on young plants. C 1978. **var. chinensis** Osborn. A taller, more open and equally beautiful geographical form. Leaves slightly larger and normally without tufts of down beneath. China. I 1907. ♀ 2002. FCC 1924. AM 1975 (for foliage). AM 1956. **'Gold Star'** Leaves with a large, central blotch of golden-yellow. In autumn the centre turns red, the margin purple. I from Japan in 1977. **'Satomi'** A Japanese selection with deep pink bracts. The leaves turn deep purple-red in autumn. C 1986. ♀ 2002. FCC 1991. **'Snowboy'** Leaves grey-green with a broad white margin. Japanese origin before 1977.

macrophylla Wall. (*Swida macrophylla* (Wall.) Soják) A small tree or tall shrub with large, glossy green leaves, making a splendid specimen. The flowers are creamy-white and borne in heads 10–15cm across, in July and August. Fruits blue-black. Himalaya, China, Japan. I 1827. AM 1899.

mas L. Cornelian cherry. A large shrub or small, densely branched tree, producing an abundance of small, yellow flowers on the naked twigs in February. Fruits bright red, cherry-like and edible; leaves reddish-purple in autumn. C and S Europe. Long cultivated. AM 1929. **'Aurea'** A large shrub; leaves suffused yellow. C 1895. **'Aureoelegantissima'** ('Tricolor') A slow-growing, medium-sized bush, best shaded from strong sun. Leaves variegated yellow and flushed pink. Originated about 1869. FCC 1872. **'Golden Glory'** A vigorous, upright form with dense clusters of bright yellow flowers and large red fruits. C 1970. ♀ 2002. **'Hillier's Upright'** A form of broadly upright habit raised in our nurseries before 1974. **'Macrocarpa'** A form with larger fruits. **'Nana'** See *C. pumila*. **'Tricolor'** See 'Aurea Elegantissima'. **'Variegata'** Leaves conspicuously white-margined; free fruiting. An outstanding, variegated shrub or small tree. C 1838. ♀ 2002. AM 1981.

'Norman Hadden' (*C. capitata* × *C. kousa*) A small, spreading tree similar to 'Porlock'. A seedling that arose in the garden of Norman Hadden near Porlock, Somerset, in the late 1960s, and was later moved to Knightshayes Court, Devon, where the original plant still grows. See also *C.* 'Porlock'. ♀ 2002. AM 1974 (for flower).

nuttallii Audubon (*Benthamidia nuttallii* (Audubon) Moldenke) Mountain dogwood. A noble, medium-sized tree from W North America. Flowers appear in May, often a few expanding in autumn. The heads usually have 6 large, white floral bracts sometimes becoming flushed pink. The flowerheads are not enclosed by bracts during the winter. Foliage turns yellow, occasionally red in autumn. Not recommended for poor, shallow chalk soils. A specimen reached 13m in the Sir Harold Hillier Gardens and Arboretum (1990). Many plants in Britain have proved to be the hybrid *C. florida* × *C. nuttallii*. Like *C. florida*, it is susceptible to anthracnose. I 1835. FCC 1920. AM 1971. **'Colrigo Giant'** A vigorous form of American origin. Upright habit with very large flowerheads up to 15cm across. Found in the Columbia River Gorge after which it is named. **'Eddiei'** See under 'Gold Spot'. **'Gold Spot'** An unusual form, the leaves splashed, spotted and mottled yellow. 'Eddiei' is perhaps the same; it sometimes produces many of its flowers in autumn. **'Monarch'** A Dutch selection of spreading habit with purple shoots and bearing large flowerheads to 12cm across, with 5–6 broad, rounded bracts. C 1970. **'North Star'** A selected form of strong, vigorous growth with dark purple young shoots and large flowerheads. C 1971. **'Portlemouth'** A selected form with large bracts; often gives good, red autumn colour. This plant first came to notice in 1969 when a party from the International Dendrological Society visited the garden of Dr and Mrs Barker at E Portlemouth near Salcombe, Devon.

obliqua See *C. amomum* subsp. *obliqua*.

†**oblonga* Wall. (*Swida oblonga* (Wall.) Soják) A rare, evergreen species making a large shrub. Leaves narrowly elliptic, dark glossy green above, grey-downy below. Flowers white, slightly fragrant, produced in late autumn or early winter in domed, terminal corymbs. Has lived for many years in a sheltered position in the Sir Harold Hillier Gardens and Arboretum. Himalaya, W China. I 1818.

officinalis Siebold & Zucc. A small tree or large shrub with attractive, peeling bark and clusters of yellow flowers borne on the naked twigs in February. Red fruits and rich autumn tints. Resembles the closely related *C. mas* but coarser growing, with exfoliating bark, and earlier flowering; the individual flowers have longer pedicels. Japan, Korea. I about 1870. AM 1970.

'Ormonde' (*C. florida* × *C. nuttallii*) A large shrub similar to 'Eddie's White Wonder' but of spreading habit. Origin unknown but grown at Kew for many years as *C. nuttallii*.

paniculata See *C. racemosa*.

paucinervis Hance (*Swida paucinervis* (Hance) Soják) A slow-growing, narrow-leaved shrub, seldom exceeding 2m; produces creamy-white flowers, in 8cm-wide, rounded clusters, during July and August; fruits black. China. I 1907 by Ernest Wilson. AM 1911.

'Porlock' (*C. capitata* × *C. kousa*) A beautiful, small tree of graceful spreading habit, developing peeling bark with age. The flowerheads have 4 taper-pointed, creamy-white bracts in June, turning to deep pink in July. In autumn, it bears large crops of hanging, strawberry-like fruits. In the Sir Harold Hillier Gardens and Arboretum some leaves usually persist over winter while others turn soft red in autumn; in milder areas the foliage is retained until spring. Arose in 1958 as a self-sown seedling at Underway, the garden of Norman Hadden in West Porlock, Somerset, where the original plant still grows. The parentage was at first thought to be *C. kousa* × *C. nuttallii*. ♀ 2002. AM 1986 (for fruit).

pubescens See *C. stolonifera* var. *occidentalis*.

pumila Koehne. A dense, rounded, bushy hummock reaching about 2m. Leaves deep red-purple when young becoming dark green, long persistent. Flowers in dense, long-stalked cymes in July. Fruits black. It has also been grown as *C. mas* 'Nana'. Origin unknown. C 1890.

racemosa Lam. (*C. paniculata* L'Hér., *C. candidissima* Marshall, *Swida racemosa* (Lam.) Moldenke) A medium-sized shrub. Panicles of creamy-white flowers are borne in June and July. Fruits white with bright rose-coloured stalks. Good autumn colour. E and C USA. I 1758.

rugosa Lam. (*Swida rugosa* (Lam.) Rydb.) An erect-growing shrub of medium size from E North America. Distinct, roundish leaves, densely grey-woolly beneath, and conspicuous clusters of white flowers in June; fruits pale blue. I 1784.

rutgersensis See *C.* Stellar Group.

sanguinea L. (*Swida sanguinea* (L.) Opiz) Common dogwood. Our native hedgerow species, greenish, red-flushed stems and rich purple autumn colour. Fruits black, bitter to the taste. Europe. **'Beteramsii'** A medium-sized shrub, the shoots yellow flushed with orange-red in winter. It is remarkable that this shrub, which has been in cultivation since before 1940, has not become better known considering the popularity of recent, very similar selections, for which see under 'Winter Beauty'. **'Compressa'** A remarkable dwarf form of narrow, congested, upright habit. Leaves small, to 3.5 × 2.5cm, down-curved and overlapping with deeply impressed veins. Does not flower. It is often grown as *C. hessei*, for which see *C. alba* 'Hessei'. **'Midwinter Fire'** See 'Winter Beauty'. **'Winter Beauty'** ('Midwinter Fire', 'Winter Flame') A Dutch selection of compact habit with the shoots bright orange-yellow and red in winter. The leaves are pale yellow-green in summer and turn orange-yellow in winter. C 1987. Another selection, distributed as 'Midwinter Fire' is more vigorous and can be distinguished in summer by its darker green leaves, flushed deep bronze when young, and the young shoots purple-pink on the exposed side. **'Winter Flame'** See 'Winter Beauty'.

sericea L. (*C. stolonifera* Michx., *Swida stolonifera* (Michx.) Rydb., *C. baileyi* Coult. & W.H. Evans) A rampant, suckering shrub, with vigorous shoots up to 2.5m, in suitable situations forming a dense thicket of dark red stems. Fruits white. North America. I 1656. **'Bud's Yellow'** (*C. alba* 'Bud's Yellow') A selection resembling 'Flaviramea' with yellow-green winter shoots but said to be more resistant to canker. **'Cardinal'** Vigorous with orange-yellow winter shoots shading to red at the tips. C 1987. **'Flaviramea'** Young shoots yellow to olive-green, very effective in winter, particularly when planted with the red-stemmed sorts. Ideal for moist or wet situations. C 1899. ♀ 2002. AM 1985. **'Hedgerow Gold'** A form found on the border of Oregon and Washington states, USA. Young leaves have a yellow margin, becoming creamy-white. **'Isanti'** Compact with deep red winter shoots. C 1987. **'Kelseyi'** ('Kelsey Dwarf') A dwarf form of dense habit with small, crowded leaves. Winter shoots yellowish-green, red towards the tips. C 1939. **'Nitida'** A form with green young shoots in winter and somewhat glossy leaves. **subsp. *occidentalis*** (Torr. & A. Gray) Fosberg (*C. pubescens* Nutt.) A taller growing form from W USA with the leaves roughly hairy beneath. **'Rosco'** (Kelsey's Gold) A sport of 'Kelseyi'; a dwarf shrub with yellow leaves, bronze when young. C 1992. **'Silver and Gold'** A sport of 'Flaviramea' of American origin; yellow shoots and white-margined leaves. C 1984. **'Silver Lining'** A striking variegated form found as a sport in the wild near Vancouver. Leaves grey-green, broadly and irregularly margined with creamy-white. **'Sunshine'** A vigorous, large shrub with red winter shoots. Leaves either yellow or margined with yellow. A selection of subsp. *occidentalis*. **'White Gold'** ('White Spot') Leaves with a white margin, resembling those of *C. alba* 'Elegantissima'. Winter stems yellow. It was found as a sport in the wild. ♀ 2002.

Stellar Group (*C. rutgersensis* hort.) (*C. florida* × *C. kousa*) A series of hybrids raised by Dr Elwin Orton at Rutgers University, New Jersey, USA. The original 6 seedlings selected are large, vigorous, and mainly upright, deciduous shrubs, which are resistant to anthracnose. They do not usually produce fruit. **Aurora** ('Rutban') Vigorous, upright habit with large, overlapping white bracts, ageing to creamy-white. Flowers profusely. **Celestial** (Galaxy, 'Rutdan') Large white bracts tinged green when young. **Constellation** ('Rutcan') Long white bracts which do not overlap. **Ruth Ellen** ('Rutlan') Spreading habit, profusely flowering with white bracts. **Stardust** ('Rutfan') Spreading habit with white bracts which do not overlap. **Stellar Pink** ('Rutgan') Soft pink, rounded and overlapping bracts.

stolonifera See *C. sericea*.

stricta See *C. foemina*.

walteri Wangerin (*Swida walteri* (Wangerin) Soják) An interesting tall shrub, or small tree. Leaves oval, slender-pointed; flowers white in 8cm wide corymbs during June; fruit globose, black. C and W China. I 1907 by Ernest Wilson.

†***COROKIA** A. Cunn.—**Escalloniaceae**—A small but interesting genus of 3 species of evergreen shrubs or small trees, natives of New Zealand. In mild areas the cultivated species make interesting, medium-sized to large shrubs with small, starry, yellow flowers and often very conspicuous red or orange fruits.

buddleioides A. Cunn. Korokio. A medium-sized shrub with slender stems and long, narrow, leathery leaves, silvery-white beneath. The small, yellow, star-like flowers are followed by dark red fruits. C 1836. North Island. **var. *linearis*** Cheesem. A form that has even narrower, linear leaves.

cotoneaster Raoul. Wire-netting bush. Making a somewhat tortuous tracery, the twiggy branchlets of this species form a curiously attractive, small to medium-sized bush with tiny, yellow flowers and orange fruits. Hardy except in cold areas. I 1875. AM 1934. North and South Islands.

macrocarpa Kirk. Attractive, tall shrub with comparatively large, lanceolate leaves, silvery beneath. Flowers in axillary racemes; large red fruits. Chatham Islands.

× *virgata* Turrill (*C. buddleioides* × *C. cotoneaster*) A medium-sized shrub of erect habit with oblanceolate leaves, white beneath, and very small, bright orange fruits. Floriferous and free fruiting. Survives most winters uninjured. In the wild, forms complex hybrid swarms with the parents. The following make excellent and unusual hedges in mild coastal areas of south and west Britain. I 1907. AM 1934. **'Cheesemanii'** ('Erecta') A very upright form with densely crowded branchlets. Fruits orange-red. Found in the wild in New Zealand before 1926. **'Red Wonder'** A form bearing masses of deep red berries. C 1968. **'Yellow Wonder'** Similar to 'Red Wonder' but more vigorous with larger leaves and equally profuse bright yellow fruits. C 1968.

CORONILLA L.—**Leguminosae**—About 55 species of deciduous and evergreen shrubs and herbs with pinnate leaves. They are native to C and S Europe, the Mediterranean region, Africa, N Asia and China. The following are free-flowering shrubs producing umbels of bright yellow, pea-flowers throughout the growing season.

emerus See *Hippocrepis emerus*. **subsp. *emeroides*** See *Hippocrepis emerus* subsp. *emeroides*.

glauca See *C. valentina* subsp. *glauca*.

†*valentina L. A charming, small, glaucous shrub producing a mass of rich yellow flowers with the fragrance of ripe peaches. C Mediterranean region. C 1596. AM 1977. **subsp. *glauca*** (L.) Batt. (*C. glauca* L.) A medium-sized shrub for a warm wall. Leaves glaucous with fewer leaflets than the typical form. Most floriferous in April but bloom is produced intermittently throughout the year. S Europe. I 1722. ♀ 2002. AM 1957. **subsp. *glauca* 'Citrina'** A form with pale lemon-yellow flowers. ♀ 2002. AM 1989. **subsp. *glauca* 'Variegata'** Leaves conspicuously and prettily variegated with creamy-white.

†***CORREA** Andrews—**Rutaceae**—A small genus of about 10 species of evergreen shrubs, native to Australia and Tasmania and suitable only for the mildest gardens or for a cool greenhouse. The attractive, showy and usually bell-shaped flowers are regularly and abundantly produced in late winter when under glass.

alba Andrews. A small shrub with oval leaves, grey beneath, and funnel-shaped, creamy-white flowers with reflexed lobes. SE Australia, Tasmania. I 1793. **'Pinkie'** White flowers flushed with pink at the tips of the petals. A form found by Graham Hutchins. ♀ 2002.

backhouseana Hook. Medium-sized shrub with clusters of drooping, greenish-white flowers. Tasmania. ♀ 2002. AM 1977.

decumbens F. Muell. A small shrub with narrow, grey-green leaves. Narrowly tubular, crimson flowers with a greenish tip. The projecting anthers are yellow. S Australia.

'Dusky Bells' A compact and wide-spreading, dwarf shrub with dark green foliage and tubular, dusky red flowers. Probably *C. pulchella* × *C. reflexa*. ♀ 2002.

'Harrisii' See *C.* 'Mannii'.

lawrenceana Hook. Mountain correa. A large shrub, sometimes tree-like, with dark green leaves, to 10cm long, covered with a velvety down beneath. The slender pendent bell-shaped flowers, to 3cm long, have conspicuously exserted stamens and vary in colour from green to pink or red. SE Australia, Tasmania.

'Mannii' ('Harrisii') (*C. pulchella* × *C. reflexa*) A beautiful, early-flowering, small shrub with rose-scarlet flowers about 2.5cm long. ♀ 2002. AM 1977.

'Marian's Marvel' A small shrub of upright habit with dark green leaves and bearing pendulous tubular flowers deep pink at the base shading to yellow-green at the tip with reflexed lobes and exserted stamens. Probably *C. backhouseana* × *C. reflexa*. ♀ 2002.

pulchella Sweet. A small shrub with leaves that are green beneath. Flowers of palest almond-pink are borne throughout the winter. S Australia. ♀ 2002.

reflexa (Labill.) Vent. (*C. speciosa* J. Donn ex Andrews) A small, variable shrub with oval-oblong leaves, green and often rough above. Flowers are red, tipped with green, or all green. SE Australia, Tasmania. C 1804. ♀ 2002.

CORYLOPSIS Siebold & Zucc.—**Hamamelidaceae**—A genus of about 30 species of deciduous or semi-evergreen shrubs and small trees, natives of the E Himalaya, China and Japan. These exquisitely beautiful plants are easily grown and should be much more widely planted. The conspicuous, drooping racemes of fragrant, primrose-yellow, cup-shaped flowers are regularly carried just before the leaves in early spring. They thrive on acid or neutral soils and, with the exception of *C. pauciflora*, will survive indefinitely on chalk given 60cm depth of soil.

glabrescens Franch. & Sav. A widespreading, medium to large shrub with broadly ovate or orbicular leaves, glaucescent beneath. Flowers in freely borne, slender tassels; fruits glabrous. Japan. I 1905. FCC 1968. AM 1960. **var. gotoana** (Makino) T. Yamanaka (*C. gotoana* Makino) This is very similar to the typical form and sometimes not separated from it. For the plant previously listed as *C. gotoana*, see *C. sinensis* var. *calvescens*.

gotoana See *C. glabrescens* var. *gotoana* and *C. sinensis* var. *calvescens*.

multiflora Hance (*C. wilsonii* Hemsl.) A large shrub or occasionally a small tree with stellately-pubescent young branches. Leaves ovate to elliptic, glaucous and pubescent beneath, mainly on the veins. Flowers in dense, pendent racemes; fruits glabrous. C and SW China. I 1900.

‡*pauciflora* Siebold & Zucc. A densely branched shrub with slender stems, slowly reaching 2m by as much across. The ovate, bristle-toothed leaves, 4–6cm long, are the smallest in the genus, and are pink when young. Primrose-yellow and cowslip-scented flowers are borne in short 2–3-flowered racemes opening in March, generally before those of other species; fruits glabrous. Japan; Taiwan. I about 1860 by Robert Fortune. ♀ 2002. FCC 1983.

platypetala Rehder & E.H. Wilson. See *C. sinensis* var. *calvescens*.

sinensis Hemsl. A large shrub or small tree to 4.5m with young branches pubescent and with scattered, stalked glands. Obovate leaves, glaucescent and densely pubescent beneath. Flowers lemon-yellow; fruits pubescent. Said to be the commonest species in China. C and W China. I about 1901. ♀ 2002. AM 1967. **var. calvescens** Rehder & E.H. Wilson (*C. platypetala* Rehder & E.H. Wilson) Leaves usually glabrous beneath. Some plants, previously listed as *C. gotoana*, have large, orbicular and slightly convex leaves, bluish-green above and pink-flushed when young, chalk-white beneath. W China. I 1907. AM 1981 (as *C. platypetala*). **f. veitchiana** (Bean) B. Morley & J.M. Chao (*C. veitchiana* Bean) A very distinct large, erect shrub with characteristic elongated, oblong-elliptic, bright green leaves, edged with incurved teeth and glaucous beneath; purplish when young. Flowers in large racemes, are primrose-yellow with conspicuous brick-red anthers. W China. I 1900 by Ernest Wilson. ♀ 2002. FCC 1974. AM 1912. **Willmottiae Group** (*C. willmottiae* Rehder & E.H. Wilson) A medium-sized to large shrub with variable, but generally obovate, leaves often purple or reddish-purple when young, glaucescent and pubescent on the veins beneath. Flowers soft yellow, in dense, showy racemes; fruits glabrous. W China. I 1909 by Ernest Wilson. FCC 1965. AM 1912. **Willmottiae Group 'Spring Purple'** A selection with most attractive, plum-purple young growths. Raised in our nurseries before 1969.

spicata Siebold & Zucc. A spreading, hazel-like shrub of medium size with densely pubescent young shoots. Broad ovate to rounded leaves are glaucous and softly pubescent beneath. Flowers, in rather narrow racemes to 15cm long, have long, bright yellow petals and dark purple anthers; fruits pubescent. Japan. I about 1860 by Robert Fortune. AM 1897.

veitchiana See *C. sinensis* var. *calvescens* f. *veitchiana*.

willmottiae See *C. sinensis* Willmottiae Group.

wilsonii See *C. multiflora*.

CORYLUS L.—**Corylaceae**—The hazels are a genus of about 10 species of large shrubs or small trees, native of temperate regions of the N hemisphere. Flowers borne in catkins, the males pendent and elongating in late winter or early spring making an attractive feature. Female catkins are bud-like with only the bright red stigmas showing. Many are cultivated for their edible nuts.

americana Walter. American hazel. A medium-sized shrub with rounded, heart-shaped leaves. Nuts 1.5cm long, slightly flattened, concealed by the long, downy husks. E North America. I 1798.

avellana L. Hazel. Our native species. A large shrub or small, many-stemmed tree, impressive when draped with its long, yellow lambs' tails in February. Useful as a tall, screening shrub. Leaves yellow in autumn. Europe, W Asia, N Africa. **'Aurea'** A soft-yellow-leaved form, excellent in contrast with the purple-leaf filbert (see *C. maxima* 'Purpurea'). C 1864. **'Contorta'** Corkscrew hazel, Harry Lauder's walking stick. Curiously twisted branches; slow-growing to about 3m. A winter feature when in catkin. Discovered by Lord Ducie in a hedgerow in Gloucestershire in about 1863. AM 1917. **'Heterophylla'** ('Laciniata', 'Quercifolia') Leaves smaller and deeply lobed. Not to be confused with *C. heterophylla*, which is the E Asian representative of *C. avellana*. C 1825. **'Laciniata'** See 'Heterophylla'. **'Quercifolia'** See 'Heterophylla'. **'Pendula'** A form with weeping branches. C 1867.

chinensis Franch. Chinese hazel. A large tree with spreading branches and light-coloured, furrowed bark. Allied to *C. colurna*. W China. I 1900 by Ernest Wilson.

colurna L. Turkish hazel. A remarkable, large tree of very symmetrical, pyramidal form. The striking, corky corrugations of the bark are an attractive feature. SE Europe, W Asia. I 1582. ♀ 2002.

cornuta Marshall (*C. rostrata* Aiton) Beaked hazel. Medium-sized shrub with slender, bristly-hairy, beaked husks covering the nuts. E and C North America. I 1745.

jacquemontii Decne. A medium-sized tree related to *C. colurna*. W Himalaya. C 1898.

maxima Mill. Filbert. A large shrub or small, spreading tree with large, rounded, heart-shaped leaves. The nuts are larger and longer than those of *C. avellana* and are concealed by a large husk. Long cultivated for its nuts, and the parent of numerous cultivars. Balkans. I 1759. **'Purpurea'** ('Atropurpurea') Purple-leaf filbert. A large shrub rivalling the purple beech (*Fagus sylvatica* Purpurea group) in the intensity of its colouring. ♀ 2002. AM 1977.

sieboldiana Blume. This species is mainly represented in gardens by the following variety. The typical form is a native of Japan and differs in the rounder leaf base and the shorter beak to the fruit. I 1904. **var. *mandshurica*** (Maxim. & Rupr.) C.K. Schneid. A large shrub related to *C. cornuta*. Leaves ovate to obovate, coarsely double-toothed and hairy beneath. Fruits in clusters of 2–4, the nut completely enclosed in the husk, which is prolonged into a ridged, tubular beak, to 3.5cm long, flushed with red on the outside and divided at the apex into finger-like lobes. The whole involucre is covered in dense, white, bristly hairs. Plants grown from seed collected in Korea by Carl Miller and Sir Harold Hillier in 1976 (M. & H. 308) produced fruit in the Sir Harold Hillier Gardens and Arboretum in 1990. NE Asia. I 1882.

'Te-Terra Red' A vigorous and upright, large shrub or small tree with deep red-purple young leaves, later dark green. Red-purple husks with conspicuous frilly margins. A hybrid of *C. colurna*.

tibetica Batalin. Tibetan hazel. A small to medium-sized tree of widespreading habit with usually numerous stems. Distinct in the spiny, burr-like husks that enclose the nuts, the whole cluster resembling that of the Spanish chestnut (*Castanea sativa*). C and W China. I 1901 by Ernest Wilson.

Corymbia See *Eucalyptus*.

COTINUS Mill.—**Anacardiaceae**—A genus of 5 species now separated from *Rhus*, natives of Europe, Asia, the southern USA and Mexico. The smoke trees are among the most attractive of the larger, summer-flowering shrubs. The leaves give rich autumn tints.

americanus See *C. obovatus*.

coggygria Scop. (*Rhus cotinus* L.) Venetian sumach, Smoke tree. This species attains 2.5–4m. The smooth, rounded, green leaves give good autumn tints. The fawn-coloured, plume-like inflorescences, 15–20cm long, produced in profusion in June and July, are persistent and turn smoky-grey by late summer. From C and S Europe to the Himalaya and China. C 1656. ♀ 2002. **'Atropurpureus'**

See f. *purpureus*. **'Daydream'** Compact habit with profuse and long-persistent fluffy, brownish-pink fruit clusters. **'Flame'** See *C*. 'Flame'. **'Foliis Purpureis'** ('Rubrifolius') The leaves, especially when young, are rich plum-purple, changing to light red shades towards autumn. AM 1921. **Golden Spirit** ('Ancot') PBR A form with yellow foliage that does not burn in sun as long as the soil is not too dry. A seedling raised in Holland. **f. *purpureus*** (Dup.-Jam.) Rehder ('Atropurpureus') Burning bush. Leaves green. The large panicles of purplish-grey flowers resemble puffs of pink smoke from a distance. AM 1948. **'Royal Purple'** A selected form with deep wine-purple leaves, translucent in sunshine, the colour reddening towards autumn. 'Notcutt's Variety' is similar. ♀ 2002. **'Rubrifolius'** See 'Foliis Purpureis'. **'Velvet Cloak'** A form with leaves that are deep red-purple, the colour being retained well into autumn, eventually turning red. Found as a seedling in the USA before 1962.

Dummer Hybrids In 1978 our propagator Peter Dummer crossed a male plant of *C. obovatus* with *C. coggygria* 'Velvet Cloak'. The following year 5 seedlings were raised as a result of this cross and have been given this collective name. They are all purple-leaved with the leaves intermediate in size between the parents and showing some of the hairs on the underside characteristic of *C. obovatus*. The fruiting plumes are purple. See also *C*. 'Grace'.

'Flame' (*C. coggygria* × *C. obovatus*) A large shrub resembling *C. coggygria* but more vigorous and tree-like with larger leaves, especially when young or on strong-growing shoots. A splendid plant for the rich colour of its autumn leaves, which turn brilliant orange-red before falling. Large, pink flower clusters are borne in summer. Originally distributed as a form of *C. obovatus*, this plant is almost certainly a hybrid between the 2 species. Leaves on young plants in the nursery are of the same size as those of *C*. 'Grace' but become smaller on old plants. The leaves also bear some of the hairs beneath, characteristic of *C. obovatus*. ♀ 2002.

'Grace' (Dummer Hybrids) A vigorous, tall shrub with large, soft purplish-red leaves, turning scarlet in autumn. Large, conical, purplish-pink flower clusters are borne in summer. This plant, one of the Dummer Hybrids and originally designated as Clone 2, was selected as the best form and named after the raiser's wife. FCC 1990. Cory Cup 1984. AM 1983.

obovatus Raf. (*C. americanus* Nutt., *Rhus cotinoides* Nutt.) Chittamwood. A rare, American shrub or small tree which, in favourable seasons and situations, is one of the most brilliantly coloured autumn shrubs. Leaves much larger than in *C. coggygria*, turning to shades of orange, red and purple in autumn. SE USA. I 1882. ♀ 2002. AM 1904 (as *Rhus cotinoides*).

szechuanensis Pénzes. A very distinct small to medium-sized, Chinese shrub with red young shoots. Leaves small, orbicular, to 4cm long, wavy-edged with a scalloped, red margin, glabrous except for conspicuous tufts of white hairs in the axils of the basal veins beneath; leaves are borne on slender, red petioles about as long as the leaf blade. I by Roy Lancaster in 1993 from below Wenchuan at 1,000m in the warm, dry valley of the Min

River in W Sichuan where it was associated with *Caryopteris incana* and *Ceratostigma willmottianum* (Lancaster 2028).

COTONEASTER Medik.—**Rosaceae**—This important genus includes among its members some of the most indispensable of hardy, ornamental shrubs. Though mainly ranging from 2–3m, they vary from prostrate creepers to small trees and, while the majority are deciduous, many are evergreen. The great variation in habit makes them suitable for many purposes from hedging and border plants to specimen and wall shrubs and plants for a rock garden or groundcover. Brilliant autumn colour, either leaf or fruit, are their main attributes. Their white or pink-tinged flowers often smother the branches in June and are very attractive to bees. They are tolerant of almost all soils and conditions but are susceptible to fireblight.

About 400 species, widely distributed in N temperate regions of the Old World. Though often thought of as hybridising freely, this only applies to a limited number of species and many are apomictic, thus breeding true. Although some plants, known only in gardens, behave as species and breed true from seed, they may have originated as hybrids in cultivation. The species are much confused in cultivation. We would like to acknowledge the assistance of Jeanette Fryer with the revision of this section.

acuminatus Lindl. Large shrub of vigorous, erect habit, related to *C. simonsii*. Leaves ovate-acuminate; fruits large, bright red. A variable, diploid species. Himalaya. I 1820.

acutifolius Turcz. Medium-sized shrub with lax branches, pointed, dull green leaves and ellipsoid, red fruits. N China. I 1883. **var. *villosulus*** See *C. villosulus*.

adpressus Bois. Dwarf, widespreading shrub, a gem for a rock garden, with bright red fruits and small, wavy-edged leaves, which turn scarlet in autumn. A variable diploid species. W China. I 1896. ♀ 2002. **var. *praecox*** See *C. nanshan*.

affinis Lindl. A large, vigorous, Himalayan shrub or small tree related to *C. frigidus*, from which it differs in its subglobose, purple-black fruits and usually more obovate leaves. I 1828. **var. *bacillaris*** See *C. bacillaris*.

'Aldenhamensis' A handsome, medium-sized to large shrub of distinctive widespreading habit. The long branches are almost fan-like and carry narrow, ribbed leaves and loose clusters of small, bright red fruits. AM 1927.

ambiguus See *C. pseudoambiguus*.

amoenus E.H. Wilson. A pretty semi-evergreen shrub, resembling *C. franchetii*, but with smaller leaves more like those of *C. pannosus*, and of more compact, bushy habit. Fruits bright red. Yunnan. I 1899 by Ernest Wilson. Several recent introductions from China are close to this species.

apiculatus Rehder & E.H. Wilson. A dwarf shrub closely related to *C. adpressus* and often confused with it on the Continent and in North America, where it is more frequently grown. It is distinguished from *C. adpressus* by its flat leaves and by having 3 not 2 nutlets in each fruit. China. I 1910 by Ernest Wilson. The identity of another plant grown under this name is not certain.

applanatus See *C. dielsianus*.

atropurpureus Flinck & Hylmö. A dwarf, spreading shrub, close to *C. horizontalis* with which it has been confused. It differs in its slightly wavy-edged leaves and lacking the characteristic herring-bone branching of that species. China. **'Variegatus'** (*C. horizontalis* 'Variegatus') Especially pleasing in autumn when the small, cream-margined leaves are suffused with red. C 1922. ♀ 2002.

'Autumn Fire' See *C.* 'Herbstfeuer'.

bacillaris Wall. ex Lindl. (*C. affinis* var. *bacillaris* (Wall. ex Lindl.) C.K. Schneid) A vigorous, large, spreading shrub with arching branches, related to *C. affinis* but leaves glabrous beneath. Blue-black, bloomy fruits, 9mm across, are borne in large clusters. Himalaya. See also *C. ignotus*.

boisianus G. Klotz. A medium-sized to large, widespreading shrub related to *C. sikangensis*. Leaves dark green and deeply veined, broadly elliptic to obovate or nearly rounded, abruptly acuminate. Fruits orange-red, rather pear-shaped. China.

bradyi E.C. Nelson & J. Fryer. A medium-sized shrub related to *C. dielsianus* with small, dark green leaves grey and hairy beneath. Flowers with pale red petals, white at the tips, are followed by striking bright red fruits. Named after the late Aidan Brady, Director of the National Botanic Gardens, Glasnevin, 1968–1993. I before 1935 by Harry Smith (12624). Sichuan, China.

bullatus Bois (*C. bullatus* f. *floribundus* (Stapf) Rehder & E.H. Wilson) Large shrub with handsome, large, conspicuously corrugated leaves that colour richly in autumn, and clusters of large, bright red fruits early in the season. The foliage assumes rich autumnal colours. One of the finest species in cultivation. W China. I 1898. ♀ 2002. **f. *floribundus*** See *C. bullatus*. **var. *macrophyllus*** See *C. rehderi*.

buxifolius Wall. ex Lindl. This species is rare in cultivation. For the plant that is often listed under this name, see *C. lidjiangensis*.

*****cashmiriensis* G. Klotz. This appears to be the identity of a plant commonly grown as *C. microphyllus* var. *cochleatus*. A dense, dwarf shrub with rigid shoots and tiny, deep green leaves, forming mats up to 60cm. Berries small, bright red. Kashmir. ♀ 2002.

cambricus J. Fryer & B. Hylmö. A low-growing shrub, usually less than 1.5m tall, with elliptic to nearly rounded, grey-green leaves, hairy above when young becoming nearly glabrous. White flowers, tinged pink, in clusters of up to 3, are followed by red fruits. Originally thought to be *C. integerrimus*, it was described as a new species in 1994. Originates from Great Orme near Llandudno, North Wales, where it was first discovered in 1783. Although originally described as plentiful, it had been reduced to only 4 plants in 1979. It is hoped to save it from extinction by fencing, propagation and reintroduction.

cavei G. Klotz. A small, semi-evergreen shrub with reddish shoots, densely covered with white, bristly hairs and red warts. Leaves glossy, blackish-green, more or less orbicular, mucronate at the apex and often wavy-edged, to 1.5cm long. Fruits bright red, to 1cm long, long-persistent. I by the Dutch botanist Harry van de Laar. A similar plant introduced by Tony Schilling of Wakehurst Place is now thought to represent a different species. Himalaya, W China.

cochleatus (Franch.) Klotz (*C. microphyllus* var. *cochleatus* (Franch.) Rehder & E.H. Wilson, *C. melanotrichus* hort.) Charming, slow-growing, prostrate shrub related to *C. microphyllus* but lower growing, with broader leaves. W China, SE Tibet, E Nepal. AM 1930. See also *C. cashmiriensis*.

congestus Baker (*C. microphyllus* var. *glacialis* Hook. f., *C. pyrenaicus* hort.) A pretty, dense, creeping evergreen forming a series of molehill-like mounds of small, bluish-green leaves. Fruits red, but not freely borne. Himalaya. A very variable species. The dwarf form described here is often referred to as 'Nanus'. I 1868.

conspicuus Marq. A graceful medium-sized, small-leaved shrub with strongly arching, widespreading branches. White flowers cover the plant in early summer, followed by equally numerous bright red fruits, which often persist well into the following year. SE Tibet. I 1925 by Kingdon-Ward. AM 1933. 'Decorus' A low-growing, free-fruiting form, excellent for covering banks. As a cultivar this name refers to the plant that was taken as the type. The name used at a varietal level is a synonym of *C. conspicuus*. ♀ 2002. FCC 1953. **'Highlight'** (L. S. and E. 13310) A spectacular shrub of medium size, forming a dense mound of arching shoots. The masses of white flowers in May are followed by large, orange-red fruits. Probably a distinct species.

cooperi Marq. A medium-sized to large shrub, allied to *C. frigidus*, with elliptic leaves, dark matt green above. Fruits dull red turning deep purple. N India. I 1914 by R.E. Cooper. **var. *microcarpus*** Marq. Differs in its smaller, reddish-purple fruits. Bhutan. Apparently introduced mixed with the typical form.

*****'Coral Beauty'** A very dense, small shrub with arching branches. Leaves ovate-elliptic, to 2cm long, glossy green. Abundant, bright orange-red fruits are borne in autumn. Excellent groundcover. C 1967. 'Royal Beauty' is similar but lower growing with salmon-red fruits. Probably *C. conspicuus* × *C. dammeri*.

'Cornubia' A vigorous semi-evergreen growing upwards of 6m high. Among tall-growing kinds its red fruits are perhaps the largest, and, borne in profusion, weigh down the branches. Raised at Exbury in 1930. ♀ 2002. FCC 1936. AM 1933.

cuspidatus Marq. ex J. Fryer & B. Hylmö. A vigorous, widespreading, medium-sized shrub with nearly rounded, glossy dark green leaves spreading on either side of the shoots, turning to red and purple late in autumn or early winter. The glossy scarlet berries are striking in autumn. It was originally grown as *C. strigosus*. Tibet, Upper Burma.

dammeri C.K. Schneid (*C. humifusus* Duthie ex Veitch) Quite prostrate, with long, trailing shoots studded in autumn with sealing-wax-red fruits. Leaves oval or obovate, prominently veined, 2.5–4cm long. An ideal shrub for covering banks and as groundcover beneath other shrubs. China. I 1900 by Ernest Wilson. ♀ 2002. **'Eichholz'** See *C. radicans*. **'Oakwood'** See *C. radicans*. **var. *radicans*** See 'Major' and *C. radicans*. **'Major'** (*C. dammeri* var. *radicans* hort. not C.K. Schneid) A vigorous and commonly grown form with large leaves up to 3.5cm long.

dielsianus Pritz. (*C. applanatus* Duthie) An elegant shrub of medium size, crowded with sub-globose, scarlet fruits and small leaves, brilliantly tinted in autumn. C China. I 1900 by Ernest Wilson. AM 1907. **var. *elegans*** See *C. elegans*.

distichus See *C. nitidus*. **var. *tongolensis*** See under *C. splendens*.

divaricatus Rehder & E.H. Wilson. A medium-sized shrub: one of the best and most reliable for autumn fruit (dark red) and foliage. Excellent for hedging. W China. I 1904 by Ernest Wilson. FCC 1912.

*****'Eastleigh'** (*C. prostratus* 'Eastleigh') A vigorous, large, much-branched shrub with dark green leaves up to 3 × 2cm and large, deep ox-blood-red fruits in profusion. Raised in our nurseries about 1960 from seed of *C. marginatus*, from which it differs in its larger, duller leaves and larger fruits.

elegans Rehder & E.H. Wilson. A medium-sized shrub related to *C. dielsianus* and differing in its smaller, more rounded, nearly glabrous leaves; coral-red berries. China. I 1908 by Ernest Wilson.

'Exburiensis' A large shrub with apricot-yellow fruits becoming pink-tinged in winter. Almost identical to *C.* 'Rothschildianus'. Raised at Exbury in 1930.

'Firebird' A medium-sized to large shrub of spreading habit. The leaves are bullate and shining dark green above; fruits large, orange-red in dense clusters. Once thought to be a hybrid of *C. bullatus* with *C. franchetii*, this plant may actually represent a new species close to *C. sikangensis*.

*****floccosus* (Rehder & E.H. Wilson) Flinck & B. Hylmö (*C. salicifolius* var. *floccosus* Rehder & E.H. Wilson) A medium-sized to large shrub with small, narrow, polished leaves, shining green above, white-woolly beneath, poised on slender, drooping, fan-like stems. Bears masses of tiny, red fruits. Some plants grown under this name are *C. salicifolius*. China. I 1908 by Ernest Wilson. AM 1920.

foveolatus Rehder & E.H. Wilson. A Chinese shrub, to 2.5m, with comparatively large leaves of shining, grass-green, turning orange and scarlet in autumn. Flowers pink; fruits black. I 1908 by Ernest Wilson.

franchetii Bois. A very graceful, medium-sized, semi-evergreen shrub with sage-green foliage and ovoid, orange-scarlet fruits. One of the most popular species. China. I 1895 by the Abbé Soulié. **var. *sternianus*** See *C. sternianus*.

frigidus Wall. This is a variable, fast-growing, small, spreading tree or large shrub, loaded with large, heavy clusters of crimson fruits in autumn and throughout winter. The true plant with its large, broad, elliptic leaves is now seldom seen; hybrid seedlings of the Watereri Group are made to do duty for it. Himalaya. I 1824. AM 1966. **f. *fructuluteo*** (Bean) Rehder ('Fructuluteo', 'Xanthocarpus') Large bunches of creamy-yellow fruits. AM 1932.

*****glabratus* Rehder & E.H. Wilson. A very distinct, medium-sized to large, spreading shrub with glossy, purplish, arching shoots bearing dark glossy green, elliptic-oblanceolate and taper-pointed leaves, to 10cm long, glaucous and reticulate beneath, purple-tinged in winter. Small, bright red fruits are borne profusely in broad clusters. W China. I 1906 by Ernest Wilson and later by Roy Lancaster and Keith Rushforth.

glaucophyllus Franch. A large, semi-evergreen shrub with oval leaves. Flowering in July, it is, correspondingly late in berrying. In all seasons a handsome species. W China. C 1915. AM 1924. **f. serotinus** See *C. serotinus* and *C. meiophyllus*. **var. vestitus** See *C. vestitus* and *C. serotinus*.

glomerulatus W.W. Sm. (*C. nitidifolius* Marq.) A medium-sized shrub of graceful habit with slender, lax stems and wavy-edged, shining green leaves. The clusters of white flowers are followed by small, crimson fruits. A distinct and attractive species often with rich crimson autumn colours. SW China. I 1924 by George Forrest.

'Gnom' See *C. salicifolius* 'Gnom'.

'Gracia' A widespreading shrub, similar to 'Valkenburg' but lower-growing, to 60cm, with broader, glossier, more deeply veined leaves, purplish in autumn.

harrovianus E.H. Wilson. A graceful, arching evergreen shrub, attaining about 3m and very conspicuous when in bloom. The attractive, red fruits are not fully coloured until late December. China. I 1899 by Ernest Wilson. AM 1905.

harrysmithii Flinck & B. Hylmö. Small shrub occasionally up to 2m, with horizontal branchlets. Closely related to *C. nitens* but less vigorous and with smaller leaves, flowers and fruits. Collected in W China in 1934 by the Swedish collector Dr Harry Smith. AM 1987.

hebephyllus Diels. Medium-sized shrub with long, arching branches, wreathed with white flowers followed by large, dark red, globular fruits. China. I 1910.

henryanus (C.K. Schneid.) Rehder & E.H. Wilson. A large, wide-growing, evergreen or semi-evergreen shrub with long, dark green, corrugated leaves that are downy on both sides, at least when young; fruits crimson. Closely related to *C. salicifolius*. The true plant is elusive in cultivation. C China. I 1901 by Ernest Wilson. AM 1920.

*'Herbstfeuer' ('Autumn Fire', *C. salicifolius* 'Autumn Fire') A small, widespreading, semi-evergreen shrub of lax, almost pendent, habit, with bright glossy green, elliptic, pointed leaves. Small, bright orange-red fruits are produced in large quantities in autumn. C 1930.

hjelmqvistii Flinck & B. Hylmö (*C. horizontalis* 'Robusta') A widespreading, small shrub with arching branches and broadly obovate to nearly orbicular, glossy green leaves, up to 2cm long, turning red in autumn. Fruits red, to 8mm across. It was found among seedlings of *C. horizontalis* in a Belgian nursery in 1954 and is occasionally seen mixed with that species. Gansu, China.

horizontalis Decne. A low-growing shrub of spreading habit, with branches in a characteristic herring-bone pattern. Invaluable for shady walls or for covering banks. Fruit and leaves rich in colour in late autumn and winter. W China. I about 1870 by Père David. ♀ 2002. FCC 1897. **var. perpusillus** See *C. perpusillus*. **'Robusta'** See *C. hjelmqvistii*. **'Saxatilis'** See *C. perpusillus*. **'Variegatus'** See *C. atropurpureus* 'Variegatus'.

humifusus See *C. dammeri*.

hummelii J. Fryer & B. Hylmö. A medium-sized shrub related to *C. moupinensis*, from which it differs in its narrower, longer-stalked, long-acuminate, glossier and less deeply veined leaves, bronze when young, and longer, duller fruits to 11mm. It is named after Dr David

Hummel (1893–1984), who collected many plants in China. He was the medical doctor of the Swedish expeditions to China 1927–31 and 1933–34. Some plants distributed as *C. moupinensis* belong here. Gansu, China. I by Hummel in 1930.

hupehensis Rehder & E.H. Wilson. A medium-sized shrub of dense yet graceful arching habit. The oval leaves are interspersed with numerous white flowers in May, followed by large, solitary, bright red fruits on long slender stalks. W China. I 1907 by Ernest Wilson.

*'Hybridus Pendulus' A very striking evergreen or semi-evergreen, with glossy leaves, and long, prostrate branches which carry brilliant red fruits in abundance during autumn and winter. When grown on a stem makes an attractive, small, weeping tree. Garden origin. Variously claimed to be a hybrid of *C. dammeri* with either *C. frigidus* or *C. salicifolius*. AM 1953.

hylmoei Flinck & Fryer (*C. rugosus* hort.) A medium-sized shrub with arching branches, related to *C. floccosus*, but with broader and darker leaves, deeply veined above, white-tomentose beneath and with larger flowers, pink in bud and fruits, which persist for a long time on the branches. One of the most ornamental species. Hubei, China. I 1907 by Ernest Wilson (Wilson. 335). AM 1912.

ignavus Wolf. Medium-sized shrub, closely related to *C. melanocarpus*, with many-flowered, drooping clusters of pink flowers. Fruits purple-black. E Turkestan. I 1880.

ignotus G. Klotz. A large, upright shrub with arching branches and conspicuously blunt, broadly elliptic to obovate leaves, rounded at the shoot tips. It is striking in flower and when carrying masses of jet-black, bloomy fruits, 11mm across. In common with related species, the fruit is open at the top exposing the nutlets. Himalaya from Afghanistan to W Nepal. Some plants grown as *C. affinis* var. *bacillaris* belong here.

'Inchmery' A large shrub or small tree raised at Exbury, Hampshire, and producing bunches of large, salmon-pink fruits, yellow at first. In general appearance closely approaches *C. frigidus*.

insignis Pojark. (*C. lindleyi* Steud., *C. nummularius* Lindl. not Fisch. & C.A. Mey.) A large shrub with nearly orbicular leaves, rounded to truncate, sometimes emarginate at the apex, which is distinctly mucronate. Fruits fleshy, black. NW Himalaya, C Asia. I 1824.

integerrimus Medik. (*C. vulgaris* Lindl.) An erect-branched shrub, usually less than 2m high, with roundish leaves, pink-tinged flowers and red fruits. C Europe, Alps.

integrifolius (Roxb.) G. Klotz. (*C. microphyllus* hort., *C. microphyllus* var. *thymifolius* (Lindl.) Koehne not hort.) Dwarf, glossy-leaved evergreen with extra large, globose, deep pink fruits. Much used for draping walls and banks. Extremely tough and hardy. Commonly cultivated as *C. microphyllus*. Himalaya. SW China. I 1824. ♀ 2002.

'John Waterer' See *C.* × *watereri* 'John Waterer'.

lacteus W.W Sm. A medium-sized shrub, distinct in its large, oval, leathery leaves, grey tomentose beneath. Red fruits are rather small but carried in broad clusters. They ripen late in the year and last well after Christmas. China. I 1813 by George Forrest. ♀ 2002. AM 1935.

laxiflorus Lindl. (*C. melanocarpus* var. *laxiflorus* (Lindl.) C.K. Schneid.) A medium-sized shrub with dark green leaves, woolly beneath, and pink flowers in large, drooping clusters; fruits black. Leaves colour early in autumn. Siberia. C 1826.

lidjiangensis G. Klotz. Dwarf shrub of dense habit with small, dull green leaves and small, persistent, late-ripening, red fruits. Suitable for a rock garden. Originally listed as *C. buxifolius*, which is very rare in cultivation. Yunnan. China.

lindleyi Steud. See *C. insignis*.

linearifolius (G. Klotz) G. Klotz (*C. microphyllus* var. *thymifolius* hort. not (Baker) Koehne) A dwarf, dainty shrub with extremely small, narrow, shining, deep green leaves and small, deep pink, persistent berries. A superb rock plant. Nepal. I 1852.

lucidus Schltdl. An upright-growing species of medium height, with pink and white flowers followed by lustrous, black fruits. The dark, glossy leaves give brilliant autumn colour. Altai Mountains. I 1840.

marginatus Lindl. ex Loud. (*C. prostratus* var. *lanatus*, *C. buxifolius* Baker not Lindl., *C. wheeleri* hort.) A medium-sized to large, spreading shrub with long, arching branches, dark glossy green leaves, up to 1.5cm long, and crimson-pink berries. Himalaya.

marquandii G. Klotz. A medium-sized, upright shrub, related to *C. nitidus*, with densely hairy young shoots and small, dark glossy green leaves turning scarlet in autumn. The very conspicuous, orange-red fruits persist well into the following year. This species was originally described from a plant grown at Bodnant under KW 6788. Himalaya, Burma, Bhutan.

meiophyllus (W.W. Sm.) G. Klotz. A medium-sized shrub related to *C. glaucophyllus* with pink-tinged young shoots. Leaves ovate-elliptic, to 5.5cm long, glabrous and glaucous beneath. Fruits small, ripening very late and long-persistent during winter. Has been confused with *C. serotinus*. China.

melanocarpus var. *laxiflorus* See *C. laxiflorus*.

microphyllus Lindl. A dwarf, stiff-branched, spreading shrub forming a low mound. Leaves elliptic to obovate, to 1cm long, rounded to notched at the apex. Tiny, white flowers are followed by small, deep reddish-pink fruits. Himalaya. Several plants are grown under this name. See also *C. integrifolius*. **var. *cochleatus*** See *C. cochleatus* and *C. cashmiriensis*. **var. *thymifolius*** See *C. linearifolius* and *C. integrifolius*.

monopyrenus (W.W. Sm.) Flinck & B. Hylmö. A large, semi-evergreen or deciduous shrub of rounded habit. Leaves elliptic, obtuse to emarginate and mucronate at the apex, sea-green and glabrous above, grey tomentose beneath when young. White flowers, with deep pink sepals, are borne profusely in small corymbs along the shoots in May. Fruits dark red becoming deep purple, bloomy. Yunnan, China.

moupinensis Franch. A medium-sized shrub similar to *C. bullatus*, but with dark red fruits, 7–9mm long, turning glossy black. Leaves broad elliptic-ovate, abruptly acuminate, matt green, giving rich autumn tints. W China. I 1907.

mucronatus Franch. An erect species of medium height with green, slender-pointed leaves and clusters of orange-red fruits. China. Closely related to *C. acuminatus*.

multiflorus Bunge. A large, spreading shrub, as free in flower as hawthorn, but more graceful; large, bright red fruits ripen in August. NW China. I 1837.

nanshan Vilm. ex Mottet (*C. adpressus* var. *praecox* (Vilm.) Bois & Berthault, *C. praecox* Vilm.) A vigorous, dwarf shrub with arching branches related to *C. adpressus* but with larger leaves and growing up to 1m high and 2m across. Fruits extra large, orange-red. Autumn colour brilliant red. W China. I 1905. **'Boer'** Lower growing and wider spreading with glossier, less wavy leaves and brighter coloured, much longer-lasting fruits. Found in Holland in the 1930s.

newryensis Barbier. A rare, erect-branched, medium to large shrub, closely related to *C. franchetii*. Conspicuous, orange-red fruits. W China. C 1900.

nitens Rehder & E.H. Wilson. A very graceful shrub, up to 2m, with slender, drooping branches. The polished leaves are disposed in an almost frond-like arrangement and give brilliant autumn colour; fruits elliptic, black. W China. I 1910 by Ernest Wilson.

nitidifolius See *C. glomerulatus*.

nitidus Jacques (*C. distichus* Lange, *C. rotundifolius* hort. not Wall. ex Lindl.) An excellent slow-growing, deciduous or semi-evergreen, medium-sized shrub with rigid, widespreading branches, small, polished leaves and large, bright scarlet, elliptic fruits persisting until spring. Himalaya. SW China. I 1825.

nummularius See *C. lindleyi*.

obscurus Rehder & E.H. Wilson. An uncommon species of medium size; leaves yellow-grey beneath; fruits obovoid, dark red. W China. I 1910 by Ernest Wilson.

orbicularis See under *C. sherriffii*.

pannosus Franch. A medium-sized shrub with long, slender, arching branches. It resembles *C. franchetii* but has smaller, sage-green leaves and small fruits which are rounded, deep red and colour later. W China. I 1888 by the Abbé Delavay.

perpusillus (C.K. Schneid) Flinck & B. Hylmö (*C. horizontalis* 'Saxatilis') A charming, dwarf shrub, related to *C. horizontalis* but with smaller leaves. W China. I 1908 by Ernest Wilson. AM 1916.

'Pink Champagne' A large, vigorous, dense shrub with slender, arching branches and narrow leaves approaching the habit of *C. salicifolius*. Fruits are small but plentifully produced, at first yellow becoming pink-tinged.

praecox See *C. nanshan*.

prostratus See *C. rotundifolius*. **'Eastleigh'** See *C. 'Eastleigh'*. **var. *lanatus*** See *C. marginatus*.

pseudoambiguus J. Fryer & B. Hylmö. A medium-sized to large shrub with arching branches and dark green, deeply veined leaves, to 8cm long, bronze when young and turning red-purple in autumn. White flowers, which barely open, are borne in clusters of up to 15 in early summer, followed by obovoid, plum-purple fruits. I by Ernest Wilson from Sichuan and originally thought to be *C. ambiguus* Rehder & E.H. Wilson, of which no seed was collected.

pyrenaicus See *C. congestus*.

racemiflorus (Desf.) Booth ex Bosse. A widely distributed species, characterised by its tall, slender, arching branches and orbicular leaves, grey-white beneath. Fruits brickred. The combination of the leaves and fruit in a

September sun is most arresting. N Africa to W and C Asia. C 1829. **var. veitchii** See *C. veitchii*.

radicans Dammer ex C.K. Schneid. (*C. dammeri* var. *radicans* C.K. Schneid not hort., *C. dammeri* 'Oakwood', *C. dammeri* 'Eichholz') A prostrate shrub related to *C. dammeri,* with which it is sometimes confused, but with smaller, generally obovate, longer-stalked leaves, which lack the deep veins of *C. dammeri*, and flowers generally in pairs. W Sichuan, China.

rehderi Pojark. (*C. bullatus* var. *macrophyllus* Rehder & E.H. Wilson) An extremely handsome, medium-sized to large shrub of open habit with large, dark green, deeply veined leaves and profuse, deep red berries. W China. AM 1912.

roseus Edgew. A small, loose-growing shrub related to *C. integerrimus*, occasionally reaching about 2m. Leaves oval, mucronate, quite smooth. Flowers pink-tinged in small clusters followed by small, red, obovoid fruits. NW Himalaya, Afghanistan. I 1882.

'Rothschildianus' A large shrub possessing a distinctive spreading habit when young. Large clusters of creamy-yellow fruits. 'Exburiensis' is very similar. Both were raised at Exbury, Hampshire. ♥ 2002.

rotundifolius Wall. ex Lindl. (*C. prostratus* Baker, *C. microphyllus* var. *uva-ursi* Lindl.) A small, vigorous, semi-prostrate species with long, arching branches clothed with small, glossy leaves; fruits large, rose-red. Himalaya. I 1825. See also *C. nitidus*.

'Royal Beauty' See under 'Coral Beauty'.

rubens W.W. Sm. Small, free-berrying shrub of spreading habit. The solitary flowers have pink-tinged petals followed by red fruits. W China. I 1927. AM 1924.

rugosus Pritz. (*C. salicifolius* var. *rugosus* (Pritz.) Rehder & E.H. Wilson) Similar to *C. salicifolius* but with broader and more deeply veined leaves. For the plant originally grown under this name, see *C. hylmoei*.

'Sabrina' See *C. splendens*.

'St Monica' A semi-evergreen hybrid with leaves that colour brightly before falling in late winter. It forms a large shrub and bears heavy crops of bright red fruits. Found in the garden of the St Monica Home for the Aged, Bristol.

salicifolius Franch. An invaluable but variable evergreen, tall and graceful, it carries heavy crops of small, bright red fruits in autumn. A parent of many hybrids. Sichuan, China. I 1908. 'Autumn Fire' See *C.* 'Herbstfeuer'. 'Avondrood' See 'Repens'. **var. floccosus** See *C. floccosus*. 'Fructu Luteo' An interesting form with yellow fruits. 'Gnom' (*C.* 'Gnom') A dwarf shrub with slender, purplish, arching shoots making a low, wide mound. Leaves are lance-shaped, up to 3cm long by 1cm wide and dark glossy green, bronze-tinged in winter. Small, bright red berries ripen in November but are not usually freely borne. Excellent groundcover. Raised in Germany about 1938. 'Parkteppich' A scrambling, partially prostrate shrub covered with small, red fruits in autumn. C 1950. 'Repens' ('Avondrood') A prostrate shrub with very narrow leaves and small, red fruits. An excellent groundcover. C 1948. **var. rugosus** See *C. rugosus*.

'Salmon Spray' A medium-sized, free-fruiting shrub producing large, leafy sprays of salmon-red fruits, akin to *C. henryanus*. Raised in our nurseries before 1940.

serotinus Hutch. (*C. glaucophyllus* f. *serotinus* (Hutch.) Stapf, *C. glaucophyllus* var. *vestitus* hort. in part not W.W. Sm.) A vigorous bush to 5m or more, related to *C. glaucophyllus* but with the blue-green leaves larger and tomentose beneath. It flowers profusely in July and it is December before the fruits take on their red colour. W China. I from Yunnan, China in 1907 by George Forrest. FCC 1919. See also *C. meiophyllus*.

sherriffii G. Klotz (*C. orbicularis* hort. not Schltdl.) A medium-sized to large, deciduous or semi-evergreen shrub of spreading habit. Leaves small, broad-elliptic, greyish-hairy beneath, turning purplish in autumn. Top-shaped, red fruits are borne singly or in pairs along the secondary twigs. Sometimes grown as *C. conspicuus*. SE Tibet.

sikangensis Flinck & B. Hylmö. Medium-sized shrub, related to *C. obscurus* and differing in its more upright habit, thicker leaves and profuse, shiny, orange-red fruits. Collected by Dr Harry Smith in W China in 1934.

simonsii Baker. A well-known, semi-evergreen, erect shrub, much used in plantations and for hedges. Fruits large, scarlet. Himalaya (Nepal to Bhutan). I 1865. ♥ 2002.

'Skogholm' See *C.* × *suecicus* 'Skogholm'.

splendens Flinck & B. Hylmö (*C. distichus* var. *tongolensis* hort. not C. K. Schneid.) A handsome species up to 2m, related to *C. dielsianus*. The arching shoots, with small, greyish-green, rounded leaves, are studded with large, obovoid, bright orange fruits in autumn. W China. I 1934 by Dr Harry Smith. 'Sabrina' is a seedling that was found in the garden of Mr Norman Hadden in Somerset. It was originally thought to be a hybrid between *C. horizontalis* and *C. franchetii* but appears identical to *C. splendens*. It received an AM in 1950.

sternianus (Turrill) Boom (*C. franchetii* var. *sternianus* Turrill, *C. wardii* hort. in part) This excellent more or less evergreen shrub is one of the best of all cotoneasters. It has sage-green leaves, silvery-white beneath, and pink flowers followed by large, sub-globose, bright orange-red fruits, produced in great abundance. In the past it has been widely distributed wrongly under the name of *C. wardii*. S Tibet, N Burma. I 1913. ♥ 2002. AM 1939 (as *C. wardii*).

*'Streib's Findling' A prostrate shrub of dense, congested growth with low, arching branches and tiny, dark green leaves. Sometimes said to be a hybrid of *C. dammeri* to which it bears no resemblance. It is possibly a form of *C. procumbens*. C 1960.

× suecicus G. Klotz (*C. dammeri* × *C. conspicuus*) Hybrids between these species have arisen several times in cultivation. They make dwarf, widespreading evergreens, useful for groundcover. 'Erlinda' A sport of 'Skogholm' found in Belgium with arching branches and small, dark green leaves, marked with grey-green and conspicuously edged with creamy-white. Fruits red, sparse. Usually grown as a weeping standard. 'Skogholm' (*C.* 'Skogholm') A dwarf, evergreen shrub of widespreading habit. Leaves small; fruits small, obovoid, coral-red in autumn but not freely produced. Selected in 1941.

tomentellus Pojark. A small to medium-sized, spreading shrub with arching branches, the young shoots grey-hairy becoming purplish. Leaves broadly elliptic to obovate, up to 3.5cm long, rounded and mucronate at the apex, grey-green and hairy on both sides. Bright red fruits contrast effectively with the foliage. W Sichuan, China. I by Ernest Wilson.

tomentosus (Aiton) Lindl. A rare, erect-branched shrub with rounded leaves, white-tomentose beneath – perhaps the woolliest of the genus. Flowers are pink; fruits large, brick-red, colouring in August. Sometimes confused with *C. nebrodensis*. Alps, SE Europe. I 1759.

*turbinatus Craib. An elegant, large, July-flowering shrub of upright habit; leaves elliptic to obovate, deep blue-green above, grey-downy beneath; fruits small, bright scarlet, top-shaped, ripening in October. China. I 1910.

'Valkenburg' A small, semi-evergreen shrub of dense habit with widespreading stems reaching 2m; leaves turn orange, scarlet and yellow in autumn. Raised by Broertjes in Holland in 1951.

veitchii (Rehder & E.H. Wilson) G. Klotz (*C. racemiflorus* var. *veitchii* Rehder & E.H. Wilson) A medium-sized to large, widespreading shrub with purplish shoots, grey-hairy when young. Leaves ovate, to 4.5cm long, tomentose beneath. Large, crimson berries with a slight bloom, like small cherries, 1.5cm across, ripen early. China. I 1900.

vestitus (W.W. Sm.) Flinck & B. Hylmö (*C. glaucophyllus* var. *vestitus* W.W. Sm.) A medium-sized shrub similar to *C. glaucophyllus* but with the leaves densely tomentose beneath. W China. See also *C. serotinus*.

villosulus (Rehder & E.H. Wilson) Flinck & B. Hylmö (*C. acutifolius* var. *villosulus* Rehder & E.H. Wilson) A large shrub with arching branches and dark glossy green, ovate, taper-pointed leaves which turn purple and red in autumn. Fruits blackish-purple covered with brown hairs. W China. I 1900.

wardii W.W. Sm. A stiff, erect-branched, deciduous shrub of moderate size. Leaves dark glossy green above, silky white tomentose beneath. Berries bright orange-red, top-shaped. *C. sternianus* has also been grown under this name. China.

*× watereri Exell. Variable, semi-evergreen hybrids between *C. frigidus*, *C. henryanus* and *C. salicifolius* and their forms. All are completely hardy, medium to large shrubs or occasionally small trees of strong, vigorous growth, with long leaves and heavy crops of normally red or orange-red fruits. There are many named forms. AM 1951. 'John Waterer' A large, semi-evergreen shrub with long spreading branches laden with bunches of red fruits in autumn. C 1928. ♀ 2002. AM 1951.

zabelii C.K. Schneid. A medium-sized, arching, spreading species. Fruits obovoid, dark red, in short-stalked, pendent clusters. China. I 1907 by Ernest Wilson. AM 1912.

Cottonwood See *Populus deltoides*.

Cottonwood, mountain See *Ozothamnus leptophyllus*.
Cottonwood, golden See *Ozothamnus leptophyllus* Fulvidus Group.
Cowberry See *Vaccinium vitis-idaea*.
Crab apple See *Malus*.
Cranberry See *Vaccinium oxycoccos*.
Cranberry, American See *Vaccinium macrocarpon*.
Cranberry, highbush See *Viburnum trilobum*.
Crape myrtle See *Lagerstroemia indica*.

+CRATAEGOMESPILUS Simon-Louis ex Bellair (*Crataegus* + *Mespilus*)—**Rosaceae**—Interesting graft hybrids (chimaeras) between hawthorn and medlar.

dardarii Simon-Louis (*C. monogyna* + *M. germanica*) Both the following originated on the same tree. They are ornamental, widespreading, small trees with attractive, comparatively large, white flowers and yellow and orange autumn tints. 'Bronvaux' Bronvaux Medlar. The original hybrid, consisting of a central core of hawthorn and an outer envelope of medlar. The shoots are occasionally thorny. Leaves like those of the medlar, but smaller. Fruits also medlar-like but smaller and in clusters. Occasional branches revert to either parent. Originated in the garden of Mons Dardar at Bronvaux, near Metz, France, about 1895. 'Jules d'Asnières' (+*C. asniersii*) Occurred at the same time and on the same tree as 'Bronvaux', but in this case the medlar forms the central core and hawthorn the outer envelope. Young shoots are woolly; leaves vary from entire to deeply lobed. Fruits similar to those of the hawthorn.

grandiflora See × *Crataemespilus grandiflora*.

CRATAEGUS L.—**Rosaceae**—The thorns are among the hardiest and most adaptable trees, giving a good account of themselves both in industrial areas and windswept coastal districts. When established they are tolerant of both dryness and excessive moisture. Most are widespreading, small trees or large shrubs with attractive autumn tints. Except where otherwise stated, the flowers are white, and open in May and June, and the fruits are red.

Although more than 1,000 species have been described from North America alone, many of these are now regarded as hybrids or forms of variable species and the true number is probably more like 200.

altaica See *C. wattiana*.

arkansana See *C. mollis*.

arnoldiana Sarg. A beautiful, small tree with shallowly lobed leaves and large fruits like red cherries. NE USA. I 1901. AM 1936.

azarolus L. Azarole. A large shrub or small tree which, although introduced in the 17th century, is still rare in cultivation. Bears dense clusters of comparatively large, white flowers with purple anthers. The edible fruits are usually orange or pale yellow. Leaves rhomboid, wedge-shaped at the base. N Africa and W Asia. C 1640. AM 1976.

calpodendron (Ehrh.) Medik. (*C. tomentosa* L.) A North American species forming a small, round-headed tree; very floriferous; bears orange-red, pear-shaped fruits. I 1765.

canbyi Sarg. Small, bushy tree with glossy green, serrate and shallowly lobed leaves; fruits dark shining crimson, almost as large as cherries. NE USA. I 1901.

× *carrierei* See *C. × lavallei* 'Carrièrei'.

champlainensis Sarg. Small tree related to *C. arnoldiana*, from which it differs in its more heart-shaped leaves. North America. I 1901.

chlorosarca Maxim. A small, normally thornless tree, notable for its pyramidal habit and dark purple-brown shoots. Leaves shallowly lobed, dark and glossy above; flowers white with pink anthers; fruits dark purple-black. Japan. C 1880.

coccinea See *C. intricata* and *C. pedicellata.*

coccinioides Ashe. A small, round-headed tree with large, red fruits. The young leaves are tinged red when opening; the foliage also provides very good autumn colour. E USA. I 1883.

collina Chapm. A small tree or large shrub related to *C. punctata.* Leaves nearly glabrous, usually unlobed except on vigorous shoots; fruits large and red. C and E USA. C 1889.

cordata See *C. phaenopyrum.*

crus-galli L. Cockspur thorn. A widespreading, small, glabrous tree, with thorns often up to 8cm long. Attractive in leaf, flower and fruits, the latter often lasting well into the New Year. Often confused with *C. prunifolia.* E and C North America. I 1691. **var. oblongata** Sarg. A horizontally branched, small tree with narrow, oblong-elliptic leaves and brighter-coloured, oblong fruits. **var. pyracanthifolia** Aiton. Forms a picturesque, small, thornless, horizontally branched tree with narrower leaves. A mature standard specimen makes a perfect umbrella shape.

dahurica Koehne. An uncommon small species. One of the earliest to come into growth; fruits orange-red. SE Siberia.

× *dippeliana* Lange (*C.* × *leeana* (Loudon) Bean) A freeflowering, small tree, a hybrid of *C. tanacetifolia.* Fruits light orange-red. Garden origin about 1830.

douglasii Lindl. (*C. rivularis* Nutt.) Small tree with slender, often drooping branches and shining, dark green, often rounded leaves. Fruits black and shining. North America. I 1828.

dsungarica Zabel. A small tree with spiny branches, large flowers and purplish-black fruits. SE Siberia, Manchuria. AM 1931.

durobrivensis Sarg. A large shrub, one of the most ornamental of North American thorns. The flowers are possibly the largest in the genus, and the large, red fruits remain until midwinter. New York State. I 1901.

ellwangeriana Sarg. Small tree with ascending branches and oval leaves. Large, bright crimson fruits. North America. C 1900. AM 1922.

flabellata (Spach) K. Koch. A large shrub or small tree with thorny stems and fan-shaped, double-toothed leaves. Fruits crimson. SE Canada, NE USA. C 1830.

flava Aiton. Yellow haw. A very distinct, small tree with small leaves and conspicuous, ellipsoid, orange-yellow fruits. SE USA.

× *grignonensis* Mouill. A small tree, a hybrid of *C. mexicana.* Late in both its flowering and the ripening of its large, bright red fruits. Leaves remain green until winter. Origin about 1873.

holmesiana Ashe. An outstanding, small tree. The large, white flowers are followed by conspicuously large, rather oblong, red fruits. NE USA. I 1903.

intricata Lange. (*C. coccinea* L. in part) Large shrub or small tree with erect or spreading branches. Fruits reddish-brown. E North America. I 1730.

jackii Sarg. Medium-sized shrub with spiny stems and large, dark red fruits. Canada. I 1903.

jonesiae Sarg. A small tree particularly noted for its large, bright, glossy, red fruits. NE USA, SE Canada. AM 1977.

korolkowii See *C. wattiana.*

laciniata Ucria (*C. orientalis* Bieb.) A beautiful, small tree, distinguished by its deeply cut, downy leaves, dark green above and grey beneath. Fruits large, coral- or yellowish-red. Orient. I 1810. FCC 1970. AM 1933.

laevigata (Poir.) DC. (*C. oxyacantha* auct. not L., *C. oxyacanthoides* Thuill.) Midland hawthorn. Less common as a native than *C. monogyna,* from which it differs in its less deeply lobed leaves and flowers with usually 2 styles (usually 1 in *C. monogyna*). Many of the following are probably hybrids (*C.* × *media*) between the 2 species, all making large shrubs or small trees, and are very showy when covered with flowers in May. NW and C Europe (incl. British Isles). **‘Aurea’** Fruits yellow. AM 1976. **‘Coccinea Plena’** See ‘Paul's Scarlet’. **‘Crimson Cloud’** See under ‘Punicea’. **‘Gireoudii’** Young leaves prettily mottled pink and white. C 1890. AM 1972. **‘Masekii’** Flowers double, pale rose. C 1899. **‘Paul's Scarlet’** (‘Coccinea Plena’) Flowers double, scarlet. Originated as a sport of ‘Rosea Flore Pleno’ in a garden in Hertfordshire in 1858. ♀ 2002. FCC 1867. **‘Plena’** Flowers double, white. C 1770. **‘Punicea’** Flowers single, scarlet, with a pronounced white eye. C 1828. ‘Crimson Cloud’ (AM 1990) is a similar selection from America. **‘Rosea’** Flowers single, pink. C 1796. **‘Rosea Flore Pleno’** Flowers double, pink. ♀ 2002.

× *lavalleei* Hérincq ex Lavallée (*C. crus-galli* × *C. mexicana, C. carrierei* Vauvel ex Carrière) The plant originally known under this name is recognised as a cultivar to distinguish it from other hybrids of the same parentage. **‘Carrièrei’** A small, dense-headed tree, distinguished by its long, glossy, dark green leaves, which often remain until December. Fruits orange-red persisting throughout the winter and very colourful against the dark foliage. Garden origin about 1870. ♀ 2002. AM 1924.

× *leeana* See *C.* × *dippeliana.*

macracantha Loudon. A tree or shrub up to 5m high with attractively coloured leaves in autumn and bright crimson fruits. Has the longest spines of all thorns sometimes up to 10–13cm in length. North America. I 1819.

maximowiczii C.K. Schneid (*C. sanguinea* var. *villosa* Maxim.) A tree forming a compact cone with shallowly lobed leaves. Its flower stalks, calyx and young fruits are bristly-hairy. Fruits smooth when ripe. NE Asia.

× *media* Bechst. (*C. laevigata* × *C. monogyna*) A large shrub or small tree, intermediate in character between the parents. It is a variable plant found both in the wild and in cultivation. Several of the cultivars listed under *C. laevigata* belong here.

mexicana DC. (*C. pubescens* auct. not Steud, *C. pubescens* var. *stipulacea* (Loudon) Stapf) A small, spreading, thorny or thornless, semi-evergreen tree with dark green leaves, to 10cm long, tapered to the base and toothed above the middle. White flowers in early summer are followed by large fruits, ripening from orange-red to yellow. The cooked fruits are preserved in syrup or used to make a drink called ponche. Mexico. I 1824.

missouriensis Ashe. A shrub or small tree having distinctive, sharply-toothed, pubescent leaves and orange-red fruits. SE USA. I 1905.

mollis (Torr. & A. Gray) Scheele (*C. arkansana* Sarg.) Red haw. One of the best of the American species, forming a widespreading tree 10–12m high. Leaves downy; fruits showy, like red cherries, carried in large clusters. C North America. Long cultivated.

monogyna Jacq. Common hawthorn, May, Quick. A familiar native, extensively planted as a hedge throughout the British Isles. A tree in full flower in May is a wonderful sight and is equal to any of the foreign species. In autumn its branches are often laden with red fruits, haws. The flowers are white and strongly fragrant. Europe. N Africa. W Asia. **'Biflora'** ('Praecox') The Glastonbury thorn produces leaves earlier than normal and occasionally an early, but smaller, crop of flowers during winter. C 1770. **'Compacta'** ('Inermis Compacta') A remarkable, dwarf form with stout, stiff, unarmed branches. C 1907. **'Flexuosa'** ('Tortuosa') A curious and striking form with twisted corkscrew branches. C 1838. **'Pendula'** Weeping thorn. A form with graceful, arching branches; flowers white. **'Pendula Rosea'** Graceful, pendent branches and pink flowers. **'Praecox'** See 'Biflora'. **'Pteridifolia'** A form with deeply lobed and toothed leaves. C 1838. **'Stricta'** ('Fastigiata') Branches erect. An excellent, small, tough tree for exposed places. **'Tortuosa'** See 'Flexuosa'. **'Variegata'** Leaves splashed and mottled creamy-white.

× *mordenensis* Boom (*C. laevigata* × *C. succulenta*) This hybrid was first raised at the Morden Experimental Station, Manitoba, Canada, one parent was *C. laevigata* 'Paul's Scarlet'. **'Snowbird'** A seedling of 'Toba' with double, white flowers. **'Toba'** A small tree with deeply lobed and toothed leaves. In May produces double flowers, opening white with a pink tinge, becoming blush.

nitida Sarg. A small tree with spreading, usually thornless, branches and elliptic to oblong, shining leaves which change to orange and red in the autumn. Fruits red. E USA. I 1883.

orientalis See *C. laciniata*. **var. *sanguinea*** See *C. schraderiana*.

oxyacantha See *C. laevigata*.

pedicellata Sarg. (*C. coccinea* L. in part) Scarlet haw. A small tree with a widespreading head of thorny branches. Leaves with glandular teeth. Large bunches of scarlet fruits and often rich autumn colour. NE North America. I 1683.

× *persimilis* Sarg. (*C. crus-galli* × *C. macracantha*) A naturally occurring hybrid mainly grown in the following form. E USA. **'Prunifolia'** An excellent small, compact, broad-headed tree, notable for its persistent, showy fruits and polished, oval leaves, which colour richly in autumn. ♛ 2002.

persistens Sarg. A small tree. Leaves remain green during early winter and are accompanied by the long-persistent, red fruits. Possibly a hybrid of *C. crus-galli*.

phaenopyrum L. f. (*C. cordata* Aiton) Washington thorn. A striking, round-headed species, up to 10m. One of the most distinct of the genus with glossy, maple-like leaves and a profusion of small, dark crimson fruits. Good autumn tints. SE USA. I 1738.

pinnatifida Bunge. A small tree with large, conspicuously lobed leaves; thorns short or absent. Fruits crimson, minutely dotted. NE Asia. C 1860. **var. *major*** N.E. Br. The Chinese variety is one of the most ornamental thorns with glossy, crimson fruits to nearly 2.5cm across.

Among the best of all small trees for its rich red autumn colour. N China. C 1880. FCC 1886.

prunifolia See *C.* × *persimilis* 'Prunifolia'.

pubescens See *C. mexicana*.

punctata Jacq. An attractive tree, up to 11m, producing great crops of white blossom. Fruits large, dull crimson with pale spots. E North America. I 1746. **'Aurea'** ('Xanthocarpa') Fruits yellow.

rivularis See *C. douglasii*.

saligna Greene. A shrub or small tree from Colorado. Fruits lustrous, at first red, finally black. I 1902.

schraderiana Ledeb. (*C. orientalis* var. *sanguinea* Loudon) A small, round-headed tree with deeply cut, grey-green, downy leaves. The masses of large, dark purple-red fruits can be spectacular after a hot summer. Greece, Crimea.

stipulacea Loudon. A small but vigorous, semi-evergreen tree, remarkable as one of the few Mexican trees hardy in the British Isles. Leaves glossy green above, pubescent beneath; fruits like yellow crab apples, very persistent. I 1824.

submollis Sarg. A small tree often grown as *C. mollis* but differing in its rather smaller leaves and bright orange-red fruits. NE USA, SE Canada. AM 1953.

tanacetifolia (Lam.) Pers. Tansy-leaved thorn. A small, usually thornless, slow-growing tree with grey, downy leaves, conspicuous in flower and fruit; the latter like small, yellow apples. SW Asia. I 1789. AM 1976.

tomentosa See *C. calpodendron*.

uniflora Münchh. A medium-sized shrub with small, rounded leaves and clusters of 1–3 flowers. Fruits yellow or greenish-yellow. E USA. I 1704.

wattiana Hemsl. & Lace (*C. altaica* (Loudon) Lange, *C. korolkowii* L. Henry) Small, often thornless tree with sharply toothed leaves and translucent yellow fruits. C Asia.

wilsonii Sarg. A small tree or large shrub. Leaves lustrous; fruits deep red. C China. I 1907 by Ernest Wilson.

× **CRATAEMESPILUS** E.G. Camus (*Crataegus* × *Mespilus*)—**Rosaceae**—A natural hybrid between the hawthorn and medlar, bearing clusters of attractive, white flowers. Not to be confused with +*Crataegomespilus*, which includes graft hybrids between medlar and hawthorn.

grandiflora (Sm.) E.G. Camus (*C. laevigata* × *M. germanica*) (*Crataegomespilus grandiflora* (Sm.) Bean) An apparently sterile hybrid found wild in France in about 1800. A small, broad-headed tree with hairy, occasionally lobed leaves. Flowers in pairs or 3s, 2.5cm across; fruits like large, glossy, brownish-orange haws. Orange and yellow autumn tints, particularly striking after a hot summer.

‡†***CRINODENDRON** Molina (*Tricuspidaria* Ruiz & Pav.)—**Elaeocarpaceae**—Both species of this genus are natives of Chile, and are worthy additions to gardens in the milder areas of Britain. They require lime-free soil and partial shade.

hookerianum Gay (*Tricuspidaria lanceolata* Miq.) Lantern tree. This shrub is one of the gems of the garden. The flowers, like long-stalked crimson lanterns, hang thickly along the branches in May. A large, dense shrub in mild localities, it survived the hard winters of the 1980s at Sir

Harold Hillier Gardens and Arboretum. I 1848 by William Lobb. ♀ 2002. FCC 1916 (as *Tricuspidaria lanceolata*).

patagua Mol. (*Tricuspidaria dependens* Ruiz & Pav.) This is a strong-growing shrub or small tree bearing white, bell-shaped flowers in late summer. Requires wall protection in cold districts. I 1901 by H.J. Elwes. AM 1984.

Crowberry See *Empetrum nigrum*.
Cucumber tree See *Magnolia acuminata*.
Cudrania tricuspidata See *Maclura tricuspidata*.
Currant, flowering See *Ribes sanguineum*.
Curry plant See *Helichrysum italicum* subsp. *serotinum*.

‡***CYATHODES** Labill.—**Epacridaceae**—About 15 species of heath-like Australian and New Zealand shrubs with tiny, white, pitcher-shaped flowers and very attractive foliage. They require lime-free soil.

colensoi (Hook. f.) Hook. f. A very beautiful, prostrate shrub, this species has glaucous foliage and white or red fruit. Proving quite hardy. New Zealand. AM 1962.

†*robusta* Hook. f. Small, erect shrub with white fruits and narrow leaves, glaucous beneath. Chatham Islands.

Cyclocarya paliurus See *Pterocarya paliurus*.

CYDONIA Mill.—**Rosaceae**—A monotypic genus related to *Chaenomeles*.

japonica See *Chaenomeles speciosa*.
maulei See *Chaenomeles japonica*.
oblonga Mill. (*C. vulgaris* Pers.) The common quince. Native of N Iran and Turkestan. A small, unarmed tree, occasionally up to 6m high, with white to pale rose flowers and golden-yellow, fragrant fruit. Leaves often turn rich yellow before falling. This and named cultivars selected for their fruit, make picturesque specimen trees for lawns. For ornamental quinces see *Chaenomeles*. '**Vranja**' The most popular fruiting selection with very fragrant, golden-yellow fruits. ♀ 2002.

‡**CYRILLA** Garden ex L.—**Cyrillaceae**—An interesting genus containing one variable species of wide distribution, sometimes regarded as several species. In the southern parts of its range it is evergreen and tree-like.

racemiflora L. Leatherwood. A small, late summer-flowering deciduous or semi-evergreen shrub. Lanceolate leaves turn crimson in autumn. White flowers are borne in whorls of slender, cylindrical racemes at the base of the current year's shoots in late summer to autumn. SE USA, West Indies, Mexico, N South America. I 1765. AM 1901.

CYTISUS Desf.—**Leguminosae**—About 35 species, native mainly to Europe but extending to W Asia and N Africa. The brooms vary from prostrate shrublets to those attaining small tree-size. All have typical pea-shaped flowers and are mostly late spring- or early summer-flowering, but there are a few that flower towards autumn. The species are natives of Europe and have yellow flowers unless otherwise stated.

The majority of species are lime-tolerant but *C. multiflorus* and *C. scoparius* and their mixed progeny, comprising the bulk of the hardy hybrid brooms, will not succeed for long on poor, shallow chalky soils nor, strangely enough, in extremely acid soils. They do best in neutral or acid soils, or deep soils over chalk, including stiff clay-loam. They are all sun-loving and reach about 1.2–2m.

The more vigorous species and hybrids may be pruned immediately after flowering to prevent legginess, taking care not to cut into the old hard wood.

albus See *Chamaecytisus albus*.
ardoinoi E. Fourn. A miniature, mat-forming alpine shrub from the Maritime Alps (S France). Flowers bright yellow, April to May. I 1866. ♀ 2002. AM 1955.
austriacus See *Chamaecytisus austriacus*.
battandieri Maire. A tall shrub. Leaves laburnum-like, grey, with a silky sheen. Cone-shaped clusters of bright yellow, pineapple-scented flowers appear in July. An excellent shrub for a high wall but being very hardy will survive in the open in many places. Morocco. I about 1922. ♀ 2002. FCC 1934. AM 1931. '**Yellow Tail**' A selected form raised in our nurseries before 1975, bearing racemes up to 15cm or more long. ♀ 2002.
× *beanii* Dallim. (*C. ardoinoi* × *C. purgans*) Charming, dwarf shrub up to 35cm high. Golden-yellow flowers in May. Garden origin 1900. ♀ 2002. FCC 1955.
'**Boskoop Ruby**' (*C.* × *praecox* × *C.* 'Hollandia') A small, rounded shrub with very profuse, deep crimson flowers. Raised in Holland, it is one of the most striking red hybrids. ♀ 2002.
'**Burkwoodii**' A vigorous hybrid bearing cerise flowers with deep crimson wings, edged yellow, in May to June. ♀ 2002. AMT 1973.
candicans See *Genista monspessulana*.
capitatus See *C. supinus*.
'**C.E. Pearson**' Flowers have crimson-flushed, creamy-yellow standards and rich flame wings. May to June.
'**Compact Crimson**' Deep crimson flowers with a yellow centre. Compact habit.
'**Cottage**' Similar to *C.* × *kewensis* in its profuse, pale creamy-yellow flowers, but upright in habit.
'**Daisy Hill**' Flowers deep rose in bud, opening to cream standards, flushed rose, and deep crimson wings. May to June. C 1912.
× *dallimorei* Rolfe (*C. multiflorus* × *C. scoparius* 'Andreanus') Medium-sized shrub raised at Kew in 1900. Flowers deep rose, flushed scarlet. A parent of some of the best hybrids. AM 1910.
decumbens (Durande) Spach. A prostrate, rock garden shrublet with bright yellow flowers in May and June. S Europe. I 1775.
demissus See *Chamaecytisus polytrichus*.
'**Donard Seedling**' Pale yellow flowers, with mauve-pink standards and red-flushed wings, in May to June.
'**Dorothy Walpole**' Dark cerise-red flowers, with velvety crimson wings, in May to June. AM 1923.
'**Dukaat**' A small, erect-branched shrub of dense habit with silky-hairy young shoots and small, narrow leaves. Small, golden-yellow flowers in May. An F$_1$ hybrid from the cross *C.* 'Burkwoodii' × *C.* × *praecox*. C 1965.
emeriflorus Reichb. (*C. glabrescens* Sart.) A dwarf, compact shrub with bright golden-yellow flowers in small clusters in May and June. Switzerland. N Italy. C 1896.
frivaldszkyanus Degen. A dwarf shrub often forming a low, compact mound of hairy, leafy stems. Pale yellow

flowers in terminal heads in June and July. Balkans.

glabrescens See *C. emeriflorus*.

'Golden Cascade' Large, yellow flowers flushed with cream on arching shoots.

'Goldfinch' A compact, medium-sized shrub grown for its creamy-yellow flowers, flushed with pink and red, in April to May.

grandiflorus (Brot.) DC. (*Sarothamnus grandiflorus* (DC.) Webb) Woolly-podded broom. In its bright yellow flowers, this species resembles the common yellow broom, but is distinguished by its grey-woolly seedpods. It grows 2.5–3m high and is quite hardy. S Spain and Portugal. I 1816.

hirsutus See *Chamaecytisus hirsutus*.

'Hollandia' Pale cream flowers, the standards with cerise backs and the wings dark cerise in May and June. ♀ 2002. AMT 1973.

ingramii Blakelock. A medium-sized, erect shrub with yellow and cream flowers in June. An interesting species discovered in the mountains of NW Spain by Capt. Collingwood Ingram.

'Johnson's Crimson' Flowers clear crimson. A fine hybrid, in habit resembling the white Spanish broom. FCCT 1973. AMT 1972.

× *kewensis* Bean (*C. ardoinoi* × *C. multiflorus*) Sheets of cream-coloured flowers in May. Growth semi-prostrate. Raised at Kew in 1891. ♀ 2002. **'Niki'** A form with golden-yellow flowers. A sport found in Holland in 1984.

'Killarney Salmon' Rich salmon-orange.

'Killiney Red' Flowers rich red with darker, velvety wings, in May to June.

'La Coquette' In May bears flowers with rose-red, standards, yellow inside, deep orange-yellow wings, veined brick-red, and pale yellow keels, faintly marked with rose-red. AMT 1972.

'Lady Moore' Large, creamy-yellow flowers, in May and June, are flushed rose on the standards and flame on the wings. Larger and richer than those of 'C.E. Pearson'. AM 1928.

'Lena' A vigorous, compact, free-flowering shrub with deep red standards, red wings with yellow margins, and pale yellow keels. Raised at Kew. ♀ 2002. FCCT 1974.

leucanthus See *Chamaecytisus albus*.

'Lord Lambourne' Pale cream standards and dark red wings from May to June. AM 1927.

'Luna' Large flowers with broad, pale creamy-yellow standards, tinged red on the back and inside, rich yellow wings, and pale yellow keels in May. C 1959. FCCT 1974. AMT 1972.

maderensis var. *magnifoliosus* See *Genista stenopetala*.

'Maria Burkwood' A vigorous shrub bearing large, red flowers with coppery wings. AMT 1972.

'Minstead' A charming hybrid derived from *C. multiflorus* producing multitudes of small flowers which are white, flushed lilac, darker on wings and in bud; May to June. AM 1949.

monspessulanus See *Genista monspessulana*.

'Mrs Norman Henry' Similar in habit to 'Minstead', but has flowers with darker wings; May to June. AMT 1972.

‡*multiflorus* (Aiton) Sweet (*C. albus* (Lam.) Link) White Spanish broom. An erect shrub of medium height, its stems studded with small, white flowers in May and June. Parent of many hybrids. Spain. Portugal, NW Africa. C 1752. ♀ 2002. AMT 1974.

nigricans L. (*Lembotropis nigricans* (L.) Griseb.) A useful and elegant, small, late-flowering shrub that produces long, terminal racemes of yellow flowers continuously during late summer. C and SE Europe to C Russia. I 1730. **'Cyni'** A form with a neat, compact habit, that flowers profusely.

'Palette' A vigorous shrub with large flowers in May. The standards shade from cerise-pink at the tip to orange-yellow at the base, the wings are rich vermilion, and the keels are pink, tipped pale yellow. C 1959. AMT 1974.

'Porlock' See *Genista* 'Porlock'.

× *praecox* Wheeler ex Bean (*C. multiflorus* × *C. purgans*) A group of hybrids popular in gardens for their compact habit and profuse flowers. The original form once listed as *C.* × *praecox* has been given the cultivar name 'Warminster', see below. **'Albus'** Flowers white. **'Allgold'** An outstanding small shrub with arching sprays of long-lasting, yellow flowers. ♀ 2002. FCCT 1974. **'Goldspeer'** ('Canary Bird', 'Gold Spear') Profuse, small, deep yellow flowers. C 1955. FCCT 1973. **'Warminster'** Warminster broom. A small shrub, a spectacular plant forming, in early May, a tumbling mass of rich cream. Garden origin about 1867. ♀ 2002.

procumbens (Willd.) Spreng. A dwarf shrub with prostrate branches. Flowers borne in the leaf axils in May and June. SE Europe. AM 1948.

purgans (L.) Spach. A dense, usually leafless shrub forming a mass of erect branches 1m high. Bears fragrant, yellow flowers in April and May. SW Europe, N Africa. C mid-18th century.

purpureus See *Chamaecytisus purpureus*.

ratisbonensis See *Chamaecytisus ratisbonensis*.

'Red Favourite' See 'Roter Favorit'.

'Red Wings' Vigorous and compact. Profuse flowers are deep velvety red with the yellow keels flushed bright red. AMT 1972.

'Roter Favorit' ('Red Favourite') Standard and wings are deep velvety red, the wings with a narrow gold line at the base; the keel is light carmine. C 1959.

scoparius (L.) Link (*Sarothamnus scoparius* (L.) K. Koch) Common broom. A familiar, medium-sized, native shrub, as conspicuous as gorse but without its spines. Flowers of rich butter-yellow in May. A parent of many cultivars. See generic description for soil requirements. Europe. Some of the following are probably hybrids. **'Andreanus'** Flowers attractively marked brown-crimson. Found wild in Normandy in about 1884. ♀ 2002. FCCT 1973. FCC 1890. **'Cornish Cream'** A most attractive form with cream-coloured flowers. FCCT 1973. AM 1923. **'Dragonfly'** Standard deep yellow, wings deep crimson; May to June. Strong-growing. **'Firefly'** Standard yellow; wings with a bronze stain. AM 1907. **'Fulgens'** A late-flowering clone of dense, compact habit. Flowers rufous in bud, opening orange-yellow; wings deep crimson; June. Raised about 1906. **'Golden Sunlight'** A strong-growing form with flowers of rich yellow. C 1929. AMT 1973. f. *indefessus* McClintock. A form that continues to flower during summer and autumn. Found in Brittany in 1962 by David McClintock. subsp. *maritimus* (Rouy) Heywood (*C.*

scoparius var. *prostratus* (C. Bailey) A.B. Jacks.) A dwarf, spreading shrub with large, yellow flowers. Found wild on sea cliffs in a few localities in the west of the British Isles. AM 1913. **var.** *prostratus* See subsp. *maritimus*. **f.** *sulphureus* (Goldring) Rehder. Flowers cream, tinged red in bud; wings and keel pale sulphur.

sessilifolius L. Elegant shrub of medium size with short racemes of bright yellow flowers in June. Leaves usually sessile on flowering stems. C and S Europe, N Africa. Long cultivated. AM 1919.

× *spachianus* See *Genista* × *spachiana*.

supinus See *Chamaecytisus supinus*.

supranubius (L. f.) Kuntze (*Spartocytisus supranubius* (L. f.) Webb & Berthel.) Tenerife broom. A medium-sized shrub resembling *Spartium junceum* in habit. Leaves small, trifoliolate. Fragrant, milky-white flowers, tinted rose, are carried in May in axillary clusters on the previous year's wood. A pretty shrub when in flower. Theoretically tender, it remained uninjured by snow and wind for several years in our relatively cold area (Romsey, Hampshire). Canary Isles. C before 1824. AM 1924.

'**Toome's Variety**' A hybrid of *C. multiflorus* with long, slender stems covered with multitudes of small, creamy-white flowers, flushed lilac on the inside of the standard, in May.

× *versicolor* See *Chamaecytisus* × *versicolor*.

'**Windlesham Ruby**' Flowers rich mahogany-crimson. Upright habit.

'**Zeelandia**' (*C.* 'Burkwoodii' × *C.* × *praecox*) The standards are lilac outside, cream inside, the wings are pinkish, and the keels are cream; May to June. ♀ 2002. FCCT 1974.

D

‡***DABOECIA** D. Don—**Ericaceae**—A genus of a single species, a low-growing, lime-hating shrub, related to *Erica*, distinguished by its flowers, with usually large, glandular, deciduous corollas, and the broader leaves.

azorica See *D. cantabrica* subsp. *azorica*.

cantabrica (Huds.) K. Koch (*Menziesia polifolia* Juss.) Connemara heath, St Dabeoc's heath. One of the most charming and useful of dwarf shrubs, producing long racemes of very showy, rose-purple, pitcher-shaped flowers from June to November. W Europe (incl. Ireland). C 1800. **'Alba'** Flowers white. 40cm. **'Atropurpurea'** Rose-purple; darker than the typical form. 40cm. †**subsp.** *azorica* (Tutin & E. F. Warb.) D.C. McClint. A very pretty plant, less hardy and dwarfer than the typical form. The flowers are darker, being rich crimson. Requires a sheltered position. Azores. I 1929 by E.F. Warburg. AM 1932. **'Bicolor'** White, rose-purple and striped flowers often on the same raceme. 35cm. ♀ 2002. **'Charles Nelson'** Double, globular and long-lasting, mauve flowers. The earliest flowers open single. Found in Co. Galway. 30cm. **'David Moss'** White, freely borne. 35cm. ♀ 2002. **'Hookstone Purple'** Large, amethyst flowers over a long period. 45cm. **'Porter's Variety'** Dwarf, compact form with small, pinched, rose-purple flowers. 30cm. **'Praegerae'** Dwarf, spreading habit; flowers curiously narrowed, rich pink. 40cm. Found by Mrs Praeger in Connemara. C 1932. AMT 1970. **subsp.** *scotica* (D.C. McClint.) E.C. Nelson (*D.* × *scotica* D.C. McClint.) (subsp. *azorica* × subsp. *cantabrica*) Hybrids between the 2 subspecies first originated in a Glasgow garden in about 1953. They are hardier than subsp. *azorica*. **subsp.** *scotica* **'Jack Drake'** Flowers ruby-red. 20cm. ♀ 2002. **subsp.** *scotica* **'Silverwells'** Flowers white. 20cm. ♀ 2002. **subsp.** *scotica* **'William Buchanan'** Flowers deep purple. 45cm. ♀ 2002.**'Waley's Red'** Deep, glowing magenta with a bluish tinge. 35cm. ♀ 2002. **'White Blum'** Upright habit with bright green foliage and erect, white flowers. Among the best of the whites. 30cm.

× *scotica* See *D. cantabrica* subsp. *scotica*.

Dahoon See *Ilex cassine*.
Daisy bush See *Olearia*.

†***DAMNACANTHUS** Gaertn. f.—**Rubiaceae**—A small genus of about 6 species of evergreen, spiny shrubs native to Asia. The following is suitable for sun or shade, and a well-drained soil.

indicus Gaertn. f. A dainty, spiny, small shrub, suitable for growing in pots. Small, fragrant, funnel-shaped, white flowers followed by coral-red berries. China, Taiwan, Japan, Himalaya. I 1868.

***DANAE** Medik.—**Ruscaceae**—A monotypic genus closely related to *Ruscus* and differing in its hermaphrodite flowers, which are borne in short terminal racemes. As in *Ruscus*, the apparent leaves are in fact flattened stems (phylloclades).

racemosa (L.) Moench (*Ruscus racemosus* L.) Alexandrian laurel. A charming, small evergreen with arching sprays of narrow, polished, green leaves. Orange-red fruits are produced after hot summers. Will grow in shade. Excellent for cutting. SW Asia to N Iran. I 1713. AM 1933.

DAPHNE L.—**Thymelaeaceae**—A genus of about 50 species of beautiful, deciduous or evergreen, usually fragrant shrubs, native to Europe, Asia and N Africa. They are mostly small and suitable for a rock garden, but vary from prostrate to large shrubs. Good, loamy soil, moisture and good drainage are essential for their success. All are toxic if eaten.

*acutiloba Rehder. A medium-sized shrub with long, leathery leaves and terminal heads of white, normally scentless flowers in July. Fruits large, bright scarlet. W China. I 1908 by Ernest Wilson.

*albowiana Woron. A close relative of *D. pontica*, which it resembles except in its red fruits. Some plants grown as *D. pontica* appear to belong here. Caucasus.

alpina L. A dwarf, deciduous species with grey-green leaves and fragrant, white flowers in May and June; fruits orange-red. Mountains of S and C Europe. C 1759.

altaica Pall. Small, upright, semi-evergreen shrub with white, slightly fragrant flowers in terminal clusters in May or June, followed by red fruits. Altai Mountains, Siberia. I 1796.

*arbuscula Celak. A dwarf, rounded, alpine shrublet with crowded, narrow leaves and rose-pink, fragrant flowers; fruits brownish-yellow. Carpathian Mountains in E Czechoslovakia. ♀ 2002. FCC 1973. AM 1915.

aurantiaca Diels. Golden-flowered daphne. A small, slow-growing, very distinct and rare Chinese species with fragrant, rich yellow flowers in May and ovate-oblong, opposite leaves, glaucous beneath. Sichuan, Yunnan. I 1906 by George Forrest. FCC 1927.

bholua Buch.-Ham. ex D. Don. A deciduous or semi-evergreen shrub, up to 2m, with stout, erect branches. Leaves oblanceolate. Flowers large, sweetly scented, deep reddish-mauve in bud, opening white, with reddish-mauve reverse, twenty or more in a terminal cluster, appearing continuously in January and February. Fruits black. Hardiness and leaf retention in winter varies according to altitude. Himalaya. C 1938. AM 1946. **'Daman Ridge'** See under 'Peter Smithers'. ***'Darjeeling'** An evergreen or semi-evergreen form deriving from a plant at Wisley raised from seed from Darjeeling in 1961. Flowers very pale pink fading to white, opening early. **'Gurkha'** (T.S.S. 132b) A very hardy, deciduous form collected by Major Tom Spring-Smyth at 3,200m on the Milke Banjyang Ridge in E Nepal in 1962. Flowers are richly scented, and purplish-pink and white. The introduction of this form greatly increased the popularity of this splendid species. ***'Jacqueline Postill'** This splendid and very hardy form originated as a seedling of 'Gurkha' raised by our propagator Alan Postill in 1982. It is evergreen or semi-evergreen, flowering when in full leaf. The flowers are larger and more showy than those of 'Gurkha' with an equally powerful fragrance. ♀ 2002. FCC 1991. ***'Peter Smithers'** An evergreen or semi-evergreen form with strongly fragrant flowers, deep purple-pink in bud. When open the lobes are purple-pink, white in the centre, and become darker as the flowers age. Selected in 1990 from plants at Wakehurst Place grown from seed of plants collected on Daman Ridge, Nepal in 1971 or 1972 by Sir Peter Smithers and grown in his garden in Switzerland. Other plants from this introduction have also been distributed as 'Daman Ridge'. AM 2000. **'Rupina La'** A form with stout shoots and large clusters of large, deep purple-pink flowers. Propagated from a plant raised from seed collected by Tony Schilling in Nepal in 1983 (Schilling 2611).

blagayana Freyer. A dwarf shrub with prostrate branches terminating in bunches of oval leaves and clusters of richly scented, creamy-white flowers from March to April; fruits whitish. A difficult plant, succeeding best in deep leaf-mould and half shade. From the mountain forests of SE Europe. I about 1875. FCC 1880.

× *burkwoodii* Turrill (*D. caucasica* × *D. cneorum*) This group of hybrids includes some of the most popular and easy-to-grow plants in the genus. For the plant usually listed as *D.* × *burkwoodii* see 'Albert Burkwood'. ♀ 2002 (to all green-leaved forms). **'Albert Burkwood'** A fast-growing, semi-evergreen shrub attaining 1m. The pale pink, deliciously fragrant flowers are borne in clusters on short leafy shoots all along the branches in May and June, and often again in autumn. Raised in 1931. AM 1935. **'Astrid'** A Dutch-raised sport of upright habit, the blue-green leaves with a pale yellow margin becoming creamy-white. **'Carol Mackie'** Leaves with a golden-yellow margin which becomes creamy-white. This form is named after the raiser in whose garden in New Jersey (USA), it occurred as a sport in 1962. Similar plants have been raised in Britain and Holland. Previously distributed as 'Variegata'. **'G.K. Argles'** A form with gold-margined leaves raised as a sport at Champernowne Nursery, Buckland Monachorum, Devon. ♀ 2002. **'Lavenirii'** Spreading habit with pale pink flowers deep pink in the centre. Raised in France about 1920. **'Somerset'** A sister seedling of 'Albert Burkwood' from which it differs in its slightly larger size, more upright habit and paler flowers. FCC 1980. AM 1937. **'Variegata'** See under 'Carol Mackie'.

caucasica Pall. A small, narrow-leaved, Caucasian shrub. Terminal clusters of fragrant, white flowers in May and June, often again in early autumn; fruits yellow. C 1893.

*cneorum L. Garland flower. A great favourite due to the fragrance of its rose-pink flowers, which are borne in clusters on prostrate branches during April and May; fruits brownish-yellow. A difficult plant to establish. C and S Europe. **'Alba'** A rare, white form of var. *pygmaea*. AM 1920. A white-flowered form of the typical variety is also in cultivation. **'Eximia'** A more prostrate form with larger leaves and flowers. The unopened flower buds are crimson opening to rich rose-pink. ♀ 2002. FCC 1967. AM 1938. var. *pygmaea* Stoker. Free-flowering with branches lying flat on the ground. AM 1983. **'Ruby Glow'** A form with very deep pink flowers. **'Variegata'** A vigorous form with leaves attractively margined with cream. var. *verlotii* (Gren. & Godr.) Meissn. A rare, lax form differing in its more prostrate growth and narrower, pointed leaves. C and S Alps. AM 1916.

*collina Dickson ex Sm. A first-rate rock-garden shrub. Forms a shapely bush 28–35cm high, each shoot clothed with blunt, deep green leaves and terminating in a cluster of fragrant, rose-purple flowers in May. One of the most rewarding of daphnes. Very close to and now usually included in *D. sericea*. S Italy. C 1752. FCC 1984. AM 1938. var. *neapolitana* See *D.* × *napolitana*.

dauphinii See *D.* × *hybrida*.

genkwa Siebold & Zucc. There can be few lovelier shrubs than this small, oriental species, but it is difficult to establish. It has light green, mostly opposite leaves and relatively large, clear lilac-blue flowers, carried all along leafless branches in April and May. China, Taiwan. I 1843 from China by Robert Fortune. Long cultivated in Japan. FCC 1885.

giraldii Nitsche. An uncommon, dwarf, erect shrub to about 75cm bearing fragrant, yellow flowers in clusters in May or June, followed by bright red fruits. NW China. I 1911 by William Purdom.

*gnidium L. A small, erect, slender shrub with fragrant, creamy-white flowers, from June to August, and red fruits. S Europe and N Africa. C since the 16th century.

× *houtteana* Lindl. & Paxton (*D. laureola* × *D. mezereum*) A small, partially evergreen shrub of erect habit, with purplish leaves similar to those of *D. laureola* in shape. Flowers dark red-purple in April. Subject to virus and now rare. C 1850.

*× hybrida Colv. ex Sweet (*D. collina* × *D. odora*) (*D. dauphinii* Loudon) This charming, small shrub with dark glossy green leaves has the beauty and fragrance of *D. odora*, and is hardier. Reddish-purple, very fragrant flowers are produced from late autumn through winter. Raised about 1820.

†**jasminea* Sm. in Sibth. & Sm. A dwarf, cushion-forming shrublet with small, narrow, glaucous leaves. Flowers rose-pink in bud, opening white, deliciously fragrant. A rare alpine gem growing on cliffs and rocks in Greece, Crete, Libya. Requires winter protection. The plant described here is often referred to as the Delphi form. An upright form, usually with white flowers, is also in cultivation. I 1954. AM 1968.

jezoensis Maxim. ex Regel (*D. kamtschatica* var. *jezoensis* (Maxim. ex Regel) Ohwi. A dwarf shrub with pale green young leaves emerging in autumn, becoming dark blue-green when mature, and deciduous in early summer. Dense clusters of fragrant, golden-yellow flowers, with exserted stamens and a green tube, are borne in winter. Best in a moist, but well-drained, peaty soil in a bright but not exposed position. Japan. I about 1960. AM 1985.

*juliae Koso.-Pol. A rare dwarf, evergreen, mound-forming shrub, closely resembling and sometimes included under *D. cneorum* but with more crowded flowerheads. S Russia. I 1959. AM 1992.

*laureola L. Spurge laurel. A useful, small, native shrub, which tolerates shade. Flowers fragrant, yellow-green in dense clusters beneath the leathery, polished green leaves. February and March. Fruits black. Can cause an allergic skin reaction. S and W Europe (incl. England), North Africa. subsp. *philippi* (Gren.) Rouy. Dwarf variety with smaller, obovate leaves and smaller flowers. A very pleasing evergreen for a rock garden. Pyrenees. C 1894.

longilobata (Lecomte) Turrill. A small, erect, deciduous or semi-evergreen shrub, up to 2m, with slender, purplish stems and narrowly elliptic leaves. White flowers during summer are followed by red berries. Closely related to *D. acutiloba*. SE Tibet, NW Yunnan. C 1928. **'Peter Moore'** A striking, variegated form with grey-green leaves margined creamy-white. A seedling found by our propagator Peter Moore in 1980.

× *manteniana* Manten ex Taylor & Vrugtman (*D. × burkwoodii × D. retusa*) This hybrid is represented by the following form. **'Manten'** A dwarf, evergreen shrub of dense, rounded habit with dark glossy green leaves to 3.5cm long. Strongly scented flowers are deep rose-purple outside, deep lilac within. They are borne in dense, terminal clusters in late April and early May and usually again in summer and autumn. Raised in 1941.

mezereum L The well-known, sweet-scented, deciduous mezereon is a small shrub flowering in February and March. The purple-red flowers, covering the previous year's shoots, are followed by scarlet fruits. Unfortunately the foliage is often poor due to virus. Thrives in chalk soils. Europe (incl. British Isles), W Asia to Siberia. C 1561. **f. alba** (Weston) Schelle. Flowers white, fruits translucent amber; branches more upright. **var. autumnalis** hort. ex Rehder. Flowers relatively large and beginning to open as early as September. Previously listed as 'Grandiflora'. **'Bowles' Variety'** ('Bowles' White') A form with white flowers and pure white fruits. AM 1947. **'Rosea'** A selected form. Large, clear rose-pink flowers.

× *napolitana* Lodd. (*D. collina* var. *neapolitana* (Lodd.) Lindl.) A beautiful, dwarf, hardy shrub, rarely more than 1m high, with blunt, ash-green leaves. Clusters of rose-pink, fragrant flowers are borne profusely from April to early June. Probably a hybrid between *D. collina* and *D. cneorum*. C 1823. ♥ 2002. AM 1984.

odora Thunb. (*D. indica* hort. not L.) This winter- and early spring-flowering, small shrub should be given some protection, but is hardy enough to withstand frost of considerable severity. It makes a bush of 1.2–2m with dark green leaves and very fragrant, reddish-purple flowers. China, Japan. I 1771. **f. alba** (Hemsl.) Hara (var. *leucantha* Makino) A form with white flowers. **'Aureomarginata'** Leaves with a narrow, yellow margin that becomes creamy-white with age. Hardier than the green form. ♥ 2002. AM 1976.

oleoides Schreb. (*D. buxifolia* Vahl) An uncommon, dwarf species with thick leaves, terminating in a bristle-like tip; cream or pale pink, fragrant flowers are in terminal clusters; fruits red. S Europe to the Himalaya. **var. brachyloba** Meissn. Differs in its leaves, which are rounded not pointed, and adpressed pilose above; also in the shorter-lobed, white flowers in a lax head.

†*papyracea* Wall. ex Steud. A little-known species, related to *D. odora* and recognised by its long, oblanceolate leaves. White flowers during winter; dark red fruits. W Himalaya. C 1881.

petraea Leyb. (*D. rupestris* Facchini) An alpine gem, only 5–7.5cm high, with small, linear leaves; fragrant, rosy-pink flowers are produced in terminal clusters in June. A choice, gnarled, little shrublet suitable for an alpine house or scree. N Italy. C 1880. AM 1906. **'Grandiflora'**

A form with larger flowers. Collected in the wild in 1914. FCC 1924. AM 1918.

pontica L. A small, free-growing, widespreading shrub, which will thrive under the drip of trees and in heavy soil. Bright green, glossy leaves and loose clusters of elusively fragrant, spidery, yellow-green flowers in April and May; fruits blue-black. SE Bulgaria, N Iran, N Turkey. I 1752. ♥ 2002. AM 1977.

pseudomezereum A. Gray. A rare species, similar in habit and leaf to *D. mezereum*, but with smaller, greenish-yellow, scentless flowers clustered around the tips of the shoots in April. Fruits red. Male and female flowers on separate plants (dioecious). Japan. C 1905.

retusa See *D. tangutica* Retusa Group.

'Rossetii' (*D. cneorum × D. laureola* subsp. *philippi*) A natural hybrid found in the Pyrenees in 1927. It forms a compact, rounded bush usually less than 60cm. The reddish flowers are rarely seen. The oblanceolate leaves are intermediate between those of its parents.

rupestris See *D. petraea*.

sericea Vahl. This small shrub differs from *D. collina* in the leaves being narrower and olive-green and the flowers paler pink. Fruits orange-red. SE Europe. AM 1931.

× *susannae* C.D. Brickell (*D. arbuscula × D. collina*) Hybrids between these species have been raised several times. The following are the result of crosses made by Robin White of Blackthorn Nurseries in 1988 and are named after Hampshire villages. They make dwarf, compact shrubs with rigid shoots, white-tomentose when young, and dark green leaves, grey-green beneath. Clusters of very fragrant flowers open at the ends of the previous year's shoots from mid- to late spring or early summer. **'Cheriton'** A dwarf shrub reaching about 40cm tall and 90cm across, with glossy leaves and bearing large clusters of rosy-purple, very fragrant flowers in mid- to late spring, and again in late summer. *D. arbuscula* was the female parent. **'Tichborne'** Similar to 'Cheriton' but with matt foliage and slightly large and paler, purple-pink flowers, not repeating in late summer. *D. collina* was the female parent. AM 2000.

tangutica Maxim. A small species closely related to and resembling *D. retusa*, but distinguishable by its longer, more acute leaves. Flowers in terminal clusters in March or April, and usually again in late summer, fragrant, white, tinged purple on the inside, rose-purple outside. China. I early 1900s by Ernest Wilson. ♥ 2002. AM 1929. **Retusa Group** (*D. retusa* Hemsl.) A slow-growing, dwarf shrub with stout, stiff branches. Clusters of fragrant, deep rose-purple flowers in May and June and often again in autumn. W China, Himalaya. I 1901 by Ernest Wilson. ♥ 2002. AM 1927.

× *thauma* Farrer (*D. petraea × D. striata*) A dwarf, compact shrub, forming a low mound, with narrow leaves densely crowding the branchlets. Bright rose-purple flowers are borne in terminal clusters in May and June. A natural hybrid introduced from the S Tyrol in 1911 by Reginald Farrer.

× *transatlantica* C.D. Brickell & A.R. White (*D. caucasica × D. collina*) This hybrid was named from a plant that has been distributed in North America as *D. caucasica* but was shown by the authors to be of hybrid origin. A controlled cross at Blackthorn Nursery by Robin White

has since produced a very similar plant. **'Jim's Pride'** A semi-evergreen, dwarf shrub of rounded habit to about 90cm tall and across with dark green leaves to 4cm long. Flowers very fragrant, in dense clusters at the ends of the shoots opening in mid- to late spring and intermittently during summer and autumn. They are purple-red in bud, opening white inside with a densely white-pubescent, purple-red tube. The yellow anthers with orange-yellow pollen form a distinct eye in the centre of the flower.

****'Valerie Hillier'** (*D. cneorum* × *D. longilobata*) A dwarf, evergreen shrub of spreading habit with downy shoots and narrowly oblong-elliptic, glossy green leaves, up to 5cm long. Fragrant flowers are borne in terminal clusters on the young growths continuously from May to autumn. They are purplish-pink in bud, opening pale pink, fading nearly to white with pink-edged lobes; the tube is pale pink shading to green at the base. A splendid hybrid raised by our propagator Alan Postill from a cross made in June 1984. It is named after the wife of John Hillier, elder son of Sir Harold Hillier. The hybrid *D. collina* × *D. longilobata* was raised at the same time.

× *whiteorum* C.D. Brickell (*D. jasminea* × *D. petraea*) Hybrids between two choice dwarf alpine species, raised by Robin White of Blackthorn Nurseries, from crosses made in 1987 between the Delphi form of *D. jasminea* and *D. petraea* 'Grandiflora'. The latter was the seed parent, except for 'Beauworth' which is a product of the reverse cross. They make dwarf, spreading shrubs of compact habit with densely arranged, grey-green leaves and clusters of fragrant flowers, often over a long period. The following cultivars are named after Hampshire villages. **'Beauworth' A dwarf, rounded shrub, about 45cm tall and 60cm across. Flowers deep purple-red in bud, opening pale pink, fading to white. They are produced from mid-spring on side shoots of the previous year and during summer on the new growths. **'Kilmeston'** A dwarf shrub, reaching about 30 by 60cm and spreading by underground runners, the leaves flushed purple when young. Profuse, purple-pink flowers open from deep crimson buds from mid-spring to summer. The least hardy form, it is usually best in an alpine house. AM 1993. **'Warnford'** A nearly prostrate shrub, about 15cm tall and 90cm across. Deep red-purple buds open to white flowers from midsummer, occasionally starting in spring and through autumn. The hardiest selection.

****DAPHNIPHYLLUM**   Blume—**Daphniphyllaceae**—A small genus of about 10 species of dioecious, evergreen trees and shrubs, natives of E and SE Asia to N Australia. This aristocratic-looking shrub has leaves recalling *Rhododendron decorum* but the flowers are not conspicuous. It thrives in half shade and a neutral, loamy soil, but is lime-tolerant.

himalaense (Benth.) Müll-Arg. A native of the E Himalaya, this species is cultivated mainly in the following form. **subsp. *macropodum*** (Miq.) T.C. Huang (*D. humile* Maxim. ex Franch. & Sav., *D. macropodum* Miq., *D. glaucescens* hort. not Blume) A large, striking, evergreen shrub with large, rhododendron-like leaves, pale green above, glaucous beneath. Pungently scented flowers are borne in clusters beneath the leaves in late spring, the males in purplish, mulberry-like clusters. Remarkably

hardy. China, Japan. I 1879 by Charles Maries. FCC 1987 (for fruit and foliage). FCC 1888 (for foliage).

humile See *D. himalaense* subsp. *macropodum*.
macropodum See *D. himalaense* subsp. *macropodum*.

Date plum See *Diospyros lotus*.
Datura See *Brugmansia*.

DAVIDIA Baill.—**Cornaceae**—Medium-sized trees recalling *Tilia*. The small, inconspicuous flowers are in dense, globular heads up to 2.5cm across. Each head is attended by an unequal pair of large, conspicuous, white bracts, which have been fancifully likened to handkerchiefs. The genus contains one species and is the only member of the family. It is perfectly winter hardy and will thrive in every kind of fertile soil.

involucrata Baill. Pocket-handkerchief tree, Dove tree, Ghost tree. This beautiful, medium-sized tree is most conspicuous in May when draped with its large, white bracts. Leaves densely hairy beneath but glabrous on young plants. C and W China. First discovered by the French missionary Père David in 1869, introduced by Ernest Wilson in 1904. ♀ 2002. AM 1972. **var. *vilmoriniana*** (Dode) Wangerin. The leaves on established trees are glabrous, not silky-hairy beneath, and the fruits are more elliptic and less russety. Horticulturally both this and the typical form are very similar and of equal merit. Most plants grown as *D. involucrata* belong here. I 1897 by the Abbé Farges from China. ♀ 2002. FCC 1911.

†**DEBREGEASIA** Gaudich.—**Urticaceae**—A small genus of about 5 species of tender trees and shrubs, native to NE Africa and tropical Asia. They are related to the nettles, but unlike them, harmless to the touch.

longifolia (Burm. f.) Wedd. A medium-sized shrub of which the long, lance-shaped leaves, pale beneath, are the most striking feature. Produces yellow, mulberry-like fruits. SE Asia.

DECAISNEA Hook. f. & Thomson—**Lardizabalaceae**—A genus of 2 species of deciduous shrubs from W China and the Himalaya. The following hardy species will grow in sun or semi-shade, and moist but well-drained soil.

fargesii Franch. A very distinct shrub attaining about 3m. Large, pinnate leaves, 0.6–1m long, are blue-tinged when young. The yellow-green flowers, often unisexual, are borne in racemes up to 50cm long in May, followed by remarkable, metallic-blue pods, like those of the broad bean in shape. W China. I 1895 by the Abbé Farges.

Deerberry See *Vaccinium stamineum*.

†****DENDROMECON** Benth.—**Papaveraceae**—A genus of 2 species related to *Romneya*, but differing in their entire, evergreen leaves and smaller, yellow flowers. Both are natives of California.

rigida Benth. Bush poppy. A large shrub, best grown against a warm, sunny wall. Leaves narrow, rigid and glaucous. Flowers poppy-like, 4-petalled, bright buttercup-yellow, produced intermittently over a long period. California. I about 1854 by William Lobb. AM 1913.

Desert olive See *Forestiera neomexicana*.
Desert sweet See *Chamaebatiaria millefolium*.

‡†*DESFONTAINIA** Ruiz & Pav.—**Potaliaceae**—A mono-typic genus found in South America, mainly in the Andes. A variable plant sometimes split into several species. Given a sheltered position and half-shade this beautiful evergreen is hardy in the Home Counties. Not successful on shallow chalk soils.

spinosa Ruiz & Pav. (*D. hookeri* Dun.) A magnificent, late summer-flowering evergreen, slowly attaining 1.8–2m. Leaves small, holly-like; flowers tubular, scarlet with a yellow mouth, opening in summer. Costa Rica to Cape Horn. I about 1843 by William Lobb. ♀ 2002. AM 1931. **'Harold Comber'** A form collected by Comber in about 1925, with 5cm-long flowers varying in colour from ver-milion to orient-red. AM 1955.

DESMODIUM Desv.—**Leguminosae**—A large genus of some 300 species of mainly tender herbs and shrubs, wide-ly distributed in tropical and subtropical regions. They dif-fer from *Lespedeza* in their many-seeded pods and leaflets with small, subulate stipules.

elegans DC. (*D. tiliifolium* (D. Don) G. Don) A small to medium-sized, semi-woody shrub with erect stems and trifoliolate leaves. In summer bears a profusion of pale lilac, pea-flowers in large panicles, followed by flattened and lobed pods. Himalaya. I 1879. ♀ 2002.

penduliflorum See *Lespedeza thunbergii*.

praestans See *D. yunnanense*.

tiliifolium See *D. elegans*.

†*yunnanense* Franch. (*D. praestans* Forrest) A large shrub with long, scandent stems and large, rounded leaves. The dense covering of silky hairs gives the whole plant a sil-very appearance. Purple flowers are borne in compact, crowded racemes during late summer. Requires a well-drained position in full sun, preferably backed by a wall. SW China. I 1914 by George Forrest.

DEUTZIA Thunb.—**Hydrangeaceae**—About 70 species of deciduous shrubs, native to the Himalaya and E and SE Asia. Mainly easily cultivated shrubs, succeeding in all types of fertile soil, they flower in June and grow 1.2–2m high, unless otherwise described. Thin out and cut back old flowering shoots to within a few centimetres of the old wood, immediately after flowering. Gardeners are indebted to Lemoine of Nancy, France, for the many, attractive hybrid clones.

'Avalanche' See *D.* × *maliflora* 'Avalanche'.

calycosa Rehder. A medium-sized shrub of upright habit when young, later spreading, with grey-green leaves and pink-tinged, white flowers. Sichuan and Yunnan, China. I 1981 by the Sino-British Expedition to the Cangshan. **'Dali'** A name given by Roy Lancaster to a selection with particularly large flowers raised from SBEC 417.

× **candelabra** (Lemoine) Rehder (*D. gracilis* × *D. sieboldiana*) This graceful shrub is similar to *D. gracilis*, but hardier and with broader and denser flower panicles. Garden origin. C 1907 (Lemoine).

chunii See *D. ningpoensis*.

compacta Craib. This rare, July-blooming, Chinese species forms a neat bush. Flowers, in 7.5cm-wide corymbs, are

pink in bud, opening to white, and strongly resemble hawthorn in size, form and sweet scent. I 1905. **'Lavender Time'** Flowers are lilac at first, turning pale lavender. This very distinct shrub, collected in the wild by Kingdon-Ward, may be a new species.

'Contraste' See *D.* × *hybrida* 'Contraste'.

corymbosa R. Br. A medium-sized shrub with ovate leaves and corymbs of white flowers in June. Not as good a garden plant as *D. setchuenensis* var. *corymbiflora*, but hardier. W Himalaya. I 1830.

crenata var. *nakaiana* **'Nikko'** See *D. gracilis* 'Nikko'.

discolor Hemsl. An attractive, small shrub with ovate leaves. Produces clusters of white or pink flowers in May and June. C and W China. For Farrer 846, which has been grown under this name, see *D. purpurascens* 'Alpine Magicien'. **'Major'** Flowers 2–2.5cm across in corymbose clusters, white, pink-tinted outside. The best form of this handsome Chinese species. I by Ernest Wilson in 1901. AM 1999.

× *elegantissima* (Lemoine) Rehder (*D. purpurascens* × *D. sieboldiana*) Rose-pink-tinted, fragrant flowers in panic-ulate corymbs. Garden origin 1909. AM 1914. **'Fasciculata'** A very beautiful form of medium size. Flowers bright rose-pink. C 1911 (Lemoine). FCC 1972. AM 1949. **'Rosealind'** A lovely clone with deep carmine-pink flowers. C 1962. ♀ 2002. AM 1972.

glomeruliflora Franch. A Chinese shrub usually less than 2m high with leaves that are grey beneath; large, white flowers are borne in dense clusters in May and June. I 1908 by Ernest Wilson. **var. *forrestiana*** See *D. subulata*.

gracilis Siebold & Zucc. An elegant, white-flowered, Japanese species, which is a parent of many good hybrids. Needs protection from late spring frosts. Previously much used for forcing. I about 1840. AM 1980. **'Nikko'** (*D.* 'Nikko', *D. crenata* var. *nakaiana* 'Nikko') A dwarf, compact shrub with narrow, pointed leaves to 6cm long. Flowers small, white, but often not freely produced in the British Isles. I to the US National Arboretum in 1976 as *D. nakaiana*. AM 1996.

'Hillieri' (*D. longifolia* 'Veitchii' × *D. setchuenensis* var. *corymbiflora*) An attractive shrub of graceful habit raised in our nurseries in 1926. The star-like flowers are purple-tinged in bud, opening pink and fading to white. They are carried in compact clusters of 20 to 30 in late June or July.

hookeriana (Schneid.) Airy Shaw. This rare species with small leaves is closely related to *D. monbeigia*. Dense corymbs of white flowers in late June. Sikkim, W China.

× *hybrida* Lemoine (*D. discolor* × *D. longifolia*) A variable, extremely floriferous hybrid of medium size. There are a number of named clones. **'Contraste'** Soft lilac-pink, star-shaped flowers in loose panicles; outside of petals rich vinous-purple. C 1928. AM 1931. **'Joconde'** A superb, strong-growing shrub with very large flowers, lined and shaded rose-purple outside. AM 1959. **'Magicien'** ('Strawberry Fields', *D.* × *magnifica* 'Rubra') Large flowers are mauve-pink, edged white and tinted purple on the reverse. ♀ 2002. **'Mont Rose'** Rose-pink flowers, with darker tints, are very freely borne in paniculate clusters. Raised by Lemoine about 1925. ♀ 2002. AM 1971. **'Perle Rose'** A medium-sized shrub with long, ovate-lanceolate leaves and soft rose flowers in long-stalked, corymbose panicles in June. C 1935 (Lemoine). **'Pink Pompon'** See 'Rosea Plena'. **'Rosea Plena'** ('Pink Pompon') A medium-sized shrub producing dense heads of double flowers, pink at first becoming white. **'Strawberry Fields'** See 'Magicien'.

hypoglauca See *D. rubens*.

'Iris Alford' (*D. longifolia* 'Veitchii' × *D. × hybrida* 'Magicien') A small shrub with purple shoots and roughly hairy leaves. Flowers 2.5cm across, deep purple-pink in bud, opening white inside, deep purple-pink on the reverse, the petals with white margins. Selected in 1994 from a group of 3 seedlings in the Sir Harold Hillier Gardens and Arboretum raised by Alf Alford and named after his wife.

'Joconde' See *D. × hybrida* 'Joconde'.

× *kalmiiflora* Lemoine (*D. parviflora* × *D. purpurascens*) A charming, floriferous shrub with large, white flowers, flushed carmine. Leaves purple in autumn. Garden origin 1900.

longifolia Franch. A handsome, medium-sized shrub with long, narrowly lanceolate leaves and large clusters of white or pink-tinted flowers in June and July. W China. I 1905 by Ernest Wilson. AM 1912. **'Veitchii'** Large clusters of rich lilac-pink-tinted flowers in June and July make this the most aristocratic of a popular group of shrubs. ♔ 2002. FCC 1978. AM 1912.

'Magicien' See *D. × hybrida* 'Magicien'.

× *magnifica* (Lemoine) Rehder (*D. scabra* × *D. vilminoriae*) (*D. crenata* var. *magnifica* Lemoine) A vigorous, medium-sized shrub with erect branches and large panicles of double, white flowers. Garden origin 1909. This and the following forms raised by Lemoine. AM 1916. **'Eburnea'** A very beautiful clone with single, white flowers in loose panicles. C 1912. **'Latiflora'** Single, white flowers up to 2.5cm across. C 1910. **'Longipetala'** White, long-petalled flowers. One of the best clones of this popular shrub. **'Macrothyrsa'** White flowers in large clusters. C 1918.

× *maliflora* Rehder (*D. × lemoinei* × *D. purpurascens*) A strong-growing, medium-sized shrub with large corymbs of purple-flushed, white flowers in June. Garden origin 1905. **'Avalanche'** The slender, erect branches are arched by the weight of the fragrant, white flowers. C 1904 (Lemoine).

mollis Duthie. Small to medium-sized shrub with leaves thickly felted beneath. White flowers, in dense corymbs, in June. W China. I 1901 by Ernest Wilson. AM 1931.

monbeigii W.W. Sm. A very pretty shrub, distinct in its small leaves, white beneath. Bears profusion of small, glistening, star-like, white flowers; late. China. I 1921 by George Forrest. AM 1936.

'Mont Rose' See *D. × hybrida* 'Mont Rose'.

'Nikko' See *D. gracilis* 'Nikko'.

ningpoensis Rehder (*D. chunii* Hu) A very beautiful and remarkable, July-blooming species. Flowers, 12mm across, have white or pink petals, reflexed to expose the yellow anthers. Panicles to 10cm long are produced all along the branches. Leaves narrow, grey beneath. This plant both in pink- and white-flowered forms is sometimes seen in cultivation under the name *D. ningpoensis*. E China. I 1935. ♔ 2002. AM 1972. **'Pink Charm'** A pink-flowered form selected in our nurseries.

'Perle Rose' See *D. × hybrida* 'Perle Rose'.

pulchra Vidal. A magnificent, hardy, medium-sized shrub with racemes of white flowers like drooping spikes of lily-of-the-valley. Philippines, Taiwan. I 1918 by Ernest Wilson.

purpurascens (L. Henry) Rehder. A graceful, medium-height species with white, sweetly scented flowers, tinted rich purplish-crimson, in early June. Parent of many hybrids. Yunnan, Upper Burma. I 1888 by the Abbé Delavay. **'Alpine Magicien'** A distinct form with dark purple filaments. Named from a plant at the National Botanic Gardens, Glasnevin originally grown as *D. discolor*, collected in Burma in 1919 (Farrer 846).

× *rosea* (Lemoine) Rehder (*D. gracilis* × *D. purpurascens*) This hybrid forms a compact shrub with arching branches and widely bell-shaped, pink flowers. Garden origin 1898. This and the following forms were raised by Lemoine. **'Campanulata'** An erect form with white petals contrasting with the purple calyx. C 1899. **'Carminea'** Very attractive form with flowers flushed rose-carmine. C 1900. **'Floribunda'** Pink-tinged flowers in dense, erect panicles. C 1901. **'Grandiflora'** Large, white flowers with pink suffusion. C 1899. **'Multiflora'** Free-flowering, with white flowers. C 1903. **'Venusta'** This leans towards *D. gracilis*, but has larger, white flowers. C 1898.

rubens Rehder (*D. hypoglauca* Rehder) A graceful shrub with arching branches bearing lanceolate leaves, white beneath, and numerous, pure white flowers in June. China. I 1910 by William Purdom.

scabra Thunb. Tall, erect-branched shrub, to 3–3.5m, producing large, paniculate clusters of white flowers in June and July. Japan, China. I 1822. **'Azaleiflora'** Flowers smaller with reflexed petals. **'Candidissima'** Tall shrub with double, pure white flowers. C 1867. AM 1980. **'Macrocephala'** Large, bell-shaped, white flowers. **'Plena'** Double flowers suffused rose-purple outside. I 1861 by Robert Fortune. FCC 1863. **'Punctata'** Leaves heavily mottled with white. Flowers single, white. **'Pride of Rochester'** Double, white flowers flushed with pink outside. **'Watereri'** Single, white flowers, tinted carmine. C 1877.

schneideriana Rehder. A medium-sized shrub producing panicles of white flowers in June or July. W China. I 1907. AM 1938. **var. laxiflora** Rehder. A variety with somewhat narrower leaves and lax panicles. I 1901.

setchuenensis Franch. A charming, slow-growing species, up to 2m, producing corymbose clusters of innumerable, small, white, star-like flowers during July and August. One of the very best summer-blooming shrubs, but not quite hardy enough for the coldest parts of the British Isles. China. I 1895. AM 1945. **var. corymbiflora** (Lemoine) Rehder. This equally beautiful and very floriferous form differs in its broader leaves. ♔ 2002. AM 1945.

sieboldiana Maxim. An elegant shrub of loose habit with ovate or elliptic leaves and panicles of white flowers in early June. Japan. C 1890.

staminea R. Br. A Himalayan species of medium height with white flowers, in 5cm-wide corymbs, in June. Requires a warm, sheltered position. I 1841.

subulata Hand.-Mazz. (*D. glomeruliflora* var. *forrestiana* Zaik.) A small to medium-sized shrub of compact habit with neat, roughly hairy leaves to 5cm long, glaucous beneath. Flowers white, tinged pale pink, the calyx becoming reddish and remaining conspicuous long after flowering. S Sichuan, NW Yunnan. I 1981 (SBEC 529).

vilmoriniae Lemoine. A rapid-growing, erect-branched species, attaining 2.5–3m. Bears white flowers in broad, corymbose panicles and long, lance-shaped leaves, grey beneath. China. I 1897 by the Abbé Farges. AM 1917.

× *wilsonii* Duthie. (*D. discolor* × *D. mollis*) A handsome natural hybrid with brown, exfoliating bark and panicles of large, white flowers in June. W and C China. I about 1901 by Ernest Wilson. AM 1908.

Devil's club See *Oplopanax horridus*.
Devil's walking stick See *Aralia spinosa*.
Dewberry See *Rubus caesius*.

†***DICHOTOMANTHES** Kurz—**Rosaceae**—A monotypic genus closely related to *Cotoneaster*, differing in the dry, capsular fruits with persistent, enlarged calyces. Suitable for a sheltered wall in any fertile soil.

tristaniicarpa Kurz. A large, cotoneaster-like shrub with white-woolly stems and dark green, oblong-elliptic leaves to 7cm long, reticulate above, tomentose beneath. White flowers in terminal corymbs during June are followed by orange-red, cotoneaster-like fruits, which only ripen after hot summers. Spring foliage prettily tinted. This rare plant has grown undamaged at the Sir Harold Hillier Gardens and Arboretum for many years. China. I 1917 by George Forrest.

DIERVILLA Mill.—**Caprifoliaceae**—A genus of 3 species of easily-grown, small, summer-flowering shrubs, allied to *Lonicera* and native to North America. Frequently confused with *Weigela* but differing in the smaller, yellow, 2-lipped flowers.

lonicera Mill. (*D. canadensis* Willd.) A small, suckering shrub with pale-yellow, honeysuckle-like flowers, opening in June and July. Good autumn leaf colour in exposed positions. North America. I 1720.

rivularis Gatt. A small shrub with lemon-yellow flowers in July and August. Attractive autumn tints. SE USA. C 1898.

sessilifolia Buckley. Sulphur-yellow flowers, in short panicles, from June to August. SE USA. I 1844.

× *splendens* (Carrière) Kirchn. (*D. Ionicera* × *D. sessilifolia*) A hybrid with short-petioled leaves and sulphur-yellow flowers. Originated about 1850.

‡†**DIOSMA** L.—**Rutaceae**—A small genus of about 30 species of evergreen, heath-like shrubs, related to *Coleonema*, natives of South Africa.

ericoides L. A dwarf shrub with arching shoots and small, densely arranged, heath-like leaves. The small, white or pale pink, star-shaped flowers are borne in clusters at the ends of the shoots in spring and summer. South Africa.
'Pink Fountain' Dark green foliage and pink flowers.
'Sunset Gold' Yellow foliage and white flowers.

pulchella See *Agathosma pulchella*.

DIOSPYROS L.—**Ebenaceae**—A large genus of nearly 500 species of mainly tropical, evergreen and deciduous, dioecious trees and shrubs, many of considerable economic importance such as *D. ebenum*, the source of ebony. Few species are hardy.

armata Hemsl. A remarkable, large, slow-growing, semi-evergreen shrub with spiny, spreading branches; leaves lustrous. China. I 1904 by Ernest Wilson.

kaki L. f. (*D. chinensis* Blume) Chinese persimmon. A large shrub or small tree, long cultivated in the East for its edible fruits, and, in the British Isles for the glorious, orange-yellow to orange-red and plum-purple autumn colour of its large, lustrous leaves. Orange-yellow, tomato-like fruits are carried here in the open most late summers. China. I 1796.

lotus L. The date plum is a perfectly hardy, small tree with tapered leaves, dark polished green above, paler below. The female trees produce purple or yellow fruits like small tomatoes. E Asia. C 1597.

virginiana L. The North American persimmon forms an elegant, widespreading, medium-sized tree with rugged, tessellated bark. Good autumn colour. I 1629.

DIOSTEA Miers—**Verbenaceae**—A genus of 3 species of shrubs or small trees native to Chile and Argentina.

juncea (Gillies & Hook.) Miers. A tall, elegant shrub, resembling Spanish broom (*Spartium junceum*) in growth, but with opposite leaves. Clusters of pale lilac, verbena-like flowers are borne in June, but seldom with sufficient profusion to be conspicuous. Andes of Chile and Argentina. I 1890.

DIPELTA Maxim.—**Caprifoliaceae**—A small genus of 4 species of tall shrubs, native of China and bearing a general resemblance to *Weigela*. They differ mainly in their showy, winged fruits.

floribunda Maxim. A large shrub of first-class garden merit. Fragrant, weigela-like, pink flowers, flushed yellow at the throat, are produced in great profusion in May. C and W China. I 1902 by Ernest Wilson. ♀ 2002. AM 1927.

ventricosa Hemsl. An attractive, large, spring-flowering shrub bearing conspicuous, lilac-rose flowers with curiously swollen bases. W China. I 1904 by Ernest Wilson.

yunnanensis Franch. Large shrub bearing cream-coloured flowers with orange markings. Related to *D. ventricosa* but flowers narrowed at base. W China. I 1910 by George Forrest.

Diplacus See *Mimulus*.

DIPTERONIA Oliv.—**Aceraceae**—A genus of 2 species in C and S China allied to *Acer* and the only other member of the family. They differ from *Acer* in that their fruit is winged all round instead of on one side.

sinensis Oliv. A large shrub with bold, pinnate leaves. The inconspicuous flowers are followed, in autumn, by large clusters of winged seeds, pale green, changing to red, like those of the wych elm (*Ulmus glabra*), but more conspicuous. China. I about 1900 by Ernest Wilson. AM 1922.

DIRCA L.—**Thymelaeaceae**—A genus of only 2 species of deciduous shrubs, native to North America and related to

Daphne, differing botanically in the exserted stamens and style. They thrive in moist soils, particularly those of a calcareous nature.

occidentalis A. Gray. Western leatherwood. A rare, medium-sized shrub similar to *D. palustris* but more upright in habit, with hairy young leaves and shoots, and broader leaves. The flowers are also slightly larger and more distinctly lobed. California. First flowered in the Sir Harold Hillier Gardens and Arboretum in March 1981.

palustris L. Leatherwood. An interesting shrub of medium size with yellow flowers, about 12mm long, usually produced in threes on the leafless branches during March. The strong, flexible stems are used for basket-making in some parts of the USA. North America. I 1750.

‡**DISANTHUS** Maxim.—**Hamamelidaceae**—A monotypic genus related to *Liquidambar*.

cercidifolius Maxim. A medium-sized shrub resembling a witch hazel (*Hamamelis*) in habit and Judas tree (*Cercis siliquastrum*) in leaf. It is valued for its beautiful, soft crimson and claret-red autumn tints. The tiny, purplish flowers are produced in October. Requires a moist but well-drained soil in semi-shade. Japan. **subsp.** *longipes* (H.T. Chang) K.Y. Pan. Occurs in SE China. I 1893. ♀ 2002. FCC 1970. AM 1936.

DISCARIA Hook.—**Rhamnaceae**—About 15 species of spiny trees and shrubs related to *Colletia* and found in South America, New Zealand, Australia and Tasmania. Like *Colletia* they have prominent, opposite spines and small, clustered flowers. They require a sunny, sheltered position and will grow in most well-drained soils.

crenata (Clos) Regel. A large, spiny shrub or small tree with drooping branches and elliptic to ovate-lanceolate, leaves, up to 4 × 1.5cm, crenate-undulate at the margin, emarginate at the apex. Small, white flowers, with 5 lobes, are borne in clusters of 2–4 in the leaf axils in June. Originally listed as *D. serratifolia*. C and S Chile, Argentina. C 1842.

serratifolia See *D. crenata*.

toumatou Raoul. Wild Irishman. A botanically interesting, small to medium-sized shrub allied to *Colletia* but less formidably armed. It has numerous, small, green-white flowers and small leaves in opposite clusters or occasionally absent. Spines in pairs, slender, green, over 2.5cm long. New Zealand. I 1975.

*****DISTYLIUM** Siebold & Zucc.—**Hamamelidaceae**—A small genus of about 12 species of evergreen shrubs and trees related to *Sycopsis* but with flowers in racemes. Native to E and SE Asia and Central America. They thrive best in the same conditions as *Hamamelis*.

racemosum Siebold & Zucc. A widespreading, but slow-growing, evergreen shrub, reaching tree size in the wild, with glossy, leathery leaves. Its petalless flowers consist of clusters of conspicuous, red stamens, produced in racemes in April and May. S Japan, Taiwan, Korea, China. I 1876. The plant previously listed as *Sycopsis tutcheri* is now considered to be the Chinese form of this species. It differs from the more commonly grown form in its much more vigorous habit, smaller, glossier leaves and its smaller flower clusters. It has been seen in flower

in late winter at the same time as *Sycopsis sinensis*, and in midsummer. The racemes, which are produced in winter, barely expand and at that time of year this plant resembles a *Sycopsis* more closely.

Dockmackie See *Viburnum acerifolium*.

DOCYNIA Decne.—**Rosaceae**—A genus of about 5 species of small, evergreen or semi-evergreen trees and shrubs resembling wild pears and allied to *Cydonia* of which the name is an anagram. Natives of the Himalaya, China and SE Asia. Rare in cultivation in the British Isles.

delavayi (Franch.) Schneid. A tree with leaves 3–5-lobed on young plants becoming lanceolate, white-tomentose beneath, persisting into winter; flowers in April, white, rose-tinted outside; fruits apple-like, yellow. SW China. C 1890.

indica (Wall.) Decne. (*D. rufifolia* (H. Lév.) Rehder) A species similar to *D. delavayi*, but with less persistent leaves, tomentose beneath when young. Young leaves reddish. E Himalaya, China, SE Asia. I 1903.

Dogwood See *Cornus*.

Dorycnium hirsutum See *Lotus hirsutus*.

Dove tree See *Davidia involucrata*.

Dracaena australis See *Cordyline australis*.

Dracaena indivisa See *Cordyline indivisa*.

†*****DRIMYS** J.R. Forst. & G. Forst.—**Winteraceae**—About 9 species of evergreen trees and shrubs, natives of Malaysia, E Australia, New Guinea and Central and South America. The cultivated species are handsome plants for favoured localities.

andina See *D. winteri* var. *andina*.

aromatica See *D. lanceolata*.

colorata See *Pseudowintera colorata*.

lanceolata (Poir.) Baill. (*D. aromatica* (R. Br.) F. Muell.) Mountain pepper. A medium-sized to large, aromatic shrub of slender, upright habit with purplish-red shoots and dark green leaves, paler green beneath and attractive copper-tinted, young growths. Numerous, small, creamy-white flowers appear in April and May; male and female on separate plants. Tasmania, SE Australia. I 1843. AM 1926.

winteri J.R. Forst. & G. Forst. Winter's bark. A very handsome, tall shrub or small tree with large, leathery leaves, glaucous beneath. Bears fragrant, ivory-white flowers in loose umbels in May. We have grown 2 forms, one with shorter, broader leaves than the other. The broad-leaved form is sometimes distinguished as var. *latifolia* Miers. Both these plants are considered to represent var. *chilensis* (DC.) A. Gray. C Chile. I 1827. ♀ 2002. AM 1971. **var.** *andina* Reiche (*D. andina* hort.) A dwarf, compact, slow-growing variety. It flowers freely at only 30cm tall. Chile, Argentina.

DRYAS L.—**Rosaceae**—A genus of 2 species of carpeting plants with small, evergreen, oak-like leaves, dark shining green above and gleaming white beneath. Natives of N temperate and Arctic regions. They are suitable for screes or wall tops, between paving or on a rock garden, in most soils.

integrifolia M. Vahl. A dwarf, matted shrublet with dark green leaves densely white-tomentose beneath, untoothed or toothed only at the base. Flowers creamy-white on tall scapes, followed by silky seedheads. Arctic North America, Greenland.

octopetala L. Mountain avens. A native species. The white, yellow-centred flowers, like little dog roses, are carried on 7.5cm stalks, and cover the whole plant during May or early June. These are followed by silky tassels which later change to fluffy, grey balls of down. North America, Europe (incl. British Isles), Asia. C 1750. ♀ 2002. AM 1955. **'Minor'** A charming miniature, smaller in all its parts. C 1930. ♀ 2002.

× *suendermannii* Kellerer ex Sünd. (*D. drummondii* × *D. octopetala*) This is an uncommon hybrid, that is similar in most respects to *D. octopetala*, but differs in its slightly larger, rather erect leaves and its nodding, creamy-white flower buds (those of the native plant are erect and white); flowering in May or early June. C 1750. ♀ 2002. AM 1955.

E

Echinopanax See *Oplopanax*.

EDGEWORTHIA Meissn.—**Thymelaeaceae**—A small genus of 2 species of shrubs related to *Daphne* and natives of the Himalaya and China.

chrysantha Lindl. (*E. papyrifera* Siebold & Zucc.) A Chinese shrub attaining 1.2–1.5m. Dense, nodding, terminal clusters of fragrant, yellow flowers, clothed on the outside with white, silky hairs, open in late winter. Used in Japan for the manufacture of a high-class paper for currency. I 1845. AM 1961. **'Red Dragon'** A form with orange-red flowers. AM 1982 (as f. *rubra*).

Edwardsia chilensis See *Sophora macrocarpa*.

EHRETIA P. Browne—**Boraginaceae**—About 50 species of evergreen and deciduous trees and shrubs, widely distributed in tropical and subtropical regions. The 2 species in cultivation thrive in any fertile soil, including chalk soils. Both have a distinctive appearance with conspicuous leaves and corymbose panicles of small, white flowers. Tender when young, ripened growth will withstand our coldest winters, but unripened growth is liable to frost damage.

acuminata R. Br. (*E. ovalifolia* Hassk., *E. thyrsiflora* (Siebold & Zucc.) Nakai, *E. serrata* hort. not Roxb.) A small and slow-growing tree with leaves smaller than those of *E. dicksonii* and glabrous, or nearly so, at maturity; it also flowers later, normally in August. China, Japan, Korea, Taiwan, SE Asia, Australia. I 1900.

dicksonii Hance (*E. macrophylla* hort. not Wall.) An interesting, fast-growing, small, sturdy tree with large, roughly hairy, lustrous leaves, to 23cm long. Broad corymbs of small, fragrant, white flowers are borne in June. E. Himalaya, China, Vietnam, Taiwan, Ryukyu Isles. I 1897 by Ernest Wilson.

ovalifolia See *E. acuminata*.

thyrsiflora See *E. acuminata*.

ELAEAGNUS L.—**Elaeagnaceae**—A genus of about 40 species of deciduous and evergreen, mostly fast-growing shrubs or small trees, natives of S Europe and Asia, with one species in North America. Excellent wind resisters, they are valuable for hedges and shelter belts particularly in maritime and exposed areas. The flowers, though small, are pleasantly scented and produced in abundance. They will thrive in any fertile soil except very shallow chalk soil.

angustifolia L. (*E. angustifolia* var. *orientalis* (L.) Kuntze) Oleaster. A large, spiny shrub or small tree with fragrant flowers in June and silvery-grey, willow-like leaves. Silvery-amber, oval fruits are 12mm long. Easily mistaken for the willow-leaved pear (*Pyrus salicifolia*). Seedlings and young plants have broader, hairy leaves. Temperate W Asia, widely naturalised in S Europe. Cultivated in England in the 16th century. AM 1978. **var. *caspica*** See *E.* 'Quicksilver'. **var. *orientalis*** See *E. angustifolia*.

commutata Bernh. (*E. argentea* Pursh not Moench) Silver berry. A medium-sized, stoloniferous shrub with intensely silver leaves, fragrant flowers in May and small, egg-shaped, silvery fruit. North America. I 1813. AM 1956.

*× ebbingei hort. (*E. macrophylla × E. pungens*) (*E. × submacrophylla* Servett.) A large, hardy, fast-growing, evergreen shrub, splendid for creating shelter, even near the sea. The leaves are large, silvery beneath. Silvery-scaly and fragrant flowers appear in autumn, and orange fruit with silvery freckles in spring. Garden origin 1929. **'Albert Doorenbos'** One of the original seedlings with large leaves, up to 12cm long and 6cm across. **'Coastal Gold'** Broad leaves, silvery when young, later pale yellow with an irregular green border and pale green blotches. **'Gilt Edge'** Leaves margined with golden-yellow. C 1961. ♀ 2002. FCC 1987. AM 1971. **'Limelight'** Leaves green above at first with silvery scales, developing a broad, central blotch of deep yellow and pale green, silvery beneath. Liable to revert. **'The Hague'** Similar to 'Albert Doorenbos' but smaller leaves, up to 10cm by 5cm. AM 1989.

*glabra Thunb. A first-class, vigorous, thornless, evergreen shrub similar to *E. macrophylla*, but with narrower leaves. Fragrant flowers in autumn followed by orange fruit with silvery freckles. China, Korea, Japan. C 1888.

*macrophylla Thunb. Eventually a large, spreading shrub. The broad, rotund leaves of this species are silvery on both surfaces, becoming green above as the season advances. Fragrant flowers in autumn. Korea, Japan. I 1879 by Charles Maries. AM 1932.

multiflora Thunb. (*E. edulis* Carrière, *E. longipes* A. Gray) A widespreading shrub of medium size with leaves green above, silvery beneath. Most decorative in July when laden with oblong, edible, ox-blood-red fruit. Fragrant flowers are produced in April and May on the new shoots. Japan, China. I 1862. AM 1976.

parvifolia Wall. ex Royle (*E. umbellata* var. *parvifolia* (Royle) Schneid.) A large shrub with arching branches and bronze-scaly shoots, silvery when young. Leaves are elliptic-lanceolate, scaly above when young becoming bright glossy green. Fragrant, creamy-white flowers in spring and early summer are followed by red fruits. Himalaya, W China. AM 1985.

*pungens Thunb. A vigorous, spreading, rarely spiny shrub up to 5m. A good shelter-making evergreen. Leaves green and shiny above, dull white, speckled with brown scales beneath. Fragrant flowers in autumn. Japan. I 1830. **'Dicksonii'** ('Aurea') A rather slow-growing, erect clone with leaves with a wide irregular margin of golden-yellow. **'Forest Gold'** Dark green leaves with a large, central yellow blotch. Found growing as 'Maculata' but differing in its more upright habit with less frequent reversion. AM 1997. **'Frederici'** A slow-growing form, the narrow leaves mainly pale creamy-yellow with a narrow, bright green border. C 1888. **'Goldrim'** A striking form with deep glossy green leaves, margined with bright yellow. The margin is brighter than that of 'Variegata' and narrower than that of 'Dicksonii'. Originated as a sport of 'Maculata'. ♀ 2002. **'Hosobafukurin'** A vigorous but compact form with spiny shoots, the leaves with a narrow, wavy yellow margin, white beneath. **'Maculata'** Leaves with a central splash of gold, giving a very bright effect. A very handsome

shrub of moderate growth but prone to reversion. FCC 1891. **var. reflexa** See *E.* × *reflexa*. **'Simonii'** A handsome, erect form with broad, elliptic-oblong leaves. C 1862. **'Variegata'** A large, vigorous shrub, leaves with a thin, creamy-yellow margin.

'Quicksilver' An outstanding, large, deciduous shrub, spreading by suckers, with narrowish leaves that are exceptionally silvery, especially when young. Until fairly recently it was grown under the name *E. angustifolia* var. *caspica*. Probably *E. commutata* × *E. angustifolia*, it resembles a plant of this parentage received by us from Poland. ♀ 2002. AM 1978 (as (*E. commutata*)).

*× **reflexa** C. Morren & Decne. (*E. glabra* × *E. pungens*) (*E. pungens* var. *reflexa* (C. Morren & Decne.) C.K. Schneid.) A tall, vigorous, nearly spineless evergreen with elongated, reddish-brown, almost scandent branches. Leaves are densely clad beneath with brown scales. Japan.

umbellata Thunb. (*E. crispa* Thunb.) A large, strong-growing, widespreading shrub with yellowish-brown shoots and soft green leaves, silvery beneath, giving a unique effect in autumn when heavily laden with its small, rounded, pale red fruits, speckled with white. Delightfully fragrant flowers appear in May and June. China, Korea, Japan. I 1830. AM 1933. **var. parvifolia** See *E. parvifolia*.

†***ELAEOCARPUS** L.—Elaeocarpaceae—A genus of about 60 species of evergreen trees related to *Aristotelia* and distributed from SE Asia to Australia and New Zealand. The following species thrive best in a peaty soil in very mild areas.

cyaneus See *E. reticulatus*.

dentatus (J.R. Forst. & G. Forst.) Vahl. An unusual species for sheltered gardens, this is mainly of botanical interest. It has tiny, yellow-red flowers in April and purplish-grey fruits. New Zealand. I 1883.

reticulatus Sm. (*E. cyaneus* Aiton ex Sims) A medium-sized shrub bearing racemes of white, fringed flowers, recalling those of *Chionanthus*, in summer, followed by conspicuous, turquoise-blue, marble-like fruits. For mildest localities only. E Australia. I 1803. FCC 1912.

Elder See *Sambucus*.
Elder, box See *Acer negundo*.

ELEUTHEROCOCCUS Maxim. (*Acanthopanax* (Decne. & Planch.) Miq.)—Araliaceae—About 50 species of trees and shrubs, sometimes climbing, related to *Fatsia* and *Aralia* and natives of E and SE Asia. Leaves are lobed to palmately compound. Umbels of small flowers are followed by clusters of black fruits.

henryi Oliv. (*Acanthopanax henryi* (Oliv.) Harms) A large shrub with bristly shoots and leaves with 5 leaflets. Large, spherical heads of black fruits resemble giant blackberries. When in flower it is besieged by insects of many kinds. C China. I 1901.

sieboldianus (Makino) Koidz. (*Acanthopanax sieboldianus* Makino, *A. pentaphyllus* hort. not (Siebold & Zucc.) Marchal, *A. spinosus* hort. not (L. f.) Miq.) A medium-sized shrub with numerous, erect stems and clusters of 3- to 5-parted leaves, each cluster with a small, curved prickle at its base. China. I 1874. **'Variegatus'** Leaflets edged creamy-white.

simonii (Schneid.) Nakai (*Acanthopanax simonii* Schneid.) A medium-sized shrub with spiny stems and bristly leaves composed of 5 sharply toothed, bristly leaflets. China. I 1901.

‡**ELLIOTTIA** Mühlenb. ex Elliott—Ericaceae—A genus of 2 species of North American deciduous shrubs. They require a moist, lime-free soil and an open sunny position.

bracteata See *Tripetaleia bracteata*.
paniculata See *Tripetaleia paniculata*.

pyroliflora (Bong.) S.W. Brim & P.F. Stevens (*Cladothamnus pyroliflorus* Bong.) An erect shrub of about 1.2m, so distinct as to be well worthy of inclusion in any collection of ericaceous plants. The curious flowers, borne in June, have 5 spreading petals of terracotta, edged with yellow. NW North America.

racemosa Mühlenb. ex Elliott. Georgia plume. A beautiful, medium-sized, erect-branched, enkianthus-like shrub, scarcely known in European gardens, with oblong-elliptic leaves, 5–10cm long, and 4-petalled, white, slightly fragrant flowers carried in erect terminal racemes or panicles during late summer. SE USA. I 1813.

Elm See *Ulmus*.
Elm, water See *Planera aquatica*.

ELSHOLTZIA Willd.—Labiatae—A small genus of about 30 species of aromatic herbs and subshrubs, natives of Asia. The following are valued for their late flowers. In cold districts or after severe frost the stems are usually cut to the ground in winter but reappear the following spring. Easily grown in any fertile soil, and an open position in full sun.

fruticosa (D. Don) Rehder (*E. polystachya* Benth.) A vigorous, pubescent shrub, up to 2m, bearing elliptic-oblong to lanceolate leaves and long, slender spikes of small, white flowers during late summer and autumn. Himalaya, W China. I about 1903.

stauntonii Benth. A small subshrub with rounded stems, the lance-shaped leaves smelling of mint when crushed. Lilac-purple flowers are freely borne in panicles from August to October making a splendid splash of late colour. N China. I 1909. **'Alba'** Flowers white.

‡***EMBOTHRIUM** J.R. Forst. & G. Forst.—Proteaceae—A small genus of about 8 species of evergreen trees or shrubs, natives of the Andes of South America. Ideally sited when growing in a sheltered border or woodland clearing in deep, moist but well-drained, lime-free soil. Particularly suitable for gardens in the west and south-west British Isles.

coccineum J.R. Forst. & G. Forst. Chilean fire bush. This glorious species, with its profusion of brilliant orange-scarlet flowers in May and early June, is one of the most desirable garden treasures. It is normally an erect, semi-evergreen, slender, tall shrub or small tree with a measured span of life, but on Valencia Island, SW Ireland, there is a giant of 15m. Chile. Forms with yellow flowers are known in the wild and have been introduced but do not appear to be in cultivation. I 1846. AM 1928. **Lanceolatum Group** (*E. coccineum* var. *lanceolatum* (Ruiz & Pav.) Kuntze) This, the least evergreen form with linear-lanceolate leaves, is perfectly hardy. Collected by Harold Comber. **'Norquinco'** (Lanceolatum Group) A selection awarded FCC 1948 and AM 1932 when exhibited by the late Lord Aberconway, who pointed out that the flower clusters touch one another, so that the whole branch is clad in scarlet. ♀ 2002. **Longifolium Group** Differs in its longer, usually persistent leaves. FCC 1948.

EMMENOPTERYS Oliv.—**Rubiaceae**—A small genus of 2 species of deciduous trees, natives of E Asia. The following is the only species in general cultivation and needs a sheltered site.
henryi Oliv. A rare, small tree or large shrub of spreading habit. Large, ovate leaves are particularly decorative in spring when the bronze-coloured young growths unfold. Ernest Wilson described it as being "one of the most strikingly beautiful trees of the Chinese forests, with its flattish to pyramidal corymbs of white, rather large flowers and still larger, white bracts". First flowered in the British Isles at Wakehurst Place, Sussex, in late summer 1987. It prefers a moist, deep loam but is chalk-tolerant. China. I 1907 by Ernest Wilson.

‡***EMPETRUM** L.—**Empetraceae**—Dwarf, carpeting shrubs, natives of moors and mountains and wild, windswept places. There are 4 or 5 species widely distributed.
atropurpureum Fernald & Wiegand. A wiry-stemmed shrub covered with a white tomentum. Fruits reddish-purple. North America. C 1890.
hermaphroditum See *E. nigrum* subsp. *hermaphroditum*.
nigrum L. The crowberry is a very widely distributed, procumbent evergreen, forming widespreading, dense carpets. Inconspicuous, purple-red flowers are followed by glossy black fruits. Requires a moist, lime-free soil. Northerly latitudes of N hemisphere (incl. British Isles). subsp. *hermaphroditum* (Hagerup) Boecher (*E. hermaphroditum* Hagerup, *E. nigrum scoticum*) A hermaphrodite form of more compact habit. Northerly latitudes of N hemisphere (incl. British Isles). **'Lucia'** A form with creamy-white, young growths.

‡**ENKIANTHUS** Lour.—**Ericaceae**—An outstanding, distinct group of shrubs. About 10 species originating from the Himalaya to Japan. The flowers, produced in May, are drooping, cup- or urn-shaped, and prettily veined, while the exquisite colouring of the fading leaves is not excelled in any other genus. They require lime-free soil.
campanulatus (Miq.) G. Nicholson. An erect-branched species attaining 2.5–3m. A splendid shrub with variable yet subtle qualities and one of the easiest to grow. Cup-shaped, sulphur to rich bronze flowers are carried in great profusion and last for 3 weeks; useful for cutting. Autumn foliage of every shade between yellow and red. Japan. I 1880 by Charles Maries. ♀ 2002. AM 1890. **Albiflorus Group** (f. *albiflorus* (Makino) Makino) Flowers creamy-white. **'Red Bells'** A form of upright habit, taller than wide. Flowers profusely borne, cream at the base, veined with pink and shading to deep pink on the lobes. Selected from plants in the Sir Harold Hillier Gardens and Arboretum about 1980.

cernuus (Siebold & Zucc.) Makino. A Japanese species mainly cultivated as the following form. **f.** *rubens* (Maxim.) Ohwi. The best form of a choice species. A small to medium-sized shrub, noteworthy for its deep red, fringed flowers and brilliant autumn colour of deep reddish-purple. ♀ 2002. FCC 1992. AM 1930.
chinensis Franch. (*E. himalaicus* var. *chinensis* (Franch.) Diels, *E. sinohimalaicus* Craib) A remarkably beautiful, small tree or tall, narrow shrub, reaching 6m under favourable conditions. Yellow and red flowers with darker veins are carried in many-flowered umbels. Comparatively large leaves usually have red petioles and give attractive autumn tints. See also *E. deflexus*. W China, NE Upper Burma. I 1900. AM 1935.
deflexus (Griff.) Schneid. A small tree related to *E. chinensis* and differing in the leaves being hairy beneath and in the larger flowers, which are cream, veined with pink. Some plants distributed as *E. chinensis* belong here. Himalaya, W China. I 1908 by Ernest Wilson.
perulatus (Miq.) Schneid. (*E. japonicus* Hook. f.) A densely leafy, slow-growing, compact shrub to 2m high. Masses of urn-shaped, white flowers appear with the leaves in spring. One of the most consistently good autumn shrubs for its intense scarlet leaves. Japan. I about 1870. ♀ 2002. AM 1979.

†***ENTELEA** R. Br.—**Tiliaceae**—A monotypic genus requiring a sheltered site or conservatory. Among cultivated plants it is most closely allied to *Sparmannia*.
arborescens R. Br. A shrub, to 3m, for the mildest localities. Leaves are large, heart-shaped and double toothed. Erect, open heads of white flowers, with a central bunch of yellow stamens, are borne in May. The wood of this plant is one of the lightest known, lighter even than cork. New Zealand. I 1820.

***EPHEDRA** L.—**Ephedraceae**—A genus of some 40 species of curious shrubs with slender, rush-like, green stems and leaves reduced to tiny scales. A genus of great botanical interest, providing a link between flowering plants and conifers. They are widely distributed in North and South America and Eurasia.
andina C.A. Mey. A dwarf, spreading species from Chile. I 1896.
distachya L. European shrubby horsetail. Dwarf shrub with slender, erect stems forming large, creeping patches. Fruits, when produced, are red. S and E Europe. Cultivated in the 16th century.
gerardiana Wall. var. *sikkimensis* Stapf. A dwarf shrub with erect, many-branched stems forming extensive patches. Himalaya (E Nepal, Sikkim, Bhutan). I 1915. The typical variety is found in the W Himalaya.

‡***EPIGAEA** L.—**Ericaceae**—A genus of 3 species of creeping, evergreen shrubs for peaty soils and semi-shade. A hybrid between the following species (*E.* × *intertexta* Mulligan) was raised in 1928. Also in cultivation is *E. gaultherioides* (Boiss. & Balansa) Takht. (*Orphanidesia gaultherioides* Boiss. & Balansa) from NE Turkey. I 1934.
asiatica Maxim. A dwarf, creeping, mat-forming evergreen for moist, peaty soils. Rose-pink, urn-shaped flowers in

terminal and axillary racemes in April. Japan. I about 1930. AM 1931.

repens L. May flower. A creeping evergreen a few centimetres high. Dense, terminal heads of fragrant, white or rose-tinted flowers in April. E North America. I 1736. AM 1931.

ERICA L.—Ericaceae—The heaths are a large genus of more than 700 species, ranging in habit from dwarf shrubs to small trees. They are natives of Europe, Turkey and Africa, with by far the largest number of species in South Africa. In *Erica*, it is the corolla that is coloured and conspicuous, not the calyx as in the closely related *Calluna*.

Heaths are now very numerous; apart from the species and older cultivars, scores of newly named cultivars are constantly swelling the ranks. Their popularity arises in part from their all-the-year-round effect when different cultivars are planted, as it is possible to have ericas in flower most months of the year. Those forms with long racemes are ideal for cutting for indoor decoration, and even when dead and brown, they are not without beauty. All but tree heaths may be pruned immediately after flowering by removing the old inflorescences. When such species as *E. arborea* and *E. lusitanica* become too large and lanky, they may be hard pruned into the old wood during April.

With few exceptions, ericas are lime-hating and thrive best in acid soils, particularly those of a sandy nature. They are generally tolerant of semi-shade but flower best in full sun, combining most effectively with callunas (heathers), daboecias, dwarf rhododendrons and dwarf conifers.

For soils containing lime, a number of mainly winter-flowering species and their cultivars are the most suitable, for example *Erica carnea*, *E. erigena*, *E. terminalis*, *E. vagans* and also the cultivars of *E.* × *darleyensis*.

‡*arborea* L. Tree heath. A medium to large shrub which occasionally grows to 5m high and wide. Fragrant, white, globular flowers are produced profusely in early spring. S Europe, SW Asia, N and E Africa. I 1658. **'Albert's Gold'** A vigorous, hardy, medium-sized form with bright yellow foliage. A sport of var. *alpina*. ♀ 2002. **var. alpina** Dieck. A more hardy form, medium-sized but more erect. Foliage brighter green. Mountains of Spain. I 1899. ♀ 2002. AM 1962. **'Estrella Gold'** A slow-growing, small to medium-sized, very hardy form with bright yellow young foliage. Found in the mountains east of Coimbra, Portugal in 1972. ♀ 2002. **'Pink Joy'** See *E.* × *veitchii* 'Pink Joy'.

‡*australis* L. Spanish heath. Medium-sized shrub with rose-purple flowers during April and May. One of the showiest of the tree heaths. Very hardy but not recommended for the coldest areas. Spain, Portugal. I 1769. ♀ 2002. FCC 1962. AM 1935. **'Mr Robert'** A beautiful, white form. Found in the mountains of S Spain in 1912. ♀ 2002. AM 1929. **'Riverslea'** A lovely, small to medium-sized cultivar with flowers of fuchsia-purple. ♀ 2002. AM 1946.

‡†*canaliculata* Andr. This beautiful tree heath has reached a height of 5.5m in Cornwall. Flowers are white or pink-tinged with protruding brown anthers, borne in January and March. Needs a warm, sheltered position. South Africa. C about 1802. ♀ 2002. AM 1986.

carnea L. (*E. herbacea* L.) Winter heath. One of the most widely planted dwarf shrubs in cultivation, forming dense hummocks and mats covered with rosy-red flowers throughout winter. Alps of C Europe.

Cultivars of *Erica carnea*

There are innumerable cultivars available in a wide range of shades through the white-pink-purple spectrum. The early cultivars begin flowering in November and the latest in April, but the majority are mid-season January to March. All are lime-tolerant but not recommended for shallow chalk soils. Heights are 15–25cm unless otherwise stated. Thanks to the efforts of Chris Brickell and David McClintock the well-known name for this popular plant can be retained. Hybrids have been raised in Germany between this species and *E. arborea*.

'Adrienne Duncan' Dark bronze-green foliage; carmine-red flowers. Mid. ♀ 2002.

'Alan Coates' Low, spreading habit; dark leaves; pale pink flowers. Mid. AMT 1965.

'Ann Sparkes' Slow-growing, spreading form; golden foliage; rich purple flowers. Late. ♀ 2002. AMT 1971.

'Atrorubra' Dark rose-pink. Late.

'Aurea' Bright gold foliage during spring and early summer; deep pink flowers, paling to almost white. Mid to late. AMT 1971.

'Bells' Extra Special' Whisky-coloured foliage flecked orange and gold. Flowers heliotrope. Mid to late. 15cm.

'Cecilia M. Beale' A free-flowering, white form with erect shoots holding the flowers well above the ground. Mid. C 1920.

'Challenger' Dark green foliage; magenta flowers with crimson sepals. Mid. ♀ 2002.

'C.J. Backhouse' Pale pink, deepening with age. Late.

'December Red' Deep green foliage and strong spikes of rose-red flowers. Mid to late. AMT 1966.

'Eileen Porter' Low-growing; rich carmine-red flowers. The dark corollas and pale calyces produce a delightful bicoloured effect. Early to late. C 1934. AM 1956.

'Foxhollow' Yellowish-green foliage becoming rich yellow tinged red in winter; pale pink flowers. Late. C 1970. ♀ 2002.

'Golden Starlet' Bright yellow foliage in winter, lime-green in summer; white flowers. Mid. ♀ 2002.

'Gracilis' Bright rose-pink; compact. Early to mid.

'Heathwood' Dark green foliage, bronze in winter; bright rose-purple flowers. Late.

'Ice Princess' ('Springwood White' × 'Snow Queen') Upright habit with bright green foliage and long racemes of white flowers. Mid. 15cm. ♀ 2002.

'Isabell' ('Springwood White' × 'Snow Queen') Bright green foliage and profuse white flowers. Mid. 15cm. ♀ 2002.

'James Backhouse' Large, soft pink flowers. Late. C 1911.

'King George' Very similar to 'Winter Beauty' but differs in bud when the sepals are pale green and the corolla pale mauve.

'Loughrigg' Dark green foliage; rose-purple flowers Mid. ♀ 2002. AMT 1966.

'March Seedling' Spreading habit; dark green foliage; rich rose-purple flowers. Late.

'Mrs Samuel Doncaster' Somewhat glaucous foliage; rose-carmine flowers. Mid to late.

Erica carnea **continued**

'Myretoun Ruby' Deep green foliage; masses of deep rose-pink flowers. Late. An excellent plant raised in 1965 at Myretoun House, Scotland. ♀ 2002. FCC 1988.
'Nathalie' Compact with bright green foliage and bright purple flowers. Raised in Germany from a cross involving 'Myretoun Ruby'. Mid. 15cm. ♀ 2002.
'Pink Spangles' Profuse pink flowers. An improvement on 'Grayswood Pink'. Mid to late. ♀ 2002.
'Praecox Rubra' Deep rose-red. Early to mid. ♀ 2002. FCCT 1968. AMT 1966.
'Prince of Wales' Bright rose-pink flowers. Late.
'Queen Mary' Deepest rose-red flowers. Early to mid.
'Queen of Spain' Pale madder-pink flowers. Late.
'R.B. Cooke' Clear pink flowers over a long period. Mid to late. 20cm. ♀ 2002.
'Rosalie' A cross involving 'Myretoun Ruby' with bronze-green foliage and bright pink flowers. Mid. 15cm. ♀ 2002.
'Rosy Gem' Neat bushy habit; bright pink flowers. Mid to late.
'Rubra' Rose-red flowers. Mid.
'Ruby Glow' Bronzed foliage; large, rich dark red flowers. Late. AMT 1967.
'Snow Queen' Large, pure white flowers well above the foliage. Mid. C 1934.
'Springwood Pink' Good habit and foliage; clear rose-pink flowers. Mid. AMT 1964.
'Springwood White' Still the finest white cultivar, its strong trailing growths packed with long, urn-shaped flowers. Mid. ♀ 2002. FCCT 1964. AM 1930.
'Startler' Soft coral-pink flowers. Mid to late.
'Sunshine Rambler' Clear yellow foliage, bronze-yellow in winter; pink flowers. Late. C 1971. ♀ 2002.
'Thomas Kingscote' Pale pink flowers. Late.
'Treasure Trove' Slow-growing with unusual and distinct salmon flowers. Late. 15cm.
'Urville' See 'Vivellii'.
'Vivellii' ('Urville') A superb cultivar with bronzy-red foliage in winter and deep, vivid carmine flowers. Mid. C 1919. ♀ 2002. FCCT 1965. AMT 1964.
'Westwood Yellow' Compact habit; golden-yellow foliage; deep pink flowers. Late. ♀ 2002.
'Whitehall' ('Snow Queen' × 'Springwood White') Compact with bright green foliage and white flowers. Mid.
'Winter Beauty' Bright rose-pink flowers start to appear in December. Sepals and corolla red-tinged in bud. See also 'King George' with which this has been confused. AM 1922.
'Wintersonne' Distinctive red-brown foliage. Flowers opening lilac-pink, deepening to magenta. Late. 15cm.
‡*ciliaris* L Dorset heath. A low, spreading species, up to 30cm high, with comparatively large, rosy-red flowers in short, terminal racemes from July to October. SW Europe (incl. British Isles). **'Corfe Castle'** Leaves bronze in winter; salmon-pink flowers. 30cm. **'David McClintock'** White flowers tipped with mauve-pink; grey foliage. Found wild in Brittany by David McClintock. AM 1972. **'Maweana'** A form with larger, long-lasting flowers borne on stiff, erect stems. Found in Portugal in 1872 by George Maw. **'Mrs C.H. Gill'** Dark green

foliage and freely produced, clear red flowers. ♀ 2002. **'Stoborough'** Long racemes of white flowers. 50–60cm. Found in Dorset. ♀ 2002. **'Wych'** Flesh-pink flowers in long racemes. 50cm. Found in Dorset.

‡*cinerea* L. The common native purple bell heather, forming mats of wiry stems, and flowering from June to September. Height 25–30cm unless otherwise stated. W Europe (incl. British Isles).

Cultivars of *Erica cinerea*

'Alba Major' White flowers in short racemes.
'Alba Minor' Small and compact, 15cm. White flowers. ♀ 2002. FCCT 1968. AMT 1967.
'Atropurpurea' Bright purple flowers.
'Atrorubens' Quite distinct, brilliant red flowers in long sprays. AM 1915.
'Atrosanguinea Smith's Variety' Flowers of an intense scarlet; dark foliage. 15cm. C 1852.
'C.D. Eason' Glowing deep pink flowers. C 1931. ♀ 2002. FCCT 1966.
'Celebration' Prostrate with deep gold foliage during summer and autumn, lime-green in winter. Flowers white. 20cm.
'Cevennes' Lavender-rose flowers, over a long period. AMT 1968.
'C.G. Best' Soft salmon-pink flowers. C 1931. ♀ 2002.
'Cindy' Large, pure pink flowers; bronze-green foliage. ♀ 2002.
'Coccinea' ('Fulgida') Dwarf habit, 10cm. Dark scarlet flowers. C 1852.
'Colligan Bridge' Long, erect racemes of vivid purple flowers.
'Domino' White flowers and ebony-coloured calyces – charming combination. AMT 1970.
'Eden Valley' Soft lilac-pink flowers, paler at base. 15cm. C 1926. ♀ 2002. AM 1933.
'Fiddler's Gold' Compact and vigorous with pale green foliage flushed yellow and red when young. Deep mauve flowers. 25cm. ♀ 2002. AMT 1970.
'Foxhollow Mahogany' Dark green foliage; profuse, deep wine-red flowers. 30cm.
'Fulgida' See 'Coccinea'.
'Golden Drop' Summer foliage golden-copper-coloured turning to rusty-red in winter. Pink flowers are rarely produced. 15cm.
'Golden Hue' Golden foliage turning red in winter. A most effective plant. 50cm. ♀ 2002.
'G. Osmond' Pale mauve flowers with dark calyces. C 1931.
'Hookstone White' Bright green foliage; large, white flowers in long racemes. 35cm. ♀ 2002.
'Knap Hill Pink' Pure carmine-pink flowers in long trusses. Vigorous. ♀ 2002. FCCT 1967. AMT 1966.
'Lilacina' Pale lilac flowers.
'Lime Soda' Lime-green foliage and profuse soft lavender flowers. 30cm. ♀ 2002.
'Mrs Dill' Very neat, compact and low-growing; bright pink flowers. 10cm.
'My Love' Striking mauve-blue flowers contrasting with the foliage.
'Pentreath' A delightful form with rich purple flowers. ♀ 2002.

Erica cinerea continued:

'Pink Ice' Compact and vigorous with bright dark green foliage and clear pale pink flowers. ♀ 2002. FCCT 1971. AMT 1968.

'P.S. Patrick' Long sprays of bright purple flowers. C 1928. ♀ 2002. AMT 1967.

'Purple Beauty' Deep rose-purple flowers; dark green foliage.

'Romiley' A smaller version of 'Atrorubens'; vivid rose-red flowers. 15–20cm.

'Rosea' Bright pink flowers. AMT 1966.

'Ruby' Rose-purple flowers.

'Sea Foam' Pale mauve flowers.

'Sherry' Glossy green foliage; profuse, clear dark red flowers.

'Startler' Bright gleaming pink flowers.

'Stephen Davis' Compact with dark green foliage. Vivid deep pink flowers. 20cm. ♀ 2002. FCCT 1971.

'Velvet Night' Blackish-purple flowers, a most unusual colour. ♀ 2002.

'W.G. Notley' (× *Ericalluna bealeana* 'W.G. Notley') Purple flowers with deeply divided corollas.

'Windlebrooke' Vigorous with golden-yellow foliage, orange-red in winter; mauve flowers. ♀ 2002.

× **darleyensis** Bean (*E. carnea* × *E. erigena*) A most useful hybrid in its several forms, and a natural companion to *E. carnea*. All the following clones flower throughout the winter. Lime-tolerant, but not recommended for shallow chalk soils. See 'Darley Dale'. **'Ada S. Collings'** White flowers contrast well with the attractive, dark green foliage. 20cm. **'Alba'** See under 'Silberschmelze'. **'Archie Graham'** Compact growth, dark foliage and racemes of deep rose flowers. 50cm. **'Arthur Johnson'** Long, dense sprays of magenta flowers, useful for cutting. 60cm. ♀ 2002. AM 1952 **'Darley Dale'** Pale pink flowers over a long period. 30cm. One of the most popular of all ericas. This, the original plant, appeared in the Darley Dale Nurseries, Derbyshire, about 1890. Originally catalogued as *E.* × *darleyensis*. AM 1905. **'Furzey'** Vigorous and compact with dark green foliage. Deep rose-pink flowers over a long period. 35cm. Raised at Furzey Gardens, Lyndhurst, Hampshire. ♀ 2002. AMT 1968. **'George Rendall'** A superb form with rich pink flowers over a long period. 30cm. **'Ghost Hills'** Bright green foliage, tipped with cream in spring; pink flowers with deeper tips. A sport of 'Darley Dale'. 30cm. ♀ 2002. **'J.W. Porter'** Mauve-pink flowers. Young shoots reddish in spring. 25cm. ♀ 2002. **'Jack H. Brummage'** Pale yellow foliage, golden tinged-red in winter. Deep pink flowers in short spikes. 30cm. AMT 1970. **'Jenny Porter'** Soft pink flowers. Vigorous, upright habit. 30cm. ♀ 2002. **'Kramer's Rote'** Deep magenta flowers; bronze-green foliage. 35cm. ♀ 2002. **'Margaret Porter'** Glossy green foliage, tipped cream when young. Clear rose flowers in short, curving racemes. 20cm. **'Silberschmelze'** ('Molten Silver') Perhaps the best winter white, certainly the most rewarding. Sweetly scented flowers over a long period. Sometimes referred to as *E.* × *darleyensis* 'Alba'. C 1937. 35cm. AMT 1968. **'White Glow'** White flowers. 25cm. **'White Perfection'** Bright green foliage and white flowers. 40cm. ♀ 2002.

erigena R. Ross (*E. mediterranea* auct. not L., *E. hibernica* (Hook. & Arn.) Syme) A dense shrub of small to medium size, covered with fragrant, rose-red flowers from March to May. Lime-tolerant but not recommended for shallow chalk soils. The wild, Irish form often referred to as *E. hibernica* differs in no way from the continental form. S France, Spain, W Eire. **'Alba'** White, free-flowering, up to 1.2m. **'Brian Proudley'** A vigorous, upright form with bright green foliage and long racemes of white flowers. 90cm. **'Brightness'** A low-growing form; buds bronzed-red, opening to rose-pink. 0.6–1m. C 1925. AM 1972. **'Coccinea'** Similar to 'Brightness' but with richer-coloured buds and flowers. 0.6–1m. **'Glauca'** An erect form of dense, compact growth with slightly glaucous foliage and pale flesh-coloured flowers. 1–1.2m. **'Golden Lady'** Golden-yellow foliage; white flowers. Compact habit. 30cm. ♀ 2002. **'Irish Dusk'** Compact habit with dark green foliage and salmon-pink flowers. 45cm. ♀ 2002. **'Irish Salmon'** Salmon-pink. 1m. **'Nana'** ('Compacta') A compact form with silvery-pink flowers. 20cm. **'Rubra'** Compact habit; dark foliage; ruby-red flowers. 40cm. **'Superba'** A fine, pink-flowered form. 2m or over. AM 1972. **'W.T. Rackliff'** A charming, dense, compact cultivar, with dark green foliage and pure white flowers with brown anthers. 1–1.2m. ♀ 2002. AM 1972.

× **griffithsii** D. McClintock (*E. manipuliflora* × *E. vagans*) A hybrid first raised by Dr John Griffiths in 1983. **'Heaven Scent'** Long sprays of fragrant, lilac-pink flowers from late summer to autumn, grey-green foliage. Vigorous, upright habit to 1m. **'Valerie Griffiths'** (*E. vagans* 'Valerie Proudley' × *E. manipuliflora* 'Aldeburgh') Bushy upright habit with yellow summer foliage turning golden-yellow in winter. Flowers pale pink, July-October. 45cm.

herbacea See *E. carnea*.

hibernica See *E. erigena*.

hybrida This name refers correctly to various hybrids of South African species, but has erroneously been used for several European hybrids, including *E.* × *darleyensis*, *E.* × *stuartii*, *E.* × *watsonii* and *E.* × *williamsii*.

‡**lusitanica** Rudolphi (*E. codonodes* Lindl.) Portugal heath. A fine tree heath, resembling *E. arborea*, but earlier flowering. Large, pale green, plumose stems, crowded with white, tubular, fragrant flowers, pink in bud, are borne over a very long period from late autumn to early spring. Portugal. ♀ 2002. FCC 1977. AM 1972. **'George Hunt'** Golden-yellow foliage.

‡**mackayana** Bab. (*E. mackaii* Hook.) Mackay's heath. A rare, dwarf species with dark green foliage and rose-crimson flowers in umbels from July to September. 15cm. W Ireland, Spain. **'Dr Ronald Gray'** Flowers white. **'Lawsoniana'** Dwarf form with small, pink flowers. Found in Connemara. **'Maura'** An upright form with grey-green foliage and profuse, semi-double, purple flowers. To 25cm. **'Plena'** ('Crawfordii') Double, rose-crimson flowers. Found in W Galway. **'Shining Light'** Profuse, large, white flowers; dark green foliage. 25cm.

manipuliflora Salisb. Whorled heath. A small, erect to spreading species with mid-green, sharply pointed leaves. The flowers resemble *E. vagans*. Late summer to autumn. Lime tolerant. E Mediterranean.

mediterranea See *E. erigena*.

× *oldenburgensis* D.C. McClint. (*E. arborea* × *E. carnea*) Hybrids between these two species were first raised in Germany by Kurt Kramer. They most resemble *E. arborea* but make smaller, hardier shrubs flowering between March and May, and are lime tolerant. **'Ammerland'** Flowers soft pink, foliage green, tipped bright orange in spring. Smaller and more compact than *E. arborea*, to 75cm. **'Oldenburg'** Flowers white, habit broad and spreading.

‡†*pageana* Bolus. A remarkable, small, South African species. Erect growth and cylindrical clusters of bell-shaped, rich yellow flowers of a waxy texture in spring. In Hampshire it survives only the mildest winters. AM 1937.

× *praegeri* See *E.* × *stuartii*.

‡*scoparia* L. Besom heath. A medium-sized shrub of loose habit. Greenish flowers appear in May and June. W Mediterranean region. I 1770. **subsp.** *azorica* (Hochst.) D.A. Webb. A taller form with smaller flowers. Azores. **'Minima'** ('Nana', 'Pumila') A dwarf form not above 60cm. C 1825.

†*sicula* Guss. (*Pentapera sicula* (Guss.) Klotzsch) A dwarf shrub with erect, downy stems clothed with linear, heath-like leaves, arranged in whorls of 4. The pitcher-shaped, white or pink flowers are borne in terminal clusters during May and June. Sicily. Malta, E Mediterranean region. I 1849. AM 1951.

spiculifolia Salisb. (*Bruckenthalia spiculifolia* (Salisb.) Rchb.) A dwarf, heath-like plant, up to 25cm high, with terminal racemes of rose-pink, bell-shaped flowers in June. SE Europe, Turkey. I 1888. Hybrids between this species and *E. carnea* have been raised by Kurt Kramer and are known as *E. krameri* D.C. McClint. f. *albiflora* (D.C. McClint.) E.C. Nelson & D.C. McClint. Flowers white.

stricta See *E. terminalis*.

‡× *stuartii* (Macfarl.) E.F. Linton (*E.* × *praegeri* Ostenf.) (*E. mackayana* × *E. tetralix*) Hybrids between Mackay's heath and the cross-leaved heath have been found where the parents come into contact in the wild. **'Charles Stuart'** (*E.* 'Stuartii') A plant found in Co Galway, Ireland, in 1890. Pinched and narrow, deep rose flowers from June-September. When a plant of this cultivar reverted it was shown to have the same parentage as *E.* × *praegeri*; unfortunately the name *E.* × *stuartii* was published first. 30cm. **'Connemara'** (*E.* × *praegeri* 'Connemara') A dwarf shrub with terminal clusters of pale pink flowers during late summer. 15cm. This is the original plant of *E.* × *praegeri* collected in the wild in Connemara in 1890. **'Irish Lemon'** Bright pink flowers; lemon-yellow young foliage in spring. ♀ 2002. **'Irish Orange'** Deep pink flowers; orange tipped young foliage.

'Stuartii' See *E.* × *stuartii* 'Charles Stuart'.

terminalis Salisb. (*E. stricta* Willd., *E. corsica* DC.) Corsican heath. Bushy, medium-sized shrub with erect branches. The rose-coloured flowers, borne in late summer in terminal heads, fade to warm brown and remain throughout winter. Excellent on chalk soils. W Mediterranean region, naturalised in N Ireland. I 1765. ♀ 2002.

‡*tetralix* L. Cross-leaved heath. A native species growing 20–50cm high. Dense heads of rose-coloured flowers are produced from June to October. N and W Europe (incl. British Isles). **'Alba Mollis'** ('Mollis') Pretty grey foliage; white flowers. ♀ 2002. AM 1927. **'Alba Praecox'** Grey foliage; white flowers; earlier than 'Alba Mollis'. **'Con Underwood'** Grey-green hummocks studded with crimson flower clusters. C 1938. ♀ 2002. **'Hookstone Pink'** Vigorous; silvery-grey foliage; pale pink flowers. C 1953. **'Lawsoniana'** See *E. mackayana* 'Lawsoniana'. **'L.E. Underwood'** Silver-grey mounds; pale pink flowers, a striking terracotta in bud. C 1937. **'Mary Grace'** Bright pink flowers set amid silvery foliage. **'Mollis'** See 'Alba Mollis'. **'Pink Glow'** Grey foliage; bright pink flowers. **'Pink Star'** An unusual form in which the lilac-pink flowers are held erect on the stems. Foliage grey-green. Low, spreading habit. Found in the wild in Cornwall. ♀ 2002. **'Rosea'** Rose-coloured flowers.

†*umbellata* L. An attractive species of dwarf habit, proving fairly hardy. Flowers throughout summer, cerise-pink, with chocolate anthers. Lime-tolerant. Spain, Portugal, Morocco. AM 1926.

‡*vagans* L. Cornish heath. A dwarf, spreading shrub, producing flowers in long sprays from July to October. SW Europe (incl. British Isles). **'Alba'** Compact form; white flowers. 60cm. **'Birch Glow'** Bright green foliage; glowing rose-pink flowers. 45cm. ♀ 2002. **'Cornish Cream'** Creamy-white flowers in slender racemes. 50cm. Found in Cornwall. ♀ 2002. **'Cream'** White flowers in long racemes, an improvement on 'Alba'. 60cm. AMT 1968. **'Diana Hornibrook'** Red flowers; dark green foliage. Compact habit. 30cm. AMT 1967. **'Fiddlestone'** A superb form, throwing up long racemes of rose-cerise flowers over a long period. 50–60cm. **'Grandiflora'** Very long sprays of rose-coloured flowers. 1m. **'Holden Pink'** Compact, mound-forming; dark green foliage. White flowers flushed mallow-purple at the tips. 35cm. AMT 1966. **'Kevernensis'** See 'St Keverne'. **'Kevernensis Alba'** A compact form with small racemes of white flowers. 30cm. ♀ 2002. AMT 1971. **'Lilacina'** Short racemes of lilac-pink flowers over a long period. 50cm. **'Lyonesse'** Pure white flowers with protruding, brown anthers. 0.5–1m. C 1925. ♀ 2002. AM 1928. **'Mrs D.F. Maxwell'** Deep cerise flowers; a superb cultivar. 50cm. ♀ 2002. FCCT 1970. AM 1925. **'Pyrenees Pink'** Long racemes of pink flowers. 50cm. **'Rubra'** Rosy-red flowers. 50cm. **'St Keverne'** ('Kevernensis') Flowers clear rose-pink. Found in the wild in Cornwall. 50cm. FCCT 1971. AM 1914. **'Valerie Proudley'** A dwarf, dense bush with bright yellow foliage and white flowers. ♀ 2002. AMT 1971 (for summer foliage). AMT 1971 (for winter foliage).

‡× *veitchii* Bean (*E. arborea* × *E. lusitanica*) A hybrid tree heath of which the following are the most common clones at present in general cultivation. **'Exeter'** A beautiful, medium-sized shrub with attractive, bright green foliage and great plumes of fragrant, white flowers in spring. Not recommended for the coldest areas. This is the original clone raised by Messrs Veitch at Exeter, before 1900. Originally catalogued as *E.* × *veitchii*. ♀ 2002. AM 1905. **'Gold Tips'** Bright yellow young

foliage becoming dark green. ♀ 2002. AM 1981. **'Pink Joy'** (*E. arborea* 'Pink Joy') Flowers deep pink in bud opening nearly white. C 1969.

vulgaris See *Calluna vulgaris*.

‡× *watsonii* (Benth.) Bean (*E. ciliaris* × *E. tetralix*) Hybrids between 2 native species. The following are grown. **'Dawn'** A spreading form with young foliage yellow in spring, and terminal clusters of large, rose-pink flowers in July to October, often continuing until November. 23cm. Found in Dorset in 1923. ♀ 2002. **'F. White'** White flowers suffused pink from July to October. 20cm. Found in Dorset before 1931. **'H. Maxwell'** An attractive clone, similar to 'Dawn' but taller and more upright in habit, and slightly paler flowers from July to October. 30cm. **'Truro'** Rose-coloured flowers in short racemes from July to October. 23cm. The original clone, found wild in Cornwall in 1839 by H.C. Watson. Originally catalogued as *E.* × *watsonii*.

‡× *williamsii* Druce (*E. tetralix* × *E. vagans*) A variable hybrid of which the following are the most common clones at present in general cultivation. **'Gwavas'** A dwarf shrub of compact habit with yellowish-green foliage in spring, and pink flowers from July to October. 50–60cm. C 1924. **'P.D. Williams'** A pretty, late-flowering heath. Young growths tipped yellow in spring, becoming bronze in winter. Rose-pink flowers in umbels from July to September. 30–60cm. This is the original clone found in the wild in Cornwall in 1910. Originally catalogued as *E.* × *williamsii*. ♀ 2002.

× **ERICALLUNA BEALEANA** Krüssm. Plants once listed here, for example 'W.G. Notley', were thought to be hybrids between *Calluna vulgaris* and *Erica cinerea*. They are now treated as cultivars of the latter.

ERINACEA Adans.—**Leguminosae**—A monotypic genus related to *Genista* and *Spartium*.

anthyllis Link (*E. pungens* Boiss.) Hedgehog broom, Blue broom. A dwarf, slow-growing, spiny shrub making a very dense, rigid hummock. Slate-blue flowers in April and May. Requires a well-drained position in full sun. A splendid sight in the mountains above Granada. SW Europe, N Africa. I 1759. ♀ 2002. FCC 1976. AM 1922.

***ERIOBOTRYA** Lindl.—**Rosaceae**—A small genus of about 27 species of evergreen trees and shrubs, related to *Photinia*, natives of the Himalaya and E Asia.

'Coppertone' A large shrub or small tree with dark green leaves to 30cm long. Large clusters of small, white flowers open from pink buds with the bronze young foliage during spring. Of uncertain origin, it has been said to be a hybrid between *Eriobotrya* and *Rhaphiolepis*.

†*deflexa* (Hemsl.) Nakai. A large shrub, similar to *E. japonica* but differing in its leaves, which are oblong, with rounded teeth, and are soon glabrous beneath. They are also not such a deep glossy green and are borne on a longer petiole of up to 5cm (up to 1cm in *E. japonica*). Creamy-white flowers are borne in panicles during spring and early summer. Taiwan.

japonica (Thunb.) Lindl. Loquat. An architectural plant normally seen as a large shrub in the British Isles, and best grown against a wall. One of the most striking evergreens because of its firm, leathery, corrugated leaves, often 30cm long, oblanceolate, with pointed teeth and a persistent, pale brown tomentum beneath. Clusters of strongly fragrant, hawthorn-like flowers, produced only after a hot summer, open intermittently from November to April, and are sometimes followed by globular or pear-shaped, yellow fruits 4–5cm across. It is commonly cultivated in warmer countries for the edible fruits. China, Japan. I 1787. ♀ 2002.

prionophylla See *Photinia prionophylla*.

†**ERYTHRINA** L.—**Leguminosae**—A large genus of more than 100 species of mainly tropical deciduous trees and shrubs with trifoliolate leaves and often prickly stems. Natives of tropical and subtropical regions in both hemispheres.

crista-galli L. Coral tree. A very beautiful, semi-woody plant with trifoliolate leaves and deep scarlet flowers, like waxen sweetpeas, in large terminal racemes during summer. Needs a warm, sunny wall, and protection for the crown in winter. Brazil. I 1771. FCC 1987. AM 1954.

***ESCALLONIA** Mutis ex L. f.—**Escalloniaceae**—About 40 species of mainly evergreen shrubs and small trees, all natives of South America, mainly in the Andes. They rank high among flowering evergreens, and are all the more valuable for giving their display during summer and early autumn. Though not all are hardy inland, most can be grown successfully near the sea, where they make perfect hedges and windbreaks. Unless otherwise stated they average 1.5–2.5m in height. None of the species have large leaves or large flowers, reference to size being comparative within the group. With rare exceptions they are lime-tolerant and drought-resistant, thriving in all types of well-drained soil. Pruning, consisting of cutting back the old flowering growths, may be carried out immediately after flowering and large, unwieldy plants may be hard-pruned at the same time.

'Alice' A first-class hybrid with large leaves and large, rose-red flowers.

alpina DC. A small to medium-sized shrub of dense, bushy habit proving extrememly hardy even in exposed positions where it is often nearly deciduous. Leaves small, to 3cm long, obovate, glossy dark green. Flowers in leafy racemes at the ends of the shoots, corolla red. Chile, Argentina. I about 1926 by Harold Comber.

'Apple Blossom' A very attractive, slow-growing hybrid with pink and white flowers. ♀ 2002. AM 1946.

bellidifolia See under *E.* × *stricta* 'Harold Comber'.

†*bifida* Link & Otto (*E. montevidensis* (Cham. & Schltdl.) DC.) Handsome, large shrub, with large leaves, requiring wall protection. White flowers in large panicles in late summer and autumn. S Brazil. Uruguay. I 1827. ♀ 2002. AM 1915.

'C.F. Ball' Vigorous, growing up to 3m, with large leaves that are aromatic when bruised; crimson flowers. Excellent for maritime exposure. A seedling of *E. rubra* var. *macrantha* raised at Glasnevin by Charles Frederick Ball before 1914. AM 1926.

'C.H. Beale' A strong-growing, medium-sized shrub with crimson-red flowers in profusion.

'Crimson Spire' See *E. rubra* 'Crimson Spire'.

'**Donard Beauty**' Exceedingly free-flowering shrub with large leaves, aromatic when bruised, and rich rose-red flowers. AM 1930.

'**Donard Brilliance**' A shrub of graceful habit with arching branches, large leaves and large, rich rose-red flowers. AM 1928.

'**Donard Gem**' Large, pink, sweetly-scented flowers. Compact growth with small leaves. AM 1927.

'**Donard Radiance**' A magnificent, strong-growing shrub of compact habit and medium size with large, shining deep green leaves and large, brilliant soft rose-red, chalice-shaped flowers. ♀ 2002. AM 1954.

'**Donard Seedling**' (*E.* 'Langleyensis' × *E.* × *virgata*) A vigorous hybrid up to 3m; flowers are flesh-pink in bud, opening white and leaves are large. AM 1916.

'**Donard Star**' Medium-sized shrub of compact, upright habit. Large leaves and large flowers of a lovely rose-pink. AM 1967.

'**Donard White**' Medium-sized shrub of compact, rounded habit with small leaves. White flowers, pink in bud, are produced over a long period.

'**Edinensis**' (*E. rubra* × *E.* × *virgata*) Neat, bushy habit, 2–2.5m high, with small leaves and flowers that are carmine in bud opening to clear shell-pink. Raised at the Royal Botanic Garden, Edinburgh before 1914. AM 1918.

'**E.G. Cheeseman**' A vigorous hybrid of which *E. revoluta* is probably one parent. Nodding, deep, bright cherry-red, bell-shaped flowers, 12mm long, are carried in terminal leafy panicles. Leaves large, ovate to rotund obovate, coarsely serrated, sage- or grey-green. Downy in all its parts.

× *exoniensis* Veitch (*E. rosea* × *E. rubra*) A vigorous shrub, to 4m high, with downy, glandular shoots and large leaves; flowers white or blush. AM 1891.

'**Gwendolyn Anley**' A small, very hardy shrub of bushy habit with small leaves and flesh-pink flowers.

'**Hopleys Gold**' See *E. laevis* 'Gold Brian'.

illinita C. Presl (*E. viscosa* Forbes) A tall, strong-smelling shrub, up to 3m, with glandular shoots, large, glossy green leaves and cylindrical panicles of white flowers. Chile. I 1830.

'**Ingramii**' See *E. rubra* 'Ingramii'.

†'**Iveyi**' (*E. bifida* × *E.* × *exoniensis*) A large, vigorous hybrid with large, handsome, glossy foliage and large panicles of white flowers in autumn. Originally found at Caerhays, Cornwall. ♀ 2002. AM 1926.

†*laevis* (Vell.) Sleumer (*E. organensis* Gardn.) A small, Brazilian shrub with large, lustrous leaves, aromatic when bruised, and large, clear pink flowers. I 1844 by William Lobb. '**Gold Brian**' (*E.* 'Hopleys Gold') PBR Golden young foliage becomes dark green. Flowers deep rose-pink. '**Gold Ellen**' Similar to 'Gold Brian' but leaves dark green, margined yellow.

'**Langleyensis**' (*E. rubra* × *E.* × *virgata*) A hardy, graceful shrub, up to 2.5m, with small leaves and rose-pink flowers wreathing the arching branches. Garden origin 1893. The same cross has occurred in the wild. ♀ 2002. AM 1897.

leucantha Remy (*E. bellidifolia* Phil.) A tall, graceful shrub, recalling *Leptospermum stellatum*, with angular stems and large, crowded panicles of white flowers in July. Chile. I 1927 by Harold Comber.

macrantha See *E. rubra* var. *macrantha*.

montana See under *E. rubra* var. *uniflora*.

montevidensis See *E. bifida*.

'**Newry**' ('Newryensis') (*E.* 'Langleyensis' × *E. rosea*) Vigorous, upright growth. Flowers white, tinged pink; leaves large, aromatic when bruised. A good windbreak. C 1912.

organensis See *E. laevis*.

'**Peach Blossom**' Medium-sized shrub, similar in habit to 'Apple Blossom' but with flowers of clear peach-pink. ♀ 2002.

'**Pink Elf**' A vigorous, compact shrub with small, glossy green leaves and profuse, deep pink, tubular flowers; early to midsummer.

'**Pink Pearl**' Soft pink flowers, stained bright rose-pink, about 20mm across when wide open, carried in short dense racemes on arching branches. Rather small, obovate leaves.

'**Pride of Donard**' Large, brilliant rose, somewhat bell-shaped flowers are carried in terminal racemes from June onwards. Leaves large, dark polished green above. ♀ 2002.

punctata See *E. rubra*.

'**Red Dream**' A compact, bushy shrub with red shoots and small, coarsely toothed, glossy green leaves. The relatively large, clear pinkish-red flowers are freely produced in summer, even on small plants; a second crop is often produced later in the year. It was originally found as an unnamed plant in the USA. C 1993.

'**Red Elf**' (*E.* 'William Watson' × *E.* 'C.F. Ball') A vigorous and free-flowering, medium-sized shrub which has dark, glossy green leaves and deep crimson flowers. C 1970.

'**Red Hedger**' A vigorous, medium-sized to large shrub bearing profuse crimson flowers throughout summer. Very wind resistant and excellent for hedging, responding well to pruning.

†*revoluta* (Ruiz & Pav.) Pers. A large shrub with grey-felted shoots and foliage and soft pink to white flowers in terminal racemes from August to September. Chile. I 1887.

rosea Griseb. (*E. pterocladon* Hook.) Medium-sized shrub with downy, angled branches and small leaves. White, fragrant flowers in slender racemes. Parent of many hybrids. Patagonia. I 1847 by William Lobb.

rubra (Ruiz & Pav.) Pers. (*E. punctata* DC., *E. microphylla* hort., *E. sanguinea* hort.) A medium-sized shrub with loose panicles of red flowers in July. Leaves aromatic when bruised. Chile. I 1827. '**Crimson Spire**' A strong-growing shrub of erect growth, up to 2m. Leaves comparatively large, dark glistening green; flowers bright crimson. An excellent hedging shrub. ♀ 2002. '**Ingramii**' An excellent maritime shrub, which grows 4m high and makes a good hedge. Flowers deep rose-pink; leaves large, aromatic when bruised. C 1833. **var. macrantha** (Hook. & Arn.) Reiche (*E. macrantha* Hook. & Arn.) Rose-crimson flowers set amid large, fine, glossy, aromatic leaves. Strong-growing, up to 4m, and one of the best hedging plants to withstand sea gales. Parent of many hybrids. Chiloe. I 1848. '**Pygmaea**' See 'Woodside'. **var. uniflora** Poepp. & Endl. A low, compact, dense-growing shrub with long leaves. Flowers deep red. Originally grown and catalogued as *E. montana*. **'Woodside'** ('Pygmaea') A small shrub, the product of a witches' broom in Ireland. It has a neat habit, but its branches spread over a considerable area; suitable for a large rock garden. Flowers small, crimson.

'St Keverne' (*E. kevernensis* hort.) Medium-sized shrub of arching habit, with small leaves and large, rich pink flowers; free-flowering.

'Slieve Donard' A medium-sized, compact shrub with small leaves and large panicles of apple blossom-pink flowers. Very hardy.

×*stricta* Remy (*E. leucantha* × *E.* × *virgata*) A variable, natural hybrid of which the following clone is grown. **'Harold Comber'** One of the hardiest of the genus. A dense shrub up to 1.5m, the slender stems crowded with small leaves and small, white flowers. Introduced in 1927 by Harold Comber from Chile as *E. bellidifolia* (Comber 988).

†*tucumanensis* Hosseus. A very distinct and beautiful species making a large shrub with widely arching branches bearing rather thin, narrowly elliptic to oblanceolate leaves, to 10cm long and toothed above the middle, and producing white flowers, 1.5cm long, in drooping panicles in July. NW Argentina. I 1961.

virgata (Ruiz & Pav.) Pers. (*E. philippiana* (Engl.) Mast.) A graceful, small-leaved, deciduous shrub with arching branches and white flowers. Not suitable for chalky soils. A hardy species and parent of many hybrids. Chile. I 1866. FCC 1888.

viscosa See *E. illinita*.

'William Watson' A medium-sized, small-leaved shrub of compact growth bearing bright red flowers over a long period.

***EUCALYPTUS** L'Hér. (*Corymbia* K.D. Hill & L.A.S. Johnson)—**Myrtaceae**—The gum trees are a large genus of some 800 species of fast-growing, evergreen trees, sometimes shrubs, mainly natives of Australia with a few species extending to New Guinea, the Philippines and Java. Not found wild in New Zealand. In common with many other plants of wide distribution, selections from high altitudes usually prove hardier than the same species from lower levels. Several species are hardy or nearly hardy in the British Isles, creating an impressive subtropical effect with their lush foliage, unusual multi-stamened flowers (which are white unless otherwise stated) and attractive stems. The leaves of adult trees are often very different from those of young specimens, many providing excellent foliage for floral decoration. The common name refers to the quantity of gum that exudes from their trunks. The tallest tree ever recorded was a specimen of *Eucalyptus regnans* in Victoria, SE Australia, estimated to have been more than 150m in 1872.

Eucalyptus will grow in a great variety of soils and many are tolerant of wet sites but some species tend to become chlorotic in very shallow chalk soils. As yet *E. parvula* is the only species which we have proved will grow indefinitely on a chalk soil.

They are best planted as small, pot-grown plants, preferably in the spring. If, due to over-rapid growth, there is a likelihood that a tall, young tree will blow over, we recommend cutting back to about 25–45cm from the ground in the spring and selecting the strongest new growth. Remove all subsidiary shoots, unless a bushy plant with several stems is preferred. Strong cold winds are a greater danger to many eucalyptus than hard frosts.

In 1995 a proposal was made to include the species known as bloodwoods and ghost gums in a new genus, *Corymbia*, containing about 120 species and differing from *Eucalyptus* in small characters such as their compound terminal inflorescences. As this has not yet been universally accepted, it is not adopted here. The species listed that would be affected are *E. citriodora* and *E. ficifolia*.

†*amygdalina* Labill. (*E. salicifolia* Cav.) Black peppermint. A large shrub or medium-sized tree with fibrous bark and long, narrow, aromatic, green leaves. E Tasmania.

archeri Maiden & Blakely. Alpine cider gum. Closely related to *E. gunnii* but smaller with wrinkled fruits. A very hardy, small tree with grey-green lanceolate leaves and smooth, grey and white bark. Flowers in clusters of 3, sessile on short peduncles. Tasmania.

camphora R.T Baker (*E. ovata* var. *aquatica* Blakely) Broad-leaved sally. One of the hardiest species. A small to medium-sized tree with rough bark, forming clumps. Leaves ovate to lanceolate. In its native habitat this species usually grows in wet areas, even in standing water. New South Wales, E Victoria. AM 1977.

†*cinerea* Benth. Argyle apple. A medium-sized tree with silver-grey leaves and fibrous bark. Only hardy in the mildest localities. New South Wales, Victoria.

†*citriodora* Hook. (*Corymbia citriodora* (Hook.) K.D. Hill & L.A.S. Johnson) Lemon-scented gum. A large tree in the wild with smooth, white bark and very slender, adult leaves. Mainly grown in its juvenile stage for its lemon-scented foliage, it is only suitable for the mildest areas but worth a place in a conservatory. Widely planted in warm countries. Queensland.

coccifera Hook. f. Mount Wellington peppermint. A large tree with striking glaucous leaves and stems, not apparent in young plants. Specimens have passed without injury all but the very severest winters in the Home Counties. Tasmania. I 1840. AM 1953.

cordata Labill. Silver gum. A dense species making a small tree with grey-silver, sessile leaves and strongly 4-angled, glaucous-bloomed shoots. The attractive, white bark is marked with green or purplish patches. Flowers in winter. It is often seen as a bedding plant, grown for its ornamental foliage. E Tasmania. C 1850.

coriacea See *E. pauciflora*.

dalrympleana Maiden. Mountain gum. A most attractive, very fast-growing species of medium size, proving one of the hardiest. Attractive, patchwork bark becoming white. Handsome, grey-green leaves are bronze coloured when young. A specimen in the Sir Harold Hillier Gardens and Arboretum was 22m in 1990. New South Wales, Victoria, Tasmania. ♀ 2002. AM 1953.

debeuzevillei See *E. pauciflora* subsp. *debeuzevillei*.

divaricata See *E. gunnii*.

†*ficifolia* F. Muell. (*Corymbia ficifolia* (F. Muell.) K.D. Hill & L.A.S. Johnson) Red-flowering gum. A superb, small tree of lax habit with broad lanceolate leaves up to 15cm long. Scarlet or flame-coloured flowers are borne in large corymbs towards the ends of the branches. They are very effective against the glossy green foliage. Very tender;

best under glass. Both flowers and foliage are cut and sold in florists' shops. SW Australia. FCC 1907.

glaucescens Maiden & Blakely. Tingiringi gum. A vigorous, large tree with smooth, grey-green, peeling bark, darker and fibrous at the base on old trees. Juvenile leaves orbicular, glaucous-green, adult leaves lanceolate, to 13cm, green or grey-green on both sides. Flowers in clusters of 3, followed by distinctive, large, glaucous fruits. SE Australia.

†*globulus* Labill. Tasmanian blue gum. In mild districts this species will make a large, noble tree but is more usually seen as a sparsely branched shrub in subtropical bedding schemes. The large leaves are blue-green, almost silvery on young specimens. Tasmania, Victoria. C 1829.

gregsoniana Johnson & Blaxell (*E. pauciflora* var. *nana* Blakely) A very hardy, large shrub related to *E. pauciflora* but differing in its shrubby habit and short-stalked leaves. It has grey and white flaking bark and lance-shaped, grey-green leaves, to 12cm long, on red shoots. Flowers in short-stalked or sessile clusters of 7–11. New South Wales.

gunnii Hook. f. (*E. divaricata* Brett) Cider gum. The best-known species in cultivation, this fine tree is also one of the hardiest. Leaves of the adult tree are sickle-shaped, sage-green; those of young trees are rounded and startling silver-blue. It will attain large tree size or will make an excellent bush if regularly pruned. Tasmania. C 1853. ♀ 2002. AM 1950.

johnstonii Maiden. Yellow gum. One of the hardier species. A large tree with reddish, peeling bark and bright, glossy, apple-green leaves. A specimen in the Sir Harold Hillier Gardens and Arboretum was 23m in 1990. C 1886. Tasmania.

mitchelliana Cambage. Mount Buffalo Sally. A small to medium-sized, weeping tree or large shrub, also known as weeping sally in Australia. Bark smooth and white with age. Leaves narrowly lanceolate, green. Victoria (Mt Buffalo).

niphophila See *E. pauciflora* subsp. *niphophila*.

nitens Maiden. Silver top. A vigorous, large, and very fast-growing tree with long, ribbon-like, glaucous leaves. Appears to be one of the more hardy species but can be damaged or even killed in the hardest winters. Victoria, New South Wales. AM 1975.

parvifolia See *E. parvula*.

parvula L.A.S. Johnson & K.D. Hill (*E. parvifolia* Cambage) An exceptionally hardy species with attractively peeling bark, making a handsome, medium-sized tree in the British Isles and surviving the severest winters. Will even tolerate chalk soils. Mature leaves are narrow, blue-green. New South Wales. ♀ 2002.

pauciflora Sieber ex Spreng. (*E. coriacea* Schauer) Snow gum. A small, high-mountain tree, and one of the hardiest species. When growing conditions are favourable will withstand up to 15°C of frost. Sickle-shaped leaves are up to 20cm long, the trunk white. C 1880. SE Australia, Tasmania. **subsp. *debeuzevillei*** (Maiden) L. Johnson & Blaxell (*E. debeuzevillei* Maiden) Jounama snow gum. Thick, lance-shaped adult leaves to 15cm long. SE Australia. **var. *nana*** See *E. gregsoniana*. **subsp. *niphophila*** (Maiden & Blakely) L.A.S. Johnson &

Blaxell (*E. niphophila* Maiden & Blakely) Snow gum. A beautiful, small tree, of comparatively slow growth, with leathery, grey-green leaves, smaller than in the typical form, on bloomy shoots. The trunk is a lovely green, grey and cream patchwork and has been likened to a python's skin. A tree in the Sir Harold Hillier Gardens and Arboretum has sustained no frost damage since it was planted in 1960. ♀ 2002. AM 1977.

pauciflora × *amygdalina* A medium-sized tree with attractive bark and long, narrow, sickle-shaped, sage-green leaves. Hardier than *E. pauciflora*.

perriniana F. Muell. ex Rodway. Spinning gum. A small, silver-leaved tree producing white stems with dark blotches. Juvenile leaves rounded; mature leaves oblanceolate, glaucous. Victoria, New South Wales, Tasmania. AM 1982.

†*pulverulenta* Sims. Silver-leaved mountain gum. A handsome, small tree or large shrub resembling *E. cordata*, with attractive, bluish, rounded leaves. Hardy in the south-west and similar areas. New South Wales. I 1819.

salicifolia See *E. amygdalina*.

subcrenulata Maiden & Blakely. A medium-sized tree, similar to *E. johnstonii* but smaller, with wavy-edged leaves and smaller leaves and fruits. It occurs at higher altitudes than *E. johnstonii*. Tasmania.

urnigera Hook. f. Urn gum. Small to medium-sized, fairly hardy species with greyish, peeling bark and dark green leaves. Distinct, urn-shaped fruits. Tasmania. C 1860.

vernicosa Hook. f. Varnished gum. A very hardy shrub or occasionally a small tree producing dense masses of thick, elliptic-lanceolate, shining green leaves. W Tasmania.

EUCOMMIA Oliv.—**Eucommiaceae**—A monotypic genus and the only member of the family. It is perfectly hardy and thrives in all types of fertile soil.

ulmoides Oliv. The only hardy tree known to produce rubber. A vigorous and ornamental Chinese tree up to 9m or more, with rather large, leathery, glossy, elm-like leaves. If a leaf is torn gently in half, the two halves eased apart, and then the stalked half held, the detached lower half will hang seemingly unconnected, but it is in fact attached by fine strands of latex almost invisible to the naked eye. I about 1896 from cultivation in China and not known in the wild.

‡**EUCRYPHIA** Cav.—**Eucryphiaceae**—A small genus of 7 species of highly ornamental shrubs or trees, flowering when sufficiently mature from July to September. All have white flowers with conspicuous stamens. They thrive best in sheltered positions and in moist loam, preferably non-calcareous. The roots should be shaded from hot sun.

billardieri See *E. lucida*.

†*cordifolia* Cav. Ulmo. A very beautiful, large, evergreen shrub or, in favoured areas, a broad columnar tree of 9–12m. Leaves oblong, wavy-edged, often heart-shaped at the base; flowers like a white Rose of Sharon (*Hypericum calycinum*). Somewhat lime-tolerant. Chile. I 1851. AM 1936.

cordifolia × *lucida* See *E.* 'Penwith'.

glutinosa (Poepp. & Endl.) Baill. (*E. pinnatifolia* Gay) One of the most glorious of woody plants. A large, erect-branched, deciduous shrub or small tree with pinnate leaves; flowers 6cm across are borne profusely in July and August. Beautiful autumn tints. It is evergreen in the wild. Chile. I 1859. ♀ 2002. FCC 1976 (for autumn foliage). FCC 1880 (for flower). **Plena Group** Flowers double or semi-double. Arises fairly frequently in seed batches.

†*× **hillieri** Ivens (*E. lucida* × *E. moorei*) An interesting chance hybrid between an Australian and a Tasmanian species. The following clone is the one in general cultivation but other plants of the same parentage have arisen independently. **'Penwith'** See *E.* 'Penwith'. **'Winton'** This hybrid originated as a self-sown seedling in our Chandler's Ford nursery. Its pinnate leaves have fewer leaflets than those of *E. moorei* and it is also considerably hardier. Its beautifully formed, cup-shaped flowers resemble those of *E. lucida*.

*× **hybrida** Bausch (*E. lucida* × *E. milliganii*) A naturally occurring hybrid, intermediate between the parents in leaf and flower size, and making a large shrub or small tree. Cultivated plants have leaves about 2cm long and 1cm wide and flowers 2–2.5cm across. Some plants grown as *E. milliganii* belong here. It was collected in Tasmania by Harold Comber and may also have arisen in cultivation.

*× **intermedia** Bausch (*E. glutinosa* × *E. lucida*) A lovely, fast-growing hybrid. Leaves variable, both simple and trifoliolate occurring on the same plant, glaucous beneath. Flowers smaller than those of *E. glutinosa*, crowding the branches. This hybrid first occurred at Rostrevor, N Ireland, the garden of the late Sir John Ross of Blandenburg, but other forms are also in cultivation.

'Rostrevor' The form in general cultivation. An extremely floriferous, free-growing, small tree of compact, broadly columnar habit. The fragrant flowers, 2.5–5cm across, smother the slender branches in August and September. Raised at Rostrevor, Co Down. ♀ 2002. FCC 1973. AM 1936. 'Grayswood' is similar.

***lucida** (Labill.) Baill. (*E. billardieri* Spach) Leatherwood. A delightful, large, densely leafy shrub or small tree with simple, oblong leaves, glaucous beneath. The charming, fragrant, pendent flowers, up to 5cm across, appear in June and July. Tasmania. I 1820. AM 1936. **var. milliganii** See *E. milliganii*. **'Ballerina'** Flowers pale pink, 3cm across with deep pink margins and red stamens. Found in W Tasmania in 1986 by Ken Gillanders. **'Leatherwood Cream'** Leaves 2.5cm long, notched at the tip with a creamy margin. **'Pink Cloud'** Flowers pale pink at the margins of the petals shading to white, red at the base. This form was discovered as a 20m tree in a remote area of NW Tasmania.

***milliganii** Hook. f. (*E. lucida* var. *milliganii* (Hook. f.) Summerh.) A delightful and very hardy, miniature species eventually a small, usually slender, shrubby tree. Leaves tiny, neat, shining dark green, glaucous beneath. Buds exceptionally sticky. Flowers cup-shaped, similar to those of *E. lucida* but smaller. Even as a small shrub it flowers freely. It has reached 6m tall by 1m across in the Sir Harold Hillier Gardens and Arboretum. Tasmania. I 1929 by Harold Comber. AM 1978.

†***moorei** F. Muell. A rare, small tree having pinnate leaves with up to 13 elegantly poised, slender leaflets. The flow-

ers are rather smaller than those of *E. glutinosa*. Suitable only for the mildest localities. SE Australia. I 1915. AM 1933.

*× **nymansensis** Bausch (*E. cordifolia* × *E. glutinosa*) A variable hybrid between 2 superb South American species. The leaves are intermediate between those of the parents, both simple and compound leaves appearing on the same plant. **'Mount Usher'** Resembling more *E. cordifolia* in general appearance. The flowers are often double. Raised at Mount Usher in Ireland. **'Nymansay'** A magnificent, small to medium-sized tree of rapid growth and dense, columnar habit. Flowers, 6cm across, wreathe the branches in August and September. Raised about 1915 at Nymans, Sussex, by James Comber, Head Gardener to the late Lt Col L.C.R. Messel. ♀ 2002. FCC 1926. AM 1924.

†*'Penwith'** (*E. cordifolia* × *E. lucida*) A large, tall-growing evergreen of vigorous growth with oblong-lanceolate, leathery leaves, dark shining green above, glaucous beneath. Resembles *E. lucida* in general appearance but differs in its larger flowers and leaves which are wavy-edged, pointed and occasionally toothed. Raised at Trengwainton. In recent years it has been incorrectly distributed as a form of *E.* × *hillieri*.

*__EUMORPHIA__ DC.—**Compositae**—About 4 species of small shrubs, natives of South Africa.

sericea Wood & Evans. A grey-leaved shrub, reaching about 1m, with smooth, yellowish-brown stems, grey-tomentose when young and small, opposite leaves, entire or 2- to 3-lobed at the apex, silky-hairy on both sides. Solitary, white daisy flowerheads, 2.5cm across, are borne on short peduncles at the tips of the shoots over a long period during summer and autumn. Has proven remarkably hardy in an open position at the Sir Harold Hillier Gardens and Arboretum.

Euodia See *Tetradium*.
Euodia hupehensis See *Tetradium daniellii*.
Euodia velutina See *Tetradium daniellii*.

EUONYMUS L.—**Celastraceae**—A genus of about 175 species ranging from dwarf shrubs to creepers, climbers and small trees, both evergreen and deciduous, and all harmful if eaten. They are natives mainly of Asia but also occur in Europe, North America, Africa and Australia. The wide range of forms makes them suitable for a variety of purposes in gardens including valuable hedging and groundcover. They thrive in almost any soil, and are particularly at home on chalk. The flowers, in early summer, are normally green or purplish and of little ornament. The chief attraction is the often very showy, lobed, sometimes winged fruits, which persist into winter and open to reveal the seeds covered by a coloured aril. It is desirable to plant several specimens in close proximity to obtain cross-pollination, as single specimens may never fruit due to imperfect flowers. Many deciduous species give attractive autumn tints.

alatus (Thunb.) Siebold. A slow-growing, much-branched shrub of medium size, under favourable conditions distinguished by broad, corky wings on the branchlets. One of the finest and most reliable of all deciduous shrubs for autumn colour, the leaves turning to brilliant crimson-pink. Reddish-purple fruits open to reveal bright orange-coated seeds. China, Japan. I 1860. ♀ 2002. **var. *apterus*** Regel. An unusual plant, differing from the typical form in its more lax habit and its wingless or scarcely winged stems. Equally colourful in autumn. **'Compactus'** A compact form, colouring equally well in autumn. Ideal for a low hedge. Raised in the USA before 1928. ♀ 2002.

americanus L. Strawberry bush. A medium-sized shrub with 4-angled branches and narrowly oval, glossy green leaves, sometimes red in autumn. The tiny flowers are succeeded by 3- to 5-lobed, red, warty capsules. E USA. C 1683.

bungeanus Maxim. A large shrub or small tree with slender, arching branches and elliptic, slender-pointed leaves. Bears yellowish-white flowers in June; 4-lobed, cream to flesh-pink fruits only produced after a hot summer. Autumn colour pale straw-yellow. N and NE China. I 1883. AM 1941. **var. *semipersistens*** (Rehder) Schneid. A distinct, semi-evergreen shrub often retaining its leaves until the New Year. Fruits pink.

cornutus Hemsl. A rare, small to medium-sized shrub of loose habit. The remarkable, pink-tinged fruits have 4 slender, horn-like extensions, giving them the appearance of jesters' caps. W and SW China. I 1908 by Ernest Wilson. **var. *quinquecornutus*** (Comber) Blakelock. In this form the fruit has 5 or 6 horns.

europaeus L. Spindle tree. This is a familiar native hedgerow shrub, particularly on chalk soils. It is vigorous, occasionally making a small tree, with green stems and an abundance of scarlet capsules, opening to reveal the orange-coated seeds. Europe, W Asia. **f. *albus*** (Weston) Rehder ('Fructu-albo') A conspicuous, white-fruited form, showy in winter. **'Atropurpureus'** Leaves green at first turning to deep purple in early summer, passing to vivid shades of red in the autumn. **'Aucubifolius'** Leaves mottled with yellow and white and attractively tinted with pink in autumn. **'Fructu-coccineo'** Capsules bright red. **'Red Cascade'** A selected form, the arching branches often drooping under the weight of the rosy-red fruits. Rich scarlet autumn colour. ♀ 2002. AM 1949.

farreri See *E. nanus.*

*****fortunei* Hand.-Mazz. An extremely hardy, trailing evergreen, suitable for groundcover in sun or shade, or as a self-clinging climber, the long stems rooting at intervals. Leaves generally elliptic, up to 6cm long, distinctly veined beneath. Like the English ivy, the creeping and climbing stems are barren and it is only when adult growths appear that flowers and fruits are produced. Small, pale green flowers, in loose cymes during summer, are followed in autumn by pinkish capsules with orange seeds. Most cultivated plants belong to var. *radicans.* China. I 1907. **Blondy** ('Interbolwji') PBR A sport of 'Sunspot' found in a Dutch nursery, the leaves with a broad yellow blotch in the centre and a narrow, green margin. Like its parent, it can revert. C 1990. **'Canadale Gold'** A small, bushy, spreading shrub the bright green leaves broadly edged with golden-yellow. A seedling from Canadale Nurseries, Canada, introduced in 1974. **'Carrièrei'** A small shrub with larger leaves, reaching 2–2.5m against a wall. This is regarded as the adult form of var. *radicans* and produces both flowers

and fruits. C 1881. AM 1936. **'Coloratus'** A trailing or climbing form, reaching 8m with support. The leaves are a beautiful, sanguineous-purple throughout winter, especially when the roots are starved or controlled. An unusual character is that the leaves that are coloured in winter may resume their summer green in spring. **'Dart's Blanket'** An improvement on 'Coloratus', this was selected in Holland where it is widely planted for groundcover. Leaves deep green turning bronze-red in autumn. C 1969. **'Emerald Charm'** An adult form of upright habit with glossy green leaves. Yellowish-white fruits open to reveal orange-coated seeds. Raised in the USA. **'Emerald Cushion'** A dwarf, mound-forming shrub of dense habit, with rich green leaves. Raised in the USA. **'Emerald Gaiety'** A small, compact, bushy shrub bearing broad, deep green leaves with an irregular white margin which becomes pink-tinged during winter. Raised in the USA. ♀ 2002. **'Emerald 'n' Gold'** A very striking form making a dense, dwarf bush. Deep green leaves have a broad, bright golden margin that becomes cream, flushed with pink, in winter. Climbs given support. Raised in the USA before 1967. ♀ 2002. AM 1979. **'Emerald Surprise'** Upright habit with large, rounded leaves edged with bright gold. ♀ 2002. **'Gold Spot'** See 'Sunspot'. **'Gold Tip'** See 'Golden Prince'. **'Golden Prince'** ('Gold Prince', 'Gold Tip') Leaves pale green, edged yellow when young, becoming dark and grey-green edged cream, later all green, flushed yellow towards the tip in winter. C 1972. **'Gracilis'** See Variegatus'. **'Harlequin'** A dwarf form with green leaves heavily mottled with white. Young growth often totally white becoming green and white later. Tends to scorch in full sun; weak constitution. C 1990. **'Kewensis'** A dainty form with slender, prostrate stems and minute leaves. Suitable for a rock garden where it will form small hummocks or cover rocks. Will climb if support is available. Possibly a sport of var. *radicans.* 'Minimus' is similar but with larger leaves. I 1893. **'Minimus'** See under 'Kewensis'. **var. *radicans*** (Miq.) Rehder. A trailing or climbing shrub with ovate or elliptic, shallowly toothed, rather leathery leaves up to 3.5cm long. This is the commonest form in cultivation with smaller leaves than the typical form. Propagation of the adult growth has resulted in various shrubby forms such as 'Carrièrei'. Japan. I about 1865. **'Sarcoxie'** Upright habit to 1.8m. Leaves dark glossy green. Large, white fruits tinged pink. Raised in the USA in 1950. **'Sheridan Gold'** A dwarf shrub with upright shoots, the young leaves suffused with yellow, later green. Not very exciting. **'Silver Pillar'** ('Versicolor Albus') Leaves narrow with a broad, marginal white variegation. Habit erect. **'Silver Queen'** A sport of 'Carrièrei', producing flowers and fruits, this is a small, compact shrub, attaining 2.5–3m against a wall. The unfolding leaves in spring are rich creamy-yellow, later becoming green with a broad, creamy-white margin. One of the loveliest of variegated shrubs. C 1914. AM 1977. **'Sunshine'** Leaves green in the centre with a broad, golden-yellow margin, which becomes creamy-yellow flushed pink with age. A sport of 'Emerald 'n' Gold' raised in Holland. **'Sunspot'** ('Gold Spot') Leaves deep green with an elongated, central, golden blotch, red-tinged underneath in winter. Stems yellowish. C 1980.

'**Tustin**' A low-growing, prostrate form, the long, narrow leaves veined with pale yellow-green. Excellent ground-cover. ♀ 2002. '**Variegatus**' ('Gracilis') A trailing or climbing form, the leaves greyish-green, margined white, often tinged pink. A sport of var. *radicans*. Now superseded by other selections. AM 1977. **var. *vegetus*** (Rehder) Rehder. A small, bushy, creeping form with both prostrate and erect stems, climbing if support is available. The leaves are quite distinct being broad ovate to orbicular, thick in texture and dull green. Flowers and fruits are normally freely produced. Probably a distinct form of var. *radicans*. I from Japan in 1876.

†****frigidus*** Wall. A rare, tender species of medium size, with small, chocolate-brown flowers, hanging on slender stalks, followed by 4-winged, red fruits, opening to show orange-coated seeds. Leaves oblanceolate. E Himalaya. W China. I 1931 by Kingdon-Ward.

grandiflorus Wall. An erect, semi-evergreen shrub, to 4m high, with conspicuous, comparatively large, straw-yellow flowers and pink capsules with scarlet-coated seeds. Leaves give rich wine-purple autumn colour. Himalaya, W China. I 1824. AM 1927. **f. *salicifolius*** Stapf & F. Ballard. The form most usually grown, with longer, narrower leaves. W China. C 1867. AM 1953.

hamiltonianus Wall. A large, deciduous or semi-evergreen shrub or small tree related to *E. europaeus*. Fruits pink with orange or red-coated seeds. A variable species of wide distribution in E Asia. The typical variety is native to the Himalaya and may not be in cultivation. '**Coral Charm**' Leaves pale yellow and green in autumn. Pale pink fruits are freely borne; the seeds have red arils. Habit spreading. Selected in the Sir Harold Hillier Gardens and Arboretum. AM 1981. '**Coral Chief**' Similar to 'Coral Charm' but of upright habit, the pink fruits opening to show red arils. Selected in the Sir Harold Hillier Gardens and Arboretum. '**Fiesta**' Leaves blotched with creamy-yellow and pink, turning purple in autumn. Raised from a sport found by our foreman Alf Alford on a plant grown as *E. yedoensis* in 1967. Shy fruiting. **var. *lanceifolius*** (Loes.) Blakelock (*E. lanceifolius* Loes.) A deciduous or semi-evergreen, small tree or large shrub; leaves, 7.5–12.5cm long, are usually lanceolate-oblong; the pink 4-lobed fruits open to disclose the scarlet-coated seeds. Unfortunately this variety fruits too infrequently in cultivation. C and W China. I 1908 by Ernest Wilson. AM 1929. **var. *maackii*** (Rupr.) Komar. (*E. maackii* Rupr.) Leaves smaller and narrower, more finely toothed. Cultivated plants have beautiful autumn colour and pink fruits with orange-coated seeds. N China, Manchuria, Korea. C 1880. '**Red Elf**' Habit similar to 'Coral Chief' but with rich deep pink fruits and red-coated seeds. Selected in the 1970s in the Sir Harold Hillier Gardens and Arboretum from plants grown as *E. hians* and originally named 'Red Cap'. AM 1981. **subsp. *sieboldianus*** (Blume) Hara (*E. hians* Komar., *E. semiexsertus* Koehne, *E. sieboldianus* Blume, *E. yedoensis* Koehne) Leaves yellow, pink or red in autumn. Fruits conspicuous, rose-pink, often abundantly produced. Japan, E China, Korea. I 1865. AM 1924.

hians See *E. hamiltonianus* subsp. *sieboldianus*.

†****ilicifolius*** Franch. A remarkable species with thick, spiny, holly-like leaves and rounded, whitish capsules with orange-coloured seeds. W China. I 1930. Only suitable for the mildest localities and now probably no longer in cultivation.

****japonicus*** Thunb. A large, densely branched shrub with dark glossy green, leathery leaves. One of the best evergreens for coastal or town planting, and succeeding in sun or shade. China, Japan. AM 1976. '**Albomarginatus**' Leaves pale green when young becoming blue-green, narrowly margined with white. '**Aureopictus**' See 'Aureus'. '**Aureus**' ('Aureopictus') Leaves with golden centre and a broad, green margin. Liable to revert. '**Bravo**' Young leaves with a broad central blotch of bright golden-yellow, ageing to creamy-white. '**Chollipo**' An excellent selection from the Chollipo Arboretum in South Korea, introduced to the USA in 1985. A large shrub of dense, upright habit, the leaves broadly edged with bright yellow. ♀ 2002. '**Duc d'Anjou**' Dark green leaves with a central splash of pale yellow or yellowish-green. See also 'Viridivariegatus'. '**Golden Maiden**' Similar to 'Aureopictus' with larger leaves and the same tendency to revert. '**Green Spire**' A compact form of vigorous, upright habit suitable for hedging. I 1978 to the US National Arboretum from a garden in Japan by John Creech, Frederick Meyer and Sylvester March. '**Hibarimisaki**' An unusual and distinct dwarf and very slow-growing shrub, 10–20cm tall, of congested habit with upright shoots. Very small, downcurved and overlapping leaves with a narrow, silvery margin. Suitable for a sheltered scree or alpine house. '**Latifolius Albomarginatus**' ('Macrophyllus Albus') Leaves with a conspicuous, broad, white margin. The most pronounced variegated form. '**Macrophyllus**' ('Latifolius') Leaves larger than those of the typical form, elliptic. FCC 1866. '**Macrophyllus Albus**' See 'Latifolius Albomarginatus'. '**Microphyllus**' ('Myrtifolius') A small, slow-growing form of dense, compact habit, with small, narrow leaves. Somewhat resembling box (*Buxus*) in general appearance. '**Microphyllus Aureovariegatus**' Similar to 'Microphyllus' but with leaves edged yellow. '**Microphyllus Pulchellus**' ('Microphyllus Aureus') This is similar to 'Microphyllus' but leaves suffused with gold. '**Microphyllus Variegatus**' Small leaves with a white margin. '**Myrtifolius**' See 'Microphyllus'. '**Ovatus Aureus**' ('Aureovariegatus') Leaves margined and suffused creamy-yellow, particularly apparent when they are young; growth rather slow and compact. Requires a sunny site to retain its colour. The most popular golden euonymus. ♀ 2002. '**Président Gauthier**' Leaves large, greygreen and dark green with a broad, creamy-white margin. '**Robustus**' A very hardy form with rather thick, round ovate leaves and stiff compact growth. Under favourable conditions the first fruiting form of the species. '**Viridivariegatus**' Leaves dark green in the centre with a pale green or yellowish-green margin. Often grown as 'Duc d'Anjou'.

****kiautschovicus*** Loes. (*E. patens* Rehder) Hardy, spreading, evergreen shrub of medium size, producing greenyellow flowers in early autumn, followed by late, pink fruits. Akin to *E. japonicus*, from which it differs in its wider inflorescence, thinner, more pointed leaves and laxer habit. This plant should replace *E. japonicus* in the coldest areas. E and C China. I about 1860. AM 1961.

lanceifolius See *E. hamiltonianus* var. *lanceifolius*.

latifolius (L.) Mill. A European species, 3–4.5m high, with larger, scarlet fruits and more brilliant autumn foliage than the common spindle tree. Similar to and has been confused with *E. planipes* but differs in the sharp-edged wings of the fruit. I 1730. AM 1916.

†*lucidus* D. Don (*E. pendulus* Wall.) A large, evergreen shrub or small to medium-sized tree, suitable only for the mildest localities. In spring the young growths are crimson, passing to coppery-salmon, finally deep green. Confused in gardens with *E. fimbriatus*, which, however, is a deciduous species. Himalaya. I 1850.

maackii See *E. hamiltonianus* var. *maackii*.

macropterus Rupr. A medium-sized to large shrub of spreading habit, with oval or obovate leaves and attractive, pink, 4-winged capsules. NE Asia, Japan. I 1905.

myrianthus Hemsl. (*E. sargentianus* Loes. & Rehder) A large, slow-growing, evergreen shrub with rather long, tough, leathery leaves. Greenish-yellow flowers, in dense, rounded heads of up to 7.5cm across, are followed by orange-yellow fruits, splitting to expose the attractive, orange-scarlet seeds. W China. I 1908 by Ernest Wilson. AM 1976.

nanus M. Bieb. (*E. farreri* hort., *E. rosmarinifolius* hort.) A useful, dwarf, semi-evergreen shrub with narrow leaves and tiny, brown-purple flowers. Ideal as a groundcover and for banks. Caucasus to China. I 1830. AM 1920. **var. turkestanicus** (Dieck) Krysht. (*E. nanus* var. *koopmannii* Koehne) A semi-erect form, up to 1m, with longer leaves. The commonest form in cultivation. Fruits bright pink with orange seeds. Tian Shan and Altai Mountains. C 1883.

obovatus Nutt. A prostrate shrub closely related to *E. americanus* but with long, trailing stems. Peculiar in its 3-lobed bright pink fruits, which are covered with prickly warts, particularly striking when they open to reveal orange-coated seeds. E North America. I 1820.

oresbius W.W. Sm. An uncommon shrub, to about 2m, with very narrow, linear leaves. The pendent, rosy-red, scarlet-seeded fruits are seldom seen in cultivation. Yunnan, W China. C 1934.

oxyphyllus Miq. A slow-growing, medium-sized to large shrub; leaves pass to rich shades of red and purple-red in autumn when the branches are also strung with rich carmine-red capsules. Japan, Korea, China. I 1892.

patens See *E. kiautschovicus*.

pendulus See *E. lucidus*.

phellomanus Loes. A large shrub with shoots conspicuously corky-winged and oval to obovate leaves, 5–10cm long. The conspicuous, 4-lobed, pink fruits are freely carried. N and W China. C 1924. ♀ 2002. FCC 1924.

planipes (Koehne) Koehne (*E. sachalinensis* hort.) A large, handsome species similar to *E. latifolius* and equally colourful in autumn. The large and showy scarlet fruits are freely borne. NE Asia. I 1892. *E. sachalinensis* (F. Schmidt) Maxim. is probably not in cultivation. It is a native of Sakhalin with a variety in Japan. ♀ 2002. AM 1954.

sachalinensis See *E. planipes*.

sanguineus Loes. A medium-sized, occasionally large shrub, rare in cultivation. The young shoots and leaves are often flushed purple beneath. The red fruits and tinted leaves are attractive in autumn. C and W China. I 1900 by Ernest Wilson.

sargentianus See *E. myrianthus*.

semiexsertus See *E. hamiltonianus* subsp. *sieboldianus*.

sieboldianus See *E. hamiltonianus* subsp. *sieboldianus*.

*tingens Wall. (L.S. & H. 17559) A large shrub or small tree with elliptic, toothed, dark green leaves. Bears creamy-white flowers, conspicuously purple-veined, in stalked clusters in May and June. Pink fruits with scarlet-coated seeds, ripen in late autumn. Proving hardy in the Sir Harold Hillier Gardens and Arboretum. Himalaya, W China. I 1850 by Sir Joseph Hooker. AM 1994 (for fruit).

vagans Wall. A prostrate, evergreen shrub with stout shoots and glossy green, broadly ovate leaves, to 6cm long and 4cm across, glossy on both sides. Flowers greenish, lying flat along the upper leaf surface. A handsome species useful for groundcover in shady places; given support it will climb, like *E. fortunei*. Himalaya, W China. I by Roy Lancaster from Mt Omei in 1980 (Lancaster 551).

velutinus (C.A. Mey.) Fisch. & C.A. Mey. A medium-sized to large shrub, related to *E. europaeus*, with grey-pubescent young shoots and leaf undersides. Small, pink-tinged flowers in July are followed by conspicuous, rich pink fruits. Autumn colour soft pink. I 1972 by Mrs Ala and Roy Lancaster from the Elburz Mountains of N Iran (A. & L. 2). W Asia.

verrucosus Scop. Medium-sized shrub with densely warty branches. Purple-brown flowers, in 3- to 7-flowered cymes, are followed, after a hot summer, by pink capsules which shed black seeds covered by an orange aril. Attractive, autumn tints. E Europe, W Asia. I 1763.

*wilsonii Sprague. A large and striking, Chinese evergreen of lax habit. The lanceolate, dark green leaves are 7–15cm long, one third as wide and tapered to a slender point. The 4-lobed fruits are set with awl-shaped spines giving a remarkable, hedgehog-like appearance. I 1904 by Ernest Wilson.

yedoensis See *E. hamiltonianus* subsp. *sieboldianus*.

Eupatorium ligustrinum See *Ageratina ligustrina*.
Eupatorium micranthum See *Ageratina ligustrina*.

EUPHORBIA L.—**Euphorbiaceae**—The spurges make up a very large genus of more than 1500 species of herbs and shrubs of cosmopolitan distribution, particularly in subtropical areas. Many species are spiny succulents resembling cacti. Several are commonly grown as indoor or conservatory plants. The species listed here are evergreen subshrubs. The individual flowers are not obvious but each inflorescence bears showy bracts and often contains conspicuous glands. Euphorbias are harmful if eaten and the sap may cause eye and skin irritation.

amygdaloides L. wood spurge. A native common in woods in southern Britain but better known in gardens as the following variety. There are attractive forms with purple leaves and stems. Europe, SW Asia. **subsp. robbiae** (Turrill) Stace (*E. robbiae* Turrill) Mrs Robb's bonnet. A dwarf subshrub spreading rapidly by underground stems. Obovate, deep glossy green, leathery leaves are borne in dense rosettes at the stem tips. Conspicuous, greenish-yellow flowerheads are produced over a long period during late winter and spring. Excellent groundcover in shade. Turkey. I in the early 1890s by Mrs Robb. ♀ 2002. AMT 1975. AM 1968.

characias L. A small subshrub bearing erect, unbranched, biennial stems. Linear, downy, bluish-green leaves are borne in dense clusters at the ends of the shoots. Flowers, in terminal panicles, have conspicuous, yellowish-green bracts and reddish-purple glands, and are attractive for several months during spring and summer. Mediterranean region. AM 1961. **'Blue Hills'** Compact and low-growing, with densely arranged blue-green leaves and lime-green flowerheads. **'Humpty Dumpty'** Low-growing with numerous shoots and oval heads of apple-green flowers. **'Portuguese Velvet'** A compact form of dome-shaped habit with velvety blue-grey foliage and bronze-yellow flowerheads. Collected in Portugal by John Fielding. ♀ 2002. **subsp. *wulfenii*** (Hoppe ex Koch) Radcl-Sm. (*E. wulfenii* Hoppe ex Koch) Differs from the typical form in the yellowish-green glands of the inflorescence. SE Europe. C 1837. ♀ 2002. FCC 1988. AM 1905. **subsp. *wulfenii* 'Emmer Green'** Leaves margined with creamy white, inflorescences lime-yellow. **subsp. *wulfenii* 'John Tomlinson'** Flowers in large heads with long upper rays making the inflorescence nearly rounded; bracts bright yellow-green. Wild-collected in former Yugoslavia in 1966 (Mathew & Tomlinson 4005). ♀ 2002. AM 1977 (as *E. characias* subsp. *wulfenii*) FCC 1996. **subsp. *wulfenii* 'Lambrook Gold'** Columnar inflorescence with bright golden-green bracts. ♀ 2002.

× martinii Rouy (*E. amygdaloides* × *E. characias*) A clump-forming subshrub producing tufts of dark green leaves, flushed purple when young. Green flowers, tinged purple, appear over a long period in spring, the inflorescences often turning to deep pink in summer. AM 1976. ♀ 2002. **Redwing** ('Charam') PBR A very hardy form with red shoots and blue-green leaves flushed red when young, inflorescences green in summer. A back-cross with *E. characias*. ♀ 2002. FCC 2000.

†**mellifera** Aiton. A medium-sized, dense, rounded shrub with stout, glabrous shoots and narrowly oblong leaves, up to 20cm long, downy only at the base of the midrib beneath. Brown, honey-scented flowers, in May, are followed by warty fruits. Madeira, Canary Islands. ♀ 2002.

robbiae See *E. amygdaloides* subsp. *robbiae*.

EUPTELEA Siebold & Zucc.—Eupteleaceae—A small genus of 2 species making large shrubs or small trees. The flowers appear in dense clusters all along the leafless branches in spring. Lacking petals, they consist of bunches of red-anthered stamens. They succeed in all types of fertile soil.

franchetii See *E. pleiosperma*.

pleiosperma Hook. f. & Thoms. (*E. franchetii* Tiegh., *E. davidiana* Baill.) A small, multi-stemmed tree or large shrub with stout, erect stems, attracting attention in spring when crowded with clusters of red anthers. Young growths are copper-tinted. Autumn leaf colour is sometimes conspicuous. E Himalaya. W China. I 1896.

polyandra Siebold & Zucc. A large shrub or small tree, differing from *E. pleiosperma* in its coarsely and irregularly toothed leaves; also notable for its pretty, red and yellow autumn colours. Japan. C 1877.

EURYA Thunb.—Theaceae—About 70 species of evergreen shrubs and trees related to and often confused with *Cleyera*, but differing in the dioecious flowers and usually toothed leaves Natives of SE Asia and the Pacific islands.

†*emarginata* (Thunb.) Makino. A small to medium-sized shrub with brown-hairy young shoots, conspicuously lined with ridges decurrent from the base of the petioles. Obovate, toothed, glossy green leaves, to 3.5cm by 1cm, are obtuse to emarginate at the apex, reddish-tinged in winter. Small, pale yellow-green flowers are borne in the leaf axils in spring. Coastal areas of S Japan. **'Microphylla'** A curious form making a small, densely branched shrub recalling *Cotoneaster horizontalis* when young. Leaves arranged in 2 ranks, obovate or orbicular, notched at the apex, 6–8mm long.

fortunei See *Cleyera japonica* 'Tricolor'.

japonica Thunb. A small, evergreen shrub with bluntly serrate, leathery leaves, dark green and lustrous above, pale green beneath. The inconspicuous, greenish-yellow flowers, formed in late summer, open in spring and smell objectionable. They are followed by purplish-black berries. Japan, Taiwan, Korea. FCC 1861. **'Variegata'** A charming, small, slow-growing shrub, compact in habit. Leaves 2 ranked, oblanceolate, toothed, pale green with a dark green margin. This name has also been applied to *Cleyera japonica* 'Fortunei'. FCC 1894.

latifolia **'Variegata'** See *Cleyera japonica* 'Fortunei'.

ochnacea See *Cleyera japonica*.

EURYOPS Cass.—Compositae—About 100 species of evergreen shrubs with conspicuous, yellow, daisy flowerheads. Natives mainly of South Africa but extending north to Arabia. The following require a warm, sunny position and well-drained soil.

acraeus M.D. Hend. (*E. evansii* hort.) A dwarf shrub of rather neat habit, forming a low, compact mound of grey stems and small, narrow, silvery-grey leaves. The canary-yellow flowerheads, 2.5cm across, smother the plant during late May and June. Ideal for a rock garden or scree; generally hardy if soil and aspect are suitable. Introduced about 1945 from the Drakensberg Mountains, Lesotho. At first confused with *E. evansii*, a related species. ♀ 2002. AM 1952.

†*chrysanthemoides* (DC.) B. Nordenst. A small shrub with purplish stems, the leaves deeply divided into oblong lobes, which become linear towards the base. The solitary flowerheads are yellow, deeper yellow in the centre, and 6cm across. They are borne on long, erect stalks from midsummer onwards. Differs from *E. pectinatus* in the nearly glabrous leaves with fewer, broader lobes. South Africa. AM 1988.

hybridus See under *E. pectinatus*.

†*pectinatus* Cass. A small shrub with erect, greyish, downy shoots up to 1m. Deeply lobed (pectinate) leaves, 5–7.5cm long, are grey-downy. Rich yellow flowerheads, 4cm across, are borne on long, slender, erect peduncles in late May and June and often again during winter. Plants we have grown under the name *E. hybridus* have proved to be this species. South Africa. I 1731. ♀ 2002.

†*virgineus* Less. A small shrub forming a dense clump of erect, glabrous shoots, 0.6–1m high. The neat, tiny,

green, pectinate leaves densely crowd the stems. Flowers, 1.25cm across, are produced on slender stalks in the axils of the upper leaves during spring. South Africa. I 1821.

Evodia See *Tetradium*.

EXOCHORDA Lindl.—**Rosaceae**—Pearlbush. A genus of 4 or 5 species of beautiful, May-blooming shrubs with long, arching branches that are festooned with conspicuous racemes of comparatively large, paper-white flowers. Generally inclined to become chlorotic on very shallow chalk soils.

giraldii Hesse. An excellent, large, free-flowering shrub, similar to *E. korolkowii*, but not so erect. NW China. I 1907. **var.** *wilsonii* (Rehder) Rehder. This variety has the largest flowers in the genus, being 5cm across. C China. I 1907. AM 1931.

korolkowii Lavallée (*E. albertii* Regel) A vigorous species from Turkestan, attaining about 4.5m; one of the best for chalky soils. I 1881. AM 1894.

× *macrantha* (Lemoine) Schneid. (*E. korolkowii* × *E. racemosa*) Large shrub similar in habit to *E. racemosa*. Abundant racemes of large flowers in late spring. Garden origin about 1900. AM 1917. **'The Bride'** A small to medium-sized, dense bush of weeping habit. Very attractive when the arching branches are wreathed in large flowers in April or May. C 1938. ♀ 2002. FCC 1985. AM 1973.

‡*racemosa* (Lindl.) Rehder (*E. grandiflora* (Hook.) Lindl.) The best-known species, a large shrub rather spreading in habit. Not suitable for shallow chalk soil. China. I 1849. AM 1979.

serratifolia S. Moore. An extremely free-flowering species which thrives in chalky soils, forming an elegant, medium-sized bush. **var.** *pubescens* Rehder. Leaves pubescent beneath.

F

*FABIANA Ruiz & Pav.—Solanaceae—About 25 species of evergreen, heath-like shrubs, belonging to the potato family and among hardy plants most closely related to *Cestrum*. Natives of South America mainly in temperate regions. One species is in general cultivation. Succeeds best in a sunny position in moist, well-drained, neutral or acid soil, but is sufficiently lime-tolerant to be well worth growing in all but very shallow soils over chalk.

†*imbricata* Ruiz & Pav. A charming shrub of medium size. In June its branches are transformed into plumes of white, tubular flowers. Chile. I 1838. AM 1934.
  'Prostrata' A small shrub, hardier than the typical form, making a dense rounded mound of feathery branchlets, usually covered with small, pale mauve-tinted flowers in May and June. Ideal for a large rock garden or wall top.
  Violacea Group (f. *violacea* hort) Similar to the typical form but with lavender-mauve flowers. ♀ 2002. FCC 1932.

FAGUS L.—Fagaceae—The beeches are a small genus containing some of the most noble of trees. About 10 species in N temperate regions. In the British Isles, the European species reach their maximum size in deep, well-drained soils. The Asiatic species also give a good account of themselves, but the American beech is disappointing as seen in cultivation and is less lime-tolerant.

americana See *F. grandifolia*.

crenata Blume (*F. sieboldii* A. DC.) A large tree closely allied to the common beech (*F. sylvatica*) from which it differs in its rather more obovate leaves. Some plants grown under this name are *F. orientalis*. Japan. I 1892.

engleriana Seemen. A rare tree of medium size with glaucous, sea-green foliage. C China. I 1907 by Ernest Wilson.

grandifolia Ehrh. (*F. americana* Sweet, *F. ferruginea* Aiton) The American beech does not form a large tree in the British Isles. Distinguished from the common beech by its suckering habit and its longer, narrower leaves, with nearly twice as many veins. E North America. I 1766. FCC 1894. **f. pubescens** Fernald & Rehder. Leaves pubescent beneath.

japonica Maxim. Japanese beech. A small, often shrubby tree in British gardens, with ovate to elliptic, bright green leaves. Japan. I 1905.

lucida Rehder & E.H. Wilson. A small tree with ovate leaves, often shining green on both surfaces. W China. I 1905.

orientalis Lipsky. Oriental beech. A large tree differing from the common beech in its rather larger, obovate leaves, which turn rich yellow in autumn. E Europe, Asia Minor. I 1904

sieboldii See *F. crenata*.

sylvatica L. Common beech. The native beech is undoubtedly the most noble large tree for calcareous soils and is excellent for hedges. The rich golden-copper of its autumn foliage is not excelled by any other tree. Given a well-drained soil and avoiding heavy clay there is perhaps no other tree that will thrive in such extremes of acidity and alkalinity. Europe. ♀ 2002.

Cultivars of *Fagus sylvatica*

'Albovariegata' ('Argenteovariegata') Leaves margined and streaked white. C 1770.

'Ansorgei' A remarkable form with very narrow lanceolate to almost linear, dark purple leaves. Originated about 1891.

'Aspleniifolia' Fern-leaved beech, Cut-leaved beech. Leaves relatively narrow, deeply cut into slender lobes. C 1804. ♀ 2002.

'Atropunicea' See under Purpurea Group.

'Atropurpurea' See under 'Riversii'.

'Atropurpurea Macrophylla' See under 'Riversii'.

'Aurea Pendula' An elegant, tall, slender form, the branches hanging down almost parallel with the main stem. Golden-yellow leaves may scorch in full sun and in deep shade lose their rich colour. Originated as a sport about 1900.

'Aureovariegata' See 'Luteovariegata'.

'Black Swan' A weeping tree with deep red-purple foliage, similar to 'Purple Fountain' but more compact with darker leaves. C 1960.

'Cochleata' A slow-growing, shrubby form with obovate leaves strongly toothed in the upper half. C 1842.

'Cockleshell' A tall, columnar form with small, rounded leaves. A sport of 'Rotundifolia' raised in our nurseries in 1960.

'Comptoniifolia' A small tree similar to 'Aspleniifolia' but with finer foliage. Leaves mainly reduced to slender threads only a few millimetres wide, with some leaves deeply pinnately lobed. C 1815.

'Cristata' Cock's comb beech. A slow-growing eventually large tree with clustered leaves, deeply lobed and curled. C 1811.

'Cuprea' See under Purpurea Group.

'Dawyck' Dawyck beech. A tall, columnar tree, broadening in maturity. Originated at Dawyck in Scotland before 1850. Sometimes incorrectly known as 'Fastigiata'. ♀ 2002.

'Dawyck Gold' A dense, columnar tree with bright yellow young foliage, pale yellow-green in summer. A seedling of 'Dawyck' probably pollinated by 'Zlatia' raised by J.R.P. van Hoey-Smith in 1969. It has reached just over 14m in the Sir Harold Hillier Gardens and Arboretum (2000). ♀ 2002.

'Dawyck Purple' A splendid, narrowly columnar tree with deep purple foliage. Originated at the same time as 'Dawyck Gold' but in this case the pollen parent was a purple beech. Narrower than 'Dawyck Gold' and not as dense. It has reached nearly 16m in the Sir Harold Hillier Gardens and Arboretum (2000). ♀ 2002. AM 1973.

'Fastigiata' See under 'Dawyck'.

'Franken' Leaves mottled with white, particularly when young. C 1993.

'Grandidentata' A form with coarsely toothed leaves and slender branches. C 1864.

Heterophylla Group (var. *heterophylla* Loudon) As used here, this name covers several forms in which the leaves are narrow and variously cut and lobed. The plant originally grown under this name is 'Aspleniifolia'

Fagus sylvatica **continued:**
while other forms include 'Incisa', 'Laciniata' and 'Quercifolia'.

'Incisa' See under Heterophylla Group.

'Laciniata' See under Heterophylla Group.

Latifolia Group (f. *latifolia* Kirchn., var. *macrophylla* Dippel) Leaves much larger, often up to 15cm long and 10cm wide. C 1864.

'Luteovariegata' ('Aureovariegata') Leaves variegated with yellow.

var. *macrophylla* See Latifolia Group.

'Mercedes' Similar to 'Comptoniifolia' but slower growing with even more slender leaves. C 1970.

'Norwegiensis' See under 'Riversii'.

'Pendula' Weeping beech. A spectacular large, weeping tree taking on various forms, sometimes the enormous branches hanging close to and perpendicular with the main stem, while in other specimens some primary branches are almost horizontal but draped with long, hanging branchlets. C 1836. ♀ 2002.

'Prince George of Crete' A striking form with very large leaves. C 1898.

'Purple Fountain' A seedling of 'Purpurea Pendula' raised in Holland making a narrowly upright tree with purple leaves and weeping branches. C 1975. ♀ 2002.

Purpurea Group (f. *purpurea* (Aiton) Schneid.) Purple beech. This name covers purplish-leaved forms normally selected from seed-raised plants. They include 'Atropunicea' and 'Cuprea'. See also under 'Riversii'.

'Purpurea Latifolia' See under 'Riversii'.

'Purpurea Pendula' Weeping purple beech. A superb, small, weeping tree with dark leaves. Usually top-worked to make a small, mushroom-headed specimen. C 1865.

'Purpurea Tricolor' ('Roseomarginata') An attractive cultivar with purple leaves edged with an irregular, pale pink border. Not very constant. C 1888.

'Quercifolia' See under Heterophylla Group.

'Riversii' Purple beech. A large tree with large, dark purple leaves. 'Atropurpurea', 'Atropurpurea Macrophylla', 'Norwegiensis' and 'Purpurea Latifolia' are similar clones. C 1880. ♀ 2002.

'Rohan Gold' Similar to 'Rohanii' but more vigorous, with the leaves yellow when young becoming green. Raised in 1970 by J.R.P. van Hoey-Smith from seed of 'Rohanii' almost certainly pollinated by 'Zlatia'.

'Rohan Obelisk' Narrow, upright habit with irregularly lobed, red-purple leaves.

'Rohan Trompenburg' Leaves red-purple, edged with triangular teeth, upright habit. A seedling of 'Dawyck' pollinated by 'Rohanii' raised at Trompenburg Arboretum, Rotterdam in 1973, and an improvement on 'Rohanii'.

'Rohanii' A purple-leaved form of the fern-leaved beech. A remarkably beautiful, rather slow-growing tree. C 1894.

'Roseomarginata' See 'Purpurea Tricolor'.

'Rotundifolia' Unusual cultivar with strongly ascending branches and small, rounded leaves. C 1872.

'Tortuosa' A low, widespreading tree with twisted and contorted branches that are pendent at their extremities. C 1861.

'Zlatia' A slow-growing tree. Leaves are soft yellow at first becoming green in late summer. The original tree grows in former Yugoslavia in a native stand of *F. moesiaca*, which is an intermediate between *F. sylvatica* and *F. orientalis*. C 1890.

Farkleberry See *Vaccinium arboreum*.

†***FASCICULARIA** Mez—**Bromeliaceae**—A small genus of about 5 species of stemless plants forming dense clumps of evergreen, strap-shaped, spiny leaves, all natives of Chile. They require a warm, sunny, sheltered position in a well-drained soil or rock fissure.

bicolor (Ruiz & Pav.) Mez (*F. pitcairniifolia* hort., *Rhodostachys bicolor* Ruiz & Pav.) A hardy plant in mild areas and, given winter protection, almost so in colder areas. Long, narrow and spine-toothed, leaves sage-green above, glaucous beneath, are produced in dense tufted rosettes. The shorter, central leaves are rich crimson creating a delightful bicolor effect. Tubular, sky-blue flowers are gathered in a dense, sessile head in the centre of the rosette. While in bud the flowerhead is surrounded and concealed by conspicuous, ivory-coloured bracts. I 1851. AM 1949.

pitcairniifolia See *F. bicolor*.

*× **FATSHEDERA** Guillaumin (*Fatsia* × *Hedera*)—**Araliaceae**—An interesting and very useful evergreen, intergeneric hybrid. A splendid shade-bearing plant, creating excellent groundcover. Tolerant of atmospheric pollution, maritime exposure and all types of soil. In constant demand as a house plant.

lizei Guillaumin (*F. japonica* × *H. hibernica*) A small to medium-sized shrub of loose habit with large, leathery, palmate leaves. Spherical heads of white flowers are borne in autumn. Said to be a hybrid between the Irish ivy and *Fatsia japonica* 'Moseri'. Garden origin 1910. ♀ 2002. **'Annemieke'** Leaves centrally blotched bright yellow-green. ♀ 2002. **'Variegata'** Grey-green leaves with an irregular, creamy-white margin. ♀ 2002.

***FATSIA** Decne. & Planch.—**Araliaceae**—A genus of 3 species, natives of Japan and Taiwan. The following succeeds in all types of well-drained soil.

japonica (Murray) Decne. & Planch. (*Aralia sieboldii* K. Koch) A handsome, medium-sized to large shrub of spreading habit. The very large, polished, dark green, palmate leaves give a subtropical effect and are an admirable foil to the panicles of milk-white, globular flowerheads, which terminate the stems in October and are followed by striking clusters of black fruits, ripe in late winter or spring. Succeeds in sun or semi-shade and is excellent for seaside gardens. Japan. I 1838. ♀ 2002. FCC 1966. **'Murakumo-nishiki'** Leaves with a central blotch of yellow-green. **'Variegata'** The leaf lobes are white at the tips. ♀ 2002. FCC 1868.

Feijoa sellowiana See *Acca sellowiana*.

†**FENDLERA** Engelm. & A. Gray—**Hydrangeaceae**—A small genus of 3 species of shrubs with opposite leaves. They require a warm, sunny position in well-drained soil.

wrightii A. Heller. A beautiful plant but difficult to grow and requiring a warm, sunny position. Forms a small to medium-sized shrub with small, lanceolate leaves, 3-nerved and roughly hairy above. The white or pink-tinted, 4-petalled flowers are produced singly or in small clusters in the leaf axils during May and June. SW USA. N Mexico. I 1879.

Fern bush See *Chamaebatiaria millefolium*.
Fetter bush See *Leucothoe racemosa*, *Lyonia lucida*, *Pieris floribunda*.

FICUS L.—**Moraceae**—The figs are a vast genus probably numbering over 800 species of trees, shrubs and woody vines found throughout tropical and subtropical regions. Only a few species may be grown outside in the British Isles but many are popular as indoor or conservatory plants.
carica L. Common fig. A very handsome, large shrub, or small, spreading tree in suitable districts. Often grown against a warm, sunny wall where its handsome, lobed leaves and delicious, edible fruits are an object of interest throughout the year. May cause skin irritation in sunlight. W Asia. Cultivated in England since early 16th century. **'Brown Turkey'** The most popular fruit-producing cultivar. ♀ 2002.
nipponica See *F. sagittata*.
†*pumila L. (*F. stipulata* Thunb.) Creeping fig. A scandent shrub; in its native habitat it climbs tree trunks like ivy. The juvenile growths bear small, neat, ovate or heart-shaped leaves, 1.25–2cm long. In time, adult growths are formed. These produce larger leaves, up to 10cm long, and also, if conditions are suitable, flowers and fruits. A tender plant for a conservatory, where it may be encouraged to cover walls or used in hanging baskets. It may also be grown in a sheltered corner outside in milder districts. Japan, Ryukyus, Taiwan, China. I 1721. ♀ 2002.
'Minima' (*F. stipulata* 'Minima') A very slender creeper, forming close carpets of minute leaves, 6mm long. It is an ideal plant for clothing shady rocks and low walls and in such a situation survived outside for over 35 years in our Winchester nursery.
radicans See *F. sagittata*.
†*sagittata Vahl (*F. nipponica* hort., *F. radicans* Desf.) Similar to *F. pumila* in habit but with longer, narrower leaves, which end in a long point. Only suitable for a conservatory or for use in hanging baskets although it may survive outside for several years in a warm, sheltered position in the milder counties. N India to SE Asia. **'Variegata'** (*F. radicans* 'Variegata') An attractive form with leaves irregularly margined creamy-white.
stipulata See *F. pumila*.

Fig, common See *Ficus carica*.
Fig, creeping See *Ficus pumila*.
Filbert See *Corylus maxima*.
Firethorn See *Pyracantha*.

†**FIRMIANA** Marsigli—**Sterculiaceae**—A small genus of about 8 species of trees with large, lobed leaves. Found from New Guinea to SE Asia and in tropical Africa.
simplex (L.) Wight (*Sterculia platanifolia* L. f.) A noble medium-sized foliage tree with large, maple-like leaves. Suitable for the mildest localities. China, long cultivated in Japan, Taiwan. I 1757.

Flannel bush See *Fremontodendron*.

FONTANESIA Labill.—**Oleaceae**—A small genus of a single privet-like shrubby species, closely related to ash (*Fraxinus*), but with simple leaves.
fortunei See *F. phillyreoides* subsp. *fortunei*.
phillyreoides Labill. A medium-sized shrub with ovate or elliptic, finely toothed leaves and greenish-white flowers in June. Sicily, SW Asia. I 1787. **subsp.** *fortunei* (Carrière) Yalt. (*F. fortunei* Carrière) A taller form making a large shrub or small tree with larger, untoothed leaves. C China. I 1845 by Robert Fortune.

FORESTIERA Poir.—**Oleaceae**—A genus of about 15 species of mainly privet-like shrubs, succeeding in any ordinary soil. They are natives of North and South America and the West Indies. The leaves are opposite and the small, unisexual, greenish flowers are of little or no ornament.
acuminata (Michx.) Poir. (*Adelia acuminata* Michx.) Swamp privet. A large shrub or small tree with narrow-oblong, dark purple fruits. SE USA. I 1812.
neomexicana A. Gray. Desert olive. Medium-sized shrub of spreading habit. Flowers inconspicuous, followed by black, egg-shaped fruits covered with a blue bloom. SW USA. C 1913.

FORSYTHIA Vahl—**Oleaceae**—The most colourful of early spring-flowering shrubs, all very hardy and easy to grow. About 10 species mainly in E Asia with one in SE Europe. The bell-shaped flowers, which wreathe the branches, are golden-yellow unless otherwise described. Several large-flowered hybrids have been raised by Dr Karl Sax at the Arnold Arboretum, Boston, USA. Thin out and cut back old flowering shoots to within a few centimetres of the old wood, immediately after flowering.
'Arnold Dwarf' (*F.* × *intermedia* × *F. japonica* var. *saxatilis*) An interesting hybrid raised at the Arnold Arboretum in 1941. It has value as a low, groundcover plant, attaining a height of only 0.6–1m, but a spread of 1.8–2.1m. The few, yellow-green flowers have no merit.
'Beatrix Farrand' This dense, upright shrub has exceptionally large, deep canary-yellow, nodding flowers, considerably more than 2.5cm across when fully expanded. Named after the American garden designer who was influenced by Gertrude Jekyll, the plant grown under this name is a tetraploid raised at the Arnold Arboretum in 1944. The original clone was a triploid hybrid between *F.* 'Arnold Giant' and *F. ovata* and is probably no longer in cultivation. AM 1961.
Boucle d'Or (Gold Curl) ('Courtacour') PBR A slow-growing very dwarf form, less than 50cm tall, suitable for a rock garden or container. The short shoots are densely covered in bright yellow flowers.
europaea Degen & Bald. European golden ball. A medium-sized shrub with long, 4-angled branches and ovate-lanceolate, usually entire leaves. Pale yellow flowers in April. Albania, former Yugoslavia, Bulgaria. I 1899.
'Fiesta' A compact small to medium-sized shrub, leaves blotched with bright lime-yellow and cream. Vigorous but shy-flowering.
giraldiana Lingelsh. A large shrub of loose, graceful habit, the first species to begin flowering, its pale yellow

blossoms sometimes appearing in late February. NW China. I 1910.

'Golden Nugget' ('Beatrix Farrand' × 'Arnold Giant') A vigorous, medium-sized shrub bearing large, golden-yellow flowers up to 5cm across. Occasionally bears flowers with 6 corolla lobes. Raised by our foreman Alf Alford from a cross made in 1964.

'Golden Times' Bright yellow young leaves later green in the centre, the margin becoming creamy-white, some leaves remaining all yellow. Shy flowering and can scorch in hot sun.

× *intermedia* Zabel (*F. suspensa* × *F. viridissima*) A vigorous hybrid of medium to large size, intermediate in habit and flower between its parents, flowering during late March and April. Leaves sometimes trifoliolate. C before 1880. AM 1894. There are several cultivars. **'Arnold Giant'** A tetraploid hybrid raised at the Arnold Arboretum in 1939. A robust shrub of medium size with exceptionally large, nodding, rich yellow flowers. **'Densiflora'** Fairly compact habit with flowers in such profusion as almost to hide the branches. Garden origin 1899. **'Karl Sax'** A strong-growing, floriferous hybrid with deep canary-yellow flowers. A few flowers open in autumn when the leaves turn purple. A tetraploid hybrid of 'Arnold Giant' and 'Spectabilis' raised at the Arnold Arboretum in 1944. **'Lynwood'** A lovely cultivar, found in a cottage garden in Northern Ireland in 1935 as a sport of 'Spectabilis'. The large, broad-petalled, rich yellow flowers are borne profusely all along the branches. With 'Beatrix Farrand' and 'Karl Sax', this is one of the most spectacular of the forsythias. ♀ 2002. FCC 1966. **'Minigold'** Compact, upright habit bearing profusions of small, deep yellow flowers with broad lobes. **'Primulina'** Pale yellow flowers. A seedling raised in the Arnold Arboretum before 1912. **'Spectabilis'** One of the most popular of early spring-flowering shrubs. The flowers are so profuse as to create a mass of golden-yellow. Garden origin 1906. FCC 1935. AM 1915. **'Spring Glory'** A sport of 'Primulina' with larger flowers more freely borne. Found in a garden in Mentor, Ohio about 1930. **'Tremonia'** See *F.* 'Tremonia'. **'Vitellina'** Strong, erect growth and deep yellow flowers. Garden origin 1899. **Weekend** ('Courtalyn') PBR A mutation of 'Lynwood' raised in 1972 retaining the colour and floriferousness of its parent, but less tall with a compact habit. ♀ 2002.

Marée d'Or (Gold Tide) ('Courtasol') PBR A dwarf shrub suitable for groundcover, reaching only 60cm tall and 1.2m across. Leaves untoothed or with sparse teeth, reddish in autumn. The early lemon-yellow flowers are borne profusely. ♀ 2002.

Melée d'Or (Gold Mix) ('Courtaneur') PBR A small shrub of upright habit, to 1m, bearing clear yellow flowers in spring a week before 'Lynwood'. Leaves often sharply toothed, sometimes entire, red in autumn.

ovata Nakai. An early-flowering, Korean species only 1.2–1.5m high with ovate leaves and amber-yellow flowers in early March. Associates well with heaths and *Rhododendron* 'Praecox'. I 1918. AM 1941. **'Tetragold'** A colchicine-induced, tetraploidal form raised in Holland. It is of dense habit with larger flowers borne slightly earlier than normal. C 1963.

'Robusta' A strong-growing shrub probably of hybrid origin, attaining 1.8–2.7m. Flowers deep yellow. In the past wrongly catalogued as *F. ovata* 'Robusta'.

suspensa (Thunb.) Vahl. A rambling shrub attaining about 3m but much higher against a wall, with slender interlacing branches. Flowers on slender pedicels are produced in late March and early April. Leaves often trifoliolate. China. I 1833. **f. atrocaulis** Rehder. Young stems almost black-purple, contrasting with the comparatively large, pale lemon-yellow flowers. AM 1934. **var. fortunei** (Lindl.) Rehder. The largest and most vigorous form with stout, arching branches. China. I about 1860. **'Nymans'** A large shrub with bronze-purple branches and large, primrose-yellow flowers. A sport of f. *atrocaulis*. C 1951. **var. sieboldii** Zabel. A variety with slender, pendent to almost prostrate branches. An excellent wall shrub for a shady aspect, or for covering an unsightly bank. China, long cultivated in Japan. I 1833.

'Tremonia' (*F.* × *intermedia* 'Tremonia') A small, compact shrub with distinct, very deeply toothed leaves. Large, pale yellow flowers, with broad petals serrate at the apex, are freely borne. A hybrid of 'Beatrix Farrand' raised at the Dortmund Botanic Garden, Germany. C 1963.

viridissima Lindl. Erect, square-stemmed shrub up to 2.4m high, with lanceolate leaves. Normally the last forsythia to flower, commencing in April, some time after *F. suspensa*. China. I 1844 by Robert Fortune. **'Bronxensis'** A dense and compact, dwarf form with masses of twiggy branchlets. Garden origin 1928. AM 1958.

'Volunteer' (*F. ovata* × *F. suspensa*) A vigorous shrub of medium size, with dark-coloured young shoots and thickly clustered, deep yellow flowers. An interesting hybrid that originated in the garden of the late Mr Arthur Simmonds VMH, at Clandon, Surrey.

FORTUNEARIA Rehder & E.H. Wilson—**Hamamelidaceae**—A monotypic genus differing from *Hamamelis* in its 5-parted flowers, and from *Corylopsis* in its tiny, narrow petals.

sinensis Rehder & E.H. Wilson. A large, rather slow-growing shrub, similar in general appearance to *Hamamelis*. but with tiny, green flowers in terminal racemes during winter. Moderately lime-tolerant but grows better in neutral or acid soil. W China. I 1907 by Ernest Wilson.

†***FORTUNELLA** Swingle—**Rutaceae**—A small genus of 4 or 5 species of evergreen shrubs or small trees formerly included under *Citrus*. Natives of SE Asia. Suitable only for a conservatory.

japonica (Thunb.) Swingle (*Citrus japonica* Thunb.) Round kumquat. A large shrub with often spineless green branches and thick, ovate leaves. White flowers are followed by cherry-sized, golden-yellow fruits. Only known in cultivation but probably native to S China. AM 1905.

margarita (Lour.) Swingle. Oval kumquat. Differs from *F. japonica* in its larger size, its slightly thorny shoots and its fruits, which are obovoid to oblong fruits up to 4.5cm long. I from China by Robert Fortune in 1846.

‡**FOTHERGILLA** Murray—**Hamamelidaceae**—The witch alders are a genus of 2 species of shrubs, native to the SE USA. Conspicuous in spring with their bottlebrush-like

flower spikes and again in autumn for the rich colouring of their leaves. They require lime-free soil.

gardenii Murray (*F. alnifolia* L. f., *F. carolina* Britton) Pretty shrub usually less than 1m high, suckering when established. Obovate, dark green leaves, to 6cm long, turn to yellow, orange and red in autumn. Conspicuous, erect, fragrant inflorescences, composed of clusters of white stamens, open in April and May. SE USA. I 1765. **'Blue Mist'** A selection with attractive, blue-green foliage, but inferior autumn colour. **'Mt. Airy'** A splendid form with blue-green foliage, colouring well in autumn, and profuse flowerheads.

major Lodd. A slow-growing shrub of medium to large size. Conspicuous, white flower clusters emerge before the leaves, which are glaucous and downy beneath. Brilliant autumn colours. Alleghany Mountains (USA). I 1780. ♀ 2002. FCC 1971. AM 1927. **Monticola Group** (*F. monticola* Ashe) This form is usually lower-growing, with the leaves green and less hairy beneath. FCC 1969. AM 1988.

monticola See *F. major* Monticola Group.

Frangula See under *Rhamnus*.

‡**FRANKLINIA** Marshall—*Theaceae*—A monotypic genus allied to *Gordonia* and sometimes included in it. A gorgeous autumn-flowering shrub given a hot continental summer, when its ripened growths will withstand a zero winter. It does not flourish in the British Isles and benefits from some glass protection.

alatamaha Marshall (*Gordonia alatamaha* (Marshall) Sarg., *G. pubescens* L'Hér.) A remarkable and rare shrub or small tree with large, lustrous green, oblong leaves that turn crimson in autumn. The large, stewartia-like, cup-shaped, snow-white flowers only open during a hot, late summer. Georgia, USA, but perhaps last seen in the wild by the American collector, Lyon, in 1803. I 1770.

FRAXINUS L.—*Oleaceae*—The ashes are an extensive genus of about 65 species of mainly hardy, fast-growing trees with pinnate leaves. They thrive in almost any soil and tolerate windswept and coastal localities, and smoke-polluted areas. Those of Sect. Ornus are attractive flowering trees.

americana L. (*F. alba* Marshall, *F. biltmoreana* Beadle) White ash. A large species soon forming a noble shade tree. One of the fastest-growing of American hardwoods. Winter buds brown. Leaves with 5-9 leaflets, often colouring well in autumn. E North America. I 1724. **'Autumn Purple'** An American selection of broadly conical habit with dark green leaves, reddish-purple in autumn. **'Rosehill'** Dark green leaves, bronze-red in autumn.

angustifolia Vahl. (*F. rotundifolia* Mill.) A large, elegant, fast-growing tree with perfectly glabrous, slender-pointed leaflets. Winter buds brown. S Europe, N Africa. C 1800. **var. *australis*** (Gay) Schneid. A geographical form with slightly hairy leaf undersides. S Europe, N Africa. C 1890. **var. *lentiscifolia*** Henry. A beautiful variety with small, graceful and semi-pendent branches. **subsp. *oxycarpa*** (M. Bieb. ex Willd.) Franco & Rocha Afonso (*F. oxycarpa* M Bieb. ex Willd.) A graceful,

small-leaved tree akin to *F. angustifolia* from which it is doubtfully distinct. Winter buds dark brown. SE Europe to SW Asia. Mainly represented in gardens by Raywood. I 1815. **'Pendula'** A handsome tree with slender, pendent branches. **Raywood** ('Flame') (*F. oxycarpa* 'Raywood') A fast-growing tree of dense, fairly upright habit. This form is especially attractive in autumn when its dark green leaves turn plum-purple. An excellent tree of relatively compact habit. C 1928. ♀ 2002. AM 1978. **subsp. *syriaca*** (Boiss.) Yalt. (*F. syriaca* Boiss.) Syrian ash. A rare, small tree with crowded, whorled leaves of bright apple-green. Winter buds brown. W and C Asia. C 1880.

berlandierana A. DC. Rare in gardens, this is a small tree with glabrous shoots; leaves to 25cm long with 3–5 leaflets, the lateral ones stalked. The leaflets are glossy green above and glabrous on both sides, tapered to the apex and the base and edged with small teeth above the middle. It has grown well in an exposed position at the Sir Harold Hillier Gardens and Arboretum. S USA, NE Mexico.

biltmoreana See *F. americana*.

bungeana DC. (Sect. Ornus) A large shrub or small tree with downy twigs and petioles but 5–7 glabrous leaflets. Flowers are produced in terminal panicles in May. Winter buds black. N China. I 1881.

caroliniana Mill. Water ash, pop ash. A variable small tree, rare in gardens, the leaves with usually 5 or 7, slightly leathery and sharply toothed leaflets to 10cm long, glossy dark green above, paler and blue-green beneath. Buds small, brown, shoots and leaf undersides glabrous or downy. It is distinct in the broadly winged fruits which taper to the base. There are small trees at the Sir Harold Hillier Gardens and Arboretum. SE USA.

chinensis Roxb. Chinese ash. A free-growing, medium-sized tree with attractive leaves which sometimes give wine-purple autumn colours. Winter buds a conspicuous grey. Flowers sweetly scented. China. I 1891. **var. *acuminata*** Lingelsh. A variety having leaflets with longer tapering points. China. I 1910. **subsp. *rhyncophylla*** (Hance) E. Murr. An outstanding, tall, Chinese variety; grows well in the British Isles and is notable for the large size of its terminal leaflets. NE Asia. I 1881.

†*dipetala* Hook. & Arn. California ash. A medium-sized to large shrub with 4-angled branches; leaves varying in number of leaflets, usually 5. This species is particularly useful for the creamy-white flowers, which are produced in conspicuous panicles on the previous year's growth in late spring. Requires a warm, sheltered position as the young growths are subject to damage by late frosts. California. I 1878.

excelsior L. Common ash. A magnificent, large tree and one of the most valuable for timber. Winter buds black. Europe (incl. British Isles), Caucasus. There are several cultivars. Forms selected in the 1940s in Holland for their suitability as street trees include 'Altena', 'Atlas' and 'Eureka'. See also 'Westhof's Glorie'. **'Aurea'** See under 'Jaspidea'. **'Aurea Pendula'** A small tree of rather weak constitution with yellow and drooping young shoots, forming an umbrella-shaped crown. **'Crispa'** Slow-growing, shrubby form of stiff, upright growth. Leaves have small, shining, dark green, curled and twisted leaflets. **'Diversifolia'** ('Monophylla') One-leaved ash. A vigorous tree with leaves simple or sometimes 3-parted and usually jaggedly toothed. C 1789. **'Erosa'** A small tree with very narrow, deeply cut leaflets. C 1806. **'Jaspidea'** A vigorous clone with golden-yellow young shoots and yellowish branches, conspicuous in winter. Leaves clear yellow in autumn. Often found in cultivation under the name 'Aurea', which is a dwarf, slow-growing tree. C 1873. ♀ 2002. **'Monophylla'** See 'Diversifolia'. **'Nana'** A densely branched, slow-growing, eventually large, rounded bush. **'Pendula'** Weeping ash. A strong-growing tree, forming an attractive, widespreading mound of divergent, weeping branches. ♀ 2002. **'R.E. Davey'** Narrow, upright habit, the leaf stalks and leaflets conspicuously twisted. More vigorous than 'Crispa'. **'Westhof's Glorie'** A vigorous tree, narrowly upright when young, later spreading. Dark green leaves open late. A common street tree in continental Europe. C 1947. ♀ 2002.

floribunda Wall. (Sect. Ornus) Striking, small tree with purplish young wood. The large leaves have a conspicuous, polished sheen and the white flowers are in large terminal panicles. Proving hardy in the Sir Harold Hillier Gardens and Arboretum. Himalaya. I 1822.

†*griffithii* C.B. Clarke (*F. bracteata* Hemsl.) A nearly evergreen species with 4-angled, green shoots and leathery, dark green and glabrous, entire leaflets. Flowers in large, loose panicles. Requires shelter in all but the mildest areas. This uncommon species has grown for many years at the Sir Harold Hillier Gardens and Arboretum. N India to SE Asia. I 1900 by Ernest Wilson.

holotricha Koehne. A small tree with downy young growths, related to *F. angustifolia*. The many narrow leaflets are decidedly greyish. Very close to *F. pallisiae*, it differs in its more open habit, and larger leaves with usually 9–11 more sharply toothed leaflets. Origin uncertain. C 1870.

latifolia Benth. (*F. oregona* Nutt.) Oregon ash. A medium-sized, fast-growing tree with large leaves. Winter buds brown. W North America. C 1870.

mandshurica Rupr. Manchurian ash. A large tree showing kinship with Britain's native species. Winter buds dark brown. The leaves often turn red and yellow in autumn. NE Asia. I 1882.

mariesii See *F. sieboldiana*.

nigra Marshall. Black ash. A small to medium-sized tree, said to grow in wet situations in the wild. Winter buds dark brown; leaves have 7–11 slender-pointed leaflets. Not one of the best species in cultivation. E North America. I 1800.

oregona See *F. latifolia*.

ornus L. (Sect. Ornus) Manna ash. A pretty tree of medium size, flowering abundantly in May. This is the type species of Section Ornus, popularly known as flowering ashes. S Europe, SW Asia. I before 1700. ♀ 2002.

oxycarpa See *F. angustifolia* subsp. *oxycarpa*. **'Raywood'** See *F. angustifolia* Raywood.

pallisiae Wilmott. A close relative of *F. angustifolia*, bearing leaves often arranged in 3s, this species makes an elegant tree eventually of large size. Leaves, as seen here, usually have 7 slender leaflets, the lateral ones sessile, tapered to a long, fine point. The shoots and leaves are covered in soft hairs. E Europe. I 1932.

paxiana Lingelsh. (Sect. Ornus) A remarkable tree of medium size with glabrous twigs and large, terminal winter buds, coated with brownish down. Leaves, about 30cm long, are composed of 7–9 lanceolate, toothed, slender-pointed leaflets, the lowest pair much smaller than the rest. Petioles often enlarged at the base. White flowers are produced in large panicles during May and June. Himalaya, W and C China. I 1901 by Ernest Wilson.

pennsylvanica Marshall (*F. pubescens* Lam.) (*F. pennsylvanica* var. *lanceolata* (Borkh.) Sarg.) Green ash, Red ash. A fast-growing, shade-giving, medium-sized tree with downy shoots and large leaves. Winter buds brown. E North America. I 1783. **'Aucubifolia'** Leaves mottled golden-yellow. **'Summit'** An American selection of broadly conical habit with glossy leaves turning golden-yellow in autumn. **'Variegata'** A brightly variegated tree; leaves silver-grey, margined and mottled cream-white.

platypoda Oliv. (*F. spaethiana* Lingelsh.) Lingelsh. A small to medium-sized tree, with conspicuously large leaves, remarkable for the large, swollen, often red-brown base of its petioles. Large panicles of flowers without petals. China, Japan. C 1873.

potamophila See *F. sogdiana*.

profunda See *F. tomentosa*.

quadrangulata Michx. Blue ash. Small tree with distinctly 4-winged, square branchlets. Leaves with 7–11 short-stalked leaflets. C and E USA. I 1823.

rotundifolia See *F. angustifolia*.

sieboldiana Blume (*F. longicuspis* var. *sieboldiana* (Blume) Lingelsh., *F. mariesii* Hook. f.) (Sect. Ornus) This is the most beautiful of the flowering ashes. A small tree with creamy-white flowers in handsome panicles during June. Leaflets 5, rarely 7, often giving autumn tints. C China. I 1878 by Charles Maries. AM 1962 (as *F. mariesii*). Japan, Korea.

sogdiana Bunge (*F. potamophila* Herder) A small tree with greenish, glabrous shoots and having leaves with 7–11 lanceolate, glabrous leaflets, conspicuously toothed, sessile or almost so. Turkestan. C 1890.

spaethiana See *F. platypoda*.

syriaca See *F. angustifolia* subsp. *syriaca*.

tomentosa Michx. f. (*F. profunda* (Bush) Bush) Pumpkin ash. A medium-sized tree with downy young shoots and petioles and large leaves with up to 9 stalked leaflets, downy beneath. E North America. C 1912.

velutina Torr. Arizona ash. A neat and pretty tree of 9–12m. Remarkable for its leaves and shoots, which are densely clothed with grey, velvety down. Winter buds brown. SW USA, N Mexico. I 1891. **var.** *coriacea* (S. Watson) Rehder. A form with leaflets more leathery and less downy. California. C 1900. **var.** *glabra* Rehder. Leaves, with 3–7 leaflets, glabrous like the branches. **var.** *toumeyi* Rehder. A distinct variety of dense habit. Leaves smaller with 3–5 downy leaflets. Arizona, New Mexico, Mexico. I 1891.

xanthoxyloides DC. The Afghan ash is a small tree or large shrub of unusual appearance, with small, rounded, close-set leaflets on winged petioles. Winter buds brown. Himalaya to Afghanistan. C 1870. **var.** *dimorpha* (Coss. & Durieu) Wenz. Algerian ash. A geographical form from N Africa differing in leaf shape and other minor characters. I about 1855. **var. _dumosa_** Carrière. A curious small bush with interlacing branches and tiny leaflets. C 1865.

†*FREMONTODENDRON** Cov. (_Fremontia_ Torr.)—Sterculiaceae—Flannel bush. A genus of 2 species of tall, evergreen shrubs, best grown on a sunny wall in all but the milder parts of the British Isles. The flowers have no petals but possess a large, coloured calyx. Requires full sun and good drainage; excellent on chalk soils. Skin and eye irritant.

'**California Glory**' (_F. californicum_ × _F. mexicanum_) A floriferous hybrid of vigorous growth, which originated at Rancho Santa Ana Botanic Garden in California in 1952. Yellow flowers, up to 6cm across, are borne over a long period. ♀ 2002. FCC 1967.

californicum (Torr.) Cov. A large, semi-evergreen shrub, with usually 3-lobed leaves, and large, yellow flowers borne freely throughout the summer and autumn. California, Arizona. I 1851. FCC 1866.

mexicanum Davidson. Similar to, but differing from _F. californicum_ in its generally 5-lobed leaves, often shiny above. Flowers have slightly narrower sepals, giving a star-like appearance. California, Mexico. I 1926. AM 1927.

'**Pacific Sunset**' Similar to 'California Glory' but with more angularly lobed leaves and a brighter yellow calyx, the lobes ending in tail-like points. A backcross of 'California Glory' raised at Rancho Santa Ana Botanic Garden. C 1984.

†*FREYLINIA** Colla—Scrophulariaceae—A small genus of about 4 species of evergreen shrubs, natives of tropical and South Africa.

lanceolata (L. f.) G. Don (_F. cestroides_ Colla) A pretty, medium-sized shrub for the mildest localities. Panicles of fragrant, creamy-white or yellow flowers appear in late summer. South Africa. I 1774.

Fringe tree See _Chionanthus_.

FUCHSIA L.—Onagraceae—Some 100 species of shrubs, small trees and climbers, natives mainly of Central and South America but also occurring in Tahiti and New Zealand. Flowers mostly pendent with a showy calyx and corolla.

Most of the kinds listed below have passed successfully many winters outdoors in our nurseries. Although the tender sorts may be cut to ground level, they usually shoot up strongly again in spring. All have red sepals except where otherwise stated, and flower freely throughout summer and autumn. These hardy fuchsias are remarkable in thriving alike in sun or shade in any well-drained soil.

'**Achievement**' Single, profuse flowers over a long period; reddish-cerise tube and recurved sepals; corolla reddish-purple becoming scarlet at the base. An excellent border plant of upright habit. ♀ 2002. C 1886.

'**Alice Hoffman**' A small shrub with small, purple-tinged leaves in dense clusters. Small flowers with a scarlet calyx and white petals. C 1911. ♀ 2002.

'**Alison Patricia**' Semi-double with a red tube and pale pink sepals; corolla violet-pink, veined red. Compact, upright habit. C 1990. ♀ 2002.

'**Army Nurse**' Semi-double with carmine tube and sepals; corolla blue-violet. Vigorous upright habit. C 1947. ♀ 2002.

†× _bacillaris_ Lindl. (_F. microphylla_ × _F. thymifolia_) A beautiful shrub bearing small flowers with a glowing crimson calyx and reflexed, coral-red petals. Mexico. Originally wrongly catalogued as _F. parviflora_. C 1832.

'**Cottinghamii**' (_F._ 'Cottinghamii') This charming shrub is taller and small flowers succeeded by glossy purple-brown, bead-like fruits.

†'**Blue Gown**' A dwarf, floriferous, compact shrub with double flowers with a deep purple corolla and scarlet calyx.

†'**Brilliant**' A small shrub bearing large flowers with a rose-scarlet calyx and broad, rose-purple petals. C 1865. AMT 1962.

'**Brutus**' Vigorous, bushy habit with arching shoots. Long-stalked, single flowers have deep rose-pink sepals and a deep purple corolla; profusely borne. C 1901. ♀ 2002.

'**Chillerton Beauty**' A beautiful, small shrub. Medium-sized flowers have white calyces, flushed deep rose and clear soft violet petals. C 1847. ♀ 2002. AMT 1977.

'**Corallina**' (_F. cordifolia_ × _F._ 'Globosa') A strong, robust shrub with large, deep green leaves and scarlet and violet flowers. Raised about 1914. Originally catalogued as _F._ 'Exoniensis', which is probably no longer in cultivation. C 1844.

'**Cottinghamii**' See _F._ × _bacillaris_ 'Cottinghamii'.

'**Dark Eyes**' Double with a red tube, broad, upturned red sepals and a dense centre of rolled, violet-blue petals. C 1958. ♀ 2002.

†'**Display**' A small shrub producing large flowers with a carmine calyx, rose-pink petals and long protruding stamens. C 1881. ♀ 2002.

'**Dollar Princess**' Vigorous and upright. Profuse, double with rich purple corollas, pink at the base, and cerise sepals and tube. C 1912. ♀ 2002.

'**Dunrobin Bedder**' Small shrub of spreading habit. Flowers similar to _F. magellanica_, scarlet and violet. AM 1890.

†'**Elsa**' Small shrub with large flowers with a white calyx flushed pink and doubled, violet-rose petals.

'**Empress of Prussia**' Single flowers with a scarlet tube and spreading sepals; corolla reddish-magenta. An excellent selection of vigorous, upright habit, flowering profusely. ♀ 2002.

†_excorticata_ (J.R. Forst. & G. Forst.) L. f. The largest of the 3 New Zealand species, making a very large, tree-like shrub in the mildest localities, but here never more than a medium-sized bush. Flowers, 2.5cm long, resembling _F. procumbens_ in colour, appearing in spring. I 1824.

'**Flash**' Single, small flowers profusely borne; slender, pale magenta-pink tube and pale pink sepals; corolla pale magenta. C 1930. ♀ 2002.

'**Foxgrove Wood**' Single with pink tube and sepals; blue corolla. Bushy, upright habit. C 1993. ♀ 2002.

'**Garden News**' A vigorous and very hardy shrub of upright habit. Large, double flowers with a pale pink calyx and tube and magenta-rose corolla. C 1978. ♀ 2002.

'**Genii**' A dwarf, upright shrub with red shoots and attractive, lime-yellow leaves. Small flowers have a violet then reddish-purple corolla and cerise calyx. Leaf colour develops best in full sun. C 1951. ♀ 2002.

gracilis See *F. magellanica* var. *gracilis*. **'Variegata'** See *F. magellanica* 'Variegata'.

'Graf Witte' A small shrub with profusely borne, small, single flowers with a carmine calyx and purple corolla shaded rosy-mauve. C 1899. AMT 1978.

'Hawkshead' (*F. magellanica* var. *molinae* × *F.* 'Venus Victrix') A small shrub, the slender pure white flowers with a slight green flush; foliage deep green. Vigorous, bushy, upright habit. C 1973. ♀ 2002.

'Heidi Ann' (*F.* 'General Monk' × *F.* 'Tennessee Waltz') Fully double flowers with a stout crimson tube and short, reflexed, crimson-cerise sepals; corolla lilac-purple veined with cerise, paler at the base. Bushy, upright habit. C 1969. ♀ 2002.

'Herald' Single flowers with a swollen scarlet tube and reflexed, scarlet sepals; corolla deep blue-purple with cerise veins, ageing to red-purple. Vigorous, upright habit. C 1887. ♀ 2002.

'Joman' (*F.* 'Blue Elf' × *F.* 'Mayfield') Single, with a short, rose-pink tube and reflexed, slightly twisted, rose-pink sepals; corolla pale blue-violet with pink veins, ageing to pale violet-pink. Bushy, upright habit. C 1984. ♀ 2002.

'Lady Thumb' A bushy, dwarf shrub with profusely borne, semi-double flowers with a light red calyx and a white corolla with red veins. C 1966. ♀ 2002. FCCT 1977.

'Lena' Semi-double flowers with a pale pink calyx and a rosy-magenta corolla, flushed pink. Good for training. C 1862. ♀ 2002. AMT 1962.

'Liebriez' Small flowers profusely borne, semi-double with pale cerise-pink tube and sepals; corolla pinkish-white with pink veins. Good in a container. C 1874. ♀ 2002.

'Lottie Hobby' Very small flowers with light crimson tubes and sepals and pale purple corollas. Vigorous, upright habit. C 1839.

†**'Madame Cornélissen'** A large-flowered hybrid of *F. magellanica*, with red calyx and white petals. C 1860. ♀ 2002. FCCT 1978. AMT 1965. AM 1941.

magellanica Lam. A graceful South American shrub of medium size. Long, slender flowers have a scarlet calyx and violet petals. Leaves generally in whorls of 3. Chile, Argentina. I 1788. **'Alba'** See *F. magellanica* var. *molinae*. **'Aurea'** Vigorous with golden-yellow foliage. **var. *gracilis*** (Lindl..) Bailey. A beautiful, floriferous shrub of slender habit, with leaves generally in pairs. Flowers small, scarlet and violet. ♀ 2002. AMT 1978. **var. *molinae*** Espinosa ('Alba') Flowers shorter, white, faintly tinged mauve. AM 1932. **'Pumila'** A charming, dwarf shrub with small, narrow and tiny flowers of scarlet and deep violet. **'Riccartonii'** See *F.* 'Riccartonii'. **'Sharpitor'** A sport of var. *molinae* in which the leaves are grey-green margined with white. Originated at the National Trust garden, Sharpitor, Devon about 1973. **'Thompsonii'** A lower-growing form of upright habit with small but profuse flowers. Sepals and tube scarlet; corolla pale purple. AMT 1965. **'Tricolor'** See 'Versicolor'. **'Variegata'** (*F. gracilis* 'Variegata') A striking variegated form with green leaves, margined creamy-yellow and flushed pink, against which the small scarlet and purple flowers appear most effectively. Less hardy than the green form. ♀ 2002. AMT 1975.

'Versicolor' ('Tricolor') A small shrub of spreading habit. Slender stems, leaves striking grey-green, rose-tinted when young and irregularly variegated creamy-white when mature. A lovely foliage shrub. AMT 1965.

'Margaret' A vigorous shrub producing an abundance of crimson and violet-purple, semi-double flowers. C 1939. ♀ 2002. AMT 1965.

'Margaret Brown' A dwarf shrub of erect, compact habit with large flowers with a crimson calyx and magenta petals. C 1949. ♀ 2002.

†*microphylla* Kunth. A small shrub with red shoots and slender leaves to 4cm or less long. The small flowers are solitary in the leaf axils with white to pink or red sepals and petals, followed by black fruits. A variable species widely distributed in Mexico and Central America. I 1828.

'Mrs Popple' A small, large-flowered, hardy hybrid with spreading, scarlet sepals, violet petals, and long protruding crimson stamens and style. C 1899. ♀ 2002. AMT 1962. AM 1934.

'Mrs W.P. Wood' Very freely borne, single flowers with a pale pink calyx of slender, upturned sepals; white corolla. C 1949. ♀ 2002.

parviflora See under *F.* × *bacillaris*.

'Peter Pan' A dwarf shrub with abundant small, red and purple flowers.

'Phyllis' Vigorous and upright, the profuse, small, semi-double flowers have a rose-pink corolla and waxy red sepals and tube. C 1938. ♀ 2002.

'Pink Fantasia' Single, with a short tube and horizontally-held, spreading, salmon-pink sepals; corolla deep magenta, flushed white. C 1989.

'Pixie' A sport of 'Graf Witte' making an upright shrub to about 90cm with yellowish-green foliage. Single flowers have a carmine tube and sepals; mauve-purple corolla, veined with carmine. C 1960.

†*procumbens* A. Cunn. A trailing, small-leaved, New Zealand species. Small, erect flowers have a yellow tube; violet and green sepals; red and blue stamens; petals absent. Comparatively large, magenta fruits. I about 1854. AM 1980.

'Prosperity' (*F.* 'Bishop's Bells' × *F.* 'Strawberry Delight') A beautiful, small shrub of upright habit and vigorous growth with large, double flowers with a white corolla, veined pink, and a deep rose-pink calyx. One of the most spectacular hardy fuchsias. C 1974. ♀ 2002.

†**'Reflexa'** A small shrub with tiny leaves and small, bright cerise flowers darkening with age; fruits black. Regarded by some authorities as a form of *F. thymifolia*. while others suggest it may belong to *F.* × *bacillaris*.

'Riccartonii' (*F. magellanica* 'Riccartonii') This common, hardy shrub attains a large size, and is often used as a hedging plant in mild districts. Differs from *F. magellanica* in its deeper coloured calyx and broader sepals. C 1830. ♀ 2002. FCCT 1977. AMT 1966.

'Rose Fantasia' Single, with pale salmon-pink, recurved sepals and pale lilac corolla. A sport of 'Pink Fantasia'. C 1991.

†**'Rose of Castile'** A vigorous, small shrub with large flowers consisting of a deep violet-purple corolla and a spreading, white calyx, tinged pink inside, tipped with green. C 1855.

'**Rose of Castile Improved**' Single with very pale pink tube and slender, pink-flushed, white sepals, tipped green; corolla red-violet, veined pink, ageing to red-purple. Vigorous, bushy, upright habit. C 1871. ♀ 2002.

'**Rufus**' Vigorous, upright growth with profuse single flowers. Tube and recurved sepals bright red; corolla dusky-red. C 1952. ♀ 2002.

'**Schneewittchen**' Single with a stout, deep pink tube and short, deep pink sepals; corolla pinkish-purple. Vigorous, bushy, upright habit. C 1878.

'**Snowcap**' A dwarf shrub bearing flowers 5cm long, with red sepals and tube, the petals white veined with red. ♀ 2002. AMT 1966 (for summer bedding).

'**Son of Thumb**' Small, single, compact flowers profusely borne over a long period. Tube and sepals cerise-pink; corolla lilac. Dwarf, bushy habit to 45cm. A sport of 'Tom Thumb'. C 1978. ♀ 2002.

'**Sunray**' Pale green and cream leaves, edged and flushed red. Small, single flowers with red sepals and tube; mauve corolla. Bushy, upright habit. C 1872.

'**Tennessee Waltz**' A low shrub of arching habit. Flowers with rich purple-violet corolla and deep glossy scarlet calyx. C 1950. AMT 1978.

'**Tom Thumb**' A very free-flowering, dwarf shrub. Flowers with rose-scarlet calyx and violet petals. C 1850. ♀ 2002. FCCT 1962. AMT 1938.

'**Tom West**' Bronze-green young leaves edged deep pink, becoming pale blue-green with pale pink margins, on red-purple shoots. Flowers small, single, with red sepals and tube; purple corolla. C 1853.

†*thymifolia* Kunth. A small shrub with opposite or whorled leaves to 6.5cm long. The small, solitary flowers have white sepals and petals, later turning red. Mexico. I 1824.

'**White Pixie**' Single flowers with a slender, red tube and broad, reflexed red sepals; corolla white with deep pink veins. Upright, bushy habit, the foliage yellow-green veined red. A sport of 'Pixie'. C 1967. ♀ 2002.

Furze See *Ulex*.
Furze, needle See *Genista anglica*.

G

GARRYA Douglas ex Lindl.—**Garryaceae**—About 13 species of evergreen, dioecious shrubs with opposite, leathery leaves. Natives of SW USA, Mexico and the West Indies. Flowers are borne in long, slender, conspicuous catkins. Excellent both in maritime exposure and atmospheric pollution and useful for furnishing shady walls. They succeed in all types of well-drained soil, but require protection in cold areas.

congdonii Eastw. A shrub, up to 1.8m, with narrowly oval leaves, rounded on juvenile plants. Male catkins up to 7.5cm long in late spring. California.

elliptica Douglas ex Lindl. The male plant of this species is a magnificent evergreen, draped, during January and February, with long, greyish-green catkins. The female plant, although uncommon, is scarcely less effective, with its long clusters of deep purple-brown fruits. California, Oregon. I 1828 by David Douglas. AM 1975 (for fruit). AM 1931. **'James Roof'** A strong, vigorous male with large, leathery leaves and extra long catkins to 20cm. Originated as a seedling in California before 1950. ♀ 2002. AM 1974.

†*flavescens* S. Watson. An erect, medium-sized shrub with leathery, elliptic, sharply-pointed leaves. Flowers in stout, pendent catkins during spring. A variable species, the leaves and stems of the typical form are clothed with yellowish hairs but in their sage-green and greyish-green appearance our plants approach the variety *pallida*. California.

glaberrima Wang. A vigorous, evergreen shrub with smooth shoots flushed with red-purple when mature. Leaves glossy dark green, paler beneath, bronze when young, elliptic-oblong, rounded at the apex with a small mucro, to 9cm long, glabrous on both sides. Shoots prominently marked with corky lenticels in the second year. A plant in the Sir Harold Hillier Gardens and Arboretum is female with short, erect spikes of flowers in spring. I by Jim Priest in 1984. Mexico.

× *issaquahensis* Talbot de Malahide ex E.C. Nelson (*G. elliptica* × *G. fremontii*) A large shrub intermediate between the parents with flat or slightly undulate leaves, dark glossy green above, green and glaucous green and only slightly hairy beneath. First raised in Seattle in about 1957, the cross later occurred accidentally in the garden of Mrs Pat Ballard at Issaquah, Washington in 1960. The following clone was raised at Malahide Castle, Ireland. **'Glasnevin Wine'** A selection similar to 'Pat Ballard' but with the inflorescences more conspicuously coloured with red-purple. **'Pat Ballard'** A male selection with reddish-purple shoots and petioles. Catkins to 22cm long in midwinter, purple-tinged at first becoming green tinged red. AM 1971.

†*laurifolia* Benth. A tender species of which the following form is cultivated. **subsp. *macrophylla*** (Benth.) G.V. Dahling (*G. fadyenii* hort. not Hook.) A vigorous, medium-sized to large shrub with large leaves up to 15cm long. Catkins, less spectacular than those of *G. elliptica*, appear in late spring. Mexico. I 1846.

× *thuretii* Carrière (*G. elliptica* × *G. laurifolia* subsp. *macrophylla*) A vigorous hybrid, rapidly attaining 5.5m and making a solid green wall. Dark green, glossy leaves about 14cm long and pendent catkins in late spring. An excellent wind resister. Garden origin about 1862.

wrightii Torr. A medium-sized shrub with slender, 5cm catkins in summer. Leaves elliptic, firm and leathery with a sharp mucro-point, sage-green and conspicuously veined. SW USA. I 1901.

× *Gaulnettya* See *Gaultheria*.

‡***GAULTHERIA** L. (× *Gaulnettya* Marchant, *Pernettya* Gaudich.)—**Ericaceae**—An interesting genus of some 170 species, related to *Vaccinium*, differing in the superior ovary. They are evergreen, mainly tufted shrubs, spreading by underground stems. The white, urn-shaped flowers are normally borne in late spring or early summer. In the majority of species, the calyx enlarges after flowering, becoming fleshy and coloured, and encloses the true fruit. Most are poisonous if eaten. They thrive in moist, lime-free, preferably peaty soil, and a shady position. Widely distributed in E Asia, Australasia, and throughout the New World.

adenothrix (Miq.) Maxim. A dainty, dwarf, creeping shrub forming a low carpet of zigzag, red-brown-hairy stems, furnished with small, leathery, dark green leaves. White flowers, suffused pink, are borne from May to July and followed by hairy, crimson fruits. Japan. I 1915.

antipoda G. Forst. An interesting New Zealand species, varying in habit between a prostrate shrub and an erect bush of 1.2m. Fruits red or white, globose, about 1.25cm across. I 1820,

caudata Stapf. A low-growing, widespreading shrub forming a dense mound. A specimen in the Sir Harold Hillier Gardens and Arboretum reached 75cm high by 2.5m across. The narrowly elliptic to elliptic-oblong, sharply serrulate leaves, which are reticulate and punctate beneath, are widely spaced along the attractively arching, reddish shoots. Flowers in axillary racemes. Yunnan.

cuneata (Rehder & E.H. Wilson) Bean. A dwarf shrub of compact habit. Leaves narrowly oblanceolate. Its white fruit smell of Germolene® when crushed. A delightful species. W China. I 1909 by Ernest Wilson. ♀ 2002. AM 1924.

forrestii Diels. An attractive, spreading, Chinese shrub with conspicuous, white-stalked, axillary racemes of white, waxy, fragrant flowers, followed by blue fruits. I about 1908. AM 1937. AM 1927.

fragrantissima Wall. A medium-sized species with narrowly elliptic, toothed, subglabrous leaves, fragrant flowers in racemes from the leaf axils and bright blue fruit. Himalaya, Mountains of Burma, India and Sri Lanka. I about 1850.

hispida R. Br. Small shrub with bristly young shoots and oblong leaves up to 6.5cm long. White flowers, in terminal panicles, are followed by succulent, berry-like, white fruit. Australia, Tasmania. C 1927. AM 1927.

hookeri C.B. Clarke (*G. veitchiana* Craib) A dwarf, dense, spreading shrub with bristly, arching stems. Leathery and glandular toothed, elliptic to obovate leaves 5–7.5cm long. Flowers white in dense, axillary terminal clusters in

May; fruit blue. Himalaya, W China. I 1907 by Ernest Wilson. FCC 1945. AM 1943.

humifusa (Graham) Rydb. (*G. myrsinites* Hook.) Alpine wintergreen. A dwarf shrub of dense, compact habit, only a few centimetres high, bearing small, rounded, wavy leaves. The small, pink-tinged, bell-shaped flowers in summer are followed by small, red fruit. NW North America. C 1830.

itoana Hayata. A rare, creeping species forming close mats of bright green, pernettya-like foliage. Fruit white. Taiwan. I shortly before 1936. AM 1982.

miqueliana Takeda. A neat, dwarf, Japanese shrub, usually not above 30cm high, with shining green, oblong leaves. The short flower racemes are conspicuous in June, and are followed by white or pink, edible fruit. I 1892. AM 1948.

mucronata (L. f.) Hook. & Arn. (*Pernettya mucronata* (L. f.) Spreng.) The showiest of all dwarf evergreens in fruit and one of the hardiest of South American shrubs. Forms dense thickets of wiry stems about 60–90cm high or occasionally more. Myriad small, white, heath-like flowers in May to June are followed by dense clusters of long-persistent, marble-like berries, ranging from pure white to mulberry-purple. Though not strictly dioecious, it is best to plant in groups of 3 or more and, to ensure berry-production, include a proven male form. A marvellous plant which should be mass-planted for groundcover. Chile to Magellan region. I 1828. AM 1961. ‘Alba’ Medium-sized, white berries with a faint pink tinge, deepening with age. FCC 1882. ‘Atrococcinea’ Large, deep, shining ruby-red berries. ‘Bell’s Seedling’ A hermaphrodite form with reddish young stems and dark, shining green leaves; berries large, dark red. ♥ 2002. AM 1928. ‘Cherry Ripe’ Similar in general appearance to ‘Bell’s Seedling’, but berries medium to large, bright cherry-red. AM 1985. ‘Crimsonia’ Very large, crimson berries. C 1968. ♥ 2002. AM 1985. Davis’s Hybrids A first-rate selection of large-berried forms in a mixture of colours. ‘Edward Balls’ A very distinct male form of erect habit. Shoots stout and stiff, reddish and shortly hispid. Leaves broadly ovate or rounded. Collected in the wild by E.K. Balls. ‘Lilacina’ A free-berrying form with medium-sized, reddish-lilac berries. FCC 1878. ‘Lilian’ Very large, lilac-pink berries. C 1968. AM 1985. ‘Mother of Pearl’ See ‘Parelmoer’. ‘Mulberry Wine’ Young stems green; large, magenta berries ripening to deep purple. ♥ 2002. ‘Parelmoer’ (‘Mother of Pearl’) Fruits pale pink. ‘Pink Pearl’ Medium-sized, lilac-pink berries. ♥ 2002. ‘Rosalind’ Large, carmine-pink berries. ‘Rosie’ Young stems red; leaves dark sea-green; large, pink berries with a deep rose flush. ‘Sea Shell’ Medium to large, shell-pink berries, ripening to rose. ♥ 2002. ‘Signaal’ Very large, long-persistent cherry-red berries. ‘Sneeuwwitje’ (‘Snow White’) Profuse brilliant white berries, slightly spotted with pink. ‘Snow White’ See ‘Sneeuwwitje’. ‘Thymifolia’ A charming, small, male form of neat habit. Leaves smaller than in the type; smothered in white flowers during late May and early June. ‘White Pearl’ A selection of ‘Alba’, with medium to large berries of gleaming white. ‘Wintertime’ Large, pure white berries. ♥ 2002.

myrsinoides Kunth (*Pernettya prostrata* (Cav.) DC., *P. prostrata* subsp. *pentlandii* (DC.) B.L. Burtt, *P. buxifolia*

Mart. & Gal., *P. ciliata* Small) A dwarf or prostrate shrub forming low mounds of arching, downy and sparsely bristly stems, and narrow, glossy, bright green leaves. Pitcher-shaped, white flowers, produced singly or in small racemes in May and June, are followed by usually black berries. Central and South America. I about 1870. AM 1957.

†*nummularioides* D. Don. A neat, creeping species with small, broadly ovate, bristly leaves arranged in 2 ranks; fruits blue-black. Suitable for a sheltered shady bank. Himalaya to SE Asia. I about 1850.

oppositifolia Hook. f. A small, densely branched shrub of spreading habit with arching, usually glabrous shoots. Leaves normally opposite, ovate to oblong, dark glossy green above and strongly reticulate. The white, bell-shaped flowers are borne in conspicuous, terminal panicles during May and June. Fruit white. An extremely ornamental New Zealand species easily recognised by its opposite leaves. It requires a sheltered position. AM 1927.

procumbens L. Checkerberry, Wintergreen. A creeping evergreen, forming carpets of dark green, aromatic leaves among which, in autumn and winter, the bright red fruits are freely intermixed. E North America. I before 1762. ♥ 2002. AM 1982.

pumila (L. f.) Middleton (*Pernettya pumila* (L. f.) Hook., *P. empetrifolia* (Lamb.) Gaudich.) A dwarf, almost prostrate, dioecious species, with slender, wiry stems and tiny leaves. Berries white or pink-tinged. Magellan Straits, Falkland Is. ‘Harold Comber’ A selection with comparatively large, attractive, deep rose berries. Originally collected by Harold Comber in the Chilean Andes. var. *leucocarpa* (DC.) Middleton (*Pernettya leucocarpa* DC.) A dwarf shrub of compact habit. Small, neat, leathery leaves are densely arranged on erect, wiry stems. Berries white, edible and sweet. S Chile. I 1926. AM 1929.

pyroloides Miq. (*G. pyrolifolia* C.B. Clarke) A dwarf, creeping species, forming mats of short stems and bright green, obovate or rounded, reticulately-veined leaves, 2.5cm long. The pink-tinged, urn-shaped flowers are borne in short, leafy racemes from mid-May often to July. Fruits blue-black. An interesting little plant recalling *Salix reticulata* in leaf. Himalaya. C 1933.

semi-infera (C.B. Clarke) Airy Shaw. A dwarf shrub with hispid shoots and obovate to oblanceolate leaves, 5–8cm long, glossy green above. White flowers, occasionally blush, are followed by obovoid fruits, variable in colour, but often indigo-blue. Himalaya, SW China. AM 1950.

shallon Pursh. Salal. A vigorous species forming thickets up to 1.8m high, and ideal undergrowth for game coverts, etc. Leaves broad and leathery; flowers pinkish-white, fruits dark purple, in large clusters. W North America. I 1826. ‘Snoqualmie Pass’ A dwarf form reaching only about 45cm tall but spreading vigorously. Found on the Snoqualmie Pass, Washington State, USA.

stapfiana Airy Shaw. A dwarf shrub with arching and erect stems and elliptic to oblanceolate leaves. White flowers followed by bright blue fruit. Closely related to *G. hookeri* under which name it is often found in gardens. It mainly differs from this species in its usually more erect, glabrous or adpressed, bristly stems. W China.

tasmanica (Hook. f.) Middleton (*Pernettya tasmanica* Hook. f.) A slender, fragile, dwarf shrub a few centimetres high, often prostrate. Leaves very small and leathery. Berries up to 1cm, solitary, normally red, produced in the axils of the upper leaves. Tasmania. AM 1971.

tetramera W.W. Sm. A dwarf shrub of compact habit, forming a wide mound of arching stems. Leaves broadly oval to lanceolate-elliptic, reticulate and dark green above. White flowers in May and June are followed by blue or violet fruit. W China. C 1933. AM 1950.

trichophylla Royle. A charming shrublet of tufted habit. Pink flowers are followed by conspicuous, large, blue fruit. Himalaya, W China. I 1897. AM 1918.

veitchiana. See *G. hookeri.*

wardii Marquand & Airy Shaw. A Kingdon-Ward introduction from SE Tibet, distinct in its bristly nature and leathery, lanceolate leaves with deeply impressed veins. In May or June bears white flowers in racemes then milky-blue fruit. C 1933. AM 1933.

× *wisleyensis* Middleton (× *Gaulnettya wisleyensis* Marchant) (*G. mucronata* × *G. shallon*) Vigorous, thicket-forming shrubs of garden origin. The first form raised was 'Wisley Pearl' (see below). **'Pink Pixie'** A dwarf, suckering shrub with pink-tinged, white flowers in May followed by purplish-red fruits. Raised in 1965 by our propagator Peter Dummer back-crossing 'Wisley Pearl' with *Gaultheria shallon.* AM 1976. **'Ruby'** A small shrub of vigorous habit forming a dense, evergreen thicket. Leaves, up to 2.5cm long, are dark green and leathery; white flowers, in late May and early June, are in dense terminal and axillary racemes. The fruits, ripening in late autumn and winter, are ruby-red, each crowned by a similarly coloured, swollen calyx like a tiny elf's cap. **'Wisley Pearl'** A small shrub with dull, dark green leaves, 3.8cm or more long and half as wide. The branches are laden during autumn and winter with short but crowded bunches of large, ox-blood-red fruits. An interesting hybrid which originated at Wisley in about 1929. This is the original selected clone distributed as × *Gaulnettya wisleyensis.* AM 1939.

‡**GAYLUSSACIA** Kunth—**Ericaceae**—The huckleberries are evergreen or deciduous shrubs closely resembling *Vaccinium,* and requiring similar conditions. There are some 40–50 species in North and South America.

baccata (Wangenh.) K. Koch. Black huckleberry. A small shrub of erect habit with leaves that are resinous beneath and dull red flowers in short dense racemes in May then lustrous black, edible fruit. Autumn tints soft crimson. E North America. I 1772.

*brachycera (Michx.) A. Gray. Box huckleberry. Dwarf shrub with thick, leathery, glossy green leaves. White flowers in May and June. E USA. I 1796. AM 1940.

Gean See *Prunus avium.*

GENISTA L.—**Leguminosae**—About 80 species of shrubs, natives of Europe, W Asia and N Africa, allied to *Cytisus* and requiring similar treatment. They range from prostrate to almost tree-like. Some of the dwarf species are indispensable alpines, while the taller ones include some invaluable summer-flowering shrubs. All have yellow flowers unless otherwise described and associate well with heathers. All succeed in acid or neutral soil and are lime-tolerant.

aetnensis (Biv.) DC. Mount Etna broom. A large, elegant shrub or small tree with slender, green, leafless shoots. Fragrant flowers are profusely borne in July and August. Sardinia and Sicily. ♀ 2002. FCC 1938.

anglica L. Needle furze, Petty whin. A dwarf, spiny, native shrub with showy flowers from May to July. W Europe.

cinerea (Vill.) DC. A medium-sized shrub with slender, silky shoots and clusters of golden-yellow flowers during June and July. SW Europe, N Africa. For the plant usually grown under this name see *G. tenera* 'Golden Shower'. AM 1924.

delphinensis See *G. sagittalis* subsp. *delphinensis.*

†*ephedroides* DC. An unusual, small, erect-branched shrub with very small leaves which soon fall, leaving the slender stems quite naked. The solitary, fragrant flowers are borne towards the end of the shoots in May and June. Sardinia, Sicily and S Italy.

†*falcata* Brot. A small, gorse-like shrub producing slender branches with spiny lateral shoots, and deep golden-yellow flowers in long panicles in May. Portugal, W Spain.

†*fasselata* Decne. (*G. sphacelata* Spach) A curious, small, rather gorse-like, spiny shrub with typical yellow flowers. E Mediterranean region.

germanica L. A dwarf, spiny shrub covered with short racemes of flowers in June. C and W Europe to C Russia. C 1588.

hispanica L. Spanish gorse. One of the best plants for sunny sites, such as dry banks, forming 60cm high, dense, prickly mounds covered unfailingly in May and June with masses of flowers. SW Europe. I 1759.

horrida (Vahl) DC. (*Echinospartium horridum* (Vahl) Rothm.) A dwarf, rigid, spiny shrub of silvery-grey hue. Flowers in small, terminal heads from July to September. SW Europe. I 1821.

januensis Viv. (*G. triquetra* Waldst. & Kit.) Genoa broom. A rare, procumbent shrub with somewhat winged branches. Flowers bright yellow in May. SE Europe. I about 1840. AM 1932.

lydia Boiss. (*G. spathulata* Spach) An outstanding dwarf shrub. Slender, pendent branchlets are smothered in golden-yellow flowers in May and June. E Balkans. I 1926. ♀ 2002. FCC 1957. AM 1937.

†*monosperma* (L.) Lam. (*Lygos monosperma* (L.) Heywood) An unusual species, up to 1.8m, with long, slender, rush-like stems. The young growths give the plant a silvery appearance. Flowers milky-white, fragrant. S Europe and N Africa. I 1690.

†*monspessulana* (L.) O. Bolós & Vigo (*Cytisus candicans* (L.) DC., *C. monspessulanus* L., *Teline monspessulana* (L.) C. Koch) Montpelier broom. This is a graceful, medium-sized, semi-evergreen species with clusters of yellow flowers from April to June. Subject to injury by severe frost. S Europe. SW Asia. N Africa. C 1735. AM 1974.

pilosa L. A dwarf, native shrub, producing cascades of golden-yellow flowers in May. W and C Europe (incl. British Isles). The forms named 'Yellow Spreader' ('Lemon Spreader') and 'Vancouver Gold' seem to differ little from the typical plant as grown here. **'Goldilocks'** A vigorous Dutch selection with ascending branches reaching 60cm. Golden-yellow flowers are profusely borne over a long period. C 1970.

†'**Porlock**' (*G. monspessulana* × *G.* × *spachiana*) (*Cytisus* 'Porlock') A vigorous shrub quickly forming a large, semi-evergreen bush. Butter-yellow, very fragrant flowers appear in profuse racemes in mild weather in spring, and during autumn and winter under glass. Remarkably hardy given a sunny wall or makes a lovely conservatory shrub. Raised about 1922. ♀ 2002. FCC 1990. AM 1931.

pulchella Gren. & Godr. (*G. villarsii* Clementi) A miniature, rock garden shrub, 7.5–10cm high, with grey-hairy young shoots and solitary, bright yellow flowers in the axils of the terminal leaves in May. SE France, W Balkans.

radiata (L.) Scop. A slow-growing species, forming a dense shrub about 1m high. Flowers in June, deep yellow. C and SE Europe. I 1758.

sagittalis L. (*Chamaespartium sagittale* (L.) P. E. Gibbs) A dwarf shrub with broadly winged, prostrate branches making it look evergreen; flowers in June. Useful for dry walls and similar sites. C and S Europe. C 1588. **subsp.** *delphinensis* (Verl.) Greuter (*G. delphinensis* Verl.) This tiny, decumbent shrub is one of the best species for a rock garden, bearing deep yellow flowers in terminal or axillary clusters in July to August. Like a miniature *G. sagittalis*. S France. ♀ 2002.

scorpius (L.) DC. A rare species, which has reached a height of 1.8m here. The branches are spiny like gorse, but grey; flowers in bright yellow masses in April and May. SW Europe.

†*×spachiana* (Webb) Kuntze (*G. fragrans* hort., *Cytisus* × *spachianus* Webb) (*G. canariensis* × *G. stenopetala*) A vigorous, large shrub with arching stems and dark green leaves with 3 leaflets, to 2cm long, covered in silky hairs beneath. Very fragrant, golden-yellow flowers are borne in slender racemes, to 10cm long, in late winter and early spring. This popular conservatory shrub is only suitable for growing outside in the mildest parts of the country. Tenerife. C 1845. ♀ 2002.

†*stenopetala* Webb & Berthel. (*Cytisus maderensis* Briq. in part not (Webb & Berthel.) Masf.) A large shrub with fragrant, bright yellow flowers in racemes in spring and early summer. A conservatory plant, except in very mild localities. Madeira.

sylvestris Scop. (*G. dalmatica* Bartl.) Dalmatian broom. A decumbent shrub forming hummocks 15–23cm high, covered with terminal racemes of flowers in June and July. An excellent plant for a well-drained ledge in a rock garden. W Balkans, C and S Italy. I 1893.

tenera (Jacq.) O. Kuntze (*G. virgata* (Aiton) Link) A beautiful, hardy shrub attaining 3.5m and as much wide, flowering in June and July. Resembles *G. cinerea*. Madeira, Tenerife. I 1777. '**Golden Shower**' A vigorous, large, arching shrub bearing masses of brilliant yellow, fragrant flowers in June. Long grown incorrectly as *G. cinerea*.

tinctoria L. Dyer's greenweed. A late-flowering native shrub of about 60cm with bright yellow flowers, in long, terminal racemes, from June to September. Europe, Turkey. **var.** *anxantica* (Ten.) Fiori. A glabrous, dwarf form. Italy. I 1818. '**Flore Pleno**' ('Plena') Floriferous, dwarf, semi-prostrate form with double flowers. A superb, dwarf shrub for a rock garden. ♀ 2002. '**Golden Plate**' A low-growing form of spreading habit up to

30cm, suitable for groundcover. Found on the island of Texel in the Waddenzee off the north-west coast of Holland. **var.** *humilior* (Bertol.) Schneid. (*G. mantica* Pollini) A distinct, downy, erect variety with purple stems and deep yellow flowers. Italy. I 1816. '**Royal Gold**' A small, free-flowering shrub, the stems thickly covered with rich yellow flowers through summer. ♀ 2002. **var.** *virgata* Koch (*G. virgata* Willd.) Habit upright, to 2m tall. SE Europe.

villarsii See *G. pulchella*.

virgata See *G. tenera* and *G. tinctoria* var. *virgata*.

Georgia plume See *Elliottia racemosa*.

Germander, shrubby See *Teucrium fruticans*.

Germander, wall See *Teucrium chamaedrys*.

‡†***GEVUINA** Molina—**Proteaceae**—A monotypic genus related to *Grevillea*.

avellana Molina. Chilean hazel. An interesting species making, in favourable localities, a large shrub or small tree. The long branches are held rather loosely and carry handsome, polished, pinnate leaves. Panicles of white flowers are followed by bright red, cherry-like fruit, rarely produced in the British Isles. It grows best in sheltered woodlands. S Chile, Argentina. I 1826. AM 1983.

Ghost tree See *Davidia involucrata*.

GLEDITSIA L. (*Gleditschia* Scop.)—**Leguminosae**—A genus of about 12 species of deciduous, spiny trees, natives of North America and Asia, one species in Argentina. Valuable in gardens for their extremely beautiful, pinnate or bipinnate foliage. Mature trunks are often formidably armed with long thorns. Insignificant, greenish flowers are followed by seeds in flattened pods of varying length. Succeeds in all types of well-drained soils and tolerant of atmospheric pollution.

aquatica Marshall. Water locust. Small, shrubby tree with large, branched spines and simply or doubly pinnate leaves. Pods, when produced, are short, less than 5cm long, and contain a solitary seed. SE USA. I 1723.

caspica Desf. Caspian locust. A small tree, old specimens with trunks formidably armed with numerous spines, 15cm or more long. Leaflets larger than in most species. Transcaucasus, N Iran. I 1822.

delavayi Franch. A Chinese tree of medium height with dark green, lustrous leaves, coppery-red young growths and enormous spines. Unripened growths are cut back in very cold winters. I 1900 by Ernest Wilson.

horrida See *G. japonica* and *G. sinensis*.

japonica Miq. (*G. horrida* (Thunb.) Makino) A graceful, medium-sized Japanese tree of somewhat pyramidal habit, its trunk armed with branched spines. The fern-like leaves are composed of up to 30 small leaflets. Quite hardy even in a young state. I 1894.

macracantha Desf. A spiny tree on the tall side of medium, particularly notable for the variable size of its leaflets; flowers in downy racemes followed by long seedpods. C China. C 1800.

sinensis Lam. (*G. horrida* Willd.) Chinese honey locust. A handsome, medium-sized tree with branched spines and fern-like foliage. China. I 1774.

× *texana* Sarg. (*G. aquatica* × *G. triacanthos*) A natural hybrid eventually making a large tree, with smooth bark and spineless branches. Similar in general appearance to *G. triacanthos*. Only found in one locality in Texas. I 1900.

triacanthos L. Honey locust. This elegant, large tree, with frond-like leaves, is very tolerant of industrially polluted atmosphere. A large specimen is quite effective when strung with its long, shining, brown seedpods. C and E USA. I 1700. **'Bujotii'** ('Pendula') A shrubby form or occasionally small tree with narrower leaflets and slender, pendent branchlets. C 1845. **'Elegantissima'** A beautiful, slow-growing shrub of dense, bushy habit, attaining 3.5–4.5m, with attractive fern-like foliage. Raised about 1880. **f. *inermis*** (L.) Zabel. A form that bears no thorns. **'Inermis Aurea'** See 'Sunburst'. **'Pendula'** See 'Bujotii'. **'Rubylace'** An American selection with deep bronze-red young foliage, later dark green. C 1961. **'Shademaster'** A vigorous, thornless form with ascending branches and dark green, long-persistent leaves. C 1954. **'Sunburst'** ('Inermis Aurea') A striking, medium-sized tree, having thornless stems and bright yellow young leaves, which contrast effectively with the older, dark green foliage. C 1953. ♀ 2002.

†**GLOCHIDION** J.R. Forst. & G. Forst.—Euphorbiaceae—A large genus of some 300 species of trees and shrubs distributed throughout tropical areas but found mainly between tropical Asia, Polynesia and Queensland.

sinicum Hook. & Arn. (*G. fortunei* Hance) A rare and interesting, shrubby Chinese member of the *Euphorbia* family, with slender, reddish shoots and ovate-lanceolate, glabrous leaves, up to 9cm by 3cm, dark glossy green above, glaucous beneath, reddish in autumn. Tiny, green flowers similar to those of *Securinega suffruticosa* hang in clusters of 1–3 on slender stalks from the leaf axils in autumn.

Glory bush See *Tibouchina urvilleana*.
Goat's thorn See *Astragalus*.
Golden rain See *Laburnum*.
Goldilocks See *Helichrysum stoechas*.

‡†***GORDONIA** Ellis—Theaceae—About 70 species of camellia-like trees and shrubs, found in warmer parts of the S USA and SE Asia. They are conspicuous both in leaf and flower and require lime-free soil.

alatamaha See *Franklinia alatamaha*.

axillaris (Ker.-Gawl.) Endl. (*G. anomala* Spreng.) A rare, evergreen, large shrub or small tree with large, leathery, dark glossy green leaves and creamy-white flowers, 7.5–15cm across, appearing from November to May. China, Taiwan. I 1818. AM 1929.

chrysandra Cowan. A large, Chinese shrub with creamy-white, fragrant, flowers, 5cm across, during late winter. Yunnan. I 1917 by George Forrest.

lasianthus (L.) Ellis. Loblolly bay. A beautiful but tender, magnolia-like species attaining small tree size in the British Isles. White flowers, 7.5cm across, are borne in July and August. SE USA. I 1768.

Gorse, common See *Ulex europaeus*.
Gorse, Spanish See *Genista hispanica*.

‡†***GREVILLEA** R. Br.—Proteaceae—A genus of some 250 species of beautiful, evergreen trees and shrubs, almost all of which are natives of Australia or Tasmania, with a few species in New Caledonia and Sulawesi (the Celebes). The flowers are superficially like those of honeysuckle, but smaller, with showy, exserted styles. They are produced over a long period. Good drainage essential and avoid overhead shade and chalk soils.

alpina Lindl. A charming, compact, low shrub for the mildest parts, freely producing curious red and cream flowers. Grey-green, needle-like leaves. An excellent pot plant. SE Australia. I before 1857. AM 1936. See also *G. rosmarinifolia*.

'Canberra Gem' A vigorous, rounded, medium-sized shrub up to about 2.5m high and potentially equally as wide. It has aromatic foliage and clusters of waxy, bright pink flowers. ♀ 2002. AM 1986.

glabrata (Lindl.) Meisn. An erect, glabrous shrub with attractive, lobed leaves and long, pyramidal panicles of white flowers, with pink stigmas, in spring. A conservatory plant except in the mildest localities. W Australia.

juniperina R. Br. A beautiful, medium-sized shrub for mild districts. Terminal racemes of bright red flowers in summer. Bright green needle-like leaves. SE Australia (New South Wales). Mainly cultivated in the following form. **'Sulphurea'** (*G. sulphurea* (A. Cunn.) Benth.) Flowers bright yellow. AM 1974.

'Olympic Flame' A small shrub of compact, rounded habit with pointed leaves. The profuse, pink and white flowers are borne in slightly pendent clusters over a long period. One of a batch of seedlings raised in 1954 by Peter Althofer in New South Wales, from *G. alpina*, probably pollinated by *G. rosmarinifolia*, and named after the 1956 Olympic Games in Melbourne.

ornithopoda Meisn. A medium-sized to large shrub for a conservatory. Has long, flat, pale green, trifid leaves and thick clusters of creamy-white flowers, which cascade down the pendent stems in April. W Australia. I 1850.

rosmarinifolia A. Cunn. A beautiful shrub for mild districts, where it will attain 1.8m. The conspicuous, crimson flowers are produced in long, terminal racemes over a long period from winter to summer. Deep green, needle-like leaves. SE Australia. Cultivated plants may be hybrids with *G. lanigera*. I about 1822. Some plants grown as *G. alpina* belong here. ♀ 2002. AM 1932.

× *semperflorens* Mulligan (*G. juniperina* 'Sulphurea' × *G. thelmanniana*) An interesting and beautiful hybrid of garden origin. The flowers are a combination of yellow suffused rose-pink and tipped at the apex with green during summer. Leaves needle-like. Attains about 1.8m in sheltered areas of SW England. Raised by Miss F.E. Briggs of Plymouth in 1926.

sulphurea See *G. juniperina* 'Sulphurea'.

victoriae F. Muell. Royal grevillea. A bushy, medium-sized shrub with lanceolate leaves to 10cm long, silvery with hairs beneath. Flowers 2.5cm long, red, in pendent terminal racemes to 7cm long, opening from rusty-red buds. This species proved very hardy at Blakedown Nursery in the West Midlands. It can be found at high altitudes in the Snowy Mountains where it is often covered by snow in winter. SE Australia.

GREWIA L.—**Tiliaceae**—A large genus of more than 150 species of trees and shrubs found in Asia and Africa, mainly in tropical and subtropical regions.

†*occidentalis* L. A little-known South African shrub or small tree allied to the limes (*Tilia*) with oval leaves and pink flowers in stalked clusters. I 1690.

†**GRINDELIA** Willd.—**Compositae**—A small genus of about 60 species of subshrubs and herbaceous plants, natives of W North America and South America.

*chiloensis (Cornel.) Cabrera (*G. speciosa* Hook. & Arn.) This surprisingly hardy, small, evergreen subshrub is a really handsome plant. The narrow leaves with undulate, toothed margins are hoary, affording a harmonious contrast with the large, cornflower-like, rich yellow flowers, which appear from June to October, singly, on stout, tall stems. Buds are covered with a milk-white, sticky varnish. Requires full sun and acute drainage. Argentina. I about 1850. AM 1931.

†*GRISELINIA G. Forst.—**Griseliniaceae**—A small genus of 7 species of trees and shrubs, natives of New Zealand, Argentina, SE Brazil and Chile. Flowers inconspicuous, dioecious.

littoralis Raoul. Broadleaf. A densely leafy, large, evergreen shrub with leathery, apple-green leaves. Succeeds in all types of fertile soil and is tree-like in mild localities. An excellent hedge plant for maritime exposure, it is liable to frost damage in cold inland areas. New Zealand. I about 1850. ♀ 2002. **'Crinkles'** A slow-growing, small, bushy shrub with small, wavy-edged leaves. **'Dixon's Cream'** An attractive form with leaves splashed and marked creamy-white. Occurred as a sport of 'Variegata' in the garden of Major W.G.M. Dixon in Jersey. Forms similar to this include 'Luscombe's Gold', which occurred as a sport of 'Variegata' in Luscombe's Nursery, Torquay in 1970, and 'Bantry Bay'. Similar sports have also occurred in New Zealand. **'Green Jewel'** Similar to 'Variegata' but with paler foliage.

'Variegata' Conspicuous, white-variegated foliage. ♀ 2002. AM 1978.

lucida G. Forst. A very handsome, tender species with large leaves that have a noticeably oblique base and an almost varnished upper surface. Usually epiphytic in the wild. New Zealand.

racemosa (Phil.) Taub. A dwarf shrub, reaching about 1m and spreading by suckers, in the wild sometimes climbing or epiphytic, with upright, red-purple young shoots. Leaves glossy green, to 8cm long, 3-veined at the base on short petioles, occasionally with one or two teeth at the margin. Small flowers open in erect racemes during winter from the axils of the terminal leaves. Only the male plant has been seen; its red-purple flowers have creamy-yellow anthers. Female plants have deep purple ovoid fruits to 8mm long. This species was received at the Sir Harold Hillier Gardens and Arboretum as *G. ruscifolia*, which differs in having leaves 3-pointed at the apex and paniculate male inflorescences. Chile, recently found in a small area of Argentina.

Groundsel bush See *Baccharis halimifolia*.
Guava, Chilean See *Ugni molinae*.
Guelder rose See *Viburnum opulus*.
Gum tree See *Eucalyptus*.

GYMNOCLADUS Lam.—**Leguminosae**—A genus of deciduous trees with a single species in North America and 3 species in E Asia. Related to *Gleditsia*, they have bipinnate leaves inconspicuous flowers and seeds borne in pods.

dioica (L.) K. Koch (*G. canadensis* Lam.) Kentucky coffee tree. This medium-sized, slow-growing tree is one of the most handsome of all hardy trees. Young twigs are light grey, almost white, especially noticeable in winter. The large, compound leaves are pink-tinted when unfolding and turn clear yellow before falling. The seeds were used as a substitute for coffee by the early settlers in North America. E and C USA. I before 1748. **'Variegata'** Leaflets with creamy-white variegation.

H

Hackberry See *Celtis*.

*HAKEA Schrad.—**Proteaceae**—A remarkable genus of about 100 species of evergreen shrubs or small trees, native to Australia and Tasmania, some suggesting kinship with the conifers. A few species are hardy and make excellent subjects for sunny, arid positions. Not good on chalk soils.

acicularis See *H. sericea*.

lissosperma R. Br. A tall, erect-branched, columnar shrub creating an effect that might be associated with the desert. The rigid, grey-green, needle-like, sharply pointed leaves, 2.5–7.5cm long, are narrowed at the base and held more or less erect on the shoots. Showy white flowers are produced in clusters in the leaf axils from April to May. Originally listed as *H. sericea*. This splendid plant has proved perfectly hardy at the Sir Harold Hillier Gardens and Arboretum, where it has reached 5.5m tall (1990). SE Australia, Tasmania.

microcarpa R. Br. An interesting, medium to large shrub of dense, rounded habit. Fragrant, creamy-white flowers are produced in clusters in the axils of the needle-like leaves in May and are followed by chestnut-brown seed capsules. SE Australia, Tasmania.

sericea Schrad. (*H. acicularis* (Sm. ex Vent.) Knight) A medium-sized to large shrub similar to *H. lissosperma* but differing in the more slender, longer-pointed, shorter, bright green leaves, which are not narrowed at the base and are more spreading on the shoot. In a form we sent to the Ventnor Botanic Garden, Isle of Wight, the flowers were deep pink in bud opening white, flushed pink at the tips of the perianth segments. The plant originally listed under this name is *H. lissosperma* (see above). SE Australia, Tasmania. C 1796.

‡HALESIA L.—**Styracaceae**—The silverbells or snowdrop trees are a small genus of 5 species of very beautiful shrubs or small trees allied to *Styrax* and natives of the SE USA with one species in E China. Pendent, snowdrop-like flowers are produced in clusters along naked branches in May, followed by small, green, winged fruits. They thrive in moist but well-drained, lime-free soil in sun or semi-shade.

carolina L. (*H. tetraptera* Ellis) Snowdrop tree. A large shrub or occasionally small, spreading tree, very beautiful in spring when the branches are draped with white, nodding, bell-shaped flowers in clusters of 3 or 5. The fruits are pear-shaped and 4-winged. SE USA. I 1756. FCC 1980. AM 1954.

diptera Ellis. This species is similar to *H. carolina*, but is more shrubby in habit and less free-flowering. It is also distinguished by its broader leaves and 2-winged fruits. SE USA. I 1758. AM 1948. **var. *magniflora*** Godfrey. A widespreading, large shrub of bushy habit differing from the typical form in its larger flowers, 2–3cm long. The best form of the species. AM 1970.

monticola (Rehder) Sarg. Mountain snowdrop tree. A magnificent, small, spreading tree, differing from *H. carolina* in its greater size and its larger flowers and fruits, the latter up to 5cm long. Mountains of SE USA. I about 1897.

AM 1930. **'Rosea'** Flowers very pale pink. FCC 1984. **var. *vestita*** Sarg. A magnificent variety that in gardens produces larger flowers up to 3cm across, white, sometimes tinged rose. Leaves more or less downy beneath at first, becoming glabrous. ♀ 2002. AM 1958.

tetraptera See *H. carolina*.

*× HALIMIOCISTUS Janch. (*Cistus* × *Halimium*)—**Cistaceae**—Pretty and interesting hybrids, 2 of which are extremely hardy; the others require a very sheltered, south-facing position. See also *Cistus*, *Halimium* and *Helianthemum*.

'Ingwersenii' (*Helianthemum clusii*) Discovered in Portugal, and believed to be *H. umbellatum* × *C. inflatus*. A free-growing, dwarf, very widespreading shrub with pure white flowers over a long period and linear, dark green, conspicuously hairy leaves. Very hardy and ideal for a large rock garden. I about 1929.

†*revolii* (Coste & Soulié) Dans. (*H. alyssoides* × *C. salviifolius*) A beautiful, low evergreen producing a long succession of pale yellow or white, yellow-centred flowers. Found in France in 1914. Very rare in cultivation, although a white-flowered form is now coming back into commerce. Most plants grown under this name are × *H. sahucii*.

sahucii (Coste & Soulié) Janch. (*H. umbellatum* × *C. salviifolius*) A fully hardy, low, spreading shrub with linear leaves and pure white flowers from May to September. S France. I about 1929. ♀ 2002. **Ice Dancer** ('Ebhals') PBR Leaves narrowly edged with creamy-white.

†*wintonensis* O. & E.F. Warb. This beautiful hybrid making a dwarf, grey-leaved shrub, originated in our nurseries and is believed to be *H. lasianthum* subsp. *formosum* × *C. salviifolius*. Pearly-white flowers, 5cm across, with a feathered and pencilled zone of crimson-maroon, contrasting with yellow stains at the base of the petals, are borne in May to June. It requires a very sheltered spot and careful cultivation but is well worth the effort. I about 1910. AM 1926 (as *Cistus wintonensis*). ♀ 2002. **'Merrist Wood Cream'** In this attractive form the base colour of the flower is pale creamy-yellow. A sport found at Merrist Wood Agricultural College in 1978. ♀ 2002.

*HALIMIUM (Dunal) Spach—**Cistaceae**—A small genus of about 7 species closely related to *Cistus*, natives of the W Mediterranean region. Mostly low, spreading shrubs, akin to *Helianthemum*, they require full sun and good drainage, and are subject to injury by severe frost. See also *Cistus*, × *Halimiocistus* and *Helianthemum*.

alyssoides See *H. lasianthum* subsp. *alyssoides*.

†*atriplicifolium* (Lam.) Spach. A very beautiful but tender, small, upright silver shrub to 1.5m, with broad, silvery-grey leaves. Bears golden-yellow flowers, up to 4cm across, in June. Requires a sheltered sunny site. C and S Spain. C in the mid-17th century.

calycinum L. (*H. commutatum* Pau, *H. libanotis* Lange in part, *H. rosmarinifolium* hort.) Dwarf shrub of semi-erect habit with linear leaves and golden-yellow flowers, 2.5cm across, in June. W Mediterranean region.

commutatum See *H. calycinum*.

†*halimifolium* (L.) Willk. & Lange. A small, erect shrub with narrow, grey leaves. From May onwards the bright yellow flowers, up to 4cm across, appear in erect, few-flowered panicles. Some forms have petals with a dark spot at the base. W Mediterranean region. C since the mid-17th century.

lasianthum (Lam.) Spach (*Cistus formosus* hort.) A low, spreading shrub, ultimately 0.6–1m high, with greyish leaves and, in May, golden-yellow flowers, sometimes with a dark blotch at the base of each petal. S Portugal, S Spain, North Africa. I 1780. ♀ 2002. AM 1951. Most plants in cultivation belong to subsp. *formosum* (Curt.) Heywood, which has a bold, purple-black blotch at the base of each petal. **subsp.** *alyssoides* (Lam.) Greuter & Burdet (*H. alyssoides* (Lam.) K. Koch) Inflorescence covered in short hairs; petals unspotted. SW Europe. **'Concolor'** Petals without blotches. **'Hannay Silver'** A very vigorous and floriferous cultivar, larger in all its parts, with unblotched yellow petals and very attractive silky-haired grey leaves. Will reach 1.5m. **'Sandling'** A form with large, crescent-shaped, maroon blotches on the petals.

libanotis See *H. calycinum*.

ocymoides (Lam.) Willk. & Lange (*Helianthemum algarvense* (Sims) Dunal) Charming, compact shrub, 0.6–1m, with small, grey leaves and bright yellow flowers usually with blackish-brown basal markings. Portugal and Spain. C 1800. ♀ 2002.

× *pauanum* Font Quer (*H. halimifolium* × *H. lasianthum*) A vigorous, upright, floriferous hybrid, reaching 2m, with unblotched, bright yellow flowers. Morocco.

'Sarah' A hybrid of the same parentage as 'Susan' raised by Eric Sammons from a later cross made in 1979, and named after his grand-daughter. It differs from 'Susan' in its more open habit, larger leaves and the smaller, deeper coloured blotches in the centre of the flower.

'Susan' (*H. lasianthum* subsp. *formosum* × *H. ocymoides*) A compact, dwarf, spreading shrub with rounded leaves. The small, golden-yellow flowers, about 2.5cm across, are blotched with chocolate-brown, edged with tan, at the base and are profusely borne. Raised by Eric Sammons in 1957. ♀ 2002.

umbellatum (L.) Spach. A dwarf species, somewhat similar to *H. calycinum*, from which it differs in its white flowers in June. Mediterranean region. I 1731.

HALIMODENDRON Fisch. ex DC.—**Leguminosae**—A monotypic genus allied to *Caragana*. Succeeds in any well-drained, open site.

halodendron (Pall.) Voss (*H. argenteum* (Lam.) DC.) Salt tree. An attractive, spiny, silvery-leaved shrub up to 1.8m. Leaves have 2–3 pairs of oblanceolate, grey-tomentose leaflets and a terminal spine. Masses of purplish-pink pea flowers are borne in June and July. An excellent seaside plant. Grows in dry saltfields in Siberia, SE Russia, C and SW Asia. I 1779.

HAMAMELIS L.—**Hamamelidaceae**—The witch hazels are a most distinct and beautiful genus of mainly winter-flowering shrubs or small trees with 5 or 6 species in E North America and E Asia. In the majority the spider-like yellow or reddish flowers appear on the normally leafless branches from December to March. The curious strap-shaped petals withstand the severest weather without injury, and the hazel-like foliage usually gives attractive autumn colour. We would like to thank Chris Lane for his assistance with this genus.

FLOWER SIZE:

Large	over 3cm (1¼in) across
Medium	2–3cm (1–1¼in) across
Small	up to 2cm (1in) across

'Brevipetala' (*H. mollis* 'Brevipetala') An upright form with rounded, softly-hairy leaves, characteristically glaucous beneath, and thick clusters of deep yellow, short-petalled flowers, appearing orange from a distance; scent heavy and sweet. Autumn colour yellow. AM 1960.

× *intermedia* Rehder (*H. japonica* × *H. mollis*) Large shrubs of variable nature, generally intermediate between the parents. Leaves often large, particularly on vigorous shoots. Medium to large flowers, rarely strongly scented, have somewhat folded and crimped petals and appear from December to March. All the following clones have arisen in cultivation. **'Adonis'** See 'Ruby Glow'. **'Advent'** A large shrub with ascending branches. Medium-sized, fragrant, bright yellow flowers, the petals red-tinged at the base, with purplish-red calyces, are abundantly produced from mid-December. Selected from plants of *H.* × *intermedia* in the Sir Harold Hillier Gardens and Arboretum in 1979. **'Allgold'** Leaves varying from elliptic to obovate-orbicular; yellow in autumn. Deep yellow, very fragrant flowers, with reddish calyces, form thick clusters on the ascending branches. **'Angelly'** Large, scented, citron-yellow flowers, late. Compact, upright habit. Raised in Holland in about 1975. AM 1991. **'Aphrodite'** A seedling of 'Vesna' raised in Holland and probably pollinated by 'Pallida'. Spreading habit with very large, slightly fragrant, deep orange flowers, autumn colour yellow. **'Arnold Promise'** A vigorous, large, widespreading bush with very freely borne, medium-sized, bright yellow flowers opening late. One of the original seedlings raised at the Arnold Arboretum in 1928 from seed of *H. mollis*. ♀ 2002. **'August Lamken'** See 'Orange Beauty'. **'Aurora'** A seedling of 'Vesna' raised in Holland and probably pollinated by 'Pallida'. Upright habit with very large and strongly fragrant, bronze-yellow flowers, shading from red at the base to yellow at the tips of the petals. Autumn colour orange-yellow to red. AM 1991. **'Barmstedt Gold'** A vigorous and upright, large shrub with large, faintly scented, deep golden-yellow flowers. C 1975. ♀ 2002. **'Carmine Red'** (*H. japonica* 'Carmine Red') A strong-growing clone of somewhat spreading habit, raised in our nurseries. Large, almost round leaves with a strongly oblique base, are dark shining green above; yellow in autumn. Large, pale bronze flowers are suffused copper at tips. **'Copper Beauty'** See 'Jelena'. **'Diane'** Claimed by its raiser to be one of the best red-flowered seedlings yet produced, and superior in this respect to 'Ruby Glow'. The large leaves colour richly in autumn. Originated in the Kalmthout Arboretum, Belgium. C 1969. ♀ 2002. AM 1969. **'Feuerzauber'** ('Magic Fire')

A vigorous clone with strong, ascending branches and large, rounded leaves. Medium to large flowers are bright coppery-orange, suffused red. C 1935. **'Georges'** A selection of upright habit with medium-sized, pale peachy-red flowers. Raised at Hemelrijk, Belgium. **'Glowing Embers'** Dense clusters of very large, slender-petalled flowers, yellow, suffused red, appearing coppery-orange from a distance. Spreading habit. **'Harry'** A sister seedling of 'Orange Peel' with large, slightly paler flowers. Named after Harry van Trier, one-time curator of Kalmthout Arboretum, Belgium. **'Hiltingbury'** (*H. japonica* 'Hiltingbury') A large shrub of spreading habit, raised in our nurseries. The large leaves give brilliant autumn tints of orange, scarlet and red. Medium to large, pale copper flowers, suffused red. **'Jelena'** ('Copper Beauty') A superb clone of vigorous, spreading habit with large, broad and softly hairy leaves turning orange, red and scarlet in autumn. Bears dense clusters of large, yellow flowers suffused rich copper-red, appearing almost orange. Raised at Kalmthout Arboretum, Belgium before 1935, and named after a great gardener, Jelena de Belder. ♀ 2002. AM 1955. **'Livia'** A superb red-flowered selection from Hemelrijk. Spreading habit. **'Luna'** Twisted, yellow petals, red at the base with a red calyx. Originated at Kalmthout Arboretum, Belgium. **'Magic Fire'** See 'Feuerzauber'. **'Moonlight'** A large shrub with ascending branches. Medium to large flowers have folded and crimpled, pale sulphur-yellow petals with a claret-red tinge at base; scent strong and sweet. As effective as *H. × intermedia* 'Pallida', but differing in its narrower, more crimpled and paler petals. Autumn colour yellow. **'Orange Beauty'** ('August Lamken') A large shrub of broad, spreading habit and large, orange-yellow, early flowers. Excellent red and orange-yellow autumn colour. **'Orange Peel'** Large, light orange flowers. Upright habit with orange-red autumn colour. Raised at Hemelrijk. **'Pallida'** (*H. × intermedia* 'Pallida') Deservedly one of the most popular witch hazels. The large, sulphur-yellow flowers are borne in densely crowded clusters along the naked stems; scent strong and sweet, but delicate. Autumn colour yellow. ♀ 2002. FCC 1958. AM 1932. **'Primavera'** A selection of broadly upright habit. Bright yellow petals are tinged purplish-red at the base. Raised at Kalmthout, Belgium. **'Ripe Corn'** Prolific deep yellow flowers. A selection of broadly upright habit raised at Hemelrijk. **'Robert'** Large, yellow flowers, suffused coppery-red. Raised at Hemelrijk and named in honour of the late Rober de Belder. **'Rubin'** A German selection similar to *H. japonica* in foliage and habit. Flowers dark red. **'Ruby Glow'** (*H. japonica* 'Rubra Superba') ('Adonis') A strong-growing cultivar of somewhat erect habit. Coppery-red flowers. Rich autumn colour. C 1935. **'Sunburst'** (*H. mollis* 'Sunburst') Large, very pale yellow flowers and yellow autumn colour. Habit upright. An improvement on 'Moonlight'. **'Vesna'** A vigorous and upright shrub with large, strongly fragrant, deep orange-yellow flowers. The hanging petals are flushed red at the base and the calyx is deep red. Excellent red and orange-yellow autumn colour. C 1970. **'Westerstede'** A vigorous, upright, large shrub with large, light yellow, faintly scented flowers opening late. **'Winter Beauty'** Large

flowers with orange-yellow petals, deeper and reddish-tinged towards the base. Originated in Japan before 1962.

japonica Siebold & Zucc. Japanese witch hazel. A variable species, commonly a large, spreading shrub. Generally obovate or somewhat diamond-shaped leaves are smaller than those of *H. mollis*, becoming glabrous and shining. Small to medium flowers with much-twisted and crimpled petals, appear from December to March. Rich autumn colour. Japan. I 1862. **'Arborea'** A tall form occasionally making a small, widespreading tree. The almost horizontal arrangement of the branches is most characteristic. Rich deep yellow flowers, with red calyces, are normally small but plentifully produced in dense clusters; sweet scent but faint. Autumn colour yellow. I 1862 by P.F. von Siebold. FCC 1881. **var. *flavopurpurascens*** (Makino) Rehder. A large shrub developing, in time, a spreading habit, similar to *H. japonica* 'Arborea'. Small to medium, sulphur-yellow flowers, suffused red at base. Autumn colour yellow. Japan. C 1919. **'Sulphurea'** A large, spreading shrub with ascending branches. Small to medium flowers with pale sulphur-yellow petals much crimpled and curved; scent sweet but faint. Autumn colour yellow. AM 1958. **'Zuccariniana'** A large shrub distinctly erect in growth, at least in the young stage, but flattening later. Small, pale sulphur-yellow flowers with greenish-brown calyces; scent variously described as sweet to pungent. One of the latest witch hazels to flower, usually in March. Autumn colour yellow. FCC 1891.

macrophylla See *H. virginiana*.

mollis Oliv. Chinese witch hazel. Perhaps the handsomest of all witch hazels and certainly the most popular. A large shrub with large, softly hairy, rounded leaves and clusters of large, sweetly fragrant, golden-yellow, broad-petalled flowers from December to March. Autumn colour yellow. China. First introduced by Charles Maries in 1879 (see 'Coombe Wood') and much later by Ernest Wilson (see 'Jermyns Gold'). ♀ 2002 to vegetatively propagated selections only. FCC 1918. **'Brevipetala'** See *H.* 'Brevipetala'. **'Coombe Wood'** A spreading form with large flowers. Scent strong and sweet. Autumn colour yellow. The original form introduced by Charles Maries in 1879. **'Goldcrest'** A selected form with large flowers of rich golden-yellow suffused claret-red at base. The red suffusion occurs also on the backs of the rolled petals in bud creating a characteristic orange cluster effect; scent strong and sweet. Generally later flowering than other *H. mollis* cultivars. Autumn colour yellow. AM 1961. **'Jermyns Gold'** Large, erect shrub, with rounded softly hairy leaves and clusters of large, sweetly fragrant, golden-yellow, broad-petalled flowers from December to March. Yellow autumn colour. We believe this could be one of Ernest Wilson's original forms, for many years grown as *H. mollis*. Some of the new collections of *H. mollis* being introduced are of inferior quality, so we decided to give this plant a name. ♀ 2002. **'Pallida'** See *H. × intermedia* 'Pallida'. **'Wisley Supreme'** Large, pale yellow, sweetly scented flowers. Selected from an old plant at Wisley.

vernalis Sarg. Ozark witch hazel. A medium-sized to large shrub producing tall, erect stems. The flowers, though very small, are produced in large quantities during

January and February, varying in colour from pale yellow to red, but generally of a pale orange or copper. The scent is heavy and pungent, but not unpleasant. Autumn tints usually butter-yellow. SC USA. I 1908. **'Red Imp'** A selection with petals claret-red at base, paling to copper at tips. Calyces claret-red. Originated in our nurseries in 1966. **'Sandra'** Young unfolding leaves suffused plum-purple, becoming green and purple flushed on undersides. In autumn the whole bush ignites into orange, scarlet and red. Flower petals cadmium-yellow. Originated in our nurseries in 1962. ♀ 2002. AM 1976. **'Squib'** A selection with petals of cadmium-yellow; calyces green. Originated in our nurseries in 1966. **f. tomentella** Rehder. Leaves glaucescent and pubescent beneath.

virginiana L. (*H. macrophylla* Pursh) The commercial source of the witch-hazel astringent. A large shrub, occasionally a small, broad-crowned tree. Often used as an understock for the larger-flowered witch hazels but produces lovely golden-yellow autumn tints and myriad small to medium-sized, yellow flowers from September to November; scent sweet but faint. E North America. I 1736.

Harry Lauder's walking stick See *Corylus avellana* 'Contorta'.
Hawthorn, common See *Crataegus monogyna*.
Hawthorn, Midland See *Crataegus laevigata*.
Hazel See *Corylus*.
Hazel, Chilean See *Gevuina avellana*.
Heath See *Erica*.
Heath, Connemara See *Daboecia cantabrica*.
Heath, St Dabeoc's See *Daboecia cantabrica*.
Heather See *Calluna vulgaris*.
Heather, bell See *Erica cinerea*.
Heather, golden See *Ozothamnus leptophyllus* Fulvidus Group.
Heather, silver See *Ozothamnus leptophyllus* Albidus Group.

*****HEBE** Comm. ex Juss. (*Veronica* L. in part)—Scrophulariaceae—100 or more species of ornamental evergreen shrubs, occasionally trees, at one time included under *Veronica*. Most are natives of New Zealand, with a few species in Australia and S South America. They flower from spring to autumn and are invaluable for seaside and industrial planting. Most of those that do not thrive inland may be safely planted along the south and west coasts, even in exposed places where few other shrubs will survive. They will succeed in all types of well-drained soil. Flowers white unless otherwise stated.

albicans (Petrie) Cockayne. A very splendid dwarf, dense, rounded, glaucous shrub. Flowers in dense spikes during summer. Perfectly hardy and very ornamental. New Zealand (South Island). I about 1880. ♀ 2002. **'Cranleigh Gem'** A compact form, making a rounded shrub, with silvery leaves. Possibly a hybrid. **'Pewter Dome'** See *H*. 'Pewter Dome'. **'Red Edge'** See *H*. 'Red Edge'. **'Sussex Carpet'** A selection of low, widespreading habit, good for groundcover.

†**'Alicia Amherst'** ('Veitchii', 'Royal Purple') A magnificent *H. speciosa* hybrid. A small shrub with long racemes of deep purple-blue flowers in late summer. Raised by Veitch in 1911.

†**'Amy'** A small, rounded shrub of compact, upright habit. The leaves are purplish when young, looking effective over a long period, eventually to 7.5cm long and dark glossy green. Racemes of violet-purple flowers are borne during summer. Raised in Dublin and named after Lady Amy Ardilaun. The plant grown as 'Purple Queen' (AM 1893) is identical.

†× *andersonii* (Lindl. & Paxton) Cockayne (*H. salicifolia* × *H. speciosa*) A vigorous shrub, to 1.8m, with leaves about 10cm long, and long racemes of soft lavender-blue flowers, fading to white, from August to September. Raised by Isaac Anderson-Henry before 1849. **'Variegata'** A very attractive form with leaves broadly margined and splashed creamy-white. C 1887.

anomala See *H. odora*.
'Aoira' See *H. recurva*.
armstrongii (J. B. Armstr.) Cockayne & Allan. A dwarf whipcord species with erect, densely branched stems of olive-green, sometimes yellow-tinged at tips. Flowers appear in July and August. The plant commonly grown under this name in gardens is *H. ochracea*. AM 1925 (possibly to *H. ochracea*). Mountains of South Island, where it is rare.

'Autumn Glory' (*H. pimeleoides* × *H.* × *franciscana* 'Blue Gem') A small shrub of loose habit with intense violet flowers continuously in short, dense racemes in late summer and autumn. C 1900.

'Baby Marie' (*H. buxifolia* 'Nana') A very dainty shrub, only 30cm by 45cm and making excellent groundcover. During mid- to late spring, its fresh green foliage is almost completely hidden by masses of tiny, pale lilac flowers fading to white. For best results, plant in free-draining soil in a sunny position.

'Balfouriana' A dwarf shrub of compact growth with small, obovate, pointed, yellowish-green leaves, purple-edged in bud, densely crowding the dark coloured stems. Purplish-blue flowers during summer. Raised at Royal Botanic Garden, Edinburgh, from New Zealand seed before 1894. It is believed to be a hybrid of *H. vernicosa* with perhaps *H. pimeleoides*.

'Blue Clouds' A small shrub with dark glossy green leaves, purplish in winter. Long spikes of wisteria-blue flowers are borne over a long period during summer and autumn. A seedling of 'Mrs Winder' raised at County Park Nursery, Essex in 1974. ♀ 2002.

'Bowles' Hybrid' ('Bowles' Variety') A charming, dwarf shrub for a rock garden. The flowers, both in spring and summer, crowd the short branches in pretty mauve-coloured racemes. Moderately hardy. Possibly *H. diosmifolia* × *H. parviflora*.

brachysiphon Summerh. (*H. traversii* hort. not (Hook. f.) Cockayne & Allan) A popular shrub, 1.5m high or sometimes much more, flowering profusely in June or July. South Island. I 1868. **'White Gem'** See *H*. 'White Gem'.

buchananii (Hook. f.) Cockayne & Allan. A dwarf shrub with tiny, rounded, leathery, closely imbricated leaves. Flowers June and July. Suitable for a rock garden. Mountains of South Island. AMT 1982. **'Minor'** An extremely dwarf form with tiny leaves. Rarely flowers.

buxifolia See *H. odora*. **'Nana'** See *H*. 'Baby Marie'.
'Caledonia' A dwarf, compact and rounded shrub with red-tinted young leaves and spikes of violet flowers from late spring to early autumn. C 1975. ♀ 2002.

canterburiensis (J.B. Armstr.) L.B. Moore. A dwarf shrub forming a neat, rounded hummock covered by short racemes of flowers in June to July. Mountains of North and South Islands. I 1910.

'Carl Teschner' See *H.* 'Youngii'.

†**'Carnea'** An attractive shrub, about 1.2m high, with long racemes of rose-pink flowers, which fade to white, produced plentifully from May to late summer. C 1881. AM 1925.

†**'Carnea Variegata'** Similar to 'Carnea' of which it is a sport, but with grey-green leaves margined creamy-white. C 1945.

carnosula (Hook. f.) Cockayne. Dwarf to prostrate in habit; leaves small, glaucous, shell-like. Flowers from July to August. Suitable for a rock garden and excellent groundcover. Possibly of hybrid origin. Mountains of South Island.

chathamica Buchanan. A prostrate shrub making a dense mat of thick, pale green leaves; dense racemes of pale lilac flowers fading to white, appear during late summer. Found on sea cliffs in its native habitat, it is suitable for groundcover except in the coldest areas. Chatham Island.

'Christabel' A neat and compact, dwarf shrub making a low mound only about 20cm tall, with small, densely arranged, bright green leaves. Found by Graham Hutchins near Lake Christabel in New Zealand in 1985. It is possibly a hybrid beyween *H. pauciramosa* and *H. lycopodioides*.

ciliolata (Hook. f.) Cockayne & Allan. A miniature shrublet with congested, greyish-green stems and closely imbricated leaves. Mountains of South Island.

colensoi (Hook. f.) Cockayne. A dwarf, bushy shrub with dark glossy green leaves, glaucous when young. Flowers in dense, short racemes during summer. North Island. **'Glauca'** A dense shrub with attractive, glaucous-blue foliage; height 0.6–1m. Flowers July to August.

cookiana See *H. stricta* 'Cookiana'.

'County Park' A dwarf shrub of spreading habit, suitable for groundcover. Grey-green leaves margined red, flushed pink in winter. Flowers violet in short racemes during summer. A seedling of *H. pimeleoides* 'Glaucocaerulea' raised at County Park Nursery, Essex in 1970.

'Cranleighensis' A small shrub with glossy leaves that are red-purple beneath when young. Long spikes of pink flowers are borne in summer.

cupressoides (Hook. f.) Cockayne & Allan. Normally a small shrub, but occasionally reaching as much as 2m, of very distinct appearance. The long, slender, green or grey branches are remarkably like those of a *Cupressus*. Small, pale blue flowers are produced quite freely in June and July. Mountains of South Island. FCC 1894. **'Boughton Dome'** A dwarf form of dense habit making a very compact, rounded bush. FCCT 1982.

darwiniana See *H. glaucophylla*.

†**'Dazzler'** PBR A compact, dwarf shrub with slender, purple-flushed shoots. The narrow leaves, to 3cm long, are grey-green with a cream and pink-flushed margin, becoming cream with age. The leaves occasionally have a sharp tooth on each side towards the apex. Excellent for a patio container or sheltered border. A sport found at Lowaters Nursery, Warsash, Hampshire.

decumbens (J.B. Armstr.) Cockayne & Allan. A low, spreading shrub with dark shoots and densely arranged,

glossy green, rather fleshy, red-edged leaves to 2cm long. White flowers open in dense racemes, to 3cm long, in summer. South Island.

†*dieffenbachii* (Benth.) Cockayne & Allan. A small, wide-spreading, irregular shrub with distinctly tiered, long, lance-shaped leaves. Flowers lilac-purple, in long showy racemes in September. Chatham Islands.

†*diosmifolia* (A. Cunn.) Cockayne & Allan. A small shrub, sometimes much larger in the wild, with slender, downy shoots. The glossy dark green, rather leathery leaves, to 3cm long, are often held upright on the shoots and have a few small teeth on the margins. Lilac-blue to nearly white flowers open in flat-topped corymbs in spring to early summer. North Island.

× *divergens* (Cheeseman) Cockayne (possibly *H. elliptica* × *H. gracillima*) Forms a neat, rounded shrub to 1.2m, characterised by its short, elliptic-oblong, flat-spreading leaves and dense racemes of white or pale lilac flowers with violet anthers. South Island.

'Edinensis' (*H. muscoidea* hort.) (possibly *H. hectoris* × *H. odora*) A charming, dwarf shrub, suitable for a rock garden, with tiny, bright green, imbricated leaves. Originated in 1904 at the Royal Botanic Garden, Edinburgh.

elliptica (G. Forst.) Pennell (*Veronica decussata* Sol., *Hebe magellanica* J.F. Gmel.) A rare, small to medium-sized shrub with oval or obovate, pale green leaves, downy at the margins. Comparatively large, fragrant flowers are borne in racemes. New Zealand (North, South and other islands). Chile, Tierra del Fuego, Falkland Isles. I 1776.

'Emerald Green' ('Green Globe') A dwarf, bun-shaped shrub of compact habit, up to 30cm tall, with upright, green shoots and tiny, densely arranged, glossy leaves. Small flowers are borne in summer. ♀ 2002.

epacridea (Hook. f.) Cockayne & Allan. A tiny, conifer-like shrublet, densely clothed with recurved, scale-like leaves. Flowers in short terminal racemes in July. A miniature carpeting evergreen suitable for a rock garden or scree. Mountains of South Island. I 1860.

'Ettrick Shepherd' A small, moderately hardy hybrid with violet-coloured flowers in long racemes.

'Fairfieldii' (*H. hulkeana* × *H. lavaudiana*) A dwarf, stiffly branched, upright shrub with deep purple shoots and broad, toothed, glossy green leaves, to 4cm long, edged with purple. Lilac-purple flowers are borne in upright panicles, to 15cm long, in late spring and early summer. Like *H. hulkeana* it benefits from dead-heading after flowering. Found in Fairfield Gardens, Dunedin, New Zealand before 1893.

× *franciscana* (Eastw.) Souster (*H. elliptica* × *H. speciosa*) (*Veronica lobelioides* Anderson-Henry) A first-rate and most popular hybrid originally raised before 1859. **'Blue Gem'** A small, compact, dome-shaped shrub producing dense racemes of bright blue flowers. One of the hardiest hebes and resistant to salt-laden winds, this is perhaps the most commonly planted and is hardy anywhere along the English coast, except in the very coldest areas. Excellent for low hedges. Raised by a Salisbury nurseryman about 1868. FCC 1869. **'Variegata'** Leaves broadly edged with creamy-white. Commonly seen in London window-boxes. ♀ 2002.

gibbsii (Kirk) Cockayne & Allan. A dwarf shrub with stout branches almost hidden by the comparatively large, glaucous, reflexed leaves, which are noticeably ciliate and densely arranged in 4 ranks. Flowers produced in short, dense racemes during late summer. An easily recognised species, rare both in the wild and in cultivation. Mountains of South Island.

glaucophylla (Cockayne) Cockayne (*H. darwiniana* hort. not (Colenso) Cockayne) A small, bushy shrub with slender branches bearing small, narrow, greyish-green leaves. Flowers in slender racemes towards the ends of the branches in July and August. Often found in gardens under the synonym. South Island. **'Variegata'** (*H. darwiniana* 'Variegata') A small, neat, attractive form with slender, wiry shoots and greyish-green leaves margined creamy-white. AMT 1982.

†**'Gloriosa'** (*H.* 'Pink Pearl') A most attractive *H. speciosa* hybrid making a small, compact shrub with bright pink flowers in conspicuous long racemes.

'Great Orme' A compact bush, to 1m high, with lance-shaped leaves, 5–7.5cm long, and bright pink flowers in long, tapering racemes. A seedling of 'Carnea'. Reasonably hardy. ♀ 2002.

'Greensleeves' A whipcord hebe making a bushy, upright, dwarf shrub with small, pale green leaves, turning outwards at the tips. White flowers are freely borne in terminal spikes in May and June. A hybrid of *H. ochracea* raised at County Park Nursery, Essex in about 1973.

haastii (Hook. f.) Cockayne & Allan. A very hardy, dwarf species, its stems densely covered with small, overlapping leaves. Flowers form a terminal head in July to August. Mountains of South Island.

'Hagley Park' (*H.* 'Hagleyensis') (*H. hulkeana* × *H. raoulii*) A dwarf, upright shrub with glossy green, red-margined, bluntly-toothed leaves. Rose-purple flowers appear in large panicles in early summer. A seedling in Hagley Park, Christchurch, New Zealand. AM 1976.

†**'Headfortii'** An attractive, purple-blue-flowered *H. speciosa* hybrid, 0.6–1m high.

hectorii (Hook. f.) Cockayne & Allan. An interesting, hardy, dwarf shrub of erect habit, having thick, rounded, stiffly cord-like branches, thickly covered by yellowish-green, closely adpressed leaves. Bears white or pale pink flowers in a crowded terminal head in July. Mountains of South Island.

'Hielan Lassie' A moderately hardy, small, compact, narrow-leaved shrub with rich blue-violet flowers, in racemes 5–7.5cm long, from July to September.

†**'Highdownensis'** A small, well-branched, spreading shrub with glossy leaves and dark stems. Slender spikes of deep purple-blue flowers open in summer.

hulkeana (F. Muell.) Cockayne & Allan. Perhaps the most beautiful species of hebe in cultivation, this is a small shrub of loose habit, occasionally reaching 1.8m against a sheltered wall, with glossy green, toothed, ovate leaves and large panicles of delicate lavender-blue flowers in May and June. At Winchester, it survived the severe winter of 1962–63, uninjured. Prune lightly to remove heads after flowering. South Island. I about 1860. ♀ 2002. FCC 1882. **'Sally Blunt'** A vigorous form with large, glossy dark green, red-edged leaves and wisteria-blue flowers in large panicles. Raised at County Park Nursery, Essex from seed collected in New Zealand by Graham Hutchins in 1985.

†**'Inspiration'** A dwarf, spreading shrub with arching, red-purple shoots and glossy green leaves to 4cm long. Dense racemes of rich violet-purple flowers open in early to midsummer, fading to nearly white. A hybrid of *H. speciosa*. C 1957.

†*insularis* (Cheeseman) Cockayne & Allan. Dwarf shrub, resembling *H. diosmifolia* but differing in its rather broader, somewhat oblong leaves and less densely branched inflorescence. Flowers pale lavender-blue in June and July. Cliffs on Three Kings Islands.

'James Stirling' See *H. ochracea* 'James Stirling'.

'Karo Golden Esk' A dwarf whipcord hebe, reaching 80cm tall, with yellow-green to golden foliage. Leaves at the tips of the shoots closely adpressed to the shoots, those at the base spreading. A natural hybrid between *H. armstrongii* and *H. odora* found by Dr Brian Molloy by a tarn on a tributary of the River Esk, Canterbury, New Zealand. C 1992.

× *kirkii* (J.B. Armstr.) Cockayne & Allan (*Veronica salicifolia* var. *kirkii* (J.B. Armstr.) Cheeseman) One of the hardiest of large-flowered hebes, similar to *H. salicifolia* but with shorter leaves. A hybrid of *H. salicifolia*, possibly with *H. rakaiensis*. South Island. I about 1870.

'La Séduisante' See *H. speciosa* 'La Séduisante'.

†*lavaudiana* (Raoul) Cockayne & Allan. A small shrublet closely related to *H. hulkeana* but with smaller leaves. Inflorescence a compact corymb of lilac-pink spikes in May. I 1880. Banks Peninsula, South Island.

leiophylla Cockayne & Allan. One of the hardiest of the New Zealand species forming a shrub about 1.2m high. Leaves narrow, resembling those of *H. parviflora*. Flowers in 10cm long racemes in July and August. Possibly a naturally occurring hybrid. South Island.

× *lewisii* (J.B. Armstr.) Cockayne & Allan. A naturally occurring hybrid, possibly *H. elliptica* × *H. salicifolia*, this is a small to medium-sized shrub of erect habit. Pale blue flowers are borne in 5–6.5cm racemes at the end of the stems in July and August. Named after a New Zealand nurseryman. South Island.

'Lindsayi' (*H. amplexicaulis* × *H. pimeleoides*) A very hardy shrub to about 1m high and of equal width. Leaves rather rotund; flowers pink in short, conspicuous racemes.

loganioides (J.B. Armstr.) Wall. (*H. selaginoides* hort.) A dwarf shrublet only a few centimetres high, its slender stems clothed with tiny, spreading, scale-like leaves. Flowers are borne in short, terminal racemes during summer. A peculiar, almost conifer-like plant, which may well be of hybrid origin. Found in New Zealand in 1869. South Island.

lycopodioides (Hook. f.) Cockayne & Allan. A dwarf shrub with slender, erect, 4-sided stems of yellow-green. Scale-like leaves with a sharp horn-like point, densely clothe the branches. Flowers in July. South Island. FCC 1894.

'Macewanii' A dwarf shrub with glaucous foliage and blue flowers. A hybrid of *H. pimeleoides*.

†*macrantha* (Hook. f.) Cockayne & Allan. A very valuable dwarf shrub, notable for its leathery, toothed leaves, and its pure white flowers, which are as much as 2cm across. Mountains of South Island. ♀ 2002. AM 1952.

macroura See *H. stricta* var. *macroura*.

'**Margret**' PBR A compact, hardy, dwarf shrub, to 60cm, with bright green leaves, producing a profusion of sky-blue flowers on short spikes in late spring or early summer, followed by several flushes in late summer and autumn. As the flowers age, they fade to pale blue and then white, producing a bicolour effect. C 1985. ♀ 2002.

'**Marjorie**' Remarkably hardy for a hebe, this forms a neat bush about 1m high, and produces racemes 5–7.5cm long of light violet and white flowers from July to September.

matthewsii (Cheeseman) Cockayne An erect shrub, to 1.2m, with thick, and leathery, oblong or oval leaves and white or pale purple flowers in racemes 5–10cm long in July. South Island. AM 1927.

'**Midsummer Beauty**' (*H.* 'Miss E. Fittall' × *H. speciosa*) A handsome, small shrub with conspicuous reddish leaf undersides. Flowers in long, lavender racemes through summer. Moderately hardy. ♀ 2002. FCC 1975. AM 1960.

'**Mrs E. Tennant**' A comparatively hardy, small shrub. Flowers light violet, in racemes 7.5–12.5cm long, from July to September.

'**Mrs Winder**' ('Waikiki') A small to medium-sized, moderately hardy hybrid with purple foliage and bright blue flowers. ♀ 2002. AMT 1982. AM 1978.

muscoidea See *H.* 'Edinensis'.

'**Neil's Choice**' A small, bushy shrub with red-purple shoots and dark green, red-edged leaves, to 8cm long, red-purple when young. Rich violet-purple flowers open in dense racemes, to 12cm long, from midsummer to early winter. Raised at County Park Nursery, Essex before 1976 and probably a seedling of 'Mrs Winder'. ♀ 2002.

'**Nicola's Blush**' A dwarf shrub bearing profuse, pale pink flowers, fading to white, over a long period from summer to late autumn or early winter. Leaves flushed purple in winter with red margins. A seedling raised at County Park Nursery, Essex before 1980. ♀ 2002.

ochracea Ashwin. A dwarf, densely branched shrub with erect, glossy, cord-like stems of characteristic ochre or old gold. Flowers appear in July and August. This plant is commonly found in gardens under the name *H. armstrongii*, which differs in its greener branches and its sharply keeled and pointed leaves. Mountains of South Island. AMT 1982. '**James Stirling**' (*H.* 'James Stirling') A dwarf form with stouter branches and bright ochre-gold foliage, which, however, lacks the grace of the typical form. ♀ 2002. AMT 1982.

odora (Hook. f.) Cockayne (*H. anomala* (Armstr.) Cockayne, *H. buxifolia* (Benth.) Cockayne & Allan) A small to medium-sized very hardy shrub with crowded leaves and white flowers during summer. Extremely variable. Mountains of North, South and Stewart Islands. '**New Zealand Gold**' A form with the young growths tipped bright yellow. I from Arthur's Pass in New Zealand by Kenneth Beckett.

'**Oratio Beauty**' Compact with deep green leaves and bicoloured flower spikes like coconut ice. ♀ 2002.

†*parviflora* (Vahl) Cockayne & Allan. A variable species in the wild mainly represented in cultivation by the following. **var. *angustifolia*** (Hook. f.) L.B. Moore. A variety with linear, grass-like leaves and purple-brown stems. Often grown as *H.* 'Spender's Seedling'. South Island. I about 1868. **var. *arborea*** (Buchanan) L.B. Moore (*Veronica arborea* Buchanan) An erect-branched shrub, to about 1.5m, but considerably taller and tree-like in its native habitat. Leaves long and narrow; white flowers, tinged lilac-pink, in July and August. North Island. I 1822.

'**Pascal**' A dwarf shrub raised by Graham Hutchins. Compact, rounded habit with deep red winter foliage turning green in summer. Violet-purple flowers open from late spring to autumn. ♀ 2002.

'**Petra's Pink**' A dwarf, spreading shrub with red-flushed young leaves becoming dark green edged red-purple. Dense spikes of pink flowers open during summer.

'**Pewter Dome**' (*H. albicans* 'Pewter Dome') A low-growing shrub, making a dense, dome-shaped bush, with grey-green leaves and short spikes of flowers in early summer. A hybrid of *H. albicans*. ♀ 2002.

pimeleoides (Hook. f.) Cockayne & Allan. A distinct but variable species making a dwarf or almost prostrate shrub with purplish shoots and glaucous rather red-edged leaves. Blue to purple flowers are borne in racemes during summer. Mountains of South Island. '**Glaucocaerulea**' A form with upright shoots, small, glaucous-blue leaves and violet-blue flowers in June and July. **var. *minor*** (Hook. f.) Cockayne & Allan. A minute shrub, forming loose mounds 5–7.5cm high, the slender stems clothed with narrow, glaucous leaves, 5mm long. A choice little plant for a scree or trough. '**Quicksilver**' A dwarf, spreading shrub with tiny, silvery-blue leaves contrasting with the very dark shoots. Flowers pale lilac. ♀ 2002.

pinguifolia (Hook. f.) Cockayne & Allan. A dwarf shrub with purplish nodes and small, glaucous, often red-margined leaves. Flowers in dense spikes during summer. Mountains of South Island. I about 1864. '**Pagei**' (*Veronica pageana* hort.) Wide mats of small, glaucous-grey leaves are attractive throughout the year. The small flowers are borne in quantity in May. Excellent ground-cover or rock garden plant. ♀ 2002. AMT 1982. AM 1958. '**Sutherlandii**' Differs from 'Pagei' in its much denser, more upright habit making a compact, rounded, dwarf bush with grey-green foliage.

'**Pink Elephant**' A compact and very hardy dwarf shrub the leaves edged with buttery-yellow and tipped pink, becoming flushed burgundy-red in winter. Spikes of white flowers open in early summer. A sport of 'Red Edge' found by Mark Walberton of Ashwood Nurseries. C 1981. ♀ 2002.

'**Pink Paradise**' PBR A Dutch-raised hybrid of unknown parentage selected in 1995. A very hardy, dwarf shrub of compact habit bearing profuse, pink flowers over a long period during spring and summer.

propinqua (Cheeseman) Cockayne & Allan. A dwarf, many-branched shrublet forming a low mound of rounded, green or yellowish-green, thread-like stems. Mountains of South Island. Sometimes found in gardens, quite wrongly under the names *H. armstrongii* 'Compacta' and *H. salicornioides* 'Aurea'.

'**Purple Picture**' A low, spreading shrub, to 60cm tall, with deep purple shoots and glossy purple young leaves, to 4cm long, later glossy dark green. Rich violet-purple flowers open in dense racemes, to 8cm long, from midsummer to early winter. A seedling of *H. speciosa* 'La Séduisante' raised at County Park Nursery, Essex before 1978.

'Purple Queen' See 'Amy'.

Purple Shamrock ('Neprock') PBR A compact sport of 'Mrs Winder' found by Doug Thomson of Irish Garden Plants, Northern Ireland. Slender leaves purple when young becoming lime-green edged yellow, on purple shoots, turning deep purple in winter. Occasional blue flowers during summer. C 1999.

'Purple Tips' See *H. speciosa* 'Variegata'.

rakaiensis (J.B. Armstr.) Cockayne (*H. subalpina* hort. not Cockayne & Allan) A dwarf, very hardy shrub forming dense, compact mounds of crowded stems bearing small, neat, pale green leaves. Flowers are borne in short, crowded racemes in June and July. A splendid ground cover in full sun. Sometimes found in gardens wrongly as *H. subalpina*. South Island. ♀ 2002. AMT 1982.

raoulii (Hook. f.) Cockayne & Allan. A dwarf shrub with spathulate leaves, toothed and often reddish at the margins. Lavender or almost white flowers are borne in crowded terminal spikes during summer. South Island.

recurva G. Simpson & J.S. Thomson. A small, slender-branched shrub of open, rounded habit up to 1m. Leaves narrow, lanceolate, glaucous above. Flowers in slender racemes. The form in general cultivation is known as 'Aoira'. South Island. I 1923. AM 1972. **'Boughton Silver'** Compact with very silvery-blue leaves. ♀ 2002.

'Red Edge' (*H. albicans* 'Red Edge') A dwarf shrub with dense, blue-grey leaves, narrowly margined with red particularly in winter. Flowers in summer, lilac becoming white. Raised at County Park Nursery, Essex in 1968 and probably *H. albicans* × *H. pimeleoides* 'Glaucocaerulea'. ♀ 2002.

'Rosie' PBR A compact, dwarf shrub, to 30cm tall, with small, blue-green leaves, to 1.5cm long. Bears profuse spikes of clear pink flowers, with purple anthers, over a long period in summer and autumn. The best dwarf pink hebe. A seedling of 'Great Orme' raised in 1985.

salicifolia (G. Forst.) Pennell. A medium-sized shrub for maritime districts. Leaves lanceolate, bright green; flowers white or lilac-tinged in long racemes; June to August. Withstands most winters with only superficial injury. A parent of many hybrids. South and Stewart Islands. S Chile. AMT 1982. **'Spender's Seedling'** See *H.* 'Spender's Seedling'. **'Variegata'** See *H.* 'Snow Wreath'.

'Sapphire' A small, upright shrub with slender, red-tinged leaves and long spikes of rose-purple flowers during summer and autumn. ♀ 2002.

'Silver Dollar' A sport of 'Red Edge' with grey-green leaves narrowly edged with cream and pink, the young leaves turning burgundy-red in winter. Short spikes of white flowers are borne in summer.

†**'Simon Delaux'** Small, rounded shrub with rich crimson flowers in large racemes. One of the best of the *H. speciosa* hybrids.

'Snow Wreath' (*H. salicifolia* 'Variegata') A small, bushy shrub with slender, pale green leaves, to 5cm long, margined with creamy-white. Racemes of small, white flowers are borne during late summer and autumn.

†*speciosa* (A. Cunn.) Cockayne & Allan. A small shrub of dense, rounded habit, with handsome, leathery leaves and dark, reddish-purple flowers. Represented in cultivation by innumerable colourful hybrids and cultivars, many of which are only suitable for seaside gardens.

North and South Islands. **'La Séduisante'** (*H.* 'Diamant', *H.* 'La Séduisante') A very pretty form. A small shrub with large, bright crimson racemes of flowers and dark glossy green leaves, purple-tinged when young. AM 1897. **'Tricolor'** See 'Variegata'. **'Variegata'** ('Tricolor') A small shrub, a sport of 'La Séduisante', with leaves that are rose-purple on the back when young, opening grey-green with deep green veins, broadly margined creamy-white and becoming rose-tinted during winter. Long racemes of magenta-purple flowers fade to white. Rather tender. C 1926.

'Spender's Seedling' (*H. salicifolia* 'Spender's Seedling') A small, very hardy, free-flowering shrub. Its fragrant flowers produced over a long period. AMT 1982. AM 1954.

'Spring Glory' An attractive, small, spreading shrub bearing deep purple flowers in spring. It does best in full sun and well-drained soil.

†*stricta* (Benth.) L.B. Moore. A variable, often large shrub, related to *H. salicifolia*. The typical form is confined to North Island. **'Cookiana'** (*H. cookiana* (Colenso) Cockayne & Allan) Small, dense, floriferous shrub with elliptic, fleshy leaves and long, dense racemes of mauve-tinged, white flowers from August to October. **var. *macroura*** (Benth.) L.B. Moore (*H. macroura* (Benth.) Cockayne & Allan) Small shrub, to 1.2m, with long, dense racemes of flowers and long, elliptic-lanceolate leaves. North Island.

subalpina (Cockayne) Cockayne & Allan. A small, very hardy shrub of dense, rounded habit. Similar to *H. rakaiensis* and confused with it in cultivation. It differs in its longer leaves, to 3cm or more (2cm in *H. rakaiensis*) and its glabrous capsules. South Island. See also under *H. rakaiensis*.

subsimilis (Colenso) M.B. Ashwin. A dwarf whipcord shrub of upright habit reaching about 25cm. Leaves tiny, green. Flowers in small spikes during summer. N and S Islands. **var. *astonii*** (Petrie) Ashwin. Miniature, much branched shrublet forming a compact hummock of thin, rounded, green stems. North Island.

tetrasticha (Hook. f.) Cockayne & Allan. A miniature shrublet forming tiny patches of green, 4-sided stems, thickly clothed with the closely adpressed, scale-like leaves. Mountains of South Island.

topiaria L.B. Moore. A small, compact, dome-shaped shrub, to 1m, with small, grey-green leaves and short clusters of flowers in summer. South Island. ♀ 2002.

traversii hort. See *H. brachysiphon*.

venustula (Colenso) L.B. Moore (*H. laevis* (Benth.) Cockayne & Allan) Dwarf or small shrub forming a rounded hummock. The small, 1.25cm long, yellowish-green leaves have a thin, yellowish margin. Short racemes of flowers crowd the branches in summer. Mountains of North and South Islands.

vernicosa (Hook. f.) Cockayne & Allan. A very hardy, dwarf shrub of spreading habit with small, bright glossy green leaves. White flowers, sometimes pale lilac at first, are in slender racemes, up to 5cm long, in late spring. South Island. ♀ 2002.

'Waikiki' See 'Mrs Winder'.

†**'Watson's Pink'** A small shrub with slender leaves and spikes of bright pink flowers throughout summer.

'White Gem' (*H. brachysiphon* 'White Gem') A dwarf, compact, hardy shrub, rarely over 50cm high, producing a profusion of flowers in June. It differs from *H. brachysiphon* in its dwarfer habit, smaller, paler leaves and earlier flowering with shorter racemes. Possibly *H. brachysiphon* × *H. pinguifolia*. C 1964. ♀ 2002.

'Wingletye' A prostrate shrub of compact habit, suitable for a rock garden, with small, glaucous leaves. Ascending shoots bear racemes of deep mauve flowers in early summer. A seedling of *H. pimeleoides* 'Glaucocaerulea' raised at County Park Nursery, Essex in 1970. ♀ 2002.

'Wiri Charm' A compact, small, bushy shrub bearing profuse spikes of bright rose-purple flowers over a long period during summer. This and the other Wiri selections were bred by Jack Hobbs, curator of the Auckland Regional Botanic Gardens.

'Wiri Cloud' A compact, dwarf shrub, to about 60cm tall and across, with bright green foliage on yellow-green shoots, the small leaves to 1.5cm long. Clusters of white flowers, flushed with pink, open in summer from pink buds. ♀ 2002.

'Wiri Dawn' A dwarf, mound-forming shrub, to about 40cm tall, with slender leaves. Spikes of rose-pink flowers open during summer. ♀ 2002.

'Wiri Image' A compact shrub of upright growth, the pale green shoots with a conspicuous red-purple band at the nodes. Leaves rich green, elliptic-oblong, to 7cm long and 2cm across. Racemes of violet flowers open in summer.

'Wiri Mist' A dwarf, rounded shrub with bright green foliage. Dense spikes of white flowers open during summer.

'Wiri Splash' A beautiful, dwarf shrub, to 90cm tall, bearing profuse spikes of lilac flowers over a long period during summer and autumn. Suitable for the border or a container.

'Youngii' (*H.* 'Carl Teschner') (*H. elliptica* × *H. pimeleoides*) A hardy, dwarf, summer-flowering shrub of compact habit with small leaves and abundant, short racemes of violet flowers, with a white throat, in June to July. Makes splendid free-growing groundcover. Garden origin. Raised in New Zealand and long known under this name, it was re-christened 'Carl Teschner' in England after the New Zealand nurseryman who sent it, unnamed, to this country. ♀ 2002. AM 1964.

HEDYSARUM L.—**Leguminosae**—A large genus of about 100 species of perennials and shrubs found throughout N temperate regions. The following is easily cultivated given full sun.

multijugum Maxim. A small Mongolian shrub of lax habit with sea-green, pinnate leaves and long racemes of rose-purple, pea-flowers throughout summer. Plants in cultivation belong to var. *apiculatum* Sprague. I 1883. AM 1898.

HEIMIA Link—**Lythraceae**—A small genus of 3 species of shrubs related to the familiar Loosestrife (*Lysimachia*) and natives of North and South America.

salicifolia (Kunth) Link. An interesting shrub, attaining 1.2m, with narrow leaves and yellow flowers, 1.25cm across, produced in the leaf axils from July to September. Central and South America. I 1821.

*HELIANTHEMUM Mill.—**Cistaceae**—The rock roses or sun roses consist of more than 100 species of mainly dwarf,

evergreen shrubs, natives of Europe, N Africa, W and C Asia, and North and South America. The following are excellent for dry sunny situations, producing a multitude of flowers in brilliant colours throughout summer.

algarvense See *Halimium ocymoides*.

alpestre See *H. oelandicum* subsp. *alpestre*.

apenninum (L.) Mill. White rock rose. A dwarf shrublet forming mats of slender, spreading shoots crowded with narrow, grey leaves. White flowers, with a yellow eye, are borne in profusion from May to July. W and S Europe. A rare native species found only in two localities, one in Devon another in Somerset. C 1768. **var. *roseum*** (Jacq.) Schneid. (*H. rhodanthum* Dunal) An attractive, dwarf form with hoary foliage and silvery-rose flowers.

canadense (L.) Michx. (*Crocanthemum canadense* (L.) Britton & A. Br.) A rare, dwarf shrublet with downy stems and small, alternate leaves, greyish-tomentose beneath. Bright yellow flowers are usually solitary in the leaf axils during early summer. We are indebted to Dr Henry Skinner of the National Arboretum, Washington, for locating this plant in the wild and sending us seeds. E USA. C 1825.

chamaecistus See *H. nummularium*.

lunulatum (All.) DC. A dainty, cushion-like alpine bearing yellow flowers, with a small, orange spot at the base of each petal, in June and July. NW Italy.

nummularium (L.) Mill. (*H. chamaecistus* Mill., *H. vulgare* Gaertn.) Common sun rose. A dwarf, spreading shrublet with ascending or prostrate stems. Leaves green above, grey or white beneath in the typical form. Most forms usually listed under this name are hybrids (see below). Splendid groundcover plants for full sun and poor dry soil. Europe (incl. British Isles). **subsp. *glabrum*** (Koch) Wilczek. Leaves nearly glabrous, green beneath. C & S Europe.

oelandicum (L.) DC. A variable and widely distributed species mainly represented in gardens by the following. **subsp. *alpestre*** (Jacq.) Breitstr. (*H. alpestre* (Jacq.) DC.) A very dwarf shrub with grey-green foliage and bright yellow flowers in June and July. Mountains of S and C Europe. I 1818. AMT 1925.

Helianthemum hybrids

The many colourful plants generally seen in cultivation are mainly hybrids of a group of 3 species *H. apenninum*, *H. nummularium* and *H. croceum*. Between them they have produced a great variety of silver- and green-leaved plants with flowers ranging in colour from orange, yellow or white, to rose, red and scarlet, both single and double.

'Alice Howarth' Double, deep pink flowers with a red and yellow centre. Open, upright habit; foliage dark green.

'Amy Baring' Deep buttercup-yellow flowers on a dwarf, compact plant; foliage green. Found in the French Pyrenees by Mrs Amy Doncaster and named after her by the nurseryman A.K. Bulley. ♀ 2002.

'Baby Buttercup' Small, golden-yellow flowers, 2.3cm across, the petals with a faint orange blotch in the centre. Very dense and low-growing with slender, dark green leaves, making excellent groundcover.

'Beech Park Scarlet' Compact and slow-growing with very large, scarlet flowers and grey foliage.

Helianthemum hybrids continued:

'Ben Afflick' Bright deep orange-bronze flowers with bronze-copper centres; foliage green.

'Ben Dearg' Deep copper-orange flowers with darker centres; foliage green.

'Ben Fhada' Golden-yellow flowers with orange centres; foliage grey-green.

'Ben Heckla' Rich orange flowers, 2.5cm across, with a deep scarlet centre and prominent yellow stamens. Vigorous, bushy, spreading habit.

'Ben Hope' Carmine flowers with deep orange centres; foliage light grey-green.

'Ben Ledi' Bright, deep tyrian-rose flowers; foliage dark green.

'Ben Macdhui' Deep scarlet flowers with a pale yellow crescent-shaped blotch towards the centre of the petals, orange-yellow at the base. Open habit with slender, bright green leaves, profuse flowering.

'Ben More' Bright, rich orange flowers with darker centres; foliage dark green.

'Ben Nevis' Deep buttercup-yellow flowers with conspicuous bronze-crimson central zones; foliage green. AM 1924. AMT 1924.

'Boughton Double Primrose' Double, primrose-yellow flowers, deeper in the centre; leaves broad, dark green.

'Cerise Queen' Scarlet, double flowers; foliage green.

'Coppernob' Deep glowing copper flowers with bronze-crimson centre; foliage grey-green.

'Fire Dragon' ('Mrs Clay') Bright orange-scarlet flowers; foliage grey-green. ♀ 2002.

'Golden Queen' Golden-yellow flowers; foliage green.

'Henfield Brilliant' Bright orange flowers; foliage grey-green. ♀ 2002.

'Jock Scott' Bright, deep rose-cerise flowers with darker centres; foliage green.

'Jubilee' Drooping, primrose-yellow, double flowers; foliage green. ♀ 2002. AMT 1970.

'Mrs Clay' See 'Fire Dragon'.

'Mrs Croft' Pink flowers, suffused orange; foliage silver-grey.

'Mrs C.W. Earle' Double, scarlet flowers with a yellow basal flush; foliage dark green. ♀ 2002.

'Old Gold' Orange with a prominent orange-scarlet blotch and yellow centre. Compact, bushy habit; grey-green foliage.

'Praecox' Lemon-yellow flowers; dense habit; grey foliage.

'Raspberry Ripple' Deep reddish-pink flowers with white-tipped petals; foliage dark green.

'Red Dragon' Scarlet flowers with yellow centres; foliage green.

'Red Orient' See 'Supreme'.

'Rhodanthe Carneum' Pale rhodamine-pink flowers with orange centres; foliage silver-grey. ♀ 2002.

'Rose of Leeswood' Rose-pink, double flowers; foliage green.

'Saint John's College Yellow' Yellow flowers, 2.7cm across, the cupped petals darker at the base. Neat, upright habit with very grey foliage, good for groundcover.

'Salmon Queen' Large flowers, 3.3cm across, pale pink with a deeper pink centre to the petals, yellow at the base. Large, dark green leaves.

'Snowball' Creamy-white, double flowers with pale yellow centres; foliage green.

'Sudbury Gem' Deep pink flowers with flame-red centres; foliage grey-green.

'Supreme' ('Red Orient') Crimson flowers; foliage grey-green.

'The Bride' Creamy-white flowers with bright yellow centres; foliage silver-grey. ♀ 2002. AMT 1924. AM 1924.

'Tigrinum Plenum' Double, bright orange flowers, paler towards the tip of the petals which have a yellow base. Dense, spreading habit with dark green foliage.

'Watergate Rose' Rose-crimson flowers with orange-tinged centres; foliage grey-green. AMT 1932.

'Wisley Pink' Soft pink with grey foliage.

'Wisley Primrose' Primrose-yellow flowers with deeper yellow centres; foliage light grey-green. ♀ 2002. AMT 1970.

'Wisley White' Pure white, single flowers with a centre of golden anthers; foliage narrow, grey.

*HELICHRYSUM Mill.—**Compositae**—A large genus of some 500 species of herbs and shrubs that are widely distributed in Europe, Asia, Africa and Australasia, particularly in South Africa and Australia. The shrubby members provide some interesting, mainly low-growing, often aromatic plants with attractive foliage. Most are reasonably hardy given full sun and well-drained, poor soil. Many of the shrubby species that are native to New Zealand and Australia and often listed under *Helichrysum* are treated under *Ozothamnus*.

angustifolium See *H. italicum*.

antennarium See *Ozothamnus antennaria*.

diosmifolium See *Ozothamnus thyrsoideus*.

ericeteum See under *Ozothamnus purpurascens*.

hookeri See *Ozothamnus hookeri*.

italicum (Roth) G. Don (*H. angustifolium* (Lam.) DC., *H. rupestre* hort.) This variable species is a superb, dwarf shrub with long, narrow, grey leaves and terminal, long-stalked clusters of bright yellow flowerheads during summer. One of the best of all silvery-grey shrubs. Mediterranean region. Many plants called *H. rupestre* actually belong here. ♀ 2002. **Korma** ('Proma') PBR A form with silvery, very aromatic foliage. **subsp. serotinum** (Boiss.) P. Fourn. (*H. serotinum* Boiss.) Curry plant. Dense, dwarf shrub bearing narrow, sage-green leaves with a strong, curry-like smell. Heads of yellow flowers in midsummer. S Europe.

ledifolium See *Ozothamnus ledifolius*.

microphyllum hort. See *Plecostachys serpyllifolia*.

†*petiolare* Hilliard & B.L. Burtt (*H. petiolatum* hort. not (L.) DC.) A dwarf, often trailing, shrublet with white-woolly stems and long-stalked, ovate, grey-woolly leaves. Yellow flowers in late summer. Normally a tender species but may overwinter in milder areas if given good drainage and overhead protection. South Africa. ♀ 2002. AM 1987. **'Limelight'** Foliage lime-green. ♀ 2002. **'Variegatum'** A form with the leaves edged creamy-white. ♀ 2002.

petiolatum See *H. petiolare*.

†*plicatum* (Fisch. & C.A. Mey.) DC. An attractive, dwarf, silvery-white shrub with long, narrow, downy leaves and terminal clusters of bright yellow flowers in July. SE Europe. I 1877.

rosmarinifolium See *Ozothamnus rosmarinifolius*.
rupestre See *H. italicum*.
scutellifolium See *Ozothamnus scutellifolius*.
selago See *Ozothamnus selago*.
serotinum See *H. italicum* subsp. *serotinum*.
splendidum (Thunb.) Less. (*H. triliniatum* hort. not DC.) (*H. aveolatum* hort. not DC.) A small, globular shrub to about 1m. Silvery-grey leaves with 3 longitudinal ridges. The everlasting flowers remain a good yellow into mid-winter. One of the very few South African plants hardy in the Home Counties. ♀ 2002.
†*stoechas* (L.) Moench. Goldilocks. A dwarf shrub with silvery-white leaves and bright yellow flowers, in corymbs, during summer. S Europe. C 1629.
thyrsoideum See *Ozothamnus thyrsoideus*.
triliniatum hort. See *H. splendidum*.

HELWINGIA Willd.—Helwingiaceae—A small genus of 3 species, interesting because of the peculiar position of the insignificant flowers which, due to the fusion of the pedicel with the petiole and leaf midrib, appear on the upper surface of the leaf. Natives of E Asia from the Himalaya to Japan.
chinensis Batalin. A strong-growing, medium-sized shrub with narrow, lanceolate, willow-like leaves, to 15cm long, coppery-red when young and edged with incurved, bristle-tipped teeth. Flowers in small clusters at the widest point of the leaf in summer, purple-red in bud, opening green-purple. Fruits black. China. I by several collectors in recent years, including Mikinori Ogisu, Roy Lancaster and Keith Rushforth.
japonica (Thunb.) F. Dietr. (*H. rusciflora* Willd.) A small shrub bearing pale green flowers, and later black berries, on the upper surface of the leaves. Japan. I 1830.

HEMIPTELEA Planch.—Ulmaceae—A monotypic genus closely related to *Zelkova* and sometimes included in it but differing in its spiny branches and winged fruits.
davidii (Hance) Planch. (*Zelkova davidii* (Hance) Hemsl.) A small, dense, shrubby tree with spine-tipped branchlets and oval, toothed leaves. China, Korea. I 1908.

HEPTACODIUM Rehder—Caprifoliaceae—A genus of a single species, a deciduous Chinese shrub related to *Abelia*.
jasminoides See *H. miconioides*.
miconioides Rehder (*H. jasminoides* Airy Shaw) Seven Son Flower of Zhejiang. A vigorous and very hardy, large, deciduous shrub of upright habit, with peeling bark. Bold, conspicuously 3-veined leaves are retained until late autumn or early winter. Small, fragrant, white flowers are borne in whorls at the ends of the shoots in late summer and autumn. Given good weather, the calyx enlarges and turns bright red after flowering. China. I to the Sir Harold Hillier Gardens and Arboretum in 1981.

Hercules' club See *Aralia spinosa*.

†***HESPERALOE** Engelm.—Agavaceae—A genus of 3 species of stemless, evergreen herbs related to *Yucca*, natives of SW USA.
parviflora (Torr.) Coult. An evergreen, spreading shrub having thick, leathery, linear leaves, 2.5cm wide and up to 1.2m long, bright green with white threads hanging

from the margins. The aloe-like, tomato-red flowers, golden within, are produced in slender panicles, up to 1.2m long, in July. Texas. I 1822. **var. *engelmannii*** (Krauskopf) Trel. Flowers more bell-shaped.

Hesperoyucca whipplei See *Yucca whipplei*.

†***HETEROMELES** M. Roem.—Rosaceae—A monotypic genus formerly included in *Photinia*.
arbutifolia See *H. salicifolia*.
salicifolia (C. Presl) Abrams (*H. arbutifolia* (Lindl.) M. Roem., *Photinia arbutifolia* Lindl.) Christmas berry, Toyon. A large shrub in favoured areas. Leaves thick and leathery, lanceolate to obovate, sharply-toothed, 5–10cm long. Flowers white, produced in flattened, terminal panicles in late summer. Fruits bright red, like haws. California. I 1796.

HIBISCUS L.—Malvaceae—A large genus of some 200 species of herbs, shrubs and trees, widely distributed in tropical and subtropical regions. Of this extensive genus, few are hardy in the British Isles but of these the following provide us with some of the most effective late summer- and early autumn-flowering shrubs They need full sun.
hamabo See under *H. syriacus* 'Hamabo'.
sinosyriacus L.H. Bailey. A very handsome and hardy, vigorous species making a medium-sized shrub more spreading in habit than *H. syriacus* and with broader, sage-green leaves. The flowers, appearing in late summer and autumn, are slightly larger, and the petals thicker. It enjoys similar conditions to *H. syriacus* and is equally hardy. C China. Introduced by us in 1936 when we received seed from the Lushan Botanic Garden from which we raised the following cultivars: **'Autumn Surprise'** Petals white with attractively feathered, cerise bases. **'Lilac Queen'** Petals lilac with garnet-red bases. **'Ruby Glow'** Petals white with cerise bases, but the flowers often not opening fully.
syriacus L. Given a position in full sun and a favourable season, no late-flowering shrub is more beautiful than this shrubby mallow. The large, trumpet-shaped flowers open in succession between July and October according to weather conditions. It is generally seen as a medium- to large-sized shrub of upright habit, occasionally a small tree. E Asia. It is not known when this species was introduced into cultivation but it existed in England in the late 16th century. **'Aphrodite'** A triploid selection from the US National Arboretum, Washington, the very large, deep pink flowers, to 13cm across, have a prominent red centre. C 1986. **'Ardens'** Pale rosy-purple flowers with maroon blotches at the base, double, large. Erect, compact habit, spreading later. 'Caeruleus Plenus' is a similar clone. C 1873. **'Blue Bird'** See 'Oiseau Bleu'. **'Bredon Springs'** Vigorous, the very large, pale purple flowers crimson-purple in the centre. C 1989. ♀ 2002. **'Cicola'** Semi-double, white flowers with feathered, deep red blotches in the centre. ♀ 2002. **'Coelestis'** Light violet-blue flowers with a reddish base, single. C 1887. AM 1897. **'Diana'** Pure white, single, large flowers with crimped petals, occasionally with a few small petaloids in the centre. The best white, a triploid selection raised at the US National Arboretum,

Washington in 1963. **'Dorothy Crane'** Large, white flowers with feathered, red centres. Raised by Notcutts before 1935. **'Duc de Brabant'** Deep rose-purple, double flowers. C 1872. **'Elegantissimus'** See 'Lady Stanley'. **'Freedom'** Semi-double, rose-pink, anemone-like flowers. **'Hamabo'** Pale blush flowers with a crimson eye, single, large. One of the best of the cultivars. Not to be confused with *H. hamabo* Siebold & Zucc., a tender species with yellow, red-centred flowers. C 1935. ♀ 2002. **'Helene'** Very large, often semi-double flowers, 9cm across, white, flushed pink when opening, the outer petals streaked with deep pink with attractively feathered, deep maroon blotches at the base, and white petaloid stamens in the centre. A sister seedling of 'Diana'. **'Hinomaru'** Pink flowers with deep cerise, anemone centres. **'Jeanne d'Arc'** White, semi-double flowers. C 1894. **'Lady Stanley'** ('Elegantissimus') White flowers shaded blush-pink with a maroon base, almost double. C 1861. **Lavender Chiffon** ('Notwoodone') PBR Large, semi-double, lilac-purple flowers, to 12cm across, have a radiating red centre with some small petals in it. C 1997. **'Lenny'** Large, pink-mauve flowers with a crimson centre, opening early. ♀ 2002. **'Marina'** Similar to 'Oiseau Bleu' but of better constitution, flowers violet-blue, up to 9cm across, with a strongly radiating red centre. C 1995. **'Meehanii'** Single, lilac-mauve flowers with a maroon eye; leaves with an irregular creamy-white margin. C 1867. ♀ 2002. **'Minerva'** A triploid selection from the US National Arboretum, Washington, with profusions of large, pale lavender-pink flowers, to 13cm across, with a large, red centre and slightly wrinkled petals. The parentage involves 'Oiseau Bleu'. C 1986. **'Monstrosus'** Single, white flowers with maroon centres. C 1873. **'Monstrosus Plenus'** Similar in colour to 'Monstrosus' but double. **'Oiseau Bleu'** ('Blue Bird') Violet-blue flowers with a darker eye, single. The best single blue, an improvement on 'Coelestis'. C 1958. ♀ 2002. AM 1965. **Pink Giant** ('Flogi') Clear pink flowers with a deep red eye. A cross of 'Red Heart' with 'Woodbridge'. It differs from the latter in the larger flowers, the basal blotches with a dark band near the apex and distinctly feathered. C 1956. **'Puniceus Plenus'** See under 'Violet Clair Double'. **'Red Heart'** Large, white flowers with a conspicuous, red eye. C1973. ♀ 2002. **Rosalbane** ('Minrosa') Large, pink flowers with purple-red centres and veins. Leaves deeply cut and wavy-edged. Raised by Claude Bellion of Minier Nurseries, France. **'Roseus Plenus'** See under 'Violet Clair Double'. **'Russian Violet'** Large, lilac-pink flowers with deep red centres. Raised by crossing 'Blue Bird' with 'Red Heart'. C 1970. **'Sanchonyo'** Double, deep purple-red flowers with anemone-like centres. **'Shintaeyang'** Vigorous, the white to very pale pink flowers have deep red centres and veins. **'Snowdrift'** White, single, large flowers appearing early. C 1909. AM 1911. 'Totus Albus' is scarcely different. **'Totus Albus'** See under 'Snowdrift'. **'Violet Clair Double'** ('Violaceus Plenus') Wine-purple, double flowers deep reddish-purple at the base within. 'Puniceus Plenus' and 'Roseus Plenus' are scarcely different. C 1921. **White Chiffon** ('Notwoodtwo') PBR Large, semi-double, pure white flowers, up to 11cm across. C 1997. ♀ 2002. **'William R. Smith'** Pure white,

single, large flowers. C 1916. ♀ 2002. **'Woodbridge'** Rich rose-pink, single, large flowers with carmine centres; basal blotches concolorous, not feathered. An improvement on 'Rubis'. C 1928. ♀ 2002. AM 1937.

Hickory See *Carya*.
Hickory, big shellbark See *Carya laciniosa*.
Hickory, bugbud See *Carya tomentosa*.
Hickory, shagbark or shellbark See *Carya ovata*.

HIPPOCREPIS L.—**Leguminosae**—A genus of about 20 species of perennial herbs and shrubs, natives of Europe and W Asia. They have pinnate leaves and yellow pea-flowers followed by slender pods divided into curved segments. The following prefers a well-drained soil in a sunny position.

emerus (L.) Lassen (*Coronilla emerus* L.) Scorpion senna. An elegant, hardy, medium-sized shrub with clusters of flowers in the leaf axils; slender and articulated seedpods, like a scorpion's tail. C and S Europe. Long cultivated. **subsp.** *emeroides* (Boiss. & Spruner) Greuter & Burdet ex Lassen (*Coronilla emerus* subsp. *emeroides* (Boiss. & Spruner) Hayek) A small shrub with leaves having 7 instead of 9 leaflets and flowerheads more crowded and longer-stalked. C and SW Europe.

HIPPOPHAE L.—**Elaeagnaceae**—A genus of 3 species of hardy shrubs or small trees with slender, willow-like leaves that are silvery or sage-green. Natives of Eurasia. Attractive, orange berries are produced on female plants. Excellent wind resisters for maritime exposure.

rhamnoides L. Sea buckthorn. A tall shrub, sometimes a small tree, succeeding in almost any soil. Attractive in summer with its narrow, silvery leaves, and in winter, with its orange-yellow berries, which contain an intensely acrid, yellow juice and which are normally avoided by birds, although pheasants are said to eat them. Plant in groups of both sexes to obtain fruits. Europe (incl. British Isles), temperate Asia. In recent years several selections have been made in E Germany and Russia for the high vitamin C content of the fruits. ♀ 2002. AM 1944. **'Leikora'** A female form with large and very profuse, late-ripening fruits high in vitamin C. **'Pollmix'** A male form selected as a pollinator.

salicifolia D. Don. A rare species making a small to medium-sized tree, and differing from *H. rhamnoides* in its taller habit, pendent branches, which are less spiny, and its sage-green leaves. Himalaya. I 1822.

HOHERIA A. Cunn.—**Malvaceae**—A genus of beautiful, floriferous, mid- to late summer-flowering shrubs or small trees belonging to the mallow family. Five species native to New Zealand. All have white flowers. The evergreen species need a specially selected site or wall protection, except in mild districts. The leaves of juvenile plants are often deeply toothed and lobed and are smaller than those of adult plants.

*angustifolia Raoul. This is an elegant, small tree of columnar habit with roundish to narrowly lanceolate leaves, that are up to 5cm long. Juvenile plants are dense and bushy with slender, interlacing branches and

minute, obovate, shallowly-toothed leaves. Masses of small, white flowers, 1.25cm across, cover the plant in July. AM 1967.

glabrata Sprague & Summerh. Mountain ribbonwood. A magnificent large shrub or small tree, possibly a little hardier than *H. lyallii*. In June and July its flexible branches are bent with the weight of masses of fragrant, almost translucent, white flowers. C 1871. FCC 1946. AM 1911.

'Glory of Amlwch' (*H. glabrata × H. sexstylosa*) A large shrub or small tree, retaining its foliage during mild winters. Flowers of pure white, 3.5cm across, are densely crowded on the stems. Originated in the garden of Dr Jones, Amlwch, Anglesey. ♀ 2002. AM 1960.

lyallii Hook. f. Mountain ribbonwood. A beautiful but variable, large shrub or small tree. The more or less glabrous juvenile leaves change to grey-tomentose adult foliage. Clusters of cherry-like, white flowers crowd the branches in July, normally later than *H. glabrata*. ♀ 2002. FCC 1964. AM 1955.

†*populnea* A. Cunn. Lacebark. Beautiful, large shrub or small tree with broadly ovate leaves. it blooms in late summer or autumn and the flowers, about 2cm across, are in dense clusters. AM 1912. **'Alba Variegata'** Leaves with a broad, creamy-white margin, often pink-tinged when young. A sport of 'Variegata' raised in New Zealand. AM 1976. **'Foliis Purpureis'** Leaves plum-purple on the lower surface. AM 1977. **var.** *lanceolata* See *H. sexstylosa*. **'Osbornei'** Flowers with blue stamens; leaves purple-tinged beneath. Named after the Osborne family on whose property on Great Barrier Island it was found in about 1910. **'Variegata'** Leaves yellow-green, edged deep green. C 1926.

†*sexstylosa* Colenso (*H. populnea* var. *lanceolata* Hook. f.) Lacebark. This splendid floriferous, tall, vigorous shrub or small tree differs from *H. populnea* in its greater hardiness, more upright growth and narrower adult leaves. Those of young trees are extremely variable. FCC 1924 (under the synonym). AM 1964. **'Crataegifolia'** The juvenile form with small, coarsely-toothed leaves, maintained as a bush by vegetative propagation. **'Stardust'** A very floriferous form with a compact, upright habit and glossy leaves. ♀ 2002.

Holly See *Ilex*.

HOLODISCUS (K. Koch) Maxim.—**Rosaceae**—A small genus of about 8 species of hardy spiraea-like shrubs natives of regions from W North America to Colombia.

discolor (Pursh) Maxim. (*Spiraea discolor* Pursh) Ocean spray. A handsome and elegant shrub, to 3.5m high, with most conspicuous, long, drooping, feathery panicles of creamy-white flowers in July. Leaves are greyish-white-tomentose beneath. W North America. I 1927 by David Douglas. AM 1978.

Honey locust See *Gleditsia triacanthos*.
Honeysuckle See *Lonicera*.
Hop hornbeam See *Ostrya carpinifolia*.
Hop tree See *Ptelea trifoliata*.
Hornbeam See *Carpinus*.
Horse chestnut See *Aesculus hippocastanum*.

HOVENIA Thunb.—**Rhamnaceae**—A small genus of 2 species of trees and shrubs, natives of E Asia.

dulcis Thunb. Japanese raisin tree. A small to medium-sized tree grown for its handsome, polished foliage. The fleshy, reddish branches of the inflorescences are edible. China, Himalaya. Cultivated in Japan and India. I 1912.

Huckleberry See *Gaylussacia*.
Huckleberry, California See *Vaccinium ovatum*.
Huckleberry, hairy See *Vaccinium hirsutum*.
Huckleberry, red See *Vaccinium parvifolium*.
Huckleberry, squaw See *Vaccinium stamineum*.
Huckleberry, thin-leaf See *Vaccinium membranaceum*.

HYDRANGEA L.—**Hydrangeaceae**—About 23 species of shrubs, small trees and climbers, natives of E Asia and North and South America. The cultivated members of this genus are easily grown, but all require generous treatment and resent dryness at the roots. For the larger-leaved species some shade is essential. Summer and autumn is the flowering period unless otherwise stated.

Most species and their forms produce flowers in a flattened or dome-shaped terminal head. These heads are composed of flowers of two kinds. The majority are fertile and, though coloured, are rather small and often insignificant. The second type are sterile but possess rather large, conspicuous, coloured sepals. These sterile flowers, or ray-florets, occur on the outside of the flowerhead and in some instances completely surround the fertile flowers, hence the popular name 'lacecap'. Some hydrangeas, in particular the Hortensia Group of *H. macrophylla*, have flowerheads composed entirely of ray-florets.

acuminata See under *H. serrata* 'Bluebird'.

arborescens L. A small shrub of loose, bushy growth, with ovate, slender-pointed, serrated leaves, usually glabrous. Flowers are in corymbs, up to 15cm across, bearing several long-stalked, creamy-white ray-florets. They are borne in succession from July to September. E USA. I 1736. **'Annabelle'** A spectacular form with huge, rounded heads of white ray-florets, up to 30cm across. ♀ 2002. AM 1978. A plant received under the name of 'Bounty' appears identical. **'Bounty'** See under 'Annabelle'. **subsp.** *discolor* (Ser.) E.M. McClint. (*H. cinerea* Small) Leaves grey-tomentose beneath; flowers with a few white ray-florets. I 1908. **'Grandiflora'** The commonly cultivated form with large, globular heads of creamy-white ray-florets. I 1907. ♀ 2002. AM 1907. **subsp.** *radiata* (Walter) E.M. McClint. (*H. radiata* Walter) (*H. nivea* Michx.) An erect shrub, up to 1.8m, remarkable for the snow-white under-surfaces of the leaves. Creamy-white, sweetly scented flowers are produced in broad corymbs in July. Carolina, USA. I 1786. **'Sterilis'** A form of subsp. *discolor* with globular heads of creamy-white ray-florets. Originated before 1908.

aspera D. Don. A magnificent but variable, large-leaved species of medium size, in June and July covered with large heads of pale porcelain-blue flowers with a ring of lilac-pink or white ray-florets. Himalaya, W and C China, Taiwan. **Kawakamii Group** (*H. kawakamii* Hayata) A medium-sized shrub, flowering very late. The deep violet flowerheads with their white sterile flowers open late during autumn. **'Macrophylla'** A form with very large leaves and flowerheads. ♀ 2002. **'Mauvette'** Hemispherical flowerheads to 15cm across. Fertile and sterile flowers mauve, turning to grey-pink. **'Peter Chappell'** A striking selection with broad heads of white fertile and sterile flowers. **subsp. *sargentiana*** (Rehder) E.M. McClint. (*H. sargentiana* Rehder) A noble medium-sized shrub with shoots thickly clothed with a curious moss-like covering of hairs and bristles and very large, velvety leaves. In July and August bears large, bluish inflorescences with white ray-florets. Suitable for a sheltered shrub border or woodland. Winter hardy, but requires shade and wind protection. China. I 1908 by Ernest Wilson. ♀ 2002. AM 1912. **subsp. *strigosa*** (Rehder) E.M. McClint. (*H. strigosa* Rehder) A striking and rare, slow-growing, medium-sized shrub. The lilac and white flowers appear in the autumn after all the other hydrangeas are over. Lance-shaped leaves are conspicuously adpressed hairy, as are the shoots. Subject to damage by late spring frosts. C China. I 1907 by Ernest Wilson. **'Taiwan'** Flowerheads to 20cm across in autumn, the pink, sharply toothed sterile florets to 2cm or more across. Fertile flowers pale purplish-pink with blue stamens. Raised by Maurice Mason from Taiwan seed. AM 1998. **'Velvet and Lace'** We propose this name for a very beautiful selection, long grown by us as *H. villosa*. Flowers in domed heads to 22cm across; fertile flowers purple-blue, sterile flowers nodding, with 4-5 pale mauve-pink, serrated sepals. Leaves lanceolate, acuminate, to 21cm long. **Villosa Group** (*H. villosa* Rehder) Close to the typical form but differing in its less coarse habit and smaller leaves and flowerheads. This is one of the loveliest of late summer-flowering hydrangeas. A medium-sized shrub of spreading habit, with stems, leaf and flower stalks densely villous. The large inflorescences are lilac-blue with prettily toothed, marginal sepals. Requires half shade. W China. I 1908. See also 'Velvet and Lace'. ♀ 2002. AM 1950.

'Ayesha' See *H. macrophylla* 'Ayesha'.

'Blue Deckle' (*H. serrata* 'Blue Deckle') Compact and slow-growing, lacecap type, with clear blue to pink, toothed ray-florets. Raised by Michael Haworth-Booth before 1970.

bretschneideri See *H. heteromalla* 'Bretschneideri'.

chinensis See *H. scandens* subsp. *chinensis*.

cinerea See *H. arborescens* subsp. *discolor*.

  'Sterilis' See *H. arborescens* 'Sterilis'.

dumicola See *H. heteromalla*.

heteromalla D. Don (*H. dumicola* W.W. Sm.) (*H. xanthoneura* Diels) A very variable, medium-sized to large shrub or small tree. The leaves are dark green above and whitish beneath. White flowers in broad corymbs, with conspicuous, marginal ray-florets. Himalaya, N and W China. I 1821. AM 1978. **'Bretschneideri'** (*H. bretschneideri* Dippel) A medium-sized July-blooming shrub with broad, flattened white lacecap flowerheads and chestnut-brown, exfoliating bark. Hardy in full exposure. I about 1882 from China. **'Jermyns Lace'** A vigorous, large shrub with broad, lacecap flowerheads, the white ray-florets turning pink. Named from a plant in the Sir Harold Hillier Gardens and Arboretum originally grown as *H. heteromalla* var. *xanthoneura*. **'Snowcap'** A superb shrub of stately habit with large, heart-shaped leaves and white flowers in large, flattened corymbs, 20–25cm across. This is a hardy shrub, tolerant of wind, sun and drought. For many years it was grown by us under the name *H. robusta*, which is now regarded as a subspecies of *H. aspera*. Collected in the Himalaya, our plant is sufficiently distinct and ornamental to deserve the above name. Flowers slightly later than 'Jermyns Lace' and the outer florets remain creamy-white. **'Yalung Ridge'** Young foliage crimson, flowerheads large, to 18cm across, pale pink at first fading to white. I by Tony Schilling from Nepal.

hirta (Thunb.) Siebold. A small, much-branched shrub with dark stems and ovate, deeply-toothed leaves. Dense, compact corymbs of blue-purple fertile flowers; ray-florets absent. Japan.

involucrata Siebold. A pretty dwarf species with blue or rosy-lilac flowers, surrounded by white or variously tinted ray-florets. Japan, Taiwan. C 1864. **'Hortensis'** A remarkable and attractive form with double, creamy-white ray-florets, which become rose-tinted in the open. ♀ 2002. AM 1956.

kawakamii See *H. aspera* Kawakamii Group.

longipes Franch. A medium-sized, spreading shrub of loose habit, remarkable in the genus for the length of the leaf stalks. White flowers with ray-florets as much as 4cm across. W China. I 1901.

macrophylla (Thunb.) Ser. This name covers a large and varied group of hydrangeas, many of which are possibly of hybrid origin, and may be divided into two groups, namely the Hortensias and the Lacecaps (see below). **var. *acuminata*** See under *H. serrata* 'Bluebird'. **var. *normalis*** E.H. Wilson (*H. maritima* Howarth-Booth) A small to medium-sized shrub producing flat corymbs of fertile flowers with a few, pink ray-florets. The wild form, a native of the coastal regions of C Japan, first introduced by Ernest Wilson in 1917. See also 'Seafoam' under Lacecaps below. **subsp. *serrata*** See *H. serrata*.

Hortensia Group

The familiar mop-headed hydrangeas. Their average height in most gardens ranges from 1.2–1.8m, but in sheltered gardens and woodlands in mild localities some cultivars will reach as much as 3.5m. They are admirable for seaside planting and many are seen at their best in coastal gardens. The florets are sterile, forming large, globular heads of white, pink, red, blue, or a combination of these colours, in some cultivars producing a wonderful almost metallic lustre. These are marvellous everlasting flowers for the floral artist.

In very shallow chalk soils *H. macrophylla* and its forms may become chlorotic; this can be counteracted by generous mulching and feeding. In alkaline soils treatment is needed if the blue flower shades are desired; Bluing Powder should be applied every seven or fourteen days during the growing season at the rate of 85g (3oz) dissolved in 13.5 litres (3 gallons) of water.

Immediately after flowering, thin out and cut back (except in cold areas) old flowering shoots to within a few centimetres of the old wood.

  'Alpenglühen' Large heads of crimson florets. C 1950.

  'Altona' Rose-coloured, large florets; blues well. Best in shade. C 1931. ♀ 2002. AM 1957.

Hortensia Group continued:

'Ami Pasquier' Deep red. Dwarf habit. C 1930. ♛ 2002. AM 1953.

'Ayesha' (*H.* 'Ayesha', 'Silver Slipper') A distinct and unusual hydrangea of puzzling origin and very different from the usual mop-headed hydrangea. The leaves are bold and glossy green above. The rather flattened dense heads are composed of thick-petalled, cup-shaped florets, resembling those of a large lilac. They possess a faint but distinct fragrance and are greyish-lilac or pink. AM 1974.

'Baardse's Favourite' Rich pink or deep purple-blue. Dwarf. C 1920.

'Benelux' A small shrub with profuse, large heads of rich blue or light red flowers, paler in the centre. C 1950.

'Blauer Prinz' ('Blue Prince') Rose-red or cornflower-blue.

'Bodensee' Pink; blues well.

'Bouquet Rose' Dense heads of closely packed, violet-blue to pink sterile flowers. Raised by Lemoine. C 1907.

'Deutschland' Deep pink; attractive autumn tints. AM 1927.

'Domotoi' Loose, irregular heads of large, double, pale pink or blue florets. An old Japanese cultivar.

'Enziandom' ('Gentian Dome') Large hemispherical heads of deep gentian-blue sterile flowers. C 1950.

'Europa' Deep pink; large florets. ♛ 2002.

'Frillibet' A sport of 'Madame Emile Mouillère', selected by Michael Haworth-Booth in about 1950. Dense heads with pale blue flowers, cream when young, with toothed sepals.

'Garten-Baudirektor Kuhnert' Rose-coloured or vivid blue.

'Générale Vicomtesse de Vibraye' Vivid rose or a good blue. C 1909. ♛ 2002. AM 1947.

'Gentian Dome' See 'Enziandom'.

'Gertrud Glahn' Deep pink to purple.

'Goliath' Deep pink or purplish-blue; very large florets in small heads. A fine cultivar for a seaside garden.

'Hamburg' Deep rose or purplish; large florets. C 1931.

'Heinrich Seidel' Glowing red to purple, large, fringed florets. Best in semi-shade.

'Holstein' Pink or sky-blue; free-flowering, very large florets with serrated sepals. C 1928.

Japanese Lady Group These forms, distinguished by their distinctive, white-edged sepals, are the result of a breeding programme in Japan by Hiroshi Ebihara. The forms released are 'Frau Katsuko' (Lady Katsuko) (red), 'Lady Fujiyo' (peach-pink), 'Lady Taiko Blue' (blue), 'Lady Taiko Pink' (pink), 'Lady Mariko (lilac-blue) and 'Lady Nobuko' (purple).

'Joseph Banks' A medium-sized, vigorous shrub of particular value for coastal planting. Very large heads are cream at first, passing to pale pink or pale hyacinth-blue. Said to be a branch sport of the wild Japanese type. I via China in 1789.

'King George' Rose-pink; large florets with serrated sepals. AM 1927.

'Kluis Superba' ('Maréchal Foch' × 'La Marne') Vigorous shrub with profuse, large heads of deep pink to purple-blue flowers. C 1932.

'La France' Phlox-pink to mid-blue in huge heads.

'La Marne' Pale pink or blue in enormous heads; sepals prettily feathered. Excellent by the sea. C 1917.

'Loreley' Carmine to deep blue, free-flowering.

'Madame A. Riverain' A vigorous shrub with dense heads of vivid pink. Upright sepals give the individual flowers a cupped appearance. C 1909.

'Madame Emile Mouillère' Large florets with serrated sepals, white with pink or blue eyes. Perhaps the best white cultivar and certainly one of the most popular. ♛ 2002. AM 1910.

'Mandshurica' See 'Nigra'.

'Maréchal Foch' Rich rosy-pink or purple to vivid deep gentian-blue. Very free flowering. AM 1923.

'Masja' Compact habit with red flowers. A sport of 'Alpenglühen'. C 1977.

'Mathilda Gutges' Broad heads of deep pink to violet or blue. AM 1996.

'Miss Belgium' Rosy-red. Dwarf.

'Münster' Florets violet, crimson or deep blue turning to bright autumn tints of red and scarlet. Dwarf.

'Niedersachsen' Pale pink or good blue. AM 1968.

'Nigra' ('Mandshurica') A distinct cultivar with black or nearly black stems. Florets rose or occasionally blue. C 1870. ♛ 2002. FCC 1895.

'Nikko Blue' Vigorous and reliable with profuse heads of lavender-blue flowers.

'Parzival' Rose-madder to crimson-pink or purple to deep blue flowers. Best in light shade. ♛ 2002. AM 1922.

'Pia' A slow-growing dwarf with long-lasting heads of purplish-red florets on any soil.

'Queen Elizabeth' A lovely shade of rose-pink; lends itself readily to bluing.

'Queen Emma' Large crimson heads.

'Silver Slipper' See 'Ayesha'.

'Sœur Thérèse' Rather flattened heads of large, white florets. Best in partial shade. C 1947.

'Souvenir de Madame E. Chautard' Clear pale pink, mauve or blue. Dwarf, early flowering.

'Souvenir de Président Paul Doumer' Dark velvety-red, purple to dark blue. Dwarf.

'Strafford' Light red.

'Westfalen' Vivid crimson or violet. ♛ 2002. AM 1958.

Lacecap Group

A smaller group than the Hortensias, but similar in growth and requirements. Produces large, flattened corymbs of fertile flowers around which are borne a ring of coloured ray-florets.

'Blauling' (Teller Group) Pale mauve-blue sterile flowers with 3–4 lobes notched at the tip. Fertile flowers blue.

'Blaumeise' (Teller Group) A vigorous, broad shrub with rather flattened heads of up to 15 large, lilac-blue florets. Also sold as Teller Blue and Teller Pink. C 1979.

'Blue Wave' See 'Mariesii Perfecta'.

'Fasan' (Teller Group) Profusely borne bright red sterile flowers in a double row. Fertile flowers deep crimson. C 1979.

'Geoffrey Chadbund' See 'Möwe'.

'Kardinal' (Teller Group) Large, deep red sterile flowers; fertile flowers pink to mauve. Dense, upright habit with healthy dark green foliage.

Lacecap Group continued:

'**Lanarth White**' A superb, compact shrub with large, flattened heads of bright blue or pink fertile flowers surrounded by a ring of white ray-florets. ♀ 2002. AM 1949.

'**Libelle**' (Teller Group) This is a very fine selection with large, pure white ray-florets and blue fertile flowers. C 1964.

'**Lilacina**' Broad heads of mauve-pink to blue. ♀ 2002.

'**Maculata**' ('Variegata') A medium-sized, erect shrub grown for its attractive leaves which have a broad creamy-white margin. Flowerheads have a few small, white ray-florets.

'**Mariesii**' Wide, flat corymbs of rosy-pink or very rich blue flowers with very large ray-florets. I 1879 by Charles Maries from Japan. FCC 1881.

'**Mariesii Alba**' See 'White Wave'.

'**Mariesii Perfecta**' ('Blue Wave') A strong-growing shrub of medium size producing beautifully shaped heads of blue fertile flowers surrounded by numerous, large ray-florets, varying in colour from pink to blue. In suitable soils, the colour is a lovely gentian-blue. Best in semi-shade. Raised by Messrs Lemoine from seed of 'Mariesii' about 1900. ♀ 2002. FCC 1965. AM 1956.

'**Möwe**' ('Geoffrey Chadbund') (Teller Group) Flowers brick-red on alkaline or neutral soils. ♀ 2002.

'**Quadricolor**' Leaves variegated dark green, pale green, cream and deep yellow. More striking than 'Tricolor'. Flowers pale pink.

'**Rotdrossel**' (Teller Group) Large, crimson, toothed sterile flowers, in several rows; fertile flowers mauve with white stamens. Dark green, slightly glossy leaves. One of the hardiest of the group.

'**Rotschwanz**' (Teller Group) Large, deep red, cross-shaped sterile flowers; fertile flowers pink and white. The dark green foliage turns deep wine-red in autumn. C 1987.

'**Sea Foam**' (*H. maritima* 'Seafoam') A small to medium-sized shrub with blue fertile flowers surrounded by white ray-florets. A handsome shrub succeeding best in seaside and sheltered gardens. Said to be a clone of the wild coastal hydrangea *H. macrophylla* var. *normalis* and to have arisen as a reversion on the Hortensia 'Joseph Banks' (see above).

'**Taube**' (Teller Group) Large heads with large, pink sterile flowers and pink fertile flowers.

Teller Group A group of lacecaps raised at Waedenswil in Switzerland in 1952, initially to provide plants for the pot plant trade, but now increasingly grown in the open ground. A total of 26 were named, mainly after birds in German, which may also appear as their English or Dutch translations. Plants grown as Teller Blue or Teller Pink are usually 'Blaumeise', as Teller Red 'Rotdrossel', as Teller White 'Libelle'.

'**Tokyo Delight**' A Japanese selection making a small slender-stemmed shrub. Tiered flowerheads open white with a pink eye, turning to pink and finally deep crimson-purple. ♀ 2002. AM 1998.

'**Tricolor**' A choice, strong-growing cultivar with leaves most attractively variegated green, grey and pale yellow. Large, freely produced flowers are pale pink to white. Said to be a branch sport of 'Mariesii'. C 1860. FCC 1882.

'**Veitchii**' A medium-sized shrub, with rich dark green leaves, growing best in semi-shade. Flowers in flattened corymbs, the ray-florets white ageing to pink. Very hardy and very lime-tolerant. I from Japan about 1880. ♀ 2002. AM 1974.

'**White Wave**' ('Mariesii Alba', 'Mariesii Grandiflora') A small shrub that originated in about 1902 in the nursery of Messrs Lemoine of Nancy, France, as a seedling of 'Mariesii'. It is a strong-growing clone with flattened heads of bluish or pinkish, fertile flowers margined by large, beautifully formed, pearly-white ray-florets. Free-flowering in an open position. ♀ 2002. AM 1948.

maritima See *H. macrophylla* var. *normalis*.

'**Seafoam**' See under Lacecaps.

paniculata Siebold. A medium-sized to large shrub with both fertile flowers and large, creamy-white ray-florets in dense terminal panicles in late summer and autumn. For large panicles, the laterals should be cut back to within 5–7.5cm of the previous year's growth in early spring (except for 'Praecox'). Japan. China, Taiwan. I 1861. AM 1964. '**Brussels Lace**' Profuse lace-like heads of creamy fertile flowers with white sterile flowers that become spotted with pink. A seedling of 'Unique' selected by Robert and Jelena de Belder in 1975. '**Burgundy Lace**' A vigorous shrub with large, conical inflorescences. The large sterile flowers are pale pink turning deeper pink and mauve. A seedling of 'Unique' selected by Robert and Jelena de Belder. '**Everest**' A splendid form with handsome, dark green foliage and large, very dense heads of ray-florets, white at first turning to pink. AM 1990. '**Floribunda**' Long, narrow panicles with numerous ray-florets from late July. C 1867. AM 1953. '**Grandiflora**' One of the showiest of hardy, large shrubs. In summer and autumn bears massive panicles of numerous, small, white ray-florets becoming deep pink. Excellent winter decoration when cut. I by P.F. von Siebold from Japan about 1867. ♀ 2002. FCC 1869. '**Greenspire**' Similar to 'Kyushu' but with green ray-florets becoming tinged with pink. A seedling of 'Unique' selected by Robert and Jelena de Belder in 1975. '**Kyushu**' Upright habit with dark glossy green, taper-pointed leaves and panicles liberally sprinkled with ray-florets. Introduced by Collingwood Ingram from Kyushu, Japan. AM 1964. ♀ 2002. '**Pee Wee**' Similar to 'Grandiflora' but with smaller flowerheads. Makes a large shrub. **Pink Diamond** ('Interhydia') Large heads of ray-florets similar to but larger than 'Unique' of which it is a seedling, white becoming pink. ♀ 2002. AM 1990. '**Praecox**' A form with smaller panicles of toothed ray-florets. The earliest form, it generally flowers in early July; hardy in the coldest areas of Europe. Hard pruning early in the year will prevent flowering. Raised at the Arnold Arboretum, Boston, USA, from Japanese seed collected by Sargent in 1893. FCC 1973. AM 1956. '**Tardiva**' Late flowering, from late August or September, producing large heads with numerous ray-florets. AM 1966. '**Unique**' Similar to 'Grandiflora' but with even larger flowerheads. A seedling of 'Floribunda', selected in 1968 by Robert and Jelena de Belder. ♀ 2002. AM 1990. '**White Moth**' A seedling of 'Unique' by Robert and Jelena de Belder. Rounded heads, with many fertile flowers, are borne over a long period; sterile flowers white, turning green in autumn.

'Preziosa' (*H. serrata* 'Preziosa') A handsome shrub with purplish-red stems, up to 1.5m high. Leaves purple-tinged when young. Bears attractive globular heads of large, rose-pink ray-florets, deepening to reddish-purple in autumn. A hybrid between *H. macrophylla* and *H. serrata*. Garden origin. ♥ 2002. FCC 1964. AM 1963.

quercifolia Bartram. Oak-leaved hydrangea. The value of this medium-sized shrub lies in the magnificent autumnal tints of its large, strongly lobed leaves. Conical heads of large, white ray-florets are borne in late summer. SE USA. I 1803. ♥ 2002. AM 1928. **'Harmony'** Large, dense clusters of all sterile, creamy-white flowers, each 2cm across, weigh down the arching branches. Found in the wild in Alabama before 1988. **'Pee Wee'** A compact and low-growing, spreading selection, wider than tall, the broadly conical flowerheads with mainly sterile flowers. Good autumn colour. **'Sikes Dwarf'** A compact, dwarf form, making a small shrub, wider than tall. **'Snow Flake'** A striking form in which several series of bracts are produced on each flower creating a doubled appearance. **Snow Queen** ('Flemygea') A medium-sized shrub bearing upright panicles of large, white ray-florets that turn pink. The dark green leaves are bronze-red in autumn.

radiata See *H. arborescens* subsp. *radiata*.

robusta hort. See under *H. heteromalla* 'Snowcap'.

sargentiana See *H. aspera* subsp. *sargentiana*.

scandens (L. f.) Ser. A small shrub related to *H. hirta* with which it has been confused but differing in the flowerheads bearing both fertile and sterile flowers. In a cultivated form the leaves are flushed with blue in summer. S Japan. **subsp. *chinensis*** (Maxim.) E.M. McClint. (*H. chinensis* Maxim.) A rare, small shrub with oval or lanceolate-oblong, denticulate leaves. Flowers are produced in corymbs composed of bluish fertile flowers and a few slender-stalked, white ray-florets. Requires a sheltered position. SE China, Taiwan. C 1934.

serrata (Thunb.) Ser. (*H. macrophylla* subsp. *serrata* (Thunb.) Makino) A charming, dwarf shrub rarely exceeding 1m. Flattened corymbs of blue or white flowers are surrounded by a pretty circle of white, pink, or bluish ray-florets, often deepening to crimson in autumn. A variable species. Japan, Korea. I 1843. **f. *acuminata*** See under 'Bluebird'. **'Amagi-amacha'** An unusual form with slender, taper-pointed leaves and lacecap heads, the sterile flowers with small, white, oval sepals. Found by Makino in Japan about 1925. **'Beni-gaku'** Lacecap heads with white sterile flowers which age to red. Long cultivated but now uncommon; an old Japanese selection possibly intorduced by Siebold. **'Bluebird'** (*H. acuminata* 'Bluebird') A small, robust shrub with stout shoots and abruptly acuminate leaves. The blue fertile flowers are borne in slightly dome-shaped corymbs surrounded by large ray-florets, reddish-purple on chalk soils and a lovely sea-blue on acid soils. Reputedly a selected form of *H. serrata* f. *acuminata*, but in our experience the two are identical. Plants seen under either name would suggest by their robust nature a hybrid origin with *H. macrophylla* as one parent. ♥ 2002. AM 1960. **'Blue Deckle'** See *H.* 'Blue Deckle'.

'Chinensis' A charming, dwarf shrub of dense habit, with rather wiry branches and short-stalked, downy leaves. Flowers in flattened corymbs; ray-florets lilac-blue on chalk soils, powder-blue on acid soils. The origin and botanical status of this shrub is something of a conundrum. It has every appearance of being a wild species although it does not fit any available description. It is sometimes found in cultivation under the name *H. chinensis acuminata*, but bears no resemblance to the plants generally grown in gardens as *H. serrata acuminata*. Our stock plant only attained 30cm by 60cm after many years. See also 'Koreana'. **'Diadem'** A very hardy, compact shrub with vivid blue or pink flowers. Leaves reddening in full sun. ♥ 2002. AM 1963. **'Golden Sunlight'** Bronze young leaves turn clear yellow then green. Flowers in flattened heads with red ray-florets. A sport of 'Bluebird' found in Holland about 1990. **'Grayswood'** An attractive, small shrub with flattened corymbs of blue fertile flowers surrounded by a ring of ray-florets, white at first, changing to rose and finally deep crimson. ♥ 2002. AM 1948. **'Intermedia'** Small shrub with flat corymbs of pinkish fertile flowers surrounded by a ring of ray-florets which are white at first turning to shades of crimson. **'Kiyosumi'** Sterile flowers are white with deep red edges; fertile flowers pinkish-white. Young foliage purple. Originally found on Mt Kiyosumi in Japan in about 1950. **'Koreana'** A delightful dwarf shrub with slender branches and slender, acuminate, almost sessile leaves. Ray-florets are lilac on chalk soils, sky-blue on acid soils. Similar in habit to 'Chinensis' but even smaller with longer, smoother, thicker-textured leaves. Our stock plant only attained 30cm by 30cm after many years. Origin unknown, possibly Korea. **'Maiko'** Loose, spherical heads of mauve sterile flowers with some fertile flowers visible. **'Miranda'** Dwarf habit with deep blue flowers. ♥ 2002. **'Preziosa'** See *H.* 'Preziosa'. **'Rosalba'** A small shrub distinguished by its larger leaves and ray-florets that are white at first, quickly turning crimson. ♥ 2002. AM 1939. **'Tiara'** Intermediate between a mophead and a lacecap with profuse sterile flowers opening blue over a long period and turning mauve-pink. Foliage crimson in full sun turning bright crimson in autumn. C 1990. ♥ 2002. AM 1996.

sikokiana Maxim. A small shrub with smooth shoots and long-stalked roughly hairy leaves, to 20cm long, conspicuously lobed and toothed in the upper half. White flowers, borne in broad, tiered, flattened heads in summer, are edged with a few small, white sterile florets. A rare species in gardens, this has grown at the Sir Harold Hillier Gardens and Arboretum for many years. Japan.

strigosa See *H. aspera* subsp. *strigosa*.

villosa See *H. aspera* Villosa Group.

xanthoneura See *H. heteromalla*.

Hymenanthera See *Melicytus*.

HYPERICUM L.—**Guttiferae**—A genus of about 400 species of herbs, shrubs and trees widely distributed. The shrubby hypericums will thrive in almost any well-drained soil. Very desirable summer- and autumn-blooming shrubs, producing their conspicuous, bright yellow flowers in great abundance, they are happy in full sun or semi-shade. Many of the Asiatic species have been mixed or mis-named in cultivation. The species described below are treated in accordance with research carried out by Dr N. K. B. Robson of the Natural History Museum.

acmosepalum N. Robson (*H. oblongifolium* hort. not Choisy) (*H. kouytchense* hort. not Lév.) A splendid, very hardy, small, semi-evergreen shrub of erect habit, distinguished by its close-set, narrowly oblong leaves, which often turn orange or scarlet in late autumn and winter. Golden-yellow flowers, 5cm across, are freely borne from June to October, followed by bright red capsules. SW China.

addingtonii N. Robson. A splendid, semi-evergreen shrub of upright habit and medium size with short-stalked, ovate-oblong leaves. The large, rich yellow flowers, 6–7.5cm across, are borne singly or in clusters at the ends of the shoots. Originally listed as *H. leschenaultii*. China (NW Yunnan). Possibly introduced by George Forrest.

androsaemum L. Tutsan. A good, shade-bearing shrub, seldom above 75cm high. It is continuous and free-flowering bearing rather small flowers with conspicuous anthers, followed in autumn by erect, red, finally black, berry-like capsules. Susceptible to mildew. W and S Europe (incl. British Isles), N Africa, W Asia. C before 1600. **'Albury Purple'** Leaves purple but subject to mildew. **'Gladys Brabazon'** A poor variegated form, with leaves irregularly blotched with white, which originated in Ireland.

augustinii N. Robson. A rare, small, densely branched shrub with arching branches and sessile, ovate to oblong-lanceolate, leathery leaves, the upper leaves amplexicaul. Golden-yellow flowers, 4–6cm across, are clustered at the ends of the branches during autumn. Named in honour of Augustine Henry who first discovered it. China (S Yunnan).

aureum See *H. frondosum*.

†*balearicum L. A dwarf, erect-branched shrub with very distinctive, winged stems and small, curiously warted leaves. Small, yellow, fragrant flowers are borne from June to September. Balearic Isles. I 1714.

beanii N. Robson (*H. patulum* var. *henryi* Veitch ex Bean) A small shrub related to *H. patulum*. Branches gracefully arching, producing slightly drooping flowers, up to 6cm across. Named in honour of W.J. Bean who first described it. China (Yunnan and Guizhou). AM 1904. **'Gold Cup'** See *H. × cyathiflorum* 'Gold Cup'.

bellum Li (L.S. & E. 15737) An elegant, small, densely branched shrub with broadly ovate to orbicular, wavy-edged leaves and deep yellow, slightly cup-shaped flowers, 3.5cm across, then puckered capsules. A rare species related to *H. forrestii*. W China, E Himalaya. I about 1908. **'Buttercup'** See *H. uralum*.

*calycinum L. Rose of Sharon. A dwarf, evergreen shrub with large leaves and large, golden flowers. Excellent as groundcover in dry and shaded places, but if left unchecked can become a weed. Occasionally naturalised. Suffers badly from rust. SE Bulgaria, N Turkey. I 1676. AM 1978.

chinense See *H. monogynum*.

choisyanum Wall. ex N. Robson (Beer, Lancaster & Morris 147) A small to medium-sized shrub with slender, arching, reddish shoots. Leaves are lanceolate, short-stalked, up to 8cm long and 3cm across, purple-tinged when young. Deep yellow, cup-shaped flowers, about 4cm across, are borne in summer. SW China, Himalaya, NE India. I 1971.

*coris L. A dwarf or prostrate, evergreen shrublet with slender stems and linear leaves, arranged in whorls of 3–6. The golden-yellow flowers, 1.25–2cm across, are borne in terminal panicles up to 12cm long during summer. Ideal for a rock garden, scree or dry wall. C and S Europe. C 1640.

× *cyathiflorum* N. Robson (*H. addingtonii* × *H. hookerianum*) This hybrid only occurs in gardens where it is represented by the following form. **'Gold Cup'** (*H. beanii* 'Gold Cup') A graceful, small shrub with attractive, lanceolate leaves arranged along the arching branches in 2 opposite rows. Flowers are deep yellow, cup-shaped and 6cm across.

densiflorum Pursh. A small, densely branched shrub with linear-oblong leaves and corymbs of small, abundant, deep yellow flowers in July and August. E USA. I 1889.

× *dummeri* N. Robson (*H. forrestii* × *H. calycinum*) The following plant was raised in 1975 by our propagator Peter Dummer at the suggestion of Dr Norman Robson in an attempt to determine the parentage of 'Hidcote'. **'Peter Dummer'** A dwarf, mound-forming shrub, reaching 80cm tall, with arching reddish shoots and ovate leaves, bronze-red when young and somewhat red or purplish-tinged in winter. Large, golden-yellow flowers, with orange anthers, are borne in summer and autumn from deep orange flushed buds, and are followed by red-tinged fruits.

'Eastleigh Gold' A small, semi-evergreen shrub of loose, spreading habit, with drooping, reddish-brown branchlets. Leaves elliptic, slightly leathery, dark shining green above, 4–5cm long. Freely bears slightly cup-shaped, golden-yellow flowers, 6cm across, with comparatively short stamens, from late June to October. Capsules puckered. This plant occurred as a seedling in our nurseries about 1964. It is probably a hybrid but the parentage is uncertain.

elatum See *H. × inodorum* Mill. **'Elstead'** See *H. × inodorum* 'Elstead'.

*empetrifolium Willd. A dwarf, evergreen shrublet with slender stems, small, linear leaves and golden-yellow flowers, 1.25–2cm across, in small, erect panicles during summer. Requires a warm, sunny, well-drained position on a rock garden or scree. Greece. I 1788. AM 1937. **var. oliganthum** Rech. f. A prostrate form found in the mountains of Crete.

forrestii (Chitt.) N. Robson (*H. patulum* var. *forrestii* Chitt., *H. calcaratum* hort., *H. patulum* var. *henryi* hort.) A hardy shrub of neat habit usually attaining 1–1.2m in height. Leaves persist into early winter giving rich autumn tints. Saucer-shaped, golden-yellow flowers, 5–6cm across, rounded in bud, are profusely borne throughout summer and autumn. SW China, NE Burma. I 1906 by George Forrest. ♈ 2002. AM 1922.

fragile hort. See *H. olympicum* f. *minus*.

frondosum Michx. An attractive shrub up to 1.2m high, often giving the effect of a miniature tree, with flaking bark. Leaves sea-green; flowers in clusters, bright yellow with a large boss of stamens, appearing in July and August. The sepals are large and leaf-like. A beautiful and unmistakable species. SE and S USA.

'Hidcote' (*H. patulum* 'Hidcote', *H.* 'Hidcote Gold') (*H.* × *cyathiflorum* 'Gold Cup' × *H. calycinum*) A superb, hardy, semi-evergreen shrub of compact habit, 2m high by 2–2.5m wide. The golden-yellow, saucer-shaped flowers, which are among the largest of any hardy *Hypericum*, are produced with gay abandon from July to October. The origin of this plant is uncertain but it probably originated at Hidcote Manor, Gloucestershire. It is now one of the most popular of all flowering shrubs. ♀ 2002. AM 1954.

'Hidcote Variegated' Leaves rather narrow, dark green with a white margin. A poor plant that tends to revert.

hircinum L. A compact shrub to about 1m with leaves that emit a strong, pungent odour when bruised. Flowers 2.5cm across, are bright yellow with conspicuous stamens, and borne freely from July to September. A variable species. The most commonly grown form is subsp. *majus* (Aiton) N. Robson which differs from the typical form (a native of Corsica and Sardinia) in its narrower leaves. S Europe, SW Asia. Naturalised in the British Isles. I 1640.

hookerianum Wight & Arn. A small, semi-evergreen shrub, distinguished by its leathery, ovate-oblong, sea-green leaves on pale green, stout, rounded branchlets, and clusters of large, cup-shaped, pale yellow flowers from August to October, which are followed by puckered fruits. Nepal to Burma and Thailand, Yunnan, S India. I before 1853. AM 1890.

× *inodorum* Mill. (*H. androsaemum* × *H. hircinum*) (*H. elatum* Aiton, *H. multiflorum* hort., *H. persistens* F. Schneid.) An erect-growing shrub, up to 1.5m, with ovate to ovate-oblong leaves. The small, pale yellow flowers are produced in terminal cymes and are followed by attractive, red fruits. A variable hybrid, some forms tending more to one parent than the other. SW Europe, naturalised in the British Isles. C 1850. **'Elstead'** (*H. elatum* 'Elstead') A selected form with brilliant salmon-red fruits. Suffers badly from rust. AM 1933. **'Rheingold'** A form selected for its brilliant orange-red fruits. Unlike other hypericums of this type, it appears to be free from mildew and rust. **'Summergold'** Golden-yellow young foliage, burns badly in sun. 'Ysella' is similar.

kalmianum L. A slender-branched shrub, up to 1m high, of dense, compact habit, the main stems often gnarled, with pale brown, flaky bark. Narrow leaves, 2.5–5cm long, are sea-green when young. Flowers, 1.25–2cm across, are bright yellow and produced in the axils of the terminal leaves. NE USA, E Canada. I 1759.

kouytchense H. Lév. (*H. penduliflorum* hort.) (*H. patulum* var. *grandiflorum* hort.) (*H. patulum* 'Sungold') A small, semi-evergreen shrub of rounded, compact habit with ovate leaves. Flowers, up to 6cm across, golden-yellow, with conspicuous, long stamens, freely borne from late June to October. The bright red, long-styled capsules resemble colourful, upturned stork's heads. China (Guizhou). ♀ 2002.

lancasteri N. Robson. An attractive and graceful, small shrub related to *H. stellatum*, with bloomy young shoots, flushed reddish on the exposed side and purple-tinged

when young. Has ovate, sea-green leaves and golden-yellow flowers, up to nearly 6cm across. The calyx is star-like, the red-margined sepals creating an attractive effect before the flowers open. Capsules attractively red-tinged. This delightful, recently named species was first collected by George Forrest in 1906, and introduced in 1980 by Roy Lancaster and Keith Rushforth. N Yunnan and S Sichuan, China.

†*****leschenaultii*** Choisy. A beautiful but tender shrub rarely cultivated. For the plant previously grown under this name see *H. addingtonii*. Indonesia. I 1853.

lysimachioides hort. See *H. stellatum*.

monogynum L. (*H. chinense* L.) A pretty semi-evergreen shrub, not above 1m high, with oblong-oval leaves and 6cm wide, golden flowers with conspicuous stamens. A choice shrub for mild localities. China, Taiwan. I 1753.

× *moserianum* André (*H. calycinum* × *H. patulum*) A first-rate, dwarf shrub, usually not more than 50cm high, making excellent groundcover with arching, reddish stems. Golden flowers, 5–6cm across, have conspicuous, reddish anthers and are borne from July to October. Garden origin about 1887. ♀ 2002. FCC 1891. **'Tricolor'** Leaves prettily variegated white, pink and green. Succeeds best in a sheltered position. AM 1896.

× *nothum* Rehder (*H. densiflorum* × *H. kalmianum*) A curious, small shrub distinguished by its slender, interlacing stems with brown, peeling bark, and its narrow leaves and numerous, small flowers in late summer. Raised at the Arnold Arboretum, Boston, USA in 1903.

olympicum L. A dwarf, erect or hummock-forming sub-shrub with small, glaucous, green leaves. Bright yellow flowers are borne in clusters at the ends of the shoots in summer. Balkan Peninsula, Turkey. I 1675. ♀ 2002. **f. minus** Hausskn. (*H. polyphyllum* hort. not Boiss. & Bal.) (*H. fragile* hort. not Heldr. & Sart.) Leaves narrowly elliptic. Habit prostrate or erect. C and S Greece. **'Sulphureum'** Flowers large, pale yellow. **f. uniflorum** Jordanov & Koz. More commonly cultivated than the typical form, this has rather broadly elliptic to obovate leaves. NE Greece, S Bulgaria, NW Turkey. **f. uniflorum** **'Citrinum'** Flowers pale sulphur-yellow, 3.5cm across. Habit upright. ♀ 2002. **f. uniflorum** **'Sunburst'** Flowers large, 6cm across, golden-yellow. Habit upright.

patulum Thunb. ex Murray. The true species of this name is a tender plant from SW China and is rare in cultivation in the British Isles. It was originally introduced from Japan (where it was widely cultivated) by Richard Oldham in 1862, and became popular in European gardens. The subsequent introduction of closely related, but hardier species from China, such as *H. beanii*, *H. forrestii* and *H. pseudohenryi* saw its gradual replacement.

penduliflorum See *H. kouytchense*.

polyphyllum hort. See *H. olympicum* f. *minus*.

prolificum L. A small, densely branched shrub of rounded, bushy habit. Main stems are often gnarled, with attractive, grey and brown, peeling bark. Leaves narrow, 2.5–5cm long, shining above. Flowers, 1.25–2cm across, are bright yellow and borne in terminal clusters from July to September. E and C USA. I about 1750.

pseudohenryi N. Robson (*H. patulum henryi* hort.) A small, mound-forming shrub with arching stems and narrowly ovate to lanceolate-oblong leaves. Golden-yellow flowers, 3–5cm across, with spreading petals and conspicuous stamens, are abundantly produced in July and August. China (Yunnan, Sichuan). Often grown under the name *H. patulum* var. *henryi*. See also *H. beanii* and *H. forrestii*. First introduced by Ernest Wilson in 1908.

reptans Hook. f. & Thoms. A slender shrublet with prostrate stems rooting at intervals and forming small mats. Leaves, 0.6–2cm long, crowd the stems and terminal, solitary, rich golden-yellow flowers, 4.5cm across, are borne from June to September. A choice alpine species for a rock garden or scree. Himalaya. C 1881.

†'**Rowallane**' (*H. hookerianum* 'Charles Rogers' × *H. leschenaultii*) This magnificent, semi-evergreen plant is the finest of the genus, but needs a sheltered site, where it might reach 2m high. It is graceful with bowl-shaped flowers, 5–7.5cm wide, which are intense rich golden-yellow, firm textured and beautifully moulded. Has been wrongly grown under the name *H. rogersii*. ♀ 2002. AM 1943.

stellatum N. Robson (*H. dyeri* hort. not Rehder) (*H. lysimachioides* hort.) An elegant, semi-evergreen species of semi-pendent habit 1–1.2m in height and greater in width. Flowers are 4cm across. The slender, pointed sepals give the prettily red-tinted calyces a delightful star-like effect. The young growths are similarly tinted. Capsules puckered. China (NE Sichuan). I 1894.

subsessile N. Robson A small shrub with upright to arching shoots and subsessile leaves to 6.5cm long. Bright yellow flowers, sometimes flushed red outside in bud, are followed by conical fruits which turn red as they ripen. N Yunnan, W Sichuan, China. I 1981.

tenuicaule Hook. f. & Thoms. ex Dyer (Beer, Lancaster & Morris 238) A small to medium-sized, elegant shrub with slender, strongly arching shoots, bloomy when young. Lanceolate leaves, up to 6cm by 2cm, are purplish at first, glaucous and gland-dotted beneath. Yellow, cup-shaped flowers are borne in terminal clusters. E Nepal, Sikkim. I 1971.

uralum Buch.- Ham. ex D. Don (*H*. 'Buttercup') A delightful, hardy, semi-evergreen shrub, attaining 0.6–1m, with arching stems and ovate or oval, often wavy-edged leaves, 2.5–4cm long, smelling faintly of oranges when crushed. The golden-yellow flowers, 2.5cm across, are borne in terminal cymes during August and September. Himalaya to NW Yunnan. I about 1820.

wilsonii N. Robson. A small shrub with spreading branches and ovate to ovate-lanceolate leaves. Flowers, 4–5cm across, are golden-yellow with spreading petals and conspicuous stamens. Discovered by Ernest Wilson in 1907. China (Hubei, Sichuan).

xylosteifolium (Spach) N. Robson (*H. inodorum* Willd. not Mill.) A small, suckering shrub, forming a dense thicket of erect, slender, usually unbranched stems, 1–1.2m high. Leaves ovate or oblong, 2.5–5cm long. Rather small flowers, 2–2.5cm across, solitary or in terminal clusters at the ends of the shoots, open intermittently from July to September. Caucasus (Georgia), NE Turkey. C 1870.

HYSSOPUS L.—**Labiatae**—A small genus of about 5 species of aromatic perennial herbs and evergreen shrubs with opposite leaves, natives from Europe to C Asia. The following is the only commonly grown species, and is suitable for any well-drained soil in full sun. To retain a compact habit, cut back after flowering.

aristatus See *H. officinalis* subsp. *aristatus*.

*officinalis L. Hyssop. A dwarf shrub of compact habit, the upright shoots bearing slender, aromatic leaves to 5cm long. Small, bright blue, 2-lipped flowers are borne in dense, upright spikes at the ends of the shoots in summer and early autumn. Pink- and white-flowered forms are also grown. S Europe. Long cultivated.

subsp. *aristatus* (Godron) Briq. (*H. aristatus* Godron) Differs in its bright green foliage and the bracts ending in fine points.

I

IDESIA Maxim.—**Flacourtiaceae**—A monotypic genus related to *Azara*. It succeeds best in a deep neutral or somewhat acid soil, but may be grown quite well given 75cm of loam over chalk. Some geographical forms are subject to damage in severe weather while others seem quite hardy.

polycarpa Maxim. An ornamental, medium-sized, sometimes dioecious tree with large, ovate, long-stalked leaves, glaucous beneath, recalling those of *Populus wilsonii*. The tiny, yellowish-green flowers are borne in large, terminal panicles in summer, but not on young trees. Large bunches of pea-like, bright red berries are borne on female trees in autumn. Japan, China. I about 1864 by Richard Oldham. AM 1934. **var. *vestita*** Diels. A particularly hardy form with leaves tomentose beneath. W China. I 1908 by Ernest Wilson.

ILEX L.—**Aquifoliaceae**—The hollies are a large genus of about 400 species of evergreen and deciduous trees and shrubs, rarely climbers, occurring in temperate and tropical regions of both hemispheres. The evergreen species and their forms provide some of the most handsome specimen trees hardy in our climate. The European and Asiatic species are adaptable to most soils and are indifferent to sun or shade, but most of the North American species require a neutral or preferably an acid soil. For assistance with this account we are indebted to Susyn Andrews of the Royal Botanic Gardens, Kew, who in recent years has carried out a great deal of work on the cultivated hollies.

Certain species are invaluable for hedging and will withstand a polluted atmosphere and maritime exposure. As a group, they display a great variety of leaf form and colour excelled by few other genera. Male and female flowers are usually borne on separate plants; in a favourable season female plants fruit abundantly. Well rooted and balled nursery stock may be moved throughout the dormant season. In a damp spring evergreen hollies move well in May. Reversions that occur on variegated hollies should be cut out.

× **altaclerensis** (hort. ex Loud.) Dallim. This name was originally used to describe the Highclere holly which was said to be the result of a cross between *I. aquifolium* (*I. balearica* Desf.) and *I. perado* (*I. maderensis* Lam.). It is now used to cover a number of similar but variable hybrids in which *I. perado* subsp. *platyphylla* also played a part. Most are large shrubs or small to medium-sized trees of vigorous growth, with handsome, normally large leaves. The majority are excellent for tall hedges or screens. They are quite tolerant of industrial conditions and seaside exposure. The name derives from *Alta Clera*, the medieval Latin name for Highclere. **'Atkinsonii'** A green-stemmed clone with large, handsome, rugose leaves, glossy dark green above and with regular spiny serrations. A bold holly with leaves among the finest in the group. Male. **'Balearica'** (*I. balearica* hort. not Desf., *I. aquifolium* var. *balearica* hort. not (Desf.) Loes.) A hardy, vigorous, medium-sized tree of erect, somewhat conical habit when young. Leaves ovate to broadly ovate, flat, leathery, shining green, entire or spiny, always spine-tipped. Red berries; free fruiting.

Both this plant and 'Maderensis' are clones of hybrid origin despite their geographical attributions. Not to be confused with *I. aquifolium* (*I. balearica* Desf.). See also 'Belgica'. **'Belgica'** A strong-growing, conical tree with stout green to yellow-green shoots. Leaves elliptic-lanceolate, dark glossy green, usually spineless to few spined. Large, orange-red fruits are profusely borne. Some plants distributed as 'Balearica' belong here. C 1874. **'Belgica Aurea'** ('Silver Sentinel', *I. perado* 'Aurea') One of the most handsome, variegated hollies. A vigorous, erect-growing, female clone. The firm, flat, sparsely spiny leaves, often 8.25–10cm long, are deep green with pale green and grey mottling, and an irregular, but conspicuous creamy-white or creamy-yellow margin. Red fruit. It is probably a sport of the clone 'Belgica' which it resembles in habit and leaf shape. ♀ 2002. AM 1985. **'Camelliifolia'** A beautiful, large-fruiting clone, pyramidal in habit with purple stems. The long, large, mainly spineless leaves are a lovely shining dark green, reddish-purple when young. Scarlet fruit. C 1865. ♀ 2002. **'Camelliifolia Variegata'** Leaves dark polished green, marbled paler green and margined gold. Sometimes half or complete leaves are gold. Large, scarlet fruit. Slow-growing to about 5m. C 1865. **'Golden King'** The broad, almost spineless leaves are green, with a bright yellow margin. One of the best golden-variegated hollies and one of the few plants to have received two awards in the same year. Female; reddish-brown fruit. A sport of 'Hendersonii' found in Edinburgh in 1884. ♀ 2002. FCC 1898. AM 1898. **'Hendersonii'** Vigorous in growth, the comparatively dull green leaves are generally entire though occasionally shortly spiny. A female clone producing often heavy crops of large, brown-red fruits. Raised in the early 1800s by Edward Hodgins of Co Wicklow, Ireland. **'Hodginsii'** ('Nobilis', 'Shepherdii') A strong, vigorous, male clone with purple stems. The large, dark green, rounded or oval leaves are variably armed, some boldly spiny others few spined; the latter more prevalent on older specimens. It forms a noble specimen tree for a lawn and is especially suitable for coastal and industrial areas. There is also a rare, unnamed female form. ♀ 2002. **'Howick'** A sport of 'Hendersonii' with dark green leaves, narrowly margined creamy-white. A vigorous female tree with red berries. **'Jermyns'** A strong-growing, green-stemmed clone with polished green, near spineless leaves. Ideal for hedging. Male. This tree was found growing in the grounds of Jermyns House when Harold Hillier moved there in 1952. **'Lawsoniana'** A very colourful branch sport of 'Hendersonii' with large, generally spineless leaves, splashed yellow in the centre. Female; reddish-brown fruit. Reverting shoots should be removed. ♀ 2002. FCC 1894. **'Maderensis'** (*I. maderensis* hort.) A vigorous, medium-sized tree with dark stems and regularly spined, flat leaves. A male clone which probably originated in a similar way to 'Balearica'. *I. maderensis* Lam. is a synonym of *I. perado*. **'Maderensis Variegata'** See *I. aquifolium* 'Maderensis Variegata'. **'Moorei'** A vigorous, large-leaved clone with green stems, tinged reddish-purple. Large leaves, approaching those of 'Wilsonii', but rather longer in outline, are polished dark green above and boldly and regularly spined. Male. **'Mundyi'** A most pleasing green-stemmed clone with large, broadly oval, concave, regularly spiny leaves with prominent venation. Male. One of the most magnificent of this group. Named after Mr Mundy of Shipley Hall, Derby. C 1898. **'N.F. Barnes'** (*I. aquifolium* 'N.F. Barnes') Distinct purple shoots and large, dark, shining green leaves. Female; bright red fruit. **'Purple Shaft'** A striking cultivar with strong, dark purple, young shoots and abundant, red fruit. Fast-growing and making a fine specimen tree. A sport of 'Balearica'. **'Silver Sentinel'** See 'Belgica Aurea'. **'W.J. Bean'** (*I. aquifolium* 'W.J. Bean') A compact clone with large, spiny, dark green leaves and bright red fruits. **'Wilsonii'** A compact, dome-shaped clone with green stems and large, evenly spiny, prominently veined leaves. Female, with large, scarlet fruits. A seedling raised by Fisher, Son and Sibray in the early 1890s. Deservedly one of the most popular of this group. FCC 1899.

*'**Ampfield King'** (*I. dipyrena* × *I. pernyi*) A small, conical tree, the dark green leaves edged with usually 2–3 spiny teeth on each side and ending in a triangular, spiny point. Profuse flowers open from purple buds in spring. A hybrid raised in our nurseries in the 1960s and originally distributed as *I. pernyi* or *I. pernyi* var. *veitchii*, the original plant is in the Sir Harold Hillier Gardens and Arboretum.

*'**Ampfield Queen'** (*I. dipyrena* × *I. pernyi*) A female tree similar to, and of the same origin as, 'Ampfield King' but with profuse scarlet berries. The leaves are also slightly different with usually fewer spines and less distinct lateral veins. The original plant is in the Sir Harold Hillier Gardens and Arboretum.

*aquifolium L. Common holly. There is no more beautiful or useful evergreen for this climate. It is usually seen as a small tree or large bush, but in favourable positions may reach 18–21m or more. Female forms produce red fruit. It is native over a wide area from W and S Europe (incl the British Isles), N Africa and W Asia. Cultivated since ancient times. ♀ 2002. **var. *chinensis*** Loes. A misapplied synonym of *I. centrochinensis* for which see under *I. corallina*.

Cultivars of *Ilex aquifolium*

Innumerable cultivars have arisen with variously shaped and coloured leaves, of different habits and with usually red fruits although some are orange or yellow. Unless otherwise stated, all make large shrubs or small trees. Both the typical form and many of its cultivars are excellent for hedging and are good in industrial and coastal areas.

'Alaska' A small, narrowly conical tree, with narrow, spiny or entire leaves. Female with bright red fruits produced even on young plants.

'Amber' An interesting clone selected in our nurseries before 1955; large, bronze-yellow fruits. ♀ 2002. FCC 1985.

'Angustifolia' A slow-growing cultivar of neat, pyramidal habit when young. Stems purple; leaves varying to nearly 4cm by 1.25cm wide, long-pointed and with 10–16 slender marginal spines. Male and female; red fruit. 'Serratifolia', 'Hascombensis' and 'Pernettyfolia' are similar clones.

'Angustimarginata Aurea' Dark purple stems and strongly spined, narrow leaves, about 5cm long, mottled dark green with a narrow, deep yellow margin. Male.

'Argentea Marginata' Broad-leaved silver holly. A handsome, free-fruiting female tree with bright red berries, green stems and white-margined leaves. Pink young growth. ♀ 2002.

'Argentea Marginata Pendula' Perry's silver weeping holly. A small, graceful tree with strongly weeping branches, eventually forming a compact 'mushroom' of white-margined leaves. Female; produces its bright red fruits freely.

'Argentea Regina' See 'Silver Queen'.

'Aurea Marginata' A small, bushy tree with purple stems and spiny, yellow-margined leaves. Female, with red fruit.

'Aurea Marginata Ovata' See 'Ovata Aurea'.

'Aurifodina' ('Muricata', 'Bicolor') An effective, green-stemmed clone. Flattened, dark green leaves with a dark old gold margin. Female; free-fruiting with scarlet berries.

'Bacciflava' Yellow-fruited holly. A handsome cultivar with heavy crops of bright yellow fruits. 'Fructu Luteo' is similar. AM 1984.

'Crassifolia' A slow-growing clone with very thick, curved, strongly spine-edged leaves and purple young shoots. Female, fruit red. Cultivated since the mid 1700s.

'Crispa' ('Tortuosa', 'Calamistrata') A peculiar sport of 'Scotica' with twisted and curled, thick, leathery leaves, each tipped with a sharp, decurved spine. Male.

'Crispa Aurea Picta' Similar to 'Crispa' but the dark green leaves have a central splash of yellow and pale green. Tends to revert. Male.

'Donningtonensis' Dark blackish-purple stems and purple-flushed, spiny young leaves. Male.

'Elegantissima' (Argentea Marginata Group) A green-stemmed clone with boldly spined, wavy-edged, green leaves, with faint marbling and creamy-white margins. Young leaves pink. Male.

'Ferox' Hedgehog holly. A distinctive clone with small leaves, the upper surfaces of which are puckered and furnished with short, sharp spines. Male. Lower and slower-growing than most, making an excellent hedge. This is said to be the oldest identifiable cultivar of holly still in cultivation, having been known at least since the early 17th century.

'Ferox Argentea' Silver hedgehog holly. Rich purple twigs and leaves with creamy-white margins and spines. A very effective combination. Male. C 1662. ♀ 2002. AM 1988.

'Ferox Aurea' Gold hedgehog holly. Leaves with a central deep gold or yellow-green blotch. Male. AM 1993.

'Flavescens' Moonlight holly. Leaves suffused canary-yellow, shaded old gold. Particularly effective on a dull winter afternoon or in spring when the young leaves appear. Best in full sun. Female; red fruit.

'Foxii' A purple-stemmed clone with shining green, ovate leaves bearing evenly spaced, marginal spines. Resembles a long-spined 'Ovata'. Male.

'Fructu Luteo' See under 'Bacciflava'.

'Golden Milkboy' A striking and most ornamental holly with large, flattened, spine-edged leaves, which are green with a large splash of gold in the centre. Reverting shoots should be removed. Male.

Ilex aquifolium continued:

'Golden Milkmaid' Similar to 'Golden Milkboy' but female with red berries.

'Golden Queen' ('Aurea Regina') A striking cultivar with green young shoots. Broad, spiny, dark green leaves have pale green and grey shading and a broad yellow margin. Male. ♀ 2002.

'Golden van Tol' A sport of 'J.C. van Tol' with attractive, golden-margined leaves and sparse red fruit.

'Green Pillar' An erect, narrow form with upright branches and dark green, spiny leaves. Female; red fruit. An excellent specimen or screening tree and suitable for growing in tubs.

'Handsworthensis' A green or dusky-stemmed cultivar of compact habit, with small, regularly and sharply spined leaves. Male.

'Handsworth New Silver' (Argentea Marginata Group) An attractive, purple-stemmed clone, distinguished by its comparatively long leaves, which are deep green mottled grey with a broad, creamy-white margin. Female; free-fruiting, bright red fruit. ♀ 2002.

'Hascombensis' Compact, narrow habit with narrow leaves and purple shoots. Male.

'Hastata' ('Latispina Minor') A remarkable, dense, slow-growing cultivar with deep purple shoots and small, rigid, undulating leaves with an occasional stout spine towards the base. Male.

f. *heterophylla* (Aiton) Loes. A name previously used to cover plants bearing both entire and spiny leaves, now regarded as a synonym of *I. aquifolium*. The plant formerly distributed by us under this name is 'Pyramidalis'.

'Heterophylla Aureomarginata' See under 'Pyramidalis Aurea Marginata'.

'Ingramii' Shoots deep purple; leaves sharply spiny and flecked and margined creamy-white. Young growth pinky-mauve. Male.

'J.C. van Tol' ('Polycarpa', 'Polycarpa Laevigata') A superb cultivar with dark, shining, almost spineless, green leaves. Produces large, regular crops of red fruits. Self-pollinating. ♀ 2002.

'Laurifolia' A striking cultivar with glossy, usually spineless leaves and deep purple shoots. Male.

'Laurifolia Aurea' ('Laurifolia Variegata') Dark green leaves, thinly edged yellow. Very effective with the deep purple twigs. Male. FCC 1883.

'Lichtenthalii' A curious form making a low, spreading bush. Leaves long, twisted and irregularly spiny with a prominent pale green midrib. Of unknown origin. Female; red fruit.

'Madame Briot' (Aureomarginata Group) An attractive purple-stemmed clone with large, strongly spiny leaves which are green, mottled and margined dark yellow. Female; scarlet fruit. ♀ 2002.

'Maderensis Variegata' (*I.* × *altaclerensis* 'Maderensis Variegata') A striking clone with reddish-purple stems. Leaves dark green, with a bold, irregular central splash of yellow and pale green. Tends to revert. Female; red fruit.

'Monstrosa' ('Latispina Major') An easily recognised cultivar of dense habit with bright green stems and broad, viciously spiny leaves. Male.

'Muricata' See 'Aurifodina'.

'Myrtifolia' A neat-growing cultivar with purple shoots and small, dark green leaves, variably edged with sharp spines or entire. Male.

'Myrtifolia Aurea' ('Myrtifolia Variegata') Purple stems. Ovate-lanceolate leaves, to 4cm long, are dark glossy green with golden-yellow margins. Male. Dense habit to about 4m.

'Myrtifolia Aurea Maculata' A dense, compact form with small, evenly spined, dark green leaves with pale green shading and an irregular central splash of gold. Male. ♀ 2002.

'N.F. Barnes' See *I.* × *altaclerensis* 'N.F. Barnes'.

'Ovata' A slow-growing cultivar with purple shoots and distinct, neat, ovate leaves, shallowly scalloped along the margin. Male.

'Ovata Aurea' ('Aurea Marginata Ovata') A strong-growing clone. The thick, short-spined leaves are margined gold, contrasting beautifully with the deep purple twigs. One of the brightest and neatest of variegated hollies. Male.

'Pendula' An elegant, free-fruiting, small tree forming a dense mound of weeping stems clothed with dark green, spiny leaves. Female; red fruit.

'Polycarpa' See 'J.C. van Tol'.

'Pyramidalis' A handsome, self-fertile, free-fruiting clone with green stems and bright green, variously spined leaves. Red fruit. Conical in habit when young, broadening in maturity. ♀ 2002. AM 1989.

'Pyramidalis Aureomarginata' A strong-growing, green-stemmed clone. Leaves are deep shining green with an irregular but conspicuous, golden margin. Female; red fruit. Plants grown by us as 'Heterophylla Aureomarginata' belong here.

'Pyramidalis Fructu Luteo' Similar to 'Pyramidalis' in habit, but with profuse, bright yellow fruits. ♀ 2002. AM 1985.

'Recurva' A slow-growing clone of dense habit with purplish twigs and strongly spined, recurved leaves, 2.5–3.75cm long. Male.

'Scotica' A distinct cultivar with thick, leathery, deep green leaves, which are spineless and slightly twisted with a cup-shaped depression below the apex. Female; red fruit.

'Silver Milkboy' See 'Silver Milkmaid'.

'Silver Milkmaid' ('Silver Milkboy') ('Argentea Mediopicta') An old, attractive cultivar with strongly spiny, dark green leaves with a central blotch of creamy-white. Female; red fruit. Plants previously grown as 'Silver Milkboy' have proved to be female. Reverting shoots should be removed. FCC 1985.

'Silver Queen' ('Argentea Regina') A striking clone with blackish-purple young shoots and broadly ovate, dark green leaves, faintly marbled grey and bordered creamy-white. Young leaves shrimp-pink. Male. ♀ 2002.

'Silver van Tol' A sport of 'J.C. van Tol' with the leaves margined creamy-white. Female.

'Smithiana' ('Smithii') A dense-growing clone with purplish twigs and narrow, often spineless leaves. Male.

'Tortuosa' See 'Crispa'.

'W.J. Bean' See *I.* × *altaclerensis* 'W.J. Bean'.

'Watereriana' ('Waterer's Gold') (Aureomarginata Group) Dense, compact, slow-growing shrub with green

Ilex aquifolium **continued:**

stems striped greenish-yellow. The small, rounded, generally spineless leaves are mottled yellow-green and grey with an irregular, yellow margin. Male.

'Weeping Golden Milkmaid' An attractive shrub with stiffly pendent branches and dark green leaves, blotched in the centre with bright green and golden-yellow. Female; red berries.

× **aquipernyi** Gable ex W. Clarke (*I. aquifolium × I. pernyi*) A group of hybrids first raised in North America where they are hardier than *I. aquifolium*. **'Aquipern'** The first form raised. A large, densely branched, conical shrub or small tree, intermediate between the parents. Leaves similar to those of *I. pernyi* but larger, usually with 5–7 prominent spines, the terminal one long and deflexed. Male. Raised in the USA in 1933.

× **attenuata** Ashe (*I. cassine × I. opaca*) (*I. × topelii*) Topal holly. A tall, slender shrub or small tree of rather conical habit, with narrow, normally entire leaves, 5–10cm long, and clusters of red fruits. A natural hybrid found with the parents in S USA. Not suitable for chalky soils. **'East Palatka'** A female clone of upright, conical habit. Pale glossy green, obovate leaves are entire except for a sharp, terminal point and an occasional spine. **Foster Group** This name covers a number of clones of the parentage *I. cassine* var. *angustifolia × I. opaca* with narrow, variously spined, glossy, green leaves, bronze when young. **'Sunny Foster'** A slow-growing form with narrow, golden-yellow leaves. Particularly attractive during winter. A sport of 'Foster no. 2', which occurred at the US National Arboretum in Washington. AM 1989.

balearica See *I. × altaclerensis* 'Balearica' and *I. aquifolium*.

× **beanii** Rehder (*I. aquifolium × I. dipyrena*) A variable hybrid with leaves generally matt green. Superficially closer to the *aquifolium* parent. Our plant is female with red fruit. C early 1900s.

*bioritsensis** Hayata (*I. pernyi* var. *veitchii* Bean) A shrubby species with leaves 3–6cm by 1.5–4cm, ovate-rhomboid with a prolonged apex and sporadic spines. Fruits red. It has been wrongly distributed in the USA as *I. ficoidea* Hemsl. Burma, SW China, Taiwan. AM 1930.

‡*cassine** L. not Walter. Dahoon. An extremely variable species making a large shrub, or rarely a small tree. The lanceolate leaves are occasionally 10cm long. Fruits red. SE USA. Unsuitable for chalky soils. I 1726. **var. angustifolia** Aiton. A form with smaller, narrower leaves.

centrochinensis See under *I. corallina*.

chinensis See *I. purpurea*.

*ciliospinosa** Loes. Large shrub bearing small, neat, leathery, weakly spined leaves, up to 5.5cm long. Fruits egg-shaped, red. Related to *I. dipyrena*, but differs in its smaller, more regularly spiny leaves and rounded shoots. W China. I 1908.

*colchica** Pojark. Black Sea holly. A small to medium-sized shrub closely related to *I. aquifolium* but with narrower, often less undulate, shorter-stalked leaves with fewer, more forward-pointing teeth. Female specimens have red fruit. Some of the plants of this species in the Hillier Gardens and Arboretum derive from introductions made by Sir Harold Hillier. N Turkey, Caucasus, SE Bulgaria.

collina Alexander (*Nemopanthus collinus* (Alexander) Clark) A large, deciduous shrub or small tree with ellip-

tic to obovate, serrate leaves and bright red fruit. Virginia and W Virginia. C 1930s. Has previously been distributed by us as *Nemopanthus mucronatus* (L.) Trel.

†*corallina** Franch. (*I. corallina* var. *pubescens* S.Y. Hu) A small, variable, graceful tree with slender stems and narrowly elliptic to elliptic-lanceolate, slender-pointed and serrated leaves. Small, red fruits are produced in axillary clusters. The juvenile form, with slender, purple twigs and shining, deep green, oblong-lanceolate, strongly spiny leaves, was originally listed as *I. centrochinensis* (*I. aquifolium* var. *chinensis* Loes.) which is not in cultivation. W and SW China. I about 1900. **var. pubescens** See *I. corallina*.

*cornuta** Lindl. & Paxton (*I. furcata* Lindl.) A dense, slow-growing species, rarely 2.4m high. Leaves of a peculiar rectangular form, mainly 5-spined. The large, red fruits are rarely abundant. China, Korea. I 1846. **'Burfordii'** A medium-sized to large shrub of compact growth with shining green, leathery leaves which, except for a short terminal spine, are entire. Long-persistent fruits are freely borne. Extensively planted as a hedge in the USA, where it can reach 4m. Female. **'Burford Variegated'** Leaves pale green with a broad, bright yellow margin. Female. **'Dazzler'** A compact bush with rich glossy green leaves and large, bright red berries. **'D'Or'** Leaves entire or nearly so; fruits yellow. **'Dwarf Burford'** ('Burfordii Nana') A dwarf female form of slow growth and dense, compact habit. Leaves varying from entire to spiny. Fruits dark red. **'Kingsville Special'** A strong-growing shrub with large, leathery, almost spineless leaves. Female. **'O' Spring'** Spiny leaves, green and grey-green in the centre margined with dull golden-yellow. Shoots deep purple above. A sport of 'Rotunda'. Female. **'Rotunda'** Dwarf selection with compact, rounded habit and strongly spined, oblong leaves. Female.

*crenata** Thunb. ex Murray. Japanese holly. A tiny-leaved holly of slow growth, reaching 4–6m. Fruits small, shining black. A variable species, particularly in cultivation. Excellent as a dwarf clipped hedge. Sakhalin Is, Korea, Japan. I about 1864. **'Aureovariegata'** See 'Variegata'. **'Convexa'** ('Bullata') A free-fruiting, small, bushy shrub, with glossy, bullate or convex leaves. A superb low hedge. C 1919. ♀ 2002. **'Fastigiata'** See under 'Sky Pencil'. **var. fukasawana** Makino. A distinct, comparatively large-leaved variety of dense, erect habit, with strong, angular shoots and lanceolate or narrowly-elliptic, blunt-toothed leaves up to 5cm long, bright or yellowish-green when young. Japan. **'Golden Gem'** A small, compact shrub with a flattened top and yellow leaves, particularly attractive during winter and spring. Female but very shy flowering. ♀ 2002. **'Helleri'** Perhaps the most attractive dwarf, small-leaved form, making a low, dense, flattened hummock. Female. Originated in the USA in 1925. **'Hetzii'** A vigorous form of broad, bushy habit with oblong-elliptic leaves to 3.5cm long. C 1943. **'Latifolia'** (*I. crenata* f. *latifolia* (Goldring) Rehder) A strong-growing form with larger, elliptic leaves, 2–3cm long. Female. I 1860. **'Mariesii'** (*I. mariesii, I. crenata* var. *nummularioides* (Franch. & Sav.) Yatabe) A dwarf, most unholly-like clone of very slow growth, with crowded, tiny, round leaves. Ideal for troughs or bonsai culture. Eventually makes a stiffly upright shrub of about 2m, most attractive when covered with its black berries in winter. Female. I 1879 by Charles Maries. A male plant with larger leaves and of faster growth has also been grown under this name. It is similar to 'Nakada', named in the USA. **var. paludosa** (Nakai) Hara (*I. radicans* Nakai) A low-growing, spreading variety of dense habit, eventually reaching 1.5m tall and twice as much across, with broad, elliptic leaves. Found in damp places in Japan. **'Shiro-fukurin'** Leaves grey-green with a cream margin. **'Sky Pencil'** A narrowly upright form. Found on Mount Daisen, Honshu, Japan by Norihiro Shibamachi and introduced to the US National Arboretum in 1985. Female. A plant grown as 'Fastigiata' is very similar. **'Stokes'** A dwarf shrub, forming a dense, compact mound of tiny leaves. Male. C 1949. **'Variegata'** ('Aureovariegata', 'Luteovariegata') Leaves irregularly blotched with gold. Male.

†*****cyrtura** Merr. A rare and tender species making a medium-sized tree in mild areas. Leaves are leathery and toothed with a long, slender tip. Female plants bear bright red fruits. A plant in the Sir Harold Hillier Gardens and Arboretum has survived for many years and derives from the trees at Trewithen, Cornwall, which were probably raised from seed collected by George Forrest. SW China (Yunnan), Upper Burma.

‡*decidua* Walter. Possum-haw. A medium-sized to large, deciduous shrub with slender stems and obovate to oblanceolate, crenately-toothed leaves. Bright orange or red fruits, last well into winter, but are not very prolific on young plants. Not suitable for chalky soils. SE USA. I 1760.

†*****dimorphophylla** Koidz. A small shrub of upright habit, proving fairly hardy given shelter. Juvenile foliage is very spiny; adult leaves dark green, to 3cm long, entire except for the apical spine. Red fruit. Ryukyu Islands. C 1976.

*****dipyrena** Wall. Himalayan holly. A large shrub or small to medium-sized tree, conical in outline, with angled young shoots. Leaves dark green, with a short purplish petiole; juvenile foliage very spiny. Fruits deep red, slightly 2-lobed. E Himalaya, W China. I 1840.

*****'Dr Kassob'** (*I. cornuta* × *I. pernyi*) A neat-growing, large shrub with conspicuous, ridged, yellow-green stems and very dark green, often somewhat convex, oblong, 5-spined leaves up to 4cm by 3cm. Female; red fruit.

*****fargesii** Franch. (*I. franchetiana* Loes.) A large shrub or occasionally a small tree, easily recognized by its narrow, oblong or oblanceolate leaves up to 12.5cm long. Fruits small, red. SW China. I 1911. AM 1926. **var. brevifolia** S. Andrews. A shrubby form with smaller leaves up to about 7cm long. Belongs to the typical subspecies. Some plants previously distributed as *I. fargesii* may belong here. China (W Hubei). I 1900s. **subsp. melanotricha** (Merr.) S. Andrews (*I. melanotricha* Merr.) Differs from the typical subspecies in the pubescent pedicels. Makes a graceful, large shrub with slender shoots and profuse, orange-red fruits. China (Yunnan), N Burma, SE Tibet. The plant previously listed as *I. fargesii* var. *sclerophylla* is a form of this with purple shoots and petioles and smaller, deep red fruits. **var. sclerophylla** hort. See under subsp. *melanotricha*.

fragilis Hook. f. Plants originally listed under this name are *Myrsine semiserrata* (Myrsinaceae).

franchetiana See *I. fargesii*.

*****geniculata** Maxim. A large, deciduous shrub or small tree, with slender, greyish branches and ovate to elliptic, shallowly toothed, thin-textured leaves. Red fruits on jointed pedicels. Japan. I 1926.

†*****georgei** Comber. A rare species, allied to *I. pernyi*, making a medium-sized to large shrub of compact habit. Leaves elliptic-lanceolate, up to 5cm long, thick and weakly spinose. Fruits small, sealing-wax-red. Not hardy in the Home Counties. Discovered by George Forrest in SW China. Upper Burma, Tibet. I 1900s.

‡*****glabra** (L.) A. Gray. Inkberry. A small to medium-sized shrub forming a dense, rounded bush with small, dark, shining green leaves, in some forms turning purple in winter. Fruits small, black. Not suitable for chalky soils. E North America. I 1759. **f. leucocarpa** F.W. Woods. An unusual form with white fruits.

hookeri King. This species is rare in cultivation. Plants previously grown by us under this name have been *I. kingiana* or *I. dipyrena*. All 3 species have very spiny juvenile foliage.

integra Thunb. A medium-sized to large shrub, tender when young. Obovate to broad elliptic, spineless and leathery leaves. Fruit 1.25cm long, red. Japan, Ryukyu Is, Korea, Taiwan. I 1864.

*****'Jermyns Dwarf'** A dwarf shrub with arching stems making a low, dense mound, eventually forming a leader and reaching about 2m. Leaves of polished dark green are strongly spine-toothed. Of hybrid origin, or a seedling of *I. pernyi*. Female; red fruits.

*****'John T. Morris'** (*I. cornuta* × *I. pernyi*) A medium-sized to large shrub of dense, compact habit with oblong, glossy green leaves, up to 5cm by 4cm, with 5 triangular lobes tipped with sharp spines. Male.

*****kingiana** Cockerell (*I. insignis* Hook. f. not Heer, *I. nobilis* Gumbleton) A remarkable species making a small tree or large shrub, with stout shoots and elliptic-lanceolate, leathery, few-toothed leaves, 12–20cm long. Leaves of juvenile plants and suckers are smaller and markedly spiny. Fruits large, red. We have long grown two forms, one of which is very hardy while the other is damaged in very cold winters. Some plants previously listed by us as *I. hookeri* belong here. E Himalaya, Yunnan. I 1880. AM 1964.

*****× koehneana** Loes. (*I. aquifolium* × *I. latifolia*) An interesting hybrid first reported in Florence, Italy. A large shrub or small tree with purple-flushed young shoots. Leaves elliptic to oblong-lanceolate, slightly undulate, dark polished green above and evenly spiny throughout. Female plants bear large, red fruits. I 1890s or earlier. **'Chestnut Leaf'** (*castaneifolia* hort.) A robust clone of French origin. The thick, leathery, yellowish-green leaves are boldly margined with strong, spiny teeth. Female; red fruit. ♀ 2002. **'San Jose'** (*I.* 'San Jose') An attractive vigorous, small tree or large shrub of North American origin. Young shoots purple-flushed; leaves elliptic to ovate-lanceolate, dark polished green above, paler beneath, conspicuously and evenly spined. Female; red fruit.

latifolia Thunb. Tarajo. A magnificent species usually making a small tree or large shrub up to 7m in the British Isles. Leaves, nearly equal in size to those of *Magnolia grandiflora*, are dark glossy green, leathery, oblong with serrated margins. Although quite hardy it is tender when young and succeeds best in a sheltered position. Orange-red fruits often abundantly produced. Japan, China. I 1840. AM 1952 (for foliage and fruit). AM 1977 (for flower).

*'**Lydia Morris**' (*I. cornuta* 'Burfordii' × *I. pernyi*) A medium-sized, compact, pyramidal shrub, up to 2.5m, with polished green, strongly spiny leaves, a little smaller than those of *I. cornuta*. Large, red fruits. A female counterpart to *I.* 'John T. Morris'.

macrocarpa Oliv. A small to medium-sized, deciduous tree with spur-like branches and ovate, serrated leaves up to 15cm long. Remarkable for the size of its fruits, which resemble small, black cherries. S and SW China. I 1907.

macropoda Miq. A large, deciduous shrub or small tree with ovate to broad-elliptic, serrated leaves. Fruits red. Related to and resembling the American *I. montana*. China, Japan, Korea. I 1894.

maderensis hort. See *I.* × *altaclerensis* 'Maderensis'.

maderensis Lam. See *I. perado*.

*× **makinoi** Hara (*I. leucoclada* × *I. rugosa*) A dwarf shrub, similar in general appearance to *I. rugosa* but larger in all its parts. Leaves narrowly oblong, less conspicuously veined. Fruits red. Japan. I early 1900s.

melanotricha See *I. fargesii* subsp. *melanotricha*.

*× **meserveae** S.Y. Hu. Blue hollies. (*I. aquifolium* × *I. rugosa*) This group of hybrids was originally raised by Mrs Kathleen Meserve of New York in an attempt to produce an ornamental holly for the eastern half of North America where *I. aquifolium* is not hardy. They are bushy, small to medium-sized shrubs up to 2m with angled, purplish shoots and softly spiny, glossy, dark blue-green leaves. Females have glossy, red fruit. They are best given a continental climate. Forms in cultivation include 'Blue Angel' (female), 'Blue Girl' (female), 'Blue Princess' (female) AM 1992. 'Blue Boy' and 'Blue Prince' (male).

‡***myrtifolia** Walter (*I. cassine* var. *myrtifolia* (Walter) Sarg.) Myrtle-leaved holly. A medium-sized to large shrub with narrow leaves, 2.5–5cm long. Fruits normally red. Not suitable for chalky soils. SE USA. I 1700s.

*'**Nellie R. Stevens**' (*I. aquifolium* × *I. cornuta*) An ornamental, small tree with green shoots and oblong-elliptic, blackish-green, often bullate leaves, up to 7.5cm long, which are spine-tipped with usually 2 spines on each side. Female, bearing profuse and long-persistent, orange-red fruits.

†***nothofagifolia** Kingdon-Ward. A very distinct and unusual, large shrub or small tree of spreading habit. The shoots are lined with longitudinal ridges of warts and glossy dark green leaves resemble those of *Nothofagus antarctica*, and are densely clustered, up to 2cm long, broadly ovate and margined with short, slender spines. Fruit scarlet. NE Upper Burma, Yunnan, Assam. I about 1919 and again in 1963.

‡***opaca** Aiton. American holly. In this country, a large shrub or small tree. Variously spiny leaves are a distinctive soft, matt olive-green or yellow-green. Not suitable for chalky soils and best in a continental climate. Fruits red. Numerous cultivars are grown in North America. E and C USA. I 1744. '**Natalie Webster**' Leaves darker

and glossier than normal. Female. The original plant was found on Fire Island, off Long Island, New York in the early 1930s by Charles Webster. I to our nursery in 1964. **f.** *xanthocarpa* Rehder. Fruits yellow. I 1811.

‡***pedunculosa** Miq. (*I. pedunculosa* f. *continentalis* Loes.) An attractive large shrub or small tree with dark, glossy green, entire, wavy-edged leaves. Fruits bright red, carried on slender stalks 2.5–3.75cm long. Not suitable for chalky soils. China, Japan. Taiwan. I 1893 by Charles Sargent. **f.** *continentalis* See *I. pedunculosa*.

†***perado** Aiton (*I. maderensis* Lam.) A small to medium-sized tree which is one parent of many of the *I.* × *altaclerensis* hybrids. It is distinguished from our native holly, mainly by its distinctly winged leaf stalks and flatter leaves, which are variously short-spined when young, occasionally entire, and rounded at the tip. Rather tender except in sheltered gardens and mild districts. Madeira. I 1760. **subsp.** *azorica* (Loes.) Tutin occurs in the Azores. **subsp.** *platyphylla* (Webb & Berth.) Tutin (*I. platyphylla* Webb & Berth.) Canary Island holly. A handsome and relatively hardy form with a bushy habit, making a small tree in mild districts. The leaves are large and broad, occasionally 12.5–15cm long by half as wide or more. They are dark green, leathery, short-stalked and short-toothed. The fruits are deep red. This remarkable plant has survived undamaged in the Sir Harold Hillier Gardens and Arboretum for many years. Canary Isles (Tenerife, Gomera). I 1842.

***pernyi** Franch. A distinguished large shrub or small tree with small, peculiarly spined, almost triangular leaves. Fruits small, bright red. C and W China. I 1900. FCC 1908. **var.** *veitchii* See *I. bioritsensis*.

platyphylla See *I. perado* subsp. *platyphylla*.

†***purpurea** Hassk. (*I. chinensis* Sims) A small tree remarkable for its bright pink young foliage. Rather thin, elliptic-lanceolate leaves, up to 13cm long, are shallowly toothed at the margin and taper-pointed at the apex. Flowers lilac, deepening with age, followed, on female plants, by glossy, scarlet fruits. Has reached 4m in the Sir Harold Hillier Gardens and Arboretum in spite of defoliation in very severe winters. Japan, China.

†***rotunda** Thunb. A small tree with ovate or broad elliptic, entire leaves up to 10cm long, recalling those of *Ligustrum japonicum*. Fruits small, red, borne in clusters on the current year's growth. Ryukyu Is, Korea, China. Taiwan. I 1848.

‡***rugosa** F. Schmidt. A dwarf, prostrate shrub forming a dense low mound. Young stems are sharply angled, almost quadrangular. Elliptic to lanceolate leaves are acute and toothed, slightly rugose above. Fruits red. Not suitable for chalky soils. It is best known as one of the parents of the Blue hollies (*I.* × *meserveae*). Japan, Sakhalin Is, Kurile Is. I 1895.

'**San Jose**' See *I.* × *koehneana* 'San Jose'.

‡**serrata** Thunb. (*I. sieboldii* Miq.) A deciduous, slow-growing, small to medium-sized shrub of dense, twiggy habit. Leaves small and thin, attractively tinted in autumn. Flowers pink. The tiny, red fruits of the female plants are produced in abundance and last throughout the winter or until eaten by birds. Not recommended for chalky soils. Japan, China. I 1893. '**Leucocarpa**' A form with pale creamy-yellowish-white berries.

sieboldii See *I. serrata*.

'Sparkleberry' (*I. serrata* × *I. verticillata*) A medium-sized to large, deciduous shrub with ovate, long-acuminate leaves, attractively purple-tinted in spring. The small, bright scarlet berries are profusely borne. 'Apollo' is a male plant of the same parentage.

*spinigera (Loes.) Loes. A large shrub or small tree close to *I. colchica* but with strongly undulate, deeply spined leaves and pubescent branches. Spines usually 3–4 on each side, the terminal one strongly deflexed. Berries orange-red. N Iran and neighbouring Russia.

*sugerokii Maxim. A rare, small to medium-sized shrub of dense, compact, upright habit with elliptic leaves, 2.5–3.75cm long, shallowly toothed in upper half, leathery and glossy dark green. Fruits red, solitary in the leaf axils of the current year's growths. Closely related to *I. yunnanensis*, differing in its generally glabrous shoots and few-toothed leaves. In the wild it is often found with *I. crenata*, and like that species is suitable for growing as a dense hedge. Japan. I 1914.

‡*verticillata* (L.) A. Gray (*Prinos verticillatus* L.) Winterberry. A deciduous, large shrub with yellow leaves in autumn. Fruits bright red and long persisting. Not suitable for chalky soils. E North America. I 1736. AM 1962. **f. aurantiaca** (Moldenke) Rehder. Fruits orange. **'Christmas Cheer'** A selected female clone of American origin, bearing masses of bright red fruits, which normally last through the winter months. **'Winter Red'** Very profuse glossy red, long persistent fruits.

†*vomitoria Aiton. Yaupon. A large shrub or small tree, to 6m, with ovate or elliptic leaves, up to 4.5cm long, often purple-tinged when young, becoming dark glossy green. Fruit bright red, or in some forms yellow, profusely borne and long persistent. Tender and little planted in the British Isles, it is very popular in S USA where many selections have been made. An infusion of the leaves was used as a drink by the North American Indians. SE USA, Mexico, naturalised in Bermuda. I before 1700.

*× wandoensis T.R. Dudley (*I. cornuta* × *I. integra*) A naturally occurring, very variable hybrid. Male and female forms occur, the females bearing red fruits. Generally tends towards *I. cornuta*. Korea. I about 1980.

*yunnanensis Franch. (*I. yunnanensis* f. *gentilis* Loes.) A medium-sized to large shrub of bushy habit with small, ovate to ovate-lanceolate, acute or obtuse, crenately toothed leaves, glossy green above, neatly arranged on the slender, densely pubescent twigs. The small, slender-stalked, bright red fruits are conspicuous on female plants. W China. I 1901 by Ernest Wilson. **f. gentilis** See *I. yunnanensis*.

*ILLICIUM L.—Illiciaceae—A genus of about 40 species of aromatic, evergreen shrubs and trees, a small, outstanding group with unusual many-petalled flowers. Natives of E and SE Asia and warm parts of America and the only genus in the family, they are allied to *Magnolia* and thrive under conditions congenial to *Rhododendron*, though tolerant of a little lime.

*anisatum L. (*I. religiosum* Siebold & Zucc.) Japanese anise. A medium-sized to large, aromatic shrub of slow growth. Leaves obovate or oval, abruptly pointed, thick and fleshy, glossy deep green. Pale yellow flowers, about 2.5cm across, are carried in spring, even on young plants. Japan, China. I 1790. AM 1930.

*floridanum Ellis. Florida anise, Stinking laurel. A medium-sized, aromatic shrub with deep green, broadly oval, leathery leaves and maroon-purple flowers in May and June. SE USA. I 1771. The Mexican *I. mexicanum* A.C. Sm. is very similar but some selections at least flower over a very long period.

*henryi Diels. A medium-sized shrub with glossy, leathery leaves and bright rose flowers. W China.

*mexicanum See under *I. floridanum*.

*parviflorum Michx. ex Vent. Proving hardy though slow-growing here, this small to medium-sized shrub has blunt-tipped, aromatic leaves. The tiny, nodding, yellow flowers are produced from the leaf axils in late summer and have perianth segments no more than 5mm long. Florida, a common landscape plant in the SE USA.

Indian bean tree See *Catalpa bignonioides*.
Indian currant See *Symphoricarpos orbiculatus*.

INDIGOFERA L.—Leguminosae—A very large genus of some 700 or more species of shrubs and herbs found mainly in tropical and subtropical regions. The following are a very attractive group of shrubs which, owing to their racemes being produced from the leaf axils of growing shoots, flower continuously throughout summer and autumn. All have elegant, pinnate leaves. Requiring full sun, they thrive in all types of soil and are especially good on dry sites. Some species may be cut back during severe winters but these usually throw up a thicket of strong shoots the following spring. Old, poorly shaped specimens may also be hard pruned to achieve the same effect. We would like to thank Dr Brian Schrire for assistance with this genus.

*amblyantha Craib. Flowers of a delightful shrimp-pink. It has been confused with *I. potaninii*. China. I 1908 by William Purdom. ♀ 2002.

†*decora Lindl. (*I. incarnata* (Willd.) Nakai) A rare and pretty dwarf shrub from China and Japan, producing long racemes of pink pea-flowers. I 1846. AM 1933. **f. alba** Sarg. An attractive form with white flowers. I about 1878. AM 1939.

*gerardiana See *I. heterantha*.

*hebepetala Benth. A medium-sized, widespreading shrub with flowers of distinct colouring, being rose with a deep crimson standard. NW Himalaya. C 1881.

*heterantha Wall. ex Brandis (*I. gerardiana* Wall. ex Baker, *I. pulchella* Roxb.) Flowers bright purplish-rose, foliage very elegant. Grows 0.9–1.2m in the open, but much higher against a wall. Plants we have received under the name *I. divaricata* are almost identical with this species and are perhaps merely a geographical form. NW Himalaya. C 1840. ♀ 2002. AM 1977.

*incarnata See *I. decora*.

*kirilowii Palib. (*I. macrostachya* Bunge) A small shrub with bright almond-pink flowers in long, dense racemes, rather hidden by the leaves. N China. Korea. I 1899.

†*pendula Franch. A vigorous upright shrub with arching branches. Leaves to 15cm long with usually 15–17 elliptic leaflets to 3.5cm long, ending in a fine point. Long pendent racemes, to 25cm long, bearing numerous flowers, open on the young shoots during late summer and

autumn. Standard lilac-grey with darker streaks outside, inside nearly white at the tip shading to deep carmine, veined white, at the base, persisting over the young fruits after the other petals have fallen. SW China.

potaninii Craib. A splendid medium-sized shrub with horizontally spreading racemes, 12–20cm long, of clear pink flowers, produced continuously from June to September. NW China. C 1925.

pseudotinctoria Matsum. A vigorous species from China and Japan, attaining about 1.5m. Related to *I. amblyantha*, it has pink flowers in dense racemes up to 10cm long. I 1897 by Augustine Henry. AM 1965.

pulchella See *I. heterantha*.

Inkberry See *Ilex glabra*.
Ironwood See *Ostrya virginiana*.

ITEA L.—**Escalloniaceae**—A small genus of about 10 species of deciduous and evergreen shrubs and small trees, natives of E Asia, from the Himalaya to the Philippines, with one species in E North America. The following make attractive and unusual, summer-flowering shrubs, thriving in half shade. The evergreen species will take full sun against a sunny wall, providing the soil is not too dry.

*ilicifolia Oliv. A lax, evergreen, holly-like shrub, up to 3m or more, charming when, in late summer, it is laden with long, drooping, catkin-like racemes of fragrant, greenish-white flowers. C China. I before 1895 by Augustine Henry. ♀ 2002. FCC 1988. AM 1911.

‡virginica L. An attractive small, erect-branched, deciduous shrub, producing upright, cylindrical racemes of fragrant, creamy-white flowers in July. Foliage often colours well in autumn, but some forms retain green leaves well into winter. E USA. I 1744. AM 1972. **'Beppu'** A name given to what was originally thought to be a form of *I. japonica* introduced to the USA from Japan. It was later shown to belong here. **'Henry's Garnet'** A form with rich red-purple autumn colour. It was found by Dr Mike Dirr on the campus at Swarthmore College, Pennsylvania in 1982.

†*yunnanensis Franch. Closely resembles *I. ilicifolia*, but has longer leaves. White flowers in racemes 15–18cm long. Yunnan, China. I about 1918 by George Forrest.

J, K

JAMESIA Torr. & A. Gray—**Hydrangeaceae**—A monotypic genus related to *Fendlera* and *Carpenteria*. Suitable for any ordinary soil in full sun.

americana Torr. & A. Gray. Cliffbush. A small to medium-sized, erect shrub with greyish leaves and slightly fragrant, white flowers produced in cymose clusters during May and June. W North America. I 1862.

Japanese angelica tree See *Aralia elata*.
Jasmine See *Jasminum*.
Jasmine, winter See *Jasminum nudiflorum*.

JASMINUM L.—**Oleaceae**—The jasmines or jessamines consist of more than 200 species of evergreen and deciduous shrubs and climbers, natives of tropical and temperate regions of mainly Asia and Africa, extending to the Pacific islands and Australia. They are popular as climbing plants but too little planted as self-supporting shrubs. All the hardy, shrubby species have yellow flowers and, although more or less deciduous in a hard winter, their usually green stems create an evergreen effect. Their soil requirements are cosmopolitan. For climbing species see under CLIMBERS at end of Manual.

fruticans L. A small to medium-sized, semi-evergreen shrub with erect stems and normally trifoliolate leaves. Yellow flowers are borne in clusters at the end of the stems from June to September. Fruits black. Mediterranean region to C Asia. C 1517.

humile L. Italian jasmine. A small to medium-sized, semi-scandent, half-evergreen shrub. The leaves normally have 3–7 leaflets. Bright yellow flowers are borne in terminal clusters in June or July. This extremely variable species is distributed over a wide area from Afghanistan to Yunnan and Sichuan, China. C 1656. **var.** *glabrum* See f. *wallichianum*. *‘Revolutum’* (*J. revolutum* Sims.) A quite remarkable and beautiful, medium-sized shrub with persistent, deep green leaves of good texture, composed of usually 5–7 leaflets. These create a splendid setting for the comparatively large, deep yellow, slightly fragrant flowers in cymose clusters during summer. I from China in 1814. ♀ 2002. AM 1976. **f.** *wallichianum* (Lindl.) P.S. Green (*J. humile* var. *glabrum* (DC.) Kobuski) A form of tall, scandent growth. The leaves normally have 7–11 leaflets, the terminal one long and acuminate. Yellow flowers are carried in pendent clusters. NE Nepal. I 1812.

nudiflorum Lindl. Winter jasmine. One of the most tolerant and beautiful of winter-flowering shrubs with bright yellow flowers appearing on the naked, green branches from November to February. Makes strong, angular growths up to 4.5m long. Excellent for covering unsightly walls and banks. When grown as a wall shrub, long growths may be cut back immediately after flowering. W China. I 1844 by Robert Fortune. ♀ 2002. **‘Aureum’** Leaves yellow-blotched or almost entirely yellow. C 1889. **‘Mystique’** Leaves edged with silvery-white.

parkeri Dunn. A dwarf or prostrate shrub, normally forming a low mound of densely crowded, greenish stems, bearing small, pinnate leaves and tiny, yellow flowers in summer. Suitable for a rock garden. W Himalaya.

Discovered and introduced by R.N. Parker in 1923. AM 1933.

revolutum See *J. humile* ‘Revolutum’.

Jerusalem sage See *Phlomis fruticosa*.
Joshua tree See *Yucca brevifolia*.

†**JOVELLANA** Ruiz & Pav.—**Scrophulariaceae**—About 6 species of herbs and subshrubs, native to New Zealand and Chile. Related to *Calceolaria*, but their flowers do not have pouched lips.

sinclairii (Hook.) Kraenzl. A very distinct New Zealand species of dwarf habit, suitable for a rock garden in a mild locality, with white or pale lavender, purple-spotted flowers in June. I 1881.

*violacea (Cav.) G. Don (*Calceolaria violacea* Cav.) A charming, small shrub with erect branches and small, neat leaves. Pale violet flowers, with darker markings, are produced in June and July. I 1853. Chile. ♀ 2002. AM 1930.

Judas tree See *Cercis siliquastrum*.

JUGLANS L.—**Juglandaceae**—The walnuts are a genus of some 20 species of deciduous trees, native to N and S America and from SE Europe to SE Asia. They are mostly fast-growing, ornamental trees that are not particular as to soil, but should not be planted in sites subject to late frosts. Their leaves are pinnate and, in some species, are large and ornamental. They are distinguished from *Carya* by the chambered pith.

ailanthifolia Carrière (*J. sieboldiana* Maxim.) An erect-growing tree of medium size with large, handsome leaves often as much as 1m long. Japan. I 1860. **var.** *cordiformis* (Maxim.) Rehder. A form differing only in the shape of its fruits.

californica S. Watson. A distinct, large shrub or small tree with attractive leaves composed of 11–15 oblong-lance-olate leaflets. S California. C 1889.

cathayensis See *J. mandshurica*.

cinerea L. Butternut. A handsome, fast-growing species of medium size, with shoots sticky to the touch, large, hairy leaves and exceptionally large fruits. E North America. C 1633.

elaeopyren Dode (*J. major* (Torr.) Heller, *J. microcarpa* var. *major* (Torr.) Benson) A very handsome, medium-sized tree differing from *J. microcarpa* in its larger size, generally larger, more coarsely toothed leaflets and larger fruits. The leaves turn butter-yellow in autumn. New Mexico to Arizona, NW Mexico. Some plants grown as *J. microcarpa* belong here. I about 1894.

hindsii (Jeps.) R.E. Sm. Medium-sized tree with handsome foliage. C California. C 1878.

× *intermedia* Carrière (*J. nigra* × *J. regia*) A vigorous tree intermediate between the parents. Leaves usually with 5 or 6 pairs of leaflets, the terminal one often missing as in *J. nigra*. Leaflets oblong, crenate at the margin, glabrous apart from axillary tufts beneath.

major See *J. elaeopyren*.

mandshurica Maxim. (*J. cathayensis* Dode) Medium-sized tree with stout, glandular, hairy young shoots. Leaves, up to 60cm long, sometimes longer on young trees, are composed of 11–19 taper-pointed leaflets. NE former USSR, NE China, Korea. I 1859.

microcarpa Berl. (*J. rupestris* Torr.) Texan walnut. A very graceful, small, shrubby tree similar to *J. californica*, but with numerous, small, thin, narrow leaflets. Some plants grown under this name are *J. elaeopyren*. Texas, New Mexico. C 1868. var. *major* See *J. elaeopyren*.

nigra L. Black walnut. A noble, large, fast-growing tree with deeply furrowed bark and large leaves. Large, round fruits are generally in pairs. E and C USA. C 1686. ♀ 2002.

regia L. (*J. sinensis* (DC.) Dode) Common walnut. A slow-growing, medium-sized to large tree with a characteristic rounded head. Cultivated in England for many centuries. The timber is highly prized and very valuable. SE Europe, Himalaya, China. Normally grown from seed, selected cultivars, propagated vegetatively, such as 'Broadview' and 'Buccaneer', are grown for their early fruiting and the quality of their nuts. ♀ 2002. **'Laciniata'** Cut-leaved walnut. A form with somewhat pendent branchlets and deeply cut leaflets. A tree on the site of our West Hill nursery in Winchester has reached 16m (1990). AM 1960. **'Purpurea'** A form with deep red-purple leaves found in Germany in 1938. It is rare in cultivation.

rupestris See *J. microcarpa*.

sieboldiana See *J. ailanthifolia*.

sinensis See *J. regia*.

Juneberry See *Amelanchier*.
Juneberry, mountain See *Amelanchier bartramiana*.

‡**KALMIA** L.—**Ericaceae**—A genus of 7 species of mainly evergreen shrubs, mostly natives of North America with one species in Cuba. Charming, spring- and early summer-flowering shrubs, with conspicuous, saucer-shaped flowers. They luxuriate under conditions similar to those required by *Rhododendron*. For maximum flowering, plant in full sun and moist soil. Harmful if eaten.

*angustifolia L. Sheep laurel. A low-growing shrub, up to 1m high, slowly spreading and forming thickets. Leaves variable in shape, normally ovate-oblong, in pairs or threes. Flowers rosy-red; June. A very poisonous plant. E North America. I 1736. ♀ 2002. var. *carolina* (Small) Fern. (*K. carolina* Small) Southern sheep laurel. Leaves grey-downy underneath; flowers purple-rose. SE USA. I 1906. var. *ovata* Pursh. A form with broader, ovate, bright green leaves. **'Rubra'** Foliage deep green; flowers deep rosy-red, carried over a long period. ♀ 2002. **'Rubra Nana'** A dwarf form with flowers of rich garnet-red.

carolina See *K. angustifolia* var. *carolina*.

cuneata Michx. White wicky. A very rare, small, deciduous or semi-evergreen shrub, rarely above 1m. The small, alternate, dark green leaves are sessile or nearly so; white flowers are borne in clusters among the stems during summer. Marshy places in N and S Carolina, USA. I 1820.

glauca See *K. polifolia*.

*latifolia L. Calico bush, Mountain laurel. A magnificent, rhododendron-like shrub of medium size. Apart from roses and rhododendrons possibly the best June-flowering shrub for acid soils. The glossy, alternate leaves, 5–13cm long, make a pleasing setting for the clusters of bright pink flowers which open in June, giving the impression of sugar-icing when in bud. E North America. I 1734. ♀ 2002. **'Alba'** Plants seen under this name have flowers that are pale pink in bud opening white, flushed pink. There seems to be a relationship between the flower colour and the number of glands in the inflorescence, the pale-coloured forms being the most glandular. **'Carousel'** Flowers white, heavily marked with bright red-purple inside. **'Clementine Churchill'** Flowers deep pink in bud opening rich pink. A lovely clone. AM 1952. **'Elf'** A selection of f. *myrtifolia*. Compact habit with small leaves, young shoots purplish-red on the exposed side. Flowers pale pink in bud opening nearly white. C 1982. **'Freckles'** Flowers creamy-white spotted purple, from pink buds. ♀ 2002. **'Goodrich'** Corolla deep red inside with a narrow, white border. Selected from wild plants in Connecticut, USA in 1972. **'Heart of Fire'** Deep pink flowers from red buds. An improvement on 'Ostbo Red' of which it is a seedling. **'Little Linda'** A dwarf form to about 1m tall and across. Flowers deep pink from red buds. ♀ 2002. **'Minuet'** A compact, dwarf form with small leaves. Flowers white, banded deep red inside. f. *myrtifolia* (Jäger) K. Koch. A very slow-growing, small bush of compact habit, with smaller leaves and flowers. C 1840. AM 1965. **'Nipmuck'** Flowers bright deep red in bud, nearly white when open; pale green foliage. Raised in 1963. **'Olympic Fire'** A seedling, and said to be an improvement, of 'Ostbo Red'. Large, red buds open to pink flowers. Leaves wavy-edged. Selected in 1971. ♀ 2002. **'Ostbo Red'** Flowers bright red in bud opening to pale pink. The first red-budded kalmia. Selected in the USA in the 1940s. **'Pink Charm'** Deep pink to red buds open rich pink flowers with a deep maroon band inside. Selected in 1974. ♀ 2002. **'Pink Frost'** Flowers silvery-pink, deeper with age, from large pink buds. **'Shooting Star'** An unusual form in which the corolla is divided into 5 lobes which reflex as the flower opens. Flowers slightly later than normal. Selected from wild plants in North Carolina, USA, in 1972. **'Silver Dollar'** Very large, white flowers, up to 4cm across, with red anther pockets and a basal ring. Selected in 1952.

microphylla (Hook.) Heller. A dwarf shrub closely related to *K. polifolia* but smaller, to 15cm tall, with broader leaves not revolute at the margin. NW North America.

*polifolia Wangenh. (*K. glauca* Aiton) Eastern bog laurel. A small, wiry shrub, 30–60cm, with narrow leaves, dark shining green above, glaucous beneath, in pairs or threes. Flowers, in large, terminal clusters, are bright rose-purple, opening in April. In its native land this species grows in swamps and boggy places. N North America. I 1767.

‡**KALMIOPSIS** Rehder—**Ericaceae**—A monotypic genus related to *Rhodothamnus*.

leachiana (Henderson) Rehder. A choice and rare, dwarf shrub of considerable beauty bearing pink, kalmia-like blooms in terminal, leafy racemes from March to May. Quite hardy. A protected plant in SW Oregon, USA. I 1931. ♀ 2002. FCC 1987. AM 1937. **'Glendoick'** A selection with profuse, deep pink flowers.

‡*× **KALMIOTHAMNUS** B.N. Starling (*Kalmia × Rhodothamnus*)–**Ericaceae**–A group of hybrids first described in 1985.

ornithomma B.N. Starling (*K. leachiana × R. chamaecistus*) A dwarf shrub with dark green, glabrous leaves to 1.5cm long. The 5-lobed, saucer-shaped flowers, to 2.8cm across, are pink to red-purple with a bright red ring in the centre and open in clusters at the shoot ends in spring. Raised by Barry Starling from a cross made in 1981.

KALOPANAX Miq.—**Araliaceae**—A monotypic genus differing from *Eleutherococcus* in its lobed but not compound leaves.

pictus See *K. septemlobus*.

septemlobus (Thunb. ex A. Murray) Koidz. (*K. pictus* (Thunb.) Nakai, *Acanthopanax ricinifolius* (Siebold & Zucc.) Seem.) A small to medium-sized tree in cultivation, superficially resembling an *Acer*. The branches and sucker growths bear scattered, stout prickles. The 5- to 7-lobed leaves are over 30cm across in young plants. Small clusters of white flowers are borne in large, flattish heads, 30–60cm across, in autumn. Japan, E Russia, Korea, China. I 1865. **var.** *maximowiczii* (Van Houtte) Hand.-Mazz. Deeply lobed leaves.

Kangaroo thorn See *Acacia armata*.

†***KECKIELLA** Straw—**Scrophulariaceae**—A small genus of evergreen shrubs and subshrubs closely related to *Penstemon* with 7 species in the W USA and N Mexico.

cordifolia (Benth.) Straw (*Penstemon cordifolius* Benth.) A semi-evergreen, slender-branched shrub reaching 2m high whe grown against a wall. Leaves heart-shaped, coarsely toothed, glossy dark green. Flowers orange-scarlet, in panicles from June to August. California. Discovered by David Douglas in 1831 and introduced by Hartweg in 1848.

corymbosa (Benth.) Straw (*Penstemon corymbosus* Benth.) A small, semi-evergreen shrub, closely related to *K. cordifolia*, differing in its smaller stature, its ovate leaves, tapered at the base and its shorter flowers in flattened racemes. California.

Kentucky coffee tree See *Gymnocladus dioica*.

KERRIA DC.—**Rosaceae**—A monotypic genus differing from *Rhodotypos* in its alternate leaves and yellow flowers. A suckering shrub which has adorned gardens since Victorian times. May be thinned and pruned immediately after flowering.

japonica (L.) DC. A graceful shrub, to 1.8m high or more against a wall. In April and May, or earlier in mild weather, its arching branches are wreathed with rich yellow flowers, like large buttercups. Its green stems are most effective in winter. China, long cultivated in Japan. I 1834.

'Albescens' Flowers white. **'Golden Guinea'** A form with very large, single flowers. ♀ 2002. **'Picta'** ('Variegata') A pleasing and elegant, creamy-white variegated form of lower spreading habit, up to 1.5m in height. C 1844. **'Pleniflora'** ('Flore Pleno') The well-known, double-flowered form, taller and more vigorous and erect than the single-flowered form. I from China by William Kerr in 1804. ♀ 2002. AM 1978. **'Variegata'** See 'Picta'.

KOELREUTERIA Laxm.—**Sapindaceae**—3 species of deciduous trees, natives of China and Taiwan. Only the following is widely grown. Easy on all soils, but flowering and fruiting best in hot, dry summers.

paniculata Laxm. (*K. paniculata* var. *apiculata* (Rehder & E.H. Wilson) Rehder) The best-known species, given such names as Pride of India, China tree, Golden rain tree. A very attractive, broad-headed tree, 9–12m high, with pinnate leaves comprising 9–15 ovate leaflets. The large panicles of small, yellow flowers in July and August are followed by conspicuous, bladder-like fruits. The leaves turn yellow in autumn. China. I 1763. ♀ 2002. AM 1932. **var.** *apiculata* See *K. paniculata*. **'Fastigiata'** A rare and remarkable, slow-growing form of narrowly columnar habit, attaining 8m high by 1m wide. Raised at Kew in 1888. **'Rose Lantern'** Named from a plant at the Arnold Arboretum, this form flowers very late, in September and October, and produces red-tinged young pods. It has also been grown as 'September', a similar form with green pods.

KOLKWITZIA Graebn.—**Caprifoliaceae**—A monotypic genus related to *Abelia*.

amabilis Graebn. Beauty bush. This lovely and graceful, very hardy and adaptable, medium-sized shrub forms a dense, twiggy bush. In May and June its drooping branches are draped with masses of bell-shaped, soft pink flowers with a yellow throat. The calyces and pedicels are conspicuously hairy. One of the many lovely shrubs introduced by Ernest Wilson. W China. I 1901. AM 1923. **'Pink Cloud'** A lovely, pink-flowered seedling, selected and raised at Wisley in 1946. 'Rosea' is similar. ♀ 2002. FCC 1963.

†***KUNZEA** Reichb.—**Myrtaceae**—A genus of some 30 species of evergreen, heath-like shrubs, natives of Australia. Closely related to *Leptospermum* but differing in having anthers that are longer than the petals.

ericoides (A.Rich.) Joy Thomps. (*Leptospermum ericoides* (A. Rich.) *L. phylicoides* (Schauer) Cheel) A medium-sized to large, evergreen shrub, sometimes tree-like, with arching shoots and slender, dark green to grey-green leaves to 1.5cm long. Small, white flowers, to 1.5cm across, with long, white stamens and a red centre, open singly or in clusters along the shoots in mid- to late summer. SE Australia.

L

Labrador tea See *Rhododendron groenlandicum.*

+LABURNOCYTISUS C.K. Schneid. (*Laburnum + Chamaecytisus*)—**Leguminosae**—A graft hybrid between a broom and *Laburnum*. Only the following form is known.
'Adamii' (*Laburnum anagyroides + Chamaecytisus purpureus*) A remarkable, small tree, a graft hybrid (chimaera) with laburnum forming the core and broom the outer envelope. Some branches bear the yellow flowers of the laburnum, while other branches bear dense, congested clusters of the purple-flowered broom. To add to the confusion, most branches produce intermediate flowers of striking coppery-pink. Originated in the nursery of M. Adam near Paris in 1825.

LABURNUM Medik.—**Leguminosae**—Golden rain. A genus of 2 species of small, easily cultivated, ornamental trees, suitable for almost all types of soil. The yellow pea-flowers are produced in drooping racemes during late spring and early summer. All parts of the plant are poisonous, particularly the seeds.
alpinum (Mill.) Bercht. & J. Presl. Scotch laburnum. A small, broad-headed tree producing long, drooping racemes of fragrant flowers in early June. Leaves trifoliolate, deep shining green above, paler and with a few hairs beneath. Pods flattened, glabrous and shining. C and S Europe. C 1596. **'Pendulum'** A slow-growing form developing a low, dome-shaped head of stiffly weeping branches. **'Pyramidale'** A form with erect branches.
anagyroides Medik. (*L. vulgare* Bercht. & J. Presl) Common laburnum. A small tree flowering in late May or early June, the drooping racemes crowded along the branches. This species differs from *L. alpinum* in its earlier flowering, shorter racemes, smaller, dull green leaves, which are grey-green and densely adpressed hairy beneath, and its rounder, adpressed, hairy pods. C and S Europe. C 1560. **'Aureum'** Golden-leaved laburnum. Leaves soft yellow during summer; sometimes liable to revert. FCC 1875. **'Autumnale'** ('Semperflorens') A form that frequently flowers for a second time in the autumn. **'Erect'** An excellent, small tree with stiffly ascending branches. Originated as a seedling in our nurseries and found by foreman Alf Alford in 1964. **'Pendulum'** A low, elegant tree with long, slender, drooping branches. **'Quercifolium'** A curious small tree with deeply lobed leaflets, occasionally numbering 4 or 5. The petals of the flower are toothed, the wings with slender lobes on the upper side.
× *watereri* (Wettst.) Dipp. (*L. alpinum × L. anagyroides*) A small tree with glossy leaves and long, slender racemes in June. Resembles *L. alpinum* in general habit, but the leaves and pods are slightly more hairy, the latter usually only partially developed. **'Alford's Weeping'** A vigorous, small tree with a widespreading head of long, drooping branches. Originated as a seedling in our nurseries and found by foreman Alf Alford in 1965. **'Vossii'** (*L. × vossii* hort.) A lovely form, very free-flowering, with long racemes. ♥ 2002.

Laburnum, Dalmatian See *Petteria ramentacea.*
Laburnum, evergreen See *Piptanthus nepalensis.*
Lacebark See *Hoheria populnea* and *H. sexstylosa.*
Lad's love See *Artemisia abrotanum.*

†LAGERSTROEMIA L.—**Lythraceae**—A genus of some 50 species of evergreen and deciduous trees and shrubs often with exotic flowers. Natives of warm parts of Asia, the Pacific Islands and Australia.
fauriei Koehne. Following the introduction of this species to the US National Arboretum, Washington, DC., by Dr John Creech in the 1950s from Japan, Dr Donald Egolf started a breeding programme with *L. indica*, which has resulted in a large number of selections. The incorporation of mildew resistance and striking red-brown bark from *L. fauriei* produced plants ranging from small shrubs to trees, in a wide variety of colours. Many are now common landscape subjects in warm parts of the USA.
indica L. Crape myrtle. A beautiful, large shrub or small tree requiring more hot sun than usually experienced in the British Isles. The main stem is attractively mottled grey, pink and cinnamon. The flowers are usually lilac-pink, with crinkled petals, and borne in terminal panicles in autumn, only opening outside after a warm, late summer. Best planted against a sunny wall. China, Korea. I 1759. ♥ 2002. AM 1924. **'Rosea'** Flowers deep rose.

Lancewood See *Pseudopanax crassifolius.*
Lancewood, toothed See *Pseudopanax ferox.*
Lantern tree See *Crinodendron hookerianum.*
Laurel, Alexandrian See *Danae racemosa.*
Laurel, bay See *Laurus nobilis.*
Laurel, Californian See *Umbellularia californica.*
Laurel, Carolina Cherry See *Prunus caroliniana.*
Laurel, Chilean See *Laurelia sempervirens.*
Laurel, common or cherry See *Prunus laurocerasus.*
Laurel, eastern bog See *Kalmia polifolia.*
Laurel, mountain See *Kalmia latifolia.*
Laurel, Portugal See *Prunus lusitanica.*
Laurel, Serbian See *Prunus laurocerasus* 'Serbica'.
Laurel, sheep See *Kalmia angustifolia.*
Laurel, sierra See *Leucothoe davisiae.*
Laurel, spotted See *Aucuba japonica.*
Laurel, spurge See *Daphne laureola.*
Laurel, stinking See *Illicium floridanum.*
Laurel, Tasmanian See *Anopterus glandulosus.*

†*LAURELIA Juss.—**Monimiaceae**—A small genus of 3 species of evergreen trees with opposite leaves, natives of Chile, Argentina and New Zealand.
sempervirens (Ruiz & Pav.) Tul. (*L. serrata* Bertero, *L. aromatica* Juss. ex Poir.) Chilean laurel. A handsome, large, evergreen shrub or small to medium-sized tree, lime-tolerant, with smooth, grey bark, cracking with age. The leathery, serrated leaves are bright green and strongly aromatic. Small, green flowers open in late spring. Proving remarkably hardy given reasonable shelter. Chile. I before 1868.
serrata See *L. sempervirens.*

***LAURUS** L.—**Lauraceae**—The true laurels are a genus of only 2 species of dioecious, evergreen shrubs or small trees. The small, yellowish-green flowers cluster the branches in April, or earlier in mild weather, and are followed, on female trees, by shining black fruits. Suitable for all types of well-drained soil.

†*azorica* (Seub.) Franco (*L. canariensis* Webb & Berth.) Canary Island laurel. In this country a large, evergreen shrub. A handsome species, differing from *L. nobilis* in its larger, broader leaves and its downy young twigs; leaves of older trees become narrower. Suitable only for the mildest gardens. There appear to be 2 forms in cultivation; one with hairy leaves and another with glabrous leaves, the latter being more tender. Canary Islands, Azores.

‘Dunloe Castle’ A large-leaved form or hybrid of *L. nobilis* making a handsome, bushy tree. The original plant grows at Dunloe Castle Hotel Gardens, near Killarney, Co. Kerry.

nobilis L. Bay laurel. The laurel of the ancients, now grown for its aromatic foliage and for its usefulness as a dense, pyramidal, evergreen shrub or tree. Stands clipping well, and thrives in coastal regions where it will form good hedges. Subject to frost damage in cold areas. Mediterranean region. C 1562. ♀ 2002. ‘Angustifolia’ (‘Salicifolia’) Willow-leaf bay. A remarkably hardy form with long, narrow, pale green, leathery, wavy-edged leaves. ‘Aurea’ Golden-yellow leaves, particularly attractive in winter and spring. ♀ 2002.

Laurustinus See *Viburnum tinus*.

***LAVANDULA** L.—**Labiatae**—About 36 species of aromatic shrubs and herbs, natives of the Mediterranean region, the Canary Islands, Cape Verde, Madeira, the Near East, N Africa, NE tropical Africa and India. Lavender is perhaps the most highly prized of all aromatic shrubs. It is a favourite for dwarf hedges, associating well with stonework or rose beds, and as a component of grey or blue borders. It succeeds in all types of well-drained soil preferably in full sun. An excellent maritime plant. We are grateful to Susyn Andrews for assistance with this genus.

†× *allardii* Hy (*L. dentata* × *L. latifolia*) Vigorous hybrids of cultivated origin making small shrubs to 1.2m tall with grey-green, toothed or entire leaves and long spikes of blue flowers on very long peduncles.

angustifolia Mill. (*L. spica* L. in part, *L. officinalis* Chaix) A dwarf, aromatic shrub of compact habit with slender grey-green leaves. The flowers are borne in dense spikes on long, slender stems. SW and SC Europe, east to Greece. The most commonly grown form, subsp. *angustifolia* is the source of true lavender oil; subsp. *pyrenaica* (DC.) Guinea occurs in the E Pyrenees. AMT 1962. ‘Alba’ See *L.* × *intermedia* ‘Alba’. ‘Ashdown Forest’ Dwarf, bushy habit, to 50cm tall, with spikes of pale purple flowers. C 1980s. ‘Beechwood Blue’ Compact, to 45cm tall, with profuse blue flowers. ♀ 2002. **Blue Cushion** (‘Schola’) PBR A dwarf, mound-forming selection with small heads of deep blue flowers becoming pale blue then grey. A seedling of ‘Hidcote’ pollinated by ‘Nana Alba’. C 1992. ‘Folgate’ A compact form with narrow, grey-green leaves and stems from 60–75cm high.

Lavender-blue flowers open in early July. Often confused in cultivation. C 1933. AMT 1963. ‘Grappenhall’ See *L.* × *intermedia* ‘Grappenhall’. ‘Grosso’ See *L.* × *intermedia* ‘Grosso’. ‘Hidcote’ A compact form with narrow, grey-green leaves and stems from 60–80cm high. Violet flowers in dense spikes, open in early July. One of the best and most popular cultivars. C 1920s. ♀ 2002 to vegetatively propagated plants. FCCT 1963. AM 1950. Many seedlings have been propagated and distributed under this name and the true plant is perhaps no longer grown. ‘Nana Atropurpurea’ is a similar, though older, clone. ‘Hidcote Giant’ See *L.* × *intermedia* ‘Hidcote Giant’. ‘Hidcote Pink’ Compact habit to 60cm with grey-green leaves. Similar to ‘Hidcote’ but with pale pink flowers. C 1950s. ♀ 2002. ‘Imperial Gem’ Similar to ‘Hidcote’, with deep purple flowers and more silvery foliage. C 1980s. ♀ 2002. **Little Lottie** (‘Clarmo’) PBR A dwarf selection to 40cm tall bearing profuse heads of pale pink flowers. C 1998. ♀ 2002. ‘Loddon Blue’ Compact, to 45cm tall, with purple-blue flowers. C 1963. ♀ 2002. ‘Loddon Pink’ A compact form with narrow leaves, greener than ‘Hidcote Pink’, and stems from 60–75cm high. Pale pink flowers open in early July. C 1950. AMT 1963. ‘Miss Katherine’ PBR Compact habit and very fragrant, with grey-green leaves and profuse deep pink flowers. ♀ 2002. ‘Miss Muffet’ (‘Scholmis’) PBR Compact with silvery foliage and lilac-blue flowers. ♀ 2002. ‘Munstead’ A compact form with narrow green leaves and stems from 60–75cm high. Lavender-blue flowers open in early July. It is often grown from seed and is confused in cultivation. C 1916. AMT 1963. ‘Nana Alba’ A dwarf, compact, and very aromatic form with comparatively broad, green-grey leaves and grey-green stems up to 30cm. White flowers open in early July. ♀ 2002. ‘Princess Blue’ Vigorous and upright with long spikes of pale blue flowers. ‘Rosea’ A compact form with narrow, strongly scented leaves, much greener than those of ‘Loddon Pink’. Stems 60–75cm high, bear lavender-pink flowers in early to mid-July. C 1930s. ‘Royal Purple’ A tall-growing form, to 75cm, with long spikes of purple flowers. C 1940s. ‘Sawyers’ See *L.* ‘Sawyers’. ‘Twickel Purple’ A vigorous form with comparatively broad, grey-green leaves and stems from 60–75cm high. Lavender-blue flowers on long spikes open in early July. AMT 1961. ‘Vera’ See *L.* × *intermedia* ‘Dutch’. ‘Wendy Carlisle’ A dwarf, compact, and quite aromatic form with grey foliage. A neater, more erect habit than ‘Nana Alba’ with slightly larger leaves. White flowers in July with distinct, silver-grey calyces. ♀ 2002.

‘Avonview’ (*L. stoechas* × *L. viridis*) A striking hybrid raised in New Zealand, growing to 60cm tall, with long spikes of deep purple flowers and large, pale purple bracts.

†*canariensis* (L.) Mill. A small shrub with glabrous shoots and downy, green leaves bipinnately cut into flattened lobes. Branched inflorescences bear slender heads of blue flowers and blue-purple bracts. Canary Islands.

†× *christiana* Gattef. & Maire (*L. canariensis* × *L. pinnata*) A very attractive but tender hybrid of cultivated origin with bipinnate, silvery-green leaves and long-stalked, slender flowerheads in branched inforesences. An excellent container plant for a patio, requiring winter protection in most areas.

†*dentata* L. A dwarf, aromatic shrub with oblong, green leaves, each one divided like the pinnae of a fern. The powdery-blue flowers are borne in dense, short spikes in late summer. S and E Spain, Balearic Islands, NW Africa, Arabia. C 1597. **var. candicans** Batt. Foliage silvery-white. **'Royal Crown'** Upright habit with dense clusters of pale violet flowers held well above the foliage. ♀ 2002.

'Fathead' (*L. stoechas* × *L. viridis*) A dwarf shrub to 45cm tall. Bears dense heads of deep purple flowers with contrasting pale pink bracts. C 1997.

'Goodwin Creek Gray' (*L. dentata* × *L. lanata*) A bushy hybrid of American origin to 75cm tall, with softly hairy, toothed leaves and long spikes of blue flowers over a long period. C 1990s.

'Helmsdale' PBR (*L. stoechas* 'Helmsdale) (*L. stoechas* × *L. viridis*) A selection introduced from New Zealand, with green-grey leaves and large, burgundy-purple bracts. Compact, to 75cm.

× *intermedia* Emeric ex Loisel. (*L. angustifolia* × *L. latifolia*) Lavandin. A vigorous shrub, to 1.5m, with a scent of camphor. Long flower stalks and flowerheads. Usually flowering later than *L. angustifolia*. There are many selections, often grown as forms of *L. angustifolia*. Spain, France, Italy. **'Alba'** (*L. angustifolia* 'Alba') A robust and very aromatic form with long, narrow, grey-green leaves producing erect stems 0.9–1.2m high. White flowers open in late July. ♀ 2002. **'Arabian Night'** Purple-blue flowers on long spikes; grey-green foliage. ♀ 2002. **'Dutch'** (*L. angustifolia* 'Vera') A robust form with comparatively broad, grey leaves and stems 1–1.2m high. Lavender-blue flowers open in late July. Usually referred to in cultivation as Dutch lavender. AMT 1962. **'Fragrant Memories'** Bushy, to 75cm, with grey foliage and pale purple flowers. C 1994. **'Grappenhall'** (*L. angustifolia* 'Grappenhall') A robust form with comparatively broad, grey-green leaves and strong stems 0.9–1.2m high. Lavender-blue flowers open in late July. **'Grosso'** (*L. angustifolia* 'Grosso') A superb, robust and very aromatic form with green leaves and stems to 90cm. Mid-blue flowers open in profusion in late July. Widely grown commercially for the oil. **'Hidcote Giant'** (*L. angustifolia* 'Hidcote Giant') Similar in habit and appearance to 'Grappenhall', but with dense, conical spikes of flowers that are a little darker in colour. C 1950. **'Seal'** Vigorous and bushy, to 1m tall, with blue-purple flowers. C 1930s. **Walberton's Silver Edge** ('Walvera') PBR Vigorous, to 90cm, with grey leaves edged with cream; long-stalked spikes of pale purple flowers. C 1999.

†*lanata* Boiss. A small, white-woolly shrub producing long-stalked spikes of fragrant, bright violet flowers from July to September. Spain. ♀ 2002.

latifolia Medik. A dwarf shrub, closely related to *L. angustifolia* but differing in its broader leaves and often branched flowerheads. It is not commonly grown but is a parent of many of the cultivated lavenders, see *L.* × *intermedia*. SW and SC Europe.

'Marshwood' PBR (*L. stoechas* 'Marshwood') (*L. stoechas* × *L. viridis*) From the same source as 'Helmsdale', but less hardy with larger, purple flowerheads with pink bracts. Compact to 90cm.

†*multifida* L. A small shrub with bipinnate, downy, green leaves and long-stalked heads of blue-violet flowers. S Spain, Italy, N Africa.

pedunculata See *L. stoechas* subsp. *pedunculata*.

†*pinnata* L. f. A dwarf, grey-hairy shrub with the leaves pinnately cut into slender lobes. Flowers blue-purple, in long-stalked branched spikes. Canary Islands, Madeira.

'Richard Gray' (*L. angustifolia* × *L. lanata*) A dwarf shrub, to 50cm tall, with grey foliage and cylindrical spikes of purple flowers. C 1980s. ♀ 2002.

'Sawyers' (*L. angustifolia* 'Sawyers') (*L. angustifolia* × *L. lanata*) Compact, bushy plant, to 60cm, with superb, silvergrey leaves and large, purple, pointed flowers. ♀ 2002.

spica See *L. angustifolia*.

stoechas L. French lavender. A dwarf, intensely aromatic shrublet with narrow leaves. Dark purple flowers are borne in dense, congested terminal heads on short peduncles during summer. It requires a warm, dry, sunny position. Mediterranean region, N Africa, with other subspecies in Madeira, the Iberian Peninsula, Turkey and N Africa. C since mid-16th century. ♀ 2002. AM 1960. **var. albiflora** See f. *leucantha*. **'Helmsdale'** See *L.* 'Helmsdale'. †**'Kew Red'** A striking but very tender form with crimson flowers and pale pink bracts. **f. leucantha** Lassaraz (var. *albiflora* Bean) White flowers and bracts on short peduncles. **'Marshwood'** See *L.* 'Marshwood'. **'Papillon'** see under subsp. *pedunculata*. **subsp. pedunculata** (Mill.) Rozeira. Shorter flower spikes on long, wispy peduncles. 'Papillon' is a name given by us to a commonly grown form of this. Spain, Portugal. ♀ 2002. AM 1981. **'Purple Emperor'** See under subsp. *sampaioana*. **subsp. sampaioana** Rozeira. A form resembling subsp. *pedunculata* with long-stalked flowerheads. Spain and Portugal. 'Purple Emperor' is a name given by us to a selection of this. The tall stems carry heads with tiny deep purple flowers and conspicuous rose-purple bracts. **'Snowman'** Compact habit with short, dense spikes of pure white flowers. **'Willow Vale'** See *L.* 'Willow Vale'.

†*viridis* L'Hér. A tender species related to *L. stoechas* with roughly hairy leaves and shoots. Foliage lemon-scented. Bracts of the inflorescence and the large upper bracts pale green; flowers white. SW Spain, S Portugal, NW Africa.

'Willow Vale' (*L. stoechas* 'Willow Vale') (*L. stoechas* × *L. viridis*) A superb lavender from Australia with grey-green foliage and long, purple, crinkly bracts. ♀ 2002.

LAVATERA L.—Malvaceae—A genus of some 25 species of herbs and shrubs, natives of Europe, W Asia, Australia and California. The shrubby mallows have typical mallow flowers and palmate leaves. Succeeds in all types of soil, preferably in full sun; excellent for maritime exposure.

bicolor See under *L. maritima*.

× *clementii* Cheek (*L. olbia* × *L. thuringiaca*) A vigorous, medium-sized to large subshrub with 3–5-lobed, grey-downy leaves. The widely funnel-shaped flowers, 7cm across, vary from pink to white with a red eye and open over a long period during summer. A largely sterile hybrid naturalised in parts of the British Isles. The cultivars described here have previously been listed as forms of either *L. olbia* or *L. thuringiaca*. The name commemorates Eric Clement who pointed out that these plants were probably of hybrid origin. **'Barnsley'** Flowers very pale, nearly white with a red eye. It has now been shown that this splendid form is a periclinal chimaera which originated as a sport of 'Rosea'. Any reversions should be removed. AM 1986. **'Blushing Bride'** Almost identical to 'Barnsley' in flower, but generally a little smaller and more compact. Found as a seedling and less likely to revert. **'Bredon Springs'** Flowers with overlapping petals, opening widely, deep dusky pink, borne in profusion over a long period. ♀ 2002. **'Burgundy Wine'** Deep purplish-pink flowers. Selected and named by Peter Catt in 1988 from a number of seedlings found in his garden. ♀ 2002. **'Candy Floss'** Very pale pink flowers. ♀ 2002. **'Eye Catcher'** Similar to 'Rosea' but with very deep pink flowers with darker veins and centre. **'Kew Rose'** More vigorous than 'Rosea' with darker, purplish stems and larger, bright pink flowers. Previously grown as *L. olbia*. AM 1988. **'Lisanne'** ('Barnsley' × *L. thuringiaca* 'Ice Cool') Similar to 'Barnsley', but a purer white. **'Mary Hope'** A compact form, reaching 1.5m, bearing profuse white flowers with a pink eye. **Memories** ('Stelav') PBR Pale pink buds opening to white flowers with a pink eye. **'Pink Frills'** Clear pink flowers with frilly edges. Found as a seedling by The Botanic Nursery, Wiltshire. **'Pavlova'** Soft pink with a white eye. **'Rosea'** (*L. olbia* 'Rosea') Deep pink flowers. ♀ 2002. AM 1920.

†*maritima* Gouan. An elegant species attaining 1.5–1.8m against a sunny wall. Both the stems and the palmate leaves are greyish and downy. Large, saucer-shaped, pale lilac flowers, with purple veins and eyes, are produced continuously from midsummer to late autumn. Needs a warm, sheltered position. The plant described here was originally known as *L. bicolor*. 'Princess de Ligne' is a selection that differs little from the typical form. SW Europe, N Africa. ♀ 2002.

oblongifolia Boiss. A semi-evergreen, upright, subshrub with grey-hairy shoots and heart-shaped leaves, to 10cm long, densely covered in softly bristly hairs on both sides; petiole to 4cm. Flowers 5cm across on short stalks in the leaf axils in late summer, mauve-pink with a carmine blotch at the base of each petal. S Spain.

†*olbia* L. A vigorous shrub up to 2.5m high, the whole plant conspicuously and softly grey-downy; leaves with 3–5 lobes. Large, pink or reddish-pink flowers appear throughout summer. Best in a warm, sunny position. W Mediterranean region. AM 1912. Rarely grown in gardens, most plants under this name belong to *L.* × *clementii*. **'Lilac Lady'** Flowers small, pale violet with darker veins. This seedling, raised by Peter Catt, has not proved hardy.

thuringiaca L. This species, native of SW Europe is herbaceous and so not described here. Most cultivars previously thought to belong under this name are hybrids with *L. olbia*, for which see *L.* × *clementii*. 'Ice Cool', ('Peppermint Ice'), is however, a white-flowered form that belongs here.

Lavender See *Lavandula*.
Lead plant See *Amorpha canescens*.
Leadwort, Cape See *Plumbago auriculata*.
Leatherleaf See *Chamaedaphne calyculata*.
Leatherwood See *Cyrilla racemiflora, Dirca palustris* and *Eucryphia lucida*.

Leatherwood, western See *Dirca occidentalis*.
× *Ledodendron* **'Arctic Tern'** See *Rhododendron* 'Arctic Tern'.
Ledum See *Rhododendron*.
Ledum buxifolium See *Leiophyllum buxifolium*.
Ledum glandulosum See *Rhododendron neoglandulosum*.
Ledum groenlandicum See *Rhododendron groenlandicum*.
Ledum latifolium See *Rhododendron groenlandicum*.
Ledum minus See under *Rhododendron tomentosum*.
Ledum palustre See *Rhododendron tomentosum*.

‡***LEIOPHYLLUM** R. Hedw.—**Ericaceae**—The single species in this genus is an evergreen shrub with small, leathery leaves. Suitable for a peat garden or similar site.

buxifolium (Bergius) Elliott (*Ledum buxifolium* Bergius) Sand myrtle. A dwarf shrub of neat, compact, rounded habit. In May and June produces clusters of white flowers, pink in bud. Leaves opposite and alternate. An attractive species requiring lime-free soil. E North America. I by Peter Collinson in 1736. ♀ 2002. AM 1955. **var.** *hugeri* (Small) C.K. Schneid. Leaves mostly alternate, longer than in the typical form. **var.** *prostratum* (Loudon) A. Gray. A very dainty prostrate or loosely spreading, dwarf shrub. Leaves mostly opposite. AM 1945.

‡**LEITNERIA** Chapm.—**Leitneriaceae**—A monotypic genus and the only member of the family, most closely related to *Myrica, Populus* and *Salix* but very different in general appearance. It requires moist, lime-free soil.

floridana Chapm. Corkwood. A rare and botanically interesting species that makes a medium-sized to large, suckering shrub, occasionally a small tree. It has narrow-elliptic to elliptic-lanceolate leaves, 12–20cm long, and small flowers appear in slender greyish catkins in spring; male and female borne on separate plants. SE USA. I 1894.

Lemon See *Citrus limon*.
Lemon verbena See *Aloysia triphylla*.

†**LEONOTIS** (Pers.) R. Br.—**Labiatae**—About 15 species of annuals, perennials and shrubs native to tropical and S Africa. The following is a shrub, easily grown in all types of soil but only suitable for a sunny wall in very mild localities. Excellent for a conservatory.

leonurus (L.) R. Br. Lion's ear. A small, square-stemmed shrub with downy, lanceolate, opposite leaves and dense, axillary whorls of 5cm long, downy, bright orange-scarlet, 2-lipped flowers in late autumn. S Africa. I 1712. AM 1982.

LEPECHINIA Willd.—**Labiatae**—A genus of 35 species of sage-like shrubs and herbaceous perennials, natives of warm parts of North and South America. The following is only suitable for the mildest areas of the British Isles but makes an excellent conservatory shrub.

chamaedryoides (Balb.) Epling (*Sphacele chamaedryoides* (Balb.) Briq., *S. campanulata* Benth.) A small shrub that has wrinkled leaves and bears loose racemes of pale blue, tubular flowers, to 2cm long, during summer. Chile. I 1875.

†**LEPTODERMIS** Wall.—**Rubiaceae**—About 30 species of deciduous shrubs, natives of the Himalaya and E Asia. The following are interesting and subtly attractive, small to medium-sized shrubs for all soils in moderately sheltered gardens.

kumaonensis Parker. An uncommon, small shrub with downy leaves. Small, trumpet-shaped, white flowers, becoming lilac or purplish, are borne in clusters in the leaf axils from July to October. NW Himalaya. I 1923.

pilosa Diels (*Hamiltonia pilosa* Franch.) A medium-sized shrub with smaller leaves than *L. kumaonensis*. Lavender flowers from July to September. Yunnan. I 1904 by George Forrest.

***LEPTOSPERMUM** J.R. Forst. & G. Forst.—**Myrtaceae**—A genus of some 80 species of attractive, small-leaved, evergreen shrubs or small trees, mainly natives of Australia, a few found in New Zealand, New Caledonia and Malaysia. They are related to the myrtles and of about equal merit to the tree heaths. In warm maritime and mild localities, many form large shrubs up to 4–6m high, but elsewhere most require the protection of a wall. They succeed best in full sun in well-drained, acid or neutral soils. Flowers are white, unless otherwise stated, and borne in May and June.

cunninghamii See *L. myrtifolium*.

ericoides See *Kunzea ericoides*.

†*grandiflorum* Lodd. (*L. rodwayanum* Summerh. & Comber) Tasmanian species with flowers as much as 3cm across, the largest of the genus, in late summer. I 1930 by Harold Comber.

humifusum See *L. rupestre*.

†*laevigatum* (Gaertn.) F. Muell. A vigorous species with comparatively large, glossy, glabrous leaves and flowers 2cm across. Coasts of SE Australia and Tasmania. I about 1788. AM 1927.

lanigerum (Sol. ex Aiton) Sm. (*L. pubescens* Lam.) A beautiful, large shrub with upright branches and silvery leaves, often bronzed towards autumn. Flowers are produced in early summer. In southern counties there are bushes that have grown splendidly in open borders for more than 20 years. SE Australia, Tasmania. I 1774 by Captain Tobias Furneaux. '**Silver Sheen**' See *L. myrtifolium* 'Silver Sheen'.

liversidgei R.T. Baker & H.G. Sm. An Australian species with numerous, small, crowded leaves, lemon-scented when crushed. Flowers in graceful sprays. One of the hardier species which has here survived many winters in the open. E Australia.

myrtifolium Sieber ex DC. (*L. cunninghamii* S. Schauer) A medium-sized shrub with attractive, silvery-grey leaves and reddish stems. Flowers in July, considerably later than *L. lanigerum*. SE Australia. '**Silver Sheen**' (*L. lanigerum* 'Silver Sheen') A selection from the plants originally grown as *L. cunninghamii*, with particularly silvery leaves. ♀ 2002.

phylicoides See *Kunzea ericoides*.

'**Pink Cascade**' An attractive, small shrub of spreading habit with arching and pendent branches. Flowers pale pink, 15mm across. Probably a hybrid of *L. polygalifolium*.

rodwayanum See *L. grandiflorum*.

rupestre Hook. f. (*L. humifusum* Cunn. ex Schauer, *L. scoparium* var. *prostratum* hort. not Hook. f.) An extremely

hardy, prostrate shrub, forming an extensive carpet of reddish stems and small, blunt, leathery leaves, which turn bronze-purple in very cold weather. Small flowers stud the branches of mature plants in early summer. A splendid specimen in the Sir Harold Hillier Gardens and Arboretum has reached 1m tall and 5m across. Tasmania. I 1930 by Harold Comber. ♀ 2002.

†*scoparium* J.R. Forst. & G. Forst. The common manuka or tea-tree of New Zealand. A variable species that has given rise to numerous forms. Australia, Tasmania, New Zealand. I 1771. AM 1972. '**Album Flore Pleno**' Double flowers. Compact and erect habit. C 1926. '**Autumn Glory**' Large, double, button-like, pink flowers in late spring and early summer, occasionally flowering again in late summer and early autumn. '**Boscawenii**' Flowers up to 2.5cm across, rich pink in bud opening white with reddish centres. Compact habit. A seedling of 'Nichollsii' raised in 1909. AM 1912. '**Chapmanii**' Leaves brownish-green; flowers bright rose. Found as a seedling by Sir Frederic Chapman on Signal Hill, near Dunedin, New Zealand in about 1890. '**Decumbens**' A semi-prostrate form with pale pink, long-lasting flowers, freely produced. '**Keatleyi**' An outstanding cultivar with large, waxy-petalled, soft pink flowers. Young shoots and leaves crimson and silky. A tetraploid form of var. *incanum* Allan found in the wild in New Zealand by Captain Keatley in 1917. ♀ 2002. AM 1961. '**Kiwi**' A dwarf form of dense habit with freely produced deep pink flowers and bronze foliage. A seedling of 'Nanum' raised in New Zealand. ♀ 2002. '**Martini**' Large, single pink flowers, deeper with age, profusely borne. C 1945. **Nanum Group** A charming, dwarf form, attaining about 30cm; rose-pink flowers are produced with great freedom. An excellent alpine-house shrub. Raised in New Zealand before 1940. AM 1952. '**Nichollsii**' Carmine-red flowers and dark purplish-bronze foliage. Seed raised from a plant found in New Zealand in 1898 and brought into cultivation there by William Nicholls in 1904. ♀ 2002. AM 1953. FCC 1912. '**Nichollsii Grandiflorum**' A selected form of 'Nichollsii' with larger flowers. '**Nichollsii Nanum**' A dwarf form with deep pink flowers with a darker centre. Foliage bronze-purple. ♀ 2002. AM 1953. **var. *prostratum*** Hook. f. Prostrate forms occur in the wild and have originated in cultivation. Plants grown under this name are usually *L. rupestre*. '**Red Damask**' Very double, deep red, long-lasting flowers. An F$_2$ hybrid from a cross between 'Nichollsii' and a plant with double, pink flowers. Raised in California in 1944. ♀ 2002. AM 1955. '**Roseum Multipetalum**' Double, rose-pink flowers in profusion. AM 1928. '**Snow Flurry**' A form with double, white flowers. A plant with single flowers has been distributed under this name. C 1946.

sericeum Labill. A moderately hardy Tasmanian shrub of medium height. Leaves small, bright green, pointed; young stems red.

stellatum See *L. trinervium*.

trinervium (Smith) Thompson (*L. stellatum* Cav.) A medium-sized shrub with bright green leaves, only injured by the severest weather. E Australia.

LESPEDEZA Michx.—**Leguminosae**—The bush clovers contain about 40 species of herbs and shrubs, natives of

North America, E Asia and Australia. The cultivated species of this extensive genus are very useful, late flowering shrubs. Their racemes of small, pea-flowers are borne profusely and continuously along the shoots, which are bowed by their weight. All have trifoliolate leaves and, given full sun, are easy to cultivate.

bicolor Turcz. A medium-sized shrub of semi-erect habit. Bright rose-purple flowers are borne in racemose inflorescences in late summer. Korea, Manchuria, China, Japan. I 1856 by Maximowicz. **'Yakushima'** A low-growing, almost prostrate form with short, upright shoots, to about 20cm tall, and very small leaves and flowers.

buergeri Miq. A medium-sized shrub of spreading habit. Bears dense racemes of purple and white flowers. Japan, China.

cyrtobotrya Miq. A small shrub throwing up erect, woody stems annually. In late summer, rose-purple pea-flowers crowd the ends of each shoot. Japan, Korea. I 1899.

kiusiana Nakai. A distinct and very attractive, small shrub with soft green, clover-like leaves, and light rose-purple flowers in large, compound, leafy panicles. Japan, Korea.

thunbergii (DC.) Nakai (L. sieboldii Miq., Desmodium penduliflorum hort. not Wall.) One of the best autumn-flowering shrubs. The arching, 1.2–1.5m stems are bowed to the ground in September by the weight of the huge, terminal panicles of rose-purple pea-flowers. Japan, China. I about 1837. ♀ 2002. FCC 1871 (as Desmodium penduliflorum). **'White Fountain'** A striking form, the long, arching shoots covered in sprays of pure white flowers.

‡***LEUCOPOGON** R. Br.—**Epacridaceae**—A large genus of about 150 species of evergreen shrubs and trees, natives mainly of Australia and New Zealand, with a few species in Malaysia and the Pacific Islands. They require the same conditions as Erica.

fraseri A. Cunn. A dwarf, New Zealand shrublet, related to Cyathodes and requiring similar treatment. The decumbent branchlets are clothed with close-set, imbricated, shining green leaves. Small, white or lavender, tubular flowers are followed by orange-yellow fruits. C 1911.

‡**LEUCOTHOE** D. Don—**Ericaceae**—An attractive and useful genus of shade-bearing shrubs for lime-free soils. There are about 45 species, natives of North and South America, the Himalaya, E Asia and Madagascar.

axillaris (Lam.) D. Don. This species is closely related to L. fontanesiana and confused with it in gardens. It differs in the smaller leaves which are less taper-pointed and on shorter stalks. In the wild it is found in low-lying and coastal areas, while L. fontanesiana is generally found in the mountains. SE USA.

catesbaei See L. fontanesiana.

***davisiae** Torr. (Andromeda davisiae C.K. Schneid.) Sierra laurel. A pretty shrub, usually less than 1m high, with dark green, glossy leaves and erect panicles of pure white flowers in June. California. I 1853 by William Lobb. FCC 1883.

***fontanesiana** (Steud.) Sleum. (L. catesbaei (Walt.) A. Gray) A small to medium-sized shrub of elegant habit, excellent groundcover for acid soils. The graceful, arching stems carry lanceolate, leathery, green leaves, which become tinged a rich beetroot-red or bronze-purple in autumn and winter, especially in exposed positions. The short, pendent racemes of white, pitcher-shaped flowers, appear all along the stems in May. For many years this plant was grown as L. catesbaei. SE USA. I 1793. ♀ 2002. AM 1972. **Carinella** ('Zebekot') Raised by Alex J. Zebehazy in Ohio, by crossing L. fontanesiana with what was believed to be L. axillaris, but may have been L. fontansesiana 'Nana'. A compact, low-growing, spreading shrub with arching shoots. The slender bright green leaves, to 10cm long and 3cm across, are flushed red at the margin when young, in winter dark green flushed with red-purple. Flowers in short racemes to 3cm long. **Lovita** ('Zebonard') From the same cross as Carinella, this differs in its smaller leaves to 7.5cm by 3.5cm, turning to deep red-purple flushed green in winter. Flowers in short racemes to 2.5cm long. **'Nana'** A lower-growing, more compact form. **'Rainbow'** Leaves variegated with cream, yellow and pink. This plant arose as a seedling in our Chandler's Ford nursery. The American-raised 'Girard's Rainbow' is the same or very similar. **Red Lips** ('Lipsbolwi') PBR A sport of Scarletta found in Holland before 1997. It has a more compact habit, smaller leaves and deep purple winter foliage. **'Rollissonii'** A selection with narrower leaves. ♀ 2002. AM 1981. **Scarletta** ('Zeblid') Of the same origin as Carinella, this has dark green leaves to 10cm long by 3.5cm wide, slightly edged with red when young, becoming deep bronze-red in winter.

grayana Maxim. A remarkable, small, semi-evergreen shrub with stout, green, ascending stems, becoming an attractive, deep polished red in winter, and large, broadly oval leaves, usually turning bronze-yellow, tinted purple, in autumn. Pale green flowers are produced in July and August in ascending one-sided racemes. Japan. I 1890. **var. oblongifolia** (Miq.) Ohwi. A slightly dwarfer variety of stiffer, more upright habit; the dark polished stems are reddish-purple in winter, and the markedly oblong, smaller and darker leaves turn yellow and flame in autumn. Japan.

***keiskei** Miq. A small, glabrous shrub with arching, red-tinged shoots and ovate to ovate-elliptic, slender-pointed leaves, 5–10cm long, glossy green above. The comparatively large, cylindrical, white flowers are borne in nodding, terminal and axillary racemes in July. Japan. I 1915 by Ernest Wilson. AM 1933. **'Royal Ruby'** Dark green foliage, rich ruby-red when young and again in winter.

populifolia See Agarista populifolia.

racemosa (L.) A. Gray. Fetter-bush. A small to medium-sized, deciduous or semi-evergreen shrub with narrow elliptic to ovate leaves. White, urn-shaped flowers are borne in one-sided, often curved racemes in June. SE USA.

LEYCESTERIA Wall.—**Caprifoliaceae**—A small genus of 6 species of hollow-stemmed shrubs, natives of the Himalaya and China. Suitable for any reasonably fertile soil.

†**crocothyrsos** Airy Shaw. An interesting and attractive, medium-sized shrub, unfortunately suitable only for mild districts. Large, slender pointed, glossy green leaves are

prominently veined. The showy yellow flowers are borne in terminal racemes in April and are followed by small, gooseberry-like, green fruits. Assam. I 1928 by Kingdon-Ward. AM 1960.

crocothyrsos × *formosa* A vigorous, small shrub with hollow stems, closest to *L. crocothyrsos* (the male parent) in foliage. Shoots glandular hairy when young, red; leaves ovate, to 12cm long, sharply toothed and taper-pointed, deep red-purple when young becoming green with red veins, stipules resembling those of the male parent but smaller. Flowers in slender, drooping, glandular-hairy spikes to 12cm long, corolla creamy-yellow, red-tinged in bud becoming creamy-white. Raised by Peter Dummer from a cross made in 1994.

formosa Wall. A medium-sized, erect shrub with stout, hollow, sea-green shoots covered at first with a glaucous bloom. White flowers are carried in dense, terminal, drooping panicles of claret-red bracts from June to September. These are followed by large, shining, reddish-purple berries which are attractive to pheasants. Himalaya. I 1824. ♥ 2002.

Ligustrina pekinensis See *Syringa reticulata* subsp. *pekinensis*.

LIGUSTRUM L.—Oleaceae—The privets consist of some 40 species of deciduous and evergreen shrubs or trees, natives of the Himalaya and E and SE Asia to Australia, with one species in Europe and N Africa. They are mostly fast-growing, shade-tolerant and not particular about soil. Many produce conspicuous flowerheads and fruits. Harmful if eaten.

acuminatum See *L. tschonoskii*.

acutissimum See *L. leucanthum*.

amurense Carrière. Amur privet. A large shrub of tough constitution. Similar in most respects to *L. ovalifolium* but with twigs and undersides of leaves pubescent. N China. C 1860.

chenaultii See *L. compactum*.

compactum Brandis (*L. chenaultii* Hickel, *L. yunnanense* Henry) A striking large, semi-evergreen shrub or small tree with glossy, bright green, lanceolate leaves, up to 12.5cm long. Bears large panicles of white flowers in June and July followed by blue-black fruits. Plants cultivated as *L. chenaultii* have leaves up to 15cm long and 6cm across, sometimes with small teeth at the margin. Himalaya, SW China. I 1874. var. *velutinum* P.S. Green (*L. yunnanense* L. Henry) This form differs in its velvety shoots.

†*confusum* Decne. A conspicuous, but rather tender, nearly evergreen species, forming a large shrub in mild districts. White flowers are very freely borne in wide panicles in June and July. The clusters of bloomy black fruits are very striking. Himalaya, SW China, SE Asia. I 1919.

delavayanum Hariot (*L. ionandrum* Diels, *L. prattii* Koehne) A rather variable, small-leaved, evergreen, spreading shrub of medium size. Dense panicles of white flowers with violet anthers are followed by black fruits. A good hedging plant but not for the colder counties. SW China. I 1890 by the Abbé Delavay.

henryi Hemsl. A medium-sized to large shrub of compact growth. Small, roundish, dark almost black-green and glossy leaves. Flowers in August. C and SW China. I 1901 by Ernest Wilson. AM 1910.

ibota See *L. obtusifolium*.

ionandrum See *L. delavayanum*.

japonicum Thunb. Japanese privet. A compact, medium-sized, very dense shrub with camellia-like foliage of shining olive-green. Bears large panicles of white flowers in late summer. An excellent evergreen for screening or hedging. China, Korea, Taiwan, Japan. I 1845 by P.F. von Siebold. 'Macrophyllum' A splendid form with broad, glossy, black-green, camellia-like leaves. Sometimes wrongly referred to as a form of *L. lucidum*. An outstanding evergreen. 'Rotundifolium' ('Coriaceum') A very slow-growing, rigid, compact form with round, leathery, black-green leaves. Introduced from cultivation in Japan by Robert Fortune in 1860. 'Silver Star' Leaves grey-green with a white margin.

leucanthum (Moore) P.S. Green (*L. acutissimum* Koehne) A Chinese shrub of medium height, akin to *L. obtusifolium*, with downy shoots and elliptic pointed leaves, downy beneath when young. Flowers in dense conical panicles. C China. I about 1900.

lucidum W.T. Aiton. Chinese privet. A large, evergreen shrub or small to medium-sized tree with large, glossy green, long-pointed leaves and large, handsome panicles of white flowers in autumn. Occasionally seen as a beautiful, symmetrical tree, up to 12m or more high, with an attractive, fluted trunk. A worthy street tree for restricted areas. It is commonly planted in warm countries where it is often confused with *L. japonicum*. S and E China. I 1794. ♥ 2002. AM 1965. 'Excelsum Superbum' A very striking variegated form, the leaves bright green marked with pale green and edged with yellow or greenish-yellow. ♥ 2002. 'Latifolium' A conspicuous form with large, camellia-like leaves. 'Tricolor' Leaves rather narrow, deep green, prominently marked with grey-green, edged with pale creamy-yellow or nearly white, tinged pink when young. It has reached 9m on the site of our West Hill nursery (1990). C 1895.

obtusifolium Siebold & Zucc. (*L. ibota* Siebold) A vigorous, medium-sized to large, deciduous shrub with dark green, elliptic-obovate leaves, often purplish in autumn. Profuse flowers in nodding panicles are borne in July, followed by blue-black fruits, bloomy at first. N China, Korea, Japan. I 1860. var. *regelianum* (Koehne) Rehder. A low-growing form with horizontally spreading branches. White flowers in terminal, nodding clusters, are very freely produced in July; leaves turn rose-madder in autumn and persist for several weeks. C 1885.

ovalifolium Hassk. Oval-leaf privet. The ubiquitous privet is one of the commonest of cultivated shrubs. It is much used for hedging, but when unpruned will reach a large size. It tolerates most soils and aspects, only losing its leaves in cold districts. Useful for game coverts. Japan. C 1885. 'Argenteum' Leaves with creamy-white margin. 'Aureum' Golden privet. A brightly coloured shrub with rich yellow, green-centred leaves, often completely yellow. C 1862. ♥ 2002. AM 1977.

quihoui Carrière. An elegant, medium-sized shrub. Florally, this species is one of the best of the genus, producing white panicles up to 50cm long, in August and September. China. I about 1862. ♥ 2002. AM 1980.

sempervirens (Franch.) Lingelsh. (*Parasyringa semper-virens* (Franch.) W.W. Sm.) This species makes a striking evergreen shrub of small to medium size, with dark green, leathery, rounded leaves. The small, white flowers are produced in conspicuous, dense panicles in August and September, followed by persistent, fleshy, black fruits which often split as they dry. W China. I 1913 by George Forrest. AM 1930. Recently reintroduced from China.

sinense Lour. This free-flowering species is perhaps the most floriferous of deciduous privets. A large shrub of spreading habit with downy stems and oval leaves. White flowers are produced in long, dense sprays in July, followed by equally numerous, black-purple fruits. China, Vietnam. I about 1852 by Robert Fortune. **var. myri-anthum** (Diels) Hoefker. An unusual form with lateral inflorescences. I 1986. **'Pendulum'** A medium-sized to large shrub with pendent branches, also distinct in its large leaves and open panicles. **'Variegatum'** An attractive form. The soft grey-green, white-margined leaves combining with the sprays of white flowers to lighten the dullest corner. **'Wimbei'** ('Wimbish') A compact form of upright habit making a medium-sized shrub with small leaves; rarely flowers. It was originally grown here as *L. sinense* sterile mutation.

strongylophyllum Hemsl. Large shrub or small tree with small, rounded or ovate-lanceolate leaves and loose panicles of white flowers in late summer. C and SW China. I 1879 by Charles Maries.

tschonoskii Decne. (*L. acuminatum* Koehne) Medium-sized shrub of upright habit, with large, slender-pointed leaves. White flowers in June are followed by lustrous, black fruits. Japan. I 1888.

'Vicaryi' Medium-sized, semi-evergreen shrub with leaves suffused golden-yellow, turning bronze-purple in winter. Said to be a hybrid between *L. ovalifolium* 'Aureum' and *L. vulgare*. Garden origin. C about 1920.

vulgare L. The partially evergreen common privet is a familiar native of our hedgerows and woodlands, particularly in chalk areas. Leaves lanceolate, dark green. Its long clusters of shining black fruits are conspicuous during autumn. Europe, N Africa, SW Asia. **'Aureum'** A form with dull yellow leaves. C 1884. **'Chlorocarpum'** Mature fruits are yellowish-green. **'Glaucum'** Leaves are metallic blue-green. C 1838. **'Insulense'** Leaves are longer; inflorescences and fruits larger. C 1883. **var. italicum** (Mill.) Vahl ('Sempervirens') (*L. vulgare* var. *sempervirens* Loud.) Leaves almost evergreen. **'Pyramidale'** ('Fastigiatum') A dense form with erect branches. C 1893. **'Sempervirens'** See var. *italicum*. **'Xanthocarpum'** A form with yellow fruits. C 1811.

yunnanense See *L. compactum* var. *velutinum*.

Lilac See *Syringa*.
Lime See *Tilia*.

‡**LINDERA** Thunb.—**Lauraceae**—A genus of about 80 species of deciduous and evergreen, aromatic trees and shrubs, related to bay (*Laurus nobilis*) and requiring lime-free soil. They are natives mainly of S and E Asia, with 2 species in E North America. Grown primarily for their attractive, variably shaped leaves which in the deciduous species give rich autumn tints. Small, unisexual flowers are sometimes conspicuous in the mass, followed by berries.

benzoin (L.) Blume (*Benzoin aestivale* Nees) Spice bush. A medium-sized to large shrub with large, obovate leaves turning clear yellow in autumn. The small, greenish-yellow flowers in spring are followed, on female plants, by red berries. SE USA. I 1683.

cercidifolia See *L. obtusiloba* and *L. praetermissa*.

glauca (Siebold & Zucc.) Blume. A large shrub with narrow-elliptic leaves, glaucous beneath, turning to purple, orange and red in November. In China, this and several other species are used in the manufacture of incense-sticks (joss-sticks). Japan, China, Korea, Taiwan.

megaphylla Hemsl. A large, handsome, evergreen shrub or small tree, recalling *Daphniphyllum*. Leaves up to 22cm long by 6.5cm wide, are dark, shining green above, glaucous beneath. Flowers dioecious, the females producing plum-like fruits. Proving remarkably hardy in the Sir Harold Hillier Gardens and Arboretum, where a specimen has reached 9.5m (1990). S China, Taiwan. I 1900 by Ernest Wilson.

obtusiloba Blume (*L. cercidifolia* Hemsl.) A magnificent, medium-sized to large shrub of erect or compact habit. The large, 3-nerved, broadly ovate to obovate leaves are entire or 3-lobed at the tip. In autumn their bright summer green turns a glorious butter-yellow with rich pink tints. The flowers, in early spring, are the colour of newly-made mustard. Japan, China, Korea. I 1880. ♀ 2002. AM 1952 (as *L. triloba*).

praecox (Siebold & Zucc.) Blume (*Parabenzoin praecox* (Siebold & Zucc.) Nakai) A large shrub or small tree of upright habit. Leaves light green turning lovely yellow in autumn. The greenish-yellow flowers occur in short-stalked clusters along the bare twigs in March or early April. Japan. I 1891.

praetermissa Grierson & D.G. Long (*L. cercidifolia* hort. not Hemsl.) A large shrub or small tree with ovate or rounded, entire leaves, bronze when young, yellow in autumn. Sulphur-yellow flowers are borne in clusters on the leafless stems in March. Berries red. Assam. SE Tibet, Upper Burma, Yunnan. I by George Forrest.

†*rubronervia* Gamble. A handsome, medium-sized shrub with oblong-elliptic leaves, shining green above, paler or glaucous below, turning orange and red in late autumn. SW China.

umbellata Thunb. A semi-erect, medium-sized shrub with slender branches and elliptic to obovate, thin-textured leaves, 6.5–14cm long, glaucescent beneath. Yellow flowers appear in short umbels with the leaves. Yellow is the dominant autumn colour. Japan, C and W China. I 1892.

Ling See *Calluna vulgaris*.
Lingberry See *Vaccinium vitis-idaea*.

‡*LINNAEA* L.—**Caprifoliaceae**—A monotypic genus named in honour of Linnaeus. It requires a peaty woodland soil.

borealis L. Twinflower. A charming, little shrublet, its slender stems carpeting the ground, in moist, acid soils forming extensive colonies. Delicate small, nodding, pinkish, bell-like flowers are carried in pairs on thread-like stems from June to early August. A large patch in full flower in a Scottish woodland, a slight breeze wafting through the pink bells, is an unforgettable sight. Throughout the N hemisphere (incl. British Isles). C 1762.

LINUM L.—**Linaceae**—About 200 species of annual and perennial herbs and small shrubs, natives mainly of S Europe and W Asia but widely distributed throughout temperate and tropical regions. Attractive plants many of which are suitable for a rock garden. The following require full sun and good drainage.

*arboreum L. Tree flax. Dwarf, spreading shrub with narrow, glaucous leaves. Golden-yellow flowers appear in loose terminal clusters during summer. E Mediterranean region. C 1788. ♀ 2002.

campanulatum L. A dwarf shrub with erect stems and glaucous, slender-pointed leaves. Yellow flowers in terminal corymbs during summer. S Europe. C 1795. FCC 1871.

Lion's ear See *Leonotis leonurus*.
Lippia citriodora See *Aloysia triphylla*.

‡**LIQUIDAMBAR** L.—**Hamamelidaceae**—A small genus of 4 species of deciduous trees with maple-like, alternate leaves that usually colour well in autumn. Not suitable for shallow chalky soil. The leaves of juvenile and adult trees are sometimes variable.

acalycina H.T. Chang. A vigorous tree, reaching 25m in the wild, similar to, but hardier than *L. formosana*, from which it differs in its smoother fruits in clusters of 15–26 (24–43 in *L. formosana*). The 3-lobed leaves, to 15cm across, are bronze-purple when young and often remain on the tree well into winter. I to the USA and Britain in the 1980s. China.

formosana Hance. A beautiful tree surviving, uninjured, all but our severest winters. The leaves are attractively red-tinted in spring and again in autumn. Differing from *L. styraciflua* in its duller, green, 3–5-lobed leaves, hairy beneath, and its normally hairy shoots. S China, Taiwan. I 1884. **Monticola Group** (var. *monticola* Rehder & E.H. Wilson) This Chinese form, discovered by Ernest Wilson, is perfectly hardy. It has remarkably large, normally 3-lobed, glabrous leaves that colour richly in autumn. I 1908. AM 1958.

orientalis Mill. A slow-growing, large bush or small, bushy tree. Small, glabrous, deeply 5-lobed leaves are attractively tinted in autumn. In warmer climates it attains large tree size. SW Turkey. I about 1750.

styraciflua L. A beautiful, large tree, conspicuous at all times, especially in autumn when, if happily placed, the deeply 5- to 7-lobed, shining green leaves assume their gorgeous crimson colouring. In winter the corky bark of the older twigs is often a feature. It is occasionally confused with the maples (*Acer*), but its alternate leaves easily identify it. Autumn colour is variable on seed-raised plants. E USA. I in the 17th century. FCCT 1975. AM 1952. **'Aurea'** See 'Variegata'. **'Burgundy'** Five-lobed leaves purple-tinged when young turn purple late in the season and remain on the tree until early winter. Selected in California before 1963. **'Globe'** See 'Gum Ball'. **'Golden Treasure'** Leaves with a conspicuous deep yellow margin turning reddish-purple, edged

yellow, in autumn. Slow-growing. **'Gum Ball'** ('Globe') A remarkable form of dense, shrubby habit with long-persistent leaves turning orange-red and purple in winter. Colours best in an open position. It was found in Tennessee. **'Lane Roberts'** A selected clone and one of the most reliable for its autumn colour, which is rich blackish-crimson-red. Bark comparatively smooth. ♀ 2002. **'Moonbeam'** Leaves pale creamy-yellow, eventually green turning red, yellow and purple in autumn. **'Rotundiloba'** Leaves with usually 3 rounded lobes, turning yellow to red or purple in autumn. The original tree was found in North Carolina about 1930. **'Silver King'** Leaves attractively margined creamy-white, flushed rose in late summer and autumn. Originally listed as 'Variegata'. **'Stared'** Leaves very deeply cut into 7 lobes, reddish when young, turning red to deep purple in autumn. **'Variegata'** Leaves striped and mottled yellow. It was originally grown as 'Aurea'. See also 'Silver King'. **'Worplesdon'** Leaves with long, narrow lobes, turning orange and yellow in autumn. Unusual in that it often bears fruit in this country, unlike many other forms. ♀ 2002. AM 1987.

LIRIODENDRON L.—**Magnoliaceae**—The North American tulip tree was considered monotypic until, at the beginning of the 20th century, a second and very similar species was discovered in China. Fast-growing trees, succeeding in all types of fertile soil, they are made conspicuous by their curiously shaped, foreshortened, 3-lobed leaves, which turn clear yellow in autumn. Hybrids between the 2 species are also in cultivation from crosses made in the USA in 1973 and 1977; the hybrid was, however, first raised in China in 1963.

chinense (Hemsl.) Sarg. A rare tree of medium size, similar to *L. tulipifera*, but leaves more glaucous beneath and narrower waisted. The smaller flowers are green outside, green with yellowish veins within. China, N Vietnam. I 1901 by Ernest Wilson. AM 1980.

tulipifera L. Tulip tree. A beautiful, large tree characterised by its distinctive, oddly shaped leaves, which turn a rich butter-yellow in autumn. The peculiar flowers, appearing in June and July, are tulip-shaped and yellow-green, banded with orange at the base of the petals, but are not produced on young trees. E North America. C 1688. ♀ 2002. AM 1970. **'Arnold'** See 'Fastigiatum'. **'Aureomarginatum'** A striking tree, the leaves bordered with bright yellow, turning greenish-yellow by late summer. C 1903. ♀ 2002. AM 1974. **'Crispum'** ('Contortum') A form with somewhat contorted, undulating leaves. **'Fastigiatum'** ('Arnold', 'Pyramidale') A magnificent, medium-sized, erect tree of broadly columnar habit, an excellent choice where height is required and space confined. **'Glen Gold'** A form with yellow leaves, raised in Australia. **'Integrifolium'** An unusual form, the leaves lacking side lobes. C 1864. **'Mediopictum'** Leaves with an irregular central yellow blotch very variable in size. Unlike 'Aureomarginatum', the colour does not fade. Lateral lobes often absent.

‡***LITHOCARPUS** Blume (*Pasania* (Miq.) Oerst.)—**Fagaceae**—A large genus of nearly 300 species of evergreen trees and shrubs, all but one natives of E and S Asia.

Differing from *Castanea* in the acorn-like fruits and from *Quercus* in the erect flower spikes. They require a lime-free soil.

†*densiflorus* (Hook. & Arn.) Rehder (*Quercus densiflora* Hook. & Arn.) Tanbark oak. A small, evergreen tree, native of California and Oregon. The shoots and the sharply toothed, oblong, leathery leaves are covered with milk-white down when young. The leaves become dark shining green above and whitish- or tawny-downy below, finally glabrous. The bark of this tree is a source of tannin. Only for the most sheltered gardens in the S and W British Isles. I 1874. **var.** *echinoides* (R. Br.) Abrams (*Quercus echinoides* R. Br.) Dwarf tanbark. A small to medium-sized, comparatively hardy shrub of open habit, with glabrous, greyish-brown twigs. Leathery, entire, ovate-elliptic to oblong-elliptic, leaves, 1.25–4cm long, are green above, paler below, with yellow petioles. California, Oregon.

edulis (Makino) Nakai (*Quercus edulis* Makino, *Pasania edulis* Makino) A small, bushy tree or large shrub with glabrous young shoots. The glabrous, leathery leaves are tapered at both ends, yellowish-green above, scaly when young. Proving hardy and free-fruiting given reasonable shelter. Japan. I early 19th century.

henryi (Seemen) Rehder & E.H. Wilson (*Quercus henryi* Seemen) An outstanding, small, evergreen tree with very long, lanceolate, slender-pointed leaves. Fruits, when produced, are borne in dense heads in autumn. This remarkable evergreen has grown slowly but successfully in the Sir Harold Hillier Gardens and Arboretum for over 40 years. C China. I 1901 by Ernest Wilson. AM 1979.

†*pachyphyllus* (Kurz) Rehder (*Quercus pachyphylla* Kurz) A small tree with a low, spreading head of branches. Elliptic to elliptic-lanceolate, abruptly acuminate leaves are 10–20cm long, dark glossy green above and pale metallic silvery-green beneath. A rare species only suitable for the milder counties. A fine tree at Caerhays, Cornwall, produces shillalah-like clusters of strangely contorted fruits, which appear to be infertile. E Himalaya, W China.

***LITHODORA** Griseb. (*Lithospermum* L. in part)—**Boraginaceae**—A genus of 7 species of dwarf shrubs, natives of Europe, N Africa and SW Asia. The following are delightful low-growing, blue-flowered plants, particularly in a rock garden. With the exception of *L. diffusa* all are lime-tolerant.

‡*diffusa* (Lag.) I.M. Johnst. (*Lithospermum diffusum* Lag., *Lithospermum prostratum* Loisel.) A prostrate shrub forming large mats covered with lovely, blue flowers in late spring and early summer. Not recommended for shallow chalky soils. SW Europe. I 1825. '**Alba**' White flowers. '**Cambridge Blue**' Flowers pale blue. '**Grace Ward**' A form with larger flowers. ♀ 2002. AM 1938. '**Heavenly Blue**' The most common form in general cultivation. The name is self-explanatory. ♀ 2002. AM 1909. '**Picos**' A compact form, to only 6cm tall, bearing rich blue flowers over a long period during summer. '**Star**' PBR A sport of 'Heavenly Blue' in which the corolla lobes are white banded with blue in the centre.

oleifolia (Lapeyr.) Griseb. (*Lithospermum oleifolium* Lapeyr.) A choice and rare, evergreen, semi-prostrate shrub for a sheltered rock garden or alpine house; beautiful, azure-blue, bell-shaped flowers are produced from June to September. Spain (E Pyrenees). I about 1900. ♀ 2002. AM 1938.

†*rosmarinifolia* (Ten.) I.M. Johnst. (*Lithospermum rosmarinifolium* Ten.) A lovely rosemary-like, dwarf, erect shrub with narrow leaves and bright blue flowers during winter and early spring. A rock garden shrub for milder counties, otherwise an excellent plant for an alpine house. S Italy, Sicily.

Lithospermum See *Lithodora*.
Lithospermum petraeum See *Moltkia petraea*.

†***LITSEA** Lam.—**Lauraceae**.—A large genus of dioecious, evergreen trees and shrubs with more than 400 species widely distributed in warm areas of Asia, the Americas and Australia. The following is hardy only in the mildest areas of the country but makes a splendid foliage plant for a container if given winter protection.

glauca See *Neolitsea sericea*.

japonica (Thunb.) Juss. A small, evergreen tree with stout shoots covered in a brown tomentum. Leaves elliptic to oblong, to 14cm long, glossy dark green above, with a brown tomentum beneath. Clusters of yellowish-white flowers in the leaf axils in autumn are followed on female plants by bloomy purple-black fruits which ripen in spring. Coastal areas of S Japan and South Korea.

Lobster's claw See *Clianthus puniceus*.
Locust, black See *Robinia pseudoacacia*.
Locust, Caspian See *Gleditsia caspica*.
Locust, honey See *Gleditsia triacanthos*.
Locust, water See *Gleditsia aquatica*.

†***LOISELEURIA** Desv.—**Ericaceae**—A monotypic genus related to *Rhododendron*.

procumbens (L.) Desv. (*Azalea procumbens* L.) Mountain azalea. A charming, prostrate, native shrub, forming large mats or low mounds of procumbent stems and tiny leaves, studded in May with clusters of small, pink flowers. Requires moist, peaty conditions; best in full exposure. Alpine and arctic regions of the N hemisphere (incl. Scotland). C 1800.

‡***LOMATIA** R. Br.—**Proteaceae**—A small genus of about 12 species of striking Australian and South American, evergreen trees and shrubs. Attractive both in foliage and flower, they should be better known and more widely planted. While hardy or near hardy in all but the coolest areas, they cannot be recommended for shallow chalky soils, and succeed best in partial shade. A splendid group of plants for the flower arranger although some are a little too slow in growth for cutting.

†*dentata* (Ruiz & Pav.) R. Br. A shrub that is medium-sized to large in cultivation. It has elliptic to obovate, holly-like leaves, coarsely toothed except at the base, shining dark green above, pale green or glaucescent beneath. Flowers are greenish-white. Chile, Argentina. I by Harold Comber. Reintroduced in 1963.

†*ferruginea* (Cav.) R. Br. A magnificent foliage plant, making a large shrub or small, erect tree, with large, deep

green, much divided, fern-like leaves and red-brown, velvety stems. Buff and scarlet flowers are in short racemes. Hardy only in mild localities. Chile, Argentina. I about 1846 by William Lobb. AM 1927.

hirsuta (Lam.) Diels (*L. obliqua* (Ruiz & Pav.) R. Br.) A little-known Chilean species, proving hardy in a sheltered woodland in the Sir Harold Hillier Gardens and Arboretum. It is a remarkable, large shrub with rather large, leathery, broadly and obliquely ovate leaves. Masses of small cream and green flowers open in racemes at the ends of the shoots in May. W South America. I 1902 by H.J. Elwes. AM 1956.

longifolia See *L. myricoides*.

myricoides (Gaertn.) Domin (*L. longifolia* R. Br.) This species has proved hardy and long-lived in the Sir Harold Hillier Gardens and Arboretum, making a well-furnished, widespreading shrub, 1.8–2.4m high. The long, narrow leaves are distantly toothed and the white, grevillea-like, very fragrant flowers are borne freely in July. An excellent evergreen for the flower arranger. SE Australia. I 1816. AM 1955.

obliqua See *L. hirsuta*.

silaifolia (Sm.) R. Br. A small, widespreading shrub with ascending stems, finely divided leaves, though less finely divided than those of the very similar *L. tinctoria*, and large panicles of creamy-white flowers in July. Both species have lived outside in the Sir Harold Hillier Gardens and Arboretum for many years. E Australia. I 1792.

tinctoria (Labill.) R. Br. Small, suckering shrub eventually forming a dense thicket. Leaves pinnate or double pinnate with long, narrow segments. Flowers, sulphur-yellow in bud changing to creamy-white, are borne in long, spreading racemes at the ends of the shoots. Tasmania. I 1822. AM 1948.

Lombardy poplar See *Populus nigra* 'Italica'.
London plane See *Platanus* × *hispanica*.

LONICERA L.—**Caprifoliaceae**—A genus of some 240 species of deciduous and evergreen shrubs and climbers with opposite leaves, widely distributed in the N hemisphere, mainly in temperate regions. The shrubby honeysuckles are very different in appearance from the climbing species to which the colloquial name properly belongs. Their flowers are borne in pairs, normally on slender peduncles, and are followed by partially or completely fused berries. All are easy to cultivate in any ordinary soil. Thin out and cut back old flowering shoots to within a few centimetres of the old wood immediately after flowering. For climbing species see CLIMBERS at end of Manual.

albertii Reg. (*L. spinosa* var. *albertii* (Reg.) Rehder) A low-growing shrub of spreading habit, attaining 0.9–1.2m, with slender, arching branches, linear, glaucous leaves and relatively large and showy, fragrant, lilac-pink flowers in May. Berries purplish-red. Turkestan. I about 1880.

alpigena L. Erect, medium-sized shrub of dense habit. Oval, oblong or obovate leaves are 5–10cm long, half as wide. Pairs of yellow, tinged-red flowers are produced in May. Berries red, drooping, cherry-like. C Europe. C since the 16th century.

× *amoena* Zabel (*L. korolkowii* × *L. tatarica*) A vigorous, floriferous shrub with grey-green leaves. 'Rosea' An

attractive, medium-sized form producing an abundance of fragrant, pink flowers in May and June. Garden origin before 1895.

angustifolia Wall. An elegant, narrow-leaved, Himalayan species of medium size. The small, fragrant, pale pink flowers, produced in April and May, are followed by red, edible berries. I about 1849 by Sir Joseph Hooker.

caerulea L. A variable species, typically a stiff, compact shrub attaining about 1.5m, with orbicular-ovate, sea-green leaves, yellowish-white flowers and conspicuous, dark blue berries. N and C Europe, N Asia, Japan. Long cultivated.

chaetocarpa (Batal. ex Rehder) Rehder. A pretty, erect shrub, 1.8–2.1m, with bristly stems and leaves. Comparatively large, primrose-yellow flowers, subtended by 2 large, conspicuous bracts, appear in May and June. Berries bright red. A shrub of quality and interest for every well-stocked garden. W China. I 1904 by Ernest Wilson.

chrysantha Turcz. A tall, hardy shrub, up to 3.75m, blooming in May and June with cream flowers becoming yellow, then coral-red berries. NE Asia. C 1880.

'Clavey's Dwarf' A small shrub of dense habit, up to 1m, possibly a hybrid of *L. xylosteum* and *L. tatarica*. Flowers creamy-white; berries large, translucent, red. C 1955.

deflexicalyx Batal. A vigorous and very distinct large shrub of elegant habit with arching shoots, red when young. Slender, lanceolate leaves are dark green with impressed veins above, downy beneath. Small, yellow flowers, often flushed with red, are borne in pairs above the shoots in late spring to early summer, followed by orange-red fruits. W China. I 1904 and several times by recent expeditions.

discolor Lindl. A medium-sized shrub with elliptic leaves, dark green above, glaucous beneath. Yellowish-white flowers may be tinged rose. Kashmir to Afghanistan. C 1847.

fragrantissima Lindl. & Paxt. A partially evergreen shrub of medium size, producing its sweetly fragrant, cream-coloured flowers during late winter and spring. Red berries in May. I by Robert Fortune from China in 1845.

gracilipes Miq. var. *glandulosa* Maxim. (*L. tenuipes* Nakai) An attractive and distinct small shrub with reddish-tinged young shoots, densely covered in red-tipped glandular hairs, and ovate, short-stalked and densely pilose leaves. Deep pink flowers, with conspicuous yellow anthers, are borne singly or in pairs on a long, slender, glandular, hairy peduncle. Fruit oblong, scarlet, glandular, hairy. Japan.

iberica Bieb. Densely branched shrub up to 3m high. Cream flowers are borne on short stalks and enclosed by the cup-shaped, united bracts. Its unusual orbicular leaves make this a distinctive species. Caucasus, Iran. I 1824. 'Microphylla' A looser-growing form with smaller leaves.

infundibulum Franch. var. *rockii* Rehder. A medium-sized to large shrub with purple-flushed shoots slightly bristly when young. Leaves ovate to obovate, dark green above, blue-green beneath, to 8cm long, roughly hairy on both sides. The slender-tubed, funnel-shaped, fragrant flowers are pale primrose-yellow, tinged pink outside, and open in late winter. China. I from Wudang Shan in 1983 by Roy Lancaster (Lancaster 1171).

insularis Nakai. A vigorous, large shrub, the young shoots densely covered with soft hairs. Leaves broadly ovate, tomentose beneath, to 6cm long. Large white flowers, each with a long, slender lower lip, open in late spring and age to creamy-yellow. South Korea. I 1976 to our nurseries by Sir Harold Hillier.

involucrata (Richardson) Spreng. A distinct, vigorous, spreading, medium-sized shrub. In June produces yellow flowers subtended by 2 conspicuous red bracts, which persist during fruiting; berries shining, black. A robust, adaptable species growing equally well in seaside gardens and industrial areas. W North America. I 1824. var. *ledebourii* (Eschsch.) Zabel (*L. ledebourii* Eschsch.) Corolla orange-yellow tinged red; leaves more hairy beneath. Coastal regions of California. I 1838.

korolkowii Stapf. A very attractive, vigorous, large shrub of graceful, arching habit, the downy shoots and pale, sea-green, downy leaves giving the shrub a striking grey-blue hue. Pink flowers are produced in June and are followed by red berries. Turkestan. C 1880. var. *zabelii* (Rehder) Rehder. Leaves usually glabrous and broader than those of the typical form. See also *L. tatarica* 'Zabelii'.

ledebourii See *L. involucrata* var. *ledebourii*.

ligustrina var. *yunnanensis*. See under *L. nitida* 'Fertilis'.

maackii (Rupr.) Maxim. A large shrub bearing fragrant, white flowers that turn yellow as they age. Berries dark red, long-lasting. Manchuria, Korea. I 1880. f. *podocarpa* Rehder. A tall, graceful, widespreading shrub, attaining 3m, beautiful when bearing its white to yellow flowers, or loaded with red berries. This form is considered superior to the typical one. I 1900 by Ernest Wilson. AM 1907.

maximowiczii (Rupr.) Maxim. A vigorous, upright, medium-sized shrub with reddish shoots and dark green, pointed leaves. Violet-red flowers in May-June are followed by red berries. Manchuria, Korea. C 1878. var. *sachalinensis* F. Schmidt (*L. sachalinensis* (F. Schmidt) Nakai) A medium-sized shrub of erect habit. Dark violet-purple flowers in May and June are followed by dark purple berries. Japan, Sakhalin Is, North Korea, Manchuria, Ussuri. C 1917.

microphylla Roem. & Schult. A small shrub of stiff habit with purplish young shoots and small, glaucous leaves, producing pale yellow flowers in pairs in spring followed by bright red berries, flowers best after a hot summer. C Asia. I 1818.

morrowii A. Gray. A vigorous, medium-sized, spreading shrub. The leaves are grey-green, those at the tips of the shoots purplish in late summer and autumn; early summer, creamy-white flowers, changing to yellow, are followed by dark red berries. Japan. I 1875.

myrtilloides Purpus. A small, slender-branched shrub with reddish young shoots. Leaves lanceolate, to 2.5cm long; flowers urn-shaped with small, spreading lobes, white, flushed purplish-pink, 5mm long, in May and June, followed by translucent, bright red fruits. E Himalaya. C 1907.

myrtillus Hook. f. & Thoms. In general appearance this remarkable Himalayan species resembles a *Ledum*. A dense, rounded shrub, about 1m high, with small, con-spicuously veined, ovate leaves, glaucous beneath, and small, fragrant, pitcher-shaped, creamy-white flowers produced in pairs in May. Berries orange-red. Himalaya, Afghanistan.

nigra L. A small to medium-sized shrub of stiff upright habit, with deep purplish young shoots. Leaves ovate, short-stalked, downy beneath. The small pink flowers in May are followed by green berries which turn purplish-black. Mountains of C and S Europe. I in the 16th century.

*nitida E.H. Wilson. This dense, small-leaved evergreen, reaching 1.5–1.8m, has long been used extensively for hedging, being quick in growth and responding well to clipping. See also 'Ernest Wilson'. W China. I 1908 by Ernest Wilson. **'Baggesen's Gold'** A form with yellow leaves during summer, turning yellow-green in autumn. C 1967. ♀ 2002. AM 1988. **'Elegant'** A small, dense, spreading shrub with arching branches bearing small, ovate, matt green leaves. A form grown in Germany since 1935 as *L. pileata yunnanensis*, it is now regarded as a hybrid between *L. nitida* and *L. pileata*. **'Ernest Wilson'** This, the commonest form, has been the one most extensively used for hedging and is the 'nitida' of the trade. Its habit is rather spreading with arching or drooping branches and tiny, ovate leaves. Flowers and fruits poorly produced in the British Isles. AM 1911 (as *L. nitida*). **'Fertilis'** A strong-growing clone of erect habit, with long arching branchlets and ovate or elliptic leaves. It differs from 'Ernest Wilson' in its more erect habit, larger, narrower-based leaves, fragrant flowers and rather more freely produced translucent, violet fruits. It has in the past been catalogued under the names *L. pileata yunnanensis* and *L. ligustrina* var. *yunnanensis*. AM 1924. **'Lemon Beauty'** A sport of 'Elegant', the glossy green leaves broadly margined with creamy-white. **'Maigrün'** ('Maygreen') A small bush of dense, spreading habit, the pale green young leaves in spring contrasting with the dark green older foliage. **'Red Tips'** Leaves broadly heart-shaped, deep red-purple when young becoming bright green. Raised in the Netherlands from seed collected on Mt Omei, Sichuan, China in 1980. **'Silver Beauty'** An attractive form with silver-margined leaves. **'Twiggy'** A dwarf shrub, a sport of 'Baggesen's Gold', the leaves broadly margined yellow or entirely yellow, bronzing in winter. **'Yunnan'** Similar to 'Ernest Wilson', but stouter and more erect in habit. Its leaves are also slightly larger and it produces both flowers and fruits rather more freely. It has in the past been distributed under the name *L. yunnanensis* which, correctly, applies to an unrelated species. Excellent for hedging.

pileata Oliv. A dwarf, semi-evergreen, horizontally-branched shrub, occasionally 1.5m high, most suitable for underplanting and groundcover, particularly in shade. Leaves small, elliptic, bright green; berries in clusters, translucent violet. Very pretty in spring with the bright green young leaves among the dark green old leaves. China. I 1900 by Ernest Wilson. AM 1910. **'Loughgall Evergreen'** A small, widespreading, evergreen shrub; excellent groundcover. Selected and named as the best low-growing form after a trial of the species at the Northern Ireland Plant Breeding Station, Loughgall. **'Moss Green'** A selection with bright green foliage. *yunnanensis* See under *L. nitida* 'Fertilis'.

× **purpusii** Rehder (*L. fragrantissima* × *L. standishii*) A vigorous hybrid of medium size, producing very fragrant, cream-coloured flowers in winter. AM 1971. '**Spring Romance**' (*L.* × *purpusii* × *L. standishii* var. *lancifolia*) Similar to 'Winter Beauty' but with longer, bristly leaves and bristly shoots. '**Winter Beauty**' A backcross of *L.* × *purpusii* with *L. standishii*. A very free-flowering form raised by our foreman Alf Alford from a cross made in 1966. Flowers when young, often from early December to early April. ♀ 2002. AM 1992.

pyrenaica L. Although perhaps the choicest shrubby honeysuckle, attaining about 1m, this is possibly the most difficult to propagate. Small, sea-green leaves and nodding, comparatively large, funnel-shaped, cream and pink flowers in May and June are followed by orange-red berries. C and E Pyrenees, Balearic Is. I 1739. AM 1928.

quinquelocularis Hardw. A large shrub with oval leaves. Flowers white, changing to yellow, freely borne from the leaf axils in June and followed by translucent, white berries. Himalaya, China. C 1840. AM 1992. **f. translucens** (Carrière) Zabel. Leaves longer, heart-shaped at base. Flowers with distinctly gibbous corolla tube. C 1870.

rupicola Hook. f. & Thoms. A low, dense, globular shrub with interlacing branches. Flowers fragrant, lilac-pink in May and June. Related to *L. syringantha*. Himalaya, Tibet, W China. C 1850.

ruprechtiana Reg. A vigorous species forming a shapely bush of 2.4m or more. The oblong-ovate to lanceolate leaves are downy beneath; flowers in axillary pairs, are white changing to yellow, May and June. NE Asia. I about 1860.

saccata Rehder. A large, bushy shrub of elegant habit, resembling a small-leaved *Symphoricarpos* in leaf. Pairs of small, creamy-white flowers are borne in the leaf axils in June. China.

sachalinensis See *L. maximowiczii* var. *sachalinensis*.

setifera Franch. (Rock 13520) A rare and beautiful shrub of medium size. The stout, erect stems are densely bristly. The tubular, sweetly scented, daphne-like, white and pink flowers appear in short clusters on the naked stems during late winter and early spring, earlier in mild weather. Berries red, bristly. Himalaya, China. This species, originally introduced by Kingdon-Ward in 1924, has recently been reintroduced. AM 1980.

spinosa var. albertii. See *L. albertii*.

standishii Jacques. A charming, deciduous or semi-evergreen, medium-sized, fragrant, winter-flowering species, resembling *L. fragrantissima*, differing in its bristly stems and more elliptic hairy leaves. White flowers tinged pink, with conspicuous yellow anthers. Red berries in June. China. I 1845 by Robert Fortune. **var. lancifolia** Rehder. A narrow-leaved form of more distinct appearance. China. I 1908 by Ernest Wilson.

syringantha Maxim. A graceful, intricately-branched shrub of rounded habit, 1.2–1.8m high. Small, sea-green leaves are borne in threes on strong shoots and tubular, soft lilac, fragrant flowers appear in May and June. Berries red. China, Tibet. I about 1890. AM 1984.

tatarica L. A vigorous, variable shrub, up to 3m, producing multitudes of pink flowers in May and June. Berries red. C Asia to Russia. I 1752. '**Alba**' A form with white flowers. C 1801. '**Arnold Red**' Flowers rose-pink; berries larger. This cultivar originated as a seedling of 'Latifolia' in the Arnold Arboretum, Boston, USA in 1945. '**Hack's Red**' A first class selection with rose-pink flowers. **f. sibirica** (Pers.) Rehder. Flowers rosy-pink. The forms *punicea*, *pulcherrima* and *rubra* are very similar. C 1882. AM 1947. '**Zabelii**' Flowers bright pink, not as deep as either 'Arnold Red' or 'Hack's Red'. This has been distributed as *L. korolkowii* var. *zabelii*.

tenuipes See *L. gracilipes*.

thibetica Bur. & Franch. A vigorous species, up to 1.8m high, resembling *L. syringantha* in its lilac-pink, fragrant flowers, but differing in its leaves, which are dark glossy green above, white-tomentose beneath. Flowering in May and June. Berries red. Tibet. I 1897.

tomentella Hook. f. & Thoms. An elegant, small to medium-sized shrub with small, neat leaves and tubular, white, pink-tinged flowers in June. Berries small, black with a blue bloom. E Himalaya, Tibet. I 1849 by Sir Joseph Hooker.

trichosantha Bur. & Franch. A medium-sized, spreading Chinese shrub. The pale yellow flowers, produced in axillary pairs, are followed by dark red berries. W China. I about 1908 by Ernest Wilson.

vesicaria Komar. A vigorous, large shrub with stout shoots densely covered with red-based bristles when young. Leaves broadly ovate, glossy green above, somewhat bristly beneath, rather leathery, up to 12cm long, and occasionally deeply lobed on vigorous shoots. Flowers in late spring, relatively large, creamy-white with yellow anthers becoming deep yellow, followed by large, succulent orange-red berries. Korea.

× **vilmorinii** Rehder (*L. deflexicalyx* × *L. quinquelocularis*) A floriferous, small-flowered hybrid, attaining 2.7m. Yellow flowers are followed by pink berries, suffused yellow and minutely speckled red. Garden origin about 1900.

xylosteum L. Fly honeysuckle. A presumed native shrub attaining about 3m with yellowish-white flowers. Attractive, red berries in late summer. Europe (incl SE England), W Siberia.

yunnanensis See under *L. nitida* 'Yunnan'.

†***LOPHOMYRTUS** Burret—Myrtaceae—A genus of 2 species of evergreen shrubs, or small trees, natives of New Zealand and related to *Myrtus*.

bullata Burret (*Myrtus bullata* Sol. ex A. Cunn. not Salisb.) Ramarama. A large bush or small tree, with distinct round, leathery, coppery-green or reddish-brown, bullate leaves. Flowers white followed by blackish-red berries. Suitable only for the mildest localities. C 1854.

obcordata (Raoul) Burret (*Myrtus obcordata* (Raoul) Hook. f.) Rohutu. A graceful, medium-sized to large shrub, the thin branches clothed with small, notched leaves. Berries dark red or violet.

× **ralphii** (Hook. f.) Burret. (*L. bullata* × *L. obcordata*) (*Myrtus* × *ralphii* Hook. f.) A medium-sized to large shrub, occasionally a small tree, with ovate or rounded, puckered leaves. Flowers almond-pink, solitary in the axils of the leaves; berries dark red. A variable hybrid ranging in character between the parents, and occuring in the wild where they grow together. '**Kathryn**' A form with puckered bronze-purple leaves. **'Purpurea'** Foliage deep purple, especially in winter. **'Variegata'** Leaves green and grey-green in the centre with a narrow cream margin.

Loquat See *Eriobotrya japonica*.

†***LOROPETALUM** R. Br. ex Rchb.—**Hamamelidaceae**—A genus of 1 or 2 species, differing from *Hamamelis* in their evergreen leaves, inferior ovary and white petals. Unsuitable for shallow chalky soils.

chinense (R. Br.) Oliv. A distinct, evergreen shrub, attaining 1.5–2m and recalling *Sycopsis*. The white, witch-hazel-like flowers are freely produced during February and March. An interesting and attractive shrub in mild localities. In recent years several forms combining pink flowers and red-purple foliage, referable to var. *rubrum* Yieh, have been selected in the USA. This form occurs in the wild in China and is also commonly cultivated there. China, Japan. I 1880 by Charles Maries. FCC 1894.

LOTUS L.—**Leguminosae**—A genus of about 100 species of annual and perennial herbs and subshrubs with pea-like flowers, widely distributed in N temperate regions. Leaves pinnate, with often 5 leaflets, the lowest pair resembling stipules. Apart from the following, the genus also contains the familiar European native, *L. corniculatus* L. (bird's foot trefoil) and the striking *L. berthelotii* Masf., from the Canary Islands, very rare in the wild but often cultivated.

hirsutus L. (*Dorycnium hirsutum* (L.) Ser.) A charming, dwarf subshrub with erect annual stems and terminal heads of pink-tinged, white pea-flowers during late summer and autumn. The whole plant is silvery-hairy, a pleasant foil for the red-tinged fruit pods. Requires a position in full sun. Mediterranean region, S Portugal. C 1683. ♀ 2002.

Louiseania ulmifolia See *Prunus triloba*.

†***LUCULIA** Sweet—**Rubiaceae**—A small genus of 5 species of very beautiful, evergreen shrubs or small trees from the temperate Himalaya and SW China. They are mainly suitable as winter-flowering shrubs for a conservatory or outdoors in the mildest gardens.

grandifolia Ghose. A beautiful shrub, to 2m, from Bhutan, where it was discovered by Kingdon-Ward growing at an altitude of 2,500m, indicating its probable greater hardiness than others of the genus. Has fragrant trusses of snow-white flowers in June or July, and large, prominently veined leaves, which give rich autumn colours. AM 1955.

gratissima (Wall.) Sweet. A semi-evergreen, free-growing shrub producing sweetly fragrant, almond-pink flowers in winter. Himalaya. I 1816. ♀ 2002. AM 1938.

pinceana Hook. A beautiful, semi-evergreen plant with deliciously scented, almond-pink flowers from May to September. Leaves narrower and flowers larger than those of *L. gratissima*. Khasia Hills (Assam). I 1843. FCC 1935. AM 1930.

***LUETKEA** Bong.—**Rosaceae**—A rare monotypic genus differing from the closely related *Spiraea* in its dissected leaves.

pectinata (Pursh) Kuntze (*Spiraea pectinata* (Pursh) Torr. & A. Gray) A dwarf, evergreen, mat-forming shrublet with tiny, pectinate leaves and small racemes of white flowers in May and June. A choice little shrublet resembling a mossy saxifrage (*Saxifraga hypnoides*). Suitable for a cool moist pocket on a rock or peat garden. W North America. C 1890.

LUMA A. Gray—**Myrtaceae**—Two species of evergreen trees or shrubs from Chile and Argentina and previously listed under *Myrtus*.

apiculata (DC.) Burret (*Myrtus luma* Mol., *M. apiculata* hort.) A lovely species attaining small tree size in mild localities. The cinnamon-coloured outer bark of even quite young trees peels off in patches, exposing the beautiful, cream-coloured inner surface. Leaves dark, dull green, oval, ending in a short abrupt point. Solitary, white flowers bedeck the branches during late summer and early autumn. The red and black fruits, when produced, are edible and sweet. In some southern Irish gardens it has become naturalised and reproduction is prolific. Chile. I 1843. ♀ 2002. AM 1978. **'Glanleam Gold'** Leaves with a conspicuous creamy-yellow margin, pink-tinged when young. Originated as a seedling at Glanleam House, Valentia Island, Co. Kerry before 1970. ♀ 2002. **'Penwith'** Leaves deep blue-green and grey-green, margined with creamy-white, strongly pink-tinged in winter and when young. A seedling found in Penlee Memorial Park, Penzance, Cornwall in 1972 by Mr E.M. Cock.

chequen (Mol.) A. Gray (*Myrtus chequen* (Mol.) Spreng.) A Chilean myrtle proving to be one of the hardiest, and ultimately forming a small, densely leafy tree, flowering in summer and autumn. Leaves aromatic, bright green, undulate. I 1847 by William Lobb.

LUPINUS L.—**Leguminosae**—The lupins are a genus of some 200 or more species of annual and perennial herbs and shrubs mainly found in W North America but also in N and S America and the Mediterranean region. The majority are herbaceous, but among the shrubby species are several worthy garden plants.

***arboreus** Sims. Yellow tree lupin. A comparatively short-lived, more or less evergreen, fast-growing shrub up to 2m. Flowers normally yellow, but variable from seed and sometimes blue, delicately scented, produced in dense racemes continuously throughout summer. Thrives in full sun in a well-drained position and easily naturalises in sandy soils, particularly by the sea. California. C 1793. ♀ 2002. **'Golden Spire'** A form with deeper yellow flowers. **'Snow Queen'** Flowers white. AM 1899.

chamissonis Eschs. A densely branched, silvery lupin up to 1m. Ideal for grey borders; clouded purple-blue flowers are borne during early summer. Requires a sunny, preferably well-drained position. Coastal regions of California. I about 1826.

†***LUZURIAGA** Ruiz & Pav.—**Philesiaceae**—A small genus of 3 species of half-hardy plants, natives of South America and New Zealand.

radicans Ruiz & Pav. A shrubby evergreen of creeping habit and but a few cm high, with ovate leaves and star-shaped, glistening white flowers, with prominent yellow anthers, in summer followed by bright orange berries. Requires shade and moist conditions. Native of Chile and Argentina where it is often found growing on the trunks of forest trees. I before 1850.

LYCIUM L.—**Solanaceae**—About 100 species of often spiny, rambling shrubs, widely distributed throughout the world. Excellent for maritime exposure and for fixing sandy banks. Flowers small, usually violet, followed by conspicuous berries.

barbarum L. (*L. halimifolium* Mill., *L. chinense* Mill., *L. europaeum* hort. not L.) Duke of Argyll's tea tree. A vigorous, medium-sized shrub with long, often spiny, scrambling, arching stems. Funnel-shaped, purple flowers appear in clusters in the leaf axils from June to September, followed by small, egg-shaped orange or scarlet berries. We have also grown 'Carnosum', with pink flowers. Excellent by the sea. China; extensively naturalised in Europe and W Asia. I about 1700.

chilense Bertero (*L. grevilleanum* Miers) A medium-sized, lax shrub with spineless, spreading branches, slender, almost linear, fleshy leaves and yellowish-white and purple, funnel-shaped flowers from June to August. Chile, Argentina.

chinense See *L. barbarum*.

europaeum hort. See *L. barbarum*.

halimifolium See *L. barbarum*.

‡**LYONIA** Nutt.—**Ericaceae**—Attractive, evergreen and deciduous shrubs or occasionally small trees, closely related to *Pieris*, and requiring lime-free soil. About 35 species in E Asia, the Malay peninsula, North America, the Greater Antilles and Mexico.

ligustrina (L.) DC. Male berry. A deciduous, small to medium-sized shrub with oval or obovate leaves. Pitcher-shaped, white flowers are carried in panicles during July and August. Thrives in a moist, peaty or sandy loam. E USA. I 1748. **var. *foliosiflora*** (Michx.) Fern. An unusual variety with leafy bracts in the flower panicles. SE USA.

lucida (Lam.) K. Koch (*Andromeda lucida* Lam.) (*Pieris lucida* (Lam.) Rehder.) Fetter bush. Small to medium-sized shrub with rather lax, sharply angled stems. Broadly elliptic to ovate, entire, leathery leaves are shining dark green above. White to pink flowers appear in axillary clusters in May and June. SE USA. I 1765.

mariana (L.) D. Don. Stagger bush. A small, deciduous shrub, somewhat resembling *Gaultheria shallon*, with erect, flexuous, shiny stem and oval, dark green, leathery leaves. White or pink-tinged, nodding flowers are borne in axillary panicles in May or early June. E USA. I before 1736.

ovalifolia (Wall.) Drude. A medium-sized to large, semi-evergreen shrub, widely distributed in E and SE Asia of which we have grown the following form: **var. *elliptica*** (Siebold & Zucc.) Hand.-Mazz. Medium-sized to large shrub with slender, reddish shoots and elliptic, slender-pointed leaves, bronze when unfolding. Small, white flowers occur in axillary racemes in June and July. Japan, Taiwan. I 1829.

‡†***LYONOTHAMNUS** A. Gray—**Rosaceae**—A monotypic genus.

floribundus A. Gray. Catalina ironwood. This species is mainly represented in cultivation by the following form. The typical form differs in its simple, entire to toothed leaves. It is rarely seen in gardens but there is a fine specimen at the Chelsea Physic Garden. Intermediates between the two forms occur in the wild. Santa Catalina Island (California, USA). **subsp. *aspleniifolius*** (Greene) Raven. A graceful, fast-growing, small tree of slender habit, soon forming a remarkable, slender trunk, like a miniature redwood, with attractive, chestnut-brown and grey, shredding bark. Fern-like, pinnate leaves, the leaflets divided to the base into oblong lobes, are glossy green above, grey hairy below. Bears creamy-white flowers in large, spiraea-like panicles in early summer. Except in the milder counties needs the shelter of a warm, sunny wall. San Clemente, Santa Rosa and Santa Cruz Islands (California, USA). I 1900.

M

MAACKIA Rupr.—**Leguminosae**—A small genus of about 11 species of attractive, very hardy, small, slow-growing, deciduous trees, related to *Cladrastis* but differing in the solitary, exposed leaf buds, opposite leaflets and densely packed, more or less erect racemes. They are natives of E Asia. The following species succeed in most soils including deep soil over chalk.

amurensis Rupr. & Maxim. (*Cladrastis amurensis* (Rupr. & Maxim.) Benth.) A small tree with pinnate leaves, glabrous beneath; white flowers, tinged palest slate-blue, with a green blotch on the standard, in erect racemes, in July and August, even on young plants. Russian Far East, N China, Korea. I 1864 by C.J. Maximowicz. **subsp.** *buergeri* (Maxim.) Kitamura. A variety with obtuse leaflets, usually pubescent beneath. Japan. I 1892 by Charles Sargent.

chinensis See *M. hupehensis*.

fauriei (Lévl.) Takeda. This species has leaves with up to 17 leaflets, glabrous beneath, and white or pink-tinged flowers. A native of Cheju Do, South Korea, it was introduced by Ernest Wilson in 1917 but is rare in cultivation. A plant received under this name at the Sir Harold Hillier Gardens and Arboretum proved to be *M. amurensis*.

hupehensis Takeda (*M. chinensis* Takeda) A small, broad-headed tree producing downy terminal panicles of dull white pea-flowers in July and August. The dark bluish young shoots which, like the young leaves, are densely covered with silvery-silky down, are particularly outstanding in late spring. W Hubei, E Sichuan, China. I 1908 by Ernest Wilson.

Machilus ichangensis See *Persea ichangensis*.
× *Macludrania hybrida* See *Maclura* 'Hybrida'.

MACLURA Nutt.—**Moraceae**—A genus of about 12 species of trees, shrubs and climbers, natives of North America, E Asia, Africa and Australia. Male and female flowers are borne in spherical clusters on separate trees. They bear a multiple fruit derived from many flowers.

'Hybrida' (*M. pomifera* × *M. tricuspidata*) (× *Macludrania hybrida* André) Small to medium-sized tree with spiny branches and long, taper-pointed leaves. Inconspicuous flowers are followed by large, orange-like fruits. Garden origin in France before 1905.

pomifera (Raf.) C.K. Schneid. (*M. aurantiaca* Nutt.) Osage orange. A hardy, free-growing, small to medium-sized tree with thorny branches and fleshy, yellow roots. Remarkable for its large, pale yellow, orange-like fruits, borne on mature trees. Yellow autumn leaf colour. Used as an impenetrable hedge in the USA. Any well-drained soil; excellent on chalky soils. S and C USA. I 1818.

tricuspidata Carrière (*Cudrania tricuspidata* (Carrière) Bureau) Chinese silkworm thorn. A large shrub or small tree with ovate, entire or 3-lobed leaves and stalked, axillary clusters of tiny flowers. Rare in cultivation. China, Korea. C 1872.

MADDENIA Hook. f. & Thomson—**Rosaceae**—A small, botanically interesting genus of 4 species of small trees and shrubs from the Himalaya and China, related to *Prunus*, but differing in the flowers having small petals similar to the calyx lobes, borne in short, dense, terminal racemes as the leaves emerge. Any fertile soil.

hypoleuca Koehne. An unusual shrub or small tree, with cherry-like leaves, bronze-tinged when young, glaucous and nearly glabrous beneath, and small, black fruits. The numerous, exserted, yellowish stamens make an attractive feature as the flowers open in small clusters with pink-tinged sepals and petals in early spring. Desmond Clarke, in the supplement to W.J. Bean's, *Trees and Shrubs Hardy in the British Isles*, attributes to Hillier Nurseries the survival of this rare plant in gardens. W Hubei, China. I 1907 by Ernest Wilson.

wilsonii Koehne. This differs from *M. hypoleuca* in that the leaves emerge green, softly hairy beneath on the veins, the young shoots are densely hairy, and sepals and petals are green. W Sichuan, China.

Madroña See *Arbutus menziesii*.

MAGNOLIA L.—**Magnoliaceae**—A genus of some 120 species of deciduous and evergreen trees and shrubs, natives of the Himalaya to E and SE Asia and from North America to Brazil. The magnolias embrace the most magnificent of flowering trees hardy in the temperate regions. On the whole their cultural requirements are not difficult to provide: they need a reasonable depth of good soil, and respond to rich living, good drainage and plenty of moisture. The early flowering kinds need a sheltered site with protection from spring frosts and cold winds; those with large leaves should be given shelter from gales, while partial shade, provided by woodland or similar sites, is beneficial to many species. The petals and sepals are usually similar and are collectively termed 'tepals'.

With the exception of *M. salicifolia*, the larger tree magnolias do not flower when small and, unless stated below, the flowers of the deciduous species appear before the leaves. The fruit clusters of some species are colourful in autumn.

Magnolias are very tolerant of heavy clay soils and atmospheric pollution. The most lime-tolerant are *M. acuminata*, *M. delavayi*, *M. kobus*, *M. × loebneri* and *M. wilsonii*. In 1987 our propagator, Peter Dummer, made several crosses using *M. campbellii* as the male parent. As this species flowers much earlier than most others, the pollen was collected, dried and stored until required for use. Crosses were carried out using *M. cylindrica*, *M. denudata* 'Purple Eye', *M. × soulangeana* 'Picture' and *M.* 'Sayonara' as female parents. The resulting seedlings all appear to be very vigorous in growth and have been distributed to several gardens including the Sir Harold Hillier Gardens and Arboretum.

acuminata (L.) L. Cucumber tree. A vigorous species rapidly growing into a large, spreading tree, conical when young. Flowers appear with the leaves, in May and June (not on young trees) and are greenish, metallic-blue and yellow. The popular name refers to the shape and colour of the young fruit clusters. E USA, SE Canada. I 1736. **var.** *cordata* See var. *subcordata*. **'Philo'** Flowers green, covered with a conspicuous blue-white bloom, and yellow autumn colour. Found by Professor Joe McDaniel near Philo, Illinois before 1964. **var.** *subcordata* (Spach) Dandy (*M. cordata* Michx., *M. acuminata* var. *cordata* (Michx.) Sarg.) Usually a smaller, compact, round-headed tree or large shrub with soft canary-yellow flowers, borne with the leaves, in summer and again in early autumn, even on young plants. SE USA. I 1801. **'Miss Honeybee'** A vigorous form with fragrant, pale yellow flowers. C 1970.

‡**'Albatross'** (*M. cylindrica* × *M.* × *veitchii* 'Peter Veitch') A small, conical tree bearing large flowers before the leaves in early spring. Flowers white, to 30cm across, with up to 12 tepals, flushed with pink towards the base. It was named from a plant grown at Lanhydrock, raised from seed of *M. cylindrica* at Trewithen in 1970. FCC 1996.

‡**'Ann'** (*M. liliiflora* 'Nigra' × *M. stellata* 'Rosea') A medium-sized to large, upright, deciduous shrub. The flowers appear in mid-spring and have 8 deep reddish-pink, upright tepals, paler on the inside. ♀ 2002.

‡**'Apollo'** (*M. campbellii* subsp. *mollicomata* 'Lanarth' × *M. liliiflora* 'Nigra') A free-flowering hybrid raised in New Zealand before 1990 by Felix Jury. The large, rather star-shaped, profusely borne flowers have spreading tepals which open deep purple-pink turning to deep rose-pink.

ashei See *M. macrophylla* subsp. *ashei*.

‡**'Athene'** (*M.* 'Mark Jury' × *M.* × *soulangeana* 'Lennei Alba') A vigorous, upright, medium-sized tree with large, fragrant flowers, resembling those of *M. campbellii*. The thick tepals are white, shading to pink at the base. Raised by Felix Jury in New Zealand.

‡**'Atlas'** (*M.* 'Mark Jury' × *M.* × *soulangeana* 'Lennei') A sister seedling of 'Iolanthe', which it resembles, but making a more vigorous tree, flowering slightly later. The very large flowers are up to 35cm across, of a cup and saucer shape, with soft pink tepals, white inside.

auriculata See *M. fraseri*.

‡**'Betty'** (*M. liliiflora* 'Nigra' × *M. stellata* 'Rosea') A vigorous, medium-sized, deciduous shrub bearing large flowers, to 20cm across, with up to 19 tepals, purplish-red outside, white inside. ♀ 2002.

biondii Pamp. A small tree with slender shoots and dark green, oblong to elliptic leaves, to 20cm long. The small, fragrant flowers open before the leaves and have 6 white tepals, to 5cm long, flushed purple towards the base, and an outer whorl of 3 small, sepal-like tepals. Related to *M. salicifolia* but with silky buds and non-aromatic shoots. C China. I to North America in 1977 where it first flowered in 1986.

× *brooklynensis* Kalmb. (*M. acuminata* × *M. liliiflora*) This hybrid was first raised at Brooklyn Botanic Garden in 1954 and later by Professor Joe McDaniel in Illinois. The several forms in cultivation make small to medium-sized trees, the flowers an interesting combination of colours derived from the parents, and opening in late spring, with and after the young leaves. **'Woodsman'** (*M. acuminata* 'Klan' × *M. liliiflora* 'O'Neill') A form raised by Professor Joe McDaniel in the 1960s. Tepals an unusual combination of green and dusky pink outside, creamy-white veined pink inside flushed green towards the base. **'Yellow Bird'** (*M.* 'Yellow Bird') A backcross of *M.* ×

brooklynensis 'Evamaria' with *M. acuminata* raised at Brooklyn Botanic Garden in 1967. The cup-shaped deep yellow flowers open in late spring.

'Butterflies' (*M. acuminata* 'Fertile Myrtle' × *M. denudata*) This is one of several crosses made by Phil Savage in Michigan, USA, looking for the perfect yellow magnolia. It is a compact, upright, medium-sized tree, flowering at an early age. The yellow flowers with red stamens are freely produced in late spring and tend to get lost among the foliage.

‡**'Caerhays Belle'** (*M. sargentiana* var. *robusta* × *M. sprengeri* 'Diva') A magnificent medium-sized tree raised at Caerhays in 1951. Very large, salmon-pink flowers with 12 broad tepals are freely borne before the leaves.

‡**'Caerhays Surprise'** (*M. campbellii* subsp. *mollicomata* × *M. liliiflora* 'Nigra') A small tree with arching shoots that bear large flowers, to 25cm across, over a long period during spring, mostly before the leaves emerge. The 9–12 tepals are soft lilac-pink, deeper beneath. Raised from a cross made at Caerhays by Philip Tregunna in 1959, the original plant flowered when 7 years old.

‡*campbellii* Hook. f. & Thoms. The giant, deciduous Himalayan pink tulip tree attains its greatest dimensions in warmer counties. The very large flowers, opening in February and continuing into March, are goblet-shaped at first, later spreading wide, like water lilies; tepals usually pink within, deep rose-pink without. Flowers are not normally produced until the tree is 20–30 years old. A large tree carrying many hundreds of blooms is an unforgettable sight. From seed the flowers are usually pink, but may vary between white and deep rose-purple. There is also considerable variation in the degree of hardiness, the deeper coloured forms being usually the least hardy. E Nepal, Sikkim, Bhutan, SW China. I about 1865. FCC 1903. **Alba Group** (f. *alba* hort.) Flowers white. This is the form most common in the wild and would have become the type had not the pink-flowered form been discovered first. First planted in western gardens by J.C. Williams, it is at its most glorious in flower in the great garden he made at Caerhays Castle, Cornwall. C 1925. FCC 1951. **'Betty Jessel'** A seedling of 'Darjeeling' raised by Sir George Jessel before 1967 and named after his wife. Large, deep crimson flowers opening late, in mid- to late spring. **'Charles Raffill'** A vigorous hybrid between the typical form and subsp. *mollicomata*, inheriting the early flowering habit of the latter. The large flowers are deep rose-pink in bud, opening rose-purple outside, white with a pinkish-purple marginal flush inside. Grown at Windsor, and one of the original seedlings raised by Charles Raffill at Kew in 1946. The same cross had also arisen many years earlier in the garden of the late Sir Charles Cave. Bart. See 'Sidbury'. FCC 1966. AM and Cory Cup 1963. **'Darjeeling'** A superb clone with flowers of the darkest rose. Our stock was vegetatively propagated from the original tree in Darjeeling Botanic Garden, India. **'Ethel Hillier'** A vigorous, hardy form raised in our nurseries from wild-collected seed. This has very large flowers with white tepals with a faint pink flush at the base on the outside. **'Kew's Surprise'** One of Charles Raffill's seedlings, grown at Caerhays, Cornwall. The magnificent flowers are larger than those of 'Charles Raffill' and the outside of the

tepals are richer pink. FCC and Cory Cup 1967. **'Lanarth'** A striking form of subsp. *mollicomata* raised at Lanarth from seed collected by Forrest (F.25655) in 1924. Very large, cyclamen-purple flowers with even darker stamens. FCC 1947. **subsp. *mollicomata*** (W.W. Sm.) Johnstone (*M. mollicomata* W.W. Sm.) Similar in many respects to the typical form, but hardier and more dependable in this climate, also flowering at an earlier age, sometimes within 10–15 years. The flowers are like large, pink to rose-purple water lilies. Differing from subsp. *campbellii* in the hairy internodes on the peduncles (those of the typical form being glabrous) and often more hairy leaves. SE Tibet, N Burma, Yunnan. I 1924 by George Forrest. FCC 1939. **'Princess Margaret'** See *M.* 'Princess Margaret'. **'Sidbury'** A medium-sized to large tree of vigorous habit, flowering earlier in life than *M. campbellii*, and equally spectacular in flower. This cross between subsp. *campbellii* and subsp. *mollicomata* was raised some years prior to 1946 at Sidbury Manor, Devon, the home of the late Sir Charles Cave. Bart. It therefore precedes those made by Charles Raffill at Kew. **'Wakehurst'** A magnificent hybrid, differing from 'Charles Raffill' in its darker flowers. **'Werrington'** A form of subsp. *mollicomata* originating from the same Forrest collection as 'Lanarth' and of similar garden merit.

'Candy Cane' Flowers white with 9 tepals, 7.5cm long, striped with rose-pink on the back. Selected by John Giordano from one of Todd Gresham's crosses.

‡**'Charles Coates'** (*M. sieboldii* × *M. tripetala*) (*M. coatesii* hort.) A distinct and interesting hybrid, making a large bush or small, spreading tree. Fragrant, creamy-white flowers with a conspicuous centre of reddish anthers, resemble those of *M. tripetala*, and are produced with the leaves in May and June. Selected from seedlings found by Charles Coates at Kew in about 1946. AM 1973.

†*coco (Lour.) DC. (*M. pumila* Andre, *Talauma coco* Merrill) A small, evergreen or semi-evergreen shrub with smooth, net-veined leaves and nodding, creamy-white, fragrant (particularly at night) flowers, produced intermittently during summer. Requires conservatory treatment except in the mildest localities. Java. I 1786.

conspicua See *M. denudata*.

cordata See *M. acuminata* var. *subcordata*.

‡*cylindrica* E.H. Wilson. A very rare, small tree or large shrub. The white flowers, very similar to those of *M. denudata* but more elegant, appear on the naked stems in April. The name refers to its cylindrical fruits. We believe we were the first to introduce this species to Britain via the USA. E China (Anhui). See also *M.* 'Pegasus'. C 1936. AM 1963.

'David Clulow' Selected from one of Todd Gresham's crosses, probably *M.* × *soulangeana* 'Lennei Alba' × *M.* × *veitchii* 'Rubra', this has large, white, cup- and saucer-shaped flowers with a pink flush at the base.

‡*dawsoniana* Rehder & E.H. Wilson. A rare and magnificent species from W China, attaining a small to medium-sized tree or large shrub. Leaves nearly 15cm long, are leathery, bright green above, rather glaucous beneath; flowers in spring, large, pale rose, suffused purple without, held horizontally (not on young trees). E Sikang, China. I 1908 by Ernest Wilson. AM 1939. **'Chyverton**

Red' Flowers bright crimson outside, white within with crimson anthers and styles. A seedling raised at Caerhays, Cornwall and planted at Chyverton garden Cornwall in 1944. AM 1974.

dealbata See *M. macrophylla* subsp. *dealbata*.

†*delavayi* Franch. With the exception of *Rhododendron sinogrande* and *Trachycarpus fortunei* and its allies, this magnificent species has probably the largest leaves of any evergreen tree or shrub grown outdoors in this country. A large shrub or bushy tree, up to 14m, it has sea-green leaves, matt above, glaucous beneath. The parchment-white, slightly fragrant flowers, in late summer and early autumn, are 18–20cm across, but the individual blossom seldom survives for more than 2 days. Requires wall protection except in favoured localities. Does well in soils over chalk. China (Yunnan, Sichuan). I 1899 by Ernest Wilson. FCC 1913.

‡*denudata* Desrouss. (*M. conspicua* Salisb.) Yulan, Lily tree. A large shrub or small, rounded tree, usually below 9m. The fragrant, pure white, cup-shaped flowers open in early spring. The broad tepals are thick and fleshy. E China. I 1789. ♛ 2002. FCC 1968. **'Forrest's Pink'** A form with pink flowers deeper at the base of the tepals. Selected at Caerhays and possibly raised from seed collected by George Forrest. **'Purple Eye'** ('Veitch's Var.') A large, widespreading shrub, one of the most beautiful of this aristocratic family. Flowers large, fragrant, pure white with a purple stain at the base of the inner tepals. Probably of hybrid origin. AM 1926.

‡**'Elizabeth'** (*M. acuminata* × *M. denudata*) A remarkable, small, conical tree raised by Eva Maria Sperbes at the Brooklyn Botanic Garden, New York and selected in 1978. It is named after Elizabeth Scholz, then Director. The clear, pale primrose-yellow, fragrant, cup-shaped flowers open before the leaves in April or May. ♛ 2002.

'Eric Savill' See *M. sprengeri* 'Eric Savill'.

‡*fraseri* Walt. (*M. auriculata* Bartr.) A rare, medium-sized tree, allied to *M. macrophylla*. The leaves, up to 40cm long, have 2 distinct auricles at the base and are clustered at the ends of the branches. Flowers, produced in May and June, with the leaves, are large, parchment-white and slightly fragrant and are followed by attractive, rose-coloured fruit clusters. Mts of SE USA. I 1786. AM 1948. **subsp. *pyramidata*** (Bartr.) E. Murray (*M. pyramidata* Bartr.) A very rare, small tree, differing in its smaller, thinner leaves and smaller flowers in June. SE USA. C 1825.

*'Freeman' (*M. grandiflora* × *M. virginiana*) A large, evergreen shrub or small tree of dense, columnar habit, with glossy green leaves, similar to but smaller than those of *M. grandiflora*, up to 20cm long and 6cm wide, thinly felted beneath. White, fragrant, globular flowers are borne in summer but rarely open fully. Raised by Oliver Freeman of the US National Arboretum, Washington, from a cross made in 1931. Hybrids of the same parentage are found in S Alabama.

fuscata See *Michelia figo*.

‡**'Galaxy'** (*M. liliiflora* 'Nigra' × *M. sprengeri* 'Diva') A vigorous, small, conical, deciduous tree with striking, purple-pink to red, slightly fragrant, tulip-shaped flowers in mid- to late spring before the leaves. It flowers when young. Raised by William Kosar at the US National Arboretum in 1963. ♛ 2002.

‡'**George Henry Kern**' (*M. liliiflora* 'Nigra' × *M. stellata* 'Rosea') A compact, medium-sized shrub bearing profuse soft pink flowers, each with 8–10 tepals, opening over a long period from mid-spring to summer. Raised in 1935 in Cincinnati, Ohio.

glauca See *M. virginiana*.

globosa Hook. f. & Thoms. (*M. tsarongensis* W.W. Sm. & Forrest) A large shrub or rarely a small tree, with rusty-felted young shoots and buds. Nodding, creamy-white, rather globular, fragrant flowers are produced on stout brown-felted stalks in June. The leaves differ from those of the related *M. wilsonii* and *M. sinensis* in having red-brown pubescence beneath. Requires a protected site in colder areas. 2 forms of this species, Indian and Chinese, are in cultivation; the Indian form is the hardier of the two. E Himalaya to W China. I 1919 by George Forrest. AM 1931. **var. sinensis** See *M. sieboldi* subsp. *sinensis*.

‡'**Gold Star**' (*M. acuminata* subsp. *subcordata* 'Miss Honeybee' × *M. stellata*) A vigorous, small to medium-sized tree with bronze-red young leaves. The soft yellow flowers are similar to those of *M. stellata*, with 14 rather slender tepals. Raised by Phil Savage in Michigan, USA.

*grandiflora L. Bullbay, Loblolly magnolia. One of the most magnificent evergreens, generally and admirably suited to being grown as a wall shrub. It is, however, hardy in the open if given shelter and full sun, making a massive, round-headed shrub or short-stemmed tree. Leaves are leathery, glossy green above, often reddish-brown beneath, at least when young. The delightfully fragrant, creamy-white flowers, sometimes up to 25cm across, are produced throughout summer and early autumn. Lime-tolerant if given a good depth of rich loam. SE USA. I 1734. '**Angustifolia**' Leaves lanceolate to oblanceolate, 15–20cm long by 3.5–5cm wide, glossy green above, cinnamon pubescent beneath, becoming glabrous. Flowers typical. '**Charles Dickens**' An American selection with broad leaves and, in the USA, large bright red fruits. '**Edith Bogue**' A selection of American origin said to be very hardy. C 1920. '**Exmouth**' ('Exoniensis', 'Lanceolata') A splendid form with elliptic to elliptic-obovate leaves, polished, soft green above, reddish-brown-felted beneath, becoming glabrous. Flowers very large, and richly fragrant, appearing at an early age. C 1768. ♥ 2002. '**Ferruginea**' A form of erect, compact habit with typical flowers and elliptic-obovate leaves, dark shining green above, richly rusty-tomentose beneath, becoming glabrous, veins indistinct. C 1804. '**Gallissonnière**' A particularly hardy form of conical habit with very large flowers and leaves that are reddish-brown beneath. I to France before 1750. '**Goliath**' A form with relatively short, broad leaves, dark glossy green above, green beneath or thinly pubescent when very young. Very large, globular flowers are produced at an early age. Selected in Guernsey before 1910. FCC 1951. AM 1931. '**Lanceolata**' See 'Exmouth'. '**Little Gem**' A form of American origin which makes a compact, small tree of narrowly columnar habit. Flowers and leaves smaller than usual, the latter dark glossy green above with a deep brown felt beneath. Slightly tender. Selected in North Carolina in 1952. '**Saint Mary**' A large, bushy shrub with lustrous, wavy-edged leaves covered beneath with a dark indumentum

when young. Cup-shaped, porcelain-white flowers are freely produced from an early age. C 1905. '**Samuel Sommer**' Dark glossy green leaves with a deep brown felt beneath. Huge flowers, up to 35cm across, are borne from an early age. Very hardy and wind resistant, good for planting away from walls. C 1952. '**Undulata**' A distinct form with typical flowers and strongly wavy-edged leaves, distinctly veined, glossy green above and green beneath, even when young. Selected in France about 1850. '**Victoria**' A very hardy form selected in Victoria, British Columbia. The glossy dark green leaves have rich brown tomentum beneath. C 1930. ♥ 2002.

grandiflora × *virginiana* See 'Freeman' and 'Maryland'.

‡**Gresham Hybrids** In 1955 Dr Todd Gresham, a noted magnolia enthusiast of Santa Cruz, California, made a series of crosses involving *M.* × *veitchii* with *M. liliiflora* on the one hand and *M.* × *soulangeana* 'Lennei Alba' on the other. Of the hundred or so seedlings produced, 24 of each cross were selected and grown on. All proved vigorous, developing into strong trees in the manner of *M.* × *veitchii*. We are indebted to Dr Gresham for several of his named selections. Although the term Gresham Hybrids will continue to be used, it is confusing as it includes hybrids of different parentage. Those such as 'Heaven Scent', 'Peppermint Stick', 'Raspberry Ice' and 'Royal Crown', all *M. liliiflora* × *M.* × *veitchii*, can be referred to the Svelte Brunettes Group, while 'Crimson Stipple', 'Delicatissima', 'Rouged Alabaster' and 'Sayonara', which are *M.* × *soulangeana* 'Lennei Alba' × *M.* × *veitchii* can be referred to the Buxom Nordic Blondes Group.

‡'**Heaven Scent**' (Svelte Brunettes Group) (*M.* × *veitchii* × *M. liliiflora* 'Nigra') A magnificent small to medium-sized tree with richly scented, narrowly cup-shaped flowers in April-May; tepals pale pink, heavily flushed deep pink towards the base with a distinct magenta-pink stripe on the back. ♥ 2002.

× *highdownensis* See *M. wilsonii*.

hypoleuca See *M. obovata*.

‡'**Iolanthe**' (*M.* × *soulangeana* 'Lennei' × *M.* 'Mark Jury') A vigorous, upright, small to medium-sized tree raised in New Zealand. Large, cup-shaped, rose-pink flowers, creamy-white inside, are borne at an early age.

‡'**Jane**' (Kosar Hybrids) (*M. liliiflora* 'Reflorescens' × *M. stellata* 'Water Lily') A medium-sized, upright shrub of compact habit. Fragrant, cup-shaped flowers open from narrow, erect, red-purple buds; tepals red-purple outside, white within. ♥ 2002.

‡'**Judy**' (De Vos Hybrids) (*M. liliiflora* 'Nigra' × *M. stellata* 'Rosea') A medium-sized, upright shrub with small, candle-like flowers, red-purple outside and creamy-white inside, in mid- to late spring.

'**Kewensis**' See *M. salicifolia* 'Kewensis'.

kobus DC. (*M. kobus* var. *borealis* Sarg.) A very hardy, Japanese, small tree or large shrub that does not produce its slightly fragrant, white flowers until it is about 12 to 15 years old, when they are regularly borne with magnificent freedom during April. Excellent for all types of soil including chalky soils. Japan, Cheju do. I 1865. AM 1942. **var. borealis** See *M. kobus*. **var. loebneri** See *M.* × *loebneri*. **var. stellata** See *M. stellata*.

× *lennei* See *M.* × *soulangeana* 'Lennei'.

‡*liliiflora* Desrouss. (*M. discolor* Venten., *M. purpurea* Curtis) A widespreading, medium-sized shrub, occasionally to 4m, with obovate to broad elliptic leaves, shining dark green above. Erect flowers, like slender tulips, gradually open wide and are purple flushed on the outside, creamy-white within. They appear in late April, continuing until early June, and intermittently during the summer. One of the best species for a small garden, thriving in all but chalky soils. C China, long cultivated in Japan. I 1790. **'Nigra'** (*M.* × *soulangeana* 'Nigra') A more compact form with slightly larger flowers, deep vinous-purple outside, creamy-white, stained purple inside, borne freely over a long period from spring to summer. I 1861 from Japan in 1861 by J.G. Veitch. ♀ 2002. FCC 1981. AM 1907.

‡*liliiflora* × *stellata* We are grateful to the US National Arboretum, Washington, for 8 named selections of the above parentage. Raised at the arboretum in 1955/56 by Dr Francis de Vos and William F. Kosar, they were named after staff there or their family. Said to be superior to their parents in size, colour, fragrance and abundance of flower, the original plants were described as being multiple-stemmed, rounded or conical, erect-growing and 2–3m in height. Having grown these clones we have found them to be very floriferous and, while they will not replace their parents, they have managed to combine the best qualities of them, inheriting the narrow tepals and profuse flowers of *M. stellata* and the colouring and long flowering period of *M. liliiflora*. Those received are as follows: 'Ann', 'Judy', 'Randy' and 'Ricki' (raised by de Vos) and 'Betty', 'Jane', 'Pinkie' and 'Susan' (raised by Kosar). They are often known as the De Vos/Kosar Hybrids or the 'eight little girls'.

× *loebneri* Kache (*M. kobus* × *M. stellata*) (*M. kobus* var. *loebneri* (Kache) Spongberg) A variable hybrid uniting the best qualities of its distinguished parents, and making a small tree or large shrub, flowering with profusion even on small plants. Fragrant flowers with numerous, white, strap-shaped tepals appear in April. Succeeds well on all types of soil including chalk soil. Garden origin prior to 1910. **'Donna'** A very promising recent selection raised in Massachusetts. The fragrant, white flowers are up to 20cm across, opening from pale pink buds. **'Leonard Messel'** A magnificent, tall shrub or small tree with lilac-pink flowers, deeper in bud. A chance hybrid between an unusual *M. kobus*, which has a pale purple line along the centre of its tepals, and *M. stellata* 'Rosea'. Originated at Nymans, Sussex, a great garden made by the late Col Messel. ♀ 2002. FCC 1969. AM 1955. **'Merrill'** An outstanding selection. A vigorous, small tree with large, white, fragrant flowers, freely produced. Named after Prof. Elmer Merrill, a former Director of the Arnold Arboretum, Boston, USA where it was raised in 1939 by Dr Karl Sax. ♀ 2002. FCC and Cory Cup 1979. **'Neil McEacharn'** A vigorous, small tree with pink-flushed flowers. A cross between *M. kobus* and *M. stellata* 'Rosea' raised at Windsor from seed received from Neil McEacharn of the Villa Taranto, Italy. AM 1968. **'Raspberry Fun'** A seedling of 'Leonard Messel' raised at Chollipo Arboretum in South Korea which contains one of the most extensive collections of magnolias in the world. Selected in 1987 by the garden's founder Carl

Ferris Miller, it differs from its parent in the more numerous tepals which are deeper pink with a deep pink stripe outside. **'Snowdrift'** We adopted this name for a form descended from one of the seedlings of the original cross made in Germany in about 1910. It has larger flowers than *M. stellata* with about 12 tepals; the leaves are also a little larger.

‡**'Lois'** A hybrid of *M. acuminata* and *M. denudata* similar to 'Elizabeth' but without the tendency to fade. Flowers opening over a long period in mid-spring are clear primrose-yellow with 9 tepals. Raised at Brooklyn Botanic Garden by Lola Koerting from a cross made in the 1960s.

‡*macrophylla* Michx. An awe-inspiring, small tree when seen alone in its grandeur – ideally in a site sheltered from the prevailing wind, but open to the sun and backed by dark evergreens. It has perhaps larger leaves and flowers than any other deciduous tree or shrub hardy in the British Isles. The leaves, sometimes exceeding 60cm long, are rather thin in texture, glaucous beneath. The very large, fragrant flowers are parchment-white with purple markings in the centre and appear in early summer. SE USA. I 1800. FCC 1900. **subsp.** *ashei* (Weatherby) Spongberg (*M. ashei* Weatherby) A large shrub, in all respects a miniature *M. macrophylla*, with smaller leaves, flowers and fruits. The flowers appear with the leaves and are produced even on young specimens. Outer 3 tepals blotched with maroon at the base. It is strange that a plant of this quality, growing in a country enjoying western civilisation was not recorded in cultivation until 1933. NW Florida. **subsp.** *dealbata* (Zucc.) J.D. Tobe (*M. dealbata* Zucc.) This differs in having larger fruits with beaked follicles and in the tepals usually not blotched with maroon at the base. A native of Mexico, it was collected by Sir Harold Hillier and introduced to our nursery in 1980.

'Manchu Fan' (Gresham Hybrids) (*M.* × *veitchii* × *M.* × *soulangeana* 'Lennei Alba') A splendid, small to medium-sized tree. The large, goblet-shaped flowers have 9 broad, creamy-white tepals, the inner ones flushed purplish-pink at the base. Similar to 'Sayonara' but flowers less goblet-shaped and less green-flushed at the base, with only the basal third of the inner tepals flushed pink.

*'Maryland'** A large shrub or small tree similar to *M.* 'Freeman', differing in its more open habit, larger leaves and flowers that open more widely. Origin as 'Freeman'.

‡**'Michael Rosse'** (*M. campbellii* Alba Group × *M. sargentiana* var. *robusta*) A beautiful tree raised at Caerhays, Cornwall and grown at Nymans, Sussex, having large, soft purple flowers. AM 1968.

‡**'Milky Way'** (*M.* 'Mark Jury' × *M.* × *soulangeana* 'Lennei Alba') A sister seedling of 'Athene' but the flowers white, with a slight pink flush at the base. ♀ 2002.

mollicomata See *M. campbellii* subsp. *mollicomata*.

nicholsoniana hort. See *M. sinensis*.

nicholsoniana Rehder & E.H. Wilson See *M. wilsonii*.

'Nimbus' (*M. obovata* × *M. virginiana*) A small, semi-evergreen tree of upright habit, with glossy green leaves, to 30cm long, glaucous beneath. Cup-shaped, ivory-white, fragrant flowers, 10cm across, open in late spring to early summer. Raised in 1956 by William Kosar, at the US National Arboretum.

‡†*nitida* W.W. Sm. An evergreen shrub or small tree of dense habit, with leathery leaves, dark shining green above. Creamy-white, scented flowers, 5–7.5cm across, are borne in late spring or early summer. The young growths have an almost metallic lustre. A charming but tender species, only suitable for the mildest localities. One of the finest specimens is growing in the woods at Caerhays, Cornwall. Upper Burma, NW Yunnan, SE Tibet. AM 1966.

'Norman Gould' See *M. stellata* 'Norman Gould'.

‡*obovata* Thunb. (*M. hypoleuca* Siebold & Zucc.) A handsome, strong-growing, medium-sized tree often with purple-tinged young shoots. Very large, obovate leaves are held in whorls at the ends of the shoots. The creamy-white, very strongly fragrant flowers, borne in May and June, are 20cm across and have a central ring of crimson stamens; fruit clusters attractive and large. Japan. I about 1880. ♀ 2002. FCC 1893.

‡*officinalis* Rehder & E.H. Wilson. A small to medium-sized tree, closely related to *M. hypoleuca*, with usually yellowish-grey young shoots and large, obovate leaves, up to 50cm long. The large, saucer-shaped, white and fragrant flowers appear at the end of leafy young growths in early summer. China, but only known in cultivation. I 1900 by Ernest Wilson. **var. biloba** Rehder & E.H. Wilson. A very rare and distinct Chinese tree, introduced by our nurseries to British gardens from the Botanic Garden, Lushan in 1936. Its large, obovate leaves are pale green above, glaucous and finely downy beneath, deeply notched at the apex. The cup-shaped flowers, 15–20cm across, scented of wintergreen are parchment-white with a maroon centre, delicately flushed outside with green and pink. AM 1975.

parviflora See *M. sieboldii*.

‡**'Pegasus'** A very beautiful, large shrub or multi-stemmed, small tree named from a plant at Trengwainton in Cornwall, supplied by us as *M. cylindrica*. The profuse, upright flowers have 6 large tepals, to 10cm long, and 3 small, outer tepals. The large tepals have distinctively reflexed margins and are white, flushed with purple at the base. It is possibly a hybrid between *M. cylindrica* and *M. denudata*. We also distributed many seed-raised plants as *M. cylindrica* and it cannot be assumed that all plants under this name are 'Pegasus'.

‡**'Peppermint Stick'** (Svelte Brunettes Group) (*M. liliiflora* × *M.* × *veitchii*) A strong-growing, medium-sized, conical tree with distinctive narrowly columnar flower buds, to 11cm long. The 9 tepals are creamy-white, flushed pink at the base with a central, deep pink line; the outer tepals spread with age; the inner tepals are erect, heavily flushed deep pink towards the base.

'Phillip Tregunna' (*M. campbellii* × *M. sargentiana* var. *robusta*) Large flowers, to 19cm across, with 11–12 tepals, are purple-pink, paler inside when fully open. Raised from seed of *M. sargentiana* var. *robusta* at Caerhays in 1960. FCC 1992.

‡**'Pinkie'** (Kosar Hybrids) (*M. liliiflora* 'Reflorescens' × *M. stellata* 'Rosea') A medium-sized shrub bearing cup-shaped flowers, up to 18cm across, with 9–12 tepals, pale red-purple becoming pink outside, white within. ♀ 2002.

‡**'Princess Margaret'** (*M. campbellii* Alba Group × *M. sargentiana* var. *robusta*) Large flowers, red-purple out-

side, cream inside. A seedling of *M. campbellii* Alba Group from Caerhays, Cornwall, raised in 1957 and grown at Windsor Great Park. FCC 1973.

‡× *proctoriana* See *M. salicifolia* 'Proctoriana'.

pumila See *M. coco*.

purpurea See *M. liliiflora*.

pyramidata See *M. fraseri* var. *pyramidata*.

‡**'Randy'** (De Vos Hybrids) (*M. liliiflora* 'Nigra' × *M. stellata* 'Rosea') A medium-sized shrub with light pink flowers, consisting of 15 narrow tepals, opening to 12cm wide.

‡**'Raspberry Ice'** (Svelte Brunettes Group) (*M. liliiflora* 'Nigra' × *M.* × *veitchii*) A small, spreading tree with profusions of large, rich pink flowers, white inside. One of the many hybrids raised by Todd Gresham who named it in 1962.

‡**'Ricki'** (De Vos Hybrids) (*M. liliiflora* 'Nigra' × *M. stellata* 'Rosea') A medium-sized shrub with large flowers, deep purplish-pink in bud, up to 15cm across when open. Tepals about 15, rather narrow, pink to deep rose-purple at the base outside.

†‡*rostrata* W.W. Sm. A rare, medium-sized, gaunt tree for woodland shelter, with broad, obovate, conspicuously veined leaves up to 50cm long. Young foliage and buds are clothed with tawny, velvety hairs. Flowers, appearing with the leaves in June, have fleshy, creamy-white or pink tepals, followed by conspicuous pink, cone-like fruits. Yunnan, SE Tibet, Upper Burma. AM 1974 (for foliage).

‡**'Royal Crown'** (Svelte Brunettes Group) (*M. liliiflora* × *M.* × *veitchii*) A small tree, the large flowers, with 12 tepals, open before the leaves, deep purplish-pink in bud, fading to white at the tips when open, white inside.

‡*salicifolia* (Siebold & Zucc.) Maxim. A small, broadly conical tree or large shrub with slender branches. Leaves usually narrow and willow-like, occasionally ovate, normally slightly glaucous beneath; flowers, usually produced on young plants, white, fragrant, with mostly 6 narrow tepals, produced on the leafless stems in April. The leaves, bark and wood are pleasantly lemon-scented when bruised. Japan. I 1892. ♀ 2002. FCC 1962. AM 1927. **'Jermyns'** A slow-growing, shrubby form with broader leaves, conspicuously glaucous beneath, and larger flowers appearing later. One of the best flowering clones of this beautiful magnolia. **'Kewensis'** (*M.* 'Kewensis') A small, slender, broadly conical tree. Flowers creamy-white, fragrant, 6cm long, very freely borne in March or April before the leaves. Originated at Kew about 1938. AM 1952. **'Proctoriana'** (*M. x proctoriana* Rehder) A large, very floriferous shrub or small tree with shortly pubescent leaf buds, and leaves that are green beneath. Flowers white, with 6–12 tepals, appear in April. Garden origin 1928.

‡*sargentiana* Rehder & E.H. Wilson. A noble medium-sized tree from W China. Flowers like enormous water lilies are rose-pink outside, paler within, produced on mature specimens in April and May in advance of the leathery, obovate leaves. I 1908 by Ernest Wilson. FCC 1935. **var. robusta** Rehder & E.H. Wilson. This magnificent variety has longer, narrower leaves and larger flowers and fruits. Flowers 23cm in diameter, rosy-crimson without, paler within, and usually with more tepals than the typical form, but not produced until tree size is

attained. W Sichuan, China. I 1908 by Ernest Wilson. FCC 1947. **var. *robusta* 'Multipetal'** Named from a seedling raised at Mount Congreve in Ireland and named in 1983, this bears flowers with up to 27 pale pink tepals.

‡**'Sayonara'** (Buxom Nordic Blondes Group) (*M. × soulangeana* 'Lennei Alba' × *M. × veitchii* 'Rubra') A small tree bearing profuse, white, goblet-shaped flowers, 10cm long, tepals 9, slightly pink and green flushed at the base, the inner tepals heavily flushed pink to above the middle. ♀ 2002. AM 1990.

‡**'Serene'** (*M. liliiflora × M.* 'Mark Jury') A vigorous, small tree with profuse, large, bowl-shaped, rose-pink flowers.

‡***sieboldii*** K. Koch (*M. parviflora* Siebold & Zucc.) A large, widespreading shrub with ovate to obovate leaves, glaucous and hairy beneath. The nodding flowers in bud are egg-shaped, but turn outwards as the tepals expand; flowers white and fragrant, appearing intermittently with the leaves from May to August. The crimson fruit clusters are spectacular. Japan, Korea. I 1865. ♀ 2002. FCC 1894. **susbp. *sinensis*** (Rehder & E.H. Wilson) Spongberg (*M. sinensis* (Rehder & E.H. Wilson) Stapf, *M. globosa* var. *sinensis* Rehder & E.H. Wilson, *M. nicholsoniana* hort.) A large, widespreading shrub, resembling *M. wilsonii* but easily distinguished by its broader, obovate leaves, tomentose beneath, and wider, more strongly lemon-scented, nodding flowers, 10–13cm wide, which appear with the leaves, in June. The paper-white flowers contrast with the central red staminal cone. Before 1930 this plant was distributed by Chenault of Orleans, France as *M. nicholsoniana*. NW Sichuan (W China). I 1908 by Ernest Wilson. FCC 1931. AM 1927.

sinensis See *M. sieboldii* subsp. *sinensis*.

'Sir Harold Hillier' A very beautiful hybrid named from a tree at Chyverton. Large, white flowers up to 30cm across.

‡**× *soulangeana*** Soulange-Bodin (*M. denudata × M. liliiflora*) In its numerous forms, the best and most popular magnolia for general planting. Usually seen as a large shrub with several widespreading stems. Flowers appear during April to early May, before the leaves. They are large, tulip-shaped, white, stained rose-purple at the base. The best magnolia for tolerating indifferent clay soils and atmospheric pollution, but only moderately lime-tolerant, and no good for shallow chalk soils. Raised by Mons. Soulange-Bodin at Fromont, near Paris, early in the 19th century but forms may have originated in Japan long before this. There are a number of cultivars all of which have the useful habit of flowering when young. For the plant usually grown under this name see 'Etienne Soulange-Bodin'. **'Alba'** See 'Alba Superba' and 'Amabilis'. **'Alba Superba'** ('Alba') One of the first of the group to produce its white, scented flowers, closely resembling those of *M. denudata*. C 1835. **'Alexandrina'** One of the most popular forms, vigorous, erect and free-flowering; the large, erect flowers are white, flushed purple at the base. C 1831. **'Amabilis'** ('Alba') A superb selection resembling *M. denudata* in general habit and flowers. The faint purplish flush at the base of the inner tepals is generally quite concealed and the beautifully formed flowers appear ivory-white. C 1865. **'Brozzonii'** The aristocrat of the "Soulangeanas". Large, elongated, white flowers, shaded purple at the

base. One of the largest-flowered and latest of the group. C 1873. ♀ 2002. FCC 1929. **'Etienne Soulange-Bodin'** The typical form described above and usually grown as *M. × soulangeana*. ♀ 2002. **'Lennei'** (*M. × lennei* hort.) One of the first clones. A vigorous, spreading, multi-stemmed shrub with large, broadly obovate leaves up to 25cm long. The flowers, like enormous goblets, have thick fleshy tepals, rose-purple outside and creamy-white, stained soft purple inside, and appear in April and May, and sometimes again in the autumn. Said to have originated in a garden in Lombardy, Italy, some time before 1850. ♀ 2002. FCC 1863. **'Lennei Alba'** Flowers ivory-white, very like those of *M. denudata*. C 1905. ♀ 2002. **'Nigra'** See *M. liliiflora* 'Nigra'. **'Norbertii'** A free-flowering clone with white flowers, flushed purple on the outside. Similar to 'Alexandrina', but flowers slightly smaller. C 1835. **'Pickard's Opal'** Goblet-shaped, white flowers with a slight purple flush at the base. A seedling of 'Picture', raised by Arnos Pickard in the 1960s. **'Pickard's Schmetterling'** Large, slender, upright flowers with creamy white tepals heavily flushed with red-purple towards the base. A seedling of 'Picture', raised by Arnos Pickard in the 1960s. **'Picture'** A vigorous, erect-branched clone of Japanese origin, with large leaves and long, erect flowers, vinous-purple outside, white inside. Flowers when quite young and said to be *M. denudata × M. liliiflora* 'Nigra'. An excellent magnolia found in a Japanese garden in about 1930. AM 1984. **'Rubra'** See 'Rustica Rubra'. **'Rustica Rubra'** ('Rubra') A vigorous clone, one of the best for general planting, with oval leaves and cup-shaped flowers of rich rosy-red. A seedling of 'Lennei'. ♀ 2002. AM 1960. **'San José'** A vigorous, large shrub with large flowers, deep pink outside, creamy-white inside. Raised in California about 1938. AM 1986. **'Speciosa'** A form with smaller leaves and abundant, nearly white flowers. C 1825. **'Sundew'** Large, creamy-white flowers, flushed pink at the base. C 1966. **'Triumphans'** Flowers white within, reddish-purple without, paling towards the tips. **'Verbanica'** Tepals pink on the outside. One of the last of the group to flower. C 1873.

‡**'Spectrum'** A sister seedling of 'Galaxy', differing in its larger, deeper pink flowers.

‡***sprengeri*** Pamp. (*M. sprengeri* var. *diva* Stapf ex Johnstone) (*M. denudata* var. *purpurascens* (Maxim.) Rehder & E.H. Wilson) A small to medium-sized tree, occasionally up to 13m, in April bearing fragrant, pink flowers resembling, and as rich as, those of *M. campbellii* but smaller. Leaves, up to 18cm long, are obovate with a wedge-shaped base. C and W China. I 1900 by Ernest Wilson from W Hubei. **'Burncoose'** Flowers to 17.5cm across, rose to red-purple. **'Claret Cup'** Flowers purplish-pink outside, white flushed pink inside. A seedling of 'Diva'. AM 1963. **'Copeland Court'** A tree of spreading habit with large flowers to 20cm across, deep pink, flushed crimson. **'Diva'** Flowers rose-carmine. Derives from a tree at Caerhays, Cornwall, which is the only Wilson seedling of the typical variety to survive. AM 1942. **var. *diva*** See *M. sprengeri*. **var. *elongata*** (Rehder & E.H. Wilson) Johnstone. Small, bushy tree or large shrub. Pure white flowers with narrower tepals. Hubei, Sichuan, China. I 1900 by Ernest Wilson. AM 1955.

'Eric Savill' (*M.* 'Eric Savill') A small, upright tree with large, cup-shaped flowers to 20cm across, rich pink outside and nearly white inside, borne in mid-spring before the leaves. A seedling of 'Diva' at the Savill gardens raised from Caerhays seed and named by John Bond in 1982. AM 1986.

‡**'Star Wars'** (*M. campbellii* × *M. liliiflora*) A small to medium-sized tree that flowers when only 4–5 years old. Deep pink buds, open to pink flowers, white inside, up to 15cm across, in late spring as the leaves emerge; they are a similar size to those of *M. campbellii*. An excellent cross from New Zealand. ♀ 2002. AM 1991.

stellata (Siebold & Zucc.) Maxim. (*M. halleana* Parsons, *M. kobus* var. *stellata* (Siebold & Zucc.) Blackburn) A distinct and charming, slow-growing, Japanese shrub, forming a compact, rounded specimen usually wider than high, seldom exceeding a height of 3m. Winter buds grey-hairy. The white, fragrant, many-tepalled flowers are profusely borne in March and April. A rare species restricted in the wild to a small area in the western Tokai district of Japan. The correct name for this plant is considered by some authorities to be *M. tomentosa* Thunb. I 1862. ♀ 2002. FCC 1878. **'Centennial'** A magnificent selection, a seedling of 'Rosea' raised at the Arnold Arboretum and named to commemorate the arboretum's 100th anniversary in 1972. A vigorous, large shrub, the large, slightly pink-tinged flowers with numerous tepals. **'Chrysanthemiflora'** Flowers with up to 25 tepals, pale pink with a deeper pink line on the reverse. A seedling of 'Rubra' selected in Japan by K. Wada. **'Dawn'** Flowers with numerous, narrow tepals, pale pink in bud opening white, banded with pink on the outside. **'Jane Platt'** Named from a plant grown as *M. stellata* 'Rosea' in the garden of Jane Platt in Portland, Oregon, this form has very profuse deep pink flowers with up to 30 tepals. **'King Rose'** A selection from New Zealand with flowers pale pink in bud, opening white, with up to 30 tepals. **'Norman Gould'** (*M.* 'Norman Gould') A distinct form making a small tree. Flowers opening early with usually 6–9 obovate tepals faintly streaked with pink outside towards the base, and up to 3 small, sepal-like tepals. A colchicine-induced polyploidal form raised in the RHS Gardens at Wisley. Norman Gould was a Wisley botanist. He died in 1960. FCC 1967. **'Rosea'** Flowers flushed pink, deeper in bud. AM 1893. **'Royal Star'** Very large flowers produced later than most other forms, pink-tinged in bud opening white, with numerous tepals. Raised on Long Island, New York in 1947. **'Rubra'** Flowers similar to those of 'Rosea', but slightly deeper in colour. AM 1948. **'Water Lily'** An outstanding form of Japanese origin with larger flowers and more numerous tepals. ♀ 2002.

'Summer Solstice' (*M. globosa* × *M. obovata*) A small tree with broad, dark green leaves glaucous beneath. The deep pink, globular flowers, creamy-white inside, are 10cm across and open in summer. A seedling of *M. globosa* from Windsor Great Park found by Maurice Foster, probably pollinated by the pink form of *M. obovata*. AM 1994.

'Sundance' (*M. acuminata* × *M. denudata*) A vigorous, small to medium-sized tree bearing barium-yellow flowers, 20cm across, before the leaves emerge in mid- to late spring. Raised by Professor Joe McDaniel.

‡**'Susan'** (Kosar Hybrids) (*M. liliiflora* 'Nigra' × *M. stellata* 'Rosea') A medium-sized shrub of upright habit. Flowers deep red-purple in bud, red-purple when open, paler within, with up to 6 tepals. ♀ 2002.

‡**'Sweetheart'** A vigorous tree of upright habit bearing fragrant, globular, purplish-pink flowers, deeper pink at the base and white or pale pink inside. The flowers have about 12 tepals and are 30cm across when fully open. A seedling of 'Caerhays Surprise' raised in New Zealand. AM 1997.

×*thompsoniana* (Loudon) C. de Vos (*M. tripetala* × *M. virginiana*) A large, widespreading shrub or small tree, resembling *M. virginiana*, but with larger leaves, up to 25cm long, which persist into early winter. The large, fragrant, parchment-white flowers are carried intermittently throughout the summer, even on young plants. Garden origin about 1808; raised by Archibald Thompson in London probably from American seed. AM 1958.

‡*tripetala* L. Umbrella tree. A very hardy, open-headed tree sometimes attaining 9–12m. Leaves large, 30–50cm long and 15–25cm wide. The cream-coloured flowers, 18–25cm across, in May and June are strongly and pungently scented. They are followed by attractive, red, cone-shaped fruit clusters. E USA. I 1752.

tsarongensis See *M. globosa*.

‡×*veitchii* Bean (*M. campbellii* × *M. denudata*) A very vigorous, medium-sized to large tree, hardy and attractive both in leaf and flower. The following cultivars are grown. 'Isca' and 'Peter Veitch' were both selected from the 6 seedlings raised by Peter Veitch who made the cross in 1907. **'Columbus'** (*M. denudata* × *M.* × *veitchii* 'Peter Veitch') Large, cup-shaped, white flowers. The name was suggested by John Bond in 1992, the 500th anniversary of Columbus's voyage. Selected by Frank Santamour from a cross made by William Kosar at the US National Arboretum, Washington, DC in 1960. **'Isca'** Flowers white in April. **'Peter Veitch'** A first class hardy magnolia with goblets of white, flushed purple-pink, on the naked branches in April, as soon as it attains small tree size. We are indebted to Veitch's nursery of Exeter for this splendid magnolia. FCC 1921.

virginiana L. (*M. glauca* L.) Sweet bay, Swamp bay. A partially evergreen shrub or small tree. The fragrant, creamy-white, rather small, globular flowers are produced from June to September. Leaves up to 13cm long, glossy above, blue-white beneath. E USA. Probably the first magnolia to be grown in England. Evergreen forms from the south of the range are sometimes referred to as var. *australis* Sarg. C late 17th century by John Banister.

‡**'Vulcan'** (*M. campbellii* subsp. *mollicomata* 'Lanarth' × *M. liliiflora*) A sister seedling of 'Apollo' making a small tree with large, deep ruby-red flowers borne at an early age.

'Wada's Memory' A selection from a number of seed-raised plants supplied in 1940 to the University of Washington Arboretum, Seattle, by Mr K. Wada of Yokohama, Japan. A small tree with large, fragrant, white flowers, borne in abundance. Variously regarded as a hybrid between *M. kobus* and *M. salicifolia*, or a form of *M. salicifolia*. It has reached 9m tall and 6.5m across at the Sir Harold Hillier Gardens and Arboretum (1990). ♀ 2002. FCC 1986.

× *watsonii* See *M.* × *wieseneri*.

× *wieseneri* Carrière (*M.* × *watsonii* Hook. f.) (*M. obovata* × *M. sieboldii*) A splendid, rare shrub or small, bushy tree with leathery, obovate leaves. Flowers, 13cm wide, opening in June and July from rounded, white buds, are upward-facing, saucer-shaped, creamy-white with prominent, rosy-crimson anthers and pink sepals, and with an almost overpowering fragrance. Garden origin in Japan. C 1889. FCC 1975. AM 1917.

wilsonii Rehder (*M. nicholsoniana* Rehder & E.H. Wilson, *M.* × *highdownensis* Dandy) A large, widespreading shrub with elliptic-lanceolate leaves, pointed at the apex. In May and June bears pendent, saucer-shaped, white flowers with crimson stamens. A lovely species differing from *M. sinensis* in its narrower leaves and rather smaller flowers. Best in a partially shaded position. W China. I 1908 by Ernest Wilson. ♀ 2002. FCC 1971. AM 1932.

'Yellow Bird' See *M.* × *brooklynensis* 'Yellow Bird'.

zenii W.C. Cheng. A small tree of conical, upright habit with slender shoots and silky buds. Leaves obovate, dark green, to 10cm or more long. Flowers very fragrant, with 9 white tepals, streaked rose-purple towards the base, opening in early spring. E China. I to North America by Stephen Spongberg in 1980. It first flowered at the Arnold Arboretum in 1988.

× **MAHOBERBERIS** Schneid. (*Mahonia* × *Berberis*)—**Berberidaceae**—Hybrids of botanical interest and some of horticultural merit between 2 closely related genera. In each case the *Mahonia* is the mother parent. Any soil and any exposure.

aquicandidula Krüssm. (*M. aquifolium* × *B. candidula*) A dwarf, slow-growing, unhappy-looking shrublet of weak growth. The densely clustered leaves are ovate to ovate-elliptic, varying in size from 1–4cm long, lustrous, dark green above and at first pruinose beneath, entire or spine toothed; many are compound, with 2 small leaflets at their base. Flowers yellow. Garden origin in Sweden, 1943.

aquisargentii Krüssm. (*M. aquifolium* × *B. sargentiana*) A really splendid and remarkable, medium-sized shrub of dense, upright habit. Leaves vary in shape and are either slender-stalked, elliptic-lanceolate, up to 21cm long, and regularly spine-toothed, or short-stalked, ovate-lanceolate and margined with 2cm long, vicious spines. Some leaves are compound, with 2 leaflets at their base. All are shining dark green above, paler beneath. Soft yellow flowers in terminal clusters, followed by black berries. Garden origin in Sweden. × *M. miethkeana* Melander & Eade (*B. ? julianae* × *M. aquifolium*) is a similar hybrid raised in the State of Washington, USA, in 1940.

miethkeana See under × *M. aquisargentii*.

neubertii (Baumann) Schneid. (*M. aquifolium* × *B. vulgaris*) (*B. ilicifolia* hort.) A small, loose-habited shrub forming a rounded bush. Leaves both simple and compound, either obovate and finely toothed, as in the *Berberis* parent, or ovate, acute and coarsely toothed. The young foliage is an attractive sea-green, becoming bronze or purple-tinged. Originated in the nursery of Mons. Baumann, at Bolwiller in Alsace, France, in 1854.

× **MAHONIA** Nutt.—**Berberidaceae**—About 70 species of evergreen shrubs, natives of the Himalaya E and SE Asia and North and Central America. They are distinguished from the closely related *Berberis* by their pinnate leaves and spineless stems. Grown for their attractive, evergreen foliage and yellow flowers in winter or spring, followed by usually blue-black berries. They thrive in most types of well-drained soils including chalk soil.

acanthifolia See *M. napaulensis*.

'Aldenhamensis' See *M.* × *wagneri* 'Aldenhamensis'.

aquifolium (Pursh) Nutt. Oregon grape. A small shrub, valuable for underplanting or for game cover, in sun or shade. Leaves pinnate, polished green, sometimes turning red in winter. Flowers rich yellow, in dense racemes, borne in terminal clusters, opening in early spring; very decorative, blue-black berries. Parent of many hybrids and very variable. W North America. I 1893. **'Apollo'** A splendid form of vigorous habit making a dense, low-growing, spreading bush. Leaves deep green with reddish stalks. Flowers bright yellow in large, dense clusters. ♀ 2002. **'Atropurpurea'** A selected form with rich reddish-purple leaves during winter and early spring. C 1915. **'Green Ripple'** Wavy-edged, pale green leaves turn deep glossy green in summer. **'Heterophylla'** See *M.* 'Heterophylla'. **'Moseri'** A small shrub with attractive, bronze-red young leaves turning to apple-green and finally dark green. C 1895. **'Smaragd'** A small, upright shrub of compact habit with glossy dark green leaves, bronze when young, and large, dense clusters of bright yellow flowers, slightly earlier than 'Apollo'. C 1979.

bealei (Fortune) Carrière (*M. japonica* 'Bealei') A medium-sized to large, winter-flowering shrub related to *M. japonica* from which it differs mainly in its stiffer, shorter, erect racemes, and its broad-based, often overlapping leaflets. Now much rarer in cultivation than *M. japonica* with which it has been confused. China. I about 1849 by Robert Fortune. AM 1916. A form of this species introduced by Mikinori Ogisu from Sichuan in 1994 has leaves with chalk-white undersides.

confusa Sprague. A small, erect, usually unbranched shrub, related to *M. fortunei*. The leaves have about 20 narrow, sea-green, spine-toothed leaflets on a purplish rachis. Slender, spike-like, upright racemes of small, pale yellow flowers open in early autumn. Berries blue-black, bloomy, ripe by spring. A form with pale green foliage is also cultivated. China (Sichuan, Hubei, Guizhou). I 1980 by Roy Lancaster.

× *decumbens* Stace (*M. aquifolium* × *M. repens*) This hybrid occurs where the parents grow together in the wild. It makes a low-growing, stoloniferous shrub to about 50cm tall, the leaves with 5–7 matt green leaflets, and is naturalised in a few places in Britain.

eutriphylla See *M. trifolia*.

fascicularis See *M. pinnata*.

fortunei (Lindl.) Fedde. A slender, erect shrub, slowly attaining 1.8–2m, with distinctive, matt green, linear-lanceolate leaflets. Bright yellow flowers are borne in erect, narrow, terminal racemes from September to November. China. I 1846 by Robert Fortune.

fremontii (Torr.) Fedde. A very beautiful, blue-green, small to medium-sized shrub for a well-drained site in full sun. The pinnate leaves are composed of small, glaucous, crisped and spiny leaflets. Small clusters of flowers in

May and June are followed by inflated, dry, yellowish or red berries. SW USA.

gracilipes (Oliv.) Fedde. A small suckering shrub forming low colonies. Leaves with 5–9 rigid, spine-toothed leaflets, dark blue-green above, brilliant chalky-white beneath. Flowers small in slender-stalked, open, branched sprays in late summer and autumn, outer petals purple-red, inner petals creamy-white. Fruits rarely produced out of doors in this country. SW China. I 1980 by Roy Lancaster from Mt Omei, Sichuan, where it was growing in moist, shady places. Hybrids between this species and *M. confusa* occur in the wild and were first raised in cultivation at the Savill Gardens. They have upright, cylindrical racemes of yellow flowers, red in bud, appearing orange from a distance.

†*haematocarpa* (Wooton) Fedde. An attractive species related to *M. fremontii*, but with smaller, plum-coloured berries and longer, narrower, greener leaflets. Requires a sunny site. SW USA, N Mexico. I 1916.

'Heterophylla' (*M. aquifolium* var. *heterophylla* hort., *M. toluacensis* Bean not J.J.) A small shrub of loose, open habit with leaves composed of 5–9 long, narrow, glossy green, wavy-edged leaflets which often turn reddish-purple during winter. Flowers are in racemes, clustered at the tips of the shoots in spring. Origin uncertain, but most likely a seedling of the original *M. toluacensis* J.J.

japonica (Thunb.) DC. This beautiful species is deservedly one of the most popular and ornamental of all evergreen shrubs. Magnificent deep green, pinnate leaves and terminal clusters of long, pendent, or lax, racemes of fragrant, lemon-yellow flowers from late autumn to early spring. Origin uncertain, long cultivated in Japan. ♀ 2002. AM 1916. 'Bealei' See *M. bealei*. *trifurca* See under *M. japonica* × *napaulensis*.

japonica × *napaulensis* An attractive hybrid with good foliage and erect racemes of yellow flowers in late winter. A plant grown as *M. japonica trifurca* was considered to be *M. japonica* 'Bealei' × *M. napaulensis*. It made a distinct shrub of upright habit, bearing large ruffs of pinnate leaves and erect, clustered racemes of yellow flowers in late winter.

× *lindsayae* P.F. Yeo (*M. japonica* × *M. siamensis*) This hybrid was raised in 1959 at the University Botanic Garden, Cambridge, from seed of the tender *M. siamensis* Takeda collected at Serre de la Madone, Menton, France, the garden of the late Major Lawrence Johnston. It was named after Nancy Lindsay who inherited the Serre in 1958. 'Cantab' A medium-sized shrub of lax habit, broader than tall. Leaves rich green, long and drooping with up to 15 widely-spaced leaflets, each bearing up to 6 sharp spines on each side, often red-tinged in cold weather, on a reddish rachis. Flowers lemon-yellow in late autumn and winter in spreading or pendent racemes, relatively large and strongly fragrant. Proving hardy.

†*lomariifolia* Takeda. A very imposing species, but only sufficiently hardy for gardens in milder counties. A large shrub, branches erect, stout, closely beset with long leaves composed of 15–19 pairs of rigid, narrow leaflets. Deep yellow flowers are borne during winter in dense, terminal clusters of erect racemes, 15–25cm long, each carrying as many as 250 small flowers. W China, Burma. I 1931. ♀ 2002. FCC 1939. AM 1938.

× *media* C.D. Brickell (*M. japonica* × *M. lomariifolia*) A vigorous shrub of medium to large size with ruffs of handsome, pinnate leaves and terminal clusters of long, lax racemes in late autumn and early winter. This magnificent hybrid has been independently raised in several places and a number of clones have been named. The flowers are generally only slightly fragrant. 'Arthur Menzies' (*M. japonica* 'Bealei' × *M. lomariifolia*) A compact, medium-sized shrub of upright habit with glaucous-bloomed young shoots. Leaves are up to 45cm long with up to 19 deep blue-green leaflets, each with 3–4 spines on each side. Lemon-yellow flowers are borne in late autumn to early winter in upright, unbranched racemes, spreading as they open. Selected in 1964 at the University of Washington Arboretum, USA and named after the Supervisor of Plant Accessions at the Strybing Arboretum, San Francisco, in whose garden the cross occurred. 'Buckland' A handsome clone raised from a deliberate cross made by Mr Lionel Fortescue at The Garden House, Buckland Monachorum, Devon. In leaf it tends towards *M. japonica*; the racemes are long and spreading. ♀ 2002. AM 1992. 'Charity' A superb, medium-sized to large shrub of upright, stately habit. Leaves, 50–60cm long, bear 2-ranked long, spiny leaflets. The slightly fragrant, deep yellow flowers are borne in long spreading and ascending racemes, in large terminal clusters during autumn and early winter. Selected by Sir Eric Savill and Mr Hope Findlay at the Savill Garden, Windsor from seedlings raised by the Slieve Donard Nursery, N Ireland, in about 1950. FCC 1962. AM 1959. 'Lionel Fortescue' Flowers bright yellow in numerous, long, upright racemes. Originated in the same batch of seedlings as 'Buckland'. ♀ 2002. FCC 1992. AM and Cory Cup 1975. 'Underway' Relatively compact, the leaves with 17–21 leaflets. Flowers bright yellow in long, upright racemes. ♀ 2002. AM 1992. 'Winter Sun' A selected form raised by the Slieve Donard Nursery, N Ireland. A compact shrub, the racemes erect, densely packed with fragrant, yellow flowers. ♀ 2002.

'Moseri' See *M. aquifolium* 'Moseri'.

†*napaulensis* DC. (*M. acanthifolia* G. Don) A magnificent, erect, large shrub, or small tree in mild areas. The enormous, pinnate leaves are arranged in dense collars at the summit of each stem, ideal backing for the bunches of long, spreading racemes of mimosa-yellow, faintly scented flowers which appear in the autumn and continue into winter. Nepal, Sikkim, Assam. I 1858. FCC 1958. AM 1953 (as *M. acanthifolia*). 'Maharajah' Flowers deep yellow. The best form of the species.

nervosa (Pursh) Nutt. A dwarf, suckering species with lustrous leaves that often turn red in winter when grown in a sunny position. Racemes 15–20cm long in May and June; berries blackish-blue. Not the best of mahonias on chalk. W North America. I 1822.

†*nevinii* (A. Gray) Fedde. A small shrub with small, pinnate leaves. Leaflets 5, flattened, grey-green above and attractively veined, pruinose beneath. Flowers in small clusters followed by small red berries. S California. I 1928.

nitens C.K. Schneid. A small shrub with glossy green, pinnate leaves, coppery-red when young, and erect terminal racemes of yellow flowers in autumn. China. I by Jelena de Belder in the 1980s from Mt Omei and by Mikinori Ogisu in 1994. It hybridises with *M. confusa* in the wild.

pallida Fedde. A small to medium-sized shrub with short-stalked leaves usually with 11–15 leaflets edged with a few small teeth, blue-green, later glossy green. Open, slender-stalked panicles, to 25cm or more long, of small flowers, the outer petals pale greenish-white, the inner petals yellow, open from midsummer to early autumn. Fruits blue-black with a white bloom, 1cm across. Mexico. I 1987 by Nigel Taylor and Sabina Knees. AM 1994 (for fruit).

pinnata (Lag.) Fedde (*M. fascicularis* DC.) A strong-growing shrub of medium size. Leaves short-stalked; leaflets prickly and sea-green. The rich yellow racemes appear in clusters along the stems during late winter. California. AM 1948. The true plant is rare in cultivation; for the plant often grown under this name see *M.* × *wagneri* 'Pinnacle'. I before 1838.

pumila (Greene) Fedde. A rare, dwarf shrub of neat habit. Leaves with 5–7, flattened, spine-edged, sea-green, somewhat glaucous leaflets; flowers in spring; fruits bloomy-black in large clusters. SW Oregon and California.

repens (Lindl.) G. Don. A dwarf, suckering shrub, eventually making small colonies. Leaflets matt green; flowers in terminal clusters; bloomy, black berries. W North America. I 1822. **'Rotundifolia'** A small shrub of distinct appearance with ovate or rounded, sea-green, spineless leaves and large plumes of rich yellow flowers in May, followed by black, bloomy berries. Probably a hybrid between *M. aquifolium* and *M. repens*. C 1875. AM 1991.

†*russellii* N.P. Taylor. A small to medium-sized shrub with upright, pinkish-red shoots. Leaves, to 40cm long, with up to 13 spine-toothed leaflets green on both sides, pink when young. Flowers nodding, in slender-stalked, upright panicles, about 25cm long, bearing leafy bracts, outer perianth segments red and white, inner yellow, opening in summer followed by blue-black, bloomy fruits to 1cm long. Mexico (Veracruz). Discovered and introduced by Jim Russell in 1984.

†*swaseyi* (Buckland) Fedde. Medium-sized shrub related to *M. fremontii*, differing in its leaflets which are pruinose beneath and closely reticulate, also in its small leaf-like bracts. Berries yellowish-red. Hybrids between this species and *M. trifoliolata* occur where the species grow together in the wild in the Texas Hill country. Texas, USA.

toluacensis See *M.* 'Heterophylla'.

trifolia Cham. & Schltdl. (*M. schiedeana* Schltdl., *M. eutriphylla* hort. not Fedde) (E.K. Balls 4618) A rare, small to medium-sized, slow-growing shrub. Leaves small, with 3–5 thick, rigidly spiny, dark green leaflets, turning plum-purple in cold winters. Dense clusters of yellow flowers in spring are followed by bloomy, black berries. C Mexico. Collected by E.K. Balls to whom we are indebted for this plant. It has reached 3m at the Sir Harold Hillier Gardens and Arboretum.

trifoliolata (Moric.) Fedde. Mainly grown as the following variety, the typical form is a native of SE Texas and differs in its green leaflets. **var. *glauca*** I.M. Johnston. An attractive, medium-sized evergreen for a well-drained,

sunny position against a warm wall, where it will each to 4–5m. Leaves composed of 3 spiny, conspicuously veined, glaucous leaflets. Clusters of flowers in spring followed by redcurrant-like berries. W Texas to Arizona, N Mexico. I 1839.

'Undulata' See *M.* × *wagneri* 'Undulata'.

veitchiorum C.K. Schneid. A dwarf, suckering shrub, the pinnate leaves with glossy-green, spine-toothed leaflets. Flowers yellow, borne in erect terminal racemes in spring. China. I by Mikinori Ogisu.

× *wagneri* (Jouin) Rehder (*M. aquifolium* × *M. pinnata*) A variable, small shrub, resembling *M. aquifolium*, producing its racemes of flowers in spring. **'Aldenhamensis'** A splendid, strong-growing, medium-sized erect shrub, with distinctive, sea-green, pinnate leaves and fascicles of rich yellow flowers along the stems in late winter. **'Hastings' Elegant'** A small shrub of compact, upright habit with bright green leaves. Flowers bright yellow in dense clusters. **'Pinnacle'** A vigorous, upright form with bright green leaves, bronze when young, and showy clusters of bright yellow flowers. A selection from plants grown as *M. pinnata*. ♀ 2002. **'Undulata'** An ornamental medium-sized shrub, taller than *M. aquifolium*, with lustrous, dark green leaves, the leaflets with undulate margins. Flowers deep yellow in spring. C 1930. AM 1971.

Maidenhair tree See *Ginkgo biloba* under CONIFERS.
Male berry See *Lyonia ligustrina*.

†**MALLOTUS** Lour.—**Euphorbiaceae**—About 140 species of interesting shrubs or small trees, natives of warm areas of the Old World. The following is lime-tolerant, requiring full sun and a well-drained soil. Only suitable for mild areas of the British Isles.

japonicus (Thunb.) Muell.-Arg. A large shrub or small tree with large, handsome, roundish leaves. Flowers small, in large pyramidal panicles; male and female on different plants. Japan, Taiwan, China, Korea.

MALUS Mill.—**Rosaceae**—The flowering crabs comprise a genus of some 25 species of deciduous trees, found throughout N temperate regions. Along with the ornamental cherries (*Prunus*), their floral charm is unexcelled by any other trees. With few exceptions they are easily grown, small to medium-sized trees and their flowering season is April and May. The flowers have 5 styles; those of *Prunus* are solitary. Many bear very attractive fruits in autumn, in several sorts persisting late into winter. Unless otherwise stated, all those listed are small trees, thriving in all types of fertile soil. Straggly or untidy specimens may be hard-pruned immediately after flowering. E indicates crabs with edible fruits most suitable for using in preserves.

'Adirondack' ('Admiration') A charming, dwarf and disease-resistant tree of upright habit. Large, waxy white flowers open in dense clusters from deep carmine buds, followed by persistent, nearly spherical, red fruits. An open-pollinated seedling of *M. halliana*, raised by Donald Egolf at the US National Arboretum, Washington, DC in 1985.

'Admiration' See 'Adirondack'.

'Aldenhamensis' (Purpurea Group) A small tree or tall

shrub of loose growth. Leaves purplish becoming bronze-green in late summer. Flowers single or semi-double, deep vinous-red, followed by reddish-purple fruits. Resembles *M.* × *purpurea*, but flowering about a fortnight later. AM 1916.

'Almey' An early, free-flowering, small tree of broad, rounded habit. Young leaves reddish-bronze. Flowers large, soft red with white centres; fruits orange-red with a crimson flush, persisting into winter. A seedling from the hybrid *M. baccata* × *M. niedzwetzkyana*. C 1945.

'American Beauty' A vigorous tree with bronze-red, later bronze-green, leaves. Flowers double, deep red. Said to be scab resistant. C 1978.

angustifolia (Aiton) Michx. An uncommon tree, up to 10m, related to *M. coronaria*. The leaves on vigorous shoots are ovate and sharply lobed; on mature shoots they are narrow and toothed. Flowers salmon-pink, violet-scented; fruits yellowish-green. E USA. I 1750.

× *arnoldiana* Sarg. (*M. baccata* × *M. floribunda*) An extremely floriferous, small, round-headed tree or large shrub with somewhat drooping branches. Flowers large, fragrant, red in bud, opening pale pink inside, deep pink outside with a red calyx, in umbellate clusters; fruits yellow, with a reddish flush. Originated in the Arnold Arboretum, Boston, USA in 1883.

× *atrosanguinea* (Späth) C.K. Schneid. (*M. halliana* × *M. sieboldii*) A small, mushroom-shaped tree with glossy green leaves. Flowers crimson in bud, opening rose; fruits yellow with a red cheek. Similar to *M. floribunda* but with darker flowers. C 1898.

baccata (L.) Borkh. The true Siberian crab is a small to medium-sized tree of rounded habit. Flowers white, fragrant, followed by small, red or yellow, berry-like fruits. Widely distributed throughout Asia. I 1784. **var. mandshurica** (Maxim.) C.K. Schneid. An extremely hardy, round-headed tree up to 12m. Flowers early, during late April and May, white, fragrant; fruits slightly larger. NE Asia. I 1824. FCC 1969. AM 1962.

'Butterball' A small, spreading tree with slightly drooping branches. Flowers pink in bud, opening white, flushed with pink; fruits, 2–3cm across, yellow with an orange flush. A seedling of *M.* × *zumi* 'Calocarpa' raised in North America. C 1961.

'Cashmere' A beautiful, small, hybrid tree having pale pink flowers followed by yellow fruits in abundance.

'Chilko' A small tree of Canadian origin, a seedling of *M. niedzwetzkyana*, developing a spreading head with large, purplish-red flowers up to 4.5cm across; fruits ovoid, 4cm long, brilliant crimson with a shiny skin. C 1920. E. AM 1967.

coronaria (L.) Mill. A beautiful, strong-growing, American crab up to 10m. Large, fragrant flowers of a delightful shade of shell-pink are produced with the foliage towards the latter end of May. Fruits green. Leaves often richly tinted in autumn. E North America. I 1724. **'Charlottae'** ('Flore Pleno') A most excellent small tree with large, lobed leaves that colour richly in the autumn. Flowers large, semi-double, shell-pink and violet-scented during late May and early June. Can fruit profusely after a hot summer. Originated about 1902.

'Cowichan' A vigorous tree, up to 9m or more, with large, light red flowers. The large, reddish-purple fruits are accompanied by red-tinted foliage. A seedling of *M. niedzwetzkyana*. C 1920.

crataegifolia See *M. florentina*.

'Crittenden' An excellent small, compact tree with attractive, pale pink flowers. Particularly notable for its heavy crops of bright scarlet fruits which persist throughout autumn and winter. E. FCC 1971. AM 1961.

'Dartmouth' An attractive hybrid producing abundant, white flowers and equally plentiful, reddish-purple, bloomy fruits. Raised before 1883. E.

diversifolia See *M. fusca*.

domestica Borkh. Orchard apple. A familiar tree of hybrid origin probably derived from *M. dasycarpa*, *M. praecox* and *M. sylvestris*, as well as several Asiatic species. It is cultivated for its fruit throughout the temperate regions of the world. Forms are often found naturalised or as garden escapees in wild situations, but they may always be distinguished from our native wild crab (*M. sylvestris*) by their larger, often sweet fruits. There are said to be over a thousand cultivars. E.

'Dorothea' A small tree, raised at the Arnold Arboretum, Boston, USA, and possibly a hybrid between *M.* × *arnoldiana* and *M. halliana* 'Parkmanii'. Flowers semi-double, 4–5cm across, pale crimson, darker in bud; fruits golden-yellow. C 1943.

'Echtermeyer' (*M.* 'Exzellenz Thiel' × *M. niedzwetzkyana*) (*M.* 'Oekonomierat Echtermeyer', *M.* × *purpurea* 'Pendula') A graceful, low, widespreading tree with weeping branches and purplish or bronze-green leaves. Flowers rose-crimson, deeper in bud, followed by reddish-purple fruits. Prone to mildew. C 1914.

'Eleyi' Resembles *M.* × *purpurea* in leaf and flower, but slightly darker in both, the flowers opening slightly later. Carries very decorative purplish-red fruits in autumn. Garden origin before 1920. FCC 1922 (for fruit). AM 1922 (for flower). See also *M.* 'Profusion', a more recent cultivar.

'Elise Rathke' (*M. pumila* 'Pendula') A small tree with stiffly pendent branches. Flowers large, pink in bud, opening white, followed by large, sweet, yellow fruits. C 1885. E.

'Evereste' A conical tree with dark green, often somewhat lobed leaves. Flowers freely borne, 5cm across, red in bud, later white. Fruits to 2.5cm across, orange to orange-yellow. C 1980. ♛ 2002.

'Exzellenz Thiel' A small, weeping tree or shrub raised by Späth about 1909. Flowers semi-double, pink in bud, opening white. Possibly *M. floribunda* × *M. prunifolia* 'Pendula'. C 1909.

florentina (Zuccagni) C.K. Schneid. (*M. crataegifolia* Koehne, × *Malosorbus florentina* (Zuccagni) Browicz) A small, round-headed tree with hawthorn-like foliage, white tomentose beneath, which turns orange and scarlet in autumn. Flowers white; fruits small, red. It has been suggested that this tree is a hybrid between *Malus sylvestris* and the Wild service tree, *Sorbus torminalis*. Italy, S former Yugoslavia, N Greece, N Turkey. C 1877. AM 1956.

floribunda Siebold ex Van Houtte. Japanese crab. A most popular, flowering, small tree or large shrub with long, arching branches. Remarkably beautiful when in flower, the crimson buds opening to white or pale blush. Fruits small, red and yellow. One of the earliest crabs to flower. I from Japan in 1862. ♀ 2002.

fusca (Raf.) C.K. Schneid. (*M. diversifolia* Roem.) (*M. rivularis* (Hook.) Roem.) Oregon crab. A small tree or large shrub of dense, vigorous growth. Leaves serrate, often 3-lobed; flowers like apple blossom; fruits red or yellow. W North America. I 1836.

'Gibbs' Golden Gage' A small tree of unusual charm when carrying masses of medium-sized, waxy, almost translucent yellow fruits. C before 1923.

glaucescens Rehder. A distinct small, round-headed tree with sometimes spiny branches. Lobed leaves are glaucous beneath, turning yellow and purple in autumn. Flowers pink; fruits waxy, green to yellow. North America. C 1902.

'Golden Hornet' A small tree producing white flowers followed by large crops of bright yellow fruits which are retained until late in the year. One of the best fruiting crabs for general planting. Probably a seedling of *M. × zumi* 'Calocarpa'. C before 1949. ♀ 2002. FCC 1961. AM 1949.

'Gorgeous' (*M. halliana × M. sieboldiana*) A small tree of dense, rounded habit with pink buds opening to single, white flowers, 3cm across. Long persistent, glossy crimson to orange-red, ovoid fruits ripen in autumn. C 1925.

halliana Koehne. A small tree up to 5m. Leaves narrow, dark, glossy green; flowers carmine in bud, opening shell-pink; small, purple fruits. Originated in China where it is known only in cultivation. I via Japan in 1863. AM 1935. **'Parkmanii'** A lovely form with pendent clusters of partly semi-double flowers, rose-red in bud, opening shell-pink, borne on deep crimson pedicels. I 1861.

× hartwigii Koehne (*M. baccata × M. halliana*) A delightful small tree, intermediate between the parents. Flowers almost semi-double, up to 5cm across, pink in bud, opening white.

'Hillieri' (Scheideckeri Group) A very attractive, late-flowering tree, like *M. × scheideckeri* but with a better constitution. Flowers, semi-double, crimson in bud, opening bright pink, wreath the arching stems in clusters of 5 to 8. C before 1928.

'Hopa' A hybrid between *M. baccata* and *M. niedzwetzkyana*, up to 10m, with large, purple-red flowers, followed by orange and red fruits. C 1920. E.

hupehensis (Pamp.) Rehder (*M. theifera* Rehder) A freegrowing, small tree with stiff, ascending branches. Flowers fragrant, soft pink in bud, opening white, produced in great abundance during May and June. Fruits small, usually deep red on cultivated plants. China, Japan. I 1900 by Ernest Wilson. ♀ 2002. AM 1928. **'Rosea'** Differs in its pale pink flowers and rather spreading branches. A lovely tree in full bloom. AM 1938.

'Hyslop' An openly branched, small tree with white flowers, 1–4cm across, followed by relatively large, red-cheeked fruits, 5–8cm across. C 1869. E.

‡*ioensis* Britton. The Prairie crab is a very attractive, North American species, closely allied to *M. coronaria*, developing ornamental peeling bark with age. Branches downy, and leaves persistently woolly beneath, turning orange-red in autumn; flowers fragrant, 4–5cm across,

white usually flushed pink, in corymbs of 4 to 6. Fruits green. C USA. **'Plena'** Bechtel's crab. Large, semi-double, soft pink, fragrant flowers. At its best perhaps the most beautiful flowering crab apple, but a tree of weak constitution and unsuitable for chalk soils. C 1888. FCC 1950. AM 1940.

'Jay Darling' (*M. baccata × M. niedzwetzkyana*) A most ornamental tree. Large, wine-red flowers produced before or with the crimson-tinted foliage; fruits purplish-red. C 1904.

'John Downie' Perhaps the best fruiting crab. Flowers white; fruit comparatively large, conical, bright orange and red, refreshing flavour. Raised in 1875. E. ♀ 2002. AM 1895.

'Kaido' See *M. × micromalus*.

kansuensis (Batal.) C.K. Schneid. A large shrub or small tree with ovate, usually 3-lobed leaves. Flowers small, creamy-white; fruits elongated, red and yellow. Good autumn colour. W China. I 1904. AM 1933.

'Katherine' (Hartwigii Group) A small tree with a regular, densely-branched, globular head. Deep pink buds open to semi-double, pink flowers, over 5cm in diameter, which gradually fade white. These many petalled flowers are followed by bright red fruits, flushed yellow. C about 1928. AM 1967.

'Lady Northcliffe' An attractive, small, densely-branched, broad-headed tree with flowers carmine-red in bud, opening blush then white. Very free-flowering. Fruits small and round, yellow. A most ornamental tree for a small garden. C before 1929.

lancifolia Rehder. A small tree with variously shaped leaves, those of the flowering shoots lanceolate. Flowers shell-pink followed by round, green fruits, 2.5cm across. USA. I 1912.

'Lemoinei' (Purpurea Group) This fine hybrid is more erect in growth than typical *M. × purpurea*, and has larger, but fewer, deep wine-red flowers. Garden origin 1922. AM 1928.

'Liset' (*M. 'Lemoinei' × M. sieboldii*) A small tree of dense, rounded habit with purplish young foliage. Flowers rose-red, opening from deep crimson buds, followed by glossy, crimson fruits. Raised in Holland before 1935.

'Magdeburgensis' A small, broad-headed tree like the domestic apple, with somewhat spreading branches and beautiful, large, semi-double flowers, deep red in bud, opening to purplish-pink-clouded white. Fruits light green to yellow. AM 1933.

× micromalus Makino (*M. baccata × M. spectabilis*) (*M. 'Kaido'*) A small, erect-branched tree with clear, deep pink flowers, very showy in the mass. Fruits small, red or yellow. I from Japan before 1856.

'Montreal Beauty' A small, tree of erect, open habit. Flowers white, slightly fragrant, freely borne along the branches and followed by comparatively large, conical, yellow to orange, scarlet-flushed fruits. E.

'Neville Copeman' (Purpurea Group) A seedling from *M. 'Eleyi'*, developing into a small tree with purple shaded, green leaves throughout summer. Flowers light purple, followed by conical orange-red fruits. AM 1953.

niedzwetzkyana Dieck (*M. pumila* var. *niedzwetzkyana* (Dieck) C.K. Schneid.) A small, tree with red young growths. Purple-red flowers in clusters are followed by large, conical, dark red fruits covered with a plum-purple bloom. Parent of many notable hybrids. SW Siberia, Turkestan. I about 1891.

orthocarpa Lavallée. A large shrub or small tree with pale pink flowers followed by orange and scarlet fruits. China.

'Pink Perfection' A small, free-flowering, densely branched tree. The flowers, red in bud, open clear pink, double, and fragrant.

× *platycarpa* Rehder (*M. coronaria* × *M. domestica*) A low-spreading tree. Flowers large, soft pink followed by large, fragrant, flattened, pale yellow fruits. North America. I 1912.

prattii (Hemsl.) C.K. Schneid. A distinct Chinese tree, up to 10m, with very pleasing large, red-veined leaves, which give good autumn colour. Flowers white, followed by red or yellow fruits. China. I 1904 by Ernest Wilson.

'Prince George's' Originating in the Arnold Arboretum, Boston, USA, this slow-growing tree is probably a hybrid between *M. angustifolia* and *M. ioensis* 'Plena'. The scented, late flowers are fully double, 5cm in diameter, and light pink. C 1919.

'Professor Sprenger' (Zumi Group) A small, dense-headed tree flowering in great profusion. Flowers pink in bud, opening white, followed by large quantities of shining, amber-yellow fruits which usually remain until late December. I 1950 by Mr Doorenbos of The Hague, Holland.

'Profusion' (*M.* 'Lemoinei' × *M. sieboldii*) A first-class hybrid flowering a little later than *M.* 'Lemoinei'. Flowers in great profusion, wine-red, slightly fragrant, about 4cm across, borne in clusters of 6 or 7. Fruits small, ox-blood-red. Young leaves coppery-crimson. Probably the best of all the crabs with wine-red flowers and red young growths, however suffers from apple canker and mildew, as do the others. C 1938.

prunifolia (Willd.) Borkh. A small tree with oval, unequally toothed leaves. Flowers, rose-crimson in bud, opening white, flushed pink, are produced in April and followed by red, conical fruits, which retain their calyces. NE Asia. C 1758. **'Fastigiata'** Branches ascending, forming a columnar head, becoming spreading with age. Fruits yellow and red. C 1906. **'Pendula'** A form with pendent branches. **var. *rinki*** (Koidz.) Rehder (*M. ringo* Siebold) A variety with almond-pink flowers and bright yellow fruits. W China. I 1850. AM 1984.

pumila Mill. This name, which correctly belongs to the Paradise apple of gardens, has long been used to cover several apples including *M. dasyphylla*, *M. domestica* and *M. sylvestris*. The latter is the wild crab of the British Isles while *M. domestica* is the orchard apple. **var. *niedzwetzkyana*** See *M. niedzwetzkyana*. **'Pendula'** See *M.* 'Elise Rathke'.

× *purpurea* (Barbier) Rehder (*M.* × *atrosanguinea* × *M. niedzwetzkyana*) A beautiful hybrid producing a wealth of rosy-crimson flowers and dark purplish-green shoots and leaves. Fruits light crimson-purple. Many clones have been named. Garden origin before 1900. We regard *M.* 'Profusion' as a tree of better constitution. AM 1914. **'Pendula'** See *M.* 'Echtermeyer'.

'Red Glow' A small tree with young foliage tinged purple.

Large, pink flowers are followed by large, red-purple fruits.

'Red Jade' A lovely, small tree or shrub with weeping branches. Young leaves bright green; flowers white and pink; fruits red, the size of cherries, long persistent. A seedling of 'Exzellenz Thiel' raised in 1935.

'Red Profusion' A vigorous, small tree with glossy dark green, occasionally 3-lobed leaves, deep red-purple when young. Flowers semi-double, red, 3.5cm across.

'Red Sentinel' An excellent fruiting tree with white flowers and large clusters of deep red fruits that remain on the branches throughout winter. ♀ 2002. AM 1959.

'Red Silver' A small tree with silvery-grey-hairy young leaves becoming purplish-red then dark green. Dark red-purple flowers are followed by small, purplish fruits. Raised in 1928.

'Red Tip' (*M. coronaria* 'Elk River' × *M. niedzwetzkyana*) An exciting hybrid, worthy of inclusion in every representative group of crabs. Flowers red-purple, leaves broad, slightly lobed, young foliage bright red, fruits red-flushed. C 1919.

ringo See *M. prunifolia* var. *rinki*.

× *robusta* (Carrière) Rehder (*M. baccata* × *M. prunifolia*) Popularly, though incorrectly, known as Siberian crab, the forms of this variable hybrid have white or pinkish flowers and more or less globular, cherry-like, red or yellow fruits, without calyces. C about 1815. AM 1957. **'Red Siberian'** Fruits red. **'Yellow Siberian'** Fruits yellow.

'Royal Beauty' A small, weeping tree with slender, hanging, reddish-purple stems; leaves reddish-purple when young, becoming dark green, purplish beneath. Deep red-purple flowers are followed by small, dark red fruits. C 1980. ♀ 2002.

'Royalty' A small tree of rather upright habit with attractive, taper-pointed, glossy, dark purple leaves, turning red in autumn. Large, purplish-crimson flowers, rather hidden in the foliage, are followed by dark red fruits. Raised in Canada in 1953.

'Rudolph' A small tree of upright habit, with glossy bronze-red, later dark bronze-green, leaves on red young shoots. Flowers rose-red, deeper in bud, 4.5cm across, followed by long-persistent, orange-yellow, oblong fruits to 18mm long. Raised in Canada in 1954.

sargentii Rehder. A delightful shrubby species, up to 2.8m high, with leaves often 3-lobed. In spring it is smothered with golden-anthered, pure white flowers, and in autumn with small, bright red, cherry-like fruits. Closely related to *M. sieboldii*; some authorities regard it as a form. Japan. I 1892. AM 1915. **'Rosea'** Flowers blush, rose in bud; slightly more vigorous. C 1921.

× *scheideckeri* Zabel (*M. floribunda* × *M. prunifolia*) A very free-flowering, slow-growing shrub or miniature tree with masses of slightly fragrant, semi-double, pink and white blossoms. Not suitable for shallow chalky soils. C 1888. AM 1896.

sieboldii (Regel) Rehder (*M. toringo* Siebold ex Miq.) A small, picturesque semi-weeping, Japanese crab, rarely more than 3m high. Leaves simple or variously lobed. Flowers pink in bud, fading to white, smaller than those of *M. floribunda*; fruits small, red or yellowish. Japan. I 1856.

sikkimensis (Wenzig) C.K. Schneid. A distinct, small, erect-branched tree from the Himalaya. Flowers white, followed by somewhat pear-shaped, dark red fruits. Easily recognised by the excessive development of stout, branching spurs on the trunk around the base of the branches. I 1849 by Sir Joseph Hooker.

'Simcoe' (*M. baccata × M. niedzwetzkyana*) A small but strong-growing tree of Canadian origin. Young growths copper-tinted. Flowers comparatively large, light purplish-pink, produced in large quantities, followed by purplish-red fruits. Best in a continental climate. C 1920. AM 1945 (for fruit). AM 1940 (for flower).

'Snowcloud' (*M.* 'Almey' × *M.* 'Katherine') A small tree of upright habit, the young leaves bronze-green, becoming dark green. Flowers pale pink in bud opening white, semi-double to double, 4cm across, long-lasting. Fruits yellow, sparse. Raised in the USA before 1978.

× *soulardii* (L.H. Bailey) Britton (*M. domestica × M. ioensis*) A very beautiful hybrid with large, clear, almond-pink flowers and yellow, red-flushed fruits. C 1868.

spectabilis (Aiton) Borkh. A small tree with upright branches. The flowers are deep rose-red in bud, opening to blush, 5cm wide. One of the loveliest flowering crabs, at its best during late April and early May. China, but not known in the wild. C 1780. **'Albiplena'** Large, semi-double, white, delicately violet-scented flowers. Probably of hybrid origin, although some authorities regard it as a form of *M. sylvestris*. **'Riversii'** ('Rosea Plena') A tree with upright branches. The semi-double flowers are deep rose-red in bud, opening rosy-pink. Raised by the English nurseryman, Thomas Rivers, before 1864.

× *sublobata* Rehder (*M. prunifolia × M. sieboldii*) A small, pyramidal tree. Leaves narrow-elliptic with an occasional lobe. Flowers pale pink; fruits yellow. Raised in the Arnold Arboretum, Boston, USA, from Japanese seed collected by Sargent in about 1892.

'Sun Rival' A small, umbrella-shaped, weeping tree with arching branches. Pink buds open to white flowers followed by large, red fruits. An improvement on 'Red Jade'.

sylvestris (L.) Mill. (*M. pumila* hort. in part, *M. acerba* Mérat) Common crab apple. A small tree or a large shrub, often with spurs. Leaves ovate to broad elliptic, shallowly toothed, glabrous at maturity. Flowers white or suffused pink followed by yellowish-green or red-flushed fruits, crowned by the persistent calyx and measuring 2–4cm across. A parent of the orchard apple (*M. domestica*), also of several ornamental crabs. Sometimes wrongly referred to in cultivation as *M. pumila*, which name rightly belongs to the Paradise apple of gardens. Europe. The true species is wild in most parts of the British Isles, but is less frequent than the forms of *M. domestica*, which are commonly planted and naturalised.

theifera See *M. hupehensis*.

toringo See *M. sieboldii*.

toringoides (Rehder) Hughes. A very beautiful, small, shrubby tree with graceful, slender, widespreading branches and deeply lobed leaves. Flowers creamy-white, slightly fragrant, in May, followed by rounded or pear-shaped, red and yellow fruits, which are particularly conspicuous. Attractive autumn tints. W China. I 1904 by Ernest Wilson. AM 1919.

transitoria (Batal.) C.K. Schneid. A slender, small tree resembling *M. toringoides* but more elegant, differing in its leaves being usually smaller, more narrowly lobed and more pubescent. Fruits smaller, rounded, yellow. Very beautiful autumn colour. NW China. I 1911 by William Purdom. ♀ 2002.

trilobata (Labill.) C.K. Schneid. A comparatively rare, erect-branched tree, to about 13m, so distinct that it is sometimes listed in a separate genus (*Eriolobus*). Leaves maple-like, deeply 3-lobed, the lobes themselves often sharply lobed and toothed, attractively tinted red in autumn. Flowers large, white; fruits green, sometimes with a red flush, most frequent after hot summers. This little-known tree is worthy of more extensive public planting, particularly where space is confined. E Mediterranean region, NE Greece. C 1877.

tschonoskii (Maxim.) C.K. Schneid. An attractive, strong-growing tree, up to 12m, of erect, conical habit. Ovate, irregularly incised leaves and white flowers, tinged pink followed by globose, yellowish-green fruits, tinged reddish-purple. One of the best trees for autumn colour, with its bold yellow, orange, purple and scarlet foliage. A splendid tree for public planting in confined spaces. Japan. I 1897 by Sargent. ♀ 2002. FCC 1983. AM 1962. (FCC and AM both for autumn colour)

'Van Eseltine' (*M. × arnoldiana × M. spectabilis*) A small tree of distinctive columnar habit, the branches stiffly erect. The semi-double flowers, 3.5–5cm across, are rose-scarlet in bud, opening shell-pink, clouded white on the inner petals; fruits yellow. An excellent crab for a small garden. C 1930.

'Veitch's Scarlet' (*M.* 'Red Pippins' × *M. × robusta* 'Red Siberian') An outstanding crab with white flowers followed by conspicuous, large, bright red fruits. E. AM 1955. AM 1904.

'White Star' A vigorous and disease-resistant, small tree bearing profuse, white, star-shaped flowers followed by large, golden crab apples that persist until December.

'Winter Gold' A shapely, small, round-headed tree with pink-budded, white flowers and an abundance of clear yellow fruits, which are carried well into winter. A hybrid of *M. sieboldii*. C 1946.

'Wisley' A vigorous seedling of *M. niedzwetzkyana*. Leaves bronzy-red; flowers large, vinous-red, slightly scented, followed by large, purple-red fruits. AM 1924.

yunnanensis (Franch.) C.K. Schneid. A notable small to medium-sized tree with ovate, occasionally lobed leaves, turning crimson and orange in autumn. Flowers white; fruits deep red. W China. I 1900 by Ernest Wilson. **var. veitchii** Rehder. A comparatively tall, erect-branched variety, distinguished by its cordate, lobulate leaves and more brightly coloured fruits. C China. I 1901 by Ernest Wilson. AM 1912.

× *zumi* (Matsum.) Rehder (*M. baccata* var. *mandshurica × M. sieboldii*) A small, pyramidal tree, resembling, and often included as a variety of, *M. sieboldii*, but differing in its rarely lobed leaves, and larger flowers and fruits. Flowers pink in bud, opening white, fragrant; fruits bright red. Japan. I 1892 by Charles Sargent. AM 1933. **'Calocarpa'** A spreading form with smaller leaves and flowers. Bright red fruits persist throughout winter. Japan. I 1890.

‡†***MANGLIETIA** Blume—**Magnoliaceae**—A small genus of about 25 species of evergreen trees, very closely related to *Magnolia* and natives of the Himalaya and SE Asia. They require a moist, lime-free soil and are only suitable for the mildest localities.

fordiana Oliv. An evergreen tree with glossy dark green, narrow, elliptic, leathery leaves, to 20cm long. Bud scales 3, glaucous green, flushed with purple when exposed to sun, persistent and tepal-like in flower. Flowers parchment-white, with 6 very thick tepals and a centre of short crimson stamens, not fragrant. This unusual tree has grown at the Sir Harold Hillier Gardens and Arboretum for nearly 20 years and first flowered in July 2000. S China, Vietnam.

insignis (Wall.) Blume. A small tree with stout twigs and leathery, oblanceolate to narrowly oval leaves, to 10–20cm long, dark glossy green above, pale green or slightly glaucous beneath. Erect, solitary, creamy-white, tinged pink or deep rose, magnolia-like flowers, 7.5cm across, are borne during May. Himalaya. Burma, W China. I about 1919.

Manuka See *Leptospermum scoparium*.
Manzanita See *Arctostaphylos*.
Maple See *Acer*.

***MARGYRICARPUS** Ruiz & Pav.—**Rosaceae**—A monotypic genus related to *Acaena* and *Alchemilla*. Any well-drained soil.

pinnatus (Lam.) Kuntze (*M. setosus* Ruiz & Pav.) Pearl berry. A charming, prostrate or slightly erect, white-berrying shrub from the Chilean Andes. Leaves deep green and finely cut. Suitable for a rock garden. I 1829.

setosus See *M. pinnatus*.

Marsdenia erecta See *Cionura erecta*.
May See *Crataegus monogyna*.
May flower See *Epigaea repens*.

***MAYTENUS** Molina—**Celastraceae**—A large genus of more than 200 species of evergreen trees and shrubs, native to the Americas, from the S USA to S South America, and tropical Africa. Few species are hardy in most parts of the British Isles. Any well-drained soil, acid or alkaline. Apart from the following we have also grown the South American *M. ilicifolia* Reiisseck ex Mart. which has not proven hardy here.

boaria Molina (*M. chilensis* DC.) A large shrub or small tree, recalling *Phillyrea latifolia* but more graceful, with slender branches and narrow elliptic, finely toothed leaves. Myriad tiny green flowers are borne in spring. An unusual species, with pleasant, shining green foliage, which is proving perfectly hardy. Variable in habit from columnar, with upright branches, to weeping. Chile. I 1829. **'Worplesdon Narrow'** A female form of narrow habit with upright branches. Male plants similar in habit have grown for many years at the Sir Harold Hillier Gardens and Arboretum.

magellanica (Lam.) Hook. f. This species is proving hardy but slow-growing, eventually making a large shrub or small tree. It has leathery, elliptic, toothed leaves and small, crimson flowers, scented strongly of orange peel,

which are produced in clusters in the leaf axils in winter or early spring. S Chile. I 1938 by Capt. Collingwood Ingram.

Mazzard See *Prunus avium*.
Meadow sweet See *Spiraea alba*.

MEDICAGO L.—**Leguminosae**—Medick. A genus of more than 50 species of mainly annual and perennial, clover-like herbs with trifoliolate leaves. Natives of Europe, W Asia and Africa. Any well-drained soil; full sun. The cultivated alfalfa or lucerne is *M. sativa*.

†*arborea L. Moon trefoil, Tree medick. A small, semi-evergreen shrub with clusters of yellow pea-flowers produced continuously, though often sparsely, from May to September; seed pods resemble snail shells. Excellent for maritime exposure; elsewhere it requires the shelter of a warm wall. Mediterranean region. I 1596.

Medlar See *Mespilus germanica*.

†***MELALEUCA** L.—**Myrtaceae**—About 150 or more species related to and resembling *Callistemon* but with the numerous stamens borne in 5 bundles. Natives of Australia to SE Asia. They make elegant shrubs when cultivated in the British Isles but some attain tree size in their native haunts. Even given protection, they are only suitable for the mildest localities, and need full sun but are wind resistant. Not tolerant of chalk soils.

alternifolia Maiden & Betche ex Cheel. A large shrub, often tree-like, of bushy habit, with slender leaves to 2.5cm long. Flowers white, in bottlebrush-like clusters during summer. Tea-tree oil is made from this species. E Australia (New South Wales, Queensland).

decussata R.Br. A large, rounded shrub of dense habit with arching branches bearing slender, grey-green, opposite leaves in 2 rows on the shoots. Flowers pink to mauve, fading to white, in bottlebrush-like clusters in summer. SE Australia (South Australia, Victoria).

gibbosa Labill. A small to medium-sized, wiry shrub, with small, crowded, opposite leaves. Flowers light purple in short dense terminal bottlebrushes during summer. Tasmania, S and SE Australia.

hypericifolia Sm. Large shrub of graceful habit. Leaves small, aptly described by the specific epithet. Flowers bright red in summer. SE Australia. I 1792.

squamea Labill. Small to medium-sized, erect shrub with narrow, alternate leaves, crowded along the branches. Flowers variable in colour, usually purplish, in dense terminal heads in late spring. Tasmania, S and SE Australia. I 1805.

squarrosa Sm. An erect, rigid shrub. Leaves ovate-lanceolate to ovate, sharply pointed; flowers pale yellow in crowded, oblong spikes during summer. Tasmania, S and SE Australia. I 1794.

wilsonii F. Muell. An elegant shrub, up to 2m, with linear-lanceolate leaves and conspicuous, red or pink flowers in clusters along the shoots during late spring or summer. W Australia. I 1861.

†**MELIA** L.—**Meliaceae**—A small genus of 5 species of sun-loving, small trees or large shrubs, natives of Asia and

Australia of which the following species is the only one that sometimes succeeds in the mildest parts of the British Isles. Its bead-like seeds are used in necklaces, etc.

azedarach L. Bead tree. A small tree or large shrub, best grown against a warm, sheltered wall or in a conservatory. Large, elegant, doubly pinnate leaves and small, fragrant, lilac flowers in loose panicles during summer. In warm countries clusters of rounded, yellow, bead-like fruits are produced in autumn. These remain long after the leaves have fallen. Commonly planted as a street tree in warmer countries, particularly in the Mediterranean region. It requires hot sun to ripen growth. Asia to Australia. C in England since the 16th century.

†*MELIANTHUS** L.—**Melianthaceae**—A small genus of about 6 species of sun-loving, evergreen subshrubs, natives of South Africa, with attractive foliage and unusual flowers. Only suitable for the mildest parts of the British Isles, they can be herbaceous in colder areas.

major L. A handsome subshrub with spreading, hollow stems. Its glaucous, deeply toothed, pinnate leaves, 30–45cm long, give a striking subtropical effect. Tubular, tawny-crimson flowers are borne in dense, erect terminal racemes, up to 15cm long, in summer. Hardy in Cornwall and S Ireland and similar favoured areas, where it will attain 2m or more. Occasionally used in subtropical bedding. South Africa. I 1688. ♚ 2002. FCC 1975.

†**MELICOPE** J.R. Forst. & G. Forst.—**Rutaceae**—A genus of about 20 species of small trees and shrubs native of Australasia, the Pacific isles and tropical Asia. One species is occasionally grown in the mildest parts of the British Isles.

ternata J.R. Forst. & G. Forst. A large, semi-evergreen shrub for the mildest localities. Leaves trifoliolate. Flowers greenish-white, in cymose inflorescences in autumn. New Zealand. I 1822.

MELICYTUS J.R. Forst. & G. Forst. (*Hymenanthera* R. Br.)—**Violaceae**—A small genus of about 20 species of dioecious trees and shrubs, natives of SE Australia, Tasmania, New Zealand and the South Pacific Islands, bearing small, clustered flowers.

angustifolius (DC.) Garn.-Jones (*Hymenanthera angustifolia* DC., *H. dentata* var. *angustifolia* (R. Br.) Benth.) A small, erect shrub with smooth, oblanceolate leaves. Small, yellow, often unisexual flowers are followed by white berries with purple markings. Tasmania, SE Australia, New Zealand. I 1820.

crassifolius (Hook. f.) Garn.-Jones (*Hymenanthera crassifolia* Hook. f.) A semi-evergreen shrub of spreading habit, usually less than 1.5m high. Leaves obovate. Insignificant flowers are followed by quantities of white berries on the underside of the branches. New Zealand C about 1875. FCC 1892.

obovatus (Kirk) Garn.-Jones (*Hymenanthera obovata* Kirk) An erect, medium-sized species, with obovate, occasionally toothed, leathery leaves up to 5cm long; berries purplish. New Zealand.

†*ramiflorus* J.R. Forst. & G. Forst. Whiteywood. As seen in the British Isles, a large shrub with lanceolate-oblong or narrow elliptic, coarsely toothed leaves. The clusters of tiny, greenish-yellow flowers are followed by violet or dark blue berries. New Zealand, Tonga, Fiji. AM 1925.

MELIOSMA Blume—**Meliosmaceae**—A genus of 20 to 25 species of evergreen and deciduous trees and shrubs, natives of SE Asia and C and S America. The following are handsome in leaf, which may be simple or compound, and produce spiraea-like, paniculate inflorescences, crowded with small, white flowers in summer, Although lime-tolerant, they succeed best in deep neutral soil.

cuneifolia See *M. dilleniifolia* subsp. *cuneifolia*.

dilleniifolia (Wall. ex Wight & Arn.) Walp. A large shrub or small tree with stout, rusty-hairy shoots. The large, prominently veined, obovate leaves, up to 20cm long and 12cm wide, are rusty-hairy on the midrib above, grey-hairy beneath. Flowers in large, upright panicles in summer, followed by small glossy black fruits. Himalaya, N Burma. **subsp. cuneifolia** (Franch.) Beusekom (*M. cuneifolia* Franch.) A large shrub with simple, obovate, bristle-toothed leaves, 8–18cm long, bearing spiraea-like plumes of creamy-white flowers, with hawthorn-like fragrance, in July. Fruit globose, about the size of a peppercorn, black. W China. I 1901 by Ernest Wilson. **subsp. flexuosa** (Pamp.) Beusekom (*M. pendens* Rehder & E.H. Wilson) A large shrub with simple, obovate, bristle-toothed leaves, up to 15cm long. Flowers fragrant, white, in pendent, terminal panicles in July. East C China. I 1907 by Ernest Wilson. **subsp. tenuis** (Maxim.) Beusekom (*M. tenuis* Maxim.) A large shrub with slender, dark brown stems and coarsely toothed, obovate leaves to 15cm long. The tiny, creamy-yellow flowers are carried in pyramidal, nodding panicles in May and June. Japan. I 1915.

meliantha See under *M. myriantha*.

myriantha Siebold & Zucc. In its typical state, this is a native of Japan. E China and South Korea, and differs from the form described below in the fewer veins of the leaf. I 1879 by Charles Maries. **subsp. pilosa** (Lecomte) Beusekom. The plants grown under this name were raised from seed received from China. A spreading shrub 1.5–2m high and more across, with downy young shoots and narrow elliptic leaves, sharply toothed in the upper half to 16cm long. Wide panicles of creamy-white flowers are borne at the tips of short, lateral branches in July. Our plants belong to var. *stewardii* (Merr.) Beusekom (*M. stewardii* Merr.) and were originally listed as *M. meliantha*. E and C China.

oldhamii See *M. pinnata* var. *oldhamii*.

parviflora Lecomte. Medium-sized shrub of semi-erect habit with small, obovate, glossy green, denticulate leaves. So far proving hardy in our nurseries. China. I 1936.

pendens See *M. dilleniifolia* subsp. *flexuosa*.

pinnata (Roxb.) Walp. A variable species, covering a wide area from the Himalaya to E and SE Asia and New Guinea. Cultivated in the following form. **var. oldhamii** (Maxim.) Beusekom (*M. oldhamii* Maxim.) A rare, small tree with handsome, pinnate, ash-like leaves, up to 50cm long. Flowers white in large, erect terminal panicles in June. China, Korea. I 1900 by Ernest Wilson.

pungens See *M. simplicifolia* subsp. *pungens*.

†*simplicifolia* (Roxb.) Walp. **subsp. *pungens*** (Wall. ex Wight & Arn.) Beusekom (*M. pungens* Wall. ex Wight & Arn.) A medium-sized, semi-evergreen shrub with greyish stems and rather leathery, oblanceolate leaves conspicuously toothed in the upper half and with a tail-like apex, decurrent at the base.

stewardii See under *M. myriantha* subsp. *pilosa*.

tenuis See *M. dilleniifolia* subsp. *tenuis*.

veitchiorum Hemsl. A rare, small tree of architectural quality, remarkable for its very large, pinnate, red-stalked leaves, stout, rigid branches and prominent winter buds. Flowers creamy-white, fragrant, in 30–45cm long panicles, in May; fruits violet. W and C China. I 1901 by Ernest Wilson.

‡**MENZIESIA** Sm.—Ericaceae—A genus of about 7 species, natives of North America and E Asia. Small, slow-growing, deciduous shrubs recalling *Enkianthus*, requiring lime-free soil and, if possible, protection from late frosts. Flowers in terminal clusters, resembling *Daboecia*, but waxy in texture. This small genus, embracing at least 3 exquisite shrubs of top quality, deserves greater recognition.

ciliicalyx (Miq.) Maxim. A beautiful, small shrub with oval or obovate, ciliate leaves and clusters of nodding, pitcher-shaped flowers in May, varying in colour from cream to soft purple. Japan. I 1915. AM 1938. **var. *multiflora*** See *M. multiflora*. **var. *purpurea*** Makino (*M. purpurea* hort. not Maxim.) A superb slow-growing variety with obovate, mucronate leaves. The striking rose-purple flowers are larger than those of the typical form and appear slightly later. Often grown in gardens wrongly as *M. purpurea*, which is doubtfully in cultivation. Some plants grown under this name appear to be forms of *M. multiflora*. Japan.

ferruginea Sm. A small to medium-sized shrub with peeling bark. The small, cylindrical, pink-tinged flowers are borne in nodding clusters during May. W North America.

glabella A. Gray. A small shrub with obovate leaves and clusters of small, orange-flushed, pitcher-shaped flowers in late May and June. North America. I about 1885.

multiflora Maxim. (*M. ciliicalyx* var. *multiflora* (Maxim.) Makino) A small shrub, similar to *M. ciliicalyx* but with shorter, more urn-shaped corollas, the colour varying from pale purple to near white, with deeper coloured lobes and very slender calyx lobes. Japan.

pilosa (Michx.) Juss. Minnie bush. A small shrub of erect habit and modest charm. Young shoots and leaves glandular downy. The pendent, urn-shaped flowers, 6mm long, are creamy-yellow, flushed red and are carried in glandular-stalked, nodding clusters during May. E USA. I 1806.

purpurea See *M. ciliicalyx* var. *purpurea*.

MESPILUS L.—Rosaceae—A monotypic genus related to *Crataegus* but differing in its solitary flowers.

germanica L. Medlar. A small, thorny, picturesque, wide-spreading tree rivalling the black mulberry as an isolated specimen for an architectural feature. The large, hairy leaves turn a warm russet in the autumn. Large, white flowers are produced singly in May and June, followed by brown fruits, 2–3cm across. SE Europe to C Asia.

Long cultivated in England and naturalised in some counties. Cultivars selected for their fruits, such as 'Nottingham', are less thorny, with much larger leaves, flowers and fruits than wild plants.

Mespilus, snowy See *Amelanchier*.

*****METAPANAX** Frodin—Araliaceae—A small genus of about 3 species of glabrous, evergreen trees and shrubs, related to *Pseudopanax*. They are natives of China and N Vietnam. The following has proven hardy but young foliage is sometimes damaged by late frosts.

davidii (Franch.) Frodin (*Pseudopanax davidii* (Franch.) Philipson, *Nothopanax davidii* (Franch.) Diels) A medium-sized to large, slow-growing shrub with variable leaves, which can be simple or divided into 2–3 lobes or leaflets. Umbels of small, green flowers in long, terminal panicles are followed by black fruits. W and C China, N Vietnam. I 1907 by Ernest Wilson.

†*****METROSIDEROS** Banks ex Gaertn.—Myrtaceae—A genus of about 20 species of handsome, evergreen trees, shrubs and aerial-rooted climbers, related to *Callistemon* and natives of Australasia to Malaysia. The brilliantly coloured 'bottlebrush' flowers, composed largely of stamens, are often spectacular. All require protection and can only be grown outside in the mildest areas of the British Isles. Moderately lime-tolerant but not suitable for shallow chalk soils.

diffusa (G. Forst.) Sm. In cultivation in this country an exceedingly slow-growing, small to medium-sized, lax or scandent shrub, with cymes of pink-petalled flowers, with long pinkish stamens, in April and May. New Zealand. I 1910. AM 1931.

excelsa Sol. ex Gaertn. (*M. tomentosa* A. Rich.) Called the Christmas tree in New Zealand, where it is abundant in parts of North Island and described as a 'noble and picturesque tree'. Its large, bottlebrush flowers are brilliant crimson and smother the branches in summer. The finest examples in the British Isles are to be found in the Tresco Abbey Gardens, Isles of Scilly, elsewhere it is more usually a conservatory plant. I 1840.

kermadecensis W.R.B. Oliv. (*M. villosa* Kirk not Sm.) Resembling *M. excelsa*, but a little smaller in all its parts; flowers scarlet. Suitable only for the very mildest areas. New Zealand (Kermadec Islands). **'Variegata'** Leaves with a broad, creamy-white margin. It was originally thought to belong to *M. excelsa*. AM 1981.

lucida See *M. umbellata*.

robusta A. Cunn. Rata. A magnificent small to medium-sized tree, for mild, maritime districts. Leaves dark green, thick and rounded, narrower on juvenile plants. Coppery-scarlet flowers appear in late summer. Flowers at an earlier age than *M. umbellata*, but less hardy. New Zealand. AM 1959.

tomentosa See *M. excelsa*.

umbellata Cav. (*M. lucida* (G. Forst.) A. Rich.) Southern rata. One of the hardiest species, thriving in Cornwall, and similarly favoured districts, where it forms a large shrub or small tree of dense, bushy habit. The small, polished, myrtle-like leaves are coppery when young. On mature specimens the clusters of bright crimsonstamened flowers are produced in late summer illuminating the dark green foliage. New Zealand.

villosa See *M. kermadecensis*.

Mexican orange blossom See *Choisya ternata*.
Meyer's lemon See *Citrus* 'Meyer'.
Mezereon See *Daphne mezereum*.

‡***MICHELIA** L.—Magnoliaceae—About 50 species of evergreen trees or shrubs, closely related to *Magnolia*, but differing most noticeably in the flowers being borne in the axils of the leaves. Natives of tropical and subtropical SE Asia. Only suitable for the milder lime-free areas.

compressa (Maxim.) Sarg. A rare, slow-growing shrub or occasionally a small tree with ovate to obovate, glossy green, leathery leaves, 5cm long. Fragrant, pale yellow or whitish flowers, with a purplish-red centre, open during late spring. Most often seen growing against a south or west wall or in the sheltered corner of a house. Uninjured by the long severe winter of 1962/63. Japan, Ryukyus, SW China, Philippines, Taiwan. I 1894.

†*doltsopa* Buch.-Ham. ex DC. A magnificent small to medium-sized, semi-evergreen tree in the South West. Leaves 15–18cm long, leathery, glaucous beneath; flowers formed in autumn, opening in spring, multi-petalled, white and heavily scented. W Yunnan, Tibet, E Himalaya. I about 1918 by George Forrest. AM 1961. 'Silver Cloud' Flowers much larger, to 20cm across, with about 30 tepals; leaves very long and leathery. Named from a seedling sent by us to New Zealand.

†*figo* (Lour.) Spreng. (*M. fuscata* (Andr.) Wall., *Magnolia fuscata* Andr.) Banana shrub. A medium to large shrub, best treated as a greenhouse plant. Leaves small, dark, glossy green; flowers small, brown-purple and strongly scented of pear drops, produced in a long succession during spring and summer. SE China. I 1789.

×*foggii* See under *M*. 'Jack Fogg'.

†'**Jack Fogg**' (*M. doltsopa* × *M. figo*) A large shrub or small tree of upright, conical habit, with glossy dark green leaves. The fragrant, white flowers are tinged with pinkish-purple at the edge of the tepals and are freely produced from an early age, opening from cinnamon-pubescent buds which form in autumn. Proving hardy in the south of England. One of several hybrids of this parentage, sometimes referred to collectively as *M*. × *foggii* hort.

maudiae Dunn. An evergreen shrub or small tree of upright habit with grey-green leaves. Early spring flowers are pure white, scented and 15cm across. Proving hardy in the south of England. E China.

yunnanensis Franch. ex Finet & Gagnep. An evergreen, large shrub, sometimes a small tree. Strongly fragrant, white flowers open from velvety buds in early spring. Leaves brown hairy beneath when young. SW China.

Microglossa albescens See *Aster albescens*.
Mimosa See *Acacia dealbata*.

MIMULUS L. (*Diplacus* Nutt.)—Scrophulariaceae—A large genus of about 150 species of mainly annual and perennial herbs, but embracing 1 or 2 woody plants suitable for favoured sunny positions. Natives mainly of W North America but also occurring in South Africa, Asia, Australia and South America. Lime-tolerant.

†*aurantiacus Curtis (*M. glutinosus* H. Wendl.) The shrubby musk is a pretty shrub for mild localities, especially near the sea, growing about 1.2m high. Stems sticky to the touch. Orange or salmon-yellow flowers are borne throughout summer and autumn. California, Oregon. I in the late 18th century. ♀ 2002. AM 1938. **var. *puniceus*** (Nutt.) A. Gray (*M. puniceus* (Nutt.) Steud.) A form differing mainly in its smaller, brick-red or orange-red flowers. California.

glutinosus See *M. aurantiacus*.
puniceus See *M. aurantiacus* var. *puniceus*.

Minnie bush See *Menziesia pilosa*.

‡***MITCHELLA** L.—Rubiaceae—A genus of only 2 species of evergreen, creeping plants, suitable for a cool spot on a rock garden, or as groundcover in shade. They require a lime-free soil.

repens L. Partridge berry. A charming, mat-forming subshrub with procumbent, rooting stems. The tiny, ovate or rounded leaves are dark glossy green and borne in pairs. The small, fragrant, white or pink flowers are borne in terminal pairs in June and July. Fruits scarlet, 12mm across. E and C North America. I about 1761. AM 1951.

†***MITRARIA** Cav.—Gesneriaceae—A monotypic genus.

coccinea Cav. A low, spreading evergreen with small, glossy, leathery leaves and large, bright orange-scarlet, tubular flowers borne singly in the leaf axils from late spring through summer. A charming plant for a partially shaded, sheltered position. Unsuitable for shallow chalk soils. Chile, Chiloe. I 1846 by William Lobb. AM 1927. A plant grown under the name Clarke's Form has bright orange flowers, pale yellow in the throat and the insides of the lobes. It appears identical to plants we have grown as *Mitraria coccinea*. '**Lago Puyehue**' We propose this name for the plant grown as Lake Puye form. It has rich scarlet flowers with a cream throat, the colour barely reaching the lobes. The calyx lobes are also more conspicuously exserted from the bracts. It was introduced to Kew in 1963 from near Lago Puyehue in Chile, where it was found growing on a tree stump in full sun. It is said to be particularly hardy.

Mockernut See *Carya tomentosa*.
Mock orange See *Philadelphus*.

MOLTKIA Lehm.—Boraginaceae—A small genus of 6 species of herbaceous perennials and subshrubs related to *Lithodora*, differing in the exserted style. Natives of S Europe to SW Asia. A well-drained site in full sun on scree or in a rock garden.

×*intermedia* (Froebel) J. Ingram (*M. petraea* × *M. suffruticosa*) A dwarf, evergreen subshrub, domed in habit and reaching 30cm by 50cm. The leaves are dark and very narrow; the bright blue, open funnel-shaped flowers are profusely borne on spikes in summer. ♀ 2002.

petraea (Tratt.) Griseb. (*Lithospermum petraeum* (Tratt.) DC.) A lovely subshrub forming a neat bush 30–45cm high. Tubular flowers are pink in bud opening to violet-blue in June and July. Balkan Peninsula. I about 1840. FCC 1871.

Mooseberry See *Viburnum edule*.
Moosewood See *Acer pensylvanicum*.

MORUS L.—Moraceae—The mulberries contain some 7 species of deciduous trees and shrubs, natives of North and South America, Africa and Asia, and generally small to medium-sized, picturesque trees. Although succeeding in any well-drained soil, they respond to liberal treatment and are particularly suitable for town or coastal gardens. In winter the twigs may be recognized by the absence of a terminal bud. The brittle, fleshy roots call for special care when planting mulberries.

acidosa See *M. alba*.
alba L. (*M. acidosa* Griff., *M. australis* Poir., *M. bombycis* Koidz., *M. kagayamae* Koidz.) White mulberry. A small to medium-sized tree of rugged appearance. Leaves heart-shaped or ovate-lanceolate, often up to 15cm wide. Fruits whitish, changing to reddish-pink or nearly black in some forms, sweet and edible. Silkworms are traditionally fed on the leaves of this tree. C Asia to E Asia. Said to have been introduced into England in 1596. **'Laciniata'** ('Skeletoniana') A curious form with leaves deeply divided into narrow, long-pointed lobes. **'Macrophylla'** A remarkable form with large, often lobed, leaves, 18–22cm long, recalling those of a fig. C 1836. **'Nana'** A small, shrubby form of compact habit. **'Pendula'** A striking small, weeping tree with closely packed, perpendicularly falling branches. Very ornamental when in full fruit. AM 1897. **'Pyramidalis'** An erect-branched form resembling a Lombardy Poplar in habit. **'Skeletoniana'** See 'Laciniata'. **var.** *tatarica* (Pall.) Ser. A small, bushy-headed geographical variety with smaller leaves and fruits. Withstands very low temperatures. **'Venosa'** Leaves slenderly tapered at both ends, green with conspicuous pale veins.
australis See *M. alba*.
bombycis See *M. alba*.
cathayana Hemsl. A remarkable, small tree with large, heart-shaped, slender-pointed leaves and black, red or white fruits, 2.5cm long. C and E China. I 1907 by Ernest Wilson.
kagayamae See *M. alba*.
†*microphylla* Buckl. In cultivation a very slow-growing, bushy shrub, differing from *M. rubra* in its tiny leaves, also smaller catkins and fruits. This distinct species has not succeeded outdoors in our nurseries. S USA and Mexico. I 1926.
nigra L. Black mulberry. A small, very long-lived, architectural tree with a widespreading head, becoming gnarled and picturesque with age. Leaves heart-shaped, rough above, downy below. Fruits dark almost black-red, with an agreeable taste. W Asia. Said to have first been grown in England early in the 16th century. ♆ 2002.
rubra L. Red mulberry. A rare species in cultivation. A small to medium-sized tree with rounded, downy leaves, turning bright yellow in autumn. Very like the White mulberry. Fruit red. E and C USA. I 1629. **'Nana'** A dwarf, slow-growing form of compact habit, broader than high. Leaves smaller and prominently 3- to 5-lobed.

Mountain ash See *Sorbus aucuparia*.
Mountain mahogany See *Cercocarpus*.
Mrs Robb's bonnet See *Euphorbia amygdaloides* subsp. *robbiae*.
Mulberry See *Morus*.
Mulberry, paper See *Broussonetia papyrifera*.

†***MUSA** L.—Musaceae—The bananas make up a genus of some 35 species of large, often tree-like, herbs, natives of tropical Asia. The commonly eaten bananas come from forms of *M. acuminata*, a native of SE Asia but widely grown in warm regions of the world.
basjoo Siebold & Zucc. ex Iinuma. A large, evergreen herb reaching about 3m, which although tree-like in habit is not woody. Closely related to the edible banana and similar to it with very large leaves. Flowers creamy-yellow in summer followed by inedible, green fruits. A handsome plant for tropical effects but will thrive only in sheltered places in South West Britain. Ryukyu Islands. I about 1881 by Charles Maries.

†***MYOPORUM** Banks & Sol. ex G. Forst.—Myoporaceae—A genus of about 30 species of evergreen trees and shrubs, native mainly of Australia but extending to New Zealand, the Pacific Islands and SE Asia. Only for the mildest localities. Lime-tolerant. *M. tenuifolium* G. Forst. is commonly planted and naturalised in S Spain. It has white flowers in spring and purple fruits in summer.
laetum G. Forst. (*M. perforatum* hort.) Ngaio. An evergreen shrub or small tree notable for its dark, sticky buds and its lanceolate leaves, conspicuously studded with pellucid glands. Flowers small, white, purple-spotted. Will survive only in the mildest parts of the British Isles. Excellent for maritime exposure. New Zealand.

‡**MYRICA** L.—Myricaceae—A genus of about 50 species of interesting aromatic shrubs, widely distributed throughout the world. Embracing species tolerant of dry, sterile soil and those which delight in an acid bog. Flowers unisexual, in small catkins.
*californica Cham. & Schltdl. California bayberry. A glossy-leaved, hardy shrub of large size, occasionally a small tree. The oblanceolate, serrated leaves are polished apple-green on both surfaces, less aromatic than in other species. Fruits dark purple, clustered like small blackberries on short spurs and persisting until mid-winter. Tolerant of both moist and acid conditions. W USA. I 1848.
*cerifera L. (*M. caroliniensis* Mill.) Candleberry, Wax myrtle. A North American shrub or small tree, with narrow, obovate or oblanceolate leaves. A pleasing subject for a damp site. The glaucous wax that covers the fruits is made into fragrantly burning candles. E USA. I 1669. **var.** *pumila* Michx. A dwarf form spreading by underground stems and making a low hummock.
gale L. Sweet gale, Bog myrtle. A small, native, deciduous shrub of dense habit. Male and female catkins are warm golden-brown and glisten in the sunlight. They are produced on separate plants in April and May. The whole plant is strongly aromatic and may be grown in acid, boggy swamps where few other plants will exist. Europe to NE Asia, North America. C 1750.

pensylvanica Lois. Bayberry. A hardy, valuable plant for acid soils, making a large, semi-evergreen shrub, sometimes spreading by suckers. The oblong or obovate, aromatic leaves fall late in autumn. Conspicuous in winter with its tiny, grey-white fruits. An excellent maritime plant, and good for arid conditions. E North America. I 1727.

MYRICARIA Desv.—**Tamaricaceae**—A small genus of about 10 species distributed from Europe to E Asia. Closely related to, and requiring the same conditions as, *Tamarix*, but differing in the flowers, which have more numerous stamens, united in the lower half.

germanica (L.) Desv. (*Tamarix germanica* L.) Wand-like stems, 1.2–2m high, carry feathery, blue-green foliage and light pink, fluffy flowers throughout the summer. Succeeds best in neutral or acid soil but is lime-tolerant. C and S Europe, W Asia. C 1582.

Myrobalan See *Prunus cerasifera*.

*****MYRSINE** L.—**Myrsinaceae**—A large genus of about 300 species of chiefly tropical evergreen trees and shrubs, primarily of botanical interest; the females sometimes produce attractive fruits. Widely distributed mainly in the tropics. Moderately lime-tolerant, but not recommended for a shallow chalky soil.

africana L. A small, upright, suckering shrub with aromatic, myrtle-like leaves. Dense clusters of tiny flowers open in the leaf axils in late spring. The most conspicuous feature of them is the deeply cut, greenish-white stigma. Blue-black, pea-like fruits are produced. Resembling in general appearance *Paxistima myrtifolia*, differing in its alternate leaves and dioecious flowers. Perfectly hardy given reasonable shelter and suitable for sun or shade. Himalaya to E Asia, Azores, Mts of E and S Africa. I 1691. AM 1927. **var. *retusa*** (Aiton) DC. A variety with more rounded-obovate leaves, notched at the tip.

†*australis* (A. Rich.) Allan (*Suttonia australis* A. Rich.) Mapau. A small to medium-sized shrub with slender, orange-red branchlets and oblong or elliptic leaves with strongly undulate margins. For a sheltered position in mild gardens. New Zealand.

nummularia Hook. f. (*Suttonia nummularia* Hook. f.) A prostrate shrub with wiry stems and densely-set, small, orbicular, brownish-green leaves. Female plants produce small, blue-purple fruits. New Zealand.

†*semiserrata* Wall. A large shrub or occasionally a small tree with thinly textured, elliptic-ovate, slender-pointed, serrated leaves up to 12cm long, prettily tinted when young. Flowers in axillary clusters, reddish to white, followed by blue to reddish-purple berries. Originally listed as *Ilex fragilis*. Only for the mildest areas. E Himalaya, W and C China.

*****MYRTEOLA** O. Berg—**Myrtaceae**—Three species of evergreen shrubs from South America, previously listed under *Myrtus*.

nummularia (Poir.) O. Berg (*Myrtus nummularia* Poir.) The hardiest myrtle is a tiny, prostrate shrublet with wiry, reddish stems. The tiny, neat, rounded leaves are borne in 2 opposite ranks. Flowers white, borne at the end of the stems in May or June, followed by white to pink or red berries up to 15mm across. Andes of South America to S Chile and Falkland Isles. I before 1927. AM 1967.

Myrtle See *Myrtus*.
Myrtle, bog See *Myrica gale*.
Myrtle, wax See *Myrica cerifera*.

†*****MYRTUS** L.—**Myrtaceae**—The myrtle is an easily cultivated and effective white-flowered, aromatic evergreen for mild climates. It succeeds best in full sun on any well-drained soil, including chalk soils, and is excellent for maritime exposure.

apiculata See *Luma apiculata*.
bidwillii See *Austromyrtus bidwillii*.
bullata See *Lophomyrtus bullata*.
chequen See *Luma chequen*.
communis L. The common myrtle, hardy in many localities, particularly by the sea. An aromatic, densely leafy shrub, attaining 3–4.5m against a sunny wall. The white flowers are borne profusely in July and August, followed by conspicuous purple-black berries. Mediterranean region, SW Europe, W Asia; thoroughly naturalised in S Europe particularly in the Mediterranean region. C in England in the 16th century. ♀ 2002. AM 1972. **'Flore Pleno'** An uncommon form with double flowers. **'Microphylla'** See subsp. *tarentina*. **'Microphylla Variegata'** A form of subsp. *tarentina* with white-margined leaves. **subsp. *tarentina*** (L.) Nyman ('Jenny Reitenbach', 'Microphylla') A very pretty, compact, free-flowering form with small, narrow leaves and white berries. Flowers in autumn with pink-tinged petals. Mediterranean region. ♀ 2002. AM 1977. **'Variegata'** Leaves grey-green, narrowly margined creamy-white. A pretty plant.

lechleriana See *Amomyrtus luma*.
luma See *Luma apiculata*.
nummularia See *Myrteola nummularia*.
obcordata See *Lophomyrtus obcordata*.
×*ralphii* See *Lophomyrtus* × *ralphii*.
ugni See *Ugni molinae*.

N, O

*NANDINA Thunb.—**Berberidaceae**—A curious monotypic genus looking somewhat like a bamboo, but related to
Berberis. Should be given a sheltered position in full sun in
any well-drained soil.

domestica Thunb. Sacred bamboo. An extremely decorative bamboo-like shrub of medium size, with long, erect,
unbranched stems. The large, compound, green leaves
are attractively tinged purplish-red in spring and autumn.
Flowers small, white, in large terminal panicles during
summer. Berries red, but rarely produced in this country
except after very hot summers. Hardy in all but the coldest districts. C China, Japan. I 1804. ♀ 2002. AM 1897.
'**Fire Power**' Similar to 'Nana Purpurea' but foliage
yellow-green in summer, orange-red in winter. ♀ 2002.
'**Nana Purpurea**' A small shrub of more compact habit,
with less compound leaves and broader leaflets. The
young foliage reddish-purple throughout the season.
'**Richmond**' A vigorous, medium-sized form with an
abundance of red fruits during winter.

NEILLIA D. Don—**Rosaceae**—A small genus of about 10
species of deciduous shrubs related to *Spiraea* and, like
them, easy to cultivate in all but very dry soils. Natives of
China and the Himalaya.

affinis Hemsl. A medium-sized shrub related to *N. thibetica* with glabrous shoots and shallowly lobed, taper-pointed leaves. Pink flowers open in racemes to 8cm long in
summer. China. I by Ernest Wilson in 1908.

longiracemosa See *N. thibetica*.

malvacea See *Physocarpus malvaceus*.

ribesoides See *N. sinensis* var. *ribesoides*.

sinensis Oliv. A medium-sized shrub with glabrous shoots
and bronze-purple young foliage. Leaves lobed and
toothed. Flowers in short, terminal racemes in June, petals
and calyx white. C China. I by Ernest Wilson in 1901. **var.
ribesoides** (Rehder) J.E. Vidal (*N. ribesoides* Rehder)
Medium-sized shrub closely related to *N. thibetica*.
Leaves deeply and incisely toothed. Flowers pink, borne
in dense racemes in early summer. W China. C 1930.

thibetica Bur. & Franch. (*N. longiracemosa* Hemsl.) A very
attractive, medium-sized shrub with erect, downy stems
bearing ovate, slender-pointed, often 3-lobed leaves and
slender, terminal racemes of pink, tubular flowers in May
and June. W China. I 1904 by Ernest Wilson. AM 1931.

thyrsiflora D. Don. Small to medium-sized shrub of spreading habit with long, arching stems. Leaves 3-lobed, slender-pointed and sharply toothed. The small, white flowers are borne on branched racemes at the ends of the
shoots during summer. E Himalaya.

torreyi See *Physocarpus malvaceus*.

†***NEOLITSEA** (Benth.) Merr.—**Lauraceae**—A genus of
some 60 species of evergreen, aromatic trees and shrubs,
with attractive foliage, mainly native of tropical Asia.
Flowers dioecious. A few species succeed in the mildest
parts of the British Isles. Not recommended for shallow
chalk soil.

sericea (Blume) Koidz. (*N. glauca* (Siebold) Koidz., *Litsea
glauca* Siebold) A rare and distinguished member of the

Lauraceae, forming a medium to large shrub. This
remarkable shrub has succeeded in the Sir Harold Hillier
Gardens and Arboretum in a sheltered position for the
past 35 years with but little frost damage. The unfolding,
fawn-brown leaves are most attractive in colour and texture, like soft suede above and white silk beneath, ageing
leathery and dark glossy green above, glaucous beneath;
aromatic when crushed. Flowers greenish-yellow in
dense clusters in October. Japan, China, Taiwan, Korea.

Neopanax See *Nothopanax*.

†***NERIUM** L.—**Apocynaceae**—A small genus of a single
species, a tender, ornamental sun-loving evergreen related
to, but very different from, the periwinkle (*Vinca*). Lime-
tolerant, but not recommended for shallow chalk soil.
WARNING: The foliage is poisonous.

indicum See *N. oleander*.

oleander L. (*N. indicum* Mill.) Oleander. This superb evergreen flourishes along the Mediterranean seaboard of S
Europe where it rivals the *Camellia japonica* of more
northern gardens. An erect-branched, medium to large
shrub, it has pairs or whorls of leathery, long, lance-
shaped leaves. Flowers like large periwinkles, appear
from June to October. Numerous forms are grown with
white, yellow, buff or pink flowers, which may be single,
double or semi-double, as well as forms with variegated
leaves. In the British Isles the oleander is one of the best
evergreens for tub culture standing out of doors in full
sun in the summer and protected in a conservatory during winter. Mediterranean region to SW Asia. I 1596.
'**Variegatum**' Leaves margined with cream. Flowers
double, pink. ♀ 2002.

Nettle tree See *Celtis*.

NEVIUSIA A. Gray—**Rosaceae**—A genus of 2 species,
mainly of botanical interest, related to *Kerria*. The white
stamens are so numerous as to be conspicuous and the sepals enlarge after flowering. Any well-drained soil.

alabamensis A. Gray. Alabama snow wreath. A spiraea-like
shrub, up to 2m, forming dense thickets with arching
branches and finely toothed, ovate leaves. During April
and May it is covered with clusters of fluffy white flowerheads which lack petals but are composed of numerous
stamens. Enjoys a sunny position where it can spread
rapidly by suckers. Alabama (USA), rare in the wild. I
about 1860.

cliftonii J.R. Shevock, B. Ertter & D.W. Taylor. Shasta snow
weath. This remarkable species was discovered Near Lake
Shasta in northern California in 1992. It differs from *N.
alabamensis* in its coarsely toothed and lobed leaves and
the small white petals. It has been suggested that *Neviusia*
was once a widespread genus, a theory supported by
recent fossil evidence. It is very rare in the wild and not
known to be in cultivation in this country.

New Jersey tea See *Ceanothus americanus*.
New Zealand flax See *Phormium tenax*.

Nine bark See *Physocarpus opulifolius.*
Norway maple See *Acer platanoides.*
Notelaea excelsa See *Picconia excelsa.*

‡**NOTHOFAGUS** Blume—**Fagaceae**—The Southern beeches are a small genus of very ornamental fast-growing, evergreen and deciduous trees or large shrubs; about 34 species from South America, Australasia, New Caledonia and New Guinea. Related to *Fagus*, but differing in the normally small leaves, closely spaced along the branchlets, and in the male and female flowers appearing singly or in clusters of 3. They vary in degree of hardiness and many grow rapidly but are poor wind-resisters. They do not survive on chalk soils. There is increasing opinion that they should be placed in a separate family – Nothofagaceae.

alpina (Poepp. & Endl.) Oerst. (*N. nervosa* (Phil.) Dim. & Mil., *N. procera* (Poepp. & Endl.) Oerst.) A fast-growing tree of large size, distinguished by its comparatively large, prominently veined leaves, 4–10cm long, resembling those of the hornbeam (*Carpinus*). Usually gives rich autumn tints. Chile, Argentina. I 1913.

alpina × *obliqua* This hybrid, which is intermediate between the parents, has arisen in cultivation where seed has been collected from the parents grown together.

antarctica (G. Forst.) Oerst. Antarctic beech. An elegant, fast-growing, deciduous tree of medium size. Leaves small, rounded and heart-shaped, irregularly toothed, dark green and glossy, turning yellow in autumn. Trunk and primary branches often curiously twisted. Chile. I 1830. **'Benmore'** ('Prostrata') A low, spreading form growing into a dense mound of interlacing branches. **var. *uliginosa*** A. DC. A variety with rather larger, somewhat pubescent leaves. Chile.

betuloides (Mirbel) Blume. A medium-sized to large, densely leafy, evergreen tree, of columnar habit at least when young. Leaves ovate or roundish, usually less than 2.5cm long, dark shining green and toothed, closely arranged on the branchlets. Chile, Argentina. I 1830.

cliffortioides See *N. solandri* var. *cliffortioides.*

†*cunninghamii* (Hook.) Oerst. A rare, small, evergreen tree in mild gardens. The wiry shoots are clothed with tiny, almost diamond-shaped, closely set, glabrous leaves, bluntly toothed in the upper half. C 1860. Tasmania.

dombeyi (Mirbel) Blume. A medium to large, evergreen tree of vigorous habit. Leaves 2.5–4cm long, doubly toothed, dark shining green. A fairly hardy tree that may lose its leaves in cold winters. In leaf very like *N. betuloides* but usually a faster-growing, wider-spreading tree with a more loosely open arrangement of its branches. Chile, Argentina. I 1916.

fusca (Hook. f.) Oerst. Red beech. Somewhat tender when young but developing into a beautiful, hardy, small to medium-sized, evergreen tree. The rounded or oval, coarsely toothed leaves, 2.5–4cm long, often turn copper in autumn. The bark on old trees becomes flaky. New Zealand.

glauca (Phil.) Krasser. Related to *N. obliqua*. Juvenile trees bear large leaves, shallowly lobed and toothed and rough on both sides. As the tree matures these are replaced by adult foliage in which the leaves are similar to those of *N. obliqua* but relatively broader. The bark is very distinct and ornamental, even on young trees, being pale orange-brown and peeling in thin flakes. This is a large tree in the wild but grows slowly in the British Isles; it has taken 10 years to reach about 5m in the Sir Harold Hillier Gardens and Arboretum. C Chile.

†*menziesii* (Hook. f.) Oerst. Silver beech. A graceful, small to medium-sized, evergreen tree akin to *N. cunninghamii*. Leaves up to 12mm long, rotund-ovate, dark-green, double-toothed. Hardy in the southern counties if well-sited. Bark of young wood cherry-like. New Zealand.

†*moorei* (F. Muell.) Krasser. Australian beech. A small to medium-sized, evergreen tree with comparatively large, hard, leathery, dark green leaves, 4–8cm long, an attractive copper colour when young. Not hardy here and only suitable for the mildest localities. New South Wales, Queensland. I 1892.

nervosa See *N. alpina.*

obliqua (Mirbel) Blume. Roble beech. A large, elegant, very fast-growing tree, forming a handsome specimen in a few years. Leaves broadly ovate or oblong, 5–8cm long, irregularly toothed, glabrous. I 1902 from Chile by H.J. Elwes. Chile, Argentina.

procera See *N. alpina.*

pumilio (Poepp. & Endl.) Krasser. Lenga. A variable plant in the wild, ranging from a shrub to a tree larger than *N. antarctica* to which it is related. Plants in the Sir Harold Hillier Gardens and Arboretum are making small trees or large shrubs with several upright branches. Leaves ovate, to 3cm by 2cm, oblique at the base, dark matt green above, margined with blunt teeth. S Chile, S Argentina. I about 1960.

solandri (Hook. f.) Oerst. Black beech. A tall, slender, medium-sized, evergreen tree with ascending, fan-like branches. Wiry branchlets bearing neatly arranged, tiny, oblong or elliptic, entire leaves. C 1917. New Zealand. **var. *cliffortioides*** (Hook. f.) Poole (*N. cliffortioides* (Hook. f.) Oerst.) Mountain beech. An elegant, small to medium-sized, fast-growing tree, differing in its generally smaller, ovate leaves with curled edges and raised tip. New Zealand.

Nothopanax arboreus See *Pseudopanax arboreus.*
Nothopanax davidii See *Metapanax davidii.*
Nothopanax laetus See *Pseudopanax laetus.*

NOTOSPARTIUM Hook. f.—**Leguminosae**—A small genus of 3 species embracing some moderately hardy, sun-loving, broom-like shrubs from the South Island of New Zealand. They succeed in full sun in any well-drained soil.

carmichaeliae Hook. f. The pink broom of New Zealand is a charming, medium-sized shrub of graceful habit, its arching, leafless stems wreathed in July with lilac-pink pea-flowers. Only injured in the coldest winters. I 1883. FCC 1889.

glabrescens Petrie. A large shrub, a tree in its native habitat. Branches long and whippy; flowers rose, carried in loose racemes during May and June. I 1930.

Nuttallia cerasiformis See *Oemleria cerasiformis.*

‡**NYSSA** L.—**Cornaceae**—A small genus of 11 species of deciduous trees noted for their rich autumn tints.

Insignificant flowers are followed by equally inconspicuous blue-black fruits. They require moist, lime-free soil, and are best planted when small as they resent disturbance.

aquatica L. (*N. uniflora* Wangenh.) Water tupelo. A rare, small tree with ovate-oblong leaves, downy beneath as are the young shoots, long-stalked and frequently with a few coarse teeth. SE USA, where it grows in swamps with *Taxodium distichum*, reaching a large size. I 1735.

sinensis Oliv. A rare, large shrub or small tree of spreading habit proving perfectly hardy in the Sir Harold Hillier Gardens and Arboretum. Leaves narrowly ovate up to 15cm long. A magnificent introduction. The young growths are red throughout the growing season and the leaves change to every shade of red in autumn. China. C 1902. ♀ 2002. FCC 1976.

sylvatica Marshall (*N. multiflora* Wangenh.) Tupelo, Sour gum. A handsome, slow-growing, medium-sized to large tree of broadly columnar outline. Leaves are variable in shape, generally obovate or oval, pointed, up to 15cm long, dark glossy green, occasionally dull green above. The foliage turns rich scarlet, orange and yellow in autumn. S Canada, E USA, C and S Mexico. I 1750. ♀ 2002. AM 1951. **var. biflora** (Walter) Sarg. Swamp tupelo, Black gum. A variety with usually narrower, more leathery leaves and bearing the female flowers in pairs (in groups of 3–4 or more in the typical variety). SE USA. **'High Beeches'** Selected at High Beeches by Anne and Edward Boscawen, this develops glossy crimson, pink and gold autumn colour but is difficult to propagate. FCC 1968. **'Jermyns Flame'** A form selected by John Hillier in 1985 from plants in the Sir Harold Hillier Gardens and Arboretum. Leaves relatively large with striking autumn colours of red, yellow and orange. **'Sheffield Park'** Selected from one of the many plants of this species raised by Arthur Soames of the National Trust gardens at Sheffield Park, East Sussex. The brilliant orange-red colouring starts 2 or 3 weeks before most other tupelos. **'Wisley Bonfire'** Named from the well-known tree at the RHS Gardens, Wisley. A vigorous conical tree with brilliant red autumn colour.

Oak See *Quercus*.

Ocean spray See *Holodiscus discolor*.

†**OCHNA** L.—Ochnaceae—A large genus of more than 80 species of evergreen and deciduous trees and shrubs, natives of warm temperate and tropical regions of the Old World. The following is the only species occasionally met with in cultivation, requiring conservatory treatment.

*serrulata (Hochst.) Walp. (*O. multiflora* hort. not DC.) A small shrub for a conservatory. Flowers yellow followed by curious, pendent, black, pea-like fruits, beautifully set-off by the bright crimson, waxy calyces. Natal (South Africa). I 1860. FCC 1879.

OEMLERIA Rchb.—Rosaceae—A monotypic genus related to, but superficially very different from, *Prunus*, with male and female flowers usually on different plants. Easily cultivated in all types of fertile soil, but sometimes inclined to become chlorotic in very poor, shallow chalk soils.

cerasiformis (Hook. & Arn.) Landon (*Osmaronia cerasiformis* (Torr. & A. Gray) Greene, *Nuttallia cerasiformis* Torr. & A. Gray) Oso berry. A suckering shrub, forming a thicket of erect stems, 2–2.5m or more high. It has pendent racemes of fragrant, white, ribes-like flowers in February and March, more attractive in the male plant. Plum-like fruits, brown at first, are purple when ripe. Leaves sea-green, conspicuous on vigorous young growths, emerging very early as the flowers open. California. I 1848. AM 1927 (as *Nuttallia cerasiformis*).

†***OLEA** L.—Oleaceae—A genus of more than 40 species of tender, evergreen trees and shrubs with opposite, leathery leaves. Natives of warm regions of the Old World. 1 or 2 species survive in the mildest localities. Any well-drained soil.

europaea L. The olive is only hardy in the mildest areas of the British Isles where it forms a large shrub or small tree, with grey-green, leathery leaves, glaucous beneath, and axillary racemes of fragrant, small, white flowers in late summer. The olive oil of commerce is extracted from the fruits. Mediterranean region, with a form extending to China. Widely cultivated and naturalised in warm-temperate countries. Cultivated from time immemorial. **subsp. africana** (Mill.) P.S. Green (*O. verrucosa* Link) A small tree or large shrub with greyish, warty shoots and linear-lanceolate leaves. South Africa. I 1814.

verrucosa See *O. europaea* subsp. *africana*.

Oleander See *Nerium oleander*.

***OLEARIA** Moench—Compositae—The daisy bushes or tree daisies are of Australasian origin, with about 130 species. As a genus they are attractive, evergreen, easy to grow, wind-resistant and sun-loving shrubs. They include some of the finest of all evergreens for maritime exposure. All have daisy-like flowerheads, which are white or creamy-white (unless otherwise stated), and the average height attained in the British Isles is 1.2–2.5m. Straggly or untidy specimens may be hard-pruned in April. Some species are very tolerant of atmospheric pollution. They will succeed in any well-drained soil and are especially recommended for chalky soils.

†*albida* Hook. f. (*O. albiflora* hort.) A medium-sized shrub of upright habit with oblong-elliptic, undulate, pale green leaves, white beneath. A tender species, hardy plants in cultivation under this name being referable to *O.* 'Talbot de Malahide', a hybrid of *O. avicenniifolia*. New Zealand.

†*arborescens* (G. Forst.) Cockayne & Laing (*O. nitida* (Hook. f.) Hook. f.) A vigorous, large shrub or small tree up to 4m. Broadly ovate leaves, shining dark green above, with a silvery, satiny sheen beneath, slightly toothed. Flowerheads in large corymbs in May or June. New Zealand.

†*argophylla* (Labill.) Benth. A medium-sized to large shrub with grey-tomentose shoots. Leaves elliptic, to 10cm long, spiny at the margins, dark glossy green above with a thin, silvery tomentum beneath. Small, 4- to 6-rayed flowers, with yellow centres, are borne in large corymbs during autumn and winter. SE Australia, Tasmania.

avicenniifolia (Raoul) Hook. f. A medium-sized to large shrub with pointed leaves, whitish or buff beneath. Flowerheads sweetly fragrant, borne in wide corymbs, in

August and September. The leaves bear a distinct resemblance to those of the white mangrove (*Avicennia alba*). A plant often erroneously grown in gardens as *O. albida* is thought to be a hybrid of this species and has been named *O.* 'Talbot de Malahide'. A good dense, hedge-making shrub, especially in maritime exposure or industrial areas. New Zealand. **'White Confusion'** A form with larger, slightly wavy leaves, and masses of white flowerheads in summer.

capillaris Buchanan. (*O. arborescens* var. *capillaris* (Buchanan) Kirk) A small, compact, rounded and very hardy shrub, up to 1.2m, with leaves similar to those of *O. arborescens*, but much smaller and entire or minutely toothed. Flowerheads in corymbs in June. New Zealand.

†**chathamica** Kirk. A beautiful, small shrub, up to 1.2m, resembling *O. semidentata*, but with broader, green leaves inclined to be obovate, 3-veined beneath. In June produces flowerheads, up to 5cm across, solitary on long stalks, pale violet with purple centres. Chatham Isles. I 1910. AM 1938.

†**cheesemanii** Cockayne & Allan (*O. rani* hort. not (A. Cunn.) Druce. A medium-sized shrub with narrow leaves, dark green above, covered with a buff or whitish tomentum beneath. Flowerheads fragrant, in large, branched corymbs, in May. New Zealand.

†**colensoi** Hook. f. A large shrub with obovate or oblong-obovate, leathery leaves, shining green above, white-woolly beneath; flowerheads brownish-purple in July. Makes an excellent tall, evergreen shrub in favoured localities. New Zealand.

cymbifolia See *O. nummulariifolia* var. *cymbifolia*.

dentata See *O. macrodonta* and *O. rotundifolia*.

†**erubescens** (DC.) Dippel. A small, spreading shrub with reddish shoots and conspicuously toothed, shining dark green leaves; flowering in May or June. Tasmania. C 1840. **var. ilicifolia** (DC.) Bean. A form with larger leaves occasionally 7.5cm long by 2.5cm wide. Flowerheads also larger. SE Australia.

†× **excorticata** Buchanan (*O. arborescens* × *O. lacunosa*) A remarkable shrub, up to 3m, with narrow, leathery leaves, up to 10cm long, shining dark green above, thickly buff-felted beneath. New Zealand.

†**floribunda** (Hook. f.) Benth. A slender, Tasmanian species up to 2m, having the appearance of a tree heath. The branches are crowded with minute, deep green leaves and, in June, wreathed with small flowerheads. Tasmania, S and SE Australia. AM 1935.

forsteri See *O. paniculata*.

†**frostii** (F. Muell.) J.H. Willis. A small, downy shrub with sage-green, shallowly toothed leaves. Flowerheads solitary on long peduncles, large, double, mauve, recalling the best forms of the modern michaelmas daisy. Has been wrongly cultivated as *O. gravis*. SE Australia.

†**furfuracea** (A. Rich.) Hook. f. A large shrub or small tree with attractive, glossy, leathery leaves, 5–10cm long, grey-white beneath. Flowerheads borne in wide corymbs in August. New Zealand.

†**glandulosa** (Labill.) Benth. A distinct, small to medium-sized, aromatic shrub with green shoots and narrowly linear, dark glossy green leaves, edged with curious, small, wart-like glands. Small flowers are borne in open corymbs in late summer and autumn. SE Australia.

gunniana See *O. phlogopappa*.

× **haastii** Hook. f. (*O. avicenniifolia* × *O. moschata*) A rounded bush of medium size with small, entire leaves, white-felted beneath, and smothered with fragrant flowerheads in July and August. Hardy almost everywhere in the British Isles, and tolerant of town conditions. An excellent, well-proven hedging plant. New Zealand. I 1858. FCC 1873.

†**'Henry Travers'** (*O. semidentata* hort. not Decne. ex Hook. f.) One of the loveliest of all shrubs for more favoured coastal gardens. A medium-sized shrub with lanceolate, grey-green leaves, silvery beneath. The large, pendent, aster-like flowerheads are lilac, with a purple centre, and appear in June. Possibly the hybrid *O. chathamica* × *O. semidentata*, which occurs in the wild in the Chatham Islands. I to Dublin in 1908.

ilicifolia Hook. f. A dense, medium-sized shrub with thick, leathery, linear-oblong, grey-green leaves, sharply and coarsely toothed, and whitish-felted beneath. Fragrant flowerheads are produced in June. The whole plant possesses a musky odour. One of the best of the hardier species. New Zealand. AM 1972.

†**insignis** Hook. f. (*Pachystegia insignis* (Hook. f.) Cheeseman) Marlborough rock daisy. A dwarf shrub of remarkably distinct appearance, suitable for mild districts, and especially for maritime exposures, where it will take the full blast of sea winds. Leaves obovate, up to 15cm long, dark green, white-felted beneath. The large, yellow-centred, white, aster-like flowers are carried singly on stiff, erect, white-tomentose stems during late summer. I 1850. AM 1915. **'Minor'** (*Pachystegia insignis* var. *minor* Cheeseman) A distinct and interesting form, smaller in all its parts and less tomentose. Suitable for a rock garden in a sunny, well-drained position.

†**lacunosa** A very distinct medium-sized to large, slow-growing shrub with stout, white-tomentose stems. Rigid, long, narrow leaves, up to 17cm long by 1cm across, taper from just above the base to a sharp point; margins revolute and not or only slightly toothed. They are loosely white floccose above at first becoming dark green with a conspicuous pale midrib. The undersurface has a persistent, silvery tomentum. Flowers small, in clusters of terminal panicles, but rarely produced outdoors in the British Isles. New Zealand.

macrodonta Baker (*O. dentata* Hook. f.) New Zealand holly. A strong-growing, medium-sized shrub, up to 3m or more, with sage-green, holly-like leaves, 6–9cm long, silvery-white beneath. Flowerheads fragrant, in broad panicles, in June. One of the best screening or hedging shrubs for exposed coastal gardens. The whole plant possesses a musky odour. New Zealand. ♀ 2002. FCC 1895. **'Major'** A form with larger leaves and flower corymbs. **'Minor'** A dwarf form, smaller in all its parts.

†**megalophylla** (F. Muell.) F. Muell. ex Benth. A small shrub with angular, pale brown-tomentose young shoots. Leaves opposite, lanceolate, up to 14cm long, dark glossy green, glabrous and reticulate above, densely pale brown-tomentose beneath. The young growth is tinged with red in some forms. Flowers in compound corymbs. SE Australia. I 1952. AM 1977.

× *mollis* hort. not (Kirk) Cockayne (*O. ilicifolia* × *O. moschata*) A small shrub of rounded, compact habit, with wavy-edged, silvery-grey, slightly toothed leaves, up to 4cm long. Flowerheads in large corymbs in May. One of the hardiest of the genus. See also *O.* 'Zennorensis'.

moschata Hook. f. A slow-growing, small to medium-sized shrub with small, flat, entire, grey-green leaves, 2cm long, white-felted beneath. Flowers in July. The whole plant possesses a musky odour. New Zealand.

†*nernstii* (F. Muell.) F. Muell. ex Benth. Both the stems and the long, narrow, shining green leaves of this plant are clammy to the touch. A plant of botanical interest. SE Australia.

nitida See *O. arborescens*.

nummulariifolia (Hook. f.) Hook. f. One of the hardiest species. A medium-sized, stiffly-branched shrub of unusual appearance, with small, thick, yellow-green leaves, thickly crowding the stems. Flowerheads small, solitary in the axils of the leaves in July, fragrant. Some plants grown under this name are hybrids. New Zealand. **var. cymbifolia** Hook. f. (*O. cymbifolia* (Hook. f.) Cheeseman) A form with rather sticky young shoots and leaves with strongly revolute margins. New Zealand.

odorata Petrie. An elegant, medium-sized, hardy shrub of loose habit, with long, wiry, arching stems and narrow-obovate leaves. Of no floral beauty, but worth growing for its fragrance in July. New Zealand. I 1908.

× *oleifolia* Kirk (*O. avicenniifolia* × *O. odorata*) A slow-growing, medium-sized shrub of compact habit, suitable for windswept coastal gardens. Leaves ovate-elliptic, matt sea-green above, white-tomentose beneath, the blade to 5cm by 1.5cm; petiole about 5mm. New Zealand. **'Waikariensis'** (*O.* 'Waikariensis') A small, attractive shrub with lanceolate leaves, the blade to 6.5cm by 1.5cm, glossy green above and white beneath with a buff midrib; petiole about 12mm. Flowerheads in axillary clusters. Origin unknown, probably New Zealand from where it was introduced in the early 1930s.

†*pachyphylla* Cheeseman. This is a medium-sized shrub with large, entire, wavy-edged leaves, brown or silvery beneath. Flowerheads in large corymbs in July. New Zealand.

†*paniculata* (J.R. Forst. & G. Forst.) Druce (*O. forsteri* (Hook. f.) Hook. f.) Large shrub or small tree. A distinct and pleasing species with bright olive-green, undulate leaves, reminiscent of *Pittosporum tenuifolium*; flower-heads inconspicuous, but fragrant in November and December. Used for hedgemaking especially in favoured maritime districts. New Zealand. I 1816.

†*phlogopappa* (Labill.) DC. (*O. gunniana* (DC.) Hook. f. ex Hook., *O. stellulata* (hort. not Labill.) DC.) The popular May-flowering Tasmanian daisy bush. An extremely variable shrub in the wild. Of medium size with aromatic, toothed and narrow leaves, 1–3.5cm long, thickly crowding the erect stems. Flowerheads, 2cm across, in crowded panicles along the stems. Tasmania, SE Australia. I 1848. FCC 1885. **Splendens Group** (*O. stellulata* 'Splendens') We owe a debt to the late Harold Comber for the introduction of several good garden plants including this lovely form with flowerheads resembling michaelmas daisies. I from Tasmania in 1930. For many years we have grown forms of this with

blue, lavender and rose flowers. 'Comber's Blue', 'Comber's Mauve' and 'Comber's Pink' are selections. **var. subrepanda** (DC.) J.H. Willis. Differs in its smaller, narrower, grey-tomentose leaves and denser habit.

†*ramulosa* (Labill.) Benth. Small, twiggy shrub with slender, arching stems and small, linear leaves. Flowerheads small, crowding the stems in August. Tasmania, S Australia. C 1822. AM 1927.

rani hort. See *O. cheesemanii*.

†**'Rossii'** (*O. argophylla* × *O. macrodonta*) A strong-growing shrub of medium size. Leaves elliptic, green above, silvery-downy beneath. Garden origin, Ireland.

†*rotundifolia* (Less.) DC. (*O. dentata* hort., *O. tomentosa* hort.) An uncommon, tender species, usually less than 1m, of special interest because of its large, mauve, aster-like flowerheads, borne singly and continuously over a long period. Leaves oval, leathery, dark green and serrated. It seldom survives a winter in our part of Hampshire. SE Australia. I 1793.

†× *scilloniensis* Dorrien-Smith (*O. lyrata* × *O. phlogopappa*) A compact, rounded, grey-leaved shrub, up to 2.5m. An exceedingly free-flowering hybrid, the plant being literally covered with bloom in May. Garden origin, Tresco, Isles of Scilly. ♀ 2002. AM 1951. **'Master Michael'** A selection with mauve flowers.

semidentata See under *O.* 'Henry Travers'.

†*solandri* (Hook. f.) Hook. f. A dense, heath-like shrub of medium size giving a yellowish effect, rather like *Cassinia fulvida*. Leaves linear, 6mm long, in clusters. Flowerheads small, sweetly scented, in August. Requires wall protection except in mild localities. New Zealand.

†*speciosa* Hutch. A small shrub with brown-woolly shoots and thick, leathery, glossy dark green leaves, thickly pale brown-felted beneath. Flowerheads large, white or blue during summer. SE Australia. I before 1883.

†*stellulata* DC. A variable, rather lax, small to medium-sized shrub recalling *O. phlogopappa* but taller and less compact and with rather longer leaves. Flowerheads in panicles in May. Tasmania. AM 1893. **'Splendens'** See *O. phlogopappa* Splendens Group.

tomentosa See *O. rotundifolia*.

†*traversii* (F. Muell.) Hook. f. Considered to be one of the best and fastest-growing evergreens for windbreaks in Cornwall and similar maritime localities, growing to 6m high, even in exposed positions on poor, sandy soils. Shoots 4-angled, covered in a dense, white felt. Leaves broad, leathery, opposite, polished green above, silvery-white-felted beneath. Flowerheads insignificant, in summer. Chatham Isles. I 1887.

virgata (Hook. f.) Hook. f. (*Eurybia virgata* Hook. f.) A variable, medium-sized to large, hardy shrub of dense habit, with long, wiry, 4-angled stems. Leaves, 1–2cm long, narrowly obovate to linear, arranged in pairs or in small clusters. Flowers in June are small and of little ornamental value. New Zealand. **var. lineata** Kirk. (*O. lineata* (Kirk) Cockayne) A large, very graceful shrub of loose habit, with long, slender, angular, pendent branches. Leaves narrowly linear. New Zealand.

viscosa (Labill.) Benth. Small shrub, up to 2m, with sticky young shoots and shiny green, lanceolate leaves, silvery-white beneath. Broad corymbs of flowers in July and August. Tasmania, SE Australia. An extremely floriferous form, introduced by Sir Harold Hillier in 1977, is proving very hardy.

'Waikariensis' See *O.* × *oleifolia* 'Waikariensis'.

†**'Zennorensis'** (*O. ilicifolia* × *O. lacunosa*) A striking foliage plant, up to 2m, with narrow, pointed, sharply toothed leaves, about 10cm long and 12mm wide, dark olive-green above, white beneath. Young stems and leaf stalks heavily coated with pale brown tomentum. Originated in the garden of that splendid gardener Arnold Foster at Zennor, Cornwall. A first class shrub for a less cold garden. Excellent in maritime exposure. It is a form of the true *O.* × *mollis*. ♀ 2002.

Oleaster See *Elaeagnus angustifolia*.
Olive See *Olea europaea*.

ONONIS L.—**Leguminosae**—About 75 species of often spiny herbs and shrubs, natives of Europe, the Canary Islands, N Africa and W Asia. The shrubby members come from S and C Europe and make useful dwarf subjects for a border or rock garden. All have trifoliolate leaves and pea-shaped flowers. They require full sun and succeed in any well-drained soil including shallow chalk soils.

arvensis L. (*O. hircina* Jacq.) A small, moderately hardy, subshrub producing in summer dense, leafy racemes of pink flowers. Europe.

fruticosa L. A splendid small shrub forming a compact mound to 1m high. Bright rose-pink flowers are borne in small clusters throughout summer. Leaflets narrow. W Mediterranean region. C 1680. AM 1926.

rotundifolia L. A vigorous but none-too-persistent, sub-shrubby species, rather dwarfer than *O. fruticosa*, and with larger, rounded leaflets. Flowers bright rose-pink, continuous during summer. C and S Europe. C in England since the 17th century.

OPLOPANAX (Torr. & A. Gray) Miq. (*Echinopanax* Decne. & Planch.)—**Araliaceae**—A genus of only 3 species, differing from *Eleutherococcus* (*Acanthopanax*) in the simple leaves. Natives of W North America, Korea and Japan.

horridus (Sm.) Miq. (*Echinopanax horridus* (Sm.) J.G. Cooper) Devil's club. A small to medium-sized shrub with stout, spiny stems and broad, palmate, maple-like leaves, which are prickly along the veins beneath. Flowers greenish-white, in panicles, followed by scarlet fruits. W North America. I 1828.

Oregon boxwood See *Paxistima myrsinites*.

ORIXA Thunb.—**Rutaceae**—A monotypic genus. Any well-drained soil.

japonica Thunb. A pungently aromatic, dioecious, medium-sized shrub with bright green leaves that change to palest lemon or white in autumn, contrasting with the more prevalent reds and purples of that season. Japan, China, Korea. I 1870. **'Variegata'** This has puckered leaves that are shaded silvery-grey, with a broad, creamy-white margin. Particularly attractive as the leaves emerge when the small, greenish, pungent flowers are also profusely borne in panicles from the old wood. We are indebted to Robert de Belder for this interesting and rare form.

Osage orange See *Maclura pomifera*.
Osier, common See *Salix viminalis*.

*****OSMANTHUS** Lour.—**Oleaceae**—A genus of about 35 species of evergreen shrubs and trees, natives of the S USA, Asia and the Pacific Islands. The following are attractive and useful, often somewhat holly-like shrubs, doing well in almost all soils. Flowers small, white or cream, usually fragrant.

†**americanus** (L.) A. Gray. Devil wood. A large shrub or small tree with obovate to oblanceolate, leathery, glossy green, entire leaves, up to 15cm long. The fragrant, white flowers are borne in short axillary panicles in spring. Fruits dark blue. Requires a warm sheltered position or conservatory. SE USA, N Mexico. C 1758.

aquifolium See *O. heterophyllus*.

armatus Diels. A handsome, large shrub of dense habit. Leaves elliptic or oblong-lanceolate, thick and rigid, up to 18cm long, edged with stout, often hooked, spiny teeth. Flowers in autumn, sweetly scented. Thrives in sun or shade. A splendid evergreen worthy of more extensive planting. W China. I 1902 by Ernest Wilson.

× **burkwoodii** (Burkw. & Skipw.) P.S. Green (× *Osmarea burkwoodii* Burkw. & Skipw.) (*O. delavayi* × *O. decorus*) This is a first class, hardy shrub of compact growth, slowly attaining 2.5–3m. Leaves oval 2.5–5cm long, dark shining green, leathery and toothed. The very fragrant, white flowers are profusely borne in April or May. Raised by Burkwood and Skipwith about 1930. ♀ 2002. AM 1978.

decorus (Boiss. & Bal.) Kasapl. (*Phillyrea decora* Boiss. & Bal., *Phillyrea decora* 'Latifolia') A dome-shaped bush, up to 3m, usually wider than high, with comparatively large, leathery leaves, which are more or less entire, glossy green above. The clusters of small, fragrant, white flowers are borne freely in spring and followed by purplish-black fruits like miniature plums. A very distinct, tough evergreen worthy of more extensive planting. W Asia. I 1866. FCC 1888. **'Baki Kasapligil'** A form with narrow leaves. Originally distributed as *Phillyrea decora*.

delavayi Franch. (*Siphonosmanthus delavayi* (Franch.) Stapf) One of China's gems. A very beautiful, small-leaved species, slowly growing to 2m high and more in diameter, and bearing fragrant, white, jessamine-like flowers profusely in April. China (Sichuan, Yunnan). I 1890 by the Abbé Delavay. ♀ 2002. FCC 1931. AM 1914. **'Latifolius'** A distinct, taller form with broader, more rotund leaves.

forrestii See *O. yunnanensis*.

× **fortunei** Carrière (*O. fragrans* × *O. heterophyllus*) A large, comparatively vigorous shrub of dense habit. Large, broad ovate, dark polished green leaves, conspicuously veined above, are edged with spiny teeth, giving them a holly-like appearance. They often become entire on mature plants. Flowers delightfully fragrant, produced during autumn. Japan. I 1862 by Robert Fortune. **'Variegatus'** The plant listed under this name is usually *O. heterophyllus* 'Latifolius Variegatus', however, a variegated form of *O.* × *fortunei* is grown in Japan.

†**fragrans** Lour. (*Olea fragrans* Thunb.) A large shrub or small tree with large, oblong-lanceolate, finely toothed

leaves. Flowers deliciously and strongly fragrant in summer. A wall shrub for growing in the mildest localities, this plant will not survive the average British winter. China, Japan. I 1771. **f. aurantiacus** (Makino) P.S. Green. This is an unusual form that produces yellowish-orange flowers.

heterophyllus (G. Don) P.S. Green (*O. aquifolium* Siebold) (*O. ilicifolius* (Hassk.) Carr.) A rather slow-growing, holly-like shrub, occasionally a small tree. Leaves almost as variable as in the common holly, entire or coarsely spine-toothed, dark shining green. Sweetly scented flowers in autumn. Often mistaken for a holly but readily distinguished by its opposite leaves. Makes a useful dense hedge. Japan, Taiwan. I 1856 by Thomas Lobb. FCC 1859. **'Argenteomarginatus'** See 'Variegatus'. **'Aureomarginatus'** ('Aureovariegatus') ('Aureus') Leaves margined deep yellow. C 1877. **'Goshiki'** A striking form in which the leaves are conspicuously mottled with yellow, bronze-tinged when young. The name means 5-coloured. **'Gulftide'** Leaves somewhat lobed or twisted and strongly spiny; of dense habit. A remarkable and well worthwhile shrub. ♀ 2002. **'Latifolius Variegatus'** (*O.* × *fortunei* 'Variegatus') Similar to 'Variegatus' but leaves broader and less deeply toothed. It appears to belong here and not to *O.* × *fortunei*. **'Myrtifolius'** A neat slow-growing, compact form with small, spineless leaves. C 1894. **'Purpureus'** Growths deep purple at first, later green, slightly tinged purple. Raised at Kew in 1860. **'Rotundifolius'** A curious slow-growing form of neat, compact habit, with short, thick, black-green, leathery leaves, which are spineless but bluntly toothed and occasionally twisted. C 1866. **'Sasaba'** A remarkable form of Japanese origin, the leaves deeply cut into numerous, spine-tipped lobes. The name means bamboo-leaf. **'Variegatus'** ('Argenteomarginatus') Leaves bordered with creamy-white. C 1861. ♀ 2002.

ilicifolius See *O. heterophyllus*.

serrulatus Rehder. A medium-sized to large shrub of compact, rounded habit. Leaves large, ovate-lanceolate, sharply toothed or entire, glossy dark green. Clusters of white, fragrant flowers are borne in the leaf axils in spring. Himalaya. I 1910.

suavis C.B. Clarke (*Siphonosmanthus suavis* (King ex C.B. Clarke) Stapf) An erect-growing shrub up to 4m, related to *O. delavayi*, but differing in its 8cm long, oblong-lanceolate, sharply toothed, shining green leaves. Fragrant flowers are borne in spring. This species has grown well in the Sir Harold Hillier Gardens and Arboretum for many years. Himalaya.

yunnanensis (Franch.) P.S. Green (*O. forrestii* Rehder) A remarkable, large shrub or small tree. Leaves lanceolate, dark olive-green, up to 15cm long, varying from undulate and coarsely toothed to flat and entire, both on the same plant. Flowers ivory-white, fragrant, produced during late winter. This splendid plant has proven hardy in the Sir Harold Hillier Gardens and Arboretum given shelter. China (Yunnan, Sichuan). I 1923 by George Forrest. AM 1967.

× *Osmarea burkwoodii* See *Osmanthus* × *burkwoodii*.
Osmaronia cerasiformis See *Oemleria cerasiformis*.

†***OSTEOMELES** Lindl.—**Rosaceae**—A genus of probably 3 species of small to medium-sized, evergreen shrubs, natives of E Asia and the Pacific Islands. They have pinnate leaves with tiny leaflets and corymbs of small, white flowers followed by small fruits. They need the protection of a sunny wall, where they will succeed in any well-drained soil.

subrotunda K. Koch. A pretty small to medium-sized, slow-growing shrub with slender, arching shoots and dainty pinnate, fern-like leaves, composed of small, glossy green leaflets. Hawthorn-like flowers appear in June, followed by reddish fruits. Requires wall protection in cold districts. The plant described may be a form of the similar and very variable *O. schweriniae*. E China. I 1894.

OSTRYA Scop.—**Corylaceae**—A small genus of medium-sized to large, deciduous trees, resembling the hornbeam (*Carpinus*) and notable in autumn when arrayed with their hop-like fruits. About 10 species, natives of the N hemisphere south to Central America. The following are easy to cultivate in any fertile soil.

carpinifolia Scop. (*O. vulgaris* Willd.) Hop hornbeam. A round-headed tree of medium size, with ovate, double-toothed leaves, 8–13cm long, which give clear yellow autumn tints. Fruits 3.5–5cm long, each nutlet contained in a flat, bladder-like husk. Enchanting in spring when the many branches are strung with numerous, long, drooping male catkins. S Europe, W Asia. I 1724. AM 1976.

japonica Sarg. Japanese hop hornbeam. A small to medium-sized tree with ovate to ovate-oblong leaves, 7–13cm long, velvety hairy beneath. Conspicuous when bearing its multitudes of green, hop-like fruits, 4–5cm long. Japan, Korea, China. I 1888.

virginiana (Mill.) K. Koch. Ironwood. A rare and attractive, small tree of elegant, rounded or pyramidal habit, differing from *O. carpinifolia* in its glandular-hairy shoots and fewer-veined leaves. Rich, warm yellow autumn tints. E North America. I 1692.

OSTRYOPSIS Decne.—**Corylaceae**—A rare genus of 2 species of medium to large shrubs of botanical interest, natives of China and Mongolia, differing from *Ostrya* in the clustered, not racemose, fruits. Any fertile soil.

davidiana (Baill.) Decne. A medium-sized, somewhat suckering shrub with the general appearance of the common hazel (*Corylus avellana*) but with sessile, red glands on the undersurface of the leaves and long-stalked fruit clusters. N and W China. I about 1865.

†**OTHONNA** L.—**Compositae**—A genus of about 150 species of shrubs and herbs, natives mainly of tropical and South Africa. The following needs a warm position in full sun and well-drained soil.

*cheirifolia L. (*Othonnopsis cheirifolia* (L.) Benth. & Hook.) A dwarf shrub with spreading stems and short, ascending branches, clothed with distinctive paddle-shaped, grey-green leaves. The golden-yellow flower-heads are borne singly at the ends of the shoots in spring and summer and intermittently through autumn and winter. Algeria, Tunisia. I 1752.

Othonnopsis cheirifolia See *Othonna cheirifolia*.
Our Lord's candle See *Yucca whipplei*.
Oxycoccus macrocarpus See *Vaccinium macrocarpum*.
Oxycoccus palustris See *Vaccinium oxycoccos*.

‡**OXYDENDRUM** DC.—**Ericaceae**—A monotypic genus succeeding in shade or sun given a lime-free soil.
arboreum (L.) DC. (*Andromeda arborea* L.) Sorrel tree. A beautiful, large shrub or small tree, grown chiefly for its exquisite crimson and yellow autumn colouring. The white flowers, in slender, drooping racemes, are produced in clusters from the tips of the shoots in July and August. The leaves possess a pleasant acid flavour. Thrives under conditions suitable for rhododendrons. E USA. I 1752. FCC 1972 (for autumn foliage). AM 1957 (for flowers). AM 1951 (for autumn colour).

†*****OXYLOBUS** (DC.) A. Gray—**Compositae**—A genus of 5 species succeeding in any well-drained soil but only in mild gardens. They are all native to Mexico.
arbutifolius A. Gray. A small shrublet with roughly glandular-hairy shoots. Flowerheads white, borne in erect, slender-stalked corymbs from June onwards. Mexico.

Oxypetalum caeruleum See *Tweedia caerulea* under CLIMBERS.

*****OZOTHAMNUS** R. Br.—**Compositae**—Evergreen, summer-flowering shrubs related to *Helichrysum*, under which name they are sometimes found. They require full sun and a well-drained position. About 50 species, natives of Australia and New Zealand.
†*antennaria* (DC.) Hook. f. (*Helichrysum antennaria* (DC.) F. Muell. ex. Benth.) A small to medium-sized, dense evergreen with narrowly obovate or spathulate, leathery leaves, grey beneath, glossy green above. Flowerheads white, in dense, terminal clusters opening in June. Tasmania. I before 1880.
ericifolius See under *O. purpurascens*.
hookeri Sond. (*Helichrysum hookeri* (Sond.) Druce) An upright or spreading small shrub, the rigid shoots densely covered in white wool. Tiny, revolute, sticky, aromatic leaves, the upper surface glossy green and closely pressed to the shoot, the lower surface densely woolly. Flowers small, white in small flowerheads clustered towards the ends of the shoots in summer. SE Australia, Tasmania.
ledifolius (DC.) Hook. f. (*Helichrysum ledifolium* (DC.) Benth.) Kerosene bush. This species makes a small, globular, dense, aromatic shrub. Leaves are broadly linear with recurved margins and yellow backs. Flowers comparatively large, their inner bracts with conspicuous, white, spreading tips, reddish in bud. Seedheads emit a sweet honey-like aroma. A superb shrub displaying its incurved terminal yellow leaves. Uninjured by the severe winters of 1962–63 and the 1980s. Tasmania. I 1930. ♥ 2002.

leptophyllus (G. Forst.) Breitw. & J.M. Ward (*Cassinia leptophylla* (G. Forst.) R. Br., *C. vauvilliersii* Hook. f.) Mountain cottonwood. Erect, greyish shrub, up to 2m, with tiny leaves, white or yellowish-downy beneath. White flowerheads in terminal corymbs in August and September. New Zealand. **Albidus Group** (*Cassinia vaulvilliersii* var. *albida* (Kirk) Cockayne) Silver heather. An attractive form with white-hoary stems and leaves. **Fulvidus Group** (*Cassinia fulvida* Hook. f.) Golden heather, Golden cottonwood. A small, erect, dense shrub. The small, crowded leaves give a golden effect; white flowers in dense, terminal heads in July. Young growths sticky to the touch.
†*purpurascens* DC. An erect, pleasantly aromatic shrub of medium size. Leaves narrow, like those of a rosemary, sticky to the touch. Flowers white, tinged with purple in bud, in terminal heads. Tasmania. Originally listed as *O. ericifolius* (*Helichrysum ericeteum*).
rosmarinifolius (Labill.) DC. (*Helichrysum rosmarinifolium* (Labill.) Steud. ex Benth.) A medium-sized shrub with white-woolly stems and dark green, linear, verrucose leaves. The dense corymbs of red buds are spectacular for 10 days or more before they open to white, scented flowers. One of the hardiest species, given hot sun and a well-drained soil it can survive for many years. Tasmania, SE Australia. I 1827. AM 1968. **'Kiandra'** A vigorous form flowering freely over a long period from spring to summer. I by Graham Hutchins in 1990. **'Silver Jubilee'** A rather tender form with silvery-grey leaves. It was selected by John May from seedlings collected in the wild in SE Tasmania in 1978 and named for the anniversary of Queen Elizabeth II. ♥ 2002.
scutellifolius (Hook. f.) Benth. (*Helichrysum scutellifolium* (Hook. f.) Benth.) A curious dwarf species reaching 120cm in the wild. Slender, antler-like shoots are clothed with white down through which the circular, grey-green, adpressed leaves peep. Flowers yellow in terminal clusters. A plant for a rock garden. Tasmania.
selago Hook. f. (*Helichrysum selago* (Hook. f.) Benth. & Hook.) A dwarf shrublet of variable growth. The slender, erect or ascending stems are rather stiffly held and much-branched. Tiny, green, scale-like leaves are closely adpressed to the stems. They are smooth on the outside, but coated white on the inside, and give the stems a chequered appearance. Small, creamy-yellow flowerheads are borne at the tips of the shoots in June. A plant for a rock garden or alpine house. New Zealand. **'Major'** A more robust selection with thicker stems and larger leaves. AM 1987.
†*thyrsoideus* DC. (*O. rosmarinifolius* hort., *Helichrysum thyrsoideum* (DC.) Willis & Morris, *H. diosmifolium* hort.) Snow in summer. This delightful plant was well known long before related species were introduced from Tasmania by Harold Comber. A medium-sized shrub with slender, spreading, angular branches and spreading, linear leaves. Flowerheads white, in large terminal corymbs during summer. Australia, Tasmania. AM 1925.

P

Pachistima See *Paxistima*.

PACHYSANDRA Michx.—**Buxaceae**—A small genus of 4 or 5 species of dwarf shrubs or subshrubs, with monoecious flowers, natives of North America and E Asia. Suitable for groundcover in moist, shaded sites. They do not luxuriate in shallow chalk soils.

*axillaris Franch. A dwarf, tufted, evergreen shrublet, with comparatively large leaves. Less spreading than *P. terminalis*. Flowers white, produced in short axillary spikes in April. China. I 1901 by Ernest Wilson.

procumbens Michx. Alleghany spurge. A dwarf, creeping, semi-evergreen subshrub bearing terminal clusters of ovate to obovate leaves. Flowers, with conspicuous pale stamens, are borne in crowded cylindrical spikes on the lower halves of the shoots during spring. SE USA. I 1800.

*terminalis Siebold & Zucc. A very useful dwarf, evergreen, carpeting shrublet for covering bare places under trees. Leaves clustered at the ends of the stems, rather diamond-shaped and toothed in the upper half. Spikes of greenish-white flowers are produced at the ends of the previous year's shoots in February and March. Japan. I 1882.'**Green Carpet**' A compact form with small leaves making good groundcover. ♀ 2002. '**Variegata**' Leaves attractively variegated white. ♀ 2002.

Pachystegia insignis See *Olearia insignis*.
Pachystima See *Paxistima*.

PAEONIA L.—**Paeoniaceae**—The peonies consist of 30 or so species of mainly herbaceous perennials, natives of the north temperate regions of Europe, Asia and W North America. The shrubby members or tree peonies come from W China and SE Tibet and are represented in gardens by a few species and their varieties and hybrids, but the term is most commonly applied to those that have originated from *P. suffruticosa*. These are among the most gorgeously coloured of all shrubs. Such species as *P. delavayi* and *P. ludlowii* have splendid foliage of architectural quality. Given full sun and a sheltered site they will thrive in any well-drained soil.

While they are winter hardy, the young growth is susceptible to damage by night frost in the spring and it is wise to provide artificial protection at this time. A sacking screen may be erected on a tripod of bamboos, the covering being positioned nightly during periods of frost, and removed after frost has gone off in the morning. Once growth has been hardened the screen may be removed entirely.

arborea See *P. suffruticosa*.

decomposita Hand.-Mazz. (*P. szechuanica* Fang) A beautiful, small shrub with purple-red young shoots and flaking bark on older stems. The large leaves are finely cut and the pink flowers up to 15cm across. Closely related to *P. suffruticosa* and *P. rockii* but with much more finely cut leaves and glabrous fruits. NW Sichuan. I by Mikinori Ogisu in 1996.

delavayi Franch. A handsome, suckering shrub, attaining 2m. Flowers, in May, deepest crimson with golden anthers, followed by large, black-seeded fruits, surrounded by conspicuously coloured, persistent sepals. The large, deeply cut leaves place this plant in the category of shrubs grown for the quality of their leaves. An excellent shrub for chalky soils. W China. I 1908. ♀ 2002. AM 1934. **var. angustiloba** See *P. delavayi* Potaninii Group. **Lutea Group** (*P. lutea* Franch.) A bold shrub of about 2m, possessing the foliage qualities of *P. delavayi*, in fact from leaf only they are difficult to tell apart. Flowers, borne in May or June, are cup-shaped, 6cm across, resembling those of the king cup or marsh marigold (*Caltha palustris*). Yunnan. I 1886. FCC 1903. **Potaninii Group** (*P. potaninii* Komar., *P. delavayi* var. *angustiloba* Rehder & E.H. Wilson) A suckering shrub, up to 60cm, forming small patches of glabrous stems and deeply divided, narrowly lobed leaves. Flowers deep maroon, 5–6cm across, nodding, appearing in May. W China. I 1904. **Potaninii Alba Group** (*P. potaninii* f. *alba* (Bean) Stern) Similar to Potaninii Group but with creamy-white flowers. **Trollioides Group** (*P. potaninii* var. *trollioides* (Stapf) Stern) Resembling Potaninii Group but habit more upright, reaching 1m. Flowers yellow, like *Trollius*. I 1914 by George Forrest from Yunnan. AM 1980.

× *lemoinei* Rehder (*P. delavayi* Lutea Group × *P. suffruticosa*) By this cross, tree peonies with enormous, yellow flowers have been produced and also cultivars showing gorgeous colour combinations. Most will reach 1.5–2m in height and flower in May or June. They appreciate a rich soil and do well on chalk. First raised by Messrs Lemoine about 1909. '**Alice Harding**' Flowers large, fully double, canary-yellow. AMT 1960. '**Argosy**' Flowers semi-double, pale yellow, streaked carmine at the base. FCC 1956. AM 1937. '**Chromatella**' Flowers large, double, sulphur-yellow. A sport of 'Souvenir de Maxime Cornu'. '**Souvenir de Maxime Cornu**' Flowers fragrant, very large, double, bright yellow, edged with carmine.

ludlowii (Stern & Taylor) D.Y. Hong (*P. lutea* var. *ludlowii* Stern & Taylor, *P. lutea* 'Sherriff's Variety') A vigorous, medium-sized to large shrub with stout, unbranched stems and bold, deeply cut leaves. This splendid species, first collected by Kingdon-Ward and subsequently by Ludlow and Sherriff in SE Tibet, has large, golden-yellow, saucer-shaped flowers, opening as the large and conspicuous leaves are beginning to expand. ♀ 2002. AM 1954.

lutea See *P. delavayi* Lutea Group. **var. ludlowii** See *P. ludlowii*.

moutan See *P. suffruticosa*.

potaninii See *P. delavayi* Potaninii Group. **f. alba** See *P. delavayi* Potaninii Alba Group. **var. trollioides** See *P. delavayi* Trollioides Group.

rockii (Haw & Lauener) Hong & Li (*P. suffruticosa* 'Rock's Variety') A beautiful species with very large, single, palest flesh-pink flowers, passing to silver-white, marked at the base of each petal with a maroon splash. We are indebted to the untiring American collector Joseph Rock for the introduction of several new species and many good hardy forms of hitherto tender subjects. China (SE Gansu, S Shaanxi, W Henan and W Hubei). I by Joseph Rock. FCC 1943.

suffruticosa Haw. (*P. moutan* Sims, *P. arborea* Donn ex K. Koch) Moutan peony. A branching shrub, up to 2m, with large flowers, 15cm or more across, in May. China (SW Shanxi and Shaanxi). Flowers white in the wild. The following is only a selection of the numerous cultivars of this species. **'Godaishu'** White with yellow centre, semi-double to double. **'Goshazaki'** Lustrous pink. **'Hana-kisoi'** Deep cherry-red, double, large. **'Higurashi'** Vivid crimson, semi-double, large. **'Hodai'** Rosy-red, double, large. **'Jitsugetsu-nishiki'** Bright scarlet with deeper sheen, semi-double to double. **'Kumagai'** Deep pink turning to magenta, double. **'Renkaku'** Pure white, irregularly cut petals, double, large. **'Rock's Variety'** See *P. rockii*. **'Sakurajishi'** Lustrous pink, irregularly cut petals, double, large. **'Shichi-fukigin'** Bright crimson, soft pink margin. **'Shunkoden'** Rosy-violet, semi-double. **'Taiyo'** Brilliant red with satin sheen of maroon, semi-double. **'Yachiyo-tsubaki'** Phlox-pink, shading to soft neyron-rose tips, long petals ruffled and fringed at edges, semi-double to double.

szechuanica See *P. decomposita*.

Pagoda tree See *Sophora japonica*.

PALIURUS Mill.—**Rhamnaceae**—A small genus of about 8 species of deciduous, spiny trees and shrubs, requiring plenty of sun and good drainage. Natives of S Europe to E Asia. *P. spina-christi* is one of the plants from which the Crown of Thorns is said to have been made. Any fertile soil.

spina-christi Mill. (*P. aculeatus* Lam.) Christ's thorn. A medium-sized to large, straggling shrub, the long thin stems armed with innumerable pairs of unequal thorns. The ovate leaves turn yellow in autumn. Flowers small, greenish-yellow in late summer. The curious circular fruits remind one of miniature cardinal's hats. S Europe to Himalaya, and N China. C 1597.

Palm, Canary Island date, See *Phoenix canariensis*.
Palm, Chusan See *Trachycarpus fortunei*.
Palm, Chinese windmill See *Trachycarpus fortunei*.
Palm, desert fan See *Washingtonia filifera*.
Palm, dwarf fan See *Chamaerops humilis*.
Palm, jelly See *Butia capitata*.
Palm, thread See *Washingtonia robusta*.
Parabenzoin praecox See *Lindera praecox*.

PARAHEBE W.R.B. Oliv.—**Scrophulariaceae**—A small genus of about 30 species of semi-woody, dwarf plants intermediate between *Hebe* and *Veronica*, formerly included under the latter. Natives of New Zealand and Australia. Suitable for a rock garden in all types of soil.

× *bidwillii* (Hook.) W.R.B. Oliv. (*P. decora* × *P. lyallii*) A naturally occurring hybrid most closely resembling and at one time confused with, *P. decora*, from which it differs in its more vigorous growth and larger leaves often with two pairs of teeth. New Zealand (South Island). **'Kea'** A prostrate shrublet with glossy dark green leaves to 6mm long and slender racemes of white flowers with crimson veins.

catarractae (G. Forst.) W.R.B. Oliv. (*Veronica catarractae* G. Forst.) A dwarf plant forming low, spreading mounds, making excellent groundcover in full sun. Leaves small,

ovate or lanceolate, acute, coarsely serrate. Flowers white to rose-purple with a crimson central zone, in slender, erect racemes in late summer. New Zealand. Blue-flowered forms are often cultivated. **'Delight'** Flowers white, veined heliotrope, profusely borne over a long period. ♀ 2002. **subsp. *diffusa*** (Hook. f.) Garn.-Jones. A smaller-leaved form, forming dense mats. Flowers white, veined rose-pink. **'Miss Willmott'** Flowers veined with mauve.

decora Aswhin. Creeping subshrub forming low hummocks and patches. Leaves tiny, to 5mm long, ovate or rounded, entire or with 1 or rarely 2 pairs of teeth. Flowers white or pink, borne in long-stalked racemes in summer. New Zealand (South Island). Sometimes grown as *P. × bidwilli* q.v.

lyallii (Hook. f.) W.R.B. Oliv. (*Veronica lyallii* Hook. f.) A low, prostrate shrublet with small, rounded or ovate leaves, which are leathery and slightly crenate. Flowers white, prettily veined pink, anthers blue, appearing in slender racemes from July to August. New Zealand (South Island). I 1870. **'Julie-Anne'** Low-growing with small leaves and profuse pale lilac flowers with deeper blotches and veins in summer and autumn. ♀ 2002. **'Snowcap'** Flowers white with brown veins. Long, dark green, toothed leaves.

'Mervyn' A dwarf, spreading shrub with small, red-edged leaves and racemes of lilac-blue flowers in summer. Probably a hybrid of *P. lyallii*.

†*perfoliata* (R. Br.) B.G. Briggs & Ehrend. (*Veronica perfoliata* R. Br.) Digger's speedwell. A dwarf subshrub, herbaceous in most areas, with erect stems usually about 30–45cm. Leaves perfoliate, greyish-green. Flowers violet-blue, borne in long axillary racemes in late summer. An unusual plant for a sunny, well-drained spot in mild areas. Australia. I 1834. ♀ 2002.

PARASERIANTHES I. Nielsen—**Leguminosae**—A small genus of 4 species of tender trees closely related to *Albizia* and *Acacia* and natives of SE Asia, New Guinea, the Solomon Islands and Australia.

lophantha (Willd.) I. Nielsen (*Albizia lophantha* (Willd.) Benth., *A. distachya* (Vent.) Macbr.) Cape Leeuwin wattle, Crested wattle. A large shrub or small tree with beautiful, pinnate or doubly pinnate leaves, to 20cm long; sulphur-yellow, bottlebrush-like racemes of flowers are produced in spring or earlier under glass. Only suitable for the mildest localities. SW Australia. I 1803.

Parasyringa sempervirens See *Ligustrum sempervirens*.

PARROTIA C.A. Mey.—**Hamamelidaceae**—A monotypic genus, remarkably lime-tolerant for the *Hamamelis* family. A Chinese tree, originally described as a species of *Hamamelis*, has recently been transferred to this genus (*Parrotia subaequalis* (H. T. Chang) R.M. Hao & H.T. Wei), it has been introduced to cultivation in Britain.

jacquemontiana See *Parrotiopsis jacquemontiana*.

persica (DC.) C.A. Mey. Persian ironwood. A large shrub or small tree of widespreading habit. Bark of older stems delightfully flaking like that of the London plane (*Platanus × hispanica*). Leaves turning crimson and gold in autumn. Flowers consisting of clusters of crimson stamens, appear in mid- to late winter and early spring. One of the finest small trees for autumn colour, even on chalk.

N Iran to the Caucasus. C 1840. ♀ 2002. FCC 1884.
'Pendula' A form with pendent branches, slowly developing into a dome-shaped mound, 1.8–3m high. Becoming a richly coloured pile in autumn. **'Vanessa'** A form of more tree-like habit. It has glossy red shoots and young leaves, conspicuously edged with bronze-red. A seedling selected in Holland in 1975.

PARROTIOPSIS (Nied.) C.K. Schneid.—**Hamamelidaceae**—A monotypic genus best in an acid or neutral soil, but moderately lime-tolerant. May be grown over chalk given 60cm of good soil.
jacquemontiana (Decne.) Rehder (*Parrotia jacquemontiana* Decne.) A large shrub of erect habit. Leaves rounded or broadly ovate, usually turning yellow in autumn. The flower clusters, reminiscent of *Cornus florida*, being subtended by conspicuous white bracts, are produced during April and May and intermittently throughout summer. W Himalaya. I 1879.

Parrot's bill See *Clianthus puniceus*.
Partridge berry See *Mitchella repens*.
Pasania edulis See *Lithocarpus edulis*.

PAULOWNIA Siebold & Zucc.—**Scrophulariaceae**—A small genus of about 6 species of E Asian trees. The species here listed are among the grandest of ornamental flowering trees. Their foxglove-shaped flowers, which are not borne on very young trees, are carried in erect panicles and, though formed in autumn, do not open until the following spring. The leaves of mature trees are large, while on vigorous, pruned plants they are enormous. Owing to the colour of their flowers, these trees are best planted where they can be viewed from above; the site should be in full sun, but sheltered from gales. All types of deep, well-drained soil.
fargesii Franch. A magnificent tree of 18–21m which, though more recently introduced, seems to be better adapted to our climate than the better known *P. tomentosa*, and flowers at a comparatively early age. Flowers fragrant, heliotrope, freely speckled dark purple in the throat and with a creamy basal stain. W China. I about 1896.
fargesii hort. See *P. tomentosa* 'Lilacina'.
fortunei (Seem.) Hemsl. A rare, small tree, similar in habit to *P. tomentosa*. Flowers fragrant, creamy-white, heavily marked with deep purple on the inside, flushed lilac on the outside. China, Taiwan.
imperialis See *P. tomentosa*.
lilacina See *P. tomentosa* 'Lilacina'.
tomentosa (Thunb.) Steud. (*P. imperialis* Siebold & Zucc.) This well-known species forms a round-topped tree, 9–12m high. The flowers are heliotrope, and, providing they come through the winter and escape a late frost, give a wonderful display in May. Alternatively, young plants may be pruned to the ground in spring and the resultant suckers thinned to a single shoot. Such is its vigour the shoot will reach 2.5–3m in a single season and clothe itself with huge leaves up to 60cm or more across. China. I via Japan in 1834. ♀ 2002. AM 1934. **'Lilacina'** (*P. lilacina* Sprague, *P. fargesii* hort. not Franch.) This differs mainly in its unlobed leaves and lilac flowers, pale yellow in the throat, in June. China. C about 1908. FCC 1944.

Pawpaw See *Asimina triloba*.

***PAXISTIMA** Raf. (*Pachistima*, *Pachystima*)—**Celastraceae**—A genus of 2 species of interesting, but not conspicuous, dwarf, evergreen shrubs of neat habit, with tiny leaves and quadrangular stems. Not recommended for shallow chalk soils. They do best in a moist shady position.
canbyi A. Gray. Leaves narrow, small greenish flowers during summer. Fruits white. Makes an unusual dwarf hedge or groundcover. E USA. C 1800.
myrsinites (Pursh) Raf. (*P. myrtifolia* (Nutt.) Wheeler) Oregon boxwood. Leaves small, leathery, toothed in upper half; opposite. Flowers tiny, 4-petalled, red, produced in March. W North America, N Mexico. C 1879.
myrtifolia See *P. myrsinites*.

Pea tree See *Caragana arborescens*.
Peach See *Prunus persica*.
Peach, Chinese See *Prunus davidiana*.
Pear See *Pyrus*.
Pear, Bollwyller See × *Sorbopyrus auricularis*.
Pear, sand See *Pyrus pyrifolia*.
Pear, willow-leaved See *Pyrus salicifolia* 'Pendula'.
Pearl berry See *Margyricarpus pinnatus*.
Pearlbush See *Exochorda*.
Pecan See *Carya illinoinensis*.

PENSTEMON Schmidel (*Pentstemon*)—**Scrophulariaceae**—A large genus of some 250 species, mostly subshrubs and herbaceous plants, mainly from NW America and Mexico. The tender species require the shelter of a sunny wall while the hardy members make excellent rock garden plants. Full sun and good drainage.
cordifolius See *Keckiella cordifolia*.
corymbosus See *Keckiella corymbosa*.
davidsonii** Greene (*P. menziesii* Hook.) A dwarf or prostrate, evergreen shrublet for a rock garden with short-stalked, entire leaves broadest above the middle and erect racemes of large, tubular, purple flowers in May and June. NW North America. **var. *menziesii (D.D. Keck) Cronquist (*P. menziesii* Hook.) Leaves toothed, broadest at or below the middle. C 1902. ♀ 2002.
fruticosus (Pursh) Greene. This species is mainly represented in gardens by the following variety. **var. *scouleri*** (Lindl.) Cronquist (*P. scouleri* Lindl.) A charming, dwarf subshrub with narrow, lanceolate leaves and large, lilac-coloured blossoms, in erect racemes, in June. Suitable for a rock garden. W North America. I 1828. ♀ 2002. AM 1951. **'Albus'** A form with white flowers. ♀ 2002.
heterophyllus Lindl. A dwarf, erect shrublet with long, narrow leaves. California. I 1828 by David Douglas. **'Blue Springs'** Glossy foliage and striking blue and mauve flowers over a long period. Possibly a hybrid. **'Blue Gem'** Lovely azure blue, tubular flowers in long racemes during summer. **'Catherine de la Mare'** Low, spreading habit with glossy dark green foliage and glowing blue-mauve flowers. Possibly a hybrid. ♀ 2002. **'Heavenly Blue'** Rich lilac-blue flowers over a long period from late spring to summer.
menziesii See *P. davidsonii* var. *menziesii*.
***newberryi** A. Gray. A variable dwarf subshrub. Plants under this name belong mainly to the following form.

♀ 2002. **f. humilior** Sealy (*P. roezlii* hort.) A dwarf shrub, suitable for a rock garden, similar to *P. davidsonii*, but with longer, pointed leaves and scarlet flowers in profusion in June. W USA.

*__pinifolius__ Greene. A dwarf, evergreen shrub with very slender, needle-like, pointed leaves. The bright scarlet, tubular flowers end in 5-pointed lobes and are borne in terminal spikes in late summer. A first-class rock garden plant. SW North America. ♀ 2002. **'Mersea Yellow'** A selection with bright yellow flowers. **'Wisley Flame'** Vigorous habit with scarlet flowers. A chance seedling raised at Wisley. ♀ 2002.

rupicola (Piper) Howell. A dwarf, mat-forming shrub with small, blue-green leaves and dense racemes of deep pink flowers, late spring to summer. An excellent rock garden plant. W. North America. ♀ 2002.

scouleri See *P. fruticosus* var. *scouleri*.

‡***PENTACHONDRA** R. Br.—**Epacridaceae**—A small genus of 3 species of low-growing, evergreen shrubs for lime-free soils.

pumila (J.R. Forst. & G. Forst.) R. Br. A tiny shrublet, a few centimetres high. Procumbent stems are crowded with bronze-tinted, very small leaves. The small, cylindrical, white flowers are produced singly in the axils of the uppermost leaves in summer and are followed by red fruits. Tasmania, SE Australia, New Zealand.

Pentapera sicula See *Erica sicula*.
Pentapterygium rugosum See *Agapetes incurvata*.
Pentapterygium serpens See *Agapetes serpens*.
Pepper tree See *Pseodowintera colorata* and *Schinus molle*.

‡**PERAPHYLLUM** Nutt. ex Torr. & A. Gray—**Rosaceae**—A monotypic genus, related to *Amelanchier* but differing in its narrow leaves, long calyx tube and rounded petals. It is hardy and grows best in a hot, sunny position. Not recommended for chalk soils.

ramosissimum Nutt. Wild crab apple. A small to medium-sized shrub with clusters of narrowly oblanceolate leaves, which are obscurely toothed in their upper halves, and umbels of pink and white flowers in April and May. The cherry-like fruits are rarely produced in the British Isles. W North America. I 1870.

†***PERICALLIS** D. Don—**Compositae**—A genus of 14 species of herbs and shrubs at one time included in *Senecio*. Natives of the Canary Islands and including the common florists' cineraria.

lanata (L'Hérit.) B. Nord. (*Senecio heritieri* DC.) The true plant of this name is herbaceous with single flowerheads composed of mauve ray florets with a purple centre. Many plants grown as this species are, however, the following. S coast of Tenerife. C 1774.

'Purple Picotee' (*Senecio heritieri* hort.) A small, loose-growing shrub with broadly ovate, toothed or shallowly lobed leaves, 10–15cm long. Young stems and leaf undersurfaces covered by dense, white tomentum. Flowerheads white and crimson with purple centres, violet-scented, recalling the popular cineraria, borne in large panicles from May to July. Only suitable for the mildest areas or conservatory. Possibly *P. appendiculata* × *P. lanata*.

Periwinkle See *Vinca*.
Pernettya See *Gaultheria*.
Pernettya buxifolia See *Gaultheria myrsinoides*.
Pernettya ciliata See *Gaultheria myrsinoides*.
Pernettya empetrifolia See *Gaultheria pumila*.
Pernettya leucocarpa See *Gaultheria pumila* var. *leucocarpa*.
Pernettya mucronata See *Gaultheria mucronata*
Pernettya prostrata See *Gaultheria myrsinoides*.
Pernettya prostrata subsp. *pentlandii* See *Gaultheria myrsinoides*.
Pernettya pumila See *Gaultheria pumila*.
Pernettya tasmanica See *Gaultheria tasmanica*.

PEROVSKIA Kar.—**Labiatae**—A small genus of 7 species of late-flowering, aromatic subshrubs with deeply toothed or finely cut leaves, natives of C Asia to the Himalaya. They associate well with lavender for a blue and grey border, and succeed in a sunny position in all types of well-drained soil.

abrotanoides Kar. Small shrub with grey-hairy, branching stems and deeply cut, grey-green leaves. Flowers violet-blue in terminal panicles during late summer and autumn. Afghanistan to W Himalaya. C 1935.

atriplicifolia Benth. A small, Himalayan shrub with long, narrow panicles of lavender-blue flowers in late summer, blending perfectly with the grey foliage and whitish stems. Afghanistan, W Himalaya to Tibet. C 1904. AM 1928. **'Blue Spire'** See *P.* 'Blue Spire'.

'Blue Spire' (*P. atriplicifolia* 'Blue Spire') A beautiful selection with deeply cut leaves and even larger panicles of lavender-blue flowers. ♀ 2002. AM 1962.

'Filigram' Similar to 'Blue Spire' but with the leaves more deeply cut, almost to the midrib.

'Hybrida' (*P. abrotanoides* × *P. atriplicifolia*) An admirable plant for late summer effect, having deeply cut, grey-green leaves and very long panicles of deep lavender-blue flowers. Originated in our nurseries before 1937.

'Little Spire' Compact upright habit to about 65cm tall. Leaves greyer than 'Blue Spire' and less deeply cut, flowers deeper purple-blue. A seedling selected in Holland in 1995.

†***PERSEA** Mill.—**Lauraceae**—A large genus of some 150 species of evergreen shrubs and trees, widely distributed through tropical and warm temperate regions. *P. americana* Mill., the avocado pear, native to C America, is the most commonly grown.

borbonia (L.) Spreng. (*P. carolinensis* Nees) Red bay. A handsome, small tree with leaves glossy above, glaucous beneath. Bears dark blue fruits on red stalks. The wood is used in cabinet making. Only possible to grow in the mildest areas. SE USA. I 1739.

ichangensis (Rehder & E.H. Wilson) Kosterm. (*Machilus ichangensis* Rehder & E.H. Wilson) A small tree, semi-evergreen in the British Isles. Oblong-lanceolate to lanceolate, leathery, long-pointed leaves, 10–20cm long, are an attractive coppery colour when young. Flowers small, white, produced in short axillary panicles in late spring or early summer, followed by small shining black fruits. A rare species from C and SW China, introduced by Ernest Wilson about 1901.

Persian ironwood See *Parrotia persica*.

PERSICARIA Mill.—**Polygonaceae**—A genus of mainly herbaceous perennials which contains several garden favourites previously listed under *Polygonum*. The following is the best-known shrubby species.

vacciniifolia (Wall. ex Meisn.) Ronse Decr. (*Polygonum vacciniifolium* Wall. ex Meisn.) A prostrate, mat-forming shrub with slender stems and small, glossy green leaves, glaucous beneath. Flowers bright rose-pink, in slender erect spikes, in late summer and autumn. Himalaya. I 1845. ♀ 2002.

Persimmon See *Diospyros virginiana*.
Persimmon, Chinese See *Diospyros kaki*.

PERTYA Sch. Bip.—**Compositae**—A small genus of about 16 species of shrubs and herbs, natives of Afghanistan to Japan. The following is hardy and succeeds in all types of soil.

sinensis Oliv. A shrub up to 1.5m high. Leaves, bitter to the taste, 2.5–7.5cm long, taper-pointed and borne in rosettes. Flowerheads purplish-pink, daisy-like, about 12mm across, produced in June and July. Hubei, China. I 1901 by Ernest Wilson.

PETTERIA C. Presl—**Leguminosae**—A monotypic genus of restricted distribution. In the wild it seldom exceeds 1.2–1.5m. It succeeds in full sun in all types of well-drained soil.

ramentacea C. Presl. Dalmatian laburnum. An unusual shrub of upright habit, about 1.8–2.5m, with trifoliolate leaves. May be likened to a shrubby, erect-flowered laburnum, producing racemes of fragrant, yellow flowers in May and June. W former Yugoslavia, N Albania. I 1838. AM 1976.

†***PEUMUS** Molina—**Monimiaceae**—A monotypic genus of economic importance in South America. This species will succeed in all well-drained soils, but only in the mildest gardens.

boldus Molina. Boldo. A small, dioecious, evergreen tree with leathery leaves and white flowers in terminal cymes in summer. The bark is used in tanning and dyeing; the leaves make an interesting tea, which is taken medicinally to aid digestion, and the fruits are sweet and edible. Chile. I 1844.

PHELLODENDRON Rupr.—**Rutaceae**—A small genus of about 10 species of small to medium-sized, widespreading trees, natives of E Asia and resembling *Ailanthus* in their large, handsome, aromatic, pinnate leaves and graceful habit. Related to *Tetradium* (*Euodia*), but differing in the enclosed winter buds and the fruit, which is a drupe. They grow well on chalky soil, their leaves usually turning clear yellow before falling. Small, yellow-green flowers, in cymes, are followed by small, black, viscid fruits.

amurense Rupr. Amur cork tree, so called because of the corky bark of older trees. Distinguished by its bright green leaves, 25–38cm long with 5–11 leaflets, glabrous beneath, and its silvery-hairy winter buds. NE Asia. I 1885. **var.** *japonicum* See *P. japonicum*. **var.** *lavalleei* See *P. lavalleei*. **var.** *sachalinense* See *P. sachalinense*.

chinense C.K. Schneid. A handsome tree with leaves up to 38cm long, composed of 7–13 acuminate, glossy leaflets, downy beneath, and densely packed fruiting clusters. C China. I 1907 by Ernest Wilson. **var.** *glabriusculum* C.K. Schneid. A variety differing in its almost glabrous leaflets. C and W China. I 1907.

japonicum Maxim. (*P. amurense* var. *japonicum* (Maxim.) Ohwi) A small tree related to *P. amurense* but without corky bark. Leaves softly downy beneath, with 9–15 leaflets. The attractive, black fruits are produced after a warm summer. Japan. I 1863.

lavalleei Dode (*P. amurense* var. *lavallei* (Dode) Sprague) A medium-sized tree similar to *P. amurense* but the bark less corky, and the dull green leaves downy beneath. Japan. I 1866.

sachalinense (F. Schmidt) Sarg. (*P. amurense* var. *sachalinense* F. Schmidt) A very hardy, medium-sized tree, the dull green leaves with 7–11 leaflets. Bark not corky. Sakhalin, Korea.

PHILADELPHUS L.—**Hydrangeaceae**—The mock oranges, often erroneously called syringa, are an indispensable genus of shrubs, comprising some 65 species in N temperate regions and giving a good display even on the poorest chalk soils. Most have fragrant flowers, produced in June and July. These are pure white unless otherwise described. Prune immediately after flowering: thin out and cut back old flowering shoots to within a few centimetres of the old wood. Many of the finest hybrids and cultivars were raised by the French nursery firm Lemoine during the early years of the 20th century. Unless otherwise stated the cultivars reach a height of 1.8–2.4m.

'Albâtre' (Virginalis Group) A small shrub with double, slightly fragrant flowers in large racemes. C 1912 (Lemoine).

'Amalthée' A medium-sized shrub with long branches and single, sweetly scented, rose-stained flowers. C 1923 (Lemoine).

argyrocalyx Wooton. A very beautiful, distinct and graceful shrub, 1.5–1.8m in height, related to *P. microphyllus*. The fragrant, evenly spaced flowers are 3.5–4cm across and have large, silky-pubescent calyces. New Mexico (USA). I 1916.

'Atlas' (Burfordensis Group) A medium-sized shrub of loose habit with long, arching branches. Large flowers, 5–6cm across, single, slightly scented. Leaves often with faint yellow mottling. C 1923 (Lemoine). AM 1927.

'Avalanche' (Lemoinei Group) A small, semi-erect shrub with small leaves. In summer the masses of small, single, richly fragrant flowers weigh down the slender branches. C 1896 (Lemoine).

'Beauclerk' (Purpureomaculatus Group) A splendid medium-sized shrub raised by the Hon Lewis Palmer in 1938, with single, broad-petalled flowers, 6cm across, milk-white with a zone of light cerise around the stamens. A cross between 'Burfordensis' and 'Sybille'. ♀ 2002. FCC 1951. AM 1947.

'Belle Etoile' (Purpureomaculatus Group) A beautiful, compact shrub up to 2m. The single, 5cm wide flowers are flushed maroon at the centre, and are delightfully fragrant. A triploid hybrid. C 1930 (Lemoine). ♀ 2002. AM 1930.

'Bicolore' (Purpureomaculatus Group) Small shrub. The single, cup-shaped flowers are creamy-white with a purple basal stain. A triploid hybrid. C 1918 (Lemoine).

'Boule d'Argent' (Virginalis Group) A small shrub with large, double, slightly fragrant, pure white flowers, freely produced in dense clusters. C 1893 (Lemoine). FCC 1895.

'Bouquet Blanc' (Virginalis Group) Small shrub with double, orange-scented flowers in large, crowded clusters. C 1903 (Lemoine). AM 1912.

brachybotrys Koehne (*P. pekinensis* var. *brachybotrys* (Koehne) Koehne) An elegant, medium-sized to large Chinese shrub with delicately fragrant, creamy-white flowers. I 1892.

'Buckley's Quill' (Virginalis Group) ('Bouquet Blanc' × 'Frosty Morn') A broadly upright shrub to 2m. The large, double flowers each have about 30 quilled petals. C 1961.

'Burfordensis' (Burfordensis Group) A magnificent, erect-branched, medium-sized shrub raised by Sir William Lawrence. The large, single flowers are cup-shaped and have conspicuous yellow stamens. Originated in 1920 as a sport of 'Virginal'. It is the typical form of the Burfordensis Group which also includes 'Atlas', 'Conquête', 'Falconeri', 'Favorite', 'Innocence', 'Norma', 'Rosace' and 'Voie Lactée'. FCC 1969. AM 1921.

'Burkwoodii' (Purpureomaculatus Group) ('Etoile Rose' × 'Virginal') A slender, medium-sized shrub with single, fragrant flowers. The long, narrow petals, arranged in windmill fashion, are white with a purple basal stain. C 1929.

californicus Benth. A vigorous, medium-sized shrub attaining 3m. Fragrant flowers, 2.5cm across, are produced in large panicles. California. I 1885.

'Conquête' (Burfordensis Group) A small shrub with slender, arching branches carrying clusters of large, fragrant, single and semi-double, pure white flowers with long, narrow petals intermixed with shorter petaloid stamens. C 1903 (Lemoine).

coronarius L. A strong-growing, medium-sized shrub with creamy-white, richly scented flowers. The most commonly cultivated species, particularly suitable for very dry soils. Origin obscure, perhaps wild in N and C Italy, Austria and C Romania. Long cultivated. **'Aureus'** (*P. caucasicus* 'Aureus') Leaves bright yellow when young, becoming greenish-yellow. ♥ 2002. AM 1983. **'Variegatus'** (*P. caucasicus* 'Variegatus') Leaves with a creamy-white margin. C 1770. ♥ 2002.

'Coupe d'Argent' (Lemoinei Group) A somewhat frail aristocrat, and a small shrub of superb quality. The large, single, fragrant flowers have a very slight stain at the base of the petals. They are rather square in outline and beautifully poised at regular intervals. C 1915 (Lemoine). AM 1922.

delavayi L. Henry. A large, vigorous shrub with large leaves, grey-felted beneath. Flowers heavily scented, 3–4cm across, in dense racemes. China, Tibet, Upper Burma. Discovered and introduced by the Abbé Delavay in 1887. **var. *calvescens*** Rehder. Leaves less hairy beneath. **f. *melanocalyx*** (Lemoine) Rehder. A delightful form with purple calyces. It is often grown as

var. *calvescens*. **'Nymans Variety'** The best form of f. *melanocalyx* with deep purple calyces. AM 1935.

'Enchantement' (Virginalis Group) A small to medium-sized shrub, producing profuse terminal clusters of double, sweetly scented flowers. C 1923 (Lemoine). AM 1966.

'Erectus' (Lemoinei Group) A small shrub of erect habit, with small leaves and flowers, extremely floriferous and richly scented. C 1890 (Lemoine).

'Etoile Rose' (Purpureomaculatus Group) Flowers large, fragrant, single, the petals elongated with a carmine-rose blotch at base. C 1908 (Lemoine).

'Falconeri' (Burfordensis Group) (*P. × falconeri* Sarg.) A large shrub. The slightly fragrant flowers, 3–4cm across, are very distinct because of their narrow, lance-shaped petals. Origin uncertain. C 1881.

'Favorite' (Burfordensis Group) An attractive cultivar up to 2m. Single, very large, cup-shaped flowers are pure white with serrated petals and a central cluster of yellow stamens. C 1916 (Lemoine).

'Frosty Morn' (Lemoinei Group) A small shrub that bears fragrant, double flowers. C 1953.

'Girandole' (Virginalis Group) A showy shrub with clusters of very double, fragrant flowers. C 1915 (Lemoine). AM 1921.

'Glacier' (Virginalis Group) A small, late-flowering shrub, that bears crowded clusters of very double, fragrant flowers. C 1913 (Lemoine).

incanus Koehne. A medium-sized to large shrub, distinguished by its hairy leaves and late blossoming. Fragrant flowers in late July. C China. I 1904 by Ernest Wilson.

'Innocence' (Burfordensis Group) Flowers single, fragrant, borne with extraordinary freedom. Leaves often with creamy-white variegation. C 1927 (Lemoine).

insignis Carrière. A vigorous shrub 3–3.6m high. Flowers about 3cm wide, rather cup-shaped, scented, produced in panicles of 15–20. One of the last to flower, the blossoms remaining until mid-July. California. AM 1929.

intectus Beadle (*P. pubescens* var. *intectus* (Beadle) A.H. Moore) A very vigorous shrub, growing 4.5m or more high. Outstanding when laden with masses of slightly fragrant flowers. SE USA. C before 1890.

'Lemoinei' (Lemoinei Group) (*P. coronarius* × *P. microphyllus*) Raised in 1884 by M. Lemoine, this was the original hybrid of which there are now numerous named clones. A small shrub, it bears very fragrant flowers 2.5cm wide, in clusters of 3–7 on short side branches. AM 1898. It is the typical form of Lemoinei Group which also includes 'Avalanche', 'Coupe d'Argent', 'Erectus', 'Frosty Morn', 'Manteau d'Hermine', 'Silberregen' and 'Velléda'.

lewisii Pursh. A medium-sized to large shrub of erect habit with racemes of white flowers. W North America. I 1823. **'Siskyou'** A large-flowered selection raised from cuttings collected by Roy Lancaster in the Siskyou Mountains in 1988. **'Snow Velvet'** Very sweetly fragrant, large, semi-double, pure white flowers, to 8cm across. Raised from seed collected in the Cascade Mountains.

maculatus See under *P. mexicanus* 'Rose Syringa'.

'Manteau d'Hermine' (Lemoinei Group) A popular dwarf, compact shrub attaining about 0.75–1.2m with fragrant, creamy-white, double flowers. C 1899 (Lemoine). ♀ 2002. AM 1956.

†*mexicanus* Schltdl. A tender species, native to Mexico and Guatemala, of which the following form is the most commonly cultivated. **'Rose Syringa'** (*P. maculatus* hort. not (Hitchc.) Hu) A beautiful, medium-sized shrub with richly fragrant, white flowers with a purple blotch in the centre. Sometimes wrongly grown in gardens under the name *P. coulteri*, which differs in its exposed buds and pure white flowers. A parent of many fine hybrids. AM 1961.

microphyllus A. Gray. A very dainty small-leaved species, forming a twiggy bush of about 1–1.2m high. Flowers are richly fragrant. SW USA. I 1883. FCC 1890.

'Minnesota Snowflake' (Virginalis Group) An American cultivar, 1.5–1.8m high, with arching branches bowed by the weight of the double, fragrant flowers. C 1935.

'Monster' A vigorous, large shrub, quickly attaining 4.5m. Flowers nearly 5cm across.

'Mrs E.L. Robinson' (Virginalis Group) Very large single to semi-double flowers with numerous petaloid stamens.

'Natchez' A medium-sized shrub, upright in habit, bearing large, slightly fragrant, single white flowers up to 5cm across.

'Norma' (Burfordensis Group) Flowers single, 5cm across, slightly fragrant, on long slender branches. C 1910 (Lemoine). AM 1913.

pekinensis var. *brachybotrys* See *P. brachybotrys*.

× *pendulifolius* Carrière. Medium-sized shrub with racemes of cup-shaped flowers. Probably a hybrid of *P. pubescens*.

pubescens Loisel. (*P. pubescens* var. *verrucosus* (Schrad.) Hu, *P. verrucosus* Schrad.) A vigorous shrub up to 3m high. Flowers about 3–4cm across, slightly fragrant, in racemes of 5–7. SE USA. **var. *intectus*** See *P. intectus*. **var. *verrucosus*** See *P. pubescens*.

purpurascens (Koehne) Rehder. A small-leaved species, making a medium-sized shrub, with spreading and arching branches, wreathed with sweet-scented flowers, the white petals contrasting with the purple calyces. W China. I 1911 by Ernest Wilson.

'Purpureomaculatus' (*P.* × *lemoinei* × *P. mexicanus* 'Rose Syringa') A small to medium-sized shrub. The arching stems are weighted with purple-stained, white, scented blossoms. It is the typical form of Purpureomaculatus Group which also contains 'Beauclerk', 'Belle Etoile', 'Bicolore', 'Burkwoodii', 'Etoile Rose' and 'Sybille'.

'Pyramidal' (Virginalis Group) Strong-growing shrub with semi-double, fragrant flowers. C 1916 (Lemoine).

'Rosace' (Burfordensis Group) Large, semi-double, fragrant flowers in large sprays. C 1904 (Lemoine). AM 1908.

satsumanus See *P. satsumi*.

satsumi Lindl. & Paxton (*P. satsumanus* Siebold & Zucc., *P. acuminatus* Lange) A slender, erect shrub with rather small, slightly scented flowers in racemes of 5–11. Japan. I 1851.

schrenkii Rupr. A large shrub of upright habit, akin to *P. coronarius*. Flowers very fragrant. E Siberia. Manchuria, Korea. I 1874.

sericanthus Koehne. A spreading shrub of medium to large size. Late flowering, with racemes of small, cupped flowers. C China. I 1897 by Paul Farges.

'Silberregen' (Lemoinei Group) ('Silver Showers') A dense, small shrub with small, pointed leaves and profusely borne, single, fragrant flowers.

'Snowbelle' (Virginalis Group) ('Manteau d'Hermine' × 'Virginal') A small shrub with double, bell-shaped flowers, each with up to 15 petals.

'Splendens' (*P.* × *splendens* Rehder.) A large, spreading shrub forming a wide mound of arching branches. Flowers large in crowded clusters, filled with bright yellow anthers. Origin unknown, possibly *P. lewisii* var. *gordonianus* × *P. grandiflorus*.

subcanus Koehne (*P. wilsonii* Koehne) A large shrub producing long racemes of fragrant, somewhat bell-shaped flowers. C and W China. I 1908 by Ernest Wilson.

'Sybille' (Purpureomaculatus Group) A superb small shrub with arching branches bearing single, squarish, purple-stained, orange-scented flowers. A triploid hybrid. C 1913 (Lemoine). ♀ 2002. AM 1954.

tomentosus G. Don. A medium-sized shrub with slender-pointed, hairy leaves, grey-felted beneath. Flowers fragrant, 2.5–3.5cm across, borne in slender racemes in June. Himalaya. I 1822.

'Velléda' (Lemoinei Group) A pretty cultivar with single, perfectly shaped, fragrant flowers, about 3–4cm across; petals crimped at the edges. C 1922 (Lemoine).

verrucosus See *P. pubescens*.

'Virginal' (Virginalis Group) A strong-growing, erect-branched shrub to 3m, with flowers 2.5–3.5cm across, richly fragrant. Still probably the best double-flowered cultivar. FCC 1911.

Virginalis Group A group of hybrids with double flowers of which the typical form is 'Virginal'. See also 'Albâtre', 'Boule d'Argent', 'Bouqet Blanc', 'Buckley's Quill', 'Enchantement', 'Girandole', 'Glacier', 'Minnesota Snowflake', 'Pyramidal' and White Rock.

'Voie Lactée' (Burfordensis Group) Flowers single, 5cm across, their broad petals having slightly reflexed edges. C 1905 (Lemoine). AM 1912.

White Rock ('Pekphil') PBR (Virginalis Group) A small to medium-sized shrub of spreading habit with pendent branches. Flowers fragrant, single to semi-double or double, very large, to 6cm across, white with up to 25 petals. Raised in France before 1992.

wilsonii See *P. subcanus*.

‡†*× **PHILAGERIA** Mast. (*Lapageria* × *Philesia*)— **Philesiaceae**—An exceedingly rare, intergeneric hybrid for a cool, moist, peaty soil in a mild garden or conservatory. A difficult plant to establish.

veitchii Mast. (*Lapageria rosea* × *Philesia magellanica*) A small, scrambling shrub with wiry branches and small, narrow, leathery leaves. Flowers solitary in the axils of the leaves, drooping, pale rose-purple outside, bright rose inside, appearing in late summer and autumn. Raised by Messrs Veitch in 1872. *Lapageria* is the mother parent.

‡†***PHILESIA** Comm. ex Juss.—**Philesiaceae**—A monotypic genus related to *Lapageria*.

magellanica J.F. Gmel. (*P. buxifolia* Lam.) One of the choicest, most remarkable and beautiful of dwarf, suckering, evergreen shrubs, forming wide thickets of wiry stems and narrow, rigid leaves, green above, glaucous beneath. Crimson, tubular flowers, 5cm long, are borne in summer and autumn. Requires a moist, peaty, half shady site, well-drained soil and a sheltered position. S Chile. I 1847 by William Lobb. AM 1937. **'Rosea'** Flowers paler, almost rose-red.

PHILLYREA L.—**Oleaceae**—Handsome, evergreen shrubs or small trees, allied to *Osmanthus* and sometimes mistaken for the Holm oak (*Quercus ilex*). 4 species in Madeira, the Mediterranean region and SW Asia. The growths of the smaller-leaved kinds develop, at maturity, into elegant, plumose masses of foliage. They succeed in all types of soil.

angustifolia L. A compact, rounded bush of medium size. Leaves narrow, normally entire, dark green and glabrous. Flowers small, fragrant, creamy-yellow, in axillary clusters in May and June. Excellent for maritime exposure. N Africa, S Europe. C before 1597. **f. *rosmarinifolia*** (Mill.) Schelle. A most attractive, neat, compact form with even narrower leaves.

decora See *Osmanthus decorus*.

latifolia L. An elegant, olive-like small tree or large shrub suitable for planting where the Holm oak would grow too large. Its branches are bowed by the weight of luxuriant masses of small, glossy, dark green, opposite leaves. Flowers dull white in late spring, followed by tiny, blue-black fruits, which are seldom produced in the British Isles. S Europe. Asia Minor. C 1597. **'Rotundifolia'** Leaves broadly ovate or rotund. **f. *spinosa*** (Mill.) Rehder (*P. latifolia* var. *ilicifolia* DC.) Narrow, serrated leaves.

PHLOMIS L.—**Labiatae**—A valuable genus of about 100 species of mainly low-growing shrubs, subshrubs and herbs, usually densely hairy or woolly and producing attractive flowers in axillary whorls. Widely distributed in Europe and Asia. They require full sun and good drainage.

chrysophylla Boiss. A pleasing, small shrub, differing from *P. fruticosa* in its sage-like foliage, which assumes a golden-yellow tinge after midsummer. Flowers golden-yellow in June, best in hot summers. Lebanon. ♀ 2002.

'Edward Bowles' An attractive, small to medium-sized subshrub with large, hoary, heart-shaped leaves, and whorls of sulphur-yellow flowers, with a distinctly paler upper lip, in late summer and autumn. Appears to be intermediate between *P. fruticosa* and the herbaceous *P. russeliana*.

fruticosa L. Jerusalem sage. A small, grey-green shrub, hardy in all but the coldest districts. Its whorls of bright yellow flowers are attractive in summer. A good plant for growing on a sunny bank. Mediterranean region. C 1596. ♀ 2002. AM 1925.

†*italica* L. This is a very desirable dwarf shrub from the Balearic Islands. Stems and leaves white-hairy; flowers pale lilac and borne in terminal spikes in summer. C 1750.

lanata Willd. A dense, dwarf, mound-forming shrub with yellow-woolly shoots and small, sage-green and scurfy, ovate leaves, to 3cm long, the veins deeply impressed above. Flowers golden-yellow with brownish hairs, borne in whorls in summer. Crete. ♀ 2002. **'Pygmy'** A dwarf form of compact habit with dense foliage and flowering over a very long period.

longifolia Boiss. & Blanche. A very attractive, small shrub, proving hardy, with white-woolly young stems and bright green, deeply veined, ovate-triangular leaves, heart-shaped at the base. Terminal clusters of deep golden-yellow flowers are borne in summer. SW Asia. **var. *bailanica*** (Vierh.) Hub.- Mor. A form with broader, darker green and more conspicuously veined leaves.

lycia D. Don. A small shrub, 1.5 to 2m tall, the leaves to about 5cm long, covered in a dense yellow-grey tomentum. Flowers deep golden-yellow in a single terminal head or with another whorl on the same stem. When the fruit forms, the calyx mouth is star-shaped with golden hairs inside. SW Turkey.

†*PHOENIX* L.—**Palmae**—A genus of about 17 species of single- or multistemmed, dioecious palms with pinnate leaves, natives of S Asia and Africa with species in the Canary Islands and Crete. The following can only be grown outside in Britain in the mildest areas but makes a handsome specimen for a large container on a patio, if given conservatory protection during winter. The genus also includes the date palm (*P. dactylifera* L.) and the rare *P. theophrasti*, endemic to Crete, and one of only two palms native to Europe.

canariensis hort. ex Chabaud. Canary Island date palm. A vigorous, medium-sized palm with a single stout trunk, prominently marked with leaf scars. The dense crown bears very large, arching leaves, up to 6m long and divided into numerous leaflets. Drooping inflorescences, to 1m long, bear numerous creamy-yellow flowers followed, on female plants in the presence of a male, by pale orange fruits about 2cm long. Canary Islands, widely cultivated in warm regions of the world. ♀ 2002.

PHORMIUM J.R. Forst. & G. Forst.—**Phormiaceae**—Two species of New Zealand evergreens with handsome, sword-like leaves. They have much the same garden value as the yuccas, with which they associate well, and they thrive in a variety of soils and are good for maritime exposure and for industrial areas. They are more or less hardy in all but the coldest areas. Many of the more recent forms are hybrids between the species.

'Apricot Queen' Low, weeping habit to 1m; leaves soft yellow, flushed apricot, margined dark green and bronze.

'Bronze Baby' Leaves bronze, drooping at the tips. Compact, to 1m with broad leaves.

'Bronze Surfer' Similar to 'Green Surfer' but with bronze foliage.

cookianum Le Jol. (*P. colensoi* Hook. f.) Differs from *P. tenax* in its smaller stature and its thinner, greener, laxer and more flexible leaves. Flowers yellowish, in panicles up to 1m, in summer. I 1848. FCC 1868. The following are forms of subsp. *hookeri* (Hook. f.) Wardle. **'Cream Delight'** Leaves with a broad cream, central band and narrower stripes of cream towards the margin. Raised in New Zealand before 1978. ♀ 2002. **'Tricolor'** Leaves conspicuously edged with creamy-yellow, narrowly margined with red. Found in New Zealand in the 1880s. ♀ 2002.

'Dark Delight' Up to 1m. Broad, upright, dark bronze-purple leaves with a reddish midrib, drooping at the tips.

'Dazzler' A striking plant, to 1m, with leaves deep red-purple striped with rose-red in the centre.

'Duet' Upright or slightly spreading leaves, up to 1m long, margined with creamy-white. ♀ 2002.

'Evening Glow' Arching leaves, to 1m tall, pink, variously striped with bronze-green in the centre, with bronze-green margins.

'Flamingo' Bright pink centre with green margins and occasional bands of green and deep pink in the centre.

'Gold Sword' Yellow leaves margined with green, occasionally with a faint pink stripe in the centre.

'Green Surfer' Slender, twisted and arching green leaves with a narrow, nearly black stripe on the margins and the midrib beneath.

'Jack Spratt' Dwarf, clump-forming, to 45cm, with slender, curled, deep bronze-purple foliage.

'Jester' Slender, arching leaves, deep pink in the centre with a bright green margin. Dwarf, growing to about 1m tall.

'Maori Chief' Leaves upright, drooping at the tips, variegated with scarlet, crimson and bronze.

'Maori Maiden' Leaves to 90cm, drooping at the tips, bronze-green striped rose-red.

'Maori Queen' Leaves upright with drooping tips, bronze-green with rose-red stripes.

'Maori Sunrise' Low-growing with slender, arching leaves, pale red to pink, margined bronze.

'Pink Panther' Ruby-red with pink margins.

'Pink Stripe' Dark bronze-green foliage narrowly edged pink and with occasional narrow pink stripes in the centre.

'Platt's Black' Slender, arching leaves of very deep purple; to 90cm tall.

'Sundowner' Leaves, to 1.5m long, bronze-green with a deep rose-red margin. ♀ 2002. AM 1978.

'Surfer' Narrow, bronzy leaves to 1m, striped bright green in the centre.

tenax J.R. Forst. & G. Forst. New Zealand flax. A striking evergreen for foliage effect, forming clumps of rigid, leathery, somewhat glaucous, sword-like leaves, from 1–3m in length. Flowers bronzy-red in panicles up to 4.5m high in summer. A superb architectural plant for creating contrasting and diverse effects. It possesses something of the subtropical, the arid desert, and the waterside. It may be grown in all types of fertile soil and in all aspects. It is tolerant of sea wind and industrial pollution. Its leaves contain one of the finest fibres known. New Zealand. Often found naturalised in the west of Ireland. I 1789. ♀ 2002. 'Nanum Purpureum' A compact, dwarf form with slender, red-purple leaves, up to 45cm long. Purpureum Group Leaves bronzy-purple to 2m long. A striking plant for contrasting with grey foliage subjects. ♀ 2002. 'Variegatum' Leaves with a creamy-white margin. ♀ 2002. FCC 1864. 'Veitchii' Leaves striped creamy-yellow in the centre.

'Thumbelina' This has very narrow, deep bronze-red leaves. Dwarf habit usually less than 45cm tall.

'Tom Thumb' Low-growing, to 45cm high, with slender, grassy, bronzy-orange to bronzy-green leaves with a darker margin.

'Yellow Wave' Leaves to 1m long, drooping, the yellowish-green central band variously striped with green. Raised in New Zealand about 1967. ♀ 2002. AM 1977.

PHOTINIA Lindl. (*Stranvaesia* Lindl., × *Stranvinia* Hillier)—**Rosaceae**—A genus of large, mainly evergreen shrubs or small trees allied to *Crataegus* and comprising about 40 species that are natives of regions from the Himalaya to E and SE Asia. The white flowers are usually produced in spring in corymbose clusters, followed in autumn by red fruits. The foliage of some deciduous species colours well before falling, and in some evergreen sorts the bronze-red, unfolding leaves rival Forrest's *Pieris*. The deciduous species are inclined to be calcifuge, while the evergreens are lime-tolerant. Unfortunately, with the exception of *P. davidiana*, the evergreen species seldom fruit with any sort of freedom presumably due to lack of sun and warmth.

arbutifolia See *Heteromeles salicifolia*.

beauverdiana C.K. Schneid. This Chinese species has proved to be a very desirable small tree, up to 6m high, conspicuous in late May or early June when it is covered with corymbs of hawthorn-like flowers, and in autumn when bedecked with dark red fruits and richly tinted leaves. Moderately lime-tolerant. W China. I 1900 by Ernest Wilson. **var. notabilis** (C.K. Schneid.) Rehder & E.H. Wilson. It is distinguished by its larger leaves, up to 12.5cm long, broader corymbs and taller habit. Excellent when in flower in late spring, and in autumn, its leaves colouring before falling, leaving clusters of orange-red fruits. C and W China. I 1908 by Ernest Wilson. AM 1960.

benthamiana Hance. This deciduous species, related to *P. villosa*, does not appear to be in cultivation. Plants grown under this name are *P. glabra*. China and Vietnam.

*davidiana (Decne.) Cardot. (*Stranvaesia davidiana* Decne.) An extremely vigorous, large shrub or small tree with erect branches and dark green, lanceolate or oblanceolate, leathery, entire leaves. The globular, brilliant crimson fruits are carried in conspicuous, pendent bunches all along the branches. In established specimens the oldest leaves turn bright red in autumn, contrasting effectively with the still green younger leaves. Unfortunately susceptible to fireblight. W China. First discovered by Père Armand David in 1869. Introduced in its typical form by George Forrest in 1917. In 1967 our propagator Peter Dummer raised a hybrid between this and *Pyracantha atalantioides*. AM 1928. 'Fructuluteo' (Undulata Group) A selected form with bright yellow fruits. AM 1986. 'Palette' A slow-growing form, the leaves conspicuously blotched and streaked with creamy-white, pink-tinged when young. Admired by some, hated by others. Raised in Holland before 1980. 'Prostrata' (Undulata Group) A low-growing, more or less prostrate form. **Salicifolia Group** (*Stranvaesia davidiana* var. *salicifolia* (Hutch.) Rehder, *S. salicifolia* Hutch.) The most commonly cultivated form. The leaves tend to narrow oblong or narrow lanceolate and are more numerously veined. W China. I 1907 by Ernest Wilson. **Undulata Group** (*Stranvaesia davidiana* var. *undulata* (Decne.) Rehder & E.H. Wilson, *S. undulata* Decne.) Less vigorous and usually seen as a shrub of medium size with widespreading branches, often twice as wide as high. Leaves generally wavy at the margin. W China. I 1901 by Ernest Wilson. AM 1922.

*davidsoniae Rehder & E.H. Wilson. A small to medium-sized, thorny tree with reddish, downy shoots and oblanceolate, dark glossy green, taper-pointed leaves, up to 15cm long. Heads of flowers in spring are followed by

orange-red fruits. The plant originally listed under this name is a form of *Photinia nussia*. W Hubei, China. I 1900 by Ernest Wilson.

*×*fraseri* Dress (*P. glabra* × *P. serratifolia*) A variable hybrid. A large vigorous, evergreen shrub with dark glossy green, leathery leaves and attractive, coppery young growths. The forms of this hybrid have proven very hardy. **'Birmingham'** An American-raised form with generally obovate, abruptly pointed leaves, bright coppery-red when young. Tending towards the *P. glabra* parent. C 1940. **Indian Princess** ('Monstock') A compact sport of 'Birmingham' found at Monrovia Nurseries, California in 1977. It has small, rather wavy-edged leaves, coppery when young, and reaches about 1.5 × 2m but can revert. **'Red Robin'** (*P. glabra* 'Red Robin') A most spectacular clone, raised in New Zealand, with sharply toothed, glossy green leaves and brilliant red, young growths, equal to the best forms of *Pieris formosa*. ♥ 2002. AM 1977. **'Robusta'** (*P. glabra* 'Robusta') A strong-growing clone, tending toward the *P. serratifolia* parent, with thick, leathery oblong to obovate leaves. Young growths brilliant coppery-red. Proving the hardiest clone. A seedling raised in Hazelwood's Nursery, Sydney, Australia. AM 1990 (for flower). AM 1974 (for foliage). **'Rubens'** See *P. glabra* 'Rubens'.

glabra (Thunb.) Maxim. A medium-sized to large shrub with oblong to obovate, dark green, minutely serrulate, leathery leaves and bronze young growths. Flowers in May or June followed by red fruits. Japan, China. C about 1903. **'Parfait'** ('Pink Lady', 'Roseomarginata', 'Variegata') Young leaves bronze, margined pink, becoming green, flecked with grey-green and with a narrow, creamy-white margin. A rather weak grower. **'Roseomarginata'** See 'Parfait'. **'Rubens'** (*P. ×fraseri* 'Rubens') A choice selection; the young leaves a brilliant sealing wax-red. FCC 1992. AM 1972.

glomerata Rehder & E.H. Wilson. This deciduous Chinese species does not appear to be in cultivation. The identity of the plant grown under this name is not certain. It has also been incorrectly referred to as *P. prionophylla*. **'Marwood Hill'** See under *P. serratifolia*.

†*integrifolia* Lindl. Medium-sized shrub with slender-pointed, entire, leathery, oblanceolate leaves, up to 15cm long. It is sad that this outstanding evergreen is too tender for our area. It is lime-tolerant. Himalaya, China, Vietnam.

koreana See *P. villosa* f. *maximowicziana*.

lasiogyna See under *P. nussia*.

niitakayamensis Hayata. Closely related to *P. davidiana*, this species differs in its thinner, glossier leaves and more compact habit. The bright pinkish-red fruits often persist well into winter,making it a valuable ornamental shrub. Taiwan. I. about 1980.

†*nussia* (D. Don) Kalkman (*Stranvaesia nussia* (D. Don) Decne., *S. glaucescens* Lindl.) A large shrub or, in mild localities, a small tree, with oblanceolate to obovate, leathery leaves, up to 10cm long, which are dark glossy green and finely toothed, white tomentose beneath when young. Flowers appearing in flattish, tomentose clusters in July, followed by downy orange fruits. Himalaya, SE Asia. I 1828. Plants grown under the name *P. lasiogyna* C.K. Schneid. may represent a form of this species. As

seen in cultivation it differs in its much faster growth, the leaves opening much earlier and nearly glabrous beneath, even when young, its glabrous flower buds and its smooth, dark red fruits. SW China.

†*prionophylla* (Franch.) C.K. Schneid. (*Eriobotrya prionophylla* Franch.) A stiff, medium-sized evergreen from China. Its hard, leathery, obovate leaves have prickly margins. The flowers, appearing in July, are borne in corymbs 5–7.5cm across; fruits crimson. Not hardy in our area. See also under *P. glomerata*. W China. I 1916 by George Forrest.

prunifolia (Hook. & Arn.) Lindl. Some plants previously grown as *P. glabra* belong here. It can be distinguished by the numerous, small black spots on the underside of the leaf and, judging by cultivated plants, has larger flowers than *P. glabra*. China, Vietnam.

'Redstart' (× *Stranvinia* 'Redstart') (*P. davidiana* 'Fructuluteo' × *P. ×fraseri* 'Robusta') A vigorous, large shrub or small tree with foliage that is bright red when young. Leaves dark green, oblong-elliptic, to 11cm long, finely and sparsely toothed above the middle, up to 14 pairs of veins, not or only slightly raised beneath. Flowers in June in dense, hemispherical corymbs with reddish-purple calyces and pedicels. Fruits orange-red, flushed yellow. Raised by our propagator Peter Dummer from a cross made in 1969.

serratifolia (Desf.) Kalkman (*P. serrulata* Lindl.) A very handsome, large, evergreen shrub or small tree. Leaves oblong, up to 15cm long, shining dark green and leathery with coarsely toothed margins. The young leaves throughout the whole of its long growing season are bright, coppery-red. Flowers, in large corymbs, during April and May, best following hot summers (they were particularly spectacular in 1990); fruits red, the size of haws. One of the most splendid lime-tolerant evergreens. It is remarkable how the young growths withstand spring frost. A plant distributed recently as *P. glomerata* 'Marwood Hill' appears to belong here. China, Taiwan. I 1804. The plant previously distributed by us as *P. serrulata* Formosan form is very distinct, with densely white-tomentose young stems and petioles, and conspicuous, red bud scales and stipules. Young foliage rich bronze.

serrulata See *P. serratifolia*.

villosa (Thunb.) DC. (*P. variabilis* Hemsl., *Pourthiaea villosa* (Thunb.) Decne.) A deciduous species forming a large shrub or small, broad-headed tree with obovate, shortly acuminate leaves. It bears hawthorn-like flowers in May, followed by small, egg-shaped, bright red fruits, and is one of the most effective autumn-colouring subjects, the leaves turning to scarlet and gold. It does not thrive on shallow chalky soil. Japan, Korea, China. I about 1865 by P.F. von Siebold. ♥ 2002. AM 1932. **var. *laevis*** (Thunb.) Dippel. The most commonly grown form, this has glabrous, finely toothed leaves, attractively margined with bronze when young and brilliant orange and red in autumn. Unlike other forms of this variable species, it tends to make a tree, with spreading rather than arching branches. **f. *maximowicziana*** (Lév.) Rehder (*P. koreana* Lancaster) Leaves almost sessile, obovate, pale green, rather leathery in texture, the veins strongly impressed above, giving the leaf a bullate appearance. Autumn colour rich golden-yellow.

Originally wrongly catalogued and distributed by us as *P. amphidoxa*. South Korea (Jeju do). I via Japan in 1897.
var. *sinica* Rehder & E.H. Wilson. A small tree or occasionally a large shrub, differing in its more spreading habit, elliptic or elliptic-oblong leaves and its larger, almost cherry-like fruits in pendent clusters. C China. I about 1901 by Ernest Wilson.

*'**Winchester**' A selection from the same cross as 'Redstart'. Differs in its thinner leaves, which are elliptic-oblanceolate, to 13.5cm long, veins in up to 18 pairs, distinctly raised beneath. Fruits orange-red, flushed yellow at the apex.

PHYGELIUS E. Mey. ex Benth.—**Scrophulariaceae**— A genus of 2 species of attractive, evergreen or semi-evergreen, penstemon-like subshrubs from South Africa. *P. capensis* is remarkable as being one of the very few South African shrubs hardy in the British Isles. They reach their greatest height against a sunny wall, but look well towards the front of a shrub or herbaceous border. They succeed in full sun in all types of well-drained but not too dry soil.

aequalis Hiern. A small subshrub up to 1m, with 4-angled stems. Flowers tubular, 2.5–4cm long, corolla slightly down-curved, regular at the mouth with spreading lobes, pale dusky-pink to red, with a yellow throat, produced in compact, one-sided panicles in late summer and early autumn. Not so hardy as *P. capensis* and requires wall protection. AM 1936. **Sensation** ('Sani Pass') PBR A striking and unusual form with magenta flowers. Discovered at the Sani Pass in the Drakensburg Mountains of South Africa. '**Trewidden Pink**' Plants under this name have dusky-pink flowers. They probably derive from an introduction by B.L. Burtt in 1973. It is now the most commonly grown form of the species. ♀ 2002. '**Yellow Trumpet**' A striking form with pale creamy-yellow flowers and broad, light green leaves. It was discovered in the wild in SW Natal and introduced to this country from cultivation in South Africa independently by B.L. Burtt and Sir Harold Hillier in 1973. ♀ 2002. AM 1984.

capensis Benth. Cape figwort. A small shrub, occasionally up to 2m in mild areas. Flowers tubular, nodding and turning back towards the stem when open, irregular at the mouth, with reflexed lobes, orange-red to deep red, with a yellow throat, elegantly borne on all sides of the stem in tall, open panicles during summer and autumn. C 1855. ♀ 2002. AM 1978. '**Coccineus**' As originally described, this form had rich red flowers, but it may no longer be in cultivation. Plants now grown under this name have large, rich orange-red flowers. AM 1926.

× *rectus* Coombes (*P. aequalis* × *P. capensis*) A group of hybrids intermediate between the parents in the shape of the corolla tube. The F₁ hybrids have pendent flowers with a more or less straight tube, whereas back-crosses tend more to one of the parents. Several forms have now been raised in various colours. Unless stated they reach about 1–1.5m. '**African Queen**' ('Indian Chief') An F₁ hybrid with pale red flowers. This was the first hybrid, raised by John May at the Wimborne Botanic Garden in 1969. ♀ 2002. '**Devil's Tears**' A back-cross between 'Winchester Fanfare' and *P. capensis* 'Coccineus' raised by our propagator Peter Dummer in 1985. Flowers deep reddish-pink, deeper in bud with orange-red lobes. The tall, open inflorescence tends to *P. capensis*. ♀ 2002.

'**Indian Chief**' See 'African Queen'. '**Moonraker**' A back-cross between 'Winchester Fanfare' and *P. aequalis* 'Yellow Trumpet' raised by Peter Dummer in 1985. It resembles 'Yellow Trumpet' but the flowers are borne on all sides of the inflorescence with a nearly straight corolla tube. '**Pink Elf**' This very distinct form is a back-cross between 'Winchester Fanfare' and *P. aequalis* 'Yellow Trumpet' raised by Peter Dummer in 1985. A compact, dwarf form of weak constitution, with narrow leaves, reaching about 75cm. Flowers very slender, pale pink with deep crimson lobes, borne on all sides of the inflorescence and spreading, not pendent. '**Salmon Leap**' A back-cross between 'Winchester Fanfare' and *P. capensis* 'Coccineus' raised by Peter Dummer in 1985. It resembles 'Devil's Tears' but has orange flowers with deeper lobes. ♀ 2002. '**Sunshine**' This is a sport of 'Winchester Fanfare' with soft yellow foliage. '**Winchester Fanfare**' (*P. aequalis* 'Yellow Trumpet' × *P. capensis* 'Coccineus') Flowers pendent with a straight corolla tube, dusky reddish-pink with scarlet lobes. It most resembles 'African Queen' but differs in its flower colour and the broader leaves inherited from 'Yellow Trumpet'. Raised by Peter Dummer in 1974.

†***PHYLICA** L.—**Rhamnaceae**—A large genus of about 150 species of evergreen shrubs mainly found in South Africa. Suitable for sunny positions in the mildest areas.

arborea Thouars (*P. superba* hort.) A remarkable, small, helichrysum-like shrub with crowded, small, silver-green leaves. Inflorescences, composed of tiny, green-white flowers, open in late autumn, emitting a strong fragrance like meadowsweet. An attractive conservatory shrub. Lime-tolerant. Islands of S Atlantic and Indian oceans.

superba See *P. arborea*.

‡*× **PHYLLIOPSIS** Cullen & Lancaster (*Kalmiopsis* × *Phyllodoce*)—**Ericaceae**—An interesting intergeneric hybrid described from a plant which originated in our nursery.

'**Coppelia**' (*Kalmiopsis leachiana* × *Phyllodoce empetriformis*) A charming, dwarf shrub of compact habit, raised by Barry Starling. Slender, green leaves and profuse, saucer-shaped, lavender-pink flowers in late spring. ♀ 2002.

hillieri Cullen & Lancaster (*Kalmiopsis leachiana* × *Phyllodoce breweri*) The following is the first hybrid to be recorded between these genera. It was noticed in our nursery in 1960. '**Pinocchio**' A dwarf shrub with glossy green, oblong-obovate leaves, up to 2cm long. Flowers deep pink, bell-shaped, about 1cm across, freely borne in long, slender racemes over a long period in spring and again in autumn. FCC 1984. AM 1976.

‡***PHYLLODOCE** Salisb.—**Ericaceae**—A genus of 6 or 7 species of dainty dwarf, heath-like shrubs, natives of N temperate and Arctic regions and thriving in cool, moist, moorland conditions, and in lime-free soil. April to July flowering.

aleutica (Spreng.) A. Heller. A dwarf, carpeting shrublet, 15–23cm high. Flowers pitcher-shaped (urceolate), creamy-white or pale yellow, in terminal umbels during May and June. Canada, S Alaska, Aleutian Isles, Kamchatka, N Japan. I 1915. AM 1939. **subsp. *glanduliflora*** (Hook.) Hultén (*P. glanduliflora* Hook.) Corolla densely covered in glandular hairs. Oregon to Alaska. AM 1978.

breweri (A. Gray) A. Heller. A dwarf, tufted species, 23–30cm high. The flowers are comparatively large, saucer-shaped and a delightful rose-purple. They are produced in long terminal racemes in May and June. California. I 1896. AM 1956.

caerulea (L.) Bab. (*P. taxifolia* Salisb.) A rare, native alpine found wild in Perthshire. A dwarf, cushion-forming shrublet, up to 15cm. Pitcher-shaped, bluish-purple flowers are borne in delicate terminal umbels in May and June. Alpine-Arctic regions of N Europe, North America, N Asia. C 1800. ♀ 2002. AM 1938.

empetriformis (Sm.) D. Don. A dwarf, tufted shrublet, 15–25cm high. Flowers are bell-shaped, bright reddish-purple, and produced in umbels during April and May. W North America. C 1830.

glanduliflora See *P. aleutica* subsp. *glanduliflora*.

× **intermedia** (Hook.) Rydb. (*P. empetriformis* × *P. aleutica* subsp. *glanduliflora*, *P. hybrida* Rydb.) A variable, dwarf hybrid of vigorous growth, soon forming large mats, up to 30cm high and four times as much wide. Often wrongly grown in gardens as *P. empetriformis*, from which it differs in its pitcher-shaped flowers, puckered at the mouth. W North America. AM 1936. **'Fred Stoker'** (*P. pseudoempetriformis* hort.) This is the form in general cultivation. Named after that keen amateur gardener the late Dr Fred Stoker. AM 1941.

nipponica Makino. One of the most perfect rock garden shrublets for peaty soils. A dwarf, erect-growing species of neat, compact habit, 15–23cm high. Flowers bell-shaped, white or pink-tinged, appearing in terminal umbels in May. N Japan. I 1915. ♀ 2002. FCC 1946. AM 1938.

‡*× **PHYLLOTHAMNUS** C.K. Schneid. (*Phyllodoce* × *Rhodothamnus*)—**Ericaceae**—An interesting intergeneric hybrid raised by Cunningham and Fraser, nurserymen of Edinburgh in about 1845. Suitable for a lime-free, moist, peaty or leafy soil.

erectus (Lindl.) C.K. Schneid. (*P. empetriformis* × *R. chamaecistus*) This is a dwarf shrublet, 30–45cm in height, its stems crowded with narrow leaves. The flowers are shallowly funnel-shaped, delicate rose and they are produced in terminal umbels in April and May. FCC 1969. AM 1958.

PHYSOCARPUS Maxim.—**Rosaceae**—A small genus of about 10 species of tall shrubs related to *Neillia* and, like them, thriving in open, moist positions. Natives of North America, Mexico and NE Asia. Tend to become chlorotic on a dry, shallow, chalk soil.

amurensis (Maxim.) Maxim. A medium-sized shrub of compact habit with rounded, 3- to 5-lobed leaves. Flowers white with reddish-purple anthers, in clusters in summer. Manchuria, Korea.

capitatus (Pursh) Greene. A medium-sized shrub with 3-lobed, double-toothed leaves and clusters of white flowers in summer. W North America. I 1827. **'Tilden Park'** A low-growing, widespreading form suitable for groundcover reaching 1 by 2.5m in 5 years. Found by James Roof in California in 1963.

malvaceus (Greene) Kuntze (*Neillia torreyi* S. Watson, *Neillia malvacea* Greene) An elegant, spiraea-like shrub

of medium size bearing umbels of white flowers in June. W North America. I 1896.

monogynus (Torr.) Coult. Small shrub with small, ovate, 3–5-lobed leaves and clusters of white or pink-tinged flowers in summer. C USA. I 1879.

opulifolius (L.) Maxim. (*Spiraea opulifolia* L.) Nine bark. Vigorous, medium-sized shrub, thriving almost anywhere. Leaves 3-lobed; flowers white, tinged pink, produced in dense clusters along the stems in June. E North America. I 1687. **'Dart's Gold'** A compact shrub, an improvement on 'Luteus' with foliage a brighter, longer-lasting yellow. C 1969. ♀ 2002. **'Diabolo'** PBR A medium-sized shrub with dark purple leaves that are bronze-green when they are young. Flowers white. ♀ 2002. AM 1998 (for flower and foliage). **'Luteus'** Young growths clear yellow, very effective when planted with purple-leaved shrubs. C 1864.

PHYTOLACCA L.—**Phytolaccaceae**—A small genus of about 25 species of herbs, shrubs and trees, natives of tropical and warm temperate regions. It is best known in gardens for *P. americana*, the pokeweed from the S USA and Mexico, and *P. clavigera* from China.

†**dioica** L. (*P. arborea* Moq.) A large, dioecious, semi-evergreen shrub of vigorous growth, making a small, heavy-limbed tree in its native habitat and the Mediterranean region, where it is often planted. Leaves poplar-like, up to 15cm long. Flowers greenish, in racemes 5–7.5cm long, followed by dark purple, berry-like fruits. A conservatory shrub, only growing outside in the mildest areas. There is, or was, a thick-trunked tree in the public gardens on Gibraltar. Native of South America.

†***PICCONIA** DC.—**Oleaceae**—2 species of large, evergreen shrubs or small trees, related to the olive (*Olea*) and natives of Madeira, the Canary Islands and the Azores. Only suitable for milder areas of the British Isles.

excelsa (Aiton) DC. (*Notelaea excelsa* (Aiton) Webb & Berth., *Olea excelsa* Aiton) A large shrub or small tree with glabrous, grey, flattened shoots. Leaves opposite, elliptic to elliptic-lanceolate, 7.5–12.5cm, long. Flowers fragrant, white, borne in short terminal or axillary racemes during spring or summer. A splendid tree like a small evergreen oak (*Quercus ilex*) grows in the Abbotsbury Subtropical Gardens, Dorset. With us, in Hampshire, it grows slowly, has survived outside for many years and flowers occasionally. The wood is extremely hard and heavy. Canary Isles, Madeira. I 1784.

PICRASMA Blume—**Simaroubaceae**—A genus of 6 species of trees and shrubs related to *Ailanthus*, natives of tropical America, E and SE Asia. Succeeding in a cool, well-drained loam, in sun or semi-shade.

quassioides (D. Don) Benn. (*P. ailanthoides* Planch.) A very ornamental small, hardy tree with attractive, pinnate leaves, 15–25cm long, turning brilliant orange and scarlet in autumn. All parts taste bitter. Flowers tiny, yellow-green, in axillary corymbs in May and June, followed by red, pea-like fruits. Lime-tolerant but succeeding best in neutral or acid soils. Japan, Taiwan, China, Korea, India.

†***PIERIS** D. Don—**Ericaceae**—Highly ornamental, dense, evergreen shrubs, requiring similar treatment to

rhododendrons. The flower panicles are formed in autumn, and those with red-tinged buds are attractive throughout winter. The flowers eventually open during April and May. They are white and pitcher-shaped, rather like lily-of-the-valley. Several have very attractive, red or bronze young growth which is vulnerable to late spring frost and, for that reason, light overhead shade and protection on the north and east sides is desirable for *P. formosa* in all its forms.

'Bert Chandler' (*P. japonica* 'Bert Chandler', *P. japonica* 'Chandleri') An unusual small shrub of Australian origin, reaching about 1.5m. The young foliage is bright salmon-pink changing to creamy-yellow then white, finally green. Given an open position the leaves are an attractive creamy-yellow throughout winter. Flowers rarely produced. Raised in Chandler's Nurseries in Victoria, Australia about 1936. AM 1977.

'Firecrest' (*P. formosa* Forrest 8945 × *P. japonica*) A vigorous, large shrub, similar to *P.* 'Forest Flame', with bright red young foliage but with broader and more deeply veined leaves. Large, white flowers are borne in dense panicles. C 1964. ♀ 2002. AM 1981 (for flower). AM 1973 (for foliage).

'Flaming Silver' A small shrub with bright red young leaves that show no variegation when young but soon develop a striking silvery-white margin, pink at first. Flowers creamy-white. A sport of 'Forest Flame' raised in Holland. The same or very similar sport has occurred in several places at about the same time, including one in our nurseries. Of these, at least **Havila** ('Mouwsvila') (AM 1993) appears to be distinct, with narrower leaves and a broader margin. ♀ 2002.

floribunda (Pursh) Benth. & Hook. (*Andromeda floribunda* Pursh ex Sims) Fetter bush. A very hardy, slow-growing shrub, forming a dense, rounded mound 1.2–2m high. Flowers are produced in numerous, erect, terminal panicles during March and April. The greenish-white buds are attractive during winter before they open. SE USA. I 1800. **'Elongata'** ('Grandiflora') A distinct form with longer panicles, also flowering later. Garden origin about 1935. AM 1938.

'Forest Flame' (*P. formosa* 'Wakehurst' × *P. japonica*) A superb large shrub, combining the hardiness of *P. japonica* with the brilliant red young growths of 'Wakehurst'. The leaves pass from red, through pink and creamy-white to green. Flowers in large, terminal, drooping panicles. Originated as a chance seedling in Sunningdale Nurseries, Berkshire, about 1946. ♀ 2002. AM 1973.

formosa (Wall.) D. Don (*Andromeda formosa* Wall.) A magnificent large, evergreen shrub for mild climates. The large leaves are leathery, finely toothed and dark glossy green. The clustered flower panicles are produced in May. Young growths copper-tinged. E Himalaya, Upper Burma, SW and C China. C 1858. FCC 1969. AM 1894. **'Charles Michael'** (Forrest 27765) A striking form raised at Caerhays Castle, Cornwall from Forrest's seed and named after the Head Gardener there. The individual flowers are the largest of any form and occur in large panicles. AM 1965. **Forrestii Group** (*Pieris formosa* var. *forrestii* (Harrow) Airy Shaw) In its best forms, this is one of the most beautiful of all shrubs, the young growths are brilliant red, and the large, slightly fragrant flowers borne in long, conical panicles. A handsome

foliage shrub, 2.5m or more high, blooming in April. Forms placed here come from SW China, NE Upper Burma and represent one extreme of a variable species. I about 1905 by George Forrest. AM 1924. **'Henry Price'** (Forrest 8945) A splendid selection from Wakehurst Place, Sussex. Leaves broad, very dark green and deeply veined, deep red when young. Flowers large in upright panicles. AM 1957. **'Jermyns'** A superb form, selected in our nursery. Young leaves deep vinous-red becoming dark glossy green. Panicles long and drooping, an attractive red over a long period in winter. The whole inflorescence, including the sepals, is of the same rich colouring as the young stems and contrasts strikingly with the white flowers. AM 1959. **'Wakehurst'** A lovely selection, strong and vigorous, with relatively short, broad leaves. The vivid red young foliage contrasts beautifully with the glistening white flowers. ♀ 2002. FCC 1930.

Havila See under *P.* 'Flaming Silver'.

japonica (Thunb.) D. Don (*Andromeda japonica* Thunb.) A medium-sized shrub with attractive, glossy foliage, coppery when young and white, waxy flowers borne in drooping panicles during March and April. Japan, E China, Taiwan. C 1870. FCC 1882. **'Bert Chandler'** See *P.* 'Bert Chandler'. **'Bisbee Dwarf'** A slow-growing and very compact dwarf eventually reaching 1m, with small dark green leaves bronze-red when young. Flowers white but rarely produced. **'Blush'** A beautiful form with dark glossy green leaves and inflorescences that are deep purplish-pink before they open. Flowers rose in bud, opening white, streaked with pink towards the apex, eventually fading to white, contrasting with the red calyx. This form, the first of the pinks, remains one of the best. C 1967. ♀ 2002. **'Cavatine'** A dwarf, compact, dome-shaped shrub spreading to 1m wide. Very free flowering. The white, pendent, scented flowers, with pale greenish-cream calyces, show up well against the dark green foliage. Raised in Holland by Mr Esveld. C 1982. ♀ 2002. **'Christmas Cheer'** An exceedingly hardy form from Japan. The flowers are flushed with deep rose at the tip, creating a delightful bicolor effect. Corolla has convex lobes, appearing crimped. Abundantly produced even on young plants and often appear during winter. The pedicels are also deep rose. C 1967. **'Crispa'** (*P. taiwanensis* 'Crispa') A small, slow-growing shrub with matt leaves, strongly curled or wavy-edged. Flowers in large, lax racemes that cover the whole bush. Young growths an attractive copper. **'Cupido'** A compact dwarf shrub, reaching about 1m tall and twice as much across, with bronze young foliage and upright panicles of white flowers. Raised in Holland from Japanese seed before 1982. **'Daisen'** ('Rosea Daisen Form') A selection from Mount Daisen in Japan. Flowers pink, deeper in bud. An improvement on 'Rosea'. C 1967. **'Debutante'** An unusual low-growing form making a compact mound. White flowers are borne in dense, strictly upright panicles. Collected in the wild on the Island of Yakushima by Mr and Mrs de Belder. C 1980. ♀ 2002. **'Dorothy Wyckoff'** Leaves dark green, deeply veined, bronzing in cold weather. Inflorescences rich purplish-red during winter. Corolla pale pink in bud, opening white, contrasting with the deep red calyx.

Raised in the USA about 1960. AM 1984. **'Flamingo'** Large panicles of flowers, deep red in bud, opening deep pink fading to rose-pink, eventually striped with white, nearly white at the mouth and base. Calyx pale green, red at the base. Raised in the USA about 1953. AM 1981. **'Grayswood'** A very distinct form making a compact, small shrub with narrow, dark green leaves. Panicles have long, spreading and drooping branches bearing numerous, densely packed, small, white flowers. ♀ 2002. AM 1981. **'Little Heath'** Similar to 'Variegata' but more compact with smaller leaves. Flowers sparse but can be freely borne when grown in a light position, buds pink. Occasionally sports to 'Little Heath Green'. C 1976. ♀ 2002. **'Little Heath Green'** A compact, dwarf shrub of mound-forming habit with small, dark green leaves, bronze-red when young and in winter on red stems. Rarely, if ever, flowers. C 1967. ♀ 2002. **'Mountain Fire'** Young leaves red, turning to deep glossy chestnut-brown. Flowers white. A selection from British Columbia. C 1967. ♀ 2002. **'Pink Delight'** Long, drooping panicles; flowers pale pink, white at the base, fading to white. Selected in New Zealand before 1964. ♀ 2002. **'Prelude'** A small, compact, dome-shaped shrub; free flowering. White flowers are shown off well against the small, dull, dark leaves. Raised in Holland by Mr Esveld. C 1982. ♀ 2002. **'Purity'** A selected seedling from Japan, making a small, compact shrub bearing trusses of comparatively large, snow-white flowers in clustered, rather upright racemes. Young foliage pale green. C 1967. ♀ 2002. AM 1977. **'Pygmaea'** A curious dwarf form of slow growth reaching about 1m tall and across, almost unrecognisable as a *Pieris*, with leaves 1.2–2.5cm long, linear-lanceolate, shallowly toothed. Resembling a rather loose-leaved *Phyllodoce*. White flowers, in simple racemes, are very sparsely produced. C 1872. **Red Mill** ('Zebris') A very hardy North American selection with dark green leaves, bronze-red when young, and drooping panicles of white flowers. C 1980. **'Sarabande'** A small, compact, dome-shaped shrub, 1m by 2m. Very free-flowering, producing pure white flowers on multi-stemmed racemes, 12cm long and wide, above dark green leaves. Raised in Holland by Mr Esveld. C 1980. ♀ 2002. **'Scarlett O'Hara'** Pure white flowers opening early and profusely borne in dense, hanging clusters. Young growths bronze. Selected in New Zealand before 1980. **Taiwanensis Group** (*P. taiwanensis* Hayata) There is no absolute distinction between the plants from Japan and Taiwan but the latter tend to have matt green, more leathery leaves with fewer teeth and the panicles are less drooping, being spreading or somewhat upright. Young growths bronze or bronze-red. I from Taiwan by Ernest Wilson in 1918. FCC 1923. AM 1922. **'Valley Rose'** ('Flamingo' × 'Deep Pink') Flowers are deep pink in bud, opening rose-pink and conspicuously streaked, white at the base, fading to white; they are freely borne in large hanging clusters. Rather like 'Blush' in flower but slightly deeper pink and lacking the attractively coloured young inflorescence. Young foliage pale green. **'Valley Valentine'** ('Flamingo' × 'Valley Rose') Flowers are deep dusky red, hardly fading, white at the base of the corolla, and borne in large drooping clusters. Calyx lobes are pale green marked with deep

red at the centre and base. ♀ 2002. **'Variegata'** The dark green leaves have a narrow creamy-white margin. A bit more vigorous than 'White Rim'. See also *P. japonica* 'White Rim'. C 1850. **'White Cascade'** Profuse white flowers are densely borne in long racemes. Raised in the USA about 1961. **'White Pearl'** Low, spreading habit with white flowers in upright clusters, freely borne even when young. A seedling selected in Holland. C 1982. **'White Rim'** A slow-growing form of medium size. The leaves are prettily variegated with creamy-white, flushed pink when young. One of the most attractive of all silver-variegated shrubs. Grown for many years as 'Variegata'. C 1948. ♀ 2002. **var. *yakushimensis*** Yamazaki. This form is dwarf with upright racemes. Yakushima, Japan.

nana (Maxim.) Mak. (*Arcterica nana* (Maxim.) Mak.) A prostrate shrublet only a few centimetres in height. Leaves in pairs or whorls of 3. The fragrant, white, urn-shaped flowers are produced in terminal clusters in April and May. Japan, Kamchatka. I 1915. AM 1924. **'Redshank'** A form in which the young growth, calyx and pedicels are red. AM 1974.

taiwanensis See *P. japonica* Taiwanensis Group.

Pignut See *Carya glabra*.

*****PIMELEA** Banks & Sol. ex Gaertn.—Thymelaeaceae—A genus of some 80 species of shrubs, natives of Australasia. Attractive, small-leaved evergreens, closely allied to *Daphne* and requiring similar cultural treatment. Not recommended for shallow chalk soils.

†*drupacea* Labill. A small, erect shrub with ovate or narrow leaves, 2.5–5cm long. Terminal clusters of white flowers in summer, followed by black fruits. SE Australia, Tasmania. I 1817.

†*ferruginea* Labill. A dwarf, erect shrub of excellent quality, flowering in late spring and early summer. The heads of clear deep peach-pink flowers are borne at the tips of the branchlets, which are continuously produced. Leaves in rows, small and neat, shining green. W Australia. I 1824. AM 1959.

prostrata (J.R. Forst. & G. Forst.) Willd. (*P. laevigata* Gaertn.) A pretty and interesting carpeting species having prostrate or sub-erect branches clothed with small, glabrous, grey-green leaves. The fragrant, white flowers, produced in clusters in summer, are followed by fleshy, white fruits. An excellent scree plant which succeeded here for many years. New Zealand. AM 1955.

Pineapple guava See *Acca sellowiana*.

PIPTANTHUS Sweet—Leguminosae—A small genus of 2 species of deciduous and evergreen, large shrubs with trifoliolate leaves and comparatively large, showy, yellow, pea-flowers. They succeed in any well-drained soil, including chalk soils.

laburnifolius See *P. nepalensis*.

*****nepalensis** (Hook.) Sweet (*P. laburnifolius* (D. Don) Stapf) Evergreen laburnum. An attractive, nearly evergreen (deciduous in severe winters), Himalayan shrub, 2.4–3.5m high, with large, bright yellow, laburnum-like flowers opening in May. May be grown in the open but an excellent wall plant. I 1821. AM 1960. A slightly more tender form collected by Ludlow and Sherriff in Bhutan (L. & S. 17394) had greyish-green, silky leaves and clusters of attractive, yellow flowers during April and May.

Pistachio See *Pistacia vera*.
Pistachio, Chinese See *Pistacia chinensis*.

PISTACIA L.—**Anacardiaceae**—A small genus of 9 species of evergreen and deciduous shrubs, or occasionally small trees, related to *Rhus*, differing in the petal-less flowers. Widely distributed in warm temperate regions of the N hemisphere. *P. chinensis* is the only fully hardy species. Best in sun, they will succeed in all types of soil.

chinensis Bunge. Chinese pistachio. A hardy, large shrub with elegant, glossy green, pinnate leaves, assuming gorgeous colours in autumn. Flowers unisexual, in dense terminal clusters; fruits, which seldom appear, are small, reddish at first then blue. C and W China. I 1897.

†*lentiscus* L. Mastic tree. A large shrub or small tree. Pinnate leaves have 8–10 ovate, glossy green leaflets on a winged rachis. Mediterranean region. C 1664.

†*terebinthus* L. Chian turpentine tree. A small tree or large shrub with aromatic, glossy, dark green, pinnate leaves. The unisexual flowers are greenish; the small fruits are reddish, turning purplish-brown. Asia Minor, Mediterranean region. C 1656.

†*vera* L. Pistachio. A small tree with pinnate leaves bearing large, downy leaflets. Dense panicles of inconspicuous flowers are followed by small, reddish fruits – the pistachio nuts of commerce, which are rarely developed outside in the British Isles. Requires a hot, dry, sheltered position, or greenhouse. W Asia, long cultivated. I 1770.

***PITTOSPORUM** Banks ex Gaertn.—**Pittosporaceae**—A large genus of some 200 species of evergreen shrubs or small trees, the majority only suitable for mild districts; they thrive especially well near the sea. Grow in any well-drained soil. Natives of Australasia to E and SE Asia, tropical and South Africa, several have small, fragrant flowers, but they are chiefly grown for their foliage, which is useful for cutting. *P. dallii* is the only species that has never been injured outside here during its stay of more than 40 years.

†*adaphniphylloides* Hu & Wang (*P. daphniphylloides* sens. Rehder & E.H. Wilson not Hayata) A remarkable, large shrub or small tree with large, dark green, obovate or oblanceolate leaves, up to 23cm long. Flowers cream, deliciously scented, in large terminal clusters from April to July. Fruits small, red. Proving hardy, given shelter. There are large specimens in Cornwall. W China. I 1904 by Ernest Wilson.

anomalum Laing & Gourlay. A small shrub similar to *P. divaricatum* but with more slender shoots and flowers with yellow petals. Some plants previously grown as *P. divaricatum* belong here. New Zealand.

†*bicolor* Hook. A large shrub or small tree of erect habit with narrow, revolute, entire leaves, dark green above, white- becoming brownish-tomentose beneath. Flowers bell-shaped, maroon and yellow in clusters during spring. A useful tall hedge in mild areas. Tasmania, SE Australia. C 1854.

chinense See *P. tobira*.

†*colensoi* Hook. f. A medium to large shrub, closely related to *P. tenuifolium*, excellent in maritime districts. Leaves 3.5–10cm long, oblong or oval, leathery and glossy, dark green above. Dark red, comparatively large flowers appear in April. New Zealand.

†*cornifolium* A. Cunn. A distinct species, to 1.8m high, with leaves 5–7.5cm long and whorled. Purple, musk-scented flowers, in terminal umbels of 2–5, appear in February and March. Normally epiphytic on tree trunks in its native habitat, but succeeds in ordinary, well-drained soil in favoured areas of the British Isles. New Zealand.

crassifolium A. Cunn. Karo. One of the hardiest species, surviving many years uninjured at the Sir Harold Hillier Gardens and Arboretum. Leaves 5–7.5cm long, oval or obovate, thick and leathery, deep green above, white-felted beneath. Flowers deep purple, in terminal clusters. An excellent dense screen or shelter-belt in coastal areas. Kermadec and North Island, New Zealand. '**Variegatum**' Leaves grey-green, attractively margined creamy-white. AM 1977.

crispulum Gagnep. A medium-sized shrub with rather thin, glossy dark green, narrow, elliptic leaves, to 18cm or more long, gradually tapered to the base and pointed at the apex with a shallowly crenate margin. They are borne on long and slender petioles, to 3cm long, and have a conspicuously undulate margin. Flowers deep golden-yellow, not fragrant, in dense clusters as the bright green young leaves emerge in late spring, followed by pear-shaped glabrous fruits, to 2.5cm long, bright green when young, turning to brown and splitting to reveal deep orange seeds. I 1980 by Harry van de Laar who collected it on Mt Omei, Sichuan, China. It was originally thought to be *P. omeiense*.

dallii Cheesem. A perfectly hardy, large, spreading shrub, or rarely a small, rounded tree. Shoots and petioles dark reddish-purple. Leaves elliptic to elliptic-lanceolate, leathery and jaggedly toothed or occasionally entire, matt green. Fragrant, creamy-white flowers, with exserted stamens, are borne in small, terminal clusters in summer. It flowered at the Sir Harold Hillier Gardens and Arboretum for the first time in August 1988 and has reached 4 by 6.5m. New Zealand (South Island), rare in the wild.

daphniphylloides See *P. adaphniphylloides*.

divaricatum Cockayne. A small to medium shrub with rigid, wiry branches forming a dense, tangled mass. Leaves variable, 12–20mm long; those of juvenile plants deeply toothed, those of adult plants entire to deeply toothed or lobed. Small, dark maroon flowers are produced at the ends of the shoots in May. A curious species reminiscent of *Corokia cotoneaster* in habit. Proving hardy. New Zealand.

†*eugenioides* A. Cunn. Tarata. A large shrub or small tree with dark twigs and oval or oblong, glossy green, undulate leaves, 5–10cm long, and pleasantly aromatic. Flowers pale yellow, honey-scented, produced in terminal clusters in spring. New Zealand. '**Variegatum**' One of the prettiest and most elegant of variegated shrubs for very mild climates. Leaves margined creamy-white. C 1882. ♀ 2002.

'**Garnettii**' (*P. tenuifolium* 'Garnettii') (*P. ralphii* × *P. tenuifolium*) A large, conical to broadly columnar shrub with grey-green leaves irregularly margined creamy-white and marked or spotted pink to red during winter. Arose in a New Zealand nursery before 1957 and named after its discoverer, Arthur Garnett. 'Saundersii' is a seedling of this and is virtually identical. ♀ 2002.

mayi See *P. tenuifolium*.

nigricans See *P. tenuifolium*.

patulum Hook. A large slender, sparsely branched, hardy shrub or small, erect tree to 4.5m. Leaves variable; those of juvenile plants are 2.5–5cm long, narrow and conspicuously lobed, those of adult plants are 12mm long, toothed or entire. Flowers bell-shaped, fragrant, dark crimson with yellow anthers, in terminal clusters during May. New Zealand (South Island).

†*ralphii* Kirk. This medium to large shrub, though not fully hardy, did survive for many years uninjured in our nursery. Related to *P. crassifolium*, from which it differs in its larger, more oblong, less obovate leaves, which are flat, not recurved, at the margins. Flowers are dark crimson with yellow anthers. New Zealand (North Island). **'Variegatum'** Leaves broadly margined with creamy-white. C 1957. AM 1979.

'Saundersii' See under *P.* 'Garnettii'.

tenuifolium Gaertn. (*P. nigrcans* hort., *P. mayi* hort.) A charming, large shrub or small tree of columnar habit, with bright, pale green, undulate leaves, prettily set on black twigs. One of the hardier species, extensively used as a cut evergreen for floristry. A good hedging plant for mild localities. Flowers small, chocolate-purple, honey-scented, appearing in spring. Many plants appear to bear only male or female flowers. New Zealand. ♀ 2002. AM 1931. **'Abbotsbury Gold'** A variegated form similar to 'Eila Keightley' but the variegation most apparent on the young foliage, becoming indistinct on mature leaves. Arose as a sport at Abbotsbury Gardens, Dorset, in about 1970. **'Arundel Green'** Compact with bright green foliage on dark shoots. **'Deborah'** A medium-sized to large shrub with small, rounded, green to grey-green leaves, the broad creamy margin flushed deep pink, particularly in winter. **'Dunloe Castle'** A narrow-leaved form named from a plant growing at Dunloe Castle Hotel Gardens, Co. Kerry. **'Eila Keightley'** ('Sunburst') Leaves conspicuously blotched in the centre with bright greenish-yellow, the variegation most conspicuous on the older foliage. Discovered in 1964 as a sport of 'Rotundifolium', a form with white-margined leaves. **'Elizabeth'** Bushy and upright, leaves to 6cm long, green and cream, edged with pink, especially in winter. **'Garnettii'** See *P.* 'Garnettii'. **'Gold Star'** Young leaves yellow-green in the centre with an irregular, narrow, dark green margin, dark green and very inconspicuously variegated with a prominent white midrib when mature except beneath where the variegation is still apparent. Compact and upright with the young shoots red. **'Irene Paterson'** A very attractive, slow-growing form, eventually reaching about 3m. The young leaves emerge creamy-white, become deep green marbled with white, and develop a pink tinge in winter. Later growth in summer is pale green. Found in the wild near Christchurch, New Zealand by Grahame Paterson when he was Deputy Director of Parks and Recreation in Dunedin, and named after his wife. Mr Paterson, who died in 1988, will be

remembered for setting up the first unit for the preservation of New Zealand endangered plants. Male. C 1970. ♀ 2002. **'James Stirling'** A charming form with small, dainty, silvery-green, rounded or oval leaves crowding the slender, blackish-purple branchlets. It was seed-raised from a plant found by James Stirling of the Government Gardens, Wellington, New Zealand. **'Katie'** Leaves grey-green with a creamy-white margin which turns to creamy-yellow, smaller and less undulate than those of 'Silver Queen'. **'Limelight'** Leaves to 5.5cm long, not wavy-edged, pale green with a dark green margin, on green young shoots. **'Purpureum'** An attractive selection in which the pale green leaves gradually change to deep bronze-purple. More tender than the green form. **'Saundersii'** See under *P.* 'Garnettii'. **'Silver Queen'** Leaves suffused silvery-grey, narrowly margined with white. Forms a neat and handsome specimen shrub. Female. ♀ 2002. AM 1914. **'Stirling Gold'** A sport of 'James Stirling' raised in New Zealand. The tiny leaves are conspicuously blotched in the centre with bright yellow. **'Tom Thumb'** A seedling of 'Purpureum', this is a dwarf shrub of dense, rounded habit. Leaves are green when young becoming deep reddish-purple. The colour is brighter and redder than 'Purpureum'. Raised in New Zealand about 1960. ♀ 2002. **'Tresederi'** Small leaves with an upturned margin and strongly hooked tip. Glossy dark green with a paler green centre, the variegation most conspicuous on the older foliage as the centre of the leaf turns to bright yellow-green. **'Variegatum'** Leaves margined creamy-white. Possibly a hybrid. **'Warnham Gold'** Young leaves greenish-yellow maturing to golden-yellow, with markedly wavy edges. It is particularly attractive during autumn and winter. A selected seedling raised at Warnham Court, Sussex, in 1959. ♀ 2002.

'Saundersii' See under *P.* 'Garnettii'.

†*tobira* Aiton (*P. chinense* Donn) A slow-growing species eventually making a large shrub. Obovate, bright, glossy green leaves in whorls. In summer, orange-blossom-scented flowers are creamy-white at first, turning to yellow. An excellent wall shrub. Used extensively in S Europe for hedging; very drought-resistant. China, Taiwan, Japan. I 1804. ♀ 2002. AM 1984. **'Variegatum'** Leaves grey-green with an irregular, but conspicuous, creamy-white margin. Plants under glass often flower during winter. ♀ 2002.

truncatum E. Pritz. A medium-sized shrub with leathery, rhombic dark green leaves, to 8cm long, usually broadest slightly above the middle, entire. Flowers white at first, ageing to deep yellow, sweetly fragrant, borne in clusters in late spring. Fruits pear-shaped, downy, to 1.5cm long. It was originally grown here as *P. heterophyllum*. Sichuan, China.

turneri Petrie. A large shrub or small tree of erect habit with obovate leaves, 2.5–4cm long, and pink or purple flowers, in terminal clusters, in May and June. On juvenile plants the slender, tortuous branches are formed in a dense, tangled mass. One of the hardier species, it has reached 5.5m in the Sir Harold Hillier Gardens and Arboretum (1990). New Zealand (North Island).

†*undulatum* Vent. A large shrub with shining, dark green, wavy-edged leaves, 7.5–15cm long. Flowers creamy-white, fragrant, produced in terminal clusters in May and

June even on young plants. Only suitable for the mildest localities. Australia. I 1789. **'Variegatum'** A very beautiful, silver-variegated form.

PLAGIANTHUS J.R. Forst. & G. Forst.—**Malvaceae**—A genus of 2 species of graceful trees or shrubs, natives of New Zealand, where they hybridise in the wild. They succeed in the South and South West of Britain, in all types of fertile soil. The flowers are very small and are usually unisexual.

betulinus See *P. regius*.

divaricatus J.R. Forst. & G. Forst. An interesting shrub forming a densely branched bush 2m high. Leaves of young plants are linear or spathulate, 2–3.5cm long; those of adult plants are spathulate or narrow obovate, 6–20mm long. Flowers small, yellow-white, solitary or in short clusters in May. New Zealand. I 1820.

lyallii See *Hoheria glabrata* and *H. lyallii*.

regius (Poit.) Hochr. (*P. betulinus* A. Cunn.) Ribbonwood. A graceful, slender, small to medium tree. Leaves ovate to ovate-lanceolate, up to 7.5cm long, toothed. Flowers inconspicuous, white, in large panicles during May. Juvenile plants present a dense bush of slender, interlacing branches with short-stalked leaves, 1–4cm long, toothed or lobed. A curious tree passing through several stages of growth. New Zealand. I 1870.

Plane See *Platanus*.

Plane, Corstorphine See *Acer pseudoplatanus* 'Corstorphinense'.

PLANERA Gmel.—**Ulmaceae**—A rare, monotypic genus that is easy to cultivate in all types of soil; related to *Ulmus*, but differs in its warty, nut-like fruits.

aquatica (Walter) Gmel. (*P. ulmifolia* Michx.) Water elm. A small to medium-sized, widespreading tree with oval, simply or doubly serrate leaves 2.5–7.5cm in length and slightly rough to the touch. Flowers monoecious, inconspicuous. A native of swampy forests in the SE USA. I 1816.

PLANTAGO L.—**Plantaginaceae**—The plantains contain more than 250 species, nearly all herbaceous, of cosmopolitan distribution. The following is interesting because of its shrubby nature.

*sempervirens Crantz (*P. cynops* L.) Shrubby plantain. A dwarf shrub with slender, erect stems, reddish-purple when young. Leaves opposite, linear, with rough margins. Tiny flowers, with exserted, cream anthers, are borne in small, dense heads, on short stalks, during summer. SW Europe. C 1596.

PLATANUS L.—**Platanaceae**—A small genus of about 6 species of magnificent large, maple-like trees with alternate leaves and attractive, flaking bark. Natives of North America and Mexico, apart from *P. orientalis* and one species in SE Asia. They may be grown in all types of fertile soil, but will not reach their maximum size in chalky soil and may become chlorotic in very shallow chalk soils.

× *acerifolia* See *P.* × *hispanica*.

'Augustine Henry' (*P. californica* hort.) A large tree similar to the London plane but with drooping lower branches and with more conspicuously flaking bark. It has large, 5-lobed leaves.

× *hispanica* Mill. ex Münchh. (*P.* × *acerifolia* (Aiton) Willd., *P.* × *hybrida* Brot.) London plane. A large, noble park tree with attractive, mottled or patchwork, flaking bark, and large, palmate leaves. The rounded, burr-like, fruit clusters are produced in strings of 2–6 and hang like baubles on the branches from early summer through to the following spring. Extensively planted as a street tree owing to its tolerance of atmospheric pollution and severe pruning. First recorded about 1663. It has long been considered a hybrid between *P. occidentalis* and *P. orientalis*, though it may be a form of the latter. ♀ 2002. **'Pyramidalis'** A large, erect form, making an excellent tree for a broad thoroughfare. C 1850. **'Suttneri'** A striking form with large leaves boldly variegated creamy-white. C 1896. **'Tremonia'** A vigorous tree of narrowly conical habit selected in the Dortmund Botanic Garden, Germany in 1951.

occidentalis L. Buttonwood, American sycamore. A difficult tree to cultivate successfully in the British Isles, this differs from *P.* × *hispanica* in its shallowly lobed leaves and smoother fruit clusters, which are normally produced singly on long stalks. S Ontario (Canada), E USA, NE Mexico. In spite of several attempts, it has proved impossible to establish any of the American species here. I 1636.

orientalis L. Oriental plane, Chennar tree. A large, stately, long-lived tree developing a widespreading head of branches. Bark attractively dappled and flaking; leaves deeply 5-lobed, the lobes reaching halfway or more to the base. Bristly fruit clusters, 2–6 on a stalk. One of the most magnificent of all large trees and attaining a great age. SE Europe. Cultivated in England in the early 16th century. ♀ 2002. AM 1966. **'Digitata'** (*P. orientalis laciniata* hort.) Leaves deeply divided into 3–5 finger-like lobes. ♀ 2002. **var. insularis** A. DC. (*P. cretica* Dode, *P. cyprius* hort.) Cyprian plane. A small tree with smaller leaves of variable shape, usually deeply divided, with narrow lobes, and cuneate at the base.

†*racemosa* Nutt. (*P. californica* Benth.) A rare species, attaining a large size in California but much smaller in the British Isles. Leaves 3- or 5-lobed to below the middle, tomentose beneath. Fruit clusters sessile, 2–7 on each stalk. California, NW Mexico. I 1870.

PLATYCARYA Siebold & Zucc.—**Juglandaceae**—A monotypic genus related to *Pterocarya*, differing in the erect inflorescences and twigs with a solid pith.

strobilacea Siebold & Zucc. (*Fortunaea chinensis* Lindl.) A beautiful, small tree with pinnate leaves composed of 7–15 sessile, lanceolate, toothed leaflets. Flowers small, the males in cylindrical catkins, the females in erect, green, cone-like clusters, at the end of the current year's growth, in July or August. Conspicuous and distinctive cone-like fruits. It reached 9m in the Sir Harold Hillier Gardens and Arboretum (1990). China, Japan, Korea, Taiwan. I 1845 by Robert Fortune.

†****PLECOSTACHYS** Hilliard & B.L. Burtt—**Compositae**—2 species of intricately branched shrubs, allied to *Helichrysum* and natives of South Africa.

serpyllifolia (Berg.) Hilliard & B.L. Burtt (*Helichrysum microphyllum* hort. not Benth. & Hook.) A dwarf, spreading, aromatic, stiffly branched shrub with white-tomentose stems. Leaves small, sessile, recurved at the apex, white-tomentose on both sides. Tiny, white flowerheads, tinged pink, are borne in terminal clusters in winter and spring. Commonly grown for summer bedding and hanging baskets; hardy only in mild areas.

†**PLUMBAGO**—**Plumbaginaceae**—The leadworts consist of some 15 species of annuals, perennials, evergreen shrubs, and scandent climbers from warm-temperate and tropical regions of the world.

auriculata Lam. (*P. capensis* Thunb.) Cape leadwort. An evergreen shrub with scandent, long, arching branches that produce masses of tubular, sky-blue flowers during summer and into late autumn. Ideal for a large conservatory or heated greenhouse. South Africa. ♛ 2002. **f. alba** (Pasq.) T.H. Peng. Flowers white. ♛ 2002.

capensis See *P. auriculata*.

Plumbago, hardy See *Ceratostigma willmottianum*.
Pocket handkerchief tree See *Davidia involucrata*.

POLIOTHYRSIS Oliv.—**Flacourtiaceae**—A monotypic genus related to *Idesia*, differing in the capsular fruits. It is quite hardy and succeeds in all types of fertile soil.

sinensis Oliv. A small, hardy tree or large shrub with red-stalked, ovate, slender-pointed leaves, 10–15cm long, red-tinged and downy on both sides when young later smooth, dark green. Flowers unisexual, fragrant, whitish in bud opening creamy-yellow, borne in terminal, conical panicles, to 25cm long, in July or August; best in hot summers. China. I 1908 by Ernest Wilson. ♛ 2002. AM 1960.

*****POLYGALA** L.—**Polygalaceae**—A large genus of more than 500 species of annual or perennial herbs and shrubs with colourful pea-like flowers; widely distributed. The woody species thrive in most types of soil but are not recommended for shallow chalk soils.

‡*chamaebuxus* L. A dwarf, evergreen, alpine shrublet forming large tufts a few centimetres high. Flowers creamy-white, tipped bright yellow, appear in profusion from April to June. Suitable for a cool, moist position in a rock or peat garden. Mts of C Europe; a common plant in the Alps. C 1658. ♛ 2002. **'Angustifolia'** A form with narrow leaves, up to 2.5cm long by 0.3cm across. Flowers purple, tipped yellow. **var. grandiflora** Neilr. (*P. chamaebuxus* var. *purpurea* Neilr., *P. chamaebuxus* var. *rhodoptera* Ball) A very beautiful form with purple wing-petals and yellow keel. ♛ 2002. AM 1896. **var. rhodoptera** See var. *grandiflora*.

†× *dalmaisiana* Bailey (*P. myrtifolia* var. *grandiflora* × *P. fruticosa* var. *cordata*) (*P. myrtifolia* var. *grandiflora* hort.) A small, almost continuously flowering shrub with bright purple flowers. Suitable for a conservatory. Both parents are natives of South Africa. ♛ 2002.

†*myrtifolia* An erect deciduous shrub, about 1.5m high, with greenish-white flowers, veined with purple, in summer. For a conservatory or a very sheltered spot in a mild area. South Africa. **var. grandiflora** (Lodd.) Hook. Larger, rich purple flowers. See also *P.* × *dalmaisiana*.

‡*vayredae* Costa. A choice, creeping alpine shrublet, resembling *P. chamaebuxus*, but with narrower leaves. Flowers reddish-purple, tipped bright yellow, in March and April. Suitable for a cool, moist position in a rock or peat garden. Spanish Pyrenees. C 1923.

†*virgata* Thunb. An erect shrub, to 2m, with reed-like stems and narrow leaves. Flowers purple, very conspicuous, in long racemes. Suitable for a conservatory. South Africa. I 1814. AM 1977.

POLYGONUM L.—**Polygonaceae**—With the splitting of this genus now generally accepted, the following is the only species of garden note. Most of the herbaceous species belong to *Persicaria*. See also *Fallopia* under CLIMBERS.

equisetiforme See under *P. scoparium*.

scoparium Req. ex Loisel. (*P. equisetiforme* hort. not Sibth. & Sm.) A small subshrub of interesting and unusual growth. The long, slender, reed-like stems are usually devoid of leaves and bear a remarkable resemblance to those of a horsetail (*Equisetum* sp.). The small, creamy-white flowers are borne in numerous, axillary clusters during late summer and autumn. Requires a warm, sunny, well-drained position. Usually cut back during a severe winter. Corsica, Sardinia. *P. equisetiforme*, a native of the Mediterranean region and Middle East, is prostrate and rarely grown.

vacciniifolium See *Persicaria vacciniifolia*.

POLYLEPIS Ruiz & Pav.—**Rosaceae**—A genus of 15 species of trees and shrubs, related to *Margyricarpus* and *Acaena* and natives of the Andes, often at very high altitudes. The generic name refers to the peeling bark.

australis Bitter. An unusual, semi-evergreen shrub of medium size, reaching 10m in the wild, with attractive, pale brown, flaking bark. Leaves congested at the ends of the shoots, pinnate, with 5- to 7-toothed, short-stalked leaflets, oblique at the base, some turning yellow in autumn. Flowers small, green, with reddish-purple stamens, borne in long, drooping racemes in May. Proving hardy at the Sir Harold Hillier Gardens and Arboretum where it has reached 3m by 4m. N Argentina.

†*****POMADERRIS** Labill.—**Rhamnaceae**—A genus of about 40 species of evergreen, small trees and shrubs, natives of Australasia. All require a warm, sheltered position or conservatory treatment. They succeed in all types of well-drained soil, but are not recommended for very shallow chalk soils.

apetala Labill. A large shrub with oblong-lanceolate, toothed leaves, wrinkled above, densely tomentose beneath; flowers small, mustard-yellow in large panicles in summer. SE Australia, Tasmania, New Zealand. I 1803.

phylicifolia Lodd. ex Link. A small, heath-like shrub having densely woolly shoots, small, narrow leaves, and cream-coloured flowers borne very abundantly in April. SE Australia, Tasmania, New Zealand. I 1819.

Pomegranate See *Punica granatum*.

PONCIRUS Raf.—**Rutaceae**—A monotypic genus related to *Citrus*. It is hardy and will succeed in all types of well-drained soil, preferably in full sun.

trifoliata (L.) Raf. (*Aegle sepiaria* DC., *Citrus trifoliata* L.) Japanese bitter orange. A stout, slow-growing, medium-sized shrub with green stems armed with stout spines and trifoliolate leaves. Beautiful in spring when carrying its white, sweetly scented flowers, like orange blossom. The individual flowers are almost as large as those of *Clematis montana*. Fruits globular, like miniature oranges, 3.5–5cm across, green ripening to yellow. N China. I 1850.

Poplar See *Populus*.

POPULUS L.—**Salicaceae**—The poplars are a genus of about 35 species of trees, distributed throughout N temperate regions. They include some of the fastest-growing of all trees. Many are well adapted for quickly forming an effective, tall windbreak, but their rapid growth and surface-rooting makes them unsuitable for small gardens, and they should not be planted near buildings as problems can be caused by the roots invading drains. Most thrive in all types of soil, even when wet or boggy, but in wet sites mound planting is desirable. With a few exceptions poplars do not thrive on shallow chalky soils and most of the black poplars tend to become chlorotic and even die within thirty years. Many are tolerant of atmospheric pollution and several are excellent in maritime exposure. Some of the poplars, especially the newer hybrids, are valuable for timber production and give comparatively quick returns. The balsam poplars have pleasantly aromatic young leaves, while many of the black poplars have attractive, copper-coloured growths in spring. The catkins of certain species are long, and drape the bare branches in spring, male and female catkins appearing on separate trees (dioecious). Some species and their hybrids are prone to canker.

× *acuminata* Rydb. (*P. angustifolia* × *P. sargentii*) A medium-sized balsam poplar with rounded twigs and ovate to rhomboid, acuminate, shining green leaves, aromatic when unfolding. W North America. I 1898.

alba L. White poplar, Abele. A large, suckering tree, conspicuous due to the white-woolly undersurfaces of the leaves, particularly noticeable when ruffled by the wind. The leaves are variable in shape, some ovate and irregularly lobed or toothed, others larger and distinctly 3- to 5-lobed like a maple. Autumn colour yellow. An excellent tree in exposed sites, particularly in coastal areas where, if cut severely and retained as a shrub, it is effective with similarly pruned, red- and yellow-stemmed willows and *Spartium junceum*. Grows well on chalky soil. C and SE Europe to C Asia. Long cultivated and naturalised in the British Isles. **'Bolleana'** See 'Pyramidalis'. **'Paletzkyana'** A form with deeply lobed and toothed leaves. **'Pyramidalis'** ('Bolleana') A large tree with erect branches, resembling in habit the Lombardy poplar (*P. nigra* 'Italica'), but slightly broader in relation to height. C 1841. **'Raket'** A very narrow tree with upright branches. Raised in Holland before 1956. **'Richardii'** A smaller-growing, less vigorous tree with leaves bright golden-yellow above, white beneath. A delightful form, very effective at a distance; best grown as a stooled plant. C 1910. AM 1912.

'Andover' (*P. nigra* var. *betulifolia* × *P. trichocarpa*) A robust, slow-growing, large tree of American origin; a hybrid between a black poplar and a balsam poplar.

'Androscoggin' (*P. maximowiczii* × *P. trichocarpa*) A large, extremely vigorous male hybrid of American origin. Specimens growing in the Quantock Forest in Somerset attained 30m in 17 years.

angulata See *P. deltoides* 'Carolin'.

'Balsam Spire' (*P.* 'T.T. 32', *P.* 'Tacatricho 32') (*P. balsamifera* × *P. trichocarpa*) A large, narrow, female tree of extremely fast growth, with white-backed leaves and fragrant buds. ♀ 2002.

balsamifera L. (*P. tacamahacca* Mill.) Balsam poplar. A large, erect-branched tree, grown mainly for the balsamic odour of its unfolding leaves. Twigs rounded, glabrous; buds large and sticky. Leaves ovate to ovate-lanceolate, whitish and reticulate beneath. The sticky buds and smell of balsam is possessed by a number of poplars, notably *P. × jackii*. North America. I before 1689. **var. *michauxii*** (Dode) Henry. A minor form with petioles and veins of leaf underside minutely hairy.

balsamifera × *trichocarpa* See *P.* 'Balsam Spire'.

× *berolinensis* Dippel (*P. laurifolia* × *P. nigra* 'Italica') Berlin poplar. A large, broadly columnar tree with slightly angled, downy twigs and ovate to rhomboid, acuminate leaves, pale beneath. Much used for street planting on the Continent and for windbreaks on the North American prairies. A male clone. **'Petrowskyana'** (*P. × petrowskyana* C.K. Schneid.) A very hardy hybrid. Branches angled and pubescent, leaves ovate, pale beneath. Raised in Russia about 1880. **'Rumford'** A moderately vigorous tree of American origin.

× *canadensis* Moench (*P. × euramericana* Guinier) A large group of hybrids between the American *P. deltoides* and forms of the European *P. nigra*. They are known collectively as hybrid black poplars. All are vigorous trees and excellent for screening purposes. The wood of several clones is used in the match industry. The first clone originated possibly in France about 1750. **'Carrièreana'** A large, erect tree of vigorous growth. Proving lime-tolerant. **'Eugenei'** A narrow, male tree with short, ascending branches; young leaves coppery in colour. Among the best poplars to grow commercially in this country. A hybrid between *P. nigra* 'Italica' and *P. × canadensis* 'Regenerata'. Ours is a canker-resistant form introduced by the late Lt Col Pratt, from Messrs Simon-Louis at Plantières, near Metz (France). **'Gelrica'** A vigorous, male tree of Continental origin, with whitish bark and coppery young growths. A cross between 'Marilandica' and 'Serotina', usually breaking into leaf after the former and before the latter. **'Henryana'** A large tree with a widespreading, rounded head of branches. A male clone. Origin unknown. **'Lloydii'** (*P.* 'Lloydii') A large, spreading, female tree of moderate growth, a hybrid between *P. deltoides* and *P. nigra* var. *betulifolia*. **'Marilandica'** A large, densely branched, female tree with a wide head. Resembles 'Serotina', but is usually earlier leafing and its young leaves are green. One of the best poplars for chalk soils. Probably *P. nigra* × 'Serotina'. **'Pacheri'** A fast-growing, large tree. **'Regenerata'** ('Marilandica' × 'Serotina') A large, female tree with twiggy branches arching outwards. Branchlets slender; young leaves green, appearing about a fortnight earlier than those of 'Serotina'. Originated in a nursery near Paris in 1814 and now universally planted in industrial areas. **'Robusta'** A large, vigorous, male tree forming an open crown with a straight bole to summit. Young twigs minutely downy; young leaves an attractive coppery-red. A hybrid between *P. deltoides* 'Cordata' and *P. nigra* 'Plantierensis' raised by Messrs Simon-Louis at Plantières, near Metz (France) in 1895. **'Serotina'** A very vigorous, large, openly branched, male tree with a usually uneven crown and glabrous twigs. Leaves appear late; copper-red when young. Catkins, 7.5–10cm long, with conspicuous red anthers. This commonly planted tree is said to have originated in France early in the 18th century. **'Serotina Aurea'** ('Van Geertii') Golden poplar. Leaves clear golden-yellow in spring and early summer, becoming yellowish-green later then golden-yellow in autumn. Originated as a sport in Van Geert's nursery at Ghent in 1871. ♀ 2002. **'Serotina de Selys'** ('Serotina Erecta') A large, columnar form raised in Belgium before 1818.

× *candicans* See *P.* × *jackii*.

× *canescens* (Aiton) Sm. (*P. alba* × *P. tremula*) Grey poplar. A medium-sized to large, suckering tree sometimes forming thickets. Mature specimens develop an attractive, creamy-grey trunk. Leaves variable in shape, rounded or deltoid, dentate and slightly toothed, more or less grey-tomentose beneath. One of the best poplars for chalk soils, giving attractive, yellow and sometimes red autumn colour. The male catkins in late winter are most decorative, being woolly and crimson, up to 10cm long. Female trees are rare in this country. W. C and S Europe (incl. England). Extensively planted and naturalised. **'De Moffart'** A male selection from Belgium with a dense, conical crown and large leaves which open early. C 1977. **'Macrophylla'** Picart's poplar. A large-leaved form, very vigorous in growth. It has reached nearly 35m in the Sir Harold Hillier Gardens and Arboretum (2000).

'Carrièreana' See *P.* × *canadensis* 'Carrièreana'.

cathayana Rehder. A rare balsam poplar of vigorous growth. A medium-sized to large tree. The upright branches with rounded twigs carry large, white-backed leaves. NW China to Manchuria and Korea. I about 1908 by Ernest Wilson. Subject to canker. Plants grown under this name are sometimes *P. trichocarpa*.

× *charkoviensis* See *P. nigra* 'Charkoviensis'.

deltoides Marshall (*P. monilifera* Aiton.) Cottonwood, Necklace poplar. A large, broad-headed, black poplar with rounded or angled twigs and broadly heart-shaped, slender-pointed, bright green leaves. Now almost displaced in cultivation by its hybrid progeny. E North America. **'Carolin'** (*P. angulata* hort.) Carolina poplar. A large, open-headed, male tree, with prominently angled twigs and large, heart-shaped leaves. Origin uncertain, probably North America. C about 1789. **'Cordata'** Similar to 'Carolin' but female. Both have been grown as *P. angulata*.

'Eugenei' See *P.* × *canadensis* 'Eugenei'.

× *euramericana* See *P.* × *canadensis*.

'Gelrica' See *P.* × *canadensis* 'Gelrica'.

× *generosa* Henry (*P. deltoides* 'Cordata' × *P. trichocarpa*) We were the first to distribute this remarkably vigorous hybrid, raised by Augustine Henry at Kew in 1912. Young trees sometimes increase in height at the rate of 2m a year. Male and female trees are grown, the males

with long, crimson-anthered catkins in April. Leaves conspicuously large on young trees, bright soft green above, turning yellow in autumn.

glauca Haines (*P. jacquemontii* var. *glauca* (Haines) Kimura) An attractive and vigorous tree with bronze young foliage emerging late, in early summer. Leaves up to 17cm long, broadly ovate, heart-shaped at the base, shallowly-toothed at the margin, blue-green above with red veins, glaucous beneath, on a flattened red petiole. I by A.D. Schilling in 1983 (Schilling 2620). E Himalaya.

grandidentata Michx. Large-toothed aspen. A medium-sized tree with rounded or ovate, deeply and broadly toothed leaves, greyish-tomentose beneath at first, later glabrous and glaucous. Differing from *P. tremula* in its downy young shoots and from *P. tremuloides* in its large-toothed leaves. E North America. I 1772.

'Henryana' See *P.* × *canadensis* 'Henryana'.

'Hiltingbury Weeping' (*P. tremula* 'Pendula' × *P. tremuloides* 'Pendula') A small tree with long, weeping branches forming a curtain of greyish-green trembling leaves. The result of a deliberate cross made in our Chandler's Ford nursery in 1962.

× *jackii* Sarg. (*P.* × *candicans* Aiton) (*P. balsamifera* × *P. deltoides*) Ontario poplar, Balm of Gilead poplar. A medium-sized, broad-headed tree with stout, angled, downy twigs and broad ovate leaves, greyish-white beneath, strongly balsam-scented when unfolding. Origin uncertain, probably North American. Only the female tree is known. C 1773. **'Aurora'** A conspicuously variegated form. The leaves, especially when young, are creamy-white, often pink-tinged. Older leaves green. To obtain the best results, hard prune the shoots in late winter. Often does not show variegation the first year after transplanting. AM 1954.

jacquemontiana var. *glauca* See *P. glauca*.

koreana Rehder. A handsome balsam poplar of medium size, with conspicuous, large, bright apple-green leaves, white beneath and with red midribs. One of the first trees to come into leaf in early spring. Korea. I 1918 by Ernest Wilson.

lasiocarpa Oliv. A magnificent, medium-sized tree with stout, angled, downy twigs. The leaves, often up to 30cm long and 23cm wide, are bright green with conspicuous, red veins and leaf stalks. C China. Discovered by Augustine Henry in 1888, introduced by Ernest Wilson in 1900. ♀ 2002. FCC 1908.

lasiocarpa × *wilsonii* This remarkable hybrid was obtained by Sir Harold Hillier in 1974 from Kornik Arboretum in Poland, where it was raised. It is a vigorous tree with large leaves to 22cm long, green beneath as in *P. lasiocarpa*, but much less hairy on the underside and with the flattened petiole and glabrous mature shoots of *P. wilsonii*. The clone grown here is male with stout green catkins in spring, the anthers flushed orange-red as they emerge, and coming into leaf much earlier than *P. lasiocarpa*.

laurifolia Ledeb. A slow-growing balsam poplar, making a medium-sized tree of elegant habit. The young shoots are strongly angled. Leaves narrowly ovate or lanceolate, whitish beneath. Siberia. I about 1830.

'Lloydii' See *P.* × *canadensis* 'Lloydii'.

'Maine' (*P.* × *berolinensis* × *P.* × *candicans*) An interesting American-raised, multiple hybrid of moderate growth.

'Marilandica' See *P.* × *canadensis* 'Marilandica'.

maximowiczii Henry. A conspicuous, rapid-growing balsam poplar of medium size, distinguished by its rounded, downy young twigs and its roundish, leathery, deeply veined leaves with white undersurfaces and a twisted tip. E Asia. I about 1890.

monilifera See *P. deltoides*.

nigra L. Black poplar. A large, heavy-branched tree with characteristic burred trunk and glabrous twigs. Leaves rhomboid to ovate, slender-pointed, bright, shining green. C and S Europe, W Asia. Long cultivated and naturalised in many countries. Often referred to as var. *typica*. **'Afghanica'** ('Thevestina') A strong-growing, columnar tree, similar to the Lombardy poplar (*P. nigra* 'Italica'), but female and with downy young shoots. In the Middle East and hotter climes than the British Isles, it is renowned for its white trunk. **subsp.** ***betulifolia*** (Pursh) Wettst. Manchester poplar, Wilson's Variety. A picturesque, bushy-headed tree, characterised by its downy shoots and young leaves. Tolerant of smoke pollution and formerly much planted in the industrial North of England. Native of E and C England. **'Charkowiensis'** A tree of Russian origin, probably a cross between *P. nigra* and *P. nigra* 'Italica'. A large tree of broadly pyramidal habit. **'Italica'** ('Pyramidalis') Lombardy poplar. A large, narrow, columnar tree with close, erect branches. A male tree and one of the most effective of its habit, particularly suitable for forming a tall screen. Origin before 1750. I 1758. ♀ 2002. **'Italica Foemina'** The female form, a broader tree than 'Italica' but of similar outline. The orange twigs are effective in winter. **'Lombardy Gold'** A striking tree with golden-yellow foliage. Discovered in 1974 as a sport on a mature Lombardy poplar near the village of Normandy in Surrey by John Whitehead. It has already (1990) reached more than 12m at Wisley. **'Plantierensis'** A fastigiate tree like the Lombardy poplar, which it has largely replaced in this country. It differs from the latter in its downy twigs, stronger, lower branching and bushier, broader head. Appears to have the amalgamated characters of var. *betulifolia* and 'Italica'. **'Pyramidalis'** See 'Italica'. **'Thevestina'** See 'Afghanica'. **var.** ***viadri*** (Rudiger) Aschers. & Graebn. A slender, erect-growing wild form. I 1893.

'Oxford' (*P.* × *berolinensis* × *P. maximowiczii*) A vigorous-growing, large tree of American origin.

'Pacheri' See *P.* × *canadensis* 'Pacheri'.

× *petrowskyana* See *P.* × *berolinensis* 'Petrowskyana'.

'Regenerata' See *P.* × *canadensis* 'Regenerata'.

'Robusta' See *P.* × *canadensis* 'Robusta'.

'Rumford' See *P.* × *berolinensis* 'Rumford'.

'Serotina' See *P.* × *canadensis* 'Serotina'.

'Serotina Aurea' See *P.* × *canadensis* 'Serotina Aurea'.

'Serotina Erecta' See *P.* × *canadensis* 'Serotina de Selys'.

sieboldii Miq. Japanese aspen. Medium-sized tree with downy shoots and ovate, minutely toothed, deep green leaves. Japan. C 1881.

simonii Carrière. A medium-sized, early-leafing balsam poplar with slender, angled, glabrous, red-brown twigs and rhomboid leaves, pale beneath. Liable to canker. N China. I 1862. **'Fastigiata'** A columnar tree with long and upright branches. Makes an excellent dense hedge or screen. I from China in 1913.

suaveolens Fisch. A very ornamental, medium-sized balsam poplar with rounded twigs and ovate-lanceolate, slender-pointed leaves, pale beneath. E Siberia. I 1834.

szechuanica C.K. Schneid. A strikingly handsome, balsam poplar making a large tree. Leaves large, whitish-glaucescent beneath, with crimson midrib, reddish when young. Fast-growing, but needs shelter from late spring frosts. W China. I 1908 by Ernest Wilson. **var.** ***tibetica*** C.K. Schneid. (*P. violascens* Dode) One of the most ornamental poplars, differing in its larger leaves, which resemble those of *P. lasiocarpa*. It reached 24m in the Sir Harold Hillier Gardens and Arboretum (1990). W China. I 1904.

'T.T. 32' See *P.* 'Balsam Spire'.

tacamahacca. See *P. balsamifera*.

tremula L. Aspen. A medium-sized, suckering tree. Leaves prominently toothed, late in appearing and hanging late in the autumn when they turn a clear butter-yellow. Petioles slender and compressed, causing the leaves to tremble and quiver in the slightest breeze. Catkins long and grey draping the branchlets in later winter or early spring. One of the commonest sources of wood for the match industry. Widely distributed in Europe and Asia extending to N Africa. ♀ 2002. **'Erecta'** An uncommon form of narrowly columnar habit. Originated in Sweden. C 1847. **'Gigas'** A very vigorous and robust, triploid form. Male. C 1935. **'Pendula'** Weeping aspen. One of the most effective, small, weeping trees, especially attractive in February with its abundance of long purplish-grey, male catkins.

tremuloides Michx. American aspen. A small to medium-sized tree, mainly distinguished from our native species *P. tremula* by the pale yellowish bark of its young trunks and branches, and by its smaller, finely and evenly toothed leaves. Its catkins are also more slender. One of the most widely distributed of North American trees, being found in the mountains of N Mexico northwards to Alaska. C 1812. **'Pendula'** Parasol de St Julien. A small, pendent, female tree which originated in France in 1865.

trichocarpa Hook. Black cottonwood. The fastest and tallest growing of the balsam poplars, reaching a height of over 30m, and up to 60m in its native habitat. Bark of young trees peeling. Buds large and sticky; leaves pale and reticulate beneath, strongly balsam-scented when unfolding. Autumn colour rich yellow. Liable to canker. W North America. I 1892.

violascens See *P. szechuanica* var. *tibetica*.

wilsonii C.K. Schneid. A highly ornamental, medium-sized species, somewhat resembling *P. lasiocarpa*. Leaves large, up to 20cm long, bright sea-green. Branchlets thick, rounded, polished violet-green. C and W China. I 1907 by Ernest Wilson.

yunnanensis Dode. A fast-growing, medium-sized balsam poplar similar to *P. szechuanica*. Leaves with white undersurfaces and reddish stalks and midribs. SW China. I before 1905.

Portugal laurel See *Prunus lusitanica*.
Possum-haw See *Ilex decidua*.

POTENTILLA L.—**Rosaceae**—A large genus of some 500 species of mainly herbs, natives largely of N temperate regions. The shrubby potentillas are rich in good qualities: they are very hardy, dwarf to medium-sized shrubs, thriving in any soil, in sun or partial shade. Their flowers, like small, single roses, are displayed over a long season, beginning in May and June and in some forms lasting until November. Though they are shade tolerant, on the whole they are best grown in full sun. The cultivars with orange, red or pink flowers tend to fade in the hottest sun and perform better if given a moister soil and a position where they receive light shade when the sun is highest. The various selections and forms are regarded as variants of *P. fruticosa*. We would like to thank Mr Wilfrid Simms for assistance with this genus.

arbuscula See *P. fruticosa* var. *arbuscula*. **var.** *bulleyana* See *P. fruticosa* 'Bulleyana'. **var.** *rigida* See *P. fruticosa* var. *rigida*. *davurica* See *P. fruticosa* var. *davurica*. **var.** *veitchii* See *P. fruticosa* 'Veitchii'.

× *friedrichsenii* See *P. fruticosa* 'Friedrichsenii'.

fruticosa L. A dense bush, averaging l–1.5m high, producing yellow flowers from May to September. Leaves small, divided into 5–7 narrow leaflets. This is generally treated as a variable species, being distributed throughout the N hemisphere, including the north of England and the west of Ireland.

Varieties and cultivars of *Potentilla fruticosa*

The cultivars listed below are mainly dwarf shrubs.

'Abbotswood' Dwarf shrub of spreading habit with dark foliage. Flowers are white, plentifully and continuously produced. ♀ 2002. AMT 1965.

'Abbotswood Silver' A sport of 'Abbotswood' with the leaflets narrowly margined creamy-white. Quickly reverts.

'Annette' A compact and dwarf form of Dutch origin with profuse orange-yellow flowers over a long period. Fades in strong sunlight.

var. *arbuscula* (D. Don) Maxim (*P. arbuscula* D. Don) A very distinct, dwarf shrub with shaggy branches due to the presence of large, brown stipules. Sage-green leaves have 5 leaflets. Large, rich yellow flowers are produced continuously from midsummer to late autumn. Himalaya. AMT 1965. AM 1925.

'Beanii' ('Leucantha') A dwarf shrub with dark foliage and white flowers tinged with cream. C 1910.

'Beesii' (*P. arbuscula* 'Beesii', *P. arbuscula* 'Nana Argentea') A delightful, dwarf shrub that displays its golden flowers on mounds of silvery foliage. Raised by Bees from Forrest 2437 collected in Tibet. AMT 1984.

'Bulleyana' (*P. arbuscula* var. *bulleyana* Balf. f. ex Fletcher) A small shrub with silky-hairy leaves and bright yellow flowers. Taller and more erect than the typical form. I by Forrest from Yunnan (Forrest 119).

'Buttercup' A small shrub of compact habit, producing small, deep yellow flowers over a long period.

'Cascade' A dwarf, rounded, spreading shrub. Flowers apricot with an ochre-pink eye. Best in partial shade.

'Chelsea Star' Profuse, small, vivid yellow, open-petalled flowers of star-like appearance, starting early in summer. Small, bright green leaves. ♀ 2002.

'Chilo' A dwarf shrub, the leaflets edged with cream. Flowers small, bright yellow. Named after a Dutch pop group. Rather weak-growing and subject to reversion.

'Dart's Cream' Large, creamy-yellow flowers. Grey-green foliage on pink-flushed shoots. Very prone to mildew.

'Dart's Golddigger' A splendid, dwarf shrub of Dutch origin. Dense and compact habit with light grey-green foliage and large butter-yellow flowers. A seedling, probably of var. *arbuscula*. C 1970.

var. *davurica* Nestl. (*P. davurica* Nestl., *P. glabra* Lodd., *P. glabrata* Schlecht., *P. fruticosa glabra*) A very variable form, rarely more than 1.5m in height, usually much less. Both stems and leaves may be glabrous or hairy, depending on the form. The flowers are usually white and freely produced. N China, Siberia. I 1822.

'Daydawn' A small shrub with flowers of an unusual peach-pink, suffused cream. A sport of 'Tangerine'.

'Eastleigh Cream' ('Gold Drop' × Sulphurascens Group) A small shrub of dense habit, spreading to form a low mound. Leaves green; flowers cream, 2.5cm across. Raised in our Eastleigh nursery in 1969.

'Elizabeth' (Sulphurascens Group) (*P. fruticosa* var. *arbuscula* × *P. fruticosa* 'Veitchii') A magnificent hybrid raised in our nurseries about 1950 and named after the younger daughter of Sir Harold Hillier. A dome-shaped bush, 1m by 1.2m, studded from late spring to early autumn with large, rich canary-yellow flowers. This plant was wrongly distributed throughout European nurseries as *P. arbuscula*. AMT 1965.

'Farrer's White' A small shrub of somewhat erect habit, with multitudes of white flowers during summer. Raised from seed collected by Farrer in Gansu. Two clones are grown under this name.

'Floppy Disc' A small weak-growing shrub with semi-double, pink flowers. I by Liss Forest Nurseries, near Petersfield, Hampshire.

'Frances Lady Daresbury' See 'Lady Daresbury'.

'Friedrichsenii' (*P.* × *friedrichsenii* Späth) (*P. fruticosa* var. *davurica* × *P. fruticosa*) A vigorous shrub, up to 2m, with slightly grey-green foliage and light yellow flowers. Originated as a seedling in Späth's Nursery in Berlin, in 1895. The form in cultivation is sometimes referred to under the name 'Berlin Beauty'. See also 'Beanii' and 'Ochroleuca' which are of the same parentage. Both the latter and the present plant are excellent when planted as informal hedges.

'Glenroy Pinkie' Dwarf habit with large pink flowers.

'Gold Carpet' See 'Goldteppich'.

'Gold Drop' A dwarf shrub of compact habit, with small, neat leaves and small, bright golden-yellow flowers. Often wrongly grown as *P. fruticosa farreri*. C 1953.

'Golden Spreader' A low-growing shrub of wide-spreading habit, very hardy and good for groundcover. Flowers bright yellow with a paler reverse. Raised in Orkney by Alan Bremner.

'Goldfinger' A dwarf, compact shrub with pinkish shoots and blue-green leaves with usually 5 leaflets. Large, rich golden-yellow flowers profusely borne. Raised in Germany about 1970.

'Goldstar' Habit rather upright, to 80cm. Very large, deep yellow flowers, up to 5cm across, are borne over a long period. Raised in Germany. C 1976.

'Goldteppich' ('Gold Carpet') Low, spreading habit with deep yellow flowers. Raised in Germany. C 1969.

'Grace Darling' Compact, dwarf and very hardy with grey-green foliage and peach-pink flowers holding their colour well.

Potentilla fruticosa **continued:**

var. *grandiflora* Schltdl. A strong-growing, erect shrub, up to 1.5m, with sage-green leaves and dense clusters of large, canary-yellow flowers.

'Groneland' A selection of bushy habit from Hungary with bright green foliage and off-white flowers. ♀ 2002.

'Hopleys Little Joker' An unusual, very dwarf form, a seedling of 'Red Ace'. Flowers pink-maroon fading to white-blotched.

'Hopleys Orange' A dwarf, spreading shrub with bright orange flowers, the petals with a narrow yellow margin. Bright green foliage with slender leaflets. ♀ 2002.

'Hersii' A free-flowering, small shrub of erect habit with the young shoots pink later purple-black. Leaves large, dark green; flowers white, often with extra petals. Raised from seed collected by Joseph Hers. See also 'Snowflake'.

'Hurstbourne' Small shrub of upright habit, with bright yellow flowers. Raised at Kew in the 1930s.

'Jackman's Variety' (*P. fruticosa jackmanii* hort.) A seedling of var. *grandiflora*. Upright with dark green foliage and large, deep yellow flowers. C 1940. ♀ 2002. FCCT 1966.

'Janet' Bushy habit with bright green foliage and broad leaflets. Flowers large, pale yellow.

'Jolina' Large, golden-yellow flowers, 4cm across, borne over a very long period. Compact, spreading habit with grey-green leaves and pink-flushed young shoots.

'Katherine Dykes' (*P. fruticosa* 'Friedrichsenii' × *P. fruticosa* var. *parvifolia*) A shrub up to 2m, producing an abundance of primrose-yellow flowers in summer. Named after the raiser's wife. C 1925. AM 1944.

'King Cup' Large, vivid yellow flowers. Large, mid-green leaves. ♀ 2002.

'Kingdon Ward' A form raised from seed collected in Tibet by Kingdon Ward in 1925. Foliage sage-green to grey; flowers yellow, large.

'Klondike' A first-rate shrub of dwarf habit, raised in Holland. Similar to 'Gold Drop', but with larger flowers. C 1950. AMT 1965.

'Lady Daresbury' ('Frances Lady Daresbury') A small shrub forming a broad, dome-shaped bush of arching branches, and foliage with a bluish hue. Flowers large, yellow, continuously produced, but especially abundant in late spring and autumn. C 1955.

'Limelight' ('Lemon and Lime') Soft yellow flowers, bright yellow in the centre, are borne over a very long period. Bright green foliage. ♀ 2002.

'Logan' (Sulphurascens Group) A small shrub, up to 1.5m, of bushy habit with pale green foliage, producing masses of pale yellow flowers during summer.

'Longacre Variety' (Sulphurascens Group) A dense, dwarf, mat-forming shrub. Flowers large, bright, almost sulphur-yellow. A seedling raised at Longacre in N Ireland. C 1956. AMT 1965.

Lovely Pink See 'Pink Beauty'.

'Maanelys' ('Moonlight') A small shrub producing a continuous succession of soft yellow flowers from May to November. Raised by Axel Olsen of Kolding, Denmark in 1930. Makes an excellent informal hedge. C 1950.

'Manchu' (*P. fruticosa* var. *mandshurica* hort. not Wolf) A charming, dwarf, low-spreading shrub bearing a continuous succession of white flowers on mats of greyish foliage. AM 1924.

Marian Red Robin (Red Robin, 'Marrob') PBR A low, spreading shrub with red flowers, slightly deeper than 'Red Ace'. ♀ 2002.

'Medicine Wheel Mountain' Compact, low-spreading habit, with red-flushed shoots and blue-green foliage. Profuse large, bright yellow flowers to 3.5cm across. Collected in the wild in the Sioux Territory, Utah. ♀ 2002.

'Milkmaid' Small shrub with slender, upright stems and leaves with 3–5 leaflets. Flowers flattened, 2.5–3cm wide, creamy-white, nodding or inclined on slender peduncles. A hybrid of *P. fruticosa* Rhodocalyx Group raised in our nurseries in 1963.

'Minstead Dwarf' A dwarf shrub forming a low hummock of green leaves and masses of bright yellow flowers.

'Mount Everest' A small, robust shrub raised in Holland, up to 1.5m and of dense, rounded habit. The flowers are white and are produced intermittently throughout summer.

'New Dawn' Pink, deeper in the centre shading to white at the edge. Fades less in sun than other pink selections.

'Northman' A small, erect shrub with sage-green leaves and small, rich yellow flowers.

'Ochroleuca' A small, erect shrub, up to 2m, similar to 'Friedrichsenii', of which it is a seedling, with cream-coloured flowers. Both make an excellent informal hedge. C 1902.

'Orange Star' ('Orange Stripe') Flowers yellow, suffused and edged orange. A chance seedling of 'Tangerine' raised by Robinson's Hardy Plants in the early 1970s.

'Orange Stripe' See 'Orange Star'.

'Orangeade' Foliage bright green; flowers orange-red. A seedling of 'Red Ace' selected at Liss Forest Nursery.

var. *parvifolia* (Lehm.) Wolf (*P. parvifolia* Fisch. ex Lehm.) A compact shrub of semi-erect habit, seldom exceeding 1m in height. Leaves small, with 7 leaflets, the lower 2 pairs forming a whorl. Flowers golden-yellow, comparatively small but abundantly produced during early summer, and more sparingly until October. Asia, Siberia, Himalaya.

'Penny White' A dwarf shrub with bright, mid-green foliage and pink-flushed shoots. Clusters of white, flattened, often semi-double flowers are freely produced. Raised by our foreman Alf Alford in the 1960s. ♀ 2002.

'Pink Beauty' (Lovely Pink) PBR A dwarf shrub, raised in Canada, with bright green foliage bearing single and semi-double, soft pink flowers over a long period. ♀ 2002.

'Pink Pearl' Soft pink flowers fading to white in the sun. Foliage grey-green.

'Pretty Polly' A low, spreading shrub with medium-sized, pale pink flowers. A seedling of 'Red Ace'.

'Primrose Beauty' A small, spreading, free-flowering shrub with arching branches, grey-green foliage and primrose-yellow flowers with deeper yellow centres. ♀ 2002. AMT 1965.

Princess ('Blink') PBR A compact, dwarf shrub of spreading habit. Flowers delicate pale pink, yellow centred, sometimes with a few extra petals. Best in partial shade.

Potentilla fruticosa continued:

'Red Ace' A compact, dwarf shrub forming a dense mound of bright green foliage. Leaves with usually 5 narrow leaflets. Flowers bright orange-red, cream on the back of the petals. Best in partial shade. C 1973. FCC 1975.

'Rhodocalyx' (*P. fruticosa rhodocalyx*) A small, upright shrub of subtle, gentle quality, the aristocrat of a popular group. Rather small, somewhat cup-shaped flowers with reddish calyces nod on slender stems.

var. rigida (Lehm.) Maxim. (*P. arbuscula* var. *rigida* (D. Don) Hand.-Mazz., *P. rigida* Wall. ex Lehm.) A small, compact shrub with bristly stems covered with conspicuous papery stipules, and leaves with only 3 leaflets. Flowers bright yellow. Himalaya. I 1906. We have also grown an attractive form with smaller, silvery leaves and slightly smaller flowers.

'Royal Flush' A seedling of 'Red Ace' with deep pink flowers. C 1980.

'Ruth' A small shrub of upright habit with nodding, slightly cup-shaped flowers, creamy-yellow at first becoming white, with red-flushed calyces. A hybrid of *P. fruticosa* Rhodocalyx Group, raised in our nurseries in 1960 and named after Sir Harold Hillier's eldest daughter.

'Sandved' A tall shrub of upright habit with light green foliage. Flowers large, white with a cream flush. A seedling selected at the Sandved Research Station, Norway, in 1949.

'Silver Schilling' Upright habit, the downy silvery-grey leaves with 5–7 leaflets, grey-white beneath. Flowers golden-yellow, 3cm across. Raised from seed collected by Tony Schilling from below the village of Braga in the Marsyandi Valley, Annapurna, Nepal in 1983 (Schilling 2704).

'Snowbird' A dwarf shrub of bushy habit, raised in Canada, with semi-double white or pink-flushed flowers.

'Snowflake' Flowers white and very similar to 'Hersii', single or sometimes semi-double. Foliage dark green. Named in 1956 but known since 1940. Raised from seed collected by Joseph Hers. ♀ 2002.

'Sommerflor' ('Summer Flower') Bushy habit with large, golden-yellow flowers. ♀ 2002.

'Stoker's Variety' A small, upright shrub up to 1.5m. Small, densely crowded leaves and abundant rich yellow flowers.

var. subalbicans Hand.-Mazz. A robust shrub, up to 1.5m, with stiff, hairy stems and clusters of comparatively large, white flowers. Gansu, Shanxi.

Sulphurascens Group (*P. × sulphurascens* Hand.-Mazz.) (*P. fruticosa* var. *arbuscula* × *P. fruticosa* var. *davurica*) A rather variable hybrid originally described from Yunnan, which has given rise to several of the best garden potentillas, including 'Elizabeth', 'Longacre' and 'Logan' (see above).

'Summer Flower' See 'Sommerflor'.

'Sunset' A small shrub with flowers of an unusual colour, varying between deep orange and brick-red. Best grown in partial shade. A sport of 'Tangerine'.

'Tangerine' A dwarf, widespreading shrub forming a dense mound. The pale coppery-yellow of the flowers is developed best on plants growing in partial shade. Raised at the Slieve Donard Nursery, N. Ireland.

var. tenuiloba Ser. Erect-growing shrub, up to 1.5m, with narrow leaflets and bright yellow flowers. The clone in cultivation is probably of North American origin.

'Tilford Cream' A dense, dwarf bush, broader than tall, with rich green foliage and large, creamy-white flowers, about 3.5cm across.

'Veitchii' (*P. davurica* var. *veitchii* (E.H. Wilson) Jesson) A small, graceful bush, about 1m high, with arching branches bearing pure white flowers. W and C China. I 1900 by Ernest Wilson.

'Vilmoriniana' A splendid, erect-branched shrub, up to 2m, with very silvery leaves and cream-coloured flowers. The best tall, erect potentilla. AMT 1965.

'Walton Park' A small, very floriferous shrub, forming a low compact bush with large, bright yellow flowers.

'Whirligig' (*P. fruticosa* var. *arbuscula* × *P. fruticosa* var. *grandiflora*) A strong-growing, small shrub. The relatively large leaves have broad, soft green, silky-hairy leaflets. Flowers bright yellow with curiously twisted and wavy-edged petals. Raised by our foreman Alf Alford from a cross made in 1969.

'White Rain' Profuse white flowers, leaves broad. A chance seedling from Jack Drake. C 1969.

'William Purdom' (*P. fruticosa purdomii* hort.) A small shrub of semi-erect growth, up to 1.5m, with an abundance of light yellow flowers. FCCT 1966.

'Yellow Bird' Compact with semi-double, yellow flowers over a very long period. ♀ 2002.

glabra See *P. fruticosa* var. *davurica*.

parvifolia See *P. fruticosa* var. *parvifolia*.

salesoviana Stephan. An unusual, dwarf shrub with erect, hollow, reddish-brown stems bearing large, dark green, pinnate leaves, white beneath. Flowers nodding, white, occasionally tinged pink, produced in terminal corymbs in June and July. Siberia, N China. Himalaya. I 1823.

tridentata Aiton. A prostrate subshrub forming low tufts or mats. Leaves trifoliolate with oblanceolate leaflets, 3-toothed at the apex. Flowers white during summer. An excellent plant for paving or scree. E North America. C 1789.

Prickly Moses See *Acacia verticillata*.
Pride of India See *Koelreuteria paniculata*.

PRINSEPIA Oliv.—**Rosaceae**—A small genus of probably only 3 species of uncommon and interesting, usually spiny shrubs, natives of E Asia. All do best in an open position, and succeed in any fertile soil.

sinensis (Oliv.) Oliv. ex Bean. A rare, lax shrub, up to 2m, with arching stems. In early spring, the leaf axils of the previous year's wood bear slender-stalked, buttercup-yellow flowers, 1.2–2cm across, in clusters of 2–5. Fruits red, produced in August. Manchuria. I 1903.

uniflora Batal. A spreading shrub, 1.5–2m high, with spiny, grey stems and linear leaves. Flowers white, in axillary clusters of 1–3 on the previous year's wood, in late April or early May. Fruits purplish-red, like short-stalked Morello cherries, rarely produced except during a hot summer. NW China. I 1911 by William Purdom. AM 1983.

utilis Royle. An attractive, vigorous, small to medium-sized shrub with strongly spiny, arching, green stems. Flowers white, in axillary racemes during late winter and early spring. Himalaya. C 1919.

Privet See *Ligustrum*.

†***PROSTANTHERA** Labill.—**Labiatae**—The mint bushes are a genus of beautiful, small to medium-sized, floriferous, aromatic shrubs, with about 50 species, natives of Australasia. Ideal for the cool conservatory or in a warm, sheltered corner in the milder counties. Inclined to become chlorotic on a shallow chalky soil. Established specimens are best pruned back hard immediately after flowering.

aspalathoides A. Cunn. ex Benth. A small, compact shrub with tiny, almost linear, dark green, aromatic leaves and red flowers. Australia.

cuneata Benth. A relatively hardy, dwarf shrub of spreading habit with small, dark glossy green leaves, toothed at the tip, wedge-shaped at the base. Flowers white, flushed lilac, marked with purple inside, borne in May. Survived the hard winters of the 1980s. SE Australia, Tasmania. C 1886, reintroduced by Capt Neil McEachern in 1943. ♀ 2002.

lasianthos Labill. Medium-sized to large shrub of erect growth. Leaves comparatively large, lanceolate. The purple-tinted, white flowers appear in branched, terminal racemes during spring. Tasmania, Australia. I 1808. FCC 1888.

melissifolia F. Muell. A native of SE Australia, this species is represented in cultivation by the following form. **var. parvifolia** Sealy. This pretty shrub has been confused with *P. sieberi*. Flowers bright lilac, nearly 2.5cm across, borne abundantly in early summer.

ovalifolia R. Br. An elegant, small to medium-sized shrub with small, olive-green leaves and soft lilac-mauve or purple flowers on long, drooping branches in spring. Australia. ♀ 2002. AM 1952.

rotundifolia R. Br. A beautiful, small to medium-sized shrub of dense habit, with tiny rounded or ovate leaves. Attractive, heliotrope flowers inundate the branches during summer. The massed effect of the flowers is quite staggering. I 1824. ♀ 2002. AM 1924. **'Chelsea Pink'** See 'Rosea'. **'Rosea'** ('Chelsea Pink') Leaves aromatic, grey-green, wedge-shaped at the base. Flowers pale pink with purple anthers. ♀ 2002. AM 1986.

PRUNUS L.—**Rosaceae**—A large genus of about 400 species of mainly deciduous trees and shrubs, found largely in N temperate regions. It encompasses many of the most beautiful flowering trees suitable for temperate regions. Under *Prunus* are included: almond (*P. dulcis*); apricot (*P. armeniaca*); bird cherry (*P. padus*); common laurel (*P. laurocerasus*); peach (*P. persica*); and Portugal laurel (*P. lusitanica*). For Japanese cherries see the end of the entry. With the exception of most of the evergreen species, all require an open, preferably sunny position, in any ordinary soil, being particularly happy in soils containing lime or chalk. The cherry laurel (*P. laurocerasus*) will tend to become chlorotic in poor, shallow chalk soils: plant the Portugal laurel (*P. lusitanica*) instead.

'Accolade' (*P. sargentii* × *P.* × *subhirtella*) An outstanding cherry; a small tree with spreading branches and semi-double, rich pink flowers, 4cm in diameter, in profuse, pendent clusters in early summer. ♀ 2002. FCC 1954. AM 1952.

americana Marshall (*P. lanata* (Sudw.) Mack. & Bush.) American red plum. A small tree of graceful habit. Flowers white, 2.5cm across, in clusters of 2–5; fruits up to 2.5cm wide, yellow, finally bright red, but not freely produced in the British Isles. USA, S Canada. I 1768.

× *amygdalo-persica* (West.) Rehder (*P. dulcis* × *P. persica*) A hybrid between the peach and almond, first recorded about 1623. The following is the most commonly grown form: **'Pollardii'** (*P.* × *pollardii* hort.) This beautiful, small tree differs from the almond in its larger, richer pink flowers. Said to have originated in Australia about 1904. Bears fruit, which leaves us in no doubt as to its hybrid origin. Susceptible to peach leaf curl, for which see under *P. dulcis*. FCC 1935.

amygdalus See *P. dulcis*.

armeniaca L. Apricot. The wild species. A small, rounded-headed tree with white or pink-tinged, single flowers in March and April, then yellow, red-tinged fruits. C Asia, China. Widely grown and naturalised in S Europe. Clones selected for their fruit are widely cultivated. **var. ansu** Maxim. (*P. ansu* (Maxim.) Komar.) A small tree with rounded leaves and pink flowers in April; fruits red. Often confused in gardens with *P. mume*, from which it differs in its darker, usually purple-flushed shoots and its larger flowers with strongly reflexed sepals. N China, long cultivated in Japan and Korea. AM 1944. **'Flore Pleno'** (*P. mume* 'Grandiflora', *P. mume* 'Rosea Plena') A beautiful form of var. *ansu* with semi-double flowers, carmine in bud opening to pink, densely clustered on purple-flushed shoots in March or April. AM 1934.

avium L. Gean, Mazzard, Wild cherry. One of the most attractive of our native woodland trees. A medium-sized to large tree with smooth, grey bark, turning mahogany-red, peeling and deeply fissured with age. The white, cup-shaped flowers are borne in clusters and open with the leaves in late April or early May. Fruits small and shiny, reddish-purple, tasting bitter or sweet. Autumn foliage crimson. From this species are derived most of the sweet cherries. Europe (incl. British Isles), W Asia. ♀ 2002. **'Decumana'** (*P. macrophylla* Poir.) An unusual form with large flowers, 2.5cm across, and very large leaves, up to 23cm long. Raised in France before 1808. **'Pendula'** A form with semi-pendent, rather stiff branches. C 1825. **'Plena'** ('Multiplex') Double gean. One of the loveliest of all flowering trees, its branches are wreathed with masses of drooping, double, white flowers. Cultivated since 1700. ♀ 2002. FCC 1964.

besseyi Bailey (*P. pumila* var. *besseyi* (Bailey) Waugh) Sand cherry. A small shrub with greyish-green leaves turning rusty-purple in autumn. Clusters of tiny, white flowers are massed along the branches in May. Fruits rounded, black with purplish bloom, rarely produced in the British Isles. C USA. I 1892.

× *blireana* André (*P. cerasifera* 'Pissardii' × *P. mume* 'Alphandii') A beautiful, large shrub or small tree with leaves of a metallic coppery-purple. Flowers double, over 2.5cm across, slightly fragrant, rose-pink, appearing with the leaves in April. Garden origin 1895. ♀ 2002. FCC 1923. AM 1914. **'Moseri'** Differs in its slightly smaller, pale pink flowers, and paler foliage. C 1894. AM 1912.

†*campanulata* Maxim. Formosan cherry. A delightful, small, round-headed tree. The dark, rose-red flowers are produced in dense clusters during early spring. Only suitable outside in the mildest areas. S China, Taiwan, S Japan. C 1899. AM 1935. **'Plena'** A form with small, double, red flowers.

canescens Bois. A shrubby, medium-sized cherry with attractive, dark mahogany, peeling bark and slender, willowy branches. The polished, dark brown inner bark is exposed on the older branches. Leaves greyish-green, downy, coarsely toothed; flowers small, pink-tinted, in early April; fruits red, pleasantly flavoured. China. I 1898.

canescens × *serrula* An unusual and not unattractive hybrid, this is a small tree, retaining the ornamental bark of *P. serrula* and possessing the long, willowy stems of *P. canescens* which, like the leaves, are downy. The flowers also resemble those of the latter, but are slightly larger. Flowering during April.

capollin See *P. serotina* subsp. *capuli*.

†*caroliniana Aiton. Carolina cherry laurel. A small, bushy-headed tree in the mildest parts of the country, attaining a large size in the wild. Leaves elliptic, up to 10cm long, dark glossy green, entire or sparsely toothed. Flowers white, in short axillary racemes in spring, followed by black fruits. SE USA. I 1759.

cerasifera Ehrh. (*P. myrobalana* (L.) Loisel., *P. korolkowii* Vilm.) Myrobalan, Cherry plum. A small tree with greenish young shoots. The myriads of small, white flowers crowd the twigs in March, sometimes earlier or later. Mature trees sometimes bear red cherry plums. An excellent dense hedging shrub. Not known in the wild. C during the 16th century. AM 1977. **'Atropurpurea'** See 'Pissardii'. **'Diversifolia'** ('Aspleniifolia') Leaves bronze-purple, varying in shape from ovate to lanceolate, often irregularly toothed or lobed. Flowers white. A sport of 'Pissardii'. **'Feketiana'** See 'Pendula'. **'Hessei'** A medium-sized shrubby form with leaves pale green on emerging, becoming bronze-purple and irregularly edged creamy-white to yellowish or pink. Flowers snow-white, crowding the slender purple shoots in late March. C 1906. **'Lindsayae'** An attractive tree of graceful habit with flat, almond-pink flowers and green leaves. I from Iran by Miss Nancy Lindsay. AM 1948. **'Nigra'** Leaves and stems blackish-purple; flowers very prolific, pink fading to blush. A very effective, small tree flowering in March and April. C 1916. 'Vesuvius' is almost, if not, identical. ♀ 2002. FCC 1939. **'Pendula'** ('Feketiana') A form with pendent, interlacing stems, green leaves and white flowers. C 1901. **'Pissardii'** ('Atropurpurea') Purple-leaved plum. A very popular form with dark red young foliage turning to deep purple. Flowers in great profusion, white, pink in bud, appearing in late March and early April; fruits purple, only occasionally produced. If grown as shrubs, both this and 'Nigra' are excellent hedging plants. Originally discovered as a sport, some time before 1880 by Mons Pissard, gardener to the Shah of Persia. FCC 1884. **'Rosea'** Leaves bronze-purple at first, becoming bronze-green, then green in late summer. Small, clear salmon-pink flowers, paling with age, crowd the slender, purple stems before the leaves emerge, after both 'Nigra' and 'Pissardii'. Distributed by Messrs B. Ruys Ltd. of Holland, who believe the plant to be of hybrid origin (*P. cerasifera* 'Nigra' × *P. spinosa*). Sometimes found in gardens under the name *P. spinosa* 'Rosea'. It is looser and more open in habit than *P. spinosa* with slightly larger flowers, less densely crowded on the branchlets, which are sparsely spiny. **'Trailblazer'** See *P.* 'Trailblazer'. **'Vesuvius'** See under 'Nigra'.

†*cerasoides* D. Don. This species is represented in gardens by the following form. **var. *rubea*** Ingram. Kingdon-Ward's carmine cherry. A lovely tree of small to medium size, related to *P. campanulata*. Flowers rose-pink, deeper in bud, but not generally free-flowering in the British Isles. W China, Upper Burma. I 1931 by Kingdon-Ward. AM 1946.

cerasus L. Sour cherry. Of interest as being one of the parents of the morello cherries. A small bushy tree with comparatively dark slender stems and producing dense clusters of white flowers in late April or May followed by acid, red or black fruits. SW Asia. Widely cultivated and naturalised in Europe. **'James H. Veitch'** See *P.* 'Fugenzo' under Japanese cherries. **'Rhexii'** (*P. cerasus* f. *ranunculiflora* Voss) A form with very showy, double, white flowers, 2.5–4cm across. Known to have been in cultivation in England since the 16th century. **'Semperflorens'** All saints' cherry. A floriferous, and somewhat pendent, small tree producing white flowers intermittently throughout the spring and summer. C 1623.

× *cistena* Koehne (*P.* 'Cistena', *P.* 'Crimson Dwarf') Purple-leaf sand cherry (*P. pumila* or *P. besseyi* × *P. cerasifera* 'Pissardii') A beautiful shrub, up to 2m, with red leaves and white flowers in spring; fruits black-purple. An excellent hedging plant. Garden origin in the USA before 1910. ♀ 2002.

'Collingwood Ingram' A small tree of upright habit resembling 'Kursar', of which it is a seedling, but with deeper coloured flowers. Raised at Kalmthout and selected in 1979. A fitting tribute to Captain Collingwood Ingram to whom we owe the presence of many ornamental cherries in our gardens.

communis See *P. dulcis*.

concinna Koehne. A very beautiful, shrubby, small-leaved cherry of medium size, producing white or pink-tinted flowers profusely before the purplish young leaves, in March or early April. China. I 1907 by Ernest Wilson.

conradinae See *P. hirtipes*.

cornuta Steud. (Subgenus Padus) Himalayan bird cherry. A medium-sized tree, differing from *P. padus* in its larger leaves and fruits, the latter being glossy, brown-crimson and carried in drooping, grape-like clusters, 10–13cm long, from mid-August onwards. Flowers white, carried in long, cylindrical racemes in May. Himalaya. I 1860.

'Crimson Dwarf' See *P.* × *cistena*.

cyclamina Koehne. A delightful cherry, forming an elegant, small tree. The bright pink flowers, profusely borne in April, have reflexed sepals. Unfolding leaves are bright copper. C China. I 1907 by Ernest Wilson.

× *dasycarpa* Ehrh. (*P. armeniaca* × *P. cerasifera*) Purple apricot, Black apricot. A small tree with purple twigs and a profusion of white flowers, appearing before the leaves in March. Fruits black, with a purple bloom, apricot-flavoured, rarely produced in the British Isles.

davidiana (Carrière) Franch. This Chinese peach is one of the earliest trees to bloom, and on that account should be given a sheltered position. A small, erect tree with finely toothed, long-pointed leaves. The white or rose-coloured flowers open any time between January and March. Like all deciduous trees and shrubs that flower early on the leafless branches, it is very desirable to select a site with a suitable background. China. I 1865 by the Abbé David. **'Alba'** Flowers white. C 1872. FCC 1892. **'Rubra'** Flowers pink. C 1867.

× *dawyckensis* Sealy. Dawyck cherry. A small tree with shining, dark brown bark and downy young shoots and leaves, glaucous beneath. Flowers pale pink in April, followed by amber-red cherries. A tree of uncertain origin, first discovered in the famous gardens at Dawyck, Scotland, and thought to have been introduced by Ernest Wilson in 1907. Rehder suggested that it might be the hybrid *P. canescens* × *P. dielsiana*.

dielsiana C.K. Schneid. (*P. dielsiana* var. *laxa* Koehne) A small, floriferous tree, related to *P. cyclamina*, but later flowering and never so tall. The trunk and primary branches are dark mahogany-red. Flowers white or pale pink, with conspicuous stamens, borne on long, downy pedicels before the leaves in April or early May; fruits red. C China. I 1907 by Ernest Wilson. **var. laxa** See *P. dielsiana*.

divaricata Ledeb. A small tree closely related to *P. cerasifera* but with smaller, yellow fruits. W to C Asia.

domestica L. Plum. A small, usually spineless tree represented in gardens by forms selected for their fruit. It is of hybrid origin and similar plants occur in the Caucasus. Widely naturalised. **subsp. insititia** (L.) Poir (*P. insititia* L.) Bullace, Damson. A small tree with occasionally spiny, brownish, pubescent branches and small, white flowers in early spring, followed by rounded, purple, red, yellow or green fruits.

dulcis (Mill.) D.A. Webb (*P. amygdalus* Batsch) (*P. communis* (L.) Arcang.) Common almond. A universal favourite and one of the best spring-flowering trees. A small tree with lanceolate, long-pointed, finely toothed leaves. Pink flowers, 2.5–5cm across, are borne singly or in pairs in March and April. The edible almonds of commerce are mainly introduced from S Europe. Distributed in the wild from N Africa to W Asia, but widely grown and extensively naturalised in the Mediterranean region. Cultivated in England since the 16th century or earlier. Susceptible to peach leaf curl for which we recommend Murphy's Traditional Copper Fungicide. **'Alba'** Flowers white, single. **'Erecta'** A broadly columnar form, up to 6m or more, with erect branches and pink flowers. **'Macrocarpa'** Flowers very pale pink or white, up to 5cm across. One of the best of the edible cultivars with large fruits. AM 1931. **'Praecox'** A form with pale pink flowers opening 2 weeks earlier than normal, very often in late February. FCC 1925. **'Roseoplena'** Double almond. Flowers pale pink, double.

× *dunbarii* Rehder (*P. americana* × *P. maritima*) A large shrub with sharply serrate, acuminate leaves, white flowers and purple fruits. Origin about 1900.

× *effusa* See *P.* × *gondouinii*.

emarginata (Hook.) Eaton. Bitter cherry. In its typical form a shrub with more or less glabrous shoots and leaves, this species is represented in cultivation by the following form. W North America. **var. mollis** (Hook.) Brewer & S. Wats. A small, elegant, deciduous tree with a dense, spreading head and downy shoots. Leaves finely toothed, downy beneath. Flowers small, creamy-white, produced in dense clusters at the end of the branches in May, followed by small, dark fruits. The bark tastes bitter. I 1862.

fenzliana Fritsch. A small, widespreading, shrubby almond, closely related to *P. dulcis*, but with narrower, sea-green leaves. The flowers, carmine in bud, opening soft pink, are conspicuous on the naked branches during March. Caucasus. C 1890.

fruticosa Pall. Ground cherry. A small, spreading shrub with small, white flowers and dark red fruits. When grown as a standard, it forms a neat mop-headed, miniature tree. C and E Europe to Siberia. C 1587. **'Pendula'** A form with slender, pendent branches. **'Variegata'** Leaves variegated yellowish-white, but not very constant.

glandulosa Thunb. Chinese bush cherry. A small, neat, bushy shrub with slender, erect shoots covered in numerous, small, pink or white flowers in April. Grows best in a warm, sunny position. C and N China, long cultivated in Japan. C 1835. **'Alba Plena'** A very beautiful shrub, each shoot pendent with a wealth of comparatively large, double, white flowers in early May. Excellent for forcing. C 1852. AM 1950. **'Rosea Plena'** See 'Sinensis'. **'Sinensis'** ('Rosea Plena', *P. japonica* 'Flore Roseoplena') Flowers double, bright pink. A very popular shrub in Victorian and Edwardian gardens. Excellent for forcing. C 1774. AM 1968.

× *gondouinii* (Poit. & Turpin) Rehder (*P. avium* × *P. cerasus*) (*P.* × *effusa* (Host) C.K. Schneid.) Duke cherry. A variable, medium-sized tree, producing white flowers in spring, followed by somewhat acid, red fruits. Several clones are grown for their fruits.

grayana Maxim. (Subgenus Padus) A small, Japanese bird cherry. Leaves coarsely toothed; flowers white in erect, glabrous racemes, 7.5–20cm long, in June; fruits small, black. Japan. I 1900.

'Hally Jolivette' ([*P. subhirtella* × *P.* × *yedoensis*] × *P. subhirtella*) A small, graceful tree or large shrub raised by Dr Karl Sax at the Arnold Arboretum, Boston, and named after his wife. Its slender, willowy stems are inundated over a long period in early spring with small, semi-double, blush-white flowers.

'Hillieri' A hybrid of *P. sargentii* raised in our nurseries before 1928, the original is now a broad-crowned tree 10m high, and in spring is like a soft pink cloud. In favourable seasons the autumn colour is gorgeous. The other parent was possibly *P.* × *yedoensis*. AM 1959. **'Spire'** See *P.* 'Spire'.

'Hilling's Weeping' A small tree with long, slender, almost perpendicularly weeping branches, wreathed with pure white flowers in early April.

hirtipes Hemsl. (*P. conradinae* Koehne) This early-flowering cherry is a small tree of elegant habit. In a sheltered position its fragrant, white or pinkish flowers, which are produced very freely, give a welcome foretaste of spring, usually during the latter half of February. China. I 1907 by Ernest Wilson. AM 1923. **'Malifolia'** Carmine buds and pink flowers, about 3cm across; slightly later flowering. C 1948. **'Semiplena'** Flowers longer lasting with a few extra petals, appearing in late February and March. C 1925. AM 1935.

†*__ilicifolia__ (Hook. & Arn.) Walp. Holly-leaved cherry. A dense, medium-sized to large shrub. Leaves broadly ovate to orbicular, undulate, leathery and edged with spreading spines. Flowers white, in short racemes 5cm long, in June and July, followed by red fruits. California. **susbp.** _lyonii_ (Eastw.) Raven (_P. lyonii_ (Eastw.) Sarg., _P. integrifolia_ Sarg.) Catalina cherry. A rare, evergreen shrub, closely related to _P. ilicifolia_, but differing in its flat, mostly entire leaves, longer racemes and nearly black fruits. California. Our stock has toothed, slightly undulate leaves and may be a hybrid with _P. ilicifolia_.

incana Batsch. Willow cherry. A small to medium-sized, erect-branched shrub of loose habit. The slender leaves are white-woolly beneath. Flowers pink, contrasting effectively with the grey-green leaves, and occasionally followed by red, cherry-like fruits. SE Europe and Asia Minor. I 1815.

incisa Thunb. Fuji cherry. A lovely Japanese species, generally shrubby, but occasionally a small tree, blooming with great freedom in March. Leaves small, incisely-toothed, beautifully tinted in autumn. Flowers small, white, pink-tinged in bud and appearing pink from a distance; fruits only occasionally produced, small, purple-black. Makes an unusual hedge. Long used by the Japanese for bonsai. C 1910. AM 1927. **'February Pink'** An early flowering form with pale pink flowers in February or earlier. **'Kojo-no-mai'** A small, slow-growing shrub with zigzag shoots and pale pink flowers. 'Mikinori' A shrubby selection with semi-double flowers, pink in bud, opening white. Named after the eminent Japanese botanist and plant collector Mikinori Ogisu. **'Moerheimii'** See _P._ 'Moerheimii'. **'Omoinoyama'** Profuse, double, pale pink flowers. **'Oshidori'** Double, pale pink flowers with numerous rather quilled petals open from deeper buds. Possibly a hybrid. **'Praecox'** A winter-flowering form with white flowers, pale pink in bud. ♀ 2002. FCC 1973. AM 1957. **'The Bride'** A small, shrubby tree of dense, spreading habit. Flowers pure white with prominent deep red stamens.

'Yamadei' A form with white flowers, lacking pink coloration even in buds. Calyx green. Discovered near Mt Fuji in 1916.

jacquemontii Hook. f. Afghan cherry. A small to medium-sized shrub of straggling habit, with small leaves. Flowers pink, opening in April. Fruits only occasionally produced, small, red. Happiest in a well-drained, sunny position. NW Himalaya, Tibet, Afghanistan. I 1879.

jamasakura Siebold (_P. serrulata_ var. _spontanea_ (Maxim.) E.H. Wilson, _P. mutabilis_ Miyoshi) Hill cherry. A medium-sized tree of spreading habit with bronze-coloured young foliage. Flowers white or pink in late April and early May. A beautiful cherry, said to be the most adored tree in Japan, one which has inspired her poets and artists and is a prototype of many of the Japanese cherries. It is extremely variable, the best forms having rich, coppery-red young foliage and pure white flowers. Fruit dark purplish-crimson. Japan. I about 1914. AM 1936.

japonica Thunb. This is a small shrub with slender, wiry branches. The small, single, white or pale pink flowers

appear with the leaves in April; fruits only occasionally produced, dark red. C China east to Korea. Long cultivated in Japan. I 1860. **var.** _nakaii_ (H. Lév.) Rehder. A geographical form introduced from Korea in 1918 by Ernest Wilson.

× _juddii_ E. S. Anderson (_P. sargentii_ × _P._ × _yedoensis_) A small tree with leaves copper-tinted when unfolding, deep crimson in the fall. Flowers pale pink in late April or early May. Originated at the Arnold Arboretum, Boston, USA in 1914.

kansuensis Rehder. A small tree akin to _P. persica_, with long, spray-like branches carrying pink-tinged, white blossoms in January or February. NW China. I 1914. AM 1957.

kurilensis See _P. nipponica_ var. _kurilensis_.

'Kursar' (_P. campanulata_ × _P. nipponica_ var. _kurilensis_) A very beautiful, small tree raised by Captain Collingwood Ingram, who was the leading Western authority on Japanese cherries. The flowers, though small, are rich deep pink and borne in great profusion with, or just before, the reddish-bronze, young leaves, in March or early April. ♀ 2002. AM 1952.

lanata See _P. americana_.

lannesiana (Carrière) E.H. Wilson (_P. serrulata_ var. _lannesiana_ (Carrière) Rehder, _P. serrulata hortensis_ hort.) Under this name Ernest Wilson described a pink, single-flowered Japanese cherry of garden origin. The wild type with fragrant, white flowers he named _P. lannesiana_ f. _albida_ (now _P. speciosa_). Japanese botanists use the name _P. lannesiana_ to cover the numerous garden cherries with large, single or double flowers, many of which are now thought to be forms of either _P. speciosa_ or _P. jamasakura_ (_P. serrulata_ var. _spontanea_). **f.** _albida_ See _P. speciosa_. **f.** _speciosa_ See _P. speciosa_.

latidentata Koehne. A small tree or shrub mainly grown in the following form. **var.** _pleuroptera_ (Koehne) Ingram. This makes a small, round-headed tree with a peculiar mottled trunk. Flowers are small and white; they are produced in drooping clusters, with the leaves in April. China. I 1908 by Ernest Wilson.

*_laurocerasus_ L. Common laurel, Cherry laurel. A vigorous, widespreading, evergreen shrub, attaining 6m or more in height, by as much, or more, across. Leaves large, leathery, dark shining green. Mainly grown for screening purposes or for shelter in game coverts, but attractive in April when bearing its erect, axillary and terminal racemes of small, white flowers, followed by cherry-like fruits, red at first, finally black. Harmful if eaten. Not at its best on shallow, chalk soils. E Europe, SW Asia. Extensively planted and naturalised in the British Isles. I 1576. ♀ 2002.

There are few other evergreens more tolerant of shade and drip from overhanging trees than the laurel in its many forms. Several of the more compact, erect cultivars make excellent tub specimens where _Laurus nobilis_, the Bay, is insufficiently hardy. **'Angustifolia'** A form with ascending branches and narrow leaves similar to those of 'Zabeliana'. C 1802. **'Camelliifolia'** A large shrub or small tree. Leaves dark green twisted and curled. C 1901. **'Castlewellan'** ('Marbled White') A slow-growing, dense bush eventually of large size. Leaves green and grey-green, marbled throughout with white. Originally grown as 'Variegata'. AM 1986. **'Caucasica'** A vigorous, upright form with rather narrow leaves. **'Cherry Brandy'** A dense, small shrub making a low mound only 60cm high. The bronze young foliage later becomes green. C 1980. **Etna** ('Anbri') PBR A seedling of 'Rotundifolia' raised in Germany, making a dense, broadly upright and very hardy, medium-sized shrub. Leaves bronze when young becoming glossy dark green. C 1993. **'Green Carpet'** See 'Grüner Teppich'. **'Greenmantle'** A medium-sized to large, widespreading shrub of open habit with dark glossy green leaves. Found in our nursery in 1965. **'Grüner Teppich'** ('Green Carpet') A dwarf form growing wide and flat with narrow, dark green leaves. Excellent for groundcover. C 1984. **'Herbergii'** Erect form of dense, compact habit, with oblanceolate, polished green leaves. Excellent for hedging. C 1930. **'Latifolia'** ('Macrophylla', 'Magnoliifolia') An imposing evergreen with glossy leaves up to 30cm long and 10cm wide. The largest-leaved laurel. C 1869. **Low 'n' Green** ('Interlo') A small, spreading shrub to about 90cm tall and twice as wide, with glossy dark green leaves. Makes dense groundcover. **'Magnoliifolia'** See 'Latifolia'. **'Marbled White'** See 'Castlewellan'. **'Mischeana'** A most ornamental clone slowly forming a dense, rather flat-topped mound of dark, lustrous green, oblong leaves. A superb lawn specimen. Attractive also when in flower, the short, erect racemes packed along the stems. C 1898. **'Mount Vernon'** A slow-growing, dwarf, shrubby laurel making a dense mound about 30cm high, covered with glossy, dark green leaves. Rarely flowers. C 1967. **'Otinii'** A large, compact bush with large, very dark green, lustrous leaves. C 1873. **'Otto Luyken'** A low, compact shrub with erect stems and narrow, shining green leaves. An outstanding clone in both leaf and flower. Raised in 1940. ♥ 2002. AM 1968. **'Reynvaanii'** A small, slow-growing form of compact habit with stiff branches. C 1913. **'Rotundifolia'** A bushy form, excellent for hedging. Leaves half as broad as long. C 1865. **'Rudolph Billeter'** Broadly upright with ascending branches. Narrow, dark green leaves are edged with small, coarse teeth. C 1930. **'Rufescens'** For many years we have grown under this name a rather slow-growing, small, rather flat-topped bush with small, neat, oval to obovate leaves. **'Schipka Holland'** ('Schipkaensis Holland') A selection made in Holland from plants grown as 'Schipkaensis'. This is a compact, medium-sized, spreading bush differing from 'Schipkaensis' in its smaller, more distinctly toothed leaves. Flowers profusely. **'Schipkaensis'** An extremely hardy, free-flowering, narrow-leaved form of spreading habit. Found in the wild near the Schipka Pass in Bulgaria. I 1888. AM 1959. **'Schipkaensis Holland'** See 'Schipka Holland'. **'Schipkaensis Macrophylla'** A German clone of open habit having ascending branches up to 2m. Leaves oblong-elliptic up to 18cm long. Free-fruiting. C 1930. **'Serbica'** Serbian laurel. More upright than 'Schipkaensis', and with obovate, rugose leaves. Originally found in former Yugoslavia. C 1877. **'Van Nes'** Broad, spreading habit with dark green foliage. **'Variegata'** See under 'Castlewellan'. **'Zabeliana'** A low, horizontally branched form, with long, narrow, willow-like leaves; very free-flowering. Makes an excellent groundcover, even under the shade and drip of trees, also useful for breaking the regular outline of a border or bed in the same way as the Pfitzer juniper. C 1898.

litigiosa C.K. Schneid. (*P. pilosiuscula* var. *barbata* Koehne) A splendid small, somewhat conical tree with small, white flowers appearing in drooping clusters with the unfolding leaves in April. Worthy of more extensive planting. Attractive autumn tints. C China. I 1907 by Ernest Wilson.

*lusitanica L. Portugal laurel. An indispensable, large, evergreen shrub or small to medium-sized tree. A beautiful specimen tree when allowed to develop naturally. Leaves ovate, dark green with reddish petioles. Flowers small, white, hawthorn-scented, carried in long slender racemes, in June. Fruits small, red turning to dark purple. Hardier than the cherry laurel (*P. laurocerasus*). Useful as game cover and a splendid hedging plant. Happy even on shallow chalk soils, where it may be used instead of *P. laurocerasus*. Spain, Portugal. I 1648. ♥ 2002. **'Angustifolia'** See 'Myrtifolia'. **subsp.** *azorica* (Mouillef.) Franco. A magnificent and very hardy, large, evergreen shrub or small tree with larger, thicker leaves of a bright green, reddish when unfolding and with reddish petioles. Azores. I about 1860. FCC 1866. **'Myrtifolia'** ('Angustifolia', 'Pyramidalis') Forms a dense cone, up to 5m, with polished, deep green leaves, smaller and neater than those of the type. In cold areas may be used as a formal evergreen to replace the conical Bay (*Laurus nobilis*). C 1892. **'Variegata'** An attractive form with leaves conspicuously white margined, sometimes pink-flushed in winter. C 1865.

lyonii See *P. ilicifolia* subsp. *lyonii*.

maackii Rupr. Manchurian cherry. A rare, vigorous, small tree with attractive, shining, golden-brown, flaking bark. Flowers small, white, carried in irregular racemes on the previous year's shoots in April; fruits small, black. Manchuria, Korea. I 1878. **'Amber Beauty'** A Dutch selection with amber-coloured bark and a narrow crown.

macradenia Koehne. A small tree or large shrub related to *P. maximowiczii*. Flowers small, white, carried in few-flowered corymbose racemes in May. China. I 1911.

macrophylla See *P. avium* 'Decumana'.

mahaleb L. St Lucie cherry. A very attractive, small to medium-sized tree of spreading or rounded habit, smothered with myriads of small, white, fragrant blossoms in late April and early May, but not very free-flowering when young. Fruits black. Cherrywood pipes and walking sticks are made from this species. C and S Europe. I 1714. **'Pendula'** An elegant form with gracefully arching branches. Raised in France in 1847. FCC 1874.

mandshurica (Maxim.) Koehne. Manchurian apricot. An uncommon, small tree. Its pale pink flowers, which open in February and March, are a lively peach-pink before expanding. Fruits rounded, yellow. Manchuria, Korea. C 1900. AM 1977.

maritima Marshall. Beach plum. A small shrub of fairly compact habit, occasionally reaching 2–2.5m. Flowers small, white produced in May. Fruits rounded, red or purple. Native of the eastern USA where it frequently grows in sandy places near the sea.

maximowiczii Rupr. A small, dense-headed tree with small,

coarsely toothed leaves and erect, corymbose racemes of small, creamy-white flowers in May. Fruits red, turning black. Manchuria, Ussuri, Korea, Japan. I 1892 by Charles Sargent.

'Moerheimii' (*P. incisa* 'Moerheimii') A small, picturesque, weeping tree of widespreading, dome-shaped habit. Flowers blush-white, pink in bud, in late March and early April.

mugus Hand.-Mazz. Tibetan cherry. Described as growing prostrate in the wild but the plant in general cultivation is a stiff, thick-stemmed, rather compact small bush. The flowers are more curious than beautiful, shell-pink with inflated reddish calyces, usually disposed singly or in pairs. W China. I by George Forrest in 1922.

mume Siebold & Zucc. Japanese apricot. A delightful small tree with green young shoots and single, almond-scented, pink flowers, paling with age. Normally in flower during March, occasionally as early as late January or as late as early April. China, Korea, extensively cultivated in Japan. I 1844. **'Alba'** A vigorous form with usually single, pure white flowers studding the branches in late March or early April. **'Alboplena'** Flowers semi-double, white, appearing in late winter and early spring. **'Alphandii'** ('Flore Pleno') A beautiful form with semi-double, pink flowers in March, sometimes earlier. C 1902. **'Beni-shidare'** A striking form with strongly fragrant, double, cup-shaped, rich madder-pink flowers, darker in bud and paling slightly with age, in late March or early April. Originally listed as 'Beni-shidon'. AM 1961. **'Grandiflora'** See *P. armeniaca* var. *ansu* 'Flore Pleno'. **'Omoi-no-mama'** A charming form with semi-double, cup-shaped, usually white flowers in late March or early April. Occasional petals and sometimes whole flowers are pink. Previously listed as 'O-moi-no-wac'. AM 1991. **'Pendula'** A small, weeping tree with single or semi-double, pale pink flowers in late February or March. **'Rosea Plena'** See *P. armeniaca* var. *ansu* 'Flore Pleno'.

munsoniana Wight & Hedr. Wild goose plum. Small tree with lanceolate, shining green leaves and clusters of white flowers in spring, occasionally followed by red fruits. SE USA. C 1911.

mutabilis See *P. jamasakura*.

myrobalana See *P. cerasifera*.

nana See *P. tenella*.

nigra Aiton. Canada plum. A small, narrow-headed tree or large shrub, producing in spring clusters of fragrant, white flowers, which later turn pink. Red or yellowish, plum-like fruits. Canada and E USA. I 1773.

nipponica Matsum. Japanese alpine cherry. A dense shrub or bushy tree, 2.5–3m, with chestnut-brown branches. Leaves coarsely toothed; flowers white or pale pink in May. Fruits small, black. Japan. I 1915. var. *kurilensis* (Miyabe) E.H. Wilson (*P. kurilensis* (Miyabe) Miyabe) A large, bushy shrub or small tree with coarsely toothed leaves, rusty-brown when young. Flowers in April, before the leaves, comparatively large, white or pink-tinged; fruits purplish-black. Japan. I 1905. **'Brilliant'** A selection of var. *kurilensis* of upright habit with large pure white flowers. **'Ruby'** A lovely form of var. *kurilensis*, making a small tree, its erect branches a mass of pale pink blossoms, with conspicuous purplish-red calyces, in early April. C 1958. AM 1997.

'Okame' (*P. campanulata* × *P. incisa*) A small tree, one of the numerous hybrids raised by Captain Collingwood Ingram. This is a very lovely cherry with masses of carmine-rose flowers throughout March. Foliage attractively tinted in autumn. ♀ 2002. AM 1947.

padus L. (Subgenus Padus) Bird cherry. A small to medium-sized, native tree, widely distributed in the N hemisphere. Flowers small, white, almond-scented, produced in slender, drooping or spreading racemes in May after the leaves; fruits black, bitter to taste. Europe (incl. British Isles). N Asia to Japan. **'Albertii'** A very free-flowering form of medium size, strong and erect in growth. C 1902. **'Colorata'** A remarkable clone with dark purplish shoots, coppery-purple young foliage and pale pink flowers. The leaves in summer are a sombre green with purple-tinged veins and undersurfaces. Found in Sweden in 1953. 'Purple Queen' is very similar. ♀ 2002. FCC 1995. AM 1974. var. *commutata* Dippel (*P. seoulensis* Nakai) A geographical form from eastern Asia. A medium-sized tree of spreading habit. One of the first heralds of spring, the fresh green leaves appearing before winter has passed. I 1880. AM 1956. **'Plena'** A form with longer-lasting, larger, double flowers. C 1892. **'Purple Queen'** See under 'Colorata'. **'Watereri'** ('Grandiflora') A medium-sized tree with conspicuous racemes up to 20cm long. C 1914. ♀ 2002. AM 1969.

'Pandora' (*P. pendula* 'Ascendens Rosea' × *P.* × *yedoensis*) A splendid, small tree with ascending branches which, in March or early April, are flooded with pale shell-pink blossoms, 2.5cm across. Leaves bronze-red when unfolding, and often colouring richly in autumn. ♀ 2002. AM 1939.

pendula Maxim. (*P.* × *subhirtella* 'Pendula') Raised from Japanese seed, this forms a lovely, slender, weeping tree of medium size, recalling the most graceful forms of weeping birch. The tiny blush flowers in late March to early April are not conspicuous. Japan. I 1862. AM 1930. f. *ascendens* (Makino) Ohwi (*P.* × *subhirtella* var. *ascendens* (Makino) Tanaka) As seen in cultivation in this country is a small, semi-erect tree, but is much larger in Japan. Flowers white or pale pink, opening towards the end of March. Japan, China, Korea. C 1916. **'Ascendens Rosea'** (*P.* × *subhirtella* 'Ascendens Rosea') A lovely form with flowers of clear shell-pink, enhanced by the red-tinged calyces. AM 1960. **'Pendula Rosea'** (*P.* × *subhirtella* 'Pendula Rosea') Weeping spring cherry. A small, weeping, mushroom-shaped tree. Flowers rich pink in bud passing to pale blush, wreathing the graceful, drooping branches in late March and early April. Often grown as *P.* × *subhirtella* 'Pendula'. ♀ 2002. **'Pendula Rubra'** (*P.* × *subhirtella* 'Pendula Rubra') Flowers single, deep rose, carmine in bud, wreathing the long, pendent branches. ♀ 2002. AM 1983. **'Stellata'** (*P.* × *subhirtella* 'Stellata') A very beautiful form with larger, clear pink, star-shaped flowers, produced in crowded clusters along the branches. I about 1955. AM 1949.

pensylvanica L. f. A fast-growing, small to medium-sized tree with bright green, finely toothed leaves and clusters of white flowers in late April and early May. Fruits small, red. North America. I 1773.

persica (L.) Batsch. Peach. A small, bushy tree or large shrub with pale pink flowers, 2.5–4cm wide, in early

April. Differing from the almond in its smaller flowers, which appear 2 or 3 weeks later, and in its fleshy, juicy fruits. Native probably of China, but cultivated since ancient times. Susceptible to peach leaf curl: for treatment see under *P. dulcis*. **'Alba'** Flowers white. C 1829. **'Alboplena'** Flowers white, double. C 1850. FCC 1899. **'Alboplena Pendula'** A weeping form with double, white flowers. **'Atropurpurea'** See 'Foliis Rubris'. **'Aurora'** Dense clusters of double, rose-pink flowers with frilled petals. AM 1950. **'Cardinal'** Flowers glowing red, semi-double, rosette-like. **'Crimson Cascade'** Weeping branches; flowers crimson, double. **'Foliis Rubris'** ('Atropurpurea') Leaves rich purplish-red when young, becoming bronze-green; flowers single; fruits reddish-purple. AM 1939. **'Helen Borchers'** A strong-growing form with large, semi-double, rose-pink flowers. AM 1949. **'Iceberg'** A very free-flowering form with large, semi-double, pure white flowers. AM 1950. **'Klara Mayer'** ('Flore Roseoplena') Flowers double, peach-pink. This is the best double peach for general planting. C 1890. **'Prince Charming'** A small, upright tree with double, rose-red flowers. **'Russell's Red'** Flowers double, crimson. AM 1933. **'Windle Weeping'** A very distinct weeping form with broad leaves and semi-double, cup-shaped, purplish-pink flowers. AM 1949.

pilosiuscula Koehne. Small tree or large shrub in April producing clusters of small, white or pink-tinged flowers, with conspicuous protruding anthers, followed by red fruits in June. W China. I 1907 by Ernest Wilson.

'Pink Shell' One of the loveliest of cherries in a genus full of floral treasures. A small, elegant tree, the slender, spreading branches drooping beneath a wealth of cup-shaped, delicate, shell-pink blossoms, which blend beautifully with the pale green of the emerging leaves in early April. Possibly a seedling of *P. × yedoensis*. ♀ 2002. AM 1969.

pleiocerasus Koehne. Small tree with small, white flowers in spring. W China. I 1907.

× *pollardii* See *P. × amygdalo-persica* 'Pollardii'.

prostrata Labill. Rock cherry. A dwarf, spreading shrub usually forming a delightful, low, gnarled hummock reaching 0.7m high by 2m wide in 25 years. The flowers are bright pink and are borne along the wiry stems in April. SE Europe. Mediterranean region. W Asia. I 1802.

pseudocerasus Lindl. A small tree, the leafless stems wreathed in clusters of white flowers in early March. N China. I 1819. **'Cantabrigiensis'** This interesting, small tree is well worth growing for its early display of fragrant, pink blossoms, commencing as early as mid-February. The original plant is growing in the University Botanic Garden, Cambridge. AM 1925.

pubigera Koehne (Subgenus Padus) A distinct and attractive bird cherry forming a medium-sized tree. Flowers small, creamy-white, in drooping racemes up to 18cm long and 2.5cm wide. W China. AM 1957.

pumila L. Sand cherry. A spreading shrub to 2m. In May the naked branches are wreathed with multitudes of tiny, white flowers. The greyish-green, narrowly obovate leaves become bright red in autumn. Fruits dark red. NE USA. I 1756. **var. *besseyi*** See *P. besseyi*. **var. *depressa***

(Pursh) Bean. A prostrate form, less than 15cm tall and good for groundcover. It is studded with white flowers in May. I 1864.

rufa Hook. f. Himalayan cherry. A small tree with rusty-hairy young shoots and small clusters of pale pink flowers. Some forms have superb, peeling, reddish-brown or amber bark. Himalaya. I 1897.

salicifolia See *P. serotina* subsp. *capuli*.

salicina Lindl. (*P. triflora* Roxb.) Japanese plum. A small, bushy tree or large shrub with shining dark twigs. Leaves turning bright red in autumn. Small, white flowers crowd the leafless branches in early April. China. Long cultivated in Japan. I 1870. AM 1926.

sargentii Rehder (*P. serrulata* var. *sachalinensis* (F. Schmidt) E.H. Wilson) Considered by many to be the loveliest of all cherries. A round-headed tree, attaining 15–18m in Japan, but rather less in the British Isles. Bark dark chestnut-brown. Young foliage bronze-red. Flowers single, pink, opening late March or early April. One of the first trees to colour in autumn, its leaves assuming glorious orange and crimson tints, usually in late September. One of the few cherries that bullfinches appear to ignore. Japan, Sakhalin, Korea. I 1890. ♀ 2002. FCC 1925. AM 1921. **'Rancho'** A narrowly upright form raised in the USA before 1962. Some plants grown under this name are poor forms of *P. sargentii*.

× *schmittii* Rehder (*P. avium* × *P. canescens*) This fast-growing, narrowly conical tree of medium size should have a great future for public planting. The polished brown trunk is a greater attraction than the pale pink flowers in spring. It has reached nearly 17m in the Sir Harold Hillier Gardens and Arboretum (2000). Garden origin in 1923.

†*scoparia* (Spach) C.K. Schneid. A remarkable, rare, large shrub, with slender, broom-like branches recalling those of *Spartium junceum*, sparsely furnished with small, narrow leaves, reddish-bronze at first becoming bronze-green and finally green. Flowers pale pink, almond-like, in early spring. Iran. I 1934.

scopulorum Koehne (*P. vilmoriniana* hort.) A rare, upright tree, 11–12m. Flowers tiny, fragrant, white flushed pink in March or April. China.

serotina Ehrh. (Subgenus Padus) In its native environs a large tree, but small to medium-sized in this country. The attractive, glossy leaves, recalling those of the Portugal Laurel (*P. lusitanica*) turn clear yellow in the autumn. Flowers white, in racemes up to 15cm long, produced during May to June. E North America. I 1629. **'Aspleniifolia'** An unusual form of graceful habit, with slender leaves strongly toothed and less than 12mm wide. C 1864. **subsp. *capuli*** (Cav. ex Spreng.) McVaugh (*P. capollin* Zucc., *P. salicifolia* Kunth, *P. serotina* var. *salicifolia* (Kunth) Koehne) Leaves lanceolate, long-pointed, glabrous and persisting well into winter, racemes stouter. Remarkably hardy considering its native distribution. Mexico to Peru. I 1820. **var. *salicifolia*** See susbp. *capuli*.

serrula Franch. (*P. serrula* var. *tibetica* (Batal.) Koehne) A small, but vigorous tree whose main attraction is the glistening surface of its polished red-brown, mahogany-like new bark. Leaves narrow, willow-like; flowers small, white, produced with the foliage in late April. W China. I 1908 by Ernest Wilson. ♀ 2002. AM 1944.

serrulata Lindl. (*P. serrulata* 'Alboplena') A small, flat-topped tree with widespreading branches, green unfolding leaves and clusters of white, double flowers in late April and early May. An interesting tree of ancient garden origin, introduced from Canton in 1822. It has been suggested by some authorities that this tree may have arisen as a branch sport on the wild Chinese Hill Cherry (*P. serrulata* var. *hupehensis*). It was the first Japanese cherry to be planted in European gardens and is the plant designated by Lindley as the type of the species. **'Alboplena'** See *P. serrulata*. **'Autumn Glory'** See *P. verecunda* 'Autumn Glory'. **f. erecta** See *P.* 'Amanogawa' under Japanese Cherries. **var. hupehensis** Ingram (*P. mutabilis stricta* hort.) Chinese hill cherry. Considered to be the prototype of the cultivated, double, white cherry, to which Lindley gave the name *P. serrulata*. A medium-sized tree with ascending branches bearing clusters of white or blush flowers in April and early May. Young leaves bronze, and autumn foliage attractively tinted. C China. I 1900 by Ernest Wilson. **var. pubescens** See *P. verecunda*. **var. sachalinensis** See *P. sargentii*. **f. sieboldii** See *P.* × *sieboldii*. **var. spontanea** See *P. jamasakura*.

'Shosar' (*P. campanulata* × *P. incisa*) A strong-growing, rather fastigiate tree with single, clear pink flowers in late March to early April. Usually good autumn colour. Raised by Captain Collingwood Ingram.

× *sieboldii* (Carrière) Wittm. (*P. apetala* × *P. speciosa*) (*P.* 'Takasago', *P. serrulata* f. *sieboldii* (Carrière) Makino, *P. pseudocerasus watereri* hort.) A small, spreading cherry with downy leaves. Flowers semi-double, pale pink, mid- to late April. Young leaves vary from yellowish-brown to reddish-bronze. I about 1864.

simonii Carrière. Apricot plum. Small tree or large shrub of erect, conical habit, producing white flowers in March and April. Fruits very conspicuous, tomato-shaped, red and yellow, fragrant, edible. N China. I 1863.

'Snow Goose' A small tree with ascending branches crowded in spring with pure white, well-formed flowers. A seedling of similar parentage (*P. incisa* × *P. speciosa*) to 'Umineko', but differing from that cultivar in its broader crown and its larger leaves, which appear after the flowers.

speciosa (Koidz.) Ingram (*P. lannesiana* f. *albida* (Makino) E.H. Wilson) Oshima cherry. A medium-sized tree producing ovate-elliptic leaves with aristate teeth and usually terminating in a slender, acuminate apex, bronze-green when unfolding soon turning bright green. In April the fragrant white flowers are carried on long pedicels. This species is regarded as the ancestor of many of the Japanese cherries, for example 'Gyoikô', 'Tai Haku' and 'Jo-nioi'. Japan. C 1909.

spinosa L. Blackthorn, Sloe. A large, dense shrub or small, bushy tree with dark, spiny branches, crowded in March or early April with small, white flowers. Fruits like small damsons, blue-bloomy at first, later shining black. A familiar native shrub in hedges, its fruits are used in preserves, in winemaking and for flavouring gin, while its branches provide the traditional blackthorn sticks and Irish shillalahs. Europe, N Africa, W Asia. Long cultivated. **'Plena'** An attractive form with double flowers. C 1770. AM 1950. **'Purpurea'** A neat, compact bush with rich purple leaves and white flowers. One of the elite of purple-leaved shrubs. C 1903. **'Rosea'** See *P. cerasifera* 'Rosea'.

'Spire' (*P.* × *hillieri* 'Spire') Possibly the best small street tree raised in the 20th century. A vase-shaped tree attaining 10m high and about 7m wide with age. Flowers soft pink; leaves with rich autumn tints. It is a sister seedling of *P.* 'Hillieri'. ♀ 2002.

× *subhirtella* Miq. (*P. incisa* × *P. pendula*) Spring cherry. A small to medium-sized tree. It includes among its forms some of the most delightful of early spring-flowering trees, and in a good year most forms produce attractive autumn tints. Flowers small, pale pink in March and April. Unknown in the wild. I 1894. AM 1930. **var. ascendens** See *P. pendula* f. *ascendens*. **'Ascendens Rosea'** See *P. pendula* 'Ascendens Rosea'. **'Autumnalis'** Autumn cherry. A small tree up to 7.5m producing semi-double, white flowers intermittently from November to March. Flowers may be found on this tree on almost any winter's day and a few cut sprays are a welcome indoor decoration. C 1900. ♀ 2002. FCC 1966. AM 1912. **'Autumnalis Rosea'** Similar to 'Autumnalis' but flowers blush-white. ♀ 2002. AM 1960. **'Flore Pleno'** A rare and splendid form with flattish, many-petalled or double flowers, about 2.5cm across, rich pink in bud, opening white. AM 1935. **'Fukubana'** This very striking, small tree, with its profusion of semi-double, rose-madder flowers, is certainly the most colourful of the spring cherries. I 1927 from California by Captain Collingwood Ingram. **'Pendula'** See *P. pendula* and *P. pendula* 'Pendula Rosea'. **'Pendula Plena Rosea'** A weeping shrub or small tree. Flowers semi-double, rosette-like, rose-madder, similar to those of 'Fukubana', but slightly paler. I 1928 by Captain Collingwood Ingram. AM 1938. **'Pendula Rosea'** See *P. pendula* 'Pendula Rosea'. **'Pendula Rubra'** See *P. pendula* 'Pendula Rubra'. **'Stellata'** See *P. pendula* 'Stellata'.

'Sunset Boulevard' A narrow, conical tree with coppery young foliage becoming green then yellow-orange in autumn. Flowers 4cm across, white flushed with pink.

tangutica (Batal.) Koehne (*P. dehiscens* Koehne) A large, bushy shrub with spiny branches. The carmine-pink, almond-like flowers appear from March onwards. W China. I 1910 by Ernest Wilson.

tenella Batsch (*P. nana* (L.) Stokes) (*Amygdalus nana* L.) The dwarf Russian almond is a charming, small shrub with long, glabrous stems. Flowers borne in April, bright pink. SE Europe, W Asia to E Siberia. I 1683. AM 1929. **'Alba'** Flowers white. C 1845. **'Fire Hill'** Perhaps the best dwarf almond. An outstanding small shrub, a selection of f. *gessleriana* from the Balkan Alps. The erect stems are wreathed with brilliant, rose-red flowers. AM 1959. **f. georgica** hort. A tall, geographical form, up to 2m, with larger leaves. Flowers pink. **f. gessleriana** (Kirchn.) Rehder. A small shrub with bright pink flowers, darker in bud.

tomentosa Thunb. Downy cherry. A very variable shrub of medium size and usually erect habit. Young shoots and leaf undersides tomentose. Flowers white or more usually pale pink, produced in late March or early April. Fruits red. N and W China, Korea, Himalaya. C 1870. **'Leucocarpa'** A form almost completely lacking the red coloration found in the typical form. Flowers white, even in bud; fruits white. C 1930.

'**Trailblazer**' A small tree of open, spreading habit with bright red-purple leaves becoming bronze-green above when mature. Profuse, white flowers are followed by edible, red fruits. Found as a seedling in an Oregon garden before 1954, it is probably a hybrid betweeen *P. cerasifera* 'Pissardii' and *P.* 'Shiro', a plum hybrid involving several species including *P. salicina* and *P. cerasifera*.

triflora See *P. salicina*.

triloba Lindl. (*P. triloba* f. *simplex* (Bunge) Rehder, *Louiseania ulmifolia* (Franch.) Pachom.) Most frequently grown as the following form, the wild plant differs in its single, pale pink flowers. China. I 1884. '**Multiplex**' (*P. triloba* f. *multiplex* (Bunge) Rehder) A medium-sized to large shrub with small, coarsely toothed, 3-lobed leaves. Flowers large, double, rosette-like, clear peach-pink, produced in great profusion at the end of March or early April. It makes a splendid wall shrub if the old flowering shoots are pruned back immediately after flowering. I 1855 by Robert Fortune from China. FCC 1981. **f. *simplex*** See *P. triloba*.

'**Umineko**' (*P. incisa* × *P. speciosa*) A narrow, upright tree of considerable merit. Flowers white, single, produced in April with the leaves, which tint beautifully in autumn. See also 'Snow Goose'. AM 1928.

verecunda (Koidz.) Koehne (*P. serrulata* var. *pubescens* (Nakai) E.H. Wilson in part) Korean hill cherry. A medium-sized tree with bronze-green young foliage and white or pink flowers in late April and early May. Often producing rich autumn tints. Intermediate between *P. serrulata* var. *hupehensis* and *P. jamasakura*, differing from both in its hairy petioles and leaf undersurfaces. China, Korea, Japan. I 1907. '**Autumn Glory**' A form selected by Captain Collingwood Ingram for its consistent, rich, deep crimson and red autumn colours. Flowers pale blush, very prolific. AM 1966.

vilmoriniana See *P. scopulorum*.

virginiana L. (Subgenus Padus) Choke cherry. A small tree or large shrub with glossy green leaves and densely packed racemes of small, white flowers in May. Fruits dark red. E North America. I 1724. **var. *demissa*** (Torr. & A. Gray) Torr. Western choke cherry. A small, bushy tree or shrub, mainly of botanical interest. W USA. I 1892. '**Schubert**' A small tree of conical habit. Young foliage green, quickly changing to deep reddish-purple. C 1950.

'**Wadae**' (*P. pseudocerasus* × *P.* × *subhirtella*) A small, twiggy tree or large shrub with bristly-hairy young shoots, the trunk inclined to produce aerial roots. The pale pink flowers, deep rose in bud, are produced in March and smell of ripe peaches. Garden origin in Japan and named after Mr K. Wada of Yokohama.

× *yedoensis* Matsum. (*P. speciosa* × *P.* × *subhirtella*) Yoshino cherry. A graceful, early flowering, small to medium-sized tree with arching branches. Highly valued for the profusion of its almond-scented, blush-white flowers in late March and early April. Unknown in the wild; introduced from Japan in 1902, possibly earlier. ♀ 2002. AM 1927. '**Ivensii**' Raised in our nurseries from seed of *P.* × *yedoensis* in 1925. A quite remarkable, small, vigorous, weeping tree with long, tortuous branches and long, slender, drooping branchlets which, in late March to early April, are transformed into snow-white cascades of delicately fragrant blossom. Named to commemorate our late Manager, Arthur J. Ivens, FLS. '**Shidare-yoshino**' (f. *perpendens* E.H. Wilson) ('Pendula') A small tree with horizontal and arching branches often weeping to the ground. Pale pink flowers in late March and early April. I 1916. ♀ 2002. '**Tsubame**' Branches spreading and slightly weeping; flowers white.

Japanese Cherries of Garden Origin

The Sato Zakura of Japan are a large group of extremely ornamental flowering cherries. Most are of obscure origin, some having been cultivated in Japan for more than 1,000 years. Some are hybrids, while others are undoubtedly derived from *P. speciosa* and *P. jamasakura* (*P. serrulata* var. *spontanea*). No doubt other species have also contributed to their development. Many of the older sorts at least are derived from trees found in the wild, in fact, forms of *P. speciosa* identical to some of the Sato Zakura have been found growing wild in Japan.

The majority are small trees, easy to cultivate, varying from low and spreading to tall and erect in habit. The leaves of some are bronze in spring, providing a delightful backing to the emerging flowers. The flowers may be single, semi-double or double, and vary in colour from rich pink to white or cream. With few exceptions, the leaves turn to shades of yellow or tawny-orange in autumn. Like the edible cherries, they succeed in all types of well-drained soils, including chalk soils. During the dormant period the buds are often subject to bird damage, so it is necessary to use a repellent to ensure blossom. Pruning of any kind is rarely necessary, but when unavoidable is best carried out in late summer so that the cuts heal before winter.

Flowering periods are indicated as follows:

Early	late March to early April
Mid	mid- to late April
Late	late April to mid-May

'**Amanogawa**' (*P. serrulata* f. *erecta* Miyoshi) A small, columnar tree with erect branches and dense, upright clusters of fragrant, semi-double, shell-pink flowers. Mid to late. Young leaves greenish-bronze. ♀ 2002. AM 1931.

'**Asagi**' (*P. serrulata* f. *luteoides* Miyoshi) Similar to 'Ukon', but flowers single or nearly so and paler in colour, opening earlier. Early to mid.

'**Asano**' (*P. serrulata* f. *geraldiniae* Ingram) A small tree with ascending branches, bearing dense clusters of deep pink, very double flowers with pointed petals. Early. Young leaves greenish-bronze. A beautiful tree, in effect an upright form of 'Cheal's Weeping'. I 1929 by Captain Collingwood Ingram and named after a 17th-century Japanese warrior.

'**Benden**' ('Bendono', *P. serrulata* f. *rubida* Miyoshi) A vigorous tree with ascending branches, similar in size and habit to 'Kanzan'. Flowers single, pale pink. Early. Young leaves and bracts reddish-brown or coppery-red. Said to have originated on Mt Nikko and probably a form of *P. jamasakura*.

'**Bendono**' See 'Benden'.

'**Benifugen**' See 'Daikoku'.

'**Botan**' (*P. serrulata* f. *moutan* Miyoshi) A small tree with ascending and spreading branches. Flowers large, nearly 5cm across, single or semi-double, fragrant, lilac-pink in bud, opening pale pink or white. Mid. Young leaves bronze-green. Similar to 'Mikuruma-gaeshi' and 'Ojochin' in flower.

'Cheal's Weeping' See 'Kiku-shidare-zakura'.

'Chôshû-hizakura' (*P. serrulata splendens* hort.) A beautiful, small tree with single, deep pink flowers, the calyces attractively tinted purplish-brown. Mid. Young leaves reddish-brown or coppery-red. Sometimes listed as 'Hisakura', a name which has been applied to several cherries.

'Daikoku' A small tree with strong, ascending branches. Flowers large, up to 5cm across, double, purplish-red in bud opening deep lilac-pink, with a central cluster of small green carpels, carried in loose, drooping clusters. Late. Young leaves yellowish-green. Originally called 'Benifugen', a name which properly applies to 'Fugenzô'. I 1899.

'Fudanzakura' (*P. serrulata* f. *semperflorens* Miyoshi) A small, round-headed tree opening its single, white flowers, from pink buds, during spells of mild weather between November and April. Especially useful for cutting for indoor decoration. Young leaves coppery-red or reddish-brown. AM 1930.

'Fugenzô' (*P. cerasus* 'James H. Veitch') (*P. serrulata* f. *fugenzo* Mak.) Resembling 'Kanzan' in some respects, but smaller and with a broader, flat-topped head. Flowers large, double, rose-pink, borne in drooping clusters. Very late. Young leaves coppery-red. A very old cultivar, commonly grown in Japan. I about 1880. FCC 1899.

'Fukubana' See *P. × subhirtella* 'Fukubana'.

'Gyoikô' (*P. serrulata* f. *tricolor* Miyoshi) A strong-growing tree with ascending branches; flowers semi-double, creamy-white, streaked green and often tinged with pink. Mid, opening a little later than 'Ukon'. Young leaves reddish-brown. I about 1914. AM 1930.

'Hata-zakura' Flag cherry. Branches ascending. Flowers fragrant, single, white or pink-flushed. Early. Young leaves green or bronze-tinged. The name refers to the peculiar tattered edges of the petals.

'Hisakura' See under 'Chôshû-hizakura' and 'Kanzan'.

'Hokusai' One of the earliest and most popular introductions. A vigorous, widespreading tree, its branches hidden in spring by the large clusters of large, semi-double, pale pink flowers. Mid. Young leaves brownish-bronze. An old cultivar of good constitution, ideally suited to English gardens. I about 1866.

'Horinji' (*P. serrulata* f. *decora* Miyoshi) A small, upright tree with ascending branches. Flowers semi-double, mauve-pink in bud opening soft pink, contrasting with the purplish-brown calyces, freely borne along the branches. Mid. Young leaves greenish-bronze. I about 1905. AM 1935.

'Ichiyo' (*P. serrulata* f. *unifolia* Miyoshi) A beautiful tree with ascending branches and double, shell-pink flowers which have a circular, frilled appearance and are borne in long-stalked corymbs. Mid. Young leaves bronze-green. ♀ 2002. FCC 1993. AM 1959.

'Imose' A free-growing tree with double, mauve-pink flowers, abundantly produced in long, loose clusters. Mid. Leaves reddish-copper when young, glossy bright green at maturity, turning yellow in November. Fruits often produced in pairs on the same stalk. I 1927 by Captain Collingwood Ingram.

'Itokukuri' (*P. serrulata* f. *fasciculata* Miyoshi) A small tree with ascending branches. Flowers semi-double, pale pink or white. Mid. Young leaves greenish-bronze. Cultivated in Japan for more than 400 years.

'Jô-nioi' (*P. serrulata* f. *affinis* Miyoshi) A strong-growing cherry of spreading habit. Single, white, deliciously scented blossoms wreathe the branches in spring. The white petals contrast very effectively with the purple-brown sepals. Mid. Young leaves pale golden-brown. I about 1900.

'Kanzan' ('Sekiyama', *P. serrulata* f. *purpurascens* Miyoshi) One of the most popular and commonly planted ornamental cherries. A strong-growing, medium-sized tree with characteristic stiffly ascending branches when young, later spreading. Flowers large and showy, double, purplish-pink. Mid. Young leaves coppery-red or reddish-brown. Often wrongly grown in cultivation under the name 'Hisakura', for which see under 'Chôshû-hizakura', from which it differs in its taller stature and double flowers, opening generally a week later. I about 1913. ♀ 2002. FCC 1937. AM 1921.

'Kiku-shidare Sakura' A small tree with arching or drooping branches, very attractive when wreathed with clear deep pink, very double flowers. Early. Young leaves bronze-green, later green and glossy. Often wrongly referred to as 'Cheal's Weeping' which has more steeply pendent branches. ♀ 2002. AM 1915.

'Kiku-zakura' (*P. serrulata* f. *chrysanthemoides* Miyoshi) A small, slow-growing cultivar. Flowers double, each flower being a congested, rounded mass of soft pink petals. Late. Young leaves bronze-green.

'Kojima' See 'Shirotae'.

'Kokonoe' (*P. serrulata* f. *homogena* Miyoshi) A small tree producing large, semi-double, shell-pink blossoms in great profusion. Early to mid. Young leaves bronze-green.

'Mikuruma-gaeshi' (*P. serrulata* f. *diversifolia* Miyoshi, *P. serrulata* 'Temari') A distinct tree with long, ascending, rather gaunt, short-spurred branches along which large, mostly single, blush-pink flowers are densely packed. Mid. Young leaves bronze-green. Similar to 'Ojochin' and 'Botan' in flower. AM 1946.

'Mount Fuji' See 'Shirotae'.

'Ojochin' A striking tree easily distinguished by its large leaves and stout growth. Flowers single, 5cm across, pink in bud opening blush, profusely borne in long-stalked clusters of as many as 7 or 8. Mid. Young leaves bronze-brown becoming rather tough and leathery when mature. Similar to 'Botan' and 'Mikuruma-gaeshi' in flower. I before 1905. AM 1924.

'Okiku' A small tree of rather stiff habit. Flowers large, double, pale pink, passing to white. Mid. Young leaves bronze-green. AM 1934.

'Oku Miyako' See under 'Shôgetsu'.

'Oshokun' (*P. serrulata* f. *conspicua* Miyoshi) A small tree of weak growth, but with very lovely, single flowers, carmine-red in bud, opening blush-pink, very freely produced. Mid to late. Young leaves bronze-green.

'Pink Perfection' A very striking cultivar raised in Britain from 'Shôgetsu', probably pollinated by 'Kanzan'. Habit is intermediate. Flowers bright rosy-pink in bud, opening paler, double, carried in long, drooping clusters. Mid to late. Young leaves bronze. C 1935. ♀ 2002. AM 1945.

'Royal Burgundy' A small tree with glossy deep purple young foliage turning bronze in autumn. Flowers double, rose-pink. In effect a purple-leaved 'Kanzan'.

'Sekiyama' See 'Kanzan'.

'Shimidsu' See 'Shôgetsu'.

'Shirofugen' (*P. serrulata* f. *alborosea* E.H. Wilson) A strong-growing, widespreading tree up to 10m. Flowers large, double, dull purplish-pink in bud, opening white, then fading to purplish-pink, produced in long-stalked clusters and contrasting superbly with the copper-coloured young leaves. Very late and long-lasting. One of the best clones for general planting. I about 1900. ♀ 2002. AM 1951.

'Shirotae' ('Mount Fuji') A beautiful cherry, one of the most distinct clones. A small vigorous tree with widespreading, horizontal or slightly drooping branches, often reaching to the ground. Flowers very large, single or semi-double, fragrant, snow-white, bursting from the soft green young foliage in long, drooping clusters. Mid. The leaves have a distinctive fringed appearance. I about 1905. ♀ 2002.

'Shôgetsu' ('Shimidsu') One of the loveliest of Japanese cherries. A small tree with widespreading branches forming a broad, flattened crown. The large, fimbriated, double flowers are pink-tinted in bud, opening to pure white, and hang all along the branches in long-stalked clusters. Mid to late. Young leaves green. Wrongly called 'Oku Miyako' in the past. ♀ 2002. FCC 1989. AM 1930.

'Shogun' A vigorous cherry with deep pink, semi-double flowers, becoming abundant as the tree ages. Mid. Rich autumn colours.

'Shosar' See *P.* 'Shosar' (p.240).

'Shujaku' (*P. serrulata* f. *campanuloides* Miyoshi) A small tree with double, slightly cup-shaped, pale pink flowers, freely produced. Mid. Young leaves yellowish-bronze. I about 1900.

'Taihaku' Great white cherry. A superb, robust tree up to 12m. Flowers very large, single, dazzling white, enhanced by the rich coppery-red of the young leaves. Mid. One of the finest cherries for general planting and perhaps the best of the whites. It is one of the many lovely cherries that owe their popularity to Captain Collingwood Ingram. It was lost to cultivation in Japan, but in 1923, he located a plant, which had been introduced from Japan in 1900, in a Sussex garden. It was reintroduced to Japan in 1932. ♀ 2002. FCC 1944. AM 1931.

'Taizanfukun' (*P. serrulata* f. *ambigua* Ingram) A distinct, erect cherry of twiggy habit, with leathery leaves. Flowers double, pale pink. Mid. Young leaves bronze.

'Takasago' See *P.* × *sieboldii*.

'Taki-nioi' (*P. serrulata* f. *cataracta* Miyoshi) A strong, vigorous, medium-sized tree with spreading branches. The honey-scented, single, white flowers are rather small, but are produced in great abundance and contrast effectively with the reddish-bronze, young leaves. Late.

'Taoyame' A floriferous, small tree of slow growth and spreading habit. Flowers fragrant, semi-double, shell-pink becoming pale blush with purplish-brown calyces, effectively backed by the reddish-brown or coppery emerging leaves. Mid. I 1929 by Captain Collingwood Ingram.

'Ukon' (*P. serrulata* f. *grandiflora* Wagner, *P. serrulata* f. *luteovirens* Miyoshi) A robust, spreading tree. Flowers semi-double, pale yellowish, tinged green, occasionally pink-flushed, freely borne and very effective against the brownish-bronze young leaves. Closely akin to 'Asagi'. Mid. The large, mature leaves turn rusty-red or purplish-brown in autumn. I about 1905. ♀ 2002. AM 1923.

'Umineko' See *P.* 'Umineko'.

'Washino-o' (*P. serrulata* f. *wasinowo* Ingram) A strong-growing tree with white, slightly fragrant, single flowers. Early. Young leaves soft bronze-green.

'Yae-murasaki' (*P. serrulata* f. *purpurea* Miyoshi) A small, free-flowering tree of slow growth. Flowers semi-double, purplish-pink. Mid. Young leaves coppery-red.

'Yedo Zakura' (*P. serrulata* f. *nobilis* Miyoshi) Small, upright tree; flowers semi-double, carmine in bud, almond-pink when expanded. Mid. Young leaves golden-coppery. I about 1905.

'Yokihi' A small tree with widely ascending or spreading branches and large, semi-double, pale pink flowers in loose clusters, freely produced. Late. Young leaves bronze-green.

PSEUDOCYDONIA (C.K. Schneid.) C.K. Schneid.—**Rosaceae**—A monotypic genus related to and sometimes included in *Cydonia*.

sinensis (Thouin) C.K. Schneid. (*Cydonia sinensis* Thouin) A small, occasionally semi-evergreen tree or large shrub with flaky bark. Shoots hairy when young, bearing obovate to ovate leaves 5–10cm long. Flowers in spring, solitary, pink, followed by large, egg-shaped, yellow fruits, 5–18cm long, which in this country are rarely fully developed. China.

†***PSEUDOPANAX** K. Koch—**Araliaceae**—A genus of about 20 species of evergreen trees and shrubs from South America, New Zealand and Tasmania, with remarkable leaves of variable form, often sword-shaped but varying depending on the age of the plant. Flowers small, greenish of little or no garden merit. Hardy in mild localities, and succeeding in all types of well-drained soil. Some make useful houseplants.

arboreus (Murray) K. Koch (*Neopanax arboreus* (Murray) Allan, *Nothopanax arboreus* (Murray) Seem.) Five finger. A handsome, large shrub in cultivation but often a small tree in its native habitat. The large, glossy green leaves are divided into 5–7 coarsely toothed, stalked leaflets. Flowers in dense, rounded clusters, followed by decorative black fruits. Only suitable for the mildest areas. New Zealand. I 1820.

crassifolius (A. Cunn.) K. Koch. Lancewood. A small, evergreen tree with leaves varying extraordinarily according to the age of the plant. In young, unbranched specimens, they are rigid and sharply toothed, up to 60cm long by 1.2cm wide, dark green with a red midrib and purple undersurface. New Zealand. I 1846.

davidii See *Metapanax davidii*.

ferox (Kirk) Kirk. Toothed lancewood. A small, slender-stemmed tree resembling *P. crassifolius* but the leaves of juvenile and mature plants are always simple; in young plants they are pendent, greyish-green, with strongly hooked teeth. New Zealand.

laetevirens (Gay) Franch. A large shrub of upright habit or a small tree, reaching about 6m tall in the wild. The leaves have slender petioles to 8cm long, and bear 5 or sometimes 3, glossy dark green leaflets, edged with small teeth. Small, greenish-white flowers are borne in panicles at the base of the young growths in summer. Fruits not seen but said to be bright blue. The species has grown at the Sir Harold Hillier Gardens and Arboretum for more than 20 years. Chile.

laetus (Kirk) W.R. Philipson (*P. daviesii* hort., *Neopanax laetus* (Kirk) Allan) (*Nothopanax laetus* (Kirk) Cheesem.) A very handsome species, related to, but differing from *P. arboreus* in its much larger, drooping, 3-lobed, glossy green leaves. New Zealand.

lessonii (DC.) K. Koch. A small tree or large shrub with bright green, compound leaves composed of 3–5, coarsely toothed or entire, leathery leaflets. New Zealand. **'Gold Splash'** Leaves conspicuously blotched with yellow. A sport found on a cut stump of *P. lessonii* in New Plymouth, New Zealand about 1969. ♀ 2002. **'Purpureus'** Foliage tinged with purple. Possibly a hybrid with *P. discolor*. ♀ 2002.

'Trident' A vigorous, large shrub of upright habit. Leaves dark glossy green, varying from simple to 3-lobed at the apex. Possibly a hybrid of *P. lessonii* with *P. crassifolius*.

†***PSEUDOWINTERA** Dandy—**Winteraceae**—A small New Zealand genus of about 3 species related to *Drimys*. Not suitable for shallow chalk soils.

colorata (Raoul) Dandy (*Drimys colorata* Raoul) Pepper tree. A small to medium-sized shrub. Unusual in the colouring of its aromatic, oval, leathery leaves, which are pale yellow-green above, flushed pink, edged and blotched with dark crimson-purple, glaucous beneath. The small greenish-yellow flowers are borne in axillary clusters. Fruits dark red to black, rarely produced in the British Isles. Grows best in sheltered woodland conditions. AM 1975.

†**PSORALEA** L.—**Leguminosae**—A genus of 20 species of herbs and shrubs with usually compound leaves, natives of North and South America and South Africa. The following species is only suitable for the very mildest areas, but makes an attractive conservatory shrub.

pinnata L. Medium-sized to large shrub with very beautiful, pinnate leaves. Masses of lovely, blue and white pea-flowers cluster the branches in May or June. South Africa. I 1690. AM 1903.

PTELEA L.—**Rutaceae**—A small genus of North American aromatic shrubs or small trees of which the hop-tree (*P. trifoliata*) is the best known. All possess gland-dotted, trifoliolate leaves and monoecious flowers. Suitable for all types of fertile soil.

baldwinii var. *crenulata* See *P. crenulata*.

crenulata Greene (*P. baldwinii* var. *crenulata* Jeps.) Large shrub related to *P. trifoliata*, but differing in its smaller leaves with narrow leaflets and its larger, individual flowers. California.

nitens Greene. A rare species with lustrous leaves, strongly aromatic when crushed. SW USA. C 1912.

polyadenia Greene. A rare species akin to *P. trifoliata*. SW USA. I 1916.

trifoliata L. Hop-tree. A low, spreading tree or large shrub. Corymbs of small, yellowish flowers open in June and are probably the most fragrant of any hardy tree, being equal to those of the best scented honeysuckle. They are followed by dense green clusters of persistent, winged, elm-like fruits. E North America, Mexico. I 1704. **'Aurea'** Soft yellow leaves, contrasting well with purple and dark green-leaved shrubs. ♀ 2002. FCC 1980. **'Fastigiata'** A form with erect branches. It has reached 8m in the Sir Harold Hillier Gardens and Arboretum.

PTEROCARYA Kunth—**Juglandaceae**—The wing nuts are fast-growing, often widespreading trees of the walnut family, with handsome, pinnate leaves and monoecious, catkin-like inflorescences. About 10 species in Asia, mainly China. The pith of the stems is characteristically chambered. They succeed in all types of fertile soil.

caucasica See *P. fraxinifolia*.

fraxinifolia (Lam.) Spach (*P. caucasica* C.A. Mey.) A large, widespreading tree, occasionally forming large thickets of suckering stems, and usually with a short trunk and deeply furrowed bark. Leaves 30–60cm long, composed of numerous, oblong, toothed leaflets. Flowers greenish, in pendent catkins, the females up to 50cm long, draping the branches in summer. Fruits winged. A hardy, fast-growing tree, happiest in a moist, loamy soil, and particularly suitable for planting by lakes or rivers. Caucasus to N Iran. I 1782. ♀ 2002. **var. dumosa** C.K. Schneid. A remarkable, medium to large shrub, with smaller leaflets. **'Heerenplein'** A selection of compact narrow habit.

paliurus Batal. (*Cyclocarya paliurus* (Batal.) Iljinsk.) A medium-sized tree, the pinnate leaves to 25cm long with usually 7–9 glossy green, taper-pointed and sharply toothed leaflets on an unwinged rachis; lateral leaflets very unequal at the base. Distinct in its fruits which have a broad, almost circular wing to 5cm or more across, notched on one side and somewhat resembling those of *Paliurus spina-christi*. C China.

×*rehderiana* C.K. Schneid. (*P. fraxinifolia* × *P. stenoptera*) A large, suckering tree, raised in the Arnold Arboretum, Boston, in 1879. In general, it is intermediate in character between its parents. The rachis of the leaf is winged but never so pronounced nor toothed as in *P. stenoptera*. It is a first-class, hardy tree, tolerant of all kinds of soils. The long, drooping catkins, which later support the fruits, are an attractive feature for several months. In the Sir Harold Hillier Gardens and Arboretum there is a specimen that was 16m in 1990, when it was less than 40 years old. **'Fern Leaf'** Leaflets pinnately cut into slender, sharply toothed lobes. Originally distributed as a form of *P. stenoptera*, it appears to belong here.

rhoifolia Siebold & Zucc. Japanese wing nut. A large, fast-growing tree with leaves about 30cm long, composed of 11–21 finely toothed leaflets; female catkins 20–30cm long. Japan. I 1888.

stenoptera C. DC. (*P. sinensis* Rehder) A large, vigorous tree. Leaves 25–40cm long, the rachis prominently winged. Female catkins 20cm long; wings of fruit narrow and erect. China. I 1860.

PTEROSTYRAX Siebold & Zucc.—**Styracaceae**—A small genus of 4 species of interesting, large Asiatic shrubs or small trees, conspicuous in their halesia-like leaves and long panicles of small, interesting, but not showy flowers.

They succeed in all types of good, deep soil, even over chalk, but cannot be recommended for poor, shallow, chalk soils.

corymbosa Siebold & Zucc. A rare, small tree or large, spreading shrub with ovate leaves and nodding, corymbose panicles of fragrant, white flowers in May and June. Fruits obovoid, 5-winged. China, Japan. I 1850.

hispida Siebold & Zucc. Epaulette tree. A large shrub or small tree with bristle-toothed, oval or obovate leaves. The fragrant, white flowers are borne in June and July, in drooping panicles up to 23cm long, followed by spindle-shaped, 5-ribbed fruits. Japan, China. I 1875. ♥ 2002. AM 1964.

†**PUNICA** L.—**Punicaceae**—A small genus of 2 species. The following is the only species in general cultivation.

granatum L. Pomegranate. A large shrub, or small bushy tree, requiring a warm, sunny wall and good drainage in southern counties. Leaves oblong, deep shining green, coppery when young, yellow in autumn. Spectacular in late summer and early autumn, when carrying its funnel-shaped, scarlet or orange-red flowers, which have crumpled petals. The familiar fruits require a long, hot summer in which to ripen. Naturalised in SE Europe; in the Mediterranean region, it is often seen as a dense hedge. W Asia. Long cultivated in S Europe. **'Albopleno'** ('Multiplex') Flowers are double and creamy-white. Young leaves green. C 1830. **'Multiplex'** See 'Albopleno'. **'Nana'** A charming, dwarf form with narrow leaves. Plants of 15–23cm produce many orange-scarlet flowers in September and October. Suitable for a selected sunny site on a rock garden. C 1806. ♥ 2002. AM 1936. **'Rubrum Flore Pleno'** ('Rubroplena') A showy form with double, orange-red flowers. ♥ 2002.

Purslane, tree See *Atriplex halimus*.

*****PYRACANTHA** Roem.—**Rosaceae**—The firethorns are related to *Cotoneaster*, but are easily distinguished by their thorny branches and toothed leaves. They are frequently grown as wall shrubs where they will attain a height of 5m or more; when grown as such, their long growths may be cut back immediately after flowering. They are equally effective, though less tall, grown as specimen shrubs. Their masses of hawthorn-like flowers are borne in early summer, and their red, orange or yellow fruits in autumn and winter. All are hardy, and include some of the best evergreen, flowering and fruiting shrubs for north and east walls. They are tolerant of all exposures and pollution and will grow in all kinds of fertile soil. Susceptible to fireblight and canker, though some are more resistant than others. In recent years a number of disease-resistant forms have been raised at the US National Arboretum, Washington DC.

'Alexander Pendula' A medium-sized, spreading shrub of arching habit with weeping shoots. Berries yellow at first turning to coral-red.

angustifolia (Franch.) C.K. Schneid. Medium-sized shrub, occasionally up to 4m high. Very distinct with its narrow, oblong leaves, grey-felted beneath, and conspicuous clusters of orange-yellow fruits retained throughout winter. W China. I 1899. FCC 1904.

atalantioides (Hance) Stapf (*P. gibbsii* A.B. Jacks.) A large, robust shrub, occasionally a small tree, with large, oval, dark glossy green leaves. Flowers in May or early June. Fruits scarlet, long-lasting. Excellent on a sunless wall. A splendid species but unfortunately very susceptible to fireblight. China. I 1907 by Ernest Wilson. FCC 1918. In 1967 a deliberate hybrid was made by our propagator Peter Dummer in which the flowers of *Photinia davidiana* were pollinated by pollen of *Pyracantha atalantioides*. It was named × *Pyravaesia* Lancaster.

'Aurea' ('Flava') Fruits rich yellow. AM 1936.

'Buttercup' A hybrid of spreading habit with small fruits of a rich yellow.

coccinea Roem. A large shrub with narrowly obovate or oval, finely toothed leaves. Flowers, in downy corymbs, in June, followed by rich red fruits in dense clusters all along the branches. S Europe, SW Asia. I 1629. **'Lalandei'** Stronger-growing and more erect, with broader leaves and larger, orange-red fruits, thickly covering the branches in autumn and winter. Raised in France in 1874 by Mons Lalande. Once the most popular variety but very susceptible to canker. **'Red Column'** A dense, bushy shrub, of upright habit, with reddish shoots and ovate to broadly elliptic, sharply toothed, glossy green leaves. Dense clusters of scarlet fruits ripen early. **'Red Cushion'** A dwarf, compact, spreading form, useful for groundcover. Bears profuse red berries.

crenatoserrata (Hance) Rehder (*P. yunnanensis* Chitt.) A large shrub related to *P. atalantioides*. The obovate to oblanceolate leaves, 2.5–8cm long, have a broad, rounded apex with shallow, rounded teeth in their upper halves. Flowers in June, followed by innumerable clusters of small, red fruits, often persisting until March. C and W China. I 1906.

crenulata (D. Don) Roem. A variable species related to *P. coccinea*, differing in its blunt-tipped leaves, and its smaller flowers and fruits, which are orange-red. Himalaya. I about 1844. AM 1915. **var. *rogersiana*** See *P. rogersiana*.

Dart's Red ('Interrada') A vigorous, medium-sized shrub with large, matt red fruits. Resistant to scab and fireblight.

'Fiery Cascade' A medium-sized shrub of upright habit with small, glossy leaves and profuse, small, orange-red fruits. Very hardy and disease-resistant.

gibbsii See *P. atalantioides*.

'Golden Charmer' (*P. coccinea* × *P. rogersiana*) A vigorous shrub with long, arching branches bearing finely toothed, bright glossy green leaves. Large, globose, orange-yellow berries are profusely borne and ripen early. C 1960. ♥ 2002.

'Golden Dome' A splendid, small shrub making a dense mound of arching branches. A mass of flowers in June is followed by an equal abundance of small, deep yellow berries. Selected in our nursery before 1973.

'Harlequin' An unusual variegated form with pink-flushed leaves, margined with cream. Best on a wall.

koidzumii (Hayata) Rehder. A rare species, akin to *P. crenulata*, with oblanceolate leaves and loose clusters of red fruits. Taiwan.

'Mohave' (*P. coccinea* 'Wyatt' × *P. koidzumii*) A dense, medium-sized to large shrub with large, deep green leaves. Masses of bright orange-red, persistent berries ripen early. Very prone to scab. Raised at the US National Arboretum, Washington in 1963. FCC 1984.

'Mohave Silver' Leaves grey-green with an irregular, narrow white margin. Bright red berries.

'Monrovia' Vigorous, upright habit with dark glossy green, pointed leaves. Large, orange-red fruits are profusely borne.

'Navaho' (a second-generation seedling of the cross *P. angustifolia* × *P.* 'Watereri') A small to medium-sized shrub of dense, spreading habit; leaves narrowly oblong-oblanceolate, to 6cm by 1cm, entire, apart from a few teeth at the apex. Berries late ripening, small but firm, distinctly flattened, orange becoming orange-red, in very dense clusters. Very resistant to fireblight. Raised at the US National Arboretum, Washington in 1966.

'Orange Charmer' A large shrub resembling 'Orange Glow' but fruits deeper orange and more flattened. C 1962.

'Orange Glow' A vigorous shrub of dense habit, its branches inundated each autumn with bright, orange-red fruits which last well into winter. Probably *P. coccinea* × *P. crenatoserrata*. ♀ 2002.

'Renault d'Or' A vigorous shrub with stout, reddish-purple shoots and dark glossy green, broad elliptic-oblong leaves, reddish when young. Bears dense clusters of clear yellow berries 11mm across.

rogersiana (A.B. Jacks.) Chitt. (*P. crenulata* var. *rogersiana* A.B. Jacks.) This is a large, free-fruiting shrub, related to *P. crenulata* but distinguished by its smaller, oblanceolate leaves and reddish-orange fruits. W China. I 1911. ♀ 2002. AM 1953. **'Flava'** Fruits bright yellow. ♀ 2002. FCC 1919.

'Rosedale' A hybrid of *P. koidzumii* selected for its resistance to fireblight and its large, bright red fruits.

'Rutgers' A small, widespreading shrub with small, dark glossy green leaves and densely grey-hairy shoots. Profuse orange-red fruits.

Saphyr Jaune ('Cadaune') A form with attractive, yellow berries.

Saphyr Orange ('Cadange') A medium-sized, upright shrub with dark green leaves, an abundance of deep orange berries and resistance to scab and canker. It is suitable for a container. ♀ 2002.

Saphyr Rouge ('Cadrou') A medium-sized, upright shrub with glossy dark green leaves and profuse, flattened, carmine-red berries that ripen to orange. It is good for hedging and resistant to scab and fireblight. ♀ 2002.

'Shawnee' A dense, spiny shrub of medium to large size, widespreading at the base. The masses of flowers are replaced by an equal abundance of yellow to light orange fruits, which begin to colour as early as August. An American cultivar raised at the US National Arboretum, Washington, as a second-generation seedling of the hybrid *P. crenatoserrata* × *P. koidzumii*. It is claimed by its raisers to be resistant to fireblight and scab.

'Soleil d'Or' A medium-sized, upright shrub with reddish stems and dark glossy green, broadly elliptic leaves. Golden-yellow berries, 1cm across, are borne in large clusters. A sport of 'Morettii' raised in France in about 1970.

†**'Sparkler'** A very striking, variegated form, the leaves heavily mottled with white, pink-tinged in autumn and winter. Unfortunately tender and best under glass.

'Teton' (*P.* 'Orange Glow' × *P. rogersiana* 'Flava') A large shrub of vigorous, upright habit with reddish shoots and small, bright glossy green, wavy-edged leaves. Berries small, yellow-orange, profusely borne. Very resistant to fireblight. Raised at the US National Arboretum, Washington in 1963. ♀ 2002.

'Victory' A vigorous shrub with arching branches and red, often sparsely spiny shoots. Leaves bronze when young, obovate to oblanceolate, sometimes narrowly so, usually truncate to emarginate and mucronate at the apex, rich glossy green, to 6.5cm by 1.7cm, entire or sparsely toothed above the middle. Berries large, distinctly flattened, in large dense clusters, pinkish-red becoming scarlet.

'Watereri' (*P. atalantioides* × *P. rogersiana*) A very free-fruiting hybrid of compact growth, smothered annually with clusters of white flowers, followed by bright red fruits. Garden origin. AM 1955.

'Waterer's Orange' A strong-growing, free-fruiting shrub with orange-yellow fruits. AM 1959.

yunnanensis See *P. crenatoserrata*.

× **PYRACOMELES** Rehder (*Pyracantha* × *Osteomeles*)—Rosaceae—A remarkable, intergeneric hybrid, succeeding in all types of fertile soil. Tolerant of maritime exposure and air pollution.

vilmorinii Rehder (*P. crenatoserrata* × *O. subrotunda*) A small, semi-evergreen shrub with slender, thornless branches. Leaves are 2–3cm long, pinnate in the lower half, pinnatisect in the upper half. White flowers, 1cm across, in corymbs in May, followed by small, coral-red fruits. Garden origin in France before 1922.

× *Pyravaesia* Lancaster. See under *Pyracantha atalantioides*.

+**PYROCYDONIA** Winkl. ex Daniel (+*Pirocydonia*) (*Pyrus* + *Cydonia*)—Rosaceae—Interesting graft hybrids (chimaeras) between pear and quince.

'Danielii' (*Cydonia oblonga* + *Pyrus communis* 'Williams Bon Chretien') A remarkable, quince-like tree or shrub with ovate, downy leaves and white flowers, succeeded by large, apple-like, brown fruits with paler spotting. First recorded in 1902 at the junction of a pear grafted onto a quince in a garden at Rennes in France.

× **PYRONIA** Veitch (*Cydonia* × *Pyrus*)—Rosaceae—A remarkable, intergeneric hybrid intermediate between a quince and a pear and succeeding in all types of fertile soil. Tolerant of polluted atmosphere.

veitchii Guill. (*C. oblonga* × *P. communis*) A large shrub or small tree with oval, entire leaves. Flowers white, nearly 5cm across, borne usually 3 together at the tips of branchlets; anthers violet. Fruit ellipsoid, 8cm long, greenish-yellow, spotted red. Raised by John Seden of Messrs Veitch about 1895. This, the original form, should be referred to as 'John Seden' to distinguish it from later forms. **'Luxemburgiana'** Leaves larger. Flowers about 4cm across, pale rose. Fruits resembling small pears. Probably raised by Veitch.

PYRUS L.—Rosaceae—The Pears are a genus of about 20 species of mainly deciduous trees and shrubs, natives of temperate regions of the Old World. The ornamental pears are small to medium-sized, deep-rooted trees with green to silvery-grey leaves, and white flowers in April. Succeeding in all types of fertile soil, they are quite tolerant of both drought and moisture, and are excellent for cold areas. They are also tolerant of smoke pollution.

amygdaliformis Vill. A rare and quaint species from the northern shores of the Mediterranean. A large shrub or small tree with occasionally spiny branches. Leaves narrow, shallowly toothed or entire, at first silvery, becoming sage-green. Fruits small, globose, yellow-brown. I 1810. **var. *cuneifolia*** (Guss.) Bean. A form with smaller, narrower leaves.

betulifolia Bunge. A graceful, slender, small tree of rapid growth. Leaves, ovate or rounded with a slender point and strongly toothed, are greyish-green at first, becoming green and glossy above. Fruits small, the size of a large pea, brown. N China. I 1882.

boissieriana Buhse. A vigorous, medium-sized tree with reddish young shoots. The small, slender-stalked leaves are broadly heart-shaped, mucronate at the apex and with a scalloped margin, silky beneath when young, glossy dark green above. White flowers with deep pink anthers open in broad, compact corymbs in late spring, followed by small, ovoid, russet-brown and heavily speckled fruits. I 1972 by Roy Lancaster and Mrs Ala (Ala and Lancaster 37). N Iran.

calleryana Decne. Medium-sized tree with normally thorny branches and oval or broadly ovate, finely toothed, glossy green, long-persistent leaves. Fruits small, like large, brown peas, on slender stalks. China. I 1908 by Ernest Wilson. **'Autumn Blaze'** A broadly conical to rounded tree selected in Oregon in 1980 for its excellent red-purple autumn colour and profuse flowering. **'Bradford'** A selected, non-thorny seedling, raised at the Plant Introduction Station, Glenn Dale, Maryland (USA) from seed collected in China in 1918. It forms a vigorous, medium-sized, dense-headed tree, flowering profusely in late March or early April. In suitable conditions the leaves colour attractively in autumn. Highly praised as an ornamental in the USA and commonly planted as a street tree. The original tree was over 15m high and 9m across after forty-four years. **'Chanticleer'** A selection made in the USA by Edward Scanlon. It is similar to 'Bradford', but much narrower, and is proving to be an excellent street tree. ♀ 2002. Other more recent selections from North America include 'Autumn Blaze', 'Redspire' and 'Trinity'.

× *canescens* Spach (*P. nivalis* × *P. salicifolia*) A small tree, attractive when in flower. Leaves lanceolate or narrowly oval, finely toothed, greyish-white, downy when young, eventually becoming green and glossy above. Fruits small, roundish, pale green. A most attractive, silvery-foliaged tree.

communis L. The common or garden pear. A medium-sized tree with oval or rounded, glossy green leaves, which often give rich autumn tints. The branches in April are smothered with blossom, followed by sweet-tasting pears. Long cultivated and said to be a hybrid of multiple parentage. Over a thousand cultivars are known. **'Beech Hill'** A narrow tree with upright branches. The glossy green leaves often turn to brilliant orange-yellow in autumn.

cossonii Rehder (*P. longipes* Coss. & Durieu) A small tree or large shrub with rounded or ovate, finely toothed leaves, glossy green above. Small, rounded, brown fruits. Algeria. I before 1875.

elaeagnifolia Pall. A small tree or large shrub with erect, thorny branches and narrow, greyish leaves. Flowers, over 2.5cm across, are followed by small, rounded or top-shaped fruits. A most attractive, grey foliage tree. SE Europe, Turkey. I 1800.

× *lecontei* Rehder (*P. communis* × *P. pyrifolia*) A small tree with glossy green, finely toothed leaves and yellow fruits. Rich autumn colour. The cultivars 'Kieffer' and 'Le Conte' originated from this cross. Originated before 1850.

longipes See *P. cossonii*.

× *michauxii* Poir. (*P. amygdaliformis* × *P. nivalis*) A small, round-headed tree with entire, ovate or oval, greyish leaves, later glossy green above. Fruits rounded or top-shaped, greenish-yellow, spotted brown.

nivalis Jacq. A small tree with stout, ascending branches, most conspicuous in April when the pure white flowers are produced abundantly and simultaneously with the white-woolly young leaves. Leaves oval or obovate, entire. Fruits small, rounded, yellowish-green, becoming sweet when over-ripe. A most attractive, silvery-foliaged tree. S Europe. I 1800.

pashia D. Don. A small, round-headed tree with ovate, finely toothed leaves sometimes 3-lobed on vigorous shoots. Flowers pink-flushed in bud, opening white with red anthers. Rounded fruits 2–2.5cm across, brown with paler speckles. Himalaya, W China. I 1825.

pyraster (L.) Burgsd. (*P. communis* var. *pyraster* L.) Wild pear. A small to medium-sized tree with occasionally thorny branches. Leaves ovate or rounded, crenulate-serrulate, glossy green above. Fruits small, globose or pear-shaped, yellow or brown. The wild counterpart of *P. communis*. Europe, W Asia, doubtfully wild in the British Isles.

pyrifolia (Burm. f.) Nakai (*P. serotina* Rehder) Sand pear. A small to medium-sized tree. Leaves ovate-oblong, toothed, glossy green above, 8–12cm long, often giving rich autumn colour. Fruits small, rounded, brown. China. I 1908 by Ernest Wilson. **var. *culta*** (Mak.) Nakai. A form with larger leaves and much larger fruits, which are hard and gritty. Long cultivated in China and Japan. I 1880.

salicifolia Pall. Willow-leaved pear. A graceful, small, often weeping tree with silvery, narrow, willow-like leaves eventually becoming greyish-green and shining above. Flowers creamy-white. Fruits small, top-shaped, brown. Caucasus. I 1780. **'Pendula'** A very elegant and attractive, silvery-grey tree with weeping branches. This is the form in general cultivation. ♀ 2002.

syriaca Boiss. A small, round-headed tree with usually thorny branches. Leaves oblong-lanceolate, finely toothed, glossy green. Fruits small, globular or top-shaped. SW Asia, Cyprus. I before 1874.

ussuriensis Maxim. A vigorous, small to medium-sized tree with ovate or rounded, bristle-toothed leaves, turning bronze-crimson in autumn. The most important of the wild Chinese pears, and one of the earliest in flower. Fruits small, yellow-green. NE Asia. I 1855.

QUERCUS L. (including *Cyclobalanopsis* Oerst.)—**Faga-ceae**—The oaks make up a large genus of some 500 species of deciduous and evergreen trees, or occasionally shrubs, widely distributed in the N hemisphere and extending from cold temperate to tropical regions. Two species are native to the British Isles and are valued for their timber. Many reach noble proportions and live to a great age. Several species possess large or attractively cut leaves, and quite a few give rich autumn tints. Oaks are monoecious, the drooping male catkins appearing with the leaves in spring. They thrive in deep, rich soils and, apart from the North American red and white oaks, are mostly lime-tolerant, given a deep soil over chalk, but very few succeed on shallow chalk soil. One may judge the quality and depth of soil by the rate of growth and ultimate size of our native oaks.

This genus was one in which the late Sir Harold Hillier was particularly interested. During the 1970s and early 1980s in his travels to many parts of the world he brought back seed of numerous species. Plants grown from this seed now form part of the National Collection of Oaks at the Sir Harold Hillier Gardens and Arboretum.

‡*acerifolia* (E.J. Palmer) Stoynoff & Hess (*Q. shumardii* var. *acerifolia* E.J. Palmer) A vigorous, medium-sized tree with bright red young foliage. Leaves densely tomentose on both sides when young. The upper surface becomes glabrous; at first the lower surface has a thin, pale brown felt, which rubs off easily; later it is glossy green, nearly glabrous. Leaves of the first flush have the blade about as broad as long, maple-like, deeply cut into bristle-tipped lobes, those of the second flush are relatively longer. Deep red-purple autumn colour. I to the Sir Harold Hillier Gardens and Arboretum in 1989. Arkansas, USA, where it is rare in the wild.

*acherdophylla Trel. A small, spreading tree with arching branches and slightly scurfy-pubescent young shoots. Leaves oblong-elliptic, short-stalked, entire, ending in a small mucro, glossy bright green and glabrous on both sides, with a bronze tinge when young. A vigorous species proving among the hardiest of recent introductions. I to the Sir Harold Hillier Gardens and Arboretum in 1995, and earlier, usually unidentified, by other collectors. Mexico.

‡*acuta Thunb. (*Q. laevigata* Blume) A small, slow-growing, evergreen tree or large, bushy shrub. Leaves leathery, elliptic, slender-pointed, glossy, dark green above. The young leaves are densely covered with a deciduous, pale brown tomentum when they emerge in late spring and early summer. Japan, Taiwan, Korea. I about 1878.

acutissima Carruth. (Cerris Section) (*Q. serrata* Siebold & Zucc.) Sawtooth oak. Medium-sized, free-growing tree with narrowly oblong, chestnut-like, polished, bright green leaves margined with bristle-tipped teeth. They are downy at first, becoming glabrous above, glossy green and glabrate beneath, with axillary tufts of hairs, and they persist into winter. It has reached 19.5m tall at the Sir Harold Hillier Gardens and Arboretum (2001). Japan, Korea, China, Thailand. I 1862 by Richard Oldham.
subsp. *chenii* See *Q. chenii*.

aegilops See *Q. macrolepis*.

*affinis Scheidw. A vigorous tree of columnar habit with oblong-lanceolate, glossy dark green leaves, bronze when young, to 10cm long, edged with forward-pointing teeth. A fast-growing tree proving to be very hardy. Widely distributed in Mexico from where it has been introduced several times in recent years.

*agrifolia Née. Coast live oak. A small, round-headed, evergreen tree or large shrub, occasionally reaching 12m, with smooth, black bark becoming rough and squared with age. Leaves oval or rounded, short-stalked, 2.5–5cm long, hard and usually convex, armed with spine-tipped, marginal teeth; smooth, shiny green above, glabrous except for axillary tufts of hair beneath, or densely downy in var. *oxyadenia* (Torr.) J.T. Howell. Acorns sessile, cone-shaped, 2.5cm long. California, Baja California. I 1849 by Hartweg.

‡*alba* L. (*Q. alba* var. *repanda* Michx.) White oak. In the British Isles, generally a medium-sized tree with obovate, deeply and irregularly lobed, soft green leaves, reddish when unfolding, turning purple-crimson in autumn. Lobing of the leaves very variable, from shallow to very deep. SE Canada, E USA. I 1724. **'Elongata'** Leaves long and drooping, strongly convex, turning deep red-purple early in autumn. **var.** *repanda* See *Q. alba*.

aliena Blume. A small tree with large, obovate to oblong-lanceolate, coarsely toothed leaves, 15–20cm long, shining dark green above, paler and pubescent beneath. Japan, Korea, China, Thailand. I 1908. **var.** *acuteserrata* Maxim. A form with smaller, narrower leaves with gland-tipped teeth. C China, Korea, Taiwan, Japan. I 1905.

*alnifolia Poech. Golden oak of Cyprus. A rare and interesting, slow-growing, medium to large shrub in cultivation. Leaves rounded or broad obovate, hard in texture, hooded at apex, dark glossy green above and yellow-felted beneath. Hardy in sheltered gardens in the Home Counties. It has reached 8m tall in the Sir Harold Hillier Gardens and Arboretum (2001). Cyprus (Troödos Mts). I 1815. AM 1989.

ambrozyana See *Q.* × *hispanica* 'Ambrozyana'.

aquatica See *Q. nigra*.

†*arizonica* Sarg. Arizona white oak. A large shrub or small tree in cultivation. Leaves long persistent, obovate to oblong-lanceolate, shortly spine-toothed, 5–10cm long. S Central USA, N Mexico.

× *benderi* See under *Q. coccinea*.

*berberidifolia Liebm. California scrub oak. An evergreen, intricately branched shrub with slender stems and tiny, dark green, oblong or rounded, spiny leaves. S California, Baja California. It has been confused with the much rarer *Q. dumosa* and grown under that name.

‡*bicolor* Willd. Swamp white oak. A medium-sized tree with characteristic flaking bark, particularly noticeable on young specimens. Leaves obovate, 13–18cm long, shallowly lobed, polished green above, thinly whitish- or greyish-felted beneath, or sometimes only inconspicuously pubescent. One of the most satisfactory of the American white oaks in cultivation. SE Canada, E USA. I 1800.

borealis See *Q. rubra*. **var. maxima** See *Q. rubra*.

boissieri Reuter. See *Q. infectoria* subsp. *veneris*.

‡× *bushii* Sarg. (*Q. marilandica* × *Q. velutina*) Medium-sized tree with leaves intermediate in character between those of the parents, generally obovate and strongly 3- to 7-lobed, glossy green above, clothed with a pale yellowish pubescence beneath. E USA. **'Seattle Trident'** A magnificent foliage plant with large, broadly obovate, glossy dark green leaves, to about 20cm long, prominently 3-lobed at the apex. We obtained this splendid form as scions from Washington Park Arboretum, Seattle in 1962. It was raised there from seed sent by the Arnold Arboretum in 1937.

calliprinos See *Q. coccifera* subsp. *calliprinos*.

canariensis Willd. (Robur Section) (*Q. mirbeckii* Durieu) Algerian oak. A handsome, large tree with very dark grey, deeply fissured bark and a dense, rounded head of branches; much narrower as a young tree. The large, obovate or oval, shallowly lobed leaves are dark shining green above, paler or slightly glaucous beneath and remain on the tree until the New Year. An excellent, fast-growing tree succeeding equally well on heavy clay or shallow chalky soil, easily recognised in winter by its bold, persistent foliage. N Africa, S Portugal, Spain. I about 1845. ♀ 2002.

canariensis × *robur* See *Q.* × *carrisoana*.

‡*canbyi* Trel. A semi-evergreen spreading tree of vigorous growth proving hardy here. Leaves elliptic in outline, to 12cm long, with usually 4 or 5 bristle-tipped lobes on each side, glossy dark green and minutely downy above, glossy beneath with a thin layer of down and conspicuous tufts of hair in the vein axils. It is unusual among red oaks in developing acorns the first autumn after flowering. Introduced to our nursery by Sir Harold Hillier from Mexico in 1979. It has reached 10.5m tall at the Sir Harold Hillier Gardens and Arboretum (2001). N Mexico.

× *carrisoana* A. Camus (*Q. canariensis* × *Q. robur*) A fast-growing tree, intermediate in character between the parents, leaves never as large as in *Q. canariensis*. When home-grown seed of *Q. canariensis* is raised, the progeny is almost invariably this hybrid. Morocco, Spain. See also *Q.* × *viveri*.

castaneifolia C.A Mey. (Cerris Section) Chestnut-leaved oak. A magnificent medium-sized to large tree, resembling the Turkey oak (*Q. cerris*) in general appearance. Leaves oblong or narrowly oval, tapered at both ends and margined with coarse, triangular, sharply pointed teeth, shining dark green above, minutely greyish pubescent beneath. Caucasus, Iran. I 1846. **'Green Spire'** A broadly columnar form of compact habit, raised in our nurseries in about 1948. A vigorous, tall tree. ♀ 2002.

cerris L. Turkey oak. A large tree and possibly the fastest-growing oak in the British Isles. Excellent on chalky soils and in maritime exposure. Leaves oval or oblong, coarsely toothed or shallowly lobed, covered with stellate hairs and slightly rough to the touch. Both the winter buds and the acorn cups are furnished with long, narrow, downy scales. The leaves of sucker shoots and vigorous growths are often variable in size and shape. In North America, the name Turkey oak is applied to *Q. laevis* Walt., a species from the SE USA, rare in this country. S Europe, SW Asia. I 1735. **var. *ambrozyana*** See *Q.* × *hispanica* 'Ambrozyana'. **'Argenteovariegata'** ('Variegata') Leaves with a conspicuous, creamy-white margin. A most effective variegated tree. Occasionally produces reverting green shoots. **'Laciniata'** Leaves pinnatisect with narrow, spreading, mucronate lobes.

chenii Nakai (*Q. acutissima* subsp. *chenii* (Nakai) A. Camus) A Chinese relative of *Q. acutissima* with obovate, glossy green leaves. Late-made, unripened growth is subject to frost damage in cold areas. Not satisfactory on shallow chalk soils. SE China.

*chrysolepis Liebm. Canyon live oak, Maul oak. A variable, small, slow-growing, evergreen tree or large shrub. Leaves oval or ovate, spine-toothed, often entire on mature trees, resembling those of *Q. coccifera*, but normally larger, yellowish-downy and minutely gland-dotted beneath when young becoming nearly glabrous and grey during the second year. SW USA, NW Mexico. I 1877 by Charles Sargent. **var. *vacciniifolia*** See *Q. vacciniifolia*.

*coccifera L. (Suber Section) Kermes oak. A very slow-growing, dense, evergreen shrub, 2m or more high. The polished, green leaves are very variable and may be small and prickly or flat and nearly smooth. This is the host plant to the Kermes insect, from which is obtained cochineal, a once common scarlet dye. It makes a splendid backcloth for a rock garden. In the south of France it may frequently be seen growing in stony, arid ground in company with scrubby *Quercus ilex*, *Phillyrea angustifolia*, *Juniperus oxycedrus* and *J. phoenicea*. Mediterranean region, Portugal. Cultivated in England since 17th century. **subsp. *calliprinos*** (Webb) Holmboe. Palestine oak. A form with larger leaves making a medium to large tree in the wild. E Mediterranean region.

‡*coccinea* Münchh. Scarlet oak. A large tree with attractive, broad, deeply lobed leaves, each lobe furnished with several bristle-tipped teeth. The leaves are glossy dark green above during summer, in autumn turning, branch by branch, to a glowing scarlet. Some leaves persist on a few lower branches until Christmas. One of the finest trees for autumn colour, but variable in this respect. Plants in cultivation are sometimes the hybrid with *Q. rubra* (*Q.* × *benderi* Baen.). SE Canada, E USA. I 1691. **'Splendens'** A selected form vegetatively propagated. Leaves rich scarlet in autumn. ♀ 2002. FCC 1893.

conferta See *Q. frainetto*.

†**crassipes* Humb. & Bonpl. Similar to *Q. mexicana*, with which it is often confused, this species differs in its more leathery and deeply veined leaves, more densely tomentose beneath and with a conspicuous reticulate venation. In fruit it can be distinguished by the incurved rim of the acorn cup. Mexico. I 1839 by Hartweg.

cuspidata See *Castanopsis cuspidata*, but some plants distributed under this name are *Q. acuta*.

densiflora See *Lithocarpus densiflorus*.

‡*dentata* Thunb. (*Q. daimio* K. Koch) Daimio oak. A rare species, generally making a small, angular tree or large, irregular shrub in the British Isles. Remarkable for its very stout shoots and very large, obovate, broadly lobed leaves, occasionally over 30cm long and 18cm wide. Japan, Korea, China. I 1830. AM 1901. **'Carl Ferris Miller'** Selected from plants grown at Hemelrijk from seed collected in South Korea in 1976 by Robert and Jelena de Belder and Sir Harold and Lady Hillier. A vigorous, rounded tree with thick leaves, no autumn colour. **'Pinnatifida'** A rare and striking but very slow-

growing form in which the leaves are deeply cut into narrow lobes. C 1879. **'Sir Harold Hillier'** A tree of the same origin as 'Carl Ferris Miller' but with deep orange to pink autumn colour.

douglasii Hook. & Arn. Blue oak. A small, Californian tree or large shrub with oblong, occasionally lobed leaves, sea-green above, paler beneath.

*dumosa Nutt. Nuttall's scrub oak. An evergreen shrub in the wild occurring only in a few localities on the coast of S California and N Baja California. It has been confused with *Q. berberidifolia* but has the leaves distinctly tomentose beneath. Plants in cultivation under this name are usually *Q. berberidifolia*.

‡*ellipsoidalis* E.J. Hill. Northern pin oak. A medium-sized to large tree, related to *Q. palustris*, usually with a short trunk and spreading head. The deeply lobed leaves, on slender petioles, turn deep crimson-purple in autumn, equal to the best forms of *Q. coccinea*. C North America. I 1902. **'Hemelrijk'** Named from a small tree at Hemelrijk, originally supplied by us. There it colours a good deep red every year.

*emoryi Torr. Emory oak. A small tree with rigid, downy shoots. Leaves elliptic to lanceolate, short-stalked and tapered to a sharp point at the apex, edged with a few sharp teeth or nearly entire, downy on both sides when young becoming glossy green on both sides. The small acorns are sweet and are eaten in areas where it is native. SW USA, N Mexico.

faginea Lam. Portuguese oak. Usually a small, broad-headed tree. Strongly toothed leaves vary from oval to obovate; grey-felted beneath. Excellent on all soil types including chalk. It has been confused with *Q. lusitanica*. Portugal, Spain. I 1824.

‡*falcata* Michx. Spanish oak, Southern red oak. A large and distinct tree with densely tomentose shoots. Leaves, long-stalked, to 20cm long, rounded at the base, glossy dark green and glabrous above when mature, grey tomentose beneath, those of the first flush usually 3–5-lobed, the lobes often long and curved, the central lobe elongated, sometimes half the total length of the blade, those of the second flush with up to 5 lobes on each side. C & E USA. **var. *pagodifolia*** See *Q. pagoda*.

frainetto Ten. (Robur Section) (*Q. conferta* Kit., *Q. farnetto* Ten., *Q. pannonica* Endl.) Hungarian oak. A magnificent large, fast-growing tree with fissured bark and widespreading, often slightly drooping branches. Leaves obovate, occasionally as much as 20cm long, with deep, regular, large, oblong lobes. This fine species ought to be more widely planted. For all types of soil including chalk soils, this exotic species, together with *Q. cerris* and *Q. canariensis* is equal to, or even superior in rate of growth to, our 2 native species. SE Europe. I 1838. **'Hungarian Crown'** This is the tree widely grown in Britain as *Q. frainetto*. A splendid vigorous tree with upright branches making a broadly oval head. ♀ 2002. **'Trump'** A form with ascending branches selected in Holland but inferior to 'Hungarian Crown'.

fruticosa See *Q. lusitanica*.

fulhamensis See *Q.* × *hispanica* 'Fulhamensis'.

gambelii Nutt. Gambel oak. A small tree or large shrub with leathery, obovate, deeply lobed, glossy leaves. Slow-growing. SW USA, N Mexico. I 1894.

× *ganderi* C.B. Wolf (*Q. agrifolia* var. *oxyadenia* × *Q. kelloggii*) A small, semi-evergreen tree bearing leathery, obovate, shallowly and irregularly lobed leaves with bristle-tipped teeth. California (San Diego Co.).

garryana Douglas ex Hook. Oregon oak. This species makes a medium-sized tree in the British Isles with a short, stout trunk and wide-spreading head. Leaves shining green, obovate, deeply cut into oblong lobes. W North America. I 1873.

‡*georgiana* M.A. Curtis. Georgia oak. A small, spreading tree or large shrub with the young shoots glabrous or nearly so. Leaves glossy green on both sides, pointed at the apex, long-tapered at the base, edged with 2–3 or up to 5 triangular lobes on each side which end in one or few bristle teeth. An attractive and rare species which has grown for many years at the Sir Harold Hillier Gardens and Arboretum, the leaves generally turn red late in autumn. SE USA.

glandulifera See *Q. serrata*.

‡*glauca Thunb. A rare, small, evergreen tree or more usually a large, bushy shrub with stout, leafy branches. Leaves bronze when young, leathery, elliptic to obovate-oblong with an abrupt point and usually several teeth, glossy green above, glaucous beneath. Very hardy but can be damaged by late spring frost. Japan, Taiwan, China, Himalaya. I 1804.

graciliformis C.H. Mull. This Texan species is extremely rare in the wild and in cultivation. Plants grown from Mexican seed under this name are usually *Q. canbyi* q.v.

‡*grisea* Liebm. Grey oak. A variable species in the wild ranging from a shrub to a medium-sized tree. Twigs densely grey-hairy. Leaves leathery, grey-green and softly downy on both sides, oblong, to 5cm long with a few small teeth, persisting well into winter. A specimen in the Sir Harold Hillier Gardens and Arboretum has reached 4m (1990). SW USA, N Mexico.

grosseserrata See *Q. mongolica* subsp. *crispula*.

‡× *heterophylla* F. Michx. (*Q. phellos* × *Q. rubra*) A medium-sized to large tree with oblong or oval leaves varying from entire to strongly toothed, glossy dark green above, glabrous except for axillary tufts beneath. Occurring with the parents in the wild. C 1822.

× *hickelii* A Camus (*Q. pontica* × *Q. robur*) A densely branched, large shrub or small tree, of upright habit, with stout shoots and buds similar to those of *Q. pontica* but smaller. Leaves obovate, edged with triangular teeth, often auriculate at the base as in *Q. robur*. Originated at the splendid Arboretum des Barres near Paris where there is a still a very fine specimen.

‡*hinckleyi C.H. Mull. Hinckley oak. A very rare, evergreen shrub, in the wild forming low thickets. Leaves glaucous, very rigid and short-stalked with 2–3 sharp spines on each side, often auricled at the base. Found only near Solitario Peak in SW Texas.

× *hispanica* Lam. (*Q. cerris* × *Q. suber*). A variable hybrid between the cork oak and the Turkey oak but always a magnificent tree and sometimes nearly evergreen, occurring with the parents in the wild in S Europe. The same hybrid has also arisen a number of times in cultivation. All are hardy, semi-evergreen trees of medium to large size, inheriting some of the Turkey oak's vigour. The bark is thick and fissured, but never as corky as that of the cork oak. A very lime-tolerant tree. **'Ambrozyana'** (*Q. cerris* var. *ambrozyana* (Simonkai) Aschers. & Graebn.) A distinct and attractive, semi-evergreen tree differing from the Turkey oak in its darker leaves, which are white beneath and remain on the tree until the following spring. When established, unless in a very exposed position or in an extremely severe winter, this tree remains evergreen. The original tree grows in Mlynany Arboretum, Czechoslovakia, the home of the late Count Ambrozy. When we visited this splendid arboretum under the guidance of the distinguished Director Bencat and his charming interpreter Dr F. Botka we were shown this tree as well as many other exciting plants. C 1909. **'Crispa'** Originated in 1792 as a seedling of 'Lucombeana', a shorter-stemmed tree with a low, broad crown and dark grey, corky bark with deep, wide fissures. The leaves are variously shaped, but in general are shorter and remain dark green on the tree until spring, except in the hardest winters. **'Fulhamensis'** (*Q. fulhamensis* ZAB.) Fulham oak. A large tree with grey, corky bark and a dense head of drooping branchlets. Leaves grey beneath, coarsely toothed. Raised at Osborne's Nursery, Fulham about 1760. Sometimes incorrectly known as 'Dentata'. **'Hemelrijk'** See under *Q. trojana*. **'Lucombeana'** (*Q. lucombeana* Sweet) Lucombe oak. A large, ornamental tree raised by Mr Lucombe in his nursery in Exeter about 1762. The original form is a tall-stemmed tree resembling *Q. cerris*, with pale grey, shallowly fissured bark and long leaves that mostly fall around the New Year. Many of the plants grown under this name appear to be seedlings. ♀ 2002. **'Wageningen'** Of upright habit, later rounded, this selection was a seedling from 'Lucombeana'. It has glossy dark green leaves up to 12cm long and 6cm across, and is probably a hybrid with another species, such as *Q. castaneifolia*.

× *hybrida* See *Q.* × *rosacea*.

hypoleuca See *Q. hypoleucoides*.

*****hypoleucoides** A. Camus (*Q. hypoleuca* Engelm.) Silverleaf oak. A very rare and remarkable, small tree with grey-tomentose branches. Leaves thick and leathery, narrowly oblong to lanceolate, entire, 5–8cm long, with a permanent silvery white tomentum beneath. A plant grown under this name at the Sir Harold Hillier Gardens and Arboretum appears to be a hybrid with *Q. emory*. It was 11.3m tall in 2001. SW USA, N Mexico.

*****ilex** L. Evergreen oak, Holm oak. A large tree with attractive, corrugated bark and a rounded head of branches, the ends of which become pendent with age. The leathery leaves are dark glossy green above, greyish-downy beneath or glabrous; they may be entire or toothed, and are extremely variable both in shape and size depending on age of tree and growing conditions. On young bushy specimens in shade and on shoots at the base of old trees, the leaves are often completely green and glabrous. Thrives in any well-drained soil, and is particularly valuable for coastal planting, but is not recommended for the very coldest inland areas. Responds well to clipping and tolerates shade.

Excepting certain conifers, this is probably the most majestic evergreen tree cultivated in the British Isles. A large specimen with its lush piles of dark green foliage is a striking sight, particularly in June when the tawny or white woolly young shoots and pendent, yellow catkins are emerging. There can be few species that exhibit such an extraordinary variation in shape, size and texture of leaf. The evergreen oak will make a magnificent rigid hedge resistant to sea winds. Mediterranean region, SW Europe. Cultivated in England since the 16th century. ♀ 2002. **var. ballota** See *Q. rotundifolia*. **'Bicton'** A form with large, broad leaves. There is a remarkable old specimen at Bicton, S Devon. Possibly the same as or a variant of 'Rotundifolia'. **'Fordii'** ('Angustifolia') A distinct, small-leaf form of dense, broadly conical habit. Leaves narrow, 2.5–4cm long by 0.8–1.2cm wide. Raised at Exeter before 1843. **var. rotundifolia** See *Q. rotundifolia*.

‡*ilicifolia* Wangenh. Bear oak. A spreading shrub or small tree, rarely exceeding 5m, with obovate, deeply lobed leaves, white-felted beneath, that persist into early winter. Young growths attractively pink-flushed. E USA. I about 1800.

‡*imbricaria* Michx. Shingle oak. A medium-sized, vigorous tree, occasionally reaching 20m. Leaves oblong or narrowly oval, 10–18cm long, usually entire, with a bristle point at the tip, shining dark green, displaying rich autumn colours. The English name refers to the use of the wood by early settlers for shingles on roofs. E USA. I 1786 by John Fraser.

incana Bartram. Bluejack oak. A small tree with deeply cracked nearly black bark and downy shoots. Leaves elliptic to oblong, to 11cm long, usually entire, occasionally with a few small, bristle-tipped lobes, densely white tomentose beneath. SE USA.

incana Roxb. See *Q. leucotrichophora*.

infectoria G. Olivier. A large, semi-evergreen shrub or small tree, closely related to *Q. faginea* from which it differs chiefly in its glabrous or nearly glabrous, spine-toothed leaves and branches. Leaves to 5cm long on petioles to 5mm. Greece, N Turkey. I 1850. **subsp. veneris** (A. Kern.) Meikle (*Q. boissieri* Reuter, *Q. infectoria* subsp. *boissieri* (Reuter) O. Schwarz) A small to medium-sized tree, differing from the typical form in its larger leaves, to 15cm long, on petioles to 2.5cm. Cyprus to SW Asia.

ithaburensis Decne. A small tree of neat habit with rugged bark and deeply cut, often fiddle-shaped leaves. Some trees grown under this name seem to be hybrids with *Q. cerris*. They are much more vigorous with larger leaves. SW Asia. **subsp. macrolepis** See *Q. macrolepis*.

‡*kelloggii* Newb. California black oak. A medium-sized to large tree with deeply lobed, bristle-toothed, shining green leaves. California and Oregon. C 1873.

*****× kewensis** Osborn (*Q. cerris* × *Q. wislizeni*) A small to medium-sized, vigorous tree, with a dense, compact head and almost persistent, small, dark green, angularly lobed leaves. Acorns rarely produced. Raised at Kew in 1914.

‡*laurifolia* Michx. Laurel oak. Medium-sized, semi-evergreen tree of dense, rounded habit. Leaves glossy green, oblong or oblong-obovate, entire or occasionally shallowly lobed. Differing from the closely related *Q. nigra* in its narrower, less obovate and usually longer leaves. E USA. I 1786.

‡*× leana* Nutt. (*Q. imbricaria* × *Q. velutina*) A medium-sized to large tree with oblong, entire or occasionally

lobed leaves, 10–18cm long, firm and leathery in texture. Occurring with the parents in the wild. C 1850.

†*****leucotrichophora** A. Camus (*Q. incana* Roxb. not Bartram) A very striking, small, evergreen tree or large shrub for the mildest areas. Leaves narrowly oval, slender-pointed and conspicuously toothed, dark green above, white-felted beneath. It attains a large size in the Himalaya where it is accompanied by *Rhododendron arboreum*. Large, old specimens are said to have attractive, flaking bark. I about 1815.

× **libanerris** Boom (*Q. cerris* × *Q. libani*) Vigorous trees eventually of large size, closest to *Q. cerris* in habit but the leaves have bristle-tipped teeth as in *Q. libani*. Acorns large and showy, more exserted from the cup than in *Q. libani*, and covered in slender, golden-green scales. First raised at Trompenburg Arboretum, Rotterdam, before 1957, seedlings grown under this name tend to be closer to *Q. cerris*. **'Rotterdam'** Leaves to 10cm long and 3.5cm across, edged with regular triangular, bristle-tipped lobes. **'Trompenburg'** Leaves larger than those of 'Rotterdam', to 13cm long and 5cm across, more irregularly lobed.

libani G. Olivier. Lebanon oak. A small, elegant tree with slender branches and persistent, long, oblong-lanceolate leaves, glossy green above and beneath, and margined with triangular, bristle-tipped teeth. Acorns large and rounded, mostly enclosed in the cup. Closely related to *Q. trojana*. E Turkey to Syria, Asia Minor. I about 1855.

lobata Née. Valley oak. A slow-growing, small to medium-sized tree in the British Isles. Leaves elliptic to obovate, with broad, rounded lobes, dark green above, pale downy beneath. A native of the lower hills and valleys of California, large areas of its native range have been cleared to make way for new housing and agriculture. I 1874.

*****longispica** (Hand.-Mazz.) A. Camus. An evergreen tree, the shoots rough with pale brown hairs. Leaves short-stalked, elliptic-oblong or slightly obovate, to 8cm long, entire or edged with sharp teeth, dark green and rough above, with a yellow felt beneath. Flowers opening in July, the male catkins to 18cm long. Female flowers on arching peduncles to 12cm long, longer than the leaves; acorns ripen in autumn of the following year, in thin-walled cups, the scales fringed with hairs. It fruits regularly in the Sir Harold Hillier Gardens and Arboretum and is proving to be extremely hardy. In the wild this and similar species are often confused with *Q. semecarpifolia*, which, in China, occurs only in Tibet. SW China. I by Roy Lancaster from the valley of the Pi River, Sichuan in 1981.

lucombeana See *Q.* × *hispanica* 'Lucombeana'.

‡× **ludoviciana** Sarg. (*Q. pagoda* × *Q. phellos*) A most attractive, large, semi-evergreen tree of vigorous habit. Leaves obovate to oblanceolate, usually with deep, irregular lobes, shining green above. Rich autumn tints. Occurs with the parents in SE USA. I 1880. The plant now commonly grown under this name is a form or hybrid of *Q. nigra*.

lusitanica Lam. (*Q. fruticosa* Brot.) A small to medium-sized, semi-evergreen shrub. Leaves short-stalked, leathery, obovate-oblong with mucronate teeth. A scrub oak in Portugal, SW Spain and N Africa. I before 1827 but still rare in cultivation. This name has been incorrectly

applied to *Q. faginea*. A plant previously grown under this name appears to be a hybrid between *Q. faginea* and *Q. canariensis*.

macedonica See *Q. trojana*.

'Macon' (*Q. frainetto* × *Q. macranthera*) A vigorous, medium-sized to large tree with stout, hairy shoots. Leaves obovate, deeply lobed, up to 17cm long, tomentose beneath, on stout, hairy petioles. Raised by J.R.P. van Hoey-Smith.

macranthera Fisch. & C.A. Mey. ex Hohen. (Robur Section) A splendid, fast-growing tree of medium size, with striking, large, broad-obovate, acute, strongly lobed leaves, up to 15cm long. It is easily distinguished from related species by its stout twigs which, like the slender-scaled winter buds and leaf under-surfaces, are clothed with pale grey, velvety tomentum. An excellent tree that may be grown in deep soils over chalk. Often hybridises with *Q. robur* in cultivation and a tree of this parentage has reached 16.7m tall at the Sir Harold Hillier Gardens and Arboretum (2001). Caucasus, N Iran. I 1873.

‡**macrocarpa** Michx. Bur oak, Mossy-cup oak. A remarkable and handsome, North American species of medium size. On vigorous, young trees the conspicuously lobed, obovate leaves are sometimes up to 40cm long. Young shoots, buds and undersurfaces of leaves are covered by a pale down. Not a tree for the plantsman who wants a perfect specimen with a gun-barrel-like stem. NE and NC North America. I 1811.

macrolepis Kotschy (*Q. aegilops* L., *Q. aegilops* subsp. *pyrami* (Kotschy) A. Camus, *Q. ithaburensis* subsp. *macrolepis* (Kotschy) Hedge & Yalt.) Valonia oak. A small to medium-sized tree with grey-tomentose twigs. Leaves somewhat greyish-olive-green, oblong, sharply lobed, the lobes bristle-tipped and occasionally toothed, grey-tomentose beneath. The acorns, ripening the second year, are set in large cups with reflexed, slender scales. S Balkans, SE Italy, W Asia. I 1731. **'Hemelrijk Silver'** A form with large, silvery-white leaves. Grown from seed collected on the island of Rhodes by Robert and Jelena de Belder. It is similar to some forms of this species grown at the Sir Harold Hillier Gardens and Arboretum. Originally distributed as *Q. macrolepis* 'Hemelrijk'. **subsp. pyrami** See *Q. macrolepis*.

‡**marilandica** (L.) Münchh. Blackjack oak. A remarkable, small, slow-growing tree of low, spreading habit, with dark, deeply cracked bark. Leaves sometimes almost triangular, broadly obovate, tapered to the base, more or less 3-lobed at the broad apex, up to 18cm long and often as much across, glossy dark green above, tawny-yellow beneath, turning yellow or brown in autumn. E USA. C 1739.

†*****mexicana** Humb. & Bonpl. An evergreen tree with scurfy-pubescent shoots. Leaves oblong, untoothed, or with a few teeth on vigorous shoots, to 8cm long, with a loose grey tomentum beneath often nearly glabrous when mature. Acorns, as in most red oaks, ripening the second year, 1.5–2cm long. Mexico. Proving relatively hardy and fast-growing from several recent introductions.

‡**michauxii** Nutt. Swamp chestnut oak, Basket oak. A medium to large, round-headed tree with pale, scaly bark and obovate, coarsely toothed, bright green leaves. Rich yellow autumn colour. It is rare in cultivation and prefers

hotter summers than we can generally provide here. SE USA. I 1737.

mirbeckii See *Q. canariensis*.

‡*mongolica* Fisch. ex Ledeb. Mongolian oak. A striking, irregular, small to medium-sized tree with thick, glabrous branches. Leaves large, short-stalked, obovate to obovate-oblong, strongly lobed, auricled at the base, borne in dense clusters at the ends of the branches. Japan, Manchuria, Korea, Mongolia, E Siberia. I 1879.

subsp. *crispula* (Blume) Menitsky (*Q. mongolica* var. *grosseserrata* (Blume) Rehder & E.H. Wilson, *Q. grosseserrata* Blume) A form bearing usually narrowly obovate, pointed leaves with rather acute, forward-pointing teeth. Japan. **var. *grosseserrata*** See *Q. mongolica* subsp. *crispula*.

*monimotricha (Hand.-Mazz.) Hand.-Mazz. A dense and slow-growing shrub, reaching medium size in the wild, with downy shoots. Leaves ovate, short-stalked and edged with sharp spiny teeth, rough above, softly downy beneath. Acorns, in short-stalked clusters among the foliage, ripen the second year. Judging by plants raised at the Sir Harold Hillier Gardens and Arboretum, it comes true from garden seed. SW China, N Burma where it forms extensive carpets. I by Roy Lancaster from above Lijiang, Yunnan in 1986.

montana Willd. (*Q. prinus* L.) Chestnut oak. Medium-sized to large tree with an open, spreading crown. Leaves obovate to oblong-obovate, crenately-toothed, turning rich yellow in autumn. SE Canada, E USA. C 1688.

‡*muhlenbergii* Englem. Chinquapin oak, Yellow chestnut oak. Medium-sized tree with oblong to oblong-lanceolate, coarsely toothed leaves, yellowish-green above, pale pubescent beneath, the midrib and petioles yellow. Rich autumn tints. E & C North America, N Mexico. I 1822.

‡*myrsinifolia Blume (*Q. bambusifolia* Fort. not Hance, *Q. vibrayeana* Franch. & Sav.) A small, and very hardy, densely branched, evergreen tree of compact habit. The smooth, somewhat shining leaves are lanceolate with finely tapered points, remotely-toothed, dark green above, paler beneath, purple-red when unfolding, much later than those of *Q. glauca* and escaping spring frosts. It has reached 10m tall at the Sir Harold Hillier Gardens and Arboretum (2001). China, Japan. I 1854 by Robert Fortune.

†*myrtifolia Willd. Myrtle oak. An evergreen or semi-evergreen shrub or small tree. Leaves up to 5cm long, rigid, glossy bright green above, usually entire or with a few short spines. This interesting species has proved hardy in a sheltered position. SE USA.

‡*nigra* L. (*Q. aquatica* Walt.) Water oak. A medium-sized tree. Leaves normally obovate, occasionally oblong, variously lobed, particularly on young plants, sometimes entire, glossy, deep rich green on both sides, often persisting into early winter. Native of SE USA, where it frequents moist areas. I 1723.

oglethorpensis W.H. Duncan. Oglethorpe oak. A large tree, very rare in the wild, with elliptic to obovate entire leaves, to 13cm long, often lobed on the second growth flush. This species was only discovered in 1940. Native to NE Georgia, W South Carolina and Mississippi, USA, it was introduced to our nurseries in 1978. At the Sir

Harold Hillier Gardens and Arboretum it has proved hardy but slow-growing and has reached 8m tall (2001).

†*oxyodon Miq. A vigorous, evergreen tree reaching a large size in the wild, the bold, prominently veined and toothed leaves to 20cm or more long. A variable, widely distributed species. Recent introductions, from Emei Shan by Roy Lancaster in 1980, and from Guizhou to RBG Kew in 1985, are proving hardy. E Himalaya to W China. I 1900 by Ernest Wilson. AM 1998 (for foliage).

‡*pagoda* Raf. (*Q. falcata* var. *pagodifolia* Elliott) Swamp Spanish oak, Cherrybark oak. A fast-growing tree closely related to *Q. falcata* but with more regularly lobed leaves, tapered to the base and less densely tomentose beneath. SE USA.

‡*palustris* Münchh. Pin oak. A free-growing, large, denseheaded tree resembling *Q. coccinea*, but more elegant with the slender branches drooping gracefully at their extremities. Leaves deeply and sharply lobed, shining green on both surfaces and with conspicuous tufts of down in the axils below. They are smaller than those of the Scarlet oak, but often turn the same rich scarlet in autumn. SE Canada, E USA. I 1800. ♛ 2002.

pedunculata See *Q. robur*.

pedunculiflora (C. Koch) Schwarz. A rare, medium-sized to large tree related to and resembling *Q. robur*, but leaves somewhat glaucous-green above, pubescent beneath. SE Europe.

petraea (Matt.) Liebl. (*Q. sessiliflora* Salisb.) Sessile oak, Durmast oak. One of our 2 large native species replacing *Q. robur* in many damper districts or soils, notably in the west. It is distinguished by its often rather larger, longstalked leaves, usually pubescent beneath along the midrib and cuneate, not auricled, at the base; also in its sessile fruits. Good for maritime exposure. W, C and SE Europe, SW Asia. ♛ 2002. **'Acutiloba'** Leaves with pronounced and regular lobes. Originally grown as 'Acutifolia'. **'Columna'** See *Q.* × *rosacea* 'Columna'. **'Insecata'** See 'Laciniata Crispa'. **'Laciniata'** See 'Laciniata Crispa'. **'Laciniata Crispa'** ('Insecata', 'Laciniata') Leaves up to 15cm long, narrow, deeply incised with forward-pointing lobes, occasionally reduced almost to the midrib. **'Mespilifolia'** A form with irregular and crinkled, narrow leaves, 15–20cm long, tapered at both ends and entire or shallowly lobed. **'Purpurea'** ('Rubicunda') Leaves very similar in colour to those of the purple beech. **'Salicifolia'** See *Q. robur* 'Salicifolia'.

‡*phellos* L. Willow oak. A large tree with slender branches and narrow, entire, willow-like leaves, glossy green above and turning yellow and orange in autumn. The leaves of young trees are often lobed. An attractive species, broad-headed when young. Requires a lime-free soil. E USA. I 1723.

*phillyreoides A. Gray. A rare, very hardy, large shrub recalling *Phillyrea latifolia*, generally seen as a dense, rounded bush up to 5m or more, but occasionally a small tree. Leaves oval or obovate, leathery, glossy green on both surfaces, sharply but minutely toothed, usually bronze-tinted when unfolding. China, Japan. I 1861 by Richard Oldham. **'Emerald Sentinel'** A fast-growing, upright selection from the J.C. Raulston Arboretum, where it has been shown to be very hardy and easy to propagate from cuttings.

‡**Pondaim Group** (*Q. pontica* × *Q. dentata*) A small, rugged tree intermediate between the parents, both of which are remarkable plants. Leaves large, obovate and sharply toothed, dark glossy green above, grey beneath. This name was never restricted to a single clone and several different forms have been distributed. Raised by J.R.P. van Hoey-Smith about 1960.

‡*pontica* K. Koch (Robur Section) Armenian oak. An unmistakable species, usually shrubby, but occasionally a small tree. Shoots stout; leaves large, oval to obovate, sometimes as much as 25cm long by 12cm wide, strongly ribbed and toothed. The midrib and petiole are yellow. Rich yellow autumn colour. NE Turkey, Caucasus. I 1885.

prinus See *Q. montana*.

× *pseudoturneri* See *Q.* × *turneri* 'Pseudoturneri'.

pubescens Willd. (*Q. lanuginosa* Lam., *Q. virgiliana* (Ten.) Ten.) A small to medium-sized tree, occasionally shrubby, with densely hairy twigs. Leaves obovate, with wavy margins, deeply lobed and covered with a thick, greyish down. A very variable and widely distributed species. Europe, Turkey.

pyrenaica Willd. (Robur Section) (*Q. toza* DC.) Pyrenean oak. A medium to large tree that develops a widespreading head of pendent branches, tomentose branchlets, and bark of pale grey, deeply fissured into knobbly squares. Leaves variable in size, obovate or broadly oblong, with long, narrow, usually pointed lobes, glossy green above, grey-felted beneath. Its long, drooping, male catkins are attractive in June, turning from grey to gold. SW Europe, N Italy. I 1822. **'Pendula'** An elegant form with drooping branches. There are good examples of this tree to be seen at Westonbirt Arboretum and in Holland Park, London.

reticulata See *Q. rugosa*.

‡***rhysophylla** Weatherby. A strong-growing, evergreen tree; ultimate height in the British Isles uncertain. The young shoots are downy and ridged and the buds have linear stipules. Elliptic, wavy-edged rigid leaves, to 25cm long by 8cm wide, are shallowly lobed to merely toothed above the middle, the lobes with bristle tips, and auricled at the base. When young downy on both sides and reddish, they mature to dark glossy green above, conspicuously bullate, nearly glabrous beneath with small tufts of hair in the vein axils. This remarkable tree was first received in our nursery in 1978 and was introduced by Sir Harold Hillier in the following year from above the Horsetail Falls near Monterrey, Nuevo Leon, Mexico. It is proving hardy and has already reached more than 13m in the Sir Harold Hillier Gardens and Arboretum (2000). Trees raised from seed produced in cultivation are usually hybrids with other red oaks.

robur L. (*Q. pedunculata* Ehrh.) Common oak, English oak. This is the better known and more widely distributed of the 2 native species, the other being *Q. petraea*. A large, long-lived tree, developing a broad head of rugged branches when growing in the open. Leaves sessile or almost so, shallowly lobed and auricled at the base. Fruits one to several on a slender stalk. Almost all the ancient named oaks in the British Isles belong to this species rather than *Q. petraea*, but it has been shown that some are hybrids between the two. Europe, Caucasus,

SW Asia, N Africa. ♀ 2002. **'Atropurpurea'** A curious, slow-growing form with leaves and shoots of a rich vinous-purple, becoming greyish-purple at maturity. **'Concordia'** Golden oak. A small, rounded tree of very slow growth. Leaves suffused golden-yellow throughout spring and summer. Raised in Van Geert's nursery at Ghent in 1843. FCC 1868. **'Cristata'** A curious form in which the short, broad, deeply lobed leaves are folded and curled. **'Cucullata'** Leaves long and relatively narrow, the margins variously lobed and inrolled. **Fastigiata Group** Cypress oak. A large, imposing tree of columnar habit. **'Fastigiata Koster'** This is the name now given to the tree previously widely grown as *Q. robur* 'Fastigiata' of narrow, columnar habit. Normally grown from seed, and variable. A splendid specimen tree where space is restricted. ♀ 2002. **'Fastigiata Purpurea'** This is smaller than 'Fastigiata Koster' with reddish-purple young leaves throughout the growing season. **'Filicifolia'** (*Q.* × *rosacea* 'Filicifolia') (*Q. robur* 'Pectinata') Leaves pinnately divided into narrow, forward-pointing segments; petioles long and undersurfaces downy as in *Q. petraea*. Fruits peduncled. As effective as the better-known Fern-leaved Beech (*Fagus sylvatica* 'Aspleniifolia'), though never so large a tree. **'Holophylla'** See 'Salicifolia'. **'Pectinata'** See 'Filicifolia'. **'Pendula'** Weeping oak. A small to medium-sized tree with pendent branches. **'Salicifolia'** ('Holophylla', *Q. petraea* 'Salicifolia') Leaves ovate-oblong to oblong-lanceolate, entire or with an occasional shallow lobe, distinctly stalked. Propagated from the tree in the Trompenburg Arboretum, Rotterdam, whose owner and director, J.R.P. van Hoey-Smith, is an authority on oaks. **'Strypemonde'** A curious form with relatively narrow, jaggedly lobed leaves, mottled yellow. **'Variegata'** Leaves with an irregular, creamy-white margin.

× *rosacea* Bechst. (Robur Section) (*Q. petraea* × *Q. robur*) (*Q.* × *hybrida* Bechst.) A variable hybrid, generally intermediate in character between the parents but sometimes leaning more to one than the other. Occurs with the parents in the wild. **'Columna'** (*Q. petraea* 'Columna') (*Q. robur* 'Fastigiata' × *Q. petraea* 'Mespilifolia') A densely branched, columnar tree of medium size. Leaves obovate, shallowly lobed at the apex, petiole up to 2cm long, acorns pedunculate. **'Filicifolia'** See *Q. robur* 'Filicifolia'.

*rotundifolia Lam. (*Q. ilex* var. *ballota* (Desf.) A. DC., *Q. ilex* var. *rotundifolia* (Lam.) Trab.) A small, evergreen tree, closely related to *Q. ilex* but differing in its rounded and glaucous, spine-toothed foliage, and large, usually sweet acorns which, in its native habitat, are used to feed the pigs that produce the famous Iberian ham. Surpisingly rare in cultivation for a species so close to home. Spain, Portugal, S France, North Africa.

‡*rubra* L. (*Q. borealis* var. *maxima* Marshall) Ashe) Red oak. This large, fast-growing, broad-headed tree thrives in most parts of the British Isles, even in industrial areas, and in some places has reached a height of over 30m. Its large, oval or obovate, lobed leaves are matt-green above, blue-green beneath and turn red and finally red-brown before falling; on some trees they turn ruby-red or mixed yellow and brown. It differs from the closely related *Q. coccinea* in its stout, more horizontal branches and

in its less deeply lobed, matt leaves. E North America. I 1724. ♀ 2002. AM 1971. **'Aurea'** A small to medium-sized tree, the young leaves bright yellow in spring, later turning to yellow-green, finally green. A lovely clone, it requires a sheltered position in partial shade otherwise the leaves are inclined to scorch in strong sun. A specimen in the Sir Harold Hillier Gardens and Arboretum has reached 17.3m tall (2000). Raised in Holland about 1878. The original form does not seem to be grown in Holland, for plants grown there under this name see 'Limelight'. AM 1971. **'Limelight'** This name has been proposed by us for the tree that is grown as 'Aurea' in continental Europe. It does not scorch in full sun.

*_rugosa_ Née. (_Q. reticulata_ Bonpl.) A rare, evergreen species. A large shrub or small, slow-growing tree of upright habit with densely hairy branches and obovate, spine-toothed, leathery leaves, sea-green above, paler, shortly pubescent and strongly reticulate beneath. Hardy given reasonable shelter. SW USA, Mexico, C America. I 1839.

‡*_sadleriana_ R. Br. Deer oak. A rare and distinct, small, stoutly branched shrub with conspicuously scaly buds and prominently veined, serrately toothed leaves. Remarkably similar to _Q. pontica_, it often produces acorns in cultivation but can cross with _Q. robur_. Siskiyou Mountains, California and SW Oregon.

‡*_salicina_ Blume. A rare, small tree related to _Q. glauca_. Leaves lanceolate to narrowly so, long-acuminate and sharply toothed towards the apex, up to 15cm long, bronze to deep bronze-purple when becoming green beneath then glaucous. S Japan, S Korea. C 1895.

‡× _schochiana_ Dieck (_Q. palustris_ × _Q. phellos_) A vigorous, large, spreading tree with glossy green, often willow-like leaves, few-toothed or lobed or occasionally entire. A most attractive hybrid, colouring bright yellow in autumn. Occurs naturally with the parents. C 1894.

*_semecarpifolia_ Sm. In cultivation a small, rounded tree proving to be very hardy and reaching a large size in mild gardens. Leaves up to 11cm long by 7cm across, leathery, broadly elliptic to oblong, rounded at the apex, heart-shaped or almost auricled at the base, undulate and spiny on the margins on young plants becoming entire, dark glossy green above with a conspicuous midrib. Male catkins can be up to 30cm long. A tree in the Sir Harold Hillier Gardens and Arboretum is just over 10m tall (2001) and derives from an old plant in a Hampshire garden introduced by J.S. Gamble in 1900. The first introduction was by C. Gilbert Rogers to Tregrehan in 1894, where it has reached 21m (1995). Afghanistan, Himalaya, Tibet.

serrata Thunb. (_Q. glandulifera_ Blume) A small, slow-growing tree. Leaves variable, oblong-obovate to ovate-lanceolate, up to 18cm long, margined with gland-tipped teeth, bright apple-green above, greyish-white beneath, remaining late in the year. Japan, Korea, China. I 1893 by Charles Sargent. This name has also been applied to _Q. acutissima_.

sessiliflora See _Q. petraea_.

‡_shumardii_ Buckley (_Q. shumardii_ var. _schneckii_ (Britton) Sarg.) Swamp red oak. A small to medium-sized tree with attractive, deeply cut leaves, glossy green on both sides with conspicuous tufts of hair in the vein axils

beneath, turning red or golden-brown in autumn. S and C USA. I 1897. var. _acerifolia_ See _Q. acerifolia_.

‡_stellata_ Wangenh. Post oak. A medium-sized tree with large, obovate, conspicuously and deeply lobed leaves, rough to the touch above, densely clothed beneath with a stellate tomentum. SE USA. I 1800.

*_suber_ L. Cork oak. Normally a short-stemmed, wide-spreading tree of medium size, but occasionally reaching 20m. Its bark is thick, rugged and corky and provides the cork of commerce. Leaves oval or oblong, broadly toothed, leathery, lustrous green above, greenish-grey-felted beneath. Though very frost-resistant, it is not satisfactory in the coldest counties. S Europe, N Africa. Extensively cultivated in Spain and Portugal. C 1699.

trojana Webb (Cerris Section) (_Q. macedonica_ A. DC.) Macedonian oak. A small to medium-sized, densely branched, usually deciduous tree. The rather shiny, obovate-oblong, taper-pointed leaves are margined with large, incurved triangular teeth, and are often retained until the end of the year. A plant distributed as _Q._ × _hispanica_ 'Hemelrijk' belongs here. Balkans, SE Italy. I about 1890.

× _turneri_ Willd. (_Q. ilex_ × _Q. robur_) Turner's oak. A distinctive, medium-sized to large, semi-evergreen tree with a compact, rounded head of dark green leaves, oblong-obovate to oblanceolate, with 4–6 broad, mucronate teeth on each margin. Good on calcareous soils. Raised in the nursery of a Mr Turner in Essex, during the late 18th century. **'Pseudoturneri'** (_Q. pseudoturneri_ Willd.) The most commonly grown form described above. **'Spencer Turner'** The form from which the hybrid was named, also raised by Turner and now uncommon in gardens. It differs in its shorter, relatively broader leaves, with mucronate teeth. A few trees still exist in some London parks and a few other gardens.

*_vacciniifolia_ Kellogg (_Q. chrysolepis_ var. _vacciniifolia_ (Kellogg) Engelm.) Huckleberry oak. A slow-growing, very hardy, small to medium-sized shrub of dense, bushy habit. Leaves 1.5–2.5cm long, pointed, undulate and spine-toothed or entire, greyish-green beneath. SW USA.

variabilis Blume (Cerris Section) A large, elegant tree that develops an attractive, corky bark. Leaves chestnut-like, narrow, oval or oblong, margined with small, bristle-tipped teeth, green above, densely greyish- or yellowish-white-pubescent beneath and persisting late into autumn. China, Korea, Taiwan, Japan. I 1861 by Robert Fortune from near Beijing.

‡_velutina_ Lam. (_Q. tinctoria_ Michx.) Black oak, Yellow-bark oak. A large tree with downy buds and young shoots. Leaves large, hard and often 30cm long, deeply and irregularly lobed, dark green and glossy above, covered by a pale pubescence beneath. The dye quercitron is extracted from the inner bark which is bright yellow. Rich autumn tints. E and C USA. I 1800. **'Rubrifolia'** One of the most striking of all oaks with its enormous, hooded leaves measuring up to 40cm long by 23cm wide. Colours in autumn warm reddish-brown and yellowish.

virgiliana See _Q. pubescens_.

†‡*_virginiana_ Mill. Live oak. A widespreading, evergreen tree with tomentose twigs and elliptic or oblong, leathery leaves, normally entire, or rarely with a few spiny teeth, glossy dark green above, greyish- or whitish-pubescent

beneath. A tender species difficult to grow in this country. It makes a large tree common in the coastal plain of the SE USA, where it is often planted in majestic avenues as in Savannah, Georgia, and is usually seen draped in Spanish moss (*Tillandsia usneoides*). SE USA, NE Mexico, W Cuba. I 1739.

× *viveri* Sennen ex A. Camus (*Q. canariensis* × *Q. petraea*) A vigorous, large, late-deciduous tree with ascending branches making an oval head with stout shoots, downy when young becoming nearly glabrous. Leaves obovate, the blade to 15cm long, rounded to broadly cuneate and often oblique at the base with 7–9 lobes on each side, dark green above, with a loose tomentum when young beneath becoming nearly glabrous and blue-green; petiole 3cm. Acorns sessile. A tree at the Sir Harold Hillier Gardens and Arboretum, originally thought to be *Q. canariensis* × *robur*, belongs here; it was 19.5m tall in 2001. N Spain.

× *warburgii* A. Camus. (*Q. robur* × *Q. rugosa*) Cambridge oak. A rare, large tree that has large, obovate, shallowly lobed leaves which are remarkably like those of *Q. robur*, but slightly longer stalked and semi-evergreen, often remaining on the branches until the following March. Our stock is propagated from one of the original trees, growing in the University Botanic Garden, Cambridge. C 1869.

*wislizeni A. DC. Interior live oak. A large shrub or small, rounded tree of slow growth. Leaves holly-like, polished, leathery, oblong to ovate, edged with slender spiny teeth. Related to and resembling *Q. agrifolia*, but leaves almost sessile, and glabrous, with acorns maturing the first (not second) autumn. California, Mexico. I 1874. **var. *frutescens*** Englem. A shrubby variety with smaller, rigidly spiny leaves. California.

Quick See *Crataegus monogyna*.

†***QUILLAJA** Molina—**Rosaceae**—A small genus of 4 species of tender, evergreen, South American trees or large shrubs, succeeding in all kinds of well-drained, fertile soil.

saponaria Molina. Soap bark tree. A small Chilean tree. Leaves oval, toothed, thick, leathery and shining green. Flowers usually solitary in April, rather large, white with purple centre. The bark contains saponin, as well as several minerals used for washing purposes in parts of Chile. Only suitable for the mildest localities. I 1832.

Quince See *Cydonia oblonga*.

R

Raisin tree, Japanese See *Hovenia dulcis*.
Raphiolepis See *Rhaphiolepis*.
Raspberry See *Rubus idaeus*.
Redbud See *Cercis*.

†***REEVESIA*** Lindl.—**Sterculiaceae**—A small genus of 3 or 4 species of evergreen, monoecious trees and shrubs, natives of the Himalaya, China and SE Asia. Only suitable for sheltered woodland gardens in the mildest areas, but excellent conservatory subjects. They require a moist, deep, preferably lime-free loam and sun or semi-shade.

pubescens Mast. A rare, small, evergreen tree with ovate, rather leathery leaves, the veins impressed above. Flowers creamy-white, fragrant, borne in terminal corymbs during summer. A splendid specimen, like a large bay tree (*Laurus nobilis*), grew for many years at Caerhays Castle, Cornwall, and a smaller specimen in a more exposed position at Wakehurst Place, Sussex, but both succumbed to the severe winter of 1962–63. A later planting at Wakehurst survived recent hard winters. E Himalaya, S China, SE Asia. I 1910 by Ernest Wilson. AM 1954.

thyrsoidea Lindl. A tall, evergreen shrub or small tree with ovate-lanceolate leaves. Flowers fragrant, creamy-white, produced in dense terminal clusters 5–7.5cm across, in July. SE Asia. I 1826.

‡**REHDERODENDRON** Hu—**Styracaceae**—This is a small genus of about 5 species of deciduous trees, natives of SW China, Myanmar and Vietnam and only known since 1930.

macrocarpum Hu. A small tree with elliptic to oblong-ovate, finely serrate leaves, 7.5–10cm long, usually attractively tinted before falling. Cup-shaped, slightly fragrant, white flowers tinged pink and with conspicuous, exserted yellow anthers, are produced in hanging clusters with the leaves in May. The pendent fruits are oblong, 8–10-ribbed and bright red. A magnificent species, in garden merit equal to the best *Styrax*. Requires a moist, lime-free soil. Discovered on Mt Omei, W China by Mr F.T. Wang in 1931, and introduced by Professor Hu in 1934. AM 1947.

RHAMNUS L.—**Rhamnaceae**—A large genus of about 160 species of deciduous and evergreen trees and shrubs, widely distributed, mainly in N temperate regions and largely grown for their foliage. The flowers, which may be perfect, dioecious or polygamous, are small but numerous; borne in axillary clusters, they are generally inconspicuous. Harmful if eaten. *Rhamnus* will grow in all types of soils in sun or semi-shade.

*alaternus L. A useful, large, bushy, fast-growing, evergreen shrub. Leaves alternate, small, dark glossy green; flowers yellowish-green in April; fruits red, becoming black. It is splendid for maritime exposure and industrial areas. In warmer, sunnier climes, it rivals the English holly in fruit. Not recommended for the coldest inland areas. Remarkable, small-leaved forms, which creep over rocks, are found in the mountains of S Spain. Mediterranean region, Portugal. I early 17th century.

'Angustifolia' A large, compact bush of dense, rounded habit, with narrow, conspicuously toothed leaves. A splendid evergreen proving extremely hardy. **'Argenteovariegata'** Leaves green, marbled grey with an irregular, creamy-white margin. One of the best of all variegated shrubs, but somewhat tender and best given some shelter in cold areas. ♀ 2002. AM 1976.

alpina L. Alpine buckthorn. A slow-growing, small to medium-sized shrub of compact habit, producing numerous, erect stems. Leaves broad-elliptic, finely toothed, glossy green and attractively veined. Fruits black. SW Europe, C Alps, Italy. I 1752.

*californica Esch. (Frangula Section) Coffeeberry. An interesting, more or less evergreen shrub of medium size, with oblong or oval leaves about 5cm long, occasionally to 10cm. Fruits red, changing to purple-black. W North America. C 1871. **subsp. crassifolia** See *R. tomentella* subsp. *crassifolia*.

cathartica L. Common buckthorn. A large, native shrub or small tree, a common hedge or woodland shrub on chalk. The spiny branches are quite attractive in autumn, when laden with masses of shining black fruits. Europe (incl. British Isles).

davurica Pall. Dahurian buckthorn. A large shrub or small tree with slender-pointed, oblong leaves and black fruits in autumn. Siberia, Manchuria, N China. I 1817.

frangula L. (*Frangula alnus* Mill.) Alder buckthorn. A large shrub or small tree with ovate leaves turning yellow in autumn. Fruits red, changing to black; the shrub is extremely ornamental when bearing berries of both colours. Its wood makes the best charcoal for gunpowder. Europe (incl. British Isles). **'Aspleniifolia'** A curious form in which the leaf blade is reduced to a mere thread 3–5mm wide. Particularly attractive in autumn when the pendent leaves turn deep yellow. **'Columnaris'** Tallhedge buckthorn. A compact form of narrowly upright habit. Found in the USA in 1936.

*× hybrida L'Hér. (*R. alaternus × R. alpina*) A medium-sized to large, usually semi-evergreen shrub of spreading habit, with dark glossy green, oblong, shallowly toothed leaves up to 10cm long. C 1788. **'Billardii'** Leaves smaller, more deeply toothed.

imeretina Kirchn. The most outstanding of the buckthorns. A medium-sized to large shrub with stout shoots and large, handsome, corrugated leaves, dark green above, downy beneath, usually becoming bronze-purple in autumn. Some leaves may be as much as 30–35cm long and 10–15cm wide. A splendid shrub for a damp, shaded site. W Caucasus. I 1858.

infectoria L. Avignon berry. A spreading shrub to 2m, with spine-tipped branches and ovate or obovate leaves. The black fruits were once used by dyers. SW Europe.

japonica Maxim. Medium-sized shrub with glossy, pale green, obovate leaves, crowded at the ends of the branchlets. The small, faintly scented, yellowish-green flowers are produced in dense clusters in May. Fruits black. Japan. I 1888.

parvifolia Bunge. A spiny, medium-sized shrub with elliptic, dark green, polished leaves and black fruits in autumn. It has not grown very successfully in the Hampshire area. NE Asia. I 1910.

*__procumbens__ Edgew. A prostrate species from the Himalaya, making a low mound of intricate stems clothed with small, shining, bright green leaves; black fruits. Most suitable for a rock garden.

__pumila__ Turra. Dwarf buckthorn. A dwarf, sometimes prostrate shrub, only a few centimetres high. Fruits blue-black. Suitable for a rock garden. Mts of S Europe, Alps. C 1752.

__purshiana__ DC. (Frangula Section) Cascara. A small tree or large shrub worthy of inclusion in a representative arboretum. The rather large leaves are prominently veined and downy beneath. Fruits red, turning black. The drug 'Cascara Sagrada' is obtained from the bark of this tree. W North America. C 1870.

__rupestris__ Scop. (Frangula Section) A small, spreading, sometimes procumbent shrub. Leaves elliptic or rounded. Fruits small, red at first, finally black. W Balkans. C 1800.

*__tomentella__ Benth. Hoary coffeeberry. A large shrub related to __R. californica__ but with downy shoots and the leaves tomentose beneath. Fruits black, to 15mm. California, New Mexico, Baja California. **subsp. *crassifolia*** (Jepson) J.O. Sawyer. (__R. californica__ subsp. *crassifolia* (Jepson) C.B. Wolf. A form with larger leaves white-tomentose on both sides.

__utilis__ Decne. A medium-sized shrub with slender branches and oblong, polished, green leaves. Fruits black. Long cultivated for the dye known as 'China Green'. C and E China, Japan.

*__RHAPHIOLEPIS__ Lindl. (*Raphiolepis* Lindl.)—**Rosaceae**—A small genus of about 15 species, natives of E Asia. The following are rather slow-growing, evergreen shrubs with firm, leathery leaves. They require a warm, sunny position in a well-drained, fertile soil.

†× __delacourii__ André (__R. indica__ × __R. umbellata__) A charming shrub, usually less than 2m, of rounded habit. Leaves obovate, glossy green, toothed in upper half. Lovely rose-pink flowers are borne in erect, terminal panicles in spring or summer. Only injured by severe frosts. It makes an attractive wall shrub. Raised by Mons Delacour, near Cannes, France, towards the end of the 19th century. AM 1932. **'Coates' Crimson'** A choice selection with rose-crimson flowers. Named after the Californian raiser. C 1952. **'Enchantress'** A compact form with large clusters of rose-pink flowers. **'Spring Song'** A form with apple-blossom-pink flowers borne over a long period.

†__indica__ (L.) Lindl. A small shrub with narrow, toothed, leathery leaves, 5–7.5cm long. Flowers white, flushed pink, borne in racemes intermittently during spring and summer. Only suitable for the mildest localities or a conservatory. S China. C 1806.

__umbellata__ (Thunb.) Makino (__R. japonica__ Siebold & Zucc.) A delightful, dense, slow-growing shrub of rounded habit, usually attaining about 1.2m in the open or higher against a wall. Leaves oval, thick and leathery, inconspicuously toothed. Terminal clusters of slightly fragrant, white flowers in June, followed by bronzy-black fruits. Normally hardy, but injured in very severe winters, such as 1962–63 when parts of the British Isles were frozen for up to 10 weeks. Japan, Korea. I about 1862. ♥ 2002.

*__RHAPHITHAMNUS__ Miers—**Verbenaceae**—Two species of evergreen shrubs or small trees, natives of Chile and Argentina.

†*__spinosus__ (A.L. Juss.) Moldenke (__R. cyanocarpus__ (Hook. & Arn.) Miers) A medium-sized to large, evergreen, myrtle-like shrub of dense habit. Each pair or cluster of small, sharply toothed leaves is accompanied by 2 or 3 sharp, needle-like spines. Flowers small, tubular, 1cm long, pale blue, in April; berries deep blue. Requires a warm sunny wall. I about 1843 by William Lobb.

RHODODENDRON L. (including *Azalea*)—**Ericaceae**—The rhododendrons are one of the most important and diverse groups of ornamental plants in cultivation. They include many of the most spectacular, as well as some of the noblest, of flowering trees and shrubs. Late spring and early summer is the height of their flowering season and about nine-tenths flower during the months of April, May and June. The remainder are, nevertheless, an important group, bringing colour to the garden sometimes as early as January or even late December, or as late as August. Many are notable for their handsome foliage and a number of deciduous kinds for their autumn tints. For landscaping, the rhododendrons are unsurpassed. When massed, no other shrub gives such a wealth of colour. The variations in form, colour, texture and size of leaf are so remarkable that even if they never flowered, some species would still be the outstanding evergreens of the temperate world. Those with large leaves are subject to wind damage and should, if possible, be planted in woodland or similar shelter. The dwarf, small-flowered species may be mass planted and are particularly effective in an open heather garden: the same is true of almost all of the Lapponica Subsection.

Rhododendrons may be grown in a moist yet well-drained, fertile soil, so long as no free lime is present. Few rhododendrons will tolerate even a trace of free lime, although applications of Iron Sequestrene to the soil often improve performance in such situations. A sheltered, semi-shaded position is appreciated by all but many, especially the alpine species and that wide range of hybrids popularly known as the Hardy Hybrids, will luxuriate in full exposure to wind and sun. They are also remarkably tolerant of atmospheric pollution. Rather than loosen the topsoil by annual forking, it is better to give an annual mulch up to 8cm deep, preferably in early autumn, to protect and nourish the root system which develops close to the soil surface. Excellent mulches include decaying leaves, bracken, peat or spent hops. Rhododendrons require no regular pruning, but the removal of the faded trusses immediately after flowering is extremely beneficial. Hardy Hybrids that have become straggly or too large may be hard-pruned in April.

Hardiness
H4 Hardy anywhere in the British Isles.
H3 Hardy in the south and west, also along the seaboard and in sheltered gardens inland.
H2 Requires protection in the most sheltered gardens.
H1 Can usually be grown only as a greenhouse plant.

Rhododendrons have been treated under 5 main headings:
Rhododendron Species (including Azaleas), see p.259.
Rhododendron Hybrids, see p.283.

Azaleodendrons, see p.304.
Deciduous Hybrid Azaleas, see p.305.
Evergreen Hybrid Azaleas, see p.308.

‡Rhododendron Species (including Azaleas)

The genus *Rhododendron* is one of the largest, containing some 800 species. It is represented mainly in the N hemisphere, reaching its greatest density in the vast expanse of mountain ranges and gorges bordering China, Tibet and Upper Burma. Men such as Sir Joseph Hooker, George Forrest, Joseph Rock, Kingdon-Ward and Ernest Wilson introduced many of these species, and it is thanks to them that our gardens have such a wide representation. However, had it not been for J.B. Stevenson, many would have been lost to cultivation during and after the First World War. Gardeners throughout the world owe to him a debt of gratitude for raising and maintaining the most complete set of rhododendron species at Tower Court, Ascot. After his death, his work was continued by his widow (who later became Mrs Harrison) assisted by the Head Gardener, Mr Keir. Fortunately, before her death, she sold the bulk of the collection to the Commissioner of Crown Lands, so that these plants have been saved for posterity in the Valley Garden made in Windsor Great Park by Sir Eric Savill, that past-master of informal gardening.

The species described below range from tiny, prostrate alpines to trees with enormous leaves. The dwarf species are charming, rock-garden shrubs, those belonging to the subsections Lapponica and Saluenensia of subgenus Rhododendron associating well with heaths. A massed planting of dwarf and alpine rhododendrons, with all their various colours, ranging from white through pink and red to yellow, purple and blue, exhibits a greater colour range than that of the finest heather garden. The large-leaved species require shelter, especially from wind, and will not tolerate very dry conditions for long periods. An ideal site for these is provided by thin, oak woodland, with some evergreen shelter.

This account follows the now widely accepted Edinburgh Revision. Subgenus Rhododendron is divided into 3 Sections: Rhododendron into which most species fall, and which is further divided into subsections, Pogonanthum, which contains *R. anthopogon* and its relatives, and Vireya, of which none of the mainly subtropical and tender species are dealt with here. Subgenus Hymenanthes contains only one section, which is divided into subsections. Subgenus Tsutsusi contains most of the Asiatic azaleas, the evergreen ones in Section Tsutsusi, the deciduous ones in Section Brachycalyx. Subgenus Pentanthera contains 4 Sections: Pentanthera containing the North American azaleas as well as the related *R. molle*; Sciadorhodion, containing 4 species of Asiatic azalea such as *R. quinquefolium*; Viscidula containing only the very distinct *R. nipponicum*; and Rhodora, containing *R. canandense* and *R. vaseyi*. The subgenus and section/subsection to which each species belongs is indicated in parentheses after the name. The section name for species in Subgenus Rhododendron, Section Rhododendron is not given.

Where certain species worthy of horticultural recognition have been relegated to synonymy in the Edinburgh Revision, the RHS Horticultural Revision has been followed in giving these Group status.

Except where otherwise stated, the following species and their forms are evergreen.

Awards. Many awards have been given to unnamed forms of species, and these are indicated in the text as follows: AM (F) or FCC (F).

We are grateful to John Bond for help with the revision of this section.

aberconwayi Cowan (Subgenus Hymenanthes, Subsect. Irrorata) A small to medium-sized shrub with loose trusses of flat, saucer-shaped, white flowers, tinged pink and usually heavily spotted maroon, in May and June. Leaves medium-sized, rather rigid and leathery. NE Yunnan. I 1937. H3. **'His Lordship'** Flowers white flashed with crimson. AM 1945.

adenogynum Diels (Subgenus Hymenanthes, Subsect. Taliensis) Small to medium-sized shrub with woolly young shoots and leathery leaves covered with a tawny, suede-like felt beneath. Flowers deep rose in bud opening white, shaded rose, funnel-shaped, April to May. W Yunnan, SW Sichuan, SE Tibet. I by George Forrest in 1910. H3. **Adenophorum Group** (*R. adenophorum* Balf. f. & W.W. Sm.) Flowers rose with scattered crimson spots, April. Yunnan. I by George Forrest in 1910. H4.

adenophorum See *R. adenogynum* Adenophorum Group.

adenopodum Franch. (Subgenus Hymenanthes, Subsect. Argyrophylla) A medium-sized shrub of rounded, spreading habit. Leaves to 20cm long, dark green above with deeply impressed veins, tomentose when young, covered beneath with a thick brown felt. Flowers funnel-campanulate, to 5cm long, pale pink sometimes with deeper spots, in trusses of up to 8, April to May. Sichuan and Hubei, China. I by Ernest Wilson in 1900. AM 1926. H3.

aechmophyllum See *R. yunnanense*.

aemulorum See *R. mallotum*.

aeruginosum See *R. campanulatum* subsp. *aeruginosum*.

aganniphum Balf. f. & Kingdon-Ward (Subgenus Hymenanthes, Subsect. Taliensia) A medium-sized to large shrub with leaves 5–10cm long, covered beneath with a smooth white or yellowish-white indumentum. Flowers bell-shaped, varying from white to deep rose, spotted crimson; May and June. SE Tibet, NW Yunnan. H4. **var.** *flavorufum* (Balf. f. & Forrest) D.F. Chamb. This differs from the typical variety in the deep red-brown, partially deciduous indumentum on mature leaves.

albrechtii Maxim. (*Azalea albrechtii* (Maxim.) Kuntze) (Subgenus Pentanthera, Sect. Sciadorhodion) A very beautiful, medium-sized, deciduous shrub of open habit. Leaves obovate or oblong-obovate, clustered at the ends of the branches, turning yellow in autumn. Flowers deep rose, 5cm across, appearing before or with the leaves in April and May. Japan. I 1914 by Ernest Wilson. AM 1943. H4.

alutaceum Balf. f. & W.W. Sm. (Subgenus Hymenanthes, Subsect. Taliensia) A medium-sized to large shrub with oblong leaves up to 15cm long, clothed beneath with a pale brown woolly indumentum. Flowers in loose trusses, bell-shaped, rose, spotted and blotched crimson within, April. SW China, SE Tibet. I 1914 by George Forrest. H4.

amagianum (Makino) Makino ex Hara (*Azalea amagiana* Makino) (Subgenus Pentanthera, Sect. Brachycalyx) An outstanding, medium-sized to large, deciduous shrub with broad obovate leaves in clusters of 3 at the ends of the branches. Flowers orange-red, funnel-shaped, 3–4 in a truss, June and July. Japan. AM 1948. H4.

ambiguum Hemsl. (Subgenus Rhododendron, Subsect. Triflora) An attractive, medium-sized to large shrub, with 5–7.5cm long leaves and clusters of 3–6 funnel-shaped flowers of greenish-yellow, spotted green, April and May. C Sichuan. I 1904 by Ernest Wilson. H4.

annae Franch. (Subgenus Hymenanthes, Subsect. Irrorata) Medium-sized to large shrub with rather small, narrow leaves. Flowers white to rose-flushed with or without purple spots, bell-shaped, June and July. W Yunnan, NE Upper Burma. H3–4.

anthopogon D. Don (Subgenus Rhododendron, Sect. Pogonanthum) A dwarf shrub of compact habit with brown, scaly branchlets and leaves up to 3cm long, densely scaly below. Flowers varying from cream to deep pink, narrowly tubular, in a tight, terminal cluster, April. Nepal, Sikkim, Assam, Bhutan, S Tibet. I 1820. AM 1955. H4. subsp. *hypenanthum* (Balf. f.) Cullen (*R. hypenanthum* Balf. f.) Small, tubular, yellow flowers in tight, rounded heads in April and May. '**Annapurna**' An attractive form with smaller, dark glossy green leaves and slightly larger flowerheads. AM 1974.

anthosphaerum Diels (*R. eritimum* Balf. f. & W.W. Sm.) (Subgenus Hymenanthes, Subsect. Irrorata) A variable, medium-sized to large shrub or small tree with leaves to 18cm long. Flowers in large trusses, bell-shaped, dark crimson with a dark basal blotch. Yunnan, SE Tibet. H3.

anwheiense E.H. Wilson (*R. maculiferum* subsp. *anwheiense*. (E.H. Wilson) D.F. Chamb.) (Subgenus Hymenanthes, Subsect. Maculifera) Medium-sized shrub with ovate-lanceolate leaves, 5–7.5cm long. Rounded heads of bell-shaped, white flowers, usually with a pink flush and reddish-purple spots, appear April and May. Anhui Province (China). AM 1976. H4.

aperantum Balf. f. & Kingdon-Ward (Subgenus Hymenanthes, Subsect. Neriiflora) A dwarf, spreading shrub with tomentose shoots and dark green, obovate leaves, up to 6cm long, glaucous beneath. Flowers usually pink or red but varying to white and yellow, often flushed pink, tubular-campanulate, in trusses of 3–6, April and May. Best in a cool, moist, open position. NE Upper Burma, NW Yunnan. I 1919 by Kingdon-Ward. AM (F) 1931. H4.

apodectum See *R. dichroanthum* subsp. *apodectum*.

arborescens (Pursh) Torr. (*Azalea arborescens* Pursh) (Subgenus Pentanthera. Sect. Pentanthera) A large, deciduous shrub with obovate or oval, glossy green leaves, pale green or glaucous beneath, usually attractively tinted in autumn. Flowers white, occasionally pink-flushed, fragrant, funnel-shaped, style red, long and protruding, June and July. E USA. I 1818. H4.

arboreum W.W. Sm. (Subgenus Hymenanthes, Subsect. Arborea) A magnificent, large shrub or small tree, in its less hardy forms requiring woodland shelter. Leaves up to 20cm long, green above, whitish to brownish-red below, primary veins conspicuously impressed. From January to April the bell-shaped, 5cm long flowers are carried in dense, globular heads and vary from white to blood-red. The flowers are usually produced very early and in cold districts are often ruined by frost. Many of its progeny are, however, hardier. This magnificent species was the first rhododendron introduced from the Himalaya and is the parent of many of our hardy hybrids. Temperate Himalaya, Kashmir to Bhutan, Khasia Hills. I about 1810. H2–4. '**Album**' Flowers white. H4. '**Blood Red**' Flowers striking blood-red. H3. subsp. *cinnamomeum* (Lindl.) Tagg. Leaves with a thick, cinnamon or rust-coloured tomentum beneath. E Nepal, NE India. I 1820. subsp. *delavayi* (Franch.) D.F. Chamb. (*R. delavayi* Franch.) Leaves glossy dark green above with a greyish-white tomentum beneath. Flowers usually blood-red, bell-shaped, in a round, compact truss, March to May. E Himalaya to SW China. I about 1884. FCC 1936. H2–3. var. *roseum* Lindl. A lovely form of subsp. *cinnamomeum*, the flowers rich pink with darker spots. AM 1973. H4. '**Sir Charles Lemon**' See *R*. 'Sir Charles Lemon' under Hybrids. '**Tony Schilling**' Deep pink flowers with darker spots. A selection of subsp. *cinnamomeum* var. *roseum*. FCC 1974. H3–4. subsp. *zeylanicum* (Booth) Tagg (*R. zeylanicum* Booth) A large shrub or small tree, superb in the milder parts of the British Isles. Leaves elliptic-oblong, bullate, very dark green, covered with dense fawn or tawny indumentum below. Flowers red, bell-shaped, in a dense truss, April and May. One of the most beautiful foliage rhododendrons. Sri Lanka. I in the 1830s. H2–3.

argenteum See *R. grande*.

argipeplum Balf. f. & R.E. Cooper (*R. smithii* Nutt. ex Hook. f.) (Subgenus Hymenanthes, Subsect. Barbata) Large shrub or small tree with attractive, plum-coloured bark and bristly-hairy shoots. Leaves oblong-lanceolate, 10–15cm long, loosely tomentose below. Flowers scarlet-crimson, bell-shaped, in compact trusses, March. NE India, Bhutan, SE Tibet, I 1850. H3.

argyrophyllum Franch. (Subgenus Hymenanthes, Subsect. Argyrophylla) A beautiful, large, densely leafy shrub of slow growth, with long leaves, silvery or white-felted beneath. Flowers white or pink with darker spots, bell-shaped, in a loose head, May. Yunnan, Sichuan, Shaanxi. I 1904 by Ernest Wilson. AM (F) 1934. H4. '**Chinese Silver**' A beautiful selection of subsp. *nankingense*. Leaves very silvery beneath, flowers pink, darker on the lobes, 5cm across. An excellent foliage plant. ♀ 2002. AM 1957. **Cupulare Group** (var. *cupulare* Rehder & E.H. Wilson) Flowers smaller, cup-shaped, white spotted with pink. subsp. *nankingense* (Cowan) D.F. Chamb. A form with larger leaves and flower trusses. W Sichuan, Guizhou. I 1931. AM 1996. '**Roseum**' Flowers clear rose.

arizelum Balf. f. & Forrest (*R. rex* subsp. *arizelum* (Balf. f. & Forrest) D.F. Chamb.) (Subgenus Hymenanthes, Subsect. Falconera) A large shrub or small tree for moist woodland with magnificent large leaves covered with a cinnamon indumentum beneath. Flowers are compact heads of creamy-yellow bells, sometimes rose-tinted, with dark crimson blotch. April. W Yunnan, NE Upper Burma. AM (F) 1963. H3–4.

atlanticum (Ashe) Rehder (*Azalea atlantica* Ashe) (Subgenus Pentanthera, Sect. Pentanthera) A charming, small, deciduous, stoloniferous shrub with obovate or oblong-obovate, bright green leaves. Flowers white or white flushed pink, occasionally with a yellow blotch, fragrant, funnel-shaped, May. Coastal plain of mid-eastern USA. I about 1916. H4.

aucklandii See *R. griffithianum*.

augustinii Hemsl. (Subgenus Rhododendron, Subsect. Triflora) A large, small-leaved shrub with blue flowers in April and May. In its best forms, this beautiful Chinese species is one of the finest of all rhododendrons. It is fairly quick-growing, making an ideal woodland shrub. The name commemorates Augustine Henry who first found it. Hubei, E Sichuan. I 1899 by Farges. AM 1926. H3–4. **subsp. *chasmanthum*** (Diels) Cullen (*R. chasmanthum* Diels) A splendid variety with pale lavender to deep lavender-mauve flowers, a little later than the typical form, and borne in rather larger trusses. Yunnan, Sichuan, SE Tibet. FCC 1932. AM 1930. H3. **'Electra'** A magnificent shrub when bearing clusters of violet-blue flowers marked with greenish-yellow blotches. The flowers are a startling colour, particularly when seen en masse on a large bush. Raised by Lionel de Rothschild at Exbury in 1937. It is a hybrid between the typical form and subsp. *chasmanthum*. ♀ 2002. AM 1940. H3–4.

aureum Georgi (*R. chrysanthum* Pall.) (Subgenus Hymenanthes, Subsect. Pontica) A prostrate or dwarf shrub up to 30cm. Leaves oblanceolate to obovate, 4–7.5cm long. Flowers pale yellow, bell-shaped, May and June. E former USSR, Korea, Japan, N China. I 1796. H4.

auriculatum Hemsl. (Subgenus Hymenanthes, Subsect. Auriculata) A large shrub, occasionally a small tree. Though very distinct and handsome in leaf, this Chinese species is chiefly remarkable for its late flowering, which occurs normally in July and August, but sometimes even later. The large, white, funnel-shaped flowers, long-tapered in bud, are borne in huge trusses and are richly scented. Hubei, Sichuan, Guizhou. I Ernest Wilson in 1901. AM 1922. H4.

†*auritum* Tagg (Subgenus Rhododendron, Subsect. Boothia) A small shrub with dark green leaves 2.5–6cm long. Flowers bell-shaped, 2.5cm long, pale yellow, slightly flushed pink on the lobes, April. SE Tibet. AM 1931. I 1924 by Kingdon Ward. H2–3.

austrinum (Small) Rehder (*Azalea austrina* Small) (Subgenus Pentanthera, Sect. Pentanthera) A small to medium-sized deciduous shrub. Flowers creamy-yellow to orange, often tinged or striped purple, to 3.5cm long, with or before the leaves in spring, May. SE USA. H4.

baileyi Balf. f. (Subgenus Rhododendron, Subsect. Baileya) A small shrub sometimes reaching 2m, the young shoots and undersides of the small leaves coated with reddish-brown scales. Flowers red-purple, usually with darker markings, saucer-shaped, May. SE Tibet, Bhutan, Sikkim. I 1913. AM 1960. H3–4.

× *bakeri* (Lemmon & McKay) Hume (Subgenus Pentanthera, Sect. Pentanthera) (*R. canescens* × *R. flammeum*) A naturally occuring hybrid which has been confused with *R. cumberlandense* q.v. H4.

balfourianum Diels (Subgenus Hymenanthes, Subsect. Taliensia) A medium-sized to large shrub with dark green leaves, to 12cm long, covered beneath with a glossy, silvery tomentum. Trusses of up to 9, bell-shaped flowers,

5cm across, are pale to deep pink, spotted with deep red, April to May. Yunnan and Sichuan, China. H4.

barbatum G. Don (Subgenus Hymenanthes, Subsect. Barbata) A beautiful, large, spreading shrub or small tree with coloured stems and attractive, peeling bark. The branchlets and petioles are clad with conspicuously impressed primary veins. Flowers glowing crimson-scarlet, bell-shaped, carried in dense, globular heads, March. N India, S Tibet, Nepal, Bhutan. C 1829. AM 1954. H3–4.

basilicum Balf. f. & W.W. Sm. (Subgenus Hymenanthes, Subsect. Falconera) A large shrub or small tree, succeeding best in woodland conditions. The large, handsome leaves have winged petioles and are rich cinnamon-brown beneath. Flowers pale yellow, sometimes crimson-tinged and with a deep crimson basal blotch, April. W Yunnan, NE Upper Burma. I 1912 by George Forrest. AM (F) 1956. H3–4.

bathyphyllum Balf. f. & Forrest (Subgenus Hymenanthes, Subsect. Taliensia) Small, densely leafy shrub, the leaves 5–7.5cm long, clothed beneath with a rust-coloured indumentum. Flowers white, spotted crimson, 4–5cm long, bell-shaped, April and May. SE Tibet, NW Yunnan. H4.

bauhiniiflorum See *R. triflorum* var. *bauhiniiflorum*.

beanianum Cowan (Subgenus Hymenanthes, Subsect. Neriiflora) Medium-sized shrub of open habit, with chestnut- or yellowish-brown, woolly tomentum on the undersides of the leaves. Flowers usually red, sometimes pink, bell-shaped, waxy, in loose trusses, March to May. Named after W.J. Bean, one of the greatest-ever authorities on woody plants. NE Upper Burma, NE India. AM (F) 1953. H3–4. **var. *compactum*** See *R. piercei*.

beesianum Diels (Subgenus Hymenanthes, Subsect. Taliensia) A large shrub or small tree with stout shoots and bold, dark green leaves, to 30cm or more long, thinly covered with a red-brown felt beneath. Flowers in large trusses are widely bell-shaped, 5cm across, and deep pink, blotched with crimson. SW China, E Himalaya. I 1906 by George Forrest and later by Kingdon-Ward and Rock. H3.

bodinieri Franch. A very hardy, medium-sized shrub with narrow, acuminate leaves. Flowers white or pale rose, with purple spots, funnel-shaped, March and April. Closely related to *R. yunnanense* and probably of hybrid origin. C 1933. H3–4.

brachyanthum Franch. (Subgenus Rhododendron, Subsect. Glauca) A dwarf or small shrub of neat habit, with aromatic leaves, sparsely scaly beneath, and bell-shaped, pale yellow flowers in June and July. C Yunnan. Discovered by the Abbé Delavay in 1884, introduced by George Forrest in 1906. AM 1966 (to 'Jaune'). H4. **subsp. *hypolepidotum*** (Franch.) Cullen. Leaves densely scaly beneath. NE Burma, NW Yunnan, SE Tibet. AM 1951 (to 'Blue Light').

brachycarpum D. Don ex G. Don (Subgenus Hymenanthes, Subsect. Pontica) An attractive, hardy species of medium size, with leaves covered with a fawn or brownish indumentum beneath. Flowers creamy-white, flushed pink, funnel-shaped, June and July. Japan, Korea. H4. **subsp. *fauriei*** (Franch.) D.F. Chamb. (*R. fauriei* Franch.) Leaves becoming glabrous beneath; white flowers with a pink flush and green spots.

brachystylum See *R. trichocladum*.

bullatum See *R. edgeworthii*.

bureaui Franch. (Subgenus Hymenanthes, Subsect. Taliensia) Medium-sized shrub with attractive, dark, glossy green leaves, covered beneath with a rich red-woolly indumentum. Flowers rose, with crimson markings, bell-shaped, 10–15 in a tight truss, April and May. This outstanding species is well worth growing if only for the attractive colours of its young growths, which vary between pale fawn and warm rusty-red. N Yunnan. I by Ernest Wilson in 1904. ♀2002. AM 1972 (for foliage). AM 1939 (for flower). H4.

burmanicum Hutch. (Subgenus Rhododendron, Subsect. Maddenia) Small shrub with scaly, dark green leaves. Flowers greenish-yellow, ageing to white, fragrant, funnel-shaped, 5cm long, April. Mt Victoria, C Burma. H3.

caeruleum See *R. rigidum*.

caesium Hutch. (Subgenus Rhododendron, Subsect. Trichoclada) Small shrub with attractive, shining, pale brown bark and aromatic leaves, green above, bluish-grey and scaly below. Flowers greenish-yellow, with green flecks within, funnel-shaped, small, 2–3 together, May. Yunnan. I 1925 by George Forrest. H4.

calendulaceum (Michx.) Torr. (*Azalea calendulacea* Michx.) (Subgenus Pentanthera. Sect. Pentanthera) Flame azalea. A medium-sized to large, deciduous shrub with elliptic or obovate-oblong leaves, turning orange and red in autumn. Flowers varying in rich colours from yellow to orange or scarlet (hence the specific epithet, like a marigold), funnel-shaped, 5cm across, May and June. One of the most vividly coloured of all wild azaleas. E USA (Appalachian Mts). I 1806. H4. **'Burning Light'** Flowers coral-red with orange throats. AM 1965.

callimorphum Balf. f. & W.W. Sm. (*R. cyclium* Balf. f. & Forrest) (Subgenus Hymenanthes, Subsect. Campylocarpa) A dainty, medium-sized shrub with small, round leaves, green above, glaucous below. Flowers deep rose in bud opening soft pink, occasionally with a crimson basal blotch, bell-shaped, in loose trusses, April to June. W Yunnan. I 1912 by George Forrest. H4. **var. *myiagrum*** (Balf. f. & Forrest) D.F. Chamb. (*R. myiagrum* Balf. f. & Forrest) Flowers white. I 1919 by George Forrest.

calophytum Franch. (Subgenus Hymenanthes, Subsect. Fortunea) One of the noblest of Chinese species and one of the hardiest of those species that have conspicuous large leaves. A large shrub or small tree with thick shoots capped with rosettes of long, narrow, oblanceolate leaves. Large trusses of white or pink, bell-shaped flowers, each with a maroon basal blotch, are borne in March and April. Sichuan, Yunnan. First found by the Abbé David, introduced by Ernest Wilson in 1904. ♀2002. FCC (F) 1933. AM (F) 1920. H4.

calostrotum Balf. f. & Kingdon-Ward (Subgenus Rhododendron, Subsect. Saluenensia) A very attractive, dwarf shrub with grey-green foliage and comparatively large, flat or saucer-shaped, bright magenta-crimson flowers in May and June. A fine rock-garden species. NE Upper Burma, W Yunnan. I 1919. AM (F) 1935. H4. **'Gigha'** ('Red Form') A very splendid selection with flowers of deep claret-red contrasting with the grey-green young leaves. The name recalls the lovely garden made by Col Sir James Horlick on the Isle of Gigha, off the coast of Argyllshire. ♀2002. FCC 1971. **subsp. *keleticum*** (Balf. f. & Forrest) Cullen (*R. keleticum* Balf. f. & Forrest) A dwarf shrub forming mats or hummocks of small, densely scaly leaves from which the saucer-shaped, purple-crimson flowers arise, singly or in pairs, in May and June. SE Tibet, Yunnan, Upper Burma. I 1919 by George Forrest. ♀2002. AM (F) 1928. **Radicans Group** (*R. radicans* Balf. f. & Forrest) Very dwarf, prostrate with normally solitary, flattish, rose-purple flowers in May and June. Suitable for a rock garden. SE Tibet. I 1921 by George Forrest. AM (F) 1926. **subsp. *riparioides*** Cullen. Similar to subsp. *riparium* but with larger leaves. NW Yunnan. A plant known as 'Rock's Form' has deep purple flowers. **subsp. *riparium*** (Kingdon-Ward) Cullen (*R. riparium* Kingdon-Ward) Habit upright, leaves not glaucous. NE India, NE Upper Burma, Yunnan, S Tibet. AM 1983. **subsp. *riparium* Calciphilum Group** (*R. calostrotum* var. *calciphilum* (Hutch. & Kingdon-Ward) Davidian) A form with very small leaves and rather later pink flowers. Grows on limestone screes in the wild. NE Upper Burma. **subsp. *riparium* Nitens Group** (*R. nitens* Hutch.) A dwarf, erect shrublet with aromatic leaves and usually deep purple flowers, widely funnel- or saucer-shaped, up to 5cm across, in June and July. The last of its series to flower. Upper Burma.

caloxanthum See *R. campylocarpum* subsp. *caloxanthum*.

campanulatum D. Don (Subgenus Hymenanthes, Subsect. Campanulata) A large shrub, the unfolding leaves covered with a suede-like, fawn or rust-coloured indumentum. Flowers varying from pale rose to lavender-blue, bell-shaped, April and May. A lovely species, said to be one of the commonest rhododendrons in the Himalayan forests. Kashmir to Bhutan. I 1825 by Wallich. H4. **subsp. *aeruginosum*** (Hook. f.) D.F. Chamb. (*R. aeruginosum* Hook. f.) A slow-growing, compact shrub with striking metallic blue-green young growths. Sikkim, Bhutan. **'Knap Hill'** An attractive selection with lavender-blue flowers. AM 1925.

campylocarpum Hook. f. (Subgenus Hymenanthes, Subsect. Campylocarpa) A small to medium-sized shrub with ovate leaves, glossy green above, glaucous green below. Flowers clear yellow, bell-shaped, April and May. The best of its colour for general planting and one of the choicest of all hardy shrubs. In common with its relatives, it does not flower when young. E Nepal, Sikkim, Bhutan, Assam, S Tibet. I by Sir Joseph Hooker about 1849. FCC 1892. H3–4. **subsp. *caloxanthum*** (Balf. f. & Farrer) D.F. Chamb. (*R. caloxanthum* Balf. f. & Farrer) (*R. telopeum* Balf. f. & Forrest) Charming, small, free-flowering shrub with small, rounded leaves and clusters of bell-shaped, citron-yellow flowers, tipped orange-scarlet in bud, in April and May. One of Reginald Farrer's prettiest introductions. NE Burma, SE Tibet, Yunnan. I 1919 by Reginald Farrer. AM (F) 1934. **subsp. *caloxanthum* Telopeum Group** (*R. telopeum* Balf. f. & Forrest) Small to medium-sized shrub with smaller leaves, about 2.5–3.5cm long, glaucous below. The bell-shaped flowers are yellow, sometimes with a faint reddish blotch, May. SE Tibet, Yunnan. H4. **Elatum Group** Taller and looser in growth. Flowers usually with a crimson basal blotch, orange-vermilion in bud. Collected at a lower elevation than the typical form.

campylogynum Franch. (Subgenus Rhododendron, Subsect. Campylogyna) A delightful, dwarf shrub with small, lustrous green leaves, glaucous beneath. Produces long-stalked, nodding, rose-purple to almost mahogany, bell-shaped, waxy flowers when only a few centimetres high, in May and June. Suitable for a rock garden. Apart from the following, a selection with the designation 'claret', is grown. It has bloomy plum-purple, thimble-shaped flowers on long stalks. Yunnan, SE Tibet, NE Burma, NE India. I 1912 by George Forrest. ♀ 2002. H3–4. **'Bodnant Red'** A selection of Cremastum Group with red flowers. AM 1971. **Charopoeum Group** (*R. charopoeum* Balf. f. & Forrest) Leaves and flowers larger. **Cremastum Group** (*R. cremastum* Balf. f. & Forrest) Habit erect; leaves green beneath. **'Crushed Strawberry'** Flowers pink, a pleasant shade of crushed strawberry. A selection made in our nurseries in about 1955. **Myrtilloides Group** (*R. myrtilloides* Balf. f. & Kingdon-Ward) A charming shrublet, with smaller, delightful, waxy, plum-purple flowers. FCC 1943. AM 1925. **'Patricia'** A form with plum-red flowers.

camtschaticum Pall. (*Therorhodion camtschaticum* (Pall.) Small) (Subgenus Therorhodion) A dwarf, spreading, deciduous shrublet, up to 30cm, with curious, comparatively large, saucer-shaped, rose-purple flowers in May. A curious feature is the corolla tube which is split almost to the base on the lower side. Leaves, up to 5cm long, give attractive autumn tints. Requires an open, well-drained situation. Alaska, E former USSR, Japan. I 1799. AM 1908. H4.

canadense (L.) Torr. (*Azalea canadensis* (L.) Kuntze, *Rhodora canadensis* L.) (Subgenus Pentanthera. Sect. Rhodora) A small, deciduous shrub of erect, twiggy habit. Leaves narrowly oval, sea-green. Flowers rose-purple, saucer- or bell-shaped, appearing before the leaves in April. Thriving in moist situations. NE North America. I 1767 AM 1928 (as *Rhodora canadensis*). H4. **'Album'** Flowers white.

canescens (Michx.) Sweet (*Azalea canescens* Michx., *R. roseum* (Loisel.) Rehder) (Subgenus Pentanthera, Sect. Pentanthera) A medium to large, deciduous shrub with oblong or oblanceolate leaves, densely hairy beneath. Flowers white or pink-flushed, with a pink or reddish gland-covered tube, sweetly scented, funnel-shaped, April and May. SE USA. I 1810. H4.

cantabile See *R. russatum*.

carolinianum See *R. minus* Carolinianum Group.

catawbiense Michx. (Subgenus Hymenanthes, Subsect. Pontica) An extremely hardy, medium-sized to large shrub of dense habit, with oval or oblong, glossy green leaves up to 15cm long. An old plant will develop into a dense thicket of layering stems. Flowers varying from lilac-purple to pink or white, bell-shaped, in large trusses, June. A parent of many hardy hybrids. SE USA (Allegheny Mts). I 1809 by John Fraser. H4.

caucasicum Pall. (Subgenus Hymenanthes, Subsect. Pontica) A slow-growing, dome-shaped shrub of medium size. Leaves elliptic to oblanceolate, clad with a thin, fawn tomentum beneath. Flowers pale sulphur-yellow with pale green markings within, widely funnel-shaped,

in a compact truss, May, occasionally again in late summer. A parent of many of the old hardy hybrids. Now rare in cultivation, the form described here is the plant previously known as 'Cunningham's Sulphur'. Caucasus, NE Turkey. I 1803. H4.

cephalanthum Franch. (Subgenus Rhododendron, Sect. Pogonanthum) A very beautiful, small, slender, aromatic shrub, with small leaves, densely scaly beneath, and dense, terminal heads of tubular, white or pinkish, daphne-like flowers in May. Yunnan, Sichuan, SE Tibet, Upper Burma. I 1908. H4. **Crebreflorum Group** (*R. crebreflorum* Hutch. & Kingdon-Ward) A choice dwarf form from Assam bearing pink flowers. A gem for a peat garden. AM 1934.

cerasinum Tagg (Subgenus Hymenanthes, Subsect. Thomsonia) A medium-sized to large shrub with elliptic leaves 5–10cm long and, in May, drooping trusses of long, bell-shaped flowers varying from white, with marginal band of cherry-red, to self red or crimson. It was to the former that Kingdon-Ward gave the name 'Cherry Brandy'. NE Upper Burma, SE Tibet. AM (F) 1938. H4.

chaetomallum See *R. haematodes* subsp. *chaetomallum*.

chamaethomsonii (Tagg & Forrest) Cowan & Davidian (*R. repens* var. *chamaethomsonii* Tagg & Forrest) (Subgenus Hymenanthes, Subsect. Neriiflora) Dwarf, semi-prostrate or spreading shrub producing trusses of 5–6 bell-shaped, crimson or rose-crimson flowers from March to April. NW Yunnan, SE Tibet. H4. **var. *chamaethauma*** (Tagg) Cowan & Davidian (*R. repens* var. *chamaethauma* Tagg) A form with smaller leaves. AM 1932.

chameunum See *R. saluenense* subsp. *chameunum*.

chapmanii See *R. minus* var. *chapmanii*.

charianthum See *R. davidsonianum*.

charidotes See *R. saluenense* subsp. *chameunum*.

charitopes Balf. f. & Farrer (Subgenus Rhododendron, Subsect. Glauca) A charming shrublet, rarely as much as 1.2m, with obovate leaves, glaucous and densely scaly below. Flowers apple-blossom-pink, speckled crimson, bell-shaped, April and May. NE Upper Burma, NW Yunnan. I 1924 by George Forrest. H4. **subsp. *tsangpoense*** (Kingdon-Ward) Cullen (*R. tsangpoense* Kingdon-Ward) A variable dwarf to small, aromatic shrub. The leaves are obovate-oblong, 2.5–5cm long, glaucous-scaly below, interspersed with pale green or pink scales which, when viewed through a lens, appear like glistening jewels set in a white satin cloth. Flowers varying from crushed strawberry to deep-crimson or violet, semi-bell-shaped, very freely produced, May and June. S Tibet. AM 1972 to 'Cowtye'.

chartophyllum See *R. yunnanense*.

chasmanthum See *R. augustinii* subsp. *chasmanthum*.

chrysanthum See *R. aureum*.

chryseum See *R. rupicola* var. *chryseum*.

chrysodoron Hutch. (Subgenus Rhododendron, Subsect. Boothia) A small shrub with often bristly shoots and bright green, ciliate leaves, blue-green and scaly beneath. Small clusters of widely bell-shaped, canary-yellow flowers, each 4cm across, open early, in March or April. A beautiful but rather tender species, suitable for mild areas or a cool greenhouse. SW China, N Burma, where it is often an epiphyte. I 1924 by George Forrest and later by Kingdon-Ward. AM 1934. H2–3.

ciliatum Hook. f. (Subgenus Rhododendron, Subsect. Maddenia) A beautiful, dome-shaped shrub, about 1.2–1.5m, with attractive, peeling bark and conspicuously ciliate leaves. Flowers rose-lilac, fragrant, bell-shaped, nodding, borne at an early age, March and April. E Nepal, Sikkim, SE Tibet, Bhutan. I 1850 by Sir Joseph Hooker. AM (F) 1953. H3–4.

cinnabarinum Hook. f. (Subgenus Rhododendron, Subsect. Cinnabarina) A beautiful, medium-sized to large shrub with obovate-elliptic, scaly leaves and tubular, bright cinnabar-red flowers in May and June. One of the choicest of the Himalayan species. Unfortunately, this species and most of the forms are prone to powdery mildew. Nepal, Sikkim, Bhutan, SE Tibet. I by Sir Joseph Hooker in 1849. H4. **'Aestivale'** Flowers later, usually in July. **'Blandfordiiflorum'** Flowers red outside, yellow within. AM 1945. **'Caerhays John'** Medium-sized shrub of erect, bushy habit. Flowers deep apricot, funnel-shaped, up to 6cm across, May and June. Flowering later than 'Caerhays Lawrence'. A cross between Concatenans and the typical form. **'Caerhays Lawrence'** Similar in habit to 'Caerhays John', and bearing waxy flowers of rich orange-yellow, April and May. A cross between Concatenans and the typical form. **'Caerhays Philip'** A beautiful, medium-sized shrub with elliptic leaves and loose trusses of funnel-shaped, yellow flowers, 6cm across, April and May. A cross between 'Blandfordiiflorum' and Concatenans. AM 1966. **Cinzan Group** ('Blandfordiiflorum' × subsp. *xanthocodon*) Flowers rich yellow, flushed pink. C 1951. **Concatenans Group** (*R. concatenans* Hutch.) A distinct and lovely shrub of medium size. Leaves oval to oblong, densely scaly beneath, 4–6cm long, glaucous blue when young. Flowers apricot-yellow faintly purple-tinged on outside and sometimes conspicuously veined, bell-shaped, waxy, April and May; less susceptible to powdery mildew. SE Tibet. I 1924 by Kingdon-Ward. FCC 1935. H3. **'Conroy'** (*R.* 'Conroy') Loose, flat-topped trusses of pendent, narrowly trumpet-shaped, waxen light orange flowers with a rose tinge, May and June. C 1937. A cross between Concatenans Group and Roylei Group. AM 1950. **'Mount Everest'** A lovely form from the Tower Court collection (see introduction). Flowers pale apricot, freely produced, less tubular than in the typical form. **Purpurellum Group** (var. *purpurellum* Cowan) A form of subsp. *xanthocodon* with plum-purple flowers. AM 1951. **Roylei Group** (*R. roylei* Hook. f.) Leaves glaucous; flowers rose-red to purple-red, shorter than those of the type. A splendid form; less prone to powdery mildew. Bhutan, SE Tibet. **subsp. *xanthocodon*** (Hutch.) Cullen (*R. xanthocodon* Hutch.) Clusters of waxy, yellow, bell- to funnel-shaped flowers in May and June. Flowers best when given some form of shelter; appears resistant to powdery mildew. NE India, Bhutan, SE Tibet. I 1924 by Kingdon-Ward. FCC 1998, AM (F) 1935.

citriniflorum Balf. f. & Forrest (Subgenus Hymenanthes, Subsect. Neriiflora) A small shrub with obovate or oblong leaves, covered with a thick fawn or dark brown tomentum. Flowers in trusses of 4–6, bell-shaped, lemon-yellow or occasionally rose-flushed, shaded orange at base, calyx coloured and conspicuous, April and May. Yunnan. I by George Forrest in 1917. H4.

clementinae Forrest (Subgenus Hymenanthes, Subsect. Taliensia) A small to medium-sized, stiffly branched shrub with matt green leaves, densely covered with a thick, pale brown tomentum beneath. Flowers bell-shaped, 5cm across, with 6–7 lobes, cream, flushed pink and spotted red. SW China, SE Tibet. I 1913 by George Forrest. H4.

concatenans See *R. cinnabarinum* Concatenans Group.

concinnum Hemsl. (Subgenus Rhododendron, Subsect. Triflora) Medium-sized to large shrub with elliptic or obovate-elliptic, scaly leaves, and clusters of funnel-shaped, purplish flowers in April and May. Sichuan, Hubei. I 1904 by Ernest Wilson. H4. **Benthamianum Group** (*var. benthamianum* (Hemsl.) Davidian) A form with lavender-purple flowers. **Pseudoyanthinum Group** (*R. pseudoyanthinum* Hutch.) A lovely variety with deep ruby-red or purple-red flowers. Appears resistant to powdery mildew. AM 1951.

coreanum See *R. yedoense* var. *poukhanense*.

coriaceum Franch. (Subgenus Hymenanthes, Subsect. Falconera) A large shrub or small tree with large, narrowly elliptic leaves, silvery beneath at first, later greyish to pale brown. Flowers white, or rose-flushed, with a crimson basal blotch, bell-shaped, in large, loose trusses, April. NW Yunnan, SE Tibet. H3–4.

coryanum Tagg & Forrest (Subgenus Hymenanthes, Subsect. Argyrophylla) A large shrub with long, leathery, cinnamon-backed leaves and lax trusses of bell-shaped, creamy-white, crimson-spotted flowers in April and May. Named after that keen amateur gardener Reginald Cory. NW Yunnan, SE Tibet. H4.

coryphaeum See *R. praestans* Coryphaeum Group.

cosmetum See *R. saluenense* subsp. *chameunum*.

cowanianum Davidian (Subgenus Rhododendron, Subsect. Lepidota) A small, deciduous shrub, the leaves covered with yellow scales beneath. Flowers reddish-purple, bell-shaped, in clusters of 2–4, large calyx, May. C Nepal. H3–4.

crassum See *R. maddenii* subsp. *crassum*.

crebreflorum See *R. cephalanthum* Crebreflorum Group.

cremastum See *R. campylogynum* Cremastum Group.

crinigerum Franch. (Subgenus Hymenanthes, Subsect. Glischra) A medium-sized shrub with glandular-hairy shoots and glossy green, rather bullate leaves covered beneath with a creamy-yellow or buff tomentum. The attractive, bell-shaped flowers are white or blush, with a blood-red basal blotch, April and May. NW Yunnan, SE Tibet, NE Upper Burma. First found by the Abbé Soulié in 1895. I by George Forrest in 1914. AM (F) 1935. H4.

croceum See *R. wardii*.

cubittii See *R. veitchianum* Cubittii Group.

cumberlandense E.L. Braun (*Azalea cumberlandense* (E.L. Braun) Copeland, *Rhododendron bakeri* auct. not (Lemmon & McKay) Hume) (Subgenus Pentanthera, Section Pentanthera) A deciduous shrub varying in height from dwarf to medium-size. Leaves obovate, glaucous beneath. Flowers varying from orange to yellow or red, funnel-shaped, in terminal clusters, June. E USA. H4. **'Sunlight'** A selection from Polly Hill with orange, deep pink and golden-yellow flowers; dark green foliage with excellent autumn colour.

cuneatum W.W. Sm. (Subgenus Rhododendron, Subsect. Lapponica) Medium-sized shrub with 2.5cm long, densely scaly leaves and 2.5cm long, widely funnel-shaped flowers, in varying shades of rose-lilac, in April. Yunnan, Sichuan. I 1913. H4. **Ravum Group** (*R. ravum* Balf. f. & W.W. Sm.) A small shrub with densely scaly shoots and small, scaly leaves. Flowers deep rose, occasionally purple, in terminal clusters, May. I 1913.

cyanocarpum (Franch.) W.W. Sm. (Subgenus Hymenanthes, Subsect. Thomsonia) A large shrub, distinguished by its rigid, rounded, glaucous leaves and trusses of widely funnel-shaped flowers, varying in colour from white, pink to soft rose, in March and April. W Yunnan. AM (F) 1933. H4.

cyclium See *R. callimorphum*.

†*dalhousiae* Hook. f. (Subgenus Rhododendron, Subsect. Maddenia) Medium-sized to large shrub with bristly shoots and deeply veined leaves. Flowers creamy-white, streaked crimson outside, highly fragrant, lily-like, April. Himalaya. H2. **var. *rhabdotum*** (Balf. f. & Cooper) Cullen (*R. rhabdotum* Balf. f. & Cooper) Corolla with red streaks on the backs of the lobes. I 1925 by Kingdon-Ward. H2.

dasycladum See *R. selense* subsp. *dasycladum*.

dauricum L. (Subgenus Rhododendron, Subsect. Rhodorastra) A charming, early flowering, semi-evergreen shrub of medium size, with elliptic leaves, 2–3cm long, and 1–3-flowered trusses of funnel-shaped, bright rose-purple flowers, 2.5–3.5cm across, from January to March. Closely related to *R. mucronulatum* differing in its smaller, blunter, partially evergreen leaves and its smaller flowers. Japan, Korea, N China, Mongolia, E Siberia. C 1780. H4. **'Hiltingbury'** An evergreen form of compact habit, leaves bronzing in cold weather. Selected by John Bond in our Chandler's Ford nursery. AM 1990. **'Midwinter'** A deciduous or semi-evergreen form with flowers of phlox-purple. ♀ 2002. FCC 1969. AM 1963. **Sempervirens Group** A form with persistent leaves. C 1817.

davidsonianum Rehder & E.H. Wilson (*R. charianthum* Hutch.) (Subgenus Rhododendron, Subsect. Triflora) A medium to large-sized shrub with lanceolate leaves. Flowers extremely variable in colour from soft pink to purplish-rose, sometimes spotted, funnel-shaped, in both terminal and axillary clusters, April and May. Sichuan. I 1904 by Ernest Wilson. ♀ 2002 (to pink forms only). FCC 1955. AM 1935 (both to a pink-flowered form from Bodnant). H3–4. **'Caerhays Pink'** Flowers pink.

decorum Franch. (Subgenus Hymenanthes, Subsect. Fortunea) This large and beautiful Chinese species should be in every representative collection. Leaves glabrous, oblong-obovate, pale beneath, up to 15cm long. Flowers white or shell-pink, sometimes spotted, large, funnel-shaped, fragrant, in lax trusses, May and June. NE Burma, Yunnan, Sichuan, Guizhou, Laos. I 1901 by Ernest Wilson. H3–4. ♀ 2002. **subsp. *diaprepes*** (Balf. f. & W.W. Sm.) T.L. Ming (*R. diaprepes* Balf. f. & W.W. Sm.) A magnificent, large woodland shrub or small tree with light green, oblong-elliptic leaves, up to 30cm long. Flowers white with a faint rose flush, slightly fragrant, bell-shaped, fleshy, in loose trusses, June and July. A parent of 'Polar Bear'. NE Burma, W Yunnan. I 1913 by George Forrest. AM 1926. H3. **subsp. *diaprepes* 'Gargantua'** (Forrest 11958) A triploid form with very

large flowers, white, flushed green at the base. FCC 1974.

degronianum Carrière (*R. pentamerum* (Maxim.) Matsum. & Nakai) (*R. metternichii* f. *pentamerum* Maxim.) (Subgenus Hymenanthes, Subsect. Pontica) A very hardy, small, dome-shaped bush with dark green leaves up to 15cm long, covered below with a fawn or rufous tomentum. Attractive flowers soft pink, bell-shaped, May. Japan. I 1870. H4. **subsp. *heptamerum*** (Maxim.) Hara (*R. metternichii* Siebold & Zucc.) Flowers rose-coloured, 7-lobed, April and May. Japan. I 1860 by Robert Fortune and Philipp von Siebold. **'Wada'** (*R. metternichii* 'Wada') An interesting form of subsp. *heptamerum*: more compact with leaves that are deep cinnamon-brown beneath.

delavayi See *R. arboreum* subsp. *delavayi*.

deleiense See *R. tephropeplum*.

desquamatum See *R. rubiginosum* Desquamatum Group.

detonsum Balf. f. & Forrest (Subgenus Hymenanthes, Subsect. Taliensia) A rather slow-growing, medium-sized shrub. Leaves cinnamon to brown below; flowers bell-shaped, rose-pink with crimson markings, May. Yunnan. H4.

diaprepes See *R. decorum* subsp. *diaprepes*.

dichroanthum Diels (Subgenus Hymenanthes, Subsect. Neriiflora) A slow-growing, dome-shaped shrub, 1.2–2m high. Leaves 6–10cm long, oblong-obovate to oblanceolate, with white or grey indumentum beneath. Bearing loose trusses of variably coloured, usually deep orange, bell-shaped flowers in May and June. Calyx large and fleshy, coloured as the corolla. Parent of many hybrids. W Yunnan. First found by George Forrest in 1906. AM (F) 1923. H4. **subsp. *apodectum*** (Balf. f. & W.W. Sm.) Cowan. A colourful variety with orange-yellow flowers flushed rose or crimson. W Yunnan, NE Upper Burma. I 1913 by George Forrest. **subsp. *herpesticum*** See subsp. *scyphocalyx*. **subsp. *scyphocalyx*** (Balf. f. & Forrest) Cowan (*R. scyphocalyx* Balf. f. & Forrest, *R. dichroanthum* subsp. *herpesticum* (Balf. f. & Kingdon-Ward) Cowan, *R. herpesticum* Balf. f. & Kingdon-Ward) Flowers unusual coppery-orange, the lobes suffused red, calyx similarly coloured in clusters of 3–5. NE Upper Burma, W Yunnan. I by George Forrest in 1919.

didymum See *R. sanguineum* subsp. *didymum*.

discolor See *R. fortunei* subsp. *discolor*.

dryophyllum See *R. phaeochrysum*.

eclecteum Balf. f. & Forrest (Subgenus Hymenanthes, Subsect. Thomsonia) An early flowering shrub of medium size with distinctive, short-stalked, oblong or obovate-oblong leaves. Flowers varying in colour from white to rose-red, bell-shaped, fleshy, in loose trusses, February to April. Differing from the closely related *R. stewartianum* in the leaves, which are glabrous beneath. Yunnan, Sichuan, SE Tibet, NE Upper Burma. AM (F) 1949. H3.

edgarianum Rehder & E.H. Wilson. A small shrub, 0.6–1m high, with small, densely scaly, sage-green leaves and a wealth of attractive, small, blue-purple flowers in May and June. A hybrid of *R. nivale*. Sichuan, Yunnan, SE Tibet. H4.

†*edgeworthii* Hook. f. (*R. bullatum* Franch.) (Subgenus Rhododendron, Subsect. Edgeworthia) Medium-sized

shrub, its branches coated with a soft fawn or brown, woolly tomentum as are the dark green, bullate leaves beneath. Flowers white or pink-tinged, richly scented, funnel-shaped, April and May. Some forms of this beautiful species may be grown in the open in very mild districts, where it forms a rather straggly shrub. N India, Yunnan, Bhutan, SE Tibet, NE Upper Burma. First found by the Abbé Delavay in 1886, introduced by George Forrest in 1904. ♀ 2002, AM (F) 1946, FCC (F) 1937, AM (F) 1923. H2–3.

elaeagnoides See *R. lepidotum*.

elegantulum Tagg & Forrest (Subgenus Hymenanthes, Subsect. Taliensia) A compact, small to medium-sized shrub, related to *R. bureaui* which it rivals in its striking foliage. Leaves to 9cm long, dark green above with deeply impressed veins, covered beneath with a thick felt, which is deep pink on young leaves, maturing to rich red-brown. Flowers funnel-campanulate, to 3.5cm long, pale purple-pink, spotted crimson, in trusses of up to 20, April and May. SW China. I 1922 by George Forrest. H3.

†*elliottii* Watt (Subgenus Hymenanthes, Subsect. Parishia) Large shrub or small tree requiring woodland conditions, with glossy green leaves and large, bell-shaped, scarlet or crimson flowers from May to July. One of the best red-flowered species and the parent of many good hybrids. Nagaland (NE India). I 1927 by Kingdon-Ward. FCC 1937. AM 1934. H1–2.

eriocarpum (Hayata) Nakai (*R. indicum* var. *eriocarpum* Hayata, *R. simsii* var. *eriocarpum* (Hayata) E.H. Wilson) (Subgenus Tsutsusi, Sect. Tsutsusi) A slow-growing, dwarf shrub of dense, compact habit. Flowers pink to lavender, large and frilled, June and July. A variable shrub with several forms. S Japan. For some cultivars often listed here, see under Evergreen Hybrid Azaleas. H3. **'Album Grandiflorum'** Very large, white flowers with green markings.

eriogynum See *R. facetum*.

eritimum See *R. anthosphaerum*.

erubescens See *R. oreodoxa* var. *fargesii*.

× *erythrocalyx* Balf. f. & Forrest (*R. selense* × *R. wardii*) A medium-sized shrub with ovate to elliptic leaves. Flowers white or pink with or without crimson spots and basal blotch, bell-shaped, April and May. ŞE Tibet, NW Yunnan. H3. **Panteumorphum Group** (*R. panteumorphum* Balf. f. & W.W. Sm.) Medium-sized to large shrub with oblong-elliptic leaves, 5–10cm long, and trusses of bell-shaped flowers of a lovely pale yellow in April and May. H4.

euchaites See *R. neriiflorum* Euchaites Group.

eximium See *R. falconeri* subsp. *eximium*.

exquisitum See *R. oreotrephes* Exquisitum Group.

faberi Hemsl. (Subgenus Hymenanthes, Subsect. Taliensia) Large shrub or small tree, the young shoots clothed with rust-red, woolly indumentum. Leaves up to 15cm or more long, pale to rusty-brown beneath. Loose trusses of white, bell-shaped flowers in May. Sichuan. H4. **subsp.** *prattii* See *R. prattii*.

†*facetum* Balf. f. & Kingdon-Ward (*R. eriogynum* Balf. f. & W.W. Sm.) (Subgenus Hymenanthes, Subsect. Parishia) A superb large shrub of tree-like habit requiring woodland conditions. Leaves glaucous below. Flowers scarlet or crimson, bell-shaped, up to 7.5cm long and

wide, June and July. The parent of many excellent hybrids. NE Upper Burma, W Yunnan. I 1914 by George Forrest. FCC 1980. AM 1938. AM 1924. H2–3.

falconeri Hook. f. (Subgenus Hymenanthes, Subsect. Falconera) This magnificent, Himalayan rhododendron may be grown in sheltered gardens in most parts of the British Isles, where it makes a large shrub or small tree. It has large, broadly obovate leaves with deeply impressed veins and huge, dome-shaped trusses of waxy, creamy-yellow, purple-blotched, bell-shaped flowers in April and May. E Nepal, Sikkim, Bhutan. I 1850 in Sikkim by Sir Joseph Hooker. ♀ 2002. AM 1922. H3–4. **subsp.** *eximium* (Nutt.) D.F. Chamb. (*R. eximium* Nutt.) A magnificent large shrub or small tree, the young growths covered with orange-brown indumentum, as are the large leaves, up to 30cm long and 7.5cm wide. In April and May bears 5cm long, bell-shaped, fleshy flowers of pink or rose. NE India. AM 1973. H3–4.

fargesii See *R. oreodoxa* var. *fargesii*.

fastigiatum Franch. (Subgenus Rhododendron, Subsect. Lapponica) A dense, small, dome-shaped bush, 0.6–1m high, with small, scaly leaves, sea-green when young. Flowers lavender-purple, funnel-shaped, April and May. Yunnan. I 1906 by George Forrest. AM (F) 1914. H4. **'Blue Steel'** A compact, dwarf shrub with striking glaucous blue-green young foliage and profuse deep lavender-blue flowers in April. ♀ 2002.

fauriei See *R. brachycarpum* subsp. *fauriei*.

ferrugineum L. (Subgenus Rhododendron, Subsect. Rhododendron) The Alpen rose of Switzerland. A small, flattish dome-shaped or spreading shrub with leaves reddish-scaly beneath. Flowers rose-crimson, tubular, in small trusses, June. Pyrenees and Alps of C Europe. C 1740. AM 1990. H4. **f.** *album* (D. Don) Zabel. Flowers white. I 1830. AM 1969. **'Coccineum'** A charming form with crimson flowers.

fictolacteum See *R. rex* subsp. *fictolacteum*.

fimbriatum See *R. hippophaeoides*.

fittianum See *R.* 'Fittianum' under Hybrids.

flavidum Franch. (*R. primulinum* Hemsl.) (Subgenus Rhododendron, Subsect. Lapponica) A pretty, erect shrub, 0.6–1m high, with small, glossy, aromatic leaves and funnel-shaped, primrose-yellow flowers in March. NW Sichuan. I 1905 by Ernest Wilson. AM 1910 (as *R. primulinum*). H4. **'Album'** Differs in its laxer habit and larger, white flowers. C 1925.

fletcherianum Davidian (Subgenus Rhododendron, Subsect. Maddenia) Small, bristly shrub with usually oblong-lanceolate, 5cm long leaves, pale brown-scaly beneath. Flowers pale yellow, widely funnel-shaped, nearly 5cm long, March and April; deeply 5-lobed calyx. Perhaps the hardiest member of the Maddenia Subsection, distinguished by its decurrent leaf base, narrowly winged petioles, and crenulate leaf margin. Collected by Joseph Rock in SE Tibet in 1932, and long grown under the name *R. valentinianum* to which species it is closely related. Named after Dr Harold Fletcher, Regius Keeper, Royal Botanic Garden Edinburgh, 1956–70. H4.

flinckii (Subgenus Hymenanthes, Subsect. Lanata) A compact, medium-sized shrub of broadly upright habit. Leaves dark green, to 10cm long, with deeply impressed veins, rusty hairy above when young. The underside of the leaf is covered with a white tomentum when young which matures to rusty-brown. Flowers bell-shaped, to 5cm long, yellow, spotted with red, April and May. Bhutan, SE Tibet. I 1915 from Bhutan by Cooper. H4.

floccigerum Franch. (Subgenus Hymenanthes, Subsect. Neriiflora) A small shrub. Leaves oblong-elliptic, glaucous below and covered with a loose tomentum. The trusses of narrowly bell-shaped flowers are usually waxy and scarlet but may vary from rose or crimson to rose-margined yellow, March and April. Yunnan, SE Tibet. I 1914 by George Forrest. H4.

floribundum Franch. (Subgenus Hymenanthes, Subsect. Argyrophylla) A pleasing, large shrub with dense foliage; leaves rich green and bullate above, white-felted beneath. Flowers usually magenta-purple, lavender-purple or rose, with crimson blotch and spots, bell-shaped, April. Sichuan. I 1903 by Ernest Wilson. H4.

formosum Wall. (Subgenus Rhododendron, Subsect. Maddenia) A medium-sized shrub with glossy green, pointed leaves, margined with long bristles when young. Broadly funnel-shaped, white or slightly pink flowers, more than 5cm long, have yellow throats and are highly fragrant, May and June. Himalaya. H2–3.

forrestii Balf. f. ex Diels (Subgenus Hymenanthes, Subsect. Neriiflora) A slow-growing, prostrate shrub forming dark green mats or low hummocks, occasionally up to 30cm high. Broadly obovate to rounded leaves are 2.5–3.5cm long and purple beneath. The comparatively large, bell-shaped, bright scarlet flowers are borne singly or in pairs from the tips of short branchlets in April and May. Requires moist soil and partial shade. SE Tibet, NW Yunnan, NE Upper Burma. Discovered by George Forrest in 1905 and introduced by him in 1914. H4. **Repens Group** (*R. repens* Balf. f. & Forrest) A choice creeping variety, differing in its leaves which are pale or glaucous-green below. A parent of the FCC cultivars 'Ethel', 'Elizabeth' and 'Little Ben'. The cultivars 'Scarlet Pimpernel' (K.W. 5845) and 'Scarlet Runner' (K.W. 5846) were both introduced by Kingdon-Ward, as was 'Seinghku' (K.W. 6832). FCC (F) 1935 (as *repens*). **Tumescens Group** (var. *tumescens* Cowan & Davidian) A dome-shaped bush, with creeping outer shoots and large leaves.

fortunei Lindl. (Subgenus Hymenanthes, Subsect. Fortunea) A large shrub or small tree, leaves elliptic. 10–18cm long. Flowers lilac-pink, fragrant, bell-shaped, in loose trusses of 6–12, May. Probably the first hardy Chinese species to be introduced. A parent of numerous hybrids. China. I 1855 by Robert Fortune. H4. **subsp.** *discolor* (Franch.) D.F. Chamb. (*R. discolor* Franch.) A superb late-flowering form making a large shrub. Leaves oblong-elliptic to oblanceolate up to 20cm long. The funnel-shaped, fragrant, pink flowers, with 7-lobed corollas, are borne in huge trusses, giving a magnificent display in June and July. This is a parent of many distinguished hybrids. Sichuan, Hubei. I 1900 by Ernest Wilson. ♀ 2002. FCC (F) 1922. AM (F) 1922. AM 1921. **Houlstonii Group** (*R. houlstonii* Hemsl. & E.H. Wilson) A choice small tree or large shrub, a form of subsp. *discolor*. Leaves oblong-oblanceolate, 7.5–15cm long. Flowers usually soft lilac or pale pink, faintly lined and spotted, bell-shaped, May. A parent of the AM hybrid

named after our late Manager Arthur J. Ivens. Hubei, Sichuan. I about 1900 by Ernest Wilson. **'Sir Charles Butler'** ('Mrs Charles Butler') Flowers blush, fading to almost white.

fulgens Hook. f. (Subgenus Hymenanthes, Subsect. Fulgensia) Medium-sized shrub with broad leaves, dark shining green above, covered with reddish-brown indumentum below. Tight, rounded trusses contain 10–12, bell-shaped bright scarlet flowers from February to April. The young shoots are adorned with attractive, crimson bracts. Bark in some forms attractively peeling. E Nepal, Sikkim, Bhutan, Assam, S Tibet. I 1850 by Sir Joseph Hooker. AM 1933. H4.

fulvoides See *R. fulvum* subsp. *fulvoides*.

fulvum Balf. f. & W.W. Sm. (Subgenus Hymenanthes, Subsect. Fulva) A large shrub or small tree, attractive because of its large, polished, dark green leaves which are clothed beneath with a conspicuous, cinnamon indumentum. Flowers blush to deep rose with or without a crimson blotch, bell-shaped, March and April. W Yunnan, NE Upper Burma, SE Tibet. Discovered and introduced by George Forrest in 1912. ♀ 2002. FCC (F) 1981. AM (F) 1933. H4. **subsp.** *fulvoides* (Balf. f. & Forrest) D.F. Chamb. (*R. fulvoides* Balf. f. & Forrest) This differs from the typical form in its matt green leaves with a yellow or pale brown tomentum beneath. I 1917 by George Forrest.

galactinum Balf. f. ex Tagg (Subgenus Hymenanthes, Subsect. Falconera) A large shrub or small tree with large, leathery leaves, clothed beneath with buff-grey or pale cinnamon indumentum. Flowers white to deep rose with a crimson blotch and spots within, bell-shaped, April and May. C Sichuan. Discovered and introduced by Ernest Wilson in 1908. H4.

× *geraldii* (Hutch.) Ivens (*R. sutchuenense* var. *geraldii* Hutch.) (*R. praevernum* × *R. sutchuenense*) (Subgenus Hymenanthes, Subsect. Fortunea) A large shrub with splendid foliage. Flowers white with a deep purplish basal blotch, February and March. Occurs in the wild with the parents. AM 1945. H3–4.

glaucophyllum Hook. f. (*R. glaucum* Hook. f.) (Subgenus Rhododendron, Subsect. Glauca) A small, aromatic shrub with lanceolate leaves, white beneath, and attractive, bell-shaped flowers of a pale old-rose to lilac shade in April and May; calyx large and leafy. E Nepal, Sikkim, Bhutan, SE Tibet. I 1850 by Sir Joseph Hooker. H3–4. **var.** *luteiflorum* See *R. luteiflorum*. **subsp.** *tubiforme* (Cowan & Davidian) D.G. Long. Flowers pale pink, flushed white, tubular with spreading lobes. I by Ludlow and Sherriff from E Bhutan.

glischroides See *R. glischrum* subsp. *glischroides*.

glischrum Balf. f. & W.W. Sm. (Subgenus Hymenanthes, Subsect. Glischra) Large shrub or small tree. Leaves oblanceolate 10–25cm long. The twigs and petioles covered with gland-tipped bristles. Flowers varying from white to deep rose with crimson blotch and spots, bell-shaped, April and May. Yunnan, Upper Burma, SE Tibet. I 1914 by George Forrest. H3. **subsp.** *glischroides* (Tagg & Forrest) D.F. Chamb. (*R. glischroides* Tagg & Forrest) Large shrub with bristly young shoots. Leaves oblong-lanceolate, 10–15cm long, bristle-clad on the undersurface. Flowers white or creamy-white, flushed rose and with a crimson basal blotch, bell-shaped, March and April. NE Upper Burma. I 1925 by George Forrest. H3–4. **subsp.** *rude* (Tagg & Forrest) D.F. Chamb. (*R. rude* Tagg & Forrest) Medium-sized shrub with bristly twigs and broad oblong to oblanceolate, dark green leaves, 13–20cm long, hispid above and covered with crisped hairs beneath. Flowers purplish-crimson with darker lines, bell-shaped, April and May. Yunnan. I 1925 by George Forrest. H4.

glomerulatum See *R. yungningense*.

†*grande* Wight (*R. argenteum* Hook. f.) (Subgenus Hymenanthes, Subsect. Grandia) A small tree or large shrub of imposing appearance. The handsome, leathery, oblong to oblanceolate leaves are 15–30cm long, dark green and shining above, silvery-white or buff tomentose beneath. Flowers are pink in bud opening ivory-white with purple basal blotch within, bell-shaped, 5–7.5cm across, in dense rounded trusses, February to April. One of the most spectacular species but only suitable for sheltered woodland gardens in the milder counties. There are some fine examples in Cornwall. E Nepal, Sikkim, Bhutan. I 1850 by Sir Joseph Hooker. FCC (F) 1901. H2–3.

griersonianum Balf. f. & Forrest (Subgenus Hymenanthes, Subsect. Griersonia) A splendid, distinct and striking, medium-sized, Chinese rhododendron. Leaves lanceolate, 10–20cm long, matt green above, buff-woolly beneath. The brilliant geranium-scarlet, narrowly bell-shaped flowers appear in June and are unlike any others in the genus. It is a prolific parent and its hybrid progeny are now innumerable. Distinct because of its long, tapered flower buds, a character possessed by only one other species – *R. auriculatum*. Yunnan, N Burma. Discovered and introduced by George Forrest in 1917. FCC 1924. H3–4.

†*griffithianum* Wight (*R. aucklandii* Hook. f.) (Subgenus Hymenanthes, Subsect. Fortunea) A magnificent, large shrub or small tree, the parent of innumerable award-winning hybrids. Unfortunately, only suitable for the most sheltered gardens in the mildest areas. Bark of branches reddish-brown, attractively peeling. Leaves up to 30cm long. Flowers white with faint green speckles, sweetly scented, widely bell-shaped, 7.5cm long and up to 15cm across, in loose trusses of 3–6, May. E Nepal, NE India, Bhutan. I 1850 by Sir Joseph Hooker. FCC 1866. H1–3.

groenlandicum (Oeder) Kron & Judd (*Ledum groenlandicum* Oeder, *L. latifolium* Jacq.) (Subsect. Ledum) Labrador tea. A dwarf, upright evergreen, occasionally to 1m. Small, white flowers produced from April to June in conspicuous terminal clusters. North America, Greenland. I 1763. H4. **'Compactum'** A compact, neat shrub, 30–45cm high, with broader leaves on shorter branches and bearing smaller flower clusters. AM 1980.

habrotrichum Balf. f. & W.W. Sm. (Subgenus Hymenanthes, Subsect. Glischra) Medium-sized to large shrub with reddish-bristly young shoots, dark green leaves, up to 18cm long, and compact trusses of funnel-shaped, white to deep rose flowers in April and May. W Yunnan, NE Upper Burma. I 1912–13. AM (F) 1933. H3.

haematodes Franch. (Subgenus Hymenanthes, Subsect. Neriiflora) Generally considered one of the finest of Chinese rhododendrons. A compact, small to medium-sized, slow-growing bush. Leaves oblong-obovate, 4–7.5cm long, dark green, thickly rufous-felted beneath. Flowers brilliant scarlet-crimson, bell-shaped, May and June. A parent of several good hybrids. W Yunnan. I about 1911 by George Forrest. FCC 1926. H4. **subsp.** *chaetomallum* (Balf. f. & Forrest) D.F. Chamb. (*R. chaetomallum* Balf. f. & Forrest) A very splendid, medium-sized shrub with obovate leaves densely covered beneath with a brown, woolly indumentum. Flowers blood-red, waxy, bell-shaped, in loose trusses, March and April. NE Upper Burma, SE Tibet, NW Yunnan. I 1918 by George Forrest. AM (F) 1959.

hanceanum Hemsl. (Subgenus Rhododendron, Subsect. Tephropepla) A dainty, small shrub with bronze-coloured young growths and ovate-lanceolate to obovate leaves, finely scaly below. Flowers creamy-white or pale yellow, slightly scented, funnel-shaped, 2.5cm long, April. C Sichuan. H4. **Nanum Group** A slow-growing shrub making a neat, compact hummock up to 35cm. A choice rock garden shrublet. 'Canton Consul', a selection of this, received an AM in 1957.

heliolepis Franch. (*R. oporinum* Balf. f. & Kingdon-Ward) (Subgenus Rhododendron, Subsect. Heliolepida) Medium-sized shrub. Leaves elliptic-oblong, 6–10cm long, truncate or rounded at the base, intensely aromatic. Flowers purple-rose, funnel-shaped, in small, loose trusses, May and June, sometimes later. Yunnan. I 1912 by George Forrest. AM (F) 1954. H4.

hemitrichotum Balf. f. & Forrest (Subgenus Rhododendron, Subsect. Scabrifolia) A small shrub with oblanceolate leaves about 2.5cm long. Very attractive in April with its numerous, small, funnel-shaped flowers, bright red in bud, opening white or pale pink with darker edges. N Yunnan, SW Sichuan. I 1919 by George Forrest. H4.

hemsleyanum E.H. Wilson (Subgenus Hymenanthes, Subsect. Fortunea) A large shrub or occasionally a small tree with auricled leaves up to 20cm long. Flowers white, trumpet-shaped, 8–10cm long, May and June. Named after the English botanist William Botting Hemsley (1843–1924) who named and described numerous plants of Chinese origin. Sichuan (Mt Omei). C 1964. H4.

× *hillieri* Davidian (Subgenus Hymenanthes, Subsect. Neriiflora) A small shrub, sometimes reaching 1.8m, with bristly-hairy shoots and leathery, dark green leaves, to 6cm long, thinly brown-hairy beneath. Flowers crimson, bell-shaped, to 4cm long, in trusses of 3–7, April to May. SE Tibet. Discovered by George Forrest in 1922 at 13,000–14,000ft and named after Sir Harold Hillier 'in recognition of his outstanding contributions to the cultivation of rhododendrons'. It is a naturally occurring hybrid, probably involving *R. catacosmum* and *R. temenium*. H4.

hippophaeoides Balf. f. & W.W. Sm. (*R. fimbriatum* Hutch.) (Subgenus Rhododendron, Subsect. Lapponica) A small, erect, leafy shrub with small, greyish-green, oblanceolate leaves and usually lavender, lilac or rose-coloured, or occasionally lilac-pink, funnel-shaped flowers in March and April. A fairly tolerant species which will grow even in semi-bog conditions. Yunnan, Sichuan. I 1913 by George Forrest. AM (F) 1927. H4. **'Haba**

Shan' Large trusses of lavender flowers. ♀ 2002.
'Inshriach' Flowers lavender-mauve, darker at margins, in comparatively large, dense clusters. A choice form raised by Jack Drake in Scotland.

hirsutum L. (Subgenus Rhododendron, Subsect. Rhododendron) Small, twiggy shrub with bristly shoots and bristle-fringed leaves. Clusters of tubular, rose-pink flowers are borne in June. Alps of C Europe. This species has the distinction of being the first rhododendron to be introduced into cultivation. I 1656. H4. **'Album'** Flowers white.

hirtipes Tagg (Subgenus Hymenanthes, Subsect. Selensia) A large shrub or small tree with bristly shoots and broadly obovate leaves, up to 12cm long. Flowers red in bud opening pink to white often spotted and streaked with red, bell-shaped, in trusses of 3–5, spring. SE Tibet. I 1924 by Kingdon-Ward. H3–4.

hodgsonii Hook. f. (Subgenus Hymenanthes, Subsect. Falconera) A large Himalayan shrub or small tree, grown for its very handsome foliage. Leaves up to 30cm long and 13cm wide, dark green above, grey- or fawn-tomentose beneath. Flowers dark magenta, bell-shaped, in dense trusses, April. E Nepal, NE India, Bhutan, SE Tibet. I 1850 by Sir Joseph Hooker. H4.

†*hookeri* Nutt. (Subgenus Hymenanthes, Subsect. Thomsonia) An unusual species of medium to large size. Leaves pale glaucous-green beneath, the veins studded with small, isolated but conspicuous tufts of hooked hairs, a character possessed by no other known species. Flowers bell-shaped, blood-red or pink, calyx often similarly coloured, March and April. NE India. I 1850. FCC (F) 1933. H3.

houlstonii See *R. fortunei* Houlstonii Group.

hunnewellianum Rehder & E.H. Wilson (Subgenus Hymenanthes, Subsect. Argyrophylla) An attractive, large shrub or small tree neat and compact in growth, the long, narrow leaves with conspicuously impressed venation above, loosely grey-felted beneath. Flowers pink-tinted white, bell-shaped, March and April. Named in honour of a well-known New England family of great gardeners. C Sichuan. I 1908 by Ernest Wilson. H4.

hypenanthum See *R. anthopogon* subsp. *hypenanthum*.

hyperythrum Hayata (Subgenus Hymenanthes, Subsect. Pontica) Small shrub with usually oblong, curiously rigid, polished green leaves, the lower surfaces dotted with reddish specks. Flowers pure white or with purple spots, funnel-shaped, April and May. Taiwan. H3–4.

impeditum Balf. f. & W.W. Sm. (*R. litangense* Balf. f. & Hutch.) (Subgenus Rhododendron, Subsect. Lapponica) A dwarf, alpine shrub forming low, tangled mounds of scaly branches only a few centimetres high. Tiny leaves. Flowers light purplish-blue, funnel-shaped, April and May. Frequently confused with *R. fastigiatum*. Most suitable for a rock garden. Yunnan, Sichuan. I 1911 by George Forrest. AM (F) 1944. H4.

imperator See *R. uniflorum* var. *imperator*.

indicum (L.) Sweet (*R. macranthum* (Bunge) D. Don, *Azalea indica* L., *A. macrantha* Bunge) (Subgenus Tsutsusi, Sect. Tsutsusi) A small, dense, semi-evergreen bush rarely reaching medium size. Leaves small, narrow, lanceolate to oblanceolate, often turning crimson or purple in autumn. Flowers varying from red to scarlet, widely funnel-shaped, single or in pairs, June. A variable species with numerous forms. Both this species and *R. simsii* and their forms are often referred to as Indian azaleas. S Japan. I about 1877. AMT 1975. H2–3. **'Balsaminiflorum'** (*R. rosiflorum* hort., *Azalea rosiflora* hort.) Charming, dwarf form with double, salmon-pink flowers. FCC 1882. **'Coccineum'** Low, spreading shrub with large, single, scarlet-red flowers. **'Double Rose'** Flowers double, rose-pink. **var.** *eriocarpum* See *R. eriocarpum*. **'Hakata Shiro'** A low shrub with very large, ivory-white flowers. Earlier flowering and more tender than the type. **'Kokinshita'** See under Evergreen Azaleas. **'Misomogiri'** A form with semi-double, salmon-coloured flowers. **'Salmonea'** Low-growing habit; large, single, salmon-red flowers. **'Zangetsu'** Flowers pale crimson with white throat.

insigne Hemsl. & E.H. Wilson (Subgenus Hymenanthes, Subsect. Argyrophylla) An exceptionally hardy and unmistakable, slow-growing, Chinese species, eventually attaining a large size. Leaves leathery, oblong-lanceolate, 6–13cm long, rich glossy green above and silvery-white beneath when young, assuming a metallic lustre. Large trusses of bell-shaped, soft pink flowers with dark markings appear in May and June. C Sichuan. I 1908 by Ernest Wilson. ♀ 2002. AM 1923. H4.

intricatum Franch. (Subgenus Rhododendron, Subsect. Lapponica) Small, densely twiggy shrub, 0.6–1m high, with small, olive-green, aromatic leaves. Flowers lavender-blue, funnel-shaped, in small, rounded trusses, April and early May. Suitable for a rock garden. A parent of the AM cultivar 'Bluebird'. N Yunnan, Sichuan. I 1904 by Ernest Wilson. FCC 1907. H4.

irroratum Franch. (Subgenus Hymenanthes, Subsect. Irrorata) A large shrub or small tree. Leaves oblanceolate or elliptic, 6–13cm long, green on both surfaces. Flowers variously coloured, usually white, pink, or creamy-yellow with a more or less broad ray of dark crimson markings or sometimes heavily spotted, narrowly bell-shaped, March to May. Yunnan, Sichuan. I about 1886 by the Abbé Delavay. AM (F) 1957. H3. **'Polka Dot'** A very remarkable form, the white flowers being densely marked with purple dots. It received an AM when exhibited by Exbury Gardens, Hampshire, in 1957.

japonicum See *R. molle* subsp. *japonicum*.

†*johnstoneanum* Watt ex Hutch. (Subgenus Rhododendron, Subsect. Maddenia) Large shrub with leaves elliptic to obovate, ciliate, 5–10cm long, densely scaly below. The large, fragrant, funnel-shaped flowers are borne in clusters of 3 or 4 in May. They are creamy-white or pale yellow with red spots and a yellow blotch. There are forms with double flowers. Manipur. I 1882. AM (F) 1934. H3. **'Double Diamond'** A form with double flowers. AM 1956. **Parryae Group** See *R. parryae*.

kaempferi Planch. (*R. obtusum* var. *kaempferi* (Planch.) E.H. Wilson) (Subgenus Tsutsusi, Sect. Tsutsusi) A very beautiful and very hardy, deciduous or semi-evergreen shrub of medium size. Leaves 4–7.5cm long and, like the young shoots, strigose pubescent. Flowers varying from biscuit to salmon- to orange-red, or rose-scarlet, funnel-shaped, in clusters of 2–4, May and June. A parent of many of the Kurume azaleas. Japan. I 1892 by Professor Sargent. AM 1953. H4. **'Daimio'** See 'Mikado'.

'Highlight' A striking form raised in our nurseries; flowers bright salmon-orange. **'Mikado'** ('Daimio') Flowers an exquisite shade of apricot-salmon, late June and July. AM 1988.

keiskei Miq. (Subgenus Rhododendron, Subsect. Triflora) A very attractive, free-flowering, semi-evergreen, dwarf species suitable for a rock garden. Leaves 2.5–7.5cm long, lanceolate. Flowers lemon-yellow, widely funnel-shaped, in trusses of 3–5, March to May. Japan. I 1908. AM 1929. H3–4. **'Ebino'** A dwarf form to 30cm tall the foliage bronze when young and in winter. **'Yaku Fairy'** A very dwarf or prostrate form of var. *ozawae* T. Yamaz., collected on Mt Kuromi, Yakushima. ♀ 2002. AM 1970. H4.

keleticum See *R. calostrotum* subsp. *keleticum*.

keysii Nutt. (Subgenus Rhododendron, Subsect. Cinnabarina) An interesting, medium-sized to large shrub with oblong-lanceolate, densely scaly leaves. Very attractive when bearing its clusters of remarkable, tubular, cuphea-like flowers, 2cm long, bright orange-red, tipped yellow, in June. SE Tibet, Bhutan, Assam. I 1851. H3–4.

kiusianum Makino (*Azalea kiusiana*) (*R. obtusum* f. *japonicum* (Maxim.) E.H. Wilson) (Subgenus Tsutsusi, Sect. Tsutsusi) Kyushu azalea. A dwarf, evergreen or semi-evergreen shrub, occasionally up to 1m, of dense, spreading habit. Leaves small, oval. Flowers varying from salmon-red to crimson or purple, but usually lilac-purple, funnel-shaped, in clusters of 2–5, May and June. This is generally regarded as one of the species from which the Kurume azaleas were developed. In the wild it is restricted to the tops of high mountains on the island of Kyushu (Japan). I 1918 by Ernest Wilson. ♀ 2002. H3–4. **'Hillier's Pink'** A lovely form with flowers of a clear lilac-pink. Raised in our nurseries about 1957.

kotschyi See *R. myrtifolium*.

lacteum Franch. (Subgenus Hymenanthes, Subsect. Taliensia) A beautiful, large shrub or rarely a small tree of slow growth. Leaves oblong to oblong-elliptic, covered with a thin, suede-like fawn or brown tomentum below. Flowers normally clear soft yellow, sometimes with a pink stain or crimson blotch, bell-shaped, April and May. Unfortunately of rather weak constitution. W Yunnan. I 1910 by George Forrest. FCC (F) 1926. H4.

lanatum Hook. f. (Subgenus Hymenanthes, Subsect. Lanata) A small to medium-sized, unusual and attractive shrub. Leaves thick, inclined to obovate, 5–10cm long, brown-felted beneath. Flowers pale yellow with crimson-purple markings, bell-shaped, April and May. NE India, Bhutan, S Tibet. Discovered by Sir Joseph Hooker in 1848. I 1850. H4.

lanigerum Tagg (*R. silvaticum* Cowan) (Subgenus Hymenanthes, Subsect. Arborea) Large shrub or small tree, the young shoots grey-tomentose and the large, oblong-lanceolate leaves, 10–23cm long, covered with white, grey or cinnamon-brown tomentum beneath. Flowers rose-purple to dark magenta, bell-shaped, up to 5cm long, in round, compact trusses of 25 or more, March and April. Assam, SE Tibet. I 1928 by Kingdon-Ward. AM 1949. AM 1951 (as *R. silvaticum*). H4. **'Chapel Wood'** Flowers bright pink. FCC 1967. AM 1961. **'Round Wood'** Flowers crimson. AM 1951. **'Silvia'** Flowers pale crimson flushed white. AM 1954.

lapponicum Wahlenb. (Subgenus Rhododendron, Subsect. Lapponica) A dwarf shrub of dense, compact habit. The tiny leaves are densely scaly. Flowers purple, funnel-shaped, in clusters of 2–3, January and February. A difficult plant to keep in cultivation. Arctic regions of Europe, Asia and America. I 1825. H4.

†**latoucheae** Franch. (*R. wilsoniae* Hemsl. & E.H. Wilson) (Subgenus Azaleastrum. Sect. Choniastrum) A medium-sized shrub with narrowly oval, glossy leaves up to 12cm long. Flowers flesh-pink, slightly fragrant, funnel-shaped, deeply 5-lobed, April and May. W Hubei. I by Ernest Wilson in 1900. AM 1971. H2–3.

ledifolium See *R.* Mucronatum Group under Evergreen Azaleas.

ledoides See *R. trichostomum* Ledoides Group.

lepidostylum Balf. f. & Forrest (Subgenus Rhododendron, Subsect. Trichoclada) A dwarf, deciduous or semi-evergreen shrub occasionally to 1m, of dense, compact habit. The small, bristly, ovate leaves are a conspicuous blue-green above until the winter months. Flowers pale yellow, funnel-shaped, produced singly or in pairs, May and June. A choice shrub for a peat garden or shady rock garden. The most glaucous-leaved of the dwarf rhododendrons. SW Yunnan. I 1924 by George Forrest. AM 1969. H4.

lepidotum G. Don (*R. obovatum* Hook. f., *R. elaeagnoides* Hook. f.) (Subgenus Rhododendron, Subsect. Lepidota) A variable dwarf shrub with conspicuously scaly, oblanceolate leaves, 2–4cm long. Flowers varying from pink to purple, occasionally yellow or white, saucer-shaped, scaly on the outside, 1–3 in a small truss, June. NW Himalaya to Yunnan. I 1829. H3–4. **'Reuthe's Purple'** See *R.* 'Reuthe's Purple'.

leucaspis Tagg (Subgenus Rhododendron, Subsect. Boothia) Dwarf shrub occasionally to 1m, with elliptic to obovate, hairy leaves, 4–6cm long, and scaly stems. The lovely saucer-shaped flowers, 5cm diameter, are milky-white with contrasting chocolate-brown anthers, and borne in clusters of 2–3 in February and March. It should be given a sheltered site. A parent of several fine hybrids. Burma–Tibet frontier. I 1925 by Kingdon-Ward. FCC 1944. AM (F) 1929. H3–4.

†**lindleyi** T. Moore (Subgenus Rhododendron, Subsect. Maddenia) A large, open shrub with bluish leaves, glaucous and scaly beneath. Flowers creamy, sometimes edged with pink and blotched with orange or yellow at the base, very strongly fragrant, widely funnel-shaped, 10cm wide, April and May. H2–3.

linearifolium See *R. stenopetalum* 'Linearifolium'. **var. macrosepalum** See *R. stenopetalum*.

litangense See *R. impeditum*.

litiense See *R. wardii* Litiense Group.

× **lochmium** Balf. f. (Subgenus Rhododendron, Subsect. Triflora) A medium-sized shrub of loose, open habit with leaves densely scaly beneath. Flowers white flushed rosy-purple, funnel-shaped, May. A natural hybrid probably of *R. davidsonianum* and *R. trichanthum*. H4.

lopsangianum See *R. thomsonii* subsp. *lopsangianum*.

lowndesii Davidian (Subgenus Rhododendron, Subsect. Lepidota) A dwarf, deciduous shrublet of compact habit. Leaves bright green, obovate, bristly, up to 2.5cm long. Flowers pale yellow with light reddish spots, widely bell-shaped, solitary or in pairs, 2.5cm across, June and July. A charming, diminutive species for a peat garden or rock garden. Discovered in C Nepal by Col Donald Lowndes in 1950. H3–4.

ludlowii Cowan (Subgenus Rhododendron, Subsect. Uniflora) A charming, dwarf shrub for a peat garden. Leaves obovate, about 12mm long. Flowers yellow with reddish-brown spots in the centre, saucer-shaped, 2.5cm long and wide, singly or in pairs, April and May; calyx large and leafy. Parent of AM cultivar 'Chikor'. SE Tibet. I 1938 by Ludlow, Sherriff and Taylor. H3–4.

luteiflorum (Davidian) Davidian (*R. glaucophyllum* var. *luteiflorum* Davidian) (Subgenus Rhododendron, Subsect. Glauca) A small to medium-sized shrub of compact habit, closely related to *R. glaucophyllum* and differing in its yellow flowers in April and May. NE Burma. I 1933 by Kingdon-Ward. H3.

lutescens Franch. (Subgenus Rhododendron, Subsect. Triflora) A lovely, but variable Chinese species up to 3.6m. Leaves lanceolate, 4–7.5cm long. Its primrose-yellow, funnel-shaped flowers, from February to April, and bronze-red young leaves are especially effective in thin woodland. Requires shelter to protect its early flowers. C Sichuan, Yunnan. Discovered by the Abbé Delavay and introduced by Ernest Wilson in 1904. H4. **'Bagshot Sands'** Flowers larger; young growth deep bronze-red. ♀ 2002. AM 1953. H3–4. **'Exbury'** Flowers lemon-yellow. FCC 1938.

luteum Sweet (*Azalea pontica* L.) (Subgenus Pentanthera, Sect. Pentanthera) The well-known, common, fragrant, yellow azalea. A medium-sized, deciduous shrub, occasionally reaching 3.5m high and as much or more across. Winter buds and young shoots sticky. Leaves oblong to oblong-lanceolate, 5–10cm long, turning to rich shades of crimson, purple and orange in autumn. Flowers yellow, viscid on the outside, richly and strongly fragrant, funnel-shaped, in a rounded truss, May. Caucasus, N Turkey, E Europe, occasionally naturalised in the British Isles. I 1793. ♀ 2002. AM 1979. H4.

× *lysolepis* Hutch. An intricately branched, small shrub of stiff, erect habit with small, bright shiny green leaves. Flowers rosy-mauve, lavender-blue or purple, funnel-shaped, in 3-flowered trusses, April and May. A natural hybrid of *R. flavidum*. Sichuan. I 1921 by Kingdon-Ward. H4.

macabeanum Watt ex Balf. f. (Subgenus Hymenanthes, Subsect. Grandia) A magnificent species for woodland conditions. A large, rounded shrub or small tree. The handsome leaves up to 30cm long are dark, shining green and conspicuously veined above, greyish- or greyish-white-tomentose beneath. The large trusses of bell-shaped, pale-yellow, purple-blotched flowers are borne in March or April. In some forms the flowers are deep canary-yellow. Assam, Manipur. I about 1928 by Kingdon-Ward. ♀ 2002. FCC 1938. AM 1937. H3–4.

macranthum See *R. indicum.*

macrophyllum G. Don (*R. californicum* Hook.) (Subgenus Hymenanthes, Subsect. Pontica) A large shrub with strong, stout stems and leaves like those of *R. ponticum*. Flowers rose-purple with reddish-brown spots, bell-shaped, up to 20 in a compact truss, May and June. W North America. I 1850 by William Lobb. H4.

macrosepalum See *R. stenopetalum*. **'Linearifolium'** See *R. stenopetalum* 'Linearifolium'.

maculiferum Franch. (Subgenus Hymenanthes, Subsect. Maculifera) A medium-sized to large shrub or small tree. Leaves 7.5–13cm long, oval to obovate, sea-green beneath. Flowers white or rose-flushed with a dark black-purple basal blotch, bell-shaped, in a loose truss, April. Sichuan, Hubei. I 1901 by Ernest Wilson. H3. **subsp. *anwheiense*** See *R. anwheiense.*

†*maddenii* Hook. f. (Subgenus Rhododendron, Subsect. Maddenia) A large shrub or small tree with very fragrant, white or pink flowers. Rather tender in its typical state, the following is more hardy. NE India, Bhutan, SE Tibet. I 1850 by Sir Joseph Hooker. H2–3. **subsp. *crassum*** (Franch.) Cullen (*R. crassum* Franch.) A medium-sized to large shrub with stout, scaly young shoots. Leaves lanceolate or oblanceolate, 5–12cm long, thick and rigid, glossy dark green above, densely rusty-scaly below. Flowers varying from white to pink with or without a yellow blotch, sweetly-scented, funnel-shaped, 5–8cm long, June and July. In some forms, one of the hardiest members of its group. A beautiful, late-flowering shrub, worth growing as a conservatory shrub in cold districts. N Vietnam, Yunnan, SE Tibet, Upper Burma, Manipur. I 1906 by George Forrest. AM 1938. AM (F) 1924. H3.

†*magnificum* Kingdon-Ward (Subgenus Hymenanthes, Subsect. Grandia) A magnificent, large shrub or small tree for a very sheltered woodland site, with leaves 30–45cm long, covered with a white or greyish-white indumentum beneath. Flowers rose-purple, bell-shaped, 5cm long, in a dense truss, February and April. Flowers not produced on young plants. Burma–Tibet frontier. I 1931. AM (F) 1950. H2–3.

makinoi Tagg (*R. metternichii* var. *angustifolium* (Nakai) Ohwi) (Subgenus Hymenanthes, Subsect. Pontica) A very hardy, medium-sized shrub. The young growths are clothed with a white- or tawny-woolly indumentum and appear in late summer. Leaves narrow lanceolate, somewhat bullate above, thickly fawn- or tawny-woolly tomentose beneath. Flowers soft pink sometimes with crimson dots, bell-shaped, June. Japan. ♀ 2002. H4.

mallotum Balf. f. & Kingdon-Ward (*R. aemulorum* Balf. f.) (Subgenus Hymenanthes, Subsect. Neriiflora) A distinct and beautiful, large shrub or small tree with obovate leaves, 7.5–15cm long, covered beneath with red-brown-woolly indumentum. Flowers dark crimson, bell-shaped, March and April. W Yunnan, NE Upper Burma. I 1919 by Reginald Farrer. AM 1933. H4.

mariesii Hemsl. & E.H. Wilson (Subgenus Tsutsusi, Sect. Brachycalyx) A medium-sized to large, deciduous shrub. Leaves 3–7.5cm long, prominently reticulate beneath, borne in clusters of 2–3 at the ends of the branches. Flowers lilac or pale rose with reddish spots on upper lobes, saucer- or shallowly funnel-shaped, 5cm across, April. SE and C China, Taiwan. I 1886 by Augustine Henry. H3.

maximum L. (Subgenus Hymenanthes, Subsect. Pontica) The great laurel or rose bay of the USA. A useful and very hardy, large shrub or small tree with leaves 10–30cm long. Flowers varying from purple-rose to white, slightly fragrant, funnel-shaped, in compact trusses, July. E North America. I 1736 by Peter Collinson. H4.

A plant previously listed as an intergeneric hybrid with *Kalmia latifolia* has lanceolate-oblong to oblanceolate leaves, 7–10cm long, sometimes twisted, the apex either retuse or mucronate, decurrent at the base into a long slender petiole. A specimen in the Sir Harold Hillier Gardens and Arboretum has not flowered though buds have been produced. It appears to be an abnormal form of *R. maximum*.

maxwellii See *R.* 'Maxwellii' under Evergreen Azaleas.

meddianum Forrest (Subgenus Hymenanthes, Subsect. Thomsonia) Medium-sized to large shrub with glaucous young shoots and obovate or oval leaves, 5–18cm long. Flowers deep crimson or bright scarlet, bell-shaped, fleshy, April. A parent of the AM cultivars 'Queen of Hearts' and 'Rocket'. W Yunnan, NE Upper Burma. I 1917 by George Forrest. H2–4. **var. *atrokermesinum*** Tagg. A variety with usually larger, darker flowers and glandular branchlets. NE Upper Burma. AM 1954.

megeratum Balf. f. & Forrest (Subgenus Rhododendron, Subsect. Boothia) A charming but fastidious, dwarf species. Leaves glaucous and scaly below. Flowers rich yellow, bell-shaped, March and April; calyx large. NW Yunnan, S Tibet, NE India, NE Burma. I 1914 by George Forrest. AM 1970. AM 1935. H3.

mekongense Franch. (Subgenus Rhododendron, Subsect. Trichoclada) A small, semi-evergreen shrub with sea-green leaves. Funnel-shaped, yellow or greenish-yellow flowers open in spring or summer. E Nepal, NE Burma, S Tibet, NW Yunnan. H4. **'Doshong La'** See *R. viridescens* 'Doshong La'. **Viridescens Group** See *R. viridescens*. **var. *melinanthum*** (Balf. f. & Kingdon-Ward) Cullen (*R. melinanthum* Balf. f. & Kingdon-Ward) Yellow, funnel-shaped flowers appear before the leaves in April and May. The best garden plant of this series. NE Upper Burma, NW Yunnan, SE Tibet.

melinanthum See *R. mekongense* var. *melinanthum*.

metternichii See *R. degronianum* subsp. *heptamerum*. **var. *angustifolium*** See *R. makinoi*. **'Wada'** See *R. degronianum* 'Wada'.

micranthum Turcz. (Subgenus Rhododendron, Subsect. Micrantha) A very distinct and interesting Chinese species with racemes of tiny, white, bell-shaped flowers in May to July. They resemble those of *Ledum* and are entirely different from nearly all other rhododendrons. A free-growing, small-leaved shrub up to 2m high. China, Korea. I 1901 by Ernest Wilson. H4.

microgynum Balf. f. & Forrest (*R. gymnocarpum* Balf. f. ex Tagg) (Subgenus Hymenanthes, Subsect. Neriiflora) Small shrub with leaves 5–7.5cm long, clad with buff tomentum beneath. Flowers soft rose, spotted crimson, bell-shaped, April. NW Yunnan, SE Tibet. AM (F) 1940 (as *R. gymnocarpum*). H4.

microleucum See *R. orthocladum* var. *microleucum*.

mimetes Tagg (Subgenus Hymenanthes, Subsect. Taliensia) A medium-sized shrub with elliptic to oblong leaves, 6–10cm long, buff-coloured beneath. Flowers funnel-shaped, white, tinged pink and flecked crimson, in loose trusses, May. SW Sichuan. H4.

minus Michx. (Subgenus Rhododendron, Subsect. Caroliniana) A medium-sized to large shrub most commonly grown in the following forms. SE USA. H4. **'Album'** (Carolinianum Group) Flowers white with a yellow blotch, May and June; leaves also narrower and more pointed. I 1895. **Carolinianum Group** (*R. carolinianum* Rehder) A very attractive, free-flowering shrub attaining 2m. Leaves densely scaly beneath. Flowers soft rose-purple, tubular, May and June. N Carolina (USA). I 1812. AM (F) 1968. **var. *chapmanii*** (A. Gray) Duncan & Pullen (*R. chapmanii* A. Gray) Small shrub of stiff habit, occasionally reaching 2m; leaves scaly below. Flowers pink with greenish spots and conspicuous chocolate-coloured anthers, funnel-shaped, in tight clusters, April and May. W Florida (USA). I 1936.

molle (Blume) G. Don (*Azalea mollis* Blume) (Subgenus Pentanthera, Sect. Pentanthera) A small to medium-sized, deciduous shrub of upright habit with bristly shoots and oblanceolate leaves, softly hairy beneath. Flowers usually yellow, funnel-shaped, in large trusses, May. Best known as a parent of the Mollis and Exbury azaleas. E and C China. I 1823. H4. **subsp. *japonicum*** (A. Gray) Kron (*R. japonicum* (A. Gray) J.V. Suringar, *R. molle* Siebold & Zucc. not G. Don) A tall shrub of medium size with ovate-oblong, ciliated leaves, 5–10cm long, often giving rich autumn tints. Flowers, usually appearing before the leaves in May, are fragrant, funnel-shaped, orange- or salmon-red with a basal blotch, and borne in conspicuous trusses of 6–12. This is a dominant parent of many named garden hybrids. Japan. I 1861.

mollyanum See *R. montroseanum*.

monosematum See *R. pachytrichum*.

montroseanum Davidian (*R. mollyanum* Cowan & Davidian) (Subgenus Hymenanthes, Subsect. Grandia) Large shrub or small woodland tree of noble proportions. Leaves inclined to oblong, 15–30cm long, silvery-white beneath. Flowers pink with a crimson basal blotch, bell-shaped, in large trusses, April and May. Named after the late Duchess of Montrose. S Tibet. I 1925 by Kingdon-Ward. H3–4.

morii Hayata (Subgenus Hymenanthes, Subsect. Maculifera) A medium-sized to large shrub. A rare and beautiful rhododendron from Taiwan. Leaves oblong-lanceolate, 7.5–13cm long, green on both surfaces. The bell-shaped flowers are white with a ray of crimson spots, April and May. I 1918 by Ernest Wilson. AM (F) 1956. H3–4.

moupinense Franch. (Subgenus Rhododendron, Subsect. Moupinensia) A delightful, early flowering, small shrub with bristly branchlets. Leaves ovate-elliptic, densely scaly below. Flowers white, pink or deep rose, sometimes spotted red, sweetly-scented, funnel-shaped, February and March. C Sichuan. It should have some shelter, especially on the east side against early morning frost while in flower. I 1909 by Ernest Wilson. It is a parent of the following AM cultivars: 'Bo-peep', 'Bric-a-brac', 'Tessa', 'Tessa Roza', 'Seta' and several others. FCC 1994 (to a white form). AM (F) 1937. AM (F) 1914. H3–4.

mucronatum (Blume) G. Don (*R. ledifolium* (Hook.) G. Don, *R.* Mucronatum Group) A very lovely, small, ever-green or semi-evergreen shrub of widespreading, dome-shaped habit. Flowers fragrant, funnel-shaped, pure white; May. Long cultivated in Japan. I 1819. AMT 1958. H4. **'Bulstrode'** A floriferous shrub; large white flowers with a faint yellowish-green stain. **'Lilacinum'** Flowers soft lilac-mauve. **'Noordtianum'** A form with slightly larger white flowers, green at the throat, occasionally red striped. **var. ripense** (Makino) E.H Wilson. Pink flowers. Occurs in the wild in S Japan.

mucronulatum Turcz. (Subgenus Rhododendron, Subsect. Rhodorastra) A slender, medium-sized, normally deciduous shrub. Leaves elliptic-lanceolate up to 5cm long. Flowers bright rose-purple, funnel-shaped, 4–5cm long, January to March. Japan, Korea, China, Mongolia, Ussuri. I 1882. AM (F) 1935. AM (F) 1924. H4. **'Cornell Pink'** Large, clear pink flowers. ♀ 2002. AM 1965. **'Winter Brightness'** Flowers rich purplish-rose. FCC 1957.

myiagrum See *R. callimorphum* var. *myiagrum*.

myrtifolium Schott & Kotschy (*R. kotschyi* Simonk.) (Subgenus Rhododendron, Subsect. Rhododendron) Dwarf shrub of dense habit, the 1cm long leaves are crenulate and are densely scaly below. Flowers rose-pink, tubular with spreading lobes, in clusters of 3–8, May to July. C Europe (Carpathians). I 1846. H3–4.

myrtilloides See *R. campylogynum* Myrtilloides Group.

nakaharae Hayata (Subgenus Tsutsusi, Sect. Tsutsusi) A very attractive and rare, dwarf shrub of creeping habit and with densely adpressed hairy shoots. Suitable for a rock garden. Leaves small, oblanceolate, persistent. Flowers unusual dark brick-red, funnel-shaped, up to 2.5cm long, in small clusters, June and July or even later. Native of mountains in N Taiwan. H4. **'Mariko'** Flowers rich orange-red with a deeper flare. AM 1970. **'Mount Seven Star'** Bright red with wavy-edged lobes and inconspicuous purple spots. Low, spreading habit to 10cm tall. Raised from seed collected on Mount Seven Star, Taiwan, by C.S. Kuo. ♀ 2002.

neoglandulosum Harmaja (*Ledum glandulosum* Nutt.) (Subsect. Ledum) A useful dwarf species, occasionally up to 1m. Leaves oblong, oval or ovate, glandular and scaly beneath; flowers white in terminal clusters, 2.5–5cm across, May. W North America. H4.

neriiflorum Franch. (Subgenus Hymenanthes, Subsect. Neriiflora) One of the most desirable species. A medium-sized shrub with narrow leaves, gleaming white beneath, and trusses of fleshy, bell-shaped flowers varying from deep rose to scarlet or crimson in April and May; calyx large, coloured like the corolla. W Yunnan, SE Tibet, NE Upper Burma. First discovered by the Abbé Delavay and introduced by George Forrest in 1910. H3–4. **Euchaites Group** (*R. neriiflorum* subsp. *euchaites* (Balf. f. & Forrest) Tagg, *R. euchaites* Balf. f. & Forrest) A lovely form, differing in its taller growth and larger, crimson-scarlet flowers in April. Often considered the finest of its series. I 1913. AM 1929. **subsp. phaedropum** (Balf. f. & Farrer) Tagg. A form with variably coloured flowers; in the form we grow they are straw-yellow, tipped scarlet. SE Tibet, NE Upper Burma, W Yunnan, NE India.

nigropunctatum See *R. nivale* subsp. *boreale* Nigropunctatum Group.

niphargum See *R. uvariifolium*.

nipponicum Matsum. (*Azalea nipponica* (Matsum.) Copeland) (Subgenus Pentanthera, Sect. Viscidula) A rare and distinct, small, deciduous shrub of stiff, erect habit; older stems with attractive, peeling, cinnamon-

brown bark. Leaves large, up to 15cm long and 7.5cm wide, obovate, turning rich orange or crimson in autumn. Flowers white, tubular in clusters, appearing with or after the leaves, May and June. Japan. I 1914 by Ernest Wilson. H4.

nitens See *R. calostrotum* subsp. *riparium* Nitens Group.

nivale Hook. f. (Subgenus Rhododendron, Subsect. Lapponica) A dwarf shrub, native of the Himalaya and most commonly grown in the following form. **subsp. boreale** Philipson & M.N. Philipson (*R. violaceum* Rehder & E.H. Wilson) A dwarf, aromatic shrub of dense, twiggy habit, with minute, densely scaly leaves. Flowers pale purple, small, widely funnel-shaped, solitary or in pairs, May and June. NW Yunnan, W Sichuan, SE Tibet. H4. **subsp. boreale Nigropunctatum Group** (*R. nigropunctatum* Franch.) Upright habit with small, glossy leaves and small, pale purple to pink flowers. **subsp. boreale Stictophyllum Group** (*R. stictophyllum* Balf. f. & Forrest) Compact with small, deep rose-purple flowers.

niveum Hook. f. (Subgenus Hymenanthes, Subsect. Arborea) An attractive, large Himalayan shrub for woodland. Leaves obovate-lanceolate, to 15cm long; young leaves covered with white indumentum, persisting and turning pale brown on the undersurfaces. Flowers smoky-blue to rich purple, bell-shaped, in tight globular heads, April and May. Sikkim, Bhutan. I 1849 by Sir Joseph Hooker. ♀ 2002. AM (F) 1951. H4. **'Clyne Castle'** A form with larger leaves and rich purple flowers.

nudiflorum See *R. periclymenoides*.

†*nuttallii* Booth (Subgenus Rhododendron, Subsect. Maddenia) A superb species, but too tender for all but the mildest areas. A medium-sized to large shrub, often epiphytic in nature, of rather straggling habit. Leaves up to 20cm long, bullate and reticulate above, densely scaly beneath, an enchanting metallic purple when unfolding. Fragrant, funnel-shaped, lily-like flowers, 13cm or more long, appear in loose trusses of 3–9, yellow or white flushed yellow within, tinged pink on the lobes, April and May. An ideal conservatory shrub. NE India, NW Yunnan, SE Tibet. I 1850. FCC 1864. H1–2.

oblongifolium See *R. viscosum*.

obtusum See *R.* Obtusum Group under Evergreen Azaleas.

occidentale (Torr. & A. Gray) A. Gray (*Azalea occidentalis* Torr. & A. Gray) (Subgenus Pentanthera, Sect. Pentanthera) Medium-sized, deciduous, summer-flowering shrub with oval or obovate, glossy green leaves, turning yellow, scarlet or crimson in autumn. Flowers creamy-white to pale pink with a pale yellow or orange-yellow basal stain, fragrant, widely funnel-shaped, normally appearing with the leaves in June. A parent of many beautiful hybrids. W North America (S Oregon to S California). I about 1851 by William Lobb. ♀ 2002. AM (F) 1944. H4.

ochraceum Rehder & E.H. Wilson (Subgenus Hymenanthes, Subsect. Maculifera) A rare, medium-sized shrub with glandular-hairy shoots and petioles. Flowers crimson, bell-shaped, in trusses of 8–12, March and April. A plant grown under this name has proved to be a hybrid between *R. arboreum* and *R. campanulatum*. Sichuan. H3–4.

†**oldhamii** Maxim. (*Azalea oldhamii* (Maxim.) Mast.) (Subgenus Tsutsusi, Sect. Tsutsusi) A medium-sized shrub with densely glandular-hairy young shoots and elliptic, glossy green leaves, thickly covered with rust-coloured hairs. Flowers bright brick-red, funnel-shaped, in clusters of 1–3, May. Taiwan. First discovered by Richard Oldham in 1864, introduced by Charles Maries in 1878 and later Ernest Wilson in 1918. H2–3.

oleifolium See *R. virgatum* subsp. *oleifolium*.

oporinum See *R. heliolepis*.

orbiculare Decne. (Subgenus Hymenanthes, Subsect. Fortunea) An outstanding Chinese species forming a symmetrical, dome-shaped bush up to 3m high. Rounded, heart-shaped leaves held rigidly horizontal are matt green above, glaucous beneath. Flowers rose-pink, sometimes with a bluish tinge, bell-shaped, 7-lobed, March and April. Sichuan, Guanxi. I 1904 by Ernest Wilson. ♀ 2002. AM 1922. H4.

oreodoxa Franch. (*R. haematocheilum* Craib) (Subgenus Hymenanthes, Subsect. Fortunea) A very floriferous, large shrub or small tree with oblanceolate-elliptic leaves, glaucous beneath. Loose trusses of funnel-shaped, pink flowers, deep red in bud, March and April. Sichuan. I about 1904 by Ernest Wilson. AM (F) 1937. H4. **var. fargesii** (Franch.) D.F. Chamb. Medium-sized to large shrub. Leaves oblong-elliptic, 7.5–12cm long. Flowers deep rose-pink on the outside, paler within, funnel-shaped, 5cm long, up to about 8 in a truss, March and April. Hubei, Sichuan, Yunnan. I 1901 by Ernest Wilson. ♀ 2002. AM (F) 1926.

oreotrephes W.W. Sm. (*R. artosquameum* Balf. f. & Forrest, *R. timeteum* Balf. f. & Forrest) (Subgenus Rhododendron, Subsect. Triflora) A free-flowering, large shrub with glaucous young growths and usually oblong-elliptic leaves, scaly and glaucous beneath. Flowers varying from mauve, mauve-pink or purple to rose, with or without crimson spots, generally funnel-shaped, April and May. Semi-deciduous in cold gardens. N Yunnan, SW Sichuan, S Tibet. I 1910 by George Forrest. AM (F) 1932 (as *R. timeteum*). H4. **Exquisitum Group** (*R. exquisitum* Hutch.) (Forrest 20489) A beautiful form with larger leaves and flowers. AM 1937.

orthocladum Balf. f. & Forrest (Subgenus Rhododendron, Subsect. Lapponica) A small, neat, Chinese shrub with densely scaly branches and small, greyish, scaly leaves. Flowers mauve, purplish-blue or lavender-blue, small, funnel-shaped, produced in great profusion, April. N Yunnan, SW Sichuan. I 1913 by George Forrest. H4. **var. microleucum** (Hutch.) Philipson & M.N. Philipson (*R. microleucum* Hutch.) Flowers white. A dwarf shrub suitable for a rock garden. Yunnan. FCC 1939.

†**ovatum** (Lindl.) Maxim. (Subgenus Azaleastrum, Sect. Azaleastrum) A medium-sized to large shrub with pale bark and broadly ovate leaves, up to 2.5cm long. Flowers white, pink or purple, with purple spots, saucer-shaped, solitary, May and June. E and C China, C Taiwan. I 1844 by Robert Fortune. H3.

†**pachypodum** Balf. f. & W.W Sm. (*R. scottianum* Hutch.) (Subgenus Rhododendron, Subsect. Maddenia) A beautiful but tender shrub of medium size with densely scaly branches. Leaves obovate, densely scaly beneath. Flowers white, occasionally flushed rose, strongly and sweetly scented, widely funnel-shaped, up to 10cm long and across, May and June. Only suitable for a conservatory. Yunnan, NE Burma. H1.

pachysanthum Hayata (Subgenus Hymenanthes, Subsect. Maculifera) A medium-sized shrub with tomentose young shoots. Leaves oblong, up to 9cm long, silvery- or brownish-tomentose above when young, densely so beneath. Flowers white to pale pink, sometimes spotted inside, broadly bell-shaped, in large trusses of up to 20, March and April. A promising species, handsome in foliage and flower. Taiwan. I 1972 by John Patrick. ♀ 2002. AM 1989. H4.

pachytrichum Franch. (*R. monosematum* Hutch.) (Subgenus Hymenanthes, Subsect. Maculifera) A slow-growing, medium-sized to large shrub, the young shoots thickly covered with shaggy, brown hairs. Leaves oblong to oblanceolate, 6–13cm long, shining green beneath. Flowers usually soft pink but varying from white to deep pink, with a purple blotch, bell-shaped, up to 5cm long, March and April. W Sichuan, NE Yunnan. I 1903 by Ernest Wilson. H4.

× **pallescens** Hutch. (*R.* 'Pallescens') (*R. davidsonianum* × *R. racemosum*) A small, slender shrub of thin, open habit with lanceolate leaves, glaucous and scaly below. Funnel-shaped flowers occur in terminal clusters and in the upper leaf axils. They are pale pink with a white or carmine flush about the margin, May and June. A natural hybrid from W China, raised at Exbury from Rock's seed. AM (F) 1933. H4.

panteumorphum See *R.* × *erythrocalyx* Panteumorphum Group.

parmulatum Cowan (Subgenus Hymenanthes, Subsect. Neriiflora) A small shrub with leaves 3.5–7.5cm long, glaucous below. Flowers about 5cm long, bell-shaped, creamy-yellow or white, sometimes tinged pink, spotted crimson, April and May. SE Tibet. H4. **'Ocelot'** Flowers pale yellow, conspicuously spotted with purple. AM 1977.

†**parryae** Hutch. (*R. johnstoneanum* Parryae Group) (Subgenus Rhododendron, Subsect. Maddenia) A large shrub related to *R. johnstoneanum*, the red-purple bark peeling on mature plants. It has scaly, dark green leaves, to 14cm long, glaucous beneath. Flowers white with orange blotches, very fragrant, broadly funnel-shaped, to 8cm long, April and May. Assam. I by Mrs A.D. Parry in 1927 and again by Cox and Hutchinson in 1965. FCC 1973, AM 1957. H1–2.

pemakoense Kingdon-Ward (Subgenus Rhododendron, Subsect. Uniflora) A beautiful dwarf, suckering, alpine species only a few centimetres high. Small leaves and comparatively large, funnel-shaped, lilac-pink or purple flowers in March and April. A very floriferous species provided the flower buds escape frost damage. NE India, SE Tibet. I 1924 by Kingdon-Ward. AM (F) 1933. H3–4.

pentamerum See *R. degronianum*.

pentaphyllum Maxim. (*Azalea pentaphylla* (Maxim.) Copeland) (Subgenus Pentanthera, Sect. Sciadorhodion) A very lovely medium-sized to large, deciduous shrub. Leaves oval to elliptic-lanceolate, in whorls of 5 at the ends of the branches, turning orange and crimson in autumn. Flowers rich clear peach-pink, saucer- or shallowly bell-shaped, singly or in pairs, appearing before the leaves in March and April. Japan. I 1914 by Ernest Wilson. AM (F) 1942. H4.

periclymenoides (Michx.) Shinners (*R. nudiflorum* (L.) Torr.) (Subgenus Pentanthera, Sect. Pentanthera) Medium-sized, deciduous shrub with oblong or obovate, bright green leaves. Flowers pale pink with reddish tube, fragrant, funnel-shaped, in clusters, May. A parent of many of the Ghent hybrid azaleas. E USA. I 1734 by Peter Collinson. H4.

phaeochrysum Balf. f. & W.W. Sm. (*R. dryophyllum* Balf. f. & Forrest) (Subgenus Hymenanthes, Subsect. Taliensia) A variable, medium-sized to large shrub or small tree, with 5–7.5cm long leaves coated on the underside with a suede-like fawn, brown or buff indumentum. Flowers varying from white through pink to rose-purple, sometimes with crimson spots or blotch, bell- or funnel-shaped, April and May. NW Yunnan, W Sichuan, S Tibet. H4.

piercei Davidian (*R. beanianum* var. *compactum* Cowan) (Subgenus Hymenanthes, Subsect. Neriiflora) A small shrub of compact, spreading habit, related to *R. beanianum* but differing in the lack of bristles on the shoots. Leaves glossy dark green, to 11cm long, with impressed veins, densely covered with a thick, brown, woolly tomentum beneath. Fleshy, tubular-bell-shaped, crimson flowers, 3.5cm long, are borne in open trusses of up to 8, March to May. S Tibet. I 1933 by Kingdon-Ward. H3.

planetum Balf. f. A large shrub with oblong leaves up to 20cm long. Flowers pink, bell-shaped, 8–10 in a truss, March and April. Not known in the wild. Raised at Caerhays from Wilson seed before 1920. H4.

pleistanthum Balf. f. ex Wilding (Subgenus Rhododendron, Subsect. Triflora) A large shrub closely related to *R. yunnanense* but differing in the absence of bristles. It has been confused with *R. yunnanense* and some plants grown under that name may belong here. Yunnan and Sichuan, China. H4.

pocophorum Balf. f. ex Tagg (Subgenus Hymenanthes, Subsect. Neriiflora) A medium-sized shrub with oblong-ovate leaves up to 15cm long, covered beneath with brown, woolly indumentum. Flowers crimson, bell-shaped, in a tight head, March and April. NE India, S Tibet, NW Yunnan. H3–4.

polycladum Franch. (Subgenus Rhododendron, Subsect. Lapponica) A small shrub of upright habit with small, scaly leaves and blue to purple flowers. Yunnan. H4. Best known in the following form: **Scintillans Group** (*R. scintillans* Balf. f. & W.W. Sm.) Flowers lavender-blue, or purple-rose, funnel-shaped, April and May. I 1913 by George Forrest. ♀ 2002. FCC (F) 1934 (now named 'Policy'). AM (F) 1924.

polylepis Franch. (Subgenus Rhododendron, Subsect. Triflora) A medium-sized to large shrub. Leaves narrowly elliptic-lanceolate, aromatic, densely scaly beneath. Flowers varying from pale to dark purple, often with yellow spots, widely funnel-shaped, April. Sichuan. I 1904 by Ernest Wilson. H4.

ponticum L. (Subgenus Hymenanthes, Subsect. Pontica) The commonest and most extensively planted rhododendron in the British Isles, where it has become naturalised, and has interbred with garden cultivars to such an extent that the true species has become obscured. It is a large shrub with mauve to lilac-pink flowers which can look lovely especially in the fading light of evening. Its floral display in May and June is a feature of many districts. Invaluable for shelter belts and forming hedges. It is one of the few shrubs that will grow even under beech trees. Bulgaria, N Turkey, Caucasus, Lebanon, SW Spain, S Portugal. I 1763. H4. **'Cheiranthifolium'** A curious form with narrow, wavy leaves. **'Flore Pleno'** An unusual form with double flowers. **'Foliis Purpureis'** Leaves turning deep purple in winter. FCC 1895. **'Lancifolium'** A relatively low-growing, compact form making a medium-sized shrub with rather short and narrow leaves but not wavy as in 'Cheiranthifolium'. **'Variegatum'** One of the few variegated rhododendrons. Leaves margined creamy-white.

poukhanense See *R. yedoense* var. *poukhanense*.

praestans Balf. f. & W.W. Sm. (Subgenus Hymenanthes, Subsect. Grandia) A large woodland shrub or small tree bearing immense, leathery, obovate-oblong leaves, dark green above and covered with a greyish-white or fawn plastered indumentum beneath, borne on large-winged petioles. Flowers deep magenta-rose or pink with a crimson basal blotch, bell-shaped, in a dense truss, April and May. NW Yunnan, SE Tibet. Originally discovered by George Forrest on the mountains between the Mekong and the Yangtze rivers in 1914. H3–4. **Coryphaeum Group** (*R. coryphaeum* Balf. f. & Forrest) Flowers creamy-white with basal crimson blotches, produced in April in heads of 20 or more. I 1918 by George Forrest.

praevernum Hutch. (Subgenus Hymenanthes, Subsect. Fortunea) An early-flowering, medium-sized to large shrub. Leaves elliptic to oblanceolate, 10–18cm long. Flowers white or rose-flushed with a large, reddish-purple basal blotch, bell-shaped, up to 6cm long, in trusses of 8–15, February to April. SE Sichuan, Hubei. AM 1954. H4.

prattii Franch. (*R. faberi* subsp. *prattii*. (Franch.) D.F. Chamb.) (Subgenus Hymenanthes, Subsect. Taliensia) Medium-sized to large shrub. Its feathery, ovate leaves, 10–15cm long, are coated beneath with a fawn or brown indumentum. Flowers white, with pink spots, bell-shaped, April and May; calyx conspicuous and leafy. Patience is needed to wait for this plant to reach flowering age. Sichuan. I 1904 by Ernest Wilson. AM 1967. H4.

primuliflorum Bureau & Franch. (Subgenus Rhododendron. Sect. Pogonanthum) A twiggy, small to medium-sized, aromatic shrub. Leaves small, oblong-elliptic, densely scaly and white beneath. The small, tubular, daphne-like flowers, borne in small, rounded heads are usually white with a yellow tube, April and May. Differing from the very similar *R. cephalanthum* in the deciduous leaf bud scales. W Yunnan, SW Sichuan, S Tibet. H4.

primulinum See *R. flavidum*.

principis Bureau & Franch. (Subgenus Hymenanthes, Subsect. Taliensia) A large shrub or small tree to 5m. Leaves silvery-white to fawn tomentose beneath. Flowers white or blush with purple or carmine spots, bell-shaped, in a compact truss, March and April. SE Tibet. H4. **Vellereum Group** (*R. vellereum* Hutch.) A large shrub or small tree to 5m. Leaves silvery-white to fawn tomentose beneath. Flowers in compact trusses, bell-shaped, white or blush with purple or carmine spots, March and April.

prinophyllum (Small) Millais (Subgenus Pentanthera, Sect. Pentanthera) A lovely medium to large, deciduous shrub with oval or obovate leaves. Flowers pale to deep pink, clove-scented, funnel-shaped, appearing in clusters with the leaves, May. E USA. I 1812, perhaps earlier. AM (F) 1955. H4.

prostratum See *R. saluenense* Prostratum Group.

proteoides Balf. f. & W.W. Sm. (Subgenus Hymenanthes, Subsect. Taliensia) Small, slow-growing shrub. Leaves small, narrowly oblong, with revolute margins, thick, woolly, rufous tomentum beneath. Flowers creamy-yellow or white with crimson spots, bell-shaped, in a compact truss, April. NW Yunnan, SW Sichuan, SE Tibet. H4.

protistum Balf. f. & Forrest (Subgenus Hymenanthes, Subsect. Grandia) A large shrub or small tree with large, dark green, broadly obovate leaves up to 45cm long, glabrous or nearly so beneath. Flowers white to deep pink with a deeper basal blotch, fleshy, with 8 lobes, in large trusses of up to 25–30, February and March. W Yunnan, NE Upper Burma. I by George Forrest in 1919. H1–3. **var. giganteum** (Tagg) D.F. Chamb. (*R. giganteum* Tagg) Leaves densely brown-tomentose beneath at least on mature plants. I by George Forrest in 1919 who discovered it as a tree 25m tall. FCC 1953.

pruniflorum Hutch. (*R. tsangpoense* var. *pruniflorum* (Hutch.) Cowan & Davidian) (Subgenus Rhododendron, Subsect. Glauca) A dwarf shrub allied to *R. brachyanthum*. Leaves obovate, dark green above, glaucous and scaly beneath. Flowers usually plum-purple, bell-shaped, May and June. NE India, NE Burma. H4.

prunifolium (Small) Millais (*Azalea prunifolia* Small) (Subgenus Pentanthera, Sect. Pentanthera) A remarkable, late-flowering, deciduous, medium-sized to large shrub. Leaves elliptic to obovate, up to 13cm long. Flowers normally brilliant orange-red, funnel-shaped, 4–5cm across, 4–5 in a truss, appearing after the leaves, July and August. Georgia–Alabama border (USA). I 1918 by Professor Sargent. H3–4.

pseudochrysanthum Hayata (Subgenus Hymenanthes, Subsect. Maculifera) A slow-growing, medium-sized, dome-shaped shrub of compact habit. Leaves ovate-elliptic, 5–7.5cm long; young foliage covered with a woolly indumentum. Flowers pale pink or white with darker lines and spots, bell-shaped, April. Taiwan. I 1918 by Ernest Wilson. ♀ 2002. AM (F) 1956. H4.

pseudoyanthinum See *R. concinnum* Pseudoyanthinum Group.

pubescens Balf. f. & Forrest (Subgenus Rhododendron, Subsect. Scabrifolia) An attractive, small shrub of straggling habit, with bristly stems and densely hairy, narrowly lanceolate leaves. Flowers pink, funnel-shaped, in clusters of 1–4, April and May. Closely related to *R. scabrifolium*. SW Sichuan, N Yunnan. H4. **'Fine Bristles'** Flowers white, suffused rose, deep pink in bud. AM 1955.

pulchrum See *R.* 'Phoeniceum' under Evergreen Azaleas. **'Maxwellii'** See *R.* 'Maxwellii' under Evergreen Azaleas. **'Tebotan'** See *R.* 'Tebotan' under Evergreen Azaleas.

pumilum Hook. f. (Subgenus Rhododendron, Subsect. Uniflora) A dwarf or prostrate shrub of neat habit with small leaves that are narrow, scaly and usually glaucous beneath. Small pink or rose, bell-shaped flowers are borne in clusters of 2–3 in May and June. E Nepal, Sikkim, Bhutan, NE Burma, S Tibet. I 1924 by Kingdon-Ward. AM (F) 1935. H4.

puralbum See *R. wardii* var. *puralbum*.

purdomii Rehder & E.H. Wilson (Subgenus Hymenanthes, Subsect. Taliensia) A medium-sized shrub with oblong-lanceolate to oblong leaves, 6–9cm long. Flowers white or pink, bell-shaped, April and May. Named after William Purdom who collected in China for the Arnold Arboretum, Boston, during 1909–11, and with Reginald Farrer in 1914. Shaanxi (China). H4.

quinquefolium Bisset & S. Moore (*Azalea quinquefolia* (Bisset & S. Moore) Olmsted) (Subgenus Pentanthera, Sect. Sciadorhodion) An exquisitely beautiful azalea, a medium-sized to large, deciduous shrub. Leaves broadly obovate or diamond-shaped, in whorls of 4 or 5 at the ends of the shoots. They are green bordered reddish-brown when young, colouring richly in autumn. Flowers pure white with green spots, pendent, saucer-shaped, 4–5cm across, in small clusters, appearing after the leaves, April and May. Japan. I about 1896. AM 1931. H4. **'Five Arrows'** Flowers white spotted with olive-green. FCC 1967. AM 1958.

racemosum Franch. (Subgenus Rhododendron, Subsect. Scabrifolia) A variable but invaluable Chinese species, normally a dense, small to medium-sized shrub, a suitable subject for a heather garden. Leaves oblong-elliptic, leathery, glaucous beneath. Flowers pale to bright pink, funnel-shaped, very numerous from axillary buds, forming racemes along the branchlets, March and April. Yunnan, SW Sichuan. I about 1889 by the Abbé Delavay. ♀ 2002. FCC 1892. H4. **'Forrest's Dwarf'** (Forrest 19404) A dwarf form with red branchlets and bright pink flowers, originally collected by George Forrest in Yunnan in 1921. Admirable shrub for a rock garden. **'Rock Rose'** (Rock 11265) An extremely floriferous, compact form with bright pink flowers. ♀ 2002. AM 1970. **'White Lace'** Flowers white. AM 1974.

radicans See *R. calostrotum* subsp. *keleticum* Radicans Group.

ramsdenianum Cowan (Subgenus Hymenanthes, Subsect. Irrorata) A tree to 10m or more in the wild, usually a small to medium-sized shrub in cultivation. Leaves dark green, to 12.5cm long, smooth beneath. Flowers tubular-bell-shaped, to 4cm long, fleshy, crimson to pink, sometimes blotched deep red at the base, April and May. SE Tibet. I 1924 by Kingdon-Ward. H3.

ravum See *R. cuneatum* Ravum Group.

recurvoides Tagg & Kingdon-Ward (Subgenus Hymenanthes, Subsect. Glischra) Small shrub of dense, compact habit. Leaves narrowly lanceolate, 5–7.5cm long, tawny-tomentose beneath, margins recurved. Flowers white or rose with darker spots, bell-shaped, in a compact truss, April and May. NE Upper Burma. I 1926 by Kingdon-Ward. AM (F) 1941. H4.

repens See *R. forrestii* Repens Group.

reticulatum D. Don (*Azalea reticulata* K. Koch, *R. rhombicum* Miq.) (Subgenus Tsutsusi, Sect. Brachycalyx) A medium-sized to large, deciduous shrub. Leaves broad obovate or diamond-shaped, conspicuously reticulate beneath, purplish when young, turning vinous-purple in autumn. Flowers bright purple, funnel-shaped, solitary or in pairs, appearing before the leaves, April and May. Japan. I 1865. AM 1894 (as *R. rhombicum*). H4.

rex Lévl. (Subgenus Hymenanthes, Subsect. Falconera) A large shrub or small tree with large, shining dark green leaves covered with grey to pale buff tomentum beneath. Flowers rose or white with a crimson basal stain and spots, bell-shaped, in large trusses, April and May. S Sichuan, NE Yunnan. ♀ 2002. AM (F) 1946, FCC (F) 1935. H4. **subsp.** *arizelum* See *R. arizelum*. **subsp.** *fictolacteum* (Balf. f.) D.F. Chamb. (*R. fictolacteum* Balf. f.) A very handsome, large shrub or small tree, with cinnamon-tomentose young shoots and long, dark green leaves, brown-tomentose beneath, occasionally as much as 30cm long. Flowers creamy-white with a crimson blotch, bell-shaped, in large trusses, April and May. One of the hardiest of the large-leaved rhododendrons. W Yunnan, SE Tibet, NE Burma. I about 1885 by the Abbé Delavay. ♀ 2002. AM (F) 1923. **'Quartz'** A form with pale pink flowers, blotched and speckled with crimson. AM 1955.

rhombicum See *R. reticulatum*.

rigidum Franch. (*R. caeruleum* Lévl.) (Subgenus Rhododendron, Subsect. Triflora) A beautiful, medium-sized shrub of twiggy habit. Leaves 2.5–6cm long, oblong-elliptic. Flowers varying from white to pink, funnel-shaped, March to May. W Yunnan, SW Sichuan. AM (F) 1939 (as *R. caeruleum*). H4. **'Album'** A form with white flowers.

riparium See *R. calostrotum* subsp. *riparium*.

ririei Hemsl. & E.H. Wilson (Subgenus Hymenanthes, Subsect. Argyrophylla) A large, early-flowering shrub with oblong-elliptic leaves, 10–15cm long, silvery-white or greyish beneath. Flowers purplish-blue, bell-shaped, February and March. Sichuan. I 1904 by Ernest Wilson. AM (F) 1931. H4.

roseum See *R. canescens*.

rosiflorum See *R. indicum* 'Balsaminiflorum'.

rothschildii Davidian (Subgenus Hymenanthes, Subsect. Falconera) A medium-sized to large, rounded shrub, usually a tree in the wild with stout shoots, thinly tomentose when young. Bold, obovate, glossy green leaves are up to 35cm long, glabrous above with deeply impressed veins and have a yellow-brown indumentum beneath when young. Flowers obliquely bell-shaped, to 4.5cm long, crimson-purple in bud, opening to pale creamy-yellow blotched crimson at the base, April and May. NW Yunnan. I 1929 by Joseph Rock. H3–4.

roxieanum Forrest (Subgenus Hymenanthes, Subsect. Taliensia) A variable, slow-growing, small to medium-sized shrub of compact habit. The narrow leaves, 5–10cm long, are coated below with a fawn or rust-red indumentum. The bell-shaped flowers are creamy-white usually rose-flushed, appearing 10–15 in a tight truss in April and May. It takes some time to reach flowering age but is well worth growing for its leaves alone. NW Yunnan, SE Tibet, SW Sichuan. I 1913 by George Forrest. H4. **var.** *oreonastes* (Balf. f. & Forrest) T.L. Ming. A form with very narrow leaves. ♀ 2002. AM 1973.

roylei See *R. cinnabarinum* Roylei Group.

rubiginosum Franch. (Subgenus Rhododendron, Subsect. Heliolepida) A floriferous, large shrub with ovate to elliptic aromatic leaves, 4–6cm long, covered with rust-coloured scales beneath. Flowers pink or rosy-lilac, with brown spots, funnel-shaped, April and May. SW Sichuan, Yunnan, SE Tibet, NE Burma. I 1889 by the Abbé Delavay. H4. **'Album'** A lovely form with white flowers. **Desquamatum Group** (*R. desquamatum* Balf. f. & Forrest) A large shrub or small tree with aromatic, oblong-elliptic leaves, dark brown-scaly beneath. Flowers mauve with darker markings, funnel-shaped or almost flat, March and April. Yunnan, Sichuan, Burma, SE Tibet. AM (F) 1938.

rude See *R. glischrum* subsp. *rude*.

rufum Batal. (Subgenus Hymenanthes, Subsect. Taliensia) Medium-sized to large shrub with elliptic-oblong to obovate leaves, red-brown beneath. Flowers white or pinkish-purple with crimson spots, narrowly bell-shaped, April. N Sichuan, Gansu. AM 1980. H4.

rupicola W.W. Sm. (Subgenus Rhododendron, Subsect. Lapponica) A dwarf shrub of spreading habit with oblong-obovate leaves, up to 2.5cm long, dark glossy green above, densely scaly on both sides, revolute at the margins. Flowers deep purple in bud opening to mauve, saucer-shaped, 3cm across, in small, dense clusters, April and May. SE Tibet, N Burma, Yunnan, SW Sichuan. I 1910 by George Forrest. H4. **var.** *chryseum* (Balf. f. & Kingdon-Ward) Philipson & M.N. Philipson (*R. chryseum* Balf. f. & Kingdon-Ward) Flowers bright yellow; calyx not scaly. NE Burma, NW Yunnan, SE Tibet. I 1918 by George Forrest.

russatum Balf. f. & Forrest (*R. cantabile* Balf. f.) (Subgenus Rhododendron, Subsect. Lapponica) A first-rate garden plant, making compact growth up to 1 or 1.2m high. Leaves oblong-lanceolate, densely scaly below and about 2.5cm long. Flowers deep blue-purple or violet with a white throat, funnel-shaped, April and May. NW Yunnan, Sichuan. I 1917 by George Forrest. ♀ 2002. FCC (F) 1933. AM (F) 1927. H4. **'Purple Pillow'** A compact dwarf shrub with amethyst-violet flowers 3cm across. C 1964.

saluenense Franch. (Subgenus Rhododendron, Subsect. Saluenensia) Small, densely matted shrub of variable habit. The small, ovate-elliptic, aromatic leaves are hidden by clusters of funnel-shaped, rose-purple or purplish-crimson flowers in April and May. SE Tibet, NW Yunnan, NE Burma. I 1914 by George Forrest. AM (F) 1945. H4. **subsp.** *chameunum* (Balf. f. & Forrest) Cullen (*R. chameunum* Balf. f. & Forrest) (*R. charidotes* Balf. f. & Farrer) (*R. cosmetum* Balf. f. & Forrest) Dwarf shrub with erect stems and bristle-clad branchlets. The small leaves are brown-scaly beneath. Flowers rose-purple, with crimson spots, saucer-shaped with wavy margin, in loose clusters of up to 6, April and May. N Yunnan, NE Burma, SE Tibet, SW Sichuan. **Prostratum Group** (*R. prostratum* W.W. Sm.) A form of subsp. *chameunum* with a prostrate habit and very small leaves. I 1910 by George Forrest.

sanguineum Franch. (Subgenus Hymenanthes, Subsect. Neriiflora) A very variable, dwarf or small shrub, with 4–6cm long, obovate or narrow oblong leaves, greyish-white beneath. Flowers bright crimson, bell-shaped, in trusses of 3–6, May; not produced on young plants. NW Yunnan, SE Tibet. I 1917 by George Forrest. H4. **var. didymoides** Tagg & Forrest. A medium-sized shrub with rose or yellowish-red flowers. **subsp. didymum** (Balf. f. & Forrest) Cowan (*R. didymum* Balf. f. & Forrest) Flowers an unusual black-crimson. A parent of several good hybrids. SE Tibet. **var. haemaleum** (Balf. f. & Forrest) D.F. Chamb. Flowers dark blackish-red. **Roseotinctum Group** (subsp. *roseotinctum* Balf. f. & Forrest) Cowan. A form of var. *didymoides* with white flowers, edged red or pink and yellow.

sargentianum Rehder & E.H. Wilson (Subgenus Rhododendron, Sect. Pogonanthum) Dwarf, twiggy shrub of dense, compact habit. Leaves small, aromatic when bruised. Flowers lemon-yellow or white, small, tubular, April and May. A gem for a cool spot in a rock garden but not an easy plant to grow. C Sichuan. I 1903–4 by Ernest Wilson. AM (F) 1923. H4. **'Maricee'** See *R.* 'Maricee'. **'Whitebait'** Flowers pale primrose-yellow. AM 1966.

scabrifolium Franch. (Subgenus Rhododendron, Subsect. Scabrifolia) A small to medium-sized, straggly shrub with oblanceolate leaves, 4–5cm long, roughly hairy above, tomentose and reticulate beneath. Flowers varying from white to deep rose, funnel-shaped, March and April. N Yunnan. I 1885. H3. **var. spiciferum** (Franch.) Cullen (*R. spiciferum* Franch.) A small, moderately hardy shrub from Yunnan with wiry, bristly stems and bristly, narrowly oblanceolate leaves. Flowers rose or pink, funnel-shaped, borne in profusion, April and May. C and S Yunnan. I 1921 by Kingdon-Ward.

†*scabrum* G. Don (Subgenus Tsutsusi, Sect. Tsutsusi) A small to medium-sized shrub of bushy habit. Leaves elliptic to oblanceolate, 6–10cm long. Flowers rose-red to brilliant scarlet, funnel-shaped, with a large, green calyx, April and May. Japan (Ryukyu Islands). I about 1909. AM 1911. H2. **'Red Emperor'** A striking form with large, scarlet flowers, usually a little later than those of the typical form.

schlippenbachii Maxim. (*Azalea schlippenbachii* (Maxim.) Kuntze) (Subgenus Pentanthera, Sect. Sciadorhodion) This exquisitely beautiful azalea, though winter hardy, is subject to injury by late spring frosts. A medium-sized to large, deciduous shrub of rounded habit, it has large, broadly obovate leaves in whorls of 5 at the ends of the branches. They are suffused purplish-red when young, turning to yellow, orange and crimson in autumn. Flowers pale pink to rose-pink, occasionally white, saucer-shaped, 7.5cm across, appearing before or with the leaves, April and May. Korea, E Russia (near Vladivostock). First discovered by Baron Schlippenbach in 1854, introduced by James Veitch in 1893. FCC (F) 1944. AM (F) 1896. H4.

scintillans See *R. polycladum* Scintillans Group.

scottianum See *R. pachypodum*.

scyphocalyx See *R. dichroanthum* subsp. *scyphocalyx*.

searsiae Rehder & E.H. Wilson (Subgenus Rhododendron, Subsect. Triflora) An attractive, medium-sized shrub with leaves densely scaly and glaucous beneath. Flowers white, rose or purplish-mauve, with pale green spots, widely funnel-shaped, freely produced, April and May. SW Sichuan. I by Ernest Wilson in 1908. H4.

selense Franch. (Subgenus Hymenanthes, Subsect. Selensia) Medium-sized shrub with oblong to obovate, dark green leaves and bell-shaped, pink or rose flowers, occasionally with a crimson basal blotch, in April and May. SE Tibet, NW Yunnan. I 1917 by George Forrest. H4. **subsp. dasycladum** (Balf. f. & W.W. Sm.) D.F. Chamb. (*R. dasycladum* Balf. f. & W.W. Sm.) Medium-sized shrub with glandular-hairy, young shoots and leaves varying from 3–8cm long. The small, funnel-shaped flowers, borne in April and May, may be white or rose with or without a dark basal stain. W Yunnan, SW Sichuan.

semibarbatum Maxim. (Subgenus Mumeazalea) Medium-sized to large, deciduous shrub, often giving rich orange-yellow and crimson autumn colour. Leaves elliptic, 2.5–5cm long. Flowers white or yellowish-white, flushed pink, spotted red, small, funnel-shaped, solitary, June. A very unusual species. Japan. H4.

semnoides Tagg & Forrest (Subgenus Hymenanthes, Subsect. Falconera) A large shrub with stout shoots densely covered in white or brown hairs. Leaves obovate, to 27cm long, dark green above with deeply impressed veins, clothed beneath with a thick, woolly, pale brown indumentum. Flowers obliquely bell-shaped, to 5cm long, creamy or pinkish-white with a crimson blotch at the base, borne in trusses of up to 20, April and May. SE Tibet, NW Yunnan. I by George Forrest in 1922. H3.

serotinum Hutch. A large, late-flowering shrub related to *R. decorum* of which it is probably a hybrid. Leaves up to 15cm long. Flowers white, flushed pink on the outside, spotted pink within and with a yellow basal stain, sweetly scented, bell-shaped, 5cm long, August and September; it is one of the last rhododendrons to flower. I by the Abbé Delavay before 1889. AM (F) 1925. H4.

serpyllifolium (A. Gray) Miq. (*Azalea serpyllifolia* A. Gray) (Subgenus Tsutsusi, Sect. Tsutsusi) A remarkable, small, deciduous shrub, in fact a true mini azalea, of dense habit with slender, interlacing stems and very tiny leaves. Flowers rose-pink, small, funnel-shaped, solitary or in pairs, appearing after the leaves, April and May. C and S Japan. I by Charles Maries about 1879. H4.

serrulatum See *R. viscosum*.

setosum D. Don (Subgenus Rhododendron, Subsect. Lapponica) A small shrub with densely bristly branches and bristly, scaly, aromatic leaves. Flowers reddish-purple, funnel-shaped, May. Nepal, Sikkim, W Bengal, SE Tibet. I 1825. H4.

sherriffii Cowan (Subgenus Hymenanthes, Subsect. Fulgensia) A medium-sized shrub with elliptic to oblong-elliptic leaves, 7.5cm long, covered with a thick, dark brown indumentum beneath. Flowers deep rich carmine, bell-shaped, March and April; crimson, bloomy calyx. S Tibet. I 1926 by Ludlow and Sheriff. AM 1966. H4.

shweliense Balf. f. & Forrest (Subgenus Rhododendron, Subsect. Glauca) Dwarf, aromatic shrub, with densely scaly twigs. Leaves oblong-obovate, 2.5–5cm long, scaly above when young and very glaucous beneath. Flowers pink with yellow flush and purple spots, bell-shaped, scaly on the outside, May. SW Yunnan. I 1924 by George Forrest. H4.

sidereum Balf. f. (Subgenus Hymenanthes, Subsect. Grandia) A large shrub or small tree, closely related to *R. grande*, with bold leaves up to 25cm long, silvery-grey to fawn beneath. Flowers creamy-white to clear yellow with a crimson basal blotch, bell-shaped, April. NE Upper Burma, W Yunnan. I 1919. H2–3. **'Glen Rosa'** Flowers primrose-yellow blotched deep crimson. AM 1964.

siderophyllum Franch. (Subgenus Rhododendron, Subsect. Triflora) A medium-sized to large shrub of upright habit. Leaves oblanceolate, glossy green and slightly scaly above, densely scaly beneath, up to 6cm long. Open funnel-shaped flowers, 4cm across, are borne in small clusters in May. They are greenish in bud, opening very pale pink with a large patch of reddish spots on the upper lobe. Yunnan, Guizhou. AM 1945. H4.

sikangense Fang (Subgenus Hymenanthes, Subsect. Maculifera) A large shrub, sometimes a small tree, the young shoots covered in loose white hairs, later glabrous. Leaves dark green with impressed veins above, to 10cm long, glabrous beneath. Bell-shaped flowers, to 4cm long, are purple, blotched with red at the base and with purple spots, opening in trusses of up to 10, May and June. SW Sichuan. H4.

silvaticum See *R. lanigerum*.

†*simsii* Planch. (*Azalea indica* Sims not L.) (Subgenus Tsutsusi, Sect. Tsutsusi) A tender evergreen or semi-evergreen shrub up to 2m high, of dense, spreading habit. Leaves up to 5cm long, broadly oval. Flowers rose-red to dark red, with darker spots, funnel-shaped, 5–6cm across, in clusters of 2–6, May. A parent of the greenhouse 'Indica' hybrid azaleas. Upper Burma to S China SE Asia and Japan. I early 19th century. FCC (IF) 1933. H2. **var. *eriocarpum*** See *R. eriocarpum*. **'Queen Elizabeth'** A beautiful form reminiscent of the greenhouse azaleas, but hardier. Flowers white, edged rose-opal, large, 7.5–9cm across, double. **'Queen Elizabeth White'** Flowers double, pure white.

†*sinogrande* Balf. f. & W.W. Sm. (Subgenus Hymenanthes, Subsect. Grandia) A large shrub or small tree for woodland. Magnificent as a foliage plant, the shining dark green leaves are sometimes as much as 80cm long and 30cm wide, the lower surface has a silvery-grey or fawn indumentum. Flowers creamy-white with a crimson blotch, in huge trusses, April. W Yunnan, NE Upper Burma, SE Tibet. Discovered and introduced by George Forrest in 1913. ♀ 2002. FCC (F) 1926. AM (F) 1922. H3.

smirnowii Trautv. (Subgenus Hymenanthes, Subsect. Pontica) A very hardy, compact, slow-growing shrub of medium to large size, with oblong-obovate leaves, 10–15cm long, grey or pale brown-felted beneath. Flowers rose-purple or rose-pink, bell-shaped, May and June. NE Turkey, Georgia (former USSR). I 1886. H4.

smithii See *R. argipeplum*.

souliei Franch. (Subgenus Hymenanthes, Subsect. Campylocarpa) A beautiful, hardy, medium-sized shrub with almost round leaves, 5–7.5cm long, and saucer-shaped, white or soft pink flowers in May and June. Said to do best in the eastern counties. Sichuan. I 1903 by Ernest Wilson. FCC (F) 1909. H4.

sperabile Balf. f. & Farrer (Subgenus Hymenanthes, Subsect. Neriiflora) A small shrub, occasionally reaching 2m. Leaves elliptic-lanceolate, 6–10cm long, with a thick, tawny or cinnamon tomentum beneath. Flowers scarlet or deep crimson, fleshy, bell-shaped, April and May. NE Upper Burma. Discovered and introduced by Reginald Farrer in 1919. AM (F) 1925. H3–4. **var. *weihsiense*** Tagg & Forrest. Leaves narrower, thinly hairy or nearly glabrous beneath. NW Yunnan. I 1924 by George Forrest.

sphaeranthum See *R. trichostomum*.

sphaeroblastum Balf. f. & Forrest (Subgenus Hymenanthes, Subsect. Taliensia) A medium-sized shrub with glabrous shoots and ovate-lanceolate leaves, up to 15cm long, densely brown-tomentose beneath. Flowers white or pink with crimson spots, bell-shaped, in trusses of up to 20, April and May. N Yunnan, SW Sichuan. H4.

spiciferum See *R. scabrifolium* var. *spiciferum*.

spinuliferum Franch. (Subgenus Rhododendron, Subsect. Scabrifolia) A quite remarkable, medium-sized shrub, one of the many discovered by the Abbé Delavay. Leaves oblanceolate and bullate, 5–7.5cm long, and like the stems softly pubescent. Flowers red, tubular, 2.5cm long, with protruding stamens, in erect clusters, in the axils of the upper leaves, April. C and S Yunnan. I 1907. H3.

stenopetalum (Hogg) Mabb. (*R. macrosepalum* Maxim., *R. linearifolium* var. *macrosepalum* (Maxim.) Makino) (Subgenus Tsutsusi, Sect. Tsutsusi) A small, semi-evergreen shrub of loose, spreading habit with often densely glandular-hairy young shoots. Leaves ovate to ovate-elliptic or lanceolate, densely hairy; often some leaves turn rich crimson in autumn. Flowers lilac-pink to rose-purple, fragrant, funnel-shaped, 5cm across, April and May; calyx lobes long and narrow. Japan. I 1863. H3. **'Linearifolium'** (*R. linearifolium* Siebold & Zucc.) An unusual form with narrower leaves, up to 7.5cm long by 6mm wide. Pink flowers are deeply divided into 5 narrow segments. Long cultivated in Japan. C 1808. H3–4.

stewartianum Diels (Subgenus Hymenanthes, Subsect. Thomsonia) An early flowering, medium-sized to large shrub with loose trusses of bell-shaped flowers, varying from white to yellow, rose or crimson from February to April. Differing from the very similar *R. eclecteum* in its leaves, the undersurfaces of which are minutely hairy and covered by a thin, creamy-yellow, farinose indumentum. SE Tibet, NW Yunnan, NE Upper Burma. I 1919 by Farrer and Cox. AM 1934. H4.

stictophyllum See *R. nivale* subsp. *boreale* Stictophyllum Group.

strigillosum Franch. (Subgenus Hymenanthes, Subsect. Maculifera) A large, Chinese shrub with bristly young shoots. Leaves oblong-lanceolate, 10–18cm long, bristly-hairy. Magnificent when bearing its trusses of brilliant crimson, bell-shaped flowers in February and March. A sheltered woodland site is necessary. Sichuan, NE Yunnan. I 1904 by Ernest Wilson. AM (F) 1923. H3–4.

subansiriense D.F. Chamb. (Subgenus Hymenanthes, Subsect. Thomsonia) A large shrub or small tree with peeling bark when mature. Leaves to 10cm long, with deeply impressed veins, nearly glabrous. Flowers tubular bell-shaped, to 4cm long, scarlet flecked with purple, in dense trusses of up to 15. Arunachal Pradesh, India. I 1965 by Cox and Hutchinson. H3.

suberosum See *R. yunnanense* Suberosum Group.

succothii Davidian (Subgenus Hymenanthes, Subsect. Barbata) A large shrub with glabrous shoots and very short-stalked oblong, glabrous leaves, to 13cm long, heart-shaped at the base. Flowers crimson, bell-shaped, in dense trusses of up to 15, March to April. Bhutan, NE India. I 1937 by Ludlow and Sherriff. H4.

sutchuenense Franch. (Subgenus Hymenanthes, Subsect. Fortunea) An outstanding, large, Chinese shrub with stout shoots and drooping, oblong-oblanceolate leaves, up to 30cm long. In favourable seasons its floral display is magnificent, the flowers, 7cm long, bell-shaped, varying from palest pink to rosy-lilac, with purple spots; February and March. China. I 1900 by Ernest Wilson. H4. **var. geraldii** See *R. × geraldii.* **'Seventh Heaven'** (Wilson 1232) Flowers white suffused pale lilac, spotted red in the throat. Raised at Borde Hill in Sussex. AM 1978.

taliense Franch. (Subgenus Hymenanthera, Subsect. Taliensia) A medium-sized shrub with tomentose shoots and dark green, broadly ovate leaves, to 10cm long, densely brown-felted beneath. Flowers creamy-white to yellow flushed pink with red spots, bell-shaped, in trusses of up to 20, April to May. W Yunnan. I about 1910 by George Forrest. H4.

tapetiforme Balf. f. & Kingdon-Ward (Subgenus Rhododendron, Subsect. Lapponica) A dwarf, scaly-branched shrub with terminal clusters of 2–3 pale mauve-pink or purple, funnel-shaped flowers in April. NE Burma, NW Yunnan, SE Tibet. H4.

tatsienense Franch. (Subgenus Rhododendron, Subsect. Triflora) A medium-sized to large shrub, related to *R. davidsonianum*, with reddish young growths and elliptic, dark green leaves, scaly on both sides. Flowers pink to pale purple, broadly funnel-shaped, in clusters of up to 6, April and May. N Yunnan, SW Sichuan. I by George Forrest. H3–4.

tebotan See *R.* 'Tebotan' under Evergreen Azaleas.

telmateium Balf. f. & W.W. Sm. (Subgenus Rhododendron Subsect. Lapponica) A small, erect shrub with small, oblanceolate, scaly leaves and branches. Flowers deep rose-purple with white throat, small, funnel-shaped, solitary or in clusters of 2–3, April and May. Suitable for a rock garden. I 1914 by George Forrest. Yunnan, SW Sichuan. H4.

telopeum See *R. campylocarpum* subsp. *caloxanthum* Telopeum Group.

temenium Balf. f. & Forrest (Subgenus Hymenanthes, Subsect. Neriiflora) A small, compact shrub with bristly shoots and nearly glabrous leaves to 8cm long. Small clusters of tubular-campanulate, red flowers, to 4cm long, with a fleshy corolla, April and May. I 1917 by George Forrest. SW China, SE Tibet. H4.

tephropeplum Balf. f. & Farrer (*R. deleiense* Hutch. & Kingdon-Ward) (Subgenus Rhododendron, Subsect. Tephropepla) A dwarf or small shrub, occasionally to 1.5m. Narrow, oblong-lanceolate leaves, 3.5–10cm long, are glaucous and dark scaly beneath. Flowers varying from pink to carmine-rose, bell-shaped, in profusion, April and May. Young leaves an attractive plum-purple beneath. NE Burma, NW Yunnan, SE Tibet, Assam. I 1921 by George Forrest. AM 1935 (as *R. deleiense*). AM (F) 1929. H3–4.

thayerianum Rehder & E.H. Wilson (Subgenus Hymenanthes, Subsect. Argyrophylla) A medium-sized shrub with sticky shoots and narrow, pointed leaves, densely clustered at the ends of the shoots and covered beneath with a dense yellow-brown tomentum. Funnel-shaped, white flowers, 3cm across, flushed pink and spotted with red, open in summer on slender, sticky peduncles. Sichuan, China. I 1910 by Ernest Wilson. H4.

thomsonii Hook. f. (Subgenus Hymenanthes, Subsect. Thomsonia) A well-known and desirable Himalayan species. A large shrub or small tree with attractive, smooth, plum-coloured or cinnamon bark and rounded or oval leaves, 3.5–8cm long, glaucous when young. Flowers deep blood-red, bell-shaped, in loose trusses, April to May; calyx large, cup-shaped. The fruiting clusters are most attractive with apple-green calyces and glaucous capsules. Because of its prodigious flowering, this magnificent species appreciates an annual feed and mulch, but is unfortunately prone to powdery mildew. A parent of many fine hybrids. E Nepal, N India, Bhutan. I 1850 by Sir Joseph Hooker. AM 1973. H3. **subsp.** *lopsangianum* (Cowan) D.F. Chamb. (*R. lopsangianum* Cowan) A small shrub up to 2m. Leaves 3–6cm long, glaucous beneath. Flowers deep crimson, narrowly bell-shaped, fleshy, April. Named after a former Dalai Lama of Tibet. SE Tibet. H3–4.

tomentosum (Stokes) Harmaja (*Ledum palustre* L.) (Subsection Ledum) Wild rosemary. A variable species, up to 1m high, closely related to *R. groenlandicum* and producing terminal clusters of small, white flowers in April and May. Arctic regions of Europe, Asia and America. I 1762. A plant previously listed as *Ledum minus* hort. may belong here. H4.

tosaense Makino (Subgenus Tsutsusi, Sect. Tsutsusi) A densely branched, semi-evergreen shrub, occasionally reaching 2m. Leaves narrow, pubescent, turning crimson-purple in autumn. Flowers lilac-purple, funnel-shaped, 2.5–3cm across, in clusters of 1–6, April to May. Japan. I 1914 by Ernest Wilson. H3–4. **'Barbara'** A lovely selection with flowers of a clear pink. Raised in our nurseries in 1958 and named after Harold Hillier's wife.

traillianum Forrest & W.W. Sm. (Subgenus Hymenanthes, Subsect. Taliensia) A large shrub or small tree related to *R. phaeochrysum*. Leaves obovate to elliptic, to 13cm long, dark green and glabrous above, brown-felted beneath. Flowers white or flushed with pink and spotted red, funnel-campanulate, in trusses of up to 15, April to May. Named after G.W. Traill, George Forrest's father-in-law. W Yunnan, SW Sichuan. H4.

trichanthum Rehder (*R. villosum* Hemsl. & E.H. Wilson) (Subgenus Rhododendron, Subsect. Triflora) Large shrub, the branches densely beset with bristles. Leaves ovate-elliptic, 5–10cm long, pubescent. Flowers usually dark violet-purple, sometimes paler, widely funnel-shaped, 3–5 in a truss, May and June. NW Sichuan. I 1904 by Ernest Wilson. H4.

trichocladum Franch. (*R. brachystylum* Balf. f. & Forrest) (Subgenus Rhododendron, Subsect. Trichoclada) Small, deciduous shrub with hairy twigs. Leaves ovate-oblong, 2.5–3.5cm long. Flowers greenish-yellow, spotted dark green, funnel-shaped, April and May. NE Upper Burma, Yunnan. I 1910 by George Forrest. H4.

trichostomum Franch. (*R. sphaeranthum* Balf. f. & W.W. Sm.) (Subgenus Rhododendron, Sect. Pogonanthum) A small, twiggy, aromatic shrub with slender shoots bearing small, narrow leaves, about 2.5cm long, and tight terminal heads of tubular, white, pink or rose, daphne-like flowers in May and June. N Yunnan, Sichuan. I 1908 by Ernest Wilson. AM 1925 (as *R. sphaeranthum*). H3–4. **'Collingwood Ingram'** (Ledoides Group) Flowers red-purple, paler in the centre. ♀ 2002. FCC 1976. **Ledoides Group** (*R. ledoides* Balf. f. & W.W. Sm.) Corolla without scales. FCC 1976. AM 1925. **Radinum Group** (var. *radinum* (Balf. f. & W.W. Sm.) Cowan & Davidian) Flowers more scaly, of equal garden merit. AM 1972.

triflorum Hook. f. (Subgenus Rhododendron, Subsect. Triflora) A slender shrub of medium to large size, with attractive, peeling bark. Leaves ovate-lanceolate, 5–7.5cm long. Flowers lemon-yellow with a ray of green spots, funnel-shaped, in trusses of 3; May and June. E Nepal, N India, Bhutan, S Tibet, NE Burma. I 1850 by Sir Joseph Hooker. H4. **var. *bauhiniiflorum*** (*R. bauhiniiflorum* Watt ex Hutch.) Flowers lemon-yellow, flat saucer-shaped. Manipur. I 1928 by Kingdon-Ward. H3–4. **Mahogani Group** (var. *mahogani* Hutch.) Flowers with a mahogany-coloured blotch or suffused mahogany. Discovered and introduced by Kingdon-Ward from SE Tibet.

tsangpoense See *R. charitopes* subsp. *tsangpoense.* **var. *pruniflorum*** See *R. pruniflorum.*

tsariense Cowan (Subgenus Hymenanthes, Subsect. Lanata) A small shrub with yellow-tomentose young shoots and obovate to elliptic-obovate leaves, covered with a dense, woolly indumentum beneath. Flowers varying from pale blush to cream or white, spotted red within, bell-shaped, in a loose truss, April and May. SE Tibet, NE India, Bhutan. I 1936 by Ludlow and Sherriff. H4.

tsusiophyllum Sugim. (*Tsusiophyllum tanakae* Maxim.) (Subgenus Tsutsusi, Subsect. Tsutsusi) Ohwi. A delightful, dwarf or small, semi-evergreen shrub of dense, twiggy habit, with myriad tiny leaves, glaucous beneath. Tiny, bell-shaped, white flowers appear in 1–3-flowered clusters during June and July. Japan. I 1915 by Ernest Wilson. AM 1965. H4.

ungernii Trautv. (Subgenus Hymenanthes, Subsect. Pontica) Large shrub, notable for its hardiness and late flowering, producing its trusses of funnel-shaped, pinky-white flowers in July. Handsome, oblong-oblanceolate, leathery leaves, 12–20cm long, greyish-white to fawn, tomentose beneath. NE Turkey, Georgia (former USSR). I 1886. AM 1973. H4.

uniflorum Kingdon-Ward (Subgenus Rhododendron, Subsect. Uniflora) A small shrub closely related to *R. pemakoense*, with oblong-elliptic, mucronate leaves, up to 2.5cm long, densely scaly on both sides. Flowers pale to rose-purple spotted red, funnel-shaped, singly or in pairs, April and May. SE Tibet. I by Kingdon-Ward in 1924. H4. **var. *imperator*** (Hutch. & Kingdon-Ward) Cullen (*R. imperator* Hutch. & Kingdon-Ward) A dwarf shrub, often creeping, with small, narrow leaves and normally solitary, funnel-shaped flowers of pink or rose-purple, 2.5cm across, appearing even on very young plants, in May. Best in an open, sunny position and very suitable for a rock garden. NE Burma. I 1926 by Kingdon-Ward. AM (F) 1934. H3–4.

uvariifolium Diels (*R. niphargum* Balf. f. & Kingdon-Ward) (Subgenus Hymenanthes, Subsect. Fulva) A large shrub or small tree with beautiful, silvery young growths in spring. Leaves up to 25cm long, oblanceolate to obovate, dark shining green above, white- or grey-tomentose beneath. Flowers white or pale rose with or without crimson spots, bell-shaped, March or April. NW Yunnan, SW Sichuan, SE Tibet. I 1913 by George Forrest. H4. **'Reginald Childs'** Flowers white, flushed and spotted red. AM 1976.

valentinianum Forrest ex Hutch. (Subgenus Rhododendron, Subsect. Maddenia) A small shrub with densely scaly and bristly young shoots. Leaves about 3cm long, oval or obovate, densely scaly beneath, clustered at the ends of the branches. Flowers bright buttercup-yellow, narrowly bell-shaped, 3.5cm long, pubescent and scaly on the outside, April. NE Burma, NW Yunnan. I 1917 by George Forrest and later by Joseph Rock. Remarkably hardy for the Maddenia Subsection. AM 1933. H3–4.

vaseyi A. Gray (*Azalea vaseyi* (A. Gray) Rehder) (Subgenus Pentanthera, Sect. Rhodora) A beautiful, medium-sized to large deciduous shrub with narrowly oval leaves up to 13cm long, often turning fiery-red in autumn. Flowers pale pink, rose-pink or white, with orange-red spots, widely funnel-shaped, 3.5–5cm across, appearing before the leaves, April and May. North Carolina (USA). I about 1880. ♀ 2002. H4.

†*veitchianum* Hook. f. (Subgenus Rhododendron, Subsect. Maddenia) A tender, small to medium-sized shrub with densely scaly leaves up to 13cm long. Flowers white with a faint green tinge, fragrant, comparatively large, widely funnel-shaped, deeply 5-cleft, with crinkled petals, May to July. Only suitable for a conservatory. Burma, Laos, Thailand. I 1850 by Thomas Lobb. H1. **Cubittii Group** (*R. cubittii* Hutch.) A medium-sized to large, spreading shrub with leaves margined with bristles and scaly beneath. Flowers deep pink, sometimes blotched with orange-yellow, fragrant, broadly funnel-shaped, March and April. H2.

vellereum See *R. principis* Vellereum Group.

venator Tagg (Subgenus Hymenanthes, Subsect. Venatora) A medium-sized shrub of bushy habit with glandular-hairy young shoots. Leaves oblong-lanceolate, 10cm long. Flowers scarlet, bell-shaped, in trusses of 4 or 6, May and June. SE Tibet. I 1924 by Kingdon-Ward. AM (F) 1933. H3.

vernicosum Franch. (Subgenus Hymenanthes, Subsect. Fortunea) A variable, large shrub with oblong-elliptic leaves, 7.5–13cm long, dull and wax-covered above, becoming shiny when rubbed, blue-green beneath. Flowers widely funnel-shaped, to 8cm across, varying in colour from white to rose-lavender, sometimes with crimson spots, April and May. Yunnan, Sichuan. I 1904 by Ernest Wilson. H4.

villosum See *R. trichanthum.*

violaceum See *R. nivale* subsp. *boreale.*

†*virgatum* Hook. f. (Subgenus Rhododendron, Subsect. Virgata) A small to medium-sized, leggy shrub with ovate leaves, 3.5–6cm long, scaly below. Flowers varying from purple through pink to white, usually lilac-purple, inclined to be tubular, April and May. E Nepal,

N India, Bhutan, S Tibet. I 1850 by Sir Joseph Hooker. AM (F) 1928 H2–3. **subsp.** *oleifolium* (Franch.) Cullen (*R. oleifolium* Franch.) Differs in its smaller, pink flowers. Yunnan, SE Tibet. I 1906. H3.

viridescens Hutch. (*R. mekongense* Viridescens Group) (Subgenus Rhododendron, Subsect. Trichoclada) A small, evergreen shrub with oblong-elliptic leaves about 2.5–3.5cm long, glaucous beneath. Flowers yellowish-green, spotted green within, funnel-shaped, June. SE Tibet. I 1924 by Kingdon-Ward. H4. **'Doshong La'** (*R. mekongense* 'Doshong La') (KW 5829) Yellow flowers are flushed pink at the tips of the lobes, flecked olive-green inside, June and July. Collected by Kingdon-Ward at the Doshong La Pass, Tibet. AM 1972.

viscosum (L.) Torr. (*Azalea viscosa* L. *R. oblongifolium* (Small) Millais, *R. serrulatum* (Small) Millais) (Subgenus Pentanthera, Sect. Pentanthera) Swamp honeysuckle. A medium-sized, deciduous, summer-flowering shrub of bushy habit. Leaves up to 3.5cm long, dark green above, glaucous green beneath. Flowers white, sometimes with a pink stain, delightfully and spicily fragrant, narrowly funnel-shaped. 2.5–3.5cm across, viscid on the outside, appearing after the leaves, June and July. E North America. I 1734. ♀ 2002. AM (F) 1921. H4.

wallichii Hook. f. (Subgenus Hymenanthes, Subsect. Campanulata) Medium-sized to large shrub with elliptic-obovate leaves, 5–10cm long, dark green and glabrous above, paler and dotted with tiny, powdery tufts of reddish-brown hair below. Flowers lilac with rose spots, bell-shaped, 6–10 in a truss, April. E Nepal, Sikkim, Bhutan, Assam, S Tibet. I 1850. Closely related to *R. campanulatum*. H4.

wardii W.W. Sm. (*R. croceum* Balf. f. & W.W. Sm.) (Subgenus Hymenanthes, Subsect. Campylocarpa) A compact, medium-sized to large, Chinese shrub with oblong-elliptic or rounded leaves, 5–10cm long. Flowers clear yellow, sometimes with a crimson basal blotch, saucer-shaped, in loose trusses, May. NW Yunnan, SW Sichuan, SE Tibet. A beautiful species discovered and introduced in 1913 by Kingdon-Ward after whom it is named. A parent of several superb hybrids. Unfortunately prone to powdery mildew. AM (F) 1931. AM (F) 1926. H4. **Litiense Group** (*R. litiense* Balf. f. & Forrest) A very beautiful shrub with widely bell-shaped or saucer-shaped, clear soft yellow flowers, without markings, in May. Leaves oblong, waxy glaucous beneath. Yunnan. FCC 1953. AM 1931. H3. **var.** *puralbum* (Balf. f. & W.W. Sm.) D.F. Chamb. (*R. puralbum* Balf. f. & W.W. Sm.) Flowers white. Leaves oblong-elliptic, 5–7.5cm long, dark green. Yunnan. I 1913 by George Forrest. H3.

wasonii Hemsl. & E.H. Wilson (Subgenus Hymenanthes, Subsect. Taliensia) A small to medium-sized shrub of compact growth with stout, greyish-white young shoots. Leaves 5–10cm long, usually oval, glossy green above, white beneath, becoming reddish-brown. Flowers varying from white to pink, rose or rarely yellow, with crimson spots, bell-shaped, May. C Sichuan. I 1904 by Ernest Wilson. H4. **f.** *rhododactylum* Flowers white, lined pink and blotched with red. I 1904 by Ernest Wilson. AM 1923.

watsonii Hemsl. & E.H. Wilson (Subgenus Hymenanthes, Subsect. Grandia) A large shrub, sometimes a small tree, with bold, dark green leaves, to 20cm long, covered beneath with a thin, white tomentum. Bell-shaped 7-lobed flowers, 5cm across, are white, blotched at the base with purple; open in large trusses, to 15cm across, February to April. W Sichuan and Gansu, China. I 1908 by Ernest Wilson. W4.

weyrichii Maxim. (Subgenus Pentanthera, Sect. Brachycalyx) A very splendid, medium-sized to large, deciduous shrub with broad-ovate or rounded leaves in clusters of 2–3 at the ends of the branches. Flowers variable in colour, usually bright brick-red, with a purple blotch, widely funnel-shaped, opening before the leaves, April and May. Japan and the island of Cheju do (Quelpaert), S Korea. I 1914 by Ernest Wilson. H4.

wightii Hook. f. (Subgenus Hymenanthes, Subsect. Taliensia) A large, usually rather lax shrub, the oblong-elliptic leaves up to 20cm long, covered with a fawn or rust-coloured, suede-like tomentum below. Flowers cream or pale yellow, spotted crimson, rarely white, bell-shaped, in a loose, one-sided truss, May. C and E Nepal, N India, Bhutan, S Tibet. I 1850 by Sir Joseph Hooker. AM (F) 1913. H3–4.

williamsianum Rehder & E.H. Wilson (Subgenus Hymenanthes, Subsect. Williamsia) A charming, Chinese shrub with attractive, bronze young growths, small, round, heart-shaped leaves and delightful, bell-shaped, shell-pink flowers in April. It is generally of dwarf, spreading habit, but may reach a height of 1–1.5m. Forms with white flowers are also grown. C Sichuan. Discovered and introduced by Ernest Wilson in 1908. A parent of several good hybrids including 'Arthur J. Ivens'. ♀ 2002. AM 1938. H4.

wilsoniae See *R. latoucheae*.

wiltonii Franch. (Subgenus Hymenanthes, Subsect. Taliensia) A medium-sized to large shrub with distinct dark green, deeply veined, oblong-obovate leaves, 7.5–13cm long, white turning to cinnamon-felted beneath. The bell-shaped flowers are usually pale pink with red markings, April and May. C Sichuan. I 1904 by Ernest Wilson. ♀ 2002. AM (F) 1957. H4.

wongii Hemsl. & E.H. Wilson (Subgenus Rhododendron, Subsect. Triflora) A rare, small shrub with densely scaly twigs and terminal clusters of pale yellow, funnel-shaped flowers in May and June. Probably the same as *R. ambiguum* but differing in its smaller stature, smaller, obtuse leaves and flowers without scales. Sichuan. H4.

xanthocodon See *R. cinnabarinum* subsp. *xanthocodon*.

yakushimanum Nakai (*R. metternichii* var. *yakushimanum* (Nakai) Ohwi) (Subgenus Hymenanthes, Subsect. Pontica) A remarkable species forming a compact, dome-shaped bush up to 1.3m high and more in width. Young growths silvery. Leaves leathery, recurved at the margins, dark glossy green above, densely brown-tomentose beneath. Flowers rose in bud, opening to apple blossom-pink and finally white, bell-shaped, in a compact truss, May. Only found on the windswept, rain-drenched, mountain peaks of Yakushima Island, Japan. I 1934. Now the parent of many new hybrids. H4. **'Koichiro Wada'** This selection of the original introduction is the best form of the species. The original plant grows at Wisley. ♀ 2002. FCC 1947.

yanthinum See *R. concinnum*.

yedoense Maxim. (*R.* 'Yodogawa') (Subgenus Anthodendron, Sect. Tsutsusi) A small, usually deciduous shrub of dense, spreading habit. Leaves narrow, 5–9cm long, often colouring prettily in autumn. Flowers rosy-purple, funnel-shaped, double, May. Long cultivated in Japan and Korea. C 1886. H4. **var.** *poukhanense* (Lévl.) Nakai (*R. poukhanense* Lévl., *R. coreanum* Rehder) Korean azalea. A small, usually deciduous shrub of dense, spreading habit. Leaves narrow, up to 8cm long, dark green, turning to orange and crimson in autumn. Flowers lilac-rose to pale lilac-purple, fragrant, funnel-shaped, 5cm wide, in clusters of 2 or more, appearing before or with the leaves, May. Korea, Japan. I 1905. AM 1961.

yungningense Balf. f. (*R. glomerulatum* Hutch.) (Subgenus Rhododendron, Subsect. Lapponica) A small shrub, 0.6–1m high, resembling *R. russatum*. Leaves ovate-elliptic, 1–2cm long, densely scaly. The clusters of light purple-mauve, funnel-shaped flowers are encircled by semi-persistent bud-scales, March to May. N Yunnan, SW Sichuan. H4.

yunnanense Franch. (*R. aechmophyllum* Balf. f. & Forrest, *R. chartophyllum* Franch.) (Subgenus Rhododendron, Subsect. Triflora) A very hardy and exceedingly floriferous, Chinese shrub, up to 4m. Leaves lanceolate or oblanceolate, bristly when young, semi-deciduous in cold or exposed gardens. Flowers usually pink with darker spots, funnel-shaped, May. Sichuan, Yunnan, Guizhou, NE Burma. I about 1889 by the Abbé Delavay. AM 1903. H4. See also *R. pleistanthum*. **Hormophorum Group** (*R. hormophorum* Balf. f. & Forrest) A small to medium-sized, floriferous shrub, the leaves lanceolate, 2.5–7.5cm long, covered with pale yellow scales below. Flowers rose-lilac or lavender, usually with a ray of brown markings, funnel-shaped, May. AM (F) 1943. H4. **'Openwood'** A hardy and extremely free-flowering shrub up to 4m high, deciduous in cold or exposed gardens. Flowers mauve-lavender, speckled with red, funnel-shaped, May. ♀ 2002. H3–4. **'Praecox'** An early flowering form. **Suberosum Group** (*R. suberosum* Balf. f. & Forrest) Dark green, very bristly leaves, corolla white spotted with green. I 1919 by George Forrest.

zaleucum Balf. f. & W.W. Sm. (Subgenus Rhododendron, Subsect. Triflora) A large shrub with lanceolate to obovate leaves, white beneath. Flowers varying from white to purple, usually lilac-mauve, with or without crimson spots, widely funnel-shaped, in terminal and axillary trusses, April. N Burma, Yunnan. I 1912 by George Forrest. AM (F) 1932. H3–4.

zeylanicum See *R. arboreum* subsp. *zeylanicum*.

‡*Rhododendron Hybrids

The earliest hybrids began to appear about 1825, when *R. arboreum* flowered for the first time in the British Isles. During the next 75 years, a large number of hybrids were raised, derived mainly from *R. catawbiense* and *R. maximum* (USA), *R. arboreum* (Himalaya), *R. caucasicum* (Caucasus), *R. ponticum* (Turkey), and to a lesser extent *R. fortunei* (China) and *R. griffithianum* (Himalaya). Most of the hybrids produced from these species have several things in common: hardiness, ample foliage, firm and full flower trusses, and an ability to withstand exposure, and hence they are often referred to as the Hardy Hybrids (HH). As a group they are indispensable for planting in cold or exposed

districts and are unsurpassed for landscape effect, while many are ideal as informal hedges or screens. More recently *R. yakushimanum* has played an important part in the development of many new hybrids suitable for smaller gardens.

With the exploration of China and the E Himalaya during the first 30 years of the 20th century, a vast wealth of new and exciting species flooded British gardens. From this glorious palette has been raised a whole range of colourful and ornamental hybrids; new hybrids are continuously being produced. They show a much greater variation in foliage, flower and habit than the older hybrids and though most are hardy, few will tolerate the extreme conditions often weathered by the Hardy Hybrids.

Among the many raisers of hybrid rhododendrons, the following names are closely associated with this great genus: the late Lord Aberconway of Bodnant, N Wales; Sir Edmund Loder of Leonardslee, Sussex; Edward Magor of Lamellan, Cornwall; Lionel de Rothschild, creator of the Exbury Gardens, Hampshire; Mr and Mrs J.B. Stevenson of Tower Court, Ascot, Berks; and J.C. Williams of Caerhays, Cornwall. In more recent years, many fine hybrids have been raised in the Savill Gardens, Windsor, and in the RHS Gardens, Wisley.

The following hybrids, all of which are evergreen, vary from prostrate alpines to small trees, and unless otherwise stated may be taken as averaging 1.8–3m in height. The date of introduction of a hybrid (when known) is given in parentheses at the end of each description. A number of the descriptions are original work done by our late manager Arthur J. Ivens. We are grateful for the assistance of Alan Hardy with the revision of this section.

Flowering seasons are indicated as follows:

Early   April
Mid   May to mid-June
Late   Mid-June onwards

'A. Gilbert' (*R. campylogynum* × *R. fortunei* subsp. *discolor*) An exceedingly free-flowering hybrid, similar to 'Lady Bessborough', but more compact. Leaves oblong-obovate, to 11cm long. Flowers 6cm across, fragrant, in loose trusses, apricot-yellow in bud, opening to pale cream with 2 small crimson flashes. Mid. (1925). AM 1925. H3.

'Adder' (*R. diphrocalyx* × *R. thomsonii*) Beautiful, blood-red, bell-shaped flowers with large petaloid calyces. Early. (1933). H3.

'Aladdin' (*R. auriculatum* × *R. griersonianum*) A very beautiful shrub with large, widely expanded, brilliant salmon-cerise flowers in loose trusses. Late. (1930). AM 1935. H3.

Albatross Group (*R. fortunei* subsp. *discolor* × *R.* Loderi Group) One of the glories of Exbury. A large, robust shrub or a small tree with terminal clusters of large leaves and magnificent, lax trusses of richly fragrant, trumpet-shaped flowers, 13cm across. Mid. (1930). AMT 1953. AM 1934. H3. **'Albatross Townhill Pink'** (*R. fortunei* subsp. *discolor* × *R.* Loderi Group 'King George') Flowers in enormous trusses, deep pink in bud, opening shell-pink. Mid. Both this and the white form were raised by Frederick Rose from seed given to him by Lionel de Rothschild. (1945). AM 1945. **'Albatross Townhill**

White' A lovely form differing only in its comparatively shorter, broader leaves and white flowers, which are pale yellowish-green within. Mid.

'Albert Schweitzer' A large shrub of upright habit with large conical trusses of rose-bengal flowers with a deeper blotch. Parentage unknown. Mid. (1960). ♀ 2002. H4.

'Alice' (HH) A hybrid of *R. griffithianum*, large, vigorous and upright in habit. Flowers funnel-shaped, rose-pink with lighter centre, borne in tall, conical trusses. Mid. (1910). ♀ 2002. AM 1910. H4.

'Alison Johnstone' (*R. cinnabarinum* Concatenans Group × *R. yunnanense*) A dainty hybrid with oval leaves and trusses of slender-tubed flowers, greenish in bud opening to pale yellow, flushed orange or pink. Mid. Prone to powdery mildew. (1945). AM 1945. H4.

'Alpine Glow' (Avalanche Group) A handsome, large shrub with long, rich green leaves, and flowers in large trusses, widely funnel-shaped, 10cm across, delicate pink with a deep crimson blotch at the base, sweetly scented. Mid. (1933). AM 1938. H3.

'America' (*R.* 'Parson's Red' × dark red hybrid) A small to medium-sized shrub bearing dense, rounded trusses of deep red flowers, flushed blue-purple, with contrasting white anthers. Extremely hardy and best in colder areas. Mid. (1920). H4.

'Amor' (*R. griersonianum* × *R. thayerianum*) A dense, bushy shrub with narrow, dark green leaves, thickly brown-felted beneath, up to 13cm long. Flowers 8–10 in a truss, scarlet in bud opening white, stained pink. Late. (1927). AM 1951. H3.

'Angelo' (*R. fortunei* subsp. *discolor* × *R. griffithianum*) A Group of magnificent hybrids raised first at Caerhays, Cornwall, and later by Lionel de Rothschild at Exbury, Hampshire. 'Exbury Angelo' makes a large shrub or small tree with handsome foliage. Huge, shapely trusses of large, fragrant, trumpet-shaped, white flowers, 14cm across, with green markings within. Mid. (1933). FCC 1948. AM 1935. H3. See also 'Solent Queen'.

'Anna Baldsiefen' (*R.* 'Pioneer' selfed) A dwarf shrub of compact, upright habit with light green leaves, bronzed-red in winter, to 2.5cm long. Flowers profusely borne, vivid phlox-pink with darker, wavy margins, funnel-shaped, 3cm across. Early. (1964). H4.

'Anna Rose Whitney' (*R.* 'Countess of Derby' × *R. griersonianum*) A vigorous, medium-sized, spreading shrub with dark green leaves, to 11cm long. Flowers in dense, rounded trusses, widely funnel-shaped, 10cm across, deep rose-pink spotted with brown on the upper lobes. Mid. (1954). AMT 1987. H4.

'Antonio' (*R. fortunei* subsp. *discolor* × *R.* 'Gill's Triumph') A splendid, large hybrid, notable for the rich scent of its beautiful, funnel-shaped, pink flowers, which are blotched and spotted crimson within, rich pink in bud. Mid. (1933). AM 1939. H3.

'Anuschka' (*R.* 'Sammetglut' × *R. yakushimanum* 'Koichiro Wada') A low-growing shrub with dark green, recurved leaves, thinly tomentose beneath. Flowers bright red outside, pink inside fading to nearly white. (1983). Mid. H4.

'April Chimes' (*R. hippophaeoides* × *R. mollicomum*) (*R.* 'Hippomum') A charming, small shrub of upright habit, similar in leaf to *R. hippophaeoides*. Flowers funnel-shaped, rosy-mauve, in the axils of the upper leaves and in terminal umbels, like compact balls. Early. A floriferous hybrid of neat habit, excellent as for cutting for indoor decoration. Raised as a chance seedling in our nurseries from seed of *R. hippophaeoides* in 1938. H3–4.

'Arborfield' (*R.* 'Crest' × *R.* Loderi Group 'Julie') Mimosa-yellow flowers with slight pink flush and deeper base with a crimson tinge, bell-shaped, on long pedicels, 11.5cm across. Mid. AM 1963. H3.

'Arctic Tern' (× *Ledodendron* 'Arctic Tern') (*R. trichostomum* hybrid) A vigorous, compact, free-flowering shrub, of upright habit, with narrowly oblong, glossy green leaves to 3.5cm long, densely scaly beneath. Flowers 1cm long, white, tinged with green, in compact, globular trusses. Mid. It has been suggested that a *Ledum* sp. is involved in the parentage. (1982). ♀ 2002. AMT 1989 (as *Rhododendron* 'Arctic Tern'). AMT 1984 (as × *Ledodendron* 'Arctic Tern'). H4.

'Argosy' (*R. auriculatum* × *R. fortunei* subsp. *discolor*) A vigorous, large shrub or small tree with handsome, large leaves and very fragrant, trumpet-shaped, white flowers with a ray of dull crimson at base of throat. Late. (1933). ♀ 2002. H3–4.

'Ariel' (*R. fortunei* subsp. *discolor* × *R.* 'Memoir') A large shrub with plentiful, pale pink flowers. Mid. (1933). H3.

'Arthur Bedford' A charming hybrid of unknown parentage, possibly *R. ponticum* × mauve seedling, making a large, very floriferous shrub. Compact, conical trusses of pale mauve flowers spotted with dark rose-madder within. Mid. Named after a head gardener at Exbury, Hampshire. (1936). FCCT 1958. AM 1936. H4.

'Arthur J. Ivens' (*R. fortunei* Houlstonii Group × *R. williamsianum*) A medium, dome-shaped bush, resembling *R. williamsianum* in leaf shape and the coppery-red tints of its young foliage. Flowers shallowly bell-shaped, 7.5cm across, deep pink in bud, opening delicate rose-pink with 2 small crimson flashes. Early. Raised by and named after our late manager. (1938). AM 1944. H4.

'Arthur Osborn' (*R. griersonianum* × *R. sanguineum* subsp. *didymum*) A small, late-flowering shrub with small, narrowly oblong leaves, pale cinnamon beneath. Flowers drooping, funnel-shaped, ruby-red with orange-scarlet tubes. Late; sometimes continuing until early autumn. A useful, low-growing shrub, flowering when quite small. (1929). AM 1933. H3.

'Arthur Stevens' (*R.* 'Coronation Day' × *R. souliei*) A lovely hybrid of rounded habit. Young shoots, petioles and buds bright yellow. The loose trusses of bell-shaped flowers are pale pink fading to white, with a deep rose-red basal stain. Mid. A seedling raised in our nurseries and named in memory of our late foreman. (1960). AM 1976. H3.

'Ascot Brilliant' A hybrid of *R. thomsonii* with an unknown garden hybrid. Lax trusses of funnel-shaped, rose-red flowers, darker at margins. Early to mid. Requires woodland treatment for the best results (1861). H4.

Augfast Group (*R. augustinii* × *R. fastigiatum*) A small, dense, rounded shrub with small, scattered leaves and scaly young shoots. Flowers small, funnel-shaped, in terminal clusters. Early. Forms of our own raising vary from dark lavender-blue to heliotrope. (1921). H4.

'**Aurora**' (*R.* Loderi Group × *R. thomsonii*) A large, fast-growing shrub or small tree of rather open habit. The fragrant, trumpet-shaped, rose-coloured flowers are borne in flat trusses, 20cm across. Early to mid. (1922). AM 1922. H3.

'**Avalanche**' (*R. calophytum* × *R.* Loderi Group) A large shrub with bold foliage and large trusses of enormous, fragrant, widely funnel-shaped, snow-white flowers with a red basal stain within, pink-flushed in bud. The conspicuous red pedicels and bracts contrast superbly with the flowers. Early. (1933). ♀ 2002. FCC 1938. AM 1934. H3. See also 'Alpine Glow'.

'**Azor**' (*R. fortunei* subsp. *discolor* × *R. griersonianum*) A large shrub bearing trusses of large, trumpet-shaped flowers of soft salmon-pink. Late. (1927). AM 1933. H3–4.

'**Azurro**' (*R.* 'Danamar' × *R.* 'Purple Splendour') This small shrub is an improvement on 'Purple Splendour' showing increased hardiness, a more compact habit and better, glossy deep green foliage. Domed trusses of large purple flowers blotched with blackish purple. Mid to late. (1986). H4.

'**Babette**' (*R. wardii* × *R. yakushimanum* 'Koichiro Wada') A compact, small shrub, to about 1m tall, with glossy dark green leaves, to 10cm long, with a thin brown indumentum beneath. Bell-shaped flowers are pale greenish-yellow with a deep red blotch. Mid. (1952). H4.

'**Bad Eilsen**' (*R.* 'Essex Scarlet' × *R. forrestii* Repens Group) Dwarf, free-flowering shrub of spreading habit. Flowers funnel-shaped, red, with waved and crinkled margins. Mid. (1965). H4.

'**Baden-Baden**' (*R.* 'Essex Scarlet' × *R. forrestii* Repens Group) Dwarf, compact, spreading shrub with small, dark glossy green, rather twisted leaves. Deep waxy-red flowers are profusely borne. Mid. (Before 1972). H4.

'**Bagshot Ruby**' A vigorous hybrid of *R. thomsonii*, raised by John Waterer, Sons & Crisp, producing dense rounded trusses of widely funnel-shaped, ruby-red flowers. Mid. (1916). AM 1916. H4.

'**Bambi**' (*R.* 'Fabia Tangerine' × *R. yakushimanum*) A small and compact shrub with dark green, deeply veined leaves, felted pale brown when young. Flowers red in bud, opening pale pink flushed yellow. (About 1964). H3.

Barclayi Group (*R.* 'Glory of Penjerrick' × *R. thomsonii*) Beautiful hybrids raised by Robert Barclay Fox at Penjerrick, Cornwall in 1913. Unfortunately, they are somewhat tender and are only seen at their best in Cornwall and similarly favourable areas. H2.
'**Barclayi Helen Fox**' Flowers deep scarlet. Early.
'**Barclayi Robert Fox**' Flowers of a glowing deep crimson. Early. AM 1921.

'**Barmstedt**' (*R.* 'Sammetglut' × *R. yakushimanum* 'Koichiro Wada') A small shrub, the leaves to 13cm long, with strongly revolute margins, white-felted beneath. Flowers to 6.5cm across, rose-pink, paler in the centre with deep red markings. Mid. H4.

'**Bashful**' (*R.* 'Doncaster' × *R. yakushimanum*) A medium-sized shrub of widespreading habit with narrow, red-tinged leaves, silvery when young. Flowers light pink with a rust-red blotch fading to white. Mid. (1971). ♀ 2002. AMT 1989. H4.

'**Beatrice Keir**' (*R. lacteum* × *R.* 'Logan Damaris') A large shrub with handsome foliage and large trusses of funnel-shaped, lemon-yellow flowers. Early. (1974). AM 1974. H3.

'**Beau Brummell**' (*R. facetum* × *R.* 'Essex Scarlet') Scarlet, funnel-shaped flowers, with conspicuous black anthers; as many as 30 in a neat globular truss. Late. (1934). AM 1938. H4.

'**Beauty of Littleworth**' (HH) One of the first *R. griffithianum* hybrids. A very striking, large shrub with immense conical trusses of crimson-spotted, white flowers. Mid. Still one of the best hardy hybrids. Raised by Miss Clara Mangles at Littleworth, Surrey, about 1900. FCCT 1953. FCC 1904. H4.

'**Beefeater**' (*R. elliottii* × *R.* 'Fusilier') A superb Wisley hybrid with well-filled, flat-topped trusses of geranium-red flowers. Mid. FCC 1959. AM and Cory Cup 1958. H3.

'**Belle Heller**' (*R.* 'Catawbiense Album' × white *R. catawbiense* seedling) A compact, small shrub with dark green leaves. Large, dense, conical trusses of white flowers marked with a gold flash. Mid. (1958). H4.

'**Ben Mosely**' A compact, small shrub bearing funnel-shaped, frilly-margined, light purplish-pink flowers, with a deep red flare, in dense, rounded trusses. Mid. (1981). H4.

'**Bengal**' (*R.* 'Essex Scarlet' × *R. forrestii* Repens Group) A very hardy, small shrub of compact habit with glossy foliage and loose trusses of deep red flowers. Mid. (1960). H4.

'**Betty Wormald**' (*R.* 'George Hardy' × red garden hybrid) (HH) A magnificent hybrid with immense trusses of large, widely funnel-shaped, wavy-edged flowers, rich crimson in bud opening deep rose-pink, lighter in the centre and with a broad pattern of blackish-crimson markings within. Mid. (Before 1922). FCCT 1964. AMT 1935. H4.

'**Bibiani**' (*R. arboreum* × *R.* 'Moser's Maroon') A large shrub with good foliage, producing compact trusses of rich crimson, funnel-shaped flowers with a few maroon spots. Mid. (1934). AM 1934. H4.

'**Billy Budd**' (*R. elliottii* × *R.* 'May Day') A Wisley hybrid with Turkey-red flowers in a loose flat-topped truss. Early. (1954). AM 1957. H3.

'**Binfield**' (*R.* 'China A' × *R.* 'Crest') A large shrub with open bell-shaped, primrose-yellow flowers, stained red in the throat, in large, rounded trusses. Mid. AM 1964. H4.

'**Biskra**' (*R. ambiguum* × *R. cinnabarinum* Roylei Group) A large, slender, floriferous shrub carrying rather flat trusses of pendent, narrowly funnel-shaped, vermilion flowers. Early. (1934). AM 1940. H3.

'**Blewbury**' (*R. anwheiense* × *R. roxieanum*) A small shrub of compact habit, named after a village in Oxfordshire. Leaves resemble those of *R. roxieanum*, narrow and pointed, to 9cm long with downcurved margins and a loose, pale brown indumentum beneath. Flowers white with reddish-purple spots, widely bell-shaped, 4cm across. Mid. (1968). ♀ 2002. FCCT 1983. AM 1968. H4.

'**Bluebird**' (*B. augustinii* × *R. intricatum*) A neat, dwarf, small-leaved shrub, suitable for a rock garden or the front row of borders. Flowers lovely violet-blue borne in small, compact trusses. Early. Raised by the late Lord Aberconway at Bodnant in 1930. AM 1943. H4.

'**Blue Chip**' (*R.* 'Blue Diamond' × *R. russatum*) A dwarf shrub with dark green leaves to 5.5cm long, scaly beneath. Flowers violet-purple, widely funnel-shaped and deeply 5-lobed. Early to mid. (Before 1978). AM 1978. H4.

'**Blue Diamond**' (*R. augustinii* × *R.* 'Intrifast') A slow-growing, compact bush, up to 1m high or more, with terminal clusters of rich lavender-blue, saucer-shaped flowers in tight clusters. Early to mid. Raised by Mr J.J. Crosfield at Embley Park, Hampshire. (1935). FCC 1939. AM 1935. H4.

'**Blue Peter**' (HH) A vigorous, very free-flowering hybrid of upright habit. Flowers in compact, conical trusses, funnel-shaped, frilled at the margin, cobalt-violet, paling to white at throat, with a ray of maroon spots. Mid. (1930). ♥ 2002. FCCT 1958. AMT 1933. H4.

'**Blue Star**' (*R. impeditum* × *R.* 'Saint Tudy') Mauve-blue, 3cm across. Mid. (1961). H4.

'**Blue Tit**' (*R. augustinii* × *R. impeditum*) A Caerhays hybrid very similar to Augfast, forming dense bushes up to 1m high and as wide. The small, widely funnel-shaped flowers are borne in clusters at the tips of branchlets. They are a lovely lavender-blue, which intensifies with age, as in 'Blue Diamond'. Early. A first class shrub for a rock or heather garden. (1933). H4.

'**Blurettia**' (*R.* 'Blue Peter' × *R. yakushimanum* 'Koichiro Wada') A compact, small shrub with pale green leaves, downy beneath. Wavy-edged flowers, borne in rounded trusses, are mallow-purple, paler in the centre and marked with red. Mid to late. (1983). H4.

'**Boddaertianum**' ('Bodartianum') (HH) A large, fast-growing hybrid, developing into a small tree. Leaves long and narrow, dark green above, slightly bronzed beneath. Flowers in a compact, rounded truss, widely funnel-shaped, lavender-pink in bud, opening very pale pink or nearly white, with a wide ray of crimson-purple markings, 6cm across. Early. Said to be *R. arboreum* × *R. campanulatum*, but in our opinion white forms of both *R. arboreum* and *R. ponticum* are the parents. (1863). AM 1992. H4.

'**Bodnant Yellow**' (Lady Chamberlain Group) A beautiful rhododendron with orange-buff flowers flushed red on the outside. Mid. FCC 1944. H3.

'**Bonito**' (*R. fortunei* subsp. *discolor* × *R.* 'Luscombei') Flowers pink in bud, opening white with a basal choco-late-coloured blotch within. Mid. (1934). AM 1934. H4.

'**Bo-peep**' (*R. lutescens* × *R. moupinense*) A small Exbury hybrid of slender, loose habit. Flowers primrose-yellow with 2 broad bands of pale orange spots and streaks, widely funnel-shaped, 4cm across, in clusters of 1 or 2. Very early (March). Very floriferous and a splendid sight when in full flower. (1934). AM 1937. H3–4.

'**Bounty**' (Calfort Group) A large shrub with large trusses of off-white flowers blotched red-purple. Mid. AM 1967. H4.

'**Bow Bells**' (*R.* 'Corona' × *R. williamsianum*) A charming shrub of bushy, compact habit, with bright coppery young growths. Flowers are widely bell-shaped, 8cm across, long-stalked and nodding, deep cerise in bud, opening to soft pink within, shaded rich pink outside, borne in loose trusses. Early to mid. (1934). ♥ 2002. AM 1935. H4.

'**Bray**' (*R. griffithianum* hybrid × *R.* 'Hawk') A Windsor hybrid with flowers deep pink in bud, opening mimosa-yellow, shaded pale pink on the outside. Mid. AM 1960. H3.

'**Bric-a-brac**' (*R. leucaspis* × *R. moupinense*) A small, neat, floriferous shrub bearing pure white, wide open flowers, 6cm across, with bright chocolate-coloured anthers. Although hardy, it is best given a sheltered position to protect its flowers which appear in March or earlier in a mild season. Raised by Lionel de Rothschild at Exbury. (1934). AM 1945. H3.

'**Britannia**' (*R.* 'Queen Wilhelmina' × *R.* 'Stanley Davies') (HH) A superb shrub of slow growth, forming a compact, rounded bush generally broader than high. Flowers glox-inia-shaped, glowing crimson-scarlet, in compact trusses backed by bold, handsome foliage. Mid. One of the most popular of all hardy hybrids and an excellent wind resister. Raised by C.B. van Nes & Sons of Boskoop, Holland. (1921). FCCT 1937. AM 1921. H4.

'**Brocade**' A dome-shaped shrub, strongly resembling 'Arthur J. Ivens' in habit and foliage. Flowers in loose trusses, bell-shaped, 7cm across, with frilly margins, vivid carmine in bud, opening to peach-pink. Early to mid. This pretty shrub was raised at Exbury and is stated to be a cross between 'Vervaeniana' and *R. william-sianum*. The latter parent is obvious, but there seems lit-tle evidence of the other. (1934). H4.

'**Brookside**' (*R.* 'Goshawk' × *R. griersonianum*) A Windsor hybrid of flamboyant appearance. The tubular, campsis-like flowers are ochre-yellow, shaded paler yellow and flame; blood-red in bud. Mid. AM 1962. H3–4.

'**Bruce Brechtbill**' A sport of 'Unique', which it closely resembles, but with pale pink flowers with a yellow throat. Early to mid. (1970). ♥ 2002. H4.

'**Butterfly**' (*R. campylocarpum* × *R.* 'Mrs Milner') A very pretty hybrid bearing rounded trusses of widely funnel-shaped, primrose-yellow flowers with a broad ray of crimson speckles. Early to mid. (1940). AMT 1940. H4.

'**Buttermint**' (*R.* 'Unique' × [*R.* Fabia Group × *R. dichroanthum* subsp. *apodectum*]) A compact, dwarf shrub with dark glossy green leaves, bronze when young. Bright yellow, bell-shaped flowers, edged with deep pink, open from orange-red buds. Mid. (1979). H3.

'**Buttersteep**' (*R.* 'Crest' × *R.* 'Jalisco') Barium-yellow flowers with a small red blotch, open funnel-shaped and 7-lobed in loose trusses. Mid. AM 1971. H4.

'**C.I.S.**' (*R.* 'Fabia' × *R.* 'Loder's White') A vigorous, free-flowering, medium-sized shrub of upright habit with dark green leaves to 12.5cm long. Flowers in compact, globular trusses, widely funnel-shaped with wavy mar-gins, 6cm across; red in bud, opening orange-yellow, flushed and veined with red, speckled orange-brown in the throat. The initials stand for Claude I. Sersanous, once President of the American Rhododendron Society. Mid. (1952). AMT 1975. AM 1973. H4.

'**Cadis**' (*R.* 'Caroline' × *R. fortunei* subsp. *discolor*) A vig-orous, medium-sized shrub with handsome, dark green leaves, red-tinged when young. Flowers large, funnel-shaped with wavy edges, lilac-pink fading to nearly white on red stalks, borne in large, rounded trusses. Mid. (1958). H4.

'**Caerhays John**' See *R. cinnabarinum* 'Caerhays John'.

'Caerhays Lawrence' See *R. cinnabarinum* 'Caerhays Lawrence'.

'Caerhays Philip' See *R. cinnabarinum* 'Caerhays Philip'.

Calfort Group (*R. calophytum* × *R. fortunei*) A vigorous, large shrub with dark glossy green leaves raised by Captain Collingwood Ingram. Flowers white to pale pink, blotched with red, in very large trusses. Several cultivars have been named. Mid. AM 1932. H4. See also 'Bounty'.

'Carex White' (*R. oreodoxa* var. *fargesii* × *R. irroratum*) A tall, pyramidal, very free-flowering hybrid from Exbury. Flowers in a lax truss, bell-shaped, fragrant, pink-flushed in bud, opening white, freely spotted maroon within. Very early (March or April). (1932). H4.

Carita Group (*R. campylocarpum* × *R.* Naomi Group) A beautiful Exbury hybrid bearing well-filled trusses of large, bell-shaped flowers of the palest shade of lemon, with a small basal blotch of cerise within. Early. (1935). AM 1945. H4. **'Carita Charm'** Deep pink in bud, opening to cream flushed and overlaid deep peach-pink. **'Carita Cream'** Pink in bud, opening pale cream. **'Carita Golden Dream'** Flowers deep cream, flushed and shaded pink, becoming ivory-white at maturity. **'Carita Inchmery'** Pink with biscuit-yellow centre, red in bud, usually with 6 lobes. **'Carita Pink'** Flowers soft lilac-pink.

'Carmen' (*R. forrestii* Repens Group × *R. sanguineum* subsp. *didymum*) A dwarf or prostrate shrub carrying waxy, bell-shaped flowers of glistening dark crimson. Mid. (1935). AMT 1989. H4.

'Caroline Allbrook' (*R.* 'Purple Splendour' × *R. yakushimanum*) A vigorous, small shrub of compact, spreading habit with dark green leaves to 11cm long. Flowers widely funnel-shaped with very wavy margins, lavender-pink with a paler centre fading with age, borne in compact, globular trusses to 12.5cm across. Mid. (1975). ♀ 2002. AMT 1977. H4.

'Cary Ann' (*R.* 'Corona' × *R.* 'Vulcan') A compact, small shrub with dark green leaves and dense, rounded trusses of coral-pink flowers. Mid. (1962). H4.

'Caucasicum Pictum' A compact, medium-sized shrub, a hybrid of *R. caucasicum* with oblanceolate leaves to 12cm long. Flowers in dense trusses, wavy-edged, pink at first, later white, flushed pink, conspicuously flared with red-brown. Early to mid. (1853). H4.

'Cetewayo' (HH) One of the darkest-flowered of all rhododendrons, making a medium-sized shrub of compact habit. Flowers bell-shaped, 5cm across, blackish-purple with white anthers, borne in dense rounded trusses. Mid. (1883). ♀ 2002. AMT 1958. H4.

'Champagne' ('Tortoiseshell Champagne') (*R.* 'Goldsworth Orange' × *R. griersonianum*) Small shrub with rich yellow, funnel-shaped flowers, fading to pale yellow, tinged pink at the margins of the lobes. Mid to late. (1945). ♀ 2002. AMT 1967. H3–4.

'Charlotte de Rothschild' (Sir Frederick Moore Group) Similar to 'Sir Frederick Moore' but flowers clear pink, spotted chocolate. Mid. (1935). FCC 1992. AM 1958. H4.

'Cheer' (*R. catawbiense* hybrid × *R.* 'Cunningham's White') A dense, medium-sized shrub with glossy green leaves. Flowers shell-pink blotched with red, freely borne in conical trusses. (1958). H4.

'Chelsea Seventy' A sister seedling of 'Vintage Rose' which it resembles. Flowers salmon-pink flushed rose-pink from purple buds. (1972). H3.

'Chevalier Félix de Sauvage' (*R. caucasicum* × hardy hybrid) (HH) A very old hybrid and still among the best. A medium-sized to large shrub of dense habit with trusses of deep rose-pink, dark-blotched flowers, 6cm across, wavy at the margin. Mid. (1870). ♀ 2002. H4.

'Chikor' (*R. rupicola* var. *chryseum* × *R. ludlowii*) A choice dwarf shrub with small leaves and clusters of yellow flowers. Mid. Raised by E.H.M. and P.A. Cox at Glendoick, Perthshire. FCCT 1968. AM 1962. H4.

'China' (*R. fortunei* × *R. wightii*) A strong-growing plant with particularly handsome foliage and large, loose trusses of creamy-white flowers with a basal blotch of rose-carmine. Mid. Prone to powdery mildew. (1936). FCCT 1982. AMT 1948. AM 1940. H4.

'China A' Similar to 'China' but flowers pale yellow and smaller. (1946). H4.

'Chink' (*R. keiskei* × *R. trichocladum*) An early flowering, dwarf shrub raised at Windsor Great Park, bearing lax trusses of drooping, bell-shaped flowers of an unusual chartreuse-green, with occasional darker spotting on the lower lobe. Very early (March). (1961). AM 1961. H4.

'Chionoides' An extremely hardy hybrid of *R. ponticum* making a medium-sized compact shrub with narrowly elliptic, acute leaves to 10cm long. Flowers funnel-shaped, 4cm across, in rounded heads, pink-tinged in bud, opening pure white apart from a conspicuous patch of yellow spots on the upper lobe. Late. Raised by John Waterer, Sons & Crisp before 1865. H4.

'Choremia' A compact, medium-sized shrub with dark green leaves, silvery-grey beneath, and bell-shaped, waxy, red flowers. March or April. (1933). ♀ 2002. AM 1993. FCC 1948. H4.

'Christmas Cheer' (HH) An old *R. caucasicum* hybrid of rather dense, compact habit. Flowers pink in bud, fading to white. Normally flowering in March, occasionally February. The name refers to the one-time practice of forcing this plant for Christmas decoration; very occasionally in mild weather it is in flower by Christmas. (1908). AM 1990. H4.

'Chrysomanicum' A small, compact, spreading shrub with glossy dark green leaves and primrose-yellow flowers. Early. (1947). AM 1947. H3.

'Cilpinense' (*R. ciliatum* × *R. moupinense*) A beautiful, free-flowering, Bodnant hybrid forming a neat, rounded bush, up to 1m high, with glossy green, bristle-margined leaves. Flowers in loose trusses, shallowly bell-shaped, 6cm across, sparkling white, flushed pink, deeper in bud. Very early (March). (1927). ♀ 2002. FCC 1968. AM 1927. H3–4.

Cinnkeys Group (*R. cinnabarinum* × *R. keysii*) A choice hybrid of upright habit with oval, glossy green leaves. Flowers tubular, 3.5cm long, bright orange-red, shading to pale apricot on the lobes, produced in dense, drooping clusters. Mid. (1926). AM 1935. H4.

'Colonel Coen' A hybrid of *R. ponticum* making a vigorous, bushy shrub with glossy foliage. Flowers deep purple with dark spots, borne in domed trusses. Mid. (1958). H4.

Colonel Rogers Group (*R. falconeri* × *R. niveum*) A large shrub of open habit with large, deeply veined leaves, thinly tomentose beneath. Flowers in large trusses, pale lilac-pink, often fading to nearly white. Mid. (1917). H3–4.

'**Concessum**' (HH) Compact trusses of widely funnel-shaped, bright pink flowers with paler centres. Mid to late. (Before 1867). H4.

'**Concorde**' (*R.* 'The Master' × *R. yakushimanum*) Flowers white with a green blotch, 10cm across, with 7 wavy-edged, recurved lobes. Mid. (1966). H4.

'**Conroy**' See *R. cinnabarinum* 'Conroy'.

'**Cool Haven**' (*R.* 'Chaste' × *R. wardii* Litiense Group) A lovely hybrid named by us and raised at Embley Park, Hampshire in 1945. A compact, leafy shrub with dark green, ovate leaves up to 10cm by 5cm. Flowers in a well-filled, rounded truss, widely funnel-shaped, pale Dresden-yellow, flushed pink on the outside, with a broad ray of crimson spots, faintly fragrant. Mid. H3.

'**Coral Reef**' (*R.* 'Fabia' × *R.* 'Goldsworth Orange') A lovely hybrid raised at Wisley. Large-lobed, narrowly bell-shaped flowers, 8cm across, in a lax, open truss, salmon-pink tinged apricot in the throat and pink at the margin. Mid. AM 1954. H4.

'**Cornish Cross**' (*R. griffithianum* × *R. thomsonii*) A large shrub of rather open habit, producing lax trusses of narrowly bell-shaped, waxy flowers, mottled rose-pink, shaded darker on the outside. Early to mid. A lovely hybrid raised at Penjerrick in Cornwall, but prone to powdery mildew. (Before 1930). H3.

'**Cornubia**' (*R. arboreum* 'Blood Red' × *R.* 'Shilsonii') A rather sparsely-leaved, large shrub or small tree. The blood-red, bell-shaped flowers are produced in compact, rounded trusses. Very early (March and April). A magnificent Penjerrick hybrid only suitable for sheltered gardens. (Before 1911). AM 1912. H3.

'**Corona**' (HH) Forms a very charming, slow-growing, compact mound. Flowers funnel-shaped, 5cm across, rich coral-pink, in rather elongated trusses. Mid. (Before 1911). AM 1911. H4.

'**Corry Koster**' (HH) A strong-growing hybrid of uncertain origin. Perfectly formed, conical trusses of frilly-edged, widely funnel-shaped flowers, are rich pink in bud opening pink, paling to white at the margin and with a ray of brownish-crimson spots. Mid. (1909). H4.

'**Cosmopolitan**' (*R.* 'Cunningham's White' × *R.* 'Vesuvius') A medium-sized shrub of dense, spreading habit with dark glossy green leaves. Flowers pale pink, flared with deep red, in rounded trusses. Mid. (1957). H3.

'**Countess of Athlone**' (*R.* 'Catawbiense Grandiflorum' × *R.* 'Geoffrey Millais') (HH) An attractive hybrid of compact growth, well furnished with glossy, olive-green leaves. Flowers widely funnel-shaped, wavy-edged, purple in bud, opening mauve with greenish-yellow markings at base, in conical trusses. Mid. (1923). H4.

'**Countess of Derby**' (*R.* 'Cynthia' × *R.* 'Pink Pearl') (HH) A large shrub bearing perfectly formed, conical trusses of large, widely funnel-shaped flowers, striking pink in bud, opening pink, paling slightly on the lobes and marked with reddish-brown spots and streaks within. Mid. (1913). AM 1930. H4.

†'**Countess of Haddington**' (*R. ciliatum* × *R. dalhousiae*) A beautiful but tender hybrid of rather straggling habit. Leaves usually 5 in a terminal cluster, glaucous-green

and gland-dotted beneath. Flowers richly fragrant, borne in umbels of 2–4, trumpet-shaped, white, flushed pale rose. Early. A charming conservatory shrub. (1862). ♀ 2002. FCC 1862. H1.

'**Cowslip**' (*R. wardii* × *R. williamsianum*) A small shrub of neat, rounded habit. Flowers bell-shaped, 5–6cm across, cream or pale primrose with a pale pink flush when young, in loose trusses. Mid. (1937). AM 1937. H4.

'**Crane**' (*R. keiskei* 'Yaku Fairy' × *R. racemosum* 'White Lace') A small shrub, similar to 'Ginny Gee', forming a dense mound, but with profuse, creamy-white flowers. Early. ♀ 2002. H4.

'**Creamy Chiffon**' (*R. campylocarpum* hybrid) A compact, small shrub bearing profusions of long-lasting, double, creamy-white flowers, from salmon-orange buds. Mid. H4.

'**Creeping Jenny**' ('Jenny') (Elizabeth Group) A prostrate shrub raised at Bodnant, carrying large, deep red, bell-shaped flowers. Mid. (1939). H4.

'**Crest**' (Hawk Group) A magnificent Exbury hybrid with reddish-purple shoots and dark glossy green leaves, up to 10cm long. Large trusses of bell-shaped, primrose-yellow flowers, with a slight darkening in the throat, open from orange buds. Each flower is 10cm across. Mid. (1953). ♀ 2002. FCC 1953. H3.

'**Crete**' (*R. smirnowii* × *R. yakushimanum*) A small, mound-forming shrub of spreading habit. Glossy dark green leaves, silvery-hairy above when young, covered with a thick, beige indumentum beneath. Flowers deep pink in bud, opening to pale rose-purple, fading to white. May. (1982). H4.

'**Cunningham's White**' (*R. caucasicum* × white-flowered *R. ponticum*) An old hybrid, once commonly planted, making a compact, medium-sized shrub with dark green leaves to 10cm long. Flowers funnel-shaped, pale mauve fading to white, spotted with yellow, brown and purple, in open trusses. Mid. Tolerates slightly alkaline soil and is excellent for shelter. H4.

'**Curlew**' (*R. fletcherianum* 'Yellow Bunting' × *R. ludlowii*) A most attractive, dwarf, spreading shrub with small, dark green, obovate leaves and profuse, widely funnel-shaped flowers, 5cm across, pale yellow, marked with greenish-brown. Mid. Best in a cool position. Raised by Peter Cox. (1970). ♀ 2002. FCCT 1986. AMT 1981. FCC 1969. H4.

'**Cutie**' A hybrid of *R. calostrotum* making a small, compact shrub, the leaves to 2.5cm long with a slight tan indumentum. Small, lilac-pink flowers are profusely borne. Mid. (1959). H4.

'**Cynthia**' (*R. catawbiense* × *R. griffithianum*) (HH) One of the best rhododendrons for general planting, thriving in a great variety of situations. A large, vigorous, dome-shaped bush bearing magnificent conical trusses of widely funnel-shaped, rose-crimson flowers, each with a narrow ray of blackish-crimson markings within. Mid. Raised by Messrs Standish and Noble of Bagshot, Surrey before 1870. ♀ 2002. H4.

'**Dairymaid**' A hybrid of *R. campylocarpum*. A dense, slow-growing shrub bearing compact trusses of pale creamy-yellow flowers streaked and spotted with red inside. Mid. (1930). AMT 1934. H4.

Damaris Group (*R. campylocarpum* × *R.* 'Dr Stocker') A broadly dome-shaped bush with oval leaves. Flowers in a lax truss, widely bell-shaped, glossy pale canary-yellow, shading to ivory at the margin. Early to mid. (1926). H3.

'Damozel' A widespreading hybrid of *R. griersonianum*. Dome-shaped trusses of funnel-shaped, ruby-red flowers up to 8cm across, with darker spots within. Mid. (1936). AM 1948. H3–4.

'David' (*R.* 'Hugh Koster' × *R. neriiflorum*) Compact, rounded trusses of funnel-shaped, frilly-margined, deep blood-red flowers, slightly spotted within. Mid. (1939). ♀ 2002. AMT 1957. FCC 1939. H4.

'Day Dream' (*R. griersonianum* × *R.* 'Lady Bessborough') A beautiful Exbury hybrid of open, spreading habit with large, loose trusses of broadly funnel-shaped flowers, rich crimson in bud, opening to pink, flushed crimson and fading to creamy-white, flushed pale pink on tube. Mid. (1936). AM 1940. H3.

'Diana Colville' A vigorous and free-flowering, large shrub of compact habit with dark matt green leaves to 5cm long. Flowers 5cm across, widely funnel-shaped with wavy edges, pale lilac-purple spotted with red and with a yellow throat are borne in dome-shaped trusses 10cm across. A seedling of *R. yunnanense* raised by Lt Col N.R. Colville in 1949. Mid. FCCT 1972. AMT 1968. H4.

'Diana Pearson' (*R.* 'Glamour' × *R. yakushimanum*) A vigorous and compact, small shrub of spreading habit bearing dense, globular trusses, to 14cm across, of funnel-shaped, very pale pink flowers, red-spotted inside. Mid. AMT 1980. AM 1978. H4.

'Doc' (*R.* 'Corona' × *R. yakushimanum*) A small, compact, free-flowering shrub with dull green leaves to 8cm long. Flowers in globular trusses, funnel-shaped, 4cm across, with wavy margins, rose-pink with deeper edges and spots, fading to creamy-white. Mid. (1972). H4.

'Doctor Stocker' (*R. caucasicum* × *R. griffithianum*) (HH) A dome-shaped bush, broader than high, bearing loose trusses of large, widely bell-shaped flowers, milk-white, tinged cream and delicately marked brown-crimson. Early to mid. (1900). AM 1900. H3.

'Doncaster' (HH) A very popular, distinct and easily recognised hybrid of *R. arboreum*. A small, broadly dome-shaped shrub with somewhat glossy, very dark green, leathery leaves, held very stiffly on the shoots. Flowers in dense trusses, funnel-shaped, brilliant crimson-scarlet, with a ray of black markings within. Mid. Prone to bud blast. Raised by Anthony Waterer at Knap Hill. H4.

'Dopey' ([*R. facetum* hybrid × *R.* Fabia Group] × [*R. yakushimanum* × *R.* 'Fabia Tangerine']) A small to medium-sized shrub of compact habit. Flowers bell-shaped, wavy-edged, bright orange-red, paler towards the margin, spotted with orange-brown, freely borne in globular trusses. Mid. (1971). ♀ 2002. FCCT 1979. AMT 1977. H4.

'Dora Amateis' (*R. minus* Carolinianum Group × *R. ciliatum*) A vigorous, compact, mound-forming shrub with ovate-lanceolate, dark dull green leaves, to 7cm long, scaly on both sides. Flowers freely produced in open clusters, funnel-shaped, pale pink in bud, opening white, faintly spotted with yellow, 5cm across. Early. (1955). ♀ 2002. FCCT 1981. AMT 1976. H4.

'Dormouse' (*R.* 'Dawn's Delight' × *R. williamsianum*) A small to medium-sized, compact, dome-shaped bush

with loose clusters of bell-shaped, delicate pink flowers amid kidney-shaped leaves, which are copper-coloured when young. Mid. (1936). H4.

'Dreamland' A compact, small shrub, raised by Waterer's and with complicated parentage involving *R. yakushimanum*, *R.* Fabia Group and *R. fortunei* subsp. *discolor*. Young foliage silvery, becoming dark green. Flowers pale pink with darker edges. Mid. ♀ 2002. H4.

'Dusky Maid' (*R. fortunei* subsp. *discolor* × *R.* 'Moser's Maroon') A tall, erect bush of robust habit. Tight rounded trusses of very attractive, dark, dusky-red flowers. Mid to late. (1936). H4.

'Dusty Miller' (*R. yakushimanum* hybrid) A compact and rather slow-growing, dwarf shrub, the leaves with a persistent silvery-white indumentum. Flowers pale pink flushed red, fading to cream. Mid. (1975). H4.

'Earl of Athlone' (*R.* 'Queen Wilhelmina' × *R.* 'Stanley Davies') A splendid hybrid from the same pod as 'Britannia', but less hardy. Compact trusses of bell-shaped glowing, deep blood-red flowers. Early to mid. FCCT 1933. H3.

'Earl of Donoughmore' A hybrid of *R. griersonianum* produced by M. Koster and Sons in 1953. Flowers bright red with an orange glow. Mid. H4.

'Egret' (*R. racemosum* 'White Lace' × *R. campylogynum*, white form) A compact and free-flowering, dwarf shrub of neat habit with dark glossy green leaves to 2.5cm long. Flowers 2cm across, widely funnel-shaped, white tinged green, in open trusses 7cm across. Mid. (1982). ♀ 2002. AMT 1987. AM 1982. H4.

'Eider' (*R. minus* Carolinianum Group 'Album' × *R. leucaspis*) A vigorous and compact, free-flowering shrub of spreading habit, the leaves to 6cm long. Flowers widely funnel-shaped, 5cm wide, white, in compact globular trusses to 7cm across. Early to mid. (1979). AMT 1981. H4.

'El Camino' (*R.* 'Anna' × *R.* 'Marinus Koster') A vigorous, large shrub with dark green leaves and very large, wavy-edged, glowing red flowers with darker spots. Mid. (1976). H4.

'Eleanore' (*R. augustinii* × *R. rubiginosum* Desquamatum Group) A large, pretty shrub with pale mauve flowers nearly 7.5cm across. Early to mid. Suitable for woodland planting. (1937). AM 1943. H3.

'Electra' See *R. augustinii* 'Electra' under species.

'Elisabeth Hobbie' (*R.* 'Essex Scarlet' × *R. forrestii* Repens Group) A dwarf shrub with loose umbels of 6–10 translucent, scarlet-red, bell-shaped flowers. Early. (1945). ♀ 2002. AMT 1986. H4.

Elizabeth Group (*R. forrestii* Repens Group × *R. griersonianum*) A dwarf or small, spreading shrub raised at Bodnant. Flowers trumpet-shaped, 7.5cm across, rich dark red, in clusters of 5–6. Early. Prone to powdery mildew. (1939). FCC 1943. AM 1939. H4. See also 'Creeping Jenny'.

'Elizabeth Lockhart' A small, mound-forming shrub with oval to oblong, deep bronze purple leaves. Loose clusters of bell-shaped, deep red flowers. Early. A sport of 'Humming Bird'. (1965). H4.

'Elizabeth Red Foliage' A small, spreading shrub with red young foliage maturing to deep olive-green. Flowers funnel-campanulate, to 9cm across, vivid red from deeper buds, the lobes speckled with deep red. Probably derived from a plant of Elizabeth Group. Early, and often again in autumn. (Before 1960). H4.

'Emasculum' (*R. ciliatum* × *R. dauricum*) A medium-sized shrub of upright habit with elliptic leaves up to 3cm long, slightly glossy above and scaly on both sides. Flowers in pairs or singly, mauve-pink in bud, opening very pale lilac-pink, broadly funnel-shaped, 4cm across. The stamens are present but are much reduced in size, not reaching above the ovary and bearing sterile anthers. Early. AM 1976. H4.

'Emerald Isle' (*R.* 'Idealist' × *R.* 'Naomi') An unusual hybrid with bell-shaped flowers of chartreuse-green. Mid. (1956). AM 1956. H4.

'Ernest Inman' (*R.* 'Purple Splendour' × *R. yakushimanum*) A dwarf shrub with dark green, slightly glossy leaves to 11cm long. Flowers funnel-shaped, 7cm across, light purple fading to silvery-white at the base, spotted with deep orange-yellow, borne in compact, globular trusses. Mid. (1963). AMT 1979. H4.

'Ethel' (*R.* 'F.C. Puddle' × *R. forrestii* Repens Group) A dwarf Bodnant hybrid of low, spreading habit. Large, trumpet-shaped flowers of crimson-scarlet. Early. (1940). FCC 1940. H3.

'Everestianum' A very old hybrid of *R. catawbiense* making a medium-sized, dense bush. Flowers widely funnel-shaped with frilly lobes, pale lilac with a broad band of brown or reddish spots. Mid. (Before 1853). H4.

Exburiense Group (*R. kyawii* × *R. sanguineum* var. *didymum*) A medium-sized, spreading shrub with dark green leaves and bell-shaped, dark waxy-red flowers. Late. (1937). H4.

'Exbury Angelo' See under 'Angelo'.

'Exbury Isabella' (*R. auriculatum* × *R. griffithianum*) A large shrub or small tree with large trusses of enormous, fragrant, trumpet-shaped, white flowers. Late. (1948). H3.

'Exbury Lady Chamberlain' Medium-sized shrub with flowers yellow, overlaid salmon-orange. Mid. FCC 1931. H3.

'Fabia' (*R. dichroanthum* × *R. griersonianum*) A beautiful, widely dome-shaped bush bearing loose, flat trusses of funnel-shaped flowers, scarlet shaded orange in the tube and freely speckled with pale brown markings. Mid. Raised at Bodnant. (1934). ♀ 2002. FCC 1989. AM 1934. H3.

'Fabia Tangerine' Vermilion flowers shaded geranium-red around the mouth and poppy-red in the throat. As in Fabia, the calyx is large and petaloid with an incised margin. Mid. AM 1940. H3.

'Fabia Waterer' Salmon-pink, with a tint of orange. Compact habit. A splendid selection. Late. H3.

'Faggetter's Favourite' A hybrid of *R. fortunei* raised by W.C. Slocock of Woking. A tall grower with fine foliage and producing large trusses of sweetly scented, shell-pink flowers with white shading. Mid. (1933). ♀ 2002. AMT 1955. AM 1933. H4.

'Fantastica' (*R. yakushimanum* 'Koichiro Wada' × *R.* 'Mars') A small, spreading and very hardy shrub of compact habit with dark green leaves, woolly beneath. Striking wavy-edged flowers are pale pink, shading to white in the centre, with a conspicuous deep pink margin, borne in large trusses. Mid to late. (1985). ♀ 2002. H4.

'Fastuosum Flore Pleno' (*R. catawbiense* × *R. ponticum*) (HH) A very hardy hybrid forming a large, dome-shaped bush. Flowers in a lax truss, funnel-shaped with wavy margins, rich mauve with a ray of brown-crimson markings within, filaments unevenly petaloid. Mid. Raised at Ghent, Belgium some time before 1846. ♀ 2002. H4.

'Fire Bird' (*R. griersonianum* × *R.* 'Norman Shaw') A tall, vigorous shrub producing large trusses of glowing salmon-red flowers with deeper orange-red eyes. The bright green young leaves are strikingly set against long crimson bracts. Mid. (1938). H3–4.

'Fireball' (*R.* 'Ascot Brilliant' × *R. barbatum*) An early flowering shrub requiring woodland conditions. Flowers bell-shaped with frilly margins, glowing carmine-scarlet, in rounded trusses. March. Raised by Richard Gill and Sons of Penryn, Cornwall, before 1925. AM 1925. H3–4.

'Fireman Jeff' (*R.* 'Jean Marie de Montague' × *R.* 'Grosclaude') A small shrub with dark green leaves and dense trusses of deep blood-red flowers. Mid. (1977). H4.

'Fittianum' (*R. fittianum* Balf. f.) A small to medium-sized shrub, sometimes considered to be a form of *R. dauricum*, but the 2.5cm wide, mauve-pink flowers not opening until mid-April. A natural hybrid of *R. racemosum* raised in 1913 at Werrington Park from Forrest 10278 and named after the then Head Gardener. H4.

'Fittra' (*R.* 'Fittianum' × *R. racemosum*) A very free-flowering, dwarf, compact shrub, raised in our nurseries. The vivid, deep rose-pink flowers are borne in dense trusses of up to 30 blooms, often completely covering the plant. Early to mid. (1938). AM 1949. H4.

Flavum Group See Volker Group.

Fortune Group (*R. falconeri* × *R. sinogrande*) A splendid hybrid raised at Exbury and, like its parents, needing a sheltered woodland situation. A large, stoutly branched shrub, the dark glossy green, deeply veined leaves with a brown indumentum beneath. Flowers pale yellow blotched with deep red, in huge trusses. Early to mid. FCC 1938. H3.

†**'Fragrantissimum'** (*R. edgeworthii* × *R. formosum*) A beautiful hybrid of medium size with attractive, dark green, corrugated leaves, paler beneath. Flowers appearing in terminal umbels of 4, extremely fragrant, widely funnel-shaped, up to 7.5cm long, white, flushed rose without and greenish within at base, stamens with brown anthers. Early. Requires conservatory treatment except in the mildest areas. (1868). ♀ 2002. FCC 1868. H2–3.

'Francis Hanger' (*R. dichroanthum* × *R.* 'Isabella') Flowers with frilly margins, chrome-yellow, edged with a delicate tinge of pale rose. Mid. Raised at Exbury and named after the late Curator of the RHS Gardens, Wisley. (1942). AM 1950. H4.

'Frank Baum' (*R.* 'Jasper' × *R.* 'Mars') A small shrub with red-stalked leaves and coral-watermelon flowers in dense, rounded trusses. Late. (1968). H4.

'Frank Galsworthy' A medium-sized shrub with narrow, slightly twisted leaves. Flowers funnel-shaped, deep purple with a large, yellow and white blotch and white anthers, in dense, rounded trusses. Late. ♀ 2002. AMT 1960. H4.

'Fred Peste' ([*R.* 'Corona' × *R. yakushimanum*] × *R. haematodes*) A low-growing, rounded shrub, to about 1m tall, producing dark green leaves, to 9.5cm long, with a dense orange-yellow indumentum beneath. Flowers broadly funnel-campanulate, 7.5cm across, rich red with darker throat and spots. Mid. (1971). H4.

'Fred Rose' (*R.* 'Gladys Swaythling' × *R. lacteum*) A medium-sized shrub with dark matt green leaves to 12.5cm long. Flowers 6cm diameter, widely bell-shaped and wavy margined, lemon-yellow spotted red in the throat, in compact, dome-shaped trusses, 12.5cm across. Mid. (1962). H4.

'Fred Wynniatt' A large shrub with large, maize-yellow flowers flushed with pink, in flat-topped trusses. Mid. FCC 1980. AM 1963. H4.

Fulgarb Group (*R. arboreum* 'Blood Red' × *R. fulgens*) A large shrub or tree bearing small, compact trusses of rich crimson flowers. Very early (February). (Before 1930). AM 1937. H3.

'Furnivall's Daughter' Similar to 'Mrs Furnivall' but stronger-growing, with larger leaves and flowers, which are widely funnel-shaped, light rose-pink with a bold splash of dark markings. Mid to late. (1957). ♀ 2002. FCCT 1961. AMT 1958. H4.

'Fusilier' (*R. elliottii* × *R. griersonianum*) A magnificent Exbury hybrid; a dense bush furnished with long, narrow leaves, brown-tomentose beneath. Large trusses of brilliant red, funnel-shaped flowers, 8cm across, darker spotted on all lobes. Mid. (1938). FCC 1942. AM 1938. H3–4.

'Gartendirektor Glocker' (*R.* 'Doncaster' × *R. williamsianum*) A compact, small shrub of domed habit with rounded, deep blue-green leaves, bronze when young. Deep rose-red, funnel-shaped flowers are borne in loose trusses. Mid. (1952). H4.

'Gartendirektor Rieger' (*R.* 'Adriaan Koster' × *R. williamsianum*) A small shrub of compact, spreading habit with rounded, dark green leaves on red-purple stalks. Widely bell-shaped flowers, 10cm across, are creamy-white, speckled with red spots on the upper lobe, profusely borne from blush-pink buds. Mid. ♀ 2002. H4.

'General Eisenhower' A hybrid of *R. griffithianum* bearing large trusses of widely funnel-shaped, deep carmine flowers with frilly lobes darker spotted within. Mid. (1946). H4.

'General Sir John du Cane' (*R. fortunei* subsp. *discolor* × *R. thomsonii*) A very fine hybrid producing large, lax trusses of fragrant, widely funnel-shaped flowers, rose-madder, fading to pink, with a dark crimson basal flash within. Mid. (1933). H4.

'George Hardy' A tall, fast-growing shrub, a hybrid of *R. griffithianum*. Leaves dark glossy green, to 15cm long. Flowers in large, conical trusses, bright rose in bud, opening to glistening, waxy-white with crimson markings, broadly bell-shaped, to 10cm across, fragrant. Mid. (Before 1922). H4.

'George Johnstone' A medium-sized shrub with aromatic leaves and loose trusses of bright orange, bell-shaped flowers. Early to mid. AM 1967. H3–4.

'Geraldii' See *R.* × *geraldii* under species.

'Germania' (*R.* 'Antoon von Welie' × *R.* 'Catherine van Tol') A small shrub with glossy dark green leaves. Flowers deep pink in large upright trusses. Mid. H4.

'Ginny Gee' (*R. keiskei* 'Yaku Fairy' × *R. racemosum*) An excellent, dwarf shrub of compact, spreading habit with

profuse, widely funnel-shaped, pale pink flowers, deeper in bud and fading to nearly white edged pink. Early to mid. (1979). ♀ 2002. H4.

'Golden Bee' (*R. keiskei* 'Yaku Fairy' × *R. mekongense* var. *melinanthum*) A dwarf, semi-evergreen shrub of compact habit bearing small, funnel-shaped, bright yellow flowers in open trusses. Early to mid. (1982). H4.

'Golden Gate' A seedling of *R. dichroanthum* subsp. *scyphocalyx* making a small shrub of compact habit. Small, reddish-pink flowers, with an orange-yellow centre, are borne in trusses of 5–6. Mid. H4.

'Golden Horn' (*R. dichroanthum* × *R. elliottii*) A brilliantly coloured, small, Exbury hybrid. Flowers drooping, bell-shaped, salmon-orange, freely speckled with brownish markings within; calyx large, double, same colour as corolla. Mid. (1939). AM 1945. H3–4.

'Golden Horn Persimmon' See *R.* 'Persimmon'.

'Golden Orfe' (Comely Group) (*R. cinnabarinum* Concatenans Group × *R.* Lady Chamberlain Group) A Tower Court hybrid resembling *R. cinnabarinum*. Flowers 5cm long, orange-yellow. (Before 1943). AM 1964. H4.

'Golden Oriole' (*R. moupinense* × *R. sulfureum*) A small shrub of upright habit with attractive, red young shoots. Leaves ovate or obovate, to 5cm long, glaucous beneath with long bristles on the margins. Flowers usually in 2s or 3s, funnel-shaped, primrose-yellow with 2 patches of orange spots inside. When newly opened they contrast effectively with the bright pink bud scales densely clustered at their bases. Early. AM 1947. H3.

'Golden Oriole Talavera' Similar to 'Golden Oriole' but flowers clear pale yellow. FCC 1963. AM 1947. H3.

'Golden Star' (*R. fortunei* × *R. wardii*) A vigorous, medium-sized to large shrub with handsome, dark glossy green leaves. Flowers pale yellow flushed with pink in bud, freely borne. Mid. (1966). H4.

'Golden Torch' (*R.* 'Bambi' × [*R.* 'Grosclaude' × *R. griersonianum*]) A small, compact shrub with leaves to 6cm long. Flowers bell-shaped, 5cm across, salmon-pink in bud, opening pale yellow, in compact trusses. The parentage is doubtful. Mid. (1972). ♀ 2002. AMT 1984. H4.

'Golden Wedding' (*R.* 'Mrs Lammot Copeland' × *R. yakushimanum*) A compact, dwarf shrub, to about 80cm tall, with elliptic leaves to 12cm long. Flowers open funnel-shaped, 7cm across, chrome-yellow with a deeper flush, from reddish-orange buds. Mid. (1969). H4.

'Goldflimmer' A slow-growing, small shrub, the dark green leaves with an irregular, slender streak of yellow. Flowers lilac, marked with brownish-yellow spots. Probably a sport of a *R. ponticum* hybrid. Mid to late. (1983). H4.

'Goldfort' (*R. fortunei* × *R.* 'Goldsworth Yellow') Flowers pink in bud, opening creamy-yellow, tinted with apricot-pink. Mid. (1937). H4.

'Goldkrone' ([*R. wardii* × *R.* 'Alice Street'] × *R.* 'Hachmann's Manna') A small shrub making a compact mound. Large trusses of golden-yellow, funnel-shaped flowers are profusely borne over a long period. One of the best small yellows. Mid. (1983). ♀ 2002. H4.

'Goldstrike' (*R. oreotrephes* × *R.* Royal Flush Group) A medium-sized shrub of upright habit, with dark green leaves. Flowers yellow, nodding, borne in open terminal clusters. Mid. (1962). H4.

'Goldsworth Orange' (*R. dichroanthum* × *R. fortunei* subsp. *discolor*) A low, spreading bush bearing large trusses of pale orange flowers, tinged with apricot-pink. Late. (1938). AMT 1959. H4.

'Goldsworth Pink' A hardy shrub raised from *R. griffithianum* crossed with an unnamed garden hybrid. Lax, conical trusses of widely funnel-shaped flowers are deep rose in bud, opening to mottled rose-pink and fading to white. Mid. (1933). FCCT 1987. AMT 1958. H4.

'Goldsworth Yellow' (*R. campylocarpum* × *R. caucasicum*) A leafy, dome-shaped bush, broader than high and very hardy. Flowers in a well-filled, rounded truss, funnel-shaped, apricot-pink in bud, opening primrose-yellow, with a large ray of warm brown markings. Mid. Usually flowering at bluebell time. Raised by W.C. Slocock at Goldsworth Nurseries, Woking. (1925). AM 1925. H4.

'Gomer Waterer' (HH) A very beautiful, medium-sized bush of dense habit, a hybrid of *R. catawbiense*. Leaves dark green, large and leathery, oval or oblong-obovate, to 13cm long, with deflexed margins. The buds in the leaf axils are reddish and rather conspicuous. Flowers, 8cm across, fragrant, in a large, dense, rounded truss, funnel-shaped but deeply divided, white, flushed pale mauve towards the edges, with a mustard-coloured basal blotch. Mid to late. (Before 1900). ♀ 2002. AM 1906. H4.

'Goosander' (*R. ludlowii* × *R. lutescens*) A vigorous and compact, free-flowering, dwarf shrub with dark green leaves to 3cm long, bronze when young. Flowers 4cm across, open funnel-shaped, pale yellow flushed green and spotted red, in compact, dome-shaped trusses up to 6cm across. Early to mid. AMT 1981. H3.

'Grace Seabrook' (*R. 'Jean Marie de Montague' × R. strigillosum*) A vigorous, tough, medium-sized shrub with dark green, pointed leaves. Flowers deep red, with paler margins, in compact, broadly conical trusses. Early to mid. (1965). H4.

'Grayswood Pink' (*R. venator* × *R. williamsianum*) A small, dense bush with obovate-oblong, dark glossy green leaves to 7.5cm long. Flowers narrowly bell-shaped, rose-pink, darker spotted within. Mid. (1949). H4.

'Grenadier' (*R. elliottii* × *R. 'Moser's Maroon'*) An Exbury hybrid. A tall shrub of compact growth bearing magnificent trusses of deep blood-red flowers. Mid to late. (1939). FCC 1943. H3.

'Gristede' A compact, dwarf shrub. A hybrid of *R. impeditum*, resembling 'Blue Diamond', with glossy green leaves and clusters of funnel-shaped, violet-blue flowers. Early to mid. (1977). ♀ 2002. H4.

'Grosclaude' (*R. facetum* × *R. haematodes*) An Exbury hybrid of neat, compact habit, producing lax trusses of bell-shaped, waxen, blood-red flowers, darker spotted within, with wavy margins; calyx petaloid. Mid. (1941). AM 1945. H4.

'Grumpy' (*R. yakushimanum* × unknown hybrid) Small shrub of very compact, spreading habit. Leaves dark dull green to 8cm long. Flowers in rounded trusses, funnel-shaped, 5cm across, cream, tinged pale pink at margins, spotted with orange-yellow, from orange buds. (1971). AMT 1979. H4.

'Gwillt-King' (*R. griersonianum* × *R. arboreum* subsp. *zeylanicum*) A vigorous and attractive shrub for woodland planting. Flowers bell-shaped, rich Turkey-red. Mid. (1938). AM 1952. H2–3.

'Hachmann's Marlis' (*R. 'Mars' × R. yakushimanum 'Koichiro Wada'*) A low, spreading shrub, the leaves to 13.5cm long, thinly white-tomentose when young, the indumentum becoming grey-white beneath. Flowers broadly funnel-shaped, to 7.5cm across, white, edged and lined with deep purple-pink, the upper lobe marked with red. Mid. (1970). ♀ 2002. H4.

'Hachmann's Polaris' (*R. yakushimanum* 'Koichiro Wada' × *R. 'Omega'*) A small shrub making a compact mound with hairy leaves. Flowers, 6cm across, are light rhodamine-pink marked with green, deeper at the margin, carmine-red in bud. Mid. (1963). ♀ 2002. H4.

'Halcyone' (*R. 'Lady Bessborough' × R. souliei*) A lovely hybrid bearing rather lax, flat-topped trusses of delicate pink, wide open flowers with a basal flash of crimson spots. Mid. (1940). AM 1994. H4.

'Halfdan Lem' (*R. 'Jean Marie de Montague' × red Loderi*) A vigorous, medium-sized shrub with dark green somewhat twisted leaves. Bright red flowers are borne in large trusses. Mid. (1974). H4.

'Hallelujah' (*R. 'Kimberley' × R. 'Jean Marie de Montague'*) A small shrub with thick, dark green leaves bent downwards from the middle. Rose-red flowers are borne in large, dense trusses. Mid. (1976). H4.

'Hampshire Belle' A distinct, small, upright and compact shrub with linear-oblong to lanceolate leaves, up to 8cm by 1cm. Dense, hemispherical trusses of about 18 funnel-shaped flowers, 5cm across, pink in bud, opening lilac-pink fading to white in the centre, heavily blotched with red. Mid. A seedling found in about 1970 in the Sir Harold Hillier Gardens and Arboretum by Head Gardener E.W. (Bill) George and probably a hybrid of *R. ponticum*. H4.

'Harkwood Premier' (*R. 'Bud Flanagan' × R. yakushimanum*) A compact, low-growing shrub, the leaves to 15cm long with an orange-yellow indumentum below. Flowers open bell-shaped, 8.5cm across, with 5 wavy lobes, lilac fading to white, with a dark red blotch, from cerise buds. Mid. (1975). H4.

'Harvest Moon' (*R. campylocarpum* hybrid × *R. 'Mrs Lindsay Smith'*) A lovely hybrid with bell-shaped, creamy-white flowers marked with a broad ray of carmine spots within. Mid. (1938). AMT 1948. H4.

Hawk Group (*R. 'Lady Bessborough' × R. wardii*) A magnificent Exbury hybrid with oblong, glossy green leaves, to 14cm long, on long, slender, purplish petioles. Bears loose, flat-topped trusses of large, sulphur-yellow, funnel-shaped flowers marked with red at the base, apricot in bud. Mid. (1940). AM 1949. H3. See also 'Crest' and 'Jervis Bay'.

'Helene Schiffner' A small, dense, rounded bush of German origin, bearing rounded trusses of widely funnel-shaped flowers, mauve in bud, opening to pure white, occasionally with an inconspicuous ray of greenish markings within. Mid. A hybrid of *R. arboreum*. (1893). ♀ 2002. FCC 1893. H4.

'High Summer' (*R. 'Inamorata' × R. 'Mrs J.G. Millais'*) A small shrub raised by E.G. Millais, the pale creamy-yellow flowers slightly deeper in the centre, borne in trusses of 8–10. Mid. (1963). AMT 1989. H4.

'Honey Bee' (*R. hanceanum* × *R. ludlowii*) A slow-growing dwarf shrub of compact habit with bronze young growths and pale yellow flowers. Mid. H4.

'Hoppy' (*R.* 'Doncaster' × *R. yakushimanum*) selfed. A vigorous, compact, free-flowering, small shrub with dark green leaves to 8cm long. Flowers, 5cm across, funnel-shaped with frilled edges, pale lilac fading to white spotted with yellow, in compact, globular trusses up to 18cm across. Mid. (1972). AMT 1977. H4.

'Horizon Monarch' (*R.* 'Nancy Evans' × *R.* 'Point Defiance') A medium-sized shrub with large, leathery, dark green leaves. Flowers in very large, upright trusses of 15 or more, red in bud opening to a mellow, warm yellow with small, vivid red flares. Raised from a cross made by Ned Brockenbrough in Seattle. ♀ 2002. H3–4.

'Hotei' (*R.* 'Goldsworth Orange' × [*R. souliei* × *R. wardii*]) A compact, medium-sized shrub with narrow, dark green leaves to 12cm long. Deep yellow, widely bell-shaped flowers. Mid. The parent of many new hybrids. (1964). ♀ 2002. AM 1974. H4.

'Hugh Koster' (*R.* 'Doncaster' hybrid × *R.* 'George Hardy') (HH) A sturdy, leafy bush with stiff, erect branches. Flowers in a well-formed truss, funnel-shaped, glowing crimson-scarlet with black markings within. Mid. A fine, hardy hybrid resembling 'Doncaster', but foliage slightly wavy at the margins and flowers lighter in colour. (1915). AMT 1933. H4.

'Humming Bird' (*R. haematodes* × *R. williamsianum*) A small, compact, dome-shaped bush of distinctive appearance. Flowers half nodding, widely bell-shaped, carmine, shaded glowing scarlet inside the tube. Early. (1933). H3.

'Hydon Dawn' (*R.* 'Springbok' × *R. yakushimanum*) A compact, dwarf shrub with dark, slightly glossy green leaves, to 10cm long, with a cream indumentum when young. Flowers 5cm across, light pink, funnel-shaped with wavy, paler margins and reddish-brown spots, borne in compact, globular trusses 12.5cm across. Mid. (1969). ♀ 2002. FCCT 1987. AMT 1986. AM 1978. H4.

'Hydon Hunter' (*R.* 'Springbok' × *R. yakushimanum*) A vigorous and compact, small shrub of upright habit with dark, slightly glossy green leaves to 10cm long. Flowers funnel-shaped, 5.5cm across, in compact dome-shaped trusses 12cm across, white flushed pale pink and spotted with yellow. Mid. (1972). ♀ 2002. FCCT 1979. AM 1976. H4.

'Idealist' (*R.* 'Naomi' × *R. wardii*) A very floriferous, large shrub or small tree, striking when in flower. Leaves broadly elliptic, bright green above, to 9cm long, on purple petioles. Large, compact, clustered trusses of flowers appear to weigh down the branches. They are widely funnel-shaped, to 8cm across, with 5–7 lobes, coral-pink in bud, opening to pale creamy-yellow with lines of reddish markings at the base. Early to mid. (1941). AM 1945. H3.

'Ilam Cream' (*R.* Loderi Group hybrid) A large shrub raised in New Zealand, producing lax trusses of fragrant, funnel-shaped, creamy-yellow flowers, to 9cm across, from pink buds. Mid. (1981). H3.

'Ilam Violet' (*R. augustinii* 'Electra' × *R. russatum*) A very free-flowering, small shrub of upright habit, with dark green leaves, to 4cm long, reddish when young. Flowers 4cm across, widely funnel-shaped with wavy margins, deep violet blue, in globular trusses 6.5cm across. Early to mid. (1947). AMT 1983. H4.

Impeanum Group (*R. hanceanum* × *R. fastigiatum*) A dwarf, spreading shrub with small, crowded leaves. Smothered with small clusters of saucer-shaped flowers of a striking cobalt-violet. Mid. Excellent for a rock or heather garden. Cross made at Kew in 1915. FCC 1934. H4.

'Impi' (*R.* 'Moser's Maroon' × *R. sanguineum* subsp. *didymum*) A medium-sized shrub of upright growth. Leaves broadly elliptic, bullate above, to 8cm long. Flowers funnel-shaped, 5cm across, in small trusses, nearly black in bud, opening to very deep, vinous-crimson, faintly black-spotted within. Brilliant when viewed by transmitted light. Late. (1945). AM 1945. H4.

Intrifast Group (*R. fastigiatum* × *R. intricatum*) A dwarf shrub of dense habit producing innumerable clusters of small, violet-blue flowers. Mid. H4.

'Isabel Pearce' (*R.* 'Anna' × *R.* 'Lem's Goal') A stiffly branched, large shrub of upright habit with long, narrow leaves. Flowers rose-red fading to pink with conspicuously blotched and spotted, deeper margins, in large trusses. Mid. (1975). H3.

'Isabella' (*R. auriculatum* × *R. griffithianum*) A beautiful Leonardslee hybrid. A large shrub or small tree with oblong-lanceolate leaves, to 20cm long, on long, yellowish-green petioles. Bears large trusses of enormous, fragrant, trumpet-shaped, frilly-edged, white flowers, 11cm across, with a patch of rose-red markings near the base. Late. (1934). H3.

'Jacksonii' (*R. caucasicum* × *R.* 'Nobleanum') (HH) A broadly dome-shaped, slow-growing, medium-sized bush. Flowers in a well-formed truss, widely funnel-shaped, 6cm across, bright rose-pink, with maroon markings and paler spotting within; normally opening in April, occasionally in March. One of the earliest raised hybrids, tolerant of industrial pollution and thriving where many other rhododendrons would fail. (1835). H4.

Jalisco Group (*R.* 'Dido' × *R.* 'Lady Bessborough') A most attractive hybrid raised at Exbury. Flowers straw-coloured, tinted orange-rose at the tips. Late. Prone to powdery mildew. (1942). H3.

'Jalisco Eclipse' Flowers primrose-yellow, streaked crimson on the outside and blotched and spotted crimson at the base within. Calyx yellow, edged with red. AM 1948. H3.

'Jalisco Elect' Flowers primrose-yellow with paler lobes, the margins slightly frilled, marked with brownish-red spots within. Calyx yellow. FCCT 1987. AM 1948. H3.

'Jalisco Emblem' Flowers very pale yellow or nearly white with a dark maroon basal blotch within. Calyx white, veined red. (1948). H3.

'Jalisco Goshawk' Mimosa-yellow flowers spotted with crimson. FCC 1954. H3.

'Jalisco Janet' Flowers apricot-yellow. (1948). H3.

'Jalisco Jubilant' Red in bud, opening buttercup-yellow, deeper in the throat. AM 1966. H3.

'James Barto' (*R. orbiculare* × *R. williamsianum*) A compact, small shrub with elliptic leaves to 7.5cm long. Flowers pink, funnel-shaped and slightly fragrant. Early to mid. (1953). H4.

'James Burchett' (*R. catawbiense* hybrid × *R. fortunei* subsp. *discolor*) A vigorous, large shrub of dense habit, with dark green leaves. Flowers white, tinged mauve, with a bronze-green flare, in compact trusses. Late. (1960). ♀ 2002. AMT 1960. H4.

'**Jenny**' See 'Creeping Jenny'.

'**Jervis Bay**' (Hawk Group) A superb, rounded, medium-sized shrub with dark green, ovate leaves to 11cm long. Widely funnel-shaped flowers, in firm, rounded trusses, are golden-yellow, tinged orange in bud, primrose-yellow when open, with a large maroon blotch at the base and maroon marks inside. Mid. AM 1951. H3.

'**John Barr Stevenson**' (*R. lacteum* × *R.* 'Logan Damaris') A splendid Tower Court hybrid bearing lemon-yellow, red-blotched, broadly bell-shaped flowers in large trusses. Early to mid. AM 1971. H4.

'**John Walter**' (HH) A shrub with semi-erect branches and a compact habit. Flowers in dense, globular trusses, cherry-red fading to lilac-red with dark spotting, funnel-shaped, wavy at the margin. Late. (1860). H4.

'**July Fragrance**' (*R. diaprepes* × *R.* 'Isabella') A strong-growing bush, with young leaves flushed bronze. Flowers in large, loose trusses, trumpet-shaped, white with a crimson basal stain within, deliciously fragrant. Late. Raised in our nurseries. (1967). H3.

'**Jutland**' (*R.* 'Bellerophon' × *R. elliottii*) Flowers in a large, dome-shaped truss, widely bell-shaped and geranium-lake, flecked darker red. Late. (1942). AM 1947. H3.

'**Kalinka**' (*R.* 'Morgenrot' × [*R.* 'Mars' × *R. yakushimanum*]) A small, spreading shrub of compact habit with glossy, dark green leaves, downy beneath. Deep pink flowers, paler inside, fade to rose-pink, spotted with yellow-green. Mid. (1985). H4.

'**Kantilene**' (*R.* 'Mars' × *R. yakushimanum* 'Koichiro Wada') A compact, low-growing shrub with glossy, dark green leaves, to 12.5cm long and thinly brown-tomentose beneath. Flowers, 5.5cm across and with 5 wavy-edged lobes, are deep purple-pink edged with vivid purplish-red, shading to white in the throat and with white spots on the upper lobe; they are borne in compact, rounded trusses. Mid. (1968). H4.

'**Karkov**' (*R. griersonianum* × *R.* 'Red Admiral') A vigorous, Exbury hybrid bearing large, globular trusses of widely funnel-shaped, frilly-edged flowers, carmine-rose, faintly and evenly spotted. Early to mid. (1943). AM 1947. H3.

'**Kate Waterer**' (HH) A medium-sized to large, dense shrub with oblong-ovate leaves to 12cm long. Flowers funnel-shaped, to 6cm across, rose-crimson passing to clear rose, the upper lobe with a ray of greenish-yellow spots on a white background. Mid. (Before 1876). ♀ 2002. H4.

'**Ken Janeck**' (*R. yakushimanum* hybrid) This is a low, spreading shrub, to about 1m tall. Leaves: upper surface dark green, with a white tomentum at first, lower surface with a thin, deciduous, pale brown tomentum. Flowers funnel-campanulate, 7cm across, pale pink fading to white with a few green spots inside. They open from rose-pink buds borne in dense trusses. Mid. (1964). AM 2001. H4.

'**Kilimanjaro**' (*R.* 'Dusky Maid' × *R. elliottii*) A superb Exbury hybrid, with compact, globular trusses of funnel-shaped, currant-red, wavy-edged flowers, spotted chocolate within. Mid to late. (1943). FCC 1947. H3.

'**Kluis Sensation**' (*R.* 'Britannia' × unnamed seedling) A hardy shrub bearing bright scarlet flowers with darker spots on upper lobes. Mid. (1948). ♀ 2002. H4.

'**Kluis Triumph**' A splendid *R. griffithianum* hybrid with outstanding deep red flowers. Mid. (Before 1958). FCCT 1971. AMT 1969. H4.

'**Lady Alice Fitzwilliam**' (*R. ciliatum* × *R. edgeworthii*) A beautiful but tender, medium-sized shrub with dark green, deeply veined leaves. Flowers 10cm across, funnel-shaped, white flushed pink with yellow markings in the throat, very fragrant. Mid. (1881). ♀ 2002. FCC 1881. H2–3.

Lady Bessborough Group (*R. campylocarpum* Elatum Group × *R. fortunei* subsp. *discolor*) A tall, erect-branched hybrid bearing trusses of funnel-shaped, wavy-edged flowers, apricot in bud, opening to creamy-white, with a flash of maroon on a deeper cream ground within. Mid. Prone to powdery mildew. Raised at Exbury. FCC 1933. H4. See also 'Roberte'.

'**Lady Bowes Lyon**' (*R.* 'Pilgrim' × *R. yakushimanum*) A vigorous, small shrub bearing large trusses of pink flowers, fading to white, flushed pink. One of the first hybrids of *R. yakushimanum*, raised at the RHS Gardens, Wisley. AM 1962. H4.

Lady Chamberlain Group (*R. cinnabarinum* Roylei Group × *R.* Royal Flush Group, orange form) Undoubtedly one of the loveliest rhododendrons grown in gardens, but tragically now very prone to powdery mildew. It forms a stiffly branched shrub with neat, sea-green leaves, and bears with the utmost freedom clusters of drooping, waxy, long, narrowly bell-shaped flowers. The typical colour is mandarin-red, shading to orange-buff on the lobes. Mid. A variable hybrid, it was raised by Lionel de Rothschild at Exbury. (1930). FCC 1931. H3.

'**Lady Chamberlain Chelsea**' Flowers orange-pink. H3.

'**Lady Chamberlain Exbury**' See 'Exbury Lady Chamberlain'. H3.

'**Lady Chamberlain Gleam**' Flowers orange-yellow with crimson-tipped lobes. H3.

'**Lady Chamberlain Ivy**' Flowers orange. H3.

'**Lady Chamberlain Salmon Trout**' Flowers salmon-pink. H3.

'**Lady Chamberlain Seville**' Flowers bright orange inside, reddish outside. H3.

'**Lady Clementine Mitford**' (HH) A large shrub, a hybrid of *R. maximum*, with large, glossy green leaves. Flowers in a firm truss, widely funnel-shaped, peach-pink, shading to white in centre, with a V-shaped pattern of pink, olive-green and brown markings within. Mid to late. (1870). ♀ 2002. AMT 1971. H4.

'**Lady Eleanor Cathcart**' (*R. arboreum* × *R. maximum*) (HH) A magnificent, large, dome-shaped bush or small tree with very distinctive, handsome foliage. Flowers in a rounded truss, widely funnel-shaped, bright clear rose with slightly darker veins and a conspicuous maroon basal blotch within. Mid to late. Said to have originated at Sandleford Park near Oxford, before 1844. H4.

'**Lady Grey Egerton**' A hybrid of *R. catawbiense*. Flowers in a loose truss, pale lilac, nearly white in the centre with a broad patch of yellow spots, funnel-shaped, 6cm across. Mid to late. (Before 1888). H4.

'**Lady Longman**' An excellent hardy hybrid bearing large, vivid rose flowers with a chocolate eye. Mid to late. H4.

'**Lady Romsey**' (*R.* 'Elizabeth de Rothschild' × *R. yakushimanum*) Medium-sized shrub. Broadly funnel-shaped, 7-

lobed flowers, to 8cm across, are white, faintly spotted with greenish yellow. Leaves to 13cm long with a sparse brown indumentum beneath. Mid. (1965). AM 1982. H4.

Lady Rosebery Group (*R. cinnabarinum* Roylei Group × *R.* Royal Flush Group, pink form) Similar to Lady Chamberlain Group, except in colour, pink shades predominating. Typical colour is deep pink, graduating to a lighter shade at the margins. Mid. Prone to powdery mildew. Raised by Lionel de Rothschild at Exbury. (1930). FCC 1932. AM 1930. H3. **'Dalmeny'** Flowers soft pink. **'Pink Beauty'** A lovely pink form. (1955). **'Pink Delight'** A beautiful shrub with flowers of a glistening pink, paler within.

'Lamplighter' (*R.* 'Britannia' × *R.* 'Mme F.R. Chauvin') A vigorous, large shrub of open habit with narrow, pointed, dark green leaves. Bright red flowers are borne in large trusses. Mid. (1955). H4.

'Lava Flow' (*R. griersonianum* × KW 13225) A late flowering hybrid of dwarf, bushy habit; the dark green leaves have a buff-coloured indumentum beneath. Flowers trumpet-shaped, 7cm across, deep scarlet with darker spots. Late. The Kingdon-Ward introduction used as one parent is similar to *R. sanguineum* subsp. *didymum*. (1955). H3.

'Lavender Girl' (*R. fortunei* × *R.* 'Lady Grey Egerton') A vigorous, free-flowering hybrid of compact habit, producing dome-shaped trusses of fragrant, funnel-shaped flowers, lilac-mauve in bud, opening pale lavender with darker margins and pinkish-yellow throats. Mid. (1950). ♛ 2002. FCCT 1967. AMT 1950. H4.

'Lee's Dark Purple' (HH) A compact, rounded bush, resembling *R. catawbiense* in habit and foliage. Flowers in a dense, rounded truss, widely funnel-shaped, royal purple with a ray of greenish-brown or ochre markings within. Mid. (Before 1955). H4.

'Lem's Cameo' (*R.* 'Anna' × *R.* 'Dido') A medium-sized, upright shrub with dark matt green leaves, to 16cm long, bronze when young. Flowers funnel-shaped, to 9cm across, red in bud, opening cream and apricot, flushed red and spotted pink, in rounded trusses. Mid. (1962). ♛ 2002. FCC 1991. H3–4.

'Lem's Monarch' (*R.* 'Anna' × *R.* 'Marinus Koster') A vigorous, large shrub of spreading habit with thick-textured, pointed leaves. Flowers pale pink fading to white, edged with pink, in very large, conical trusses. Mid. (1971). ♛ 2002. H4.

'Letty Edwards' (*R. campylocarpum* Elatum Group × *R. fortunei*) (Gladys Group) Free-flowering shrub of compact habit. Flowers pale pink in bud, opening funnel-shaped, pale sulphur-yellow with a deeper flush. Mid. FCCT 1948. AMT 1946. H4.

'Linda' (*R.* 'Britannia' × *R. williamsianum*) A small, compact shrub with pale green, oval leaves and upright trusses of deep rose-pink, frilly-edged, bell-shaped flowers. Mid. Best in a sunny position. ♛ 2002. H4.

'Lionel's Triumph' (*R. lacteum* × *R.* 'Naomi') An outstanding Exbury hybrid with long leaves and large trusses of bell-shaped flowers, 10cm across, Dresden-yellow, spotted and blotched crimson at the base within. Early to mid. (1954). FCC 1974. AM 1954. H3.

'Little Ben' (*R. forrestii* Repens Group × *R. neriiflorum*) A dwarf, spreading shrub producing an abundance of waxy,

bell-shaped, brilliant flowers 4cm long. March or April. (1937). FCC 1937. H4.

'Loch o' the Lowes' A hybrid from Glendoick raised by Peter Cox, with the same parentage as 'Loch Rannoch' and making a small, spreading shrub with glossy green, obovate leaves to 12cm long. Pale yellow-green, unspotted, funnel-campanulate flowers, 6cm across, have a large, similarly-coloured petaloid calyx and are borne in rounded trusses. Mid. (1976). H4.

'Loch Rannoch' ([*R.* 'Tidbit' × *R. caucasicum*] × [*R. wardii* × (*R. yakushimanum* × *R.* 'Crest')]) Raised by Peter Cox at Glendoick Gardens, this makes a compact, small, spreading shrub, free-flowering even when young. Profuse, deep yellow flowers with a small, red blotch in the throat. Mid. (1976). H4.

Lodauric Group (*R. auriculatum* × *R.* Loderi Group) Magnificent in leaf and flower, this is a large shrub or small tree, bearing nodding trusses of richly scented, trumpet-shaped, pure white flowers, 13cm across, with 2 streaks of brownish-crimson at the base within. Late. (1939). H4.

'Lodauric Iceberg' Similar to Lodauric but with more flowers in the truss. (1936). ♛ 2002. AM 1958. H3–4.

Loderi Group (*R. fortunei* × *R. griffithianum*) Generally considered to be the finest hybrid rhododendron. A strong-growing, large, rounded bush or small tree bearing enormous trusses of very large, lily-like, trumpet-shaped, richly scented flowers, 13–15cm across, varying from white to cream and soft pink. Early to mid. Raised by Sir Edmund Loder at Leonardslee in 1901. H3–4. From the original and subsequent crosses a great number of slightly different clones have been raised. **'Loderi Game Chick'** Pink in bud, opening white in the centre, pink at the edges of the lobes, blotched green at the base with brownish-red spots. ♛ 2002. **'Loderi Julie'** Cream, suffused sulphur. The nearest to a yellow Loderi. AM 1944. **'Loderi King George'** Perhaps the best of the bunch. Flowers soft pink in bud, opening to pure white with a basal flash of pale green markings within. ♛ 2002. FCC 1970. AM 1968. **'Loderi Patience'** Flowers carmine-rose in bud, opening to white with a faint flash of crimson and green at the base within. H3–4. **'Loderi Pink Diamond'** Flowers similar to those of 'King George', but slightly smaller and a delicate pink with a basal flash of crimson, passing to green flushed brown. ♛ 2002. FCC 1914. **'Loderi Pink Topaz'** Soft pink with a basal flush of green. ♛ 2002. **'Loderi Venus'** Deep pink in bud, opening rhodamine-pink, passing to pale pink with a very faint greenish flash at the base within. ♛ 2002. **'Loderi White Diamond'** Pure white, pink-flushed in bud. FCC 1914.

'Loder's White' (*R.* 'Album Elegans' × *R. griffithianum*) (HH) A large, dome-shaped shrub, clothed to the ground with handsome foliage. Flowers in a magnificent, conical truss, widely funnel-shaped, mauve-pink in bud, opening pure white edged with pink and marked with a few scattered crimson spots. Mid. Raised by J.H. Mangles before 1884. ♛ 2002. AM 1911. H4.

'Logan Damaris' ('Damaris Logan') (Damaris Group) A lovely form with Dresden-yellow flowers admirably set off by the rich green, glossy foliage. Early to mid. (1948). AM 1948. H4.

'**Lord Roberts**' (HH) An old hybrid of erect growth. Flowers in a dense, rounded truss, funnel-shaped, dark crimson with an extensive V-shaped pattern of black markings. Mid to late. ♀ 2002. H4.

'**Lori Eichelser**' (*R. forrestii* Repens Group × *R.* 'Bowbells') This is a free-flowering, dwarf shrub of compact, spreading habit with glossy green, rounded leaves. Cherry-red flowers in loose trusses. Mid. (1966). H4.

'**Lucy Lou**' (*R. leucaspis* × [*R. ciliatum* × *R. leucaspis*]) A free-flowering, dwarf shrub of compact habit with attractive, dark green, hairy leaves and pure white flowers. Early. (1956). H3.

'**Luscombei**' (*R. fortunei* × *R. thomsonii*) A large shrub forming a broadly dome-shaped bush. Flowers in a loose truss, trumpet-shaped, deep rose, with a well-defined ray of crimson markings within. Early to mid. (1875). H3.

'**Madame de Bruin**' (*R.* 'Doncaster' × *R.* 'Prometheus') (HH) A vigorous, leafy hybrid with dark green leaves marked by a conspicuous pale green midrib. Conical trusses of cerise-red flowers. Mid. (1904). H4.

'**Madame Masson**' (*R. catawbiense* × *R. ponticum*) (HH) An old hybrid bearing trusses of white flowers, deeply cut into 5 lobes, with a yellow basal blotch within. Mid. (1849). H4.

'**Maharani**' (*R.* 'Harvest Moon' × *R.* 'Letty Edwards') Medium-sized shrub. Creamy-white flowers, 9cm across, are flushed pale lilac-pink, red and yellow in the centre. Mid. (1964). H4.

'**Manderley**' (*R.* 'Fabia' × *R.* 'Scandinavia') A compact, small shrub with dark matt green leaves, to 9cm long, reddish when young. Flowers funnel-shaped, 9cm across, cardinal-red with darker spots. Mid. (1965). AMT 1983. H4.

'**Marchioness of Lansdowne**' This medium-sized to large shrub, is an old hybrid of *R. maximum* raised by Waterer, Sons & Crisp before 1879. Dense trusses of pale magenta-pink, funnel-shaped flowers, 7cm across, with a very dark flare, are borne over a long period. Late. H4.

'**Mardi Gras**' (*R.* Vanessa Group FCC form × *R. yakushimanum* 'Koichiro Wada') A dwarf to small shrub of dense habit, the dark green leaves with a reddish-brown indumentum beneath. Soft pink flowers with ruffled edges, fade to blush white, purple-pink on the reverse. Mid. (1975). H4.

'**Maricee**' (*R. sargentianum* 'Maricee') A hybrid of *R. sargentianum* making a dwarf shrub with small, glossy, dark green leaves and clusters of small, daphne-like, creamy-white flowers. Mid. (1960). AMT 1983. H4.

'**Mariloo**' (*R.* 'Doctor Stocker' × *R. lacteum*) A handsome woodland rhododendron with bold foliage and large trusses of lemon-yellow flowers, flushed green. Early to mid. Named after Mrs Lionel de Rothschild, one of the greatest experts on rhododendron hybrids, a passion she shared with her most distinguished husband. (1941). H3.

'**Marinus Koster**' A magnificent, hardy, free-flowering shrub, a hybrid of *R. griffithianum*. Flowers 10cm across, in large trusses, deep pink in bud, opening white shading to pink at the margins, with a large purple blotch within. Mid. (1937). FCCT 1948. AMT 1937. H4.

'**Marion Street**' (*R.* 'Stanley Davies' × *R. yakushimanum*) A vigorous, small shrub of dense, spreading habit with

dark green leaves, to 10cm long, brown-felted beneath. Flowers widely funnel-shaped, up to 7cm across, white-edged and flushed pale pink, fading to white. Mid. (1965). ♀ 2002. AMT 1989. AM 1978. H4.

'**Markeeta's Prize**' (*R.* 'Loderi Venus' × *R.* 'Anna') A medium-sized to large shrub of upright habit with excellent, dark green foliage. Scarlet flowers, with darker spots, are freely borne in large, flat-topped trusses. Mid. (1967). ♀ 2002. H4.

'**Mary Fleming**' (*R.* Keisrac Group × *R. keiskei*) A very hardy, dwarf shrub of compact habit, the foliage bronzing in cold weather. Bears small clusters of buff-yellow flowers flushed with pink at the margins. Early to mid. (1967). H4.

'**Matador**' (*R. griersonianum* × *R. strigillosum*) A Bodnant hybrid making a large shrub of spreading habit with leaves densely rusty-hairy beneath. Flowers 5cm across, in large, loose trusses, funnel-shaped, brilliant dark orange-red. Early to mid. (1945). FCC 1946. AM 1945. H4.

'**May Day**' (*R. griersonianum* × *R. haematodes*) A magnificent, comparatively low, widespreading shrub bearing loose trusses of slightly pendent, funnel-shaped flowers, brilliant signal-red or orange-red; calyces large and similarly coloured. Mid. ♀ 2002. AM 1932. H3–4.

'**Merganser**' (*R. campylogynum*, white form × *R. luteiflorum*) A vigorous, free-flowering, dwarf shrub of compact, upright habit, with dark green leaves to 3.5cm long. Flowers funnel-shaped, 3cm across, pale primrose-yellow, in compact conical trusses, 6cm across. Early to mid. (1967). ♀ 2002. H4.

'**Michael Waterer**' (HH) A slow-growing, compact, free-flowering *R. ponticum* hybrid. Flowers in a well-formed truss, funnel-shaped, crimson-scarlet, fading to rose-crimson. Mid to late. (Before 1894). H4.

'**Michael's Pride**' (*R. burmanicum* × *R. dalhousiae*) Tubular, lily-like, creamy-yellow, waxy and fragrant flowers open from lime-green buds. Bronze young foliage. (1964). H2.

'**Midsummer Snow**' (*R. decorum* subsp. *diaprepes* × *R.* 'Isabella') A handsome hybrid, raised in our nurseries. Buds and young shoots bright yellow-green. Large, trumpet-shaped, pure white, richly fragrant flowers in large, loose trusses. Late. (1967). H3.

'**Moerheim**' A dwarf shrub of compact habit with glossy green leaves turning maroon in winter. Clusters of small, aster-violet flowers are freely produced. Mid. Probably a hybrid of *R. impeditum*. (1966). ♀ 2002. H4.

'**Moerheim's Pink**' (*R.* 'Genoveva' × *R. williamsianum*) A very attractive, small, dome-shaped bush of dense habit with broadly ovate leaves to 8cm long. Flowers funnel-shaped, deep pink in bud, opening pale lilac, spotted rose inside with slightly frilled lobes. Mid. Raised by Dietrich Hobbie. (1973). AMT 1972. H4.

'**Mohamet**' (*R. dichroanthum* × *R. facetum*) An Exbury hybrid producing brilliant rich orange flowers, with frilly margins and large, coloured, petaloid calyces. Mid. AM 1945. H3.

'**Moonshine Crescent**' Similar to 'Moonshine Supreme' but with clear yellow flowers. (1962). AMT 1960. H4.

'**Moonshine Supreme**' (*R.* 'Adriaan Koster' × *R. wardii* Litiense Group) A Wisley hybrid with compact, dome-shaped trusses of saucer-shaped, primrose-yellow flowers, with a darker staining on upper segment and indistinct spotting. Early to mid. (1953). AM 1953. H4.

'Moonstone' (*R. campylocarpum* × *R. williamsianum*) A small, dome-shaped bush bearing attractive, bell-shaped flowers, rose-crimson in bud, opening cream or pale primrose. Early to mid. (1933). H3.

'Morgenrot' ('Morning Red') (*R.* 'Spitfire' × *R. yakushimanum* 'Koichiro Wada') A small shrub of compact, rounded habit with dark green leaves. Flowers in large trusses, deep red in bud, opening rose-red. Mid. (1983). H4.

'Morning Cloud' (*R.* 'Springbok' × *R. yakushimanum*) A dwarf, compact shrub with leaves woolly-felted beneath and rounded trusses of white flowers, heavily flushed rich pink, fading to cream. Mid to late. (1970). ♀ 2002. AM 1971. H4.

'Morning Red' See 'Morgenrot'.

'Moser's Maroon' A vigorous, tall-growing hybrid of French origin, with copper-red young growths. Flowers maroon-red with darker markings within. Mid to late. Used by the late Lionel de Rothschild as a parent for many of his hybrids. AM 1932. H4.

'Mother of Pearl' A lovely hybrid, a sport of 'Pink Pearl' with flowers rich pink in bud, opening delicate blush and fading to white, with a few external pink streaks. Mid. Raised in the Bagshot nursery of Messrs Waterer, Sons & Crisp, before 1914. AM 1930. H4.

'Mount Everest' (*R. campanulatum* × *R. griffithianum*) A large, vigorous, very free-flowering shrub. Conical trusses of narrow, bell-shaped flowers of pure white, with reddish-brown speckling in throat; large yellow stigma. Early. (1930). FCCT 1958. AMT 1953. H4.

'Mrs A.M. Williams' (HH) A superb *R. griffithianum* hybrid. A large shrub of dense habit with dark green leaves, up to 15cm long, and well-filled, rounded trusses of bright crimson-scarlet, funnel-shaped flowers with wavy margins and a broad ray of blackish spots. Mid. (1896). FCCT 1954. AMT 1933. AM 1926. H4.

'Mrs A.T. de la Mare' (*R.* 'Halopeanum' × *R. fortunei* 'Sir Charles Butler') (HH) A free-flowering hardy hybrid of vigorous, upright, compact habit. Flowers in a compact, dome-shaped truss, pink-tinged in bud, opening white, funnel-shaped with frilly margins, greenish-yellow spotting in the throat. Mid. ♀ 2002. AMT 1958. H4.

'Mrs Charles Butler' See *R. fortunei* 'Sir Charles Butler' under species.

'Mrs Charles E. Pearson' (*R.* 'Catawbiense Grandiflorum' × *R.* 'Coombe Royal') (HH) A robust hybrid with stout, erect branches. Flowers in a large, conical truss, widely funnel-shaped, 10cm across, mauve-pink in bud, opening pale pinky-mauve passing to nearly white, with a burnt-sienna ray within. Mid. (1909). ♀ 2002. FCCT 1955. AMT 1933. H4.

'Mrs Davies Evans' (HH) A vigorous, free-flowering hybrid of upright, compact habit. Flowers in a compact, globular truss, funnel-shaped with frilly margins, imperial-purple with a white basal blotch and yellow spots within. Mid. (Before 1915). ♀ 2002. AMT 1958. H4.

'Mrs E.C. Stirling' (HH) A widely dome-shaped hybrid of *R. griffithianum*, bearing handsome, conical trusses of flattened, crinkly-edged, mauve-pink flowers with a paler centre, rich rose in bud. Mid. AM 1906. H4.

'Mrs Edwin Hillier' (*R. griffithianum* hybrid × *R.* 'Monsieur Thiers') A medium-sized shrub of lax habit with dark matt green leaves to 19cm long. Flowers vivid pink in rounded trusses, funnel-shaped, 7cm across. Mid. (1933). H4.

'Mrs Furnivall' (*R. caucasicum* hybrid × *R. griffithianum* hybrid) (HH) A magnificent, dense bush, producing compact trusses of widely funnel-shaped, light rose-pink flowers, each with a conspicuous blotch of sienna and crimson markings within. Mid to late. One of the finest hardy hybrids ever produced. (1920). ♀ 2002. FCCT 1948. AMT 1933. H4.

'Mrs G.W. Leak' (*R.* 'Chevalier Felix de Sauvage' × *R.* 'Coombe Royal') (HH) A splendid hybrid of Dutch origin, making a large, dense shrub with dark green leaves to 15cm long. Flowers in a rather lax, conical truss, widely funnel-shaped, 8cm across, mottled light rosy-pink, darkening in tube and with a conspicuous splash of blackish-brown and crimson markings within; nectaries blood-red. Mid. (1916). FCCT 1934. H4.

'Mrs J.C. Williams' A tall, rounded bush with narrowly elliptic to oblanceolate leaves to 22cm long. Bears compact, rounded trusses of white flowers with a ray of crimson markings within, pink in bud. Mid to late. ♀ 2002. AMT 1960. H4.

'Mrs Lionel de Rothschild' A compact, erect-branched shrub with large, firm trusses of fleshy, widely funnel-shaped, white flowers 7cm across, edged with apple blossom-pink and marked with a conspicuous ray of dark crimson. Mid. (1931). ♀ 2002. FCC 2001. AM 1931. H4.

'Mrs P.D. Williams' A free-flowering hybrid. Flowers in a compact flattened truss, ivory-white with a large brown blotch on the upper lobes. Mid to late. AMT 1936. H4.

'Mrs R.S. Holford' (HH) A Knap Hill hybrid of vigorous growth, apt to become leggy with age. Flowers in a large truss, widely funnel-shaped, salmon-rose with a small pattern of crimson spots within. Mid to late. (1866). ♀ 2002. H4.

'Mrs T.H. Lowinsky' A vigorous, tall hardy hybrid with broad elliptic-obovate leaves to 9cm long. Flowers open funnel-shaped, 7–8cm across, lilac, whitish towards the centre, heavily spotted orange-brown. The parentage includes *R. ponticum*, *R. maximum*, and *R. catawbiense*. Not to be confused with 'Mrs Tom Lowinsky', a tender hybrid of *R. griffithianum*. Raised at Knap Hill before 1917. ♀ 2002. AM 1919. H4.

'Mrs W.C. Slocock' A dense bush, a hybrid of *R. campylocarpum*. Flowers apricot-pink, shading to buff. Mid. (1929). AM 1929. H4.

'Nancy Evans' (*R.* 'Hotei' × *R.* 'Lem's Cameo') A compact, small shrub with glossy dark green foliage, bronze when young. Rounded trusses of amber-yellow flowers with a petaloid calyx are freely borne from orange-red buds. Mid. (1981). ♀ 2002. H3–4.

Naomi Group (*R.* 'Aurora' × *R. fortunei*) A wonderful Exbury hybrid. A large shrub or small tree producing large, shapely trusses of fragrant, widely-expanded flowers of lovely soft lilac-mauve shading to greenish-yellow in the tube, with a ray of faint brown markings. Early to mid. Prone to powdery mildew. (1926). AM 1933. H3–4.

'Naomi Astarte' Pink shaded yellow with a yellow

throat. AM 1997. **'Naomi Early Dawn'** Pale soft pink, deeper outside, yellowish towards the base, slightly rose spotted inside, 6cm across. **'Naomi Exbury'** Lilac, tinged yellow. **'Naomi Glow'** Bright pink, deepening in throat. **'Naomi Hope'** Pink, tinged mauve. **'Naomi Nautilus'** Large, frilled flowers of deep rose, flushed pale orange-yellow on the tube, becoming paler with age. AM 1938. **'Naomi Nereid'** Lavender and yellow. **'Naomi Pink Beauty'** Satiny-pink. **'Naomi Stella Maris'** Buff, shaded lilac-pink, slightly larger and fuller in the truss than other forms and longer in leaf. FCC 1939.

'New Comet' (*R.* 'Idealist' × *R.* 'Naomi') An attractive hybrid producing large, heavy, globular trusses of shallowly funnel-shaped, mimosa-yellow flowers flushed pale pink, mauve-pink in bud, 9cm across, slightly scented. Early to mid. AM 1957. H3.

'Nicoletta' (*R.* 'Fantastica' × [*R.* 'Hachmann's Ornament' × *R.* 'Furnivall's Daughter']) A dwarf shrub of flattened, spreading habit, making only about 50cm tall in 10 years, with dark green leaves to 11cm long. Broadly funnel-shaped flowers, to 8cm across, are deep purple-pink at first, fading to white with purple-pink veins and a red blotch. Mid. (1977). H4.

'Night Sky' (*R.* 'Moerheim' × *R. russatum*) A dwarf shrub of neat, compact habit and good foliage. Bright violet-blue flowers. Early to mid. H4.

Nobleanum Group (*R. arboreum* × *R. caucasicum*) (HH) A large, slow-growing shrub or small tree with dull, dark green leaves covered beneath with a thin, plastered, buff indumentum. Flowers in a compact truss, widely funnel-shaped, brilliant rose-scarlet in bud, opening to rich rose, flushed white within and with a few crimson spots; nectaries dark crimson. One of the earliest rhododendron hybrids, first raised by Anthony Waterer at Knap Hill about 1832. It is also one of the first to flower, opening from January to March, or earlier in sheltered gardens. H4. **'Nobleanum Album'** (*R. arboreum* 'Album' × *R. caucasicum*) (HH) A dense bush of compact habit. Flowers in a compact truss, pink in bud, opening white or blush with purplish spots inside and reddish-purple nectaries, faintly marked with a small ray of yellowish-green. January to March. Raised by Messrs Cunningham & Fraser of Edinburgh. **'Nobleanum Coccineum'** (HH) A large, conical bush bearing trusses of bell-shaped flowers of deep rose, marked with a few dark crimson spots at the base within. January to March. **'Nobleanum Venustum'** (*R. arboreum venustum*) (HH) A very old hybrid, a densely leafy bush of broadly dome-shaped habit, up to 2m high and 3m across. Flowers in a compact truss, funnel-shaped, glistening pink, shading to white in the centre, with a small pattern of dark crimson markings at base within; nectaries crimson. Flowering in late winter, but occasionally opens in December in a mild season. Raised by William Smith at Norbiton Common, near Kingston, Surrey in 1829. AM 1973.

'Nova Zembla' (*R.* 'Parson's Grandiflorum' × red-flowered hybrid) An excellent and very hardy, medium-sized shrub of rather upright habit with dark green, deeply veined leaves. Deep red flowers with a conspicuous dark blotch are borne in compact trusses. Mid. (1902). H4.

'Odee Wright' (*R.* 'Idealist' × *R.* 'Mrs Betty Robinson') A small to medium-sized, compact shrub with dark glossy green leaves. Flowers widely funnel-shaped with frilled lobes, pale yellow tinged with pink and spotted red. Mid. (1964). H4.

'Old Copper' (*R.* Fabia Group × *R.* 'Vulcan') A medium-sized to large shrub of compact, upright habit. The large, bell-shaped flowers in loose trusses are an unusual coppery colour, opening from red buds. Mid to late. (1958). H4.

'Old Port' (HH) A vigorous, leafy, dome-shaped bush with very glossy foliage; a hybrid of *R. catawbiense*. Rich plum-purple flowers, up to 6.5cm across, in a dense truss, widely funnel-shaped, with frilled lobes and a well-defined pattern of blackish-crimson markings. Mid to late. Raised at Knap Hill in 1865. ♥ 2002. H4.

'Olga' ('Dido' × 'Mrs Lindsay Smith') A compact, medium-sized shrub of spreading habit with striking and long-lasting, pale apricot-orange flowers fringed pink with deeper spots. Good foliage. Mid to late. (1982). ♥ 2002. AM 1986. H4.

'Olive' (*R. dauricum* × *R. moupinense*) An attractive, floriferous, small to medium-sized shrub of upright habit. Leaves ovate-elliptic, to 4cm long, bright fresh green above. Flowers in 2s or 3s, funnel-shaped, mauve-pink with deeper spots, up to 4cm across. Very early. (1936). AM 1942. H4.

'Olympic Lady' (*R.* 'Loderi King George' × *R. williamsianum*) A small shrub of compact habit with dark green leaves 5cm long. Flowers bell-shaped, 6cm across, pink in bud, opening white, in lax conical trusses to 11cm wide. Mid. (1960). AMT 1977. H4.

Oreocinn Group (*R. cinnabarinum* × *R. oreotrephes*) A delightful Lamellen hybrid of slender, twiggy habit, with sea-green leaves and soft apricot pastel flowers. Mid. We were fortunate to obtain the original plant for our collection. (1926). H4.

'Osmar' (*R. williamsianum* hybrid) A small shrub with nearly orbicular leaves to 5cm long, heart-shaped at the base. Bell-shaped flowers, to 8cm across, open pale lilac-purple, fading to pale purple-pink. Early. (Before 1965). ♥ 2002. H4.

'Ostara' A hybrid of *R. mucronulatum*, of Japanese origin. It differs in its smaller leaves and deep rose-pink flowers. Early. (Before 1982). H4.

'Oudijk's Sensation' A small shrub forming a dense mound, the young foliage attractively bronze-tinged. Flowers in open, flat-topped trusses, bell-shaped, striking bright pink with a few deeper spots on the upper lobe, 7cm across. Mid. (1965). H4.

'Pallescens' See *R.* × *pallescens* under species.

'Patty Bee' (*R. fletcherianum* × *R. keiskei* 'Yaku Fairy') A compact and vigorous, dwarf shrub; dark green leaves to 4.5cm long bronzing in winter. Flowers pale yellow, funnel-shaped with wavy margins, 4.5cm across, borne in compact trusses. Early. (1977). ♥ 2002. AMT 1989. H4.

'Peace' (*R. cinnabarinum* Concatenans Group × *R. rigidum*) A very attractive Bodnant hybrid making a densely branched, medium-sized shrub with broadly elliptic leaves, to 6cm long, densely brown-scaly beneath. Flowers funnel-shaped, in loose trusses, yellowish in bud, opening white marked yellow inside, 6cm across. Mid. Has flowered at Christmas in the Sir Harold

Hillier Gardens and Arboretum in mild weather. AM 1946. H4.

'Peeping Tom' (*R. wardii* × *R.* 'Mrs Furnivall') A small, spreading shrub of compact habit. Flowers pure white with a prominent plum-purple flare. Considering the flower colour, the parentage has been questioned. Mid. (1966). H4.

'Penheale Blue' (*R. concinnum* Pseudoyanthinum Group × *R. russatum*) A small, compact, rounded shrub with dark glossy green leaves to 2.5cm long. Flowers freely borne in small, dense clusters, widely funnel-shaped, 3.5cm across, deep violet-blue flushed red. One of the best of the deep blues. Early. (1975). ♀ 2002. FCCT 1981. AMT 1974. H4.

Penjerrick Group (*R. campylocarpum* Elatum Group × *R. griffithianum*) One of the choicest of all hybrid rhododendrons. Loose trusses of bell-shaped, fragrant, creamy-yellow or pale pink flowers, with crimson nectaries. Early. One of the many fine hybrids raised by Mr Smith, Head Gardener at Penjerrick, Cornwall. AM 1923. H3.

'Percy Wiseman' (*R.* Fabia Group 'Tangerine' × *R. yakushimanum*) selfed. A small, compact shrub with dark glossy green leaves to 7.5cm long. Flowers funnel-shaped, 5cm across, cream flushed with pink, fading to creamy-white, in globular trusses. Mid. (1971). ♀ 2002. AMT 1982. H4.

'Persimmon' (Golden Horn Group) A colourful hybrid of medium size, more compact in habit than 'Golden Horn'. Flowers orange-red with a large calyx of similar colour. Mid. (1939). H3–4.

'Peter John Mezitt' (*R. minus* Carolinianum Group × *R. dauricum*) A small, free-flowering shrub with broad elliptic leaves, to 5cm long, blackish-green above, purple-tinged in cold weather, with a bronzy lustre beneath, densely scaly on both sides. Flowers in small, dense clusters, saucer-shaped, up to 4cm across, lilac with 2 patches of indistinct pink spots. Early. It is a selection of the P.J.M. Group raised in Massachusetts in 1943 and popular for their extreme hardiness in North America where several selections have been made. ♀ 2002. AM 1972. H4.

'Peter Koster' (*R.* 'Doncaster' hybrid × *R.* 'George Hardy') (HH) A handsome shrub of sturdy, bushy habit. Flowers in a firm truss, trumpet-shaped, rosy-crimson, paling towards the margins, darker in bud. Mid to late. (1909). AMT 1946. H4.

'Pink Cherub' (*R.* 'Doncaster' × *R. yakushimanum*) A vigorous, small shrub of compact habit with dark green leaves to 9cm long. Flowers very freely borne in large, compact, rounded trusses, funnel-shaped, wavy-margined, pink in bud, opening to nearly white flushed pale pink, throat with greenish spots. ♀ 2002. FCCT 1988. AMT 1968. H4.

'Pink Drift' (*R. calostrotum* × *R. polycladum* Scintillans Group) A dwarf shrub of neat, compact habit with small, aromatic leaves and clusters of soft lavender-rose flowers. Mid. Resembles an evergreen azalea. Suitable for a rock garden. (1955). H4.

'Pink Pearl' (*R.* 'Broughtonii' × *R.* 'George Hardy') (HH) One of the most popular of all rhododendrons. A strong-growing shrub, ultimately tall and bare at the base.

Flowers in magnificent, large, conical trusses, widely funnel-shaped, rose in bud, opening to deep lilac-pink, fading to white at the margins, with a well-defined ray of crimson-brown markings. Mid. Raised by J. Waterer & Sons at Bagshot. (Before 1897). FCC 1900. AM 1897. H4.

'Pink Pebble' (*R. callimorphum* × *R. williamsianum*) A free-flowering, dense, small shrub bearing loose trusses of widely bell-shaped, rose-pink flowers from red buds. Mid. (1954). ♀ 2002. H4.

'Polar Bear' (*R. auriculatum* × *R. decorum* subsp. *diaprepes*) A superb, late-flowering hybrid forming a large shrub or small tree with handsome, large leaves. Flowers in large trusses, trumpet-shaped, richly fragrant, like pure white lilies, with a light green flash within. Late. This lovely rhododendron is most suitable for woodland conditions. Unfortunately, flowers are not produced on young specimens. Raised by J.B. Stevenson at Tower Court, Ascot in 1926. ♀ 2002. FCC 1946. H3–4.

'Pook' A hybrid of *R. williamsianum* making a small shrub with rounded leaves and bell-shaped, white flowers. Mid. (Before 1975). H4.

'Praecox' (*R. ciliatum* × *R. dauricum*) An extremely popular, small, early flowering hybrid of compact growth. Leaves sometimes partially deciduous, aromatic when crushed. Flowers produced in 2s and 3s at the tips of the shoots. They are widely funnel-shaped, purplish-crimson in bud, opening to glistening rosy-purple, slightly darker on the outside. February to March. Raised by Isaac Davies of Ormskirk, Lancashire, about 1855. (1860). ♀ 2002. FCC 1978. H4.

'Princess Alice' (*R. ciliatum* × *R. edgeworthii*) A small shrub of open habit with dark green leaves to 10cm long. Flowers white flushed pink from pink buds, very fragrant, 7.5cm across, borne in clusters of 3. Mid. Tender but worth trying on a wall except in very cold areas. Raised by Veitch and named after one of Queen Victoria's daughters. FCC 1862. H2.

'Princess Anne' (*R. hanceanum* × *R. keiskei*) A very attractive, dwarf shrub of dense habit with light matt green, elliptic, pointed leaves to 6cm long. Flowers greenish in bud, opening pale yellow with faint greenish spots, funnel-shaped, 3cm across. Early to mid. Sometimes grown as 'Golden Fleece'. (1974). ♀ 2002. FCCT 1983. AMT 1978. H4.

'Professor Hugo de Vries' (*R.* 'Doncaster' × *R.* 'Pink Pearl') Similar in habit to 'Countess of Derby'. Flowers in a large, conical truss, widely funnel-shaped, rich rose in bud, opening lilac-rose with a ray of reddish-brown markings on a light ground. Mid. ♀ 2002. AM 1975. H4.

'Prostigiatum' (*R. fastigiatum* × *R. prostratum*) A dwarf shrub of dense habit resembling *R. impeditum*, producing clusters of violet-purple flowers. Early. (1924). AM 1924. H4.

'Ptarmigan' (*R. leucaspis* × *R. orthocladum* var. *microleucum*) A floriferous, low, spreading shrub of compact habit with scaly leaves, 1–2cm long. Flowers usually in 3s, saucer-shaped, 3cm across, pure white. Early. ♀ 2002. FCC 1965. H3–4.

'Purple Splendour' (HH) A sturdy, leafy bush with erect branches; a hybrid of *R. ponticum*. Flowers in a well-formed truss, widely funnel-shaped, rich royal purplish-blue with a well-defined ray of embossed black markings on a purplish-brown ground. Mid to late. A fine hybrid, looking well against 'Goldsworth Yellow', which flowers about the same time. (Before 1900). ♀ 2002. AM 1931. H4.

'Queen Elizabeth II' (*R.* 'Crest' × *R.* 'Idealist') A medium-sized shrub with lanceolate to narrowly elliptic leaves up to 14cm long. The 7-lobed, pale chartreuse-green flowers are widely funnel-shaped and 11cm across, borne in trusses of up to 12. Mid. ♀ 2002. AM 1967. H3.

'Queen of Hearts' (*R. meddianum* × *R.* 'Moser's Maroon') A striking shrub, producing dome-shaped trusses of widely funnel-shaped flowers of deep, glowing crimson, speckled black within, enlivened by white filaments. Early to mid. One of the last hybrids raised by Lionel de Rothschild. (1949). AM 1949. H4.

'Racil' (*R. ciliatum* × *R. racemosum*) A small, free-flowering shrub with obovate leaves, to 6cm long, and clusters of funnel-shaped flowers, 2.5cm across, pink in bud, opening lilac-pink, darker on the margins. Early. (1937). H4.

'Ramapo' (*R. fastigiatum* × *R. minus* Carolinianum Group) A dwarf, very hardy, compact shrub with attractive, blue-grey young foliage. The clusters of small, violet-purple flowers are freely borne. Best in sun. Early to mid. (1940). ♀ 2002. H4.

'Razorbill' (*R. spinuliferum* hybrid) A very ornamental, small shrub of compact habit, with dark green leaves, to 5cm long, scaly beneath. Flowers tubular, 2cm long, deep pink in bud, opening rose-pink outside, paler inside, held upright in dense trusses. Early to mid. (1976). ♀ 2002. FCCT 1983. AMT 1981. AM 1978. H4.

'Red Carpet' (*R.* 'Amerika' × *R. forrestii* Repens Group) A dwarf shrub of compact, spreading habit with leaves to 6.5cm long. Bright red, bell-shaped flowers, 5.5cm across, with wavy margins, are borne in lax trusses. Mid. (1967). AMT 1983. H4.

'Red Riding Hood' (*R.* 'Atrosanguineum' × *R. griffithianum*) A tall-growing shrub bearing large, conical trusses of brilliant deep red flowers. Mid. (1933). H4.

'Remo' (*R. lutescens* × *R. valentinianum*) A Tower Court hybrid of compact habit making an attractive, small bush; scaly leaves to 7cm long. Flowers 3.5cm across, in loose trusses, bright yellow with darker spots inside. Early. (1943). H3.

'Rendezvous' (*R.* 'Marinus Koster' × *R. yakushimanum* 'Koichiro Wada') A small shrub with dark green leaves that have a silvery tomentum above when young. Red flowers fade to white in the centre with red spots and a deep pink margin. Mid to late (1985). ♀ 2002. H4.

'Renoir' A small, compact, upright shrub with rounded trusses of crimson-spotted, rich rose flowers, fading to nearly white. Mid to late. ♀ 2002. AM 1961. H4.

'Repose' (*R. fortunei* subsp. *discolor* × *R. lacteum*) A beautiful hybrid raised at Exbury. The deeply bell-shaped flowers are whitish-cream with a faint greenish suffusion and greenish-crimson speckling in the throat. Mid. (1956). AM 1956. H4.

'Reuthe's Purple' (*R. lepidotum* 'Reuthe's Purple') A dwarf shrub with deep rose-purple flowers, freely borne. AM 1967. H4.

'Review Order' (*R. neriiflorum* Euchaites Group × *R.* 'May Day') A dense, medium-sized shrub of spreading habit. Leaves densely tomentose beneath; flowers in a lax truss, bell-shaped, blood-red, faintly brown-spotted within. Mid. (1954). AM 1954. H3.

Riplet Group (*R. forrestii* Repens Group × *R.* 'Letty Edwards') A small shrub bearing rounded trusses of bell-shaped, bright pink flowers, white in the throat with crimson spots. Early to mid. AM 1961. H4.

'Robert Keir' A large shrub with dark green foliage and dense, rounded trusses of pale yellow flowers flushed with pink. Mid. (1951). AM 1957. H4.

'Roberte' (Lady Bessborough Group) A beautiful form with loose trusses of daintily fringed flowers of bright salmon-pink, tinged with apricot and spotted with crimson in the throat. Mid. FCC 1936. H4.

'Romany Chai' (*R. griersonianum* × *R.* 'Moser's Maroon') A lovely hybrid raised at Exbury; the name means 'gypsy children'. Large, compact trusses of rich terracotta flowers with a dark maroon basal blotch. Mid to late. (1912). AM 1932. Cory Cup 1932. H3–4.

'Romany Chal' (*R. facetum* × *R.* 'Moser's Maroon') Another Exbury hybrid, the name meaning 'gypsy girl'. A tall bush bearing lax trusses of bell-shaped, cardinal-red flowers with a ray of black markings within. Mid to late. Magnificent in a woodland setting. (1932). FCC 1937. AM 1932. H3.

'Roseum Elegans' (HH) A very old hybrid of *R. ponticum* making a large shrub. Funnel-shaped flowers, 6cm across, are rosy-lilac with a small pattern of brown markings, in rounded trusses. Mid to late. (1851). H4.

'Rosy Dream' (*R.* 'Britannia' × *R. yakushimanum*) A dwarf, spreading shrub with narrow leaves to 14cm long, the underside with a silvery indumentum ageing to cinnamon. Flowers open funnel-shaped, 6.5cm across, with wavy-edged lobes, deep purple-pink slightly spotted with red, from red buds. Mid. (1975). H4.

'Roza Stevenson' ('Roza Harrison') (*R.* 'Loderi Sir Edmund' × *R. wardii*) A superb hybrid raised by, and named in memory of, a great lover of rhododendrons (see note under Rhododendron Species). Flowers saucer-shaped, 10–12cm across, deep lemon-yellow, darker in bud, in attractive trusses. FCC 1968. H4.

'Rubicon' (*R.* 'Kilimanjaro' × *R.* 'Noyo Chief') A medium-sized shrub with handsome, dark glossy green, deeply veined leaves. Bright red flowers, spotted with black, are produced in dense, rounded trusses. Mid. (1979). H3.

'Ruby Hart' ([*R.* 'Carmen' × *R.* 'Elizabeth'] × *R. elliottii*) A promising small shrub with glossy green leaves, to 7cm long, with a thin brown indumentum beneath. Bell-shaped, waxy, very deep red flowers, to 4.5cm long, are borne in open trusses. Mid. (1976). AM 1988. H3–4.

Russautinii Group (*R. augustinii* × *R. russatum*) A first class, compact shrub of upright habit, combining the best features of its distinguished parents. Leaves obovate, dull bluish-green, aromatic, to 4cm long. Flowers in clusters of 5–6, deep lavender-blue, reddish on the ribs, with brownish spots on the upper lobes. Early to mid. In very mild weather can be in flower at Christmas. (1936). H4.

'Sacko' (*R.* 'Moerheim' × *R. russatum*) A dwarf shrub of spreading habit with small leaves. Deep purple-blue flowers are profusely borne in rounded trusses. Among the best of the new dwarf blue rhododendrons and an improvement on 'Sapphire'. Early to mid. H4.

'**Saffron Queen**' (*R. burmanicum* × *R. xanthostephanum*) A beautiful hybrid with narrowly elliptic leaves, glossy green above, with scattered brown scales beneath. Flowers tubular, sulphur-yellow with darker spotting on the upper lobes. Mid. (1948). AM 1948. H3.

'**Saint Breward**' (*R. augustinii* × *R. impeditum*) A beautiful, small, compact, rounded shrub bearing tight, globular trusses of shallowly bell-shaped flowers, soft lavender, darker at the margins; anthers pale blue. Early to mid. (1963). FCC 1962. H4.

'**Saint Merryn**' (*R. impeditum* × *R.* 'Saint Tudy') A free-flowering, compact, dwarf shrub of spreading habit with dark glossy green leaves, 1cm long. Flowers broadly funnel-shaped with wavy margins, 3cm across, deep violet-blue, darker at the margins, in trusses 5cm across. Mid. (1971). ♀ 2002. FCCT 1986. AMT 1983. FCC 1973. AM 1970. H4.

'**Saint Minver**' A small, compact shrub with clusters of violet-blue flowers. Early to mid. (1973). H4.

'**Saint Tudy**' (*R. augustinii* × *R. impeditum*) A small, dense, bushy shrub bearing dense trusses of shallowly bell-shaped, lobelia-blue flowers. Early to mid. Raised by Maj Gen Harrison at Tremeer, St Tudy, Cornwall. FCCT 1973. AM 1960. H4.

'**Sapphire**' (*R.* 'Blue Tit' × *R. impeditum*) A dwarf, small-leaved shrub of open habit, resembling *R. impeditum*. Flowers pale, lavender-blue. Early. (1969). AMT 1967. H4.

'**Sappho**' (HH) A very free-growing bush of rounded or dome-shaped habit, with dark glossy green leaves to 18cm long. Flowers in handsome, conical trusses, widely funnel-shaped, mauve in bud, opening pure white with a conspicuous blotch of rich purple overlaid black. Mid. Raised by Anthony Waterer at Knap Hill, before 1867. AMT 1974. H4.

'**Sarita Loder**' (*R. griersonianum* × *R.* Loderi Group) An outstanding hybrid producing loose trusses of large, bright pink flowers, deep crimson in bud. Mid. (1934). AM 1934. H3.

Sarled Group (*R. sargentianum* × *R. trichostomum* Ledoides Group) A dwarf shrub, suitable for a rock garden, with tiny leaves and rounded trusses of small flowers, pink in bud, opening creamy-white. Mid. (1942). ♀ 2002. AM 1974. H4.

'**Scarlet Wonder**' (*R.* 'Essex Scarlet' × *R. forrestii*) A very hardy, dwarf shrub forming a compact mound of dense foliage. Flowers trumpet-shaped, frilly-margined, ruby-red, borne in loose trusses at the ends of the shoots. Mid. This very useful shrub was raised by Dietrich Hobbie of Germany. (1965). ♀ 2002. AMT 1989. H4.

'**Schneekrone**' (*R.* 'Humboldt' × *R. yakushimanum* 'Koichiro Wada') A small, very hardy shrub of compact, rounded habit with dark green, cupped leaves. Dense, rounded trusses of white flowers, slightly flushed pink and spotted red, open from deep pink buds. Mid to late. H4.

'**Scintillation**' A hybrid of *R. fortunei* raised in North America making a medium-sized shrub with glossy dark green foliage. Pink flowers with a bronze flare are borne in large, rounded trusses. Mid to late. (1959). H4.

'**Sennocke**' A dense, dwarf shrub with funnel-shaped, deep waxy-red flowers. Mid. H4.

'**September Song**' (*R.* Didi Group × *R.* 'Fawn') A compact, small shrub with slightly glossy, dark green leaves to 11cm long. Flowers widely bell-shaped to funnel-campanulate, to 8cm across, red in bud, opening brilliant orange-yellow, margined deep pink and spotted reddish-orange. Mid. (1988). H4.

'**Seta**' (*R. moupinense* × *R. spinuliferum*) An exceedingly pretty, medium-sized Bodnant hybrid of erect habit, producing umbels of unspotted, narrowly bell-shaped flowers, 4cm long, white at base, shading to vivid pink in the lobes. March and April, one of the first hybrids to flower. (1933). FCC 1960. AM 1933. H3.

'**Seven Stars**' (*R.* 'Loderi Sir Joseph Hooker' × *R. yakushimanum*) A large, vigorous, free-flowering hybrid, raised at Windsor Great Park. Flowers bell-shaped with wavy margins, white, flushed pink, reddish in bud. Mid. This plant is best grown in woodland shade. (1966). FCCT 1974. AM 1967. H4.

'**Shamrock**' (*R. keiskei*, dwarf form × *R. hanceanum* Nanum Group) A dwarf shrub of compact, spreading habit with glossy green leaves. Pale yellow flowers open from yellow-green buds. Early to mid. (1978). H4.

'**Shilsonii**' (*R. barbatum* × *R. thomsonii*) A strong-growing, rounded, symmetrical bush or small tree; intermediate in habit and foliage between the parents. Attractive, metallic-coloured stems. Flowers in loose trusses, bell-shaped, blood-red with darker veins and inconspicuous dark brown markings; calyx large, cup-shaped, pale green, flushed crimson. Early. Raised by Richard Gill before 1900. AM 1900. H3–4.

'**Shrimp Girl**' (*R.* 'Fabia Tangerine' × *R. yakushimanum*) A compact, small shrub with blue-green foliage, downy beneath. Flowers salmon-pink with a petaloid calyx, in open trusses. Mid. (1971). H4.

'**Silberwolke**' ('Silver Cloud') (*R.* 'Album Novum' × *R. yakushimanum* 'Koichiro Wada') A dwarf shrub of dense, rounded habit, with dark green leaves. Flowers pale purple, darker outside, spotted with yellow-green and with frilled margins. (1963). H4.

'**Silver Cloud**' See 'Silberwolke'.

'**Silver Jubilee**' (*R.* 'Coronation Day' × *R. yakushimanum*) A small shrub with glossy green leaves and large trusses of pale greenish-yellow flowers fading to pale yellow-green and marked with crimson. Mid. (1967). H4.

'**Silver Sixpence**' A small, upright shrub bearing cream flowers spotted with yellow; green buds, tinged mauve. Mid. (1975). H4.

'**Sir Charles Lemon**' (*R. arboreum* 'Sir Charles Lemon') A magnificent, large shrub or small tree with handsome leaves, rusty-brown beneath. Flowers white in dense trusses. Early. Probably *R. arboreum* × *R. campanulatum*. C 1868. ♀ 2002. H3–4.

'**Sir Frederick Moore**' (*R. fortunei* subsp. *discolor* × *R.* 'St Keverne') A tall, hardy hybrid with long leaves and large, compact, rounded trusses of large, widely funnel-shaped, wavy-edged flowers, clear pink, heavily spotted crimson at the base within. Mid. (1935). FCCT 1972. AM 1937. H3–4.

'**Sneezy**' (*R.* 'Doncaster' × *R. yakushimanum*) A compact and very hardy, small shrub of vigorous growth, with dark green leaves that are silvery-hairy when young. Deep pink flowers, paler in the centre with red spots, open in large, dense trusses. Mid to late. (1971). AMT 1986. H4.

'Snipe' A dwarf, dense shrub with pale green leaves and pale pink to white flowers, flushed violet and purple and with deeper spots. Early to mid. AM 1975. H4.

'Snow Lady' (*R. ciliatum × R. leucaspis*) A compact, small shrub of spreading habit with bristly-hairy leaves to 7.5cm long. Fragrant, white flowers are borne in lax trusses. Mid. (1955). H4.

'Snow Queen' (*R.* 'Halopeanum' × *R.* Loderi Group) A lovely, free-flowering Leonardslee hybrid. A large, compact bush, bearing dome-shaped trusses of large, funnel-shaped flowers, dark pink in bud, opening pure white with a small red basal blotch within. Mid. (1926). FCCT 1970. AMT 1946. AM 1934. H4.

'Solent Queen' (Angelo Group) A large Exbury hybrid producing magnificent trusses of large, widely funnel-shaped, fragrant flowers each about 13cm across; white flushed pink at margins and with a central ray of green. Mid. AM 1939. H3.

'Solidarity' (*R.* 'The Honourable Jean Marie de Montague' × *R. yakushimanum*) A medium-sized shrub, the leaves to 12.5cm long with a light tan indumentum beneath. Flowers open funnel-shaped, 7.5cm across, with wavy-edged lobes, light purple-pink with deeper margins, fading to pale pink spotted with deep purple-red. Mid. (1969). H4.

'Songbird' (*R.* 'Blue Tit' × *R. russatum*) A charming, small shrub producing clusters of violet, bell-shaped flowers. Early. Raised by Col Sir James Horlick at Gigha, Argyllshire, Scotland. (1954). AM 1957. H4.

'Souvenir de Doctor S. Endtz' (*R.* 'John Walter' × *R.* 'Pink Pearl') A compact bush showing the influence of the former parent in its habit and that of the latter parent in its foliage and flowers. Flowers in a dome-shaped truss, widely funnel-shaped, rich rose in bud, opening rich, mottled pink, paler in the centre and marked with a ray of crimson; nectaries crimson. Mid. Raised by L.J. Endtz & Co. of Boskoop before 1924. ♀ 2002. FCCT 1970. AM 1924. H4.

'Souvenir of Anthony Waterer' A vigorous, upright, large shrub bearing dark rose-red flowers, with a prominent yellow eye, in domed trusses. Mid. (Before 1924). ♀ 2002. H4.

Spinulosum Group (*R. racemosum × R. spinuliferum*) An erect shrub bearing compact trusses of narrowly bell-shaped, deep pink flowers with protruding anthers. Mid. Raised at Kew. (1926). AM (F) 1944. H4.

'Spring Magic' (*R.* 'Essex Scarlet' × *R. forrestii* Repens Group) A compact, spreading, small shrub with dark green leaves. Flowers deep currant-red with darker spots. Mid. AMT 1969. H4.

'Streatley' (*R. aberconwayi × R. yakushimanum*) A small shrub with white flowers flushed rose-pink and spotted red, from magenta buds. Mid. (1965). AM 1965. H4.

'Surrey Heath' ([*R. facetum × R.* Fabia Group] × [*R. yakushimanum × R.* 'Britannia']) Small, bushy shrub of spreading habit, with narrow leaves, white-tomentose above when young. Flowers funnel-shaped, 4.5cm across, in globular trusses, pale rose-pink, deeper at the margins with brownish spots inside. Mid. (1975). AMT 1982. H4.

'Susan' (*R. campanulatum × R. fortunei*) A tall, bushy hybrid bearing large trusses of bluish-mauve flowers, darker at margins and spotted purple within. Early to mid. (1930). ♀ 2002. FCC 1954. AMT 1948. AM 1930. H4.

'Sweet Simplicity' A medium-sized, bushy shrub with large, glossy leaves. Flowers ruffled, white with pink edges and olive spots, in rounded trusses. Mid to late. (Before 1922). AM 1970. H4.

'Sweet Sue' ([*R. facetum × R.* 'Fabia'] × [*R. yakushimanum × R.* 'Fabia Tangerine']) A vigorous, small shrub of upright habit, with leaves to 11cm long. Flowers bell-shaped, 7cm across, with wavy margins, orange-red, spotted red and margined pale pink, in compact, dome-shaped trusses 14cm across. Mid to late. (1972). H4.

'Talavera' See *R.* 'Golden Oriole Talavera'.

'Tally Ho' (*R. facetum × R. griersonianum*) A broadly dome-shaped bush bearing compact, rounded trusses of brilliant scarlet, funnel-shaped flowers. Mid to late. A superb woodland plant raised by J.J. Crosfield at Embley Park. (1933). FCC 1933. H3.

'Tatjana' (*R.* 'Nachtglut' × [*R.* 'Mars' × *R. yakushimanum*]) A small, compact shrub, with dark green leaves that have a woolly indumentum beneath. Flowers red, paler in the centre, in trusses of up to 16. Mid to late. (1985). ♀ 2002. H4.

'Taurus' (*R.* 'Jean Marie de Montague' × *R. strigillosum*) A stout-branched, large shrub of upright growth, with handsome, dark green, prominently veined leaves. Vivid red, widely funnel-shaped flowers, with frilled margins, are borne in large, rounded trusses. Early to mid. (1972). ♀ 2002. H4.

'Teal' (*R. brachyanthum* var. *hypolepidotum × R. fletcherianum*) A compact, dwarf shrub of rather upright habit, with pale green leaves, to 5.5cm long; develops peeling bark with age. Flowers primrose-yellow, broadly bell-shaped, to 3.5cm across. Mid. Best in a cool position. (1977). AM 1977. H4.

'Teddy Bear' (*R. bureaui × R. yakushimanum*) A small shrub making an excellent foliage plant, the glossy dark green leaves with brown felt above when young and a persistent brown indumentum beneath. Large and showy pale pink flowers fade to white. Mid. H4.

'Temple Belle' (*R. orbiculare × R. williamsianum*) A charming shrub of neat, rounded habit, much resembling the former parent. Rounded leaves are attractively glaucous beneath. Flowers in a loose cluster, bell-shaped, uniform Persian-rose without markings. Early to mid. (1916). H3.

'Tessa' (*R. moupinense × R.* Praecox Group) A small bush up to 1m. Flowers in loose flattened umbels, soft, slightly purplish-pink, with a ray of crimson spots, opening in March or early April. (1935). AM 1935. H4.

'Tessa Roza' A selection from 'Tessa', which it resembles, but with deeper pink flowers. Early. ♀ 2002. AM 1953. H4.

'The Hon. Jean Marie de Montague' A vigorous, medium-sized shrub of compact, spreading habit, with dark green leaves to 15cm long. Flowers widely funnel-campanulate with wavy margins, 8cm across, deep scarlet-crimson with darker spots in the throat, borne in compact, dome-shaped trusses to 15cm wide. Mid. A hybrid of *R. griffithianum*. (1921). ♀ 2002. AMT 1989. H4.

'**The Master**' (*R.* 'China' × *R.* 'Letty Edwards') Huge, globular trusses of large, funnel-shaped, pink flowers with a dark red basal blotch within. Mid. (1955). ♀ 2002. AMT 1966. H4.

'**Thomwilliams**' (*R. thomsonii* × *R. williamsianum*) A compact, medium-sized shrub with broadly ovate or nearly orbicular leaves, deeply cordate at the base, to 7.5cm long. Flowers widely bell-shaped, 7.5cm across, deep crimson in bud, opening deep reddish-pink, unspotted, in open trusses. Early. (1927). AM 1935. H4.

'**Thor**' (*R. haematodes* × *R.* 'Felis') A compact, small shrub of rounded habit; dark green leaves are covered beneath with a thick indumentum. Flowers bright scarlet with a showy, petaloid calyx, in open trusses. Mid. (1962). H3.

'**Thunderstorm**' A medium-sized shrub with glossy dark green leaves. Flowers wavy-edged, dark red, darker-spotted with white stamens, in neat, dome-shaped trusses. Mid to late. (1930). AMT 1955. H4.

'**Tibet**' (*R.* 'Bismark' × *R. williamsianum*) A compact, small shrub of neat habit with deep green, ovate leaves to 8cm across. Bell-shaped, white flowers, 5.5cm across, open from pink buds. Mid. (1966). ♀ 2002. H3–4.

'**Tidbit**' (*R. dichroanthum* × *R. wardii*) A small shrub of dense, spreading habit with dark glossy green leaves to 7cm long. Bell-shaped flowers, 3cm across, with wavy margins, straw-yellow, red in the throat, in compact, domed trusses. Mid. (1957). ♀ 2002. H4.

'**Titian Beauty**' ([*R. facetum* × *R.* Fabia Group 'Tangerine'] × [*R.* Fabia Group 'Tangerine' × *R. yakushimanum*]) A small shrub of compact, rather upright habit; dark green leaves have a thin brown indumentum beneath. Flowers waxy-red. Mid. (1971). H4.

'**Too Bee**' (*R. campylogynum* 'Patricia' × *R. keiskei* 'Yaku Fairy') This is a most attractive, compact, dwarf shrub of spreading habit, with dark green leaves, to 4cm long, slightly scaly beneath. Flowers tubular to bell-shaped, 3cm long, deep pink outside, pale pink to white inside, borne in clusters of 3–4. Early to mid. (1983). AM 1988. H4.

'**Tortoiseshell Champagne**' See *R.* 'Champagne'.

'**Tortoiseshell Orange**' (*R.* 'Goldsworth Orange' × *R. griersonianum*) A Goldsworth hybrid bearing large, deep orange flowers. Mid to late. (1945). ♀ 2002. H3–4.

'**Tortoiseshell Wonder**' (*R.* 'Goldsworth Orange' × *R. griersonianum*) Salmon-pink. (1945). ♀ 2002. AM 1947. H3–4.

'**Tottenham**' A dwarf shrub, an old hybrid of *R. ferrugineum*, with dark green leaves and clusters of small, pale pink flowers. Mid to late. H4.

'**Treasure**' (*R. forrestii* Repens Group × *R. williamsianum*) Dwarf, mound-forming shrub with gnarled branches and neat, oval or rounded leaves, bronze when young. Flowers bell-shaped, deep rose, 5cm across. Early to mid. (1937). H3–4.

'**Trewithen Orange**' (*R. cinnabarinum* Concatenans Group × *R.* 'Full House') A remarkable hybrid bearing loose, pendent trusses of deep orange-brown flowers with a faint rosy blush. Early to mid. Raised at Trewithen, near St Austell, Cornwall. FCC 1950. H3–4.

'**Trude Webster**' (*R.* 'Countess of Derby' selfed) A strong-growing, medium-sized to large shrub, the winner of several awards in North America. Flowers clear pink, white on the lobes with darker spots, in very large, rounded trusses. Mid to late. (1961). H4.

'**Tyermannii**' An upright, medium-sized, tender shrub with glossy leaves and fragrant, lily-like, cream flowers, fading to white inside, tinged green and brown outside. Mid. (1925). FCC 1925. H2.

'**Unique**' A leafy, dense bush, a hybrid of *R. campylocarpum*. Flowers in a dense, dome-shaped truss, funnel-shaped, creamy-white with a faint blush and marked by scattered, faint, crimson spots within. Early to mid. (1934). ♀ 2002. FCCT 1935. AMT 1934. H4.

Vanessa Group (*R. griersonianum* × *R.* 'Soulbut') A spreading, rather shapely bush bearing loose trusses of soft pink flowers, 9cm across, spotted carmine at the base within. Mid to late. Raised at Bodnant, this was the first hybrid of *R. griersonianum* to be exhibited at the RHS. Cross made in 1924. FCC 1929. H4. '**Vanessa Pastel**' A lovely clone with flowers, 10cm across, of soft rose-pink, flushed biscuit with a deep crimson eye. Mid to late. (1946). ♀ 2002. FCCT and Cory Cup 1971. AM 1946.

'**Venetian Chimes**' ([*R. facetum* × *R.* 'Fabia'] × [*R.* 'Britannia' × *R. yakushimanum*]) A vigorous, small shrub of compact, spreading habit. Flowers bell-shaped, 5cm across, in compact, globular trusses, to 13cm across, brick-red, flushed scarlet towards the base and spotted with blackish-red. Mid to late. (1971). AMT 1979. H4.

'**Veryan Bay**' (*R. pseudochrysanthum* × *R. williamsianum*) A medium-sized, compact shrub raised by J.C. Williams. It bears profuse, nodding bell-shaped, shell-pink flowers on red stalks. Mid. (1929). H4.

'**Vintage Rosé**' (*R. yakushimanum* × [*R.* 'Jalisco Eclipse' × *R.* 'Fusilier']) A small, vigorous shrub with dark matt green leaves to 10cm long, with a thick indumentum beneath. Funnel-shaped, wavy-margined flowers, 6cm across, are rose-pink, deeper in the centre, in large, conical trusses 13cm across. Mid to late. (1974). ♀ 2002. H4.

'**Virginia Richards**' ([*R. wardii* × *R.* 'F.C. Puddle'] × *R.* 'Mrs Betty Robertson') A small shrub of vigorous, upright habit. Leaves to 9cm long. Flowers in large, globular trusses, up to 16cm across, funnel-shaped, wavy-margined, pale orange in the centre flushed rose-pink at the margins, deeper at the base with red spots inside. Mid. Unfortunately prone to powdery mildew. (1962). AMT 1985. H4.

'**Viscy**' (*R.* 'Diane' × *R. viscidifolium*) A small shrub of open habit with bold, glossy dark green foliage. Large, bell-shaped flowers of an unusual and striking orange, age to coppery-yellow, conspicuously spotted with dark red. Mid to late. (1980). ♀ 2002. H4.

Volker Group (Flavum Group) (*R. wardii* × *R. yakushimanum* 'Koichiro Wada') A compact, small shrub with dark glossy green leaves. Flowers bell-shaped, to 6cm across, pale yellow sometimes blotched with red, in dense, dome-shaped trusses. Mid. This hybrid has been raised many times and several cultivars have been named. (1953). H4.

'**Vulcan**' (*R. griersonianum* × *R.* 'Mars') A medium-sized shrub of compact habit. Funnel-shaped, wavy-margined, bright red flowers 6cm across are borne in dome-shaped trusses. Mid. (1938). ♀ 2002. AMT 1957. H4.

'W.F.H.' (*R. haematodes* × *R.* 'Tally Ho') A small, spreading shrub bearing clusters of brilliant scarlet, funnel-shaped flowers. Mid. Named after Mr W.F. Hamilton, one-time Head Gardener at Pylewell Park near Lymington, Hampshire. (1941). ♥ 2002. H4.

'Wee Bee' (*R. campylogynum* 'Patricia' × *R. keiskei* 'Yaku Fairy') A dwarf shrub making a low, spreading mound of neat habit. Tubular, frilled, rose-pink flowers, deeper in the throat, with red spots, open from red buds. Early to mid. ♥ 2002. H4.

'White Swan' (*R. decorum* × *R.* 'Pink Pearl') A tall shrub with dark greyish-green foliage. Flowers pale pink fading to white with a green eye in throat. FCCT 1957. AMT 1937. H3–4.

'Wigeon' (*R. calostrotum* 'Gigha' × *R. minus* Carolinianum Group) A compact, free-flowering, dwarf shrub, with dark green leaves to 4.5cm long. Flowers open funnel-shaped with wavy margins, 4cm across, deep lavender-pink with darker spots, in dome-shaped trusses 7cm across. Mid. (1982). AMT 1987. H4.

'Wilgen's Ruby' (*R.* 'Britannia' × *R.* 'John Walter') A popular and very hardy, medium-sized, compact shrub. Bears handsome, large, rounded trusses of funnel-shaped, deep red flowers, with darker spots. Mid to late. (1951). H4.

'Willbrit' (*R.* 'Britannia' × *R. williamsianum*) A small shrub of compact, rounded habit with dark green leaves, to 8cm long, reddish when young. Deep pink, bell-shaped flowers, paler at the margin are borne in open trusses. Mid to late. (1960). H4.

'Windlesham Scarlet' (*R.* 'Britannia' × *R.* 'Doncaster') A vigorous, medium-sized shrub of compact habit. Dome-shaped trusses bear widely bell-shaped, deep crimson, frilly-margined flowers speckled with black inside. Mid to late. (1950). FCCT 1971. AMT 1968. H4.

'Windsor Lad' A hybrid of *R. ponticum* making a medium-sized shrub. Widely funnel-shaped flowers, 6–7cm across, open lilac-purple with a prominent green patch, from deep purple buds. Mid to late. (1958). H4.

'Winsome' (*R. griersonianum* × *R.* 'Humming Bird') A lovely Bodnant hybrid, making a small bush, with deep coppery young growths. Leaves, to 9cm long, are dark green above with a thin, rusty tomentum beneath. Flowers funnel-shaped, 6cm across, in loose, pendent clusters, scarlet in bud, opening deep rose-pink, reddish towards the base, contrasting effectively with the young leaves. Mid. (1939). ♥ 2002. AM 1950. H3–4.

'Wishmoor' (*R. wardii* Litiense Group × *R. yakushimanum*) A compact, small shrub with glossy green leaves. Flowers 7-lobed, bell-shaped, 8cm across, open pale primrose-yellow, deeper in the throat, from orange-red buds. Mid. (1972). FCC 1987. AM 1972. H4.

'Woodcock' (*R.* 'Elizabeth' × *R. hyperythrum*) A very distinct, small, rounded shrub of compact habit raised at Wisley. Leaves rich green, to 10cm long, deeply veined and with recurved margins. Flowers in flat-topped trusses of about 10, funnel-shaped, clear pale pink with a few red spots, contrasting effectively with the deep strawberry-pink buds. (1972). AMT 1986. H4.

'Wren' (*R. ludlowii* × *R. keiskei* 'Yaku Fairy') A prostrate, mound-forming, dwarf shrub with deep glossy green leaves, scaly beneath, and reddish young growths. Flowers clear yellow. Early to mid. AM 1970. H4.

'Yaku Princess' (*R.* 'King Tut' × *R. yakushimanum* 'Koichiro Wada') A small, very hardy shrub of dense, rounded habit; leaves have a pale brown indumentum beneath. Flowers apple blossom-pink with greenish spots, in dense, rounded trusses. Mid to late. (1977). H4.

'Yellow Hammer' (*R. flavidum* × *R. sulfureum*) A charming, rather slender hybrid raised at Caerhays, Cornwall. Flowers in pairs from terminal and axillary buds, tubular or narrowly bell-shaped, bright yellow. Early. (Before 1931). ♥ 2002. H3–4.

‡Azaleodendrons

A group of attractive hybrids between deciduous azaleas and evergreen species of other subgenera. Very hardy, mostly semi-evergreen shrubs of small to medium size, flowering in May or June. H4.

****'Azaleoides'** (*R. periclymenoides* × *R. ponticum*) A dense, slow-growing shrub with slender branches. Leaves oblanceolate, dull, dark green above, pale green or faintly glaucous beneath. Flowers in rounded trusses, funnel-shaped, deliciously scented, purplish-lilac in bud, opening white, edged purplish-lilac and faintly spotted within; June. The first recorded rhododendron hybrid, it occurred as an accidental cross in the nursery of a Mr Thompson, at Mile End, London, about 1820.

'Broughtonii Aureum' ([*R. maximum* × *R. ponticum*] × *R. molle*) ('Norbitonense Broughtonianum') A small shrub of rounded habit. Leaves elliptic to oblanceolate, persistent, 7.5–10cm long, dark green above, paler beneath, often bronze-flushed in winter. Flowers in a compact truss, widely funnel-shaped, deep creamy-yellow with light brown markings, flushed pink in bud; June. Raised in the village of Broughton, Peeblesshire, Scotland, about 1830. FCC 1935.

'Dot' Small to medium-sized shrub. Leaves green, oblanceolate to elliptic-obovate, 6–10cm long. Large clusters of rose-crimson flowers. May and June. AM 1945.

'Galloper Light' A most pleasing, leafy bush, raised at Exbury. Bears loose trusses of funnel-shaped flowers, cream in the tube shading to soft salmon-pink in the lobes, with a chrome-yellow blotch (general effect creamy-pink); late: May to early June. AM 1927.

'Gemmiferum' A small shrub of loose, open habit. Leaves elliptic to obovate, 3–5cm long, leathery, dark green above, paler beneath. Flowers in a compact, rounded truss, funnel-shaped, dark crimson in bud, opening to rose, heavily flushed crimson; late May to early June. Brought into cultivation by T. Methven & Son of Edinburgh, in 1868. Of similar origin to 'Azaleoides'.

'Glory of Littleworth' A superb, small, azalea-like shrub of stiff, erect habit. Leaves oblong to oblong-lanceolate, 7.5–11cm long, often curled and undulate. Flowers funnel-shaped, cream at first becoming milk-white with a conspicuous coppery blotch, fragrant; May. Raised by H.J. Mangles. AM 1911.

'Govenianum' An erect, densely branched bush up to 2m or more in height. Leaves crowded at the tips of the shoots, elliptic to oblanceolate, leathery, 5–6cm long, smooth, dark green and reticulate above, pale green beneath. Buds red in winter. Flowers funnel-shaped, fragrant, delicate lilac-purple, slightly paler on lobes, stained crimson on the ridges outside and faintly green-spotted within; June. Brought into cultivation by T. Methven & Son of Edinburgh, about 1868. Said to be a hybrid rhododendron (*R. catawbiense* × *R. ponticum*) crossed with an unknown azalea.

'**Hardijzer Beauty**' (Kurume azalaea × *R. racemosum*) A small shrub with glossy bright green leaves to 4.5cm long. Flowers funnel-shaped, 3cm long, bright pink with deeper spots, borne in compact heads of several small trusses. (1964). AMT 1970.

'**Jill Dolding**' A small, stiffly upright shrub with oblanceolate leaves to 9cm by 3cm, turning deep purple above in winter. Flowers funnel-shaped, rose-purple shading to lilac with orange and rose-red spots on the upper lobe, borne in a rather open truss; May. Occurred as a chance seedling in our nurseries and is probably *R. ponticum* hybrid × *R.* (deciduous azalea) 'Marconi'.

'**Martha Isaacson**' (*R.* 'Mrs Donald Graham' × *R. occidentale*) A small, semi-evergreen shrub of upright habit with bronze-red foliage. White, pink-striped flowers are borne in dense trusses. (1956). ♔ 2002.

'**Martine**' (*R. racemosum* × ? *R.* 'Hinomayo') A small, densely branched shrub of Dutch origin. Leaves elliptic to elliptic-oblong. 1–2cm long, bright glossy green. Flowers funnel-shaped, shell-pink, abundantly produced; May to mid-June.

'**Nellie**' (*R. occidentale* × *R.* 'The Monitor') A small, azalea-like shrub, resembling the former parent in habit, but much broader in outline. Leaves narrowly elliptic to oblanceolate, dull green above, paler beneath. Flowers in a rounded truss, fragrant, funnel-shaped, pure white with a conspicuous deep yellow blotch; May.

'**Norbitonense Aureum**' See 'Smithii Aureum'.

'**Norbitonense Broughtonianum**' See 'Broughtonii Aureum'.

*'**Odoratum**' (*R. nudiflorum* × *R. ponticum*) A small, dense, bushy shrub. Leaves obovate to obovate-elliptic, 5–6cm long, green above, glaucous at first beneath. Flowers blush or pale lilac, fragrant. May and June. I before 1875. AM 1994.

*'**Ria Hardijzer**' (*R.* 'Hinode-giri' × *R. racemosum*) A dwarf shrub, to about 70cm tall, with dark green leaves to 2.5cm long. Flowers broadly funnel-shaped, to 2.3cm across, purple-red, deeper in the throat, borne in compact, globular trusses. (1958). FCCT 1980. AMT 1974.

'**Smithii Aureum**' ([*R. maximum* × *R. ponticum*] × *R. molle*) ('Norbitonense Aureum') A small shrub resembling 'Broughtonii Aureum', but differing in the leaves, which are oblanceolate, 7–9cm long, glaucous beneath, and the paler yellow flowers; late May to early June. The leaves assume a distinctive purplish or plum-colour in winter. Raised by W. Smith at Norbiton, Surrey, in 1830.

'**Torlonianum**' An azalea-like shrub to 2m high. Leaves elliptic, 5–10cm long, dark shining green. Flowers in a neat rounded truss, funnel-shaped, lilac-rose, darker at the margins, with a conspicuous orange blotch; late May to early June.

Deciduous Hybrid Azaleas

The first deciduous hybrid azaleas began to appear in the early 19th century; today they number in hundreds. Their average height varies from 1.5–2.5m, but many clones may reach greater heights in moist, woodland gardens. Flowers are normally trumpet-shaped and single, though a number have double flowers. Colours range from the delicate pastel shades of the Occidentale Hybrids to the riotous reds, flames and golds of the Mollis Azaleas and Knap Hill Hybrids. Some groups, including the Ghent Azaleas and the Occidentale Hybrids, have flowers that are deliciously fragrant, particularly in the evening. Many exhibit rich autumn colours.

Ghent Hybrids (Gh)—A popular group, first raised in Ghent, Belgium in the early 19th century, later (1830 and 1850) in England, and more recently in the USA. Among the species involved are *RR. atlanticum, calendulaceum, canescens, flammeum, luteum, periclymenoides*, and *arborescens*. They are distinguished by their usually fragrant, long-tubed, honeysuckle-like flowers. They are taller and more twiggy than the Mollis Azaleas, and their flowering season is later, commencing about the end of May. Average height in an open position 1.8–2.5m. H4.

Knap Hill Hybrids (Kn)—A large and colourful group probably derived from *R. calendulaceum* × *molle*, Ghent Hybrids × *R. molle* as well as *R. occidentale* and *R. arborescens*. Originally developed in the Knap Hill Nursery by Anthony Waterer, and more extensively by the late Lionel de Rothschild at Exbury, Hampshire (the latter are often referred to as the Exbury Azaleas and are marked Kn-Ex). Further development by the late Edgar Stead at Christchurch, New Zealand produced the Ilam Hybrids. New cultivars from several sources continue to appear. Members are characterised by their trumpet-shaped, usually scentless flowers in a wide range of colours, opening in May. Average height in an open position 1.8–2.5m. H4.

Mollis Azaleas (M)—This attractive group originated as selections of *R. molle* subsp. *japonicum*, made by L. van Houtte in 1873, and later on by other Belgian nurserymen. Later this species was crossed with *R. molle* to produce a range of seedlings with flowers of more intense and diverse colouring. Their large, scentless flowers are borne in handsome trusses usually in early May, before the leaves. Average height in an open position 1.2–1.8m. H4.

Occidentale Hybrids (O)—A group derived mainly from *R. molle* × *R. occidentale*. All have delicate pastel-coloured, fragrant flowers, opening in late May, usually a fortnight later than the Mollis Azaleas. Average height when growing in an open position 1.8–2.5m. H4.

Rustica Hybrids (R)—(Rustica Flore Pleno Hybrids) A double-flowered group produced by crossing double-flowered forms of Ghent azaleas with *R. molle* subsp. *japonicum*. They are compact in habit, with attractive, sweetly scented flowers, opening in late May and early June. Average height in an open position 1.2–1.5m. H4.

'**Aida**' (R) Deep peach-pink with a deeper flush, double. (1888).

'**Altaclerense**' (M) Orange-yellow with darker flash, flushed pink in bud, fragrant, in large, globular heads. FCC 1862.

'**Annabella**' (Kn) Orange and yellow in bud, opening to golden-yellow, overlaid and flushed orange-rose. (1947). ♀ 2002.

'**Babeuff**' (M) Bright salmon, shaded orange. (1918).

'**Ballerina**' (Kn-Ex) White with an orange flush, suffused flesh-pink in bud, large with frilled edges.

'**Balzac**' (Kn-Ex) Nasturtium-red with orange flash, fragrant. AM 1934.

'**Basilisk**' (Kn-Ex) Rich creamy-yellow in bud, opening to cream with bright orange flare. AM 1934.

'**Beaulieu**' (Kn-Ex) Deep salmon-pink in bud, opening soft salmon-pink with a deep orange flush; young foliage bronze-red.

'**Berryrose**' (Kn-Ex) Rose-pink with a yellow flash; young foliage coppery. ♀ 2002. AM 1934.

'**Bouquet de Flore**' (Gh) Vivid red blotched with yellow. C 1869. ♀ 2002.

'**Brazil**' (Kn-Ex) Bright tangerine-red, darkening with age, frilly margins. (1934).

'**Buzzard**' (Kn) Pale straw-yellow, edged and tinted pink, with a deep yellow flare. (1947).

'**Cannon's Double**' (Kn-Ex) Fully double, pale yellow flushed pink on the outside of the lobes, with deep pink veins and tube. Good autumn colour. (1983). ♀ 2002.

'**Cecile**' (Kn-Ex) Dark salmon-pink in bud, opening to salmon-pink with a yellow flare, large. (1947). ♀ 2002.

'**Christopher Wren**' (M) ('Goldball') Orange-yellow flushed flame, with dark orange spotting, flushed red in bud.

'**Coccineum Speciosum**' (Gh) Brilliant orange-red. Still one of the best of the old azaleas. (Before 1846). ♀ 2002.

'**Comte de Gomer**' (M) Rose-pink with orange flare. (1872). FCC 1879.

'**Comte de Papadopoli**' (M) Bright pink, illuminated orange. (1873).

'**Corneille**' (Gh) Cream, flushed deep pink on outside, pink in bud, double. Especially good autumn leaf colour. ♀ 2002. AMT 1958.

'**Coronation Lady**' (Kn-Ex) Yellowish-pink with an orange-yellow blotch.

'**Corringe**' (Kn-Ex) Flame.

'**Daviesii**' (Gh) White with a yellow flare, fragrant; a hybrid between *R. molle* and *R. viscosum*. (About 1840). ♀ 2002. AM 1989.

'**Delicatissimum**' (O) Fragrant, pale yellowish white, flushed pink, with a yellow blotch.

'**Devon**' (Kn) Orange-red. AMT 1952.

'**Diorama**' ([*R. viscosum* × *R.* 'Koster's Brilliant Red'] × *R.* 'Fireglow') Deep red, fragrant.

'**Directeur Moerlands**' (M) ('Golden Sunlight') Golden-yellow, deepening in throat, with an orange flare, buds Chinese-white.

'**Doctor M. Oosthoek**' (M) Deep orange-red. (1920). ♀ 2002. AMT 1940. AM 1920.

'**Double Damask**' (Kn) One of the few double Knap Hill azaleas. Flowers are cream-white, double and fragrant. ♀ 2002.

'**Dracula**' (Kn) An unusual colour: blackish-red in bud opening to a smouldering nasturtium-red, overlaid crimson, margins frilled; young leaves bronze-tinted. Raised in our nurseries. (1970).

'**Drury Lane**' (Kn-Ex) Semi-double, to 8.5cm across, with 9 lobes, light orange-yellow tipped deep yellowish-pink. (1970s). AM 1989.

'**Embley Crimson**' (Kn) Crimson; compact habit. A seedling from Embley Park, Hampshire.

'**Exbury White**' (Kn-Ex) White blotched orange-yellow, large.

'**Exquisitum**' (O) Flesh-pink, flushed deep pink on outside, orange flare, frilly margins, fragrant. (1901). FCCT 1968. AMT 1950. ♀ 2002.

'**Fanny**' See 'Pucella'.

'**Fawley**' (Kn-Ex) Flushed pink in bud, opening white flushed pink at margins with an orange flare. (1947).

'**Fireball**' (Kn-Ex) Deep orange-red; young foliage deep copper-red. (1951). ♀ 2002.

'**Firefly**' (Kn-Ex) Rose-red with a faint orange flare. (1947).

'**Floradora**' (M) Orange-red, deeply spotted. (1910). AM 1910.

'**Freya**' (R) Pale pink, tinted orange-salmon, double. (1888). AMT 1953. AM 1897.

'**Frills**' (Kn-Ex) Orange-red, semi-double with frilly margins. (1951).

'**Frome**' (Kn) Saffron-yellow, overlaid fiery-red in throat, margins waved and frilled. (1958). AMT 1958.

'**Gallipoli**' (Kn-Ex) Rose-red buds, opening pale tangerine, flushed pink with a warm yellow flare, very large. (1947).

'**George Reynolds**' (Kn) Deep butter-yellow with chrome-yellow and green spotting, pink-flushed in bud. A tall clone with large flowers. AM 1936.

'**Gibraltar**' (Kn-Ex) Large, flame-orange flowers with warm yellow flash and crinkly petals; deep crimson-orange in bud. (1947). ♀ 2002.

'**Ginger**' (Kn-Ex) Orange-carmine in bud, opening to brilliant orange with warm golden upper petal. (1947).

'**Gloria Mundi**' (Gh) Bright orange with yellow flare, frilled at the margins. (1846).

'**Glowing Embers**' (Kn-Ex) Vivid reddish-orange with orange blotch.

'**Gog**' (Kn) Orange-red with yellow flash, flushed dark red on the outside. (1926).

'**Gold Dust**' (Kn-Ex) Pale yellow with gold flare. (1951).

'**Goldball**' See 'Christopher Wren'.

'**Golden Eagle**' (Kn) Reddish-orange with orange-yellow veins, blotched vivid orange. A hybrid of *R. calendulaceum*.

'**Golden Flare**' (Kn) Vivid yellow blotched reddish-orange, to 6.5cm across. A seedling of 'Altaclerense'. (Before 1966).

'**Golden Horn**' (Kn-Ex) Flowers straw-yellow with a deep yellow flash, tinged rose on the outside, and in bud, fading to ivory; leaves bronze-tinted, greyish, hoary. (1947).

'**Golden Lights**' Golden-yellow, fragrant flowers. One of the very hardy Northern Lights azaleas.

'**Golden Oriole**' (Kn) Deep golden-yellow with orange flare; young leaves bronze-tinted. (1939). AM 1947.

'**Golden Sunset**' (Kn) Vivid yellow. AM 1956.

'**Harvest Moon**' (Kn) Straw-yellow with chrome-yellow flare, slightly scented. (1938). AMT 1953.

'**Homebush**' (Kn) Rose-madder with paler shading, semi-double, in tight rounded heads. A most attractive azalea. (1926). ♀ 2002. AMT 1950.

'**Hortulanus H. Witte**' (M) Bright orange-yellow, red-tinged in bud. (1892).

'**Hotspur**' (Kn-Ex) Dazzling flame-red with darker markings on upper petals. AM 1934.

'**Hotspur Red**' (Kn-Ex) Rich reddish-orange with an orange blotch. ♀ 2002.

'**Hugh Wormald**' (Kn-Ex) Deep golden-yellow with a darker flare.

'**Igneum Novum**' (Gh) Deep yellowish-orange with an orange blotch. C 1876.

'**Il Tasso**' (R) Rose-red, tinted salmon, double. Good orange-red autumn leaf colour. (1892).

'**Irene Koster**' (O) Rose-pink with a small yellow blotch; late. ♀ 2002.

'**Kathleen**' (Kn-Ex) Salmon-pink with an orange blotch; darker in bud. (1947).

'**Klondyke**' (Kn-Ex) A wonderful glowing orange-gold, large, tinted red on outside, flushed red in bud; young foliage coppery-red. One of the most striking of its group. (1947). ♀ 2002.

'**Koningin Emma**' ('Queen Emma') (M) Deep orange with a salmon glow.

'**Koster's Brilliant Red**' (M) Glowing orange-red. Perhaps the best of its colour. Very close to typical *R. molle* subsp. *japonicum*. (1918).

'**Lapwing**' (Kn) Pale yellow tinged orange and pink, upper lobe deeper with a greenish blotch. C 1935. AMT 1953.

'**Lemonara**' (M) Apricot-yellow, tinged red on outside. (1920).

'**Magnificum**' (O) Creamy-white, flushed pink, with an orange flare; rose-flushed in bud, fragrant. (1910).

'**Marion Merriman**' (Kn) Chrome-yellow with a large orange flash, petals with crimped margins. AMT 1950. AM 1925.

'**Mrs Peter Koster**' (M) Deep red with an orange glow. AMT 1953.

'**Multatuli**' (M) Deep glowing orange-red. (1918).

'**Nancy Buchanan**' (Kn-Ex) Pale straw-yellow, flushed pink with an orange flare. (1947).

'**Nancy Waterer**' (Gh) Brilliant golden-yellow, large. (Before 1876). ♀ 2002.

'**Narcissiflorum**' (Gh) Pale yellow, darker in centre and on outside, double, sweetly scented; vigorous, compact habit. (Before 1871). ♀ 2002. AMT 1954.

'**Norma**' (R) Rose-red with a salmon glow, double. (1888). ♀ 2002. AMT 1959. AM 1891.

'**Orange Truffles**' (Kn) Apricot, illuminated chrome-yellow within, flushed nasturtium-red on the outside, double, with frilly margins, borne in a tight compact, rounded truss. Young foliage coppery-red. Raised in our nurseries in 1966.

'**Oxydol**' (Kn-Ex) White with a yellow blotch. C 1947.

'**Pallas**' (Gh) Orange-red with an orange-yellow flare. (Before 1875).

'**Peregrine**' (Kn) Rich orange-red, darker in bud. (1949).

'**Persil**' (Kn) White with an orange-yellow flare. ♀ 2002.

'**Pink Ruffles**' Pink with an orange blotch.

'**Princess Margaret of Windsor**' (Kn-Ex) Large, glowing deep yellow flowers, May and June. C 1981. H4.

'**Pucella**' ('Fanny') (Gh) Deep rose-magenta with a darker tube and orange flare, becoming rose with age. ♀ 2002.

'**Queen Emma**' See 'Koningin Emma'.

'**Raphael de Smet**' (Gh) White, flushed rose, double; excellent autumn colour. (Before 1889). AM 1893.

'**Rosata**' (*R. viscosum* × *R.* 'Koster's Brilliant Red') Deep pink with darker veins, fragrant. ♀ 2002.

'**Royal Command**' (Kn-Ex) Vivid reddish-orange.

'**Royal Lodge**' (Kn-Ex) Deep vermilion-red, becoming crimson-red with age, long protruding stamens. (1947).

'**Sang de Gentbrugge**' (Gh) Bright signal-red. (1873).

'**Satan**' (Kn) Geranium-red, darker in bud. (1926). ♀ 2002.

'**Scarlet Pimpernel**' (Kn-Ex) Flowers dark red in bud, opening red with a faint orange flare; young foliage coppery-tinted. (1947).

'**Silver Slipper**' (Kn-Ex) White flushed pink with an orange flare; young foliage copper-tinted. (1948). ♀ 2002. FCCT 1963. AMT 1962.

'**Soir de Paris**' (*R. viscosum* hybrid) Purplish-pink with an orange blotch, fragrant. C 1965.

'**Spek's Orange**' (M) Orange, deeper in bud. Late flowering for its group. ♀ 2002. FCCT 1953. AMT 1948.

'**Strawberry Ice**' (Kn-Ex) Flesh-pink, mottled deeper pink at margins with a gold flare, deep pink in bud. (1947). ♀ 2002. AMT 1963.

'**Sugared Almond**' (Kn-Ex) Pale pink. C 1951.

'**Summer Fragrance**' (O) (*R. luteum* × *R. occidentale*) Pale yellow with vivid yellow blotch, fragrant; June. A compact, small shrub with good autumn colour. ♀ 2002.

'**Sun Chariot**' (Kn-Ex) Vivid yellow with an orange-yellow blotch. FCCT 1967. AMT 1963.

'**Sunbeam**' (M) A hybrid of 'Altaclerense' with larger flowers which are bright yellow with an orange blotch. (1895). AMT 1952.

'**Sunte Nectarine**' (Kn-Ex) Deep orange flowers blotched with yellow. ♀ 2002.

'**Tangiers**' (Kn-Ex) Tangerine, flushed pink, large, with frilly margins.

'**Tay**' (Kn) Chinese-yellow with an orange blotch, crinkled margins. (1959). AMT 1959.

'**Toucan**' (Kn) Pale straw-yellow with a saffron-yellow flare, fading with age, pink-tinged margins. (1941).

'**Trent**' (Kn) Chrome-yellow, tinged salmon at margins, with a golden-yellow flare, buds pink-tinged. (1958). AMT 1958.

'**Tunis**' (Kn) Deep crimson with an orange flare, darker in bud. (1926).

'**Unique**' (Gh) Vivid orange-red in bud, opening yellowish-orange, in a dense, ball-like truss. (Before 1875). AMT 1952.

'**Washington State Centennial**' Fragrant, frilly-edged, orange-yellow flowers, from orange-red buds, fade to white, edged pink with a bright yellow flare. Glossy leaves turn red to yellow in autumn.

'**Westminster**' (O) Clear rich almond-pink with a faint orange flash, fragrant.

'**White Lights**' A very hardy, small, rounded shrub bearing profuse, fragrant, white flowers yellow in the centre, opening from pink buds. May. C 1983. ♀ 2002.

'**White Swan**' (Kn-Ex) White with a yellow flare.

'**Whitethroat**' (Kn) Pure white, double, with frilly margins; compact habit. (1941). ♀ 2002. AMT 1962.

'**Wryneck**' (Kn) Straw-yellow, darker at margins, deeper yellow flash, darker and pink-tinged in bud.

'Wye' (Kn) Apricot-yellow, darker in throat, with an orange flare and crinkled margins, pink-flushed in bud.

'Yellow Cloud' (Kn) Large, very fragrant, bright yellow flowers, deeper on the upper lobe. C 1980.

‡*Evergreen Hybrid Azaleas

The hardy, evergreen and semi-evergreen species of the Azalea Series have given rise to a prodigious number of hybrids, many of which have arisen in Europe and the USA. The majority, however, have come from Japan, from where Ernest Wilson introduced the beautiful Kurume azaleas. In woodland glades, a close planting of dwarf, evergreen Kurume azaleas creates a spectacular effect, like a colourful patchwork quilt.

Evergreen azaleas will thrive in full sun if their roots are kept moist, but some shelter from cold winds is desirable and partial shade should be provided if possible as the flowers are liable to bleach in some clones. The flowering season is April and May (the majority in May) and the blossom is often produced so freely that the foliage is completely hidden. Individual flowers are normally single but certain clones possess 'hose-in-hose' flowers (one flower within another). Unless otherwise stated, their average height is 0.6–1.2m. Where known, the date of introduction of a hybrid is given in parentheses at the end of each description.

The main groups are as follows:

Exbury Hybrids (E)—Hybrids between various species raised by Lionel de Rothschild at Exbury, about 1933. Flowers normally large – 6–7.5cm across. Previously listed as Oldhamii Hybrids.

Gable Hybrids (G)—A large group of hybrids developed by Joseph B. Gable at Stewartstown, Pennsylvania, USA, and introduced about 1927. Many are the result of *R. kaempferi × R. yedoense* var. *poukhanense* but several other species and named hybrids have been used. Flowers medium-sized – 4–6cm across.

Glenn Dale Hybrids (GD)—A large and varied group of hybrids in which innumerable species and hybrids have been used. They were developed after 1935 through the work of B.Y. Morrison of the USA Department of Agriculture at Glenn Dale, Maryland. Flowers vary from medium to very large – 5–10cm across.

Indian or Indica Azaleas (I)—A large group of mainly tender hybrids developed in Belgium and England and to a lesser extent in France and Germany during the 19th century. Several species are involved in their parentage including *R. indicum*, *R. mucronatum* and *R. simsii*. The numerous greenhouse azaleas forced for Christmas and offered by florists belong here. Flowers large – 6–7cm across.

Kaempferi Hybrids (Kf)—A large group of hybrids that originated in Holland about 1920. They were produced by crossing *R. kaempferi* with *R.* 'Malvaticum'. At a later date several new clones were raised using *R.* 'Maxwellii'. Flowers usually medium size – 4–5cm across.

Kurume Azaleas (K)—The Kurume azaleas originated in Kurume, Japan, during the 19th century. Ernest Wilson was responsible for their arrival in the west, introducing his famous 'Wilson's Fifty' in 1920. Numerous other clones have since been raised, particularly in the USA. The main species responsible for the original Kurumes

are *R. kaempferi*, *R. kiusianum* and *R.* 'Obtusum'. Flowers characteristically small – 2.5–3.5cm across.

Oldhamii Hybrids See Exbury Hybrids.

Sander Hybrids (Sr)—Hybrids between Indian azaleas and Kurume azaleas. Originally developed in 1890 by Charles Sander of Brookline, Massachusetts. Flowers medium to large – 4–7.5cm across.

Satsuki Hybrids (S)—Introduced by the Chugai Nursery, Kobe, Japan to America during 1938–39. They are mainly the result of *R. indicum × R. simsii*, but various Belgian hybrids have also played a part. They are notorious for their tendency to sport and produce flowers of various colours. Flowers medium to large – 4–7.5cm across.

Vuyk Hybrids (V)—A group of hybrids that originated in the Vuyk van Nes Nursery, Boskoop, Holland, in 1921. Flowers normally large – 5–7.5cm across.

Wada Hybrids (W)—Hybrids of mixed parentage raised by K. Wada of Yokohama, Japan, before 1940. Flowers medium to large – 4–7.5cm across.

'Addy Wery' (K) (*R.* 'Malvaticum' × *R.* 'Flame') Deep vermilion-red. (1940). ♀ 2002. AMT 1950. H4.

'Adonis' (K) White, hose-in-hose, with frilly margins. H4.

'Advance' (GD) Rosy-red, 5cm across. H4.

'Aladdin' (K) (*R. kaempferi* hybrid × *R.* Kurume hybrid) Intense geranium-red fading to salmon. H4.

'Alexander' (*R. nakaharae* × *R.* 'Kin-no-sai') Deep reddish-orange with a purplish-red blotch. Dwarf, spreading habit. ♀ 2002. H4.

'Alice' (Kf) (*R.* 'Malvaticum' × *R. kaempferi*) Salmon-red with a dark flash. (1922). H4.

'Appleblossom' See 'Ho-o'.

'Atalanta' (Kf) (*R.* 'Malvaticum' × *R. kaempferi*) Soft lilac. H4.

'Azuma-kagami' (K) Phlox-pink with darker shading, hose-in-hose. Up to 1.8m; best in semi-shade. (Wilson 16). AMT 1950. H4.

'Beethoven' (V) Orchid-purple with a deeper blotch, petals fringed. (1941). ♀ 2002. H4.

'Bengal Beauty' (*R. kaempferi* 'Daimio' × *R. simsii*) Purplish-pink with wavy margins. C 1964. H4.

'Bengal Fire' (E) (*R. kaempferi × R. oldhamii*) Fieryorange; ultimately 1.8m high. (1934). H4.

'Beni-giri' (K) Bright crimson. (1910). H4.

'Betty' (Kf) (*R.* 'Malvaticum' × *R. kaempferi*) Salmon-pink with deeper centre. (1922). FCCT 1972. AMT 1940. H4.

'Bijou de Ledeberg' (I) Rose-red; leaves dark green with white margins. (1865). H3.

'Blaauw's Pink' (K) Salmon-pink with paler shading, early. (1953). ♀ 2002. H4.

'Blue Danube' (Kf) A most distinctive and striking bluish-violet. ♀ 2002. FCCT 1975. AMT 1970. H4.

'Buccaneer' (GD) (*R.* 'Hinode Giri' × *R.* 'Late Salmon') Vivid reddish-orange. Vigorous. H4.

'Bungo-nishiki' (W) Orange-scarlet, semi-double; late (June). H4.

'Canzonetta' (*R.* 'Signalglühen' × [*R.* 'Rubinetta' × *R.* 'Vuyk's Scarlet']) A compact, slow-growing, dwarf shrub. Flowers semi-double, with 5–8 lobes, to 4.5cm across, rich purple-red with deeper spots. Dark green foliage turns light purple-red in winter. (1974). ♀ 2002. H4.

'**Chanticleer**' (GD) Amaranth-purple, brilliant in effect, very floriferous. Bushy, dense habit. H4.

'**Chippewa**' Purplish-red with darker blotch. H4.

'**Christina**' (Kf) (*R.* 'Florida' × *R.* 'Louise Gable') Red, hose-in-hose or double, large. H4.

'**Christmas Cheer**' See 'Ima-shojo'.

'**Commodore**' (GD) Vivid red, blotched purple, 7cm across. H4.

'**Connie**' (Kf) Reddish-orange. H4.

Diamant Group Hybrids raised by Carl Fleischmann in Germany before 1969 by crossing an evergreen azalea named 'Multiflorum' with *R. kuisianum*. They make dense, mound-forming, very hardy dwarf shrubs and are grown in a range of colours. H4.

'**Double Beauty**' (*R.* double seedling × *R.* 'Vuyk's Scarlet') Purplish-red, hose-in-hose; low, compact habit. C 1966. H4.

'**Eddy**' (E) (*R.* 'Apollo' × *R. kaempferi*) Deep salmon-red; ultimately 1.5m high. (1933). AM 1944. H3.

'**Elsie Lee**' (*R.* 'Desirée' × *R.* 'Rosebud') Dwarf, with profuse funnel-shaped, pale mauve flowers to 7cm across with a flare of reddish spots and numerous petaloid stamens in the centre. Neat compact habit to 60cm tall. Late May. ♀ 2002. H4.

'**Everest**' (GD) (*R. mucronatum* × *R.* 'Shinnyo-no-tsuki') Profuse large white flowers with green blotch. H4.

'**Favorite**' (*R.* 'Hinodegiri' × *R. kaempferi*) Deep rosy-pink. (1920). H4.

'**Fedora**' (Kf) (*R.* 'Malvaticum' × *R. kaempferi*) Pale pink with a darker flash. (1922). FCCT 1960. AM 1931. H4.

'**Firefly**' See 'Hexe'.

'**Florida**' (V) (*R.* unknown seedling × *R.* 'Vuyk's Scarlet') Deep red, hose-in-hose with some petaloid stamens. C 1962. ♀ 2002. H4.

'**Gaiety**' (GD) (*R. indicum* × *R.* 'Hazel Dawson') Purplish-pink with a darker blotch, large. H4.

'**Geisha Lilac**' A dwarf, mound-forming, very hardy shrub with small leaves. Flowers lilac. Raised by George Arends in Germany about 1950. H4.

'**Geisha Orange**' Similar to 'Geisha Lilac' but with orange flowers. ♀ 2002. H4.

'**Geisha Purple**' Similar to 'Geisha Lilac' with purple flowers. H4.

'**Geisha Red**' Similar to 'Geisha Lilac', flowers deep purple-red, hose-in-hose. H4.

'**General Wavell**' (S) Deep yellowish-pink, flushed yellow at the base with red spots, large. H4.

'**Girard's Hot Shot**' (*R.* 'Aladdin' × *R.* 'El Capitan') Large, deep orange-red to scarlet flowers, to 8cm across, with wavy-edged lobes, profusely borne. Foliage orange-red in autumn. H4.

'**Greenway**' (K) Pink. C 1975. H4.

'**Gumpo**' (S) Large, wavy-petalled, white, occasionally flecked red. AM 1934. H3.

'**Hana-asobi**' (K) Bright rose-carmine with white anthers. (Wilson 50). H4.

'**Hardy Gardenia**' Double, white, 6cm across. Dwarf, spreading habit. H4.

'**Hatsugiri**' (K) Bright crimson-purple, dwarf. FCCT 1969. AMT 1956. H4.

'**Helen Close**' (GD) White blotched with pale yellow, to 7.5cm across. H4.

'**Hexe**' (I) ('Firefly') Glowing crimson, hose-in-hose. Used in some European nurseries as an understock. (1885). AM 1907. H4.

'**Hino-crimson**' (K) Crimson-scarlet. ♀ 2002. AMT 1974. H4.

'**Hinode-giri**' (K) Bright crimson. A popular selection. (Wilson 42). AMT 1965. H4.

'**Hinode-no-taka**' (K) Crimson with red anthers. (Wilson 48). H4.

'**Hinomayo**' (K) Clear pink; a most lovely clone up to 1.5m in height. Obtained by C.B. van Nes & Sons from the Emperor's Garden in Tokyo, Japan about 1910. ♀ 2002. FCCT 1945. AM 1921. H4.

'**Ho-o**' (K) ('Appleblossom') Pale pink with a white throat. (Wilson 9). AMT 1950. H4.

'**Ima-shojo**' (K) ('Christmas Cheer') Bright red, hose-in-hose. (Wilson 36). AMT 1959. H4.

'**Irohayama**' (K) White with pale lavender margins and a faint chestnut-brown eye. (Wilson 8). ♀ 2002. AMT 1952. H4.

'**Ivette**' (Kf) Brilliant rose-pink; low, compact habit. H4.

'**Jeanette**' (Kf) Phlox-pink with a darker blotch. (1920). AMT 1948. H4.

'**Jitsugesuse**' (S) Pale mauve. H4.

'**Johanna**' (*R.* 'Florida' × *R.* unnamed seedling) Deep red. ♀ 2002. FCCT 1988. H4.

'**John Cairns**' (Kf) Dark orange-red. AMT 1940. H4.

'**Kermesinum**' Vivid purplish-red; low, compact habit. A hybrid of *R. kiusianum*. H4.

'**Kermesinum Rose**' Rose-pink flowers with a white picotee edge. H4.

'**Killarney**' (GD) White, blotched with greenish-yellow, to 7.5cm across; broad, spreading habit. H4.

'**Kirin**' (K) Deep rose, shaded silvery-rose, hose-in-hose. (Wilson 22). AMT 1952. AM 1927. H3.

'**Kiritsubo**' (K) Rosy-mauve. (Wilson 24). AMT 1974. H4.

'**Koningin Wilhelmina**' ('Queen Wilhelmina') (V) Vermilion-red; dwarf; best in semi-shade. H4.

'**Kumo-no-ito**' ('Sugi-no-ito') (K) Lavender-pink with white throat. (Wilson 31). AMT 1952. H4.

'**Kure-no-yuki**' ('Snowflake') (K) White, hose-in-hose. Dwarf habit. (Wilson 2). AMT 1952. H4.

'**Lemur**' (*R. nakaharae* 'Mariko' × *R.* 'Vuyk's Scarlet') Deep pink; dwarf, prostrate habit with red winter buds. Raised by Peter Cox. H4.

'**Leo**' (E) (*R.* 'Malvaticum' × *R. kaempferi*) Bright orange; late (June); dwarf and spreading in habit. (1933). AM 1997. H4.

'**Louise Dowdle**' (GD) Brilliant Tyrian-pink with a Tyrian-rose blotch, large. FCCT 1976. AMT 1974. H4.

'**Louise Gable**' (*R. indicum* × [*R. yedoense* var. *poukhanense* × *R. kaempferi*]) Deep pink with a darker blotch. Low, compact, spreading habit. H4.

'**Madame van Hecke**' Small, rosy-pink. H4.

'**Martha Hitchcock**' (GD) White with a reddish-purple margin, 7.5cm across. Tends to revert. Spreading habit. H4.

'**Mary Helen**' ([*R.* 'Mucronatum' × *R.* 'Vittata Fortunei'] × *R.* 'Kagetsu') White with yellow spotting and wavy margins. H4.

'**Maxwellii**' (*R. pulchrum* 'Maxwellii') Similar to 'Phoeniceum' but with larger flowers of bright rose-red with a darker blotch. AMT 1960. H4.

'**Merlin**' (GD) A semi-evergreen hybrid of *R. poukhanense*. Large mauve flowers, 7.5cm across. H4.

'**Michael Hill**' A shrub with a dwarf, spreading habit and soft pink, frilled flowers, darker in the throat, good for ground cover. A hybrid of *R. nakaharae* raised by Polly Hill. H4.

'**Mimi**' (Kf) Pale purplish-pink with a darker blotch. C 1962. H4.

'**Mother's Day**' Deep red, 6.5cm across, with a small flare of obscure dark red blotches, and occasional petaloid stamens. A cross between a Kurume hybrid and an Indian azalea. ♀ 2002. FCCT 1970. AMT 1959. H4.

Mucronatum Group See *R. mucronatum* under species.

'**Naomi**' (Kf) (*R.* 'Malvaticum' × *R. kaempferi*) Salmon-pink, very late; ultimately to 1.8m high. Raised at Exbury. (1933). H4.

'**Niagara**' (GD) ([*R.* 'Lilacinum' × *R.* 'Willy'] × [*R.* 'Mrs Carmichael' × *R.* 'Willy']) White with a yellow-green blotch, frilly margins. ♀ 2002. H4.

'**Nico**' Soft cherry-red with reddish foliage. (Before 1986).

Obtusum Group (*R. obtusum* (Lindl.) Planch., *Azalea obtusa* Lindl.) Kirishima azalea. A dwarf, densely branched, evergreen or semi-evergreen, widespreading shrub, seldom reaching 1m. Branches densely hairy, clothed with small, oval, glossy green leaves and flowering with prodigious freedom in spring. Flowers in clusters of 1–3, funnel-shaped, 2.5cm across, bright red, scarlet or crimson; May. Said by some authorities to be wild on a few high mountains on the island of Kyushu (Japan), but now generally regarded as being of hybrid origin. Long cultivated both in Japan and China, and a parent of many of the Kurume azaleas. I 1844 from China by Robert Fortune. AM 1898. H4. '**Amoenum**' (*Azalea amoena* Lindl.) The hardiest form. A rather taller, widespreading shrub. Flowers hose-in-hose, brilliant magenta or rose-purple. I 1845 from Japanese gardens. AMT 1965. AM 1907. '**Amoenum Coccineum**' A branch sport of 'Amoenum' with carmine-rose, hose-in-hose flowers. Tends to revert. '**Amoenum Splendens**' A low, widespreading shrub with single, pale mauve flowers. '**Kokinshita**' A dwarf shrub with rose-salmon flowers in June and July. '**Macrostemon**' Low spreading bush with single, salmon-orange flowers 4cm wide.

'**Orange Beauty**' (Kf) (*R.* 'Hinode Giri' × *R. kaempferi*) Salmon-orange. (1920). ♀ 2002. FCC 1958. AMT 1945. H4.

'**Palestrina**' (V) White, with a faint green ray; very distinct and attractive. (1926). ♀ 2002. FCC 1967. AM 1944. H3–4.

'**Panda**' (*R.* 'Everest' × *R. kiusianum* white) A dwarf shrub raised by Peter Cox and making a neat mound, to 40cm tall, smothered with pure white flowers, 3cm across, in May. ♀ 2002. H4.

'**Phoeniceum**' (*R. pulchrum* Sweet) A small to medium-sized shrub with densely hairy twigs and elliptic to obovate leaves. Flowers in clusters of 1–4, funnel-shaped, 5–6cm across, rose-purple with dark spots; May. Unknown in the wild and possibly of hybrid origin, perhaps *R. scabrum* × *R.* Mucronatum Group. Long cultivated in Japan and China. I early 19th century. H3.

'**Pink Gumpo**' (S) Large, peach-pink with deeper flecks. H4.

'**Pink Pancake**' Large, bright pink flowers. Vigorous, low, spreading habit to 25cm tall and 90cm or more across. A hybrid of *R. nakaharae* raised by Polly Hill. ♀ 2002. H4.

'**Pippa**' A low, spreading shrub with large, red flowers. H4.

'**Prinses Juliana**' (V) Light orange-red. H4.

'**Purple Splendor**' (*R. yedoense* var. *poukhanense* × *R.* 'Hexe') Vivid reddish-purple. H4.

'**Purple Triumph**' (V) Deep purple. (1951). ♀ 2002. AMT 1960. H4.

'**Purpurtraum**' A very hardy, compact, dwarf shrub with attractive foliage and deep reddish-purple flowers to 3.5cm across, profusely borne in May–June. ♀ 2002. H4.

'**Queen Wilhelmina**' See 'Koningin Wilhelmina'.

'**Racoon**' (*R.* 'Chippewa' × *R.* 'Squirrel') Compact, dwarf habit, the funnel-shaped, vivid red flowers, 4cm across, with darker spots. Raised by Peter Cox. (1979). ♀ 2002. H4.

'**Rashomon**' (K) Scarlet. (Wilson 37). H4.

'**Rose Greeley**' White with a yellow-green blotch, hose-in-hose, fragrant. Low, compact, spreading habit. H4.

'**Rosebud**' (K) Rose-pink, hose-in-hose; late. Low spreading habit. ♀ 2002. AMT 1972. H4.

'**Royal Pink**' (Kf) Rich purplish-pink. C 1969. H4.

'**Sakata Red**' (Kurume hybrid × *R. kaempferi*) Fiery red. AMT 1952. H4.

'**Salmon's Leap**' Large, clear salmon-pink flowers contrast well with the striking silver-white-margined leaves. H4.

'**Satsuki**' (I) Pink with a dark blotch. H4.

'**Shin-seikai**' (K) White, hose-in-hose; dwarf habit. (Wilson 3). AMT 1952. AM 1921. H4.

'**Silver Moon**' (GD) White with a pale green blotch, frilled. Broad spreading habit. H4.

'**Silvester**' (K) (*R.* 'Aladdin' × *R.* 'Amoenum') Purplish-red with paler margins; early. C 1964. H4.

'**Sir William Lawrence**' (E) (*R.* 'Hinode-giri' × *R. kaempferi*) Pale pink. H4.

'**Snowflake**' See 'Kure-no-yuki'.

'**Squirrel**' (*R.* 'Galathea' × *R. nakaharae*) Bright scarlet, holding the colour well. A dwarf, compact and very hardy shrub. ♀ 2002. H4.

'**Stewartsonian**' (G) Vivid red; foliage reddish in winter. H4.

'**Sugi-no-ito**' See 'Kumo-no-ito'.

'**Surprise**' (K) Light orange-red. (1939). H4.

'**Takasago**' (K) Cherry blossom-pink, hose-in-hose. (Wilson 11). H4.

'**Tebotan**' (*R. pulchrum* 'Tebotan') Double, soft purple with tiny, undeveloped, green leaves in centre. H4.

'**Terra-cotta Beauty**' Small, terracotta-pink flowers.

'**Ukamuse**' (K) Pale salmon-rose with a darker flash, hose-in-hose. (Wilson 47). AMT 1952. H4.

'**Vida Brown**' (K) Clear rose-pink, hose-in-hose. AMT 1960. H4.

'**Violetta**' (GD) (*R.* 'Malvaticum' × *R. indicum*) Light purplish-pink blotched purplish-red, to 5cm; early. H4.

'**Vuyk's Rosyred**' (V) Deep satiny-rose with a darker flash. (1954). ♀ 2002. AMT 1962. H4.

'**Vuyk's Scarlet**' (V) Bright red with wavy petals. (1954). ♀ 2002. FCCT 1966. AMT 1959. H4.

'**Willy**' (Kf) Bright pink with red spots and veins, 6cm across. H4.

'Wombat' A prostrate shrub good for groundcover with profusely borne pink flowers. A hybrid of *R. nakaharae*. 🏆 2002. H4.

Rhododendron maximum* × *Kalmia latifolia See under *Rhododendron maximum*.

‡†***RHODOLEIA** Champ. ex Hook.—**Hamamelidaceae**—A small genus of 10 species of evergreen trees that are native to SE Asia. A warm, sheltered position in woodland conditions is preferred, but they are only suitable for growing in the mildest areas.

championii Hook. A beautiful shrub or occasionally a small tree with the general habit of a rhododendron and large, thick, shining green leaves, glaucous beneath, crowding the tips of the stems. The drooping flower clusters consist of numerous silky-hairy, multi-coloured bracts through which emerge the bright, rose-madder petals and black anthers. These are borne in the axils of the leaves in spring. A superb conservatory shrub. S China. First introduced in 1852 and more recently by Kingdon-Ward.

Rhodora canandensis See *Rhododendron canadense*.

‡***RHODOTHAMNUS** Rchb.—**Ericaceae**—This is a genus of 2 species, dwarf shrubs related to *Phyllodoce* and requiring a cool, moist pocket on a rock garden. *R. sessilifolius* P.H. Davis, a rare native of Turkey was introduced for the first time in 2000.

chamaecistus (L.) Rchb. A charming, dwarf, evergreen shrublet, rarely above 25cm high. The pale rose, saucer-shaped flowers resemble those of *Rhododendron calostrotum*, and are produced during April and May. In common with others of the family, it is not suited to chalky soil in cultivation, though it grows on hard limestone formations in the wild. E European Alps. I 1786. AM 1925.

RHODOTYPOS Siebold & Zucc.—**Rosaceae**—A monotypic genus most closely related to *Kerria*, differing, among other things, in its opposite leaves and white flowers. All types of soil, in sun or half-shade.

scandens (Thunb.) Makino (*R. kerrioides* Siebold & Zucc.) A free-flowering shrub with erect branches to 1.2m. The paper-white flowers, like white dog roses, are 4–5cm across and appear from May to July, followed by conspicuous, shining black fruits which are often still present when the flowers appear. China, Korea, Japan. I 1866.

RHUS L.—**Anacardiaceae**—The sumachs are a genus of easily cultivated shrubs and trees, thriving in any fertile soil and mainly grown for their often striking foliage and rich autumn colours. There are about 200 species, a few of them climbers, widely distributed in temperate regions, with some in the tropics. They are dioecious or monoecious and the individual flowers are small and rarely of merit, but in several species are succeeded by fruits that are colourful in the mass. The sap of some species is a severe skin irritant in some people. The genus includes the poison ivy of North America (*Rhus toxicodendron*). Both *R. glabra* and *R. typhina* make handsome foliage plants when pruned to the ground each or every other year in February.

aromatica Aiton (*R. canadensis* Marshall) Fragrant sumach. A small, spreading, downy shrub with coarsely toothed, trifoliolate leaves, aromatic when bruised, giving attractive, orange and purple-red tints in autumn. The yellowish flowers, though small, are produced in conspicuous clusters in April. E USA. I 1759.

canadensis See *R. aromatica*.

chinensis Mill. (*R. javanica* auct., *R. osbeckii* (DC.) Carrière) A small, dioecious, broad-headed tree or large, irregular shrub, attaining about 6m in the British Isles. The pinnate, coarsely toothed leaves colour richly in autumn, and have a peculiarly winged rachis. Flowers yellowish-white, produced in large, terminal panicles in late summer. Late made, unripened growths are often cut back by winter frosts. Manchuria, Japan, China, Korea to Malaysia. I 1737.

copallina L. Dwarf sumach. A small to medium-sized, downy shrub. The lustrous leaves are pinnate, the usually entire leaflets being attached to a strongly winged rachis. Dense, erect clusters of small, greenish-yellow flowers are of little beauty, but the autumn foliage colour is rich red or purple and combines well with the red fruit clusters. E North America. I 1688. AM 1973.

coriaria L. Tanner's sumach. A small to medium-sized shrub or small tree. Leaves pinnate, with 7–21 ovate to oblong, coarsely-toothed leaflets, the rachis winged or partially so. The greenish-white, female flowers are followed by brownish-purple, hispid fruits. This species is extremely rare in cultivation in Britain. The sumach of commerce is obtained from the leaves, and tannin from both leaves and shoots is used in the preparation of Morocco leather. It requires a warm, sunny position in a well-drained soil. S Europe.

cotinoides See *Cotinus obovatus*.

cotinus See *Cotinus coggygria*.

glabra L. Smooth sumach. A widespreading, medium-sized shrub with glabrous, glaucous stems and attractive, glabrous, pinnate leaves which are glaucous beneath and usually turn an intense red or orange-yellow in autumn. The erect, scarlet, hairy, plume-like fruit-clusters of the female plant are also conspicuous in autumn. E North America. C 1620. **'Laciniata'** A form with deeply cut leaflets. See also *R.* × *pulvinata* 'Red Autumn Lace' from which it differs in its weaker growth and glabrous bloomy shoots. FCC 1867.

potaninii Maxim. (*R. henryi* Diels) A small, round-headed tree which, planted at the beginning of the 20th century, reached 6m on chalk soil in our Winchester nursery. Leaves pinnate, colouring richly in autumn. The greenish-white flowers and red fruits have not yet appeared on our tree. C and W China. Discovered by Augustine Henry in 1888 and introduced by Ernest Wilson in 1902. AM 1932.

× ***pulvinata*** Greene (*R. glabra* × *R. typhina*) (*R.* × *hybrida* Rehder) A medium-sized to large shrub with downy stems, intermediate between the parents. Leaves turning to rich scarlet, orange and flame in autumn. Occurs with the parents in the wild. I 1923. **'Red Autumn Lace'** A fine foliage plant, the large fern-like leaves with deeply cut leaflets that turn orange, yellow and red in autumn. Fruiting clusters red. Shoots green or red-flushed, not bloomy, with sparse hairs. Commonly grown as *R.*

glabra 'Laciniata' and first noticed in the Sir Harold Hillier Gardens and Arboretum. ♥ 2002.

†*succedanea* L. Wax tree. A small tree with large, pinnate leaves, lustrous, dark green above, paler beneath, colouring richly in autumn. Succeeds only in the mildest areas. The fruits of the female tree yield a wax that was once used for making candles in Japan. Taiwan, China, Japan, Malaysia, India. I 1862.

sylvestris Siebold & Zucc. A small to medium-sized, shrubby tree with pinnate leaves, giving conspicuous autumn colour. Fruits brownish-yellow. Taiwan, China, Korea, Japan. I 1881.

trichocarpa Miq. A splendid large shrub or small tree with large, pinnate, downy leaves, coppery-pink when young, turning deep orange in autumn. Yellow, bristly fruits are borne in drooping clusters on female plants in autumn. Japan, Korea, China. I 1894. AM 1979.

trilobata Torr. & A. Gray. Skunkbush. A small shrub occasionally to 2m, closely related to *R. aromatica*, but more erect and with leaves with smaller leaflets and an unpleasant scent. W North America. I 1877.

typhina L. Stag's-horn sumach. A widespreading, sparsely branched, small tree or an irregular large shrub, developing a gaunt, flat-topped appearance, particularly noticeable in winter. The thick, pithy branches are covered, when young, with a dense coat of reddish-brown hairs. The large, pinnate leaves turn to rich orange, yellow, red or purple in autumn. Large, erect, green clusters of male flowers and smaller, female clusters are borne on separate plants. The dense conical clusters of crimson, hairy fruits are most decorative at the end of the year. Sometimes forming small thickets of suckering stems. E North America. C 1629. ♥ 2002. **'Dissecta'** A striking, female form with deeply incised leaflets, creating a fernlike effect; orange and yellow autumn colours. Often grown as 'Laciniata'. ♥ 2002. AM 1910.

'Laciniata' See 'Dissecta'.

verniciflua Stokes. Varnish tree. Medium-sized tree with large, handsome, pinnate leaves. Flowers in large, drooping panicles, followed on female trees by yellowish fruits. This is the source of the famous varnish or lacquer of Japan where it is cultivated in warmer areas. The sap has been known to cause a severe rash when applied to the skin. Japan, China, Himalaya. C before 1862. FCC 1862.

Ribbonwood See *Plagianthus regius*.
Ribbonwood, mountain See *Hoheria glabrata* and *H. lyallii*.

RIBES L.—Grossulariaceae—About 150 species natives of temperate regions of the N hemisphere and South America. The flowering currants and ornamental gooseberries are a group of evergreen and deciduous, mainly spring-flowering shrubs that are easy to cultivate in all types of soil. Some are very showy in flower. The majority are extremely hardy. Leaves mostly 3- or 5-lobed, rarely of special merit. Straggly or untidy specimens may be hard-pruned immediately after flowering.

alpinum L. A small to medium-sized, semi-erect shrub of neat, densely twiggy habit, suitable for hedging. Flowers greenish-yellow, small, usually dioecious; berries red.

Extremely shade-tolerant. N and C Europe (including British Isles). **'Aureum'** A small shrub, usually wider than high, with yellow young leaves. FCC 1881. **'Pumilum'** A very dense, compact, rounded bush slowly reaching up to 1m, wider than high, with small, neat leaves. C 1827.

ambiguum Maxim. A small, sparsely branched shrub with shortly lobed or toothed, orbicular leaves. Flowers greenish, solitary or in pairs in spring. Fruits rounded, green and glandular, hispid. In the wild it is found as an epiphyte on tree trunks and branches in mountain forests, but it is growing quite happily, though slowly, in an open border in our garden. Japan. I 1915.

americanum Mill. American blackcurrant. A small shrub, up to 1.8m, resembling the common blackcurrant in habit, leaf and smell, but differing in its longer, funnel-shaped, rather insipid yellowish flowers. The foliage turns to gorgeous crimson and yellow shades in autumn. E North America. I 1729. **'Variegatum'** Leaves mottled pale green and cream.

aureum See under *R. odoratum*.

bracteosum Hook. Stink currant. A medium-sized shrub of upright habit, with large, 5- to 7-lobed, aromatic leaves up to 20cm across on petioles to 20cm. Flowers pinkish-green in bracteate racemes to 25cm, pendent in fruit. Berries blue-black conspicuously bloomed with white. W North America. I 1895.

× *culverwellii* Macfarl. (*R. uva-crispa* × *R. nigrum*) A small, thornless shrub, of spreading habit, with leaves and flowers resembling those of the gooseberry. Fruits like small, rounded gooseberries, green becoming dark red. Scarlet-purple autumn colour. First raised by Mr Culverwell of Yorkshire, about 1880.

emodense See *R. himalense*. **var. verruculosum** See *R. himalense* var. *verruculosum*.

fasciculatum Siebold & Zucc. A small to medium-sized, dioecious shrub with coarsely toothed leaves. Flowers fascicled, creamy-yellow and fragrant but not showy; female plants bear scarlet berries which persist well into winter. Japan, Korea, China. C 1884. **var. chinense** Maxim. A taller, more vigorous variety with larger, more persistent leaves of a distinctive bright green. N China to Korea. C 1867. AM 1976.

gayanum (Spach) Steud. A small, suckering, evergreen shrub with soft green, velvety leaves. The bell-shaped, pale yellow flowers are honey-scented and densely packed into erect, cylindrical racemes in early June. Chile. C 1858.

glutinosum See *R. sanguineum* var. *glutinosum*.

× *gordonianum* LEM. (*R. odoratum* × *R. sanguineum*) An extremely hardy, vigorous and rather pleasing shrub, intermediate in habit between its parents. Drooping racemes of flowers, deep red in bud, open yellow, the calyx pale yellow, flushed with red at the base and on the margins. Very distinct and unusual. Garden origin 1837. AM 1989.

henryi Franch. A rare and very worthy, almost prostrate, evergreen, dioecious shrub with glandular-bristly young shoots and large, obovate to orbicular, pale green leaves. Flowers in drooping racemes, greenish-yellow, produced with the new growths in February and March. It is related to *R. laurifolium*, differing in its dwarfer habit, hairy shoots and broader, thinner-textured leaves. Native of C China. I inadvertently by Ernest Wilson in 1908, with seed of *Sinowilsonia henryi*.

himalense Royle ex Decne. (*R. emodense* Rehder) Small shrub with leaves glandular beneath; flowers greenish with a purplish tinge; berries red or black. Himalaya to C China. I 1908. **var. verruculosum** (Rehder) L.T. Lu (*R. emodense* var. *verruculosum* Rehder) Rehder. Differs in its smaller leaves, which are dotted on the petiole and on the veins beneath with small, wart-like glands. Berries red. N China. I 1921.

lacustre (Pers.) Poir. Swamp currant. A subtly attractive, small shrub with slender, erect stems, closely beset with rich brown bristles. Flowers disc-like, small, but numerous, in long, drooping racemes; petals pale yellow or white, spotted with red or pink, opening from late May to June or July. Growing in wet situations in its native environs. North America. I 1812.

*laurifolium Jancz. A dwarf, evergreen, dioecious shrub with large, leathery, narrow-elliptic, glabrous leaves and drooping racemes of dioecious, greenish-white flowers in February and March. Berries red then blackish. An interesting early flowering shrub making excellent groundcover in a shady position. The male form is sometimes referred to as *R. vicarii*. W China. Discovered and introduced by Ernest Wilson in 1908. AM 1912.

menziesii Pursh. A small shrub with erect, bristly and spiny stems to 2m. The small, fuchsia-like flowers appear in pairs in the axils of the leaves in May, petals white, calyx reddish-purple, a delightful contrast; berries reddish, bristly. W North America. I 1830.

odoratum H.L. Wendl. (*R. aureum* hort. not Pursh) Buffalo currant. A small to medium-sized shrub of loose, erect habit. Leaves glabrous, shining green, colouring richly in autumn. Lax racemes of golden-yellow flowers in April, deliciously clove-scented. Berries black. Long cultivated in gardens as *R. aureum*, which is rarer and less ornamental with smaller flowers. C USA. I 1812.

roezlii Regel. A small, spiny, loosely branched shrub with pubescent young shoots. Flowers 1–3 in the leaf axils, petals rosy-white, calyx purplish, pubescent. Berries globular, purple, densely beset with slender bristles. California and S Oregon (USA). C 1899.

sanguineum Pursh. The popular flowering currant, extensively planted throughout Britain. A medium-sized shrub with a characteristic pungent smell. Flowers deep rose-pink, petals white, produced during April in racemes which are drooping at first, later ascending. Berries black, bloomy. Useful for cutting for the home and easily forced, but tending to pale in colour. W North America. First discovered by Archibald Menzies in 1793 and introduced in 1817. **'Albescens'** Flowers whitish, tinged pink. **'Album'** Flowers white. **'Atrorubens'** ('Atrosanguineum') Flowers deep blood-crimson. C 1837. **'Brocklebankii'** A small, slower-growing shrub with attractive, golden-yellow leaves and pink flowers. Tends to burn in full sun. AM 1914. **'Carneum Grandiflorum'** Flowers of a deep flesh-pink. **var. glutinosum** (Benth.) Loudon (*R. glutinosum* Benth.) A Californian variety, differing little from the typical form, but flowering 2–3 weeks earlier in cultivation. I 1832. AM 1988. **var. glutinosum 'Albidum'** Flowers

white, tinged pink, similar in effect to *R. sanguineum* 'Albescens', but earlier. C 1840. **'King Edward VII'** Flowers of an intense crimson. Rather lower-growing than the typical form. AM 1904. **'Lombartsii'** Flowers larger, rose-pink with a white centre. **'Plenum'** Flowers double. **'Poky's Pink'** Large clusters of pink flowers, flushed white. Vigorous, upright habit. **'Pulborough Scarlet'** A selected form with deep red flowers the same colour as *Spiraea japonica* 'Anthony Waterer'. ♀ 2002. AM 1959. **'Red Pimpernel'** A compact bushy shrub with profuse pinkish-red flowers over a long period. C 1984. **'Splendens'** Flowers rosy-crimson, in larger, longer racemes. C 1900. **'Tydeman's White'** An improvement on 'Album' with larger racemes and individual flowers. **White Icicle** ('Ubric') Large racemes of pure white flowers open early. ♀ 2002.

speciosum Pursh. An attractive, medium-sized, semi-evergreen shrub with reddish-bristly stems and fruits, and shining green leaves. The beautiful, slender, fuchsia-like, rich red flowers are borne in pendent clusters during April and May. In cold areas it is best grown against a sunny wall. California. I 1828. ♀ 2002.

†*viburnifolium A. Gray. A medium-sized, evergreen shrub with long, scandent stems. Leaves shining green, emitting a pleasant turpentine-like odour when crushed. Flowers small, terracotta-red, in short, erect racemes in April; berries red. Requires a warm wall in all but the mildest areas. California. I 1897.

vilmorinii Jancz. A medium-sized, densely branched, dioecious shrub closely related to and resembling *R. alpinum*. The greenish or brown-tinted flowers are followed by black berries. W China. I 1902.

‡**RICHEA* R. Br.—**Epacridaceae**—A small genus of some 10 species of very distinct and subtly attractive, evergreen shrubs, mainly natives of Tasmania with one species in SE Australia. The following require a moist, preferably acid soil.

†dracophylla R. Br. An erect, small to medium-sized shrub, with long, thick, spreading, lanceolate leaves crowded at the ends of the bare stems almost suggesting Liliaceae. Bears white flowers in terminal, crowded panicles in summer, the branches subtended by brown, rigidly pointed bracts. Tasmania.

scoparia Hook. f. An unusual, hardy, small, spreading shrub, resembling a dwarf, shrubby monkey puzzle. The stems are clothed with stiff, sharply pointed leaves. Pink flowers are produced in erect, terminal, spike-like panicles, 5–10cm long, in May, but varying on other forms from white to orange and maroon. Tasmania. AM 1942.

ROBINIA L.—**Leguminosae**—A small genus of about 10 species of fast-growing trees and shrubs, confined in the wild to the USA and N Mexico. They are characterised by their attractive, pinnate leaves, often spiny stems and pendent racemes of pea-flowers. All are hardy and suitable for any ordinary soil, being especially useful in dry, sunny situations. All species are tolerant of atmospheric pollution. As suckering trees and shrubs, they are useful for fixing sand banks and shifting soil. To avoid damage to the brittle branches we recommend that small trees are hard-pruned after flowering.

× *ambigua* Poir. (*R. pseudoacacia* × *R. viscosa*) A small tree with slightly viscid young shoots and racemes of pale pink flowers in June. Garden origin before 1812. **'Bellarosea'** An elegant form with slightly stickier shoots and rather large, pink flowers. Raised about 1860. **'Decaisneana'** (*R. pseudoacacia* 'Decaisneana') A vigorous form of medium size, producing large racemes of pale pink flowers. FCC 1865.

boyntonii Ashe. Medium-sized shrub generally with smooth, spineless branches and loose racemes of pink flowers in May and June; pods glandular-bristly. E USA. I 1914.

elliottii Ashe. A small to medium-sized shrub. Large, rose-lilac flowers appear in May and June; pods bristly. Branches rather brittle. SE USA. I about 1901.

fertilis Ashe. A small to medium-sized, suckering shrub with bristly stems and rosy-pink flowers in June; pods densely bristly. Closely related to *R. hispida*, differing in its smaller flowers and pubescent leaflets. Branches rather brittle. SE USA. C 1900. **'Monument'** A more compact form up to 3m.

hartwigii Koehne. A large shrub with downy shoots liberally sprinkled with glandular hairs. Flowers varying from pale lilac to soft rose, borne 20–30 together in dense racemes during June and July; pods glandular-bristly. SE USA. C 1904.

× *hillieri* See *R.* × *slavinii* 'Hillieri'.

hispida L. Rose acacia. A medium-sized, suckering shrub of irregular habit, with long, glandular-bristly branches. Short racemes of large, deep rose flowers, 2.5–4cm long, in May and June; pods, when produced, glandular-bristly. An excellent, small tree when grafted onto stems of *R. pseudoacacia*, but rather brittle and requires a sheltered position. It may also be grown effectively against a sunny wall. SE USA. I 1743. AM 1934. **'Macrophylla'** A less bristly form with larger leaflets and larger flowers, resembling a pink wisteria. **'Rosea'** A confused name which has been applied to *R. boyntonii*, *R. elliottii* and *R. hispida*.

× *holdtii* Beissn. (*R. luxurians* × *R. pseudoacacia*) Resembling the latter parent in habit and vigour and bearing long, loose racemes of pale pink flowers in June or July, often continuing almost to autumn, followed by attractive, red, bristly seed pods. Garden origin about 1890. **'Britzensis'** A form with nearly white flowers. Raised in 1893.

kelseyi Cowell ex Hutchins. A graceful shrub or small tree with slender branches and elegant foliage, producing its slightly fragrant, lilac-pink flowers in June; pods glandular-bristly. Branches somewhat brittle. S Allegheny Mts (USA). I 1901. FCC 1917. AM 1910.

luxurians (Dieck) C.K. Schneid. A vigorous, large shrub or small tree with spiny stipules. Short racemes of pale rose flowers in June, frequently again in August; pods bristly. SE USA, N Mexico. I 1887.

× *margaretta* Ashe (*R. hispida* × *R. pseudoacacia*) A large, suckering shrub or small tree occurring in the wild with the parents. Generally resembles *R. pseudoacacia* but with the leaflets downy beneath and with pink flowers. **'Pink Cascade'** ('Casque Rouge') A vigorous form with profuse, large, purplish-pink flowers. Raised in the USA about 1934.

pseudoacacia L. Common acacia, False acacia, Black locust. A large, suckering tree, often of picturesque oriental appearance. Bark rugged and deeply furrowed, twigs with spiny stipules. Flowers slightly fragrant, white, with a yellow stain at the base of the standard, produced in long racemes in June; pods smooth. A commonly planted tree, thriving in any well-drained soil and tolerant of industrial pollution. Its flowers are especially attractive to bees. Native of the E USA, introduced to France in 1601 and now widely naturalised both in that country and elsewhere in Europe especially in the vicinity of railways. **'Aurea'** Leaves soft yellow in early summer, becoming green later. C 1864. FCC 1873. Now superseded by 'Frisia'. **'Bessoniana'** A small to medium-sized, compact, round-headed tree, usually spineless. Perhaps the best clone for street planting. C 1871. **'Coluteoides'** A small tree of dense habit. Flowers and racemes smaller but abundantly produced. **'Decaisneana'** See *R.* × *ambigua* 'Decaisneana'. **'Erecta'** See 'Monophylla Fastigiata'. **'Fastigiata'** See 'Pyramidalis'. **'Frisia'** An outstanding, small to medium-sized tree with rich golden-yellow leaves from spring to autumn, creating a brilliant splash of colour. It associates very well with large, purple-leaved shrubs, such as *Cotinus coggygria* 'Royal Purple'. Also good if stooled each spring as a shrub. Raised at the nursery of W. Jansen in Holland, in 1935. ♀ 2002. AM 1964. **var. *inermis*** DC. Shoots without thorns. For the mop-head acacia grown under this name see 'Umbraculifera'. **'Microphylla'** ('Angustifolia') A small to medium-sized, slow-growing tree with small, dainty, fern-like leaves with small leaflets; flowers rarely produced while young. **'Monophylla'** See 'Unifoliola'. **'Monophylla Fastigiata'** ('Erecta') A medium-sized tree of narrow, upright habit; leaves with 1–3 leaflets. **'Pyramidalis'** ('Fastigiata') A slender, columnar tree of medium size with spineless closely erect branches. C 1843. **'Rehderi'** A large bush or small bushy tree with rather erect, spineless branches. Raised in 1859. **'Rozynskiana'** An elegant and beautiful, large shrub or small, spreading tree, the branches drooping at their tips and bearing large, drooping leaves. C 1903. **'Semperflorens'** Flowers produced intermittently throughout summer. C 1874. **'Tortuosa'** A picturesque, slow-growing, small to medium-sized tree with somewhat contorted branches. **Twisty Baby** ('Lace Lady') PBR A small shrub with zigzag shoots and tightly curled leaves. Young foliage emerging lime-green, becoming darker with age. Excellent in a container and sometimes top-grafted to make a miniature tree. **'Umbraculifera'** A small tree with a compact, rounded head of spineless branches. A commonly planted street tree, but requires protection from strong winds. Flowers are rarely produced. Usually grown as 'Inermis'. C 1811. **'Unifoliola'** ('Monophylla') A curious form with leaves reduced to a single large leaflet or accompanied by 1 or 2 normal-sized leaflets. Raised about 1855.

× *slavinii* Rehder (*R. kelseyi* × *R. pseudoacacia*) This hybrid was first raised in the USA in 1914. The following form was raised in our nurseries in about 1930. **'Hillieri'** (*R.* × *hillieri* hort.) An elegant, small tree with delicate foliage, developing a rounded head of branches. Flowers slightly fragrant, lilac-pink in June. An excellent tree for a small garden. ♀ 2002. AM 1962.

viscosa Vent. Clammy locust. A small tree, occasionally to 12m, with characteristic viscid young shoots and leaf stalks. Flowers in short racemes towards the end of June, pale rose, stained yellow on the standard. SE USA. I 1791.

Rock rose See *Helianthemum* and *Cistus*.

ROMNEYA Harv.—**Papaveraceae**—The tree poppy or Matilija poppy is a subshrubby Californian perennial with glaucous stems and deeply cut leaves, producing large, white, poppy-like flowers with a central mass of golden-yellow stamens. Sometimes difficult to establish, but once settled spreads quickly by underground stems (rhizomes). Best in a warm, sunny position.
coulteri Harv. Small to medium-sized perennial bearing large, solitary, fragrant flowers, 10–15cm across, from July to October. Flower buds smooth, slightly conical and somewhat beaked. I 1875. ♥ 2002. FCC 1888. **var. trichocalyx** (Eastw.) Jeps. (*R. trichocalyx* Eastw.) Stems more slender, peduncles leafy, and buds bristly and rounded here, not beaked. Some plants grown as *R. coulteri* belong here. **'White Cloud'** (*R.* × *hybrida* 'White Cloud', *R.* 'White Cloud') A strong-growing, large-flowered hybrid between var. *coulteri* and var. *trichocalyx*, of American origin. ♥ 2002.
× *hybrida* hort. See *R. coulteri* 'White Cloud'.
trichocalyx See *R. coulteri* var. *trichocalyx*.
'White Cloud' See *R. coulteri* 'White Cloud'.

ROSA L.—**Rosaceae**—The wild rose species possess a beauty and charm rarely to be found in the vast assemblage of popular garden hybrids. Indeed their often graceful elegance, plus their floral and fruiting qualities, are a refreshing change from the comparatively vivid blowsiness of many Hybrid Tea and Floribunda roses. Not that the species are without colour. Their flowers vary from the most delicate pastels, to reds and scarlets of exceptional brilliance, and colourful fruits bring a welcome bonus which sometimes lasts well into winter, brightening the doleful days that follow Christmas. The flowers are borne in June and July, unless otherwise stated. Their leaves are normally pinnate and deciduous and their stems are armed with prickles. There are about 150 species mainly in N temperate regions. They are easy to cultivate, thriving in most soils except those that are wet and acid. Most flower better when planted in full sun and the more ornamental species react favourably to an annual or bi-annual manuring.

The species and hybrids described here range in habit from trailing, or low, suckering shrubs (excellent as ground-cover) to large shrubs and tall climbers. The more vigorous shrubs are best planted as isolated specimens in lawns or borders, while the climbing species are useful for training over fences, pergolas, against walls and into trees. Once established the species require very little pruning, except to remove dead wood or to thin out dense and overcrowded specimens that threaten to destroy their support. This may be carried out immediately after flowering unless fruits are expected, in which case prune in February.

We would like to record our appreciation of the work done by Graham Thomas in popularising these roses. He is the author of several books on the subject, which we have freely consulted.

acicularis Lindl. A small, vigorous shrub, rarely above 1.3m high, with densely bristly stems and leaves with 5–9 sea-green leaflets. Flowers 5–6cm across, bright rose-pink; fruits 2.5cm long, pear-shaped, bright rose. North America, N Europe, NE Asia, Japan. I 1805.
'Agnes' (*R. foetida* 'Persiana' × *R. rugosa*) An erect shrub of Canadian origin, with arching branches and densely arranged, bright green leaves. The amber-tinted, double, butter-yellow flowers are deliciously and intriguingly scented. C 1922. ♥ 2002. AM 1951.
× *alba* L. The origin of this famous rose is still a source of argument. Its hybrid origin is generally agreed and probably involves *R. gallica*, *R. arvensis* and a relative of *R. canina*. It is known to have been in cultivation since before 1600 and research by the late Dr C.C. Hurst confirms that it was grown by the Greeks and Romans. During the Wars of the Roses it was traditionally adopted as an emblem by the Yorkists. It is the type of a group of old hybrids and in one or more of its forms is cultivated in SE Europe for Attar of Roses. **'Alba Maxima'** Jacobite rose. A small shrub with pure white, very double flowers, in upright clusters, and occasional red hips. **'Alba Semiplena'** White rose of York. A medium-sized shrub with strong, prickly stems. Leaves with 5–7 broad, greyish-green leaflets. Flowers 7.5cm across, white, usually semi-double, richly scented; fruits oblong, red. ♥ 2002.
'Albert Edwards' (*R. hugonis* × *R. pimpinellifolia* 'Grandiflora') A medium-sized shrub with arching branches that are wreathed with fragrant, lemon-yellow flowers, 5–6cm across, in May. A choice hybrid raised in our Sarum Road nursery, Winchester in about 1938 and named after our then Rose Foreman.
alpina See *R. pendulina*.
'Andersonii' A medium-sized, strong-growing shrub with arching, prickly stems and leaves with usually 5 long-pointed leaflets, downy beneath. Flowers rich, clear, rose-pink, scented, 5–7.5cm across, freely produced and showy over a long period. Fruits urn-shaped, scarlet, similar to those of the Dog rose (*R. canina*). A hybrid of unknown origin possibly *R. canina* × *R. gallica*. C 1912.
'Anemone' (*R.* 'Anemonoides', *R. laevigata* 'Anemonoides') A lovely rose, a hybrid of *R. laevigata* with a Tea Rose. Over several weeks it produces single, 10cm wide, silver-pink flowers shaded rose, like a pink 'Mermaid'; April–May. Less vigorous than *R. laevigata*, but requiring similar conditions. Garden origin about 1895. AM 1900.
anemoniflora See *R.* × *beanii*.
anemonoides See *R.* 'Anemone'.
arkansana Porter. Arkansas rose. A small, densely prickly shrub usually less than 1m high. Leaves with 5–11 leaflets. Flowers 3–4cm across, pink, followed by small, globular, red fruits. C USA. C 1917.
'Arthur Hillier' (*R. macrophylla* × *R. moyesii*) A vigorous, large shrub with semi-erect branches. The multitudes of large, rose-crimson flowers are followed, in autumn, by conspicuous, bright red, flask-shaped fruits. Occurred in our Sarum Road nursery, Winchester in about 1938. AM 1977.
arvensis Huds. Field rose. A trailing or climbing species forming dense mounds or drapes of slender stems. Leaves with 5–7 shining green leaflets persist late into winter. Flowers 4–5cm across, white, with little or no

fragrance; fruits rounded or oval, dark red. A common native species of woodlands and hedgerows. Europe. **'Splendens'** Myrrh-scented rose. A charming form, or possibly a hybrid, with long-persisting leaves. The small, double, soft pink flowers are myrrh-scented.

banksiae R. Br. Banksian rose, Lady Banks' rose. A tall, vigorous, semi-evergreen climber reaching 7.5m or above in a suitable position. The slender shoots are thornless or nearly so and the leaves are composed of 3–5 leaflets. Flowers in May, but this beautiful and well-known rose and its several forms do not flower when young. They thrive best on a warm wall in full sun which is needed to ripen growths. Plants grown in cold areas or in shady positions elsewhere are liable to frost damage which reduces, if not prevents, flowering. Named (from 'Alba Plena') after Lady Banks, wife of Sir Joseph Banks, one of the greatest Directors of the Royal Botanic Gardens, Kew. **'Alba Plena'** Flowers 3cm across, double and rosette-like, white and delicately fragrant of violets, borne in densely packed umbels during May and June. I 1807 to Kew from a garden in Canton, China by William Kerr. **'Lutea'** Yellow banksian rose. Flowers double, yellow, rosette-like. A few sensitive noses are reputed to detect in this beautiful rose a delicate fragrance. It was introduced from China via the Calcutta Botanic Garden by J.D. Parks some time before 1824. ♀ 2002. AM 1960. **'Lutescens'** Flowers single, yellow, sweetly fragrant. I before 1870. **'Normalis'** Flowers single, creamy-white, sweetly fragrant. The wild form, said to have been introduced to Megginch Castle, Strathtay, Scotland, by Robert Drummond in 1796. It remained in obscurity until 1909 when cuttings E.H. Woodall had obtained 4 years previously, flowered in his garden in Nice. Ernest Wilson described finding of this plant in C and W China, where it is abundant in glens and ravines, forming tangled masses on low trees and scrub.

banksiopsis Bak. A vigorous, medium-sized shrub with leaves composed of 7–9 leaflets. Flowers 2.5cm across, rose-red, borne in corymbs and followed by flask-shaped, orange-red fruits. W China. I 1907 by Ernest Wilson.

× *beanii* Heath (*R. anemoniflora* Fort. ex Lindl., *R. triphylla* Roxb.) A rambling or climbing shrub, the leaves with 3–5 leaflets. Flowers double, anemone-like, blush-white, 2.5–4cm across. It is subject to frost damage and is best grown against a sunny wall. It is not known in the wild and is most probably a hybrid of the group *R. banksiae*, *R. laevigata*, *R. multiflora*. I 1844 from a garden in Shanghai by Robert Fortune.

bella Rehder & E.H. Wilson. An attractive, small to medium-sized shrub with slender-spined stems and leaves with 7–9, small, glaucescent leaflets. The bright, cherry-red flowers, 3–4cm across, are slightly fragrant and appear singly or in clusters along the branches in June. Fruits small, orange-scarlet. N China. I 1910.

biebersteinii Lindl. (*R. horrida* Fisch., *R. ferox* Bieb.) A dwarf, dense shrub with rigid, prickly stems. Leaves small, composed of 5–7 rounded, coarsely toothed leaflets. The white flowers, 2.5–4cm across, are followed by globose, red fruits. The curious nature of this species is reminiscent of a small gooseberry bush. SE Europe, W Asia. I 1796.

'Blanche Double de Coubert' (*R. rugosa* 'Blanc Double de Coubert') A hybrid of *R. rugosa* with more open, taller growth. Flowers semi-double, white, blush-tinted in bud, over a long period from June to October. Garden origin in 1892. ♀ 2002. AM 1895.

blanda Aiton. Smooth rose, Meadow rose. A small shrub with nearly thornless stems and leaves with 5–7 pale green leaflets. Flowers 6–7.5cm across, rose-pink. Fruits small, globular or pear-shaped, red. North America. I 1773.

†*bracteata Wendl. Macartney rose. A medium-sized to large evergreen shrub with rambling thick, stout stems, clothed with prickles and dense, brownish down. Leaves deep green, composed of 5–11 closely-set, shining leaflets. Flowers 7.5–10cm across, lemon-scented, white, with attractive, golden anthers; each head surrounded by conspicuous leaf-like bracts; June to September. Fruits globose, orange-red. A most ornamental species, requiring a warm, sunny, sheltered wall. SE China, Taiwan. I 1795 by Lord Macartney.

brunonii Lindl. (*R. moschata* hort. not Herrm.) Himalayan musk rose. A rampant climbing species, reaching 9–12m on a building or tree. Leaves limp, composed of 5–7 narrow, sea-green leaflets. (Plants found in E Nepal, 1972, possess glossy, dark green leaflets.) The richly fragrant, white flowers, 2.5–5cm across, are carried in tight, downy-stalked corymbs. This vigorous species thrives best in full sun and a warm climate. Often wrongly grown in cultivation as *R. moschata*. Himalaya. I 1822. **'Betty Sherriff'** A very vigorous form. Flowers reddish-pink in bud, opening white, flushed pink towards the tips of the petals. Probably introduced from Bhutan by Ludlow and Sherriff in 1949. AM 1985. **'La Mortola'** (*R. moschata* 'La Mortola') A superb hardier selection raised at the celebrated Hanbury garden, La Mortola, in Italy. Its leaves are larger and more greyish-downy and the larger pure white flowers are borne in more ample clusters. Richly fragrant. It requires a sheltered position and full sun to ripen growth.

'Burgundiaca' (*R.* 'Parvifolia', *R. centifolia* 'Parvifolia') Burgundian rose. A slow-growing, almost thornless, small rose of erect habit, its stems densely leafy. Small, flat, pompon flowers are deep rose, suffused claret. Cultivated since at least 1764.

californica Cham. & Schltdl. A medium-sized shrub with stout-prickled stems and leaves composed of 5–7 leaflets. Flowers 3cm across, pink, borne in corymbs. Fruits red, globose, usually with a prominent neck. W USA. C 1878. **'Plena'** See *R. nutkana* 'Plena'.

'Canary Bird' A beautiful, medium-sized shrub with arching stems and small, fresh green, fern-like leaves. Bright canary-yellow flowers wreathe the branches during April and May. The parents of this hybrid are almost certainly *R. hugonis* × *R. xanthina*. ♀ 2002.

canina L. Dog rose. This is a familiar native rose of hedgebanks and downs. It makes a medium-sized to large shrub with strong prickly stems and leaves with 5–7 leaflets. Flowers are 4–5cm across, white or pink, scented, followed by bright red, egg-shaped fruits. Perhaps the most variable of all roses, countless varieties and subspecies having received names. Europe, W Asia.

'Cantabrigiensis' (*R. hugonis* × *R. sericea*) A medium-sized shrub with densely bristly, arching stems and fragrant, fern-like leaves composed of 7–11 leaflets. Flowers 5cm across, soft yellow, passing to cream, in May and June. A lovely hybrid raised in the University Botanic Garden, Cambridge. ♀ 2002. AM and Cory Cup 1931.

carolina L. A small, suckering shrub forming dense thickets of erect stems. Leaves composed of 5–7 leaflets. The fragrant, rose-pink flowers, 5–6cm across, are produced in clusters from June to August. Fruits orange-shaped, red and glandular-hairy. E North America. C 1732.

× centifolia L. Cabbage rose, Provence rose. A small shrub with erect, prickly stems and fragrant leaves with 5–7, broadly oval leaflets. Flowers large, double, rose-pink and richly fragrant. *R.* × *centifolia* or a form of it is also known as the 'rose des peintres', in recognition of its association with the old Dutch painters. The cabbage rose had long been regarded as the most ancient of roses until the late Dr C.C. Hurst proved otherwise. It appeared in its present familiar form in the 18th century. Dr Hurst further proved that it was of complex hybrid origin in which the following species played a part: *R. canina*, *R. gallica*, *R. moschata* and *R. phoenicea*. There are many forms of *R. centifolia* and it is a parent of numerous hybrids. **'Cristata'** ('Chapeau de Napoleon') Crested cabbage rose, Crested moss rose. A charming form in which the sepals are beautifully crested to such an extent that the flower buds are completely enveloped. Flowers large, rosy-pink. Said to have been found in the crevice of a wall at Fribourg, Switzerland in 1820. ♀ 2002. **'Muscosa'** (*R. muscosa* Aiton) Common moss, Moss rose. Differs in the dense, moss-like, glandular-bristly covering of the stems, branches, petioles, flower stalks and calyx tubes. This unusual and characteristic clothing is sticky to the touch and gives off a resinous or balsam-like odour when bruised. The clear pink, globular, double flowers later open flat and are richly scented. C 1720. **'Parvifolia'** See *R.* 'Burgundiaca'.

chinensis Jacq. (*R. indica* W.T. Aiton not L.) China rose. A small to medium-sized shrub with stout branches and leaves with 3–5 shining green leaflets. Flowers 5cm across, crimson or pink, occasionally white, appear continuously from June to September. Fruits scarlet, obovoid. This rose, more than any other, holds claim to being the ancestor of most of our modern garden hybrids. It was first introduced in the late 1700s and early 1800s in several garden forms and not until about 1900 was the wild form discovered in C China by Dr Augustine Henry. **'Minima'** Miss Lawrence's rose. A miniature shrub up to 15cm high, bearing small leaves and small, single, pink flowers, 2–3cm across. **'Mutabilis'** See *R.* × *odorata* 'Mutabilis'. **'Old Blush'** See *R.* × *odorata* 'Pallida'. **'Viridiflora'** See *R.* × *odorata* 'Viridiflora'.

cinnamomea See *R. majalis*.

'Complicata' A lovely, medium-sized shrub which will, if allowed, clamber into small trees, or cover fences and hedges. The multitudes of very large, clear, deep peach-pink, white-eyed flowers are delicately fragrant. This hybrid of *R. gallica* is a flowering shrub of unsurpassed beauty. ♀ 2002. FCC 1958. AM 1951.

'Cooperi' (*R. gigantea* 'Cooperi', *R. laevigata* 'Cooperi') Cooper's Burmese rose. A beautiful rose, reaching 12m in a suitable position. Flowers large, slightly fragrant, pure white, occasionally with a pink stain, and with golden anthers. Best grown against a sunny wall. I 1921.

'Coryana' A strong-growing, medium-sized shrub, resembling *R. roxburghii* of which it is a seedling, the other parent possibly being *R. macrophylla*. Flowers 5–6cm across, deep pink, in June. Raised at the University Botanic Garden, Cambridge in 1926 and named after Mr Reginald Cory.

corymbifera Borkh. (*R. dumetorum* Thuill.) A medium-sized shrub with stout-prickled stems and leaves with 5–9, hairy leaflets. Flowers 4–5cm across, white or pale pink; fruits ovoid, orange-red. Closely related to *R. canina*, but differing mainly in its rather more sea-green, hairy leaves. Europe, W Asia, N Africa. C 1838.

corymbulosa Rolfe. A small shrub that produces erect or somewhat climbing, almost spineless stems and leaves with 3–5 downy leaflets, often reddish-purple beneath in autumn. Flowers 4–5cm across, rose-pink with a whitish eye; fruits globose, coral-red. C and W China. I 1908.

× damascena Mill. Damask rose. This is a small shrub with densely thorny stems and greyish-green leaves with 5–7 leaflets. Flowers large, usually in corymbs, fragrant, varying from white to red, followed by obovoid, red, bristle-clad fruits. An ancient rose probably of garden origin in SW Asia, introduced to Europe in the 16th century. Its petals are used in the perfume industry, particularly those of 'Trigintipetala', which are used more than any other in the production of Attar of Roses in Bulgaria. It is represented in cultivation by numerous named forms and hybrids. **'Professeur Emile Perrot'** A form with rather small, loosely double, richly scented, soft pink flowers. Grown as 'Tringintipetala'. **var. semperflorens** (Loisel.) Rowley. Autumn damask, Four seasons rose. Forms that flower more than once during the growing season. **'Tringintipetala'** See 'Professeur Emile Perrot'. **'Versicolor'** York and Lancaster rose. An unusual form with loosely double flowers which are white, irregularly but lightly flaked pink or blotched rose. Often confused with *R. gallica* 'Versicolor'. Cultivated prior to 1629.

davidii Crép. A strong-growing, medium-sized shrub of erect, open habit. Leaves composed of 7–9, conspicuously veined leaflets. Flowers 4–5cm across, bright rose-pink, carried in large, many-flowered corymbs. The ovoid, scarlet, pendent fruits have a distinctly long neck. Originally discovered in W Sichuan, China by the great French missionary and naturalist Armand David, it was introduced by Ernest Wilson in 1903. AM 1929. **'Acicularis'** (*R. persetosa* Rolfe, *R. davidii* var. *persetosa* (Rolfe) Boulenger) An attractive, medium-sized shrub with densely bristly stems and leaves with 5–9 leaflets. Flowers pink, 2–3cm across, borne in corymbs, followed by red fruits. I 1895. **var. elongata** Rehder & E.H. Wilson. A variety with rather longer leaflets, fewer flowers and larger fruits. W China. I 1908. **'Glaucescens'** (*R. macrophylla* 'Glaucescens') (Forrest 14958) In this form the flowers are rose-purple and the leaves conspicuously glaucous on both surfaces. The leaflets are more narrowly elliptic than those of 'Rubricaulis'. The stems are also glaucous. A form of var. *elongata*. I 1917. **var. persetosa** See 'Acicularis'.

'Rubricaulis' (*R. macrophylla* 'Rubricaulis') (Forrest 15309) A very distinct form of var. *elongata*, conspicuous by its red stems overlaid with a plum-like bloom. The peduncles, petioles, bracts and primary veins are also usually red. The flowers have more lilac-blue in them and the plant is noticeably glaucous. Unfortunately it is less hardy. I 1917.

dumetorum See *R. corymbifera*.

'Dupontii' (*R. moschata* var. *nivea* (Dupont) Lindl.) A strong-growing, medium-sized shrub of loose habit, sometimes needing a little support, with leaves composed of 3–7 leaflets, downy beneath. Flowers large, fragrant, 7.5cm across, blush, passing to creamy-white, borne in corymbose clusters in July. A magnificent rose of hybrid origin possibly *R. gallica* crossed with *R. moschata* or one of its old hybrids. C 1817. AM 1954.

'Earldomensis' (*R. hugonis* × *R. sericea* f. *pteracantha*) A quite distinct and pleasing, medium-sized, rather wide-spreading shrub with conspicuously flattened reddish thorns, small, fern-like leaves and canary-yellow flowers in early June.

ecae Aitch. A small, comparatively compact shrub of dainty appearance with very prickly, slender, arching, dark chestnut-brown branches. Small leaves, 2–2.5cm long, are composed of 5–9 oval leaflets. The small, buttercup-yellow flowers, 2.5cm across, are borne along the branches during late May and June. Fruits small, globular, red. Afghanistan. I 1880 by Dr Aitchison and named after his wife, using her initials E.C.A. AM 1933. 'Helen Knight' See *R*. 'Helen Knight'.

eglanteria See *R. rubiginosa*.

elegantula Rolfe (*R. farreri* Stapf ex Stearn) A charming species, up to 2m high, with spreading branches and dainty, fern-like leaves composed of 7–9 leaflets. Pale pink or white flowers, 2–2.5cm across, in June are followed by bright coral-red, ovoid fruits which are effectively set against the purple and crimson autumn foliage. S Gansu (China). I 1915 by Reginald Farrer, one of the greatest and most descriptive of horticultural writers. 'Persetosa' Threepenny-bit rose. The form in general cultivation, originally selected from a batch of Farrer's seedlings by the great gardener and plantsman, E.A. Bowles. It differs in its smaller leaves and smaller flowers, which are coral-red in bud opening soft pink.

ernestii See *R. rubus*.

fargesii See *R. moyesii* 'Fargesii'.

farreri See *R. elegantula*. **var. *persetosa*** See *R. elegantula* 'Persetosa'.

fedtschenkoana Regel. An erect, medium-sized shrub with sea-green leaves composed of 5–7 leaflets. The white flowers, 5cm across, are produced continuously throughout summer, and are then replaced by orange-red, bristly, pear-shaped fruits. An interesting and ornamental species with distinctive foliage. Turkestan.

filipes Rehder & E.H. Wilson A strong-growing, rambling or climbing species forming large curtains over suitable support. Leaves with 5–7 leaflets. The fragrant, white flowers, 2.5cm across are borne in large panicles in late June and July. Fruits globose, red. W China. I 1908 by Ernest Wilson. 'Kiftsgate' An extremely vigorous clone with light green foliage, richly copper-tinted when young. Its panicles may contain as many as a hundred or

more sweetly scented flowers, and it is almost as spectacular when bearing its numerous small, red fruits. It should be grown wherever space allows. C 1938. ♀ 2002.

foetida Herrm. (*R. lutea* Mill.) Austrian yellow rose, Austrian briar. A small shrub with erect, slender, prickly, chestnut-brown stems and bright green leaves composed of 5–9 leaflets. Flowers rich yellow, 5–6cm across, in May and June. Plant in full sun and in a well-drained site. Cultivated since the 16th century, this species, and its forms, has figured in the ancestry of many of our modern garden roses. Though naturalised in S and C Europe (incl. Austria), it is a native of SW Asia. 'Bicolor' Austrian copper. A remarkably beautiful plant requiring plenty of sun and a good, rich, well-drained soil. The flowers are brilliant coppery-red, with brilliant yellow reverse. Very rarely, completely yellow flowers are produced on the same bush. Cultivated since at least 1590. 'Persiana' Persian yellow rose. A beautiful form with golden-yellow, double flowers. First introduced to the West in 1837, it has since been used as a parent for innumerable garden hybrids.

foliolosa Torr. & A. Gray. A low-growing, suckering shrub rarely exceeding 1m. Leaves have 7–9 narrow, glossy green leaflets. Flowers fragrant, bright pink, 4–5cm across, usually appear in late July and often continue into September. Fruits orange-shaped, red. Often good autumn colour. SE USA. C 1888.

forrestiana Boulenger. A strong-growing, medium-sized shrub with arching stems up to 2m. Leaves with 5–7 oval or rounded leaflets. The rose-crimson, strongly fragrant flowers, 3–4cm across, are borne in clusters surrounded by leafy bracts. These are followed by equally attractive, pillarbox-red, bottle-shaped fruits, which appear like highly coloured nuts encircled by the persistent green bracts. W China. I 1918 by George Forrest.

× *fortuneana* Lindl. A tall climber, reputedly a hybrid between *R. banksiae* and *R. laevigata*. It resembles the former in general appearance, but differs in its larger leaflets and bristly pedicels. The flowers, too, are larger, 6–7.5cm across, double and white. This rose seldom flowers with sufficient freedom to be conspicuous. It requires a sunny wall. I 1850 by Robert Fortune from Chinese gardens.

'Fru Dagmar Hastrup' A hybrid of *R. rugosa* making a compact shrub up to 1.8m with lush dark green foliage and flowers of pale rose-pink with cream stamens, from June to the frosts. Large crops of rich crimson fruits. Makes an excellent hedge. Garden origin 1914. ♀ 2002. AM 1958.

gallica L. (*R. rubra* Lam.) French rose. A small, suckering shrub with erect, slender stems, densely covered with prickles and bristles, and leaves composed of 3–7 leaflets. Flowers deep pink, 5–7cm across, followed by rounded or top-shaped, brick-red fruits. A native of C and S Europe, but cultivated in one form or another from time immemorial. It is a parent of countless hybrids and is the probable ancestor of the modern garden rose in Europe. **var. *officinalis*** Thory. Apothecary's rose, Red rose of Lancaster. A small shrub producing richly fragrant, semi-double, rosy-crimson flowers with prominent yellow anthers. An old rose known in cultivation since at least 1310. Its petals retain their fragrance even when dried and powdered and gave rise to a once important industry in preserves and confections. The centre of this industry was the town of Provins in France where the apothecaries were instrumental in its development. Sometimes referred to as the 'old red damask'. ♀ 2002.

'Versicolor' ('Rosa Mundi') An old and well-loved rose which arose as a branch sport of the Apothecary's rose. Flowers semi-double, usually rose-red, striped white, and carrying a few entirely red blossoms. Some seasons all the flowers may be self-red. Sometimes confused with *R.* × *damascena* 'Versicolor'. ♀ 2002. AM 1961.

gentiliana Lévl. & Van. (*R.* 'Polyantha Grandiflora') A climbing or rambling rose reaching 6m on a suitable support. Leaves glossy, deep green. Flowers strongly fragrant, creamy-white with orange-yellow stamens, followed by oval, orange-red fruits lasting well into winter. A fine free-flowering rose. China. FCC 1888.

'Geranium' (*R. moyesii* 'Geranium') A hybrid of *R. moyesii* which it resembles, but slightly more compact in habit and with flowers of brilliant geranium-red. The fruits too are slightly larger and smoother. Raised at Wisley in 1938. ♀ 2002. AM 1950.

gigantea Collett (*R. odorata* var. *gigantea* (Crép.) Rehder) A vigorous, tall, semi-evergreen climber. Leaves with 5–7 leaflets. Flowers white, 5–7.5cm across, fragrant followed by globose, bright red fruits. SW China, Burma. I 1889. **'Cooperi'** See *R.* 'Cooperi'.

giraldii Crép. A strong-growing, medium-sized shrub with leaves composed of 7–9 leaflets. Flowers pink, 1.5–2.5cm across, followed by globular or ovoid, red fruits. N and C China. C 1897.

glauca Pourr. (*R. rubrifolia* Villars) A most useful and ornamental species, forming a medium-sized shrub with reddish-violet, almost thornless stems. The great attraction of this rose is its foliage, which is glaucous purple in a sunny position and greyish-green, with a mauve tinge, in shade. Flowers clear deep pink, white in the centre, 2.5–5cm across, followed by ovoid, red fruits. Invaluable for coloured foliage schemes. Mts of C and S Europe. C before 1830. ♀ 2002. AM 1949.

'Golden Chersonese' (*R.* 'Canary Bird' × *R. ecae*) A beautiful shrub of medium size with slender, arching stems and delightful, small, frond-like leaves. The deep buttercup-yellow, sweetly scented flowers wreath the branches during late May. Raised in 1963 by the distinguished rosarian E.F. Allen. AM 1966.

× *hardii* Cels (*R. clinophylla* × *R. persica*) (× *Hulthemosa hardii* (Cels) Rowley) One of the most remarkable and beautiful of all roses, this is a small to medium-sized shrub with slender stems, and leaves composed of 1–7 oblanceolate leaflets. Flowers 5cm across, yellow with a red blotch at the base of each petal. Requires a warm, sunny position and perfect drainage; ideal for a sunny wall or sprawling over rock in a scree garden. A difficult plant to establish. Garden origin, Paris in 1836.

× *harisonii* Rivers (*R. foetida* × *R. pimpinellifolia*) (*R. lutea* var. *hoggii* D. Don) **'Harison's Yellow'** Hogg's double yellow. A small, free-flowering shrub occasionally reaching 2m. It bears brilliant yellow, semi-double flowers, which possess a similar odour to those of *R. foetida*, in May and June. These are followed by small,

blackish fruits. Raised by George Harison of New York in 1830. AM 1949. **'Lutea Maxima'** (*R.* 'Lutea Maxima', *R. pimpinellifolia* 'Lutea') One of the best single yellow roses. A small shrub with a few scattered thorns and bright green leaves, nestling among which are the buttercup-yellow flowers, 5cm across, in May and June. **'William's Double Yellow'** (*R. pimpinellifolia* 'William's Double Yellow') Rather taller in habit than *R. pimpinellifolia*, bearing fragrant, double, yellow flowers with a central cluster of green carpels, in May and June.

'Headleyensis' A vigorous but graceful, medium-sized shrub, thought to be the hybrid *R. hugonis* × *R. pimpinellifolia* 'Grandiflora'. Leaves neat and fern-like. The primrose-yellow, fragrant flowers are carried along the arching branches in May. Garden origin about 1922. Raised by the distinguished botanist and amateur gardener Sir Oscar Warburg.

'Helen Knight' (*R. ecae* × *R. pimpinellifolia* 'Grandiflora') Similar to *R. ecae* but reaching a larger size with larger flowers in April and May. Raised at Wisley in 1966.

helenae Rehder & E.H. Wilson. A vigorous rambling or climbing species reaching 6m or more in a tree. Leaves with 7–9 leaflets. The creamy-white, fragrant flowers, 2–4cm across, are borne in dense corymbs and are followed in autumn by large, drooping bunches of narrowly ovoid, orange-red fruits. W and C China. I 1907 by Ernest Wilson and named after his wife.

hemisphaerica Herrm. (*R. sulphurea* Aiton, *R. glaucophylla* Ehrh.) The sulphur rose is a rare, medium-sized shrub of rather loose growth, requiring a little support. The leaves are composed of 5–9 sea-green leaflets. Flowers double, sulphur-yellow and sweetly scented, 5cm across. This beautiful rose does best when given a warm, sheltered wall and even then it only flowers well during a warm summer. W Asia. C before 1625.

hemsleyana Täckh. A vigorous, medium-sized shrub, related to *R. setipoda*, with leaves composed of 7–9 leaflets. Flowers rose-pink, 4–5cm across, in several-flowered corymbs, followed by hispid, bottle-shaped, red fruits. C China. I 1904.

× *hibernica* Sm. (*R. canina* × *R. pimpinellifolia*) A vigorous, medium-sized shrub producing delightful, clear, bright shell-pink flowers, 5cm across, followed by globose, red fruits. First found near Belfast in 1802.

'Highdownensis' A medium-sized shrub, a seedling of *R. moyesii,* which it resembles in general appearance. The dainty leaves are somewhat glaucous beneath. Flowers 6cm across, light velvety crimson, with a ring of pale buff anthers, freely borne in May and June on the stout, semi-erect branches. Fruits flagon-shaped, orange-scarlet. Raised by the great amateur gardener the late Sir Frederick Stern at Highdown, near Goring, Sussex before 1925. AM 1928.

'Hillieri' (*R.* × *pruhoniciana* 'Hillieri') A very beautiful rose, a seedling of R. *moyesii* raised in our nurseries in about 1924. It resembles *R. willmottiae* in its elegant habit, while its flowers in May and June recall those of *R. moyesii*, but are a darker shade of crimson. It is perhaps the darkest coloured of all single roses.

hispida See *R. pimpinellifolia* 'Hispida'.

horrida See *R. biebersteinii*.

hugonis Hemsl. (*R. xanthina* Crép. not Lindl.) A very graceful shrub up to 2m. The long, arching branches are clothed with neat, fern-like leaves composed of 5–11 fresh green leaflets, often becoming bronze-hued in autumn. By mid-May the branches are wreathed with hundreds of soft yellow flowers, 5cm across. These are followed by small, rounded, dark red fruits. Deservedly the most popular single, yellow rose, it may be used to make a most delightful, informal hedge. C China. I 1899. ♀ 2002. AM 1917. **'Flore Pleno'** Double flowers on a plant that is not so graceful as the single form.

indica See *R. chinensis*.

jundzillii Besser (*R. marginata* auct. not Wallr.) A vigorous, erect shrub of medium size, with few-prickled stems and leaves composed of 5–11 glandular toothed leaflets. Flowers 5–7.5cm across, pink changing to white, followed by dark scarlet fruits. Europe, W Asia. C 1870. AM 1964.

'Lady Penzance' (*R. × penzanceana* Rehder) (*R. foetida* 'Bicolor' × *R. rubiginosa*) A medium-sized shrub with arching branches, fragrant leaves and single flowers, copper-tinted with bright yellow centres. ♀ 2002. AM 1891.

laevigata Michx. (*R. sinica* Aiton not L.) Cherokee rose. A strong-growing, semi-evergreen rambler or climber with beautiful, dark glossy green leaves composed of 3 coarsely toothed, glabrous leaflets. Flowers white, fragrant, 7.5–10cm across, borne singly on bristly stalks during late May and June. Fruits large and bristly. An attractive species with impressive foliage. Requires a warm, sheltered wall. A native of China, but long naturalised in the S USA where the common name arose. AM 1954. **'Anemonoides'** See *R.* 'Anemone'. **'Cooperi'** See *R.* 'Cooperi'.

latibracteata Boulenger. A medium-sized shrub, which has been confused with *R. multibracteata* from which it differs in its larger, cherry-pink flowers, 4cm across, carried in many-flowered corymbs. The conspicuous leafy flower bracts are 3 times bigger than those of *R. multibracteata*. The leaves, sepals and thorns are also distinctly larger. W China. I 1936.

longicuspis hort. See *R. mulliganii*.

lucida See *R. virginiana*.

lutea See *R. foetida*.

'Lutea Maxima' See *R. × harisonii* 'Lutea Maxima'.

lutescens See *R. pimpinellifolia* 'Hispida'.

'Macrantha' A small, variable, widespreading shrub with prickly, arching branches neatly set with conspicuously veined leaves composed of 5–7 leaflets. Large, deliciously fragrant flowers, 7–10cm across, pink in bud opening clear almond-pink, changing to almost white and with conspicuous stamens. Fruits rounded, red. A magnificent rose of mound-like habit with loose, often procumbent stems, ideal for clothing banks, covering stumps, and so on. A hybrid of uncertain origin. C 1888.

macrophylla Lindl. A vigorous, distinctive, medium-sized to large shrub with large leaves composed of 5–11 leaflets. Flowers 5–7.5cm across, bright cerise-pink, carried singly or in clusters of 2–3. Fruits pear-shaped, glandular-bristly, bright red. Himalaya. I 1818. AM 1897. **'Glaucescens'** See *R. davidii* 'Glaucescens'.

'Master Hugh' A superb form collected in the wild by Stainton, Sykes and Williams under the number 7822. The deep pink flowers are followed by large, orange-red fruits, changing to bright red, possibly the largest fruited rose in cultivation. ♀ 2002. AM 1966. **'Rubricaulis'** See *R. davidii* 'Rubricaulis'.

majalis Herrm. (*R. cinnamomea* L.) Cinnamon rose. A strong-growing, medium-sized shrub with leaves composed of 5–7, coarsely toothed leaflets, glaucous beneath. Flowers 5cm across, deep lilac-pink but variable, spicily fragrant. Fruits small, red. Europe, N and W Asia. C before 1600.

marginata See *R. jundzillii*.

'Mariae-graebneriae' A beautiful, low, spreading shrub reputedly a hybrid between *R. virginiana* and, possibly, *R. palustris*. Leaves with shining, coarsely toothed leaflets often colouring well in autumn. Flowers bright rose-pink, 5cm across, often carried in many-flowered corymbs from June to August. Fruits orange-shaped, red. C 1880.

'Max Graf' (*R. rugosa* × *R. wichurana*) A superb rose with long, trailing stems, excellent as a groundcover for sunny banks. The fragrant, rose-pink, golden-centred flowers, 5cm across, are borne over a long period from June onwards. C 1919. AM 1964.

*'Mermaid'** A beautiful, free-growing, evergreen rose of rambling habit with long stems and glossy green, ample foliage. Flowers 13–15cm across, sulphur-yellow with deep amber stamens, coloured even after the petals have fallen. Seen at its best in warmer, southern areas of the British Isles. A hybrid of *R. bracteata* and, like that species, best grown on a warm sheltered wall. Raised by Messrs W. Paul of Waltham Cross. ♀ 2002. AM 1917.

microphylla See *R. roxburghii*.

× micrugosa Henkel (*R. roxburghii* × *R. rugosa*) Medium-sized shrub of dense bushy habit resembling *R. rugosa* in its foliage. Flowers pale pink, followed by bristly, rounded, orange-red fruits. Garden origin before 1905.

mollis Sm. An erect-stemmed, native shrub up to 2m. Leaves composed of 5–7 downy leaflets. Flowers rose-red, 4–5cm across, in short clusters, followed by rounded, scarlet, bristle-clad fruits. Europe (incl. British Isles), Caucasus.

'Morletii' (*R. pendulina* 'Morletii') A medium-sized shrub with long, arching branches. Flowers double, magenta, opening flat and revealing petaloid stamens. Young foliage tinted in spring.

moschata Herrm. Musk rose. A strong-growing, rather lax shrub up to 3.5m. Leaves composed of 5–7 dark green, polished leaflets. The sweetly musk-scented, creamy-white flowers, 5cm across, are carried in large, branching heads during late summer and autumn. A rare species in cultivation, other roses often bearing its name (see *R. brunonii*). It is a parent of many old garden hybrids, in particular the group known as Hybrid Musks. It is notable for its richly fragrant flowers in autumn. Origin uncertain, perhaps W Asia.

moschata hort. See *R. brunonii*. **'La Mortola'** See *R. brunonii* 'La Mortola'.

moyesii Hemsl. & E.H. Wilson. A medium-sized to large, erect-branched shrub of rather loose, open habit with few-prickled stems and leaves with 7–13 leaflets.

Flowers rich blood-crimson, 6–7.5cm across, 1–2 terminating each short spur in June and July. They are followed by equally beautiful, large, flagon-shaped, bright crimson fruits. One of the most beautiful species in cultivation and a parent of several lovely hybrids. W China. I 1894 by A.E. Pratt and again by Ernest Wilson in 1903. FCC 1916. AM 1908. **var. *fargesii*** Rolfe. Flowers glowing, vivid colour, perhaps best described as shining carmine. AM 1922. **'Geranium'** See *R.* 'Geranium'.

mulliganii Bertol. (*R. lucens* Rolfe) A remarkable, semi-evergreen rambler or climber of rampant growth. Leaves 12–28cm long, composed of 5–9 slender-pointed, glabrous, dark glossy green leaflets. The white, banana-scented flowers, 5cm across, are borne in large terminal panicles. Fruits ovoid, scarlet or orange-red. A distinguished species with bold foliage, polished, dark reddish-brown shoots and copper-tinted young growths. E Nepal, NE India and W China. C 1915. Originally listed as *R. longicuspis* and often confused with the closely related and similar *R. sinowilsonii*. ♀ 2002. AM 1964.

multibracteata Hemsl. & E.H. Wilson. A very graceful shrub of medium size with stout, prickly stems and attractive, fragrant, fern-like leaves composed of 7–9 leaflets. The bright rose-lilac flowers, 2.5–4cm across, are produced intermittently between June and August. The small, rounded, red fruits are covered with glandular bristles. W China. I 1908 by Ernest Wilson. AM 1936.

multiflora Thunb. (*R. polyantha* Siebold & Zucc.) A vigorous, large shrub or rambler with long stems that will clamber 6m into trees if suitably placed. Leaves composed of 7–9 leaflets. Flowers fragrant, white, 2–3cm across, abundantly borne in large, conical heads followed by small, pea-like, bright fruits that last into winter. A dense-growing species suitable for hedging and covering banks. An ancestor of the Hybrid Polyantha roses. Japan, Korea. I 1804. **'Carnea'** Flowers double, pink. A sport of var. *cathayensis* Rehder & E.H. Wilson from China. I 1804 from China. **'Grevillei'** ('Platyphylla') Seven sisters rose. Flowers double, cerise-purple at first changing to mauve-pink and fading to white. An old favourite, vigorous and free-flowering. I about 1816 from Japan by Sir Charles Greville. **'Platyphylla'** See 'Grevillei'.

mutabilis See *R.* × *odorata* 'Mutabilis'.

nitida Willd. A charming, dwarf shrub of suckering habit producing numerous, slender, reddish stems, densely clothed with fine prickles and bristles. Leaves have 7–9 slender, shining green leaflets which turn crimson and purple in autumn. Flowers rose-red, 5cm across, followed by slightly bristly, scarlet fruits. An excellent carpeting shrub. E North America. I 1807.

nutkana Presl. Nootka rose. A strong-growing, medium-sized shrub, the leaves with 5–9 leaflets. Flowers bright pink, 5cm across, followed by globose, red fruits which persist into winter. W North America. I about 1876. **'Plena'** A most attractive, free-flowering form bearing corymbs of semi-double, rich dark pink flowers, fading to rose and purple, in June. Often grown as *R. californica* 'Plena'. ♀ 2002. AM 1958.

× *odorata* (Andr.) Sweet (*R. chinensis* × *R. gigantea*) Tea rose. A group of old and variable hybrids raised in Chinese gardens. They are best grown against a sunny, sheltered wall where they will reach several metres high.

'Fortune's Double Yellow' See 'Pseudindica'. **var. gigantea** See *R. gigantea*. **'Mutabilis'** (*R. chinensis* 'Mutabilis') (*R.* 'Tipo Ideale') A vigorous, small to medium-sized, few-spined shrub of slender habit with deep purplish young shoots and coppery young foliage. The slender-pointed, vivid-orange buds open to buff, shaded carmine flowers, changing to rose and finally crimson, borne from June to October. They are richly tea-scented and spaced to 7.5–10cm. An unusual and very versatile rose. ♀ 2002. AM 1957. **'Pallida'** (*R. chinensis* 'Old Blush') Monthly rose. An old favourite of compact habit and small to medium size. Flowers double, sweet pea-scented, pink with darker veins, deepening with age. They are produced over a very long period and after a mild autumn may even be present at Christmas. **'Pseudindica'** ('Fortune's Double Yellow') Also known as 'Beauty of Glazenwood' and 'Gold of Ophir'. An old rose, up to 3m, with semi-double flowers, salmon-yellow or coppery-yellow, flushed coppery-scarlet, richly scented, in May and June. As it flowers on the second-year wood, it should not be pruned like an ordinary climber. Discovered by Robert Fortune in a mandarin's garden at Ningpo in China and introduced by him in 1845. **'Viridiflora'** (*R. chinensis* 'Viridiflora') Green rose. A curious small shrub with double flowers consisting of numerous crowded, greenish, petal-like scales. Said to have been in cultivation as early as 1743.

omeiensis See *R. sericea* var. *omeiensis*.

oxyodon See *R. pendulina* var. *oxyodon*.

'Parvifolia' See *R.* 'Burgundiaca'.

'Paulii' (*R. arvensis* × *R. rugosa*) A low-growing, mound-forming shrub with extremely thorny, procumbent stems, reaching 3–4m long. Leaves and flowers like those of *R. rugosa*, the latter white and slightly clove-scented. A vigorous shrub excellent as groundcover in sun, or for growing beneath taller shrubs. Garden origin before 1903.

'Paulii Rosea' Similar to 'Paulii' but with pink flowers. C 1910.

pendulina L. (*R. alpina* L.) A small, semi-erect shrub with smooth or few-thorned green or purplish stems and leaves with 5–11 leaflets. Flowers magenta-pink, 4–5cm across, followed by red, flask-shaped fruits. Mts of C and S Europe. **'Morletii'** See *R.* 'Morletii'. **var. oxyodon** (Boiss.) Rehder (*R. oxyodon* Boiss., *R. haematodes* Crép.) Flowers deep pink; fruits dark red, conspicuous during late summer. Caucasus. C 1896.

× *penzanceana* See *R.* 'Lady Penzance'.

persetosa See *R. davidii* 'Acicularis'.

persica Michx. ex Juss. (*R. berberifolia* Pall., *Hulthemia persica* (Michx.) Bornm.) A rare species of dwarf habit with slender, suckering shoots and simple, greyish-green, downy leaves. The solitary flowers, 2.5cm across, are brilliant yellow, each petal with a scarlet blotch at its base. The small, globose, green fruits are clothed with minute prickles. A difficult plant to establish. It requires perfect drainage and a dry, sunny position. Iran, Afghanistan, C Asia. C 1790.

pimpinellifolia L. (*R. spinosissima* L.) Scotch rose, Burnet rose. A small, native, suckering shrub producing dense, low thickets of slender, erect stems, thickly beset with bristles and tiny prickles. Leaves composed of 5–9 deep green and glabrous leaflets. The small, white or pale pink flowers, 4–5cm across, are borne in profusion during May and June, followed by rounded, shining black or maroon-black fruits. A common native shrub of coastal sand dunes. Europe, N Asia. This species has given rise to many forms and hybrids. A form with double white flowers is also grown. **var. *altaica*** See 'Grandiflora'. **'Andrewsii'** A form with deep pinkish-red and cream, semi-double flowers with yellow stamens. Sometimes repeats in autumn. ♀ 2002. **'Canary'** A small, compact shrub intermediate in habit between 'Grandiflora' and *R.* 'Lutea Maxima', with comparatively large, single, clear yellow flowers. **'Dunwich'** Dunwich rose. Dense, spreading habit with creamy-white flowers. Found at Dunwich, Suffolk. **'Glory of Edzell'** A very beautiful, early-flowering shrub reaching 2m. Clear pink, lemon-centred flowers garland the slender branches in May. Possibly of hybrid origin. **'Grandiflora'** (var. *altaica* Rehder not (Willd.) Thory, *R. altaica* hort. not Willd.) A stronger-growing variety up to 2m high and more across. The large, creamy-white flowers, 5–6cm across, crowd the branches and are replaced by shining maroon-black fruits. An excellent free-flowering rose which, because of its dense, suckering habit makes a useful hedge. I about 1820 from Siberia. **'Hispida'** (*R. lutescens* Pursh) An unusual variety with densely bristly stems up to 1.5m. Flowers creamy-yellow, 5–6cm across. Siberia. I before 1781. **'Lutea'** See *R.* × *harisonii* 'Lutea Maxima'. **'William III'** A dwarf, suckering shrub of dense, bushy habit with short branches and greyish-green leaves. Flowers semi-double, magenta-crimson changing to rich plum colour, paler on the reverse. Fruits black. **'Williams' Double Yellow'** See *R.* × *harisonii* 'William's Double Yellow'.

pisocarpa A. Gray. A dense-growing, medium-sized shrub with leaves composed of 5–7 coarsely toothed leaflets. Flowers fragrant, lilac-pink, 2.5–3cm across, borne in corymbose clusters from June to August. Fruits rounded to ellipsoid, red. W North America. I about 1882.

× *polliniana* Spreng. (*R. arvensis* × *R. gallica*) A rambling shrub forming a low mound up to 1m high and 3m across, clambering into trees and shrubs if allowed. Flowers slightly fragrant, 6–7.5cm across, rose-pink in bud, opening blush, with yellow anthers. C 1820.

polyantha See *R. multiflora*.

'Polyantha Grandiflora' See *R. gentiliana*.

pomifera See *R. villosa*.

prattii Hemsl. An exceedingly attractive shrub of medium size with dainty foliage and clusters of deep rose flowers, 2.5–3cm across, in July. The crimson, bottle-shaped fruits are very ornamental. W China. I 1903 by Ernest Wilson.

primula Boulenger. A beautiful, medium-sized shrub with arching stems and leaves composed of 7–13 dark glossy leaflets which emit a strong incense-like odour when crushed. Flowers fragrant, 4cm across, primrose-yellow passing to white, opening in mid-May. Fruits globose, red. Turkestan to N China. I 1910. ♀ 2002. AM 1962.

× *pruhoniciana* **'Hillieri'** See *R.* 'Hillieri'.

Red Max Graf ('Kormax') PBR Similar to 'Max Graf' but with scarlet flowers.

× *reversa* Waldst. & Kit. (*R. pendulina* × *R. pimpinellifolia*) A small, suckering shrub resembling the Burnet rose in general appearance. Small, semi-double, carmine flowers, white at base, are followed by scarlet fruits. Occurs in the wild with the parents. C 1820.

'Rosa Mundi' See *R. gallica* 'Versicolor'.

'Rose d'Amour' (*R. virginiana* 'Plena') St Mark's rose. A medium-sized shrub with almost thornless stems, up to 2m, and leaves with 5–7 leaflets. Flowers double, fragrant, deep pink with paler outer petals, continuing over several weeks from mid to late summer. A vigorous, free-flowering rose, a hybrid between *R. virginiana* and another species, possibly *R. carolina*. Garden origin before 1820. ♀ 2002. FCC 1980.

'Roseraie de l'Haÿ' A hybrid of *R. rugosa*. The long, pointed buds are dark purplish-red opening to rich crimson-purple with cream stamens, expanding 10–12cm across, double, very fragrant, from June to the frosts. A superb rose of vigorous growth, making an excellent hedge. Garden origin in 1901. ♀ 2002.

roxburghii Tratt. (*R. microphylla* Roxb. ex Lindl.) Burr rose, Chestnut rose. A very distinct, viciously-armed shrub of medium to large size. Flowers composed of 9–15 neatly paired leaflets. Flowers fragrant, 6–7.5cm across, shell-pink, with prickly receptacles, calyces and pedicels, in May and June, followed by orange-yellow, tomato-shaped fruits covered with stiff prickles. The twisted, spreading, grey to cinnamon-coloured stems with their flaky bark give a gnarled effect to this interesting rose. I from China in 1908 by Ernest Wilson. **'Plena'** The double-flowered form from which the species was named. I before 1814.

rubiginosa L. (*R. eglanteria* L.) Sweet briar, Eglantine. A strong-growing, medium-sized shrub with stout, erect, densely prickly and glandular stems. Deliciously aromatic leaves are composed of 5–7 rounded leaflets and clear pink, fragrant, beautifully formed flowers, 3–4cm across, stud the arching branches during summer. Fruits bright red, oval, lasting well into winter. A lovely native species, famed for its fragrance, both flower and foliage. It makes a pleasant if vigorous hedge. Europe. It is a parent of innumerable hybrids and has given rise to several hundred forms, few of which are now in cultivation. AM 1975.

rubra See *R. gallica*.

rubrifolia See *R. glauca*.

rubus Lev. & Vaniot (*R. ernestii* Stapf ex Bean) A strong-growing, vigorous rambler with good foliage. The long stems possess large prickles and the leaves are composed of usually 5 leaflets. Flowers fragrant, 3cm across, pinkish in bud, opening creamy-white with orange anthers, borne in dense corymbs and replaced by dark scarlet, oval fruits. Related to *R. helenae*, but even more vigorous, reaching 9m in a suitable position. C and W China. I 1907 by Ernest Wilson.

rugosa Thunb. Ramanas rose. A strong-growing, perpetual-flowering shrub with stout, densely prickly and bristly stems, 1.5–2m high. Leaves up to 18cm long, composed of 5–9 oblong, conspicuously veined, rugose leaflets, downy beneath. Flowers fragrant, 8–9cm across, purplish-rose, followed by bright red, tomato-shaped fruits, 2.5cm across, intermittently from June to the frosts. The fruits appear when the plant is still flowering. A well-known rose, parent of innumerable hybrids. Its vigorous, suckering habit enables it to form dense thickets and it is an excellent hedge plant. In Japan it grows on sandy seashores and it is occasionally found naturalised in similar situations in the British Isles. NE Asia. I 1796. AM 1896. **'Alba'** Flowers white, blush-tinted in bud. Very vigorous. Exceptional in fruit. ♀ 2002. **'Blanc Double de Coubert'** See *R.* 'Blanche Double de Coubert'. **'Fru Dagmar Hastrup'** See *R.* 'Fru Dagmar Hastrup'. **'Roseraie de l'Haÿ'** See *R.* 'Roseraie de l'Haÿ'. **'Rubra'** Flowers wine-crimson, fragrant. Fruits large and conspicuous. ♀ 2002. AM 1955. **'Scabrosa'** See *R.* 'Scabrosa'.

'Scabrosa' A vigorous hybrid of *R. rugosa* with excellent foliage. Enormous violaceous-crimson flowers are up to 14cm across, from June to the frosts. Fruits large, like small tomatoes, with persistent sepals. ♀ 2002. AM 1964.

serafinii Viv. A dwarf shrub, occasionally up to 1m, with densely prickly stems and leaves composed of 5–7 rounded glandular and aromatic leaflets. The small, bright pink flowers are followed by small, bright red, rounded fruits. Mediterranean region, SE Europe. C 1914.

sericea Lindl. This is an extremely variable species, forming a dense shrub of medium size with usually conspicuously bristly and thorny stems and leaves with generally 7–15 leaflets. The white to yellow, usually 4-petalled flowers, 2.5–5cm across, rather resemble a Maltese cross and are borne all along the branches in May and early June. They are followed by bright, parti-coloured crimson and yellow, edible, pear-shaped fruits, which fall during summer. Himalaya to W and C China. I 1822. **'Atrosanguinea'** This has fruits of deep crimson. **'Chrysocarpa'** Fruits yellow. **'Lutea'** An attractive form with yellow flowers and translucent crimson thorns. **subsp. *omeiensis*** (Rolfe) A.V. Roberts (*R. omeiensis* Rolfe) Mount Omei rose. Pedicel fleshy in fruit; leaflets more than 11. **subsp. *omeiensis* f. *pteracantha*** Franch. Stems furnished with flat, broad-based, translucent crimson thorns, which are particularly pleasing when illuminated by the rays of a winter sun. They are especially conspicuous on young and vigorous, basal shoots and may be encouraged by an annual or bi-annual pruning. Himalaya, W China. I 1890. AM 1976. FCC 1905. **var. *polyphylla*** Rowley. A form with more numerous leaflets and smoother, less spiny stems.

setigera Michx. Prairie rose. A small, widespreading shrub with long, trailing stems and trifoliolate leaves, the leaflets deep green, coarsely toothed and 5–7.5cm long. Flowers 5cm across, rose-pink, fading to blush, fragrant, appearing in July and August. Fruits small, globose, red. Useful as a groundcover or for training over bushes and low walls. E USA. I 1800.

setipoda Hemsl. & E.H. Wilson A free-growing, medium-sized shrub with stout, erect, few-thorned stems. Leaves composed of 7–9 leaflets, glandular beneath and possessing a delightful sweet briar-like fragrance when crushed. The clear pink, beautifully-formed flowers, 5–6cm across, are borne on contrasting purplish pedicels all along the branches and are followed by large, flagon-shaped, crimson, glandular-bristly fruits. W China. I 1901 by Ernest Wilson.

'Silver Moon' A vigorous, rambling rose, up to 9m, with glossy, dark green leaves and large, creamy-white, richly scented flowers, butter-yellow in bud. Usually regarded as *R. laevigata* × *R. wichurana*, but the magnolia rose (*R.* 'Devoniensis') may have also played a part.

sinica See *R. laevigata*.

sinowilsonii Hemsl. & E.H. Wilson. A magnificent climbing species, related to *R. mulliganii*. Its shining, reddish-brown stems are clothed with attractive leaves composed of usually 7 long-pointed, corrugated leaflets, deep glossy green above, purple-flushed beneath. The white flowers, 5cm across, are borne in panicles during summer. Superb foliage plant requiring a warm sunny wall in a sheltered garden. I 1904 by Ernest Wilson from W China: the name refers to his nickname 'Chinese Wilson'.

soulieana Crép. A large shrub with long, scandent, pale spiny stems forming great mounds. Leaves grey-green with 7–9 leaflets. Flowers 2.5–4cm across, creamy-yellow in bud opening white, borne on well-established, mature plants in large corymbs followed by small, ovoid, orange-red fruits. A strong-growing species requiring plenty of space in which to develop. It looks well covering an old, decrepit tree. W China. I 1896. ♀ 2002.

spinosissima See *R. pimpinellifolia*.

× *spinulifolia* Dematra. A hybrid between *R. pendulina* and probably *R. tomentosa*. A small shrub of stiff habit with leaves that are glaucous at first, becoming green. Flowers fragrant, 4–5cm across, bright cherry-pink, followed by bright red, bottle-shaped fruits. Occurs in the wild with the parents.

stellata Woot. A dwarf shrub with wiry, greyish-green stems forming dense, low thickets. Leaves trifoliolate, with wedge-shaped, coarsely toothed leaflets. Flowers 5–6cm across, deep pink with yellow anthers. Fruits small, dull red. Mts of SW USA. I 1902. **var. *mirifica*** (Greene) Cockerell. Sacramento rose. A rare shrub, slightly more robust than the typical form. It also differs in its hairless stems clothed with ivory-coloured prickles and its generally glabrous leaves with 3–5, or occasionally 7, leaflets. Flowers rose-purple, paling with age, followed by red, top-shaped fruits. It requires a warm, sunny position in well-drained soil. New Mexico. I 1916. AM 1924.

stylosa Desv. A medium-sized, native shrub with long, arching stems and leaves with 5–7 leaflets. Flowers 3–5cm across, pale pink to white followed by ovoid, red fruits. Europe.

sweginzowii Koehne. A strong-growing shrub, 3–4m high, with strongly thorny stems and leaves with 7–11 leaflets, in general appearance very like *R. moyesii*. Bright rose-pink flowers, 4cm across, often in clusters, on glandular, bristly stalks, are followed by flagon-shaped, bright red, hispid fruits. The latter are about equal in size and colour to those of *R. moyesii*, but ripen earlier. NW China. I 1903 by Ernest Wilson. AM 1922.

triphylla See *R.* × *beanii*.

villosa L. (*R. pomifera* Herrm.) Apple rose. A vigorous, medium-sized shrub with leaves composed of 5–7 bluish-green, downy leaflets, fragrant when crushed. Flowers 5cm across, carmine in bud, opening clear pink followed in early autumn by large, apple-shaped, bristle-clad, crimson fruits. C and S Europe. W Asia. I 1771. AM 1955. **'Duplex'** See *R.* 'Wolley-Dod'.

virginiana Mill. (*R. lucida* Ehrh.) A small, suckering shrub forming thickets of slender, erect stems. The leaves are composed of 7–9 glossy green leaflets, which turn first to purple then to orange-red, crimson and yellow in autumn. Flowers 5–6cm across, bright pink, deeper in bud, appearing continuously from June to July into August. Fruits small, orange-shaped, bright glistening red. A most attractive species, excellent in sandy soils, particularly by the sea. E North America. I before 1807. ♀ 2002. AM 1953. **'Plena'** See *R.* 'Rose d'Amour'.

wardii Mulligan. The typical form of this rare Tibetan species is thought not to be in cultivation and is represented by the following form: **'Culta'** A lax-growing shrub, up to 2m, with arching branches and leaves similar to those of *R. moyesii*. Flowers also similar to those of the latter, but petals are creamy-white with a mahogany-red disc surrounded by yellow stamens. SE Tibet. I 1924 by Kingdon-Ward.

webbiana Royle. A graceful and slender shrub, up to 2m, with arching branches and leaves composed of 7–9 small, rounded leaflets. The clear, almond-pink flowers, 4–5cm across, are carried along the stems creating a charming effect in June. They are followed in late summer by bottle-shaped, shining sealing wax-red fruits. W Himalaya. I 1879. AM 1955.

'Wedding Day' A vigorous climbing or rambling shrub with red-thorned, green stems reaching 10m in a suitable tree. Leaves rich green and glossy. Flowers richly scented, in large trusses, deep yellow in bud, opening creamy-white with vivid orange-yellow stamens, fading to pink. Raised before 1950 by the late Sir Frederick Stern at Highdown, Sussex, by selfing a hybrid from the cross *R. sinowilsonii* × *R. moyesii*. AM 1950.

White Max Graf ('Korgram') PBR Large, single, pure white flowers. Prostrate or climbing to 2m.

wichurana Crép. A vigorous, semi-evergreen species with trailing stems up to 6m long. Leaves small, dark shining green, composed of 7–9 leaflets. Flowers 4–5cm across, white, richly scented, borne in small, conical clusters during late summer, followed by tiny, globose, red fruits. An excellent groundcover, the stems rooting as they grow. Also suitable for clothing tree-stumps and unsightly objects. A parent of numerous hybrids including 'Alberic Barbier', 'Albertine' and 'Dorothy Perkins'. E Asia. I 1891 from Japan. AM 1985. **'Grandiflora'** A splendid form with larger flowers. **'Variegata'** Leaves blotched and mottled creamy-white.

'Willam's Double Yellow' See *R.* × *harisonii* 'Williams' Double Yellow'.

willmottiae Hemsl. An elegant, medium-sized shrub with gracefully arching branches and small, sea-green, fern-like leaves composed of 7–9 leaflets, pleasantly fragrant when crushed. Flowers 3–4cm across, lilac-pink, with cream-coloured anthers, in May and June. Fruits pear-shaped, orange-red. One of the loveliest species when in flower. I 1904 from the Tibetan border region of W China by Ernest Wilson and named after the great gardener and rosarian, Miss Ellen Willmott. AM 1958. **'Wisley'** Flowers of a deeper shade of lilac-pink.

'Wintonensis' (*R. moyesii* × *R. setipoda*) A beautiful hybrid raised in our nurseries in 1928. In general appearance it shows a leaning towards *R. setipoda*, which is apparent in the sweet briar-like fragrance of the foliage. Flowers rich rose-pink, several in a cluster, with long leafy sepals and very glandular-hairy receptacles.

'Wolley-Dod' (*R. villosa* 'Duplex') Wolley-Dod's rose. An attractive, medium-sized shrub resembling *R. villosa*. Flowers semi-double, clear pink; fruits dark red. Raised in the garden of the Rev Wolley-Dod. AM 1954.

woodsii Lindl. A very variable shrub, up to 2m, the leaves with 5–7 leaflets. Flowers 3–4cm across, lilac-pink, followed by red, globose fruits. C and W North America. I 1815. **var. *fendleri*** Rydb. The most beautiful form of this species and a truly first-class garden shrub. It forms a densely leafy bush, to about 1.5m high, and carries bright lilac-pink flowers, followed by conspicuous sealing wax-red fruits, which persist long into winter. W North America. C 1888.

xanthina Lindl. (*R. xanthina* 'Flore Pleno') A beautiful, medium-sized shrub with gracefully arching branches and small, dainty, fern-like leaves composed of 7–13 rounded leaflets. Flowers semi-double, 4cm across, golden-yellow, May and June. A garden form, said to have been cultivated in N China and Korea for over 100 years. Reintroduced to the Arnold Arboretum, Boston in 1907 by the indefatigable collector Fredrick N. Meyer. AM 1945. **f. *spontanea*** Rehder. The wild form, reaching 3m in time, the branches clothed with pale sea-green foliage and bedecked in May and early June with single, comparatively large, yellow flowers, followed by dark red fruits. A parent of 'Canary Bird'. N China, Korea. I 1907. AM 1945.

Rose, apothecary's See *R. gallica* var. *officinalis*.
Rose, apple See *R. villosa*.
Rose, Arkansas See *R. arkansana*.
Rose, Austrian briar See *R. foetida*.
Rose, Austrian copper See *R. foetida* 'Bicolor'.
Rose, Austrian Yellow See *R. foetida*.
Rose, Banksian See *R. banksiae*.
Rose, Burgundian See *R.* 'Burgundiaca'.
Rose, burnet See *R. pimpinellifolia*.
Rose, burr See *R. roxburghii*.
Rose, cabbage See *R.* × *centifolia*.
Rose, cabbage, crested See *R.* × *centifolia* 'Cristata'.
Rose, Cherokee See *R. laevigata*.
Rose, chestnut See *R. roxburghii*.
Rose, China See *R. chinensis*.
Rose, cinnamon See *R. majalis*.
Rose, Cooper's Burmese See *R.* 'Cooperi'.
Rose, crested moss See *R.* × *centifolia* 'Cristata'.
Rose, damask See *R.* × *damascena*.
Rose, dog See *R. canina*.
Rose, eglantine See *R. rubiginosa*.
Rose, field See *R. arvensis*.
Rose, Fortune's Double Yellow See *R.* × *odorata* 'Pseudindica'.
Rose, green See *R. chinensis* 'Viridiflora'.
Rose, Himalayan musk See *R. brunonii*.
Rose, Jacobite See *R.* × *alba* 'Alba Maxima'.
Rose, Lady Banks See *R. banksiae*.
Rose, Macartney See *R. bracteata*.
Rose, monthly See *R.* × *odorata* 'Pallida'.

Rose, moss See *R. centifolia* 'Muscosa'.
Rose, musk See *R. moschata*.
Rose, myrrh-scented See *R. arvensis* 'Splendens'.
Rose, Nootka See *R. nutkana*.
Rose, Persian yellow See *R. foetida* 'Persiana'.
Rose, prairie See *R. setigera*.
Rose, Provence See *R. centifolia*.
Rose, Ramanas See *R. rugosa*.
Rose, red, of Lancaster See *R. gallica* var. *officinalis*.
Rose des peintres See under *R. centifolia*.
Rose, Sacramento See *R. stellata* var. *mirifica*.
Rose, Scotch See *R. pimpinellifolia*.
Rose, seven sisters See *R. multiflora* 'Grevillei'.
Rose, sweet briar See *R. rubiginosa*.
Rose, tea See *R.* × *odorata*.
Rose, threepenny bit See *R. elegantula* 'Persetosa'.
Rose, white, of York See *R.* × *alba*.
Rose, yellow Banksian See *R. banksiae* 'Lutea'.
Rose, York and Lancaster See *R. damascena* 'Versicolor'.
Rose of Sharon See *Hypericum calycinum*.
Rosemary See *Rosmarinus officinalis*.
Rosemary, wild See *Rhododendron tomentosum*.

***ROSMARINUS**—Labiatae—A genus of 3 species of evergreen, aromatic shrubs, with romantic associations, long cultivated in W European gardens, thriving in all types of well-drained soil in full sun. We would like to thank Dr Tim Upson of the University Botanic Garden, Cambridge for his assistance with this genus.

†*eriocalyx* Jord. & Fourr. A small shrub, rare in cultivation, to 1.5m, usually with a sprawling habit. Calyx densely pubescent with long, simple non-glandular and glandular hairs. Flowers blue-violet, the lower lip marked with a purple 'V' and with a white blotch at the base. S Spain, N Africa.

× *lavandulaceus* Noë (*R. officinalis* × *R. eriocalyx*) This hybrid occurs in S Spain and N Africa where the parents grow together. A number of varieties are recognised. For the plant often grown as *R. lavandulaceus* see *R. officinalis* var. *prostratus*.

officinalis L. Common rosemary. A dense shrub, up to 2m and as much through, with stems thickly clothed with linear, green or greyish-green leaves, white beneath. Flowers blue, produced in numerous axillary clusters along the branches of the previous year, in May or earlier. Makes an attractive, informal hedge which may be lightly pruned if necessary, immediately after flowering. S Europe, Asia Minor. Cultivated in Britain for over 400 years. 'Albus' Flowers white. 'Aureus' Leaves blotched with yellow; not very attractive. †'**Benenden Blue**' A smaller-growing, distinct form with very narrow, dark green leaves and bright blue flowers. A selection of var. *angustissimus*. ♀ 2002. AM 1933. '**Corsican Blue**' Low-growing with deep blue flowers. '**Fastigiatus**' See under 'Miss Jessopp's Upright'. '**Fota Blue**' Very deep blue flowers with a white throat, arching habit. '**Frimley Blue**' See 'Primley Blue'. '**Lady in White**' Pure white flowers. Spreading habit and light green foliage. An improvement on 'Albus', which is not always a clear white. '**Majorca**' A lovely clone, with flowers of bluebird-blue, with a dark spot on the lower petals. AM 1961. †'**Majorca Pink**' A form with arching stems and bright

pink flowers. '**McConnell's Blue**' See 'Mrs McConnell'. '**Miss Jessopp's Upright**' A strong-growing form of erect habit. Several forms are grown under this name. 'Fastigiatus' and 'Pyramidalis' are similar selections. ♀ 2002. '**Mrs McConnell**' ('McConnell's Blue') A dwarf shrub of low, spreading habit with dark green leaves and dark blue flowers. ♀ 2002. '**Primley Blue**' ('Frimley Blue') Upright habit, hardy with mid-blue flowers. †**var. *prostratus*** Pasquale (*R. lavandulaceus* hort. not Noë) A low-growing form making large, dense, prostrate mats, studded with clusters of blue flowers in May and June. Ideal for draping sunny wall-tops, but somewhat tender. Several forms of this variety are cultivated. '**Pyramidalis**' See under 'Miss Jessopp's Upright'. '**Roseus**' A small shrub with lilac-pink flowers. '**Severn Sea**' A dwarf shrub with arching branches and brilliant blue flowers. Raised by that dedicated gardener Norman Hadden at West Porlock, Somerset. ♀ 2002. AM 1989. '**Sissinghurst Blue**' A form of upright habit with narrow leaves and profuse rich blue flowers. A chance seedling raised at Sissinghurst Castle about 1958. ♀ 2002. AM 1983. †'**Tuscan Blue**' A small shrub with broader leaves and brighter coloured, deep blue flowers. Often flowers in winter.

tomentosus Huber-Morath & Maire. A dwarf, tender shrub, rare in cultivation, to 50cm tall, with densely clustered leaves distinctively grey-white-tomentose. Calyx densely pubescent with stalked glandular hairs. Flowers blue-violet, the lower lip marked with a purple 'V' and with a pale yellow blotch at base. Endemic to S Spain where it hybridises with *R. officinalis* to produce *R.* × *mendizabalii* Sagredo ex Rosua.

ROSTRINUCULA Kudô—Labiatae—A genus of 2 species, natives of China.

dependens (Rehder) Kudô. An erect, deciduous shrub with stout purple shoots often dying back to ground level in winter. Leaves opposite, narrowly elliptic, to 15cm long, shallowly toothed except at the base, smooth above, grey-tomentose beneath. Flowers in the axils of grey-felted bracts, in dense, pendulous terminal spikes, to 20cm long, in early to mid-autumn, pink, with long-exserted pink stamens and styles. I 1985.

Rowan See *Sorbus aucuparia*.

RUBUS L.—Rosaceae—A large genus of more than 250 species widely distributed as well as numerous apomicts in Europe and North America. The ornamental brambles are a varied throng, many species thriving in the poorest of soils and other adverse conditions. Several species have attractive flowers and foliage, while others have striking white stems in winter; all have prickles unless otherwise stated. Those grown for their ornamental stems should have the old flowering stems cut down to ground level each year, immediately after flowering. See also under CLIMBERS.

amabilis Focke. A small shrub of graceful habit, usually less than 1.2m. Leaves pinnate, with 7–9, deeply toothed leaflets, borne along the slender, fairly erect stems. Flowers solitary, 4–5cm across, white, in June and July. Fruits large, red, edible but sparingly produced. W China. I 1908 by Ernest Wilson.

australis J.R. Forst. An evergreen, dioecious climber with long, wiry, prickle-clad stems. Leaves with 3–5 leaflets, variable in shape and size. Flowers small, white, in long panicles, only produced on adult plants, in summer. Juvenile plants creep along the ground, forming dense hummocks. Requires a well-drained, sheltered position. New Zealand.

'Benenden' (*R.* Tridel 'Benenden') (*R. deliciosus* × *R. trilobus*) A beautiful hybrid raised by Capt Collingwood Ingram in 1950. A vigorous shrub producing erect, peeling, thornless shoots up to 3m high. Leaves 3- to 5-lobed. Flowers 5cm across, glistening white, with a central boss of golden-yellow stamens, produced singly all along the arching branches in May. ♀ 2002. FCC 1963. AM 1958.

*'Betty Ashburner'** A prostrate, evergreen shrub with glossy green, rounded, more or less 3-lobed leaves with wavy margins. It is a good groundcover plant, more compact, and lower growing than *R. tricolor*, which can be too invasive. In summer bears white flowers, which are rather concealed by the foliage, followed by a few red fruits.

biflorus Buch.-Ham. ex Sm. A vigorous, medium-sized shrub producing semi-erect, prickly, green stems covered with a vivid white, waxy bloom. Leaves composed of 5, occasionally 3, leaflets, white-felted beneath. The small, white flowers are produced in small, terminal clusters in summer and are followed by edible, yellow fruits. Himalaya. I 1818. ♀ 2002.

caesius L. Dewberry. A native species of little ornamental merit, with long, slender, creeping stems, forming extensive carpets. Leaves usually trifoliolate. Flowers small, white, followed by bloomy-black fruits. Europe to N Asia.

calycinoides See *R. pentalobus*.

cissoides var. *pauperatus* See *R. squarrosus*.

cockburnianus Hemsl. (*R. giraldianus* Focke) A strong-growing species of medium size with striking, purple, arching stems overlaid with a vivid white bloom. The attractively pinnate, fern-like leaves, white or grey beneath, are composed of 7–9 leaflets. Small, rose-purple flowers of little merit are borne in dense terminal panicles in summer and followed by bloomy-black fruits. N and C China. I 1907 by Ernest Wilson. **Goldenvale** ('Wyego') PBR A form with equally striking white shoots in winter but with the added bonus of yellow foliage in summer. It is also lower growing and much less invasive. ♀ 2002. AM 1996.

deliciosus Torr. A medium-sized, thornless shrub bearing arching branches with peeling bark. Leaves 3- to 5-lobed. Flowers like white dog roses, 5cm across, borne in May and June. Fruits purplish but seldom maturing. A delightful flowering shrub and for this purpose, one of the best in the genus. Native of the Rocky Mountains, Colorado (USA). I 1870. FCC 1881.

fockeanus hort. See *R. pentalobus*.

×*fraseri* Rehder (*R. odoratus* × *R. parviflorus*) A vigorous, medium-sized, suckering shrub with palmate leaves and comparatively large, fragrant, rose-coloured flowers from June to August. Particularly useful for covering shady areas beneath trees. Garden origin in 1918.

fruticosus L. Bramble, Blackberry. A common and familiar scrambling native which may be found growing in just about every type of soil and situation. It is immensely variable and in the British Isles alone several hundred species or microspecies are recognised. Only a few are of any ornamental merit, for which see *R. laciniatus* and *R. ulmifolius* 'Bellidiflorus'. **var. *laciniatus*** See *R. laciniatus*.

giraldianus See *R. cockburnianus*.

idaeus L. Raspberry. A vigorous, thicket-forming shrub with biennial, prickly and bloomy shoots. Leaves with 3–5 or 7 leaflets, white-hairy beneath. Clusters of white flowers in summer are followed by the familiar, edible, red, or sometimes yellow, fruits. Europe (incl. British Isles), Asia. **'Aureus'** A form that has bright yellow foliage.

illecebrosus Focke. Strawberry-raspberry. A dwarf sub-shrub with a creeping, woody rootstock. Erect stems bear pinnate leaves and solitary or terminal clusters of white flowers, 2.5–4cm across, in July. Fruits large, red, sweet, but rather insipid. Japan. C 1895.

*'Kenneth Ashburner'** A prostrate, vigorous, evergreen shrub with glossy, green, pointed leaves. It is suitable for groundcover.

laciniatus Willd. (*R. fruticosus* var. *laciniatus* Weston) Fern-leaved bramble, Cut-leaved bramble. This bramble is not known in a wild state and yet it breeds true from seed. It is a vigorous species with long, scrambling, prickly stems. The leaves are composed of usually 5 pinnately-lobed leaflets, the lobes incisely toothed, creating an attractive, fern-like effect. The rather insignificant flowers are replaced by prolific, sweet, black fruits. Origin before 1770. There is also a similar form with thornless stems.

leucodermis Torr. & A. Gray. A species of medium size with both erect and spreading, glaucous blue stems. Leaves with 3–5 coarsely toothed leaflets, white-felted beneath. Flowers small, white, borne in terminal clusters in June; fruits purplish-black, edible. W North America. I about 1829 by David Douglas.

†*lineatus* Reinw. A deciduous or semi-evergreen shrub with rambling, silky-hairy stems, usually less than 1.2m. The leaves are unique and beautiful, having 5 leaflets dark green above, covered with a shining, silvery, silky down beneath, conspicuously veined. Prickles few or absent. Flowers white in small axillary clusters in summer. Fruits small, red or yellow. Requires a warm sheltered position. E Himalaya, W China, Malaya. I 1905 by George Forrest.

linkianus Ser. (*R. thyrsoideus* 'Plenus') A robust, medium-sized shrub with long, scrambling stems. Leaves with 5 leaflets. Flowers double, white, in large, erect, conical panicles in July and August. A conspicuous shrub for a wild garden, also useful in semi-shade. C before 1770.

mesogaeus Focke. A strong-growing shrub producing erect, velvety stems up to 3m high. Leaves trifoliolate with large, coarsely toothed leaflets, grey-tomentose beneath. Flowers small, pinkish-white in June. Fruits black. C and W China. I 1907.

microphyllus 'Variegatus' A small, suckering shrub producing dense mounds of slender, prickly, glaucescent stems. Leaves 4–7.5cm long, prettily 3-lobed, green, mottled cream and pink. The typical form is a native of Japan.

nepalensis (Hook. f.) Kuntze (*R. nutans* Wall. ex Edgew.) A dwarf, evergreen, creeping shrub with densely soft-bristly stems and short-stalked, trifoliolate leaves. Attractive, nodding, white flowers, 2.5–4cm across, are borne on erect, leafy shoots in June, followed by purple, edible fruits. A charming carpeting shrub for a shady border or bank. Himalaya. I 1850, reintroduced in 1971 (BL & M 152). A hybrid between this species and *R. tricolor* was raised in 1976 by our propagator Peter Dummer; on this plant the leaves varied from broadly ovate to 3-lobed or trifoliolate.

×*nobilis* Regel (*R. idaeus* × *R. odoratus*) A small, thornless shrub with erect, peeling stems and large, downy, trifoliolate leaves. Flowers purple-red, in terminal clusters in June and July. A vigorous hybrid with the same potential as *R. odoratus*. C 1855.

nutans See *R. nepalensis*.

odoratus L. A vigorous, suckering shrub with erect, peeling thornless stems up to 2.5m high. Young shoots densely glandular-hairy. Leaves large and velvety, palmate. Flowers in branched clusters, 4–5cm across, fragrant, purplish-rose, opening from June to September. Fruits flat and broad, red, edible. An excellent shrub for a wild garden or semi-shade beneath trees. E North America. I 1770. '**Albus**' A form with white flowers.

parviflorus Nutt. (*R. nutkanus* Moç ex Ser.) Thimbleberry. A strong-growing shrub with erect, peeling thornless stems, 1.8–2.5m high. Leaves large, palmate, softly downy. Flowers white, 4–5cm across, in terminal clusters in May and June. Fruits large and flattened, red. W North America. I 1827 by David Douglas.

†*parvus Buch. A low-growing shrub with long, creeping or semi-climbing stems. Leaves narrow and prickly-toothed, dark or bronze-green above, paler beneath. Flowers white, unisexual, solitary or in small panicles, in May and June. Fruits red. Related to *R. australis*, forming attractive groundcover in sheltered places. New Zealand. C 1916.

peltatus Maxim. A remarkable, vigorous, small shrub of spreading and suckering habit. Shoots zigzag, and are conspicuously glaucous-bloomed in winter. Leaves shallowly 5-lobed and coarsely toothed, about 25cm across with large, glaucous stipules. Flowers white, to 6cm across, pendent on short pedicels, borne singly at the tips of short shoots in May. Japan.

*pentalobus Hayata. (*R. calycinoides* Hayata not Kuntze, *R. fockeanus* hort.) A creeping alpine evergreen, forming dense mats of short-jointed, rooting stems. The small, 3–5-lobed, mallow-like leaves are glossy green and bullate above, grey-felted beneath. White flowers are borne singly or in short clusters in summer, but are usually concealed beneath the leaves, sometimes followed by edible orange fruits. A most useful groundcover for a rock garden, scree or peat wall, even in shade. Taiwan. The Chinese *R. fockeanus* is very similar.

phoenicolasius Maxim. Wineberry. A conspicuous shrub with reddish, glandular-bristly stems 2.5–3m high. Leaves large, trifoliolate, the leaflets coarsely toothed, white-felted beneath. Flowers in July, in terminal glandular-bristly clusters, small, pale pink. Fruits bright orange-red, sweet and edible. Japan, China, Korea. I about 1876. FCC 1894.

rosifolius Sm. In its typical form this vigorous, semi-evergreen bramble has stout, angled shoots bearing dark green pinnate leaves with up to 11 leaflets. White flowers, about 3cm across, followed by bright red edible

fruits. SE Asia. C 1887. '**Coronarius**' A striking form with large, double, creamy-white flowers, flushed with green, up to 10cm across. Unusually a second flower is sometimes produced from the centre of the first after the petals have fallen. C 1813.

spectabilis Pursh. Salmonberry. A vigorous, suckering shrub, producing erect, finely prickly stems, 1.2–1.8m high. Leaves trifoliolate. Flowers solitary or in small clusters, 2.5–4cm across, bright magenta-rose, fragrant, in April. Fruits large, ovoid, orange-yellow, edible. Excellent in a wild garden or as groundcover beneath trees. W North America. I 1827 by David Douglas. '**Olympic Double**' A striking form with large, double flowers. AM 1995.

†*squarrosus* Fritsch (*R. cissoides* var. *pauperatus* Kirk) A curious species, forming a dense, tangled mass of dark, slender stems, bearing numerous, scattered, tiny, ivory-white prickles. Leaves usually thread-like but variably shaped, sparse. Flowers in racemes or panicles, small, yellowish, in summer. Fruits seldom seen in the British Isles, orange-red. Normally found in cultivation as a congested mound or scrambling over neighbouring shrubs, but in its native habitat it develops into a tall climber. New Zealand.

thibetanus Franch. (*R. veitchii* Rolfe) An attractive species with semi-erect, purplish-brown stems, 1.8–2m high, covered with a blue-white bloom. Leaves pinnate, fern-like, with 7–13, coarsely toothed leaflets, greyish silky-hairy above, white- or grey-felted beneath. Flowers small, purple; fruits black or red, in summer. W China. I 1904 by Ernest Wilson. It has also been distributed as *R. thibetanus* 'Silver Fern'. ♀ 2002. AM 1915. '**Silver Fern**' See under *R. thibetanus*.

*tricolor Focke (*R. polytrichus* Franch.) An attractive, evergreen shrub with long, trailing, densely bristly stems. Leaves cordate, 7.5–10cm long, dark glossy green above, white-felted beneath. Flowers white, 2.5cm across, produced singly in the leaf axils in July, sometimes followed by large, bright red, edible fruits. An excellent groundcover in shady places, forming extensive carpets even under beech trees. W China. Discovered by the Abbé Delavay; introduced by Ernest Wilson in 1908.

Tridel See *R.* 'Benenden'.

trilobus Ser. A lovely medium-sized shrub with strong, spreading, thornless stems. Leaves resembling those of *R. deliciosus*, but larger and cordate-ovate. Flowers 5cm across and pure white with yellow stamens are borne intermittently along the arching stems from May to July. Mexico. I 1938. AM 1947.

ulmifolius Schott. A vigorous shrub with long, scrambling, rambling, plum-coloured stems and leaves with 3–5 leaflets, white-felted beneath. This is a common native bramble of which the following is the only form in general cultivation: '**Bellidiflorus**' Large panicles of showy, double pink flowers in July and August. Too vigorous for all but a wild garden.

Rue See *Ruta graveolens*.

RUSCUS L.—**Ruscaceae**—A small genus of about 6 species of evergreen subshrubs distributed from Madeira to Iran and spreading by underground stems. The apparent leaves are really flattened stems (cladodes), which carry out the functions of the true leaves, these being reduced to tiny, papery scales. The flowers are minute and are borne, during winter to spring, on the surface of the cladodes, male and female on separate plants, followed by attractive fruits on the females. Useful plants for dry shady places in all soils.

aculeatus L. Butcher's broom. A small, erect shrub forming thick clumps of green, thick but flexible stems 0.5–1m high. Cladodes small, spine-tipped, densely borne on the branches in the upper parts of the stems. Berries resembling bright, sealing wax-red cherries, sometimes abundantly produced when plants of both sexes are present. Tolerant of dense shade, where few other plants will grow. S Europe (incl. S England).

colchicus P.F. Yeo. A dwarf shrub with arching stems closely related to *R. hypoglossum* but with the flowers borne on the underside of the cladode. Cladodes leathery, variable in size – up to 17cm long and 8cm across on a form introduced by Roy Lancaster. Black Sea region, NE Turkey.

hypoglossum L. A dwarf shrub forming broad clumps of green 'leafy' stems. The comparatively large, leaf-like cladodes carry a tiny, green flower on their upper surface and on female plants large, red, cherry-like fruits. Excellent groundcover in shade. S Europe. C since 16th century.

× *microglossus* Bertoloni (*R. hypoglossum* × *R. hypophyllum*) An interesting hybrid forming extensive suckering patches of erect or ascending stems up to 60cm high. Cladodes elliptic to obovate, petioled and slender-pointed, smaller and more elegantly posed than those of *R. hypoglossum*. The flower bracts are also much smaller and scale-like. The plants in general cultivation are female and probably all belong to a single clone. N Italy and adjacent parts of France and former Yugoslavia.

racemosus See *Danae racemosa*.

RUTA L. —**Rutaceae**—A small genus of about 8 species of aromatic shrubs and perennial herbs, natives of Europe and SW Asia. They thrive in a sunny, well-drained position in almost any soil.

*chalepensis L. Similar to *R. graveolens* and sometimes confused with it, this species is most easily distinguished by the fringe of yellow hairs on the margins of the petals and the narrower leaf lobes. S Europe.

*graveolens L. Rue. A small, evergreen shrub, up to 1m, with glaucous, much-divided, fern-like leaves and terminal corymbs of small, mustard-yellow flowers from June to August. A popular herb, long cultivated for its medicinal properties. The foliage can cause a severe blistering on the skin when handled in sunlight. S Europe. Cultivated in England since about 1652, perhaps earlier. **'Jackman's Blue'** A striking form with vivid, glaucous-blue foliage and compact, bushy habit. **'Variegata'** Creamy-white-variegated leaves.

S

†***SABAL** Adans.—**Palmae**—Palmetto. A genus of about 15 hermaphrodite species of single-stemmed or sometimes stemless palms with fan-shaped leaves, natives of the southern USA to Central Americ, N South America and the West Indies. The following makes a handsome foliage plant, suitable for growing outside in the mildest parts of the country but otherwise requiring conservatory protection in winter.

mexicana Mart. (*S. texana* (O.F. Cook) Becc.) Mexican palmetto, Texan palmetto. A medium-sized to large palm with a stout trunk, the old leaf bases persistent for several years. Leaves large, to 3m long, fan-shaped, the blade divided half the way or more to the base into numerous, drooping segments. Inflorescences about as long as the leaves bearing fragrant, white flowers followed by black fruits about 2cm long. S Texas, Mexico, Guatemala.

texana See *S. mexicana*.

Sacred bamboo See *Nandina domestica*.
Sage, common See *Salvia officinalis*.
Sage, Mexican red See *Salvia fulgens*.
Sage, mountain See *Buddleja loricata*.
Sage, pineapple-scented See *Salvia elegans*.
Sage brush See *Artemisia tridentata*.
Sage brush, **grey** See *Atriplex canescens*.
Sage wood, South African See *Buddleja salviifolia*.
St John's bread See *Ceratonia siliqua*.
St John's wort See *Hypericum*.
Salal See *Gaultheria shallon*.

SALIX L.—**Salicaceae**—The willows are a numerous and diverse genus of 300 or more species, varying from tiny, creeping alpines from high, northern altitudes, to large, noble lowland trees scattered throughout the temperate regions of the world, mainly in the N hemisphere. All may be grown in ordinary, loamy soils and many flourish in damp sites. Only a few are happy on chalky uplands, but almost all, except the alpine species, are at home in water meadows, chalky or otherwise. Few waterside trees are as beautiful as the weeping willows, despite the attentions of various diseases. Several willows, including *S. alba* 'Britzensis', *S. alba* var. *vitellina*, *S. daphnoides* and *S. irrorata*, have attractive young stems in winter; to encourage the production of these it is necessary to hard-prune each year or alternate years in March. For an effective winter garden, plant coloured-stemmed willows with silver birches, white-stemmed brambles, red and yellow-stemmed dogwoods, snakebark maples and the mahogany-barked *Prunus serrula*. A number of creeping species and their hybrids are excellent as groundcover, hiding large, bare or unsightly areas with their dense, leafy stems.

Willows are normally dioecious, male and female catkins being borne on separate plants. They generally appear in late winter or early spring, before or with the young leaves. The catkins of *S. bockii* are unusual in appearing in autumn. In the majority of species the male catkins are the more showy.

Site large shrubs and trees away from drains, which can be invaded by the root systems.

acutifolia Willd. (*S. daphnoides* var. *acutifolia* (Willd.) Doell., *S. pruinosa* Bess.) A very graceful, large shrub, occasionally a small tree, with lanceolate, long-pointed leaves and slender, damson-coloured shoots overlaid with a white bloom. Catkins appear before the leaves. Closely related to *S. daphnoides* from which it differs in its more slender, darker twigs, smaller, narrower catkins and narrower, longer-tapered and more numerously veined leaves. Russia. C 1890. **'Blue Streak'** A male form of Dutch origin, with polished, blackish-purple stems covered with a vivid blue-white bloom. ♀ 2002. **'Pendulifolia'** A beautiful, male form with conspicuously drooping leaves.

adenophylla See *S. cordata*.

aegyptiaca L. (*S. medemii* Boiss., *S. muscina* hort.) Musk willow. A large shrub or occasionally a small tree with densely grey-pubescent twigs. Leaves lanceolate, grey-pubescent beneath. Its large, conspicuous, bright yellow, male catkins occur in February and March, making this a very beautiful, early spring-flowering tree. SW to C Asia. C 1820. AM 1925 (as *S. medemii*). AM 1957 (as *S. aegyptiaca*).

alba L. White willow. A familiar, native species of water meadows and riversides. A large, elegant tree of conical habit, with slender branches, drooping at the tips. The lanceolate, silky-hairy leaves occur in great, billowy masses, creating a characteristic silvery appearance from a distance. The slender catkins appear with the young leaves in spring. A vigorous, fast-growing tree, much planted in moist, sandy areas by the sea. Europe, W Asia. **f. argentea** See var. *sericea*. **'Aurea'** A less vigorous tree with yellowish-green branches and pale yellow leaves. **'Britzensis'** ('Chermesina') Scarlet willow. A remarkable form, most conspicuous in winter when the branches are brilliant orange-scarlet, especially if pruned severely every second year. The clone 'Chrysostela' is similar, if not identical. ♀ 2002. AM 1976. **var. caerulea** (Sm.) Sm. (*S.* 'Caerulea', *S. × caerulea* Sm.) Cricket-bat willow. A large tree of conical habit, with spreading branches and lanceolate leaves, sea-green above and somewhat glaucous beneath. The best willow for cricket bats and long planted for this purpose in E England. The original tree is said to have been found in Norfolk about 1700. The female form is most commonly grown. **'Chermesina'** See 'Britzensis'. **'Chrysostela'** See under 'Britzensis'. **'Dart's Snake'** See *S. × sepulcralis* 'Dart's Snake'. **'Liempde'** A vigorous, male form with upright branches, making a narrowly conical tree. Selected in Holland where it is commonly planted. C 1968. **var. sericea** Gaudin (f. *argentea* Wimm., 'Sericea', 'Regalis') A smaller, less vigorous, rounder-headed tree with leaves of an intense silvery hue, striking when seen from a distance. ♀ 2002. **'Tristis'** See *S. × sepulcralis* 'Chrysocoma'. **var. vitellina** (L.) Stokes (*S. vitellina* L.) Golden willow. A smaller tree than the typical form. The brilliant egg-yolk-yellow shoots are made more conspicuous by severe pruning every second year. ♀ 2002. AMT 1967. **'Vitellina Pendula'** See *S. × sepulcralis* 'Chrysocoma'.

alpina Scop. A dwarf shrub, related to *S. myrsinites*, with slender, creeping, glabrous shoots and small, glossy green, usually untoothed leaves to 2cm long, bronze when young. Small catkins with bronze-purple scales open with the young leaves in spring. E Alps, Carpathians. AM 1956 (to a male form).

amygdalina See *S. triandra*.

apoda Trautv. A dwarf species with prostrate stems closely hugging the ground and glossy green leaves, paler beneath. The erect, silvery-furry, male catkins appear all along the branches in early spring, before the leaves, and gradually elongate until 2.5–3cm long, when they are decked in bright yellow anthers. A superb plant for a rock garden or scree. Both *S. retusa* and *S. uva-ursi* are occasionally wrongly grown under this name. Caucasus, Turkey. C before 1939. AM 1948.

arbuscula L. (*S. formosa* Willd.) A dwarf, creeping shrub forming close mats of green leaves, glaucous beneath. Catkins long and slender, produced with the young leaves in spring. Scandinavia, N Russia, Scotland. **'Erecta'** See *S. waldsteiniana*.

arbutifolia Pall. (*S. eucalyptoides* C.A. Mey. ex C.K. Schneid., *Chosenia arbutifolia* (Pall.) Skvorts., *Chosenia bracteosa* (Turcz.) Nakai) Said to attain large tree size in its native habitats, this is a rare tree or large shrub of elegant habit. Long, willowy stems are covered by a conspicuous, white bloom. Leaves lanceolate, bright green and bloomy at first. It is distinct among the willows in its pendulous, not erect, male catkins, its glandless flowers and other botanical characters. N Asia. I 1906.

atrocinerea See *S. cinerea* subsp. *oleifolia*.

aurita L. Eared willow. A small to medium-sized, native shrub with small, wrinkled, dull green leaves, grey-woolly beneath. Catkins produced before the leaves in early April. A common willow of bogs and streamsides on acid soils. N and C Europe (incl. Britain).

babylonica L. Weeping willow. An attractive tree of medium size with a wide-spreading head of long, pendulous, glabrous, brown branches. Leaves long and narrow, green above, bluish-grey beneath; catkins slender, appearing with the young leaves in spring. A native of China, but long cultivated in E Europe, N Africa and W Asia. Believed to have been introduced to W Europe during the late 17th century and into England about 1730. Most of the trees cultivated in Britain are said to be female. At one time widely cultivated as a waterside tree, it has now largely been superseded by *S.* × *sepulcralis* 'Chrysocoma' and other similar hybrids. **'Crispa'** ('Annularis') A curious form in which the leaves are spirally curled. **var. pekinensis** Henry (*S. matsudana* Koidz.) Pekin willow. A medium-sized, graceful tree of conical habit, with slender stems and long, narrow, slender-pointed leaves, green above and glaucous beneath. Catkins appear with the leaves in spring. Only the female form is in general cultivation. N China. Manchuria, Korea. I 1905. **'Pendula'** A very graceful tree and one of the best weeping willows, showing resistance to scab and canker. **'Tortuosa'** Dragon's claw willow. A curious form with much-twisted and contorted branches and twigs. ♥ 2002. **'Ramulis Aureis'** See *S.* × *sepulcralis* 'Chrysocoma'.

× *balfourii* Linton (*S. caprea* × *S. lanata*) A splendid, strong-growing, medium-sized to large bush, intermediate in character between the parents. Young leaves grey-woolly later green and downy. Catkins appear before the

leaves in early April, yellowish and silky-hairy, with tiny, red bracts. A remarkable and useful shrub, especially for damp sites. Said to have originated in Scotland. Ours is a male clone.

'Basfordiana' See *S.* × *rubens* 'Basfordiana'.

bicolor See *S. schraderiana*.

× *blanda* See *S.* × *pendulina* 'Blanda'.

bockii Seemen. An attractive, small to medium-sized shrub, usually seen as a neat, spreading bush 1–1.2m high. The numerous, slender, reddish twigs are greyish-downy when young, and in spring are thickly peppered with the bright green, emerging leaf-clusters. The numerous, small, greyish catkins appear along the current year's growth in late summer and autumn, the only willow in general cultivation to flower at this time of the year. W China. I 1908 by Ernest Wilson. A female form was introduced by Roy Lancaster from 1,000m in the Min Valley, W Sichuan in 1993 (Lancaster 2027).

× *boydii* Linton (*S. lapponum* × *S. reticulata*) A dwarf, erect, slow-growing shrub of gnarled appearance, with rounded, grey-downy leaves becoming green above. A female clone, with rarely produced small, dark grey catkins. An ideal shrub for a trough or for a pocket on a rock garden or scree. Found in the 1870s, only on a single occasion, in the mountains of Angus in Scotland. ♀ 2002. AM 1958.

'Caerulea' See *S. alba* var. *caerulea*.

× *calliantha* Kern. (*S. daphnoides* × *S. purpurea*) A small tree or large shrub with non-bloomy stems and lanceolate to oblanceolate, serrated leaves, glossy dark green above, sea-green beneath. Ours is a female clone. C 1872.

caprea L. Goat willow, Great sallow. A common and familiar, native species particularly noticeable in early spring when the large, yellow, male catkins are gathered as 'palm' by children. The female form known as pussy willow has silver catkins. A large shrub or small tree with stout twigs and oval or obovate leaves, grey-tomentose beneath. Europe, W Asia. **'Curly Locks'** A sport of 'Kilmarnock' found in Holland in 1990 and normally grown as a weeping standard. It has arching, twisted branches and bears silvery-grey catkins in late winter. **'Kilmarnock'** ('Pendula' in part) Kilmarnock willow. A small, umbrella-like, male tree, rarely reaching 3m, with stiffly pendent branches. Attractive, silvery catkins studded with golden anthers in late winter. Discovered on the bank of the River Ayr about 1850. AM 1977. **'Pendula'** See 'Kilmarnock' and 'Weeping Sally'. **'Weeping Sally'** ('Pendula' in part) Similar to 'Kilmarnock' but female. More vigorous but less effective in flower. C 1880.

caspica Pall. A large shrub or small tree with long, whip-like, pale grey stems and linear-lanceolate leaves. A rare species from SE Russia, W and C Asia.

× *chrysocoma* See *S.* × *sepulcralis* 'Chrysocoma'.

cinerea L. Grey sallow. A large shrub or occasionally a small tree. It has stout, pubescent twigs and obovate leaves, grey-tomentose beneath. Catkins appear before the leaves in early spring. Europe (including British Isles), W Asia, Tunisia. **subsp. oleifolia** Macreight (subsp. *atrocinerea* (Brot.) Silva & Sobr., *S. atrocinerea* Brot.) Common sallow. Similar in general habit, but branches more erect and leaves more leathery, glaucous beneath and with rust-coloured hairs. Perhaps its only claim to cultivation is its toughness and usefulness for planting in derelict areas, such as slag heaps, where it will help in the task of reclamation and reforestation. Both this species and *S. caprea* are familiar, hedgerow shrubs throughout the British Isles. Europe, S Russia. **'Tricolor'** ('Variegata') Leaves splashed and mottled yellow and creamy-white. Perhaps the only form of this species which can claim garden merit.

cordata Michx. (*S. adenophylla* Hook.) Furry willow. A loosely branched, large shrub or small tree producing densely grey-downy twigs clothed with ovate, finely-toothed, silky-hairy leaves up to 5cm long. Catkins before the leaves in early spring. NE North America. C 1900.

× *cottetii* Lagger ex Kern (*S.* × *gillotii* hort.) (*S. myrsinifolia* × *S. retusa*) A vigorous, low-growing shrub with long, trailing stems forming carpets several metres across. Leaves dark, shining green above, paler beneath; catkins before the leaves in early spring. Our plant is a male clone. Too vigorous for a small rock garden, but excellent groundcover. European Alps. C 1905.

dahurica See *S. miyabeana*.

daphnoides Vill. Violet willow. A fast-growing, small tree with long, purple-violet shoots, attractively overlaid with a white bloom. Catkins before the leaves in spring. Extremely effective in winter especially when hard-pruned each or every other year in late March. Female trees are narrower and more columnar in habit than the male. N Europe, C Asia, Himalaya. C 1829. AM 1957. **var. *acutifolia*** See *S. acutifolia*. **'Aglaia'** A male form with large, handsome, silvery then bright yellow catkins in early spring. Stems not bloomed, red in winter.

× *dasyclados* Wimm. A large shrub or small tree with downy stems and ovate to oblong-lanceolate, sharply pointed leaves, glaucescent and downy beneath. A willow of obscure origin, possibly the hybrid *S. caprea* × *S. cinerea* × *S. viminalis*. **'Grandis'** A particularly vigorous form.

'Decipiens' See *S. fragilis* var. *decipiens*.

discolor Muhl. A strong-growing, large shrub, occasionally a small tree, with stout, downy shoots, glabrous in the third year. Leaves grey-tomentose beneath. Catkins appear before the leaves in March or early April. E North America. I 1811.

× *doniana* G. Anderson ex Sm. (*S. purpurea* × *S. repens*) A small to medium-sized shrub with oblong or lanceolate leaves, glaucous beneath. Catkins before the leaves in spring, the males with red anthers, ripening to yellow. Occurs with the parents in the wild, including Britain. C 1829.

× *ehrhartiana* Sm. (*S. alba* × *S. pentandra*) A large shrub or small to medium-sized tree with polished, olive-brown twigs and oblong-lanceolate, shining green leaves. Catkins appear with or after the leaves. Europe (including British Isles). C 1894.

elaeagnos Scop. (*S. incana* Schrank) Hoary willow. A vigorous, large shrub or small tree with slender, arching shoots, grey-downy when young, and glossy dark green leaves, to 20cm long and 2cm across, white-tomentose beneath. Mainly grown as the following form. C and S Europe, Asia Minor. I about 1820. AM 1989 (for foliage). **susbp. *angustifolia*** (*S. rosmarinifolia* hort. not L.) A beautiful, medium-sized to large shrub of dense,

bushy habit. Leaves linear, like elongated leaves of rosemary, greyish-hoary at first becoming green above and white beneath, thickly clothing the slender, reddish-brown, wand-like stems. Catkins slender, appearing with the young leaves in spring. One of the prettiest willows for waterside planting. ♀ 2002.

'Elegantissima' See *S.* × *pendulina* 'Elegantissima'.

× *erdingeri* Kern. (*S. caprea* × *S. daphnoides*) An attractive, large shrub or small tree, its greenish stems covered with bluish-white bloom. Leaves obovate to oblong, glossy green above, appear after the catkins in spring. Ours is a female clone. Europe. C 1872.

eriocephala Michx. (*S. missouriensis* Bebb) Small to medium-sized tree with slender, spreading, reddish-brown branches, pubescent when young, and narrowly lanceolate leaves, hairy at first, later almost glabrous. Catkins before the leaves. E and C North America. I 1898.

× *erythroflexuosa* See *S.* × *sepulcralis* 'Erythroflexuosa'.

eucalyptoides See *S. arbutifolia*.

exigua Nutt. Coyote willow. A beautiful, large, erect shrub or a small tree with long, slender, greyish-brown branches clothed with linear, silvery-silky, minutely toothed leaves. Slender catkins appear with the leaves. W North America, N Mexico. I 1921.

fargesii Burkh. A medium-sized to large shrub of rather open habit, with stout, glabrous shoots, polished, reddish-brown in their second year. Winter buds reddish, large and conspicuous. Leaves elliptic to oblong-elliptic, up to 18cm long and deep glossy green with impressed venation. Catkins appear with or after the leaves, slender and ascending, the females 10–15cm long. C China. I 1911 by Ernest Wilson. Closely related to *S. moupinensis*.

× *finnmarchica* Willd. (*S. myrtilloides* × *S. repens*) A dwarf shrub, forming a low, widespreading patch, with slender, ascending shoots and small leaves. The small catkins crowd the stems before the leaves in early spring. Ours is a female clone. Excellent for a rock garden or as groundcover. Found in the wild with the parents in N and C Europe.

foetida Schleich. ex Lam. A dwarf shrub with trailing stems and dark green, sharply toothed leaves. Catkins produced with the leaves in spring. Mts of Europe (W and C Alps, C Pyrenees).

formosa See *S. arbuscula*.

fragilis L. Crack willow. A large tree with widespreading branches, as familiar as the White Willow, the two often growing together by rivers and streams. Bark rugged and channelled, twigs brittle at their joints. Leaves lanceolate, glabrous, sharply toothed, glossy dark green above, green or sometimes bluish-green beneath. Slender catkins appear with the leaves in spring. Europe. N Asia. **'Basfordiana'** See *S.* × *rubens* 'Basfordiana'. **var. *decipiens*** (Hoffm.) Koch (*S.* 'Decipiens') White Welsh willow. A small tree or large bush with polished, yellowish-grey branches, orange or rich red on the exposed side when young. The lanceolate, toothed leaves are shining green above. Usually male.

'Ginme' See *S.* × *tsugaluensis* 'Ginme'.

glaucosericea Flod. An attractive, grey, dwarf shrub, suitable for a rock garden. Leaves narrowly elliptic to elliptic-lanceolate, densely grey-hairy at first, less so by autumn. European Alps, Pyrenees.

gracilistyla Miq. A very splendid, vigorous, medium-sized shrub with stout, densely grey-pubescent young shoots. Leaves silky grey-downy at first, gradually becoming green and smooth, remaining late in the autumn. Catkins appearing before the leaves in early spring, the young males are grey and silky, through which the reddish, unopened anthers can be seen; later they are bright yellow. One of the most effective, catkin-bearing shrubs. Japan, Korea, Manchuria, China. I 1895. AM 1925. **'Melanostachys'** (*S. gracilistyla* var. *melanostachys* (Makino) C.K. Schneid.) (*S.* 'Melanostachys', *S. melanostachys* Makino, *S.* 'Kureneko', *S.* 'Kurome', *S.* 'Kuroyanagi') An attractive and unusual form. Quite outstanding in the remarkable colour combination of its catkins, which are very dark with blackish scales and brick-red anthers, opening to yellow, and appear before the leaves. The stout twigs are thickly clustered with oblanceolate leaves, glaucous beneath at first and sharply serrate. A male clone, known only in cultivation. Differs from the typical form in its glabrous twigs, non-silky catkins, longer, darker-coloured bracts, shorter glands, and so on. AM 1976.

× *grahamii* Borrer ex Bak. (*S. aurita* × *S. herbacea* × *S. repens*) A dwarf, procumbent shrub forming large patches of slender stems and broad, elliptic to oblong-elliptic, shining green leaves, 2.5–4cm long. Erect catkins appear with or after the leaves. Ours is a female clone. Occurring wild with the parents in Sutherland, Scotland, originally found about 1830 by Prof Robert Graham. **'Moorei'** (*S.* × *moorei* F.B. White) A dwarf shrub for a rock garden or scree, forming a low, wide-spreading mound of slender stems. Leaves small, shining green; catkins before the leaves in spring. Excellent groundcover, not too vigorous. A female form found by David Moore in Co Donegal in 1886.

hastata L. A small shrub with obovate to elliptic leaves, sea-green beneath. Catkins produced before or with the leaves in spring. C and S Europe to NE Asia and Kashmir. I 1780. **'Wehrhahnii'** (*S. wehrhahnii* Bonstedt) A slow-growing, small to medium-sized shrub of spreading habit. In spring the stout twigs are alive with pretty, silvery-grey, male catkins which later turn yellow. Found in Switzerland about 1930. ♀ 2002. AM 1964.

helvetica Vill. Swiss willow. A small, bushy shrub, the young stems, leaves and catkins clothed in a soft, greyish pubescence. The small, oblanceolate leaves are grey-green above, white beneath. Catkins appear with the young leaves in spring. An attractive foliage shrub for a rock garden. European Alps. C 1872. ♀ 2002.

herbacea L. Dwarf willow. A tiny, alpine species and one of the smallest British shrubs, forming mats of creeping, often underground stems. Leaves rounded, up to 2cm long, glossy green and prominently reticulate, borne in pairs or in 3s at the tips of each shoot. Catkins up to 2cm long, appear with the leaves in spring. Suitable for a moist position in a peat garden or rock garden. Arctic and mountainous regions of Europe and North America.

hibernica See *S. phylicifolia*.

'Hippophaifolia' See *S.* × *mollissima* var. *hippophaifolia*.

hookeriana Barratt. Coastal willow. A medium-sized to large shrub or small tree with glossy, reddish-brown branches, tomentose when young. Leaves oblong, acute, glossy green above, densely felted beneath. Catkins with the leaves. W North America. C 1891.

humilis Marshall. Prairie willow. A vigorous, medium-sized shrub. Leaves obovate or oblong-lanceolate, dark green above, glaucous and tomentose beneath. Catkins appearing before the leaves, the males with brick-red, later yellow anthers, the females with brick-red stigmas. E North America. I 1876.

incana See *S. elaeagnos*.

integra Thunb.. (*S. purpurea* L. var. *multinervis* (Franch. & Sav.) Koidz., *S.* 'Axukime') A fast-growing, large shrub or small tree of elegant habit, ideal for waterside planting. Branches long and slightly drooping, leaves generally in pairs, oblong, bright green, almost sessile. Slender catkins grace the polished stems in early April, before the leaves. Japan, Korea. **'Hakuro-nishiki'** ('Albomaculata') Leaves conspicuously blotched with white. Pretty when in young leaf but has a rather weak constitution. I from Japan in 1979 by the Dutch botanist Harry van de Laar.

irrorata Andersson. A vigorous, medium-sized shrub with long shoots, green when young, then purple and covered with a striking white bloom, particularly noticeable in winter. Leaves lanceolate or oblong-lanceolate, glossy green above, glaucous beneath. Catkins appear before the leaves, the males with brick-red anthers turning to yellow. An attractive species for contrasting with the red and yellow-stemmed clones. SW USA. I 1898. AMT 1967.

japonica Thunb. A large, elegant shrub with long, slender, pale stems. Leaves slender-pointed, serrulate, bright green above, glaucous beneath. Slender catkins appear with the leaves. Japan. C 1874.

kinuyanagi Kimura (*S.* 'Kishu') A strong-growing, large shrub or small tree with long, stout, greyish-brown-felted shoots and long, narrow leaves, silky-hairy beneath. Catkins bright yellow, closely arrayed along the stems in March. Only the male form is known. Native of Korea and introduced to Japan where it is widely cultivated. It is related to osier (*S. viminalis*), which it closely resembles.

'Kishu' See *S. kinuyanagi*.

koriyanagi Kimura (*S. purpurea* L. var. *japonica* Nakai) A large, erect-growing shrub or small tree closely related to *S. purpurea* with slender, whip-like stems. The slender, sub-opposite, bright green leaves are suffused an attractive orange-red on emerging. Catkins slender, in rows along the stems, the males with orange anthers. Korea; widely cultivated in Japan for basket-making and furniture. AM 1990.

'Kureneko' See *S. gracilistyla* 'Melanostachys'.

'Kurome' See *S. gracilistyla* 'Melanostachys'.

'Kuroyanagi' See *S. gracilistyla* 'Melanostachys'.

lanata L. Woolly willow. An attractive, slow-growing shrub usually 0.6–1.2m high, or occasionally more, with ovate to rounded, silvery-grey-downy leaves and stout, erect, yellowish-grey-woolly catkins in spring. The female catkins elongate considerably in fruit, sometimes measuring 10cm long. A rare native alpine species suitable for a rock garden. N Europe (incl. Scotland). ♀ 2002.

'Stuartii' See *S.* 'Stuartii'.

lapponum L. Lapland willow. A small, densely branched shrub with grey, downy leaves, 2.5–5cm long. Silky, grey catkins are produced before the leaves in spring. Mts of Europe (including British Isles), Siberia. C 1789.

lasiandra Benth. Pacific willow. A large, strong-growing tree with the general appearance of *S. fragilis*. Leaves lanceolate, sharply glandular-toothed, glaucous at first beneath. Catkins with the leaves in spring. W North America. C 1883.

lasiolepis Benth. Arroyo willow. A large shrub or small tree with linear, toothed leaves dull green above, glaucous beneath. An elegant species, with attractive, grey, female catkins before the leaves in early spring. W USA, N Mexico.

livida See *S. starkeana*.

lucida Muhl. Shining willow. A large shrub or small to medium-sized tree with glossy young shoots and lanceolate, slender-pointed, glossy green leaves. Catkins produced with the leaves in spring. NE North America. C 1830.

mackenzieana Barratt ex Hook. A small tree of upright habit, with long, slender, pale yellow-green stems and lanceolate leaves. W North America.

magnifica Hemsl. A large shrub or small tree of sparse habit, bearing large, oval or obovate, magnolia-like leaves up to 20cm long and 13cm wide. Catkins are produced with the leaves in spring, the females often 15–25cm in length. A most impressive and unusual species, native of W China, introduced by Ernest Wilson in 1909 who, when he first found it, thought he had discovered a new magnolia. ♀ 2002. AM 1913.

'Mark Postill' (*S. hastata* 'Wehrhahnii' × *S. lanata*) A dwarf shrub of spreading habit with purplish-brown winter shoots. Leaves pale green when young becoming sparsely white-hairy then dark green. Stout, green catkins, silvery as they emerge, are produced over a long period with and after the leaves. Raised by our propagator Alan Postill in 1967 and named after his son.

matsudana See *S. babylonica* var. *pekinensis*.

medemii See *S. aegyptiaca*.

medwedewii Dode. A small shrub, related to *S. triandra*, of which it is possibly only a form. Leaves long and narrow, vividly glaucous beneath. Catkins produced with the leaves in spring. Asia Minor. C 1910.

'Melanostachys' See *S. gracilistyla* 'Melanostachys'.

× *meyeriana* Rostk. ex Willd. (*S. fragilis* × *S. pentandra*) A vigorous, medium-sized to large tree with oval, glossy green leaves, glaucescent beneath. Catkins appear with the leaves in spring. Europe (incl. British Isles). C 1829.

missouriensis See *S. eriocephala*.

miyabeana Seem. (*S. dahurica* Turcz. ex Kakschewitz) A large shrub or small tree with long, slender, polished brown stems which, in spring and summer, are heavily clothed with narrow, pale green leaves. Catkins before the leaves. NE Asia. I 1897.

× *mollissima* Hoffm. ex Elwert (*S. triandra* × *S. viminalis*) (*S. trevirani* Spreng.) A variable hybrid forming a large shrub or small tree, the catkins appearing with the young leaves in spring. Occurs with the parents in the wild, though the typical form has not been found in Britain. **var. hippophaifolia** (Thuill.) Wimm. A large shrub or small tree with olive-brown twigs and long, narrow leaves. Catkins similar to those of *S. triandra* but with reddish anthers. Ours is a male form. England.

× *moorei* See *S.* × *grahamii* 'Moorei'.

moupinensis Franch. A very beautiful, medium-sized shrub of great quality, related to and generally resembling *S.*

fargesii with which it has long been confused in gardens. It differs from that species mainly in its slightly smaller, normally glabrous leaves. Both species are extremely ornamental at all times of the year. China. I 1869 by Armand David and 1910 by Ernest Wilson.

muscina hort. See *S. aegyptiaca*.

myrsinifolia Salisb. (*S. nigricans* Sm.) A medium-sized to large, native shrub with downy twigs and downy, variably shaped leaves, dark green above, generally glaucous beneath. Catkins appearing before the leaves. N and C Europe.

myrsinites L. Whortle willow. A prostrate, native species forming dense carpets of shortly ascending stems clothed with shining, bright green leaves and bearing large, attractive catkins in April. An ideal species for a rock garden. N Europe. N Asia.

myrtilloides L. Swamp willow. A dwarf shrub, spreading by underground stems and making a low mound about 60cm tall, with stout, smooth shoots and glossy dark green leaves to 4cm long. Catkins emerging with the leaves in spring, males to 2cm long, with red anthers turning yellow as they open. N and C Europe, N Asia. **'Pink Tassels'** A striking male form, the catkins with maroon filaments and purple anthers.

nigricans See *S. myrsinifolia*.

nitida See *S. repens* var. *argentea*.

× *pendulina* Wender. (*S. babylonica* × *S. fragilis*) A small to medium-sized, normally female, weeping tree similar to *S. babylonica* but of better constitution. Originated in Germany in the early 19th century. **'Blanda'** (*S.* × *blanda* Andersson) A small to medium-sized tree with a widespreading head of weeping branches. Leaves lanceolate, glabrous, bluish-green beneath. Catkins produced with the leaves. C 1830. **'Elegantissima'** (*S.* × *elegantissima* C. Koch) Thurlow weeping willow. Similar to 'Blanda' in habit but more strongly weeping. Both trees are sometimes found in cultivation under the name *S. babylonica*.

pentandra L. Bay willow. A beautiful, small to medium-sized tree, or occasionally large shrub, with glossy twigs and attractive, bay-like, lustrous green leaves, pleasantly aromatic when unfolding or when crushed. Catkins produced with the leaves in late spring, the males bright yellow. Found wild in N parts of the British Isles, planted elsewhere. Used as a substitute for bay in Norway. Europe, N Asia.

phylicifolia L. (*S. hibernica* Rech. f.) Tea-leaf willow. A medium-sized shrub with dark, glabrous twigs and leaves, shining green above and glaucous beneath. Catkins appearing before the leaves. N Europe.

× *pontederiana* Willd. (*S.* × *sordida* A. Kerner) (*S. cinerea* × *S. purpurea*) A medium-sized to large shrub with branches hairy at first. Leaves obovate-lanceolate, silky-hairy and glaucous beneath. Catkins produced in March, before the leaves. Ours is a male form with yellow anthers prettily red-tinted when young. Europe. C 1820.

pruinosa See *S. acutifolia*.

purpurea L. Purple osier. A graceful, medium-sized to large shrub with long, arching, often purplish shoots. Leaves narrowly oblong, dull green above, paler or glaucous beneath, often in opposite pairs. Catkins slender, produced all along the shoots in spring before the leaves.

The wood of the young shoots is bright yellow beneath the bark, a character which is normally present in its hybrids. Europe (including British Isles), C Asia. **'Eugenei'** See *S.* × *rubra* 'Eugenei'. **'Gracilis'** See 'Nana'. **var. *japonica*** See *S. koriyanagi*. **'Nana'** ('Gracilis') A dwarf, compact, slender-branched cultivar. A useful low hedge for a damp site. **'Nancy Saunders'** An elegant female form, making a small tree, with slender, glossy red shoots and blue-green leaves, glaucous beneath. **'Pendula'** An attractive form with long, pendent branches; trained as a standard it forms a charming, small, weeping tree. ♀ 2002.

pyrifolia Andersson (*S. balsamifera* Barratt ex Bebb) Balsam willow. A large shrub, or occasionally small tree, with shining reddish-brown twigs and red winter buds. Leaves ovate-lanceolate, glaucous and reticulate beneath. Catkins appearing with the leaves in spring. Canada, NE USA. I 1880.

rehderiana C.K. Schneid. A large shrub or small tree with lanceolate, bright green leaves, grey-silky beneath. W China. I 1908 by Ernest Wilson.

repens L. Creeping willow. Normally a small, creeping shrub, but in some forms occasionally 1.8–2.5m high, forming large patches or dense clumps of slender, erect stems clothed with small, greyish-green leaves, silvery-white beneath. Catkins small, crowding the naked stems in spring. A common native species of heaths, bogs and commons, particularly on acid soils. Europe, N Asia. AM 1988 (for flower). **var. *argentea*** (Sm.) Wimm. & Grab. (var. *nitida* Wender., *S. arenaria* L., *S. nitida* Ser.) A more vigorous and taller form with the leaves densely hairy on both sides. Abundant in moist, sandy areas by the sea. Grown as a standard it makes an effective miniature, weeping tree. Atlantic coasts of Europe. ♀ 2002. **var. *subopposita*** See *S. subopposita*. **'Voorthuizen'** A charming little plant of Dutch origin, the slender, prostrate stems bearing small, silky leaves and tiny, female catkins. Suitable for a small rock garden or scree.

reticulata L. A dwarf, native shrub with prostrate stems forming dense mats. Leaves small, orbicular or ovate, entire, dark green and attractively net-veined above, glaucous beneath. Catkins erect, appearing after the leaves. A dainty, pretty little willow suitable for a moist ledge on a rock garden. Arctic and mountain areas of North America, Europe and N Asia. C 1789. ♀ 2002. AM 1981 (to a male plant).

retusa L. A prostrate species forming extensive carpets of creeping stems and small, notched, polished green leaves. Erect catkins, 1.2–2cm long, appear with the leaves. Mts of Europe. I 1763.

rosmarinifolia See *S. elaeagnos* subsp. *angustifolia*.

× *rubens* Schrank (*S. alba* × *S. fragilis*) (*S.* × *viridis* Fries) A common and variable, native hybrid generally intermediate in character between the parents, with some clones leaning more to one than the other. A large, fast-growing tree with lanceolate leaves, green or glaucous beneath. Occurring in the wild either with or without the parents, including British Isles. **'Basfordiana'** (*S.* 'Basfordiana', *S. fragilis* 'Basfordiana') A medium-sized to large tree with long, narrow leaves and conspicuous, orange-red twigs in winter. A male clone with long, slender, yellow catkins appearing with the leaves in spring.

Said to have been found in the Ardennes, about 1863, by Mr Scaling, a nurseryman of Basford, Nottinghamshire. **'Sanguinea'** A female clone similar to 'Basfordiana' but with smaller leaves and redder shoots.

× *rubra* Huds. (*S. purpurea* × *S. viminalis*) A large shrub or small tree with glossy, yellow-brown shoots and narrow, dark glossy green leaves. Catkins borne before the leaves. Commonly found with the parents. Europe. **'Eugenei'** (*S. purpurea* 'Eugenei') An erect-branched, small tree of slender, conical habit producing an abundance of subtly attractive, grey-pink, male catkins.

sachalinensis See *S. udensis*. **'Sekka'** See *S. udensis* 'Sekka'.

× *salamonii* See *S.* × *sepulcralis* 'Salamonii'.

schraderiana Willd. (*S. bicolor* Willd.) A medium-sized shrub, closely related to *S. phylicifolia*. Shoots stout, with yellowish buds in winter. Leaves glossy green above, glaucous beneath. Catkins with reddish anthers, opening to yellow. Mts of Europe, but not the Alps.

× *sepulcralis* Simonk. (*S.* × *salamonii* Carrière ex Henry) (*S. alba* × *S. babylonica*) Hybrids between these two species have arisen fairly frequently. For the plant previously grown under this name see 'Salamonii'. **'Chrysocoma'** (*S. alba* var. *vitellina* × *S. babylonica*) (*S.* × *chrysocoma* Dode, *S. alba* 'Vitellina Pendula', *S. alba* 'Tristis', *S. babylonica* 'Ramulis Aureis') Possibly the most beautiful, weeping tree hardy in the British Isles. A medium-sized, widespreading tree producing vigorous, arching branches which terminate in slender, golden-yellow, weeping branchlets, ultimately of great length. Leaves lanceolate; catkins appearing with the leaves in April, both male and female flowers in the same catkin, or occasionally catkins all male or all female. Frequently seen planted in small gardens for which it is not suitable. Unfortunately subject to scab and canker, which may be controlled on young trees by spraying with a suitable fungicide. C 1888. **'Dart's Snake'** (*S. alba* var. *argentea* × *S. babylonica* 'Tortuosa') (*S. alba* 'Dart's Snake') A small to medium-sized, conical tree with twisted shoots and pendent branches. Leaves slightly twisted, glossy green above, with silky, grey hairs beneath. Male. **'Erythroflexuosa'** (*S.* × *erythroflexuosa* Ragonese) (*S.* × *sepulcralis* 'Chrysocoma' × *S. babylonica* 'Tortuosa') A curious, ornamental, small tree discovered in Argentina. The vigorous, orange-yellow, pendulous shoots are twisted and contorted, as are the narrow leaves. **'Salamonii'** A medium-sized tree of weeping habit with long, slender, pendulous stems and linear-lanceolate, glossy green leaves, glaucous beneath at first. Catkins appear with the leaves in spring. A vigorous tree resembling *S. babylonica*, but less pendulous. Garden origin before 1864.

× *seringeana* Gaud. (*S. caprea* × *S. elaeagnos*) (*S. salviifolia* Link) A large shrub or small tree of erect habit, with grey-tomentose stems and lanceolate or narrowly oblong, softly grey-downy leaves, pale beneath. A most ornamental, grey-leaved hybrid. C 1872.

serpyllifolia Scop. A dwarf shrublet making low mounds of slender shoots. Leaves obovate, small, to 8mm long, without teeth. A miniature, alpine species suited to a trough garden. Alps to SE Europe.

'Setsuka' See *S. udensis* 'Sekka'.

× *smithiana* Willd. (*S. cinerea* × *S. viminalis*) A strong-growing, variable, large shrub or small tree, with long, stout branches, tomentose when young. Leaves lanceolate, silky-hairy beneath. Catkins produced before the leaves in spring. Ours is a female form. Found in the wild only in the British Isles. The most commonly used stem for top-working.

× **sordida** See *S.* × *pontederiana*.

'Spaethii' A small tree with stout, densely hairy shoots, long leaves and female catkins. Of Continental origin.

starkeana Willd. (*S. livida* Vahl) Small to medium-sized shrub with broad, elliptic leaves, glossy green above, glaucous green beneath. Catkins appearing before the leaves. N and C Europe, N Asia. C 1872.

× **stipularis** Sm. (*S. aurita* × *S. caprea* × *S. viminalis*) A vigorous, small tree or large shrub with tomentose shoots and lanceolate leaves, glaucous and downy beneath. It has conspicuous, large, foliaceous stipules. N Europe, including British Isles.

'Stuartii' (*S. lanata* 'Stuartii') A dwarf, gnarled shrublet, conspicuous in winter with its yellow shoots and orange buds. Its leaves are smaller, but its catkins larger than those of *S. lanata*. Probably *S. lanata* × *S. lapponum*.

subopposita Miq. (*S. repens* var. *subopposita* (Miq.) Seem.) A rare and very distinct, dwarf shrub with slender, erect and spreading stems and small leaves which are opposite or nearly so. Catkins before the leaves in early spring, the males with brick-red anthers turning to yellow. This unusual little willow has the stance of a *Hebe*. Japan, Korea.

× **tetrapla** Walker ex Sm. (*S. myrsinifolia* × *S. phylicifolia*) A small to medium-sized shrub of stiff habit with stout, glossy, yellowish-green twigs and oblong-elliptic leaves, glossy green above, glaucous beneath. Occasionally found with the parents in the wild. C 1829.

trevirani See *S.* × *mollissima*.

triandra L. (*S. amygdalina* L.) Almond-leaved willow. A large shrub or small tree with flaky bark and lanceolate, glossy green, serrated leaves, glaucous beneath. Catkins produced with the leaves in spring, the males fragrant and almost mimosa-like. Europe to E Asia. Long cultivated in Europe for basket-making. **var. hoffmanniana** Bab. An uncommon variety with smaller, oblong-lanceolate leaves, green beneath.

× **tsugaluensis** Koidz. (*S. integra* × *S. vulpina*) This hybrid occurs in the wild in Japan. The following is considered to belong here. **'Ginme'** A medium-sized to large shrub of vigorous, spreading habit. Leaves oblong, bright green, paler beneath and orange-tinged when young. Catkins silvery, slender and recurved appearing all along the naked stems in spring. A female clone of Japanese origin.

udensis Trautv. & Mey. (*S. sachalinensis* F. Schmidt) A large shrub or small tree of spreading habit with polished, chestnut-brown young shoots. Leaves lanceolate, slender-pointed, shining green above, pale or glaucous beneath. Catkins appear before the leaves, the males large and conspicuous. NE Asia. I 1905. A vigorous, ornamental willow usually seen in the following clone.

'Sekka' ('Setsuka') A male clone of Japanese origin, noted for its occasional curiously flattened and recurved stems, which may be encouraged by hard pruning. Useful when cut for 'Japanese' floral arrangements.

uva-ursi Pursh. Bearberry willow. A prostrate shrub forming dense carpets of creeping stems clothed with small,

glossy green leaves. Catkins appear with the young leaves in spring. A superb plant for a rock garden or scree. Has been confused with *S. apoda* and *S. retusa*. Canada, NE USA. I 1880.

viminalis L. Common osier. A large, vigorous shrub or small tree with long, straight shoots thickly grey-tomentose when young. Leaves long and narrow, tapering to a fine point, dull green above, covered with silvery-silky hairs beneath. Catkins appear before the leaves. A very common species of rivers, streamsides, lakes and marshes. Long cultivated for basket-making. Europe to NE Asia and Himalaya.

× **viridis** See *S.* × *rubens*.

vitellina See *S. alba* var. *vitellina*.

waldsteiniana Willd. (*S. arbuscula* 'Erecta') A medium-sized, upright-branched shrub, that is closely related to *S. arbuscula*. Leaves glossy green, longer than in *S. arbuscula*, entire or slightly toothed. Catkins about 2.5cm long, borne with the leaves on leafy peduncles to 1.5cm long. SE Europe.

wehrhahnii See *S. hastata* 'Wehrhahnii'.

wilhelmsiana Bieb. A large, elegant shrub with slender, wand-like stems and narrow, obscurely toothed leaves which, like the stems, are silky-hairy at first, later shining green. Catkins appear with the leaves in spring. SE Russia to SC Asia. C 1887.

× **wimmeriana** Gren. & Godr. (*S. caprea* × *S. purpurea*) A medium-sized shrub with slender branches and oblong to lanceolate leaves, glaucescent beneath. Catkins borne all along the stems before the leaves in early April. The male catkins are very pretty when both brick-red emerging anthers and yellow ripened anthers are apparent at the same time. Ours is a male form. Occurs with the parents in the wild. C 1872.

yezoalpina Koidz. A prostrate shrub with long, trailing stems bearing attractive, long-stalked, rounded or obovate, glossy green leaves with reticulate venation. Catkins appear with the leaves in spring. A rare alpine species, suitable for a rock garden or scree. Now considered to be a variety of the Japanese *S. nakamurana*. Japan.

Sallow See *Salix caprea* and *S. cinerea*.
Salmonberry See *Rubus spectabilis*.
Salt tree See *Halimodendron halodendron*.

SALVIA L.—Labiatae—A large genus of some 900 species of often aromatic, flowering plants containing mainly herbs and numerous subshrubs, of which all but *S. officinalis* are tender in varying degrees. Widely distributed, with more than 275 species in Mexico. They require a warm, dry, well-drained position in full sun. The more tender species make excellent cool-house subjects. The two-lipped flowers are normally borne in whorls along the stems during late summer or early autumn.

ambigens See *S. guaranitica*.

†**aurea** L. A small species with round, hoary leaves and rusty-yellow flowers. S. Africa. I 1731.

bethellii See *S. involucrata* 'Bethellii'.

caerulea See *S. guaranitica*.

†**elegans** Vahl (*S. rutilans* Carrière) Pineapple-scented sage. A small species, up to 1m, suitable for a sunny wall,

with softly downy, heart-shaped, pineapple-scented leaves and loose, leafy panicles of magenta-crimson flowers throughout summer. C Mexico. C before 1873. **'Scarlet Pineapple'** A vigorous form with large flowers; originally grown as *S. rutilans*.

†*fulgens* Cav. Mexican red sage. A small species, up to 1m, with heart-shaped leaves and long racemes of showy, densely hairy, scarlet flowers, 5cm long, in late summer. C Mexico. I 1829. ♀ 2002. AM 1937.

†*gesneriiflora* Lindl. & Paxton. An attractive, small species related to *S. fulgens*, but with even larger, showier flowers of an intense scarlet. Mexico. I 1840. AM 1950.

grahamii See *S. microphylla*.

†*greggii* A. Gray. A small, slender species up to 1.2m, suitable for a sunny wall. Similar in some respects to *S. microphylla* but with smaller and narrower leaves and rose-scarlet flowers. Texas, Mexico. C 1885. AM 1914. **'Alba'** White flowers. **'Peach'** A particularly hardy form, the profuse flowers with a yellowish-pink upper lip and a deep red lower lip. **'Sparkler'** Leaves edged with creamy-white, flowers bright red. 'Desert Blaze', a sport found in a nursery in Phoenix, Arizona in 1990 is similar.

guaranitica St.-Hil. ex Benth. (*S. ambigens* Briq., *S. caerulea* hort.) A small shrub with erect stems up to 1.5m. Softly downy, heart-shaped leaves and long racemes of deep, azure-blue flowers about 5cm long, during summer and autumn. S America. I 1925. AM 1926. **'Black and Blue'** Flowers deep blue, calyx black. Originally grown as *S. caerulea*. AM 1989. **'Blue Enigma'** Shorter, with smaller, paler flowers, calyx green. Originally grown as *S. ambigens*. ♀ 2002.

†*interrupta* Schousb. A small, glandular, hairy subshrub up to 1m. Leaves varying from entire, with two basal lobes, to pinnate, with 2 pairs of leaflets. Flowers violet-purple with a white throat, produced in loose, terminal panicles from late spring to midsummer. Morocco. I 1867.

†*involucrata* Cav. A small species with ovate, long-pointed leaves and spike-like racemes of rose-magenta flowers, sticky to the touch. Late summer to autumn. Mexico. I 1824. ♀ 2002. **'Bethellii'** (*S. bethellii* hort.) A robust form with large, heart-shaped leaves and stout racemes of magenta-crimson flowers from midsummer onwards. Garden origin. ♀ 2002. FCC 1880. **'Boutin'** Flowers pale pink. ♀ 2002.

†×*jamensis* J. Compton (*S. greggii* × *S. microphylla*) A small shrub intermediate between the parents, discovered in 1991 by James Compton, John D'Arcy and Martyn Rix near the village of Jame, Coahuila, Mexico. The hybrid had previously been raised in cultivation. Several forms are cultivated with flowers ranging from red to yellow. NE Mexico. **'James Compton'** A form with large, deep crimson flowers raised by James Compton in 1987. **'La Luna'** (CDR 1151) Flowers creamy-yellow. **'Los Lirios'** Flowers have a purplish-pink upper lip and a paler lower lip with darker blotches at the base. ♀ 2002. **'Maraschino'** Vivid cherry-red flowers over a long period. **'Pat Vlasto'** Flowers peach-red. Raised by James Compton in 1986.

lavandulifolia Vahl. A dwarf species with narrow, grey, downy leaves and spike-like racemes of blue-violet flowers in early summer. Spain.

†*mexicana* L. This species from C and S Mexico is most frequently grown in the following form. **var.** *minor*

Benth. ex DC. A vigorous, small to medium-sized subshrub with large, ovate leaves and terminal, spike-like racemes of showy, violet-blue flowers in late winter. Differing from the typical variety in its smaller flowers. Only suitable for a cool greenhouse. Mexico. I 1720.

†*microphylla* Kunth (*S. grahamii* Benth., *S. microphylla* var. *neurepia* (Fern.) Epling, *S. neurepia* Fern.) A variable, small shrub up to 1.2m with leaves up to 5cm long. Flowers bright red to pink, fading to bluish-red, 2.5cm long, from June into late autumn. Mexico. I 1829. **'Cerro Potosi'** (CDR 1283) Flowers vivid magenta. I from Nuevo Leon, Mexico by James Compton, John D'Arcy and Martyn Rix. **'Kew Red'** Vivid red flowers with darker lips. ♀ 2002. **var.** *neurepia* See *S. microphylla*. **'Newby Hall'** Flowers rich scarlet. A form originally grown *as S. grahamii*. ♀ 2002. **'Pink Blush'** Flowers rose-magenta with a bright pink lower lip flushed violet-pink. ♀ 2002. **'Pleasant View'** Flowers purple-pink with a velvety bright pinkish-red lower lip. ♀ 2002.

neurepia See *S. microphylla*.

officinalis L. Common sage. A well-known, dwarf, semi-evergreen species long cultivated as a herb. Leaves grey-green and strongly aromatic. Flowers bluish-purple, during summer. S Europe. Cultivated in England since 1597, possibly before. **'Aurea'** See under 'Icterina'. **'Albifora'** Flowers white. **'Berggarten'** A form of compact, spreading habit with broad, silvery-grey leaves. 'Herrenhausen' is possibly the same. Originates from the famous Royal Gardens of Herrenhausen, Hanover, Germany. **'Herrenhausen'** See 'Berggarten'. **'Icterina'** Leaves variegated green and gold. Low, spreading habit. Sometimes grown as 'Aurea'. ♀ 2002. **'Kew Gold'** Leaves golden-yellow. A sport of 'Icterina' raised at Kew. Sometimes reverts. **'Purpurascens'** Purple-leaf sage. Stems and young foliage suffused purple. Particularly effective in coloured foliage groups for blending or contrasts. ♀ 2002. **'Tricolor'** A compact form with grey-green leaves, splashed creamy-white, suffused purple and pink. Rather tender but well worth planting each year.

'Raspberry Royale' A compact, small shrub of upright habit with narrow, elliptic to ovate, sticky and very aromatic, untoothed, grey-green leaves to 3cm long. The deep velvety carmine-pink flowers open during summer. Close to *S. greggii* but said to be a sport of a suspected hybrid between *S. greggii* 'Alba' and *S. microphylla* var. *wilsizeni*. C 1984. ♀ 2002.

rutilans See *S. elegans*.

SAMBUCUS L.—**Caprifoliaceae**—The elders are a genus of about 20 species of shrubs, small trees and perennial herbs widely distributed in temperate and subtropical regions. The cultivated species are hardy and tolerant of almost all soils and situations. Few are eye-catching in flower, but many have ornamental foliage and fruits. All species possess pinnate leaves and serrated leaflets. To encourage the production of large flowerheads or lush foliage the lateral branches may be cut back to within a few centimetres of the previous year's growth in March. Ideal subjects for a wild garden.

caerulea Raf. Blue elder. A very vigorous, large shrub, sometimes a small tree, with stout shoots and glossy green leaves with up to 9 leaflets. Heads of creamy-white flowers in summer are followed by large, drooping clusters of blue-black, bloomy fruits. W North America. AM 1928.

callicarpa Greene. A small to medium-sized shrub, the leaves with 5–7 leaflets. Flowers whitish, in a round head, 7–10cm across, in June to July, followed by small, scarlet fruits. W North America. I about 1900.

canadensis L. American elderberry. A stout, strong-growing shrub of medium to large size, the leaves with 5–11, usually 7, large leaflets. Flowers white in convex heads, 13–20cm across, appearing in July, followed by purple-black fruits. SE Canada, E USA. I 1761. AM 1905 for flower. AM 1948 for fruit. **'Aurea'** An unusual form with yellow foliage and red fruits. **'Maxima'** A handsome form with leaves 30–45cm long and enormous flower-heads 30cm or more across. The rosy-purple flower stalks, which remain after the flowers have fallen, are an added attraction. A bold shrub which should be pruned each spring to encourage the production of new shoots. A bold subject for a wild garden. AM 1951. **'Rubra'** An unusual form with red fruits. **var. *submollis*** Rehder. A variety with leaflets softly greyish-pubescent beneath.

ebulus L. Dane's elder. An unusual, herbaceous species, throwing up stout, grooved stems 1–1.2m high, in time forming dense colonies. Leaves with 9–13 leaflets. Flowers white, tinged pink, in flattened heads, 7.5–10cm across, during late summer. Fruits black. Europe, N Africa, naturalised in the British Isles.

nigra L. Common elder. A familiar, native, large shrub or small tree, with a rugged, fissured bark and leaves with 5–7 leaflets. The flattened heads of cream-coloured, sweetly fragrant flowers in June are followed by heavy bunches of shining, black fruits. Both flowers and fruits are used in country winemaking. A useful plant for extremely chalky sites. Europe, N Africa, W Asia. Long cultivated. **'Albovariegata'** See 'Marginata'. **'Aurea'** Golden elder. Leaves golden-yellow, deepening with age. One of the hardiest and most satisfactory of golden-foliaged shrubs. C 1883. ♀ 2002. **'Aureomarginata'** Leaflets with an irregular, bright yellow margin. **Black Beauty** ('Gerda') PBR Dark blackish-purple foliage and fragrant, pink flowers followed by black berries. The individual flowers have a white centre and lobed tipped with deep pink. Raised at Horticulture Research International, East Malling, Kent. ♀ 2002. **Black Lace** ('Eva') PBR A medium-sized shrub, reaching 3m, with dark purple, deeply cut leaflets and pale pink flowers. Raised at Horticulture Research International, East Malling. **'Fructuluteo'** An unusual form with yellow fruits. **'Guincho Purple'** ('Purpurea', 'Foliis Purpureis') Leaves green when young becoming deep blackish-purple, red in autumn. Flowers contrasting well with the foliage, pink in bud opening white, flushed pink on the backs of the lobes, stalks stained with purple. AM 1977. **'Heterophylla'** See 'Linearis'. **f. *laciniata*** (L.) Zabel. Fern-leaved elder. An attractive form with finely divided, fern-like leaves. ♀ 2002. AM 1988 (for flower and foliage). **'Linearis'** ('Heterophylla') A curious shrub with leaflets of variable form, often reduced to thread-like segments. **'Madonna'** Similar to 'Aureomarginata' but leaflets with a broader margin

and occasional yellow blotches. **'Marginata'** ('Albovariegata', 'Argenteomarginata') Leaflets with an irregular, creamy-white margin. AM 1892. **'Plena'** A form with double flowers. **f. *porphyrifolia*** E.C. Nelson. This name covers all forms with purple leaves. **'Pulverulenta'** A slow-growing but very effective form in which the leaves are striped and mottled white. AM 1991 (for foliage). **'Purpurea'** See 'Guincho Purple'. **'Pyramidalis'** A form of stiff, erect habit, wider above than below; leaves densely clustered on the stems. **'Thundercloud'** A pink-flowered form, similar to 'Black Beauty' but with foliage of a brighter red-purple.

pubens Michx. A large shrub related to *S. racemosa*. The leaves have 5–7 leaflets, and, like the stems, are pubescent when young. Flowers cream-coloured, borne in rounded or conical heads during May. Fruits red. North America. I 1812.

racemosa L. Red-berried elder. A medium-sized to large shrub, the leaves with 5–7 coarsely toothed leaflets. Flowers yellowish-white in conical heads, crowding the branches in April, followed in summer by dense clusters of bright scarlet fruits. Europe, W Asia. Planted as game cover in parts of N England and Scotland. Cultivated in England since the 16th century. AM 1936. **'Plumosa Aurea'** ('Serratifolia Aurea') A colourful shrub with beautiful, deeply cut, golden foliage. One of the elite of golden-foliaged shrubs; slower-growing and best in light shade. Rich yellow flowers. AM 1895. **'Sutherland Gold'** An excellent plant, similar to 'Plumosa Aurea' but slightly coarser in texture and less liable to scorching in sun. Raised in Canada. ♀ 2002. **'Tenuifolia'** A small, slow-growing shrub forming a low mound of arching branches and finely divided, fern-like leaves. As beautiful as a cut-leaved Japanese maple and a good substitute on chalky soils. A good plant for a rock garden. AM 1917.

Sand myrtle See *Leiophyllum buxifolium*.

***SANTOLINA** L.—**Compositae**—The lavender cottons are low-growing, mound-forming, evergreen subshrubs with dense, grey, green or silvery, finely divided foliage, and dainty, button-like flowerheads on tall stalks in July. They require a sunny position and well-drained soil. About 5 species, natives of the Mediterranean region.

chamaecyparissus L. (*S. incana* L.) A charming, dwarf species, valued for its woolly, silver-hued, thread-like foliage. Flowerheads bright lemon-yellow. S France, Pyrenees. Cultivated in England since the 16th century. ♀ 2002. **var. *corsica*** See 'Nana'. **'Lambrook Silver'** Silvery-grey, feathery foliage and lemon-yellow flowerheads. **'Lemon Queen'** A compact form with lemon-yellow flowerheads. **'Nana'** (var. *corsica* hort. not Fiori) A dwarfer, denser, more compact variety, ideal for a rock garden. ♀ 2002. **'Pretty Carol'** A compact form with soft, grey foliage. **'Small-Ness'** A very compact, dwarf form with dark green, aromatic foliage and butter-yellow flowerheads.

incana See *S. chamaecyparissus*.

neapolitana See *S. pinnata* subsp. *neapolitana*.

pinnata Viv. A dwarf subshrub, related to *S. chamaecyparissus*. Differing in its longer, finely divided, green leaves and off-white flowerheads. NW Italy. Mainly grown in the following forms. **subsp.** *neapolitana* (Jord. & Fourr.) Guinea (*S. neapolitana* Jord. & Fourr.) A dwarf subshrub similar to *S. chamaecyparissus*, but rather looser in growth and with longer, more feathery leaves. Flowers bright lemon-yellow. NW and C Italy. ♀ 2002. **'Edward Bowles'** A charming form, originally given to us by E.A. Bowles, after whom we named it. It is similar to 'Sulphurea', but the foliage is more grey-green and the flowerheads paler primrose, almost creamy-white. **'Sulphurea'** Foliage grey-green; flowerheads pale primrose-yellow.

rosmarinifolia L. (*S. virens* Mill., *S. viridis* Willd.) An attractive, dwarf species with thread-like, vivid green leaves. Flowerheads bright lemon-yellow. SW Europe. C 1727. **subsp.** *canescens* (Lag.) Nyman. Foliage grey-green. S Spain. **'Primrose Gem'** A lovely form with pale primrose-yellow flowerheads. Originated as a seedling in our nursery before 1960. ♀ 2002.

virens See *S. rosmarinifolia*.

viridis See *S. rosmarinifolia*.

SAPINDUS L.—**Sapindaceae**—A small genus of about 13 species of mainly tropical trees and shrubs of which the following are relatively hardy. They require well-drained soil in sun or semi-shade.

drummondii Hook. & Arn. Soapberry. An interesting, small tree with pinnate, robinia-like leaves. The tiny, cream-coloured flowers are borne in dense, conical panicles in June. Central S USA, N Mexico. C 1900.

†*mukorossi* Gaertn. A large shrub or small tree with late-persisting, pinnate leaves, consisting of 8–12 leathery, reticulately veined leaflets. The yellowish-green flowers are borne in terminal panicles. Japan, Taiwan, China to India. C 1877.

SAPIUM P. Browne—**Euphorbiaceae**—A large genus of 100 or more species of trees and shrubs almost all of which are found in the tropics.

japonicum (Siebold & Zucc.) Pax. & Hoffm. A rare, small tree or shrub, proving hardy, with greyish, glabrous branches and smooth, dark green, elliptic or obovate-elliptic, entire leaves, that turn to a glowing crimson in autumn. The flowers are unisexual and inconspicuous, appearing in June in slender, axillary, catkin-like, greenish-yellow racemes. Capsules like large capers, 3-lobed, green, finally brown, pendent. Japan, China, Korea.

†*sebiferum* (L.) Roxb. Chinese tallow tree. A small tree with broadly ovate or rounded, abruptly-pointed leaves and slender racemes of greenish-yellow flowers. The waxy coating of the seeds is used in the manufacture of candles in China. The leaves often turn a brilliant red in autumn. Only suitable for the mildest gardens in the British Isles. Commonly naturalised in SE USA. China, Taiwan. C 1850.

†*SARCANDRA* Gardner—**Chloranthaceae**—A small genus of about 15 species of mainly tropical shrubs, natives of E and SE Asia.

glabra (Thunb.) Nakai (*Chloranthus brachystachys* Blume) Small, evergreen shrub with oblong leaves and spikes of bright orange fruits. A conservatory plant in most areas. S India to SE Asia.

SARCOCOCCA Lindl.—**Buxaceae**—The Christmas boxes make up a genus of about 14 species, natives of E and SE Asia. Attractive, shade-tolerant, dwarf or small shrubs, with evergreen, glossy foliage suitable for cutting. The small, white, fragrant, male flowers open during late winter, the tiny female flowers occurring in the same cluster. Succeeding in any fertile soil, being especially happy in chalk, they slowly attain 1.2–1.5m high unless otherwise indicated.

confusa Sealy. A useful, hardy shrub of dense, spreading habit. Leaves elliptic, taper-pointed; flowers with cream-coloured anthers, very fragrant; fruits shining black. Similar in general appearance to *S. ruscifolia* var. *chinensis* and often confused with it in gardens, but the stigmas vary from 2 to 3 and the berries are black. Origin uncertain, probably China. C 1916. ♀ 2002. AM 1989.

hookeriana Baill. A rare, erect-growing species with shortly pubescent, green stems, lanceolate leaves and white flowers, the female flowers with 3 stigmas. Berries black. Not quite so hardy as var. *digyna*. Himalaya. ♀ 2002. AM 1983 (to Schilling 1260). AM 1936. **var.** *digyna* Franch. More slender, with narrower leaves. Female flowers with only 2 stigmas; berries black. W China. I 1908 by Ernest Wilson. ♀ 2002. AM 1970. **'Purple Stem'** An attractive form with the young stems, petioles and midribs flushed purple. **var.** *humilis* Rehder & E.H. Wilson (*S. humilis* (Rehder & E.H. Wilson) Stapf) A dwarf, densely branched shrub, suckering to form extensive clumps and patches seldom exceeding 60cm high. Leaves elliptic, shining deep green. Male flowers with pink anthers; berries black. W China. I 1907 by Ernest Wilson.

humilis See *S. hookeriana* var. *humilis*.

orientalis C.Y. Wu. A strong-growing, upright, small shrub with stout, green shoots. Leaves ovate-lanceolate, to 9cm long, 3-veined and cuneate at the base, slenderly taper-pointed at the apex. Male flowers with pink-tinged anthers and sepals, females with 2–3 stigmas. Fruits black. Jiangxi, E China. I 1980 by Roy Lancaster.

ruscifolia Stapf. A small, slow-growing shrub. Leaves broad-ovate, thick, shining dark green. Berries dark red. Uncommon in cultivation. C China. I 1901 by Ernest Wilson. AM 1908. **var.** *chinensis* (Franch.) Rehder & E.H. Wilson. A more vigorous shrub, commoner in cultivation, differing in its comparatively longer, narrower leaves. It is very similar in general appearance to *S. confusa* having the same long, slender-pointed leaves and attaining the same dimensions, but the berries are dark red and the female flowers have 3 stigmas. C and W China. ♀ 2002. **var.** *chinensis* **'Dragon Gate'** A selection introduced by Roy Lancaster from Dragon Gate in the mountains above Kunming, Yunnan in 1980. It has narrow and long-pointed, rich green leaves.

†*saligna* (D. Don) Muell.-Arg. (*S. pruniformis* Lindl. in part) A small shrub with erect, glabrous, green stems. Leaves tapering, lance-shaped, up to 13cm long. Flowers greenish-white with little if any scent; berries purple. W Himalaya. C 1908.

wallichii Stapf. A vigorous species reaching 1.8m tall with handsome foliage and black fruits. Nepal.

Sarothamnus scoparius See *Cytisus scoparius*.

‡**SASSAFRAS** Trew—**Lauraceae**—A small genus of 3 species of deciduous trees requiring a lime-free loam and a slightly sheltered position such as in woodland. Natives of North America, China and Taiwan.

albidum (Nutt.) Nees (*S. officinale* var. *albidum* (Nutt.) Blake) An attractive and very distinct, aromatic, medium-sized, suckering tree of broadly conical habit with flexuous twigs and branches, particularly noticeable in winter. Leaves vary from ovate to obovate, entire or with 1 or 2 conspicuous lobes, some resembling those of the fig in outline, dark green above, rather glaucous or pale green beneath, colouring attractively in autumn. Flowers greenish-yellow, inconspicuous, appearing in short racemes in May. E USA. I 1633. var. *molle* (Raf.) Fern. Leaves and young shoots downy.

†***SCHEFFLERA** J.R. Forst. & G. Forst.—**Araliaceae**—A large genus of some 200 species of trees and shrubs confined to warm and tropical regions of the world. Several are popular houseplants.

impressa (C.B. Clarke) Harms. A large, stoutly branched, spreading shrub or small tree. Leaves palmately compound with 7–9 oblanceolate leaflets, up to 20cm long, on petioles to 50cm. This remarkable plant lived for many years in front of Jermyns House in the Sir Harold Hillier Gardens and Arboretum but was badly damaged in the 1978–79 winter and eventually died in 1981. Yunnan, China.

‡†***SCHIMA** Reinw. ex Blume—**Theaceae**—A genus of a single, variable species requiring lime-free soil in a sheltered position such as woodland. Widely distributed from the Himalaya to China and SE Asia.

argentea See *S. wallichii* subsp. *noronhae* var. *superba*.
khasiana See *S. wallichii* var. *khasiana*.
noronhae See *S. wallichii* subsp. *noronhae*.
wallichii (DC.) Korthals. A small tree in cultivation with elliptic-oblong leaves, pubescent and reticulate beneath. Flowers white, fragrant, 4–5cm across, produced on the young wood in late summer. Not hardy in our area. The typical form is found from the E Himalaya to Yunnan, China. var. *khasiana* (Dyer) Bloemb. (*S. khasiana* Dyer) A large shrub to medium-sized tree bearing lustrous, dark green, elliptic, serrated leaves, 15–18cm long. Flowers white, 5cm across, with a central mass of yellow stamens, produced on the young wood during September and October. There are splendid examples in Cornwall, but it is not hardy in Hampshire. Assam, Burma, China. AM 1953. subsp. *noronhae* (Blume) Bloemb. (*S. noronhae* Blume) A small to medium-sized shrub in cultivation producing oblanceolate or narrow-elliptic, acuminate leaves, with a bluish bloom above when mature. Flowers 4–5cm across, cream-coloured, with a central boss of golden stamens produced in the axils of the terminal leaves during late summer and autumn. Only for the mildest areas, but a suitable conservatory shrub. Java, SE Asia. I 1849. var. *superba* (Gardner & Champion) Bloemb. (*S. argentea* Pritz) The hardiest form, a medium-sized to large shrub of erect, bushy habit. Leaves elliptic to elliptic-oblong, tapering to both ends, polished dark green above, usually glaucous beneath. Flowers, like small camellias, creamy-white, about 4cm across, produced on the young wood in late summer. This distinct and attractive member of the camellia family has been growing successfully in woodland conditions in the Sir Harold Hillier Gardens and Arboretum for nearly 50 years. S China. AM 1955.

SCHINUS L.—**Anacardiaceae**—A small genus of 28 species of usually dioecious shrubs and trees with simple or compound leaves. Natives of Mexico and S America.

dependens See *S. polygamus*.
†**molle* L. Pepper tree. A small, evergreen tree with gracefully drooping branches and attractive, pinnate leaves. The small, yellowish-white flowers are borne in short panicles in spring, followed, on female trees, by rosy-red, pea-shaped fruits. Commonly planted as a street tree in S Europe and best grown as a conservatory tree in the British Isles. Mexico to S America.
**polygamus* (Cav.) Cabrera (*S. dependens* Ort.) A medium-sized to large, evergreen shrub, the shoots often being spine-tipped. Leaves small, obovate, 1–2cm long. Tiny, yellow-green flowers crowd the branches in May; fruits purplish-black, the size of peppercorns. Chile. I 1790.

Sea buckthorn See *Hippophae rhamnoides*.
Scorpion senna See *Hippocrepis emerus*.

SECURINEGA Comm. ex Juss—**Euphorbiaceae**—A small genus of botanical interest related to *Andrachne* with about 25 species in temperate and subtropical regions.

suffruticosa (Pall.) Rehder (*S. ramiflora* (Aiton) Muell.-Arg.) A small, densely branched shrub with slender, arching stems and oval leaves, 2.5–5cm long. Flowers small, greenish-yellow, produced during late summer and early autumn. NE Asia to C China, Taiwan. I 1783.

SEDUM L.—**Crassulaceae**—A large genus of more than 300 species of mainly herbs, natives of N temperate regions and mountains in the tropics and well represented in herbaceous borders and rock gardens. The following is one of the few hardy, shrubby species.

populifolium L. A dwarf subshrub of erect habit with reddish-brown bark, peeling on old stems. Leaves with slender stalks, ovate, coarsely toothed, cordate at base, pale green and fleshy. Flowers sweetly hawthorn-scented, white or pink-tinged, with purple anthers, borne in small, dense, flattened heads in July and August. Siberia. I 1780.

SENECIO L.—**Compositae**—A very large genus of 1500 or more species of annual and perennial herbs, shrubs and climbers, widely distributed throughout the world.

bidwillii See *Brachyglottis bidwillii*.
compactus See *Brachyglottis compacta*.
Dunedin Hybrids See *Brachyglottis* Dunedin Group.
elaeagnifolius See *Brachyglottis elaeagnifolia*. **var. *buchananii*** See *Brachyglottis buchananii*.
greyi See *Brachyglottis greyi*.

hectoris See *Brachyglottis hectoris*.
heritieri See *Pericallis lanata* and *P.* 'Purple Picotee'.
huntii See *Brachyglottis huntii*.
kirkii See *Brachyglottis kirkii*.
laxifolius See *Brachyglottis laxifolia*.
'Leonard Cockayne' See *Brachyglottis* 'Leonard Cockayne'.
leucostachys See *S. viravira*.
'Moira Read' See *Brachyglottis* 'Moira Read'.
monroi See *Brachyglottis monroi*.
perdicioides See *Brachyglottis perdicioides*.
reinoldii See *Brachyglottis rotundifolia*.
rotundifolius See *Brachyglottis rotundifolia*.
'Sunshine' See *Brachyglottis* 'Sunshine'.
†**viravira* Hieronymus (*S. leucostachys* hort. not Baker, *S. argentinus* Baker) A striking and beautiful, lax, silvery-white shrub of medium size with finely divided, pinnate leaves. Its almost scandent branches and tender nature demand a sunny wall. Flowers whitish in summer, not very ornamental. Argentina. I 1893. ♀ 2002. AM 1973.

†**SENNA** (K. Bauhin) Mill. (*Cassia* L. in part)—**Leguminosae**—A large genus of about 240 species of trees, shrubs and herbs with a wide tropical and subtropical distribution. Leaves evenly pinnate. The pods of several species produce the senna of medicine. The following species require a warm, sheltered, sunny site or conservatory.

corymbosa (Lam.) Irwin & Barneby (*Cassia corymbosa* Lam.) Less robust than *S.* × *floribunda*, with more slender growths. A medium-sized shrub, the leaves with 2 or 3 pairs of narrow, acuminate leaflets, flowers also smaller and paler yellow, in late summer and autumn. Uruguay, Argentina and widely naturalised in warm countries. I 1796. AM 1933.

× *floribunda* (Cav.) Irwin & Barneby (*S. multiglandulosa* × *S. septemtrionalis*) A very handsome and vigorous wall shrub, the pinnate leaves with 4–5 pairs of leaflets. Flowers large, rich deep yellow, in terminal clusters during late summer and autumn. This plant is often grown as *Cassia corymbosa* or *C. obtusa*. The true *Cassia obtusa*, a native of Chile and now correctly known as *Senna candolleana*, is rarely cultivated. C 1800. ♀ 2002.

septemtrionalis (Viv.) Irwin & Barneby. This species has also been grown as both *Cassia corymbosa* and *C. obtusa*. It makes a large shrub or small tree, the leaves with 3–4 pairs of ovate, taper-pointed leaflets. Bright yellow flowers open from summer to winter. Mexico, C and northern South America, widely naturalised and a weed in many tropical areas.

Service tree See *Sorbus domestica*.
Service tree of Fontainbleau See *Sorbus latifolia*.
Service tree, wild See *Sorbus torminalis*.
Seven son flower of Zhejiang See *Heptacodium miconioides*.
Sheepberry See *Viburnum lentago*.

SHEPHERDIA Nutt.—**Elaeagnaceae**—A small genus of 3 species of dioecious shrubs related to *Elaeagnus* and *Hippophae*, differing from both in the opposite leaves. Shrubs for full exposure, excellent in coastal areas.

argentea (Pursh) Nutt. Buffalo berry. A slow-growing, occasionally spiny shrub of medium size with oblong, silvery, scaly leaves. Tiny, yellow flowers appear in small, dense clusters during March or earlier and are followed, on female plants, by scarlet, edible berries, which are used to make a sauce to accompany buffalo meat. C & W North America. I 1818.

canadensis (L.) Nutt. A dense, bushy shrub of medium size with brownish, scaly shoots and elliptic to ovate leaves, which are silvery-hairy and speckled with brown scales below. The inconspicuous flowers in spring are followed, on female plants, by yellowish-red berries. North America. I 1759.

SIBIRAEA Maxim.—**Rosaceae**—A genus of 2 species closely related to and sometimes included in *Spiraea*, but differing in the entire leaves and various small botanical characters. The following species is best in a well-drained, sunny position.

laevigata (L.) Maxim. (*S. altaiensis* (Laxm.) C.K. Schneid., *Spiraea laevigata* L.) An erect shrub, occasionally up to 1.8m, with stout, glabrous branches clad with narrowly obovate, sea-green leaves, 7.5–10cm long. Panicles of whitish flowers are produced from the tips of the shoots in late spring and early summer, but they are of little ornament. Mts of C Asia. I 1774. **var. croatica** (Degen) C.K. Schneid. In cultivation smaller in its parts. Former Yugoslavia.

Silk tree See *Albizia julibrissin*.
Silver berry See *Elaeagnus commutata*.

SINOCALYCANTHUS Cheng & Chang—**Calycanthaceae**—A monotypic genus closely related to *Calycanthus* and originally included in it.

chinensis (Cheng & Chang) Cheng & Chang (*Calycanthus chinensis* Cheng & Chang) A medium-sized, deciduous shrub reaching about 3m. Leaves opposite, broadly elliptic to obovate, abruptly acuminate, up to 15cm long, glossy green turning yellow in autumn. Nodding flowers, 7cm across, are borne singly at the ends of the shoots in June. They have numerous tepals in 2 whorls of about 10 each. The outer tepals are white, sometimes flushed pink, the smaller inner tepals are pale yellow, white at the base, with maroon markings. This remarkable plant first flowered in Britain in the garden of Roy Lancaster in 1989 and in the Sir Harold Hillier Gardens and Arboretum the following year. Zhejiang (E China). I 1983. FCC 1996.

‡**SINOJACKIA** Hu—**Styracaceae**—A small genus of 5 species of Chinese, deciduous, small trees or large shrubs, requiring a moist, lime-free soil.

rehderiana Hu. A very rare, small, styrax-like, loosely branched, small tree or large shrub with thin, elliptic, alternate leaves. Flowers white, the corolla divided to the base into 4–6 lobes, appearing singly or in short, axillary racemes in May and June. Alfred Rehder, after whom this species is named, was a giant among botanists. We all owe him a tremendous debt for his *Manual of Cultivated Trees and Shrubs*, one of his many works, but like so many botanists he was not 'good company' in the garden. E China. I 1930.

xylocarpa Hu. A small tree differing from *S. rehderiana* in its broader leaves, longer-stalked flowers and curious, ovoid fruits. E China. I 1934.

‡**SINOWILSONIA** Hemsl.—**Hamamelidaceae**—A rare, monotypic genus related to the witch hazels (*Hamamelis*) and mainly of botanical interest. Introduced from China by Ernest Wilson ('Chinese Wilson'), in whose honour it is named. A walk round the nurseries with Ernest Wilson revealed that there was virtually no tree, shrub or herbaceous plant with which he was not familiar. He was a first-class botanist, perhaps the greatest of the plant hunters and, like W.J. Bean, a tremendous companion in the garden.

henryi Hemsl. A large shrub or occasionally a small, spreading tree. The large, bristle-toothed leaves, 7.5–15cm long, recall those of a lime (*Tilia*) and are covered beneath with stellate pubescence. Flowers in May, monoecious, small and greenish, the males in slender, pendent catkins, the females in pendent racemes lengthening to 15cm in fruit. C and W China. I 1908.

***SKIMMIA** Thunb.—**Rutaceae**—A small genus of 4 species of slow-growing, aromatic, evergreen shrubs or trees, natives of the Himalaya and E Asia. *S. japonica* subsp. *japonica*, *S.* × *confusa* and *S. anquetilia* bear male and female flowers on separate plants: both sexes are required for the production of the brightly coloured fruits, which persist through the winter. All are tolerant of shade and are excellent shrubs for industrial areas and seaside gardens. Plants once thought to be hybrids between *S. japonica* and *S. reevesiana* are considered to belong to *S. japonica* subsp. *japonica*. We would like to thank Chris Lane for his assistance with this genus.

anquetilia N.P. Taylor & Airy Shaw. A small shrub of open habit with oblanceolate, taper-pointed leaves, 7.5–15cm long, clustered at the ends of the shoots in the manner of *Daphne laureola*. When crushed they emit a strong, pungent smell. Small, terminal clusters of greenish-yellow flowers, with upright petals, are borne in spring. These are followed on female plants by bright red fruits. Himalaya. I 1841. AM 1977.

× *confusa* N.P. Taylor (*S. anquetilia* × *S. japonica*) (*S. melanocarpa* hort.) A small, mound-forming shrub, thriving in sun or shade, with oblanceolate, pointed, aromatic leaves. The large, conical clusters of very fragrant, creamy-white flowers make it the best of the genus for flower. Previously distributed as *S. laureola* male. The male form is commonest in cultivation. **'Chelsea Physic'** A male form, similar to 'Kew Green' but lower-growing with smaller leaves and inflorescences. Found in the Chelsea Physic Garden. AM 1996 (for flower). **'Isabella'** A female form reaching 3m. Berries bright red. **'Kew Green'** A splendid form selected at Kew with broad leaves and very large flower clusters. Male. ♀ 2002. AM 1991.

fortunei See *S. japonica* subsp. *reevesiana*.

japonica Thunb. A variable, small, dome-shaped shrub of dense habit, with leathery, obovate to elliptic leaves. Terminal panicles of white, often fragrant flowers in April and May are followed, on female plants, by clusters of globular, bright red fruits. A most adaptable shrub in all its forms, equally at home on chalk or acid soils.

China, Japan. C 1838. FCC 1863. **'Bowles Dwarf Female'** A dwarf, slow-growing shrub of compact habit to about 30cm tall. A female selection with red berries. **'Bowles Dwarf Male'** Similar to 'Bowles Dwarf Female' but male, with red winter flower buds. **'Bronze Knight'** A male selection making a small shrub to about 1m tall, the flowers buds bronze-red in winter. **'Emerald King'** Bushy, upright habit. A male form with the flower buds green-tinged bronze-purple in broad panicles. **'Fisheri'** See 'Veitchii'. **'Foremanii'** See under 'Veitchii'. **'Fragrans'** A free-flowering male clone of broad, dome-shaped habit with dense panicles of white flowers scented of lily-of-the-valley. ♀ 2002. **'Fragrantissma'** A broad-leaved male form, with large, widely branched heads of scented flowers. **'Fructoalbo'** A rather weak, low-growing female clone of compact habit. Leaves small, fruits white. **'Highgrove Redbud'** A vigorous female form with red flower buds. Similar to 'Veitchii' but smaller, with narrower leaves and smaller fruits. **var. intermedia** Komatsu (var. *repens* (Nakai) Ohwi) A very slow, low-growing, often creeping form from the mountains of Japan, Sakhalin and Kuriles. **'Kew White'** A slow-growing female form with creamy-white fruits. **'Nymans'** An extremely free-fruiting form with oblanceolate leaves and comparatively large fruits. ♀ 2002. **'Red Princess'** A female selection with red winter flower buds and bright red berries. **'Redruth'** A vigorous, upright female form with large leaves and fruits. **subsp. reevesiana** (Fortune) N.P. Taylor & Airy Shaw (*S. reevesiana* (Fortune) Fortune) (*S. fortunei* Mast.) A dwarf shrub, rarely reaching 90cm, forming a low, compact mound. Leaves narrowly elliptic, often with a pale margin. Flowers hermaphrodite, white, produced in short, terminal panicles in May, followed by obovoid, matt crimson-red fruits which last through the winter and are usually present when the flowers appear again in spring. It is not satisfactory on chalky soils. S China, SE Asia. I 1849. AM 1982. **subsp. reevesiana 'Chilan Choice'** A form introduced from Taiwan with spherical fruits and the leaves pink-crimson on the backs. **subsp. reevesiana 'Robert Fortune'** This name has been given to the commonly grown clone deriving from the original introduction and described above. **var. repens** See var. *intermedia*. **'Rogersii'** A dense, compact, dwarf female clone of slow growth with somewhat curved or twisted leaves and large, red fruits. **'Rogersii Nana'** A free-flowering male clone, resembling 'Rogersii' but more dwarf and compact, slower-growing and with smaller leaves. **'Rubella'** (*S. rubella* Carrière) A male form with large, open panicles of red buds throughout the winter which open in the early spring into white, yellow-anthered flowers. ♀ 2002. AM 1962. **'Rubinetta'** A compact male form of low, spreading habit, the leaves and petioles flushed red in winter. Bronze-red buds open to white flowers flushed pink. **'Ruby Dome'** An excellent male form making a dense bush with small, sharp-pointed leaves. Buds red but not as dark as 'Rubella', in short, rounded panicles. **'Ruby King'** Narrow, taper-pointed, dark green leaves and large, conical panicles of flowers from deep red buds. Male. **'Snow Dwarf'** A dense, low-growing bush with small, short-pointed leaves. A male, with profuse flowers in small, rounded panicles, from green buds. **'Stoneham Red'** A vigorous male, more spreading than 'Rubella' with larger leaves and darker buds in larger, more open panicles. **'Tansley Gem'** A female selection of low, spreading habit with narrow, bright green leaves and profuse red berries. Named from a plant in a Bolton Garden. C 1950. **'Veitchii'** ('Fisheri') A vigorous female clone with distinctly broad-obovate leaves and large bunches of brilliant red fruits. FCC 1888. Often grown as 'Foremanii'. **'Wakehurst White'** A dwarf shrub bearing dense clusters of white fruits 7mm long. AM 1996 (for fruit).

laureola (DC.) Siebold & Zucc. ex Walpers. The true plant of this name has been introduced but is rare in cultivation. It is a small, creeping shrub with very dark green leaves, fragrant, hermaphrodite or unisexual flowers and black fruits. E Himalaya, W China. For the plant distributed as *S. laureola* male, see *S.* × *confusa*; for the plant distributed as *S. laureola* female, see *S. anquetilia*.

melanocarpa See *S.* × *confusa*.

reevesiana See *S. japonica* subsp. *reevesiana*.

rubella See *S. japonica* 'Rubella'.

Skunkbush See *Rhus trilobata*.

Sloe See *Prunus spinosa*.

Smoke tree See *Cotinus coggygria*.

Snowball See *Viburnum opulus* 'Roseum'.

Snowball, Japanese See *Viburnum plicatum* 'Sterile'.

Snowberry See *Symphoricarpos albus*.

Snowdrop tree See *Halesia carolina*.

Snowy mespilus See *Amelanchier*.

SOLANUM L.—**Solanaceae**—A very large genus of about 1500 species of mainly herbaceous plants, widely distributed throughout the world and containing several species of economic importance such as the potato (*Solanum tuberosum*). The following semi-woody species are only suitable for the mildest localities. See also under CLIMBERS.

crispum See under CLIMBERS.

jasminoides See under CLIMBERS.

†*laciniatum* W.T. Aiton. Kangaroo apple. A beautiful subshrub with purple stems up to 1.8m high. Leaves lanceolate, usually deeply cut. Flowers comparatively large and very attractive, violet, with a yellow staminal beak, borne in loose, axillary racemes during summer, followed by small, egg-shaped fruits which change from green to yellow. A vigorous species for very mild areas or a conservatory. Generally confused in cultivation with *S. aviculare*, which differs in its lilac or white flowers with pointed (not notched) lobes. Poisonous in all its parts. Australia, New Zealand. I 1772.

†*rantonnetii* Lesc. A medium-sized, open shrub with arching shoots and ovate to lanceolate, often wavy-edged, dark green leaves. Saucer-shaped, violet-blue flowers, to 2.5cm across, paler or yellow in the centre and with a cluster of yellow anthers, open in small clusters over a long period during summer and autumn, followed by egg-shaped, red fruits, 2.5cm long. Requires conservatory protection in most areas. Paraguay, Argentina. **'Royal Robe'** A selection with fragrant, deep violet flowers, yellow in the centre.

†*valdiviense* Dunal. A vigorous, more or less climbing shrub for a sunny, sheltered wall. The arching shoots, to 2.5 or 3m, bear entire, pointed leaves. Flowers usually pale mauve or lavender, with a central beak of yellow anthers, borne in axillary racemes during May. Valdivia (Chile). I 1927 by Harold Comber. AM 1931.

SOPHORA L.—**Leguminosae**—A genus of about 50 species of deciduous and evergreen, sun-loving trees, shrubs and herbs. The following are much valued for their elegant, pinnate leaves and floral display. Succeeding in all well-drained, fertile soils.

davidii (Franch.) Pavol. (*S. viciifolia* Hance) A medium-sized to large shrub with grey-downy, later spiny branches and leaves with 7–10 pairs of leaflets, silky-hairy beneath. Small, bluish-white pea-flowers are borne in short, terminal racemes in June. SW China. I 1897. AM 1933. **'Hans Fliegner'** A form with deep blue flowers raised at Kew from seed collected in Sichuan in 1988. A lower-growing, spinier form, typical of the species as it is found in the western part of its range.

japonica L. Japanese pagoda tree. A medium-sized to large tree, normally of rounded habit. Leaves up to 30cm long, composed of 9–15 leaflets. Creamy-white pea-flowers are produced in large, terminal panicles during late summer and autumn but, unfortunately, not on young trees. It flowers prodigiously in the hot, dry summers of SE Europe. Native of China, widely planted in Japan. I 1753. ♀ 2002. **'Pendula'** A picturesque, small, weeping tree with stiffly drooping branches. An admirable lawn specimen, also suitable for forming a natural arbour. **var. pubescens** (Tausch) Bosse. Leaflets, up to 8cm long, softly pubescent beneath. Flowers tinged lilac. **'Regent'** A vigorous form selected in North America with dark glossy green leaves and flowering at a relatively early age. **'Variegata'** Leaflets mottled creamy-white. **'Violacea'** A late-flowering form with wing and keel-petals flushed rose-violet.

†*macrocarpa* Sm. (*Edwardsia chilensis* Miers ex Lindl.) An attractive shrub of medium size, flowering at an early age. Leaves up to 13cm long with 13–25 leaflets. Flowers comparatively large, rich yellow, borne in short, axillary racemes in May. Chile. I 1822. AM 1938.

†*microphylla* Aiton (*S. tetraptera* var. *microphylla* (Aiton) Hook. f.) A large shrub or occasionally small tree, closely related to and resembling *S. tetraptera*, but with smaller, more numerous leaflets and slightly smaller flowers. Juvenile plants are dense and wiry in habit. New Zealand, Chile. I 1772. AM 1951. **'Dragon's Gold'** Flowers rather small, lemon-yellow, flushed orange. Leaves with up to 31 leaflets. Raised by Graham Hutchins from a cutting collected on Stephens Island in the Cook Strait, in 1985. **Sun King** ('Hilsop') PBR An extremely hardy form of bushy habit with large, bright yellow flowers profusely borne over a long period during late winter and spring. A selection of Chilean origin which has survived several cold winters in an exposed position in the Sir Harold Hillier Gardens and Arboretum. ♀ 2002.

†*prostrata* Buch. (*S. tetraptera* var. *prostrata* (Buch.) Kirk) A small shrub, occasionally prostrate, usually forming a broad, rounded hummock of tangled, interlacing, wiry stems. Leaves with 6–8 pairs of tiny leaflets. The small, brownish-yellow to orange pea-flowers are

produced singly or in clusters of 2–3 during May. New Zealand.

†***tetraptera** J.F. Mill. The New Zealand kowhai is best grown against a south-west-facing, sunny wall in the British Isles. It forms a large shrub or small tree with spreading or drooping branches covered, when young, by a fulvous tomentum. Leaves with 20–40 ovate to elliptic-oblong leaflets. Flowers pea-shaped, but rather tubular, yellow, 4–5cm long, produced in drooping clusters in May. The curious seedpods are beaded in appearance and possess 4 broad wings. I 1772. ♀ 2002. AM 1943. 'Grandiflora' A form with large leaflets and slightly larger flowers. AM 1977.

viciifolia See *S. davidii*.

SORBARIA (DC.) A. Braun—**Rosaceae**—Handsome, vigorous shrubs with elegant, pinnate leaves which distinguish them from *Spiraea*, with which they are commonly associated. All bear white or creamy-white flowers in terminal panicles during summer and early autumn. Even in winter their brownish or reddish stems and seedheads possess a sombre attraction. They thrive in most soils, flowering best in full sun. The old flowering stems may be hard-pruned in late February or March, to encourage the production of strong, vigorous shoots with extra-large leaves and flower panicles. They look good in association with water.

aitchisonii See *S. tomentosa* var. *angustifolia*.

arborea See *S. kirilowii*.

assurgens See *S. kirilowii*.

kirilowii (Regel) Maxim. (*S. arborea* C.K. Schneid., *S. assurgens* M. Vilm. & Bois, *Spiraea arborea* (C.K. Schneid.) Bean, *Spiraea assurgens* (M. Vilm & Bois) Bean) A large, robust shrub with strong, spreading stems and large leaves composed of 13–17 slender-pointed leaflets which are downy beneath. Flowers produced in large, conical panicles at the end of the current year's growths in July and August. An excellent, large specimen shrub for lawn or border. C and W China. I 1896 (as *S. assurgens*) and 1908 by Ernest Wilson. AM 1963.

sorbifolia (L.) A. Braun (*Spiraea sorbifolia* L.) A small to medium-sized, suckering shrub with erect stems and leaves composed of 13–25 sharply toothed, glabrous leaflets. Flowers produced in narrow, stiffly erect panicles, in July and August. N Asia. I 1759.

tomentosa (Lindl.) Rehder (*S. lindleyana* (Wall. ex Lindl.) Maxim., *Spiraea lindleyana* Wall. ex Lindl.) A large, strong-growing shrub of spreading habit. Leaves large, composed of 11–23 deeply toothed leaflets, hairy beneath. Flowers in large, terminal, downy panicles, from July to September. Himalaya. C 1840. var. *angustifolia* (Wenz.) Rahn (*S. aitchisonii* (Hemsl.) Rehder) A very elegant shrub of medium size, closely related to *S. tomentosa*, the branches long and spreading, reddish when young. Leaves glabrous, with 11–23 sharply toothed and tapered leaflets. Flowers in large, conical panicles in July and August. Afghanistan, Kashmir. I 1895. ♀ 2002. AM 1905.

× **SORBARONIA** C.K. Schneid. (*Sorbus* × *Aronia*)—**Rosaceae**—Hardy, slow-growing shrubs or small, spreading trees of a certain quality, intermediate in character between *Sorbus* and *Aronia*. Though not of outstanding ornamental merit, they add autumn tints to the garden and are interesting because of their unusual origin. Any ordinary soil, in sun or semi-shade.

alpina (Willd.) C.K. Schneid. (*S. aria* × *A. arbutifolia*) A large shrub or small tree with oval or obovate, finely toothed leaves, usually attractively tinted with soft orange in autumn. Flowers white, borne in terminal clusters during May; fruits 1.5cm long, rounded, dark reddish-purple, speckled brown. Garden origin before 1809.

dippelii (Zabel) C.K. Schneid. (*S. aria* × *A. melanocarpa*) Similar to × *S. alpina* in general appearance, but leaves narrower in outline and permanently grey-felted beneath. Fruits dark reddish-purple with an orange pulp. Garden origin before 1870.

fallax (C.K. Schneid.) C.K. Schneid. (*S. aucuparia* × *A. melanocarpa*) A medium-sized shrub or small tree with widespreading branches. Leaves elliptic, obtuse or acute, deeply divided below into 2 or 3 pairs of serrulate lobes or leaflets, turning to orange and red in autumn. Flowers white; fruits purplish. Garden origin before 1878.

hybrida (Moench) C.K. Schneid. (*S. aucuparia* × *A. arbutifolia*) A widespreading shrub or small tree. Leaves vary from ovate to elliptic, broader and larger than those of × *S. fallax*, rounded at the apex, deeply divided into 2 or 3 pairs of broad, overlapping leaflets; autumn colours of red and orange. Flowers white, hawthorn-like in spring; fruits purplish-black. Garden origin before 1785.

sorbifolia (Poir.) C.K. Schneid. (*S. americana* × *A. melanocarpa*) A medium-sized to large shrub or small tree similar to × *S. fallax* in general appearance, but with leaves shortly acuminate and young growths less downy. Fruits blackish. Garden origin before 1893.

× **SORBOCOTONEASTER** Pojark. (*Sorbus* × *Cotoneaster*)—**Rosaceae**—A rare, intergeneric hybrid of slow growth, originally found with the parents in pine forests in Yakutskland, E Siberia. Two forms are said to occur, one tends towards the *Sorbus* parent and the other to the *Cotoneaster* parent.

pozdnjakovii Pojark. (*S. sibirica* × *C. melanocarpus*) A medium-sized shrub of somewhat erect habit. Leaves ovate, deeply cut into 1–3 pairs of oval lobes or leaflets, dark green above, densely hairy beneath. Flowers white, up to 10 in a corymb. Fruits red. We are indebted for this interesting plant to Dr D.K. Ogrin of the Faculty of Agriculture, Ljubljana, former Yugoslavia who was instrumental in having scions sent to us from Siberia in 1958.

× **SORBOPYRUS** C.K. Schneid. (*Sorbus* × *Pyrus*)—**Rosaceae**—A rare, intergeneric hybrid usually forming a small to medium-sized tree. Any ordinary soil in an open position.

auricularis (Kroop) C.K. Schneid. (*S. aria* × *P. communis*) Bollwyller pear. A remarkable, small to medium-sized tree of rounded habit, with oval or ovate, coarsely toothed leaves, grey-felted beneath. Flowers white, in corymbs in May. Fruits pear-shaped, 2.5–3cm long, green then reddish, edible. Garden origin before 1619. AM 1982. 'Malifolia' (× *S. malifolia* (Spach) C.K. Schneid.) Probably a seedling of × *S. auricularis*, differing in its broader, often rounded leaves, heart-shaped at base, its larger flowers in late April and May and its larger pear-shaped fruits, 5cm long, which are yellow when ripe. Garden origin in Paris before 1834.

SORBUS L.—**Rosaceae**—A large and horticulturally important genus ranging from dwarf shrubs to large trees. There are 100 or more species in N temperate regions; the majority of these are quite hardy. Although attractive in flower, they are mainly grown for their ornamental foliage, which in many species colours richly in autumn, and for their colourful, berry-like fruits. On average the forms with white or yellow fruits retain their attractions further into winter than those with red or orange fruits. Unless otherwise stated, the flowers are white and appear in May and early June. Easily grown in any well-drained, fertile soil. Some of the species and clones of the Aucuparia Section are not long-lived on shallow chalk soils. Like many of their relatives in this family *Sorbus* are susceptible to fireblight.

The majority of *Sorbus* may conveniently be referred to the first two of the following three groups:
Aria Section Leaves simple, toothed or lobed. Excellent on chalky soil.
Aucuparia Section Leaves pinnate with numerous leaflets.
Micromeles Section A smaller group differing from the Aria Section in the fruits having deciduous calyces. Sometimes regarded as a distinct genus.

alnifolia (Siebold & Zucc.) K. Koch (Aria Section) A small to medium-sized tree with a dense head of purplish-brown branches. Leaves ovate to obovate, strongly veined, double-toothed, recalling those of the hornbeam (*Carpinus betulus*). Rich scarlet and orange tints in autumn. Fruits small, oval, bright red. Japan, Korea, China. I 1892. AM 1924. **'Skyline'** A columnar form of upright habit, the leaves turning yellow in autumn. A seedling selected by Hillier foreman Alf Alford in our Eastleigh nursery in 1962. **var. *submollis*** Rehder. Leaves broader, softly pubescent beneath, particularly when young. Japan, Korea, Manchuria, China and Ussuri.

alnifolia × *aria* A small to medium-sized tree with glabrous, reddish-brown shoots. Leaves elliptic to oblong-elliptic, doubly serrate, dark green and glabrous above, paler and thinly tomentose beneath, grey-downy when young.

americana Marshall (Aucuparia Section) American mountain ash, Roundwood. A small tree of vigorous growth with ascending branches and long-pointed, red, sticky buds. Leaves with 13–17 sharply toothed, long-acuminate leaflets. Rich autumn tints. Fruits small, bright red, borne in large, densely packed bunches. E North America. I 1782. AM 1950. **'Nana'** See *S. aucuparia* 'Fastigiata'.

anglica Hedl. (Aria Section) A medium-sized shrub or small, bushy tree, related to the whitebeam (*S. aria*). Leaves inclined to obovate, shallowly lobed and toothed, glossy green above, grey-tomentose beneath, turning golden-brown in autumn; flowers white with pink anthers, followed in autumn by globose, crimson fruits. Found only in western parts of the British Isles (except Scotland) and Co. Kerry.

'Apricot Lady' (Aucuparia Section) A small tree, a seedling of *S. aucuparia* originating in our nurseries.

Fruits apricot-yellow, large, in bold corymbs, contrasting with the neatly cut, bright green foliage, which colours richly in autumn. AM 1973.

aria (L.) Crantz. Whitebeam. A small to medium-sized tree with a compact, usually rounded head of branches. Leaves oval or obovate, greyish-white at first, later bright green above, vivid white-tomentose beneath, turning to gold and russet in autumn, when the bunches of deep crimson fruits are shown to advantage. A familiar tree, particularly on chalk formations in the south of England, where it usually accompanies yew (*Taxus*). One of the best trees for windswept or maritime districts and industrial areas. Europe. **'Aurea'** Leaves tinted soft yellow-green. **'Chrysophylla'** Leaves yellowish throughout summer, particularly effective in late spring, becoming a rich butter-yellow in autumn. **'Cyclophylla'** A form with broad-oval or orbicular leaves. **'Decaisneana'** See 'Majestica'. **'Lutescens'** Upper surface of leaves covered by a dense, creamy-white tomentum, becoming grey-green by late summer. An outstanding tree in spring. ♀ 2002. AM 1952. **'Magnifica'** An upright form with large, glossy green leaves and large clusters of red fruits. C 1916. **'Majestica'** ('Decaisneana') A handsome form with larger, elliptic leaves, 10–15cm long, and slightly larger fruits. ♀ 2002. **'Pendula'** A delightful, small, weeping tree, usually less than 3m high, with slender branches and smaller, narrower leaves. Tends to revert. **'Quercoides'** A slow-growing shrub or small tree of dense, compact, twiggy and congested growth. Leaves oblong, sharply and evenly lobed, the margins curving upwards. **'Salicifolia'** An attractive, graceful form with lax branches and leaves relatively narrow and long.

arranensis Hedl. (Aria Section) A large shrub or small tree of upright habit. Leaves ovate to elliptic, deeply lobed, green above, grey-tomentose beneath. Fruits red, longer than broad. A rare species only found wild in two glens on the Isle of Arran.

aucuparia L. Mountain ash, Rowan. A familiar, native tree of small to medium size, with greyish-downy winter buds. Leaves pinnate with 11–19 sharply toothed leaflets. Fruits bright red, carried in large, dense bunches during autumn, but soon devoured by hungry birds. An easily grown species, quite the equal to its Chinese counterparts, but not long-lived on very shallow, chalk soils. Very tolerant of extreme acidity. A parent of numerous hybrids. Europe. AM 1962. **'Aspleniifolia'** ('Laciniata') An elegant tree with deeply cut and toothed leaflets giving the leaves a fern-like effect. **'Beissneri'** An interesting tree with a dense head of erect branches. Young shoots and sometimes the leaf petioles are dark coral-red. Leaves yellow-green, particularly when young, the leaflets varying from deeply incised to pinnately lobed, many having an attractive, fern-like appearance. The trunk and stems are a warm copper or russet colour. C 1899. **'Cardinal Royal'** A form of upright habit with profuse, bright red fruits. **'Dirkenii'** Leaves yellow when young, becoming yellowish-green. Raised about 1880. **'Edulis'** ('Moravica', 'Dulcis') A strong-growing, extremely hardy tree, differing in its larger leaves with longer, broader leaflets, toothed mainly near the apex, and its larger fruits, which are edible and sweet, carried in heavier bunches. Originated about

1800. **'Fastigiata'** (*S. scopulina* hort. not Greene, *S. americana* 'Nana', *S. decora* 'Nana') A remarkable, slow-growing, columnar shrub or small tree up to 5.5m, with stout, closely erect stems. Leaves large, up to 11–15 dark green leaflets. Fruits sealing-wax-red, large, borne in large, densely-packed bunches. A distinct plant with a confusing history. AM 1924 (as *S. americana* 'Nana'). **'Fructu Luteo'** ('Xanthocarpa', 'Fifeana') Fruits amber-yellow. ♀ 2002. AM 1895. **'Moravica'** See 'Edulis'. **'Pendula'** A small, ungainly, widespreading tree with weeping branches. **'Rossica Major'** Similar to 'Edulis', but leaflets with stronger and more regular teeth. Originally grown as 'Rossica'. **'Sheerwater Seedling'** A vigorous, upright, small tree with a compact, ovoid head of ascending branches, and large clusters of orange-red fruits. Excellent as a street tree. ♀ 2002. **'Streetwise'** A vigorous selection with a neat and compact, upright habit. The large clusters of bright orange berries are borne very profusely. Selected in our nurseries in the early 1980s. I in 1998. **'Xanthocarpa'** See 'Fructu Luteo'.

'Autumn Glow' (Aucuparia Section) (*S. commixta* 'Embley' × *S. vilmorinii*) A small tree of upright habit, the pinnate leaves turning to purple and orange-red in autumn. Fruits pinkish-white then yellow flushed red. Raised in our Eastleigh nursery by our foreman Alf Alford in 1967.

bakonyensis (Jáv.) Karpati (Aria Section) A small tree related to *S. latifolia*. Leaves broadly elliptic-ovate, coarsely double-toothed above the middle, glossy green above, densely grey-tomentose beneath. Fruits large, scarlet, speckled with lenticels. Hungary.

bristoliensis Wilmott (Aria Section) A small tree with a compact, often rounded head of branches. Leaves oval or rhomboidal, shortly lobed above a wedge-shaped base, green above, grey-downy beneath. Fruits orange-red, carried in dense clusters. Only found wild in the Avon Gorge near Bristol.

caloneura (Stapf) Rehder (Micromeles Section) A large shrub or small tree with erect stems. Leaves oval to oblong, double-toothed and boldly marked by 9–16 pairs of parallel veins. Fruits small, brown, globular with a flattened apex. C China. I 1904 by Ernest Wilson.

cascadensis G.N. Jones. A medium-sized to large shrub of upright habit with stout shoots. Leaves usually have 9–11 broadly oblong leaflets, glossy green above. Large, bright orange fruits ripen early. Plants previously listed as *S. sitchensis* belong here. W North America.

cashmiriana Hedl. (Aucuparia Section) A beautiful, small tree of open habit. Leaves composed of 17–19 strongly serrated leaflets. Flowers soft pink in May. Fruits gleaming white, 12mm across. A distinct species with its loose, drooping clusters of fruits like white marbles, remaining long after the leaves have fallen. Kashmir. C 1934. ♀ 2002. FCC 1971. AM 1952.

chamaemespilus (L.) Crantz (Aria Section) A small, slow-growing shrub of dense, compact habit up to 1.8m. Twigs stout, bearing elliptic, sharply toothed leaves, glossy dark green above, paler beneath, turning rich yellow, orange and russet in autumn. Flowers pink, densely packed in terminal corymbs. Fruits 12mm long, red. A distinct species of neat appearance. Mts of C and S Europe. I 1683.

'Chinese Lace' (Aucuparia Section) A small tree of upright habit, leaves with deeply cut and divided leaflets producing a charming, lace-like effect and turning red-purple in autumn. Fruits dark red. Possibly *S. aucuparia* 'Aspleniifolia' × *S. esserteauana*.

commixta Koehne (Aucuparia Section) (*S. discolor* hort., *S. randaiensis* hort.) A small, variable tree of columnar habit when young, broadening somewhat in maturity. Winter buds long-pointed and sticky. Leaves glabrous with 11–15 slender-pointed, serrated leaflets, bright glossy green above, coppery when young, colouring richly in autumn. Fruits small and globular, red or orange-red, borne in large, erect bunches. One of the best species for autumn colour. Japan, Sakhalin, Korea. C 1880. AM 1979. **'Embley'** (*S.* 'Embley') A superb, small tree, with its leaves consistently glowing red in autumn, colouring generally later and remaining on the branches longer. Large, heavy bunches of glistening orange-red fruits. ♀ 2002. AM 1971. **'Jermyns'** (*S.* 'Jermyns') A splendid form giving good autumn tints. Fruits in large bunches, deep amber turning to orange-red. Originated in our nursery from a batch of seed received as *S. sargentiana*. **var. rufoferruginea** Shirai ex C.K. Schneid. (*S. rufoferruginea* (C.K. Schneid.) C.K. Schneid.) Differs in its slightly villous buds and the presence of soft brown hairs on the inflorescence and along the leaf midrib beneath. Japan. I 1915. AM 1958 (as *S. matsumurana*). **'Serotina'** (*S. serotina* Koehne) Leaves composed of 15–17 sharply toothed leaflets colouring richly in late autumn. Fruits small, bright orange-red.

× *confusa* See *S.* × *vagensis*.

conradinae Koehne See *S. esserteauana*.

conradinae hort. See *S. pohuashanensis*.

cuspidata See *S. vestita*.

danubialis (Jáv.) Karpati. A small tree related to *S. umbellata*. Leaves broadly elliptic to obovate to 8cm by 6cm, broadly cuneate at the base, coarsely double-toothed above the middle, glossy green above, grey-tomentose beneath. Fruits scarlet with few lenticels, about 12mm across. SE Europe.

decora hort. (Aucuparia Section) An attractive, medium-sized shrub of loose, open growth. Leaves with 13–17 sea-green, obtuse leaflets. Fruits, borne in dense clusters, are a conspicuous orange when young, later turning to red. The plant grown under this name is possibly of hybrid origin. The true species is a close relative of *S. americana*. **'Nana'** See *S. aucuparia* 'Fastigiata'.

decurrens See *S.* × *thuringiaca* 'Decurrens'.

discolor Hedl. (Aucuparia Section) A small tree with an open head of ascending branches. Leaves glabrous with 11–15 toothed leaflets, colouring richly in autumn. Flowers opening generally earlier than the others of the group, in some years by 2–3 weeks. Fruit creamy-yellow, tinged pink, ovoid to obovoid, on red stalks in rather loose clusters. It is doubtful whether the true species is in cultivation. The plant described here is probably of hybrid origin. N China. I about 1883.

discolor hort. See *S. commixta*.

domestica L. Service tree. A medium-sized tree, with open, spreading branches, rough-scaly bark and sticky, shining winter buds. Leaves pinnate, turning orange-red or yellow in autumn, composed of 13–21 leaflets. Fruits pear-

or apple-shaped, 2.5–3cm long, green, tinged red on the sunny side, edible when bletted. S and E Europe. Long cultivated. **var. pomifera** Hayne (var. *maliformis* (Hayne) Lodd.) Fruits apple-shaped, pedicel 1.5cm, leaves with 6–7 pairs of leaflets. AM 1983. **var. pyrifera** Hayne (var. *pyriformis* (Hayne) Lodd.) Fruits pear-shaped, pedicel 2.5cm, leaves with 8–9 pairs of leaflets.

'Eastern Promise' (Aucuparia Section) (*S. commixta* 'Embley' × *S. vilmorinii*) A small oval-headed tree of upright habit, the pinnate leaves with 15–19 leaflets, dark green above, on a red-tinged rachis, turning to purple then fiery-orange in autumn. Fruits deep rose-pink in dense, hanging clusters that weigh down the branches. Raised in our nurseries in 1967. AM 1994 (for fruit). Cory Cup 1994.

'Edwin Hillier' A slow-growing shrub or small tree. The mother plant was raised in our nursery from seed received as *S. poteriifolia*, and has the appearance of having a member of the Aria Section as the pollinator. Winter buds rounded and ferruginous. Leaves ovate to elliptic or lanceolate, the lower half divided into 1–3 pairs of serrated leaflets or lobes, the upper half strongly lobed and toothed, dark green above, densely grey- or brownish-grey-tomentose beneath. Flowers pink in terminal corymbs. Fruits oval, rose-red.

'Embley' See *S. commixta* 'Embley'.

epidendron Hand.-Mazz. (Micromeles Section) A very rare shrub or small tree inclined to the equally rare *S. rhamnoides*, with slightly glaucous shoots. Leaves obovate to narrowly elliptic, long-pointed, serrulate dark green above, rusty pubescent beneath. Fruits globose, brownish-green. W China. I 1925 by George Forrest.

esserteauana Koehne (Aucuparia Section) (*S. conradinae* Koehne not hort.) A small tree of open habit, occasionally up to 11m. Stipules large and leafy. Leaves composed of usually 11–13 sharply toothed leaflets, dark matt green above, grey-downy beneath. The small, scarlet fruits colour later than most other species and are borne in dense, broad clusters. The foliage gives rich autumn tints. W China. I 1907. AM 1954. **'Flava'** Fruits rich lemon-yellow in crowded, flattened corymbs. A superb clone. AM 1954.

'Ethel's Gold' (Aucuparia Section) A small tree with bright green, sharply serrated leaflets and bunches of golden-amber fruits. A seedling of hybrid origin which originated in our nurseries before 1959. Probably a seedling of *S. commixta*, which it resembles in leaf. The attractively coloured fruits persist into the New Year if the birds allow. Named after Sir Harold Hillier's mother. AM 1989.

fennica See *S. hybrida*.

folgneri (C.K. Schneid.) Rehder (Micromeles Section) A graceful, small tree of variable habit, usually with spreading or arching branches. Leaves variable, oval to narrowly oval, double-toothed, dark green above, white- or grey-tomentose beneath, often assuming rich autumnal colours. Fruits variable in size, ovoid or obovoid, dark red or purplish-red, in drooping clusters. C China. I 1901. AM 1915. **'Lemon Drop'** A graceful tree with slender, arching and drooping branches. Fruits bright yellow, set amid deep green leaves which are white beneath. Originated in our nurseries before 1950.

forrestii McAllister & Gillham (Forrest 19583) (Aucuparia Section) A very graceful, small tree of open habit related to *S. hupehensis*. Leaves blue-green with usually 13–15 oblong leaflets, toothed above the middle. Fruits small, white, tinged with pink on the calyx. An excellent tree for a small garden. Yunnan, China. I by George Forrest in 1921 but not named until 1980. AM 1992.

'Golden Wonder' (Aucuparia Section) A small tree of upright habit with stout shoots and grey-hairy buds. Leaves with 13–15 deep blue-green leaflets, sharply toothed nearly to the base and turning yellow and red in autumn. Golden-yellow fruits are borne in large clusters.

gracilis (Siebold & Zucc.) K. Koch (Aucuparia Section) A small tree or medium-sized shrub. Leaves with 7–11 matt green leaflets, toothed at the apex, stipules persistent, large and leafy. Flowers in few-flowered corymbs, fruits elongated pear-shape, oblong or obovoid, 15mm long, orange-red. Japan. C 1934.

graeca (Spach) Kotschy (Aria Section) (*S. umbellata* var. *cretica* (Lindl.) C.K. Schneid.) A medium-sized shrub or small tree of dense, compact habit. Leaves obovate or rounded, double-toothed, green above, greenish-white-tomentose beneath. Fruits crimson. SE and EC Europe. C 1830.

†*harrowiana* (Balf. f. & W.W. Sm.) Rehder (Aucuparia Section) Related to *S. insignis*, this is perhaps the most remarkable and distinct of the pinnate-leaved species. A large shrub or small tree of compact habit with stout ascending branches. Leaves 20–30cm long and as much across, pinnate with 2–4 pairs of sessile leaflets and a long-stalked terminal leaflet; leaflets 15–18cm long by 4–4.5cm across, the lateral ones conspicuously uneven at base, glossy dark green above, pale glaucous-green and slightly reticulate beneath. Small flowers in large, flattened corymbs are followed by equally small, pink or pearly-white fruits. Discovered by George Forrest in Yunnan in 1912, and later reintroduced by Kingdon-Ward. Plants of the latter survived with little injury the severe winters of 1962–63 and the 1980s, while those of Forrest's introduction have been killed by severe winters except in the mildest localities. AM 1971.

hedlundii C.K. Schneid. (Aria Section) A strikingly handsome, medium-sized tree related to *S. vestita*, with large leaves, silvery-white-tomentose beneath, with rust-coloured midribs and veins. E Himalaya.

hemsleyi Rehder. A small to medium-sized tree with grey-green young leaves, white-downy beneath. White flowers in late spring to early summer are followed by small, brown fruits, green at first. China. I to the USA in 1980 by the Sino-American Expedition to China, and from the Arnold Arboretum to Britain in 1992.

× *hostii* (Jacq.) K. Koch (*S. chamaemespilus* × *S. mougeotii*) A small tree or large shrub of compact habit. Leaves oval or obovate, sharply toothed, green above, grey-pubescent beneath. Flowers pale pink, followed by bright red fruits which open early. Occurs with the parents in the wild. C 1820. AM 1974.

hupehensis C.K. Schneid. (Aucuparia Section) A small, but strong-growing tree developing a bold, compact head of ascending, purple-brown branches. Leaves large, with a distinctive bluish-green cast, easily recognisable from a distance. Leaflets 11–17, sharply toothed in the upper half. Stipules large and leafy. Fruits white or sometimes pink-tinged. Borne in loose, drooping bunches and lasting late into winter. The leaves turn a glorious red in autumn. W China. I 1910 by Ernest Wilson. ♀ 2002. AM 1955. **var. obtusa** C.K. Schneid. A most attractive form with pink fruits. Leaves with usually 11 leaflets, toothed only near the obtuse apex. Various selections have been named including 'Pink Pagoda', 'Rosea' and 'Rufus', all with pink fruits. ♀ 2002. FCC 1977.

hybrida L. (Aria Section) (*S. fennica* (Kalm) Fries) A small to medium-sized, compact tree. Leaves broad ovate, one to one and a half times as long as broad, divided at the base into one or two pairs of long leaflets, the upper half variously toothed and lobed, green above, grey-tomentose beneath. Fruits red, globose, almost 12mm across, in large clusters. Probably originated as a hybrid between *S. aucuparia* and *S. rupicola*. Wild in Scandinavia. **'Fastigiata'** See *S.* × *thuringiaca* 'Fastigiata'. **'Gibbsii'** (*S. pinnatifida* 'Gibbsii') A selected clone of more compact habit and with larger fruits. ♀ 2002. AM 1953. AM 1925 (as *Pyrus firma*). **var. meinichii** See *S. meinichii*.

× *hybrida* hort. See *S.* × *thuringiaca*.

insignis (Hook. f.) Hedl. (KW 7746) (Aucuparia Section) A magnificent, small tree for a reasonably sheltered site, with stout, stiffly ascending, purplish-brown branches. Leaves pinnate, up to 25cm long, composed of 11–15 oblong-lanceolate, shallowly toothed leaflets, dark polished green and reticulate above, glaucous beneath. They are retained long on the tree and turn red in early winter. Petioles with a large, conspicuous, clasping base. Fruits small, oval, pink, borne in large heads. They seem to hold little attraction for birds and persist almost to Easter. In winter the large buds are conspicuous. Related to *S. harrowiana*, but hardier, this tree has grown in the Sir Harold Hillier Gardens and Arboretum for many years where it has reached 5.5m. I 1928 by Kingdon-Ward from the Naga Hills (Assam). Also found in E Nepal.

intermedia (Ehrh.) Pers. (Aria Section) Swedish whitebeam. A small to medium-sized tree with a dense, usually rounded head of branches. Leaves ovate to broad-elliptic, lobed in the lower half, coarsely toothed above, dark green and glossy above, grey-tomentose beneath. Fruits 12mm across, orange-red, in bunches. NW Europe. **'Brouwers'** A selected form with ascending branches making an oval crown. An excellent street tree.

japonica (Decne.) Hedl. (Micromeles Section) A rare tree of medium size, the young branches, inflorescence and leaves beneath covered with a dense, white pubescence. Leaves ovate-orbicular to broadly ovate, shallowly lobed and toothed. Fruits obovoid, red, with brown speckles. Attractive autumn tints. Japan. **var. calocarpa** Rehder. An attractive form with leaves whiter beneath and fruits larger, orange-yellow, without speckles. Rich yellow autumn tints. C Japan. I 1915.

'Jermyns' See *S. commixta* 'Jermyns'.

'John Mitchell' See *S. thibetica* 'John Mitchell'.

'Joseph Rock' (Rock 23657) (Aucuparia Section) An outstanding, small tree up to 9m or more high, with an erect, compact head of branches. Leaves composed of 15–19, narrowly oblong, sharply toothed leaflets, turning to shades of red, orange, copper and purple in autumn. The

rich autumn tints provide an ideal setting for the clusters of globular fruits, which are creamy-yellow at first deepening to amber-yellow at maturity, remaining on the branches well after leaf fall. The origin of this tree remains a mystery. It is probably a form of a variable Chinese species. Unfortunately very susceptible to fireblight. FCC 1962. AM 1950.

keissleri (C.K. Schneid.) Rehder (Micromeles Section) A very rare and quite distinct, small tree, up to 12m, or a large shrub, with stiffly ascending branches. Leaves obovate, leathery, glossy green. Flowers greenish-white, sweetly scented, borne in dense, terminal clusters and followed by small, crab-apple-like green fruits with bloomy, red cheeks. C and W China. I 1907 by Ernest Wilson.

× *kewensis* Hensen (Aucuparia Section) (*S. pohuashanensis* hort. not Hedl.) A first-class, hardy, free-fruiting rowan, a hybrid between *S. aucuparia* and the best of the Chinese species (*S. pohuashanensis*). The orange-red fruits are borne in large, heavy bunches, and severely test the strength of the branches, providing in autumn a feast both for the eyes and the birds. It is commonly grown in gardens under the name *S. pohuashanensis* from which it differs mainly in that the leafy stipules below the inflorescence are normally shed before the fruits develop. Raised originally at Kew Gardens. FCC 1973 (as *S. pohuashanensis*). AM 1947.

koehneana C.K. Schneid. (Aucuparia Section) A medium-sized shrub or small, elegant tree. Leaves with 17–33, narrow, toothed leaflets. The small, porcelain-white fruits are borne in slender, drooping clusters. C China. I 1910 by Ernest Wilson. ♀ 2002.

lanata See *S. vestita*.

latifolia (Lam.) Pers. (Aria Section) Service tree of Fontainbleau. A small to medium-sized tree with downy young shoots and shaggy, peeling bark. Leaves ovate or broad-elliptic, sharply lobed, glossy green above, grey-felted beneath. Fruits globular, russet-yellow with large, brownish speckles. An apomictic species derived from a hybrid between *S. torminalis* and a species of the Aria Section. EC Portugal to SW Germany. FCC 1987. AM 1973.

'Leonard Messel' (Aucuparia Section) (*S. aucuparia* × *S. harrowiana*) A splendid, but unfortunately rather neglected, small tree with upright branches making a dense, oval crown. Winter buds conical, red with brown hairs at the apex. Leaves large with usually 9–11 leaflets on a pink rachis, turning red and purple in autumn. Leaflets oblong, to 11cm by 2.8cm, sharply toothed above the middle, blue-green above, glaucous beneath. Distinctive, bright pink fruits are borne in broad, hanging clusters. Raised in 1949 by Col L.C.R. Messel. It has reached 9m in the Sir Harold Hillier Gardens and Arboretum. FCC 1987. AM 1973.

megalocarpa Rehder. A remarkable, large shrub of loose, spreading habit. Twigs brown-purple, stout, bearing large, oval to obovate, deep glossy green, coarsely toothed leaves, which sometimes turn to crimson in autumn. The large flower buds open before the leaves in early spring, producing a conspicuous corymb of cream flowers with too pungent a smell for indoor decoration. These are followed by hard, brown fruits the size and colour of small partridge eggs. The large, red, sticky bud scales and red young leaves in spring are very striking. W China. I 1903 by Ernest Wilson. **var. *cuneata*** Rehder. More vigorous, making a small tree with arching branches. Leaves matt green, short-stalked and finely toothed, with white tufts of hair in the vein axils beneath. I by Ernest Wilson in 1910.

meinichii (Hartm.) Hedl. (*S. hybrida* var. *meinichii* (Hartm.) Rehder) A small, erect tree with a compact head of fastigiate branches. Leaves with 4–6 pairs of distinct leaflets and a deeply toothed or lobed terminal portion, green above, grey-tomentose beneath. Fruits rounded, red. An apomictic species said to have originated as a hybrid between *S. aucuparia* and *S. hybrida*, though it resembles more the former. S and W Norway.

meliosmifolia Rehder (Micromeles Section) A small tree or large, bushy shrub with stiffly ascending, purplish-brown branches, spreading with age. Leaves up to 18cm long, bright green, with 18–24 pairs of parallel veins. One of the first trees to flower once winter has passed. Fruits 12mm long, brownish-red. A rare species sometimes confused in cultivation with *S. caloneura*, from which it differs in its larger, shorter-stalked, more numerously veined leaves. W China. I 1910 by Ernest Wilson.

minima (Ley) Hedl. (Aria Section) A slender-branched, native shrub of medium size. Leaves elliptic or oblong-elliptic, 5–7.5cm long, shallowly lobed, green above, grey-tomentose beneath. Fruits small, scarlet, with a few speckles. Only found in the wild on limestone crags near Crickhowell, Brecon, Wales.

'Mitchellii' See *S. thibetica* 'John Mitchell'.

mougeotii Soy.-Will. & Godron (Aria Section) Generally a large shrub or small tree with ovate or obovate, shallowly lobed leaves, green above, whitish-grey-tomentose beneath. Fruits slightly longer than wide, red, with a few speckles. European Alps (mainly in the west), Pyrenees. C 1880. AM 1984.

pallescens Rehder (Aria Section) A beautiful, small tree of upright growth. Leaves narrowly elliptic to elliptic-lanceolate, acuminate, sharply double-toothed, green above, silvery-white-tomentose beneath, with conspicuous veins. Older trees have shreddy bark and elliptic to oblong leaves. Fruits pear-shaped or rounded, up to 12mm long, green with a red cheek, borne in loose clusters. W China. I 1908. Reintroduced by Roy Lancaster from W Sichuan in 1981 (Lancaster 957).

'Pearly King' (Aucuparia Section) A small, slender-branched tree with pinnate, fern-like leaves composed of 13–17 narrow, sharply toothed leaflets. Fruits 15mm across, rose at first, changing to white with a pink flush, borne in large, loosely pendent bunches. A hybrid of *S. vilmorinii* originating in our nurseries.

'Pink-Ness' (*S. aucuparia* × *S. discolor* Forrest 22622) A striking and vigorous, small tree bearing clusters of creamy-white flowers in late spring, followed by profuse, showy, pink berries.

'Pink Pearl' (Aucuparia Section) A small tree of upright habit, the attractive, pinnate leaves with sharply toothed leaflets. Fruits white, heavily flushed and spotted pink, borne in heavy clusters. A seedling raised in our Eastleigh nursery in 1958 by our foreman Alf Alford.

pinnatifida See *S.* × *thuringiaca*. **'Gibbsii'** See *S. hybrida* 'Gibbsii'.

pohuashanensis (Hance) Hedl. (Aucuparia Section) (*S. conradinae* hort. not Koehne, *S. sargentiana warleyensis* hort.) A splendid tree, possibly the best Chinese rowan, attaining up to 11m with a dense head of spreading and ascending branches. Leaves with usually 11–15, sharply toothed leaflets, green above, grey-pubescent beneath. Stipules large and leafy, persistent, especially below the inflorescence even when fruiting. Fruits red, borne in conspicuous bunches, causing the branches to bow under their concentrated weight. One of the most reliable and spectacular of *Sorbus* in fruit. Easily grown and very hardy. A parent of several hybrids, the true plant is rare in cultivation, its place most often being taken by the hybrid *S.* × *kewensis*. N China. I 1883. AM 1946.

pohuashanensis hort. See *S.* × *kewensis*.

poteriifolia Hand.-Mazz. (*S. pygmaea* hort.) (Aucuparia Section) The smallest-known *Sorbus*. A very rare, tiny shrublet, difficult to cultivate. Leaves composed of 9–15 sharply toothed leaflets. Flowers pale rose to crimson in terminal clusters, followed by globular, white fruits. Related to *S. reducta* it is best given a moist, peaty soil. Until recently the only plants in cultivation grew in the Sir Harold Hillier Gardens and Arboretum. N Burma, NW Yunnan. I from Burma in 1926 by Kingdon-Ward and again in 1953.

poteriifolia hort. See *S.* sp. McLaren D. 84.

prattii Koehne (Aucuparia Section) (*S. prattii* f. *subarachnoidea* (Koehne) Rehder) An elegant, large shrub or occasionally a small tree, with slender branches and leaves composed of 21–29 coarsely toothed leaflets. Fruits small, globose, pearly-white, borne in small, drooping clusters all along the branches. W China. I by Ernest Wilson in 1910. AM 1971. **f. *subarachnoidea*** See *S. prattii*.

pygmaea hort. See *S. poteriifolia* Hand.-Mazz.

randaiensis (Hayata) Koidz. (Aucuparia Section) A small tree closely related to *S. commixta* and differing in the narrower leaflets. Plants previously grown under this name are *S. commixta*. The true species has now been introduced to cultivation. Taiwan. AM 1993.

'Red Marbles' (Aucuparia Section) A small tree with stout twigs which originated in our Eastleigh nurseries in 1961. Leaves with purple stalks and 13–15 large, broadly and boldly toothed leaflets. Fruits red with pale spots, 12–17mm across, borne in loose, heavy bunches. A magnificent fruiting tree, believed to be *S. aucuparia* 'Edulis' × *S. pohuashanensis*.

reducta Diels (Aucuparia Section) An unusual, small, suckering shrub forming thickets of slender, erect stems, 60cm to 1m high. Leaves with red petioles, composed of 13–15 sharply serrate, dark, shining green leaflets, bronze and reddish-purple in autumn. Fruits small, globular, white, flushed rose. A charming species when associated with heathers, dwarf conifers and other dwarf shrubs. Some plants under this name are similar in leaf and fruit but grow on a single stem and do not sucker. N Burma, W China. I 1943 by Kingdon-Ward. ♀ 2002. AM 1974.

rhamnoides Rehder. The true species of this name, a native of the E Himalaya, belongs to the Micromeles Section and is not in cultivation. The plant grown under this name is of uncertain identity. A small tree of loose habit. Leaves elliptic, 13–15cm long, serrate, slender-stalked, green above, thinly grey-downy beneath at first. Fruits green becoming yellowish-brown flushed red with persistent calyx, remaining on the tree until late winter.

'Rose Queen' (Aucuparia Section) (*S. commixta* 'Embley' × *S.* sp. McLaren D. 84) An attractive, small tree raised in our Eastleigh nurseries in 1963. Leaves composed of 13–17 sharply serrate leaflets. Fruits bright rose-red, in large, loose bunches.

'Rosi-Ness' A very attractive, small tree of open habit. Profuse, soft pink flowers in spring are followed by large, pink-flushed berries. Reddish bark with silvery markings.

rufoferruginea See *S. commixta* var. *rufoferruginea*.

rupicola (Syme) Hedl. (Aria Section) (*S. salicifolia* (Myrin) Hedl.) A medium-sized shrub of rather stiff habit. Leaves obovate or oblanceolate, tapering to the base, coarsely toothed, green above, white-tomentose beneath. Fruits broader than long, carmine, with scattered, brown speckles. British Isles, Scandinavia.

sargentiana Koehne (Aucuparia Section) A magnificent species, slowly developing into a rigidly branched tree up to 9m and as much across. Winter buds large and sticky, like those of a horse chestnut (*Aesculus*), but crimson. Leaves large and attractive, up to 30cm long, composed of 7–11 slender-pointed leaflets, each 7.5–13cm long. Leaf stalks red, stipules large, leafy and persistent. Fruits small, scarlet, late in ripening, produced in large, rounded heads up to 15cm across. Rich red autumn colour. W China. Discovered by Ernest Wilson in 1903, and introduced by him in 1908. ♀ 2002. FCC 1956. AM 1954.

'Savill Orange' (Aucuparia Section) A small tree bearing dense clusters of large, orange-red berries. A seedling of *S. aucuparia* 'Xanthocarpa', it originated in the Valley Gardens, Windsor Great Park about 1970. AM 1979.

scalaris Koehne (Aucuparia Section) A small tree of distinct appearance with widespreading branches and neat, attractive, frond-like leaves composed of 21–33 narrow leaflets, dark glossy green above, grey-downy beneath, turning to rich red and purple late in autumn. Fruits small, red, densely packed in flattened heads. W China. I 1904 by Ernest Wilson. AM 1934.

scopulina hort. See *S. aucuparia* 'Fastigiata'.

serotina See *S. commixta* 'Serotina'.

'Signalman' (Aucuparia Section) A small tree of columnar habit raised in our Eastleigh nursery in 1968 as the result of crossing *S. domestica* with *S. scopulina*. Leaves similar to those of the former parent, but slightly smaller and more densely arranged. Fruits large, bright orange, borne in dense clusters.

sitchensis Roem. (Aucuparia Section) This species is rare in cultivation. Plants previously listed under this name are *S. cascadensis*.

sp. Ghose (Aucuparia Section) A superb, small tree of upright habit showing some affinity to *S. insignis* but hardier. Probably a new species and worthy of extensive planting. Leaves large, composed of 15–19 sharply serrate leaflets, dark, dull green above, glaucescent beneath and rusty-pubescent, at least along the midrib. Fruits small, rose-red, produced in large, densely packed bunches which remain on the branches until late in the season. I by us from Himalayan seed.

sp. Lowndes See *S. ursina*.

sp. McLaren D. 84 (*S. poteriifolia* hort.) (Aucuparia Section) A beautiful, slow-growing, small tree with erect, purplish-brown branches. Leaves composed of 15–19 sharply serrate, dark green, downy leaflets. Fruits globular, delightful deep rose-pink, carried in large, loose bunches. China. AM 1951.

sp. Yu 8423 See under *S. thibetica*.

× *splendida* Hedl. (Aucuparia Section) (*S. americana* × *S. aucuparia*) A small, robust tree intermediate in character between its parents. Buds sticky but rusty-pubescent at tips. Fruits orange-red, in large, dense bunches. Garden origin before 1850.

subcuneata Wilmott. A small, British, endemic tree with glossy brown, white-hairy shoots. Leaves glossy green above, thinly grey-tomentose beneath, sharply toothed or lobed to about one-quarter of the way to the midrib, truncate or shallowly cuneate at the base. Fruits bright red. Somerset, N Devon.

'Sunshine' (Aucuparia Section) A small tree of erect habit when young. Leaves dark glossy green with 7–8 pairs of sharply toothed leaflets. Fruits golden-yellow, in large, dense clusters, and colouring before 'Joseph Rock' of which it is a seedling. Raised in our nurseries in 1968.

'Theophrasta' (Aria Section) A small, round-headed tree with broadly ovate, double-toothed leaves, grey-tomentose beneath. Fruits relatively large, brownish and conspicuously lenticelled at first becoming dull orange. Origin unknown.

thibetica (Cardot) Hand.-Mazz. This species is mainly represented in gardens by 'John Mitchell' described below. For the Kingdon-Ward introduction previously distributed under this name (KW 21175) see *S. wardii*. **'John Mitchell'** (*S.* 'Mitchellii', *S.* 'John Mitchell') A handsome, medium-sized to large tree, eventually developing a broad, rounded head. The mature leaves are large, about 15cm long by as much across, and remarkably rounded, green above, white-tomentose beneath. Fruits apple-shaped, russet-brown. The original tree from which our stock was raised is growing in Westonbirt Arboretum, Gloucestershire. ♀ 2002. **Yu 8423** A distinct, slow-growing form making an erect, small tree of narrow, columnar habit. Leaves oval to obovate, 10–13cm long, toothed, green above, grey-tomentose beneath. Winter buds green and viscid. Fruits pear-shaped, orange, flushed red. China.

× *thuringiaca* (Ilse) Fritsch (*S. aria* × *S. aucuparia*) (*S. pinnatifida* hort., *S.* × *hybrida* hort.) A small tree with a dense head of ascending branches. Leaves narrowly oval to oblong, lobed and toothed, divided at the base into 1–3 pairs of leaflets, dull green above, grey-tomentose beneath. Fruits scarlet with a few brown speckles. Occurs rarely with the parents in the wild. Frequently confused with *S. hybrida* in cultivation, it differs in its stricter, more compact habit, and in its slightly larger, more elongated leaves with smaller, oval leaflets. AM 1924 (as *S. pinnatifida*). **'Decurrens'** Leaves pinnate except for the terminal 3 leaflets which are often joined. C 1834. **'Fastigiata'** (*S. hybrida* 'Fastigiata') A most distinctive, small tree with an ovoid head of closely packed, ascending branches. Leaves and fruits as in type. A first-class tree possessing most of the qualities sought by those interested in public planting. **'Neuillyensis'** Leaves with several of the upper pairs of leaflets joined. C 1893.

tianschanica Rupr. A slow-growing shrub or low, rounded tree up to 4m high. Leaves pinnate with 9–15 sharply toothed, glossy green leaflets, colouring in autumn. Flowers and fruits are rarely carried on trees in the British Isles, though they are said to be conspicuous on specimens growing in more suitable climes. Flowers 2cm across followed by globular, red fruits. Turkestan. I 1895.

torminalis (L.) Crantz (Aria Section) Chequer tree, Wild service tree. An attractive, medium-sized, native tree with ascending branches, spreading with age, scaly bark and brown twigs, woolly-pubescent when young. Leaves maple-like, ovate, sharply and conspicuously lobed, glossy dark green above, pubescent beneath at first, turning bronzy-yellow in autumn; fruits longer than broad, russet-brown. Europe including England, Asia Minor, N Africa.

'Tundra' (Aucuparia Section) A small, upright tree with fern-like, dark green leaves composed of about 10 pairs of sharply toothed leaflets, turning reddish-purple in autumn. Fruits pale chartreuse-green at first becoming creamy-white providing an effective contrast as the leaves colour. A seedling of 'Joseph Rock' raised in our nursery in 1968.

umbellata **var.** *cretica* See *S. graeca*.

ursina Schauer (*S.* Sp. Lowndes) (Aucuparia Section) An attractive, small, erect tree with stout, ascending, greyish branches. Buds red, ferruginous-hairy at the tips. Leaves composed of 15–21 sharply toothed, elliptic-oblong, conspicuously reticulated leaflets. Fruits white or pink-tinged, borne in dense bunches. A very distinct and beautiful species. I 1950 from the Himalaya by Col Donald Lowndes. AM 1973.

× *vagensis* Wilmott (Aria Section) (*S. aria* × *S. torminalis*) (*S.* × *confusa* Gremli ex Rouy) A small to medium-sized tree of compact habit. Leaves ovate to elliptic, sharply lobed, not as deeply as in *S. torminalis*, glossy green above, thinly grey-tomentose beneath. Fruits obovoid, greenish-brown with numerous, brown speckles. Occurs with the parents in the wild, in England only in the Wye Valley.

vestita (G. Don) Lodd. (Aria Section) (*S. cuspidata* (Spach) Hedl.) (*S. lanata* hort. not (D. Don) Schauer) Himalayan whitebeam. A medium-sized tree of erect habit when young, later spreading. Leaves broad-elliptic, decurrent onto the petiole, 15–25cm long, green above, silvery-white- or buff-tomentose beneath. Fruits green, speckled and flushed warm brown, 15–20mm across, resembling small crab apples or miniature pears, borne in loose bunches. A magnificent species with bold foliage, one of the most handsome of all hardy trees. Himalaya. I 1820.

'Sessilifolia' Large, elliptic leaves tapering towards base and apex, sea-green above, grey-white-tomentose beneath, sessile or very shortly stalked.

vilmorinii C.K. Schneid. (Aucuparia Section) A beautiful, small tree or medium-sized shrub of elegant, spreading habit. Leaves often in clusters, fern-like, composed of 11–31 small leaflets, each 12–20mm long, turning to red and purple in autumn. The loose, drooping clusters of fruits are rose-red at first, gradually passing through pink

to white flushed with rose. A charming species suitable for a small garden. W China. I 1889 by the Abbé Delavay. ♀ 2002. AM 1916.

wardii Merr. (KW 21127) (Aria Section) A specimen of this rare species in the Sir Harold Hillier Gardens and Arboretum is growing strongly and is over 9m high. Its branches are rather stiff and erect giving the tree a distinct, columnar habit. Leaves elliptic to obovate, green and ribbed above, thinly hairy beneath; young leaves grey-downy. Fruits in loose corymbs, globular, 12mm in diameter, amber, speckled greyish-brown. A splendid silvery whitebeam for sites where space is limited. Tibet, Bhutan. I by Kingdon-Ward. Originally listed as *S. thibetica*.

'White Wax' (Aucuparia Section) A small tree with a conical head of branches and blackish buds covered with grey down. Leaves fern-like with up to 23 oblong, sharply toothed leaflets. Fruits pure white, 1cm across, in drooping clusters.

'Wilfrid Fox' (Aria Section) (*S. aria* × *S. vestita*) Named in memory of a generous friend and great gardener who did much to beautify the roadside plantings of England and was the creator of the famous Winkworth Arboretum in Surrey. This handsome hybrid tree has been growing in our nurseries for more than 50 years. It forms a round-headed tree, 12m high, broadly columnar when young with densely packed, ascending branches. Leaves are elliptic, 15–20cm long, with a slender petiole, 2.5–4cm long, shallowly lobed and doubly serrate, dark glossy green above, greyish-white-tomentose beneath. Fruits are marble-like, green at first turning to grey-speckled deep amber.

'Winter Cheer' (Aucuparia Section) (*S. esserteauana* 'Flava' × *S. pohuashanensis*) A seedling raised in our Eastleigh nursery in 1959. A small to medium-sized, open-branched tree. The large, flat bunches of fruits are a warm, chrome-yellow at first, ripening to orange-red. They begin to colour in September and last well into winter. AM 1971.

yuana Spongberg. A handsome, small tree, the branches upright to ascending when young, later spreading. Ornamental, ribbed leaves are green on both sides turning yellow in autumn. Fruits similar to those of *S. alnifolia* but larger, dark red, in drooping clusters. China. I from the Shennongjia Forest Reserve to the USA in 1980 by the Sino-American Expedition to China and named after the Chinese botanist T.T. Yu.

zahlbruckneri hort. See *S. alnifolia*.

Southernwood See *Artemisia abrotanum*.
Sparkleberry See *Vaccinium arboreum*.

†**SPARRMANNIA** L. f.—**Tiliaceae**—A small genus of 3 species of tender shrubs and trees, natives of tropical and South Africa.

africana L. f. African hemp, House lime. A large, stellately hairy, apple-green shrub of vigorous habit. Leaves large, often 30cm or more across, palmately-lobed. Flowers white, 4cm wide, with sensitive, yellow stamens, borne in conspicuous, cymose umbels during spring. An excellent conservatory shrub. This marvellous plant not only tolerates but appears to thrive on the cigarette- and cigar-ends and tea and coffee dregs of second class Continental cafés. South Africa. I 1790. ♀ 2002. AM 1955.

SPARTIUM L.—**Leguminosae**—A monotypic genus that is closely related to *Cytisus* and *Genista*, differing in its one-lipped, spathe-like calyx. Thrives in a well-drained, sunny position. An excellent seaside shrub. Specimens in sheltered gardens are apt to become tall and leggy. These may be hard-pruned in March, taking care not to cut into the old, hard wood.

junceum L. Spanish broom. A strong-growing shrub of loose habit, with erect, green, rush-like stems, to 3m. Leaves small and inconspicuous. The comparatively large, fragrant, yellow, pea-flowers, 2.5cm long, are borne in loose, terminal racemes throughout summer and early autumn. A wonderful shrub when kept low and bushy by the sea wind's blast. Mediterranean region, SW Europe. I to England about 1548. ♀ 2002. FCC 1977. AM 1968.

Spartocytisus nubigenus See *Cytisus supranubius*.
Sphacele chamaedryoides See *Lepechinia chamaedryoides*.

SPHAERALCEA St.-Hil.—**Malvaceae**—A genus of about 60 species of herbs, shrubs and subshrubs, natives mainly of North and South America with a few species in South Africa. The following requires a warm, sunny site and well-drained soil.

†*fendleri* A. Gray. A dwarf subshrub with downy shoots and 3-lobed leaves. The 2.5cm-wide, mallow-like flowers are pale reddish-orange and are borne in axillary clusters during summer and autumn. A pretty shrublet, suitable for a sunny border. N Mexico.

Spice bush See *Lindera benzoin*.
Spindle tree See *Euonymus europaeus*.

SPIRAEA L.—**Rosaceae**—A varied and useful genus of hardy, flowering shrubs, many of which are graceful in habit and pleasing in foliage. About 80 species in N temperate regions. They are easily grown in any ordinary soil and a sunny position though a few become chlorotic in very shallow chalk soils. Those of the *japonica-douglasii* type, which flower on the current year's shoots, may be pruned to the ground in March, while those of the *henryi-nipponica-veitchii* type, which flower on shoots of the previous year, may require thinning out and the old flowering shoots cut to within a few centimetres of the old wood, immediately after flowering. Untidy specimens of *S.* 'Arguta' and *S. thunbergii* may be hard-pruned immediately after flowering. *S. douglasii*, *S. salicifolia*, *S. tomentosa* and other thicket-forming species should only be planted where space permits.

aitchisonii See *Sorbaria tomentosa* var. *angustifolia*.

alba Du Roi. Meadow sweet. A small, upright, thicket-forming shrub, related to *S. salicifolia*, with yellow-brown stems and finely toothed leaves, to 7cm long. White flowers are borne in downy, terminal panicles in late summer. NE North America. **var.** *latifolia* (Aiton) Ahles (*S. latifolia* (Aiton) Borkh., *S. salicifolia* var. *latifolia* Aiton) A form with reddish shoots, broader, coarsely toothed leaves and white or pink flowers in

glabrous panicles. Not suitable for growing on shallow chalk soils. C 1789.

albiflora See *S. japonica* 'Albiflora'.
arborea See *Sorbaria kirilowii*.
arcuata Hook. f. A medium-sized shrub, related to *S. gemmata*, with pubescent, angular stems and entire leaves. Flowers white, carried in small umbels all along the arching branches in May. Himalaya. C 1908.

'**Arguta**' (*S. × multiflora × S. thunbergii*) Bridal wreath, Foam of May. A dense-growing, medium-sized shrub with graceful, slender branches. Leaves oblanceolate to narrowly oval, entire or few-toothed, usually glabrous. Flowers pure white, produced in small clusters all along the branches in April and May. One of the most effective and free-flowering of the early spiraeas. Resembles *S. × cinerea*. C before 1884. ♀ 2002.

assurgens See *Sorbaria kirilowii*.

baldshuanica B. Fedtsch. A dwarf shrub of rounded, compact habit, with slender, glabrous, twiggy branches. Leaves small, obovate, sea-green, toothed at the apex. Flowers white, in small, terminal corymbs in summer. SE Russia.

bella Sims. A small shrub, occasionally 1.5m high, with angular branches, downy when young. Leaves broadly ovate, toothed at apex, glaucous beneath. Very attractive when carrying its bright rose-pink flowers in terminal corymbs in June. Not happy in really shallow chalk soils. Himalaya. I 1818.

betulifolia Pall. A dwarf shrub occasionally up to 1m high, forming mounds of reddish-brown, glabrous branches and broadly ovate to rounded leaves, 2–4cm long. Flowers white, borne in dense corymbs, 2.5–6.5cm across, in June. Suitable for a rock garden. NE Asia, Japan. I about 1812. **var.** *aemiliana* (C.K. Schneid.) Koidz. A compact, dwarf form with smaller, rounded leaves.

× *billiardii* Herinq (*S. alba × S. douglasii*) Medium-sized, suckering shrub with erect, hairy stems. Leaves oblong to oblong-lanceolate, sharply toothed, greyish-pubescent beneath. Flowers bright rose, borne in narrow, densely crowded panicles throughout summer. Not happy on shallow chalky soils. C before 1854. '**Triumphans**' (*S. menziesii* 'Triumphans') A beautiful shrub with dense, conical panicles of purplish-rose flowers during summer. Not happy on shallow chalky soils.

× *brachybotrys* Lange (*S. canescens × S. douglasii*) A strong-growing, medium-sized shrub with gracefully arching branches. Leaves oblong or ovate, toothed at apex, grey-downy beneath. Flowers pale rose, borne in dense, terminal panicles during summer. Not recommended for very shallow chalky soils. C before 1867.

bracteata See *S. nipponica*.
bullata See *S. japonica* 'Bullata'.

× *bumalda* See *S. japonica* 'Bumalda'. '**Anthony Waterer**' See *S. japonica* 'Anthony Waterer'. '**Coccinea**' See *S. japonica* 'Coccinea'. '**Froebelii**' See *S. japonica* 'Froebelii'. '**Goldflame**' See *S. japonica* 'Goldflame'.

calcicola W.W. Sm. A small, graceful shrub with angular, glabrous stems. Leaves very small, fan-shaped, prettily 3-lobed and toothed, borne on slender petioles. Flowers white, tinted rose without, produced in numerous, small umbels along the arching stems in June. China. I 1915.

canescens D. Don. A graceful, medium-sized shrub with long, angular, downy branches. Leaves oval or obovate, 1–2.5cm long, toothed at apex, grey-downy beneath. Flowers in corymbs, white, wreathing the arching stems in June and July. Himalaya. I 1837. **'Myrtifolia'** Leaves oblong, dark green above, glaucescent beneath.

cantoniensis Lour. (*S. reevesiana* Lindl.) A widespreading, graceful shrub, up to 1.8m high, with slender, arching, glabrous branches. Leaves rhomboidal, deeply toothed or 3-lobed, glaucous beneath. Flowers white, in rounded clusters along the branches in June. China, long cultivated in Japan. I 1824. **'Flore Pleno'** ('Lanceata') An attractive form with lanceolate leaves and double flowers.

chamaedryfolia L. A suckering shrub producing erect, angular, glabrous shoots up to 1.8m high. Leaves ovate to ovate-lanceolate, coarsely toothed, glaucescent beneath. Flowers white, borne in corymbs along the stems in May. Widely distributed in the wild from C and E Europe to Siberia. C 1789. **var. ulmifolia** (Scop.) Maxim. A more robust form with taller stems and ovate, double-toothed leaves. Flowers in large, fluffy heads in late May or June.

× *cinerea* Zabel (*S. cana* × *S. hypericifolia*) A small, densely branched shrub with downy, arching stems and narrow, entire leaves, grey-downy when young. The small, white flowers are abundantly produced in dense clusters all along the branches in late April and early May; resembles *S.* 'Arguta' in general effect. **'Grefsheim'** A fine, flowering clone of Norwegian origin. ♀ 2002.

crispifolia See *S. japonica* 'Bullata'.

decumbens Koch. A dwarf, compact, alpine shrub with procumbent, glabrous stems and ascending branches, up to 20cm high. Leaves narrow, elliptic, toothed at apex. Flowers white in small, terminal corymbs, from June to September. A choice little shrub for a rock garden or scree. SE European Alps. **subsp. tomentosa** (Poech) Dostál (*S. hacquetii* Fenzl & K. Koch, *S. lancifolia* Hoffmanns.) Stems greyish-pubescent, leaves grey-tomentose beneath. I 1885.

densiflora Nutt. A small shrub with dark red branches and oval or oblong, sharply toothed leaves. Flowers rose-pink, in dense corymbs in June. W USA. C 1861. **var. splendens** (Baumann) Abrams (*S. splendens* Baumann) Differs from the typical form in its downy shoots. C 1875.

discolor See *Holodiscus discolor*.

‡*douglasii* Hook. A rampant, suckering shrub, forming in time dense thickets of erect, reddish shoots 1.5–1.8m high. Leaves narrowly oblong, coarsely toothed, grey-felted beneath. Flowers purplish-rose, produced in dense, terminal panicles in June and July. Not recommended for shallow chalk soils. W North America. Discovered and introduced by David Douglas in 1827. Naturalised in parts of N and C Europe. **subsp. menziesii** (Hook.) Calder & Roy L. Taylor (*S. menziesii* Hook.) A small to medium-sized, vigorous shrub of suckering habit with erect, brown stems and lanceolate to oval, coarsely toothed leaves. Flowers bright purplish-rose, borne in dense, terminal, pyramidal panicles in July and August. W North America. I 1838.

fritschiana C.K. Schneid. A small, mound-forming shrub with glabrous, yellowish or orange-brown young shoots.

Leaves ovate, glabrous, blue-green on both sides. Flowers white, tinged-pink, in broad, dense, terminal corymbs in June. I to our nurseries from Korea in 1976 by Carl Miller and Sir Harold Hillier. E China, Korea.

gemmata Zabel. An elegant shrub of medium size with glabrous, angular stems and characteristic, long, slender leaf buds. Leaves are narrowly oblong, entire or 3-toothed at apex, glabrous. Flowers white, borne in small corymbs along the arching branches in May. Mongolia. C 1886.

hacquetii See *S. decumbens* subsp. *tomentosa*.

henryi Hemsl. A strong-growing, medium-sized to large shrub of arching habit with reddish-brown, sparsely hairy stems. Leaves 4–8cm long, narrowly oblong or oblance-olate, coarsely toothed at apex. Flowers white, produced in rounded corymbs all along the arching branches in June. C China. Discovered by Augustine Henry, introduced by Ernest Wilson in 1900. AM 1934.

hypericifolia L. A dense, bushy shrub producing graceful, arching branches up to 1.5–1.8m high. Leaves obovate, entire or 3-toothed at apex. Flowers white, produced in small clusters along the branches during May. The form in general cultivation is subsp. *obovata* (Waldst. & Kit.) H. Huber. SE Europe. Naturalised in parts of North America. C 1640.

japonica L. f. (*S. callosa* Thunb.) A small, erect shrub with lanceolate to ovate, coarsely toothed leaves. Flowers pink, borne in large, flattened heads, midsummer onwards A variable species, very popular in gardens. Japan, Korea, China to the Himalayas. Naturalised in parts of C Europe. C 1870. **'Alba'** See 'Albiflora'. **'Albiflora'** ('Alba') (*S. albiflora* (Miq.) Zabel) A dwarf, front-row shrub of compact habit. Flowers white, in dense, terminal corymbs. I before 1864. **'Alpina'** See 'Nana'. **'Anthony Waterer'** (*S.* × *bumalda* 'Anthony Waterer') Flowers bright crimson. An excellent, dwarf shrub for the front of borders or for mass effect. The foliage is occasionally variegated cream and pink. C 1875. FCC 1893. **'Atrosanguinea'** Young growths red; flowers crimson. A selection of var. *fortunei*. C 1893. **'Bullata'** (*S. crispifolia* hort., *S. bullata* Maxim.) A dwarf, slow-growing shrub of compact habit. Leaves small, broadly ovate, bullate above. Flowers rose-crimson, in terminal, flat-topped clusters in summer. A splendid companion for 'Nana'. Garden origin in Japan. C before 1881. FCC 1884. **'Bumalda'** (*S.* × *bumalda* Burv.) A dwarf shrub with glabrous stems and sharply toothed, ovate-lanceolate leaves. Flowers deep pink, in broad, flattened, terminal panicles on the current year's shoots, continuously throughout summer. The leaves are often variegated with pink and cream. C before 1890. **'Candlelight'** A dwarf, compact, bushy shrub with buttery-yellow young leaves that gradually turn deeper and make a good foil for the pink flowers. It has good autumn leaf colour and is free from reversion. It was found as a seedling by Peter Catt. C 1990. ♀ 2002. **'Coccinea'** (*S.* × *bumalda* 'Coccinea') Flowers rich crimson. Originated in Japan. C 1950. **'Crispa'** Leaves dark glossy green, reddish-purple when young, deeply and sharply toothed. A sport of 'Anthony Waterer' often grown as var. *fortunei*. **'Dart's Red'** Similar to 'Anthony Waterer' in flower, with green foliage. C 1970. ♀ 2002. **'Fastigiata'** A vigorous, small shrub of stiff, erect habit. Flowers white in exceptionally wide, flat heads. **'Fire Light'** A dwarf shrub with arching branches and rich orange-red young leaves, deeper in colour than 'Goldflame', of which it is a seedling. The leaves turn orange-yellow, pale green, and a stunning, fiery red in autumn. Flowers deep rose-pink. Free from reversion. **var. *fortunei*** Rehder. The common Chinese form, differing chiefly in its much larger, glabrous, incisely toothed leaves. E and C China. I about 1850. **'Froebelii'** (*S.* × *bumalda* 'Froebelii') Flowers bright crimson in July. C 1894. **'Genpei'** An unusual, dwarf form producing a mixture of deep pink and white flowers on the same and different heads. Usually grown incorrectly as 'Shirobana' or 'Shibori'. I from Japan in 1970. **'Gold Mound'** ('Nana' × 'Goldflame') A dwarf shrub of compact habit with yellow foliage. Bears small heads of pale pink flowers. Subject to mildew. Raised in Canada before 1984. **'Golden Dome'** A compact, dome-shaped, dwarf shrub, the foliage golden-yellow in spring and early summer. **Golden Princess** ('Lisp') PBR A dwarf shrub with bronze-red young foliage becoming bright yellow and turning red in autumn. Flowers deep pink. Found as a seedling by Peter Catt before 1985 and possibly 'Goldflame' × 'Little Princess'. ♀ 2002. **'Goldflame'** (*S.* × *bumalda* 'Goldflame') A very popular, dwarf shrub, a sport of 'Anthony Waterer'. Young leaves in spring emerging reddish-orange becoming bright yellow and eventually green. Flowers deep rose-red. It can produce green, reverting shoots. **'Little Princess'** A compact form making a low mound with rose-crimson flowers. C 1964. **'Macrophylla'** An old French selection, not the best form in flower, but perhaps the best *Spiraea* for autumn leaf colour. Leaves large and bullate, reddish-purple when young. A selection of var. *fortunei*. C 1866. **Magic Carpet** ('Walbuma') PBR A compact, dwarf shrub of spreading habit with bright red young foliage early in spring, later golden-yellow. Flowers bright pink in heads to 6cm across. A third generation seedling of 'Goldflame' raised at Walberton Nursery. It is of dwarfer habit with smaller leaves, comes into growth and flowers earlier than its parent and does not revert. ♀ 2002. **'Nana'** ('Alpina', 'Nyewoods') A superb, dwarf shrub forming a dense, compact mound, 45–60cm high and rather more across, with proportionately smaller leaves and flowerheads. Spectacular when closely studded with tiny heads of rose-pink flowers. Worthy of a position in every garden and windowbox, and should be mass-planted where space permits. Originated in Japan. C 1879. ♀ 2002. **'Ruberrima'** A dense, rounded shrub with rose-red flowers. A selection of var. *fortunei*. C 1893. **'Shirobana'** See 'Genpei'. **'White Gold'** PBR A form raised by Peter Catt, the golden young foliage becoming green then gold again in autumn. Flowers white.

laevigata See *Sibiraea laevigata*.
lancifolia See *S. decumbens* subsp. *tomentosa*.
latifolia See *S. alba* var. *latifolia*.
lindleyana See *Sorbaria tomentosa*.
'Margaritae' (*S.* × *margaritae* Zabel) (*S. japonica* × *S.* 'Superba') A small shrub with erect, downy, reddish shoots and narrowly oval or oblong, coarsely toothed

leaves. Flowers bright rose-pink, in large, flattened heads from July onwards. Foliage brightly tinted in autumn. C before 1890.

media F. Schmidt (*S. confusa* Regel & Körn.) A small shrub of compact habit, with erect, rounded, glabrous stems and ovate to oblong leaves, toothed at the apex or entire. Flowers white, in long racemes in late April and May. Widely distributed from E Europe to Siberia and Japan. I 1789. **f. *glabrescens*** (Simonk.) Zabel. Differing only in its glabrous or sparsely hairy nature.

menziesii See *S. douglasii* subsp. *menziesii*. **'Triumphans'** See *S.* × *billiardii* 'Triumphans'.

micrantha Hook. f. A small to medium-sized shrub related to *S. amoena*. Leaves ovate-lanceolate, 7.5–15cm long, acuminate and toothed. Flowers pale pink, borne in loose, leafy corymbs in June. E Himalaya. I 1924.

mollifolia Rehder. A pretty, grey-leaved shrub with strongly angled, purplish shoots 1.2–1.8m high. Leaves oval or obovate, silky-hairy. Flowers creamy-white, in small corymbs along the arching branches in June and July. W China. I 1909.

nipponica Maxim. (*S. bracteata* Zabel) Among the best June-flowering shrubs. A strong-growing, glabrous, medium-sized shrub of dense, bushy habit. Stems long and arching. Leaves oval or broadly obovate or rounded, toothed at apex. Flowers white, borne in clusters which crowd the upper sides of the branches in June. Each tiny flower is subtended by a small, green bract. A bush in full flower is a lovely sight. Japan. I about 1885 by Siebold. **'Halward's Silver'** Compact with upright, not arching shoots, and profuse, white flowers. **'Rotundifolia'** One of the best June-flowering shrubs, and excellent on chalky soils. Strong-growing with broader, almost orbicular leaves and slightly larger flowers than the type. This is the form most frequently seen in older British gardens. I 1830. AM 1955. **'Snowmound'** (*S. nipponica* var. *tosaensis* hort. not (Yatabe) Makino) A small shrub of dense, mound-like habit. Leaves oblong to oblanceolate, entire or crenate at apex. Flowers smaller than those of the type, but just as freely produced, smothering the branches in June. Japan. ♀ 2002. AM 1982. **var. *tosaensis*** See 'Snowmound'.

× ***nobleana*** See *S.* × *sanssouciana* 'Nobleana'.

× ***oxyodon*** Zabel (*S. chamaedryfolia* × *S. media*) A small, suckering shrub developing large patches of erect stems. Leaves small, obovate, toothed at apex, thickly crowding the branches. Flowers white, in small umbels along the stems during summer. C before 1884.

pectinata See *Luetkia pectinata*.

prunifolia Siebold & Zucc. (*S. prunifolia* f. *simpliciflora* Nakai) The single-flowered form of this species is of little horticultural merit. It was not discovered until after the double-flowered form had been introduced. China. **'Plena'** A dense shrub with arching branches up to 1.8m high. Leaves ovate, finely toothed, turning orange or red in autumn. Flowers white, double, borne in tight, button-like, stalkless clusters along the branches in April and May. I about 1845 from Japan by Siebold. AM 1980.

× ***pseudosalicifolia*** Silverside (*S. douglasii* × *S. salicifolia*) A vigorous, thicket-forming shrub with ovate leaves toothed except in the basal one-third. Cylindrical clusters of pink flowers are borne in summer. It has been confused with *S. salicifolia* and *S.* × *billiardii*, and plants grown under these names may belong here. Naturalised in the British Isles.

reevesiana See *S. cantoniensis*.

salicifolia L. Bridewort. A vigorous, suckering shrub eventually producing dense thickets of erect stems. Leaves lanceolate to elliptic, sharply toothed, green and glabrous on both surfaces. Flowers pink, in dense, cylindrical, downy panicles in June and July. A good plant for stabilising poor soils subject to erosion but not satisfactory on shallow chalk soils. C and EC Europe, NE Asia, Japan. C 1586. **var. *latifolia*** See *S. alba* var. *latifolia*.

× *sanssouciana* K. Koch (*S. douglasii* × *S. japonica*) This hybrid is grown mainly in the following form.

  'Nobleana' (*S.* × *nobleana* Hook.) A small shrub with erect, brown, grey-felted stems and oblong to narrowly oval, coarsely toothed leaves, grey-downy beneath. Flowers bright rose, borne in broad, flattened heads in July. Not recommended for shallow chalk soils. Garden origin before 1857.

sargentiana Rehder. A graceful, medium-sized shrub with arching shoots and 2.5cm-long, narrowly oval to narrowly obovate leaves, toothed near the apex. Flowers creamy-white, in dense corymbs all along the branches in June. W China. I 1908 by Ernest Wilson. AM 1913.

× *semperflorens* Zabel (*S. japonica* × *S. salicifolia*) This hybrid is represented in gardens by the following form in which the *S. japonica* parent was 'Albiflora'. **'Syringiflora'** (*S.* × *syringiflora* Lemoine) A small shrub of spreading habit with lanceolate leaves and terminal, corymbose panicles of rose-pink flowers. Garden origin before 1885.

'Snowmound' See *S. nipponica* 'Snowmound'.

sorbifolia See *Sorbaria sorbifolia*.

splendens See *S. densiflora* var. *splendens*.

× *syringiflora* See *S.* × *semperflorens* 'Syringiflora'.

thunbergii Siebold ex Blume. A popular, small to medium-sized, spreading shrub of dense, twiggy habit with slender, angular, downy stems and narrow, glabrous, sharply toothed leaves, 2.5–3cm long. Flowers white, in numerous clusters along the branches during March and April. Generally the earliest of the spiraeas in bloom, the pure white flowers often smothering the wiry stems. Native of China, but widely cultivated and naturalised in Japan, from which country it was first introduced about 1863. ♀ 2002. **'Mount Fuji'** Leaves edged pink when young, later creamy-white. Tends to revert badly.

tomentosa L. Hardhack, Steeplebush. A small, vigorous, suckering shrub, eventually forming a dense thicket of erect, brownish stems clothed with brownish felt when young. Leaves ovate, coarsely toothed, yellowish-grey-felted beneath. Flowers purplish-rose, in dense, terminal panicles during late summer. E USA. I 1736.

trichocarpa Nakai. A vigorous, graceful shrub with glabrous, angular shoots up to 1.8m high. Leaves apple-green, oblong or oblanceolate, entire or toothed at apex. Flowers white, in rounded corymbs along the arching branches in June. Korea. I 1917 by Ernest Wilson. AM 1942.

trilobata L. A small shrub of dense, compact habit. Leaves up to 2.5cm long, rounded in outline and coarsely toothed, occasionally shallowly 3- to 5-lobed. Flowers

white, in crowded umbels on the previous year's shoots in June. N Asia. I 1801.

× *vanhouttei* (Briot) Zabel (*S. cantoniensis* × *S. trilobata*) A vigorous, semi-evergreen shrub with gracefully arching branches up to 1.8m high. Leaves obovate to rhomboidal, coarsely toothed, sometimes 3- to 5-lobed. Flowers white, in dense umbels along the branches in June. Excellent for early forcing. Garden origin before 1866. AM 1984. **'Pink Ice'** A small shrub with the foliage conspicuously flecked with creamy-white. Often produces reverted shoots.

veitchii Hemsl. A strong-growing shrub, up to 3m high, with long, arching, reddish branches. Leaves oval to oblong, 2.5–5cm long, entire. Flowers white, in dense corymbs all along the branches in June and July. A superb species well worth a place in the garden, where space permits. C and W China. I 1900 by Ernest Wilson. AM 1909.

× *watsoniana* Zabel (*S. densiflora* var. *splendens* × *S. douglasii*) An attractive shrub with erect, downy shoots to 1.5–1.8m high. Leaves elliptic to oblong, toothed towards the apex, grey-downy beneath. Flowers rose, in dense, terminal panicles in June and July. Has occurred both in cultivation and with the parents in the wild (Oregon).

wilsonii Duthie. A medium-sized shrub with long, arching shoots. Leaves oval to obovate, 2.5–5cm long, entire or toothed near apex. Flowers white, in dense corymbs, crowding the branches in June. Closely related to *S. veitchii*, but never as large and with glabrous corymbs and leaves downy above. C and W China. I 1900.

yunnanensis Franch. An elegant shrub up to 1.8m high, with orbicular-ovate to obovate leaves which are double-toothed or shallowly lobed, white- or grey-tomentose beneath. Flowers white, borne in small, densely pubescent umbels in May or June. W China. C 1923.

Spurge, Alleghany See *Pachysandra procumbens*.
Spurge, wood See *Euphorbia amygdaloides*.

STACHYURUS Siebold & Zucc.—**Stachyuraceae**—The sole representative of its family, embracing 5 or 6 species, natives of E Asia, only 2 of which are hardy throughout the British Isles. The stiffly pendent inflorescences are formed in the leaf axils before the leaves fall in autumn, but the flowers do not open until the early spring. The individual flowers are normally hermaphrodite, but there are in cultivation clones possessing unisexual flowers. *Stachyurus* will grow in all fertile soils and in sun or semi-shade.

chinensis Franch. A medium-sized to large shrub of spreading habit, with purplish branchlets. Leaves ovate-oblong to elliptic-oblong or oblong-lanceolate, narrowing into a long taper point, dull green and slightly bullate above, shining pale green beneath. Racemes drooping, 10–13cm long, composed of 30–35 soft yellow, cup-shaped flowers, at Winchester generally opening two weeks later than *S. praecox*. A rare species of considerable merit. I from China by Ernest Wilson in 1908. AM 1925. **'Magpie'** See *S. praecox* 'Magpie'.

†*himalaicus* Hook. f. & Thoms. ex Benth. A strong-growing shrub producing long, yellowish-brown shoots up to 3m high or more. Leaves oblong-lanceolate, slightly bullate above, 13–23cm long, with a long taper point and

reddish petiole and midrib. Racemes 4–5cm long, flowers cup-shaped, wine-purple to rose-pink, opening in early April. A rare and unusual species of extremely vigorous habit, worthy of a wall in all but the mildest areas. E Himalaya, N Burma, W and C China.

japonicus See *S. praecox*.

lancifolius See *S. praecox* var. *matsuzakii*.

praecox Siebold & Zucc. (*S. japonicus* Steud.) A medium-sized to large shrub with reddish-brown branchlets. Leaves ovate-oblong to elliptic or broad-elliptic, shortly taper-pointed, larger and broader than those of *S. chinensis*. Racemes stiffly drooping, 4–7cm long, composed of 15–24 cup-shaped, pale yellow flowers, opening in March or earlier in mild weather. Differing from *S. chinensis* in its stouter growths, larger leaves and usually shorter racemes. Japan. I 1864. ♀ 2002. FCC 1976. AM 1925. **'Gracilis'** A form with female flowers, otherwise differing little. **'Magpie'** (*S. chinensis* 'Magpie') Leaves grey-green above with an irregular, creamy-white margin, splashed pale green and tinged rose. Tends to produce shoots of all-white foliage. Originated in our nurseries about 1945. †**var. *matsuzakii*** (Nakai) Makino (*S. lancifolius* Koidz.) Differs in its stouter, pale green, glaucescent stems and its long-stalked, larger and longer leaves. Flowers yellow, opening in early April. A tender shrub usually cut back to ground level each year by frost and, therefore, only suitable for the mildest areas. Coastal areas of Japan. **'Rubriflorus'** A selection with pink-tinged flowers from red buds is grown under this name.

salicifolius Franch. A graceful, medium-sized, spreading shrub with arching shoots and bronze young foliage. Narrowly linear, willow-like, finely toothed and short-stalked leaves are up to 20cm long and 1.5cm across, tapering to a long, slender point. Flowers pale yellow, in pendent racemes. An excellent foliage plant but inferior to *S. praecox* in flower. China. I by Mikinori Ogisu from Sichuan in the 1990s.

Stagger bush See *Lyonia mariana*.

STAPHYLEA L.—**Staphyleaceae**—The Bladder nuts are a small genus of 11 species of mainly hardy, flowering shrubs, natives of temperate regions of the N hemisphere, whose seeds are enclosed in curious, inflated, 2- or 3-celled, bladder-like capsules. Easily grown in any fertile soil, in sun or semi-shade.

bumalda DC. A spreading shrub with glabrous, greyish-brown branches, usually less than 1.8m high. Leaves trifoliolate. Flowers white, borne in short, racemose panicles in May and June. Foliage usually giving attractive, red tints in autumn. Japan, Korea, China, Manchuria. I 1812.

colchica Stev. A strong-growing shrub with erect branches, 2.5–3.6m high. Leaves composed of 3–5 ovate-oblong leaflets, shining green beneath. Flowers white, in conspicuous, erect panicles up to 13cm long, in May. Capsules up to 10cm long. S Caucasus. I 1850. FCC 1879. **'Coulombieri'** See *S. × coulombieri*. **'Hessei'** (*S. × elegans* 'Hessei') An attractive form with red-purple-flushed flowers. AM 1927. **var. *kochiana*** Medw. A minor form distinguished by its hairy filaments.

× *coulombieri* André (*S. × elegans* Zabel) (*S. colchica × S. pinnata*) A vigorous, large shrub, intermediate between the parents. Leaves with 3–5 leaflets. Panicles compact, more or less erect. Fruits smaller than in *S. colchica*. C 1872. AM 1927.

× *elegans* See *S. × coulombieri*. **'Hessei'** See *S. colchica* 'Hessei'.

holocarpa Hemsl. A beautiful, large shrub or small, spreading tree. Leaves trifoliolate with oblong-lanceolate leaflets. Flowers white, rose in bud, produced in short, dense, drooping panicles in April and May. Discovered by Augustine Henry in C China; introduced by Ernest Wilson in 1908. AM 1924. **'Rosea'** A lovely, spring-flowering shrub or small tree, its spreading branches strung with drooping clusters of soft pink flowers. Young leaves bronze. C 1908. AM 1953.

pinnata L. A large shrub of vigorous, erect habit. Leaves pinnate, composed of usually 5, sometimes 7 or 3 leaflets, pale dull green beneath. Flowers white, borne in long, narrow, drooping panicles in May and June. C Europe. First recorded in cultivation in 1596.

trifolia L. A large shrub with glabrous shoots and trifoliolate leaves. Leaflets broadly ovate, acuminate, finely toothed, more or less glabrous above, downy beneath. Flowers creamy-white in short, drooping panicles in May, followed by 3-celled fruits. E USA. C 1640.

Steeplebush See *Spiraea tomentosa*.

STEPHANANDRA Siebold & Zucc.—**Rosaceae**—A small genus of 4 species of shrubs allied to *Spiraea* and natives of E Asia. Though of subtle beauty in flower, their graceful habit and attractive foliage qualifies them for a place in the garden. They are happy in most soils, in sun or semi-shade. The leaves often give rich tints in autumn. Untidy specimens may be hard-pruned in March.

incisa (Thunb.) Zabel (*S. flexuosa* Siebold & Zucc.) A small to medium-sized shrub of dense habit, with slender, warm brown, zigzag stems. Leaves 2.5–7.5cm long, ovate, incisely toothed and lobed. Flowers greenish-white in crowded panicles in June. Japan, Korea. I 1872. **'Crispa'** A dwarf shrub with small, crinkled leaves forming dense, low mounds. Excellent as groundcover especially in full exposure.

tanakae (Franch. & Sav.) Franch. & Sav. A medium-sized shrub producing long, arching, rich brown stems. Leaves broadly ovate or triangular, 7.5–13cm long, 3- to 5-lobed and incisely toothed. An elegant shrub with stouter growths and larger leaves than *S. incisa*, the flowers also are a little larger though not showy. Japan. I 1893.

Sterculia platanifolia See *Firmiana simplex*.

STEWARTIA L.—**Theaceae**—(*Stuartia*) A small but valuable genus of ornamental shrubs and trees allied to *Camellia*, requiring a semi-shaded position and a moist, loamy, lime-free soil, revelling in woodland conditions. All have white or cream flowers which, although soon falling, are produced in continuous succession over several weeks in July and August. Rich autumn colour is another attribute, while the beautiful trunks and flaking bark of the older trees is no less attractive. They resent disturbance and, once planted, are best left alone. Like *Eucryphia*, *Oxydendrum* and *Cornus nuttallii*, they enjoy having their roots shaded from hot sun.

gemmata See *S. sinensis*.

koreana See *S. pseudocamellia* var. *koreana*.

malacodendron L. A large shrub or occasionally a small tree, with ovate to obovate leaves, hairy beneath. Flowers solitary in the leaf axils, 6–8.5cm across, white, with purple stamens and bluish anthers in July and August. A beautiful shrub. SE USA. C 1742. ♀ 2002. FCC 1934.

monadelpha Siebold & Zucc. A large shrub or small tree with ovate to ovate-lanceolate, acuminate leaves which yield attractive autumn tints. Solitary flowers are produced in the leaf axils. They are 2.5–4cm across, white with spreading petals, the stamens with violet anthers. Japan, Cheju Do, Korea (Quelpart Island). C 1903.

ovata (Cav.) Weatherby (*S. pentagyna* L'Hér.) A large, bushy shrub with ovate to elliptic, acuminate leaves. Flowers solitary in the leaf axils, 6–7.5cm across, cup-shaped, with conspicuous, orange anthers. SE USA. I before 1785.

pseudocamellia Maxim. (*S. grandiflora* Carrière) Small to medium-sized tree with attractive, flaking bark and glabrous shoots. Leaves ovate to obovate, shortly acuminate. Flowers white, solitary in the leaf axils, 5–6cm across, cup-shaped, anthers bright yellow. The leaves turn to yellow and red in autumn. A free-growing tree of open habit, one of the best for general planting. Japan. C before 1878. ♀ 2002. FCC 1888. **Koreana Group** (*S. koreana* Rehder, *S. pseudocamellia* var. *koreana* (Rehder) Sealy) This is a splendid form giving exceptionally bright autumn colour. Flowers similar but opening wider, the petals spreading. The bark on the trunk and main branches flakes, giving the effect of beautifully marked snakeskin. Korea. I 1917 by Ernest Wilson. ♀ 2002.

†**pteropetiolata* Cheng (*Hartia sinensis* Dunn) A very interesting, large, semi-evergreen woodland shrub. Leaves dark glossy green, glandular serrate. Stems softly bristly. Flowers white, 3–4cm across, resembling those of *Camellia sinensis*. Only suitable for the mildest localities. Yunnan. I 1912 by George Forrest.

serrata Maxim. A small tree with attractive, warm brown stems and ovate-elliptic or elliptic, acuminate leaves, rather leathery in texture. Flowers solitary in the leaf axils, 5–6cm across, cup-shaped, white, stained red on the outside at base, anthers yellow, opening in June, earlier than other species. Rich autumn tints. Japan. C before 1915. AM 1932.

sinensis Rehder & E.H. Wilson (*S. gemmata* Chien & Cheng) A large shrub or small tree with attractive, flaking bark. Leaves elliptic to elliptic-oblong, acuminate. Flowers solitary in the leaf axils, 4–5cm across, cup-shaped, fragrant. Crimson autumn colour. C China. I 1901 by Ernest Wilson. ♀ 2002.

Stranvaesia See *Photinia*.

× *Stranvinia* See *Photinia*.

Strawberry bush See *Euonymus americanus*.

Strawberry tree, Grecian See *Arbutus andrachne*.

Strawberry tree, Killarney See *Arbutus unedo*.

Stuartia See *Stewartia*.

‡**STYRAX** L.—**Styracaceae**—A genus of some 120 species of trees and shrubs widely distributed in temperate and tropical regions of the N hemisphere. The cultivated species are very distinguished and beautiful trees and shrubs, thriving in a moist, loamy, lime-free soil, in sun or semi-shade. The name snowbell has been given to them in America, an allusion to their pure white, pendent flowers which appear in late spring and summer.

americanus Lam. A medium-sized shrub with ascending branches and narrowly oval or obovate, minutely toothed leaves. The slender-stalked, narrow-petalled, bell-shaped flowers hang from the branchlets in June and July. Not one of the easiest species to grow. SE USA. I 1765.

calvescens Perkins. A rare, small tree or large shrub with minutely and stellately-hairy shoots. Leaves elliptic, acuminate, serrate, lustrous green on both surfaces, rather thin in texture. Flowers borne in short racemes in June or July. China.

†*dasyanthus* Perkins. A large shrub or small tree. Leaves obovate to broad-elliptic, minutely toothed in the upper half. Flowers pendent, in slender, terminal racemes in July. Not the hardiest species and best grown against a wall except in the mildest areas. C China. First discovered by Augustine Henry. I 1900 by Ernest Wilson. **var. cinerascens** Rehder. Leaves grey- or white-downy beneath. We originally distributed this plant as *S. philadelphoides* or *S. serrulata*.

hemsleyanus Diels. An attractive, small, open-branched tree. Leaves broad, elliptic or almost orbicular, oblique at base, 10–13cm long. Flowers white, with a central cone of yellow anthers, borne in long, lax, downy racemes in June. A lovely species, similar in some respects to *S. obassia*, but differing in its less downy leaves and exposed, chocolate-brown leaf buds. C and W China. I 1900 by Ernest Wilson. ♀ 2002. FCC 1942. AM 1930.

japonicus Siebold & Zucc. A very beautiful, large shrub or small tree, with widespreading, fan-like branches, often drooping at the slender tips. Leaves ovate to narrowly oblong, acuminate. Flowers bell-shaped, white, with yellow staminal beak, coating the undersides of the branches in June. The commonest species in cultivation and deservedly the most popular, combining daintiness and elegance with a hardy constitution. Best planted where the flowers can be admired from beneath. Japan, Korea. I 1862 by Richard Oldham. ♀ 2002. FCC 1885. **Benibana Group** Flowers pink. ♀ 2002. **'Fargesii'** This is more tree-like with slightly larger leaves. I 1924. FCC 1971. AM 1945. **'Pink Chimes'** (Benibana Group) A very floriferous form with pale pink flowers deeper at the base. Branches pendent on young plants. Raised in Japan before 1976.

obassia Siebold & Zucc. A beautiful, large shrub or small, round-headed tree with handsome, large, broadly ovate to orbicular leaves, 10–20cm long and clothed beneath with a soft, velvety tomentum. The petioles are enlarged at the base enclosing the leaf buds. Bark of second-year shoots is chestnut and exfoliating. Flowers fragrant, bell-shaped, 2.5cm long, in long, lax, terminal racemes in June. Japan. I 1879 by Charles Maries. ♀ 2002. FCC 1888.

officinalis L. A medium-sized to large shrub bearing ovate leaves 7–9cm long. The short, drooping clusters of comparatively large, fragrant flowers are borne at the tips of the shoots in June. It requires a warm, sheltered position. The gum-like sap is used as incense and the seeds for rosaries. Mediterranean region. AM 1984.

serrulatus See under *S. dasyantha* var. *cinerascens*.

shiraianus Makino. A large shrub or small tree with stellately-hairy young shoots. Leaves obovate to orbicular, coarsely toothed or lobed in upper half, downy beneath. Petioles swollen at base, enclosing the leaf buds. Flowers funnel-shaped, in short, densely hairy racemes in June. Japan. I 1915.

veitchiorum Hemsl. & E.H. Wilson. A very rare, large, spreading shrub or a small tree with greyish, hairy young shoots. Leaves downy, lanceolate, taper-pointed, 7.5–13cm long. Flowers pendent, borne in slender panicles up to 20cm long in June. China. I 1900.

wilsonii Rehder. A beautiful, medium-sized shrub of dense, twiggy habit. Leaves tiny, ovate, 1–2.5cm long, toothed or occasionally 3-lobed at apex, glaucous and downy beneath. Flowers pendent, solitary or in clusters, opening in June. A pretty shrub, flowering when quite young, but requiring a sheltered position. W China. I 1908. AM 1913.

SUAEDA Forssk. ex Scop.—**Chenopodiaceae**—About 110 species of herbs and subshrubs widely distributed in both hemispheres, the majority of no horticultural merit.

fruticosa See *S. vera*.

*vera Forssk. ex J. Gmel. (*S. fruticosa* auct. not Forssk.) A small, maritime subshrub of dense habit. Leaves narrow, blue-green and fleshy, semi-evergreen. Flowers inconspicuous. The whole plant sometimes turns bronze-purple in autumn. It grows best in a sandy soil in full sun and is most suitable for seaside gardens. Sea coasts of S and W Europe, N Africa to India (including the British Isles).

Sumach, smooth See *Rhus glabra*.
Sumach, stag's horn See *Rhus typhina*.
Sumach, Venetian See *Cotinus coggygria*.
Summer holly See *Arctostaphylos diversifolia*.
Sun rose See *Helianthemum* and *Cistus*.

†**SUTHERLANDIA** R. Br.—**Leguminosae**—A small genus of 5 species of South African shrubs of which one species is occasionally seen in the British Isles.

frutescens R. Br. A medium-sized to large shrub with downy shoots and pinnate leaves composed of 13–21 narrow leaflets. The large, conspicuous, terracotta, pea-flowers are carried in axillary racemes in June. Seedpods inflated as in *Colutea*. Suitable for a warm, sunny wall in the mildest areas. South Africa. C 1683.

Swamp bay or Sweet bay See *Magnolia virginiana*.
Sweet briar See *Rosa eglanteria*.
Sweet chestnut See *Castanea sativa*.
Sweet fern See *Comptonia peregrina*.
Sweet gale See *Myrica gale*.
Sweet gum See *Liquidambar styraciflua*.
Sweet pepper bush See *Clethra alnifolia*.
Sycamore See *Acer pseudoplatanus*.
Sycamore, American See *Platanus occidentalis*.

× **SYCOPARROTIA** Endress & Anliker (*Parrotia* × *Sycopsis*)—**Hamamelidaceae**—An interesting, intergeneric hybrid between 2 outstanding plants. Unfortunately the following has not proved to be an improvement on either of its parents.

semidecidua Endress & Anliker (*P. persica* × *S. sinensis*) A medium-sized to large, semi-evergreen, open, spreading shrub with the habit of *Parrotia* and foliage resembling *Sycopsis*. Leaves ovate, elliptic or obovate, acuminate, toothed above the middle, glossy green but lighter and thinner than *S. sinensis*. Some of the leaves turn yellow and fall in autumn while others remain on the shrub until winter. Flowers resembling *Sycopsis* with dense clusters of yellow anthers tinged orange-red in late winter. Raised in Switzerland in about 1950.

****SYCOPSIS** Oliv.—**Hamamelidaceae**—A small genus of 7 species of evergreen shrubs and trees, natives of Himalaya, China and SE Asia. The following requires the same conditions as *Hamamelis*. Only one species is in general cultivation.

sinensis Oliv. A medium-sized to large, evergreen, monoecious shrub or small tree of dense, upright habit. Leaves elliptic-lanceolate, acuminate, somewhat bullate, leathery and glabrous. Flowers without petals, consisting of small clusters of yellow, red-anthered stamens, enclosed by chocolate-brown, tomentose scales, opening in February and March. C China. I 1901 by Ernest Wilson. AM 1926.

tutcheri See under *Distylium racemosum*.

SYMPHORICARPOS Duhamel—**Caprifoliaceae**—A small genus of about 17 species of deciduous shrubs, natives of North America and Mexico with one species in China. Their flowers are bell-shaped, but small and relatively insignificant. They are mainly grown for their often abundant display of white or rose-coloured berries, which appear in autumn and generally last well into winter, being untouched by birds. Several forms are excellent for hedging and all grow well in shade even among the roots and drip of overhanging trees. They are quite hardy and will grow in all types of soils. Untidy specimens may be hard-pruned in March.

albus (L.) Blake (*S. racemosus* Michx.) Snowberry. A small shrub with slender, erect, downy shoots, forming dense clumps. Leaves oval to ovate-oblong, downy beneath, lobed on sucker shoots. Berries globose or ovoid, 12mm across, white. E North America. I 1879. **var. *laevigatus*** (Fern.) Blake (*S. rivularis* Suksd.) Snowberry. A strong-growing shrub forming dense thickets of erect, glabrous stems up to 1.8m high. Leaves elliptic to elliptic-oblong, 4–7.5cm long, commonly lobed on vigorous, suckering shoots. Berries in great profusion, like large, glistening, white marbles. The common snowberry of English plantations. Ideal for game cover and for poor soils or dark, shaded corners. W North America. I 1817. FCC 1913.

× *chenaultii* Rehder (*S. microphyllus* × *S. orbiculatus*) A dense-growing shrub, 0.6–1m high, resembling *S. microphyllus* in general habit. Berries purplish-red on the exposed side, pinkish-white elsewhere, carried in clusters or spikes. Garden origin in 1910. **'Hancock'** An outstanding form of dwarf, widespreading habit. An excellent groundcover, particularly beneath trees. Raised about 1940.

×*doorenbosii* See *S.* Doorenbos Group.

Doorenbos Group A very useful group of attractive hybrids raised in The Hague by Mr Doorenbos, one of the greatest Dutch horticulturists of the 20th century, and involving *S. albus* var. *laevigatus*, *S.* × *chenaultii* and *S. orbiculatus*. **'Erect'** A vigorous, but compact shrub of erect habit producing trusses of rose-lilac berries. Excellent as a small hedge. **'Magic Berry'** A small shrub of compact, spreading habit, bearing large quantities of rose-pink berries. **'Mother of Pearl'** The first named clone, probably *S. albus* var. *laevigatus* × *S.* × *chenaultii*. A small, dense shrub, the branches weighed down by heavy crops of white, rose-flushed, marble-like berries. AM 1971. **'White Hedge'** A small shrub of strong, upright, compact growth, freely producing small, white berries in erect clusters. An excellent, small, hedging shrub.

occidentalis Hook. Wolfberry. A small shrub of dense, erect habit with rounded leaves and clusters of globular, white berries. North America. C 1880. AM 1910.

orbiculatus Moench (*S. vulgaris* Michx.) Indian currant, Coral berry. A dense, bushy shrub up to 2m high, with thin, downy, densely leafy stems. Leaves oval or ovate, glaucescent beneath. Berries purplish-rose, rounded to ovoid, very small but borne in dense clusters along the stems. E USA. I 1730. **'Foliis Variegatis'** ('Variegatus') Leaves smaller, irregularly yellow-margined. A graceful plant and one of the most pleasing variegated shrubs of medium size but inclined to revert if planted in shade. **'Taff's Silver Edge'** Leaves margined with white. **'Variegatus'** See 'Foliis Variegatis'.

rivularis See *S. albus* var. *laevigatus*.

vulgaris See *S. orbiculatus*.

SYMPLOCOS Jacq.—**Symplocaceae**—A large genus of some 250 species of evergreen and deciduous trees and shrubs, widely distributed in tropical and subtropical regions excluding Africa. Only one is generally hardy in the British Isles.

‡*paniculata* (Thunb.) Miq. (*S. crataegoides* Buch.-Ham. ex D. Don) A deciduous shrub or occasionally a small tree of dense, twiggy habit. Leaves variable in shape, 1.5–4.5cm long. Flowers small, white, fragrant, in panicles in May and June, followed by brilliant ultra-marine-blue fruits in autumn which persist into winter. It is usually necessary to plant two or more specimens in order to achieve successful fertilisation; fruits are most abundant after a long, hot summer. Himalaya, China, Taiwan, Japan. I 1871. FCC 1954. AM 1947 (fruit). AM 1938 (flower).

SYRINGA L.—**Oleaceae**—The lilacs are a genus of hardy, deciduous, flowering shrubs and small trees, containing about 20 species, distributed from SE Europe to China and Japan and including some of the most elegant and colourful of May- and June-flowering, woody plants. The flowers of many species and hybrids are accompanied by a delicious fragrance, an inseparable part of their magic. The numerous, large-flowered garden lilacs, hybrids and cultivars of *S. vulgaris*, need no introduction and their continued popularity is ensured. The species are perhaps less well known, and their good qualities deserve much wider recognition. Lilacs are happy in most well-drained soils, especially so in those of a chalky nature, and revel in full sun. Unless otherwise stated, it may be assumed that they are strong-growing shrubs of large size, often tree-like, and that they flower in May and June. Pruning consists of removing the old flowering wood immediately after flowering. Summer pinching of extra-strong shoots is often desirable. For mock orange, often wrongly referred to as syringa, see *Philadelphus*.

affinis See *S. oblata* Alba Group.

afghanica hort. See *S. protolaciniata*.

amurensis See *S. reticulata* subsp. *amurensis*. **var. japonica** See *S. reticulata*.

×*chinensis* Willd. (*S.* × *laciniata* × *S. vulgaris*) Rouen lilac. A medium-sized shrub of dense, bushy habit with ovate leaves and large, drooping panicles of fragrant, soft lavender flowers in May. Raised in the Botanic Garden at Rouen about 1777. **'Alba'** Flowers very pale lilac, nearly white. C 1885. **'Metensis'** Flowers a charming shade of pale lilac-pink. C 1871. **'Saugeana'** ('Rubra') Flowers lilac-red. Raised about 1809.

+*correlata* Braun (*S.* × *chinensis* + *S. vulgaris*) This interesting lilac is a periclinal chimaera, composed of an outer layer of *S. vulgaris* (white-flowered form), and an inner core of *S.* × *chinensis*. Its erect panicles of flowers are normally very pale lilac, nearly white, but occasional shoots of typical *S.* × *chinensis* are produced.

×*diversifolia* Rehder (*S. oblata* × *S. pinnatifolia*) A medium-sized to tall shrub with both entire, ovate-oblong leaves and pinnatifid, 3- to 5-lobed leaves. Raised at the Arnold Arboretum, Boston, USA in 1929. **'William H. Judd'** Flowers white, scented; early May.

emodi Wall. ex Royle. Himalayan lilac. A distinct, large shrub of robust habit. Leaves ovate to obovate, 10–20cm long, pale or whitish beneath. Flowers pale lilac in bud fading to white, not very pleasantly scented, borne in erect panicles in June. A noteworthy species claiming a position in every well-stocked shrub garden. W Himalaya. I 1838. **'Aurea'** Leaves suffused soft yellow. Best when grown in semi-shade. **'Aureovariegata'** Leaves yellow with green centre.

'Ethel M. Webster' A medium to large-sized shrub of compact habit. Flowers flesh-pink, borne in broad, loose panicles in May and June. Possibly a *S.* × *henryi* hybrid. C 1948.

formosissima See *S. wolfii*.

×*henryi* C.K. Schneid. (*S. josikaea* × *S. villosa*) A tall, variable hybrid raised by Mons Louis Henry at the Jardin des Plantes, Paris, in 1896. **'Alba'** A graceful shrub more lax in habit than 'Lutèce'. Flowers white. **'Floréal'** See *S.* × *nanceiana* 'Floréal'. **'Lutèce'** A large, erect shrub with leaves resembling the *villosa* parent. Flowers violet, paling as they age, fragrant, in large panicles in June. **'Prairial'** See *S.* 'Prairial'.

×*hyacinthiflora* (Lemoine) Rehder (*S. oblata* × *S. vulgaris*) An attractive, but variable hybrid first raised by Lemoine in 1876. More recently, several clones have been raised by W.B. Clarke of San Jose, California. The flowers appear quite early, usually in late April or early May. **'Alice Eastwood'** Claret-purple in bud, opening cyclamen-purple, double. C 1942 (Clarke). **'Blue Hyacinth'** Mauve to pale blue, single. C 1942 (Clarke). **'Buffon'** Soft pink, petals slightly reflexed, faintly scented; single, late April to early May. C 1921 (Lemoine). AM 1961. **'Clarke's Giant'** Rosy-mauve in bud, opening lilac-blue, large florets and large panicles up to 30cm long, single. C 1948 (Clarke). AM 1958. **'Esther Staley'** Buds red, opening pink, very floriferous, single. C 1948 (Clarke). ♀ 2002. AM 1961. **'Lamartine'** Flowers blue-lilac, in large panicles, single. Young growths flushed bronze. C 1911 (Lemoine). AM 1927. **'Plena'** Victor Lemoine's original hybrid (*S. vulgaris* 'Azurea Plena' × *S. oblata*). Flowers in dense, erect panicles, double, bright purple in bud, opening to a delicate shade of violet. Leaves bronze-tinged when unfolding. **'Purple Heart'** Deep purple flowers, large florets. C 1949 (Clarke).

japonica See *S. reticulata.*

× *josiflexa* I. Preston ex J.S. Pringle (*S. josikaea* × *S. komarovii* subsp. *reflexa*) A very beautiful race of hybrids raised in Ottawa by Miss Isabella Preston. Medium-sized to large shrubs with fine, deep green leaves and, in May or June, loose, plume-like panicles of fragrant, rose-pink flowers. **'Bellicent'** An outstanding clone, the best of this excellent hybrid, with enormous panicles of clear rose-pink flowers. ♀ 2002. FCC 1946.

josikaea Jacq. f. ex Rchb. Hungarian lilac. A large shrub related to *S. villosa.* Leaves ovate to obovate, 5–13cm long, glossy dark green above, paler beneath. Flowers fragrant, deep violet-mauve, borne in erect panicles in June. C and E Europe. I 1830.

julianae See *S. pubescens* subsp. *julianae.*

'Kim' See *S.* × *prestoniae* 'Kim'.

komarowii C.K. Schneid. (*S. sargentiana* C.K. Schneid.) A vigorous, tall shrub, related to *S. reflexa*, with large, deep green, oval or ovate-lanceolate leaves up to 18cm long. Flowers deep rose-pink, in nodding, cylindrical panicles during May and early June. China. I 1908 by Ernest Wilson. **subsp. reflexa** (C.K. Schneid.) P.S. Green & M.C. Chang (*S. reflexa* C.K. Schneid.) A distinct, large shrub of considerable quality, bearing large, oval leaves, up to 20cm long and rough to the touch. Flowers rich purplish-pink outside, whitish within, densely packed in long, narrow, drooping panicles, 15–20cm long, in late May and June. One of the best of the species and very free-flowering. C China. Discovered and introduced by Ernest Wilson in 1904. AM 1914.

× *laciniata* Mill. (*S. protolaciniata* × ? *S. vulgaris*) A graceful, small shrub with prettily dissected, 3- to 9-lobed leaves and small panicles of lilac flowers in May. Not to be confused with the wild *S. protolaciniata*, a species that is rare in cultivation, this shrub probably originated in cultivation in SW Asia. I 17th century from Turkey. AM 1965.

meyeri C.K. Schneid. A dense, compact, rather slow-growing, small-leaved shrub, to about 1.8m high. Leaves oval or obovate, about 4–5cm long. Flowers violet-purple, in short, dense panicles in May, even on young plants. Sometimes a second crop of flowers appears in September. The typical form is known only in cultivation, but a wild variety from N China has been described. I 1908. **'Palibin'** (*S. palibiniana* hort., *S. patula* hort., *S. velutina* hort.) A slow-growing, eventually medium-sized shrub of dense habit. Flowers pale lilac-pink in numerous, elegant panicles even on young plants. A lovely form suitable for a small garden. ♀ 2002. AM 1984.

microphylla See *S. pubescens* subsp. *microphylla.*

× *nanceiana* McKelvey (*S.* × *henryi* × *S. sweginzowii*) A variable hybrid raised by Lemoine in 1925 and mainly grown in the following form. **'Floréal'** (*S.* × *henryi* 'Floréal') A graceful shrub of lax habit, with panicles of fragrant, lavender-mauve flowers in May.

oblata Lindl. (*S. oblata* var. *giraldii* (Lemoine) Rehder) A large shrub or small tree, related to *S. vulgaris*, with broadly heart-shaped or reniform leaves up to 10cm wide and 7.5cm long. Flowers lilac-blue, produced in broad panicles in late April or early May. The unfolding leaves are bronze-tinted. Liable to damage by late spring frost. N China. I 1856 by Robert Fortune from a garden in Shanghai. **Alba Group** (var. *alba* hort. ex Rehder, *S. affinis* L. Henry) A form with smaller leaves and white flowers. **subsp. dilatata** (Nakai) P.S. Green & M.C. Chang. A form of medium height. Leaves ovate-acuminate, bronze when unfolding, richly tinted in autumn. Flowers violet-purple, in loose panicles. Korea. I 1917 by Ernest Wilson. **var. giraldii** See *S. oblata.* **'Nana'** A dwarf form with bluish flowers.

palibiniana hort. See *S. meyeri* 'Palibin'.

palibiniana Nakai. See *S. pubescens* subsp. *patula.*

patula hort. See *S. meyeri* 'Palibin'.

patula (Palibin) Nakai. See *S. pubescens* subsp. *patula.*

pekinensis See *S. reticulata* subsp. *pekinensis.*

× *persica* L. Persian lilac. A charming, slender-branched shrub of rounded, bushy habit, 1.8–2.5m high and as much across. Leaves lanceolate, entire, 2.5–6cm long. Flowers lilac, fragrant, borne in small panicles in May. Said to have been cultivated in England in 1640. It is possibly a backcross between *S.* × *laciniata* and *S. vulgaris.* ♀ 2002. **'Alba'** White flowers. ♀ 2002. **'Laciniata'** See *S.* × *laciniata.*

pinetorum See *S. yunnanensis.*

'Pink Pixie' A seedling of *S. pubescens* subsp. *julianae* 'Hers Variety' raised in 1980 by Max Peterson. In growth and habit it resembles *S. meyeri*, which grew nearby and with which it is probably a hybrid. Flowers closer to the seed parent, dark garnet-red in bud, opening deep pink, fading to pale pink. A beautiful lilac becoming very popular.

pinnatifolia Hemsl. An unusual species reaching about 2.5m. Leaves 4–8cm long, pinnate with 7–11 separate leaflets. Flowers white or lavender-tinted, in small, nodding panicles in May. So unlike a lilac as to create an amusing conundrum for the uninitiated. NC China. I 1904 by Ernest Wilson.

potaninii See *S. pubescens* subsp. *microphylla.*

'Prairial' (*S.* × *henryi* × *S. tomentella*) (*S.* × *henryi* 'Prairial') An elegant shrub producing large panicles of soft lavender flowers in May. Raised by Lemoine about 1933.

× *prestoniae* McKelvey (*S. komarovii* subsp. *reflexa* × *S. villosa*) An extremely hardy race of late-flowering hybrid lilacs, first raised by Miss Isabella Preston at the Central Experimental Farm Division of Horticulture, Ottawa, Canada, in 1920. Usually referred to as Canadian or Preston hybrids, they are vigorous, medium-sized to large shrubs, producing large, erect or pendent flower panicles in late May and June, on shoots of the current year. Red-purple is the dominant colour. **'Audrey'** Flowers deep pink in June. C 1927. AM 1939. **'Elinor'**

Flowers dark purplish-red in bud, opening to pale lavender, borne in rather erect panicles. C 1928. ♀ 2002. AM 1951. **'Hiawatha'** Flowers rich reddish-purple in bud, opening pale pink. C 1934. **'Isabella'** Flowers mallow-purple, borne in rather erect panicles. C 1927. AM 1941. **'Juliet'** Flowers lilac-pink. **'Kim'** (*S.* 'Kim') An elegant, medium-sized shrub with dark green, oblong-lanceolate leaves and large, freely-branching panicles of mallow-purple flowers. C 1934. AM 1958. **'Redwine'** Single, bright magenta. **'Royalty'** Flowers violet-purple. **'Virgilia'** Flowers deep lilac-magenta in bud, opening pale lilac. Compact habit. **'W.T. Macoun'** Lilac-pink flowers in large panicles.

protolaciniata P.S. Green & M.C. Chang (*S. laciniata* hort. not Mill.) A beautiful, small shrub with dark, slender stems and dainty, small, pinnately-cut leaves. Flowers lilac in slender panicles in May. N China. The form in cultivation was probably introduced from a garden in Afghanistan and has been named 'Kabul'.

pubescens Turcz. A vigorous, large shrub or small tree with ovate, nearly glabrous leaves to 5cm long. Fragrant, lilac to white flowers are produced in terminal panicles (opening from lateral buds) to 12cm long in spring as the young leaves emerge. It can be damaged by late frosts. N China. I 1881 and originally confused with *S. villosa*. **subsp. *julianae*** (Schneider) M.C. Chang & X.L. Chen (*S. julianae* C.K. Schneid.) A graceful shrub, 1.8–2.5m high by as much wide. Leaves oval, privet-like, grey-downy beneath. Flowers in slender, upright panicles, fragrant, pale lilac, in May and early June. A choice shrub of free-flowering habit. Ideal for a small garden. C China. I 1900 by Ernest Wilson. AM 1924. **subsp. *microphylla*** (Diels) Chang & Chen (*S. microphylla* Diels, *S. potaninii* C.K. Schneid.) A very pretty, small-leaved shrub, to 2m high. Leaves ovate, usually pointed at apex, 1–5cm long. Flowers rosy-lilac, darker externally, fragrant, borne in small panicles in June and again in September. N and W China. I 1910 by William Purdom. AM 1937. **subsp. *microphylla* 'Superba'** A form of free-flowering habit. Flowers rosy-pink, in May and intermittently until October. ♀ 2002. AM 1957. **subsp. *patula*** (Palib.) M.C. Chang & X.L. Chen (*S. palibiniana* Nakai, *S. patula* (Palib.) Nakai, *S. velutina* Komarov) A medium-sized to large shrub with purple young shoots and panicles of lilac flowers. Korea, N China. **subsp. *patula* 'Miss Kim'** A small to medium-sized shrub with fragrant flowers, purple in bud and on first opening, fading to blue-ice white, in late spring to early summer. Leaves dark green with wavy edges. A selection from wild source seed collected in 1947 as *S. patula* in Korea. ♀ 2002.

reflexa See *S. komarovii* subsp. *reflexa*.

reticulata (Blume) H. Hara (*S. amurensis* var. *japonica* (Maxim.) Franch. & Sav., *S. japonica* Decne.) A robust, large shrub readily trained to a stout, short tree with an attractive trunk. Leaves broad rotund-ovate, reticulate and pubescent beneath. Flowers creamy-white, fragrant, borne in large, dense panicles in late June. Japan. I 1878. FCC 1887. **subsp. *amurensis*** (Rupr.) P.S. Green & M.C. Chang (*S. amurensis* Rupr., *S. reticulata* var. *mandschurica* (Maxim.) Hara) Amur lilac. An elegant shrub with ovate, taper-pointed leaves and large, loose panicles of white

flowers in June. The older bark peels, revealing the dark, chestnut-brown, new bark marked with horizontal lenticels. Subject to injury by late spring frost after growth has commenced. NE China, Siberia, Korea. I 1855. **'Ivory Silk'** A compact form, flowering profusely. Selected in Ontario, Canada in 1973. **var. *mandschurica*** See subsp. *amurensis*. **subsp. *pekinensis*** (Rupr.) P.S. Green & M.C. Chang (*S. pekinensis* Rupr., *Ligustrina pekinensis* (Rupr.) Dieck) A small tree with ovate to ovate-lanceolate, long-tapered leaves. Flowers creamy-white, densely crowded in large panicles in June. N China. Discovered by the Abbé David. I 1881 by Dr Bretschneider. **'Pendula'** A graceful form with drooping branches.

× *swegiflexa* Hesse ex J.S. Pringle (*S. komarovii* subsp. *reflexa* × *S. sweginzowii*) A beautiful, strong-growing, variable hybrid of open habit with large, dense, cylindrical panicles of usually pink flowers, red in bud. Raised by Messrs Hesse of Weener, NW Germany about 1934. AM 1977. **'Fountain'** A medium-sized shrub of compact habit. Flowers pale pink, fragrant, in long, drooping panicles in May and June.

sweginzowii Koehne & Lingelsh. (*S. tigerstedtii* H.L. Sm.) A vigorous, medium-sized shrub of elegant habit. Leaves ovate, acute or acuminate, 5–7.5cm long. Flowers flesh-pink, sweetly fragrant, in long, loose panicles in May and June. W China. I 1894 by G.N. Potanin. AM 1915. **'Superba'** A selected form with larger panicles. AM 1918.

tigerstedtii See *S. sweginzowii*.

tomentella Bur. & Franch. (*S. wilsonii* C.K. Schneid.) A strong-growing, widespreading species up to 3.6–4.5m high. Leaves ovate to elliptic, 5–13cm long, dark green and corrugated above, grey-downy beneath. Flowers sweetly scented, deep lilac-pink, white inside, paling with age, in broad, terminal panicles in late May and June. SW China. I 1904. AM 1928.

velutina hort. See *S. meyeri* 'Palibin'.

velutina Komarov See *S. pubescens* subsp. *patula*.

villosa Vahl (*S. bretschneideri* Lemoine) A medium-sized to large, erect-branched shrub of compact habit. Leaves oval to oblong, 5–15cm long, dull dark green above, glaucous beneath. Flowers lilac-rose, in stiff, compact, erect panicles in late May and early June. N China. I 1882. AM 1931.

vulgaris L. Common lilac. A large, vigorous shrub or small tree of suckering habit. Leaves ovate or heart-shaped. Flowers richly scented, lilac, borne in dense, erect, pyramidal panicles in May. Plants that are raised from seed are variable in flower colour. Mountains of E Europe. A common garden escape readily naturalised. I 16th century.

Cultivars of *Syringa vulgaris*

Probably no other shrub or tree has given rise to so many cultivars, but as with other plants that have become the victims of the specialist, far too many – over 500 – have been selected and named. Their differences are confined almost entirely to the colour of their single or double flowers and it requires a highly cultivated imagination to distinguish the various shades, which alter from hour to hour, making naming very difficult. After transplanting, it takes 2–3 years before full flower and truss size are achieved.

Syringa vulgaris continued:

Those mentioned below are medium to large shrubs or occasionally small trees of strong, erect habit.

The flowers appear in dense, erect, conical panicles in May or early June. They vary from white through creamy-yellow to red, blue or purple, single or double. All are sweetly scented.

The garden lilacs will always be associated with the names of Victor Lemoine and his son Emile, who raised so many lovely cultivars at their nursery at Nancy, France, towards the end of the 19th century and in the early part of the 20th century. The lilac lover also owes a great deal to Alice Harding for her great work and magnificent book on this genus.

Single

'Alba' Flowers white; leaves and winter buds pale green. Long cultivated.

'Ambassadeur' Azure-lilac with a white eye; large, broad panicles. C 1930 (Lemoine).

'Andenken an Ludwig Späth' ('Souvenir de Louis Spaeth') Wine-red. Perhaps the most popular lilac, one of the most consistent and reliable. C 1883 (Späth). ♥ 2002. FCC 1894.

'Arch McKean' Single, deep magenta-purple, very showy. C 1983.

'Aurea' Leaves yellow when young, later yellowish-green.

'Blue Hyacinth' See *S.* × *hyacinthiflora* 'Blue Hyacinth'.

'Buffon' See *S.* × *hyacinthiflora* 'Buffon'.

'Capitaine Baltet' Light carmine-pink, blue-tinged in bud; large panicles. C 1919 (Lemoine).

'Charles X' Purplish-red; long, conical panicles. A very popular lilac. C before 1830 and named after the King of France.

'Clarke's Giant' See *S.* × *hyacinthiflora* 'Clarke's Giant'.

'Congo' Rich lilac-red, paling with age; large, compact panicles. C 1896 (Lemoine).

'Esther Staley' See *S.* × *hyacinthiflora* 'Esther Staley'.

'Etna' Deep claret-purple fading to lilac-pink; late. C 1927 (Lemoine).

'Firmament' Clear lilac-blue; early May. C 1932 (Lemoine). ♥ 2002.

'Glory of Horstenstein' Rich lilac-red, changing to dark lilac. C 1921 (Wilke).

'Hugo Koster' Purple-crimson. C 1913 (Koster). AM 1913.

'Jan van Tol' Pure white; long, drooping panicles. C about 1916 (van Tol). AM 1924.

'Lamartine' See *S.* × *hyacinthiflora* 'Lamartine'.

'Lavaliensis' ('Lavanensis') Pale pink. C 1865 (Leroy).

'Madame Charles Souchet' Soft lilac-blue; large florets and broad panicles; early May. C 1924 (Lemoine).

'Madame Florent Stepman' Creamy-yellow in bud, opening white. C 1908 (Stepman).

'Madame Francisque Morel' Mauve-pink; large florets, enormous panicles. Erect habit. C 1892 (Morel).

'Marceau' Claret-purple; broad panicles. C 1913 (Lemoine).

'Maréchal Foch' Bright carmine-rose; large flowers in broad, open panicles. C 1924 (Lemoine). AM 1935.

'Marie Legraye' White, creamy-yellow in bud; inflorescences rather small. Popular and much used for forcing. C 1879 (Legraye). FCC 1880.

'Masséna' Deep reddish-purple; large florets, broad panicles; late. C 1923 (Lemoine). AM 1928.

'Maud Notcutt' Pure white; large panicles up to 30cm long. C 1956 (Notcutt). AM 1957.

'Mont Blanc' Greenish-white in bud, opening white; long, well-filled panicles. C 1915 (Lemoine).

'Pasteur' Claret-red; long, narrow panicles. C 1903 (Lemoine). AM 1924.

'President Lincoln' Purple in bud, opening light bluish-violet; early May. C about 1916 (Dunbar).

'Primrose' Pale primrose-yellow; small, dense panicles. Originated as a sport in Holland. C 1949 (Maarse). AM 1950.

'Prodige' Deep purple, large florets. C 1928 (Lemoine).

'Purple Heart' See *S.* × *hyacinthiflora* 'Purple Heart'.

'Réaumur' Deep carmine-violet; broad panicles; late. C 1904 (Lemoine). AM 1916.

'Sensation' Purplish-red florets edged white; large panicles. A sport of 'Hugo de Vries'. Inclined to revert and lose its marginal variegation. C 1938 (Maarse).

'Souvenir de Louis Spaeth' See 'Andenken an Ludwig Späth'.

'Vestale' Pure white; broad, densely-packed panicles. A magnificent lilac. C 1910 (Lemoine). ♥ 2002.

Double

'Alice Eastwood' See *S.* × *hyacinthiflora* 'Alice Eastwood'.

'Ami Schott' Deep cobalt-blue with paler reverse. C 1933 (Lemoine).

'Beauty of Moscow' See 'Krasavitsa Moskvy'.

'Belle de Nancy' Purple-red in bud, opening lilac-pink; large panicles. C 1891 (Lemoine).

'Charles Joly' Dark purplish-red; late. A reliable and popular lilac. C 1896 (Lemoine). ♥ 2002.

'Condorcet' Lavender; long, massive panicles. C 1888 (Lemoine).

'Edith Cavell' Creamy-yellow in bud, opening pure white; large florets. C 1918 (Lemoine).

'Ellen Willmott' Cream in bud opening pure white; long, open panicles. C 1903 (Lemoine). AM 1917.

'General Pershing' Purplish-violet; long panicles. C 1924 (Lemoine).

'Hope' See 'Nadezhda'.

'Katherine Havemeyer' Purple-lavender, fading to pale lilac-pink; broad, compact panicles. First class. C 1922 (Lemoine). ♥ 2002. AM 1933.

'Krasavitsa Moskvy' ('Beauty of Moscow') Profuse, delicate, pale pink buds opening white; vigorous upright habit.

'Lois Utley' Very pale pink, from deeper buds. C 1985.

'Madame Abel Chatenay' Pale greenish-yellow in bud, opening milk-white; broad panicles; late. C 1892 (Lemoine). FCC 1900.

'Madame Antoine Buchner' Rose-pink to rosy-mauve; loose, narrow panicles; late. C 1900 (Lemoine). AM 1982.

'Madame Casimir Perier' Cream in bud, opening white. C 1894 (Lemoine).

Syringa vulgaris continued:

'Madame Lemoine' Creamy-yellow in bud, opening pure white. An old and popular lilac. C 1890 (Lemoine). ♥ 2002. FCC 1894. AM 1891.

'Michel Buchner' Pale rosy-lilac; large, dense panicles. C 1885 (Lemoine). AM 1891.

'Monique Lemoine' Pure white; large panicles; late. C 1939 (Lemoine). AM 1958.

'Mrs Edward Harding' Claret-red, shaded pink; very free-flowering; late. A superb and popular lilac. C 1922 (Lemoine). ♥ 2002.

'Nadezhda' ('Hope') Large panicles of blue flowers. C 1970.

'Paul Thirion' Carmine in bud, opening claret-rose, finally lilac-pink; late. C 1915 (Lemoine).

'Président Grévy' Lilac-blue; massive panicles. C 1886 (Lemoine). AM 1892.

'Président Poincare' Claret-mauve; large florets. C 1913 (Lemoine).

'Princesse Clementine' Creamy-yellow in bud, opening white; very floriferous. C about 1908 (Mathieu).

'Souvenir d'Alice Harding' Alabaster-white; tall panicles. C 1938 (Lemoine).

wilsonii See *S. tomentella*.

wolfii C.K. Schneid. (*S. formosissima* Nakai) This is an extremely hardy species related to *S. villosa*. It makes a medium-sized to large shrub with pale ash-grey branches and elliptic-lanceolate, taper-pointed leaves, 8–12cm long. Flowers fragrant, pale violet-purple, borne in long, wide, loose panicles in June. NE China, Korea. I 1904.

yunnanensis Franch. (*S. pinetorum* hort.) Yunnan lilac. A beautiful, medium-sized to large shrub, occasionally up to 4m, of loose, open habit. Leaves elliptic to oblong-lanceolate, glaucous beneath. Flowers fragrant, pink in bud, opening lilac-pink, paling with age, carried in slender panicles in June. China (Sichuan, Yunnan). Discovered by the Abbé Delavay in 1887; I by George Forrest in 1907. AM 1928. **'Alba'** Flowers white. A distinct plant, possibly of hybrid origin. **'Rosea'** A superior form selected in our nurseries. Flowers rose-pink, in long, slender panicles. In foliage, too, it is distinct and attractive.

T

Talauma coco See *Magnolia coco*.
Tamarisk See *Tamarix*.

TAMARIX L.—**Tamaricaceae**—About 50 species of shrubs or small trees, natives of Europe, Asia and N Africa. The tamarisks are excellent wind-resisters and are most commonly planted near the sea, but will thrive inland in full sun, and any soil, except shallow chalk soils. All have graceful, slender branches and plume-like foliage. The tiny, pink flowers are borne in slender racemes towards the ends of the branches, the whole creating large, plumose inflorescences which contribute a colourful splash to any landscape. As plants can become straggly in habit, pruning is usually necessary in order to maintain a balance. Those species that flower on growths of the current year should be pruned in late February or March, while those that flower on the previous year's wood should be pruned immediately after flowering.

anglica See *T. gallica*.

caspica hort. See *T. tetrandra*.

chinensis Lour. (*T. japonica* hort. ex Dipp., *T. juniperina* Bunge, *T. plumosa* hort. ex Carrière) A large shrub or small tree of dense habit. Branches extremely slender, clothed with distinctive, pale green foliage. Flowers bright pink, opening in May on shoots of the previous year. E and C Asia. C 1877.

gallica L. (*T. anglica* Webb) A large, spreading, glabrous shrub or small tree with dark purple-brown branches and sea-green foliage. Flowers during summer, pink, crowded into lax, cylindrical racemes on shoots of the current year. SW Europe. Naturalised along many stretches of the English coast.

germanica See *Myricaria germanica*.

japonica See *T. chinensis*.

juniperina See *T. chinensis*.

odessana See *T. ramosissima*.

parviflora DC. (*T. tetrandra* var. *purpurea* (DC.) Boiss.) A large shrub or small tree with long, brown or purple branches, clothed with bright green foliage. Flowers deep pink, borne in May on shoots of the previous year. SE Europe, W Asia. Long cultivated and naturalised in C and S Europe. C 1853.

pentandra See *T. ramosissima* and *T. ramosissima* 'Rosea'.

plumosa See *T. chinensis*.

ramosissima Ledeb. (*T. odessana* Stev. ex Bunge, *T. pentandra* Pall. in part) A large, glabrous shrub or small tree with reddish-brown branches. Flowers pink in slender racemes during summer, on shoots of the current year. W and C Asia. I about 1885. AM 1903. **'Pink Cascade'** A vigorous form with large plumes of rich pink flowers. **'Rosea'** Flowers rose-pink, borne in late summer and early autumn. One of the finest late-flowering shrubs, the whole bush becoming a feathery mass of rose-pink, intermingled with the delightful foliage. C 1883. AM 1933. Originally listed as *T. pentandra*. **'Rubra'** A splendid selection with darker flowers. ♀ 2002.

tetrandra Pall. (*T. caspica* hort.) A large shrub of loose, open growth, with long, dark branches and green foliage. Flowers in May or early June, light pink, borne in slender racemes on the branches of the previous year, the whole forming long, large panicles. SE Europe, W Asia. I 1821. ♀ 2002. **var. *purpurea*** See *T. parviflora*.

Tea tree See *Leptospermum scoparium*.
Teaberry See *Gaultheria procumbens*.

‡***TELOPEA** R. Br.—**Proteaceae**—A small Australasian genus of 3 or 4 species that enjoy conditions similar to those that suit embothriums but welcoming more sun. The Australian waratah (*T. speciosissima* (Sm.) R. Br.) requires a warmer climate.

truncata R. Br. Tasmanian waratah. A remarkably hardy, medium-sized to large shrub or occasionally a small tree with stout, downy shoots and rather thick, oblanceolate, evergreen leaves. Flowers rich crimson in dense terminal heads in June. Hardy when planted among other evergreens in moist, but well-drained soil. Thrives in conditions suitable to *Rhododendron*. A specimen in the Sir Harold Hillier Gardens and Arboretum reached 4.5m tall and 2.5m across before being killed by honey fungus. I 1930 by Harold Comber from Tasmania. FCC 1938. AM 1934. **f. *lutea*** A.M. Gray. An unusual form with pale yellow flowers. Occurs rarely in the wild and mostly gives red-flowered plants when grown from seed, due to open pollination. A selection of this, named 'Essie' in Tasmania, first flowered in the Sir Harold Hillier Gardens and Arboretum in May 1989; it should only be propagated vegetatively. We received cuttings from the original plant in Miss Essie Huxley's garden in Tasmania in 1975.

‡***TERNSTROEMIA** Mutis ex L. f.—**Theaceae**—A genus of about 85 species of evergreen trees and shrubs mainly native to tropical regions. They differ from the closely related *Eurya* in their entire leaves and hermaphrodite flowers and from *Cleyera* in various small floral characters.

gymnanthera (Wight & Arn.) Sprague (*T. japonica* Thunb. in part) A medium-sized shrub with stout branches. The thick, leathery, obovate leaves are blunt-tipped and generally clustered towards the ends of the shoots. Flowers white, borne in the leaf axils in July. Only suitable for mild areas, requiring a sheltered position in semi-shade. In the southern USA where this species is commonly grown it is often called *Cleyera japonica*. E and SE Asia. **'Burnished Gold'** A selection from the J.C. Raulston Arboretum, with bronze young foliage becoming bright yellow then green. **'Variegata'** A beautiful form. The dark green leaves are marbled grey and possess a creamy-white margin that turns to rose in autumn.

TETRACENTRON Oliv.—**Tetracentraceae**—A rare, monotypic genus of disputable allegiance, included under both *Magnoliaceae* and *Trochodendraceae* in the past. It bears a superficial resemblance to *Cercidiphyllum*, but its leaves are alternate and its hermaphrodite flowers are borne in catkins. It thrives in woodland conditions, but makes an elegant lawn specimen. It is lime-tolerant and has grown for many years on the site of our West Hill nursery in Winchester but prefers an acid or neutral soil.

sinense Oliv. A large shrub or small to medium-sized tree of widespreading habit. Leaves ovate or heart-shaped with a long, slender point, red-tinted when young. Flowers minute, yellowish, borne in dense, pendent, catkin-like spikes, 10–15cm long, which drape the leafy branches in summer. A graceful tree from C and W China and the Himalaya where it was seen by C.R. Lancaster in E Nepal in 1971. First discovered by Augustine Henry. I 1901 by Ernest Wilson in 1901.

TETRADIUM Lour.—**Rutaceae**—9 species of trees with pinnate leaves (with not more than 3 leaflets in *Euodia*), natives of the Himalaya, E and SE Asia. Related and similar in general appearance to *Phellodendron* but differing in the exposed winter buds and the fruits consisting of dehiscent pods. Flowers unisexual, in terminal corymbs (bisexual in axillary corymbs in *Euodia*). The hardy species in cultivation are deciduous trees succeeding in all soils.

daniellii (Benn.) T.G. Hartley (*Euodia daniellii* (Benn.) Hemsl., *Euodia hupehensis* Dode, *Euodia velutina* Rehder & E.H. Wilson) A variable, fast-growing, small to medium-sized tree with large, pinnate leaves and corymbs of small, white, pungently scented flowers, with yellow anthers, in late summer and early autumn, succeeded by red to purplish or black fruits. China, Korea. I 1905. FCC 1976. AM 1949 (both as *Euodia hupehensis*).

†***TETRAPANAX** K. Koch—**Araliaceae**—A genus of a single species related to *Fatsia*. A spectacular foliage plant for mild gardens, it will also survive in colder ones in a protected position.

papyrifer (Hook.) K. Koch. A sparsley branched, large shrub or small tree, spreading by rhizomes, with stout shoots covered with a dusty brown tomentum when young. Huge leaves, to 60cm or more across, are deeply lobed, with some of the larger lobes forked. They are borne on stout petioles, to 75cm long, clasping the stem at their base, near to which are 2 large, slender-pointed stipules. Infloresences terminal, bearing numerous umbels of small, white flowers in autumn. Taiwan.

TEUCRIUM L.—**Labiatae**—A genus of about 300 species of herbs, shrubs and subshrubs, widely distributed in warm temperate regions of the world, particularly in the Mediterranean region. The shrubby members are useful flowering and foliage plants, requiring a sunny, well-drained position. All have square stems and two-lipped flowers.

***chamaedrys** L. Wall germander. A dwarf, bushy, aromatic subshrub with creeping rootstock and erect, hairy stems, densely clothed with small, prettily toothed leaves. Flowers rose-pink with darker veins, produced in axillary whorls from July to September. Suitable for walls. C and S Europe. C in England about 1750.

†***fruticans** L. Shrubby germander. A small shrub, the stems and the undersides of the ovate leaves covered with a close white tomentum. Flowers pale blue, in terminal racemes, throughout the summer. It requires a sunny, well-drained position with the shelter of a wall. S Europe, N Africa. I 1714. AM 1982 (for foliage). **'Azureum'** A slightly more tender form with darker blue

flowers contrasting better with the foliage. ♀ 2002. AM 1936. **'Compactum'** A neat, compact form.

***polium** L. A dwarf shrub with procumbent stems forming low hummocks a few centimetres high. Leaves narrow and grey-felted. Flowers white or yellow in terminal heads during summer. Suitable for a rock garden. Mediterranean region. C 1562.

***subspinosum** Pourr. ex Willd. A dwarf, grey-spiny shrublet of unusual appearance. Flowers mauve-pink, produced in late summer. A worthy plant for a rock garden or scree. Balearic Islands (Mallorca).

Thea sinensis See *Camellia sinensis*.
Thimbleberry See *Rubus parviflorus*.
Thorn See *Crataegus*.
Thorn, Christ's See *Paliurus spina-christi*.
Thorn, Glastonbury See *Crataegus monogyna* 'Biflora'.

†**TIBOUCHINA** Aublet—**Melastomataceae**—A large genus of some 350 species of mainly trees and shrubs, natives of tropical America. None are hardy though several are suitable for walls or pillars in a conservatory.

***urvilleana** (DC.) Cogn. (*T. semidecandra* hort.) Glory bush. A large shrub with four-angled stems and velvety-hairy, prominently veined leaves. Large, vivid royal-purple flowers are produced continuously throughout summer and autumn. Old plants tend to become straggly and should be pruned in early spring. S Brazil. I 1864. ♀ 2002. FCC 1868 (as *T. semidecandra*).

TILIA L.—**Tiliaceae**—The limes or lindens make up a genus of about 45 species of deciduous trees, widely distributed in N temperate regions. They are all very amenable to cultivation, many growing into stately trees. Because of their tolerance of hard pruning, they have been widely used in the past for roadside planting and 'pleaching'. They will grow in all types of fertile soils and situations. Sticky honey-dew produced by aphids is a problem with *T. × europaea* and *T. platyphyllos* and their forms. Unless otherwise stated, small, fragrant, creamy-yellow flowers are common to all the species and are borne in numerous clusters in July; in *T. tomentosa* and its forms they are toxic to bees. They hybridise readily when grown from seed.

alba See *T. tomentosa*.

americana L. American lime, Basswood. A medium-sized tree with glabrous shoots and huge, broad leaves, up to 30cm long. They are coarsely toothed, green on both sides, and glabrous, except for minute axillary tufts beneath. Like the American beech (*Fagus grandifolia*), does not luxuriate in the British Isles. The bark of old trees is rough, almost corky in appearance. E and C North America. I 1752. **'Dentata'** Leaves coarsely toothed; a striking plant, particularly when young. **'Fastigiata'** A narrow, conical form with ascending branches. Raised in New York about 1927. **'Pendula'** See *T. tomentosa* 'Petiolaris'. **'Redmond'** A selected form said to be of dense, conical habit. Garden origin, Nebraska, about 1926. Originally introduced as a form of *T. × euchlora*.

amurensis Rupr. A small to medium-sized tree related to *T. cordata*, with broadly ovate, coarsely toothed leaves. It is unlikely to prove an outstanding tree in the British Isles. Manchuria, Korea. C 1909.

argentea See *T. tomentosa*.

begoniifolia See *T. dasystyla* subsp. *caucasica*.

caroliniana Mill. A medium-sized tree with tomentose, reddish-brown or yellowish twigs. Leaves broad-ovate and coarsely toothed, dark yellowish-green above, stellate-tomentose beneath. SE USA. **subsp. *floridana*** (Small) E. Murr. Mature leaves nearly glabrous. C 1915.

caucasica See *T. dasystyla* subsp. *caucasica*.

chinensis Maxim. A distinct, small to medium-sized tree with glabrous, glossy shoots and ovate to broadly ovate, sharply toothed, slender-pointed leaves, thinly pubescent beneath. Bark of older trees flaking. W and C China. I 1925.

cordata Mill. (*T. parvifolia* Ehrh.) Small-leaved lime. A medium-sized to large tree of rounded habit. Leaves heart-shaped, 5–7.5cm long, rather leathery, glossy dark green above, pale green, with reddish-brown axillary tufts beneath. The characteristic spreading inflorescences appear in late July, generally after those of the Common Lime and Large-leaved Lime; flowers ivory-coloured and sweetly scented. Europe (including the British Isles). ♀ 2002. **'Greenspire'** A fast-growing American selection of upright habit making a narrowly oval crown. C 1961. ♀ 2002. **'Rancho'** A small to medium-sized tree of dense, conical habit with small, glossy green leaves. Neater and smaller-leaved than 'Greenspire'. C 1961. **'Streetwise'** Similar to the popular 'Greenspire' with a compact, broadly conical habit, but much more vigorous. Selected in our nurseries in the early 1980s; I in 1998. **'Swedish Upright'** A most attractive, columnar form with spreading branches. Suitable for planting in broad thoroughfares and city squares. I 1906 by Alfred Rehder from Sweden to the Arnold Arboretum, Boston, USA. **'Winter Orange'** A selection with red buds and orange winter shoots. Ivory-white, sweetly scented flowers in July. Autumn colour butter-yellow. Found as a chance seedling in Zundert, Holland in 1977.

dasystyla Steven. This species, a native of the Crimea, is rare in cultivation. Plants grown under this name are usually subsp. *caucasica* or *T. × euchlora*. It differs from the following form in its nearly rounded, glossy green leaves. **subsp. *caucasica*** (V. Engl.) Pigott (*T. begoniifolia* Steven, *T. caucasica* Rupr.) A medium-sized tree with greenish twigs, pubescent at first, and orbicular-ovate, sharply and conpicuously bristle-toothed leaves, dull green above, paler with yellow axillary tufts beneath. Caucasus to N Iran. C 1880. An introduction was also made in 1972 by Mrs Ala and Roy Lancaster from N Iran as *T. begoniifolia* (Ala & Lancaster 16). It has reached 9m in the Sir Harold Hillier Gardens and Arboretum (1990).

× euchlora K. Koch (*T. × dasystyla* hort.) (*T. cordata × T. dasystyla*) A medium-sized tree with generally glabrous green twigs. Leaves orbicular-ovate, intermediate in size between those of the parents, shining dark green above, paler almost glaucous, with brown axillary tufts beneath. An elegant tree when young with glossy leaves and arching branches, becoming dense and twiggy with pendent lower branches in maturity. It is a "clean" lime, being free from aphids, but its flowers tend to have a narcotic effect on bees. Possibly a form of *T. caucasica*. C 1860. ♀ 2002. FCC 1890.

× europaea L. (*T. cordata × T. platyphyllos*) (*T. × vulgaris* Hayne, *T. × intermedia* DC.) Common lime. A familiar avenue tree and, at least in the past, the most commonly planted lime. A large, vigorous tree with glabrous, greenish zig-zag shoots. Leaves broadly ovate or rounded, obliquely heart-shaped at base, sharply toothed, glabrous except for axillary tufts beneath. A long-lived tree, easily recognised by its densely suckering habit. Occasionally found with its parents in the wild. The honey-dew produced by aphids on this tree is a problem in late summer. **'Pallida'** Kaiser linden. Branches ascending forming a broadly conical crown, reddish in winter. Leaves yellowish-green beneath. This is the lime of the famous lime-planted avenue, Unter den Linden, in Berlin. **'Wratislaviensis'** Leaves golden-yellow when young becoming green with age. A splendid tree whose young growths give the effect of a yellow halo. A sport of 'Pallida'. ♀ 2002.

floridana See *T. caroliniana* subsp. *floridana*.

grandifolia See *T. platyphyllos*.

'Harold Hillier' (*T. insularis × T. mongolica*) A handsome and vigorous, medium-sized tree, of narrowly conical habit, with glabrous shoots. Leaves variable in size, up to 15cm long, usually less, maple-like and 3-lobed, edged with bristle-tipped teeth, dark green above, grey-green and glabrous beneath except for pale brown tufts of hair in the vein axils. Autumn colour a lovely butter-yellow. A clean lime with good potential as a street tree. Raised in 1973 by Nigel Muir who kindly suggested we name it after the late Sir Harold Hillier.

henryana Szysz. A very rare, medium-sized tree with broadly ovate leaves up to 13cm long, oblique at the base and edged with conspicuous, bristle-like teeth. They are softly downy on both surfaces with axillary tufts beneath and are often conspicuously carmine-tinged when young. Flowers in autumn. Very slow-growing in cultivation. C China. Discovered by Augustine Henry in 1888. I 1901 by Ernest Wilson.

heterophylla Vent. (*T. heterophylla* var. *michauxii* (Nutt.) Sarg.) A medium-sized tree with glabrous branches and large, broadly ovate, coarsely toothed leaves, dark green above and covered on the undersides by a close, silvery tomentum. E USA. C 1755. **var. *michauxii*** See *T. heterophylla*.

insularis Nakai. A small to medium-sized tree in cultivation with heart-shaped, coarsely toothed, green leaves, tufted in the vein axils beneath. Fragrant flowers are profusely borne in summer. Cheju Do (Quelpart), S Korea. I 1919 by Ernest Wilson.

japonica (Miq.) Simonk. A distinct and attractive, medium-sized, small-leaved tree, related to and resembling *T. cordata*, but its leaves slightly larger and abruptly acuminate. Japan, E China. I 1875.

kiusiana Makino & Shiras. A remarkable, unlime-like, slow-growing shrub, rarely a small tree, with slender stems and small, ovate leaves about 4–6cm long, oblique at base, serrately toothed, thinly downy on both surfaces and with axillary tufts beneath. One of the most distinct of all limes. S Japan. I 1930.

mandshurica Rupr. & Maxim. A striking, small to medium-sized tree with downy young shoots and large, heart-shaped, coarsely toothed leaves, equal in size to those of

T. americana but greyish beneath, both surfaces stellately-downy. Subject to injury by late spring frosts. NE Asia. I about 1860.

maximowicziana Shiras. This is a medium-sized to large tree with downy, yellowish shoots and broadly ovate to rounded leaves, 10–18cm long and edged with broad, mucronate teeth. They are stellately-hairy above, greyish-tomentose beneath with conspicuous axillary tufts. The flowers appear in June. N Japan. C 1880. AM 1976.

miqueliana Maxim. A very distinct, slow-growing tree of small to medium size with grey-felted shoots. Leaves ovate, tapering to an acuminate apex, coarsely toothed or slightly lobed, grey-felted beneath, long persisting. Flowers appearing in August, conspicuous and fragrant. Jiangsu, E China. Long cultivated in Japan, particularly around temples. I before 1900.

'Moltkei' A strong-growing tree of medium to large size with arching, slightly pendent branches. Leaves broad ovate or rounded, 15–20cm long, greyish-downy beneath. Flowers fragrant, in large clusters, July. Raised by Messrs Späth in Berlin.

mongolica Maxim. Mongolian lime. A small tree of compact, rounded habit and dense, twiggy growth with glabrous, reddish shoots. Leaves 4–7.5cm long on red stalks, coarsely toothed or 3- to 5-lobed, particularly on young trees, glossy green and glabrous except for axillary tufts beneath, turning bright yellow in autumn. An attractive species with prettily lobed, ivy-like leaves. E Russia, Mongolia, N China. I 1880.

monticola Sarg. Medium-sized tree with reddish young twigs. Leaves ovate, acuminate, deep lustrous green above, pale beneath. Closely related to and, by some authorities, united with *T. heterophylla.* SE USA. C 1888.

neglecta Spach. A large tree with red, glabrous shoots and broadly ovate, green leaves, stellately-hairy beneath. Closely related to *T. americana.* E and C North America. C 1830.

oliveri Szysz. An elegant, medium-sized to large tree with glabrous shoots inclined to be pendent. Leaves broadly ovate or rounded, finely toothed, dark green above, silvery-white-tomentose beneath. Closely related to *T. tomentosa* and like it free from aphids, differing in its glabrous young shoots. C China. Discovered by Augustine Henry in 1888. I 1900 by Ernest Wilson.

'Orbicularis' See *T. tomentosa* 'Orbicularis'.

parvifolia See *T. cordata.*

petiolaris See *T. tomentosa* 'Petiolaris'. **'Chelsea Sentinel'** See *T. tomentosa* 'Chelsea Sentinel'.

platyphyllos Scop. (*T. grandifolia* Ehrh.) Broad-leaved lime. A large, vigorous, rounded tree with downy shoots. Leaves roundish-ovate, sharply toothed, shortly pubescent above, densely so beneath, especially on veins and midrib. Flowers appear in late June or early July. A commonly planted tree, especially in parks. Suckers are produced, though not as prolifically as in *T. × europaea,* but it still has the same aphid problems. C and S Europe to N France and SW Sweden. Possibly native in the Wye Valley and S Yorkshire. FCC 1892. **'Aspleniifolia'** An elegant, small to medium-sized tree with leaves deeply and variously divided into narrow segments. Perhaps a

sport of the variable 'Laciniata'. **'Aurea'** ('Aurantiaca', *T. grandifolia* 'Aurantia') Young shoots yellow, becoming olive-green. Most conspicuous in winter. **'Corallina'** See 'Rubra'. **'Fastigiata'** ('Pyramidalis') An erect-branched form of broadly conical habit. **'Laciniata'** A small to medium-sized tree of dense, conical habit. Leaves deeply and irregularly cut into rounded and tail-like lobes. **'Örebro'** A large tree of upright habit, forming a broad, conical crown. Found in Sweden in 1935. **'Pendula'** Branches spreading, branchlets pendent. **'Prince's Street'** A vigorous form of upright habit, the young shoots bright red in winter. **'Rubra'** ('Corallina') Red-twigged lime. Young shoots bright brownish-red, particularly effective in winter. The best cultivar for street planting owing to its uniformly semi-erect habit of branching. Excellent in industrial areas. ♥ 2002. **'Streetwise'** A striking, large tree of upright habit with glossy dark green leaves and outstanding red winter shoots. Selected in our nurseries in the early 1980s; I in 1998.

× spectabilis See *T.* 'Moltkei'.

tomentosa Moench. (*T. argentea* DC., *T. alba* Aiton in part) Silver lime. A handsome, but variable, large, stately tree. Branches erect, often pendent at their tips, shoots white-felted. Leaves shortly-stalked, ovate-orbicular, sharply toothed, dark green above, silvery-white-tomentose beneath. They are particularly effective when disturbed by a breeze. Free from aphid problems but flowers toxic to bees. SE and EC Europe. I 1767. **'Brabant'** A Dutch selection of upright habit developing a dense, broadly conical crown. C 1970. ♥ 2002. **'Chelsea Sentinel'** Resembles 'Petiolaris' in its long-stalked leaves and attractively weeping branches, but has a distinctly columnar habit. The original tree grew in the grounds of the Royal Hospital, Chelsea until it was destroyed in the hurricane of October 1987. Fortunately we had already propagated it and were happy to present a replacement, which H.M. the Queen planted to commemorate the 75th Chelsea Flower Show. **'Orbicularis'** (*T. × orbicularis* (Carrière) Jouin) A vigorous, medium-sized tree of conical habit, with somewhat pendent branches. Leaves large, orbicular, glossy green above, grey-tomentose beneath; flowers fragrant. Raised by Messrs Simon-Louis, near Metz, NE France, about 1870. **'Petiolaris'** (*T. petiolaris* DC., *T. americana* 'Pendula') Weeping silver lime. One of the most beautiful of all large, weeping trees. A round-headed tree with graceful, downward-sweeping branches. Leaves long-stalked, broadly ovate to rounded, sharply toothed, dark green above, white-felted beneath, especially attractive when ruffled by a breeze. Flowers richly scented, but narcotic to bees. Uncertain origin. C 1840. ♥ 2002.

× vulgaris See *T. × europaea.*

TOONA (Endl.) M. Roem.—**Meliaceae**—A small genus of 6 species of trees, natives of China, SE Asia and N Australia. Distinct from the genus *Cedrela,* which is restricted to 8 species in tropical America.

sinensis (A. Juss.) M. Roem. (*Cedrela sinensis* A. Juss., *Ailanthus flavescens* Carr.) A medium-sized, fast-growing tree with handsome, large, pinnate leaves, often bronze when young, in which the terminal leaflet is

sometimes absent, and small, fragrant, white flowers in drooping panicles up to 70cm long in late summer. Lovely yellow tints in autumn. N and W China. I 1862.
'**Flamingo**' (*Cedrela sinensis* 'Flamingo') Young foliage brilliant pink turning to cream then green. Raised in Australia before 1930.

Toothache tree See *Zathoxylum americanum*.
Toyon See *Heteromeles arbutifolia*.

***TRACHYCARPUS** H. Wendl.—**Palmae**—A small genus of 8 species of usually dioecious palms with very large, fan-shaped leaves, natives of the Himalaya and E Asia. *T. fortunei* is hardy in the British Isles but it deserves a sheltered position to protect its leaves from being shattered by strong winds.
fortunei (Hook.) H. Wendl. (*T. excelsus* hort., *Chamaerops excelsa* Mart. not Thunb.) Chusan palm, Chinese wind-mill palm. A remarkable species of small to medium size, developing a tall, single trunk, thickly clothed with the fibrous remains of the old leaf bases. Leaves large, fan-shaped, 1–1.5m across, with 40–50 segments, borne on long, stout petioles in a cluster from the summit of the trunk, persisting many years. Flowers yellow, small, numerously borne in large, terminal, decurved panicles in early summer, sometimes both sexes on the same tree; fruits marble-like, bluish-black. C China. Introduced by Philipp von Siebold in 1830 and by Robert Fortune in 1849. ♀ 2002. AM 1970.
martianus (Wall.) H. Wendl. An elegant, medium-sized tree with a slender trunk, usually without persistent fibres. Leaves regularly divided to about halfway into numerous (65–80) segments, glaucous beneath and drooping at the tips. N India, Nepal, N Burma. I by Wallich about 1817.
takil Becc. Kumaon fan palm. A large tree, similar to *T. fortunei*, and possibly hardier, with larger leaves divided into as many as 60 segments and a trunk which is sometimes bare of fibres. Discovered and introduced in the 1850s by Major Madden. Rare in cultivation and in the wild. N India.
wagnerianus Becc. A slow-growing, small tree reaching about 5m tall. It differs from *T. fortunei* in its smaller stature and its much smaller leaves, to about 60cm across, divided into very rigid segments, edged with white fibres. The relatively small leaves make it much more suitable for exposed positions than *T. fortunei*. Described from a plant cultivated in Japan, it is unknown in the wild.

Tree daisy See *Olearia*.
Tree flax See *Linum arboreum*.
Tree of Heaven See *Ailanthus altissima*.

Tree lupin See *Lupinus arboreus*.
Tree poppy See *Romneya*.
Trefoil, moon See *Medicago arborea*.

‡**TRIPETALEIA** Siebold & Zucc.—**Ericaceae**—A genus of 2 species of slow-growing, deciduous shrubs attaining 1.5 to 2m, occasionally more. They require a moist, lime-free soil in semi-shade. The flowers are normally 3-petalled.
bracteata Maxim. (*Elliottia bracteata* (Maxim.) Benth. & Hook. f.) A small, slender shrub with reddish-brown, rounded stems and glabrous, entire, obovate leaves. Greenish-white or pink-tinged flowers are borne in erect, terminal racemes in July and August. Japan. I 1893.
paniculata Benth. & Hook. f. (*Elliottia paniculata* (Benth. & Hook. f.) Siebold & Zucc.) A small, erect shrub with reddish-brown, angular stems. Obovate leaves are minutely pubescent beneath. White or pink-tinged flow-ers, with usually 3 petals, are borne in erect, terminal panicles from July to September. Japan. I 1879 by Charles Maries.

‡***TROCHOCARPA** R. Br.—**Epacridaceae**—A small genus of about 12 species of evergreen shrubs and small trees dis-tributed from Tasmania to Borneo.
thymifolia (R. Br.) Spreng. A dwarf or prostrate, heath-like shrub with downy shoots and tiny, densely arranged, nar-rowly ovate, dark green leaves, 3-veined beneath. Small, deep pink flowers, white within, are borne in short, pen-dent spikes in early spring and often again in autumn, followed by fleshy, bluish fruits. Tasmania. C 1940. AM 1995 (for flower).

‡***TROCHODENDRON** Siebold & Zucc.—**Trocho-dendraceae**—A monotypic genus growing in most fertile soils except shallow chalky soils, in sun or shade. During the severe winter of 1962/63 when most evergreens looked bedraggled, this species was unharmed and quite outstanding.
aralioides Siebold & Zucc. A large, glabrous, slow-grow-ing, evergreen shrub or small tree of spreading habit, the bark aromatic. The long-stalked, obovate, leathery leaves are bright apple- or yellowish-green and prettily scal-loped at the margins. Flowers green, in erect, terminal racemes during spring and early summer. A striking and unusual shrub desired by flower arrangers. Japan, Taiwan, S Korea. C 1894. AM 1976.

Tsusiophyllum tanakae See *Rhododendron tsusiophyllum*.
Tulip tree See *Liriodendron tulipifera*.
Tupelo See *Nyssa sylvatica*.
Tutsan See *Hypericum androsaemum*.
Tweedia caerulea See under CLIMBERS.
Twinflower See *Linnaea borealis*.

U

UGNI Turcz.—**Myrtaceae**—A genus of up to 15 species of evergreen shrubs natives of South America.

molinae Turcz. (*Eugenia ugni* Mol.) Hook. f., *Myrtus ugni* (Mol.) Chilean guava. A slow-growing, small to medium-sized, leathery-leaved shrub, rather stiff and erect in habit, bearing nodding, waxy, pink bells followed by edible and delicious, aromatic, mahogany-red berries. Chile. I 1844 by William Lobb. AM 1925. **'Variegata'** Leaves green, shaded grey, with a creamy-yellow margin.

ULEX L.—**Leguminosae**—About 20 species of spiny shrubs, natives of W Europe and N Africa. Variously known as furze, gorse or whin. The 3 species native to the British Isles are usually found on poor, dry heath or downland, and are valuable for covering dry banks, and for windswept, maritime sites.

If Britain's native gorses were rare exotics, they would be sought by connoisseur and garden designer alike. It is impossible to imagine in any landscape a richer mass of chrome-yellow, intermixed with the occasional splash of deep lemon-yellow, than one sees covering the downs around Slieve Donard in Northern Ireland in April. This dazzling feast of colour is provided by *U. europaeus*. In August and September along the Welsh mountainsides, as one approaches C Wales from Herefordshire, the countryside is enriched by lower-growing masses of *U. gallii*.

Many of us have roved those lovely downs that rise from Salcombe harbour in S Devon and which, in late summer, become a patchwork quilt of golden gorse and purple heather. In parts of the New Forest *U. minor*, the third native species, also flowers in the autumn with the heather.

Gorse should be pot grown, otherwise it is difficult to establish. Strong-growing plants are apt to become leggy and bare at the base. They may be cut to the ground after flowering. Like heather, gorse grows best in poor, dry, acid soil. It is not recommended for shallow chalk soils.

europaeus L. Common gorse. A densely-branched, green, viciously spiny shrub, 1.2–1.8m high, much more in sheltered or shaded sites. Chrome-yellow pea-flowers crowd the branches from March to May and intermittently throughout the year. W Europe extending eastwards to Italy. Extensively naturalised in C Europe. **'Flore Pleno'** ('Plenus') A superb shrub in April and May, when its lower-growing, compact hummocks are smothered in long-lasting, semi-double flowers. C 1828. ♀ 2002. AM 1967. **'Strictus'** ('Hibernicus', 'Fastigiatus') A slow-growing, unusual form with erect, slender, shortly and softly spiny shoots forming a dense, compact bush. It resembles more a form of *U. gallii* than *U. europaeus* and, though it rarely flowers, makes an excellent low hedge.

gallii Planch. A dwarf shrub, often prostrate in maritime areas, usually more robust and stronger-spined than *U. minor*, but much less so than *U. europaeus*. Flowers smaller than those of the common gorse, deep golden-yellow, opening in late summer to autumn from August to October. W Europe (including the British Isles). **'Mizen Head'** A prostrate shrub with shoots spreading along the ground. Flowers deep yellow in July and August. A useful, spiny groundcover plant.

minor Roth (*U. nanus* T.F. Forst. ex Symons) A dwarf, often prostrate shrub with slender, softly spiny shoots. Flowers half the size of those of the common gorse, golden-yellow, opening during autumn and particularly spectacular in September. A low-growing species which must be given a 'starvation diet' to prevent it becoming tall and lanky. SW Europe northwards to the British Isles, but not Ireland.

Ulmo See *Eucryphia cordifolia*.

ULMUS L.—**Ulmaceae**—The elms are a genus which included, until recently, some of the noblest, deciduous, hardy trees in the British Isles. They all thrive in almost any type of soil and in exposed positions, the Wych Elm being one of the few trees that may be planted near the sea in full exposure to Atlantic gales. The golden and variegated forms are colourful trees in the landscape, while the weeping forms are picturesque and useful for the shade they give. In most species the leaves turn glowing yellow in the autumn. The flowers are small, reddish and hermaphrodite; unless otherwise stated, they are borne on the naked twigs in early spring. The fruits (samaras) are greenish, winged and disc-like.

The English elm (*U. procera*) was an inseparable part of the English landscape. Unfortunately, its presence in certain areas has been drastically reduced due to the depredations of Dutch elm disease (the name refers to the fact that early work on the disease was carried out in Holland, not that it is connected with the Dutch elm or that it originated in Holland), which is caused by a fungus (*Ceratocystis ulmi*), spores of which are transmitted from diseased trees to healthy trees through the agency of various elm-bark beetles (*Scolytus scolytus* and *S. multistriatus*). Death is caused by the blockage of the vessels that transport water from the roots. It was first reported in 1918 and reached epidemic proportions in the 1930s. After this it died down but returned in the early 1970s in a very aggressive form. Most of the forms mentioned here as being resistant were only resistant to earlier introductions of the disease. At present most disease-resistance is shown by Asiatic species such as *U. japonica*. It has been estimated that the disease has killed more than 80 per cent of the United Kingdom elm population.

In dealing with this serious disease, landowners and gardeners are asked to cooperate by checking the condition of all elms (whatever the species) growing on their property. Badly infected trees should be completely removed; where isolated branches are infected these should be dealt with in the same manner and burnt. To prevent the disease from spreading, it is necessary to remove all possible breeding sites for the elm-bark beetles, and to this end all dead or dying trees and branches should be destroyed. Elm logs or stumps left in the open should have their bark removed.

alata Michx. Winged elm. A small to medium-sized tree developing a rounded head. Branches glabrous or nearly so, with 2 opposite, corky wings. Leaves narrowly obovate or ovate-oblong, glabrous above. Fruits hairy. SE USA. I 1820.

americana L. White elm. A large, vigorous, attractive tree with ash-grey bark and a widespreading head of graceful branches. The ovate to obovate, slender-pointed leaves, 10–15cm long, are double-toothed along the margins and unequal at the base. Fruits ciliate. E and C North America. I 1752.

angustifolia See *U. minor* subsp. *angustifolia*. **var. cornubiensis** See *U. minor* subsp. *cornubiensis*.

belgica See *U.* × *hollandica* 'Belgica'.

campestris L. A confused name that has been applied to several species, in Britain mainly to *U. procera*. **'Major'** See *U.* × *hollandica* 'Major'. **var. stricta** See *U. minor* subsp. *angustifolia*. **var. sarniensis** See *U. minor* subsp. *sarniensis*.

carpinifolia See *U. minor*. **var. cornubiensis** See *U. minor* subsp. *angustifolia*. **'Dampieri'** See *U.* × *hollandica* 'Dampieri'. **'Italica'** See *U.* × *hollandica* 'Australis'. **f. sarniensis** See *U. minor* subsp. *sarniensis*. **'Variegata'** See *U. minor* 'Variegata'.

chinensis See *U. parvifolia*.

crassifolia Nutt. A slow-growing, small, round-headed tree in cultivation, with downy young shoots and occasionally opposite or subopposite winter buds. Leaves ovate to oblong, blunt-tipped, leathery, 2.5–5cm long, rough above, downy beneath. Flowers produced in axillary clusters in late summer and early autumn. Fruits downy. S USA, NE Mexico. I 1876.

davidiana Planch. A medium-sized tree, related to *U. minor*, with downy shoots and broad, obovate or ovate leaves, pubescent beneath. Fruits hairy in the centre. NE Asia. I 1895. **var. japonica** See *U. japonica*.

'Dodoens' A large, fast-growing tree of broadly upright habit with dark green leaves. It is suitable for exposed positions. Raised at Wageningen in Holland and selected for resistance to Dutch elm disease.

effusa See *U. laevis*.

× *elegantissima* Horw. (*U. glabra* × *U. plottii*) A naturally occurring hybrid found in central England where the parents grow together. **'Jacqueline Hillier'** A slow-growing, medium to large, suckering shrub of dense habit. Slender, brown-pubescent twigs are neatly clothed with small, double-toothed, scabrid leaves 2.5–3.5cm long. An unusual elm found in a garden in Birmingham. Its neat, dense habit lends itself to planting as a low hedge or for bonsai.

exoniensis See *U. glabra* 'Exoniensis'.

foliacea See *U. minor*.

fulva See *U. rubra*.

glabra Huds. (*U. montana* Stokes) Wych elm, Scotch elm. A large tree, usually developing a dome-shaped crown with spreading branches, arching or pendent at their extremities. Leaves shortly-stalked, large and rough to the touch above, coarsely toothed, markedly unequal at base, abruptly acuminate. Fruits downy at apex, effective in early spring when they crowd the branches. It is said to be the only native elm that reproduces itself freely and regularly from seed. An excellent tree for planting in exposed situations either inland or along the coast. Probably the only elm native to Britain, the others having been introduced by man. Many forms have been named. Europe, N and W Asia. **'Camperdownii'** (*U. pendula* 'Camperdownii') Camperdown elm. A small, neat and compact tree with pendent branches forming a globose or dome-shaped head in marked contrast to the more spreading, stiffer-looking crown of the equally common 'Horizontalis'. Suitable as an isolated specimen on a lawn. C 1850. **'Crispa'** ('Aspleniifolia', 'Urticifolia') An unusual form, of slow growth and generally loose habit, with narrow leaves that are curiously infolded, with jaggedly toothed margins. **'Exoniensis'** ('Fastigiata', *U. scabra* 'Pyramidalis', *U. exoniensis* hort.) An erect tree of medium to large size, narrowly columnar when young, broadening with age. Leaves broad, jaggedly toothed, occurring in clusters on the ascending branches. Found near Exeter in about 1826. **'Fastigiata'** See 'Exoniensis'. **'Horizontalis'** See 'Pendula'. **'Lutescens'** (*U. americana* 'Aurea') Leaves soft cream-yellow in spring, becoming yellowish-green. A very beautiful, free-growing tree. **'Pendula'** ('Horizontalis') Weeping wych elm. A small tree occasionally reaching 9m, developing a wide head of spreading branches with long, pendent branchlets. Suitable as an isolated specimen for a large garden or park. **'Vegeta'** See *U.* × *hollandica* 'Vegeta'.

× *hollandica* Mill. (*U. glabra* × *U. minor*) An extremely variable, natural hybrid widespread in W Europe. According to Dr R. Melville this hybrid, in its numerous forms, constitutes almost the entire elm population of Germany, Holland, Belgium and France, as well as being quite abundant in East Anglia and the Midlands. R.H. Richens has more recently expressed the view that it is less common but occurs where the parents grow together.

The cultivars described below under this name are of similar parentage, but independent origin. The majority are very vigorous and, unless otherwise stated, attain a large size. **'Australis'** (*U. procera* 'Australis', *U. carpinifolia* 'Italica') An interesting tree with conspicuously and numerously veined leaves, rather leathery in texture. It is said to occur in the wild in SE France, Switzerland and Italy. **'Bea Schwarz'** A Dutch selection raised for its resistance to Dutch elm disease. First introduced in 1948. **'Belgica'** (*U. belgica* Weston) Belgian elm. A natural hybrid strongly resembling *U. glabra*. A vigorous tree forming a broad crown with almost glabrous twigs and obovate-elliptic leaves with a long, serrated point. This was usually grown as *U.* × *hollandica* in Belgium and Holland, where it was commonly planted in parks and along roads. C 1694. **'Christine Buisman'** An attractive, disease-resistant selection of Dutch origin. Introduced in 1937. **'Commelin'** A disease-resistant form of Dutch origin differing in its narrower habit and smaller leaves. **'Dampieri'** A narrow, conical tree with broadly ovate, double-toothed leaves, densely crowded on short branchlets. **'Dampieri Aurea'** ('Wredei', 'Wredei Aurea') A narrowly conical tree in which the crowded broad leaves are suffused golden-yellow. A sport of 'Dampieri'. FCC 1893. **'Hillieri'** A graceful, compact, slow-growing, miniature, weeping tree to shrub, usually less than 12m high. It originated as a chance seedling in our Pitt Corner nursery, Winchester in 1918. The slender branchlets carry small leaves which, under favourable conditions, turn crimson and yellow in autumn. **'Major'** (*U. major* Smith) Dutch elm. A large, suckering tree with a short trunk and widespreading branches. Young shoots glabrous or almost so. Leaves broad-elliptic with a long, serrated point and markedly unequal at base. Branchlets often prominently ridged. This is the *U.* × *hollandica* of England, where it was commonly planted. **'Pendula'** See 'Smithii'. **'Serpentina'** A remarkable, small tree with curved and twisted, zig-zag, pendent branches, forming a dense, conical or globose crown. **'Smithii'** ('Pendula') Downton elm. An elegant, small to medium-sized tree with ascending branches and long, pendent branchlets. Leaves dark green, smooth and shining above. **'Vegeta'** (*U. vegeta* (Loudon) Ley, *U. glabra* 'Vegeta') Huntingdon elm, Chichester elm. A magnificent, large tree with a short trunk and long, ascending branches. Young shoots sparsely hairy. Large, elliptic, jaggedly toothed and conspicuously veined leaves are very unequal at base, long-pointed, smooth, and shining dark green above. One of the most vigorous elms, raised from seed of trees growing in Hinchingbrook Park, Cambridgeshire about 1750. **'Wredei'** See 'Dampieri Aurea'.

japonica (Rehder) Sarg. (*U. davidiana* var. *japonica* (Rehder) Nakai) Japanese elm. A graceful tree with downy twigs and elliptic or obovate leaves, rough to the touch above. Fruits glabrous. Japan.

laciniata (Trautv.) Mayr (*U. montana* var. *laciniata* Trautv.) A small tree, closely related to *U. glabra*, with large, thin, obovate leaves, usually 3- to 9-lobed at the apex, rough to the touch above and sharply double-toothed. Fruits glabrous. NE Asia. I 1905.

laevis Pall. (*U. effusa* Willd., *U. pedunculata* Foug.) European white elm. A large tree with a widespreading head and rounded to ovate or obovate, double-toothed leaves, softly downy below, markedly unequal at base. Fruits ciliate. CE and SE Europe to W Asia.

'Lobel' A large, fast-growing tree of narrowly upright habit. It is very wind-resistant and suitable for planting close to buildings. Raised at Wageningen in Holland and selected for resistance to Dutch elm disease.

macrocarpa Hance. Large-fruited elm. A small, bushy tree with corky-winged branches and roughly hairy leaves. Distinguished from other elms by the large, winged fruits, up to 3cm long, which are bristly, like the leaves. N China. I 1908.

major See *U.* × *hollandica* 'Major'.

minor Mill. (*U. carpinifolia* Gled., *U. nitens* Moench, *U. foliacea* Gilib.) Field elm, Smooth-leaved elm. A large tree of graceful, open habit, with slender, often pendent shoots. Leaves narrowly oval to oblanceolate, markedly unequal at base, double-toothed and rather leathery, glabrous, shining dark green above, hairy in the vein axils beneath. Fruits glabrous. An attractive but variable species, usually developing a conical head, or spreading and round-topped when exposed to gales near the coast, where it is invaluable as a windbreak. Europe, N Africa, SW Asia. It was possibly introduced to England during the Bronze Age. **subsp. *angustifolia*** (Weston) Stace (var. *cornubiensis* (Weston) Richens, *U. angustifolia* (Weston) Weston, *U. stricta* (Aiton) Lindl., *U. angustifolia* var. *cornubiensis* (Weston) Melv., *U. carpinifolia* var. *cornubiensis* (Weston) Rehder) Cornish elm. A familiar elm, easily recognised by its dense, conical head of ascending branches, eventually attaining a large size and then more open and looser in growth. Leaves small, obovate or ovate; fruits glabrous. Occurs wild in Dorset, Devon and

Cornwall in England, and in Brittany in France, from where it probably came to Cornwall in Anglo-Saxon times. An excellent maritime tree. **'Argenteovariegata'** See *U. procera* 'Argenteovariegata'. **var. *cornubiensis*** See subsp. *angustifolia*. **'Dicksonii'** (*U. sarniensis* 'Dicksonii', *U. sarniensis* 'Aurea', *U.* 'Wheatleyi Aurea') Dickson's golden elm. A very slow-growing tree with leaves of a beautiful bright golden-yellow. **'Jacqueline Hillier'** See *U.* × *elegantissima* 'Jacqueline Hillier'. **var. *lockii*** See *U. plottii*. **subsp. *sarniensis*** (C.K. Schneid.) Stace (*U. minor* var. *sarniensis* (Loudon) Druce, *U. sarniensis* (C.K. Schneid.) Bancroft, *U. carpinifolia* f. *sarniensis* (C.K. Schneid.) Rehder, *U. wheatleyi* (Bean) Druce) Guernsey elm, Wheatley elm. A large tree of conical habit with strictly ascending branches, developing a narrower, denser crown than the Cornish elm. Leaves small, ovate to obovate, broader than those of the Cornish elm. Fruits glabrous. One of the finest of all trees for roadside planting, especially near the coast. Occurs in Guernsey and the other Channel Islands. Commonly planted elsewhere. Probably a selection from N France. R.H. Richens, in his book *Elm*, has pointed out that we were instrumental in the early distribution of this tree. **'Purpurea'** (*U. sarniensis* 'Purpurea') A medium-sized tree with spreading branches. The leaves and shoots are suffused dull purple when young. Strong, vigorous shoots on young plants bear large, roughly hairy leaves. **'Variegata'** (*U. carpinifolia* 'Variegata') Leaves densely mottled white, giving a silvery-grey effect. **'Viminalis'** See *U.* × *viminalis*. **'Viminalis Aurea'** See *U.* × *viminalis* 'Aurea'. **'Viminalis Marginata'** See *U.* × *viminalis* 'Marginata'. **var. *vulgaris*** See *U. procera*.

montana See *U. glabra*.

'New Horizon' (*U. japonica* × *U. pumila*) PBR A vigorous, large tree of upright habit with a straight central leader and a dense, conical crown. Leaves dark green, ovate-elliptic, acuminate at the tip, unequal at the base, with a sharply toothed margin, to 9cm long. One of the new range of Resista elms, bred for their resistance to Dutch elm disease. The original tree has reached a large size at the University of Wisconsin.

nitens See *U. minor*. **var. *wheatleyi*** See *U. minor* subsp. *sarniensis*.

parvifolia Jacq. (*U. chinensis* Pers., *U. sieboldii* Daveau) Chinese elm. A medium-sized tree with densely pubescent young shoots. Leaves small, 2.5–8cm long, leathery and glossy green. Flowers produced in early autumn. One of the most splendid elms, having the poise of a graceful *Nothofagus*, with small, rich green leaves that persist halfway through winter. We have never seen this tree affected by disease. N and C China, Korea, Taiwan, Japan. I 1794. **'Frosty'** A charming, slow-growing, shrubby form, eventually 6m or more tall, the small, neatly-arranged leaves bearing white teeth. **'Geisha'** A dwarf shrub with tiny, dark green leaves, edged white. **'Hokkaido'** A slow-growing, compact, dwarf form with small leaves. Develops corky bark with age. **'Yatsubusa'** Meaning dwarf in Japanese, this name may cover several forms popular for use in bonsai, with very small leaves on corky shoots.

'Pinnatoramosa' (*U. pumila* var. *arborea* hort. not *U. pumila* var. *arborescens* Litv.) A small tree, recognisable by the pinnate arrangement of its small, bright green leaves. C 1894.

plotii Druce (*U. minor* var. *lockii* (Druce) Richens) Lock's elm, Plot's elm. A large, erect tree with short, horizontal or ascending branches and long, pendent branchlets. Leaves small, smooth above. Differs from the Cornish elm in its looser habit and arching leader, particularly noticeable when young. A native of C and N England, most common in Lincolnshire.

procera Salisb. (*U. minor* var. *vulgaris*. (Aiton) Richens, *U. campestris* L. in part) English elm. A large, stately tree inseparably associated with the English landscape. Shoots downy; leaves appearing earlier than those of the wych elm (*U. glabra*), oval or rounded, acute, rough above, sharply double-toothed. Fruits glabrous, but rarely produced. There are few more pleasing sights than a tall, mature tree in autumn when the clear butter-yellow of its fading leaves is intensified by the rays of the setting sun and a background mist. SW Europe. Probably introduced to England from NW Spain. It does not produce seed in this country but spreads extensively by suckers. **'Argenteovariegata'** Leaves green, splashed and striped silvery-grey and white. A large tree is particularly conspicuous. Long cultivated. **'Louis van Houtte'** ('Van Houttei') A handsome tree with golden-yellow foliage throughout summer. **'Silvery Gem'** Leaves with irregular but conspicuous, creamy-white margins. **'Viminalis'** See *U. × viminalis*.

pumila L. Dwarf elm, Siberian elm. A species varying from a large shrub to a medium-sized tree, the latter being the form in general cultivation. Leaves ovate to ovate-lanceolate, 2.5–3.5cm long, thin in texture, simply toothed. Fruits glabrous. N Asia. I 1770. **var. arborea** See *U.* 'Pinnatoramosa'.

racemosa See *U. thomasii*.

rubra Muhl. (*U. fulva* Michx., *U. elliptica* Koehne) Slippery elm, Red elm. A striking, medium-sized tree with a spreading head of branches. Twigs densely pubescent. Leaves large, oval or obovate, velvety-hairy beneath, rough above. Fruits reddish-brown. Its large, velvety leaves make this one of the most distinct elms. C and E North America. C 1830.

'Sapporo Autumn Gold' (*U. japonica × U. pumila*) PBR A fast-growing, medium-sized tree of spreading habit, with glossy green leaves, red-tinged when young, turning yellow-green in autumn. Selected at the University of Wisconsin from plants grown from seed of *U. pumila* sent from Japan where it had crossed with *U. japonica*. Proving resistant to the aggressive strain of Dutch elm disease.

sarniensis See *U. minor* subsp. *sarniensis*.

serotina Sarg. A large tree forming a spreading head of drooping branches. Leaves oblong to obovate, slender-pointed, markedly unequal at base, bright glossy green above. Flowers produced during early autumn; fruits ciliate with silvery-white hairs. SE USA. C 1903.

sieboldii See *U. parvifolia*.

stricta See *U. minor* subsp. *cornubiensis*.

thomasii Sarg. (*U. racemosa* D. Thomas) Rock elm. A slow-growing, small to medium-sized tree, conical when young. Winter buds large and, like the young shoots, downy. Leaves oval to obovate, unequal at base and abruptly pointed, glabrous and glossy green above, downy beneath. Flowers in short racemes; fruits downy all over. E North America. I 1875.

vegeta See *U. × hollandica* 'Vegeta'. **'Commelin'** See *U. × hollandica* 'Commelin'.

villosa Brandis ex Gamble. A large, noble tree of vigorous growth and widespreading habit with smooth, silvery-grey bark, becoming fissured and greyish-brown. Leaves fresh pale green and softly downy. W Himalaya. AM 1974.

× *viminalis* Lodd. (*U. minor* 'Viminalis', *U. procera* 'Viminalis', *U. antarctica* Kirchn.) (*U. minor × U. plottii*) An extremely graceful, medium-sized tree, recalling *Zelkova × verschaffeltii*, of slow growth with arching and drooping branches. Leaves small, oblanceolate to narrowly oval, tapered at base, the margins deeply toothed. E and C England. Long cultivated. **'Aurea'** (*U. minor* 'Viminalis Aurea', *U. campestris* 'Rosseelsii', *U. campestris* 'Aurea') A picturesque form with leaves suffused golden-yellow when young, becoming yellowish-green. C about 1865. **'Marginata'** ('Argentea', *U. minor* 'Viminalis Marginata') This has leaves mottled with greyish-white, especially near the margins.

wallichiana Planch. A rare, medium-sized to large tree with downy, red-tinged young shoots and obovate, coarsely toothed leaves ending in a slender point. Himalaya.

wheatleyi See *U. minor* subsp. *sarniensis*.

'Wredei Aurea' See *U. × hollandica* 'Dampieri Aurea'.

***UMBELLULARIA** (Nees) Nutt.—**Lauraceae**—A monotypic evergreen genus resembling the bay (*Laurus nobilis*) in general appearance and requiring a warm, sunny position in well-drained soil.

californica (Hook. & Arn.) Nutt. California laurel, California bay. A strongly aromatic, large shrub or small to medium-sized tree of dense, leafy habit. Leaves oblong to oblong-lanceolate, entire, bright green or yellowish-green. Flowers small, yellowish-green, in small umbels during April, occasionally followed by oval, green fruits, 2.5cm long, turning dark purple when ripe. In exposed positions the young shoots are subject to injury by late spring frosts. The pungent aroma emitted by the leaves when crushed can cause a headache if inhaled. The 'old school' of gardeners indulged in extravagant stories of prostrate dowagers overcome by the powerful aroma. California and Oregon. Introduced by David Douglas in 1829.

Umbrella tree See *Magnolia tripetala*.

V

‡**VACCINIUM** L.—**Ericaceae**—A large genus of some 450 species of evergreen and deciduous shrubs, widely distributed over the N hemisphere, also occurring in SE Africa and on mountains in South America. They require much the same conditions as heathers, but are more tolerant of shade and moisture – in fact some species demand these conditions. While autumn colour of leaf and berry is their most notable attribute, their flowers and modest beauty at other seasons qualify them for inclusion in any representative collection of shrubs. Excellent subjects for extremely acid soils.

angustifolium Aiton (*V. pensylvanicum* var. *angustifolium* (Aiton) A. Gray) Low-bush blueberry. A dwarf shrub of compact habit with thin, wiry twigs and bristle-toothed, lanceolate leaves, richly tinted in autumn, sometimes earlier. Flowers cylindrical or bell-shaped, white or red-tinted, produced in dense clusters in April and May. Berries blue-black, bloomy, sweet and edible. Grown commercially for its fruits in North America. NE North America. **var.** *laevifolium* House (*V. pensylvanicum* Lam. not Mill.) A variable, taller-growing form with larger, lanceolate to narrowly oval or oblong leaves. I 1772. FCC 1890.

arboreum Marshall. Farkleberry, Sparkleberry. A medium-sized to large, deciduous or semi-evergreen shrub, sometimes a tree up to 10m high in some of its native haunts. Leaves ovate to obovate, up to 5cm long, leathery, glabrous and dark glossy green above, giving rich autumn tints. Flowers white, bell-shaped, in small racemes during summer, followed by black, inedible berries. S and E USA. I 1765.

arctostaphylos L. Caucasian whortleberry. A splendid, slow-growing shrub of medium size and loose, wide-spreading habit with reddish young shoots. Leaves large, up to 10cm or even 13cm long, narrowly elliptic to obovate, reticulately veined and finely toothed, turning purplish-red in autumn and often remaining until Christmas. The waxy, white or crimson-tinted, bell-shaped flowers are carried in conspicuous racemes in summer and again during autumn, followed by rounded, shining black berries. Caucasus. I 1800. AM 1970.

atrococcum (A. Gray) A. Heller. Black highbush blueberry. A small to medium-sized shrub with oval, entire leaves, densely pubescent beneath. Flowers urceolate, greenish-white, tinged red, carried in dense racemes during May, often before the leaves. Berries black and shining. It is closely related to *V. corymbosum* and, like that species, gives rich autumn colours. E North America. I before 1898.

*bracteatum Thunb. A charming, evergreen shrub, up to 2m high, with narrowly oval, glabrous leaves, copper-red when young. The cylindrical or ovoid, fragrant, white flowers are borne in numerous leafy racemes during late summer and autumn, sometimes earlier. Berries red. Easily recognised in flower by the presence of small, leaf-like bracts on the main flower stalk. Japan, Korea, China, Taiwan. I 1829.

caespitosum Michx. Dwarf bilberry. A dwarf, spreading shrub with green or reddish shoots and small, finely toothed leaves. Flowers pinkish-white, borne singly in April-May, followed by blue-black, bloomy berries. North America. I 1823.

corymbosum L. Swamp blueberry, High-bush blueberry. A colourful, small to medium-sized shrub forming a dense thicket of erect, branching stems. Leaves ovate to ovate-lanceolate, up to 8.5cm long, bright green and reticulate, turning vivid scarlet and bronze in autumn. Clusters of pale pink or white, urn-shaped flowers are borne in May. Berries comparatively large, black with a blue bloom, sweet and edible, like small grapes. Extensively commercially cultivated in the USA for its fruit. Several cultivars selected for fruit quality are also available. E North America. I 1765. ♀ 2002. AM 1990 (for fruit).

*crassifolium Andr. Creeping blueberry. A dwarf, evergreen shrub of creeping habit with slender, reddish stems up to 15cm high. Leaves oval, shining green and leathery, densely crowding the twigs. Small, bell-shaped, rose-red flowers are borne in terminal racemes in May and June. Berries black. SE USA. I 1787.

cylindraceum Sm. (*V. longiflorum* Wikstr.) A superb, semi-evergreen species. An erect, medium-sized to large shrub with bright green, finely toothed and reticulate leaves, often green until well into the New Year. Flowers cylindrical, 12mm long, densely packed in short racemes along the previous year's branchlets during late summer and autumn, red in bud, opening to pale yellow-green, tinged red, recalling *Agapetes serpens*. Berries cylindrical blue-black, bloomy. Azores. ♀ 2002. AM 1990 (for fruit).

*delavayi Franch. A neat, compact, evergreen shrub slowly reaching 1.8m, densely set with small, box-like, leathery leaves, usually notched at the apex. Tiny, pink-tinged, whitish flowers are borne in small racemes terminating the shoots in late spring or early summer. Berries purplish-blue, rounded. In its native state it grows on cliffs and rocks and as an epiphyte on trees. Discovered by the Abbé Delavay in Yunnan. I before 1923 by George Forrest. AM 1950.

deliciosum Piper. Cascade bilberry. A dwarf, tufted, glabrous shrub with oval or obovate leaves. Solitary, pinkish, globular flowers in May are replaced by sweet, edible, black, bloomy berries. NW USA. I 1920.

*floribundum Kunth (*V. mortinia* Benth.) A beautiful, small, evergreen shrub with attractive, red young growths and small, ovate, dark green leaves, purplish-red when young, densely crowding the spray-like branches. Flowers cylindrical, rose-pink, carried in dense racemes in June. Berries red, edible. Although its native haunts are close to the equator, it is remarkably hardy in the southern counties of England. Ecuador. I about 1840. AM 1935 (as *V. mortinia*).

†**gaultheriifolium* (Griff.) Hook. f. ex C.B. Clarke. A small to medium-sized, evergreen shrub of loose habit, with bloomy young shoots. Leaves elliptic, 7.5–13cm long, acuminate, glossy green and attractively veined above, paler and covered by a blue-white bloom beneath, entire or minutely toothed. Flowers white, in corymbs in late summer. Berries black. Related to *V. glaucoalbum*, but more graceful in habit, and with larger, slender-pointed leaves. E Himalaya, W China.

*glaucoalbum Hook. f. ex C.B. Clarke. An attractive, evergreen shrub, suckering and forming clumps 1.2–1.8m in

height. Leaves comparatively large, oval or ovate, grey-green above, vividly blue-white beneath. Flowers cylindrical, pale pink, borne among conspicuous, rosy, silvery-white bracts in racemes during May and June. Berries black, blue-bloomy, often lasting well into winter. Liable to damage by frost in cold areas of the British Isles. E Himalaya, S Tibet. C 1900. ♀ 2002. AM 1931.

hirsutum Buckley. Hairy huckleberry. A small, suckering shrub producing dense thickets of slender, hairy stems with ovate or elliptic, entire leaves, often colouring well in autumn. Flowers cylindrical, white, tinged-pink, in short racemes during May. Berries blue-black, rounded, covered with tiny, glandular hairs, sweet and edible. SE USA. I 1887.

longiflorum See *V. cylindraceum*.

***macrocarpon** Aiton (*Oxycoccus macrocarpus* (Aiton) Pursh) American cranberry. A prostrate shrublet with slender, creeping, wiry stems and small, delicate, oval or oblong leaves, glaucous beneath. Flowers small, drooping, pink, the petals curving back to reveal a beak of yellow anthers, carried in short racemes during summer. Berries red, globular, 12–20mm across, edible but acid in flavour. Selected forms of this species are the commercially grown cranberry of the USA. It requires a moist, peaty or boggy soil in which to thrive. E North America. I 1760.

membranaceum Douglas ex Torr. Thin-leaf huckleberry. A small, erect-growing shrub with glabrous, angular branches and ovate to oblong, bright green leaves. Flowers urn-shaped, greenish-white or pink-tinged, produced singly in the leaf axils in June, followed by purplish-black, edible berries. Closely related to the native bilberry (*V. myrtillus*), which it much resembles. C and E North America. I 1828.

mortinia See *V. floribundum*.

***moupinense** Franch. A neat-growing, dwarf, evergreen shrub of dense habit. Leaves narrowly obovate or ovate, 12mm long, leathery and usually entire, densely crowding the branches. Flowers urn-shaped, mahogany-red, borne on similarly coloured stalks in dense racemes during May and June. Berries purplish-black, rounded. Resembling *V. delavayi* in many ways, differing in its leaves, which are rounded, not notched at the apex, and in its glabrous inflorescence. W China. I 1909 by Ernest Wilson.

***myrsinites** Lam. Evergreen blueberry. A dwarf, spreading, evergreen shrub of compact habit, with small, neat, oval, finely toothed leaves. Flowers white or pink-tinged, rose in bud, in terminal and axillary clusters during April and May. Berries blue-black. SE USA. C 1813.

myrtillus L. Bilberry, Whortleberry, Whinberry, Blaeberry. A familiar British native species of heaths and moorland, forming a dense, suckering patch of slender, bright green, angular stems. Leaves ovate, finely toothed. Flowers globular, greenish-pink, singly or in pairs in the leaf axils from late April to June, followed by bloomy, black, edible berries. Europe to Caucasus and N Asia.

†***nummularia** Hook. f. & Thoms. ex C.B. Clarke. This is probably the most attractive dwarf species in cultivation. A compact, evergreen shrub with bristly-hairy, arching shoots neatly clothed with a double row of small, leathery, dark glossy green, orbicular-ovate leaves. The small,

cylindrical rose-red flowers are borne in small, dense clusters at the ends of the shoots in May and June, followed by globular, black, edible berries. Although hardy only in mild localities, this choice little shrub makes an ideal alpine house plant. It is excellent for a not too dry, sheltered, shady bank. Himalaya. I about 1850. AM 1932.

***ovatum** Pursh. Box blueberry, California huckleberry. An attractive, evergreen shrub of medium size and dense, compact habit. Leaves, thickly crowding the downy branches, are 1–4cm long, ovate to oblong, leathery, bright coppery-red when young, becoming polished, dark green. Flowers bell-shaped, white or pink, in short racemes during May and June. Berries red at first, ripening black. A useful evergreen for cutting. W North America. I 1826 by David Douglas. AM 1993 (for flower).

***oxycoccos** L. (*Oxycoccus palustris* Pers.) Cranberry. A prostrate, evergreen shrublet of moorland and mountain bogs, producing far-reaching wiry stems bearing tiny, silver-backed leaves. The tiny, nodding flowers with pink, recurved petals and a yellow staminal beak are borne on short, erect, thread-like stems and recall those of a *Dodecatheon* (Shooting Star), but are much smaller. They appear during May and June and are followed by edible, red, rounded fruits that possess an agreeable acid taste. Requires a moist, peaty soil to thrive. Widely distributed in the cooler regions of the N hemisphere from North America eastwards to Japan, including British Isles. C 1789.

padifolium Sm. (*V. maderense* Link) Madeiran whortleberry. A strong-growing, medium-sized, semi-evergreen shrub of rather stiff, erect habit. Leaves ovate, 2.5–6cm long, reticulately veined. Flowers bell-shaped, greenish, with a pale brown "eye" of stamens, appearing in clusters in June. Berries globular, purplish-blue. The leaves often remain green until the New Year. Remarkably hardy in view of its origin. Mts of Madeira. I 1777.

pallidum Aiton A small shrub with arching branches and oval, slender-pointed, wavy-edged leaves, glaucous beneath. The pale pink, cylindrical flowers in June are followed by round, purplish-black, bloomy berries, which are sweet and edible. Rich autumn colours. E USA. C 1878.

parvifolium Sm. Red bilberry, Red huckleberry. A variable, small to medium-sized shrub, usually of erect habit, with sharply angled stems densely furnished with variably shaped, entire leaves. Flowers globular, pinkish, borne singly in the leaf axils in May and June, followed by conspicuous, red berries, edible but acid. W North America to Alaska. I 1881.

pensilvanicum See *V. angustifolium* var. *laevifolium*.

praestans Lamb. A creeping shrub forming dense patches of shortly ascending shoots 3–10cm high. Leaves are obovate to broadly ovate, 2.5–6cm long. Flowers bell-shaped, white to reddish, borne singly or in clusters of 2–3 in June. Comparatively large, edible berries are globular, 12mm across, bright glossy red, fragrant and sweet. A choice little species for growing in a moist, cool place. Its leaves colour richly in autumn. NE Asia, Japan. I 1914 by Ernest Wilson.

***retusum** (Griff.) Hook. f. ex C.B. Clarke. A dwarf, evergreen shrub, slowly reaching 0.6–1m, with stiff, downy shoots and small, bright green, oval, leathery leaves, retuse and mucronate at the apex. Small, urn-shaped, pink flowers are carried in short, terminal racemes in May, followed by black berries. Rare and shy-flowering. E Himalaya. I about 1882.

smallii A. Gray. A small, erect-branched shrub with elliptic to broadly ovate leaves. Flowers bell-shaped, greenish-white to pinkish, borne 1–3 together in clusters in May and June. Berries purple-black, globular. Japan. I 1915.

stamineum L. Deerberry, Squaw huckleberry. A delightful, small to medium-sized shrub with thinly downy young shoots and oval, blue-green leaves to 9cm long. Small, dainty, white flowers are borne in open racemes in late spring. The individual flowers are open bell-shaped with exserted stamens, nodding on a slender pedicel, and sub-tended by a small, leaf-like bract. Fruits usually purple to black. Among the most distinct and attractive of the genus but uncommon in gardens. E North America. I 1772.

uliginosum L. Bog whortleberry. An uncommon, dwarf shrub of bushy habit with small, obovate or oval, blue-green leaves. Flowers pale pink, singly or in clusters in the leaf axils, in May and June. Globular, black, bloomy, sweet berries are said to produce headache and giddiness if eaten in quantity. Cool moorland and mountainous regions of the N hemisphere including N England and Scotland.

†*urceolatum* Hemsl. An evergreen shrub producing strong, downy shoots, 1.2m or occasionally to 1.8m high. Leaves thick and leathery, ovate-elliptic to oblong-elliptic, slender-pointed. Flowers urn-shaped, red-tinged, in axillary clusters in June. Berries globular, black. W China. I 1910.

virgatum Aiton. Rabbiteye blueberry. An attractive, small to medium-sized, graceful shrub of elegant habit. The long, slender branches arch at their extremities and bear narrow, ovate to lanceolate leaves, rich shades of red in autumn. Flowers white or pink-tinged, in axillary clusters in May and June. Berries black. E North America. I 1770.

*vitis-idaea L. Cowberry, Lingberry. A dwarf, creeping, evergreen shrub, native of moors and woods in the north and west of the British Isles. Leaves small, box-like, glossy dark green above, paler and gland-dotted beneath. Flowers bell-shaped, white, tinged pink, borne in short, terminal racemes from June to August, followed by globular, red, edible but acid berries. An excellent groundcover plant in shade. Northern regions of North America, Europe and Asia, and mountains of C and S Europe. **'Koralle'** An attractive, free-fruiting form bearing relatively large, bright red berries. C 1969. ♀ 2002. AM 1976. **subsp.** *minus* (Lodd.) Hultén ('Nana') An interesting miniature shrub with leaves half the size of the typical form. N USA, Canada. C 1825. **'Variegata'** A form with creamy-white-margined leaves, not very constant.

†*VALLEA Mutis ex L. f.—Elaeocarpaceae*—A monotypic genus.

stipularis L. f. An unusual, large shrub or small tree. Leaves glabrous, somewhat fleshy and very variable, ovate and entire to 3-lobed and ivy-like, deeply cordate at base, grey and reticulate beneath, with small, kidney-shaped

stipules. The deep pink flowers, with 5, 3-lobed petals and numerous stamens are usually borne in early summer. Best against a wall in most areas. Andes, from Colombia to Bolivia. C 1928. AM 1978.

Varnish tree See *Rhus verniciflua*.

VELLA L. (*Pseudocytisus* Kuntze)—**Cruciferae**—A small genus of 4 species of deciduous and evergreen shrubs, natives of the W Mediterranean region, some of the few shrubby members of the cabbage family.

*pseudocytisus L. (*Pseudocytisus integrifolius* (Salisb.) Rehder) A small, evergreen shrub, suitable for maritime exposure, with spiny, bristly stems and small, obovate, bristly leaves. Long, erect, terminal racemes of small, yellow, 4-petalled flowers in late May to early June. Requires a hot, dry, well-drained position to succeed. Spain. C 1759.

†**VERBENA** L.—**Verbenaceae**—A large genus of some 250 species of mostly annual and perennial herbs, widely distributed but largely in South America. The following woody species is fairly hardy in most areas of the British Isles, enjoying a warm, sunny position in a well-drained soil.

*tridens Lag. This very unusual shrub looks like an ungainly tree heath with its stiffly erect, rigid stems thickly crowded with tiny, downy, often spiny leaves. It attains a height of 1–1.5m. Flowers white to rosy-lilac, strongly vanilla-scented, in terminal spikes in July. In its native land it is often collected and used as fuel. Patagonia. I 1928 by Clarence Elliott. AM 1934.

VERONICA The shrubby members of this genus are featured under *Hebe* and *Parahebe*.

†*VESTIA* Willd.—**Solanaceae**—A monotypic genus related to *Cestrum*, requiring the same conditions.

foetida (Ruiz & Pav.) Hoffmanns. (*V. lycioides* Willd.) A small, evergreen shrub of erect habit, foetid when bruised. Leaves oblong to obovate, 2.5–5cm long. Flowers nodding, tubular, pale yellow, profusely borne in the axils of the upper leaves from April to July, followed by small, yellow fruits. Only suitable for the milder areas of the British Isles where it requires a warm, sunny position in well-drained soil. It has succeeded with us for several years planted against a south-east wall. Chile. I 1815. ♀ 2002.

lycioides See *V. foetida*.

VIBURNUM L.—**Caprifoliaceae**—A large genus of about 150 species of evergreen and deciduous shrubs and small trees, widely distributed mainly in N temperate regions, extending into Malaysia and South America. Most have white flowers, some very fragrant, in flat heads or round corymbs, often followed by brightly coloured fruits. Several of the evergreen species are most effective in leaf, while many of the deciduous species give rich autumn colour. Those species grown for their fruits often give the most satisfactory results when planted 2 or more together to assist cross-pollination.

acerifolium L. Dockmackie. A small shrub, to 2m high, bearing maple-like, 3-lobed, coarsely toothed leaves, covered with black dots beneath. Flowers white, borne in terminal corymbs in June, but not particularly attractive. Fruits ovoid, red at first turning purplish-black. The foliage becomes rich dark crimson in autumn. E North America. I 1736.

alnifolium See *V. lantanoides*.

'Anne Russell' See *V. × burkwoodii* 'Anne Russell'.

*atrocyaneum C.B. Clarke. An attractive, evergreen shrub of medium to large size and dense, bushy habit. Leaves ovate, acute, glandular-toothed, dark green above, copper-tinted when young. Fruits small, steely-blue, effective in winter. Sometimes grown under the name *V. wardii*. Himalaya. I 1931 by Kingdon-Ward.

awabuki See *V. odoratissimum* var. *awabuki*.

betulifolium Batalin. A large, erect shrub with ovate to rhomboid, coarsely toothed leaves and corymbs of white flowers in June to July. A magnificent sight in autumn when the long, swaying branches are heavy with innumerable bunches of redcurrant-like fruits which persist into winter. Unfortunately, they are none too freely borne on young plants. One of the finest fruiting shrubs but to ensure fruiting, plant several in a group from different sources. W and C China. I 1901 by Ernest Wilson. FCC 1957. AM 1936.

bitchiuense Makino (*V. carlesii* var. *bitchiuense* (Makino) Nakai) A medium-sized shrub of slender, open habit, similar to *V. carlesii*, to which it is closely related, but rather taller and more lax. Leaves ovate-elliptic, dark metallic green. The sweetly scented, flesh-pink flowers are produced in clusters during late April and May, followed by inconspicuous black fruit. Japan. I 1911.

× *bodnantense* Stearn (*V. farreri* × *V. grandiflorum*) A medium-sized to large shrub of strong, upright habit with densely packed clusters of sweetly scented, rose-tinted flowers, freely produced over several weeks from October onwards. Its flowers are remarkably frost-resistant and provide a cheering sight on a cold winter's day. A splendid hybrid, first raised at the Royal Botanic Garden, Edinburgh in 1933 and later at Bodnant in 1935. **'Charles Lamont'** Similar in vigour and habit to 'Dawn' but with flowers of a purer pink resembling *V. farreri*. One of the original seedlings raised at Edinburgh. ♀ 2002. **'Dawn'** The first-named form, a vigorous, hardy shrub with leaves approaching those of *V. grandiflorum* and ample clusters of richly fragrant flowers during late autumn and winter. Anthers pink. ♀ 2002. AM 1947. **'Deben'** A lovely selection producing clusters of sweetly scented flowers, pink in bud, opening white during mild spells from October to April. Anthers cream. ♀ 2002. FCC 1965. AM 1962.

bracteatum Rehder. A rare shrub of medium size which is related to *V. dentatum*, with rounded leaves and cymose clusters of white flowers in May and June, followed by bluish-black fruits. The name refers to the conspicuous bractlets that accompany the flowers. SE USA (Georgia). C 1904.

buddlejifolium C.H. Wright. This is a medium-sized, nearly evergreen shrub of distinctive appearance. Leaves oblong-lanceolate, up to 20cm long, pale green and softly pubescent above, thickly grey-felted beneath. Flowers white, in clusters 7.5cm across, in June. Fruits red at first, finally black. C China. I 1900 by Ernest Wilson.

burejaeticum Regel & Herder. A large shrub with downy young shoots and ovate or elliptic leaves, pubescent beneath. Flowers white, in downy, cymose clusters during May. Fruits bluish-black. A rare species akin to *V. lantana*. Manchuria, N China. C 1900.

*× burkwoodii Burkwood & Skipwith ex Anon. (*V. carlesii × V. utile*) A medium-sized, evergreen shrub, taller than *V. carlesii*, from which it inherits its clusters of fragrant, pink-budded, white flowers, produced from January to May. Its ovate leaves are dark shining green above and brownish-grey-felted beneath. Raised by Messrs Burkwood and Skipwith in 1924. AM 1929. **'Anne Russell'** A lovely hybrid with clusters of fragrant flowers. The result of a backcross with *V. carlesii*. Raised about 1951. ♀ 2002. AM and Cory Cup 1957. **'Chenaultii'** A medium-sized, semi-evergreen shrub, similar in general appearance to *V. × burkwoodii* and with the same qualities. **'Conoy'** The result of a backcross of 'Park Farm Hybrid' with *V. utile* made at the US National Arboretum, Washington in 1968. It was selected for its profuse and long-persistent, glossy red fruits which later turn black. **'Fulbrook'** A medium-sized shrub producing clusters of comparatively large, sweetly scented flowers, pink in bud opening white. Like 'Anne Russell', the result of a backcross with *V. carlesii*. ♀ 2002. AM 1957. **'Mohawk'** A backcross with *V. carlesii* raised at the US National Arboretum, Washington and selected in 1959. Flowers bright red in bud opening white, red on the outside, strongly fragrant. Leaves glossy green, orange-red in autumn. AM 2001. **'Park Farm Hybrid'** A strong-growing shrub of more spreading habit than typical *V. × burkwoodii*, and with fragrant, slightly larger flowers produced in April and May. ♀ 2002. AM 1949.

*calvum Rehder (*V. schneiderianum* Hand.-Mazz.) A medium-sized to large, evergreen shrub, akin to *V. tinus*, with ovate or elliptic, wavy-edged, sage-green leaves. Corymbs of small, white flowers appear in June and July, followed by glossy, bluish-black fruits. W China. C 1933.

canbyi See *V. dentatum*.

× *carlcephalum* Burkwood & Skipwith ex A.V. Pike (*V. carlesii × V. macrocephalum*) A splendid, medium-sized shrub of compact habit, producing rounded corymbs, 10–13cm across, of comparatively large, very fragrant, pink-budded, white flowers in May. The leaves often colour richly in autumn. Raised about 1932. ♀ 2002. AM 1946. **'Cayuga'** A backcross with *V. carlesii* raised at the US National Arboretum, Washington and selected in 1960. It is more compact than the typical form with smaller but more profuse heads of fragrant, white flowers, pink in bud.

carlesii Hemsl. One of the most popular of all shrubs. A medium-sized shrub of rounded habit, with ovate, downy leaves, dull green above, greyish beneath, often colouring in autumn. Rounded clusters of pure white flowers are pink in bud and emit a strong, sweet, daphne-like fragrance during April and May. Fruits jet black. Korea. I 1902. FCC 1909. AM 1908. **'Aurora'** An outstanding selection made by the Slieve Donard Nursery, with red flower buds opening to pink and deliciously fragrant. ♀ 2002. **var. *bitchiuense*** See *V. bitchiuense*. **'Charis'** Another Donard selection, extremely vigorous in growth, bearing flowers that are red in bud, passing to pink and finally white, and richly scented. **'Diana'** A strong-growing form of compact habit with flower buds opening red, passing to pink, strongly fragrant. Young foliage with a distinct, purple tinge.

‡***cassinoides*** L. Blue haw, Withe-rod. A medium-sized shrub of rounded habit with scurfy young shoots. The ovate-elliptic, leathery, dull dark green leaves are bronze when unfolding and in autumn change to crimson and scarlet. The small, creamy-white flowers in June are replaced by rounded, red fruits changing to metallic blue, finally black. E North America. Not satisfactory on thin soils over chalk. I 1761. **'Nanum'** ('Bullatum') A remarkable, slow-growing shrub, having large, peculiarly formed, wavy leaves that colour richly in autumn. In spite of growing here for many years it has never flowered. It may be a form of *V. lentago*.

'Chenaultii' See *V.* × *burkwoodii* 'Chenaultii'.

'Chesapeake' (*V.* × *carlcephalum* 'Cayuga' × *V. utile*) A small shrub forming a dense mound broader than tall with dark glossy green, long-persistent leaves. Flowers pink in bud opening white, followed by red fruits turning black.

****cinnamomifolium*** Rehder. A large, handsome, evergreen shrub with large, dark glossy, leathery leaves, similar to those of *V. davidii*, but thinner and entire, or almost so. Flowers small, dull white, carried in cymose clusters, 10–15cm across, in June, followed in autumn by small, shining, egg-shaped, blue-black fruits. An imposing species when well grown, it requires a more sheltered position than *V. davidii* and is equally happy in semi-shade. China. I 1904 by Ernest Wilson. 🏆 2002.

coriaceum See *V. cylindricum*.

‡***corylifolium*** Hook. f. & Thoms. A medium-sized shrub with reddish-brown, hairy shoots and broad, ovate or rounded, hairy leaves which colour attractively in autumn. Flowers white, in flattened heads during May and June. Fruits bright red, long-lasting. E Himalaya, C and W China. I 1907.

cotinifolium D. Don. A medium-sized to large shrub with densely hairy young shoots and leaf undersurfaces. Leaves broadly ovate to rounded, up to 13cm long, sometimes turning crimson in autumn and hanging for several weeks. Flowers are white, flushed pink. They are borne in terminal cymes in May; fruits ovoid, red then black. Related to *V. lantana*. Afghanistan, Himalaya. I 1830.

****cylindricum*** Buch.-Ham. ex D. Don (*V. coriaceum* Blume) A large, evergreen shrub or occasionally a small tree, with glabrous, warty shoots and comparatively large, narrowly oval or oblong, to broadly ovate, dull green leaves, paler beneath, older leaves tending to hang. The upper surface is covered by a thin, waxy film which cracks and turns grey when bent or rubbed. The characteristic, tubular, white flowers have protruding, lilac stamens and are carried in conspicuous, flattened heads from July to September. Fruits egg-shaped, black. Subject to injury in severe winters. Himalaya, W China. I 1881.

dasyanthum Rehder. A medium-sized shrub of upright habit with ovate, slender-pointed leaves, glabrous except for hairs on the veins and in the vein axils beneath. Flowers white, borne in branched corymbs in June and July, followed by showy bunches of bright red, egg-shaped fruits. Closely related to *V. hupehense*. C China. I 1907 by Ernest Wilson. AM 1916.

****davidii*** Franch. A small, evergreen shrub of compact habit, generally forming a low, widespreading mound and creating good groundcover. The large, narrowly oval, leathery leaves are conspicuously 3-nerved and are glossy dark green above, paler beneath. Flowers small, dull white, borne in terminal cymes in June. The bright turquoise-blue, egg-shaped fruits are never too plentiful but are particularly striking during winter, combining effectively with the lustrous green foliage. Several plants should be planted together to effect cross-pollination. Some plants seem dominantly male and others female while others are possibly mules: it is all in the luck of the draw. A popular, widely planted species introduced from W China by Ernest Wilson in 1904. 🏆 2002. AM 1971 (for fruit). AM 1912 (for flower).

dentatum L. (*V. canbyi* Sarg., *V. pubescens* var. *canbyi* (Rehder) Blake) Southern arrow wood. A medium-sized to large shrub, bearing broad-ovate to rounded, coarsely toothed leaves, hairy beneath at least on the veins. Flowers white, borne in slender-stalked cymes during May and June. Fruits egg-shaped, blue-black. The strong, straight basal shoots are said to have been used for making arrows by the native Indians. E North America. I 1736. **var. *lucidum*** See *V. recognitum*. **var. *pubescens*** Aiton (*V. pubescens* (Aiton) Pursh) Leaves thicker and more hairy beneath. I 1731.

dilatatum Thunb. ex Murray. An excellent shrub of medium size with downy young shoots and ovate to obovate or rounded, coarsely toothed leaves, hairy on both surfaces. Flowers pure white, pungently scented, produced in numerous trusses in late May and June. Fruits vivid red, borne in heavy bunches and often lasting well into winter. Does particularly well in the eastern counties. Japan. I before 1875. AM 1968. **'Catskill'** A seedling selected at the US National Arboretum in 1958. Dense, mound-like habit to 1.5m tall and twice as much across. Leaves smaller, colouring well in autumn. **'Erie'** A selection raised at the US National Arboretum from Japanese seed, making a medium-sized, spreading shrub, the leaves turning orange, red and yellow in autumn. Profuse, orange-red fruits, turning to coral-red, persist well into winter. **f. *xanthocarpum*** Rehder. A form with yellow fruits. AM 1936.

edule (Michx.) Raf. (*V. pauciflorum* (Raf.) Torr. & A. Gray) Mooseberry. A small, straggling shrub with broad, oval or rounded leaves, weakly 3-lobed at apex. Flowers white, in small clusters during May. Fruits red. Requires a moist, shaded position. North America. I 1880.

erosum Thunb. ex Murray. A medium-sized, compact shrub with sharply toothed, rounded, almost sessile leaves. Flowers white, produced in cymes during May, followed in autumn by red fruits. Not free-fruiting as a rule. Japan. I 1844 by Robert Fortune.

†***erubescens*** Wall. ex DC. A medium-sized shrub or occasionally a small tree with ovate to obovate, acuminate leaves. Flowers fragrant, white, tinted pink, borne in loose, pendent clusters in July. One of the few viburnums with paniculate flower clusters. Fruits red then black. A lovely shrub, but too tender for cold or exposed gardens.

A form of this species introduced by Harry van de Laar (as *V. grandiflorum*) has white flowers tipped with deep pink. Himalaya. **var. gracilipes** Rehder. A perfectly hardy form with elliptic, usually glabrous leaves and longer panicles of fragrant flowers. Free-fruiting. C China. I 1910 by Ernest Wilson. FCC 1988.

'Eskimo' A small, semi-evergreen shrub of dense habit with leathery, dark glossy green leaves. Compact, snow-ball-like inflorescences, 7.5cm across, of white flowers open from creamy buds tinged with pink. The result of self-pollination of a seedling from the cross *V.* × *carlcephalum* 'Cayuga' × *V. utile*.

farreri Stearn (*V. fragrans* Bunge not Loisel.) A medium-sized to large shrub with the primary branches stiff and erect but as the shrub ages it forms a broad, rounded outline. Leaves oval or obovate, strongly toothed and with conspicuous, parallel veins, bronze when young. Flowers produced in both terminal and lateral clusters, pink in bud, opening white, sweetly-scented. Fruits red, only occasionally produced in cultivation. One of the most popular of all shrubs and a favourite for the winter garden. Its flowers appear in November and continue through winter. N China. First introduced by William Purdom in 1910, later by Reginald Farrer. ♥ 2002. AM 1921 (as *V. fragrans*). **'Candidissimum'** ('Album') A distinct form with green unfolding leaves and pure white flowers. AM 1926. **'Farrer's Pink'** Deep pink in bud opening white, flushed pink. Flowers profusely in late autumn and early winter. **'Nanum'** ('Compactum') A dwarf form of dense, mound-like habit, not free-flowering. AM 1937.

foetens See *V. grandiflorum* f. *foetens*.

foetidum Wall. A medium-sized to large, semi-evergreen shrub with oval to oblong leaves, entire or coarsely-toothed and often 3-lobed at the apex. Flowers white with purple anthers, in rounded clusters in July. Fruits scarlet-crimson. Large specimens in full fruit are extremely effective in autumn. Himalaya, W China. I 1901 by Ernest Wilson. AM 1934.

fragrans See *V. farreri*.

'Fulbrook' See *V.* × *burkwoodii* 'Fulbrook'.

‡*furcatum* Blume. A large shrub closely related to and resembling *V. lantanoides*, but of more upright habit. Leaves broadly ovate or rounded, up to 15cm long, conspicuously veined and colouring richly over a long period during late summer and autumn. Flowers in May, in flattened, terminal corymbs, surrounded by several sterile ray-florets, resembling a lacecap hydrangea. Fruits red, becoming black at maturity. A beautiful species of elegant charm; an excellent woodland plant. Japan, Taiwan. I 1892. ♥ 2002. AM 1944.

× **globosum** Coombes (*V. calvum* × *V. davidii*) A medium-sized, evergreen shrub of dense, rounded habit. Leaves leathery, narrowly-elliptic to lanceolate, 8–12cm long, shallowly and distantly toothed, sometimes twisted or undulate, dark green and reticulate above, on slender, reddish petioles. Small, white flowers are produced in flat-topped clusters in late spring and often at other times of the year. Fruits ovoid, bluish-black. An interesting hybrid that occurred in our West Hill nursery, Winchester in 1964. It was raised from seed collected from *V. davidii* which grew close to a specimen of *V. calvum*. The habit is intermediate between those of the parents, but much more compact than either. **'Jermyns Globe'** The best form, of dense, rounded habit, selected from the original seedlings.

grandiflorum Wall. ex DC. (*V. nervosum* auct. not D. Don) A medium-sized shrub of stiff, upright habit and related to *V. farreri*. Leaves elliptic to ovate, of firm texture with parallel veins. Flowers fragrant, carmine-red in bud, opening deep pink, fading to blush, produced in dense clusters during February and March. It differs from *V. farreri* in its more hairy, multi-veined leaves and slightly larger individual flowers. Himalaya. I 1914. AM 1937. **f. foetens** (Decne.) N.P. Taylor & Zappi (*V. foetens* Decne.) A beautiful, fragrant, winter-flowering shrub of medium size. It is closely related to *V. grandiflorum*, differing in its looser, more spreading habit, large, smoother leaves and its white flowers, occasionally pale pink in bud, opening from January to March. Fruits are said to be red turning to black. It is not one of the easiest plants to make happy. It seems to appreciate a good deep moist loam in half shade and grows well on chalk on the site of our West Hill nursery in Winchester. C 1937. W Himalaya. **'Snow White'** (Lowndes 1409) Flowers deep pink in bud, nearly white inside when open, flushed pink on the backs of the lobes. I from Nepal by Col Donald Lowndes in 1950. FCC 1974. AM 1970.

*harryanum Rehder. A medium-sized shrub of dense, bushy growth. A species that is distinctive because of its small, neat, orbicular leaves, dark green above and 1–2cm long. They appear in whorls of 3 on strong shoots. The small, white flowers appear in late spring; fruits ovoid, shining black. Introduced by Ernest Wilson from China in 1904, and named after Sir Harry Veitch who did more than any other nurseryman to introduce new plants to western gardens.

*henryi Hemsl. A medium-sized, evergreen shrub of open, erect habit with rather stiff branches and narrowly elliptic, glossy green, leathery leaves recalling those of *Ilex fargesii*. Flowers white, fragrant, carried in pyramidal panicles in June followed by colourful, bright red, then black, ellipsoid fruits. C China (Hubei). First discovered by Augustine Henry in 1887. I 1901 by Ernest Wilson. FCC 1910.

hessei See *V. wrightii* 'Hessei'.

× **hillieri** Stearn (*V. erubescens* × *V. henryi*) A semi-evergreen shrub of medium size with spreading and ascending branches and narrowly oval leaves, copper-tinted when unfolding and suffused bronze-red in winter. Flowers creamy-white, profusely borne in panicles in June. Fruits red, finally black. An attractive hybrid which originated in our nurseries in 1950. Wilson also reports having seen this hybrid in W Hubei (China). **'Winton'** The original selected clone. ♥ 2002. AM 1956.

hupehense Rehder. A very tough shrub of medium size with broadly ovate, coarsely toothed leaves, which change colour early in autumn. Flowers white in clusters during May and June. Egg-shaped, orange-yellow, finally red fruits are conspicuous in autumn. C China. I 1908 by Ernest Wilson. AM 1952.

ichangense Rehder. A small to medium-sized shrub with slender branches and ovate to ovate-lanceolate, slender-pointed leaves. Flowers white, fragrant, borne in clusters during May. Fruits bright red. C and W China. I 1901 by Ernest Wilson.

japonicum (Thunb. ex Murray) Spreng. (*V. macrophyllum* Blume) A handsome, medium-sized, evergreen shrub with firm, leathery, often bullate leaves, up to 15cm long and 10cm wide. They may be entire or undulately toothed in the upper half and are glossy dark green above, paler and minutely punctate beneath; petioles stout, grooved above. Flowers white, fragrant, borne in dense, rounded trusses in June, but not on young plants. Fruits red, long-persistent. Japan. I about 1879 by Charles Maries.

'Jermyns Globe' See *V.* × *globosum* 'Jermyns Globe'.

× *juddii* Rehder (*V. bitchiuense* × *V. carlesii*) A delightful, small to medium-sized shrub of bushy habit, freely producing its terminal clusters of sweetly scented, pink-tinted flowers during April and May. A plant of better constitution than *V. carlesii* and less susceptible to aphid attack. Raised in 1920 by William Judd, one-time propagator at the Arnold Arboretum, Boston, USA. ♀ 2002.

kansuense Batalin. A medium-sized, loose-growing shrub with deeply lobed, maple-like leaves. Pink-flushed, white flowers in June and July are followed by red fruits. Succeeds best in half shade. Not very lime-tolerant. W China. I 1908 by Ernest Wilson.

lantana L. Wayfaring tree. A large, native shrub, a familiar hedgerow plant, particularly on the chalk downs of Southern England. Leaves broadly ovate, covered beneath, as are the young shoots, with a dense, stellate tomentum, sometimes turning dark crimson in autumn. Flowers creamy-white in May and June, followed by oblong fruits which slowly mature from red to black. C and S Europe, N Asia Minor, N Africa. 'Aureum' ('Auratum') Young growths yellowish; not very exciting. var. *discolor* Huter (*V. maculatum* Pant.) An interesting, geographical form from the Balkans with smaller, neater leaves, white- or pale grey-tomentose beneath. 'Mohican' A form of dense habit with dark green foliage and orange-red fruits. Selected in 1956 at the US National Arboretum, Washington.

‡*lantanoides* Michx. (*V. alnifolium* Marshall) Hobble bush. A distinct and attractive shrub of medium size, with comparatively large, strongly veined leaves. In shape they are broadly ovate or orbicular, 10–20cm long, downy above at first, more densely so beneath, turning deep claret in autumn. The first inflorescences appear in May and June and recall those of a lacecap hydrangea, having a marginal row of conspicuous, white, sterile florets. Fruits red, turning blackish-purple. Thrives in woodland conditions. A low, suckering shrub as seen in the forests of New England but reaching 2–2.5m in cultivation in the British Isles. E North America. I 1820. AM 1952.

lentago L. Sheepberry. A strong-growing, large shrub or small tree of erect habit with ovate to obovate leaves, dark shining green above, giving rich autumn tints. Flowers creamy-white, produced in terminal cymes during May and June. Fruits blue-black and bloomy, like small Merryweather damsons. E North America. I 1761.

lobophyllum Graebn. A medium-sized shrub allied to *V. betulifolium* and *V. dilatatum*. Leaves variable, usually ovate or rounded with an abrupt point and coarsely

toothed. Flowers white in June followed by bright red fruits. W China. I 1901 by Ernest Wilson. AM 1947.

macrocephalum Fortune (*V. macrocephalum* f. *keteleeri* (Carrière) Rehder) A semi-evergreen, medium-sized shrub of rounded habit. Leaves ovate to elliptic, 5–10cm long. Flowers white, in lacecap-like heads margined with large, sterile florets, in May. China. 'Sterile' Flowers sterile, gathered together in large, globular heads, 7.5–15cm across, like the sterile forms of *Hydrangea macrophylla*, giving a spectacular display in May. Best grown against a warm, sunny wall in cold districts. A garden form, introduced from China in 1844 by Robert Fortune. AM 1927.

molle Michx. A medium-sized shrub with broadly ovate to rounded, coarsely toothed leaves. Flowers white in flattened heads in June. Fruits blue-black. The bark of older stems is flaky. N USA. I 1923.

nervosum See *V. grandiflorum*.

‡*nudum* L. A medium-sized shrub of upright growth, related to *V. cassinoides*, but differing in its dark glossy green leaves, colouring attractively in autumn. Flowers yellowish-white, borne in long-stalked cymes in June. Fruits oval, blue-black. E USA. I 1752.

obovatum Walt. A large, semi-evergreen shrub or small tree with rigid shoots and small, obovate, entire or shallowly toothed leaves, to 5cm long, glossy green above, dotted with small, red-brown glands beneath. Small, white flowers open in unstalked clusters, to 6cm across, during summer. An unusual species which has grown at the Sir Harold Hillier Gardens and Arboretum for many years. SE USA.

†*odoratissimum* Ker Gawl. A large, evergreen shrub of noble aspect, bearing striking, glossy green, oval to obovate, leathery leaves with 5–8 pairs of veins and red-flushed petioles. They vary in size from 10–20cm long and are shallowly serrate in the upper half. Older leaves often colour richly during winter and early spring. Fragrant, white flowers, in large, conical panicles during late summer, fruits red turning black. A magnificent species for gardens in mild areas. India, Burma, S China, Taiwan, Japan. I about 1818. var. *awabuki* (K. Koch) Zabel (*V. awabuki* K. Koch) The commonly cultivated form described above. The typical form differs in its duller green leaves with green petioles and 4–6 pairs of veins.

'Oneida' (*V. dilatatum* × *V. lobophyllum*) An erect, medium-sized shrub with dark green leaves of variable shape and size. Creamy-white, pungently scented flowers are abundantly produced in May and intermittently throughout summer and are followed by glossy, dark red fruits, which persist well into winter. A hybrid of American origin.

opulus L. Guelder rose, Water elder. A large, vigorous shrub of spreading habit with 3- to 5-lobed, maple-like leaves, which colour richly in autumn. The flattened corymbs in June or July are edged with showy white ray-florets, the effect being similar to that of a lacecap hydrangea. Followed in autumn by glistening red, translucent fruits, which persist long into winter. A familiar native of hedgerows and woods, particularly rampant in wet or boggy situations. Europe, N and W Asia, N Africa (Algeria). 'Aureum' A striking form of compact habit with bright yellow leaves. Tends to burn in full sun. **'Compactum'** A small shrub of dense, compact habit which flowers and fruits freely. ♀ 2002. AM 1962. **'Fructuluteo'** Fruits lemon-yellow with a strong, pink tinge, maturing to chrome-yellow with a faint hint of pink. **'Nanum'** A curious, dwarf form of dense, tufted habit; seldom, if ever, flowering but often colouring in autumn. **'Notcutt's Variety'** A selected form with larger flowers and fruits. ♀ 2002. AM 1930. **'Roseum'** ('Sterile') Snowball. One of the most attractive and popular, hardy, flowering shrubs. The flowers are all sterile and gathered into conspicuous, globular, creamy-white heads. ♀ 2002. **'Sterile'** See 'Roseum'. **'Xanthocarpum'** Fruits differing from those of 'Fructuluteo' in being clear golden-yellow at all stages, becoming a little darker and almost translucent when ripe. ♀ 2002. FCC 1966. AM 1932.

'Park Farm Hybrid' See *V.* × *burkwoodii* 'Park Farm Hybrid'.

parvifolium Hayata. A rare, small shrub with small, ovate to obovate, toothed leaves up to 2.5cm in length. Flowers white, followed by globular, red fruits. Taiwan.

pauciflorum See *V. edule*.

phlebotrichum Siebold & Zucc. A medium-sized shrub of slender habit with strong, erect shoots and narrow, ovate-oblong, acuminate, bronze-green leaves which, in the adult state, have spiny teeth and are prettily net-veined. Flowers white or pink-tinged in small, nodding trusses. Fruits crimson-red. Rich autumn tints. Japan. C 1890.

plicatum Thunb. (*V. plicatum* f. *tomentosum* (Thunb.) Rehder, *V. tomentosum* Thunb. not Lam.) A widespreading, medium-sized to large shrub of architectural value with a distinctive mode of branching. The branches are produced in layers creating, in time, an attractive and characteristic, tiered effect. The bright green, pleated, ovate to oval leaves are followed in May and early June by 7.5–10cm-wide umbels of small, fertile, creamy-white flowers surrounded by conspicuous, white ray-florets. The inflorescences sit in double rows along the upper sides of the branches giving the appearance, from a distance, of icing on a cake. Fruits red, finally black. The leaves are often attractively tinted in autumn. China, Japan, Taiwan. I about 1865. **'Dart's Red Robin'** A form of spreading habit, flowering and fruiting profusely. A seedling of 'Rowallane' raised in Holland before 1985. **'Grandiflorum'** Similar to 'Sterile' with larger heads of sterile, white florets flushed pink at the margins. AM 1961. **'Lanarth'** A very fine form, resembling 'Mariesii' but stronger in growth and less horizontal in branching habit. AM 1930. **'Mariesii'** A superb shrub with a tabulate arrangement of branching. Its abundance of flower gives the effect of a snow-laden bush. The ray florets are also relatively large and the leaves colour well in autumn. ♀ 2002. **'Nanum Semperflorens'** ('Watanabe') A slow-growing form of dense habit with white flowers produced over a long period during summer and autumn. It was found as a seedling in the wild in Japan by Kenji Watanabe about 1956. Dwarf plants reaching 50cm and found in the wild at the foot of Mt Fuji in Japan have been described as f. *watanabei* (Honda) Hara. **'Pink Beauty'** A charming selection in which the ray-florets age to a delightful pink. Free-fruiting. ♀ 2002. **'Rosace'** Similar to 'Sterile' but bearing both white and pink flowerheads. **'Rowallane'** Similar to 'Lanarth', but a little less vigorous. The marginal ray-florets are larger and it has the added attraction of usually producing a conspicuous show of fruits which very seldom occur on 'Mariesii'. Good autumn colour. FCC 1956. AM 1942. **'Shasta'** A profusely flowering, widespreading form, similar to 'Lanarth' but with larger ray-florets. Fruits bright red, turning black. Raised at the US National Arboretum in 1970. AM 1988. **'Sterile'** Japanese snowball. This popular shrub of medium size and dense, spreading habit is in the front rank of hardy, ornamental shrubs. The conspicuous, white, sterile florets are gathered into globular heads 5–7.5cm across. They are produced in late May and early June, in a double row along the length of each arching branch, and persist for several weeks. This is a garden form, long cultivated in both China and Japan. It was introduced from the former by Robert Fortune in 1844, several years before the wild form. Previously listed as *V. plicatum* of which it is a selected form. FCC 1893. **'Summer Snowflake'** A medium-sized shrub with tiered branches and lacecap-like flowerheads in May and through summer. Leaves red to purple in autumn. Similar to and possibly the same as 'Nanum Semperflorens'. **f. tomentosum** See *V. plicatum*. **'Watanabe'** See 'Nanum Semperflorens'.

*'Pragense'** (*V. rhytidophyllum* × *V. utile*) An attractive, spreading, evergreen shrub of medium to large size. Elliptic, corrugated leaves, 5–10cm long, are lustrous dark green above, white-felted beneath. Flowers creamy-white, buds pink, produced in terminal branched cymes during May. This hybrid was raised in Prague and is extremely hardy. ♀ 2002.

*propinquum Hemsl. A small to medium-sized, evergreen shrub of dense, compact habit. Leaves 3-nerved, ovate to elliptic, polished dark green above, paler beneath. Flowers greenish-white, borne in umbellate cymes during summer, followed by blue-black, egg-shaped fruits. C and W China, Taiwan. I 1901 by Ernest Wilson. **'Lanceolatum'** A form with narrower leaves.

prunifolium L. Black haw. A large, erect shrub or small tree, with shining, bright green, ovate to obovate leaves which colour richly in autumn, and clusters of white flowers in April and May. Fruits comparatively large, bloomy, blue-black, sweet and edible. E North America. I 1731.

pubescens See *V. dentatum* var. *pubescens*. **var. canbyi** See *V. dentatum*.

rafinesquianum Schult. Downy arrow wood. A medium-sized to large shrub with ovate to elliptic, coarsely toothed, polished leaves, often colouring richly in autumn. Flowers white, borne in cymes during May and June. Fruits blue-black. NE USA, E Canada. C 1883.

recognitum Fern. (*V. dentatum* var. *lucidum* Aiton) Arrow wood. A medium-sized to large shrub, related to *V. dentatum* but with the leaves glossy green and glabrous except for occasional axillary tufts beneath. Some plants grown as *V. dentatum* belong here. SE USA.

*× rhytidocarpum Lemoine (*V. buddlejifolium* × *V. rhytidophyllum*) A large, more or less evergreen shrub, intermediate in habit and leaf between its parents. C 1936.

× **rhytidophylloides** J.V. Suringar (*V. lantana* × *V. rhytido-phyllum*) A very vigorous, large shrub with elliptic-ovate to oblong-ovate, rugose leaves and stout cymes of yellowish-white flowers in May. In general effect intermediate between the parents. A splendid shrub for screen planting. **'Alleghany'** Leaves leathery and dark green, fruits brilliant red ripening to black. Selected at the US National Arboretum, Washington in 1958 from a batch of seedlings obtained from a plant raised by crossing *V. rhytidophyllum* with *V. lantana* 'Mohican'. **Dart's Duke** ('Interduke') A Dutch selection flowering in late spring to early summer and again in early autumn, followed by profuse red fruits. C 1971. **'Holland'** The name given to the original clone, raised about 1925 and described above. **'Willowwood'** A form with glossy deep green, deeply veined leaves on arching shoots. Raised from a cross made at Willowwood Farm, New Jersey.

****rhytidophyllum** Hemsl. A large, fast-growing, handsome, evergreen shrub with large, elliptic to oblong, attractively corrugated leaves, dark glossy green above, densely grey-tomentose beneath. Small, creamy-white flowers are produced in stout, tomentose cymes during May. Fruits oval, red, finally black. It is necessary to plant 2 or more in close proximity, as single specimens do not fruit freely. A magnificent foliage shrub and a splendid chalk plant, creating the effect of a large-leaved *Rhododendron*. C and W China. I 1900 by Ernest Wilson. FCC 1907. **'Roseum'** A form with rose-pink-tinted flowers. The plant we grow originated in our nurseries. **'Variegatum'** Leaves conspicuously blotched with pale yellow when young turning to creamy-white. Of curiosity value only. C 1935.

rigidum See *V. tinus* subsp. *rigidum*.

rufidulum Raf. Southern black haw. A large shrub of rigid habit with rusty-tomentose young shoots. Leaves elliptic-obovate, leathery, polished green, often colouring in autumn. Flowers white in May and June; fruits blue-black. SE USA. I 1883.

rugosum See *V. tinus* subsp. *rigidum*.

sargentii Koehne. A large, vigorous shrub related to and resembling *V. opulus*, but the maple-like leaves are larger, the bark corky and the flowers, in June, have purple anthers (not yellow). The fruits also are a little larger, bright, translucent red and last well into winter. Rich autumn tints. NE Asia. I 1892. AM 1967. **f. *flavum*** Rehder ('Fructuluteo') An unusual form with translucent, yellow fruits. The flowers have yellow anthers. **'Onondaga'** A splendid form with deep maroon young leaves, reddish-purple in autumn. Fertile flowers, deep red in bud, are surrounded by a ring of white, sterile flowers, the inflorescence contrasting effectively with the young foliage. A seedling raised at the US National Arboretum, Washington and selected in 1959. Although originally described as globose, it has retained a strong upright habit here. ♀ 2002.

scabrellum Chapm. Medium-sized shrub related to *V. dentatum* with scabrous shoots and ovate to ovate-oblong leaves. White flowers in June are followed by blue-black, rounded fruits. E USA. C 1830.

schensianum Maxim. A medium-sized to large shrub with downy young shoots and ovate to elliptic leaves, downy beneath. Flowers creamy-white, borne in flattened cymes in May or June followed by red, finally black, egg-shaped fruits. It belongs to the same group as *V. lantana*. NW China. I about 1910.

schneiderianum See *V. calvum*.

setigerum Hance (*V. theiferum* Rehder) A distinct and attractive shrub of medium size and open, lax growth. From time of unfolding until early winter, the ovate-lanceolate to oblong, slender-pointed leaves are constantly changing colour from metallic-blue-red through shades of green to orange-yellow in autumn. Its corymbs of white flowers in early summer are followed by conspicuous clusters of comparatively large, orange-yellow, finally brilliant red, somewhat flattened, oval fruits. C and W China. I 1901 by Ernest Wilson. AM 1925.

sieboldii Miq. A vigorous shrub of medium to large size. The unfolding foetid leaves in spring, and the falling leaves in autumn, are attractively bronze-tinted, but emit an objectionable smell if crushed. They have a conspicuous, impressed venation and throughout the summer are soft yellow-green. Flowers creamy-white in May and June. The oval, comparatively large fruits are pink, changing to red then blue-black. Japan. C 1880. **'Seneca'** A form raised and selected at the US National Arboretum, Washington for its large, drooping clusters of long-persistent, red fruits.

†****suspensum*** Lindl. (*V. sandankwa* Hassk.) A medium-sized, evergreen shrub bearing leathery, ovate or rotund, glossy green leaves, 7.5–13cm long. The domed panicles of fragrant, rose-tinted flowers are produced in early spring. Fruits, when produced, globular, red. An attractive species for mild localities where it is best grown against a warm, sheltered wall. Ryukyus, Taiwan. Long cultivated in S Japan from where it was introduced about 1850.

theiferum See *V. setigerum*.

****tinus** L. Laurustinus. One of the most popular evergreens. A medium-sized to large shrub of dense, bushy habit with luxurious masses of dark glossy green, oval leaves. Flattened cymes of white, pink-budded flowers appear continuously from late autumn to early spring. Fruits ovoid, metallic-blue, finally black. An excellent winter-flowering shrub for all but the coldest areas. Makes an attractive informal hedge. Tolerant of shade and succeeds well in maritime exposure. Mediterranean region, SE Europe. Cultivated in Britain since the late 16th century. **'Eve Price'** A selected form of dense, compact habit with smaller leaves than the type and very pretty, carmine buds and pink-tinged flowers. ♀ 2002. AM 1961. **'French White'** A strong-growing form with large heads of white flowers. ♀ 2002. **'Gwenllian'** A compact form with small leaves. Flowers rich, deep pink in bud opening to white, flushed pink on the backs of the lobes. Raised at Kew. ♀ 2002. **f. *hirtum*** hort. (*V. hirtulum*) A distinct form with larger, thicker, densely ciliate leaves. Shoots, petioles and leaf bases are clothed with bristly hairs. Less hardy than the typical form, but an excellent shrub for mild maritime areas. AM 1939. **'Lucidum'** A vigorous form with comparatively large, glossy green leaves. The flowerheads are also larger than those of the type, opening white in March and April. AM 1972. **'Pink Prelude'** Flowers opening white then turning through pale to deep pink. C 1966. **'Purpureum'** A form with

very dark green leaves, purple-tinged when young. **'Pyramidale'** ('Strictum') A selected form of more erect habit. †**subsp. rigidum** (Vent.) P. Silva (*V. rigidum* Vent., *V. rugosum* Pers.) Differs in its more open habit and larger leaves, 7.5–15cm long, hairy on both surfaces. Flowers white, in flattened corymbs from February to April. A tender form for a specially favoured position. Canary Isles. I 1778. **Spirit** ('Anvi') PBR A selection bearing profuse, white flowers over a long period from October to March followed by blue then black fruits. **'Variegatum'** Leaves conspicuously variegated creamy-yellow. Not recommended for cold districts.

tomentosum See *V. plicatum*. **'Sterile'** See *V. plicatum* 'Sterile'.

trilobum Marshall (*V. americanum* auct. not Mill.) Highbush cranberry. A large shrub, related to and closely resembling *V. opulus*, from which it differs in the usually long terminal lobe of the leaf, the petiole of which is only shallowly grooved and bears small glands. The petioles of *V. opulus* are broadly grooved and bear large, disc-like glands. The red fruits colour in July and persist throughout winter. Rich autumn tints. N North America. I 1812. **'Compactum'** A small form of dense, compact growth.

utile Hemsl. A graceful, evergreen shrub of medium size and elegant, rather sparingly branched habit. Long, slender stems bear narrowly ovate or oblong, glossy dark green leaves, white-tomentose beneath. White, sweetly-scented flowers are produced in dense, rounded clusters in May. Fruits bluish-black. C China. I 1901 by Ernest Wilson. AM 1926.

veitchii C.H. Wright. A shrub of medium to large size, related to *V. lantana*. Leaves ovate, wrinkled above. Flowers white, borne in flattened heads during May and June. Fruits bright red at first, passing through purple to black. C China. I 1901 by Ernest Wilson.

wilsonii Rehder. A medium-sized shrub, related to *V. hupehense*, with oval leaves. Flowers white, appearing in corymbs in June, followed by bright red, downy, egg-shaped fruits. W China. I 1908 by Ernest Wilson.

wrightii Miq. A medium-sized shrub with broadly ovate to obovate, abruptly pointed leaves. Flowers white, borne in corymbs in May, followed in autumn by glistening red fruits. The metallic green leaves often colour richly in autumn. Closely related to *V. dilatatum*, from which it differs in its almost glabrous nature. Japan, Sakhalin, Korea, China. I 1892. **'Hessei'** A dwarf form with broad, ovate, attractively veined leaves. The flowers are followed by conspicuous, sealing wax-red fruits which appear each autumn with remarkable consistency. An excellent shrub for the border front.

Victoria rosemary See *Westringia fruticosa*.
Villaresia mucronata See *Citronella mucronata*.

*VINCA L.—Apocynaceae—The periwinkles are a genus of 7 species of herbs and shrubs, natives of Europe, N Africa and W and C Asia. The following are vigorous, evergreen, trailing shrubs forming extensive carpets and ideal as groundcover in both shade or full sun. Growing in all fertile soils.

difformis Pourr. (*V. acutiflora* Bertol., *V. media* Hoffmanns. & Link) An uncommon species usually herbaceous in cold areas. Leaves ovate, 4–7.5cm long. Flowers solitary in the leaf axils, pale lilac-blue, with rhomboid lobes, resembling a 5-bladed propeller, produced during autumn and early winter. In general appearance it resembles the hardier *V. major*, but is quite glabrous in all its parts. W Mediterranean region. ♥ 2002. **'Alba'** Flowers white. Plants grown as Greystone form are similar but have broad, overlapping corolla lobes. ♥ 2002. **'Jenny Pym'** Flowers with deep lilac lobes, narrowly edged white and with a white centre. **'Ruby Baker'** A vigorous form of trailing habit with olive-green foliage and rich pinkish-purple flowers. Found by Ruby and David Baker in southern Europe.

major L. Greater periwinkle. A rampant species with shortly ascending shoots which later lengthen and trail along the ground, rooting only at their tips. Leaves ovate, 2.5–7.5cm long, dark glossy green and ciliate. Flowers bright blue, 4cm across, borne in the leaf axils, produced continuously from late April to June. An excellent shrub for covering unsightly banks or waste ground. C and S Europe, N Africa. Long cultivated and naturalised in the British Isles. **'Elegantissima'** See 'Variegata'. **subsp. hirsuta** (Boiss.) Stearn. A more pubescent form. N Turkey, Georgia. See also 'Oxyloba'. **'Jason Hill'** A vigorous form, the deep blue flowers with a white eye. **'Maculata'** ('Surrey Marble') Leaves with a central splash of greenish-yellow, more conspicuous on young leaves in an open position. **'Oxyloba'** (var. *hirsuta* hort. not Boiss.) A form with narrower, somewhat pubescent leaves and violet-blue flowers with narrower, pointed lobes. **'Reticulata'** Leaves conspicuously veined with yellow when young, later green. **'Surrey Marble'** See 'Maculata'. **'Variegata'** ('Elegantissima') Leaves blotched and margined creamy-white; a conspicuous plant, as vigorous as the green-leaved form. ♥ 2002. AMT 1982. AM 1977.

minor L. Lesser periwinkle. A familiar cottage-garden plant with long, trailing stems rooting at intervals. Leaves oval or elliptic-lanceolate, 2.5–5cm long. Bright blue flowers, 2.5cm across, are borne singly in the leaf axils of short, erect, flowering shoots. They appear continuously from April to June and intermittently until autumn. There are numerous named selections. Europe, W Asia. Doubtfully a British native, though frequently found in woods, copses and hedgebanks. **'Alba'** Flowers white. ♥ 2002. **'Alba Variegata'** Leaves grey-green edged with creamy-white. Flowers white. **'Argenteovariegata'** Leaves variegated creamy-white; flowers blue. Originally listed as 'Variegata'. ♥ 2002. **'Atropurpurea'** Flowers deep plum-purple. ♥ 2002. AMT 1983. **'Aureovariegata'** Leaves blotched yellow; flowers blue. **'Azurea Flore Pleno'** Flowers sky-blue, double. ♥ 2002. AMT 1983. **'Bowles' Variety'** See 'La Grave'. **'Gertrude Jekyll'** A selected form with glistening white flowers. ♥ 2002. AMT 1983. **'Illumination'** PBR Leaves with a large, bright golden-yellow centre and a narrow green margin. Flowers blue. A striking selection found in a nursery in Washington State, USA. It produces sports with the leaves all green or green blotched with yellow. **'La Grave'** ('Bowles' Variety') Flowers azure-blue, larger than those of the type. ♥ 2002. AMT 1983. **'Multiplex'** Flowers plum-purple, double. **'Persian Carpet'** Broad, grey-green leaves edged with white. Low-growing, making good groundcover, but does not flower. **'Silver Service'** Double, blue flowers; leaves edged with grey-green. **'Variegata'** See 'Argenteovariegata'.

Virgilia See *Cladrastis kentukea*.

VITEX L.—**Verbenaceae**—A large genus of some 250 species of mainly evergreen trees and shrubs, widely distrubuted mostly in the tropics and subtropics. The species grown in temperate climes are deciduous shrubs which succeed better in a continental climate. In the British Isles *Vitex* need good drainage and full sun to ripen growth and produce flower, hence they make excellent subjects for a sunny wall. Pruning consists of the removal of the old flowering shoots in late February or March.

agnus-castus L. Chaste tree. An attractive, spreading, aromatic shrub of medium size. The compound leaves, composed of 5–7, ovate-lanceolate leaflets on short stalks, are borne in pairs along the elegant, grey-downy shoots. Flowers violet, fragrant, in slender racemes at the ends of the current year's shoots in September and October. Mediterranean region to C Asia. Said to have been cultivated in the British Isles since 1570. AM 1934. **f. *alba*** (Weston) Rehder. Flowers white. AM 1959. **f. *latifolia*** (Mill.) Rehder (*V. macrophylla* hort.) A more vigorous and hardy form with broader leaflets. AM 1964.

macrophylla See *V. agnus-castus* f. *latifolia*.

†***negundo*** L. This is a graceful shrub of medium to large size, with long, 4-angled stems. The leaves are compound, with 3–5, stalked, ovate-lanceolate leaflets. Lavender flowers are borne in loose panicles during late summer or early autumn. India, China, Taiwan. I about 1697. **var. *heterophylla*** (Franch.) Rehder. Leaflets finely cut.

W

Walnut See *Juglans*.
Waratah, Tasmanian See *Telopea truncata*.

†***WASHINGTONIA** H. Wendl.—**Palmae**—Two species of single-stemmed palms with large, fan-shaped leaves and hermaphrodite flowers. In both species the dead leaves, unless removed, remain attached for many years, densely covering the stem. They may be grown outside in the mildest parts of Britain; in cooler areas they are effective in a large container and given conservatory protection in winter. They are commonly grown in warm regions of the world.

filifera (Linden) H. Wendl. Desert fan palm. A medium-sized to large tree with a stout trunk marked with closely spaced rings, if the thatch of dead leaves has been removed. Leaves large, fan-shaped, on a long, spine-edged petiole to 2m long, the grey-green blade to 2m long divided into numerous segments which droop at the tips and are edged with white threads. Large inflorescences, to 5m long, bear white flowers followed by small dark brown fruits to 6mm long. SW USA, NW Mexico. ♀ 2002.

robusta H. Wendl. Thread palm. A large tree, similar to *W. filifera* but differing in its taller, slender stem, which is conspicuously swollen at the base on mature trees. NW Mexico.

Water elm See *Planera aquatica*.
Wattle See *Acacia*.
Wattle, Cape Leeuwin See *Paraserianthes lophantha*.
Wattle, Crested See *Paraserianthes lophantha*.
Wax myrtle See *Myrica cerifera*.
Wax tree See *Rhus succedanea*.
Wayfaring tree See *Viburnum lantana*.

WEIGELA Thunb.—**Caprifoliaceae**—A small genus of about 10 species of hardy, flowering shrubs, natives of temperate E Asia and differing from the closely related *Diervilla* in the almost regular corolla (two-lipped in *Diervilla*), which is larger and varies in colour from white to pink and red. Very decorative and easily grown shrubs, growing to an average of 2m high and excellent for town gardens, particularly in industrial areas. The tubular, foxglove-like flowers appear in May and June all along the shoots of the previous year. Occasionally a small, second crop is produced in late summer or early autumn. Thin out and cut back old flowering shoots to within a few centimetres of the old wood immediately after flowering.

coraeensis Thunb. (*W. grandiflora* (Siebold & Zucc.) K. Koch) An elegant shrub of medium size with glabrous shoots and oval to obovate, abruptly pointed leaves. Flowers bell-shaped, white or pale rose at first, deepening to carmine, June. Japan. C 1850. **'Alba'** Flowers cream changing to pale rose.

decora (Nakai) Nakai (*W. nikoensis* Nakai) A medium-sized shrub related to *W. japonica*. Leaves obovate-elliptic, abruptly acuminate, slightly glossy above. Flowers white, becoming reddish with age, May and June. Japan. C 1933.

florida (Bunge) A. DC. (*W. rosea* Lindl.) A medium-sized shrub with ovate-oblong to obovate, acuminate leaves. Flowers funnel-shaped, reddish or rose-pink on the outside, paler within, May and June. Perhaps the most popular species in cultivation. A parent of many attractive hybrids. Japan, Korea, N China, Manchuria. I 1845 by Robert Fortune. **'Foliis Purpureis'** A slower-growing, dwarfer form of compact habit with attractive, purpleflushed leaves and pink flowers. ♀ 2002. **'Variegata'** See *W.* 'Florida Variegata'. **var.** *venusta* (Rehder) Nakai. A free-flowering form, the flowers being a little larger and a brighter rose-pink. Korea. I 1905. **'Versicolor'** Flowers creamy-white changing to red. 'Dart's Colourdream' is very similar.

hortensis (Siebold & Zucc.) K. Koch. A small to medium-sized shrub with ovate-elliptic to obovate, acuminate leaves, densely white pubescent beneath. Flowers reddish, May and June. The typical form is rare in cultivation and is less hardy than most other species. Japan. C 1870. **'Nivea'** ('Albiflora') A lovely form with comparatively large, white flowers. FCC 1891.

japonica Thunb. Medium-sized shrub with ovate or oval, taper-pointed leaves. The flowers in May are pale rose or nearly white at first, later changing to carmine. Japan. I 1892. **var.** *sinica* (Rehder) Bailey. A taller-growing variety with pale pink flowers deepening with age. C China. I 1908 by Ernest Wilson.

maximowiczii (S. Moore) Rehder. A small shrub of spreading habit with ovate-oblong to obovate, abruptly pointed, rather narrow leaves. Greenish-yellow or pale yellow flowers open in April and May. Japan. I 1915.

middendorffiana (Carrière) K. Koch. A small shrub of no mean quality, with exfoliating bark and broader ovate leaves than those of *W. maximowiczii*. They are also more abruptly pointed. Flowers bell-shaped, sulphur-yellow often with dark orange markings on the lower lobes, April and May. This is an ornamental species of compact growth, best grown in a sheltered and partially shaded position. Japan, N China, Manchuria. I 1850. AM 1931.

nikoensis See *W. decora*.

praecox (Lemoine) Bailey. A vigorous, medium-sized shrub with ovate to ovate-oblong leaves. The comparatively large, honey-scented flowers are rose-pink with yellow markings in the throat. They commence opening in early May. Japan, Korea, Manchuria. C 1894. **'Variegata'** See *W.* 'Praecox Variegata'.

rosea See *W. florida*.

Cultivars and hybrids of *Weigela*

A colourful selection of hardy hybrids of medium size, flowering on the old wood during May and June and often a second time in early autumn. Pruning consists of the shortening or removal of the flowering stems immediately after flowering.

'Abel Carrière' Free-flowering cultivar with large, bright rose-carmine flowers, flecked gold in the throat; buds purple-carmine. C 1876.

'Avalanche' A vigorous cultivar with numerous panicles of white flowers.

'Ballet' A hybrid between 'Boskoop Glory' and 'Newport Red'. Flowers dark pinkish-red.

Cultivars and hybrids of *Weigela* continued:

Briant Rubidor ('Olympiade', 'Rubidor') Flowers of carmine-red. Leaves yellow or green with a broad, yellow margin. Tends to burn in full sun.

'Bristol Ruby' Vigorous, erect-growing cultivar, free-flowering with flowers of a sparkling ruby-red. A hybrid between *W. florida* and *W.* 'Eva Rathke'. AM 1954.

'Bristol Snowflake' Pink-flushed white flowers over a long period. C 1961.

'Buisson Fleuri' Early-flowering cultivar with large, fragrant, rose flowers spotted yellow in throat.

'Candida' Flowers pure white, even in bud. Foliage bright green.

Carnaval ('Courtalor') PBR A triploid hybrid between 'Abel Carrière' and 'Bristol Ruby' raised in France. A small shrub flowering profusely and bearing a mixture of pink-and-white bicoloured flowers and pink flowers.

'Conquête' An old favourite with very large flowers, almost 5cm long, of deep rose-pink. C 1907.

'Espérance' An early-flowering cultivar with large flowers of pale rose-salmon, white within. C 1906.

'Eva Rathke' An old favourite and still one of the best reds. A slow-growing cultivar of compact growth. Flowers bright red-crimson with straw-coloured anthers, opening over a long season. FCC 1893.

'Eva Supreme' Growth vigorous; flowers bright red. A cross between 'Eva Rathke' and 'Newport Red'.

'Evita' A dwarf shrub of low, spreading habit. Bright red flowers are borne over a long period.

'Féerie' Flowers large and numerous, rose-pink, in erect trusses.

Feline ('Courtamon') PBR Raised in France from a cross between 'Bristol Ruby' and 'Abel Carrière', this makes a small shrub of upright habit to 1.6m tall, the erect branches arching with age. Distinct, long-trumpet-shaped, white and pink flowers are profusely borne over a long period.

'Fiesta' A hybrid between 'Eva Rathke' and 'Newport Red'. Growth lax. Flowers shining, uniform red, produced in great abundance.

'Fleur de Mai' Flowers salmon-rose inside, marbled purple-rose outside, purple in bud. Usually the first to bloom.

'Florida Variegata' (*W. florida* 'Variegata') A compact shrub, the leaves edged creamy-white; flowers pink. One of the best variegated shrubs for general planting. ♥ 2002. AM 1968 (for foliage).

'Gracieux' Erect-growing, free-flowering cultivar with large flowers of salmon-rose with sulphur-yellow throats. Said to be a selection of *W. praecox*.

'Gustave Malet' Very floriferous, with long-tubed, deep red flowers. Said to be a selection of *W. florida*.

'Héroine' An erect-growing cultivar with large, pale rose flowers.

'Idéal' Flowers carmine-rose inside, bright carmine outside, in large clusters, early and free-flowering.

'Java Red' A compact, small shrub with bronze young foliage, later bronze-green. Deep pink flowers open from red buds.

'Kosteriana Variegata' A compact, small shrub with cream-edged leaves and rose-pink flowers. The leaves turn to shades of pink and red in autumn.

'Lavalléei' Crimson flowers with a protruding, white stigma.

'Le Printemps' Large, peach-pink flowers, very floriferous.

'Looymansii Aurea' Very pleasing in spring and early summer, when the pink flowers enhance the effect of the light golden foliage. Best in partial shade. Found as a seedling in 1873.

'Majestueux' An erect, early-flowering cultivar, producing masses of large, erect flowers, madder-pink flushed carmine in the throat.

'Minuet' A compact, dwarf shrub with dark green foliage, flushed purple. Flowers rich red with a yellow throat.

'Mont Blanc' Vigorous cultivar with large, white, fragrant flowers. Perhaps the best of the whites. C 1898.

Nain Rouge ('Courtanin') PBR A compact, dwarf shrub of rounded habit, only about 80cm tall. Flowers red, flushed orange, with a prominent, white stigma. A sport of 'Eva Supreme' raised in France.

'Nana Variegata' Compact, to 1.2m, with fresh green foliage, edged with cream; pale pink flowers from deep pink buds.

'Newport Red' ('Vanicek') A superb cultivar, more upright than 'Eva Rathke', with larger flowers of a lighter red.

'Perle' Vigorous cultivar with large flowers in rounded corymbs, pale cream with rose edges, the mouth clear yellow.

'Praecox Variegata' (*W. praecox* 'Variegata') An attractive shrub that has leaves variegated creamy-white. Flowers rose-pink and honey-scented. ♥ 2002.

'Red Prince' An excellent, American selection with narrow, tubular, bright red flowers. ♥ 2002.

'Rubidor' See Briant Rubidor.

'Rumba' Compact with purple-tinged foliage; red flowers with a yellow throat.

'Samba' A compact, dwarf shrub with dark green leaves edged bronze-red. Rosy-red flowers, yellow in the throat.

'Styriaca' Vigorous cultivar with abundant, carmine-red flowers. C 1908.

'Suzanne' Small shrub with pale pink to white flowers; leaves with white margins.

'Tango' Low, compact, spreading habit with purple foliage. Funnel-shaped, red flowers with a yellow throat open profusely in spring and sometimes again in summer.

'Victoria' A small, upright shrub with deep bronze-purple foliage and purple-pink flowers.

Wine and Roses ('Alexandra') PBR Dense, spreading habit with deep red-purple foliage veined with green, becoming bronze-green edged purple, then deep purple in autumn. Reddish-pink flowers. Raised in Holland.

†***WEINMANNIA** L.—**Cunoniaceae**—A large genus of nearly 200 species of mainly tropical, evergreen trees and shrubs, widely distributed. The following species require loamy soil and are only suitable for sheltered gardens in the mildest areas of the British Isles.

racemosa L. Kamahi. A small, graceful tree or large shrub with remarkably variable leaves – on adult trees are simple, ovate to oval and coarsely toothed and on juvenile specimens varying from simple to 3-lobed, or trifoliolate with coarsely toothed leaflets. Flowers white, produced in slender racemes during summer. New Zealand.

trichosperma Cav. A slender, small to medium-sized tree or large shrub, with pinnate leaves composed of 9–19 small, neat, oval or obovate, toothed leaflets. The rachis in between each leaflet bears a pair of small, triangular wings. The white flowers, in dense racemes during May and June, are succeeded by small, coppery-red capsules. Chile. AM 1927.

†***WESTRINGIA** Sm.—**Labiatae**—A small genus of about 25 species of tender, evergreen shrubs, natives of Australia.
fruticosa Sm. (*W. rosmariniformis* Sm.) Victoria rosemary. A small to medium-sized shrub bearing whorls of narrow, rosemary-like leaves which, like the shoots, are silvery-hoary beneath. Flowers white, borne in axillary clusters in July. An interesting shrub for a wall in a warm, sunny, well-drained position in mild areas. E Australia. I 1791. ♀ 2002.
rosmariniformis See *W. fruticosa*.

Whinberry See *Vaccinium myrtillus*.
White wicky See *Kalmia cuneata*.
Whitebeam See *Sorbus aria*.
Whitebeam, Swedish See *Sorbus intermedia*.
Whiteywood See *Melicytus ramiflorus*.
Whortleberry See *Vaccinium myrtillus*.
Whortleberry, bog See *Vaccinium uliginosum*.
Whortleberry, Caucasian See *Vaccinium arctostaphylos*.
Whortleberry, Madeiran See *Vaccinium padifolium*.

WIKSTROEMIA Endl.—**Thymaeleaceae**—A genus of some 70 species of deciduous and evergreen trees and shrubs closely related to *Daphne*. Natives of E Asia to the Pacific Islands. Few species are cultivated.
canescens Meissn. Small, deciduous shrub with slender, arching, downy shoots. Leaves elliptic, to 8 cm long, short-stalked, alternate or sub-opposite. The small yellow-green flowers, purple in bud, have a slender, slightly curved tube 1.5 cm long, and 4 short lobes, flushed reddish on the backs with finely cut margins. They open in clusters at the ends of the shoots in late summer and early autumn. Himalayas. I 1985 by Ron McBeath.

Wild Irishman See *Discaria toumatou*.
Willow See *Salix*.
Willow-leaved jessamine See *Cestrum parqui*.
Wineberry See *Rubus phoenicolasius* and *Aristotelia serrata*.
Wineberry, mountain See *Aristotelia fruticosa*.
Wing nut See *Pterocarya*.
Winter jasmine See *Jasminum nudiflorum*.
Wintersweet See *Chimonanthus*.
Winterberry See *Ilex verticillata*.
Wintergreen See *Gaultheria procumbens*.
Wintergreen, alpine See *Gaultheria humifusa*.
Winter's bark See *Drimys winteri*.
Witch alder See *Fothergilla*.
Witch hazel See *Hamamelis*.
Withe-rod See *Viburnum cassinoides*.
Wolfberry See *Symphoricarpos occidentalis*.
Wych elm See *Ulmus glabra*.

X, Y, Z

XANTHOCERAS Bunge—**Sapindaceae**—A monotypic genus related to *Koelreuteria*, but very different in general appearance. The erect flower panicles recall those of the horse chestnut.

sorbifolium Bunge. A beautiful, large shrub or small tree of upright growth. Leaves pinnate, composed of 9–17 sessile, lanceolate, sharply toothed leaflets. Flowers 2.5cm wide, white with a carmine eye, borne in erect panicles in May on the shoots of the previous year. Fruit a top-shaped, 3-valved, walnut-like capsule containing numerous, small, chestnut-like seeds. It may be grown in all types of fertile soil; its thick, fleshy, yellow roots take kindly to a chalk formation. N China. I 1866. ♀ 2002. FCC 1876.

XANTHORHIZA Marshall (*Zanthorhiza* L'Hér.)—**Ranunculaceae**—A monotypic genus related to buttercups but very different in general appearance from other members of the family.

simplicissima Marshall (*Zanthorhiza apiifolia* L'Hér.) Yellow root. A small, suckering shrub forming in time a thicket of erect stems up to 1m. Very attractive, pinnate leaves are composed of 3–5 sessile, deeply toothed leaflets which turn the colour of burnished bronze, often with a purple cast, in autumn. Tiny, delicate, deep purple flowers are produced in loose, drooping panicles with the emerging leaves during March and April. The roots and inner bark are coloured a bright yellow and taste bitter. Thrives in a moist or clay soil but is not at home on shallow chalk. E USA. I 1776. AM 1975 (for foliage effect).

Xanthoxylum See *Zanthoxylum*.

†***XYLOSMA** G. Forst.—**Flacourtiaceae**—A genus of evergreen trees and shrubs, normally with spiny branches and dioecious flowers. About 85 species, found mainly in the tropics and subtropics.

japonica (Thunb.) A. Gray (*X. racemosa* (Siebold & Zucc.) Miq.) A large, dioecious shrub or small, bushy tree sparsely armed with axillary spines when young. Leaves ovate to oblong-ovate, leathery and dark glossy green. Flowers small, yellow, fragrant, produced in short, axillary racemes in late summer. Berries blackish-purple. Japan, Ryukyus, Taiwan, China. **var. pubescens** Rehder & E.H. Wilson. Shoots hairy. Most cultivated plants belong here. I by Ernest Wilson.

Yaupon See *Ilex vomitoria*.
Yellow root See *Xanthorhiza simplicissima*.
Yellowwood See *Cladrastis kentukea*.

***YUCCA** L.—**Agavaceae**—These remarkable evergreens, with rosettes or clumps of narrow, usually rigid leaves and tall racemes or panicles of drooping, bell-shaped, lily-like flowers, are of great architectural value and help to create a subtropical effect in gardens. There are about 40 species, natives of C America, Mexico and S USA. Several species are hardy in the British Isles where they prefer a hot, dry, well-drained position in full sun.

angustifolia See *Y. glauca*.

†**arizonica** McKelvey. A stemless species bearing narrow, rigidly recurved leaves, channelled above and clothed with white threads along the margins. Flowers creamy-white, in attractive panicles in late summer. Arizona.

†**brevifolia** Engelm. Joshua tree. A small, tree-like species with an erect trunk ending in several stout branches. Leaves green, narrow and recurved, channelled above, margined with fine teeth. Flowers cream to greenish-white, borne in a dense panicle during late summer. SW USA. **var. jaegeriana** McKelvey. Differs in its shorter stature, smaller leaves and panicles. SW USA.

filamentosa L. A stemless species producing dense clumps of spreading or erect, lanceolate, slightly glaucous leaves. The leaf margins are clothed with numerous, curly, white threads. The creamy-white flowers, each 5–7.5cm long, are borne in erect, glabrous, conical panicles 1–2m tall, in July and August, even on young plants. SE USA. C 1675. ♀ 2002. **'Bright Edge'** Leaves with a narrow, golden-yellow margin. ♀ 2002. **'Variegata'** Leaves margined with creamy-white. ♀ 2002.

flaccida Haw. A stemless species forming tufts of long, lanceolate, green or glaucous leaves. The terminal portion of each leaf bends down and the margins are furnished with curly, white threads. Flowers creamy-white, 5–6.5cm long, borne in erect, downy panicles, 0.6–1.2m tall in July and August. As in the related *Y. filamentosa*, this species spreads by short basal side-growths. SE USA. I 1816. **'Golden Sword'** Leaves with a broad central band of creamy-yellow. ♀ 2002. **'Ivory'** Large panicles of green-stained, creamy-white flowers. ♀ 2002. FCC 1968. AM 1966.

glauca Nutt. (*Y. angustifolia* Pursh) A low-growing, short-stemmed species producing a rounded head of linear, greyish leaves, margined white and edged with a few threads. Greenish-white flowers, 5–7.5cm long, are carried in an erect raceme, 1–1.5m tall, in July and August. The species is hardy in our part of Hampshire but young plants do not flower. S Central USA. I 1696.

gloriosa L. Adam's needle. A small, tree-like species with a stout stem, 1.2 to 2.5m tall, and few or no branches. Leaves straight and stiff, almost dangerously spine-tipped, glaucous green, 30–60cm long, by 7.5–10cm wide, gathered into a dense, terminal head. Flowers creamy-white, sometimes tinged red on the outside, borne in an erect, crowded, conical panicle, 1–2m or more high, from July to September. SE USA. I about 1550. ♀ 2002. AM 1975. **'Variegata'** Leaves margined and striped creamy-yellow, fading to creamy-white on older leaves. ♀ 2002. FCC 1883.

× **karlsruhensis** Graebn. (*Y. filamentosa* × *Y. glauca*) A hardy, stemless plant with long, linear, greyish leaves and panicles of creamy-white flowers during late summer. It resembles *Y. glauca* in general appearance, but the leaves possess numerous marginal threads.

parviflora var. engelmannii See *Hesperaloe parviflora* var. *engelmannii*.

recurvifolia Salisb. A medium-sized species, usually with a short stem and several branches. The tapered leaves, 0.6–1m long, are glaucous at first becoming green with

age. All but the upper, central leaves are characteristically recurved. Flowers creamy-white, in dense, erect panicles, 0.6–1m high during late summer. Perhaps the best species for town gardens. Similar to *Y. gloriosa*, but differing in the recurved leaves. SE USA. I 1794. ♀ 2002.
'Variegata' Leaves with a pale green, central band.

†*whipplei* Torr. (*Hesperoyucca whipplei* (Torr.) Trel.) Our Lord's candle. A stemless species developing a dense, globular clump of long, narrow, rigid, spine-tipped leaves, finely toothed and glaucous. Flowers large, fragrant, greenish-white, edged with purple, produced in a densely packed panicle at the end of an erect, 1.8–3.6m scape, in May and June. Though able to withstand frost, this magnificent species can only be recommended for sunny places in the mildest counties and requires a very well-drained position. California. I 1854. AM 1945.

Yulan See *Magnolia denudata*.

ZANTHOXYLUM L. (*Xanthoxylum* Mill.)—**Rutaceae**—A large and rather neglected genus of some 200 species of mainly deciduous trees and shrubs widely distributed particularly in warm regions of the world. Branches normally spiny, leaves aromatic when crushed. The flowers are small but the diversity of the usually compound leaves is always attractive: in some species they are as beautiful as the fronds of a fern, and in others as spectacular as those of the Tree of Heaven (*Alianthus altissima*). The fruits, which may be jet-black or bright red, also have a subtle quality. Easily grown in any ordinary soil, sun or shade.

ailanthoides Siebold & Zucc. A very vigorous, sparsely branched, large shrub or small tree with thorny branches and stout, glaucous young shoots. Leaves pinnate, 30–60cm long, composed of 11–23 ovate to ovate-lanceolate, acuminate leaflets. Greenish-yellow flowers are produced in flattened heads, 13cm or more across, during early autumn. An extremely attractive foliage tree of subtropical appearance. It reached 7.5m tall with a spread of 12m in the Sir Harold Hillier Gardens and Arboretum (1990). Japan, Korea, China, Ryukyus, Taiwan.

alatum **var.** *planispinum* See *Z. armatum*.

americanum Mill. Toothache tree, Prickly ash. A large, rather gaunt shrub or short-stemmed tree with short, stout spines and pinnate leaves composed of 5–11 ovate or oval leaflets. Small, yellowish-green flowers are produced in short, axillary clusters in spring, followed by conspicuous, capitate clusters of jet-black fruits. The twigs and fruits are said to have been chewed by the native North Americans to alleviate toothache, the acrid juice having a numbing effect. E North America. I about 1740.

armatum DC. (*Z. planispinum* Siebold & Zucc., *Z. alatum* var. *planispinum* (Siebold & Zucc.) Rehder & E.H. Wilson) A large, spreading shrub with a pair of prominently flattened spines at the base of each leaf. Leaves with 3 or 5 ovate or lanceolate, sessile leaflets and a conspicuously winged petiole. Small, yellow flowers in spring, followed by small, red, warty fruits. Himalaya to E and SE Asia. C 1880.

bungei See *Z. simulans*.

piperitum (L.) DC. Japan pepper. A medium-sized shrub of neat, compact habit with pairs of flattened spines. The attractive, pinnate leaves are composed of 11–19 sessile,

broadly lanceolate or ovate leaflets. Small, greenish-yellow flowers are produced on the old wood in May or June and are followed by small, reddish fruits. The black seeds are crushed and used as a pepper in Japan. Leaves turn rich yellow in autumn. Japan, Korea, N China. C 1877.

planispinum See *Z. armatum*.

schinifolium Siebold & Zucc. A graceful, medium-sized shrub, the branches bearing single thorns and fern-like leaves, which are pinnate and composed of 11–21, lanceolate leaflets. Small, flat clusters of green-petalled flowers, in late summer, are followed by red fruits. A pretty shrub, resembling *Z. piperitum*, but with solitary spines and later flowers on the current year's shoots. Japan, Korea, E China. C 1877.

simulans Hance (*Z. bungei* Planch.) A medium-sized to large shrub or small tree of spreading habit with spiny branches. Leaves pinnate, composed of 7–11, broadly ovate, shining green leaflets. Greenish-yellow flowers in early summer followed by small, reddish fruits. Large stout prickles are a prominent feature of the trunks of mature specimens. China, Japan. I 1869.

†**ZAUSCHNERIA** C. Presl—**Onagraceae**—A small genus of 4 species of perennials or dwarf subshrubs natives of W USA and N Mexico and requiring a warm, sunny, well-drained position. Excellent subjects for a rock garden. In the wild they are pollinated by hummingbirds.

californica C. Presl. California fuchsia. A bushy subshrub with several erect, green or grey-downy, more or less glandular stems, densely clothed with narrow, downy, grey-green leaves. Tubular, fuchsia-like, red flowers, with a scarlet tube, are borne in long, loose spikes during late summer and autumn. California. I 1847. **'Dublin'** ('Glasnevin') Flowers borne over a long period from August to October. Selected at Glasnevin Botanic Garden. ♀ 2002. AM 1983. **subsp.** *latifolia* (Hook.) Keck (*Z. canescens* Eastw.) More herbaceous in nature, with broader leaves. SW USA. AM 1928. **subsp.** *mexicana* (Presl) Raven. Similar to the typical form and equally floriferous but with broader, green leaves. **'Olbrich Silver'** Bright scarlet flowers and very silvery foliage. **'Western Hills'** Scarlet flowers borne over a very long period from June until the frosts. ♀ 2002.

cana Greene (*Z. microphylla* (A. Gray) Moxley) A grey, dwarf subshrub with linear leaves crowding the stems, and loose spikes of red, scarlet-tubed flowers during late summer and autumn. California. AM 1928 (as *Z. microphylla*).

canescens See *Z. californica* subsp. *latifolia*.

microphylla See *Z. cana*.

ZELKOVA Spach—**Ulmaceae**—A small genus of 5 species of smooth-barked trees or rarely shrubs, natives of Asia with one species in Crete. They are allied to the elms (*Ulmus*), differing in their simple (not double), toothed leaves and unwinged fruits. The small, greenish flowers (male and bisexual on the same tree) and the fruits that follow are of little ornament. They thrive in deep, moist, loamy soils and are fairly tolerant of shade. Zelkovas are trees of considerable quality; their garden value may be paralleled with the deciduous *Nothofagus*.

abelicea (Lam.) Boiss. (*Z. cretica* Spach) A large, wide-spreading shrub with slender twigs and small, ovate to oblong, coarsely toothed leaves up to 2.5cm long. Flowers small, whitish, scented. A rare species in cultivation and the wild. Mts of Crete. I about 1924.

acuminata See *Z. serrata*.

carpinifolia (Pall.) K. Koch (*Z. crenata* (Michx. f.) Spach, *Planera richardii* Michx.) A long-lived, slow-growing tree eventually attaining a large size. The bark is smooth and grey like a beech, but flakes with age. As seen in the British Isles the trunk is generally comparatively short, soon giving way to numerous, erect, crowded branches which form a characteristic dense, conical head. On old trees the trunk is often buttressed. The hairy shoots bear 4–7.5cm-long, ovate to elliptic, coarsely toothed leaves, rough to the touch above. Caucasus, N Iran. I 1760.

crenata See *Z. carpinifolia*.

cretica See *Z. abelicea*.

serrata (Thunb.) Makino (*Z. acuminata* (Lindl.) Planch.) (*Z. keaki* (Siebold) Maxim. *Planera acuminata* Lindl.) Keaki. A medium-sized, occasionally large tree of graceful, widespreading habit, forming a rounded crown, with smooth, grey, later flaky bark. The attractive, ovate to ovate-lanceolate, acuminate leaves are 5–12cm long and edged with slender-pointed, coarse teeth. In autumn they turn to bronze or red. In 1951 we supplied a specimen of this tree for the Festival of Britain. It was the largest tree planted on the Thames embankment site, weighing over 2 tons and with a branch spread exceeding 10m. Throughout its journey from Winchester to London, it was honoured by a police escort. Japan, Korea, Taiwan, China. I 1861. ♥ 2002.

sinica C.K. Schneid. A medium-sized tree with smooth, grey bark, flaking with age. Twigs slender and short-pubescent. Leaves small and neat, ovate to ovate-lanceolate, coarsely toothed, 2.5–6cm long, harsh to the touch. The young growths are pink-tinted in spring. C and E China. I 1908 by Ernest Wilson.

× *verschaffeltii* (Dippel) Nichols. (*Z. carpinifolia* × *Z. serrata*) Normally a splendid, large shrub or small, bushy-headed tree of graceful habit, with slender shoots and oval to ovate, conspicuously toothed leaves, rough to the touch above, and in shape recalling those of *Ulmus* × *viminalis*. There is a large tree in Westonbirt Arboretum with grey and rich brown, mottled bark and deeply lobed leaves. Origin unknown. C 1886. FCC 1886 (as *Ulmus pitteursii pendula*).

‡**ZENOBIA** D. Don—**Ericaceae**—A monotypic genus requiring lime-free soil and preferably semi-shade. One of the most beautiful and most neglected of early summer-flowering shrubs. One suspects that this glorious little shrub flowers during the "London Season": how else can it have been so unnoticed.

pulverulenta (Bartr. ex Willd.) Pollard. A beautiful, small, deciduous or semi-evergreen shrub of loose habit with bloomy young shoots. The oblong-ovate, shallowly toothed leaves are covered by a conspicuous, glaucous bloom which tends to fade above as the leaves age. The white, bell-shaped flowers, resembling those of a large lily-of-the-valley, are aniseed-scented and appear in pendent, axillary clusters in June and July. E USA. I 1801. FCC 1934. AM 1932. **'Blue Sky'** A selection with striking, glaucous-blue young foliage. **f. *nitida*** (Michx.) Fern. (var. *nuda* (Vent.) Rehder) A form with green leaves. This variety is said to occur with the typical form in the wild. Some authorities regard it as a distinct species, but seed-grown plants in cultivation contain forms that appear intermediate between the two. AM 1965. **var. *nuda*** See f. *nitida*.

CLIMBERS

Only true climbers are listed here. For other wall plants see TREES AND SHRUBS. Climbers may roughly be divided into three main categories, based on their mode of growth, namely:

Group 1 consists of those climbers which, owing to the presence of aerial roots (as in ivy), or adhesive tendril tips (as in Virginia creeper), are self-clinging and have the ability to scale a wall or tree trunk without added support.

Group 2 consists of climbers with twining stems (as in honeysuckle), curling tendrils (as in vine), or curling petioles (as in Clematis), which require support other than that of a flat surface up which to grow.

Group 3 consists of climbers with hooked thorns (as in climbing roses) or with long scandent stems (as in Berberidopsis), which require the support of a wall or tree over or into which to scramble.

All climbers require careful attention on a support until established. Even the self-clingers of group 1 usually require the help of some string or wire until their adhesive organs establish permanent contact with the wall or tree surface. In the absence of trees or suitable walls, the climbers of groups 2 and 3 may be trained up specially constructed wooden supports or over hedges. Many climbers, particularly those in groups 1 and 3, may be used as groundcover, particularly on unsightly banks, producing a rapid and often ornamental effect. Several climbers are dioecious, the females often bearing attractive fruits. Where fruits are required, plants of both sexes are best planted together over or against the same support.

ACTINIDIA Lindl.—**Actinidiaceae**—About 60 species of climbers, natives of E Asia. Vigorous, generally hardy, twining climbers with simple leaves, unisexual, bisexual or polygamous flowers and sometimes edible, juicy berries. They are excellent for covering old walls or tall stumps and will grow in most fertile soils in sun or semi-shade. Those grown for their fruits are best planted in pairs.

arguta (Siebold. & Zucc.) Miq. A strong-growing species climbing to the tops of lofty trees in its native land. Leaves broadly ovate, 7.5–13cm long, bristly-toothed. Flowers white with purple anthers, slightly fragrant, 1–2cm across, opening in June and July. Fruits oblong, greenish-yellow, 2.5cm long, edible but insipid. Japan, Korea, NE China. C 1874. var. *cordifolia* Dunn. A form with heart-shaped leaves.

chinensis Planch. Plants grown under this name are usually *A. deliciosa* q.v. The true species differs in its sharply toothed, taper-pointed leaves and its usually rounded, smooth or shortly downy fruits. It is commonly eaten in China and selected forms grown for their edible fruits are cultivated in New Zealand, to where it was introduced in 1977. It is in cultivation in this country but is rare in gardens. China.

†*coriacea* Dunn. A vigorous, almost evergreen species with leathery, slender-pointed leaves to 13cm long. Flowers 12mm across, fragrant, attractive rose-pink, in May and June. Fruits brown, spotted white, egg-shaped, to 2.5cm long. Requires a warm, sunny sheltered position. On a west-facing wall in Winchester it survived the severe winter of 1962–63, although it was injured. W China. I 1908 by Ernest Wilson.

deliciosa C.S. Liang & A.R. Ferguson (*A. chinensis* hort. not Planch.) Chinese gooseberry, Kiwi fruit. A vigorous species, reaching 9m, with densely reddish-hairy shoots and large, heart-shaped leaves, 15–23cm long and up to 20cm wide. Flowers creamy-white, turning to buff-yellow, 4cm across, fragrant, produced in axillary clusters in late summer. Fruits edible, green then brown, 4–5cm long, resembling a large, elongated gooseberry and with a similar flavour. To obtain fruit it is necessary to plant both sexes; only one male is needed for several females in reasonable proximity. Selected clones are cultivated for their fruits, notably in New Zealand to where the species was first introduced in 1904. China. I 1900 by Ernest Wilson. AM 1907. **'Aureovariegata'** Leaves splashed and marked with cream and yellow. Tends to revert. **'Hayward'** The large fruits of this selection, which store well, have made it by far the most popular fruiting cultivar. Raised in New Zealand before 1935. **'Jenny'** A self-fertile form not requiring a pollinator to produce fruit. **'Tomuri'** A male form grown as a pollinator.

giraldii Diels. A strong-growing species, related to *A. arguta*, with ovate or elliptic leaves, and white flowers during summer. C China. C 1933.

kolomikta (Maxim. & Rupr.) Maxim. A striking, slender, dioecious climber reaching 4.5–6m. Remarkable on account of the tri-coloured variegation of many of its leaves, the terminal half being creamy-white, flushed pink. The variegation is not apparent on very young plants. Flowers white, slightly fragrant, 12mm across, opening in June; fruits ovoid, 2.5cm long, yellowish and sweet. The form in general cultivation appears to be a male plant. Japan, N China, Manchuria. I about 1855. ♀ 2002. AM 1931.

melanandra Franch. A vigorous species, reaching a great height in a tree. Leaves oblong or narrowly oval, 7.5–10cm long, glaucous beneath. Flowers unisexual, white with purple anthers, in June and July. Fruits egg-shaped, 2.5–3cm long, reddish-brown with a plum-like bloom. C China. I 1910 by Ernest Wilson.

pilosula (Finet. & Gagnep.) Stapf ex Hand.-Mazz. A vigorous climber with smooth shoots. Leaves lance-shaped, ending in a fine, tapered point and edged with bristle-like teeth, dark green with a conspicuous silvery-white botch at the tip or covering half to most of the leaf. Flowers pink, about 2cm across, borne singly or in small clusters in the leaf axils in spring. China.

polygama (Siebold & Zucc.) Maxim. Silver vine. A slender-branched species up to 4.5–6m in a tree. Leaves broadly ovate to elliptic, 7.5–13cm long, bronze tinted when unfolding, becoming blotched with silvery-white. Fragrant white flowers, 2cm across, are produced in June. Fruits ovoid, beaked, 2.5–4cm long, yellow and edible. C Japan.

purpurea Rehder. Strong-growing species, related to *A. arguta*, reaching 6–7.5m in a tree. Leaves oval to ovate-oblong, 7.5–13cm long. Flowers white, 1–2cm across, open in June. Fruit ovoid or oblong, 2.5cm long, purple, edible and sweet. W China. I 1908 by Ernest Wilson.

AKEBIA Decne.—**Lardizabalaceae**—A genus of 5 species of vigorous, hardy, semi-evergreen, monoecious, twining plants from E Asia with attractive foliage and flowers. Succeeding in most soils, in sun or shade, they are excellent for training over hedges, low trees, bushes or old stumps. A mild spring (for the flowers) and a long hot summer are usually required before the conspicuous and unusual fruits are produced.

lobata See *A. trifoliata*.

× *pentaphylla* (Makino) Makino (*A. quinata* × *A. trifoliata*) A strong-growing, rare hybrid, the leaves with usually 5 oval leaflets. Flowers similar to those of *A. trifoliata*. Japan.

quinata (Houtt.) Decne. A semi-evergreen climber up to 9 or 12m in a tree. Leaves composed of normally 5 oblong or obovate, notched leaflets. Flowers fragrant, red-purple, male and female in the same racemes in April. Fruits 5–10cm long, sausage-shaped, turning dark purple, containing numerous black seeds embedded in a white pulp. Japan, Korea, China. I 1845 by Robert Fortune. AM 1956.

trifoliata (Thunb.) Koidz. (*A. lobata* Decne.) An elegant climber up to 9m in a tree. Leaves trifoliolate, with broadly ovate, shallowly lobed or undulate leaflets. Flowers dark purple, male and female produced in a drooping raceme in April. Fruits sausage-shaped, often in groups of 3, 7.5–13cm long, pale violet, containing black seeds in a white pulp. Japan, China. I 1895.

AMPELOPSIS Michx.—**Vitaceae**—A small genus of about 25 species of ornamental vines climbing by means of curling tendrils; natives mainly of North America and E Asia. At one time they were included under *Vitis*, but differ in having free (not united) petals and usually compound leaves. They are excellent subjects for covering walls, fences, hedges, and so on, and with initial support will clamber into trees. Valuable for their attractive foliage and for their fruits which, however, require a long, hot summer and a mild autumn in which to develop. The inconspicuous flowers appear in late summer or early autumn. They will grow in any ordinary soil and in sun or semi-shade, but for those species with attractive fruits a warm, sunny, sheltered position is recommended. See also *Parthenocissus* and *Vitis*.

aconitifolia Bunge (*Vitis aconitifolia* (Bunge) Hance) A vigorous, luxurious climber. Leaves variable in shape, composed of 3 or 5 sessile, lanceolate or rhomboid, coarsely toothed or lobed leaflets. The whole leaf is 10–13cm across and deep glossy green above. Fruits small, orange or yellow. N China. C 1868. **'Chinese Lace'** We propose this name for an attractive form with leaves cut to the base into 3–5 pinnately cut lobes, turning orange and yellow to red in autumn.

bodinieri (Lév. & Vaniot) Rehder (*Vitis micans* (Rehder) Bean) A slender climber up to 6m with smooth, often purplish stems. Leaves simple, triangular-ovate or rounded, 7.5–13cm long, coarsely toothed and occasionally 3-lobed, dark shining green above, somewhat glaucous beneath. The small, rounded fruits are dark blue. C China. I 1900 by Ernest Wilson.

brevipedunculata (Maxim.) Trautv. (*Cissus brevipedunculata* Maxim.) A vigorous, luxuriant climber with 3-lobed or occasionally 5-lobed, cordate leaves, 5–15cm across, resembling those of the hop (*Humulus*). After a hot summer the small fruits vary between verdigris and deep blue but *en masse* are porcelain-blue and exceedingly attractive. NE Asia. C 1870. **'Citrulloides'** Leaves more deeply 5-lobed. An attractive foliage plant. Fruits similar to those of the typical form. C 1875. **'Elegans'** ('Variegata', 'Tricolor') An attractive form with leaves densely mottled white and tinged pink. Relatively weak-growing and therefore useful for planting where space is restricted. An excellent patio plant. I before 1847 by Siebold. **'Tricolor'** See 'Elegans'. **'Variegata'** See 'Elegans'.

chaffanjonii (Lév.) Rehder (*Ampelopsis watsoniana* E.H. Wilson) A large-leaved climber, suitable for walls and wooden supports. Leaves pinnate, 15–30cm long, composed of 5 or 7 oval or oblong, deep glossy green leaflets, purple-tinted beneath, and often colouring richly in autumn. Fruits red, later black. C China. I 1900 by Ernest Wilson. AM 1907.

megalophylla (Veitch) Diels & Gilg (*Vitis megalophylla* Veitch) A strong but rather slow-growing, aristocratic climber of considerable quality, reaching 9m or more in a suitable tree. Leaves bipinnate, 30–60cm long, with ovate to ovate-oblong leaflets usually glaucous beneath, coarsely toothed and 5–15cm in length. Loose bunches of top-shaped fruits, purple at first, finally black. W China. I 1894. AM 1903.

orientalis (Lam.) Planch. (*Cissus orientalis* Lam.) A bushy shrub of loose growth or occasionally climbing. Leaves variable, pinnate, bipinnate or bi-ternate with ovate to obovate, coarsely toothed leaflets. After a hot summer bears bunches of attractive, redcurrant-like fruits. SW Asia, Syria. I 1818.

sempervirens hort. See *Cissus striata*.

veitchii See *Parthenocissus tricuspidata* 'Veitchii'.

†***ARAUJIA** Brot.—**Asclepiadaceae**—A small genus of 4 species of mainly tropical, twining climbers requiring full sun. Natives of S America.

sericifera Brot. Cruel plant. A vigorous, evergreen climber with pale green, ovate-oblong leaves. Slightly fragrant, creamy-white, salver-shaped flowers are borne in short racemes close to the leaf axils during late summer. These are followed after a long, hot summer by large, grooved, yellowish-green pods, 10–13cm long, containing numerous, silky-tufted seeds. Only suitable for the mildest areas of the British Isles. The common name refers to the peculiar fact that in its native habitats, night-flying moths visiting the flowers are held trapped by their long probosces until daytime when they are usually able to release themselves. S Brazil. I 1830. AM 1975.

ARISTOLOCHIA L.—**Aristolochiaceae**—A large genus of about 300 species of shrubs, climbers and herbaceous plants with cordate leaves and peculiarly shaped flowers; widely distributed especially in warm regions. The species described here are excellent, twining plants for covering unsightly walls, fences or stumps and equally effective in trees and on wooden supports such as arbours, archways, and so on, and will grow in most fertile soils, in sun or shade.

altissima See *A. sempervirens*.

durior See *A. macrophylla*.

chrysops (Stapf) Hemsl. A rare species, up to 6m, with hairy shoots and hairy, auricled, ovate leaves, 5–13cm long. Flowers shaped like a small, tubby, greyish saxophone, 4cm long, with a flared, purplish-brown mouth and a mustard-yellow throat, appear singly on long, slender, pendent stalks during late May and June. W China. I 1904.

macrophylla Lam. (*A. sipho* L'Hér., *A. durior* Rehder not Hill) Dutchman's pipe. A vigorous species reaching 9m in a suitable tree. Leaves heart-shaped or kidney-shaped up to 30cm long. Flowers tubular, bent in the lower half, like a siphon, 2.5–4cm long, yellowish-green, the flared mouth brownish-purple, produced in June in axillary pairs. E USA. I 1763 by John Bartram.

†*sempervirens L. (*A. altissima* Desf.) An evergreen species with long, lax stems up to 3m, trailing along the ground unless trained. Leaves glossy green, heart-shaped and slender-pointed to 10cm long. Flowers yellowish-brown to dull purple, funnel-shaped and curved, produced singly in the leaf axils during late spring or early summer. May be cut to ground level in a cold winter, but invariably appears the following spring, particularly if given winter protection. E Mediterranean region, N Africa. I 1727.

sipho See *A. macrophylla*.

tomentosa Sims. A vigorous species, related to and somewhat resembling *A. macrophylla*, but downy in almost all its parts. Its leaves are also smaller and its flowers possess a distinctly 3-lobed, yellowish, flared mouth. SE USA. I 1799.

†**ASTERANTHERA** Klotzsch & Hanst.—**Gesneriaceae**—A monotypic genus related to *Mitraria* and climbing by means of aerial roots. It requires a cool, leafy soil, preferably neutral or acid, and is happiest in a sheltered woodland or against a north wall in milder areas of the British Isles.

ovata (Cav.) Hanst. A beautiful, evergreen, trailing creeper that will climb up the trunks of trees or the surface of a wall where conditions are suitable, otherwise it makes a charming ground cover. Leaves opposite, rounded or ovate, 1–4cm long. Tubular, 2-lipped flowers are 5cm long and appear in June. They are red, the lower lip having blood-red veins, accentuated by a white throat. In the forests of the Chilean Andes, it adheres closely to the trunks of trees and attains a height of 3–6m. Chile. I 1926 by Harold Comber in 1926. AM 1939.

†**BERBERIDOPSIS** Hook. f.—**Flacourtiaceae**—A genus of 2 species requiring an open or sandy loam and a sheltered position in shade, succeeding best in an acid or neutral soil. Correctly sited it is moderately hardy. A shaded site and a moist soil are essential.

corallina Hook. f. Coral plant. A beautiful, evergreen, scandent shrub attaining a length of 4.5–6m on a shaded wall. Leaves heart-shaped or ovate, thick and leathery, the margins set with spiny teeth, dark green above, glaucous beneath. Flowers deep crimson, 12mm across, borne singly on slender stalks or in pendent racemes during late summer. Chile. I 1862 by Richard Pearce. AM 1901.

BERCHEMIA Necker ex DC.—**Rhamnaceae**—A small genus of about 12 species of twining climbers, natives of E Asia, E Africa and North America. They have rather insignificant white or greenish flowers and small fruits which are rarely freely produced in British gardens. Their elegant foliage makes them unusual climbers for walls, hedges, or bushy-headed trees. Easy to grow in most fertile soils in sun or semi-shade.

giraldiana C.K. Schneid. A graceful species attaining 4.5–6m, with reddish-brown shoots and ovate-oblong, parallel-veined leaves, 2.5–6cm long, dark sea-green above, glaucous beneath. Fruits sausage-shaped, 8mm long, red at first, then black. C and W China. C 1911.

lineata DC. An elegant climber with neat, elliptic, parallel-veined leaves, 6–40mm long. The tiny fruits ripen to blue-black. China, Taiwan, Himalaya.

racemosa Siebold & Zucc. A strong-growing, scandent shrub, up to 4.5m, with pretty ovate, parallel-veined leaves, 4–7.5cm long, pale or glaucescent beneath. Fruits small, oblong, changing from green to red, then black. A spreading species ideal for growing over hedges, low trees and bushes. The leaves turn clear yellow in autumn. Japan. I 1880. **'Variegata'** Leaves, particularly when young, conspicuously variegated creamy-white.

BIGNONIA L.—**Bignoniaceae**—As now understood this is a monotypic genus, but at one time it included *Campsis* and *Tecoma*.

capreolata L. (*Doxantha capreolata* (L.) Miers) Cross vine. A vigorous, evergreen or semi-evergreen shrub, climbing by means of twining leaf tendrils. Leaves composed of 2 oblong to ovate-lanceolate leaflets, 5–13cm long. Tubular flowers, 4–5cm long, are orange-red, paler within, carried in axillary clusters in June. A rampant climber for a sunny, sheltered wall or tree. Hardy in the southern counties. SE USA. C 1653. AM 1958.

†**BILLARDIERA** Sm.—**Pittosporaceae**—A small genus of about 8 species of low-growing, Australasian, twining plants. The following is suitable for a warm, sunny position in milder areas of the British Isles. It makes an unusual conservatory subject.

longiflora Labill. A slender climber, up to 2m. Leaves lanceolate, 2.5–4cm long. Solitary, bell-shaped flowers hang on slender stalks from the leaf axils during summer and autumn. Greenish-yellow and 2cm long, they are replaced by brilliant deep blue, oblong fruits, 2–2.5cm long. A charming plant against a wall or clambering over a large boulder on a rock garden or scrambling through a low bush. Tasmania. I 1810. ♀ 2002. AM 1924. **'Cherry Berry'** This has fruits like large, red cherries. **'Fructualbo'** ('Alba') The fruits are white.

Bittersweet See *Celastrus scandens*.

Bluebell creeper See *Sollya heterophylla*.
Bridgesia spicata See *Ercilla volubilis*.

CAMPSIS Lour.—**Bignoniaceae**—A genus of only 2 species of attractive, deciduous, scandent shrubs related to *Bignonia*, and equally brilliant in flower. Both require a position in full sun to ripen growth and produce flowers. They are excellent when trained over walls or the roofs of outhouses or tree stumps. Specimens that have become too large and tangled may be pruned in late February or March.

chinensis See *C. grandiflora*.

grandiflora (Thunb.) K. Schum. (*C. chinensis* (Lam.) Voss) This beautiful oriental climber will attain a height of 6m or more in a suitable position. Leaves pinnate, composed of 7 or 9 ovate, coarsely toothed, glabrous leaflets. Flowers trumpet-shaped, 5–9cm long, deep orange and red, carried in drooping panicles from the tips of the current year's growths during late summer and early autumn. China. I 1800. AM 1949. **'Thunbergii'** A form with shorter-tubed, red trumpets and reflexed lobes. I 1856 by Siebold.

radicans (L.) Seem. Trumpet vine. A tall, strong-growing species that normally climbs by aerial roots, but is best given a little support until established. Leaves pinnate, composed of 9 or 11, coarsely toothed leaflets, downy beneath, at least on the veins. Flowers trumpet-shaped, 5–8cm long, brilliant orange and scarlet, produced in terminal clusters on the current year's growths in August and September. SE USA. C 1640. AM 1990. **'Flava'** ('Yellow Trumpet') An attractive form with rich yellow flowers. ♀ 2002. AM 1969.

× *tagliabuana* (Vis.) Rehder (*C. grandiflora* × *C. radicans*) A variable hybrid intermediate in habit between the parents. Leaflets varying from 7–11, slightly downy on the veins beneath. **'Madame Galen'** A vigorous climber with panicles of salmon-red flowers in late summer. Requires support up which to clamber. C 1889. ♀ 2002. AM 1959.

CELASTRUS L.—**Celastraceae**—A genus of some 30 widely distributed species. Vigorous, twining and scandent climbers with tiny, insignificant flowers, followed in autumn by attractive, long-persistent capsules containing brightly coloured seeds. The flowers are often unisexual; therefore, when grown for fruit, the species are best planted in pairs. Sometimes male and female clones are available. All species are tall-growing, rampant climbers and are best accommodated in an old tree or tall bush. They are also excellent for covering large stumps, hedges, unsightly walls, and so on, in full sun or shade.

articulatus See *C. orbiculatus*.

hypoleucus (Oliver) Loes. (*C. hypoglaucus* Hemsl.) A large climber, the young shoots covered with a purplish bloom. Leaves oblong or obovate, up to 15cm long, strikingly glaucous beneath. Yellow-lined, green capsules split to reveal red seeds. A handsome species distinguished by its terminal inflorescences and the glaucous undersurfaces of its leaves. C China. I about 1900 by Ernest Wilson.

orbiculatus Thunb. (*C. articulatus* Thunb.) A strong-growing climber reaching a height of 12m or more in a tree. The twining, young shoots are armed with a pair of short spines at each bud. Flowers in terminal clusters. Leaves varying from obovate to orbicular, 5–13cm long, turning clear yellow in autumn. Also in autumn the brownish capsules split open to reveal a yellow lining containing red seeds. A beautiful climber in autumn, when the scarlet and gold-spangled fruits glisten against a backcloth of yellow. The most consistent species for fruiting. NE Asia. Commonly naturalised in parts of the SE USA. I 1860. ♀ 2002 (to hermaphrodite forms). FCC 1958 (to a hermaphrodite form). AM 1914.

rosthornianus Loes. A vigorous, scandent shrub reaching 5–6m in a tree. Leaves ovate to ovate-lanceolate, 4–8cm long, glossy green above. Capsules orange-yellow, containing scarlet seeds, long-persistent. W China. I 1910 by Ernest Wilson.

rugosus Rehder & E.H. Wilson. A vigorous climber, up to 6m, with warty shoots and ovate or elliptic, strongly toothed and wrinkled leaves, up to 15cm long. Capsules orange-yellow, containing bright red seeds. W China. I 1908 by Ernest Wilson.

scandens L. Bittersweet. Vigorous climber, up to 7m, with ovate to ovate-oblong, sharply pointed leaves. Flowers in small, axillary clusters. Female plants produce orange-lined capsules containing scarlet-coated seeds. Not very free-fruiting in the British Isles. North America. I 1736 by Peter Collinson.

†**CISSUS** L.—**Vitaceae**—A large genus of 350 species of shrubs and herbaceous plants, widely distributed, mainly in tropical regions, the majority climbing by means of twining tendrils. Only the following species may be grown outdoors in the British Isles, and then only in the mildest areas.

*antarctica Vent. Kangaroo vine. A strong-growing, vine-like climber with ovate-oblong, cordate leaves, rather leathery in texture, glossy green and 8–10cm long. An excellent climber or trailer for a conservatory and a popular house plant, succeeding in sun or shade. E Australia. I 1790. ♀ 2002.

*striata Ruiz & Pav. (*Vitis striata* (Ruiz & Pav.) Miq., *Ampelopsis sempervirens* hort.) A luxuriant, evergreen climber for a sunny wall. Leaves 5–7.5cm across, composed of 5 obovate or oblanceolate, dark glossy green leaflets, coarsely toothed towards the apex. Fruits like reddish-purple currants. Chile and S Brazil. I about 1878.

CLEMATIS L.—**Ranunculaceae**—A genus of about 300 species of deciduous and evergreen climbers, shrubs, sub-shrubs and herbaceous perennials, widely distributed. The species of this most popular genus are, on the whole, much easier to establish than the large-flowered hybrids, though, like the latter, they thrive best in full sun, with their roots in cool, moist, well-drained soil. The climbing species support themselves by means of their petioles, which twine round any slender support available. The stronger-growing species are ideal for growing into trees or over large bushy shrubs and most others are very effective on walls, fences or wooden supports. As well as flowers, some species have attractive, silken seedheads. The flower of a clematis is composed of 4–8 sepals which are usually large and colourful and sometimes incorrectly referred to as tepals. The true petals are absent or in a few species (Atragene Section) reduced to small petaloid staminodes.

The only pruning needed is the removal of dead or useless wood, and the shortening of shoots that have extended beyond their allotted space, but, if necessary, the later summer-flowering species may be pruned hard every spring. See also **Large-flowered garden clematis** p.398.

aethusifolia Turcz. Parsley-leaved clematis. A slender-stemmed climber, reaching about 2m, with deeply and finely divided leaves. Flowers in late summer, bell-shaped, 2cm long, with recurved lobes, pale primrose-yellow and fragrant, nodding on slender stems. N China, Mongolia. I about 1875. AM 1992.

afoliata Buchanan (*C. aphylla* Kuntze) A curious species with slender, leafless, green stems up to 3m long, clambering into bushes or, when no support is available, forming dense mounds. Worth growing for its unusual form and for the fragrance of its small, unisexual, greenish-white flowers in May. Requires a warm, sunny, sheltered position. New Zealand. AM 1915.

akebioides (Maxim.) Veitch (Sect. Meclatis) A relative of *C. tibetana* growing to about 4m. Leaves pinnate, with up to 7, glaucous and rather fleshy, crenately toothed leaflets. Flowers bell-shaped, yellow or tinged with green to purple outside, borne on long stalks in late summer and early autumn. W China.

alpina (L.) Mill. (Sect. Atragene) A lovely species with slender stems up to 2.5m long. Leaves with 9 ovate-lanceolate, coarsely toothed leaflets. Flowers solitary, 2.5–4cm long, blue or violet-blue with a central tuft of white staminodes, borne on long, slender stalks during April and May, followed by silky seedheads. Superb when grown over a low wall or scrambling over a large rock or small bush. Mts of C and S Europe. I 1792. ♀ 2002. AM 1894. **'Burford White'** Creamy-white flowers. **'Blue Dancer'** Pale blue flowers with long, slender sepals. Raised by Raymond Evison before 1985. **'Columbine'** Pale grey-blue. C 1937. **'Columbine White'** See 'White Columbine'. **'Constance'** A seedling of 'Ruby' with semi-double, deep pink flowers. C 1992. ♀ 2002. **'Foxy'** Pale pink, staminodes pink. A sport of 'Frankie' introduced by Raymond Evison in 1996. ♀ 2002. **'Frances Rivis'** ('Blue Giant') A vigorous, free-flowering clone with larger flowers, up to 5cm long, with a contrasting sheaf of white stamens and staminodes in the centre. Raised by Sir Cedric Morris before 1961 and possibly a hybrid with *C. ochotensis*. ♀ 2002. AM 1965 (as 'Blue Giant'). **'Frankie'** Blue, the white staminodes tipped with blue. C 1991. ♀ 2002. **'Helsingborg'** See *C.* 'Helsingborg'. **'Jacqueline du Pré'** See *C.* 'Jacqueline du Pré'. **'Pamela Jackman'** Large, rich blue flowers; outer staminodes tinged blue, inner staminodes white. C 1960. **'Pink Flamingo'** Profuse double pink flowers. C 1993. ♀ 2002. **'Rosy Pagoda'** Pale pink flowers in profusion. Greenish-white staminodes. A seedling of *C. alpina* 'Ruby' raised by Magnus Johnson of Sweden in 1974. **'Ruby'** Flowers rose-red with creamy-white staminodes. Raised by Ernest Markham in 1935. **var. *sibirica*** See *C. sibirica*. **'White Columbine'** ('Columbine White') A seedling of 'Columbine' with pure white flowers. C 1986. ♀ 2002. **'White Moth'** See *C. macropetala* 'White Moth'. **'Willy'** Flowers mauve-pink with a deep pink blotch at the base of each sepal. C 1971.

'Anita' White flowers, each with 6 sepals and white stamens, from creamy buds during late summer and early autumn. A seedling of *C. potaninii* subsp. *fargesii*, possibly pollinated by *C. tangutica*, raised in Holland in 1989.

'Annamieke' A seedling raised in Holland before 1991 and possibly a hybrid between *C. serratifolia* and *C. tanguti-ca*. Small, yellow flowers with twisted, recurved sepals open in late summer and early autumn.

aphylla See *C. afoliata*.

*armandii Franch. A strong-growing, evergreen climber with stems 4.5–6m long. Leaves composed of 3, long, leathery, glossy dark green leaflets. Fragrant, creamy-white flowers, 5–6.5cm across, are carried in axillary clusters during April or early May. A beautiful species, subject to injury in severe winters and best planted on a warm, sunny wall. Seed-raised plants often produce smaller, inferior flowers. C and W China, N Burma, N Vietnam. I 1900 by Ernest Wilson. FCC 1914. **'Apple Blossom'** The true plant is a superb form with broad sepals of white shaded pink, especially on the reverse. Leaves bronze-green when young. A poor form that is easy to propagate has been distributed under this name. ♀ 2002. FCC 1936. AM 1926. **'Snowdrift'** Flowers are pure white. FCC 1996.

× *aromatica* Lenné & Koch (*C. flammula* × *C. integrifolia*) A small subshrub, dying back to near ground level each winter. Leaves pinnate with 3–7 short-stalked leaflets. Flowers fragrant, dark bluish-violet, in terminal cymes from July to September.

'Aureolin' (*C. tangutica* 'Aureolin') A hybrid of *C. tangutica* making a medium-sized climber selected for its large, nodding, bright yellow flowers, with sepals to 4cm long, often opening widely, followed by showy seedheads.

*australis Kirk. A slender-stemmed, usually dioecious, scrambling species, the dark glossy green, trifoliolate leaves with deeply cut leaflets. Flowers creamy to greenish-yellow with 5–8 sepals, very fragrant, females about 3.5cm across, males slightly smaller, profusely borne either singly or in small panicles, April–May. New Zealand (South Island).

'Betty Corning' A hybrid growing to about 2m. Small, slightly fragrant, pale lilac, bell-shaped flowers, 5cm long, open from midsummer to late autumn. Found in the USA in 1932 and possibly *C. crispa* × *C. viticella*. ♀ 2002.

'Bill Mackenzie' (*C. tangutica* × *C. tibetana* subsp. *vernayi*) A vigorous, floriferous climber, the bright green leaves with sharply toothed leaflets. Flowers long-stalked, up to 6cm across, with 4 widespreading, rather thick sepals, bright yellow with purple filaments. Unfortunately, seedlings that have little resemblance to the true plant are being distributed under this name. ♀ 2002. AM 1976.

'Blue Bird' (*C. alpina* × *C. macropetala*) A vigorous hybrid between 2 popular species which it resembles. Flowers 7.5cm across, purple-blue, semi-double. C 1965.

†*brachiata* Thunb. A tender species only suitable for the mildest areas or a conservatory. Flowers greenish-white, deliciously fragrant. South Africa. AM 1975.

campaniflora Brot. A vigorous climber, up to 6m, with pinnate leaves, the leaflets in groups of 3. Small, bowl-shaped, blue-tinted flowers, borne profusely from July to September; most effective in the mass. Portugal, S Spain.

I 1810. **'Lisboa'** Large, mauve-blue flowers. Selected in Sweden in 1993 from seed from Lisbon Botanic Garden, Portugal.

'Carmen Rose' See *C. ochotensis* 'Carmen Rose'.

†*× *cartmanii* hort. (*C. marmoraria* × *C. paniculata*) Several forms of this hybrid between 2 evergreen New Zealand species have been raised in cultivation. They are slender-stemmed, trailing plants, like the parents dioecious and suitable for growing over low shrubs or in a container. **Avalanche** ('Blaaval') PBR A vigorous male form reaching 5m and bearing profuse white flowers, to 9cm across, with yellow stamens and usually 6 sepals. Leaves leathery, dark green, with 3 deeply toothed and cut leaflets. Raised by Robin White about 1989. ♀ 2002. AM 1999. **'Joe'** A male selection raised in 1983, with purplish shoots, growing up to 2m, and finely cut foliage. Profuse flowers open in clusters of up to 30; they are white, 4cm across, with 5–8 sepals and creamy-white stamens.

chiisanensis Nakai. A slender-stemmed climber, related to *C. alpina*, the leaves with 3 coarsely toothed leaflets. Pendent, bell-shaped flowers in summer are creamy-yellow with prominently ridged sepals, spurred at the base, and a centre of creamy staminodes. They open in summer and are followed by conspicuous silky seedheads. South Korea. **'Lemon Bells'** Flowers pale yellow on red-purple stalks, with thick sepals flushed red at the base. Selected at the University of British Columbia from South Korean seed in 1992.

chrysocoma Franch. A small subshrub, reaching 2m or less, the stems scrambling through low shrubs and often dying back to the ground in winter. Leaves with 3 leaflets densely covered in yellow hairs. Pale to deep pink flowers, to 5cm across, open in summer or autumn. I 1910.

chrysocoma hort. See *C. spooneri*.

*cirrhosa L. An evergreen species, up to 3m, with leaves varying from simple to compound, with 3–6 leaflets. Flowers 4–6.5cm across, yellowish-white, opening during winter and followed by silky seedheads. Best grown in a sheltered spot. S Europe, North Africa, SW Asia. I 1596. **var. balearica** (Rich.) Willk. & Lange (*C. balearica* (Rich.) Juss.) Fern-leaved clematis. An elegant, evergreen climber with slender stems, 3.5–4.5m long. Leaves prettily divided into several segments, becoming bronze-tinged in winter. Flowers pale yellow, spotted reddish-purple within, 4–5cm across, produced throughout winter. Balearic Isles, Corsica, Sardinia. I before 1783. AM 1974. **'Freckles'** Flowers large, very heavily spotted and streaked with red, opening from early autumn. Raised in the late 1980s by Raymond Evison from seed collected in the Balearic Islands. AM 1989. ♀ 2002. **'Wisley Cream'** Large, creamy-white, unspotted flowers. Leaves leathery, the 1–3 leaflets with rounded teeth, sometimes entire. ♀ 2002.

colensoi See *C. hookeriana*.

connata DC. A vigorous species allied to *C. rehderiana* and distinguished by the flattened bases of the petioles that surround the stem. Flowers nodding, bell-shaped, pale yellow and slightly fragrant, borne in panicles in early autumn. Himalaya, W China. C 1885.

crispa L. A slender-stemmed, semi-woody climber, to about 2.5m, with angled stems and pinnate leaves with up to 5 entire leaflets. Flowers borne during summer, bell-shaped, the reflexed lobes with crisped margins, pale to deep blue, solitary at the ends of the shoots. SE USA. I 1726.

× *durandii* Kuntze (*C. integrifolia* × *C.* 'Jackmanii') A lovely hybrid up to 3m. Leaves simple, entire, 7.5–15cm long. Dark blue, 4-sepalled flowers, borne from June to September, sometimes exceed 10cm in diameter and have a central cluster of yellow stamens. Garden origin in France about 1870. ♀ 2002.

× *eriostemon* Decne. (*C. integrifolia* × *C. viticella*) The original hybrid was raised in France before 1852. **'Blue Boy'** Purple-blue flowers, the sepals edged with white. Stems 2.5m high. Raised in Canada in 1947. **'Hendersonii'** A beautiful clematis, semi-herbaceous in habit, each year throwing up slender stems of 2–2.5m. Leaves simple or pinnate. Flowers deep bluish-purple, widely bell-shaped, slightly fragrant, 5–6.5cm across, nodding, borne singly on slender peduncles from July to September. It is best given some support. Raised by Messrs Henderson of St John's Wood in about 1830. AM 1965.

†***'Early Sensation'** A beautiful hybrid of *C. paniculata*, raised by Graham Hutchins. Finely cut, leathery, glossy green leaves and, in mid- to late spring, profuse white flowers, greenish-white at first, with yellow-green stamens, followed by abundant, attractive seedheads.

'Edward Prichard' (*C. recta* × *C. tubulosa*) A subshrubby scrambling plant reaching about 1.5 m tall. The small, creamy-pink, fragrant flowers, up to 4cm across, are profusely borne in summer and early autumn. Raised in Australia in 1950.

fargesii See *C. potaninii* subsp. *fargesii*. **var. souliei** See *C. potaninii*.

* *fasciculiflora* Franch. A very distinct evergreen climber, to 6m tall, with red-purple young shoots. Leathery leaves, with 3 untoothed, taper-pointed leaflets, are deep bronze-red when young, later dark green and often with a silvery blotch in the centre. Clusters of small, fragrant, white, bell-shaped flowers open during winter and early spring. SW China, N Burma, N Vietnam. I 1910 by George Forrest and more recently by Roy Lancaster.

†*finetiana Lévl. & Vaniot (*C. pavoliniana* Pamp.) An evergreen climber up to 5m, related to *C. armandii*, but differing in its smaller flowers. Leaves composed of 3 dark green, leathery leaflets. Flowers white, fragrant, 2.5–4cm wide, borne in axillary clusters in June. Best grown on a warm, sheltered wall except in milder areas. C to E China. I 1908 by Ernest Wilson.

flammula L. A strong-growing climber, 4–5m high, forming a dense tangle of glabrous stems clothed with bright green bipinnate leaves. From August to October, the loose panicles of small, white, sweetly scented flowers are abundantly scattered over the whole plant, followed by silky seedheads. An ideal climber for clothing tall, unsightly walls or hedges. S Europe, N Africa, SW Asia. Has been cultivated in England since the late 16th century. AM 1984.

†*florida* Thunb. An elegant species with wiry stems, 3–5m long, and glossy green, compound leaves. Flowers, opening in June and July, are 6–10cm across, solitary on long, downy stalks, sepals creamy-white with a greenish stripe

on the reverse, stamens dark purple. A native of S and SE China and a parent of many garden hybrids. Best grown in a sheltered position or conservatory. I 1776.
'Alba Plena' See var. *plena*. **var. *plena*** D. Don ('Alba Plena', 'Plena') In this striking form each flower is fully double, a dense mass of greenish-white sepals, long-lasting and borne over a long period. **'Sieboldii'** See var. *sieboldiana*. **var. *sieboldiana*** Morren ('Bicolor', 'Sieboldii') A beautiful and striking form recalling a passion flower (*Passiflora*). Flowers white, 8cm across, with a conspicuous central boss of violet-purple petaloid stamens. I before 1836 from Japan. AM 1914.

forrestii See *C. napaulensis*.

*forsteri J.F. Gmel. A usually dioecious, scrambling species related to *C. indivisa* but differing in its thinner leaves which are bright apple-green. Flowers verbena-scented, star-like, the males up to 4cm across with 5–8 white to creamy-yellow sepals, females smaller. New Zealand.

glauca See *C. intricata*.

Golden Tiara ('Kugotia') A seedling of 'Golden Harvest', raised in Holland in 1994. Climbing to 2.5m, with bipinnate leaves; flowers, upright to arching, with 4 thick golden-yellow sepals and black-purple stamens, opening in late summer to autumn, followed by profuse silky seedheads. ♀ 2002.

grandidentata (Rehder & E.H. Wilson) W.T. Wang (*C. grata* var. *grandidentata* Rehder & E.H. Wilson) A strong-growing climber reaching 9m in a suitable position. Leaves 15cm long, composed of 3–5, coarsely toothed leaflets. Flowers white, 2.5cm wide, borne in small axillary and terminal panicles during May and June. It is a hardy species related to *C. vitalba*. I 1904 by Ernest Wilson from W China.

grata Wall. A vigorous climber, 8m, with pinnate to bipinnate leaves and panicles of profuse, fragrant, creamy-white flowers in summer and early autumn. Himalaya, S China, Taiwan. I 1830. **var. *grandidentata*** See *C. grandidentata*.

'Helios' See *C. tangutica* 'Helios'.

'Helsingborg' (*C. alpina* × *C. ochotensis*) Raised in 1972 by Tage Lundell of Helsinborg, Sweden. Similar to *C. alpina* with long, mauve sepals. ♀ 2002.

heracleifolia DC. A deciduous, semi-shrubby species to 1m. Leaves composed of 3 leaflets, 5–13cm long and wide. Flowers nodding, often fragrant, 2–2.5cm long, tubular, deep blue. Plants grown under this name may be *C. tubulosa*. C and E China. I 1837. **var. *davidiana*** See *C. tubulosa*. **'Wyevale'** See *C. tubulosa* 'Wyevale'.

*hookeriana Allan (*C. colensoi* Hook. f. 1864 not 1852) An unusual species of subtle charm similar to *C. forsteri*. Up to 3m, it has fern-like, compound leaves with glossy green leaflets. Delightfully fragrant, star-shaped flowers, 4cm across, have yellowish-green, silky sepals and are borne in profusion during May and June. Succeeds best against a sunny wall. New Zealand. I 1935 by Capt. Collingwood Ingram. AM 1961.

indivisa See *C. paniculata* J.F. Gmel.

intricata Bunge (*C. glauca* Turcz. not Willd.) (Sect. Meclatis) A slender climber, up to 6m, with pinnate or bipinnate, glaucous leaves. Slender-stalked, bell-shaped flowers are 5cm across when fully open and deep orange-yellow. They are produced during August and

September and are followed by silky seedheads. S Mongolia, N China.

× *jackmanii* See C. 'Jackmanii' under Large-flowered garden clematis p.398.

'Jacqueline du Pré' (*C. alpina* 'Jacqueline du Pré') Large, mauve-pink flowers, the sepals narrowly edged with white. Probably a hybrid of *C. alpina*, reaching 3m. C 1985. ♀ 2002.

'Jan Lindmark' (*C. macropetala* 'Jan Lindmark') Mauve-pink flowers with deeper stripes. A seedling of *C.* 'Blue Bird' raised in Sweden in 1981.

× *jouiniana* C.K. Schneid. (*C. tubulosa* × *C. vitalba*) A vigorous, somewhat shrubby climber up to 3.5m high. Leaves composed of 3–5 coarsely toothed leaflets. Effective in autumn with its profusion of small, white, lilac-tinted flowers. An excellent plant for covering low walls, mounds or tree stumps. Garden origin before 1900. **'Côte d'Azur'** A charming form with azure-blue flowers. **'Mrs Robert Brydon'** See *C.* 'Mrs Robert Brydon'. **'Praecox'** A vigorous, early-flowering form with slightly larger, pale blue flowers. ♀ 2002.

ladakhiana C. Grey-Wilson. A scrambling climber, 4m, with shoots often purple-flushed and blue-green leaves divided into slender, taper-pointed and mostly untoothed leaflets. Flowers pendent, the sepals 2.5cm long, deep yellow blotched with red, opening widely with age. NW India, Tibet.

'Lambton Park' (*C. tangutica* 'Lambton Park'). A vigorous climber resembling *C. tangutica*. Very large, yellow flowers, with tepals to 8cm long, followed by attractive seedheads. ♀ 2002.

lasiandra Maxim. An uncommon species bearing leaves with 3–9, ovate-lanceolate, coarsely toothed leaflets, 5–10cm long. Purple, bell-shaped flowers, 12mm long, are borne in short axillary cymes during autumn. White-flowered forms occasionally appear. S Japan, China, Taiwan. I 1900 by Ernest Wilson.

'Last Dance' See *C. tibetana* subsp. *vernayi* 'Last Dance'.

macropetala Ledeb. (Sect. Atragene) A charming, slender-stemmed climber, up to 2.5m, with prettily divided leaves. Flowers 6.5–7.5cm across, violet-blue with conspicuous paler petaloid staminodes, giving the effect of doubling, produced from May or June onwards. Seedheads silky, becoming fluffy and grey with age. A beautiful species for a low wall or fence. Mongolia, N China, SE Siberia. I 1910 by William Purdom. AM 1923. **'Ballet Skirt'** Large, deep pink flowers. **'Blue Bird'** See *C.* 'Blue Bird'. **'Blue Lagoon'** See 'Lagoon'. **'Jan Lindmark'** See *C.* 'Jan Lindmark'. **'Lagoon'** ('Blue Lagoon') Similar to 'Maidwell Hall' but with slightly deeper blue flowers. C 1959. ♀ 2002. **'Maidwell Hall'** Flowers deep lavender-blue. C 1956. **'Markham's Pink'** ('Markhamii') A lovely form with flowers the shade of crushed strawberries. ♀ 2002. AM 1935. **'Pauline'** Profuse large, deep blue flowers with blue staminodes. ♀ 2002. **'Wesselton'** A selection with very large, blue flowers. ♀ 2002. **'White Moth'** (*C. alpina* 'White Moth') Flowers pure white. C 1955. **'White Swan'** See *C.* 'White Swan'.

†**marmoraria* Sneddon. The smallest clematis species, this is a prostrate, suckering, dioecious plant, forming clumps reminiscent of parsley. The trifoliolate glossy, evergreen

leaves are deeply and closely divided. Flowers to 2cm across on long, erect stalks, greenish-white becoming cream-white. Best in the alpine house. New Zealand. ♀ 2002.

maximowicziana See *C. terniflora*.

'Mayleen' (*C. montana* 'Mayleen') A vigorous climber resembling *C. montana*. Very fragrant satiny rose-pink flowers and bronze young foliage. ♀ 2002.

†***meyeniana** Walp. A strong-growing evergreen species, up to 6m or more, resembling *C. armandii* in leaf. Flowers white, 2.5cm across, borne in large, loose panicles during spring. A rare species for a warm, sheltered wall in milder areas. S Japan, Ryukyus, Taiwan, S China, Laos, Vietnam. C 1821. AM 1920.

montana Buch.-Ham. ex DC. A popular species of vigorous, often rampant growth and strong constitution. Stems 6–9m long with trifoliolate, almost glabrous leaves. Flowers white or pink-tinged, 5–6.5cm across, borne on long stalks in great profusion during May. A lovely climber for any aspect, excellent for growing in trees, over walls, outhouses and arbours, particularly those with a northern aspect. Himalaya, China, Taiwan. I 1831 by Lady Amherst. **'Alexander'** A lovely form with creamy-white, sweetly scented flowers. Introduced from N India by Col R.D. Alexander. **'Broughton Star'** ('Marjorie' × 'Picton's Variety') A very attractive form with double, pink flowers. C 1988. ♀ 2002. **'Elizabeth'** A desirable clone with large, slightly fragrant, soft pink flowers in May and June. ♀ 2002. **'Freda'** Deep cherry-pink, the sepals with darker edges; young foliage bronze. A seedling of 'Pink Perfection' raised by and named after Mrs Freda Deacon. ♀ 2002. **var. grandiflora** Hook. A strong-growing variety, occasionally up to 12m, producing an abundance of large white flowers in May and June. Excellent on a shady wall. Himalaya, China. ♀ 2002. **'Marjorie'** Semi-double, creamy-pink with salmon-pink centres. A seedling of var. *wilsonii*. **'Mayleen'** See *C.* 'Mayleen'. **'Picton's Variety'** Deep rosy-mauve with up to 6 sepals. **'Pink Perfection'** Fragrant flowers similar to but slightly deeper coloured than 'Elizabeth'. **'Primrose Star'** ('Freda' × 'Starlight') Compact with semi-double creamy-yellow flowers fading to white flecked with pink. **var. rubens** E.H. Wilson. A beautiful variety with bronze-purple shoots and leaves and rose-pink flowers during May and June. W and C China. I 1900 by Ernest Wilson. AM 1905. **'Tetrarose'** A tetraploid form of Dutch origin with bronze foliage and, during May and June, lilac-rose flowers up to 7.5cm across. ♀ 2002. **'Warwickshire Rose'** A seedling of var. *rubens* with deep pink flowers and red-purple foliage. **var. wilsonii** Sprague. A Chinese variety producing masses of fragrant, rather small, white flowers in late June.

†***'Moonbeam'** (*C.* × *cartmanii* 'Moonbeam') (*C.* 'Fairy' × *C. foetida*) An evergreen trailing plant, climbing to 2m with support, with deeply cut leaves and large clusters of small, greenish-yellow flowers in spring. Raised by Graham Hutchins of County Park Nursery in 1990, it is rather tender, requiring a sheltered position or cool greenhouse.

'Mrs Robert Brydon' (*C.* × *jouiniana* 'Mrs Robert Brydon') (*C. tubulosa* × *C. virginiana*) A scrambling subshrub close to *C. heracleifolia*, reaching 2m. Flowers very pale blue with white stamens from midsummer to late autumn.

'My Angel' A small, slender-stemmed climber, 2.5m high, with blue-green foliage, leaves with usually 5 leaflets, the basal pair divided into 3. Flowers small, profusely borne over a long period during late summer and autumn, dusky purple-pink outside becoming flushed yellow with a yellow margin, yellow inside with contrasting purple stamens. The flowers open widely with age, the sepals spreading horizontally, followed by conspicuous silky seedheads. Raised in Holland and said to be a hybrid between *C. orientalis* and *C. intricata*.

†**napaulensis** DC. (*C. forrestii* W.W. Sm.) A semi-evergreen climber reaching 6–9m, with leaves composed of 3–5 glabrous leaflets. Flowers cup-shaped, 1–2.5cm long, creamy-yellow with conspicuous purple stamens, produced in axillary clusters on the young growths during winter. Only suitable for the milder areas. Himalaya, SW China. Collected by George Forrest in 1912. AM 1957.

nutans hort. See *C. rehderiana*.

ochotensis (Pall.) Poir. A deciduous climber to 3m tall, closely related to *C. alpina* but with broader sepals and longer staminodes. The flowers open in April and May and vary in colour from deep blue to purple. NE Asia. **'Carmen Rose'** (*C.* 'Carmen Rose') Profusely borne, large pale pink flowers with wavy-edged sepals, staminodes white tipped pink. Selected in Sweden in 1950 from seed collected in Kamchatka.

orientalis L. (Sect. Meclatis) Graceful climber to 5m with downy shoots. Leaves pinnate with up to 3 pairs of widely spaced, glaucous grey leaflets, toothed or lobed. Flowers small, nodding, with 4 strongly reflexed, pale yellow sepals, slightly streaked with red towards the base and contrasting with the deep purplish-red filaments of the clustered stamens. Flowers late September to October, best after a hot summer. SE Europe to W China. The true species is rare in cultivation. For the plant commonly grown under this name see *C. tibetana* subsp. *vernayi*.

†***paniculata** J.F. Gmel. (*C. indivisa* Willd.) A usually dioecious New Zealand species, to 4m high, the trifoliolate leaves with dark glossy green, entire or shallowly lobed or toothed leaflets. Flowers often fragrant, the males larger than the females, up to 10cm across, 6–8 white sepals, yellow stamens with pink anthers. I 1840. FCC 1934. **'Bodnant'** A particularly hardy selection, raised at Bodnant by Lord Aberconway, with lush, bright green foliage and a conspicuous centre of pink anthers. **'Lobata'** A juvenile form with coarsely toothed or lobed leaflets and slightly larger flowers.

paniculata Thunb. See *C. terniflora*.

patens Morr. & Decne. A slender species, up to 3m, closely related to and resembling *C. florida*. The form we grow has flowers 10–15cm across with creamy-white sepals, during late summer and early autumn. Several of the large-flowered garden hybrids are derived from this species. NE China, Korea. I 1836 by Siebold from cultivation in Japan.

'Paul Farges' (*C. potaninii* subsp. *fargesii* × *C. vitalba*) A vigorous climber to 7m or more. Profusely borne and fragrant, creamy-white flowers, 4cm across, have 4–6 sepals and a centre of white stamens; they open during late summer and autumn. ♀ 2002.

pavoliniana See *C. finetiana*.

†*phlebantha* L.H.J. Williams. A species discovered and introduced by O. Polunin, W. Sykes and L.H.J. Williams from W Nepal in 1952 (under the number P.S. & W. 3436). Described as a trailing shrub in the wild, the greatest attraction of this lovely climber is its glistening silvery-silky, pinnate leaves. The flowers are 2.5–4.5cm across, with 5–7 creamy-white, prettily veined sepals. They are borne singly in the leaf axils of the young growths during summer. It is sad that this beautiful plant is not proving more hardy. Planted against a south-east wall here it survived for many years but was cut back most winters. It is certainly worthy of a selected site in full sun against a sunny wall or on a well-drained sunny bank. An excellent conservatory climber. I 1952. AM 1968.

pitcheri Torr. & A. Gray. A relative of *C. texensis* reaching about 3–4m, the leaves with up to 9 entire or lobed, reticulate leaflets. Flowers pitcher-shaped, purplish-blue, deeper inside, with recurved sepals, solitary on long stalks. Named after its discoverer, Zina Pitcher. C USA. I 1878.

potaninii Maxim. (*C. fargesii* Franch. var. *souliei* Finet. & Gagnep.) A strong-growing climber, up to 6m, with comparatively large, compound leaves. Flowers white, 4–5cm across, produced in the leaf axils continuously from June to September. W China. I 1911. **subsp.** *fargesii* (Franch.) Grey-Wilson (*C. fargesii* Franch.) A less vigorous form, with smaller flowers and the leaves with fewer leaflets. W China.

rehderiana Craib (*C. nutans* hort. not Royle) A charming species, reaching 7.5m in a tree. Leaves pinnate or bipinnate with 7–9, coarsely toothed leaflets. Nodding, bell-shaped flowers, up to 2cm long, are soft primrose-yellow and deliciously scented of cowslips. They are carried in erect panicles, 15–23cm long, during late summer and autumn. W China. I 1898. ♀ 2002. AM 1936.

'**Rosy O'Grady**' A hybrid between *C. alpina* and *C. macropetala* with large, rose-pink, semi-double flowers. C 1967. ♀ 2002.

serratifolia Rehder (Sect. Meclatis) A slender species, up to 3m, related to *C. tangutica*, with prettily divided green leaves. Flowers 2.5cm long, yellow with purple stamens, borne very profusely in August and September, followed by attractive, silky seedheads. N Japan, N Korea, NE China, SE Russia. I about 1918.

sibirica (L.) Miller (*C. alpina* var. *sibirica* Maxim., *C. alpina* var. *alba* Davis) A close relative of *C. alpina* differing mainly in the flowers which are creamy-white. Norway, Finland, Siberia, Mongolia, N China. I 1753.

songarica Bunge. A low, rambling shrub of greyish-green hue, with narrow, simple leaves up to 10cm long. Flowers 2.5cm across, creamy-white, produced during summer and autumn, followed by feathery seedheads. Afghanistan to N China and Mongolia. I before 1880.

spooneri Rehder & E.H. Wilson. (*C. chrysocoma* hort., *C. chrysocoma* var. *sericea* Schneid.) A beautiful species resembling the well-known *C. montana*, but less rampant. Leaves trifoliolate, covered, as are the shoots and flower stalks, with a thick yellowish down. White or soft pink flowers are 4–6cm across, generally smaller than those of *C. montana*, and carried on usually longer and stouter peduncles. They are profusely borne from early May to June and successively on the young growths in late summer. Intermediate between *C. chrysocoma* and *C. montana* and possibly a hybrid. W China. I about 1890. AM 1936.

tangutica (Maxim.) Korsh (Sect. Meclatis) A dense-growing climber, up to 4.5m, closely related to *C. orientalis*. A delightful, easily grown species with prettily divided sea-green leaves and rich yellow, lantern-like flowers, 4–5cm long. They are nodding at first, produced on long, downy stalks during autumn, the later ones intermingled with masses of silky seedheads. Perhaps the best yellow-flowered species, excellent for low walls, fences, trellises, large boulders and banks. Kazakstan, Kashmir, NW China. C 1890. '**Aureolin**' See *C.* 'Aureolin'. '**Helios**' (*C.* 'Helios') A compact selection to 2m tall, the bright yellow flowers opening widely and borne over a very long period. Inferior seedlings have been sold under this name. Raised in Holland in 1988. '**Lambton Park**' See *C.* 'Lambton Park'. **subsp.** *obtusiuscula* (Rehder & E.H. Wilson) Grey-Wilson. A free-flowering, strong-growing variety differing in having fewer teeth on the leaves and the flowers opening more widely with blunt sepals. W China. I by Ernest Wilson in 1908. AM 1913.

terniflora DC. (*C. maximowicziana* Franch. & Sav., *C. paniculata* Thunb. not J.F. Gmel.) A vigorous species, up to 10m, often forming a dense tangle of growth. Leaves with 3–5 long-stalked leaflets. Hawthorn-scented, white flowers, 2.5–4cm wide, are borne in panicles on the current year's growth in autumn. In the British Isles this species only flowers in profusion after a hot summer. Korea, China, Japan. I about 1864.

texensis Buckl. (*C. coccinea* Engelm. ex A. Gray) A distinct species with pinnate leaves, composed of 4–8, stalked, glaucous leaflets. Red, pitcher-shaped, nodding flowers, 2.5cm long, are produced on peduncles 13–15cm long during the summer and autumn. In the British Isles this attractive climber is usually semi-herbaceous and requires some form of protection in winter. It is a parent of several hybrids. Texas (USA). I 1868.

tibetana Kuntze (Sect. Meclatis) The typical form of this species, a native of N India and SW Tibet, is rare in cultivation. Most plants grown under this name are the following form. **subsp.** *vernayi* (C.E.C. Fisch.) Grey-Wilson (*C. orientalis* hort.) A vigorous and graceful climber with finely divided, glaucous leaves. Flowers nodding, yellow to greenish-yellow or purple-flushed with purple stamens, bell-shaped at first, the sepals later spreading; borne singly or up to 3 together. Remarkable in its thick, spongy sepals, which have given it the name of 'orange peel clematis', but inferior seedlings are often sold under this name. Nepal, Tibet, W China. I from SE Tibet in 1947 by Ludlow and Sherriff (L. & S. 13342), to which the awards refer. AM 1950. **subsp.** *vernayi* '**Last Dance**' (*C.* 'Last Dance') A selection flowering profusely over a long period and with attractive foliage.

× *triternata* DC. (*C. flammula* × *C. viticella*) (*C.* × *violacea* A. DC.) A vigorous climber, up to 5m, with pinnate or bipinnate leaves. Flowers up to 3cm wide, pale violet, borne in terminal panicles during late summer. Origin before 1840. **'Rubromarginata'** The fragrant flowers are white margined with reddish-violet; when borne in masses during late summer they give the effect of dark, billowing clouds. ♀ 2002.

tubulosa Turcz. (*C. heracleifolia* var. *davidiana* (Verl.) Hemsl.) Hyacinth-flowered clematis. A small subshrub closely related to *C. heracleifolia* but taller with larger and longer, upright, indigo-blue, very fragrant flowers. N China, North Korea. I 1863 by Père David. **'Wyevale'** (*C. heracleifolia* 'Wyevale') A selection with deep blue, fragrant flowers. ♀ 2002. AM 1976.

†***uncinata*** Benth. An evergreen climber, up to 4.5m, with compound leaves, the leaflets up to 10cm long, glaucous beneath. Flowers about 2.5cm across, white, fragrant, borne in large panicles in June and July. A beautiful species requiring a warm, sheltered wall. China, S Japan, Taiwan, N Vietnam. First discovered by Augustine Henry in 1884. I 1901 by Ernest Wilson. AM 1922.

× ***vedrariensis*** Vilm. (*C. montana* var. *rubens* × *C. spooneri*) A strong-growing climber up to 6m. Leaves trifoliolate with coarsely toothed, dull purplish-green leaflets. Flowers 5–6.5cm wide with 4–6, broad, delicate rose sepals, surrounding the bunched yellow stamens, from late May onwards. Raised by Mons Vilmorin prior to 1914. AM 1936.

× ***violacea*** See *C.* × *triternata*.

vitalba L. Traveller's joy, Old man's beard. A rampant, familiar native climber of hedgerows and roadsides, especially in chalk areas, often clambering high into trees, its rope-like stems forming long columns or dense curtains. Leaves variable in size, pinnate. Small, greenish-white, faintly scented flowers, in late summer and early autumn, are followed by glistening silky seedheads which become fluffy and grey with age, remaining throughout winter. Too vigorous for all but the wild garden. S, W and C Europe (incl. British Isles), N Africa, Caucasus.

viticella L. Virgin's bower. A slender climber, to 3.5m, with pinnate leaves. Violet, reddish-purple or blue flowers, 4cm across, profusely borne on slender stalks in summer and early autumn. S Europe, SW Asia. Cultivated in England since the 16th century. Small-flowered hybrids of this species are included here. ♀ 2002. **'Abundance'** Delicately veined flowers of soft purpler. ♀ 2002. **'Alba Luxurians'** Flowers white, tinted mauve. ♀ 2002. **'Kermesina'** Flowers crimson. ♀ 2002. **'Little Nell'** White with pale pink margins, 5 cm across, very profuse. C 1900. **'Minuet'** Flowers erect, larger than those of the type, creamy-white, with a broad stripe of purple terminating each sepal. ♀ 2002. **'Purpurea Plena Elegans'** Flowers double, to 6cm across, with numerous sepals, lilac-purple, paler in the centre. ♀ 2002. FCC 1987. **'Royal Velours'** Flowers deep velvety purple. ♀ 2002. AM 1948.

'White Swan' (*C. macropetala* 'White Swan') (*C. sibirica* × *C. macropetala*) A hybrid raised in Canada and selected in 1961. Pure white, double flowers up to 12cm across.

Large-flowered garden clematis

Along with the rose, the large-flowered clematis, a selection of which is described here, share a special place in the garden. They are among the most colourful of flowering plants and, when well placed, their effect is charming and often spectacular. Like the species from which they are derived, they are fairly adaptable, but being less easy to establish, require and fully deserve more care in the selection of the site and preparation of the soil.

They are most happy planted where their 'heads' are in the sun and their roots are shaded. They do best in a good loamy soil in which well rotted manure plus lime in some form have been mixed. Good drainage is essential. They may be trained to wires on a wall or grown over pergolas, trellises, or tripods or into shrubs or small trees. They may also be encouraged to grow with wall shrubs or climbing roses, their flowers often combining effectively. When considering training a clematis over or into a tree or bush, take care to plant it, where practicable, well away from the roots of the intended host.

Clematis are gross feeders and respond to an annual mulch of well rotted manure or compost, plus an ample supply of water.

Generally speaking, clematis flower most abundantly in full sun, but many are almost as prolific in a shady or north-facing position. The paler and more delicately coloured cultivars, such as 'Nelly Moser', tend to bleach when they are exposed to hot sun.

The large-flowered clematis are sometimes subject to a puzzling disease known as clematis wilt, for which, at present, there seems to be no cure. Young plants are mainly affected, the sudden collapse of a single shoot or of the whole plant while in full growth being the usual symptom. Plant new acquisitions deeply so that they reshoot from the base, should they suffer from this disease. Cut back wilted shoots and treat the soil with a recommended fungicide.

Pruning. For pruning purposes the large-flowered clematis can be divided into 2 groups.

(a) Applies to the FLORIDA (F), LANUGINOSA (L) and PATENS (P) groups which bloom on the previous year's wood. These normally flower in May and June and the only pruning required is to trim back the old flowering growths immediately after flowering. Old, dense plants may also be hard-pruned in February, but the first crop of flowers will thus be lost.

(b) Applies to the JACKMANII (J), TEXENSIS (T) and VITICELLA (V) groups which bloom on the current year's shoots. These normally flower in late summer and autumn and may be hard-pruned to within 30cm of the ground in February or March. Old unpruned plants tend to become bare at the base.

Alabast ('Poulala') PBR (F) Large creamy-white flowers, flushed green when they first open. Raised in Denmark in 1970. ♀ 2002.

'Aljonushka' (*C. integrifolia* × *C.* 'Nezhdannyi') A semi-herbaceous, non-climbing hybrid to 2m tall. Pendent, bell-shaped, rose-pink, slightly fragrant flowers, to 8cm across, have 4, sometimes up to 6 sepals, opening in late summer to early autumn. C 1961. ♀ 2002.

Anna Louise ('Evithree') PBR (P) Large, velvety purple flowers, each sepal with a broad red stripe. A seedling raised by Raymond Evison. C 1993. ♀ 2002.

'Arabella' A semi-woody hybrid of *C. integrifolia* reaching 2m; profuse purple-blue flowers, with 5–6 sepals and a centre of white stamens, are produced over a long period during summer and autumn. C 1991. ♀ 2002.

Arctic Queen ('Evitwo') PBR (F) Large, double, white flowers with creamy stamens, late summer and early autumn. A seedling raised by Raymond Evison in 1989. ♀ 2002.

'Asao' (P) Large with 6–7 broad, rose-carmine sepals.

'Ascotiensis' (V) Azure-blue, to 13cm across, with pointed sepals, very floriferous; July to September. C 1871.

'Bagatelle' See 'Dorothy Walton'.

'Barbara Dibley' (P) Pansy-violet with a deep carmine stripe along each sepal, to 20cm across or more; May and June and again in September.

'Barbara Jackman' (P) Deep violet, striped magenta, to 15cm, with cream stamens. C 1952.

'Beauty of Worcester' (L) Blue-violet, to 15cm, with contrasting creamy-white stamens, occasionally produces double flowers; May to August. C 1900.

'Bee's Jubilee' (P) Blush-pink, striped carmine, to 18cm. C 1958.

'Belle Nantaise' Large, pale lavender flowers, to 20cm across in early summer, with 6 pointed sepals and a conspicuous centre of creamy stamens. C 1887.

'Belle of Woking' (F) Pale mauve, double, 10cm.

'Blekitny Aniol' ('Blue Angel') Pale sky-blue flowers in mid- to late summer, the 4 sepals paler in the centre with wavy margins. Stamens greenish. Raised in Poland in 1990. ♀ 2002.

'Blue Belle' (V) Deep purple flowers with 6 broad sepals and a centre of creamy stamens, late summer to early autumn. Raised by Ernest Markham before 1949.

'Blue Gem' (L) Sky-blue, large, to 15cm; June to October.

Blue Moon ('Evirin') PBR Large, pale blue flowers with wavy-edged sepals, striped in the centre with greenish-white, and with conspicuous, reddish stamens. Flowers in late spring to early summer, blooming again in early autumn and best in semi-shade. Raised by Raymond Evison before 1997.

'Blue Ravine' (P) Large, pale mauve-blue flowers, to 20cm across, the 7–8 wavy-edged sepals striped with mauve in the centre; stamens purple-red. Raised in Canada in 1978 and best in semi-shade.

'Capitaine Thuilleaux' See 'Souvenir du Capitaine Thuilleaux'.

'Carmencita' (V) Satin-textured, deep carmine flowers to 10cm across, the 4–6 sepals darker at the margin; stamens deep red-purple. A seedling of *C. viticella* 'Grandiflora Sanguinea' raised in Sweden in 1952.

'Carnaby' (L) Deep raspberry-pink with a deeper bar. Good in shade. Compact and free-flowering. C 1983.

'Charisissima' (P) Large, pink flowers, the broad, wavy-edged, pointed sepals striped with deep pink in the centre. Raised by Walter Pennell in 1962 from a cross between 'Nelly Moser' and 'Kathleen Wheeler'.

'Comtesse de Bouchaud' (J) Beautiful soft rose-pink with yellow stamens, to 15cm across, vigorous and free-flowering; June to August. C 1903. ♀ 2002. AM 1936.

'Corona' (P) Purple suffused pink with orange highlights, 18cm across, dark red anthers; May–June and August. C 1972.

'Countess of Lovelace' (P) Double and single, bluish-lilac with cream anthers, 15cm across; May–July. C 1876.

'Daniel Deronda' (P) Large violet-blue, paler at centre with creamy stamens, up to 20cm across, often double; June to September. ♀ 2002.

'Dawn' (L/P) Pale pink shading white towards the base with conspicuous red anthers, 15cm across. Best in shade. C 1969.

'Doctor Ruppel' (P) Deep pink with a carmine bar and yellow stamens, up to 20cm across. C 1975.

'Dorothy Walton' ('Bagatelle') (J) Pale mauve with pink flush, paler in the centre of the taper-pointed sepals.

'Duchess of Albany' ('Star of India' × *C. texensis*) (T) Flowers tubular, nodding, bright pink, shading to lilac-pink at margins; July to September. AM 1897.

'Duchess of Edinburgh' (F) Large, double, rosette-like, white with green shading, scented, to 10cm across; May and June. C 1875.

'Duchess of Sutherland' (V) Petunia-red with a darker bar on each tapered sepal, to 15cm across, often double; July and August.

'Edith' (L) This is similar to 'Mrs Cholmondeley', of which it is a seedling, but its flowers are white with red anthers. ♀ 2002.

'Edouard Desfossé' (*C. lanuginosa* × *C. patens*) (P) Compact with large, pale blue flowers, profusely borne, the sepals striped with mauve-blue; anthers red-purple. Raised in France about 1880.

'Elsa Späth' (P) Large, lavender-blue with red stamens, to 20cm; May–June and September.

'Emilia Plater' (V) Bright blue, the 4 sepals conspicuously veined with deeper blue. Raised in Poland in 1989.

'Ernest Markham' (V) Glowing petunia-red with a velvety sheen, to 15cm across, sepals rounded; June to September. C 1938. ♀ 2002.

'Etoile Rose' ([*C. scottii* × *C. texensis*] × *C. viticella*) (T) Flowers nodding, bell-shaped, 5cm long, deep cherry-purple with a silvery-pink margin; summer. Semi-herbaceous. AM 1959.

'Etoile Violette' (V) Deep purple, to 10cm across, 4–6 sepals; July–September. Vigorous and free-flowering. C 1885. ♀ 2002.

Evening Star ('Evista') PBR A striking hybrid raised by Raymond Evison in 1997. Large, mauve flowers with slender, rather wavy-edged and pointed sepals. Flowers early summer to early autumn.

'Fair Rosamond' (L) Fragrant, to 15cm across, pale blush-pink with a carmine bar fading to white, purple anthers. C 1871. FCC 1873.

'Fairy Queen' (L) Pale flesh-pink with bright central bars, 18cm across. FCC 1875.

'Fireworks' (L) Violet flowers, striped with red; long, slender, twisted sepals.

'Fuji-musume' ('Asagiri' × 'The President') (L) Sky-blue flowers profusely borne on a compact plant. Raised in Japan in 1952. ♀ 2002.

'Général Sikorski' (L) Mid-blue, reddish at the base of the sepals, to 15cm across; June–July. Raised in Poland.

'Gillian Blades' (J) Very large, pure white flowers, up to 22cm across, with frilled edges; midsummer. Little or no pruning is required. ♀ 2002.

'Gipsy Queen' (J) Rich velvety violet-purple, to 12cm across, broad, rounded sepals, July to September. Vigorous and free-flowering. C 1871. ♀ 2002.

'Gravetye Beauty' (T) Flowers bell-shaped at first, the sepals later spreading, cherry-red; July to September. AM 1935.

'Guernsey Cream' (P) Large, single, creamy-yellow flowers 12cm across during summer. Fades if planted in full sun.

'H. F. Young' (P) A good blue, up to 20cm across, broad, overlapping sepals and white stamens; May–June and September. C 1962.

'Hagley Hybrid' (J) Shell-pink with contrasting chocolate-brown anthers, to 15cm across; June to September. Free-flowering. C 1956.

'Henryi' (L) Large, creamy-white, to 18cm across, pointed sepals and dark stamens; May and June and again in August and September. Vigorous and free-flowering. Raised by and named after Isaac Anderson-Henry. C 1858. ♆ 2002.

'Haku-ôkan' (L) Large, violet-purple flowers with usually 8 taper-pointed sepals and a prominent centre of creamy-white stamens. Raised in Japan

'Horn of Plenty' (L) Cup-shaped, rose-purple with darker stripes and a centre of plum stamens; early summer.

'Huldine' (V) Pearly-white, the pointed sepals with a mauve bar on the reverse; July to October. Vigorous and free-flowering; requires full sun. ♆ 2002. AM 1934.

'Jackmanii' (*C.* × *jackmanii* Moore) (*C. lanuginosa* × *C. viticella*) A superb, large-flowered hybrid, raised in the nursery of Messrs Jackman of Woking in 1858. A spectacular climber, 3–4m high, with pinnate leaves. Flowers 10–13cm across, consisting of normally 4 conspicuous, rich, violet-purple sepals. They are borne in great profusion singly or in 3s from July to October on the current year's growth. ♆ 2002. FCC 1863.

'Jackmanii Alba' (J) White, veined with blue, to 13cm across, early flowers double, later single. Very vigorous. C 1878. FCC 1883.

'Jackmanii Rubra' (J) Flowers semi-double, 12cm across, crimson-purple with yellow anthers. Later flowers are usually single.

'Jackmanii Superba' (J) Large, rich violet-purple with broad sepals; July to September. Vigorous and free-flowering. C 1878.

'John Huxtable' (J) An excellent late-flowering white; July to August. A seedling of 'Comtesse de Bouchaud', which it resembles in all but flower colour. ♆ 2002.

'John Warren' (L) Pinkish-lilac with deeper bar and margins and red stamens, fading after opening, to 25cm across.

Josephine ('Evijohill') PBR Large, striking, fully double flowers consisting of numerous pale mauve-pink sepals, each with a deeper stripe, flushed and tipped green, and with a rosette-like centre; late spring to early summer and again in early autumn. C 1980. ♆ 2002.

'Kakio' ('Pink Champagne') ('Star of India' × 'Crimson King') (P) Large flowers, the pink sepals striped in the centre with white. Raised in Japan about 1980.

'Kathleen Wheeler' (P) Deep mauve-blue, the prominent stamens with lilac filaments, large, 18cm across; May to June, with smaller flowers in autumn. C 1967.

'Ken Donson' (P) Blue flowers with golden anthers; late summer. ♆ 2002.

'King George V' (L) Flesh-pink, each sepal with a dark central bar, 15cm across; July and August.

'Kiri Te Kanawa' ('Beauty of Worcester' × 'Chalcedony') Large, double, rich blue flowers in May and June and again in September. Raised by Barry Fretwell in 1986.

'Lady Betty Balfour' (V) Deep velvety purple, 12cm across, with golden stamens; August to October. Very vigorous, best in full sun. C 1910. AM 1912.

'Lady Londesborough' (P) Pale mauve at first, becoming silvery-grey, to 15cm across, with dark stamens and broad, overlapping sepals. Free-flowering. FCC 1869.

'Lady Northcliffe' ('Beauty of Worcester' × 'Otto Froebel') (L) Rich violet-blue with broad, wavy sepals and cream stamens, to 15cm across; June–September and later. AM 1906.

'Ladybird Johnson' ('Bee's Jubilee' × *C. texensis*) (T) Upright, deep dusky-red flowers, flushed purple; summer and autumn. Raised by Barry Fretwell in 1984.

'Lasurstern' (P) Deep lavender-blue, to 18cm across, with conspicuous white stamens and broad, tapering, wavy-margined sepals; May and June and again in early autumn. ♆ 2002.

'Lemon Chiffon' (P) Large, lemon-yellow flowers, the sepals deeper in the centre. Retains its colour best in semi-shade. C 1993.

Liberation ('Evifive') PBR Large, rich pink flowers, sepals each with a deeper pink, central stripe; conspicuous creamy-white stamens. Raised before 1995 by Raymond Evison.

'Lincoln Star' (P) Brilliant raspberry-pink, 15cm across, with dark red stamens; May–June and September. Later flowers paler with a deep pink bar. C 1954.

'Lord Nevill' (P) Flowers deep purplish-blue, to 18cm across, with darker veins; June and September. Vigorous with bronze young foliage. C 1878.

'Louise Rowe' ('Marie Boisselot' × 'William Kennett') (F) Large, fully double, very pale lilac flowers with broad, overlapping sepals. Summer and early autumn, the later flowers semi-double or single. C 1984.

'Madame Baron Veillard' (J) Vigorous, to 4m, with pale lilac-pink flowers 13cm across, 6 sepals; July to September. C 1885.

'Madame Edouard André' (J) Rich crimson with yellow stamens, 12cm across, pointed sepals; June to August. Very free-flowering. C 1893.

'Madame Grangé' (J) Velvety deep purplish-red, to 12cm across; July–September. C 1873. ♆ 2002. FCC 1877.

'Madame Julia Correvon' (V) A hybrid of *C. viticella* and 'Ville de Lyon'. Flowers rose-red, up to 13cm across with cream stamens, very freely borne; July–September. C 1900. ♆ 2002.

'Madame Le Coultre' See 'Marie Boisselot'.

'Marcel Moser' (P) Mauve, to 20cm across, each tapered sepal with a deep carmine central bar. AM 1897.

'Margot Koster' (V) A hybrid of *C. viticella*. Flowers deep rose-pink, to 10cm across with up to 6 reflexed sepals; July–September.

'Marie Boisselot' ('Madame Le Coultre') (P) Large, to 20cm across, pure white, with cream stamens and broad, rounded, overlapping sepals; May to October. Vigorous and free-flowering. C 1900. ♆ 2002.

'Miss Bateman' (P) Large, white, 15cm across, striped pale green when first open. C 1869. ♆ 2002.

'Moonlight' ('Yellow Queen') (P) Large, pale creamy-yellow with yellow stamens; June–August.

'Mrs Cholmondely' (J) Large, pale blue, 20cm across, with long-pointed sepals; May to August. Vigorous and free-flowering. ♆ 2002. FCC 1873.

'**Mrs George Jackman**' (P) White, to 18cm across, with broad, overlapping sepals; May–June and September. Similar to 'Marie Boisselot' but the sepals have a cream bar and the darker anthers are more prominent. C 1873. ♀ 2002.

'**Mrs Hope**' (L) Pale blue with deeper bar and purple anthers, to 18cm across with overlapping sepals.

'**Mrs N. Thompson**' (P) Violet with a scarlet stripe, 12cm across; May–June and September. C 1961.

'**Mrs Spencer Castle**' (V) Large, pale heliotrope, sometimes double; May and June and again in early autumn.

'**Multi Blue**' (P) A sport of 'The President' bearing large, double, blue flowers, the centre a dense mass of smaller, blue and white sepals. Raised in Holland in 1983

'**Nelly Moser**' (L) One of the most popular. Large, pale mauve-pink, to 20cm across, each sepal with a carmine central bar; May and June and again in August and September. Very free-flowering, but best on a north wall or in a shady position to prevent bleaching. C 1897. ♀ 2002.

'**Niobe**' (J) Deep red, to 15cm across, with yellow anthers. The best red. Raised in Poland in 1970. ♀ 2002.

'**Pagoda**' (V) ('Etoile Rose' × *C. viticella*) Nodding, lilac-pink flowers, the 4 sepals broadly striped white in the centre. Raised by John Treasure about 1980. ♀ 2002.

Patricia Ann Fretwell ('Parfar') PBR A striking selection raised by Barry Fretwell in 1999. Large, double flowers in late spring and early summer, the pale pink sepals striped with deep pink in the centre; stamens creamy-white. Single flowers are borne in early autumn.

'**Perle d'Azur**' (J) Light blue, with broad sepals; June to August. Vigorous and free-flowering. C 1885.

Petit Faucon ('Evisix') ('Daniel Deronda' × *C. integrifolia*) PBR A non-climbing subshrub, the somewhat nodding flowers with 4 rather twisted violet-blue sepals appear midsummer to early autumn. Anthers yellow on violet-blue filaments. Raised by Raymond Evison in 1989. ♀ 2002.

'**Piilu**' ('Hagley Hybrid' × 'Mahrovyi') (P) Large, double, mauve-pink flowers in May and June, the numerous wavy-edged sepals each with a deep pink stripe. Stamens yellow. Later flowers are single. Raised in Estonia in 1984.

'**Pink Champagne**' See 'Kakio'.

'**Pink Fantasy**' (J) Pale pink, single flowers, the taper-pointed sepals striped deep pink; anthers deep pink. Raised in Canada before 1975.

Pistachio ('Evirida') PBR (F) Large, single, creamy-white flowers, with a centre of grey-purple anthers, borne over a long period during summer and early autumn.

'**Polish Spirit**' (V) Purple flowers with deep red stamens; July to November. Fast-growing; requires hard pruning. ♀ 2002.

'**Prince Charles**' (J) Profuse pale blue flowers, compact plant to 2.5m. Raised in New Zealand in 1975. ♀ 2002.

'**Princess Diana**' (T) ('Bee's Jubilee' × *C. texensis*) Bright pink, upright, tulip-shaped flowers, the recurved sepals with a white margin. Raised by Barry Fretwell in 1984. ♀ 2002.

'**Proteus**' (F) Deep mauve-pink, to 15cm across, double with numerous sepals; June and September; later flowers single. FCC 1876.

'**Rhapsody**' Deep blue, single flowers, with evenly spaced, overlapping sepals ending in a short point; stamens cream. Flowers midsummer to early autumn. ♀ 2002.

'**Richard Pennell**' (P) Lavender flushed white, to 20cm across, with wavy-margined sepals, red filaments and cream anthers; May–June and September. Raised from a cross between 'Vyvyan Pennell' and 'Daniel Deronda'. C 1974. ♀ 2002.

'**Romantika**' (J) Deep blackish-purple fading slightly when open with 4–6 sepals, late summer to early autumn. Raised in Estonia in 1983.

'**Rouge Cardinal**' (J) Crimson velvet, to 15cm across, with brown anthers; June–August. C 1968.

'**Royalty**' (P) A vigorous and compact plant with double flowers, single in autumn. Similar to 'Vyvyan Pennell' but darker blue-purple. ♀ 2002.

Royal Velvet ('Evifour') PBR Compact with profuse, large, velvety blue-purple flowers, to 15cm across, in late spring and early summer, the sepals each with a darker stripe in the centre. Stamens red-purple. Raised by Raymond Evison before 1993.

'**Ruby Glow**' (L) Large, mauve-red flowers, the broad, overlapping and wavy-edged sepals striped deep red in the centre. Raised in Canada before 1975.

'**Scartho Gem**' ('Lincoln Star' × 'Mrs N. Thompson') (P) Bright pink, the wavy-edged sepals with pale pink margins. Raised by Walter Pennell in 1963.

'**Sealand Gem**' (L) Pale mauve-pink with a carmine bar, to 15cm across; May–June and September. Tends to fade in sun. C 1950.

'**Sensation**' (L) Bright satiny mauve. FCC 1867.

'**Silver Moon**' (L) A vigorous and bushy plant with large, pale lavender flowers borne over a long period. Good on a shady wall.

'**Sir Trevor Lawrence**' ('Star of India' × *C. texensis*) (T) An attractive hybrid from the same cross as 'Duchess of Albany'. Flowers red-purple, the 4 spreading and recurved sepals striped with red in the centre. Raised in 1890 by Arthur George Jackman.

'**Snow Queen**' Large, single flowers to 18cm across, the pointed, white sepals, tinged pink, with red anthers. A seedling found in New Zealand in 1956.

'**Souvenir du Capitaine Thuilleaux**' ('Capitaine Thuilleaux') (P) Creamy-pink with a deeper bar, to 16cm across.

'**Star of India**' (J) Red-purple becoming violet-purple with a redder central bar, up to 16cm across, with broad sepals; June–September. FCC 1867.

Sugar Candy ('Evione') PBR (P) Large, mauve-pink flowers in summer and early autumn, the abruptly pointed sepals striped with deep pink; anthers yellow. Raised by Raymond Evison before 1994.

'**Sunset**' (J) Single, bright mauve-red flowers, to 12cm across, with yellow anthers. C 1992. ♀ 2002.

'**Sylvia Denny**' (F) Pure white, semi-double and rosette-like. From the cross 'Duchess of Edinburgh' × 'Marie Boisselot'.

'**The President**' (P) A popular clematis. Deep purple-blue with silvery reverse, to 18cm across; June to September. Flowers are freely produced. ♀ 2002. FCC 1876.

'**Twilight**' Semi-double with deep magenta-pink, overlapping and pointed sepals, ageing to lilac-pink with a pale margin. Flowers in late spring and early summer.

'Venosa Violacea' (V) A very distinct hybrid of *C. viticella* possibly with *C. florida*. Flowers up to 10cm across, the 5 or 6 sepals with a white centre, veined and edged purple, anthers blackish-purple; June–September. C 1910. ♀ 2002.

'Veronica's Choice' ('Percy Lake' × 'Vyvyan Pennell') (L) Large, semi-double flowers, to 15cm across, in early summer, the sepals pale lavender-blue and mauve. Later flowers are often single. Best in semi-shade. Raised by Walter Pennell in 1963.

'Victoria' (J) Rose-purple with 3 darker ribs on each sepal, to 15cm across, white stamens; June to September. Vigorous and free-flowering. FCC 1870. ♀ 2002.

'Ville de Lyon' (V) Bright carmine-red, deeper at margins, with golden stamens; July to October. AM 1901.

Vino ('Poulvo') ('Daniel Deronda' × 'Lasurstern') PBR (J) Large, single, purple-red flowers to 15cm across, anthers yellow. Raised in Denmark in 1970.

'Voluceau' (V) Large, to 14cm across, petunia-red with yellow stamens. C 1970.

'Violet Charm' (L) Large, single, violet-blue flowers with pointed, overlapping sepals; stamens red. Raised in 1966.

'Vyvyan Pennell' (P) Described by its raisers as the best double clematis yet produced. Deep violet-blue, suffused purple and carmine in centre, to 15cm across, fully double; from May to July. Single, lavender-blue flowers are also produced in autumn. A cross between 'Daniel Deronda' and 'Beauty of Worcester'. C 1959.

'Wada's Primrose' (P) Pale creamy-yellow. Best in shade. C 1979.

'Walter Pennell' ('Daniel Deronda × 'Vyvyan Pennell') Large, double, grey-purple flowers with creamy-white stamens in late spring-early summer. Also bears single flowers in early autumn. Raised by Walter Pennell in 1962.

'Warszawska Nike' (J) Profuse, velvety purple flowers, to 10cm across, with yellow anthers, midsummer. ♀ 2002.

'W.E. Gladstone' (L) Very large, to 25cm across, silky lavender with purple anthers; June to September. Vigorous and free-flowering. FCC 1881.

'Will Goodwin' (P) Large, pale lavender flowers with broad, overlapping, wavy-edged sepals and a centre of golden stamens. ♀ 2002.

'William Kennet' (L) Lavender-blue with dark stamens and sepals with crimped margins; June to August.

'Yellow Queen' See 'Moonlight'.

CLEMATOCLETHRA Maxim.—**Actinidiaceae**—About 25 species of twining climbers, natives of China. They are related to *Actinidia*, but differ in the solid pith and the flowers having 10 stamens and a single style (numerous in *Actinidia*). Useful subjects for a wall or tree in sun or semi-shade.

integrifolia Maxim. A climber up to 7.5m, with ovate-oblong leaves, 4–7cm long, bristle-toothed, glaucous beneath. Flowers solitary or in clusters, small, white and fragrant, in June. NW China. I 1908 by Ernest Wilson.

lasioclada Maxim. Up to 6m, with downy shoots. Leaves ovate, 5–10cm long, bristle-toothed. Flowers white, borne in axillary cymes in July. W China. I 1908 by Ernest Wilson.

strigillosa Franch. A rare and distinct species with comparatively broad leaves. China.

Climbing hydrangea See *Hydrangea anomala* subsp. *petiolaris*.

COCCULUS DC.—**Menispermaceae**—A small genus of twining climbers suitable for growing into trees and hedges or on trelliswork in sun or semi-shade. About 11 species, widely distributed, mainly in the tropics.

orbiculatus (L.) DC. (*C. trilobus* (Thunb.) DC.) A variable species up to 4.5m, with long-persistent leaves, entire or 3-lobed, orbicular to ovate-acuminate. Flowers small and inconspicuous, in axillary clusters in August. Fruits rounded, black, with a blue bloom. Japan, China. I before 1870.

trilobus See *C. orbiculatus*.

Coral pea See *Hardenbergia violacea*.
Coral plant See *Berberidopsis corallina*.
Cross vine See *Bignonia capreolata*.
Cruel plant See *Araujia sericifera*.

DECUMARIA L.—**Hydrangeaceae**—A genus of 2 perfectly hardy species of shrubs climbing by means of aerial roots. They are related to *Hydrangea*, but differ in that all their flowers are fertile. Like the climbing hydrangeas and schizophragmas, they succeed in sun or shade on a wall or tree trunk.

barbara L. A semi-evergreen climber up to 9m. Leaves ovate, 7.5–13cm long. Small, white flowers are carried in small corymbs in June and July. Native of SE USA where it climbs the trunks of trees. I 1785.

*sinensis Oliv. A rare, evergreen species, up to 5m, with obovate or oblanceolate leaves, 2.5–9cm long. Small, green and white flowers are profusely carried in corymbs in May and are deliciously honey-scented. C China. I 1908 by Ernest Wilson. AM 1974.

†DREGEA E. Meyer (*Wattakaka* (Decne.) Hassk.)—**Asclepiadaceae**—A genus of 3 species from warm regions of the Old World. The following may be grown outside on a warm, sheltered wall, or in a conservatory.

sinensis Hemsl. (*Wattakaka sinensis* (Hemsl.) Stapf) A moderately hardy species with slender stems up to 3m long requiring some support. Leaves ovate, grey-felted beneath. Deliciously scented flowers, which bear a close resemblance to those of a *Hoya*, are white, with a central zone of red spots. They are borne in long-stalked, downy umbels during summer. China. I 1907 by Ernest Wilson. AM 1954.

Dutchman's pipe See *Aristolochia macrophylla*.

ECCREMOCARPUS Ruiz & Pav.—**Bignoniaceae**—A small genus of 3 species of evergreen or nearly evergreen climbers, natives of the Andes of South America, from Chile to Colombia, climbing by means of coiling leaf tendrils. They have opposite, bipinnate leaves and tubular flowers which are pollinated by hummingbirds. The following is hardy in a sheltered corner in southern gardens, but in colder areas may be treated either as a conservatory subject or as a half-hardy annual.

scaber Ruiz & Pav. A vigorous, fast-growing climber, quickly covering a support with its angular stems 3–4.5m long. Leaves bipinnate ending in a slender tendril. Scarlet to orange or yellow, tubular flowers, 2.5cm long, are borne in racemes, continuously produced throughout summer and autumn. Fruit a capsule, packed with small, winged seeds. Forms selected for flower colour include **f. aureus** (yellow), **f. carmineus** (carmine-red) and **f. roseus** (pink). Chile and adjacent S Argentina. I 1824.

†***ELYTROPUS** Müll.-Arg.—**Apocynaceae**—A rare monotypic genus.

chilensis Müll.-Arg. A strong-growing, twining, evergreen climber 3–4.5m high, with slender, bristly stems. Leaves opposite, elliptic to elliptic-oblong, acuminate, bristly-hairy and conspicuously fringed. Small, white, lilac-flushed flowers are produced singly, or in pairs, in the axils of the leaves in spring. Fruits when produced are green, ripening to yellow. A rare climber suitable for a small tree or trellis or against a sheltered wall in milder areas of the British Isles, perhaps preferring semi-shade to full sun. Chile, Argentina.

***ERCILLA** A. Juss.—**Phytolaccaceae**—A genus of 2 species of evergreen climbers supporting themselves by means of aerial roots; natives of Chile. May be grown on a wall in sun or shade, or as a groundcover.

volubilis Juss. (*E. spicata* (Hook. & Arn.) Moq., *Bridgesia spicata* Hook. & Arn.) A self-clinging, evergreen climber with rounded, leathery leaves and dense, sessile spikes of small, purplish-white flowers during spring. Chile. I 1840 by Thomas Bridges, and more recently by Harold Comber. AM 1975.

FALLOPIA Adans.—**Polygonaceae**—A genus of 9 species of perennial herbs and woody climbers, natives of N temperate regions. The species described here is a hardy, twining climber of vigorous, rampant growth, ideal for covering and concealing unsightly objects. They also look effective when trained into trees and are among the best plants for clothing old stumps and bare banks.

aubertii See *F. baldschuanica*.

baldschuanica (Reg.) Holub (*Polygonum baldschuanicum* Reg., *P. aubertii* L. Henry, *Bilderdykia baldschuanica* (Reg.) Webb, *B. aubertii* (L. Henry) Dumort.) Russian vine. A rampant climber with stems up to 12m long. Leaves ovate or heart-shaped, pale green. Flowers white to pink-tinged. Though individually small, they are borne in conspicuous, crowded panicles on terminal and short lateral branches throughout summer and autumn. When in flower, covering a 12m high tree, it creates a remarkable picture. SE Russia (Tadzhikistan). C 1883. AM 1899. **'Summer Sunshine'** A vigorous sport with red shoots and yellow leaves and bearing profuse white flowers.

†***GELSEMIUM** Juss.—**Loganiaceae**—A genus of 2 or 3 species of tender evergreen, twining shrubs producing attractive flowers; natives of North America and SE Asia. The following species requires a sunny, sheltered wall.

sempervirens (L.) J. St.-Hil. Yellow jessamine. A species with stems to 6m long bearing oblong or ovate-lanceolate, glossy green leaves, 3.5–5cm long. Fragrant, yellow, funnel-shaped flowers, 2.5cm long, late spring or early summer. S USA. ♀ 2002. **'Gene Cline'** A particularly hardy form selected in the USA.

Granadilla See *Passiflora edulis*.

†***HARDENBERGIA** Benth.—**Leguminosae**—A genus of 3 species of climbers and sub-shrubs, natives of Australia. They have pinnate leaves, sometimes reduced to a single leaflet, and pea-like flowers in axillary racemes. The following requires a conservatory except in the mildest areas.

violacea (Schneev.) Stearn. Coral pea. A vigorous climber to 2m or more, or a creeper, with wiry shoots, the dark green, ovate to lance-shaped leaves with a single leaflet to 12cm long. Violet-purple flowers, marked with yellow in the centre, open in racemes to 12cm long from late winter to early summer. E Australia. ♀ 2002.

***HEDERA** L.—**Araliaceae**—The ivies are a small genus of about 12 species of evergreen climbers attaching themselves to walls or tree trunks by aerial roots or covering the ground with a dense carpet; native from Europe and N Africa to Japan. No other self-clinging evergreens are comparable with the ivies, thriving as they do in almost any soil, or situation, climbing without artificial aid to great heights or clothing bare ground under trees or shrubs where not even grass would grow. When large specimens on walls are becoming too dense, they may be pruned severely. Ivies are excellent for industrial sites, and withstand atmospheric pollution. The leaves of the climbing (sterile) shoots are often markedly different from those of the flowering (fertile) shoots; this is particularly noticeable in the common ivy (*H. helix*). The flowers are small and inconspicuous, borne in greenish umbels and replaced by usually black, berry-like fruits. Ivy is harmful if eaten and may cause allergic skin reactions.

algeriensis Hibberd. A strong-growing species with large, dark green leaves up to 15cm or even 20cm across. Those of the climbing shoots are kidney-shaped, sometimes obscurely 3-lobed, those of the flowering shoots rounded with a cordate base. They are bright green during summer, often turning deep bronze with green veins in winter, particularly if growing in a dry situation. Usually grown as *H. canariensis*. N Africa. C 1833. **'Gloire de Marengo'** (*H. canariensis* 'Gloire de Marengo', *H. canariensis* 'Variegata') An attractive and colourful form with large leaves, deep green in the centre, merging into silvery-grey and margined white. Admirably suitable for patio gardens, low walls, and so on. Less hardy than green-leaved forms. It is a popular houseplant. ♀ 2002. FCC 1880. AMT 1979. **'Marginomaculata'** (*H. canariensis* 'Marginomaculata') Leaves deep green and pale green mottled creamy-white, often producing shoots bearing leaves similar to 'Gloire de Marengo' but with a mottled margin. Often grown as a houseplant; outside the leaves become heavily mottled with creamy-white. A sport of 'Gloire de Marengo'. C 1942. ♀ 2002. **'Ravensholst'** A large-leaved form, but slightly tender. ♀ 2002.

amurensis See *H. colchica*.

azorica Carrière (*H. canariensis* 'Azorica') A distinct and hardy species with broad leaves of a light matt green; those of the climbing shoots have 5–7 blunt lobes. Azores.

†*canariensis* Willd. (*H. helix* var. *canariensis* (Willd.) DC.) Canary Island ivy. The true species of this name is a vigorous ivy with stout, reddish shoots. Leaves often large, deep bronze when young becoming mid- to dark green and matt or only slightly glossy above. They are rounded and almost entire to shallowly lobed or angled, deeply

heart-shaped at the base. The most tender species, it can be killed by frost in hard winters, even in S England, but climbs vigorously when established. Canary Islands. For the plant usually grown under this name see *H. algeriensis*. **'Azorica'** See *H. azorica*. **'Gloire de Marengo'** See *H. algeriensis* 'Gloire de Marengo'. **'Marginomaculata'** See *H. algeriensis* 'Marginomaculata'. **'Variegata'** See *H. algeriensis* 'Gloire de Marengo'.

chrysocarpa See *H. helix* f. *poetica*.

colchica K. Koch (*H. amurensis* Hibberd, *H. roegneriana* Hibberd) Persian ivy. A handsome, strong-growing species with the largest leaves in the genus. They are ovate or elliptic and 15–20cm long or more on the climbing shoots, smaller and oblong-ovate on the flowering shoots; all are dark green, thick and leathery. Caucasus. C 1850. Several introductions of this species with unlobed leaves were made from the Caucasus in 1979 by Roy Lancaster. ♀ 2002. **'Arborescens'** A shrubby form developing into a small, densely leafy mound with large, oblong-ovate leaves. Raised from a cutting of the flowering growth; free-fruiting. **'Batumi'** A form with broadly ovate, shallowly lobed, glossy dark green leaves on long petioles. Collected by Roy Lancaster near Batumi Botanic Garden at the eastern end of the Black Sea in 1979. **'Dentata'** A spectacular climber with leaves even larger and somewhat more irregular in outline, slightly softer green and with occasional teeth. ♀ 2002. AMT 1979. **'Dentata Variegata'** A most ornamental ivy with large, broad, ovate to elliptic, often elongated leaves, bright green shading to grey and conspicuously margined creamy-yellow when young, creamy-white when mature. Hardier than *H. algeriensis* 'Gloire de Marengo', and just as effective in patio gardens, on walls, and so on. ♀ 2002. FCCT 1979. AM 1907. **'Sulphur Heart'** ('Gold Leaf', 'Paddy's Pride') An impressive variegated ivy. The large, broadly ovate leaves are boldly marked by an irregular central splash of yellow, merging into pale green and finally deep green. Occasionally almost an entire leaf is yellow. On old leaves the yellow splash becomes pale yellow-green. ♀ 2002. AMT 1979.

cypria McAllister. An attractive and vigorous species that is related to *H. pastuchovii*. The thick, blackish-green, triangular leaves are borne on long, red petioles and are prominently marked with silvery veins. Excellent for covering a wall. Mts of Cyprus. I 1977.

helix L. Common ivy. One of the most adaptable plants, making excellent groundcover and useful where little else will grow. Several forms are commonly grown as houseplants and in windowboxes. Leaves of climbing shoots variable, 3- to 5-lobed, those of the flowering shoots ovate to rhomboidal, entire. Europe, Asia Minor to N Iran.

Forms and cultivars of *Hedera helix*

'Adam' Leaves rather small, shallowly 3-lobed, green and grey-green in the centre, margined creamy-white. C 1968.
'Angularis Aurea' A large climber with broad, glossy leaves flushed with bright yellow. Not suitable for groundcover. ♀ 2002.
'Anita' Compact with small, deeply cut, arrow-shaped leaves with pointed lobes. C 1983.
'Anna Marie' Grey-green, often shallowly lobed, sometimes unlobed leaves narrowly margined with creamy-

white. Selected in Denmark in the 1960s.
'Arborescens' A shrubby form developing into a broad, densely leafy mound. Originated as a cutting from flowering shoots.
'Atropurpurea' Leaves entire or with 2 short lateral lobes. Dark purplish-green, darker in winter, often with bright green veins. C 1884. AMT 1979.
'Bird's Foot' See 'Pedata'.
'Buttercup' The best golden form of the common ivy. Leaves rich yellow becoming yellowish-green or pale green with age. Slow-growing. C 1925.
'Caecilia' Similar to 'Parsley Crested' with crisped leaf margins but edged creamy-white. ♀ 2002.
'Caenwoodiana' See 'Pedata'.
'Cavendishii' A pretty form with small, angular, green leaves mottled grey and broadly margined creamy-white. C 1867.
'Ceridwen' Leaves with 3 pointed lobes, broadly edged with bright yellow, sometimes all yellow. ♀ 2002.
'Chicago' A form with small, dark green leaves that are frequently stained or blotched bronze-purple. C 1962.
'Chicago Variegated' See 'Harald'.
'Chrysophylla' Leaves irregularly suffused soft yellow, but liable to revert.
'Cockle Shell' An unusual sport found in California with rounded and cupped, shell-like, often unlobed leaves with pale green veins. Popular for hanging baskets. C 1976.
'Congesta' An upright, non-climbing form, similar to 'Erecta' but differing in its more congested habit and smaller leaves. C 1887. ♀ 2002.
'Conglomerata' A dense, slow-growing form with rigid stems forming a low hummock. Leaves with or without lobes, obtuse at the apex and with a distinct wavy margin. Excellent for a rock garden or woodland garden. AMT 1979. FCC 1872.
'Cristata' See 'Parsley Crested'.
'Deltoidea' See *H. hibernica* 'Deltoidea'.
'Digitata' See *H. hibernica* 'Digitata'.
'Duckfoot' Leaves small, 3-lobed and pale green, shaped like a duck's foot. Often grown as an indoor plant. ♀ 2002.
'Elfenbein' Leaves with twisted and wavy, white margins.
'Erecta' ('Conglomerata Erecta') A slow-growing form with stiffly erect shoots. Leaves 3-lobed, arrow-shaped with an acute apex. An excellent plant for growing by a boulder on a rock garden or against a low tree stump. C 1898. It has been confused with 'Congesta' q.v. ♀ 2002.
'Eva' Leaves green and grey-green with a broad, creamy-white margin. A popular houseplant. A sport of 'Harald'. C 1966.
'Fantasia' Five-lobed, bright green leaves that are heavily mottled with creamy-white, on purple shoots. Best as an indoor plant.
'Feastii' See 'Köniter's Auslese'.
'Francis' Similar to 'Green Ripple' with right green leaves but with 5–7 or sometimes 9 wavy-edged lobes. Good as groundcover or in a hanging basket. C 1999.
'Glacier' Leaves silvery-grey with a narrow, white margin. C 1950. ♀ 2002. AMT 1979.
'Glymii' ('Tortuosa') Leaves ovate, somewhat curled or twisted, especially during cold weather. Often turning reddish-purple in winter. C 1867.

Hedera helix continued:

'Goldchild' Leaves bright green and pale green in the centre with a broad, golden-yellow margin when young, becoming blue-green and grey-green margined creamy-yellow. A very attractive ivy but best as a houseplant. ♀ 2002. AM 1971.

'Golden Ingot' Similar to 'Kolibri' but with leaves heavily, irregularly mottled or edged grey-green and cream-yellow, sometimes mostly yellow. C 1987. ♀ 2002.

'Goldheart' A most striking form of neat growth, the leaves with a large, conspicuous central splash of yellow. Reverts with age. It has been wrongly called 'Jubilee'. C about 1950. AM 1970.

'Goldstern' Arrow-shaped leaves with 5 lobes, the central lobe long-pointed; lime-green with a dark green central blotch. Selected in Germany in 1979.

'Gracilis' See *H. hibernica* 'Gracilis'.

'Green Feather' ('Meagheri') An unusual cultivar with small, pointed, deeply cut leaves. C 1939.

'Green Ripple' An attractive form with small, jaggedly lobed leaves, the central lobe long and tapering. A sport found in 1939. AMT 1979.

'Harald' ('Chicago Variegated') Leaves shallowly 5-lobed, green and grey-green in the centre margined creamy-white. C 1958.

'Heise' Grey-green, 3-lobed leaves, mottled and edged with creamy-white. C 1963.

'Hibernica' See *H. hibernica*.

'Ivalace' A compact ivy with bright green, shallowly 5-lobed leaves, stiffly curled at the margins. Very good for groundcover. C 1955. ♀ 2002. FCCT 1979.

'Kolibri' A striking ivy, the leaves dark green, broadly and conspicuously blotched and streaked creamy-white. Best grown under cover. A sport of 'Harald' raised in Germany in the 1970s. See also 'White Knight'.

'Königer's Auslese' ('Feastii') A neat-growing form with 5-lobed leaves, the central lobe large and triangular. Frequently grown as 'Sagittifolia'.

'Lalla Rookh' Pale green, deeply cut leaves with 5 irregularly toothed lobes. Useful in hanging baskets or for groundcover.

'Lightfinger' A selection with arrow-shaped, yellow leaves, showing the colour best in a bright position.

'Little Diamond' A dwarf, bushy plant of dense growth. Leaves diamond-shaped, entire or 3-lobed, green mottled grey with a creamy-white margin. C 1970. AMT 1979.

'Luzii' An attractive form popular as a houseplant. Leaves shallowly 5-lobed, green mottled with pale green, often developing a pale green margin when grown outdoors. Originally listed as 'Marmorata Minor'. C 1951.

'Manda's Crested' ('Curly Locks') An attractive ivy suitable for groundcover. Leaves with 5 pointed lobes which point upwards while the sinuses point down, giving a wavy-edged effect, bronzing in winter. C 1940. ♀ 2002. FCCT 1979.

'Maple Leaf' Deeply cut leaves, with 5 irregularly toothed lobes, the central lobe the longest, the basal lobes very short. C 1956. ♀ 2002.

'Marginata' ('Argentea Elegans') Leaves triangular-ovate, broadly margined white, often tinged pink in winter.

'Marginata Elegantissima' See 'Tricolor'.

'Marmorata Minor' See 'Minor Marmorata' and 'Luzii'.

'Meagheri' See 'Green Feather'.

'Melanie' Similar to 'Parsley Crested', of which it is a sport, but the leaves with pink to purple margins. Found by Melanie Nicholas in Beth Chatto's nursery in 1980. ♀ 2002.

'Midas Touch' A medium-sized climber with golden-yellow leaves splashed lime-green and dark green; some are edged with bright green. ♀ 2002.

'Minor Marmorata' ('Marmorata Minor') An unusual form with small leaves mottled and marbled cream and grey, occasionally pink-tinged during winter. C 1868. ♀ 2002. See also 'Luzii'.

'Minty' Small, 3-lobed, grey and mint-green leaves, mottled and sometimes margined with white.

'Misty' Small, grey-green, 3-lobed leaves, edged with creamy-yellow. Best as a houseplant.

'Palmata' A rather slow-growing form with palmately lobed leaves. C 1846.

'Parsley Crested' ('Cristata') A distinct and unusual form making good groundcover with pale green, often rounded leaves, attractively twisted and crimped at the margin. C 1956. ♀ 2002. AMT 1979.

'Pedata' ('Bird's Foot', 'Caenwoodiana') A charming form with small leaves regularly divided into narrow lobes, of which the middle lobe is longest. C 1863.

'Persian Carpet' A vigorous form, good for groundcover or a wall, with green shoots and light green, shallowly lobed leaves. Found in a public park in Tehran by John Whitehead in 1978.

f. *poetica* (Nyman) McAllister & Rutherford (*H. chrysocarpa* Walsh) Poets' ivy, Italian ivy. An ivy distinguished by its bright green, shallowly lobed leaves and the yellow fruits of the adult growth. In winter, the older leaves often turn a bright copper colour with green veins. Greece and Turkey (naturalised in Italy and France), N Africa, SW Asia. 'Emerald Gem' is a named clone. AM 1999 to the arborescent state (for fruit).

subsp. *rhizomatifera* McAllister. A neat form with small, silver-veined leaves and producing white underground stems. S & SE Spain. I 1974.

var. *rhombea* See *H. rhombea*.

'Ritterkreuz' Leaves 5-lobed and irregularly toothed, the basal lobes very small, at least the terminal lobe narrowed to the base and appearing diamond-shaped.

'Sagittifolia' Leaves bluntly and shallowly 3-lobed, arrow-shaped. C 1872. Now rarely seen, plants grown under this name are often 'Königer's Auslese' or 'Caenwoodiana'.

'Sagittifolia Variegata' Similar to 'Königer's Auslese' but leaves grey-green, margined creamy-white. C 1965.

'Schäfer Three' ('Calico') Small, dark green, 3-lobed leaves, mottled and veined creamy-white. A hardy selection making dense groundcover.

'Shamrock' Clover-leaf ivy. A distinct form with small, bright green leaves, entire or with up to 3 deep, overlapping lobes, bronzing in winter. C 1954.

'Silver Queen' See 'Tricolor'.

'Spetchley' A dense, prostrate and congested form with very small leaves. Good for a rock garden, low wall or tub. ♀ 2002.

'Sunrise' Golden-yellow, 5-lobed leaves.

'Tortuosa' See 'Glymii'.

Hedera helix continued:

'Très Coupé' Small, deeply cut leaves with 3 taper-pointed lobes, often with 2 smaller lobes at the base. A good plant for hanging baskets, groundcover in small areas or for a low wall. C 1968.

'Tricolor' ('Marginata Elegantissima', 'Marginata Rubra', 'Silver Queen') A pretty form that has small, greyish-green leaves, margined white, and edged rose-red in winter.

'Ursula' Similar to 'Shamrock' but with yellow-green leaves.

'White Knight' A selection from the now very variable 'Kolibri', with leaves more conspicuously variegated white. ♀ 2002.

'Yellow Ripple' Similar to 'Green Ripple' with red stems and maple-like leaves strikingly edged with bright yellow.

hibernica Bean (*H. helix* 'Hibernica') Irish ivy. The common ivy of W England and the only species native to Ireland. It is closely related to *H. helix* but often produces larger leaves and is further distinguished by the rays of the scale hairs lying parallel with the leaf surface (upright in *H. helix*). The commonly grown form or forms of this species have large, dark green, usually 5-lobed leaves, 7.5 to 15cm across. A vigorous ivy particularly useful as groundcover. ♀ 2002. AMT 1979.

'Deltoidea' (*H. helix* 'Deltoidea') A distinct form of neat, close growth, making an excellent groundcover plant. The leaves possess 2 basal lobes which are rounded and overlapping. Bronze-tinged in winter. C 1872. ♀ 2002. 'Digitata' (*H. helix* 'Digitata') Leaves broad, divided into 5 finger-like lobes. Originally found in Ireland. C 1826. 'Gracilis' (*H. helix* 'Gracilis') A slender form with prettily lobed leaves. C 1864.

'Hamilton' Leaves deeply 5-lobed, with small basal lobes, slightly twisted and wavy-edged, and with a thickened margin; shoots green. C 1978.

maderensis Rutherford. This ornamental and vigorous species is proving very hardy. Most closely resembling *H. hibernica* and with potential as a groundcover plant. Leaves broad, slightly glossy, bronzing in cold weather, attractively held above the ground on long, pink stalks. Madeira. **subsp. iberica** McAllister. A form with smaller leaves from SW Spain and Portugal.

maroccana McAllister. A vigorous species with large, bright green, 3–5-lobed leaves, often with red veins, up to 16cm across and on long, stout petioles. Morocco. 'Spanish Canary' A very fast-growing selection with particularly large, deeply 5-lobed leaves. Commonly cultivated in Spain.

nepalensis K. Koch (*H. cinerea* (Hibberd) Bean, *H. himalaica* Tobler) Himalayan ivy. A strong-growing species with greyish-green, ovate to ovate-lanceolate, taper-pointed leaves, 5–13cm long, occasionally with 2 basal lobes and several blunt teeth. Fruits usually yellow or rarely red. Himalaya. C 1880. **var. sinensis** (Tobler) Rehder. Leaves unlobed or nearly so. E Himalaya, SW China.

pastuchovii Woronow. A vigorous species with leaves from entire to shallowly lobed or toothed. Mrs Ala and Roy Lancaster introduced plants to our nurseries in 1972 from the Caspian Forest in N Iran (Ala & Lancaster 26). These have dark blackish-green, heart-shaped and unlobed leaves with pale green veins, the midrib red beneath. Roy Lancaster also collected it in the Caucasus in 1979. Caucasus, N Iran. 'Ann Ala' The form introduced by Ala and Lancaster in 1972, with dark, blackish green, elongated leaves. The name commemorates Mrs Ann Ala, who helped many botanists and plantsmen visiting Iran in the 1970s.

rhombea (Miq.) Bean (*H. helix* var. *rhombea* Miq.) Japanese ivy. The Japanese equivalent of our native ivy, differing from the common species in its ovate or triangular-ovate leaves with sometimes 2 shallow lobes. Japan. 'Variegata' Leaves with a narrow creamy-white margin. C 1867.

*HOLBOELLIA Wall.—Lardizabalaceae—A small genus of some 5 species, related to *Stauntonia*, of luxuriant, evergreen, monoecious, twining plants with compound leaves; natives of the Himalaya and China. They will grow in any fertile soil in sun or shade, but require sun for flower and fruit. Differs from *Stauntonia* in the free stamens.

coriacea Diels. A vigorous, hardy species up to 6m or more. Leaves composed of 3, stalked, glossy green leaflets, 7.5–15cm long. Flowers in April and May, the purplish male flowers in terminal clusters, the greenish-white, purplish-tinged, female flowers in axillary clusters. Fruits are purplish, fleshy pods, 4–7.5cm long, filled with rows of black seeds. A useful climber for growing on walls, drainpipes or into trees. C China. I 1907 by Ernest Wilson.

latifolia Wall. (*Stauntonia latifolia* (Wall.) Wall.) An attractive but slightly tender species with leaves consisting of 3–7, stalked leaflets, 7.5–18cm long. Fragrant flowers are borne in short racemes during March, the male flowers greenish-white, the female flowers purplish. Fruit an edible, purple, sausage-shaped, fleshy pod 5–7.5cm long. Hand-pollination is usually required to ensure fruiting. It may be distinguished from *H. coriacea* by the more pronounced reticulate venation. Himalaya. I 1840.

Honeysuckle See *Lonicera*.
Honeysuckle, Cape See *Tecoma capensis*.
Hop See *Humulus*.

HUMULUS L.—Cannabaceae—A small genus of 3 species of dioecious, annual and perennial, herbaceous climbers, natives of Europe and Asia. Though herbaceous, the following species and its attractive, golden-leaved form are vigorous plants and useful for giving summer clothing to unsightly objects, hedges, and so on.

lupulus L. Hop. A familiar, native climber with long, twining stems 3–6m long. Commonly seen scrambling in hedges and thickets. Leaves 7.5–15cm long, deeply 3- to 5-lobed and coarsely toothed. The female flowers are borne in drooping, yellowish-green, cone-like clusters during late summer, enlarging in fruit. The fruit clusters are a valuable constituent of the best beers, for which purpose this plant is extensively cultivated in certain districts. Europe, W Asia. 'Aureus' An attractive form with soft yellow leaves. Best grown in full sun. It is most effective when trained on a pergola or a wooden tripod. ♀ 2002.

HYDRANGEA L.—**Hydrangeaceae**—The species that are described here are climbing shrubs, attaching themselves to trees or walls by means of aerial roots. They are splendid in such positions and are equally happy in sun or semi-shade in all types of soils. Excellent for industrial sites and withstand atmospheric pollution.

altissima See *H. anomala*.

anomala D. Don (*H. altissima* Wall.) A vigorous climber reaching a height of 12m or above in a suitable tree. Mature bark brown and peeling. Leaves ovate or elliptic, coarsely toothed. Flowers in slightly domed corymbs, 15–20cm across, in June, small, yellowish-white with several conspicuous, white, sterile florets along the margin. Himalaya to W China. I 1839. **subsp.** *petiolaris* (Siebold & Zucc.) McClintock (*H. petiolaris* Siebold & Zucc., *H. scandens* Maxim. not (L. f.) Ser.) Climbing hydrangea. A strong-growing, self-clinging climber reaching 18–25m in suitable trees and excellent on a north-facing or otherwise shady wall, in addition it is very picturesque when grown as a shrub. Leaves broadly ovate, abruptly pointed and finely toothed. Flowers in corymbs, 15–25cm across, in June, dull, greenish-white, with several large, conspicuous, white, sterile florets along the margin. Vigorous enough when once established, it may require initial support until its aerial roots become active. Japan, Kuriles, Sakhalin, S Korea. I 1865. ♀ 2002.

integerrima See *H. serratifolia*.

petiolaris See *H. anomala* subsp. *petiolaris*.

*seemannii Riley. A vigorous evergreen climber, related to *H. serratifolia* and clinging by aerial roots. Leaves glossy dark green, to 20cm long. Domed white flowerheads open from buds enclosed by conspicuous bracts in summer. Most flowers are fertile, each flowerhead edged by a few large sterile florets. Mexico. C 1973.

*serratifolia (Hook. & Arn.) F. Phil. (*H. integerrima* (Hook. & Arn.) Engler) An evergreen species with stout, elliptic to obovate, leathery leaves which are entire and usually marked with curious, tiny pits in the vein axils beneath. Flowers small, creamy-white, borne in crowded, columnar panicles, 7.5–15cm long, in late summer. Best grown against a wall in sun or shade, though in its native forests it is known to reach 15m or more in suitable trees. Chile. I 1925/27 by Harold Comber. AM 1952.

Ivy See *Hedera*.

Ivy, Boston See *Parthenocissus tricuspidata*.

Jasmine See *Jasminum*.

Jasmine, Chilean See *Mandevilla laxa*.

JASMINUM L.—**Oleaceae**—The climbing jasmines or jessamines are easily grown in most fertile soils, preferring a sunny position. They are excellent for training up walls or pergolas and several are useful for covering unsightly banks. The hardy species are excellent for withstanding industrial sites. See also TREES AND SHRUBS.

†**angulare* Vahl (*J. capense* Thunb.) A choice but tender species with rather thickish, dark green, trifoliolate leaves. Sweetly scented, white flowers, 5cm long, are borne in large panicles during late summer. Only suitable for the mildest localities, but a beautiful conservatory subject. South Africa. ♀ 2002. AM 1956.

†**azoricum* L. (*J. trifoliatum* Moench) A beautiful twining species with trifoliolate leaves and clusters of white, sweetly scented flowers, purple-flushed in bud, opening in summer and winter. Only suitable for the mildest localities. An excellent conservatory plant. Madeira, where it is very rare. I late 17th century. ♀ 2002. AM 1934.

capense See *J. angulare*.

beesianum Forrest & Diels. A vigorous, scandent shrub developing a dense tangle of slender stems, 2.5–3.5m long. Leaves tapering to a long point, dark, dull green. Flowers fragrant, rather small, an unusual deep velvety red, appearing in May and June, followed by shining black berries which often last well into winter. SW China. I 1907 from Yunnan by George Forrest.

†*dispermum* Wall. A delightful climber with twining stems and leaves varying from trifoliolate to pinnate on the same plant. Fragrant, white, pink-flushed flowers are borne in axillary and terminal cymes during summer. Only suitable for the mildest localities, but admirable as a conservatory plant. Himalaya, W China. C 1849. AM 1937.

diversifolium See *J. subhumile*.

†**floridum* Bunge. (*J. giraldii* Diels) An evergreen species of scandent growth with angular shoots and alternate, usually trifoliolate leaves. Flowers yellow, appearing in terminal clusters during late summer and early autumn. Requires a warm, sunny wall. W and C China. I 1850.

giraldii See *J. floridum*.

humile See TREES AND SHRUBS.

†**mesnyi* Hance (*J. primulinum* Hemsl.) Primrose jasmine. A singularly beautiful, evergreen species with 4-angled shoots and opposite, trifoliolate leaves, 2.5–7.5cm long. Flowers bright yellow, 4cm long, semi-double and produced in succession from March to May. A strong-growing species with scandent stems up to 4.5m long. Best grown against a warm, sheltered sunny wall in favoured localities or in a conservatory. I 1900 from SW China by Ernest Wilson. ♀ 2002. FCC 1903.

†**nitidum* Skan. Angel-wing jasmine. A bushy, twining shrub with simple, glossy dark green, opposite leaves to 8cm long. Flowers star-like, in small clusters in the leaf axils, sweetly scented, white from red-purple buds, 4cm across, with up to 11 slender lobes. Flowering almost continuously in good conditions but suitable for the mildest areas or conservatory only. Admiralty Islands, near New Guinea.

nudiflorum See TREES AND SHRUBS.

officinale L. Common white jasmine, Poets' jasmine. A strong-growing, scandent or twining climber, reaching 6–9m in a suitable tree. Leaves pinnate, composed of 5–9 leaflets. Flowers white, deliciously fragrant, borne in terminal clusters from June to September. An old favourite cottage-garden plant, said to have been introduced into Britain as long ago as 1548. It requires a sheltered corner in cold northern districts. Caucasus, N Iran and Afghanistan, through the Himalaya to China. ♀ 2002. **f.** *affine* (Lindl.) Rehder ('Grandiflorum') A superior form with slightly larger flowers, usually tinged pink on the outside. Not to be confused with *J. grandiflorum* L., a tender species for a greenhouse. **'Argenteovariegatum'** A very striking form, the leaves grey-green, margined creamy-white. C 1770. ♀ 2002. **'Aureum'** ('Aureovariegatum') Leaves variegated and suffused yellow; a very effective plant. C 1914. **Fiona Sunrise** ('Frojas') PBR A form with yellow-flushed leaves found as a seedling by Dave West in 1989 and launched by us at Chelsea Show, 1995. **'Grandiflorum'** See f. *affine*. **'Inverleith'** A form with the flowers bright red in bud, and on the tube and backs of the lobes when open. ♀ 2002.

†*polyanthum* Franch. A beautiful, vigorous, twining species up to 7.5m, related to *J. officinale*, but tender. Leaves pinnate, composed of 5–7 leaflets. Intensely fragrant, white flowers, flushed rose on the outside, are borne in numerous panicles from May until late summer, earlier under glass. Requires a warm wall or trellis in mild localities, but makes an excellent conservatory subject elsewhere, providing it is kept under control by rigorous pruning. A form with deep pink flowers is also in cultivation. SW China. I 1891. ♀ 2002. FCC 1949. AM 1941.

primulinum See *J. mesnyi*.

†*sambac* (L.) Aiton. Arabian jasmine. Vigorous climber with angled shoots and undivided, opposite, dark green leaves, sometimes borne in 3s. Clusters of large, white, very fragrant flowers open mainly in summer, often fading to pink. Suitable for the conservatory. Long cultivated, of uncertain origin. ♀ 2002. **'Grand Duke of Tuscany'** Flowers double, large and very fragrant. **'Maid of Orleans'** Compact with semi-double, extremely fragrant flowers over a long period. ♀ 2002.

†*simplicifolium* subsp. *suavissimum* (Lindl.) P.S. Green (*J. suavissimum* Lindl.) A tall-growing conservatory species with slender twining stems and linear leaves 2.5–6cm long. White, sweetly fragrant flowers are borne in loose panicles during late summer. They will perfume the whole conservatory. E Australia.

× *stephanense* Lemoine (*J. beesianum* × *J. officinale*) A vigorous climber, up to 7.5m, with slender green, angular shoots. Leaves simple or pinnate, with 3–5 leaflets. Flowers fragrant, pale pink, borne in terminal clusters in June and July. The leaves of young or vigorous shoots are often flushed creamy-yellow. Interesting on account of it being the only known hybrid jasmine. It is a beautiful plant where space permits its full development, such as when covering an outhouse. It was raised at Saint-Etienne in France just prior to 1920 and occurs with the parents in the wild in W China including Yunnan, where it was found by Delavay in 1887. AM 1937.

suavissimum See *J. simplicifolium* subsp. *suavissimum*.

†*subhumile* W.W. Sm. (*J. diversifolium* Kobuski, *J. heterophyllum* Roxb.) A scandent shrub with purplish young shoots and alternate, dark glossy green, leathery, privet-like leaves, simple or occasionally with 1 or 2 small, slender subsidiary leaflets. Flowers small, yellow, star-like, in slender, glabrous cymes during late spring. The form we grow is sometimes distinguished as var. *glabricymosum* (W.W. Sm.) P.Y. Bai, differing little from typical form. E Himalaya, SW China. I 1820.

†***KADSURA** Juss.—**Schisandraceae**—A small genus of evergreen, monoecious, twining plants related to *Schisandra*. About 20 species natives of E and SE Asia.

japonica (L.) Dunal. A slender climber, up to 3.6m, with dark green, oval or lanceolate leaves, 5–10cm long,

glossy green, often turning red in autumn. Flowers solitary, cream-coloured, 2cm across, appearing during summer and early autumn. Fruits scarlet, in clusters. Requires a warm, sheltered wall; best in mild localities. Japan, China, Taiwan. I 1860. **'Variegata'** Leaves with a broad margin of creamy-yellow.

Kangaroo vine See *Cissus antarctica*.
Kudzu vine See *Pueraria lobata*.

†***LAPAGERIA** Ruiz & Pav.—**Philesiaceae**—A monotypic genus requiring cool, moist, lime-free soil in shade or semi-shade. Succeeds best on a sheltered wall. It is an excellent conservatory plant, but detests long exposure to strong sunlight.

rosea Ruiz & Pav. Chilean bellflower. One of the most beautiful of all flowering climbers, the national flower of Chile. An evergreen with strong, wiry, twining stems reaching 3–4.5m on a suitable wall. Leaves ovate-lanceolate to cordate, leathery. Rose-crimson, fleshy, bell-shaped flowers, 7.5cm long by 5cm wide, are borne singly or in pendent clusters from the axils of the upper leaves during most of summer and autumn. A lovely plant for a shaded sheltered wall in the milder counties. Chile, Argentina. I 1847. ♀ 2002. FCC 1974. **var. albiflora** Hook. Flowers white. **'Flesh Pink'** Flowers flesh-pink. **'Nash Court'** Flowers soft pink marbled with deeper pink. FCC 1884.

†***LARDIZABALA** Ruiz & Pav.—**Lardizabalaceae**—A genus of a single species, an evergreen, twining plant with compound leaves and unisexual flowers; natives of Chile. Suitable for a sheltered wall in sun or semi-shade, but only in mild localities.

biternata See *L. funaria*.

funaria (Molina) Looser (*L. biternata* Ruiz & Pav.) A fairly vigorous climber with leaves composed of 3–9 dark green, glossy, oblong leaves. Flowers chocolate-purple and white, the males in pendent racemes, the females solitary, appearing during late autumn and winter. Fruits sweet, sausage-shaped, edible, dark purple, 5–7.5cm long. Chile. I 1844.

LONICERA L.—**Caprifoliaceae**—The climbing honeysuckles include some of the loveliest and most popular of all twining plants. All are worth cultivating, though none surpasses the fragrance of the common native hedgerow species *L. periclymenum*. They are probably seen at their best when scrambling over other bushes, or tree stumps, trellises or pergolas, but are very adaptable to other purposes and some are even occasionally grown as small standards. Although some flower best with their 'heads' in full sun, many honeysuckles luxuriate in half-shade or even complete shade and in such positions are less susceptible to aphids. They are happy in almost all soils. The tubular, funnel-shaped or trumpet-shaped flowers are pollinated by hawk-moths, bumble-bees and so on.

*acuminata Wall. The true plant under this name has now been introduced to cultivation. For a plant previously grown under this name see *L. japonica* 'Dart's Acumen'.

*alseuosmoides Graebn. An evergreen species with glabrous shoots and narrowly oblong, ciliate leaves.

Flowers small, funnel-shaped, 12mm long, yellow outside, purple within, in short, broad panicles on the young growths from July to October. Berries black, blue-bloomy. W China. I by Wilson about 1904.

× **americana** (Mill.) K. Koch (*L. grata* Aiton) A climbing, semi-evergreen shrub. Leaves obovate, short-stalked or sessile, dark green; the uppermost pairs of leaves connate. Inflorescences in terminal spikes, often in groups of 3, from midsummer to autumn; corolla 4–6cm long, purple, inside white, ageing to yellow, fragrant. Fruits: none; a sterile hybrid. For the plant commonly grown under this name see *L.* × *italica*.

× **brownii** (Regel) Carrière (*L. hirsuta* × *L. sempervirens*) Scarlet trumpet honeysuckle. A deciduous or semi-evergreen climber of moderate vigour. Leaves up to 8.5cm long, downy and glaucous beneath, the upper leaves perfoliate. Flowers 2.5–4cm long, orange-scarlet, borne in whorls at the ends of the branches in late spring, and again in late summer. Garden origin, before 1850. **'Dropmore Scarlet'** A tall-growing climber, producing clusters of bright scarlet, tubular flowers, from July to October. Now the commonest form of *L.* × *brownii* in cultivation but very susceptible to attack by aphids. See *L. sempervirens*. **'Fuchsioides'** This clone of equal beauty is scarcely distinguishable from the typical form. **'Plantierensis'** Flowers coral-red with orange lobes.

calcarata Hemsl. A vigorous, high-climbing species with large leaves united at the base by dish-like stipules. Flowers borne in pairs in the leaf axils in June to July, creamy-white ageing to yellow then flame, the corolla with a distinct spur, 1cm long, near the base. Sichuan, China. I by Mikinori Ogisu from Mt Omei to Japan in 1994 and to Britain in 1997.

caprifolium L. (*L.* 'Early Cream') Perfoliate honeysuckle. A fairly vigorous climber, up to 6m, with obovate or oval, glaucous leaves, the upper pairs of which are perfoliate. Flowers 4–5cm long, fragrant, creamy-white, usually tinged pink on the outside, borne in whorls at the ends of the shoots in June and July. Berries orange-red. A popular species commonly planted in cottage gardens. The perfoliate upper leaves easily distinguish it from *L. periclymenum*. C and S Europe, Caucasus, Asia Minor. Long cultivated and occasionally naturalised in the British Isles. ♀ 2002. **'Anna Fletcher'** Flowers creamy-white with no pink tinge. **'Pauciflora'** See *L.* × *italica*.

ciliosa (Pursh) Poir. Western trumpet honeysuckle. An American honeysuckle related to *L. sempervirens*, but differing in its ciliate leaves, the upper pairs of which are perfoliate. Flowers 2.5–4cm long, yellow, tinged purple on the outside, in whorls at the ends of the shoots in June. W North America. I 1825. AM 1919.

dioica L. A bushy, twining shrub with ovate or elliptic, glabrous leaves, to 7cm long, glaucous beneath. Flowers deep yellow tinged red, fragrant, borne in dense groups of terminal whorls above a pair of perfoliate leaves in June. Corolla, 2-lipped, about 2.5cm long and across. Berries red. E North America. I 1776.

'Dropmore Scarlet' See *L.* × *brownii* 'Dropmore Scarlet'.

etrusca Santi. A very vigorous, deciduous or semi-evergreen climber with purplish young shoots and oval or obovate, glaucous, usually downy leaves, perfoliate at the ends of the shoots. Flowers 4cm long, fragrant,

opening cream, often flushed red, deepening to yellow, borne in whorls at the ends of the shoots in June and July, but not on young plants. A superb species revelling in sun and seen at its best in the drier counties. Mediterranean region. I about 1750. **'Donald Waterer'** Young shoots red, bloomy, flowers red outside white inside, becoming orange-yellow followed by bright orange fruits. Found in the French Pyrenees about 1973 by Donald Waterer. ♀ 2002. AM 1985. **'Michael Rosse'** Flowers are pale yellow at first deepening with age; foliage grey bloomy. Derived from a plant in the National Trust garden at Nymans, West Sussex. AM 1982. **'Superba'** A large, vigorous variety with red young shoots and red flowers, white inside, turning orange-yellow. ♀ 2002.

flexuosa See *L. japonica* var. *repens*.

giraldii Rehd. An evergreen species forming a dense tangle of slender, hairy stems. Leaves narrowly oblong, heart-shaped at base, 4–9cm long and densely velvety-hairy. Flowers 2cm long, purplish-red with yellow stamens, yellowish pubescent on the outside, in terminal clusters in June and July. Berries purplish-black. Useful for growing over a low wall or parapet. NW China. I 1899.

glabrata Wall. A very vigorous, evergreen climber with densely hairy shoots and dark glossy green, lanceolate leaves, cordate at the base and hairy on both sides. Flowers slightly fragrant, opening yellow, tinged-red, becoming white, tinged deep pink, borne in terminal clusters and in pairs from the axils of young leaves in early summer and again in autumn. Berries black. Himalaya. I by Dutch botanist Harry van de Laar from E Nepal in 1973 (VdL 4120).

glaucescens Rydb. A bushy shrub with twining stems and obovate to narrow elliptic leaves, green above, glaucous and pubescent beneath. Flowers 2cm long, orange-yellow, borne in terminal whorls in June and July followed by dense clusters of orange-red fruits. North America. C 1890.

grata See *L.* × *americana*.

× **heckrottii** Rehder. (*L.* × *americana* × *L. sempervirens*) A shrubby plant with scandent branches. Leaves oblong or elliptic, glaucous beneath, the upper ones perfoliate. Flowers 4–5cm long, fragrant, yellow, heavily flushed purple, abundantly borne in whorls at the ends of the shoots from July to August or September. Origin uncertain, before 1895. **'Gold Flame'** According to Dutch botanist Harry van de Laar this is a distinct clone. It differs from the plant described above in being less evergreen and more of a climber, with deeper green leaves turning blue-green in autumn; it also has shorter racemes and brighter flowers. The name 'American Beauty' has been proposed for the form described above.

henryi Hemsl. (*L. henryi* var. *subcoriacea* Rehder) A vigorous, evergreen or semi-evergreen species with downy shoots and oblong, slender-pointed, ciliate leaves, 4–10cm long, dark green above, paler and glossy beneath. Flowers yellow, stained red, 2cm long, borne in terminal clusters in June and July, followed by black berries. W China. I 1908 by Ernest Wilson. A handsome plant introduced by Keith Rushforth is close to this species but has bristly shoots, leaves that are very large and glossy, deep bronze when young and flowers opening white with a pink tube becoming deep yellow, followed by blue-black berries. **var. subcoriacea** See *L. henryi*.

†*__hildebrandiana__ Collet & Hemsl. Giant honeysuckle. This magnificent species is a giant in every respect. A strong-growing, evergreen climber, in its native forests reaching into lofty trees. Leaves broadly oval, 7.5–15cm long. Flowers 9–15cm long, fragrant, creamy-white at first, changing to rich yellow occasionally flushed orange-yellow, produced in the terminal leaf axils from June to August; berries 2.5–3cm long. This wonderful species is only suitable for the very mildest localities of the British Isles, but makes a spectacular, if rampant, climber for a conservatory. Shy-flowering when young, it is the largest in size, leaf, flower and fruit of all the honeysuckles. Burma, Thailand, SW China. First discovered in the Shan Hills (Burma) by Sir Henry Collett in 1888. FCC 1901.

'Honey Baby' (_Lonicera japonica_ 'Halliana' × _L. periclymenum_ 'Belgica Select') A scandent shrub, to 2m, with dark green foliage. Flowers fragrant, red-purple in bud opening creamy-yellow, ageing to orange-yellow from midsummer to autumn.

*__implexa__ Sol. An evergreen or semi-evergreen climber with glabrous shoots and ovate to oblong leaves, glaucous beneath, the upper ones perfoliate. Flowers fragrant, 4–5cm long, yellow, flushed pink on the outside, borne in whorls at the ends of the shoots from June to August. In 1934 our propagator was most surprised when he received this species as cuttings by air from Mr H.G. Hillier who was on his honeymoon. S Europe. I 1772.

× __italica__ Tausch (_L. caprifolium_ × _L. etrusca_) (_L._ × _americana_ hort., _L. caprifolium_ 'Pauciflora') A magnificent extremely free-flowering, vigorous climber, reaching 9m under suitable conditions. Leaves broad elliptic to obovate. Flowers 4–5cm long, fragrant, white, soon passing to pale and finally deep yellow, heavily tinged purple outside, appearing in whorls at the ends of the shoots and providing one of the most spectacular floral displays of late spring and early summer. C before 1730. ♀ 2002. AM 1937. **Harlequin** ('Sherlite') PBR A medium-sized form bearing green leaves edged with cream and pink variegation in various shades.

*__japonica__ Thunb. A rampant, evergreen or semi-evergreen species, reaching 6–9m on a suitable support. Leaves ovate to oblong, often lobed on young or vigorous shoots. Flowers fragrant, 2.5–4cm long, white, changing to yellow with age, produced continuously from June onwards. An excellent climber or creeper for covering and concealing unsightly objects. As a groundcover it must be kept under control; it is a serious weed in parts of North America. Japan, Korea, Manchuria, China. I 1806. **'Aureoreticulata'** A delightful form of var. _repens_, the neat, bright green leaves with a conspicuous golden reticulation. I by Robert Fortune before 1862. **'Dart's Acumen'** A vigorous, even rampant, evergreen or semi-evergreen plant, excellent as a rapid groundcover. This form has been commonly grown as _L. acuminata_. **'Halliana'** Flowers white, changing to yellow, very fragrant. Considered by some authorities to be the typical form. ♀ 2002. **'Hall's Prolific'** Selected in Holland from plants grown as 'Halliana', this flowers profusely even when young. **var. _repens_** Rehder (_L. flexuosa_ Thunb.) A distinct variety making excellent groundcover, the leaves and shoots flushed purple; flowers

flushed purple on the outside, very fragrant. Japan, China. Introduced early in the 19th century. ♀ 2002.

__periclymenum__ L. Woodbine. The common honeysuckle of hedgerows and woods. A vigorous species climbing, scrambling or trailing in habit. Leaves ovate to oblong, glaucous beneath. Flowers 4–5cm long, strongly and sweetly fragrant, creamy-white within, darkening with age, purplish or yellowish outside, appearing in terminal clusters from June to September. Berries red. A pretty climber, long connected with old cottage gardens. Europe, N and C Morocco. **'Belgica'** Early Dutch honeysuckle. Flowers reddish-purple on the outside fading to yellowish, produced during May and June and again in late summer. Cultivated since the 17th century. **'Graham Thomas'** Flowers white in bud and when first open, becoming yellow, borne over a long period. Found in Warwickshire about 1960. ♀ 2002. **Harlequin** See _L._ × _italica_ Harlequin. **'Munster'** Flowers deep pink in bud, opening white, streaked-pink on the tube and the backs of the lobes, fading to cream. **'Red Gables'** A free-flowering form similar to 'Serotina' but neater and more compact. Found on a house near Pershore. **'Serotina'** ('Late Red') Late Dutch honeysuckle. Flowers rich reddish-purple outside, from July to October. ♀ 2002. AM 1988. **'Sweet Sue'** A form found on a Swedish beach by Roy Lancaster and named after his wife. Very fragrant, creamy-white flowers age to yellow. The inflorescences are larger than those of 'Graham Thomas'.

__pilosa__ Willd. ex Kunth. A twining shrub with glabrous, purple shoots, bloomy when young, and blue-green, glabrous leaves, glaucous beneath. The terminal 2 pairs of leaves are united around the stem; from the upper pair are borne pendent clusters of bright orange-red, tubular flowers, 5–6cm long, pilose and glandular outside, orange-yellow inside, in May-June. NE Mexico.

__prolifera__ (Kirchn.) Rehder. A vigorous, twining shrub with glaucous-bloomed shoots. Leaves glaucous green above, glaucous beneath. Upper leaves perfoliate, intensely glaucous forming a rounded disk. Flowers creamy-yellow, pink-tinged with exserted yellow anthers, borne in several terminal whorls in May, not fragrant. Fruits red. Has been confused with _L. glaucescens_. North America.

*__sempervirens__ L. Trumpet honeysuckle. A high-climbing, usually semi-evergreen species with elliptic to obovate, rich green leaves, glaucous and slightly downy beneath, the upper ones perfoliate. Flowers 4–5cm long, rich orange-scarlet outside, yellow within, borne in axillary whorls towards the ends of the shoots during summer. A striking and very hardy species which does not seem to be troubled by aphids like _L._ × _brownii_ 'Dropmore Scarlet'. E USA. I 1656. ♀ 2002. AM 1964. **f. _sulphurea_** (Jacques) Rehder. Flowers yellow.

*__similis__ Hemsl. This species is represented in cultivation by the following variety. **var. _delavayi_** (Franch.) Rehder (_L. delavayi_ Franch.) A slender half-evergreen climber with ovate-lanceolate leaves, white and downy beneath. Flowers fragrant, 3–4cm long, white changing to pale yellow, produced in the axils of the terminal leaves during late summer and early autumn. W China. I 1901. ♀ 2002.

†*__splendida__ Boiss. A rather fastidious, evergreen or sometimes semi-evergreen species with oval or oblong, very glaucous leaves, the upper ones perfoliate. Flowers

4–5cm long, fragrant, reddish-purple outside, yellowish-white within, borne in dense, terminal clusters during summer. A beautiful climber, succeeding best in the milder areas of the British Isles. Spain. I about 1880.

× *tellmanniana* Späth (*L. sempervirens* × *L. tragophylla*) A superb hybrid with oval or ovate leaves, the upper ones perfoliate. Flowers 5cm long, rich coppery-yellow, flushed red in bud, borne in large terminal clusters in June and July. Succeeds best in semi-shade or even in full shade. Raised at the Royal Hungarian Horticultural School, Budapest some time prior to 1927. AM 1931. **'Joan Sayers'** Selected in 1988 as the best form of this hybrid for flower.

tragophylla Hemsl. A climber of great ornamental merit. Leaves 7.5–10cm long, oblong to oval, glaucous and downy beneath. Flowers 6–9cm long, bright golden-yellow, produced in June and July, in large, terminal clusters. Berries red. An extremely showy species, requiring almost complete shade. Best grown into a tree. W China. Discovered by Augustine Henry. I 1900 by Ernest Wilson. ♀ 2002. AM 1913.

†**MANDEVILLA** Lindl.—**Apocynaceae**—More than 100 species of mainly twining climbers of the periwinkle family with characteristic, milky sap; natives of tropical America. The following require a warm, sheltered wall and a well-drained soil in the milder counties or make attractive conservatory plants.

*× amabilis (hort. Buckl.) Dress. A hybrid of *M. splendens* making a vigorous, evergreen climber with glossy dark green, deeply veined leaves. Bears racemes of large, funnel-shaped, pink flowers, deepening in colour as they age, over a long period from spring to autumn. For a conservatory. **'Alice du Pont'** (*M.* × *amoena* 'Alice du Pont') A form with more abundant, darker flowers. ♀ 2002.

laxa (Ruiz & Pav.) Woodson (*M. suaveolens* Lindl.) Chilean jasmine. An elegant, sun-loving climber with slender stems 3–4.5m long or more. Leaves heart-shaped, slender-pointed, bearing tufts of white down in the vein axils beneath. Fragrant, white, periwinkle-like flowers, 5cm across, are borne in corymbs from the leaf axils during summer. Well worth growing for its sweetly scented flowers. Bolivia, N Argentina. I 1837 by H.J. Mandeville. ♀ 2002. AM 1957.

suaveolens See *M. laxa*.

MENISPERMUM L.—**Menispermaceae**—A genus of 2 species of semi-woody, twining, dioecious plants, suitable for growing into small trees or over walls, sheds, and so on, best in full sun. In cold districts they may be cut to the ground each winter, but will invariably produce new shoots in spring. They are distinctive in leaf, but to obtain fruit, plants of both sexes are required.

canadense L. Moonseed. A climber spreading by suckers and making a dense tangle of slender shoots up to 4.5m long. Conspicuous, long-stalked leaves, 10–18cm across, are ovate to heart-shaped, with 5–7 angular lobes. Inconspicuous, greenish-yellow flowers are borne in slender axillary racemes in summer and on female plants are followed by blackcurrant-like fruits, each containing a single, crescent-shaped seed (hence the common name). E North America. C 1646.

Moonseed See *Menispermum canadense*.

MUEHLENBECKIA Meisn.—**Polygonaceae**—A small genus of about 15 species of dioecious, creeping or climbing plants, natives of Australasia and South America. They are of little beauty in flower, but amusing and interesting botanically. *M. complexa* is useful for covering and concealing unsightly objects in mild areas.

axillaris (Hook. f.) Walp. A hardy, slow-growing, prostrate species forming dense carpets of intertwining, thread-like stems clothed with small, ovate to orbicular leaves, 2–5mm long. Fruits white, bearing a shiny black nutlet. Useful as groundcover on rock gardens and screes. New Zealand, Australia, Tasmania.

†*complexa* (Cunn.) Meisn. A twining species with slender, dark, interlacing stems, occasionally up to 6m or more, forming dense tangled curtains or carpets. Leaves variable in shape and size 3–20mm long and from roundish or oblong to fiddle-shaped. Minute, greenish flowers in autumn are followed on female plants by small, white, fleshy fruits, enclosing a single, black, shining nutlet. New Zealand. I 1842. **var.** *trilobata* (Col.) Cheesem. (*M. varians* Meisn., *M. trilobata* Col.) A curious and amusing form in which the larger leaves are distinctly fiddle-shaped. In habit it is just as vigorous and as twining as the typical variety and makes excellent cover for old stumps, walls and banks in mild areas.

varians See *M. complexa* var. *trilobata*.

***MUTISIA** L. f.—**Compositae**—The climbing gazanias are a genus of about 60 species of erect or climbing evergreens, the climbing species attaching themselves to a support by means of leaf tendrils; natives of South America, particularly Chile. They may be grown on a wall, but are perhaps best planted near an old or unwanted shrub or small bushy tree, so that their stems may be encouraged to grow into the support provided. They require a warm, sunny position in rich but well-drained soil. The colourful, gazania-like flowerheads are produced singly on long stalks.

†*clematis* L. f. A strong-growing species for a conservatory. Leaves pinnate, composed of 6–10 oblong-ovate leaflets, white-woolly beneath. Flowerheads pendent, cylindrical at base, 5–6cm across, with brilliant orange petals, produced in summer and early autumn. Andes of Colombia and Ecuador I 1859. AM 1926.

decurrens Cav. A rare species, up to 3m, with narrowly oblong, sessile leaves, 7.5–13cm long. Flowerheads 10–13cm across, with brilliant orange or vermilion petals, are borne continuously during summer. A superb species but difficult to establish. It succeeds in a warm, sheltered position such as a partially shaded west wall and in a rich friable sandy loam. Chile. I 1859 by Richard Pearce. FCC 1861.

ilicifolia Cav. A vigorous, hardy species with stems 3–4.5m long. Leaves sessile, ovate-oblong, the margins strongly toothed, dark green above, pale woolly beneath. Flowerheads 5–7.5cm across, yellow, with lilac-pink petals, borne in summer and early autumn. Chile. I 1832.

oligodon Poepp. & Endl. A very beautiful, suckering species, usually easy to establish by growing through a sparsely branched shrub. It forms a low thicket of straggling stems rarely reaching 1.5m. Leaves oblong, sessile, coarsely toothed, auriculate at base. Flowerheads 5–7.5cm across with salmon-pink petals, appear continuously throughout summer and intermittently into autumn. A lovely species more compact in habit than *M. ilicifolia* and with shorter stems. In a sunny site supported by a low trellis or a low or small shrub, it is a most attractive plant except that in winter it can look almost dead, with only an occasional green shoot. Chile. I 1927 by Harold Comber. AM 1928.

Oxypetalum caeruleum See *Tweedia caerulea*.

PAEDERIA L.—**Rubiaceae**—A small genus of some 20 species of twining plants emitting a foetid smell when bruised; natives of temperate and tropical Asia and S America. The following requires a sunny, sheltered position in any fertile soil.

scandens (Lour.) Merr. (*P. chinensis* Hance) A strong-growing climber, up to 5m, with ovate, slender-pointed, dark green leaves, often rather downy beneath. Flowers tubular, white with a purple throat, carried in slender terminal panicles throughout summer, followed by small, orange fruits. China, Taiwan, Japan, Korea. I 1907.

†*__PANDOREA__ (Endl.) Spach—**Bignoniaceae**—A small genus of about 6 species of evergreen, twining plants with opposite, pinnate leaves; natives of SE Asia and Australia. The following require a warm, sheltered position in very mild localities and are best grown in a conservatory.

jasminoides (Lindl.) Schum. (*Bignonia jasminoides* hort., *Tecoma jasminoides* Lindl.) The bower plant of Australia, a beautiful climber, the pinnate leaves composed of 5–9 slender-pointed leaflets. Attractive, funnel-shaped flowers, 4–5cm long, pale pink, stained crimson in the throat, are borne in terminal panicles during summer. E Australia. **'Charisma'** Leaves bright green, the leaflets with a broad, irregular cream margin, sometimes half or nearly all cream. **'Rosea Superba'** Flowers large, to 6cm long, very deep pink in the throat with purple spots. ♀ 2002.

pandorana (Andr.) Steenis. Wonga-wonga vine. A vigorous climber, the glossy green leaves with up to 19 leaflets. Large clusters of fragrant, tubular flowers, to 3cm across, open at the ends of the shoots in spring and summer. The flowers are variable in colour, usually creamy-yellow flushed with red in the throat. Papua New Guinea, E Australia. **'Golden Rain'** Flowers golden-yellow flushed red, from deep red buds.

PARTHENOCISSUS Planch.—**Vitaceae**—A small genus of about 10 species of high-climbing vines, related to *Vitis* and attaching themselves to supports by means of leaf tendrils which either twine or adhere by adhesive pads. They are natives of the USA, Mexico, E Asia and the Himalaya. The self-clinging species are excellent on walls or tree trunks while those with twining tendrils may be trained over hedges, large coarse shrubs or small, bushy trees. The leaves are often richly coloured in autumn. The attractive, small fruits are only produced following a hot, dry summer. See also *Ampelopsis* and *Vitis*.

henryana (Hemsl.) Diels & Gilg (*Vitis henryana* Hemsl.) A beautiful, self-clinging species. Leaves are digitate,

composed of 3–5 obovate or narrowly oval leaflets, dark green or bronze with silvery-white veinal variegation, particularly when growing in half-shade, turning red in autumn. Fruits dark blue. Best grown on a wall. C China. First discovered by Augustine Henry about 1885. I 1900 by Ernest Wilson. ♀ 2002. AM 1906.

himalayana (Royle) Planch. (*Vitis himalayana* Brandis) A strong-growing, more or less self-clinging climber, differing from the Virginia creeper mainly in its larger leaflets, which turn rich crimson in autumn. Fruits deep blue. Himalaya. C 1894. **var. rubrifolia** (Lév. & Vaniot) Gagnep. An attractive variety, leaflets smaller, purple when young. W China. I 1907.

inserta See *P. quinquefolia* and *P. vitacea*.

quinquefolia (L.) Planch. (*Parthenocissus inserta* (A. Kern.) Fritsch not auct., *Vitis quinquefolia* (L.) Lam., *Vitis hederacea* Ehrh.) Virginia creeper. A tall-growing, more or less self-clinging vine excellent for high walls, trees, towers, and so on. Leaves composed of usually 5, oval to obovate, stalked leaflets, dull green and glaucescent beneath, turning brilliant orange and scarlet in autumn. Fruits blue-black. Reaching to the tops of lofty trees in its native habitats. The plant often incorrectly referred to as Virginia creeper is *P. tricuspidata*, the Boston ivy. E USA, Mexico. I 1629. ♀ 2002.

sinensis See *Vitis piasezkii*.

thomsonii (M.A. Lawson) Planch. (*Vitis thomsonii* M.A. Lawson) A beautiful vine of slender habit. Leaves composed of 5, oval or obovate, glossy green leaflets. The young growths in spring are purple; in autumn the foliage turns to rich crimson and scarlet. Fruits black. Himalaya, China. I 1900 by Ernest Wilson. FCC 1903 (as *Vitis thomsonii*).

tricuspidata (Siebold & Zucc.) Planch. (*Vitis inconstans* Miq.) Boston ivy. A vigorous, self-clinging vine, almost as ubiquitous as the common ivy. Leaves extremely variable, broadly ovate and toothed, or trifoliolate on young plants, ovate and conspicuously 3-lobed on old plants, rich crimson and scarlet in autumn. Fruits dark blue and bloomy. A commonly planted vine, densely covering walls in urban districts and a familiar sight in many older cities and towns. Japan, Korea, China, Taiwan. I 1862 from Japan by J.G. Veitch. ♀ 2002. FCC 1868. **'Beverley Brook'** Rather small, bright green leaves, to 10cm across, bronze when young and deep red in autumn. C 1950. **'Green Spring'** A very vigorous form with large leaves to 25cm across, bronze when young and red-purple in autumn. C 1965. **'Lowii'** A selection with small, curiously crisped, palmate, 3- to 7-lobed leaves and rich autumn colour. AM 1907. **'Veitchii'** (*Ampelopsis veitchii* hort., *Vitis inconstans* 'Purpurea') A selected form with slightly smaller, ovate or trifoliolate leaves, purple when young.

vitacea (Knerr) Hitchc. (*P. inserta* auct. not (A. Kern.) Fritsch, *Vitis vitacea* (Knerr) Bean) A vigorous vine with twining tendrils climbing into small trees or scrambling over hedges. Leaves with 5, stalked, ovate to obovate leaflets, shining green beneath, colouring richly in autumn. Fruits blue-black. Ideal for covering unsightly objects, differing most markedly from the closely related Virginia creeper in its non-adhesive tendrils and bright green leaves. E USA. C before 1800.

†**PASSIFLORA** L.—**Passifloraceae**—The passion flowers make up a large genus of some 350 species of evergreen or deciduous, mainly climbers, attaching themselves to a support by means of twining tendrils. Natives mainly of tropical South America, the majority are too tender for planting outside in the British Isles, but the few that will survive are among the most beautiful and exotic of flowering creepers. They are best planted on a sunny, sheltered, south-facing wall. The beautiful and fascinating flowers, usually borne singly on long stalks, are composed of a tubular calyx with 5 lobes or sepals. These are often the same size, shape and colour as the 5 petals and are referred to collectively as tepals. Inside the tepals are rings of filaments which are usually thread-like and coloured, referred to collectively as the corona. The 5 stamens are carried on a long central column and are topped by the ovary and 3 nail-like stigmas. The fruits vary in size and shape and contain numerous seeds in an edible, jelly-like pulp. Outdoors they are normally only produced after a long, hot summer.

According to Dr Masters the name 'passion flower' was used originally by the Spanish priests in South America because of the resemblance their piety led them to detect between the various parts of the flower and the instruments of Christ's Passion: the 3 stigmas representing the 3 nails; the 5 anthers representing the 5 wounds; the corona representing the crown of thorns or the halo of glory; the 10 tepals representing the apostles—Peter and Judas being absent; the lobed leaves and the whip-like tendrils representing the hands and scourges of His persecutors.

alata Dryand. A vigorous climber, related to *P. quadrangularis*, with winged shoots and undivided leaves, to 15cm long. Flowers fragrant, to 12cm across, with red sepals and a corona striped with white and purple; they are followed by yellow, edible fruits to 15cm long. Brazil, Peru. ♥ 2002.

× *allardii* Lynch (*P. caerulea* 'Constance Elliot' × *P. quadrangularis*) A strong-growing climber with large, 3-lobed leaves. Flowers 9–11.5cm across, through summer and autumn: tepals white, shaded pink, corona white and deep cobalt-blue. May be grown outside in the milder counties. Raised at the University Botanic Garden, Cambridge.

'**Amethyst**' (*P. amethystina* Mikan., *P.* 'Lavender Lady') A large, vigorous climber with 3-lobed leaves. Flowers 8cm across, from spring to summer: bell-shaped calyx and pointed sepals are blue inside, deeper blue petals and dark purple corona. For a conservatory only. ♥ 2002.

amethystina See 'Amethyst'.

antioquiensis Karst. (*Tacsonia vanvolxemii* Lem.) A beautiful climber with slender, downy stems and leaves of 2 kinds: lanceolate, unlobed leaves, and deeply 3-lobed leaves, the lobes long and slender-pointed, downy beneath. Flowers pendent, 10–13cm across, tube 2.5–4cm long, rich rose-red, with a small violet corona, borne singly on long peduncles during late summer and autumn. May be grown outside only in the most favoured localities, otherwise a plant for a conservatory. Colombia. I 1858. ♥ 2002.

caerulea L. Blue passion flower. A vigorous, usually rampant species often forming a dense blanket of tangled stems, evergreen in mild localities. Leaves palmately 5- to 7-lobed. Flowers slightly fragrant, 7.5–10cm across appear continuously throughout summer and autumn, often until the first frosts: tepals white or occasionally pink-tinged; the conspicuous corona has the outer filaments blue at the tips, white in the middle and purple at the base. Fruits ovoid, orange-red, 2.5–4cm long. Hardy on a warm, sunny wall in the south and often surviving many winters in the Home Counties. S Brazil, Argentina. I 1609. ♥ 2002. '**Constance Elliot**' A superb clone with ivory-white flowers. FCC 1884.

× *caeruleoracemosa* See *P.* × *violacea*.

edulis Sims. Purple granadilla. A tender, vigorous climber with angular stems and ovate, deeply 3-lobed leaves. Flowers 6cm across produced throughout summer: tepals white, green without, corona with curly, white filaments, striped with purple. Fruits ovoid, 5cm long, yellow or dull purple, pulp edible. Commonly cultivated in warmer countries for its fruit, sometimes produced in the mildest gardens of the British Isles. Brazil. I 1810.

'**Exoniensis**' (*P. antioquiensis* × *P. mollissima*) (*Tacsonia* 'Exoniensis') A beautiful hybrid with downy stems and deeply 3-lobed, downy leaves. Flowers pendent, 10–13cm across, appear during summer: tube 6cm long, tepals rose-pink, corona small, whitish. Only for a conservatory. Raised by Messrs Veitch of Exeter about 1870. ♥ 2002.

'**Incense**' (*P. cincinnata* × *P. incarnata*) A vigorous climber with exquisitely fragrant, violet-mauve, lace-like flowers, 12cm across, gathered in the centre to produce a striping effect of alternate white and deep purple, early to midsummer. Fruits edible but slightly acid. For a conservatory only. ♥ 2002.

'**Lavender Lady**' See 'Amethyst'.

mollissima (Kunth) L.H. Bailey. A vigorous climber with softly downy shoots and deeply 3-lobed, toothed leaves, densely hairy beneath. Flowers solitary, pendent, to 7.5cm across, in late summer: tube 7–9.5cm long, petals and sepals pink; the corona is a warty, purple ridge. Fruits yellow, edible up to 12cm long. Northern Andes of South America. C 1843. ♥ 2002.

quadrangularis L. Granadilla. A vigorous climber with 4-angled, winged stems and unlobed leaves up to 20cm long. Flowers fragrant, 8cm across, in summer: greenish outside, white, pink, red or violet within, the corona striped with reddish-purple, blue and white. Fruit edible, yellow, 20–30cm long. Origin unknown but widely grown in tropical America for its fruit. ♥ 2002.

racemosa Brot. (*P. princeps* Lodd.) Red passion flower. A climber with ovate, usually 3-lobed leaves. Flowers vivid scarlet with purple, white-tipped outer filaments, borne in drooping, terminal racemes during summer. A magnificent species requiring conservatory treatment. Brazil. I 1815. ♥ 2002.

'**Star of Bristol**' A large, slender, vigorous climber with 3- to 5-lobed leaves. Flowers in summer: green sepals, purple above, and mauve petals; the filaments are mauve, striped lilac. For a conservatory only. ♥ 2002.

umbilicata (Griseb.) Harms (*Tacsonia umbilicata* Griseb.) A fast-growing species with small, violet flowers in late summer and round, yellow fruits. Proving one of the hardiest, thriving in the open in the SW counties of England. Bolivia, Paraguay, N Argentina. I 1954.

× *violacea* Loisel. (*P.* × *caeruleoracemosa* Sabine) (*P. caerulea* × *P. racemosa*) A vigorous climber with deeply

5-lobed leaves. Flowers borne singly throughout summer and autumn: tepals deeply flushed violet, corona deep violet-purple, column apple-green, stigmas purple and green. A free-flowering hybrid, rampant when established. Only suitable for the mildest localities. Raised by Thomas Milne in 1819. ♀ 2002.

vitifolia Kunth. A vigorous climber with cylindrical, downy shoots and dark green, 3-lobed and sharply toothed leaves. The large, fragrant flowers, to 15cm or more across, are bright scarlet with a yellow to red corona and are followed by dark green, edible fruits to 6cm long. Central America to N South America.

Passion flower See *Passiflora*.

PERIPLOCA L.—**Asclepiadaceae**—A small genus of about 10 species of deciduous and evergreen shrubs and twining climbers, exuding a poisonous, milky juice when cut. Suitable for growing on pergolas, fences, and so on, in any fertile soil in a sunny position.

graeca L. Silk vine. A vigorous climber, to 9–12m on a suitable support. Leaves ovate or lanceolate, long-persistent. Flowers 2.5cm across, greenish outside, brownish-purple within, possessing a heavy odour, borne in cymes during July and August. Seedpods in pairs, 12cm long, packed with small silky-tufted seeds. SE Europe, W Asia. C 1597.

†*laevigata* Aiton. A tender, strong-growing, semi-evergreen climber, differing from *P. graeca* in its lanceolate, sessile leaves, subsessile cymes and smaller, greenish-yellow flowers. Canary Islands. I 1770.

*PILEOSTEGIA Hook. f. & Thoms.—**Hydrangeaceae**—A small genus of 4 species of evergreen shrubs climbing by means of aerial roots; natives of E Asia. The following species, the only one in general cultivation, requires a wall or tree trunk in sun or shade and will grow in all types of fertile soil.

viburnoides Hook. f. & Thoms. A rather slow-growing, evergreen, self-clinging species, reaching 6m on a suitable surface. Leaves entire, leathery, narrow-oblong to ovate-lanceolate, 7.5–15cm long, strongly veined and minutely pitted beneath. Flowers in crowded, terminal panicles, creamy-white, appearing during late summer and autumn. One of the best climbers for any aspect including shady walls. Khasia Hills (India), S China, Ryukyus. The first meeting Mr H.G. Hillier had with this plant was in 1922 in Orleans when the leading French nurseryman of the time, Mons Chenault, proudly pointed to a plant covering the front of his house. I 1908 by Ernest Wilson. ♀ 2002. AM 1914.

Plumbago capensis See *Plumbago auriculata* in TREES AND SHRUBS.
Polygonum aubertii See *Fallopia baldschuanica*.
Polygonum baldschuanicum See *Fallopia baldschuanica*.

†PUERARIA DC.—**Leguminosae**—A small genus of about 20 species of herbaceous and woody, twining climbers with trifoliolate leaves and often attractive pea-flowers. Natives of E and SE Asia.

lobata (Willd.) Ohwi (*P. thunbergiana* (Siebold & Zucc.) Benth.) Kudzu vine. A vigorous species, up to 6m, woody at base, stems climbing or trailing. Leaves trifoliolate, the middle leaflets 15–18cm long. Flowers fragrant, violet-purple, in long racemes in July and August. The long stems are often cut back during winter, but grow again from the base. Useful for training over large, unwanted shrubs or old hedges, in full sun. A very serious weed in the SE USA. Japan, Korea, China. I 1885.

Purple bells See *Rhodochiton atrosanguineum*.

†RHODOCHITON Zucc. ex Otto & Dietr.—**Scroph-ulariaceae**—A monotypic genus requiring conservatory treatment. It makes an unusual summer creeper.

atrosanguineum (Zucc.) Rothm. (*R. volubile* Zucc.) Purple bells. A slender plant with stems up to 3m long, climbing by means of its twining petioles and peduncles. Leaves cordate, few-toothed. The curious flowers, consisting of a broadly bell-shaped, almost black-purple calyx and a long tubular, purplish-red corolla are borne in endless succession during summer. Mexico. ♀ 2002. AM 1985.

RUBUS L.—**Rosaceae**—The climbing members of this large genus are fairly vigorous shrubs with long, prickly, scandent stems. They may be trained up wooden supports or into small trees or hedges. Of little beauty in flower or fruit, they are mainly grown for their ornamental foliage. Thriving in all types of well-drained soil. See also TREES AND SHRUBS.

bambusarum See *R. henryi* var. *bambusarum*.

*flagelliflorus Focke. An evergreen species with long, white-felted, minutely prickly stems. Leaves broad ovate to ovate-lanceolate, 10–18cm long, shallowly lobed and toothed, felted beneath. Small, white flowers are borne in axillary clusters in June, followed by black, edible fruits. Mainly grown for its striking ornamental foliage. China. I 1901 by Ernest Wilson.

*henryi Hemsl. & Kuntze. An evergreen species with long, scandent stems, reaching a height of 6m on a suitable support. Leaves deeply 3-lobed, 10–15cm long, glossy dark green above, white-felted beneath. Flowers pink, borne in slender racemes during summer, followed by black fruits. Both the species and the following variety are grown for their habit and attractive foliage. C and W China. First discovered by Augustine Henry. I 1900 by Ernest Wilson.

var. *bambusarum* (Focke) Rehder (*R. bambusarum* Focke) An elegant variety with leaves composed of 3 distinct, lanceolate leaflets. C China. I 1900. FCC 1907.

hupehensis See *R. swinhoei*.

lambertianus Ser. A semi-evergreen species with scandent, 4-angled, prickly stems, viscid when young. Leaves ovate, 7.5–13cm long, shallowly 3- to 5-lobed and toothed, glossy on both surfaces. Flowers small, white, borne in terminal panicles during summer, followed by red fruits. C China. I 1907 by Ernest Wilson.

*parkeri Hance. An evergreen species with slender, scandent, biennial stems, densely clothed with greyish hairs. Leaves oblong-lanceolate with wavy, finely toothed margins, densely reddish-brown-downy beneath. Flowers small, white, in panicles during summer, followed by black fruits. C China. I 1907 by Ernest Wilson.

swinhoei Hance (*R. hupehensis* Oliv.) A vigorous, scandent shrub with erect branches that can reach 3m or more in one season. Shoots purplish and loosely floccose when young, later glabrous and reddish-green with a few small spines. Leaves glossy green above, grey-felted beneath at first, oblong-lanceolate, to 18cm long. Flowers in terminal racemes, white, the filaments spreading and turning red, forming a conspicuous corona around the small, blackberry-like, insipid fruits. Hubei, China. I 1907 by Ernest Wilson.

Russian vine See *Fallopia baldschuanica*.

SCHISANDRA Michx.—Schisandraceae—Some 25
species of deciduous and evergreen, monoecious or dioecious, twining shrubs of considerable charm and quality; natives of E and SE Asia with a single species in North America. Flowers borne in clusters in the leaf axils, followed on female plants by long, pendent spikes of attractive berries. They are suitable for growing on walls or fences or over shrubs and into trees.

chinensis (Turcz.) Baill. A high-climbing species reaching 9m on a suitable support. Leaves obovate to oval, 5–10cm long. Flowers fragrant, 1–2cm across, usually white or palest pink, produced on slender, drooping stalks during late spring. Berries scarlet. Usually dioecious. E China, Korea, Japan. I 1860.

grandiflora (Wall.) Hook. f. & Thoms. A rare species with obovate, somewhat leathery leaves and conspicuous venation, 7.5–10cm long. Flowers 2.5–3cm across, white or pale pink, borne on drooping stalks during May and June. Berries scarlet. Temperate Himalaya. **var. cathayensis** See *S. sphaerandra*. **var. rubriflora** See *S. rubriflora*.

propinqua (Wall.) Baill. The typical form of this species is a native of the Himalaya. It is mainly grown as the following form. **var. sinensis** Oliv. This Chinese variety is hardier and is notable for bearing its short-stalked, yellowish-terracotta flowers during late summer and autumn. Leaves oblong to lanceolate, persistent, 5–10cm long. Berries scarlet. C and W China. I 1907.

rubriflora Rehder & E.H. Wilson (*S. grandiflora* var. *rubriflora* (Rehder & E.H. Wilson) C.K. Schneid.) Closely related to *S. grandiflora* but flowers deep crimson, borne on pendent stalks during late spring. Berries scarlet. W China, N India, N Burma. I 1908. AM 1925 (for fruit).

sphaerandra Stapf (*S. propinqua* var. *cathayana* C.K. Schneid. in part.) An uncommon species with glossy dark green leaves, rather glaucous beneath, and red flowers. Fruits red. SW China. I 1907.

sphenanthera Rehder & E.H. Wilson. A strong-growing climber with warty shoots. Leaves obovate, 5–10cm long, green beneath. Flowers a distinct shade of orange-red or terracotta, borne on slender stalks during May and June. Berries scarlet. W China. I 1907 by Ernest Wilson.

SCHIZOPHRAGMA Siebold & Zucc.—Hydrangeaceae—
A small genus of 4 species of ornamental climbers, supporting themselves by means of aerial roots. Small, creamy-white flowers are densely borne in large, flattened cymes, each cyme attended by several conspicuous, cream-coloured, marginal bracts (really enlarged sepals of sterile flowers). Their requirements are similar to those of *Hydrangea anomala* subsp. *petiolaris* and they are suitable for north-facing or otherwise shady walls, though flowering

best on a sunny wall. They are most effective when allowed to climb a large tree or old stump. Although eventually tall, they are slow starters and need cultural encouragement in their early years.

hydrangeoides Siebold & Zucc. A superb climber, reaching 12m. Leaves broadly rotund-ovate and coarsely toothed (by which it is distinguished from *S. integrifolium*). Flowerheads 20–25cm across, appearing in July, bracts 2.5–4cm long. Native of Japan where it is found in woods and forests in the mountains often accompanied by *Hydrangea anomala* subsp. *petiolaris*. C 1880. FCC 1885. **'Moonlight'** A selection with silvery blue-green foliage, yellow in autumn. **'Roseum'** A lovely form with rose-flushed bracts. AM 1939. ♀ 2002.

integrifolium (Franch.) Oliv. A climber that reaches 12m or more under suitable conditions. Leaves broad ovate to elliptic-oblong, slender-pointed, entire or thinly set with small, narrow teeth. Flowerheads often as much as 30cm across, the bracts 6–9cm long, borne freely in July. A magnificent species, larger in all its parts than *S. hydrangeoides*. Native of C China where it is said to grow on rocky cliffs. I 1901 by Ernest Wilson. ♀ 2002. FCC 1963. AM 1936.

SENECIO L.—Compositae—Probably the largest genus of
flowering plants in the world. Only a few are climbers and of these the following is the only hardy species likely to be met with in cultivation.

†*scandens* G. Don. A fairly vigorous, semi-evergreen, semi-woody climber with scandent stems 4.5–6m long. Leaves narrowly triangular or ovate, coarsely toothed, sometimes lobed at the base. Small, bright yellow, groundsel-like flowerheads are produced in large panicles during autumn. Best planted where it may scramble over bushes and hedges or into small, densely branched trees. It requires a sunny, sheltered site and though in cold areas it is frequently cut to ground level in winter, it will normally spring up again from the base. Given mild weather, a well established specimen is one of the most conspicuous flowering plants in the garden during October and November. Japan, Taiwan, China, Philippines, India, E Nepal. I 1895.

Silk vine See *Periploca graeca*.
Silver vine See *Actinidia polygama*.

SINOFRANCHETIA Hemsl.—Lardizabalaceae— A mono-
typic genus related to *Holboellia* but deciduous and dioecious. It requires a sunny or semi-shady position in any ordinary soil.

chinensis (Franch.) Hemsl. A vigorous, hardy, twining climber reaching 9m in a suitable tree or on a high wall. Leaves trifoliolate, glaucous beneath. Flowers white, inconspicuous, borne in drooping racemes during May. These are followed, on female plants, by conspicuous, large, elongated bunches of lavender-purple, rounded fruits. C and W China. I 1907 by Ernest Wilson. AM 1948.

SINOMENIUM Diels—Menispermaceae—A monotypic
genus related to *Cocculus*. Suitable for growing into a tree or against a large wall in sun or semi-shade and in any ordinary soil.

acutum (Thunb.) Rehder & E.H. Wilson. A hardy, twining climber up to 12m. Shining green leaves vary from ovate and entire to kidney-shaped, often shallowly lobed or with 3–5 lanceolate lobes. Flowers small, yellowish, borne in long, slender, pyramidal panicles in June, followed, on female plants, by small globular, bloomy black fruits. E Asia. I 1901 by Ernest Wilson. **var.** *cinereum* (Diels) Rehder & E.H. Wilson. The form occasionally seen in cultivation with leaves greyish-pubescent beneath. I 1907 by Ernest Wilson.

SMILAX L.—**Smilacaceae**— A large genus of 200 or more species of evergreen and deciduous, mainly climbing plants. Their often prickly stems are tough and wiry, bearing stipular tendrils by which they are able to support themselves, scrambling over bushes, hedges or similar support. They are normally grown for their rich, often glossy green foliage and are excellent for covering stumps, low walls, and so on. Sun or shade in any ordinary soil. They are normally dioecious, with flowers of little beauty.

†*aspera L. An evergreen climber with prickly, angular zigzag stems and ovate-lanceolate to heart-shaped, glossy green, leathery leaves, often attractively blotched with grey. Racemes of small, fragrant, pale green flowers are produced in late summer and early autumn, often followed by small, red fruits. An established plant forms a dense tangle of thorny stems. It requires a warm sunny position and is not suitable for cold areas. S Europe, N Africa, Canary Isles. C 1648. AM 1903.

biflora Siebold ex Miq. This remarkable species is not a climber but makes a dwarf, congested bush about 10cm tall, spreading by suckers. Stems zigzag, somewhat spiny. Leaves glossy green above, glaucous beneath, three-nerved, broadly ovate, mucronate, about 1cm long. Flowers in few-flowered umbels, followed by red fruits. S Japan.

china L. China root. A deciduous shrub with rounded, prickly scrambling stems. Leaves variable in shape, usually roundish-ovate with a heart-shaped base, often turning red in autumn. Flowers greenish-yellow in May. Fruits bright red. The large, fleshy root is said to be eaten by the Chinese. It also contains a drug known as China Root, once valued as a cure for gout. China, Japan, Korea. I 1759.

discotis Warb. A deciduous species with generally prickly stems up to 3–4.5m long. Leaves ovate, heart-shaped at base, glaucous beneath. Fruits blue-black. W China. I 1908.

*excelsa L. A vigorous, evergreen or semi-evergreen climber with 4-angled stems and glossy green, heart-shaped leaves, purple-tinged in winter. Fruits bright red, in axillary umbels in autumn. SE Europe, W Asia. Our stock was introduced by Mrs Ala and Roy Lancaster from the Caspian Forests of N Iran in 1972 (A. & L. 15).

hispida Muhl. Hag brier. A vigorous, deciduous climber with slightly angled, densely bristly-spiny stems. Leaves broadly ovate, heart-shaped at the base, acuminate at the apex, 5- to 7-nerved, minutely toothed at the margin. Fruits blue-black. E North America.

megalantha C.H. Wright. A very vigorous, evergreen climber with stout, green, spiny shoots. Young leaves bronze-pink when they emerge in early spring, glabrous.

Mature leaves to 18 × 8cm, or more, dark green above with 3 prominent veins, blue-grey and tomentose beneath. Flowers pale green, with long-exserted anthers, in stalked, drooping clusters from the base of the young shoots in March to early April. The plant grown here appears to be male. W China. I by Ernest Wilson in 1907.

*pumila Walt. An unusual, low, trailing species with slender, rounded, spineless stems. Leaves glossy above with a dense, white tomentum beneath, 5-veined with conspicuous secondary veins, ovate, cordate at the base, to 13cm long, red-tinged in winter. Flowers yellowish, fruits red. SE USA.

SOLANUM L.—**Solanaceae**—The climbing members of this large genus make spectacular wall climbers for sheltered gardens. They require full sun and a south or west aspect and are not fastidious about soil.

crispum Ruiz & Pav. A vigorous, semi-evergreen shrub with scrambling, downy, normally herbaceous stems 4.5–6m long. Leaves ovate to ovate-lanceolate, variable in size, minutely downy. Flowers very slightly fragrant, 2.5–3cm across, resembling those of a potato, but rich purple-blue, with a bright yellow staminal beak, borne in loose corymbs very freely from July to September. Fruits small, yellowish-white. A pleasing species suitable for training on a wall and equally effective when allowed to scramble over small fences, sheds and similar structures. It is hardier than *S. jasminoides* and luxuriates in a chalky soil. Chile. I about 1830. AM 1989. **'Glasnevin'** ('Autumnale') A selected form with a longer flowering season. ♥ 2002. AM 1955.

jasminoides See *S. laxum*.

†*laxum* Spreng. (*S. jasminoides* Paxton) A slender, fast-growing, semi-evergreen climber with twining stems, in mild areas reaching 6–9m long. Leaves ovate-acuminate, glossy green and thin in texture. Flowers 2cm across, pale slate-blue with a yellow staminal beak, profusely borne in loose clusters from midsummer until checked by autumn frosts. This species needs the protection of a sunny wall. Brazil. I 1838. **'Album'** Flowers white with a yellow staminal beak. ♥ 2002.

†***SOLLYA** Lindl.—**Pittosporaceae**—A genus of 3 species of extremely beautiful, evergreen, twining plants only suitable for the mildest localities or for the conservatory; natives of SW Australia. They require a sunny, sheltered position and a well-drained soil. The following are delightful when grown against a low wall or allowed to scramble over low shrubs.

drummondii See *S. parviflora*.

heterophylla Lindl. (*S. fusiformis* Payer) Bluebell creeper. A beautiful plant with slender stems up to 2m or more. Leaves variable, usually ovate to lanceolate, 2.5–5cm long. The nodding clusters of delicate bell-shaped, sky-blue flowers are freely borne during summer and autumn. I 1830. ♥ 2002. **'Pink Charmer'** Flowers pink.

parviflora Turcz. (*S. drummondii* Morr.) This is a delightful species, differing from *S. heterophylla* in its even more slender shoots, smaller, linear leaves and its smaller, darker blue flowers, which are produced usually singly or in pairs during summer and autumn. I 1838. AM 1922.

*STAUNTONIA DC.—**Lardizabalaceae**—A genus of about 16 species of evergreen, twining shrubs, closely related to *Holboellia* but monoecious and with united stamens (free in *Holboellia*). The following requires a warm, sheltered wall in full sun or semi-shade.

hexaphylla (Thunb.) Decne. A strong-growing climber up to 10m or more. Leaves large, composed of 3–7, stalked, leathery, dark green leaflets. Flowers 2cm across, fragrant, male and female in separate racemes, white, tinged violet, appearing in spring. Egg-shaped, pulpy, purple-tinged fruits, 2.5–5cm long, are edible, but are only produced after a warm, dry summer. Japan, Korea, Ryukyus, Taiwan. I 1874. AM 1960.

latifolia See *Holboellia latifolia*.

Tacsonia See *Passiflora*.
Tecomaria capensis See *Tecoma capensis*.

†TECOMA Juss.—**Bignoniaceae**—A genus of about 15 species of trees, shrubs and climbers, natives of warm regions of the New World from the southwest USA to South America, and only suitable for mild localities. The following requires a warm, sunny wall in a sheltered position.

capensis (Thunb.) Lindl. (*Tecomaria capensis* (Thunb.) Spach. Cape honeysuckle. A vigorous, self-clinging, twining or scandent shrub with glabrous stems up to 4.5m long. Leaves pinnate, composed of 5–9 toothed leaflets. Brilliant scarlet, trumpet-shaped flowers, 5cm long, are borne in terminal racemes during late summer. In colder districts it makes an excellent conservatory climber. E and South Africa. I 1823. ♀ 2002.

*TRACHELOSPERMUM Lem.—**Apocynaceae**—A genus of about 20 species, natives of E and SE Asia with a single species in the SE USA. Given a sunny, sheltered wall, these beautiful, evergreen, twining shrubs may be successfully grown in all but the coldest localities. Their attractive, sweetly scented, jasmine-like flowers are borne in July and August. The stems and leaves exude a milky juice when cut.

asiaticum (Siebold & Zucc.) Nakai (*T. divaricatum* Kanitz, *T. crocostemon* Stapf, *T. majus* Nakai not hort.) A very beautiful species. When grown on a wall, it produces a dense leafy cover up to 6m high or more and as much across. Leaves oval, 2.5–5cm long, dark glossy green. Flowers 2cm across, creamy-white with a buff-yellow centre, changing to yellow, fragrant. Hardier than *T. jasminoides* and neater and more compact in growth. It also differs from that species in its smaller leaves and flowers, the latter with exserted stamens and longer-pointed in bud. E and SE Asia. ♀ 2002.

divaricatum See *T. asiaticum*.
japonicum See *T. jasminoides* 'Japonicum'.
jasminoides (Lindl.) Lem. (*Rhyncospermum jasminoides* Lindl.) A lovely, rather slow-growing climber up to 7m high or more and as much across. Leaves narrowly oval, 5–7.5cm long, dark polished green. Flowers 2.5cm across, very fragrant, white, becoming cream with age. It requires a warm, sheltered wall. In cold areas it is a very worthy candidate for a conservatory. C and S China, Vietnam, Korea, Taiwan. I 1844 by Robert Fortune from Shanghai. ♀ 2002. AM 1934. **'Japonicum'** (*T. japonicum* Hort., *T. majus* Hort. not Nakai) A vigorous selection, a

form of var. *pubescens* Mak., which is taller-growing with larger leaves than the typical form. When established it will clothe a wall as effectively as ivy. The leaves are downy beneath and often colour richly in winter. **'Variegatum'** Leaves margined and splashed creamy-white, often with a crimson suffusion in winter. A very pretty plant. ♀ 2002. **'Wilsonii'** An unusual form introduced from China by Ernest Wilson under his number W.776. Leaves vary from ovate to almost linear-lanceolate, attractively veined, often turning crimson in winter.

majus See *T. asiaticum* and *T. jasminoides* 'Japonicum'.

TRIPTERYGIUM Hook. f.—**Celastraceae**—A small genus of 2 interesting species of deciduous, scandent shrubs, requiring moist, loamy soil and best planted to clamber into a suitable tree or large bush or over a pergola or outhouse. They flower best in full sun, but grow freely in shade.

forrestii See *T. wilfordii*.

regelii Sprague & Takeda. A large, scandent shrub with long, reddish-brown conspicuously warty branches, reaching 6m in a suitable tree. Leaves ovate or elliptic, slender-pointed, up to 15cm long, dark green above, paler beneath. Flowers small, greenish-white, in large, brown-pubescent panicles in late summer, followed by pale green, 3-winged fruits. Japan, Korea, Manchuria. I 1905.

wilfordii Hook. f. (*T. forrestii* Loes.) A large, scandent shrub with long, angular, downy stems up to 6m long. Leaves ovate or elliptic, 5–15cm long, green above, glaucous beneath. Flowers small, greenish-white, in large, rusty-tomentose panicles in early autumn. Fruits 3-winged, purplish-red. Proving hardy here. S China, Taiwan, Japan, Burma. I 1913 from Yunnan by George Forrest. AM 1952.

Trumpet vine See *Campsis radicans*.

†TWEEDIA Hook. & Arn.—**Asclepiadaceae**—A genus of a single species. It may be grown outside only in the very mildest localities, but makes an exceptionally attractive conservatory climber.

caerulea D. Don. (*Oxypetalum caeruleum* (D. Don) Decne. A beautiful subshrub with twining stems and oblong or heart-shaped, sage-green leaves. The remarkable flowers are powder-blue at first and slightly tinged green, turning to purplish and finally lilac. They are freely borne in erect, few-flowered cymes during summer. Temperate SE South America. I 1832. ♀ 2002. AM 1936.

Vine, ornamental See *Ampelopsis*, *Parthenocissus* and *Vitis*.
Vine, Russian See *Fallopia baldschuanica*.
Vine, silk See *Periploca graeca*.
Vine, trumpet See *Campsis radicans*.
Virginia creeper See *Parthenocissus quinquefolia*.

VITIS L.—**Vitaceae**—The ornamental vines are a genus of 65 species of woody climbers, supporting themselves by twining tendrils and widely distributed throughout N temperate regions, particularly North America. They are variable in leaf and several species give rich autumn colour. The majority are vigorous and are most effective when allowed to clamber into a large tree or cover an old hedge or stump. They may also be trained to cover walls, pergolas, bridges and fences. The small, greenish flowers are carried in panicles or racemes during summer and though of little beauty are followed after a hot, dry season by bunches of small grapes. See also *Ampelopsis* and *Parthenocissus*.

aconitifolia See *Ampelopsis aconitifolia*.

amurensis Rupr. A strong-growing species with reddish young shoots. Leaves broadly ovate, 10–25cm across, 3- to 5-lobed, sometimes deeply so. Fruits small, black. Autumn colours rich crimson and purple. Manchuria, Amur region. I about 1854.

betulifolia Diels & Gilg. A high-climbing vine with ovate to oblong-ovate leaves, 5–10cm long, toothed and occasionally slightly 3-lobed, covered with white or tawny floss when young. Rich autumn tints. Fruits small, blue-black. C and W China. I 1907. AM 1917.

'Brant' (*V. vinifera* 'Brant') One of the most popular of hardy fruiting vines. A vigorous grower, reaching 9m high or more on a suitable support. It produces numerous, cylindrical bunches of sweet, aromatic grapes, dark purple-black and bloomy when ripe. In addition the attractive, deeply 3- to 5-lobed leaves turn shades of dark red and purple, with greenish or yellow veins. Often wrongly regarded as a form of the common grape vine (*Vitis vinifera*), it is in fact a seedling of multiple parentage, *V.* 'Clinton' (*V. labrusca* × *V. riparia*) crossed with *V. vinifera* 'Black St Peters'. It was raised at Paris, Ontario (Canada) in the early 1860s by Charles Arnold. ♀ 2002. AM 1970.

Claret Cloak ('Frovit') PBR A vigorous climber with purple-red young foliage later dark olive-green. Leaves white-tomentose beneath when young, shallowly to rather deeply 3–5 lobed, turning scarlet in autumn. Fruits 1cm across, purple and bloomy. Discovered at Fromefield Nurseries near Romsey in Hampshire in 1988, growing in a batch of seedlings of *V. coignetiae* of which it is thought to be a hybrid.

coignetiae Pulliat ex Planch. Perhaps the most spectacular of all vines, a strong-growing species climbing to the tops of lofty trees. The broadly ovate or rounded leaves, often 30cm across, possess a heart-shaped base and 3–5 obscure lobes, clothed with rust-coloured tomentum beneath. Fruits 12mm across, black with a purple bloom. Large, handsome leaves turn crimson and scarlet in autumn, giving a magnificent display. Best colours are obtained in poor soils or when the root run is restricted, such as against a wall. Japan, Korea, Sakhalin. C 1875. ♀ 2002.

davidii (Rom. Caill.) Foëx (*V. armata* Diels & Gilg) (*Spinovitis davidii* Rom. Caill.) A vigorous climber, its shoots covered with gland-tipped, hooked spines. Leaves heart-shaped, coarsely toothed, 10–25cm long, shining dark green above, glaucous and glandular-bristly beneath turning rich crimson in autumn. Fruits black, edible. A luxuriant vine easily recognised by its spiny shoots. China. C 1885. AM 1903. **var. *cyanocarpa*** (Gagnep.) Sarg. A variety with less prickly shoots, rather larger leaves and bluish, bloomy fruits. Rich autumn colour. AM 1906.

flexuosa Thunb. An elegant species with slender stems. Leaves roundish-ovate, 5–9cm across, rather thin in texture, glossy green above. Fruits black. Japan, Korea, China. **var. *major*** See *V. pulchra*. **var. *parvifolia*** (Roxb.) Gagnep. A pretty variety with smaller leaves which are a pleasing shade of bronze-green with a metallic sheen

above, purple beneath when young. Himalaya to C China. I 1900 by Ernest Wilson. AM 1903.

henryana See *Parthenocissus henryana*.

himalayana See *Parthenocissus himalayana*.

inconstans See *Parthenocissus tricuspidata*. **'Purpurea'** See *Parthenocissus tricuspidata* 'Veitchii'.

labrusca L. Fox grape. A vigorous, luxuriant vine with woolly young shoots. Leaves broadly ovate or rounded, 7.5–18cm wide, varying from shallowly toothed to 3-lobed, normally rather thick in texture, dark green above, white- then rusty-pubescent beneath. Fruits black-purple, edible and musky-flavoured. A parent of most of the cultivated American grapes. E USA. I 1656.

megalophylla See *Ampelopsis megalophylla*.

micans See *Ampelopsis bodinieri*.

orientalis See *Ampelopsis orientalis*.

piasezkii Maxim. (*Parthenocissus sinensis* (Diels & Gilg) C.K. Schneid.) A vigorous, but slender species with remarkably variable leaves, 7.5–15cm long. They vary from 3-lobed to compound with 3–5 oval or obovate leaflets. All are dark green above, brown-tomentose beneath. Fruits black-purple. Rich spring and autumn tints. C China. I 1900. AM 1903.

pulchra Rehder (*V. flexuosa major* hort.) A handsome, vigorous, hardy vine, possibly a hybrid between *V. coignetiae* and *V. amurensis*, with reddish shoots and roundish-ovate, coarsely toothed leaves, 7.5–15cm across. Young leaves reddish, autumn foliage brilliant scarlet. C about 1880.

quinquefolia See *Parthenocissus quinquefolia*.

riparia Michx. (*V. vulpina* hort.) Riverbank grape. A vigorous, high-climbing species with ovate to broadly ovate, coarsely toothed and usually 3-lobed leaves, 7.5–20cm across. Fruits purple-black with an intense blue bloom. A useful species, worth growing for its attractive, bright green foliage and delightfully mignonette-scented male flowers. E North America. C 1656.

striata See *Cissus striata*.

thomsonii See *Parthenocissus thomsonii*.

vinifera L. Grape vine. The grape vine has been cultivated for so long that its native country is now a matter of conjecture. Most authorities regard it as having originated in Asia Minor and the Caucasus region. Many vines grown for their fruits are hybrids between this and other species. The following clones are particularly useful for their ornamental foliage as well as fruits. **'Apiifolia'** ('Laciniosa') Parsley vine. An attractive form with deeply divided leaves recalling *Ampelopsis aconitifolia*. **'Brant'** See *V.* 'Brant'. **'Fragola'** An unusual form with small fruits with a distinct musky flavour, to some palates reminiscent of strawberries and to others gooseberries. **'Incana'** Dusty Miller grape. Leaves grey-green covered with white, cobwebby down, 3-lobed or unlobed. Fruits black. A most effective form when grown with purple-leaved shrubs. **'Laciniosa'** See 'Apiifolia'. **'Purpurea'** Teinturier grape. Leaves at first claret-red, later deep vinous-purple, particularly effective when grown with grey or silver foliage shrubs. An attractive combination may be achieved by training a specimen into a weeping willow-leaved pear (*Pyrus salicifolia* 'Pendula'). ♀ 2002. AM 1958.

vitacea See *Parthenocissus vitacea*.

vulpina See *V. riparia*.

Wattakaka sinensis See *Dregea sinensis*.

WISTERIA Nutt. (*Wistaria*)—**Leguminosae**—A small genus of about 6 species of deciduous twiners, natives of E Asia and North America. When draped with a multitude of long racemes of white, pink, blue or mauve pea-flowers, there is no climber more beautiful. May and June is the normal flowering season, but later blooms are often produced. The attractive leaves are pinnate. Wisterias are harmful if eaten. Planting in full sun is advised, and if the soil is chalky, some good loam should be added. They are excellent subjects for walls and pergolas or for growing into old trees. They may even be trained into small standards by careful cultivation. Large, vigorous specimens on walls, and so on, may require an annual hard pruning in late winter to keep them within bounds. A second pruning consists of shortening the leafy shoots in August. We would like to thank Chris Lane for his assistance with this genus.

brachybotrys Siebold & Zucc. (*W. venusta* Rehder & E.H. Wilson) A strong-growing climber, up to 9m or more and twining anticlockwise. Leaves with 9–13 oval to ovate, downy leaflets. Flowers, the largest in the genus, violet-blue to white, slightly fragrant, borne in racemes 10–15cm long. Seedpods velvety. Japan. **'Murasaki-kapitan'** (*W. venusta* f. *violacea* Rehder) Violet-blue, very fragrant flowers. Young leaves often mottled, turning yellow in autumn. This form twines in a clockwise direction and may be a hybrid with *W. floribunda*. **'Shiro-kapitan'** The form most commonly grown, usually as *W. venusta*. Large, very fragrant, white flowers. It was to this plant that the name *W. venusta* was originally given. Long cultivated in Japan. C 1912. FCC 1948. AM 1945. **'Showa-beni'** Mauve-pink flowers with a small yellow blotch. The pinkest wisteria raised so far.

'Burford' A vigorous climber, resembling *W. floribunda* in twining clockwise, but possibly of hybrid origin. Leaves with up to 13 leaflets; racemes to 40cm or more long, the sweetly scented, pale violet flowers with deeper wings and keel.

'Caroline' (*W. floribunda* 'Caroline') An early-flowering hybrid with rather short racemes to 21cm long. Flowers densely borne, slightly fragrant, with a pale violet standard, blotched green at the base shading to yellow then white, and deeper violet keel and wings. The stems twine clockwise.

chinensis See *W. sinensis*.

floribunda (Willd.) DC. Japanese wisteria. A lovely climber up to 4m or more. Leaves composed of 13–19 ovate, dark green leaflets. Flowers fragrant, violet-blue or bluish-purple, in slender racemes, 13–25cm long with the leaves and opening successively from the base onwards. Seedpods velvety. The stems twine in a clockwise direction. Japan. I 1830 by Philipp von Siebold. AM 1894. **'Alba'** See 'Shiro Noda'. **'Caroline'** See *W.* 'Caroline'. **'Domino'** ('Issai') Flowers lilac-blue, in short trusses 18–25cm long, even on young shoots. Possibly a hybrid between *W. floribunda* and *W. sinensis*, the trusses resembling the latter while the stems twine in a clockwise direction like the former. **'Honbeni'** ('Rosea', *W. multijuga* 'Rosea') Flowers pale rose, tipped purple, in long racemes. ♀ 2002. **'Kuchi-beni'**

('Lipstick', 'Peaches and Cream') Flowers pale mauve-pink, the wings and keel purple at the tips, in racemes to 45cm long. Young foliage pale green, yellow in autumn. **'Lawrence'** Pale violet-blue flowers with deep violet-purple wings and keel, in long dense racemes of numerous blooms. Young foliage pale green, yellow in autumn. Discovered in Canada in 1970. **'Macrobotrys'** ('Multijuga') Racemes very long, to 1m or more. Flowers fragrant, lilac, tinged blue-purple. Best grown on a wooden bridge, pergola or high arch to allow for the drop of the long racemes. I from Japan to Belgium by Siebold, and thence to England in 1874. ♀ 2002. **'Multijuga'** See 'Macrobotrys'. **'Rosea'** See 'Honbeni'. **'Shiro Noda'** ('Alba', *W. multijuga* 'Alba') Flowers white, tinted lilac on keel, in racemes 45–60cm long. ♀ 2002. AM 1931. **'Violacea'** Flowers violet-blue. **'Violacea Plena'** Flowers violet-blue; double.

× *formosa* Rehder (*W. floribunda* 'Alba' × *W. sinensis*) An attractive hybrid of American origin. Shoots silky downy, flowers pale violet-pink, opening almost simultaneously on racemes 25cm long. Raised in the garden of the late Professor Sargent of the Arnold Arboretum, Boston in 1905.

frutescens (L.) Poir. A rare species in cultivation with long, climbing stems and leaves composed of 5–17 ovate leaflets. Flowers fragrant, pale lilac-purple with a yellow spot, crowded into racemes 10–15cm long, borne on the current year's shoots during summer. Seedpods glabrous. Less vigorous in cultivation than the Asiatic species. SE USA. I 1724.

'Lavender Lace' This beautiful selection from New Zealand has bronze-green young foliage, the leaves with up to 15 leaflets, and twines clockwise. The long racemes, to 50cm, can have more than 100 flowers, each with a pale violet standard and deeper wings and keel. It is possibly a hybrid between *W. floribunda* and *W. sinensis*.

multijuga See *W. floribunda* 'Macrobotrys'. **'Alba'** See *W. floribunda* 'Alba'. **'Rosea'** See *W. floribunda* 'Rosea'.

sinensis (Sims) Sweet (*W. chinensis* DC.) Chinese wisteria. Perhaps the most popular of all wisterias and one of the noblest of all climbers, reaching 18–30m in a suitable tree. Leaves with 9–13, mostly 11 elliptic to elliptic-oblong leaflets. Fragrant, mauve or deep lilac flowers, 2.5cm long, are carried in racemes 20–30cm long before the leaves; the flowers open simultaneously. Seedpods velvety. A large specimen in full flower against an old house wall is one of the wonders of May. The stems twine in an anti-clockwise direction. China. First introduced in 1816 from a garden in Canton. ♀ 2002. **'Alba'** Flowers white. ♀ 2002. FCC 1892. **'Amethyst'** A vigorous form with deep bronze young foliage and strongly fragrant, reddish-violet flowers blotched yellow inside. **'Black Dragon'** The plant grown under this name has proved to be *W. floribunda* 'Violacea Plena'. **'Plena'** Flowers double, rosette-shaped, lilac. **'Prolific'** A selection with long racemes bearing numerous flowers. C 1968.

venusta See *W. brachybotrys*. **f. *violacea*** See *W. brachybotrys* 'Murasaki Kapitan'.

Wonga-wonga vine See *Pandorea pandorana*.

CONIFERS

There are few hardy, evergreen trees apart from the conifers. Their beauty, wide range of shape, form and colour, and their adaptability and valuable timber qualities render them indispensable for forest, shelter and ornamental planting. Climatic conditions being suitable, they will grow in most soils except very shallow chalky land, pure sand, barren peat or waterlogged ground; but there are species adaptable even to these extreme conditions. Some are excellent for maritime exposures and others, in particular those that respond well to clipping such as *Platycladus*, *Thuja* and *Taxus*, lend themselves to hedgemaking.

Species that start into growth very early and are, therefore, subject to injury by spring frosts are unsuitable for low-lying land and similar frost pockets. This includes several conifers from extremely cold Arctic regions. On other sites the risk of injury may be reduced by planting on the west side of shelter trees, where they are screened from the early morning sun.

The term 'conifer', as used in gardens, has a different meaning to its use botanically. In horticulture, the term is generally regarded as including all the Gymnosperms with the exception of *Ephedra* (a course that is followed here). Botanically, the conifers also exclude *Ginkgo* and the rarely cultivated *Gnetum* and *Welwitschia*.

The conifers are mainly distributed in the temperate and subtropical regions of the world (a small proportion occur at high elevations in the tropics). Only 3 species, namely *Juniperus communis* (juniper), *Pinus sylvestris* (Scots pine) and *Taxus baccata* (yew) are native to the British Isles, though many foreign species are commonly planted and sometimes naturalised.

The leaves of conifers are, with few notable exceptions, evergreen. They vary from the long, bundled needles of the Pines (*Pinus*) to the shorter, often sharp-pointed leaves of the Firs (*Abies*), Spruces (*Picea*) and Junipers (*Juniperus*). Very different in appearance are the small, scale-like leaves of the cypresses (*Cupressus*), False cypresses (*Chamaecyparis*) and Arborvitae (*Platycladus*, *Thuja*). Of the deciduous conifers the following genera are described here: *Larix*, *Pseudolarix*, *Metasequoia*, *Taxodium*, *Ginkgo* and *Glyptostrobus*.

The flowers of conifers are small and primitive and are borne in usually short, catkin-like structures known as strobili. The male and female are borne on separate strobili on the same or on different plants. Pollination is by wind. The fruits vary from a woody cone, as in pine and larch, to a fleshy, berry-like fruit as in juniper and yew.

A great deal of work on the growth and heights of conifers in the British Isles was carried out by the late Alan Mitchell, of the Forestry Commission and the author of several books on trees in this country.

Dwarf Conifers Recent years have witnessed a tremendous upsurge in the development and interest in miniature to semi-dwarf conifers. Few species are truly dwarf, they include the creeping or low-growing junipers, particularly *Juniperus horizontalis* and its cultivars, *Podocarpus nivalis* and *Lepidothamnus laxifolius* (*Dacrydium laxifolium*). Used in a broad sense the term includes all those cultivars that have originated both in the wild and in cultivation as seedling variants, or as sports or mutations; quite a few have come into being as propagations from witches' brooms, while some prostrate cultivars are the result of vegetative reproduction of horizontally growing side branches

With the reduction in size of the modern garden there is not room for the large, timber-producing species, but a miniature forest is a thing of beauty and infinite interest for every day of the year and is easy to plant to suit the size of any garden. Dwarf conifers are available in the complete range of evergreen colours and contours that exists in the full-size trees in the great pinetums and natural forests of the temperate world. They associate well with heathers and many are suitable for planting as specimens on a small lawn or a rock garden. The miniature bun forms make excellent subjects for an alpine house or for growing in troughs and similar containers.

*ABIES Mill.—**Pinaceae**—The silver firs are a genus of about 50 species of evergreen trees, widely distributed in the Northern hemisphere, reaching as far south as Central America and N Vietnam. Many of them reach a great size, particularly in the wild. They differ from *Picea* in the disc-like leaf-scars and their erect cones which break up while still on the tree. The majority of species are conical in outline, at least when young, the branches borne in more or less regular whorls, flattened in a horizontal manner. The leaves are linear and usually flattened, bearing several greyish or white lines of stomata on their lower surface and, in some species, on the upper surface too. Male and female strobili are produced on the same tree during spring. The cones are borne on the upper sides of the branchlets and, in many species, are an attractive blue-purple or violet when young. The firs require a deep, moist soil for best development. Most dislike industrial atmosphere and shallow chalk soils, the chief exceptions being *A. cephalonica*, *A. pinsapo*, and their hybrid *A.* × *vilmorinii*.

alba Mill. (*A. pectinata* (Lam.) Lam. & DC.) European silver fir. The common species of C Europe, being particularly predominant in the mountains of France, Switzerland and Germany. A large or very large tree with smooth, grey bark when young. Leaves 2–3cm long, in 2 usually horizontal ranks, dark shining green above, marked with 2 glaucous bands beneath. Cones cylindrical, 10–16cm long, greenish-brown when young, with exserted reflexed bracts. Subject to injury from late spring frosts and one of the least satisfactory species for the southern counties of the British Isles. Europe. I about 1603. **'Pendula'** An unusual tree of medium size with long, weeping branches, often hanging down the trunk. Originated as a seedling in France about 1835. **'Pyramidalis'** ('Pyramidalis Compacta') A medium-sized tree of conical habit, narrower and fastigiate when young, the crowded, ascending branches bearing short, dark shining green leaves. C 1851.

‡*amabilis* Douglas ex J. Forbes. Pacific silver fir, Red silver fir. A beautiful, large tree with silvery-white bark when

young, and small, very resinous winter buds. Leaves 2.5–3cm long, dark shining green above, white beneath, smelling of oranges when crushed, crowded on the upper sides of the branchlets, pectinate below. Cones 8–15cm long, purplish when young; bracts hidden. A rare tree in the British Isles and unsuitable for chalky or dry soils. W North America. I 1830. **'Spreading Star'** ('Procumbens') A low-growing cultivar, up to 1m high, with widespreading, horizontally arranged branches. Raised in Holland. C 1960.

arizonica See *A. lasiocarpa* var. *arizonica*.

‡*balsamea* (L.) Mill. Balsam fir, Balm of Gilead. A medium-sized tree common in North America and extending into the Arctic regions, but not well adapted for our climate. It is one of the species from which Canada Balsam is obtained. Winter buds very resinous. Leaves 1.5–3cm long, strongly balsam-scented, glossy dark green above except for a patch of glaucous stomata at tip, and with 2 narrow greyish bands beneath, spreading upwards on the upper sides of the branchlets, parted beneath. Cones 6–10cm long, violet-purple when young. I 1696. **Hudsonia Group** Dwarf shrubs of compact habit with a flattish top. Leaves short and densely arranged on the branchlets. A specimen in our nursery attained 0.75m by 1.2m in about 30 years. More lime-tolerant than the typical form. Originally found in the White Mountains of New Hampshire, USA. I before 1810. ♀ 2002. **'Nana'** A rounded, dwarf shrub of compact habit bearing short, densely arranged leaves radially on the shoots. C 1867.

borisii-regis Mattf. A strong-growing, large tree. Leaves 2.5–3cm long, dark glossy green above, marked with 2 glaucous bands beneath, crowded on the upper surfaces of the branchlets, pectinate below. Cones cylindrical, 10–15cm long, bracts exserted and reflexed. A variable species more or less intermediate between *A. alba* and *A. cephalonica*, from which it is perhaps derived as a hybrid. Balkan Peninsula. AM 1974.

× *bornmuelleriana* Mattf. (*A. cephalonica* × *A. nordmanniana*) A naturally occurring hybrid making a large tree resembling *A. nordmanniana* in habit, with branches down to the ground. Leaves densely arranged on the upper sides of the branchlets, up to 2–3cm long, green above, often with stomata at the tip, marked with 2 white bands of stomata beneath. Cones 12–15cm long; bracts exserted and reflexed. W Turkey.

brachyphylla See *A. homolepis*.

bracteata (D. Don) A. Poit. (*A. venusta* (Douglas ex Hook.) K. Koch) Santa Lucia fir, Bristlecone fir. One of the most outstanding and beautiful of the firs, forming a large tree. It is distinguished by its pale brown, spindle-shaped winter buds, up to 2.5cm long, and its 3.5–5cm long, rigid, spine-tipped, dark green leaves, in 2 ranks on the branchlets. Cones 7–10cm long; bracts long-exserted, spine-tipped, giving the cones a whiskery appearance. Succeeds on deep soil over chalk. Mts of S California. I 1852 by William Lobb. FCC 1915.

cephalonica Loudon. Greek fir. A large, handsome tree reaching 30m in the wild. Leaves rigid, sharp-pointed, shining green, 1.5–2.5cm long, white beneath, spreading more or less all round the branchlets but not as noticeably so as *A. pinsapo*. Cones 12–16cm long, with exserted, reflexed bracts. One of the best species for chalky soils

and for freedom from disease, but breaks into growth early and, therefore, should not be planted in frost pockets. Mts of S Greece. I 1824. **'Meyer's Dwarf'** ('Nana') A dwarf cultivar with horizontally spreading branches, rigid branchlets and shorter leaves. C 1963.

chengii Rushforth. A medium-sized tree related to *A. forrestii* and described in 1984 from a specimen at Westonbirt. Leaves dark glossy green, up to 6cm long, notched at the apex and with 2 pale green bands of stomata beneath, adpressed beneath the shoots, parted above. Cones pale violet when young, to 9cm long, the tips of the bracts slightly exserted. It has reached 19m in the Sir Harold Hillier Gardens and Arboretum (2000). Probably introduced from Yunnan in 1931 by George Forrest.

chensiensis Tiegh. A medium-sized tree with conspicuous rough, grey bark. Leaves 1.5–3.5cm long, thick and rigid, shining dark green above, marked with 2 grey or bluish stomatic bands beneath, arranged in a V-shaped formation. Cones 8–10cm long, greenish when young; bracts hidden. Very rare in cultivation. C and W China. I 1907 by Ernest Wilson.

cilicica (Antoine & Kotschy) Carrière. Cilician fir. Medium to large tree. Bark greyish, deeply fissured on old trees. Leaves 2–3.5cm long, light green above, marked with 2 narrow, greyish stomatic bands beneath, arranged on the branchlets in a V-shaped formation. Cones cylindrical, 16–25cm long; bracts hidden. S Turkey, NW Syria, Lebanon. I 1855.

concolor (Gordon) Lindl. ex Hildebr. Colorado white fir. A very beautiful, large tree with smooth, grey bark, grooved and scaly on old trees. Leaves up to 5.5cm long, thick, almost round in section, attractive blue-green or grey-green, arranged mainly in 2 ranks, but also standing above the shoot. Cones 8–14cm long, pale green when young sometimes purplish bloomy; bracts hidden. W USA, Baja California. I 1873. ♀ 2002.

'Candicans' A striking cultivar with vivid grey or silvery-white leaves. Raised in France before 1929.

'Compacta' ('Glauca Compacta') A dwarf shrub of compact but irregular habit, leaves attractive greyish-blue. A wonderful plant, the most outstanding dwarf silver fir, suitable for a large rock garden or as an isolated lawn specimen. A specimen in the Sir Harold Hillier Gardens and Arboretum has exceeded 2m in height and width. C 1891. ♀ 2002. **'Hillier's Dwarf'** A dwarf shrubby form, propagated from a witches' broom collected by Sir Harold Hillier during the IDS tour to the western USA in 1971. **Lowiana Group** (var. *lowiana* (Gord.) Lemm., *A. lowiana* (Gord.) A. Murr.) Pacific white fir. A large tree, the side-branches very even in length and short in comparison with the height of the tree and diameter of the trunk. It has greyish-green young shoots and smaller winter buds with the leaves pectinate above or arranged in a V-shaped formation. I 1851 by William Lobb. **'Violacea'** Leaves glaucous-blue. C 1875. **'Wattezii'** A small to medium-sized tree, leaves creamy-yellow when young, becoming silvery-white later. Raised in Holland before 1900.

delavayi Franch. A medium-sized, handsome tree of somewhat variable nature. Densely set leaves, 2–3cm long, are revolute, bright shining green above and gleaming silvery-white beneath. Cones barrel-shaped, 6–10cm long, dark bluish-violet with very slightly exserted bracts. W Yunnan, China, N Burma, N India. I 1918. AM 1980 (to K.W. 21008). **var. fabri** See *A. fabri.* **var. faxoniana** See *A. fabri* subsp. *minensis* and *A. fargesii* var. *faxoniana.* **var. forrestii** See *A. forrestii.* **var. georgei** See *A. forrestii* var. *georgei* and *A. forrestii* var. *smithii.* **'Major Neishe'** ('Nana') A dwarf, slow-growing form. Winter buds orange-brown. Leaves more or less radially arranged, 1–1.5cm long, the margins recurved. **'Nana'** See 'Major Neishe'.

ernestii See *A. recurvata* var. *ernestii.*

fabri (Mast.) Craib (*A. delavayi* var. *fabri* (Mast.) D.R. Hunt) A medium-sized tree with brown, scaly bark. Leaves 2–3cm long, dark green above, gleaming white beneath, with recurved margins, often rather loosely and irregularly arranged. Cones 6–8cm long, bluish-black; bracts exserted and reflexed. W Sichuan, China. I 1901. **subsp.** *minensis* (Bordères & Gaussen) Rushforth. A more vigorous form with longer, flatter leaves. W Sichuan. Plants grown as *A. delavayi* var. *faxoniana* belong here.

fargesii Franch. A strong-growing, medium-sized tree with glossy, purple young shoots. Leaves, scented of orange when crushed, are loosely 2-ranked, 3–5cm long, notched, dark green above, marked with 2 glaucous bands beneath. Cones 6–10cm long, purplish-brown when young; bracts shortly exserted and reflexed. A splendid species and one of the best of the Asiatic silver firs in cultivation. N China. First discovered by Père Farges and introduced by Ernest Wilson in 1901. **var.** *faxoniana* (Rehder & E.H. Wilson) Tang S. Liu (*A. faxoniana* Rehder & E.H. Wilson, *A. delavayi* var. *faxoniana* (Rehder & E.H. Wilson) A.B. Jacks.) A form with more hairy, red-brown shoots. See also *A. fabri* subsp. *minensis.* **var.** *sutchuenensis* Franch. (*A. sutchuenensis* (Franch.) Rehder & E.H. Wilson) Sichuan fir. This form differs in its shorter, pungently scented leaves and more exserted bracts. W China. I 1911 by William Purdom and again by Joseph Rock in 1925.

faxoniana See *A. fabri* subsp. *minensis* and *A. fargesii* var. *faxoniana.*

‡*firma* Siebold & Zucc. Japanese fir, Momi fir. A large tree which can reach 40m or more in the wild. The comparatively broad, stiff, leathery leaves, 1.5–4cm long, are yellowish-green above, with 2 greyish-green, stomatic bands beneath. They are conspicuously notched on the lateral branches, densely crowded, with a V-shaped parting, on the upper sides of the shoots, loosely pectinate below. The cones are 8–15cm long and are yellowish-green when young; the bracts are slightly exserted. Japan. I 1861. FCC 1863.

forrestii Coltm.-Rog. (*A. delavayi* var. *forrestii* (Coltm.-Rog.) A.B. Jacks.) A very distinct and beautiful, small to medium-sized tree. Leaves variable in length and arrangement, but usually 2–4cm long and almost radial, dark green above, conspicuously silvery-white beneath. Cones barrel-shaped, 8–15cm long, sloe-black with exserted bracts. NW Yunnan, SW Sichuan, SE Tibet. I 1910 by George Forrest. AM 1930. **var.** *georgei* (Orr) Farjon (*A. delavayi* var. *georgei* (Orr) Melville) This variety is probably not in cultivation. For plants previously grown under this name see *A. forrestii* var. *smithii.*

var. *smithii* Viguié & Gaussen. This form differs in its stout, densely hairy shoots. Plants that have been grown previously as *A. delavayi* var. *georgei* belong here.

fraseri (Pursh) Poir. Medium-sized tree with a slender, conical crown. Leaves short, 1–2cm long, crowded on the upper sides of the twigs, pectinate below, dark shining green above, with a few short lines of stomata near the tip, marked with 2 white stomatic bands beneath. Cones 3–5cm long, purple when young; bracts long-exserted and reflexed. One of the least satisfactory of the North American silver firs in cultivation and very prone to disease. SE USA, rare in the wild. I 1811 by John Fraser.

gamblei See *A. pindrow* var. *brevifolia.*

georgei See *A. forrestii* var. *georgei.*

grandis (Douglas ex D. Don) Lindl. Giant fir. This remarkably fast-growing tree quickly attains a large size. Leaves from 2–6cm long, dark shining green above, marked with 2 glaucous-grey bands beneath, spreading horizontally on either side of the shoot; they are delightfully fragrant when crushed. Cones 7.5–10cm long, bright green when young. Grows best in areas with a heavy rainfall and prefers a moist but well-drained soil. A good shade-tolerant species and moderately lime-tolerant. W North America. I 1830 by David Douglas. **'Aurea'** Leaves yellowish. C 1890.

†*hickelii* Flous & Gaussen **var.** *oaxacana* (Martínez) Farjon & Silba (*A. oaxacana* Martínez) A rare, medium-sized tree with conspicuous glabrous, orange-brown young shoots. Leaves 2–4cm long, dark green above, marked with 2 glaucous stomatic bands beneath. Cones 8–11cm long; bracts exserted. Resembles both *A. religiosa* and *A. vejarii,* at least when young. S Mexico.

holophylla Maxim. Manchurian fir. A large tree, rare in cultivation. Leaves 2.5–4cm long, bright green above, with 2 greyish-green stomatic bands beneath, densely arranged on the upper sides of the shoots, pectinate below. Cones 10–13cm long, green when young. Closely related to *A. homolepis.* NE Asia. I 1908.

homolepis Siebold & Zucc. (*A. brachyphylla* Maxim.) Nikko fir. A splendid, large tree, very tolerant of atmospheric pollution. Leaves 1.5–3cm long, green above, with 2 chalk-white stomatic bands beneath, crowded on the upper sides of the branchlets, pectinate below. Cones 7.5–10cm long, purple when young. Japan. I 1861.

× *insignis* Carrière ex Bailey (*A. nordmanniana* × *A. pinsapo*) A vigorous, large, conical tree, the foliage appearing blue-green from a distance. Leaves mainly upswept from the shoots, some spreading below, glossy dark green above with a prominent white stomatal band towards the apex and with two broad white bands beneath. Cones similar to those of *A. pinsapo.* First raised in France before 1890.

kawakamii (Hayata) T. Itô. A very rare, small to medium-sized tree with very pale or whitish, corky bark. Leaves 1.5–3cm long, bloomy at first above, later green, marked with 2 pale bands beneath, crowded and curved on the upper sides of the branchlets, loosely spreading below. Cones 5–7.5cm long, purple when young. Mts of Taiwan. I before 1930.

koreana E.H. Wilson. A small, slow-growing tree of neat habit. Leaves 1–2cm long, dark green above, gleaming white beneath, radially arranged on strong shoots, loosely arranged on others. An interesting species, producing its violet-purple, cylindrical cones, 5–7.5cm long, even on specimens only 50cm high. A tall-growing but very poor form is in cultivation. S Korea. I 1905. AM 1993. **'Compact Dwarf'** A small, compact form, spreading horizontally, without a leader. Non-coning. C 1964. **'Flava'** Cones green becoming yellow-brown, lacking the normal blue coloration. Raised in Poland in 1933. **'Horstmann's Silberlocke'** See 'Silberlocke'. **'Piccolo'** A slow-growing dwarf form differing from 'Compact Dwarf' in its much shorter leaves, mainly pointing forwards and upwards on the shoots and not radially arranged. Raised in Holland before 1979. **'Silberlocke'** ('Horstmann's Silberlocke') A slow-growing form, the leaves twisted upwards revealing their white undersides. Raised in Germany before 1983. ♀ 2002.

lasiocarpa (Hook.) Nutt. Subalpine fir. A medium-sized tree with distinctive pale greyish-green leaves, 1.5–3.5cm long, densely but irregularly arranged on the branchlets in 2 ranks. Cones 5–10cm long, purple when young. Moderately lime-tolerant. W North America. **var. *arizonica*** (Merriam) Lemmon (*A. arizonica* Merriam) Cork fir. A medium-sized tree with greyish or buff-coloured, shortly pubescent branchlets and thick, soft, corky bark. Leaves 2.5–3.5cm long, silvery-grey. Cones smaller. SW USA. I 1903. **var. *arizonica* 'Compacta'** (*A. arizonica* 'Compacta') A slow-growing shrub of compact, conical habit, leaves a conspicuous blue-grey. C 1927. ♀ 2002.

lowiana See *A. concolor* Lowiana Group.

‡*magnifica* A. Murray. California red fir. A beautiful, large tree of slender, cone-shaped habit, attaining 60m in its native habitats. Young trees have whitish bark. Leaves long and curved, 2–4cm long, grey- or blue-green on both surfaces, densely clothing the upper sides of the branchlets, pectinate below. Cones 15–22cm long, purple when young. Not suitable for chalk soils. Oregon, California. I 1851. **'Glauca'** Leaves deep glaucous-green. C 1891. **'Prostrata'** ('Nana') A dwarf form with widespreading branches.

‡*mariesii* Mast. Maries' fir. Medium-sized to large tree with persistently reddish-brown, downy young shoots. Winter buds very resinous. Leaves 1.5–2.5cm long, shining dark green above, with 2 conspicuous white bands of stomata below, crowded on the upper sides of the branchlets, pectinate below. Cones 1.5–10cm long, violet-purple when young. Japan. I about 1879 by Charles Maries.

marocana See *A. pinsapo* var. *marocana*.

nebrodensis (Lojac.) Mattei. A small to medium-sized tree, related to *A. alba*, but differing in its smaller size and the broader, flatter crown of mature specimens. The leaves are also stiffer and slightly shorter and densely arranged on the upper sides of the branchlets. Cones to 15cm long with exserted bracts. A very rare species at one time almost extinct in the wild and restricted to a few trees in the mountains of N Sicily. A specimen in the Sir Harold Hillier Gardens and Arboretum reached 12m. Coning material from this tree received the Award of Merit in 1990.

nephrolepis (Trautv.) Maxim. A large tree in the wild, smaller in cultivation with densely arranged leaves to 2.5cm long, dark green above, green or with faint stom-

atic lines beneath. Cones purple, to 7cm long, the tips of the bracts exserted from the scales. Subject to damage by late spring frosts. Korea, NE Asia. I 1908 by Ernest Wilson.

nobilis See *A. procera*.

nordmanniana (Steven) Spach. Caucasian fir. A noble species of great ornamental value. A large to very large tree, reaching 50–60m in its native habitats, with tiered branches sweeping downwards. Winter buds reddish-brown. Leaves 2–3cm long, shining green above, marked with 2 white stomatic bands beneath, densely arranged on the branchlets, pointing forwards and overlapping above, pectinate below. Cones 15–20cm long, greenish when young, scales long-exserted and reflexed. A very satisfactory, generally disease-resistant species. W Caucasus, N Turkey. I 1840. ♀ 2002. **'Aureospica'** Growth irregular. Leaves tipped golden-yellow. C 1891. **'Golden Spreader'** ('Aurea Nana') A dwarf, slow-growing cultivar with widespreading branches. Leaves 1–2.5cm long, light yellow above, pale yellowish-white beneath. C 1960. ♀ 2002. **'Pendula'** A widespreading, semi-prostrate form, the branchlets with pendent tips. C 1870.

numidica de Lannoy ex Carrière. Algerian fir. A large tree of conical habit. Leaves radially arranged, but all curving upwards, 1–2cm long, dark green above with a greyish stomatic patch near the apex, marked with 2 white bands beneath. Cones 12–18cm long, brown. Only native in a small mountainous area of E Algeria. I 1861. AM 1976. AM 1987 (for both foliage and cones). **'Pendula'** A slow growing form with pendent branchlets.

oaxacana See *A. hickelii* var. *oaxacana*.

pectinata See *A. alba*.

pindrow Royle. West Himalayan fir. A rare and beautiful, large tree of slender, conical habit. Leaves normally 3–6cm long, bright shining green above, with 2 greyish-white stomatic bands beneath, loosely arranged but concealing the branchlets above, pectinate below. W Himalaya, where it forms mixed forests with *Cedrus deodara* and *Picea smithiana* and ranges into *A. spectabilis*. I about 1837 by Dr Royle. **var. *brevifolia*** Dallim. & A.B. Jacks. (*A. gamblei* Hickel) A very distinct tree with pale brown or reddish-brown shoots and leaves 2–3.5cm long. Cones up to 12cm long, violet-blue when young. N India. C 1860. **var. *intermedia*** See *A. spectabilis* var. *intermedia*.

pinsapo Boiss. Spanish fir. A medium-sized to large tree, easily recognised by its short, rigid, dark green leaves, up to 1.5cm long, which radiate from all sides of the branchlets. Cones 10–15cm long, purplish-brown when young. One of the best species for chalk soils and one of only 2 species with radially spreading leaves, the other being *A. cephalonica* although *A. numidica* and some forms of *A. forrestii* approach this condition. Mts of S Spain near Ronda, where it is planted in the streets. Pinsapo is the Spanish name of the tree. I 1839. **'Aurea'** Leaves suffused golden-yellow. Usually a medium-sized to large shrub or small tree of rather poor constitution. C 1868. **'Glauca'** A large tree selected for its striking blue-grey leaves. C 1867. ♀ 2002. **'Horstmann'** A compact dwarf form with glaucous foliage. Originated from a witches' broom on 'Glauca' It was originally distributed as 'Horstmann's Nana' and can revert to form a tree.

'Kelleriis' A vigorous form with glaucous foliage.

var. marocana (Trab.) Ceballos & Bolaño (*A. marocana* Trab.) Moroccan fir. A medium-sized tree closely related to *A. pinsapo*. Young shoots yellowish-grey and glabrous. Winter buds resinous. Leaves 1–1.5cm long, green above, with white stomatic bands beneath, arranged in 2 horizontal ranks. Cones cylindrical, 12–15cm long, pale brown. Rare in cultivation. Morocco. I about 1905.

‡**procera** Rehder (*A. nobilis* (Doug. ex D. Don) Lindl.) Noble fir. A most beautiful, large to very large tree. Leaves 2.5–3.5cm long, bluish-green above, with 2 narrow, glaucous bands beneath, crowded on the upper sides of the branchlets, pectinate and decurved below. The magnificent cylindrical cones are 16–25cm long, green when young, with long-exserted, reflexed bracts. W USA. I 1830 by David Douglas. ♀ 2002. AM 1986 (for flower). FCC 1979. AM 1973 (for foliage). **'Glauca'** A selection with blue-grey leaves. C 1863. **'Glauca Prostrata'** ('Prostrata') A low bush with spreading or prostrate branches and glaucous leaves. Originated in our Shroner Wood Nursery in about 1895.

recurvata Mast. Min fir. A medium-sized tree closely resembling *A. chensiensis* but with shorter leaves. Leaves 1.5–2.5cm long, thick and rigid, those on the upper sides of the terminal branchlets strongly recurved, dark shining green or sometimes slightly glaucous above, paler beneath. Cones 5–10cm long, violet-purple when young. NW Sichuan, China. I 1910. **var. ernestii** (Rehder.) C.T. Kuan (*A. ernestii* Rehder) Differs in its longer, notched leaves. Some plants grown as *A. chensiensis* belong here.

religiosa (Kunth.) Schltdl. & Cham. Sacred fir. A rare tree of small to medium size with down-sweeping stems. Leaves 1.5–3.5cm long, peculiarly tapered and curved, dark green above, marked with 2 greyish stomatic bands beneath, densely arranged and forward-pointing on the upper sides of the branchlets, pectinate below. Cones 10–15cm long, bluish when young; bracts exserted and reflexed. In Mexico the branches are used to decorate mission buildings during religious festivals. Reasonably lime-tolerant, it grew in our nursery for more than 50 years and a specimen in the Sir Harold Hillier Gardens and Arboretum has reached nearly 18m (2000). C Mexico. I 1838.

sachalinensis (F. Schmidt) Mast. Sachalin fir. A medium-sized tree with leaves very densely arranged, 1.5–3.5cm long, light green above, marked with 2 greyish bands beneath. Cones 7–8cm long, olive-green when young; bracts exserted and reflexed. Less susceptible to spring frosts. Differs from the closely related *A. sibirica* in its furrowed shoots which are not densely white-pubescent. N Japan, Sakhalin, Kurile Isles. I 1878. **var. mayriana** Miyabe & Kudô. A variety differing mainly in its shorter leaves, 1.5–2.5cm long, and slightly larger cones.

spectabilis (D. Don) Spach (*A. webbiana* (Wall. ex D. Don) Lindl.) Himalayan fir. A magnificent, large, tree, closely resembling forms of *A. delavayi*. Young shoots reddish-brown, stout and rough, downy in the grooves. Winter buds large and globular, very resinous. The densely 2-ranked leaves, 1.5–5cm or occasionally 6cm long, are shining dark green above and gleaming silvery-white beneath. Cones cylindrical, 14–18cm long, violet-purple when young; bracts hidden or slightly exserted. Unfortunately, this striking species is susceptible to spring frosts. Nepal, Sikkim, Bhutan. I 1822. AM 1974. **var. intermedia** Henry (*A. pindrow* var. *intermedia* Henry) A very distinct, striking variety with leaves 4.5–6cm long, dark green above, gleaming silvery-white beneath, loosely 2-ranked. Uncertain origin. C 1870. AM 1944.

squamata Mast. Flaky fir. A very rare, small to medium-sized tree with conspicuous shaggy, peeling, purplish-brown bark. Leaves 1–2.5cm long, greyish-green above with 2 greyish bands beneath, sharply pointed, densely arranged on the upper sides of the branchlets. Cones 5–6cm long, violet; bracts with exserted, reflexed tips. It has reached 19m on the site of our Chandler's Ford nursery (1990). I from W China in 1910 by Ernest Wilson.

sutchuenensis See *A. fargesii* var. *sutchuenensis*.

× **vasconcellosiana** Franco (*A. pindrow* × *A. pinsapo*) A very rare, medium-sized tree which occurred in a park in Portugal in 1945. Resembling *A. pindrow* in general habit. Leaves 1–3cm long, slightly curved, glossy dark green above, prominently marked with 2 greyish stomatic bands beneath. Cones 12–15cm long, dark purple when young.

‡**veitchii** Lindl. A beautiful, large, fast-growing tree. Densely arranged, up-curved leaves, 1–2.5cm long, are glossy dark green above and silver-white beneath. Cones 5–7cm long, bluish-purple when young, tips of bracts exserted. This handsome species thrives better in the vicinity of large towns than most others. C Japan. First discovered by John Gould Veitch on Mt Fuji in 1860; introduced by Charles Maries in 1879. AM 1974.

vejarii Martínez. A small to medium-sized, fast-growing tree of relatively recent introduction. Leaves up to 3.5cm long, dark green above, marked with 2 grey stomatic bands beneath. Cones 5–8cm long, purple when young, bracts with exserted tips. Young specimens resemble *A. religiosa*. Mexico. I 1964.

venusta See *A. bracteata*.

× **vilmorinii** Mast. (*A. cephalonica* × *A. pinsapo*) A medium-sized to large tree. Leaves 2–3cm long, marked with 2 grey bands beneath, radially arranged but more densely so on the upper sides of the branchlets. Cones 14–20cm long; bracts exserted and reflexed at tips. An intentional cross raised in 1867 by Maurice L. de Vilmorin, whose arboretum at Des Barres was and still is one of the largest and richest in Europe. It was to M. Vilmorin that the plant-collecting French missionaries, such as David, Delavay and Farges, sent seed of so many new and exciting woody plants from China. This same hybrid frequently occurs where the parent species are growing in close proximity.

webbiana See *A. spectabilis*.

†***AFROCARPUS** (J. Buchholz & N.E. Gray) C.N. Page—**Podocarpaceae**—A genus of 6 species of tender trees, natives of E and South Africa, previously included in *Podocarpus*.

falcatus (Thunb.) C.N. Page (*Podocarpus falcatus* (Thunb.) Endl.) A small to medium-sized tree; leaves long and narrow, up to 13cm long on young plants but variable in length and arrangement. Suitable only for the mildest areas or for a conservatory. S Africa.

gracilior (Pilg.) C.N. Page (*Podocarpus gracilior* Pilg.) An attractive and elegant, small to medium-sized tree with willow-like leaves, up to 10cm long on young plants. Only suitable for the mildest gardens in the British Isles or a conservatory. An important timber tree in its native E Africa.

†***AGATHIS** Salisb.—**Araucariaceae**—A genus of 21 species of large, usually monoecious, evergreen trees with massive trunks, related to *Araucaria*, natives of SE Asia to Queensland and New Zealand. The following is the hardiest species but is only suitable for the mildest localities. The thick, scaly, resinous bark emits a thick, milky liquid when wounded.

australis (D. Don) Loudon. Kauri pine. An exotic-looking tree with thick, spreading branches. Leaves variable: on young trees they are narrowly lanceolate, 2.5–8cm long, spreading, leathery and lime-green in colour, on old trees they are shorter, oblong and sessile. Young plants are bronze or purple-flushed. Cones 6–8cm across, sub-globose. These were produced on a tree which grew for many years on chalk soil in our West Hill nursery in a cold house. Outside it grew for several years at the Ventnor Botanic Garden. It attains small tree size in the British Isles, but in New Zealand giants of 45m high, with trunks 6–7m in diameter, are recorded. Native of New Zealand (North Island) where it is of economic importance for its timber and resin. I 1823.

***ARAUCARIA** Juss.—**Araucariaceae**—A genus of about 19 species of evergreen trees found in Oceania, Queensland and S America. Young trees are remarkable for their symmetrical habit, with branches usually borne in whorls down to ground level. The long-persistent, spirally arranged leaves are usually leathery and overlapping, but vary in size and shape, often on different parts of the same tree. Male and female strobili normally borne on different trees, occasionally on different branches of the same tree. The globular or ovoid cones break up while still on the tree. Apart from the following, the only hardy species, the Norfolk Island pine (*A. heterophylla* (Salisb.) Franco) is a commonly grown conservatory plant.

araucana (Molina) K. Koch (*A. imbricata* Pav.) Chile pine, Monkey puzzle. A medium-sized to large tree of unique appearance with long, spidery branches and densely overlapping, rigid, spine-tipped, dark green leaves. Cones globular, 11–18cm long, taking 3 years to mature. One of the few S American trees hardy in the British Isles and an excellent wind resister. It grows best in moist, loamy soil. In industrial areas it loses its lower branches and becomes ragged in appearance. Extensively planted in Victorian times. S Chile, S Argentina. First introduced by Archibald Menzies in 1795 and later by William Lobb in 1844. AM 1980.

***ATHROTAXIS** D. Don—**Cupressaceae**—The Tasmanian cedars, with their small cones and usually short, thick, imbricated leaves, are unique in appearance and slow-growing. Male and female strobili borne on the same tree. Cones small, ripening the first year. Leaves of the main branchlets

are larger than those of the subsidiary branchlets. All 3 species are native to Tasmania and require a warm, sheltered position. *A. cupressoides* and *A. laxifolia* have grown here without injury for more than 55 years, but *A. selaginoides* is less hardy and can be injured or killed in a very severe winter.

cupressoides D. Don. A small, erect tree with very small, closely imbricated, dark green, scale-like leaves, obtuse at the tips and pressed close to the stems. Cones 8–12mm across. I 1848.

laxifolia Hook. A small to medium-sized tree differing from *A. cupressoides* in its laxer habit and larger, usually pointed leaves which are slightly spreading. Cones 16–18mm across, often profusely borne and then very ornamental. I 1857.

†*selaginoides* D. Don. A small to medium-sized tree larger in all its parts than the other 2 species. Closer to *A. laxifolia*, but leaves larger, up to 12mm long, more spreading, conspicuous, glaucous bands above, and a long-pointed apex. Cones up to 18mm long and broad. I about 1857. AM 1931.

***AUSTROCEDRUS** Florin & Boutelje—**Cupressaceae**—A monotypic genus closely related to and sometimes united with *Libocedrus*. Leaves scale-like, borne in unequal opposite pairs, marked with glaucous stomatic bands, forming flattened sprays. Male and female strobili are usually borne on the same tree. Cones small, solitary.

chilensis (D. Don) Pic. Serm. & Bizzarri (*Libocedrus chilensis* (D. Don) Endl.) Chilean cedar. A remarkably beautiful and distinct species, slow-growing here, but hardy and making a small, columnar tree. The branchlets are flattened and beautifully moss-like or fern-like in their ultimate divisions. Leaves in V-shaped pairs, pleasant shade of sea-green. This tree grew successfully in our nursery for more than 40 years. S Chile, SW Argentina. I 1847. **'Viridis'** Leaves bright green, lacking the glaucous stomatic bands. Similar forms can sometimes be found among seedlings.

†***CALLITRIS** Vent.—**Cupressaceae**—With about 15 species, the Cypress pines of Australia and New Caledonia are evergreen trees and shrubs thriving in dry, arid conditions. Their branchlets are long and thread-like, densely clothed with small, narrow or scale-like leaves arranged in whorls of 3. Male and female strobili borne on the same tree. The globular, ovoid or conical cones, with 6–8 scales, are often borne in clusters and persist for several years. All species are tender and should be grown in a conservatory or in sheltered woodland in mild localities.

oblonga Rich. & A. Rich. Tasmanian Cypress pine. An erect bush of medium size. Densely arranged, spray-like branchlets bear short, adpressed, scale-like leaves. Cones up to 2.5cm long, woody, with clawed scales; produced singly or in clusters. New South Wales, Tasmania. AM 1931.

rhomboidea R. Br. ex Rich. & A. Rich. (*C. cupressiformis* Vent., *C. tasmanica* (Benth.) R.T. Baker & H.G. Smith) Oyster Bay pine. A rare species that has reached 15m in Irish gardens. Branchlets finely divided, clothed with bright green or glaucous scale-like leaves. Cones ovoid, 8–13mm across, purplish-brown. E Tasmania,

Australia (Queensland, New South Wales, South Australia, Victoria).

tasmanica See *C. rhomboidea*.

*CALOCEDRUS Kurz—Cupressaceae—A small genus of 3 species of evergreen trees allied to *Thuja* and, by some authorities, united with *Libocedrus*; natives of SE Asia and North America. The branchlets are arranged in broad, flattened sprays. Leaves scale-like, flattened, densely borne in opposite pairs. Male and female strobili borne on different branches of the same tree. Cones woody, ripening the first year.

decurrens (Torr.) Florin (*Libocedrus decurrens* Torr.) Incense cedar. A large tree with a conical head of spreading branches in the wild state. Most cultivated trees belong to the form 'Columnaris' ('Fastigiata'). The characteristic columnar habit renders it unmistakable among cultivated trees and ideal as a single specimen or for grouping for skyline or formal effect. The dark green leaves are crowded into dense, fan-like sprays. Cones ovoid, pendent, up to 2.5cm long. W North America I 1853. ♀ 2002. 'Aureovariegata' A cultivar in which sprays of golden leaves occur irregularly about the branches. An attractive, slow-growing, medium-sized tree. C 1894. 'Berrima Gold' A slow-growing form with orange bark and pale yellow-green foliage, tipped with orange in winter. Ultimate height uncertain. I 1977 by Sir Harold Hillier from an Australian nursery. 'Fastigiata' See under *C. decurrens*. 'Intricata' A remarkable, dwarf form making a dense, rigid column with thick, flat and twisted recurving branchlets. 1.2m high by 0.6m wide after 20 years it has reached 3.7m tall in the Sir Harold Hillier Gardens and Arboretum (2001). Originally listed as 'Nana'. Seed raised by James Noble of San Francisco in 1938. 'Nana' See under 'Intricata'.

†*formosana* (Florin) Florin (*Libocedrus formosana* Florin) A distinct species. A small tree of open habit showing kinship with *C. macrolepis*, but differing in its more slender branchlets and bright green leaves, yellowish-green beneath. Only suitable for the mildest localities. Plants have survived several winters here, growing among shelter trees. Taiwan.

†*macrolepis* Kurz (*Libocedrus macrolepis* (Kurz) Benth. & Hook. f.) A beautiful, small, open-branched tree with broad, elegant, fan-like sprays of flattened branchlets. Large, flattened leaves are sea-green above and glaucous beneath. Only suitable for the mildest localities. SW China to Vietnam. I 1900 by Ernest Wilson. FCC 1902 (as *Libocedrus macrolepis*).

*CEDRUS Trew—Pinaceae—The Cedars are a small genus of 4 species of evergreen trees renowned for their grandeur and longevity. Young trees are conical in outline, developing often a massive trunk and large, horizontal branches as they age. They are among the most popular of all trees for specimen plantings but owing to their eventual size are only suitable for parks, open areas and large gardens.

The narrow, needle-like leaves are sparsely arranged in spirals on the terminal shoots and borne in rosettes on the numerous, spur-like side growths. Male and female strobili are borne usually on the same tree, the bright yellow males peppering the flattened branchlets in autumn. Cones barrel-

shaped, erect, maturing in 2 years and breaking up while still on the tree. *C. atlantica*, *C. brevifolia* and *C. libani* are very closely related and differ only in small details.

atlantica (Endl.) Manetti ex Carrière. Atlas cedar. A large or very large tree of rapid growth when young. Leaves 2–3.5cm long, green or grey-green, thickly covering the long branches which, though somewhat ascending at first, eventually assume the horizontal arrangement generally associated with *C. libani*. Cones 5–7cm long. The Atlas cedar is said to differ from the Cedar of Lebanon in a number of characters such as hairier shoots, larger leaf rosettes, and so on, but these minor differences are not consistent, varying from tree to tree. It is perhaps best considered as a geographical subspecies of *C. libani*. Atlas Mts in Algeria and Morocco (N Africa). I about 1840. 'Aurea' A medium-sized tree; leaves shorter than in the type, distinctly golden-yellow. Not always a satisfactory grower. C 1900. 'Fastigiata' A large, densely branched tree of erect habit, the branches sharply ascending, branchlets short and erect. Leaves bluish-green. C 1890. **Glauca Group** (f. *glauca* Beissn.) Blue cedar. Perhaps the most spectacular of all blue conifers and a very popular tree for specimen planting. Leaves silvery-blue, extremely effective. ♀ 2002. FCC 1972. 'Glauca Pendula' A superb small tree with weeping branches and glaucous leaves. Most effective when well positioned. C 1900. 'Pendula' A small, weeping tree with green or greyish-green leaves. C 1875.

brevifolia (Hook. f.) A. Henry. Cyprian cedar. A rare species of slow growth, but eventually making a tree of medium size. The arrangement of the branches is similar to that of *C. libani*, but the usually green leaves are much smaller – 1–1.25cm long, or up to 2cm on young trees. Mts of Cyprus. I 1881. 'Hillier Compact' ('Compacta') A dwarf, spreading selection with densely arranged, glaucous leaves. It was originally found in the garden of W. Archer as a plant 30cm tall and 70cm across after 20 years.

deodara (Roxb.) G. Don. The deodar is a most beautiful, large tree of somewhat pendent habit. The leaves are glaucous when young, soon deep green. It is readily distinguished from all other species by its drooping leader and by its longer leaves which occasionally measure 5cm long. Cones 7–10cm long. W Himalaya. I 1831. ♀ 2002. 'Albospica' Tips of young shoots creamy-white. An elegant tree, particularly effective in late spring. C 1867. 'Aurea' Golden deodar. A tree with leaves golden-yellow in spring, becoming greenish-yellow later in the year. C 1866. ♀ 2002. 'Aurea Pendula' Branches weeping; leaves yellow during late spring and summer, yellow-green during winter. 'Cream Puff' A large shrub or small tree with white-tipped young foliage. 'Feelin' Blue' A shrubby form with grey-blue foliage. C 1987. 'Golden Horizon' A Dutch-raised selection of spreading habit with golden-yellow foliage. C 1975. 'Karl Fuchs' An extremely hardy form with good blue foliage. Raised in Germany from seed collected by Karl Fuchs in Paktia province, Afghanistan. C 1979. 'Pendula' ('Prostrata') A form with pendent branches spreading over the ground eventually growing too large for a rock garden. Attractive as a widespreading low bush if controlled by pruning, but if permitted to develop unchecked it tends to produce a leader and lose its dwarf habit. C 1866. **'Pygmy'** ('Pygmaea') An extremely slow-growing, dwarf form increasing at about 1.5cm per year. It is of American origin, making a tiny hummock of blue-grey foliage and is best suited to the alpine-house. C 1943. **'Robusta'** A widespreading tree of medium height with irregular drooping branches and long, stout, dark blue-green leaves up to 8cm long. C 1850. **'Verticillata Glauca'** A dense-growing, small, bushy tree with horizontal branches and almost whorled (verticillate) branchlets. Leaves dark glaucous-green. C 1867.

libani A. Rich. Cedar of Lebanon. A large, widespreading tree, slower-growing than *C. atlantica* and, like that species, conical when young, gradually assuming the familiar, picturesque, flat-topped and tiered arrangement of a mature tree. Leaves green or greyish-green, 2–3.5cm long. Cones 8–10cm long. This interesting tree has innumerable sculptural and historical associations. It is a native of SW Asia and Syria and is thought to have been first introduced into England sometime before 1650, possibly 1645. ♀ 2002. **'Aurea Prostrata'** See 'Golden Dwarf'. **'Comte de Dijon'** A slow-growing, conical form of dense, compact growth, eventually making a medium-sized bush. C 1867. **'Golden Dwarf'** ('Aurea Prostrata') A slow-growing, horizontal, dwarf bush with yellow leaves. Stems sometimes prostrate. C 1960. **'Nana'** A very slow-growing, dense, conical bush of medium size, similar to 'Comte de Dijon', but with slightly broader, shorter leaves, 1–2.5cm long. C 1838. **'Sargentii'** ('Pendula Sargentii') A slow-growing, small bush with a short trunk and dense, weeping branches; leaves blue-green. A superb plant, ideal for a rock garden. C 1919. **subsp. *stenocoma*** (O. Schwarz) P.H. Davis. A conical or broadly columnar tree, intermediate in leaf and cone between *C. atlantica* and *C. libani*. A geographical form native to SW Turkey. I about 1938.

*****CEPHALOTAXUS** Siebold & Zucc. ex Endl.—**Cephalotaxaceae**—A small genus of some 10 species of shrubs or shrubby trees, best described as large-leaved yews; natives of the Himalaya and E Asia. Like the yews (*Taxus*), they grow well in shade and in the drip of other trees, even conifers, and thrive on calcareous soils. The plants are normally dioecious, the females producing large, olive-like fruits ripening the second year. They differ from *Taxus* both in their fruits and in their longer leaves which have 2 broad, silvery bands beneath. They are distinguished from the closely related *Torreya* by their non-spine-tipped leaves.

drupacea See *C. harringtonii* var. *drupacea*.

fortunei Hook. Chinese plum yew. A handsome, large shrub or small, bushy tree, wider than high, with dark glossy green, lanceolate leaves, 6–9cm long, arranged spirally on the erect shoots and in 2 opposite rows along the spreading branchlets. Fruits ellipsoid or ovoid, 2–3cm long, olive-brown. An excellent shade-tolerant evergreen. C and SW China. I 1849 by Robert Fortune. AM 1975. **'Grandis'** An attractive female form with long leaves. C 1928. **'Prostrata'** See 'Prostrate Spreader'. **'Prostrate Spreader'** ('Prostrata') A low-growing shrub with widespreading branches and large, deep green leaves. A superb groundcover plant, eventually covering

several metres. It originated in our nurseries before the First World War as a side cutting. The original plant reached 0.8m high by 4.5m across.

harringtonii (Knight ex Forbes) K. Koch (*C. pedunculata* Siebold & Zucc., *C. drupacea* var. *pedunculata* (Siebold & Zucc.) Miq.) A large shrub or small bushy tree of dense growth. Leaves 3.5–6.5cm long, densely arranged along the spreading branchlets in 2 irregular ranks, usually shorter and stiffer than those of *C. fortunei*, also rather paler green. Fruits are ovoid to obovoid, 2–2.5cm long and olive-green. They are borne on drooping peduncles 6–10mm long. Origin unknown, probably China, but cultivated in Japan for many years. I 1829. **var. *drupacea*** (Siebold & Zucc.) Koidz. (*C. drupacea* Siebold & Zucc.) Cow's tail pine, Japanese plum yew. In cultivation a medium-sized shrub, rarely above 3m, of dense, compact habit. This is the wild form, native to Japan and C China. It differs from var. *harringtonii* in its smaller size (in cultivation) and in its smaller leaves, 2–5cm long, which are ascending, creating a V-shaped trough on the upper sides of the branchlets. Large plants develop into beautiful, large mounds with elegant, drooping branchlets. Fruits obovoid, 2–3cm long, olive-green. I 1829. **'Fastigiata'** An erect-branched shrub of medium to large size, resembling the Irish yew (*Taxus baccata* 'Fastigiata') in habit. Leaves almost black-green, spreading all round the shoots. Probably derived as a sport from *C. harringtonii*. Garden origin in Japan. I 1861. **'Gnome'** A dwarf form with shortly ascending stems, and radially arranged leaves, forming a flat-topped dome. A sport from 'Fastigiata', raised in our Crook Hill nursery in 1970. **'Prostrata'** (*C. drupacea* 'Prostrata') A dwarf form with low spreading branches. Similar to var. *drupacea* except in habit. Originated in our West Hill nursery as a sport from 'Fastigiata' before 1920.

pedunculata See *C. harringtonii*.

*****CHAMAECYPARIS** Spach—**Cupressaceae**—The false cypresses are a small genus of 5 species of evergreen trees, natives of North America, Japan and Taiwan. They differ from *Cupressus* in their flattened, frond-like branchlets and smaller cones. Young trees are conical in outline, broadening as they mature. Leaves opposite, densely arranged, awl-shaped on seedling plants, soon becoming small and scale-like. Male and female strobili borne on the same tree, the males minute but usually an attractive yellow or red. Cones small, globose, composed of 6–12 shield-like scales, usually maturing during the first year. They thrive best in a moist, well-drained soil, being slower-growing on a dry, chalk soil. Unlike *Cupressus* they do not resent disturbance and may be moved even as small specimen trees.

The few species have given rise in cultivation to an astonishing number of cultivars covering a wide range of shapes and sizes, with foliage varying in form and colour. A few are really dwarf, others are merely slow-growing, while many are as vigorous as the typical form. Forms with juvenile foliage (awl-shaped leaves) were at one time separated under the genus *Retinispora*.

formosensis Matsum. Taiwan cypress, Taiwan cedar. In its native land up to 60m; in the British Isles a slow-growing, medium-sized tree of loose conical or bushy habit. Young trees have attractive, bright green foliage which becomes darker and bronzed in autumn. Leaves sharp-pointed making the sprays rough to the touch, sometimes whitish beneath, smelling of seaweed when bruised. Established trees are proving hardy. Taiwan. I 1910.

funebris See *Cupressus funebris*.

henryae See *C. thyoides* var. *henryae*.

lawsoniana (A. Murray) Parl. Lawson cypress. A large, conical tree with drooping branches and broad, fan-like sprays of foliage, arranged in horizontal though drooping planes. Leaves pointed, green or glaucous green, marked with indistinct white streaks beneath. Male strobili usually pinkish or red in spring. First introduced in 1854 when seeds were sent to Lawson's nursery, Edinburgh. Native of SW Oregon and NW California where trees of 60m have been recorded. A most useful and ornamental tree making an excellent hedge or screen even in exposed positions and shade.

Cultivars of *Chamaecyparis lawsoniana*

The numerous cultivars of this species vary from dwarf shrubs suitable for a rock garden to stately, columnar trees in many shades of green, grey, blue and yellow, also variegated.

'Albospica' A slow-growing, small, conical tree. Foliage green, speckled white, with tips of scattered shoots creamy-white. C 1884. FCC 1869.

'Alumigold' A sport of 'Alumii'; more compact with the young foliage tipped with golden-yellow. C 1968.

'Alumii' A medium-sized tree of columnar habit. Branches dense, compact and ascending; foliage blue-grey, soft, in large, flattened sprays. A popular and commonly planted cultivar. C 1891.

'Argenteovariegata' A strong-growing, broadly columnar tree of medium size with green foliage interspersed with creamy-white patches C 1862.

'Aurea Densa' A small, slow-growing, conical bush of compact habit, eventually up to 2m. Foliage golden-yellow in short, flattened, densely packed sprays, stiff to the touch. One of the best golden conifers for a rock garden. Raised at Rogers', Red Lodge Nurseries, Southampton, who produced many excellent dwarf conifers during the early 20th century. C 1939. ♀ 2002.

'Aureovariegata' A small to medium-sized tree. Foliage in flattened sprays, green with scattered patches of creamy-yellow. C 1864.

'Backhouse Silver' See 'Pygmaea Argentea'.

'Bleu Nantais' A slow-growing, small shrub of conical habit with striking, silvery-blue foliage. Raised in France and a sport of 'Ellwoodii'. C 1965.

'Blom' A dense, columnar, medium-sized bush with ascending branches and vertically flattened sprays of glaucous foliage. A sport of 'Alumii', raised in Holland about 1930.

'Blue Surprise' A slow-growing form of Dutch origin making a narrowly conical bush with striking, silvery-blue juvenile foliage. C 1968.

'Bowleri' A small, dense, globular bush. Branches very slender, spreading, drooping at the tips; foliage dark green. C 1883.

'Broomhill Gold' Similar in habit to 'Erecta Viridis', of which it is a sport, but slower growing with golden-yellow foliage. C 1972.

'Caudata' A small, rather flat-topped shrub. The crowded branches bear apical tufts of green stems and occasional long, tail-like stems. Raised in Holland before 1934.

'Chilworth Silver' A slow-growing, broadly columnar bush, with densely packed, silvery-blue juvenile foliage. A sport that originated on a plant of 'Ellwoodii' at Chilworth near Southampton before 1956. ♀ 2002.

'Columnaris' ('Columnaris Glauca') A small, narrow, conical tree with densely packed, ascending branches and flattened sprays, glaucous beneath and at the tips. One of the best narrow-growing conifers for a small garden, although 'Pelt's Blue' is proving more popular. Raised by Jan Spek of Boskoop about 1940.

'Darleyensis' A medium-sized tree of conical habit. Foliage green with a glaucous flush. Some plants grown under this name are 'Lutea Smithii'. C 1874.

'Depkenii' Medium-sized tree of slender, conical habit. Branches slender; foliage yellowish-white, becoming green in winter. Raised in Germany in 1901.

'Dow's Gem' A large bush of dense, rounded habit with bluish-green foliage in drooping sprays. Similar to 'Knowefieldensis' but larger. Seed-raised in California. C 1964.

'Duncanii' A small, compact bush forming a wide-based, flat-topped dome. Branches narrow, thread-like; leaves glaucous green. A specimen in the Sir Harold Hillier Gardens and Arboretum has reached 2.5m tall and more across after 30 years. Raised in New Zealand before 1922.

'Elegantissima' A beautiful, small tree of broadly conical habit, with pale yellow shoots and broad, flattened, drooping sprays of silvery-grey or greyish-cream foliage. Raised in our nurseries before 1920.

'Ellwoodii' A slow-growing, columnar bush of medium to large size. Short, feathery sprays of grey-green foliage are densely arranged and become steel-blue in winter. A deservedly popular and commonly planted conifer, excellent as a specimen for a lawn or large rock garden. A juvenile form raised in Swanmore Park, Bishops Waltham about 1925 and named after the head gardener G. Ellwood. ♀ 2002. AM 1934.

'Ellwood's Gold' A neat, compact, columnar form of slow growth. The tips of the sprays are yellow-tinged giving the whole bush a warm glow. A sport of 'Ellwoodii'. C 1968. ♀ 2002.

'Ellwood's Nymph' A small, columnar shrub with densely arranged, upright branches. C 1988.

Ellwood's Pillar ('Flolar') This is a narrow and compact form of 'Ellwoodii' with feathery, blue-grey foliage. C 1977.

'Ellwood's White' ('Ellwoodii Variegata') A sport of 'Ellwoodii' with creamy-white or pale yellow patches of foliage. Slow-growing. C 1965.

'Erecta' See 'Erecta Viridis'.

'Erecta Alba' A medium-sized to large, conical tree with shortly spreading, stout branches; foliage grey-green, tips of young growths white. FCC 1882.

'Erecta Aurea' A slow-growing, eventually medium-sized or large bush of dense, compact habit with erect sprays of golden foliage which tends to scorch in full sun. Raised in Holland in 1874.

***Chamaecyparis lawsoniana* continued:**

'Erecta Filiformis' Medium-sized tree of dense, conical habit. Branches ascending with long, spreading and drooping thread-like tips; foliage bright, rich green. C 1896.

'Erecta Viridis' A medium-sized to large tree of dense, compact growth, columnar when young, broadening in maturity. Foliage bright, rich green, arranged in large, flattened, vertical sprays. It normally forms numerous long, erect branches which require tying-in to prevent damage by heavy snow. An old but still very popular cultivar, often grown as 'Erecta', which is a different cultivar. FCC 1870.

'Erecta Witzeliana' See 'Witzeliana'.

'Filifera' A large shrub or small tree of loose habit, with slender, green, drooping, filiform branchlets. Less strong-growing than 'Filiformis' and without the long, projecting terminals. C 1887. AM 1896.

'Filiformis' A medium-sized to large tree of broadly conical habit. Branches whip-like, drooping with thread-like sprays of green foliage and long, slender, projecting terminals. The branches of mature trees form enormous hanging curtains. C 1877.

'Filiformis Compacta' ('Globosa Filiformis') Dwarf bush of globular habit. Branchlets thread-like, drooping, with dark green foliage. C 1891.

'Fleckellwood' Similar to 'Ellwoodii' but slower growing, the grey-green foliage irregularly flecked with white. C 1970.

'Fletcheri' A well-known and commonly planted cultivar, forming a dense, compact column up to 5m or more. Normally seen as a broad, columnar bush with several main stems. The semi-juvenile foliage is similar to that of 'Ellwoodii', but more greyish-green, becoming bronzed in winter. Because of its slow growth it is often planted on a rock garden where it soon becomes too large. A specimen in the Bedgebury Pinetum was 11m high in 1971. Named after Fletcher Bros who introduced it. ♀ 2002. FCC 1913.

'Fletcheri Somerset' See 'Somerset'.

'Fletcher's White' ('Fletcheri Variegata') A large, columnar bush with greyish-green, close foliage, boldly variegated white or creamy-white. C 1965.

'Forsteckensis' A small, slow-growing bush of dense, globular habit. Branchlets short, in congested fern-like sprays; foliage greyish-blue-green. A specimen in our nursery reached 90cm by 1.2m after 30 years. Recalling 'Lycopodioides' but branchlets not so cord-like and twisted. Raised at Forsteck near Kiel, Germany before 1891.

'Fraseri' Medium-sized tree of narrowly conical or columnar habit. Branches erect; foliage grey-green, in flattened, vertically arranged sprays. Similar to 'Alumii' and, like that cultivar, commonly planted. It differs, however, in its greener foliage and neater base. C 1891.

'Gimbornii' A dwarf, dense, globular bush of slow growth; foliage bluish-green, tipped mauve. Suitable for a rock garden. Named after van Gimborn on whose estate in Holland it arose before 1938. ♀ 2002.

'Glauca' A dense, broadly columnar tree with glaucous foliage. Similar forms commonly turn up in seedbeds and occur in the wild. C 1852. A selected form is known as 'Blue Jacket'.

'Gnome' A dwarf, very slow-growing, rounded bush suitable for a rock garden. Foliage in flattened sprays and densely branched tufts. Raised at Warnham Court, Surrey before 1968.

'Golden King' A medium-sized, conical tree with sparse, spreading branches and large, flattened sprays of golden-yellow foliage, becoming bronzed in winter. A seedling of 'Triomf van Boskoop', raised in Holland before 1931.

'Golden Pot' ('Pot of Gold') A slow-growing sport of 'Pottenii' with golden-yellow foliage. C 1968.

'Golden Wonder' A medium-sized, broadly conical tree with bright yellow foliage. Raised as a seedling in Holland about 1955.

'Gracilis Nova' Medium-sized tree of conical habit with slender branches slender and bluish-green foliage in whorled sprays. C 1891.

'Gracilis Pendula' Small tree with slender, thread-like, pendent branches; foliage dark green with a bluish bloom. C 1881.

'Grayswood Feather' A small tree of slender, columnar habit with upright sprays of dark green foliage. C 1978.

'Grayswood Gold' Similar to 'Grayswood Feather' but with golden-yellow foliage.

'Grayswood Pillar' A medium-sized tree of narrow columnar habit with tightly packed, ascending branches and grey foliage. It occurred as a sport of 'Blue Jacket' in about 1952; the original tree reached about 9m × 50cm after 16 years. ♀ 2002. AM 1969.

'Green Globe' A very dense, dwarf bush of rounded habit becoming more irregular with age. Foliage deep bright green in short, tightly congested sprays. Cut out occasional reversions. Raised in New Zealand before 1973.

'Green Hedger' An erect, medium-sized to large tree of dense, conical habit with branches from the base; foliage rich green. Excellent for hedges and screens. A seedling raised by Jackman's Nursery, Woking, Surrey, before 1949. ♀ 2002.

'Green Pillar' ('Green Spire') Conical tree of upright habit, the ascending branches clothed in bright green foliage, tinted gold in early spring. C 1940.

'Green Spire' See 'Green Pillar'.

'Headfortii' ('Headfort') A medium-sized tree of graceful habit with spreading branches and large, loosely borne, flattened sprays of blue-green foliage, silvery-white beneath. Named after the late Lord Headfort, one of the most enthusiastic growers of the 20th century, who planted a very complete pinetum at Kells, County Meath and staged an outstanding exhibit at Westminster at the Conifer Conference of 1930.

'Hillieri' Medium-sized tree of dense, conical habit. Foliage in large, floppy, feathery sprays, bright golden-yellow. Selected by Edwin Hillier before 1920.

'Hollandia' A medium-sized to large tree of conical habit. Branches thick, spreading, bearing flattened sprays of dark green foliage. Raised in Holland before 1895.

'Intertexta' A superb large tree of open, ascending habit. Branches loosely borne, with widely spaced, drooping branchlets and large, thick, flattened, fan-like sprays of dark glaucous green foliage. A most attractive conifer of distinct growth resembling a columnar form of *Cedrus deodara* from a distance. Raised at Lawson's Nursery, Edinburgh about 1869. ♀ 2002.

Chamaecyparis lawsoniana continued:

'Kilmacurragh' A medium-sized to large tree of dense, narrow, columnar habit. Short, ascending branches bear irregular sprays of dark green foliage. A superb tree, similar to the Italian cypress (*Cupressus sempervirens*) in effect, perfectly hardy and, owing to the angle of branching, remarkably resistant to snow damage. Raised at Kilmacurragh, Co Wicklow before 1951. ♀ 2002.

'Knowefieldensis' A dwarf, dense, flat-topped, dome-shaped bush. Foliage deep sea-green, in short, overlapping, plumose sprays. C 1911.

'Kooy' ('Glauca Kooy') Medium-sized, conical tree with spreading branches and fine sprays of glaucous blue foliage. Raised in Holland about 1925.

'Krameri' A semi-dwarf, globular, rather flat-topped bush with densely and irregularly arranged branches, cord-like terminal growths and dark green foliage. C 1909.

'Krameri Variegata' A sport of 'Krameri', with silver or cream variegated growths.

'Lanei Aurea' ('Lane') A medium-sized, columnar tree with thin, feathery sprays of golden-yellow foliage. One of the best golden cypresses. Named after Lane's Nurseries, Berkhampstead who introduced it. C 1938. ♀ 2002.

'Lemon Queen' A form with pale yellow young foliage. C 1980.

'Little Spire' A slow-growing, small tree of narrowly conical habit with the distinctive foliage of 'Wisselii'. From a cross between 'Wisselii' and 'Fletcheri'. Bears numerous small, brownish-red cones in spring. C 1972. ♀ 2002. AM 1995 (for flower and foliage).

'Lutea' A medium-sized tree of broad, columnar habit, with a narrow, drooping spire-like top. Foliage golden-yellow in large, flattened, feathery sprays. An old and well-tried cultivar. ♀ 2002. FCC 1872.

'Lutea Nana' A small, slow-growing bush of narrowly conical habit, eventually attaining 2m in height. Foliage golden-yellow, densely arranged in short, flattened sprays. Raised at the Red Lodge Nursery, Eastleigh. C 1930. ♀ 2002.

'Lutea Smithii' ('Smithii', 'Smithii Aurea') Medium-sized conical tree of slow growth. Branches spreading; foliage golden-yellow, in large, drooping, horizontal sprays. C 1898.

'Luteocompacta' A small to medium-sized tree of dense, conical habit. Foliage golden-yellow in loosely held sprays. C 1938.

'Lycopodioides' A slow-growing, broadly conical, medium-sized to large bush, eventually a small, fat tree. The curious grey-green branchlets are cylindrical in form and become twisted and tangled like whipcord. Seed-raised in Holland about 1890.

'Minima' A small, slow-growing, globular bush, eventually about 2m high with numerous ascending stems and densely packed, often vertically arranged, neat sprays of green foliage. Suitable for a rock garden. C 1863.

'Minima Aurea' A dense-growing, dwarf, conical bush with often vertically held sprays of golden-yellow foliage, soft to the touch. One of the best golden conifers for a rock garden. Specimens in our nursery attained 1.1m by 80cm in 30 years. Raised at the Red Lodge Nursery. C 1929. ♀ 2002.

'Minima Glauca' A dense, globular, small bush of slow growth. Foliage sea-green, in short, densely packed, often vertically arranged sprays. A specimen in our nursery attained 1m by 1.2m in 25 years. C 1863. ♀ 2002.

'Naberi' Medium-sized tree of conical outline. Foliage green with sulphur-yellow tips, paling to creamy-blue in winter, a very distinct colour shade. Raised by Naber & Co. of Gouda, Holland. C 1929.

'Nana' A small, dense, semi-globular bush, slowly growing to 2m and developing a thick central trunk in later years. Foliage dark glaucous green, in short, generally horizontal sprays. A specimen in our nursery attained 2m by 1.5m in about 35 years. It differs from the rather similar 'Minima' in its generally pointed top, thick and obvious central trunk (on old plants) and rather horizontally held branchlets. Raised in France in 1861.

'Nana Argentea' A remarkably attractive, dwarf, slow-growing bush. The inner previous year's foliage is cream, while the current season's growth is silver-grey with an occasional cream fleck. C 1884.

'Nana Rogersii' ('Rogersii') A small, slow-growing bush of dense, globular habit, old specimens are broadly conical. Foliage grey-blue, in thin, loose sprays. Eventually attains a height of about 2m. Raised at the Red Lodge Nursery. C 1930.

'Nidiformis' A slow-growing form of dense habit, ultimately a small tree. Foliage green, borne in large, horizontally flattened sprays, drooping gracefully at the tips. A specimen in the Sir Harold Hillier Gardens and Arboretum reached 6m by 3.5m. Not to be confused with 'Nidifera' which is a form of *C. nootkatensis*. C 1901.

'Parsons' A beautiful, dense, compact, dome-shaped bush, eventually of medium size. Foliage green in large, flattened, arching and drooping, overlapping, fern-like sprays. One of the most graceful of the smaller Lawson cultivars. C 1964.

'Patula' A graceful, conical tree of medium size with greyish dark green foliage in narrow, outward-curving sprays. C 1903.

'Pelt's Blue' ('Van Pelt') A narrowly conical, small tree with deep blue-grey foliage, later blue-green. An improvement on 'Columnaris'. ♀ 2002.

'Pembury Blue' A medium-sized, conical tree with sprays of silvery-blue foliage. A very striking cultivar. Perhaps the best blue Lawson cypress. C 1963. ♀ 2002.

'Pena Park' An attractive, slow-growing, widespreading bush with glaucous green foliage. The original plant in Portugal was stated to measure 2.5m high by nearly 35m in circumference after approximately 80 years.

'Pendula' A medium-sized, rather open tree of conical shape. Branches pendent; foliage dark green. C 1870. FCC 1870.

'Pot of Gold' See 'Golden Pot'.

'Pottenii' A medium-sized, columnar tree of dense, slow growth with sea-green partly juvenile foliage, in soft, crowded, feathery sprays. Very decorative. AM 1916.

'Pygmaea Argentea' ('Backhouse Silver') A dwarf, slow-growing bush of rounded habit. Foliage dark bluish-green with silvery-white tips. Suitable for a rock garden. Perhaps the best dwarf, white variegated conifer. Raised by James Backhouse and Son of York before 1891. ♀ 2002. AM 1900.

Chamaecyparis lawsoniana **continued:**

'**Pyramidalis Alba**' A small to medium-sized tree of narrow, columnar habit. Branches erect; foliage dark green with creamy-white tips. C 1887.

'**Robusta Glauca**' A large tree of broadly columnar habit. Branches stout, rigid and spreading; foliage in short, thick, greyish-blue sprays. C 1891.

'**Rogersii**' See 'Nana Rogersii'.

'**Shawii**' Dwarf, globular bush of slow growth with light glaucous green foliage in loose sprays. Suitable for a large rock garden. C 1891.

'**Silver Queen**' Medium-sized to large, conical tree with elegantly spreading branches. Foliage greyish-green, creamy-white when young, in large, flattened sprays. Not one of the best variegations; 'Elegantissima' is much better. C 1883.

'**Silver Threads**' A large shrub or small tree; foliage marked in cream and silver. A sport of 'Ellwood's Gold'. C 1974.

'**Smithii**' See 'Lutea Smithii'.

'**Snow White**' PBR A dwarf, compact shrub; juvenile foliage tipped with white. C 1982.

'**Somerset**' ('Fletcheri Somerset') A densely columnar, small tree or large bush, a sport of 'Westermannii'. Blue-grey, feathery foliage is yellowish-tinged during summer, becoming bronze-tinged in winter. C 1967.

'**Springtime**' PBR A sport of 'Ellwoodii', making a small to medium-sized, rounded bush with soft, yellow-green foliage, particularly attractive when in young growth.

'**Stardust**' An outstanding, columnar or narrowly conical tree raised in Holland. Yellow foliage is suffused bronze at the tips. C 1960. ♀ 2002.

'**Stewartii**' A medium-sized to large tree of elegant, conical habit. Branches slightly erect bearing large, flattened sprays of golden-yellow foliage, changing to yellowish-green in winter. A very hardy, popular cultivar and one of the best golden Lawsons for general planting. Raised by Stewart and Son of Bournemouth. C 1890.

'**Summer Snow**' A small shrub of bushy habit with white young growth turning to green. C 1965.

'**Tabuliformis**' A small to medium-sized shrub of dense, spreading habit with overlapping, flattened sprays of green foliage.

'**Tamariscifolia**' Slow-growing, eventually medium-sized to large bush with several ascending and spreading main stems, flat-topped when young, eventually umbrella-shaped. Foliage sea-green in horizontally arranged, flattened, fan-like sprays. One of many fine conifers raised by James Smith and Son at their Darley Dale nursery, near Matlock in Derbyshire. There are several large, attractive specimens in the Bedgebury Pinetum including one at 5.5m high and 4.5m across. C 1923.

'**Tharandtensis Caesia**' A large bush of globular habit when young, broadly conical and sometimes flat-topped when older. Branches short; foliage glaucous, in dense, curly, moss-like sprays. C 1890.

'**Treasure**' An upright sport of 'Ellwoodii' the yellow-green foliage flecked with creamy-yellow. C 1970.

'**Triomf van Boskoop**' ('Triomphe de Boskoop') At one time a very popular cultivar, growing into a large tree of open, conical habit. Foliage glaucous blue, in large, lax sprays. Needs trimming to obtain density. Raised in Holland about 1890.

'**Van Pelt**' See 'Pelt's Blue'.

'**Versicolor**' A medium-sized tree, broadly conical in outline with spreading branches and flattened sprays of green foliage, mottled creamy-white and yellow. Raised in Holland about 1882.

'**Westermannii**' Medium-sized tree of broadly conical habit with loose and spreading branches. Foliage in large sprays, light yellow when young becoming yellowish-green. Raised in Holland about 1880.

'**White Spot**' Foliage grey-green, the young growth flecked creamy-white. C 1943.

'**Winston Churchill**' A dense, broadly columnar tree of small to medium size. Foliage rich golden-yellow all year round. One of the best golden Lawsons. Raised in Sussex before 1945.

'**Wisselii**' A most distinct and attractive, fast-growing tree of medium to large size. Slender and conical with widely spaced, ascending branches. Stout, upright branchlets bear crowded, short, fern-like sprays of bluish-green foliage. The rather numerous red male strobili are very attractive in the spring. Named after the raiser, F. van der Wissel of Epe, Holland. C 1888. ♀ 2002. AM 1899.

'**Witzeliana**' ('Erecta Witzeliana') A small, narrow, columnar tree, like a slender green flame, with long, ascending branches and vivid green, crowded sprays. An effective cultivar. Probably a sport of 'Erecta'. C 1931.

'**Yellow Transparent**' Young foliage yellowish, transparent in summer with the sun behind it, bronzing in winter. A slow-growing sport of 'Fletcheri' raised at Boskoop in Holland in about 1955.

'**Youngii**' A beautiful, medium-sized to large, conical tree, with loosely spreading branches and long, frond-like, firm sprays of shining dark green foliage. One of the best of the green forms. Raised by and named after Maurice Young of Milford. C 1874.

nootkatensis (D. Don) Spach. Nootka cypress. A large tree of conical habit, often broadly so. Branchlets drooping, with long, flattened sprays of green foliage, rough to the touch owing to the sharp-pointed, scale-like leaves. A handsome specimen tree differing from *Chamaecyparis lawsoniana* in its coarser stronger-smelling, duller green foliage and the yellow male strobili in May, and perhaps more closely related to *Cupressus*. W North America. First discovered by Archibald Menzies in 1793. I about 1853. AM 1978. '**Aurea**' Medium-sized, conical tree; foliage yellow when young, becoming yellowish-green. C 1891. '**Aureovariegata**' A medium-sized tree with conspicuous deep yellow variegated foliage. Raised by Maurice Young of Milford before 1872. FCC 1872. '**Compacta**' A medium-sized to large bush of dense, globular habit; foliage light green, in crowded sprays. C 1872. '**Glauca**' A medium to large, conical tree with dark sea-green foliage. C 1858. '**Lutea**' Conical with bright yellow foliage and pendent branchlets. C 1896. '**Pendula**' A superb specimen tree of medium to large size. Branchlets hanging vertically in long, graceful streamers. There are 2 forms of this tree in cultivation. C 1884. ♀ 2002. AM 1988. '**Variegata**' ('Argenteovariegata') A medium-sized tree, foliage with splashes of creamy-white. C 1873.

obtusa (Siebold & Zucc.) Endl. Hinoki cypress. A large tree of broad, conical habit. Branches spreading horizontally, foliage deep shining green, in thick, horizontally flattened sprays. Differing from other species in its unequal pairs of usually blunt-tipped leaves, with white, X-shaped markings below and in its larger cones. One of the most important timber trees in Japan and held to be sacred by followers of the Shinto faith. I 1861 by Philipp von Siebold and J.G. Veitch.

Cultivars of *Chamaecyparis obtusa*

The garden cultivars of this species, including many of Japanese origin, are almost as numerous as those of *C. lawsoniana* and include several excellent dwarf or slow-growing forms.

'Albospica' Small tree of compact habit; young shoots creamy-white changing to pale green. C 1863.

'Aurea' A conical tree with flattened sprays of golden-yellow foliage. Introduced by Robert Fortune in 1860. See also 'Crippsii'.

'Bassett' ('Nana Bassett') A very dwarf bush similar to 'Juniperoides', but taller-growing with darker green foliage. A rock garden plant. C 1914.

'Caespitosa' ('Nana Caespitosa') A slow-growing, miniature bush of dense, bun-shaped habit, a gem for an alpine garden or trough. Foliage light green, in short, crowded, shell-like sprays. One of the smallest conifers, raised in the Rogers' Red Lodge Nursery, Southampton, sometime before 1920, from seed of 'Nana Gracilis'.

'Chabo Yadori' A most attractive, dwarf or small bush of dome-shaped or conical habit. Both juvenile and adult foliage are present in irregular fan-like sprays. Imported from Japan.

'Compacta' Medium-sized to large bush of dense, compact, conical habit; foliage deep green. C 1875.

'Compact Fernspray' ('Filicoides Compacta') A miniature, rather stunted form of 'Filicoides'. C 1964.

'Coralliformis' Small to medium-sized bush with densely arranged, twisted, cord-like, brown branchlets and dark green foliage. A specimen in the Sir Harold Hillier Gardens and Arboretum has reached 2.5m by 2.5m. C 1903.

'Crippsii' A small, slow-growing, loosely conical tree with spreading branches and broad, frond-like sprays of rich golden-yellow foliage. One of the loveliest and most elegant of small, golden conifers. Raised by Thomas Cripps and Sons of Tunbridge Wells before 1899. ♥ 2002. FCC 1899.

'Densa' See 'Nana Densa'.

'Fernspray Gold' A small to medium-sized shrub similar to 'Filicoides' but with golden-yellow foliage in fern-like sprays. Originally grown in New Zealand as 'Tetragona Aurea'. C 1970.

'Filicoides' Fernspray cypress. A bush or small tree of open, irregular, often gaunt habit, branches long and straggly, clothed with dense pendent clusters of fernspray, green foliage. A specimen in our nursery reached 2.4m high by as much through in 25 years. I by Philip von Siebold to Germany from Japan about 1860.

'Filicoides Compacta' See 'Compact Fernspray'.

'Flabelliformis' ('Nana Flabelliformis') A miniature, globular bush with small, fan-shaped branchlets of slightly bloomy, light green foliage. Very similar to 'Juniperoides'. Suitable for an alpine house or trough. Raised at the Rogers' Nursery before 1939.

var. *formosana* (Hayata) Hayata. A rare, small to medium-sized tree in cultivation, smaller in all its parts than the typical form. Distinct in its *Thuja*-like foliage, green beneath. One of the most important timber trees in Taiwan where it reaches a large size. I 1910.

'Golden Fairy' A dwarf, bun-shaped plant of rounded habit to about 50cm tall, with golden-yellow foliage.

'Golden Sprite' A very slow-growing, bun-shaped, dwarf plant, the foliage sprays tipped with yellow, shading to green at the base. Suitable for a rock garden or trough. A seedling of 'Gracilis Aurea' raised before 1967.

'Graciosa' See 'Loenik'.

'Hage' Dwarf, slow-growing bush of dense, compact, conical habit. Foliage bright green in crowded, twisted sprays. A seedling of 'Nana Gracilis' raised by the Hage Nursery in Holland before 1928.

'Intermedia' ('Nana Intermedia') A miniature, slow-growing bush of slightly loose, conical habit, with short, loose sprays of green foliage. Regarded as intermediate between 'Caespitosa' and 'Juniperoides'. Suitable for an alpine house or trough. A seedling of 'Nana Gracilis' raised at the Rogers' Nursery before 1915.

'Juniperoides' ('Nana Juniperoides') A miniature, slow-growing, globular bush with loose branches and small, cupped sprays of foliage. Suitable for an alpine house or trough. Raised at the Rogers' Nursery about 1915. AM 1980.

'Juniperoides Compacta' Similar to 'Juniperoides' in general appearance, but slightly more compact and dense as an old plant. Raised at the Rogers' Nursery about 1920.

'Kosteri' ('Nana Kosteri') A dwarf bush, intermediate in growth between 'Nana' and 'Pygmaea'. Conical with flattened and mossy sprays of bright green foliage, bronzing in winter. Suitable for a rock garden. C 1915.

'Loenik' ('Graciosa') A large shrub of compact, conical habit with bright green foliage. A sport of 'Nana Gracilis' raised in Holland about 1935.

'Lycopodioides' A medium-sized bush of informal habit often gaunt with age. Branches sparse, heavy with masses of dark bluish-green, mossy foliage becoming particularly congested towards the ends of the branches. A specimen in our nursery attained 1.8m by 2.4m in about 30 years. I 1861 from Japan by Philip von Siebold.

'Lycopodioides Aurea' A slower-growing form of 'Lycopodioides' with soft, yellow-green foliage. I about 1890 from Japan.

'Magnifica' Small, broadly conical tree with broad, fan-shaped, heavy sprays of deep green leaves. C 1874.

'Mariesii' ('Nana Variegata') Small, slow-growing bush of cone-shaped habit and open growth. Foliage in loose sprays, creamy-white or pale yellow during summer, yellowish-green during winter. In the Sir Harold Hillier Gardens and Arboretum it has reached 1.8m tall by 1.4m across. C 1891.

'Minima' ('Nana Minima') Miniature bush, forming a moss-like, flat pin-cushion. Foliage green, in tightly packed, erect, quadrangular sprays. Perhaps the smallest conifer of its kind. Suitable for an alpine house or trough. Raised at the Rogers' Nursery before 1923.

Chamaecyparis obtusa **continued:**

'Nana' A miniature, flat-topped dome, comprising tiers of densely packed, cup-shaped fans of black-green foliage. One of the best dwarf conifers for a rock garden. A specimen in our nursery attained 75cm high by 1m wide at base in 40 years. The stronger-growing plant found under this name in many collections throughout Europe is 'Nana Gracilis'. I about 1861 from Japan by Philip von Siebold. ♀ 2002.

'Nana Aurea' A looser, slightly taller-growing plant than 'Nana' with golden-yellow foliage. Perhaps the best dwarf golden conifer. Ideal for a rock garden. I from Japan by J.G. Veitch. C 1867. ♀ 2002.

'Nana Densa' ('Densa') A slow-growing, miniature bush of dense, dome-shaped habit. Foliage in densely crowded and congested cockscombs. Suitable for a rock garden or trough. A specimen in our nursery attained 60cm high by a little greater width after 35 years. C 1923.

'Nana Gracilis' A conical bush or small tree of dense, compact habit. Foliage dark green, in short, neat, shell-like sprays. Perhaps the most commonly planted dwarf conifer, eventually attaining several metres in height. It was from seeds of this cultivar that the Rogers' Nursery, Southampton, raised a selection of dwarf and miniature bun-shaped conifers, including 'Caespitosa', 'Intermedia', 'Juniperoides' and 'Minima'. C 1874. ♀ 2002.

'Nana Lutea' A sport of 'Nana Gracilis' with golden-yellow foliage, raised in Holland. C 1966.

'Nana Pyramidalis' Dwarf bush of dense, conical habit with dark green foliage in short, shell-like sprays. Suitable for a rock garden. A seedling of 'Nana Gracilis' raised in Holland about 1905.

'Nana Rigida' See 'Rigid Dwarf'.

'Pygmaea' A small, widespreading bush with loose sprays of bronze-green foliage, tinged reddish-bronze in winter, arranged in flattened tiers. I 1861 from Japan by Robert Fortune.

'Pygmaea Aurescens' Resembling 'Pygmaea' in growth, but foliage permanently yellow-bronze, richer in winter. A sport of 'Pygmaea' which occurred in Holland before 1939.

'Pygmaea Densa' A smaller, more compact form of 'Pygmaea'.

'Repens' ('Nana Repens') Dwarf bush with prostrate branches and loose sprays of bright green foliage, yellow-tinged in winter. A sport of 'Nana Gracilis'. A most attractive cultivar of spreading habit. C 1929.

'Rigid Dwarf' ('Nana Rigida') A small, slow-growing bush of stiff, rigid, almost columnar habit. Foliage almost black-green, with conspicuous white markings beneath, in shell-like sprays. Most effective among the bun-shaped clones. C 1964.

'Sanderi' See *Platycladus orientalis* 'Sanderi'.

'Spiralis' ('Contorta', 'Nana Spiralis') A dwarf, ascending bush with attractively twisted branchlets, resembling 'Nana' as a young plant. A specimen in our nursery attained 75cm by 45cm in about 30 years. Raised at the Rogers' Nursery before 1930.

'Suiroya-hiba' Medium-sized shrub of loose habit with long cord-like branchlets, often curiously twisted and contorted. C 1971.

'Tempelhof' A dense, conical bush of small to medium size. Foliage deep green, in broad, dense, shell-like sprays. Found in the Tempelhof nurseries in Holland before 1965.

'Tetragona Aurea' An unusual, large shrub or small tree of angular appearance. Branches sparse, usually wide-spreading, thickly covered with golden-yellow, moss-like sprays of foliage. A very distinct and attractive cultivar which associates well with heathers. The green form 'Tetragona', which is said to have been introduced at the same time, now appears lost to cultivation. In our opinion both may have arisen as sports of 'Filicoides', the Fernspray cypress. I about 1870 from Japan. FCC 1876.

'Tonia' A dwarf sport of 'Nana Gracilis'. A dense, small bush of irregular habit, the shoots occasionally white-tipped. Raised in Holland about 1928.

'Tsatsumi' A small, globular bush of loose habit, with slender, thread-like branchlets and drooping sprays of foliage. C about 1910.

pisifera (Siebold & Zucc.) Endl. Sawara cypress. A large tree of broadly conical habit, with spreading branches and horizontally flattened sprays of dark green foliage. The sharply pointed, scale-like leaves, with white markings below, plus its small cones, 6mm across, distinguish it from other species. Japan. I 1861 by Robert Fortune. FCC 1861.

Cultivars of *Chamaecyparis pisifera*

This species has given rise to numerous cultivars, many of which have juvenile foliage.

'Argenteovariegata' ('Albovariegata') A medium-sized tree with foliage speckled silvery-white. I 1861 from Japan by Robert Fortune.

'Aurea' Young foliage yellow, passing to soft green during summer. I 1861 from Japan by Robert Fortune. FCC 1862.

'Aurea Nana' See 'Strathmore'.

'Aureovariegata' A slow-growing, small tree or large bush with golden variegated foliage. C 1874.

'Boulevard' ('Cyanoviridis') An outstanding, medium-sized bush of dense, conical habit. Foliage steel-blue, soft to the touch, becoming attractively purple-tinged in winter. A juvenile form which originated as a sport of 'Squarrosa' in the Boulevard nurseries, USA about 1934. It has become one of the most popular of all conifers. ♀ 2002.

'Cyanoviridis' See 'Boulevard'.

'Filifera' A small to medium-sized tree or large shrub of broadly conical habit, usually broader than high. Branches spreading, with long, drooping, whip-like branchlets and string-like sprays of green foliage. I 1861 from Japan by Robert Fortune.

'Filifera Aurea' Smaller and slower-growing than 'Filifera', making a medium-sized to large bush with attractive, golden-yellow foliage. Can burn in full sun. See also 'Sungold'. C 1889. ♀ 2002.

'Filifera Aureovariegata' A small to medium-sized bush. The whip-like branches, and branchlets are splashed with sections of yellow foliage. C 1891.

'Filifera Nana' A dense, rounded, flat-topped, dwarf bush with long, string-like branchlets. Suitable for a rock garden. C 1897.

Chamaecyparis pisifera **continued:**

'**Filifera Nana Aurea**' See 'Golden Mop'.

'**Golden Mop**' ('Filifera Nana Aurea', 'Filifera Aurea Nana') Small, dense-growing, bright golden form of 'Filifera Nana'. ♀ 2002.

'**Gold Spangle**' Small, densely conical tree with both loose and congested sprays of golden-yellow foliage. A sport of 'Filifera Aurea'. Reverting shoots should be removed. C 1900.

'**Nana**' A dwarf, slow-growing bush forming a flat-topped dome with crowded, flattened sprays of dark green foliage. Old specimens will form a top tier, resembling a cottage loaf. A very consistent cultivar. A specimen in our nursery attained 60cm by 1.4m after about 30 years. C 1891.

'**Nana Aureovariegata**' Similar in habit to 'Nana', but foliage possessing a golden tinge. Excellent for a rock garden. C 1867.

'**Nana Variegata**' Similar to 'Nana', but foliage flecked with a creamy-white variegation. C 1867.

'**Parslorii**' ('Nana Parslorii') A dense, dwarf shrub of flattened, bun-shaped habit, with foliage in short, crowded sprays. Suitable for a rock garden.

'**Plumosa**' A small to medium-sized, conical tree or large, compact bush with densely packed branchlets and plumose sprays of bright green, juvenile foliage, soft to the touch. I 1861 from Japan by J.G. Veitch. FCC 1866.

'**Plumosa Albopicta**' Foliage speckled with white, otherwise similar to 'Plumosa'. C 1855.

'**Plumosa Aurea**' Young growths bright yellow deepening with age to soft yellow-green, stained bronze-yellow. I 1861 from Japan by Robert Fortune.

'**Plumosa Aurea Compacta**' Dwarf, dense, conical bush of slow growth. Foliage soft yellow, more especially in spring. C 1891.

'**Plumosa Aurescens**' A small conical tree with plumose branchlets, the tips of which are light yellow in summer, bluish-green in autumn. C 1900.

'**Plumosa Compressa**' A dwarf, slow-growing, rather flat-topped bush, usually forming a tight, rounded bun with both 'Plumosa' and 'Squarrosa' foliage which, on young plants, is crisped and moss-like. A sport of 'Squarrosa' raised in Holland before 1929. AM 1925.

'**Plumosa Compressa Aurea**' Similar to 'Plumosa Compressa', but foliage gold-tinged in summer.

'**Plumosa Flavescens**' A small, conical bush with foliage similar to 'Plumosa' but pale sulphur-yellow when young. I about 1866 by Philip von Siebold from Japan.

'**Plumosa Juniperoides**' Similar to 'Plumosa Compressa' but more vigorous and open. Foliage golden-yellow when young, later green. C 1963.

'**Plumosa Pygmaea**' ('Pygmaea') Small, slow-growing bush of compact, conical habit with densely crowded juvenile foliage. C 1939.

'**Plumosa Rogersii**' A small, upright bush with golden-yellow foliage which in its long needles is closer to 'Squarrosa'. A sport of 'Plumosa Aurea' raised by the Rogers' Nursery about 1930.

'**Pygmaea**' See 'Plumosa Pygmaea'.

'**Snow**' ('Squarrosa Snow') A dwarf, bun-shaped bush with mossy, blue-grey foliage tipped creamy-white,

green in winter. Tends to burn in full sun or cold wind. It has reached 60cm tall by 1m across in the Sir Harold Hillier Gardens and Arboretum. Raised in Japan before 1971.

'**Squarrosa**' A small to medium-sized tree of broadly conical outline, with spreading branches and dense, billowy sprays of glaucous juvenile foliage, soft to the touch. A commonly planted cultivar. I 1861 from Japan by J.G. Veitch. FCC 1862.

'**Squarrosa Aurea Nana**' A dwarf, slow-growing form of dense, compact habit with yellow foliage, paling in winter.

'**Squarrosa Boulevard**' See 'Boulevard'.

'**Squarrosa Dumosa**' Foliage similar to 'Squarrosa' but a compact, dwarf, rounded bush; foliage grey-green, bronzing in winter. It was found in Berlin Botanic Garden before 1891.

'**Squarrosa Intermedia**' ('Squarrosa Minima', 'Squarrosa Argentea Pygmaea', 'Dwarf Blue') A dense, dwarf, globular bush with dense, congested, greyish-blue, juvenile foliage through which occasional longer shoots protrude. An unsatisfactory plant unless trimmed annually. C 1923.

'**Squarrosa Lombarts**' A dwarf rounded shrub with pale blue juvenile foliage. C 1970.

'**Squarrosa Sulphurea**' Similar to 'Squarrosa' in habit; foliage sulphur-yellow, especially in spring. C before 1894. AM 1894.

'**Strathmore**' Dwarf, slow-growing form of flattened, globular habit. One of the most consistent, rich yellow, dwarf conifers; suitable for a rock garden. Origin uncertain, long grown as 'Aurea Nana' which is probably no longer in cultivation.

'**Sungold**' Similar to 'Filifera Aurea' but not as bright yellow and withstands full sun. C 1969.

‡*thyoides* (L.) Britton, Sterns & Poggenb. White cypress. A conical tree, small to medium-sized in the British Isles. Branchlets bearing erect, fan-shaped sprays of aromatic, glaucous green foliage. Cones small and bloomy. Unsuitable for shallow chalk soils. E USA. I 1736 by Peter Collinson. '**Andelyensis**' ('Leptoclada') A medium-sized to large, slow-growing bush of dense, narrowly columnar habit, with short sprays of dark bluish-green adult and juvenile foliage. Attractive in late winter when peppered with tiny, red male strobili. A specimen in the Bedgebury Pinetum was 6m high in 1971. Raised at Les Andelys, France about 1850. FCC 1863. '**Andelyensis Nana**' ('Leptoclada Nana') A small shrub of slow growth with mostly juvenile foliage, forming a dense, rather flat-topped bush. A specimen in our nursery attained 1.1m by 90cm after about 30 years. C 1939. '**Aurea**' A slow-growing form, the foliage bright yellow in summer, bronzing in winter. C 1872. '**Conica**' A slow-growing, dwarf bush of dense, conical habit with both sea-green adult and some juvenile foliage which turns bronze-purple in winter. Differs from 'Andelyensis' in its much slower growth and from 'Andelyensis Nana' in its conical habit. C 1949. '**Ericoides**' An attractive, small, compact, conical form with sea-green juvenile foliage, soft to the touch, becoming bronze or plum-purple in winter. C 1840. ♀ 2002. '**Glauca**' ('Kewensis') Foliage glaucous-blue. C 1847. '**Heatherbun**' ('Purple

Heather') A slow-growing, dwarf bush of bun-shaped habit. Grey-green juvenile foliage turns to deep plum-purple in winter. **var.** *henryae* (H.L. Li) Little (*C. henryae* H.L. Li) An interesting medium-sized tree, differing in its smoother bark, less flattened branchlets and the much lighter yellowish-green foliage, especially pronounced on young specimens. Leaves also differ in being slightly larger and more adpressed. Juvenile leaves are green, not glaucous beneath. Male strobili are pale, not dark, and the cones are slightly larger and green, or only slightly glaucous. Large specimens are said to resemble more *C. nootkatensis* than *C. thyoides*. Named after that indefatigable traveller and collector of American plants the late Mrs J. Norman Henry, who first collected it and from whom we received this plant in 1968. Coastal plains of Florida, Alabama and Mississippi. **'Purple Heather'** See 'Heatherbun'. **'Red Star'** See 'Rubicon'. **'Rubicon'** ('Red Star') A dwarf, upright bush of compact habit. The juvenile foliage turns plum-purple in winter. C 1972. **'Variegata'** Foliage speckled with yellow. C 1831.

*CRYPTOMERIA** D. Don—**Cupressaceae**—A monotypic genus. Male and female strobili borne on the same tree, the males orange or reddish in March. Cones solitary, globular, maturing the first year.

fortunei See *C. japonica*.

japonica (Thunb. ex L. f.) D. Don (*C. japonica* var. *sinensis* Siebold & Zucc., *C. fortunei* Hooibr. ex Otto & Dietr.) Japanese cedar. A large, fast-growing, broadly columnar tree with reddish, shredding bark and spreading or decurved branches. Leaves awl-shaped, densely crowded on long, slender branchlets. It resembles the wellingtonia (*Sequoiadendron giganteum*), but its leaves are longer and its bark has not the spongy thickness of the American tree. Easily cultivated and thriving best in moist soils. There are many cultivars. Japan, cultivated in China. I 1842. ♀ 2002. **'Araucarioides'** See under 'Viminalis'. **'Bandai-sugi'** A small, slow-growing, compact bush becoming more irregular in old age. Foliage in congested, moss-like clusters with intermittent normal growth, turning bronze in very cold weather. C 1939. ♀ 2002. **'Compressa'** A dwarf bush of very slow growth similar to 'Vilmoriniana', forming a compact, rather flat-topped globe. Foliage densely crowded, turning reddish-purple in winter. Suitable for a rock garden or scree. 'Birodo-sugi' appears identical. I from Japan to Holland in 1942. **'Cristata'** A conical bush eventually making a small to medium-sized tree. Many of the branches are flattened (fasciated) into great cockscomb-like growths. C 1901. **'Elegans'** A beautiful form of tall, bushy habit, eventually making a small tree. Soft, feathery juvenile foliage is retained throughout its life and becomes an attractive red-bronze during autumn and winter. I 1854 by Thomas Lobb from Japan. FCC 1862. **'Elegans Aurea'** A large shrub similar to 'Elegans' but slower-growing with yellow-green foliage, bronzing only in very cold weather. C 1935. **'Elegans Compacta'** A very dense, slow-growing, small shrub with juvenile foliage, bronze in winter. Differs from 'Elegans Nana' in its tighter habit and straight leaves, which are fairly stiff to the touch. C 1923. ♀ 2002. **'Elegans Nana'** A slower-growing, smaller

shrub than 'Elegans', with even softer, more plumose foliage, forming a medium-sized billowy bush. Leaves turn rich purple in winter. A sport of 'Elegans'. C 1881. **'Globosa'** A small, dense, dome-shaped bush of neat and compact habit. Foliage adult, rust-red in winter. Ideal for a large rock garden attaining about 60cm by 80cm in 15 years. C 1923. **'Globosa Nana'** A dwarf, dense, flat-topped bush of slow growth. Branchlets and foliage similar to 'Lobbii'. Numerous, somewhat arching branchlets fan out to make a perfect low dome. Originally listed as 'Lobbii Nana'. ♀ 2002. **'Jindai-Sugi'** A small, dense, slow-growing bush developing an irregular but rather flattened top. Foliage cheerful bright green, densely crowded. A specimen in our nursery attained 1.2m by 1.2m in 25 years. I from Japan before 1932. **'Knaptonensis'** See under 'Nana Albospica'. **'Lobbii'** A very desirable, medium-sized to large, conical tree, differing from the type in its longer branchlets more clustered at the ends of the shorter branches. Leaves deep rich green and more adpressed to the shoots. I about 1850 by Thomas Lobb. **'Lobbii Nana'** See under 'Globosa Nana'. **'Lycopodioides'** See under 'Viminalis'. **'Midare-sugi'** A small bush of loose growth resembling 'Elegans' in foliage, except for the scattered bunches of congested growths at the base of the shoots. **'Monstrosa'** A medium-sized bush up to 3m. Growth irregular, shoots long at first, then becoming dense and crowded, forming large, congested clusters over the whole plant. C 1909. **'Nana'** A small, slow-growing, compact bush with slender branchlets ending in recurved tips. C 1850. **'Nana Albospica'** ('Albovariegata', 'Argenteovariegata') A dwarf, slow-growing, flat-topped bush. Foliage green, young growths creamy-white. The creamy tips are often browned by sun or frost and a sheltered position is desirable. 'Knaptonensis' is very similar in general appearance, being perhaps a little more compact and slower-growing. **'Pygmaea'** A slow-growing, eventually compact, small bush of dense, irregular habit. Branchlets short and drooping, borne in congested clusters at the shoot tips. Has been confused with 'Nana' but differs in its much more compact growth and its outer foliage turning rich bronze-red in winter. C 1850. **'Pyramidata'** A conical bush or small tree of rather open growth, with small, densely packed leaves concealing the slender branchlets. C 1891. **'Rasen-sugi'** Similar to 'Spiraliter Falcata' but much more vigorous with more tightly curled leaves and lacking the normal foliage often found on the shoots. **'Sekkan-sugi'** A small tree with pale creamy-yellow young foliage. **'Selaginoides'** See under 'Viminalis'. **var.** *sinensis* See *C. japonica*. **'Spiralis'** Grannies' ringlets. There is a large tree of this cultivar in the gardens at Nymans in Sussex and at Fota in SW Ireland, but as grown in general cultivation, it forms a small, slow-growing bush of dense, spreading habit. The leaves are spirally twisted around the stems. The whole bush is a pleasant, bright green. I 1860 from Japan. **'Spiraliter Falcata'** ('Spiralis Elongata') Similar in effect to 'Spiralis', but with longer, thinner, almost whip-cord-like branchlets with pendent tips. A medium-sized bush of loose growth. C 1876. **'Vilmoriniana'** An exceedingly slow-growing, dwarf bush with very small, crowded branchlets and leaves, forming a dense, rigid globe. Turning reddish-purple in winter. This is one of the most popular dwarf conifers for rock gardens. It is very similar to 'Compressa', but its leaves are a little shorter and more congested on the branchlets. A specimen in our nursery attained 60cm by 1m in about 30 years. Raised in France by M de Vilmorin in 1890 from Japanese seed. ♀ 2002. **'Viminalis'** A large, irregular bush with long, whip-like branches bearing terminal whorls of elong-ated branchlets. A specimen in our nursery attained 4.6m × 4.6m in about 40 years. 'Araucarioides', 'Athrotaxoides', 'Lycopodioides' and 'Selaginoides' are very similar, some appearing identical.

***CUNNINGHAMIA** R. Br. ex Rich. & A. Rich.—**Cupress-aceae**—A small genus comprising 2 species of very distinct trees recalling *Araucaria.* They are fairly hardy, but thrive best in a sheltered position. Male and female strobili are borne on the same tree. The whorled branches are densely clothed with spirally arranged leaves, twisted at the base so as to appear in 2 ranks.

†*konishii* Hayata. A small tree mainly differing from *C. lanceolata* in its smaller leaves and cones. Young plants of both species are very similar. As may be expected this tree is less hardy than the Chinese fir and is not suitable for the colder areas of the British Isles. Taiwan, S China to Vietnam. I 1910. AM 1980.

lanceolata (Lamb.) Hook. (*C. sinensis* R. Br. ex Rich. & A. Rich.) Chinese fir. A small to medium-sized, exotic-looking, hardy tree. Leaves lanceolate, 3–7cm long, irregularly arranged, emerald-green above, marked with 2 white bands of stomata beneath, becoming dark and bronzy by autumn. Cones usually in clusters, ovoid or rounded, 3–4cm across. It would be unwise to plant this tree in a windswept site. C and S China, Vietnam. I 1804 by William Kerr. AM 1977. **'Glauca'** Leaves with a conspicuous glaucous bloom. A particularly hardy form with very lush foliage.

*× **CUPRESSOCYPARIS** Dallim. (*Cupressus* × *Chamaecyparis*)—**Cupressaceae**—Interesting intergeneric hybrids, all of which have arisen in cultivation. They are extremely fast-growing trees with many uses, and include some of the most popular conifers. Their requirements are similar to those of *Chamaecyparis.*

leylandii (Dallim. & A.B. Jacks.) Dallim. (*Chamaecyparis nootkatensis* × *Cupressus macrocarpa*) Leyland cypress. A large, noble tree of dense, columnar habit, extremely vigorous in growth. Foliage borne in flattened or irregular, slightly drooping sprays, similar to those of *C. nootkatensis*, but less strong-smelling when bruised. In general appearance it resembles more the *C. nootkatensis* parent; the cones are intermediate. It is the fastest-growing conifer in the British Isles, indeed the fastest-growing evergreen, apart from some *Eucalyptus* species. Even on a relatively poor site plants from cuttings have reached 15m in 16 years. Such is its vigour and adaptability that it is unsurpassed for tall screens but is generally too vigorous to be used for hedging in a small garden. When trimmed it is important that only the young growth is cut into. It is tolerant of a wide range of conditions including coastal areas and chalk soils. May cause a skin allergy. ♀ 2002. **'Castlewellan'** ('Galway Gold')

Young foliage golden-yellow on small plants tending to become bronzy-green with age. Slower-growing and more suitable for hedging than the green forms. A seedling raised at Castlewellan, Co Down in 1962. The female parent was *Cupressus macrocarpa* 'Lutea' while the male parent was *Chamaecyparis nootkatensis* 'Lutea'. **'Galway Gold'** See 'Castlewellan'. **'Gold Rider'** Raised from a sport found in Holland, this has foliage of a much better yellow than other forms such as 'Castlewellan'. It stands full sun and does not burn. ♀ 2002. **'Green Spire'** (Clone 1) A dense, narrow column of bright green foliage, arranged in irregular sprays. Eventually very similar to 'Haggerston Grey'. Raised at Leighton Hall in 1888. **'Haggerston Grey'** (Clone 2) Perhaps the commonest clone in cultivation and more open in growth than 'Leighton Green'. Foliage green or with a slight pale grey cast, arranged in dense, irregular sprays. Raised at Leighton Hall in 1888. **'Harlequin'** A sport of 'Haggerston Grey' which occurred at Weston Park, found by the late Lord Bradford in 1975. Foliage flecked with creamy-white. **'Hyde Hall'** The first dwarf Leyland and the best form for small gardens. A conical shrub of upright habit with bright green foliage. **'Leighton Green'** (Clone 11) One of the clones most commonly propagated. It forms a tall column of green foliage arranged in more or less flattened fern-like sprays. Cones often present. Raised at Leighton Hall in 1911. **'Naylor's Blue'** (Clone 10) A narrow, columnar tree with greyish-green foliage, most noticeably glaucous during winter, arranged in more or less irregular sprays. Raised at Leighton Hall in 1911. **'Olive's Green'** A form of dense, bushy habit, with soft green foliage. A sport of 'Castlewellan' discovered by the late Olive Greeves in Northern Ireland in 1984. **'Picturesque'** An unusual form of vigorous growth with twisted branches. It was originally grown as *Cupressus macrocarpa* 'Tortuosa'. **'Robinson's Gold'** Similar to 'Castlewellan' but a better colour. The foliage resembles 'Leighton Green'. A seedling raised at Belvoir Castle, Co Down in about 1962 and named after the head gardener who found it. ♀ 2002. **'Rostrevor'** A form similar to 'Leighton Green' but more vigorous. It is now believed to be the earliest form of the hybrid. It derives from a tree that used to grow at Rostrevor, Co Down, Ireland and probably originated about 1870. The cross later occurred at Leighton Hall, Powys, Wales in 1888 (6 seedlings) and again in 1911 (2 seedlings), also in a garden at Ferndown, Dorset in 1940 (2 seedlings). AM 1941. **'Silver Dust'** Foliage conspicuously blotched with creamy-white. Originated at the US National Arboretum, Washington, DC in 1960 as a sport of a plant of 'Leighton Green' which had been supplied by us. I to England in 1966. **'Stapehill'** A dense columnar tree with flattened sprays of green foliage.

notabilis A.F. Mitch. (*Cupressus arizonica* var. *glabra* × *Chamaecyparis nootkatensis*) An attractive, medium-sized tree, raised at the Forestry Commission's Research Station at Alice Holt Lodge, Surrey. The original seed was collected in 1956 from a specimen of *Cupressus arizonica* var. *glabra* growing at Leighton Hall, Powys. In 1970 the original 2 seedlings were reported as being 9m and 7.5m tall respectively, and growing fast. Trees have since reached 12m and are described by A.F. Mitchell as having sinuous, upswept branches draped with flattened sprays of dark grey-green foliage. AM 1986.

ovensii A.F. Mitch. (*Cupressus lusitanica* × *Chamaecyparis nootkatensis*) An interesting hybrid raised by Mr H. Ovens in his nursery at Talybont, Dyfed, from seed collected in 1961 from a specimen of *Cupressus lusitanica* growing in Silkwood, Westonbirt Arboretum, Gloucestershire. This hybrid exhibits a strong influence of the Nootka parent and produces large, flattened sprays of drooping, dark, glaucous green foliage. It promises to reach a medium size and has exceeded 10m in cultivation.

*CUPRESSUS L.—**Cupressaceae**—The cypresses are a genus of about 17 or so species of evergreen trees of mostly conical or columnar habit. Male and female strobili borne on the same tree, the males often quite effective in the mass. Cones globular, composed of 6–12 shield-like scales, maturing during their second year, becoming woody and remaining on the branches often for several years. They do not take kindly to clipping. The species of *Cupressus* differ from those of *Chamaecyparis* in their irregular, rounded or quadrangular branchlet systems and larger cones, and on the whole they are less hardy. They do not transplant easily from the open ground, hence young trees are pot-grown. They are tolerant of a wide range of soil conditions (excepting wet soils) and several species will grow even in shallow chalk soils.

abramsiana See *C. goveniana* var. *abramsiana*.

arizonica Greene. Arizona cypress. A small to medium-sized tree of dense conical or broadly columnar habit with grey and brown, stringy and slightly ridged bark. Foliage green. Cones 1–2.5cm across, globose, the scales with prominent bosses. SW USA, N Mexico. A rare and graceful species in cultivation, most trees grown under this name are var. *glabra*. **'Arctic'** A small tree with emerald-green foliage, the young growth silvery-white. Originated in New Zealand before 1983. **var. *bonita*** See *C. arizonica* var. *glabra*. **var. *glabra*** (Sudw.) Little (*C. arizonica* hort. not Greene, *C. arizonica* var. *bonita* Lemmon) Smooth Arizona cypress. A small to medium-sized tree of dense, conical habit with ascending branches and attractive, peeling, red bark, blistering and purple with age. Foliage greyish-green or grey, resin-speckled. Cones globular, 2–3cm long, with prominent bosses. A common tree in cultivation, usually under the name *C. arizonica*, which differs mainly in its usually green foliage and less attractive bark. C Arizona. I 1907. **var. *glabra* 'Aurea'** A broadly conical form. Leaves suffused yellow during summer, paling towards winter. Originated in Australia. C 1957. **var. *glabra* 'Blue Ice'** A small, slow-growing, conical tree with striking blue-grey foliage. Originated in about 1984 in New Zealand. ♛ 2002. **var. *glabra* 'Compacta'** ('Nana', *C. arizonica* 'Compacta') A beautiful, dwarf, globular bush with attractive, grey-green adult foliage and red-brown branchlets. Suitable for a rock garden or scree. C 1913. **var. *glabra* 'Hodginsii'** A strong-growing tree with ascending and spreading branches covered with silvery-grey foliage which is conspicuously resin-speckled, strong-smelling when bruised and rough to the touch.

Raised in Australia in about 1940. **var. *glabra* 'Pyramidalis'** (*C. arizonica* 'Pyramidalis') A dense, compact, conical tree of medium size, with blue-grey foliage. Small, yellow male strobili pepper the branchlets during late winter. Cones freely produced. One of the best formal blue conifers in cultivation. C 1928. ♛ 2002. **var. *glabra* 'Variegata'** A slow-growing, conical tree with blue-green foliage interspersed with creamy-white growths. Requires a sheltered position. **var. *stephensonii*** (C.B. Wolf) Little (*C. stephensonii* C.B. Wolf) Cuyamaca cypress. A rare, small tree with smooth, cherry-like bark and grey-green foliage. Cones globose, scales with inconspicuous bosses. This tree has been growing successfully in the Sir Harold Hillier Gardens and Arboretum for more than 30 years. California.

assamica See *C. cashmeriana*.

atlantica See *C. dupreziana* var. *atlantica*.

bakeri Jeps. Modoc cypress, Siskyou cypress. (*C. bakeri* subsp. *matthewsii* C.B. Wolf) A small to medium-sized tree of loose, conical habit, with reddish-grey, flaking bark. Branches spreading, branchlets drooping, much divided into greyish-green, thread-like sections, liberally speckled with resin. Cones globular 1.25cm across, scales with prominent bosses. Small specimens grown as subsp. *matthewsii* passed the severe winter of 1962–63 without injury and have proven hardy ever since. N California, S Oregon. I 1917. **subsp. *matthewsii*** See *C. bakeri*.

†*cashmeriana* Royle ex Carrière (*C. assamica* Silba, *C. darjeelingensis* (Silba) Silba, *C. himalaica* Silba, *C. pendula* Griff.) Weeping cypress of Bhutan. One of the most graceful and beautiful of all conifers. In cultivation, a small to medium-sized tree of conical habit, reaching a large size in the wild. The branches are ascending and are draped with long, pendent branchlets. Foliage a conspicuous blue-grey, in flattened sprays. We have grown this plant outdoors here for 20 years, but it is seen at its best outdoors only in the mildest parts of the British Isles, making an excellent specimen for a large conservatory. Some recent introductions have green foliage and appear hardier. It has variously been regarded as a juvenile form of both *C. funebris* and *C. torulosa*. Bhutan. I 1862. ♛ 2002. FCC 1971.

corneyana Knight & Perry ex Carrière (*C. torulosa* var. *corneyana* (Knight & Perry ex Carrière) Carrière) The identity of the plant originally described under this name is not certain but most plants in cultivation have proved to be *C. lusitanica*. A more recent introduction under this name from Bhutan is *C. cashmeriana*.

duclouxiana Hickel. A graceful, small to medium-sized species forming a conical tree, with reddish-brown bark. Branchlets finely divided into greyish-green, thread-like segments. Cones globular and smooth, 2–2.5cm across, like miniature footballs. SW China, SE Tibet.

dupreziana A. Camus. An extremely rare relative of *C. sempervirens*, of which it is sometimes regarded as a geographical form, differing from that species in a few minor points, including its flattened branchlets and smaller, longer cones. Only found in the Tassili Mountains in the Sahara of Algeria, where it is now almost extinct, only 14 or so ancient trees surviving in a remote valley. It has grown outside in the Sir Harold

Hillier Gardens and Arboretum for many years where it has reached 5.5m (1990). **var. *atlantica*** (Gaussen) Silba (*C. atlantica* Gaussen) A large, conical tree, reaching 35m in the wild, restricted to a few populations in the High Atlas Mountains where some trees have been estimated to be 2000 years old. It has been introduced to cultivation and is proving hardy. Young trees are narrowly columnar with bright green foliage. Morocco.

forbesii See *C. guadalupensis* var. *forbesii*.

funebris Endl. (*Chamaecyparis funebris* (Endl.) Franco) Mourning cypress, Chinese weeping cypress. An elegant, small to medium-sized tree, erect in growth when young, becoming more open and pendent with age. Branches spreading, eventually drooping, branchlets pendent. Adult foliage sage-green in flattened sprays. Until it forms its adult leaves it makes a very attractive pot-plant with soft, glaucous-green juvenile foliage. In this form, before the Second World War, it was often used as the central table piece in cafes and restaurants in London and other large cities and was dispensed by growers as *Juniperus bermudiana*. A native of C China where it reaches a large size and is commonly found near temples and monasteries. I 1849.

gigantea W.C. Cheng & L.K. Fu (L. & S. 13345) A large tree in the wild, a species related to *C. duclouxiana* and only described in 1975. In cultivation it has made a medium-sized tree of narrowly columnar habit with grey-green foliage. Cones not yet produced in this country. It reached 8.5m in the Sir Harold Hillier Gardens and Arboretum (1990). Originally listed as *Juniperus indica*. SE Tibet. I by Ludlow and Sherriff.

glabra See *C. arizonica* var. *glabra*.

goveniana Gordon (*C. pigmaea* (Lemmon) Sarg., *C. goveniana* var. *pigmaea* Lemmon) Gowen cypress, California cypress, Mendocino cypress. A small to medium-sized tree of conical or broadly columnar habit with loosely arranged, ascending branches and long, drooping, irregularly divided branchlets. Foliage dark green, fragrant when crushed. Cones globular, 2cm long, the scales with prominent bosses. Restricted in the wild to Monterey (California) where it occurs with *C. macrocarpa*. I 1846. **var. *abramsiana*** (C.B. Wolf) Little (*C. abramsiana* C.B. Wolf) Santa Cruz cypress. A fast-growing, symmetrical tree of dense, columnar habit. Branches ascending bearing both ascending and spreading, finely divided branchlets clothed with green foliage. Similar in general effect to a narrow-growing Monterey cypress. Cones irregularly globose, 2–2.5cm long, scales with a slight boss. A specimen in the Sir Harold Hillier Gardens and Arboretum was 25.8m in 2000. Santa Cruz Mts (California). C 1935. **var. *pigmaea*** See *C. goveniana*.

guadalupensis S. Watson. Tecate cypress. A very beautiful, fast-growing tree of medium-size, with attractive, peeling, cherry-red bark. Branches ascending, with finely divided, crowded branchlets and greyish-green foliage. Cones globular, 3–4.5cm across, the scales with conspicuous bosses. Proving hardy in the Home Counties. Guadalupe Island (Baja California), SW California. I 1880. AM 1978 (for foliage and fruit). **var. *forbesii*** (Jeps.) Little (*C. forbesii* Jeps.) A rare and little-known form proving hardy here. A small, slender tree with attractive, brown and red, flaking bark, resembling a *Stewartia* in this respect. Branches spreading, with loose and irregular branchlet systems and green foliage. Cones irregularly globose, 2–2.5cm across. Baja California, California. C 1927.

himalaica See *C. cashmeriana*.

lindleyi See *C. lusitanica*.

lusitanica Mill. (*C. lindleyi* Klotzsch ex Lindl.) Mexican cypress, Cedar of Goa. A medium-sized to large, graceful tree with rich brown, peeling bark. Branches spreading, with pendent branchlets and greyish-green foliage. Cones glaucous, globular, 12mm across, the scales with slender, pointed bosses. Though surprisingly hardy, it cannot be recommended for cold districts. Mexico, Guatemala, Honduras. There is currently some doubt concerning the correct name for this tree. It is possible that *C. lusitanica* is a distinct species originally native to Goa, in which case the Mexican and more commonly cultivated plant should be called *C. lindleyi*. C 1682. **var. *benthamii*** (Endl.) Carrière. A very distinct tree of narrowly conical habit, in which the bright, shining green branchlet systems are decidedly flattened, giving an attractive, fern-like appearance. Not recommended for cold areas. Mexico. I about 1838. **'Brice's Weeping'** A dense, mound-forming, small shrub, the pendent branches weeping to the ground. Foliage glaucous, heavily resin-dotted and strongly aromatic. A seedling found by the late Jack Brice, Head Gardener at the Sir Harold Hillier Gardens and Arboretum 1961–1978. **'Flagellifera'** A rare form. A small to medium-sized tree with long, pendent, cord-like, green branchlets. Cones up to 2cm across. C 1927. **'Glauca'** Foliage an attractive bluish-green. Found in Portugal before 1910. **'Glauca Pendula'** A beautiful form selected by Edwin Hillier, with a spreading crown and graceful, drooping, glaucous blue branchlets. Makes a small, wide-spreading tree. C 1925. AM 1944.

lusitanica × *macrocarpa* A strong-growing tree of graceful habit with spreading branches, drooping branchlets and green foliage. Hardier than *C. lusitanica* and eventually attaining a large size. We received this plant in 1966 from the E African Agriculture and Forestry Organisation in Kenya.

macnabiana A. Murray. McNab's cypress. A small tree or large shrub with comparatively widespreading branches, conspicuous, red-tinged branchlets and pale glaucous green foliage. Cones 2–2.5cm across, the scales with conical, curved bosses. A rare tree in cultivation and one of the hardiest cypresses, even on shallow chalk soils. N California. I 1854 by William Lobb.

macrocarpa Hartw. ex Gordon (*C. lambertiana* hort. ex Carrière) Monterey cypress. A popular, very fast-growing tree of medium to large size, conical or broadly columnar in habit when young, becoming broad-crowned with age when it resembles almost a Lebanon cedar (*Cedrus libani*) in outline. Foliage bright green, in densely packed sprays. Cones 2.5–3.5cm across, the scales with a short boss. A valuable shelter tree in coastal districts. Young plants are subject to damage in cold areas. The yellow-foliaged forms colour best in an open position, becoming green in shade. California. I about 1838. **'Compacta'** ('Globosa', 'Globe') A dwarf, globular bush of dense, compact habit, with scale-like leaves. If reversions occur they should be removed. C 1920. **'Conybearii Aurea'** ('Conybearii') A small, wide-spreading tree of loosely conical habit, bearing drooping branches and long, filiform, yellow or yellowish-green branchlets. An unusual form of Australian origin, recalling *Chamaecyparis pisifera* 'Filifera' in habit. **'Crippsii'** ('Sulphurea') A form with stiffly spreading, horizontal branches and short, stiff branchlets, cream-yellow at the tips when young. C 1850. **'Donard Gold'** A conical or broadly columnar tree of medium size. Foliage rich, deep golden-yellow. An improvement on 'Lutea'. Raised in the Slieve Donard Nursery in 1935. **'Globe'** See 'Compacta'. **'Goldcrest'** A medium-sized tree of narrowly columnar form and dense, compact habit. Feathery, rich yellow juvenile foliage. Raised by Messrs Treseder of Truro about 1948. One of the best of its colour. ♀ 2002. **'Golden Cone'** A dense, conical tree with golden-yellow foliage. C 1971. **'Golden Pillar'** A small tree of narrow habit, with golden-yellow foliage. A seedling raised in Holland before 1950. ♀ 2002. **'Gold Spread'** ('Horizontalis Aurea') A very distinct and ornamental form of compact, widespreading habit reaching about 1m tall with bright golden-yellow foliage. Excellent groundcover except in the coldest areas and the brightest conifer for this purpose. Raised in Australia in the 1950s. **'Horizontalis Aurea'** See 'Gold Spread'. **'Lutea'** A tall, broadly columnar tree of medium size and compact growth. Foliage soft yellow, becoming green. C before 1893. FCC 1893. **'Minimax'** ('Minima') A dwarf, slow-growing, low bush of mainly juvenile foliage. If reversions occur they should be cut away. Raised by Mr R. Menzies at the Golden Gate Park, San Francisco before 1962, and sent to the late Alfred Nisbet of Brooker's Farm, Gosport, Hants, who, until his death, had gathered together one of the best collections of dwarf conifers in the British Isles. **'Pendula'** A broad tree of medium size. The widespreading branches droop at their extremities. The original tree at Glencormac, Bray, Co Wicklow was 15m tall in 1971. C 1952. **'Pygmaea'** A very slow-growing, dwarf form, differing from 'Woking' in having mainly adult foliage at least on older plants. Raised in 1929 by the late Mr Marcham of Carshalton Nursery, Surrey. **'Tortuosa'** See × *Cupressocyparis leylandii* 'Picturesque'. **'Variegata'** ('Lebretonii') Foliage with irregular creamy-white variegation. C 1866. FCC 1867. **'Wilma'** A small, narrow tree with nearly upright branches bearing bright yellow spring and summer foliage. A sport of 'Goldcrest'. C 1987. **'Woking'** The best miniature of the species. Tiny, scale-like leaves are in 4 ranks, very closely set, concealing the stem and recalling *Pilgerodendron*. This remarkable dwarf originated in Jackman's nursery near Woking before 1962.

pigmaea See *C. goveniana*.

sargentii Jeps. Sargent cypress. A small to medium-sized tree, with dark-coloured bark and soft green foliage. Cones 2–2.5cm long, scales with inconspicuous bosses. This tree has been growing at the Sir Harold Hillier Gardens and Arboretum for more than 30 years. California. C 1908.

sempervirens L. Italian cypress, Mediterranean cypress. The cypress of the ancients. A medium-sized tree of narrow, columnar habit, with strictly ascending branches and dark green foliage. Cones 2–3cm across, the scales with small bosses. A familiar tree in the Mediterranean region where it is widely distributed and cultivated. Young plants are prone to injury in cold areas. The form described here, sometimes known as 'Fastigiata' or 'Stricta', is unknown in the wild state. Mediterranean region, W Asia. **'Gracilis'** A narrowly columnar form of dense, compact growth raised in New Zealand. **'Green Pencil'** A very slender and hardy form with bright green foliage selected in our nurseries. The original plant in the Sir Harold Hillier Gardens and Arboretum stood at 12.2m tall in 2001. Tends to open up when fruiting starts. It was originally distributed as 'Green Spire'. **var. horizontalis** (Mill.) Loudon. The wild form, differing from the above in its more spreading branches, forming a conical crown. E Mediterranean region. **Stricta Group** (var. *stricta* Aiton) The commonly grown form of narrow habit. ♀ 2002. **'Swane's Gold'** A compact, columnar form with golden-tinged foliage. One of the best tree-sized, golden conifers for small gardens. Raised in Australia. **'Totem Pole'** A very narrow upright column of deep green foliage. Selected in New Zealand before 1983.

stephensonii See *C. arizonica* var. *stephensonii*.

torulosa D. Don. A graceful, usually small to medium-sized tree, but occasionally attaining large proportions. Conical in habit, with horizontal branches and flattened sprays of whip-like branchlets and dark green foliage. Cones 1–2cm across, dark brown with a violet bloom, the scales with small bosses. Himalaya. I 1824. **var. corneyana** See under *C. corneyana*. **'Majestica'** A distinct, slow-growing form with thickened branches and rather congested moss-like foliage. C 1855.

Cypress See *Cupressus* and *Chamaecyparis*.

†***DACRYCARPUS** (Endl.) de Laub.—**Podocarpaceae**—A genus of 9 species of trees natives of W China and Myanmar to New Guinea and New Zealand. They were previously included in *Podocarpus*.

dacrydioides (A. Rich.) de Laub. (*Podocarpus dacrydioides* A. Rich.) Kahikatea, White pine. An extremely beautiful tree in the mildest areas of the British Isles, but reaching 45m and above in its native habitat. The long, slender, gracefully drooping branchlets are clothed with small, narrow, bronze-green, 2-ranked leaves, which on young trees are scale-like, spirally arranged on older trees. An elegant species which makes an attractive conservatory specimen. New Zealand.

†***DACRYDIUM** Sol. ex G. Forst.—**Podocarpaceae**—A small genus of about 21 species of evergreen trees and shrubs allied to *Podocarpus*; natives of SE Asia to Australasia. The leaves are scale-like on adult trees and awl-shaped on juveniles. Male and female strobili are normally borne on different trees. Fruits consist of an ovoid, nut-like seed seated in a cup-like aril.

biforme See *Halocarpus biformis*.

colensoi See *Manoao colensoi*.

cupressinum Sol. ex G. Forst. Rimu, Red pine. A small, graceful, conical tree with arching branches and pendent, string-like branchlets. Considered by the botanist

Cheeseman to be 'as beautiful and attractive as any tree in New Zealand'. Slow-growing in the British Isles even in a sheltered position. It makes a charming specimen for a conservatory. New Zealand.

franklinii See *Lagarostrobos franklinii*.
intermedium See *Lepidothamnus intermedius*.
laxifolium See *Lepidothamnus laxifolius*.

*DISELMA Hook. f.—**Cupressaceae**—A monotypic, Tasmanian genus related to *Fitzroya*. Male and female strobili are borne on separate plants. The cones are small and composed of 2 pairs of scales.

archeri Hook. f. A beautiful, medium-sized to large bush of lax habit. Leaves scale-like, adpressed to and concealing the slender branchlets. This species was lost to cultivation until reintroduced by Lord Talbot de Malahide to whom we are indebted. W Tasmania.

Fir See *Abies*.

*FITZROYA Lindl.—**Cupressaceae**—A monotypic genus, closely allied to *Diselma*. Male and female strobili borne on the same or separate plants.

cupressoides (Molina) I.M. Johnst. (*F. patagonica* Hook. f. ex Lindl.) A beautiful, large tree of cypress-like habit, in cultivation a surprisingly hardy, graceful, large shrub or small, dense tree with scale-like leaves borne in 3s, banded white, carried on drooping branchlets. Cones small, consisting of 9 scales. There is a splendid specimen at Killerton near Exeter, where a magnificent collection of trees was planted by the late Sir Francis Acland and is now maintained by the National Trust. In the wild it can reach 70m tall and live for 3,600 years, but unfortunately large forests of it have now been cleared to provide land for agriculture. S Chile, Argentina. I by William Lobb in 1849 and later by Richard Pearce.

*FOKIENIA A. Henry & H.H. Thomas—**Cupressaceae**— A genus of a single species, related to *Cupressus* and *Calocedrus* and resembling *Calocedrus macrolepis* in foliage. Male and female strobili are borne on the same plant. The cones, up to 2.5cm long, are similar to those of *Chamaecyparis*, ripening the second year. The following species is best given a sheltered position in woodland.

hodginsii (Dunn) A. Henry & H.H. Thomas. A small to medium-sized shrub of very slow growth. The very distinct and characteristic spine-tipped, paired, scale-like leaves are bright, glossy green above, marked with conspicuous silvery-white bands of stomata beneath. They are borne in large, flattened sprays somewhat resembling those of *Thujopsis*, but more delicate and graceful. Probably the best specimen in cultivation is at Borde Hill, planted by the great amateur gardener the late Col Stephenson Clarke. This rare and remarkable conifer is a native of SE China, N Laos and N Vietnam and was first discovered in the province of Fujian (previously Fokien or Fukien) by Captain Hodgins in 1908, and was introduced the following year by Sir Lewis Clinton-Baker. AM 1911.

GINKGO L.—**Ginkgoaceae**—A remarkable and distinct, monotypic genus of great ornamental, botanical and geographical interest. *G. biloba* is the sole survivor of an ancient family whose ancestors occurred in many parts of the world (including the British Isles) about 190 million years ago. Male and female strobili occur on separate plants. The yellow, plum-shaped fruits are produced in pairs or 3s at the end of a slender stalk, ripening and falling in autumn, when, if crushed, they emit a strong, offensive odour. It is regarded as a sacred tree in the East and is commonly planted in the vicinity of Buddhist temples. Long considered to be extinct in the wild, it is known to have survived in Zhejiang and Anhui Provinces, SE China.

biloba L. (*Salisburia adiantifolia* Sm.) Maidenhair tree. A medium-sized to large, deciduous, tree, conical when young. Easily recognised by its peculiar fan-shaped, undivided leaves, which turn a beautiful clear yellow before falling in autumn. Perfectly hardy and suitable for most soils. It is tolerant of industrial areas and is magnificent either as a single specimen or as an avenue tree. It was first introduced into Europe about 1727 and to England in 1754. ♀ 2002. '**Autumn Gold**' A broadly conical male form with excellent golden-yellow autumn colour. C 1955. '**Fastigiata**' A columnar form with semi-erect branches. C 1906. '**Pendula**' A remarkable selection with spreading or weeping branches. C 1855. '**Saratoga**' A male form making a compact, small tree with excellent yellow autumn colour. '**Tremonia**' A very narrowly columnar form raised as a seedling in Dortmund Botanic Garden in 1930. We are indebted for this form to the late Dr G. Krussmann, once Director of the celebrated gardens at Dortmund. Dr Krussmann was a very rare example of a botanist who was also a horticulturist. '**Variegata**' Leaves streaked with creamy-white. Slow-growing and very prone to reversion. C 1855.

†GLYPTOSTROBUS Endl.—**Cupressaceae**—A monotypic genus related to *Taxodium*. Male and female strobili are borne on the same plant. Cones pear-shaped, 2cm long, borne on long stalks. Not recommended for cold localities.

lineatus See *G. pensilis*.

pensilis (Staunton ex D. Don) K. Koch (*G. lineatus* auct. not (Poir.) Druce, *G. sinensis* A. Henry ex Loder) This is an extremely rare, deciduous conifer, making a large bush or small tree. Soft, sea-green, narrow leaves turn rich brown in autumn. This remarkable species has grown slowly in the Sir Harold Hillier Gardens and Arboretum without protection for many years. It is a native of S China and N Vietnam, where it is often found on the banks of streams and in similarly moist situations.

†*HALOCARPUS—**Podocarpaceae**—A genus of 3 species of evergreen shrubs, native to New Zealand, previously included in *Dacrydium*.

biformis (Hook.) Quinn (*Dacrydium biforme* (Hook.) Pilger. A rare species received by us from Messrs Duncan & Davies of New Plymouth, New Zealand, who describe it as a slow-growing, alpine conifer up to 6m. The leaves of juvenile plants are likened to those of a yew, spreading in 2 opposite ranks. Leaves of adult plants are smaller and scale-like. New Zealand.

Hemlock See *Tsuga*.

*JUNIPERUS L.—Cupressaceae—The junipers are a genus of about 54 species of trees and shrubs, ranging from prostrate or creeping alpines to dense, bushy shrubs and tall, conical or columnar trees. They are widely distributed almost throughout the N hemisphere from Mexico to China and from the Arctic Circle to the mountains of tropical E Africa.

The leaves of juvenile plants are awl-shaped and usually pointed; those of adult plants are normally scale-like and crowded, although in some species they retain their juvenile form. The awl-shaped leaves have white or glaucous stomatal bands above (i.e. on the inner surface) but because of the often horizontal disposition of the branches the bands appear to be on the lower surface. Male and female strobili are borne on the same or on separate plants. The fruits are usually rounded or ovoid, becoming fleshy and berry-like.

Juniperus is a very versatile genus, containing plants for most soils and situations and having among the most suitable conifers for calcareous soils. They range in colour from green to yellow, grey and steel-blue. The prostrate forms are excellent as groundcover in sun and several of the small, columnar forms are effective in a heather garden.

†*ashei* J. Buchholz. A large, slow-growing, dioecious shrub or occasionally a small tree of conical habit. Foliage awl-shaped and sage-green on young plants, scale-like and dark green on mature plants. Fruits rounded, 6–8mm across, deep blue and covered with a glaucous bloom, tasting sweet and aromatic. A rare species for a sheltered site in the milder counties. It occurs with *J. virginiana* in the wild. S USA, NE Mexico. I 1926.

'Blue Cloud' See *J. virginiana* 'Blue Cloud'.

†*californica* Carrière. California juniper. A large bush or small tree; foliage yellowish-green, scale-like. Fruits reddish-brown, bloomy. Only for mild areas. California, Oregon. I 1853 by William Lobb.

canadensis See *J. communis* var. *depressa*.

†*cedrus* Webb & Berthel. Canary Island juniper. An erect-growing, dioecious, small tree of graceful habit, with slender, drooping, whitish branchlets, densely clothed with sharply pointed, awl-shaped leaves, arranged in whorls of 3. Fruits 10–12mm across, reddish-brown, bloomy. A tender species closely related to *J. oxycedrus*. Native of the Canary Isles where it is now very rare. Large trees are still to be found on the island of La Palma growing in inaccessible parts of the volcanic crater. It has been grown outside in the Home Counties for many years.

chinensis L. (*J. sheppardii* (Veitch) Van Melle) Chinese juniper. An extremely variable, dioecious species widespread in the wild. In cultivation it is typically a tall, conical or columnar, grey or greyish tree of medium size and dense, compact habit, with both awl-shaped juvenile and scale-like adult foliage on the same plant. Fruits rounded or top-shaped, 5–7mm across, glaucous, ripening in the second year. See also *J. × pfitzeriana*. Myanmar, China, Japan, Korea. Originally introduced before 1767. I into England by William Kerr in 1804.

Cultivars of *Juniperus chinensis*

'Albovariegata' See 'Variegata'.

'Ames' Medium-sized to large bush of rather spreading growth; leaves awl-shaped, bluish-green at first, later green. Selected in the USA in 1935.

'Armstrongii' See *J. × pfitzeriana* 'Armstrongii'.

'Aurea' Young's golden juniper. A tall, slender, slow-growing conical or columnar tree with golden foliage, inclined to burn in full sun. A male clone exhibiting both juvenile and adult foliage Raised as a sport at Milford, Surrey about 1855. ♀ 2002. FCC 1871.

'Blaauw' (*J. × media* 'Blaauw') A strong-growing shrub, up to 1.5m, with strongly ascending main branches and shorter outer branches, all densely clothed with feathery sprays of mainly scale-like, greyish-blue leaves. It is often confused in gardens with 'Globosa Cinerea', which it resembles as a young plant, but it is stronger and much more irregular in habit when older. C 1924. ♀ 2002.

'Blue Alps' A vigorous, large shrub with striking steel-blue foliage. Found in a garden in Austria in 1968.

'Columnaris' Similar in habit to and of the same origin as 'Columnaris Glauca'. It differs in its slightly coarser, green foliage.

'Columnaris Glauca' Small tree of dense, columnar habit, slightly broader at base and tapering gradually to summit. Leaves awl-shaped, sharply pointed and glaucous. Sometimes wrongly referred to under the name 'Pyramidalis Glauca'. A seedling selected at the US Dept of Agriculture from seed collected by Frank N. Meyer in Hubei, China in 1905.

'Echiniformis' A dwarf, tight ball of prickly leaves. Originally thought to be a form of *J. communis*. Not an easy plant to grow. C 1850. AM 1961.

'Excelsa Stricta' See 'Stricta'.

'Expansa' See 'Parsonsii'.

'Expansa Aureospicata' (*J. davurica* 'Expansa Aureospicata') Smaller and slower-growing with predominantly juvenile leaves. Greyish-green with scattered yellow splashes. C 1938.

'Expansa Variegata' (*J. chinensis* 'Parsonsii Variegata', *J. davurica* 'Expansa Variegata') Similar in habit and foliage but with scattered, creamy-white sprays. C 1938.

'Fairview' Small to medium-sized tree of narrow habit; leaves bright green, mostly juvenile. Raised from seed in the USA in about 1930.

'Globosa Cinerea' (*J. × media* 'Globosa Cinerea') A strong-growing, small to medium-sized shrub with ascending branches, clothed with blue-grey, mostly adult leaves. C 1915. It is very similar to 'Blaauw'.

'Helle' See 'Spartan'.

'Iowa' Medium-sized shrub of spreading habit; leaves green, slightly bluish, both scale-like and awl-like present on the same plant. Female. C 1934.

'Japonica Oblonga' See 'Oblonga'.

'Japonica Variegata' ('Kaizuka Variegata') A compact, medium-sized, bushy shrub of conical habit. Foliage mainly adult, flecked with creamy-yellow and silvery-white. C 1867.

'Kaizuka' (*J. chinensis* var. *torulosa* hort., *J. sheppardii* var. *torulosa* (Eastwood) Melle) Hollywood juniper. A large, erect-growing shrub, eventually a small tree, with long, spreading branches clothed with characteristic dense clusters of scale-like, bright green foliage. A very distinct form, particularly effective in a heather garden or as an isolated lawn specimen. I about 1920 from Japan. ♀ 2002.

'Kaizuka Variegata' See 'Japonica Variegata'.

Juniperus chinensis continued:

'Keteleeri' (*J. virginiana* 'Keteleeri') Small, conical tree of dense habit with crowded masses of vivid green, scale-like leaves and an abundance of small, light green fruits. C 1906.

'Kuriwao Gold' (*J. × media* 'Kuriwao Gold') A large, dense, shrub with an upright, branching habit, yellow-green foliage and spreading, bright yellow shoots. A seedling of 'Keteleeri' raised in New Zealand before 1975.

'Maney' Medium-sized shrub with ascending branches; leaves bluish bloomy, awl-shaped. C 1935.

'Monarch' An upright, conical bush of open habit, with ascending or spreading, arm-like branches bearing a mixture of adult and juvenile foliage. Raised from seed of Japanese origin. C 1935.

'Mountbatten' Medium-sized bush or small tree of columnar habit; leaves greyish-green, awl-shaped. Raised by the Sheridan Nurseries, Ontario, Canada. C 1948.

'Obelisk' Medium-sized shrub of erect, columnar habit; foliage bluish-green, awl-shaped, densely packed. Raised from Japanese seed in Holland in 1930. ♀ 2002.

'Oblonga' ('Japonica Oblonga') A small shrub of irregular, rounded habit, with densely crowded branches, those in the lower part of the bush bearing prickly, dark green, awl-shaped leaves, those in the upper part projecting and clothed with scale-like leaves. A sport of 'Japonica' raised in the USA. C 1932.

'Olympia' Medium-sized shrub or small tree of columnar habit; leaves glaucous both scale-like and awl-shaped. Raised in Holland from Japanese seed in the 1930s.

'Parsonsii' (*J. chinensis* 'Expansa', *J. davurica* 'Expansa') A dwarf shrub with rigid, widespreading, almost horizontal, thick branches, eventually developing into a low mound up to 1m high in the centre and 3m or more across. Scale-like, sage-green leaves are arranged in attractive, dense, spray-like, heavy clusters along the branches. I from Japan by the Parsons Nursery of New York State in the 1930s.

'Pfitzeriana' See *J. × pfitzeriana* 'Wilhelm Pfitzer'.

'Plumosa' (*J. × media* 'Plumosa', *J. japonica* hort.) A low-growing male shrub with widespreading branches bearing crowded, plume-like sprays of densely set, green, scale-like leaves. Occasionally a few sprays of juvenile awl-shaped leaves are present in the centre of the bush. Originally introduced from Japan as *J. japonica*, under which name it was commonly grown in cultivation. *J. japonica* of Carrière is *J. chinensis* 'Japonica'. C before 1920.

'Plumosa Albovariegata' (*J. × media* 'Plumosa Albovariegata', *J. japonica* 'Albovariegata') Dwarf, spreading shrub of slow growth; foliage scale-like, deep green, speckled with white. C 1867.

'Plumosa Aurea' (*J. × media* 'Plumosa Aurea', *J. japonica* 'Aurea') An attractive and ornamental form of 'Plumosa', with ascending branches arching at the tips, densely clothed with plumose sprays of yellow, scale-like leaves which ripen to bronze-gold in winter. C 1885. ♀ 2002.

'Plumosa Aureovariegata' (*J. japonica* 'Aureovariegata', *J. × media* 'Plumosa Aureovariegata') Similar in habit to 'Plumosa Aurea' but lower and slower growing, its green foliage irregularly variegated deep yellow. C 1873.

var. *procumbens* See *J. procumbens*.

'Pyramidalis' A dense, slow-growing, columnar bush with almost entirely juvenile, prickly, glaucous leaves. I from Japan to Holland by Philip von Siebold in 1843. ♀ 2002.

'Reptans' See *J. virginiana* 'Reptans'.

'San José' Dwarf shrub with prostrate branches; leaves grey-green, mostly juvenile. Selected in California in 1935.

var. *sargentii* A. Henry (*J. sargentii* (A. Henry) Takeda) A prostrate shrub slowly forming dense carpets 2m across. Leaves mostly scale-like, green and bloomy. Fruits blue. A pleasing groundcover in an open position. Native of Japan, S Kuriles and Sakhalin where it inhabits rocky mountain cliffs and seashores. I 1892 by Prof. Sargent.

var. *sargentii* 'Glauca' A slower-growing form with glaucous, grey-green foliage. A good small 'rug' for a scree garden.

'Sheppardii' (*J. sheppardii* (Veitch) Van Melle, *J. chinensis fortunei* hort., *J. fortunei* C. de Vos) A large, usually multi-stemmed shrub with orange-brown, peeling bark and loose, bushy growth. Branches ascending and gracefully spreading at the tips. The branches of older plants become rather congested, with characteristic projecting filiform shoots. Leaves green, mainly adult with occasional small sprays of juvenile leaves. There may be more than one form in cultivation. Ours is a male clone and in late winter and early spring is rendered easily recognisable by its multitudes of male strobili. SE China. According to Van Melle, probably first introduced by Robert Fortune in about 1850.

'Shimpaku' A slow-growing dwarf selection with tufted, grey-green adult foliage. It is commonly used for bonsai. C 1966.

'Spartan' ('Helle') A narrowly conical, erect-branched, large shrub or small tree of dense habit, with rich green foliage. C 1961.

'Stricta' A large shrub of compact, conical habit, with erect branches. Foliage juvenile, soft to the touch and glaucous. FCC 1868 (as *J. excelsa stricta*). C 1862.

var. *torulosa* See 'Kaizuka'.

'Variegata' ('Albovariegata') Usually a large conical bush of dense, compact habit. Leaves mostly juvenile, glaucous, with scattered sprays of white variegation. I about 1860 from Japan.

'Variegated Kaizuka' A sport of 'Kaizuka' which it resembles but with foliage flecked with creamy-yellow. C 1950.

communis L. Common juniper. A variable species, usually found as a medium-sized to large shrub. Its silver-backed leaves are awl-shaped, prickly to the touch and arranged in whorls of 3. Fruits rounded, 5–6mm across, black, covered by a glaucous bloom, ripening during the second or third year and sometimes used to flavour gin. This species has probably a wider distribution than any other tree or shrub, occurring from North America eastwards through Europe and Asia to Korea and Japan. It is one of the 3 British native conifers, being particularly plentiful on the chalk downs of the south of England. One of the most accommodating of conifers, its prostrate forms are especially useful as groundcover in sun, while the slender columns of the Irish Juniper ('Hibernica') are a conspicuous feature of many gardens. AM 1890. **subsp. alpina** See var. *saxatilis*. **'Compressa'** A gem for a rock garden or scree. A dwarf, compact, slow-growing column. Resembling a miniature Irish Juniper. Several specimens planted with variously coloured, prostrate junipers create a charming miniature landscape. C 1855. ♀ 2002. **'Corielagan'** A slow-growing, prostrate form with grey-brown foliage, the leaves bronze beneath and with a conspicuous white stripe above. Found in Corrie Lagan on the Isle of Skye in the 1970s. **'Cracovia'** A conical or broadly columnar geographical form of Polish origin, with ascending branches and branchlets with drooping tips. C 1855. **var. depressa** Pursh (*J. canadensis* Lodd. ex Burgsd.) Canadian juniper. A widespreading dwarf to about 60cm, forming large patches of dense, slightly ascending stems clothed with comparatively broad, yellowish or brownish-green, silver-backed leaves, bronze-coloured above during winter. A wild variety from the mountains of North America and one of the best of all dwarf, carpeting conifers, excellent as groundcover in sun. **'Depressa Aurea'** Leaves and young shoots golden-yellow during early summer. Growth as in var. *depressa*. Very prone to needle blight. C 1887. **'Dumosa'** A dwarf, spreading shrub forming large patches. Leaves green, silvery-white beneath, turning coppery bronze or brown in winter. A form of var. *depressa* which originated in Holland. A splendid groundcover for an open situation. A specimen in the Sir Harold Hillier Gardens and Arboretum attained 60cm by 1.5m in 15 years. Raised in Holland about 1934. **'Effusa'** A widespreading, semi-prostrate form. Leaves green above, silvery-white beneath, pointing forward and lying along the branches, which they more or less conceal. An excellent dwarf, carpeting conifer, its leaves usually remaining green in winter contrasting effectively with the bronze of var. *depressa* and 'Dumosa'. Raised in Holland about 1944. **'Gold Cone'** ('Suecica Aurea') Similar to Suecica Group in habit but slower-growing and with golden-yellow foliage. **'Green Carpet'** Dense, low-growing and widespreading with bright green foliage. Found in Norway before 1975. ♀ 2002. **'Hibernica'** ('Stricta', *J. hibernica* hort.) Irish juniper. A dense, compact form of slender, columnar habit, attaining 3m or occasionally 5m. Leaves densely arranged. A very popular conifer, excellent for use in formal gardens. To some extent the counterpart of the Italian cypress of the warmer S European gardens though never so tall. C 1838. ♀ 2002. **'Hornibrookii'** ('Prostrata') A dwarf, creeping groundcover taking on the shape of the object over which it creeps. Leaves comparatively small, loosely spreading, sharply pointed, silvery-white beneath. A seedling collected in Co Galway, Ireland, by the great authority on dwarf conifers, Murray Hornibrook. C 1923. ♀ 2002. **var. jackii** See var. *saxatilis*. **var. montana** See var. *saxatilis*. **subsp. nana** See var. *saxatilis*. **'Oblonga Pendula'** An elegant, erect shrub of compact habit up to 3–5m, with slightly ascending branches drooping at the tips, branchlets pendent. Leaves sharply pointed, bronze during winter. Recalling *J. oxycedrus*, but with rounded shoots. C 1838. **'Prostrata'** See 'Hornibrookii'. **'Repanda'** A dwarf, carpet-forming shrub with densely-packed, semi-prostrate stems and forward-pointing, loosely arranged leaves, sometimes slightly bronze-tinged in winter. Although of different origin, this cultivar is, for garden purposes, identical with 'Effusa'. Both make excellent groundcover in full sun. Discovered in Ireland by the late Maurice Prichard. C 1934. ♀ 2002. **var. saxatilis** Pall. (subsp. *alpina* (Suter) Celak, subsp. *nana* (Willd.) Syme, var. *jackii* Rehder, var. *montana* Aiton, *J. nana* Willd., *J. sibirica* Burgsd.) A slow-growing, prostrate form, its densely packed stems hugging the ground and forming mats or carpets of dark green leaves. In the wild it is found on rocks, mountains and moors and in the north of Scotland may be seen draping sea-cliffs in the teeth of cold, briny winds. W North America, Greenland, British Isles and through Europe, the Himalaya to Japan. **'Schneverdingen Goldmachangel'** Similar in habit to 'Hibernica' but slower growing with golden-yellow foliage. Raised in Germany about 1970. **'Sentinel'** A very narrowly columnar form with dense, erect branches. Deep bluish-green leaves contrast well with the reddish-purple shoots. Reaches 4m tall and 50cm wide in 30 years. Raised in Canada before 1961. **'Stricta'** See 'Hibernica'. **Suecica Group** (f. *suecica* (Mill.) Beissn., *J. suecica* Mill.) Swedish juniper. A medium-sized shrub, similar to 'Hibernica' in habit, but the ascending branches are open and drooping at the tips. Occurs wild in Scandinavia. C 1768. **'Vase'** ('Vase Shaped') Dwarf shrub up to 70cm with low, obtusely spreading branches and leaves turning bronze in winter. C 1936.

conferta See *J. rigida* subsp. *conferta*.

davurica 'Expansa' See *J. chinensis* 'Parsonsii'. **'Expansa Aureospicata'** See *J. chinensis* 'Expansa Aureospicata'. **'Expansa Variegata'** See *J. chinensis* 'Expansa Variegata'. **'Parsonsii Variegata'** See *J. chinensis* 'Expansa Variegata'.

deppeana Steud. A small, dioecious tree of conical habit, with reddish-brown bark that is deeply furrowed into square plates. Leaves glaucous. Fruits globular 10–12mm across, reddish-brown and bloomy. I 1904. **var. pachyphlaea** (Torr.) Martínez (*J. pachyphlaea* Torr.) Chequer-barked juniper, Alligator juniper. Particularly conspicuous as a young plant when it is the most vividly silver-blue of all junipers. Not easy to cultivate coming as it does from the dry mountain slopes of the SW USA and NE Mexico. C 1873.

distans See *J. tibetica*.

drupacea Labill. Syrian juniper. A striking and distinctive, dioecious species of narrow, columnar habit, at least in cultivation. A small tree, branches short and densely crowded with sharply pointed, awl-shaped leaves, fresh green, broadly banded white on the inner surface. Fruits ovoid or globose, 2–2.5cm across, bluish-black and bloomy, ripening during the first season when they are edible. Fruits have been borne on a tree in the Sir Harold Hillier Gardens and Arboretum. A remarkable species, easily recognised in gardens by its habit, together with its comparatively broad, prickly leaves. SW Asia, Greece. I about 1854.

excelsa M.-Bieb. Greek juniper. Small tree or large shrub of conical or loosely columnar habit, with long sprays of thread-like branchlets densely clothed with tiny grey-green leaves spreading at tips. Fruits ripening the second year, globose, 9–12mm across, deep purplish-brown and

bloomy. SE Europe, SW Asia, to Pakistan. I 1806.
'Stricta' A columnar form with mainly juvenile foliage. Unfortunately this name has been erroneously used in gardens for *J. chinensis* 'Pyramidalis'.

flaccida Schltdl. Mexican juniper. A small tree with attractive, scaly bark, slender branches and pendent branchlets. Leaves scale-like, grey-green, bright grass-green on mature trees. Fruits ripening the second year, globose, 10–15mm across, reddish-brown, bloomy. This species has grown in the Sir Harold Hillier Gardens and Arboretum for more than 30 years. Mexico, Texas. I 1838.

†*formosana* Hayata. Prickly cypress. A beautiful, small, dioecious tree of loose, elegant habit, with drooping branchlets. Leaves awl-shaped, in whorls of 3, sharp-pointed, glaucous above. Fruits subglobose, 6–12mm across, olive-green, with 3 conspicuous, white grooves at the apex, ripening to dark brown the second year. A graceful but tender species similar in aspect to *J. oxycedrus*. China, Taiwan. I about 1844.

'Grey Owl' (*J. virginiana* 'Grey Owl') A splendid, medium-sized, vigorous shrub with widespreading branches. Foliage soft silvery-grey. It is thought to be a hybrid between *J. virginiana* 'Glauca' and *J.* × *pfitzeriana* 'Wilhelm Pfitzer', possessing a habit similar to the latter but in other respects appears typical *J. virginiana*. Originated in 1938. ♀ 2002. AM 1968.

hibernica See *J. communis* 'Hibernica'.

'Holger' See *J. squamata* 'Holger'.

horizontalis Moench. Creeping juniper. A dwarf or prostrate shrub with long, sometimes procumbent branches, in time forming carpets several metres across. Leaves on cultivated plants mostly juvenile crowding the branchlets, glaucous green, grey-green or blue, varying in intensity and often plum-purple in winter. Fruits rarely produced in cultivation. One of the best species for use as groundcover, contrasting effectively with the green prostrate forms of *J. communis*. It is a native of North America where it inhabits sea cliffs, gravelly slopes, even swamps. C 1830. **'Alpina'** A form with prostrate branches and ascending branchlets up to 60cm high. Leaves greyish-blue, purple-tinged during autumn and winter. C 1838. **'Andorra Compact'** Similar to but an improvement on 'Plumosa', of denser habit with bronze-purple winter foliage. C 1955. **'Banff'** A low-growing form, the short, arching shoots clothed with bright blue-grey foliage. Found in the Banff National Park near Calgary, Alberta, Canada before 1975. **'Bar Harbor'** A prostrate form with branches closely hugging the ground and spreading in all directions. Shortly ascending branchlets are clothed with glaucous, grey-green, scale-like leaves. C 1930. **'Blue Chip'** A prostrate form with bright blue foliage throughout the year. Raised in Denmark about 1945. **'Blue Rug'** See 'Wiltonii'. **'Coast of Maine'** Low-growing form making flattened mounds. Leaves awl-shaped, grey-green, purple-tinted in winter. **'Douglasii'** Waukegan juniper. A low-growing, procumbent form up to 50cm high with long, spreading branches and sprays of both adult and juvenile leaves. The whole plant is a bright, glaucous, grey-green in summer, purple-tinged in autumn and winter. C 1916. **'Emerald Spreader'** Very low-growing, forming dense mats of bright green foliage. C 1973. **'Glauca'** Prostrate

with long branches with slender whipcord tips hugging the ground. Leaves steel-blue in slender sprays. C 1939. **'Golden Carpet'** A sport of 'Wiltonii' with yellow-green foliage. C 1992. **'Grey Pearl'** A compact form with short, upright shoots and densely arranged, grey-green juvenile foliage. A sister seedling of 'Blue Chip', raised in Denmark about 1945. **'Hughes'** A vigorous form with ascending branches and grey-green foliage. Raised in the USA. **'Jade River'** A vigorous, prostrate form with blue-green foliage. C 1960. **'Montana'** A prostrate form with long branches, slender and filiform at their tips. Branchlets shortly ascending, plumose and densely packed, bearing scale-like leaves of an intense glaucous blue. One of the best forms. **'Plumosa'** A dense, procumbent form of compact habit, with ascending, plumose branchlets up to 60cm high. Leaves awl-shaped, grey-green, becoming purple-tinged in winter. C 1919. **'Prince of Wales'** A low-growing form of dense habit forming mats up to 15cm tall. Foliage bright green tinged blue, flushed with purple in winter. Found in Alberta in 1931. **'Prostrata'** A prostrate form with shortly ascending branchlets clothed with awl-shaped and scale-like, glaucous leaves, bronze-tinged in winter. C 1938. **'Turquoise Spreader'** Low and widespreading with densely arranged, juvenile, turquoise-blue foliage. C 1973. **'Wiltonii'** ('Blue Rug') One of the best forms, its branches long and prostrate, forming flattened, glaucous blue carpets. C 1914. ♀ 2002. **'Youngstown'** Similar to 'Andorra Compact' but usually greener in winter.

'Hunnetorp' See *J. squamata* 'Hunnetorp'.

indica Bertol. (*J. wallichiana* Parl. *J. pseudosabina* Hook. f. not Fisch. & Mey.) A dioecious, large shrub or small tree of densely, narrowly conical habit when young. Branches ascending and closely packed, bearing dense bunches of scale-like, green leaves and scattered sprays of juvenile leaves, the latter more apparent on young plants. Fruits ripening the second year, ovoid, 6mm long, black when mature. Sometimes found in cultivation under the name *J. pseudosabina* which is an irregular shrub with smaller, often rounded fruits. For another plant once grown under this name see *Cupressus gigantea*. Himalaya. I 1849 by Sir Joseph Hooker.

japonica hort. See *J. chinensis* 'Plumosa'.

macrocarpa See *J. oxycedrus* subsp. *macrocarpa*.

× *media* See *J.* × *pfitzeriana*. **'Armstrongii'** See *J.* × *pfitzeriana* 'Armstrongii'. **'Blaauw'** See *J. chinensis* 'Blaauw'. **'Blue and Gold'** See *J.* × *pfitzeriana* 'Blue and Gold'. **'Blue Cloud'** See *J. virginiana* 'Blue Cloud'. **'Carbery Gold'** See *J.* × *pfitzeriana* 'Carbery Gold'. **'Globosa Cinerea'** See *J. chinensis* 'Globosa Cinerea'. **'Gold Coast'** See *J.* × *pfitzeriana* 'Gold Coast'. **'Hetzii'** See *J. virginiana* 'Hetzii'. **'Kosteri'** See *J. virginiana* 'Kosteri'. **'Kuriwao Gold'** See *J. chinensis* 'Kuriwao Gold'. **Mint Julep** See *J.* × *pfitzeriana* Mint Julep. **'Mordigan Gold'** See *J.* × *pfitzeriana* 'Mordigan Gold'. **'Old Gold'** See *J.* × *pfitzeriana* 'Old Gold'. **'Pfitzeriana'** See *J.* × *pfitzeriana* 'Wilhelm Pfitzer'. **'Pfitzeriana Aurea'** See *J.* × *pfitzeriana* 'Pfitzeriana Aurea'. **'Pfitzeriana Compacta'** See *J.* × *pfitzeriana* 'Pfitzeriana Compacta'. **'Pfitzeriana Glauca'** See *J.* × *pfitzeriana* 'Pfitzeriana Glauca'. **'Plumosa'** See *J. chinensis* 'Plumosa'. **'Plumosa Albovariegata'** See *J. chinensis* 'Plumosa Albovaeriegata'. **'Plumosa**

Aurea' See *J. chinensis* 'Plumosa Aurea'. **'Plumosa Aureovariegata'** See *J. chinensis* 'Plumosa Aureovariegata'. **'Reptans'** See *J. virginiana* 'Reptans'. **'Sulphur Spray'** See *J. virginiana* 'Sulphur Spray'.

†*monosperma* (Engelm.) Sarg. Cherrystone juniper. A large, densely branched shrub or small tree, with fibrous, reddish-brown bark and greyish-green, scale-like foliage. SW USA, N Mexico. I about 1900.

morrisonicola Hayata. Mount Morrison juniper. A medium-sized to large shrub of usually dense, erect habit with bluish-green, awl-shaped leaves crowding the short branchlets. Fruits single-seeded, 6mm long, black when ripe. A rare species restricted in the wild to Mount Morrison, Taiwan, where it forms impenetrable scrubby thickets on rocky slopes, reaching small tree size in more sheltered ravines. Botanically it is close to *J. squamata*.

nana See *J. communis* var. *saxatilis*.

†*osteosperma* (Torr.) Little (*J. utahensis* (Engelm.) Lemmon) Utah juniper. Small, monoecious, conical tree with brown, fibrous bark, and green, scale-like leaves. Fruits rounded, 6–16mm long, reddish-brown and bloomy. W USA. I 1900.

oxycedrus L. Prickly juniper. A large, dioecious shrub or small tree of open, drooping habit. Leaves in 3s, awl-shaped, ending in a sharp point, green above, marked with 2 white stomatic bands beneath. Fruits ovoid or globose, 9–13mm long, shining reddish-brown when ripe in the second year. The fragrant wood produces an oil of Cade which is used medicinally, particularly in the treatment of certain skin diseases. Mediterranean region, W Asia. C 1739. **subsp. *macrocarpa*** (Sibth. & Sm.) Neilr. (*J. macrocarpa* Sibth. & Sm.) A large shrub or small tree, occasionally prostrate in the wild. It differs in its larger fruits.

pachyphlaea See *J. deppeana* var. *pachyphlaea*.

× *pfitzeriana* (Späth) P.A. Schmidt (*J.* × *media* Melle) (*J. chinensis* × *J. sabina*) A variable hybrid which occurs in the wild in NE Asia. Van Melle was of the opinion that 4 commonly cultivated junipers previously regarded as forms of *J. chinensis* belonged to this hybrid group and existed in a wild state. While agreeing with his concept of their hybrid origin, we prefer here to treat them as cultivars originally selected from wild material rather than varieties having a distinct geographical distribution. We also regard *J. chinensis* in its broader concept as a parent rather than Van Melle's *J. sphaerica*. **'Armstrongii'** (*J.* × *media* 'Armstrongii') In habit resembling a dense and compact 'Wilhelm Pfitzer'. Leaves mainly scale-like, greyish. The juvenile leaves are mostly confined to the centre of the bush. A sport of 'Wilhelm Pfitzer' introduced in 1932 by the Armstrong Nurseries of California. **'Blue and Gold'** (*J.* × *media* 'Blue and Gold') A small, spreading shrub, reaching about 1.5m. Foliage blue-grey flecked creamy-yellow. C 1972. **'Carbery Gold'** (*J.* × *media* 'Carbery Gold') A prostrate shrub with striking bright creamy-yellow foliage all year. C 1987. **'Gold Coast'** (*J.* × *media* 'Gold Coast') A flat-topped, low-growing and widespreading form with golden foliage. **Gold Sovereign** ('Blound') PBR A sport of 'Old Gold' differing in its slower growth and more persistently golden-yellow foliage. C 1983. **'Golden Saucer'** A small shrub of spreading habit with golden-yellow young

foliage. **Mint Julep** ('Monlep') (*J.* × *media* Mint Julep) A spreading, flat-topped bush with arching shoots resembling 'Wilhelm Pfitzer' but with bright green foliage. C 1960. **'Mordigan Gold'** (*J.* × *media* 'Mordigan Gold') Similar to 'Pfitzeriana Aurea' of which it is a sport, but more compact. Bright golden summer foliage. **'Old Gold'** (*J.* × *media* 'Old Gold') A sport of 'Pfitzeriana Aurea', from which it differs in its more compact habit, and bronze-gold foliage which does not fade in winter. C 1958. ♀ 2002. **'Pfitzeriana Aurea'** (*J.* × *media* 'Pfitzeriana Aurea') Golden Pfitzer. Terminal shoots and foliage suffused golden-yellow in summer, becoming yellowish-green in winter. A sport of 'Wilhelm Pfitzer' which originated in the USA in 1923. **'Pfitzeriana Compacta'** (*J.* × *media* 'Pfitzeriana Compacta') A sport of 'Wilhelm Pfitzer', more dense and compact in habit, with mainly juvenile awl-shaped leaves. C 1930. ♀ 2002. **'Pfitzeriana Glauca'** (*J.* × *media* 'Pfitzeriana Glauca') A sport of 'Wilhelm Pfitzer' raised in the USA. It is a little denser in habit with mainly awl-shaped, grey-glaucous leaves. It may be described as a glaucous 'Pfitzeriana Compacta'. C 1940. **'Saybrook Gold'** A low, widespreading shrub with bright golden-yellow young foliage bronze in winter. C 1980. **'Wilhelm Pfitzer'** (*J. chinensis* 'Pfitzeriana', *J.* × *media* 'Pfitzeriana') Pfitzer juniper. One of the most popular and commonly planted of all conifers. An eventually medium-sized, widespreading shrub with stout, ascending, arm-like branches, drooping at the tips. Leaves mainly green and scale-like, but with scattered sprays of juvenile leaves with glaucous upper surfaces, particularly in the centre of the bush. An excellent conifer either as a lawn specimen or when used to break the regular outline of a border or bed. It is often used effectively to cover unsightly structures of low stature such as manhole covers and inspection pits. C 1896.

Its true origin has given rise to much wrangling among botanists and horticulturists. It was first mentioned by the great German nursery firm of Späth who named it after Wilhelm Pfitzer, a nurseryman of Stuttgart. Van Melle suggested that it was a wild form from the Ho Lan Shan Mountains, Inner Mongolia, and may possibly have been introduced by the French missionary, Armand David in about 1866.

phoenicea L. Phoenicean juniper. A large shrub or small tree of dense, rounded or broadly conical habit. Leaves green, awl-shaped on juvenile plants. Fruits rounded, 6–14mm across, ripening the second year. It has been growing successfully here for several years without protection. Mediterranean region. I 1683. **subsp. *turbinata*** (Guss.) Nyman. Differs in its egg-shaped or top-shaped fruits. Occurs on hills and by the sea in the W Mediterranean region.

†*pinchotii* Sudw. Red berry juniper. A rare, large shrub with widespreading branches. Leaves dark yellowish-green, awl-shaped on juvenile plants, scale-like on adult plants. SW USA, N Mexico.

pingii W.C. Cheng ex Ferré. A Chinese species closely related to *J. squamata* and including some plants previously included under that species. C & W China. **'Glassel'** A dwarf shrub of vase-shaped habit with ascending shoots, nodding at the tip. C 1958. **'Loderi'**

(*J. squamata* 'Loderi') A small, slow-growing shrub of dense, compact, usually conical habit, eventually reaching 3m. The branchlets nod at their tips and are densely set with short, awl-shaped leaves, which are marked with 2 white bands above. As a young plant it is an ideal subject for a rock garden. Raised by Sir Edmund Loder at Leonardslee, Sussex, in 1925. It has been confused in gardens with plants grown as var. *wilsonii* of which it is probably a selection. **'Pygmaea'** (*J. squamata* 'Pygmaea') A low-growing plant which forms a dwarf, dense, spreading little bush with shortly ascending branches. **var.** *wilsonii* (Rehder) Silba (*J. squamata* 'Wilsonii') Similar in foliage to 'Loderi' but making a rounded bush to about 2m tall and as much across. This is one of several seedlings raised from seed, collected by Ernest Wilson in W China in 1909.

†*procera* Hochst. ex Endl. East African juniper. A tall tree in E Africa, where it occurs at high elevations in the mountains. In cultivation it is usually seen as a large shrub or small tree with green, scale-like leaves, awl-shaped on juvenile plants. Fruits rounded, 5mm across, glaucous. Only suitable for the mildest localities. E Africa to Saudi Arabia and Yemen, the only juniper extending to the S hemisphere.

procumbens (Siebold ex Endl.) Miq. (*J. chinensis* var. *procumbens* Siebold ex Endl.) Creeping juniper. A dwarf, procumbent species with long, stiff branches, forming carpets up to 30cm high (in the centre) and several metres across. The tightly packed branchlets are crowded with awl-shaped, glaucous green, sharply pointed leaves. Excellent groundcover for an open, sunny position on a well-drained soil. A native of Japan where it is said to inhabit seashores. I 1843. **'Bonin Isles'** Similar to 'Nana' but more vigorous. **'Nana'** A more compact plant with shorter branches. I from Japan in about 1900. ♛ 2002.

recurva Buch.-Ham. ex D. Don. Drooping juniper. A large shrub or small tree of broadly conical habit, with stringy, shaggy bark and drooping branchlets. Leaves awl-shaped, in 3s, green or greyish-green, usually with white stomatal bands above, occasionally green. Fruits ovoid, 7–10mm long, glossy olive-brown, ripening to black, containing a single seed. It is an extremely variable species and in the wild appears to intergrade with *J. squamata*. Some forms in cultivation seem intermediate in character between the 2 species though they always retain their characteristic drooping habit. The wood of *J. recurva*, particularly that of the variety *coxii*, is burned for incense in Buddhist temples in the E Himalaya. Himalaya, from Afghanistan, Nepal, NE India, Yunnan and Upper Burma. I about 1822. **'Castlewellan'** A small tree of loose open habit, the branches lax, like fishing rods, the branchlets drooping in long, slender sprays of soft, thread-like foliage. **var.** *coxii* (A.B. Jacks.) Melville. An elegant, small tree with gracefully drooping branchlets which are longer and more pendulous. Leaves are also more loosely arranged, sage-green in colour. I from Upper Burma in 1920 by E.H.M. Cox and Reginald Farrer. **'Embley Park'** (*J. squamata* 'Embley Park', *J. recurva* var. *viridis* hort.) A very distinct, small, spreading shrub with reddish-brown, ascending branches clothed with rich grass-green, awl-

shaped leaves. Raised at Exbury and Embley Park, Hampshire, from seed collected by George Forrest in China. **'Nana'** A dwarf form of spreading habit, the branches strongly decurving; foliage greyish-green. **var.** *viridis* See 'Embley Park'.

rigida Siebold & Zucc. An elegant, large, dioecious shrub or small tree, bearing spreading branches and gracefully drooping branchlets. Leaves rigid, awl-shaped and sharply pointed, marked with glaucous bands above, bronze-green during winter. Fruits globose, 6–8mm across, black and bloomy, ripening the second year. A lovely species, native of Japan, Korea and N China. I 1861 by J.G. Veitch. **subsp.** *conferta* (Parl.) Kitam. (*J. conferta* Parl., *J. litoralis* Maxim.) Shore juniper. A prostrate species with shortly ascending branches, forming large patches of bright green, prickly leaves which have a white stomatal band on their upper surface. Fruits globose, 8–12mm across, purplish-black and bloomy. An invaluable groundcover species, its dense prickly carpets of apple-green foliage contrasting effectively with the prostrate dark green forms of *J. communis* and the blue and grey forms of *J. horizontalis*. A native of Japan and Sakhalin where it is found on sandy seashores. I 1915 by Ernest Wilson. **subsp.** *conferta* **'Blue Pacific'** (*J. conferta* 'Blue Pacific') Leaves broader and less prickly, darker green and not bronzing in winter.

sabina L. Savin. A common and extremely variable, usually dioecious species of spreading or procumbent habit. In its typical form it is a low, spreading shrub, with branches extending 2–3m and slender, ascending, plumose branchlets. Its pungent, disagreeable smell usually separates it from forms of *J. virginiana*. All but the exclusively juvenile forms are harmful if eaten. Leaves green or grey-green, mostly scale-like, but scattered sprays of paired, awl-shaped leaves occur even on old plants. Fruits ovoid or globose, 5–7mm across, bluish-black and bloomy. Widely distributed in the wild, from the mountains of S and C Europe to Caucasus. It is said to have been cultivated since ancient times and has been known in England since 1548. **'Arcadia'** A dense, dwarf shrub with short branchlets clothed with predominantly scale-like, greyish-green leaves. Similar in effect to 'Tamariscifolia'. A specimen in the Sir Harold Hillier Gardens and Arboretum attained 30–45cm by 1m in 10 years. Raised in the USA from seed imported from the Ural Mts in 1933. **'Blaue Donau'** ('Blue Danube') A low-growing shrub with spreading branches and crowded branchlets. Leaves mostly scale-like, grey-blue. C 1956. **'Blue Danube'** See 'Blaue Donau'. **'Cupressifolia'** A low-growing form throwing out long, more or less horizontal branches seldom exceeding 60cm above ground, clothed with mostly adult, dark green leaves. Female. C 1789. **'Erecta'** A strong-growing, medium-sized, female shrub with ascending branches clothed with predominantly scale-like, green leaves. This is the form usually distributed as *J. sabina*. It is also sometimes wrongly grown as 'Cupressifolia' which is lower-growing. C 1891. **'Fastigiata'** An unusual large shrub of dense, columnar habit with tightly packed, ascending branches. Leaves dark green, mainly scale-like. C 1891. **'Hicksii'** A strong-growing shrub with spreading or ascending, later procumbent branches and semi-erect, plumose branchlets crowded with greyish-blue, awl-shaped leaves. A most splendid and vigorous, semi-prostrate shrub, to all practical intents and purposes a blue Pfitzer. It soon reaches 1.2m and sends out its 3–4m long, plumose, steely grey-blue branches. C 1940. **'Mas'** A male clone, similar in habit to 'Cupressifolia'. Leaves mainly awl-shaped, dark green. C 1940. **'New Blue'** See 'Tam no Blight'. **'Rockery Gem'** A vigorous, widespreading dwarf shrub of dense habit with grey-green juvenile foliage. A seedling selected in Holland in 1966. **'Skandia'** ('Scandens') An excellent, low, creeping shrub with dark green, mainly awl-shaped leaves. A plant in the Sir Harold Hillier Gardens and Arboretum attained 20cm by 2m after 10 years. C 1953. **'Tamariscifolia'** A low-growing, compact variety with horizontally packed branches, forming, in time, a wide-spreading, flat-topped bush. Leaves mostly awl-shaped, bright green. An extremely popular juniper of architectural value, equally suitable for clothing dry banks, wall tops or the edges of lawns. Mts of S Europe. Large carpets several metres across can be found in the Spanish Pyrenees. Long cultivated. **'Tam no Blight'** ('New Blue') Similar to 'Tamariscifolia' but with bluer foliage and resistant to juniper blight. C 1970. **'Tripartita'** See *J. virginiana* 'Tripartita'. **'Variegata'** A small shrub with low, slightly ascending branches and dark green, adult foliage flecked with white. C 1855. **'Von Ehren'** A strong-growing shrub, eventually reaching up to 2.5m high, with wide, horizontally spreading, slender branches forming a unique plateau 5m or more across. Branchlets ending in slender sprays; leaves awl-shaped green. C 1912.

sanderi See *Platycladus orientalis* 'Sanderi'.

sargentii See *J. chinensis* var. *sargentii*.

scopulorum Sarg. Rocky Mountain juniper. A small, cypress-like tree of conical habit, often with several main stems. Bark red-brown and shredding. Branches stout and spreading with slender branchlets and tightly adpressed, scale-like leaves, varying in colour from light green to bluish-green and glaucous. Fruits rounded, 6mm across, dark blue and bloomy. A native of the Rocky Mountains from British Columbia to Arizona, Texas and New Mexico. It has given rise to many forms. I 1839. **'Blue Arrow'** A compact, small tree of narrow, upright habit with blue-grey foliage, steel-blue in autumn. An improvement on 'Skyrocket' C 1980. **'Blue Heaven'** A small, conical tree with striking blue foliage. C. 1955. **'Erecta Glauca'** An erect, loosely columnar form with ascending branches and both scale-like and awl-shaped, silvery-glaucous leaves becoming purple-tinged in winter. C. 1958. **'Glauca Pendula'** Dwarf to medium-sized shrub of loose, open habit, branches ascending, branchlets drooping; foliage awl-shaped, greyish-green. With us forming a plant of rather weak constitution. **'Hillborn's Silver Globe'** Small, dense shrub of irregular, rounded habit with silvery-blue, mainly awl-shaped leaves. **'Hill's Silver'** A compact, narrowly columnar form with silvery, grey-blue foliage. C 1922. **'Moonglow'** A small tree of compact, conical habit with blue-grey foliage. C 1971. **'Pathfinder'** A small, narrow, conical tree with flat sprays of bluish-grey foliage. C 1937. **'Repens'** A dwarf, carpeting shrub with prostrate

branches clothed with bluish-green, awl-shaped leaves. C 1939. **'Skyrocket'** (*J. virginiana* 'Skyrocket') A spectacular form of extremely narrow columnar habit. The tallest specimen in the Sir Harold Hillier Gardens and Arboretum measured 5m high by 30cm in diameter in 1970; it reached 7.5m tall in 26 years. Foliage blue-grey. One of the narrowest of all conifers and as such an excellent plant for breaking up low or horizontal planting schemes. Particularly effective in a heather garden. It was found in the wild as a seedling. C 1949. **'Springbank'** Small tree of erect, columnar habit with ascending and spreading branches and slender branchlets; foliage silvery grey-green. C 1965. **'Tabletop'** A compact, small to medium-sized shrub of spreading habit with silvery-blue foliage. C 1951. **'Tolleson's Weeping'** A small tree of open, spreading habit with arching branches from which hang long, thread-like shoots clothed in silvery-grey foliage. C 1973. **'Wichita Blue'** A small tree of compact, broadly upright habit with bright silvery-blue foliage. C 1976.

sheppardii See *J. chinensis* 'Sheppardii'. **var. *torulosa*** See *J. chinensis* 'Kaizuka'.

sibirica See *J. communis* var. *saxatilis*.

silicicola See *J. virginiana* var. *silicicola*

sp. Yu 7881 See *J. squamata* 'Chinese Silver'.

squamata Buch.-Ham. ex D. Don (*J. squamata* var. *fargesii* Rehder & E.H. Wilson) An extremely variable species ranging from a prostrate shrub to a small, bushy tree. Approaching some forms of *J. recurva* in character. All forms have characteristic nodding tips to the shoots and short, awl-shaped leaves which are channelled and white or pale green above. Fruits ellipsoid, 6–8mm across, reddish-brown becoming purplish-black, containing a single seed. The old leaves tend to persist, turning brown. It is widely distributed in the wild throughout Asia, from Afghanistan eastwards to China and Taiwan. I 1824. **'Blue Carpet'** A low-growing form with spreading branches and blue-grey foliage. C 1962. ♀ 2002. **'Blue Spider'** A dwarf shrub, a sport of 'Meyeri', highest in the centre, the spreading branches with silvery-blue foliage. C 1980. **'Blue Star'** A low-growing bush of dense habit making a compact, dwarf bun with comparatively large, silvery-blue, awl-shaped leaves. A very desirable cultivar. Found as a witches' broom on 'Meyeri' before 1950. ♀ 2002. **'Chinese Silver'** (Yu 7881) A beautiful, medium-sized to large, multi-stemmed shrub of dense habit with recurved terminal shoots. Leaves awl-shaped, intense silvery blue-green. **'Embley Park'** See *J. recurva* 'Embley Park'. **var. *fargesii*** See *J. squamata*. **'Filborna'** A vigorous, spreading shrub with ascending shoots and green foliage. A seedling of 'Meyeri' raised in Sweden in 1946. **'Holger'** (*J.* 'Holger') A small, spreading shrub with glaucous, blue foliage, creamy-yellow when young. Raised in 1946 by Holger Jensen in Sweden. ♀ 2002. See also *J.* 'Hunnetorp'. **'Hunnetorp'** (*J.* 'Hunnetorp') A sister seedling of 'Holger' under which name it has been distributed. It differs in its permanently glaucous-blue foliage. **'Loderi'** See *J. pingii* 'Loderi'. **'Meyeri'** A popular and easily recognised juniper of semi-erect habit, with stout, ascending, angular branches and densely packed, glaucous blue, awl-shaped leaves. Although usually seen as a small to medium-sized shrub it will eventually reach a large size. I from a Chinese garden by Frank N. Meyer in 1914. AM 1931. **'Pygmaea'** See *J. pingii* 'Pygmaea'. **'Wilsonii'** See *J. pingii* 'Wilsonii'.

suecica See *J. communis* Suecica Group.

taxifolia Hook. & Arn. (*J. lutchuenensis* Koidz.) A prostrate shrub making a low mound, excellent for groundcover. Leaves in 3s, to 5mm long, densely overlapping, glaucous when young becoming bright green on the lower surface, with a single, broad, glaucous band on the upper surface. Some plants grown under this name are *J. rigida* subsp. *conferta* which differs in its much longer, spreading needles. S Japan (Islands).

thurifera L. Spanish juniper. A large, dioecious shrub or small tree of tight, columnar habit. In the wild developing a rounded or spreading head and stems with a large girth. Adult leaves scale-like, greyish-green borne on slender, thread-like branchlets. Fruits globose, 7–11mm across, blue, ripening to black, bloomy. A rare species in cultivation and unsuitable for the coldest areas. Mts of S. C and E Spain, French Alps, NW Africa (Atlas Mts). C 1752.

tibetica Kom. (*J. distans* Florin) A rare, large shrub or small tree of loosely columnar habit, with drooping branchlets. Leaves mainly juvenile, awl-shaped, grey-green. Fruits ovoid, 8–12mm long, reddish-brown. SW China. I 1926.

virginiana L. Pencil cedar. One of the hardiest and most accommodating of conifers, forming a medium-sized to large tree of broadly conical habit. Branchlets slender, clothed with small, sharp-pointed, scale-like leaves and scattered patches of awl-shaped, glaucous, juvenile leaves. Fruits rounded or ovoid, 5mm across, brownish-purple and bloomy, ripening the first year. A variable species which can be confused with *J. chinensis* but the latter has broader juvenile leaves. There are numerous cultivars. E and C North America. C 1664. **'Blue Cloud'** (*J.* 'Blue Cloud', *J.* × *media* 'Blue Cloud') A wide-spreading, medium-sized shrub, similar in habit to *J.* × *pfitzeriana* 'Wilhelm Pfitzer' but lower-growing and less vigorous, with slender, almost thread-like branchlets and glaucous, blue foliage. Possibly a hybrid. C 1955. **'Burkii'** An excellent columnar form of dense, compact habit, with ascending branches and both scale-like and awl-shaped, steel-blue leaves, bronze-purple in winter. C 1930. **'Canaertii'** Small, conical tree of rather dense habit. Foliage bright green, very attractive when peppered with small, cobalt-blue to purple-bloomed, violet fruits. C 1868. **'Chamberlaynii'** See 'Pendula Nana'. **'Cupressifolia'** See 'Hillspire'. **'Elegans'** See 'Elegantissima'. **'Elegantissima'** ('Elegans') A small tree of graceful habit. Branches ascending, drooping at the tips; branchlets spreading or arching. Leaves scale-like, bright green. FCC 1875. **'Glauca'** A dense, columnar form with spreading branches clothed with silvery-grey, mainly scale-like leaves. A most attractive, small to medium-sized tree. C 1855. **'Globosa'** Dwarf shrub of dense, rounded habit. Densely packed branches are clothed with mainly scale-like, bright green leaves. C before 1904. **'Grey Owl'** See *J.* 'Grey Owl'. **'Hetzii'** (*J.* × *media* 'Hetzii') A medium-sized to large, widespreading shrub, similar to *J.* × *pfitzeriana* 'Wilhelm Pfitzer', but stems more ascending. The glaucous, mainly adult foliage is also softer to the touch. C 1920. **'Hillii'**

('Pyramidiformis Hillii') A slow-growing, columnar form of dense, compact habit, up to 4m. Leaves awl-shaped, glaucous or bluish-green, turning to purplish-bronze in winter. C 1914. **'Hillspire'** ('Cupressifolia') A dense, conical or columnar form with densely packed, slender, fastigiate branches clothed with dark green, scale-like foliage. Raised in Illinois, USA about 1925. **'Keteleeri'** See *J. chinensis* 'Keteleeri'. **'Kosteri'** (*J.* × *media* 'Kosteri') A small shrub with prostrate and ascending, plumose branches, clothed with grey-green, scale-like and awl-shaped leaves, sometimes purple-tinged in winter. C 1884. **'Manhattan Blue'** A small, conical, male tree of compact habit; foliage bluish-green. C 1963. **'Nana Compacta'** Dwarf shrub, similar to 'Globosa', but less regular in shape and bearing mainly juvenile leaves of greyish-green, becoming purple-tinged in winter. C 1887. **'Pendula'** An elegant, small tree with spreading or arching branches and drooping branchlets. Leaves mainly awl-shaped, green. C 1850. **'Pendula Nana'** A female clone of dense habit. A dwarf, spreading or prostrate shrub with drooping branchlets and glaucous, mainly awl-shaped leaves. It is sometimes trained to make a weeping tree. C 1850. Originally distributed as 'Chamberlaynii'. **'Pseudocupressus'** Slender, columnar form of compact habit. Leaves awl-shaped, light green, bluish-green when young. C 1932. **'Pyramidiformis Hillii'** See 'Hillii'. **'Reptans'** (*J.* × *media* 'Reptans', *J. chinensis* 'Reptans') A low-growing shrub with rigid, slightly ascending branches. Leaves both scale-like and awl-shaped, grey-green. The foliage is rough to the touch. C 1896. **'Schottii'** Small tree of dense, narrowly conical habit; foliage scale-like, light green. C 1855. **var. silicicola** (Small) E. Murray (*J. silicicola* (Small) L.H. Bailey) A medium-sized tree which it differs in its more slender shoots and smaller cones. SE USA (coastal regions). **'Skyrocket'** See *J. scopulorum* 'Skyrocket'. **'Sulphur Spray'** (*J.* × *media* 'Sulphur Spray') A sport of 'Hetzii', resembling it in habit but slower growing, to about 2m tall and across. Foliage a striking pale sulphur-yellow. C 1962. ♀ 2002. **'Tripartita'** (*J. sabina* 'Tripartita', *J. lusitanica* hort.) A strong-growing, medium-sized shrub, with strongly ascending, nearly erect branches densely clothed with both green, scale-like leaves and glaucous, awl-shaped leaves. It is a juniper of rather heavy, ponderous habit which has now been superseded by the many forms of the Pfitzer Juniper (*J.* × *pfitzeriana*). C 1867.

wallichiana See *J. indica*.

*KETELEERIA Carrière—**Pinaceae**—A genus of 3 species of evergreen trees native to S China and SE Asia, related to *Abies* and resembling them in general appearance. Young trees are rather conical in habit, gradually becoming flat-topped with age. The oblong-lanceolate or linear leaves are arranged in 2 ranks on the lateral shoots, leaving a circular scar (as in *Abies*) when they fall. Leaves of juvenile plants are usually spine-tipped. Male and female strobili are borne on the same tree, the males in clusters. The erect cones ripen during the second year, falling intact.

davidiana (Bertr.) Beissn. A small to medium-sized tree, old specimens developing buttress-like roots. Leaves sharply pointed and 4–6cm long on young trees, blunter and 2–4cm long on adult trees. Cones cylindrical, 12–20cm long, reddish when young, maturing pale brown. Perhaps the hardiest species, although the young shoots are subject to damage by late spring frosts. C and W China, with a variety in Taiwan. Discovered by Père David in 1869. I 1888 by Augustine Henry.

†*fortunei* (A. Murr.) Carrière. A small tree in cultivation, resembling *K. davidiana*, but with shorter leaves and larger seeds. It needs a sheltered position and may be damaged by late spring frosts. SE China. I 1844 by Robert Fortune.

†*LAGAROSTROBOS** Quinn—Podocarpaceae—A genus of a single species from Tasmania, previously included in *Dacrydium*.

franklinii (Hook. f.) Quinn (*Dacrydium franklinii* Hook. f.) Huon pine. In the milder parts of the British Isles this forms a large, graceful shrub or small, conical tree. The slender, drooping branches are clothed with bright green, scale-like leaves. Subject to injury in severe winters. The wood is highly prized for furniture and cabinet work in Tasmania.

LARIX Mill.—Pinaceae—The larches make up a small genus of some 11 species of mostly fast-growing, deciduous, monoecious trees combining utility and beauty. The branches are borne in irregular whorls ending in long, slender, flexible branchlets which, on older trees, tend to droop or hang in a graceful manner. Leaves linear, borne in dense rosettes on short spurs on the older wood, bunched on short side shoots and spirally arranged on the young growing shoots. They are generally bright green or occasionally blue-green during spring and summer, turning to butter-yellow or old gold in autumn. In early spring the attractive, red, pink, yellow or green female strobili and the more numerous but small, yellow male strobili stud the, as yet, leafless branchlets. The small, erect, rounded or oblong cones which follow, shed their seed usually in the autumn of the first year, but remain intact for an indefinite period and as such are commonly used for indoor Christmas decorations.

Several of the larches are extremely valuable for their timber which is strong, heavy and durable. They are adaptable to most soils, though wet sites and dry, shallow chalk soils are best avoided. There is no more refreshing tint of spring than the pale green of their awakening buds, nor a more mellow shade than the autumn colour of their foliage.

americana See *L. laricina*.

dahurica See *L. gmelinii*.

decidua Mill. (*L. europaea* Lam. & DC.) European larch, Common larch. A large tree with a slender, cone-shaped crown when young. Branches and branchlets drooping on old specimens. Shoots yellowish or grey, glabrous. Rosette leaves 1.5–3.5cm long, light green. Cones ovoid, 2–4cm long, bracts hidden. One of the most important reforestation trees. Native of the European Alps and Carpathians. Commonly planted elsewhere. Long cultivated; perhaps first introduced into the British Isles in about 1620. ♀ 2002. **'Corley'** A slow-growing, small, leaderless bush of rounded habit. Propagated from a witches' broom found by Mr R.F. Corley. **'Fastigiata'** A narrow, conical form with short, ascending branches. C

1868. **'Pendula'** A tall tree of irregular habit; branches arching downwards, branchlets pendent. C 1836. **'Puli'** An attractive, weeping form grown as a standard with slender, pendent branches. Raised in Hungary about 1972. **'Repens'** A form in which the lower branches elongate and spread out along the ground. C 1825.

× *eurolepis* See *L.* × *marschlinsii*.

europaea See *L. decidua*.

gmelinii (Rupr.) Kuzen. (*L. dahurica* Turcz. ex Trautv.) Dahurian larch. A variable species of medium size in cultivation, with usually glabrous, yellowish shoots which may be reddish during winter. Leaves 2–3cm long, bright green. Cones 1.5–3cm long. Not one of the best species for the British Isles, being liable to damage by spring frosts. It occurs further north than any other tree. NE Asia. I 1827. **var.** *japonica* (Maxim. ex Regel) Pilg. Kurile larch. A medium-sized tree differing in its denser branching system, shorter leaves and smaller cones. Shoots reddish-brown and downy. Slow-growing and liable to injury by late spring frosts. Sakhalin, Kurile Isles. I 1888. **var.** *olgensis* (A. Henry) Ostenf. & Syrach. Similar growth to var. *japonica*, but shoots even more densely reddish-hairy and both leaves and cones smaller. Like its relatives. this larch is conditioned to much longer and severer winters than are experienced in the British Isles and is too easily tempted into premature growth by warm periods and then damaged by subsequent inclement conditions. NE Asia. I about 1911. **var.** *principis-rupprechtii* (Mayr) Pilg. A more vigorous form with reddish-brown, glabrous shoots, much longer bright green leaves, up to 10cm long, on vigorous shoots, and larger cones. Korea, Manchuria, NC China. I 1903.

†*griffithii* Hook. f. (*L. griffithiana* hort. ex Carrière) Himalayan larch. A beautiful tree of medium size, with long, drooping branchlets and downy shoots which turn reddish-brown the second year. Leaves 2.5–3.5cm long, bright green. Cones large, cylindrical, 7–10cm long, with exserted, reflexed bracts. A graceful species for milder districts, easily distinguished by its weeping branchlets and large cones. E Himalaya. I 1848 by Sir Joseph Hooker. AM 1974.

kaempferi (Lamb.) Carrière. (*L. leptolepis* (Siebold & Zucc.) Gordon) Japanese larch. A vigorous, large tree with reddish shoots. Leaves 2–3.5cm long, sea-green, broader than those of *L. decidua*. Cones ovoid, 2–3cm long with scales turned outward and downward at tips. A commonly planted larch used extensively for reforestation, withstanding exposure well. The reddish twigs appear to create a purple haze above a plantation on a sunny afternoon in late winter. Japan. I 1861 by J.G. Veitch. ♀ 2002. **'Blue Dwarf'** A dwarf shrub with short blue-green leaves on red shoots. C 1982. **'Blue Haze'** A selection with attractive, glaucous blue leaves. **'Blue Rabbit Weeping'** Pendent branchlets and glaucous-blue foliage. Normally grown as a weeping standard. C 1986. **'Diana'** A graceful, upright tree with contorted branches and fresh green foliage. Selected in Germany in 1974. **'Hobbit'** A compact, slow-growing, dwarf form found as a witches' broom by our salesman Stan Dolding in 1960. **'Pendula'** A beautiful, tall, elegant tree with long, weeping branches. A tree in the Sir Harold Hillier Gardens and Arboretum was 17m tall in 1992. C 1896. 'Dervaes' is very similar. **'Wolterdingen'** A dense, dwarf, bun-shaped bush of slow growth with blue-grey foliage. Found in a park in Wolterdingen, Germany in 1970.

laricina (Du Roi) K. Koch (*L. americana* Michx.) Tamarack. A small to medium-sized tree, vigorous when young. Shoots glabrous and glaucous at first, later reddish-brown. Leaves 2–3cm long, bright green. Cones cylindric-ovoid, 1–1.5cm long. Though of great value in North America it is less successful in the British Isles and has been little planted. It is interesting on account of its small, neat cones. N North America. I about 1760, possibly before (see note under *L. × pendula*).

leptolepis See *L. kaempferi*.

lyallii Parl. A small to medium-sized tree in its native habitat, often forming a gnarled, windswept, small tree or shrub. It is easily recognised by its densely felted young shoots and its 4-angled, greyish-green leaves, 2.5–3.5cm long. Cones oblong-ovoid, 3.5–5cm long with conspicuous, long-pointed, exserted bracts. Regarded by some authorities as an alpine form of *L. occidentalis*. One of the least adaptable species for the British Isles, it appears to require a colder climate. W North America. I about 1904.

× *marschlinsii* Coaz (*L. × eurolepis* A. Henry) (*L. decidua × L. kaempferi*) Hybrid larch, Dunkeld larch. A vigorous, large tree of great commercial value. It differs from *L. decidua* in its faintly glaucous shoots and its slightly broader, somewhat glaucous leaves, and from *L. kaempferi* in its less glaucous, brown or pale orange shoots and shorter, less glaucous leaves. This important hybrid forest tree is less susceptible to disease than the common larch. It arose at Dunkeld, Perthshire, in about 1904; the same hybrid had already occurred in Switzerland although it was originally considered to be *L. kaempferi × L. sibirica*.

occidentalis Nutt. Western larch. A large tree, attaining 60m in its native habitat. Young shoots pale straw, hairy in the grooves, pale orange-brown and glabrous the second year. Leaves 2.5–4cm long, greyish-green. Cones ovoid, 2.5–3.5cm long, with long-pointed, exserted bracts. North America. Discovered by David Douglas. C 1880.

× *pendula* Salisb. Weeping larch. A large tree with long branches, pendent branchlets and shoots that are glabrous and pinkish when young, becoming purple in summer.

The origin of this attractive larch has long been obscure. It was first recorded in cultivation in Peter Collinson's garden at Peckham, where it had been planted in 1739. At that time it was claimed to be growing wild in America, but no one since then has found any evidence of this. Most authorities favour the explanation of its origin as a hybrid between *L. decidua* and *L. laricina*. Mr Desmond Clarke has pointed out that the tree originally described by the botanist Solander was not the Peckham tree but a tree growing in Collinson's garden at Mill Hill, which some authorities assumed was the same tree, simply transplanted from one garden to another by Collinson. From this it seems highly probable that Collinson's original tree at Peckham was in fact *L. laricina* and that the later, Mill Hill tree (*L. × pendula*) was a seedling, the result of a cross with *L. decidua*.

potaninii Batalin (*L. thibetica* Franch.) Chinese larch. A beautiful, medium-sized tree with comparatively long, blue-green leaves and graceful, drooping branchlets and orange-brown or purplish, usually glabrous shoots. Leaves 4-angled, 2–3cm long. Cones oblong-ovoid, 2.5–5cm long, with long-pointed, exserted bracts; the common larch of W Sichuan and said to be the most valuable coniferous timber tree in W China. Unfortunately, it is not of robust constitution in the British Isles. I 1904 by Ernest Wilson.

russica See *L. sibirica*.

sibirica Ledeb. (*L. russica* (Endl.) Sabine ex Trautv.) Siberian larch. A medium-sized tree, conical when young. Shoots yellow, hairy or glabrous. Leaves 2–4cm long, sharply pointed. Cones conical, 3–4cm long. Like several of its relatives, this species requires a colder, more even climate than can be expected in the British Isles The young shoots are very subject to damage by spring frost. Russia, N China. I 1806.

thibetica See *L. potaninii*.

***LEPIDOTHAMNUS** Phil.—Podocarpaceae—A genus of 3 species of shrubs or small trees from South America and New Zealand previously included in *Podocarpus*.

intermedius (Kirk) Quinn (*Dacrydium intermedium* Kirk) A small tree or large bush with spreading branches. Widely distributed in New Zealand where its wood is used for railway sleepers, boat building and telegraph poles.

laxifolius (Hook. f.) Quinn (*Dacrydium laxifolium* Hook. f.) Mountain Rimu, Pygmy pine. A prostrate or scrambling conifer forming mats of slender, wiry stems and tiny, scale-like leaves which turn plum-purple in winter. Perhaps the smallest conifer in the world, coning at just 8cm high. When it was first discovered, it was mistaken for a moss; it is found in mountain districts of New Zealand. **'Blue Gem'** A form with blue foliage, selected in the wild near Homers Tunnel, New Zealand.

Leyland cypress See × *Cupressocyparis leylandii*.

***LIBOCEDRUS** Endl.—Cupressaceae—A small genus of 5 species allied to *Thuja*. Evergreen trees and shrubs from the S hemisphere, occurring in New Caledonia and New Zealand. The branches are regularly divided into flattened, fern-like sprays of scale-like leaves. Male and female strobili occur on the same plant. Cones short-stalked, ripening the first year. The following species are only suitable for the mildest areas of the British Isles.

bidwillii Hook. f. Pahautea. A rare species differing from *L. plumosa* in its smaller leaves and cones and the 4-sided character of the branchlets. This fastigiate tree is hardier than *L. plumosa* and has survived uninjured in the Sir Harold Hillier Gardens and Arboretum for many years. New Zealand.

chilensis See *Austrocedrus chilensis*.

decurrens See *Calocedrus decurrens*.

doniana See *L. plumosa*.

formosana See *Calocedrus formosana*.

macrolepis See *Calocedrus macrolepis*.

plumosa (D. Don) Sarg. (*L. doniana* (Hook.) Endl.) Kawaka. A small tree, often shrubby in cultivation, with peculiar flattened, fern-like branchlets, clothed with bright green, scale-like leaves. Cones ovoid, 1–2cm long. New Zealand.

tetragona See *Pilgerodendron uviferum*.

Maidenhair tree See *Ginkgo biloba*.

†**MANOAO** Molloy—**Podocarpaceae**—A genus of a single species previously included in *Dacrydium*, or more recently, in *Lagarostrobos*.

colensoi (Hook.) Molloy (*Dacrydium colensoi* Hook.) Westland pine. A small, conical tree of rather loose habit, branchlets long and slender. Native to New Zealand where its wood is highly prized.

METASEQUOIA Hu & W.C. Cheng—**Cupressaceae**—The first specimen of this monotypic genus was found by Mr T. Kan in a village in C China in 1941. It was not until 1944 that further trees were discovered and specimens collected, and in the following year the sensational news was released that a living relic of a fossil genus had been discovered. Not unlike *Taxodium* in general appearance, it differs in several botanical characters, including its leaves and ultimate branchlets, both of which are oppositely arranged.

glyptostroboides Hu & W.C. Cheng. Dawn redwood. A strong-growing, vigorous, deciduous tree of conical habit when young, with shaggy, cinnamon-brown bark. Leaves linear, flattened, borne in 2 opposite ranks on short, deciduous branchlets, the whole resembling a pinnate, feathery leaf. They are bright larch-green during summer, becoming tawny-pink and old gold in autumn. Male and female strobili borne on the same tree, the males in large racemes or panicles. Cones pendent, on long stalks, globose or cylindrical, 15–20mm across, dark brown and mature the first year.

The ease with which it is propagated and its rapid growth, plus its ornamental qualities, have combined to make this perhaps the most popular coniferous species in the shortest possible time. It thrives best in moist but well-drained conditions. On chalk soils it is slower-growing. It has proved quite hardy and is equally successful in industrial areas. After only 40 years in cultivation some plants in North America are more than 30m. Trees growing in the British Isles from seeds received from the Arnold Arboretum in 1948 have already exceeded 25m in height. Mature trees in its native habitat were reported to be 28–35m high with rounded crowns. Native of C China (Hubei, NE Sichuan and W Hubei). I 1947. ♀ 2002. AM 1969. **'Emerald Feathers'** A fine tree of regular, conical habit with lush green foliage. Selected by the US National Arboretum, Washington, before 1972. **'Gold Rush'** A form with soft yellow foliage, originally raised in Japan and introduced to Europe in 1993. **'National'** A more narrowly conical form, selected by the US National Arboretum, Washington, USA in 1958.

*MICROBIOTA** Kom.—**Cupressaceae**—A monotypic genus related to *Juniperus*, differing in its fruits which possess hardened, almost woody scales, breaking up when mature. Male and female strobili are on separate plants.

decussata Kom. A densely branched, prostrate, evergreen shrub with widespreading branches bearing small, opposite, almost scale-like leaves, although awl-shaped leaves are present on some branches. Leaves are pale green in summer, turning bronze-red or purple in winter. Fruits very small, berry-like, 3mm long. In the wild it is confined to the Valley of the Suchan, to the east of Vladivostock in E Siberia, where it was discovered in 1921. ♀ 2002. AM 1973.

*MICROCACHRYS** Hook. f.—**Podocarpaceae**—A monotypic genus related to *Podocarpus*, with slender stems and scale-like leaves. Male and female strobili are borne on the same plant.

tetragona (Hook.) Hook. f. A splendid and hardy, dwarf bush with snake-like, 4-angled, arching branches clad with minute, scale-like leaves arranged in 4 ranks. Both male and female strobili are conspicuous when present. Fruits egg-shaped, bright red, fleshy and translucent. A rare conifer, restricted in the wild to the summits of 2 mountains in Tasmania. I 1857. FCC 1977. AM 1971.

*MICROSTROBOS** J. Garden & L.A.S. Johnson—**Podocarpaceae**—2 species of very rare, evergreen shrubs related to *Microcachrys*. The adult leaves are scale-like and spirally arranged along the slender stems. Male and female strobili are borne on the same plant. Cones about 2mm long, containing several pale brown or greyish seeds. Both species are found in moist conditions in the wild.

fitzgeraldii (F. Muell.) J. Garden & L.A.S. Johnson (*Pherosphaera fitzgeraldii* (F. Muell.) Hook. f.) A small, semi-prostrate, densely branched shrub with slender stems clothed with tiny, olive-green, scale-like leaves. Differs from *M. niphophilus* in its looser growth and longer, less congested leaves. Usually only found at the foot of waterfalls in the Blue Mountains of New South Wales, Australia. It has grown successfully in the Sir Harold Hillier Gardens and Arboretum for many years.

niphophilus J. Garden & L.A.S. Johnson (*Pherosphaera hookeriana* W. Archer) A slender-branched, small to medium-sized shrub with short, stiff branches densely clothed with tiny, green, overlapping scale-like leaves. Resembles *Lagarostrobos franklinii* in general appearance. Only found in high alpine regions in Tasmania, normally frequenting the margins of lakes, streams and waterfalls. Rare, even in the wild.

Monkey puzzle See *Araucaria araucana*.

†**NAGEIA** Gaertn.—**Podocarpaceae**—A genus of 6 species of tender trees natives of Asia from India to Japan and SE Asia to New Guinea, previously included in *Podocarpus*.

nagi (Thunb.) Kuntze (*Podocarpus nagi* (Thunb.) Pilg.) A small, slow-growing tree or large, bushy shrub. Leaves opposite or nearly so, ovate or broadly lanceolate, 4–5cm long, leathery, dark green above, paler below. Not hardy enough to survive long in the Home Counties. Japan, China, Taiwan.

*PHYLLOCLADUS** Rich. ex Mirb.—**Phyllocladaceae**—A small genus of 4 species of evergreen trees and shrubs of unusual appearance, suggesting a primitive origin. The branches are normally arranged in whorls and bear peculiar and attractive, leaf-like, flattened branchlets (cladodes), which perform the functions of the true leaves, these being scale-like and found mainly on seedlings. Male and female strobili are found on the same or on separate plants, the males produced in clusters at the tips of the shoots, the females borne on the margins of the cladodes. Fruits consisting of one to several seeds, each in a cup-like, fleshy receptacle. Suitable only for the mildest districts, except *P. trichomanoides* var. *alpinus*, which has grown successfully in the Sir Harold Hillier Gardens and Arboretum for more than 40 years and was uninjured by the severe winter of 1962–63, when we lost all other species of the genus.

alpinus See *P. trichomanoides* var. *alpinus*.

†*aspleniifolius* (Labill.) Hook. f. (*P. glaucus* hort. ex Carrière, *P. rhomboidalis* Rich. & A. Rich.) Celery-topped pine. A small tree with glaucous, fan-shaped cladodes up to 2.5–5cm long, usually toothed or lobed. Suitable only for a conservatory or sheltered corners in the mildest areas. Tasmania.

glaucus See *P. aspleniifolius* and *P. toatoa*.

rhomboidalis See *P. aspleniifolius*.

†*toatoa* Molloy (*P. glauca* Kirk) Toa toa. An attractive, small tree bearing cladodes of 2 kinds: those of the main stem are solitary and fan-shaped with coarsely toothed margins; those on the branchlets are arranged in whorls and resemble pinnate leaves 10–25cm long, with 9–17 coarsely toothed, fan-shaped or diamond-shaped "leaflets". Male and female strobili are borne on separate plants. New Zealand (North Island).

†*trichomanoides* D. Don. Tanekaha. A large shrub or small tree with fan-shaped or ovate, entire or lobed, green cladodes, pinnately arranged in attractive 'fronds'. The young emerging cladodes are reddish-brown. New Zealand. **var.** *alpinus* (Hook. f.) Parl. (*P. alpinus* Hook. f.) Alpine celery-topped pine. A small to medium-sized shrub, often dwarf and stunted, usually with a single main stem. Its habit here is erect and narrowly conical bearing numerous, small, green, diamond-shaped cladodes up to 3.5cm long. The clusters of reddish male strobili are small, but attractive. This species is perfectly hardy here and is a splendid miniature tree for a rock garden. New Zealand. **var.** *alpinus* 'Silver Blades' A small to medium-sized shrub of slow growth. Small, neat, diamond-shaped cladodes of silvery-blue. The best colour is retained on plants under glass.

*PICEA A. Dietr.—Pinaceae—The spruces form a genus of about 35 species found throughout N temperate regions, particularly in E Asia. Evergreen trees, usually of conical habit, with branches borne in whorls. The shoots and branchlets are rough to the touch due to numerous, tiny, peg-like projections left by the fallen leaves. The leaves are short and needle-like, flattened or quadrangular and arranged spirally or in 2 ranks. Male and female strobili are produced on the same tree, the male axillary and the often colourful females, terminal. Cones pendent varying from ovoid to cylindrical, ripening in the autumn of the first year, remaining intact and falling usually late in the second year. The spruces are an extremely ornamental group of trees, containing a wide range of shapes and sizes with foliage varying in shades of green and grey. They thrive in a variety of soils, but cannot be recommended for really poor, shallow, chalky or dry soils, nor as single isolated specimens or narrow shelterbelts in very exposed places. They differ from the superficially similar *Abies* in their plug-like leaf scars and pendent cones, which fall intact. There are numerous dwarf forms, particularly of the Norway spruce, *P. abies*.

abies (L.) H. Karst. (*P. excelsa* (Lam.) Link) Common spruce, Norway spruce. The commonest spruce in general cultivation and the species popularly known as the Christmas tree. A large tree with orange or reddish-brown, usually glabrous shoots. Leaves 1–2.5cm long, shining dark green, densely clothing the upper sides of the branchlets, pectinate below. Cones cylindrical, 10–15cm long. This species is extensively used for reforestation and the white or cream-coloured wood for a wide variety of articles. The young shoots and leaves are the basis of spruce beer. Widely distributed in the wild over N and C Europe, often in large forests. I to the British Isles about 1500.

Cultivars of *Picea abies*

Under cultivation it has given rise to numerous forms, differing mainly in size and habit. Most of the dwarf forms are very slow-growing and suitable for a large rock garden.

'Acrocona' A large, spreading bush or small tree with semi-pendent branches which, even at an early age, usually terminate in a precocious cone. C 1890.

'Argenteospica' Young foliage tipped with creamy-white. Raised in Germany by Hesse before 1891.

'Aurea' Unfolding leaves bright yellow, changing as they age to soft yellow-green. C 1838. FCC 1862.

'Capitata' Dense, small, globular bush with clustered terminal branches. Terminal buds large, more or less concealed by the erect leaves. A specimen in our collection reached 1.2m by 1.2m after 35 years. C 1889.

'Cincinnata' A small tree with weeping branches. C 1897.

'Clanbrassiliana' A dense, small, flat-topped bush, wider than high. In the dormant season it is conspicuous by its innumerable brown winter buds and small, crowded leaves on branchlets noticeably variable in vigour. A specimen in our collection attained 1.2m by 2.4m after 40 years. One of the oldest cultivars, originally discovered in N Ireland about 1790.

'Cranstonii' A curious, small, irregular tree of loose, open habit, with long, lax branches often without branchlets. C 1855.

'Cupressina' A medium-sized tree of columnar habit, with ascending branches. An attractive form of dense growth. C 1855.

'Doone Valley' A remarkable, extremely slow-growing bush forming a minute bun of tightly congested growth. Almost unrecognisable as a spruce. Suitable for a scree or alpine trough garden. Named after "Doone Valley", the one-time garden of Mr W. Archer.

'Echiniformis' An exceedingly slow-growing, little hummock of dense, congested growth. It may be confused with 'Gregoryana', but is slower-growing, never so large and its leaves are more rigid and prickly. A specimen in our collection attained 23cm by 53cm after 20 years. Most suitable for a rock garden. C 1875.

'Effusa' A dense, compact, dwarf bush of irregular dome-shaped habit. Suitable for a rock garden.

Picea abies continued:

'Fastigiata' See 'Pyramidata'.

'Finedonensis' ('Argentea') Small tree with spreading branches and silver young foliage. Tends to scorch in strong sun. Originally found as a seedling at Finedon Hall, Northamptonshire. C 1862.

'Gregoryana' A dense, compact, dwarf bush developing into a somewhat billowy, rounded, flat-topped dome with conspicuous, radially arranged, sea-green leaves. A specimen in our collection attained 50cm by 1.2m after 30 years. One of the most popular dwarf forms. C 1862.

'Humilis' A dwarf, slow-growing bush of dense, compact, conical habit with crowded and congested branchlets. Suitable for a rock garden. Differs from the similar 'Pygmaea' in its pale or yellowish-brown winter buds. C 1891.

'Inversa' ('Pendula') An unusual form usually seen as a large shrub with depressed branches. It is taller, less rigid and softer to the touch than 'Reflexa'. There is a magnificent specimen, exceeding a hundred years old, in the celebrated arboretum and garden at Kalmthout, Belgium. C 1855.

'Little Gem' A dwarf, slow-growing bun of globular habit with tiny, densely crowded leaves. Originated as a sport of 'Nidiformis' in the nurseries of F.J. Grootendorst of Boskoop. ♥ 2002.

'Maxwellii' A squat, dwarf, rounded, slow-growing dome with coarse, rigid, spine-pointed, sea-green leaves. C about 1860.

'Nana' A slow-growing, dwarf bush of conical habit, with densely crowded branches and sharply pointed, small leaves. C 1855.

'Nana Compacta' A dwarf, very compact and slow-growing, rounded bush with spreading branches and erect upper shoots. Leaves sharp-pointed, densely arranged on stout shoots. C 1950.

'Nidiformis' A very popular and commonly planted form of German origin, making a dwarf, dense, flat-topped bush of spreading habit, the branches forming a series of tight, horizontal layers. A specimen in our collection attained 60cm by 1.8m after 30 years. C 1907. ♥ 2002.

'Ohlendorffii' Small, conical bush of dense habit; leaves yellowish-green, rather small, recalling those of *P. orientalis*. Freer-growing than most, it will reach 1.8m by 1.2m after 30 years. C about 1845.

'Pachyphylla' Dwarf, slow-growing bush with few short, stout branches and exceptionally thick, forward-directed, rigid leaves. An excellent specimen of this distinct cultivar is growing at Glasnevin Botanic Garden, Ireland. C 1923.

'Pendula' See 'Inversa'.

'Pendula Major' A strong-growing, conical tree with mainly spreading branches, some decurving and pendent, bearing branchlets which are also decurving or pendent. C 1868.

'Phylicoides' A slow-growing, medium-sized to large shrub of irregular growth, conspicuous by its short, thick, distantly spaced leaves. A specimen in our collection attained 1.8m by 1.5m after 30 years C 1855.

'Procumbens' A dwarf, flat-topped, widespreading bush with densely layered branches, the branchlets ascending at the tips. A specimen in our collection attained 60cm by 3m after 30 years. C 1850.

'Pseudoprostrata' ('Prostrata') Dwarf, broad-spreading shrub with a flattened top. Denser growing than 'Procumbens'. A specimen in our collection attained 60cm by 1.5m after 25 years. C 1923.

'Pumila' A dwarf, slow-growing, flat-topped bush of spreading, compact but irregular habit. Branches and branchlets densely packed and congested. A specimen in our collection attained 60cm by 1.5m after 30 years. C 1874.

'Pumila Nigra' Dwarf bush, similar to 'Pumila', but leaves shining dark green. 'Pumila Glauca' is almost, if not wholly, identical.

'Pygmaea' A dwarf, extremely slow-growing form of globular or broadly dome-shaped habit, with tightly congested branchlets forming a neat, compact but irregular outline. It is one of the slowest-growing of all *P. abies* cultivars, attaining 45cm by 30cm in about 30 years. It is also one of the oldest, having been known since about 1800.

'Pyramidata' ('Fastigiata', 'Pyramidalis') A strong-growing, narrowly conical tree with ascending branches. Excellent where space is limited. C 1853.

'Reflexa' A dense, rigid, more or less prostrate or creeping bush of irregular habit, with normal-sized branchlets and leaves. Unless it is trained to a single, upright stem, it forms a low dome with long, prostrate branches extending carpet-like for several metres. A specimen in our collection measured 50cm high at the raised centre and 4m across after 25 years. Excellent groundcover. C 1890.

'Remontii' A dense, slow-growing, conical bush, similar to *P. glauca* var. *albertiana* 'Conica' in shape, eventually attaining 2–2.5m. C 1874.

'Repens' A slow-growing, dwarf, flat-topped bush with branches in layers. A low, widespreading clone, suitable for a large rock garden. It appears very similar to 'Pseudoprostrata'. C 1898.

'Rubra Spicata' A form with red young growths is grown under this name.

'Tabuliformis' A small, slow-growing bush with tabulated growth and flattened top. A specimen in our collection attained 1.75m by 3.5m after 30 years. C 1865.

'Virgata' A medium-sized tree of curious habit, with long, whorled, sparsely produced branches. They are undivided and snake-like in appearance or with a few pendent branchlets. The leaves are radially arranged. C 1853. AM 1978.

'Waugh' Medium-sized, sparsely branched bush with thick shoots and thick, widely spaced leaves.

'Will's Zwerg' An attractive, slow-growing form of dense, conical habit, eventually a medium-sized bush.

alba See *P. glauca*.

alcoquiana (Veitch ex Lindl.) Carrière (*P. bicolor* (Maxim.) Mayr) A medium-sized to large tree of broad conical shape, with long branches, upcurved at tips, and with yellowish-brown to reddish-brown, glabrous or hairy young shoots. Leaves 1–2cm long, green or bluish-green above, somewhat glaucous beneath, densely crowded on the upper surfaces of the branchlets. Cones to 12cm long, reddish-purple when young. Japan. I 1861 by J.G. Veitch.

var. acicularis (Maxim. ex Beissn.) Fitschen (*P. bicolor* var. *acicularis* (Maxim. ex Beissn.) Shiras.) An uncommon variety differing in its more densely arranged leaves. Japan. I 1868. **var. reflexa** (Shiras.) Fitschen (*P. bicolor* var. *reflexa* Shiras.) An obscure variety from Japan in which the cone scales are elongated and reflexed. It is the most ornamental form, with more conspicuous stomatic lines on the leaves. Japan.

asperata Mast. A medium-sized tree similar to *P. abies*, which it resembles in general appearance, with pale yellowish-brown young shoots. Leaves 1–2cm long, 4-angled, dull greyish-green sometimes bluish-green, rigid and sharply pointed. Cones cylindrical, to 13cm long. This very hardy, lime-tolerant species is the Chinese counterpart of the European *P. abies*. W China. I 1910 by Ernest Wilson. AM 1981. **var. notabilis** Rehder & E.H. Wilson. A variety with slightly longer, glaucous green leaves and rhombic-ovate cone scales. W Sichuan. **var. retroflexa** See *P. retroflexa*.

bicolor See *P. alcoquiana*. **var. acicularis** See *P. alcoquiana* var. *acicularis*. **var. retroflexa** See *P. alcoquiana* var. *reflexa*.

brachytyla (Franch.) Pritz. (*P. sargentiana* Rehder & E.H. Wilson) A beautiful, medium-sized to large tree, conical when young but developing a rounded head in maturity. The long, spreading branches are gracefully ascending, then arching at the tips. Young shoots shining pale brown, bearing attractive, chestnut-brown buds in winter. Leaves to 20mm long, vividly white beneath, crowded on the upper surface of the branchlets. Cones oblong-cylindrical, 6–9cm long, greenish or purple-tinged when young. A most ornamental species with its slenderly upcurved branches and drooping branchlets. W and C China. I 1901 by Ernest Wilson. **var. complanata** (Mast.) W.C. Cheng. Differs in its slightly longer, sharply pointed leaves, up to 2.5cm, and its brown or purplish-brown young cones. W. China, NE India.

breweriana S. Watson.. Brewer's weeping spruce. Perhaps the most beautiful of all spruces and one of the most popular of all ornamental conifers. A small to medium-sized, broadly conical tree with spreading or decurved branches from which hang slender, tail-like branchlets, 1.8–2.5m long. Leaves to 3cm long, shining dark blue-green above, marked with 2 white bands beneath. Cones up to 10cm long, green at first, turning purple later.

There are few more breathtaking sights than a fine specimen of this spruce with its curtained branches, rising like a majestic green fountain. It is sometimes confused with *P. smithiana*, particularly when young, but differs in its smaller, flattened, dark blue-green leaves, smaller, dome-shaped buds and hairy shoots. It is a rare tree in the wild, confined to a few isolated localities in the Siskiyou Mountains of NW California and SW Oregon. I 1897. ♛ 2002. FCC 1974. AM 1958.

‡*engelmannii* Parry ex Engelm. Engelmann spruce. A small to medium-sized tree with pale yellowish-brown young shoots. Leaves 4-angled, 1.5–2.5cm long, sharply pointed, greyish-green, emitting a pungent odour when bruised, crowded on the upper surfaces of the branchlets. Cones to 7.5cm long. W North America with a variety in N Mexico. I 1862. **Glauca Group** (f. *glauca* Beissn.) A very attractive form with glaucous leaves.

excelsa See *P. abies*.

glauca (Moench) Voss (*P. alba* Link) White spruce. A large tree of dense, conical habit, with decurved branches, ascending at the tips. Leaves 4-angled, to 20mm long, glaucous green, emitting a foetid odour when bruised, densely arranged and standing above the upper surfaces of the branchlets. Cones to 6cm long. A very hardy species, useful for planting in cold, exposed positions. Canada, NE USA. I 1700. **var. albertiana** (S. Br.) Sarg. Alberta white spruce. An uncommon variety, differing in its less upright habit, slightly longer leaves, which are less glaucous beneath, and its smaller cones. C North America. Introduced by H.J. Elwes in 1906. AM 1920. **var. albertiana Alberta Blue** ('Haal') PBR A sport of 'Conica' found at Hagthorne Cottage Nurseries near Woking, Surrey in 1976. It has a similar habit but differs in the blue foliage. **var. albertiana 'Alberta Globe'** Raised in Holland, this is a form of very dense habit, making a compact, rounded bun. C 1968. **var. albertiana 'Conica'** A slow-growing, perfectly cone-shaped bush of dense, compact habit with bright grass-green leaves. A deservedly popular cultivar, in 30 years making a pointed cone of symmetrical shape, 2m high by 1.2m at base. Originally found in the Canadian Rockies, near Alberta in 1904 by Dr J.G. Jack and Prof. Alfred Rehder. AM 1933. **var. albertiana 'J.W. Daisy's Wjite'** PBR A sport of 'Conica' raised in Belgium before 1977 with pale creamy-yellow young foliage later turning green. **var. albertiana 'Laurin'** A slow-growing sport of 'Conica' of conical habit with slender needles. C 1950. **var. albertiana 'Lilliput'** A very slow-growing form, similar in habit to 'Conica' but more dwarf. **var. albertiana 'Piccolo'** A dwarf, conical selection, a sport of 'Conica' raised in Holland. C 1987. **var. albertiana 'Tiny'** A very compact, slow-growing form, with densely arranged, short needles and red buds. Raised from a witches' broom at the Red Lodge Nursery, Chandler's Ford. C 1961. **'Caerulea'** An attractive form with densely arranged, silvery, grey-blue leaves. C 1866. **'Densata'** (var. *densata* L.H. Bailey) A slow-growing, eventually large shrub or small tree of dense habit. C 1920. **'Echiniformis'** Dwarf, slow-growing, globular bush of dense habit; leaves glaucous grey-green, forward-pointing, concealing both branchlets and buds. A first-class miniature conifer for a rock garden. C 1855. ♛ 2002. **'Nana'** A dwarf or small, slow-growing bush of dense, globular habit, with radially arranged, greyish-blue leaves. A specimen in our collection attained 1.4m by 1.8m after 30 years. C 1828.

glehnii (F. Schmidt) Mast. Sakhalin spruce. A small to medium-sized, slender, conical tree with reddish or chocolate-brown, flaking bark. Young shoots conspicuously reddish-orange. Leaves bluish-green above, glaucous beneath, 1.5cm long, densely arranged on the upper surfaces of the branchlets. Cones to 8cm long, violet when young. Similar in effect to *P. abies*, but less vigorous and with shorter leaves. S Sakhalin, E and N Hokkaido (Japan). I 1877.

× *hurstii* De Hurst (*P. engelmannii* × *P. pungens*) A vigorous, medium-sized tree, more or less intermediate in character between the parents. Young shoots pale orange, usually glabrous. Buds slightly resinous. Leaves 4-sided,

10–12mm long, greyish-green, spreading all round the branchlets or loosely parted below. C 1938.

jezoensis (Siebold & Zucc.) Carrière. Yezo spruce. A medium-sized to large tree with deflexed branches and shining, pale brown to yellowish-brown young shoots. Leaves flattened, 1–2cm long, glossy dark green above, silvery-white beneath, densely crowded and overlapping on the upper surfaces of the branchlets. Cones to 7.5cm long, reddish when young. The young growths are prone to injury by late spring frosts. NE Asia, Japan. I 1861 by J.G. Veitch. **subsp. *hondoensis*** (Mayr) P.A. Schmidt. Hondo spruce. A form with shorter leaves, dull green above. In cultivation less susceptible to damage by spring frosts. Mts of Hondo (Japan). I 1861. AM 1974.

koyamae Shiras. A small to medium-sized tree of narrowly conical habit, with reddish-orange young shoots. Leaves to 12mm long, green or slightly glaucous, densely packed on the upper surfaces of the branchlets. Cones to 10cm long, pale green when young. A rare tree both in the wild and in cultivation. Distinguished from all other Japanese species by its resinous buds. Found in the wild only on Mount Yatsuga in C Japan. Discovered by Mitsua Koyama in 1911. A tree in the Sir Harold Hillier Gardens and Arboretum was 24m tall in 1994. I 1914 by Ernest Wilson.

likiangensis (Franch.) E. Pritz. A most ornamental, vigorous and accommodating tree of medium size, showing considerable variation within the species. Upper branches with ascending terminals. Young shoots pale brown or reddish. Leaves flattened, 1–2cm long, green or bluish-green above, glaucous beneath, loosely packed on the upper surfaces of the branchlets. Cones to 10cm long, reddish-pink when young, freely produced. In April and May, when loaded with its male flowers and brilliant red young cones, it is spectacularly beautiful. W China. C 1910. FCC 1974. AM 1961. **subsp. *balfouriana*** (Rehder & E.H. Wilson) Rushforth. A form with densely hairy branchlets, dark green or glaucous, obtuse leaves and violet-purple young cones. **var. *purpurea*** See *P. purpurea*.

× *lutzii* Little (*P. glauca* × *P. sitchensis*) A medium-sized tree, intermediate in character between the parents. Young shoots yellowish and glabrous. Leaves greyish-green. Cones to 6cm long. Found in the wild with the parents in S Alaska in 1950. It has also been artificially raised in cultivation in Europe.

mariana (Mill.) Britton et al. (*P. nigra* (Aiton) Link) Black spruce. A medium-sized, rather narrowly conical tree with brown, densely hairy young shoots. Leaves to 12mm long, dark bluish-green, densely crowding the upper surfaces of the branchlets. Cones to 3.5cm long, produced in large quantities, dark purple when young. N North America. C 1700. **'Aurea'** Leaves yellow when young, becoming glaucous green later. Tends to lose its colour when growing in shade. C 1891. **'Doumetii'** Eventually a large bush of dense, rather irregular but somewhat globular habit. C 1850. **'Nana'** A slow-growing, dwarf, mound-forming bush of dense habit, with grey-green leaves. A good dwarf conifer, suitable for a rock garden. C 1884. ♀ 2002.

× *mariorika* Boom (*P. mariana* × *P. omorika*) A medium-sized tree, intermediate in character between the parents,

with some forms closer to one parent than the other. Resembles *P. omorika* in general appearance, but is usually broader in habit, with narrower, more sharply pointed leaves, and smaller cones 3.5–4.5cm long. Raised in the nurseries of G.D. Boehlje at Westerstede, Germany in 1925.

maximowiczii Regel ex Mast. A small to medium-sized, densely branched tree of conical habit, with yellowish-brown or reddish, glabrous young shoots and white, resinous buds in winter. Leaves 4-sided, 10–15mm long, dark shining green, densely arranged above, pectinate below. Cones to 6cm long, pale green when young. It resembles an intermediate between *P. abies* and *P. orientalis*. Mts of Japan. First discovered on Mt Fujiyama in 1861. I 1865.

morinda See *P. smithiana*.

morrisonicola Hayata. Mount Morrison spruce. A rare and graceful, small to medium-sized tree with white or pale brown, glabrous shoots. Leaves 4-sided, 1–2cm long, green, very slender, sharply pointed, crowded forward on the upper surfaces of the shoots. Cones to 8cm long. Taiwan.

nigra See *P. mariana*.

obovata Ledeb. Siberian spruce. A medium-sized to large tree often a large bush, closely related to *P. abies*, but differing in its usually shorter duller leaves and smaller cones, 6–8cm long. Rare in cultivation. Hybrids between this species and *P. abies* occur where their distributions meet. N Europe, N Asia. I 1852.

omorika (Pancic) Purk. Serbian spruce. One of the most beautiful and adaptable spruces in cultivation, quickly forming a tall, graceful, slender tree. A medium-sized to large tree with relatively short, drooping branches which curve upwards at the tips. Young shoots pale brown. Leaves flattened, 1–2cm long, dark green above, glaucous beneath, densely arranged on the upper surfaces of the branchlets, loosely parted below. The leaves of young plants are narrower, sharply pointed and more spreading on the shoots than those of the adult. Cones ovoid-conic, 4–6cm long, bluish-black when young. It is one of the best spruces for industrial areas and chalk soils and would make an excellent evergreen street tree. A superb species, native of former Yugoslavia where it inhabits limestone rocks on both sides of the River Drina. It was discovered in 1875 and introduced to England in 1889. ♀ 2002. **'Expansa'** A low, widespreading bush with shortly ascending branches up to 80cm. Tends to revert. C 1940. **'Nana'** A medium-sized, densely conical bush of compact habit. The conspicuous stomatal bands add considerably to its attraction. A specimen in our collection attained 1.2m by 1.2m after 15 years. C 1930. ♀ 2002. **'Pendula'** A very beautiful, slender tree with drooping, slightly twisted branches displaying the glaucous upper surfaces of the leaves. C 1920. ♀ 2002. **'Pimoko'** A slow-growing dwarf, making a dense, rounded bun with numerous brown buds and silver-blue foliage. Originally found as a witches' broom. C 1984.

orientalis (L.) Link. Oriental spruce. A large, densely branched tree of broadly conical habit, with branches to ground level. Young shoots pale brown. Leaves to 8mm long, with blunt tips, dark shining green, densely pressed on the upper surfaces of the branchlets. Cones to 9cm long, purple when young. One of the best and most adaptable species in cultivation, easily recognised by its dense, conical habit and small, closely pressed leaves. N Turkey, Caucasus. I about 1839. ♀ 2002. **'Aurea'** ('Aureospicata') Young shoots creamy-yellow, becoming golden-yellow, finally green. A spectacular tree in spring. C 1873. ♀ 2002. FCC 1893. **'Gracilis'** ('Nana Gracilis') A slow-growing, rounded bush of dense habit, eventually developing into a small, conical tree up to 5–6m. A specimen in our collection attained 2.4m by 1.8m after 22 years. C 1923. **'Pendula'** See 'Weeping Dwarf'. **'Skylands'** A beautiful, slow-growing small tree similar to 'Aurea' but the foliage golden-yellow throughout the year. **'Weeping Dwarf'** ('Pendula') A compact, slow-growing form with weeping branches.

polita See *P. torano*.

pungens Engelm. Colorado spruce. A medium-sized to large tree of conical habit, with stout orange-brown young shoots, glaucous at first. Leaves rigid, to 3cm long, sharply pointed, green to grey, spreading all round the branchlets, but denser on the upper surfaces. Cones to 10cm long, green when young. The typical form is uncommon in cultivation due to the popularity of its glaucous-leaved forms of which there are a considerable number. W USA (Rocky Mountains). I about 1862. FCC 1877. **'Compacta'** A medium-sized, flat-topped bush of dense, compact habit, with horizontally spreading branches and grey-green leaves. C 1874. **'Eric Frahm'** A form of conical habit with good, silvery blue foliage. Found in Germany before 1950. **'Fat Albert'** A dense, conical large shrub with striking blue foliage. C 1981. **Glauca Group** (f. *glauca* (Reg.) Beissn.) Blue spruce. A medium-sized to large tree with glaucous leaves. A variable form, occurring both in the wild and in cultivation. The leaves tend to lose their intensity as they age, those at the base of the branches being greyish-green or green. In cultivation the most glaucous forms are usually small to medium-sized trees. FCC 1890. **'Glauca Prostrata'** A prostrate form with glaucous-blue foliage, often producing a leading shoot and forming a tree. C 1906. **'Globosa'** ('Glauca Globosa') (Glauca Group) Dwarf, flat-topped, globular bush of dense habit; leaves glaucous blue. C 1937. ♀ 2002. **'Hoopsii'** (Glauca Group) An excellent, small to medium-sized tree of densely conical habit, with vividly glaucous blue leaves. C 1958. ♀ 2002. **'Hoto'** (Glauca Group) A Dutch selection. Not the best for colour but strong-growing with a dense, conical habit. Foliage blue-grey. C.1972. **'Iseli Fastigiate'** A form of strongly upright habit making an excellent accent plant. C 1963. **'Koster'** (Glauca Group) The most popular form of Blue spruce. A small to medium-sized, conical tree with intense silver-blue leaves. C 1885. ♀ 2002. **'Moerheimii'** (Glauca Group) A small to medium-sized tree of dense, conical habit with intensely glaucous blue leaves. One of the most satisfactory of the group. C 1912. **'Montgomery'** (Glauca Group) A dwarf, slow-growing bush of compact habit. The sharply pointed leaves are greyish-blue. C 1934. **'Oldenburg'** A German selection of dense, broadly conical habit, with striking blue-grey foliage. C. 1976. **'Pendula'** (Glauca Group) A slow-growing, small tree with downswept branches and glaucous blue leaves.

FCC 1898. **'Procumbens'** ('Glauca Procumbens') (Glauca Group) Dwarf shrub with low branches, spreading in all directions; branchlets pendent. Leaves glaucous blue. If terminal reversions occur they should be removed. C 1910. **'Spekii'** (Glauca Group) Small to medium-sized, conical tree with glaucous blue leaves. I about 1925 by the Jan Spek nurseries of Boskoop. **'Thomsen'** (Glauca Group) A beautiful, conical tree of small to medium-size, bearing leaves of a striking silvery-blue. C 1928.

purpurea Mast. (*P. likiangensis* var. *purpurea* (Mast.) Dallim. & A.B. Jacks.) Previously regarded as a variety of *P. likiangensis* but developing a narrower, more pointed upper crown, the upper branches with erect terminals. Leaves also darker green, smaller and more closely pressed on the upper surfaces of the branchlets. Cones smaller, violet-purple. W China. I 1910.

retroflexa Mast. (*P. asperata* var. *retroflexa* (Mast.) W.C. Cheng) A medium-sized tree, related to *P. asperata* and differing in its greyer bark, yellow shoots and the leaves green and pectinate below. W China. I about 1910 by Ernest Wilson.

‡*rubens* Sarg. (*P. rubra* (Du Roi) Link not A. Dietr.) Red spruce. A medium-sized to large tree with reddish-brown, scaly bark. Young shoots light reddish-brown. Leaves to 1.5cm long, twisted, densely set on the upper surfaces of the branchlets. Cones to 5cm long, green or purple when young. At its best in moist conditions and unsuitable for chalk soils. NE North America. I before 1755.

rubra See *P. rubens*.

schrenkiana Fisch. & C.A. Mey. Schrenk's spruce. A medium-sized tree with greyish young shoots and resinous buds. Leaves to 3cm long, sage-green, rigid and sharply pointed, arranged all around the branchlets, but more densely above than below. Cones to 9cm long. It resembles *P. smithiana* in its leaves which, however, are slightly shorter, more glaucous and less radially arranged. C Asia. I 1877.

sitchensis (Bong.) Carrière. Sitka spruce. A fast-growing, large to very large, broadly conical tree primarily of economic importance. Leaves 18mm long, rigid, and sharply pointed, green above marked with 2 glaucous bands beneath, spreading all round the branchlets, or sometimes loosely parted below. Cones to 10cm long, yellowish-brown when young. A remarkable, prickly-leaved spruce, thriving particularly well in damp sites.

This is one of the most important reforestation trees and is the most commonly planted conifer for this purpose in the British Isles, particularly in the north and in Wales. W North America, from California to Alaska. Originally discovered by Archibald Menzies in 1792, and introduced by David Douglas in 1831. **'Papoose'** Although commonly cultivated, the Sitka spruce has given rise to surprisingly few cultivars. This form makes a very slow-growing dwarf with blue-grey foliage. C 1982.

smithiana (Wall.) Boiss. (*P. morinda* Link) West Himalayan spruce. A large and extremely beautiful tree with branches upcurved at tips and long, pendent branchlets. Leaves to 4cm long, dark green, needle-like and flexible, spreading all round the branchlets. Cones to

17cm long, green when young, becoming purplish. An attractive and ornamental tree, recognisable at all ages by its drooping branches, long leaves and glabrous shoots. Young plants are occasionally subject to injury by late spring frosts, but established trees are quite hardy and develop into a specimen second only in elegance to *P. breweriana*. W Himalaya. I 1818. AM 1975.

spinulosa (Griff.) A. Henry. A medium-sized to large tree, reaching 60m and above in its native environs. Branches spreading, branchlets pendent. Leaves to 3.5cm long, green below, glaucous above, spreading all round the branchlets. Cones to 10cm long, green or reddish-grey when young. A rare and remarkable, semi-weeping tree but perhaps a little gaunt and sparsely branched when compared with *P. breweriana* or *P. smithiana*. E Himalaya. I about 1878.

torano (Siebold ex K. Koch) Koehne (*P. polita* (Siebold & Zucc.) Carrière) Tiger-tail spruce. A medium-sized to large tree of dense, broadly conical habit, with nearly horizontal branches. Young shoots stout, shining yellowish-brown, often white. Leaves to 2cm long, green, sickle-shaped and spine-pointed, stiffly spreading all round the branchlets. Cones to 10cm long, yellowish-green when young. A distinct species, easily recognised by its stout, prickly leaves which are more difficult to handle than any other species. Japan. I 1861 by J.G. Veitch. FCC 1873.

wilsonii Mast. (*P. watsoniana* Mast.) A small tree, remarkable for its conspicuous, marble-white, glabrous, young shoots, attractive buds and narrow leaves. Leaves to 2cm long, dark green, densely clothing the upper surfaces of the branchlets. Cones to 5cm long. C and W China. I 1901 by Ernest Wilson.

*PILGERODENDRON Florin—**Cupressaceae**—A monotypic genus differing from the closely related *Libocedrus* in its uniformly 4-ranked leaves. Male and female strobili are borne on the same plant.

uviferum (D. Don) Florin (*Libocedrus uvifera* Pilg.) Alerce. A rare, small, slow-growing tree of stiff, upright habit when young. Small, green, scale-like leaves are borne in 4 ranks, giving the shoots a quadrangular appearance. Cones ovoid, 8–13mm long, with 4, woody, brown scales. This remarkable tree, a native of Chile, has proven hardy here. In the wild it occurs further south than any other conifer. I 1849.

*PINUS L.—**Pinaceae**—The pines make up a genus of about 110 species of evergreen trees, widely distributed mainly in temperate regions of the N hemisphere, south to Central America and Indonesia. Young trees are normally conical in habit, broadening and becoming bushy or flat-topped with age. The leaves are long and needle-like, borne in bundles of 2–5. Male and female strobili are borne on the same tree and are often attractive in late spring and early summer. Cones vary in shape from rounded and conical to banana-shaped, and ripen at the end of the second year. In most species the cones release their seed on ripening, but in a few the cones remain intact until they fall. Under natural conditions certain species such as *P. radiata* retain their cones intact on the tree for many years until forced to open by forest fires.

The pines serve a great variety of purposes, many being highly ornamental as well as useful. Some species will succeed in the poorest soils whether alkaline or acid but as a rule the 5-needled species are not long satisfactory on shallow chalk soils, while others are invaluable as windbreaks, especially in coastal districts. All species dislike shade and very few will tolerate smoke-polluted air. Numerous dwarf or slow-growing forms have appeared in cultivation, many of which are suitable for a rock garden where they combine effectively with dwarf spruces, firs and junipers.

albicaulis Engelm. Whitebark pine. A small tree related to *P. flexilis* from which it differs in its dense, short leaves and its cones which do not open when ripe. Young shoots reddish-brown, sparsely downy or glabrous. Leaves in 5s, to 6.5cm long, green or greyish-green. Cones to 7.5cm long, falling intact. Seeds edible. A rare species in cultivation. W North America. I 1852 by John Jeffrey. **'Nana'** See 'Noble's Dwarf'. **'Noble's Dwarf'** ('Nana') A dwarf, shrubby form of compact habit. Our plant was propagated from material received from the late Mr Nisbet of Gosport, who in turn received his plant from the late Mr Noble of California.

aristata Engelm. Bristlecone pine. A small tree or large shrub, with stout, reddish-brown, hairy young shoots. Leaves in 5s, to 4cm long, flecked with white resin, tightly bunched and closely pressed to the branchlets. Cones to 9cm long, the scales with slender-spined, bristle-like bosses. Native of the SW USA (Colorado, Arizona, New Mexico), where trees aged up to 2,000 years have been recorded. I 1863. See also *P. longaeva*.

arizonica Engelm. (*P. ponderosa* var. *arizonica* (Engelm.) Shaw) Arizona pine. A large tree, closely related to *P. ponderosa*, with deeply fissured, almost black bark, glaucous young shoots and rather rigid leaves to 20cm long in bundles of 5 or occasionally in 3s or 4s. SW USA, N Mexico. **var. cooperi** (C.E. Blanco) Farjon (*P. cooperi* C.E. Blanco) This variety is attractive in its shorter, grey-green leaves to 12cm long in dense clusters. NW Mexico.

armandii Franch. Armand's pine. An attractive tree of medium size. Leaves in 5s, 10–15cm long, glaucous. Cones usually borne in clusters of 2 or 3, barrel-shaped, to 19cm long, becoming pendent. A very ornamental species with its drooping, glaucous leaves and decorative cones. It grows well in the British Isles. SE Tibet, W China, with a variety in Taiwan. I 1895.

attenuata Lemmon (*P. tuberculata* Gord.) Knobcone pine. A small to medium-sized tree with an open, upswept crown of long branches. Leaves in 3s, 10–18cm long, greyish-green. Cones to 13cm long, the scales armed with sharp prickles, appearing singly or in whorls of 2–4. They remain intact for many years and in the wild are usually opened as a result of forest fires. Closely related to *P. radiata*. SW USA. I about 1847.

ayacahuite Ehrenb. Mexican white pine. A large, attractive tree with a spreading head of branches and stout, pale brown or greyish young shoots. Leaves in 5s, slender and spreading, to 20cm long, glaucous green. Cones, resin-smeared, to 20cm long, sometimes longer, pendent, and borne singly or in clusters of 2 or 3 towards the ends of the branches, even on quite young trees. Mexico and Central America. I 1840. FCC 1961. AM 1960. **var. veitchii** (Roezl) Shaw. Some plants grown under the above name belong here. It differs in its larger seeds and cones with larger, thicker scales. C Mexico.

‡*banksiana* Lamb. Jack pine. A very hardy tree of medium size, occasionally gnarled and shrubby. Leaves in pairs, to 4cm long, curved or twisted. Cones usually in pairs, to 5cm long. It is adaptable to most soils except shallow chalk soils and is particularly good in moist soils. Easily recognised by its crooked branches and uneven cones. It occurs further north than any other American pine. N USA, Canada. C 1783.

brutia Ten. (*P. halepensis* var. *brutia* (Ten.) A. Henry) A medium-sized tree in cultivation differing from *P. halepensis* mainly in its green young shoots, leaves to 16cm long and almost sessile, spreading or forward-pointing cones. E Mediterranean.

bungeana Zucc. ex Endl. Lace-bark pine. A small to medium-sized tree or a large shrub, typically branching from near the base. On trees in cultivation the smooth, grey-green bark flakes away creating a beautiful patchwork of white, yellow, purple, brown and green. Leaves in 3s, 5–10cm long, rigid. Cones to 7cm long. One of the most ornamental of all pines. Closely allied to *P. gerardiana*. China. First discovered by Dr Bunge in a temple garden near Peking in 1831. I 1846 by Robert Fortune.

†*canariensis* C. Sm. Canary Island pine. A very beautiful tree reaching a large size in its native habitats, but smaller and only suitable for the mildest localities in the British Isles. A graceful pine with spreading branches and drooping branchlets. Leaves in 3s, 20–30cm long, conspicuously glaucous on very young plants, bright green later. Cones to 23cm long, solitary or in clusters, deflexed. Small plants in pots are excellent for conservatory decoration. Canary Isles.

†*caribaea* Morelet. Caribbean pine. In the British Isles a small tree suitable only for the most sheltered positions in the mildest areas. Leaves in 3s, occasionally in 4s or 5s, 15–23cm long, crowded at the ends of the branchlets. Cones to 10cm long. Cuba, S Mexico, Central America.

cembra L. Arolla pine. A small to medium-sized tree of characteristic, dense, conical or columnar habit in cultivation. Leaves in 5s, 5–8cm long, densely crowded and dark blue-green with blue-white inner surfaces. Cones deep blue, to 8cm long, never opening, the seeds being liberated when the scales rot or by the attentions of squirrels or birds. An ornamental tree of almost formal aspect which has distinct landscape possibilities. Mts of C & E Europe. C 1746. **'Aureovariegata'** A pleasing form with yellow-tinged leaves. C 1865. **'Jermyns'** An exceedingly slow-growing, compact bush of dwarf, conical habit, raised in our nurseries. **'Stricta'** ('Columnaris') A columnar form with closely ascending branches. C 1855.

cembroides Zucc. Mexican nut pine. A small, short-stemmed tree or large bush with a dense, rounded head of branches. Leaves normally in 3s, but varying from 2–5 on some trees, sickle-shaped, to 5cm long. Cones to 6cm long, containing large, edible seeds. S Arizona to Mexico. **var. edulis** See *P. edulis.* **var. monophylla** See *P. monophylla.*

chihuahuana See *P. leiophylla* var. *chihuahuana.*

‡*contorta* Douglas ex Loudon. Beach pine. A medium-sized to large tree, occasionally a large bush, with short branches. Leaves in pairs, to 5cm long, twisted and yel-

lowish-green. Cones to 5cm long, occurring in pairs or clusters, the scales bearing a slender recurved spine. Not adaptable to chalky soils, but a suitable species for light stony or sandy land. It is a vigorous species, used for fixing sand dunes in maritime areas. W North America. I 1831 by David Douglas. **var. latifolia** Engelm. Lodgepole pine. A medium-sized tree, less vigorous than the type and with slightly broader leaves, 6–8.5cm long, and larger cones. The common name derives from its use by the North American Indians as the central pole of their huts. Mountains of W North America. I about 1853 by John Jeffrey. **'Spaan's Dwarf'** ('Minima') A slow-growing dwarf form producing numerous upright and spreading shoots, densely clothed with short, dark green leaves.

cooperi See *P. arizonica* var. *cooperi.*

coulteri D. Don. Big-cone pine. A remarkable and striking tree of medium to large size, with very stout shoots. Leaves in 3s, to 30cm long, stiff and curved, pale bluish-grey-green. Cones very large and long-persistent, to 35cm long. The largest cones may weigh up to 2kg. S California, Baja California. Discovered by Dr Coulter in 1832 and introduced by David Douglas in the same year. ♀ 2002. AM 1961.

culminicola Andresen & Beaman. A small, slow-growing shrub of spreading habit. Leaves in 5s, densely clustered, grey-green and up to 5cm long. This remarkable species was introduced to our nursery by Sir Harold Hillier from the high sierra near Saltillo, Mexico in 1979. There he found several thousand bushy plants on average 1–1.2m tall. It is proving perfectly hardy in cultivation. N Mexico (Coahuila, Nuevo Leon).

‡*densiflora* Siebold & Zucc. Japanese red pine. A medium-sized to large tree. Leaves in pairs, to 12cm long, twisted. Cones shortly-stalked, solitary or in clusters of 2 or 3, to 5cm long. It is the Japanese counterpart of the native Scots pine and has similar reddish young bark. Japan. I 1852. **'Alice Verkade'** A bun-shaped plant of dwarf, spreading habit with densely arranged foliage. A seedling of 'Tanyosho' raised in New Jersey. C 1961. **'Aurea'** Foliage yellow-green turning golden yellow in winter. C 1890. **'Oculus-draconis'** Dragon-eye pine. A curious form whose branches, when viewed from above, show alternate yellow and green rings, hence the name. C 1890. **'Pendula'** A dwarf shrub with prostrate branches. C 1890. **'Umbraculifera'** A miniature tree of extremely slow growth, with a dense umbrella-like head of branches, bearing tiny cones. Our largest specimen attained 2m by 2.4m in 30 years. C 1890.

†*devoniana* Lindl. (*P. michoacana* Martínez) A small to medium-sized tree in the mildest areas of the British Isles, closely related to *P. montezumae.* Leaves in 5s, 25–43cm long, spreading and drooping. Cones oblong-ovoid, 25–30cm long. Mexico.

‡*echinata* Mill. Short-leaf pine. A small to medium-sized tree with green, violet-flushed young shoots. Leaves usually in pairs, sometimes in 3s or 4s, to 13cm long, twisted, dark grey-green. Cones usually clustered, to 6cm long, normally remaining on the branches after the seeds have been shed. Best suited to well-drained soils. E and SE USA. I 1739.

edulis Engelm. (*P. cembroides* var. *edulis* (Engelm.) Voss) Colorado pinyon, Two-leaved nut pine. A small to medium-sized, compact tree, in the wild related to *P. cembroides*. Leaves normally in pairs, occasionally in 3s or single. Cones rounded, with large, edible seeds. SW USA. I 1848.

‡‡†*elliottii* Engelm. Slash pine. A small tree in cultivation, only suitable for the mildest areas of the British Isles. Young shoots orange-brown at first. Leaves in pairs or 3s, to 25cm long, occasionally longer. Cones to 14cm long, the scales armed with a stout prickle. SE USA.

engelmannii Carrière. Apache pine, Arizona long-leaf pine. A large tree in the wild with a rounded crown and deeply furrowed bark when mature. The very stout shoots, rough with persistent leaf bases, bear foliage mainly clustered at the tips that has been likened to a chimney-sweep's brush. Leaves dark green, thick and rigid, to 35cm or more long, in clusters of 3–5, the margins rough with small, coarse teeth. Cones ovoid, to 14cm long, ripe in 2 years. A magnificent species, related to *P. ponderosa* and first introduced to our nursery from Mexico in 1965. SW USA, N Mexico.

excelsa See *P. wallichiana*.

flexilis E. James. Limber pine. A medium-sized tree of conical outline. Leaves in 5s, 3.5–7.5cm long, crowded towards the ends of the branches, entire, or almost so. Cones to 15cm long, spreading. Rocky Mts of W North America, N Mexico. I 1861.

gerardiana Wall. ex D. Don. Gerard's pine. A rare, small tree in cultivation, its main attraction being the beautiful patchwork bark which is greyish-pink, flaking to reveal green, yellow and brown new bark. Leaves in 3s, 5–10cm long. Cones to 20cm long. An extremely ornamental tree, allied to *P. bungeana* from which it mainly differs in its longer leaves and larger cones. NW Himalaya, Afghanistan, to SE Tibet. First discovered by Captain Gerard of the Bengal Native Infantry. I 1839 by Lord Auckland.

greggii Engelm. A medium-sized tree, thriving best in a sheltered position. Leaves in 3s, bright green, 7.5–15cm long. Cones ovoid-conic, shining creamy-brown, 8–15cm long, borne in reflexed clusters and persisting for many years. A beautiful pine rendered conspicuous at all times of the year by the bright grass-green of the younger leaves. It has grown in the Sir Harold Hillier Gardens and Arboretum for many years without winter damage. NE Mexico.

griffithii See *P. wallichiana*.

halepensis Mill. Aleppo pine. A medium-sized tree with glaucous, glabrous young shoots. Leaves in pairs, very distant, sparse, slightly twisted, 5–10cm long, bright fresh green. Cones deflexed, to 10cm long. Naturally found in warm, dry regions, this species is suitable for maritime areas in the south. It will also grow on dry, shallow chalk soils. Mediterranean region, W Asia. C 1683.

hartwegii Lindl. (*P. lindleyana* Gordon, *P. montezumae* var. *hartwegii* (Lindl.) Shaw, *P. montezumae* var. *rudis* (Endl.) Shaw, *P. rudis* Endl.) A large tree related to *P. montezumae*. Leaves green to grey-green in clusters of 3–5, to 15cm long. Cones very dark, to 16cm. It grows at higher altitudes than *P. montezumae* and is hardy. Mexico, Central America.

heldreichii H. Christ (*P. heldreichii* var. *leucodermis* (Antoine) Markg. ex Fitschen, *P. leucodermis* Antoine)

Bosnian pine. A very distinct, medium-sized tree with smooth, greenish-grey bark and a dense, ovoid habit. Young shoots glaucous. Leaves in pairs, to 9cm long, rigid and erect, dark almost black-green. Cones to 7.5cm long, bright blue the first year. Particularly suitable for dry soils and shallow soils over chalk. Italy, Balkan Peninsula. I 1864. ♀ 2002. **'Compact Gem'** A very slow-growing, eventually medium-sized bush, of compact, rounded habit, with dark green leaves. C 1964. **'Pygmy'** See under 'Schmidtii'. **'Satellit'** A narrowly conical form with the leaves densely clustered and pressed against the shoots on the young growths, later spreading. A seedling of Dutch origin. **'Schmidtii'** A slow-growing, dwarf or small form developing into a dense, compact mound. Discovered in the wild by the late Mr Schmidt of Czechoslovakia. C 1952. Originally listed as *P. leucodermis* 'Pygmy'. ♀ 2002.

× *holfordiana* A.B. Jacks. (*P. ayacahuite* var. *veitchii* × *P. wallichiana*) A large, fast-growing tree with widespreading branches. In leaf and cone characters it is close to *P. wallichiana* and resembles that species in general appearance. A most ornamental hybrid with long, silvery-green leaves and long, banana-shaped, resin-flecked cones. Originated in the Westonbirt Arboretum about 1906. AM 1977.

× *hunnewellii* A.G. Johnson (*P. parviflora* × *P. strobus*) A vigorous, medium-sized tree of loose, open habit, similar in some respects to *P. strobus*, but with larger cones and hairy young shoots. Leaves 7.5–8.5cm long, grey-green. Originated in the Hunnewell Arboretum, Wellesley, Massachusetts in 1949.

insignis See *P. radiata*.

jeffreyi Balf. (*P. ponderosa* var. *jeffreyi* (Balf.) Vasey) Jeffrey pine. A large, imposing tree with a conical or spire-like crown. Young shoots stout, glaucous. Leaves in 3s, to 22cm long, dull bluish-green or pale grey, crowded towards the ends of the branchlets. Cones terminal and spreading, conical-ovoid, 13–20cm long, the scales with a slender, recurved spine. Differs from *P. ponderosa* mainly in its black or purple-grey bark and its stouter, longer, bluish-green leaves, invariably in 3s. SW USA, Baja California. I 1852, possibly earlier. ♀ 2002.

†*kesiya* Royle ex Gord. (*P. khasia* Engelm) A small tree in cultivation, with pale brown young shoots. Leaves in 3s, very slender, green or greyish-green, to 23cm long. Cones to 7.5cm long. A rare species only suitable for the mildest areas. SE Asia, Philippines.

koraiensis Siebold & Zucc. Korean pine. A medium-sized tree of loose, conical habit. Young shoots green, covered by a dense, reddish-brown pubescence. Leaves usually in fives, to 12cm long, stiff and rough to the touch, blue-green. Cones short-stalked, to 14cm long. Closely related to *P. cembra* from which it differs in its openly branched habit and its usually longer, more glaucous leaves which are toothed to the apex and possess 3 as against 2 resin canals. E Asia. Introduced by J.G. Veitch in 1861. **'Compacta Glauca'** (*P. cembra* 'Compacta Glauca') A strong-growing, compact form with short, stout branches and attractive, densely packed, conspicuously glaucous leaves. C 1949. **'Winton'** A large, bushy form, wider than high, with glaucous leaves. It possesses characters intermediate between the above species and *P. cembra*.

The leaves are not toothed to the apex and the resin canals vary from 2 to 3. A specimen in our collection attained 2m by 4.5m in 30 years.

lambertiana Douglas. Sugar pine. The largest of all pines, attaining a height of 75m or more in its native habitats. In the British Isles it is a medium-sized tree. Leaves in 5s, to 14cm long, sharply pointed and conspicuously twisted. Cones pendent, to 50cm long (the longest in the genus). A sweet exudation from the heartwood has in the past been used as a substitute for sugar. Oregon and California. I by David Douglas in 1827 and later by William Lobb in 1851.

‡†*leiophylla* Schiede ex Schltdl. & Cham. Smooth-leaved pine. A small tree in the mildest areas of the British Isles. Young shoots glaucous. Leaves in 5s, 7.5–10cm long, slender and greyish-green. Cones stalked, solitary or in clusters, ovoid, 4–6cm long. Mexico. **var. *chihuahuana*** Engelm. (*P. chihuahuana* Engelm.) A small to medium-sized, tender tree, closely related to *P. leiophylla*, and resembling it in most characters. Leaves in 3s or 4s, occasionally in pairs or 5s, 7–10cm long. S Arizona and New Mexico, Mexico.

leucodermis See *P. heldreichii*.

lindleyana See *P. hartwegii*.

longaeva D.K. Bailey. Western bristlecone pine. This species, only described in 1970, is closely related to *P. aristata* but it differs in its leaves, which lack the white specks of resin present in that species. Specimens in the White Mountains of California have been proved to be up to 5,000 years old, the oldest living plants. California, Nevada and Utah. Both these species are known as bristlecone pines.

longifolia See *P. palustris* and *P. roxburghii*.

‡†*luchuensis* Mayr. Luchu pine. A rare, small to medium-sized tree with characteristic smooth, greyish bark. Leaves in pairs, 15–20cm long. Cones ovoid-conic, 5cm long. Ryukyu Islands (Japan).

maritima See *P. pinaster*.

†*massoniana* Lamb. A small to medium-sized tree with reddish young bark and glabrous young shoots; winter buds conic-cylindric, resinous. Leaves in pairs, 14–20cm long, very slender. Cones ovoid, 3.5–6cm long. C & SE China, N Taiwan. I 1829.

michoacana See *P. devoniana*.

monophylla Torr. & Frém. (*P. cembroides* var. *monophylla* (Torr. & Frém.) Voss) One-leaved nut pine. An unusual large shrub or small tree related to *P. cembroides*. Leaves borne singly or occasionally in pairs, stiff, glaucous green, up to 5cm long. Cones up to 8cm, with large, edible seeds. Hardy but best in a hot, dry position. SW USA to Mexico (Baja California). I 1848.

montana See *P. mugo*.

montezumae Lamb. (*P. montezumae* var. *lindleyi* Loudon) Montezuma pine. A magnificent medium-sized to large tree with rough and deeply fissured bark and a large, domed crown. Young shoots glabrous, stout, orange-brown; winter buds ovoid, pointed. Leaves usually in 5s but varying from 3–8 on some trees, 18–25cm long, bluish-grey, spreading or drooping. Cones varying from ovoid-conic to cylindrical, 7.5–25cm long. A bold and imposing tree, hardy given reasonable shelter. Mts of Mexico. I 1839. **var. *hartwegii*** See *P. hartwegii*.

var. *lindleyi* See *P. montezumae*. **var. *rudis*** See *P. hartwegii*.

‡*monticola* Douglas ex D. Don. Western white pine. A medium-sized to large tree of narrowly conical habit. Leaves in 5s, to 10cm long, dark blue-green with white inner surface. Cones solitary or in clusters, to 25cm long, pendent after the first year. W North America. I 1831.

mugo Turra (*P. mughus* Scop., *P. montana* Mill.) Mountain pine. A very hardy, large shrub or small tree of dense, bushy habit. Leaves in pairs, 3–4cm long, rigid and curved, dark green. Cones solitary or in clusters, to 6cm long. A variable species in the wild, all forms succeeding in almost all soils. Very lime-tolerant. Several of the smaller forms are excellent in association with heathers, while the dwarf, slow-growing cultivars are suitable for a rock garden or scree. Mts of C & W Europe. **'Corley's Mat'** A dwarf, widespreading form with stout shoots and densely arranged, long, bright green and twisted needles. Raised by R.S. Corley before 1979. **'Gnom'** A small, compact selection forming a dense, dark green, globular mound. C 1890. **'Humpy'** Very dwarf and slow-growing with very short needles. Raised in Holland and selected in 1970. **'Jacobsen'** A slow-growing dwarf, broader than tall, with dark green, congested foliage. C 1960. **'Mops'** Dwarf, globular bush of dense, slow growth. C 1951. ♀ 2002. **'Ophir'** A compact, bun-shaped dwarf with golden-yellow winter foliage. C 1975. **'Pal Maleter'** A compact form with creamy-white young foliage. C 1960. **Pumilio Group** (*P. mugo* var. *pumilio* (Haenke) Zenari) A dwarf form, often prostrate, but occasionally reaching 2m. ♀ 2002. **var. *rostrata*** See *P. mugo* subsp. *uncinata*. **'Trompenburg'** A dwarf, spreading form making a dense, hemispherical mound about twice as broad as it is tall. Found as a seedling in the Trompenburg Arboretum on the outskirts of Amsterdam. **subsp. *uncinata*** (Ramond ex DC.) Domin. (*P. mugo* var. *rostrata* (Antoine) Hoopes, *P. uncinata* Ramond ex DC.) Mountain pine. A medium-sized tree differing in both its habit and its larger cones, 5–7cm long. Its splendid dense, bushy, broadly conical habit makes it ideal for creating shelter against the coldest winds. Succeeds in all types of soil including shallow chalk. Pyrenees to E Alps. **'Winter Gold'** A dwarf, spreading bush of open habit. Foliage golden-yellow during winter. C 1967. **'Zundert'** Low-growing, compact habit with long needles bright gold in winter. C 1977.

‡*muricata* D. Don. Bishop pine. A very picturesque, medium-sized to large tree, forming a dense, rather flat head of branches. Leaves in pairs, to 15cm long, stiff and curved or twisted, dark bluish-grey or yellowish-grey-green. Cones solitary or in clusters, to 9cm long, often remaining unopened on the branches for many years. In the wild the cones have been known to remain intact for 30 or 40 years, the seeds eventually being liberated by forest fires. This species is suitable for exposed areas. California, Baja California. I 1848. ♀ 2002.

nigra J.F. Arnold. (*P. nigra* var. *austriaca* (Höss) Badoux) Austrian pine. A commonly planted and familiar, large tree with rough, greyish-brown or dark brown bark and a dense head of large branches. Leaves in pairs, dark green, 8–12cm long, stiff and stout, densely crowded on the branchlets. Cones solitary or in clusters, to 8cm long.

All forms of *P. nigra* are excellent for maritime areas and are tolerant of most soils. It thrives better than any other in chalky soils and in bleak exposures and makes an excellent windbreak. Europe, from Austria to C Italy, Greece and former Yugoslavia. I by Messrs Lawson of Edinburgh in 1835. ♀ 2002. **'Black Prince'** A low-growing, dwarf rounded bush of very compact habit with dark green foliage. **'Bright Eyes'** A dwarf conical bush with light green foliage and conspicuous white buds. Found as a witches' broom on Horsell Common, Woking, Surrey. C 1979. **var. calabrica** See subsp. *laricio*. **var. caramanica** See subsp. *pallasiana*. **var. cebennensis** See subsp. *salzmannii*. **'Hornibrookiana'** A dwarf form of very slow growth. Originated from a witches' broom on an Austrian pine in Seneca Park, Rochester (USA) before 1932. **subsp. laricio** (Poir.) Maire (*P. nigra* var. *calabrica* (Loudon) C.K. Schneid., *P. nigra* var. *maritima* (Aiton) Melville) Corsican pine. A large tree with a straight main stem to the summit of the crown, more open and with fewer, shorter, more level branches than the Austrian pine. It also differs in the more slender and flexible, grey-green leaves, which occur less densely and more spreading on the branchlets. The Corsican pine is extensively used for forestry purposes and is happy in almost any soil or situation. The wood is used throughout the Mediterranean region, especially for general construction purposes. S Italy and Corsica. I 1759 by Philip Miller. ♀ 2002. **var. maritima** See subsp. *laricio*. **'Moseri'** (*P. sylvestris* 'Moseri') A very slow-growing, miniature tree of dense, globular or ovoid shape, the leaves turning yellow or yellow-green in winter. Originally listed as *P. nigra* 'Pygmaea'. C 1900. ♀ 2002. **subsp. pallasiana** (Lamb.) Holmboe (*P. nigra* var. *caramanica* (Loudon) Rehder) Crimean pine. A large tree of broad, conical habit, with usually many long, stout, erect branches; leaves to 18cm long. Cones to 10cm long. Rarer in cultivation than the Austrian pine (*P. nigra* subsp. *nigra*) from which it mainly differs in its more compact, conical habit, longer, thicker leaves and usually larger cones. Cyprus, Black Sea coast, Turkey. I 1798. **'Pygmaea'** See *P. sylvestris* 'Moseri'. **subsp. salzmannii** (Dunal) Franco (*P. nigra* var. *cebennensis* (Godr.) Rehder) Pyrenean pine. A medium-sized tree with drooping branches forming a widely-spreading, low-domed crown. Leaves 10–15cm long, greyish-green, very slender and soft to the touch. Cones 4–6cm long. Cevennes, Pyrenees and C and E Spain, North Africa. I 1834.

oaxacana See *P. pseudostrobus* var. *apulcensis*.

†*oocarpa* Schiede ex Schltdl. A rare and beautiful, small to medium-sized tree, allied to *P. patula*. Young shoots glaucous. Leaves variable in number, in 3s, 4s or 5s, to 30cm long, sea-green. Cones long-stalked, to 9cm long. A tender species only suitable for the very mildest areas. Mexico, Central America.

‡*palustris* Mill. (*P. longifolia* Salisb.) Southern pitch pine. A low, erect-growing, small to medium-sized tree requiring a warm, moist soil. Young shoots stout, orange-brown. Leaves in 3s, to 25cm long, up to 45cm long on young, vigorous plants, flexible, densely crowded on the branchlets. Cones cylindrical, to 25cm long, the scales with a reflexed spine. E USA. I 1730.

parviflora Siebold & Zucc. Japanese white pine. A small to medium-sized tree or large shrub, conical when young, flat-topped in maturity. Leaves in 5s, 5–7.5cm long, slightly curved, deep blue-green with blue-white inner surfaces. Cones solitary or in clusters, erect or spreading, 5–8cm long. This picturesque Japanese species is the pine of the willow pattern used to decorate china and is commonly cultivated in Japan, particularly for bonsai purposes. I 1861 by J.G. Veitch. ♀ 2002. AM 1977. **'Adcock's Dwarf'** A slow-growing, eventually medium-sized bush of rather compact, upright habit. Leaves 1.5–2.5cm long, greyish-green, produced in congested bunches at the tips of the shoots. A seedling raised in our Jermyns Lane Nursery in 1961, it reached 2.5m tall and 1.3m across at the Sir Harold Hillier Gardens and Arboretum (1990). Named after our propagator, Graham Adcock. ♀ 2002. **'Bergman'** A slow-growing, dwarf, spreading shrub of dense habit with twisted, blue-green twisted needles. Selected by Bergman's Nurseries, Philadelphia in 1965. **'Brevifolia'** A small tree with tight bunches of short, stiff, blue-green leaves. C 1900. **Glauca Group** A small to medium-sized tree of spreading habit, with rigid, twisted needles. C 1909. **'Negishi'** A Japanese selection of upright habit, the twisted, blue-green needles to 4.5cm long. **'Tempelhof'** A vigorous form with glaucous blue foliage.

‡†*patula* Schiede ex Schltdl. & Cham. An extremely beautiful, small to medium-sized tree of graceful habit, with reddish bark, long spreading branches and pendent, glaucous green, glabrous young shoots. Leaves bright green, usually in 3s, occasionally in 4s or 5s, to 30cm long. Cones in clusters, curved, to 10cm long. An elegant species with gracefully drooping foliage. This lovely tree has grown uninjured in our nurseries for more than 40 years, but is not recommended for the coldest northern areas. Mexico. ♀ 2002.

‡*peuce* Griseb. Macedonian pine. An attractive, medium-sized to large tree, recalling *P. cembra* in its narrowly conical habit. Young shoots shining green and glabrous. Leaves in 5s, to 10cm long, deep blue-green with white inner surfaces, densely packed on the branchlets. Cones to 15cm long. Balkan Peninsula. I 1864.

pinaster Aiton (*P. maritima* Lam.) Maritime pine, Bournemouth pine. Usually a sparsely branched, medium-sized tree but occasionally a large tree with a bare stem and thick, reddish-brown or dark purple bark in small squares. Leaves in pairs, to 25cm long, rigid and curved, dull grey. Cones to 18cm long, rich shining brown, often remaining intact on the branches for several years. An excellent species for sandy soils and seaside districts, particularly in the warmer parts of the British Isles. It is commonly planted along the South Coast, especially in the Bournemouth area. It is an important source of resin and the chief centre of the industry is in W France, from where large quantities of turpentine and resin are distributed. W Mediterranean region. C since the 16th century. ♀ 2002.

pinea L. Umbrella pine, Stone pine. A very distinct tree of small to medium size developing a characteristic dense, flat-topped or umbrella-shaped head. Leaves in pairs, to 15cm long, stiff and slightly twisted, sharply pointed. Cones stalked, to 15cm long, shining nut-brown. Seeds large and edible. A picturesque pine, particularly suitable for sandy soils and maritime areas. Mediterranean region. ♀ 2002.

ponderosa Douglas ex C. Lawson (*P. washoensis* Mason & Stockw.) Western yellow pine. A large tree of striking appearance with usually a tall, clear trunk, scaly cinnamon bark and stout, spreading or drooping branches. Young shoots stout, orange-brown or greenish, glabrous. Leaves in 3s, to 25cm long, stiff and curved, spreading and crowded at the ends of the branchlets. Cones to 16cm long, the scales armed with a small spine. A variable species with several named varieties. W North America. I 1826 by David Douglas. ♀ 2002. AM 1980. **var.** *arizonica* See *P. arizonica*. **var.** *jeffreyi* See *P. jeffreyi*. **var.** *scopulorum* Engelm. A form with usually drooping branches, shorter leaves, 7.5–15cm long, and smaller cones, to 7.5cm long. Rocky Mountains to North Mexico.

‡*pseudostrobus* Lindl. A tender tree of small to medium size, only suitable for the mildest areas of the British Isles. Young shoots glaucous. Leaves usually in 5s, apple-green, to 25cm long, pendent. Cones to 14cm long. It is closely allied to *P. montezumae*, differing in its glaucous shoots and smooth bark. Mexico, Central America. Recent introductions of this species, some received as *P. montezumae*, are proving hardy and very fast growing. I 1839. **var.** *apulcensis* (Lindl.) Shaw (*P. oaxacana* Mirov, *P. pseudostrobus* var. *oaxacana* (Mirov) S.G. Harrison) A tender tree related to *P. pseudostrobus*. Leaves 20–30cm long; cones 13–14cm long. S Mexico, Central America. **var.** *oaxacana* See *P. pseudostrobus var. apulcensis*.

‡*pumila* (Pall.) Regel (*P. cembra* var. *pumila* Pall.) Dwarf Siberian pine. Variable in habit, usually a dwarf shrub of spreading growth, occasionally a dense, medium-sized or large bush. Leaves in 5s, to 7cm or occasionally 10cm long, blue-white on the inner surfaces, densely bundled and crowding the branchlets. Cones 5cm long. Closely related to *P. cembra* and often difficult to distinguish from dwarf forms of that species. *P. pumila* and its forms are excellent conifers for a heather garden and a large rock garden. Widely distributed in E Asia, usually growing in cold, exposed places high in the mountains. I about 1807. **'Compacta'** A small shrub, up to 2m, of dense, erect, bushy habit; the branches crowded with large bunches of glaucous leaves. Very effective on a large rock garden or border edge. **'Glauca'** A bushy, small to medium-sized shrub with bright grey-blue leaves in 5s. Should be grown in lime-free soil. ♀ 2002.

‡*pungens* Lamb. Hickory pine. A small to medium-sized tree, often of bushy habit, with thick, reddish-brown bark. Leaves in pairs or occasionally in 3s, to 7.5cm long, rigid and twisted, sharply pointed, densely crowded on the branchlets. Cones to 9cm long, viciously spiny, often remaining intact on the tree for several years. E North America. I 1804.

quadrifolia Sudw. A small tree in the wild, slow-growing and extremely rare in cultivation, with smooth grey bark which cracks into scaly plates on mature trees. Needles to 4.5cm long, in dense bundles of 4 or sometimes 3 or 5, blue-green on the outer surface, glaucous on the inner surfaces, sharp-pointed. Cones ovoid, often broadly so

and wider than long, to 8cm long, ripening in 2 years. A plant in the Sir Harold Hillier Gardens and Arboretum was raised from seed received from E.K. Balls in 1956 and has reached 3m tall (2000). S California, Baja California.

‡*radiata* D. Don (*P. insignis* Douglas ex Loudon) Monterey pine. A large tree with deeply fissured, dark brown bark and a dense head of branches. Leaves in 3s, to 15cm long, bright green, densely crowded on the branchlets. Cones to 15cm long, borne in whorls along the branches, often remaining intact for many years. An attractive, rapid-growing tree for mild inland and coastal areas. Excellent for withstanding sea winds. Monterey Peninsula (California). I 1833 by David Douglas. ♀ 2002. **Aurea Group** Foliage golden-yellow. Raised in New Zealand. C 1910.

‡*resinosa* Aiton. Red pine. A small to medium-sized tree of rather heavy appearance, with a broad, conical head of branches. Leaves in pairs, 12–18cm long, slender and flexible. Cones to 6cm long. An important timber tree in North America. E Canada, NE USA. C 1736.

‡*rigida* Mill. Northern pitch pine. A medium-sized tree with strongly ridged young shoots. Leaves in 3s, to 10cm long, thick, stiff and spreading. Cones usually in clusters, to 9cm long. A peculiarity of this species is the tendency to produce tufts of leaves on the trunk. E North America. C 1759.

†*roxburghii* Sarg. (*P. longifolia* Roxb. ex Lamb.) Long-leaved Indian pine. A small tree in cultivation, closely related to *P. canariensis*. Young shoots clothed with scale-like leaves. Leaves in 3s, to 35cm long, light green. Cones to 20cm long, borne on short, stout stalks. A rare species, only suitable for the milder areas of the British Isles. Himalaya. I 1807.

rudis See *P. hartwegii*.

sabineana Douglas ex D. Don. Digger pine. A remarkable pine, related to *P. coulteri*. A medium-sized tree usually of gaunt open habit, with straggly branches. Leaves in 3s, to 30cm long, spreading or drooping, glaucous green, sparsely arranged on the branchlets. Cones to 25cm long. The edible seeds were once an important food for the American Indians. California. I 1832 by David Douglas.

‡× *schwerinii* Fitschen (*P. strobus* × *P. wallichiana*) A large tree resembling *P. wallichiana* in general appearance. Leaves in 5s, to 13cm long, loose and pendent, glaucous green. Cones slightly curved, to 15cm long. It differs from *P. wallichiana* mainly in its densely hairy shoots and shorter leaves. An attractive hybrid which originated on the estate of Dr Graf von Schwerin, near Berlin, in 1905.

‡*strobus* L. Weymouth pine, White pine. A large tree, conical habit when young, later developing a rounded head. Leaves in 5s, to 15cm long, somewhat glaucous green. Cones to 20cm long, pendent on slender stalks liberally flecked with resin. Once the most commonly planted of the 5-needled pines, due to its ornamental habit and fast growth. It owes its English name to Lord Weymouth, who made extensive plantings of this species at Longleat, Wiltshire, in the early 1700s. E North America. C since the mid-16th century. **'Blue Shag'** A slow-growing dwarf shrub of dense, rounded habit with intensely silver-blue needles. **'Compacta'** A dwarf, slow-growing

bush of dense habit. **'Contorta'** ('Tortuosa') A curious form, developing twisted branches and densely set, conspicuously twisted leaves. C 1932. **'Densa'** This is a dwarf bush of dense habit. **'Fastigiata'** An erect-branched form of conical or broadly columnar habit. C 1884. **Nana Group** A small form developing into a dense bush. There are several slight variations of this form, some of which are more vigorous and larger-growing. **'Nivea'** An attractive form in which the glaucous leaves are tipped milky-white, giving the whole tree an unusual silver-white appearance. **'Pendula'** A form with long, drooping branches. **'Prostrata'** A remarkable, prostrate form, the branches lying flat on the ground or shortly ascending and forming a low mound. Originally found by Alfred Rehder in the Arnold Arboretum, Boston, USA. C 1893.

sylvestris L. (*P. sylvestris* var. *lapponica* Hartm., *P. sylvestris* var. *rigensis* Loudon) Scots pine. The only pine native to Britain. A familiar tree usually seen as a large, tall-stemmed and, occasionally, a low, picturesque, spreading tree. It is easily recognised by its characteristic and attractive, reddish young bark. Leaves in pairs, 3–10cm long, twisted, grey-green or blue-green. Cones to 7.5cm long, on short stalks. W Europe to NE Asia.

A commonly planted tree which combines beauty with utility. In the British Isles, truly wild stands of this species are only found in parts of N Scotland, but it once grew naturally throughout England and Wales. Due to extensive planting in the past, it has become naturalised in many areas, particularly on heaths and moors. There are numerous geographical variants of which our native form has been called var. *scotica* Beissn.. Many garden forms have arisen, several of which are suitable for a rock garden. The Scots pine may be grown in all types of soil but does not reach its maximum proportions or maximum age in damp acid soils or shallow dry chalk soils. ♀ 2002. **'Argentea'** See 'Edwin Hillier'. **Aurea Group** A slow-growing, small tree with striking golden-yellow leaves in winter. ♀ 2002. AM 1964. **'Beuvronensis'** This miniature Scots pine forms a small, compact, dome-shaped shrublet. A superb subject for a rock garden. C 1891. ♀ 2002. AM 1968. **'Chantry Blue'** A vigorous form of upright habit with foliage a good blue. **'Compressa'** A dwarf bush of conical habit, with short, crowded, glaucous leaves. C 1867. **'Doone Valley'** A dwarf form of compact, somewhat conical habit. Leaves glaucous. Named after "Doone Valley", the one-time garden of Mr W. Archer. **'Edwin Hillier'** A beautiful form selected by Edwin Hillier with silvery-blue-green leaves and reddish stems. Originally listed as 'Argentea', it has no connection with f. *argentea* Steven (*P. sylvestris* var. *hamata* Steven) described from the Caucasus. **'Fastigiata'** A remarkable Scots pine, the shape of a Lombardy poplar. C 1856. **'Frensham'** A slow-growing, dwarf, bun-shaped plant of congested habit with blue-green foliage. Originally found as witches' broom. **'Gold Coin'** Similar to 'Aurea' but smaller with brighter yellow foliage. C 1979. **'Gold Medal'** A slow-growing dwarf with bright yellow foliage in winter and spring. C 1979. **'Inverleith'** A form with the leaves variegated creamy-white. The original is an old tree in the Royal Botanical Garden in Edinburgh.

var. *lapponica* See *P. sylvestris*. **'Lodge Hill'** A dwarf form of dense habit with blue-grey foliage. Originated as a witches' broom in Surrey. C 1981. **'Moseri'** See *P. nigra* 'Moseri'. **'Nana'** Dwarf, bushy form of slow growth; differing from the very similar 'Beuvronensis' in its non-resinous winter buds. C 1855. **'Pumila'** See 'Watereri'. **'Pygmaea'** A rare, slow-growing, dwarf form of dense, rounded habit. C 1891. var. *rigensis* See *P. sylvestris*. **'Viridis Compacta'** Dwarf bush of conical habit, superficially resembling a dwarf form of *P. nigra*, with its long, vivid, grass-green leaves. C 1923. **'Watereri'** ('Pumila') A slow-growing, medium-sized bush or rarely a small tree, conical in habit at first, later becoming rounded. It is suitable for a heather garden, but eventually becomes too large for a normal rock garden. Found on Horsell Common, Surrey by Mr Anthony Waterer in about 1865. The original plant in the Knap Hill Nursery is about 8m high. **'Windsor'** Dwarf, bun-shaped form of slow growth. Leaves very small, greyish-green. Originated as a witches' broom.

tabuliformis Carrière (*P. sinensis* Mayr not D Don) Chinese pine. An uncommon species, usually a small to medium-sized, flat-headed tree in cultivation. Leaves in pairs or 3s, 10–15cm long, densely crowding the branchlets. Cones to 6.5cm long. N China. C 1862. var. *yunnanensis* See *P. yunnanensis*.

taeda L. Loblolly pine. A small to medium-sized tree with glabrous and glaucous young shoots. Leaves in 3s, to 25cm long, slender and flexible and slightly twisted. Cones to 10cm long. A distinct and effective tree which should be in every pinetum. Suitable for southern and drier parts of the British Isles. SE USA. I 1741.

†*taiwanensis* Hayata. A rare tree of small to medium size; leaves in pairs. Only suitable for a conservatory or sheltered sites in mild areas. Taiwan.

thunbergii Parl. Black pine. A distinct and splendid, large tree with stout, twisted branches. Leaves in pairs, 7–18cm long, rigid and twisted. Cones to 6cm long, borne singly or in large clusters. The black pine is one of the most important timber trees in Japan, where it often occurs by the seashore. In the British Isles it is useful as a windbreak in maritime areas and for growing in poor, sandy soils. Japan, S Korea. I 1852. **'Globosa'** ('Compacta') A dense-growing, large bush. **'Oculus-draconis'** An unusual form in which the leaves are marked with two yellowish bands.

†*torreyana* Parry ex Carrière. Torrey pine. A small tree or a gnarled bush, sometimes prostrate in the wild. Leaves in 5s, 20–30cm long, borne in dense bunches at the ends of the branchlets. Cones to 13cm long, stalked. Seeds sweet and edible. Only suitable for milder, drier areas of the British Isles. S California. I 1853.

tuberculata See *P. attenuata*.

uncinata See *P. mugo* subsp. *uncinata*.

‡*virginiana* Mill. Scrub pine. Small to medium-sized tree with purplish, bloomy young shoots. Leaves in pairs, to 6cm long, stiff and twisted. Cones to 7cm long, the scales ending in a short, recurved prickle. It dislikes shallow chalk soils. E USA. I 1739.

wallichiana A.B. Jacks. (*P. griffithii* M'Clelland not Parl., *P. excelsa* Wall. ex D. Don not Lamb.) Bhutan pine. An elegant, large, broad-headed tree, retaining its lowest branches when isolated. Leaves in 5s, to 20cm long, blue-green, slender and drooping with age. Cones stalked, solitary or in bunches, banana-shaped, 15–25cm long. A most attractive species with its graceful foliage and ornamental, resin-smeared, pendent cones. It is moderately lime-tolerant but not recommended for shallow chalk soils. Temperate Himalaya. I about 1823. ♀ 2002. AM 1979. **'Nana'** See under 'Umbraculifera'. **'Umbraculifera'** A small, dome-shaped, glaucous bush of slow growth and dense habit. Previously listed as 'Nana'. **'Zebrina'** Leaves with a creamy-yellow band below the apex. C 1889.

washoensis See *P. ponderosa*.

yunnanensis Franch. (*P. tabuliformis* var. *yunnanensis* Dallim. & A.B. Jacks.) A medium-sized tree related to *P. tabuliformis* and differing in its stout, glabrous, shining pink shoots, its longer, more slender and drooping leaves, 20–30cm long, borne usually in 3s, and in the larger, darker brown cones up to 9cm long. A very distinct, rather sparsely branched tree creating the effect of *P. montezumae*. SW China. I 1909 by Ernest Wilson.

*PLATYCLADUS Spach—**Cupressaceae**—A monotypic genus previously included in *Thuja* but very distinct in its formal habit, erect branches, its foliage being less aromatic than others and its cone scales, which have conspicuous recurved hooks.

orientalis (L.) Franco (*Thuja orientalis* L., *Biota orientalis* (L.) Endl.) Chinese arbor-vitae. A large shrub or small tree of dense, conical or columnar habit when young. Branches erect, the leaves borne in frond-like, vertical sprays. There are several forms suitable for a rock garden. N and W China, E Russia, Korea. I about 1690. **'Athrotaxoides'** An extremely slow-growing, small shrub with noticeably thick branches and branchlets, lacking the spray-like foliage typical of the species. Originated in the Jardin des Plantes, Paris in 1867. **'Aurea Nana'** A dwarf, globular bush of dense habit, with crowded, vertically arranged sprays of light yellow-green foliage. C 1804. ♀ 2002. **'Compacta'** See 'Sieboldii'. **'Conspicua'** A medium-sized to large bush of dense, compact, conical habit. The golden foliage is retained longer than in most other forms of similar colour. C 1804. **'Decussata'** See 'Juniperoides'. **'Elegantissima'** A medium-sized to large bush of dense, columnar habit. Foliage golden-yellow, tinged old-gold, becoming green in winter. C 1858. ♀ 2002. **'Filiformis Erecta'** An unusual form of ovoid habit, forming a large bush or small tree, with erect, whip-like stems, clothed with yellowish-green leaves, bronzed in winter. C 1868. **'Hillieri'** A small to medium-sized bush of dense, compact, ovoid habit. Leaves soft yellow-green, becoming green in winter. Raised in our nurseries prior to 1924. **'Juniperoides'** ('Decussata') A dwarf, rounded bush with soft, juvenile foliage, greyish-green in summer turning a rich, purplish-grey in winter. It is a most attractive form, requiring shelter from cold winds. C 1850. AM 1973. **'Meldensis'** A dwarf bush of dense, globular habit. The semi-juvenile foliage is sea-green in summer turning plum-purple in winter. Raised in 1852. **'Minima Glauca'** A beautiful, dwarf bush of dense, globular habit. Foliage semi-juvenile, sea-green in summer, turning

warm yellow-brown in winter. C 1891. **'Rosedalis'** ('Rosedalis Compacta') A dense, ovoid bush with soft juvenile foliage which, in early spring, is a bright canary-yellow, changing by midsummer to sea-green, and in winter glaucous plum-purple. In 15 years it will attain 80cm in height. Its soft-to-the-touch foliage and its spring colour distinguish it from 'Meldensis'. C 1923. **'Sanderi'** (*Chamaecyparis obtusa* 'Sanderi', *Juniperus sanderi* hort.) A dwarf, slow-growing, juvenile form with short, thick leaves. The whole bush is delightfully sea-green in summer, becoming plum-coloured in winter. It is somewhat wind-tender and requires a sheltered, well-drained position or a pot in an alpine house. It was originally introduced from Japan in 1894 and for many years was considered to be a juniper. H.J. Welch and the late L.J. Gough, using gas chromatography to analyse leaf extracts, have shown that it belongs here. AM 1899. **'Semperaurea'** A dense, rounded bush of medium size, with yellow foliage throughout summer, becoming bronzed later. C 1870. FCC 1870. **'Sieboldii'** ('Nana', 'Compacta') A small, rounded bush of dense, compact habit. Foliage golden-yellow at first, turning mid-green later, borne in delicate lace-like, vertical sprays. C 1859.

*PODOCARPUS L'Hér. ex Pers.—**Podocarpaceae**—A large genus of 106 species of evergreen trees and shrubs mainly confined in the wild to the S hemisphere in warm temperate and tropical countries. Leaves are variable in shape, usually spirally arranged. Fruits consist of a fleshy, coloured, usually red, receptacle in which the seed is inserted. Several species are suitable for milder areas of the British Isles and a few may be classed as hardy. They succeed in most types of soil whether acid or alkaline. It has recently been proposed that *Podocarpus* be divided into several genera. Both male and female plants are needed to produce fruits.

acutifolius Kirk. Needle-leaved Totara. A small to medium-sized, moderately hardy shrub usually of dense, prickly habit. Leaves linear, 1–2.5cm long, sharply pointed, bronze-green. Although it reaches small tree size in its native habitat, it remains dense and slow-growing in cultivation and, as such, is an interesting plant for a prominent position on a large rock garden. This plant has grown successfully on the scree at the Sir Harold Hillier Gardens and Arboretum for many years. New Zealand (South Island).

acutifolius × *lawrencei* Seedlings of this parentage have arisen at the Sir Harold Hillier Gardens and Arboretum from the female *P. lawrencei* 'Alpine Lass' pollinated by a nearby male *P. acutifolius*. They are taller than the female parent with longer needles that are spine-tipped but not as sharply pointed as those of the male parent. The foliage turns deep bronze-purple in winter, unlike either parent.

alpinus See *P. lawrencei*.

andinus See *Prumnopitys andina*.

chilinus See *P. salignus*.

'County Park Fire' (*P. lawrencei* × *P. nivalis*) PBR A low, spreading mound-shaped shrub. Creamy young foliage turns to salmon-pink, bronze-red in winter. Produces fruits with fleshy red receptacles if a suitable pollinator is nearby. Raised by Graham Hutchins of County Park Nursery. 'Flame' is similar but male.

†*cunninghamii* Colenso (*P. hallii* Kirk, *P. totara* var. *hallii* (Kirk) Pilg.) A small tree or large, bushy shrub, related and similar to *P. totara*, but differing in its longer leaves, 2.5–5cm on young plants, and its thin, papery, peeling bark. There is a good specimen growing very well at Castlewellan, N Ireland, in the splendid pinetum planted by Mr Gerald Annesley. New Zealand.

dacrydioides See *Dacrycarpus dacrydioides*.

†*elatus* R. Br. ex Endl. A small to medium-sized tree of elegant habit, its branches clothed with narrowly oblong, bright green leaves varying from 5–15cm long, or longer on young vigorous specimens. Only survives outdoors in the mildest areas, but suitable for a conservatory. E Australia.

falcatus See *Afrocarpus falcatus*.

ferrugineus See *Prumnopitys ferruginea*.

'Flame' See under 'County Park Fire'.

gracilior See *Afrocarpus gracilior*.

hallii See *P. cunninghamii*. 'Aureus' See *P. totara* 'Aureus'.

lawrencei Hook. f. (*P. alpinus* R. Br. ex Hook. f.) A remarkably hardy, dwarf species, forming a low, densely branched mound or a creeping carpet extending 1–2m or more across, sometimes a small bush of upright or pendent habit. Leaves yew-like, narrow, blue or grey-green, crowding the stems. Suitable for a rock garden or as groundcover. In its native habitat it is often found on stony mountainsides where it helps to prevent erosion. SE Australia, Tasmania. 'Alpine Lass' The commonly grown female form, usually grown as *P. alpinus*. Dark green leaves and low, spreading or pendent habit. The red-based fruits are a conspicuous feature in summer. 'Blue Gem' A vigorous form of spreading habit with blue-green foliage. A female selection good for groundcover.

‡*macrophyllus* (Thunb.) Sweet. Kusamaki. One of the hardiest species, forming a shrub or small tree of very distinct appearance. Leaves 10–13cm long, up to 18cm on vigorous plants, 12mm wide, bright green above, glaucous beneath, arranged in dense spirals on the stems. Not suitable for chalky soils. It has withstood 28 degrees of frost in the Sir Harold Hillier Gardens and Arboretum. Native of China and of Japan where it is occasionally grown as an unusual and effective hedge. 'Angustifolius' A form with narrower leaves. C 1864. 'Argenteus' A slow-growing form, its narrower leaves with an irregular white border. C 1861. FCC 1865.

nagi See *Nageia nagi*.

nivalis Hook. Alpine totara. One of the hardiest species, succeeding throughout the British Isles and doing well in chalky soils. Normally seen as a low, spreading mound of shortly erect and prostrate stems, densely branched and crowded with small, narrow, leathery, olive-green leaves, 6–20mm long. An excellent groundcover. A large plant growing in shade in the Bedgebury Pinetum, Kent, formed a carpet 2–3m across. Native of New Zealand where it is found on mountain slopes. 'Bronze' ('Aureus') Leaves bronze-tinged, more noticeable in the young growths.

nubigenus Lindl. A distinct, slow-growing, beautiful shrub rarely reaching the size of a small tree. The usually spirally arranged, sharply pointed, narrow leaves are 3.5–4.5cm long, deep green above and glaucous beneath. In the Sir Harold Hillier Gardens and Arboretum injured only in the coldest winters. Mts of S Chile and S Argentina.

†*salignus* D. Don (*P. chilinus* Rich. & A. Rich.) A most attractive and elegant, small tree or large shrub with drooping branches and long, narrow, bright grey-green leaves, 5–15cm long. A well-grown specimen creates an almost tropical effect with its lush piles of evergreen, glossy, willow-like foliage. Hardy in the South West when given the shelter of other evergreens. S Chile. ♛ 2002.

spicatus See *Prumnopitys taxifolia*.

totara G. Benn ex D. Don. A tall tree in New Zealand, but usually a slow-growing large shrub in the British Isles. Leaves yellowish-green, scattered or 2-ranked, up to 2cm long on adult plants, 2.5cm long on young plants, leathery, stiff and sharply pointed. Correctly sited among sheltering evergreens this unusual shrub is more or less hardy in the Home Counties. 'Aureus' (*P. hallii* 'Aureus') Leaves yellow-green. var. *hallii* See *P. cunninghamii*.

*PRUMNOPITYS** Phil.—Podocarpaceae—A genus of 9 species of trees, natives of C and S America, New Zealand and E Australia.

andina (Poepp. ex Endl.) de Laub. (*Podocarpus andinus* Poepp. ex Endl., *Prumnopitys elegans* Phil.) Plum-fruited yew, Chilean yew. A small to medium-sized tree or large shrub, somewhat resembling a yew in habit. Leaves linear, 1–2.5cm long, bright green above, twisted to reveal the glaucous green undersurface. Fruits like small damsons, glaucous black, borne on slender scaly stalks. This species grows excellently on good soils over chalk. Andes of S Chile and Argentina. I by Robert Pearce for Messrs Veitch in 1860. FCC 1864.

elegans See *P. andina*.

†*ferruginea* (G. Benth. ex D. Don) de Laub. (*Podocarpus ferrugineus* G. Benth. ex D. Don) Miro. A graceful, small tree. Leaves rather yew-like in shape but a softer yellow-green, arranged in irregular ranks along the slender branches, which are pendent at their extremities. This rare and attractive species is doing well in the beautiful garden made by Mrs Vera Mackie at Helen's Bay, N Ireland. Native of New Zealand where it is an important timber tree.

†*taxifolia* (Banks & Sol. ex G. Don) de Laub. (*Podocarpus spicatus* R. Br.) Matai, Black pine of New Zealand. An interesting small tree in the mildest areas of the British Isles. Young trees possess numerous, slender, drooping branches and branchlets, towards the tips of which occur the small, narrow, bronze-tinted leaves.

‡**PSEUDOLARIX** Gordon—Pinaceae—A monotypic genus superficially resembling *Larix* but differing in several characters. The linear leaves, which are borne in dense clusters on short spurs on the older wood, are spirally arranged on the young shoots. Male and female strobili are borne on the same tree. It requires a lime-free soil. Fossil records show that it was once widely distributed in the N hemisphere.

amabilis (J. Nelson) Rehder (*P. fortunei* Mayr, *P. kaempferi* auct. not Gordon) Golden larch. A beautiful and very hardy, slow-growing, deciduous, medium-sized tree of broadly conical habit. The long, larch-like, light green leaves, 3–6cm long, turn clear golden-yellow in autumn. Cones ripen the first year. On a large tree they stud the long, slender branches, resembling small, pale green artichokes, bloomy when young, reddish-brown when ripe. E China. I by Robert Fortune in 1852. ♀ 2002. AM 1976.

‡***PSEUDOTSUGA** Carrière—**Pinaceae**—A small genus of 4 or more species of evergreen trees of broadly conical habit, with whorled branches and spindle-shaped buds recalling those of the common beech (*Fagus sylvatica*), natives of E Asia, W North America and Mexico. The leaves are linear, soft to the touch and marked with 2 glaucous stomatic bands beneath. Male and female strobili are borne on the same tree. Cones are pendent and ripen in one season. The members of this genus may be distinguished from *Abies* by the pendent cones which fall intact, and from *Picea* by the 3-lobed cone-bracts. The majority of species dislike chalky soils, thriving best in moist, but well-drained soils. *P. menziesii* is of great economic importance.

douglasii See *P. menziesii*.

glauca See *P. menziesii* var. *glauca*.

japonica (Shiras.) Beissn. The Japanese douglas fir is rare in cultivation and makes a small, bushy tree. Leaves to 2.5cm long, notched, pale green, arranged on the branchlets in 2 ranks. Cones to 5cm long. Distinguished from other species by its glabrous shoots, smaller cones and shorter leaves. SE Japan. I 1898. AM 1984.

macrocarpa (Vasey) Mayr. Large-coned douglas fir. A rare, medium-sized tree with reddish-brown young shoots. Leaves to 3cm long, arranged on the branchlets in 2 ranks. Cones 10–18cm long, the largest in the genus. Native of S California. There is a specimen 16m tall in the Sir Harold Hillier Gardens and Arboretum (2001). I 1910 by H. Clinton-Baker.

menziesii (Mirb.) Franco (*P. taxifolia* (Lamb.) Britton, *P. douglasii* (Sabine ex G. Don) Carrière) Douglas fir. A fast-growing, large tree. The lower branches of large specimens are downswept and the bark is thick, corky and deeply furrowed. Leaves to 3cm long, arranged on the branchlets in 2, usually horizontal ranks, fragrant when crushed. Cones to 10cm long, with conspicuous exserted bracts. This well-known conifer is an important timber tree both in Britain and in North America. It is one of the stateliest conifers, being particularly effective when planted in groups, as in the New Forest and at Knightshayes Court in Devon. It is unsatisfactory on chalk soils. A native of W North America, it reaches its finest proportions in Washington and British Columbia, where specimens of 90m and above are recorded. It was originally discovered by Archibald Menzies in about 1792 and introduced by David Douglas in 1827. Measured in November 1999, the douglas fir at Dunans, Argyll, was 65m tall, the tallest tree in Britain at the millennium, and probably the tallest since the last ice age. ♀ 2002. AM 1984. **'Brevifolia'** A small, shrubby form, occasionally a miniature tree up to 2m, with leaves only 6–15mm long, densely spreading all round the shoots. It differs from the similar 'Fretsii' in its narrower leaves, and is less lime-tolerant. FCC 1886. **var. caesia** See var. *glauca*. **'Densa'** Dwarf, slow-growing, shrubby

form of dense habit, with spreading branches and green leaves to 2cm long. C 1933. **'Elegans'** See under 'Glauca Pendula'. **'Fletcheri'** (*P. glauca* 'Fletcheri') A slow-growing, shrubby form developing into an irregular, flat-topped, globular bush, eventually 1.5–2m in height. Leaves blue-green, 2–2.5cm long, loosely arranged. Originated as a seedling of var. *glauca* in 1906. AM 1912. **'Fretsii'** An unusual, slow-growing form. The short, broad, obtuse leaves, 10–12mm long, resemble those of a *Tsuga*, but the arrangement is radial. Specimens in our nurseries had made irregular bushes about 1.2m high by 1.8m across at 30 years old. More lime-tolerant than 'Brevifolia'. The colour of the leaves suggests kinship with var. *caesia*. C 1905. **var. glauca** (Beissn.) Franco (*P. glauca* (Beissn.) Mayr) Blue douglas fir. A medium-sized tree of narrow, conical habit. Leaves shorter, glaucous above, smelling of turpentine when crushed. Cones 6–7.5cm long, the bracts reflexed. Hardier but slower-growing and more lime-tolerant. Native of the Rocky Mountains, from Montana to C Mexico. **'Glauca Pendula'** A small, weeping tree of graceful habit. Branchlets ascending, clothed with bluish-green leaves, 3–5cm long. Plants we have received under the name 'Elegans' appear identical. C 1891. FCC 1895. **'Holmstrup'** A small to medium-sized shrub or miniature tree of rather compact, upright habit, with green leaves to 1.5cm long, densely and radially arranged on the branchlets. **'Nana'** (*P. glauca* 'Nana') Small to medium-sized bush, conical when young. Leaves 2–2.5cm long, glaucous-green, almost radial. Originated as a seedling of var. *glauca* in 1915. **'Pendula'** An unusual form with weeping branches, a form of var. *glauca*. C 1868.

sinensis Dode. A small tree in cultivation, with reddish-brown, young shoots. Leaves to 3.5cm long, notched at apex, arranged in 2 ranks. Cones to 5cm long. This rare, slow-growing species is susceptible to damage by spring frost. China, Taiwan. I 1912.

taxifolia See *P. menziesii*.

Redwood See *Sequoia sempervirens*.

RETINISPORA Siebold & Zucc. An obsolete generic name which was at one time used to cover those forms of *Chamaecyparis* with permanently juvenile (awl-shaped) foliage.

***SAXEGOTHAEA** Lindl.—**Podocarpaceae**—A monotypic genus resembling *Prumnopitys andina* in general appearance. The branchlets are arranged in whorls of 3 or 4. Male and female strobili are borne on the same plant. The genus is named in honour of Prince Albert, consort of Queen Victoria, after the Prussian province from which he came. A connecting link between Podocarpaceae and Araucariaceae, it resembles a *Podocarpus* in foliage and an *Araucaria* in the female strobili. It occurs in dense forests in S Chile and S Argentina.

conspicua Lindl. Prince Albert's yew. An unusual large shrub or small tree of loose habit, with laxly spreading branches and drooping branchlets. Leaves linear, 1.5–2cm long, dark green above, marked with 2 glaucous bands beneath, rather twisted and arranged on the lateral branches in 2 ranks. Fruits 12–20mm across, soft and prickly. An attractive conifer and botanically very interesting. I 1847 by William Lobb.

‡*SCIADOPITYS Siebold & Zucc.—**Sciadopityaceae**—A monotypic genus of unique appearance, and the only member of its family. Thriving in a lime-free soil, it should be planted in every representative collection of conifers. It does well in partial shade.

verticillata Siebold & Zucc. Umbrella pine. A slow-growing, very hardy, monoecious tree of medium size. Dense and conical when young usually with a single trunk, sometimes with several main stems. Bark peeling to reveal the reddish-brown new bark. Branches horizontal, bearing lush clusters of rich, glossy green foliage. The apparent single linear leaves, up to 13cm long, are, in fact, fused pairs and are arranged in characteristic dense whorls like the spokes of an umbrella, hence the English name. The attractive cones, 6–10cm long, are green at first, ripening to brown the second year. Native of Japan. First introduced as a single plant by Thomas Lobb in 1853, later more successfully by both Robert Fortune and J.G. Veitch in 1861. ♀ 2002. AM 1979.

*SEQUOIA Endl.—**Cupressaceae**—A well-known monotypic genus named after Sequoiah (1770–1843) of Georgia, who was half Cherokee and invented the Cherokee alphabet. The butt of a felled tree will produce a sheaf of suckers, which is unusual in a conifer. Given 60cm depth of soil, it will succeed in chalk areas.

gigantea See *Sequoiadendron giganteum*.

sempervirens (D. Don) Endl. (*Taxodium sempervirens* D. Don) California redwood. A very large, evergreen, monoecious tree, reaching over 100m tall in its native forests, possessing a thick, fibrous, soft and spongy, reddish-brown outer bark. Branches slightly drooping, yew-like, bearing 2-ranked, linear-oblong leaves, 1–2cm long, dark green above, marked with 2 white stomatic bands beneath. Leaves on leading shoots and fertile shoots smaller and spirally arranged. Cones pendent, ovoid to globose, 2–3cm long, ripening the first season.

This majestic tree is a native of California and Oregon where it is found on the seaward side of the coastal mountain range. It was discovered by Archibald Menzies in 1794 and first introduced into Europe (St Petersburg) in 1840. Three years later Hartweg sent seed to England. The Redwood has the distinction of being the world's tallest living tree, the record at present being held by the 'Harry Cole' tree in the Humbolt State Redwood Park which, in 1988, measured 113m (371ft). (The tallest tree ever recorded was a specimen of *Eucalyptus regnans* in Victoria, SE Australia, estimated to have been more than 150m in 1872.). The tallest redwood in the British Isles is found at Bodnant and measured 47m (153ft) in 1984. It is also a long-lived tree, the average age being 500–700 years. Several trees have reached 2,000 years and the oldest known specimen, felled in 1934, was dated at 2,200 years. ♀ 2002. **'Adpressa'** ('Albospica') The tips of the young shoots are creamy-coloured, and the short leaves regularly disposed in one plane. It is often grown as a dwarf shrub but unless frequently cut back will eventually make a large tree. C 1867. FCC 1890. **'Cantab'** A remarkable form with the distinctive foliage of 'Prostrata' but making a strong-growing tree. Occasionally originates when 'Prostrata' produces vigorous, upright shoots. A specimen in the Sir Harold Hillier Gardens and Arboretum has reached 17m (2000). **'Prostrata'** A most remarkable, dwarf form with spreading branches thickly clothed with comparatively broad, glaucous green, 2-ranked leaves. Originated as a branch sport on a tree at the University Botanic Garden, Cambridge. See also 'Cantab'. C 1951. AM 1951.

wellingtonia See *Sequoiadendron giganteum*.

*SEQUOIADENDRON J. Buchholz—**Cupressaceae**—A monotypic genus, once included under *Sequoia*, differing in its naked winter buds, awl-shaped leaves and larger cones, ripening during the second year. It is quite hardy and reasonably lime-tolerant but will not succeed on thin chalky soils.

giganteum (Lindl.) J. Buchholz (*Sequoia gigantea* (Lindl.) Decne., *Sequoia wellingtonia* Seem.) Wellingtonia, Mammoth tree. The 'big tree' of California attains a very large size. The deeply furrowed, reddish-brown outer bark is similar to that of *Sequoia sempervirens* in texture. As a young tree it has a densely branched, conical habit. On older trees the branches are more widely spaced and conspicuously downswept. Sometimes the lower part of the trunk is clear of branches for several metres, revealing the ornamental bark. Leaves awl-shaped, 6–12mm long, bright green, spirally arranged, persisting for up to 4 years. Cones ovoid, 5–7.5cm long, green at first, maturing to reddish-brown the second year. It is a familiar tree of parks and estates and resembles no other hardy cultivated conifer, except perhaps *Cryptomeria japonica*, which has similar leaves and similarly coloured bark.

It is a native of California where it grows on the western slopes of the Sierra Nevada. Although never as tall as the redwood, in its native state it attains a greater girth and the "General Sherman" tree, with a height of 84m (275ft), a girth of 25m (82ft) at 1.4m, and a total trunk volume of 1400m³ (50,000 cubic feet), is generally acknowledged to be the world's largest living thing. It is estimated to weigh 2,500 tonnes and be up to 3,000 years old. Specimens of 30m and above are not uncommon in the British Isles, among the tallest was one at Endsleigh, Devon which, in 1970, measured 49m (165ft), with a girth (at 1.5m or 5ft) of 6.71m (22ft). The Wellingtonia is regarded as one of the oldest living things in the world (see also *Pinus longaeva*). The oldest authenticated age of a felled tree is about 3,200 years, while several standing trees appear to be about 1,500–2,000 years old. I 1853. ♀ 2002. **'Glaucum'** A form of narrowly conical habit with glaucous leaves. It has reached 13.5m in the Sir Harold Hillier Gardens and Arboretum. C 1860. **'Hazel Smith'** A selection with blue-grey foliage, not as intense as 'Glaucum' but more vigorous. C 1988. **'Pendulum'** A tree of unique appearance often assuming the most fantastic shapes, but usually forming a narrow column with long branches hanging almost parallel with the trunk. C 1863. FCC 1882. **'Pygmaeum'** Small to medium-sized bush of dense, conical habit. If reversions occur they should be removed. C 1891. **'Variegatum'** Leaves flecked with a white variegation. Not a beauty. C 1890.

Spruce See *Picea*.

*****TAIWANIA** Hayata—**Cupressaceae**—A genus of a single species. A remarkable conifer that is rare in cultivation. It is related to and somewhat resembles *Cryptomeria* in general appearance. Male and female strobili are borne on the same tree.

†*cryptomerioides* Hayata. A rare tree of conical habit, attaining 50m or more in its native habitats. In cultivation it forms a small, sparsely branched tree with slender, drooping, whip-like branchlets, densely clothed with glaucous green, linear, sickle-shaped, sharply pointed leaves, shorter and more scale-like on adult trees. Cones cylindrical, 12mm long. This unusual conifer requires a moist but well-drained soil and a sheltered site to succeed. Western slopes of Mount Morrison, Taiwan. I 1920 by Ernest Wilson. AM 1931.

flousiana Gaussen Coffin tree. This is an attractive species closely resembling *T. cryptomerioides*, but with greener, slightly longer, less rigid leaves, softer to the touch. It has also proved a hardier tree. A specimen in our Chandler's Ford nursery grew slowly for many years uninjured by severe winters. It is a native of SW and C China and also N Burma, where it was discovered by Kingdon-Ward. Its wood is used in China for making coffins and it is this species rather than *J. recurva* var. *coxii* which is in danger of extinction through over-felling.

‡**TAXODIUM** Rich.—**Cupressaceae**—A genus of 2 species of deciduous trees. Leaves linear and flattened or awl-shaped, arranged alternately in 2 opposite ranks on short, deciduous branchlets, the whole resembling a pinnate leaf. On persistent branchlets they are radially arranged. Male and female strobili are borne on the same tree, the males in long, drooping, terminal panicles. Cones short-stalked, with thick, woody, shield-like scales, ripening during the first year. These beautiful North and Central American trees, with their attractive, frond-like foliage, can be successfully grown in all soils other than chalky soils. They are remarkable for their adaptability for growing in waterlogged conditions, but it is essential that they are mound planted in such sites.

ascendens See *T. distichum* var. *imbricarium*.

distichum (L.) Rich. Deciduous cypress, Swamp cypress, Bald cypress. A strikingly beautiful tree and the most suitable conifer for wet soils. A large tree with fibrous, reddish-brown bark and a strongly buttressed trunk. Leaves linear and flattened, 1–1.5cm long, grass-green, pectinate on short, deciduous shoots, spirally arranged on the persistent branchlets, turning bronze-yellow in autumn. When grown by water, large specimens produce peculiar knee-like growths (cypress knees), which project above ground, from the roots. Native of wet places, rivers and swamps in S USA, and the dominant tree in the Everglades of Florida. I by John Tradescant about 1640. ♀ 2002. AM 1973. **'Hursley Park'** A dwarf, dense bush which originated from a witches' broom on a tree at Hursley Park, Hampshire, in 1966. **var. *imbricarium*** (Nutt.) Croom (*T. ascendens* Brongn.) A small to medium-sized tree of narrowly conical or columnar habit, with spreading branches and erect branchlets. Leaves awl-shaped, 5–10mm long, incurved and adpressed, bright green. In cultivation in the British Isles it tends to be slower-growing than *T. distichum*, but it is worth cultivating for its habit and rich brown autumn foliage. Native of swampy places in SE USA. **'Nutans'** A beautiful, columnar tree with shortly spreading or ascending branches. The thin, crowded branchlets are erect at first, later nodding, clothed with adpressed, awl-shaped leaves up to 5mm long. C 1789. ♀ 2002. **'Pendens'** A form with drooping branchlets and branch tips. C 1855.

†*mucronatum* Ten. Mexican cypress. A small to medium-sized tree, closely resembling *T. distichum*, but leaves semi-persistent in warm areas. In its native habitat it grows along riverbanks and rarely produces cypress knees. It is too tender for all but the mildest areas of the British Isles. A famous specimen in the town of Tule, Oaxaca, Mexico has the largest girth of any tree. In 1982 it had a circumference of 36m (118ft) at 1.5m (5ft) and was 41m (135ft) tall. Mexico.

sempervirens See *Sequoia sempervirens*.

*****TAXUS** L.—**Taxaceae**—The yews are a small genus of about 10 species of evergreen trees and shrubs, widely distributed in N temperate regions, south to Central America and Indonesia. They bear linear, 2-ranked or radial leaves, marked by 2 yellowish-green or greyish-green bands beneath. Male and female strobili are borne during spring, usually on separate plants. Fruits with a fleshy, often brightly coloured cup (aril) containing a single poisonous seed. The yews are of great garden value, tolerant of most soils and situations, including dry chalk soils and heavy shade. They are very useful for hedges; the columnar forms are ideal for formal planting.

baccata L. Common yew, English yew. One of Britain's 3 native conifers, usually found in the wild on chalk formations. A small to medium-sized tree or large shrub with dark, almost black-green leaves, to 3cm long. Fruits with a red aril. A well-known tree, a common and familiar resident of churchyards where specimens of great age are occasionally found. Given good drainage the yew will grow on almost pure chalk or in very acid soils. Europe, W Asia, North Africa. ♀ 2002.

Cultivars of *Taxus baccata*

The yew has given rise to numerous forms varying in habit and colour. The low, prostrate forms make wonderful groundcover plants, even in dense shade.

'Adpressa' A large shrub or small tree. A female clone of dense, spreading habit, with ascending branches and short, crowded branchlets clothed with small, dark green leaves, 5–10mm long. C 1828.

'Adpressa Aurea' See under 'Adpressa Variegata'.

'Adpressa Erecta' ('Adpressa Stricta') A taller, female form with more ascending branches, forming a broad shrub with dark green leaves up to 1.5cm long. C 1886. FCC 1886.

'Adpressa Variegata' A male form of 'Adpressa'. The unfolding leaves are old-gold passing to yellow, a colour that is confined to the margin as the leaves age. This is the form usually grown wrongly under the name 'Adpressa Aurea'. C 1866. ♀ 2002. FCC 1889.

Taxus baccata continued:

'Amersfoort' A curious, small to medium-sized shrub of open habit. The stiffly ascending branches are clothed with numerous, small, radially arranged, oblong-ovate leaves, 5–7mm long. A botanical conundrum quite un-yew-like in appearance, and recalling *Olearia nummula-riifolia*. The mother plant, of French origin, is growing at the Psychiatric Hospital of Amersfoort, Holland.

'Argentea' See 'Variegata'.

'Argentea Minor' See 'Dwarf White'.

Aurea Group (*T. baccata* f. *aurea* Pilg.) Golden yew. A large shrub of compact habit, with golden-yellow leaves turning green by the second year. This name is used to cover all golden or gold-margined forms, the most popular of which is 'Elegantissima'. C 1855.

'Cavendishii' A low-growing, female form, less than 1m high, with widespreading branches drooping at the tips. In time forming a semi-prostrate mound several metres across. An excellent groundcover, even in heavy shade. C 1932.

'Cheshuntensis' An erect-growing, female clone, in habit intermediate between common yew and Irish yew. It was raised as a seedling of the latter in Messrs Paul's Nursery at Cheshunt about 1857.

'Corley's Coppertip' A compact, low growing shrub of spreading habit. Leaves with bronze tips when young, later with a golden-yellow margin, becoming dark green. A seedling of 'Dovastonii Aurea'. C 1983.

'Decora' A dwarf, slow-growing shrub forming a low, flat-topped hummock with arching branches and dark, polished green, upward-curving leaves, 3cm long and 3–4mm broad.

'Dovastoniana' Westfelton yew. A very distinct, wide-spreading, small, elegant tree with tiers of long, horizontal branches and long, weeping branchlets. Leaves blackish-green. It is normally female. The original tree, planted in 1777, is at Westfelton, Shropshire. Plants that have lost their leader when young form widespreading, shallowly vase-shaped bushes several metres across. ♀ 2002.

'Dovastonii Aurea' ('Dovastonii Aurea Pendula') Similar to 'Dovastoniana' in habit, but leaves margined bright yellow. A splendid male form raised in France. C 1891. ♀ 2002.

'Dwarf White' ('Argentea Minor') A delightful small, slow-growing, female shrub with drooping branchlets. The leaves have a narrow, white margin.

'Elegantissima' The most popular of the golden yews. A dense-growing, large bush with ascending branches. The yellow of the young leaves becomes straw-yellow and confined to the margin. Female. C 1852.

'Erecta' Fulham yew. An erect-branched, broadly columnar, open-topped, female bush, eventually of large size. Raised from seed of the Irish yew ('Fastigiata'). C 1838.

'Ericoides' A medium-sized to large, slow-growing bush of erect habit; leaves narrow and spreading. C 1855.

'Fastigiata' Irish yew. A female clone of erect habit, forming a dense, compact, broad column of closely-packed branches. As a young specimen it is narrowly columnar. Leaves black-green, radially arranged. A very popular yew and a familiar resident of churchyards.

Originally found as 2 plants on the moors in County Fermanagh in 1780. There is also a male form of slightly broader habit. ♀ 2002. FCC 1863.

'Fastigiata Aurea' Similar to 'Fastigiata' but young foliage deep yellow. C 1888.

'Fastigiata Aureomarginata' Golden Irish yew. A male form, similar to 'Fastigiata', but leaves with yellow margins. C 1880. ♀ 2002.

'Fastigiata Robusta' Similar to 'Fastigiata' but with a more robust and upright habit with lighter green leaves. C 1949.

'Fructoluteo' See 'Lutea'.

'Glauca' ('Nigra') Blue John. A male form of loose yet upright habit with leaves a characteristic dark bluish-green almost black-green above, paler below. One of the most easily recognised forms, particularly in early spring when the male strobili crowd the sombre foliage. C 1855.

'Lutea' ('Fructoluteo', 'Xanthocarpa') Yellow-berried yew. An unusual and attractive form, the fruits, with yellow arils, are often abundant and then quite spectacular. C about 1817. AM 1929.

'Nana' A dwarf, slow-growing bush of compact habit. C 1855.

'Nigra' See 'Glauca'.

'Nutans' A small, flat-topped bush. Leaves irregular in shape, often small and scale-like. A specimen in our collection attained 1m by 80cm after 30 years. C 1910.

'Pygmaea' An extremely slow-growing, dwarf shrub of dense conical or ovoid habit, bearing small, polished, black-green, radially arranged leaves. C 1910.

'Repandens' A low-growing, often semi-prostrate, female bush, with long, spreading branches, drooping at the tips. A splendid groundcover plant doing well in sun or dense shade. C 1887. ♀ 2002.

'Repens Aurea' A low, spreading, female bush with leaves margined with yellow when young, turning to cream later. Recalls a low form of 'Dovastonii Aurea'. Like all golden foliaged plants it loses its colour when in deep shade. ♀ 2002.

'Semperaurea' A slow-growing, male bush of medium size, with ascending branches and short, crowded branchlets well clothed with foliage. The unfolding leaves are old-gold, passing with age to rusty-yellow, a colour they retain throughout the year. C 1908. ♀ 2002. AM 1977.

'Standishii' ('Fastigiata Standishii') A slow-growing, female form of 'Fastigiata Aurea'. It is of dense, columnar habit with erect, tightly packed branches and radially arranged, golden-yellow leaves. The best of its colour and habit, but slow in growth. C 1908. ♀ 2002.

'Summergold' A low shrub with broadly spreading branches. Foliage yellow in summer becoming green with a yellow margin. Does not burn in full sun.

'Variegata' ('Argentea') A female form with obtusely ascending branches, in habit simulating the pfitzer juniper. The unfolding leaves are creamy-yellow, maturing to a slender marginal band of greyish-white. C 1770.

'Washingtonii' A vigorous, female form with ascending branches forming a broad, medium-sized bush. Young leaves rich yellow, ageing to yellowish-green, becoming bronzed during winter. C 1874.

'Xanthocarpa' See 'Lutea'.

canadensis Marshall. Canadian yew. A small, erect-growing, monoecious shrub, up to 1.8m high, with crowded branches and irregularly arranged, often 2-ranked leaves, 1–2cm long. Fruits with a red aril. In the wild the main shoots are loose, often becoming semi-prostrate and taking root, in time forming extensive carpets. Canada, NE USA. I 1800.

celebica See *T. chinensis* var. *mairei*.

chinensis (Pilg.) Rehder. This species, a native of China and Taiwan, is mainly grown as the following form. **var. *mairei*** Lemée & Lév. (*T. celebica* auct. not (Warb.) H.L. Li) Chinese yew. A splendid, large shrub or small tree of loose, spreading habit, easily confused with *Torreya grandis*. Leaves 2-ranked, 1–3cm long, a characteristic yellowish-green or pale green. Fruits with a red aril. China, Vietnam.

cuspidata Siebold & Zucc. Japanese yew. In its native habitats a small to medium-sized tree, but usually shrubby in cultivation. Leaves 1–2.5cm long, dark green above, yellowish-green beneath, ascending from the branchlets. Fruits with a red aril. In colder climes it proves hardier than *Taxus baccata*. NE Asia. I 1855 by Robert Fortune. **'Aurescens'** A low-growing, compact form with deep yellow young leaves changing to green the second year. C 1920. **'Densa'** A dwarf, compact, female shrub forming a mound of crowded, erect stems. C 1917. **'Minima'** An extremely slow-growing, dwarf bush of irregular habit. C 1932. **var. *nana*** hort. ex Rehder. A dense, small bush with ascending branches, nodding at the tips. Leaves radially arranged. Old specimens in cultivation have attained 1.2–1.5m high by 3m or more across. Japan. C 1861.

floridana Nutt. ex Chapm. Florida yew. Medium-sized to large shrub with crowded, ascending branches and dark green, sickle-shaped leaves, 2–2.5cm long. Fruits with a red aril. Rare in cultivation. Florida.

× *hunnewelliana* Rehder. (*T. canadensis* × *T. cuspidata*) A vigorous, large, very widespreading shrub with obtusely ascending branches and an open centre. It resembles one of the widespreading forms of *T.* × *media*, from which it differs in its longer, narrower, deep green leaves. A specimen in our collection planted in 1954 reached 3m high by 6m across in 15 years. Raised in the Hunnewell Pinetum, Wellesley, Massachusetts. C 1900.

× *media* Rehder. (*T. baccata* × *T. cuspidata*) A vigorous, medium-sized to large shrub of spreading habit, more or less intermediate between the parents. Leaves usually 2-ranked. Raised by T.D. Hatfield at the Hunnewell Pinetum, Wellesley, Massachusetts about 1900. There are several named forms in cultivation. Some of the widespreading cultivars develop a peculiar twisting character in the branches, shoots and older leaves. **'Brownii'** A broadly columnar, male form with semi-erect branches. Excellent as a hedge. C 1950. **'Hatfieldii'** A dense, compact, male form with sharply ascending branches. An excellent subject for hedging. C 1923. **'Hicksii'** A broadly columnar, female bush. It makes an excellent hedge. C 1900. ♀ 2002. **'Nidiformis'** A dense, broad, open-centred, male bush with obtusely ascending branches. C 1953. **'Sargentii'** An erect, female form of dense habit, excellent for hedging. **'Thayerae'** A broad, vigorous, male shrub with widely ascending branches and

open centre. In habit somewhat like *T.* × *hunnewelliana* but with shorter, broader leaves and probably not so tall. C 1930.

†***TETRACLINIS** Mast.—**Cupressaceae**—A monotypic genus related to *Callitris*, only suitable for the conservatory or outside in the mildest localities. Male and female strobili borne on the same plant.

articulata (Vahl) Mast. A rare, evergreen species attaining tree size in its native environs, but generally shrubby in the British Isles. Branches dense and ascending, terminating in flat, jointed, spray-like branchlets clothed with scale-like leaves, decurrent at the base and arranged in 4s. Cones solitary, rounded, 8–12mm across, composed of 4, thick, woody, glaucous scales. Both the wood and resin are of commercial importance. Native to the Atlas Mountains of Algeria and Morocco, also in Malta and SE Spain, in which countries it grows in dry places and withstands considerable periods of drought.

***THUJA** L. (*Thuya* L.)—**Cupressaceae**—Popularly known as arbor-vitae, these comprise a small genus of 5 species of hardy, evergreen trees and shrubs, widely distributed in N temperate regions. They differ from the superficially similar *Chamaecyparis* in the usually pleasantly aromatic foliage and cones with overlapping scales. Most form trees of attractive, conical habit, with small, scale-like, overlapping leaves arranged in 4 ranks and borne in often large, flattened, fan-like sprays. Male and female strobili are borne on the same tree in early spring, the males reddish. Cones small, oblong or subglobose and composed of 3–10 pairs of woody, overlapping scales, which are attached at their base, maturing the first year. Harmful if eaten. The Thujas will thrive in almost any soil, providing it is well-drained. *T. occidentalis* and *T. plicata* are invaluable for hedges and screens, while a good number of cultivars are dwarf or slow-growing and thus suitable for a rock garden. There are several excellent coloured forms though the range is less than in *Chamaecyparis*.

japonica See *T. standishii*.

koraiensis Nakai. Korean arbor-vitae. A striking species, usually densely shrubby in habit but occasionally a small tree, with decurved branches and dark brown, peeling bark. Foliage borne in large, flattened, frond-like sprays, green or sea-green above, conspicuously white beneath, pungently aromatic when crushed. NE China, Korea. I 1917 by Ernest Wilson.

lobbii See *T. plicata*.

occidentalis L. American arbor-vitae. An extremely hardy, medium-sized, columnar tree with reddish-brown, peeling bark. Branches spreading, upcurved at the tips. Leaves with conspicuous resin glands, dark green above, pale green beneath, borne in numerous, flattened sprays, usually bronze during winter. The foliage exudes a pleasant fruity odour when crushed. An important timber tree in the USA. E North America. I about 1534.

Cultivars of *Thuja occidentalis*
Innumerable forms of this species have arisen in cultivation.

'Aurea' ('Mastersii Aurea') A broadly conical, medium-sized to large bush with golden-yellow leaves. C 1857.

Thuja occidentalis **continued:**

'Aureospicata' An erect-growing form with young shoots becoming yellow, intensified in winter to a rich burnished old-gold.

'Beaufort' An open, slender-branched, large shrub or small tree with white-variegated leaves. C 1963.

'Bodmeri' Medium-sized bush of open, conical habit. Branches thick and stout; foliage dark green, in large, monstrous sprays. C 1877.

'Buchananii' Small tree of narrow, conical habit, with ascending branches and long branchlets with sparse foliage. C 1887.

'Caespitosa' A dwarf, slow-growing bush forming a rounded hummock, wider than high. Foliage irregular and congested. Excellent for a rock garden. C 1923.

'Cristata' A slow-growing, dwarf bush with short, flattened, crest-like branchlets, recalling those of the fernspray cypress (*Chamaecyparis obtusa* 'Filicoides'). C 1867.

'Danica' A dwarf bush of dense, compact, globular habit. Foliage held vertically in erect, flattened sprays. ♀ 2002.

'Ellwangeriana Pygmaea Aurea' See under 'Rheingold'.

'Ericoides' A small, dense, rounded or cone-shaped bush with soft, loose branchlets and dull green, juvenile foliage, donkey-brown in winter. Very liable to damage by snow. C 1867.

'Europa Gold' A Dutch selection of narrowly conical habit, making a large shrub or small tree with golden-yellow foliage. C 1974.

'Fastigiata' ('Columnaris', 'Pyramidalis', 'Stricta') A narrowly conical or columnar form of dense, compact growth. An excellent, small, formal tree. C 1865.

'Filiformis' A slow-growing, fairly compact bush with drooping 'whipcord' branchlets. In 30 years reaching 2m by 1.2m. C 1901.

'Globosa' A compact, globular bush, slowly reaching about 1.3m high by 2m wide. C 1875. 'Globularis' and 'Tom Thumb' are almost, if not wholly, identical.

'Golden Globe' A small shrub of dense, rounded habit with year-round golden-yellow foliage. C 1965.

'Hetz Midget' An extremely slow-growing, dwarf bush of globular habit. Perhaps the smallest form of all. C 1928.

'Holmstrup' ('Holmstrupii', 'Holmstrupensis') A slow-growing, medium-sized to large, narrowly conical bush of dense, compact habit, with rich green foliage throughout the year in vertically arranged sprays. C 1951. ♀ 2002.

'Holmstrup Yellow' A sport of 'Holmstrup' with golden-yellow foliage. Raised in Denmark before 1951.

'Hoveyi' A slow-growing bush of globular or ovoid habit, reaching 3m. The yellowish-green foliage is arranged in vertically held sprays. C 1868.

'Indomitable' A large shrub or small tree with spreading branches and dark green foliage, rich reddish-bronze in winter. C 1960.

'Little Gem' A dwarf, globular bush of dense, slightly flat-topped habit. Foliage deep green, in crowded, crimped sprays. The clone 'Recurva Nana' is very similar. C 1891.

'Lutea Nana' A small, conical bush of dense habit, with deep golden-yellow winter foliage, yellow-green in summer. C 1891. ♀ 2002.

'Malonyana' A striking, small to medium-sized tree of narrow, columnar habit, leaves uniform rich green, borne in short, dense, crowded sprays. This architectural tree forms a perfect avenue in the late Count Ambroze's garden, Mlynany Arboretum, Czechoslovakia.

'Mastersii' ('Plicata') A small, conical tree with large, flat sprays of foliage, arranged in a vertical plane and tipped old-gold in spring. C 1847.

'Ohlendorffii' ('Spaethii') One of the most distinct and curious of dwarf or semi-dwarf conifers, carrying dense clusters of soft juvenile foliage, and long, erect, slender, whipcord-like branches, clothed with adult foliage. C 1887.

'Pendula' Weeping American arbor-vitae. A small tree with openly ascending branches and pendent branchlets. C 1857.

'Pygmaea' ('Plicata Pygmaea', 'Mastersii Pygmaea') A dwarf bush of dense but irregular growth, with crowded sprays of sea-green foliage.

'Recurva Nana' A low-growing, flat-topped dome, the branchlets noticeably recurved at the tips. 'Little Gem' is very similar.

'Rheingold' A slow-growing bush of ovoid or conical habit eventually making a large shrub. Foliage mainly adult, a rich deep old-gold, shaded amber. A very popular plant, perhaps the richest piece of radiant old-gold in the garden in the dead of winter. It is an excellent companion to heathers and heaths and contrasts most effectively with darker conifers. The name 'Rheingold' is sometimes retained for small plants raised from cuttings of juvenile shoots. In the course of time these revert to the plant described here and appear inseparable from the cultivar 'Ellwangeriana Aurea'. C before 1902. ♀ 2002. AM 1902 (as *T. occidentalis* 'Ellwangeriana Pygmaea Aurea').

'Smaragd' ('Emerald') A narrowly conical, small tree with bright green foliage. ♀ 2002.

'Spiralis' A narrowly columnar, small tree of densely branched habit with short, pinnately arranged sprays of dark green foliage. A splendid formal tree. C 1923.

'Sunkist' A dense, small shrub of broadly conical, round-topped habit, with golden-yellow foliage in summer.

'Tiny Tim' A very slow-growing dwarf bush of rounded habit. Raised in Canada.

'Vervaeneana' A large bush or small tree of dense, conical habit, with crowded sprays of light green and yellow foliage, becoming bronzed in winter. C 1862.

'Wansdyke Silver' An attractive, small, slow-growing bush of conical habit, the foliage conspicuously variegated creamy-white. C 1966.

'Wareana' ('Robusta') A compact, slow-growing, small bush of conical habit with short, thickened sprays of green foliage. Raised in the nursery of Messrs Weare at Coventry in about 1827.

'Wareana Lutescens' ('Lutescens') Similar to 'Wareana', but more compact and with pale yellow foliage. C 1884.

'Wintergreen' ('Lombarts' Wintergreen') Small to medium-sized tree of columnar habit, with foliage green throughout the year.

Thuja occidentalis **continued:**

'Woodwardii' A dense, ovoid bush, taller than broad, eventually reaching 1m in height, with typical *T. occidentalis* foliage remaining green in winter.

'Yellow Ribbon' A distinct form making a large shrub of narrow conical habit with golden yellow foliage throughout the year.

orientalis See *Platycladus orientalis*.

plicata Donn ex D. Don (*T. lobbii* hort. ex Gordon, *T gigantea* Nutt.) Western red cedar. A large, fast-growing, ornamental tree with shredding bark and spreading branches. Leaves bright glossy green above, faintly glaucous beneath, carried in large, drooping sprays and with a pleasant, fruity odour when crushed. An important timber tree in North America. It makes a splendid hedge or screen, withstanding clipping well; it is also tolerant of shade and shallow chalk soils. W North America. I 1853 by William Lobb. The most commonly grown clone is sometimes listed under the name 'Atrovirens'. **'Atrovirens'** Foliage glossy dark green. C 1874. ♀ 2002. **'Aurea'** An outstanding form with foliage of a rich, old-gold. ♀ 2002. FCC 1897. **'Aureovariegata'** See 'Zebrina'. **'Collyer's Gold'** A slow-growing form similar to 'Stoneham Gold' but with brighter yellow foliage. **'Copper Kettle'** A slow-growing, shrubby form of upright habit. Foliage golden-bronze, particularly in winter. C 1978. **'Cuprea'** A dense, very slow-growing, conical bush, the growths tipped in various shades of deep cream to old-gold. A splendid plant for a rock garden. Raised at the Red Lodge Nursery, Southampton about 1930. **'Doone Valley'** A slow-growing form, eventually a small, broadly conical tree. Foliage tipped creamy-yellow when young, bronze in winter. C 1970. **'Fastigiata'** ('Stricta') A tall-growing, narrowly columnar form with densely arranged, slender, ascending branches. Excellent as a single specimen tree or for hedging when a minimum of clipping is necessary. C 1867. ♀ 2002. **'Gracilis'** A large bush of conical habit with finely divided sprays of green foliage. C 1923. **'Gracilis Aurea'** Medium-sized, slow-growing bush with slender branchlets and yellow-tipped foliage. A sport of 'Gracilis'. C 1949. **'Hillieri'** ('Nana') A slow-growing, dense, compact, rounded bush of medium size. The green foliage is arranged in curious moss-like clusters on branchlets, which are thick and stiff, with irregular crowded growths. Our original plant, which occurred in our Shroner Wood nursery c.1880, had attained 2.4 × 2.1m when the nursery was sold in about 1925. In the Sir Harold Hillier Gardens and Arboretum a specimen measured in 1990 when it was about 35 years old was 3m tall and 4m across. **'Irish Gold'** Similar to 'Zebrina' but the foliage more strongly flecked with deeper yellow. ♀ 2002. **'Rogersii'** ('Aurea Rogersii') A slow-growing, dwarf, compact bush of conical habit, with densely crowded gold and bronze-coloured foliage. It will attain about 1.2m by 1m in 30 years. Raised by the Rogers' Nursery, Southampton about 1928. **'Semperaurescens'** An extremely vigorous, large tree worthy of inclusion in any pinetum, or for use as a tall screen where colour variation is desired. Young shoots and leaves tinged golden-yellow, becoming bronze-yellow by winter. C 1923. **'Stoneham Gold'** A slow-growing, eventually large bush of dense, narrowly conical habit. Foliage bright gold, tipped coppery-bronze. A superb plant for a large rock garden. C 1948. ♀ 2002. **'Zebrina'** ('Aureovariegata') A conical tree, the sprays of green foliage banded with creamy-yellow. A strong-growing, large tree, certainly one of the best variegated conifers, the variegations being so crowded as to give a yellow effect to the whole tree. C 1868. FCC 1869.

standishii (Gordon) Carrière (*T. japonica* Maxim.) Japanese arbor-vitae. A small to medium-sized tree of conical habit, with loosely spreading or upcurved branches and drooping branchlets. Leaves yellowish-green above, slightly glaucous beneath, carried in large, gracefully drooping sprays. An attractive species, easily recognised by its characteristic yellowish-green appearance and loose habit. The crushed foliage smells of lemon verbena. C Japan. I by Robert Fortune to the Standish Nurseries, Bagshot in 1860.

*THUJOPSIS Siebold & Zucc. ex Endl.—**Cupressaceae**—A monotypic genus related to *Thuja*, differing in its broader, flatter branchlets and larger leaves. It thrives in all types of well-drained soil including shallow chalk soils. Male and female strobili are borne on the same tree.

dolabrata (Thunb. ex L. f.) Siebold & Zucc. (*Thuja dolabrata* Thunb. ex L. f.) Hiba. A distinct and attractive, small to medium-sized tree or large shrub of dense, broadly conical habit. Branchlets flattened, bearing sprays of large, 4-ranked, scale-like leaves, shining dark green above, marked with conspicuous silver-white bands beneath. Cones to 20mm long. Japan. I 1853. ♀ 2002. FCC 1864. **'Aurea'** Leaves suffused golden-yellow. A splendid yellow conifer which deserves to be much more frequently planted. C 1866. **var. hondae** Makino. The northern form of the species, attaining 30m in its native habitat. It tends to be more compact in habit, with smaller, blunter leaves. N Japan. **'Nana'** (var. *laetevirens* (Lindl.) Mast.) A dwarf, compact, spreading, flat-topped bush, smaller in all its parts I 1861. **'Variegata'** A strong-growing clone with scattered patches of creamy-white foliage. Not very stable. I 1859.

Thuya See *Thuja*.

*TORREYA Arn.—**Taxaceae**—A small genus of about 5 species of evergreen trees and shrubs, allied to *Taxus*; natives of E Asia and North America. Leaves linear, rigid and spine-tipped, marked with 2 glaucous bands beneath, spirally arranged on leading shoots, twisted to appear in 2 ranks on the lateral shoots. Male and female strobili borne on the same or different trees. Fruits plum-like, fleshy, containing a single seed. They are excellent trees for chalk soils and are good shade-bearers.

californica Torr. (*T. myristica* Hook.) California nutmeg. A small to medium-sized, broadly conical tree, well furnished to ground level, like a majestic yew. Leaves rigid, 3–7.5cm long, shining dark green above, spine-tipped. Fruits ovoid or obovoid, 3–4cm long, green, streaked with purple when ripe. California. Discovered and introduced by William Lobb in 1851. **'Spreadeagle'** A low-growing form with long, spreading branches. Originated in our Crook Hill nursery in 1965.

grandis Fortune ex Lindl. A rare, small tree or large shrub in cultivation. Leaves spine-tipped, to 2.5cm long, yellowish-green above. Fruits to 3cm long, brownish when ripe. A species similar to *T. nucifera*, differing in its paler green, slightly smaller leaves which lack the familiar aromatic scent of the Japanese species and may be confused with those of the Chinese yew (*Taxus chinensis*). China. I 1855 by Robert Fortune.

nucifera (L.) Siebold & Zucc. Kaya nut. Although a large tree in its native habitat, in the British Isles it is usually seen as a large shrub or occasionally a small slender, thinly-foliaged tree. Leaves smaller than those of *T. californica*, to 3cm long, sickle-shaped and spine-tipped and rather more consistently in a flat plane, pungent when crushed. Fruits to 2.5cm long, green, clouded purple when ripe. Japan. I 1764.

taxifolia Arn. Stinking cedar. A small tree, rare in cultivation. It most resembles *T. californica* but has smaller leaves, 2–4cm long. Fruits to 4cm long. SW Georgia, NW Florida, very rare and declining in the wild. I 1840.

*TSUGA (Endl.) Carrière—**Pinaceae**—A small genus of about 9 species of extremely elegant, evergreen trees of broadly conical habit, with spreading branches and gently drooping or arching branchlets; natives of E Asia and North America. The leaves are short and linear, arranged on the branchlets so as to appear 2-ranked, except in *T. mertensiana*. Male and female strobili are borne on the same tree. The cones are small and pendent, ripening during the first year, but remaining until the second year. They are good shade-bearers and thrive best in a moist, but well-drained, loamy soil. *T. canadensis* may be grown in moderately deep soils over chalk.

albertiana See *T. heterophylla*.

brunoniana See *T. dumosa*.

canadensis (L.) Carrière. Eastern hemlock. A large tree, often with several main stems from near the base. The best species for limy soil. Leaves to 15mm long, marked with 2 whitish bands beneath. Cones ovoid, slender-stalked, 1.5–2.5cm long. It differs from the closely related *T. heterophylla* in its usually forked trunk and its leaves which are more tapered to the apex and not so noticeably banded beneath. Another characteristic is the line of the leaves lying undersides uppermost, along the uppersides of the branchlets. E North America. I 1736.

Cultivars of *Tsuga canadensis*

This species has given rise to innumerable cultivars, a selection of which are listed here. Many of them are suitable for a rock garden or stone trough.

'Abbot's Pigmy' A very dwarf form similar to 'Minuta' but smaller and slower growing with shorter leaves. Found as a seedling in Vermont, USA by Frank Abbott in 1933.

'Albospica' A slower-growing, more compact form in which the growing tips of the shoots are creamy-white. Particularly effective during spring and summer. C 1884.

'Armistice' A slow-growing, dwarf form developing into a flat-topped mound. C 1965.

'Aurea' A slow-growing, dwarf form of compact, conical habit. Leaves rather broad and crowded, golden-yellow when unfolding, becoming yellowish-green later. C 1866.

'Bennett' ('Bennett's Minima') A slow-growing, dwarf shrub of spreading habit and dense, crowded growth. C 1920.

'Branklyn' ('Prostrata') A rather slow-growing, prostrate form with stems which press themselves to the ground and lie in all directions, eventually forming large mats. C 1933.

'Cinnamomea' Dwarf, slow-growing bush of dense, congested, globular habit. Young stems densely covered with a cinnamon pubescence. C 1929.

'Cole's Prostrate' ('Cole') A remarkable, prostrate plant with long branches flattened along the ground, in time forming extensive carpets. Similar in habit to 'Branklyn'.

'Compacta' Dwarf bush with short, crowded branchlets. C 1868.

'Curly' A curious, small shrub in which the young leaves are crowded and curled around the shoots.

'Dwarf Whitetip' A small, broadly conical bush, the young shoots creamy-white, changing to green in late summer. C 1939.

'Fantana' A small bush as broad as high, with wide-spreading branches. C 1913.

'Fremdii' A small, slow-growing, eventually broadly conical tree of compact, bushy habit, with crowded branchlets and leaves. C 1887.

'Globosa' Dwarf, globose bush with pendent tips to the branchlets. C 1891.

'Greenwood Lake' Slow-growing, medium-sized to large bush with crowded branchlets and no definite leader. C 1939.

'Horsford' ('Horsford's Dwarf') A dwarf, slow-growing, globular bush with congested branchlets and small, crowded leaves.

'Hussii' Medium-sized to large bush of slow growth. Habit dense and irregular with no definite leader. C 1900.

'Jeddeloh' A reliably dwarf bush of compact habit with the branches arching from a depressed centre. Selected in W Germany. C 1965. ♀ 2002.

'Jervis' ('Nearing') An extremely slow-growing, dwarf bush of compact but irregular habit, with crowded, congested growths. A gem for a rock garden.

'Lutea' A slow-growing tree, the golden foliage conspicuous in winter.

'Macrophylla' Large, bushy shrub or small, densely branched tree with relatively large leaves. Inclined to revert to typical growth. C 1891.

'Many Cones' A slow-growing bush of open habit with gracefully arching branches, free-coning.

'Microphylla' ('Parvifolia') A distinct and interesting large bush or small tree with tiny, heath-like leaves. C 1864.

'Minima' A slow-growing, widespreading, small bush with arching and drooping branches. C 1891.

'Minuta' An extremely slow-growing, miniature bun of tightly congested growth, with small, crowded leaves. I 1927.

'Nana' This is a small, slow-growing bush of graceful, spreading habit. Suitable for growing in a large rock garden. C 1855.

'Nana Gracilis' Dwarf, mound-forming bush of graceful habit with slender, arching stems.

'Nearing' See 'Jervis'.

Tsuga canadensis **continued:**

'Pendula' A most attractive form developing into a low mound of overlapping, drooping branches. A superb plant for a prominent position on a large rock garden or isolated on a lawn. In 40 years it reached about 2m by 3.7m in the Sir Harold Hillier Gardens and Arboretum. I before 1876. ♀ 2002.

'Prostrata' See 'Branklyn'.

'Pygmaea' A dwarf, irregular globe with short, congested growths.

'Rugg's Washington Dwarf' A dwarf, globular or mound-forming bush with dense, congested growth.

'Stranger' Small, slow-growing tree of compact habit; leaves rather broad and thick. C 1939.

'Taxifolia' Dwarf to medium-sized, irregular, compact bush, the leaves crowded at the ends of each year's growth, longer than in the type. C 1938.

'Verkade Recurved' A slow-growing, dwarf, conical shrub with unusual, recurved needles. Found in New Jersey in 1962.

'Warner's Globe' ('Warner Globosa') A globular bush with relatively short, broad leaves.

'Warnham' A vigorous prostrate form raised from a witch's broom found at Warnham Court, Surrey. C 1985.

‡*caroliniana* Engelm. Carolina hemlock. Although a handsome, large, conical tree in its native habitats, it is rarely more than a compact, small tree or large shrub in the British Isles. Young shoots grey, yellow-brown or red-brown and shining, with short pubescence scattered along the grooves. Leaves 1–1.2cm long, soft yellowish-green, marked with 2 white bands beneath. Cones ovoid or oblong, 2–3.5cm long. SE USA. I 1881. **'La Bar Weeping'** A very compact, dwarf form of spreading habit, making a dense mound of arching shoots.

chinensis (Franch.) E. Pritz. (*T. formosana* Hayata) Usually a small tree in cultivation. Leaves to 2.5cm long, comparatively broad, marked with 2 inconspicuous, greyish-green bands beneath. Cones to 2.5cm long. A distinct hardy species not subject to damage by spring frost and to a considerable degree lime-tolerant. It most resembles *T. heterophylla*. C and W China, Taiwan. I 1902 by Ernest Wilson.

‡*diversifolia* (Maxim.) Mast. Northern Japanese hemlock. In cultivation a small, horizontally branched tree. Leaves glistening deep green, 5–15mm long, notched at the apex, marked with 2 chalk-white bands beneath, oblong, very regular. Cones ovoid, 2cm long. An attractive species, easily distinguished by its combination of hairy shoots and leaves with entire margins. Japan. I 1861 by J.G. Veitch.

†*dumosa* (D. Don) Eichl. (*T. brunoniana* Carrière, *T. yunnanensis* (Franch.) E. Pritz) Himalayan hemlock. A distinct tender species, scarcely more than shrubby in most districts, but it has attained about 21m in Cornwall. Branches gracefully drooping. Leaves to 3cm long, marked with 2 vivid, silvery-white bands beneath. Cones to 2.5cm long. A beautiful species when growing well, but very subject to injury by spring frosts. It is moderately lime-tolerant. Native of SW China, N Myanmar and SE Tibet where it attains heights of over 30m in sheltered valleys. I 1838 by Captain Webb. AM 1931.

formosana See *T. chinensis*.

forrestii Downie. The tree received under this name from Borde Hill is quite different from *T. chinensis*, a species to which it is referred by some botanists. In its longer, narrower leaves, white beneath, it approaches *T. dumosa*, but is decidedly hardier. It has reached 5.5m in the Sir Harold Hillier Gardens and Arboretum. I 1923 by George Forrest.

‡*heterophylla* (Raf.) Sarg. (*T. albertiana* (A. Murray) Sénécl.) Western hemlock. A large, fast-growing tree with gracefully spreading branches. Leaves to 20mm long, marked with 2 bright white bands beneath. Cones to 2.5cm long. A beautiful conifer, particularly when grown as a single specimen, developing into an elegant tree with a spire-like crown. It is an important timber tree in North America and is extensively planted in the British Isles. It is not suitable for chalk soils but is tolerant of shade. It makes a better specimen tree than the allied *T. canadensis*, but has given rise to few cultivars. W North America. First discovered by David Douglas in 1826, it was introduced by John Jeffrey in 1851. ♀ 2002. **'Conica'** A medium-sized bush of dense, conical or ovoid habit, the branches ascending, drooping at the tips. Raised in the arboretum of van Gimborn, Doorne, Netherlands, about 1930. **'Greenmantle'** A graceful, tall, narrow tree with pendent branches, which originated at Windsor Great Park. **'Laursen's Column'** A striking tree of loosely columnar habit, recalling *Prumnopitys andina* in general appearance. Leaves irregularly, almost radially arranged on the ascending branches. A seedling found by Mr Asger Laursen in 1968. It has reached 6.5m in the Sir Harold Hillier Gardens and Arboretum (1990).

× *jeffreyi* See *T. mertensiana* var. *jeffreyi*.

mertensiana (Bong.) Carrière (*T. pattoniana* (Balf.) Sénécl.) A beautiful species, a large tree of spire-like habit. Young shoots brownish-grey and densely pubescent. Leaves radially arranged, 1–2.5cm long, pointing forwards, greyish-green or blue-grey on both surfaces. Cones sessile, oblong-cylindrical, 5–8cm long. A distinct species easily recognised by its radially arranged leaves and comparatively large cones. W North America. I 1851 by Jeffrey. **'Glauca'** A beautiful, slow-growing form with glaucous leaves. C 1850. **var. jeffreyi** (A. Henry) C.K. Schneid. (*T.* × *jeffreyi* (A. Henry) A. Henry) A comparatively slow-growing, eventually medium-sized to large tree, first raised at Edinburgh in 1851. It has been considered to be a hybrid between *T. heterophylla* and *T. mertensiana*. NW North America.

pattoniana See *T. mertensiana*.

sieboldii Carrière. Japanese hemlock. In the British Isles usually a small to medium-sized, dense tree or large bush, but reaching greater proportions in the wild. Leaves to 2.5cm long, glossy green above, marked with white bands beneath. Cones ovoid, 2.5–3cm long. S Japan. I about 1850 by Philipp von Siebold.

yunnanensis See *T. dumosa*.

Wellingtonia See *Sequoiadendron giganteum*.

†*****WIDDRINGTONIA** Endl.—**Cupressaceae**—A genus of 4 species of evergreen, cypress-like trees from C and S Africa. Male and female strobili are normally borne on the same tree. Leaves are spirally arranged and linear on young plants, scale-like on adult trees. The erect, woody cones

remain for some time after shedding their seed. All are tender and require conservatory treatment except in the mildest areas. They are excellent conifers for hot, dry climes.

cedarbergensis J.A. Marsh. Clanwilliam cedar. A small tree with elegant sprays of linear, glaucous green juvenile leaves, 1–2cm long, soft to the touch. Adult leaves scale-like, closely pressed to the shoot. S Africa (Cedarberg Mts, SW Cape Province).

cupressoides See *W. nodiflora*.

nodiflora (L.) Powrie (*W. cupressoides* (L.) Endl.) Sapree wood. A tree of conical habit when young, reaching 42m with a spreading crown in Malawi, smaller and sometimes shrubby in S Africa. Juvenile leaves linear, up to 2.5cm long, sea-green and soft to the touch. Adult leaves scale-like and closely pressed. S and E Africa.

schwarzii (Marloth) Mast. Willowmore cedar. An attractive, small tree in cultivation, but reaching 27m in its native habitat. Leaves scale-like, glaucous, in closely pressed pairs. Young plants growing under glass differ strikingly from the other species described here, in their conspicuously glaucous and scale-like leaves. S Africa (Willowmore district, Cape Province).

whytei Rendle. Mlanji cedar. A small tree of conical habit when young, reaching 42m with a spreading crown in its native habitat. Juvenile leaves linear, to 2.5cm long, sea-green and soft to the touch. Adult leaves scale-like and closely adpressed. Malawi.

†***WOLLEMIA** W.G. Jones et al.—**Araucariaceae**—A genus of a single species, related to *Araucaria* and *Agathis*. The discovery of this new genus, by David Noble in 1994, created worldwide interest, particularly as it was found only 150km from Sydney, Australia. Less than 40 trees exist in two stands in a narrow canyon in the Wollemi Wilderness.

nobilis W.G. Jones et al. Wollemi pine. A large monoecious tree to 40m tall, with a single trunk when young, and spongy, nodular bark; older trees often have multiple trunks from coppice shoots. Leaves opposite or sub-opposite, 4-ranked, long-persistent, retained until whole branches are shed, narrowly oblong, to 4cm long on adult shoots. Cones borne at the ends of the shoots, the females to 12.5cm long, breaking up when ripe. New South Wales.

Yew See *Taxus*.

BAMBOOS
(Gramineae)

Members of the Grass family, some of the most beautiful and elegant of all evergreens, are included under this heading.

The majority of the species described below are perfectly hardy, but they are not suitable for windswept sites and it is a mistake to imagine that, because they are moisture-lovers, they will grow in permanently wet land. Many are excellent for growing in shade and all succeed in good soils over chalk. Though the transplanting period need not be restricted, early autumn and late spring are usually the most satisfactory times. It is important to avoid using near bamboos any selective weed killer designed to destroy couch grass or other grasses.

When skilfully placed, bamboos are among the most ornamental features of any planting scheme, but it is as waterside plants that they are shown to their best advantage.

The leaves of most species are long and narrow, rich green above, pale green or greyish-green beneath. The flowering of bamboos is still not completely understood. Most species will live a great many years before flowering, while some flower over a period of years. Contrary to what is often said, death does not always follow flowering. Several popular species have flowered in recent years and many new selections are being made from their seedlings.

In their native habitats many of the following species reach great heights, but the ultimate sizes quoted below are approximate under average conditions of soil and aspect in the British Isles.

ARUNDINARIA Michx. While this genus at one time contained many of the cultivated bamboos, these have now been transferred to other genera, with only the following species remaining. *Arundinaria* differs from *Phyllostachys* and *Sasa* in the usually more numerous branches to each cluster and also from *Phyllostachys* in the rounded (terete) internodes, those of the latter being flattened or broadly grooved on alternate sides.

amabilis See *Pseudosasa amabilis*.

anceps See *Yushania anceps*.

angustifolia See *Pleioblastus chino* f. *angustifolius*.

auricoma See *Pleioblastus auricomus*.

chino See *Pleioblastus chino.*

    f. *angusifolia* See *Pleioblastus chino* f. *angustifolius*.

chrysantha See *Pleioblastus chrysanthus*.

disticha See *Pleioblastus pygmaeus* var. *distichus*.

falconeri See *Himalayacalamus falconeri*.

fastuosa See *Semiarundinaria fastuosa*.

fortunei See *Pleioblastus variegatus*.

'Gauntletti' See *Pleioblastus humilis* var. *pumilus*.

gigantea (Walt.) Chapm. (*A. macrosperma* Michx.) Cane reed. A strong-growing bamboo, forming dense thickets under suitable conditions, but rarely invasive. Canes 4.5–6m or above in sheltered gardens, but usually 2.5–3m and dull greenish-yellow. Leaves variable in size, 10–30cm long by 2–4cm wide, glabrous or nearly so above, sheaths deciduous. Native of the SE United States where it frequently forms dense thickets known as 'cane brakes' on the swampy margins of rivers. It requires a sheltered position and is not suitable for cold areas. **subsp. *tecta*** (Walt.) McClure (*A. tecta* (Walt.) Muhl.) Canes up to 2m high bearing coarsely textured leaves up to 25cm long by 2cm wide, hairy on both sides, sheaths persistent.

graminea See *Pleioblastus gramineus*.

hindsii hort. See *Pleioblastus hindsii* hort.

hookeriana See *Himalayacalmus hookerianus*.

humilis See *Pleioblastus humilis*.

intermedia See *Sinarundinaria intermedia*.

japonica See *Pseudosasa japonica*.

jaunsarensis See *Yushania anceps*.

macrosperma See *A. gigantea*.

maling See *Yushania maling*.

marmorea See *Chimonobambusa marmorea*.

murieliae See *Fargesia murieliae*.

nitida See *Fargesia nitida*.

nobilis See *Himalayacalamus falconeri*.

pumila See *Pleioblastus humilis* var. *pumilus*.

pygmaea See *Pleioblastus pygmaeus*.

    var. *disticha* See *Pleioblastus pygmaeus* var. *distichus*.

quadrangularis See *Chimonobambusa quadrangularis*.

racemosa hort. See *Yushania maling*.

ragamowskii See *Indocalamus tessellatus*.

simonii See *Pleioblastus simonii*.

    var. *chino* See *Pleioblastus chino*.

spathiflora See *Thamnocalamus spathiflorus*.

tecta See *A. gigantea* subsp. *tecta*.

tessellata See *Thamnocalamus tessellatus*.

vagans See *Sasaella ramosa*.

variegata See *Pleioblastus variegatus*.

veitchii See *Sasa veitchii*.

viridistriata See *Pleioblastus auricomus*.

Bambusa albostriata See *Pleioblastus simonii* 'Variegatus'.

Bambusa angustifolia See *Pleioblastus chino* f. *angustifolius*.

Bambusa metake See *Pseudosasa japonica*.

Bambusa vilmorinii See *Pleioblastus chino* f. *angustifolius*.

CHIMONOBAMBUSA Makino. A genus of about 12 species, native to E and SE Asia.

marmorea (Mitf.) Makino (*Arundinaria marmorea* (Mitf.) Makino) A normally low-growing bamboo forming clumps or patches of 1–2m canes, green at first maturing to deep purple when grown in a sunny position. New shoots are an attractive, pale green, mottled brown and silvery-white, tipped and striped pink. Leaves 5–15cm long by 1–1.5cm wide. A few canes have flowered on old clumps in recent years. Japan. I 1889. **'Variegata'** Leaves striped with white.

quadrangularis (Fenzi) Makino (*Arundinaria quadrangularis* (Fenzi) Makino, *Tetragonocalamus quadrangularis* (Fenzi) Makino) Square-stemmed bamboo. A rare species with a creeping rootstock. The bluntly 4-angled canes reach 2.5–3m high and are dark green, occasionally splashed purple. The young spring shoots are edible. Leaves 7.5–23cm long by 2.5–3cm wide. An attractive and unusual bamboo, only succeeding in a sheltered position. Not suitable for cold areas. China. Long cultivated and naturalised in Japan.

tumidinoda See *Chimonobambusa tumidissinoda*.

tumidissinoda D. Ohrnb. (*C. tumidinoda* (Hsueh & Yi) T.H. Wen, *Qiongzhuea tumidinoda* Hsueh & Yi) An elegant, thicket-forming bamboo, reaching 6m in the wild and spreading very vigorously. It has slender, bright green leaves, lighter in sun, grey-green beneath, to 14cm long, and is remarkable for its canes, which are green when young, maturing to yellow-brown with curiously thickened nodes. In China they are used for making walking sticks. Best in semi-shade. SW China. I 1980 by Peter Addington.

CHUSQUEA Kunth. A genus of about 95 species of graceful, mainly South American bamboos, distinct in their numerous, densely clustered branches and solid stems. This latter characteristic makes chusqueas useful for cutting, as their leaves do not flag as easily as do those of the hollow-stemmed bamboos.

breviglumis hort. See *C. culeou* 'Tenuis'.

culeou E. Desv. A hardy species forming broad, dense clumps. Deep olive-green canes, 2.5–3.5m high or occasionally up to 9m, produce dense clusters of slender, short, leafy branches along their entire length, giving them a characteristic, bottlebrush effect. The first-year canes possess conspicuous white sheaths at each node. Edible young shoots in spring. Leaves 2.5–7.5cm long by 6–10mm wide, slender-pointed. Chile. I 1890 and again by Harold Comber in 1926. ♀ 2002. AM 1974. 'Tenuis' (*C. breviglumis* hort. not Phil.) A very distinct and ornamental form with numerous, spreading, olive-green canes to 1.2m. This rare bamboo was introduced from Chile by Harold Comber.

FARGESIA Franch. An increasingly large genus of Chinese bamboos forming dense clumps.

dracocephala T.P. Yi. A vigorous species making dense clumps of arching shoots to 5m high; the bright green culms have persistent, creamy sheaths. Leaves to 12cm long and 2cm across, rough with fine teeth at the margin, ending in a fine, tapered point. China.

murieliae (Gamble) T.P. Yi (*Arundinaria murieliae* Gamble, *Sinarundinaria murieliae* (Gamble) Nakai, *Thamnocalamus spathaceus* hort. not. (Franch.) Söderstr.) An elegant species forming graceful, arching clumps, 2.5–3.5m high or more. Canes bright green at first, maturing to dull yellow-green. Leaves 6–10cm long by 1–2cm wide, bright pea-green. Excellent as an isolated specimen or in a large tub. This beautiful bamboo, which is undoubtedly one of the best species in cultivation, was introduced from China in 1913 by Ernest Wilson and was named after his daughter Muriel. ♀ 2002. 'Jumbo' A vigorous and very hardy form of dense, upright growth with bright green foliage. A seedling raised in Denmark in 1976. 'Simba' A form of compact habit with densely packed culms to 2m tall. ♀ 2002.

nitida (Mitford) Keng f. ex T.P. Yi (*Arundinaria nitida* Mitford, *Sinarundinaria nitida* (Mitford) C.S. Chao & Renvoize) This beautiful, clump-forming species is often confused with *F. murieliae* but differs most noticeably in its purple-flushed canes and narrower leaves. It is one of the most elegant and ornamental of all bamboos, with canes 3–3.8m high, or more, arching at the summit under the weight of foliage. Leaves 5–8cm long by 6–12mm wide, thin and delicate. It thrives best in a little shade and makes an excellent specimen plant. It may also be grown most effectively in a large tub. China. C 1889. FCC 1898. 'Eisenach' A form with upright branches and more conspicuously purple culms. 'Nymphenburg' A compact form with small, slender leaves and arching shoots. ♀ 2002.

robusta T.P. Yi. A very decorative and hardy bamboo forming dense clumps of erect culms, to 4m high, deep blue-green when young, paler when mature. The contrasting and persistent creamy-white sheaths are a conspicuous feature of this species, those at the base densely overlapping and covered with bristly brown hairs. Leaves bright glossy green above, blue-green beneath, to 15cm long and 2cm across. China.

Hibanobambusa tranquillans See × *Phyllosasa tranquillans*.

†**HIMALAYACALAMUS** Keng f. Beautiful but tender, Himalayan bamboos for the mildest gardens.

falconeri (Munro) Keng. f. (*Arundinaria falconeri* (Munro) Benth. & Hook. f., *A. nobilis* Mitford, *Thamnocalamus falconeri* Munro) A strong-growing, but tender species, forming dense clumps, normally 1.8–3m but up to 6m or more in sheltered gardens. Canes olive-green, maturing to dull yellow in a sunny position, thin and pliable. Leaves 5–10cm long by 12mm wide, delicate and paper-thin. Flowered 1875–77, 1903–07 and again profusely during 1966 and 1967 producing large, gracefully branched panicles of chocolate-red spikelets. All clumps subsequently died, but produced seed from which fresh stocks were grown. This beautiful species grew for many years in a sheltered position in the Sir Harold Hillier Gardens and Arboretum. Originally distributed wrongly as *Arundinaria pantlingii*. NE Himalaya. I 1847 by Col Madden. 'Damarapa' A striking form, the culms pink when young becoming green striped with pink and yellow.

hookerianus (Munro) Stapleton (*Arundinaria hookeriana* Munro, *Sinarundunaria hookeriana* (Munro) C.S. Chao & Renvoize) An attractive, but tender bamboo for a conservatory or may be grown outside in the mildest localities. Canes up to 6m or more, blue-green and with a glaucous bloom when young, with long, taper-pointed sheaths, yellow-green to purple-red when mature. Leaves to 18cm long. Sikkim, Nepal to Bhutan. I to Kew in 1896, the plants flowered, seeded then died shortly afterwards. Descendants of this introduction flowered again and produced seed in the early 1990s.

INDOCALAMUS Nakai. A genus of about 15 species, natives of China; only the following is generally grown.

tessellatus (Munro) Keng f. (*Arundinaria ragamowskii* (Nicholson) Pfitzer, *Sasa tessellata* (Munro) Nakai) Not to be confused with the rare South African *Thamnocalamus tessellatus* q.v. This remarkable species forms dense thickets of slender, bright green canes up to 2m tall. The shining green leaves, up to 60cm long by 5–10cm wide, are the largest of all hardy bamboos and such is their collective weight that the canes bend down, giving the clump an almost dwarf habit. China. I 1845. ♀ 2002.

× **PHYLLOSASA** Demoly (× *Hibanobambusa* Maruy. & H. Okamura) Originally described as a species of *Semiarundinaria*, this bamboo, which was found growing in the wild in Japan, is now believed to be a naturally occurring hybrid between a *Phyllostachys* and a *Sasa*.

tranquillans (Koidz.) Demoly (× *Hibanobambusa tranquillans* (Koidz.) Maruy. & H. Okamura) A vigorous, spreading bamboo of dense habit, with upright culms, 3m high, grooved on one side as in *Phyllostachys*. The bold, dark green leaves are up to 23cm long and 5cm across. **'Shiroshima'** Bold, dark green leaves conspicuously streaked with creamy-white. One of the most attractive variegated bamboos. ♀ 2002.

PHYLLOSTACHYS Siebold & Zucc. Tall, graceful bamboos with usually zig-zag stems, the internodes of which are flattened or shallowly grooved on alternate sides. Branches normally in pairs at each node. Some 75 species, natives of China.

aurea (Carrière) Rivière & C. Rivière. A very graceful species, forming large clumps 2.5–3.5m high. Canes bright green at first, maturing to pale creamy-yellow, dull yellow in full sun. Leaves 7.5–18cm long by 1–2cm wide. A hardy bamboo characterised by the peculiar crowding of the nodes at the base of each cane and the curious swelling beneath each node. Edible young shoots in spring. The canes are used in the Far East for walking sticks, umbrella handles, etc, and in America for fishing rods. It has flowered on several occasions. China. Long cultivated in Japan. I before 1870. ♀ 2002. **'Albovariegata'** Leaves striped with white. **'Flavescens Inversa'** Culms green, striped with yellow in the groove. **'Holochrysa'** A form with golden-yellow culms. **'Koi'** Culms golden-yellow striped with bright green in the groove.

aureosulcata McClure. Yellow-groove bamboo. A vigorous and very hardy species to 5m or more, with arching green culms, broadly banded with yellow in the groove, often zig-zag at the base. Shoots rough with hairs and bloomy beneath the nodes, particularly when young. Sheaths streaked with pink and cream. E China. I (to the USA) 1907. **f. alata** T.H. Wen. A form with green culms. **'Aureocaulis'** Culms reddish when young, maturing to pale golden-yellow. ♀ 2002. **'Spectabilis'** A striking form, the new shoots rich pink becoming yellow with a narrow, green band on the groove. ♀ 2002.

bambusoides Siebold & Zucc. (*P. quilioi* (Carrière) Rivière) A very hardy and highly ornamental bamboo forming large clumps. Canes 3–4.5m high, deep shining green at first becoming deep yellow-green and finally brown at maturity. Leaves 5–19cm long by 1.5–3cm wide. In warmer countries canes are known to grow as much as 23m high and almost 15cm in diameter. In China, Japan and the United States it is cultivated on a commercial scale and its canes put to a wide range of uses. Edible young shoots in spring. China. I 1866. **'Allgold'** ('Sulphurea') A very attractive bamboo, differing in its generally smaller leaves and its rich yellow canes, which are sometimes striped with green along the internodal grooves. I 1865. **'Castillonis'** A form with golden-yellow stems striped with a distinctive green in the grooves. **'Castillonis Inversa'** Culms green with a yellow groove. **'Sulphurea'** See 'Allgold'.

bissetii McClure. A very vigorous and hardy species making dense thickets of upright, dark green culms, to 6m or more high, bearing lush, glossy dark green leaves. Excellent for shelter, hedging or as a clump. It can spread vigorously. China.

boryana See *P. nigra* 'Boryana'.

decora McClure. A vigorous and elegant, very hardy species forming a dense clump of upright, bright green canes, rough to the touch and up to 6m high. Leaves dark green, to 12cm long and 2cm across, ending in a tapered point. Useful for making a dense screen. China.

edulis (Carrière) J. Houz. (*P. heterocycla* var. *pubescens* (J. Houz.) Ohwi, *P. mitis* hort. not Rivière & C. Rivière, *P. pubescens* J. Houz.) A strong-growing bamboo with bright green, later dull yellow canes up to 4.5m high. The young shoots are much prized for eating in warmer climes. Leaves 7.5–10cm long by 2cm wide. Best grown in a sheltered position. China. **'Heterocycla'** (*P. heterocycla* (Carrière) Mitford, *P. pubescens* 'Heterocycla', *P. pubescens* 'Kikkochiku') Tortoise-shell bamboo. An unusual form of vigorous growth, differing in the curious appearance of the cane bases caused by the alternate swelling of the internodes. China. I 1893.

flexuosa Rivière & C. Rivière. A graceful bamboo, 2.5–3m high, throwing up slender, somewhat wavy canes, bright green at first, becoming darker at maturity. Forming large thickets in time. Young shoots in spring edible. Leaves 5–13cm long by 1–2cm wide. Extensively cultivated in France for use as fishing rods. Excellent as a screening plant. Strong shoots are noticeably zig-zag at base. N China. I 1864.

henonis See *P. nigra* var. *henonis*.

heterocycla See *P. edulis* 'Heterocycla'. **var. pubescens** See *P. edulis*.

mitis hort. See *P. edulis*.

nidularia Munro. A rare, Chinese species with tall canes up to 6m in sheltered positions.

nigra (Lodd.) Munro. Black bamboo. A beautiful, clump-forming bamboo of gracefully arching habit. Canes normally 2.5–3.5m, green the first year becoming mottled dark brown or black and finally an even jet black. In colder gardens the canes often remain a mottled brownish-green. Edible young shoots in spring. Leaves 5–13cm long by 6–12mm wide. This distinct and attractive species enjoys a sunny position. China. I 1827. ♀ 2002. AM 1975. **'Boryana'** ('Bory', *P. boryana* Mitford) An elegant bamboo producing luxuriant masses of arching, leafy stems. Canes 2.5–4m high, green at first, changing to yellow and splashed purple. Edible young shoots in spring. Leaves 5–9cm long by 6–12mm wide. A magnificent specimen plant in isolation. Originated in Japan. **var.** *henonis* (Mitford) Rendle ('Henon', *P. henonis* Mitford) A handsome bamboo throwing up tall, graceful canes, 2.5–4m high, swathed in dark green clouds of shining leaves. Canes bright green at first, maturing to brownish-yellow. Edible young shoots in spring. Leaves 7.5–11cm long by 1–2cm wide. One of the best for planting as a specimen in a lawn or similarly prominent position. The common wild form of the species. C about 1890. ♥ 2002. '**Punctata**' Canes 2.5–3.5m high, green, mottled black, never wholly black as in *P. nigra*. Edible young shoots in spring. Leaves 5–10cm long by 6–12mm wide. Originated in China.

quilioi See *P. bambusoides*.

ruscifolia See *Shibataea kumasaca*.

violascens Rivière & C. Rivière. A very vigorous, large species spreading rapidly. Culms 8m high, stout, sea-green, bloomy and flushed red-purple when young, with purple-flushed sheaths, becoming greenish-brown when mature. Leaves glossy green, to 15cm long and 5cm across. China.

viridiglaucescens (Carrière) Rivière & C. Rivière. A graceful, extremely hardy and very vigorous, clump-forming species. Canes 4–6m high, green at first changing to dull yellowish-green. Leaves 7.5–15cm long, 1–2cm wide, brilliant green above, glaucous beneath. Forms a thicket in ideal conditions, but otherwise an attractive specimen plant in isolation. E China. I 1846.

vivax McClure. An erect species of compact, clump-forming habit. The tall, green, thin-walled canes will attain 8m in mild areas and bear heavy drooping foliage. It resembles *P. bambusoides*, but is faster-growing. E China. I 1908 (to North America). '**Aureocaulis**' A beautiful selection, the culms golden-yellow, striped with green. ♥ 2002.

PLEIOBLASTUS Nakai. Slender-stemmed, clump-forming or spreading bamboos.

auricomus (Mitford) D.C. McClint. (*Arundinaria auricoma* Mitford, *A. viridistriata* (Makino) Nakai, *Pleioblastus viridistriatus* (Makino) Makino) A very hardy species with erect, purplish-green canes, 1–2m high, forming small patches. Leaves variable in size, 7.5–20cm long, 1–4cm wide, dark green, striped rich yellow, often more yellow than green. The best of the variegated bamboos, quite small when grown in shade and an excellent tub plant. Old canes may be cut to ground level in autumn to encourage the production of new canes with brightly coloured young foliage. It has flowered at the tips of the canes in several localities over a considerable period (since 1898) without any ill effect. Japan. I about 1870. ♥ 2002. AM 1972. '**Chrysophyllus**' A form with yellow foliage occasionally originating as a sport from the typical form. It can burn in full sun.

chino (Franch. & Sav.) Nakai (*Arundinaria chino* (Franch. & Sav.) Makino, *Arundinaria simonii* var. *chino* (Franch. & Sav.) Makino) An erect-growing bamboo with a creeping rootstock and dark green, purple-flushed canes, 3–4m high. Leaves 10–25cm long by 2–2.5cm wide, borne in stiff, plume-like clusters. Has flowered

several times in cultivation without any ill effect. Japan. I 1876. **f.** *angustifolius* (Mitford) Muroi & Okamura (*Arundinaria chino* f. *angustifolia* (Mitford) C.S. Chao & Renvoize, *Arundinaria angustifolia* (Mitford) J. Houz., *Bambusa angustifolia* Mitford, *Bambusa vilmorinii* hort.) A narrow-leaved form reaching 2m tall. I about 1895. '**Elegantissimus**' Leaves attractively striped with white.

chrysanthus (Mitford) D.C. McClint. (*Arundinaria chrysantha* Mitford, *Sasa chrysantha* (Mitford) Camus) A fast-growing species forming dense thickets. Canes 1–2m high, deep olive-green. Leaves 7.5–18cm long by 1.5–2.5cm wide, bright green, striped yellow, not very consistent. A vigorous bamboo, useful as groundcover. Japan. I 1892.

gramineus (Bean) Nakai (*Arundinaria graminea* (Bean) Makino) A fast-growing species, forming dense clumps or patches. Canes up to 3m tall, pale green, maturing to dull yellowish-green. Leaves very narrow in proportion to their length, 10–25cm long by 8–12mm wide. An excellent screening plant and one of the few hardy bamboos that prefers shade. It has flowered in several localities in recent years and good seed is usually produced. Ryukyu Islands (Japan). I 1877.

hindsii hort. not (Munro) Nakai (*Arundinaria hindsii* hort. not Munro) A strong-growing species forming dense thickets of erect, olive-green canes, 2.5–3.5m high. Leaves variable in size, 15–23cm long by 1.5–2.5cm wide, rich sea-green, thickly clustered towards the summits of the canes. A useful bamboo, equally happy in sun or dense shade and making an excellent hedge or screen. Origin probably Japan. I 1875.

humilis (Mitford) Nakai (*Arundinaria humilis* Mitford) A rampant species forming low patches or thickets. Canes slender, dark green, 0.6–1.8m high, but usually under 1.2m. Leaves 5–20cm long by 1–2cm wide, slightly downy beneath. An excellent groundcover beneath trees or for covering unsightly banks or waste places. A few canes have flowered at their tips in several localities in recent years without any apparent ill effect. Japan. I about 1892. **var.** *pumilus* (Mitford) D.C. McClint. (*Arundinaria pumila* Mitford, *Pleioblastus pumilus* (Mitford) Nakai) A very hardy, dwarf bamboo forming dense carpets of slender, dull purple canes 30–80cm high, with conspicuously hairy nodes. Leaves 5–18cm long by 1–2cm wide. A far-creeping species, useful as groundcover. Japan. I late 19th century.

linearis (Hack.) Nakai. An elegant species, similar to *P. gramineus*, with arching, pale green culms bearing rich green foliage. Leaves to 20cm long and 7mm across. Best in a shady, woodland situation. Ryukyu Islands.

pygmaeus (Miq.) Nakai (*Arundinaria pygmaea* (Miq.) Mitford) A dwarf species with far-reaching rhizomes forming carpets of slender stems up to 25cm long, taller in shade. Leaves up to 13cm long by 2cm wide. An excellent groundcover plant. Japan. **var.** *distichus* (Mitford) Nakai (*Arundinaria disticha* (Mitford) Pfitzer) A more vigorous form, to 1m, with larger, distinctly 2-ranked leaves. I about 1870 from Japan where it is known only in cultivation.

shibuyanus See *P. variegatus* f. *humilis*. '**Tsuboi**' See *P. variegatus* 'Tsuboi'.

simonii (Carrière) Nakai (*Arundinaria simonii* (Carrière) Rivière & C. Rivière) A vigorous bamboo of erect habit, forming dense clumps or patches of tall, olive-green canes, up to 4.5m high or more. The first-year canes are liberally dusted with a white bloom, and the young spring shoots are edible. Leaves 7.5–30cm long by 1–3cm wide. The leaf undersurface is green along one side, greyish-green along the other. A hardy species with luxuriant foliage, useful as a hedge or screen. It has flowered in several localities in recent years and produced good seed. China. I 1862. **var. *chino*** See *Pleioblastus chino*. **'Variegata'** (*Bambusa albostriata* hort.) Some of the smaller leaves striped creamy-white, not consistent.

variegatus (Miq.) Makino (*Arundinaria fortunei* (Van Houtte) Nakai, *Arundinaria variegata* (Miq.) Makino) A low, tufted species forming dense thickets of erect, zigzag, pale green canes, 0.8–1.2m high. Leaves 5–20cm long by 1–2.5cm wide, dark blue-green, with white stripes, fading to pale green. The best of the white-variegated bamboos and suitable for a rock garden or tub. Japan. C 1863. ♀ 2002. **f. *humilis*** (Makino ex Tsuboi) Makino & Nemoto (*Pleioblastus shibuyanus* Makino ex Nakai) A form with green leaves. **'Tsuboi'** (*P. shibuyanus* 'Tsuboi') This differs from the typical form in the bright green, not blue-green, leaves striped with cream, often all cream towards the end of the leaf.

viridistriatus See *Pleioblastus auricomus*.

PSEUDOSASA Nakai. A genus of 4 species of bamboos from E Asia.

amabilis (McClure) Keng f. (*Arundinaria amabilis* McClure) A little-known species suitable for sheltered gardens in the mildest parts of the British Isles, where it will reach a height of 2.5–4.5m. Leaves vary between 10cm and 35cm long by 1–4cm wide. China.

japonica (Steud.) Nakai (*Arundinaria japonica* Steud.) (*Bambusa metake* Miq.) This extremely adaptable and very hardy species is the bamboo most commonly cultivated in the British Isles. It forms dense thickets of olive-green canes, about 3–4.5m high occasionally up to 6m, arching at the summit and bearing lush masses of dark glossy green leaves, 18–30cm long by 2–5cm wide. The greyish undersurface of the leaves has a characteristic, greenish marginal strip. Branches borne singly from each of the upper nodes. Isolated plants and odd canes have flowered sporadically in cultivation. Japan, S Korea. I 1850. ♀ 2002. **'Akebono'** Leaves yellow, shading to green at the base. It occasionally arises as a sport of 'Akebonosuji'. **'Akebonosuji'** Leaves conspicuously streaked with creamy-yellow, sometimes producing sports with all-yellow leaves. **'Tsutsumiana'** A form of compact habit, the culms with conspicuous bulbous swelling above the nodes.

Qiongzhuea tumidinoda See *Chimonobambusa tumidissinoda*.

SASA Makino & Shibata. A genus of about 50 species of small, thicket-forming bamboos with a typically low habit, usually solitary branches arising from each node and relatively broad, oblong or ovate-oblong leaves. Natives of Japan, Korea and China.

albomarginata See *S. veitchii*.

chrysantha See *Pleioblastus chrysanthus*.

kurilensis (Rupr.) Makino & Shibata. An extremely hardy and very invasive species with slender, yellow-green culms to 2.5m tall. The glossy dark green leaves, to 20cm long and 5cm across, are clustered at the tips of the shoots. Kurile islands, Sakhalin. **'Shimofuri'** A much less vigorous form, the leaves conspicuously striped with white. Best in partial shade.

palmata (Burb.) E.G. Camus (*Bambusa palmata* Burb.) A rampant, large-leaved bamboo forming extensive thickets of bright green canes 2–2.5m high. Leaves up to 35cm long by 9cm wide, the margins often withering during a hard winter. It has been flowering profusely for several years now. Although too invasive for a small garden it makes an excellent shelter plant where space permits. Japan. I 1889. FCC 1896. **f. *nebulosa*** (Makino) Suzuki. The commonly grown form distinguished by its purple-blotched stems.

ramosa See *Sasaella ramosa*.

tessellata See *Indocalamus tessellatus*.

veitchii (Carrière) Rehder (*S. albomarginata* (Franch. & Sav.) Makino & Shibata, *Arundinaria veitchii* (Carrière) N.E. Brown) A small, dense-growing species forming large thickets of deep purplish-green, later dull purple canes 0.6–1.2m high. Leaves 10–25cm long by 2.5–6cm wide, withering and becoming pale straw-coloured or whitish along the margins in autumn, providing an attractive and characteristic, variegated effect that lasts throughout winter. Japan. I 1880. AM 1898.

SASAELLA Makino. A genus of about 12 species of Japanese bamboos related to *Sasa*.

masamuneana (Makino) Hatusima & Muroi. A vigorous and hardy thicket-forming species, reaching 1.5–2m tall, with slender, upright culms, bloomy when young, becoming purple. Leaves to 16cm long and 3cm across, rich green with a distinct, reticulate venation, very rough at the margins, on a short, bloomy petiole. Japan. **'Albostriata'** A striking, variegated form, the leaves with conspicuous, longitudinal streaks of creamy-yellow and grey-green.

ramosa (Makino) Makino (*Arundinaria vagans* Gamble, *Pleioblastus viridistriatus* var. *vagans* (Gamble) Nakai, *Sasa ramosa* (Makino) Makino & Shibata) A dwarf, creeping species, quickly forming extensive carpets of bright green foliage. Canes 0.4–1.1m high, bright green at first, becoming deep olive-green, bearing solitary branches from each node. Leaves 5–15cm long by 1–2cm wide, downy on both surfaces. Too rampant for most gardens, but an excellent groundcover where little else will grow, even in dense shade. Japan. I 1892. It flowered at Kew in 1981, the first time outside Japan.

SEMIARUNDINARIA Nakai. A genus of about 20 species of bamboos, natives of E Asia.

fastuosa (Mitford) Makino (*Arundinaria fastuosa* Mitford) An extremely hardy, vigorous bamboo of stiff, erect habit, forming tall, dense clumps of deep glossy green canes, becoming flushed red-purple in a sunny position, 4.5–7.5m high, which are useful as stakes. Leaves 10–25cm long by 1.5–2.5cm wide. A handsome species of distinct habit which has been flowering sporadically in cultivation for several years. The young shoots in spring are edible. An excellent screen or tall hedge. Japan. I 1892. ♀ 2002. AM 1953.

yashadake (Makino) Makino. A vigorous bamboo making a dense thicket of erect, rich green culms to 6m or more tall. The glossy green leaves are up to 25cm long and 4cm across. Japan. **'Kimmei'** Culms yellow with a green stripe, sometimes red-flushed in a sunny position.

SHIBATAEA Nakai. A genus of 5 species, natives of Japan and China. Low-growing bamboos with a creeping rootstock. Stems flattened on one side between the nodes. Branches short and leafy, borne in clusters of 3–5 at each node.

kumasasa (Zoll.) Nakai (*Phyllostachys ruscifolia* (Munro) Satow) A very distinct bamboo of dwarf, compact habit. Canes 50–80cm high, characteristically zig-zag and almost triangular in outline, pale green at first, maturing to dull brownish. Leaves broadly lanceolate to ovate-oblong, 5–10cm long by 2–3cm wide. It has flowered in recent years with no apparent ill effect. A charming species forming dense, leafy clumps, particularly happy in a moist soil. Japan. I 1861. FCC 1896.

SINARUNDINARIA A genus of some 50 species, natives of Asia, Central America and Africa.

anceps See *Yushania anceps*.

hookeriana See *Himalayacalamus hookerianus*.

†*intermedia* (Munro) C.S. Chao & Renvoize (*Arundinaria intermedia* Munro) A vigorous but tender species with erect, green canes, 2.5–3.5m high, forming a dense clump. Leaves 7.5–20cm long by 1.5–2.5cm wide. Only suitable for the mildest localities, but an attractive tub plant for a conservatory. Flowered and died at Kew in 1899. E Himalaya.

maling See *Yushania maling*.

murielae See *Fargesia murieliae*.

nitida See *Fargesia nitida*.

Tetragonocalamus quadrangularis See *Chimonobambusa quadrangularis*.

THAMNOCALAMUS Munro. Six species, natives of China, the Himalaya and Africa.

crassinodus (T.P. Yi) Demoly. An elegant bamboo of graceful, spreading habit. The erect, then arching culms, often zig-zag at the base, are olive-green and slightly swollen just above the nodes, glaucous-bloomed beneath them when young. Sheaths bristly, leaves small and slender, to

6cm long and 1cm across. China. **'Kew Beauty'** A selection with even smaller leaves and erect culms, white-bloomed when young.

falconeri See *Himalayacalamus falconeri*.

spathaceus See *Fargesia murieliae*.

spathiflorus (Trin.) Munro (*Arundinaria spathiflora* Trin.) A beautiful, clump-forming species of neat, erect habit. Canes densely packed, up to 4.5m high, but more usually 2.5–3m, bright green ripening to a pinkish-purple shade on the exposed side, white-bloomy during their first season. Leaves 7.5–15cm long by 6–12mm wide. A lovely bamboo, thriving best in a little shade and shelter. NW Himalaya. I 1882.

tessellatus (Nees) Söderstr. & Ellis (*Arundinaria tessellata* (Nees) Munro) A rare species, not to be confused with *Indocalamus tessellatus*, forming clumps or patches. Canes 2.5–3.5m high, pale green at first, darkening and maturing to deep purple. Cane sheaths conspicuous, white the first year, cream later. Leaves 5–14cm long by 1cm wide. The only bamboo native to South Africa, where it occurs in the mountains from Table Mountain northwards. The canes are said to have been used by the Zulus in the construction of shields and so on.

YUSHANIA Keng f. Vigorous bamboos, often of spreading habit, native from the Himalayas to E Asia.

anceps (Mitford) C.S. Chao & Renvoize (*Arundinaria anceps* Mitford, *A. jaunsarensis* Gamble) A beautiful, but rampant species, ideal for screens and hedges, with straight, erect, deep glossy green canes reaching a height of 3–3.5m or more in mild localities. The arching tips bear arching masses of glossy green leaves, 10–15cm long by 12mm wide. Has flowered in various parts of the British Isles. The mature canes can be used for staking in the garden. NW Himalaya. I 1865. **'Pitt White'** A vigorous form which reached 9m high in the garden of Dr Mutch at Pitt White, Lyme Regis, Dorset. The canes bear great plumes of small, narrow leaves, 7.5cm long by 1.25cm wide. It was originally misidentified as *Arundinaria niitakayamensis*, a dwarf species, native to Taiwan and the Philippines, which is not in cultivation.

maling (Gamble) C.S. Chao & Renvoize (*Arundinaria maling* Gamble, *A. racemosa* hort. not Munro) A rare bamboo with a creeping rootstock. Canes brownish-green at first, maturing to dull brown, 2.5–3.5m high or more. Leaves 5–15cm long by 12mm wide. Similar to *Thamnocalamus spathiflorus* in general appearance, but habit more robust and foliage of a darker green. The internodes are extremely rough to the touch. Nepal, Sikkim.

GLOSSARY

Acicular Needle-shaped

Acuminate Tapering at the end, long pointed

Acute Sharp pointed

Adpressed Lying close and flat against a surface

Anther The pollen-bearing part of the stamen

Aristate Awned, bristle-tipped

Articulate Jointed

Ascending Rising somewhat obliquely and curving upwards

Auricle An ear-shaped projection or appendage

Awl-shaped Tapering from the base to a slender and stiff point

Axil The angle formed by a leaf or lateral branch with the stem, or of a vein with the midrib

Axillary Produced in the axil

Bearded Furnished with long or stiff hairs

Berry Strictly a pulpy, normally several-seeded, indehiscent fruit

Bifid Two-cleft

Bipinnate Twice pinnate

Bisexual Both male and female organs in the same flower

Blade The expanded part of a leaf or petal

Bloomy With a fine powder-like waxy deposit

Bole Trunk, of a tree

Bract A modified, usually reduced leaf at the base of a flower stalk, flower cluster, or shoot

Bullate Blistered or puckered

Calcareous Containing carbonate of lime or limestone, chalky or limy

Calcifuge Avoiding calcareous soils

Calyx The outer part of the flower, the sepals

Campanulate Bell-shaped

Capitate Head-like, collected into a dense cluster

Capsule A dry, several-celled pod

Catkin A normally dense spike or spike-like raceme of tiny, scaly-bracted flowers or fruits

Ciliate Fringed with hairs

Cladode Flattened leaf-like stems

Clone See under Nomenclature and Classification (p. 7)

Columnar Tall, cylindrical or tapering, column-like

Compound Composed of two or more similar parts

Compressed Flattened

Conical Cone-shaped

Cordate Shaped like a heart at the base of the leaf

Coriaceous Leathery

Corolla The inner, normally conspicuous part of a flower, the petals

Corymb A flat-topped or dome shaped flowerhead with the outer flowers opening first

Corymbose Having flowers in corymbs

Crenate Toothed with shallow, rounded teeth, scalloped

Cultivar See under Nomenclature and Classification (p. 7)

Cuneate Wedge-shaped

Cuspidate Abruptly sharp pointed

Cyme A flat-topped or dome-shaped flowerhead with the inner flowers opening first

Cymose Having flowers in cymes

Deciduous Soon or seasonally falling, not persistent

Decumbent Reclining, the tips ascending

Decurrent Extending down the stem

Deltoid Triangular

Dentate Toothed, with teeth directed outward

Denticulate Minutely dentate

Depressed Flattened from above

Diffuse Loosely or widely spreading

Digitate With the members arising from one point (as in a digitate leaf)

Dioecious Male and female flowers on different plants

Dissected Divided into many narrow segments

Distichous Arranged in two vertical ranks, two-ranked

Divaricate Spreading far apart

Divergent Spreading

Divided Separated to the base

Double Flowers with more than the usual number of petals, often with the style and stamens changed to petals

Doubly serrate Large teeth and small teeth alternating

Downy Softly hairy

Elliptic Widest at or about the middle, narrowing equally at both ends

Elongate Lengthened

Emarginate With a shallow notch at the apex

Entire Undivided and without teeth

Evergreen Remaining green during winter

Exfoliating Peeling off in thin strips

Exserted Projecting beyond (eg stamens from corolla)

Falcate Sickle-shaped

Fascicle A dense cluster

Fastigiate With branches erect and close together

Fertile Stamens producing good pollen or fruit containing good seeds, or of stems with flowering organs

Ferruginous Rust-coloured

Filament The stalk of a stamen

Filiform Thread-like

Fimbriate Fringed

Flexuous Wavy or zig-zag

Floccose Clothed with flocks of soft hair or wool

Florets Small, individual flowers of a dense inflorescence

Floriferous Flower-bearing, usually used to indicate profuse flowering

Gibbous Swollen, usually at the base (as in corolla)

Glabrous Hairless

Glandular With secreting organs

Glaucous Covered with a bloom, bluish-white or bluish-grey

Glutinous Sticky

Hermaphrodite Bisexual, both male and female organs in the same flower

Hirsute With rather coarse or stiff hairs

Hispid Beset with rigid hairs or bristles

Hoary Covered with a close whitish or greyish-white pubescence

Hybrid A plant resulting from a cross between different species

Imbricate Overlapping, as tiles on a roof

Impressed Sunken (as in veins)

Incised Sharply and usually deeply and irregularly cut

Indehiscent Fruits which do not (burst) open

Indumentum Dense hairy covering

Inflorescence The flowering part of the plant

Internode The portion of stem between two nodes or joints

Involucre A whorl of bracts surrounding a flower or flower cluster

Keel A central ridge

Lacerate Torn, irregularly cut or cleft

Laciniate Cut into narrow, pointed lobes

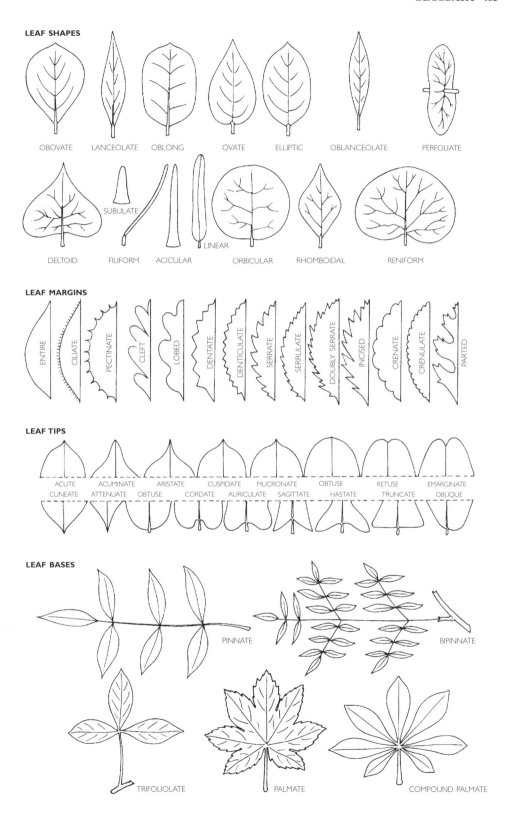

LEAF SHAPES

OBOVATE LANCEOLATE OBLONG OVATE ELLIPTIC OBLANCEOLATE PERFOLIATE

SUBULATE

DELTOID FILIFORM ACICULAR LINEAR ORBICULAR RHOMBOIDAL RENIFORM

LEAF MARGINS

ENTIRE CILIATE PECTINATE CLEFT LOBED DENTATE DENTICULATE SERRATE SERRULATE DOUBLY SERRATE INCISED CRENATE CRENULATE PARTED

LEAF TIPS

ACUTE ACUMINATE ARISTATE CUSPIDATE MUCRONATE OBTUSE RETUSE EMARGINATE

CUNEATE ATTENUATE OBTUSE CORDATE AURICULATE SAGITTATE HASTATE TRUNCATE OBLIQUE

LEAF BASES

PINNATE BIPINNATE

TRIFOLIOLATE PALMATE COMPOUND PALMATE

Lanceolate Lance-shaped, widening above the base and long tapering to the apex

Lanuginose Woolly or cottony

Lateral On or at the side

Lax Loose

Leaflet Part of a compound leaf

Linear Long and narrow with nearly parallel margins

Lip One of the parts of an unequally divided flower

Lobe Any protruding part of an organ (as in leaf, corolla or calyx)

Membranous Thin and rather soft

Midrib The central vein or rib of a leaf

Monoecious Male and female flowers separate, but on the same joint

Monotypic Of a single species (genus)

Mucronate Terminated abruptly by a spiny tip

Nectary A nectar-secreting gland, usually a small pit or protuberance

Node The place on the stem where the leaves are attached, the 'joint'

Nut A non-splitting, one-seeded, hard and bony fruit

Oblanceolate Inversely lanceolate

Oblique Unequal-sided

Oblong Longer than broad, with nearly parallel sides

Obovate Inversely ovate

Obtuse Blunt (as in apex of leaf or petal)

Orbicular Almost circular in outline

Oval Broadest at the middle

Ovary The basal 'box' part of the pistil, containing the ovules

Ovate Broadest below the middle (like a hen's egg)

Ovule The body which, after fertilization, becomes the seed

Palmate Lobed or divided in hand-like fashion, usually 5- or 7-lobed

Panicle A branching raceme

Paniculate Having flowers in panicles

Parted Cut or cleft almost to the base

Pea-flower Shaped like a sweet-pea blossom

Pectinate Comb-like (as in leaf margin)

Pedicel The stalk of an individual flower in an inflorescence

Peduncle The stalk of a flower cluster or of a solitary flower

Pellucid Clear, transparent (as in gland)

Pendulous/pendent Hanging, weeping

Perfoliate A pair of opposite leaves fused at the base, the stem appearing to pass through them

Perianth The calyx and corolla together; also commonly used for a flower in which there is no distinction between corolla and calyx

Persistent Remaining attached

Petal One of the separate segments of a corolla

Petaloid Petal-like (as in stamen)

Petiole The leaf-stalk

Pilose With long, soft, straight hairs

Pinnate With leaflets arranged on either side of a central stalk

Pinnatifid Cleft or parted in a pinnate way

Pistil The female organ of a flower comprising the ovary, style and stigma

Plumose Feathery (as the down of a thistle)

Pollen Spores or grains contained in the anther, containing the male element

Polygamous Bearing bisexual and unisexual flowers on the same plant

Procumbent Lying or creeping

Prostrate Lying flat on the ground

Pruinose Bloomy

Puberulent Minutely pubescent

Pubescent Covered with short, soft hairs, downy

Punctate With translucent or coloured dots or depressions

Pungent Ending in a stiff, sharp point, also acid (to the taste) or strong-smelling

Pyramidal Pyramid-shaped (broad at base tapering to a point)

Raceme A simple elongated inflorescence with stalked flowers

Racemose Having flowers in racemes

Rachis An axis bearing flowers or leaflets

Recurved Curved downward or backward

Reflexed Abruptly turned downward

Reniform Kidney-shaped

Reticulate Like a network (as in veins)

Revolute Rolled backwards, margin rolled under (as in leaf)

Rib A prominent vein in a leaf

Rotund Nearly circular

Rufous Reddish-brown

Rugose Wrinkled or rough

Runner A trailing shoot taking root at the nodes

Sagittate Shaped like an arrow-head

Scabrous Rough to the touch

Scale A minute leaf or bract, or a flat gland-like appendage on the surface of a leaf, flower or shoot

Scandent With climbing stems

Scarious Thin and dry, not green

Semi-evergreen Normally evergreen but losing some or all of its leaves in a cold winter or cold area

Sepal One of the segments of a calyx

Serrate Saw-toothed (teeth pointing forward)

Serrulate Minutely serrate

Sessile Not stalked

Setose Clothed with bristles

Sheath A tubular envelope

Shrub A woody plant that branches from the base with no obvious trunk

Simple Said of a leaf that is not compound or an unbranched inflorescence

Sinuate Strongly waved (as in leaf margin)

Sinus The recess or space between two lobes or divisions of a leaf, calyx or corolla

Spathulate Spoon-shaped

Spicate Flowers in spikes

Spike A simple, elongated inflorescence with sessile flowers

Spine A sharp, pointed end of a branch or leaf

Spur A tubular projection from a flower; or a short stiff branchlet

Stamen The male organ of a flower comprising filament and anther

Staminode A sterile stamen, or a structure resembling a stamen, sometimes petal-like

Standard The upper, normally broad and erect petal in a pea-flower; also used in nurseries to describe a tall single-stemmed young tree

Stellate Star-shaped

Stigma The summit of the pistil which receives the pollen, often sticky or feathery

Stipule Appendage (normally two) at the base of some petioles

Stolon A shoot at or below the surface of the ground which produces a new plant at its tip

Striate With fine, longitudinal lines

Strigose Clothed with flattened, fine, bristle-like, hairs

Style The middle part of the pistil, often elongated, between the ovary and stigma

Subulate Awl-shaped

Succulent Juicy, fleshy, soft and thickened in texture

Suckering Producing underground stems; also the shoots from the stock of a grafted plant

Tendril A twining thread-like appendage

Ternate In threes
Tessellated Mosaic-like (as in veins)
Tomentose With dense, woolly
    pubescence
Tomentum Dense covering of matted
    hairs
Tree A woody plant that produces
    normally a single trunk and an
    elevated head of branches
Trifoliate Three-leaved
Trifoliolate A leaf with three separate
    leaflets

Turbinate Top-shaped
Type Strictly the original (type)
specimen, but often used in a general
    sense to indicate the typical form in
    cultivation
Umbel A normally flat-topped inflo-
    rescence in which the pedicels or
    peduncles all arise from a common
    point
Umbellate Flowers in umbels
Undulate With wavy margins
Unisexual Of one sex

Urceolate Urn-shaped
Velutinous Clothed with a velvety
    indumentum
Venation The arrangement of veins
Verrucose Having a wart-like or
    nodular surface
Verticillate Arranged in a whorl or
    ring
Villous Bearing long and soft hairs
Viscid Sticky
Whorl Three or more flowers or
    leaves arranged in a ring

INFLORESCENCES (SIMPLIFIED)

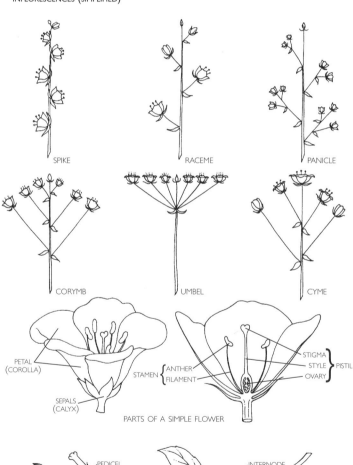

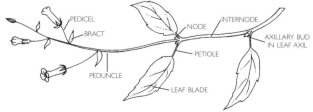

BOTANICAL NAMES

The study of botanical plant names is fascinating and rewarding. Knowledge of the derivation and meaning of names makes them and the plants they apply to easier to remember. To the uninitiated these names, which are in Latin, can be confusing, but there is a good reason why they are used. Latin botanical names are accepted the world over. Vernacular or common names may be easier to learn and pronounce but they can be a source of much confusion and misunderstanding. For example, the names 'bilberry', 'whortleberry', 'blaeberry', 'huckleberry' and 'whinberry' are all English names used in different parts of the British Isles for the same plant, called *Vaccinium myrtillus* in Latin. Mention 'huckleberry' to an American gardener and he would probably think you were referring to a *Gaylussacia*. Talk of any of the above to a Russian, Chinese, French or any other non-English-speaking horticulturist and he would shake his head in confusion, but use the botanical name and there is every chance that he would understand. Botanical names usually tell us something about a plant.

Generic names

Generic names are always nouns. Their origins and meanings are occasionally obscure, but the majority are derived from older names in Greek, Latin, Arabic and other languages. Some are based on characters in Greek mythology: *Daphne* after the river god's daughter, *Andromeda* after the daughter of Cepheus and Cassiope, *Phyllodoce* a sea nymph. Others commemorate people, such as botanists, patrons, and so on: *Buddleja* after Rev Adam Buddle, *Deutzia* after J. Deutz, *Escallonia* after Signor Escallon, *Fuchsia* after Leonard Fuchs, *Lonicera* after Adam Lonicer.

Specific epithets

The term epithet is used here rather than name because, unlike generic names, species names will not stand on their own. Words used to describe species are varied and fall into four main categories (see also under Nomenclature and Classification, page 6–8) namely: epithets that indicate the origin of a plant, eg. continent, country, region; epithets that describe the habitat of a plant (where it grows in the wild), eg. in woods, on mountains, by rivers; epithets that describe a plant or a particular feature, such as size, habit, leaf shape, colour of flower; epithets that commemorate people, eg. botanists, plant collectors, patrons, famous horticulturists.

The following lists are a selection of the most commonly used specific epithets and their meanings.

Geographical epithets

atlantica(um)(us) (*Cedrus atlantica*) – of the Atlas Mountains – (North Africa)
australe(is) (*Cordyline australis*) – southern
boreale(is) (*Linnaea borealis*) – northern
californica(um)(us) (*Fremontodendron californicum*) – of California
capense(is) (*Phygelius capensis*) – of the Cape (South Africa)
europaea(um)(us) (*Euonymus europaeus*) – of Europe
himalaica(um)(us) (*Stachyurus himalaicus*) – of the Himalaya
hispanica(um)(us) (*Genista hispanica*) – of Spain
japonica(um)(us) (*Camellia japonica*) – of Japan
lusitanica(um)(us)(*Prunus lusitanica*) – of Portugal
nipponica(um)(us) (*Spiraea nipponica*) – of Japan
occidentale(is) (*Thuja occidentalis*) – western
orientale(is) (*Platycladus orientalis*) – eastern
sinense(is) (*Wisteria sinensis*) – of China

Epithets describing habitat

alpina(um)(us) (*Daphne alpina*) – alpine, of the Alps or growing in alpine regions
arvense(is) (*Rosa arvensis*) – of fields or cultivated land
aquatica(um)(us) (*Nyssa aquatica*) – of water, or growing by water
campestre(is) (*Acer campestre*) – of plains or flat areas
littorale(is) (*Griselinia littoralis*) – of sea shores
maritima(um)(us) (*Prunus maritima*) – by the sea
montana(um)(us) (*Clematis montana*) – of mountains
palustre(is) (*Dirca palustris*) – of swamps or marshes
sylvatica(um)(us) (*Fagus sylvatica*) – of, or forming, woods

Epithets describing habit

arborea(um)(us) (*Rhododendron arboreum*) – tree-like
fastigiata(um)(us) (*Cassiope fastigiata*) – erect, the branches
fruticosa(um)(us) (*Bupleurum fruticosum*) – shrubby
horizontale(is) (*Cotoneaster horizontalis*) – horizontally spreading
humile(is) (*Chamaerops humilis*) – low-growing
major(us) (*Vinca major*) – greater
minor(us) (*Vinca minor*) – lesser
nana(um)(us) (*Betula nana*) – dwarf
pendula(um)(us) (*Betula pendula*) – pendulous, weeping
procera(um)(us) (*Abies procera*) – very tall, high
procumbens (*Juniperus procumbens*) – procumbent, creeping
prostrata(um)(us) (*Ceanothus prostratus*) – prostrate, hugging the ground
repens (*Salix repens*) – creeping and rooting
suffruticosa(um)(us) (*Paeonia suffruticosa*) – woody at base

Epithets describing leaves
(phylla(um)(us) and folia(um)(us) – leaf)

Many names describe shape and toothing of leaves, eg ovata, lanceolata, rotundifolia, serrata, crenata, laciniata for which see Glossary pp.482–485.
angustifolia(um)(us) (*Phillyrea angustifolia*) – narrow-leaved
arguta(um)(us) (*Spiraea* 'Arguta') – sharp
coriacea(um)(us) (*Holboellia coriacea*) – coriaceous, leathery
crassifolia(um)(us) (*Melicytus crassifolius*) – thick-leaved

decidua(um)(us) (*Larix decidua*) – deciduous, dropping its leaves

glabra(um)(us) (*Elaeagnus glabra*) – glabrous, without hairs

heterophylla(um)(us) (*Osmanthus heterophyllus*) – variably leaved

hirsuta(um)(us) (*Vaccinium hirsutum*) – hairy

incana(um)(us) (*Alnus incana*) – grey-downy

integrifolia(um)(us) (*Schizophragma integrifolium*) – without teeth

laevigata(um)(us) (*Rosa laevigata*) – smooth and polished

latifolia(um)(us) (*Ilex latifolia*) – broad-leaved

macrophylla(um)(us) (*Acer macrophyllum*) – large-leaved

maculata(um)(us) (*Elaeagnus pungens* 'Maculata') – spotted, blotched

microphylla(um)(us) (*Azara microphylla*) – small-leaved

molle(is) (*Hamamelis mollis*) – soft

nitida(um)(us) (*Lonicera nitida*) – shining

parvifolia(um)(us) (*Ulmus parvifolia*) – small-leaved

picta(um)(us) (*Kerria japonica* 'Picta') – painted, coloured

pinnata(um)(us) (*Psoralea pinnata*) – pinnate

platyphylla(um)(us) (*Tilia platyphyllos*) – broad- leaved

reticulata(um)(us) (*Salix reticulata*) – net-veined

sempervirens (*Buxus sempervirens*) – always green, evergreen

splendens (*Cotoneaster splendens*) – glittering, shining

tomentosa(um)(us) (*Tilia tomentosa*) – covered with a short, dense pubescence

variegata(um)(us) (*Cornus mas* 'Variegata') – variegated, two-coloured

velutina(um)(us) (*Fraxinus velutina*) – velvety

Epithets describing flowers
(**flora**(um)(us) – flower)

campanulata(um)(us) (*Rhododendron campanulatum*) – bell-shaped

floribunda(um)(us) (*Dipelta floribunda*) – free-flowering

grandiflora(um)(us) (*Viburnum grandiflorum*) – large-flowered

macropetala(um)(us) (*Clematis macropetala*) – large-petalled

nudiflora(um)(us) (*Jasminum nudiflorum*) – naked, without leaves

paniculata(um)(us) (*Koelreuteria paniculata*) – flowering in panicles

parviflora(um)(us) (*Aesculus parviflora*) – small-flowered

pauciflora(um)(us) (*Corylopsis pauciflora*) – few-flowered

polyantha(um)(us) (*Jasminum polyanthum*) – many-flowered

racemosa(um)(us) (*Berchemia racemosa*) – flowers in racemes

spicata(um)(us) (*Corylopsis spicata*) – flowers in spikes

stellata(um)(us) (*Magnolia stellata*) – starry

triflora(um)(us) (*Abelia triflora*) – flowers in threes

umbellata(um)(us) (*Berberis umbellata*) – flowers in umbels

uniflora(um)(us) (*Crataegus uniflora*) – one-flowered

Epithets describing colours

alba(um)(us) (*Populus alba*) – white

argentea(um)(us) (*Shepherdia argentea*) – silvery

aurantiaca(um)(us) (*Mimulus aurantiacus*) – orange

aurea(um)(us) (*Salvia aurea*) – golden

bicolor (*Quercus bicolor*) – two-coloured

carnea(um)(us) (*Aesculus × carnea*) – flesh-coloured

caerulea(um)(us) (*Passiflora caerulea*) – blue

cinerea(um)(us) (*Erica cinerea*) – ash-grey

coccinea(um)(us) (*Quercus coccinea*) – scarlet

concolor (*Abies concolor*) – of the same colour

discolor (*Holodiscus discolor*) – two-coloured

ferruginea(um)(us) (*Rhododendron ferrugineum*) – rusty-brown

flava(um)(us) (*Rhododendron flavum*) – pale yellow

glauca(um)(us) (*Picea glauca*) – sea-green

lactea(um)(us) (*Rhododendron lacteum*) – milk-white

lilacina(um)(us) (*Erica cinerea* 'Lilacina') – lilac

lutea(um)(us) (*Rhododendron luteum*) – yellow

nigra(um)(us) (*Sambucus nigra*) – black

punicea(um)(us) (*Clianthus puniceus*) – crimson

purpurea(um)(us) (*Malus × purpurea*) – purple

rosea(um)(us) (*Lapageria rosea*) – rose-coloured

rubra(um)(us) (*Quercus rubra*) – red

sanguinea(um)(us) (*Ribes sanguineum*) – blood-red

tricolor (*Rubus tricolor*) – three-coloured

variegata(um)(us) (*Weigela* 'Florida Variegata') – variegated, two-coloured

versicolor (*Chamaecytisus × versicolor*) – variously coloured or changing colour

violacea(um)(us) (*Jovellana violacea*) – violet

viride(is) (*Alnus viridis*) – green

Epithets describing aromas and scents

citriodora(um)(us) (*Eucalyptus citriodora*) – lemon-scented

foetida(um)(us) (*Viburnum foetidum*) – strong-smelling, unpleasant

fragrantissima(um)(us) (*Lonicera fragrantissima*) – most fragrant

graveolens (*Ruta graveolens*) – smelling unpleasantly

odorata(um)(us) (*Rubus odoratus*) – sweet-scented

odoratissima(um)(us) (*Viburnum odoratissimum*) – sweetest scented

moschata(um)(us) (*Olearia moschata*) – musk-scented

suaveolens (*Brugmansia suaveolens*) – sweet-scented

Epithets alluding to other plants

bignonioides (*Catalpa bignonioides*) – bignonia-like

jasminea (*Daphne jasminea*) – jasmine-like

liliiflora(um)(us) (*Magnolia liliiflora*) – lily-flowered

pseudoplatanus (*Acer pseudoplatanus*) – false plane

salicifolia(um)(us) (*Cotoneaster salicifolius*) – willow-leaved

tulipifera(um)(us) (*Liriodendron tulipifera*) – tulip-bearing

Commemorative epithets

armandii (*Pinus armandii*) – after Armand David

davidii (*Viburnum davidii*) – after Armand David

delavayi (*Abies delavayi*) – after the Abbé Delavay

harryana(um)(us) (*Viburnum harryanum*) – after Sir Harry Veitch

henryana(um)(us) (*Parthenocissus henryana*) – after Dr Augustine Henry

hookeri (*Berberis hookeri*) – after Sir Joseph Hooker

thunbergii (*Spiraea thunbergii*) – after Carl Peter Thunberg

williamsiana(um)(us) (*Rhododendron williamsianum*) – after Mr J. C. Williams
willmottiana(um)(us) (*Ceratostigma wilmottianum*) – after Miss Ellen Willmott
wilsoniae (*Berberis wilsoniae*) – after Mrs E.H. Wilson

Miscellaneous epithets

affine(is) (*Cotoneaster affinis*) – related (to another species)
alata(um)(us) (*Euonymus alatus*) – winged
amabile(is) (*Kolkwitzia amabilis*) – lovely
ambigua(um)(us) (*Ribes ambiguum*) – doubtful (identity)
amoena(um)(us) (*Lonicera × amoena*) – charming, pleasing
bella(um)(us) (*Spiraea bella*) – pretty
commune(is) (*Juniperus communis*) – common, occurring in plenty
confusa(um)(us) (*Sarcococca confusa*) – confused (identity)
dulce(is) (*Prunus dulcis*) – sweet

edule(is) (*Passiflora edulis*) – edible
florida(um)(us) (*Cornus florida*) – flowering
formosa(um)(us) (*Leycesteria formosa*) – handsome, beautiful
hybrida(um)(us) (*Deutzia × hybrida*) – hybrid
insigne(is) (*Sorbus insignis*) – outstanding
intermedia(um)(us) (*Eucryphia × intermedia*) – intermediate
media(um)(us) (*Mahonia × media*) – middle, midway between
officinale(is) (*Rosmarinus officinalis*) – of the shop (herbal)
praecox (*Chimonanthus praecox*) – early
pulchella(um)(us) (*Agathosma pulchella*) – beautiful
speciosa(um)(us) (*Callistemon speciosus*) – showy
sativa(um)(us) (*Castanea sativa*) - sown, planted or cultivated
utile(is) (*Viburnum utile*) – useful
vernale(is) (*Hamamelis vernalis*) – spring
vulgare(is) (*Calluna vulgaris*) – common

GENERA INCLUDED BY FAMILY

(including intergeneric and graft hybrids)

ACERACEAE
Acer
Dipteronia

ACTINIDIACEAE
Actinidia
Clematoclethra

AGAVACEAE
Beschorneria
Cordyline
Hesperaloe
Yucca

ALANGIACEAE
Alangium

ANACARDIACEAE
Cotinus
Pistacia
Rhus
Schinus

ANNONACEAE
Asimina

APOCYNACEAE
Elytropus
Mandevilla
Nerium
Trachelospermum
Vinca

AQUIFOLIACEAE
Ilex

ARALIACEAE
Aralia

Eleutherococcus
× Fatshedera
Fatsia
Hedera
Kalopanax
Metapanax
Oplopanax
Pseudopanax
Schefflera
Tetrapanax

ARAUCARIACEAE
Agathis
Araucaria
Wollemia

ARISTOLOCHIACEAE
Aristolochia

ASCLEPIADACEAE
Araujia
Cionura
Dregea
Periploca
Tweedia

ASTELIACEAE
Astelia

AUCUBACEAE
Aucuba

BAUERACEAE
Bauera

BERBERIDACEAE
Berberis
× Mahoberberis

Mahonia
Nandina

BETULACEAE
Alnus
Betula

BIGNONIACEAE
Bignonia
Campsis
Catalpa
× Chitalpa
Eccremocarpus
Pandorea
Tecoma

BORAGINACEAE
Ehretia
Lithodora
Moltkia

BROMELIACEAE
Fascicularia

BUDDLEJACEAE
Buddleja

BUXACEAE
Buxus
Pachysandra
Sarcococca

CALYCANTHACEAE
Calycanthus
Chimonanthus
Sinocalycanthus

CANNABACEAE
Humulus

CAPRIFOLIACEAE
Abelia
Diervilla
Dipelta
Heptacodium
Kolkwitzia
Leycesteria
Linnaea
Lonicera
Sambucus
Symphoricarpos
Viburnum
Weigela

CASUARINACEAE
Allocasuarina

CELASTRACEAE
Celastrus
Euonymus
Maytenus
Paxistima
Tripterygium

CEPHALOTAXACEAE
Cephalotaxus

CERCIDIPHYLLACEAE
Cercidiphyllum

CHENOPODIACEAE
Atriplex
Camphorosma
Suaeda

CHLORANTHACEAE
Sarcandra

CISTACEAE
Cistus
× *Halimiocistus*
Halimium
Helianthemum

CLETHRACEAE
Clethra

CNEORACEAE
Cneorum

COMPOSITAE
Ageratina
Artemisia
Aster
Baccharis
Brachyglottis
Chiliotrichum
Eumorphia
Euryops
Grindelia
Helichrysum
Mutisia
Olearia
Othonna
Oxylobus
Ozothamnus
Pericallis
Pertya
Plecostachys
Santolina
Senecio

CONVOLVULACEAE
Convolvulus

CORIARIACEAE
Coriaria

CORNACEAE
Cornus
Davidia
Nyssa

CORYLACEAE
Carpinus
Corylus
Ostrya
Ostryopsis

CRASSULACEAE
Sedum

CRUCIFERAE
Vella

CUNONIACEAE
Caldcluvia
Weinmannia

CUPRESSACEAE
Athrotaxis
Austrocedrus
Callitris
Calocedrus
Chamaecyparis
Cryptomeria
Cunninghamia
× *Cupressocyparis*
Cupressus
Diselma
Fitzroya
Fokienia
Glyptostrobus
Juniperus
Libocedrus
Metasequoia
Microbiota
Pilgerodendron
Platycladus
Sequoia
Sequoiadendron
Taiwania
Taxodium
Tetraclinis
Thuja
Thujopsis
Widdringtonia

CYRILLACEAE
Cyrilla

DAPHNIPHYLLACEAE
Daphniphyllum

EBENACEAE
Diospyros

ELAEAGNACEAE
Elaeagnus
Hippophae
Shepherdia

ELAEOCARPACEAE
Aristotelia
Crinodendron
Elaeocarpus
Vallea

EMPETRACEAE
Empetrum

EPACRIDACEAE
Cyathodes
Leucopogon
Pentachondra
Richea
Trochocarpa

EPHEDRACEAE
Ephedra

ERICACEAE
Agapetes
Agarista
Andromeda
Arbutus
Arctostaphylos
Bryanthus
Calluna
Cassiope
Chamaedaphne
Daboecia
Elliottia
Enkianthus
Epigaea
Erica
Gaultheria
Gaylussacia
Kalmia
Kalmiopsis
× *Kalmiothamnus*
Leiophyllum
Leucothoe
Loiseleuria
Lyonia
Menziesia
Oxydendrum
× *Phylliopsis*
Phyllodoce
× *Phyllothamnus*
Pieris
Rhododendron
Rhodothamnus
Tripetaleia
Vaccinium
Zenobia

ESCALLONIACEAE
Anopterus
Carpodetus
Corokia
Escallonia
Itea

EUCOMMIACEAE
Eucommia

EUCRYPHIACEAE
Eucryphia

EUPHORBIACEAE
Andrachne
Euphorbia
Glochidion
Mallotus
Sapium
Securinega

EUPTELEACEAE
Euptelea

FAGACEAE
Castanea
Castanopsis
Chrysolepis
Fagus
Lithocarpus
Nothofagus
Quercus

FLACOURTIACEAE
Azara
Berberidopsis
Carrierea
Idesia
Poliothyrsis
Xylosma

GARRYACEAE
Garrya

GESNERIACEAE
Asteranthera
Mitraria

GINKGOACEAE
Ginkgo

GRAMINEAE
Arundinaria
Chimonobambusa
Chusquea
Fargesia
Himalayacalamus
Indocalamus
× *Phyllosasa*
Phyllostachys
Pleioblastus
Pseudosasa
Sasa
Sasaella
Semiarundinaria
Shibataea
Sinarundinaria
Thamnocalamus
Yushania

GRISELINIACEAE
Griselinia

GROSSULARIACEAE
Ribes

GUTTIFERAE
Hypericum

HAMAMELIDACEAE
Corylopsis
Disanthus
Distylium
Fortunearia
Fothergilla
Hamamelis

Liquidambar
Loropetalum
Parrotia
Parrotiopsis
Rhodoleia
Sinowilsonia
× Sycoparrotia
Sycopsis

HELWINGIACEAE
Helwingia

HIPPOCASTANACEAE
Aesculus

HYDRANGEACEAE
Carpenteria
Decumaria
Deutzia
Fendlera
Hydrangea
Jamesia
Philadelphus
Pileostegia
Schizophragma

ICACINACEAE
Citronella

ILLICIACEAE
Illicium

JUGLANDACEAE
Carya
Juglans
Platycarya
Pterocarya

LABIATAE
Ballota
Colquhounia
Elsholtzia
Hyssopus
Lavandula
Leonotis
Lepechinia
Perovskia
Phlomis
Prostanthera
Rosmarinus
Rostrinucula
Salvia
Teucrium
Westringia

LARDIZABALACEAE
Akebia
Decaisnea
Holboellia
Lardizabala
Sinofranchetia
Stauntonia

LAURACEAE
Cinnamomum
Laurus
Lindera
Litsea
Neolitsea
Persea
Sassafras
Umbellularia

LEGUMINOSAE
Acacia
Adenocarpus
Albizia
Amicia
Amorpha
Anagyris
Anthyllis
Astragalus
Caesalpinia
Calophaca
Caragana
Carmichaelia
× Carmispartium
Ceratonia
Cercis
Chamaecytisus
Chordospartium
Cladrastis
Clianthus
Colutea
Coronilla
Cytisus
Desmodium
Erinacea
Erythrina
Genista
Gleditsia
Gymnocladus
Halimodendron
Hardenbergia
Hedysarum
Hippocrepis
Indigofera
+ Laburnocytisus
Laburnum
Lespedeza
Lotus
Lupinus
Maackia
Medicago
Notospartium
Ononis
Paraserianthes
Petteria
Piptanthus
Psoralea
Pueraria
Robinia
Senna
Sophora
Spartium

Sutherlandia
Ulex
Wisteria

LEITNERIACEAE
Leitneria

LINACEAE
Linum

LOGANIACEAE
Gelsemium

LYTHRACEAE
Heimia
Lagerstroemia

MAGNOLIACEAE
Liriodendron
Magnolia
Manglietia
Michelia

MALVACEAE
Abutilon
Hibiscus
Hoheria
Lavatera
Plagianthus
Sphaeralcea

MELASTOMATACEAE
Tibouchina

MELIACEAE
Melia
Toona

MELIANTHACEAE
Melianthus

MELIOSMACEAE
Meliosma

MENISPERMACEAE
Cocculus
Menispermum
Sinomenium

MONIMIACEAE
Atherosperma
Laurelia
Peumus

MORACEAE
Broussonetia
Ficus
Maclura
Morus

MUSACEAE
Musa

MYOPORACEAE
Myoporum

MYRICACEAE
Comptonia
Myrica

MYRSINACEAE
Ardisia
Myrsine

MYRTACEAE
Acca
Amomyrtus
Austromyrtus
Callistemon
Eucalyptus
Kunzea
Leptospermum
Lophomyrtus
Luma
Melaleuca
Metrosideros
Myrteola
Myrtus
Ugni

OCHNACEAE
Ochna

OLEACEAE
Abeliophyllum
Chionanthus
Fontanesia
Forestiera
Forsythia
Fraxinus
Jasminum
Ligustrum
Olea
Osmanthus
Phillyrea
Picconia
Syringa

ONAGRACEAE
Fuchsia
Zauschneria

PAEONIACEAE
Paeonia

PALMAE
Butia
Chamaerops
Phoenix
Sabal
Trachycarpus
Washingtonia

PAPAVERACEAE
Dendromecon
Romneya

PASSIFLORACEAE
Passiflora

PHILESIACEAE
Lapageria
Luzuriaga
× *Philageria*
Philesia

PHORMIACEAE
Phormium

PHYLLOCLADACEAE
Phyllocladus

PHYTOLACCACEAE
Ercilla
Phytolacca

PINACEAE
Abies
Cedrus
Keteleeria
Larix
Picea
Pinus
Pseudolarix
Pseudotsuga
Tsuga

PITTOSPORACEAE
Billardiera
Bursaria
Pittosporum
Sollya

PLANTAGINACEAE
Plantago

PLATANACEAE
Platanus

PLUMBAGINACEAE
Ceratostigma
Plumbago

PODOCARPACEAE
Afrocarpus
Dacrycarpus
Dacrydium
Halocarpus
Lagarostrobus
Lepidothamnus
Manoao
Microcachrys
Microstrobos
Nageia
Podocarpus

Prumnopitys
Saxegothaea

POLEMONIACEAE
Cantua

POLYGALACEAE
Polygala

POLYGONACEAE
Atraphaxis
Fallopia
Muehlenbeckia
Persicaria
Polygonum

POTALIACEAE
Desfontainia

PROTEACEAE
Banksia
Embothrium
Gevuina
Grevillea
Hakea
Lomatia
Telopea

PUNICACEA
Punica

RANUNCULACEAE
Clematis
Xanthorhiza

RHAMNACEAE
Berchemia
Ceanothus
Colletia
Discaria
Hovenia
Paliurus
Phylica
Pomaderris
Rhamnus

ROSACEAE
Amelanchier
× *Amelasorbus*
Aronia
Cercocarpus
Chaenomeles
Chamaebatiaria
Cotoneaster
+ *Crataegomespilus*
Crataegus
× *Crataemespilus*
Cydonia
Dichotomanthes
Docynia
Dryas
Eriobotrya

Exochorda
Heteromeles
Holodiscus
Kerria
Luetkea
Lyonothamnus
Maddenia
Malus
Margyricarpus
Mespilus
Neillia
Neviusia
Oemleria
Osteomeles
Peraphyllum
Photinia
Physocarpus
Polylepis
Potentilla
Prinsepia
Prunus
Pseudocydonia
Pyracantha
× *Pyracomeles*
+ *Pyrocydonia*
× *Pyronia*
Pyrus
Quillaja
Rhaphiolepis
Rhodotypos
Rosa
Rubus
Sibiraea
Sorbaria
× *Sorbaronia*
× *Sorbocotoneaster*
× *Sorbopyrus*
Sorbus
Spiraea
Stephanandra

RUBIACEAE
Bouvardia
Cephalanthus
Coprosma
Damnacanthus
Emmenopterys
Leptodermis
Luculia
Mitchella
Paederia

RUSCACEAE
Danae
Ruscus

RUTACEAE
Acradenia
Agathosma
Boenninghausenia
Choisya
× *Citrofortunella*

× *Citroncirus*
Citrus
Coleonema
Correa
Diosma
Fortunella
Melicope
Orixa
Phellodendron
Poncirus
Ptelea
Ruta
Skimmia
Tetradium
Zanthoxylum

SALICACEAE
Populus
Salix

SAPINDACEAE
Koelreuteria
Sapindus
Xanthoceras

SCHISANDRACEAE
Kadsura
Schisandra

SCIADOPITYACEAE
Sciadopitys

SCROPHULARIACEAE
Bowkeria
Calceolaria
Freylinia
Hebe
Jovellana
Keckiella
Mimulus
Parahebe
Paulownia
Penstemon
Phygelius
Rhodochiton

SIMAROUBACEAE
Ailanthus
Picrasma

SMILACACEAE
Smilax

SOLANACEAE
Brugmansia
Cestrum
Fabiana
Lycium
Solanum
Vestia

STACHYURACEAE
Stachyurus

STAPHYLEACEAE
Staphylea

STERCULIACEAE
Firmiana
Fremontodendron
Reevesia

STYRACACEAE
Halesia
Pterostyrax
Rehderodendron
Sinojackia
Styrax

SYMPLOCACEAE
Symplocos

TAMARICACEAE
Myricaria
Tamarix

TAXACEAE
Taxus
Torreya

TETRACENTRACEAE
Tetracentron

THEACEAE
Camellia
Cleyera
Eurya
Franklinia
Gordonia
Schima
Stewartia
Ternstroemia

THYMELAEACEAE
Daphne
Dirca
Edgeworthia
Pimelea
Wikstroemia

TILIACEAE
Entelea
Grewia
Sparrmannia
Tilia

**TROCHODEN-
DRACEAE**
Trochodendron

ULMACEAE
Aphananthe
Celtis
Hemiptelea
Planera
Ulmus
Zelkova

UMBELLIFERAE
Bupleurum

URTICACEAE
Debregeasia

VERBENACEAE
Aloysia
Callicarpa
Caryopteris
Citharexylum
Clerodendrum
Diostea
Rhaphithamnus
Verbena
Vitex

VIOLACEAE
Melicytus

VITACEAE
Ampelopsis
Cissus
Parthenocissus
Vitis

WINTERACEAE
Drimys
Pseudowintera

TREES AND SHRUBS IN GARDEN AND LANDSCAPE DESIGN

The approach to choosing trees and shrubs varies according to the nature of the landscaping job – public or private, town or country – the taste of the landscape designer or garden maker, the labour available for maintenance. All these factors, and more, have an affect on which trees and shrubs to use, and all must also be influenced by the soil and situation. Having produced a wide range of woody plants since 1864, we are anxious that our expertise should be presented to give the best possible advantage. As in most other walks of life, fashions and production methods change, therefore, you are strongly advised to check availability of all the plants before launching too far into your final plans.

In addition to the symbols used in the text indicating the likes and dislikes of the plants, the following lists should serve as a guide to or reminder of trees and shrubs suitable for some of the many different soils and situations found in the British Isles, and even within one site. We wish to emphasise that the plants mentioned in each list are merely a selection and there are numerous other examples. We would also point out that we have listed plants that are suitable for a particular situation, but that we are not necessarily recommending them only for that situation: a great many will grow quite happily in a variety of other sites.

For further details of the plants in these lists, please refer to the individual descriptions in the text. cvs – cultivars (see under Nomenclature and Classification, pages 6–8).

TREES and SHRUBS suitable for CLAY SOILS (neutral to slightly acid)

TREES
Acer (all)
Aesculus (all)
Alnus (all)
Betula (all)
Carpinus (all)
Crataegus (all)
Eucalyptus (all)
Fraxinus (all)
Ilex (all)
Laburnum (all)
Malus (all)
Platanus (all)
Populus (all)
Prunus (all)
Quercus (all)
Salix (all)
Sorbus (all)
Tilia (all)

SHRUBS
Abelia (all)
Aralia elata and cvs
Aronia (all)
Aucuba japonica and cvs
Berberis (all)
Brachyglottis 'Sunshine'
Chaenomeles (all)
Choisya (all)
Colutea (all)
Cornus (all)
Corylus (all)
Cotinus (all)
Cotoneaster (all)
Cytisus (all)
Deutzia (all)

Escallonia (all)
Forsythia (all)
Genista (all)
Hamamelis (all)
Hibiscus syriacus and cvs
Hypericum (all)
Lonicera (all)
Mahonia (all)
Magnolia (all)
Osmanthus (all)
Philadelphus (all)
Potentilla (all)
Pyracantha (all)
Rhododendron Hardy Hybrids
Ribes (all)
Rosa (all)
Skimmia (all)
Spiraea (all)
Symphoricarpos (all)
Viburnum (all)
Weigela (all)

CONIFERS
Abies (all)
Chamaecyparis (all)
Juniperus (all)
Larix (all)
Pinus (all)
Taxodium (all)
Taxus (all)
Thuja (all)

BAMBOOS
Phyllostachys (all)
Pleioblastus (all)
Pseudosasa japonica
Sasa (all)
Thamnocalamus

TREES and SHRUBS suitable for DRY ACID SOILS

TREES
Acer negundo and cvs
Ailanthus altissima
Betula (all)
Castanea (all)
Cercis (all)
Gleditsia (all)
Ilex aquifolium and cvs
Populus alba
Populus tremula
Robinia (all)

SHRUBS
Acer tataricum subsp. *ginnala*
Berberis (all)
Calluna vulgaris and cvs
Caragana arborescens
Cistus (all)
Colutea arborescens
Cotoneaster (all)
Elaeagnus angustifolia
Elaeagnus commutata
Erica (all)
Gaultheria mucronata and cvs
Genista (all)
Hakea lissosperma
Halimodendron halodendron
Helianthemum (all)
Hibiscus (all)
Ilex crenata and cvs
Indigofera (all)
Kerria japonica and cvs
Lonicera (all)
Lycium barbarum
Physocarpus opulifolius and cvs
Rosa pimpinellifolia and cvs
Salix caprea

Salix cinerea
Salix repens var. *argentea*
Tamarix (all)
Ulex (all)

CONIFERS

Cupressus arizonica var. *glabra* and
  cvs
Juniperus (all)
Pinus (all)

TREES and SHRUBS suitable for SHALLOW SOIL OVER CHALK

TREES

Acer campestre
Acer negundo and cvs
Acer platanoides and cvs
Acer pseudoplatanus and cvs
Aesculus (all)
Carpinus betulus and cvs
Cercis siliquastrum
Crataegus laevigata and cvs
Fagus sylvatica and cvs
Fraxinus excelsior and cvs
Fraxinus ornus
Malus (all)
Morus nigra
Populus alba
Prunus (Japanese cherries)
Sorbus aria and cvs
Sorbus hybrida cvs
Sorbus intermedia

SHRUBS

Aucuba japonica and cvs
Berberis (all)
Brachyglottis (all)
Buddleja davidii and cvs
Buxus sempervirens and cvs
Caragana arborescens and cvs
Ceanothus (all)
Cistus (all)
Colutea (all)
Cornus mas and cvs
Cotoneaster (all)
Cytisus nigricans
Deutzia (all)
Dipelta floribunda
Elaeagnus (deciduous species)
Euonymus (all)
Forsythia (all)
Fuchsia (all)
Genista cinerea
Hebe (all)
Hibiscus syriacus and cvs
Hypericum (all)
Laurus nobilis
Ligustrum (all)
Lonicera (all)
Mahonia aquifolium and hybrids

Olearia (all)
Paeonia delavayi and forms
Philadelphus (all)
Phillyrea (all)
Photinia × *fraseri* cvs
Photinia serratifolia
Potentilla (most)
Rhus (most)
Rosa (most)
Rosmarinus (all)
Rubus tricolor
Sambucus (all)
Sarcococca (all)
Spartium junceum
Spiraea japonica and cvs
Spiraea nipponica and forms
Stachyurus (all)
Symphoricarpos
Syringa (all)
Vinca (all)
Weigela (all)
Yucca (all)

CONIFERS

Juniperus communis and cvs
Juniperus × *pfitzeriana* and cvs
Pinus mugo and forms
Pinus nigra
Taxus baccata and cvs
Thuja occidentalis and cvs
Thuja plicata and cvs
Thujopsis dolabrata and cvs

BAMBOOS

Pseudosasa japonica
Sasaella ramosa

TREES and SHRUBS tolerant of both extreme ACIDITY and ALKALINITY

TREES

Betula papyrifera and forms
Betula pendula and cvs
Betula platyphylla and vars
Betula pubescens
Crataegus monogyna and cvs
Fagus sylvatica and cvs
Populus alba
Populus tremula
Quercus cerris
Quercus robur and cvs
Sorbus hybrida
Sorbus intermedia

SHRUBS

Ilex aquifolium and cvs
Ligustrum ovalifolium and cvs
Lycium barbarum
Rhamnus frangula
Salix caprea
Salix cinerea

Sambucus nigra and cvs
Sambucus racemosa and cvs
Viburnum opulus and cvs

CONIFERS

Juniperus communis and cvs
Pinus nigra
Pinus sylvestris and cvs
Taxus baccata and cvs

TREES and SHRUBS suitable for DAMP SITES

TREES

Alnus (all)
Amelanchier (all)
Betula nigra
Betula pendula and cvs
Betula pubescens
Crataegus laevigata and cvs
Magnolia virginiana
Mespilus germanica cvs
Populus (all)
Pterocarya (all)
Pyrus (most)
Quercus palustris
Salix (all)
Sorbus aucuparia and cvs

SHRUBS

Amelanchier (all)
Aronia (all)
Calycanthus floridus
Clethra (all)
Cornus alba and cvs
Cornus sericea and cvs
Gaultheria shallon
Hippophae rhamnoides
Lindera benzoin
Myrica cerifera
Myrica gale
Neillia thibetica
Photinia villosa
Physocarpus opulifolius
  and cvs
Prunus spinosa and cvs
Salix caprea
Salix humilis
Salix purpurea and cvs
Salix repens and cvs
Sambucus (all)
Sorbaria (all)
Spiraea × *vanhouttei*
Spiraea veitchii
Symphoricarpos (all)
Vaccinium (all)
Viburnum opulus and cvs

CONIFERS

Metasequoia glyptostroboides
Picea sitchensis
Taxodium distichum and forms

BAMBOOS

Phyllostachys (all)
Pleioblastus (all)
Pseudosasa japonica
Sasa (all)
Thamnocalamus (all)

TREES and SHRUBS suitable
for INDUSTRIAL AREAS

TREES

Acer (many, but not Japanese maples)
Aesculus (all)
Ailanthus altissima
Alnus cordata
Alnus glutinosa and cvs
Alnus incana and cvs
Amelanchier (all)
Betula papyrifera and forms
Betula pendula and cvs
Betula platyphylla and vars
Betula pubescens
Carpinus betulus and cvs
Catalpa bignonioides and cvs
Crataegus (most)
Davidia involucrata
Eucalyptus (most)
Fagus (all)
Fraxinus (all)
Ilex × altaclerensis and cvs
Ilex aquifolium and cvs
+ *Laburnocytisus adamii*
Laburnum (all)
Ligustrum lucidum and cvs
Liriodendron tulipifera and cvs
Magnolia acuminata
Magnolia denudata
Magnolia kobus
Magnolia × loebneri and cvs
Magnolia × soulangeana and cvs
Malus (all)
Mespilus germanica cvs
Morus nigra
Platanus (all)
Populus (most)
Prunus avium
Prunus cerasifera and cvs
Prunus Japanese cherries
Prunus padus and cvs
Pterocarya (all)
Pyrus (most)
Quercus × hispanica
Quercus ilex
Quercus × turneri 'Pseudoturneri'
Rhus (most)
Robinia pseudoacacia and cvs
Salix (most)
Sorbus aria and cvs
Sorbus aucuparia and cvs
Tilia × euchlora
Tilia × europaea and cvs
Tilia platyphyllos and cvs

SHRUBS

Amelanchier (all)
Aralia elata
Arbutus unedo and cvs
Aucuba japonica and cvs
Berberis (all)
Brachyglottis monroi
Brachyglottis 'Sunshine'
Buddleja davidii and cvs
Buxus sempervirens and cvs
Camellia japonica and cvs
Camellia × williamsii cvs
Ceanothus × delileanus cvs
Ceratostigma willmottianum
Chaenomeles (all)
Cistus (all)
Clethra (all)
Colutea arborescens
Colutea × media
Cornus alba and cvs
Cornus sericea and cvs
Cotoneaster (most)
Cytisus (most)
Daphne mezereum
Deutzia (many)
Elaeagnus × ebbingei and cvs
Elaeagnus pungens and cvs
Escallonia (all)
Euonymus fortunei and cvs
Euonymus japonicus and cvs
Fatsia japonica
Forsythia (all)
Garrya (all)
Gaultheria mucronata and cvs
Genista (all)
Hibiscus sinosyriacus and cvs
Hibiscus syriacus and cvs
Hydrangea macrophylla and cvs
Hypericum (all)
Ilex aquifolium and cvs
Ilex cornuta and hybrids
Kerria japonica and cvs
Leycesteria formosa
Ligustrum japonicum and cvs
Ligustrum ovalifolium
Lonicera pileata
Lycium barbarum
Magnolia grandiflora and cvs
Magnolia × soulangeana and cvs
Magnolia stellata and cvs
Mahonia aquifolium and hybrids
Mahonia japonica
Mahonia lomariifolia
Mahonia × media and cvs
Mahonia repens 'Rotundifolia'
Olearia avicenniifolia
Olearia × haastii
Osmanthus (all)
Philadelphus (all)
Phillyrea (all)
Photinia davidiana
Physocarpus (all)

Prunus laurocerasus and cvs
Pyracantha (all)
Rhododendron Hardy Hybrids
Rhododendron Knap Hill Azaleas
Rhododendron luteum
Rhododendron ponticum
Rhodotypos scandens
Rhus glabra
Rhus typhina
Ribes (all)
Rosa (most)
Salix (most)
Sambucus canadensis 'Maxima'
Sambucus nigra and forms
Sarcococca (many)
Skimmia japonica and cvs
Sorbaria (all)
Spartium junceum
Spiraea (all)
Staphylea (all)
Symphoricarpos (all)
Syringa (all)
Tamarix tetrandra
Ulex (all)
Viburnum (many)
Vinca major and cvs
Vinca minor and cvs
Weigela florida and cvs
Weigela hybrids

CLIMBERS

Ampelopsis (most)
Hedera (all)
Parthenocissus (all)

CONIFERS

Cephalotaxus fortunei and cvs
Cephalotaxus harringtonii
    and forms
Fitzroya cupressoides
Ginkgo biloba
Metasequoia glyptostroboides
    and cvs
Taxus baccata and cvs
Taxus × media and cvs
Torreya californica

TREES and SHRUBS suitable
for COLD EXPOSED AREAS

TREES

Acer pseudoplatanus and cvs
Betula (most)
Crataegus monogyna and cvs
Fagus sylvatica and cvs
Fraxinus excelsior and cvs
Laburnum (all)
Populus × canadensis 'Robusta'
Populus × canadensis 'Serotina'
Populus tremula
Quercus robur and cvs
Sorbus aria and cvs

Sorbus aucuparia and cvs
Sorbus intermedia and cvs
Tilia cordata and cvs

SHRUBS

Arctostaphylos uva-ursi
Calluna vulgaris and cvs
Cornus alba and cvs
Cornus sericea and cvs
Cotinus coggygria and cvs
Elaeagnus commutata
Euonymus fortunei
   and cvs
Gaultheria mucronata and cvs
Gaultheria shallon
Gaultheria × wisleyensis cvs
Hippophae rhamnoides
Hydrangea paniculata
   and cvs
Kalmia angustifolia and cvs
Kalmia latifolia and cvs
Kerria japonica 'Picta'
Lavatera × clementii cvs
Leucothoe fontanesiana
Lonicera pileata and cvs
Mahonia aquifolium
   and cvs
Myrica gale
Pachysandra terminalis
Philadelphus (many)
Pieris floribunda and cvs
Prunus spinosa and cvs
Rhododendron groenlandicum
Rhododendron Hardy Hybrids
Rhododendron ponticum
Rhododendron yakushimanum
Salix (most)
Spiraea (most)
Tamarix (all)
Ulex (all)
Viburnum opulus and cvs

CONIFERS

Chamaecyparis nootkatensis
   and cvs
Chamaecyparis obtusa and cvs
Chamaecyparis pisifera and cvs
Cryptomeria japonica and cvs
Ginkgo biloba
Juniperus communis and cvs
Juniperus × pfitzeriana
   and cvs
Larix decidua
Picea abies and cvs
Pinus banksiana
Pinus nigra and forms
Pinus ponderosa
Pinus sylvestris and cvs
Taxus baccata and cvs
Thuja occidentalis and cvs
Thuja standishii
Tsuga canadensis and cvs

TREES and SHRUBS suitable for SEASIDE AREAS

TREES

Acer pseudoplatanus
Arbutus unedo and cvs
Castanea sativa
Crataegus (all)
Eucalyptus (many)
Fraxinus angustifolia and cvs
Fraxinus excelsior and cvs
Griselinia littoralis
Ilex × altaclerensis and cvs
Ilex aquifolium and cvs
Laurus nobilis and cvs
Phillyrea latifolia and cvs
Populus alba
Populus tremula
Quercus cerris
Quercus ilex
Quercus petraea
Quercus robur
Quercus × turneri 'Pseudoturneri'
Salix (most)
Sorbus aria and cvs
Sorbus aucuparia and cvs

SHRUBS

Atriplex halimus
Brachyglottis (most)
Bupleurum fruticosum
Chamaerops humilis
Choisya (all)
Colutea (all)
Cordyline australis and cvs
Corokia cotoneaster
C. × virgata and cvs
Cotoneaster (many)
Cytisus (many)
Elaeagnus × ebbingei and cvs
Elaeagnus pungens and cvs
Erica arborea 'Alpina'
Erica lusitanica
Erica × veitchii
Escallonia (most)
Euonymus fortunei and cvs
Euonymus japonicus and cvs
Fabiana imbricata 'Prostrata'
Fuchsia magellanica and cvs
Garrya elliptica and cvs
Genista (most)
Halimium (all)
Halimodendron halodendron
Hebe (all)
Helianthemum (most)
Helichrysum (many)
Hippophae rhamnoides
Hydrangea macrophylla and cvs
Ilex aquifolium and cvs
Lavandula (all)
Lavatera × clementii cvs
Leycesteria formosa

Lonicera pileata and cvs
Lycium barbarum
Myrica cerifera
Olearia (most)
Ozothamnus (many)
Parahebe (all)
Phlomis (most)
Phormium (all)
Pittosporum (most)
Prunus spinosa and cvs
Pyracantha (all)
Rhamnus alaternus and cvs
Rosa (many species)
Rosmarinus officinalis and cvs
Salix (many)
Sambucus racemosa and cvs
Santolina (all)
Spartium junceum
Spiraea (many)
Tamarix (all)
Ulex (all)
Viburnum (many) especially
   evergreen spp.
Yucca (all)

CLIMBERS

Fallopia baldschuanica
Muehlenbeckia complexa

CONIFERS

× Cupressocyparis leylandii
Cupressus (many)
Juniperus (most)
Pinus cortorta
Pinus mugo and forms
Pinus muricata
Pinus nigra
Pinus nigra subsp. *laricio*
Pinus pinaster
Pinus pinea
Pinus radiata
Pinus thunbergii
Podocarpus lawrencei
Podocarpus nivalis

BAMBOOS

Pleioblastus (many)
Sasa (all)

SHRUBS suitable for HEAVY SHADE

Arctostaphylos uva-ursi
Aucuba japonica and cvs
Buxus sempervirens and cvs
Camellia japonica and cvs
Camellia × williamsii and cvs
Cornus canadensis
Daphne laureola
Daphne pontica
Elaeagnus (evergreen)
Euonymus fortunei and cvs
× Fatshedera lizei

Fatsia japonica
Gaultheria (all)
Hedera helix 'Arborescens'
Hypericum androsaemum
Hypericum calycinum
Ilex × *altaclerensis* and cvs
Ilex aquifolium and cvs
Leucothoe fontanesiana and cvs
Ligustrum (many)
Lonicera nitida and cvs
Lonicera pileata
Mahonia aquifolium and cvs
Osmanthus decorus
Osmanthus heterophyllus and cvs
Pachysandra terminalis and cvs
Prunus laurocerasus and cvs
Prunus lusitanica and cvs
Rhododendron Hardy Hybrids
Rhododendron ponticum
Rhodotypos scandens
Ribes alpinum
Rubus 'Betty Ashburner'
Rubus odoratus
Rubus tricolor
Ruscus (all)
Sarcococca (all)
Skimmia (all)
Symphoricarpos (all)
Vaccinium vitis-idaea and cvs
Viburnum davidii
Vinca (all)

CONIFERS

Cephalotaxus (all)
Juniperus × *pfitzeriana* 'Wilhelm Pfitzer'
Podocarpus lawrencei
Podocarpus nivalis
Prumnopitys andina
Taxus (all)

BAMBOOS

Phyllostachys (most)
Pleioblastus (most)
Sasa (all)

SHRUBS and CLIMBERS suitable for NORTH- and EAST-FACING WALLS

SHRUBS

Azara microphylla
Azara petiolaris
Berberis × *stenophylla*
Camellia (most – north walls only)
Chaenomeles (most)
Choisya ternata
Crinodendron hookerianum
Crinodendron patagua
Daphne gnidium
Daphne × *hybrida*
Daphne odora

Desfontainia spinosa
Drimys winteri
Eriobotrya japonica
Eucryphia cordifolia
Eucryphia × *intermedia* cvs
Eucryphia × *nymansensis* and cvs
Euonymus fortunei and cvs
Garrya elliptica and cvs
Garrya × *thuretii*
Grevillea rosmarinifolia
Ilex latifolia
Illicium anisatum
Jasminum humile and forms
Jasminum nudiflorum
Kerria japonica and cvs
Lomatia myricoides
Mahonia japonica
Mahonia lomariifolia
Mahonia × *media* and cvs
Mitraria coccinea and forms
Osmanthus yunnanensis
Photinia × *fraseri* and cvs
Photinia serratifolia
Piptanthus nepalensis
Pyracantha (all)
Ribes laurifolium
Rubus lambertianus
Schima argentea
Viburnum foetens
Viburnum grandiflorum

CLIMBERS

Akebia quinata
Celastrus orbiculatus
Hedera (most)
Hydrangea anomala subsp. *petiolaris*
Muehlenbeckia complexa
Parthenocissus (all)
Pileostegia viburnoides
Rubus henryi var. *bambusarum*
Schizophragma hydrangeoides
Schizophragma integrifolium

SHRUBS suitable for GROUND COVER

Arctostaphylos nevadensis
Arctostaphylos uva-ursi
Artemisia 'Powis Castle'
Aucuba japonica 'Nana Rotundifolia'
Berberis tsangpoensis
Berberis wilsoniae
Buxus microphylla
Buxus sempervirens 'Prostrata'
Calluna vulgaris and cvs
Ceanothus 'Blue Cushion'
Ceanothus griseus 'Yankee Point'
Ceanothus 'Pin Cushion'
Ceanothus prostratus
Ceanothus thyrsiflorus var. *repens*
Cornus canadensis
Cornus sericea 'Kelseyi'

Cotoneaster, several, including
Cotoneaster 'Coral Beauty'
Cotoneaster dammeri
Cotoneaster horizontalis
Cotoneaster integrifolius
Cotoneaster nanshan
Cotoneaster radicans
Cotoneaster salicifolius 'Gnom'
Cotoneaster × *suecicus* 'Skogholm'
Cotoneaster 'Valkenburg'
Cytisus × *beanii*
Cytisus scoparius subsp. *maritimus*
Daboecia cantabrica and cvs
Erica (most)
Euonymus fortunei and cvs
Gaultheria (most)
× *Halimiocistus* 'Ingwersenii'
× *Halimiocistus sahucii*
Hebe many, especially
Hebe albicans
Hebe pinguifolia 'Pagei'
Hebe rakaiensis
Hebe 'Youngii'
Hedera (most)
Helianthemum (all)
Hypericum calycinum
Hypericum × *moserianum*
Jasminum nudiflorum
Jasminum parkeri
Leptospermum rupestre
Leucothoe fontanesiana and cvs
Leucothoe keiskii
Lithodora diffusa and cvs
Lonicera pileata
Mahonia aquifolium 'Apollo'
Mahonia nervosa
Mahonia repens
Mitchella repens
Muehlenbeckia (all)
Pachysandra terminalis
Pimelea prostrata
Potentilla fruticosa 'Abbotswood'
Potentilla fruticosa 'Longacre'
Potentilla fruticosa 'Medicine Wheel Mountain'
Prunus laurocerasus 'Green Carpet'
Prunus laurocerasus 'Low 'n' Green'
Prunus laurocerasus 'Mount Vernon'
Rhododendron (many, especially members of the Subsections Lapponica and Saluenensia)
Rhododendron Evergreen Azaleas (most)
Ribes laurifolium
Rosa 'Max Graf'
Rosa nitida
Rosa 'Paulii'
Rosa 'Raubritter'
Rosa wichurana
Rosmarinus officinalis var. *prostratus*
Rubus 'Betty Ashburner'

Rubus pentalobus
Rubus tricolor
Salix, several, including
Salix × *cottetii*
Salix repens and cvs
Salix uva-ursi
Salix yezoalpina
Santolina (all)
Sarcococca hookeriana
  var. *humilis*
Stephanandra incisa 'Crispa'
Symphoricarpos × *chenaultii*
  'Hancock'
Ulex gallii 'Mizen'
Vaccinium, many, especially
Vaccinium delavayi
Vaccinium glaucoalbum
Vaccinium myrtillus
Vaccinium vitis-idaea
Viburnum davidii
Vinca (all)

CONIFERS

Cephalotaxus fortunei 'Prostrate
  Spreader'
Juniperus communis, several forms,
  including *Juniperus communis*
  var. *depressa*
Juniperus communis 'Hornibrookii'
Juniperus communis 'Repanda'
Juniperus 'Grey Owl'
Juniperus horizontalis and cvs
Juniperus × *pfitzeriana* (several cvs)
Juniperus rigida subsp. *conferta*
Juniperus sabina 'Tam no Blight'
Juniperus sabina 'Tamariscifolia'
Juniperus squamata 'Blue Carpet'
Picea abies 'Reflexa'
Pinus strobus 'Prostrata'
Podocarpus lawrencei
Podocarpus nivalis
Taxus baccata 'Repandens'
Taxus baccata 'Repens Aurea'
Tsuga canadensis 'Bennett'
Tsuga canadensis 'Branklyn'

BAMBOOS

Indocalamus tessellatus
Pleioblastus humilis var. *pumilus*
Sasa veitchii
Shibataea kumasaca

TREES of PENDULOUS HABIT

Acer saccharinum Laciniatum Group
Betula pendula 'Dalecarlica'
Betula pendula 'Tristis'
Betula pendula 'Youngii'
Cercidiphyllum japonicum
  'Pendulum'
Crataegus monogyna 'Pendula Rosea'
Fagus sylvatica 'Aurea Pendula'
Fagus sylvatica 'Pendula'

Fagus sylvatica 'Purple Fountain'
Fraxinus excelsior 'Pendula'
Gleditsia triacanthos 'Bujotii'
Malus 'Red Jade'
Malus 'Sun Rival'
Populus tremula 'Pendula'
Prunus pendula 'Pendula Rosea'
Prunus 'Pendula Rubra'
Prunus × *yedoensis* 'Shidare-yoshino'
Pyrus salicifolia 'Pendula'
Quercus robur 'Pendula'
Robinia pseudoacacia 'Rozynskiana'
Salix babylonica 'Pendula'
Salix × *sepulcralis* 'Chrysocoma'
Salix × *sepulcralis* 'Erythroflexuosa'
Sophora japonica 'Pendula'
Tilia tomentosa 'Petiolaris'

The ultimate height of the underlisted
trees is largely dependent on the stem
height at which they are grafted or to
which they are trained.
Caragana arborescens 'Pendula'
Caragana arborescens 'Walker'
Cotoneaster 'Hybridus Pendulus'
Fagus sylvatica 'Purpurea Pendula'
Ilex aquifolium 'Argenteomarginata
  Pendula'
Ilex aquifolium 'Pendula'
Laburnum alpinum 'Pendulum'
Laburnum anagyroides 'Pendulum'
Malus 'Royal Beauty'
Morus alba 'Pendula'
Prunus 'Cheal's Weeping'
Prunus × *yedoensis* 'Ivensii'
Salix caprea 'Kilmarnock'
Salix purpurea 'Pendula'

CONIFERS

Cedrus atlantica 'Glauca Pendula'
Cedrus atlantica 'Pendula'
Chamaecyparis lawsoniana
  'Filiformis'
Chamaecyparis lawsoniana 'Pendula'
Chamaecyparis nootkatensis
  'Pendula'
Cupressus lusitanica 'Glauca
  Pendula'
Fitzroya cupressoides
Lagarostrobus franklinii
Larix decidua 'Pendula'
Larix kaempferi 'Pendula'
Picea abies 'Inversa'
Picea breweriana
Picea omorika 'Pendula'
Picea smithiana
Picea spinulosa
Taxodium distichum 'Pendens'
Taxus baccata 'Dovastoniana'
Taxus baccata 'Dovastonii Aurea'
Tsuga canadensis 'Pendula'
Tsuga heterophylla 'Greenmantle'

TREES and SHRUBS of UPRIGHT or FASTIGIATE HABIT

TREES and SHRUBS

Acer campestre 'William Caldwell'
Acer × *lobelii*
Acer platanoides 'Columnare'
Acer pseudoplatanus 'Erectum'
Acer rubrum 'Scanlon'
Acer saccharinum 'Pyramidale'
Betula pendula 'Fastigiata'
Carpinus betulus 'Fastigiata'
Carpinus betulus 'Frans Fontaine'
Corylus colurna
Crataegus monogyna 'Stricta'
Fagus sylvatica 'Cockleshell'
Fagus sylvatica 'Dawyck'
Fagus sylvatica 'Dawyck Gold'
Fagus sylvatica 'Dawyck Purple'
Ilex aquifolium 'Green Pillar'
Liriodendron tulipifera 'Fastigiatum'
Malus tschonoskii
Malus 'Van Eseltine'
Populus alba 'Pyramidalis'
Populus nigra 'Italica'
Prunus 'Amanogawa'
Prunus lusitanica 'Myrtifolia'
Prunus 'Pandora'
Prunus × *schmittii*
Prunus 'Snow Goose'
Prunus 'Spire'
Prunus 'Sunset Boulevard'
Pyrus calleryana 'Chanticleer'
Quercus castaneifolia 'Green Spire'
Quercus frainetto 'Hungarian
  Crown'
Quercus robur 'Fastigiata Koster'
Quercus robur 'Fastigiata Purpurea'
Quercus × *rosacea* 'Columna'
Robinia pseudoacacia 'Pyramidalis'
Sorbus aucuparia 'Fastigiata'
Sorbus aucuparia 'Sheerwater
  Seedling'
Sorbus commixta
Sorbus 'Joseph Rock'
Sorbus × *thuringiaca* 'Fastigiata'
Tilia cordata 'Greenspire'
Ulmus 'Dodoens'
Ulmus × *hollandica* 'Dampieri Aurea'
Ulmus 'Lobel'
Ulmus 'New Horizon'

CONIFERS

Calocedrus decurrens
Cephalotaxus harringtonii 'Fastigiata'
Chamaecyparis lawsoniana 'Alumii'
Chamaecyparis lawsoniana
  'Columnaris'
Chamaecyparis lawsoniana 'Ellwoodii'
Chamaecyparis lawsoniana 'Erecta'
Chamaecyparis lawsoniana
  'Grayswood Feather'

Chamaecyparis lawsoniana
'Kilmacurragh'
Chamaecyparis lawsoniana
'Pottenii'
Chamaecyparis lawsoniana
'Wisselii'
Chamaecyparis lawsoniana
'Witzeliana'
× *Cupressocyparis leylandii*
and cvs
Cupressus arizonica var. *glabra*
'Pyramidalis'
Cupressus sempervirens and cvs
Ginkgo biloba 'Tremonia'
Juniperus chinensis 'Keteleeri'
Juniperus chinensis 'Pyramidalis'
Juniperus communis 'Compressa'
Juniperus communis 'Hibernica'
Juniperus communis 'Sentinel'
Juniperus drupacea
Juniperus scopulorum 'Skyrocket'
Juniperus virginiana 'Burkii'
Picea omorika
Pinus sylvestris 'Fastigiata'
Taxodium distichum 'Nutans'
Taxus baccata 'Fastigiata'
Taxus baccata 'Fastigiata
Aureomarginata'
Taxus baccata 'Standishii'
Taxus × *media* 'Hicksii'
Thuja occidentalis 'Europa Gold'
Thuja occidentalis 'Fastigiata'
Thuja occidentalis 'Holmstrup'
Thuja occidentalis 'Malonyana'
Thuja occidentalis 'Smaragd'
Thuja plicata 'Fastigiata'
Tsuga heterophylla 'Laursen's
Column'

TREES and SHRUBS with ORNAMENTAL BARK or TWIGS

TREES

Acer capillipes
Acer × *conspicuum* cvs
Acer davidii 'George Forrest'
Acer griseum
Acer grosseri var. *hersii*
Acer negundo var. *violaceum*
Acer palmatum 'Sango-kaku'
Acer pensylvanicum and cvs
Acer tegementosum
Acer 'White Tigress'
Arbutus × *andrachnoides*
Arbutus menziesii
Betula (most)
Carya ovata
Eucalyptus (most)
Fraxinus excelsior 'Jaspidea'
Luma apiculata
Lyonothamnus floribundus subsp.
aspleniifolius

Parrotia persica
Platanus (all)
Prunus maackii
Prunus maackii 'Amber Beauty'
Prunus × *schmittii*
Prunus serrula
Salix acutifolia
Salix acutifolia 'Blue Streak'
Salix alba 'Britzensis'
Salix alba var. *vitellina*
Salix babylonica 'Tortuosa'
Salix daphnoides and cvs
Salix × *sepulcralis* 'Chrysocoma'
Salix × *sepulcralis*
'Erythroflexuosa'
Stewartia (most)
Tilia cordata 'Winter Orange'
Tilia platyphyllos 'Aurea'
Tilia platyphyllos 'Rubra'

SHRUBS

Abelia triflora
Arctostaphylos (most)
Clethra barbinervis
Cornus alba and cvs
Cornus officinalis
Cornus sanguinea 'Winter Flame'
Cornus sericea 'Flaviramea'
Corylus avellana 'Contorta'
Deutzia (several spp.)
Dipelta floribunda
Euonymus alatus and cvs
Euonymus phellomanus
Hydrangea aspera and forms
Hydrangea heteromalla
'Bretschneideri'
Jasminum nudiflorum
Kerria japonica and cvs
Leucothoe grayana
Leycesteria formosa
Philadelphus (several)
Rhododendron
Rhododendron barbatum
Rhododendron thomsonii
Rosa sericea f. *pteracantha*
Rosa virginiana
Rubus biflorus
Rubus cockburnianus
Rubus phoenicolasius
Rubus thibetanus
Salix irrorata
Salix moupinensis
Stephanandra tanakae
Vaccinium corymbosum

CONIFERS

Abies squamata
Cryptomeria japonica
Pinus bungeana
Pinus sylvestris
Sequoia sempervirens
Sequoiadendron giganteum

TREES and SHRUBS with BOLD FOLIAGE

TREES

Acer japonicum 'Vitifolium'
Acer macrophyllum
Ailanthus altissima
Aralia (all)
Catalpa (all)
Cordyline australis and cvs
Gymnocladus dioica
Idesia polycarpa
Juglans cinerea
Kalopanax pictus
Magnolia hypoleuca
Magnolia macrophylla
Magnolia officinalis var. *biloba*
Magnolia tripetala
Meliosma veitchiorum
Paulownia (all)
Platanus (all)
Populus lasiocarpa
Populus szechuanica var. *tibetica*
Populus wilsonii
Pterocarya (all)
Quercus dentata
Quercus frainetto 'Hungarian Crown'
Quercus macrocarpa
Quercus pontica
Quercus velutina 'Rubrifolia'
Sorbus insignis
Sorbus thibetica 'John Mitchell'
Sorbus vestita
Tilia americana 'Redmond'
Tilia × *moltkei*
Toona sinensis
Trachycarpus fortunei

SHRUBS

Aralia (all)
Chamaerops humilis
Eriobotrya japonica
× *Fatshedera lizei*
Fatsia japonica
Hydrangea aspera subsp. *sargentiana*
Hydrangea quercifolia and cvs
Ilex × *koehneana* and cvs
Ilex latifolia
Magnolia delavayi
Magnolia grandiflora and cvs
Mahonia acanthifolia
Mahonia japonica
Mahonia lomariifolia
Mahonia × *media* and cvs
Melianthus major
Metapanax davidii
Osmanthus armatus
Osmanthus yunnanensis
Phormium (all)
Rhododendron, several including
Rhododendron grande
Rhododendron macabeanum

Rhododendron rex and forms
Rhododendron sinogrande
Sambucus canadensis 'Maxima'
Sorbaria (all)
Tetrapanax papyrifer
Viburnum rhytidophyllum
Yucca gloriosa
Yucca recurvifolia

CLIMBERS

Actinidia deliciosa
Ampelopsis megalophylla
Aristolochia macrophylla
Hedera algeriensis and cvs
Hedera colchica and cvs
Holboellia latifolia
Vitis amurensis
Vitis coignetiae

BAMBOOS

Indocalamus tessellatus

TREES and SHRUBS for AUTUMN COLOUR

TREES

Acer, many, especially
Acer capillipes
Acer davidii and cvs
Acer × freemanii cvs
Acer griseum
Acer maximowiczianum
Acer platanoides and cvs
Acer rubrum and cvs
Acer triflorum
Aesculus, several, including
Aesculus 'Dallimorei'
Aesculus glabra
Aesculus × neglecta
Amelanchier laevis
Amelanchier lamarckii
Betula (most)
Carpinus (all)
Carya (all)
Cercidiphyllum japonicum
Cercis canadensis
Cladrastis (all)
Cornus controversa
Crataegus, many, especially
Crataegus crus-galli
Crataegus pinnatifida var. *major*
Crataegus persimilis 'Prunifolia'
Fagus (most)
Fraxinus angustifolia 'Raywood'
Fraxinus excelsior 'Jaspidea'
Gymnocladus dioica
Liquidambar (all)
Malus, several, including,
Malus coronaria 'Charlottae'
Malus transitoria
Malus trilobata
Malus tschonoskii

Malus yunnanensis var. *veitchii*
Nothofagus antarctica
Nyssa (all)
Parrotia persica
Phellodendron (all)
Photinia beauverdiana
Photinia villosa
Picrasma quassioides
Populus, several, including
Populus alba
Populus × canadensis 'Serotina Aurea'
Populus canescens 'Macrophylla'
Populus tremula
Populus trichocarpa
Prunus, many, including
Prunus 'Hillieri'
Prunus × juddii
Prunus sargentii
Prunus verecunda 'Autumn Glory'
Quercus, many, including
Quercus coccinea 'Splendens'
Quercus palustris
Quercus phellos
Quercus rubra
Rhus trichocarpa
Sassafras albidum
Sorbus, many, including
Sorbus alnifolia
Sorbus americana
Sorbus commixta
Sorbus commixta 'Embley'
Sorbus 'Joseph Rock'
Sorbus scalaris
Stewartia (all)
Toona sinensis

SHRUBS

Acer, many, especially
Acer japonicum and cvs
Acer palmatum and cvs
Acer tataricum subsp. *ginnala*
Aesculus parviflora
Amelanchier canadensis
Aronia (all)
Berberis, many, including
Berberis aggregata
Berberis dictyophylla
Berberis × media 'Parkjuweel'
Berberis morrisonensis
Berberis thunbergii and cvs
Berberis wilsoniae
Callicarpa (all)
Ceratostigma willmottianum
Clethra (all)
Cornus alba and cvs
Cornus 'Eddie's White Wonder'
Cornus florida and cvs
Cornus officinalis
Corylopsis (all)
Cotinus (all)
Cotoneaster, many, including
Cotoneaster bullatus

Cotoneaster divaricatus
Cotoneaster horizontalis
Cotoneaster nanshan
Cotoneaster splendens
Disanthus cercidifolius
Enkianthus (all)
Eucryphia glutinosa
Euonymus, many, including
Euonymus alatus and cvs
Euonymus europaeus and cvs
Euonymus latifolius
Euonymus oxyphyllus
Euonymus planipes
Fothergilla (all)
Hamamelis (all)
Hydrangea 'Preziosa'
Hydrangea quercifolia
    and cvs
Lindera (most)
Prunus, several, including
Prunus incisa
Prunus pumila var. *depressa*
Ptelea trifoliata
Rhododendron several Azaleas
    including
Rhododendron arborescens
Rhododendron calendulaceum
Rhododendron 'Coccineum
    Speciosum'
Rhododendron 'Corneille'
Rhododendron luteum
Rhododendron 'Nancy Waterer'
Rhododendron quinquefolium
Rhus, several, especially
Rhus copallina
Rhus glabra
Rhus × pulvinata 'Red Autumn
    Lace'
Rhus typhina and cvs
Ribes odoratum
Rosa nitida
Rosa rugosa and cvs
Rosa virginiana
Sorbaria aitchisonii
Spiraea thunbergii
Stephanandra (all)
Vaccinium several,
Vaccinium corymbosum
Vaccinium praestans
Viburnum, many, including
Viburnum carlesii and cvs
Viburnum furcatum
Viburnum × hillieri 'Winton'
Viburnum opulus and cvs
Viburnum plicatum cvs
Zanthoxylum piperitum

CLIMBERS

Ampelopsis (all)
Celastrus (all)
Parthenocissus (all)
Vitis (all)

CONIFERS

Ginkgo biloba
Larix (all)
Metasequoia glyptostroboides and cvs
Pseudolarix amabilis
Taxodium (all)

TREES and SHRUBS with RED or PURPLE FOLIAGE

TREES

Acer campestre 'Schwerinii'
Acer platanoides 'Crimson King'
Acer platanoides 'Deborah'
Acer platanoides 'Schwedleri'
Betula pendula 'Purpurea'
Catalpa × erubescens 'Purpurea'
Cercidiphyllum japonicum 'Rotfuchs'
Cordyline australis (several cvs)
Fagus sylvatica 'Dawyck Purple'
Fagus sylvatica Purpurea Group
Fagus sylvatica 'Purple Fountain''
Fagus sylvatica 'Riversii'
Fagus sylvatica 'Rohanii'
Fagus sylvatica 'Roseomarginata'
Malus 'Lemoinei'
Malus 'Liset'
Malus 'Profusion'
Malus × purpurea
Malus 'Red Profusion'
Malus 'Royal Beauty'
Malus 'Royalty'
Malus 'Rudolph'
Prunus × blireana
Prunus cerasifera 'Nigra'
Prunus cerasifera 'Pissardii'
Prunus cerasifera 'Rosea'
Prunus padus 'Colorata'
Prunus 'Royal Burgundy'
Prunus virginiana 'Schubert'
Quercus petraea 'Purpurea'
Quercus robur 'Atropurpurea'

SHRUBS

Acer palmatum, many, including
Acer palmatum Atropurpureum Group
Acer palmatum 'Bloodgood'
Acer palmatum 'Crimson Queen'
Acer palmatum 'Dissectum
    Atropurpureum'
Acer palmatum 'Hessei'
Acer palmatum 'Linearilobum
    Atropurpureum'
Acer palmatum 'Red Pygmy'
Acer palmatum 'Trompenburg'
Berberis × ottawensis 'Superba'
Berberis thunbergii Atropurpurea
    Group
Berberis thunbergii 'Atropurpurea
    Nana'
Berberis thunbergii 'Bagatelle'
Berberis thunbergii 'Harlequin'

Berberis thunbergii 'Helmond Pillar'
Berberis thunbergii 'Pink Queen'
Berberis thunbergii 'Red Chief'
Berberis thunbergii 'Red Pillar'
Berberis thunbergii 'Rose Glow'
Cercis canadensis 'Forest Pansy'
Corylopsis sinensis Willmottiae Group
    'Spring Purple'
Corylus maxima 'Purpurea'
Cotinus coggygria 'Royal Purple'
Cotinus coggygria 'Velvet Cloak'
Cotinus 'Grace'
Phormium tenax 'Purpureum Group
    and others
Physocarpus opulifolius 'Diabolo'
Pittosporum tenuifolium 'Purpureum'
Pittosporum tenuifolium 'Tom
    Thumb'
Prunus × cistena
Salvia officinalis 'Purpurascens'
Sambucus nigra Black Beauty
Sambucus nigra 'Guincho Purple'
Sambucus nigra 'Thundercloud'
Weigela florida 'Foliis Purpureis'
Weigela 'Victoria'
Weigela 'Wine and Roses'

CLIMBERS

Vitis vinifera 'Purpurea'

TREES and SHRUBS with GOLDEN or YELLOW FOLIAGE

TREES

Acer cappadocicum 'Aureum'
Acer negundo 'Auratum'
Acer negundo 'Kelly's Gold'
Acer platanoides Princeton Gold
Acer pseudoplatanus 'Worley'
Alnus incana 'Aurea'
Catalpa bignonioides 'Aurea'
Fagus sylvatica 'Aurea Pendula'
Fagus sylvatica 'Zlatia'
Gleditsia triacanthos 'Sunburst'
Ilex aquifolium 'Flavescens'
Laurus nobilis 'Aurea'
Liquidambar styraciflua 'Moonbeam'
Populus alba 'Richardii'
Populus × canadensis 'Serotina Aurea'
Quercus robur 'Concordia'
Quercus rubra 'Aurea'
Robinia pseudoacacia 'Frisia'
Sorbus aria 'Chrysophylla'
Tilia × europaea 'Wratislaviensis'
Ulmus × hollandica 'Dampieri Aurea'

SHRUBS

Acer shirasawanum 'Aureum'
Berberis thunbergii 'Aurea'
Berberis thunbergii Bonanza Gold
Calluna vulgaris 'Beoley Gold'
Calluna vulgaris 'Gold Haze'

Calluna vulgaris 'Golden Carpet'
Calluna vulgaris 'Golden Feather'
Calluna vulgaris 'Guinea Gold'
Calluna vulgaris 'Joy Vanstone'
Calluna vulgaris 'Orange Queen'
Calluna vulgaris 'Robert Chapman'
Calluna vulgaris 'Sir John Charrington'
Choisya Goldfingers
Choisya ternata Sundance
Cornus alba 'Aurea'
Cornus mas 'Aurea'
Corylus avellana 'Aurea'
Cotinus coggygria Golden Spirit
Erica carnea 'Ann Sparkes'
Erica carnea 'Aurea'
Erica carnea 'Foxhollow'
Erica cinerea 'Golden Drop'
Erica cinerea 'Golden Hue'
Erica × darleyensis 'Jack H.
    Brummage'
Erica vagans 'Valerie Proudley'
Escallonia laevis 'Gold Brian'
Fuchsia 'Genii'
Fuchsia magellanica 'Aurea'
Ilex aquifolium 'Flavescens'
Ligustrum ovalifolium 'Aureum'
Ligustrum 'Vicaryi'
Lonicera nitida 'Baggesen's Gold'
Philadelphus coronarius 'Aureus'
Physocarpus opulifolius 'Dart's Gold'
Pittosporum tenuifolium 'Warnham
    Gold'
Ptelea trifoliata 'Aurea'
Ribes alpinum 'Aureum'
Ribes sanguineum 'Brocklebankii'
Rubus cockburnianus Goldenvale
Sambucus canadensis 'Aurea'
Sambucus nigra 'Aurea'
Sambucus racemosa 'Plumosa Aurea'
Sambucus racemosa 'Sutherland Gold'
Spiraea japonica 'Candlelight'
Spiraea japonica 'Golden Princess'
Viburnum opulus 'Aureum'
Weigela Briant Rubidor
Weigela 'Looymansii Aurea'

CLIMBERS

Hedera helix 'Buttercup'
Humulus lupulus 'Aureus'
Jasminum officinale Fiona Sunrise

CONIFERS

Abies nordmanniana 'Golden
    Spreader'
Calocedrus decurrens 'Berrima Gold'
Cedrus atlantica 'Aurea'
Cedrus deodara 'Aurea'
Cedrus deodara 'Aurea Pendula'
Chamaecyparis lawsoniana, many cvs,
    including
Chamaecyparis lawsoniana 'Aurea
    Densa'

Chamaecyparis lawsoniana 'Lanei Aurea'
Chamaecyparis lawsoniana 'Lutea'
Chamaecyparis lawsoniana 'Lutea Nana'
Chamaecyparis lawsoniana 'Minima Aurea'
Chamaecyparis lawsoniana 'Stardust'
Chamaecyparis lawsoniana 'Stewartii'
Chamaecyparis lawsoniana 'Winston Churchill'
Chamaecyparis obtusa, several cvs, including
Chamaecyparis obtusa 'Crippsii'
Chamaecyparis obtusa 'Fernspray Gold'
Chamaecyparis obtusa 'Nana Aurea'
Chamaecyparis obtusa 'Tetragona Aurea'
Chamaecyparis pisifera, several cvs, including
Chamaecyparis pisifera 'Filifera Aurea'
Chamaecyparis pisifera 'Gold Spangle'
Chamaecyparis pisifera 'Golden Mop'
Chamaecyparis pisifera 'Plumosa Aurea'
Cryptomeria japonica 'Sekkan-sugi'
× *Cupressocyparis leylandii* 'Castlewellan'
× *Cupressocyparis leylandii* 'Gold Rider'
× *Cupressocyparis leylandii* 'Robinson's Gold'
Cupressus macrocarpa, several cvs, especially
Cupressus macrocarpa 'Gold Pillar'
Cupressus macrocarpa 'Goldcrest'
Cupressus sempervirens 'Swanes Golden'
Juniperus chinensis 'Aurea'
Juniperus chinensis 'Plumosa Aurea'
Juniperus communis 'Depressa Aurea'
Juniperus × *pfitzeriana*, several, including
Juniperus × *pfitzeriana* 'Gold Coast'
Juniperus × *pfitzeriana* 'Mordigan Gold'
Juniperus × *pfitzeriana* 'Old Gold'
Juniperus × *pfitzeriana* 'Pfitzeriana Aurea'
Juniperus × *pfitzeriana* 'Saybrook Gold'
Metasequoia glyptostroboides 'Gold Rush'
Picea orientalis 'Aurea'
Pinus sylvestris 'Aurea'
Platycladus orientalis, several cvs, especially
Platycladus orientalis 'Aurea Nana'
Taxus baccata, several cvs, including
Taxus baccata 'Adpressa Variegata'
Taxus baccata 'Dovastonii Aurea'

Taxus baccata 'Elegantissima'
Taxus baccata 'Standishii'
Taxus baccata 'Summergold'
Thuja occidentalis 'Europa Gold'
Thuja occidentalis 'Rheingold'
Thuja plicata 'Aurea'
Thujopsis dolabrata 'Aurea'

TREES and SHRUBS with GREY or SILVER FOLIAGE

TREES
Eucalyptus, many, including
Eucalyptus coccifera
Eucalyptus gunnii
Eucalyptus pauciflora subsp. *niphophila*
Populus alba
Populus × *canescens*
Pyrus, several, especially
Pyrus nivalis
Pyrus salicifolia 'Pendula'
Salix alba var. *sericea*
Sorbus aria 'Lutescens'
Sorbus thibetica 'John Mitchell'

SHRUBS
Artemisia (all)
Atriplex halimus
Berberis dictyophylla
Berberis temolaica
Brachyglottis 'Sunshine'
Buddleja alternifolia 'Argentea'
Buddleja fallowiana
Calluna vulgaris 'Silver Queen'
Calluna vulgaris 'Sister Anne'
Caryopteris × *clandonensis* cvs
Cistus × *argenteus* 'Peggy Sammons'
Cistus × *argenteus* 'Silver Pink'
Convolvulus cneorum
Cytisus battandieri
Elaeagnus angustifolia
Elaeagnus commutata
Elaeagnus macrophylla
Elaeagnus 'Quicksilver'
Erica tetralix 'Alba Mollis'
Euryops acraeus
Euryops pectinatus
Feijoa sellowiana
× *Halimiocistus wintonensis*
Halimium lasianthum
Halimium ocymoides
Halimodendron halodendron
Hebe, several, including
Hebe albicans
Hebe colensoi 'Glauca'
Hebe pimeleoides 'Quicksilver'
Hebe pinguifolia 'Pagei'
Helianthemum 'Rhodanthe Carneum'
Helianthemum 'Wisley Pink'
Helianthemum 'Wisley White'
Helichrysum (all)

Hippophae rhamnoides
Lavandula (many)
Leptospermum lanigerum
Lotus hirsutus
Olearia, several, including
Olearia × *mollis*
Olearia moschata
Olearia × *scilloniensis*
Ozothamnus leptophyllus Albidus Group
Perovskia atriplicifolia 'Blue Spire'
Pittosporum tenuifolium 'James Stirling'
Potentilla fruticosa 'Beesii'
Potentilla fruticosa 'Manchu'
Potentilla fruticosa 'Silver Schilling'
Potentilla fruticosa 'Vilmoriniana'
Romneya coulteri
Rosa glauca
Ruta graveolens and cvs
Salix elaeagnos subsp. *angustifolia*
Salix exigua
Salix gracilistyla
Salix lanata
Salix repens var. *argentea*
Salvia officinalis
Santolina chamaecyparissus
Santolina pinnata subsp. *neapolitana*
Teucrium fruticans and cvs
Zauschneria californica 'Olbrich Silver'
Zauschneria californica 'Western Hills'
Zauschneria cana

CONIFERS
Abies concolor 'Candicans'
Abies concolor 'Compacta'
Abies lasiocarpa var. *arizonica*
Abies magnifica 'Glauca'
Abies pinsapo 'Glauca'
Cedrus atlantica Glauca Group and forms
Chamaecyparis lawsoniana, many cvs, including
Chamaecyparis lawsoniana 'Columnaris'
Chamaecyparis lawsoniana 'Ellwoodii'
Chamaecyparis lawsoniana 'Fletcheri'
Chamaecyparis lawsoniana 'Pembury Blue'
Chamaecyparis lawsoniana 'Triomf van Boskoop'
Chamaecyparis lawsoniana 'Van Pelt'
Chamaecyparis pisifera 'Boulevard'
Chamaecyparis pisifera 'Squarrosa'
Cupressus arizonica var. *glabra* 'Pyramidalis'
Cupressus cashmeriana
Cupressus lusitanica 'Glauca Pendula'

Juniperus chinensis (several cvs)
Juniperus 'Grey Owl'
Juniperus horizontalis 'Bar Harbor'
Juniperus horizontalis 'Wiltonii'
Juniperus × *pfitzeriana* 'Pfitzeriana Compacta'
Juniperus procumbens
Juniperus sabina 'Hicksii'
Juniperus scopulorum 'Blue Heaven'
Juniperus scopulorum 'Skyrocket'
Juniperus scopulorum 'Springbank'
Juniperus squamata 'Blue Carpet'
Juniperus squamata 'Blue Star'
Juniperus squamata 'Meyeri'
Juniperus virginiana 'Glauca'
Picea glauca
Picea pungens Glauca Group and cvs
Pinus koraiensis 'Glauca Compacta'
Pinus parviflora 'Glauca'
Pinus pumila 'Compacta'
Pinus sylvestris 'Edwin Hillier'
Pinus wallichiana
Pseudotsuga menziesii var. *glauca*
Tsuga mertensiana f. *argentea*

CLIMBERS
Lonicera caprifolium and cvs
Vitis vinifera 'Incana'

TREES and SHRUBS with VARIEGATED FOLIAGE

TREES
Acer negundo 'Elegans'
Acer negundo 'Flamingo'
Acer negundo 'Variegatum'
Acer platanoides 'Drummondii'
Acer pseudoplatanus 'Leopoldii'
Acer pseudoplatanus 'Nizetii'
Acer 'Silver Cardinal'
Castanea sativa 'Albomarginata'
Cornus controversa 'Variegata'
Crataegus monogyna 'Variegata'
Fagus sylvatica 'Albovariegata'
Fraxinus pennsylvanica 'Variegata'
Ilex × *altaclerensis* 'Belgica Aurea'
Ilex × *altaclerensis* 'Golden King'
Ligustrum lucidum 'Excelsum Superbum'
Ligustrum lucidum 'Tricolor'
Liquidambar styraciflua 'Silver King'
Liquidambar styraciflua 'Variegata'
Liriodendron tulipifera 'Aureomarginatum'
Platanus × *hispanica* 'Suttneri'
Populus × *candicans* 'Aurora'
Quercus cerris 'Argenteovariegata'
Quercus robur 'Variegata'

SHRUBS
Abelia × *grandiflora* Hopleys
Abutilon megapotamicum 'Variegatum'

Acca sellowiana 'Variegata'
Acer campestre 'Carnival'
Acer palmatum, several cvs, especially
Acer palmatum 'Butterfly'
Acer palmatum 'Kagiri-nishiki'
Acer palmatum 'Ukigumo'
Acer pseudoplatanus 'Esk Sunset'
Aralia elata 'Aureovariegata'
Aralia elata 'Variegata'
Aucuba japonica, several cvs, especially:
Aucuba japonica 'Crotonifolia'
Aucuba japonica 'Gold Dust'
Aucuba japonica 'Golden King'
Aucuba japonica 'Variegata'
Azara integrifolia 'Variegata'
Azara microphylla 'Variegata'
Berberis thunbergii 'Rose Glow'
Berberis thunbergii 'Pink Queen'
Buddleja davidii 'Harlequin'
Buxus sempervirens 'Elegantissima'
Buxus sempervirens 'Latifolia Maculata'
Clerodendrum trichotomum 'Carnival'
Cleyera japonica 'Tricolor'
Cordyline australis 'Torbay Dazzler'
Cornus alba 'Elegantissima'
Cornus alba 'Sibirica Variegata'
Cornus alba 'Spaethii'
Cornus alba 'Variegata'
Cornus alternifolia 'Argentea'
Cornus florida 'Rainbow'
Cornus florida 'Welchii'
Cornus mas 'Aurea Elegantissima'
Cornus mas 'Variegata'
Cornus sericea 'White Gold'
Coronilla valentina 'Variegata'
Cotoneaster atropurpureus 'Variegatus'
Crataegus laevigata 'Gireoudii'
Daphne × *burkwoodii* 'Carol Mackie'
Daphne cneorum 'Variegata'
Daphne longilobata 'Peter Moore'
Daphne odora 'Aureomarginata'
Elaeagnus × *ebbingei* 'Gilt Edge'
Elaeagnus × *ebbingei* 'Gold Coast'
Elaeagnus × *ebbingei* 'Limelight'
Elaeagnus pungens 'Dicksonii'
Elaeagnus pungens 'Frederici'
Elaeagnus pungens 'Goldrim'
Elaeagnus pungens 'Maculata'
Elaeagnus pungens 'Variegata'
Euonymus fortunei 'Emerald Gaiety'
Euonymus fortunei 'Emerald 'n' Gold'
Euonymus fortunei 'Silver Pillar'
Euonymus fortunei 'Silver Queen'
Euonymus fortunei 'Variegatus'
Euonymus japonicus 'Aureus'
Euonymus japonicus 'Chollipo'
Euonymus japonicus 'Latifolius Albomarginatus'

Euonymus japonicus 'Microphyllus Pulchellus'
Euonymus japonicus 'Microphyllus Variegatus'
Euonymus japonicus 'Ovatus Aureus'
× *Fatshedera lizei* 'Annemieke'
× *Fatshedera lizei* 'Variegata'
Fatsia japonica 'Variegata'
Forsythia 'Fiesta'
Forsythia 'Golden Times'
Fuchsia magellanica 'Sharpitor'
Fuchsia magellanica 'Variegata'
Fuchsia magellanica 'Versicolor'
Fuchsia 'Sunray'
Fuchsia 'Tom West'
Griselinia littoralis 'Dixon's Cream'
Griselinia littoralis 'Variegata'
Hebe × *andersonii* 'Variegata'
Hebe 'Dazzler'
Hebe × *franciscana* 'Variegata'
Hebe 'Glaucophylla Variegata'
Hebe 'Pink Elephant'
Hebe 'Purple Tips'
Hedera helix 'Little Diamond'
Hoheria populnea 'Alba Variegata'
Hydrangea macrophylla 'Quadricolor'
Hypericum × *moserianum* 'Tricolor'
Ilex aquifolium 'Argenteomarginata'
Ilex aquifolium 'Golden Milkboy'
Ilex aquifolium 'Golden Queen'
Ilex aquifolium 'Handsworth New Silver'
Ilex aquifolium 'Ovata Aurea'
Ilex aquifolium 'Silver Milkmaid'
Kerria japonica 'Picta'
Leucothoe fontanesiana 'Rainbow'
Ligustrum sinense 'Variegatum'
Luma apiculata 'Glanleam Gold'
Myrtus communis 'Variegata'
Osmanthus heterophyllus 'Aureomarginatus'
Osmanthus heterophyllus 'Goshiki'
Osmanthus heterophyllus 'Latifolius Variegatus'
Osmanthus heterophyllus 'Variegatus'
Pachysandra terminalis 'Variegata'
Philadelphus coronarius 'Variegatus'
Phormium (many)
Photinia davidiana 'Palette'
Pieris 'Flaming Silver'
Pieris japonica 'Little Heath'
Pieris japonica 'Variegata'
Pieris japonica 'White Rim'
Pittosporum eugenioides 'Variegatum'
Pittosporum 'Garnettii'
Pittosporum tenuifolium 'Irene Paterson'
Pittosporum tenuifolium 'Silver Queen'
Pittosporum tenuifolium 'Variegatum'
Pittosporum tobira 'Variegatum'

Prunus laurocerasus 'Castlewellan'
Prunus lusitanica 'Variegata'
Rhamnus alaternus
  'Argenteovariegata'
Rhododendron ponticum 'Variegatum'
Rhododendron 'President Roosevelt'
Rubus microphyllus 'Variegatus'
Salvia officinalis 'Icterina'
Salvia officinalis 'Tricolor'
Sambucus nigra 'Aureomarginata'
Sambucus nigra 'Madonna'
Sambucus nigra 'Pulverulenta'
Symphoricarpos orbiculatus
  'Variegatus'
Viburnum tinus 'Variegatum'
Vinca major 'Variegata'
Vinca minor 'Argenteovariegata'
Vinca minor 'Illumination'
Weigela 'Florida Variegata'
Weigela 'Kosteriana Variegata'
Weigela 'Praecox Variegata'
Yucca filamentosa 'Bright Edge'
Yucca filamentosa 'Variegata'
Yucca flaccida 'Golden Sword'
Yucca gloriosa 'Variegata'

CONIFERS

Calocedrus decurrens
  'Aureovariegata'
Chamaecyparis lawsoniana 'Pygmaea
  Argentea'
Chamaecyparis lawsoniana 'White
  Spot'
Chamaecyparis nootkatensis
  'Aureovariegata'
Chamaecyparis pisifera 'Nana
  Aureovariegata'
Chamaecyparis pisifera 'Snow'
× Cupressocyparis leylandii 'Silver
  Dust'
Thuja plicata 'Irish Gold'
Thuja plicata 'Zebrina'

CLIMBERS

Actinidia kolomikta
Actinidia pilosula
Ampelopsis brevipedunculata
  'Elegans'
Hedera algeriensis 'Gloire de
  Marengo'
Hedera algeriensis
  'Marginomaculata'
Hedera colchica 'Dentata Variegata'
Hedera colchica 'Sulphur Heart'
Hedera helix 'Adam'
Hedera helix 'Caecilia'
Hedera helix 'Cavendishii'
Hedera helix 'Eva'
Hedera helix 'Glacier'
Hedera helix 'Goldchild'
Hedera helix 'Golden Ingot'
Hedera helix 'Goldheart'

Hedera helix 'Harald'
Hedera helix 'Kolibri'
Hedera helix 'Luzii'
Hedera helix 'Marginata'
Hedera helix 'Midas Touch'
Hedera helix 'Sagittifolia Variegata'
Jasminum officinale
  'Argenteovariegatum'
Jasminum officinale 'Aureum'
Kadsura japonica 'Variegata'
Lonicera japonica 'Aureoreticulata'
Trachelospermum jasminoides
  'Variegatum'

BAMBOOS

Pleioblastus auricomus
Pleioblastus variegatus
Sasa veitchii

TREES and SHRUBS bearing ORNAMENTAL FRUIT

TREES

Ailanthus altissima
Arbutus unedo
Catalpa bignonioides
Cercis siliquastrum
Crataegus laciniata
Crataegus × lavalleei
Crataegus mollis
Crataegus × persimilis 'Prunifolia'
Diospyros kaki
Fraxinus ornus
Halesia (all)
Ilex (most females), including
Ilex aquifolium 'Amber'
Ilex aquifolium 'Bacciflava'
Ilex aquifolium 'Pyramidalis'
Ilex aquifolium 'Pyramidalis
  Fructu-luteo'
Koelreuteria paniculata
Magnolia campbellii subsp.
  mollicomata
Magnolia obovata
Magnolia officinalis var. biloba
Magnolia tripetala
Malus 'Butterball'
Malus 'Crittenden'
Malus 'Evereste'
Malus 'Golden Hornet'
Malus 'Gorgeous'
Malus hupehensis
Malus 'John Downie'
Malus 'Red Jade'
Malus 'Red Sentinel'
Malus transitoria
Pterocarya (all)
Sorbus aucuparia and cvs
Sorbus commixta
Sorbus 'Joseph Rock'
Sorbus 'Kewensis'
Sorbus scalaris

Sorbus vilmorinii
Sorbus 'Winter Cheer'
Tetradium daniellii

SHRUBS

Aucuba japonica (female cvs)
Berberis (most, especially deciduous)
Callicarpa (all)
Chaenomeles (most)
× Citrofortunella microcarpa
Citrus (most)
Clerodendrum trichotomum
Colutea (all)
Coriaria (all)
Cornus, many, especially
Cornus amomum
Cornus mas
Cornus mas 'Variegata'
Cornus 'Porlock'
Cotinus (all)
Cotoneaster (all)
Daphne mezereum
Daphne tangutica
Decaisnea fargesii
Euonymus europaeus 'Red Cascade'
Euonymus hamiltonianus 'Coral
  Charm'
Euonymus latifolius
Euonymus oxyphyllus
Euonymus planipes
Gaultheria cuneata
Gaultheria forrestii
Gaultheria miqueliana
Gaultheria procumbens
Gaultheria mucronata and cvs
Hippophae rhamnoides
Ilex cornuta 'Burfordii'
Leycesteria formosa
Mahonia aquifolium
Mahonia japonica
Mahonia lomariifolia
Mespilus germanica cvs
Myrica pennsylvanica
Photinia davidiana and forms
Poncirus trifoliata
Prunus laurocerasus and cvs
Ptelea trifoliata
Pyracantha (all)
Rosa 'Arthur Hillier'
Rosa glauca
Rosa 'Highdownensis'
Rosa macrophylla and cvs
Rosa moyesii and forms
Rosa rugosa and cvs
Rosa webbiana
Rubus phoenicolasius
Ruscus aculeatus
Sambucus (most)
Skimmia japonica (female forms)
Staphylea (all)
Symphoricarpos (most)
Symplocos paniculata

Vaccinium corymbosum and cvs
Vaccinium cylindraceum
Vaccinium vitis-idaea
Viburnum betulifolium
Viburnum davidii
Viburnum opulus and cvs
Viburnum setigerum
Viburnum wrightii 'Hessei'

CLIMBERS

Actinidia deliciosa
Akebia quinata
Akebia trifoliata
Ampelopsis brevipedunculata
Billardiera longiflora
Celastrus (all)
Clematis, several, especially
Clematis tangutica
Clematis tibetana subsp. vernayi
Parthenocissus himalayana
Passiflora caerulea
Passiflora edulis
Schisandra (all)
Stauntonia hexaphylla
Vitis 'Brant'

CONIFERS

Abies forrestii
Abies koreana
Abies procera
Picea abies 'Acrocona'
Picea likiangensis
Picea purpurea
Picea smithiana
Pinus ayacahuite
Pinus wallichiana
Taxus baccata 'Lutea'

TREES and SHRUBS with FRAGRANT or SCENTED FLOWERS

The scents of flowers are a wonderful part of garden enjoyment as well as being a delightful extra attraction in a flowering plant. Just as a sense of smell differs from person to person, so scents vary from flower to flower. Siting a plant is important so that its scent is not lost to the wind. Even if the position is right, weather conditions can make all the difference to the strength or carrying power of delicate scents.

TREES

Acacia dealbata
Aesculus hippocastanum
Azara microphylla
Cladrastis lutea
Cladrastis sinensis
Crataegus monogyna
Drimys winteri
Eucryphia × intermedia 'Rostrevor'

Eucryphia lucida
Fraxinus sieboldiana
Gordonia axillaris
Laburnum alpinum
Laburnum × watereri 'Vossii'
Luma apiculata
Magnolia fraseri
Magnolia grandiflora and cvs
Magnolia kobus
Magnolia macrophylla
Magnolia obovata
Magnolia salicifolia
Malus baccata var. mandshurica
Malus coronaria 'Charlottae'
Malus floribunda
Malus 'Hillieri'
Malus hupehensis
Malus 'Profusion'
Malus × robusta
Michelia doltsopa
Pittosporum eugenioides
Prunus 'Amanogawa'
Prunus 'Jo-nioi'
Prunus lusitanica and cvs
Prunus × yedoensis and cvs
Robinia pseudoacacia and cvs
Styrax japonica
Tilia × euchlora
Tilia oliveri
Tilia platyphyllos
Tilia tomentosa and cvs

SHRUBS

Abelia chinensis
Abelia × grandiflora
Abelia triflora
Abeliophyllum distichum
Azara petiolaris
Berberis microphylla
Berberis sargentiana
Brugmansia (most)
Buddleja alternifolia
Buddleja crispa
Buddleja davidii and cvs
Buddleja fallowiana
Buddleja 'Lochinch'
Buxus sempervirens and cvs
Camellia sasanqua cvs
Ceanothus × delileanus 'Gloire de Versailles'
Chimonanthus praecox and cvs
Chionanthus virginicus
Choisya 'Aztec Pearl'
Choisya ternata
Citrus × meyeri 'Meyer'
Clerodendrum bungei
Clerodendrum trichotomum
Clethra (most)
Clethra barbinervis
Clethra fargesii
Colletia hystrix 'Rosea'
Colletia paradoxa

Corokia cotoneaster
Coronilla valentina subsp. glauca
Corylopsis (all)
Cytisus battandieri
Cytisus × praecox and cvs
Cytisus supranubius
Daphne, many, including
Daphne arbuscula
Daphne bholua and cvs
Daphne blagayana
Daphne × burkwoodii and cvs
Daphne cneorum and forms
Daphne collina
Daphne × hybrida
Daphne × manteniana 'Manten'
Daphne mezereum and cvs
Daphne × napolitana
Daphne odora and cvs
Daphne pontica
Daphne tangutica
Deutzia compacta
Deutzia × elegantissima and cvs
Edgeworthia chrysantha
Elaeagnus (all)
Erica arborea 'Alpina'
Erica × darleyensis and cvs
Erica lusitanica
Erica × veitchii
Escallonia 'Donard Gem'
Eucryphia glutinosa
Eucryphia milliganii
Euonymus planipes
Fothergilla gardenii
Fothergilla major
Gaultheria forrestii
Gaultheria fragrantissima
Genista aetnensis
Genista 'Porlock'
Hakea lissosperma
Hamamelis (most)
Hoheria glabrata
Hoheria lyallii
Itea ilicifolia
Itea virginica
Jasminum humile 'Revolutum'
Ligustrum, all, including
Ligustrum quihoui
Ligustrum sinense
Lomatia myricoides
Lonicera fragrantissima
Lonicera × purpusii and cvs
Lonicera standishii
Lonicera syringantha
Luculia gratissima
Lupinus arboreus
Magnolia denudata
Magnolia grandiflora and cvs
Magnolia × loebneri and cvs
Magnolia sieboldii
Magnolia sieboldii subsp. sinensis
Magnolia × soulangeana and cvs
Magnolia stellata and cvs

Magnolia × *thompsoniana*
Magnolia virginiana
Magnolia × *wieseneri*
Magnolia wilsonii
Mahonia japonica
Myrtus communis and cvs
Oemleria cerasiformis
Olearia × *haastii*
Olearia ilicifolia
Olearia macrodonta and cvs
Osmanthus (all)
Paeonia × *lemoinei* and cvs
Philadelphus, many, including
Philadelphus 'Belle Etoile'
Philadelphus 'Bouquet Blanc'
Philadelphus coronarius and cvs
Philadelphus 'Erectus'
Philadelphus microphyllus
Philadelphus 'Sybille'
Philadelphus 'Virginal'
Philadelphus White Rock
Pimelea prostrata
Pittosporum tenuifolium
Pittosporum tobira
Poncirus trifoliata
Prunus mume and cvs
Ptelea trifoliata
Pterostyrax hispida
Pyracantha (all)
Rhododendron, many, including
Rhododendron Albatross and forms
Rhododendron arborescens
Rhododendron auriculatum
Rhododendron calophytum
Rhododendron canescens
Rhododendron 'Countess of
  Haddington'
Rhododendron decorum
Rhododendron fortunei
Rhododendron 'Fragrantissimum'
Rhododendron Lodauric Group
Rhododendron Loderi Group and cvs
Rhododendron luteum
Rhododendron periclymenoides
Rhododendron 'Polar Bear'
Rhododendron viscosum
Rhododendron Deciduous Azaleas,
many, especially
Rhododendron 'Daviesii'
Rhododendron 'Exquisitum'
Rhododendron 'Irene Koster'
Ribes alpinum
Ribes gayanum
Ribes odoratum
Romneya coulteri
Rosa, many, including
Rosa 'Albert Edwards'
Rosa 'Andersonii'
Rosa 'Anemone'
Rosa banksiae (single forms)
Rosa bracteata
Rosa brunonii

Rosa filipes 'Kiftsgate'
Rosa foliolosa
Rosa helenae
Rosa longicuspis
Rosa 'Macrantha'
Rosa moschata
Rosa × *odorata* 'Pseudindica'
Rosa primula
Rosa rugosa and cvs
Rosa wichurana
Sarcococca (all)
Skimmia × *confusa* and cvs
Skimmia japonica 'Fragrans'
Skimmia japonica 'Rubella'
Spartium junceum
Syringa, many, including
Syringa × *chinensis* 'Saugeana'
Syringa × *josiflexa* 'Bellicent'
Syringa × *persica* and cvs
Syringa pubescens subsp. *julianae*
Syringa sweginzowii 'Superba'
Syringa vulgaris cvs
Ulex europaeus
Viburnum, many, including
Viburnum × *bodnantense* cvs
Viburnum × *burkwoodii* and cvs
Viburnum × *carlcephalum*
Viburnum carlesii and cvs
Viburnum 'Chesapeake'
Viburnum erubescens var. *gracilipes*
Viburnum farreri
Viburnum grandiflorum
Viburnum japonicum
Viburnum × *juddii*
Yucca filamentosa
Yucca flaccida
Zenobia pulverulenta

CLIMBERS

Actinidia deliciosa
Akebia quinata
Clematis armandii and cvs
Clematis cirrhosa var. *balearica*
Clematis flammula
Clematis montana and forms
Clematis rehderiana
Decumaria sinensis
Dregea sinensis
Holboellia latifolia
Jasminum azoricum
Jasminum beesianum
Jasminum officinale and cvs
Jasminum polyanthum
Jasminum × *stephanense*
Lonicera caprifolium and cvs
Lonicera etrusca
Lonicera × *heckrottii*
Lonicera × *italica*
Lonicera japonica and cvs
Lonicera periclymenum and cvs
Mandevilla laxa
Stauntonia hexaphylla

Trachelospermum (all)
Wisteria

TREES and SHRUBS with
AROMATIC FOLIAGE

TREES

Cercidiphyllum japonicum (in autumn)
Clerodendrum (all)
Eucalyptus (all)
Juglans (all)
Laurus nobilis and cvs
Phellodendron (all)
Populus balsamifera
Populus trichocarpa
Salix pentandra
Salix triandra
Sassafras albidum
Umbellularia californica

SHRUBS

Aloysia triphylla
Artemisia arborescens
Artemisia 'Powis Castle'
Caryopteris (all)
Cistus, many, including
Cytisus × *aguilarii*
Cytisus × *cyprius*
Cytisus ladanifer
Cytisus × *purpureus*
Clerodendrum bungei
Comptonia peregrina
Elsholtzia stauntonii
Escallonia (many)
Gaultheria procumbens
Hebe cupressoides
Helichrysum italicum subsp. *serotinum*
Helichrysum plicatum
Illicium (all)
Lavandula (most)
Lindera (all)
Myrica (all)
Myrtus communis and cvs
Olearia ilicifolia
Olearia mollis
Perovskia (all)
Prostanthera (all)
Ptelea trifoliata
Rhododendron, many, including:
Rhododendron augustinii
Rhododendron cinnabarinum forms
  and hybrids
Rhododendron Mollis Azaleas
Rhododendron 'Pink Drift'
Rhododendron saluenense
Ribes sanguineum and cvs
Rosmarinus officinalis and cvs
Ruta graveolens
Salvia (all)
Santolina (all)
Skimmia anquetilia
Skimmia × *confusa* and cvs

CONIFERS

Most conifers, particularly
Calocedrus decurrens
Chamaecyparis (all)
Cupressus (all)
Juniperus (all)
Pseudotsuga menziesii and forms
Thuja (all)

FLOWERING TREES and SHRUBS for EVERY MONTH

A month by month selection of flowering trees and shrubs. Many subjects flower over a long period, but are only mentioned under the months during which they provide a reasonable display.

JANUARY
TREES

Acacia dealbata

SHRUBS

Camellia sasanqua cvs
Chimonanthus praecox and cvs
Erica carnea and cvs
Erica × darleyensis and cvs
Garrya elliptica and cvs
Hamamelis (many)
Jasminum nudiflorum
Lonicera fragrantissima
Lonicera × purpusii and cvs
Lonicera standishii
Sarcococca (several)
Viburnum × bodnantense and cvs
Viburnum farreri
Viburnum tinus and cvs

FEBRUARY
TREES

Acacia dealbata
Magnolia campbellii and forms
Populus tremula
Prunus incisa 'Praecox'
Prunus mume and cvs
Rhododendron arboreum and forms
Sorbus megalocarpa

SHRUBS

Camellia sasanqua cvs
Cornus mas
Cornus officinalis
Daphne bholua and cvs
Daphne mezereum
Daphne odora and cvs
Erica carnea and cvs
Erica × darleyensis and cvs
Garrya elliptica and cvs
Hamamelis (many)
Jasminum nudiflorum
Lonicera fragrantissima
Lonicera × purpusii and cvs
Lonicera setifera

Lonicera standishii
Mahonia japonica
Pachysandra terminalis and cvs
Rhododendron dauricum 'Midwinter'
Rhododendron mucronulatum
Sarcococca (several)
Ulex europaeus and cvs
Viburnum × bodnantense cvs
Viburnum farreri
Viburnum tinus and cvs

MARCH
TREES

Acer opalus
Acer rubrum
Magnolia (several)
Maytenus boaria
Prunus (several)
Rhododendron (several)
Salix (many)
Sorbus megalocarpa

SHRUBS

Camellia japonica (several cvs)
Camellia sasanqua and cvs
Chaenomeles (several)
Corylopsis pauciflora
Daphne bholua and cvs
Daphne mezereum
Erica carnea and cvs
Erica × darleyensis cvs
Erica erigena and cvs
Erica lusitanica
Erica × veitchii cvs
Forsythia (several)
Lonicera setifera
Magnolia stellata
Mahonia aquifolium
Mahonia japonica
Osmanthus (several)
Pachysandra terminalis and cvs
Prunus (several)
Rhododendron (several)
Salix (many)
Stachyurus praecox
Ulex europaeus and cvs
Viburnum tinus and cvs

APRIL
TREES

Acer platanoides and cvs
Amelanchier (several)
Magnolia kobus
Magnolia × loebneri and cvs
Magnolia salicifolia
Malus (several)
Prunus (many)

SHRUBS

Amelanchier (several)
Berberis darwinii
Berberis × lologensis

Berberis trigona
Camellia japonica and cvs
Camellia × williamsii and cvs
Chaenomeles (many)
Corylopsis (several)
Cytisus (several)
Daphne (several)
Erica (several)
Forsythia (many)
Kerria japonica and cvs
Magnolia × soulangeana and cvs
Magnolia stellata
Mahonia aquifolium
Mahonia pinnata
Osmanthus × burkwoodii
Osmanthus decorus
Osmanthus delavayi
Pieris (most)
Prunus (many)
Rhododendron (many)
Ribes (many)
Spiraea 'Arguta'
Spiraea thunbergii
Viburnum (many)

CLIMBERS

Clematis alpina and cvs
Clematis armandii and cvs
Holboellia coriacea

MAY
TREES

Aesculus (many)
Cercis (several)
Cornus nuttallii
Crataegus (many)
Davidia involucrata
Embothrium coccineum and cvs
Fraxinus ornus
Halesia (all)
Laburnum anagyroides
Laburnum × watereri 'Vossii'
Malus (many)
Paulownia tomentosa
Prunus (many)
Pyrus (all)
Sorbus (many)

SHRUBS

Azara serrata and cvs
Callistemon (several)
Camellia japonica cvs (several)
Ceanothus (several)
Chaenomeles (many)
Choisya (all)
Cornus florida and cvs
Cotoneaster (many)
Crinodendron hookerianum
Cytisus (many)
Daphne (many)
Dipelta floribunda
Enkianthus (all)

Erica (several)
Exochorda (all)
Genista (many)
Halesia (all)
Helianthemum (all)
Kerria japonica and cvs
Kolkwitzia amabilis
Lonicera (many)
Magnolia liliiflora
Magnolia × soulangeana cvs
Menziesia (all)
Paeonia (many)
Piptanthus nepalensis
Potentilla (many)
Pyracantha (many)
Rhododendron (many)
Rosa (many)
Xanthoceras sorbifolium

CLIMBERS
Clematis (many)
Lonicera (many)
Schisandra (all)
Wisteria (all)

JUNE
TREES
Aesculus (several)
Crataegus (many)
Embothrium coccineum and forms
Laburnum alpinum
Laburnum × watereri 'Vossii'
Magnolia acuminata var. subcordata
Magnolia 'Charles Coates'
Magnolia fraseri
Magnolia obovata
Malus trilobata
Robinia (several)
Styrax (several)

SHRUBS
Abelia (several)
Buddleja globosa
Cistus (many)
Colutea (all)
Cornus kousa
Cornus 'Porlock'
Cotoneaster (many)
Cytisus (many)
Deutzia (most)
Erica ciliaris and cvs
Erica cinerea and cvs
Erica tetralix and cvs
Escallonia (many)
Genista (many)
× Halimiocistus (all)
Halimium (all)
Hebe (many)
Helianthemum (all)
Hydrangea (several)
Kalmia (all)

Kolkwitzia amabilis and cvs
Lonicera (several)
Magnolia × thompsoniana
Magnolia virginiana
Neillia (several)
Olearia (several)
Ozothamnus (all)
Paeonia (all)
Penstemon (several)
Philadelphus (many)
Potentilla (all)
Rhododendron (many)
Rosa (many)
Rubus (many)
Spartium junceum
Spiraea (many)
Staphylea (several)
Syringa (many)
Viburnum (many)
Weigela (all)
Zenobia pulverulenta

CLIMBERS
Clematis (many)
Jasminum (several)
Lonicera (many)
Schisandra (several)
Wisteria (all)

JULY
TREES
Aesculus indica
Castanea sativa
Catalpa (all)
Cladrastis sinensis
Eucryphia (several)
Koelreuteria paniculata
Liriodendron tulipifera
Magnolia delavayi
Magnolia grandiflora and cvs
Stewartia (several)

SHRUBS
Aster albescens
Buddleja davidii and cvs
Calluna vulgaris and cvs
Cistus (many)
Colutea (all)
Daboecia cantabrica and cvs
Desfontainia spinosa
Deutzia setchuenensis
Erica ciliaris and cvs
Erica cinerea and cvs
Erica vagans and cvs
Escallonia (many)
Fuchsia (many)
Grevillea juniperina 'Sulphurea'
Halimodendron halodendron
Hebe (many)
Hoheria (several)
Holodiscus discolor

Hydrangea (many)
Hypericum (many)
Indigofera (several)
Lavandula (most)
Magnolia virginiana
Olearia (several)
Penstemon (several)
Philadelphus (several)
Phygelius (all)
Potentilla (many)
Rhododendron (several)
Romneya (all)
Yucca (several)
Zenobia pulverulenta

CLIMBERS
Clematis (many)
Eccremocarpus scaber
Fallopia baldschuanica
Jasminum (several)
Lonicera (many)
Mutisia oligodon
Passiflora (several)
Schizophragma (all)
Solanum (all)
Trachelospermum (all)

AUGUST
TREES
Catalpa bignonioides
Eucryphia (several)
Koelreuteria paniculata
Ligustrum lucidum and cvs
Magnolia delavayi
Magnolia grandiflora and cvs
Oxydendrum arboreum

SHRUBS
Buddleja (many)
Calluna vulgaris and cvs
Caryopteris (several)
Ceanothus (several)
Ceratostigma willmottianum
Clerodendrum (all)
Clethra (several)
Colutea (all)
Daboecia cantabrica and cvs
Desfontainia spinosa
Deutzia setchuenensis
Elsholtzia stauntonii
Erica ciliaris and cvs
Erica cinerea and cvs
Erica tetralix and cvs
Erica vagans and cvs
Fuchsia (many)
Genista tinctoria and cvs
Grevillea juniperina 'Sulphurea'
Hibiscus (several)
Hydrangea (many)
Hypericum (many)
Indigofera (several)
Itea ilicifolia

Lavandula (most)
Leycesteria formosa
Myrtus (several)
Olearia (several)
Perovskia (all)
Phygelius (all)
Potentilla (all)
Romneya (all)
Rosa (many)
Yucca (several)
Zauschneria (all)
Zenobia pulverulenta

CLIMBERS
Berberidopsis corallina
Campsis (all)
Clematis (many)
Eccremocarpus scaber
Jasminum (several)
Lonicera (many)
Lapageria rosea cvs
Mutisia oligodon
Passiflora (several)
Pileostegia viburnoides
Fallopia (all)
Solanum (all)
Trachelospermum asiaticum

SEPTEMBER
TREES
Eucryphia × nymansensis
Magnolia grandiflora and cvs
Oxydendrum arboreum

SHRUBS
Abelia chinensis
Abelia × grandiflora and cvs
Abelia parvifolia
Aralia elata
Buddleja (several)
Calluna vulgaris and cvs
Caryopteris (several)
Ceratostigma griffithii
Ceratostigma willmottianum
Clerodendrum bungei
Clerodendrum trichotomum
Colutea (several)
Daboecia cantabrica and cvs

Elsholtzia stauntonii
Erica ciliaris and cvs
Erica cinerea (several cvs)
Erica terminalis
Erica tetralix and cvs
Erica vagans and cvs
Fuchsia (several)
Genista tinctoria and cvs
Grevillea juniperina 'Sulphurea'
Hebe (several)
Hibiscus (several)
Hydrangea (several)
Hypericum (several)
Indigofera (several)
Lespedeza thunbergii
Leycesteria formosa
Perovskia (all)
Potentilla (most)
Romneya (all)
Vitex (all)
Yucca gloriosa
Zauschneria (all)

CLIMBERS
Campsis (all)
Clematis (several)
Eccremocarpus scaber
Fallopia baldschuanica
Jasminum (several)
Lapageria rosea cvs
Mutisia oligodon
Passiflora (several)
Pileostegia viburnoides
Polygonum baldschuanicum
Solanum crispum 'Glasnevin'

OCTOBER
TREES
Magnolia grandiflora and cvs

SHRUBS
Abelia × grandiflora and cvs
Calluna vulgaris (several cvs)
Ceratostigma griffithii
Ceratostigma willmottianum
Erica carnea 'Eileen Porter'
Erica vagans (several cvs)
Fatsia japonica

Fuchsia (several)
Hibiscus (several)
Hydrangea (several)
Hypericum (several)
Lespedeza thunbergii
Mahonia × media and cvs
Potentilla (several)
Vitex (all)
Zauschneria (all)

CLIMBERS
Clematis (several)
Eccremocarpus scaber
Lapageria rosea cvs

NOVEMBER
TREES
Prunus × subhirtella 'Autumnalis'

SHRUBS
Erica carnea 'Eileen Porter'
Jasminum nudiflorum
Lonicera standishii
Mahonia acanthifolia
Mahonia × media and cvs
Viburnum × bodnantense cvs
Viburnum farreri

DECEMBER
TREES
Prunus × subhirtella 'Autumnalis'
Prunus × subhirtella 'Autumnalis
  Rosea'

SHRUBS
Erica carnea (several cvs)
Erica × darleyensis 'Silberschmelze'
Hamamelis × intermedia (some)
Hamamelis mollis
Jasminum nudiflorum
Lonicera fragrantissima
Lonicera × purpusii and cvs
Lonicera standishii
Mahonia × media and cvs
Viburnum × bodnantense and cvs
Viburnum farreri
Viburnum grandiflorum
Viburnum tinus and cvs

PLANTS RAISED OR SELECTED BY HILLIER NURSERIES

(Dates in parentheses represent the approximate year of raising or selection)

Abies procera 'Glauca Prostrata' (1895)

Abutilon × suntense 'Jermyns' (1967)
♀ 2002

Abutilon × suntense 'White Charm'
(1975)

Acer campestre 'Streetwise' (1998)

Acer × conspicuum 'Silver Vein' (1961)

Acer × hillieri (before 1935)

Acer palmatum 'Lutescens'
(before 1935)

Aucuba japonica 'Hillieri'
(before 1930)

Berberis 'Blenheim'

Berberis 'Goldilocks' (1978)
FCC 1991, Cory Cup 1991

Berberis × stenophylla 'Etna'
(before 1935)

Berberis × wintonensis (before 1955)

Buddleja 'West Hill' (before 1967)

Camellia 'Barbara Hillier' (1960)

Camellia × williamsii 'Jermyns' (1960)

Carpinus betulus 'Streetwise' (1998)

Caryopteris incana 'Peach Pink'
(1960)

Ceanothus 'Blue Mound' (1960)
♀ 2002

Cephalotaxus fortunei 'Prostrate
Spreader' (before 1920)

Cephalotaxus harringtonii 'Gnome'
(1970)

Cephalotaxus harringtonii 'Prostrata'
(before 1930)

Chamaecyparis lawsoniana
'Elegantissima' (before 1930)

Chamaecyparis lawsoniana 'Hillieri'
(before 1930)

Chamaecytisus × versicolor 'Hillieri'
(1935)

Choisya 'Aztec Pearl' (1982) ♀ 2002,
AM 1990

Chrysanthemum 'Hillier's Apricot'
(1919) AM 1921

Cistus × argenteus 'Silver Pink'
(1910) AM 1919

Corylopsis Willmottiae Group 'Spring
Purple' (1969)

Cotinus Dummer Hybrids (1978)

Cotinus 'Grace' (1978) FCC 1990,
Cory Cup 1984, AM 1983

Cotoneaster 'Eastleigh' (1960)

Cotoneaster 'Salmon Spray' (before
1940)

Cupressus lusitanica 'Glauca
Pendula' (before 1914) AM 1944

Cytisus battandieri 'Yellow Tail'
(before 1975) ♀ 2002

Daphne bholua 'Jacqueline Postill'
(1982) FCC 1991

Daphne longilobata 'Peter Moore'
(1980)

Daphne 'Valerie Hillier' (1984)

Deutzia 'Hillieri' (1926)

Deutzia ningpoensis 'Pink Charm'
(1960)

Escallonia 'Wintonensis' (before 1921)

Eucryphia × hillieri 'Winton' (1953)

Euonymus hamiltonianus subsp.
sieboldianus 'Coral Charm'
AM 1981

Euonymus hamiltonianus subsp.
sieboldianus 'Coral Chief'

Euonymus hamiltonianus subsp.
sieboldianus 'Fiesta' (1967)

Euonymus hamiltonianus subsp.
sieboldianus 'Red Elf' AM 1981

Fagus sylvatica 'Cockleshell' (1960)

Forsythia 'Golden Nugget' (1964)

Gaultheria mucronata 'Cherry Ripe'
(1965) AM 1985

Gaultheria mucronata 'Mulberry Wine'
(1965) ♀ 2002

Gaultheria mucronata 'Pink Pearl'
(1965) ♀ 2002

Gaultheria mucronata 'Rosie' (1965)

Gaultheria mucronata 'Sea Shell'
(1965) ♀ 2002

Gaultheria mucronata 'White Pearl'
(1965)

Gaultheria × wisleyensis 'Pink Pixie'
(1969) AM 1976

× Halimiocistus wintonensis (1910)
♀ 2002, AM 1926

Hamamelis × intermedia 'Carmine
Red' (1934)

Hamamelis × intermedia 'Hiltingbury'
(1934)

Hamamelis vernalis 'Red Imp' (1966)

Hamamelis vernalis 'Sandra' (1962)
♀ 2002, AM 1976

Hamamelis vernalis 'Squib' (1966)

Helianthemum 'Coppernob' (1968)

Helleborus Hillier Hybrids (2000)

Hibiscus sinosyriacus 'Autumn
Surprise' (1936)

Hibiscus sinosyriacus 'Lilac Queen'
(1936)

Hibiscus sinosyriacus 'Ruby Glow'
(1936)

Hypericum × dummeri 'Peter Dummer'
(1975)

Hypericum 'Eastleigh Gold' (1964)

Ilex × altaclerensis 'Purple Shaft'
(1965)

Ilex aquifolium 'Amber' (1950)
♀ 2002, FCC 1985

Ilex 'Jermyn's Dwarf' (before 1955)

Iris chrysographes 'Purple Wings'
(1962)

Kniphofia 'St Cross' (before 1935)

Laburnum anagyroides 'Erect' (1965)

Laburnum × watereri 'Alford's
Weeping' (1968)

Larix kaempferi 'Hobbit' (1960)

Leucothoe fontanesiana 'Rainbow'

Linum flavum 'Saffron' (1967)

Lonicera × purpusii 'Winter Beauty'
(1966) ♀ 2002, AM 1992

Lupinus 'Broadgate Yellow' (1962)

Magnolia campbellii 'Darjeeling'

Magnolia campbellii 'Ethel Hillier'
(1927)

Magnolia salicifolia 'Jermyns' (1935)

Malus domestica 'Easter Orange'
(before 1897) AM 1897

Nyssa sylvatica 'Jermyns Flame' (1985)

Perovskia 'Hybrida' (before 1937)

Photinia 'Redstart' (1969)

Photinia 'Winchester' (1969)

Phygelius × rectus 'Devil's Tears'
(1985) ♀ 2002

Phygelius × rectus 'Moonraker' (1985)

Phygelius × rectus 'Pink Elf' (1985)

Phygelius × rectus 'Salmon Leap'
(1985) ♀ 2002

Phygelius × rectus 'Winchester
Fanfare' (1974)

Phyllocladus trichomanoides var.
alpinus 'Silver Blades' (1968)

× Phylliopsis hillieri 'Pinocchio' (1960)
AM 1976, FCC 1984

Pieris formosa 'Jermyns' (1950)
AM 1959

Pinus cembra 'Jermyns' (1929)

Pinus koraiensis 'Winton' (1929)

Pinus parviflora 'Adcock's Dwarf'
(1965) ♀ 2002

Pinus sylvestris 'Edwin Hillier' (1920)

Platycladus orientalis 'Hillieri' (1920)

Populus 'Hiltingbury Weeping' (1962)

Potentilla fruticosa 'Eastleigh Cream'
(1969)

Potentilla fruticosa 'Elizabeth' (1950)
AMT 1965

Potentilla fruticosa 'Milkmaid' (1960)

Potentilla fruticosa 'Penny White'
♀ 2002

Potentilla fruticosa 'Ruth' (1960)

Potentilla fruticosa 'Whirligig'
(1969)

Primula sinensis 'Annie Hillier' (1875)
FCC 1880

Prunus 'Hillieri' (before 1928)
AM 1959

Prunus incisa 'Praecox' (before 1938)
♀ 2002, FCC 1973, AM 1957

Prunus laurocerasus 'Greenmantle'
(1965)

To clarify this further, I consider a universal concept one that possesses universal validity and is the perfect representative of a system or function. It can be a well-conceived, well-balanced idea with immediate universal connotations, that communicates directly and will yield further inquiries while it can withstand the stress of experimentation (see Figs 1–18).

Universal concepts seeking analogies and new associations are not easily subjected to the analysis of symbolic logic. It takes a new type of logic and perhaps a new philosophy to categorize their symmetries and consequences.

When these hidden patterns and processes are realized in visual form ambiguities can be clarified, misconceptions reexamined and the subjective self-state of a system can be studied to seek the imperfection or restate the perfection in its design. Processes can be held still for analysis, their intricacies brought into perspective and all that is unseen, undiscovered or guessed at but feasible can gain recognition until it can establish its own validity.

Pattern finding is a symmetry operation. It is the purpose of the mind and the construct of the universe. There are an infinite number of patterns and only some are known. Those that are still unknown hold the key to unresolved enigmas and paradoxes. Thus formal and exclusively visual information can be refined to such an extent as to impart the most precise and significant information in addition to visual gratification.

These thoughts are further clarified by quoting from my lecture entitled "Evolution and the Creative Mind". This lecture was first delivered at the Smithsonian Institution, Washington, D.C., 1976.

> My art exists in a dynamic, evolutionary world of rapidly changing concepts and measures, where the appearances of things, facts and events are assumed manifestations of reality and distortions are the norm. . . .
>
> Although I deal with difficult concepts, my work remains visual. The process of "visualization" is doubly important since aspects of the work explore invisible systems, underlying structures and patterns inherent in our existence. . . .
>
> I incorporate science, philosophy and all those disciplines that enrich my work and are so necessary to any worthwhile human activity in the world today.
>
> I communicate my ideas in whatever form is most true to the concept. It is the concept that dictates the mode of presentation. My projects take several years to complete and they are in a constant state of flux. The work follows an evolutionary attitude and process. It

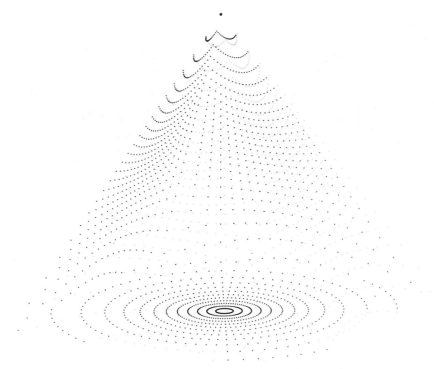

Fig. 9. Isometric Systems in Isotropic Space—Map Projections. The Pyramid—Fragmentation. 1976. Ink on vellum, 24 × 30″. © Agnes Denes 1976.

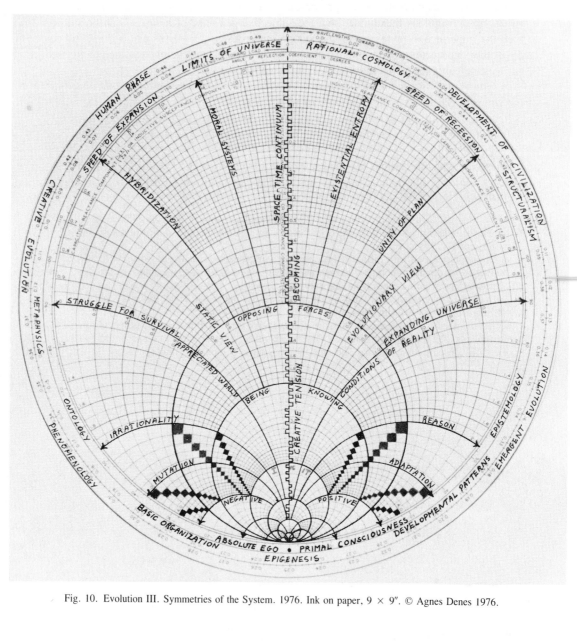

Fig. 10. Evolution III. Symmetries of the System. 1976. Ink on paper, 9 × 9″. © Agnes Denes 1976.

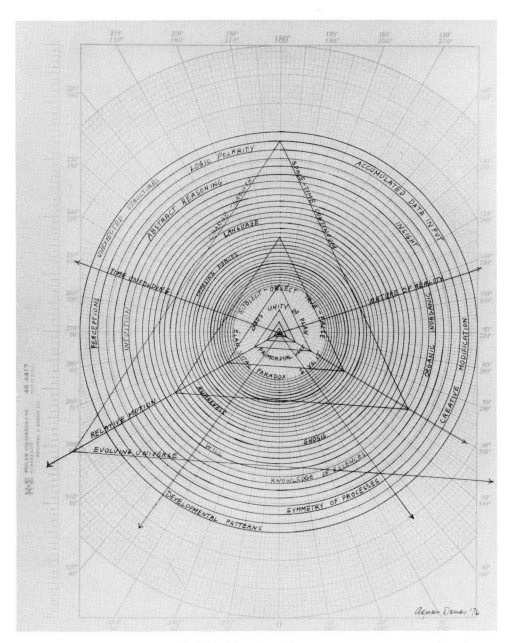

Fig. 11. Evolution II. Paradox and Essence. Spiral Evolution. 1976. Ink on graph paper, 17 × 14½''. © Agnes Denes 1976.

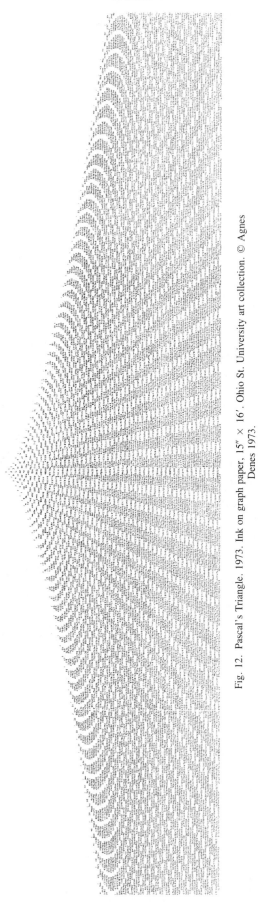

Fig. 12. Pascal's Triangle. 1973. Ink on graph paper, 15" × 16'. Ohio St. University art collection. © Agnes Denes 1973.

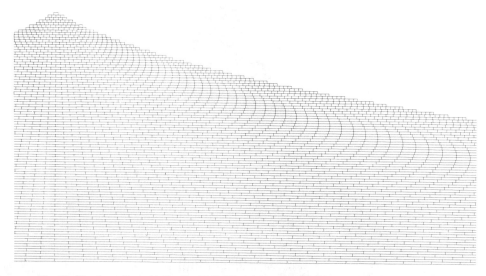

Fig. 13. The Stone Pyramid (detail). 1976. Silver ink on mylar, 28″ × 16′. © Agnes Denes 1976.

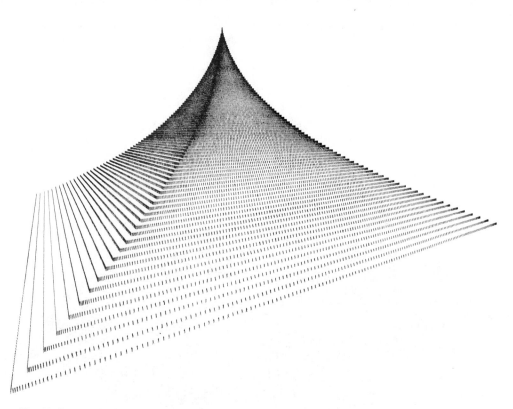

Fig. 14. Pascal's Perfect Probability Pyramid & the People Paradox—The Predicament. 1980. Ink on silk vellum, 32 × 43″. © Agnes Denes 1980.

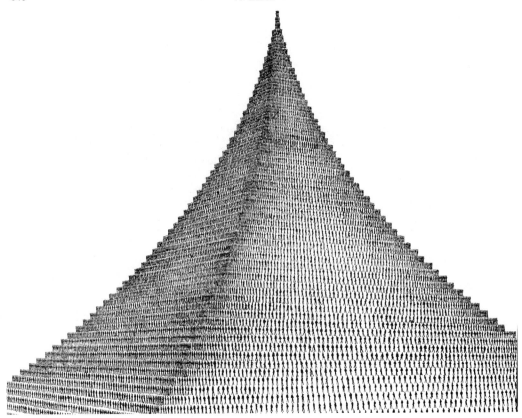

Fig. 15. Pascal's Perfect Probability Pyramid & the People Paradox—The Predicament (detail). 1980. Ink on silk vellum, 32 × 43″. © Agnes Denes 1980.

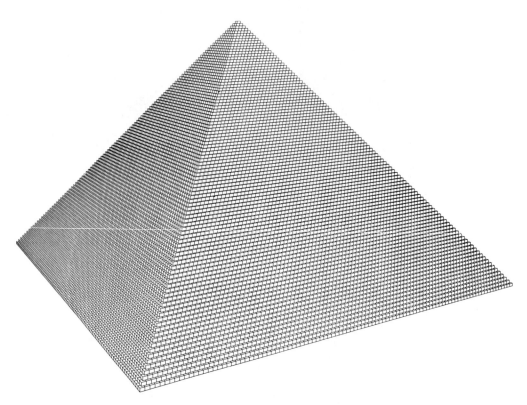

Fig. 16. The Straight Pyramid. 1974. Ink on vellum, 34 × 48″. © Agnes Denes 1974.

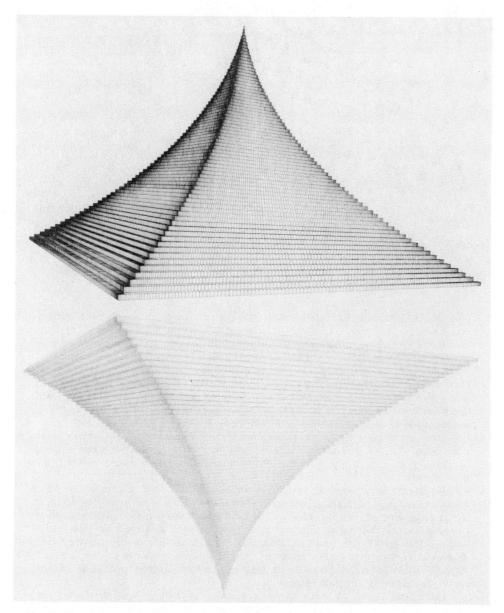

Fig. 17. The Reflection. 1978. Ink on vellum, 48″ × 26½″. Collection: Kunshalle, Nurnberg, F.R.G. © Agnes Denes 1978.

Fig. 18. Tree Mountain (study for environmental work)—1.5 mile × 285 ft high, 10,000 trees (detail). 1983. Metallic ink on mylar, $34\frac{1}{4} \times 96\frac{1}{2}''$. © Agnes Denes 1983.

questions, dissects, reevaluates and reconstructs through the conscious use of instinct, intellect and intuition.

. . . By questioning our existence as well as existence itself, we create an art universal in terms of all humanity. Personally, I am fascinated by our human position of being somewhere in the middle of this "existence." We live on an average galaxy; we can't see too far or too close, can't stand too much cold or too much heat. We don't live too long, and yet, we can look out to the edge of the universe into light years and penetrate the atom chasing quarks and another world within. The world seems to begin at the surface of our skin; there is a world beyond it and a world within, and the distance is about the same. I like that.

Once we abandon Newtonian static physics and accept Einstein's four-dimensional principles of relativity, we question reality and know that even the laws of nature may undergo evolutionary changes. We even invented the uncertainty principle, although we use it for other reasons.

We haven't begun to understand the implications of this new, relativistic existence, where everything we had known and had believed now seems to be wrong. In this new dynamic world, objects become processes and forms are patterns in motion. Matter is a form of energy and our own human substance is but spinning velocity. There is no solid matter and no empty space; time becomes an earthbound reality but remains an enigma in the fourth dimension. We must create a new language, consider a transitory state of new illusions and layers of validity and accept the possibility that there may be no language to describe ultimate reality, beyond the language of visions.

In our limited existence, evolution provides answers as to where we've been and where we are going: a future prediction based on previous phenomena. The universe contains systems, systems contain patterns. The purpose of the mind is to locate these patterns and to seek the inherent potential for new systems of thought and behavior.

My work touches on the various stages of the development of my species, reevaluates and makes new comparisons in order to enhance perception and awareness, to form new insights and new methods of reasoning. . . .

This analytical attitude probes the structural and philosophical significance of an invisible world where elusive processes, transformations and interactions of phenomena go unseen, buried in the substance of time and space. I am referring to known or unknown events hidden from recognition either by their nature of spatio-temporal limitations or by our being unaware of their existence and functions.

I believe that art is the essence of life, as much as anything can be a true essence. It is extracted from existence by a process. Art is a reflection on life and an analysis of its structure. As such, art should be a great moving force shaping the future.

Comp. & Maths. with Appls. Vol. 12B, Nos. 3/4, pp. 849–857, 1986
Printed in Great Britain.

0886-9561/86 $3.00 + .00
© 1986 Pergamon Press Ltd.

SYMMETRY IN POLYMER SCIENCE

Riichirô Chûjô

Department of Polymer Chemistry, Tokyo Institute of Technology, 12-1 Ookayama 2-chome,
Meguro-ku, Tokyo 152, Japan

Abstract—Stereoregularity and conformation of high polymers are reviewed in relation to symmetry. Stereoregularity of polypropylene is analyzed with two kinds of Bernoullian stochastic processes, while conformation of poly(vinylidene fluoride) in solution is related to that in the crystalline state. In both studies nuclear magnetic resonance spectroscopy is applied. A historical survey is also sketched for the relationship between the concept of symmetry and organic (including polymeric) molecules.

1. ISOMERS AND DIMENSION

In 1848 Pasteur found that racemic acid is a mixture of D- and L-tartaric acids, in which D and L denote dextrorotatory and levorotatory, respectively. Dextro and levo correspond to right and left, respectively, in Latin. This finding is the dawn of the concept "symmetry" in organic chemistry. In Fig. 1 are shown the chemical structures of two kinds of tartaric acids. Both compounds are composed of four carbons (C), six hydrogens (H), and six oxygens (O). Such compounds are called *isomers* with each other in chemistry. Iso means "the same" in Greek; isomer means the body with the same constituents. In Japanese, isomer is called *iseitai*, in which *i* means different, *sei* means property, and *tai* means body. Japanese terminology means the body with different properties. It is very interesting that "the same" appears in English (and also other Western languages) while "different" appears in Japanese. This difference is, however, not curious, because a more precise definition of isomer should be a body with different properties in spite of the same constituents.

The existence of such isomers is closely related to the fact that we are living in a three-dimensional space. In 1874 van't Hoff and LeBel independently proposed that four bonds of carbon atom (strictly speaking, saturated carbon atom) are arranged tetrahedrally as shown in Fig. 2. This proposal strongly struck the brains of theoretical chemists in 19th century, who had considered everything in a two-dimensional space such as books, papers and blackboards. For instance, a famous German chemist, Kolbe, attacked this proposal with a violent tone. If one thinks of the fact that he is living (not thinking) in three-dimensional space, the rationality of this proposal should easily be recognized. This has already been established experimentally; the Japanese chemist Nitta crystallographically analyzed the tetrahedral arrangement of four bonds in an organic molecules, pentaerythrit, $C(CH_2OH)_4$ in 1926.

If one tries to label the four vertices in a tetrahedron with four letters, A, B, D, and E, respectively, there are $4! = 24$ possibilities. Among these a majority of them are redundant and can be generated from one another by rotation. There are only two independent arrangements, as shown in Fig. 3. In the gaseous phase such a rotation is frequently induced after receiving thermal energy. This is the reason why there are two isomers in racemic acid, in which A=COOH, B=OH, D=H, and E=CH(OH)COOH.

The number of isomers depends on the dimension of space in which a molecule is moving. In zero-dimensional space a point is the only body which is allowed to exist there. There is no concept of isomers in this space. In one-dimensional space a segment can exist besides a point. Two segments $\overline{AB}$ and $\overline{BA}$ cannot overlap with each other by any rotation in one-dimensional space, while they can in two-dimensional space. We who are living in three-dimensional space do not distinguish two molecules AB and BA with each other. If we are living in one-dimensional space, we must distinguish these two as isomers.

An equilateral triangle is the simplest body which is not allowed to exist in one-dimensional but allowed in two-dimensional space. This is constructed with one segment where each segment is attached to each vertex in the former. In two-dimensional space △ABD and △ADB must be distinguished as isomers, while in three-dimensional space such a distinction is not required.

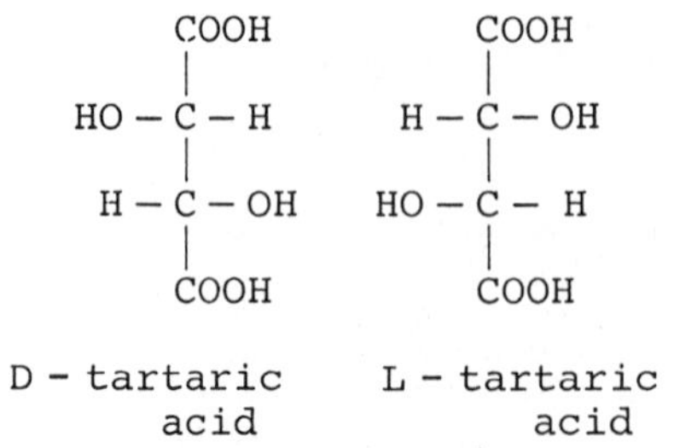

COOH   COOH
 | |
HO − C − H   H − C − OH
 | |
H − C − OH   HO − C − H
 | |
COOH   COOH

D − tartaric   L − tartaric
   acid   acid

Fig. 1. Molecular structure of D- and L-tartaric acids.

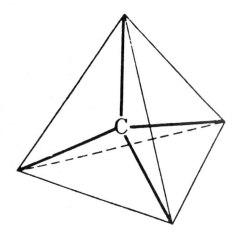

Fig. 2. Tetrahedral model of a methane-like molecule.

The regular tetrahedron is the simplest body which is not allowed to exist in two-dimensional but allowed in three-dimensional space. This is constructed with one equilateral triangle with each triangle attached to each side in the former.

As a natural extension of the above consideration, we can easily imagine a regular pentahedron (in the four-dimensional sense) as the simplest body which is not allowed to exist in three-dimensional but allowed in four-dimensional space. This is constructed with one regular tetrahedron (in the three-dimensional sense) and four regular tetrahedra attached to each of its four planes; here a tetrahedron, ABDE, as a hypersurface of a pentahedron (in the four-dimensional sense) rotates around the axis (in the four-dimensional sense, for instance △ABD), ABDE is turned inside out, and ABED is produced. This situation is quite similar to the rotation of △ABD around the axis AB. By this process we can easily obtain △ADB. This means that the two tetrahedra in Fig. 3 are not isomers with each other in four-dimensional space.

In some cases, two kinds of molecules which can overlap with each other by rotation are called *rotational isomers*. In order to distinguish the above-mentioned isomer from this rotational isomer, the term *optical isomer* is used. This is due to the existence of optical activity in the latter; if polarized light is incident on optical isomers, the signs of their polarizing angles are opposite. This is the origin of the terminologies D and L. Rotational isomers are characterized by the difference of forms, while optical ones are characterized by the difference of figures. Due to these differences, other terms, *conformation* and *configuration*, are also used respectively.

For the statistical description of rotational isomers statistical mechanics is most appropriate, in which Lebesgue measure (after a normalization procedure this quantity should become probability) is given by the Boltzmann factor $\exp(-E/kT)$, where E is the energy, k the Boltzmann constant and T the temperature. For optical isomers a quite similar factor is also used, in which E is the activation energy and T the reaction temperature. This author believes (but cannot

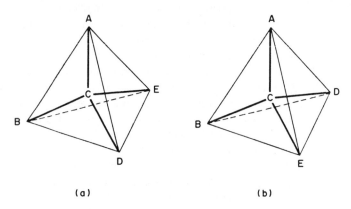

(a)   (b)

Fig. 3. Two optical isomers of the molecule C=ABDE.

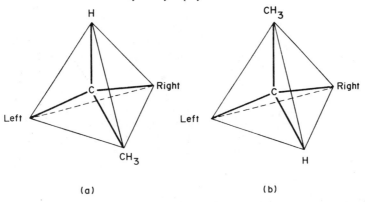

Fig. 4. Two optical isomers of polypropylene around C*.

verify as yet) that such a similarity is due to only one difference between rotational isomers in three- and four-dimensional spaces.

2. STEREOREGULARITY IN POLYPROPYLENE

High polymers, both synthetic and natural, are made by sequential chemical linkage of small elements called *monomers*. This process is called *polymerization*. Polypropylene, for instance, is obtained by the polymerization of propylene, $H_2C=CHCH_3$. Under appropriate conditions, the double bond is severed to a $—CH_2—CHCH_3—$ unit; the units are connected to form the polymer chain

$$\cdots—CH_2—\overset{*}{C}H—CH_2—\overset{*}{C}H—CH_2—\overset{*}{C}H—\cdots.$$
$$\qquad\qquad\underset{CH_3}{|}\qquad\quad\underset{CH_3}{|}\qquad\quad\underset{CH_3}{|}$$

In this polymer the carbons with asterisks are in the same situation as those in Fig. 3 (i.e. as shown in Fig. 4). We must, therefore, address the configuration of this polymer. If the polymer chain is stretched to make a planar zigzag skeleton, the configuration of this polymer can be expressed in terms of whether CH_3 groups are situated the above or below the plane containing the skeletal carbons (i.e. to a D or L configuration). Sequential pairs of similar and opposite configurations are called *mesic* (*m*) and *racemic* (*r*), respectively. These definitions are shown schematically in Fig. 5.

Polymers with consecutive *m* sequences in the polymer chain can be compared with a queue of schoolboys with knapsacks [Fig. 6(a)], in which the knapsack corresponds to the CH_3 group. In this case we require a space between two queues having a width on the order of the size of one knapsack. Polymers with consecutive *r* sequences require a similar lateral spacing when the knapsacks are interdigitated [Fig. 6(b)]. These two kinds of stereoregular polymers were named isotactic and syndiotactic polymers, respectively, by Natta. If monomer units have

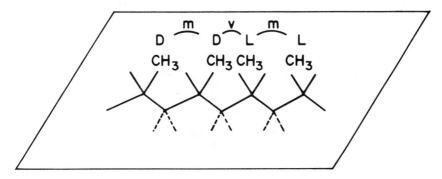

Fig. 5. Schematical representation of mesic and racemic arrangements in polypropylene.

R. CHŪJŌ

Fig. 6. Illustration of (a) isotactic, (b) syndiotactic and (c) atactic polymers with queues of schoolboys.

random stereoregularity, the situation regarding lateral packing is different from the above-mentioned polymers. As seen from the illustration of Fig. 6(c), we require a space the size of two knapsacks. In this space there are zero, one or two knapsacks. This lateral spacing is very important for stabilizing the crystalline structure of the polymers via the formation of secondary (van der Waals, hydrogen bonding, etc.) interactions between two adjacent chains. Crystalline polymers such as fibers necessitate good stereoregularity of the chains, while amorphous polymers such as rubbers accommodate stereoirregular polymers. For plastics the situation is intermediate between fibers and rubbers.

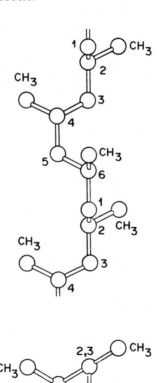

Fig. 7. Helical structure of isotactic polymers.

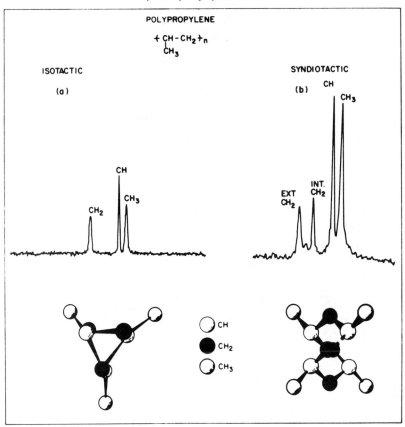

Fig. 8. Solid-state high-resolution NMR spectra of (a) isotactic and (b) syndiotactic polypropylenes.

The illustration in Fig. 6 was in two-dimensional space. In three-dimensional space the polymer is not arranged like a queue, but helically, as shown in Fig. 7. Solid-state high-resolution nuclear magnetic resonance (NMR) can facilitate the study of polymer conformation. In Fig. 8 are shown the NMR spectra of isotactic (a)[1] and syndiotactic (b)[2] polypropylene (this figure was arranged by Jelinski[3]). The conformation of the former is tgtg . . ., which makes the helical form as shown in Fig. 7 (side and top views) and in Fig. 8(a) (top view). In this polymer, all methyl (CH_3) groups are located in identical electronic environments. For the CH_2 and CH groups the situation is the same. As a result there are only one CH_2 peak, one CH peak, and one CH_3 peak in Fig. 8(a). (The peak position, the chemical shift reflects the electronic environment of the corresponding atom or group). For syndiotactic polypropylene the shape of the helix is different from that for the isotactic molecule. This is due to the tgtg conformation [Fig. 9(b)]. In this helical form, we can expect two CH_2 peaks, one CH peak, and one CH_3 peak. NMR confirms these expectations [Fig. 8(b)]. The different conformations between isotactic and syndiotactic polymers are interpreted in terms of van der Waals interactions between skeletal and sidechain atoms; the most stable conformation is realized in the solid state.

The energy differences between the most stable and other stable conformers are usually comparable to the thermal energy. This means that when these polymers are dissolved, each group rapidly changes from one stable conformer to another conformer. As a result, NMR peak positions are an average of the chemical shift values corresponding to each conformer. Such an averaging process induces the other kind of effect, narrowing of the peak due to rapid motion. If the spacings between adjacent peaks are smaller than peak widths in solution and larger than those in solids, coalesced adjacent peaks can split into each component peak after dissolving. The spacing due to the difference of configuration is just the above situation.

In Fig. 9 is shown the CH_3-region peaks of the polypropylene NMR spectrum in o-dichlorobenzene[4]. Each peak can be assigned to a corresponding pentad (four consecutive *m* or *r* letters) as shown in Table 1.

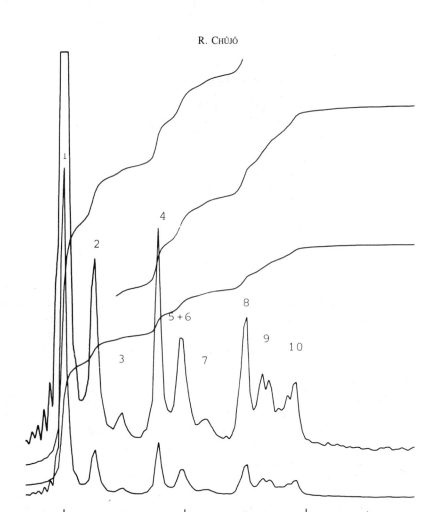

Fig. 9. Solution high-resolution NMR spectrum of highly isotactic polypropylene (only C̲H₃ region is shown).

As completely isotactic or syndiotactic polymers do not exist, we have to analyze the stereoregularity of the polymers in probabilistic terms. For polypropylene we should expect two kinds of Bernoullian processes; one is the selection of D or L (α denotes the probability of D selection) and the other is the selection of m or r (σ denotes the probability of m selection). A third parameter ω is introduced to describe the mole fraction of the polymer obtained by the former stochastic process. The mole fraction of ten pentads by these three parameters are summarized in Table 2. The values of these three parameters were determined from the relative intensities of NMR peaks and are summarized in Table 3. The samples LH-5402 and XY-S701 are commercial products produced in Liao Hua Chemical Factory (Liao Yang, China) and Xiang Yang Chemical Factory (Beijing, China), respectively. The sample LH-atac is a part of LH-5402, which is soluble in boiling heptane and insoluble in boiling pentane. Both in LH-5402 and XY-S701 ω is close to unity and α is also close to unity. These findings mean that these two samples are highly (but not completely) isotactic.

Table 1. Calculated chemical shifts (ppm) of methyl carbons in polypropylene

Pentad	Calcd	Pentad	Calcd
mmmm	0.000	*rmrr*	−0.957
mmmr	−0.255	*mrmr*	−1.123
rmmr	−0.447	*rrrr*	−1.524
mmrr	−0.749	*mrrr*	−1.706
mmrm	−0.900	*mrrm*	−1.846

Table 2. Equations for pentads using three parameters, α, σ and ω

$$A_1 = mmmm = \omega(1 - 5\beta + 5\beta^2) + (1 - \omega)\sigma^4$$
$$A_2 = mmmr = \omega(2\beta - 6\beta^2) + 2(1 - \omega)\sigma^3(1 - \sigma)$$
$$A_3 = rmmr = \omega\beta^2 + (1 - \omega)\sigma^2(1 - \sigma)^2$$
$$A_4 = mmrr = \omega(2\beta - 6\beta^2) + 2(1 - \omega)\sigma^2(1 - \sigma)^2$$
$$A_5 = mmrm = 2\omega\beta^2 + 2(1 - \omega)\sigma^3(1 - \sigma)$$
$$A_6 = rmrr = 2\omega\beta^2 + 2(1 - \omega)\sigma(1 - \sigma)^3$$
$$A_7 = rmrm = 2\omega\beta^2 + 2(1 - \omega)\sigma^2(1 - \sigma)^2$$
$$A_8 = rrrr = \omega\beta^2 + 2(1 - \omega)(1 - \sigma)^4$$
$$A_9 = mrrr = 2\omega\beta^2 + 2(1 - \omega)\sigma(1 - \sigma)^3$$
$$A_{10} = mrrm = \omega(\beta - 3\beta^2) + (1 - \omega)\sigma^2(1 - \sigma)^2$$

* $\beta = \alpha(1 - \alpha)$.

3. CONFORMATION IN POLY(VINYLIDENE FLUORIDE)

Poly(vinylidene fluoride), $(CH_2{=}CF_2)_n$ has been considered to have three crystal modifications depending on the crystallization condition (i.e. the precipitation solvent, the concentration of the polymer and the annealing temperature during crystallization). The difference between these crystal modifications at the molecular level is that of chain conformation. In this section we will clarify the relationship between conformations in solution and in solution-grown crystals.

The three stable conformers that are relevant are shown in Fig. 10 in a Newman projection. In the left one the skeletal bonds are composed of the segment started from CH_2, the segment which is perpendicular to the plane of the paper, started from the terminal of the above segment and the segment terminated at CF_2. In this conformer CH_2 and CF_2 are the most separated; such a conformer is called *trans* (T). The remaining two conformers are called *gauche*. If these two must be distinguished with each other, the notations G and $\overline{G}$ are used (Fig. 10).

In the proton NMR spectrum of this polymer the $C\underline{H}_2$ peak splits into five peaks with equal spacings. This spacing is called the indirect spin–spin coupling constant, and the notation J is usually used. This splitting is due to coupling between protons and four vicinal fluorine nuclei, i.e. $—C\underline{F}_2—C\underline{H}_2—C\underline{F}_2—$ ("vicinal" means atoms separated by three consecutive bonds ($\underline{H}—C—C—\underline{F}$)). The magnitude of J depends on the conformation. In the T conformer there are four vicinal H—F pairs in which two are *trans* between H and F, and two are *gauche*. We can, therefore, write

$$J_T = (J_t + J_g)/2,$$
$$J_G = J_{\overline{G}} = (J_t + 3J_g)/4, \tag{1}$$

where capital subscripts T, G, and $\overline{G}$ stand for the conformation of skeletal bonds, and small subscripts t and g stand for the conformation between H and F atoms.

Due to the rapid interconversion of the conformers, we can observe only an average value of eqn (1):

$$J_{obs} = \frac{2J_G + J_T \exp(-\Delta E/kT)}{2 + \exp(-\Delta E/kT)}, \tag{2}$$

in which ΔE is the energy difference between G and T conformers, k is the Boltzmann constant and T is the temperature.

Table 3. The calculated α, σ, and ω values for various polypropylenes

Sample	Crude tacticity	α	σ	ω
LH-atac	*atactic*	0.894	0.239	0.822
LH-5402	*isotactic*	0.984	0.164	0.987
XY-S701	*isotactic*	0.980	0.014	0.986

R. Chûjô

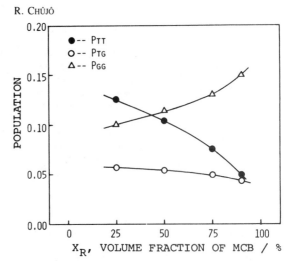

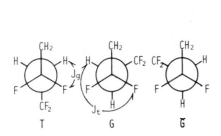

Fig. 10. Three stable conformers in poly-(vinylidene fluoride).

Fig. 11. Dependence of the populations P_{TT}, P_{TG}, and P_{GG} on the volume fraction of monochlorobenzene in poly(vinylidene fluoride).

From experimental NMR data J_t and J_g are determined to be 35.7 Hz and 6.5 Hz irrespective of temperature and the type of solvent. The value of ΔE depends on the solvent[5].

It is well known that when the crystal of this polymer is precipitated from the mixed-solvent system, monochlorobenzene (MCB) and dimethyl sulfoxide (DMSO), the conformation in the crystal depends on the composition of the solvent. In order to apply NMR data to the study of the relationship between crystalline and solution conformations, we must use the precipitation temperature in eqn (2). This yields the result of Fig. 11. We can see from this figure that the population, P_{GG}, of the GG conformer ($P_{GG}=P_{G\bar{G}}=P_{\bar{G}G}=P_{\bar{G}\bar{G}}$) is large over a wide range of X_R, the volume fraction of MCB. We nevertheless cannot find these conformers in the crystalline state. Perhaps these conformers have insufficient intermolecular interaction. Proceeding to the comparison between P_{TT} and P_{TG} ($=P_{T\bar{G}}=P_{GT}=P_{\bar{G}T}$), except for X_R close to unity, P_{TT} is always larger than P_{TG}. The conformation of the corresponding crystalline structures is also TT, as shown in Fig. 12(I). If X_R is close to unity, P_{TT} and P_{TG} are close to each other. There are two kinds of conclusions about the corresponding crystalline structure: TGT$\bar{G}$ [Fig. 12(II)] and TGTTT$\bar{G}$TT [Fig. 12(III)]. From the results of NMR the latter seems to be reasonable.

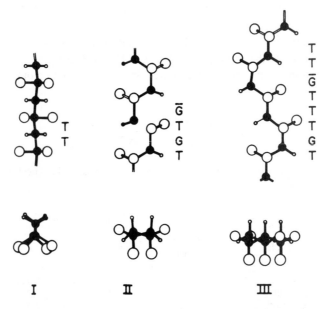

Fig. 12. Three crystal modifications in poly(vinylidene fluoride).

In this article the concept of symmetry was reviewed for polymers. Only two examples were introduced relating to the polymer configuration and conformation. Of course, this concept is widely accepted in polymer science.

REFERENCES

1. W. W. Fleming, C. A. Fyfe, R. D. Kendrick, J. R. Lyerla, Jr., H. Vanni and C. S. Yannoni, Variable-temperature magic-angle spinning carbon-13 NMR studies of solid polymers, in *Polymer Characterization by ESR and NMR*, pp. 193–217. ACS Symposium Series **142** (1980).
2. A. Bunn, E. A. Cudby, R. K. Harris, K. J. Packer and B. J. Say, *Chem. Commun.* 15–16 (1981).
3. F. A. Bovey and L. W. Jelinsky, *Chain Structure and Conformation of Macromolecules*, pp. 223–249. Academic Press, New York (1982).
4. S.-N. Zhu, X.-Z. Yang and R. Chûjô, *Polym. J.* **15**, 859–867 (1983).
5. I. Ando, H. Kobayasi and R. Chûjô, *"Contemporary Topics in Polymer Science"*, Vol. 4, pp. 173–182. Plenum, New York (1984).

Comp. & Maths. with Appls. Vol. 12B, Nos. 3/4, pp. 859–876, 1986
Printed in Great Britain.

0886–9561/86 $3.00 + .00
© 1986 Pergamon Press Ltd.

KEKULÉ STRUCTURES AND THEIR
SYMMETRY PROPERTIES

S. J. CYVIN

Division of Physical Chemistry, The University of Trondheim, N-7034 Trondheim-NTH, Norway

and

I. GUTMAN

Faculty of Science, University of Kragujevac, YU-34000 Kragujevac, Yugoslavia

Abstract—After a short historical introduction the role of Kekulé structures in theoretical chemistry is summarized. The present work concentrates upon conjugated hydrocarbons with six-membered rings. In a mathematical treatment they are represented by benzenoid systems, which consist of congruent regular hexagons. The vertices represent carbon atoms. Relations are given between certain characteristic numbers, viz. the number of vertices of different kinds (secondary, tertiary, external, internal), number of edges and of the rings. Kekuléan and non-Kekuléan benzenoids are exemplified. The latter class consists of mathematical constructions without any possible Kekulé structure.

A great amount of work has been done in the area of graph theory applied to benzenoids. Some of the most important theorems are summarized. Another approach employs group theory in the studies of the symmetry of Kekulé structures. A benzenoid or one of its Kekulé structures may belong to one of the following eight symmetry groups: $\mathscr{D}_{6h}$, $\mathscr{C}_{6h}$, $\mathscr{D}_{3h}$, $\mathscr{C}_{3h}$, $\mathscr{D}_{2h}$, $\mathscr{C}_{2v}$, $\mathscr{C}_{2h}$, $\mathscr{C}_s$. Examples are given.

Cata-condensed benzenoids are defined by having no internal vertices. Especially simple are the single straight and single zig-zag chains. The number of Kekulé structures and their symmetries are treated in these two cases. In the latter case the Fibonacci numbers come in.

Some classes of reticular benzenoids are defined, and the multiple zig-zag chains are considered in some detail. A recurrence formula for the number of Kekulé structures with relevance to this class of benzenoids is presented for the first time, along with several deductions from it.

INTRODUCTION

Historical

The history of Kekulé structures began in 1865, when August Kekulé invented the structural formula of benzene[1]. Based on intuitive chemical reasoning Kekulé concluded that benzene is a cyclic molecule, having the form of a regular hexagon [Fig. 1 (I)]. This structure was much later confirmed by various diffraction and spectroscopic measurements; see, for example, [2]. Formula I, however, had a serious drawback. The carbon atoms became trivalent, contrary to the fact that in all other structural formulas known at that time the valency of the carbon atoms was 4. Kekulé resolved this problem by inserting three additional carbon–carbon bonds in I. This resulted in the formulas II and III, which are nowadays known under the name of the Kekulé structures of benzene. In simplified drawings (see the bottom part of Fig. 1) the hydrogen atoms are omitted. The representation of the structure of benzene by means of the formulas II and/or III was far from satisfactory. For instance, neither II nor III reflects the correct $\mathscr{D}_{6h}$ symmetry of the benzene molecule. In addition, it was difficult for 19th century chemistry to accept the fact that the structure of a molecule need not be represented by a unique structural formula.

A similar situation occurred with a great number of other organic compounds, the so-called unsaturated conjugated systems, and especially the aromatics. In particular, there exist a great number of condensed aromatic molecules, which consist of fused six-membered (benzenoid) rings. They belong to the benzenoids according to a usual definition (see below). As an example, there are four distinct Kekulé structures of anthracene (Fig. 2), none of which possesses the correct $\mathscr{D}_{2h}$ symmetry. A Kekulé structure has (loosely speaking) alternating single and double carbon–carbon bonds throughout. The discussions concerning the structure of conjugated molecules continued until the middle of our century. A more or less satisfactory solution of the "Benzolproblem" was not obtained before the rise of quantum chemistry and, in particular, resonance theory[3,4] and molecular-orbital theory[4,5].

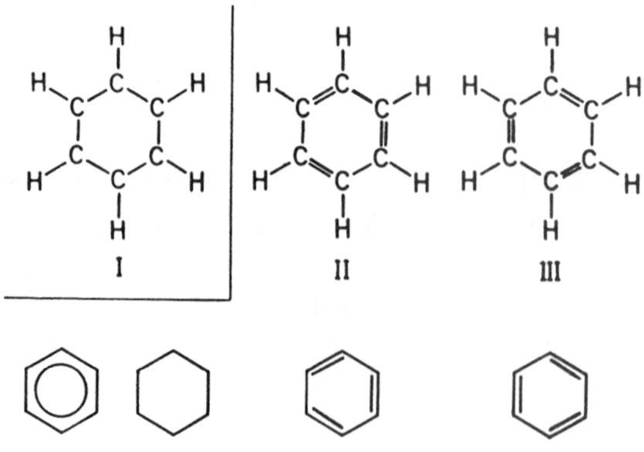

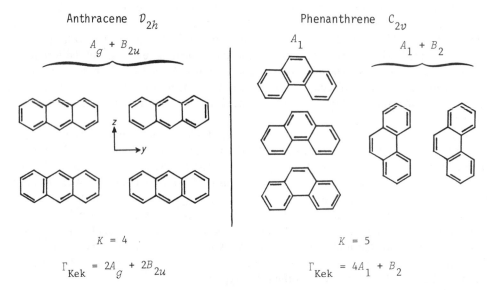

Fig. 1. Structural formulas for benzene, C_6H_6.

According to the resonance-theoretical interpretation[3,4] the ground state of the benzene molecule is described as involving both structures II and III (Fig. 1). Sometimes one speaks of benzene as resonating between the structures II and III. As a consequence, benzene is stabilized (relative to II or III) by a certain amount of energy, the resonance energy. Figure 1 (bottom part, left) includes a modern representation of the benzene molecule. It is frequently simplified to a single hexagon.

In the language of resonance theory the real ground state of anthracene (having $\mathscr{D}_{2h}$ symmetry) resonates between its four Kekulé structures (Fig. 2) and has a lower energy than each of them. It should be emphasized, however, that the quantum-chemical resonance does not imply actual alternating between different structures during the time period[3,4]. This point has been a source for many misunderstandings.

The role of Kekulé structures in theoretical chemistry

Recent developments in resonance theory[6–10] revealed the great role of the number of Kekulé structures (K), especially in the theoretical chemistry of benzenoid hydrocarbons. Some of the most important practical applications of the Kekulé structures, and their number K in particular, are the following.

(a) The total π-electron energy of a benzenoid hydrocarbon C_vH_s is a linear function of K and can be calculated by means of the semiempirical formula[11,12]

$$E = (0.201v - 0.049s + 0.043K \cdot 0.795^{v-s}) \cdot E\{\text{benzene}\}. \tag{1}$$

Fig. 2. The K Kekulé structures for anthracene ($K = 4$) and phenanthrene ($K = 5$), classified according to symmetry.

(b) The resonance energy (RE) can be estimated as [9]

$$RE = 114.3 \ln K \quad [kJ \cdot mol^{-1}].\tag{2}$$

(c) The rate constant of the reaction of a benzenoid hydrocarbon with maleic anhydride is well reproduced by the expression[13]

$$k = 0.002(K_P/K_R)^{16} \quad [dm^3 \cdot mol^{-1} \cdot s^{-1}],\tag{3}$$

where K_P and K_R denote the number of Kekulé structures of the reactant (i.e. benzenoid hydrocarbon) and of the product, respectively.

(d) If among the K Kekulé structures of a benzenoid hydrocarbon K_{rs} structures have a double bond between the atoms r and s, then the simple formula

$$d_{rs} = 146.5 - 13.0(K_{rs}/K) \quad [pm]\tag{4}$$

reproduces the interatomic distances with an error of only 1 pm[8,10]. The relation is connected with one of the different definitions of bond order for carbon–carbon bonds.

(3) Kekulé structures have been employed in vibrational-force-field developments of aromatics in the area of molecular spectroscopy[14,15].

Many qualitative deductions from Kekulé structures can be done. A simple consideration tells us, for instance, that phenanthrene is chemically more stable than anthracene. This is correctly predicted just from the number of Kekulé structures, four and five, respectively, for these two isomers of $C_{14}H_{10}$ (cf. Fig. 2). Another interesting fact is that no conjugated hydrocarbons without Kekulé structures have been found in nature, and all the numerous attempts to prepare such compounds have failed[16].

Mathematical treatments

In principle all the Kekulé structures for a given molecule may be derived by systematical drawings of alternating single and double bonds. With increasing size of the molecule this method soon becomes practically impossible. However, different methods are open for computer programming[17]. The mathematical problems of Kekulé structures for benzenoids reduce to topological properties of congruent regular hexagons. A great amount of work has been done in this area, where graph theory has been used extensively. The literature is too voluminous to be cited here; we only refer to a previous review[18], which contains 104 references, and a modern textbook (two volumes) entitled *Chemical Graph Theory*[19]. Much less work has been done in applications of group theory to the symmetry of Kekulé structures[20]. The intensive work in the area of Kekulé structures in mathematical chemistry has led to many interesting results, but still a great deal of even fundamental problems have remained unsolved.

BENZENOID SYSTEMS: BASIC CONCEPTS

Definition

Many studies of the conjugated hydrocarbons are concentrated upon six-membered (benzenoid) ring systems. In a restricted sense we define a benzenoid system as represented by congruent regular hexagons in the plane so that two hexagons are either disjoint or possess a common edge. (Many other names have been proposed for these systems in the literature.) The systems correspond to condensed aromatic molecules of six-membered rings (which are not exactly regular in reality). We include the single hexagon (corresponding to benzene) among the benzenoids.

Characteristic numbers

A benzenoid is characterized (but not defined) by several integers[21,22]. The number of rings is here denoted by h. It is uniquely determined by counting the centers of all six-membered rings. The number of vertices, v, corresponds to the number of carbon atoms. In analogy with secondary and tertiary carbon atoms we will refer to secondary and tertiary vertices (also said to have the graph-theoretical valency 2 and 3, respectively). Let their number be s (secondary) and t (tertiary). Then $v = s + t$, and also

$$s = v - 2(h - 1), \quad t = 2(h - 1). \tag{5}$$

The vertices are also divided into internal and external ones in a way which is easily grasped by intuition. (The external vertices lie on the contour or perimeter of the benzenoid.) Let the numbers be designated v_{int} (internal) and v_{ext} (external). One has $v = v_{int} + v_{ext}$, and

$$v_{int} = 2(2h + 1) - v, \quad v_{ext} = 2v - 2(2h + 1). \tag{6}$$

The tertiary vertices alone may be divided into internal and external ones ($t = t_{int} + t_{ext}$). One obviously has $v_{int} = t_{int}$ and $v_{ext} = s + t_{ext}$. These relations manifest the fact that all internal vertices are tertiary and all secondary vertices are external. Finally we introduce the number of edges, e, which is

$$e = v + h - 1. \tag{7}$$

It appears from eqn (5) that t always is an even integer (or zero for $h = 1$). v_{ext} is always even in accord with eqn (6).

Coloring of vertices

The vertices may be "colored" by two colors (say black and white) in a unique way so that two adjacent vertices never have the same color. The black and white external vertices are evidently equal in number:

$$v_{ext}^{(b)} = v_{ext}^{(w)} = v_{ext}/2 = v - (2h + 1). \tag{8}$$

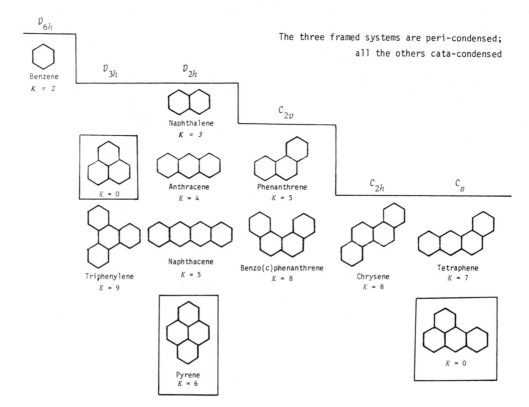

Fig. 3. All benzenoid systems with number of rings up to 4.

Classification of benzenoids

Cata-condensed benzenoids have no internal vertices. The single hexagon is included in this class (although the term "condensed" is inappropriate in this case). The remaining benzenoids are called peri-condensed (cf. Fig. 3). Here we have not worried about special classes of benzenoids (e.g. corona-condensed), which may be excluded by a more sophisticated definition.

The symbol K is used to denote the number of Kekulé structures. A precise definition reads: A Kekulé structure (of an unsaturated conjugated hydrocarbon) is a structural formula in which every carbon atom is tetravalent and incident to exactly one double bond. Benzenoids with $K = 0$ can be constructed (cf. Fig. 3) and are termed non-Kekuléan. For Kekuléan benzenoids $K > 0$.

Characteristic numbers for Kekuléan benzenoids

A Kekuléan benzenoid hydrocarbon must have an equal number of vertices of the two colors:

$$v^{(b)} = v^{(w)} = v/2 = 2h + 1 - (t_{int}/2). \tag{9}$$

In this case v must be an even integer. In fact, most of the characteristic numbers, viz. v, s, t, v_{int}, v_{ext}, t_{int}, t_{ext}, are even (or zero) for a Kekuléan benzenoid. e is even when h is odd and vice versa. It is also clear that the internal vertices of the two colors must be equal in number for a Kekuléan benzenoid. It is found that

$$v_{int}^{(b)} = v_{int}^{(w)} = t_{int}^{(b)} = t_{int}^{(w)} = 2h + 1 - v/2. \tag{10}$$

Finally, we may enumerate the single (e_-) and double ($e_=$) carbon–carbon bonds in a Kekulé structure. One has $e_- + e_= = e$, and separately,

$$e_- = \frac{s}{2} + t = \frac{v}{2} + h - 1, \quad e_= = \frac{1}{2}(s + t) = \frac{v}{2}. \tag{11}$$

KEKULÉAN AND NON-KEKULÉAN SYSTEMS

Figure 4 shows the coloring of vertices in two benzenoids. In one case (left-hand part) we find unequal numbers of black and white vertices (either total or internal). This system must necessarily be non-Kekuléan. The right-hand side of Fig. 4 exhibits equal number of black and white vertices in pyrene, which is a Kekuléan benzenoid.

It was sometimes believed that the condition $v^{(b)} = v^{(w)}$, and consequently $t_{int}^{(b)} = t_{int}^{(w)}$, is a sufficient condition for a benzenoid to be Kekuléan. Ten years ago, however, non-Kekuléan benzenoids possessing the condition of equality were depicted[21]. The smallest ones have 11 rings (cf. Fig. 5). No criterion is yet known which easily decides whether a given benzenoid is Kekuléan or not.

KEKULÉ STRUCTURES AND GRAPH THEORY

If the carbon–atom skeleton of an unsaturated conjugated hydrocarbon is represented by a graph, then it is easy to see that the (chemical) concept of a Kekulé structure is fully equivalent to the (graph-theoretical) concept of a 1-factor. A 1-factor of a graph G is a spanning subgraph of G whose all components have two vertices. More on 1-factors and 1-factorization of graphs can be found, for example, in [23]. As a convincing example one should compare the four Kekulé structures of anthracene (Fig. 2) with the four 1-factors of the corresponding graph (see Fig. 6).

The coincidence between 1-factors in graph theory and Kekulé structures in chemistry enables one to exploit various mathematical techniques in chemical investigations and, in particular, provides powerful means for the enumeration of Kekulé structures. We shall mention here a few typical results[6,18]. Let **A** be the adjacency matrix of the molecular graph, defined

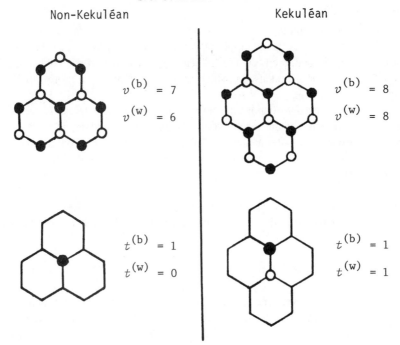

$v^{(b)} = 7$

$v^{(w)} = 6$

$v^{(b)} = 8$

$v^{(w)} = 8$

$t^{(b)} = 1$

$t^{(w)} = 0$

$t^{(b)} = 1$

$t^{(w)} = 1$

Fig. 4. Colored vertices in two benzenoids, one non-Kekuléan and one Kekuléan (pyrene).

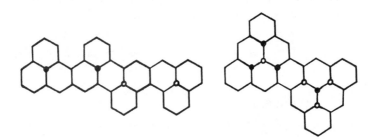

Fig. 5. Colored internal vertices in the two smallest ($h = 11$) non-Kekuléan benzenoids ($K = 0$) with equal number of black and white vertices (total or internal).

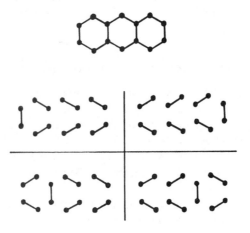

Fig. 6. The anthracene graph and its four 1-factors.

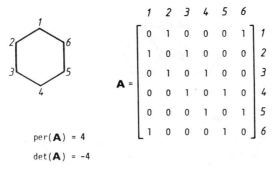

per(**A**) = 4

det(**A**) = -4

Fig. 7. The adjacency matrix for benzene.

as $A_{rs} = 1$ if the vertices x_r and x_s are adjacent, and $A_{rs} = 0$ otherwise. The zeros include also the diagonal elements A_{rr}. Figure 7 shows the example for benzene.

THEOREM 1

For alternate hydrocarbons (which possess no odd cycles),

$$\text{per}(\mathbf{A}) = K^2, \tag{12}$$

where "per" denotes permanent.

THEOREM 2

For benzenoid hydrocarbons with v carbon atoms,

$$\det(\mathbf{A}) = (-1)^{v/2}K^2, \tag{13}$$

where "det" denotes determinant.

THEOREM 3

If G is a molecular graph, x_r and x_s are its two adjacent vertices, and y_{rs} is the edge connecting x_r and x_s, then

$$K\{G\} = K\{G - y_{rs}\} + K\{G - x_r - x_s\}. \tag{14}$$

THEOREM 4

If G is a molecular graph, x_p and x_q are its two adjacent vertices, and x_p is primary (it has the graph-theoretical valency 1), then

$$K\{G\} = K\{G - x_p - x_q\}. \tag{15}$$

Figure 8 gives an illustration of Theorems 3 and 4 for phenanthrene (see also Fig. 2). These theorems provide an efficient method for the calculation of the number of Kekulé structures. An illustrative example concerning the zig–zag chain benzenoids is treated in a subsequent section.

SYMMETRY OF KEKULÉ STRUCTURES

The benzenoids considered here may belong to the symmetry group $\mathscr{D}_{6h}$ or a subgroup of $\mathscr{D}_{6h}$ which includes the reflection in the horizontal plane: $\mathscr{C}_{6h}$, $\mathscr{D}_{3h}$, $\mathscr{C}_{3h}$, $\mathscr{D}_{2h}$, $\mathscr{C}_{2v}$, $\mathscr{C}_{2h}$, or $\mathscr{C}_s$. Figure 3 shows examples of most of these symmetries. The $\mathscr{C}_{3h}$ symmetry occurs for $h \geq 6$. It is represented by one non-Kekuléan structure for $h = 6$ and one Kekuléan for $h = 17$ (see Fig. 9). The $\mathscr{C}_{6h}$ symmetry does not appear before $h = 19$, and for one single structure in that case (Fig. 9).

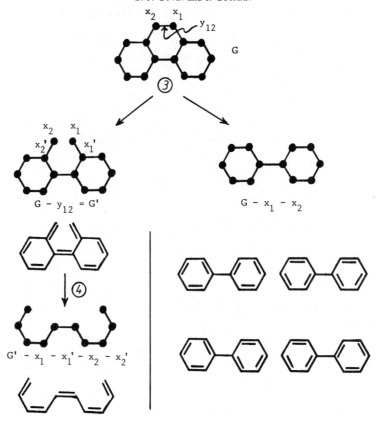

Fig. 8. Illustration of Theorems 3 and 4 (encircled numerals) for phenanthrene.

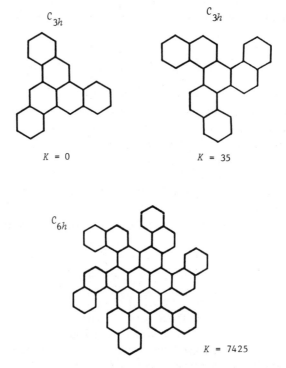

Fig. 9. The benzenoids of $\mathscr{C}_{3h}$ symmetry with $h = 6$ and $h = 7$, along with the smallest ($h = 19$) benzenoid of $\mathscr{C}_{6h}$ symmetry.

Table 1. Character table of $\mathscr{C}_{2v}$ with the characters χ_{Kek} for five benzenoids. (x is chosen perpendicular to the molecular plane)

C_{2v}		E	C_2	$\sigma(zx)$	$\sigma(yz)$
irreducible representations	A_1	1	1	1	1
	A_2	1	1	-1	-1
	B_1	1	-1	1	-1
	B_2	1	-1	-1	1
Phenanthrene		5	3	3	5
Benzo(c)phenanthrene		8	2	2	8
Pentaphene		10	4	4	10
Dibenzophenanthrene		13	5	5	13
Picene		13	5	5	13

The Kekulé structures themselves may possess the full symmetry of the molecule (then they are said to be totally symmetrical), or their symmetry may be lower, and again belong to one of the groups mentioned above. A group-theoretical treatment appears as if it was designed for an analysis of these symmetries. The whole set of Kekulé structures may be used as a basis of a representation of the molecular symmetry group. If the characters of this representation, say χ_{Kek}, are obtained in one way or another, the standard group-theoretical techniques[24] readily give the corresponding symmetrical structure,

$$\Gamma_{Kek} = \sum_{\substack{i \\ \text{(direct} \\ \text{summation)}}} n_i \Gamma_i, \quad n_i = \frac{1}{g} \sum_R \chi_i^*(R) \chi_{Kek}(R). \tag{16}$$

Here Γ_i and χ_i pertain to the irreducible representations, and g is the number of symmetry operations R (the order of the group). It is an embarrassing fact that no general methods are known for deducing χ_{Kek} for a given benzenoid. This goal of the group-theoretical treatment would at the same time solve the enumeration of Kekulé structures, since one has

$$K = \chi_{Kek}(E), \tag{17}$$

i.e. the character of the identity operation is equal to the number of Kekulé structures. In order to exemplify this problem we must resort to the opposite approach: to set up the characters after having drawn all the Kekulé structures for a given molecule. Table 1 shows the characters for five benzenoids of symmetry $\mathscr{C}_{2v}$ (cf. Figs. 3 and 10).

The application of eqn (16) is exemplified for phenanthrene below.

$$n(A_1) = \tfrac{1}{4}(1 \cdot 5 + 1 \cdot 3 + 1 \cdot 3 + 1 \cdot 5) = 4,$$

$$n(A_2) = \tfrac{1}{4}(1 \cdot 5 + 1 \cdot 3 - 1 \cdot 3 - 1 \cdot 5) = 0,$$

$$n(B_1) = \tfrac{1}{4}(1 \cdot 5 - 1 \cdot 3 + 1 \cdot 3 - 1 \cdot 5) = 0,$$

$$n(B_2) = \tfrac{1}{4}(1 \cdot 5 - 1 \cdot 3 - 1 \cdot 3 + 1 \cdot 5) = 1.$$

The result is consistent with the given Γ_{Kek} in Fig. 2. For benzo(c)phenanthrene (Fig. 3) one finds

$$\Gamma_{Kek} = 5A_1 + 3B_2.$$

For the three remaining benzenoids of Table 1 the Γ_{Kek} expressions are given in Fig. 10.

Coronene was considered in order to exemplify highly symmetrical molecules as well. It

S. J. CYVIN and I. GUTMAN

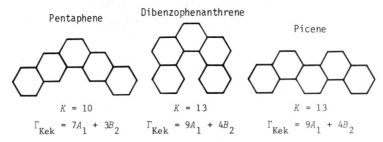

Fig. 10. Examples of benzenoids with $h = 5$ and belonging to the $\mathcal{C}_{2v}$ symmetry.

is the simplest $\mathcal{D}_{6h}$ benzenoid apart from benzene itself. Figure 11 shows representatives of the 20 coronene Kekulé structures, classified according to symmetry[20,25].

CATA-CONDENSED BENZENOIDS

Introduction

Recursive algorithms have been derived for the enumeration of Kekulé structures in cata-condensed benzenoids[18,19,26,27]. For certain classes of such molecules algebraic formulas have also been given for K as well Γ_{Kek} (see below; also Ref. [28], which gives a general treatment for K). Especially simple are the series of single straight chains (polyacenes) and zig–zag chains. We will designate these structures by L(h) and A(h), respectively. Naphthalene, anthracene and phenanthrene (cf. Fig. 3) are simple examples. They are to be designated L(2) ≡ A(2), L(3) and A(3), respectively. It is advantageous to include benzene to these classes as L(1) ≡ A(1).

Single straight chain

For the polyacenes, L(h), you can readily derive the number of Kekulé structures just from systematical drawings. You will soon discover that the Kekulé structures each contain exactly one double bond among the "vertical" edges (see Fig. 2), whose number is one more than the number of rings. Hence for the K number

$$K\{L(h)\} = h + 1. \tag{18}$$

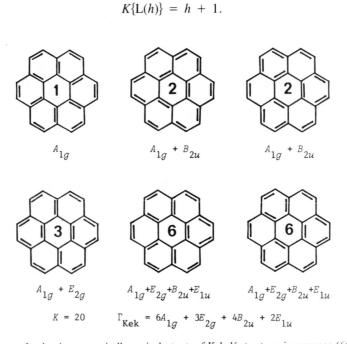

Fig. 11. Representants for the six symmetrically equivalent sets of Kekulé structures in coronene ($\mathcal{D}_{6h}$). The number of structures (k) within each set is indicated in the central ring. They may be derived by reflections, rotations of 120° or rotations of 60° in the cases $k = 2$, 3 and 6, respectively.

The symmetry is $\mathscr{D}_{2h}$ for all cases of $h \geq 2$. For the symmetrical structures the following formulas have been given[20]:

$$\Gamma_{\text{Kek}}\{L(h)\} = \left(\frac{h}{2} + 1\right)A_g + \frac{h}{2}B_{2u}, \quad h = 2, 4, 6, \ldots; \tag{19}$$

$$\Gamma_{\text{Kek}}\{L(h)\} = \tfrac{1}{2}(h + 1)(A_g + B_{2u}), \quad h = 3, 5, 7, \ldots. \tag{20}$$

Equation (20) is seen to be consistent with the result from Fig. 2 (anthracene) for $h = 3$.

Single zig–zag chain and the Fibonacci numbers

Consider the benzenoid $A(h)$ of Fig. 12 ($h \geq 3$). Apply Theorem 3 to the edge indicated by an arrow. Then

$$K\{A(h)\} = K\{A'\} + K\{A''\} \tag{21}$$

The vertices x_1 and x_2 (still referring to Fig. 12) are primary. Applying Theorem 4 twice one obtains

$$K\{A'\} = K\{A(h - 1)\}. \tag{22}$$

Similarly, a repeated application of Theorem 4 to A'' gives

$$K\{A''\} = K\{A(h - 2)\}. \tag{23}$$

Equations (21)–(23) give the recurrence formula

$$K\{A(h)\} = K\{A(h - 1)\} + K\{A(h - 2)\}, \quad h \geq 3. \tag{24}$$

One has the initial conditions $K\{A(1)\} = 2$ (the case of benzene) and $K\{A(2)\} = 3$ (naphthalene). With the definition $K\{A(0)\} = 1$, eqn (24) is also valid for $h = 3$. In conclusion, the K values are found to be ($h \geq 0$)[26,29]

$$K\{A(h)\} = F_{h+1}, \tag{25}$$

where F_n is the $(n + 1)$th Fibonacci number;

$$F_0 = F_1 = 1, \quad F_{n+1} = F_n + F_{n-1}; \quad n = 1, 2, 3, \ldots. \tag{26}$$

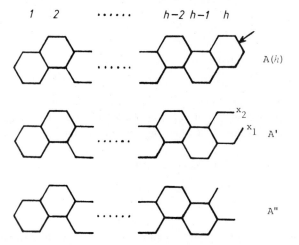

Fig. 12. The benzenoid $A(h)$, and illustration of Theorem 3.

The first Fibonacci numbers are: 1, 1, 2, 3, 5, 8, 13, 21, ... Equation (25) is alternatively given (in closed form) by

$$K\{A(h)\} = \frac{1}{\sqrt{5}} \left[\left(\frac{1 + \sqrt{5}}{2} \right)^{h+2} - \left(\frac{1 - \sqrt{5}}{2} \right)^{h+2} \right]. \tag{27}$$

The first members of this class of molecules are $A(1) \equiv$ benzene (Figs. 1, 3), $K = 2$; $A(2) \equiv$ naphthalene (Fig. 3), $K = 3$; $A(3) \equiv$ phenanthrene (Figs. 2, 3), $K = 5$; $A(4) \equiv$ chrysene (Fig. 3), $K = 8$; $A(5) \equiv$ picene (Fig. 10), $K = 13$.

For $h \geq 3$ the symmetry alternates between $\mathscr{C}_{2v}$ and $\mathscr{C}_{2h}$ for odd and even values, respectively. It has been found[20,29] that

$$\Gamma_{\text{Kek}}\{A(h)\} = \tfrac{1}{2}(F_{h+1} + F_{(h+3)/2})A_1 + \tfrac{1}{2}(F_{h+1} - F_{(h+3)/2})B_2, \quad h = 3, 5, 7, \ldots; \tag{28}$$

$$\Gamma_{\text{Kek}}\{A(h)\} = \tfrac{1}{2}(F_{h+1} + F_{h/2})A_g + \tfrac{1}{2}(F_{h+1} - F_{h/2})B_u, \quad\quad h = 4, 6, 8, \ldots. \tag{29}$$

Equation (28) is consistent with the result from Fig. 2 (phenanthrene) and Fig. 10 (picene) for $h = 3$ and 5, respectively.

SOME CLASSES OF RETICULAR BENZENOIDS

Algebraic formulas have also been derived for the number of Kekulé structures of multiple chains (reticular benzenoids). Figure 13 shows three examples, which have been studied. For two of the classes the expressions of K are known in closed form[30]:

$$K\{T(m, n)\} = (m + 1)^n, \tag{31}$$

$$K\{L(m, n)\} = \binom{m + n}{m} = \binom{m + n}{n}. \tag{32}$$

For $n = 1$ the three classes of Fig. 13 coincide; $T(m, 1) \equiv L(m, 1) \equiv A(m, 1) \equiv L(m)$. Moreover, the formulas (31) and (32) both give $K = m + 1$ ($n = 1$) in consistence with eqn (18). Equation (31) also applies to $m = 1$, which corresponds to polyphenylenes (cf. Fig. 14), although these molecules are not (condensed) benzenoids. One obtains $K = 2^2 = 4$ for $T(1, 2) \equiv$ biphenyl, in consistence with Fig. 8. $T(2, n)$ for $n \geq 2$ are called polyrylenes. The simplest example is perylene, $T(2, 2)$; cf. Fig. 15, which also gives the number of Kekulé structures (3^2) and the deduced Γ_{Kek}[20]. The multiple zig–zag chain $A(m, n)$ is identical with $L(m, n)$ for $n = 2$: $A(m, 2) \equiv L(m, 2) \equiv L(2, m)$. The smallest Kekuléan peri-condensed benzenoid, pyrene (Fig. 3), is equivalent to $A(2, 2) \equiv L(2, 2)$. No general formula is known for the number of Kekulé structures of the $A(m, n)$ benzenoids. In the subsequent section we report some new findings in this area.

MULTIPLE ZIG–ZAG CHAINS

Augmented structure

In our studies we have augmented the $A(m, n)$ structure by an auxiliary row on top of it, consisting of k rings, where $0 \leq k \leq m$ (cf. Fig. 16). The augmented structure is designated $A(m, n, k)$. For the limiting values of k one has, by virtue of the definitions,

$$A(m, n, 0) \equiv A(m, n), \tag{33}$$

$$A(m, n, m) \equiv A(m, n + 1). \tag{34}$$

Recurrence formulas

Using a reasoning similar to, but slightly more complex than, that which led to eqn (24),

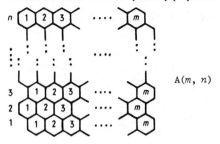

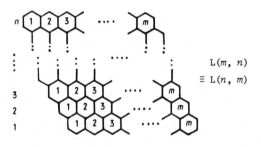

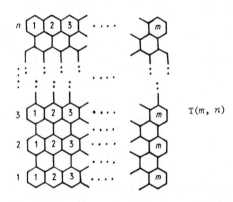

Fig. 13. Three classes of reticular benzenoids.

a recurrence formula for the number of Kekulé structures, $K\{A(m, n, k)\}$, has been derived. It is communicated here for the first time:

$$K\{A(m, n, k)\} = K\{A(m, n, k - 1)\}$$
$$+ K\{A(m, n - 1, m - k)\}; \quad m \geq k > 0, \quad n \geq 1. \quad (35)$$

A similar formula for $k = 0$ is obtained on combining (35) with eqns (33) and (34):

$$K\{A(m, n, 0)\} = K\{A(m, n)\} = K\{A(m, n - 1, m)\} = K\{A(m, n - 1, m - 1)\}$$
$$+ K\{A(m, n - 2, 0)\}, \quad m \geq 1, \quad n \geq 2. \quad (36)$$

T(1, n)
K = 2^n

Fig. 14. Polyphenylenes.

S. J. Cyvin and I. Gutman

Perylene $\quad D_{2h}$

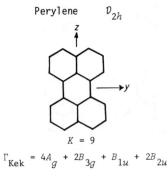

$K = 9$

$\Gamma_{Kek} = 4A_g + 2B_{3g} + B_{1u} + 2B_{2u}$

Fig. 15. Perylene.

The integer n is also allowed to have the value of zero. Hence we have an initial condition as

$$K\{A(m, 0, k)\} = k + 1, \quad k \geq 0. \tag{37}$$

This is the case of L(k), for which the K number is given by eqn (18). It is convenient to include $k = 0$ by virtue of the definition $K\{A(m, 0, 0)\} = 1$, although this trivial case of "no rings" is inadequate for benzenoids. Another initial condition reads

$$K\{A(m, 1, 0)\} = m + 1, \quad m \geq 0, \tag{38}$$

where the appropriate structure is L(m). The formula (38) may also be derived from (37) with the aid of (33) and (34); one has A(m, 1, 0) ≡ A(m, 1) ≡ A(m, 0, m). Finally, we extend the trivial case of "no rings" to be described by $m = 0$ as well as $n = 0$. Hence, for arbitrary m and n,

$$K\{A(m, 0)\} = K\{A(0, n)\} = 1. \tag{39}$$

Single zig–zag chain
    Consider the structures represented by A(1, n) ≡ A(n). Equation (36) gives

$$K\{A(1, n + 1)\} = K\{A(1, n, 0)\} + K\{A(1, n - 1, 0)\} = K\{A(1, n)\}$$
$$+ K\{A(1, n - 1)\}, \quad n \geq 1, \tag{40}$$

which is consistent with eqn (24). In the present notation one attains

$$K\{A(1, n)\} = F_{n+1}, \quad n \geq 0 \tag{41}$$

[cf. eqn (25)].

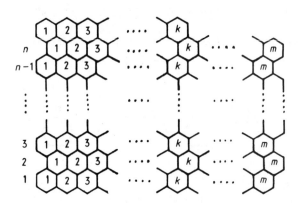

Fig. 16. The reticular A(m, n) benzenoid augmented with a row of k rings at the top: A(m, n, k).

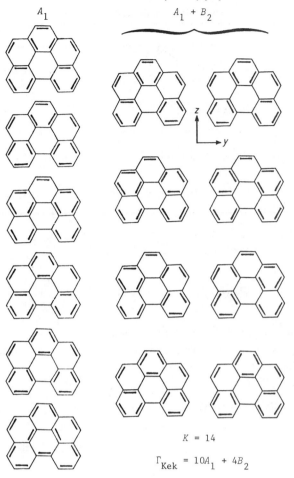

Fig. 17. The Kekulé structures of A(2, 3) ≡ benzo(g, h, i)perylene ($\mathscr{C}_{2v}$), classified according to symmetry.

Double zig–zag chain

For the structures A(2, n) repeated application of eqns (35) and (36) lead to

$$K\{A(2, n + 2)\} = 2K\{A(2, n + 1)\} + K\{A(2, n)\} - K\{A(2, n - 1)\}, \quad n \geq 1. \quad (42)$$

As initial conditions we have $K\{A(2, 0)\} = 1$, $K\{A(2, 1)\} = 3$ and $K\{A(2, 2)\} = 6$ (the case of pyrene). Hence all K numbers for higher values of n may be found successively; $K\{A(2, n)\} = 14, 31, 70, 157, \ldots$ for $n = 3, 4, 5, 6, \ldots$. The example of A(2, 3) is shown in Fig. 17, where the 14 Kekulé structures are classified according to their symmetries.

Algebraic formulas

Not only recurrence formulas, but algebraic formulas (in closed form) are obtainable by repeated use of eqn (35). First, one obtains the summation formula

$$K\{A(m, n)\} = K\{A(m, n - 1, m)\} = \sum_{i=0}^{m} K\{A(m, n - 2, i)\}, \quad n \geq 2. \quad (43)$$

For $n = 2$ the above relation gives

$$K\{A(m, 2)\} = \sum_{i=0}^{m} K\{A(m, 0, i)\} = \sum_{i=0}^{m} (i + 1) = \frac{1}{2} (m + 1)(m + 2). \quad (44)$$

Table 2. Survey of some summation formulas for the number of Kekulé structures of A(m, n) benzenoids

$K\{A(m, n)\}$	n
$\displaystyle\sum_{i=0}^{m} K\{A(m, n-2, i)\}$	$n \geq 2$
$\displaystyle\sum_{i=0}^{m} (i + 1)K\{A(m, n-3, i)\}$	$n \geq 3$
$\displaystyle\sum_{i=0}^{m} (i + 1)\left(m + 1 - \frac{i}{2}\right)K\{A(m, n-4, i)\}$	$n \geq 4$
$\displaystyle\sum_{i=0}^{m} \frac{1}{2}(i + 1)\left[(m + 1)(m + 2) - \frac{i}{3}(i + 2)\right]K\{A(m, n-5, i)\}$	$n \geq 5$

As expected, this result is consistent with eqn (32); one has

$$K\{A(m, 2)\} = K\{L(m, 2)\} = \binom{m + 2}{2}. \tag{45}$$

Further applications of eqn (35) give a series of summation formulas similar to eqn (43), and applicable to $n \geq 3, 4, 5, \ldots$. Table 2 gives a survey up to $n \geq 5$. The formula for $n \geq 3$ therein, when applied to $n = 3$, gives

$$K\{A(m, 3)\} = \sum_{i=0}^{m} (i + 1)K\{A(m, 0, i)\} = \sum_{i=0}^{m} (i + 1)^2$$

$$= \frac{1}{6} (m + 1)(m + 2)(2m + 3). \tag{46}$$

Also, this result had been known previously[19]. For $m = 2$ eqn (46) gives $K\{A(2, 3)\} = 14$ in consistence with Fig. 17. New equations are obtained upon application of the two bottom formulas of Table 2 to $n = 4$ and 5, respectively. The corresponding results of $K\{A(m, 4)\}$ and $K\{A(m, 5)\}$ are found in Table 3.

Cases with $k \neq 0$ may also be treated in a similar way. Equation (35) has already been found very useful. A further exploitation of it has given the summation formula

$$K\{A(m, n, k)\} = \sum_{i=0}^{k} K\{A(m, n - 1, m - i)\}, \quad m \geq k \geq 0, \quad n \geq 1. \tag{47}$$

Table 3. Algebraic expressions for the number of Kekulé structures of some A(m, n) benzenoids with fixed values of n

$K\{A(m, n)\}$	Expression
$K\{A(m, 0)\}$	1
$K\{A(m, 1)\}$	$m + 1$
$K\{A(m, 2)\}$	$\frac{1}{2}(m + 1)(m + 2)$
$K\{A(m, 3)\}$	$\frac{1}{6}(m + 1)(m + 2)(2m + 3)$
$K\{A(m, 4)\}$	$\frac{1}{24}(m + 1)(m + 2)\left[5(m + 1)(m + 2) + 2\right]$
$K\{A(m, 5)\}$	$\frac{1}{30}(m + 1)(m + 2)(2m + 3)\left[2(m + 1)(m + 2) + 1\right]$
$K\{A(m, 6)\}$	$\frac{1}{720}(m + 1)(m + 2)\left\{5m(m + 1)(m + 2)(m + 3)\right.$ $\left. + 2(2m + 3)^2\left[7(m + 1)(m + 2) + 6\right]\right\}$

Table 4. Algebraic expressions for the number of Kekulé structures of some A(m, n, k) benzenoids with fixed values of n

$K\{A(m, n, k)\}$	Expression
$K\{A(m, 0, k)\}$	$k + 1$
$K\{A(m, 1, k)\}$	$(k + 1)\left(m + 1 - \dfrac{k}{2}\right)$
$K\{A(m, 2, k)\}$	$\dfrac{1}{2}(k + 1)\left[(m + 1)(m + 2) - \dfrac{k}{3}(k + 2)\right]$
$K\{A(m, 3, k)\}$	$\dfrac{1}{6}(k + 1)\left\{\dfrac{k}{4}(k + 1)(k + 2)\right.$
	$\left. + \left[(m + 1)(m + 2) - \dfrac{k}{2}(k + 2)\right](2m + 3)\right\}$

When applied to $n = 1$ one finds

$$K\{A(m, 1, k)\} = \sum_{i=0}^{k} K\{A(m, 0, m - i)\} = \sum_{i=0}^{k} (m - i + 1)$$

$$= (k + 1)(m + 1 - k/2). \quad (48)$$

On inserting $k = 0$ and $k = m$ one obtains immediately the previous results for $K\{A(m, 1, 0)\} = K\{A(m, 1)\}$ and $K\{A(m, 1, m)\} = K\{A(m, 2)\}$, respectively (cf. Table 3). That covers the cases of A(m, n) for $n = 1$ and $n = 2$. Now we may apply the simple summation formula (43) for $n = 3$ along with eqn (47). It gives

$$K\{A(m, 3)\} = \sum_{i=0}^{m} K\{A(m, 1, i)\} = \sum_{i=0}^{m} (i + 1)(m + 1 - i/2), \quad (49)$$

which leads to the same result as above in eqn (46). In a similar way the summation formulas for $n \geq 3$, 4 and 5 (cf. Table 2) may be used to give $K\{A(m, n)\}$ for $n = 4$, 5 and 6, respectively. The new result for $K\{A(m, 6)\}$ was entered into Table 3. We have continued this procedure to evaluate the expressions of $K\{A(m, n, k)\}$ for $k = 2$ and 3. The results are found in Table 4. An application of these relations with the summation formulas of Table 2 might give the expressions of $K\{A(m, n)\}$ for still higher values of n, actually up to $n = 8$. Such analytical derivations rapidly become very complicated.

Finally, we wish to give some examples of A(m, n, k) benzenoids with $k \neq 0$. One has the A(2, 1, 1) and A(3, 1, 1) equal to phenanthrene and tetraphene, respectively (cf. Table 3). Equation (48) correctly gives $K\{\text{phenanthrene}\} = 5$ and $K\{\text{tetraphene}\} = 7$. Two five-ring ($h = 5$) molecules not belonging to any of the classes considered above are shown in Fig. 18.

Acknowledgement—SJC is grateful for the helpful consultation of Professor Jan Bakke and Professor Vernon Parker (Division of Organic Chemistry, The University of Trondheim).

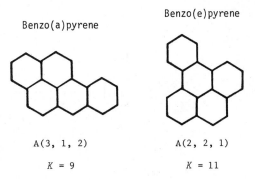

Benzo(a)pyrene

Benzo(e)pyrene

A(3, 1, 2)

$K = 9$

A(2, 2, 1)

$K = 11$

Fig. 18. Two benzenoids of A(m, n, k) with $k \neq 0$.

REFERENCES

1. R. Wizinger-Aust, J. B. Gillis, B. Helferich and C. Wurster, *Kekulé und seine Benzolformel.* Verlag Chemie, Weinheim (1966).
2. G. M. Badger, *Aromatic Character and Aromaticity.* Cambridge University Press, Cambridge (1969).
3. L. Pauling, *The Nature of the Chemical Bond.* Cornell University Press, Ithaca, NY (1945).
4. C. A. Coulson, *Valence.* Oxford University Press, Glasgow (1952).
5. E. Hückel, *Grundzüge der Theorie ungesättigter und aromatischer Verbindungen.* Verlag Chemie, Berlin (1940).
6. W. C. Herndon, Resonance theory and the enumeration of Kekulé structures. *J. Chem. Educ.* **51**, 10–15 (1974).
7. W. C. Herndon and M. L. Ellzey, Resonance theory. V. Resonance energies of benzenoid and nonbenzenoid π systems. *J. Am. Chem. Soc.* **96**, 6631–6642 (1974).
8. W. C. Herndon, Resonance theory. VI. Bond orders. *J. Am. Chem. Soc.* **96**, 7605–7614 (1974).
9. R. Swinborne-Sheldrake, W. C. Herndon and I. Gutman, Kekulé structures and resonance energies of benzenoid hydrocarbons. *Tetrahedron Lett.* 755–758 (1975).
10. W. C. Herndon and C. Párkányi, π bond orders and bond lengths. *J. Chem. Educ.* **53**, 689–692 (1976).
11. G. G. Hall, Eigenvalues of molecular graphs. *Inst. Math. Appl.* **17**, 70–72 (1981).
12. I. Gutman and S. Petrović, On total π-electron energy of benzenoid hydrocarbons. *Chem. Phys. Lett.* **97**, 292–294 (1983).
13. B. A. Hess, L. J. Schaad, W. C. Herndon, D. Biermann and W. Schmidt, Diels–Alder reactivity of polycyclic aromatic hydrocarbons 5. *Tetrahedron* **37**, 2983–2987 (1981).
14. J. R. Scherer, Modified Urey–Bradley force field for condensed aromatic rings. *J. Chem. Phys.* **36**, 3308–3321 (1962).
15. N. Neto, M. Scrocco and S. Califano, A simplified force field of aromatic hydrocarbons I. *Spectrochim. Acta* **22**, 1981–1998 (1966).
16. E. Clar, *The Aromatic Sextet.* Wiley, London (1972).
17. B. Džonova-Jerman-Blažič and N. Trinajstić, Computer-aided enumeration and generation of the Kekulé structures in conjugated hydrocarbons. *Comput. Chem.* **6**, 121–132 (1982).
18. I. Gutman, Topological properties of benzenoid molecules. *Bull. Soc. Chim. Beograd* **47**, 453–471 (1982).
19. N. Trinajstić, *Chemical Graph Theory*, Vols. I and II. CRC Press, Boca Raton, FL (1983).
20. S. J. Cyvin, Symmetry of Kekulé structures. *J. Mol. Struct.* **100**, 75–85 (1983).
21. I. Gutman, Some topological properties of benzenoid systems. *Croat. Chem. Acta* **46**, 209–215 (1974).
22. O. E. Polansky and D. H. Rouvray, Graph-theoretical treatment of aromatic hydrocarbons I. *Commun. math. chem. (match)* **2**, 63–90 (1976).
23. F. Harary, *Graph Theory.* Addison-Wesley, Reading (1969).
24. F. A. Cotton, *Chemical Applications of Group Theory*, 2nd Edn. Wiley-Interscience, New York (1971).
25. S. J. Cyvin, B. N. Cyvin, J. Brunvoll, J. C. Whitmer and P. Klaeboe, Condensed aromatics. XX. Coronene. *Z. Naturforsch.* **37a**, 1359–1368 (1982).
26. M. Gordon and W. H. T. Davison, Theory of resonance topology of fully aromatic hydrocarbons I. *J. Chem. Phys.* **20**, 428–435 (1952).
27. D. Cvetković and I. Gutman, Kekulé structures and topology. II. Cata-condensed systems. *Croat. Chem. Acta* **46**, 15–23 (1974).
28. A. T. Balaban and I. Tomescu, Algebraic expressions for the number of Kekulé structures of isoarithmic cata-condensed benzenoid polycyclic hydrocarbons. *Commun. math. chem. (match)* **14**, 155–182 (1983).
29. S. J. Cyvin, Kekulé structures and the Fibonacci series. *Acta Chim. Hung.* **112**, 281–290 (1983).
30. T. F. Yen, Resonance topology of polynuclear aromatic hydrocarbons. *Theoret. Chim. Acta* **20**, 399–404 (1971).

Comp. & Maths. with Appls. Vol. 12B, Nos. 3/4, pp. 877–881, 1986
Printed in Great Britain.

0886-9561/86 $3.00 + .00
© 1986 Pergamon Press Ltd.

THE GAPON FORMALISM

RAANAN LIEBERMANN

Laboratory for Advanced Studies, P.O. Box 1226, New Haven, CT 06505, U.S.A.

Abstract—The symmetry in donor and acceptor states in crystals is utilized to formulate a new particle-like state called gapon. The relation of gapons and SU(2) symmetry is studied and symmetry breaking of the ground state in crystals is discussed.

INTRODUCTION

Noting that the two electronic particles, electron and hole, display similarities in their properties, that in recombination processes the two electronic particles seem to play a symmetric role, and that in the case of compensated materials the number of holes equals that of electrons (i.e. donor–acceptor pairs), it suggests itself that some symmetry principle be employed to account for such systematics.

The isobaric space provides us with the proper background for such a scheme, which proves to be invariant under certain symmetries. We start by considering the donor and acceptor with an electron and hole, respectively, as two possible states of one and the same particle, for which we coin the name "gapon." The name is only fitting since the origin of the particle when the formalism is extended to all possible combinations of donor–acceptor pairs is naturally the energy gap in the crystal. The state function of the gapon will depend on the usual variables (coordinate $\mathbf{r}$, spin $\mathbf{S}$) and on a third intrinsic variable that can assume only two values: $\pm i$.

A classification of electronic states in the crystal is given in terms of gapon states in the appropriate Hilbert space and the degree of freedom in the definition is discussed in Section 1. In Section 2 the formalism is found to be useful in describing higher-order states of pairs, like dipairs, and proves to have the additional feature of accounting for the history of the system. The Hamiltonian that can produce multiplets is discussed in Section 3, as well as the construction of the gapon state with broken symmetry. Finally, reproducing Goldstone's modes is discussed, observing the symmetry breaking of the ground states in the formalism.

1. CLASSIFICATION OF ELECTRONIC STATES

To establish notations, the regular notation of the isospin of the nucleon[1] is employed; that is τ_1, τ_2, τ_3 would be the Pauli matrices, ψ_p and ψ_n would be ψ_D, ψ_A respectively (D for donor, A for acceptor) and under the operation of τ_1, τ_2, τ_3, ψ_D and ψ_A transform exactly like ψ_p and ψ_n. The operators $\frac{1}{2}i\tau_k$ form a representation of the infinitesimal operators of the rotation group and as a consequence the two components of the gapon state function form an elementary spinor under rotations, i.e.

$$g = \begin{bmatrix} |D\rangle \\ |A\rangle \end{bmatrix}.$$

To specify the state of the donor and acceptor (i.e. with or without an electron or hole) we carefully define the relevant spaces. In the case of an electron on the donor and hole on the acceptor the gapon is defined as a one-particle state:

$$g_e = \begin{bmatrix} 1 \\ 0 \end{bmatrix}, \quad g_h = \begin{bmatrix} 0 \\ 1 \end{bmatrix}, \tag{1}$$

$$g = g_e \otimes g_h = \begin{bmatrix} 0 \\ 1 \\ 0 \\ 0 \end{bmatrix}, \tag{2}$$

or in the language of a two-particle state as

$$G = \begin{bmatrix} 1 \\ 0 \end{bmatrix} \otimes \begin{bmatrix} 0 \\ 1 \end{bmatrix}. \tag{3}$$

Subsequently, if we have a donor with a hole and an acceptor with an electron, then depending on the language used (which has nothing to do with the formalism, and is important only for the interpretation as described below), the gapon is given by

$$g = \begin{bmatrix} 0 \\ 0 \\ 1 \\ 0 \end{bmatrix} \quad \text{or} \quad G = \begin{bmatrix} 0 \\ 1 \end{bmatrix} \otimes \begin{bmatrix} 1 \\ 0 \end{bmatrix}. \tag{4}$$

These states, however, are found to be unphysical and would not be dealt with. The Hilbert space for (2), (3), or (4) is H_2 and the symmetry group is $D(\frac{1}{2}) \otimes D(\frac{1}{2}) = D(0) + D(1)$. In reality there is no reason why one should prefer one definition (language) over the other, and in general each of the two definitions (g or G), or rather the degree of freedom that exists in choosing the definition used, should be employed according to the information we have for the system and the information we wish to obtain from the system. In other words, if we define the gapon as a two-particle state G, we can feed information on one-particle states and obtain information on two-particle states. For example, insert information on the donor state and acceptor state, and obtain information on the pair. On the other hand, if we define the gapon as a one-particle state g, we can insert information on a one-particle state (e.g. the unit D–A) and obtain information on a higher particle state (e.g. two D–A pairs, or a dipair).

As to the associated Hilbert space,

$$H = H_0 + H_1 + H_2 + H_3 + H_4,$$

where H_0 is the subspace for the ground states, $|D^+A^-\rangle$ or $g = G = (1)$, H_1 represents a one-particle state, and H_2 serves as the space for a two-particle state (e.g. the case $|D^0A^0\rangle$). Obviously, in g language $H = H_0 + H_1$, while in G language $H = H_0 + H_2$. When extended to a case where one pair goes into another (e.g. $D^+A^- \rightarrow D^0A^0$) we have H_3 for the other pair (which is actually H_0 in this case) and H_4 will be the joint space of both; that is, $H_4 = H_2 \otimes H_3$ and the Hilbert space is then $H = H_0 + H_2 + H_4$.

The classification of all possible electronic states in such crystals is given in Table 1.

Note that the last three possibilities have no physical meaning (i.e. they are antibonding states) and therefore would not be considered. Also, states can be defined, for example, as $|D^+A^0\rangle = \begin{bmatrix} 0 \\ 1 \end{bmatrix}$ and it is up to the reader to decide what definition to adopt and consistently stay with.

2. PAIRS OF HIGHER ORDER

We turn next to examining the extension of the systematics given to the classification of higher pair combinations such as pairs of pairs (dipairs), etc. It turns out that not only is it possible in principle to extend the gapon formalism to any order, and if desired even to account for construction mechanisms (e.g. in three-body associates[2]), but also that there is an additional feature to it. Namely, the use of gapon formalism for classification of a higher pair state enables us to write the higher pair such that it contains information about the history of the constructed system, as can be seen when tracing back the electronic states to the starting point. It should be quickly remarked, however, that at the present time it is actually immaterial how dipairs are prepared, and one is only concerned with their presence and behaviour. Thus no immediate usage seems to have any advantage from knowledge relating to the history of the final electronic states in the system. With such a disclaimer in mind we proceed to discuss construction preferences.

Table 1. Different possibilities for electronic states

Description of state	Symbol of state	Hilbert space	g Language	G Language	Rotation group $O(3)$
Donor *no* electron Acceptor *no* hole	$|D^+A^-\rangle$	H_0	(1)	(1)	$D(0)$
Donor *and* electron Acceptor *and* hole	$|D^0A^0\rangle$	H_2	$\begin{bmatrix}0\\0\\1\\0\end{bmatrix}$	$\begin{bmatrix}0\\1\end{bmatrix} \otimes \begin{bmatrix}1\\0\end{bmatrix}$	$D(\tfrac{1}{2}) \otimes D(\tfrac{1}{2}) = D(0) \oplus D(1)$
Donor *no* electron Acceptor *and* hole	$|D^+A^0\rangle$	H_1	$\begin{bmatrix}1\\0\end{bmatrix}$	$\begin{bmatrix}1\\0\end{bmatrix}$	$D(\tfrac{1}{2})$
Donor *and* electron Acceptor *no* hole	$|D^0A^-\rangle$	H_1	$\begin{bmatrix}0\\1\end{bmatrix}$	$\begin{bmatrix}0\\1\end{bmatrix}$	$D(\tfrac{1}{2})$
Donor *and* hole Acceptor *and* electron	$|D^-A^+\rangle$	H_2	$\begin{bmatrix}0\\0\\1\\0\end{bmatrix}$	$\begin{bmatrix}1\\0\end{bmatrix} \otimes \begin{bmatrix}0\\1\end{bmatrix}$	$D(\tfrac{1}{2}) \otimes D(\tfrac{1}{2}) = D(0) \oplus D(1)$
Donor *and* hole Acceptor *and* hole	$|D^-A^0\rangle$	H_2	$\begin{bmatrix}1\\0\\0\\0\end{bmatrix}$	$\begin{bmatrix}1\\0\end{bmatrix} \otimes \begin{bmatrix}1\\0\end{bmatrix}$	$D(0) \oplus D(1)$
Donor *and* electron Acceptor *and* electron	$|D^+A^+\rangle$	H_2	$\begin{bmatrix}0\\0\\0\\1\end{bmatrix}$	$\begin{bmatrix}0\\1\end{bmatrix} \otimes \begin{bmatrix}0\\1\end{bmatrix}$	$D(0) \oplus D(1)$

There are different ways to construct dipairs. It can be done by pairs, by three-body associates, by a combination of the latter and the former, etc. We choose to discuss the three-body associates approach, being the less direct and obvious one. Let us consider the respective energies of formation of the associates (DAD) and (ADA) and the equilibrium eqn (2):

$$2(\text{DAD})^+ + 2(\text{ADA})^- \underset{}{\overset{\Delta E}{\rightleftharpoons}} 3(\text{DA})_2, \qquad (5)$$

where $\Delta E = 1.76E_p$ favours symmetrical plannar pairs over three-body associates.

It would seem that when considering the higher-order associates the forms of three-body associates and dipairs given in (5) are at a disadvantage with respect to the gapon formalism, as the forms (DAD) or (ADA) do not give any information about the state of excitation of the electrically balanced pair. Thus we can have for (DAD) either

$$(\text{DAD})^+ = \text{D}^+(\text{AD}) = |D^+\rangle|D^0A^0\rangle$$

or

$$(\text{DAD})^+ = \text{D}^+(\text{AD}) = |D^+\rangle|D^+A^-\rangle,$$

which are two different physical situations. Also, as will be related shortly, the final dipair $(\text{DA})_2$ has a similar disadvantage. To achieve the desired electrical situation, it seems that cases such as

$$|D^+A^0\rangle|D^+A^-\rangle, \quad |D^+A^0\rangle|D^0A^0\rangle, \quad |D^0A^-\rangle|D^+A^-\rangle, \quad |D^0A^-\rangle|D^0A^-\rangle$$

are unfit because they do not yield the correct number of constituents. It is recognized that to write three-body associates in the gapon language is somewhat difficult as there is a single unpaired state. However, this is exactly reflected in setting Eq. (5) into equilibrium† by mul-

---

†Statistical properties and electronic states are usually treated independently of each other as the electronic structure of the system and its statistical properties are two separate problems which do not seem to affect each other. However, sometimes it is useful to view one problem with reservations for the other, as for example the case of Einstein's derivation of the domain $kT \gg h$ where Maxwell's equations are still proper, starting from the statistical distribution expressed in Planck's equation.

tiplying the three-body associates and dipairs by the appropriate coefficients without which (5) is meaningless. It tells us that one has to consider two (DAD)s, for example, as the basic constituent for the gapon when writing a single member. This result is also seen[2] when looking at ΔE in eqn (5), where symmetric planar dipairs are favored over three-body-associates.

As to the construction of the allowed dipairs, using three-body associates we study the following cases:

$$
\text{(i)} \quad \begin{bmatrix}1\\0\end{bmatrix} \otimes \begin{bmatrix}1\\0\end{bmatrix} \otimes \left[\begin{bmatrix}0\\1\end{bmatrix} \otimes \begin{bmatrix}1\\0\end{bmatrix}\right] + \begin{bmatrix}0\\1\end{bmatrix} \otimes \begin{bmatrix}0\\1\end{bmatrix} \otimes \left[\begin{bmatrix}0\\1\end{bmatrix} \otimes \begin{bmatrix}1\\0\end{bmatrix}\right]
$$

$$
= \begin{bmatrix}1\\0\\0\\0\end{bmatrix} \otimes \begin{bmatrix}0\\0\\1\\0\end{bmatrix} + \begin{bmatrix}0\\0\\0\\1\end{bmatrix} \otimes \begin{bmatrix}0\\0\\1\\0\end{bmatrix} = \begin{bmatrix}0\\0\\1\\0\\\vdots\\0\end{bmatrix} + \begin{bmatrix}0\\\vdots\\0\\1\\0\end{bmatrix}, \text{ (16 entities);}
$$

$$
\text{(ii)} \quad \begin{bmatrix}1\\0\end{bmatrix} \otimes \begin{bmatrix}1\\0\end{bmatrix} \otimes [1] + \begin{bmatrix}0\\1\end{bmatrix} \otimes \begin{bmatrix}0\\1\end{bmatrix} \otimes [1] = \begin{bmatrix}1\\0\\0\\0\end{bmatrix} + \begin{bmatrix}0\\0\\0\\1\end{bmatrix};
$$

$$
\text{(iii)} \quad \begin{bmatrix}1\\0\end{bmatrix} \otimes \begin{bmatrix}1\\0\end{bmatrix} \otimes \left[\begin{bmatrix}0\\1\end{bmatrix} \otimes \begin{bmatrix}1\\0\end{bmatrix}\right] + \begin{bmatrix}0\\1\end{bmatrix} \otimes \begin{bmatrix}0\\1\end{bmatrix} \otimes [1] = \begin{bmatrix}1\\0\\0\\0\end{bmatrix} \otimes \begin{bmatrix}0\\0\\1\\0\end{bmatrix} + \begin{bmatrix}0\\0\\0\\1\end{bmatrix};
$$

$$
\text{(iv)} \quad \begin{bmatrix}1\\0\end{bmatrix} \otimes \begin{bmatrix}1\\0\end{bmatrix} \otimes [1] + \begin{bmatrix}0\\1\end{bmatrix} \otimes \begin{bmatrix}0\\1\end{bmatrix} \otimes \left[\begin{pmatrix}0\\1\end{pmatrix} \otimes \begin{pmatrix}1\\0\end{pmatrix}\right] = \begin{bmatrix}1\\0\\0\\0\end{bmatrix} + \begin{bmatrix}0\\0\\0\\1\end{bmatrix} \otimes \begin{bmatrix}0\\0\\1\\0\end{bmatrix}.
$$

While it is clear that (i)–(iv) are the different constituents of the dipairs $3(DA)_2$, it is not so manifested in the approach given in (5). It is observed that cases (iii) and (v) cannot form a dipair in the same way (i) and (ii) can, which overrules existence of dipairs in which one pair, the electrically neutral pair in the three-body associates, is a D–A in an excited state $(DAD)^+ = D^+(D^0A^0)$ and the other such pair in the ground state $(ADA)^- = A^-(D^+A^-)$, and *vice versa*. Both are either in the excited state or in the ground state.

Thus the system expressed in the gapon formalism provides us with information about its history, the type of constituents, their grouping and the minimal amount needed.

3. SYMMETRY BREAKING AND MULTIPLETS

The usefulness of the approach becomes apparent when the experiment is considered. Here we find the gapon to be a conserved observable that commutes with a Hamiltonian. Resulting from SU(2) symmetry the Hamiltonian of the gapon is invariant under certain operations. We write the gapon Hamiltonian as

$$
H = U(\mathbf{r}, \mathbf{S}) + V(\mathbf{r}, \mathbf{S})\boldsymbol{\tau}^{(1)} \cdot \boldsymbol{\tau}^{(2)}, \tag{6}
$$

where U, V are operators constructed from position and spin operators and

$$
\boldsymbol{\tau}^{(1)} \cdot \boldsymbol{\tau}^{(2)} = \tau_1^{(1)}\tau_1^{(2)} + \tau_2^{(1)}\tau_2^{(2)} + \tau_3^{(1)}\tau_3^{(2)}.
$$

The origin of the Hamiltonian is from a potential in the SU(2) × SU(2) space that has the form of

$$V = V_0 \otimes I(4) \otimes I(4) + v_1 \otimes \boldsymbol{\sigma}^{(1)} \cdot \boldsymbol{\sigma}^{(2)} \otimes I(4) \otimes I(4)$$
$$+ V_2 \otimes I(4) \times \boldsymbol{\tau}^{(1)} \cdot \boldsymbol{\tau}^{(2)} \otimes I(4)$$
$$+ V_3 \otimes (\boldsymbol{\sigma}^{(1)} \cdot \boldsymbol{\sigma}^{(2)})(\boldsymbol{\tau}^{(1)} \cdot \boldsymbol{\tau}^{(2)}) \otimes I(4) + V_4 S_{12} \otimes I(4)$$
$$+ V_5 \otimes S_{12} \otimes \boldsymbol{\tau}^{(1)} \cdot \boldsymbol{\tau}^{(2)}, \tag{7}$$

where $S_{12} = 3/r^2(\boldsymbol{\sigma}^{(1)} \cdot \mathbf{r})(\boldsymbol{\sigma}^{(2)} \cdot \mathbf{r}) - \boldsymbol{\sigma}^{(1)} \cdot \boldsymbol{\sigma}^{(2)} \otimes I(4)$ and where τ_i are the SU(2) matrices of the gapon, and though similar in form should not be taken as the isotropic spin matrices for the nucleon, as for example V_2 is different from the strong interaction potential.‡

Once the potential is known, the Hamiltonian follows and can be applied to the states

$$H|G_S\rangle = (U + V)|G_S\rangle, \tag{8}$$

$$H|G_A\rangle = (U - 3V)|G_A\rangle, \tag{9}$$

where the subscripts S, A indicate symmetric, antisymmetric combinations respectively.

Obviously triplet states are obtained from eqn (8) and a singlet state with a different energy from eqn (9).

A possible combination for G_S, G_A can for example be

$$1/\sqrt{2}(|D^+A^0\rangle|D^0A^-\rangle \pm |D^0A^-\rangle|D^+A^0\rangle). \tag{10}$$

It is easy to see that the two states constituting (10) are degenerate in energy if the donor and acceptor levels lie equidistantly from the corresponding bands (e.g. in compensated materials). Thus, not surprisingly it seems appropriate to build an SU(2) symmetry for such states, which even though degenerate in energy and therefore $|D^0A^0\rangle$ is a state of a singlet or a triplet, should not have the multiplets separated. If on the other hand their distance from the band is not equal then we focus our attention first on those which are only slightly perturbed from the former case. There we have an almost SU(2) symmetry, or as is frequently called, a broken symmetry, and the multiplets are separated. It is noted that in the real physical world the latter case is more likely to exist, so that most of the impurity crystals have *a priori* split states which is for the experiment to verify.

Finally, the symmetry breakdown, when the ground states in the formalism are considered, is of additional speculative interest. Namely, if we note the analogy between Goldstone's theorem [(4)] and our formalism,† then with the ground states violating the symmetry should be associated a zero-mass particle or some lattice modes.

Acknowledgments—It is a pleasure to thank my old colleague Dave Berry for stimulating discussions back in 1970 when this formalism was developed, and Fred Williams as well.

REFERENCES

1. D. Roman, *Advanced Quantum Mechanics*. Adison Wesley (1965).
2. M. Martens *et al.*, *Phys. Rev.* **186**(3), 757–760 (1969).
3. R. Liebermann, The gapon formalism II (unpublished).
4. J. Goldstone, *Nuovo Cimento* **19**(1), 154–164 (1961).

‡It is obviously not claimed that the usual SU(2) symmetry for baryons is invariant under the electrostatic potential, nor is the breakdown of SU(2) symmetry under electromagnetic interactions of baryons being disregarded. It is rather speculated that there exists an SU(2) symmetry for the donors and acceptors and the potential which is left invariant is yet to be found. For further discussion the reader is referred to [3].

†It should be noted that the asymmetry of the ground states as considered by Goldstone had some different meaning than the case discussed here.

Comp. & Maths. with Appls. Vol. 12B, Nos. 3/4, pp. 883–893, 1986
Printed in Great Britain.

0886–9561/86 $3.00 + .00
© 1986 Pergamon Press Ltd.

ON SYMMETRIES IN THE GRAPHIC ART
OF HORST BARTNIG

PETER SCHARFENBERG†

Institute for Pharmacological Research, 1136 Berlin-Friedrichsfelde, G.D.R.

Abstract—Part of the artist's graphic work appears as the result of experiments with operations such as rotation, translation, and color exchange (occasionally), performed on elementary figures of square shape. By means of nine examples, some theoretical framework underlying the figures is discussed in the light of symmetry. Combinatorial as well as graph-theoretical problems are touched.

Common features of science and art, as well as in the practice of apparently such different professions as scientist and artist, are often denied. Moreover, specious arguments are frequently evaluated with reference to results (work of art *vs.* work of science) and become seemingly supported by specific prerequisites of both fields, like strong rationalism on the one hand and dominance of aesthetic aspects on the other. At least art that is classified as constructivistic, however, is subject to technical, sometimes even abstract (mathematical) influences. Consequently, whether or not constructivistic works belong to art is the question, one such that anyone, as an unbiased viewer, might even conclude that he could do the work as well. Here H. Bartnig (who is discussed in this article), at least as far as his work is involved and, perhaps more importantly, in contrast to many other artists, expresses satisfaction about its impact and his fulfilled intentions[1]. Thus giving a viewer the opportunity to reproduce visual processes and to find the rational core of the artistic means is much more important to him than that somebody becomes defeated by ingeniousness, striving after effects (usually concealed), or means of veiling. The questioning of art was the beginning of Bartnig's philosophy, from where finally he came to nonobjectivity in pictorial art. While considering himself obliged to the constructivistic tradition, especially to Malevich, and so-called "concrete painting" as represented by Van Doesburg, he is said[2] to be closely related to the "visual research"[3]. This study is an attempt to elucidate the theoretical framework underlying his graphic art, its systematic manner and order, if any, and patterns of repetition or variation. Only some such repetitions can be described by symmetry operations. As will be seen, most of them can already be understood by permutations.

We know about artists being aware of symmetry (although not always fully), while designing a work in which they make use of it. Hinterreiter is such an example[4], but Bartnig apparently belongs to another group whose representatives produce symmetric compositions somewhat more randomly. On the one hand, these are products of chance, insofar as a single figure is concerned. On the other hand, the occurrence of nontrivial symmetry elements is a necessary concomitant of complete sets of combinations. The artist, however, will usually not arrive at this by deduction. As an experimentalist in permutations, rotations, and translations as well as the exchange of colours, Bartnig passively produces symmetric patterns, thereby preserving the capability to wonder at and enjoy them as they appear.

The only basic element that persistently pervades Bartnig's graphic art is the square. In 1969 he designed a mechanical model, consisting of square fibreboard plates and alternating in black and white. In its normal position the arrangement approaches a pyramid (in Fig. 1 viewed from above) with symmetry C_{4v} [Fig. 1(a)], while synchronous twisting of the plates against each other lets the reflection plane vanish and thus reduces the symmetry to C_4 [Fig. 1(b)]. Symmetry was probably not in the foreground of this construction. It is an object to be touched. Everyone is allowed to experience how a pattern changes quasidynamically under twisting of the pyramid. If it is in its twisted form, e.g. with constant and small angles between

†On leave from the Institute for Drug Research of the Academy of Sciences (G.D.R.), 1136 Berlin-Friedrichsfelde, G.D.R.

(a) (b)

Fig. 1. Object—changeable squares with central point; fibreboard; 62 × 62 × 20 cm (1969–1974); left: normal position, right: twisted.

neighbouring plates, one seems to see four spirals [Fig. 1(b)]. Such an effect has its explanation in the positions (R_i, ϕ_i) of the corners of each individual square i. They all can be found on Archimedes' spirals (described by the function $R_i = \text{const} \times \phi_i$); therefore one side of the square always approximates the tangent through the point (R_i, ϕ_i) of the curve. Here R_i is the distance from the central point to the corner of the ith square and ϕ_i is the angle of torsion of that square, relative to the normal position [Fig. 1(a)]. The construction built by Bartnig is such that $R_{i+1} - R_i = \text{const}$.

So far we have considered a three-dimensional model, but there are also many examples of drawings where, again, the basic element is a square figure. Together with translations one finds rotations such that either local point symmetry, e.g. C_{2v} or C_4 [Fig. 2(a)] or glide reflection [Fig. 2(b)] occur, if deformations on a nonlinear scale, which the whole system undergoes, are neglected. These examples are selections from the artist's experiments of filling a plane area by drawing repeatedly an elementary figure like ◣, thereby regularly changing its position, primarily with the aim to achieve a specific impression rather than an emphasis on the use of symmetry groups. Thus, for example, one may ask about the origin of curved lines that the viewer can imagine by looking at Fig. 2(a) [but not at Fig. 2(b)] and following the diagonals of the basic squares. As the reduction of the neighbouring elements was chosen by Bartnig such that $a_{i+1}/a_i = a_i/a_{i-1}$, where a_i is the length of a side of the ith square, one "sees" straight

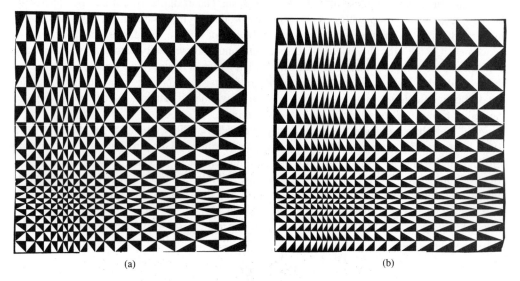

(a) (b)

Fig. 2. Yellow and black triangles; acrylic; combined technique; canvas; 98 × 98 cm (1975–1976). Left: 7/1, right: 7/2.

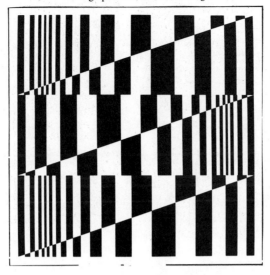

Fig. 3. Composition for Albert Einstein; screen printing; 46×46 cm (1979).

lines $y = \text{const} \times x$ as well as hyperbolae $y = \text{const} \times x^{-1}$, where x, y denote a cartesian system, located in the origin of expansion of Fig. 2(a). Figure 3 shows another example of local point symmetry C_2, combined with translation, whereas in Fig. 4 use is made of glide reflection combined with colour exchange.

Figure 5 is the latest example of translation symmetry in Bartnig's art. With screen prints (blue on black ground) of this graphic representation he won the Biennial Prize of the Seventh Norwegian International Print Biennial, held in Fredrikstad in 1984. Although in all cases of Figs. 5(a–f) translation and rotation operations are the same, the general impression depends enormously on the local symmetry and structure of the object that undergoes these operations. For example, compare Figs. 5(a) and 5(d) with their different periodicities, originating from the square with its fourfold axis perpendicular to the paper plane, whereas that of the stroke is only a twofold one. The viewer tends to search for patterns and then to follow these (e.g. the diagonal paths), thereby intuitively interpolating. Thus Figs. 5(d) and 5(e) seem to have similarities at a first glimpse. After precise inspection, however, it becomes obvious that they have none. The reason for the fallacy is that intersecting rectangular figures of twice the size of the square look in this specific arrangement somewhat like the squares themself. With longer rectangles, as in Fig. 5(f), the fallacy vanishes.

In 1975 Bartnig created his "variable systems." In doing so, one basic square figure (the variable) is necessary, occasionally together with its negative (colour exchange). With two such

Fig. 4. Black and white squares I (detail); screen printing; 87×47 cm (1973–1978).

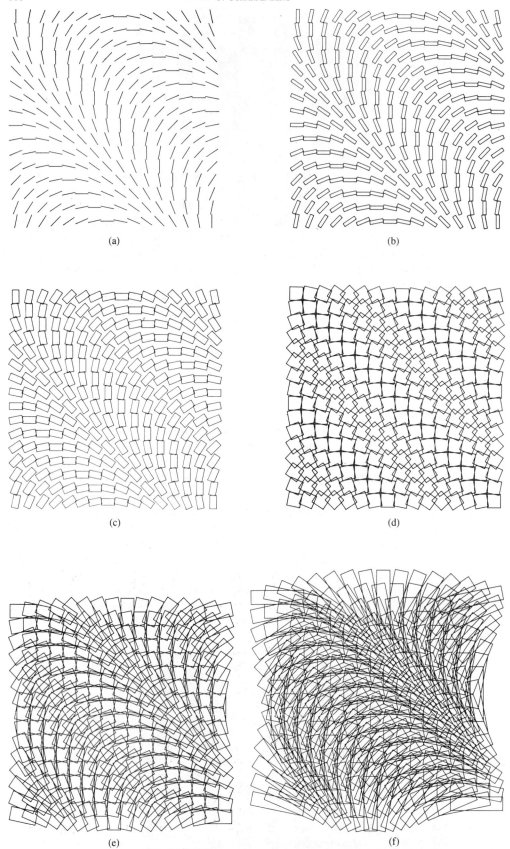

Fig. 5. Computer graphics series: 256 strokes (a), 256 small rectangles (b), 256 small rectangles (c), 256 squares (d), 256 rectangles (e), 256 long rectangles (f); between 24 × 24 cm and 28.5 × 28.5 cm (1982–1983) (programmed by D. Garling).

squares rectangles can be composed while four pieces allow supersquares. The artist's intention was to study visual relations between the basic elements in the larger figures, as offered differently in each of them. Therefore he had two intentions, namely the individual composition and the complexity of them all. To achieve this, two variants were offered. One, for example, resulted in the design of a special exhibition catalogue[5], consisting of four separate squares. These allow everyone to practice "constructivistic art," i.e. to attempt his "own" compositions, but one figure after the other. Only the second variant enables us to study all variations simultaneously because here the artist has compiled all possible combinations of four identical squares to form a supersquare. The following analysis of accompanying combinatorial problems touches some elementary symmetry considerations.

It is easily derived that four identical squares can form not more than $4^4 = 256$ different supersquares. The actual limit depends on the symmetry of the basic element, but is further reduced by Bartnig, who excludes all but one supersquare, being interconvertible by rotation and, in some cases, by reflection as well. To put this more precisely, consider for example Fig. 6, which is a first step towards supersquares. Here $4^2 = 16$ rectangles, formed by combining two identical squares in all four positions, were reduced to 10 rotationally invariant figures. This reduction may be derived as follows: Denote the four different rotational positions of a basic square A relative to a fixed rectangle B by

$$A_i \ (i = 0, 1, 2, 3),$$

whereby $\pi i/2$ is the angle of rotation of A. Analogously we have

$$B_i \ (i = 0, 2),$$

with the rectangle B in an external coordinate system. We define

$$B_0 \equiv (A_k, A_l)_0 = A_k, A_l.$$

Then

$$B_2 = (A_k, A_l)_2 = A_{l+2}, A_{k+2},$$

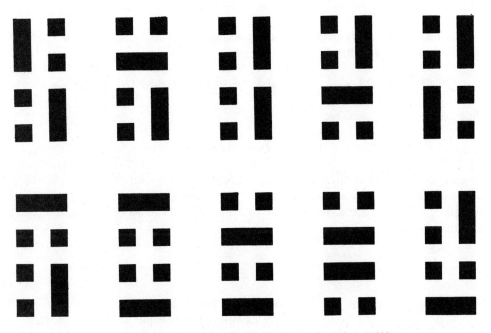

Fig. 6. Relations 3(2); line etching; hand print; 13.5 × 18 cm (1980).

and either B_0 or B_2 has to be eliminated from the set of combinations in order to obtain a set of rotational invariant rectangles (only rotations within the plane of the rectangle allowed). Hence, using the periodicity of rotations, which results in

$$A_i = A_{i \bmod 4}, \quad B_i = B_{i \bmod 4},$$

Table 1 can be set up. The latter four cases therein (separated by a dashed line) satisfy

$$B_2 = (A_k, A_l)_2 = A_k, A_l.$$

This equation formally describes the existence of a C_2 axis and that these figures appear only once in the set of combinations from the very beginning. No other nontrivial element of point symmetry occurs generally, i.e. independently of the presence of symmetry elements in the basic squares.

Let the formation of a supersquare D formally be written as

$$D_0 = \begin{pmatrix} A_j & A_m \\ A_k & A_l \end{pmatrix}_0,$$

and let its four rotational positions

$$D_i (i = 0, 1, 2, 3)$$

correspond to those of the basic squares. Accordingly

$$D_i = D_{i \bmod 4}.$$

Then

$$D_1 = \begin{pmatrix} A_{m+1} & A_{l+1} \\ A_{j+1} & A_{k+1} \end{pmatrix}, \quad D_2 = \begin{pmatrix} A_{l+2} & A_{k+2} \\ A_{m+2} & A_{j+2} \end{pmatrix}, \quad D_3 = \begin{pmatrix} A_{k+3} & A_{j+3} \\ A_{l+3} & A_{m+3} \end{pmatrix}$$

may be proved easily (anticlockwise rotation). Presence of a C_2 axis results in

$$D_0 = D_2, \quad D_1 = D_3,$$

which allows for the (k, j) and (l, m) pairs given in the last four rows of Table 1, provided that $k = l$ and $j = m$. Otherwise

$$k = (j - 1) \bmod 4, \quad l = (k - 1) \bmod 4, \quad m = (l - 1) \bmod 4, \quad j = (m - 1) \bmod 4,$$

while existence of a C_4 axis means

$$D_0 = D_1 = D_2 = D_3.$$

Table 2 lists the 16 symmetrical supersquares. Consequently, the set of rotational invariant 4-membered supersquares is composed of $(4^4 - 16)/4$ figures with a trivial rotational axis C_1, then $(16 - 4)/2$ with C_2 axis, and 4 with C_4 axis; i.e. the total number of supersquares accepted by Bartnig is

$$\frac{4^4 - 16}{4} + \frac{16 - 4}{2} + 4 = 70.$$

As in the case of rectangles (Fig. 6), however, this maximum number may be further reduced if the basic squares have special symmetry elements. For example, if they are identical with their mirror image (reflection plane perpendicular to the plane of the figure) then Bartnig reduces

Table 1. All 16 rectangles (A_k, A_l) composed of two squares. Select one combination in each row to obtain a rotational-invariant set (in the sense of Bartnig). The last four cases have no pendant to be eliminated but are the only ones showing *a priori* a nontrivial element of point symmetry (C_2).

B_0	B_2
A_0, A_0	A_2, A_2
A_1, A_1	A_3, A_3
A_0, A_1	A_3, A_2
A_1, A_0	A_2, A_3
A_1, A_2	A_0, A_3
A_2, A_1	A_3, A_0
- - - - -	- - - - -
A_0, A_2	
A_2, A_0	
A_1, A_3	
A_3, A_1	

the set of supersquares by excluding mirror images, so that the total number finally becomes 39 instead of 70. Otherwise, for example with the absence of a reflection plane in the basic square, this would not work. Two examples are shown in Fig. 7, where the elementary square is ▬ and its negative.

Note also that the whole problem of determining a rotational invariant set of combinations is related to the analysis of chemical reactions. The basic square may represent a molecule with four different binding sites where the supersquare is one of the isomers (actually a tetramer) of the reaction. Despite this analogy, however, reflection planes must be treated differently from the above in a chemically reacting system.

Bartnig also replaced basic squares within the supersquares by their negative, successively one after the other. In this way he arrived at 1044 rotational invariant compositions. Figure 8 shows a selection of 5 from his 70 sheets. The blank spaces therein [Figs. 8(c)–(e)] are a tribute

Table 2. All 16 symmetrical 4-membered supersquares. The four combinations with C_4 axes are separated by a dashed line. Select one combination in each row to obtain a rotational-invariant subset.

D_0	D_1
$\begin{pmatrix} A_0 & A_0 \\ A_2 & A_2 \end{pmatrix}$	$\begin{pmatrix} A_1 & A_3 \\ A_1 & A_3 \end{pmatrix}$
$\begin{pmatrix} A_2 & A_0 \\ A_2 & A_0 \end{pmatrix}$	$\begin{pmatrix} A_1 & A_1 \\ A_3 & A_3 \end{pmatrix}$
$\begin{pmatrix} A_3 & A_0 \\ A_2 & A_1 \end{pmatrix}$	$\begin{pmatrix} A_1 & A_2 \\ A_0 & A_3 \end{pmatrix}$
$\begin{pmatrix} A_0 & A_1 \\ A_3 & A_2 \end{pmatrix}$	$\begin{pmatrix} A_2 & A_3 \\ A_1 & A_0 \end{pmatrix}$
$\begin{pmatrix} A_3 & A_1 \\ A_3 & A_1 \end{pmatrix}$	$\begin{pmatrix} A_2 & A_2 \\ A_0 & A_0 \end{pmatrix}$
$\begin{pmatrix} A_0 & A_2 \\ A_0 & A_2 \end{pmatrix}$	$\begin{pmatrix} A_3 & A_3 \\ A_1 & A_1 \end{pmatrix}$
- - - - -	- - - - -
$\begin{pmatrix} A_1 & A_0 \\ A_2 & A_3 \end{pmatrix}$	
$\begin{pmatrix} A_2 & A_1 \\ A_3 & A_0 \end{pmatrix}$	
$\begin{pmatrix} A_3 & A_2 \\ A_0 & A_1 \end{pmatrix}$	
$\begin{pmatrix} A_0 & A_3 \\ A_1 & A_2 \end{pmatrix}$	

to invariance. In his latest work the artist has changed the arrangement so that now there are 70 supersquares per sheet instead of 16 (see Fig. 9). Although the variations are systematic in a certain sense, they are not governed by symmetry.

Compact presentations of intersecting supersquares of rectangles, such that the set of figures is complete but none appears two or more times, have been tried without success. At least in the case of rectangles it can be proved that any attempt must fail. The task is similar to the graph-theoretical classic "Königsberger Brückenproblem" and therefore closely connected with the existence of so-called Eulerian lines[6]. Making use of a theorem due to Euler it can be proved that, for example, there exists neither a loop nor a line on which the 10 rectangles shown in Fig. 6 can be placed in an overlapping manner. This, however, becomes possible if the degeneracy of the figures is not eliminated; in other words, if all those contained in Table 1 are used. A detailed analysis of these problems would probably be out of place in this study, but will perhaps soon be done elsewhere.

Bartnig's ambitions with his "variable systems" are focused on the generation of super-square patterns in dependence on the variable design of its elements, with the realization that the visual impression of a supersquare can become either complex or simple as the symmetry of basic squares changes, and also depends on the graphic structure of their edges. So one must consider the match inside a supersquare, taking into account that a viewer usually distinguishes between smooth and abrupt changes and values this aesthetically. On the other hand, it is difficult or even impossible to work out general criteria on how to solve such artistic problems; otherwise they could be treated by nearly anyone who was able to obey the rules, and then it would become questionable whether or not any graphic art would remain. Bartnig, while experimenting with colour exchanges (positive *vs.* negative), easily recognized that this process should not govern the impression of a composition, as perhaps demonstrated in Figs. 9(a)–(f). Contrary to these, Fig. 9(h) is an example of internally well-balanced coloured areas in the basic element (black:white = 1:1). He lays emphasis on the evaluation of new and ingenious patterns, not easily deduced from that of an isolated basic square alone, or its rotation as well as colour exchange. According to his present conviction, the role of highly symmetrical su-persquares, as they appear in limited numbers, is the following: Their perfect regularity becomes especially pronounced by an environment of less symmetrical figures, the other supersquares. In a quasidynamical consideration (looking from one to the other) there suddenly rises much clarity and, in a certain sense, despite simplicity, also beauty. The colour exchange, by also increasing the complexity, helps avoiding monotony that otherwise would occur. It may also be considered a perturbation that penetrates the set of supersquares, thereby generating new compositions, among them some new symmetrical ones.

Technically, Bartnig has the image of a computer-graphical artist. This, however, has not been cultivated in this study because it means, in his case, computer-aided generation of some

Fig. 7. Seventy eight times four squares with striae; line etching; 12 × 26.5 cm (1982).

(a)

(b)

(c)

(d)

(e)

Fig. 8. One thousand fourty four variations; 70 sheets (yellow on white ground); lino-cut; 37.2 × 37.2 cm.
Sheet 7, variations 97–112 (a); sheet 34, variations 529–544 (b); sheet 62, variations 971–980 (c); sheet 64,
variations 991–1000 (d), sheet 69, variations 1033–1038 (e) (1975–1979).

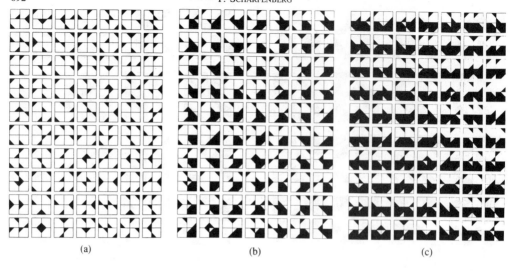

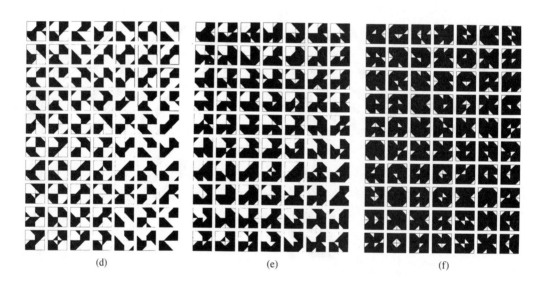

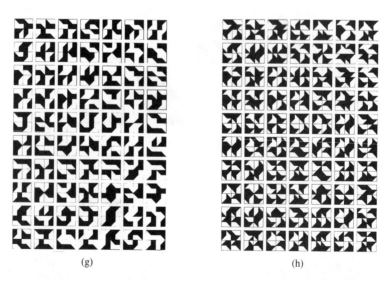

Fig. 9. Three thousand six hundred twenty two variations; 55 sheets; series of computer-supported graphics; line etching; hand print; 36 × 25 cm. Sheet 8 (a), sheet 9 (b), sheet 11 (c), sheet 14 (d), sheet 15 (e), sheet 23 (f), sheet 24 (g), sheet 47 (h) (1984). (Programmed by M. Fischer; adviser: R. Koch.)

primary steps only, e.g. contours (using an X, Y-plotter), or simply a facility for easily achieving completeness of combinations. All these things could otherwise be done by hand but do not necessarily require a new technique. (By the way, the underlying programs were written by others; see, for example, Figs. 5, 9.) With today's term "computer graphics" the reader would have immediately associated colour displays, connected with supercomputers, and perfect real-time "dynamical" compositions, impossible to make with an artist's traditional equipment. Finally, those readers not only interested in the graphic art of Bartnig but also in the whole "constructivistic" scene, in which he has a well-established place, may be referred to [7,8].

Acknowledgment—The author wishes to thank H. Bartnig for valuable discussions and for granting permission to reproduce the works underlying Figs. 1–9.

REFERENCES

1. K. Werner (Ed), *Horst Bartnig* 1976. Catalogue of the gallery Arkade, Berlin (1976).
2. H. W. Franke, Computergraphik–Galerie: Horst Bartnig. *Angew. Informatik* **3**, 120–122 (1983).
3. H. W. Franke, *Computergraphik–Galerie*. DuMont, Köln (1984).
4. E. Makovicky, The crystallographic art of Hans Hinterreiter. *Z. Kristallogr.* **150**, 13–21 (1979).
5. K. Werner (Ed), *Horst Bartnig, Konkrete Malerei, Grafik*. Catalogue of the Clara Mosch gallery, Adelsberg (1981).
6. H. Sachs, *Einführung in die Theorie der endlichen Graphen*. Teubner, Leipzig (1970).
7. J. Erpenbeck (Ed), *Hermann Glöckner, Ein Patriarch der Moderne*. Der Morgen, Berlin (1983).
8. L. Lang and H. Marquardt, *Graphische Etüden*. Reclam, Leipzig (1982).

Comp. & Maths. with Appls. Vol. 12B, Nos. 3/4, pp. 895–911, 1986
Printed in Great Britain.

0886–9561/86 $3.00 + .00
© 1986 Pergamon Press Ltd.

COLORED SYMMETRIES IN SPACE–TIME

JĒKABS ZVILNA

University of Waterloo, School of Architecture, Faculty of Environmental Studies, Waterloo, Ontario
N2L 3G1, Canada

Abstract—The paper displays a single objective: to show the emergence of symmetries as a universal, archetypal, self-organizing phenomenon which originates in an infinite number of forms all having the same trihedral innate structure. These forms have been generated by the use of a single-type, right-handed element containing three spatial dimensions plus one temporal dimension.

At an exhibition at the Waterloo School of Architecture in March 1984, a single element was used as a building block to generate all of the various forms displayed—on a flat plane, as low and high reliefs, and structures in space[1]. The theme of the exhibition was "A Doctrine of One," for it was constructed using one type of element, and manifested various symmetries—rotational, translational and combinations of both as the only one ordering concept[2] (see Fig. 1).

The concept of "one" is an essential idea of the elective course Arch. 194, Interdisciplinary Language[3]. The course engages students in the theory and practice of visual literacy based on formative processes, hierarchies and natural order (nature plus man)[4,5]. The emphasis is on the domestication of time, an issue of importance in understanding form[6]; in this case, in making the element that would grow in various forms exhibiting symmetries[7,8].

I am most grateful to the following: The UW Social Sciences and Humanities Research Council Grant Committee, the Dean, F.E.S. and the Director, School of Architecture, for the continuous support; Mrs. Kathleen Close for typing; Edward Chrzanowski for assistance with the movie and BYU graphics package; and Alison Brooks for editing. Without the advice, help and enthusiasm from my teachers, friends, and colleagues and authors on this continent and in my homeland (Latvia), there would be no addiction to the search for the new alchemy (to tame time) and, the subsequent witness of the marriage between time and symmetry[9–11].

INTRODUCTION

The following material was prepared in a school of architecture. Therefore, as in architecture, where the centre of investigation is form in space–time, the essence of this inquiry also is the genesis of visual form possessing the language of symmetry[12].

The organizing principles adopted in this exercise are economics, ecology and ecoethics.

The ultimate *economy* is achieved using the dictum "with the minimum to gain the maximum." Only one type of element is used; the number of possible forms generated by the use of this element is infinite.

Ecology (*oikos*, Gr., home) has been practised since the beginning. Man used to cooperate with nature while not knowing it. On a hot midday one rested in the shade of a tree; a house was cool, surrounded by trees planted by man. No definition for "natural order" was needed; it was lived. "Nature's order" was and still is unknown. In rare moments a poet, a scientist or an artist can get a glimpse of it. In this project the cooperation with nature is conceived by inviting real time to participate in the form-generating process, thus achieving an infinite number of solutions differing not only in size but also in kind[13].

Ecoethics advises me to let the element that has been mentioned become what it wants to be. Thus it is my obligation in the processes of individuation and of coding the nature of the element to find the ways in which it tends to connect and interrelate with additional elements. The surprise and astonishment at the end of each separate investigation is the same: the discovery that the elements prefer to be arranged into orders of various symmetries, except bilateral symmetries.

Fig. 1. A part of the exhibition "A Doctrine of One," March 1984, at the Waterloo School of Architecture.

All three principles are synchronous: man practising ecoethics—himself part of nature—cooperates with nature using the most economical means.

FORM FOLLOWS PROCESS

It has been said today in many ways, that to understand something is to understand its evolution in history—the development in space–time of the previously unknown event or unseen image[14]. In the search to understand my obsession with the generation of visual form during the last few decades, I went back as far as possible in my memory towards my beginnings.

As a child, I lived out in the country with my grandmother, whom I never saw read or write. She had knowledge, however, and recounted to me myths and folktales in unlimited numbers. She believed that stones were growing. When we walked to the local town, this was another time for listening, imagining, being in strange, impossible places; and seeing on the roadside the large stones, still growing!

Since that time, I have not changed much. I still believe in myths, where the impossible is made possible. When solving a problem one starts with the impossible, a myth, even in adventurous experiments with form. One is compelled to ask fundamental questions. How does a form occur? Through imitation, borrowing from the past? By chance? Necessity? Or does it grow from a radical (*radix*, Gr. root) idea, in the process absorbing space–time, like a crystal, a tree, a mind? Does the emerging form embrace any values? Is it a product of the present? Does it display economy of means? Does the form exhibit—simultaneously—restraint, wonder, surprise?

Through a mysterious transformation the list of questions became the program. At that time I was already on this continent inquiring into the complexities of the new environment. In my investigations I learned to think and act in terms of process–pattern; time–space; movement as one of the form-determinants; form as the biography of the process: "form follows process"[15,16].

My works at that time were three dimensional—two spatial dimensions plus one temporal. The chosen direction was to see the reality as a dynamic process generating various patterns in space–time. On another level I felt the need to integrate all I knew and felt: man–nature, science–art, East–West, conscious–unconscious. To do all that, I developed my own technique[3,19].

Figure 2 shows three images. They are developed by coating a glass sheet with carbon black. In (a) and (b) oil has been used to distribute the carbon: in (b) the oil has been supplied in limited quantity, resulting in a closed system; in (a) the supply is unlimited. In both cases the glass sheet, in uninterrupted motion, has been subjected to gravity. In Fig. 2(c) the carbon-covered glass sheet is placed in a container with a liquid (an industrial thinner), which is slowly rising. The spiral pattern, through vibrations, generates itself. In all three cases the matter is organized through symmetry transformations: change of size (growth) and rotation[17].

My next question was how to join real time with three spatial dimensions. In search of

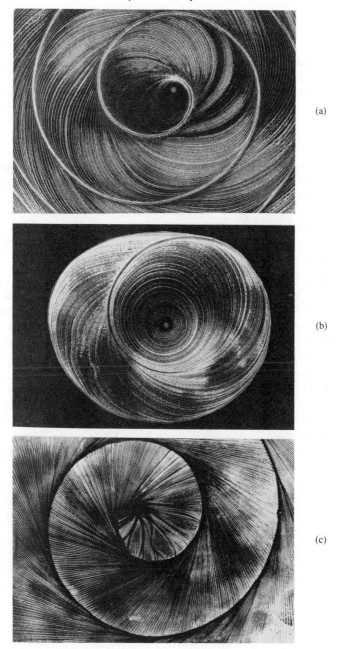

Fig. 2. (a)–(c) Three images from a selection presented at MIT, 1965.

the answer a myth emerged:

> I came to the conclusion that everything I see, feel, think and touch has a common archetypal beginning, a primal seed, the ONE[18]. At the same time I managed to convince myself that the ONE would never be found and the mystery of becoming will be preserved forever.

And yet, in my desire to show that it was at least possible to approach the myth, I became obsessed with the studies of nature's form-generating methods. In the attempt to find a method applicable to designing universal four-dimensional forms, one must come to terms with the rotation in space–time[20] (see Fig. 3).

The phenomenon of rotation is observed across the whole spectrum of the known, from the infinitely small to the world observable with the unaided eye, and further yet, to the large and distant—the solar system, the Milky Way, other galaxies and cluster of galaxies. Our 24 hr rhythm, consciousness during the period of daytime, and unconsciousness during the night, are the result of rotation.

Nature, as shown above, uses rotation on many levels to achieve infinite variety, while at the same time displaying great economy: if the earth would not rotate, one sun would not be enough to sustain life as it is now. Therefore, in this study the method (rotation in space-time) is adopted and used to develop a system of visual forms all grown from a right-handed element.

GENESIS OF THE ELEMENT

To verify the applicability of a method, rotation, in designing and making a viable primary element, four alternatives have been tested since the late 1960s. The symmetries in the forms shown here emerged by the use of the fourth type of element as the one which promised the most connections.

The element (Fig. 4) is cut off from a plank (material is of no importance), having cross-section dimensions 1 and $\sqrt{2}$: 1 for the rational and measurable in man, $\sqrt{2}$ for the irrational and immeasurable—that part of man that could not be described in whole numbers. After the first cut [Fig. 4(b)] the plank is simultaneously rotated and translated [Fig. 4(d)]. The second cut is made, resulting in a right-handed element [Fig. 4(e)], which is a volume between two stages in the generating process—between "before" and "after" in the rotational–translational movement—thus experiencing real time. My conjecture is that the element now has time as the fourth dimension. At the same time, the element has acquired memory (the helical movement) and behavior that could be predicted to grow in helical configurations. After the first element is made, a consequential single movement and cut would produce the next element.

The right-handed element contains a promise of the opposite handedness. The computer image in Fig. 5 is ambidextrous: if the plane KLMN is chosen in the foreground, a right-handed element is seen, while plane KOPN in the foreground displays a left-handed element. The promise of opposite handedness becomes real after a 180° rotation towards the right or left. The result in both cases is the same (Fig. 6). Indeed, as Fig. 7 shows, the mark of 180° could be achieved both ways—travelling from the zero point towards the left or right. As shown in Fig. 8, two different components, using two elements, are possible. They appear to display bilateral symmetry, but in this system it is an illusion. Each of the components has a single rotational symmetry axis; each one of them could be cut in half with a result of two left- or right-handed elements, thus exhibiting an ambidextrous inner nature.

A triple-element building block is arrived at in two ways: rotating the plank towards right 270° or rotating towards left 90°. Larger building blocks are possible. For example, a unit consisting of four elements is the result of a 360° rotation or no rotation at all. A unit of five elements has all the properties of one element, generating only longer components.

TRIHEDRAL FORMATION

In the inquiry only one formation, "trihedral," is investigated [Fig. 9(e)]. It consists of forms [outer appearance, Fig. 10(a)] all having the same internal structure, a tri-hedron—a

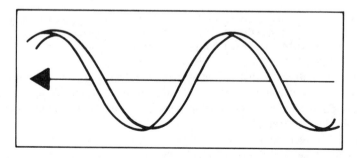

Fig. 3. Simultaneous rotational and translational movement.

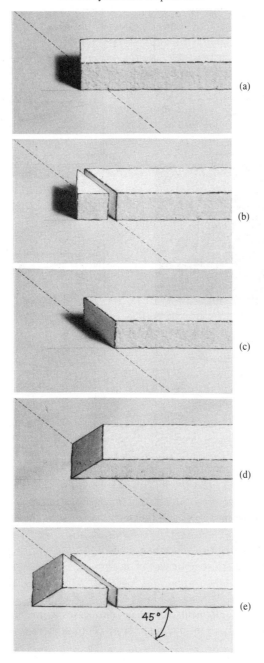

(a)

(b)

(c)

(d)

(e)

45°

Fig. 4. The making of the element.

volume enclosed by three surfaces, arrived at by connecting 14 points in space [Fig. 10(b)]. The number of ways to arrive at the same structure is infinite; one could say at the same time that the number of forms is infinite.

All the forms have the same properties.

(1) They are the result of crossing 12 helical configurations in space–time.
(2) They have projections (''buds'') for further growth.
(3) They display three-way rotational symmetry.
(4) In further growth, new symmetries emerge in clusters of forms.
(5) There are no bilateral symmetries.

J. ZVILNA

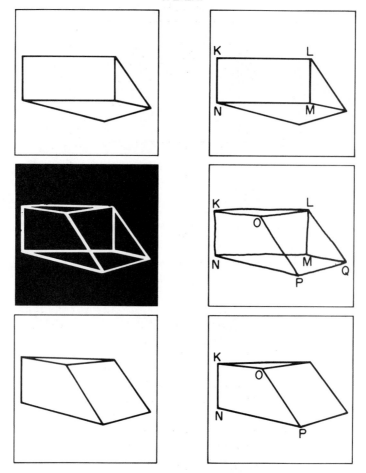

Fig. 5. Ambidextrous computer image.

The connections, used here, are as follows.

(1) Surface, or part of it, to surface or part of it.
(2) Edge, or part of it, to edge or part of it.
(3) Vertex to vertex[21].

The arrangements of components, or as in some cases elements to elements, have been emerging, thus giving rise to an infinite number of configurations through the variety of connections.

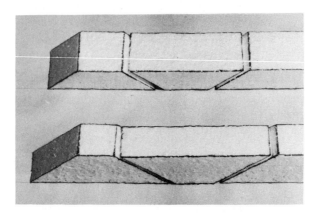

Fig. 6. Two different double-element components.

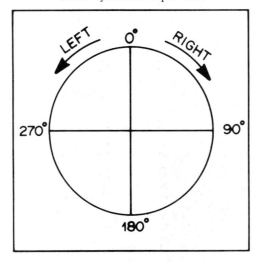

Fig. 7. Diagram of rotations.

THE NEED FOR COLOR

I have described, up to this point, the genesis of the right-handed element, and the peculiar nature of the double element. A short preview has been given of the predictable properties in the forms grown by the use of the element and its various connections, thus preparing for the ways in which the symmetries emerge. Then there is the question: how does a form grow?

One of the planes enclosing the element is square. This leads one to use six elements to embrace a cubic void. The result is a component with three-way rudiments ("buds") that would invite three other similar components to join. Continuing the growth process, a single form emerges with different spatiotemporal patterns or symmetries (Fig. 11).

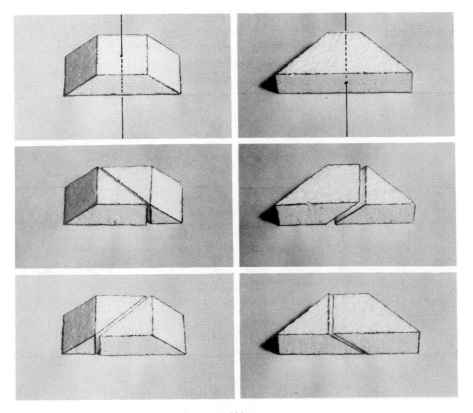

Fig. 8. Two ambidextrous components.

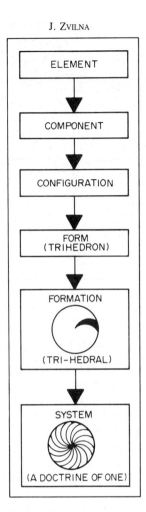

Fig. 9. Hierarchy of a system.

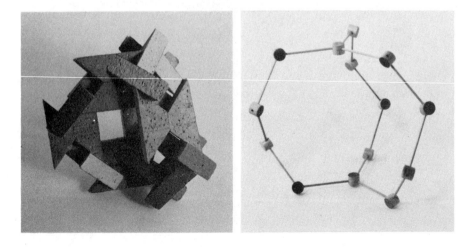

Fig. 10. Form and structure.

Fig. 11. The trihedral pattern emerging from single-color elements.

There is an unexpected variety. For example, it is possible, using imagination and abstraction, to count various helical configurations in different directions. What is lacking is a visible hint of the dynamic nature of the element, for it is generated through a dynamic process in space–time. Therefore, an additional color is included in the next exercise.

EMERGENCE OF A DECAGON

The same growth process of the elements is repeated as in Fig. 11. The only difference is that the top three elements are in color. In the final form all blue elements join in the same manner as the white ones, creating continuities. The blue bands twist around the whites, and the whites around the blues, testify to an inborn dynamic. The blue–white form will be used to analyse the trihedral formation, one of the subsystems for the system "A Doctrine of One." The reason for choosing this two-color form, in comparison with other forms, is its simplicity, as it is possible to illustrate it on a flat plane by photographs and computer graphics. It is still possible to illustrate this form on a flat plane by photographs and computer graphics. The use of the concept of stereopsis is the next best way as described later in this paper.

A ten-sided polygon (Fig. 12, lower centre) is abstracted from the blue–white pattern. By connecting the centres of cubes with straight lines, a decagon emerges—a two-way curved polygon. To simplify the presentation of the twisted decagon, it is assumed that it consists of straight planes, keeping the original centre of the polygon. Since the decagon could be built with the components consisting of double elements, enantimorphic polygons are possible, as shown in a diagrammatic view (Fig. 13).

Figure 14 leads to the next spatiotemporal pattern.

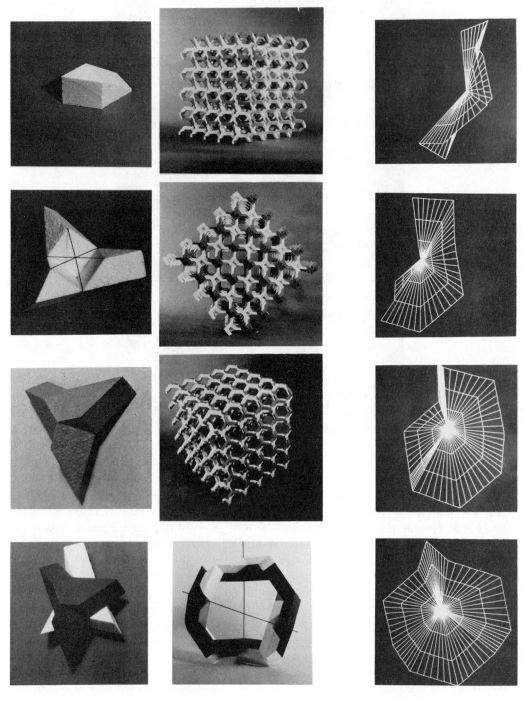

Fig. 12. The trihedral pattern emerging from two-color elements.

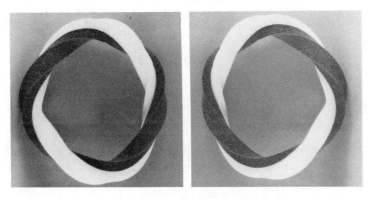

Fig. 13. Diagram of opposite handedness.

Fig. 14. The genesis of trihedral form.

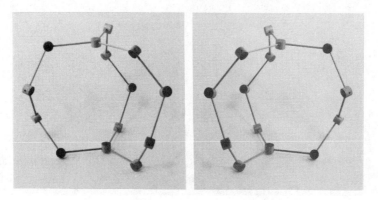

Fig. 15. Enantiomorphic trihedron structures.

Fig. 16. Growth of trihedral form.

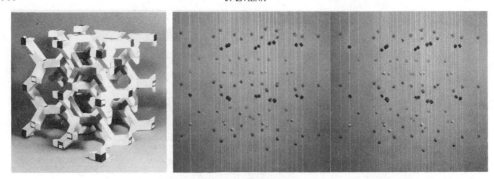

Fig. 17. Trihedral lattice.

EMERGENCE OF TRIHEDRON

The trihedron, a volume enclosed by three decagons, is also abstracted from the blue–white pattern. It has one rotational symmetry axis possible in its enantimorphic structure (Fig. 15). Since each of the three decagons have two symmetry axes (one to form a primary trihedron, the other to form a secondary), the trihedron grows infinitely (Fig. 16). As a stereogram, Fig. 16 is viewed by slightly crossing the eyes (observing the left image with right eye and right image with the left eye). The third image, a fusion of the two, will appear three dimensional, in the centre.

In Fig. 17, a cubic structure is abstracted from the blue–white pattern and translated in a trihedral lattice, typical to all further forms in this paper (see Fig. 18). Inscribed in the cube

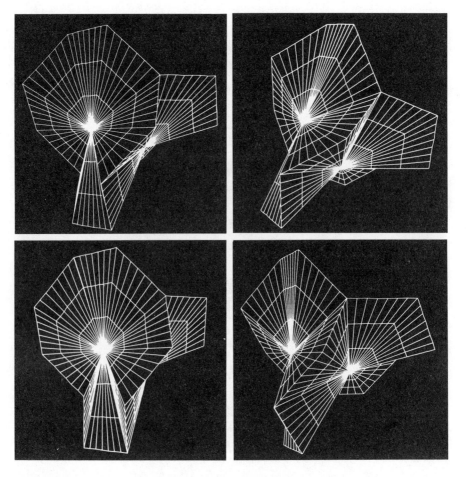

Fig. 18. Views of trihedron; computer image.

Fig. 19. Thirteen axes of symmetry.

in a dodecahedron, enclosed by 12 decagons. The analysis of the trihedral formations unfolds 13 axes of symmetry (Fig. 19): (a) four 9-sided helical configurations; (b) three octagonal and tetragonal helical configurations; and (c) six hexagonal helical configurations (see Fig. 20).

COLORED SYMMETRIES IN SPACE–TIME

The true nature of the element fully unfolds in colored symmetries[22].
The plank, the same as in Fig. 4, is painted in four different colors and cut as in Fig. 4.

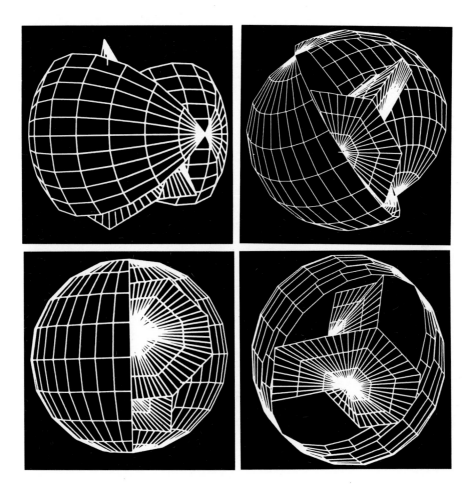

Fig. 20. Trihedron enscribed in a sphere; computer image.

Fig. 21. The same form, different color codings; elements A, B, C, D.

Fig. 22. Genesis of points (from top down): center of cube (invisible), center of hole, as crosspoint of lines.

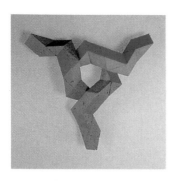

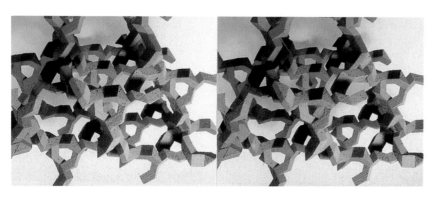

Fig. 23. Genesis of spatiotemporal pattern (form) displaying colored symmetries.

Fig. 24. Helical configurations and the arrangement of elements.

Fig. 25. Stereogram of a trihedron.

Fig. 26. Selected trihedrons (views from above).

The form of the element has not changed, while the color coding gives four different elements: A, B, C, and D (Figs. 21,22). Only one component is shown expanded, to display the growth of color symmetries through various transpositions in space–time. At the same time, additional information emerges, e.g. another color combination (Fig. 23). The same form could be arrived at by first growing helical configurations with selected color coding A, B, C, D. Figure 24, top, shows the helical configuration. It starts with A (left side):

A B C D A B C D A B C D A

Only in the 13th position has A returned to its original position. The helical configurations in other spatiotemporal patterns demonstrate the same property (Fig. 24, middle, bottom; see also Figs. 25–27).

CONCLUSION

This work is a prologue only. The future development is towards further complexity and the transposition of trihedral spaces using the same single-type right-handed element[23].

REFERENCES

1. L. A. Cummings, *The Labyrinth of Daedalus*. Waterloo School of Architecture, Waterloo (1984).
2. W. Heisenberg, *Across the Frontiers*. Harper & Row, New York (1974).
3. J. Zvilna, *An Introduction to the Study of Interdisciplinary Language*. J. Zvilna, Toronto (1979).
4. Lancelot Law Whyte, *Structural Hierarchies: A Challenging Class of Physical and Biological Problems; Hierarchical Structure*. (Edited by Whyte, Wilson and Wilson. Elsevier, New York, London, Amsterdam (1969).
5. G. Bateson, *Mind and Nature*. E. P. Dutton, New York (1979).
6. Paul A. Weiss, *Dynamic of Development: Experiments and Inferences*. Academic Press, New York, London (1968).
7. H. Weyl, *Symmetry*. Princeton University Press, Princeton, NJ (1952).
8. A. V. Shubnikow and V. A. Koptsik, *Symmetry in Science and Art*. Plenum Press, New York, London (1974).
9. J. T. Fraser, *Of Time, Passion, and Knowledge*. George Braziller, New York (1975).
10. G. J. Whitrow, *The Natural Philosophy of Time*. Clarendom Press, Oxford (1980).
11. Joseph Campbell (Ed.), *Man and Time*. Papers from the Eranos Yearbooks, Bollingen Series XXX. 3, Priceton University Press (1983).
12. Constantinos A. Doxiadis, *Architecture in Transition*. Oxford University Press, New York (1963).
13. A. Eddington, *Space, Time and Gravitation*. Harper & Row, New York, Evanston (1920).
14. Gyorgy Kepes, *The New Landscape in Art and Science*. Paul Theobald and Co., Chicago (1956).
15. Cyril Stanley Smith, *A Search for Structure*. M.I.T. Press, Cambridge (1981).
16. Julian Rowan, *Tetrahedron Modeling: Art/Science Metaphors for Order in Space*. *Leonardo*, **17**(4) (1984).
17. J. Rosen, *Symmetry Discovered*. Cambridge University Press, Cambridge (1973).
18. Norman E. Emerton, *The Scientific Reinterpretation of Form*. Cornell University Press, Ithaca, London (1984).
19. H. Yukawa, *Creativity and Intuition*. Kodensha International Ltd., Tokyo, New York, San Francisco (1973).
20. J. Zvilna, *Rotation and Form*. Proceedings, International Association for Shell and Spatial Structures, Concordia University, Montreal (1976).
21. A. F. Wells, *The Third Dimension in Chemistry*. Oxford University Press, London (1956).
22. Arthur L. Loeb, *Color and Symmetry*. Wiley-Interscience, New York (1971).
23. J. Zvilna, A Doctrine of One (unpublished).

Comp. & Maths. with Appls. Vol. 12B, Nos. 3/4, pp. 913–948, 1986
Printed in Great Britain.

0886–9561/86 $3.00 + .00
© 1986 Pergamon Press Ltd.

A COURSE IN THE MATHEMATICS OF DESIGN

JAY KAPPRAFF
New Jersey Institute of Technology, Newark, NJ 07102, U.S.A.

Abstract—A project-oriented course on the Mathematics of Design taught for the past six years to freshman architecture students at the New Jersey Institute of Technology is described. The course uses mathematics as the organizing force linking scientific, artistic and cultural subject areas together. The sequence of topics is graph theory with application to planning a floor plan; polyhedra applied to Platonic solids; tilings of the plane with application to lattice designs; tiling of three-dimensional space and space-filling polyhedra; similarity, proportion and the golden mean with application to architectural design; transformations; mirrors and symmetry; and vectors applied to analysis of polyhedra and ruled surfaces. The mathematical elements of each topic lead students to carry out a two- or three-dimensional construction. Students are helped to focus on the ideas behind their work by writing a series of essays.

1. INTRODUCTION

Seven years ago several mathematicians, architects and computer scientists at the New Jersey Institute of Technology began to explore areas of common interest. The architects were trying to find ways to break out of their limited repertoire of forms and shapes and they wished their students to develop the mathematical skills necessary to make design tasks more operational. The mathematicians were trying to find interesting applications for otherwise abstract branches of mathematics such as group theory, topology and graph theory, and in addition they wanted to rediscover the geometrical roots of their subject. The computer scientists saw the architecture students as potential users of computers—in particular, of computer graphics. As a result of this interaction, the group decided that a new course on the Mathematics of Design was needed for the following reasons:

● Most disciplines have become overspecialized. It is important to rediscover the connections between subject areas.
● The computer has gained a preeminent position in all subject areas. It is important to develop courses dealing with computer-applicable mathematics.
● Most subject areas emphasize analysis at the expense of synthesis. Courses are needed to redress this imbalance.

A course addressing these needs would have to encompass a wide range of mathematical ideas and include topics applicable to disciplines not recognized as mathematical. The ideas would have to be made active; a mere survey of mathematics as a culture or use of mathematics as a tool for analysis would not suffice. The course would have to demonstrate how ideas originating in the realm of mathematics could lead to fresh approaches in nonmathematical areas such as art, architecture, biology and chemistry. I knew about a project-oriented course that responded well to these points that was taught by an engineer, artist and geometer, Professor Mary Blade at Cooper Union College. Professor Blade's work formed the early inspiration for the course that I will describe in this article.

The course is based on geometrical ideas. By geometry we do not mean the vehicle of axiomatics that conditions most students' first approach to the subject. Rather, we refer to geometry as the matrix of ideas contained within a study of symmetry, proportion, tilings of the plane and three dimensions, perspective and the theory of graphs.

The course prepares students to carry out a construction or project rather than just conveying information and perfecting computational technique. Within this format each topic has a tight mathematical structure. The pedagogical approach is to "tell the truth, nothing but the truth—but not the whole truth." Airtight mathematical language would soon lose an audience untrained in this arcane form of expression. A primary goal of the course is to present material in plain language.

In the process of teaching nonmathematically oriented students, the problem of math anxiety

913

must be faced. Many students are not able to manipulate mathematical symbols or follow the narrow paths of lengthy mathematical arguments. Nevertheless, they are capable of understanding complex ideas and applying them to practical problems. Even though these students might not do well on exams emphasizing computation, they can gain satisfaction from applying mathematical ideas to design projects. We also feel that these students can be made more receptive to mathematical ways of thinking if mathematics is shown to be a key to understanding a wider realm of ideas. To stimulate this reappraisal of thought in the light of mathematical revelations, after each project the students write a one- or two-page essay exploring the higher-level ideas behind the project.

The course was originally organized as an experimental seminar, part of the third-year design studio of the School of Architecture at NJIT. Each week a faculty member gave a lecture focusing on the mathematical content of his subject. The architecture students and their professors then met to suggest a design project based on the lecture. The following week the lecturer returned and was presented a set of completed constructions. Often the students related to the original lecture in ways the lecturer had not imagined. There was always the element of surprise in this transaction between students and faculty. We knew at this point that we had the makings of an unusual course.

The new course was made a requirement for all students from the School of Architecture and would be taken by about 100 students in the second half of the freshman year. Now the task was more difficult. We no longer had the luxury of communicating with a highly motivated, self-selected group of upperclassmen, but the needs of wider and less experienced audience had to be met. As a result, some of the spontaneity and self-motivation of the experimental seminar was sacrificed in favor of the greater structure and formality.

Since the content of the course was spread through numerous reference books, the members of the group collaborated on a set of lecture notes. With the help of a grant from the Graham Foundation for Architecture and the Fine Arts, I was able to write the first draft of a text for the course[1].

The course has steadily evolved over the past six years. Due to the constructive nature of the course, every time a new project is carried out, it can be used to illustrate mathematical ideas that would otherwise be lifeless. Finally, after several cycles of teaching the course, one of the collaborators, Professor Alan Stewart, recognized that graph theory provided an underlying structure to the course that unified the topics. Since the theory of graphs constitutes the least constrained of all geometries and all other geometries gain their form and structure from graphical notions, it made sense to employ graph theory as the central element of the course and show how more constrained geometries arise by adding additional structure to graphs. Also, Prof. Stewart saw that the mathematical notions of duality, symmetry, combinatorial properties, space filling, vectors and transformations arose in several topics so that ideas appeared and reappeared throughout the course.

This article will describe the major topics of the course and illustrate them with examples of students' work. Not all of the topics in this survey can be covered in a three-credit course, but all the material has been covered at some time. The sequence of topics is graph theory with application to planning a floor plan; polyhedra applied to the Platonic solids; tilings of the plane with application to lattice designs; tiling of three-dimensional space and space-filling polyhedra; similarity, proportion and the golden mean with application to architectural design; transformations; mirrors and symmetry; and vectors applied to analysis of polyhedra and ruled surfaces.

2. GRAPH THEORY

Each topic of the course begins informally with constructive exercises, experiments, game playing or puzzle solving. The theory of graphs lends itself particularly well to this approach. True to the origin of this subject in 1736 by Leonhard Euler we consider the famous Konigsberg bridge problem and the Utilities problem[2]. The first of these problems makes it clear that graphs with different outward appearances are structurally identical so long as their "connectivities" are the same and that, in fact, graphs are completely defined in terms of their connectivities rather than length, angle or other familiar geometric properties. Thus we are justified in considering graphs to describe the least constrained of all geometries. In addition, the

Konigsberg bridge problem introduces the notion of Euler paths, i.e. a path through the graph that traverses each edge without retracing.

The lesson to be learned from the Utilities problem is that while some graphs, the planar graphs, can be redrawn while preserving their connectivities with no edge intersections, others cannot. Since the students are from the School of Architecture, we try to have them visualize a connected planar graph as a floor plan as shown in Fig. 1(a). By placing a vertex in each room and connecting two vertices by an edge if the rooms share all or part of a wall, we arrive at another graph known as the connectivity graph shown in Fig. 1(b). Later, we show that the floor plan is in some sense "dual" to the connectivity graph.

Problem. Draw a floor plan with four rooms so that each room borders the other three. Can you do this for a floor plan with five rooms? Why not? Draw connectivity graphs for each of these graphs. Are they planar?

The previous problem demonstrates one of the important ideas of the course, namely that spatial design is not as freewheeling as students imagine but is constrained by mathematical properties of space. In fact the connectivity graph for the five-room plan, the complete graph with five vertices, K_5, along with the utilities graph, the bipartite graph $K_{3,3}$, are in a sense described by a theorem of Kuratowski contained in all nonplanar graphs[3]. This problem also gives insight as to why four colors are sometimes needed to color a map where adjacent countries must have different colors, but five colors are never needed.

A final introductory problem, the "Handshake Lemma," introduces the subject of the combinatorial properties of graphs. The class is divided into groups of five students and the students are told to shake hands with whomever they wish from the group and draw a graph to illustrate their pattern of handshakes. They must verify the Lemma which states that the number of people in the group that shake hands an odd number of times is even.

At this point we have laid the groundwork for a more serious study of graphs. Notions of graph isomorphism, cycles, planar and nonplanar graphs, duality, map coloring and combinatorial properties have been introduced in an informal manner.

The principal application for this section of the course is the application of graphs to designing complex floor plans[4]. To carry out this program we must first specialize to connected nonplanar graphs called maps. Maps have well-defined sets of edges, vertices and faces where the faces are topologically equivalent to discs, possibly with pendant edges. It is important to our application for students to first think of the maps as being drawn on a sphere, in which case each face has finite extent. A map in the plane is then obtained by puncturing an arbitrary face, widening the hole, and deforming the map until it fills the plane, as shown in Fig. 2. The punctured face then becomes the exterior face of the map.

Again, combinatorial properties of maps are discussed and the students are asked to draw many maps in search of a relation between the number of edges (E), faces (F) and vertices (V). It is always a surprise for students to discover another constraint on space, the Euler–Poincare number:

$$\chi = F + V - E = 2.$$

The students then begin to explore maps on other surfaces such as cylinders, tori and Möbius strips and to discover the different values of χ for each of these surfaces. The Szilassi polyhedron shown in the student construction of Plate 1 shows that as many as seven colors

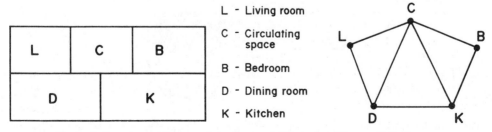

Fig. 1. A floor plan and its connectivity diagram. (a) Floor plan; (b) connectivity diagram.

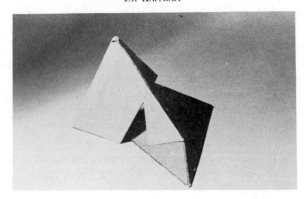

Plate 1. A Szilassi Polyhedron. Each face borders on the other six faces, demonstrating the need for seven colors to color a figure with the connectivity of a torus.

may be needed to color a map drawn on a surface with the connectivity of a torus[5]. Finally, we show students that graphs which are nonplanar in the plane and on a sphere may be planar when drawn on a torus, a fact that may prove useful for drawing floor plans for two-story houses.

By using the combinatorial properties of maps we are able to prove that there exist, aside from several trivial cases, only five regular maps, i.e. maps with vertices and faces surrounded identically by edges[3]. The students begin a search for these maps. This search will be borne out in the next section when the students encounter them as planar projections of the Platonic solids.

The notion of the dual map is introduced and students are now ready to carry out their first project:

> Design a one-story floor plan of a hypothetical house given a well-stated set of client con-
> straints.

Here, constraints on the floor plan are imagined to be communicated verbally from client to architect. Based on these constraints the architect constructs a connectivity graph which includes partial information about the organization of rooms in the house. The connectivity graph is redrawn as a planar map. The dual of the connectivity map constitutes the first approximation to the floor plan. However, the exterior region to the house may appear in the dual map as an interior face at this stage of the design process. If this is so, the map is placed on a sphere and punctured so that the exterior region becomes the outside face. Finally the map is topologically deformed, preserving adjacencies until the desired floor plan obtains. This process is illustrated in Plate 2 by a student's project to design an office.

After completion of the design, the students are asked to write a one- or two-page essay in response to the following statement.

Writing Project
Christopher Alexander, in his book *Notes on the Synthesis of Form*, makes a case for there being a stage in the design process prior to the concrete planning stage, e.g. formal

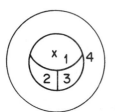 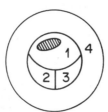 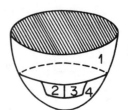 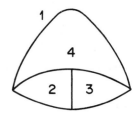

Fig. 2. Transformation of a map on a sphere to a map in the plane. (a) Map on the sphere with face 1 punctured. (b,c) The puncture is widened. (d) Map in the plane with face 1 external.

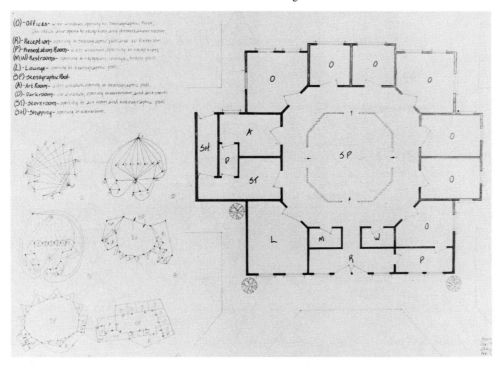

Plate 2. Design of a floor plan using graphs.

presentation of a floor plan or community development project. In this primitive stage linkages or connections are drawn between the various components of the design.

Whereas in primitive societies change occurred so slowly that this stage of the design was unconscious, in a more dynamic society such as our own, where design changes more radically, the process must be more self-conscious. Graphs are the appropriate tool to understand the linkages or connections.

What do you think? Write a response to this statement in one or more pages. (A student response is included in the Appendix.)

Other topics covered in this section of the course have been application of directed graphs to planning a job by critical path analysis[6] and application of bipartite graphs to determining the minimum number of rods needed to brace a planar and three-dimensional space frame[4,7].

3. POLYHEDRA

We are now ready to apply some of the graph-theoretic results of the last section to three-dimensional structures. Polyhedra, and in particular the Platonic solids shown in Fig. 3, provide a source of interesting structures to study[8,9]. In fact, we began their study in the previous chapter when we attempted to find the five regular maps on the plane. Each of these maps can be drawn as the projection of one of the five Platonic solids onto the plane from a projection point above one of its faces, as shown in Fig. 3. Moreover, if the regular maps are placed on a sphere they result in surfaces topologically equivalent to the Platonic solids.

The Platonic solids also constitute a subject rich in connections to the worlds of art, architecture, chemistry and biology. For example, in Plato's *Timaeus* four of the solids were related to the four elements: earth, air, fire and water. The fifth solid, the dodecahedron, represented the cosmos. These solids also served as Kepler's model for the orbits of the planets, inspired the art of M. C. Escher[10], served as the basis of Buckminster Fuller's geodesic domes[11], serve as a starting point in the study of inorganic crystals[12] and the carbon–hydrogen bonds that make up the chemistry of life and finally arise as the form of microscopic organisms known as radiolaria[13], as shown in Fig. 4.

Again, we begin this section of the course in a constructive way. The students build polyhedral forms from miniature marshmallows and toothpicks. The resulting structures can be

JAY KAPPRAFF

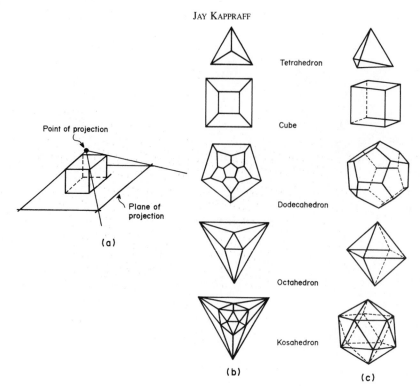

Fig. 3. The Platonic solids and their projections (Schlegel diagrams). (a) Schlegel diagram of cube formed by projection onto plane of bottom face (courtesy Dover[8]). (b) Schlegel diagram of Platonic solids. (c) Platonic solids.

thought of as three-dimensional graphs in which the marshmallows represent vertices and toothpicks play the role of edges, with the additional constraint that all edges have the same length. After some introductory puzzles which lead students to discover the tetrahedron and octahedron, the students create patterns by connecting tetrahedra vertex to vertex, edge to edge and face to face. This leads naturally to construction of octet space frames from combinations of tetrahedra and octahedra, as shown in the student constructions of Plate 3, where modulation of edge lengths results in curvature.

Another construction with marshmallows and toothpicks leads to the discovery of the Platonic solids. The students create regular polyhedra defined by the constraint that each vertex and face must have the same number of incident edges. In the process of constructing these polyhedra it becomes evident that whereas the tetrahedron, octahedron and icosahedron, with triangular faces, are all rigid, the cube and dodecahedron collapse. Thus students discover the importance of the triangle as a source of rigidity in structures.

By placing the octahedron inside the cube, the icosahedron within the dodecahedron and the tetrahedron inside another tetrahedron, the duality of these polyhedral pairs is made visually evident. Also, by tabulating F, E and V the Euler–Poincare number $\chi = 2$ is rediscovered.

The Platonic solids are considered to be a family because they relate to each other in many ways aside from duality. In fact, the golden mean, $\phi = (1 + \sqrt{5})/2$, is a number which ties this family together[14] as shown by Euclid in Book XIII of *The Elements*. The golden mean will play a major role in the portion of the course dealing with proportion. Here we demonstrate the remarkable internal structure of the icosahedron in which the vertices lie at the corners of three mutually orthogonal golden mean rectangles. Plate 4 shows a student construction of a tensegrity structure illustrating this fact.

After studying the combinatorial properties of the Platonic solids, it is natural to consider their metric properties. The cube constitutes the natural coordinate system in which to investigate metric properties since the Platonic solids can all be related to a cube. In fact, a complete characterization of the metric properties of any polyhedron related to a cube can be made in terms of the cube's three principal directions: the edge, face-diagonal and body-diagonal directions. We have found the "universal node system" of Peter Pearce[15] to be an excellent

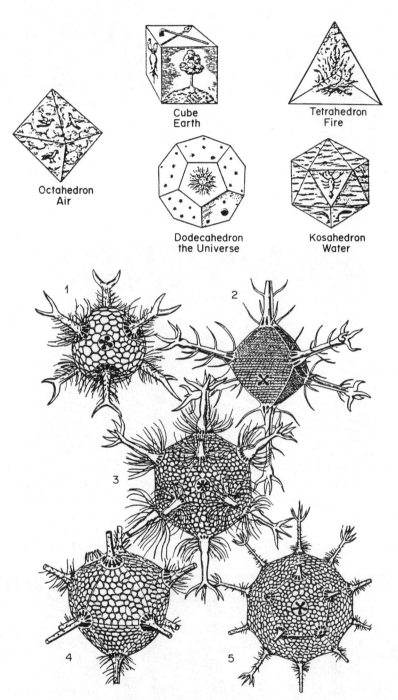

Fig. 4. (a) The Platonic solids depicted by Johannes Kepler in *Harmonices Mundi, Book II* (1619). (b) The Platonic solids in the form of Radiolaria (courtesy Cambridge Press[13]).

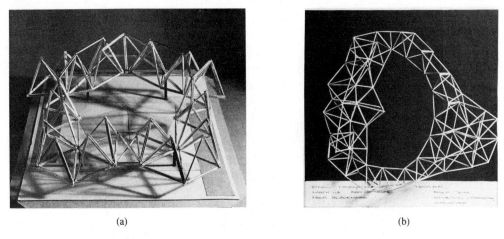

(a)   (b)

Plate 3. Two examples of octet space frames. Curvature is the result of modulated edge lengths.

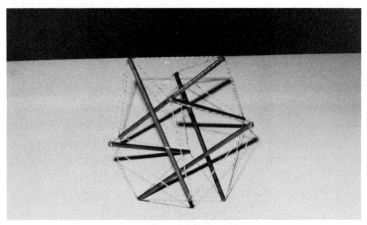

Plate 4. Tensegrity of an icosahedron illustrating inner structure of three intersecting golden mean triangles.

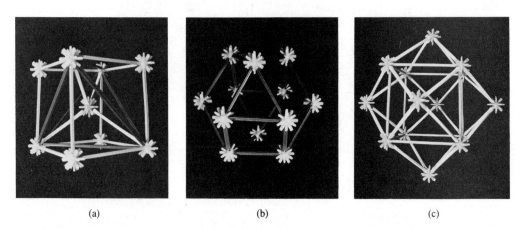

(a)   (b)   (c)

Plate 5. Three polyhedra constructed with the universal node system of Peter Pearce. (a) A cube showing principal directions. (b) Cuboctahedron constructed with face-diagonal directions. (c) Rhombic dodecahedron surrounding a cube constructed with body-diagonal directions.

tool for constructing and demonstrating at a glance the structure of polyhedra. In this system the edges are color and shape coded according to the principal directions of the cube and connect to equivalently shape-coded connectors. This enables polyhedra to be built with great ease. A cube with a tetrahedron embedded on its surface and four edges connecting the cube's center to each of the four vertices of the tetrahedron, constructed with the universal node system along with two polyhedra related to a cube, the cuboctahedron and rhombic dodecahedron, are shown in Plate 5. If we imagine a carbon atom to lie at the center of the cube and hydrogen atoms at the vertices of the tetrahedron, this system provides a model of the carbon–hydrogen bond found in organic molecules.

Symmetry will be discussed in great detail later in the course. In this section the topic is introduced by illustrating the 13 axes of rotational symmetry and the 9 planes of reflection symmetry of a cube using a cube constructed with the universal node system. The axes of rotational symmetry lie in the principal directions of the cube and can be detected by projecting the cube onto a plane perpendicular to the axes and then by finding the symmetry of the plane projections, as in Fig. 5.

The geodesic properties of the Platonic solids are introduced as the final topic of this section by posing the following problem:

Find a way to cut an orange into four congruent pieces other than the usual breakfast way.

The solution is found by projecting the tetrahedron to a circumscribed sphere from its centroid. This divides the sphere into four congruent solid angles. In the process the edges project to arcs of geodesics of the sphere. Of course, similar results obtain from other Platonic solids and their circumscribed spheres. This gives an opportunity to define geodesics and assign problems to compute shortest distances between points lying on a cube, parallelopiped, cylinder, torus, shell and cone.

Besides the circumscribed sphere, two other spheres are associated with the Platonic solids: the inscribed sphere tangent to polyhedral faces and the intersphere through the midpoints of the edges. These spheres are related to the symmetry of the Platonic solids in a striking way illustrated by the dihedral kaleidoscope of the cube shown in Plate 6[16]. Here the 9 planes of reflective symmetry divide the cube into 48 congruent tetrahedra, known as orthoschemes, defined by the radii of the three spheres[8]. These tetrahedra also form an excellent set of building blocks from which to construct polyhedral sculptures as shown.

Three additional surfaces satisfying the criteria for Platonic solids were introduced by Coxeter[17] in 1937. They differ from the five already introduced by having an infinite number of faces. Two of them are duals since four hexagons surround each vertex in one while six squares surround a vertex in the other, as shown in the student project of Plate 7.

Finally, the three regular star polyhedra discovered by Kepler have been explored by several students and give entree to the visually fascinating area of star polyhedra[18].

4. TILINGS OF THE PLANE

Tiling a region of space is the concern of many disciplines. The architect fills open spaces with buildings and partitions the inside of a building with rooms. The artist subdivides a canvas into spaces in which to portray the subjects that make up a painting. The chemist and crystallographer deal with well-ordered patterns of molecules in the form of chemical compounds or crystals. The botanist studies regular orderings of stalks, or paristichies, of a plant. Electrical engineers consider breakdowns of space into close-packed spheres representing the coding of messages. In this section, we study the mathematics of tiling a plane and indicate how mathematics addresses the concerns of other subject areas. In the next section we consider tilings of three-dimensional space.

The previous section was devoted to a study of polyhedra, and in the introductory exercises students constructed octet space frames. Now these space frames are projected, by a light source, onto a plane, and triangles, squares and hexagons are observed in the resulting patterns. The

Plate 6. Dihedral kaleidoscope based on the symmetry of the cube.

mathematics of planar tilings begins with a study of these patterns of triangles, squares and hexagons.

As an introductory exercise, students are asked to observe patterns of triangles, parallelograms and hexagons formed by the grid lines of triangular-grid graph paper. The possibilities are noted for constructing unusual designs with this grid by circumscribing a circle about a large hexagon defined by the grid and shading the grid contained within the hexagon, as shown in Fig. 6.

After creating their own hexagonal design, the students construct designs using the entire grid, in a manner reminiscent of Islamic patterns[19]. A student project is shown in Plate 8.

Now that the students have had the opportunity to try their hand at some free-form planar designs, they learn that as a consequence of the combinatorial properties of graphs, triangles, squares and hexagons are the only regular maps that tile the plane with an infinity of faces[20]. Thus once again a mathematical property of space forbids other polygons, such as pentagons, from tiling regularly.

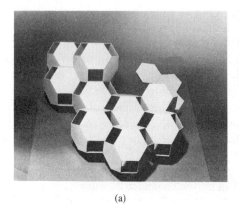

(a)   (b)

Plate 7. Two additional Platonic solids discovered by Coxeter. They are duals.

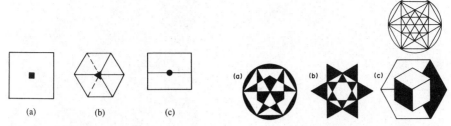

Fig. 5. Projection of a cube onto the plane along its axes of rotation. (a) Four-fold axis; (b) three-fold axis; (c) two-fold axis.

Fig. 6. A triangular grid with three hexagonal patterns (courtesy Creative Publications).

This result was proven for maps whose faces need not be congruent, or for that matter, have linear edges. If we now consider regular tilings made of congruent polygons, the three permissible tilings were already inherent in the triangular grid of the introductory exercise. However, any quadrilateral, convex or nonconvex, and hexagons with parallel opposite sides also tile the plane regularly.

Next we define semiregular tilings of the plane in which more than one polygon is used. For example, Fig. 7(a) shows a semiregular tiling with triangles and squares, five around a vertex. Next to it, in Fig. 7(b) is a tiling with pentagons. We try to get the students to explain why this tiling does not violate the proscriptions of regular pentagonal tilings. In fact, Fig. 7(a) is dual to Fig. 7(b) and brings up an important aspect of duals: although dual figures are structurally identical they are nevertheless visually quite different. Thus a single mathematical idea can serve as a carrier of a variety of visual patterns, a recurring theme in this course.

Parallelograms and hexagons with parallel opposite sides play a special role in tiling, namely they tile the plane by translation only. These polygons are members of a class of polygons known as zonagons[21], generated by stars of vectors. In order to study zonagons we first introduce the subject of vectors, which will find great utility throughout the course. The 3-zonagon is then defined by a vector star of three vectors as shown in Fig. 8.

The value of this construction to design is that vectors of the star can be altered in length to form zonagons changed in size and shape but with the same interior angles. Thus a space-filling array of hexagons continues to tile the plane, as shown by the student construction of Plate 9. From a design point of view, joints are the most difficult part of a structure to fabricate and zonagons enable structures to be "fitted" to their "function" in terms of size and shape without altering the joints.

In the regular grid tilings that introduced this section the focus was on edges and faces. Now we consider the vertices of those grids which constitute a planar lattice. Some exploratory exercises help students gain an understanding of the invariance of planar lattices under translations in two nonparallel directions characterized by vectors, and the notion of the fundamental domain of a lattice. It is not surprising that a structure as rich as the lattice in mathematical ideas is also a rich source of two- and three-dimensional tilings. A design idea suggested by William J. Gilbert[22] describes how patterns with lattice symmetry can be generated. The designs shown in Plate 10 illustrate some results of Gilbert's method. One of the tilings incorporates 90° rotations in addition to translation, while another applies Gilbert's ideas to three-dimensional lattice designs.

Up to now the plane has been tiled with polygons of identical size and shape. Now tilings

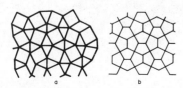

Fig. 7. A semiregular tiling and its dual (courtesy Addison Wesley[20]). (a) Semiregular tiling; (b) dual tiling.

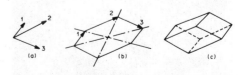

Fig. 8. Construction of a 3-zonagon. (a) 3-Vector star; (b) 3-zonagon (note: opposite sides are equal and parallel and zonagon is centrally symmetric); (c) 3-zonagon is the plane projection of a parallelopiped.

Plate 8. A design based on tiling the plane with triangles,
squares and hexagons.

Plate 9. Tiling the plane with hexagons constructed from
a 3-zonagon.

are considered with polygons that may be irregularly shaped, known as Dirichlet domains
(DDs)[20]. Dirichlet domains have applications in biology, chemistry and architecture. They
are generated by a set of points in which the regions of the tiling satisfy the following minimum
principle: all points nearer to a given point of the generating set than any other point of the set
belongs to the DD of the given point.

   Subdivision of the plane into DDs can be carried out by compass-and-straightedge construction. For example, the boundary of the two points is clearly the perpendicular bisector of

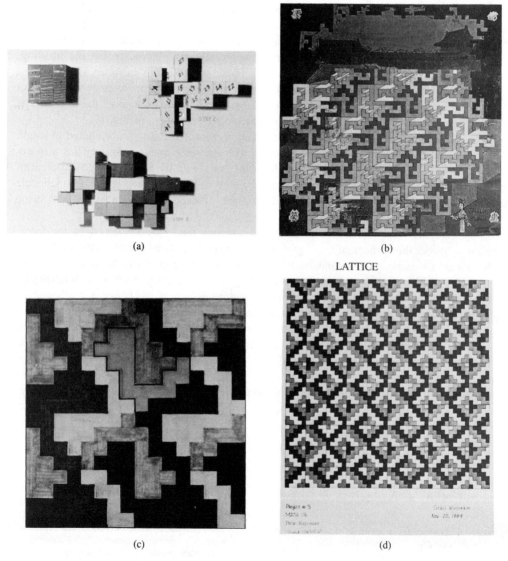

(a)

(b)

LATTICE

(c)

(d)

Plate 10. Some designs based on two- and three-dimensional lattices using Gilbert's method.

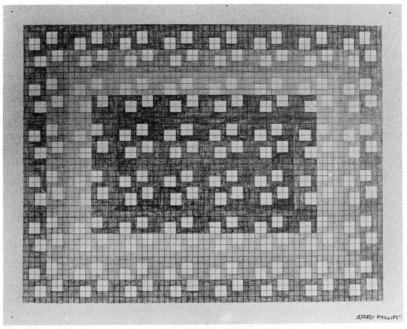

(e)

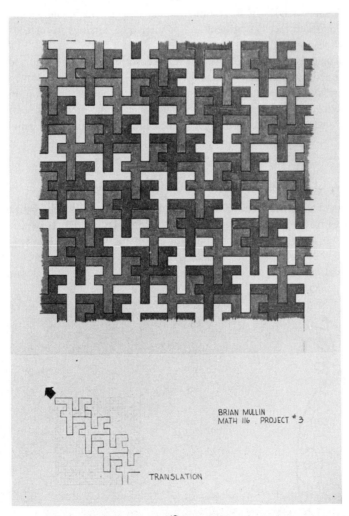

(f)

Plate 10. (Continued).

the line joining the two points. The DDs of three points are formed by the perpendicular bisectors of the sides of the triangle. The construction of the DDs of four points is more of a challenge and leads to an algorithm for constructing DDs for *n* points.

The purpose of introducing DDs is to exploit their connection to space filling in the plane, and more importantly in three-dimensional space, by congruent modules. These space-filling properties of DDs lie at the base of their applications to biology, chemistry and architecture.

The DDs of a plane lattice are either hexagons or rectangles. Coxeter[23] showed that the growth of plants can be studied by mapping the surface of the plant onto a planar lattice and identifying the stalks of the plant with the DDs of the lattice as shown in Fig. 9 for a pineapple.

> *Writing Project*
> In his paper entitled ''Perception and Modular Coordination,'' Christopher Alexander suggests that we enjoy symmetric themes in design because our minds recoil at chaos but are put at ease by the repetition of a simple motif. We like to see things that look familiar, that we have seen before, and structure and order in art and architecture help us to feel secure and comfortable with our surroundings. On the other hand, people react adversely to mindless, monotonous order. To a great extent, it is the job of the artist and architect to supply, through their work, a solution to the problem of satisfying the needs of people for both order and novelty.
> Comment on this statement. Do you agree or disagree? The Design Project on Lattices certainly satisfies the criterion of design based on order and repetition. Is it also capable of producing designs interesting enough to appeal to our need for surprise and novelty? (A student response is included in the Appendix.)

In the next section DDs of three-dimensional lattices will be shown to be space-filling polyhedra with opposite faces congruent and parallel, i.e., analogs in three dimensions of the zonagons known as zonahedra[24].

Additional material is included in the *Notes* describing an algebraic method of tiling a rectangle with noncongruent squares[25] and a class of nonperiodic tilings of the plane discovered by Roger Penrose[26]. Student projects illustrating these tilings are shown in Plate 11 and Plate 12. Also, following up on the star polyhedra introduced in the preceding section, the students explore regular star polygons, a source of both interesting patterns and number-theoretic results[27].

5. TILING OF THREE-DIMENSIONAL SPACE

This section extends the ideas of the last section to tilings of three-dimensional space. The section begins with two introductory exercises showing the relation between two- and three-dimensional tilings and the use of soap bubbles as a natural way to fill space with curvilinear polyhedra. A study of close packing of spheres leads to the subject of three-dimensional lattices, networks and dual networks[15]. The Archimedean solids are seen to be semiregular tilings of

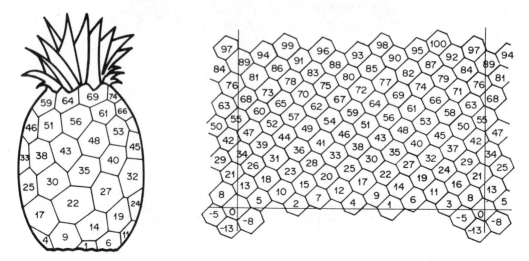

Fig. 9. Relation of pineapple phyllotaxis to a period lattice (courtesy Wiley[23]).

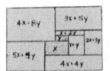
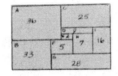

SCALE - ¼" = 1 UNIT

- THE SHADED AREAS WERE FIRST INITIALIZED, THE VALUES X & Y
  THE FURTHER SUBDIVISIONS WERE THEN DIMENSIONED
  BY BASE X, Y. - A COMPARISON WAS THEN MADE BETWEEN A+C = B+G
  THE INEQUALITY WAS THEN SOLVED AND THE VALUES Y=2, X=5 WERE DERIVED
  THE NUMERICAL DIMENSIONS WERE THEN CALCULATED -

(a)   (b)

Plate 11. Tiling a rectangle with noncongruent squares.

the sphere, and they lead to additional space-filling possibilities. Finally, prisms and antiprisms are studied and the latter are used as the basic module of a design with architectural applications.

The first introductory exercise involves using a soap solution to study what appears to be the structureless formation of bubbles making up a soap froth much like a three-dimensional graph drawn with curvilinear edges. In fact, closer study of the froth reveals a precise structure. Three bubbles always meet at an edge and four edges meet at each vertex. Also, the average number of faces in the polyhedra formed by the froth is approximately 14. Later we shall see that this state of affairs also prevails in the space-filling array of one of the Archimedean solids, the truncated octahedron.

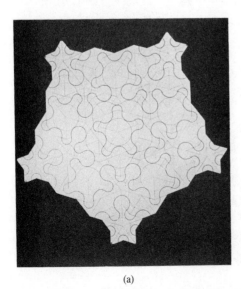
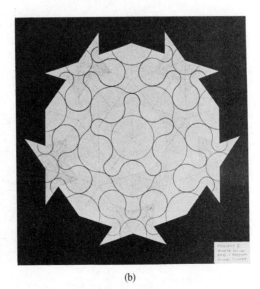

(a)   (b)

Plate 12. A nonperiodic tiling of the plane by kites and darts, based on the golden mean.

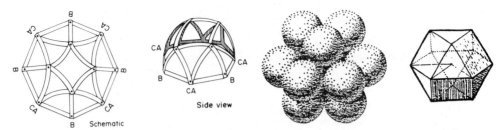

Fig. 11. The cuboctahedron as a figure of cubic close packing of spheres (courtesy Dover[8]).

Fig. 10. Pattern for a dome constructed from paper strips using the method of Gerald Segal (courtesy Gerald Segal).

Last semester I made use of a second constructive exercise, devised by Gerald Segal[28] to make the transition from tilings of the plane to polyhedra. Ninety-six heavy cardboard strips measuring 10 in. by $1\frac{1}{2}$ inches and paper connectors were distributed to groups of students. Their job was to place strips around a central square to make the square rigid. They realized that surrounding the square by triangles would do the job. At this point we presented them with the patterns shown in Fig. 10 to construct. The results are shown in Plate 13.

At a certain point in the construction, the two-dimensional pattern of strips is forced into the third dimension to form a dome. Once again the students are confronted with a mathematical property of space which forces a move from the second into the third dimension, namely, that the sum of the angles around a vertex is less than the 360° required to lie flat in a plane. The difference between 360° and this sum, known as the spherical deviation, is characteristic of all polyhedra.

Thinking back to the octet space frame of the section on polyhedra, we now visualize the marshmallows at the vertices to be spheres that expand to form a close-packed array of spheres.

Plate 13. Some domes constructed with papers strips by Segal's method.

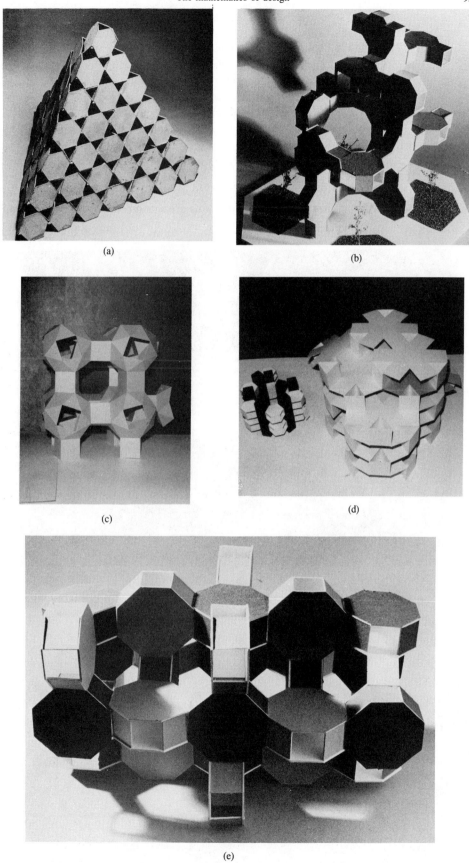

(a)

(b)

(c)

(d)

(e)

Plate 14. Some infinite regular surfaces based on a network and its dual, using **Burt**, **Kleinmann** and **Wachman's** method.

In this configuration, 12 spheres surround a central sphere, 6 in a plane, with 3 spheres lying in the interstices above and below with opposite orientations. The centers of these spheres lie at the vertices of another Archimedean solid known as the cuboctahedron (shown in Fig. 11). Also, the sphere centers of these close-packed spheres constitute one of the 14 Bravais lattices that make up the subject of crystallography, namely the face-centered cubic (FCC) lattice.

In addition to FCC we study two other lattices, the basic cubic lattice (C) and the body-centered cubic lattice (BCC), which are related, along with the FCC, to a cube. In particular, directions from point to point in these lattices occur in the edge (E), body diagonal (BD) and face diagonal (FD) directions respectively.

If lattice points are connected with edges, a network is formed made up of E, BD and FD directions. These edges also divide space into sets of space-filling polyhedra, namely, cubes, tetrahedra with curvilinear faces and octahedra and tetrahedra respectively. We can also define dual networks that connect the polyhedral centers of adjacent polyhedra through their common

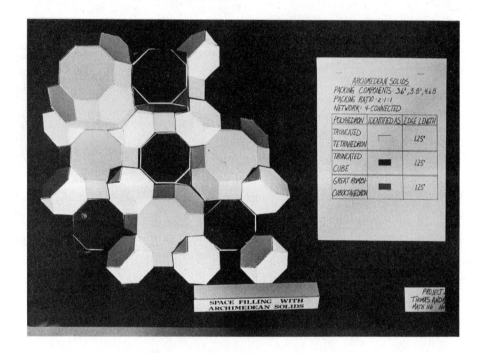

(a)

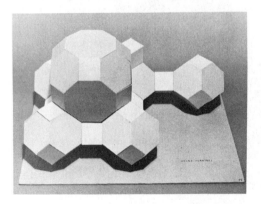

(b)

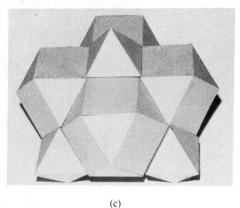

(c)

Plate 15. Two examples of space filling by combinations of Archimedean solids. (a) Cuboctahedra and octahedra; (b) great rhombicuboctahedron, truncated octahedron and cube; (c) truncated tetrahedron, truncated cube and great rhombic dodecahedron.

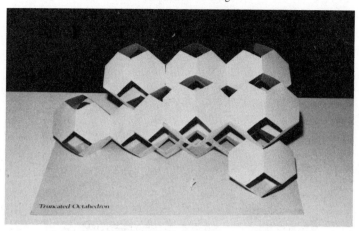

Plate 16. Space-filling truncated octahedra.

faces. Burt, Wachman and Kleinmann[17] have catalogued numerous examples of infinite rectangular surfaces with the structure of the network and its dual corresponding to a particular lattice. Student projects illustrating some of these structures are shown in Plate 14. The surface separates two connected labyrinths of tunnels[15,29].

Next we study Archimedean solids, which are the three-dimensional analogues of the semiregular tilings of the previous section. They each have more than one kind of polygonal face but surround vertices identically[11]. As for the Platonic solids, they can each be circumscribed by a sphere and through a projection from the center result in tilings of the sphere along arcs of geodesics. Several combinations of Archimedean polyhedra served as modules for the infinite regular surfaces. Many combinations of Archimedean solids combine to fill space. Two examples are shown in the student constructions of Plate 15.

In this section we focus on only the cuboctahedron shown in Plate 5(a) and the truncated octahedron shown in Plate 7(a), the former because of its relation to close-packed spheres and the latter because it is the only space filler by itself among the Archimedean solids and serves as a model for soap froths as shown in Fig. 11 and Plate 16. We also study the dual of the cuboctahedron, known as the rhombic dodecahedron and shown in Plate 5(c), because it too fills space by itself, serves as the structure of beehives[13] as shown in Fig. 12 and has possibilities as an architectural module to rival the parallelopiped[21]. In fact, the cube, rhombic dodecahedron and truncated octahedron are all zonahedra and constitute the Dirichlet domains of the C, FCC and BCC lattices—all of which connects this section strongly to the previous one. The lattices and their Dirichlet domains also have connections to the structure of metallic crystals, where two species of atoms lie at the lattice points and the vertices of the DDs-[30–32].

We have used the prescription of Anthony Pugh[32] to construct tensegrity models of polyhedra. Tensegrities, discovered by the sculptor Mark Snelson, are described to the students as discrete analogues of the balloon in which the skin is tensed under the enclosed gas. They combine both tension and compression to an even degree, much like the body with its skeleton and tendons, and always result in light, airy strucctures. A tensegrity model of a cuboctahedron is shown in Plate 17.

Prisms and antiprisms are the final two classes of solids studied in this section. Since the lateral faces of the prism are parallelograms, prisms are not rigid. However, they can be made rigid to lateral forces by rotating the top face relative to the bottom and connecting top vertices to bottom ones to form antiprisms with triangulated lateral faces.

Many of the students have incorporated the hexagonal antiprism into models of prefabricated paper housing consisting of sequences of vaults, semidomes and domes[33]. These models are fabricated by folding paper into a pattern of congruent isosceles triangles. The vaults can be joined together by intersection structures which enable them to be continued to tile the plane. Student models are shown in Plate 18.

(a)

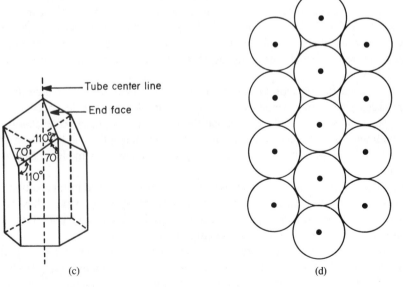

(b)

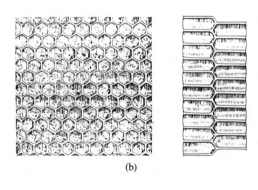

(c)

(d)

Fig. 12. The geometry of a beehive. (a) Plane section of a close-packed configuration of bees. (b) Edges of neighboring chambers are flattened to form a hexagonal pattern. (c) Detail of rhombic dodecahedron ends attached to hexagonal prisms. (d) Close packing of beehives. (Courtesy Cambridge Press[13]).

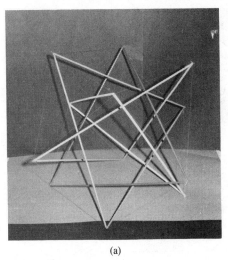

(a)

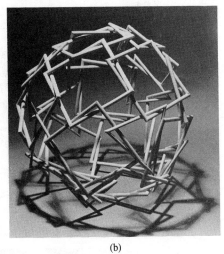

(b)

Plate 17. A tensegrity model of a cuboctahedron with inner structure of four interlocking equilateral triangles.

Writing Project
    It is stated in the Kaballah, a book of Jewish mysticism, that there are actually two bibles or torahs handed to man by God: the one of the written words and the one made up of the space between those words.
    Give your opinion as to whether the space left empty within a design has equal importance to the space that is filled. Use the example of infinite regular polyhedra in which space is divided into two congruent sets as an example of positive and negative space. (A student response is included in the Appendix).

Additional material is included in the *Notes* on the structure of soap bubbles and curved surfaces in general[34,35]. In particular, we concentrate on surfaces of rotation and translation and ruled surfaces. We return to this material in the last section of the course and apply some of the ideas to constructing ruled surfaces. It has also served as an inspiration to the students to show a film at this point in the course by a master designer, Ron Resch, entitled *The Ron Resch Paper and Stick Thing Film*[36].

6. SIMILARITY, PROPORTION AND THE GOLDEN MEAN

    The mathematical concept of similarity holds one of the keys to understanding processes of growth in the natural world. After all, as a member of a species grows to maturity it generally

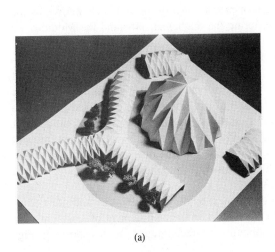

(a)

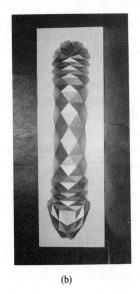

(b)

Plate 18. Two folded-paper structures made of vaults, semidomes, domes and intersecting vaults.

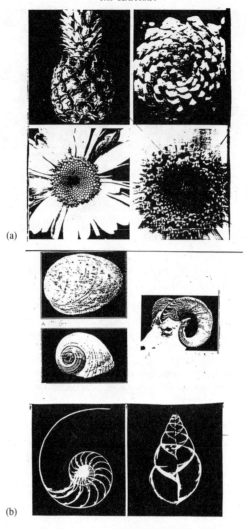

Fig. 13. The logarithmic spiral in nature. (a) Logarithmic spirals as they appear on the surface of a pineapple, pinecone and sunflowers (courtesy Dover[43]). (b) Logarithmic spirals in shells and horns (courtesy Little, Brown[37]).

transforms in such a way that its parts maintain approximately the same proportion with respect to each other. In this section of the course we show how shells, horns of horned animals and plants exhibit self-similar spiral growth[37]. In the case of plant growth, or phyllotaxis, the proportions are related to the golden mean, φ. The architect Le Corbusier took his cue from observations of plant growth to create a system of proportionality for architects known as the Modulor based on the golden mean. After mastering the mathematics behind the Modulor we apply it to creating designs[38,39].

As usual, the topic begins with a game, Fibonacci Nim[40]. Through this game students discover the Fibonacci series: 1,1,2,3,5,8, . . . , which is well known to lie at the heart of plant growth[41,42]. In fact, the number of spirals from the clockwise and counterclockwise sets of logarithmic spirals that appear on the surfaces of sunflowers, pine cones and pineapples are generally successive numbers from this series (as shown in Fig. 13(a)[37]) and the angular placement of stalks around the base of the plant is well known to depend on φ, the most frequent angle being $2\pi/\phi^2 = 136.5°$ shown in Fig. 9 of Section 3 for the pineapple. More discussion of the mathematics and mythology of the golden mean and its applications to art, architecture and biology is included in the course notes[43,44].

We begin the mathematical exposition of this subject by defining similarity and illustrating families of similar figures. We show the right triangle to be the embodiment of self-similarity by cutting a right triangle along its altitude to obtain the three similar triangles shown in Fig. 14.

From this dissection follow both the Pythagorean theorem and the mean proportionality of the altitude to the sections of the hypotenuse:

$$\frac{a}{b} = \frac{b}{c}. \tag{1}$$

Both of these theorems were considered by Kepler to be the most important truths of all geometry. From eqn (1) it follows that a geometric series of points on the logarithmic spiral can be constructed as vertices of a series of right triangles, as shown in Fig. 15. The remaining points can then be densely constructed with compass and straightedge using the growth principle: as the central angle doubles, the radius squares.

It is not surprising that the logarithmic spiral shares with the right triangle the property of self-similarity. In fact, all arcs subtending the same angle are similar. This is the same self-similarity that appears in the spiral structure of shells, horns, and other living forms shown in Fig. 13(b).

Next we show how eqn (1) governs the breakdown of rectangles into similar elements known as Gnomons and one unit similar to the original and tied together by a log spiral, as shown in Fig. 16[44]. As a result of this construction it follows that a square removed from a rectangle with golden mean proportions leaves another golden rectangle. We also discover that the golden mean ϕ forms a series

$$\ldots \frac{1}{\phi^2}, \frac{1}{\phi}, 1, \phi, \phi^2, \phi^3, \ldots$$

that is both double geometric and Fibonacci, i.e.

$$\frac{1}{\phi} + 1 = \phi, \quad 1 + \phi = \phi^2, \quad \phi + \phi^2 = \phi^3, \quad \text{etc.}$$

Artists have known that the golden mean modulates the parts of the human body. Figure 17 shows LeCorbusier's symbol of the Modulor, a 6 ft British policeman with arm outstretched and a Botticelli Venus with sections of the body modulated by powers of ϕ.

For ages architects have searched for systems of proportionality[45] to help them subdivide the inner space and facades of buildlings and the open sites upon which they placed buildings. A useful system of proportionality had to help the architect satisfy the following three design criteria. Good designs must

    (i) be repetitive (made up of a small set of modules);

    (ii) have parts that fit together;

    (iii) be nonmonotonous (not completely predictable)[45,46].

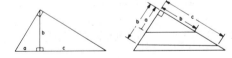

Fig. 14. Dissection of a right triangle into a family of three similar right triangles.

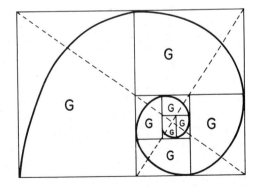

Fig. 16. Breakdown of a rectangle into a proportional unit and gnomons and spanned by a logarithmic spiral. In this example, the unit, U, has proportion $\sqrt{2}:1$ and the gnomon, G, has same proportions as the unit. For a golden mean rectangle, G is a square and U has proportion $\phi:1$.

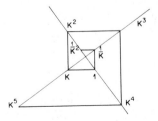

Fig. 15. Vertex points of a logarithmic spiral lie at a double geometric series of distances from the center.

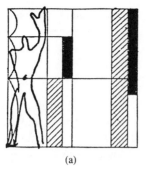

(a)

The "trademark" of LeCorbusier's proportional system, the *Modulor*. "A man-
with-arm-upraised provides, at the determining points of his occupation of space—
foot, solar plexus, head, tips of fingers of
the upraised arm—three intervals which give
rise to a series of golden sections, called
the Fibonacci series."

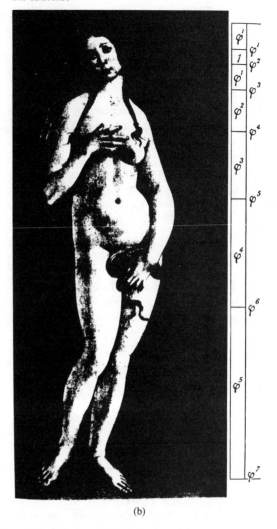

(b)

Fig. 17. (a) The "trademark" of LeCorbusier's proportional system, the Modulor. Three intervals give rise to
a Fibonacci series of golden sections (courtesy M.I.T. Press[38]). (b) Analysis of a Botticelli Venus, using the
golden mean (courtesy of Dover Press).

To satisfy these canons of architecture, Palladio used a system based on the proportions inherent
in the musical scale[45,46]. Another system, used during the Renaissance, was based on
geometric series. In this section we study the Modulor of Le Corbusier and show how it meets
these architectural criteria.

The Modulor uses a double series of lengths known as the Red and Blue series. Each series
is a geometric series with common ratio ϕ, in which for each element of the Red series there
is an element of the Blue series twice as long (as shown in Fig. 18). Thus the elements of the
two series complement each other by each filling in gaps between successive lengths of the
other. In fact, each element of the Blue series divides the gap of two adjacent elements of the
Red series in the golden section $\phi:1$. Finally, the ratio of the British policeman's upraised arm
to his height in the Modulor symbol of Fig. 17(a) is $2:\phi$, a length taken from each series.

Le Corbusier used lengths from this double series to serve as dimensions of a set of
rectangular tiles, as shown in Plate 19(a). The fact that any one of these tiles can be broken
down into other tiles from the series by using the Fibonacci property enables tilings of a rectangle
by Modulor tiles to be rearranged in many different ways to satisfy the interests of the architect.
Plates 19(b) and (c) show two student projects exploring the capabilities of the Modulor system.
In Plate 19(c) the same set of tiles is used to tile a rectangle three different ways.

The class of infinite self-similar curves known as fractals[47] has also been introduced in
the *Notes*. Coastlines, lightning and many other forms from the natural world are fractals and
these curves have potential for interesting designs (see The Geometry of Coastlines by J. Kappraff
in this issue).

7. TRANSFORMATIONS

Children explore a new object by turning it first one way and then another, touching, smelling, tasting and examining it in different shadings of light. Similarly, scientists try to understand physical reality by mapping it onto abstract constructs that are easier to study and manipulate than the actual realities. Artists help others to understand the world by transforming familiar forms and objects so that the commonplace can be seen in new ways. On a more abstract plane, dancers use their bodies to transform both space and time, connecting to natural rhythms and forms inherent in the deeper levels of being. Finally, poets transform language and ideas, bringing to light deeper meanings and connections between things otherwise inaccessible to more mundane analysis.

As an introductory assignment to this section of the course, the students show through art

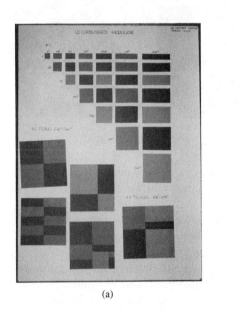

(a)

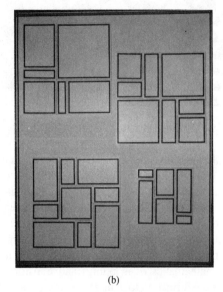

(b)

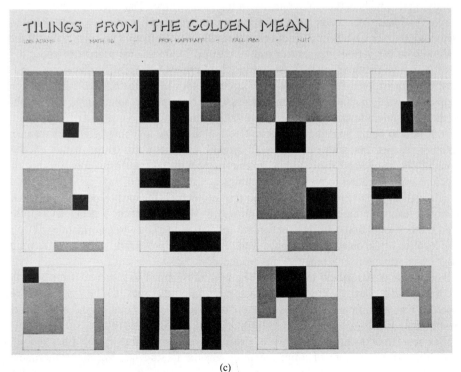

(c)

Plate 19. Tiling of a square with the Modulor.

Plate 20. The panels of metamorphisis by M. C. Escher (courtesy the World of M. C. Escher[62]).

or photography how a familiar object in their everyday experience undergoes transformations. For example, they might show the tree in front of their house before and after its leaves fall or its appearance in morning and evening light, etc.

Transformation played an important but unstated role in previous sections of the course. Floor plans were transformed into graphs which were then easier to manipulate. Polyhedra were studied in planar projections. Lattice designs were constructed invariant under transformation by translation. Natural forms transformed themselves by self-similar growth. In this section, the mathematics of mappings and transformations is presented. Our immediate purpose is to use transformation to gain deeper insight into the structure of geometry and to lay the framework for studying the mathematics of symmetry in the next section. This section is organized into a hierarchy of ideas: sets, mappings, transformations in general, particular transformations associated with various kinds of projections and finally transformation by rubber-sheet topology. We show how the various geometries can be defined by invariance properties under different classes of transformations such as isometries, similarities, affinities, projectivities and topological transformations. An appendix to this section introduces matrices to carry out transformations. As usual, mathematical completeness and rigor play a subordinate role in showing how the ideas relate to concepts familiar to the students.

It is best to begin with the most primitive notion of the mapping of objects from one set to another, carried out with objects found around the classroom. Through this exercise the notions of one-to-one and many-to-one inverse mappings and transformations are described in a concrete way. Notation to represent mappings is also introduced.

It is well known to geometers that projective geometry is the most general geometry dealing with point, line and plane. It is also a natural way to show students how geometry is intimately related to transformations. In this section we specialize to planar transformations. Depending on the location of the object plane, image plane and point of projection, either projective, affine, similar transformations or isometries are produced.

For example, a road on the ground plane is transformed to a canvas from a projection point located at the artist's eye to render a scene as the artist sees it. The road which recedes in parallel lines to infinity converges on the canvas to a single point on the horizon line, (as shown in Fig. 19).

Besides demonstrating a principle of projective geometry, this example has the effect of making the elusive concept of infinity comprehensible to students. We also experiment with projecting objects by a flashlight to their shadows. In particular, conic sections are shown to

				$\dfrac{1}{\phi^2}$	$\dfrac{1}{\phi}$		1		ϕ		ϕ^2		
Red	1	1	1	1	1		1		1		1		1
Blue	1	1	1	1		1		1		1		1	
				$\dfrac{2}{\phi^3}$	$\dfrac{2}{\phi^2}$		$\dfrac{2}{\phi}$		2		2ϕ		

Fig. 18. The Red and Blue series.

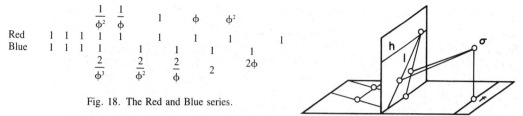

Fig. 19. A road receding to infinity depicted as converging to a point on the horizon line of an artist's canvas.

arise from circles. Finally, it is pointed out that although metric properties and even parallelism are not, in general, preserved under projective transformations, a quantity known as cross ratio is.

Projection from a point at infinity is within everyone's experience since it is the way the sun transforms objects to shadows. These so-called affine transformations generally do not preserve metric properties, unless the sun is directly overhead, but do preserve parallel lines.

If the sun is directly overhead, as it is two days per year between the tropics of Cancer and Capricorn, objects transform to their shadows under isometries preserving length and angle.

Similarity transformations, which were the subject of the previous section, map objects to enlarged or contracted similar images by means of a projection point that can be represented by the lens of a camera, overhead projector, etc. These similarity transformations preserve angle but not length.

A final class of transformations that played an important role in the design of the floor plans in Section 2 are topological transformations, which continue to be represented as transformations stretching on a rubber sheet without cutting. These transformations could be applied to design by distorting lattice tilings, such as the ones in Plate 10, by modulating the units on the coordinate axes. We have not yet tried this with our students, but the results should be reminiscent of some of Escher's prints as shown in Plate 20.

Thus we have defined a hierarchy of transformations: isometry $\rightarrow$ similarity $\rightarrow$ affinity $\rightarrow$ projectivity $\rightarrow$ topological. The corresponding geometries study the

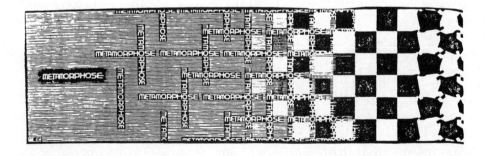

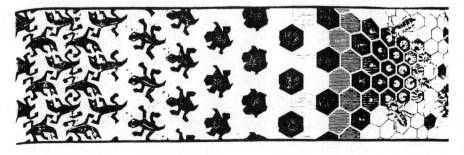

Plate 20. The panels of metamorphisis by M. C. Escher (courtesy the World of M. C. Escher[62]).

properties of figures that are invariant under these classes of transformations. Within each geometry, figures are considered "equivalent" or "congruent" if they can be transformed one to the other by transformations within that geometry. We find that even though it is beyond the scope of the course to study any one of these geometries in detail, it is nevertheless valuable for students to discover, through simple explanations, demonstrations and examples within their experience the overall structure of geometry.

The emphasis of this section of the course on projective transformations is an attempt to compensate for the complete absence of projective geometry in the educational background of students. Perspective drawing[48], an example of which is shown in Fig. 20, should be a precondition to studying geometry and should be introduced in the early grades. It creates the necessary links between what we observe in the real world and the abstractions of this world that make up the subject of Euclidean geometry[49].

The remainder of this section is devoted to studying the distance-preserving transformations or isometries. It is essential to think of isometries as rigid body movements which, in the plane, must be either translations, rotations, reflections or glide reflections. For application of isometries to the study of symmetry, it is important to classify these transformations as proper or improper. The proper transformations corresond to rigid-body motions entirely within the plane. Improper transformations require the transformed points to be removed from the plane, inverted in three-dimensional space and replaced in a manner similar to mirror images. In fact, in the next section we show that mirrors and isometries are intimately related subjects.

Writing Project

Transformation lies at the base of how people learn. For example, children learn about their world by manipulating or transforming the objects around them. Through the use of metaphor, poets and artists map the world of ideas onto their work, enabling the rest of us to sharpen our understanding of these ideas by seeing them in a different light.

Comment on this statement. Since mathematics deals primarily with transformations, state your opinion about whether mathematics can serve as a useful metaphor for architectural design. Cite ideas that you have been exposed to in Math 116 that may be applicable to architectural design. (A student response is included in the Appendix.)

Much of the material of this section is made concrete by a section in the *Notes* in which homogeneous coordinates and matrices are introduced to transform planar figures by rotation,

Fig. 20. An example of perspective in Renaissance art.

reflection, translation, similarity and projection of three-dimensional figures to a plane from a point representing the eye[50].

8. SYMMETRY

Symmetry is a concept that inspires the creative work of both artists and scientists and serves as the common root of artistic and scientific endeavors[51]. Considered naively, symmetry conjures up feelings of order, balance, harmony, and an organic relation between the whole and its parts. Artists and architects have a finely tuned sense of the symmetry of visual form without having consciously considered a precise definition of this concept from the mathematical standpoint. The objective of this section is to help students see greater possibilities for symmetry in design by exposing them to a mathematical treatment of the subject. In the process we show how the subject of symmetry is intimately connected to mirrors, as already illustrated in Section 3 with dihedral kaleidoscope. The key organizing factor for the mathematics of symmetry lies in the concept of a group of isometries[4,52].

The symmetry of a cube and the translational symmetry of lattices have already been considered in Sections 3 and 4. In this section we study bilateral symmetry, point or kaleidoscope symmetry, line or frieze symmetry and planar or wallpaper symmetry.

Before we begin to study the mathematics of symmetry it is important for students to develop an active awareness of the subject. The students are shown schematic representations and examples of the seven possible frieze patterns usable for ornamenting the edges of buildings and the patterns of wallpaper, including prints of M. C. Escher[52–54]. As an introductory exercise, the students are asked to collect as many different types of point-, line- and plane-symmetry patterns as they can from books or magazines and identify them by their symbols.

Mirrors are at once among the most familiar and puzzling of human artifacts. Why do mirrors reverse

S	but do not alter:	W	?
L		A	
E		I	
E		T	
P			

Why do mirrors seem to reverse left and right, but not up and down? How do images appear in curved mirrors[55]? The students are asked to look at the following objects in a mirror and record their observations: a pear, banana, glove, box, spiral form, conical cup, etc.

The mystery behind mirrors was already hinted at in the previous section where reflections were shown to be improper transformations and thus constructible by rigid-body movements into a higher-dimensional space, a reversal and replacement to the lower-dimensional space. For a two-dimensional world, such a program can be physically implemented. However, in three dimensions the movement and reversal must take place in the fourth dimension. Such ideas do not reside in common experience. However, they are within the intellectual domain of mathematicians, artists and philosophers, and they have been described beautifully by E. A. Abbot[56] and Rudolph Rucker[57]. Thus mirrors give an entree to the subject of higher-dimensional space, although we have not yet explored this realm in the course.

For our purposes, mirrors are fundamental to an understanding of symmetry. In fact, the subject of symmetry begins with bilateral symmetry. Bilateral symmetry pervades natural forms as nature's response to the force of gravity, which distinguishes up from down but not left from right[58].

It gives valuable insight into the structure of isometries to learn how they are generated by mirrors[4,59]. In fact, the students learn that any isometry of the plane can be generated by one, two or three mirrors; intersecting mirrors generate rotations, parallel mirrors generate translations and three mutually intersecting mirrors generate glide reflections.

What the students learn about mirrors they apply to exploring the principle behind the kaleidoscope made up of two intersecting mirrors. They learn the relationship between the angle between the mirrors and the number of images of an object placed between the mirrors. Thus the region between the mirrors can be thought of as the fundamental region of the kaleidoscope symmetry. The students also construct kaleidoscope patterns by paper cutting.

After these concrete experiences with symmetry, the students are ready for a precise mathematical definition and treatment of the subject:

Definition. A symmetry of a figure is the group of isometries that keeps the figure invariant.

The definition is applied to several examples of point symmetry. In particular, the symmetry of the equilateral triangle, the dihedral group with three mirrors, D_3, is examined in great detail. In the process of this examination, the mathematical concept of a group is defined and applied to showing, algebraically, that all the isometries of the group can be generated by two mirrors (the kaleidoscope principle) and that symmetry patterns of D_3 are generated by transforming points from the fundamental domain between two mirrors by all the elements of the group. If the mirrors are removed from D_3, the subgroup C_3 remains. C_3 is a symmetry with rotations only that arises in floral patterns.

Finally, what we learn from studying the structure of point groups applies also to frieze and wallpaper symmetries. The fact that only two-, three-, four- and sixfold rotations occur in wallpaper patterns is the result of another constraint on the properties of space, the "crystallographic restriction," which states that the images of any point of a symmetry pattern under all the transformations of the group do not accumulate at a point (i.e. there is a finite minimum distance separating them).

The emphasis of this section of the course is not on mastery of group concepts or complete cataloguing of the symmetries. An entire course could be based on this[60–62]. Rather, we are interested in conveying the idea that visually diverse symmetry patterns can have the same mathematical structure and that by understanding this structure the student can generate his or her own pattern. Some examples of student projects are shown in Plate 21.

9. VECTORS

The subject of Euclidean geometry is primarily concerned with the mathematical properties of figures constructed from points, lines and planes. These elements are the abstract primitives upon which the axiomatic structure of geometry is built. Although structures of the natural world are irregular as far as we can see, points, lines and planes are nevertheless idealizations in the mind of the geometer of certain features of experience with the natural world. For example, two islands on the horizon may appear as points, while the horizon where sea meets sky is imagined to be a line. Yet we know that, unlike mathematical points, islands have extent while

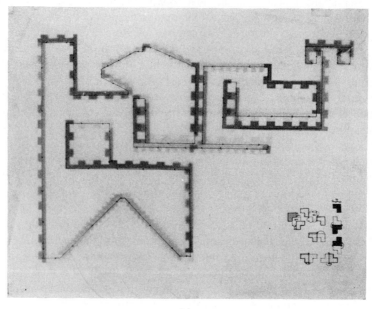

(a)

Plate 21. Some examples of point, line and wallpaper symmetries.

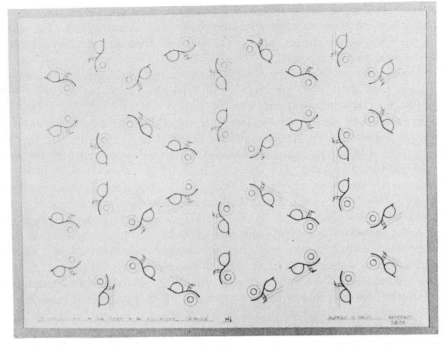

(b)

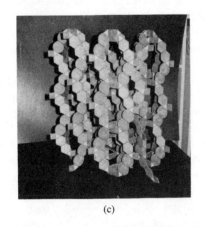

(c)

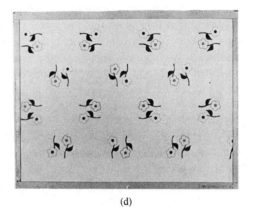

(d)

(e)

(f)

Plate 21. (Continued).

the horizon follows the curvature of the earth. Likewise, open prairies are not planes even though it is often convenient to imagine them to be. Beyond geometry, point, line and plane make up the fabric of civilization: they are the building blocks of cathedrals, skyscrapers, bridges, communication linkages, etc.

In this section we use the notion of vector to describe points, lines and planes mathematically and use these elements to study the geometry of polyhedra and a class of curved surfaces enveloped by lines known as ruled surfaces.

As an introductory exercise we ask students to find at least three examples each of configurations or objects from the natural world that can be described approximately by points, lines and planes. The students repeat the exercise for figures and objects from the world of civilization and human artifacts.

Geometrical vectors were introduced in Section 4 as vector stars to characterize the edge directions of zonagons. They were also used in that section to specify the translation directions of two- and three-dimensional lattices. In this section, since we wish to use vectors to analyze polyhedra, it is convenient to employ a unit cube as the basis of a three-dimensional cartesian coordinate system. In fact, a cube, built from the universal node system, with a tetrahedron embedded in it along with edges from the center of the cube to the vertices of the tetrahedron (as shown in Plate 5(b)) gives a sufficiently rich system of edges to begin analyzing the angles between pairs of edges and pairs of faces of polyhedra. There is educational value in using an actual cube at this stage of instruction. Any vertex of the cube can serve as the origin, while the three edge directions incident to this vertex correspond to the coordinate axes. Since the representation of a vector in this coordinate system depends only on the labeling of axes it is easily seen that representation is independent of the orientation of the axes, and that computation of angle and length are independent of any particular choice of a cartesian coordinate system, although we shall later see that the vector operation of cross product will require a choice, by convention, of a right-handed coordinate system. Finally, once an orientation of the cube is established, we represent vectors by the notation (a, b, c) in which the coordinate pairs $(\pm 1, 0, 0)$, $(0, \pm 1, 0)$ and $(0, 0, \pm 1)$ are described by the dualisms front-back, left-right and up-down with respect to a viewer centered at the origin. I find that this approach to vectors makes representation natural and avoids the difficulty students have in comprehending the invariance properties of vectors under translation and various coordinate transformations.

Once students are able to represent vectors with confidence, they are taught the usual vector operations of addition, scalar multiplication, scalar product and cross product, with stress on the computational aspect of these operations. We have found it useful to have students compute scalar product and cross product between vectors (a_1, a_2, a_3) and (b_1, b_2, b_3) as $\mathbf{a} \cdot \mathbf{b} = a_1b_1 + a_2b_2 + a_3b_3$ and $\mathbf{a} \times \mathbf{b} = (a_2b_3 - a_3b_2, a_3b_1 - a_1b_3, a_1b_2 - a_2b_1)$ initially and then show how these computations can be made easier by introducing the $\hat{\mathbf{i}}, \hat{\mathbf{j}}, \hat{\mathbf{k}}$ system.

The principal application of vectors in this section is the calculation of angles between edges and computation of the dihedral angles between faces of polyhedra related to a cube. Dihedral angles are particularly difficult for students to conceptualize, no less compute, even though the architecture students are familiar with the concept through their drafting experience. However, we have found that the vector approach makes the subject understandable. The importance of the dihedral angle was already shown in Section 5, where information about the dihedral angle between faces of the infinite regular surfaces (shown in Plate 14) were needed in order to score the paper properly in the construction. Also, as a necessary condition for polyhedra to fill space, it was shown that the sum of the dihedral angle around each edge of a space-filling array must sum to 360°. The students can now verify this condition for some of the space-filling polyhedra that have been previously mentioned.

An additional construction that requires sophisticated vector computation asks students to construct a sculpture of linear segments out of wooden dowels to form a closed cycle. The students must work out a procedure to cut the dowels so that adjacent segments match in cross section.

Finally, the representation of lines and planes in three dimensions using vectors is introduced. Three skew lines are used to generate two classes of ruled surfaces, the hyperboloid of revolution and the hyperbolic paraboloid, both of which have architectural applications[35,63,64]. These curved surfaces have already been introduced to the students in Section

5. Here we present students with practical ways to construct sculptures suggestive of architectural structures using ruled surfaces. Some student constructions are shown in Plate 22.

10. CONCLUSION

We feel that the course summarized in this article successfully fulfills the objectives set for it by the interdisciplinary group. We have been able to convey to students a sense of mathematics as the organizing force linking scientific, artistic and cultural subject areas. We have also made the course alive by involving students in the application of what they learn to constructing designs and projects and writing essays.

The results of teaching this course are always tangible. Each semester an exhibition of the students' best work is organized, and they share some of their writing with fellow students through school publications.

Perhaps more important to the life of this course is its steady growth in terms of subject matter and educational ideas. By no means do we wish to convey the idea that the sequence of topics in this article is either complete or the only natural ordering. Inevitably a course such as this must involve the instructor as an active participant in the formulation of curriculum. Actually, it is the creative process entered into by not just the students but the faculty that makes an exciting course possible. Much of the material of the course was unfamiliar to me when I began to work on this project. It was my own revelation that there lies rich untapped resources that has encouraged me to write this article as a suggestion of the possibilities. Beyond all the objectives that we set in organizing the course, it is most important to convey the idea that teaching a course like this is just plain fun for both teacher and students.

There are many avenues along which the work that we have begun can continue. First of all, work on a text for the course should be completed, since lack of such a book is the greatest impediment to replication of courses such as this by others. The course also should have a laboratory component in which portions now dealt with through lectures are conveyed by hands-on experience. Finally, we are giving thought to collaborating on a second course which develops computer applications for ideas generated by this course. After all, the technology and much

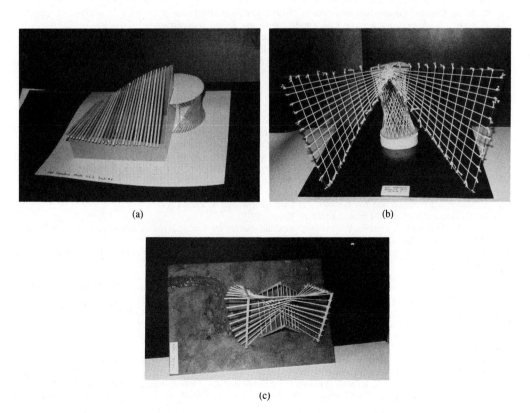

(a) (b)

(c)

Plate 22. Ruled surface sculptures suggestive of architectural structures.

of the software is presently available to do graph-theory analysis; tile the plane; design polyhedra; transform figures by isometries and projection; experiment with symmetry; and utilize vectors, lines and planes in imaginative ways. We feel strongly, however, that unless a course such as ours is undertaken first, without computers, students will not fully appreciate the ways in which computers can enhance their design experiences.

Acknowledgments—I would like to acknowledge the vision of Professor Mary Blade who showed me by her example that courses such as this can be taught. Professor Alan Stewart helped to shape many of the ideas of the course and has been an able collaborator in teaching it each year. Professor Diana Bryant added her professional touch to the preparation of many of the photographs. Finally, Ms Rebeca Daniels provided her patience and skill to the preparation of the manuscript.

REFERENCES

1. J. Kappraff, Jay and D. Blackmore, *The Mathematics of Design*. NJIT Lecture Notes (1982).
2. O. Ore, *Graphs and Their Uses*. Random House (1963).
3. R. Trudeau, *Dots and Lines*. Kent State University (1976).
4. J. A. Baglivo and J. Graver, *Incidence and Symmetry in Design and Architecture*. Cambridge Press (1983).
5. A. Beck *et al.*, *Excursions into Mathematics*. Worth Publishers (1969).
6. L. Bellman, K. Cooke and J. Lockett, *Algorithms, Graphs, and Computers*. Academic, New York (1972).
7. H. Crapo and E. D. Bolker, Bracing rectangular frameworks I. *SIAM J. Appl. Math.* **36**(30), 473–490 (1979).
8. R. W. Williams, *The Geometrical Foundation of Natural Structures*. Dover (1972).
9. A. Holden, *Shapes, Space and Symmetry*. Columbia University Press, New York (1971).
10. B. Ernst, *The Magic Mirror of M. C. Escher*. Ballantine Books, New York (1976).
11. A. Pugh, *Polyhedra: A Visual Approach*. University of California Press (1976).
12. A. F. Wells, *The Third Dimension in Chemistry*. Oxford University Press (1956).
13. D'Arcy Thompson, *On Growth and Form*. Cambridge Press (1966).
14. M. Ghyka, *A Practical Handbook of Geometrical Composition and Design*. Tiranti, London (1952).
15. P. Pearce, *Structure in Nature: A Strategy for Design*. M.I.T. Press (1978).
16. H. S. M. Coxeter and W. O. J. Moser, *Symmetries of a Cube*. International Film Bureau, Chicago.
17. A. Wachman, M. Burt, and M. Kleinmann, *Infinite Polyhedra*. Technion, Haifa (1974).
18. H. M. S. Coxeter, *The Fifty-Nine Icosahedra*. Springer-Verlag, New York (1982).
19. K. Critchlow, *Islamic Patterns*. Schocken Books, New York (1976).
20. A. L. Loeb, *Space Structures, Their Harmony and Counterpoint*. Addison Wesley, Reading, MA (1976).
21. J. Baracs *et al.*, *Polyhedral Habitat. Structural Topology*, No. 2 (1978).
22. W. J. Gilbert, *Structural Topology*, No. 1 (1978).
23. H. S. M. Coxeter, *Introduction to Geometry*. Wiley, New York (1961).
24. H. Crapo, *Mathematical Questions Concerning Zonohedral Spacefilling. Structural Topology*. No. 2.
25. S. Stein, *Mathematics: The Man-Made Universe*. Freeman Press (1963).
26. M. Gardner, *Scientific American*. 110–121 (January 1978).
27. P. A. Davis and W. G. Chinn, 3.1416 *And All That*. Simon and Schuster, New York (1969).
28. G. Segal, *Synergy*. Board of Education of the City of New York, Center for Curriculum Development.
29. *Zodiac* **21** (1971).
30. B. Fuller, *Synergetics* (Appendix by Arthur L. Loeb). Macmillan (1975).
31. L. Pauling and R. Hayward, *The Architecture of Molecules*. W. H. Freeman (1964).
32. A. Pugh, *An Introduction to Tensegrity*. University of California Press, Berkeley (1976).
33. V. Sedlek, *Paper Shelters*. Structural Plastics Research Unit, University of Surrey, Guildford, England.
34. R. Courant and H. Robbins, *What is Mathematics?* Oxford University Press (1941).
35. D. Hilbert and S. Cohn-Vossen, *Geometry and the Imagination*. Chelsea Press, New York (1956).
36. R. Resch, *The Ron Resch Paper and Stick Thing Film*. Environmental Communication, Venice, California.
37. P. Stevens, *Patterns in Nature*. Little, Brown, Boston (1974).
38. LeCorbusier. *Modulor*. M.I.T. Press (1955).
39. L. March and P. Steadman, *The Geometry of Environment*. M.I.T. Press (1971).
40. M. Gardner, *Mathematical Circus*. Alfred A. Knopf (1979).
41. J. M. Kappraff and C. Marzec, Properties of maximal spacing on a circle relate to phyllotaxis and to the golden mean. *J. Theor. Biol.* **103**, 201–226 (1983).
42. R. O. Erickson, The geometry of phyllotaxis. In *The Growth and Functioning of Leaves* (Edited by J. E. Dale and F. L. Milthorpe). Cambridge University Press (1983).
43. M. Ghyka, *The Geometry of Art and Life*. Dover (1978).
44. G. Doczi, *Power of Limits: Proportional Harmonies in Nature, Art and Architecture*. Shambhala Publ. (1981).
45. P. H. Scholfield, *The Theory of Proportion in Architecture*. Cambridge Press (1958).
46. R. Wittkower, *Architectural Principles in the Age of Humanism*. Tiranti, London (1962).
47. B. Mandelbrot, *The Fractal Geometry of Nature*. Freeman Press (1982).
48. R. Vero, *Understanding Perspective*. Van Nostrand Rheinhold (1980).
49. W. M. Ivins, *Art and Geometry*. Harvard University Press, Cambridge (1946).
50. M. Keller, *Computer Graphics and Applications of Matrix Methods*. EDC/UMAP, Newton, MA (1977).
51. H. Weyl, *Symmetry*. Princeton University Press (1952).
52. A. V. Shubnikov and V. A. Koptsik, *Symmetry in Science and Art*. Plenum Press, New York (1974).
53. C. H. McGillavry, *Fantasy and Symmetry: The Periodic Drawings of M. C. Escher*. Harry Abrams, New York (1976).
54. M. C. Escher and J. L. Locher, *The World of M. C. Escher*. Abrams Publishers, New York (1971).

55. D. E. Thomas, Mirror images. *Sci. Am.* 206–228 (December 1980).
56. E. A. Abbott, *Flatland*. Dover (1952).
57. R. Rucker, *Geometry, Relativity and the Fourth Dimension*. Dover (1977).
58. M. Gardner, *The Ambidextrous Universe*. Books, New York (1964).
59. S. Shuster and W. O. J. Moser, *Isometries*. International Film Bureau, Inc., Chicago, IL.
60. D. Schattschneider, The plane symmetry groups: Their recognition and notation. *M.A.A. Monthly* **85**, 439–450 (1978).
61. P. Stevens, *A Handbook of Regular Patterns: An Introduction to Symmetry in Two Dimensions*. M.I.T. Press (1981).
62. B. Rose and R. Stafford, An elementary course in mathematics symmetry. *M.A.A. Monthly* **88**, 59–64 (1981).
63. M. Salvador and R. Heller, *Structure in Architecture*. Prentice-Hall (1975).
64. A. Gheorghiu and V. Dragomir, *Geometry of Structural Forms*. Applied Science Publishers, London (1978).

APPENDIX
STUDENT RESPONSES TO WRITING PROJECTS

Graph Theory

In considering Christopher Alexander's thesis on the stages of design and the evolution of the design process from the unconscious instincts of primitive society to self-conscious decision making in a dynamic society, one comes to the realization that this is inevitable: the design process must have evolved parallel to all other stages of civilization's growth.

In an ideal, Hobbesian "state of nature" where man's only instinct is for survival, the concept of design must have been part of that unconscious instinct, appearing as a search for shelter. The beginnings of agricultural society and civilization were accompanied by complex needs for many types of shelter and settled communities whose designs required conscious planning with respect to function. It must be noted, however, that design of shelter, at this stage, was a skill of "everyman," passed down as a fundamental tool for survival.

With the evolution of specialization in crafts and professions in more complex economies, design probably began to emerge as a studied process. The use of architecture for the deification of both man and gods exemplifies this point of view. Inherent in the quest for more magnificent tributes to these deities is an increasing complexity of plan and structure followed by the emergence of design as a specialized art incorporating tools of math and engineering. The synthesis of complex demands and needs into a plan has become a structured "self-conscious" process.

Finally, in a dynamic technological society, the need for rapid design change is an effect of constant discovery and innovation in all facets of that society. Industrialization, space exploration, and socio-economic change heap new demands on the designer and engineer. The use of graphs as a tool for understanding linkages is certainly an appropriate step in the planning process as it facilitates and organizes the designer's thoughts at a crucial stage.

Rachel Stettler
Second-Year Architecture Student

Order and Symmetry

In his paper entitled "Perception and Modular Coordination," Christopher Alexander suggests that we enjoy symmetric themes in design because our minds recoil at chaos but are put at ease by the repetition of a simple motif. I think that this is true to a certain extent because human beings are very sensitive to their surroundings. Things like heat, lighting, color, smell and texture can have tremendous effects upon a human's mood.

In the areas of art and architecture, designs which are very intricate or haphazard cause mental stress because they demand more intense concentration. Although a high level of intricacy can cause mental stress, I feel that what makes design chaotic is a lack of cohesiveness as a whole. Intricacy is necessary to a certain extent in order to appease our appetite for new things. An artist or architect is faced with organizing and subduing his work while at the same time making it interesting. An artist does not want every part of his painting to jump out and demand equal attention. Similarly, the architect does not want his building to look like it was designed by more than one architect.

Design Project #2, which involved lattices, was a good example of repetition. I feel that there are many ways of making lattices appeal to our sense of surprise and novelty. Also, because they are on a small scale—that is, a picture or a model—I feel they can be very intricate. The level of intricacy can be increased because the viewer is not confined when viewing a picture. The level is more limited for three-dimensional lattices because they cause more mental stress in demanding that the viewer imagine three-dimensional objects twisted and intertwined.

Stephen Oliver
First-Year Architecture Student

Space Filling

Probably the most important feature of shape, the one that allows us to identify an object, is its contour, its general outline. Yet the perception of contour involves a differentiation of inside from outside, in front from behind, and, if necessity, figure from ground. In two dimensions, normally the figure stands out from the background because of a number of factors: convexity, position, texture, enclosure. The ground, whether because of lower energy or little contrast, blends into a continuous surface behind the figure. While our attention focuses on the figure, the ground is just as important because both are necessary to allow perception.

Figure is often quite different, then, in its visual qualities to make it stand out as figure. Since the artist or designer is creating both the figure and the ground, he must be aware of both to allow the differentiation to become clear. On the other hand, it is possible to create an ambiguity of figure and ground, when the ground becomes as important visually as the figure. This can be done by deliberately confusing some of the signals, the clues that we use to perceive figure as distinct from ground. The use of poché, for example, in architectural drawings, the blackening of the walls in plan, makes the thickness of the walls read as a kind of figure, when usually we think of the spaces between the walls as the figure.

In three dimensions, contour does not divide space into figure and ground, but into object and space. Sculptors, architects and dancers must all be aware of the effect their object, whether statue, building or body, has on the space around it. They are in a sense giving shape to space by placing their object in it.

Infinite polyhedra form a kind of contour, not a wiggly line as in two dimensions, but a wiggly plane separating space into two parts, inside and outside, two parts that happen to be congruent. Unlike the statue, the building or the body, there is no object which activates the space around it. There is simply the boundary between two spaces. Perhaps this is more analogous to the ambiguity it is possible to achieve in two dimensions when figure and ground can be made to have equal weight.

Allison Baxter
Fifth-Year Architecture Student

Transformation

Architecture is the manipulation of forms and the creation of space through the use of those forms. Certainly, mathematics is always present in an architectural design; however, the emphasis placed on the mathematical relationships is, more often than not, secondary to the aesthetic considerations of a project. This fact is a sad one, for appreciation of the mathematical relationship within the forms and among the forms goes unnoticed. It is often true that the aesthetic choices are also the ones that offer the best mathematical metaphors, yet the aesthetic reasoning always receives the most emphasis.

While the idea of mathematics being a useful metaphor for architectural design is an intriguing one, few architects have practiced the theory to its fullest. Le Corbusier's Le Modulor epitomized the use of traditional mathematical relationships as architectural ideas while also allowing for aesthetic qualities of an outstanding calibre.

The metaphors of traditional mathematics are largely unnoticed in the current products of architecture, but the ideas of symmetry and graphing are more readily recognized as mathematical metaphors in architecture, though the field of mathematics from which they are generated is less understood by the populace than traditional mathematics. Perhaps the well-trained eye can search out and find the traditional mathematical relationships in a facade, such as ratios of window heights to the spaces between floors. It is the common eye, however, that can easily find the relationships of symmetry and graphs. These metaphors may be easily recognized, but seldom are they properly labeled. An untrained person may recognize symmetry and describe it as "the same on one side as it is on the other." The proper terminology may be lacking, but the mathematical condition known as symmetry is easily recognized by one and all.

Architects must use both traditional and nontraditional mathematical metaphors in their work; these mathematical ideas are a source of orientation and identification for users of architectural designed spaces. When done properly, the inclusion of these metaphors can create splendid architectural spaces and allow everyone an insight into the world of architecture; without mathematical metaphors, spaces become plain and lackluster.

Douglas Gruninger
First-Year Architecture Student

Comp. & Maths. with Appls. Vol. 12B, Nos. 3/4, pp. 949–980, 1986
Printed in Great Britain.

0886–9561/86 $3.00 + .00
© 1986 Pergamon Press Ltd.

SYMMETROLOGY OF ART: COLOURED AND GENERALIZED SYMMETRIES

EMIL MAKOVICKY

University of Copenhagen, Institute of Mineralogy, Østervoldgade 10, DK-1350 Copenhagen K,
Denmark

Abstract—The paper describes general features and analyses a number of examples of various categories of colored and generalized symmetries used in visual arts. After a thorough discussion of the problems of symmetry analysis and construction of dichroic and colored patterns, examples of South American, Mexican, Egyptian, Celtic, New Guinean, Australian Aboriginal and Moorish, as well as 20th century ornamental art are analysed. It is shown that with the exception of the modern creations by Hinterreiter and Escher, colored symmetry has been used much less than dichroic symmetry and has remained largely limited to unidirectional color modulation of uncolored or originally dichroic patterns.

From among the categories of generalized symmetry, similarity, affine- and perspective-projective transformations are discussed and illustrated as well as catamorphy and the plane groups in non-Euclidean planes. Finally, the notions of submotif, submesh, supermesh, twinning, pseudosymmetry, noncommensurability of patterns, positional and "occupational" order–disorder phenomena, local high symmetry, dissymmetry, enhancement of symmetry, dichotomy, modulation, antiphase boundaries and the hierarchy and superposition of symmetries are applied to the world of visual arts.

INTRODUCTION

Symmetrological analysis of art belongs to the realm of formal analysis of art. Nevertheless, it is capable of making a number of profound observations about artistic personalities, schools or styles, or about the subject of art itself. Symmetry coexists in art with other formal aspects: the overall design, geometric elements and their interconnection, tonal and coloring schemes. It interacts with all of them and it has to be defined for each of these levels.

Together with all these aspects, symmetry can describe in fairly exact terms the canons or preferences exhibited in the visual (primarily ornamental) art created by a given person or school. Their nature and their changes, or succession in time, appear to this author to reflect very explicitly the basic features of all human thoughts and creativity either in an individual or in entire groups/schools: observation and abstraction, reproduction (copying) and invention (creativity, originality), fashions (schools) in their progressive development and refinement, subsequent mannerism and, finally, breakdown at saturation. In this development, progressive or abrupt succession of opposites takes place: symmetry versus asymmetry or dissymmetry, functionalism versus formalism, simplicity and general geometric clarity versus mannerism and richness of ornamentation.

The clarity of symmetrological definitions is advantageous when compared to many other fields of analysis of visual art. However, the richness of approaches chosen by visual artists parallels in all respects the richness of mathematical and scientific apparatus developed to describe the symmetry phenomena. It is the purpose of the present contribution to illustrate this broad spectrum of types of symmetry and to go beyond the usual application of band and plane symmetry groups to ornamental art. It is oriented toward the general public (i.e. primarily nonmathematicians and noncrystallographers) and an attempt has been made to refrain from the usage of too many specialized expressions and symbols; the definitions were adjusted to this level as well.

Many of the more complicated fields of symmetry are in development and several points of view as well as several systems of notation exist. I have adhered to the simpler ones here and I hope for the understanding of colleagues whose approaches might be more complete but also more complicated. References to the symmetrology of art grow at an accelerated rate; they are thinly spread over a range of scientific journals. Consequently, I have to apologize for possibly having omitted a number of them.

SOME FUNDAMENTAL REMARKS

It is beyond the scope of this paper to explain the basic grammar of art symmetrology—the symmetry operations, respective operators (i.e. symmetry elements) and their contradiction-free combinations, and symmetry groups in Euclidean space. The same holds for the definition of basic translation vectors and the choice of unit mesh. We shall only point out some (often omitted or overlooked) problems which ought to be taken into consideration during the symmetrological analysis. For the explanation of basic notions the reader is referred to the books by Shubnikov and Koptsik[1], Smith[2], Buerger[3] and the papers by Schattschneider[4] and Donnay and Donnay[5].

One of the important questions to be understood in the process of symmetrological analysis of a pattern is the spatial relation of its individual elements to the elements of symmetry. The elements (topological discs) of the pattern can either be positioned outside the symmetry operators, i.e. their local symmetry is 1 (total asymmetry; these are so-called general positions), or on a symmetry operator, or on an intersection of several symmetry operators (the so-called special positions). Such elements ought to display the local symmetry in their shape and also in their coloring, as described in the following chapters. The placing of asymmetric elements (discs) on symmetry operators reduces the total symmetry; the placing of highly symmetric objects into positions with lower or low local symmetry in the symmetry group leads to the local enhancement of symmetry and, as described below, potentially also to order–disorder phenomena. Finally, a large number of man-made patterns contain only elements in special positions, those in general positions being reduced to mere field boundaries.

It is at this point that the unity of the entire pattern should be stressed, both for the uninitiated beholder and the symmetrologist. Except for the patterns with discrete elements (topological discs of any possible shape) placed over a neutral, featureless background, all patterns represent a combination of linear segments, lines, areas, angles, polygons, and colors, as well as "objects with meaning," which will be alternatively selected and suppressed in the process of pattern recognition. The human mind progresses from the simple, obvious elements of the pattern to the more intricate and subdued ones; good ornamental art must contain both of these categories. Therefore such a pattern cannot be classified solely on the basis of its segments, or only of its polygons—its entire complexity ought to be grasped by the classification.

The influence of material on the resulting symmetry of the pattern should be emphasized. For example, although Islamic art is known for its profusion of hexagonal, trigonal and tetragonal patterns, it is practically only the tetragonal (and lower-symmetry) patterns which can be found in the extensive family of Islamic patterns obtained by combining together unmodified building bricks. It was the basic techniques of brick laying, basketry and weaving (with auxiliary techniques like knitting) that taught people two-dimensional symmetry. The simplest examples are given in Figs. 1–3. The two-sidedness of many of the patterns, which appears later in the interlaced designs of Islamic, Celtic, Viking, and other artists, is obvious.

In performing the symmetrological analysis, we should stay on the same level of accuracy on which the creator of the pattern worked. The free-hand creations by a Papuan or Pueblo artist must be abstracted from numerous geometrical deviations, quite unlike the creations of Renaissance or constructivist artists who worked according to the rules of geometry and with proper drawing aids. It certainly brings a certain subjectiveness into the process; we should not shun away from it because such a degree of abstraction from imperfections of certain degrees and kinds underlies the entire practice of natural sciences wherefrom the science of symmetry originated. However, we must try (1) to perceive the level of the artist's accuracy, (2) to understand, and not to exceed, the space in which he or she worked, and (3) to define possible ambiguities in our conclusions which stem from (1) and (2). Only in this way we can avoid the sterility which will inevitably arise by a strict, very exact and inflexible application of the abstract categories of the science of symmetry.

THE CATEGORY OF COLOR

By now the notion of plane group symmetry is becoming accepted in artistic and art-historian's circles (e.g. Gombrich[6]. At least two geometrical artists, Hinterreiter[7] and Escher (MacGillavry[8]) worked out their own versions of this theory, albeit incomplete. Escher's contacts with mathematicians (Coxeter) and crystallographers (MacGillavry) enabled him to complete his collection of plane group patterns and embark on other types of symmetry as well.

Fig. 2. Basic knitting patterns: the "stocking stitch" from both sides (layer group *pbm*2) and the garter stitch (*pbma*).

Fig. 1. Layer symmetry groups for the products of some basic basketry techniques. Leftmost column, plain plaiting (*p4/nbm*), twill plaiting (*pban*) and wicker plaiting (*cmma*); rightmost column, plain twine (*p222*), one-rod coiling (*p22₁2*) and three-rod stacked coiling (*c222*). Adapted with changes from various sources. The one-sided patterns produced in these cases are p4gm, pgg, cmm, p2, ~cmm, ~cmm in the above order. When black weft and white warps are used in the first two cases, the dichroic one-sided patterns are p4'g'm and pg'g' (both are also used as basic weaving techniques).

However, both of these artists, together with a number of their predecessors back to Neolithic times of the Middle East and of the Americas, realized that two or more symmetrically fully equivalent elements (i.e. topological discs) of the motif can be assigned two (or more) nongeometrical properties, in these cases usually colors, in order to produce new, artistically more expressive patterns. The duality of black (resp. dark) and white (often only light, buff or off-white) already had been recognized by Neolithic artisans and has been used in pottery, mosaics, painting, clothes, wood carving and plaster, as well as in projecting or recessed brickwork and stone masonry until the present (Figs. 4–10). It should be stressed that a great number of designs painted in black and white use the two colors for *symmetrically distinct* positions (parts, elements, discs). Although these patterns are often ingenious and beautiful (Figs. 8–10), they do not really represent color symmetry and belong to the category of simple, "uncolored" plane groups.

In contrast to the relative abundance of dichroic patterns, it appears that only exceptional human minds perceived the beauty of color symmetry in polychromatic patterns, other than the simple sequences of *n* colors along one direction or similarly simple block designs. Ornaments with three-, four- and six-colored rotation axes and other color-changing symmetry elements

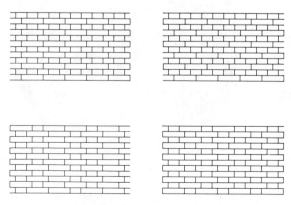

Fig. 3. Selected examples of masonry with the one-sided plane groups. Top row, pmm and *c*mm; bottom row, pmg and *c*mm.

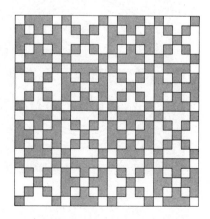

Fig. 4. A checkerboard Roman floor mosaic at Fishbourne, S. England (end of 1st century A.D.). The dichroic plane group is p$_c$4mm.

Fig. 5. Opus *E* 45 (1958–72) by H. Hinterreiter, reproduced from [45]. A dichroic p$_{a'}$2 pattern mapped onto a curvilinear net.

Fig. 6. A dichroic pattern from a dress fabric by Katja (Sweden) with the symmetry *cm'*.

are correspondingly rare or absent. We often stand perplexed in front of ornaments where only two colors are used or with the simplest color schemes applied inspite of the fact that they would offer much more refined and spectacular results if their true potential for color symmetry were properly exploited. Usually no (great) additional material expense is required. The royal palace of Alhambra, Granada, is full of examples of such "failures." The large majority of these can be described as black-and-white (i.e. dichroic) patterns with the dark elements (discs) modulated by a simple sequence of colors. The presence of 50% white tiles in the pattern seemed to be a requirement in the cases where no white boundaries were present. They are not without aesthetic appeal and their simplicity contrasts with the adjacent patterns in which colors are applied to morphologically different elements and which contain white boundaries with complex interlacing that one can study for hours. What then was the factor which held the artisans back from the full application of color symmetry, the elements of which they held in hand? Below we shall try to elaborate upon our final conclusion, which is as follows: *the artisans still understood these patterns in terms of black-and-white symmetry, with the color changes superimposed on the dichroic pattern.*

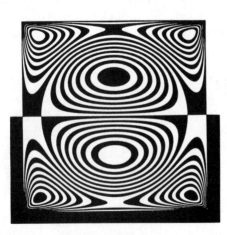

Fig. 7. A dichroic, computer-generated point-group pattern with the symmetry 2'm'm by Aldo Giorgini, reproduced from [37].

Fig. 8. Opus *E* 73 (1968–72) by H. Hinterreiter, reproduced from [45]. A nondichroic pattern in black and white, plane group p4, mapped onto a curvilinear net with a singular point. Antiphase boundaries intersect in one set of fourfold axes.

Fig. 9. A tetragonal pattern, p4, of white and red bricks from the gate of Alhaquem II, The Mosque of Córdoba.

Fig. 10. A pattern of protruding and recessed bricks from a tomb at Hamadan, Gunbad-i'Alaviyan (13th century); uncoloured plane group p4.

DICHROIC (BLACK-AND-WHITE) GROUPS

Reviews of these groups for the zero-, one- and two-dimensional cases can be found in Shubnikov and Koptsik[1] and Vainshtein[9]. In these groups not all symmetry operators need to change color. In general only some of them do, whereas the rest preserve the original color when the operation of symmetry is performed. Thus, several dichroic groups can be generated from each plane group by changing the selection of color-changing operators, the so-called operators of *antisymmetry*. The inversion center, the reflection and glide-reflection planes and translations can be operators of antisymmetry. From the rotation axes, those with multiplicity divisible by 2 can become operators of antisymmetry as well. In the plane group notation the antisymmetry operators are primed.

Fig. 11. Dichroic plane group p4′g′m worked out on a pattern from Ribat-i-Sharaf, Iran (Khurasan) (12th century A.D.). *d* denotes general positions, *a–c′* special positions. Numerals indicate the number of color permutations.

Fig. 12. Dichroic plane group p4'gm'. For explanations see Fig. 11.

The elements in general positions (i.e. neither being on nor straddling any symmetry operator) are "black" and "white" (i.e. have 2 colors which obey the operators of antisymmetry). The elements which lie on the operators of antisymmetry contain both colors and are "grey" as a consequence. If we consider fields positioned on the fourfold axes of antisymmetry and those on the "antireflection" plane in Fig. 12, their "grey" is generated by different mechanisms of color overlap. Therefore they can be differently colored in the pattern, but will share the common property—their colors remain unchanged in the respective antisymmetry operations. The elements positioned on operators of symmetry will assume their types ("shades") of "black" and "white" when the element, together with the operator of symmetry on which

Fig. 13. Pattern of glazed bricks from the entrance gate of Timur's palace Ak-sarai at Shahrisabz (1380–1405), south of Samarkand. Dichroic plane group p4'mg' with neutral background.

Fig. 14. The interlaced pattern of white borders from the Arabic mosaic in La Capella Palatina, Palermo. Layer group p622; the corresponding dichroic group is p6m'm'.

it is positioned, is moved around by the action of a primed, antisymmetry operator (Fig. 11).

As can be observed in Figs. 11 and 12, profusion of "grey" special positions limits the expressivity or immediacy of design. Therefore, extensive grey fields are rarely used in dichroic designs, and only as a sort of background to the dichroic pattern (Fig. 13). The vast majority of dichroic patterns only contain elements which undergo the color change.

Antisymmetry as well as color symmetry applies to all types of symmetry groups without regard to dimensionality: to the point, band and plane groups, as well as to all the more complicated types of symmetry mentioned below.

The one- and two-dimensional interlaced ornaments, describable by two-sided band and layer groups, were already mentioned. As shown by Grünbaum and Shephard[10] they can be described equally successfully by the application of black and white symmetry if the overlap of ribbon A over ribbon B is denoted as "white" and of B over A as "black," and the two colors are propagated through the motif. This ambivalence is based on the one-to-one correspondence between the one-sided plane groups of antisymmetry and the two-sided plane (layer) groups without a color change (e.g. Shubnikov and Koptsik[1]). The two colors correspond to the upper and to the lower side of the layer (Fig. 14).

As noted by Wondratschek[11], the black-and-white principle can be used not only for the cases with two alternating colors but for any antisymmetry observable in an ordered arrangement of objects with certain "nongeometric" characteristics that are placed in the same fields of a mosaic pattern (animal figures alternating with human figures, birds *vs.* animals, two kinds of point-group geometric patterns, etc.). Such a description is natural for the pattern because it encompasses both its highly symmetric and regular nature and the discrete nature of the "complicating" elements. There may exist several kinds of antisymmetries in the pattern: alternation of filling figures, of their colors, orientation, etc. Plane groups of multiple, mutually independent antisymmetries were worked out in crystallography for the cases of coincident unit mesh (Zamorzaev and Palistrant[12]) and may be applied here. Finally, it should be noted that the "uncolored" groups of symmetry can be understood in the language of antisymmetry as one-colored (white only) or as "grey" (neutral) with all the positions displaying the combined color.

COLORED SYMMETRY

The idea of antisymmetry was worked out for the first time by Heesh[13]. The idea of colored symmetry was described in the papers of Niggli[14] and Indebom[15] for point groups and of Belov and Tarkhova[16] for plane groups. A series of papers on further, more general types of color groups by a number of authors followed (Shubnikov and Koptsik[1]). However, they all were preceeded in certain aspects by the artists. By 1936 Escher had correctly worked out a number of colored patterns with colored rotational symmetry which gave description problems to crystallographers as late as 1965 (MacGillavry[8]). His use of plane groups with colored translations might even date back to 1927. The most systematic approach was undertaken by Hinterreiter, who already in 1941, in a manuscript not published until 1978, systematically derived the color groups based on the plane groups p4 and p6 using color permutations. He had a perfect understanding of the role of general positions and of the special positions on the four-, six-, three- and twofold axes in the coloring process. He has been flawlessly applying these principles to various plane symmetries since at least 1932 until the present.

As in the case of dichroic groups, all symmetry operators can become operators of colored symmetry, with the colors of the pattern elements changing in a predesigned sequence when all the steps of the symmetry operation are performed. Again, from each uncolored group of symmetry several colored groups can be derived if different choices of color-changing symmetry operators are made. In perhaps the most straightforward notation for the simpler cases (Shubnikov and Koptsik[1]), all the color-changing elements are in the symmetry group symbol designated by superscripts in parentheses that state directly the number of colors that alternate when the complete set of steps for the particular operator are performed and coloring of an element in a *general position* is examined. For example, $a^{(3)}$ denotes (as a subscript) a tripled translation along the a axis with the color sequence ABC, $m^{(2)}$ a two-colored reflection plane ($A \rightleftarrows B$), and $6^{(6)}$, $6^{(3)}$ and $6^{(2)}$ denote the six-, three- and two-colored sixfold axes with the cyclic color sequences ABCDEF. . ., ABCABC. . ., and ABABAB. . ., respectively. The total number of

Fig. 15. Coloured symmetry group $c_{a(2)b(2)}4^{(4)}d^{(4)}$m, based on a pattern from Ribat-i-Sharaf, Iran (Khurasan) (12th century A.D.). d denotes general positions, a–c' various sets of special positions. Numerals indicate the number of color permutations.

Fig. 16. Coloured symmetry group $c_{a(2)b(2)}4^{(4)}d^{(4)}m^{(2)}$. For explanations see Fig. 15.

colors in the group (its *color index*) may be equal to or exceed the highest color index of a single symmetry operation.

There is not enough space here for any systematic analysis of colored groups of symmetry. Let us therefore concentrate onto the illustrated examples (Figs. 15–17) on which some general features, potentially important for ornamental art, will be explained. These dichroic and poly-chromatic examples are based on an (apparently uncolored) Islamic pattern of protruding bricks and recessed fields from the Ribat-i-Sharaf caravanserai from mid-12th century Iran (Khurasan). The plane group is tetragonal, p4gm, with the fields in general position (*d*), and in the following special positions: on mirror planes (*c* and *c'*), on fourfold axes (*a*) and on the intersections of three symmetry elements, 2mm (denoted as *b*). This pattern was selected because of the rich spectrum of positions on which the action of different choices of colored symmetry elements can be studied. In all figures the general positions are illustrated by colors (hatching) while the special positions by a less conspicuous background; all color variations are indicated by numbers. This approach was chosen because it was realized that the full gamut of color permutations over all positions becomes incomprehensible. This is the direct explanation of the fact that in the majority of cases the artists used only a limited number of types of fields (colored elements, discs) for their colored patterns or point-group designs. Often it has only one type of field (i.e. position) and often the same position was repeated twice or more times as a superposition or juxtaposition of fields of different sizes or shapes. These repetitions of the same position are then differently colored but they obey the same sequence of permutations.

The special position (*a*) on $4^{(4)}$ axes is a would-be composite of four colors. For $4^{(2)}$ this position can be understood as a composite of two colors only, invariant in dichroic groups but bivariant over the two sets of $4^{(2)}$ axes in Fig. 17. The glide planes can be $g^{(4)}$ or $g^{(2)}$ according to the color group, whereas mirrors are either color changing ($m^{(2)}$) or color preserving (m). A special kind of mirror planes can be envisaged, transitional between the above two types, that changes only certain colors out of their total number, leaving the rest unchanged during the reflection operation (e.g. $1 \rightleftarrows 2$, $3 \rightleftarrows 3$ and $4 \rightleftarrows 4$ in the general *d* position). This *partial chromaticity* of some of the symmetry operations was for the first time defined by van der Waerden and Burckhardt[17]. It was used by Hinterreiter in a number of pictures (the only

Fig. 17. Colored symmetry group $(p4^{(2)}g^{(2)}m^{(2)})^{(4)}$. For explanations see Fig. 15.

dated one from 1942) in the portfolio *Geometrische Schönheit*[18] and by Escher in his first compositions based on colored translations (Jung[19]).

Further complications of the simple concept of colored symmetry elements exist which appear to transgress the boundary towards defects in design. They may be found in Koptsik[20]. Cases like $4^{(AABB)}$ or $4^{(ABCB)}$ can be handled equally well by understanding the symmetry reduced to $2^{(2)}$ in a pseudotetragonal motif.

After the general considerations and the pessimistic statement on the use of color groups in mosaics discussed above, let us examine some of the cultures known for their polychromatic ornamental art.

The first such cultures are the Precolumbian cultures of South America. The greatest flowering of polychromatic symmetry occurs in the Paracas textiles. The Nazca and Tiahuanaco cultures used mostly dichroic groups. One-sided bands predominate, followed by fabrics often interpretable as a (sometimes modified) juxtaposition of band ornaments to yield a two-dimensional pattern (Fig. 18). A great variety of often sophisticated symmetries are observed. In linear patterns four- to sixfold colored translations (**a**) occur, e.g. $p_{a^{(4)}}1$, $p_{a^{(5)}}1$ or $p_{a^{(6)}}1$. Among more sophisticated arrangements, $p_{a^{(5)}}2$ may be quoted in which the twofold axis alters four of the colors pairwise, leaving one color unchanged. In other cases, the color periodicity is a large multiple of the basic pattern (p1 or p2) but between the two consecutive color-changing elements 1–3 such elements repeat with another, "background" color (often yellow), e.g. $p_{A^{(2)}}1$ with the superperiod $A = 8a$.

In agreement with their parallel-striped design (or the stripe-like arrangement of discrete elements on a one-colored background) the periodicity along the stripes is short whereas that across the stripes is a multiple of the basic one due to color modulation [e.g. $p_{b^{(5)}}2^{(2)}$]. A complicated example in Fig. 18 represents a pattern with two-colored asymmetric stripes (yet with approximate twofold, colored rotation axes) arranged along the b direction with the full colored period $B = 6b$ but with a color-changing centration, i.e. perhaps $c^{(2)}{}_{B/2^{(3)}}2^{(2)}$. Some two-dimensional striped patterns may have one-colored stripes interspersed between those with color changes, reminding one of the problems encountered in the mosaics of Alhambra. If intercalated in 1:1 ratio, they can be regarded as color-neutral special positions between the color-changing general positions.

The Mexican codices offer another family of designs. In them, besides a number of dichroic friezes (usually p2′ or pa′ with a dichroic glide plane a), polychromatic bands with up to eight consecutive colors occur: $p_{a^{(5-8)}}1$; very frequent are stepped-pyramidal designs $p_{a^{(3)}}m^{(2 \times 2,2)}a^{(2)}$, $p_{a^{(2)}}m^{(2,2)}2^{(2)}$ with the "diamond" glide $d^{(4)}$ (Fig. 19). Rarely simple patterns occur with reflection planes both parallel and perpendicular to the translation direction. The most intriguing designs are pa designs in which the glide plane acts on blocks of striped design, seven stripes in length, but the periodicity of color change represents only six stripes, out of step with the geometrical motif (Fig. 19). In the stepped-pyramidal designs, the cores of pyramids have the color of the adjacent (glide-plane-related) pyramid, i.e. a phase shift in color. The same phase shift was often created between the main objects and their details in the Peruvian textiles.

As can be ascertained from the large collection of Egyptian ornamented art by Fořtová-Šámalová[22], the majority of two-dimensional patterns are dichroic in nature, whereas there

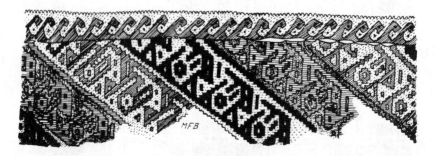

Fig. 18. Peruvian striped fabric, a complex juxtaposition of band ornaments. Details in the text of the paper. Drawing reproduced from [21].

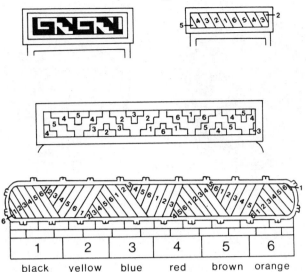

Fig. 19. Selected ornaments from Codex Vindobonensis Mexicanus I, pp. 3–4 (ornamented temple facades and platforms). Colour numbering is valid for all objects illustrated; the dichroic pattern is in red and white.

is a smaller percentage of monochromatic (from the symmetry point of view) and several colored-symmetry patterns. Many dichroic (Fig. 47 but not Fig. 48) and all the polychromatic patterns are based on the principle of parallel juxtaposition of colored stripes (simple, zig-zag or disjoint) that are parallel or diagonal to the usually square submesh. The checkerboard pattern is widely used for dichroic cases. Colored striped patterns that color the square patterns with color periodicities equal to $2 \times$, $4 \times$, $6 \times$ and even $11 \times$ the basic b period are documented, the latter with the repetition of some colors in different roles. The statue of a maiden from 2050 B.C. (now at The Metropolitan Museum of Art), with a scaly "fabric" of the dress (symmetry cm) four colored in horizontal stripes, and Egyptian jewelry illustrate these principles as well. Neutral, one-colored tiles or (zig-zag) lines without color change are often interspersed between color-changing elements. Similar to the Alhambra patterns, "dichroic" checkerboard patterns occur in which only the dark tiles are color modulated (see below) in one direction. Groups of all these designs can be described as $p_{b^{(m)}}m$, with additional m and twofold axes with partial chromaticity to be added.

One-dimensional friezes may display alternation of up to four basic colors. They are usually based on simple, pm (m is perpendicular) and pmm2 friezes. One to three neutral elements are common among the color-changing elements, especially in dichroic friezes. Elaborate floral friezes are mostly monochromatic, although up to three alternating motifs ("colors") may be present.

The king and the officials in the murals of sacrificial ceremonies in the audience hall of the royal palace of Mari (18th century B.C., middle Euphrates, Syria) have their (apparently woolen) garments colored according to exactly the same principle as the just-described Egyptian square-based patterns. Three- or four-colored modulation waves run diagonally across the (approximately) rectangular grid created by the structure of the rich garment. On other murals, disordered sequences are common. The white color is used on equal footing with the other colors in all instances. An attempt for a four-colored diamond pattern of an altar base, reminiscent of the Australian Aboriginal paintings described further below, dissolves into chaos before completing a full length of the colored translation[23].

In Celtic illuminated manuscripts the majority of linear or two-dimensional knotwork designs are either monochromatic or dichroic. Trichroic or tetrachroic linear designs are relatively rare, although they occur both in the knotwork and in the zoomorphic bands. The color-changing element in the majority of cases is a colored translation, rarely a colored glide plane in linear motifs; it is the standing dichroic mirror planes and (often rather freely intermixed with these planes) dichroic twofold axes lying in the plane of the interlaced, two-sided two-dimensional designs. The horizontal twofold axes often represent the only dichroic symmetry operator in

Fig. 20. The threefold and twofold spiral brooches from the *Book of Durrow* and *Book of Lindisfarne*, worked out as $3^{(3)}$ and $2^{(2)}$ in the originals. Reproduced from [24].

point-group designs. The most prominent application of these principles occurs in the *Book of Durrow* and the *Book of Lindisfarne*; many mistakes occur in the *Canterbury Codex Aureus* and in the famous *Book of Kells*, in which nearly irregular multicolor sequences can occur in the border designs.

Almost always it is the individual "complex knots" which form subunits of the complex linear knotwork that become colored differently, in a bead-like fashion; only rarely it is the individual threads that receive different coloring. In the normal situation the colors of each single thread change from knot to knot.

In zoomorphic point-group designs (often imperfect) $4^{(2)}$ axes play a role. Another design type based on rotation axes are the spiral "brooches" which usually form the nodes of the topologically (whenever possible) trifurcate scrollwork so typical for Irish manuscripts and rock carvings. The majority of them are three colored, $3^{(3)}$, sometimes extending to adjacent scroll-work, often with some errors in coloring. Again, the most perfect work is found in the *Book of Lindisfarne*. $2^{(2)}$ and $4^{(2)}$ axes occur in the spiralwork as well (Fig. 20).

One of the most refined color patterns is found in the Incarnation initial in the *Gospels of St. Chad*. It is a zoomorphic linear design with a homeometric (see below) glide plane parallel to the periodicity of the design (the underlying uncolored symmetry is pa) that is three-colored, $p_{a^{(3)}}a$, resulting in a complex, dynamic sequence of birds within the confines of the initial.

Our unpublished study of the material collected by Prof. A. Forge (The Australian National University, Canberra) from the Abelam region of the Sepik area, New Guinea, and very kindly offered to the author's disposal, enables us to make certain conclusions about the problem of colored symmetry in the flat-surface painting in this region of New Guinea. As stated by Forge[25], this highly stylized painting manipulates a set of elements which possess certain ritual and spiritual values in order to make effective and meaningful communication to the initiated. The latter is heightened by the aesthetic effect; hence the importance of symmetry in these four-colored images and designs.

The gables of the famous tall ceremonial houses with consecutive rows of staring faces in the region of northern Abelam gain their expressivity also by means of (1) pseudosymmetry of the oval faces, with the upper and lower halves made similar to each other and often enhanced by the color antisymmetry of the approximately corresponding fields in the two halves (Fig. 21) and (2) the dichroic contrast between the stark red triangles of "headdresses" and the intercalated triangles with black and yellow stripes (with white interspaces) which stand for "bodies" to the faces immediately above them. In many instances, abstracted from the plentiful technical irregularities, it is a rhombic (pseudotrigonal) arrangement $cmm^{(2)}2^{(2)}$. Sometimes the pattern is changed, the "bodies" being red as well.

Except for the above dichroic striped pattern, with the above-mentioned white interspaces (special positions) and the frequent modification by twinning (see below) to a zig-zag form, two-dimensional patterns are rare. They (especially those with pseudohexagonal metrics) are simply obtained by juxtaposition of individual bands of linear pattern. Except for the rare cases of $3^{(3)}$ and $4^{(2)}$ correctly applied, they usually contain such defective color sequences that no two-dimensional color periodicity results. Often there is a loss of coherence between adjacent stripes. Thus, the Abelam ornaments are essentially one dimensional. Even the huge gable areas are filled with the pattern of staring faces in this way. All the designs are drawn by free hand and the resulting uncertainties must be allowed for.

The principal band ornament is a stripe of triangles, pma2, often representing borders around the schematized figures with extremely enhanced symmetry (Fig. 22). Surprisingly enough, the basic color scheme is three colored with a glide plane, $p_{a^{(3)}}m^{(2,1)}a2^{(2)}$. The simple sequences [uncolored pma2, dichroic $pma'2'$, $p_{a'}m$ and trichroic $p_{a^{(3)}}m^{(2,1)}$ (in both cases all triangles on a single side are white)] are rare, as is the tetrachroic ABCADC, perhaps denoted $p_{a^{(3)}}a^{(1,2)}$, the latter glide plane changing only one color. The number of faults in the sequences is in most cases considerable. The successful composites of triangular stripes give $p6'mm'$, and two cases of cm, with the centering optionally dichroic and additional partly chromatic m and 2 possibly present. Surprisingly, the simple and effective color sequence which generates $6^{(3)}$ was obtained only as rare "point defects" in the design. Rarely, the triangles in the linear stripes may be separated from each other by color-neutral white rims positioned on twofold axes.

The second ubiquitous linear element are the parallelhatched, one-dimensional patterns (bands) with the lines slanting (or symmetrically V-shaped) towards the periodicity direction. They have purely translational color symmetry, the non colored elements being either twofold axes or the mirror plane in the periodic direction. Their basic color scheme is black-red-black-red, i.e. dichroic, mostly with a white (neutral) line between every two consecutive colored lines, i.e. $p_{a^{(2)}}2$ with the white lines being on $2^{(2)}$. However, it can be modified by moving the white lines close to one of the two colored sets of lines, by regularly multiplying the number of white lines, by leaving out half of the white lines in order to obtain the three-colored sequence white-red-black or, finally, by introducing a yellow line flanked by white as the color opposite of black flanked by red. Colors are filled in consecutively; hence many errors and many friezes can be characterized as almost completely random sequences of lines.

Errors are also abundant in the true striped patterns. Up to four distinct colors can build a sequence, an $a^{(4)}$ translation. By varying the width of the stripes they get reduced to "uncolored" p1 (b nonperiodic) with a group of three narrow colored stripes regularly spaced over the white-hatched background.

Fig. 21. The ceremonial face painting by Abelam, the Sepik area, New Guinea. An approximate horizontal reflection plane runs through the eyes of the figure, with colour (resp. object) antisymmetry for a number of fields. Material of Prof. A. Forge, A.N.U., Canberra.

Fig. 22. A ceremonial painting by Abelam, the Sepik area, New Guinea. A highly schematized human figure, with enhanced symmetry, is flanked by a three-colored band ornament with the symmetry $p_{a^{(3)}}m^{(2,1)}a2^{(2)}$. Material of Prof. A. Forge, A.N.U., Canberra.

Horizontal friezes can often be sequentially dichroic (also as carved masks) and they can display the same tantalizing approximate color antisymmetry of certain upper and lower fields as do the point-group designs.

Ornamental aspects of the Aboriginal bark painting from the northeastern Arnhem Land were studied on the material collected and kindly offered for our research by Dr H. Morphy, A.N.U., Canberra. The bark paintings represent rectangular pieces of specially prepared tree bark, usually divided by the painter into several compartments. As a rule, the background of the painting represents a clan design (with a number of meanings), usually large enough to deduce a complete two-dimensional pattern. On this background, figures of humans, animals, objects and plants are painted. Sometimes, especially in the case of the Riratjingu clan, they result in beautiful antisymmetry, most often $2'$.

The Aborigines of the Arnhem Land, similar to the Abelam of New Guinea, have two categories of color: plain black and other colors (excl. white) on the one hand, and shimmering colors obtained by cross hatching (one of the hatching directions is white) on the other hand. The white fields are of this type. The majority of clan designs are parallel-striped patterns made with the cross-hatched version of colors. Most of them are two colored, usually white and brown-red, or expanded two colored (black and brown) intercalated by the "neutral" white stripes (which represent here special positions on $m^{(2)}$). Only rarely three-colored sequences of these colors occur. The striped patterns can be obliquely cross cut and slightly offset by another system of dark lines, yielding Moiré patterns.

The diamond designs (Fig. 23) represent a minority and in the material studied they were limited almost entirely to three clans, i.e. Dhalwangu, Madarrpa and Gumatj. The diamonds always represent a $cmm2$ pattern and vary in shape from nearly square, as in the case of the Dhalwanga design, to much narrower lozenges in the creations of Gumatj (Morphy[26]). The majority of complex coloring patterns came from the Gumatj artists, but we could ascertain that the color distribution schemes in general transcend the clan boundaries and are not clan specific.

Upon coloring, the diamond pattern is divided into rows of diamonds with plain colors parallel to the shorter axis of the centered mesh, which are separated by the intervening rows of diamonds with shimmering colors. The simplest case, with only one kind of diamonds in each row type, has the same mesh size and the dichroic plane group $p_{c'}mm$; it is rare. Many more examples have only one color in the plain-colored rows, whereas they have two-colored sequences for the cross-hatched lozenges, i.e. $p_{b'}mm$; the uniform plain color rows then represent special positions without color change. The same holds for the cases when both the plain and the hatched-color rows display two-color sequences, $p_{b'}m$. The known case with a trichroic cross-hatched sequence, $p_{b^{(3)}}mm^{(2,1)}2^{(2,1)}$, concerns only that system of rows; the small primitive mesh of the plain-colored rows has to be considered separately (Fig. 24).

All the other cases can best be described as superposition of two dichroic groups, one valid for the plain-colored array of diamonds, the other one for the cross-hatched array. With the first one being $p_{b'}mm2$ for all cases, the latter will be characterized by either a single or a double periodicity in the a direction. If white cross-hatched lozenges are present as well, they run through the pattern unchanged (a color-neutral special position). Then they simply expand the patterns along the b direction without changing its symmetry. Thus, an expanded cross-hatched version of the partial mesh $p_{b'}mm2$ exists. The cross-hatched patterns with the doubled a axis either are $p_{a'}mm2$ (expanded) or $c_{a^{(2)}b^{(2)}}mm2$ (both in the unexpanded and expanded versions) (Fig. 24). The most complicated case of this kind is trichroic and has the strings (stripes) of shimmering colors parallel to one diagonal of the unit mesh of the basic diamond pattern. They form a regular threefold sequence of cross-hatched white, reddish brown and black. If the axes of this mesh are selected parallel to those of the plain-colored cell ($p_{b'}mm2$) they will be tripled in both directions: $p_{a^{(3)}b^{(3)}}m^{(2,1)}m^{(2,1)}2^{(2,1)}$. The color modulation vector (perpendicular to the color modulation wave) is (**3b-a**) (Fig. 24).

Thus, in the entire material from the northeastern Arnheim Land available for our inspection, there were no groups of colored symmetry beyond the cases of unidirectional triple modulation of one of the two (usually independent) submotifs typical for this region.

Finally, we should elaborate on our introductory remarks that concerned the Moorish tile patterns of Alhambra and the Arabic patterns in general. In the mosque of Córdoba (785–987

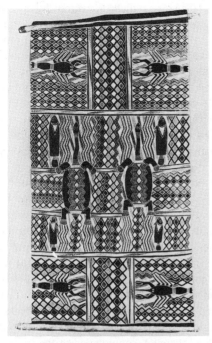

Fig. 23. A Dhalwangu bark painting by Yangarriny with the diamond clan design forming the background of the picture. Material of Dr. H. Morphy, A.N.U., Canberra.

Fig. 24. Schematized diamond patterns from the Aboriginal bark paintings from N.-E. Arnhem Land. Plain colours are indicated by capital letters (Red and Black), cross-hatched coloring by the lower-case letters (red, black and white). Outlines of the respective unit mesh are given as full and dashed lines; centration is indicated when present. Based on the material collected by Dr H. Morphy.

A.D.) none of the major red-and-white brick patterns (Fig. 9) appear to be dichroic. The ceramic tile mosaics of Alhambra can—without a claim for completeness—be divided into three groups.

(1) The first group are the large-scale three-colored modulations of uncolored or of truly dichroic (i.e. black-and-white) patterns. A "collosal" superstructure of the basic, simple uncolored square pattern in the Court of Myrtles represents $c_{b^{(3)}}mm^{(2,1)}2^{(2,1)}$. There is a large-scale linear superstructure of the tetragonal pattern based on a "Thor's hammer" design that itself is black and white in nature (Fig. 25). First, the white positions are left out. Then every second row of "hammers" remains black (special positions), whereas the other subset is color modulated to yield the expanded pattern $p_{a^{(3)}}1m$, not unlike those in the Australian designs.

The famous trigonal "propeller" patterns from Alhambra are there mostly altered from dichroic into uncolored by introducing distinct centration elements into the dark and the white sets of propellers. (The uncentered, simple dichroic design p6', without centrations, can be found both in Alhambra (color modulated) and in the Alcazar of Sevilla). Two kinds of color modulations are present: a three-colored modulation wave for the "dark propellers," parallel to one set of trigonal planes, and another color modulation wave for the "dark" stars in the centers of white propellers. The second wave is parallel to a set of trigonal planes 120° apart from the first one. The other large-scale modulation superstructure reminds us again of that found in the diamond patterns of the Australians: horizontal rows of green diamonds separate rows of alternating yellow and blue diamonds, $p_{b'}mm2$, with green as special positions, and only for the color scheme, disregarding the purely axial character of the underlying geometric design. The stars again give a pattern different from that of propellers—$p_{c'}mm$. Finally, in the long square pattern of "affine" sixfold stars in the Mexuar chamber, four distinct colors are used for the dark subset of stars and they are applied at random.

(2) The second group is represented by the dichroic, black-and-white patterns and several dichroic patterns (usually blue and black) in which the white color is absent or applied to the elements nonequivalent to the colored ones. Rather complicated pseudohexagonal rectangular patterns can be quoted in this category. Furthermore, even a doubly dichroic pattern with two distinct unit meshes for the respective black-and-white symmetries was created (Fig. 26): $p_{a^{(2)}}mm$ for small, respectively four- and eightfold centers of otherwise fully equivalent fourfold rosettes and $c_{a^{(2)}b^{(2)}}4mm$ for the light and dark coloring of these rosettes. In some simpler dichroic patterns,

the white tiles are first omitted from consideration and then a new dichroic pattern (with lower symmetry) is created over the dark tiles only.

(3) The last group are the dichroic designs which are color modulated by a point-group scheme, in a way used by Vasarely in many of his pictures centuries later. As a rule, the color modulation represents smaller and smaller "frames" superimposed over the design. They copy the shape of the outer frame of the panel. It can either represent a progression of colors or a (periodic) two-colored ripple. Another, less frequent case is a division of a long panel into zones by applying a different color to some widely spaced rows of pattern elements.

The above review of several periods of most colorful ornamental art leaves us with the pessimistic conclusion that only rudiments of two-dimensional colored symmetry were mastered by the old artists and artisans. They were those based on colored translations, usually in one direction, applied to triangular, scaly, square, diamond and rectangular patterns. Besides the cultures described in some detail, such patterns are also found in the Minoan, Persian, Roman, and later art epochs. The art of colored plane-group symmetry has come of age only in modern times, primarily through the efforts of Hinterreiter and Escher already mentioned above. It is interesting to see that the early compositions of Escher, (post)dated to 1928, still represent the groups based on three-colored translations, $p_{a^{(3)}b^{(3)}}2^{(2,1)}$ and $p_{a^{(3)}}g^{(2,1)}g$ (with errors), perhaps witnessing his study of historical examples. Escher's colored symmetry was studied by MacGillavry[8] and Weitzel (in Jung[19]) and further substantial contributions might only come from the study of his unpublished material. A detailed study of Hinterreiter's art was made in 1979 by the present author[27] and the newly available additional material appears to amplify but not substantially change the overall picture outlined there. A composition in the trichroic plane group $p_{a^{(3)}b^{(3)}}6^{(2)}$, with only the colors describing the special positions on the sixfold axes used, is shown in Fig. 27.

GENERALIZATIONS OF SYMMETRY

The ornamental artists have not failed to recognize that there exist more general forms of symmetry than the hitherto described congruence in the Euclidean plane with unchanged size and shape of individual motifs throughout the pattern. However, the conscious application of generalized forms of symmetry in art is much less frequent than that of congruence. The

Fig. 25. A ceramic tile mosaic from Alhambra, Granada. A unidirectional threefold color modulation of the black-and-white pattern p4′g′m.

Fig. 26. A ceramic tile mosaic from Alhambra, Granada. A doubly dichroic pattern; details in the text of the paper.

Fig. 27. Opus 115 (1960) by H. Hinterreiter, reproduced from [45]. A composition in the trichroic plane group $p_{a^{(3)}b^{(3)}}6^{(2)}$ with only the colors for special positions on the $6^{(2)}$ axes applied (in form of two concentric 'discs').

unconscious applications, however, are as widespread as the means of overcoming the nonlinearity or nonplanarity of space to be utilized.

Similarity or homeometry

The similarity operations preserve the shape of the motif unchanged and change only its size. The basic operation is homothety, in which equivalent points of similar objects are connected by rays intersecting in one singular point (or axis) and their dimensions and spacing are related by the equation $\overline{A'B'} = k\overline{AB}$, where k is the similarity coefficient ($k = 1$ reduces to congruence). Homothety can be combined with a rotation or reflection operation. Thus, three basic types of similarity transformations exist in a one-sided plane: (1) homothety, (2) spiral rotation (Drehstreckung), combining rotation with homothety, and (3) homothetic reflection (*Spiegelstreckung*), a similarity analogue of a glide reflection operation. On a two-sided plane a similar analogue of an ordinary two-fold axis can also occur.

In the similarity groups the similarity operators are combined with the symmetry elements we have already met in symmetry groups, some of them in a modified form. First of all, there are the n-fold axes through the singular point, often combined with mirror planes intersecting in these axes. Then there are mirror (resp. glide) planes and twofold axes excentric to the singular point, with the coordinate values subject to the similarity relationship. The planes are planes of circular inversion, concentric around the singular point. Finally, homeometry involves potential monotonous changes of the value of k with the distance from the singular point[28–30].

One- and two-dimensional homeometric band patterns are found in Irish and Celtic art, primarily in braided knotwork (Fig. 28), on brooches, and in initial letters of the illustrated manuscripts. Similar applications exist in Minoan art and numerous minor applications in the vegetal ornament in the triangular spaces of Renaissance, Muslim and other buildings. The calligraphic application of homothety, in which the design surrounds the singular point, is shown in Fig. 29.

Rich circular patterns, both those involving spiral rotation and those based on homothetic reflection, and also those based on 15-fold axes and radial mirror planes with homothety adorn

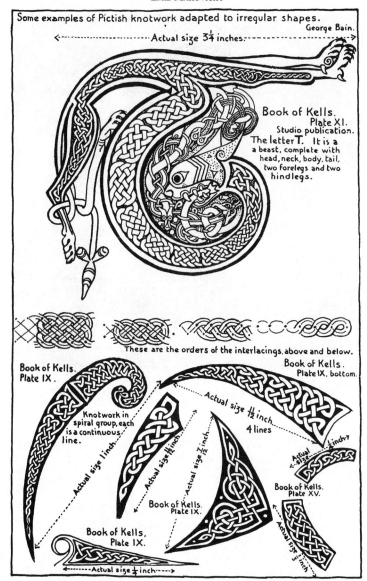

Fig. 28. Curvilinear homeometric and catametric patterns from Irish illuminated manuscripts. Drawings by G. Bain, reproduced from [24].

the floor of the interior of the Basilica of St. Marc in Venice (Fig. 30). The floor mosaics originate from the 12th century, with later additions. A magnificent example of spiral rotation combined with the point symmetry 12mm is represented by Michelangelo's design of pavement for Campidoglio, Rome (Fig. 31), whereas the dome of St. Peter's basilica as well as the domes of other churches and of Islamic religious buildings (e.g. Iranian mosques) are often applications of homothety or homothetic reflection (adjusted to the curvature of the surface). Already in the 1st century A.D., on a bronze "box lid" from Cornalagh, Ireland, a perfect openwork combination of spiral rotation with the point symmetry 38mm was executed by the La Tène masters[31].

Modern art has rather frequently exploited the similarity principle as well. In the majority of cases, similar motifs (or their simplified elements, or similar outlines) are used side by side with affine transformations to construct nonperiodic pictures, which are prevalent in modern art. Homothetic reflection has been directly employed by Camille Graeser (Fig. 32) and homothety (usually with some allowances) by Josef Albers (1961–62), Jacques Villon (1932) and Vasarely (1968) for their pictures based on a series of nested squares (pyramids). Several masterly concentric designs based on similarity were made by Escher (Fig. 33).

Fig. 29. A Quranic inscription from Ulu Cami, Bursa, Turkey, reproduced from [44]. The word *wa* has been repeated by means of homothety.

Fig. 30. Two circular patterns from the Cosmatesque floor mosaics of the Basilica of St Marc in Venice. The left-hand pattern is based on the combination of homothety with a three-colored 15-fold axis and radial mirror planes. The right-hand pattern (drawn in accordance with the outer portions of the actual pattern which changes its multiplicity half-way from the center) combines spiral rotation with the central rotation, and radial mirrors for the black tesserae. The uncolored pattern will combine homothetic reflection with a 32-fold rotation axis and radial mirror planes.

Fig. 31. Michelangelo's design of pavement for Campidoglio, Rome. Spiral rotation combined with the point-group symmetry 12mm. Drawing by G. Bain, reproduced from [24].

Fig. 32. ''Progression in red, blue and yellow'' (1944) by Camille Graeser, reproduced from [32]; a design based on homothetic reflection (except for the central rod of finite thickness).

Fig. 33. A woodprint by M. C. Escher (1958) based on a combination of homothety with eightfold rotation. Reproduced from [19]; ©M. C. Escher Heirs c/o Cordon Art-Baarn-Holland.

Accumulation (distribution) of similar motifs (resp. outlines) represents one of the chief principles of the Gothic ornamental architecture (Wolf and Wolff[28]). Similar means of expressivity are used by mannerist Renaissance artists.

Affine transformations

The next more general type of symmetry is represented by affine transformations under which only the parallellity of lines, and not the angles or the area of a polygon, remain preserved.

Except for the world of modern art, in which accumulation/distribution of affine objects (outlines) represents an important method in abstract painting, we do not have many illustrations of the conscious application of affinity. A magnificent example (Fig. 34) comes from Iran. Similar to some Chinese lattice designs (Grünbaum and Shephard[10]) and Japanese designs (Fig. 35), it represents a conscious affine transformation of a clearly tetragonal motif. It also suggests that the ideas of affine transformation can result from purely practical experience, executing a design with bricks with altered dimensional ratios or/and interspaces. Many brick, basketry and weaving patterns have to be idealized from such minor affine changes caused by technical reasons.

A striking use of affinity was made by Vasarely in his picture "Homage to Malevich" (1953) (Hahn[34]). The upper and lower halves are affinely related, the square and the approximate diamond transforming respectively into a diamond and an approximate square. The expressivity of the picture is heightened by the apparent (oppositely directed) similarity relationship of squares and lozenges, as well as by the skillful application of color antisymmetry (Fig. 36).

Perspective–projective transformations

The perspective–projective transformations have been clarified in the Renaissance times and used extensively, e.g. by Baroque artists in their *trompe-l'oeil* compositions. Their use in

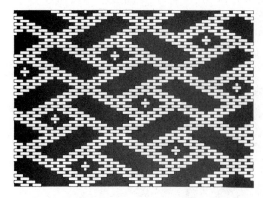

Fig. 34. A design of protruding bricks from the Jami' Mosque minaret, Gurgan, Iran (12th century). Plane group p2 as a conscious affine transformation of a tetragonal (p4) design.

Fig. 35. A Japanese design from [33]. Affine transformation of a tetragonal, p4gm, design akin to the Egyptian design in Fig. 48. Figure 9 is related to the tetragonal archetype of Fig. 35 and to Fig. 48 by minor out-of-phase shifts of blocks that destroy mirror planes.

modern art has been particularly propagated by Hans Hinterreiter (Fig. 37). It is he who also used, and worked out in detail (Hinterreiter[7]), more complicated transformations (mapping) of congruent patterns onto a series of tangential, curvilinear, elliptic and other nets (Figs. 5 and 8), often with a (series of) singular point(s). From the representatives of Op Art it was especially Bridget Riely, Enrico Castellani and Angel Duarte (Barret[35]) who used to modify in their pictures the periodicities of the underlying congruent pattern. V. Vasarely followed a different course, i.e. local distortions of periodicity and symmetry by superposition of periodic design and objects (defects) with point-group symmetries.

Catamorphy

The notion of catamorphy was introduced by Wolf and Wolff[28] as the lowest category of symmetry. Catametric figures are neither congruent, nor similar, affine or projective–perspective, but their shapes still demonstrate certain mutual relationships and they can form a

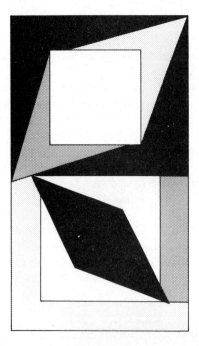

Fig. 36. *Homage to Malevich* by Vasarely (1953), an abstract painting based on affinity as well as approximate similarity and color antisymmetry.

Fig. 37. Opus *E* 94 (1959–1972) by H. Hinterreiter, reproduced from [45]. A dichroic $p_{a'}2$ pattern mapped onto a perspective net.

progression according to their consecutive changes according to a given rule. A sequence of regular polygons ordered according to increasing number of vertices was quoted as an example.

This interesting concept has not yet been used in practice. However, we found a number of examples in ornamental art, some of which are quoted here.

Islamic artists who adorned the domes in the mausoleum No. 13 in Shah-i-Zinda, Samarkand (1405) and the madrasa of Abdullah-khan in Bukhara (1588–1590) employed the nets based on corner-connected polygons to create catametric annuli in which, over the central row (circle) of n-pointed stars, the $(n - 1)$ stars are reflected into $(n + 1)$ pointed stars (Fig. 38). By this time the creators of these nets realized that these annuli cannot be extended into an infinite catametric net in which the order of polygons would regularly grow from its centre, preserving the same connectivity pattern throughout the net. The only modern approach to this problem seems to be Escher's composition *Snakes* from 1969, in which a similar net of sixfold interconnected rings alters into seven- and eightfold rings at the terminal stage.

Another type of catamorphy occurs in rectilinear or curvilinear tapering designs. After an interval of one type of linear pattern with dimensions decreasing according to the rules of similarity, the pattern is altered into a simpler one in order to avoid its excessive miniaturization. For example, the six-strand interlacing knotwork will be successively reduced to four strands, three strands and finally into a two-strand lace in Celtic manuscripts (Fig. 28). The same principle was applied to cobra designs on an Egyptian mummy (Fig. 39). Catametric change of the motif served to compensate for the change in the circumference of a Pueblo jar (Fig. 40) instead of the usually employed similarity. In the world of computer graphics simple catamorphy in its original sense was used by Norton Starr (Franke[37]).

The most extensive use of catamorphy was made by Escher in some of his two-dimensional patterns. In some patterns he used progressive catamorphic alteration of geometric tiles that completely fill the plane into interlocking animal shapes, preserving the same color group. In other designs, however, the discrete topological discs in the shape of animals gradually become the background (interdisc space) of the picture, whereas the original ''background discs'' alter into animal-shaped discs in the same process. The overall black-and-white symmetry of the pattern (if the shapes of discs are disregarded) remains preserved in this process, which we suggest calling ''anticatametry.''

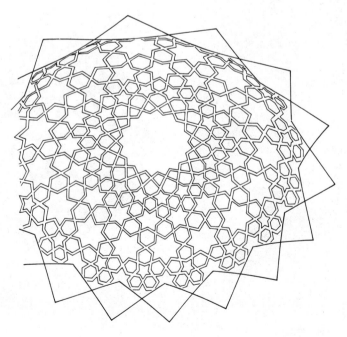

Fig. 38. The dome of the madrasa of Abdullah-khan in Bukhara (1588–1590). A catametric annulus combining vertex-connected five-, six- and sevenfold stars in one net. Drawn after a photograph in [36].

Fig. 39. Catametric adjustment of snake designs to the changes in available space. An Egyptian coffin lid, provenience unknown.

Non-Euclidean symmetry

Besides the Euclidean plane, with the sum of angles at the vertices equal to 180° (i.e. π rad) we can have a spherical plane with this sum greater than π and a hyperbolic plane with the sum of these angles less than the value of π (Coxeter [38,39]). The spherical cases give a limited number of symmetry groups on the surface of the sphere identical with point groups in three-dimensional space; the hyperbolic cases give an infinite number of new hyperbolic "plane"

Fig. 40. Catametric adjustment of zig-zag motifs to the change in the area. Pueblo pottery, The Museum of American Indian–Heyes Foundation, New York.

Fig. 41. Hyperbolic plane group (7,3,2) with antireflection planes in a circular conformal model. Reproduced from Coxeter [38].

groups. They can combine any types of rotation axes, giving combinations forbidden in Euclidean plane.

If we realize that the unit mesh of any plane group higher than rectangular can be divided into triangles with angles π/p, π/q, and π/r at the vertices which respectively coincide with the p-, q- and r-fold axes of symmetry of the plane group, a new notation (which, however, omits reflection operations) can be introduced, e.g. (4,4,2) for the plane group p4 (and higher) or (6,3,2) for p6 (and higher groups). Similarly, higher groups of symmetry on hyperbolic plane can exist such as (6,4,2), (4,3,3), (7,3,2), etc., which offer nice ornamental possibilities.

Naturally, they required the cooperation of mathematician with artist to be materialized. It was Escher aided by Coxeter who in his *Circle Limits* I–V (1958–60) utilized several hyperbolic space groups (Jung[19], Coxeter[39]). They were followed by the computer graphics of Christopher Pöppe, an artist-mathematician (Franke[37]). Figure 41 shows the hyperbolic plane group (7,3,2) with the expressive reflection antisymmetry added by Coxeter[38]).

It might be best to close this chapter by quoting the generalized definition of symmetry by Vainshtein([9], p. 28): "Symmetry is invariance of objects under some of their transformations in the space of the variables describing them." This definition not only includes all the cases which were used and described so far but it also holds a promise for new, exciting concepts which will enrich both science and visual arts.

ADDITIONAL CATEGORIES AND COMPLICATIONS

A number of features of various ornaments exceed the simple question of symmetry group. Nearly all these complications have their counterparts in inorganic nature, especially in crystal structures, and much of the nomenclature developed in natural sciences can be applied to the man-made ornaments as well. The most important examples are described in the following paragraphs.

The basic motif (submotif) and submesh; superstructure and supermesh (supercell)

In a number of cases a simpler, nearly repetitive basic motif (submotif) can be discerned in a complicated pattern which possesses long-range periodicities. The approximate submesh repeats several times in the complete unit mesh. If the basic motif is very pronounced in the resulting pattern and it is only slightly modified (e.g. only by color variations) in the resulting pattern, the long-range product can also be called a superpattern (superstructure in crystallography) of the basic pattern; the resulting supermesh is often a complicated multiple of the basic mesh (Fig. 42). As in crystal structures, the modification of the submotif may increase in intensity until only an overall division into regularly repeating moduli can be discerned hidden beyond artist's design. Many works of geometric art, from the old mosaics to Mondrian and beyond, have been based on a modular principle (Figs. 43 and 44). One-dimensional superperiods represent a common feature of Greek vases. I wonder whether anybody has attempted to correlate the length of the superperiod of the meander design with the periods and pottery workshops of Classical Greece.

Fig. 42. A ceramic tile mosaic in blue, green and black from the Alcazar, Sevilla. A large $3a \times 4b$ supermesh results from the zig-zag colour modulation.

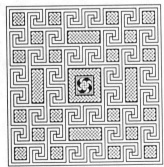

Fig. 43. A Roman floor mosaic from Chedworth, Gloucestershire, England. The braided knots and the meander design are based on a $1/8 \times 1/8$ square submesh (modulus). Drawn for the author by Ragna Larsen.

Fig. 44. A series of computer-generated designs by Chihaya Shimomura, reproduced from [37]. They display variable degree of dependence on the underlying $1/5 \times 1/5$ modulus.

Twinning

Twinning represents a common phenomenon in crystalline nature. Several blocks of crystal structure intergrow in a perfectly defined orientation and contact to yield a twin crystal. Artists have not failed to recognize and use the beauty of the principle. It started with an ornamental match of two simple brick patterns oriented 90° towards each other and very similar seams in basketry. Later it led to consciously created ornamental basketry designs, evolving all the way

(a)

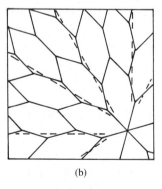

(b)

Fig. 45. (a), (b) Opus *SW-ME* 25 (1935–1978) by H. Hinterreiter, reproduced from [40], together with the underlying geometric construction (from [7]). Cyclic sixfold twinning of a pseudohexagonal pattern with further twinning on glide-reflection planes (indicated by dashed lines), giving a total of 12 orientations.

Fig. 46. Opus *ME* 376 (1940) by H. Hinterreiter, re-produced from [46]. Three portions of a cyclically twinned striped pattern (a sixfold twin), further twinned, by means of a dichroic twofold axis.

Fig. 47. A painted dichroic geometric pattern from the ceiling of a XXVIth dynasty tomb in Thebes (El Assasif). Diagonal rows with turquoise background and yellow stars (A) alternate with rows with red background and turquoise stars (B). Stippled lines indicate twin reflection planes which, when periodically applied, lead to the de-sign in Fig. 48. Reproduced from [33], color scheme from [22].

to the striking designs by Hinterreiter (Figs. 45 and 46). To a lesser extent it is also used by other modern artists. The most extensive collection of Hinterreiter's twinned designs is in the book by Albrecht & Koella[40]. Hinterreiter usually resorted to the procedure which is common in crystals: the high-symmetry structure (or pattern) is deformed to lower symmetry and then multiply twinned to restore the original higher symmetry, although only as a point-group symmetry. The planes of twin symmetry (twin planes) are mostly glide-reflection planes (as already shown in the brick design) or sometimes mirror-reflection planes; twinning around rotation axes of twin symmetry (twin axes) is also possible (Fig. 46). The composition planes, on which the two parts of the pattern meet, may be identical with, or distinct from, the twin planes. Adding of black-and-white (= anti-) symmetry to the twin operations adds to the expressivity of the design (Fig. 46).

If new twin planes are densely spaced in the unit mesh of the pattern, new patterns will be obtained (Figs. 47 and 48) similar to the situation in nature (Makovicky[41]). Should you consider this approach purely academic, consult Mucha *et al.* (1900, reprinted as [42]) where such a procedure is directly recommended for the creation of new designs.

Pseudosymmetry

If the crystals have certain symmetry but their geometry (lattice, often even the structure) is only slightly deformed when compared to that of higher symmetry, they are often called pseudosymmetric, e.g. orthorhombic-pseudohexagonal. The same holds for a great number of man-made patterns: those with lower (= oblique) symmetries are mostly pseudosymmetric, pseudorectangular or pseudosquare (-tetragonal), and less frequently pseudohexagonal; i.e. their mesh has a geometry more regular than required by the symmetry of the pattern. Reasons are obviously the dictate of the material (weaving, basketry, masonry), of space (in architecture) and of straightforward and easy geometric construction (woodcarving, mosaics). These reasons are probably often joined by artistic canons, usage patterns and subconscious imprinting. Ex-amples are taken from Hinterreiter[7] (Figs. 49 and 50).

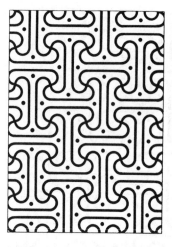

Fig. 48. A painted geometric pattern from the ceiling of a tomb in Thebes (Abd el Qurneh) (XVIIIth–XXIInd dynasty). It can be derived from the pattern in Fig. 47 by twinning on unit mesh scale. Reproduced from [33].

Fig. 49. A pseudohexagonal orthorhombic pattern constructed with the use of hexagonal metrics. Reproduced from Hinterreiter[7].

Noncommensurability

Noncommensurability occurs in all ages of the world of band ornaments. The periodicity of one band often is different from that of the other, adjacent band, without disturbing the eye of the beholder. Examples come from Greek pottery, hand-woven carpets and architectural friezes. In a number of cases the two bands or patterns can be semicommensurate, with the periodicities tied to each other in a simple, low ratio of 1:2, 1:3, 2:3, etc.

Order-disorder phenomena

If the local adjacency (neighborhood) conditions between one motif element and the adjacent element fail to unambiguously determine the position of the third consecutive (etc.) element in respect to the first one, a (potentially) disordered pattern results instead of a strictly ordered one. This can happen when the pattern can be divided into stripes with two equivalent positions of stripe No. 2 in respect to the previous stripe (Fig. 51) or when it can be divided into finite blocks with similar multiple possibilities. Figure 51 shows two of the fully *maximally ordered patterns* obtained in this situation; a number of more complicated or completely disordered patterns (sequences) are infinite. Faults of this kind exist in real ornaments.

Fig. 50. A monoclinic pattern constructed on a square mesh. Reproduced from Hinterreiter[7].

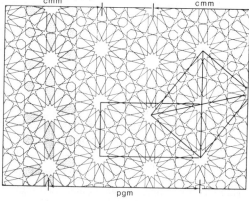

Fig. 51. An Arabic pattern with 14-fold rosettes as centers of local high symmetry. Ambiguity in the position of consecutive vertical layers results in two maximally ordered patterns, pgm and cmm. From [43].

Occupational disorder

A different type of disorder is the occupational disorder in which the same positions of a periodic pattern are occupied by different elements or colors. Early Mondrian, Klee and Vasarely works often utilize this principle, based on a rectangular net. Op Art pictures of this type (Barrett[35]) are almost identical with the computer models of scientists studying such phenomena in crystals.

Local high symmetry

The above positional disorder is caused by local symmetry higher than that of the appropriate site in the plane group in question. The preference for the high-symmetry elements (from regular triangles and squares to the manyfold stars of Islamic ornaments) represents the embedding of such elements into an environment with much lower symmetry. The elements attached to their adjacent vertices are different and may eventually lead to order–disorder phenomena.

Dichotomy/branching

Dichotomy/branching is rarely observed in the world of crystals (dendrites) but it represents the main principle in the world of higher plants, combined with similarity. It is a frequent biological analogue of translation. Its possibilities were not extensively used in art, perhaps because of the inevitable cluttering or excessive diminution of elements after merely a small number of steps. A two-dimensional design built on a combination of dichotomy with similarity (plus twinning of the overall pattern) was created by Escher in his *Square Limit* (1964) and corresponding computer graphics by Kolomyjec (Franke[37]). Two patterns of this category created by the present author are in Figs. 52(a) and (b). Kolomyjec and Schott attempted to use artistically two- to fourfold branching in linear patterns (Franke[37]).

Modulation

Modulation is a new way of describing more-or-less continuous long-range variations/changes in crystal structures, or in patterns, which proceed as a wave in one direction. These changes may be geometrical in nature (transversal or longitudinal modulations) or "compositional" (changes of shape, size, color or other properties of topological discs). Geometric modulation, e.g. the sinusoidal one, has been used by Hinterreiter and a number of Op artists (Hinterreiter[7,18]; Barrett[35]). The striped color patterns of many cultures, especially including those from Moorish Alhambra, not readily describable as color groups, can be understood as color-modulated monochroic or dichroic designs. In the latter case, it is the black component that is color modulated. Color modulations (or gradations) were frequently used by Vasarely.

Fig. 52. (a), (b) Two patterns based on dichotomy combined with similarity. The right-hand design, with antisimilarity, can be twinned by means of a sixfold rotation axis.

Hierarchy and superposition/overlay of symmetries

These categories may have just a few counterparts in nature. In order to avoid monotony, artists or artisans often combine quite opposite types of symmetries, e.g. those based on reflection and those with rotation or glide-reflection components only. They organize them into a hierarchy which develops from local (often point-group) symmetries through fragments of band or plane patterns toward the general layout of the entire design. The "carpet pages" of Irish religious manuscripts or Oriental hand-woven carpets present ample examples for this hierarchy, as do Baroque and Rococo interiors.

The most important hierarchy of symmetries occurs during the creative work of the artisan or artist. Most often the first stage is a linear design with uncolored high symmetry. This will often be reduced when the boundaries are worked out into an interlacing pattern, as in Arabic or Celtic designs. Finally, one of the possible black-and-white or colored symmetries is selected from the ones possible in the given case.

Superposition of symmetries (Shubnikov and Koptsik[1]) represents a very expressive artistic tool, especially in modern art. One widely used method in some schools is the dissymmetrization by addition of a small asymmetric element(s) into the otherwise perfectly symmetrical design. Among the masters of this method belonged New Zealand Maoris (Donnay & Donnay[5]) and the artists of the Art Noveau period (e.g. Mucha *et al.*[42]). Not so "destructive" in terms of symmetry are the symmetry-reducing elements such as bands, fields, flowers, etc., introduced into highly symmetrical designs in ancient Egypt and elsewhere. They lead to lower symmetries with pseudosymmetry of a higher system (often tetragonal or hexagonal).

Another type of superposition of symmetries is typified by Vasarely's pictures from the 1960s. A highly symmetrical plane pattern (usually a square grid or a pattern of parallel lines) is transferred onto an object with a point-group symmetry or, alternatively, "convoluted" with a nonperiodic function (an array of geometric shapes) of a certain kind. Vasarely maps plane patterns even onto animal figures, Pierrots and ladies, and "wraps" them around the axonometric projections of three-dimensional geometric bodies. Yet another sort of superposition of symmetries is the above-mentioned mapping of congruent patterns onto most variegated types of nets by Hinterreiter.

Antiphase boundaries

Antiphase boundaries is probably the best name for the method very often used by modern artists working in black-and-white (i.e. "opposite-phase") designs; they represent planes of often irregular shape and not coincident with the mirror or glide-reflection planes of symmetry of the pattern (motif) on which the color of stripes or blocks is changed to its opposite (Fig. 8). In this way, a very expressive pattern can be achieved without introducing additional symmetry. In multicolored patterns similar *out-of-phase* boundaries can exist which displace colors of stripes (blocks) within the existing geometric pattern.

Enhancement of symmetry

Enhancement of symmetry, as the opposite of dissymmetrization, heightens the symmetry of the design. In this process an artist or artisan will consciously heighten the symmetry of an object in which certain elements suggest such a possibility. Often it is a human figure in which the body and the limbs are schematized into a symmetric arrangement, the problem of the head being treated in different ways. Numerous examples come from Papua–New Guinea and the Melanesian region. Another example, undoubtedly with a narrative behind it, comes from New Zealand (Fig. 53). The above tropical regions abound with the examples of symmetry enhancement of schematized faces, with the horizontal pseudo-mirror plane through the eyes (Fig. 21). Although symbolism undoubtedly plays a role, enhancement of symmetry is evident. Enhancement of symmetry and periodicity of inscriptions and texts was a clear driving force in Islamic calligraphy (Fig. 54) and in the development of Gothic script.

EPILOGUE

In the present paper I have attempted to make you acquainted with the more complicated categories of symmetry as applied to the visual arts. Furthermore, I have tried to stress some

Fig. 53. A Maori woodcarving with a double-headed figure as an example of the enhancement of symmetry. Courtesy The Chicago Museum of Natural History.

Fig. 54. An Islamic inscription from the Bu-Inaniyyah madrasa in Meknés, Morocco (1358). Enhancement of apparent symmetry and periodicity by means of letter spacing and floral scrolls.

general observations on the topic of symmetrology in the arts and to bring factual observations in this field which I have accumulated over a number of years. None of the topics given here can be considered complete; the paper was quickly assuming the proportions of a book and had to be cut off at many points. However, if I have succeeded in stirring your interest in this subject and in revealing its inherent beauty, it has fulfilled its purpose.

Acknowledgments—I would like to extend my thanks to Mrs R. Larsen and Mr J. Tomáš, who labored on a number of drawings, to Mr O. B. Berthelsen for the photographic work, and to Mrs U. Koester, who typed the manuscript. Thanks are extended to Professor A. Forge and Dr H. Morphy, A.N.U., Canberra, for generously sharing their research material, as well as to the authors, publishers and other copyright holders who allowed the reproduction of selected figures from the quoted books. I want to thank my family for putting up with the books and manuscripts strewn all over the living room and for having their father turned into a draftsman every evening for a couple of months. Finally may thanks go to the editor, Professor I. Hargittai, for this opportunity and for his patience with my slow progress.

REFERENCES

1. A. V. Shubnikov and V. A. Koptsik, *Symmetry in Science and Art*. Plenum Press, New York–London (1974).
2. J. V. Smith, *Geometrical and Structural Crystallography*. John Wiley & Sons, New York (1982).
3. M. J. Buerger, *Elementary Crystallography*. John Wiley, New York (1956).
4. D. Schattschneider, The plane symmetry groups: their recognition and notation. *Am. Math. Monthly* **85**, 439–450 (1978).
5. J. D. H. Donnay and G. Donnay, Symmetry and antisymmetry of Maori rafter designs. *Empirical Studies of the Arts* **3**, 23–45 (1985).
6. E. H. Gombrich, *The Sense of Order*. Phaidon Press, Oxford (1979).
7. H. Hinterreiter, *Die Kunst der reinen Form*. Facsimile edition of manuscripts from 1936 to 1948. Ediciones Ebusus, Ibiza-Amsterdam (1978).
8. C. M. MacGillavry, *Symmetry Aspects of M. C. Escher's Periodic Drawings*. IUC, Utrecht (1965).
9. B. K. Vainshtein, *Modern Crystallography I. Symmetry of Crystals. Methods of Structural Crystallography*. Springer-Verlag, Berlin (1981).
10. B. Grünbaum and G. C. Shephard, Tilings, patterns, fabrics and related topics. *Jahresber. d. Deutsch. Math. Verein.* **85**, 1–32 (1983).
11. H. Wondratschek, Symmetrie in der Ornamentik. *Schriftenreihe d. Techn. Univ. Wien* **16**, 43–59 (1980).
12. A. M. Zamorzaev and A. F. Palistrant, The two-dimensional Shubnikov groups. *Sov. Phys.-Cryst.* **5**, 497–503 (1961).
13. H. Heesch, Zur Strukturtheorie der ebenen Symmetriegruppen. *Z. Krist.* **71**, 95–102 (1929).
14. A. Niggli, Zur Systematik und gruppentheoretischen Ableitung der Symmetrie, Antisymmetrie und Entartungs-symmetriegruppen. *Z. Krist.* **111**, 288–300 (1959).
15. V. L. Indebom, Relation of the antisymmetry and colour symmetry groups to one-dimensional representations of the ordinary symmetry groups. Isomorphism of the Shubnikov and space groups. *Sov. Phys.-Cryst.* **4**, 578–580 (1960).
16. N. V. Belov and T. N. Tarkhova, Colour symmetry groups. *Sov. Phys.-Cryst.* **1**, 5–11, 478–488 (1956).
17. B. L. van der Waerden and J. J. Burckhardt, Farbgruppen. *Z. Krist.* **115**, 231–234 (1961).
18. H. Hinterreiter, *Geometrische Schönheit*. Hostmann–Steinbergschen Farbenfabriken, Celle (1958).
19. J. Jung (Ed.), *Die Welten des M. C. Eschers*, 3rd Edn. M. Pawlak Verlaggess. mbH, Herrsching (1971).

20. V. A. Koptsik, Advances in theoretical crystallography. Colour symmetry of defect crystals. *Kristall und Technik* **10**, 231–245 (1975).
21. F. Boas, *Primitive Art*. Dover, New York (1955).
22. P. Fořtová-Šámalová, *Egyptian Ornament*. A. Wingate Ltd., London (1963).
23. A. Parrot, *Sumer*. Gallimard (1960).
24. G. Bain, *Celtic Art. The Methods of Construction*. Dover, New York (1973).
25. A. Forge, Style and meaning in Sepik art. In *Primitive Art and Society* (Edited by A. Forge). Oxford University Press, London and New York (1973).
26. H. Morphy, The art of Northern Australia. In *Aboriginal Australia* (Edited by C. Cooper *et al.*), Austral. Gallery Dir. Council Ltd., Sydney (1981).
27. E. Makovicky, The crystallographic art of Hans Hinterreiter. *Z. Krist.* **150**, 13–21 (1979).
28. K. L. Wolf and R. Wolff, *Symmetrie*. Böhlau-Verlag, Münster-Köln (1956).
29. A. V. Shubnikov, Symmetry of similarity. *Sov. Phys.-Cryst.* **5**, 469–476 (1961).
30. A. M. Zamorzayev, E. I. Galyarskiy and A. F. Palistrant, *Colored Symmetry, Its Generalizations and Applications* (in Russian). Shtiintsa, Kishinev (1978).
31. M. Ryan (Ed.), *Treasures of Ireland*. Royal Irish Academy, Dublin (1983).
32. M. Staber (Ed.), *The Non-Objective World* 1914–1955. Annely Juda Fine Art, London (1973).
33. W. and G. Audsley, *Designs and Patterns from Historic Ornament*. Dover, New York (1968).
34. O. Hahn, *Vasarely* 1930–1970. Tudor, New York (1970).
35. C. Barret, *Op Art*. Studio Vista, London (1970).
36. M. Hrbas and E. Knobloch, *Umění Střední Asie*. State Publ. House for Letters and Arts, Prague (1965).
37. H. W. Franke, *Computergrafik-Galerie: Bilder nach Programm*; *Kunst in elektronischen Zeitalter*. Du Mont, Köln (1984).
38. H. S. M. Coxeter, Regular compound tessellations of the hyperbolic plane. *Proc. R. Soc. A* **278**, 147–167 (1964).
39. H. S. M. Coxeter, The non-Euclidian symmetry of Escher's picture "Circle Limit III." *Leonardo* **12**, 19–25 (1979).
40. H. J. Albrecht and R. Koella *Hans Hinterreiter* (Edited by I. Schlégl). Waser Verlag Buchs, Zürich (1982).
41. E. Makovicky, The building principles and classification of bismuth–lead sulphosalts and related compounds. *Fortschr. Miner.* **59**, 137–190 (1981).
42. A. Mucha, M. Verneuil and G. Auriol, *Art Nouveau Designs in Color*. Dover, New York (1974).
43. E. Makovicky and M. Makovicky, Arabic geometrical patterns—a treasury for crystallographic teaching. *N. Jb. Miner. Mh.*, **1977**, 58–68 (1977).
44. Y. M. Safadi, *Islamic Calligraphy*. Shambhala, Boulder (1979).
45. R. Koella, *Ausstellung Hans Hinterreiter*. Kunstverein, Winterthur (1973).
46. I. Schlégl and C. van der Voort (Eds.), *Hans Hinterreiter*. Galerie Schreiner, Basel (1977).

Comp. & Maths. with Appls. Vol. 12B, Nos. 3/4, pp. 981–997, 1986
Printed in Great Britain.

0886-9561/86 $3.00 + .00
© 1986 Pergamon Press Ltd.

A RECURRING GEOMETRICAL PATTERN IN THE EARLY RENAISSANCE IMAGINATION

L. A. CUMMINGS
University of Waterloo, Waterloo, Ontario, Canada

Abstract—In 15th century Italy, a group of new imaginative devices appeared which we recognize as typifying what we call the Renaissance, many of which share a common, usually hidden characteristic— a meeting or crossing of axes of information at a focal point which in turn radiates its power outward into a circular pattern. This quasisymmetrical motif appears in artistic theory, certain paintings, plans and details of architecture, in renovations of townscapes, in the planning of new towns, in political tendencies, and in philosophical and theological beliefs. On a deep level, it becomes one of the hallmarks of much contemporary and later human expression.

Chartres Cathedral (1194–1220) may well have been constructed on the geometrical ideas garnered out of close reading of Plato's Timaeus, since it was in the famous Cathedral School of Chartres that these studies were pursued. But whether or not the theories pondered there were part of the design of the church, the mathematics apparent in the edifice displayed clearly the use of chalkline, compass, and plumbline in its visible features according to some code. The splendid geometry of the Gothic cathedral, primarily a creation of mastermasons and designers within the royal domains in and surrounding Paris, was largely inspired by the Chartrain triumph, and this French style spread across much of Europe (Fig. 1). Through a number of transformations and incrustations, it remained the dominant style in Europe until a new mode emerged in the 15th century which announced a simpler mathematics in architectural design. The "modern" forms, before the revisionist reaction which we call the Renaissance, had, as one feature, an organizing around movement, around time, and around narrative that is found not only in architecture but also in numerous other imaginative creations ranging from manuscript illuminations to the makeup of towns. This contemporary concern was in large part unawares. A treatment of this imaginative figure will be reserved for another essay to be published shortly. Today a figure that seems almost a replacement of the Medieval one will be our subject.

One place where this Gothic narrative was not an expected commitment of an architect was in Tuscany, which managed to maintain a local building style throughout the Middle Ages and the Renaissance. With a renewal of interest in old Roman remains, Florentine architects modified the indigenous forms with Roman motifs. It is this mode, touched by the supple brilliance of Filippo Brunelleschi (1377–1446), which was the first expression in visual art of what we now recognize as a starting point of the Early Renaissance. The new style was not merely a concern with pillars and pilasters rather than piers, colonnades rather than giant nave arcades, round instead of pointed arches, linteled windows, pediments, the four orders and all the other Vitruvian trappings of imperial Rome, not merely with an attempt to render static the dynamic swoops of the Gothic by means of rectangularities, not merely the reduction in building size nor the treatment of buildings as monuments, nor the interest in reestablishing the wall after its Medieval mason had opened it up until he produced a vaulted, stone cage. A belief in the Pythagorean harmonies encouraged by a Platonic revival moved architects to erect buildings in a new system of proportions and modularity culled out of Vitruvius (1st century B.C.) and out of direct archeological investigation of Roman ruins as exemplars of Vitruvian mathematical orderings, and also, I believe, out of the medieval university *quadrivium* an interrelated group of cosmic ideas was announced. Its earliest voice was the Florentine Leon Battista Alberti (1404?–1472), who, in his *De pictura* (1435), *De re aedificatoria* [*On Architecture*] (written between 1443 and 1452), and *De statua* (1464) puts forth the manifestos and handbooks of the new art. Out of musical theory, we can abstract the mathematical ratios and propositions that are present in musical harmony and that are capable of arithmetical and geometrical description and hence may be used in the ordering of architecture. These musical and mathematical elements are universal, and our approbation of an artwork designed according to them is because of our very makeup as humans. But these discussions of the geometry of

Fig. 1. The choir vaults at the cathedral church of Our Lady at Amiens (begun in 1220 by Robert de Luzarches and completed after 1258 by Thomas de Cormont), hanging 144 ft overhead, display pointed arch, rib vaults, the stone cage of glass, the restless motion of line, the dynamism of thrust and counterthrust, the patterning of light and dark, and the episodic entry into new, unrevealed spaces.

things and the artifacts that men and women made because of their belief in them had as a byproduct (or perhaps as an unrecognized cause) a stylistic mark which appeared not merely in architecture but in other human designs—artistic, literary, civic, political, philosophical, theological.

The new involvement with geometric ordering of mental and physical objects, which arose first in 15th century Florence and expanded from Tuscany to all of Europe, has been studied so frequently that I shall not try to rehearse the scholarship here; Wittkower provides a record of earlier discussions. My interest is with a single pervasive imaginative model that was structured by crossing axes of information making a strong definition of their intersection, imparting added energy to the center of the construct, which then served as a focus to the generally radial arrangement that resulted. Often the figure developed out of an initial center point and radius, inverting the former sequence. The forms sometimes becomes a star or a half-circular or spherical form or other less-clear manifestations, but what is always present is the multiaxial symmetry about the point. The ubiquity of the image suggests to me that it is an ordering device basic to the Renaissance imagination. While the arrangement occurs before this period and since, it is so widespread and often unconscious as to be one of the hallmarks of many a Renaissance thing, just as narrative movement in time is a hallmark of many a Medieval thing.

The radial axes are found in connection with other recognizably Renaissance motifs. There is, for instance, the Renaissance belief in man as a free-standing metaphysical object rather than a figure in a spiritual niche on the skin of a huge architectural synthesis dedicated to God. While was not ready to defy the heavens like Byron's Childe Harold and to call destruction down on himself like the 20th century man—for he still thought of himself as a Christian (indeed, as a refined and more advanced one than his ordinary, modern, Gothic neighbor)— he began to enjoy more luxuriously than men had heretofore the notion that he was somehow the epitome of the universe, containing existence (like a stone), growth and vitality (like a vegetable), mobility and spirit (like an animal), and intelligent spirituality (like an angel). He was the microcosm, the bearer of the image of God. Pico della Mirandola went so far as to claim that men could become gods. Since he was made in God's image and was a summary of the cosmos, he was not surprised to see himself physically as the measure of all things, however superficial such literalness might seem (Figs. 2, 3). That this was a distorted view of the anatomy is irrelevant; what was in his head—the image—was of his own central position at which all modes of existence crossed and around which the astronomical universe rotated. He depicted his body as some kind of cosmic yardstick by drawing himself as inscribed in a circle with his arms and legs radiating out to act as the definers of the circle. He reaches out to be the measure of geometric form, of the arrangement of the world and of the stars: the cosmos radiates from him, he is its center—with the implication that he orders or begets it in some sense. The harmony of the universe is found in its suitability to himself (Fig. 4). This geometric man was not limited to such diagrams. In his idealization of himself, he examined his own body and found it most satisfactory—so satisfactory that the nude became a frequent object for the painter and the sculptor. Like the nudes of other ages, the new nude was not an attempt to imitate the human physiology in any photographic way but instead developed into some ideal form—an aesthetic model, a genre; the ideal Renaissance form conformed to the geometric pattern which we are investigating. As Sir Kenneth Clark remarked of nude sculpture,

> . . . the antique male nude is like a Greek temple, the flat frame of the chest being carried on the columns of the legs; whereas the Renaissance nude is related to the architectural system that produced the central-domed church; so that instead of the sculptural interest depending on a simple, frontal plane, a number of axes radiate from one center. Not only the elevation but, so to say, the ground plans of these figures would have an obvious relationship to their respective architectures [11, p. 45].

We shall return to the architectural parallels. Just for a moment we might move from the consideration of the figure of man within the circle to consideration of the circle itself.

The circle which man's body defined was also a talisman. Alberti says,

> It is manifest that Nature delights principally in round Figures, since we find that most Things which are generated, made or directed by Nature, are round. Why need I instance the Stars, Trees, Animals, the Nests of Birds, or the like Parts of the Creation, which she has chosen to make generally round?

He goes on to derive several polygons from the circle which inscribes them; all the polygonal buildings that are implied would be based on the radii of such circles, that is, they are constructed out of the circle—are derivatives of it[3, p. 138]. Circular plans, as we shall see, became an

Fig. 2. Instead of the usually depicted Leonardo figure, it is instructive to see Francesco Giorgio's flaccid effort in his *De Harmonia Mundi* (1525) and Cesariano's monstrous one (Fig. 3) in his 1521 edition of Vitruvius to organize the geometry of the circle around man's belly button.

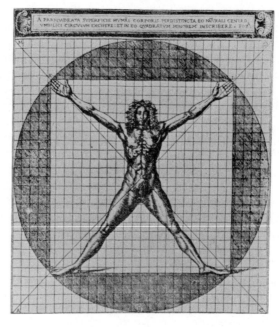

Fig. 3. See caption to Fig. 2.

admired form, and architectural critics begin to argue for the superiority of the circular church and the centrally planned church rather than the usual cruciform one, even though the latter was more functional for Catholic ritual. Instead of vaulting or polygonal towers at the crossing of the transepts, round domes—hemispherical or vaulted—were used. Painters, I find, did not use the circle as a compositional device to any extraordinary extent. However, the painting or the sculptural relief or casting were more often designed for and placed in a round frame than ever before. Moritz Hauptmann in his study of such rotondos finds dozens of 15th century exemplars, Italian and Florentine. We can recall readily the work of the Della Robbias and of Fra Filippo Lippi. Piero della Francesca and Botticelli often depicted the human head as rounded into a regular egg shape (Figs. 5 and 6), and Botticelli in addition often provided carrot-like limbs to his figures, as the *Venus on the Half-shell* (Fig. 7) and his *Primavera*. The regularization of the human shape into Albertian rounded shapes is the generation of a circular cross section, which reduces the human to an underlying geometrical demand.

Besides the subservience to the intersecting axes of the circle, sphere, and cylinder, we may notice the painter's discovery of vanishing point perspective. The Medieval illuminator knew of the three-dimensional modelling of a shape and of the lighting of such a shape, of aerial perspective, of recession by size and by colors and by height in the composition, and of the overlapping of planes. All of these imitate "reality," how we see. But the theorists, delighting in yet another use of geometry, produced geometric perspective—a device which postulates a picture plane and at least one vanishing point which gathers at one place all the linear rays from that plane into a simulation of life. This artistic trick had two interesting effects. It locked the observer to a particular place in relation to the picture plane if he was to enjoy the full effect of the view; his eye became a mirror of the vanishing point, with all the rays of the depiction gathering together in his eye. The second effect was that the artist attempts to assert that space is volumetric; it is no longer merely a transparent medium, or a place, or a series of stations, but it has definable area (this is the first great cartographic age) and depth— it has length, width, and height and can be boxed in. If the artist's view of the world is an imitation of the world, then man beholds the painting trapped at a focal point looking into volumetric space with all the points on the objects of nature radiating lines toward his eye and his judicious intelligence. He is imagined as being created at the center of a universe which radiates out from him, as if he is in some way its generator, or at least, the justification of its generation, and its sole upholder. He is the intersection of all streams of information, he is the center and perhaps the source of the universe. Unavoidably Pico, following a verbal track rather than a pictorial one, ended in heresy. Such new dogmas of man's place in the universe were

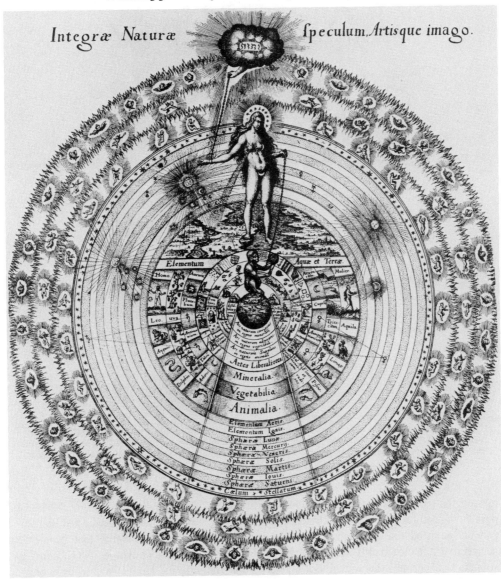

Fig. 4. A convenient if late rendition of an orderly universe in Robert Fludd's *Utriusque cosmi maioris scilicet et minoris metaphysica, physica atque technica historia* (Oppenheim, 1617) in which the geocentric cosmos, the planetary influences, the metals, the elements, everything is ordered according to the convenience of that paragon of animals—man; Mother Nature is but his servitor.

confirmed in these excited Italian minds because of the way the nature of space and of vision affirmed for them man's harmonious place in the universe. Why one would want to be the center of the universe is a puzzle until we have explored this desire for the array of other such centerings. Even the vanishing point is placed on the central vertical axis of the painting, often near the central horizontal axis, and often at their intersection. Geometric perspective also sees space not as lighted or infinite or circumstantial but as volumetric; by it space was captured, conquered, controlled. The mere notion of treating the objects in the Renaissance perspective box as if they assumed shape in volume (rather than mere space) and, like dolls in a child's playhouse, stood erect and were seen to behave like live things in that fully captured volume was the source of power over matter. Later, in the High Renaissance, Raphael (1483–1520) modified the geometry of painterly penetration of the surface by using a spiral to organize the figures on the flat plane, by showing a single figure twisting into a spiral or by arranging a number of bodies or elements into an upward swirling helix. Here more complicated geometries are seen to occur within the perspective geometry (often repressed), a tableau not denied until the 17th century Northern artists Rubens and Rembrandt denied it (Rubens by explosions of virtuoso color splashes and Rembrandt by a Manichean confrontation of light and dark) to

Fig. 5. A detail from Piero della Francesca's fresco in the Church of St. Francis in Arezzo depicting some of the retinue of the Queen of Sheba on her visit to Solomon. Hairdo, nose, and hat are affixed to eggs. If God did not arrange heads thus, we can provide what is deficient with the circle's perfecting touch. This cubistic abstraction was usual in Piero, Paolo Uccello, Sandro Botticelli, and other 14th century painters.

reassert the pictorial and two-dimensional quality, even though both preserve the illusionistic push by the painter into the wall. There are other ways in which High Renaissance and Mannerist painters adjusted the optimistic Early Renaissance models, but this belief that geometrical perspective reflected reality was so steadfast that all the later manipulations play against this strongly converging axial vector. But the use of our figure in the High Renaissance is beyond our search in this essay.

In passing, we might notice that one effect of such centralizing symmetries and near symmetries is to give the composition a certain balance, a *stasis* on a point of rest, a calm moment. Either as a result of this, or as a mutual effect of the theory of harmonies, which would focus on fixed proportional relationships rather than the onflowing of the melody or the story, there is a frequent treatment of instants in time. Medieval artists were not averse to a serial presentation in a succession of united panels or in a single frame which presented connected events differing in time in one universal vision (Fig. 8). Instead of a narrative view chronologically arranged, the new artist (Fig. 9) often gives us a selected crucial moment of his legend around which other undepicted acts which we are expected to recall are balanced as cause or as result. To dramatize this instantaneousness, the artist often displays a fragment of a great story, whose importance is as yet unrecognized by the spectators, who casually go about their business without awareness.

Ordinarily builders as builders would not have been interested in perspective drawings because such a technique would not present mensurated drawings from which masons and carpenters could work. Wolfgang Lotz in a classic essay discussing extant drawings and statements[23, pp. 1–18] allows that perhaps such a rendering might have been useful to help a client understand a proposed structure, but there is little evidence of such a use for perspectives as working documents. According to Lotz, the 14th century Florentine architect built a largish wooden model, apparently after he had explained his drawing of the plan to the client's sat-

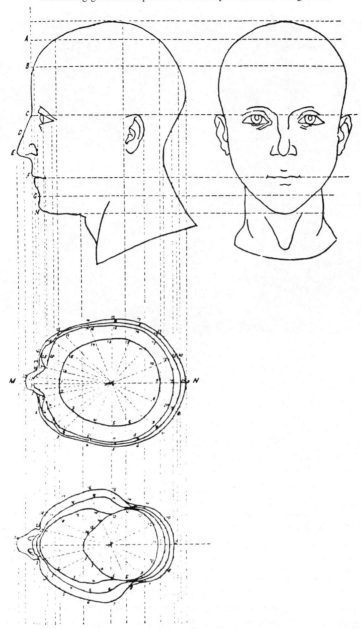

Fig. 6. That Piero was serious about radial centricity is shown in this sketch from his *De perspectiva pingendi* (*On Perspective in Painting*), written between 1480 and 1490. By perspective in his title he means geometry and little else. These drawings suggest that Piero sought out a radialism to give structure, just as Kenneth Clark speaks of cross sections of nudes.

isfaction. It seems that the model and plan and the direction of the architect on the site were sufficient. There are the stories of Brunelleschi's locking up his large model for the dome of S. M. del Fiore in a building to prevent his rival Ghiberti from seeing its solution and on another occasion of his angry destruction of his model for a proposed palazzo when Cosimo de'Medici declined it as so elaborate that it would arouse envy. Alberti prefers the use of the model as the principal tool of design[3, pp. 22–23]. Despite its lack of technical accuracy, perspective drawing and the imaginary control it gave to the presentation of a space had its appeal for architects. Antonio Manetti (1423–1491) describes Brunelleschi's constructing gadgets to give the illusion of perspective space. On one occasion, he painted on a panel an exact depiction of the piazza in front of the cathedral in the middle of whose square sits the Baptistry church S. Giovanni, but for the sky he contrived a mirrored surface of burnished silver meeting the edges of the buildings in his rendition. When viewed through another mirror held at arm's length and

Fig. 7. Botticelli abstracts from and regularizes the human form to reach some level of Platonic transcendent forms; as the principal device for these idealizations, he employs the roundures of the circle—the sphere, the tube or tubular, the egg, the arc, and such—in his painting of the Birth of Venus (after 1482), now in the Uffizi in Florence.

looked at through a hole in the panel, the beholder saw an apparently exact reproduction with clouds moving over the buildings. But the mirror had to be held in proportion to the distance that the painter was from S. Giovanni.

> Since in such a painting it is necessary that the painter postulate beforehand a single point from which his painting must be viewed, taking into account the length and width of the sides as well as the distance, in order that no error would be made in looking at it (since any point outside of that single point would change the shapes to the eye), he made a hole in the painted panel . . .[24, p. 44].

This is the reason, Manetti adds, that the hole was made—to compel the beholder to be in the right place. A requirement of perspective painting is that the observer is obliged to be on-line at an ideally fixed focus of the converging rays from the object. He is captured in space by the very device that creates the effect, just as beholders of perspective paintings are. The author of the anonymous *Life* describes how Alberti amazed his Roman friends with scenic perspective boxes which put the observer's eye at the focus of all the lines coming from the painting [according to John Spencer[1], pp. 105–106, note 27]. An architecture that was often based on a typology of small- or middle-sized works elevated on a pedestal and freestanding as a monument or art object, might be set off from other buildings by perspective alignments; likewise, those Early Renaissance paintings that weighted down streets with elongated massive masonry (boxed in the form of palazzi) would naturally provide perspective effects, being foreshortenings of the rectangular and rectilinear. But when the architect shaped larger parts of the city above the scale of the single building, he might (but did not always) resort to a playing with perspective. The Belvedere Gardens in the Vatican were deliberately ordered to emphasize geometrical perspective so that it would perform as an organizing device, but here we are already in High Renaissance design.

However intrigued Early Renaissance architects were with geometrical axes giving a focused perspective, in their actual drawings and structures we can see frequent displays of centralizing devices (the circle, the round arch and vault, the dome) all inviting analysis into a continuum of radial axialities intersecting at a central point. The circle (or derivatives—the pentagon, the octagon, etc.) in plan was not an invention of the Florentine architects, nor was it merely an aping of pagan Roman practice. Constantinian Christian rotundas were still in use in Rome, as were several Carolingian examples in the North; the form was in use in Italy in baptistries. Brunelleschi used it for the sacristy of San Lorenzo in Florence, and for a free-standing church in Santa Maria degli Angeli (1434) (Fig. 10), though it was never completed. Alberti, Filarete (writing between ca. 1457 and 1464) Francesco di Giorgio Martini (writing between 1482 and 1492) all commended its appropriateness for churches, and the form was widely used in Italy in the 15th century. Wittkower[31, p. 20] names 13 such designs, excluding mere chapels and sacristies, which were also numerous; Wolfgang Lotz[22] and Staale Sinding-Larsen[30] also trace the form, the latter adding several more to Wittkower's list (Appendix I). Sinding-Larsen[30] especially reveals the opposition of the clergy to such designs as being inconvenient to ritual and custom and as being copies of pagan temples, but so strong was the architect's advocacy of the circle and its derivatives that these plans flowered even more in the next century. In such churches, the architects preferred the high altar to be at the center, though they often agreed to place it on the circumference opposite the main entrance. The Greek cross was also recommended and built, sometimes as a compromise form for the more desirable circular form, but it also displays a multiple axial arrangement around a common point, from which all other parts of the church (in an ideal plan) might be visible. Such circular or Greek-cross architectural interiors are best understood by standing at the focus and looking in each direction to discover

Fig. 8. Completed in 1423, this altarpiece by Gentile da Fabriano is in the International Gothic style. Its narrative character is seen in the main picture of the Adoration of the Magi which shows in the background two stages of their approach to the final episode of the Adoration. But this large picture is but an episode in a larger narrative: underneath in the predella, we witness the Nativity before the Magi's appearance and simultaneously the *Gloria in excelsis* to the shepherds on the hills, the Flight into Egypt (after their appearance), and the Circumcision. But before all this, we see up in the gables the angel Gabriel announcing across to the filigree and the face of God the Father to Mary that she is to be the mother of God the Son through the agency of God the Holy Ghost. The story goes even further back into the writings of the prophets who support the rondels which frame angel, Father, and Mother. Not an instant merely, but the whole intercausal myth is laid out.

Fig. 9. Piero's *The Flagellation* (between 1458 and 1466) provides examples of geometrical perspective carefully, even intricately (see R. Wittkower and B. A. R. Carter, *The Perspective of Piero della Francesca's
"Flagellation"*, *Journal of Warburg and Courtauld Institutes*, Vol. 16, pp. 292–302, London, 1953) worked
out, and advertised by the pavement patterns and the foreshortening of pictured architecture. The instant of time
is at the moment before the first whip descends; the torturer to Christ's left lifts his whip and leans back, Christ
looks at his whip hand as does the second torturer who also holds his whip ready; Christ's body is as yet
unmarked. Three modern men, who occupy half the painting, stand in casual conversation, oblivious to the
Passion of Jesus; they seem to be the three tormentors in the dress of contemporary Urbino, the one on the left
even assuming the posture of the turbaned tormentor.

the symmetrical disposition of the members (Fig. 11). Moving off this point obscures this view
somewhat. As with geometrical perspective, the beholder is ideally locked at one point to realize
the work, which then reveals its design instantaneously. As with the paintings, the architecture
produces a fixity, a calm, that is much unlike the Gothic activity and dynamism, and the Gothic
concealments. The intense interest in circles is also seen in elevations, especially in the interiors,
where the rounded floor plan is reflected by the circle molding at the edge of the central dome
floating over the hemispherical arches niched into the circumference, the pendentives and other
open spaces being marked by circular *oculi* or by *tondi* (Fig. 12). As with many Early Renaissance
motifs, the use of the round arch rather than the contemporary, Gothic pointed arch provided
the triple satisfactions of the perfection of the circular, of the learned classical reference, and
of the rejection of the "Medieval." Antonio Averlino, called Filarete (1400?–1465?) in his
imaginary dialogue with Francesco Sforza explains to his patron that round arches are superior
to pointed ones—"poor, modern" rather than the *arte antica*; they do not arrest the eye from
continuous movement along their circular outline[13, pp. 102–103]. As elsewhere in the expressions of the day we find a conscious attempt to foster a rejection of the traditional European
imaginative patterns and an acceptance of a new way of imagining, based, as can be seen, upon
ancient Roman exemplars and Greek philosophy. Filarete's argument for the round arch may
entail the round vault, and where a flat timber ceiling under a large timber gabled roof was not
applied (a traditional Italian practice) a large oblong room might be vaulted with the simplicity
and immediate availability of the barrel vault rather than the interdependencies and excitement
of the "Medieval" rib vault. Over circular and related forms, over the center of the Greek
cross, and over the crossing of the traditional Latin-type cross the architect preferred to place
a dome, which was sometimes hemispherical and sometimes a rounded octagon, curving upward
to give an interior that appeared hemispherical to the beholder standing at his fixed-point focus
below.

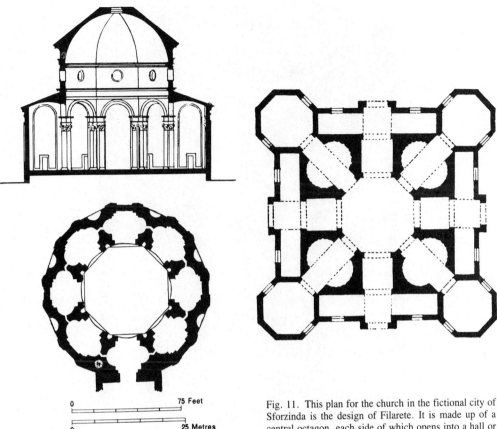

Fig. 10. Brunelleschi's S. Maria degli Angeli in Florence was begun in 1434 but discontinued in 1437; this reconstruction from the ground floor walls and contemporary engravings based on lost drawings was by Nicholas Pevsner[27, Fig. 127]. It is possibly the first Renaissance rotunda church.

Fig. 11. This plan for the church in the fictional city of Sforzinda is the design of Filarete. It is made up of a central octagon, each side of which opens into a hall or nave connecting with a further room or chapel. Thus, a Greek cross is formed, and then rotated 45° to form a second cross. The ensemble is crowned by a central dome and four corner towers. Only the corridors connecting the towers (forming a perfect square) are largely invisible from the central focus in the octagon, which controls the complex.

The concern with centricity is discernible in the organization of spaces larger than a single building. Medieval urban spaces had been developed into what is felt by the pedestrian as a series of episodes—narrow spaces turning and curving away fore and aft, followed by movement out of shadow into broad, sunlit open spaces into which debouch other streets, sometimes by means of almost slit-like entries. In the street, one cannot anticipate what is around the next turn, and in the piazza, the ordering is without a strong concern for symmetry or other geometrical ordering. To turn to a later but much admired example of the new vision, when Michelangelo reordered the buildings on top of the Capitoline Hill, he ignored the circumstantial history of the place by removing the easy connection with the Santa Maria in Ara Coeli by appliquing facades onto the Palazzi Senatorio and Conservatori, by erecting a third building to satisfy a desire to enclose his space and to block out the old church from the new square, by stationing the equestrian statue of Marcus Aurelius at a focus of the now inwardly turned space, and by paving the area with instructional, directional lines. When the Florentine Bernardo Rosselino (1409–1464) came to redesign the home village of Pope Pius II (regn. 1458–1464) at Pienza (Fig. 13) he also sought to cut out of the infinitude of earth and sky a controllable space by means of his buildings—cathedral, residences, palazzi—so as to contain the interest of the beholder by walling him in, as it were, into a geometrically designed space (an urban interior, as it were) arranged subtly and brutally to focus the lines of attraction on the west front of his church. As Guilio Argan said of Pienza,

The novelty in the Renaissance concept of space lay in the fact that perspective was no longer considered as the law of our vision but as a constructive rule of space itself; consequently, it was important as a principle of distribution of buildings in the design of the city[4, p. 21].

Fig. 12. The Pazzi Chapel was designed by Brunelleschi at once as a private chapel for the Pazzi family and as the chapter house for the monks of Santa Croce; it was erected ca. 1440–1461. An oblong, from its center at the intersection of its diagonals, the altar (here to the right) is set before one, set back in a square, identical right and left views, with the entrance at one's back. Round arches, rondels, oculi abound, and a ribbed dome floats overhead. The church is immediately understood from this focal point.

Such adjustments of common space according to some hitherto unrecognized rhetoric intimates that there may have been some pattern or figure of an ideal city in the minds of the architects. Indeed, Alberti describes the proper ordering for each element of the city piece by piece, as if he had a perfect city in mind, while Filarete unambiguously sets out to design such a city as a whole. Not surprisingly, his Sforzinda is composed of converging symmetrical axes into a common center, making an eight-pointed star inscribed in a circle (Fig. 14). Di Giorgio Martini provides several plans of ideal cities—all more or less octagonal, usually with axial streets radiating out to the walls from the center point or a central square (Fig. 15). When the Englishman St. Thomas More writes his dialogue of Utopia early in the next century, the whole island is a circle with an inland bay. It is possible to trace this concern with multiaxial symmetry in literature, but the examplars that occur to me most readily are in the 16th century, and beyond our present scope; I shall deal with them in another place.

Later, actual towns in Italy were constructed in the 16th century, when several were also established in the rest of Europe, and these generally form star shapes with streets radiating out from a central focus (e.g. Palmanova in Fruili) or stellated grid patterns with a central square at the meeting of transversing avenues (e.g. Villeneuve at Nancy). Almost always present in any adjustments in an old town or in the founding of a new town was an assertion of a center for the whole, from which pathways led to the periphery, springing out like the rays from a man's eye as he commanded the perspective scene. The ideal visual appearance of the urbanscape is depicted by painters, sometimes as background but sometimes as an object for itself (Fig. 16). It is usually a view of a piazza whose pavement is marked with a checkerboard pattern or lines to emphasize its ordering in the picture panel by geometric perspective with buildings

Fig. 13. This view of the cathedral square and the west front of the Cathedral of Pienza, an urban space that was erected at a stroke around 1460 by Bernardo Rossellino for Pope Pius II Piccolomini. The buildings have enclosed a space on four sides, forming a fifth room or shape. The palazzo to the left and right are axially tilted so as to draw together as they extend past the Cathedral, thus foreshortening the piazza and emphasizing the Cathedral front. An example of use of perspective lines to design urban space and to control the beholder.

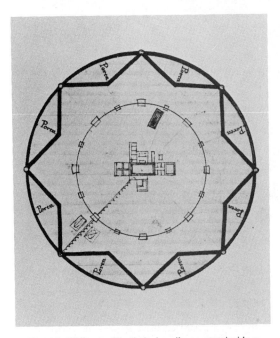

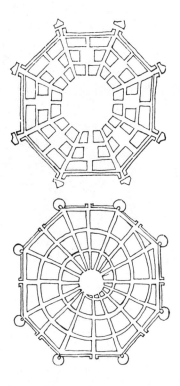

Fig. 14. Filarete's Sforzinda inscribes a star inside a circular wall and focuses in their center principal buildings. Faint radii (perhaps visible in the photograph) connect the center in the central building with the 16 points of the star, as if the power there generated this secondary wall, which blocks off a direct access by an invader fortunate enough to capture one of the ports.

Fig. 15. Two ideal cities by Francesco di Giorgio Martini showing radial streets whose axes cross the central piazza, which is the focus of interest. The bottom of the pair is a hill city.

Fig. 16. A late 15th century view of an imaginary city attributed to Piero or his "school," made for the ducal palace at Urbino. The sterility of this urban setting is only partly a result of the absence of people. The piazza's center is asserted by a monumental building, raised from the level of the pavement; it is a circular structure.

imagined after the new fashion set as geometric blocks in an almost stage-set frigidity and stillness. The onlooker is held at his focal point as one center while the painting itself recedes to another center (Fig. 17).

Beyond the realm of art and of theory, and the planning of townscapes and towns, in the domain of politics we can see further examples of this centralizing movement. The history of Florence in the 15th century can be seen as the gradual capture of power by the Medici from the oligarchic republic ruled by the councils of merchant burghers—in fact if not in title—until in 1478 the Pazzi conspiracy caused Lorenzo to make his control of the city overt; his son was able to "inherit" his primal position, and despite many vicissitudes in the first half of the next century actual titular power over Florence was centered in the head of the family. Elsewhere in Italy republican communes fell to strong men, who established hereditary princedoms. In

Fig. 17. One of the wall frescoes of the Sistine Chapel is by Pietro Perugino, *Giving the Keys to St. Peter* (1481). This central act, justifying the Sistine Chapel, Sixtus IV as pope, and the supremacy of the Chair of Peter and of the Church of Rome, is depicted in processions of figures left and right: all heads on the same level except Peter's; they stand in a checkerboard land declaring geometrical perspective and containing an elevated, octagonal, absolutely symmetrical building with a nearly hemispherical dome flanked at a distance by two triumphal arches. The buildings float over the heads of Christ and the passive apostles and modern Italians who witness the giving of the keys. In the space between the three edifices and the line of heads tiny figures flit, unaware of the great event or the monuments; they play games, a tiny saint addresses a casually collected crowd of young gentlemen, and a miniscule Stephen Protomartyr is being stoned to death. The three bands are pictorially united only by the recession of the squares of the checkerboard. Though this Renaissance piazza is peopled, it is cold and somehow void of energy other than the impulsions of geometry. The narrative structure—several related events (the preaching of the word and the beginning of the testimony of martyrs' blood coming from the giving of the keys) reported in the picture—is still Gothic.

France, after the disunity between the king and fractious nobles who sided with the English in the Hundred Years War against their chief amongst peers, Anjou and Provence came into the royal domain upon the death of the last male inheritor in 1481, and the next year saw the lordship of Picardy and Burgundy passed to Louis XI, while Charles VIII won Brittany by arms and marriage in 1491. Instead of a disunified, even warring internal arrangement, much of what we call France was now centralized under the direct control of the crown, with "the most productive tax system and the best organized military establishment in Europe," according to J. R. Hale[15, p. 68]. In Spain, the early part of the century saw "as monarchs of Castile and Aragon . . . men of mediocre competence whose reigns had been plagued by the revolts of dissident nobles and a widespread lawlessness"[15, p. 70]. In 1479, Isabella was able to end a five-year resistance to her succession to the throne of Castile, while her husband in the same year became King of Aragon, so that the union of the two crowns was announced. The history of their lives is one of subjecting independently minded nobles to the central power of the crowns. The fall of Granada in 1492, the discovery of America and the rapid response to that challenge by Castile, the success of the Aragonese policies and armies in the south of Italy are all emblems of the growing strength of Spain as the capable pair focused authority in the throne. In England, the jarring nobles had exhausted themselves in the War of the Roses, when the claimant Henry Tudor, fresh from his victory at Bosworth Field in 1485, was able to secure as great a power over his people as any English king had ever had, which he solidified capably so that the next century was ruled rigidly by his son and grandchildren. Whatever the varying circumstances, the common character of all of these was a centralization of authority in the Renaissance prince, and outside Italy, with the formation of the national state. As Eugene Rice wrote,

> Before 1453, we properly speak of the feudal state or feudal monarchy; after 1559, we speak more properly . . . of sovereign states[29, p. 92].

That is to say, the movement is from an assemblage of power by the nobility in some allegiance to a king to a focusing of power in a prince with noble but subordinate lieutenants to begin to constitute what we understand as the national state.

Amongst philosophers and theologians, the same concentration is noticeable. Marsilio Ficino (1433–1499), the founder of the so-called Florentine Neoplatonic Academy, and his able follower Giovanni Pico della Mirandola (1463–1494), in their desire for simplicity, for an intelligible and beautiful design and for a unifying focus through the harmonies, are led to attempts at unifying all the virtues in the union with the One God, thereby suggesting that here once more we have not merely a hierarchy but a model centering by collecting all the lines of speculation in a single point—God, and God in man, and indeed, man as God. In his *Oration on the Dignity of Man* (1486), Pico takes us up the Platonic ladder of successive revelations until

> . . . at last, smitten by the ineffable love as by a sting, and, like the Seraphim, born outside ourselves, filled with the godhead, we shall be, no longer ourselves, but the very One who made us[28, p. 27],

as the Christian dissolves into some Alexandrian oversoul that is the One which he becomes. But if this is Pico's course, and it is also yours, and mine, and all mankind's then all our courses ascend along our personal lines of Neoplatonic forms until we are all united in the One, centered in the Center, having become the Center (a figure of axial focus). Among the natural philosophers, the aspiration was not quite so overwhelming, and its clearest statement chronologically belongs more properly in the next century, for even though Nicolaus Copernicus (1473–1543) was lecturing on his heliocentric theory in Rome in 1500, his *On the Revolutions of the Celestial Spheres* was not published until 1543. This important though overrated book was the effusion of the desire to have a simple, clear design to the universe rather than the complicated, multimotional, nook-and-cranny cosmos the Medieval man accepted from Ptolemy. Instead of cumbersome cycles and epicycles, Copernicus desired (erroneously) simple spheres, and if that meant rearranging the universe, why then the universe would have to be arranged anew, and he would provide the mathematics—largely geometric—to permit it. Copernicus can be seen in as ridiculous a light as Pico in their obsession with focal centricity. The best minds of the day, if they touched Italy, were infected. Nicholas of Cusa on the Moselle (1401–1464) was at Padua (as Copernicus and possibly Pico later were to be, and as was Alberti earlier) in 1417 where he took his doctorate in canon law in 1423; by 1437 he was a papal diplomat and in 1448 a cardinal himself. Cusanus taught that a triangle infinitely expanded is a circle, so that the Trinity is an infinite Unity[12, I.xxi] and that

> Only in God are we able to find a centre which is with perfect precision equidistant from all points, for He alone is infinite equality. God, ever to be blessed, is, therefore, the centre of the world: He it is who is centre of the earth, of all spheres and of all things in the world; and at the same time He is the infinite circumference of all[12, II.xi].

Of course, like St. Augustine of Hippo and Pythagorus, Cusanus believed that the universe was designed, that mathematics was part of the design, that mathematics would reflect that design and God's hand in it, and that he was speaking by way of analogy. Nevertheless, it is curious that such a subtle intelligence as his would also find himself using the crossing of axes into a focal center that then radiated its power—here extended infinitely—as if it would be a way of describing the nature of God.

Before closing this all-too-quick survey, we must be reminded that the Early Renaissance concern with centricity was not the only "hidden" figure with geometrical properties. The triangle and the square and their three-dimensional expressions were ubiquitous organizing devices, as were indeed the other Platonic planar and solid shapes. Out of these a certain unawares principle of rectilinear arrest is produced. But my space is used up.

REFERENCES

1. L. B. Alberti, *On Painting* (Translated and edited by John R. Spencer). Yale University Press, New Haven (1956).
2. L. B. Alberti, *On Painting and On Sculpture: the Latin Texts of "De Pictura" and "De Statua"* (Translated and Edited by Cecil Grayson). Phaidon Press, London (1972).
3. L. B. Alberti, *Ten Books on Architecture* [Translated by James Leoni (1739), edited by Joseph Rykwert]. Alec Tiranti, London (1955). *De re aedificatoria* was written between 1443 and 1452 and circulated in manuscript; it was first printed in 1485.
4. G. C. Argan, *The Renaissance City* (Translated by S. E. Bassnett). George Braziller, New York (1969).
5. E. N. Bacon, *Design of Cities*. The Viking Press, New York (1967).
6. M. Baxandall, *Painting and Experience in Fifteenth Century Italy: a Primer in the Social History of Pictorial Style*. Oxford University Press, London (1972).
7. P. Bianconi, *All the Paintings of Piero della Francesca* (Translated by Paul Colacicchi). Hawthorne Books, New York (1962).
8. A. Blunt, *Artistic Theory in Italy* 1450–1600. Oxford University Press, London (1960, 1968).
9. E. Cassirer, P. O. Kristeller and J. H. Randall, Jr. (Eds), *The Renaissance Philosophy of Man: Petrarca, Valla, Ficino, Pico, Pomponazzi, Vives* (Translated by various hands). University of Chicago Press, Chicago (1948).
10. Sir Kenneth Clark, *The Art of Humanism*. John Murray Publishers, London (1983).
11. Sir Kenneth Clark, *The Nude: a Study in Ideal Form*. Pantheon, New York (1956, 1964).
12. N. Cusanus, *Of Learned Ignorance* (Translated by Germain Heron, introduction by D. J. B. Hawkins). Routledge and Kegan Paul, London (1954).
13. Il Filarete, *Treatise on Architecture, Being the Treatise by Antonio de Piero Avertino, known as Filarete* (Translated and edited by John R. Spencer), Vol. i. Yale University Press, New Haven (1965).
14. F. M. Godfrey, *Early Italian Painting* 1250–1500, Second edition. Taplinger Publishing, New York (1965).
15. J. R. Hale, *Renaissance Europe* 1480–1520. Collins, London (1971).
16. F. Hartt, *Art: A History of Painting, Sculpture, Architecture* (Edited by J. P. O'Neill), 2 vols. Harry N. Abrams, New York (1976).
17. M. Hauptmann, *Der Tondo: Ursprung, Bedeutung und Geschichte des Italianischen Rundbildes in Relief und Malerei*. Vittorio Klostermann, Frankfurt am Main (1936).
18. E. G. Holt (Ed), *Literary Sources of Art History: an Anthology of Texts from Theophilus to Goethe*. Princeton University Press, Princeton, NJ (1947).
19. L. H. Heydenreich and W. Lotz, *Architecture in Italy* 1400 to 1600 (Translated by M. Hottinger). Penguin Books, Harmondsworth, Middlesex (1974).
20. W. M. Ivins, Jr., *On the Rationalization of Sight, with an Examination of Three Renaissance Texts on Perspective*. Da Capo Press, New York (1938, 1973).
21. M. A. Lavin, *Piero della Francesca: The Flagellation*. Allen Lane/The Penguin Press, London (1972).
22. W. Lotz, Notes on the centralized Church of the Renaissance, in *Studies in Italian Renaissance Architecture*, pp. 66–73. The MIT Press, Cambridge, MA (1977).
23. W. Lotz, The Rendering of the Interior in Architectural Drawings of the Renaissance, in *Studies in Italian Renaissance Architecture*, pp. 1–65. The MIT Press, Cambridge, MA (1977).

24. A. di Iuccio Manetti, *The Life of Brunelleschi* (Translated by Catherine Enggass, edited by Howard Saalman). Pennsylvania State University Press, University Park, PA (1970).
25. T. More, *Utopia* (Translated by P. Turner). Penguin Books, Harmondsworth, Middlesex (1965).
26. P. Murray, *The Architecture of the Italian Renaissance*. Schocken Books, New York (1963).
27. N. Pevsner, *The Outline of European Architecture*, 7th Edn. Penguin Books, Harmondsworth, Middlesex (1968).
28. G. Pico della Mirandola, *Oration on the Dignity of Man* (Translated by A. R. Caponigri). Henry Regnery, Chicago (1956).
29. E. F. Rice, Jr., *The Foundations of Early Modern Europe* 1460–1559. W. W. Norton, New York (1970).
30. S. Sinding-Larsen, Some functional and iconographical aspects of the centralized Church in the Italian Renaissance, in *Acta ad Archaeologiam et Artium Historiam Pertinentia*, (Edited by H. P. L'Orange and H. Torp) Vol. ii, pp. 203–252. University of Oslo, Rome, (1965).
31. R. Wittkower, *Architectural Principles in the Age of Humanism*, Third revised edition. Alec Tiranti, London (1962).
32. R. Wittkower, Brunelleschi and ''Proportions in Perspective,'' in *Idea and Image, Studies in the Italian Renaissance* (Edited by Margo Wittkower), pp. 125–136. Thames and Hudson, London (1978).
33. R. Wittkower, The changing concept of proportion, in *Idea and Image, Studies in the Italian Renaissance* (Edited by Margo Wittkower), pp. 109–124. Thames and Hudson, London (1978).

Comp. & Maths. with Appls. Vol. 12B, Nos. 3/4, pp. 999–1020, 1986
Printed in Great Britain.

0886-9561/86 $3.00 + .00
© 1986 Pergamon Press Ltd.

SYMMETRY IN CHEMICAL STRUCTURES AND REACTIONS

ALEXANDRU T. BALABAN

Department of Organic Chemistry, Polytechnic Institute, Splaiul Independenţei 313,
76206 Bucharest, Roumania

Abstract—Symmetry is analyzed at the atomic level (periodic system, chemical bonding, hybridization), at the molecular level (polyhedral organic molecules and their rearrangement products; isomerism and Polya's theorem; Jahn–Teller effects) and at the supramolecular level (reaction graphs for rearrangements and automerizations; repeating sequences in polymer chains; conservation of orbital symmetry in chemical reactions). A few excursions into mathematics involve solid angles, heuristics of (3, γ)-cages, and visualization of symmetry operations for graphs in three- and four-dimensional Euclidean spaces.

Mottos:

Tiger! Tiger! Burning bright
In the forests of the night,
What immortal hand or eye
Could frame thy fearful symmetry?
W. Blake

An odd-looking girl from Devizes
Had eyes of two different sizes
The one was so small
It was nothing at all
But the other took several prizes.

INTRODUCTION

In order to arrive at an understanding of, and to be able to live in, a crooked world, human reason needs the representation of perfection in the universe; likewise, in order to understand the behaviour of real gases, physico-chemists had first to discover the laws of perfect or ideal gases. Perfection involves, in many cases, higher symmetry than the extant one.

Symmetry may be either fearful (awesome) or beautiful. It is a well-known fact that no human face is exactly symmetrical, yet some symmetry is required for a beautiful or even a normal countenance; this is the meaning of the above limerick. Escher's drawings[1–3] have a haunting, ominous symmetry. The symmetry of a tulip or of a pineapple is beautiful, yet the symmetry of the spider, shark's teeth, the snake, the octopus or the atomic bomb's mushroom appear to us as frightening; we have been conditioned to experience these reactions by biological or cultural heritage. Psychological tests (the "ink blot" butterfly, or the two human profiles versus the flower vase between them) identify such conditioning and constitute clues for diagnosis and treatment.

By contrast, in the serene world of mathematical, physical and chemical sciences, symmetry is always associated with the lofty majesty of the most basic laws. How beautiful is a planar, perfectly hexagonal benzene, an adamantane, or a dodecahedrane molecule! Or, at the supramolecular level, a snowflake! At the intermediate level, let us think about an infinite planar sheet of carbon atoms in graphite, or an infinite lattice of the same atoms in diamond. All properties of these last two materials, so different in strength, electrical conductivity, colour, transparency and price, are due to the different packing symmetry, owing to different types of bonding in the huge molecule which is the crystal in the latter case, or a sheet in the former case: σ bonds in diamond, (σ + π) bonds in graphite.

As Heisenberg had said, "Physicists learned from mathematicians that the symmetry of a problem as a rule produces a conservation law. All the conservation laws that we know in physics [and of course these are important in chemistry also]—the conservation of energy, momentum, angular momentum, etc.—rest upon fundamental symmetries in the underlying natural law'' (cited from Coulson's paper entitled *Symmetry*[4a]).

Whereas physics deals especially with the abstract symmetries of mathematically formulated laws (either expressing the nature of fundamental particles, or the connection between measurable variables), chemistry deals with both ''palpable'' symmetries of molecules or crystals, and with more abstract symmetries of electronic orbitals or of chemical reactions.

One can discuss symmetry in chemistry at various levels: (a) atomic (symmetry of electronic orbitals and the Periodic Table of Elements; hybridization, molecular geometry, and stereo-chemistry of organic and inorganic compounds), (b) molecular (symmetry of small numbers of atoms held together by strong covalent bonds; polyhedra, solid angles, and organic or inorganic compounds with polyhedral structures; isomerism and Polya's theorem, Jahn–Teller effect; tunneling), and (c) supramolecular level (symmetry of large collections of atoms which may or may not be bonded by chemical bonds; examples for the former case are polymers, proteins, polynucleotides, silicates; examples for the latter case are various types of molecular crystals such as the ice of the snowflake). Polyhedral viruses or the quaternary structure of proteins also belong here, as do liquid crystals, membranes, bilayers, etc. There is still another type of more abstract symmetry, namely the symmetry of chemical reactions: conservation of orbital symmetry and aromaticity of transition states; valence isomerizations, automerizations, and regular graphs; heuristics of $(3, \gamma)$-cages.

It should be noted that the interface with mathematics and physics is present at all levels (atomic, molecular, supramolecular). From the rich bibliography on symmetry in the physico-chemical sciences we list only a few books[5–15].

Crystallographic aspects are presented in this volume in detail by other contributors (Fichter, Mackay, Senechal and Shafranovskii), polymers are discussed by Chujo, symmetry in chemical reactions is analyzed by Pearson, and isomerism is exposed both by Slanina and by Sokolov, while graph-theoretical aspects are contained in the contribution of Hosoya. Therefore, the present selection of topics, which may appear truncated, was imposed by this framework of other contributions and by space limitations. From the preceding listings we shall pick only a few topics.

SYMMETRY AT THE ATOMIC LEVEL: ATOMS, ELECTRONS AND THE PERIODIC SYSTEM

Quantum chemistry is based on quantum mechanics. Heisenberg, Schrödinger, Dirac, Pauli and others assembled the puzzle bits uncovered by Planck, Einstein and Bohr, and formulated the laws governing the behaviour of electrons around atomic nuclei. The quantum numbers and Pauli's Exclusion Principle explain why the electronic configurations around nuclei with $Z = 1$–109 positive charges (by 1984's count†) give rise to periodically similar behaviour *versus* Z.

The principal quantum number $n = 1, 2, 3, 4, 5, 6, 7$ and the secondary quantum number $l = 0, 1, 2, \ldots, n$ (or equivalently expressed by letters s, p, d, $\ldots$, respectively) obey the $(n + l)$ laws according to the Aufbau Principle: electronic orbitals in the ground state of an atom are occupied in the order of increasing $(n + l)$ values; for equal $n + l$ values, the occupancy order is by increasing n values. These simple laws explain naturally the beautiful symmetry of Mendeleev's Periodic Table of Elements, which is puzzling at first glance (Fig. 1) because some inner shells become filled later (d- or f-type orbitals) and because the periodicity is geared according to completion of p-type orbitals. The ''atomic magic numbers of electrons'' (in opposition to the nuclear magic numbers of nucleons) are $Z_0 = 2, 10, 18, 36, 54, 86, (118)$, i.e. the atomic numbers of the six elements (rare gases) which may exist as free atoms in condensed state: these are the only elements which satisfy simultaneously the electrons' requirement for closed electronic shells, and the urge of the nucleus to group around it Z electrons for attaining electrical neutrality. A simple formula[16] for the ''magic number Z_0 of the rare gases'' is

$$Z_0 = n[(n + 3)^2 + 5]/6 - (n + 2)[1 - (-1)^n]/4.$$

†We look forward to hearing Tom Lehrer's reaction when the news about the IUPAC naming of elements with $Z \geq 104$ will come to Harvard!

Fig. 1. The Aufbau principle explaining the periodic system of elements; if one ignores the small irregularity of 5d and 6d elements at the beginning of the lanthanide and actinide series, one can note the symmetry in filling sequentially the orbitals: s; s; p, s; p, s; d, p, s; d, p, s; f, d, p, s; f, d, p, s.

$n = 1$	2	3	4	5	6	7	Z : Element
s							1,2 : H, He
	s						3,4 : Li, Be
	p						5–10 : B–Ne
		s					11,12 : Na, Mg
		p					13–18 : Al–Ar
			s				19,20 : K, Ca
		d					21–30 : Sc–Zn
			p				31–36 : Ga–Kr
				s			37,38 : Rb, Sr
			d				39–48 : Y–Cd
				p			49–54 : In–Xe
					s		55,56 : Cs, Ba
			f				58–71 : Ce–Lu (lanthanides)
				d			57,72–80 : La, Hf–Hg
					p		81–86 : Tl–Rn
						s	87,88 : Fr, Ra
				f			90–103 : Th–Lw (actinides)
					d		89,104–112 : Ac, 104–112

For comparison, the general formula[16] of the nuclear magic numbers ξ_0 is

$$\xi_0 = n(n^2 + 5)/3$$

for any $n > 3$; for $n \leq 3$ one has to introduce an additional term, $+n(n - 1)$.

The data of Fig. 1 are obtained immediately, taking into account that each atom may contain at most 1, 3, 5, and 7 s, p, d, and f-type orbitals, respectively, and that according to Pauli's principle, one orbital is filled with two electrons.

In all the other 103 elements, a compromise must be reached by the nucleus and the electrons. This compromise is called "chemical bonding"; therefore all these 103 elements exist (as such or combined with other elements) in their ground states as condensed matter, in chemically bonded forms. Ionic, covalent or metallic bonds are the most common types of bonding.

The symmetry of molecular orbitals is closely connected with the symmetry of atomic orbitals: s-orbitals have spherical symmetry, p-orbitals have reflection symmetry with respect to the three planes determined by the cartesian coordinates, and d- and f-orbitals have more elaborate symmetries. The sign of the wave function ψ changes on traversing a nodal surface: there are $n - 1$ nodal surfaces for orbitals with the principal quantum number n. The probability of finding an electron at a given point is $|\psi|^2$.

Covalent bonds, formed by two atoms having one electron each in a "jointly owned molecular orbital" are of σ type (cylindrical symmetry around the bonding axis) if the overlap between atomic orbitals (AOs) is frontal, or π type if the overlap is lateral (Fig. 2).

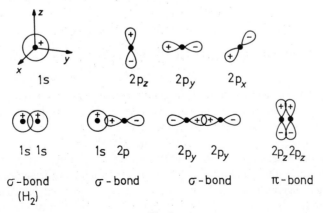

Fig. 2.

Pauling[17] introduced the idea of hybridization of AOs in order to account for molecular geometries. A tetracovalent carbon atom (as in methane or diamond) does not form one bond of one type and three of another type, but four equivalent bonds with sp^3 hybridization, oriented towards the corners of a tetrahedron having the carbon atom in its centre. The normal bond angle is 109.5°. A tricoordinated carbon atom as in ethene, benzene or graphite forms three equivalent sp^2-hybridized σ bonds at 120° and a fourth, weaker π bond using the nonhybridized $2p_z$ AO. A dicoordinated carbon atom as in acetylene forms two sp-hybridized σ bonds at 180° and two π bonds using the remaining nonhybridized 2p orbitals. Of course, the idea of tetrahedral carbon atoms explains the stereochemistry of organic compounds, following Van't Hoff and Le Bel.

One should stress the fact that it is symmetry, and symmetry alone, which makes the distinction between σ and π electrons. This distinction plays a fundamental role in organic chemistry because the σ bonds, with their cylindrical symmetry, ordinarily allow an easy rotation around the bonds at room temperature, whereas the π bonds under the same conditions do not allow such rotations and hence give rise to one type of stereoisomerism called diastereoisomerism or *cis–trans* isomerism. The second type of stereoisomerism, called enantiomerism, appears when a molecule is not superimposable on its mirror image; a common type of such isomerism appears in organic compounds having a chirotopic and stereogenic carbon atom[18], i.e. a carbon atom bonded to four different atoms or groups of atoms[19]. Such molecules are also called chiral. Most of their properties are identical, but they interact differently with polarized light or with other chiral molecules.

The geometries of molecules centered around heavier atoms possessing d orbitals can be similarly understood: trigonal bipyramids with 5-coordination around phosphorus(V) atoms; octahedral symmetry around many 6-coordinated transition metals or sulphur(VI) atoms. Gil-lespie's rules VSEPR[20] explain the geometry and symmetry of many chemical compounds by postulating various degrees of repulsion between electron pairs in shared MOs or nonshared AOs. Of course, the stereoisomerism of such 5- or 6-coordinated compounds is richer than that of the tetrahedrally 4-coordinated carbon, silicon or nitrogen compounds: whereas an asymmetric 4-coordinated atom (such as carbon, or ammonium nitrogen) gives rise to one pair of enan-tiomers, for trigonal bipyramids with 5 different ligands there exist 10 pairs of enantiomers, and for octahedral molecules with 6 different ligands there exist 15 pairs of enantiomers. If bidentate or tridentate ligands replace 2 or 3 unidentate ligands, then the number of stereoisomers may be smaller owing to steric strain[21–23].

The importance of stereochemical ideas is attested by the fact that both Van't Hoff (1901) and Werner (1913) were awarded the Nobel Prize at the beginning of this century, and that more recently Barton and Prelog (1976) attained the same distinction for contributions to stereochemistry.

During recent years, the presence of molecular chirality (either due to stereogenic atoms or to hindered rotation) is easily tested in racemic mixtures by nuclear magnetic resonance in molecules possessing diastereotopic groups, as indicated by Mislow[18].

Recently, Mislow and Siegel reformulated in mathematically rigorous form the conditions for chirality[18].

A rich bibliography exists on stereochemistry; only a few recent books are highlighted [24–43].

SYMMETRY AT THE MOLECULAR LEVEL: POLYHEDRA, SOLID ANGLES AND CHEMISTRY

The five regular polyhedra, whose faces are all a single type of regular polygons (*n*-gons) have fascinated the human imagination since Theaetetus, Euclid, Pappus, Platon and Kepler assigned them a transcendental significance; the latter associated them with the ancient "ele-ments" (fire, air, water, earth and the universe) and with the planets known at that time. One of the reasons for this fascination was the fact that unlike the infinity of regular polygons, there exist only five Platonic solids and three regular plane tesselations (6 triangles, 4 squares, or 3 hexagons meeting at a vertex), which can be considered as polyhedra having an infinite curvature radius. Another reason is their exquisite symmetry, approaching that of the sphere.

One can calculate in sterradians the solid angle 2θ at a vertex of each regular polyhedron according to the following formula[44] for a trihedral solid angle formed from three planar angles $2\alpha_1$, $2\alpha_2$, $2\alpha_3$:

$$\cos \theta = \left(\sum_{i=1}^{3} \cos^2 \alpha_i - 1 \right) \Big/ 2 \prod_{i=1}^{3} \cos \alpha_i.$$

Alternatively, the formula for 2θ may be given in terms of the three dihedral angles, φ_1 to φ_3, between the faces:

$$2\theta = \varphi_1 + \varphi_2 + \varphi_3 - \pi.$$

For the maximal solid angle 2θ formed by four planar angles $2\alpha_i$ $(i = 1\text{–}4)$ meeting at a vertex, the formula is

$$\cos \theta = \left(2 - \sum_{i=1}^{4} \sin^2 \alpha_i - 2 \prod_{i=1}^{4} \sin \alpha_i \right) \Big/ 2 \prod_{i=1}^{4} \cos \alpha_i.$$

Among all trigonal pyramids **A** having as base an equilateral triangle, the regular tetrahedron has the smallest sum of solid angles; among all tetrahedra **B** having four equal isosceles triangles as faces, the regular tetrahedron where the faces become equilateral triangles has the largest sum of solid angles (Fig. 3).
For regular polyhedra, all planar angles $2\alpha = (n - 2)/n$ are equal; when the degree of each vertex (number of edges meeting at that vertex) is d, the maximal solid angle $2\theta_d$ is given by

$$2\theta_d = 2\pi - 2d \arccos \frac{\cos(\pi/d)}{\sin(\pi/n)}.$$

For $d = 3$, $\cos \theta_3 = (2 - 3 \sin^2 \alpha)/2 \cos^3 \alpha$, i.e. a rigid trihedral solid angle with no degree of freedom allowed. In all subsequent cases the maximal solid angle 2θ formed by d planar angles α is

$$\sin(\theta_4/2) = tg^2\alpha,$$

$$\cos \theta_4 = (2 - 4 \sin^2 \alpha - 2 \sin^4 \alpha)/2 \cos^4 \alpha,$$

$$\cos \theta_5 = [2 - 5 \sin^2 \alpha - (5 + 5\sqrt{5}) \sin^4(\alpha/2)]/2 \cos^5 \alpha,$$

$$\cos \theta_6 = (2 - 6 \sin^2 \alpha - 21 \sin^4 \alpha - 2 \sin^6 \alpha)/2 \cos^6 \alpha.$$

According to the value of the solid angle the following order of regular polyhedra may be established (after each polyhedron, the solid angle is given both in sterradians and in the more usual sexagesimal degrees for comparison): tetrahedron (0.5513, 31° 35′); octahedron (1.3593, 77° 53′) cube or hexahedron (1.5708, 90°); icosahedron (2.635, 150° 58′); and dodecahedron (2.96, 169° 41′). This is the order of increasing "perfection," in agreement with the order of increasing numbers of vertices, or of increasing ratios between the radii of inscribed or circumscribed spheres and the length of the edge, or of the angle between an edge and the corresponding

A   B

Fig. 3.

radius of the circumscribed sphere. Curiously, the names of the Platonic solids are derived from the number of faces, which is the only parameter varying in a different order for the two reciprocal (dual) pairs: cube–octahedron, and icosahedron–dodecahedron.

In addition to the five Platonic regular polyhedra, there exist semiregular polyhedra having at each vertex more than one type of regular polygon; to this class belong the infinity of prisms and antiprisms, and the 13 Archimedean solids which so far have attracted less attention from organic chemists, but are important for inorganic, particularly silicate, chemistry.

The synthesis of hydrocarbons having the skeletons of Platonic solids with degree 3 (tetrahedrane, cubane and dodecahedrane) has been an interesting challenge during the last 20 years. Owing to steric strain, tetrahedrane $(CH)_4$ is too elusive to be isolated, like its valence isomers cyclobutadiene. However, the same two hydrocarbons become stable when they bear four tertiary-butyl groups, as demonstrated by Maier and his coworkers[45]. This stabilization is due to a ''straight-lace effect,'' due to the high steric constraints imposed by the bulky t-butyl groups.

Cubane [$(CH)_8$, Fig. 4(**1**)] was synthetized by Eaton[46]. It was shown that it undergoes interesting transition metal–ion-catalyzed rearrangements yielding either cuneane [Fig. 4(**2**)] with Ag(I) or the syn-cyclobutadiene dimer [Fig. 4(**3**)] with Rh(III)[47]. As will be seen in a later section, such rearrangements are symmetry-forbidden as thermal reactions because they involve the concerted migration of four electrons (indicated by distinct lines in the formulas).

Dodecahedrane $(CH)_{20}$ was obtained after considerable effort by Paquette and coworkers[48]. It has an unusually high melting point for a hydrocarbon. Dodecahedrane can also be obtained via metal–ion-catalyzed isomerizations[50]. In Paquette's words:

> Little did Plato realize in 400–350 B.C. when he composed his *Timaeus* that the most complex of the five regular polyhedra described therein was to evolve as a major synthetic challenge of organic chemistry later in the 20th century.

Pentaprismane $(CH)_{10}$ was synthesized by Eaton via an elaborated synthesis[50]; benzprismane (triprismane) is very strained[51], yet its isomerization to benzene has a sizable activation barrier owing to the thermally forbidden character of this isomerization.

It will be of interest to synthesize other polyhedral molecules, e.g. the semiregular solids with vertex degrees 3 (valence isomers of annulenes) such as the truncated tetrahedron [Fig. 5(a)-(**4**)] (the faces are 3- and 6-membered rings), the truncated octahedron (**5**) (4- and 6-membered rings), the isomeric, more strained truncated cube (**6**) (3- and 8-membered rings), or the truncated cuboctahedron (**7**); unlike the previous polyhedra (**4**)–(**6**) which each have two types of regular polygonal faces, the last one (**7**) has three types of faces: 4-, 6-, and 8-gons. Other polyhedral molecules which are neither regular nor semiregular polyhedra, such as Fig. 5(b)-(**8**), $(CH)_{16}$, are also interesting [(**8**) has 4- and 5-membered rings].

One should also note that there exist polyhedral molecular skeletons in which one edge of a regular polyhedron corresponds to a chain of two or more covalent bonds. Thus the very stable adamantane or hexamethylenetetramine molecules are regular tetrahedra with edges replaced by a chain of two $CH–CH_2–CH$ or $N–CH_2–N$ bonds, respectively. Schleyer[52] discovered that adamantane [Fig. 5(c)-(**9**)] is the ''bottom of the potential energy pit'' and is therefore formed by isomerization under the catalytic action of $AlCl_3$ or Rh(I) from any $C_{10}H_{16}$ hydrocarbon; likewise $C_{11}H_{18}$ hydrocarbons yield 1-methyladamantane[53], $C_{14}H_{20}$ hydrocarbons yield diamantane (**10**)[54], and so on for other ''inhabitants of Adamantaneland.'' The graph-theoretical systematic enumeration of polymantanes was published by Balaban and Schleyer[55].

After organic-chemical counterparts of polyhedra, we shall now discuss highly symmetrical inorganic or elemento-organic molecules with polyhedral skeletons. Although 12 carbon atoms

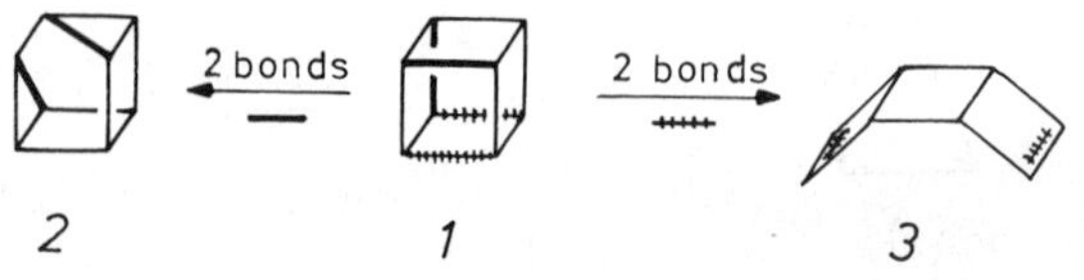

Fig. 4.

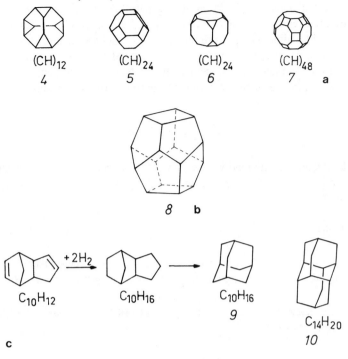

Fig. 5.

cannot be grouped together as icosahedra, boron atoms can; the dodecahedrane anion $(BH)_{12}^{2-}$ is extremely stable. By replacing two BH by CH groups, one can obtain neutral carboranes[56] which preserve their icosahedral skeleton; they exist in three isomeric forms with the two CH groups adjacent, once removed or twice removed. They are quite stable and undergo a variety of substitutions, and therefore they may be regarded as representatives of tridimensional aromatic molecules. The bonding in such electron-deficient systems is different from normal covalent bonds where a line symbolizes a shared electron pair. In boranes there exist two-electron three-centre bonds. Topological rules for the borane structure were developed by Lipscomb[57]. The bonding in polyhedral boranes was investigated, using quantum calculations, by Lipscomb and Hoffmann[58], and using graph-theoretical methods by King and Rouvray[59] and by Balaban and Rouvray[60].

ISOMERISM AND PÓLYA'S THEOREM

Molecules with the same composition (i.e. the same molecular formula) but with different structures (i.e. different arrangements of atoms) are isomeric. Constitutional isomerism is given by different skeletons or adjacencies; stereoisomerism is either enantiomerism (mirror-image nonsuperposability) or diastereomerism. Mislow[61] proposed a different dichotomy based on the isometric operations (identity of scalar properties I_1, or mirror reflection I_2). One thus groups isometric structures (homomers and enantiomers differing by I_1 or I_2) distinctly from anisometric structures which have neither I_1 nor I_2 operations, and which are represented by diastereomers and by constitutional isomers.

Both constitutional and sterical isomerism depend on the symmetry operations of the molecular frame, as shown by Pólya[62] who discovered his famous theorem: the isomer-counting series is obtained by substituting in the symmetry expression (cycle index) the figure-counting series.

It is simple to explain Pólya's theorem by a few examples. The benzene molecule is a planar regular hexagon whose symmetry operations (rotations about proper axes) are represented by the cycle index

$$Z(D_6) = (x_1^6 + 2x_6 + 2x_3^2 + 3x_1^2x_2^2 + 4x_2^3)/12. \qquad (1)$$

The formula is obtained on the basis of the character table for benzene, D_{6h}, where only the proper axes are taken into account: $I(x_1^6)$, $2C_6(2x_6)$, $2C_3(2x_3^2)$, $C_6^3 \equiv C_2''(x_2^3)$, $3C_2(3x_2^3$ for the three in-plane axes bisecting two opposite bonds), $3C_2'(3x_1^2x_2^2$ for the three in-plane axes through two opposite atoms). The C_6, C_6^3 and C_3 axes are perpendicular to the plane of the molecule.

For obtaining the numbers of isomers with one type of substituent (e.g. the numbers of mono-, di-, and trichlorobenzenes) the figure-counting series to be substituted in the above formula (1) is

$$x_i = r^i + s^i. \tag{2}$$

By simple algebraic manipulations we obtain the isomer-counting series (ICS) (only constitutional isomerism is involved here because of the planarity due to sp²-hybridization of the six carbon atoms)

$$ICS(D_6) = (r^6 + s^6) + (r^5s + rs^5) + 3(r^2s^4 + r^4s^2) + 3(r^3s^3). \tag{3}$$

The coefficients indicate the numbers of isomers, namely one nonsubstituted or hexasubstituted, one mono- or pentasubstituted, three di- or tetrasubstituted, and three trisubstituted benzenes.

Similarly, for benzene substituted with two types of halogen, say chloro-bromobenzene, the figure-counting series is

$$x_i = r^i + s^i + t^i, \tag{4}$$

leading to ICS terms such as $3rst^4$, $3r^2s^4$, $6rs^2t^3$, $11r^2s^2t^2$, etc., which indicate that there are 6 bromodichlorobenzenes, and 11 dibromodichlorobenzenes.

If two labels can be attached to the same atom, as in isotopically carbon- and hydrogen-labelled benzenes, the figure-counting series is[63]

$$x_i = r^i + s^i + r^is^i + t^i, \tag{5}$$

leading to such ICS terms as $3r^2s^4$, $4rst^4$, $9rs^2t^3$, $12rs^3t^2$, $24r^2s^2t^2$, etc., which indicate that there are four isomers of $^{13}C^{12}C_5$, $^2H^1H_5$, etc.

Similarly, for carbon-labelled toluene PhMe

$$Z(PhMe - *C) = (x_1^7 + x_1^3x_2^2)/2, \tag{6}$$

because in addition to the identity operation (x_1^7) we have one proper in-plane binary axis passing through three atoms $(x_1^3x_2^2)$. The result is the isomer-counting series by substituting (2) into (6):

$$ICS(PhMe - *C) = r^7 + 5r^6s + 16r^5s^2 + 21r^4s^3 + \cdots, \tag{7}$$

indicating that there exist 5 constitutional isomers of toluene labeled with one ^{13}C atom, 16 with two ^{13}C atoms, etc. When, however, we wish to enumerate hydrogen-labelled toluenes or the chlorotoluenes, the cycle index must take into account the free rotation of the methyl group. This is done by multiplying the symmetry groups of the three methyl and five phenyl hydrogens:

$$Z(B)Z(S_3) = \frac{x_1^5 + x_1x_2^2}{2} \cdot \frac{x_1^3 + 3x_1x_2 + 2x_3}{6} =$$

$$= (x_1^8 + 3x_1^6x_2 + 2x_1^5x_3 + x_1^4x_2^2 + 3x_1^2x_2^3 + 2x_1x_2^2x_3)/12. \tag{8}$$

On substituting the figure-counting series (2) we obtain the counting polynomial

$$ICS(PhMe - *H) = r^8 + 4(rs^7 + r^7s) + 10(r^2s^6 + r^6s^2) + 16(r^3s^5 + r^5s^3) + \cdots.$$

Cycloalkanes present stereoisomerism, in addition to constitutional isomerism. We shall illustrate the problem by examining hydrogen-labelled or chlorine-substituted cyclopropane. Three different graphs must be considered[64]. For all isomers, including stereoisomers, one has to consider the prism-like geometry Fig. 6(a)-(11); for counting only constitutional and geometrical (E/Z or diastereoisomers) by ignoring enantiomerism, one has to consider a "planar" system (12); finally, for counting only constitutional isomers, one has to consider the symmetry of (13) (these $2m$-membered cubic graphs, wherein each vertex is connected to the two vertices adjacent to its opposite vertex, were called Balaban graphs by Mallion[65a]).

Cycle indices and isomer-counting series are (note that $Z(12)$ and (1) are identical):

$$Z(\mathbf{11}) = (x_1^6 + 2x_3^2 + 3x_2^3)/6,$$

$$ICS(\mathbf{11}) = r^6 + r^5s + 4r^2s^4 + 4r^3s^3 + \cdots,$$

$$Z(\mathbf{12}) = (x_1^6 + 2x_3^2 + 4x_2^3 + 3x_1^2x_2^2 + 2x_6)/12,$$

$$ICS(\mathbf{12}) = r^6 + r^5s + 3r^2s^4 + 3r^3s^3 + \cdots,$$

$$Z(\mathbf{13}) = (x_1^6 + 8x_3^2 + 7x_2^3 + 9x_1^2x_2^2 + 8x_6 + 3x_1^4x_2 + 6x_1^2x_4)/48,$$

$$ICS(\mathbf{13}) = r^6 + r^5s + 2r^2s^4 + 2r^3s^3 + \cdots.$$

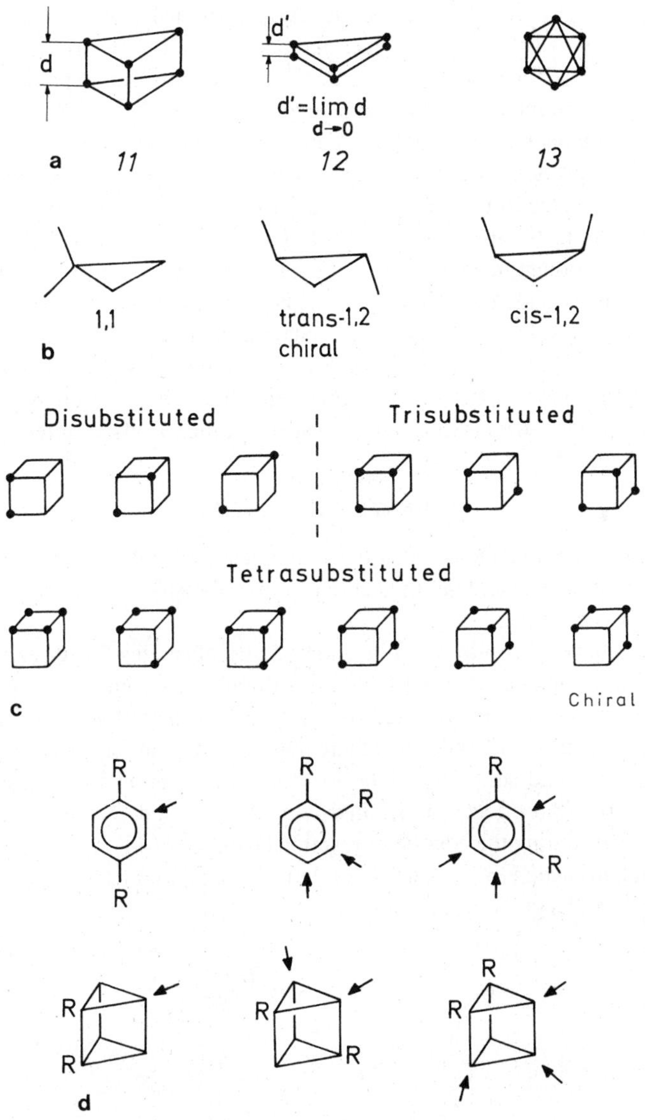

Fig. 6.

Indeed, there are four molecules if all types of stereoisomerism for dichlorocyclopropane are considered; if enantiomerism is ignored we are left with three isomers: 1,1; cis-1,2; and trans-1,2; finally, if we disregard stereoisomerism, only two constitutions remain, namely 1,1 and 1,2 [Fig. 6(b)].

Cubane (1) also presents stereoisomerism which can be taken into account or ignored. The two corresponding cycle indices and counting series are

$$Z(1) = (x_1^8 + 8x_1^2x_3^2 + 9x_2^4 + 6x_4^2)/24,$$

$$ICS(1) = r^8 + r^7s + 3r^6s^2 + 3r^5s^3 + 7r^4s^4 + \cdots,$$

$$Z'(1) = (x_1^8 + 6x_1^4x_2^2 + 8x_1^2x_3^2 + 13x_2^4 + 12x_4^2 + 8x_2x_6)/48,$$

$$ICS'(1) = r^8 + r^7s + 3r^6s^2 + 3r^5s^3 + 6r^4s^4 + \cdots.$$

The mono-, di-, and tri-substituted cubanes are all achiral, but one of the six tetrasubstituted cubane constitutions is chiral; this accounts for the difference between the two counting series indicated above [Fig. 6(c)].

We end this chapter by mentioning two relevant items of historical interest, linked with the symmetry of substituted benzenes.

(i) The polemic between Kekulé and Ladenburg about the hexagonal and the benzprismane formulas, respectively, was based on the fact that both structures give rise to the same numbers of constitutional isomers for mono-, di-, trisubstituted systems, etc. This is a consequence of the fact that the two graphs have the same cycle index $Z(G)$, i.e. the two structures are coisomeric[65b]. Only later did Baeyer bring conclusive evidence for the Kekulé formula which (a) is strain-free, (b) gives the right pattern for ortho-substitution (see below), which must be vicinal as is known from the formation of phthalic anhydride, and (c) does not lead to enantiomers in agreement with the facts, and in opposition to Ladenburg's formula.

(ii) Körner's "absolute method" for assigning ortho(1,2), meta(1,3), and para(1,4) structures to benzenes with two identical substituents R is based on their conversion into trisubstituted compounds as follows: para → 1,2,4 (one compound); ortho → 1,2,3 + 1,2,4 (two compounds); meta → + 1,2,3 + 1,2,4 + 1,3,5 (three compounds, irrespective of the relative amounts), according to the symmetry axes of the initial disubstituted systems. It can be observed that Ladenburg's "ortho"-disubstituted benzprismane which leads to three tri-substituted derivatives is not vicinal [Fig. 6(d)].

JAHN–TELLER EFFECTS

In 1937, Jahn and Teller showed that for a nonlinear molecule or ion, a situation of orbital degeneracy cannot be stable, and the molecule or ion will distort in such a way as to break the degeneracy due to symmetry.

The cyclobutadiene molecule which is antiaromatic illustrates this effect: the geometry of the ground state is rectangular, but the bond shift through a symmetrical square excited state takes place rather easily, as demonstrated by Carpenter et al.[66], Masamune et al.[67] and Mayer et al.[68]; Carpenter[66] argued that there must exist a quantum-mechanical tunneling[69] for the intramolecular bond shift despite the fact that the CR groups in cyclobutadiene [CBD, Fig. 7(14)] are heavy (the effect was studied with R = H and D); they travel a very short distance, about 0.2 Å, during the bond-shift reaction (14A) ⇌ (14B). Calculations had indicated that the square antiaromatic CBD is unstable relative to a second-order Jahn–Teller distortion, leading to a singlet rectangular ground state[70].

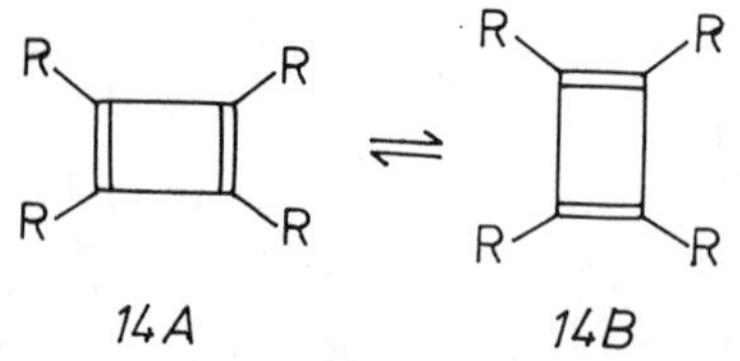

Fig. 7.

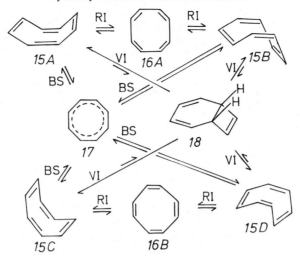

Fig. 8.

A similar process occurs in cyclooctatetraene [COT, Fig. 8(**15**)]. This molecule is, however, nonplanar (tub shaped) so that, in addition to bond-shift (BS) process, ring-inversion process (RI) also occur. The activation energies for these processes were measured by Paquette *et al.*[71] for substituted, and by Anet for unsubstituted, COT[72].

For the ring-inversion (**15A**) ⇌ (**15B**) or (**15C**) ⇌ (**15D**) a very low activation barrier ($\Delta G^\ddagger = 9.5$ kcal/mol) was measured; the transition state is the planar localized molecule (**16A**) or (**16B**), respectively. For the bond-shift reactions (**15A**) ⇌ (**15C**) or (**15B**) ⇌ (**15D**) the transition state is the planar antiaromatic (delocalized) molecule (**17**) and the activation barrier $\Delta G^\ddagger = 13.3$ kcal/mol.

The difference between these two values is in good agreement with the Dewar resonance energy (-4 kcal/mol) calculated by Dewar and Gleicher[73]. In sterically congested or chiral COT derivatives (1,3- or 1,4-di-*t*-butyl- and 1,3,5,7- or 1,2,3,4-tetramethyl-COT) the BS activation barriers increase enormously, attaining 35 kcal/mol, but the difference $\Delta H^\ddagger_{RI} - \Delta H^\ddagger_{BS}$ remains practically constant between -3.4 and -5.4 kcal/mol.

For the valence isomerization (VI) to the bicyclic isomer (**18a**) a much larger activation barrier was determined by Vogel *et al.*[75] and by Huisgen *et al.*[74], namely about 28 kcal/ mol.

There exists at present an ongoing debate about the hydrogen bond in β-diketones: is the proton centered [Fig. 9(**19**)] or oscillating [(**20A**) ⇌ (**20B**)]? Many facts are included in an excellent recent review[76].

A somewhat related problem concerns the onset of bond alternation in Hückel-type [$4n + 2$]-annulenes, predicted by Longuet-Higgins and Salem[77]. The fact that [18]-annulene (Fig. 10) has unequal bond lengths is due to its geometry and not to this electronic effect, as indicated by the fact[78] that the unequal bonds do not alternate (. . . *abab* . . .) but follow the symmetry of the molecule (. . . *abbabb* . . .) with bond distances $a = 1.419$ Å and $b = 1.382$ Å (for conversion to picometers, 1 Å $= 100$ pm).

However, it was found recently that in Nakagawa's tetra-*t*-butyl-bisdehydroannulenes (IUPAC tetradehydroannulenes) the polyene-chain bond lengths are equalized in the dehydro-[18]-annulenic system with $m = 1, n = 4$[79a] but they alternate in the dehydro-[22]-annulenic system with $m = 2, n = 5$[79b]; the number of π-electrons is $4n + 2$.

On the other hand, the fact that $C_6N_6O_6$ has neither a structure of hexanitrosobenzene, nor

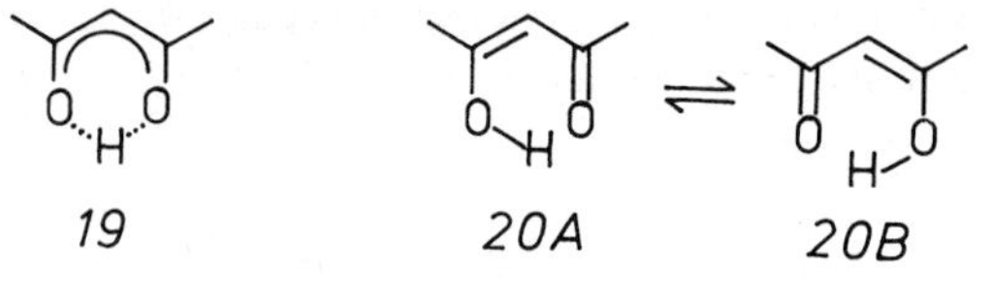

19   20A   ⇌   20B

Fig. 9.

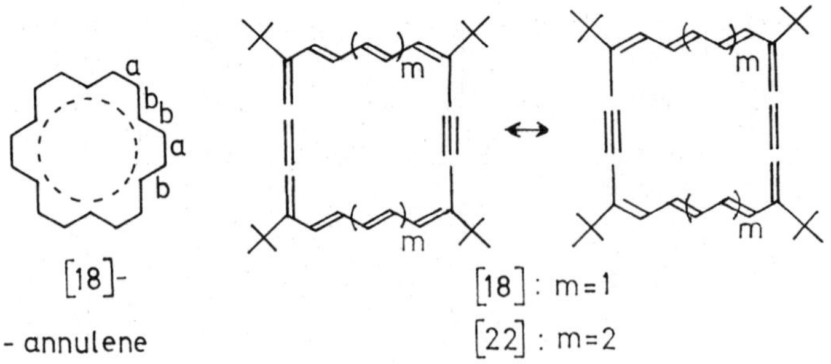

Fig. 10.

with each nitrogen atom being singly bonded to a carbon atom (both these structures would have sixfold symmetry), but rather the threefold symmetrical structure of benzotrifuroxan[79c] is probably due to the lower energy of the last structure relative to the two former ones, and not to the Jahn–Teller effect.

To quote again from Coulson[4b]:

> It is as if Nature said to us: "I have some important principles, and they do indeed dominate whole areas of chemistry, and of physics too. But I am subtle: I cannot always be treated as if I only had one idea in my head. You must use your experimental and theoretical tools carefully. Mother Nature has some feminine characteristics which from time to time will reveal themselves—perhaps to your discomfiture!"

In the field of metallic xomplexes, Jahn–Teller effects play an important role. Determinations of Jahn–Teller coupling constants for octahedral complexes are rationalized theoretically[80]. There also exist second-order Jahn–Teller effects, and pseudo-Jahn–Teller effects[80].

SYMMETRY OF LINEAR MACROMOLECULES

The geometrical single-strand helical symmetry of proteins adumbrated by H. Vasiliu[81] and demonstrated by Pauling and Corey, as well as the double helix structure discovered by Crick and Watson, are too well known to be mentioned more than cursorily here.

We shall discuss the symmetry in linear infinite polymer chains consisting of repeating units. An example is the stereochemistry of vinylic polymers resulting from regular head-to-tail polymerization of $H_2C = CHX$ (X = CH_3, Cl, Ph, OAc, etc.); the constitution is fixed but the stereochemical configuration of each –CHX– group may be either R or S. An isomorphic problem arises when considering the constitution of binary copolymers formed from two monomers, say R and S.

The repeating unit in the simplest case is R (isotactic vinylic polymers, or homopolymer R without incorporation of the second comonomer). The next higher case is of repeating units RS (syndiotactic vinylic polymer, or alternating copolymer). Most textbooks do not consider any further situation, although present-day NMR spectrometric methods "see" beyond the dyad regularity, namely one may observe heterotactic triads (. . . RRSRRS . . .), various tetrads, etc. A systematic enumeration of such possibilities is presented in Table 1. In order to avoid repetitions or duplications, the number of R configurations/monomers is considered to be equal to, or higher than, that of S counterparts, and the sense in which one goes along the chain is arbitrary; therefore RRS is considered to include RSS by the R/S reversal, whereas RSRRS is considered to include both RSRRS (in the opposite sense of going along the chain) and RSSRS (by R/S reversal).

Interestingly, for a given number n of monomer molecules in the repeating unit, the number N of solutions is seen to form the Fibonacci sequence ($F_i = F_{i-1} + F_{i-2}$) for $n \leqslant 8$ (but not for higher n values):

$$N_n = F_{n-2} \quad \text{with } F_0 = F_1 = 1.$$

Table 1. Linear infinite chains of binary copolymers and the number N of discrete solutions in terms of repeating units which are irreducible to solutions with lower n (where n is the number of monomer molecules in the unit)

n	Chain	Unit	N	n	Unit	N
1	. . . RRRRRR . . .	R	1		RRRRRS	
					RRRRSS	
2	. . . RSRSRS . . .	RS	1	6	RRRSRS	5
					RRRSSS	
3	. . . RRSRRSRRS . . .	RRS	1		RRSRSS	
4	. . . RRRSRRRS . . .	RRRS	2		RRRRRRS	
	. . . RRSSRRSS . . .	RRSS			RRRRRSS	
					RRRRSRS	
5	. . . RRRRSRRRRS . . .	RRRRS	3	7	RRRSRRS	8
	. . . RRRSSRRRSS . . .	RRRSS			RRRRSSS	
	. . . RRSRSRRSRSRS . . .	RRSRS			RRRSRSS	
					RRSRRSS	
					RRSRSRS	

Earlier connexions between Fibonacci numbers and chemistry were observed in enumerating Kekulé structures and in other theoretical problems: the numbers of Kekulé structures for [n]-helicenes or other catacondensed benzenoid aromatic hydrocarbons without any anthracenic (linearly) condensed portion from the Fibonacci sequence[82].

Table 1 may be translated in the binary enumeration system. The analogous problem for ternary copolymers corresponds to enumerating different repeating patterns in the ternary enumeration system, and so on. A computer program was devised for compiling all these cases[83].

SYMMETRY AT THE SUPRAMOLECULAR LEVEL: CONSERVATION OF ORBITAL SYMMETRY, AND REACTIONS WITH AROMATIC TRANSITION STATES

The Woodward–Hoffmann rules[84] explain the stereochemistry and the allowed/forbidden character of concerted reactions (pericyclic reactions) which involve the cyclic permutation of σ and/or π electrons. These rules are therefore on the same fundamental level as those which explain why some thermodynamically allowed reactions do not occur in practice owing to electronic or steric factors.

Observations of several research groups[85–94] converged to show the fact that in thermal reactions pericyclic processes involving *three* electron pairs occurred easily; on the contrary, photochemical processes involving *two* electron pairs are favored. Evans[85] had formulated the hypothesis that reactions such as the Diels–Alder cycloaddition and its reversal (retrodiene ring-opening) proceed thermally because they have an aromatic transition state. Dewar[86] added to this the fact that photochemical $2\pi + 2\pi$ cycloadditions must have antiaromatic transition states.

Mathieu and Valls[92] reviewed all reactions with six-membered transition states known until 1956; Balaban[93] continued this review and included reactions which had not yet been observed but were theoretically possible.

Woodward and Hoffmann formulated their rules in the most general terms based on the idea that the frontier molecular orbitals [MOs; highest occupied, HOMO, and lowest unoccupied, LUMO] determine the course and stereochemistry of such reactions.

We shall exemplify by showing three related thermal processes: the Diels–Alder cycloaddition, the Cope rearrangement (a [3,3]-sigmatropic process) and the 1,5-hydrogen shift (a [1,5]-sigmatropic reaction) (Fig. 11).

The correlation diagram† for the Cope rearrangement and its transition state has the following constraints: (i) according to the symmetry element of the process (a plane for the boat-shaped transition state) electronic levels are symmetrical or antisymmetrical; (ii) in the correlation, no levels of the same symmetry may cross (noncrossing rule); (iii) the electronic oc-

†Correlation diagrams are not reproduced here because they are well known[84,90].

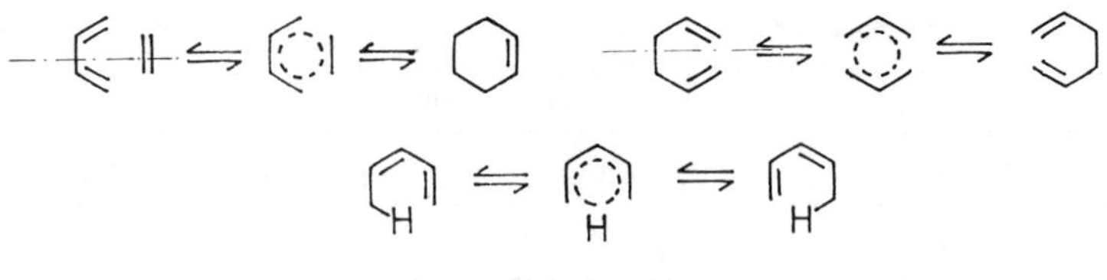

Fig. 11.

cupancy in the initial state is transferred to the transition state and the final state according to the correlation lines; and (iv) if the electronic occupancy of the transition state or final product corresponds to a higher-energy state, the reaction is forbidden, and it is allowed if the latter states have equal or lower energy than the initial state.

Correlation diagrams show that the Cope rearrangement and the $4\pi + 2\pi$ cycloaddition are thermally allowed; the former reaction is an automerization, and therefore could also be allowed photochemically, had the activation barrier for the first excited state lain lower in energy than the initial/final product (this is not the case). It is easy to see that in the Diels–Alder reaction the first excited state would have yielded the second excited state, so that this reaction is also forbidden photochemically. On the other hand, the $2\pi + 2\pi$ cycloaddition is photochemically allowed; the corresponding thermal reaction which would lead to a doubly excited state is strongly forbidden as a concerted reaction. It should be noted that in the latter case there are two symmetry elements (mutually orthogonal planes).

The stereochemical consequences of the Woodward–Hoffmann rules may be seen for the thermal electrocyclic reactions of 1,3-butadiene yielding cyclobutene and of 1,3,5-hexatriene yielding 1,3-cyclohexadiene. The symmetry element in a conrotatory process is a two-fold axis, while in a disrotatory process it is a symmetry plane; one can see that both processes are thermally allowed. If one constructs the correlation diagrams for a disrotatory $(2 + 2)$-process or a conrotatory $(2 + 2 + 2)$-process one can see that such processes are forbidden. Many known reactions have been thus rationalized; the few exceptions are probably due to the reactions proceeding in a totally nonconcerted fashion (actually Dewar maintains that no reaction may be exactly concerted). The topic is related to Pearson's rules[95] which are reviewed in more detail by Pearson in a previous issue.

For this reason, and because correlation diagrams are available in many books, the correlation diagrams pertinent to the above discussion have not been reproduced here.

REACTION GRAPHS; HEURISTIC SYMMETRY OF $(3, \gamma)$-CAGES; SYMMETRY IN HYPERSPACES E_3, E_4

Reaction graphs present all theoretically possible reactions occurring in a given system so as to enable chemists to choose the actual path followed during the course of the reaction. Vertices of a reaction graph are molecules or ions, and edges represent elementary reaction steps. The first reaction graph was published in 1966 to depict the degenerate rearrangement (automerization or topomerization) of ethylcarbenium ions with five different substituents[96]. If the two carbon atoms are distinguishable (e.g. by isotopic substitution) the reaction graph has 20 vertices and is called the Desargues–Levi graph [Fig. 12(**21**)]; if they cannot be distinguished, pairs of antipodal vertices became equivalent and the Petersen graph (**22**) results with ten vertices. In both cases the graph is cubic (regular graph of degree 3, where three lines meet at each vertex), because in each case there are three possibilities of rearrangement.

Interestingly, soon afterwards the same two graphs were published in another context, namely the pseudorotation of pentacoordinated phosphorus compounds or of other trigonal-bipyramidal molecules with five different ligands: the Desargues–Levi graph results when enantiomerism is taken into account[97] and the Petersen graph when it is disregarded[98]. Mislow[99] recognized that in both cases the substituents were grouped in a set of two and a set of three substituents; therefore the resulting graphs are isomorphic.

The Petersen graph occupies a privileged place in graph theory and is displayed on the cover of several books on graph theory[100,101]. Its "magic attraction" may be due to the relationship with the pentagram in the usual representation (**22**), and is probably connected with

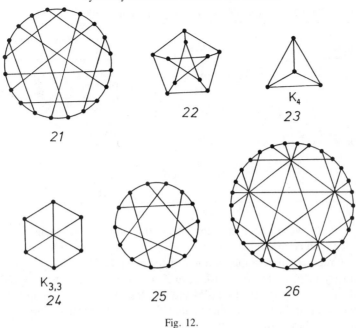

Fig. 12.

its high order of the symmetry group (though this is not readily apparent); this will be presented in more detail below when the cages will be discussed. The Petersen graph is the (3,5)-cage, so-called because it is the smallest cubic graph with girth $\gamma = 5$, i.e. the cubic graph with the smallest number of vertices wherein no cycle is smaller than 5-membered. The $(3,\gamma)$-cages were reviewed by Wong[102]. The (3,3)-cage is the tetrahedron graph K_4, (23) (4 vertices), the (3,4)-cage is the Thomsen graph $(K_{3,3})$, (24) with 6 vertices (one of the two graphs described by Kuratowsky in connection with his graph planarity theorem), the (3,6)-cage is the Heawood graph (25) (14 vertices), the (3,7)-cage is the McGee graph (24 vertices, vertex- and edge-intransitive), the (3,8)-cage is the Tutte graph (26) (30 vertices)[103] and the (3,12)-cage is the Benson graph (126 vertices)[104].

Balaban[105], and later O'Keefe and Wong, and Harries, described three (3,10)-cages with 70 vertices[106]. By observing relationships among the above cages (cages of even girth afford the next lower cage of odd girth by excision of a branched tree) Balaban removed a maximal branched tree from Benson's graph and obtained the conjectured unique (3,11)-cage with 112 vertices[107]. The same procedure, however, failed to yield the presumed (3,9)-cage but afforded instead a cubic graph with 60 vertices. About 30 other different graphs with 60 vertices and girth 9 were found by Balaban, Foster, Frucht, Biggs, Evans and Harries, but they were not the (3,9)-cage because Biggs and Hoare, and then Evans, found two smaller graphs of girth 9, having only 58 vertices[108]. The surprising fact about these two graphs is their very low symmetry. By analogy with all $(3,\gamma)$-cages so far known it can be conjectured that these are not the (3,9)-cages, and that one has to look for other cubic graphs of girth 9 with ≤58 vertices.

Thus symmetry is a heuristic criterion for assessing whether a conjecture is likely to be true or false.

The symmetry of graphs is measured by the order of their automorphism group. Unlike the symmetry of polyhedra, which is apparent from their rotations/reflections, the symmetry of graphs must consider all permutations of edges because graphs must be viewed as floppy[109], not rigid, geometrical realizations of the abstract definition of graphs (a superposition of the nonempty set of vertices on itself), so that an edge is actually an unordered pair of vertices. As a consequence, graphs may have much higher symmetries than polyhedra, for comparable numbers of vertices and vertex degrees. Thus, the orders of the symmetry group $\Gamma(G)$ of the regular dodecahedron as a polyhedron, and of the Desargues–Levi graph (both are cubic graphs with 20 vertices) are 60 and 240 respectively. Table 2 presents in more detail the orders $\Gamma(G)$ of the automorphism groups of polyhedra and cages; the tetrahedron graph is the (3,3)-cage.

s-Unitransitive (s-regular) graphs were defined as graphs which have exactly one auto-morphism mapping any path of length s on any other path of the same length (but not for a

Table 2. s-Unitransitive or s-regular graphs with v vertices and girth γ

| Polyhedra (geometrical objects) | | | | $(3,\gamma)$-Cages (graphs) | | | | |
Denomination	v	s	$\Gamma(G)$	γ	Graph	v	s	$\Gamma(G)$
Tetrahedron	4	2	12	3	K_4 (**23**)	4	2	24
Cube (**1**)	8	2	24	4	Thomsen $K_{3,3}$ (**24**)	6	3	72
Pentagonal prism	10	0	20	5	Petersen (**22**)	10	3	120
Dodecahedron	20	2	60	6	Heawood (**25**)	14	4	336
Truncated tetrahedron (**4**)	12	1	36	7	McGee	24	—	32
Truncated cuboctahedron (**7**)	48	0	144	8	Tutte (**26**)	30	5	1440

path of length $s + 1$). Vertex-transitive and edge-intransitive graphs such as the prisms are 0-uniregular; vertex- and edge-transitive graphs are 1-uniregular. The order of the automorphism group of an s-uniregular cubic graph with n vertices is $3n \times 2^{s-1}$[103].

The symmetry of reaction graphs for several automerizations was analyzed by Balaban, then Randić: the Petersen graph[96,104,105] and the Desargues–Levi graph[96,106] mentioned above, the homotetrahedryl cation automerization[113,114], and the automerization of tetragonal pyramidal complexes[115,116].

The graphs of the polyhedra have twice-higher orders of automorphism groups than those of the corresponding polyhedra because the steric configurations are defined for the polyhedra but undefined for their floppy graphs; thus, the graph K_4 of the tetrahedron has $\Gamma(G) = 24$, twice as much as for the tetrahedron as polyhedron.

An interesting problem is to speculate on how to visualize plastically the high symmetries of the cages. One can think of a game in which vertices are articulated mechanical devices, edges are colored flexible tubes with telescopically variable lengths, and the aim is to obtain the automorphisms maintaining the shape but varying the colours. Or one can think about a dynamical ''sculpture'' which automatically performs these automorphic interconversions.

An alternative idea is even more interesting: it is clear that all cages with $\gamma > 3$ in Table 2 are nonplanar graphs. The Thomsen graph $K_{3,3}$ with six vertices and the complete graph K_5 with five vertices can have no geometrical realizations in our tridimensional Euclidean space E_3 such that all edges and vertices are equivalent; however, in the four-dimensional space E_4 this is possible for the above two graphs: K_5 is the four-dimensional hypertetrahedron, which we may visualize as a tetrahedron whose four vertices are connected to a fifth vertex in E_4 exterior to E_3 where for convenience we represent the fifth vertex embedded *inside* the tetrahedron [because we cannot see another point equidistant to the other four and equivalent to them, just as the people in E. A. Abbott's *Flatland*[110] cannot represent a tetrahedron other than as a flat K_4 (**23**)]. $K_{3,3}$ is to be viewed as a bipartite graph with a set V_1–V_3 of three disconnected vertices at the corners of equilateral triangle; they are connected to a set v_1–v_3 of three disconnected vertices. Now, if v_1 and v_2 occupy equivalent positions above and below the plane of V_1–V_3, the last vertex v_3 must be in a place in the fourth dimension so as to be equivalent to v_1 and v_2 and form with them an equilateral triangle, and to be at the same time equidistant from V_1–V_3 (Fig. 13). Again we have to put up with our ''three-dimensional Flat-landness,'' and to project conventionally vertex v_3 from the fourth dimension into the centre of the figure. The

K_5

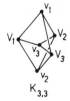

$K_{3,3}$

Fig. 13.

resulting object should have six equivalent vertices and nine equivalent edges, but we can only visualize their projections in our three-dimensional space.

It is quite easy to see that for a two-dimensional Flatlander the edges and vertices of K_4 on a plane are not equivalent, yet we know that the tetrahedron has equivalent vertices and edges. We can therefore easily see that a similar equivalence holds in the fourth dimension for K_5. It is, however, more difficult to see the equivalence of vertices and edges in $K_{3,3}$, but after some thought and imaginative effort one realizes the beautiful symmetry of the smallest nonplanar cage from Table 2 in the multidimensional space. It is an open question whether for the other cages from Table 2 it will be enough to go to E_4, or higher (E_5, etc.) for imagining "objects" displaying the equivalence of vertices and edges, which surpasses by far in richness (and beauty?) the same kind of equivalence in polyhedra.

The fascination exerted on the human mind by the five regular polyhedra is associated with the equivalence (i.e. transitivity) of vertices and edges and faces. We quote from Coxeter's book[118]: "Sir D'Arcy W. Thompson once remarked to me that Euclid never dreamed of writing an Elementary Geometry: what Euclid did was to write a very excellent (but somewhat long-winded) account of the Five Regular Solids, for the use of Initiates." It is appropriate to recall within the context of symmetry the fascinating book *On Growth and Form*[119].

On the applied side, Buckminster Fuller's idea of the geodesic dome has been elaborated rigorously from first principles by Emde (Darmstadt) who proposed an interesting 4×4 square matrix for characterizing any homogeneous polytope[120].

What artist will find a means of making visible or palpable to the senses rather than to the mathematically trained mind the tremendous 5-unitransitivity of the Tutte graph, or of other highly symmetrical graphs? If he or she succeeds, another step will be taken along the path described by Hermann Weyl: "Symmetry, as wide or as narrow as you may define its meaning, is one idea by which man through the ages has tried to comprehend and create order, beauty, and perfection"[5].

SPHERES AND CHEMISTRY

Most people will agree that the most symmetrical object in our world is the sphere; indeed, any movement which conserves its center is an automorphism, and there is an infinity of such moves. It may seem difficult to imagine something with a higher symmetry, yet this can be done. If one thinks about the circle and the sphere, then the reply is obvious. Since the sphere has one extra degree of freedom corresponding to its three-dimensionality (3D) relative to the circle, the reply is a 4D-hypersphere. Of course, Cantor showed that the intuitively obvious is out of place when discussing infinities, but this is an opportunity to discuss N-dimensional (ND hyperspheres. We shall denote by A_N the $N - 1$ dimensional content, and by V_N the N-dimensional content, of the ND-hypersphere (e.g. for $N = 3$ the area A_3 and the volume V_3 of the sphere; for $N = 2$, the perimeter A_2 and the surface V_2 of the circle). We recall the recurrences[118] where R is the radius:

$$A_{N+2} = 2\pi N R^2 A_N = 2\pi R V_N,$$

and we obtain therewith Table 3.

Is there any connexion between spheres and chemistry? Yes, indeed, and we shall mention two such connexions.†

Table 3. The N- and $(N - 1)$-dimensional content of the ND-hypersphere

N	1	2	3	4	5
V_N	$2R$	πR^2	$4\pi R^3/3$	$\pi^2 R^4/2$	$8\pi^2 R^5/15$
A_N	2	$2\pi R$	$4\pi R^2$	$2\pi^2 R^3$	$8\pi^2 R^4/3$

† A third one is also well known: the two possible types of close packing of equal spheres corresponding to the cubic and the hexagonal closest packings[39].

(1) The "gear effect" of three-pronged substituents such as alkyl groups was demonstrated by Roussel, Metzger, and coworkers[121]. Unlike a halogen substituent, whose Van der Waals "envelope" is spherical, a methyl or an isopropyl group are pronged so that their intramolecular rotation angle changes the free energy of the molecule. There exists a lowest energy conformation where vicinal substituents are geared like cogwheels. The topic was the subject of some controversies[122], and was recently reviewed[123].

(2) The spontaneous formation of bilayer vesicles from surfactant molecules on ultrasonic dispersion in water is a "membrane mimetic chemistry"[124]. The surfactant, like the biological constituents of membranes or of liposomes, must have two long tails (nonpolar alkyl chains) and a polar ammonium or phosphate headgroup. The spherical structure of the vesicle can be frozen by photochemical or radical-initiated polymerization if one uses surfactants with double bonds in the tail chains or attached to the head group. Interestingly, many membrane studies using spin labels are made with "erythrocite ghosts" (red blood corpuscles whose hemoglobin content has been removed); in such cases it is possible to know whether the sphere conserves its initial structure or has been turned inside out.

This brings us to the conclusion of this paper, which raises some problems on the topology of N-dimensional objects. A Flatlander cannot visualize a Möbius band or a Klein bottle [Fig. 14(a)-(27)], and Escher's ants crawling across the Möbius band [Fig. 14(b)] illustrate this point (it would have better suited our purpose if the band had been opaque and much larger, and the ants much flatter). Now, thinking about Plato's reflections about the shadows that we see on the walls of our cave, and about the modelling of the real world after these shadows, let us imagine (if we can) four-dimensional analogs of a Möbius band and of a Klein bottle (which are 3D projections of the 4D objects), as well as other topological oddities which have no counterpart in our three-dimensional world.

A being in a 4D world would be able to see at the same time the exterior and the interior of a sphere, both of which are open towards the fourth dimension, just as the circle is open to a 3D being like us but is a closed to a coplanar Flatlander. Thus we end with another limerick:

> A mathematician named Klein
> Thought the Möbius bands were divine.
> Said he, "If you glue
> The edges of two
> You'll get a weird bottle like mine.

Acknowledgements—I am grateful to my son, Teodor-Silviu Balaban and my daughter-in-law, Carmen Balaban, for assistance in the preparation of this manuscript.

27 **a**

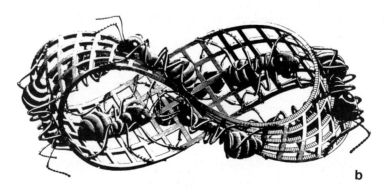

b

Fig. 14. (© M. C. Escher Heirs c/o Cordon Art, Baarn, Holland).

REFERENCES

1. *The World of M. C. Escher*. H. N. Abrams, New York (1971).
2. C. H. MacGillavry, *Symmetry Aspects of M. C. Escher's Periodic Drawings*. Bohn, Scheltema and Holkema, Utrecht (1976).
3. K. Levitin, *Geometricheskaya rapsodiya* (*Geometric Rhapsody*). Znanie, Moscow (1976).
4. C. A. Coulson
   (a) Symmetry. *Chem. Brit.* **4**, 113–120 (1968).
   (b) Mathematics in modern chemistry. *ibid.* **10**, 16–18 (1974).
5. H. Weyl, *Symmetry*. Princeton Univ. Press, Princeton (1952).
6. R. McWeeny, *Symmetry*. Pergamon Press, London (1962).
7. H. H. Jaffé and M. Orchin, *Symmetry in Chemistry*. Wiley, New York (1965).
8. P. B. Dorain, *Symmetry in Inorganic Chemistry*. Addison-Wesley, Reading, MA (1965).
9. I. Hargittai, *Szimmetria—egy kémikus szemével*, Akademiai Kiado, Budapest (1983); I. Hargittai and M. Hargittai, *Symmetry through the Eyes of a Chemist*, V. C. H. Verlagsgesselschaft, Weinheim (in press).
10. I. S. Dimitriev, *Symmetry in the World of Molecules*, Mir Publishers, Moscow (1979); I. S. Dimitriev, *Molekuly bez khimicheskikh sviazei* (*Molecules without chemical bonds*), Khimiya, Leningrad (1980); German translation, *Verlag für Grundstoffindustrie*, Leipzig (1980).
11. T. Roman, *Simetria*, (in Roumanian), Editura Tehnică, Bucureşti (1963); I. S. Zheludev, *Simmetria i eë prilozheniya*, Atomizdat, Moscow (1976) (Roumanian translation, Editura Tehnică, Bucureşti, 1979); J. Nicolle, *La symétrie et ses applications*, Albin Michel, Paris (1950) (also German translation); A. V. Shubnikov, *Simmetria i antisimmetria konechnykh figur*, Izd. Akad. Nauk, Moscow (1951); *Problema dissimetrii materialnykh obiektov*, Izd. Akad. Nauk, Moscow (1961); S. Jaskowski, *O symetrii w zdrobnictwie i przyrodzie*, Panstwowe zaklady wydawnictw szkolnych, Warszwa (1952); F. M. Jaeger, *Le principe de la symétrie et ses applications*, Gauthier-Villars, Paris (1945); R. Bentley, *Molecular Asymmetry in Biology*, Academic, New York (1970).
12. Yu. A. Urmandev, *Simmetria prirody i prirodnaya simmetria* (*Symmetry of Nature and Natural Symmetry*), Moscow (1974); R. Khochshtrasser, *Molekulyarnye aspekty simmetrii* (*Molecular Aspects of Symmetry*), Mir Publishers, Moscow (1968); F. Bakhman, *Postroenie geometrii na osnova ponyatiya simmetrii* (*Construction of Geometry Based on the Notion of Symmetry*), Nauka, Moscow (1969); I. D. Akopian, *Simmetria i asimmetria v poznanii* (*Symmetry and Asymmetry in Knowledge*), Izd. Akad. Nauk Armyanskoi S.S.R., Erevan, 1980; B. Douglas and C. A. Hollingsworth, *Symmetry in Bonding and Spectra*, Academic Press, New York (1985); G. S. Ezra, *Symmetry Properties of Molecules*, Lecture Notes in Chemistry No. 28, Springer-Verlag, Berlin (1982).
13. J. C. Slater, *Symmetry and Energy Bands in Crystals*. Dover, New York (1972) [1st Edn, McGraw-Hill, New York (1965)].
14. D. C. Harris and M. D. Bertolucci, *Symmetry and Spectroscopy: An Introduction to Vibrational and Electronic Spectroscopy*. Oxford Univ. Press, Oxford (1978).
15. A. N. Shubnikov and V. A. Koptsik, *Symmetry in Science and Art*. Plenum, New York (1974).
16. A. T. Balaban, Numere magice de electroni şi de nucleoni. *Revista de Chimie*, Bucureşti **14**, 158–160 (1963).
17. L. Pauling, *The Nature of the Chemical Bond*, 3rd Edn, Cornell Univ. Press, Ithaca, New York (1960); L. Pauling and E. B. Wilson, *Introduction to Quantum Mechanics*, McGraw-Hill, New York (1935).
18. K. Mislow and J. Siegel, Stereoisomerism and local chirality. *J. Am. Chem. Soc.* **106**, 3319–3331 (1984).
19. S. B. Elk, An application of geometry to the discovery of new classes of chemical compounds, *Caribbean J. Sci. Math.* **1**, 1–30 (1968); *Chem. Eng. News*, July 16 (1984).
20. R. J. Gillespie, *Molecular Geometry*. Van Nostrand-Reinhold, London (1972).
21. M. Gielen, in *Chemical Applications of Graph Theory* (Edited by A. T. Balaban), Academic Press, New York–London (1976); *Stéréochimie dynamique*, Freund Publ., Tel-Aviv, Israel (1974). (Edited by M. Gielen), *Advances in Dynamic Stereochemistry*, vol. 1, Freund Publ., London (1985).
22. J. Brocas, M. Gielen and R. Willem, *The Permutational Approach to Dynamic Stereochemistry*. McGraw-Hill, New York (1983).
23. R. Luckenbach, *Dynamic Stereochemistry of Phosphorus and Related Elements*. Georg Thieme Verlag, Stuttgart (1973).
24. I. Ugi, J. Dugundji, R. Kopp and D. Marquarding, *Perspectives in Theoretical Stereochemistry*, Lecture Notes in Chem. No. **36**, Springer-Verlag, Berlin (1984).
25. E. L. Eliel, *Stereochemistry of Carbon Compounds*. McGraw-Hill, New York (1962).
26. K. Mislow, *Introduction to Stereochemistry*. Benjamin, New York (1965).
27. H. Kagan, *Organic Stereochemistry*. Wiley, New York (1979).
28. M. Nogradi, *Stereochemistry*. Pergamon Press, Oxford (1981).
29. J. Dale, *Stereochemie und Konformationsanalyse*. Verlag Chemie, Weinheim (1978).
30. F. Badea and F. Kerek, *Stereochimie*, (in Roumanian). Editura Stiinţifică, Bucureşti (1974).
31. V. M. Potapov, *Stereokhimiya*. Khimiya, Moscow (1976).
32. J. D. Donaldson and S. D. Ross, *Symmetry and Stereochemistry*. Halsted Press Division, Wiley, New York (1972).
33. W. Bähr and H. Theobald, *Organische Stereochemie*. Springer-Verlag, Berlin (1973).
34. V. I. Sokolov, *Vvedenie v teoreticheskuyu stereokhimiyu* (*Introduction to Theoretical Stereochemistry*), Nauka, Moscow (1979); *Khimicheskaya topologiya* (*Chemical Topology*), Znanie, Moscow (1981).
35. G. Natta and M. Farina, *Stereochemistry*. Longmans, London (1972).
36. J. Pearce, *Stereochemistry: An Introductory Programme with Models*. Wiley-Interscience, New York (1978).
37. F. D. Gunstone, *Stereochemistry. A Programme Course*. English Univ. Press, London (1974).
38. O. B Ramsay, *Stereochemistry*. Heyden, London (1981).
39. A. F. Wells, *The Third Dimension in Chemistry*, Clarendon Press, Oxford (1956); *Three-Dimensional Nets and Polyhedra*, Wiley-Interscience, New York (1977).
40. N. S. Zefirov, S. S. Tratch and O. S. Chizhov, *Itogi nauki i tekhniki, Organicheskaya Khimia* Vol. 3, *Karkasnye i politsiklicheskie soedineniya. Molekulyarnyi design na osnove printsipa izomorfnogo zamescheniya* (*Frameworks and Polycyclic Compounds; Molecular Design Based on the Principle of Isomorphic Substitution*). Akad. Nauk. SSSR, Moscow (1979).

41. S. Mager and M. Horn, *Stereochimia Compusilor Organici*. Editura Dacia, Cluj-Napoca, Roumania (1984).
42. B. Testa, *Principles of Organic Stereochemistry*. Marcel Dekker, New York (1979).
43. W. Döpke, *Dynamische Aspekte der Stereochimie organischer Verbindungen*. Akademie-Verlag, Berlin (1979).
44. A. T. Balaban, unpublished data.
45. G. Maier *et al.*, Tetra-tert-butyltetrahedran, *Chem. Ber.* **114**, 3965–3987 (1981); *idem*, Spectroskopische Eigenschaften von Tetra-tert-butyltetrahedran, 3988–3996 (1981).
46. P. E. Eaton and T. N. Cole, The cubane system. *J. Am. Chem. Soc.* **86**, 962–964 (1964).
47. (a) A. T. Balaban and M. E. Banciu, Schemes and transformations in the $(CH)_{2k}$ series. Valence isomers of [8]- and [10]annulene. *J. Chem. Educ.* **61**, 766–770 (1984).
    (b) M. Banciu, C. Popa and A. T. Balaban, Schemes and transformations in the $(CH)_{2k}$ series. Valence isomers of [12]annulene, *Chem. Scripta* **24**, 28–37 (1984).
    (c) A. T. Balaban, M. Banciu and V. T. Ciorba, *Annulenes, Benzo-, Hetero-, Homo-Derivatives and Their Valence Isomers*. CRC Press, Boca Raton, Florida (1986).
48. L. A. Paquette *et al.*, Total synthesis of dodecahedrane, *J. Am. Chem. Soc.* **105**, 5446–5450 (1983); L. A. Paquette, In quest of the most complex of platonic hydrocarbons. The dodecahedrane story, *Chem. Aust.* **50**, 138–142 (1983).
49. P. von R. Schleyer, H. Prinzbach and W. Roth, (to be published).
50. P. E. Eaton, Yat Sun Or and S. J. Branca, Pentaprismane, *J. Am. Chem. Soc.* **103**, 2134–2136 (1981).
51. J. F. M. Oth, Kinetics and thermochemistry of the thermal rearrangement of hexamethyl-Dewar-benzene and hexamethyl-benzprismane. *Angew. Chem. Int. Ed. Engl.* **7**, 646–647 (1968). The kinetics and thermochemistry of the thermal rearrangement of hexamethylbicyclo[2.2.0]-hexa-2,5-diene (hexamethyl-Dewar-benzene) and of hexamethyltetracyclo[2.2.0.0^{2,6}, 0^{3,5}]-hexane(hexamethylprismane), *Rec. Trav. Chim.* **87**, 1185 (1969).
52. P. von R. Schleyer *et al.*, The degenerate 9-homocubyl cation, *J. Am. Chem. Soc.* **89**, 698–699 (1967); R. E. Leone and P. von R. Schleyer, Degenerate carbonium ions, *Angew. Chem. Int. Ed. Engl.* **9**, 860–891 (1970).
53. E. Osawa, K. Aigami, N. Takaishi, Y. Inamoto, F. Yoshiaki, Z. Majerski, P. von R. Schleyer, E. M. Engler and M. Farcaşiu, The mechanism of carbonium ion rearrangements of tricycloundecanes elucidated by empirical force field calculations. *J. Am. Chem. Soc.* **99**, 5361–5373 (1977).
54. T. M. Gund, P. von R. Schleyer, P. H. Gund and W. T. Wipke, Computer assisted graph theoretical analysis of complex mechanistic problems in polycyclic hydrocarbons. The mechanism of diamantane formation from various pentacyclotetradecanes. *J. Am. Chem. Soc.* **97**, 743–745 (1975).
55. A. T. Balaban and P. von R. Schleyer, Systematic classication and nomenclature of polymantanes. *Tetrahedron* **34**, 3599–3609 (1978).
56. R. N. Grimes, *Carboranes*, Academic Press, New York (1970); E. L. Muetterties and W. N. Knoth, *Polyhedral Boranes*, Marcel Dekker, New York (1968); T. Onak, *Adv. Organomet. Chem.* **3**, 263, 306 (1965); R. Köster and M. A. Grassberger, Strukturen und Synthesen von Carboranen, *Angew. Chem.* **6**, 97–219 (1967); R. E. Williams, *Progress Boron Chem.* **2**, 37 (1970).
57. W. N. Lipscomb, *Boron Hydrides*. Benjamin, New York (1963).
58. R. Hoffmann and W. N. Lipscomb, Theory of polyhedral molecules. I. Physical factorizations of the secular equation, *J. Chem. Phys.* **36**, 2179–2189 (1962); Theory of polyhedral molecules. III. Population analysis and reactivities for the carboranes, *ibid.*, 3489–3413 (1962); Boron hydrides: LCAO–MO and resonance studies, *ibid.*, **37**, 2872–2883 (1962); R. Hoffmann, An extended Hückel theory. I. Hydrocarbons, *ibid.* **39**, 1397–1412 (1963).
59. R. B. King and D. H. Rouvray, Chemical applications of group theory and topology. 7. A graph-theoretical interpretation of the bonding topology in polyhedral boranes and metal clusters. *J. Am. Chem. Soc.* **99**, 7834–7840 (1977).
60. A. T. Balaban and D. H. Rouvray, Graph-theoretical analysis of the bonding topology in polyhedral organic cations, *Tetrahedron* **36**, 1851–1855 (1980).
61. K. Mislow, On the classification of pairwise relations between isomeric structures. *Bull. Soc. Chim. Belges* **86**, 595–601 (1977).
62. G. Pólya, Kombinatorische Anzahlbestimmungen für Gruppen, Graphen und chemische Verbindungen, *Acta Math.* **68**, 145–254 (1937); Tabelle der Isomeren für die einfacheren Derivate einiger cyclischen Stammkörper, *Helv. Chim. Acta* **19**, 22–24 (1936); Algebraic calculation of the numbers of some organic compounds, *Z. Kristallogr.* (A) **93**, 415–443 (1936); Un problème combinatoire général sur les groupes de permutation et le calcul du nombre des isomères des composés organiques, *Compt. rend.* **201**, 1167–1169 (1935); Sur le nombre des isomères de certains composés chimiques, *Compt. rend.* **202**, 1554–1556 (1936).
63. A. T. Balaban, D. Farcaşiu and F. Harary, Chemical graphs. IX. Isotopic isomerism of multiply labelled compounds. *J. Labelled Comp.* **6**, 211–223 (1970).
64. A. T. Balaban, Chemical graphs. XXXII. Constitutional and steric isomers of substituted cycloalkanes. *Croatica Chem. Acta* **51**, 35–42 (1978).
65. R. B. Mallion, An analytical illustration of the relevance of molecular topology to the Aufbau process, *Croatica Chem. Acta* **56**, 477–490 (1983); A. T. Balaban, Chemical graphs. XXII. Valence isomers of heteroannulenes or of substituted annulenes. Coisomeric cubic multigraphs, *Rev. Roum. Chim.* **19**, 1323–1342 (1974).
66. B. K. Carpenter, Heavy atom tunneling as dominant pathway in a solution-phase reaction. Bond shift in antiaromatic annulenes, *J. Am. Chem. Soc.* **105**, 1700–1701 (1983); D. W. Whitman, S. W. Capon, E. R. Grant and D. K. Carpenter, *ibid.* (in press).
67. T. Bally and S. Masamune, Cyclobutadiene, *Tetrahedron*, **36**, 343–370 (1980); S. Masamune, Some aspects of strained systems: [4]Annulene and its CH$^+$ adduct, *Pure Appl. Chem.* **44**, 861–884 (1975).
68. T. Bally and S. Masamune, The cyclobutadiene problem, *Angew. Chem. Int. Ed. Engl.* **13**, 425–438 (1974); G. Maier *et al.*, Cyclobutadien—ein quadratisches Singulett-Molekül?, *ibid.* **15**, 226–229 (1976); Diradikal-artiges Verhalten von Tri-tert-butylcyclobutadien, *Angew. Chem.* **89**, 49–50 (1977).
69. R. P. Bell, *The Tunnel Effect in Chemistry*. Chapman and Hall, London (1980).
70. C. A. Coulson, The fundamentals of conjugation in ring systems. *Chem. Soc. Spec. Publ.* **12**, 85–113 (1958).
71. L. A. Paquette *et al.*, Bond fixation in annulenes. 14. Synthesis of and bond shifting equilibrium between 1,4- and 1,6-di-tert-butylcyclooctatetraenes, *J. Org. Chem.* **47**, 265–272 (1982); Bond fixation in annulenes. 11.

Synthesis and absolute configuration of the enantiomeric 1,3-di-tert-butylcyclooctatetraenes. Quantitative kinetic assessment of the effect of nonvicinal tert-butyl groups on [8]annulene. Ring inversion and bond shifting barriers, *J. Am. Chem. Soc.* **103**, 2262–2269 (1981); Bond fixation in annulenes. 8. Assessment of the ring inversion and bond shifting. Barriers in 1,2,3-trimethylcyclooctatetraene. Resolution, absolute configuration, circular dichroic behaviour of an [8]annulene hydrocarbon, *ibid.* **102**, 5016–5025 (1980); Bond fixation in annulenes. 9. Equalisation of ring and bond shifting. Energetics in 1,2,3,4-tetramethylcyclooctatetraene. Asymmetric synthesis, direct resolution and absolute configuration of the optically active hydrocarbon, *ibid.* **102**, 5026–5032 (1980); Bond fixation in annulenes. 6. Equalisation of ring inversion and bond shifting. Energetics in methyl-substituted cyclooctatetraenes. Use of buttressing effects for comparing transition-state geometries, *J. Am. Chem. Soc.* **101**, 1617–1620 (1979).

72. F. A. L. Anet *et al.*, The rate of bond change in cyclooctatetraene, *J. Am. Chem. Soc.* **84**, 671–672 (1962); Ring inversion and bond shift in cyclooctatetraene derivatives, *ibid.* **86**, 3576–3577 (1964); Photochemical interconversion of cyclooctatetraene bond shift isomers, *ibid.* **90**, 7130–7132 (1968).

73. M. J. S. Dewar and G. J. Gleicher, Ground states of conjugated molecules; allowance for molecular geometry, *J. Am. Chem. Soc.* **87**, 685–692 (1965).

74. R. Huisgen and F. Mietzsch, Valence tautomerism of cyclooctatetraene, *Angew. Chem. Int. Ed. Engl.* **3**, 83–88 (1964); R. Huisgen, W. E. Konz and G. E. Gream, Evidence for different valence tautomers of bromocyclooctatetraene, *J. Am. Chem. Soc.* **92**, 4105–4106 (1970).

75. E. Vogel, H. Kiefer and W. R. Roth, Bicyclo[4.2.0]octa-2,4,7-triene (Z). *Angew. Chem. Int. Ed. Engl.* **3**, 442–443 (1964).

76. J. Emsley, The composition, structure and hydrogen bonding in the β-diketones. *Structure and Bonding* **57**, 147–191 (1984).

77. L. C. Longuet-Higgins and L. Salem, Alternation of bond lengths in long conjugated chain molecules, *Proc. Roy. Soc. London A* **251**, 172–185 (1959); The alternation of bond lengths in large conjugated molecules. III. The cyclic polyenes $C_{18}H_{18}$, $C_{24}H_{24}$ and $C_{30}H_{30}$, *ibid.* **257**, 445–456 (1960); H. C. Longuet-Higgins, Paramagnetic ring currents in [4n]annulenes, *Aromaticity, Chem. Soc. Spec. Publ.* **21**, 109–111 (1967).

78. J. Bregman, F. L. Hirshfeld, D. Rabinovich and G. M. J. Schmidt, Crystal structure of [18]annulene. (I). X-ray study, *Acta Cryst.* **19**, 227–234 (1965); F. L. Hirshfeld and D. Rabinovich, Crystal structure of [18]annulene, *ibid.* **19**, 235–244 (1965).

79. (a) C. Kabuto, Y. Kitahara, M. Iyoda and M. Nakagawa, The crystal and molecular structure of 3,9,12,18-tetra-tert-butyldidehydro-[18]annulene. *Tetrahedron Lett.* 2791–2794 (1976).
(b) *idem*, The crystal and molecular structure of 3,11,14,22-tetra-tert-butyldidehydro-[22]annulene, *ibid.* 2787–2790 (1976).
(c) N. Bacon, A. J. Boulton and A. R. Katritzky, Structure of "hexanitrosobenzene" from vibrational spectroscopy, *Trans. Faraday Soc.* **63**, 833–835 (1967); H. H. Cady, A. C. Larson and D. T. Cromer, Crystal structure of benzotrifuroxan ("hexanitrosobenzene"), *Acta Cryst.* **20**, 336–341 (1966); R. R. McGuire, Properties of benzotrifuroxan, Report UCRL-52353 (1977), *Chem. Abstr.* **89**, 131857 (1978), *Energy Res. Abstr.* 26846 (1978).

80. K. D. Warren, Calculations of the Jahn–Teller coupling constants for d^x systems in octahedral symmetry via the angular overlap model, *Structure and Bonding* **57**, 119–145 (1984); B. J. Hathaway, A new look at the stereochemistry and electronic properties of complexes of the copper(II) ion, *ibid.* **57**, 55–118 (1984); D. Reinen and C. Friebel, Local and cooperative Jahn–Teller interactions in model structures. Spectroscopic and structural evidence, *ibid.* **37**, 1–53 (1977).

81. H. Vasiliu, On the molecular configuration of proteins, lipids and carbohydrates (in Roumanian), *Bull. Facult. Stiinte Agricole Chisinău* **1**, 5–21 (1936/7); *Chimie Agricolă*, Vol. 1, p. 36, Tiparul Moldovenesc, Chişinău (1937).

82. A. T. Balaban and I. Tomescu, Algebraic expressions for the number of Kekulé structures of isoarithmic cata-condensed benzenoid polycyclic hydrocarbons, *Math. Chem.* **14**, 155–182 (1983); *idem*, Chemical graphs. XL. Three relations between the Fibonacci sequence and the numbers of Kekulé structures for non-branched cata-condensed polycyclic aromatic hydrocarbons, *Croat. Chim. Acta* **57**, 391–404 (1984).

83. A. T. Balaban and M. Gaspar, unpublished.

84. R. B. Woodward and R. Hoffmann, *The Conservation of Orbital Symmetry*, Verlag Chemie, Weinheim (1970); Die Erhaltung der Orbitalsymmetrie, *Angew. Chem.* **81**, 797–869 (1969).

85. M. G. Evans, Activation energies of reactions involving conjugated systems, *Trans. Faraday Soc.* **35**, 824–834 (1939).

86. M. J. S. Dewar, A molecular orbital theory of organic chemistry. VIII. Aromaticity and electrocyclic reactions, *Tetrahedron Suppl.* **8**, Part I, 75–92 (1966); *The Molecular Orbital Theory of Organic Chemistry*, McGraw-Hill, New York (1969).

87. H. C. Longuet-Higgins and E. W. Abrahamson, The electronic mechanism of electrocyclic reactions, *J. Am. Chem. Soc.* **87**, 2045–2046 (1965).

88. W. T. A. M. von der Lugt and L. J. Oosterhoff, Quantum chemical interpretation of photoinduced electrocyclic reactions, *Chem. Commun.* 1235–1238 (1968).

89. K. Fukui, Stereoselectivity associated with noncycloaddition to unsaturated bonds. *Tetrahedron Lett.* 2427–2732 (1965).

90. N. Trong Anh, *Les règles de Woodward-Hoffmann*. Ediscience, Paris (1970) (German translation, Verlag Chemie, 1972).

91. I. Fleming, *Frontier Orbitals and Organic Chemical Reactions*. Wiley, Chichester (1976).

92. J. Mathieu and J. Valls, Le tranfert électronique circulaire dans l'interprétation de certaines réactions de la chimie organique. *Bull. Soc. Chim. France* 1509–1541 (1957).

93. A. T. Balaban, Chemical graphs. III. Reactions with cyclic six-membered transition states. *Rev. Roum. Chim.* **12**, 875–898 (1967).

94. H. E. Zimmermann, On molecular correlation diagrams; the occurrence of Möbius systems in cyclization reactions, and factors controlling ground- and excited-state reactions, *J. Am. Chem. Soc.* **88**, 1564–1565 (1966).

95. R. G. Pearson, Symmetry rules for chemical reactions, *Chem. Brit.* **12**, 160–165 (1976); *Acc. Chem. Res.* **4**,

152–160 (1971); *Top. Curr. Chem.* **41**, 75 (1973); *Symmetry Rules for Chemical Reactions: Orbital Topology and Elementary Processes*, Wiley-Interscience, New York (1976).

96. A. T. Balaban, D. Farcaşiu and R. Bănică, Chemical graphs. II. Graphs of multiple 1,2-shifts in carbonium ions and related systems. *Rev. Roum. Chim.* **11**, 1205–1227 (1966).
97. P. C. Lauterbur and F. Ramirez, Pseudorotation in trigonal bipyramidal molecules. *J. Am. Chem. Soc.* **90**, 6722–6726 (1968).
98. J. D. Dunitz and V. Prelog, Ligand reorganisation in trigonal bipyramids. *Angew. Chem. Int. Ed. Engl.* **7**, 725–726 (1968).
99. K. Mislow, Role of pseudorotation in the stereochemistry of nucleophilic displacement reactions, *Acc. Chem. Res.* **3**, 321 (1970), footnote 13; G. Zon and K. Mislow, *Top. Curr. Chem.* **19**, 61 (1971).
100. F. Harary, *Graph Theory*. Addison-Wesley, Reading, MA (1969).
101. H. Sachs, H.-J. Voss and H. Walther, *Beiträge zur Graphentheorie*. Teubner Verlagsges., Leipzig (1968).
102. P. K. Wong, Cages—A survey. *J. Graph Theory* **6**, 1–22 (1982).
103. W. T. Tutte, *Connectivity in Graphs*. Univ. of Toronto Press, Toronto (1966).
104. C. T. Benson, Minimal regular graphs of girths eight and twelve. *Can. J. Math.* **18**, 1091–1094 (1966).
105. A. T. Balaban, A trivalent graph of girth ten. *J. Comb. Theory* **B12**, 1–5 (1972).
106. M. O'Keefe and P. K. Wong, A smallest graph of girth 10 and valency 3. *J. Comb. Theory* **B29**, 91–105 (1980).
107. A. T. Balaban, Trivalent graphs of girth nine and eleven and relationships between cages. *Rev. Roum. Math. Pures Appl.* **18**, 1033–1043 (1973).
108. N. L. Biggs and M. J. Hoare, A trivalent graph with 58 vertices and girth 9. *Discrete Math.* **20**, 299–301 (1980).
109. M. Gordon and W. Temple, in *Chemical Applications of Graph Theory* (Edited by A. T. Balaban), p. 299. Academic Press, London (1976).
110. A. T. Balaban, Chemical Graphs. XIII. Combinatorial patterns. *Rev. Roum. Math. Pures Appl.* **17**, 3–16 (1976).
111. M. Randić, On discerning symmetry properties of graphs. *Chem. Phys. Lett.* **42**, 283–287 (1976).
112. M. Randić, Symmetry properties of graphs of interest in chemistry. II. Desargues–Levi graph. *Int. J. Quantum Chem.* **15**, 663–682 (1979).
113. A. T. Balaban, Chemical graphs. XXX. Reaction graphs for degenerate rearrangements of homovalenium cations. *Rev. Roum. Chim.* **22**, 243–255 (1977).
114. M. Randić, Symmetry properties of graphs of interest in chemistry. III. Homotetrahedryl rearangement. *Int. J. Quantum Chem., Sanibel Quantum Chem. Symp.* **14**, 557–577 (1980).
115. A. T. Balaban, Chemical graphs. XXXIII. Graphs for intramolecular rearrangements of tetragonal–pyramidal complexes. *Rev. Roum. Chim.* **23**, 733–746 (1978).
116. M. Randić and V. Katorić, *Int. J. Quantum Chem.* **21**, 647 (1982).
117. E. A. Abbott, *Flatland: A Romance in Many Dimensions, by A Square*. Boston (1928).
118. H. S. M. Coxeter, *Regular Polytopes*, Methuen, London (1948); *Trans. Roy. Soc. Canada* **51**, Section III (1957).
119. D'Arcy W. Thompson, *On Growth and Form*, Cambridge Univ. Press (1943); *Proc. Roy. Soc. A* **107**, 181 (1925).
120. H. Emde, *Homogene Polytope*, Abhandlungen-Neue Folge-Heft 89, Verlag der Bayrischen Akad. Wiss., München (1958); *Geometrie der Knoten-Stab-Tragwerte*, Strukturforschungszentrum, Würzburg (1977).
121. C. Roussel, A. Lidén, M. Chanon, J. Metzger and J. Sandström, The gear effect. V. A model for conformational transmission, *J. Am. Chem. Soc.* **98**, 2847–2852 (1976); U. Berg and C. Roussel, Gear effect. Steric anisotropy of space through "Janus-like" substituents. A dynamic ¹H- and ¹³C-NMR study of dibenzyl-4,5-diisopropylimidazoline-2-thione, *ibid.* **102**, 7848–7858 (1980).
122. W. D. Hounshell, L. D. Iroff, D. J. Iverson, R. J. Wroczynski and K. Mislow, Is the effective size of an alkyl group a gage of dynamic gearing? *Israel J. Chem.* **20**, 65–74 (1980).
123. U. Berg, T. Liljefors, C. Roussel and T. Sandström, Steric interplay between alkyl groups bonded to planar frameworks. *Acc. Chem. Res.* **18**, 80–86 (1985).
124. J. H. Fendler, *Membrane Mimetic Chemistry*, Wiley-Interscience, New York (1982); *Chem. Brit.* **20**, 1098–1100 (1984); Surfactant vesicles as membrane mimetic agents: characterization and utilization, *Acc. Chem. Res.* **13**, 7–13 (1980); J. H. Fendler and P. Tundo, Polymerized surfactant aggregates: characterization and utilization, *ibid.* **17**, 3–8 (1984).

Comp. & Maths. with Appls. Vol. 12B, Nos. 3/4, pp. 1021–1038, 1986
Printed in Great Britain.

0886-9561/86 $3.00 + .00
© 1986 Pergamon Press Ltd.

THE VSEPR MODEL OF MOLECULAR GEOMETRY

I. Hargittai[†] and B. Chamberland
Department of Chemistry and Institute of Materials Science, University of Connecticut,
Storrs, CT 06268, U.S.A.

Abstract—The valence shell electron-pair repulsion model successfully accounts for geometrical variations in extensive classes of compounds. According to its basic postulate the geometry of a molecule is determined by the space requirements of all electron pairs in the valence shell of the central atom. The compatibility of a structure with this model must be tested by examining the variations of all angles of all electron pairs in the valence shell.

1. INTRODUCTION

"There is no more basic enterprise in chemistry than the determination of the geometrical structure of a molecule. Such a determination, when it is well done, ends all speculation as to the structure and provides us with the starting point for the understanding of every physical, chemical and biological property of the molecule"[1]. The geometry of the molecule is in fact the spatial arrangement of its constituting atomic nuclei. The qualitative characterization of the molecular geometry is the shape and symmetry of the molecule, i.e. those of the ensemble of the atomic nuclei. A more quantitative characterization consists of the metrical expression of the relative three-dimensional positions of the nuclei, or more descriptively, of the bond distances, bond angles and angles of internal rotation.

The molecular geometry is only one aspect of molecular structure. There are two other major aspects, viz. the intramolecular motion, which is the relative displacements of the atomic nuclei with respect to their equilibrium positions, and the electronic structure of the molecule, which is the electron density distribution. We shall be concerned primarily with the qualitative aspects of molecular geometry, i.e. with molecular shape and symmetry.

In order to determine the molecular shape and symmetry, various experiments and/or theoretical, mainly quantum-chemical calculations can be carried out. Beyond establishing the structures of individual molecules, it is equally important to understand the reasons for the occurrence of this or that molecular structure and structural changes in series of molecules.

Various physical techniques are available today to determine the molecular geometry, i.e. to measure distances between atoms or atomic nuclei and angles between chemical linkages very accurately. The accuracy may be a few thousands of an ångstrom and a few tenths of a degree, respectively. An interatomic and an internuclear distance, however, are not the same except under rigorously defined conditions. If the electron density distribution in an atom has spherical symmetry, then interatomic and internuclear distances express the same thing. Intramolecular motion may also change the apparent structure of a molecule when measured by various physical techniques. Consider the simple case of a linear symmetrical triatomic molecule B—A—B. Suppose that this molecule is performing bending vibrations, as is shown in Fig. 1. If the B—A—B bond angle is determined from the time-averaged A—B and B . . . B distances,

$$BAB = 2 \arcsin\left[\frac{(B \ldots B)/2}{A—B}\right],$$

then even for a linear $D_{\infty h}$ symmetry AB_2 molecule the measurements may yield a bent structure with C_{2v} symmetry. Intramolecular motion usually, though not always, leads to a decrease of molecular symmetry. This obviously cannot happen if the molecule is completely motionless. There is no such molecule in reality, but the structure of such molecules can be calculated. This is the so-called equilibrium structure versus the so-called average structure influenced by

†Visiting Professor, on leave from the Hungarian Academy of Sciences, Budapest, POB 117, H-1431.

the motion. The theoretical calculations, which are mostly quantum-chemical calculations, in fact produce this very equilibrium structure. A careful comparison between experimental and calculated structures has to be considered and corrected for these differences.

All things considered, a large body of experimental and theoretical structural information has accumulated during the past years, and forms a fairly consistent pattern. For consistency we are referring to various good correlations between structural and other properties in relatively large classes of substances. It is also remarkable how well modern structural information lends itself to be discussed in those qualitative terms and ideas, most of which had been developed before the advent of modern structural chemistry. These traditional ideas and terms include items such as chemical bond, multiple bond, and electronegativity, to mention some of the most fundamental ones.

It is also remarkable how some simple and qualitative models can explain and account for large amounts of experimental and calculated data. Of course, the real test of any model and theory is its predictive power, and it is remarkable how turstworthy some of these qualitative models of molecular structure are in this respect as well. In fact, for known data, we have to expect these models to be 100% foolproof within their scopes. On the other hand, as soon as "exceptions to the rule" seem to emerge, if they prove correct, the scope or limits of applicability of the model have to be changed accordingly.

The electron-pair description of the chemical bond by Lewis[2] is perhaps the most important discovery in the chemistry of this century. The significance of this discovery was amply demonstrated during the recent Lewis anniversary[3]. The electron-pair description of the chemical bond is also the natural link between the most important discoveries in chemistry of the last century as, for example, between the Periodic Table of the elements by Mendeleev and the tetrahedral carbon configuration by van't Hoff on the one hand, and our present-day knowledge of chemical structures on the other. The cubical atom of Lewis, illustrated in Fig. 2, helped to develop the shared-electron-pair concept. Then Sidgwick and Powell[4] correlated the number of electron pairs in the valence shell of the central atom in a molecule and the bond configuration of this central atom. The valence shell is the outermost shell of the electron cloud surrounding the atomic nucleus. It is the electrons of this shell which participate in the chemical bonding. Of course, not all the electrons of the valence shell participate in bonding. Some electrons in the valence shell of the central atom may belong exclusively to the central atom. However, such unshared or "lone" pairs of electrons have also their space requirement, so it was an important realization that all electron pairs—both shared and lone—are to be considered when the bond configuration is predicted. Another important step was made by Gillespie and Nyholm[5] in the development of this model. They introduced allowances for the differences

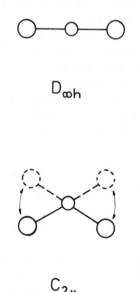

Fig. 1. The consequences of bending vibrations on the shape and symmetry of the linear symmetric triatomic molecule AB_2.

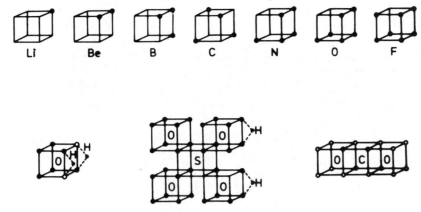

Fig. 2. Cubic atoms and molecules by Lewis in 1916.

between bonding pairs and lone pairs. It was at this point that these ideas were taking shape as a distinct model and the name VSEPR (Valence Shell Electron Pair Repulsion) model was coined by Gillespie (e.g. [6]). He has also popularized this model very effectively over the years (cf. [7–9]). The model has found its way into most introductory chemistry texts in addition to being a research tool.

The VSEPR model is presented here briefly because it has a simple and attractive way to deduce the shapes and symmetries of molecules in relatively large classes of substances. There have been reports of structures which were found to be incompatible with the predictions of the VSEPR model. Whenever these structures were within the real scope and limits of the model, they invariably turned out to be either wrong experimental results or were erroneously tested against the predictions of the model. Whereas the basic postulates of the VSEPR model have remained unchanged over the years, the way of testing its applicability has been generalized[10,11]. We shall discuss examples for all these.

2. THE BASIC POSTULATE

The VSEPR model is based on the following postulate (cf., for example, [9]): *The geometry of the molecule is determined by the repulsions among the electron pairs in the valence shell of its central atom.* This postulate implicitly emphasizes the importance of both bonding pairs and lone pairs in establishing the molecular geometry. The bond configuration around the atom A in the molecule AX_n, and, accordingly, the geometry of the AX_n molecule is such that the electron pairs of the valence shell must be at maximum distances from each other, as if the electron pairs were mutually repelling each other. Thus the situation may be visualized so that the electron pairs occupy well-defined parts of the space around the central atom, corresponding to the concept of the localized molecular orbitals.

If it is assumed that the valence shell of the central atom retains its spherical symmetry in the molecule, then the electron pairs will be at equal distances from the nucleus of the central atom. In this case the arrangements at which the distances among the electron pairs are at maximum will be the following:

Number of electron pairs in the valence shell	Arrangement
2	linear
3	equilateral triangle
4	tetrahedron
5	trigonal bipyramid
6	octahedron

Let the electron pairs be represented by points on a sphere. Then the shapes shown in Fig. 3 are obtained by connecting these points. Of the three polyhedra shown in this figure, only two

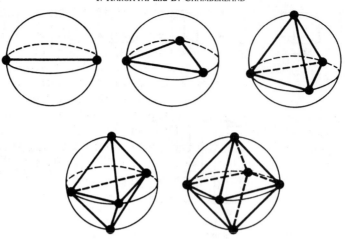

Fig. 3. Molecular shapes from a points-on-the-sphere model.

are regular, viz. the tetrahedron and the octahedron. The trigonal bipyramid is not a regular polyhedron; although its six faces are equivalent, its edges and vertices are not. Incidentally it is not so unique a solution to our problem. Another, only slightly less advantageous arrangement is the square pyramidal configuration and numerous intermediate ones between the trigonal bipyramid and square pyramid.

The repulsions considered in the VSEPR model may be expressed by the potential energy terms

$$V_{ij} = K/r_{ij}^n,$$

where K is a constant, r_{ij} is the distance between the points i and j, and the exponent n is large for strong or "hard" repulsion interactions and small for weak or "soft" repulsion interactions. Experience shows[12] that n is much larger than that which would correspond to simple electrostatic Coulomb interactions. Incidentally, as n gets larger than 3, the results become insensitive to the value of n. That is very fortunate because n is not really known. This insensitivity to the choice of n is what provides the wide applicability of the VSEPR model.

There have been attempts to provide quantum-mechanical foundations for the VSEPR model (cf., for example, [13]). Roughly speaking, these attempts have developed along two lines. One was concerned with assigning a rigorous theoretical basis to the model, primarily involving the Pauli exclusion principle. At some point it has even been suggested to call the model Pauli mechanics[12]. However, the VSEPR model is a qualitative one. It overemphasizes some interactions and ignores many others. It is thus not expected that rigorous quantum-mechanical treatment may parallel it in its entirety. On the other hand, numerous quantum-chemical calculations (e.g. [10,14]) have already produced a large amount of structural information which are in complete agreement with the VSEPR predictions. This shows again that the model captures some very important effects which appear to be dominant in some structural classes.

Thus, for example, the model emphasizes electron-pair repulsions while it ignores ligand–ligand interactions. With large central atoms and small ligands, this works well. However, with increasing ligand size relative to the size of the central atom, the nonbonded interactions gradually become more important. Obviously, both effects may be commensurable in some structures and eventually the ligand–ligand interactions become dominant. Another assumption in the VSEPR model refers to the spherical shape of the valence shell of the central atom. With decreasing validity of this assumption, again, the applicability of the predictions by the model will diminish. It is by investigating and establishing the limitations of applicability of the model that its usefulness and reliability will be enhanced.

3. MOLECULAR SHAPES AND BOND ANGLES

Using the VSEPR model, it is easy to predict the shape and symmetry of a molecule from the total number of bonding pairs, n, and lone pairs, m, of electrons in the valence shell of its central atom. The molecule may then be written as AX_nE_m, where E denotes a lone pair of electrons. An AX_2 molecule will then have two electron pairs in the valence shell of the central atom and, accordingly, a linear X—A—X configuration. However, if there is an additional lone electron pair in the valence shell (thus the molecule is AX_2E) the three electron pairs will have a trigonal planar arrangement, and, accordingly, the X—A—X configuration will be bent. These structures are illustrated in Fig. 4 along with the equilateral triangular configuration of AX_3. Consider now in some more detail molecules with four electron pairs in the valence shell of the central atom; for example, the series of methane (CH_4), ammonia (NH_3) and water (H_2O) molecules. Originally there were four electrons in the carbon valence shell, and forming four C—H bonds, the hydrogens contributed altogether four electrons. Thus methane is expressed by AX_4 and its symmetry is, accordingly, regular tetrahedral. In ammonia there were originally five electrons in the nitrogen valence shell, and the formation of the three N—H bonds added three more. With the three bonding pairs and one lone pair in the nitrogen valence shell, ammonia may be written as AX_3E and, accordingly, the arrangement of the molecule is related to a tetrahedron. However, only in three of its four directions do we find bonds, and consequently ligands, while in the fourth there is a lone pair of electrons. Hence the pyramidal geometry of the ammonia molecule. The bent configuration of the water molecule can be similarly deduced.

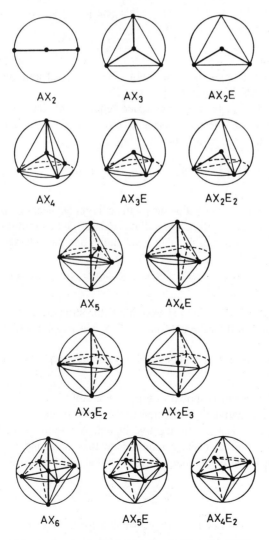

Fig. 4. Structural models for some simple molecules[7].

In order to establish the total number of electron pairs in the valence shell, the number of electrons originally present and the number of bonds formed need to be considered. A summary of geometrical arrangements for a series of various types of simple molecules is shown in Fig. 4.

The molecular shape to a large extent determines the bond angles. Thus the bond angle X—A—X is 180° in the linear AX_2 molecule, 120° in the trigonal planar AX_3 molecule and 109° 28′ in the tetrahedral AX_4 molecule. The arrangements shown in Fig. 4 correspond to the assumption that the strengths of the repulsions from all electron pairs are equal. In reality, however, the space requirements and accordingly, the strengths of the repulsions from various electron pairs may be different depending on various circumstances as described in the following three subrules[9].

1. A lone pair, E, has a greater space requirement in the vicinity of the central atom then a bonding pair. Thus it exercises stronger repulsion towards the neighboring electron pairs than a bonding pair, b. The repulsion strengths decrease in the following order:

$$E/E > E/b > b/b.$$

This is well illustrated by the various angles of the sulfur difluoride molecule as determined by *ab initio* molecular orbital calculations[10]:

$$SF_2 \text{ or } SF_2E_2: \quad E—S—E \ 135.8°$$
$$E—S—F \ 104.3°$$
$$F—S—F \ \ 98.1°.$$

This is also why, for example, the bond angles H—N—H of ammonia are smaller than the ideal tetrahedral, viz. 106.7°[15] instead of 109.5°.

2. Multiple bonds, b_m, have greater space requirement than single bonds and exercise stronger repulsions towards the neighboring electron pairs than single bonds. The repulsion strengths decrease in the following order:

$$b_m/b_m > b_m/b > b/b.$$

The consequence for bond angles is that they will be larger between multiple bonds than between single bonds. The structure of dimethyl sulfate, $(CH_3O)_2SO_2$, provides a good example. This molecule has three different types of OSO bond angles and they change in the following order:

$$S{=}O/S{=}O > S{=}O/S—O > S—O/S—O$$

(viz. 122°, 109°, and 98°)[16]. Another example is the structure of the sulfuric acid molecule, or more generally, the configurations of the XSO_2Y sulfones for which

$$S{=}O/S{=}O > S{=}O/S—X \text{ (or } S{=}O/S—Y) > S—X/S—Y.$$

The general molecular model is shown in Fig. 5. For sulfuric acid X = Y = H.

3. A more electronegative ligand decreases the electron density in the vicinity of the central atom as compared with a less electronegative ligand. Accordingly the bond to a less electronegative ligand, b_x, has greater space requirement than the bond to a more electronegative ligand, b_y. The repulsion strengths then decrease in the following order:

$$b_x/b_x > b_x/b_y > b_y/b_y.$$

The consequence is that the bond angles are smaller for more electronegative ligands than for less electronegative ligands. Examples are provided by the bond angles X—A—X of some

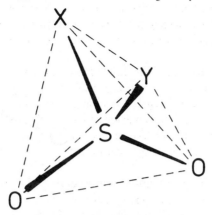

Fig. 5. The molecular model of XSO_2Y sulfones.

AX_3, i.e. AX_3E molecules (for references, see [15]):

X	NX_3	PX_3	AsX_3	SbX_3
F	102.4(3)°	97.8(2)°	96.2(2)°	95.0(8)°
Cl	107.1(5)°	100.3(1)°	98.6(4)°	97.0(12)°
Br		101.0(4)°	99.7(3)°	98.2(10)°
I		102(2)°	100.2(4)°	99(1)°

The parenthesized uncertainties are cited as units of the last digit.

A fourth subrule in the VSEPR model concerns the relative availability of space in the valence shell.

4. There is less space available in a completely filled valence shell than in a partially filled valence shell. Accordingly, the repulsions are stronger and the possibilities for angular deviations are less in the filled valence shell than in partially filled one. Thus, for example, the bond angles of the NX_3 molecules are less different from the ideal tetrahedral angle than those of the PX_3 molecules, as can be seen in the above data.

It has been shown that the differences in the electron-pair repulsions may account for the bond-angle variations in series of molecules. The question arises whether these differences have any effect on the symmetry choice of the molecules. In the four-electron-pair systems the AX_4, EBX_3, and E_2CX_2 molecules have T_d, C_{3v}, C_{2v} symmetries, respectively. The symmetry is preserved within each series upon substitution, provided that all X ligands in a molecule are the same.

Ligand electronegativity changes may have decisive effects, however, in the symmetry choices of various bipyramidal systems, of which the trigonal bipyramidal configuration is the simplest.

4. TRIGONAL BIPYRAMIDAL CONFIGURATIONS

With five electron pairs in the valence shell of the central atom, trigonal bipyramidal (Fig. 6) configurations usually occur, although the square pyramidal cannot be excluded in some cases. Even intermediate arrangements between the two may appear to be the most stable in some special cases. The trigonal bipyramidal configuration with an equilateral triangle in the equilateral plane has D_{3h} symmetry and the square pyramidal has C_{4v}. The intermediate ones have C_{2v}, or nearly so. Indeed, rearrangements often occur in the trigonal bipyramidal structures performing low-frequency large-amplitude motion[17]. Such rearrangements are illustrated in Fig. 7.

Generally speaking, the positions in the D_{3h} trigonal bipyramid are not equivalent. Their equality occurs only at a special exponent value $n = 3.4$ in the potential energy term

$$V = K/r^n.$$

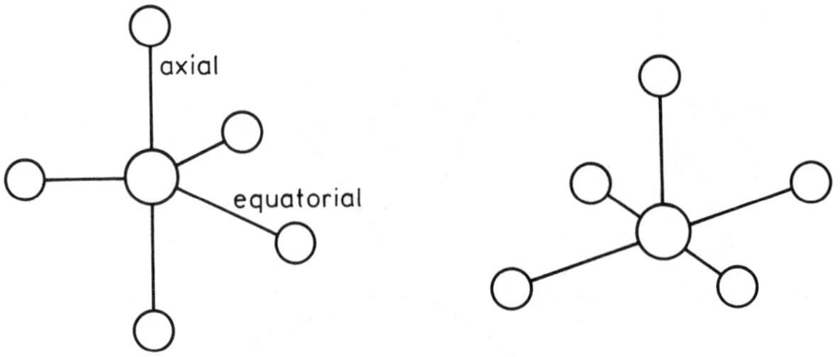

Fig. 6. Trigonal bipyramidal and square pyramidal configurations.

For n values larger than 3.4 the axial ligand position is further away from the central atom than the equatorial one, and the reverse is true for n values smaller than 3.4. These variations, however, have no effect on the symmetry of the AX_5 structures and this is comforting from the point of view of the applicability of the VSEPR model in establishing the point group symmetries of such molecules.

On the other hand, when inequality among the electron pairs occurs, the differences in the axial and equatorial positions are important for symmetry considerations. While the PF_5 molecule as an AX_5 system has unambiguously D_{3h} symmetry for its trigonal bipyramidal configuration, it is not so obvious to predict the symmetry of the SF_4 molecule (which may be written as AX_4E, and thus also has trigonal bipyramidal arrangement). The question is which position will the lone pair of electrons occupy?

There are three nearest neighbors, at 90° from any axial position in the trigonal bipyramidal configuration, and one more neighbor at 180° and that is the other axial position. For an equatorial position there are two nearest neighbors at 90° and two further ones at 120°. As the closest electron pairs exercise by far the strongest repulsion, the axial positions are effected more than the equatorial ones. It is then in agreement with this reasoning that the axial bonds are usually longer than the equatorial ones. If there is then a lone pair of electrons with a relatively large space requirement, it is to be found in the more advantageous equatorial position. Accordingly, the SF_4 structure has C_{2v} symmetry, as has the ClF_3 molecule, which is indeed AX_3E_2, and finally the XeF_2 molecule, which is AX_2E_3, having all three lone pairs in the equatorial plane; hence its symmetry is $D_{\infty h}$. All these structures are depicted in Fig. 8.

A double bond also takes an equatorial position, for similar reasons as the lone pair. Thus the point group may easily be established for the molecules $O{=}SF_4$, $O{=}ClF_3$, XeO_3F_2, and XeO_2F_2, as also seen in Fig. 8.

Lone pairs and/or double bonds replaced single bonds in the above examples. Similar considerations are applicable when ligand electronegativity changes take place. Typical and very simple examples are the structures of PF_2Cl_3 and PF_3Cl_2[18]. The chlorine atoms are less

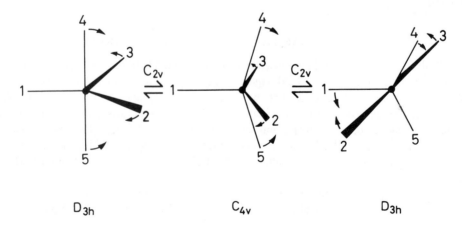

Fig. 7. The intramolecular rearrangements of the PF_5 molecule.

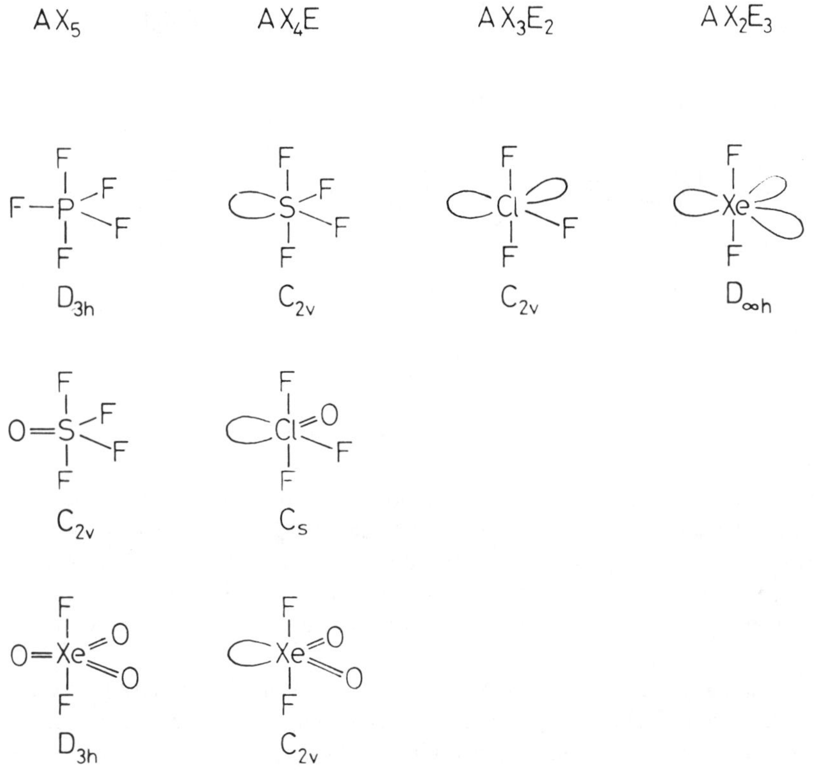

AX_5 AX_4E AX_3E_2 AX_2E_3

Fig. 8. Trigonal bipyramidal structures.

electronegative ligands than the fluorine atoms, and the former will be in equatorial positions in *both* structures, as seen in Fig. 9. The point groups are C_{2v} for PF_3Cl_2 and D_{3h} for PF_2Cl_3. If the chlorine atoms were in the axial positions in PF_3Cl_2, this molecule would also have the higher symmetry D_{3h}.

5. MORE THAN FIVE ELECTRON PAIRS

All six electron pairs are equivalent in the AX_6 molecule, as the six X ligands will be found at the vertices of a regular octahedron around the central atom A. The molecular symmetry will unambiguously be O_h. An example is SF_6. The IF_5 molecule, however, corresponds to AX_5E and its square pyramidal configuration has C_{4v} symmetry. There is no question here as to the preferred position for the lone pair as any of the six equivalent sites may be selected. When, however, a second lone pair is introduced, then the arrangement in which the two lone pairs find themselves at the maximum distance is favored. Thus for XeF_4 (i.e. AX_4E_2) the bond configuration is square planar, and the point group is D_{4h}. These molecular structures are illustrated in Fig. 10.

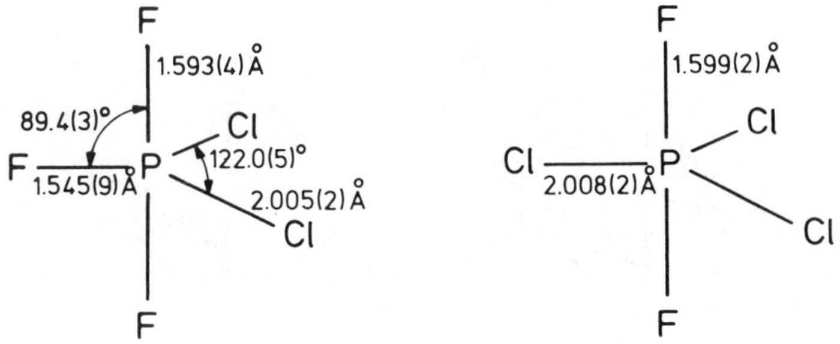

Fig. 9. The structure of PF_3Cl_2 and PF_2Cl_3.

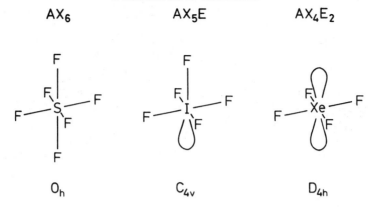

Fig. 10. Octahedral structures.

The difficulties encountered in the discussion of the five electron-pair valence shells are intensified for the seven-electron-pair case. Here again the ligand arrangements are less meritorious than for the nearest coordination neighbors, i.e. six and eight. It is not possible to arrange seven points to describe a regular polyhedron, while the number of nonisomorphic polyhedra with seven vertices is large. None of them is distinguished, however, with high relative stability.

One of the early successes of the VSEPR model was that it correctly predicted the non-octahedral structure of XeF_6, as it is indeed a seven-coordination example, AX_6E. Its possible distorted octahedral configurations are shown in Fig. 11. Experimental data are consistent with the proposed distorted octahedral models.

6. TESTING THE APPLICABILITY OF THE MODEL

From the very beginning of the history of the VSEPR model, its applicability usually has been examined for the molecular shapes and bond-angle variations. While the influence of the lone pairs on the bond angles has been correctly assessed, it has been largely ignored that the bond angles represent only part of the geometrical characterization of the entire valence shell configuration.

There have been noted some seemingly incompatible bond-angle variations with the model which were puzzling since they occurred among such simple molecules that were supposed to be well within the scope of the model. Some examples will be discussed below. First, however, a generalized approach for testing the applicability of the VSEPR model is formulated. This formulation stems directly from the basic idea of the VSEPR model[11].

As the shape and the geometry of a molecule is assumed to be determined by the repulsions among all electron pairs of the valence shell, the compatibility of a structure or structural variations with the VSEPR model has to be tested by examining the variations of *all angles of all electron pairs* rather than those of the bond angles only!

The reason that the variations of only the bond angles are usually considered is very trivial. The bond angles are the ones directly determined from the experiment. Sometimes, though by far not always, the angles made by the lone pairs are also attainable from the bond angles by

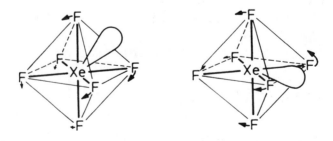

Fig. 11. The structure of XeF_6 (i.e. $EXeF_6$).

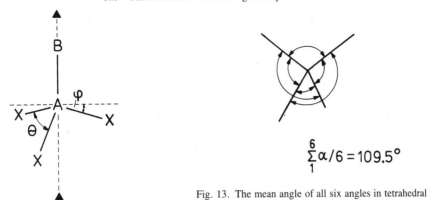

$$\sum_{1}^{6}\alpha/6 = 109.5°$$

Fig. 13. The mean angle of all six angles in tetrahedral configurations.

Fig. 12. The bond arrangement of an AX_3B molecule with C_{2v} symmetry.

virtue of the molecular symmetry. For example, the E—P—F angle of the PF_3 (i.e. EPF_3) molecule can be calculated from the F—P—F bond angle by virtue of the C_{3v} symmetry of this molecule. This is the same as in any AX_3B molecule with a C_{3v} point group; one of the two angles of the structure determines the other (cf. Fig. 12). If, for example, the angle B—A—X is $\phi + \pi/2$ and the angle X—A—X is θ, then $\cos\theta = 1 - 3/2\cos^2\phi$. On the other hand, the angles involving the lone pairs of the SF_2 (i.e. E_2SF_2) molecule with a C_{2v} point group cannot be calculated from the bond angle alone. The bond angle F—S—F and the C_{2v} symmetry do not determine the angles E—S—E and E—S—F. However, the mean value of all the angles in either the C_{3v} or the C_{2v} structures is always the ideal tetrahedral angle. The mean value is obtained, of course, by averaging all six angles in these structures. This is illustrated in Fig. 13.

The characteristic mean angle for the five-electron-pair cases is 108°. This is obtained by averaging all 10 angles in these structures, regardless whether they are trigonal bipyramidal (D_{3h}, C_{2v}, or C_s), square pyramidal (C_{4v}), or pentagonal planar (D_{5h}). This is seen in Fig. 14. The angles of the lone pair in the equatorial position of the SF_4 (i.e. ESF_4) molecule are determined by the bond angles by virtue of the C_{2v} symmetry. The same is true, for example, for the $SF_2(CF_3)_2$ molecule (also an ESX_4 system). However, the individual angles of the lone pair are not determined by the bond angles in the $ECIF_3O$ molecule, which has C_s symmetry (Fig. 8). The mean of the 10 angles is 108° here as well.

Even when the angles made by the lone pairs can easily be calculated from the experimentally determined bond angles, or when they may be deduced from the results of quantum-chemical calculations, they are often ignored. The proper application of the VSEPR model, however, should direct at least as much attention to the angles of the lone pairs and their variations as to those of the bond angles themselves.

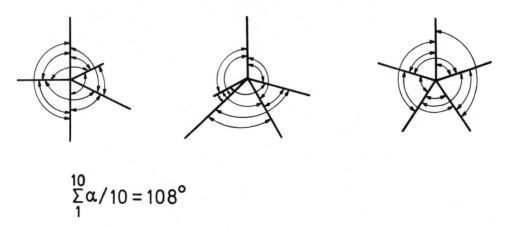

$$\sum_{1}^{10}\alpha/10 = 108°$$

Fig. 14. The mean angle of all ten angles in trigonal bipyramidal, square pyramidal, and pentagonal planar configurations.

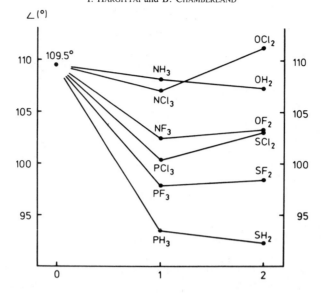

Fig. 15. Bond-angle variations in a series of tetrahedral molecules, AX_4, EBX_3, and E_2CX_2. The number of lone pairs of electrons in the valence shell of the central atom is 0, 1, and 2, respectively.

Let us consider first in some detail the experimental bond-angle variations in some AX_4, EBX_3, E_2CX_2 series of molecules shown in Fig. 15. Originally it was stated that ''. . . in the series CH_4, NH_3, and H_2O the bond angle decreases . . . as the number of nonbonding pairs increases''[9]. While it was invariably observed that going from AX_4 to EBX_3 the bond angles decreased, the replacement of yet another bond by a second lone pair did not lead to further decrease of the bond angle in E_2CX_2, except for the hydride molecules[19].

The interpretation of the changes in the bond angles, as going from the three ligand plus one lone pair case to the two ligand plus two lone pair case, is rather complicated since in addition to the bonding pair–bonding pair and bonding pair–lone pair repulsions, there are also lone pair–lone pair repulsions present. The resulting configuration depends, in the final analysis, on the relative magnitudes of the three different types of interactions.

To further examine the above changes, a simple point-charges-on-the-sphere model was constructed in which bonding and nonbonding electron pairs are represented by smaller (q_x) and larger (q_E) charges, respectively. The configuration was then determined in which only radial forces acted on the charges. At the same time it was strongly emphasized that using the

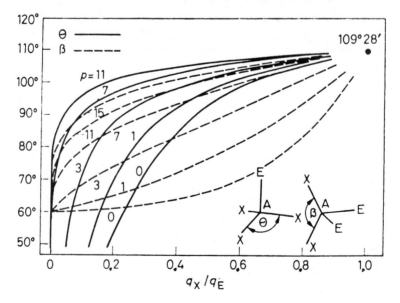

Fig. 16. Variations of the bond angles X—A—X in the AX_3E (θ) and AX_2E_2 (β) systems versus the ratio of the two charges employing various values for the repulsion exponent in the expression of the potential energy[20].

Table 1. Calculated angles for a series of isoelectronic tetrahedral fluoride molecules

	SiF_4[†]	$PF_3(EPF_3)$[‡]	$SF_2(E_2SF_2)$[‡]	$ClF(E_3ClF)$[§]	$Ar(E_4Ar)$[†]
FAF	109.5°	96.9°	98.1°	—	—
FAE	—	120.2°	104.3°	101.6°	—
EAE	—	—	135.8°	116.1°	109.5°

[†]By virtue of T_d symmetry.
[‡]Ref. [10].
[§]Ref. [21].

charges q_x and q_E by no means implied that the origin of repulsion in the systems under discussion could be considered to be simply electrostatic. In the expression of the force affecting the charges, the force and the distance between the charges were inversely proportional, of course, and the power of this distance varied over a wide range (between 1 and 15) in the calculations.

The results of these calculations are illustrated in Fig. 16. The variations of the bond angles are shown for different values of the repulsion exponent p against the ratio of the two different charges. It is seen that the bond angle θ of the AX_3E configuration is always smaller than the regular tetrahedral angle, while the bond angle β of the AX_2E_2 configuration may be smaller, as well as larger, than θ depending on the repulsion exponents. Thus the direction of the changes in the bond angles in going from AX_4 to AX_3E is well understood and is independent of the choice of the repulsion exponent. On the other hand, the relationship between the bond angles of molecule pairs AX_3E and AX_2E_2 strongly depends on the choice of the repulsion exponents. In these instances, the rules constituting the VSEPR model would seem to lose their usefulness in predicting the trends in the structural changes, since the predictions are no longer invariant to the choice of the repulsion exponents in the potential employed. Thus testing the applicability of the VSEPR model on the basis of only the bond angles is indeed contrary to the basic premises of the model. The angle made by the lone pairs must also be considered.

As not all angles made by the lone pairs in the tetrahedral systems were attainable from the experimental data, *ab initio* molecular orbital calculations have been carried out for a series of molecules[10,21]. The position of the lone pair was characterized by the center of its charge distribution. All angles in the isolectronic series SiF_4, PF_3, SF_2, ClF, and Ar are listed in Table 1. This series of molecules may be expressed by the following general formulae, AX_4E_0, AX_3E_1, AX_2E_2, AX_1E_3, AX_0E_4, respectively. It is to be noted that the differences in the angles within each structure are in accordance with the VSEPR model. The calculated bond angles in the series will parallel the changes observed in the experimental values, which are shown in Fig. 15.

There is a decrease from F—Si—F to F—P—F and the latter is smaller than F—S—F. On the other hand, the E—P—F angle is much larger than the E—S—F angle. The origin of this difference is determined by the relative strength of the repulsive interactions which decrease in the order

$$E/E > E/b > b/b,$$

where b represents the bonding pair. There are four E/b interactions and only one b/b interaction in the sulfur valence shell of SF_2. The situation is, of course, complicated by the presence of a strong E/E interaction.

Another example is provided by the experimental bond angles of SF_2, 98.0°[22] and SH_2, 92.2°[15]. The bond angle difference here has the opposite sign from what would follow from the electronegativity subrule. Again, however, the other structural changes in the rest of the valence shell configuration should not be ignored. The calculated angles (all angles, regardless of whether they involve bonds or lone pairs) are shown in Fig. 17. First of all, it is noted that the E—S—E, E—S—b, and b—S—b angles are related to each other in each molecule exactly as is predicted by the VSEPR model, considering the different space requirements of lone pairs and bonds. Furthermore, in agreement with the electronegativity subrule, the E—S—H angle is larger than the E—S—F angle. In both molecules there are four stronger E/b interactions and only one weaker b/b interaction. The former are obviously prevailing.

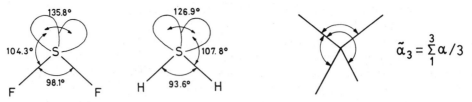

Fig. 17. All angles in the structures SF_2 (i.e. E_2SF_2) and SH_2 (i.e. E_2SH_2).

Fig. 18. Triple-average angles in tetrahedral configurations.

$$\tilde{\alpha}_3 = \sum_{1}^{3} \alpha/3$$

The general space requirements of various bonds and lone pairs can be conveniently characterized by the so-called triple-average angles[10], as illustrated in Fig. 18. The triple-average angle is the mean of the three angles made by a bond or a lone pair in a tetrahedral configuration. Whereas the formerly introduced mean angle was the average of all angles in a configuration and characterized the whole configuration, here the angular space requirement of an individual bond or lone pair is characterized. A typical triple-average angle of a bond is, say, 103° and that of a lone pair is, say, 114° in a tetrahedral configuration.

It has been noted[10] that the triple-average angles of a bond or that of a lone pair in various molecules appear to be rather constant. The space requirements of the fluorine bonds are somewhat smaller than those of the respective bonds to hydrogen atoms. The space requirement of the $S{=}O$ double bond is considerably larger than those of the single bonds and only slightly smaller than those of the lone pairs. The remarkable constancy of the general space requirements further facilitates the understanding of the bond angle changes displayed, for example, by the SF_2 and SH_2 molecules.

Let us also consider some examples from among trigonal bipyramidal structures. Comparison of the SF_4[23] and $SF_2(CF_3)_2$[24] molecular geometries (Fig. 19) by their bond angles only would again suggest incompatibility with the VSEPR model. The general configuration of these molecules is unambiguously predicted by the VSEPR model to be trigonal bipyramidal. For the bis-(trifluoromethyl) derivative it is also predicted correctly that the less electronegative CF_3 ligands should be found in the equatorial positions. According to the electronegativity subrule, then, the C—S—C bond angle of $S(CF_3)_2F_2$ could be expected to be larger than the equatorial F—S—F (F_e—S—F_e) bond angle of SF_4. This could be expected if the other interactions would be ignored. Incidentally, if steric effects rather than electron-pair repulsions would be the determining factor, then again the bulky CF_3 groups could be expected to cause an increase in the C—S—C bond angle as compared to the F_e—S—F_e bond angle. As is seen, the C—S—C bond angle is smaller than the F_e—S—F_e bond angle.

Fortunately, the angles involving the lone pairs can be easily calculated from the bond angles in these structures by virtue of the C_{2v} symmetry of the sulfur bond configuration. There are two kinds of interactions in the equatorial place, viz. E/b_Y and b_Y/b_Y in one and E/b_X and b_X/b_X in the other molecule. The stronger E/b interaction occurs twice and the weaker b/b interaction only once in both structures. Both the E—S—b and b—S—b angles are in the equatorial plane. Thus one of the two will determine the other. As the stronger and twice-occurring E/b interaction is obviously prevailing over the b/b interaction, the real question will be whether or not the difference in the E—S—b angles of the two molecules is consistent with

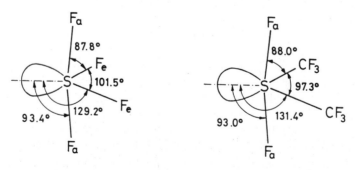

Fig. 19. The structure of the SF_4[23] and $SF_2(CF_3)_2$[24] molecules.

the VSEPR model. It is seen that the E—S—C angle is larger than the E—S—F$_e$ angle, exactly as predicted from the VSEPR model if all interactions are properly considered. The observed change in the bond angles then is the consequence of the outcome in the changes of the prevailing interactions. In the present comparison the angles involving the bonds to the axial fluorine ligands (F$_a$) are ignored as they are equal in the two structures within experimental error.

It is also instructive to consider the so-called quadruple-average angles in the trigonal bipyramidal molecules (of Fig. 20) for characterizing the general space requirements[25]. The quadruple-average angle is the mean of the four angles made by Q—A in QAX$_4$, where Q may be a ligand or a lone pair and the X ligands may all be the same or they may be different. The quadruple-average angles of the lone pairs in the two molecules considered above are

$$SF_4 \qquad\qquad 111.4°,$$
$$S(CF_3)_2F_2 \qquad\qquad 112.2°.$$

Although the difference is small, its direction is in complete agreement with the prediction of the VSEPR model postulating the E/b repulsions to be stronger when involving bonds to less electronegative ligands. It is again remembered that the E/S—F$_a$ interactions may be assumed to be equal in the two molecules.

7. CONCLUDING REMARKS

The VSEPR model of molecular geometry is an effective research tool and an excellent educational device. Its basic principles have withstood the tests of time while its applications have considerably increased. Its beauty lies in its simplicity and its reliability is mainly due to the well-defined boundaries of its applicability. The correct way of testing the applicability of the model has been given ample emphasis in the preceding section. Let us now enumerate the basic limitations of the model.

One of the most important assumptions used in the VSEPR model is the spherical symmetry of the valence shell. The less this assumption is valid, the more deviation from the simple rules of the model may be anticipated. This limitation is obviously very important for molecules in which the central atom is a transition metal, since its valence shell may be far from having spherical symmetry. It is the five-electron-pair structures where it is most likely to have differences from the VSEPR predictions, since the trigonal bipyramidal model is not very much superior to the tetragonal pyramidal model to start with. Thus it is a telling example that the molybdenum pentachloride molecule has been found to coexist in an equilibrium of trigonal bipyramidal and square pyramidal structures in the vapor phase[26], as illustrated in Fig. 21. Another example in which the relationship between the bond angles of the central atom is not in agreement with the VSEPR predictions is the structure of chromyl chloride, CrO$_2$Cl$_2$[27]. The reason is not clear, but here again the central atom is a transition metal and the model simply may not be applicable to such molecules. The structures of CrO$_2$Cl$_2$ and SO$_2$Cl$_2$ are illustrated in Fig. 22. The bond angles of sulfuryl chloride[28], of course, follow beautifully the VSEPR predictions.

An implicit assumption in the VSEPR model is that the electron pairs have cylindrical symmetry. On the examples of some trigonal bipyramidal structures some directional effects

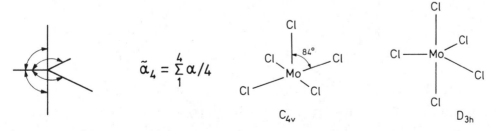

Fig. 20. Quadruple-average angles in trigonal bipyramidal configurations.

Fig. 21. The trigonal bipyramidal and square pyramidal configurations of molybdenum pentachloride found in equilibrium in the vapor phase[26].

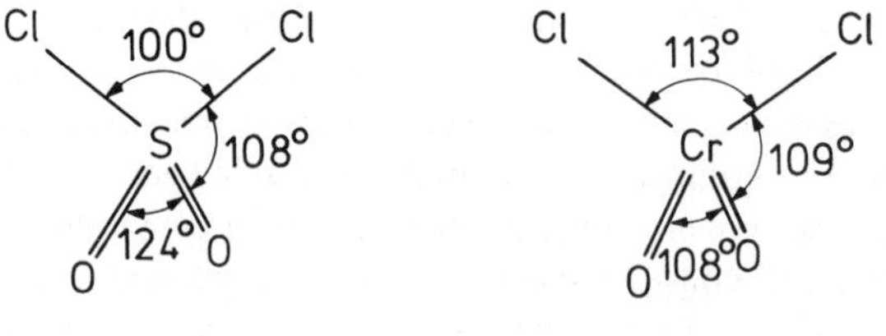

Fig. 22. The bond angles in the analogous molecules of sulfuryl chloride[27] and chromyl chloride[28].

have been clearly detected[29]. These directional effects, however, were not in conflict as regards the general shapes and angular variations in the series of structures examined from the point of view of the applicability of the VSEPR model. They were introduced to account for some subtle angular changes.

A striking example for demonstrating the importance of these directional effects is the molecular geometry of XeO_2F_2 determined in the crystalline phase[30], which is shown in Fig. 23. The molecule is of EAX_4 type and the lone pair as well as the two double bonds are found in equatorial positions, as predicted by the VSEPR model. The $O=Xe=O$ bond angle is considerably smaller than 120°, even though this angle is between two double bonds. Obviously the two $E/Xe=O$ interactions are prevailing in the equatorial plane. It is then surprising at first sight that the axial Xe—F bonds are bent towards the xenon lone pair of electrons rather than away from it. This indicates, however, that the repulsions in the axial directions are dominated by the directional effect from the $Xe=O$ double bonds. Thus structures in which the electron pairs strongly deviate from having cylindrical symmetry may not be accounted for by the original VSEPR model.

It is worth mentioning that XeO_2F_2 is the only compound in the present discussion of the VSEPR model for which the crystal-phase molecular structure is considered. For all the others, the structures of the free molecules were available. XeO_2F_2 has a layer structure in the crystal resulting from the Xe . . . O intermolecular bridging shown in Fig. 23. These contacts might be thought to decrease somewhat the repulsive strength of the xenon lone pair as well as that of the $Xe=O$ double bonds. Lacking vapor-phase data for comparison, we have no way to judge the extent of such an effect, if there is any at all. What is important in our discussion is

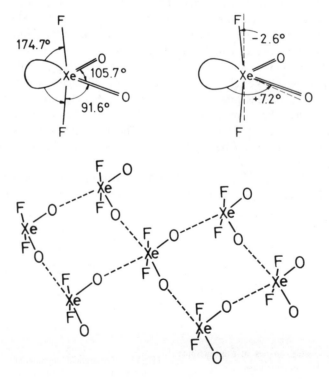

Fig. 23. The crystalline molecular structure of XeO_2F_2[30].

the opposite sign in the deviations from the "ideal" angles in the equatorial and axial directions. This certainly points to the difference in the directional repulsion strengths of the xenon lone pair and the Xe=O double bond.

It may be safe to state that the "ideal" territory for the application of the VSEPR model is the free molecule. A free molecule is unperturbed by any intermolecular interaction and its structure is determined exclusively by intramolecular forces. In the case of crystal structures the VSEPR model is less reliable since it does not consider the packing forces between molecules.

Finally, the relative importance of the electron-pair repulsions *versus* nonbonded atom–atom interactions diminishes with increasing ligand size relative to the size of the central atom. Thus the best results from the VSEPR model are expected for structures with small ligands relative to the central atom, i.e. where the steric factors are minimal.

Acknowledgment—We wish to acknowledge the University of Connecticut Research Foundation for the financial assistance which made this project possible.

REFERENCES

1. R. Hoffmann (Foreword), L. V. Vilkov, V. S. Mastryukov and N. I. Sadova, *Determination of the Geometrical Structure of Free Molecules*. Mir, Moscow (1983).
2. G. N. Lewis, The atom and the molecule. *J. Am. Chem. Soc.* **38**, 762–785 (1916).
3. a. W. B. Jensen, Abegg, Lewis, Langmuir, and the octet rule. *J. Chem. Educ.* **61**, 191–200 (1984).
   b. A. N. Stranges, Reflections on the electron theory of the chemical bond: 1900–1925. *J. Chem. Educ.* **61**, 185–190 (1984).
   c. L. Pauling, G. N. Lewis and the chemical bond. *J. Chem. Educ.* **61**, 201–203 (1984).
4. N. V. Sidgwick and H. M. Powell, Stereochemical types and valency groups. *Proc. R. Soc. London Ser. A* **176**, 153–180 (1940).
5. R. J. Gillespie and R. S. Nyholm, Inorganic stereochemistry. *Quart. Rev. Chem. Soc.* **11**, 339–380 (1957).
6. R. J. Gillespie, This week's citation classic. *Current contents PC&ES* **24**, 14–16 (1984).
7. R. J. Gillespie, The valence-shell electron-pair repulsion (VSEPR) theory of directed valency. *J. Chem. Educ.* **40**, 295–301 (1963).
8. R. J. Gillespie, *Angew. Chem. Int. Ed. Engl.* **6**, 819 (1967).
9. R. J. Gillespie, *Molecular Geometry*. Van Nostrand Reinhold, London (1972).
10. A. Schmiedekamp, D. W. J. Cruickshank, S. Skaarup, P. Pulay, I. Hargittai, and J. E. Boggs, Investigation of the basis of the valence shell electron pair repulsion model by ab initio calculation of geometry variations in a series of tetrahedral and related molecules. *J. Am. Chem. Soc.* **101**, 2002–2010 (1979).
11. I. Hargittai, Trigonal bipyramidal molecular structures and the VSEPR model. *Inorg. Chem.* **21**, 4334–4335 (1982).
12. L. S. Bartell, Pauli-Mechanics, a simple model for the molecular structure and force field (in Hungarian). *Kém. Közlem.* **43**, 497–510 (1975).
13. L. S. Bartell, Do the VSEPR points-on-a-sphere repulsions simulate quantum interactions? *Croatica Chem. Acta* **57**, 927–939 (1984).
14. R. F. Bader, P. J. MacDougall and C. D. H. Lau, Bonded and nonbonded charge concentrations and their relation to molecular geometry and reactivity. *J. Am. Chem. Soc.* **106**, 1594–1605 (1984).
15. Landolt-Börnstein, *Numerical Data and Functional Relationships in Science and Technology (New Series)*. Vol. 7: *Structure Data of Free Polyatomic Molecules* (Edited by K.-H. Hellwege and A. M. Hellwege). Springer-Verlag, Berlin–Heidelberg–New York (1976).
16. J. Brunvoll, O. Exner and I. Hargittai, Geometry and conformation of dimethyl sulphate as investigated by electron diffraction and dipolometry. *J. Mol. Struct.* **73**, 99–104 (1981).
17. See, for example, R. S. Berry, A general phenomenology for small clusters, however floppy, in *Quantum Dynamics of Molecules: The New Experimental Challenge to Theorists* (Edited by R. G. Woolley), pp. 143–195. Plenum Press, New York and London (1980).
18. R. J. French, K. Hedberg and J. M. Shreeve, Trifluorodichlorophosphorane, PF_3Cl_2, by electron diffraction. *Tenth Austin Symposium on Molecular Structure, Abstracts*, Austin, Texas, 1984, p. 51.
19. I. Hargittai, Electron pairs as architects of molecules. The Gillespie model of molecular geometry (in Hungarian). *Természet Világa* **104**, 78–82 (1973).
20. I. Hargittai and A. Baranyi, On the applicability of the VSEPR model for the molecular geometries of some tetrahedral and related molecules. *Acta Chim. Hung.* **93**, 279–288 (1977).
21. P. Scharfenberg, L. Harsányi and I. Hargittai, unpublished calculation, 1984.
22. Y. Endo, S. Saito, E. Hirota and T. Chikaraishi, Microwave spectrum of sulfur difluoride in the first excited vibrational states. Vibrational potential function and equilibrium structure. *J. Mol. Spectrosc.* **77**, 222–234 (1979).
23. M. W. Tolles and W. D. Gwinn, Structure and dipole moment for SF_4. *J. Chem. Phys.* **36**, 1119–1121 (1962).
24. H. Oberhammer, R. C. Kumar, G. D. Knerr, and J. M. Shreeve, Gas-phase structures of $(CF_3)_2S{=}O$, $(CF_3)_2S{=}NCl$, and $(CF_3)_2SF_2$. An electron diffraction study. *Inorg. Chem.* **20**, 3871–3874 (1981).
25. I. Hargittai, On the puzzle of the OSF_4 structure. *J. Mol. Struct.* **56**, 301–303 (1979).
26. J. Brunvoll, A. A. Ischenko, V. P. Spiridonov and T. G. Strand, Composition and molecular structure of gaseous molybdenum pentachloride by electron diffraction. *Acta Chem. Scand. A* **38**, 115–120 (1984).

27. M. Hargittai and I. Hargittai, The molecular structure of sulphuryl chloride: An electron diffraction reinvestigation. *J. Mol. Struct.* **73**, 253–255 (1981).
28. C. J. Marsden, L. Hedberg and K. Hedberg, Molecular structure and quadratic force field of chromyl chloride, CrO_2Cl_2. *Inorg. Chem.* **21**, 1115–1118 (1982).
29. K. O. Christe and H. Oberhammer, Evidence for the existence of directional repulsion effects by lone valence electron pairs and π bonds in trigonal bipyramidal molecules. *Inorg. Chem.* **20**, 296–297 (1981).
30. S. W. Peterson, R. D. Willett and J. L. Huston, Symmetry and structure of XeO_2F_2 by neutron diffraction. *J. Chem. Phys.* **59**, 453–459 (1973).

Comp. & Maths. with Appls. Vol. 12B, Nos. 3/4, pp. 1039–1045, 1986
Printed in Great Britain.

0886–9561/86 $3.00 + .00
© 1986 Pergamon Press Ltd.

THE MATHEMATICAL THEORY OF CHAOS

Denis Blackmore

Department of Mathematics, New Jersey Institute of Technology, Newark, NJ 07102, U.S.A.

Abstract—The basic concepts of the mathematical theory of chaos are presented through a brief analysis of some interesting dynamical systems in one-, two- and three-dimensional space. We start with a discussion of interval maps and observe that when such maps are monotonic, their iterates behave in an orderly fashion. Then, by way of contrast, we study a well-known quadratic map whose iterates clearly manifest the archetypal characteristics of chaos, such as period-doubling bifurcations and the existence of a strange attractor. As a means of indicating that mappings in two dimensions yield a richer variety of chaotic regimes than do interval maps, we next discuss the horseshoe and solenoidal mappings of the two-disk. Dizzying forms of chaos emerge from these mappings, but there is an irony—the chaotic behavior can be characterized in an orderly way. We conclude with a cursory examination of the Lorenz differential equation in three-space: a primary source of the recent interest in chaos theory.

The two most widely used definitions of chaos are the following: a state of nature completely devoid of order, and intense confusion or disorder associated with unpredictable activity. Of the two, the latter—the dynamic as opposed to the static—is the more popular and most apropos of the mathematical theory of chaos. The lure of chaos theory is the way in which simple mechanisms can lead to startling complexity; the promise is that in its mastery lies the key to unlocking the secrets of physical phenomena, such as turbulence, which have eluded satisfactory scientific analysis. Our purpose in this note is to introduce several concepts of chaos theory by a cursory examination of some models in one, two and three dimensions.

1. ONE-DIMENSIONAL CHAOS: INTERVAL MAPS

The iterates of interval maps (functions $f:I \rightarrow I$, where $I = [0, 1]$ is the unit interval of the real line) provide a rich source of chaotic behavior. For a given point x of I the iterates are $f(x), f(f(x)) = f^2(x), f(f^2(x)) = f^3(x), \ldots, f(f^{n-1}(x)) = f^n(x), \ldots$, etc. A point x satisfying $f(x) = x$ is called a *fixed point* of f. Note that if x is a fixed point, all the iterates stay at x. If the iterates stray from x but return after a minimum of $n > 1$ iterations, we say x is a *periodic point of period n*; the set of iterates $\{x, f(x), \ldots, f^{n-1}(x)\}$ is called a *periodic orbit of period n* or just an *n-cycle*, for short. A subset S of I is called an *invariant set* if the iterates of every point in S stay in S. For example, fixed points and periodic orbits are easily seen to be invariant sets. An invariant set is said to be an *attractor* or a *repellor* if the iterates of points near, but not in, S eventually approach or recede from S, respectively.

For convenience we restrict ourselves to smooth maps (functions having continuous derivatives of all orders). As a nice contrast to chaos, we first consider monotonic interval maps; these are functions $f:I \rightarrow I$ whose derivative f' does not vanish. An interval map with positive derivative is illustrated in Fig. 1. The points at which $y = f(x)$ intersect $y = x$ are the fixed points of f; these consist of the points $x^{(1)} = 0$, $x^{(2)} = \frac{3}{10}$, $x^{(5)} = \frac{4}{5}$ and the interval $J = [\frac{1}{2}, \frac{3}{5}]$. Given x_0, there is an easy way to locate $f(x_0)$: simply draw a vertical line through x_0 until it hits the graph at p, then draw a horizontal line through p until it intersects $y = x$ at q—the x coordinate of g is $f(x_0)$. By repeating this process the *orbit* or *itinerary* $x_0, x_1 = f(x_0), x_2 = f^2(x_0), \ldots$ can be traced. This construction is shown for two starting points x_0 and x_0' in Fig. 1. The reader can easily verify that $x^{(1)}$ and $x^{(3)}$ are attractors and $x^{(2)}$ is a repellor, while J attracts nearby points on its left and repels nearby points on its right. Perhaps the reader can now postulate and prove a general statement about the iterates of monotone increasing interval maps? For example, it is not difficult to see that the only possible invariant sets are composed of fixed points, and the iterates behave in an orderly way—no chaos exists.

Monotonically decreasing interval maps do not produce chaos either. Consider the map shown in Fig. 2. This function has a single fixed point at $x^{(1)} = \frac{3}{5}$. As a matter of fact, every decreasing interval map has a unique fixed point. The fixed point $x^{(1)}$ is a repellor and f has a

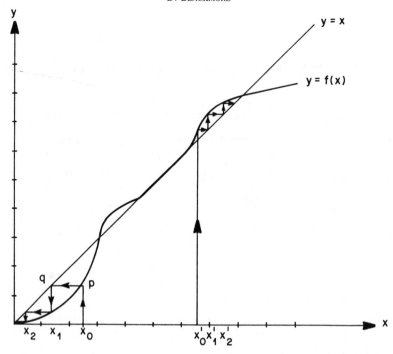

Fig. 1. Graph of function with $f' > 0$.

2-cycle $\{x^{(2)} = \frac{2}{5}, x^{(3)} = \frac{4}{5}\}$ which is an attractor. These properties can be checked by following the itineraries of x_0 and x_0'. At this point the reader might like to try to prove a general theorem about decreasing interval maps; toward this end it is useful to observe that if f is decreasing, f^2 is increasing. Certainly, apart from the unique fixed point of a decreasing f, all other invariant sets must consist of 2-cycles. Before going on to chaos, one last observation is in order: in both of the foregoing examples the attractors are characterized by $|f'| < 1$ and the repellors by $|f'| > 1$; this is not an accident, but a general rule.

    If we want chaos, we now see that monotonic interval maps will not do. A family of interval maps which is quite simple, but produces chaos nevertheless, is the following:

$$f_\lambda(x) = 4\lambda x(1 - x),$$

with $0 < \lambda < 1$. This family has been studied extensively by a host of mathematicians and scientists. In Fig. 3 the graphs for the cases $\lambda = .5$, $\lambda = .8$ and $\lambda = .9$ are drawn. The

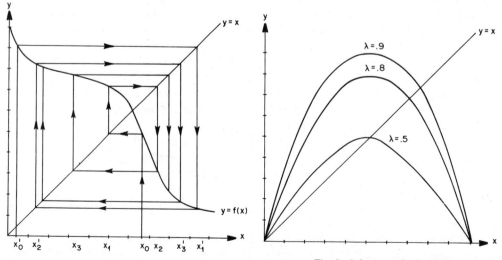

Fig. 2. Graph of function with $f' < 0$.

Fig. 3. f_λ for $\lambda = .5$, .8 and .9.

function f_λ achieves its maximum value of λ at $x = .5$, as can be shown by solving $f'_\lambda = 0$. The behavior of the iterates for these three cases differ markedly: $f_{.5}$ has but two invariant sets $x = 0$ and $x = .5$, where the first is a repellor and the second fixed point is an attractor; $f_{.8}$ has fixed-point repellors $x = 0$ and $x = \frac{11}{16}$, and a 2-cycle $\{x \simeq .51, x \simeq .80\}$ which is an attractor; $f_{.9}$ has periodic orbits of all periods 2^n and much more—the iterates are chaotic.

To see how f_λ goes from order to chaos, first note that the fixed points are $x = 0$ and $x_\lambda^{(1)} = (4\lambda - 1)/4\lambda$, as can be seen by solving

$$f_\lambda(x) = x.$$

We note that $|f'_\lambda(x_\lambda^{(1)})|$ is less than 1 when $0 < \lambda < \lambda_1 = \frac{3}{4}$ and greater than 1 when $\lambda_1 < \lambda < 1$. The equation

$$f_\lambda^2(x) = x$$

has just two real roots, $x = 0$ and $x_\lambda^{(1)}$ for $0 < \lambda < \lambda_1$. But as λ passes through λ_1, the root $x_\lambda^{(1)}$ becomes a root of multiplicity 3 at λ_1 and then splits or *bifurcates* into three real roots $x_\lambda^{(11)} < x_\lambda^{(1)} < x_\lambda^{(12)}$. The set $C_\lambda^{(1)} = \{x_\lambda^{(11)}, x_\lambda^{(12)}\}$ is a 2-cycle of f_λ for $\lambda > \lambda_c$. This phenomenon is known as *period doubling*, and is illustrated in Fig. 4. The fixed points $x = 0$ and $x_\lambda^{(1)}$ are repellors and $C_\lambda^{(1)}$ is an attractor. Replacing f_λ by f_λ^2 and tracing the roots of $f_\lambda^4(x) = x$, we find there exists $\lambda_2 \simeq .86$, at which each of the roots $x_\lambda^{(21)}$ and $x_\lambda^{(2)}$ bifurcates into a pair of new roots. For $\lambda > \lambda_2$, $x = 0$, $x_\lambda^{(1)}$ and $C_\lambda^{(1)}$ are joined by the 4-cycle $C_\lambda^{(2)} = \{x_\lambda^{(21)}, x_\lambda^{(22)}, x_\lambda^{(23)}, x_\lambda^{(24)}\}$. Continuing in this way we find a sequence $\lambda_1 < \lambda_2 < \lambda_3 \ldots$ (converging to $\lambda_c \simeq .89$) of values at which period doubling takes place; more precisely, for $\lambda_n < \lambda < \lambda_{n+1}$, f_λ has repellors $x = 0$, $x_\lambda^{(1)}$, $C_\lambda^{(1)}$, $\ldots$, $C_\lambda^{(n-1)}$ and a 2^n-cycle

$$C_\lambda^{(n)} = \{x_\lambda^{(n1)}, x_\lambda^{(n2)}, \ldots, x_\lambda^{(n2^n)}\}$$

which is an attractor. For $\lambda > \lambda_c$ the iterates of f_λ are chaotic: there are 2^n-cycles for every $n > 0$, aperiodic points arbitrarily close to periodic points, and nearby points yield widely separated points after only a few iterations.

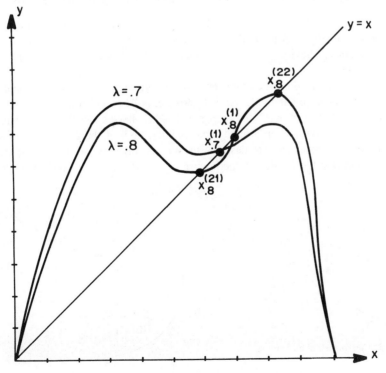

Fig. 4. f_λ^2 for $\lambda = .7$ and .8.

Feigenbaum observed the following convergence properties for this model:

$$\frac{x_{\lambda_n}^{(n-1,1)} - x_{\lambda_n}^{(n-1,2)}}{x_{\lambda_{n+1}}^{(n1)} - x_{\lambda_{n+1}}^{(n2)}} \longrightarrow \alpha \simeq 2.50$$

as $n \longrightarrow \infty$.

$$\frac{\lambda_n - \lambda_{n-1}}{\lambda_{n+1} - \lambda_n} \longrightarrow \delta \simeq 4.67$$

Moreover, these convergence properties persist for graphs of the same basic shape as that of f_λ; this so-called *metric universality* has since been proved by Lanford. The fact that this metric universality occurs in a number of mathematical models of important physical phenomena (the Navier–Stokes equations, for example) is largely responsible for the recent activity in chaos theory.

Another interesting feature of the f_λ model is the appearance of a *strange attractor* in the chaotic regime $\lambda_c < \lambda < 1$. A strange attractor is, roughly speaking, an attractor with a very complicated structure; an n-cycle, for example, is far too simple to qualify for strangeness. More precisely, a strange attractor is one that is composed of Cantor sets. A typical Cantor set may be described as follows: Let $I_0 = [0, 1]$ be the unit interval. Divide I_0 into five equal subintervals and denote the second and fourth subinterval by I_{11} and I_{12}, respectively. Note that $I_{11} = [.2, .4]$ and $I_{12} = [.6, .8]$. Now repeat this process with each of the new intervals, thereby creating I_{21}, I_{22}, I_{23}, and then continue *ad infinitum*. These intervals are shown in Fig. 5.

At the nth state of the construction we have the following set:

$$C_n = I_{n1} \cup I_{n2} \cup \cdots \cup I_{n2}n.$$

The intersection of all these sets is a Cantor set, and its structure is rather complicated. If the reader now studies the way in which new cycles are created for f_λ by period doubling, a strong resemblance to the Cantor-set construction should be manifest. It is then plausible to assume that the attractors $C_\lambda^{(n)}$ converge, in some sense, to an attractor which is a Cantor set as $\lambda \to \lambda_c$. It can actually be proved via this line of reasoning that f_λ has a strange attractor when $\lambda_c < \lambda < 1$.

2. TWO-DIMENSIONAL CHAOS: HORSESHOES AND SOLENOIDS

By the disk D we mean the subset of the plane consisting of all points on and inside a circle. We now graduate from interval maps to disk maps $f:D \to D$, thereby tapping an even richer vein of chaotic behavior. Just two examples will be considered: Smale's horseshoe and Blackmore's solenoid.

The horseshoe can be described by simply specifying the image $f(D)$ under the map f. To this end, it is convenient to subdivide the disk into pieces A, Q and B as shown in Fig. 6. The shape of $f(D)$ makes it clear why this map is called the horseshoe. This map has a strange invariant set and its iterates jump around rather wildly; both of these conditions characterize chaos. Actually, it is rather easy to describe the strange invariant set (which is a product of Cantor sets) as follows: Let f^{-1} denote the inverse of f and f^{-n} be the n-fold composition of f^{-1}

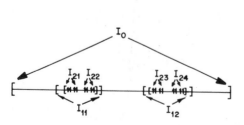

Fig. 5. Construction of a Cantor set.

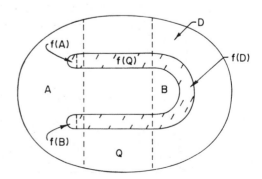

Fig. 6. The horseshoe.

with itself. The set of points Λ common to all of the sets $Q_m = Q \cap f^m(Q)$, $m = 0, \pm 1$, $\pm 2, \ldots$ is an invariant set—and this set is quite strange. A blown-up portion of Q shown in Fig. 7 illustrates several of these Q_m. The Cantor set structure of Λ can be readily discerned from this diagram.

We conclude our discussion of the horseshoe with two observations. First, if f is restricted to Λ, the map $f{:}\Lambda \to \Lambda$ can be identified with the *shift map* $\sigma{:} S \to S$, where S consists of all doubly infinite binary sequences $\{a_n : a_n = 0, 1; -\infty < n < \infty\}$ and $\sigma\{a_n\} = \{b_n\}$ with $b_n = a_{n-1}$. In this setting, for example, the sequences consisting of all zeroes or ones are fixed points and ...000100010001... represents a periodic point of period 4. Here we have a chaotic situation which can be completely described in simple terms—one person's chaos is another's order, and vice versa. Second, the chaos of the horseshoe is stable in the following sense: If the map f is perturbed slightly, the qualitative behavior of the iterates remains the same. For example, if f^* is the perturbed horseshoe, there is a strange invariant set Λ^* such that $f^*{:}\Lambda^* \to \Lambda^*$ can be identified with the shift map.

A more exotic form of chaos occurs in the $\{m_n\}$-*solenoid*. We start with a disk, then select an increasing sequence of integers: $m_0 = 1 < m_1 < m_2 \cdots$ which need to satisfy certain technical requirements in order to guarantee smoothness of the solenoid map. We shall refer to Fig. 8 in order to describe the solenoid.

Associated with the sequence $m_0 < m_1 < m_2 < \cdots$ is a nested sequence of disks $D_0 \supset D_{11} \cup D_{12} \cup \cdots \cup D_{1,m_0 m_1} \supset D_{21} \cup D_{22} \cup \cdots \cup D_{2,m_0 m_1 m_2} \supset \cdots$, whose intersection Δ is an invariant set for the solenoid map g. This set Δ is a very strange attractor for g in that its structure is even more complicated than that of a Cantor set. The map g is essentially

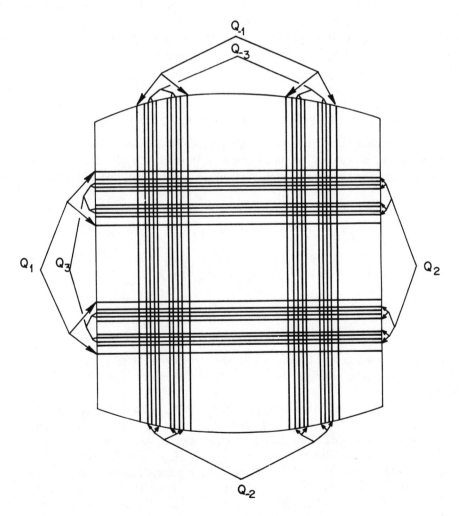

Fig. 7. Description of the invariant set Λ.

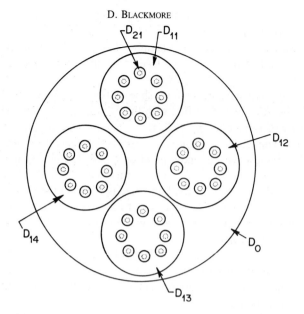

Fig. 8. The $\{m_n\}$-solenoid with $m_0 = 1 < m_1 = 4 < m_2 = 8 < \cdots$.

a rotation of $2\pi/m_1$ radians about the center of D_0 composed with rotations of $2\pi/m_1 m_2$ about the centers of $\{D_{11}, D_{12}, \ldots, D_{1,m_0 m_1}\}$ composed with rotations of $2\pi/m_1 m_2 m_3$ about the centers of $\{D_{21}, D_{22}, \ldots D_{2,m_0 m_1 m_2}\}$, and so on. In contrast to the horseshoe, the qualitative behavior of the iterates of g is not stable—it varies drastically with small perturbations of g. However, there is a fairly simple representation of the restriction map $g: \Delta \to \Delta$ analogous to that of the horseshoe.

3. THREE-DIMENSIONAL CHAOS: THE LORENZ EQUATION

There are a number of differential equations which have chaotic solutions. One of these, Duffing's equation, is treated nicely in an article by Hofstadter[5]. We shall consider just one such example, the Lorenz equation, which is actually a system of first-order differential equations of form

$$\frac{dx}{dt} = -10x + 10y,$$

$$\frac{dy}{dt} = -y + 200z - xz, \tag{L}$$

$$\frac{dz}{dt} = -\tfrac{8}{3}z + xy.$$

This system was introduced by Lorenz as a simple meteorological model. He observed erratic behavior in the computer solutions, and this led to the discovery of the chaotic nature of the solutions.

A careful analysis of (L) is too difficult to go into here, so we shall simply point out some interesting properties. Notice that (L) is nonlinear, as it must be: a linear system cannot exhibit chaos (as can be readily verified by anyone who has mastered undergraduate differential equations). The Lorenz equation has three stationary points: $(x, y, z) = (0, 0, 0)$, $\simeq (.015, .015, .000084)$, $\simeq (199.97, 199.97, 14995.5)$. Each of these points is an invariant set; that is, if a solution of (L) starts in the set, it stays in the set for all time. There are far more interesting invariant sets of (L), namely two strange attractors which are sketched in Fig. 9. The two strange attractors are like two competing solar systems, and the solution curves behave like

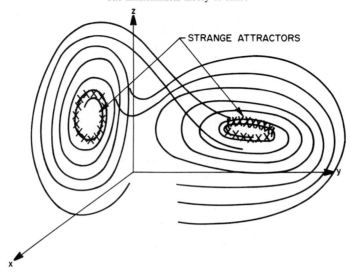

Fig. 9. The solution curves of the Lorenz equation (L).

trajectories of comets: If a comet passes too close to either system it gets sucked in; otherwise it oscillates back and forth between the two systems in an erratic way.

This concludes our introduction to chaos. For the reader whose appetite has only been whetted, we offer the following reading list.

REFERENCES

1. D. Blackmore, Exceptional minimal sets of diffeomorphisms and flows. *Abst. Am. Math. Soc.*, **5**(2), 186 (1984).
2. J. Chandra, *Chaos in Nonlinear Dynamical Systems*. SIAM, Philadelphia (1984).
3. P. Collet and J. Eckmann, *Iterated Maps on the Interval as Dynamical Systems*. Birkhauser, Boston (1980).
4. J. Guckenheimer and P. Holmes, *Nonlinear Oscillations, Dynamical Systems, and Bifurcations of Vector Fields. Appl. Math. Sci.* **42**. Springer-Verlag, New York (1983).
5. D. Hofstadter, Metamagical themas. *Scient. Am.*, **245**(5), 22–43 (1981).
6. S. Newhouse, *Entropy and smooth dynamics, Dynamical Systems and Chaos, Lecture Notes in Physics* **179**. Springer-Verlag, New York, 165–180 (1983).
7. C. Sparrow, *The Lorenz Equations: Bifurcations, Chaos and Strange Attractors*. Springer-Verlag, New York (1982).